CONTEMPORARY COMPOSERS

CONTEMPORARY COMPOSERS

WITH A PREFACE BY
BRIAN FERNEYHOUGH

EDITORS
BRIAN MORTON
PAMELA COLLINS

St J
ST. JAMES PRESS
CHICAGO AND LONDON

For information, write:
ST. JAMES PRESS
233 East Ontario Street
Chicago, Illinois 60611
U.S.A.
or
2-6 Boundary Row
London SE1 8HP
England.

British Library Cataloguing in Publication Data
Contemporary composers.
I. Morton, Brian, *1954-* II. Collins, Pamela, *1954-*
780.922

ISBN 1-55862-085-0

CONTENTS

EDITORS' FOREWORD

In the very early stages of this project, the editors contacted the director of a leading American composers' organisation. He wanted to know how many entries we hoped to include. We said that, optimistically, there would be 600, from all around the world. "But that's absurd!" he replied. "Why, there are 20,000 composers in the United States alone."

It's fair to say at the outset that somewhat over 19,000 of these will be disappointed by what follows. *Contemporary Composers* does not set out to be a comprehensive or exhaustive survey of new composition in the early 1990s; nor should it be seen as a league table of the "top" 500 composers — 500 was a logistical compromise, given the amount of material to be processed — at work today. It is intended rather as a listener's guide to the broadest spectrum of contemporary composition. It includes artists from all over the world and ranging in age from a handful of figures born in the last century to emerging composers who have not yet turned 30. Future editions will have to take account both of natural wastage and new trends, but also of any significant omissions from the present trawl.

Though the final selection is the responsibility of the editors, it reflects the suggestions and strictures of an expert advisory panel. It is also tinged with simple contingency. Where reliable information was not forthcoming, either by means of a standard questionnaire sent to all potential entrants, or else from a composer's publisher or agent, no entry was compiled. Though the initial selection was strictly limited to living composers (we resisted considerable pressure to include recently deceased figures such as Giacinto Scelsi or Kaikhosru Sorabji), a number of senior figures who died in the course of the project have been retained: Sir Lennox Berkeley, Leonard Bernstein, Aaron Copland, Peter Racine Fricker, Jean Langlais, Luigi Nono, Andrzej Panufnik, Virgil Thomson.

Entries consist of three main sections. Each begins with a brief biography containing details of birth, education, marriage(s), posts and positions held, awards and distinctions gained, together with a contact address and music publisher(s). The bulk of each entry consists of a list of works — usually but not always comprehensive — with instrumentation, date of completion and place and date of first performance (where only premiere dates are known, it is assumed that this is also the "completion" date of a piece). The final part of each entry is a short assessive article which attempts to locate each composer within contemporary styles and movements, discussing particular influences and innovations, and analysing one or more major works. Bibliographies and discographies are selective and in the latter case offer no indication as to what recordings are currently available.

In addition (and a feature of St James Press reference titles), each composer was invited to contribute a short personal statement introducing his or her work. Perhaps inevitably, a proportion of entrants preferred silence.

Further information about scores and holdings should be requested directly from composers, their agents or publishers. A list of the main international publishers is published in an appendix, together with details of national music information centres, composers' organizations and other groups.

For help and advice over and above the call of duty, we would like to thank all the advisers, Robin Anderson of Universal, Susan Bamert of Novello, Richard Barrett, Susan Bradshaw, Tracy Chevalier of St James Press, Jenny Dawson, Giles Easterbrook, Keith Howard of the University of Durham, Rosemary Johnson of Chester Music, Daniel Kirkpatrick of St James Press, Joyce Lawler of Meet the Composer (New York), Gerard McBurney, Victoria Pope of Peters Edition, Jane Williams of United Music Publishers (and subsequently of Chester Music), staff at the Danish, Finnish, Norwegian and Swedish Music Information Centres, Alan Sugar of Amstrad, the inventors of instant coffee and Optrex, and the man who turned the heating down to "Tropical" in the British Library music reading room.

This, the editors' second joint production, is dedicated with love to their first; Fiona Mary Morton was born 26 April 1990, the only deadline we didn't miss. It is also dedicated to the memory of Robert Morton, who died in March 1991, and who is much missed.

BRIAN MORTON
PAMELA COLLINS

EDITORS' FOREWORD

PREFACE

In recent years contemporary music has been undergoing sweeping change more rapidly, both socially and stylistically, than at perhaps any previous period in living memory. At the same time that composition has tended towards a greater internationality (and thus becoming less the province of a smaller group of "traditional" new music-producing nations) the accelerating revolution in the electronic media has come to make the world seem both more densely populated and more claustrophobic than hitherto. Most recently, the opening up of Eastern Europe has significantly increased contact and opportunities for interaction and will surely produce many as yet unpredictable changes in our perspective as to where contemporary compositional practice may be heading.

Given the complexity and multifariousness characteristic of the present juncture it would be invidious to attempt to simplify matters with the aid of a few prefabricated categories; nevertheless some important central issues have become clear, not the least pressing of which is the issue of stylistic diversity. Musical style in the 20th century has never been as conveniently monolithic — even in the 1950s — as many commentators would like to pretend; the current sea change may arguably reflect transformed modes of cultural perception rather than realities of stylistic hegemony. Nevertheless, much ink has been spilled of late over the question of the "total availability" of musical history as a valid object of compositional invention. It seems characteristic of our "Alexandrine" epoch that such a dehistoricising attitude towards material and context should coincide with the attempt to make new music more accessible to larger audiences by couching it in stylistic traits and aesthetic stances characteristic of a much earlier (and perhaps — at least when "creatively misunderstood" — more simple) period. It is a sign of the social power of the newer media that we should have come to appreciate the past as a function of its symbolic transmission, thus robbing it of its perspectival potential. I suppose that many if not most composers today on the threshold of their careers have come to contemporary music via popular, commercial music of one kind or another; this is certainly true on the North American continent. It is extremely interesting to see how such artists manage to grapple with the thicket of issues surrounding such "crossover" phenomena, where "History" is in any case an extremely relative concept.

The remarkable acceleration in the field of music technology has impinged directly on the current state of composing, not least the increasing isolation of composers from organs of public reproduction, the rapid internationalization of research activity and a new focus beginning to emerge in the important area of musical perception and cognition. The instrumental palette, meanwhile, has been rejuvenated through the use of commercially developed electronic equipment (although much remains to be done to persuade the industry to take heed of the specific needs of the non-commercial artist) and major advances have been made in the combination of pre-recorded tape materials and live instruments. Entire new perspectives are being opened with the application of most recent computer technology to real-time manipulation of instrumental and vocal signals, and there are signs that many composers are once more becoming actively involved with the performance of their own works on this basis. While this may indeed represent one major trend, it is also disturbing to the extent that the gap between experimental art forms and those amenable to assimilation by existing vehicles (such as the symphony orchestra) may finally become unbridgeable.

Hand-in-hand with the progressive internationalization of contemporary music comes the notable increase in the number of women composers active in the mainstream. Many women now in their thirties and forties have succeeded in establishing themselves as regular and integral parts of present-day concert life, and a significant number of them come from countries until quite recently not particularly identified as centres of new music activity. Their contribution is certain to grow even more rapidly in the coming decade, in spite of the tendency of music publishers to abdicate from their traditional role as disseminators of new works and artists. That this is an enforced abdication is clear, stemming as it does both from the economic marginality of new music and the sheer impossibility of keeping up with the expansion in the number of composers now active on the professional scene. Although a few major publishers do indeed maintain this traditional role as best they may, there is little hope for the vast majority of young composers to be adopted and supported in this fashion. One immediate result of this change has been the tendency of many individuals to set themselves up as the publishers of their own music — something that has become a practical possibility only in the last few years. Even major publishers are beginning to resort to electronic means of servicing large catalogues, thus eliminating the need to maintain costly storage space for products that typically sell very slowly.

The primary advantage of this situation from the point of view of composers is that most income from the hire, sales and performance of works remains in their own hands. Problematic, on the other hand, is the sheer effort involved in publicizing oneself, in making individual voices heard to the degree necessary for a career to "take off". *Contemporary Composers* may well address this issue by making available work lists and personal statements, not only by already established figures, but by many individuals having as yet insufficient access to broader avenues of professional communication.

Several pressing issues continue to concern those active, in whatever capacity, in new music circles. One of the most weighty of these is the tendency, already far advanced, for recent works to be eliminated from the programming of the majority of radio stations. To be sure, there are notable exceptions, especially in smaller countries, where the creative artist is often in more direct and active contact with those responsible for planning. Unfortunately they remain exceptions, and the compact for mutual support that carried much new music programming since World War II has been eroded to the point where a thoroughgoing redefinition of goals and possibilities seems unavoidable. Another concern has been the parallel dilution of journals actively propagating contemporary issues, in particular those aimed at a non-specialist readership. Music, ephemeral by definition, is in great need of support by the written word to maintain a constant profile in the public eye.

On the positive side, official support for young composers seems to be growing, to judge by the plethora of competitions and scholarships on offer. At the same time, it is difficult not to see the present juncture as extremely difficult for such individuals in view of the "New Unclearness" of both aesthetic and economic situations. Composers from Eastern Europe in particular will surely come to feel this when suddenly freed from socio-political constraints and exposed to the tender mercies of the market at large.

Few generally recognized "hubs" of contemporary music pretend any longer to the sort of hegemony prevalent a decade or two ago. The major festivals of the 1970s and early 1980s have, by and large, made way for a decentralized network of lower-key events, often supported by local rather than national institutions. Although several names are still current — Donaueschingen, Darmstadt, Holland Festival, Metz, Warsaw, ISCM, etc. — their status has come to be seen as increasingly problematic in a time of general belt-tightening and reduced expectations. It might be argued that this is a wholly positive phenomenon, insofar as the future belongs to a different species of internationalization (by implication more modest, realistic and egalitarian). My own feeling, though, is that the elimination of the sort of collision of resources and vision which such major events have often occasioned would ultimately prove a serious impoverishment, leaving the field of large-scale productions to opera and smorgasbords of "personality cult"-influenced television spectacles, themselves often enough the instruments of political or industrial interests.

In spite of all these cavils, the scope of contemporary music making has never been wider, its role and its application never more open to negotiation in the public forum. This is surely all to the good. In any event, I wish this present attempt to map, however provisionally, the essential contours of current creative activity all the best. A book of these dimensions and scope has been absent for all too long.

BRIAN FERNEYHOUGH

ADVISERS

Susan Bradshaw
Reginald Smith Brindle
Gavin Bryars
Chou Wen-chung
Jenny Dawson
Simon Emmerson
Akin Euba
Brian Ferneyhough
Keith Howard
Gerard McBurney
Odaline de la Martinez
David Revill
Yukiko Sawabe
Paul R. Schulman
Richard Steinitz

CONTRIBUTORS

Byron Adams
Julian Anderson
Virginia Anderson
Enrique Alberto Arias
Hans Åstrand
Tico Bann
Richard Barrett
Richard Rodney Bennett
Björn Billing
Kenneth Birkin
Michael Blake
Amanda Botha
Paul Boursin
Meirion Bowen
Susan Bradshaw
Lidia Bramani
Peter Brask
Andres Briner
Cynthia Clark Brown
Gavin Bryars
Eleanor Caldwell
Costin Cazaban
Chen Yi
Chew Shyh-ji
Thomas Clark
Hugo Cole
Pamela Collins
Sten Dahlstedt
Lyn Davies
Michael Dawney
Jenny Dawson
Jan Dehner
Corazon C. Dioquino
P.A.F. Dixon
David Drew
Roderic Dunnett
Giles Easterbrook
Stephen W. Ellis
Ronald F. Erin
Alan Feinberg
Oleg Felzer
Aloys Fleischmann
Henry Fogel
Curd Frosak
Anthony Gilbert
Patrick Gillis
Nikša Gligo
Loretta Goldberg
Frederic Goossen
Ian Grey
Aleksandr Grinberg
Max Harrison
Harald Herresthal
Howard Hersh
Christian Hertzog
Pierre Heureux
Malcolm J. Hill
Christiane ten Hoopen
Paul Horner
Keith Howard
Andrew Hugill
Bernard Jocobson
Jan Jacoby
Lana Kay Johns
Rosemary Johnson
Richard Elfyn Jones
Russell Kane
Ivan Karp
Oleg Karp
Rolf Klein
Werner Klüppelholz
Hartmut Krones
Charles Lao
Margaret Lion
Graham Lock
Nicola Losseff
Emmanuelle Loubet
Henk Maarten
Signe Maarten
Neil Mackay
Kyril Maslin
Kenny Mathieson
Nouritza Matossian
Robert Matthew-Walker
Michael Matthews
James W. May
Robert Maycock
Sally Mays
Gerard McBurney
Hamish Milne
William Mival
Sukphal Mody
Brian Morton
R. Peter Mueller
Isaac Musa
Rachel Myers
Severine Neff
Karl Neumann

Michael Newman
Joachim Noller
Margit Nonbo
Helmer Norgaard
Paul Norman
Denise Ondishko
Stefan Orgass
Christine Paquelet
Vivian Perlis
James E. Perone
Lionel Pike
Anthony Pople
Keith Potter
Cergio Prudencio
Thérèse Radic
Caroline A. Rae
Basil Ramsey
Sven Ravnkilde
Lennart Reimers
Gena Renk
David Revill
Renée Reznek
Alan Rich
Guy Rickards
Hans Roosenschoon
Mary Elizabeth Rörich
Sean Rourke
C. Bryan Rulon
Michael Sahl
A. Sanin
Svetlana Sarkisyan
Yukiko Sawabe
Guido Scarpone
Dieter Schoof
Ciro G. Scotto
Ian Shanahan
Ivan Shearer
Miyuki Shiraishi
Mark Sinker
Geoff Smith
Nicola Walker Smith
Richard Stein
Richard Steinitz
Robert Stevenson
Andrew Stewart
Roderick Swanston
William Sweeney
Kathleen Thomerson
Richard Townend
David Tsang
Mário Vieira de Carvalho
Richard Washington
Bea Weir
Ian Weir
James Weir
Judith Weir
Lawrence Whiffin
Nicholas Williams
Michael Wolpe
Ronald Woodley
David Wright
Velia Yedra
Zhou Long
Jean Zurabian

ENTRANTS

Komei Abe
Hans Abrahamsen
John Adams
Kalevi Aho
William Albright
Haim Alexander
Franghiz Ali-Zadeh
Carlos Roqué Alsina
Gilbert Amy
Beth Anderson
Louis Andriessen
Boris Arapov
Violet Archer
Dominick Argento
Malcolm Arnold
Vyacheslav Artyomov
Robert Ashley
Larry Austin

Milton Babbitt
Sven-Erik Bäck
Simon Bainbridge
Sándor Balassa
Claude Ballif
Alain Bancquart
Elsa Barraine
Richard Barrett
Gerald Barry
Leslie Bassett
Alison Bauld
François Bayle
Irwin Bazelon
Janet Beat
Betty Beath
David Bedford
George Benjamin
Richard Rodney Bennett
Nils Viggo Bentzon
Erik Bergman
Luciano Berio
Lennox Berkeley
Michael Berkeley
Pierre Bernard
Leonard Bernstein
Antonio Bibalo
Harrison Birtwistle
David Blake
Howard Blake
William Bolcom
Pierre Boulez
Brian Boydell
Glenn Branca
Henry Brant
Anthony Braxton
Martin Bresnick
Reginald Smith Brindle
Alexander Brott
Christopher Brown
Earle Brown, Jr
Colin Brumby
Gavin Bryars
Gunnar Bucht
Harold Budd

John Buller
Anthony Burgess
Geoffrey Burgon
Francis Burt
Alan Bush
Geoffrey Bush
Sylvano Bussotti
Martin Butler

John Cage
Charles Camilleri
Edwin Carr
Elliott Carter
John Casken
Friedrich Cerha
Joel Chadabe
Luciano Chailly
Levon Chaushian
Charles Chaynes
Chen Yi
Barney Childs
Chou Wen-chung
Aldo Clementi
Johann Cloete
Barry Conyngham
Arnold Cooke
Aaron Copland
Roque Cordero
John Corigliano
Edward Cowie
Lyell Cresswell
Gordon Crosse
George Crumb
Curtis O. B. Curtis-Smith

Peter Maxwell Davies
Norman Dello Joio
David Del Tredici
Edison Denisov
Luís de Pablo
David Diamond
Peter Dickinson
Emma Lou Diemer
James Dillon
Violeta Dinescu
Lucia Dlugoszewski
Georgy Dmitriev
Friedhelm Döhl
Franco Donatoni
James Drew
George Dreyfus
Jacob Druckman
Hugues Dufourt
Zsolt Durko
Pascal Dusapin
Henri Dutilleux

David Earl
Petr Eben
Mikael Edlund
George Edwards
Ross Edwards
Gottfried von Einem

Brian Elias
Anders Eliasson
Simon Emmerson
Einar Englund
Donald Erb
Ivan Eröd
Akin Euba

David Farquhar
Ivan Fedele
Richard Felciano
Jindřich Feld
Howard Ferguson
Brian Ferneyhough
Luc Ferrari
Vivian Fine
Ross Lee Finney
Michael Finnissy
Elena Firsova
Jacqueline Fontyn
Lukas Foss
Jennifer Fowler
Erika Fox
Jean Françaix
Peter Racine Fricker
James Fulkerson

Blas Galindo
John Gardner
Ge Gan-ru
John Maxwell Geddes
Rolf Gehlhaar
Michael Gielen
Helen Gifford
Anthony Gilbert
Janice Giteck
Philip Glass
Vinko Globokar
Alexander Goehr
Henryk Górecki
Morton Gould
Ulf Grahn
Gérard Grisey
Eric Gross
HK Gruber
Sofia Gubaidulina
Pelle Gudmundsen-Holmgreen
Alexander Gugel

Cristobal Halffter
Haflidi Halgrimsson
Bengt Hambraeus
Iain Hamilton
John Harbison
Edward Harper
Lou Harrison
Jonathan Harvey
Sorrel Hays
He Lu-ting
Åse Hedstrøm
Paavo Heininen
Hans Henkemans
Hans Werner Henze
Anders Hillborg
Lejaren A. Hiller, Jr
Christopher Hobbs
Alun Hoddinott

York Höller
Heinz Holliger
Robin Holloway
Vagn Holmboe
Simon Holt
Bo Holten
Toshio Hosokawa
Simon Hovanessian
Alan Hovhaness
Egil Hovland
Vic Hoyland
Leonid Hrabovsky
Hsu Tsang-houei
Nicolaus A. Huber
Keith Humble
Michael Hurd
Karel Husa
Ketil Hvoslef
Hwang Byung-ki

Toshio Ichiyanagi
Andrew Imbrie
Martin Israelyan

Carlos Jiménez-Mabarak
Betsy Jolas
Daniel Jones
Wilfred Josephs
John Joubert

Mauricio Kagel
Jouni Kaipainen
Viktor Kalabis
Giya Kancheli
Kang Sukhi
Dmitri Kapyrin
Faraj Karayev
Nikolai Karetnikov
Maurice Karkoff
Yuri Kasparov
Roland Kayn
Milko Kelemen
Rudolf Kelterborn
Kent Kennan
Aaron Jay Kernis
Otto Ketting
Tristan Keuris
Earl Kim
Kim Young Dong
Leon Kirchner
Peter Klatzow
Alexander Knaifel
Oliver Knussen
Gottfried Michael Koenig
Joonas Kokkonen
Barbara Kolb
Jo Kondo
Elena Konshina
Marek Kopelent
Nikolai Korndorf
Petr Kotik
Ernst Krenek
Ladislav Kupkovič
György Kurtág
Johan Kvandal
Otomar Kvěch

Joan La Barbara
Helmut Lachenmann
Ezra Laderman
Marcel Landowski
Jean Langlais
Paul Lansky
Libby Larsen
Alexander Lasoń
Anne LeBaron
Roman Ledenyov
Noel Lee
Benjamin Lees
Ton de Leeuw
Nicola LeFanu
Michaël Levinas
Ingvar Lidholm
Rolf Liebermann
György Ligeti
Douglas Lilburn
Magnus Lindberg
George Lloyd
Jonathan Lloyd
Vassily Lobanov
Annea Lockwood
Theo Loevendie
Anestis Logothetis
Fernando Lopes-Graça
Bent Lorentzen
Ivana Loudová
Alvin Lucier
Otto Luening
David Lumsdaine
Gudrun Lund
Witold Lutosławski

Ma Shui-long
Jose Maceda
François-Bernard Mâche
Tod Machover
James MacMillan
Elizabeth Maconchy
Jan Maegaard
Mary Mageau
Mesias Maiguashca
Ivo Malec
Tigran Mansurian
Giacomo Manzoni
Bunita Marcus
Roger Marsh
Donald Martino
Steve Martland
Tauno Marttinen
William Mathias
Yori-Aki Matsudaira
Yoritsune Matsudaira
Teizo Matsumura
Colin Matthews
David Matthews
Bernadetta Matuszczak
Nicholas Maw
Toshiro Mayuzumi
John McCabe
Edward McGuire
Wilfrid Mellers
Arne Mellnäs
Gian Carlo Menotti
Olivier Messiaen

Krzysztof Meyer
Costin Miereanu
Richard Mills
Anthony Milner
Edvard Mirzoyan
Akira Miyoshi
Meredith Monk
Stephen Montague
Xavier Montsalvatge
Dominic Muldowney
Gordon Mumma
Tristan Murail
Thea Musgrave

Conlon Nancarrow
Marc Neikrug
Stefan Niculescu
Tage Nielsen
Serge Nigg
Marlos Nobre
Luigi Nono
Pehr Henrik Nordgren
Arne Nordheim
Per Nørgård
Ib Nørholm
Emmanuel Nunes
Knut Nystedt

Maurice Ohana
Stephen Oliver
Pauline Oliveros
Julián Orbón
Cecilie Ore
Robin Orr
Nigel Osborne

Paik Byung-dong
Priti Paintal
Andrzej Panufnik
Graciela Paraskevaídis
Ian Parrott
Arvo Pärt
Paul Patterson
Stephen Paulus
Anthony Payne
Jorge Peixinho
Georgy Peletsis
Krzysztof Penderecki
Goffredo Petrassi
Ivo Petrić
Daniel Pinkham
Hubert du Plessis
Andrew Poppy
Henri Pousseur
Mel Powell
Folke Rabe
Phillip Ramey
Bernard Rands
György Ránki
Alexander Raskatov
Karl Aage Rasmussen
Einojuhani Rautavaara
Steve Reich
Aribert Reimann
Michèle Reverdy
Roger Reynolds
Vittorio Rieti

Wolfgang Rihm
George Rochberg
Hans Roosenschoon
Ned Rorem
Niels Rosing-Schow
Stepan Rostomian
Poul Ruders
Zbigniew Rudzinski
Daryl Runswick
Terje Rypdal
Frederic Rzewski

Kaija Saariaho
Harald Saeverud
Aulis Sallinen
Erkki Salmenhaara
Jan Sandström
Guido Santorsola
Ramon Santos
Somei Satoh
David Sawer
Robert Saxton
R. Murray Schafer
Peter Schat
Tona Scherchen
Dieter Schnebel
Alfred Schnittke
Gunther Schuller
Andrew Schultz
William Schuman
Gerard Schurmann
Elliott Schwartz
Wolfgang von Schweinitz
Kurt Schwertsik
Salvatore Sciarrino
Peter Sculthorpe
Leif Segerstam
Harold Shapero
Ralph Shapey
Rodion Shchedrin
Alexander Shchetinsky
Robert Sheff
Robert Sherlaw Johnson
Makoto Shinohara
Vladislav Shoot
Robert Simpson
Ezra Sims
Alvin Singleton
Howard Skempton
Synne Skouen
Klement Slavický
Denis Smalley
Dmitri Smirnov
Naresh Sohal
Stephen Sondheim
Bent Sørensen
Carolyn Steinberg
Roger Steptoe
Karlheinz Stockhausen
Richard Stoker
Morton Subotnick

Carlos Surinach
Viktor Suslin
Georgy Sviridov
Giles Swayne
William Sweeney
Richard Swift
Sándor Szokolay
Pawel Szymanski

Toru Takemitsu
Karen Tanaka
Vladimir Tarnopolsky
John Tavener
Boris Tchaikovsky
Virgil Thomson
Michael Tippett
Boris Tishchenko
Ton-That Tiet
Joan Tower
Harold Truscott
Mark-Anthony Turnage

Chinary Ung
Galina Ustvolskaya
Joshua Uzoigwe

Nancy Van de Vate
Aurelio de la Vega
Gerard Victory
Anatol Vieru
Alejandro Viñao
Carl Vine
Kevin Volans
Klaas de Vries

Judith Weir
Karl-Erik Welin
Richard Wernick
John White
Gillian Whitehead
Malcolm Williamson
Olly Wilson
Thomas Wilson
Trevor Wishart
Christian Wolff
John Woolrich
Wu Zuqiang
Charles Wuorinen

Iannis Xenakis

Yi Sanggyu
Yi Sŏngch'ŏn
Julian Jing-Jun Yu
Isang Yun

Jeanne Zaidel-Rudolph
Zhou Long
Ján Zimmer
Ashot Zohrabian
Ellen Taaffe Zwilich

CONTEMPORARY COMPOSERS

ABE, Komi [Komei]. Japanese. Born in Hiroshima, 1 September 1911. Educated at Tokyo Academy of Music (cello under H. Werkmeister), 1929–33, (postgraduate composition study under Klaus Pringsheim), 1933–6; conducting (privately) with Joseph Rosenstock, 1935–9. Served as Able Seaman, Japanese Navy, September 1944–August 1945. Married Midori Abe in May 1939; 1 daughter. Professor, 1953–77, dean of music department, 1969–74, and since 1977 Professor Emeritus, Kyoto Municipal University of Arts. Recipient: F. Weingartner Prize; Mainich Music Prize; Education Minister's Art Encouragement Prize (for Symphony No 1), 1958. Mailing address: 2-7-12 Shakujiidai Nerima-ku, 177 Tokyo, Japan.

Publishers: Ongaku no Tomo Edition, 6-30 Kagurazaka Shijuku-ku, Tokyo; Kyodo Music Publishing, 1-16-15 Kitasenzaku Ota-ku, Tokyo; Zen-On, Tokyo.

Symphonies/orchestral:

Kleine Suite 1935; first performed Shanghai, 1936.
Theme and Variations 1936; first performed Tokyo, 8 February 1936.
Concerto for Cello and Orchestra 1940; first performed Tokyo, 31 March 1942.
Pastoral (piano, orchestra) 1946; first performed Tokyo, 27 March 1947.
Divertimento (alto saxophone, orchestra) 1951, orchestrated 1953; first performed Tokyo, 1952.
Symphony No 1 1956; first performed Tokyo, 9 May 1957.
Symphony No 2 1958–9; first performed Tokyo, 10 October 1960.
Serenade 1962; first performed Tokyo, 7 October 1963.
Sinfonietta 1965; first performed Tokyo, 14 January 1965.
Piccola Sinfonia (strings) 1984; first performed Hiroshima, 1985.

Chamber/instrumental:

String Quartet No 1 1935; first performed Tokyo, 1935.
String Quartet No 2 1937; first performed Tokyo, 1937.
String Quartet No 3 1939; first performed Tokyo, 1939.
String Quartet No 4 1943; first performed Tokyo, 1943.
Flute Sonata No 1 (flute, piano) 1942; first performed Tokyo, 1942.
Clarinet Quintet 1945; first performed Tokyo, 1946.
String Quartet No 5 1946; first performed Tokyo, 1947.
Flute Sonata No 2 (flute, piano) 1948; first performed Tokyo, 1949.
String Quartet No 6 1948; first performed Tokyo, 1949.
String Quartet No 7 1950; first performed Tokyo, 1950.
Divertimento (alto saxophone, piano) 1951; first performed Tokyo, 1951.
String Quartet No 8 1952; first performed Tokyo, 1955.
Divertimento for Nine Instruments (flute, oboe, clarinet, bassoon, 2 violins, viola, cello, piano) 1954; first performed Tokyo, 1955.
String Quartet No 9 1956; first performed Tokyo, 1956.
Sextet (flute, clarinet, violin, viola, cello, piano) 1964; first performed Tokyo, 1964.
A Picture Book for Children (piano) 1967.
Three Sonatinas for Children (piano) 1971.
Variations on a Subject by Grieg (4 trumpets, 4 horns, 3 trombones, tuba) 1972.
String Quartet No 10 1978; first performed Tokyo, 1980.
String Quartet No 11 1982; first performed Washington, D.C., 1983.
String Quartet No 12 1987; first performed Tokyo, 1989.
String Quartet No 13 1989; first performed Tokyo, 1990.
String Quartet No 14 1990; first performed Tokyo, 1991.

* * *

Komei Abe belongs to the generation of composers who, except for few cases, were not affected by the second wave of new music starting with serialism in the 1950s. Especially in Japan the reception of contemporary western music has been difficult if not, until 1945, almost impossible. The distinct conservatism of Japan's musical life, which was already completely occupied with coping with the advent of 19th-century European music, prevented any interest in the development of modern music. Additionally, the sheer geographical distance of a country to be reached only by a several months' ship voyage did not exactly invite qualified composition teachers from the West. Again, as the most advanced contemporary style of the first half of the century, atonality and twelve-note technique of the Second Viennese School, was not really accepted in the West itself until the 1950s, no one of the few teachers who actually came to Japan, could be expected to mediate anything other than his own traditional background. Abe studied with one of these teachers, K. Pringsheim, who worked in Japan during the 1930s and World War II. Pringsheim came from the neoromantic Munich school around Louis and Thuille and his musical horizon went hardly beyond Wagner, Mahler and Strauss. Born in the same year as Webern he was one of the many opponents to Schoenberg's music.

Thus it is not surprising that Abe never took part in any of the progressive movements which arrived in Japan after the war. Throughout the long time of his compositional vita beginning with his first string quartet in 1935 he remained faithful to the German academism of his teacher. Although some of his works tackle atonality, most of them stay within the limits of an expanded tonality. Since he adhered to his style with almost no change for the largest part of his life, a look at some of his string quartets—No. 9 to No. 12—reveals the basic characteristics of his music.

Following the classical scheme most of the works consist of four movements. Their order of tempos is the conventional one of fast outer movements and a slow movement either in the second or third place. The first movements present two themes which are exposed and developed in conformity with the standards of the sonata form. The slow movements use the ternary song form. Scherzos with very fast tempos precede final movements employing free rondo sonata form. These formal principles do not necessarily mean traditionalism since composers like Schoenberg, Berg and Webern used the same formal repertory of classic music. However, the structural elements of Abe's compositions are treated in a way, which, except for tonality, do not exceed the limits reached, say, by Haydn. Abe's melodic lines mainly use narrow intervals provided by a given scale. However, one can observe his preference for chromatic progressions. This is connected to the harmonic style, which relies on construction in thirds. The impression of an expanded tonality at the edge of its suspension is mainly due to the strong alteration the notes undergo within the tertian texture of chords.

Abe's rhythmical settings generally start with the articulation of the underlying metre, which is always even (based on two or four beats) except for the scherzos (based on three beats). Irregular divisions of beats are restricted to triplets in the faster movements. No rhythmical intricacies like frequent changes of metre, syncopations or unusual note values are allowed to interrupt the regularly structured flow of time. The treatment of the voices changes from homophony to polyphony according to the formal function but in most cases one or two leading voices, preferably the outer parts, are accompanied by subordinate parts.

—Rolf Klein

ABRAHAMSEN, Hans. Danish. Born in Copenhagen, 23 December 1952. Educated at Royal Danish Conservatory of Music, Copenhagen (under Yngve Trede and Bjorn Hjelmborg); also studied horn and composition (under Pelle Gudmundsen-Holmgreen and Per Norgard). Mailing address: c/o Danish Music Information Centre, Vimmelskaftet 48, DK 1161 Copenhagen K, Denmark.

Publishers: Wilhelm Hansen, Copenhagen; Chester Music, London.

Symphonies/orchestral:

Skum / Foam (chamber orchestra) 1970.
Symphony in C 1972.
Stratifications 1973–5.
Symphony No 1 1974.
Nacht und Trompeten 1981; first performed Berlin, 25 March 1982.

Chamber/instrumental:

Fantasy Pieces after Hans-Jorgen Nielsen (flute, horn, piano/triangle, cello) 1969, revised 1976.
October (piano, left hand) 1969, revised 1976.
Focus (horn, piano, viola) 1970.
Salut-Salut (brass ad lib, 3 percussion) 1970.
Her (string quartet) 1970.
Femblok (flute, bassoon) 1970.
Rundt og imellen / Round and In Between (horn/sheep bells, 2 trumpets/triangles, trombone, tuba) 1971.
Magnolie Satser (flute, oboe, horn, percussion, violin) 1971.
Duet (horn, violin) 1972.
Landskaber / Landscapes (woodwind quintet) 1972.
Four Nocturnes (flute, piano) 1972.
Flowersongs (3 flutes) 1972.
Glansbilleder / Scraps (cello, piano) 1973.
Ten Preludes (string quartet) 1973.
Flush (alto saxophone) 1974, revised 1979.
Double (flute, guitar) 1975.
Winternacht (flute/alto flute/piccolo, clarinet, horn, cornet, piano, violin, cello) 1976–9.
Canzone (accordion) 1978.
Walden (woodwind quintet) 1978.
Puslespil (also given as *Geduldspiel*) (flute, oboe, clarinet, horn, trumpet, piano, 2 violins, viola, cello) 1980.
String Quartet No 2 1981.
Two Small Studies (piano) 1983.
Four Studies (piano) 1983.
Maerchenbilder (flute, oboe, clarinet, bassoon, trumpet, horn, trombone, piano, percussion, 2 violins, viola, cello, double bass) 1984.
Six Pieces (violin, horn, piano) 1984.
Three Studies (piano) 1984.
Two Snow Dances (soprano, alto, tenor, bass recorders; or flute, clarinet, violin, cello) 1985.
Le Trombe del Mattino (piano) 1986.
Winternacht (later version for flute, clarinet, guitar, percussion, piano, violin, cello) 1987.
Lied in Fall (cello solo, flute, cor anglais, clarinet, bassoon, horn, trumpet, trombone, piano, 2 violins, viola, double bass) 1987.
Fanfare (2 violins) 1988.
Storm og stille (cello) 1989; first performed Copenhagen, May 1989.

Vocal/choral:

Somewhere (mezzo-soprano, alto recorder, percussion, cello) 1970.
Under min gronne plante (soprano, flute, horn, percussion, violin, cello) 1970.
Efterar (voice, flute, guitar, cello) 1970–2.
Sangen om os, skoven og trolden (mixed choir) 1971.
Universe Birds (10 sopranos; Holk) 1973.
Songs of Denmark (soprano, flute, clarinet, piano, percussion, viola) 1974, revised 1976.
Aria (soprano, flute, alto saxophone, guitar, percussion; version for soprano, flute, vibraphone/crotales, harp, cello) 1979.
Two Grundtvig Motets (SATB, SSAATTBB choirs) 1983–4.

Other:

Erik Satie: *Trois Gymnopédies* (arranged for oboe, string quartet) 1988.
Carl Nielsen: *Fantasy Pieces* (arranged for oboe, violin, viola, cello) 1988.
Maurice Ravel: *Le Tombeau de Couperin* (arranged for woodwind quintet) 1989.
Carl Nielsen: *Three Pieces for Ten Instruments* (arranged for woodwind quintet, string quartet, double bass) 1989.

* * *

When Hans Abrahamsen completed his *Symphony in C* in 1972, it must have seemed an act of folly at best, critical suicide at worst, to have published such a work at such a time, when tonal writing was at a low ebb and the classical forms subject to only hostile scrutiny.

At first glance it is an extremely simple piece, far removed from the ironies and antagonisms of late modernism. However, that is to read it out of immediate context, for Abrahamsen's early orchestral work was part of a loosely federated musical movement in Denmark known as the New Simplicity. There was nothing regressive about the movement (nor has there been any sign of regression in Abrahamsen's most recent reworkings of work by Satie, Nielsen and Ravel) nor did its adherents subject themselves to any doctrinaire demands. As Abrahamsen interprets it, it is an alternative to modernism, and in particular to the post-serial strain that leads inexorably to what is conveniently known as the New Complexity. In the *Symphony in C*, Abrahamsen utilises the very simplest musical materials; what is distinctive about his style, here and in *Skum*, is that he sees no pressing need to impose any overall harmonic code to the piece, but leaves the components in an "open" relation (this, despite the vigorous counterpoint of the Symphony) which is closer to quilting or dry-stone building (unfortunate that the method should have been christened Concretism) than to collage.

Abrahamsen's music works by very simple oppositions. In his next symphony, numbered one, he contrasts two very different movements, one good generic sonata-form, the other altogether more fugitive, in such a way as to suggest that the second is not just a modulation of the first, but a reworking of it; as if to prove the point, the dominant rhythm of the first movement reasserts itself towards the end of the symphony, in a manner curiously reminiscent of Shostakovitch (though it may come from nearer at hand, in Sibelius or even Vagn Holmboe). There are clear oppositions at work in the wind piece *Walden*, inspired by the American Transcendentalist Henry David Thoreau, whose moody and occasionally rancorous pastoralism is expertly caught in Abrahamsen's sardonic homage, which takes the "concretist" manner very much further, and even further from its origins, than either *Landscapes*, an earlier woodwind quintet, or the big *Stratifications*, finished three years before. Here, the original material is so transformed as to disappear, much as the fundamental musical information disappears in the young British composer George Benjamin's recent *Cascade*. The difference between them is striking, for whereas Benjamin is all movement, Abrahamsen seems to prefer a steady, almost geological, accretion and mass which nonetheless sits lightly on the orchestra.

Unlike Benjamin, who has only recently moved away from a chordal style heavily dependent on Messiaen, Abrahamsen is a fine composer of chamber and vocal music. Apart from the two woodwind quintets, there are two powerful string quartets, and very striking music for combinations of flute with other instruments. The best of these is *Double* which pairs flute, doubling alto flute, with guitar; some of Abrahamsen's deceptive naiveté remains, but there is a new complexity, independent of the language of that movement, but intriguingly anticipative of some of Brian Ferneyhough's recent work for flutes. The guitar—like the accordion in *Canzone*—remains to remind us that this is music on a human scale.

Abrahamsen called his first composition for string quartet *Ten Preludes*, a curiously down-played and tentative title (that again intriguingly recalls Ferneyhough's *Sonatas* for string quartet). Abrahamsen's second numbered quartet for strings moves as far as possible from the light manner of its predecessor. For it he adopted a drastically revised style, in which the typical three-note cells of his earlier style are subjected to all manner of curious interventions and transformations; the music hockets dramatically, dances away down false corridors, and climaxes furiously (and repeatedly). Nothing that Abrahamsen has written since quite matches the second String Quartet for sheer power, though *Maerchenbilder* of 1984, for chamber ensemble, has something of its unifying energy and brilliant handling of disparate material.

By appearing to look backwards, Abrahamsen has achieved more than he might had he embraced a more self-conscious progressivism. Along with Per Norgard and Pelle Gudmundsen-Holmgreen, his one-time teachers, he is one of the most significant Danish composers since Nielsen.

—Henk Maarten

ADAMS, John (Coolidge). American. Born in Worcester, Massachusetts, 15 February 1947. Educated: studied clarinet with father and under Felix Viscuglia; Dartmouth College, Hanover, New Hampshire; (conducting under Mario di Bonaventura, 1965); Harvard University, Cambridge, Massachusetts, (composition under Leon Kirchner), B.A., 1969; M.A., 1971. Freelance clarinetist, since 1967. Composer in residence, Marlboro Festival, 1970; teacher, director, New Music Ensemble, San Francisco Conservatory, 1972–82; new music advisor, San Francisco Symphony Orchestra, since 1978; composer in residence, 1982–5. Creative chair, St Paul Chamber Orchestra, since 1988. Recipient: Guggenheim Fellowship, 1982; "Grammy" Award for Best Contemporary Composition (for *Nixon in China*), 1989. Mailing address: c/o Boosey & Hawkes, 24 East 21st Street, New York, New York 10010, U.S.A.

Publishers: Associated; Boosey & Hawkes.

Symphonies/orchestral:

Common Tones in Simple Time 1979.
Grand Pianola Music (2 soprano voices, 2 pianos, small orchestra) 1981–2. Recorded HMV CDC7 47331–2.
Shaker Loops (arranged for string orchestra) 1983. Recorded Philips 412 214–2.
Harmonielehre 1984–5. Recorded col legno 0647 288.
Short Ride in a Fast Machine 1986; first performed Mansfield, Massachusetts, 13 June 1986.
Tromba lontana 1986; first performed Houston, Texas, 4 April 1986.
The Chairman Dances 1986.
Fearful Symmetries (orchestra or chamber orchestra) 1988; first performed New York City, 29 October 1988.
Eros Piano (piano, orchestra or chamber orchestra) 1989; first performed London, 24 November 1989.

Chamber/instrumental:

Piano Quintet 1970.
American Standard (unspecified instrumentation) 1973.
China Gates (piano) 1977.
Phrygian Gates (piano) 1977. Recorded TROY 038–2; New Albion Records 007.
Shaker Loops (string septet) 1978. Recorded New Albion Records 007.
Light over Water (part of dance piece *Available Light*; brass, synthesizers) 1983. Recorded New Albion Records NA 005.

Vocal/choral:

Christian Zeal and Activity (speaker on tape, orchestra) 1973; first performed San Francisco, 23 March 1973.
Grounding (3 solo voices, instruments, electronics) 1975.
Harmonium (SATB choir, orchestra; Donne, Dickinson) 1980.
The Wound Dresser (baritone, orchestra or chamber orchestra; Whitman) 1989; first performed St Paul, Minnesota, 24 February 1989.

Opera:

Nixon in China (Goodman) 1987; first performed Houston, Texas, 22 October 1987. Recorded Nonesuch 979 193 4.

Other:

Onyx (tape) 1976.
Saxophone (video tape collaboration with M. Fisher) 1976.
Matter of Heart (film score), 1982.
Available Light (dance music to choreography by Lucinda Childs) 1983.

Liszt: *Berceuse Elégiaque* (arranged for chamber orchestra) 1989; first performed St Paul, Minnesota, 9 June 1989.
Liszt: *La Lugubre Gondole No 2* (arranged for orchestra or chamber orchestra) 1989; first performed St Paul, Minnesota, 27 October 1989.
Liszt: *Wiegenlied* (arranged for orchestra or chamber orchestra) 1989; first performed London, 24 November 1989.

PUBLICATIONS

On Adams: A. Porter, "Bay Laurels", in *New Yorker*, 10 August 1981; Tim Page, "Framing the River: a Minimalist Picture", in *HiFi*, 31 (11), 1981; M. Walsh, "The Heart Is Back in the Game", in *Time*, 20 September 1982; G. Sandow, "Tasting the New Era", in *Village Voice*, 29 January 1985.

* * *

While the so-called Minimalist or Systems mode has been the subject of much critical suspicion, it has also attracted the largest audience of any style of serious contemporary composition. Although he emerged a full decade later, John Adams has been bracketed with Steve Reich (whose influence he acknowleges) and Philip Glass, almost as though their music was in some way interchangeable. In fact, each of the main composers involved in this field has evolved a quite distinct voice within a broadly shared language.

While the classification Minimalism is as useless as most of the piecemeal terminology which has been allowed to attach itself to musical forms, Adams undoubtedly employs the principal constituents of the style, notably repetition and the use of tonal harmony, but his music is by no means minimal in a harmonic or textural sense.

Adams's early works were in a quite different style, although *American Standard* clearly foreshadowed the parodistic approach he would bring to the more substantial (and controversial—the composer considered withdrawing the work at one point, but wisely retained his faith in it) *Grand Pianola Music*. Following a period of experiment with electronic music, Adams turned to the style which he has developed since.

His first significant work, *Shaker Loops*, was initially written for a seven-piece string ensemble, but was subsequently rescored for the San Francisco Symphony in 1983. The composer played with the idea of trills and loops in the four-movement piece, inspired (if in rather parodic fashion) by the ecstatic shaking and trembling practised by members of the Millenial Church, or Shakers, whose plaintive hymn *'Tis a Gift to Be Simple* provided a memorable theme for Aaron Copland's *Appalachian Spring*.

Phrygian Gates, a piece for solo piano, explored the circle of fifths, but revealed his concern with large-scale structural planning in its arch-like construction. Most of his subsequent work has been written for large orchestras, although the multi-referential *Grand Pianola Music*, with its gently mocking nods toward musical touchstones from gospel and marches to Beethoven, is scored for a smaller orchestra, while the shifting, beautifully integrated textural patterns of *Light over Water* are shared by synthesizer (an instrument which Adams plays on the recording, and which he has used with increasing frequency in an orchestral context) and brass.

If his first large orchestral work, *Common Tones in Simple Time*, fell comfortably enough into a pure and literally minimal mode, *Harmonium*, a setting of poems by John Donne and Emily Dickinson scored for a massive orchestra and choir, employed its steady pulse and harmonic repetition in an unprecedentedly expansive context which defies the minimalist tag.

Huge, ecstatic choruses leap out from brooding, introspective passages; the effect is genuinely symphonic in scope and texture, while the work is freighted with the (occasionally almost Romantic) expressivity which many detractors find missing in the work of the allegedly minimalist composers.

Adams has commented that his more serious, darker works like *Harmonium* seem to oblige him to compose a lighter companion piece, which he characterises as his "Trickster", an "ironic wild card that threatens to lose me whatever friends the previous composition might have gained".

Just as *Harmonium* required a *Grand Pianola Music*, so the later *Harmonielehre*, another massive, intensely dramatic orchestral work, called out the playful *The Chairman Dances*.

The latter was a precursor to his first opera, *Nixon in China*, based on a heroic rather than satirical treatment (the libretto in rhyming couplets is by poet Alice Goodman) of President Richard Nixon's six-day visit to China in 1972, which followed on the success of Philip Glass's large-scale stage works.

The complex music is something of a summation of Adams's various shifts and emphases of style to that point, and exhibits the by now customary subtlety of harmonic effects and instrumental timbre and colour, allied to a strong rhythmic directness.

His orchestral setting of part of Walt Whitman's Civil War poem *The Wound Dresser* concentrates on the poet's poignant evocation of tending the sick and injured. As in *Harmonium*, the composer remains vividly aware of the need to respect the integral rhythms of the poetry within the music.

The Wound Dresser also has its own "Trickster" companion piece in the jagged, quirky burlesque *Fearful Symmetries* which, like *Grand Pianola Music*, draws on a wide range of musical references to good musical and comic effect. Adams is at work on another large operatic project. His music should not be confused with that of the Alaskan composer of the same name.

—Kenny Mathieson

AHO, Kalevi. Finnish. Born in Forssa, 9 March 1949. Educated at Sibelius Academy, Helsinki (under Einojuhani Rautavaara), 1968–1971, diploma in composition; Staatliche Hochsschule für Musik und Darstellende Kunst, Berlin (under Boris Blacher), 1971–2. Lecturer, department of musicology, University of Helsinki, since 1974. Recipient: Leonie Sonning Award (Denmark), 1974. Mailing address: Taivaskalliontie 15, SF-00600 Helsinki, Finland.

Publisher: Finnish Music Information Centre.

Symphonies/orchestral:

Symphony No 1 1969; first performed Helsinki, 18 February 1971.
Symphony No 2 1970; first performed Helsinki, 17 April 1973.
Symphony No 3: Sinfonia concertante (violin, orchestra) 1971–3; first performed Helsinki, 20 February 1975.
Symphony No 4 1972–3; first performed Helsinki, 12 March 1974.
Symphony No 5 1975–6; first performed Helsinki, 19 April 1977.
Chamber Symphony 1976; first performed Helsinki, 22 August 1976.
Symphony No 6 1979–80; first performed Helsinki, 13 February 1980.
Concerto for Violin and Orchestra 1981; first performed Helsinki, 29 September 1982.
Hiljaisuus/Silence 1982; first performed Helsinki, 9 October 1985.
Concerto for Cello and Orchestra 1983–4; first performed Helsinki, 1 September 1984.
Fanfare for YS (4 horns, 4 trumpets, 2 trombones, tuba) 1986; first performed Helsinki, 18 April 1986.
Symphony No 7: "Hyonteissinfonia/Insect Symphony" 1988; first performed Helsinki, 26 October 1988.
Concerto for Piano and Orchestra 1989.

Chamber/instrumental:

String Quartet No 2 1970; first performed Helsinki, 18 November 1970.
String Quartet No 3 1971; first performed Helsinki, 6 October 1971. Recorded Finlandia FA 348.
Quintetto per oboe e quartetto archi (oboe, string quartet) 1973; first performed Jyväskylä, Finland, 2 July 1974. Recorded Finlandia FA 320.
Sonata (violin) 1973; first performed Helsinki, 17 April 1978.
Prelude, Toccata and Postlude (cello, piano) 1974; first performed Helsinki, 14 February 1977.
Solo I (Tumultos) (violin) 1975; first performed Kaustinen, Finland, 26 January 1986.
Quintet (flute, oboe, violin, viola, cello) 1977; first performed Helsinki, 24 March 1983.
Quintet (bassoon, string quartet) 1977; first performed Helsinki, 16 January 1978. Recorded Finlandia FA 340.
Ludus Solemnis (organ) 1978; first performed Forssa, Finland, 3 June 1979.
Sonata (piano) 1980; first performed Helsinki, 6 September 1980. Recorded Finlandia FA 332.
In Memoriam (Juha Mannerkorpi) (organ) 1980; first performed Honkanummi, Finland, 27 September 1980.
Quartet (flute, alto saxophone, guitar, percussion) 1982; first performed Amsterdam, 1 October 1982.
Sonata (accordion) 1984.
Hamaran laulu (Das Lied der Dämmerung) (violin, harp) 1984.
Three Melodies (1–4 kanteles) 1984; first performed Kaustinen, Finland, June 1985.
Sonata (oboe, piano) 1984–5; first performed Helsinki 26 March 1985.
Solo II (piano) 1985; first performed Helsinki, 27–8 February 1986. Recorded SALP-5.
Inventions (oboe, cello) 1986.

Vocal/choral:

Lasimaalaus/Stained Glass (female choir; Meriluoto) 1975; first performed Forssa, Finald, 16 May 1975. Recorded Finnlevy SFX 52; Forssa Fo Na 40–1; Campanella Cam-02.
Kolme laulua elamasta/Three Songs about Life (tenor, piano; Lehmonen) 1977; broadcast Finnish Broadcasting Company, 23 October 1978.
Hiljaisuus/Silence (mixed choir; Manninen) 1978; first performed Helsinki, 23 April 1986.
Sheherazade (mixed choir; Manninen) 1978; first performed Tampere, Finland, 2 June 1979.

Opera:

Avain/The Key (chamber opera for solo singer, chamber orchestra; Mannerkorpi) 1978–9; first performed Helsinki, 4 September 1979.
Hyonteiselamaa/Insect Life (after Karel and Josef Capek) 1985–7.

Other:

Modest Mussorgsky: *Songs and Dances of Death* (arranged and orchestrated) 1984; first performed Minneapolis, Minnesota, 1 October 1984.
J.S. Bach: *Contrapunctus XI* (arranged and orchestrated) 1984; broadcast 21 March 1985; first concert performance Helsinki, 24 August 1985.
Leevi Madetoja: *Lauluseppele* (arranged for male choir; text by Pohjanpaa) 1987; first performed Joensuu, Finland, 23 June 1988.
Uuno Klami: Act I of ballet *Pyorteita* (arranged and orchestrated) 1988; first performed Turku, Finland, 19 August 1988.

PUBLICATIONS

By Aho: *Suomalainen musiikki ja Kalevala/Finnish Music and the Kalevala*, Manttaa, 1985; "Modest Mussorgsky under the Orchestrator's Knife", in *Finnish Music Quarterly*, 1, 1987; articles on music and musical theory.

On Aho: Tarasti Eero, "The Key to KA", in *Finnish Music Quarterly*, 2, 1987; Kimmo Korhonen, "Tyyli ja sen kehittyminen KA sonfonoissa", dissertation, Helsinki, 1988.

* * *

Kalevi Aho's main works follow a polyphonic elaboration of traditional sonata movements. He frequently gives solo roles to his own instrument, the violin, while many of his pieces relate to irony, nostalgia, humour and even the insect world. Aho's compositions prior to 1975 show the influence (sometimes in the form of direct parody) of Mahler, Shostakovitch, the fugal forms of the neo-baroque as well as his teachers; after

1975 the influence of György Ligeti has been most apparent.

The first movement of Aho's *Symphony No 1* was originally a student-work string quartet, but following the advice of Einojuhani Rautavaara, his teacher at the Sibelius Academy, it was orchestrated in a quasi-Shostakovitch manner, with lines frequently doubled to display the counterpoint. Aho subsequently augmented the movement into a full symphony. The outer movements are fugues built upon a single small-intervalled theme, which becomes transformed into a waltz melody in the ironic second movement. The third movement followed by the waltz's recapitulation becomes the central section of the whole work. With this symphony, Aho created a blueprint for many subsequent compositions: an arch-form with polyphonic outer sections and an emotional climax falling in a late-central section, the whole piece being built on tonal simplicity and frequent repetition. Hence the triple-fugue *Symphony No 2*, with its Mahleresque finale funeral march; and even more typically the *String Quartet No 3* where the sole movement starts simply but gradually incorporates complex polyphony. The arch-form with emotional climax is used here: the most complex area being the fifth of eight sections, later sections progressively develop material from the corresponding earlier section; with this development comes a partial return to the earlier section's degree of simplicity. Aho likened the form to "a horseshoe with the ends bent in different directions".

After further study under Boris Blacher in Berlin, Aho produced a series of compositions featuring the violin, notably a 22-minute *Sonata* for solo violin containing a chaconne and a B-A-C-H fugue; and *Symphony No 3* (Sinfonia concertante), written at the same time as *Symphony No 4*. Aho's style here seems to be overshadowed by Mahlerian ironic twists and sudden changes of atmosphere, various dance rhythms, and extended if riotous climaxes which now become more emotionally charged, if with simpler musical ideas.

With *Symphony No 5*, Aho turned from his earlier polyphony of individual lines to a counterpoint of very disparate musical planes. Here he mixed diverse elements to such an extent that clusters resulted which he then exploited. Thereafter, the highly characterized lines exploiting ethereal voicing are set against Ligeti-like sound-blocks. After the Beethovenian trilling of the piano *Sonata*, sound-blocks are found in Aho's *Symphony No 6* and in *Hiljaisuus* ("Silence"). The latter, generally static and tonal, is rudely interrupted by clusters on brass and organ before quieter music returns and dies away. This five-minute piece was written to serve as a prelude or postlude to his *Concerto for Violin* of the previous year, where a fairly tonal Bergian opening gradually becomes freer during its three movements. In the *Sonata* for oboe and piano, Aho offsets rather than juxtaposes disparate styles, producing a variety of parodying episodes which include microtones and multiphonics. The satirical opera *Hyonteiselamaa* ("Insect Life"), with libretto reconstructed by the composer, demonstrates his stylistic breadth by making various insect species represent different human types. Again Aho is able to produce a work where the change from one style to the next presents one of its basic unities. The opera's orchestral part was later reworked to form *Symphony No 7*, subtitled the "Insect Symphony".

—Malcolm J. Hill

ALBRIGHT, William (Hugh). American. Born in Gary, Indiana, 20 October 1944. Educated at Juillard School Preparatory Department, New York, 1959–1962; University of Michigan, Ann Arbor (under Ross Lee Finney and George Rochberg for composition, Marilyn Mason for organ), 1963–70, B.Mus. 1966, M.Mus. 1967, D.M.A. 1970; Conservatoire de Paris (under Olivier Messiaen), 1970. Has one son and one daughter. Instructor of music, 1970–1, assistant professor of music, 1971–5, associate professor, 1975–82, and professor of music, since 1982, University of Michigan, Ann Arbor; also associate director, electronic music studio, University of Michigan; director of music, First Unitarian Church of Ann Arbor, 1966–85; professional concert and recording pianist/organist. Recipient: Fulbright Fellowship, 1968, 1986; Guggenheim Fellowship, 1976, 1986; American Academy of Arts and Letters Award, 1970; National Endowment for the Arts Fellowships, 1976, 1981, 1984; Queen Marie Jose Prize; Distinguished Teaching Award, University of Michigan. Mailing address: 2555 Roseland Drive, Ann Arbor, Michigan 48103, U.S.A.

Publishers: C.F. Peters, New York; Editions Jobert, Paris.

Symphonies/orchestral:

Alliance (in 3 parts) 1967–70; first performed Buffalo, New York, 1969.
Night Procession (chamber orchestra) 1972; first performed St Paul, Minnesota, 1972.
Gothic Suite (organ, strings, percussion) 1973; first performed Syracuse, New York, 1973.
Introduction, Passacaglia and Rondo Capriccioso 1974; first performed River Falls, Wisconsin, 1974.
Heater (saxophone, band) 1977; first performed Wapinger Falls, New York, 1977.
Bacchanal (organ, orchestra) 1980; first performed Lincoln, Nebraska, 1981.
Chasm; Symphonic Fragment 1988; first performed New York City, 1989.

Chamber/instrumental:

Foils (wind, percussion) 1963–4.
Frescos (woodwind quartet) 1964.
Juba (organ) 1965.
Pianoagogo (piano) 1965–6; first performed Ann Arbor, Michigan, 1967. Recorded CRI.
Two Pieces for Nine Instruments 1965–6.
Pneuma (organ) 1966.
Caroms (8 instruments) 1966; first performed Tanglewood, Massachusetts, 1966.
Organbook I 1967; first performed Ann Arbor, Michigan, 1967. Recorded CRI; Gothic.
Three Original Rags (piano) 1967–8.
Grand Sonata in Rag (piano) 1968; first performed Paris, 1969. Recorded MHS.
Three Novelty Rags (piano) 1968.
Marginal Worlds (12 instruments) 1969–70; first performed Ann Arbor, Michigan, 1970.
The Dream Rags (piano) 1970; first performed Ann Arbor, Michigan, 1971. Recorded MHS.
Organbook II 1971; first performed Ann Arbor, Michigan, 1971. Recorded Nonesuch.
Danse Macabre (violin, cello, flute, clarinet, piano) 1971; first performed New York City, 1971.
Take That (4 drummers) 1972; first performed Ann Arbor, Michigan, 1972.
Stipendium Peccati (organ, piano, percussion) 1973; first performed Hartford, Connecticut, 1973.

Introduction, Passacaglia and Rondo capriccioso (solo tack piano, 8 instruments) 1974.
Dream and Dance (organ, percussion) 1974.
Seven Deadly Sins (7 instruments) 1974; first performed Portland, Oregon, 1974.
Doo-Dah (3 alto saxophones) 1975; first performed Ann Arbor, Michigan, 1975.
Sweet Sixteenths (piano) 1975.
Jericho: Battle Music for Trumpet and Organ (trumpet, organ) 1976; first performed Portland, Oregon, 1976.
Five Chromatic Dances (piano) 1976.
Peace Pipe (2 bassoons) 1976.
Saints Preserve Us (clarinet) 1976.
Shadows (guitar) 1977.
Organbook III 1978; first performed Evansville, Illinois, 1979. Recorded Gothic.
King of Instruments (organ, narrator) 1978; first performed South Bend, Indiana, 1978. Recorded Crystal Records.
Halo (organ, metal instruments) 1978.
Four Fancies (harpsichord) 1979; first performed Evanston, Illinois, 1979. Recorded Gasparo; Kingdom.
De Spiritum (organ, 2 assistants) 1980–1; first performed Denver, Colorado, 1986.
Romance (horn, organ) 1981; first performed Washington, D.C., 1981.
Bacchanal (organ, orchestra) 1981.
The Enigma Syncopations (flute, percussion, organ, double bass) 1982; first performed Wilmington, Delaware, 1982. Recorded Titanic.
That Sinking Feeling (organ) 1982.
In memoriam (organ) 1983.
1732: In memoriam Johannes Albrecht (organ) 1984.
Canon in D (double bass, harpsichord) 1984.
Sonata (alto saxophone, piano) 1984; first performed Ann Arbor, Michigan, 1984. Recorded Capstone Records.
Sphaera (piano, 4-track tape) 1985; first performed Cambridge, Massachusetts, 1985. Recorded Wergo.
Chasm (organ) 1986; first performed Ann Arbor, Michigan, 1986.
Symphony (organ) 1987; first performed Evansville, Illinois, 1987.
Quintet for Clarinet and String Quartet 1987; first performed Portland, Oregon, 1987.
Abiding Passions (woodwind quintet) 1988; first performed Las Vegas, 1988. Recorded Cambria Records.
Whistler Nocturnes (organ) 1989; first performed Cambridge, Massachusetts, 1989.

Vocal/choral:

An Alleluia Super-Round (8 voices, or more) 1973.
Six New Hymns (unison voices, keyboard) 1974–83.
Mass in D (chorus, congregation, organ, percussion) 1974.
Chichester Mass (unaccompanied SATB chorus) 1974. Recorded Gothic.
Pax in terra (alto, tenor, SATB chorus) 1981; first performed Ann Arbor, Michigan, 1981.
David's Songs (soprano, alto, tenor bass/SATB chorus, organ; Psalms) 1982; first performed Minneapolis, Minnesota, 1982.
A Song to David (2 choruses, solo voices, organ, narrator; Smart) 1983.
Take Up the Song (SATB chorus, piano) 1986; first performed Rochester, New York, 1986.
Antigone's Reply (SATB chorus, piano) 1987.
Deum de Deo (SATB chorus, organ) 1989; first performed Lansing, Mississippi, 1989.

Opera:

Cross of Gold (actors, chorus, instruments) 1975; first performed Chicago, 1975.
The Magic City (Garrett) 1978.

Other:

Tic (soloist, 2 ensembles, tape, films) 1967.
Beulahland Rag (narrator, jazz quartet, improvisation ensemble, tape, films, slides) 1967–9; first performed Ann Arbor, Michigan, 1968.
Full Moon in March (incidental music to Yeats) 1978.

PUBLICATIONS

By Albright: "Ross Lee Finney", in *Grove's Dictionary of Opera*, London, 1990; "The Complete Rags of Scott Joplin", liner notes, Music Heritage Society, 1990.

On Albright: E. Hantz, "An Introduction to the Organ Music of WA", in *Diapason*, June 1964, 1973; D. Reed, "The Organ Music of WA", dissertation, University of Rochester, 1976; D. Burge, "An Interview with WA", in *Contemporary Keyboard*, 3 March 1977; James E. Perone, "Pluralistic Strategies in Musical Analysis: A Study of Selected Works of WA", dissertation, State University of New York, Buffalo.

William Albright comments:

My music is generous, eclectic and maximal. I enjoy and prefer messy diversity to boring unity. Many works are public; many are private. I enjoy lively rhythm and ecstatic beauty.

* * *

Shifting from ragtime to improvisatory theater pieces and organ works to fully notated and sometimes serial chamber works, William Albright's compositional output might best be described as eclectic. Within these disparate works, however, five traits serve to define Albright's compositional style: (1) the exploration of one primary musical idea or mood in each single-movement piece or movement within a multi-movement composition; (2) the quasi-improvisatory treatment of small, cellular collections of pitches; (3) the extensive use of particular pitch-class set types for extra-musical reasons; (4) tonal movement by descending semitone motion; and (5) a tendency toward tightly controlled background structures with each succeedingly more foreground level being less tightly structured.

Concerning his *Organbook II*, Albright writes, "The generic title Organbook is an adaptation of the popular French Baroque term *livre d'orgue* and like the centuries-old model, is a collection of several pieces, each of which explores a single idea or sonority". Not only does the composer explore one primary mood or exploit one particular technique in each of the *Organbook I, Organbook II* and *Organbook III* pieces, he also does so in other organ works, such as *That Sinking Feeling*, and in non-organ works such as *Four Fancies* and *Doo-Dah*. Among the musical parameters which Albright has used as organizing factors are: (1) varying degrees of heterophony and the interplay of heterophony and strict unison (*Doo-Dah, Jericho: Battle Music for Trumpet and Organ*, the "Mirror Bagatelle" of *Four Fancies* and others, particularly of the mid- to late-1970s); (2) textural contrast (*Organbook, Caroms, Take That* and other works of the 1960s and early 1970s); (3) motivic relationships (*That Sinking Feeling*, with its near total concentration on the descending semitone both at the foreground and background levels is the clearest example); and (4) number series and twelve-tone rows (including the Fibonacci Series in the *Symphony* for organ and twelve-tone relationships in *Sphaera* and *Quintet for Clarinet and String Quartet*).

Possible due to his activity as a pianist and organist, Albright makes use of small collections of pitches and pitch-classes for use in an improvisatory, almost "noodling" manner, particularly in his keyboard works. Although in some works, such as *Organbook* and *Introduction, Passacaglia and Rondo cappriccioso*, the pitches are notated with the instruction to improvise rhythm and pitch order, in many of Albright's works exploiting this technique, rhythm and pitch order are fully notated, but sound improvised and almost random (see *De Spiritum*, *Caroms*, *Pianoagogo*, and "Mirror Bagatelle" from *Four Fancies*).

Albright makes extensive use of pitch-class set types 3–5 (the collection C-C#-F#, for example) and 4–9 (the collection C-C#-F#-G, for example). Albright describes these set-types as symbolic of the conflict between good and evil, on the basis of their interval-class content. Both collections contain an equal number of perfect intervals and tritones. Extra-musical considerations such as this have played a significant role in works from throughout Albright's career. Aside from the use of good versus evil metaphor, extra-musical considerations affect the humor of *King of Instruments* and *Seven Deadly Sins*.

Pieces such as *Caroms*, *Sweet Sixteenths*, *Quintet for Clarinet and String Quartet*, *Pax in terra*, *Stipendium Peccati*, and *Jericho: Battle Music for Trumpet and Organ*, rely heavily on tonal motion by descending semitone. Since the composition of *Caroms* in 1966, Albright has actively exploited this tonal relationship, sometimes only at local and middleground structural levels, but more usually at the background level.

Within each of the previously discussed areas of his compositional style, Albright consistently firmly controls background structure, while allowing foreground material to evolve in a significantly freer manner. While this trend is particularly strong in early theater pieces such as *Beulahland Rag* and *Tic*, it persists in recent works such as the *Quintet for Clarinet and String Quartet*, dating from 1986 (in which twelve-tone rows control background tonal relationships, but are freely treated on the more local levels of structure), and is the one consistent over-riding trait of the composer's style—a characteristic which differentiates Albright's concept of structure from strict adherents to any rigorous compositional doctrine (such as serialism), and places him in the company of a composer such as Lukas Foss, who shares Albright's tendencies toward both eclecticism and the combination of a strict background and free foreground.

—James E. Perone

ALEXANDER, Haim [Heinz]. Israeli. Born in Berlin, Germany, 9 August 1915. Educated at Konig-Stadtische-Oberreal-Schule; Stern'sches Konservatorium, Berlin (piano, theory under Willibald Tschiersch), interrupted by Nazi takeover, 1933; Palestine Conservatoire and Academy of Music (composition under Stefan Wolpe, piano under Irma Wolpe-Schoenberg; later with Hanoch Jacoby and Ilona Vincze-Kraus), 1936–45, B.Mus.; higher study, Freiburg, Germany. Military service: Haganah and special duties, Palestine. Married Ruth Alexander in January 1942; 2 sons. Teacher of piano, 1945–71, of theoretical subjects, since 1945, professor of composition, 1971–1982 (retired but continues part-time, Rubin Academy of Music, Jerusalem; master courses in improvisation, Dalcroze Institute, Geneva, 1971, 1977; master degree courses, New York University, 1974, 1978; visiting professor of analysis, department of musicology, Tel Aviv University, 1972–88; master courses, Trossingen and Remscheid Academy, 1982, 1988; visiting professor of analysis, department of musicology, Hebrew University, Jerusalem, 1990. Recipient: Zimriah Prize (for *Vekibaeti Etchem* and *Le Ma'an Zion Lo Echesche*) 1952, 1955; Engel Prize (for *Six Israeli Dances*), 1956; 1st prize (for *Sound Figures*), Israel Music Institute, 1966; 1st prize (for *Patterns*), International Rubinstein Master Competition, Israel, 1974; ACUM Prize (for vocal work) 1980. Mailing address: 55 Tschernichowsky Street, 92587 Jerusalem, Israel.

Publishers: Israel Music Institute, P.O.B. 3004, Tel Aviv, Israel; Israel Music Publications, 25 Keren Hayessod Street, Jerusalem; Schott, Mainz.

Symphonies/orchestral:

Artza (symphonic overture) 1951; first performed Israel, 1951.
Let Us Praise His Name in Dance 1954; first performed Israel, 1954.
Six Israeli Dances 1956; first performed Israel, 1956.
Journey to the Present (orchestra, with narrator) 1971; first performed Israel, 1971.
Nabot (Stick) (orchestral dance) 1974; first performed Israel, 1974.
Sheeya (suite for plucked instruments) 1977; first performed Haifa, 1977.
Heritage (suite for chamber orchestra) 1980.
Concerto for Piano (chamber orchestra) 1982; first performed Tel Aviv, 1982.

Chamber/instrumental:

If I Forget Thee, O Jerusalem (piano) 1947; first performed Jerusalem, 1947.
Variations (piano) 1947.
Quartet (2 flutes, piano, cello) 1947; first performed Jerusalem, 1947.
Suite (2 pianos, 4 hands) 1951; first performed Jerusalem, 1951.
Six Israeli Dances (piano; version for 2 pianos) 1951; first performed Jerusalem, 1951.
Sonata Brevis (2 pianos) 1960; first performed Jerusalem, 1960.
Bnot Kol (Sound Figures) (piano) 1965; first performed Tel Aviv, 1965.
Improvisation on a Yemenite Song (recorder, harpsichord) 1967; first performed Tel Aviv, 1967.
Metamorphoses (violin) 1970; first performed Jerusalem, 1970.
Shur Dodi (trombone, piano) 1970; first performed Jerusalem, 1970.
De Profundis (organ) 1972; first performed Jerusalem, 1972.
Tavniyot (Patterns) (piano) 1974; first performed Tel Aviv, 1974.
Tekyo (Tie): Jazz versus Classic (violin, flute, piano—4 hands) 1981; first performed Jerusalem, 1981.

You Are the Earth (trombone quartet) 1986; first performed Bielefeld, 1986.
D'Après une Mazurka (piano) 1987; first performed Rottenburg, 1987.
Metamorphosis on a Theme by Mozart (piano) 1989; to be performed at radio competition, Israel, 1991.
Trio—The Call of the Dervishes (piano, violin, cello) 1989; first performed Jerusalem, 1990.

Vocal/choral:

Vekibaeti Etchem (SATB choir) 1952; first performed Tel Aviv, 1952.
Ashira La'Adonai (soprano, children's choir) 1952; first performed Jerusalem, 1952.
La Ma'an Zion Lo Echesche (SATB choir) 1955; first performed Tel Aviv, 1955.
"Rubaiyat" of Omar Khayam (baritone/mezzo-soprano, 6 intruments) 1963; first performed Jerusalem, 1963.
I Have Not Said Everything Yet (alto solo, SATB choir; Zach) 1976; first performed Jerusalem, 1976.
Seven Songs (baritone/mezzo-soprano, 7 instruments; Zach) 1976; first performed Jerusalem, 1976.
A Nice Surprise: Nine Children's Songs (mezzo-soprano/baritone, piano) 1980; first performed Jerusalem, 1980.
The Nicest Girl in the Nursery: Five Duets (2 sopranos, piano) 1980; first performed Jerusalem, 1980.
My Absent Minded Friend: Three Children's Songs (voice, piano) 1983; first performed Jerusalem 1983.
Songs of Love and Expectation (voice, chamber orchestra; version for voice and piano) 1984, 1986; first performed Be'er Sheva, 1984; Jerusalem, 1986.
Three Bird Songs (children's choir) 1984; first performed Tel Aviv, 1984.
Three Nature and Two Love Songs (voice, piano, flute ad lib) 1985; first performed Jerusalem, 1985.
Three Songs by Chr. Morgenstern (8 women's voices) 1986; first performed Stuttgart, 1986.
Psalm 146 (soprano, organ) 1986; first performed Jerusalem, 1986.
Mein blaues Klavier (8 women's voices, percussion; Elsa Lasker-Schuler) 1990; first performed Frankfurt, 1990.

PUBLICATIONS

By Alexander: "Improvisation am Klavier" (German), Mainz, 1987; "Essay on Schubert" (Hebrew), Opus II/Association of Artists and Music Teachers, Israel, 1989; "Essay on My Piano Works" (Hebrew), Opus III/Association of Artists and Music Teachers, 1990.

On Alexander: Michael Wolpe, "HA", in *Music in Time*, Jerusalem, 1988–9; Alice Tischler, in *Descriptive Biography of Art Music by Israeli Composers*, Michigan, 1988.

Haim Alexander comments:

My work is tonal in general, although I have also several dodecaphonic pieces. Of the tonal pieces I would like to mention the *Nabot*, the *Concerto for Piano* and my *Six Israeli Dances*.

The piano pieces *Sonata Brevis*, *D'Après une Mazurka* and the *Metamorphosis on a Theme by Mozart* are also tonal. Most of my choral works are tonal as well, even my last piece *Mein blaues Klavier*, which is extremely difficult.

Of the dodecaphonic pieces, I would like to mention the *Sound Figures* for piano, the *"Rubaiyat" of Omar Khayam*, but the *Patterns* are tonal, even if they sound dodecaphonic. Some pieces are in more "popular" vein, like the *Three Nature and Two Love Songs*, but the bulk of my compositions have different attitudes. A recently written piece is not necessarily more modern in style than a piece composed 25 years ago.

* * *

Haim Alexander is perhaps the youngest of the generation of composers who came to Palestine in the 1930s. Born in Berlin, he studied piano and theory with Willibald Tschiersch, and sang in a prominent Berlin boys' choir. He began to study at the Berlin conservatory, but was unable to complete his course because of the Nazi "Nürnberg Laws", which denied educational opportunity to German Jews. In 1936, with the help of the violinist Emil Hauser, Alexander moved to Palestine—an independent Israel was still some dozen years away—to complete his studies together with several other young musicians at the Palestine Academy of Music.

He completed the main part of his musical education in Jerusalem, his main teachers being the Berlin-born composer Stefan Wolpe and his wife the pianist Irma Wolpe-Schoenberg. After the couple moved to America in 1939, Alexander continued to study composition with Hanoch Jacoby and piano with Ilona Vincze-Kraus. The fruitful tension between on the one hand a broadly dodecaphonic approach (Wolpe had been a pupil of Arnold Schoenberg) and Jacoby's Hindemith-influenced tonal style) is felt in all of Alexander's music, from his earliest compositions to the present day. An additional element was provided by the folk-influenced Mediterranean style, developed by such emigré composers as Paul Ben-Haim, Marc Lavry, both refugees from Nazi oppression, and the Hungarian Ödön Partos (who became director of the Israel Rubin Academy in 1956). Alexander was in turn to make a significant contribution to this style, though in time he broadened his interest into the fields of jazz and improvisation, which also helped mould his distinctive style.

Alexander's composition can be divided into a number of periods. Between 1945 and 1958, the Mediterranean style dominated composition in Israel and Alexander contributed several modal works with shades of jazz and folklore; among the most prominent of these were the piano *Variations*, the *Six Israeli Dances* which exist in more than one arrangement, the symphonic overture *Artza*, the choral *Vekibaeti Etchem* and the orchestral piece *Let Us Praise His Name in Dance* (1954).

During the ensuing 10 years, from 1958 to 1968, the Mediterranean style lost its central position in Israeli music and Alexander found a new form of expression in strict dodecaphony, and other progressive techniques originating in Central European serialism. The two outstanding works of this period are the *"Rubaiyat"* settings, which are dodecaphonic but veer close to tonality, and the piano piece *Bnot Kol*, which won first prize in the Israeli Music Institute Competition, and is considered a very important piano composition in Israel.

Since the late 1960s, Alexander has written in a freer style in which he utilises a variety of musical styles and materials. The *Sonata Brevis* for two pianos is mainly modal and is dedicated to the memory of the English composer Ralph Vaughan Williams. *Seven Songs* is in highly contrastive style, while *Tekyo* presents a contrast between classical chamber elements and jazz. The *Concerto for Piano* is mainly a modal composition, very free in style and form, while the *Songs of Love and Expectation* for female voice and chamber orchestra are based on modal material inspired by Olivier Messiaen.

Though in recent years it is Alexander's vocal music that has been particularly outstanding—the *Three Songs by Chr.*

Morgenstern most notably—he has continued to compose in a wide range of forms. During his whole career, he has been a lecturer, pianist and teacher for generations of the Rubin Music Academy, the department of musicology, Tel Aviv University, as well as abroad at such places as the Dalcroze Institute. His outstanding qualities are his approaches to research and his teaching of analysis and improvisation.

—Michael Wolpe

ALI-ZADEH, Franghiz. Azerbaijani. Born in Baku, Azerbaijan, 28 May 1947. Educated at Music School, Baku (piano under U. Khalilov), 1954–65; Azerbaijan State Conservatory, Baku (composition under Kara Karayev, piano, musical criticism, musicology), 1965–72; post-graduate research in composition, Azerbaijan State Conservatory, 1974–6, candidate degree, 1989. Married the filmmaker Dzhangir Gasanaga Zeinalov in 1982; 1 son. Lecturer and assistant to Kara Karayev, 1970–6, assistant professor, 1976–89, and Professor, since 1989, Azerbaijan State Conservatory, Baku. Secretary, Union of Composers of Azerbaijan, 1979–85, and since 1989. Concert pianist and recitalist. Recipient: Prize Laureate, Union of Composers of Azerbaijan, 1980; elected to membership, Friends of Arnold Schoenberg Institute, Los Angeles, 1988. Mailing address: U1. F. Amirova 1 Kv 63, Baku 37000, Azerbaijan.

Publisher: c/o Union of Composers of Azerbaijan, Baku.

Symphonies/orchestral:

Piano Concerto 1972; first performed Baku, 1974.
Symphony 1976; first performed Baku, 1977.
Concerto for Chamber Orchestra 1986.

Chamber/instrumental:

Sonata: To the Memory of Alban Berg (piano) 1970; first performed Pesato, Italy, 1976.
String Quartet 1974; first performed Baku, 1974.
"Zu den Kindertotenlieder"; To the Memory of Gustav Mahler (violin, clarinet, percussion) 1977; first performed Zurich, 1989.
Gabil-Sajahy (cello, piano) 1979; first performed Leningrad, 1979. Recorded Melodia, 1983; Ambitus (Hamburg), 1990.
Fantasy (organ) 1982; first performed Baku, 1983.
Partita (organ) 1985; first performed Baku, 1986.
Dilogia I (string quartet) 1988; first performed Bonn, 1989.
Music for Piano 1989; first performed Los Angeles, 1989.
Dilogia II (string quartet, wind quintet) 1990; first performed Zurich, 1990.

Vocal/choral:

Songs about Motherland (3 soloists, chorus, orchestra) 1978; first performed Baku, 1985.
Three Water-Colours (soprano, flute, piano) 1987; first performed Baku, 1987.
From Japanese Poetry (soprano, flute, piano/celeste, vibraphone) 1990.

Opera:

Legend about White Rider (rock opera) 1985.

Other:

Music for documentary and artistic films, Azerbaijan Film Studio, 1982–90.

PUBLICATIONS

On Ali-zadeh: M. Willenbrink, "Was kommt nach Schostakowitsch?", in *Neue Zurcher Zeitung*, 14 October 1986; A. Dumling, "Von Ausgegragter Individualitat", in *Tagesspiegl*, 21 September 1986; E. Schwinger, "Kurz Cerichtet", in *Musik und Gesellschaft*, 11, 1986; T. Pozwol, "Mugam und Aleatorik", in *Musik Texte*, 26 October 1988; T. Mangan, "FA-z at Schoenberg Institute", in *Los Angeles Times*, 27 October 1989; A. Rich, "FA-z" in Los Angeles *Herald-Examiner*, 29 October 1989; M. Bentley, F. Kaiman, "Azerbaijan Pianist Sojourns in Madison", in *The Daily Cardinal*, 25 September 1990.

Franghiz Ali-zadeh comments:

A person's need to write music is just as inexplicable as the appearance of life on earth. The very appearance of the first shoot of new music in a contemporary world of ruin, wars, blood and suffering, seems to me a matter worthy of wonder. And it is marvellous that man, in spite of everything which obstructs him on all sides, throws down a challenge to this awfulness by passing over it to converse with the stars.

Baku—the tragic year of 1990.

(translated by Gerard McBurney)

* * *

Azerbaijan, the country to which Franghiz Ali-zadeh belongs, is a large area in the Eastern Caucasus on the shores of the Caspian Sea. The people speak a language related to Turkish and their religion is Islam. Their loyalties therefore are to the cultures of the Middle East and Central Asia. They differ from the other two Caucasian republics of Armenia and Georgia, who have strong European sympathies and Christian backgrounds.

Ali-zadeh's music is deeply rooted in these eastern loyalties. Her music is not just influenced by the folk instruments and music of her native land, but, more and more as she goes on, seems a virtual recreation of the sounds that surrounded her as she grew up. For example, the title of her work for cello and piano, *Gabil-Sajahy*, is the name of an Azeri instrument and the music which is played on it; and her piece is, to an uninformed ear, almost exactly an imitation of what that music sounds like. Less specifically, in her *Music for Piano*, written for the Schoenberg Institute in 1989, the composer prepares the piano by throwing metal bangles (of the sort a woman of her country might wear) on to the piano strings in order to create a sound that might well be that of another folk instrument with which she would be familiar. *Music for Piano* is of indeterminate length too, not notated in the usual way and capable of enormous extension just like the improvisation of a folk musician.

But there is a complex paradox here. Ali-zadeh herself is someone steeped in the techniques of Western music and fascinated by the procedures of the post-war avant-garde. She is well acquainted with all the traditions her music appears at first glance to reject, and she feels deeply nourished by them.

She does not see herself as cutting herself off from the West but as enriching Western music with sounds and ideas it has not yet taken sufficient account of.

And yet at the same time there is no doubt that Ali-zadeh's music does not sound to her own people simply like an imitation of their folk music; for them and for her in her music a subtle recreative process is at work, which at once distances and objectifies and even idealises the native music of Azerbaijan. An Azeri listener, as the composer herself is quick to make clear, would be far more aware than a Western listener of the many ways in which her music is actually different from the folk music that we in the West think she is imitating. In her native land it would be clear that what Ali-zadeh is doing is appropriating, ordering and maybe sometimes distorting. One might add too that the very act of making a Western instrument sound like an Eastern one is fraught with ironies, both musical and political.

Ali-zadeh herself points out in conversation that when Cage and Stockhausen and others of their generation began their various musical explorations half a century ago or so, they were often looking to or inspired by traditions from outside Europe. "When Cage first prepared his piano, he wanted it to sound like something that was alien to him. But that same prepared piano sounds like something very familiar to us, very close to home. So when we prepare a piano, we may be said to be taking a Western instrument and trying to bring it closer to what we know."

Ali-zadeh is deeply interested in the "different perceptions of time and space" to be found in European music and in Middle Eastern and Central Asian music. European music is, she says, an ordered and "vertical" process, while "Eastern music is . . . horizontal". In the latter, she says, "every second of time is saturated with meaning . . . and this ability to experience a single voice and listen to its every detail is . . . what is most precious in Eastern music".

—Gerard McBurney

ALSINA, Carlos Roqué. Argentinian. Born in Buenos Aires, 19 February 1941. Educated: piano lessons (privately), 1951–9; Estudio de Fonologia Musical, National University of Buenos Aires (under Kropfl), 1962–4. Composer/performer, Agrupacion Nueva Musica, Buenos Aires, 1959–64; assistant conductor, Teatro Colon, 1960–4; Ford Foundation artist in residence, Berlin, 1964–6; assistant to Bruno Maderna, Deutsche Oper, Berlin, 1966; member, Center of Creative and Performing Arts, State University of New York, Buffalo, 1966–8; visiting professor, State University of New York, Buffalo, 1968; co-founder, New Phonic Art group, 1969; performing pianist. Recipient: Guggenheim Award (for *Uberwindung* and *Schichten*), 1971. Mailing address: c/o Edizioni Suvini Zerboni, via Quiltiliano 40, Milan, Italy.

Publisher: Edizioni Suvini Zerboni.

Symphonies/orchestral:

Three Pieces Op 13 (string orchestra) 1961.
Symptom Op 21 1969.
Uberwindung Op 25 (4 instruments, orchestra) 1970; first performed Donaueschingen, 18 October 1970.
Schichten Op 27 (chamber orchestra) 1971; first performed Royan, France, 7 April 1971.
Omnipotenz Op 28 (2 instruments, chamber orchestra) 1972; first performed Royan, France, 26 March 1972.
Approach Op 30 (piano, percussion, orchestra) 1973; first performed Berlin, 14 March 1973.
Stücke 1977; first performed Royan, France, 4 April 1977.
Señales (piano, chamber orchestra) 1977; first performed La Rochelle, France, 3 July 1977.
Decisions (chamber orchestra) 1977; first performed Metz, France, 19 November 1977.
Etudes (orchestra, tape) 1979; first performed Metz, France, 17 November 1979.
Prima sinfonia (flute, soprano, cello, orchestra) 1983; first performed Metz, France, 20 November 1983.
Concerto (piano, orchestra) 1985; first performed Paris, 16 November 1985.

Chamber/instrumental:

Klavierstück (Estudio) No 1 Op 3 (piano) 1958.
Klavierstück (Estudio) No 2 Op 6 (piano) 1960; first performed Berlin, January 1965.
Wind Quintet Op 9 1961.
Klavierstück No 3 Op 8 (piano) 1962–5; first performed Berlin, 23 March 1966.
Funktionen Op 14 (flute, clarinet, bassoon, trumpet, piano, 2 percussion, violin, cello) 1965; first performed Paris, April 1966.
Consecuenza Op 17 (trombone) 1966.
Auftrag Op 18 (flute, clarinet, bassoon, horn, percussion, violin, viola, cello, double bass) 1967; first performed Tanglewood, Massachusetts, 13 August 1967.
Trio 1967 (trombone, percussion, cello) 1967.
Jeu de cloches (3 or more instruments, tape) 1969; first performed Berlin, 1969.
Klavierstück No 4 Op 23 (piano) 1969; first performed Radenci, Yugoslavia, 4 October 1969.
Rendez-vous Op 24 (clarinet/saxophone, trombone/alphorn, piano, piano/organ/percussion) 1970.
Unity Op 31 (clarinet, cello) 1973; first performed La Rochelle, France, 19 April 1973.
Etude Op 32 (zarb) 1973.
Themen (percussion) 1974; first performed La Rochelle, France, 1974.
Themen II (12 strings, percussion) 1974; first performed Royan, France, 26 March 1975.
A Letter (wind quintet) 1976; first performed Hilversum, April 1976.
Klavierstück No 5 (piano) 1982.
Hinterland (piano, percussion, tape) 1982; first performed Paris, 22 February 1982.
Voie avec Voix (string quartet) 1984; first performed Strasbourg, France, 21 September 1984.

Vocal/choral:

Consecuenza II Op 26 (female voice) 1971; first performed Berlin, January 1971.
Cantata (tenor, choir, orchestra) 1977; first performed Paris, 22 April 1977.
Harmonies (teenage choir, 2 readers, reciter, soloists, tape, orchestra) 1979; first performed 22 December 1979.
Cinq à la une (choir, flute, 3 percussion) 1984; first performed Aix en Provence, France, 30 July 1984.

Opera:

La Muraille (Raffaelli, Dorst) 1981; first performed Avignon, France, 28 July 1981.

Other:

Textes 1967 (theatre piece; soprano, flute, trumpet, trombone, piano, percussion, violin, cello, double bass) 1967.
Fusion Op 33 (ballet; 2 pianos, 2 percussion) 1974; first performed Royan, France, 29 March 1974.
Del Tango (theatre piece; 2 sopranos, 4 actors, flute, tenor saxophone/bass clarinet/soprano saxophone, piano) 1982; first performed Paris, 1 December 1982.
Introductions (for students of piano and clarinet) 1985.

* * *

Almost inevitably, if a little unfairly, Carlos Roqué Alsina's reputation is bound up with that of his older compatriot, Mauricio Kagel. The main points of likeness are immediately evident. There is Alsina's innate theatricality; like Kagel, he worked as an assistant conductor at the Teatro Colon. And there is his almost obsessive concern for new expressive and phonic resources (usually by means of integrating instrumental voices, as in the 1973 piece *Unity* for clarinet and cello, one of his finest—and most demanding—chamber works).

However, where Kagel used chance techniques and a species of gestural conceptualisation to increase the range of his radical serialism, Alsina's use of improvisatory techniques is altogether more organic and apriorist. Perhaps in consequence, he has been less inclined to experiment with instrumental exotica, though the 1974 *Themen* for zarb, a small membrane drum which originates in Persia, is an effective examination of both an unfamiliar tonality and performative manner.

The second *Themen* piece, from the same year, shows how adept and effective an orchestrator Alsina is, a talent that is not high among Kagel's admittedly long list of credits. Early pieces such as the *Three Pieces* for strings and the later *Schichten* gave full rein to his organisational intelligence and yielded convincing structures which lack the disturbing alienation effects of *Themen II* but which are nonetheless deserving of greater exposure.

It is, though, on Alsina's chamber and instrumental compositions that his distinctive nature rests. The solo trombone piece *Consecuenza* stands alongside Berio's *Sequenza V*—also written in 1966—and anticipates Kagel's marvellous *Atem* for solo wind. The four *Klavierstück* (Piano Pieces), written over a decade, range over effects that hover between out-and-out serialism and an extreme chromaticism that suggests microtonal voicing. *Trio 1967* explores similar territory, but with a much wider timbral range.

That was the ethos of New Phonic Art, the improvising group Alsina co-founded in 1969 with Jean-Pierre Drouet, Michel Portal and the virtuosic French/Slovak trombonist and composer Vinko Globokar, with whom Alsina had overlapped at the Centre of the Creative and Performing Arts in Buffalo, New York. Perhaps oddly, perhaps inevitably, the most obvious repercussion of this very demanding collaboration was in increased awareness of the possibilities of vocal music; *Consecuenza II* for soprano and the 1977 *Cantata* are among Alsina's finest works.

He is also an accomplished pianist, with a technique very much adapted to his own demanding scores. His premiere performance of the 1985 *Concerto* for piano on O.R.T.F (Radio France), together with his Donaueschingen and Royan commissions of the early 1970s helped consolidate him as a composer on the world stage, who nonetheless retains enough of his Argentinian background to guarantee him a place in both European and Latin American musical history.

—James Weir

AMY, Gilbert. French. Born in Paris, 29 August 1936. Educated: piano lessons from age 6; Baccalauréat, and national prize in philosophy, 1954; Conservatoire National Supérieur de Musique, Paris (composition and analysis under Olivier Messiaen, composition under Darius Milhaud, also accompaniment, and counterpoint and fugue), 1955–1960; also lessons in piano and harmony with Yvonne Loriod, 1956–8; classes with Pierre Boulez, Basle, 1965. Conductor (debut 1962) and composer; director, Domaine Musical, Paris (in succession to Pierre Boulez) 1967–73, disbanded; founder/director, Nouvel Orchestre Philharmonique de Radio France, 1976–81; professor of analysis and composition, Yale University, New Haven, Connecticut, 1982. Recipient: Paris Biennale prize (for *Trajectoires*), 1967; Grand Prix de la Promotion Symphonique de la SACEM, 1971. Mailing address: c/o Universal Edition, Bösendorferstrasse 12, A-105 Vienna, Austria.

Publisher: Universal Edition.

Symphonies/orchestral:

Mouvements 1958; first performed Paris, 1958.
Diaphonies 1962.
Antiphonies (2 orchestras) 1964.
Triade 1965.
Trajectoires (violin, orchestra) 1966.
Chant (large orchestra) 1968–9, revised 1980; first performed Donaueschingen, 20 October 1968.
Refrain (large orchestra) 1972.
Adagio et Stretto 1977–8.
Praeludium 1984.

Chamber/instrumental:

Piece (organ) 1954.
Variations (flute, clarinet, cello, piano) 1956.
Sonata (piano) 1957–60; first performed Darmstadt, 1960.
Inventions I–II (flute, vibraphone/marimbaphone, harp, piano/celeste) 1959–61.
Epigrammes (piano) 1961.
Alpha-Beth (wind sextet) 1963–4.
Cahier d'épigrammes (piano) 1964.
Cycle (6 percussion) 1964–6.
Relais (brass quintet) 1967.
Jeux (1–4 oboes) 1970.
Jeux et formes (oboe solo, flute, oboe, 2 clarinets, bassoon, horn, 2 trumpets, 2 trombones, tuba, marimbaphone, harp, celeste, piano, 2 violins, viola, cello) 1971.
Seven Sites (flute/piccolo, clarinet, horn, trumpet, 2 percussion, harp, piano/celeste, 2 violins, 2 violas, 2 cellos) 1975.
Sept Bagatelles (organ) 1975.
Echos XIII (horn, trombone, harp, piano, 2 flutes/1 piccolo,

clarinet, bass clarinet, bassoon, violin, viola, cello, double bass) 1976.
Trois Etudes (flute) 1977.
Quasi scherzando (cello) 1981.
Quasi una toccata (organ) 1981.
La Variation ajoutée (17 instruments, tape) 1984–5.

Vocal/choral:

Oeil de fumée (soprano, piano; Parrot) 1957.
Cantate brève (soprano, flute, marimba, vibraphone; Lorca) 1957.
Strophe (soprano, orchestra; Char) 1965–77.
Cette Etoile enseigne à s'incliner (male chorus, 2 pianos, tape, 3 trombones, vibraphone, 2 harps, guitar, 3 cellos, 3 double basses; Dante) 1970.
Récitatif, air et variation (12 unaccompanied voices; Daumal) 1970.
. . . D'un Désastre obscur (mezzo-soprano, clarinet; Mallarmé) 1971.
D'un Espace déployé (soprano, 2 pianos, 2 orchestral groups) 1972–3; first performed Paris, 10 March 1973.
Sonata pian'e forte (soprano, mezzo-soprano, flute/alto flute, cor anglais, bass clarinet, horn, harp, piano/tam tam, piano/crotales, xylorimba/percussion, mandolin, guitar, viola, cello) 1974.
Après " . . . D'un Désastre obscur" (mezzo-soprano, flute/piccolo, clarinet, piano, violin, cello, mezzo-soprano/gongs/whip, harp, horn, bass clarinet ad lib; Mallarmé) 1976.
Shin'anim Sha'ananim (mezzo-soprano, cello, clarinet, instrumental ensemble; Ibn Gabirol) 1979.
Une Saison en enfer (soprano, piano, percussion, tape; Rimbaud) 1981.
Messe (soprano, alto, tenor, bass, children's choir ad lib, mixed choir, orchestra; Latin) 1982–3.
Ecrits sur toiles (reciter, flute/piccolo, clarinet/bass clarinet, horn, violin, cello, piano/celeste; Rilke) 1983.

Other:

Comment s'en débarrasser (incidental music to Ionesco) 1957.
La Vie est un songe (incidental music to Calderón) 1958.
Le Cadavre encerclé (incidental music to Yacine) 1958.
La Femme sauvage (incidental music to Yacine) 1958–63.
Biederman et les incendiaires (incidental music to Frisch) 1960.
Oedipe Roi (incidental music to Sophocles) 1961–2.
Travelling (film score; E.B. Weil) 1962.
Images du monde visionnaire (film score; Michaux) 1963.
Le Grand Cérémonial (incidental music to Arrabal) 1965.
La Soif et la faim (incidental music to Ionesco) 1966.
L'Alliance (film score; Challonges) 1970.

PUBLICATIONS

By Amy: "L'espace sonore", in *Esprit*, 1, 1960; "Sur quelques problèmes récents . . . et futurs", in *Phantomas*, 15, 1960; "Musique pour 'Misérable miracle' d'Henri Michaux", in *Tel quel*, 17, 1964; "Redécouvrir l'écoute", in *Preuves*, 177, 1965; "Sur Henri Michaux", in *L'Herne*, 8, 1966; "Formes et liberté", in *Lettres françaises*, June 1967.

On Amy: M. Fauré, (interview) in *Lettres nouvelles*, 11, 1961; D. Jameux, (interview) in *Musique en jeu*, 3, 1971; *Silon*, October 1971, dedicated to GA; A. Durel, "Diriger 'Carré': débat avec GA", in *Musique en jeu*, 15, 1974; E. Walter, (interview) in *Harmonie*, 103, 1975; Richard Dufallo, (interview) in *Trackings*, Oxford, 1990.

* * *

Gilbert Amy's mature music is polyphonic, complex and instrumentally virtuosic. Both qualities are a function of his "second"—but no less significant—career as a conductor. Much of his work appears to be "in dialogue" with the classics of the modern repertoire which he has performed with his orchestras, but more importantly, it is in dialogue with itself, constantly refining its language.

His roots are in the serialist movement of the early part of the century (notably Webern), filtered through the example and advice of Pierre Boulez, whom he succeeded as head of the influential Domaine Musical in Paris in 1967. However, Amy is also deeply interested in early and Baroque musics, and is by no means an orthodox serialist. He set out on a relatively conventional course with the piano Sonata which was completed, after much revision under Boulez's critical eye, in 1960. It is a complex, rather sunless work, and by no means a good benchmark even for Amy's later solo instrumental style; by comparison, the later *Epigrammes*, with the short *Cahier d'épigrammes* which is intended as a "sandwich" piece between two performances, opens out his sense of form quite dramatically. Though he has shown no great liking for chance operations, the mobility of *Epigrammes* freed him considerably from early constraints.

At the same time as he was revising the piano Sonata, Amy was fulfilling a first orchestral commission from Boulez. *Mouvements*, which was first given at the Domaine in 1958, is a strikingly powerful piece, full of vigorous tempos in relaxed but also precise counterpoint. It indicated a way forward and instituted a cycle of orchestral work which only ended with the incredibly complex and elaborate *Chant*, which betrays some signs of being a summation of all his work to date. *Mouvements* was followed by the relatively slight *Diaphonies* and, in 1964, by *Antiphonies*, a work much influenced by Stockhausen's work on spatial distribution of sound, notably in *Gruppen* which he heard in 1958. (Over a decade later, in The Hague, Amy was to co-conduct an unforgettable performance of Stockhausen's four-orchestra *Carré*.) *Antiphonies* requires two orchestras and conductors, working in perfect co-ordination. There is no gestural looseness in the conception; it is left to a small intervening group to generate the concertante effects which have become such a distinctive part of Amy's work.

He turned again to spatial distribution in 1972 with *D'un Espace déployé*, an altogether more sophisticated (but also more backward-looking) work with parts for two sopranos, two pianos and two smaller orchestral groups in which the interplay of voices is very much clearer. Amy's only excursion into concerto writing, albeit of unorthodox sort, is the remarkable *Trajectoires* for violin and orchestra, which betrays the same obsession with countervailing melodic development, harmonic complexity (it makes extensive use of quarter-tones) and an apparent freedom-within-constraint generated by chance coincidences in the development. *Trajectoires* is a haunting work, suggesting an interest not just in scientific theories, but also in a more poetic programme.

Its immediate predecessor, *Triade*, had been developed from music Amy wrote for a film by Henri Michaux, *Images du monde visionnaire*. Allied to Amy's strict-serialist background had been an interest in mystical or visionary writings and painting. What is interesting about Michaux's drug-induced reveries is their absolute control, and this is the quality Amy has exploited. His choice of texts—Lorca, Char, Mallarmé,

Daumal, Ibn Gabirol, Rimbaud and Rilke—has always tended to follow a line of highly structured romantic reverie. There is no obvious autobiographical component in Amy's music; it inhabits a world whose hierarchies are as rigidly and vividly stratified as Dante's.

His writing for voice follows the concertante approach of his orchestral pieces. *Strophe* is a large orchestral work, with a powerful soprano part; the orchestra plays in distinct halves (but with no spatial separation), which leaves the singer, like the "concertino" group in *Antiphonies* as the fulcrum of the piece. It is interesting to compare the static quality of *Cette Etoile enseigne à s'incliner*, inspired by Paul Klee, for men's voices, ensemble and tape with *Récitatif, air et variation* from the same year. The latter treats Daumal's lines almost as if they were no more than some sketched musical material; it is closest in conception to a piece of electronic music or *musique concrète*. Though both "uncharacteristic"—as Betsy Jolas wrote in *Grove's* about the former piece—they are nonetheless typical of Amy's ability to assimilate very different procedures and materials to his own usually distinctive style.

He has continued to make the freest use of the whole modern idiom. *Sonata pian'e forte* borrows Cage's "prepared" piano; in *Ecrits sur toiles*, he borrows harmonic material and some of the rhythmic coding from Stravinsky's *Symphony in Three Movements*, and the instrumentation from *Pierrot Lunaire*; in the recent *Praeludium*, he attempts to rework Webern's superb use of instrumental colour on the largest scale. Amy's chamber instrumental work has largely been concerned with the interplay of voices in concertante manner. The *Inventions* of 1959–61 establish his interest in using monophonic instruments in a polyphonic setting. He develops this to extremes in the skittish pair *Jeux* for one to four oboes and the companion *Jeux et formes* in which the solo oboe plays a ringmaster's (or conductor's) role.

In 1983, Amy finished his large-scale Mass, again an uncharacteristic enterprise for someone of his background and disposition, but typical nonetheless of his constant desire to write himself into the wider tradition of European music. This he has done determinedly and undogmatically. His work is a running commentary, by a brilliant practitioner, on the practice of music.

—James Weir

ANDERSON, Beth (professional name of Barbara Elizabeth Anderson). American. Born in Lexington, Kentucky, 3 January 1950. Educated at University of Kentucky (piano, performance), 1966–8; University of California, Davis (under Larry Austin, John Cage and Richard Swift), 1969–71, B.A.; Mills College, Oakland, California (piano and composition under Robert Ashley and Terry Riley), M.F.A. in piano performance, 1973, M.A., composition, 1974; New York University, Ph.D. programme in creative arts, 1977–8; also taught by Helen Lipscomb, Kenneth Wright, John B. Chance, Nate Rubin. Married Michael Scott Cooper 27 June 1976 (dissolved 1978). Freelance composer/pianist/organist, 1960–7, 1974; founder/co-editor, *Ear* magazine, 1973–9; performing member, Hysteresis, women composers group, 1973–5; manager, the Ensemble, new music performance organization, 1973–4; organizer of "Women Composers Festival", Mills College, 1973; secretary, board of directors, Cat's Paw Palace of Performing Arts, 1974–5; music teacher/Meet the Woman Composer, New School for Social Research, New York City, 1976; research assistant to Professors Leightner and Karp, New York University, 1977; music teacher, College of New Rochelle, campuses in New York City and New Rochelle, 1978–86; music critic, *SoHo News*, 1979–80; composer in residence, Young Audiences, schools in New York City and New Rochelle, 1982–3; dance accompanist, Alvin Ailey School of Theatrical Dance, New York City, since 1987; previously, dance accompanist at Mills College, YWCA, Berkeley, California, YMHA, 92nd Street, New York City, Neighbourhood Playhouse, American Dance Studio, Martha Graham School of Dance, New York University, Performing Arts High School, Ballet Hispanico, Harlem School of the Arts, Brearley School, The Clark Center, New Dance Group Studios, Nassau Community College, Montclair State College, 1973–84; film music editor, Eleuthyva Films and Cinema Mistral, 1986; piano teacher, Brooklyn Music School, New York, since 1987; piano teacher, Greenwich House Music School, New York City, since 1989. Recipient: Elizabeth Mills Crothers Awards, 1972, 1974; ZBS Media Residency, 1975; National Federation of Music Clubs' Award of Merit, 1977. Mailing address: 26 Second Avenue, Apt 5F, New York, New York 10003, U.S.A.

Publishers: American Composers Editions, 170 W. 74th Street, New York, New York 10023, U.S.A; Screen Gems—EMI Music Inc.

Symphonies/orchestral:

Overture (band) 1981.
Revelation 1981, revised for chamber orchestra as *Revel*.
Suite for Winds and Percussion 1981; first performed Staten Island, New York, 1981.

Chamber/instrumental:

Tulip Clause (alto flute, clarinet, bass clarinet, tenor saxophone, organ, cello, string bass, timpani, tenor, tape) 1973.
Valid for Life (large strung things and large soft instruments; first realised for 2 pianos and percussion) 1973.
Tower of Power (organ, tape) 1973.
I Am Uh Am I (string quartet) 1973.
Goodbye, Brigitte Bardot, or Hello, Charlotte Moorman (cello, tape) 1974.
She Wrote (2 violins, tape, mezzo-soprano) 1974; first performed New York City, 1974.
He Said (2 clarinets, video, person) 1975.
They Did It (piano, tape) 1975–6.
Promised Church Beautiful River (trombone, tape) 1977.
Eighth Ancestor (violin, flute, cello, piano; or flute, oboe, cello, piano; or flute, clarinet, cello, piano; or baroque flute, alto recorder, cello, harpsichord; or flute, clarinet, organ, piano, string bass, percussion) 1979; first performed Morristown, New Jersey, 1979.
Preparation for the Dominant; Outrunning the Inevitable (flute/violin/ocarina) 1979.
Skate Suite (violin, cello, electric bass, mezzo-soprano) 1979; first performed New York City, 1979.
Water-Strider Courrente (from *Skate Suite*; flute, clarinet, piano, organ, string bass, percussion) 1979.
Lullaby of the Eighth Ancestor (flute, piano; also for piano) 1979–80.

The Praying Mantis and the Bluebird (flute, piano) 1979.
Skater's Suite (violin, cello, flute, piano; or flute, oboe, cello, piano; or flute, clarinet, cello, piano; or baroque flute, alto recorder, cello, piano; or violin, cello, voice, string bass) 1980.
Dream (Trio: Dream) (piano, flute, cello) 1980.
Dr Blood's Mermaid Lullaby (flute, piano) 1980.
Net Work (saxophone quartet, 2 keyboards; also for piano) 1981, longer version 1984.
Shakuhachi Run (flute/violin/ocarina) 1981.
Quilt Music (piano) 1982; first performed New York City, 1982.
Manos Inquietas (piano) 1982; first performed New York City, 1982.
Taking Sides (piano) 1983.
Revel (electric violin, B♭ clarinet, E♭ saxophone, B♭ trumpet, trombone, piano, percussion, string bass) 1984; first performed Richmond, Virginia, 1985. Recorded Opus One Records.
Belgian Tango (piano) 1984.
Little Trio (flute, violin, guitar) 1984.
Pennyroyal Swale 1985; first performed New York City, 1985.
Rosemary Swale (string quartet) 1986; first performed New York City, 1986.
Brass Swale (brass quartet) 1988; first performed Redlands, California, 1988.

Vocal/choral:

Swatches (5 song cycle; soprano, piano) 1966.
A Day (song) 1967.
A Postcard (song) 1967.
An Argument (3 voices) 1969.
Paranoia (song) 1969.
WomanRite (soprano, piano) 1972.
Music for Myself (song) 1973.
Joan (oratorio; 4 singers, orchestra, tape, electronics) 1974; first performed Aptos, California, 22 August 1974.
Incline Thine Ear to Me (chant) 1975.
Black / White (chant) 1976.
He Says He's Got (song) 1977.
Twinkle Tonight (soprano, piano) 1978.
Time Stands Still (song) 1978.
Beauty Runs Faster (soprano, piano) 1978.
If You Have a Thought (round) 1978.
In Six (song) 1979.
Alleluia (2 tenors and 2 cellos or 2 trumpets) 1979.
Knots (soprano, piano; Laing) 1981.
The Only One I Want (song) 1981.
Junk Love (song) 1981.
Eric Jessawalla Says (song) 1982.
Talks to Teachers (song; Miller) 1982.
Dreaming Fields (song cycle; soprano, piano; Field) 1987.
Wynken, Blynken and Nod (SATB chorus) 1987.

Opera:

Queen Christina 1973; first performed Oakland, California, 1 December 1973.

Other:

Music for Charlemagne Palestine (graphic score; 2 string instruments, 2 lighting technicians) 1973.
Torero Piece (text-sound; 2 voices) 1973; first performed Berkeley, California, 1973. Recorded 1750 Arch Records 1752.
Tulip Clause and Buchla Bird Hiss Down the Road of Life (tape) 1973.
Peachy Keen-O (organ, electric guitar, vibraphone, percussion, voices, dancers, lights, tape) 1973.
Hallophone (musical environment; 2 saxophones, steel guitar, voice, tapes, slides, dancers) 1973.
Thus Spake Johnston (text-sound) 1973.
The Messiah Is Come (human sculpture, with internal and external sound sources, tape, string bass, flute, voices, speakers, piano, percussion, slides) 1974, revised 1976 as *The Bridegroom Is Hear*.
The People Rumble Louder (text-sound) 1975. Published in *Assemblings*, 1975.
Poem to Michael, John and Allison (text-sound) 1975. Published in *Ear* magazine, Summer 1975.
If I Were a Poet (text-sound) 1975; Recorded Black Box 15; published in *Ear* magazine, February 1976.
I Can't Stand It (text-sound; voice, percussion) 1976. Recorded New Music Production, 1980.
Non-Governmental Process (text-sound) 1976. Published in *Poetry Mailing List*, December 1976.
Ode (tape) 1976.
Soap Tuning (theatre piece) 1976. Published in *Dramatika*, Spring 1978.
Zen Piece (theatre piece) 1976.
Joan (tape) 1977.
I Wish I Were Single Again (text-sound) 1977.
Crackers and Checkers (text-sound) 1977. Published in *Text-Sound Texts*, 1980.
Morning View and Maiden Spring (speaker, slides, light, tape) 1978.
Yes Sir Ree (text-sound) 1978.
Six Stories in Series (text-sound) 1979.
Ocean Motion Mildew Mind (text-sound) 1979. Recorded New Music Production, 1980.
Sally's Success (text-sound) 1979.
Kitchy Kichin (text-sound) 1979.
World Honeymoon (film score) 1980.
Nirvana Manor (musical; Morely) 1981; first performed New York City, 1981.
Country Time (text-sound) 1981.
Elizabeth Rex; or the Well-Bred Mother Goes to Camp (musical; Kreston) 1983; first performed New York City, 1983.
Riot Rot (text-sound opera) 1984.
Avon (musical) 1990; first performed New York City, 1990.
German Swale (tape) 1990; first performed Germany, 1990.

PUBLICATIONS

By Anderson: "Ode for the Bicentennial", and "Copyright Amazement", in *Ear*, May 1975; Non-Performing Jobs in Music", in *Paid My Dues*, October 1979; "What's Happening in New Music?", in *SoHo Weekly News*, 27 December 1979; "My Personal Approach to Music", in *Heresies*, 10, 1980; articles and reviews in *Ear* magazine, *SoHo Weekly News* and elsewhere.

On Anderson: Naomi Sinai, "Women Composers", in *Prisma: A Magazine on Alternative Education*, October 1974; Julie Cheever, "Composing From Life", in *San Francisco Chronicle*, 23 June 1974; Donna Handly, "Yes, Virginia, There are Women Composers", in *Ms*, August 1974.

Beth Anderson comments:
To make something beautiful is revolutionary (not low class,

not easy, not a sign of low intelligence). I once said that "the relationship of feminism to my work and the evolution of the form of my music are in violent flux". They still are, but the dust is settling.

The idea that beauty is revolution is a revelation to me. I once believed that the concept of the music was more important than the sound, that the politics of the notation was more important than the time limits of the rehearsals and therefore more important than the sound of the performance; that the numerological equivalents for the instruments were the determining factor for instrumentation; that pitch must be explicit and rhythm improvised; that if the composer says it is so, two string players and two lighting technicians can be a string quartet; that any composition must be consistent throughout and that internal change in the piece showed lack of compositional concentration; that more than three chords in one piece meant confusion or commercial music, or both; and on, and on.

It is a very liberating feeling to come back to my childhood definition of composition: writing down inspirations. I've rediscovered the part of my brain that can't decode anything, that can't add, that can't work from a verbalised concept, that doesn't care about stylish notation, that makes melodies that have pitch and rhythm, that doesn't know anything about zen eternity and gets bored and changes, that isn't worried about being commercial or avant-garde or serial or any other little category. Beauty is enough.

* * *

Although Beth Anderson's work spans diverse forms and even sounds (electronic, vocal, tape collage, instrumental, noise-like, "pretty", "primitive" and "traditional") her music falls into two basic aggregates, one before 1978 and one after. She began early as a convinced modernist in Lexington, Kentucky and was devoted to John Cage long before she left Kentucky in 1969 for the University of California at Davis. First at Davis and then in the heart of the San Francisco Bay Area's modernist sanctuary, she became loved/hated as a charming/outrageous apostle/practitioner of the most radical new music techniques, both for voice—in *Joan* and in *Queen Christina*, and in many instrumental compositions and tape collages—*Goodbye, Brigitte Bardot, or Hello, Charlotte Moorman* and *She Wrote*. Those were the years of modernist euphoria, especially in the Bay Area. As a survivor of those times has said—"If you had a mayonnaise jar full of vodka and somebody to make out with in the back, it didn't make any difference how boring the music was—the concert was a success." Listening to those old pieces in the 1980s, their method of construction is not the most salient thing about them. They seem characterized by an apparent Cage-modernism in which there lurks a suspicious taint of melody or harmony as indeed it does in the *Sonatas and Amores* of Cage himself. The structure of all these pieces is basically serial, in that elements, be they pitches, noises, parts of words, are manipulated by a randomized series. One might say that they are constructed of broken repetitions which Anderson calls "cut-ups", meaning that the results could be achieved by literally cutting up the written music and laying it out in a random or serial, or, at any rate in a non-improvisational way. This method is also used in her text-sound/sound poetry/poésie sonore, in which a poem emerges out of a single line or a pair of lines which are "cut-up" and reset by some order until the permutations are all "used up" and the piece is over. All this makes the best kind of modernist sense, and would have continued to do so were it not for secret elements in the artist's character—her childhood, where she grew up, etc. Hovering beneath the otherwise glassy modernist surface of her taste were memories of beloved music, which reached as far as the "tacky": revivalist hymns, Disney songs (particularly those of Frank Churchill), Hank Williams songs, and most anti-modernist of all—"standard" popular songs and "parlor music" of a time already vanished in 1950 when she was born. This repertoire kept alive in her a sensibility for harmony, that most forbidden of modernist bogeymen. And circumstances came together to exacerbate this. Desirous to make a name in the great world Anderson left for New York, where the two inevitable twin scourges, obscurity and poverty, took over, not immediately, but as soon as her National Endowment for the Arts grant ran out. Reduced to accompanying modern dance classes (not masochistic enough to accompany ballet) Anderson had to think on her feet when a pattern was called out, and she had to improvise something plausible in a hurry. This meant as a consequence tonal-modal music and regular rhythmic patterns. After many hours of this employment the insidious message of the 1960s ("Why not?") got into her head and she began, around 1978, to make serious music out of tonal-modal elements, maintaining all the while her philosophical commitment to random serialism and collage, meaning that the pieces were made of "cut-ups" of newly composed non-modernist material.

The most recent pieces use fewer "cut-ups" but they are still present in the *Swales* and in *Revel*. In the songs, the show music and "The Angel" "cut-ups" are much less evident. In what happened to Anderson can be seen traces of a pattern by which many of her generation changed the sound of modernism while continuing to fly the official banners and adhering to some of its formal precepts. When a critic wrote that her music was "as if the twentieth century never happened", she was appalled. Anderson and others like her feel and demonstrate by their work that more happened in the 20th century than dissonance, chromaticism and noise. To wit: the influence of "World Music", the serious focus on popular music, the different concepts of modes and scales and different attitudes towards repetition. These elements entered simultaneously into rock music and art music, and by so doing, created a potentially new listening climate, in which audiences no longer come to concerts to measure American composers by pre-existing European art music. So the voyage of Anderson's music begins to look more like the beginning of something, rather than the tail of early 20th-century music.

—Michael Sahl

ANDRIESSEN, Louis. Dutch. Born in Utrecht, 6 June 1939. Educated at Royal Conservatory, The Hague (under Hendrik Andriessen and Kees van Baaren), 1957–62; further study in Milan and Berlin (under Luciano Berio), 1962–3. Professor of composition, Royal Conservatory, The Hague, since 1978; founder/performer, wind ensemble Volharding, 1972; founder/pianist, Hoketus ensemble, 1977; co-founder, Charles Ives Society, Amsterdam. Recipient: Royal Conservatory composition prize, The Hague, 1962; Matthijs Vermeulen Prize, and 1st prize, Rostrum of Composers (for *De Staat*), 1977. Mailing address: c/o Donemus Publishing, Paulus Potterstraat 14, 1971 CZ Amsterdam, Netherlands.

Publisher: Donemus.

Symphonies/orchestral:

Ittrospezione II 1963.
Anachronie I (to the memory of Charles Ives) 1965–6; first performed Rotterdam, 18 January 1968.
Contra-tempus (winds, 2 percussion, 4 pianos, 4 violas) 1968.
Anachronie II (oboe, 4 horns, piano, harp, chamber orchestra) 1969.
Hoe het is / How It Is (live electronics, 52 strings) 1970; first performed Rotterdam, 14 September 1970.
The Nine Symphonies of Beethoven (promenade orchestra, ice cream bell) 1970.
Symphonieen der Nederlanden (2 or more wind orchestras) 1974.
Worker's Union (symphonic movement for loud instruments) 1975.
Nederland, let op uw schoonheyt (brass band, wind band) 1975.
Hymne (to the memory of Darius Milhaud) 1978.
Symfonie voor losse snaren / Symphony for Open Strings 1978.

Chamber/instrumental:

Sonata (flute) 1956.
Series (2 pianos) 1958–64.
Percosse (flute, trumpet, bassoon, percussion) 1958.
Aanloop en sprongen / Rincorsi e salti (flute, oboe, clarinet) 1961.
Trois Pièces (piano, left hand) 1961.
Ittrospezione I (2 pianos) 1961.
Triplum per chitarra (guitar) 1962.
A Flower Song (cello) 1963.
A Flower Song II (oboe) 1963.
Registers (piano) 1963.
Ittrospezione III (Concept I) (2 pianos, chamber ensemble) 1964.
A Flower Song III (cello) 1964.
Sweet (recorder or flute, tape) 1964.
Double (clarinet, piano) 1965.
Ittrospezione II (Concept II) (2 pianos, chamber ensemble) 1965.
Ittrospezione III (fragment; 2 pianos, tenor saxophone ad lib) 1965.
Paintings (recorder or flute, piano) 1965.
Souvenirs d'enfance (collaboration with J. Bernlef; piano, tape) 1966.
Choralvorspiele (barrel organ) 1969.
Spektakel / Uproar (16 winds, 6 percussion, electronic instruments) 1970.
Vergeet mij niet (oboist who also plays piano) 1970.
Volkslied / National Anthem (unlimited number of any instrument) 1971.
De Volharding / Persistence (3 trumpets, 3 saxophones, 3 trombones, piano) 1972.
On Jimmy Yancey (chamber/jazz group) 1973.
Melodie (recorder, piano) 1974.
Hoketus (2 panpipes, 2 alto saxophones, 2 pianos, 2 electric pianos, 2 bass guitars, 2 congas) 1977.
Felicitatie (3 trumpets) 1979.
La Voce (cello) 1981.
Overture to Orpheus (harpsichord) 1982.
Disco (violin, piano) 1982.
Trepidus (piano) 1983.
De Snelheid / Velocity (large ensemble) 1984.
De Stijl (large ensemble; part of opera *De Materie*) 1985; first performed Holland, 1985.
Dubbelspoor (piano, harpsichord, glockenspiel, celeste) 1986.
De Lijn (3 flutes) 1986.
Widow / Song Lines (saxophone orchestra) 1990; first performed Maastricht, November 1990.

Vocal/choral:

Nocturnen (soprano, chamber orchestra) 1959.
De Staat (4 women's voices, 27 instruments) 1973–6.
Il Principe (2 choirs, winds, piano, bass guitar; Machiavelli) 1974.
Mausoleum (2 high baritones, large ensemble) 1979.
De Tijd / Time (female choir, orchestra) 1981.

Opera:

Reconstructie (collaboration with Reinbert de Leeuw, Misha Mengelberg, Peter Schat, Jan van Vlijmen; soloists, 3 choirs, orchestra, electronics) 1968–9; first performed The Hague, 29 June 1969.
De Materie (4-movement opera, incorporating *De Stijl*; soloists, large ensemble) 1989; first performed Holland, 1989.
Nietzsche redet (reciter, woodwinds, 2 pianos, strings) 1989.

Other:

In memoriam (electronic) 1971.
Il Duce (electronic) 1973.
The Family (film music; orchestra) 1973.
Mattheus Passie / St Matthew's Passion (theatre music) 1976.
Orpheus (music-theatre) 1977.
George Sand (music-theatre; 8 voices, 4 pianos) 1980.
Doctor Nero (theatre music) 1984.

PUBLICATIONS

By Andriessen: (with Elmer Schonberger) *Het Apollinisch Uurwerk* [on Stravinsky], Amsterdam, 1983, translated as *The Apollonian Clockwork*, Cambridge, 1990.

* * *

Louis Andriessen—along with the somewhat more erratic Misha Mengelberg, with whom he collaborated on the opera *Reconstructie*—is perhaps the most interesting of the post-war Dutch composers.

Andriessen was, indeed, born on the very cusp of World War II. Within a very few years, Dutch life and culture was all but dismantled by a brutal Nazi occupation and by the systematic bombing of Holland's industrial and commercial infrastructure. When the war ended, it was necessary to begin afresh and to articulate a new musical language that had little to do with the prevailing Germanic models of previous generations. Andriessen studied at the Royal Conservatory in The Hague under his father Hendrik Andriessen, from whom he drew a powerful combination of "influences" (which are only discernible as such at a considerable distance from individual works and in the most general terms) such as polytonality and a late-Romantic interest in melodies pitched at the very limits of tonal coherence. Andriessen doubtless also came under the influence of his uncle, the pianist and composer Willem Andriessen, who died in 1964, but perhaps the most significant encounter of his student and apprentice years were his two periods of study with Luciano Berio in Milan and Berlin.

Despite the artistic success of *In memoriam* and *Il Duce*, both interesting experiments, Andriessen has not been especially drawn to electronics (which may rank as elitist appurtenances in his determinedly democratic and even preterite style). What he did draw from Berio was a strong sense of voice, which becomes evident in such works as *De Staat*, a superbly scored vocal piece which underlines Andriessen's curiously chastened but defiant political standpoint; the same qualities are evident in *Volkslied* and in the collaborative opera *Reconstructie*.

Andriessen has combined composing and an academic career with performance; he is a fine, perhaps underrated pianist, with all of his uncle's formal control. Andriessen has been co-founder and keyboard player with two significant ensembles, De Volharding and Hoketus, both of which draw their names from his own compositions. The first was a strong piece for winds and piano that drew strongly—though not quite as explicitly as the later *On Jimmy Yancey*—on his interest in the polytonal possibilities of jazz ensemble and a jazz idiom. The latter exploited the interesting timbral possibilities of panpipes and saxophones set over acoustic and electric pianos, and a powerful amplified bass and conga rhythm.

Andriessen has written little non-dramatic orchestral music since the late 1970s. Unlike his father, he does not seem to be an entirely confident composer for orchestra—though the 1978 *Symphony for Open Strings* is an intriguing effort—and works much more comfortably in smaller, non-canonical ensembles, often with a particularly uniform sonority, such as the piano, harpsichord, celesta and glockenspiel *Dubbelspoor*, or the barrel-organ piece *Choralvorspiele*. An exception, at least in regard to scale, is *Widow / Song Lines*, scored for saxophone orchestra and premiered at the Maastricht Music Days in 1990, which follows the wind orchestra concept developed by Andriessen for *Symphonieen der Nederlanden* in 1974.

Andriessen's somewhat ironic response to the classical canon is suggested in the earlier *Nine Symphonies of Beethoven*, for light orchestra and ice cream bell, a satirical work that still conveys a measure of respect absent in the daringly confrontational *Worker's Union*. Though Andriessen is also a founder of the Charles Ives Society, there is less evidence of Ives than of Milhaud in the fine *Ittrospezione II* and the explicit tribute of *Hymne*, a threnody written in the year of Milhaud's death. There is also his remarkable book on Stravinsky, *Het Apollinisch Uurwerk*, one of the most profound studies of one composer by another ever published.

A proportion of Andriessen's output now seems somewhat ephemeral, including, sadly, the opera *Reconstructie*, but he has produced a remarkable body of work in a personal, but not solipsistic, idiom that is remarkable testimony to Dutch culture's powers of recovery and synthesis.

—Henk Maarten

ARAPOV, Boris (Alexandrovich). Russian. Born in St Petersburg, 12 September 1905. Educated at Leningrad Conservatoire (under V.V. Scherbachev), graduated 1930. Married Tatiana Pavlovna Todorova 1933; 2 daughters. Instructor, 1930–4, docent, 1934–40; professor, 1940–51 (faculty evacuated to Tashkent, Uzbekistan, 1941–4, head of instrumental department, 1951–74, and Head of composition, since 1974, Leningrad Conservatoire. Professor of composition and analysis, Tbilisi, Georgia, 1937–8; secretary, Leningrad section, Soviet Composers' Union. Recipient: Honoured Worker of the Uzbek S.S.R., 1944; Order of the Red Banner of Labour, 1953; Honoured Worker of the R.S.F.S.R., 1957; People's Artist of the R.S.F.S.R., 1976; Order of Lenin, 1986. Mailing address: Prospekt Y. Gagarina 35, kv.65, St Petersburg 196135, U.S.S.R.

Publishers: Sovetskii kompozitor, St Petersburg; Sikorski, Germany; Editio Musica, Budapest; Boosey & Hawkes, London.

Symphonies / orchestral:

Fugatto 1928; first performed Leningrad, 1928.
Tadzhik Suite 1938; first performed Moscow, 1939.
Russian Suite 1951; first performed Moscow, 1952.
Symphony No 2 "Svobodniy Kitay" / Free China 1959; first performed Moscow, 1960.
Symphony No 3 1962; performed Moscow, 1963.
Concerto for Violin and Orchestra 1964; first performed Leningrad, 1965.
Concerto for Full Symphony Orchestra 1969; first performed Leningrad, 1969.
Concerto for Violin, Piano, Percussion and Chamber Orchestra (In Memory of Igor Stravinsky) 1973; first performed Leningrad, 1973.
Symphony No 4 (reciter, baritone, mezzo-soprano, 2 mixed choirs, orchestra; Briusov, Mayakovsky, Orlov, Shchipachev, Vloshin) 1975; first performed Leningrad, 1977.
Symphony No 5 1981; first performed Leningrad, 1982.
Choreographic Poem on "The Picture of Dorian Gray" 1983.
Symphony No 6 1983; first performed Leningrad, 1985.
Symphonic Poem (after the novel by Hitmatov) 1988; first performed Leningrad, 1989.

Chamber / instrumental:

Variations (piano) 1929.
Sonata (violin) 1930.
Humoresque (piano) 1937; first performed Leningrad, 1945.
Three Pieces on Mongol Themes (clarinet, violin, piano) 1943; first performed Tashkent, 1943.
Ten Uzbek Pieces (piano) 1944.
Six Pieces on Chinese Themes (piano) 1955; first performed Beijing, 1956.
Etude-Scherzo (piano) 1967; first performed Leningrad, 1969.
Sonata (piano) 1970; first performed Philadelphia, 1971.
Three Pieces (piano) 1970; first performed Leningrad, 1978.
Sonata No 2 (piano) 1976; first performed Leningrad, 1978.
Sonata (violin, piano) 1978; first performed Leningrad, 1979.
Five Small Pieces on the Same Theme (flute, clarinet, 2 bassoons) 1979; first performed Leningrad, 1980.
Quintet (oboe, horn, harp, viola, cello) 1980; first performed Leningrad, 1980.
Sonata (horn, piano) 1981; first performed Leningrad, 1982.
Five Pieces (piano) 1982; first performed Leningrad, 1984.
Sonata (cello, piano) 1983; first performed Tashkent, 1985.
Dezimetto (2 clarinets, bassoon, trumpet, horn, tuba, piano, celesta, percussion, trombone) 1983; first performed Leningrad, 1987.
Sonata No 3 (piano) 1986; first performed Leningrad, 1988.

Vocal/choral:

Pokhodnaya pesnya geologov/Marching Song of the Geologists (voices, orchestra; Prokofyev) 1933.
Vocal-Symphonic Cycle (voices, orchestra; Pushkin) 1937.
Negro Protest Songs (bass, jazz orchestra) 1940; first performed Leningrad, 1940.
Dzhelal-Eddin (voices, orchestra; with Kozlovsky) 1944.
Four Romances (soprano, piano; Blok) 1947–63; first performed Leningrad, 1972.
Four Songs (voice, piano) 1949.
Monologue (baritone, trumpet, percussion, piano; Voznesensky) 1969; first performed Leningrad, 1969.
Four Sonnets by Petrarch (mezzo-soprano, piano) 1975; first performed Leningrad, 1976.
Four Seasons of a Year (soprano, tenor, instrumental nonet; Japanese texts by Chokku) 1977; first performed Leningrad, 1978.
Two Monologues (baritone, piano; Pasternak) 1980; first performed Leningrad, 1982.
Vocal Cycle (mezzo-soprano, cello, piano; Mandelstam, Akhmatova, Dudin) 1987; first performed Leningrad, 1989.

Opera:

Hodja Nasreddin (Uzbek comic opera; Vitkovitshan, Soloviev) 1944; first performed Tashkent, 1944.
Frigate "Victory" (Rozdestvensky, Ivanovsky; after Pushkin) 1957; first performed Leningrad, 1958.
The Rain (Todorova, after Maugham) 1965; first performed Leningrad, 1968.

Other:

Conquerors of the Night (film music) 1932.
The Moonstone (film music) 1933.
His Name Is Su'he Bator (film music) 1943.
Nasreddin in Buchura (film music) 1944.
The Click (film music) 1954.
The Portrait of Dorian Gray (ballet; orchestra) 1971; first performed Leningrad, 1981.

Bach: *Four Preludes and Fugues* (orchestration).

PUBLICATIONS

By Arapov: "Former Years", in *Leningrad Conservatoire in Retrospect*, Leningrad, 1962; "The Tenth Symphony of D. Shostakovitch", in *The Soviet Symphony over 50 Years*, Leningrad, 1967; "Some words about Leningrad School of Composition", in *Young Composers in Leningrad*, Leningrad, 1972; "The Stronghold of the High Arts", in *Leningrad Philharmonia*, Leningrad, 1972.

On Arapov: E. Bontsch-Osmolorskaya, "In Defence of Peace", in *Soviet Music*, 11, 1963; A. Konigsberg, in *BAA*, 1965; M. Byalik, "In a Chamber Genre", in *Stranitsi muzikal'nay Leniani*, Leningrad, 1970; E. Finkel'shteyn, "On the Specifics of Genre", in *Muzika i zhizn*, 1972; "Towards a New Musical Theatre", in *Muzika i zhizn*, 1974.

Boris Arapov comments:

Living in the stormy epoch of the 20th century, the composer cannot reflect the complicated phenomena of life by turning to old methods. It is necessary to equip oneself with all the technical riches of the age. The artist and his time have to be in accord. If one lives in keeping with the rhythm of the time, if one is concerned with the events of that time, then old age is conquered and one is ever young and purposeful.

* * *

Brought up in a family with eclectic intellectual interests, Boris Arapov imbibed a spirit of undogmatic and exploratory enthusiasm from his very earliest years. His mature career represents the almost perfect embodiment of a Soviet cultural ideal untouched by Stalinist narrowness. Arapov's work draws on a Russian classical tradition, mixes it generously with folk and ethnic materials, and even admits elements of advanced Western musical thinking (notably serialism), without allowing any single component to disrupt the organic coherence of the whole or to leave it vulnerable to ideological manipulation.

As a child, he showed prodigious talent as a pianist and composer, studying first with his mother and then with Zaytseva-Zhukovich, who moulded him into a promising concert soloist. A serious disorder of the hand cut short his performing career and reinforced his commitment to composition. He matured early and quickly developed a style that was sufficiently receptive to idiomatic and even structural change to keep it virtually intact in essentials for nearly 30 years. Arapov's music is large-scale, generous in conception, and eminently listenable. His ability to integrate material from other musical cultures—Korean, Chinese, Western—is impressive and unflagging.

It was his double good fortune to be evacuated during the war to the conservatory at Tashkent. There he was exposed to Uzbek music and to echoes (which he was to pursue later) of Far Eastern music. These had a clearly discernible influence on his subsequent work; the opera *Hodja Nasreddin* is based on Uzbek themes. Inevitably, he was not immune to the wider political complexities of the age. *Symphony No 2*—subtitled "Free China"—barely predates the final split between European and Asian communism, and the tension is palpable amid his mainly affirmative conception and confident scoring. The 1940 *Negro Protest Songs*, based on Black American texts, conform to a late Popular Front confidence in the vitality of all "proletarian" sub-cultures; the songs are brilliantly arranged, with all the dramatic sense that informs the earlier *Marching Song of the Geologists* and the post-war ballet *Frigate "Victory"*.

Almost as important for his teaching as for his composition—Alexander Knaifel and Sergei Slonimsky were his pupils—Arapov is an important presence in middle-generation Soviet music, and a distinctive exponent of the Leningrad style. In November and December 1965, there was a Festival of Leningrad Music in the "new" capital, Moscow. Arapov's *Concerto for Violin* was performed and helped underline the diversity of a musical culture which, under the rhetorical control at least of the latter-day commissars constantly threatened to become monolithic and undifferentiated. It was an important symbolic and prophetic moment.

—James Weir

ARCHER, Violet (Balesteri). Canadian. Born in Montreal, 24 April 1913. Educated: teacher's licentiate in piano, 1936;

McGill University, Montreal, B.Mus. (composition), 1936; composition scholarships, 1940–4; Royal Canadian College of Organists, associate diploma in organ, 1938; studied composition under Béla Bartók, New York, 1942; Bradley Keeler Memorial Scholarship and Charles Ditson Fellowship, Yale University School of Music, New Haven, Connecticut (under Richard Donovan and Paul Hindemith), B.Mus. (composition) 1947–8, M.Mus. (composition), 1949. Music instructor, McGill University, 1943–7; music instructor, University of Alberta, summers 1948, 1949; resident composer, North Texas State College, 1950–3; visiting lecturer, Cornell University, summer 1952; assistant professor, University of Oklahoma, 1953–61; Canada Council Senior Fellowship, 1958–9; associate professor, 1962–7, chair, division of theory and composition, 1962–78, professor, 1970–78 (and thereafter emerita), University of Alberta, Edmonton; resident composer, Banff School of Fine Arts, summers 1978, 1979. Recipient: composition trophy, Quebec Music Festival, 1938; Woods Chandler Prize for Composition, Yale University, 1949; citation, Yale School of Music, 1968; Merit Award, Government of Alberta, 1970; honorary D.Mus., McGill University, 1971; Creative and Performance Award, City of Edmonton, 1972; Queen's Jubilee Silver Medal, 1978; life academic member, Accademica Tiberina, Rome, 1979; Performing Rights Organization of Canada Ltd Award, 1981; Award of Merit, McGill University Alma Mater Fund, 1982; special award in honour of outstanding contribution to cultural life of Alberta, presented by Celebration of Women in Arts, 1983; honorary life member, Latitude 53, Society of Artists, December 1983; "Composer of the Year", Canadian Music Council, March 1984; Order of Canada, April 1984; "Women in the Arts" award, Edmonton YWCA Tribute to Women, May 1985; "Violet Archer Festival", Edmonton, October 1985; fellow, Royal Canadian College of Organists, July 1985; honorary D.Mus., University of Windsor, 1986; inducted, Culture Hall of Fame, Edmonton, 1987; Frederick Haultain Award, 1987; honorary LL.D., University of Calgary, June 1989; composition scholarship, University of Alberta named Violet Archer Scholarship. Mailing address: 10805 85th Avenue, Edmonton, Alberta T6E 2L2, Canada.

Publishers: Mercury; Boosey & Hawkes; Peer Southern; Berandol; Waterloo; Jaymar; Gordon V. Thompson; Dorn; Canada Music Centre.

Symphonies/orchestral:

Intermezzo 1936; first performed Edmonton, June 1936.
Scherzo Sinfonico 1939; first performed Montreal, February 1940.
Capriccio (hand tympani, orchestra) 1939.
Poem (based on *The Nun*, by Wolfe) 1940; first performed Oklahoma, 1960.
Variations on "A la claire fontaine" (orchestra or piano) 1940.
Britannia: A Joyful Overture 1941; first performed BBC, 1942.
Fantasia Concertante (flute, oboe, clarinet, strings) 1941; first performed Edmonton, 20 October 1974.
Fantasy (clarinet, strings) 1942; first performed Montreal, 1942.
Themes and Variations (string orchestra; arranged from string quartet version) 1942.
Symphony 1945; first performed Vancouver, 11 November 1973.
Fantasy on a Ground 1946, revised 1956; first performed Austin, Texas, 1956.
Concertino (A clarinet, orchestra) 1946, revised 1956; first performed Winnipeg, Manitoba, 1972.
Fanfare and Passacaglia 1948–9; first performed Boston, 1949. Recorded CBC Programme 130.
Concerto No 1 for Piano and Orchestra 1956.
Divertimento 1957; first performed Oklahoma, 1958.
Concerto for Violin and Orchestra 1959; first performed Montreal, 1960.
Three Sketches for Orchestra 1961; first performed Montreal, 1961. Recorded CBC SM 119.
Prelude-Incantation 1964; first performed Edmonton, 28 November 1964.
Suite (string orchestra) 1968.
Sinfonietta 1968; first performed Saskatoon, Saskatchewan, 2 March 1969. Recorded CBC SM226; RCI ACM 17.
Sinfonia 1969; first performed Edmonton, Alberta, 18 March 1970.
Mini Divertimento (piano, string orchestra) 1984; first performed London, 7 April 1986.
Improvisation on a Name (chamber orchestra) 1987; first performed Redcliffe, 4 February 1988.
Evocations (2 pianos, orchestra) 1987; first performed Edmonton, 11–12 March 1988.

Chamber/instrumental:

Six Pieces (piano, timpani) 1939.
String Quartet No 1 1940.
Aeterna Christi Mundi (organ) 1940, revised 1976.
Chorale Prelude: "Aeterna Christi Munera" (organ) 1940.
Eight Chorale Preludes (organ) 1940–8.
Variations on a Canadian Folk Tune: "Isabeau s'y promène" (piano) 1941.
Sonata (flute, A clarinet, piano) 1942; first performed Montreal, 1942.
Habitant Sketches / Three scenes (piano) 1942; first performed Montreal, 1942.
Three Scenes (piano) 1942.
Theme and Variations (string quartet; also arranged for string orchestra) 1942; first performed Edmonton, Alberta, 1943.
Sonatina (organ) 1944; first performed Montreal, 1944.
Sonata (flute, clarinet, piano) 1944.
Sonta (piano) 1945, revised 1957 as *Sonata No 1*.
Sonatina No 1 (piano) 1945.
Quartet (flute, oboe, clarinet, bassoon) 1945.
Birthday Fugue à la Weinberger (2 pianos) 1946; first performed Edmonton, Alberta, 3 June 1985.
Sonatina No 2 (piano) 1946. Recorded CBC RCI 132.
Fantasy (violin, piano) 1946; first performed Montreal, 1946.
Suite (violin, cello or clarinet, bassoon) 1947.
Suite (piano) 1947.
Three Sketches (2 pianos) 1947; first performed Saskatoon, Saskatchewan, 20 March 1974.
Two Pieces (flute) 1947.
Four Vignettes (piano) 1947, revised 1983; first performed Edmonton, Alberta, November 1984.
Six Preludes (piano) 1947 or 1949; first performed Winnipeg, Manitoba, 21 October 1979.
Fantasy (piano) 1947.
Suite (violin, cello) 1948.
Three Two-Part Inventions (piano) 1948.
Two Chorale Preludes (organ) 1948.
Chorale Prelude: "Dominus Regit Me" (organ) 1948, revised 1960.
Chorale Prelude: "Henlein" (organ) 1948, revised 1960.
Chorale Prelude III: Ibant Magi (organ) 1948, revised 1976; first performed Quebec City, 1983.

Chorale Prelude IV: Durch Adam's Fall Is Ganz Verderbt (organ) 1948, revised 1976; first performed Edmonton, Alberta, 1978.

Chorale Prelude V: Von Himmel Hoch, da Komm'Ich her (organ) 1948, revised 1976; first performed Edmonton, 1978.

Concerto for Organ (arranged from J.G. Walther) 1949.

Divertimento No 1 (oboe, clarinet, bassoon) 1949; first performed Boston, 1949. Recorded CBC RCI 192.

String Quartet No 2 1949; first performed Montreal, 1954.

Fugue Fantasy (string quartet) 1949.

Pavan (arranged from *The Royal Consorte*, by William Lawes; 2 trumpets, 2 horns, 3 trombones) 1949.

Ricercare (arranged from Pachelbel; woodwinds, brass) 1949.

Fantasy in the Form of a Passacaglia (4 horns, 3 trumpets, 3 trombones, baritone horn, tuba, timpani) 1951; first performed Denton, Texas, 1951.

Theme and Variations on La-haut sur ces montagnes (piano) 1952. Recorded Canadian Music Centre Centrediscs CMC 1684.

String Trio No 1 1953; first performed Lac-à-la-Outre, Quebec, 1953.

Ten Folk Songs (piano, 4 hands) 1953; broadcast, 1954.

Prelude and Allegro (violin, piano) 1954; first performed Lac-à-la-Loutre, Quebec, 1954. Recorded RCI 136.

Trio No 1 (violin, cello, piano) 1954; first performed Montreal, 1954. Recorded CBC SM 119; ACM 17.

Three Duets (2 violins) 1955; first performed Oklahoma, 1956.

Rondo (piano) 1955.

Prelude and Allegro (organ) 1955.

Introduction and Allegro (organ) 1955; first performed Norman, Oklahoma, 1955.

Sonata (cello, piano) 1956; first performed Montreal, 1957. Recorded CBC Programme 139; ACM 17.

Sonata No 1 (violin, piano) 1956; first performed Norman, Oklahoma, 1958. Recorded RCI Programme 196; ACM 17.

Trio No 2 (piano, violin, cello) 1957; first performed Washington, D.C., 1958.

Minute Music for Small Hands (piano) 1957.

Divertimento No 2 (oboe, violin, cello) 1957; first performed Norman, Oklahoma, 17 May 1960.

Variations on an Original Theme (carillon) 1958.

Divertimento (oboe, clarinet, bass clarinet) 1960s. Recorded CBC MG 838/39.

Eleven Short Piano Pieces 1960; first performed Oklahoma City, 1966. Recorded—3, 4, 5, 6, 7, 9—Contemporary Canadian Music 1.

String Trio No 2 1961; first performed Winnipeg, Manitoba, 1961. Recorded RCI 241; ACM 17.

Divertimento (brass quintet) 1963; first performed Montreal, 22 April 1963.

Four Little Studies (piano) 1963.

Themes and Variations (piano) 1963; first performed Edmonton, Alberta, 22 November 1970.

Introduction, Dance and Finale (2 trumpets, horn, trombone, tuba, harp/piano, snare drum, timpani) 1963.

Three Miniatures (piano) 1963. Recorded Contemporary Canadian Music 1.

Sonata (horn, piano) 1965; first performed Regina, Saskatchewan, 20 May 1965. Recorded RCI 412; ACM 17.

Chorale Improvisation on "O Worship the King" (organ) 1967; first performed Montreal, 28 July 1967. Recorded ST-56722/23.

Improvisations (piano) 1968; first performed Edmonton, Alberta, 20 November 1968. Recorded Melbourne SMLP 403.

Dance (violin, cello) 1970.

Two Miniatures (piano) 1970.

Holiday (piano) 1970.

Three Little Studies (violin, piano) 1970.

Sonata (clarinet, piano) 1970; first performed Beaumont, Texas, 1972. Recorded RCI 412; ACM 17.

Suite (4 violins) 1971; first performed Edmonton, Alberta, 1972.

Lydian Mood (piano) 1971.

Black and White (piano) 1971.

A Quiet Chat (piano) 1971.

Sonata (alto saxophone, piano) 1972; first performed Toronto, 30 August 1972. Recorded RCI 412; ACM 17.

Sonata (oboe, piano) 1973; first performed Edmonton, Alberta, 16 February 1975.

Sonatina No 3 (piano) 1973.

Three Inventions (piano) 1974.

Little Suite (trumpet or clarinet, piano) 1975; first performed Edmonton, Alberta, 1976.

Simple Tune (soprano recorder, piano) 1975.

Suite (flute) 1976; first performed Edmonton, Alberta, 3 February 1976.

Sonata (viola, cello, piano) 1976; first performed Edmonton, Alberta, 20 February 1978.

Four Bagatelles (piano) 1977; first performed Edmonton, Alberta, 28 February 1978.

Sonatina (oboe, piano) 1977; first performed Toronto, 17 May 1980.

Sonatina (bassoon, piano) 1978; first performed London, 1979.

Thirteen Fughettas (piano) 1978.

Four Contrapuntal Moods (piano) 1978.

Eight Little Canons (piano) 1978.

Sonatina (clarinet, piano) 1978; first performed Edmonton, Alberta, 27 November 1988.

Prelude and Little Fantasy on "Winchester New" (organ) 1978.

Fantasy on "Blanche comme la neige" (guitar) 1978; first performed Edmonton, Alberta, 31 March 1980.

Divertimento (saxophone quartet) 1979; first performed Edmonton, Alberta, 1979.

Three Preludes (piano) 1979; first performed London, 24 March 1980.

Sonata No 2 (piano) 1979; first performed Calgary, Alberta, 22 February 1980.

Four Duets (violin, cello) 1979; first performed Banff, Alberta, 25 July 1980.

Festive Fantasy on Pangue Lingua (organ) 1979; first performed Edmonton, Alberta, 1979.

Sonata (bassoon, piano) 1980; first performed Vancouver, February 1980.

Here and Now (piano; 10 educational pieces) 1980.

Capriccio (cello, piano) 1981; first performed London, 1981.

Twelve Miniatures (violin, piano) 1981; first performed Matsumoto, Japan, 17 July 1983.

Sonata (cello) 1981; first performed Banff, Alberta, 9 July 1982.

String Quartet No 3 1981; first performed Edmonton, Alberta, 1 October 1982. Recorded ACM 17.

Soliloquies (A and B♭ clarinet) 1982; first performed Edmonton, Alberta, 1982.

Statements (C and G flute) 1982; first performed Edmonton, Alberta, 17 January 1985.

Improvisation (cello) n.d.; first performed New York City, 18 October 1983.

Celebration (brass quintet) 1983; first performed Edmonton, Alberta, 15 November 1983.

Six Miniatures (2 for cello, piano; 2 for cello duet, with optional piano; 2 for cello trio) 1984; first performed Edmonton, Alberta, August 1985.
Variations on Aberystwyth (organ) 1984; first performed Calgary, Alberta, 23 November 1984.
Six Miniatures (viola, piano) 1984; first performed Edmonton, Alberta, August 1985.
Signatures (alto flute, C flute) 1984.
The Dancing Kitten (violin, piano) 1986.
Six Miniatures (string bass, piano) 1986.
Moods (clarinet, alto saxophone) n.d.; first performed Grand Prairie, Texas, April 1986.
I va vari (brass quintet) n.d.; first performed Calgary, Alberta, 13 November 1987.
Four Miniatures (classical accordion) 1988; first performed Edmonton, Alberta, 23 November 1988.
Carillon for a Festal Day (carillon) 1988.
Four Miniatures (classical guitar) n.d.; first performed Venice, n.d.
String Quartet No 4 n.d.

Vocal/choral:

Choruses from The Bacchae (SSA choir, orchestra; Euripides) 1938.
Leaves of Grass (SATB choir, orchestra; Whitman) 1940; first performed Montreal, 1940.
Psalm 150: Anthem (SATB/men's and boys' voices, organ) 1941.
Psalm 141 (SATB choir, organ; SA parts can be taken by boys) 1942.
Moon Songs (baritone/mezzo-soprano, piano; Lindsay) 1942–4, revised 1976; first performed Banff, Alberta, May 1979.
Lamentations of Jeremy (SATB choir, orchestra) 1947.
Some One (unison choir, piano; de la Mare) 1949, revised 1959.
Under the Sun (soprano, piano; Bourinot) 1949; first performed New Haven, Connecticut, 1949. Recorded RCI ACM 17.
The Bell (SATB choir, orchestra; Donne) 1949; first performed Montreal, 1953. Recorded CBC RCI 130; ACM 17.
Snow Shadows (mezzo-soprano; Bourinot) 1949; first performed St. Catharines, Ontario, 8 March 1989.
Landscapes (choir; Eliot) 1950; first performed Denton, Texas, 1952. Recorded CBC SM 274; RCI 10/70; ACM 17.
April Weather (medium voice, piano; England) 1950; broadcast 1953. Recorded Canadian Broadcasting Corporation RCI 108; ACM 17.
Three Biblical Songs (medium voice, piano) 1950.
Cradle Song (mezzo-soprano, piano; England) 1950; first performed Denton, Texas, 1952. Recorded Radio Canada International ACM 17; RCI 108.
The Twenty-Third Psalm (mezzo-soprano, piano) 1952; first performed Montreal, 1952. Recorded ACM 17.
Proud Horses (unaccompanied SATB choir; Sampley) 1953; first performed Montreal, 1953. Recorded RCI 189; ACM 17.
Three French Canadian Folk Songs (unaccompanied SATB choir; tr. Osborne) 1953; first performed Osaka, Japan, 17 April 1961. Recorded Vox PL 11.860; Turnabout CTC 320023.
Songs of Prayer and Praise (unaccompanied SATB choir; Donne) 1953.
Christmas (SSA choir, oboe, harp; Bass) 1955; first performed Norman, Oklahoma, 1955. Recorded TCC D003.
The Storm (mezzo-soprano, piano; Morris) 1955.
The Mater Admirabilis Chapel (SSA choir, oboe, harp; Bass) 1955; first performed Norman, Oklahoma, 1955.
The Gulls (medium voice, piano; Fletcher) 1955.
Irradiations (mezzo-soprano, piano; Fletcher) 1955.
Sky and Sea (mezzo-soprano, piano) 1955; first performed Norman, Oklahoma, 1955.
Two Songs for Women's Voices (SSAA choir, oboe, piano/harp; Bass) 1955.
Two Songs (soprano, clarinet; "The Lamb", "The Fly", Blake) 1958; first performed Montreal, 1958.
Apocalypse (soprano, SATB choir, 2 trumpets, 2 horns, 2 trombones, timpani; Revelation) 1958; first performed Montreal, 1959.
Four Canadian Folk Songs (mezzo-soprano, piano; Barbeau) 1958.
The Forty-Second Psalm (medium voice, piano) 1959; first performed Edmonton, Alberta, 1975.
Souls of the Righteous (SATB choir, optional soprano or tenor solo; Wisdom of Solomon) 1960.
Two Latin Motets (unaccompanied SATB choir) 1962; first performed Montreal, 1962.
In Nomine Jesu (Introits and Anthems) (unaccompanied SATB choir; English hymnal no 729) 1962.
Introit and Choral Prayer (SATB choir, organ; hymnal, Campbell) 1962; first performed Edmonton, Alberta, October 1979.
Sing, the Muse: a Chorale Cycle (unaccompanied SATB choir; Marston, Shakespeare, Drummond, Raleigh) 1964.
Paul Bunyan (SATB choir, piano; Bourinot) 1966; first performed Edmonton, Alberta, 15 February 1967.
Three Folk Songs of Old Manitoba (medium voice, piano; Murray, Riel, Falcon) arranged 1966.
Life in a Prairie Shack (voice, piano) arranged 1966.
Cantata Sacra (soprano, alto, tenor, baritone, bass, orchestra; Archer, Reeves, medieval) 1966–7; first performed Winnipeg, Manitoba, 14 March 1967.
Sweet Jesu, King of Bliss (unaccompanied SATB/SA choir; 13th-century English, anon.) 1967.
Centennial Springtime (unison/SATB choir, piano; Alexander) 1967.
Harvest (unison choir, piano; melody, Ferretti, text, Hetherington) arranged 1967.
I Will Lift Up Mine Eyes (SATB choir, organ; Psalm 121) 1967.
Amens for Church Use (SATB choir, organ) 1968–74.
A la Claire Fontaine (SA choir, piano; Barbeau, tr. Osborne) arranged 1968.
O Lord, Thou Hast Searched Me and Known Me (SATB choir, organ; Psalm 139) 1968.
O Sing unto the Lord (SA choir, 2 trumpets, organ; Psalm 96) 1968. Recorded CMC SNE 528.
Où vas-tu, mon petit garçon (SA choir, piano; Barbeau) 1968.
A Simple Anthem (Old 100th) (SATB choir, organ) 1969.
The Glory of God (unaccompanied SSAA choir; Psalm 67, Isaiah) 1971; first performed Edmonton, Alberta, 1971.
My Hands (medium voice, piano) 1971; first performed Edmonton, Alberta, 1972.
Green Rain (mezzo-soprano, piano; Livesay) 1971; first performed Edmonton, Alberta, 1972.
Gold Sun (alto, piano; Livesay) 1971; first performed Edmonton, Alberta, 1972.
Daffodils (medium voice, piano; Wordsworth) 1972; first performed Edmonton, Alberta, 1972.
Proclamations; Offertory Acclamations; Doxologies (SATB choir, optional organ; King James Bible) 1974.
Sing a New Song to the Lord (choir; Psalm 98) 1974.
Four Newfoundland Folk Songs (unaccompanied TTBB

choir; tenors only in no 2) 1975.
Three Sailors from Groix / Trois Marins de Groix (SSA choir, piano; tr. Cockshott) 1975.
Moods in Miniatures (SSAA choir, piano; arranged from Olsen) 1976; first performed Edmonton, Alberta, 1 June 1976.
Shout with Joy (SATB choir, organ; Psalm 100) 1976.
I Corinthians 13 (mezzo-soprano, piano) 1976; first performed Edmonton, Alberta, May 1979.
Separation (alto/baritone, piano; 10th-century Chinese) 1976.
In Just Spring (medium voice, piano; cummings) 1977; first performed Edmonton, Alberta, 28 February 1979.
Plain Songs (mezzo-soprano, piano; Livesay) 1977; first performed Edmonton, Alberta, 28 February 1978.
Two Songs of Praise (unaccompanied SSAA choir) 1978; first performed Edmonton, Alberta, 1978.
Together and Apart (mezzo-soprano, piano; Elliott) 1978.
Two Songs (high voice, piano; Longworth) 1978; first performed Edmonton, Alberta, 1978.
Northern Landscape (medium voice, piano; Smith) 1978; first performed Canada, 1980. Recorded Canadian Music Centre Centrediscs CMC 1083.
Psalmody (baritone, SATB choir, orchestra; Psalms 130, 46, 103, 148) 1978; first performed Edmonton, Alberta, May 1979.
Introit (unaccompanied SATB choir) 1979; first performed Lynchburg, Virginia, 7 October 1979.
Sprig of Flowers (tenor, flute, piano; Ch'ing) 1979; first performed Edmonton, Alberta, 19 February 1980.
Prairie Profiles (baritone, horn, piano; Carter) 1980; first performed Edmonton, Alberta, 23 February 1981. Recorded RCI ACM 17.
Primeval (tenor, piano; American Indian, translated Densmore, Neihardt) 1980; first performed Banff, Alberta, 1981.
Psalm 145 (unaccompanied SATB choir) 1981; first performed Edmonton, Alberta, 1981. Recorded World Records WRC1-1601.
Caleidoscopio (soprano, piano; Azzi) 1981; first performed Edmonton, Alberta, 1982. Recorded Canadian Music Centre CMC 1173/1183.
Rest in Thee (unaccompanied SATB choir; a Kempis) 1981.
Birds at Daybreak (tenor, piano; Layton) 1982; first performed Banff, Alberta, 1983.
Green Jade (baritone, flute/alto flute, piano; Liu, Lo) 1982; first performed Edmonton, Alberta, 28 March 1983.
Snippets (mezzo-soprano, piano; Ottman) 1982; first performed Edmonton, Alberta, 1983.
Songs of Summer and Fall (unaccompanied SATB choir; Carter) 1982; first performed Edmonton, Alberta, 30 March 1984.
Reflections (unaccompanied SSAATB choir; Carter) 1983; first performed Cork, Ireland, 2–6 May 1984.
The Cat and the Moon (SATB choir, piano; Yeats) 1983; first performed Calgary, Alberta, 29 October 1983.
Ikpakhuaq (mezzo-soprano, piano, flute, clarinet, violin, viola, cello; Eskimo, translated Roberts, Jenness) 1984; first performed Montreal, 14 January 1985.
Epigrams (baritone/tenor, piano; Johnson, Bentley, Erskine, Follansbee, anon.) 1985; first performed Edmonton, Alberta, 19 October 1985.
Miniatures from the Chinese (tenor/soprano, piano; Chang, Walmsley, Lo) 1985; first performed Edmonton, Alberta, 19 October 1985.
Two Hymns (SATB choir, congregation, organ; O'Driscoll) 1986.
Gay Is the Rose (voice, piano) 1987; first performed Alberta, 26 November 1988.
If the Stars Are Burning (mezzo-soprano, clarinet, piano; Buske) 1987; first performed Fairbanks, Alaska, 16 April 1987.
Northern Journey (song cycle for baritone, piano) 1990.
Danny Boy (arranged for SSAA choir, optional piano) n.d.

Opera:

Sganarelle (9 soli, small orchestra; Molière, Eliot) 1973; first performed Edmonton, Alberta, 5 February 1974.
The Meal (tenor, baritone, chamber orchestra; Wilson) 1983–4; first performed Edmonton, Alberta, 19 October 1985.

Other:

Episodes (electronic) 1973; first performed Edmonton, Alberta, 18 November 1973. Recorded Melbourne Records AMLP 4024.
Someone Cares (film score) 1976; first performed Edmonton, Alberta, 17 December 1976.
Whatsoever Things Are True (film score; trumpet, violin, glockenspiel, piano) 1980.

PUBLICATIONS

On Archer: *Music in Canada*, by Sir Ernest Macmillan, 1955; *A History of Music in Canada*, by Helmut Kallman, 1960; *The Encyclopaedia of Music in Canada*, 1981; *Canada's Music*, by Clifford Ford, 1982.

* * *

Violet Archer's early works date from 1938–1942, when her music was influenced by her two teachers at McGill University, Douglas Clarke and Claude Champagne; they show a significant modal influence, drawn especially from her study of the works of Vaughan Williams and Walton.

Her music becomes more chromatic between 1942 and 1948, and shows a new interest in a more driving rhythmic style; this is probably a result of her study with Bartók in 1942. The major work of this period is the four-movement *Symphony* of 1945, a piece which is laced with dissonant counterpoint and whose third movement exhibits the playful character which would become a hallmark of her style.

Archer's music from the period 1948–66 is marked by two stylistic tendencies. The first is an increasing concern with formal structures and less use of chromaticism. This seems to stem from her studies with Hindemith at Yale (1948–9). Secondly, in the early 1950s she began to move more in the direction of the Viennese school, being especially taken with Schoenberg's variation techniques, though never adopting the twelve-tone method. A large number of Archer's most significant works are from this period, including the *Fanfare and Passacaglia*, an orchestral work whose melodic shapes and contrapuntal structures are reminiscent of both Copland and Hindemith, and the *Concerto No 1 for Piano and Orchestra*, deservedly one of her most respected works. Her cantata for chorus and orchestra *The Bell*, is an early and not completely successful large-scale dramatic work. Important chamber music includes the *Sonata* for cello and piano, and the *Sonata No 1* for violin and piano, two string trios, two piano trois and the *Sonata* for horn and piano.

During the period 1966–78 the composer took a turn towards a more expressionistic and chromatic aesthetic, beginning with the *Cantata Sacra* of 1966. Most of Archer's works from this period are for smaller performing forces.

These include the *Sonata* for clarinet and piano, the *Sonata* for alto saxophone and piano, and the *Sonata No 2* for piano; the latter work has been one of her most successful. This period also marks her first venture into opera, with the comic opera *Sganarelle*. Its tangy minor 2nds/major 7th-based harmonies are set against recitative-like vocal lines which are well structured to deliver the caustic Molière text.

Since 1978 Archer has explored a wider stylistic gamut than in her earlier periods, with the emphasis still on chromatic harmonies. Highlights of the more recent music include the *String Quartet No 3*, a well-crafted and dramatic work, full of dissonance and angularity, and *Caleidoscopio*, an evocative setting of the poetry of her sister Gisella Azzi. With the song cycles *Sprig of Flowers* and *Green Jade* Archer begins to explore the poetry of China, writing music that is much more impressionistic in tone than in any of her previous works. These works also lack the rhythmic drive that has been one of the composer's trademarks. 1983 brings her second opera *The Meal*, with a libretto by Rowland Wilson which portrays a wartime encounter by two enemy soldiers. This is a well-fashioned dramatic work whose frequent changes of texture are effectively orchestrated; it is deserving of additional productions. Her most recent large work is *Evocations* for two pianos and orchestra, whose three movements are based on Inuit and Tsimshian melodies. It is one of the composer's most powerful works. Archer has previously used native Canadian musical sources, as in her *Three Sketches for Orchestra*; they lead her into a rhythmic and melodic style which makes greater use of ostinato figures. The harmonic language however remains distinctively hers, replete with 4ths and major 7ths.

In surveying Archer's work to date, several observations can be made. Stylistically she has remained, like her most important teacher Hindemith, a traditionalist. Her writing is heavily contrapuntal, usually based on the development of a germinal idea; it is linear and goal-oriented, with clear cause/effect relationships. Her rhythmic motives are straightforward and downbeat-oriented, and her metric structures are generally regular; notable exceptions to this include *The Meal* and *Caleidoscopio*. In her orchestral writing she uses strings as the dominant sonority and does not use a large percussion section. Archer has moved in her own time: examining influences, taking from them what she desires, and subsuming the chosen material into her own compositional visions.

—Michael Matthews

ARGENTO, Dominick. American. Born in York, Pennsylvania, 27 October 1927. Piano lessons from age 16; self-taught theory and orchestration; after 2 years as army cryptographer in North Africa educated at Peabody Conservatory, Baltimore, Maryland, (piano under Alexander Sklarewski, composition under Nicolas Nabokov), 1947–51, (later under Henry Cowell) 1954, B.M., M.M.; additional private composition study with Hugo Weisgall; Fulbright Fellowship, Conservatorio Cherubini, Florence (piano under Pietro Scarpini, composition under Luigi Dallapiccola), 1951–2; Eastman School, Rochester, New York (under Bernard Rogers, Alan Hovhaness, Howard Hanson), Ph.D. 1957. Married the soprano Carolyn Bailey, 6 September 1954. Teacher, Hampton Institute, Virginia, 1952–5; music director, Hilltop Opera, Baltimore; faculty, since 1958, and Regents Professor, since 1980, University of Minnesota, Minneapolis; co-founder with John Olon-Scrymgeour, Center Opera Co, later Minnesota Opera, 1963. Recipient: Guggenheim Fellowship, 1957–8; Pulitzer Prize (for *From the Diary of Virginia Woolf*), 1975; honoured by American Academy and Institute of Arts and Letters, 1976; honourable mention (for *Fire Variations*), Kennedy Center Friedheim Competition, 1982. Honorary Doctorate of Humane Letters, York College, 1976; honorary doctorate, Valparaiso University, 1982. Mailing address: 1919 Mount Curve Avenue, Minneapolis, Minnesota 55403, U.S.A.

Publisher: Boosey & Hawkes.

Symphonies/orchestral:

Divertimento (piano, string orchestra) 1955; first performed 11 July 1956.
The Resurrection of Don Juan (ballet suite) 1955; first performed New York City, 24 May 1959.
Overture to "The Boor" 1957.
Royal Invitation (Homage to the Queen of Tonga) (chamber orchestra) 1964; first performed St Paul, Minnesota, 20 March 1964. Recorded Louisville First Edition LS 764.
Variations for Orchestra (The Mask of Night) (soprano in last movement only; text from *Romeo and Juliet*) 1965; first performed Minneapolis, 27 January 1966.
Bravo Mozart! An Imaginary Biography (oboe, violin, horn, orchestra; incorporating Mozart K.1, 3, 355, 574, 399, 236) 1969; first performed Minneapolis, 3 July 1969.
A Ring of Time (orchestra, bells) 1972; first performed St Paul, Minnesota, 5 October 1972.
In Praise of Music 1977; first performed Minneapolis, Minnesota, 23 September 1977.
Fire Variations (8 variations and finale based on blacksmith's song in *Miss Havisham's Fire*) 1982; first performed Moorhead, Minnesota, 24 April 1982.
Le Tombeau d'Edgar Poe (orchestral suite—with offstage voice—from the opera *The Voyage of Edgar Allan Poe*) 1985; first performed Baltimore, Maryland, 27 February 1986.
Capriccio "Rossini in Paris" (clarinet, orchestra) 1985; first performed St Louis, Missouri, 16 May 1986.

Chamber/instrumental:

String Quartet 1956.
From the Album of Allegra Harper (2 pianos; arrangement of dance suite from *Colonel Jonathan the Saint*) 1962.

Vocal/choral:

Songs about Spring (soprano, piano; cummings) 1950–5; first performed, 1–3, Baltimore, Maryland, 22 May 1951.
Ode to the West Wind (concerto for soprano and orchestra; Shelley) 1956; first performed Rochester, New York, 29 April 1957.
Six Elizabethan Songs (high voice, piano or small baroque ensemble consisting of flute, oboe, violin, cello, harpsichord; Nashe, Daniel, Shakespeare, Constable, Jonson) 1957, 1962; first performed, Rochester, New York, 6 May 1958; ensemble version, Minneapolis, Minnesota, 8 March 1963. Recorded (ensemble version) CRI SD 380.

Songs About Spring (high voice, chamber orchestra; cummings) 1960; first performed Rochester, New York, 14 July 1960.
Gloria (from *The Masque of Angels*; mixed chorus, piano or organ) 1963. Recorded Plymouth Music Series PMS 002.
Sanctus (from *The Masque of Angels*; double chorus, piano or organ) 1963.
The Revelation of Saint John the Divine (tenor, male chorus, brass, percussion) 1966; first performed Minneapolis, Minnesota, 16 May 1966.
Letters from Composers (high voice, guitar; Chopin, Mozart, Schubert, Bach, Debussy, Puccini, Schumann) 1968; first performed St Paul, Minnesota, 23 October 1968. Recorded CRI SD 291.
A Nation of Cowslips (unaccompanied SATB chorus; Keats) 1968; first performed Minnesota, Minneapolis, 13 April 1969.
Tria Carmina Paschalia (SSA voices, harp, guitar or harpsichord) 1970; first performed St Paul, Minnesota, September 1970. Recorded Augsburg Publishing House 23–1454.
Jonah and the Whale (tenor, bass, narrator, mixed chorus, 3 trombones, timpani, percussion, harp, piano, organ; anon., traditional, biblical) 1973; first performed Minneapolis, Minnesota, 9 March 1974. Recorded Plymouth Music Series 001.
To Be Sung upon the Water (high voice, clarinet/bass clarinet, piano; Wordsworth) 1973; first performed Minneapolis, Minnesota, 20 October 1974. Recorded Desto Records DC 6443.
From the Diary of Virginia Woolf (medium voice, piano) 1974; first performed Minneapolis, Minnesota, 5 January 1975.
A Thanksgiving to God, for His House (unaccompanied SATB chorus; Herrick) 1979; first performed Minneapolis, Minnesota, 6 May 1979.
Let All the World in Every Corner Sing (SATB chorus, 2 trumpets, 2 trombones, timpani, organ; Herbert) 1980; first performed Minneapolis, Minnesota, June 1980.
Peter Quince at the Clavier (mixed chorus, piano concertante; Stevens) 1981; first performed Pennsylvania, 11 April 1981.
I Hate and I Love (mixed chorus, percussion; Catullus) 1982; first performed Minneapolis, Minnesota, 14 March 1982.
The Andrée Expedition (bariton, piano; Swedish explorers Andrée, Strindberg, Fraenkel) 1982; first performed St Paul, Minnesota, 15 February 1983.
Casa Guidi (mezzo-soprano, orchestra or piano; E.B. Browning) 1983; first performed Minneapolis, Minnesota, 28 February 1983; piano version, Los Angeles, 6 January 1984.
Te Deum (Berba Domini cum verbis populi) (SATB chorus, orchestra; Latin, Middle English anon.) 1987; first performed Buffalo, New York, 4 March 1988.

Opera:

The Boor (Olon-Scrymgeour, after Chekhov) 1957; first performed Rochester, New York, 6 May 1957.
Colonel Jonathan the Saint (Olon-Scrymgeour) 1958–61; first performed Denver, Colorado, 31 December 1971.
Christopher Sly (Manlove, after Shakespeare) 1962; first performed Minneapolis, Minnesota, 31 May 1963.
The Masque of Angels (Olon-Scrymgeour) 1963; first performed Minneapolis, Minnesota, 9 January 1964.
The Shoemaker's Holiday (Olon-Scrymgeour, after Dekker) 1967; first performed Minneapolis, Minnesota, 1 June 1967.
Postcard from Morocco (Donahue) 1971; first performed Minneapolis, Minnesota, 14 October 1971. Recorded Desto Records DC 7137–8.
A Water Bird Talk (monodrama; after Chekhov: *On the Harmful Effects of Tobacco*) 1974; first performed Minneapolis, Minnesota, 1 May 1981.
The Voyage of Edgar Allan Poe (Nolte) 1975–6; first performed Minneapolis, Minnesota, 24 April 1976.
Miss Havisham's Fire (Olon-Scrymgeour, after Dickens) 1977–8; first performed New York City, 22 March 1979.
Miss Havisham's Wedding Night (monodrama; Olon-Scrymgeour, after Dickens) 1980; first performed Minneapolis, Minnesota, 1 May 1981.
Casanova's Homecoming 1984; first performed St Paul, Minnesota, 12 April 1985.

Other:

The Resurrection of Don Juan (ballet) 1956; first performed Karlsruhe, Germany, 24 May 1959.
St Joan (incidental music to Shaw) 1964.
Volpone (incidental music to Jonson) 1964.
"S.S. Glencairn" (incidental music to O'Neill) 1966.
Oresteia (incidental music to Aeschylus) 1967.

PUBLICATIONS

On Argento: M. Steele, "DA", in *High Fidelity / Musical America* 25 (9), 1975; P. Altman, "The Voyage of DA", in *Opera News* 40 (21), 1976; Gunther Schuller, "Amerikas Avantgarde—zwischen Tradition und Experiment", in *Osterreisches Musikzeitung*, 31, 1976; *Commemorating the World Premiere of The Voyage of Edgar Allan Poe*, edited by D.J. Speer, St Paul, Minnesota, 1976; M. Steele, "DA", in *ASCAP Today*, 8(1), 1976; T.M. Sabatino, "A Performer's Commentary on *To Be Sung upon the Water* by DA", dissertation, Ohio State University, 1980; A.T. Brewer, "Characterization in DA's Opera *The Boor*", dissertation, University of Texas, Austin, 1981; L.E. Swales, "Characterization in DA's opera *Postcard from Morocco*: A Director's Guide", dissertation, University of Iowa, 1983.

* * *

There is a limit to what can be inferred from biography. That Dominick Argento was, until his post-war enrolment at Peabody, largely self-taught is perhaps evident in the unproblematic quality of his compositional style. On the other hand, the fact that he spent two of the war years as an army crytographer is not. There is little of the abstractionist about him and no sense that he regards music essentially as a problem-solving exercise.

His first exposure to music was by reading the biographies of great composers, from which he inferred enough to realise that composition was his vocation; the 1968 *Letters from Composers* was a later homage to Bach, Mozart and Chopin. Two periods of study in Italy introduced him to opera and to the independently articulated serialism of Luigi Dallapiccola (an influence he seems to have absorbed without undue anxiety). In between, he had married the distinctive young soprano Carolyn Bailey, for whose voice he had already written the beautifully offbeat cummings settings *Songs About Spring*.

In contrast to the bulk of modern composers (though there are important exceptions like Berio), Argento regards the voice as primary and instruments as dim Platonic shadows. His chamber and instrumental output is remarkably attenuated and such of his orchestral work as is not for voice or adapted from opera and vocal work (such as the *Fire Variations*) betrays a fundamental vocalism in its underlying structure.

Argento's connection with the Minnesota Opera and its predecessor Center Opera afforded him a ready outlet for stage music and he combined the composition of incidental music with three major operatic works, the superb *Masque of Angels*, the vivacious Elizabethan *Shoemaker's Holiday* and *Postcard from Morocco*, like the first a one-act piece of considerable substance. Argento's ability to concentrate large amounts of musical and dramatic material into remarkably small compass is one of his most striking qualities.

As early as 1957 and *The Boor*, he had demonstrated a considerable facility for both straightforward bel canto invention and for more complex ensemble composition with, as in *Postcard*, considerable profundity embedded in deceptively user-friendly forms. Only in the hotch-potch *Jonah and the Whale* does his grasp of idiom falter; it is his most schematic piece, too consciously wrought, and too dependent on format/thematic effects like the insistent manipulation of threes and triples.

What *Jonah* does demonstrate (more clearly, perhaps, *because* of its relative failure) is that Argento is by no means an anti-modernist, any more than Leonard Bernstein was. The interpolated classical idioms of *Casanova's Homecoming*, which features an opera-within-an-opera, extends the stylistic focal length considerably and underlines the degree to which Argento is writing not pastiche Mozart, but a genuine extension of Mozart's *buffa* and *seria* styles. His romanticism is altogether subtler than initially appears and marked by a subtle and sometimes dark scepticism (audible in the harmony) about the nature of human identity that is occasionally reminiscent of David Del Tredici's in his "Alice" works. There is a more surprising affinity between Argento's quirky monodramas, *A Water Bird Talk* and *Miss Havisham's Wedding Night*, written in 1974 and 1978 respectively, and those of Sir Peter Maxwell Davies. If *Miss Havisham's Wedding Night*, linked to an earlier opera, is superficially less disturbing than Davies's *Miss Donnithorne's Maggot* (Miss Donnithorne was the original of Dicken's jilted spinster), it is also far more moving and lacks Davies's *grand guignol* effects.

Argento is an original, with a completely individual voice and a style which, if by no means blandly populist, has proved to be durably popular with audiences and critics alike.

—Eleanor Caldwell

ARNOLD, Malcolm. British/English. Born in Northampton, 21 October 1921. Educated at Royal College of Music, London, 1938–40; Mendelssohn Scholarship, Italy, 1948. Married; 2 sons and 1 daughter. Principal trumpet, London Philharmonic Orchestra, 1941–44, 1945–8; interrupted by military service, 1944–5. Full-time composer and conductor, since 1948; president, Inner London Schools Music Association, since 1985. Recipient: Cobbett Prize, 1941; Academy Award (for *Bridge over the River Kwai* soundtrack), 1958; Ivor Novello Award (for *Inn of the Sixth Happiness* soundtrack), 1959; Bard of the Cornish Gorsedd, 1969; C.B.E., 1970; Ivor Novello Award (for "Outstanding Services to British Music"), 1986; Honorary Freedom of the Borough of Northampton, 1989. Honorary degrees: University of Exeter, D.Mus., 1969; University of Durham, D.Mus., 1982; Fellow, Royal College of Music, London, 1983; University of Leicester, D.Mus., 1984; Miami University, Ohio, Doctorate of Arts and Humane Letters, 1990; also honorary fellow, Royal Academy of Music, London. Lives in Cornwall. Mailing address: c/o Georgina Ivor, 66 Alderbrook Road, London SW12 8AB, England.

Publishers: Faber; EMI, Woodford Green, Essex; Lengnick, South Croydon, Surrey; Molenaar, Wormerveer, Netherlands; Novello, Borough Green, Kent; Paterson's Publications Ltd, London; Robertson Publications, Wendover, Buckinghamshire; Studio Music Co., London.

Symphonies/orchestral:

Divertimento No 1 Op 1 early 1940s; first performed London, 29 May 1945.

Larch Trees Op 3 1943; first performed London, 1 October 1943.

Overture: Beckus the Dandipratt Op 5 1943; first performed Illinois, 29 March 1952. Recorded Philips NBL 5021; HMV ASD 3823.

Concerto No 1 for Horn and Orchestra Op 11 1945; first performed London, 8 December 1946.

Symphony for Strings Op 13 1945–6; first performed London, 29 April 1947.

Festival Overture Op 14 1945–6; first performed Ipswich, Suffolk, 1946.

To Youth 1947–8; first performed Bath, 21 April 1948.

Concerto for Clarinet and Strings Op 20 1948; first performed Edinburgh, 29 August 1949. Recorded EMI EL 27 0264 1.

Overture: The Smoke Op 21 1948; first performed London, 24 October 1948.

Symphony No 1 Op 22 1949; first performed Cheltenham, Gloucestershire, 6 July 1951.

Divertimento No 2 Op 24 1950; first performed Brighton, Sussex, 19 April, 1950.

Serenade Op 26 (small orchestra) 1950; first performed London, 4 June 1950.

English Dances (Set 1) Op 27 (also in arrangements for piano duet and wind band) 1950; first performed London, 14 April 1951. Recorded EMI/HMV CDC 749513-2.

Symphonic Study: Machines Op 30 1951; first performed Glasgow, 5 October 1984.

A Sussex Overture Op 31 1951; first performed Brighton, Sussex, 29 July 1951.

Concerto for Piano Duet and Strings Op 32 1951; broadcast BBC, 17 August 1951; first concert performance London, 31 July 1953.

English Dances (Set 2) Op 33 (also arranged for piano duet) 1951; first performed London, 5 August 1952. Recorded EMI/HMV CDC 749513-2; Chandos CHAN 8867.

Rhapsody: The Sound Barrier Op 38 (based on film music of same name) 1952; broadcast BBC, 23 May 1984. Recorded Cloud Nine CDCNS 5466.

Concerto for Oboe and Strings Op 39 1952; first performed London, 26 June 1953. Recorded EMI EL 27 0264 1.

Symphony No 2 Op 40 1953; first performed Bournemouth, 25 May 1953. Recorded EMI/HMV 290461-4/749513-2.

Homage to the Queen Op 42a (ballet suite; also arranged for piano and, in part only, military band) 1953; first performed Northampton, 19 July 1953.

Concerto for Flute and Strings Op 45 1954; first performed London, 11 April 1954. Recorded HMV ASD 3868; Conifer MCFC 172; EMI CDM 7634912.

Concerto for Harmonica and Orchestra Op 46 1954; first performed London, 14 August 1954. Recorded Argo ZRG 905.

Concerto for Organ and Orchestra Op 47 1954; first performed London, 11 December 1954. Recorded CBC SM 129.

Sinfonietta No 1 Op 48 1954; first performed London, 7 March 1955. Recorded Hyperion KA 66332.

Serenade for Guitar and Strings Op 50 1955; first performed Richmond, Surrey, Summer 1955.

Tam O'Shanter Op 51 1955; first performed London, 16 August 1955. Recorded Chandos CHAN 8301/8379.

Little Suite No 1 Op 53 (also arranged for military band—part only) 1955.

A Grand, Grand Overture Op 57 (orchestra, 4 rifles, 3 vacuum cleaners, 1 floor polisher) 1956; first performed London, 13 November 1956. Recorded Decca CD 425401-2.

Concerto No 2 for Horn and Strings Op 58 1956; first performed Cheltenham, Gloucestershire, 17 July 1957. Recorded EMI CDM 7634912.

Four Scottish Dances Op 59 (also arranged for brass band) 1957; first performed London, 8 June 1957. Recorded Chandos CHAN 8867.

HRH The Duke of Cambridge Op 60 (military band) ?1957; first performed Twickenham, 28 June 1957.

Toy Symphony No 62 (12 toy instruments, strings or string quartet) 1957; first performed London, 28 November 1957.

Symphony No 3 Op 63 1957; first performed London, 2 December 1957. Recorded Phoenix PHCD 102.

Commonwealth Christmas Overture Op 64 1957; broadcast BBC, 25 December 1957.

Sinfonietta No 2 Op 65 1958; first performed London, 15 June 1958. Recorded Hyperion KA 66332.

United Nations (4 military bands, organ, orchestra) ?1958; first performed London, 21 November 1958.

Concerto for Guitar and Chamber Orchestra Op 67 1958–9; broadcast BBC, 18 June 1959; first concert performance Aldeburgh, Suffolk, 25 June 1959. Recorded RCA GK 13883; CBS 76715.

Sweeney Todd Op 58a (concert suite from the ballet) 1959.

Symphony No 4 Op 71 1960; first performed London, 2 November 1960.

Carnival of Animals Op 72 1960; first performed London, 31 October 1960.

Symphony No 5 Op 74 1961; first performed Cheltenham, Gloucestershire, 3 July 1961. Recorded EMI/HMV 290461-4/749513-2.

Divertimento No 2 Op 75 1961; first performed London, 26 March 1962.

Grand Concerto Gastronomique Op 76 (eater, waiter, food, large orchestra) 1961; first performed London, 28 November 1961.

Leonora No 4 (Beethoven-Strasser) (orchestra, street band: banjo, guitar, bass drum, clarinet, cornet or trumpet, trombone) 1961; first performed London, 28 November 1961. Recorded Decca CD 425401-2.

Concerto for Two Violins and String Orchestra Op 77 1962; first performed Bath, 24 June 1962. Recorded Conifer MCFC172.

Little Suite No 2 Op 78 1962; first performed Farnham, Surrey, 13 May 1963.

Little Suite No 1 for Brass Band Op 80 (also arranged for symphonic band) 1963; first performed Aberdeen, July 1963.

A Sunshine Overture Op 83 1963–4; first performed London, 14 July 1964.

Water Music Op 82 (wind, percussion; also arranged for full orchestra) 1964; first performed on River Avon, Stratford, 11 July 1964; first performance of orchestral version, Manchester, 21 March 1965.

Sinfonietta No 3 Op 81 1964; first performed Croydon, Surrey, 30 January 1965. Recorded Hyperion KA66332.

Four Cornish Dances Op 91 (also arranged for concert band, brass band; or orchestra with brass band) 1966; first performed London, 13 August 1966.

Theme and Variation 1966; first performed Swansea, 11 January 1967.

Little Suite No 2 for Brass Band Op 93 (also arranged for military band) 1966–7; first performed Cornwall, Spring 1967.

The Padstow Lifeboat Op 94 (brass band) 1966–7; first performed London, 10 June 1967.

Symphony No 6 Op 95 1967; first performed Sheffield, 28 June 1968.

Overture: Peterloo Op 97 1968; first performed London, 7 June 1968. Recorded EMI/HMV CDC 74513-2.

Anniversary Overture Op 99 1968; first performed Hong Kong, 8 December 1968.

Concerto for Two Pianos and Orchestra Op 104 (2 pianos, 3 hands, orchestra) 1969; first performed London, 16 August 1969. Recorded HMV ASD 2612.

Concerto for 28 Players Op 105 1970; first performed London, 25 April 1970.

Fantasy for Audience and Orchestra Op 106 1970; first performed London, 12 September 1970.

Concerto for Viola and Chamber Orchestra Op 108 1971; first performed Carlisle, Cumberland, 13 October 1971.

Popular Birthday (also reduced version) 1972; first performed London, 28 March 1972.

Overture: The Fair Field Op 110 1972; first performed Croydon, Surrey, 27 April 1973.

Concerto No 2 for Flute and Orchestra Op 111 1972; first performed Aldeburgh, Suffolk, 28 June 1973.

A Flourish for Orchestra Op 112 1973; first performed Bristol, 26 September 1973.

Symphony No 7 Op 113 1973; first performed London, 5 May 1974. Recorded Conifer, 1990.

Fantasy Op 114 (brass band) 1973; first performed London, 5 October 1974.

Concerto No 2 for Clarinet and Orchestra Op 115 1974; first performed Denver, Colorado, 17 August 1974.

Fantasy on a Theme of John Field Op 116 (piano, orchestra) 1975; first performed London, 26 May 1977.

Philharmonic Concerto Op 120 1976; first performed London, 31 October 1976.

Variations on a Theme of Ruth Gipps Op 122 1977; first performed London, 22 February 1978.

Symphony for Brass Instruments Op 123 1978; first performed Cheltenham, 8 July 1979.

Symphony No 8 Op 124 [also sometimes quoted as Op 121 but wrongly] 1978; first performed New York City, 5 May 1979. Recorded Conifer, 1990.

Concerto for Trumpet and Orchestra Op 125 1982; first performed Northampton 1982. Recorded EMI CDM 7634912.

Four Irish Dances Op 126 1986. Recorded Chandos CHAN 8867.

Symphony No 9 Op 128 1987; first performed Poole, Dorset, October 1991.

Four Welsh Dances 1989.

Concerto for Recorder and Orchestra Op 133 1989.

Concerto for Cello and Orchestra 1989.

A Manx Suite 1990.

Battle of Britain Suite (military band) 1990.

Overture: Robert Kett 1990; first performed Norwich, Norfolk, July 1990.

Chamber/instrumental:

Haile Selassie (piano) 1936.
Allegro in E minor (piano) 1937.
Three Piano Pieces 1937.
Serenade in G (piano) 1937.
Day Dreams (piano) 1938.
Phantasy (string quartet) 1941.
Two Piano Pieces 1941.
Sonata in B minor (piano) 1942; first performed London, 15 May 1984.
Sonata (flute, piano) 1942.
Wind Quintet Op 2 (flute, oboe, clarinet, horn, bassoon) 1942–3; first performed London, 7 June 1943.
Three Piano Pieces 1943.
Three Shanties Op 4 (wind quintet) 1943; first performed Bristol, Summer 1943. Recorded Hyperion 66173.
Trio Op 6 (flute, viola, bassoon) 1943; first performed London, 18 January 1944. Recorded Hyperion 66172.
Quintet Op 7 (flute, violin, horn, bassoon) 1943–4, later revised; first performed London, 21 December 1944; revised version first performed London, 8 March 1960. Recorded Hyperion 66173.
Variations on a Ukrainian Folk Song Op 9 1944; first performed London, 19 November 1946. Recorded Musica Nova, 1990.
Duo Op 10 (flute, viola) 1945; first performed London, 3 December 1946. Recorded Hyperion 66173.
Prelude (piano) 1945.
Sonata No 1 Op 15 (violin, piano) 1947; first performed London, 2 October 1951. Recorded Hyperion 66171.
Children's Suite Op 16 (piano) 1947.
Sonata Op 17 (viola, piano) 1947; broadcast BBC Latin American Service, 1948. Recorded Hyperion 66171.
Sonatina Op 19 (flute, piano) 1948; broadcast BBC, 20 October 1952. Recorded Hyperion 66172.
String Quartet No 1 Op 23 1949; first performed London, 26 October 1951.
Sonatina Op 28 (oboe, piano) 1951; first performed Manchester, 15 January 1952. Recorded Hyperion 66172.
Sonatina Op 29 (clarinet, piano) 1951; first performed London, 20 March 1951. Recorded Chandos ABRD 1237; Hyperion 66172.
Eight Children's Pieces Op 36 (piano) 1952.
Divertimento Op 37 (flute, oboe, clarinet) 1952; first performed London, 1953. Recorded Hyperion 66173.
Katherine, Walking and Running (2 violins; for the composer's daughter and a friend) 1952.
Sonatina Op 41 (recorder or flute, or oboe, piano) 1953; broadcast BBC, 14 July 1953. Recorded Hyperion 66172.
Homage to the Queen Op 42b (piano) 1953.
Sonata No 2 Op 43 (violin, piano) 1953; first performed London, 21 October 1953. Recorded Hyperion 66171.
Flourish for a 21st Birthday Op 44 (brass, percussion) 1953; first performed London, 7 October 1953.
Fanfare for a Festival (brass, percussion) 1955.
Piano Trio Op 54 1955–6; first performed London, 30 April 1956. Recorded Hyperion 66171.
Fanfare for a Royal Occasion (3 trumpets, 3 trombones) 1955–6; first performed London, 19 November 1956.
Oboe Quartet Op 61 1957; first performed Cambridge, 2 May 1957. Recorded Hyperion 66173.
Richmond (3 trumpets, 3 trombones) 1957; first performed Richmond, Surrey, December 1957.
Concert Piece for Percussion (3 percussion, piano) 1958.
Four Pieces for Chamber Ensemble (recorder, 3 violins) 1958.
Kingston Fanfare (3 trumpets, 3 trombones) 1958–9.
A Hoffnung Fanfare (36 trumpets, percussion) 1960.
Quintet for Brass Op 73 (2 trumpets, horn, trombone, tuba) 1961; first performed New York City, 1961. Recorded Nimbus NI5004.
Five Pieces Op 84 (violin, piano) 1964; first performed Bamburgh, Northumberland, 24 July 1965. Recorded Hyperion 66171.
Duo Op 85 (2 cellos; also arranged for 2 violas) 1965. Recorded Hyperion 66171.
Fantasy for Bassoon Op 86 [*Fantasies Opp 86–90* composed for 1966 Birmingham International Wind Competition] 1966; first performed Birmingham, May 1966.
Fantasy for Clarinet Op 87 1966; first performed Birmingham, May 1966. Recorded Hyperion 66172.
Fantasy for Horn Op 88 1966; first performed Birmingham, May 1966. Recorded Hyperion 66172.
Fantasy for Flute Op 89 1966; first performed Birmingham, May 1966. Recorded Hyperion 66172.
Fantasy for Oboe Op 90 1966; first performed Birmingham, May 1966. Recorded Hyperion 66172.
Trevelyan Suite Op 96 (3 flutes, 2 oboes, 2 clarinets, 2 horns, cello or 2 bassoons) 1967; first performed Durham, 12 March 1968.
Fantasy for Trumpet Op 100 1969.
Fanfare for Louis (2 trumpets in B♭; for Louis Armstrong's 70th birthday) 1970; first performed London, 4 July 1970.
Fantasy for Guitar Op 107 1970–1; first performed London, 16 May 1971.
Popular Birthday (reduced version for flute, piano, 2 percussion, string quartet) 1972; broadcast BBC2, 29 March 1972.
Railway Fanfare (6 fanfare trumpets) 1975.
Fantasy for Harp Op 117 1975; first performed London, 27 January 1976.
String Quartet No 2 Op 118 1975; first performed Dublin, 9 June 1976.
Sonata Op 121 (flute, piano) 1977; first performed Cardiff, 19 March 1977.
Fantasy for Descant Recorder Op 127 1986. Recorded RCA/BMG RD 87946.
Fantasy for Cello Op 130 1987. Recorded ASV 952.
Brass Quintet No 2 1990.

Vocal/choral:

Kensington Gardens (medium voice, piano; Wolfe) 1938.
Two Part-Songs (Dowson) 1939.
Two Songs Op 8 (voice, piano; Mei Sheng, translated Waley/Carpenter) 1946; first performed London, 25 February 1947.
Psalm 150: Laudate Dominum Op 25 (SATB chorus, organ) 1950; first performed Northampton, 1950.
Two Ceremonial Psalms Op 35 (treble voices) 1952; first performed London, 1952.
John Clare Cantata Op 52 (SATB chorus, piano duet) 1954–5; first performed Dartington, Devon, 5 August 1955.
Song of Praise Op 55 (unison voices, optional descant, piano; Clare) 1955–6.
Five William Blake Songs Op 66 (alto, strings) 1958; first performed Richmond, Surrey, 26 March 1959.
The Pilgrim Caravan (excerpt from *The Song of Simeon Op 69*; unaccompanied SATB chorus) 1959.
The Peacock in the Zoo (unison voices, piano; Katherine Arnold) 1962–3.

Jolly Old Friar (unison voices; Richards) 1966–7.

This Christmas Night (unaccompanied mixed voices; Mary Wilson) 1967.

St Endellion Ringers (canon for voices) 1968.

The Song of Accounting Periods Op 103 (voice, piano; 1965 Finance Act) 1969; first performed London, 4 May 1969.

Song of Freedom Op 109 (SA chorus, brass band; Parr, Truzka, Selwyn, McLean, Henry, Richardson, Porter, Thompson) 1972; first performed Harlow, Essex, 12 May 1973.

Two John Donne Songs Op 114b (tenor, piano) 1974; first performed Bristol, 23 June 1977.

The Return of Odysseus Op 119 (SATB chorus, orchestra; Dickinson) 1976; first performed London, 24 April 1977.

Opera:

Henri Christophe (Mendoza) 1950; unfinished.

Up at the Villa (Mendoza, after Browning) 1951; unfinished.

The Dancing Master Op 34 (Mendoza, after Wycherley) 1952; first performed London, 1 March 1962.

The Open Window Op 56 (Gilliat, after Saki; 6 soloists, flute, clarinet, bassoon, horn, harp, percussion, 2 violins, viola, cello, double bass) 1956; broadcast BBC TV, 14 December 1956.

Other:

Solitaire (ballet for orchestra; incorporating *English Dances Sets 1 & 2* and other pieces) 1956; first performed London, 7 June 1956.

Sweeney Todd Op 68 (ballet for orchestra) 1959; first performed Stratford upon Avon, 10 December 1959.

Song of Simeon Op 69 (nativity masque for mimes, soloists, mixed chorus, orchestra; Hassall) 1959; first performed London, 5 February 1960.

Electra Op 79 (ballet for small orchestra) 1963; first performed London, 26 March 1963.

The Three Musketeers (ballet sketches; piano) 1976.

Film scores: *Avalanche Patrol* (Swain), 1947; *Seven RAF Flashes*, 1947; *Charting the Seas* (Lowenstein) 1948; *Two RAF Flashes*, 1948; *Gates of Power / Stairway to the Sea* (Squire), 1948; *Hydrography*, 1948; *Report on Steel* (Orrom), 1948; *Badger's Green* (Irwin), 1948; *Mining Review* (Orrom), 1948; *Metropolitan Water Board*, 1948; *Hawick, Queen of the Border*, 1948; *Women in Our Time*, 1948; *Cotton—Lancashire's Time for Adventure*, 1948; *The Struggle for Oil*, 1948; *EVWs* (Orrom), 1948; *This Farming Business*, 1949; *Britannia Mews*/(U.S.) *The Forbidden Street* (Negulesco), 1949; *The Frazers of Cabot Cove / An Island Story* (Swingler), 1949; *Drums for a Holiday* (Taylor), 1949; *Terra Incognita*, 1949; *The Beautiful County of Ayr*, 1949; *Fight for a Fuller Life*, 1949; *Trieste: Problem City*, 1949; *Dollars and Sense* (Pine), 1949; *Your Witness*/(U.S.) *Eye Witness* (Montgomery), 1949; *Julius Caesar*, 1949; *Anthony and Cleopatra*, 1949; *When You Went Away*, 1949; *Science of the Orchestra* (Strasser), 1949; *Oil Review No 5*, 1950; *ECA Productivity Team*, 1950; *Fifty Acres* (Plaskitt), 1950; *Up for the Cup* (Raymond; music co-composed with Percival Mackey), 1950; *Airways*, 1950; *The Riddle of Japan*, 1950; *Where Britain Stands*, 1950; *This Is Britain*, 1950; *Let's Go For'ard*, 1950; *Alien Orders / Malaya*, 1951; *No Highway*/(U.S.) *No Highway in the Sky* (Koster), 1951; *Home to Danger* (Fisher), 1951; *Power for All* (Wallace, Squire) 1951; *Men and Machines*, 1951; *Wings of Danger* (Fisher), 1951; *Local Newspapers*, 1951; *Home at Seven*/(U.S.) *Murder on Monday* (Richardson), 1951; *Stolen Face* (Fisher), 1952; *The Holly and the Ivy* (O'Ferrall), 1952; *The Sound Barrier* (Lean), 1952; *Channel Islands* (Orrom), 1952; *The Island* (Pickering, Ingram), 1952; *Curtain Up* (Smart), 1952; *The Ringer / Gaunt Stranger* (Hamilton), 1952; *It Started in Paradise* (Bennett), 1952; *Four-Sided Triangle* (Fisher), 1952; *Invitation to the Dance* (Kelly), 1952; *Gilbert and Sullivan* (arrangements of Sullivan), 1953; *The Captain's Paradise / Paradise* (Kimmins), 1953; *Man of Africa / Kigusi Story* (Frankel), 1953; *Copenhagen, City of Towers*, 1953; *Albert R.N.* (Gilbert), 1953; *Powered Flight: The Story of the Century*, 1953; *Devil on Horseback* (Frankel), 1953; *Hobson's Choice* (Lean), 1953; *The Royal Tour: New Zealand*, 1954; *The Sleeping Tiger* (Losey), 1954; *Welcome the Queen*, 1954; *Beautiful Stranger*/(U.S.) *Twist of Fate* (Miller), 1954; *The Belles of St Trinians* (Launder), 1954; *The Sea Shall Not Have Them* (Gilbert), 1954; *The Constant Husband* (Gilliat), 1954; *A Prize of Gold* (Robson), 1954; *The Night My Number Came Up* (Norman), 1955; *I Am a Camera* (Cornelius), 1955; *Value for Money* (Annakin), 1955; *The Deep Blue Sea* (Litvak), 1955; *The Woman for Joe* (O'Ferrall), 1955; *1984* (Anderson), 1955; *Port Afrique* (Mate), 1956; *Trapeze* (Reed), 1956; *Wicked as they Come*/(U.S.) *Portrait in Smoke* (Hughes), 1956; *The Barretts of Wimpole Street* (not used), 1956; *Tiger in the Smoke* (Baker), 1956; *Roses Tattoo*, 1956; *Island in the Sun* (Rossen), 1957; *Blue Murder at St Trinians* (Launder), 1957; *The Bridge on the River Kwai* (Lean), 1957, recorded Columbia CL 1100, many others; *Dunkirk* (Norman), 1957; *The Key* (Reed), 1958; *The Roots of Heaven* (Huston), 1958; *The Inn of the Sixth Happiness* (Robson), 1958; *Coupe des Alpes* (Armstrong), 1958; *The Boy and the Bridge* (McClory); *Solomon and Sheba* (Vidor), 1959; *Suddenly Last Summer* (Mankiewicz), 1959; *The Angry Silence* (Forbes), 1960; *Tunes of Glory* (Neame), 1960; *The Pure Hell of St Trinian's* (Launder), 1960; *No Love for Johnnie* (Thomas), 1960; *Whistle Down the Wind* (Forbes), 1961; *On the Fiddle*/(U.S.) *Operation Snafu* (Frankel), 1961; *The Inspector*/(U.S.) *Lisa* (Dunne), 1962; *The Lion* (Cardiff), 1962; *Nine Hours to Rama* (Robson), 1962; *Tamahine* (Leacock), 1963; *The Chalk Garden* (Neame), 1963; *The Thin Red Line* (Marton), 1964; *The Heroes of Telemark* (Mann), 1966; *Sky West and Crooked*/(U.S.) *Gypsy Girl* (Mills), 1966; *The Great St Trinian's Train Robbery* (Launder, Gilliat), 1966; *Africa—Texas Style*/(U.S.) *Cowboy in Africa* (Marton), 1966; *North Sea Strike* (Kelly), 1967; *The Reckoning / A Matter of Honour* (Gold), 1969; *The Battle of Britain* (Hamilton; incorporating music by Walton), 1969; *David Copperfield* (Mann), 1969.

Incidental music: *Purple Dust* (to play by O'Casey), 1953; *The Tempest* (Shakespeare), 1954; *Paddy's Nightmare* (Joyce Grenfell), 1954; *War in the Air* (BBC television) 1954; *Candlemas Night* (BBC radio), 1955; *Electra* (to play by Sophocles), 1955; *Fanfare* (fanfare for ABC Television), 1956; *For Mr Pye an Island* (BBC radio; Peake), 1956; *Royal Prologue* (BBC television), 1957; *Music for You* (signature tune, BBC television), 1959; *Parasol* (musical for BBC television; Brahms/Sherrin), 1960; *Espionage* (ATV television series), 1963; *Gala Performance* (signature tune for BBC television series), 1963; *The Turtle Drum Op 92* (children's play for BBC television), 1967; *The First Lady* (theme music for BBC television series), 1968; *Hard Times* (ITV adaptation of Dickens), 1977.

Arrangements of: Anon., 13th-century *Motet—Marie Assumptio*, 1943; Guillaume de Machaut: *Double-Hoquet*, 1943; Fred Leigh: *Only a Little Box of Soldiers*, 1948; Isaac

Albeniz: *Tango in D*, 1953; Henry Purcell: *On the Brow of Richmond Hill*, 1959; Thomas Merritt: *Coronation March, Anthems and Carols*, 1967, 1968; William Walton: *Sonata for String Orchestra*, 1971.

PUBLICATIONS

By Arnold: "On the Birth of a Dandipratt", in *Winter Gardens Society Magazine*, Winter 1950; "The Serious Composer's Approach to Film Music", lecture in Royal Festival Hall, 11 March 1954; "I Think of Music in Terms of Sound", in *Music and Musicians*, July 1956; "Music", in *The Listener*, 14 October 1971.

On Arnold: Alan Poulton, *The Music of Malcolm Arnold: A Catalogue*, Faber, 1986; Hugo Cole, *MA: An Introduction to His Music*, Faber, 1988.

* * *

Malcolm Arnold is an "original": one whose musical character declares itself equally in the symphonies and in the lightest occasional instrumental pieces; only in a few very early instrumental and in a few later vocal works would it be possible to mistake the composer. Like other distinguished originals (Berlioz and Elgar among them) he gained little benefit from formal musical education. Though he profited from Gordon Jacob's teaching on orchestration during his two years at the Royal College of Music, the greatest influence on his development as a musician was that of his trumpet teacher Ernest Hall. Thereafter, he was virtually self-taught, and was little influenced by any of the main post-war compositional trends, preferring to go his own way rather than to ally himself with any group of composers.

Between 1942 and 1948 Arnold became known as one of the finest orchestral trumpet players in the country. During these years he came to know the symphonic repertory from the inside, playing under many of the world's greatest conductors, and acquiring intimate knowledge of the characters and potentialities of instruments, individually and in ensemble. It is from this time that the first entirely characteristic works date. The *Three Shanties* for wind quintet and the overture *Beckus the Dandipratt* bear the unmistakeable Arnold imprint.

In 1948 Arnold gave up orchestral playing for a career as a full-time professional composer, at first supporting himself largely by writing film music. Since then, he has composed in every genre, though his output of vocal music is relatively small. His popular reputation has rested largely on his ability to write delightful tunes, and to present them in apt and original harmonic and orchestral dress.

Of Arnold's earlier works the lyrical Second Symphony stands out for ease and fluency of movement and classical sense of proportion. Here and elsewhere, Arnold makes the process of listening so painlessly agreeable that the aptness and originality of forms and treatments often go unremarked. Nor has much attention been paid to his resourcefulness in adapting known techniques and compositional procedures to his own purposes. Serial procedures of considerable complexity may be used in predominantly tonal movements (as in the Fifth Symphony and the *Concerto for 28 Players*). Systematic retrogrades and intricate canons, in the Bartókian manner, are not uncommon. Arnold makes frequent use of ground-bass, favouring a bass-line modulating at each new entry—a procedure which possibly derives from the *Te Deum* of Berlioz, a composer by whom he has been much influenced. It should be said, however, that except in the case of one or two vocal works, influences have been so well absorbed that the listener is rarely aware of any indebtedness.

In most technical matters, in his orchestration and in the demands he makes on his performers, Arnold has remained loyal to traditional principles. Where he has shown daring, often outraging conventionally-minded critics, is in introducing popular elements into concert works: as when a 1950s-style pop tune, with its appropriate textures and harmonies puts in an appearance in the Fourth Symphony, or in the raucous marches which break into the finales of the First and Fourth symphonies.

In composing for film and in his ballet scores he proved himself an accomplished musical illustrator, master of many idioms, able to provide music apt for every sort of dramatic situation, including the darkest and most tragic. But the early concert music, up to the life-affirming Fourth Symphony of 1960, was almost free of darker shadows. Arnold has often maintained that his main purpose in writing music is to give delight. Yet in later works, violent and disturbing episodes appear with increasing frequency. Sometimes it is easy to find dramatic reason for the intervention, as in the Peterloo Overture which commemorates the Manchester massacre of 1819 or in the grimmer numbers in the *Song of Freedom* which deal with injustice and privation. Sometimes there may be musico-historical reasons why the overall tone should be grave and sombre, as in the fine *Symphony for Brass Instruments*. But often, the storms will erupt unexpectedly, as in the Seventh Symphony and the John Field Variations. The anger and grief in these episodes is not always clearly articulated, and is often all the more disturbing for that very reason. What has become increasingly clear, is that Arnold's musical character is more complex than was apparent in early days, and that he is far more than the gifted entertainer he was once thought to be.

Arnold's skills as an orchestrator ensure that the more vigorous and ebullient climaxes of his music are scored with the utmost brilliance. But many of the most original and delightful passages are those in which a handful of instruments are used with chamber-music finesse. In latter years, he has refined his processes still more, pruning away subsidiary parts and indulging his love for pure, unmixed colours by reducing doublings to a minimum. The extreme economy in the use of instruments in the *Concerto for Trumpet* and the Ninth Symphony has disconcerted some listeners. Arnold, however, has always trusted his own instincts and is unlikely to pay much attention to critical opinion. Like all true originals, he goes his own way, not in order to prove his independence, but because it is impossible for him go down any other path.

—Hugo Cole

ARTYOMOV, Vyacheslav (Wjatscheslaw Artjomow). Russian. Born in Moscow in 1940. Educated at University of Physics, Moscow; P. I. Tchaikovsky Conservatory, Moscow (under Nikolai Sidelnikov), graduated 1968. Married to the poet Valeria Lyubezkaya. Editor, Musyka publishing house, Moscow; founder (with composers Sofia Gubaidulina and Viktor Suslin), improvisation group Astreia, 1975. Freelance composer, since 1979. Mailing address: c/o Internationale Musikverlage Hans Sikorski, Postfach 132001, 2000 Hamburg, Germany.

Publisher: Hans Sikorski.

Symphonies/orchestral:

In Memoriam (violin, orchestra) 1968–84.
Tempo Costante 1970, revised 1980.
A Garland of Recitations (flute, oboe, clarinet or saxophone, bassoon, percussion, harp, celesta, piano, strings) 1975–81.
A Symphony of Elegies (2 solo violins, 6 percussion, 16 strings) 1977. Recorded Melodiuya C 10 20271 72.
Way to Olympus 1978–84.
Tristia (trumpet, piano, vibraphone, organ, 46 strings) 1983. Recorded Modern Fidelity Sound Lab Inc MFCD 906.
Lamentations (3 percussion ad lib, piano ad lib, organ, strings) 1985.
Ghourian Hymn (3 solo violins, 4 percussion, strings) 1986.

Chamber/instrumental:

Sonata (clarinet) 1966.
Scenes (violin, clarinet, percussion, piano, double bass) 1970.
Confession (clarinet) 1971.
Variations: Nestling Antsali (flute, piano) 1974. Recorded Melodiya C10 18981 82.
Five Pieces (clarinet, piano) 1975.
Autumn Sonatina (piano, saxophone or flute or oboe or clarinet) 1975.
Capriccio for New Year's Eve, 1975 (soprano saxophone, baritone saxophone, vibraphone) 1975.
Recitation I (clarinet or saxophone) 1975.
Romantic Capriccio (horn, piano) 1976.
Totem (6 percussion) 1976. Recorded Melodiya C10 18981 82.
Recitation III (flute) 1977.
Recitation IV (flute or oboe or clarinet or saxophone) 1977.
Recitation V (bassoon) 1977.
Sunday Sonata (bassoon, piano) 1977.
Litany I (soprano saxophone, alto saxophone, tenor saxophone, baritone saxophone) 1977.
Woodland Sketches (2 pianos) 1977–8.
Awakening (2 violins) 1978. Recorded Melodiya C10 18981 82.
Sonata Ricercata (percussion, 1 player) 1978.
A Sonata of Meditations (4 percussion) 1978.
Mattinate/Morning Songs (flute, violin, guitar) 1979–83. Recorded Mobile Fidelity Sound Lab Inc MFCD 918.
Recitation IX (flute or oboe or clarinet or saxophone) 1980.
Recitation X (flute or oboe or clarinet or saxophone) 1980.
Litany II (3 flutes, alto flute) 1981.
All'Rondo (alto saxophone, piano) 1981.
Recitation II (flute solo) 1981.
Preludes to Sonnets (piano) 1981. Recorded Mobile Fidelity Sound Lab MFCD 918.
Star Wind (violin, cello, flute, horn, piano, carillons) 1981.
Romantic Capriccio (horn, string quartet, piano) 1982. Recorded Mobile Fidelity Sound Lab Inc MFCD 918.
Hymns of Sudden Wafts (soprano/alto/tenor saxophone, celesta, harpsichord, piano, 8 strings) 1983–5. Recorded Mobile Fidelity Sound Lab Inc MFCD 918.
Litany III (organ) 1986.

Vocal/choral:

Funny Songs (soprano, piano; folk texts) 1964.
Four Duets (soprano, mezzo-soprano, piano; Ghrashi) 1966.
Northern Songs (mezzo-soprano, percussion, piano; folk texts) 1966.
A Hymn to Jasmine Nights (soprano, piano) 1979.
Invocations (soprano, 4 percussion) 1979–81. Recorded Melodiya C10 18981 82.
Moonlight Dreams (mezzo-soprano, alto flute, cello, piano; Wan Wei, Li Po, Ssu-K'ung Shu, translated Cheetham) 1982. Recorded Mobile Fidelity Sound Lab Inc MFCD 918.
Lamentations (SATB chorus, 3 percussion ad lib, piano ad lib, organ, with or without strings) 1986.
Requiem (2 sopranos, tenor, baritone, SATB chorus, orchestra) 1986–7. Recorded Melodiya A10 00547 006.
Ave Maria (soprano, chamber chorus, strings, organ ad lib) 1989.

Other:

Erwartung/Expectation ("nostalgic ballet") 1984.
Sola fide/By Faith Alone (ballet; after Tolstoy) 1985–7.

PUBLICATIONS

On Artyomov: N. Surkowa, "WA [VA]", in *Moskauer Komponisten*, Moscow, 1976; Vincenzo Maddaloni, "Ein Requiem fur die Opfer von Stalin", in *Famiglia Christiana*, 51, 1988; Olga Martinenko, "Der Komponist WA [VA]: der schwere Weg zum Olympus", in *Moscow News*, 5, 1989.

Vyacheslav Artyomov comments:

Sound is not something one can be deceitful with. A composer's whole personality is evident in it. One need but know how to perceive it. An artist is an exposed nerve, a light, a conscience. He must not obscure himself, but rather must change the world along with himself. As the Apostle says: "But we are all with an open face beholding as in a glass the Glory of the Lord, and are changed into the same image from glory to glory, even as by the Spirit of the Lord."

I believe in the transfiguration of the created world through music.

* * *

The main trajectory of Vyacheslav Artyomov's creative development is an interesting one and one which sets him slightly apart from his contemporaries among other Moscow composers. Where Russian music has traditionally favoured narrative structures built on strong contrasts, Artyomov has tended in his mature music to gravitate towards more abstract concepts which derive from a single unfolding process; often in his music that process will be clearly set out at the beginning of a movement and the piece will continue until the process has come to an end.

This may sound like a description of a minimalist composer, but that would be to give a misleading impression. The raw material of Artyomov's music is not like that usually associated with minimalism; it is typically loosely intonational and open-ended, rather than being powered by any recognisable melodic, harmonic or rhythmic tag. And the processes to which Artyomov's material is subjected are unpredictable in local detail however one-directional they may come to seem later, once the piece is over.

A good example of this can be found in this composer's

short but powerful *Awakening* for two violins. In this work the two instruments are like the voices of a two-part invention (both parts in the same register), which both treat of the same ideas, with much play of simple canonic and other imitative devices. The clear and somewhat fragile lines are subjected to gradually more elaborate decoration, which however never obscures their fundamental sense of direction. The overall impression is one of a linear journey, a journey in principle from low to high, from soft to loud, from plain to decorated. Indeed there is here, as so often with Artyomov, an almost visual quality to his musical thinking; it frequently seems to be made of lines, rather than notes.

In the late 1970s Artyomov joined with two other distinguished composers, Sofia Gubaidulina and Viktor Suslin, to form the improvisation group Astreia. The private sessions and occasional public concerts that resulted were an important experience not only for those composers but also for a number of others who heard their work. All three members of Astreia had travelled in the East and South of the Soviet Union and had collected a number of interesting folk instruments from some of the hundreds of different national and tribal cultures contained within that country. A completely untutored performance on these instruments was the basis of their improvisations. What such work did was to encourage a fresh approach to sonoric and acoustic questions in a country where there are practically no possibilities of working in electronics.

Perhaps Artyomov's most important and intriguing compositions are those which, drawing on his own experience as a performer in Astreia, were written for the celebrated Soviet percussionist Mark Pekarsky and his ensemble of young players. Pekarsky himself has a colossal collection of percussion instruments, mostly of folk origin, and many composers have written for him. Artyomov's works for his ensemble include the extremely refined four-movement *Invocations*, for soprano and four players, and the violent and powerful *Totem* for the complete ensemble of six. Both these pieces reveal an almost calligraphic precision which is capable of effects that are disturbingly hypnotic and indeed strongly suggestive of the Asiatic religious rituals in which the instruments in Pekarsky's collection (and indeed in Artyomov's own collection) may originally have been used. And in *Invocations* in particular Artyomov makes memorable play in the soprano part with the rhythmic possibilities of made-up words suggesting a fictive language. Alfred Schnittke has commented of this piece that "it suggests to an astonishing degree a sort of primaeval magic".

Many of Artyomov's earlier works were for chamber combinations and the finest of them are admirable in their economy and often in their delicacy. In more recent years, however, and partly under the influence of his wife Valeria Lyubezkaya, Artyomov has moved towards a more ambitious programme of large-scale symphonic composition including such works as *Way to Olympus*, the *Requiem* and an enormous ballet *By Faith Alone* based on the writings of Alexei Tolstoy. Faced with a huge orchestra Artyomov has moved away from the clarity and acoustic originality of his earlier music in favour of a heavy and very Soviet style of orchestration. These works also come encumbered with his wife's extravagent commentaries. This is a pity because such things distract from the fact that even underneath these works there is still a distinctive and impressive sense of outline and direction which has much to recommend it.

—Gerard McBurney

ASHLEY, Robert (Reynolds). American. Born in Ann Arbor, Michigan, 28 March 1930. Educated at University of Michigan (music theory), 1948–52, B.Mus.; Manhattan School of Music (piano, and composition under Wallingford Riegger), 1952–3, M.S.; further research (acoustics and composition under Leslie Bassett and Ross Lee Finney, psychoacoustics under Roberto Gerhard) University of Michigan, 1957–60. Married (1) the artist Mary Ashley; (2) the performer Mimi Johnson. Composer/performer Space Theater, 1957–64; co-founder, ONCE Group/Festivals, 1958–69, and Co-operative Studio for Electronic Music, 1958–66; research assistant, acoustics, University of Michigan, 1960–1; member/participant, Sonic Arts Union, 1966–76; director, Center for Contemporary Music, Mills College, Oakland, California, 1970–81. Composer, performing, film and video-maker, recording artist. Mailing address: 10 Beach Street, New York, New York 10013, U.S.A.

Publisher: Visibility.

Instrumental/electronic works:

Christopher Columbus Cross to the New World in the Nina, the Pinta and the Santa Maria Using Only Dead Reckoning and a Crude Astrolabe (piano sonata) 1959, revised 1979.
The Fourth of July (tape) 1960.
Manoeuvres for Small Hands (piano) 1961.
Something for Clarinet, Pianos and Tape 1961.
Complete with Heat (instruments, tape) 1962.
Detroit Divided (tape) 1962.
Fives (2 pianos, 2 percussion, string quintet) 1962.
Details (2 pianos) 1962.
In Memoriam . . . Crazy Horse (20+ wind/string/sustaining instruments) 1963.
In Memoriam . . . Esteban Gomez (4 instrumentalists/performers) 1963.
In Memoriam . . . John Smith (3 instrumentalists/performers, assistants) 1963.
In Memoriam . . . Kit Carson (8-part ensemble) 1963.
White on White (trios) 1963.
Big Danger in Five Parts (tape) 1964.
The Wolfman Tape (tape, amplified voice) 1964.
Waiting Room (wind/string quartet) 1965, revised 1978.
Untitled Mixes (tape) 1965.
The Entrance (organ) 1965.
String Quartet Describing the Motions of Large Real Bodies (string quartet, electronics) 1972.
In Sara, Mencken, Christ and Beethoven There Were Men and Women (violin electronics; studio work) 1972. Recorded Cramps 6103.
Revised, Finally, for Gordon Mumma (bells) 1973.
How Can I Tell the Difference (violin/viola, electronics, tape) 1974.
Automatic Writing (violin, electronics; studio work) 1979. Recorded Vital 1002.

Opera/music-theatre:

 # + Heat (performer, tape) 1961; first performed Ann Arbor, Michigan, December 1962.
Public Opinion Descends upon the Demonstrators 1961; first performed Ann Arbor, Michigan, 18 February 1962.
Boxing (sound-producing dance) 1963; first performed Detroit, 9 April 1964.

Combination Wedding and Funeral 1964; first performed New York City, 9 May 1965.
Interludes for the Space Theater (sound-producing dance) 1964; first performed Cleveland, Ohio, 4 May 1965.
Kitty Hawk: An Antigravity Piece 1964; first performed St Louis, Missouri, 21 March 1965.
The Lecture Series (collaboration with Mary Ashley) 1964; first performed New York City, 9 May 1965.
Night Train 1965; first performed Waltham, Massachusetts, 7 January 1967.
Orange Dessert 1965; first performed Ann Arbor, Michigan, 9 April 1966.
Unmarked Interchange 1965; first performed Ann Arbor, Michigan, 17 September 1965.
That Morning Thing (stage opera) 1967; first performed Ann Arbor, Michigan, 8 February 1968. Recorded, excerpt "She Was a Visitor", Odyssey 32 16 0156.
Purposeful Lady Slow Afternoon 1968; first performed New York City, 1968. Recorded Mainstream MS/5010.
The Trial of Anne Opie Wehrer and Unknown Accomplices for Crimes Against Humanity 1968; first performed Shegboyan, Wisconsin, 30 April 1968.
The Wolfman Motorcity Revue 1968; first performed Newport Beach, California, 11 January 1969.
Fancy Free 1970; first performed Ann Arbor, Michigan, April 1971.
Illusion Models (imaginary programmes for computer operator) 1970.
It's There 1970; first performed Brussels, April 1970.
Night Sport (monologues) 1975; first performed L'Aquila, Italy, April 1975.
Over the Telephone (installations) 1975; first performed New York City, March 1975.
Music with Roots in the Aether (television opera) 1976; first performed Paris, 1976.
Title Withdrawn (television opera) 1976; first performed Paris, 1976.
Perfect Lives (Private Parts) (television) 1977–83; broadcast United Kingdom, 1984. Recorded, complete, Lovely Music LMC 4913, 4947; excerpts on Lovely Music LML 1001, VR 4904/4908.
The Lessons [television opera; part of *Perfect Lives) (Private Parts)*] 1981; first performed New York City, 1981.
Atalanta (Acts of God) (television opera) 1982; first performed Paris, 1982.
Atalanta Strategy (television opera) 1984; first performed New York City, 1985.

Film/video:

The Image in Time (film; collaboration with G. Manupeli) 1957.
Bottleman (film; collaboration with G. Manupelli) 1960.
The House (film; collaboration with G. Manupelli) 1961.
Jenny and the Poet (film; collaboration with G. Manupelli) 1964.
My May (film; collaboration with G. Manupelli) 1965.
Overdrive (film; collaboration with G. Manupelli) 1967.
Dr Chicago (film; collaboration with G. Manupelli) 1968–70.
Portraits, Self-Portraits and Still Lifes (film; collaboration with G. Manupelli) 1969.
Battery Davis (film; collaboration with P. Makanna) 1970.
The Great Northern Automobile Presence (videotaped lighting) 1975.
What She Thinks (videotape) 1976.

PUBLICATIONS

By Ashley: "The ONCE Group", in *Arts in Society*, 5, 1968; "The ONCE Group", in *Source*, 3 1968. *And So It Goes, Depending* [notes on *Perfect Lives (Private Parts)*], unpublished photostats, copyright 1980.

On Ashley: W. Zimmermann, (interview) in *Desert Plants: Conversations with Twenty-Three American Musicians*, Vancouver, 1976; N. Osterreich, "Music with Roots in the Aether", in *Perspectives of New Music*, 16 (1), 1977; J. Howell, "RA's *Perfect Lives (Private Parts)*", in *Live: Performance Art*, 3, 1980; C. Gagne and T. Caras, (interview) in *Soundpieces: Interviews with American Composers*, Metuchen, New Jersey, 1983; John Rockwell, "Post Cageian Experimentation and New Kinds of Collaboration: RA", in *All-American Music: Composition in the Late Twentieth Century*, New York, 1983; T. DeLio, *Circumscribing the Open Universe: Essays on Cage, Feldman, Wolff, RA, and Lucier*, Washington, D.C., 1984.

* * *

"Music with roots in the aether": the title of Robert Ashley's television opera of 1976 comes close to defining his significance. He is the first opera composer of the television and video age, or the post-proscenium age. His work from the mid-1970s onward has been dedicated to a series of complex, episodic works, mostly collaborative (continuing an ethos developed with the celebrated ONCE Group in the late 1950s), and marked by shuttering imagery, textual information so fleeting as to be almost subliminal, and a close attention to speech acts as an alternative to the totalising effects of traditional composition. *Perfect Lives (Private Parts)*, his most successful work to date, is certainly too ambiguous to be totalised or summarised; it was greeted with some bafflement when shown on British television in 1984 (on the then-innovative Channel 4) but it also struck a chord with a younger rock- and movie-oriented audience just beginning to be aware of the more upmarket end of performance art (as represented by Laurie Anderson, Meredith Monk and Robert Wilson's collaborations with Philip Glass).

Ashley's musical world is antithetical to the *auteurism* of conventional composition. The actual music of *Perfect Lives* (it seems of late to have shed the second half of its title) is composed by others, notably "Blue" Gene Tyranny, alias the composer Robert Sheff, with whom Ashley worked at Mills College. If there is any significance in the fact that "opera" is a plural noun, Ashley has managed to restore it. His role in *Perfect Lives* is somewhere between ringmaster and chorus; as the speaker, he delivers a drawled repetitive monologue, suggestive of a heavily sedated patient or a victim of autism.

Ashley has not merely attempted to adjust the borders of what can be considered authentic operatic practice. For much of his career, he has been levelling questions at the nature of music itself, and of the special subset of cognitive functions dedicated to "art". There is about his work a mixture of sheer affront and sober philosophical probing. His experiments are related in effect to such profoundly alienating modern classics as Samuel Beckett's drama, John Cage's mesostic "lectures", Andy Warhol's chronicles of ennui, but also more structured narrative films like Wim Wenders's *Kings of the Road* (in which one of the characters is a theoretical linguist). Ashley's background in psychoacoustics emerges in his obsession with the reception of his work. On occasions, his intention is clearly (but not merely) to shock. A monologue to *The Wolfman Tape* has him ranting uncontrollably, but the piece has a complex resonance; as well as being a stock figure in horror cinema, the Wolfman was a patient of Freud; in addition, "Wolfman Jack" was a popular disc jockey in the early 1960s—do electromagnetic waves work on us like moonlight, a kind of lycanthropy of the aether? *Purposeful Lady Slow Afternoon* and the recorded *Automatic Writing* feature soundtracks that resemble phone-in sex lines. The excerpt "She Was a Visitor", from the opera *That Morning Thing*, shocks in a more subtle way. While a voice intones the title repeatedly and without inflection, "choral" groups, on instruction from a precentor in each group, steadily deconstruct its syllables.

It is as well to remember that Ashley had a vigorous musical education and produced some remarkable instrumental music, notably a massively titled piano sonata on the theme of Columbus, and a sequence of *In memoriam . . .* pieces that took a similarly slanted look at the icons of American history. Though Cage is undoubtedly his biggest single influence, Ashley has drawn some inspiration from the radical Wallingford Riegger, his teacher at the Manhattan School, from Roberto Gerhard, and from his friend and sometime collaborator, the composer Gordon Mumma. In combination, they instilled a sense that music is about interrelations which are in no way separable from the interrelations of people, and of people with the physical and cybernetic environment. These are not always sexual, though there is a post-Kinsey obsession with minute response-recording in much of Ashley's work. In *Kitty Hawk*, Ashley continued his examination of American history by diverting into male/female antagonisms; typically, it is the performers who generate the foreground of the piece. *The Trial of Anne Opie Wehrer and Unknown Accomplices for Crimes Against Humanity* pits "live" witnesses against a taped prosecutor. If this is parabolic of Ashley's convictions about the ways in which language calcifies and stiffens, it is also in keeping with his heterodox Freudianism.

Ashley belongs to the "hidden stream" of American culture. He has used technology to level important questions at a technological society, just as he uses language to demonstrate how phatic and empty most conventional language, and the emotions and situations it expresses, really are. If composer he be, Ashley is one of the major figures of the late 20th century.

—Brian Morton

AUSTIN, Larry (Don). American. Born in Duncan, Oklahoma, 12 September 1930. Educated at Vernon High School, Texas, 1944–7; University of North Texas, Denton (with Violet Archer), 1947–51, B.M.E., 1951–2, M.M.; San Antonio College, Texas (French and German courses), 1952–5; Mills College, Oakland, California (composition under Darius Milhaud), Summer 1955; University of California, Berkeley (composition under Andrew Imbrie), 1955–8; San Francisco Tape Music Center (electronic music), 1965–6; Stanford University, California (computer music workshop), Summer 1969; Massachusetts Institute of Technology, Cambridge, (computer music workshop), Summer 1978. Served in the United States Army, 1952–5: Sergeant. Married Edna Navarro 31 October 1953; 2 sons and 3 daughters. Teaching assistant/associate, University of California, Berkeley, 1956–8; assistant director, University of California bands, Berkeley, 1956–8; assistant professor of music, 1958–64, co-director, New Music Ensemble, 1963–8, associate professor, 1964–70, and professor, 1970–2, University of California, Davis; director, University of California bands, 1958–72; founder/editor (first 8 issues), *SOURCE: Music of the Avant Garde*, 1966; composer-associate, Broadcast Music Inc., since 1964; professor of music, Trinity University, San Antonio, Texas, Summer 1970; founder/director, SYCOM/Systems Complex for the Studio and Performing Arts, University of South Florida, 1972–8; advisory council, American Composers Alliance, since 1975; professor of music, University of South Florida, Tampa, 1972–8; professor of music, since 1978, director, Electronic Music Center, 1981–2; and director/founder, CEMI/Center for Experimental Music and Intermedia, since 1982, University of North Texas, Denton; advisory board, Composers Forum, since 1980; director, International Computer Music Conference, Denton, Texas, November 1981; board of directors, since 1980, and vice-president, 1988–90, Texas Composers Forum; guest composer in residence, Center for Computer Music, Brooklyn College, City University of New York, 1986; board of directors, 1984–8, president, 1990–2, and on advisory council, Computer Music Association. Recipient: distinguished alumnus award, North Texas State University, 1968; presentations award, Institute for Creative Arts, University of California, 1968; distinguished composer award (for *Quadrants: Event/Complex No 9*), Music Teachers National Association, 1974; first prize (for *Second Fantasy on Ives' Universe Symphony*), Florida Festival of New Music, Fine Arts Council of Florida, 1976; elected to membership of Pi Kappa Lambda, National Honorary Music Fraternity, 1979; CEMI nominated for G. Theodore Mitau Award for Innovation and Change in Higher Education, 1987; third prize (for *Sinfonia Concertante: a Mozartean Episode*), International New Music Composers' Association, 1988. Mailing address: 2109 Woodbrook, Denton, Texas 76205, U.S.A.

Publishers: ACA; Composer Performer; MJQ; Peer-Southern.

Symphonies/orchestral:

Concertino (flute, trumpet, strings) 1952; first performed San Antonio, Texas, 1952.
Prosody (chamber orchestra, narrator) 1953; first performed San Antonio, Texas, 1953.
Fanfare and Procession (concert band) 1957; first performed Bethlehem, Pennsylvania, 1959.
Men of California (band) 1957.
Music Galore (outdoor suite for marching band) 1958; first performed Stanford, California, 1958.
Suite for Massed Bands 1961; first performed California, Autumn 1961.
Improvisations (jazz soloists, orchestra) 1961; first performed Washington, D.C., 31 May 1961. Recorded Columbia Masterwork MS6733.
In Memoriam, J.F.K. (concert band) 1964; first performed Eugene, Oregon, 8 November 1964.
Open Style for Orchestra with Piano Soloist 1965; first performed Buffalo, New York, 29 September 1968.
Quadrants: Event/Complex # 1 (symphonic wind ensemble, tape) 1972; first performed Berkeley, California, 11 February 1972. Recorded IRIDA 0022.
Phantasmagoria: Fantasies on Ives' Universe Symphony (orchestra, narrator, tape, digital synthesizer) 1977, revised 1981; first performed Denton, Texas, 18 February 1982.

Sinfonia Concertante: A Mozartean Episode (chamber orchestra, computer music narrative) 1986; first performed Cleveland, Ohio, 19 October 1986. Recorded Centaur Records CRC 2029.

Chamber/instrumental:

Woodwind Quartet 1948; first performed Denton, Texas, 1948.
Woodwind Quintet 1949; first performed Denton, Texas, 1949.
Brass Quintet 1949; first performed Denton, Texas, 1949.
Sonatina (violin, piano) 1950; first performed Denton, Texas, 1951.
Wind Quartet (flute, clarinet, trumpet, bassoon) 1950.
Three Violin Duets 1951; first performed Denton, Texas, 1951.
String Trio 1952; first performed San Antonio, Texas, 1955.
String Quartet 1955; first performed Utah, 1956.
Fanfare (9 brass instruments) 1958; first performed Berkeley, California, 1958.
Homecoming (alto saxophone, jazz quintet; originally for soprano, jazz quintet) 1958–9.
Fantasy on a Theme by Berg (jazz band) 1960; first performed Davis, California, 1960.
Piano Variations 1960; first performed Chicago, 1962. Recorded Advance Records FGR1OS.
A Broken Consort (flute, clarinet, trumpet, horn, piano, double bass, drum set) 1962; first performed New York, 14 March 1963.
Collage (11 fragments for several instruments) 1963; first performed Davis, California, 31 July 1963.
Continuum: Open Style for a Number of Instruments (flute, oboe, bassoon, trumpet, bass, percussion, harpsichord) 1964; first performed Davis, California, March 1964.
Current (clarinet, piano) 1964; first performed Venice, 10 September 1964. Recorded Advance Records FGR9S.
Piano Set in Open Style 1964; first performed 2 December 1964. Recorded Advance Records FGR10S.
Quartet in Open Style (string quartet) 1964; first performed Davis, California, 7 February 1965.
Changes: Open Style (trombone, tape) 1965; first performed Davis, California, 24 October 1965.
Agape Set (suite for jazz band) 1971.
Quadrants: Event/Complex #3, 4, 5, 6, 7 (violin, piano, cello, clarinet, flute, tape) 1973; first performed #4, Birmingham, England, 11 February 1977.
Quadrants: Event/Complex #8 (viola, tape) 1973; first performed Denton, Texas, 17 April 1990.
Quadrants: Event/Complex #9 (percussion, tape) 1974.
The Life Pulse Prelude for Percussion Orchestra: A Realization for Modern Performance (20 percussionists) 1974–84; first performed Buffalo, New York, 14 April 1984.
First Fantasy on Ives' Universe Symphony—The Earth (double brass quintet, narrator, tape) 1975; first performed Tampa, Florida, 23 February 1975.
Charley's Cornet (cornet, piano) 1976.
Second Fantasy on Ives' Universe Symphony—The Heavens (clarinet, viola, keyboards, percussion, tape) 1976; first performed Tampa, Florida, 8 May 1976. Recorded IRIDA 0022.
Quadrants: Event/Complex #10 (trombone, tape) 1976; first performed Birmingham, England, 11 February 1977.
Organ Mass (organ solo) 1977; first performed Tampa, Florida, 1 May 1977.
Quadrants: Event/Complex #11 (double bass, tape) 1977; first performed London, Ontario, 30 September 1977.
Catalogo Sonoro: "Narcisso" (viola, tape) 1978; first performed Bloomington, Illinois, 29 September 1978.
Protoforms: Fractals for Cello Choir and Computer Band (13 cellos, tape) 1981; first performed Paris, 20 February 1981.
Canadian Coastlines: Canonic Fractals for Musicians and Computer Band (8 musicians: strings, winds, percussion, voices, etc; and tape) 1981; first broadcast, Toronto, Winnipeg, Manitoba and Halifax, Nova Scotia, 10 May 1981. Recorded Folkways Records FTS37475.
art is self-alteration is Cage is . . . (4 double basses, optional bass ensemble in multiples of 4) 1982; first performed New York City, 11 April 1983.
Sonata Concertante (piano, tape) 1983–4; first performed Buffalo, New York, 12 April 1984. Recorded Centaru Records CRC 2029.
Tango Violento (para piano solo) 1984; first performed Denton, Texas, 28 January 1985.
Clarini! (20 trumpets) 1985; first performed Albuquerque, New Mexico, 29 May 1985.
Montage: Themes and Variations (violin, computer tape) 1985; first performed Denton, Texas, 26 January 1987.
Violets's Invention (piano) 1988.
Snare Drum Cycles (solo snare drum) 1989.

Vocal/choral:

Song 1948; first performed Denton, Texas, 1948.
Mass (chorus, orchestra) 1955–8.
Homecoming (cantata for soprano, jazz quintet; also version for alto saxophone, jazz quintet) 1958–9; first performed San Francisco, 1960.
Triptych (chorus, string quartet) 1961.
Quadrants: Event/Complex # 2 (chorus, tape) 1972; first performed Los Angeles, 28 April 1972.
Maroon Bells (voice, piano, tape) 1976; first performed London, Ontario, 30 September 1977. Recorded IRIDA 0020.
Protoforms: Hybrid Musics (3 sopranos, computer) 1980; first performed Dallas, Texas, 23 April 1980.
Ceremony (voice, organ) 1980.
Euphonia 2344: An Intermezzo in 5 Scenes (voices, computer tape) 1988; first performed Denton, Texas, 16 February 1988.
Transmission Two: The Great Excursion (chorus, computer music ensemble, recorded dialogue) 1990; broadcast Berkeley, California, 26 February 1990.

Opera:

Catalogo Voce (mini-opera for bass-baritone, tape and slides) 1979; first performed New York City, 13 June 1979. Recorded IRIDA 0022.
Euphonia: A Tale of the Future (soloists, chorus, chamber orchestra, tape, digital synthesizer; Holliday) 1982; first performed Potsdam, New York, 1 April 1982.

Other:

Music for Electra; A Fantasy on the First Delphic Hymn (incidental music on tape) 1963; first performed Davis, California, 9 April 1963.
Music for Richard II (incidental music to Shakespeare) 1963; first performed Davis, California, 7 December 1964.
Catharsis: Open Style (2 improvisation ensembles, tape) 1965; first performed 6 December 1965.
Roma: A Theatre Piece in Open Style for Improvisation Ensemble and Tape 1965; first performed Davis, California, 9 January 1966.

Bass: A Theatre Piece in Open Style for String Bass, Player, Tape and Film 1966; first performed Davis, California, 1967.
The Maze: A Theatre Piece in Open Style for Three Percussionists, Dancer, Tapes, Machines, and Projections 1966; first performed Davis, California, 3 March 1966.
Amphitryon 38 (tape music for Giraudoux play) 1967; first performed Davis, California, June 1967.
Brass (electronically prepared brass, slides, film) 1967; first performed Davis, California, 6 November 1967.
Duet Amphitryon (electronic tape) 1967.
Accidents (electronically prepared piano, tape, mirrors, actions, projections) 1967; first performed Rome, 13 May 1967. Recorded Source Records SR13.
Cyclotron Stew (tape montage) 1968; first performed Davis, California, 10 April 1967.
The Magicians (theatre piece for children, tape, films, slides) 1968; first performed Davis, California, 28 May 1968.
Twomanshow (tape) 1969.
Black / White Study (electronic music film) 1969.
Color Study (electronic music film) 1969.
Transmission One (video/audio electronic composition for color television broadcast) 1969; first performed Oakland, California, 6 October 1969.
California 99 (collaboration with Harold Budd; several instruments) 1969.
Caritas: Symphony of the Gigantic Hammered Welded Aluminum Imitation Earth Volumes—Raisin, Stone, Stalk, Potato, God, Nut, Shoot, Germ, Rock (computer tape) 1969; first performed Pasadena, California, 24 May 1970. Recorded Source Records SR17.
Agape (celebration for priests, soprano and baritone soloists, rock band, chorus, actors, dancers and celebrants with films, ritual, sculpture, tapes) 1970; first performed Buffalo, New York, 25 February 1970.
Walter (film composition and theatre piece for viola, viola d'amore, tape, films) 1970–1; first performed New York City, 21 November 1971.
Quartet Three (4-channel electronic tape) 1971; first performed Albany, New York, 26 February 1971.
Prelude and Postlude to Plastic Surgery (film and theatre piece for keyboards, film and tape) 1971; first performed Davis, California, 8 July 1971.
Quartet Four (electronic tape) 1971; first performed Hanover, New Hampshire, 10 November 1971.
Primal Hybrid (electronic tape) 1972; first performed Albany, New York, 15 March 1972.
Tableaux Vivants (4–6 musicians, tape, slides; with graphic artist Charles Ringness) 1973, revised 1981.
"1976" (text-sound composition on tape) 1973. Recorded Deep Listening LA-R-3.
Chivalry (sonograph on tape; collaboration with Charles Ringness) 1974; first performed Tampa, Florida, January 1975.
Phoenix (computer tape) 1974; first performed Tampa, Florida, 27 September 1974. Recorded Deep Listening LA-R-3.
Catalogo Gesto / Timbro (percussionist, dancer) 1978; first performed New York City, 6–7 October 1978.
Protoforms: Fractals for Computer Band with Improvisors (computer tape) 1980; first performed Paris, 20 February 1981. Recorded Deep Listening LA-R-3.
Stars (computer tape) 1982; first performed Venice, 26 September 1982. Recorded Deep Listening LA-R-3.
Beachcombers (live electronic music for 4 musicians, tape, to be performed with dance work and film "Coast Zone" by Merce Cunningham) 1983; first performed New York City, 18 March 1983.
Ludus Fractalis (video composition; Cybernetic Arts Project) 1984. Recorded Deep Listening LA-R-3.
Concertante Cybernetica: Interactions for Performer and Synclavier Digital Music System 1987; first performed Denton, Texas, 30 November 1987.

PUBLICATIONS

By Austin: "Conversation: Karlheinz Stockhausen, Robert Ashley, LA", in *Source*, 1 (1), 1967; "Is the Composer Anonymous?", in *Source*, 1 (2), 1967; "Is the Concerto Dead? Yes", in *New York Times*, 10 March 1968; "Music Only for the Privileged?", in *New York Times*, 1 September 1968; "Groups", in *Source*, 2 (1), 1968; "Music and Light", in *Artscanada*, December 1968; (co-authored with John Cage and Lejaren Hiller) *"HPSCHD"*, in *Source*, 2 (2), 1968; "Music Is Dead, Long Live Music", in *New York Times*, 6 July 1969; "Can Electronic Music Be Romantic?", in *New York Times*, 17 September 1971; "New Romanticism: An Emerging Aesthetic for Electronic Music" (parts I and II), in *Mundus Artium*, 6 (1), 1973; "SYCOM—Systems Complex for the Studio and Performing Arts", in *Numus West*, May 1974; (with Barney Childs) "Forum: Improvisation", in *Perspectives of New Music*, 21 (1–2), 1982–3; "To Arms . . . Be Uncommon: LA Interviews LA", in *Ear Magazine*, 8 (6), 1984; "Charles Ives's *Life Pulse Prelude*: A Realization for Modern Performance from Sketches for the Universe Symphony", in *Percussive Notes: Research Edition*, 23 (2), 1985; "Electro-Acoustic Music in the USA", festival booklet for the Elektronmusic Festival 1987, Skinnskatteberg/Uttersberg, 1987; *Learning to Compose: Modes, Materials and Models of Musical Invention*, Dubuque, Iowa, 1989; "Live-Electronic Music on the Third Coast", in *Contemporary Music Review*, 1990.

On Austin: A. Kennedy, "Sound-Script Relations and the New Notation", *Artforum*, 12 (1), 1973; D. Ernst, in *The Evolution of Electronic Music*, New York, 1976; W. Zimmermann, in *Desert Plants: Conversations with 23 American Musicians*, Vancouver, 1976; Thomas Clark, "Duality of Process and Drama in LA's *Sonata Concertante*", in *Perspectives of New Music*, 23 (1), 1984; Thomas Clark, "Coasts: On the Creative Edge with Composer LA", in *Computer Music Journal*, 13 (1), Spring 1989.

Larry Austin comments:

Three things run through my work as a composer. First, I believe that the musics of mankind are concomitant with a pluralist world, one where human rights are freely experienced and expressed. In that ideal reference, I experience and assimilate all kinds of music. But, in spite of my apparent proclivity for tasting the fruits of man's musical cultures, the influence they have on the actual nature of my work is, to my ear, elusive. For instance, I grew up as a jazz musician, continue to enjoy jazz, but only occasionally, consciously make the idiom an overt part of my musical language. I'm told my music has a distinctive profile. If so, there must be a process of synthesis taking place inside me among these musics I constantly absorb.

Second, I like combining seemingly disparate compositional processes, materials and mediums, exemplified in much of my work and notably in my *Sinfonia Concertante: A Mozartean Episode*: " . . . the interplay of the chamber orchestra and the computer music narrative . . . of sweet consonance and angry dissonance, of innocence and duplicity, of pleasure and sorrow." My program note continued: "These dualities in the piece intrigue me, precisely because they are never completely reconciled, just as extreme polarities in the fortunes of life are never completely understood."

Third, I am happiest in my work when I am exploring fresh concepts, new materials and complex interactions. If my explorations take me to what turns out to be a rich vein of musical material, I experiment intensely with the possibilities. The material instructs me in how to form the piece and I'm off and running on a piece or even a series of pieces with kindred properties. Sometimes, explorations lead nowhere, experiments fail. I learn from all, assimilating the musical implications. On balance, I've been gratified by the new musical ground I've discovered for my pieces to take root and the sometimes surprisingly successful—to my ear—musical inventions that grow from my experiments with musical material.

Always at the base of this approach is the essence of the piece I am imagining. My explorations and experiments come about for technical reasons, not stemming so much from the newly developed music technology for its own sake as from musical imperatives that—it turns out—often cannot be achieved without advanced music technology to use as my *modus operandi*. Thus, when I am sometimes introduced as an "electronic composer", I flinch a bit but try to mind my manners. They confuse the way I explore the *way* I explore the materials or modes of making music with the substance of my work. I am simply—and certainly—a composer of music, not a kind of organism interfaced with a machine. On the other hand . . . that's not necessarily a flawed concept . . . I wonder if . . .

* * *

Throughout his career, Larry Austin has engaged in a broad spectrum of musical pursuits. An experimenter, he has composed highly original musical works. An entrepreneur, he has organized performances and founded institutions of artistic collaboration. An observer of contemporary musical thought, he has contributed to professional societies and journals. A mentor to emerging composers as a professor at universities in California, Florida, and since 1978 in Texas, he co-authored a 1989 composition textbook.

Theatrical avant garde works brought Austin early notoriety. Later works in advanced computer music media draw from a background of experience with analog electro-acoustic sound sources, especially combined with "live" performers of conventional instruments, voice and dance (as in *Beachcombers*). Traditional ensembles have also figured prominently in the compositional output, approached (as in *Open Style* for orchestra with piano soloist) in a way free from preconceptions of idiom. *Sinfonia Concertante* merges a traditional Mozartean chamber orchestra with computer music and dramatic narration on tape.

The *Musical Quarterly*'s 1968 review of Austin's *SOURCE* magazine pointed to the primacy of experimental process as the essence of the avant garde. Austin's own works invariably focus on a single exploratory process, setting up a problem or volatile situation ripe with contrast and surprise (as in *Accidents*). Sound relationships are modeled after natural or mathematical patterns or by the nature of sound itself. The resulting works are strongly unified, defining their own idioms with singular persistence.

Musical ideas and characters often combine in the form of collage, as in American composer Charles Ives's music. *The Life Pulse Prelude* and *Phantasmagoria* are based on Ives's unfinished compositional sketches. Drawing energy from dramatic juxtapositions, Austin's works are dense with sound activity, transforming gradually in a single, extended thrust of form.

Improvisations shows an early influence, incorporating jazz soloists into an orchestral medium. A jazz trumpet player in his youth, Austin typically structures the flow of events by constantly establishing then disintegrating pulses. As in jazz, the "beats" can be cool and languorous, almost at a standstill, or relentlessly red-hot.

Other musical structures are generated systematically by unconventional processes. *Canadian Coastlines: Canonic Fractals* traces actual map contours for compositional data. Word strings and mathematical fractals are other favored non-musical pattern models. The process is first tested intuitively "by ear", then turned loose to fill in the substance of a carefully planned architecture. Specially designed computer algorithms may assist this approach for structuring pitch, register, density, loudness and timbre choice.

An interest in musical color has led Austin to exotic sound sources offered by percussion sounds (*Quadrants* no 9), extended instrumental techniques (*Current*), and digitally synthesized sound (*Montage*). Subtle shadings of sound color play an interesting role in some works, such as *Sonata Concertante*, which pits the piano against larger-than-life synthetic piano sounds, juxtaposing and eventually merging their distinct but kindred timbres.

A drive to share accumulated musical resources and ideas had led Austin personally to found several institutions for experimental music and composition: the periodical, *SOURCE: Music of the Avant Garde*; SYCOM, Systems Complex for the Studio and Performing Arts; CEMI, Center for Experimental Music and Intermedia; and CDCM, Consortium to Distribute Computer Music. A leader in the computer music field, Austin hosted the 1981 International Computer Music Conference in Denton, Texas and in 1989 was elected President of the Computer Music Association.

Austin's work exemplifies avant garde traditions of public activism and personal exploration. His music, whether intensely dramatic or dreamlike, delights in discovery through dynamic processes, contributing to a heightened appreciation of new media and modes of expression.

—Thomas Clark

B

BABBITT, Milton (Byron). American. Born in Philadelphia, 10 May 1916. Educated at University of Pennsylvania, Philadelphia (mathematics), 1931; New York University (music under Philip James and Marion Bauer), 1932–5, B.A.; Princeton University, New Jersey (under Roger Sessions, also privately), M.F.A., 1942. Married Sylvia Miller in 1939; 1 daughter. Teacher, music faculty, 1938–42, 1948–60, mathematics faculty, 1943–5, Conant Professor of Music, since 1960, and Professor Emeritus, since 1981, Princeton University; president, ISCM American Section, 1951–2; director, Columbia-Princeton Electronic Music Center, since 1959; composition faculty, Juillard School, New York City, since 1973; courses at Darmstadt, Tanglewood, Salzburg, New England Conservatory of Music; member, editorial board, *Perspectives of New Music*. Recipient: Joseph Bearns Prize (for *Music for the Mass I*), 1942; New York Critics' Circle citations (for *Composition for Four Instruments* and *Philomel*), 1949, 1964; National Institute of Arts and Letters Award, 1959; Guggenheim Fellowship, 1960–1; membership, National Institute of Arts and Letters, 1965; Brandeis University Gold Medal, 1970; fellowship, American Academy of Arts and Sciences, 1974; Pulitzer Prize Special Citation for life's work, 1982; numerous honorary degrees. Mailing address: Department of Music, Princeton University, Woolworth Center of Musical Studies, Princeton, New Jersey 08544–1007, U.S.A.

Publishers: Associated; Peters; Boelke-Romart.

Symphonies/orchestral:

Generatrix 1935; incomplete, withdrawn.
Composition (string orchestra) 1940; incomplete, withdrawn.
Symphony 1941; incomplete, withdrawn.
Relata I 1965; first performed Cleveland, Ohio, 3 March 1966.
Correspondences (string orchestra, tape) 1967.
Relata II 1968; first performed New York City, 16 January 1969.
Concerti (violin, small orchestra, tape) 1974–6; first performed New York City, 13 March 1976.
Ars combinatoria (small orchestra) 1981; first performed Bloomington, Indiana, 16 July 1981.
Concerto for Piano and Orchestra 1985; first performed New York City, 19 January 1986.

Chamber/instrumental:

String Trio 1941; withdrawn.
Three Compositions (piano) 1947.
Composition for Four Instruments (flute, clarinet, violin, cello) 1948.
Composition for 12 Instruments (trumpet, harp, celeste, wind quintet, violin, viola, cello, double bass) 1948, revised 1954.
String Quartet No 1 1948; withdrawn.
Composition (viola, piano) 1950.
Woodwind Quartet (flute, oboe, clarinet, bassoon) 1953.
String Quartet No 2 1954.
Duet (piano) 1956.
Semi-Simple Variations (piano) 1956.
All Set (alto saxophone, tenor saxophone, trumpet, trombone, double bass, piano, vibraphone, percussion) 1957.
Partitions (piano) 1957.
Post-Partitions (piano) 1966.
Sextets (violin, piano; title refers to structure of work, not to instrumentation) 1966.
String Quartet No 3 1969–70.
String Quartet No 4 1970.
Tableaux (piano) 1972.
Arie da capo (flute, clarinet/bass clarinet, piano, violin, cello) 1973–4.
Reflections (piano, tape) 1975.
Minute Waltz (3/4 + 1/8) (piano) 1977.
Playing for Time (piano) 1977.
My Complements to Roger (piano) 1978.
My Ends Are My Beginnings (clarinet) 1978.
Paraphrases (flute, oboe/cor anglais, clarinet, bass clarinet, bassoon, horn, trumpet, trombone, tuba, piano) 1979.
Images (saxophone, tape) 1980.
Dual (cello, piano) 1980.
Don (piano, 4 hands) 1981.
About Time (piano) 1982.
Melismata (violin) 1982.
String Quartet No 5 1982.
Cononical Form (piano) 1983.
Groupwise (piccolo/flute/alto flute, violin, viola, cello, piano) 1983.
Playing for Time (piano) 1983.
Four Play (clarinet, violin, cello, piano) 1984.
It Takes Twelve to Tango (piano) 1984.
Sheer Pluck (guitar) 1984.
Lagniappe (piano) 1985.

Vocal/choral:

Music for the Mass I (unaccompanied SATB chorus) 1940; withdrawn.
Music for the Mass II (unaccompanied SATB chorus) 1941; withdrawn.
Three Theatrical Songs (from *Fabulous Voyage*; voice, piano; Koch, Childs, MB) 1946.
The Widow's Lament in Springtime (soprano, piano; Williams) 1950.
Du (soprano, piano; Stramm) 1951.
Vision and Prayer (soprano, piano) 1954.
Two Sonnets (baritone, clarinet, viola, cello; Hopkins) 1955.
Composition (tenor, flute, oboe, violin, viola, cello, harpsichord) 1960.
Sounds and Words (soprano, piano) 1960.
Vision and Prayer (soprano, tape; Dylan Thomas) 1961.
Philomel (soprano, tape; Hollander) 1964.
Four Canons (after Schoenberg; women's voices) 1968.
Phenomena (soprano, piano) 1969–70, version for tape 1975.
A Solo Requiem (soprano, 2 pianos; Shakespeare, Hopkins,

Meredith, Stramm, Dryden) 1976–7; first performed New York City, 10 February 1979.
More Phenomena (12 voices) 1978.
An Elizabethan Sextette (6 female voices) 1979.
The Head of the Bed (soprano, flute, clarinet, violin, cello; Hollander) 1982.

Opera/music-theatre:

Fabulous Voyage 1946.

Other:

Into the Good Ground (film score for orchestra) 1949; incomplete, withdrawn.
Composition for Synthesizer (tape) 1961.
Ensembles for Synthesizer (tape) 1962–4.
Occasional Variations (tape) 1971.

PUBLICATIONS

By Babbitt: "Some Aspects of Twelve-Tone Composition", in *Score and IMA Magazine*, 12, 1953; "Twelve-Tone Invariants as Compositional Determinants", in *Musical Quarterly*, 46, 1960, reprinted in Lang (ed.), *Problems of Modern Music*, New York, 1962; "Set Structure as a Compositional Determinant", in *Journal of Music Theory*, 5, 1961, reprinted in Boretz and Cone (eds), *Perspectives on Contemporary Music Theory*, New York, 1972; "Twelve-Tone Rhythmic Structure and the Electronic Medium", in *Perspectives of New Music*, 1 (1), 1962, reprinted in Boretz and Cone (eds), *Perspectives on Contemporary Music Theory*, New York, 1972; "Who Cares If You Listen?", reprinted in Schwartz and Childs (eds), *Contemporary Composers on Contemporary Music*, New York, 1967; "Contemporary Music Composition and Music Theory as Contemporary Intellectual History", in Brook, Downes and van Solkema, *Perspectives in Musicology*, New York, 1971; "Since Schoenberg", in *Perspectives of New Music*, 12 (2), 1974; "The Next Thirty Years", in *High Fidelity*, 21 (4), 1981.

On Babbitt: George Perle, in *Serial Composition and Atonality*, Berkeley, California, 1962; Richard Kostelanetz, "The Two Extremes of Avant-Garde Music", in *New York Times Magazine*, 15 January 1967; E. Salzman, "B and Serialism", in *Twentieth Century Music: An Introduction*, Englewood Cliffs, New Jersey, 1967; "An Interview with MB", in *Music Educators Journal*, 55 (3) 1968; S. Arnold and G. Hair, "MB", in *Music and Musicians*, 17 (10), 1969; D. Ewen, "MB", in *Composers of Tomorrow's Music*, New York, 1972; H. Wiley Hitchcock, "Systematic Serial Composition", in *Music in the United States*, Englewood Cliffs, New Jersey (2nd edition) 1974; Lieberson, Lundborg and Peel, "Conversation with MB", in *Contemporary Music Newsletter*, 8 (1), 1974; special issue on MB, containing reply "Responses: A First Approximation", *Perspectives of New Music*, 14 (1–2), 1976; J. Machlis, "Four Representative American Composers", in *Introduction to Contemporary Music*, New York, 1979; Rosenberg and Rosenberg, "MB", in *The Music Makers*, New York, 1979; Gagne and Caras, "MB", (interview) in *Soundpieces: Interviews with American Composers*, Metuchen, New Jersey, 1982; John Rockwell, "The Northwestern Academic Establishment and the Romance of Science", in *All American Music: Composition in the Late Twentieth Century*, New York, 1983; A. Mead, "Recent Developments in the Music of MB", in *Musical Quarterly*, 70, 1984.

* * *

The emotion in Milton Babbitt's music has become more perceptible as the years have passed, and so have its elegance and distinction. This is reassuring because nearly all of the large quantity of writing about his music, instead of giving consideration to its aesthetic qualities, has dealt almost exclusively with its theoretical foundation. True, Babbitt is one of the 20th century's major compositional theorists and his contribution in that direction can no more be ignored than can that of Schoenberg or Messiaen. Yet readers of most of what has been written on Babbitt—including by the composer himself—can easily go away with the impression that he is of interest solely for his very elaborate extension of the Schoenbergian serial method into an actual system of composition (a concept to which Schoenberg had always objected). There have even been those, including among his admirers, who maintain that Babbitt's theoretical work is more important creatively than his composing.

No doubt this is partly due to the strong influence this leading figure of the northeastern academic serial establishment has exerted through his highly original writings and his teaching. This has been reinforced by the fact that much of the new terminology his theoretical explorations forced Babbitt to introduce into music from mathematics, such as "combinatoriality", "aggregate", "source set" etc., has been widely adopted.

His starting point was scores such as Webern's Symphony Op 21 (1928) in which the tone row influences some aspects of phrase-structure, counterpoint, rhythm, dynamics, orchestration and even form. This led Babbitt to a complete reconsideration—and hence to a restructuring—of musical relationships. Trained as a mathematician (unlike Webern, or Schoenberg), he thought of the tone row not as a series but as a *set* in the mathematical sense. It became a group—a set—of relationships determined through systematic pre-compositional planning both with regard to structure and process. Hence the complete serialisation not only of linear pitch succession but also of rhythm, timbres, registers, articulation, dynamics, durations. The composition becomes an unfolding which, through processes of permutation, makes all potential relationships apparent.

This began to emerge in the late 1940s with Babbitt's *Three Compositions* for piano, *Composition for Four Instruments* and *Composition for 12 Instruments*. The keyboard work is generally reminiscent of Schoenberg and its three movements cover a wide range of expression while in the *Composition for 12 Instruments* a durational set was for the first time derived from the tone row so that it was written with a 12-duration set as well as a 12-pitch set. The listener's abiding problem with this and ever more with Babbitt's later music is not only that it is so complicated—the orchestral *Relata I*, for example, sometimes has as many as 48 independent simultaneous lines—but that events, such as switches of register and dynamics, modes of note-production etc., pass in such rapid succession. Consider the abrupt registral changes in *Partitions* or the shifts in dynamics which range from *ppppp* to *fffff* in *Post-Partitions*.

These two works for the piano highlight the extreme demands Babbitt has always made on his performers. It follows that he was greatly interested in the vast potential of the RCA Electronic Music Synthesizer Mark II which, partly under his supervision, was installed at the Columbia-Princeton Electronic Music Centre in 1959. This allowed an absolutely precise determination of intensity, duration, quality of attack and decay, tone colour etc., of both pitched and non-pitched sounds, and hence Babbitt could add exactly controlled (recorded) performance to exactly controlled composition. The synthesizer also eliminated the labourious processes of recording and re-recording on tape and then manually cutting and splicing tape during the business of composing. Pieces such as his *Composition for Synthesizer* and *Ensembles for Synthesizer* bring forward his extremely original sense of colour and texture, and show great lucidity of form, and even a renewed vitality of musical thought.

Babbitt retained his interest in live performance, however, and his continuing work in this sphere was naturally affected by his electronic pieces. An early instance, dating from before the installation of the RCA Synthesizer, is *All Set* for jazz ensemble, which is derived melodically, rhythmically, metrically and to some extent harmonically from late-1940s bop. He also combined live performers with electronic sound, as in such pieces as *Vision and Prayer, Philomel, Correspondences* for string orchestra and tape, *Reflections* for piano and tape, and *Images* for saxophone and tape.

Vision and Prayer and *Philomel* are both for soprano and tape, the former being a setting of Dylan Thomas's poem. Here the four-track tape carries only electronic sounds whereas in *Philomel* electronic sounds are mixed with electronically altered vocal sounds. The latter sets a poem by John Hollander based on Ovid's version of the Greek legend of Philomela, who was raped and her tongue torn out but on whom the gods took pity, transforming her into a nightingale. Going much further than the constant interplay between text and vocal and piano lines in the song cycle *Du*, there are marvellous correspondences in *Philomel* between Babbitt's music and the structural and musical qualities of Hollander's poem. Music and language to an extent take on each other's qualities, as is suggested by the line, "I am becoming my own song". Rationality fuses with live performance conditions in the virtuosity of the performer in a particularly intense way here, although that is always true of really perceptive interpretations of Babbitt's music.

Arguments against such difficult works usually point out that composers have been ever more employed by universities in the United States, where all kinds of additional funding always seem available, and that hence they are able to write without consideration for even the limited audience that contemporary music has. Yet Babbitt is likely to be seen eventually as a rather extreme case of what must always be the central issue with significant new music, the devising of new forms for new material; and his electronic works as the "music invigorated by science" that Varèse dreamt of.

Persistent listeners to his works have already found that the balance between compositional instinct and intellectual adventure is better—which is to say more musical—than once appeared. The mind of a real composer has emerged unimpaired from among the structures and processes set up by the mathematician. Indeed, Babbitt's finest music works so well as music that it will eventually quite outrun the fearsome theorising which shapes it from within. There is a contribution here to the expansion of man's perceptual and intellectual capacities, and this comes not from the theories but from the music.

—Max Harrison

BÄCK, Sven-Erik. Swedish. Born in Stockholm, 16 September 1919. Educated at Royal Academy of Music, Stockholm (violin under Sven Karpe), 1938–43; studied composition under Hilding Rosenberg, 1940–5; studied medieval music, Schola Cantorum, Basle, 1948–50; Accademia di Santa Cecilia, Rome (advanced composition under Goffredo Petrassi), 1951. Professional violist, Lilla Kammarorkester, 1943–8; violist in string quartet led by Charles Barkel, 1944–53; member (with Ingvar Lidholm and Karl-Birger Blomdahl), Monday Group, 1944; conductor, Kammarorkester '53, 1953–7; head of Swedish Radio music school, Edsberg, since 1959. Mailing address: Ulrikagatan 13, S-115 24 Stockholm, Sweden.

Publisher: Wilhelm Hansen, Copenhagen.

Symphonies / orchestral:

Fantasy on "Dies sind die Heiligen Zehn Gebot" 1954, revised 1957.
Chamber Symphony 1955.
Violin Concerto 1957.
A Game Around a Game (piano, celeste, percussion, strings) 1959; first performed Donaueschingen, 17 October 1959. Recorded Philips AL 8213.
Arkitektur 60 (2 wind orchestras, piano, double bass, percussion) 1960.
Ikaros (ballet suite; 3 string orchestras, piano, celeste, percussion) 1963.
Intrada (small orchestra) 1964; first performed Stockholm, 26 April 1964.
Movements (ballet suite; small orchestra) 1965.
Arkitektur 65 (2 wind orchestras, piano, double bass, percussion) 1965.
Cello Concerto 1965.
O Altitudo II (orchestra, piano, 2 harps, organ) 1966.
Ruoli per orchestra 1968.
Aperio (3 orchestral groups, 4-channel tape) 1973.
Ciklos (concerto for piano, strings, percussion) 1975.
Four Motets (orchestra or string orchestra) 1978.
Three Dialogue Motets (cello, string orchestra) 1984.

Chamber / instrumental:

String Quartet No 1 1945.
String Quartet No 2 1947.
String Quintet (2 violins, 2 violas, cello) 1948.
Expansive Preludier (piano) 1949.
Préambule pour Pierre (string quartet) 1949.
Sonata (flute) 1949.
Sonata alla ricercare (piano) 1950.
Danssuit (2 pianos) 1951.
Nocturne (3 recorders, percussion, lute, viola da gamba, violin) 1953.
Elegy (alto saxophone or viola or clarinet, piano) 1954.
String Trio No 1 (violin, cello, double bass) 1954.
Nature morte (viola, bassoon, percussion) 1955.
Sonata (2 cellos) 1957.
Impromptu (piano) 1958. Recorded HMV EBS 15.
Favola (clarinet, percussion, piano) 1962.
String Quartet No 3 1962.
Nuovo su vecchio (old instruments) 1962.
For Eliza (organ, tape ad lib) 1966.
Postludium (flute, piano, percussion) 1967.
O Altitudo (organ) 1967.
Five Preludes (flute or clarinet or violin or viola or cello or bassoon, percussion ad lib) 1968.
Sentire (flute, cello, piano) 1969.
String Trio No 2 (violin, viola, cello) 1970.
Nat for Ing (flute, violin, viola) 1970.

Decet (wind quintet, string quintet) 1972.
Fa-Ce (bassoon, harpsichord or piano) 1975.
Recercare (cello) 1978.
Signos (6 percussion) 1979.
Sonata in Two Movements and Epilogue (piano) 1980.
String Quartet No 4 1981.
Time Present. . . (2 violins) 1982.
Tollo (2 pianos) 1982.
Trio in One Movement (piano, violin, cello) 1984.
Wither (organ) 1984.

Vocal/choral:

Ur Johannes 3 (voices, organ ad lib) 1944.
Three Chinese Songs (soprano, piano) 1945.
Ur Johannes 9 (voices, organ) 1947.
Svanesang (chamber choir, flute, viola, timpani) 1947.
Gladje i Gud (cantata for solo voice, voices, organ) 1948.
Dithyramb (female voice, unison choir, chamber orchestra; Ekelof) 1949.
Kattresan (unison children's voices, 2 recorders, violin, percussion) 1951. Recorded HMV SCLP 1079.
Himlaljusens fader (solo voice, voices, string, organ) 1952.
Sinfonia sacra (voices, orchestra) 1953.
Darkness is soonover (unaccompanied mixed choir) 1959. Recorded Cantate 64–224, SR RAEP 23; SR RMLP 1096.
I Am the Bread of Life (unaccompanied mixed choir) 1959. Recorded Artist ALP 103.
Jesus, Think of Me (unaccompanied mixed choir) 1959. Recorded Cantate 640224; SR RAEP 23.
The Word Was Made Flesh (unaccompanied mixed choir) 1959.
Lo, We Go Up to Jerusalem (unaccompanied mixed choir) 1959. Recorded Artist ALP 103.
Visa (unaccompanied mixed choir) 1962. Recorded HMV SCLP 1043.
Varen (unaccompanied mixed choir) 1962.
Herr, Zu wem soller wir gehen (unaccompanied mixed choir) 1965.
The Transfiguration (unaccompanied mixed choir) 1966. Recorded Artist ALP 103; SR RMLP 1096.
Uppbrottets massa (solo voice, unison voices, organ, percussion) 1967.
Humlan / The Bumble Bee (mixed choir, cello, piano, percussion) 1968.
Behold, I Am Making All Things New (unaccompanied mixed choir) 1968. Recorded SR RMLP 1096.
Neither Nor (soprano, piano, percussion) 1971. Recorded Caprice LP 59.
Fragments 1971.
Dar fanns en brunn (chorus, flute, clarinet, cello, percussion, piano or organ) 1973.
Just da de langsta skuggorna . . . (4 singers, 10 instruments) 1974.
Naktergalen och Hoken (mixed choir, string orchestra, piano, percussion) 1975.
Te Deum (mixed choir, brass ensemble, organ) 1980.
Annus Solaris (2 sopranos, electronic tape) 1980.

Opera:

Tranfjädrarna / The Twilight Crane / Crane Feathers (4 soloists, mixed choir, children's choir, small orchestra; Noh) 1957; broadcast Swedish Radio, 28 February 1957; first stage performance Stockholm, 12 November 1958. Recorded SWD SLT 33 183.
Gastabudet / The Banquet (8 soloists, small orchestra) 1958; first performed Stockholm, 12 November 1958.
Fageln / The Bird (3 soloists, mixed choir, small orchestra, loudspeakers) 1960; broadcast Swedish Radio, 14 February 1961. Recorded SWD SLT 33196.
Ett Spel om Maria, Jesu Moder (4 soloists, mixed choir, children's choir, orchestra) 1968.

Other:

Ikaros (ballet) 1963; first performed Stockholm, May 1963.
Movements (television ballet) 1966; broadcast Swedish Television, 27 February 1966.
In Principio (electronic music) 1970.
Genom Jorden, Genom Havet / Through the Earth, Through the Sea (ballet for tape; also concert version) 1971–2; first performed Stockholm, June 1972.
Mur och Port / Wall and Gate (electronic music for ballet) 1971; first performed Stockholm, 17 January 1971.
Nox Lucebit / Psalm 139 (electronic music) 1971.
Muri (electronic music) 1972.

PUBLICATIONS

On Bäck: "Verkerforteckning, 1945–66" [catalogue raisonné of works], in *Nutida Musik*, 1966–7.

* * *

Sven-Erik Bäck was one of the earliest Swedish composers to incorporate the Italian lyrical serialism of Nono and Dallopicolla into the melodic polyphony of the Monday Group, Bäck became known first as a quartet member (1940–53) and then as a teacher-composer.

His early works (for example *String Quartet No 2*, 1947) favour mirror-writing, simple subdivisions of the beat, with over-the-beat triplet crotchets preceding a phrase's final note. Melodic lines were built on modal conjunct movement or on arpeggios of stacked thirds; instruments were used traditionally. The *Chamber Symphony* won Bäck fame with its exploitation of the melodious qualities of a single note row while incorporating Baroque elaborations. The chamber opera *Twilight Crane* (*Tranfjädrarna*) in five tableaux follows a Japanese fairytale. Two twelve-note rows symbolise continuum versus interference. While the singers have simplistic octatonic lines, and held pitches are based on perfect intervals, the rhythmic drive is maintained by accompanying repeated chords. Although the tableaux use formulae from earlier sections, their overall structure presents a textural arch where the central tableau is very sparsely accompanied while the mirroring outer sections are much thicker. Voices are seldom heard together; the opera is almost continuous monologue.

Bäck's three-movement *Violin Concerto* displays pointillistic yet lyrical lines against a large percussion section. Other typical works from this time include the pointillistic *A Game Around a Game, Favola* for clarinet and percussion, and *Intrada* for orchestra. *Sentire*, written for piano, flute and cello, demonstrates Bäck's superb instrumentation, with effects such as glissando around a pitch held by another player.

Although a string player rather than church musician, Bäck has produced one of the most significant series of church works in post-war Sweden. When a fellow music student in Basle, Eric Ericson, founded The Stockholm Chamber Choir in 1945, Swedish choral singing was given a new impetus to which Bäck immediately responded by producing the motet *Ur Johannes 3*. 12 years later, the Church of Sweden commissioned a series of modern liturgical motets for the whole church year. Bäck produced several neo-Renaissance and neo-Baroque motets, often on a grand scale and demanding complex handling of forces and technique from the singers (e.g., "These Are They Which Come Out of Great Tribulation", which is deliberately neither easy to sing nor easy to understand—more a proclamation of a difficult text).

Bäck's motet-style carried over into the neo-Baroque gestures found in *String Quartet No 3*, where generally slow-moving notes are joined by florid ornamentation, and harmony is voiced to imply tonal organisation. The slow first movement of *Decet*, for wind quintet plus string quintet, starts in motet style with a descending minor third which is filled in during the third movement. Both chamber works include passages where instruments play out of synchronisation. Each player of the Quartet has a different speed in a *collage alla cadenza*, culminating in a *tutta forza* resolution onto sets of trills. *Decet* has two such passages, the latter employing graphic notation. Typical of the Monday Group aesthetic, both works end as they begin. Bäck's return to his earlier influences can be heard even more clearly in *Fragments*, songs where the lucid accompaniment (lines of octaves, scalic movement and voicing of chords) of Rosenberg's Chinese songs (1945) are very much in evidence. Bäck returned to his own style in *Annus Solaris*, where two female voices are subjected to electronic devices while performing against a pre-recorded tape, perhaps his greatest contribution to electronic music.

—Malcolm J. Hill

BAINBRIDGE, Simon (Jeremy). British/English. Born in London, 30 August 1952. Educated at Central Tutorial School for Young Musicians (now Purcell School), 1965–6; Royal College of Music, London (under John Lambert), 1969–72; Berkshire Music Centre, Tanglewood, Massachusetts (under Gunther Schuller), 1973, 1974. Freelance composer, since 1972; Forman Fellow in composition, University of Edinburgh, 1976; composer in residence, Southern Arts, 1983–5; conductor with various orchestras and ensembles, including BBC Symphony Orchestra, BBC Scottish Symphony Orchestra, Bournemouth Symphony and Sinfonietta, London Sinfonietta, Nash Ensemble, Capricorn, Divertimenti; member, executive committee, Society for the Promotion of New Music. Recipient: Margaret Lee Crofts Composition Prize, 1973; US/UK Bicentennial Fellowship, 1978–9; Gemini Fellowship, 1987. Mailing address: 38 Constantine Road, London NW3 2NG, England.

Publisher: United Music Publishers Ltd.

Symphonies/orchestral:

Heterophony 1970.
Viola Concerto (viola, chamber orchestra) 1976; first performed Manchester, 12 March 1978. Recorded Unicorn RHD 400; Continuum CCD 1020.
Fantasia (double orchestra) 1983–4; first performed London, 2 November 1984. Recorded Continuum CCD 1020.
Ceremony and Fanfare (brass, percussion) 1985; first performed London, 3 December 1985.
Cantus Contra Cantum 1989; first performed London, February 1991.

Chamber/instrumental:

Spirogyra (septet) 1970; first performed, as first of *Three Pieces for Chamber Ensembles* (for flute, soprano saxophone, horn, piano, harp, 2 mandolins, 3 percussion, violin, viola, cello, double bass) London, 21 October 1982.
Wind Quintet 1970–1, revised 1974; first performed London, December 1971.
String Quartet 1972; first performed London, 14 August 1972.
Flugal (ensemble; second of *Three Pieces for Chamber Ensembles*) 1973; first performed London, 21 October 1982.
Wind Quartet (flute, clarinet, horn, bassoon) 1974; first performed York, April 1974.
Music for Mel and Nora (oboe or soprano saxophone, piano) 1976; first performed London, January 1980. Recorded Continuum CCD.
Voicing (flute/piccolo, oboe, clarinet/bass clarinet, bassoon, horn, piano muted with rubber, 2 violins, viola, cello, double bass) 1982; first performed London, 27 June 1982.
Path to Othona (ensemble, 4-track tape; third of *Three Pieces for Chamber Ensembles*) 1982; first performed London, 21 October 1982.
Concertante in Moto Perpetuo (oboe solo, flute, clarinet, horn, piano, 2 violins, viola, cello, double bass) 1983; first performed London, 13 April 1983. Recorded Continuum CCD.
Three Players (cello, bass clarinet, piano) 1985; first performed U.K., October 1986.
Metamorphosis (flute, oboe, clarinet, horn, trumpet, trombone, percussion, piano, 2 violins, viola, cello, double bass) 1988; first performed Amsterdam, 6 June 1988.
Sextet (2 violins, 2 violas, 2 cellos) 1988; first performed Bishop's Stortford, Essex, 4 January 1989.

Vocal/choral:

People of the Dawn (soprano, 3 clarinets/1 soprano saxophone, percussion, piano/celeste) 1975; first performed London, 15 September 1975.
Landscapes and Magic Words (amplified soprano, oboe, cor anglais, soprano saxophone/bass clarinet, clarinet/bass clarinet, horn, electric organ/amplified piano, electric guitar, percussion, violin, viola, cello, double bass, tuned bottles and glasses) 1981; first performed Edinburgh, 18 August 1981.
A Capella (2 sopranos, mezzo-soprano, tenor, baritone, bass) 1985; first performed London, 14 February 1985.
The Devil's Punchbowl (children's voices, chamber orchestra) 1987; first performed Yeovil, Somerset, 3 November 1987.
Folksong (soprano) 1988; first performed Ilkley, Yorkshire, September 1988.
A Song from Michelangelo (soprano, 2 clarinets, viola, cello, double bass) 1989; first performed Brighton, Sussex, 13 May 1989.

Other:

Trace (dance music; 2 flutes, oboe, 2 clarinets, horn, trumpet, percussion, 2 violas, 2 cellos, electric bass guitar, electronics) 1987; first performed Manchester, 28 April 1988.

* * *

It is almost impossible to associate Simon Bainbridge with any school or tendency. Still under 40, he is too individual to be pigeon-holed. Each of his works has its own particular logic and though there are common threads in his concern with musical space and micro-processes within larger structures, even these concerns vary considerably from piece to piece.

Born in London, Bainbridge did his postgraduate study with the inexhaustible Gunther Schuller at Tanglewood, from whom he seems to have derived something of Schuller's highly individual interest in rather heterodox combinations and permutations—ultimately derived from Milton Babbitt—on a basic serial set (this was later modified by Bainbridge's examination of minimalism). Schuller may also have fostered Bainbridge's skilful handling of instrumental colour; there are few better young orchestral composers working today and the massive *Fantasia* for double orchestra, probably his best work to date, is evidence of an imaginative technique in full possession of itself.

The *Fantasia* and the innovative *Viola Concerto* (which was commissioned by Walter Trampler) carefully layer their musical material. As the orchestra absorbs tonal and melodic information from the solo instrument, the surface of the music is transformed into an extended interference pattern involving microtonal interventions and unfamiliar sonorities (mandolin, metal percussion) in which individual procedures are no longer discernible, but out of which the solo material can rise in a series of leaps and beautifully judged cross-textures that are both dazzlingly well conceived and immensely satisfying. As if to underline the violas, but possibly also to subvert it, Bainbridge has the solo instrument shadowed by two offstage players, a most effective coup perfectly consistent with the temper of a piece which is remarkably fugitive and reticent, certainly in relation to the *Fantasia* or the open-hearted *Concertante in Moto Perpetuo*, a relatively light piece by Bainbridge's normally demanding standard, but none-theless very effective in its dynamic progress.

Bainbridge has recently been heard on commercial record for the first time and has attracted a good deal of positive attention for recent work such as the large ensemble *Metamorphosis*, an intriguing contrast with the earlier *Spirogyra, Flugal* and *Path to Othona*, which were much less sure-footed, and somewhat one-dimensional in conception. He has also shown an interest recently in composition for voice, either solo or accompanied. These works are re-markably fresh. If *Metamorphosis* and *A Song from Michel-angelo* have brought Bainbridge to a crossroads in his career, there is sufficient in his early output to suggest that his navigation will be impeccable.

—Pamela Collins

BALASSA, Sándor. Hungarian. Born in Budapest, 20 January 1935. Educated: musical studies from age 17 (while working as engine-fitter); self-taught; thereafter, studied choral leadership at Bela Bartók Music Secondary School; Ferenc Liszt Academy of Music, Budapest (composition under Endre Szervánszky), graduated 1965. Married Iren Balogh, 18 August 1957; 1 daughter and 1 son. Music producer, Hungarian Radio, 1964–80; professor of scoring, Academy of Music, Budapest, since 1981. Recipient: third prize (for *Legend Op 12*), UNESCO International Rostrum of Composers, Paris, 1971; Distinguished Composition of the Year (for *Requiem for Lajos Kassak Op 15*), International Rostrum of Composers, Paris, 1972; Critics Prizes (for *Tabulae* and *Quartetto per percussioni*), Hungarian Radio, 1972, 1974; Erkel Prize, 1972; Listeners' Prize, Hungarian Radio, 1976; Merited Artist, Hungarian People's Republic, 1980; Kossuth Prize, 1983; Bartók-Pasztory Award, 1988; Outstanding Artist, Hungarian People's Republic, 1989. Mailing address: Bicske Vorosmarty utca 11, 2060 Budapest Hungary.

Publisher: Edition Musica Budapest, Vorosmarty ter 1, 1051 Budapest, Hungary.

Symphonies/orchestral:

Violin Concerto Op 3 1965; first performed Budapest, 1965.
Requiem for Lajos Kassák Op 15 1969; first performed Budapest, 1970. Recorded SLPX 11681.
Cantata Y, Op 21 1970; first performed Budapest, 1971. Recorded SLPX 11681.
Lupercalia Op 24 1971; first performed Budapest, 1973. Recorded SLPX 11732.
Iris Op 22 1972; first performed Budapest, 1972. Recorded SLPX 11732.
Tabulae Op 25 (chamber orchestra) 1972; first performed Budapest, 1972. Recorded SLPX 11732.
Glarusiének / Chant of Glarus Op 29 1978; first performed Miskolc, 1978. Recorded SLPX 12223.
The Island of Everlasting Youth Op 23 1979; first performed Budapest, 1979. Recorded SLPX 12223.
Calls and Cries Op 33 1980; first performed Boston, 1982. Recorded SLPX 12557.
A Daydreamer's Diary Op 35 1983; first performed Washing-ton, D.C., 1983. Recorded SLPX 12942.
Three Fantasies Op 36 1984; first performed York, 1984. Recorded SLPX 12942.
Little Grape and Little Fish Op 40 1987; first performed Szeged, 1987.

Chamber/instrumental:

Bagatelles and Sequences Op 17 (piano) 1957; first performed Jaszbereny, 1957.
Dimensioni Op 8 (flute, viola) 1966; first performed Budapest, 1966.
Wind Quintet 1966.
Quartetto per percussioni Op 18 1969; first performed Budapest, 1975. Recorded SLPX 12557.
Xenia Op 20 (nonet) 1970; first performed Budapest, 1970. Recorded SLPX 11732.
Trio Op 19 (violin, viola, harp) 1971; first performed Budapest, 1971.
The Last Shepherd Op 30 (cello) 1978; first performed Budapest, 1978. Recorded SLPX 12557.
Quintetto d'ottoni Op 31 (brass) 1979; first performed Budapest, 1980. Recorded SLPX 12557.
The Flowers of Hajta Op 38 (cimbalom) 1984; first performed Budapest, 1985. Recorded SLPX 12755.

Vocal/choral:

Songs from Rottenbiller Street Op 1 (voice, piano) 1954; first performed Budapest, 1954.

Two Songs Op 16 (voice, piano) 1964; first performed Budapest, 1964.
Legenda Op 12 (mixed choir) 1967; first performed Budapest, 1970. Recorded SLPX 11681.
Five Children's Choruses Op 11 1968; first performed Budapest, 1968. Recorded SLPX 31128.
Summer Night Op 13 (female choir) 1968; first performed Esztergom, 1969.
Antinomia Op 14 (soprano, clarinet, cello) 1968; first performed Budapest, 1968. Recorded SLPX 11494.
Motet Op 26 (mixed choir) 1973; first performed Budapest, 1973. Recorded SLPX 12223.
Tresses Op 2 (soprano, chamber orchestra) 1979; first performed Budapest, 1979. Recorded SLPX 12223.
Chick of the Reed Op 28 (female choir) 1979; first performed Budapest, 1979.
Kyrie Op 34 (female choir) 1982; first performed Budapest, 1982.
Chants About Birds Op 37 ("The Path of the Wild Geese", "Tits"; children's choir) 1989; first performed Budapest, 1990.
Banatomtol szabadulnek / If I Got Rid of My Sorrow Op 42 (female choir) 1989; first performed Budapest, 1989.

Opera:

Az Ajton Kivul / The Man Outside Op 27 (libretto by Fodor, after Borchert) 1979; first performed Budapest, 1979. Recorded SLPX 12052/3.
The Third Planet Op 39 1986; first performed Budapest, 1989. Recorded SLPD 31186.

PUBLICATIONS

By Balassa: *Thoughts About National Music*, Budapest, 1989; *Thoughts About Nature*, Gyor, 1990.

Sándor Balassa comments:

I am only an outside, unengaged onlooker of the professional mafias, those tendentious associations for the protection of common interests grouping around the ideologies of art.

I don't join them. I also refuse the fashionable slogans which confer an absolute importance only on modernity. All other artefacts—goods, weapons, inventions of all sorts—eventually become obsolete, but real art is ageless, capable of expressing feeling irrespective of passing time and without losing its richness of content.

Nowadays, as in the past, we have to transform musical material into an art that contains both beauty and a heightened moral awareness. This is not only my ambition, but my duty, too.

Life on earth can only possibly be saved by the conscious actions of people awakened and ennobled by a sense of community. Art cannot serve policy and science, which divest it of its original character, put it off its intended course, despoil it of its cathartic force. In such unmerited service, music cannot fulfil its original creative vocation: the promotion of beauty, the elevation and purification of human nature, dialogue between the everyday and the transcendent.

It is interesting that scientists turn adoringly to Bach and Mozart. For the future rather depends on us, on contemporary composers. It is no longer viable that a tiny elite should make its mighty enunciations and thus stipulate how to compose today or tomorrow. We each have to find our own way.

The different ways, the tinged variety of possible truth, the diversity of national roots, all promise rich produce. In the immense chorus of humanity all original voices are needed. Contemporary artists weave that marvellous collective homespun which is none other than the voice of the earth. It is an honour to me to be able to participate.

* * *

Sándor Balassa came late to music study; being 30 before he graduated under Endre Szervánszky (who had initiated an ante-1950s stylistic revolution). Within a free twelve-tone style, Balassa deals primarily with melodically conceived themes accompanied by evocative harmony. His lyrical response to strong emotions and images keep him from structures based on timbre or complexity. The most important stages of Balassa's early post-studentship development are a cantata to words by Apollinaire, the choral work *Legenda* (text by the poet Jenö Dsida), the trio *Antinomia* for treble voice, clarinet and cello (words by Gustafsson and Dsida), and the Kodály-inspired *Cantata Y* (setting Beney's poem "Music"). All of these demonstrate Balassa's natural feeling for poetry and the voice.

For his *Requiem for Lajos Kassák*, Balassa compiled images, individual words and lines from poems by Kassák. The resulting libretto, moods and forces follow traditional large Romantic Requiems. Soloists engulfed in orchestral writing alternate with block-like choral writing or with instrumental cadenzas. When fast-moving, the chorus exploits aleotorism and effect-techniques. The libretto for the opera *The Man Outside* came from Wolfgang Borchert's autobiographical short stories (later a radio play) written following his internment under Hitler. Balassa's lyrical stage drama in five "movements" (rather than acts) shows influences of Berg's *Wozzeck* and Bartók's *Cantata Profana*. The orchestra supports the text by ensuring the conditions for free declamation throughout. A "Greek chorus" is used in the first movement which becomes a whispering chorus in the third part of the opera, continuing ideas from the Kassák Requiem III. An epilogue elevates the hero's death by using a B-A-C-H motif.

The opera *The Man Outside* also displays important structural elements from Balassa's instrumental works: a slow "Lassu" continues with an Andante passage which climaxes in the inevitable scherzoid "Friska"; unlike the Hungarian prototype, however, the "Lassu" is then recapitulated. This structural formula applies to works such as the nonet *Xenia* (where a note-row is treated freely); also to the one-movement *Iris* and the slow sections of the Kassák Requiem. The *Quintetto d'ottoni* uses the formula for both the first movement and for the whole work, each recapitulation being subdued.

Without the crook of poetry, Balassa's instrumental works often seem comparatively uninspired. The Wind Quintet is more "late-Romantic" than "atonal", employing melodic hoquet-technique and focusing on homophonically-grouped diads and triads. In the orchestral *Glarusiének / Chant of Glarus* (written for the Koussevitzky Foundation) development is restricted to transposition and slight re-orchestration, and seldom alters any main motif. While the last three movements all climax in Regeresque chorale writing, the blatantly fanfare-like Finale has a long repetitive build-up reminiscent of Panufnik's opening to *Symphonia Sacra*.

Although in the opera several motives are linked, leitmotif-technique is not employed. With *Glarusiének*, dialogue is employed between three distinct single-bar ideas [1) a repeating note; 2) widely-spread and loud texture; 3) slow nearby pitch-movement; (the first and third ideas often being related)]. Similarly, each motif of the Brass Quintet's last movement has a specific rhythmic character which combines in the development section. While the opera uses speech-rhythm, the Wind Quintet employs some complex temporal subdivisions (11:12) which seldom become polyrhythmic. This work also features an often-repeated pitch coupled with written-out rubatos which eventually become extended trills. Meanwhile, the implication of a somewhat random, slow pulse is achieved in both the Wind Quintet and *Glarusiének* by Balassa's starting the more unusual subdivisions of the beat with a rest.

—Malcolm J. Hill

BALLIF, Claude (André François). French. Born in Paris, 22 May 1924. Educated at Bordeaux Conservatoire (under J.-F. Vaubourgoin), 1942–8; in Paris (under Olivier Messiaen, Tony Aubin, Noel Gallon), 1948–51; in Berlin (under Boris Blacher and H. H. Stuckenschmidt), 1953–5; also Darmstadt summer schools (under Hermann Scherchen), late 1950s. Military service, infantryman 2nd class, 1945–6. Married Elisabeth Gèze, 14 September 1963; 4 children. Lecturer, Institut Français, Berlin, 1955–7; lecturer, Institut Français, Hamburg, 1957–8; research assistant, Radio-Télévision Française, Paris, 1959–63; professor of analysis and history of music, Ecole Normale de Musique, Paris, 1963–5; professor of pedagogy and musical analysis, Conservatoire de Région de Reims, 1964–71; founding member, and head of music department, 1968, University of Paris VIII; Professor of musical analysis 1971–90, and of composition, 1982–90, Conservatoire National Supérieur de Musique, Paris; seconded to McGill University, Montreal, Canada, as professor of composition and advanced harmony, 1978–9; to the Shanghai Conservatory, 1985; professor of composition, Conservatoire de Sevran, 1990. Recipient: ler Prix Pédagogique, Bordeaux, 1946; lèr Prix Composition, Berlin, 1955; ler Prix Internationale Composition, Berlin, 1955; Prix Arthur Honegger, 1974; Prix Florent Schmitt, 1976; Grand Prix Composition de la Ville de Paris, 1980; Commandeur des Arts et des Lettres, 1984; Grand Prix de SACEM, 1986. Mailing address: 69 rue de Chabrol, 75010 Paris, France.

Publishers: Durand, Paris; Transatlantiques, 151 Avenue J. Jaurès, 75019 Paris, France; Bote und Bock, Berlin.

Symphonies/orchestral:

Lovecraft Op 13 1955; first performed Venice, 1955.
Voyage de mon oreille Op 20 1957.
Fantasio Op 21 1957; first performed Strasbourg, 1962.
Fantasio grandioso Op 21b 1962; first performed Paris, 1977.
A Cor et à cri Op 39 1962; first performed Paris, 1965.
Ceci et cela Op 26 1965; first performed Paris, 1967.
Cinquième Imaginaire Op 41 No 5 (chamber orchestra) 1968, revised 1978; first performed Paris, 1978.
Sixième Imaginaire Op 41 (chamber string orchestra) 1974; first performed Rouen, 1975.
Ivre, moi, immobile Op 49 (clarinet, orchestra) 1976; first performed Nice, 1977.
Haut les Rêves Op 49 No 2 (violin, small orchestra) 1984.

Chamber/instrumental:

Cendres Op 1 (3 percussion) 1946; first performed Paris, 1960.
Airs comprimés Op 5 (piano) 1952–3; first performed Berlin, 1954. Recorded Inédits ORTF 995003.
Pièces détachées Op 6 (piano) 1952–3; first performed Bilthoven, 1955. Recorded Arion CBS 30 A.
Trio Op 8 (oboe, clarinet, bassoon) 1952–3.
Quintet Op 9 (brass) 1952.
Quintet No 2 Op 10 (flute, oboe, clarinet, bassoon, horn) 1954.
String Quartet No 1 Op 12 1955.
Four Sonatas Op 14 (organ) 1956.
Trio Op 16 (violin, viola, cello) 1956.
Sonata Op 17 (violin, piano) 1957.
Sonata No 1 Op 18 (piano) 1957.
Sonata No 2 Op 19 (piano) 1957.
String Quartet No 2 Op 22 1958.
Sonata Op 23 (flute, piano) 1958.
Quintet No 3 Op 24 (flute, oboe, string trio) 1958.
Sonata No 3 Op 29 (piano) 1958.
Mouvement pour deux Op 27 (flute, piano) 1959.
Trio No 2 Op 28 (violin, viola, cello) 1959.
String Quartet No 3 Op 30 1959.
Sonata No 4 Op 31 (piano) 1959.
Sonata No 5 Op 32 (piano) 1960.
Quintet No 4 Op 34 (bassoon, string quartet) 1960.
Trio Op 35 (flute, harp, bassoon) 1961.
Mouvements (flute, piano) 1961.
Solfegietto No 1 Op 36 (flute) 1961; first performed Paris, 1975.
Solfegietto No 2 Op 36 (cor anglais) 1961.
Bloc Note Op 37 (piano) 1961.
Passe temps No 1 Op 38 (piano) 1962; first performed Reims, 1962.
Passe temps No 2 Op 38 (piano) 1962.
Sonata Op 40 (cello) 1962.
Premier Imaginaire Op 41 No 1 (violin, cello, harp, flute, clarinet, trumpet, trombone) 1962.
Cahier de violon Op 42 (violin) 1963.
Solfegietto No 3 Op 36 (violin) 1963; first performed Prague, 1963.
Deuxième Imaginaire Op 41 No 2 (piccolo trumpet, trumpet, bugle or horn, horn, tenor trombone, bass trombone, tuba, double bass) 1967.
Solfegietto No 4 Op 36 (oboe) 1968; first performed Paris, 1973.
Solfegietto No 5 Op 36 (clarinet) 1968; first performed Japan, 1968.
Quatrième Imaginaire Op 41 No 4 (organ, trumpet, bass trumpet, trombone, bugle, horn, tuba) 1968.
Trio Op 43 (flute, viola, harp) 1968.
Trio Op 43 No 2 (violin, viola, cello) 1969.
Troisième Imaginaire Op 41 No 3 (2 violas/1 violin, cello, double bass, clarinet, horn, bassoon) 1969.
Quatuor Op 48 (violin, viola, cello, percussion) 1975; first performed Paris, 1977.
Solfegietto No 6 Op 36 (guitar) 1976; first performed Paris, 1977.
Le Jouet de jeu Op 4b No 3 (oboe, piano or harpsichord) 1976.
Timbres et postes Op 51 (6 percussion) 1977; first performed Adelaide, Australia, 1977.
Chant de charme (ondes martenot) 1977; first performed Paris, 1977.
Chant de l'innocent (flute) 1977; first performed Paris, 1980.

Sonata Op 52 (clarinet, piano) 1978; first performed St Louis, Missouri, 1979.
L'Habitant du labyrinthe Op 54 (2 percussion) 1980; first performed Paris, 1981.
Réveries Op 55 (violin, clarinet, piano) 1980.
Solfegietto No 7 Op 36 (tuba) 1980.
Solfegietto No 8 Op 36 (saxophone) 1981; first performed Aix-les-Bains, 1982.
Apostrophes et jubilations Op 56 (organ) 1981; first performed Chartres, 1982.
Solfegietto No 9 Op 36 (harp) 1982; first performed Paris, 1983.
Solfegietto No 10 Op 36 (harpsichord) 1982; first performed Paris, 1983.
Solfegietto No 11 Op 36 (bassoon) 1984.
Solfegietto No 12 Op 36 (percussion) 1984.
Solfegietto No 13 Op 36 (cello) 1985.
Solfegietto No 14 Op 36 (trumpet) 1986.
Un Moment de printemps Op 60 (flute, clarinet, violin, cello, piano) 1987.
String Quartet No 4 Op 61 1987.
Rondes nocturnes Op 62 (piano) 1988.
Solfegietto No 15 Op 36 (horn) 1988.
String Quartet No 5 Op 63 1989.
Le Taille-Lyre Op 64 (flute, clarinet, viola, cello, trombone, accordion, piano) 1990.
Vitrine (no opus number; clarinet, double bass, contrabassoon, trombone, celesta, harp) n.d.

Vocal/choral:

Le Cortège d'Orphée Op 1b (soprano or baritone, piano; Apollinaire) 1948.
Apparitions Op 2 (contralto, piano; Michaux) 1949.
Chansons bas Op 3 (soprano, piano; Mallarmé) 1949.
Minuit pour géants Op 4 (mezzo-soprano, piano; Tzara) 1951.
Quatre Antiennes à la Sainte Vierge Op 7 (soprano, light soprano, mezzo-soprano, counter-tenor, tenor, bass, orchestra) 1952–3.
La Vie du monde qui vient: première symphonie mystique Op 11 (requiem for 2 sopranos, mezzo-soprano, contralto, 2 tenors, baritone, bass, 3 mixed choirs, 2 female choirs, men's choir, orchestra) 1953–5, revised 1972.
Musik im Mirabel Op 15 (soprano, piano; Trakl) 1956.
Phrases sur le souffle Op 25 (alto, mixed chorus, flute, oboe, horn, trombone, viola, cello, double bass; version for alto, piano) 1958; first performed Avignon, 1968; piano version, Nuremberg, 1962. Recorded Inédits ORTF 995003.
Retrouver la parole Op 33 (coloratura soprano, lyric soprano, mezzo-soprano, counter-tenor, tenor, bass, 2 flutes, 2 clarinets; Giroux) 1960.
Prière à la Sainte Vierge Op 44 (6-voice mixed chorus) 1971; first performed Reims, 1972. Recorded Arion ARN 37166.
Chapelet / Rosary Op 44 No 2 (4-voice mixed chorus) 1971; first performed Reims, 1972. Recorded Arion ARN 37166.
Les Battements du coeur de Jesus Op 46 (double chorus, trumpet, trombone) 1971; first performed Reims, 1972. Recorded Arion ARN 37166.
Prière au Seigneur Op 45 (mixed chorus, cornet, trombone) 1972; first performed Reims, 1972. Recorded Arion ARN 37166.
Fragment d'une ode à la faim Op 47 (12 mixed voices) 1974; first performed Paris, 1978.
Poèmes de la félicité Op 50 (soprano, coloratura soprano, contralto, guitar, 2 percussion; Trahern) 1977; first performed Paris, 1978.
Un Coup de dés Op 53 (mixed chorus, 2 percussion, 2 timpani, 2 double basses, tape; Mallarmé) 1980; first performed Paris, 1981. Recorded Harmonia Mundi HM 5141.
Poèmes lents Op 57 (solo or trio vocal; lyric soprano/dramatic soprano/bass, piano; Brochu) 1981.
Le Livre du Seigneur Op 59 (baritone, 3 choruses, orchestra; St Paul/Quesnel) 1985.

Opera:

Dracoula Op 58 ("nocturnal drama" for high tenor, baritone, 3 sopranos, mezzo-soprano, chorus, orchestra; Stephan) 1982, revised 1983; first performed Paris, 19–20 September 1984.
Il suffit d'un peu d'air Op 65 (lyric farce; Tremblay) 1990; first performed Montreal, 11–12 December 1991.

Other:

Notes et menottes (piano music for children) 1949–79.
Musique d'Erik Zahn (incidental music) 1964; broadcast 1967.
Alice au pays des merveilles (incidental music to Caroll) 1965.
Les Troyennes (incidental music to Sartre) 1967.

Berlioz: *Nuits d'Eté: "l'absence"* (orchestration; soprano, ensemble).
Satie: *Sports et Divertissements* (orchestration) 1950; first performed Perpignan, 1986.
Gabrielli: *Canzone Ottavitoni* (orchestration; 2 orchestras) 1960; first performed Paris, 1960.

PUBLICATIONS

By Ballif: *Introduction à la métatonalité*, Paris, 1956; *Berlioz*, Paris, 1968; *Voyage de mon oreille*, Paris, 1979; *Economie musicale—souhaits entre symboles*, Paris, 1979.

On Ballif: M. Fleurat, D. Charles, "CB", in *Revue musicale*, 263, 1968; Fleurat/Charles, "CB", in *Revue Musicale*, 370/371, 1984; Michèle Tosi, *L'Ouverture métatonale*, Paris, 1990; Michèle Tosi, *CB* (biography), Bezières, 1991.

Claude Ballif comments:

I belong to that generation active immediately after World War II. The years between 1945 and 1950 were critical in my development and artistic priorities. I discovered the Second Viennese School of Schoenberg, Webern, Berg; French music in Satie, Messiaen, Machaut, Ockeghem; Italian music in Gesualdo, Vicentino; Russian music in Scriabin and Mussorgsky; and an American music of global significance (Ives, Cowell, Cage, jazz). I came to understand the two centuries of musical renewal brought about by Machaut; that of Bach, which lasted until Bartók; and finally, the dodecaphonic revolution of Webern. I pondered the aesthetic impact of Satie on Les Six and on Stravinsky, that of Haba and Wyschnegradsky on micro-tonality. I also sensed the importance of Hegel's *Aufhebung* in detecting false dichotomies (tonality/atonality), the psychological implications of Bergson's *La pensée et le mouvant*, and the scientific spirit expressed by Bachelard in *Le dialectique et la durée*. Deep friendships with Jean Wahl, Bartók's pupil Andreas Ronan, Schoenberg's pupil Josef Rufer, and with the *musique concrète* genius Pierre Schaeffer, encouraged me after 1949 in my ideas on metatonality.

All of which meant that I could pursue my work without

conflict and in freedom, knowing that if one really has something to say, one cannot be deflected from it.

* * *

Claude Ballif is a fierce individualist, an independent composer who has drawn on a wide range of influences and traditions out of which he has synthesised a highly idiosyncratic style. His training was unusual in that, having received a full musical education at the Conservatoires of Bordeaux and Paris (where he attended Messiaen's analysis class), he chose to further his studies at the Berlin Conservatory, studying analysis and composition with Josef Rufer and Boris Blacher.

He has thus digested both French and German musical thought from some of their most eminent representatives, while not being strictly bound to either. He remained in West Germany from 1955 to 1959, lecturing on music at the French Institutes in Berlin and Hamburg and attending the Darmstadt summer courses, where he studied with Hermann Scherchen; although stimulated by the music he heard at Darmstadt, he remained aloof from the most extreme tendencies and was never a strict serialist. Ballif returned to France in 1959 and studied *musique concrète* until 1963 as an assistant at Pierre Schaeffer's Groupe de Recherches Musicales.

He was relatively slow to attract widespread attention as a composer, perhaps due to his refusal to subscribe to any compositional doctrine or school. The only technique he has admitted to using is one of his own devising, which he calls "metatonality", a system which mediates between extremes of diatonicism and chromaticism, orbiting around stable pitch centres. Ballif is equally at home in the transparent simplicity of his predominantly monodic *Chapelet/Rosary* for a capella choir, as in the polyphonic complexity of his later choral and orchestral works. Whatever the genre, Ballif's harmonic consistency is clearly audible and has a curious inevitability to it. This versatility accounts for the size of Ballif's output, which includes a large quantity of chamber music—five string quartets, three string trios—orchestral works, vocal and choral music, and the "nocturnal drama" *Dracoula*.

Ballif has also explored the most advanced electro-acoustic media with typical fluency and ease. His large-scale cantata *Un Coup de dés*, composed in 1980, on Mallarmé's poem of the same name, combines computer-synthesised sound with the dark timbres of two double basses, two percussionists and mixed chorus, creating a vast meditative canvas of nearly 50 minutes, during which a single basic texture is maintained with endless internal variation—a radical gesture which might be expected of a much younger composer. The oratorio *Le Livre du Seigneur*, setting texts of St Paul, demonstrates Ballif's willingness to tackle the most ambitious subject matter on an appropriate scale (over one and three-quarter hours of music for baritone, chorus and large orchestra, again incorporating electronics in the form of a part for synthesiser). This work also testifies to the religious fervour which lies at the root of Ballif's creative impulses, evident in numerous sacred or liturgical works of smaller dimensions such as the *Prière au Seigneur* and the *Prière à la Sainte Vierge*, both for chorus and brass.

Ballif has recently achieved considerable eminence in his native country, both through his music and through his teaching at the conservatoire.

—Julian Anderson

BANCQUART, Alain. French. Born in Dieppe, 20 June 1934. Educated at Conservatoire National Supérieur de Musique, Paris (studying solfege, violin, viola, chamber music, counterpoint, fugue, composition), 1947–58. Married to Marie-Claire Bancquart. Third viola, Orchestre National de France, Radio France, 1960–73; musical director, ORTF regional orchestras, 1973–4; musical director, Orchestre National de France, 1975–6; principal inspector of music, Ministry of Culture, 1977–84 (responsible after 1982 for orchestras and training); producer, Radio France "Perspectives du XXème Siècle" concerts of contemporary music. Professor of composition and analysis, Conservatoire National Supérieur de Musique, Paris, since 1984. Recipient: Grand Prix National de la Musique, 1986. Mailing address: c/o Maison de Radio France, 116 Avenue du Président Kennedy, 75786 Paris Cédex 16, France.

Publisher: Jobert.

Symphonies/orchestral:

La Naissance du geste (piano, strings) 1961.
Viola Concerto 1964.
Symphonie en trois mouvements 1965; broadcast Radio Luxembourg, 1965.
Passages 1966; first performed Strasbourg, 1967.
Jeux pour lumière (violin, viola, cello, orchestra) 1969; broadcast Radio France, 1969.
Simple 1972; first performed Lille, 1973.
Baroques (viola, orchestra) 1972; first performed Colonne, 1973.
Iles (violin, orchestra) 1973; broadcast Radio France, 1973.
Symphonie No 1 1975; broadcast Radio France, 1981. Recorded Erato; Radio France cassettes.
D'une fougère bleue, les veines (cello, orchestra) 1977; first performed Paris, 1978.
Symphonie No 2 1979; broadcast Radio France, 1981. Recorded Radio France cassettes.
Symphonie de chambre (chamber orchestra) 1980.
Symphonie concertante (harp, orchestra) 1981.
Symphonie No 3: Fragments d'apocalypse 1983; first performed Metz, 1983.
Nocturne (violin, viola, cello, orchestra) 1986; broadcast Radio France, 1987.
Symphonie No 4 1986; first performed Strasbourg, 1987.
Symphonie No 5: Partage de midi (text by Claudel) 1990.

Chamber/instrumental:

Ecorce III (violin, clarinet, horn, piano) 1966; first performed Avignon, 1966.
Possibles (clarinet, piano, violin) 1967; first performed Paris, 1968.
Thrène I (violin, viola, cello) 1967; first performed Paris, 1968. Recorded Sappho.
Made in USA (clarinet, bassoon, horn, 2 violins, viola, cello, double bass) 1970.
Unie et désunie (2 string trios) 1970; first performed Royan, 1970.
Explosante fixe (harp, flute, oboe, clarinet/A clarinet, bassoon, horn) 1972; first performed Aix en Provence, 1972.
Rosace (string quartet) 1972; broadcast Radio France, 1973.
L'arbre au regard de chant (12 strings) 1974.
Thrène II (violin, viola, cello) 1976; first performed Bordeaux, 1977. Recorded Sappho.

Immobile (horn, 2 trumpets, 2 trombones/1 bass trombone or tuba) 1977.
Ma Manière d'oiseau (solo flute, oboe, clarinet, piano, percussion, harp, violin, viola, cello) 1977; first performed Divonne-les-Bains, 1978.
L'Amant déserté (instrumental version of chamber opera; electronic instruments) 1978.
Ma Manière de chat (harp) 1978. Recorded Erato.
Ma Manière de double (violin) 1979; first performed Aix-en-Provence, 1980.
Duo (flute, cello; version of *Symphonie de chambre*) 1980; first performed Nice, 1980. Recorded Erato.
Sonata (viola) 1982.
Cérémonial I (flute) 1984; first performed Darmstadt, 1984.
Mémoire (string quartet) 1984; first performed Orléans, 1985.
Cérémonial III (violin, viola, cello) 1985; first performed Saint-Etienne, 1986.
Duo (viola, harp) 1985; first performed Paris, 1985.
Sonata (2 pianos) 1985; first performed Paris, 1985.
Sonata (piano) 1987; broadcast Radio France, 1988.
Diurne (flute, string quartet/11 strings) 1988.
Grande Mélodie (flute) 1988; broadcast Radio France, 1988.
Sonata (flute; new version of *Sonata* for viola) 1989; first performed Prague, 1989.

Vocal/choral:

Ombre éclatée (mezzo-soprano, orchestra) 1965.
Etude pour quinze (contralto, 2 horns, 2 trumpets, 2 trombones, piano, percussion, strings, plus technician) 1969.
Proche (bass, cello or viola) 1972.
Erotique voilée (soprano, flute/G flute, clarinet/bass clarinet, piano, strings, cimbalom; St Juan de la Cruz) 1975; first performed Strasbourg, 1975.
A la mémoire de ma mort (48 mixed voices) 1975; first performed Royan, 1976.
Magique circonstancielle (reciter, mezzo-soprano, orchestra) 1975.
Animal, Mal . . . (contralto, flute, trumpet, percussion, harp, violin; Cros) 1977.
Voix (12 mixed voices; Marie-Claire Bancquart) 1981; first performed Paris, 1981.
Les Tarots d'Ulysse (soprano, tenor, baritone, harpe, 2 percussion, 2 synthesizers, cimbalom, tape; Marie-Claire Bancquart) 1984.
Cérémonial V (reciter, flute, string trio) 1985; broadcast Radio France, 1985.
Les Cinq Dits de J. Cl. Renard (soprano, 3 clarinet, string trio) 1986; broadcast Radio France 1987.
Suite au Dieu lune (6 male voices; Marie-Claire Bancquart) 1988; broadcast Radio France 1988.
Entre Désert et ange (mezzo-soprano, ensemble) 1990.

Opera:

L'Amant déserté (chamber opera; reciter, 2 sopranos, percussion, violin, cello, electronic ensemble; Marie-Claire Bancquart, Nogare) 1977; first performed Metz, 1978.

* * *

Alain Bancquart trained at the Paris Conservatoire as a viola player and composer, studying with Darius Milhaud. After leaving the conservatoire, Bancquart became a violist with the Orchestre National, remaining there for 12 years until 1973. His earliest works were influenced by Messiaen, Jolivet and Boulez. Because of his career as a violist, Bancquart remained relatively isolated from fellow composers and it was not until 1967 that he composed the first work that he regards as representative, *Thrène I* for string trio.

In this piece, Bancquart made extensive use of quarter-tones for the first time; since then, quarter-tones have become the focus of his compositional thought. He has developed a form of quarter-tone serialism, applying serial procedures of inversion, rotation and multiplication to quarter-tone rows and chords. The complexity of pitch material that this throws up results in a number of performance problems, which Bancquart has solved either by using electronic instruments or by tuning certain instruments in an ensemble or orchestra down a quarter tone.

Bancquart's output is dominated by his five symphonies, composed between 1975 and 1990; Bancquart is almost the only living French composer to be a prolific symphonist. Each of the symphonies has a different technical preoccupation, form and mood, although all are of substantial duration. The First has three movements lasting about 30 minutes; it is an intense and striving work whose core is found in the central movement for strings alone, in which Bancquart's professional expertise as a string player is put to telling use. The Second Symphony is an essay in the dense textures resulting from what Bancquart terms "multiple polyphonies", different strata of complex polyphony superimposed upon one another.

The Third, subtitled "Fragments d'Apocalypse", dates from 1983; it is closer in scoring and manner to an oratorio; there are several different ensembles each with its own type of music, whose superimposition is constantly varied, with prominent parts for tenor solo, male chorus, and six percussionists. The Fourth Symphony is a return to the multiple polyphonies of the Second, with the difference that the polyphonies are much more complex and the overall result thicker. The Fifth Symphony is the longest so far, and is something of a synthesis of Bancquart's preoccupations: like the First it has three movements and like the Third, it has a vocal element, in the form of a baritone solo who, in the final movement, sings a text from Paul Claudel's "Partage de midi". The scoring includes very prominent, almost soloistic parts for two cimbaloms.

Bancquart's other works include a large number of solo pieces exploring the monophonic possibilities of quarter-tones and several vocal works, many setting texts by his wife Marie-Claire Bancquart, such as the chamber opera *L'Amant déserté*.

Bancquart's position in the French musical scene remains hard to define. On the one hand, he has held a succession of administrative posts of increasing importance: Inspector of Music at the Ministry of Culture, producer at Radio France, where he was in charge of the important series "Perspectives du Vingtième Siècle", and, since 1984, professor of music and analysis at the Conservatoire. On the other, there is nothing stereotypically "French" about his music, with its austere, sometimes brutal orchestration and his Maxwell Davies-like insistence on the renewal of German symphonic structures articulated over large time spans. This may account for the fact that, while he is regularly played in France, he remains something of an outsider and has never founded or formed part of a compositional clique. Indeed, influences of any sort except the most general are difficult to determine in the harrowing but frequently impressive world of Bancquart's mature music.

—Julian Anderson

BARRAINE, Elsa. French. Born in Paris, 13 February 1910. Educated at Conservatoire National Supérieur de Musique, Paris (composition under Paul Dukas, harmony under Jean Gallon, fugue under Caussade, and score reading under Estyle), 1919–1929. Chef de chant, Orchestre National de France, 1936–9; head of sound, Orchestre National de France, 1944–6; musical director, Chant du Monde, 1944–6; professor of musical analysis, Conservatoire de Paris, 1953–74; teacher/conductor (with François Vercken), Fédération Musicale Populaire; inspector of national theatres, 1972–4. Recipient: harmony prize, Conservatoire de Paris, 1925; score reading prize, Conservatoire de Paris, 1927; 2nd place, Grand Prix de Rome (for *Heracles à Delphes*), 1928; Grand Prix de Rome (for *La Vierge guerrière*), 1929. Mailing address: 3 passage Saillenfait, 94000 Creteil, France.

Publishers: Schott; Le Chant du Monde; Salabert; Billandot; Enoch; Durand; Editions Transatlantiques; Jobert; SOFIRAD (Radio France).

Symphonies/orchestral:

Trois Esquisses 1931.
Symphony No 1 1931.
Pogromes 1933.
Fantaisie concertante (piano, orchestra) 1935.
Symphony No 2 1938.
Harald Harfagar (symphonic variations) 1945.
Le Fleuve rouge 1945.
Hommage à Prokofiev 1953.
Trois Ridicules 1955.
Les Jongleurs 1959.
Les Tziganes 1959.

Chamber/instrumental:

Prélude et fugue No 1 (organ) 1928.
Prélude et fugue No 2 (organ) 1930.
La Nuit dans les chemins de rêve (piano) 1930.
Wind Quintet 1931.
Hommage à Paul Dukas (piano) 1936.
Aria (trumpet, piano) 1938.
Aria (3 pianos) 1938.
Nocturne (piano) 1938.
Marche du printemps sans amour (piano) 1946.
Improvisation (alto saxophone, piano) 1947.
Variations (piano, percussion) 1950.
Suite juive (violin, piano) 1951.
Fantaisie (piano or harpsichord) 1961.
Reflets magyars (organ) 1961. Recorded ARDAM CD.
Atmosphère (oboe, 10 instruments) 1966.
Chiens de paille (tuba, tenor trombone, bass trombone, bassoon or ondes martenot) 1966.
Musique rituelle (organ, tam-tam, xylophone) 1968.

Vocal/choral:

Heracles à Delphes (cantata) 1928.
Il y a quelqu'un auquel je pense (voice, piano) 1931.
Je suis ici pour chanter les chansons (voice, piano; Tagore) 1931.
Pastourelle (voice, piano; Fouche) 1931.
La Lumière (voice, piano) 1932.
Dans la sable (voice, piano; Camus) 1938.
Avis (chorus, orchestra; Eluard) 1944.
La Marche au monde (voice, piano; Reizine) 1946.
La Poésie interrompue (3 voices, orchestra; Eluard) 1948.
La Nativité (soloists, chorus, orchestra; Masson) 1951.
Les Cinq Plaies (soloists, chorus, orchestra; Manol) 1952.
Cantate de vendredi saint (soloists, chorus, orchestra; Emmanuel) 1955.
Les Paysans (soloists, chorus, orchestra; Fenaud) 1958.
Christine (soloists, chorus, orchestra; Superveille) 1959.

Opera:

Le Roi bossu (Carré) 1932.

Other:

Le Vierge Guerrière 1929.
Le Roi Lear (incidental music to Shakespeare, translated by Jolivet) 1945.
Au Coeur de l'orage (film score) 1946.
Le Mur (ballet) 1947.
Madame Bovary (incidental music to adaptation of Flaubert) 1948.
Pattes blanches (film score) 1948.
Elisabeth d'Angleterre (incidental music to F. Bruckner) 1949.
Brand (incidental music to Ibsen) 1949.
Le Chanson de mal-aimé (ballet after Apollinaire) 1950.
Claudine à l'école (ballet) 1950.
Coeur d'amour épris (film score) 1951.
Penthesilea (incidental music to Kleist) 1955.
Le Sabotier du Val de Loire (film music) 1956.
La Tragédie des bonnes intentions (incidental music to Ustinov) 1957.
Ars (theatre music) 1960.

* * *

A senior figure on the French music scene, Elsa Barraine's music is sadly little heard today. She is, nonetheless, a remarkable composer, who has bridged the generations and who was still capable of causing considerable excitement in the 1960s, when younger luminaries like electronic composer Pierre Henry were powerfully attracted by her *Musique rituelle*, a meditation on the Tibetan Book of the Dead, the Bardo Thodol.

Barraine grew up in a musical family. Her mother was a fine singer and her father a principal cellist in the orchestra of the Opera Grand. She shone as a student, winning prizes for fugue and score reading, and blossoming as a composer under the tutelage of Paul Dukas, a patient and unprolific composer with a tremendous eye for detail. Barraine's first works showed great promise. At only 21 she completed her first symphony. Less successful than the second which took a further seven years to complete, it is nonetheless an impressive work, basically conventional in conception, but marked by ringing harmonies and a shimmering string sound.

Her work gradually became more daring, and the war clearly had a chastening effect on her imagination, introducing a darker and more philosophical edge to her music. The piano and percussion *Variations* of 1950 is still fresh and vital 40 years later, and looks forward to Barraine's later, more experimental use of percussion effects. There is a new rawness of texture at this time; it is first noticeable in the cantata *La Poésie interrompue* (in itself a good description of the tinge of surrealism she had taken from Eluard's text), one of her finest vocal works. At the same period, she wrote an effective *Improvisation* for saxophone and piano accompaniment, which broadened her instrumental range somewhat; its effect can be heard in the altered tonality of *Suite juive*.

Her *Cantate de vendredi saint*, from 1955, contains some wonderful solo and choral writing, and is her most finished statement in a religious idiom. During the same post-war period, she also wrote very effectively for the theatre and for dance, her best known ballet being the elegant *Chanson de mal-aimé*.

In the 1960s, before her retirement from the Conservatoire, Barraine enjoyed a new flowering of composition. *Musique rituelle* is one of the forgotten classics of modern French music, and the offbeat *Chiens de paille*, scored for low-pitched brass, bassoon or ondes martenot, is a small masterpiece that merits revival.

—Eleanor Caldwell

BARRETT, Richard. British. Born in Swansea, 7 November 1959. Educated at University College, London, 1977–80, B.Sc. (genetics); private composition study with Peter Wiegold, 1980–3; Darmstadter Ferienkurse, 1984 (guidance from Brian Ferneyhough and Hans-Joachim Hespos). Joint artistic director, Ensemble Expose, 1984–90; dozent, Internationale Ferienkurse, Darmstadt, 1986, 1988; lecturer, Middlesex Polytechnic, since 1989, involved in electronic free improvisation; composition seminars, Melbourne, Sydney, Brisbane, Spring 1989. Recipient: Kranichsteiner Musikpreis, Darmstadt, 1986; Gaudeamus Prize, Amsterdam, 1989. Mailing address: 15 Brighton Road, London N16 8EQ, England.

Publisher: United Music Publishers Ltd.

Chamber/instrumental:

Essay in Radiance (piccolo/bass flute, soprano saxophone/tenor saxophone, E♭ clarinet/bass clarinet, electric organ, 1 or 2 percussion, violin/viola, cello) 1981–3; first performed London, 5 February 1984.
Invention 6 (piano) 1982; first performed Darmstadt, 31 July 1984.
I Open and Close (part of sequence *Fictions*; amplified string quartet) 1983–8; first performed London, 15 December 1988.
Ruin (16 instruments) 1983–90; first performed Amsterdam, 5 March 1991.
Illuminer le temps (part of sequence *After Matta*; piccolo/flute, bass clarinet/B♭ clarinet, percussion, harpsichord, 2 electric guitars, violin, double bass; all amplified) 1984–7; first performed Maastricht, 4 March 1990.
Heard (piano) 1985; first performed London, 17 December 1985.
Anatomy (part of sequence *Fictions*; flute, cor anglais, bass clarinet, bassoon, horn, percussion, 2 violins, viola, cello, double bass; all amplified) 1985–6; first performed Darmstadt, 20 July 1986.
Ne songe plus à fuir (part of sequence *After Matta*; cello) 1985–6; first performed London, 27 January 1987.
Temptation (part of sequence *Fictions*; alto saxophone/baritone saxophone/contrabass saxophone, trumpet/piccolo trumpet/cornet/slide trumpet, cello, synthesiser, percussion, live electronics) 1986; first performed London, 8 February 1987.
Alba (part of sequence *Fictions*; bassoon, electronics) 1986–7.
Nothing Elsewhere (part of sequence *Fictions*; viola) 1987; first performed Darmstadt, 13 August 1988.
Earth (trombone, percussion) 1987–8; first performed Amsterdam, 14 June 1988.
Dark Ages (cello) 1987–90; first performed Amsterdam, 8 September 1990.
Reticule (violin) 1988; first performed London, 24 May 1989.
Another Heavenly Day (E♭ clarinet, electric guitar, double bass) 1989–90; first performed Melbourne, 22 April 1990.

Vocal/choral:

Principia (baritone, piano; Jones) 1982–4; first performed London, 17 February 1985.
Coigitum (part of sequence *After Matta*; mezzo-soprano, alto flute, oboe d'amore, piano, percussion; Leopardi) 1983–5; first performed Paris, 11 May 1985.
Lieder vom wasser (soprano, bass clarinet, double bass, percussion; Borchers) 1989–90; first performed Strasbourg, 22 September 1990.

Other:

The Unthinkable (tape) 1988–9; first performed London, 27 January 1989. Recorded ADDA, released late 1990.

PUBLICATIONS

By Barrett: "The Music of Peter Wiegold", in *Contact*, Autumn 1983; "Cornelius Cardew", in *New Music '87*, Oxford, 1987; "Giacinto Scelsi", in *Wire*, June 1990; "To Answer", in *Complexity?—An Inquiry into Its Nature, Motivation and Performability*, edited by Joel Bons, JoB Press, 1990; reviews, articles, etc, in *Contact*, *New Music*, *Contemporary Music Review*, *Tempo*, *Wire*.

On Barrett: Richard Toop, "Four Facets of 'The New Complexity'", in *Contact*, Spring 1988; Paul Brown, "RB", in *Ossia* (journal of the Federation of Australian Composers), 1990.

Richard Barrett comments:

Musical form for me is (from one angle) a narrative of the implacably widening chasm between what one at first perceives as possible/necessary/beautiful and its collapse into impoverishment and equivocation at the point of emergence into actuality. Such musical structures spin out a precarious continuity from the interaction of proposition and negation, of order and disorder, of the futility of continuation and the implausibility of closure.

From another angle: form is the process of dissecting and nullifying the fiction of an initial "vision", like hacking at a block of stone to set free a feverishly-imagined shape until nothing is left. The texture of the stone is: each work-specific apprehension of the potential of particular human and instrumental resources.

My interest is in the power, complexity, directness of sound in a raw, nascent state, rather than in manipulation of "pitch", etc., as abstract values separate from the intimacies, frictions, possibilities of the player/instrument conjunction. Music is potentially a vital point of contact with ourselves and others, and must constantly readdress fundamentals and oppose itself to normative and sanitising pressures in society, as part of a wider political engagement (and not a substitute for it).

* * *

The music of Richard Barrett occupies territory which, if no longer unexplored, still battens at the outer limits of notation and technique. Barret is a lavish user of microtones and multiphonics; he requires string players to perfect a variety of bow and finger pressures, or to play with two bows. In his string quartet *I Open and Close*, he uses polytempos, synchronising precisely by utilising whole number ratios between the five tempos (quaver 108, 81, 72, 67.5, and 54, each standing in proportion to the first 3:4, 2:3, 5:8 and 1:2). The cello piece *Dark Ages* employs five tempos, each having whole-number fractional relations to the others.

Barrett also makes extensive and meticulously specific use of live electronics, for example in *Temptation*.

The greatest challenge in his music comes not at the level of technique, but of reading. Following a Barrett score is a major task, requiring the fast pace and multiple attention of a jet pilot. *Dark Ages*, for solo cello, is written over four staves. However imperfect one's own reading may be, what any musician can tell is that performers fare at least as badly. This difficulty is a source of criticism, and the pretext for labelling him as an exponent, along with his teacher Ferneyhough, of the "New Complexity". It is suggested that the minute attention to notational detail leads not to clarity, but an overload of information that the performer cannot accurately render, nor the listener properly process. Barrett has opined that difficult notation and textural complexity lends an exhilarating physicality to performance. The opposite has also been proposed—that players are not invigorated by this challenge to their concentration and virtuosity, but are expressively paralysed by its impracticality. Barrett's main hope seems to be that performance practice will improve to such an extent that performance accuracy improves.

Barrett could be dismissed as a dry rationalist composer. There are two reasons not to leap to this conclusion. The first is the psychology and architecture of his written instructions. For all the formidable logic of his noteheads, his music is not abstract. His scores are littered with poetic suggestion at every level. Rather than using traditional Italian instructions, or blunt numerical specification, he writes allusive, almost theatrical directions—"turbulent and brutal", "morbidly sensual"—which direct the performer's psychological approach. Barrett also sets the mood for the whole piece (in *I Open and Close*, an atmosphere of chaos, failure and obsessive circling), often by literary reference.

The title *Temptation* refers to Flaubert's *La Tentation de Saint Antoine*, and it is that dissociated phantasmagoria which sets its mood. "Isa" is in seven large sections corresponding to quoted paragraphs of the *Isa Upanishad*, "understood as the authoritative guide to shaping the piece and approaching its individual passages". The significance of specific gestures is contextualised by their tension in relation to such global moods. Barrett's most extensive literary reference is to the novels (rather than plays) of Beckett, quoted as performance directions at various levels. Many individual pieces are grouped into series. *Temptation* is part of a sequence called *Fictions*; another series is *After Matta*, half-a-dozen pieces for various forces named after works by the Chilean painter Roberto Matta.

Another reason not to dismiss Barrett's work as cerebral is that arguably it has an effect, a drama, and a surprising strength and simplicity of gesture. Pieces such as *Temptation*, or *Earth* for trombone and percussion, have a gripping immediacy, an earthiness and power in common with the foremost examples of many other idioms. If (and that remains a conditional) that is a listener's experience, arguments about Barrett's notational mannerisms are misplaced. Our discernment might better concentrate on the musicality of the result, rather than on the merits of means.

Composers have always found mental crutches to aid their writing—programmes, extra-musical references, pre-compositional methods. One might say music manifests itself in spite of compositional method. Analysis and criticism best commences from the result, not from criticism of the process. If one listens to the aural results of Barrett's approach, one can judge whether or not he has found a right way to music, rather than taking the universal path which everyone could sight-read.

—David Revill

BARRY, Gerald. Irish. Born in County Clare, in 1952. Educated at University College, Dublin, B.Mus., 1973, M.A., 1975; further study in Holland (under Peter Schat), Cologne, Germany (under Karlheinz Stockhausen and Mauricio Kagel), and Austria (under Friedrich Cerha). Teacher of composition, University College, Cork, Ireland, 1982–6. Recipient: 1st prize, Dublin Symphony Orchestra Composers' Competition (for student piece *Lessness*), 1975. Mailing address: c/o Oxford University Press, 7–8 Hatherley Street, London SW1, England.

Publisher: Oxford University Press.

Symphonies/orchestral:

A Piano Concerto 1977; first performed Dublin, February 1986.
Diner 1980; first performed Belfast, 5 August 1988.
Of Queen's Gardens (chamber orchestra) 1986; first performed Ballinteer, Dublin, 29 September 1986.
Chevaux-de-frise 1987–8; first performed London, August 1988.
Reflections on Guinness 1988.
Children Aged 10–17 (young people's orchestra) 1989; first performed Dublin, 11 January 1990.

Chamber/instrumental:

"   " [sic] (3 clarinets/2 bass clarinets, 2 violas, 2 cellos, piano/harpsichord; or 2 clarinets/1 bass clarinet, viola, cello, piano, marimba) 1979; first performed London, 24 February 1980.
"Ø" (2 pianos) 1979; first performed Dublin, 9 January 1981.
Sur les pointes (piano or harpsichord or organ or instrumental ensemble) 1981, revised version for 2 clarinets, 2 bassoons, 2 saxophones, 2 horns, 2 trumpets, 2 trombones, piano, 1985; first performed London, March 1981; revised version first performed Dublin, 12 April 1986.
Au Milieu (piano) 1981; first performed London, March 1981.
Handel's Favourite Song (clarinet, flute, clarinet, trumpet, trombone, guitar, piano, double bass) 1981; first performed Dublin, 27 January 1985.

Four Chorales (2 pianos; from *The Intelligence Park*) 1984; first performed London, July 1984.
Cork (string quartet) 1985; first performed London, 8 September 1985.
Sweet Punishment (2 trumpet, horn, trombone, tuba; or 2 clarinets, bass clarinet, bassoon, contrabassoon) 1987; first performed Cork, 18 February 1987.
Oboe Quartet 1988; first performed Kerry, 17 April 1988.
Bob (2 clarinets, violin, cello, piano, marimba) 1989; first performed London, 21 March 1989.
Triorchic Blues (piano) 1990; first performed Dublin, 20 April 1991.

Vocal/choral:

Beethoven Wo080 (5 singers, 3 pianos) 1976; withdrawn.
Things That Gain by Being Painted (singer, speaker, cello, piano, screen, table, 2 books, 3 spotlights; *Pillow Book of Sei Shonagon*, Japanese, 10th century) 1977; first performed London, 24 February 1980.
What the Frog Said (soprano, bass speaker, flute, oboe, clarinet, bassoon, piano, violin, viola, cello, double bass) 1984; first performed Kenmore, Kerry, June 1984.
Carol (treble voice, keyboard) 1985.
Sweet Cork (soprano, bass, recorder, viol, harpsichord) 1985; first performed Cork, 10 September 1985.
Water Parted (counter-tenor, piano) 1988; first performed Brighton, Sussex, 25 May 1988.

Opera:

The Intelligence Park (Vincent Deane) 1982–7.

PUBLICATIONS

On Barry: Kevin Volans, (interview) in *Summer Gardeners: Conversations with Composers*, Durban, 1985; Kevin Volans and Hilary Bracefield, "A Constant State of Surprise: GB and *The Intelligence Park*", in *Contact*, 31, Autumn 1987.

* * *

During his student years in Cologne, at a time when the choice for a young composer was between the currently fashionable serialism and the newly arrived minimalism, Gerald Barry adopted neither, instead setting out at once on his own highly individual path. For his sources, he went back to the 18th century for which he has always had a great passion, and there lie the roots of his style, in three particular spheres: an 18th-century feeling for the theatre; the creation of a music not bound to a particular instrument or instrumentation; and a fondness for the textures of baroque music, in particular their clarity and transparency. With his passion for the 17th and 18th centuries, Barry could not fail to have been touched by the merging period performance movement of the later 1970s and early 1980s and as a viol player, singer and organist, he also participated in the performance of this music.

The theatre has occupied Barry since he was a student of Mauricio Kagel, one of Europe's foremost composers in the music-theatre genre, from his earliest piece, *Beethoven Wo080*, a witty parody of operatic convention, through to his most important work, the opera *The Intelligence Park*. Apart from being the first opera by an Irish composer since the 18th century, Barry's work is probably the most important new opera of recent years. Set to a libretto by Vincent Deane, it is an opera about opera, the plot partly based on fact—the elopement and eventual incarceration of an 18th-century castrato. It has all the theatrical ingredients of 18th-century opera, but in literary and musical terms it constantly breaks new ground. The work occupied Barry between 1981 and 1987, and he continued to work on the orchestration until its much delayed premiere in 1990. It also bore great fruit in terms of satellite works, notably *Four Chorales* and *What the Frog Said*, both of which actually rework material from the opera and, in the case of the latter, from the libretto.

Unlike most contemporary composers, Barry has consciously set out to create a music which is independent of any instrumentation, not governed by instrumental colour as such. A particular example is *Sur les pointes* (a ballet term) which exists in versions for piano, harpsichord, organ, and instrumental ensemble, and which can be further arranged as required. As a result, players have sometimes viewed his instrumental writing as unidiomatic, but it presents fresh challenges, in the keyboard writing in particular, deriving as it does from Barry's method of composition, which is to improvise frenetically at the keyboard. His approach to orchestration has undoubtedly been influenced by his organ playing, functioning rather like the registration of the instrument. This is especially apparent in the 1988 BBC Promenade Concerts orchestral commission *Chevaux-de-frise* where the instrumental families and sections are treated rather like organ stops to articulate a frenzied 20-minute movement of great orchestral virtuosity and invention.

Clarity of texture and absolute accuracy of pitch and rhythmic articulation are all crucial to the performance of Barry's music, because the transparency of his instrumental textures is so important to its sound and ultimately its appreciation. This is what he admires so much about Handel, probably Barry's favourite composer, and like him, an organist and theatre composer. He loves, too, Handel's passion which he feels is a passion of abandon, a quality Barry considers to be at the root of his own music, which is extreme, manic and verging sometimes on hysteria. Both composers' music has a spontaneous, almost improvisatory quality, which probably reflects their somewhat less studied approaches to composition.

Irish traditional music does have some part in Barry's musical make-up, though like other influences, it is not overt. Take, for example, the wild, rhythmically irregular jig in the ensemble piece *Bob*, one of his finest works, which depicts some of the activities that take place in a "Bower o'Bliss", or the derivation of pitch material from the Irish folktune "Bonny Kate" for his two-piano piece bearing the non-verbal title "*Ø*". For *The Intelligence Park*, Barry derives his material from 17th-and 18th-century sources: the chorales of J.S. Bach, as well as Arne, Buxtehude, C.P.E. Bach, Dowland and Handel. But his music does not depend on quotations, and the listener does not need the earlier music in order to understand Barry's own, nor will s/he recognise it as such.

Viewed overall, Barry's style owes little to the main streams of thought we have inherited from the 19th century. One of the most important aspects of his style is the fact that the music is not necessarily going anywhere; it does not need to. This is a positive feature, and something he has in common perhaps with the so-called "experimental" composers (Cage in the U.S., or Howard Skempton and Chris Newman in Britain). The listener derives satisfaction from what s/he experiences on the way and the composer's treatment of the material, rather than feeling the onward thrust of a goal and the inevitable arrival. Therefore in the musical argument we find an elaboration rather than the conventional development of ideas, in a music which is episodic rather than lyrical. In the process of forging his unique style, Barry has made one of the few significant contributions to the development of new music.

—Michael Blake

BASSETT, Leslie (Raymond). American. Born in Hanford, California, 22 January 1923. Educated at Fresno State College, California, B.A., 1947; University of Michigan, Ann Arbor (under Ross Lee Finney), M.Mus., 1949, A.Mus.D., 1956; Ecole Normale de Musique, Paris (as Fulbright scholar), 1950–2; private lessons with Nadia Boulanger and Arthur Honegger, 1950–1, Roberto Gerhard, 1960, Mario Davidovsky (electronic music), 1964. Military service with 13th Armored Division Band, United States Army, 1942–6. Married Anita Elizabeth Denniston 20 August 1949; 2 sons (1 deceased) and 1 daughter. Music instructor, schools in Fresno, California, 1951–2; faculty, School of Music, since 1952, Albert A. Stanley Distinguished University Professor, since 1977, and Henry Russel Lecturer, 1984, University of Michigan, Ann Arbor; Rome Prize Fellow, American Academy, Rome, 1961–3. Recipient: award, Society for the Publication of American Music, 1960; Rome Prize, 1961; award, National Institute for Arts and Letters, 1964; UNESCO Composers' Rostrum, Paris, 1966; Guggenheim Fellowships, 1973, 1980; Pulitzer Prize (for *Variations for Orchestra*), 1966; Koussevitzky Foundation awards, 1971, 1990; Naumburg Foundation Recording Award (for *Sextet* for piano and strings), 1974; elected member, Institute of the American Academy, National Institute of Arts and Letters, 1976; Distinguished Alumnus, California State University, Fresno, 1978; award, ISCM—League of Composers, 1980; Distinguished Artist, Michigan Council for the Arts, 1981. Mailing address: 1618 Harbal Drive, Ann Arbor, Michigan 48105, U.S.A.

Publishers: ACA; King; Merion; Peters.

Symphonies/orchestral:

Symphony 1949; withdrawn.
Symphony 1956; withdrawn.
Five Movements 1961; first performed Rome, 5 July 1962.
Variations for Orchestra 1963; first performed Rome, 6 July 1963. Recorded CRI SD 203.
Designs, Images and Textures (band) 1964; first performed Ithaca, New York, 28 April 1965. Recorded Golden Crest CRS 4214.
Colloquy 1969; first performed Fresno, California, 23 May 1969.
Forces (violin, cello, piano, orchestra) 1972; first performed Des Moines, Iowa, 1 May 1973.
Echoes from an Invisible World 1975; first performed Philadelphia, 27 February 1976. Recorded CRI 429.
Concerto for Two Pianos and Orchestra 1976; first performed Midland, Michigan, 30 April 1977. Recorded Advance FGR 26S.
Sounds, Shapes and Symbols (band) 1977; first performed Ann Arbor, Michigan, 17 March 1978.
Concerto Grosso (brass quintet, wind, percussion) 1982; first performed Ann Arbor, Michigan, 4 February 1983.
Concerto Lyrico (trombone, orchestra) 1983; first performed Toledo, Ohio, 6–7 April 1984.
Colors and Contours (band) 1984; first performed Boulder, Colorado, 1 March 1985.
From a Source Evolving 1985; first performed Midland, Michigan, 1 November 1986.
Lullaby for Kirsten (band) 1985; first performed Ann Arbor, Michigan, 4 October 1985.
Fantasy (clarinet, wind ensemble) 1986; first performed Ann Arbor, Michigan, 2 October 1987.

Chamber/instrumental:

Trombone Quartet 1949; first performed Ann Arbor, Michigan, 22 February 1949.
String Quartet 1949; withdrawn.
String Quartet 1951; withdrawn.
Six Piano Pieces 1951; first performed Los Angeles, 27 April 1952.
Sonata (horn, piano) 1952; first performed Ann Arbor, Michigan, 4 May 1953.
Brass Trio 1953; first performed Ann Arbor, Michigan, 15 November 1953.
Trio (viola, clarinet, piano) 1953; first performed Ann Arbor, Michigan, 15 November 1953. Recorded CRI 148.
Quintet (string quartet, double bass) 1954; first performed Ann Arbor, Michigan, 5 December 1955.
Sonata (trombone, piano) 1954; first performed Ann Arbor, Michigan, 23 April 1954.
Clarinet Duets 1955; first performed Ann Arbor, Michigan, 26 April 1956. Recorded Mark MES 57590.
Toccata (organ) 1955; withdrawn.
Sonata (viola, piano) 1956; first performed Ann Arbor, Michigan, 13 December 1957.
Five Pieces (string quartet) 1957; first performed Ann Arbor, Michigan, 29 July 1958.
Suite (trombone) 1957; first performed Decatur, Indiana, 27 May 1964. Recorded Crystal 5381; Fermat FLPS 49.
Woodwind Quintet 1958; first performed Ann Arbor, Michigan, 16 July 1958.
Three Voluntaries (organ) 1958; first performed Ann Arbor, Michigan, 2 November 1958.
Sonata (violin, piano) 1959; first performed Ann Arbor, Michigan, 17 November 1960.
Cello Duets 1959; first performed Interlochen, Michigan, 13 November 1966.
Mobile (piano) 1961; first performed Rome, 23 December 1962.
Piano Quintet 1962; first performed Rome, 10 June 1962.
String Quartet No 3 1962; first performed Rome, 22 May 1963.
Four Statements (organ) 1964; first performed Ann Arbor, Michigan, 13 February 1965.
Elaborations (piano) 1966; first performed Warrensburg, Missouri, 2 November 1970.
Music for Cello and Piano 1966; first performed Fresno, California, 20 November 1966. Recorded CRI 311.
Nonet (wind quintet, trumpet, trombone, tuba, piano) 1967; first performed Ithaca, New York, 16 April 1968.
Music for Saxophone and Piano 1968; first performed Tempe, Arizona, 1 August 1968. Recorded New World NW 209.
Sextet (piano, viola, string quartet) 1971; first performed Washington, D.C., 27 April 1972. Recorded CRI 323.
Sounds Remembered (violin, piano) 1972; first performed Washington, D.C., 8 December 1972. Recorded Desto DC 7142.
Music for Four Horns 1974.

Twelve Duos (2/4 trombones) 1974; first performed Boston, 2 May 1975.
Wind Music (flute, oboe, clarinet, alto saxophone, horn, bassoon) 1975; first performed River Falls, Wisconsin, 5 May 1976.
Soliloquies (clarinet) 1976; first performed Ann Arbor, Michigan, 18 February 1976. Recorded Mark MES 38084.
String Quartet No 4 1978; first performed Ann Arbor, Michigan, 26 March 1980.
Sextet (flute, alto flute, clarinet, bass clarinet, cello, double bass) 1979; first performed Ann Arbor, Michigan, 23 February 1980.
Five Temperaments (guitar) 1979–83; first performed Ann Arbor, Michigan, 26 March 1983.
A Masque of Bells (carillon; with or without dancers) 1980; withdrawn.
Liturgies (organ) 1980; first performed Ann Arbor, Michigan 20 October 1980.
Trio (violin, clarinet, piano) 1980; first performed Notre Dame, Indiana, 6 October 1981. Recorded Leonarda LE 326.
Sonata da Camera (flute, clarinet, trumpet, violin, cello, piano, percussion) 1981; first performed DeKalb, Illinois, 8 April 1982.
Duo Concertante (alto saxophone, piano) 1984; first performed New York City, 21 May 1985. Recorded ACA Digital CD.
Seven Preludes (piano) 1984; first performed Michigan, 16 February 1985.
Salute (5 trumpets) 1985; first performed Albuquerque, New Mexico, 31 May 1985.
Five Configurations (piano) 1987; first performed San Jose, California, 6 July 1987.
Dialogues (oboe, piano) 1987; first performed Pennsylvania, 6 April 1988. Recorded Crystal CD 326.
Duo Inventions (2 cellos) 1988; first performed Gainesville, Florida, 3 February 1989. Recorded Crystal CD 325.
Brass Quintet 1988; first performed Philadelphia, 27 March 1989.
Illuminations (flute, piano) 1989.

Vocal/choral:

The Lamb (SATB choir, piano; Blake) 1952; first performed Ann Arbor, Michigan, 16 November 1952.
Four Songs (solo voice; Blake, Herbert, Robinson) 1953; first performed Ann Arbor, Michigan, 15 November 1953.
Out of the Depths (SATB choir, organ) 1957; first performed Ann Arbor, Michigan, 9 February 1958.
Easter Triptych (tenor, 15 brass, 5 percussion; Bible) 1958; first performed Ann Arbor, Michigan, 15 February 1960.
For City, Nation, World (cantata for tenor, SATB choir, children's chorus ad lib, congregation, 4 trombones, organ) 1959; first performed Buffalo, New York, 21 February 1960.
Moonrise (SSA chorus, violin, 2 violas, cello, flute, piccolo, alto flute, piano, 2 percussion; Lawrence) 1960; first performed Detroit, Michigan, 6 May 1960.
Remembrance (SATB choir, organ; Rupert) 1960; first performed Ann Arbor, Michigan, 2 October 1960.
Eclogue, Encomium and Evocation (SSA, 4 instrumentalists playing piano, harp, bass drum, vibraphone, celesta, cymbals) 1962; first performed Ypsilanti, Michigan, 13 January 1966.
To Music (3 solo songs; Jonson, Herrick, Billings) 1962; first performed Rome, 17 April 1962.
Follow Now That Bright Star (SATB chorus; carol) 1962; first performed Rome, 1962.
Prayers for Divine Service (TTBB chorus, organ; Latin) 1965; first performed Williamstown, Massachusetts, 24 April 1966.
Psalm LXIV/Hear My Prayer, O Lord (SA chorus, organ) 1965; first performed Ann Arbor, Michigan, 13 November 1966.
Notes in the Silence (SATB chorus, piano; Hammarskjold) 1966; first performed Ann Arbor, Michigan, 22 January 1967.
Collect (SATB chorus, tape) 1969; first performed East Orange, New Jersey, 23 March 1969.
Moon Canticle (amplified narrator, SATB chorus, cello) 1969; first performed New York City, 10 December 1969.
Celebration: In Praise of Earth (amplified narrator, SATB chorus, orchestra) 1970; first performed Berea, Ohio, 14 October 1971.
Of Wind and Earth (SATB chorus, piano; Shelley, Bryant, St Francis) 1973; first performed Columbus, Ohio, 8 February 1974.
The Jade Garden (solo voice; oriental texts) 1973; first performed Ypsilanti, Michigan, 8 February 1976.
Time and Beyond (bass, clarinet, cello, piano; Emerson, Tagore, Van Doren) 1973.
Love Songs (solo voice; Greek, Landor, Bradstreet, Emerson, Harrington) 1975; first performed Dallas, Texas, 31 March 1976.
A Ring of Emeralds (SATB chorus, piano; Irish poets) 1979; first performed Cork, Ireland, 27 April 1979.
Psalm XCV/Sing to the Lord (SATB chorus, organ) 1981; first performed Brevard, North Carolina, 31 January 1982.
A Family History (SATB choir, piano) 1981.
Lord, Who Hast Formed Me (SATB chorus, organ; Herbert) 1981; first performed Ann Arbor, Michigan, 14 March 1982.
Whoe'er She Be (3-part women's chorus, piano; Crashaw) 1986; first performed Ann Arbor, Michigan, 4 April 1987.
Pierrot Songs (soprano, flute, clarinet, violin, cello, piano; Giraud) 1988; first performed Los Angeles, 25 January 1989.

Other:

Three Studies in Electronic Sound 1965; first performed Ann Arbor, Michigan 10 October 1965.
Triform (electronic) 1966; first performed Ann Arbor, Michigan, 3 December 1966.

Editions of Gio. M. Cesare: *La Hieronyma* (trombone, continuo), 1972; Biagio Marini: *Sonata for Two Bass Trombones and Continuo*, 1973; Gio. Batt. Riccio: *Three Canzonas* (violin or trumpet, trombone, continuo), 1979; Daniel Speer: *Sonata and Gigue* (2 violins, trombone, continuo), 1979.

PUBLICATIONS

By Bassett: *Manual of 16th Century Counterpoint*, New Jersey, 1967–78.

On Bassett: A. Brown, "LB", in *Asterisk*, 2 (2), 1976; Larry Rachleff, "Colors and Contours", in *CBDNA Journal*, Winter 1986; "LB" (composer profile), in *NACWPII Journal*, Autumn 1987; Charles Young, "Some Insights into the Compositional Process of LB", in *The Saxophone Symposium*, Summer 1990.

Leslie Bassett comments:

The more we know of music and the more we live with it, the more elusive and mysterious it becomes, always changing, capable of a thousand indescribable moods, a strange and somewhat mystical power in our lives, a fascination, a challenge, a craft, a language, a house of cards—the echo from an invisible world.

* * *

Fluent composer and respected leader, Leslie Bassett has enjoyed the double recognition of prestigious prizes and commissions and of academic honors. He has had a long and distinguished career serving in the university both as a personal mentor to composition students and as an artistic model. His own compositions in turn reflect and draw upon the stimulating university atmosphere of inquiry, exploration and achievements of colleagues. As with many other modern American composers, the symbiotic relationship of composer to university has been especially nourishing to both sides.

Adept at most compositional genres and media, Bassett is equally comfortable working in a chamber music medium or writing for large ensemble. He could be described neither as a traditionalist nor an experimentalist but as a progressive bringing under his compositional command serviceable possibilities from both approaches. He agrees: "A few years ago many composers felt that they had to become avant-garde or remain hopelessly behind. I would call the present time a period of musical consolidation, a time when the best music will be written with the means that have been now firmly established as common practice rather than far out."

Although the thrust of his compositional focus is mainly instrumental, his choral works are good examples of stylistic and structural features common to all his music. *Collect* and *Notes in the Silence* take a traditional approach by portraying the moods and emotional meanings of their profound texts while settings vocal rhythms true to the natural declamation of the words. On the other hand, bold textures of unusual spacing, vocal effects such as whispering and inflected speech, and intense, complex harmony evidence an adventuresome attitude. *Collect* utilizes an electronic tape part with the choir, for Bassett a rare use of this experimental medium.

More of the important works are for traditional instrumental media. Most come in multiple movements presenting diverse but coherent ideas, making their challenging content easier for listeners to assimilate. Many works use vivid imagery for titles, setting an active context for listening without being specifically visual or narrative (*Designs, Images and Textures*).

While keenly aware of listeners' imaginations and interests, Bassett also clearly composes for performers. Most pieces are done on commission; beyond that, they use instruments' idioms and natural qualities, challenging performers to contribute technique, intensity and subtlety to the prescribed musical expression (*Music for Saxophone and Piano*). Some works (*Sounds Remembered*) are virtuosic, others more pedagogical (*Duo Inventions*); all balance a respect for performers' musicality with demands on their technique. "I write for people who want my music and who will play it with zeal and commitment."

In structural characteristics, Bassett's works are strongly similar, reflecting a singular and intense aural concept. A reviewer observed that *Sonata da Camera* "succeeds because it is guided by a musical intelligence whose focus is consistently on clarity of structural design". A primary dimension of each work is the variety of textures presented, each a vividly etched landscape of running scale figures, assertive repeated impulses, trills and tremolos, or soaringly lyric lines. Another reviewer recognized that "although careful thought has gone into pitch and registral selection, *Liturgies* is dependent upon gesture and texture to make its point". Describing *Variations for Orchestra*, Bassett confirms that he was "fascinated by orchestral texture, and conceived each section from a textural point of view long before pitches were considered".

Most textures are in flux, transformed by distinctly rising or falling, accumulating or disintegrating, settling or taking off (*Sounds, Shapes and Symbols*). Large-scale temporal form typically concatenates contrasting textures, while variation processes tie together the material. In *Sounds Remembered*, Bassett describes a process of "unfolding key sounds, which become transformed, then return periodically to reassert themselves, as in memory". In *Echoes from an Invisible World*, he also acknowledges "the principle of unfolding and growth from small elements". In *Variations for Orchestra*, he "found the process of continuous statement with developmental or reflective overtones to be very exciting".

Rapid events strive toward goals in continual motion. Slower textures in gradual metapmorphosis seem nearly timeless (*Sextet*). These polarities of rhythmic pace take shape visually in his scores by contrasting notational means. Traditional metric complexities of modern music are employed: odd and changing meters, syncopation, frequent special subdivisions of metric units often opposed in simultaneous rhythmic dissonance. Also appearing in most works, newer non-metric notation represents passage of time by visual analog of spatial extensiveness (*Colors and Contours*). By avoiding regular pulses, it can create a free flight of frenetic figures or altogether freeze motion and time.

Bassett's harmonies freely explore intense, all-chromatic sonorities often emphasizing sonorous thirds juxtaposed with cluster-derived dissonant semitones (*Soliloquies*). The pitch language, intense and perhaps opaque to the less educated ear, may at times seem static. Strongly independent lines in fluid contrapuntal motion balance this with passages of sweeping, unceasing progression. Both trio works and the string quartets are reminiscent of Bartók in their force of contrapuntal flow.

That all these qualities are revealed in most Bassett compositions without any apparent distinction of stylistic periods or genres underscores the essence of his work "striving to evoke something of the mystery of music": eloquent expression of a personal musical vision, one of energy, intensity, poignancy and lyricism.

—Thomas Clark

BAULD, Alison. Australian; resident in United Kingdom. Born in Sydney in 1944. Educated at National Institute of Dramatic Art, 1961–2; University of Sydney, 1964–7, B.Mus.; Sydney Moss Scholarship (further study under Elisabeth Lutyens and Hans Keller), 1969–71; University of York, 1972–4, D.Phil. Married; 2 children. Musical director, Laban Centre for Dance, Goldsmiths' College, University of London, 1975–8; composer in residence, New South Wales Conservatorium, Sydney, 1978; collaborator with Graham

Dudley, Cockpit Theatre. Freelance composer; part-time teacher, Hollins College, London. Mailing address: c/o Novello & Co, 8 Lower James Street, London W1, England.

Publisher: Novello.

Chamber/instrumental:

Piece (piano) 1971.
Piece (violin) 1971.
Concert (piano, tape) 1974; first performed Sydney, December 1974. Recorded RCA VRLI 0083.
The Busker's Story (alto saxophone, bassoon, trumpet, violin, double bass) 1978; first performed Sydney, 25 September 1978.
Monody (flute) 1985; first performed Sydney, 1 October 1985.

Vocal/choral:

Three Songs of Love (soprano, flute, oboe, bassoon, violin, cello, percussion) 1968; first performed Adelaide, 1968.
Withdrawal I (soprano, violin, cello, piano, vibraphone, percussion, narrator, taped animal noises) 1968.
Withdrawal II (soprano, violin, cello, piano, vibraphone, percussion, narrator, tape of animal noises) 1970.
In a Dead Brown Land (tenor, soprano, chorus, violin, cello, alto melodica, flute, piccolo, pipes, drums) 1971, revised 1974.
Piece (soprano, speaker, flute, oboe) 1971.
On the Afternoon of the Pigsty (female speaker, piano, alto melodica, percussion) 1971; first performed London, 1973.
Humpty Dumpty (tenor, flute, guitar) 1972; first performed York, 1972.
Dear Emily (soprano, harp or harpsichord or piano) 1973; first performed York, 1973.
Egg (soprano or tenor, flute, cello, percussion) 1973.
Mad Moll (soprano) 1973; first performed Barcelona, February 1973.
One Pearl (soprano or counter-tenor, string quartet) 1973; first performed Southampton, Hampshire, 11 November 1973.
Van Diemen's Land (unaccompanied SATB chorus) 1976; first performed London, 8 November 1976.
One Pearl II (soprano, alto flute, string orchestra) 1976; first performed London, 30 April 1976.
I Loved Miss Watson (soprano, piano, tape) 1977; first performed Barcelona, 19 October 1977.
Banquo's Buried (soprano, piano; Shakespeare) 1982; first performed Sydney, 22 October 1982.
Richard III (voice, string quartet; Shakespeare) 1985; broadcast BBC, 4 July 1985.
Once Upon a Time (5 vocal soloists, 3 optional child roles, small chamber orchestra) 1986; broadcast BBC, 29 December 1986.

Opera:

Nell (soprano, mezzo-soprano, tenor, baritone, chorus, flute, oboe, clarinet, alto melodica, bassoon, piano, percussion, 2 violins, viola, cello, double bass) 1988; first performed London, 1988.

Other:

Pumpkin (2 dancers, 2 actors, ensemble) 1973.
Exiles (actors, singers, alto melodica, string quartet, percussion) 1974.
Inanna (tape) 1975.

* * *

Virtually all of Alison Bauld's compositional output can be described as music drama of one form or another. This is perhaps not surprising, given her initial training as an actress; it was only after writing some incidental music for plays that she undertook tertiary music studies. Early recognition of her talent as a composer—her *Three Songs of Love* were performed at an International Society for Contemporary Music (ISCM) concert at the 1968 Adelaide Festival of Arts, and subsequently at another ISCM concert in Sydney—confirmed her in her move towards composing.

The problem of the notational aspects of combining speech with music in dramatic works has occupied Bauld's attention, and she has experimented with a number of methods. The possibilities range from meticulously-notated forms, which tend to stifle the performer's spontaneity, through to a vaguely-indicated impression, which may only approximately convey the composer's intent. A compromise, which she prefers, is proportional notation: the closer the notes are written together, the more quickly the sounds are to be spoken.

Although she has set existing texts, such as the Shakespearean *Banquo's Buried* for soprano and piano, Bauld frequently writes her own words. Sometimes, as in *I Loved Miss Watson*, they are inspired by a particular personal experience. Another such piece is *The Busker's Story*, which although an instrumental work is nevertheless based upon a fairly specific programme. By shaping the libretto or scenario to suit her dramatic purposes, the composer can thus determine the musical directions of the work; her choice of words gives her rhythmic and atmospheric inspiration.

Like many other composers, Bauld reworks ideas that seem to her to have several musical possibilities. This may consist of a fairly simple rescoring, such as the metamorphosis through which *One Pearl* for soprano or counter-tenor and string quartet became *One Pearl II* for soprano, alto flute and string orchestra, or through which *Humpty Dumpty* for tenor, flute and guitar became *Egg* for tenor, flute, cello and percussion. On the other hand, it has led to a whole network of pieces of music theatre: from *In a Dead Brown Land*—a work involving singers, actors, instrumentalists and mimes—a character was extracted and expanded to become the protagonist of *Mad Moll*, a set of three songs for unaccompanied soprano. This character then became the focal point of the ballad opera *Nell*; the ancestors of the characters in this opera had previously appeared also in the choral work *Van Diemen's Land*. Bauld was able to achieve this "historical" continuity by writing the librettos for *Mad Moll*, *Nell* and *Van Diemen's Land* herself.

Along with the dramatic element in Bauld's works there is frequently evidence of a quirky sense of humour. Her *Concert*, prompted by a conversation with the pianist Roger Woodward and ostensibly a reasonably conventional piece for piano, relies heavily upon the performer's skills as an actor-mime; during the performance, the piano sound is surreptitiously replaced by that of a pre-recorded tape, and the spotlight finally reveals nothing but a tiny toy piano on stage. Another work from the same year, *Exiles* for actors, singers, alto melodica, string quartet and percussion, also has a strong visual impact, with the staging carefully detailed by the composer; the score is a mixture of original music counterpointed with an unmodified Haydn quartet. This parallel sounding of diverse musical elements can also be heard in *The Busker's Story*: the busker—with his alto saxophone—and the ensemble of orchestral instruments play independently of each other, only rarely and seemingly randomly achieving harmony.

—Jenny Dawson

BAYLE, François. French. Born in Tamatave, Madagascar, 27 April 1932. Educated from age 14 in Bordeaux (literature and mathematics); originally self-taught, piano lessons from Georges Elocegui; Conservatoire National Supérieur de Musique, Paris (under Olivier Messiaen), 1959; summer composition courses at Darmstadt (with Karlheinz Stockhausen), 1960, 1961, 1962; training course at Groupe de Recherches Musicales (under Pierre Schaeffer), 1959–61. Military service, 1958–9. Married (1) Janine Emile in 1955, 1 daughter; (2) Genevieve Mache in 1984. Secretary general, research division, Radiodiffusion Française, 1961–2; assistant, 1962–6, chief of research, 1966–75, and director, since 1975, Groupe de Recherches Musicales; Paris; director, since 1975, Institut National de L'Audiovisuel, Paris; founder (with Ivo Malec and J.C. Eloy), Musique Plus, 1973–8; founder/producer, Acousmatique/Acousmathèque, INA/GRM recordings, since 1977. Recipient: Chevalier, Ordre National du Mérite, 1976; Grand Prix des Compositeurs, SACEM, 1978; Grand Prix du Disque Français, 1981; Commandeur, Ordre National des Arts et des Lettres, 1986; Prix Ars Electronica, Linz, 1989. Mailing address: 31 rue de la Harpe, 75005 Paris, France.

Publisher: Association Magison (self).

Symphonies/orchestral:

Cristal (35 instruments, tape, sound projection) 1977; first performed Paris, March 1977.

Chamber/instrumental:

Points critiques (piano, cello, horn, percussion) 1960; first performed Paris, 1960.
Echiquier (oboe, flute, trombone, tubular bells, claves) 1960.
Ereignis (flute, violin, trombone, contrabass clarinet, 2 percussion) 1961; first performed Paris, 1961.
L'Objet captif (2 trumpets, 3 wooden percussion, 3 metal percussion) 1962.
L'Archipel (string quartet, tape) 1963; first performed Paris, January 1963. Recorded Philips 836.895.
Pluriel (17 instruments, tape) 1963; first performed Paris, March 1963. Recorded Philips 836.895.

Electro-acoustic (including "Musique Acousmatique" for Acousmonium, an orchestra of loudspeakers, invented by Bayle):

Lignes et points 1966; first performed Royan, April 1966. Recorded Philips 836.895.
Espaces inhabitables 1967; first performed Paris, May 1967. Recorded Philips 836.895; INA/GRM 9101.
Jeita ou murmure des eaux 1969–70; first performed Bordeaux, 1970. Philips 836.895.
L'Aventure du cri (Expérience acoustique I) 1970; first performed Lisbon, 1970.
L'Expérience acoustique (complete) 1970–2; first performed Avignon, August 1972.
Le Langage des fleurs (Expérience acoustique II) 1971; first performed Paris, February 1971.
La Preuve par le sens (Expérience acoustique III) 1971; first performed Avignon, 1971.
L'Epreuve par le son (Expérience acoustique IV) 1971; first performed Paris, 1971.
Purgatoire 1972; first performed Paris, 1972.
Trois Rêves d'oiseau 1972; first performed Paris, 1972. Recorded Philips; INA/GRM 9101.
La Philosophie du non (Expérience acoustique V) 1972; first performed Avignon, August 1972.
Exercices sons 1973.
Vibrations composées 1973; first performed Ossiach, Austria, August 1973.
Paradis (with Bernard Parmegiani) 1974.
Electrucs 1974.
La Grande Polyphonie 1974; first performed Paris, 7 April 1975. Recorded INA/GRM 727.04.
Personnages et intervalles bleus 1976; first performed Paris, 23 February 1976.
Camera Oscura 1976; first performed Metz, November 1976.
Cristal (35 instruments, loudspeakers, tape) 1977; first performed Paris, March 1977.
Tremblement de terre très doux (Erosphère II) 1978; first performed Paris, 19 March 1979. Recorded INA/GRM CD C300.
Camera Lucida 1979; first performed Paris, November 1982.
Toupie dans le ciel (Erosphère III) 1979; first performed Paris, 1980. Recorded INA/GRM CD C300.
La Fin du bruit (Erosphère I) 1979; first performed Paris, 1980. Recorded INA/GRM CD C300.
Erosphère (Eros bleu, rouge, noir) 1980; first performed Paris, January 1980.
Son Vitesse-Lumière I & II 1980.
Voyage au centre de la tête (Son Vitesse-Lumière III) 1981; first performed Paris, August 1981.
Aéroformes 1982–3; first performed Paris, 1984.
Les Couleurs de la nuit 1982; first performed Paris, March 1983. Recorded INA/GRM.
Le Sommeil d'Euclide / Lumière ralentie (Son Vitesse-Lumière IV & V) 1983; first performed Metz, August 1983. Recorded Wergo W2023.
Motion, émotion 1986; first performed Paris, 1986. Recorded INA/GRM CD C1001.
Aer (aéroformes—faim, peur, amour, aurora) 1987; first performed Paris, 1987.
Théâtre d'ombres 1988; first performed Linz, 1989. Recorded INA/GRM CD C3003.
Mimameta 1989; first performed Sao Paulo, 1989. Recorded INA/GRM CD C3003.

Vocal/choral:

Rebus (soprano, reciter, ondes martenot, percussion) 1968; first performed Paris, 1968.
L'Accent du secret (mezzo-soprano, flute, clarinet, piano, violin, cello) 1968; first performed Paris, 1968.
Nadir (soprano, tenor, bass, bass clarinet, guitar, ondes martenot, percussion) 1968; first performed Beirut, 1969.

Rumeurs (12 voices, tape) 1968; first performed Vaison-la-Romaine, 1968.
Cantate profane (5 voices, tape) 1969; first performed Amiens, 1969.

Other:

Trois-Portraits-d'un-oiseau-qui-n'éxiste-pas (music to abstract images by Robert Lapoujade; no 3, *L'Oiseau chanteur*, performed separately) 1963; broadcast 1963.
Fautrier l'engage (music to film by Baraduc) 1964.
Galaxie (music to film by Kamler) 1964.
Meurtre (music to film by Kamler) 1964.
Portrait poème de Léonore Fini (music to television film by J. E. Jeanneson) 1967; broadcast 1968.
La Belle Cérébrale (music to film by P. Foldes) 1967; broadcast 1967.
Coeurs de secours (music to film by Kamler) 1973; broadcast 1973.

PUBLICATIONS

By Bayle: "Musique et expérience", in *Musique en jeu*, 1972; "Support-Espace", in *Cahiers recherche / Musique*, 5, 1978; "Répertoire acousmatique", in *Cahiers recherche / Musique*, 7, 1980; "Ecouter et comprendre", in *La Revue musicale*, 394, 1986; "Voyage en aéroforme", in *Papiers du XXe siècle*, Paris, 1986; "L'image du son et i-son", in *Music and Cognitive Sciences*, 1989; "L'Odysse de l'espace", in *Lieu*, Brussels, 1989; *Savoir-Faire*, Marseille, 1989; *Penser-Créer*, Lyon, 1990.

On Bayle: Claude Rostand, "FB", in *Larousse*, 1970; Antoine Golea, in *Carrefours*, 1970–5; Jacques Lonchampt, "Métamorphose, transfert, voyage", in *Le Monde*, 1980; Claude Samuel, in *Le Matin*, 1980–4; Michel Chion, "FB", in *Larousse*, 1982, new edition 1989; Jean-Yves Bousseur, in *Minerve*, 1986; Bernard Vendier, in *Musique et culture*, 1989.

François Bayle comments:

So the incidental sounds of day-to-day experience—bangs, rubbings, whirlings, reverberations, echos, their distance and brightness, relationships of texture and scale and so on—usually constrained and confined to the function of index (1), become pure abstractions, auditory objects, values of speed and space, of colours and contours, harmony and noise, through acousmatic projection (2).

We are offered new relations with the old world. And our mental capacities for observation, evoked by these impressions, free themselves, opening up an Aladdin's cave, full of flowing drives and imaginary forces, imprisoned by archetypes. I believe it is fair to consider that the remit of musical art becomes the liberation of formal sources like these, so their properties can be tested and organised.

It seems to me there is nothing better to do as the 20th century runs its course than to learn to face the explosion of the crucible!

To live in a world that is multi-racial, polytheistic and turbulent

under-developed and over-equipped

oceanic and technological

musical and trivial.

(1) *Index* is used in the semiotic sense where, for example, smoke is the index of a distant fire (tr).
(2) *Acousmatic projection* is a term employed by Pierre Schaeffer for a sound-object made available for musical use by divorcing it from its cause and its context—in the same way as, apocryphally, Aristotle delivered his seminars unseen behind a veil (tr).

* * *

François Bayle has specialised in electronic music, developing a skill in juxtaposing natural and synthesised sounds. *Jeita* consists of short, precisely-constructed studies using recordings from a Lebanese cave. Sometimes concrete sounds are used alongside other sources; *L'Oiseau-chanteur* uses unmodified instrumental sounds, combined with electronic and concrete sounds for new timbral shades. Other pieces process sound material; the instrumental sounds of *Vapeur* are initially unaltered, but gradually taped transformations modify and extend their colour and range.

Bayle's formative influences include Messaien, and Stockhausen, with whom he studied at the Darmstadt summer courses. Most significant was Pierre Schaeffer; Bayle was a member of his Groupe des Recherches Musicales (GRM) in the early 1960s and later took over leadership. The group had a collective spirit of discovery, but also an independence from other musical developments; and within this affiliation, Bayle strove to avoid sectarianism.

The breakdown of meaning and transcendent systems implicit in Modernism forms the cultural problematic in which Bayle situates his work. The foundations of culture are exhausted, and all systems, even the most recent, have been pulverised. Bayle's aim is to explore this new world—facing up, as one may read above, to the explosion of the Modernist crucible. He saw his involvement with the GRM as one way to hasten the processing of our new cultural context, and to avoid the complementary dangers of over-intellectual or crudely gestural writing.

In his commentaries, he draws on literary and philosophical references of many kinds, albeit predominantly French (Lefebvre, Breton, Lacan); his own verbal style is typically French in its complexity. However, Bayle's aims in writing music have an essentialist, if not mystical, edge: he once said that his aim is to cause the listener to feel the motion and vibration of energy in the Universe.

—David Revill

BAZELON, Irwin (Allen). American. Born in Evanston, Illinois, 4 June 1922. Educated: piano lessons with Magdalen Messman and Irving Harris; studied composition with Leon Stein; De Paul University, Chicago, B.A., 1945, M.A., 1946; Yale University, New Haven, Connecticut (composition under Paul Hindemith), 1946; Mills College, Oakland, California (composition under Darius Milhaud), 1946–8; University of California, Berkeley (under Ernest Bloch), 1947. Writer of advertising jingles, since 1948; MacDowell Fellow, 1948, 1950, 1951; incidental music for American Shakespeare Theatre, Stratford, Connecticut, 1950s; Yaddo

Festival Fellow, 1969; composer in residence, Wolf Trap Farm Park, Virginia, 1974. Mailing address: 147 East 71st Street, New York, New York 10021, U.S.A.

Publishers: Novello; Boosey & Hawkes.

Symphonies/orchestral:

Concert Overture 1951–2, revised 1960.
Adagio and fugue (strings) 1956.
Suite (small orchestra) 1956.
Overture: The Taming of the Shrew 1959.
Ballet-centauri 17 1960.
Symphony No 1 1962.
Symphony No 2: Testament to a Big City 1962.
Symphony No 3 (bass, percussion, piano, string sextet) 1962.
Symphony concertante (clarinet, trumpet, marimba, orchestra) 1963.
Symphony No 4 1964–5.
Dramatic Movement 1964–5.
Excursions 1965.
Symphony No 5 1967.
Symphony No 6 1969.
Chamber Concerto: Churchill Downs (brass, percussion, string sextet) 1970–1.
A Quiet Place—For a Violent Time (chamber orchestra) 1975.
De-tonations (brass quintet, orchestra) 1975–6.
Spirits of the Night 1976.
Symphony No 7 1980.
Memories of a Winter Childhood 1981.
Spires (trumpet, small orchestra) 1981.
Tides (clarinet, orchestra) 1982.
Fusions (chamber orchestra) 1983.
Piano Concerto 1983.
Symphony No 8 1986.

Chamber/instrumental:

String Quartet No 1 1947.
String Quartet No 2 1947.
Ballet Suite (small ensemble) 1949.
Suite for Young People (piano) 1950.
Five Pieces (piano) 1950.
Five Pieces (cello, piano) 1950.
Sonatina (piano) 1951.
Movimento da camera (flute, bassoon, horn, harpsichord) 1955.
Chamber Symphony (7 instruments) 1957.
Brass Quintet 1963.
Duo (viola, piano) 1963, revised 1970.
Early American Suite (woodwind quintet, harpsichord) 1965.
Dramatic Fanfare for 1970 (brass) 1970.
Propulsions (percussion ensemble) 1974.
Woodwind Quintet 1975.
Concatenations (percussion quartet, viola) 1976.
Double Crossings (trumpet, percussion) 1976.
Sound Dreams (flute, clarinet, viola, cello, piano, percussion) 1977.
Triple Play (2 trombones, percussion) 1977.
Imprints (piano) 1978.
Three Men on a Dis-course (clarinet, cello, percussion) 1979.
Cross Currents (brass quintet, percussion) 1980.
Partnership (timpani, marimba) 1980.
For Tuba with Strings Attached (tuba, string quartet) 1982.
Re-percussions (2 pianos) 1983.

Vocal/choral:

Phenomena (soprano, ensemble) 1972.
Junctures (soprano, orchestra) 1979.

PUBLICATIONS

By Bazelon: *Knowing the Score: Notes on Film Music*, New York, 1975.

On Bazelon: D. H. Cox, "A World of Violent Silence: A Note on AB", in *Musical Times*, 123, 1982.

* * *

A list of the works of Irwin Bazelon and the basic facts of his professional career would place him more or less exactly in his generation and in his country: he studied with Hindemith and Milhaud, wrote many scores for documentary films and TV commercials and his works have such titles as *Testament to a Big City, Double Crossings, De-tonations* and *Churchill Downs* (the name of a race-track). He has written a book on film music entitled *Knowing the Score* and his main interest outside music is horse-racing. However this brief sketch would give little indication of his remarkable individuality as a composer, nor of his isolation from the musical establishment.

Nothing in his early musical life would suggest the totally personal world of his later, mature music. Hindemith gave him a strict academic base from which to work, but Bazelon found him lacking in warmth and understanding and described him as "a Prussian task-master". Milhaud was very much more stimulating and sympathetic; his love of the rhythms and harmonies of jazz and South American music and his interest in the music of Stravinsky and the Schoenberg of *Pierrot Lunaire* must have seemed fascinating to an immature and musically unawakened young man from an unmusical Chicago background. Bazelon's early works, piano sonatas, string quartets and other small chamber works were competent and disciplined, lacking facility and a truly personal voice.

In 1948, the year he completed his studies with Milhaud, he came to New York and earned his living for the next seven years as a railroad reservations clerk. He had long been suffering from an inner-ear affliction which was distressing and incapacitating, causing partial deafness and a certain introversion of character. Treatment from an ear surgeon produced dramatic results. "The violent silent world inside me erupted," he says, "I came out of my shell". There can be no doubt that his arrival in the electric, vital world of New York City contributed as much, or more to Bazelon's development as a person and as a musician.

From the early 1950s until the 1970s he supported himself as a writer of music for television commercials, documentary films and plays. But far from writing scores which were bland and self-effacing, he spoke the language of mid-20th century music in these brief fragments of applied music. At the same time he was developing a quite personal, even eccentric voice in his concert works. This is characterized by an increasingly atonal melodic and harmonic style, with elements of serial technique, by a stylized use of the language of jazz and above all by an extraordinary rhythmic energy. This propulsion of rhythm is almost never motoric; it depends rather on violent dislocations and cross accents set over an implied pulse. A typical fast movement suggests a piece of atonal modern jazz without the rhythm section, the underpinning of all popular music. The slower music tends to be brooding, unlyrical, with Bazelon's usual rhythmic energy merely held at bay, though never far beneath the surface.

His list of works includes eight symphonies and many pieces for unconventional chamber combinations, notably featuring the brass and percussion families. He recently started to write for the voice, introducing a quite new and typically unpredictable element of lyricism into his music.

He says of himself: "I like fast music over slow, high over low, loudness to softness. I'm a dramatic composer. My music snarls rather than caresses . . . " Bazelon's later music is a totally personal statement, influenced by nothing but his own nervous, sometimes violent interior world.

—Richard Rodney Bennett

BEAT, Janet (Eveline). British. Born in Streetly, Staffordshire, 17 December 1937. Educated at University of Birmingham, 1956–60, M.Mus.; 1961–4, part-time research, M.A., 1968. Freelance horn player, Midlands, 1960–5; lecturer in music, Madely College of Education, 1965–7; lecturer in music, Worcester College of Education, 1967–1971; lecturer, Royal Scottish Academy of Music and Drama, since 1972; founder member, Scottish Society of Composers, 1980–4; founder member and a director, Scottish Electro-Acoustic Music Society, 1987; founder, electro-acoustic music ensemble, Soundstrata, 1988. Recipient: G. D. Cunningham Award, 1962. Mailing address: 5 Letham Drive, Glasgow G43 2SL, Scotland.

Publisher: Novello.

Symphonies/orchestral:

Iter Temporis (small orchestra; for amateur players) 1970; first performed Worcester, 1970.
Synchronism 1977.

Chamber/instrumental:

Essays (oboe) 1968, 1974; first performed Glasgow, 1973.
Pentad (piano) 1969.
Apollo and Marsyas (clarinet, tape) 1972; first performed Glasgow, 1973.
Le Tombeau de Claude (flute, oboe, harp) 1973; first performed Glasgow, 1980.
Five Projects for Joan (cello) 1974; first performed Glasgow, 1974.
Circe (viola) 1974; first performed Glasgow, 1982.
After Reading "Lessons of the War" (violin, piano) 1976; first performed Poznan, Poland, 1976.
Inventions for Woodwind (flute, oboe, clarinet) 1977; first performed Glasgow, 1983.
Hunting Horns Are Memories (horn, tape) 1977; first performed Glasgow, 1978.
Seascape with Clouds (clarinet) 1978; first performed London, 1979.
Piangam (piano, tape) 1978–9; first performed Glasgow, 1979.
Pastore d'Aria (oboe/oboe d'amore/cor anglais, tape) 1979; first performed Edinburgh, 1980.
Noctuary (clarinet, piano, bongos) 1979; first performed Glasgow, 1982.
"Vincent" Sonata (violin) 1979–80.
Dreamscapes (bassoon, tape) 1980.
Mestra (flute/piccolo/alto flute/bass flute) 1980–1; 1st movement, Kirkcaldy, 1980; Glasgow, 1982.
Ongaku (harpsichord, tape) 1981; first performed Glasgow, 1982.
Cross Currents and Reflections (volume 1, piano; see electronic for volume 2) 1981–2.
A Willow Swept by Rain (guitar, tape) 1982; first performed Edinburgh, 1986.
Aegean Nocturne (violin, piano) 1983; first performed Edinburgh, 1985.
Alexa's Comet (harpsichord) 1984; first performed Glasgow, 1989.
Arabesque (guitar) 1985; first performed Glasgow, 1986.
Sonata No 1 (piano) 1985–6; first performed Edinburgh, 1988.
Rousseau's Snake Charmer (tenor recorder) 1986.
Hunza Aubade (treble recorder, tape) 1987.
Fireworks in Steel (trumpet) 1987; first performed Glasgow, 1987.
A Vision of the Unseen No 1 (improvising trio—acoustic or electronic—tape) 1988; (flute, violin, piano) first performed Kingston-upon-Thames, 1989.
Mandala (flute, WX7, computer-controlled synthesizers) 1989–90; first performed Glasgow, 1990.

Vocal/choral:

Summer Poem No V (unaccompanied voices) 1970.
Hide-and-Seek (music for amateur players; reciter/singer, female chorus, instruments, 1970; first performed Worcester, 1970.
Study of the Object No 3 (unaccompanied voices) 1970; first performed Worcester, 1970.
The Fiery Sunflower (3 sopranos, melodica, piano, percussion) 1972; first performed Glasgow, 1972.
The Leaves of My Brain (soprano/tenor, guitar) 1974; first performed Edinburgh, 1981.
Mitylene Mosaics (soprano, 3 clarinets) 1983–4; first performed Glasgow, 1984.
Nomoi Aulodoki (soprano, 3 clarinets) 1984; first performed Glasgow, 1984.
Sylvia Myrtea (SSAA choir) 1985.
Aztec Myth (mezzo-soprano, tape) 1987; first performed London, 1988.
Kist o'Ayres (mezzo-soprano [improvising], flute, lute, computer-controlled synthesizer) 1989; first performed Glasgow, 1989.
Puspawana (mezzo-soprano, gong, computer-controlled synthesizers) 1989; first performed Glasgow, 1990.
A Springtime Pillow Book (mezzo-soprano, flute, synthesizer, computer and synthesizers) 1990; first performed Glasgow, 1990.

Other:

Cymbalis No 1 (tape) 1969; withdrawn.
Piece for JR (tape) 1972; withdrawn.
The Gossamer Web (dance drama; soprano, piano, percussion, tape) 1975; first performed Edinburgh, 1975.
Dancing on Moonbeams: An Electronic Fantasy 1980. Recorded Scottish Society of Composers, SSC 001.
The Cranes Call: An Electronic Tone Poem (tape) 1981; first performed Tokyo, 1981.

Cross Currents and Reflections (see also instrumental; piano, mono synthesizer, electric piano, tape) 1981–2; first performed Glasgow, 1984.
Second Glance: Clocks, Times Past (electronic film music) 1983; broadcast Channel 4 (UK), 1986.
Second Glance: Lighthouse (electronic film music) 1983; broadcast Channel 4 (UK), 1986.
Journey of a Letter (electronic ballet music) 1986; first performed Cumbernauld, Scotland, 1986.
Echoes from Bali (computer-controlled synthesizer) 1988; first performed Newcastle-upon-Tyne, 1988.
A Vision of the Unseen No 2 (tape) 1988; first performed Glasgow, 1990.
Lydian Mix (computer-controlled synthesizer) 1989; first performed Edinburgh, 1990.

Editions of Carrissimi: *Jephte* and *Nisi dominus*, 1974; A. Scarlatti: *Suite from "Il Tigrane"* (2 descant, 1 treble recorders) 1975; Handel: *Let God Arise*, 1978; M.-A. Charpentier: *Filius Prodigus*, 1987.

PUBLICATIONS

By Beat: "Monteverdi and the Opera Orchestra of His Time", in *The Monteverdi Companion*, 1968; "An Extension of Vocal Accompaniment to Dance", in *The Laban Art of Movement Guild Magazine*, November 1970; "Two Problems in Carissimi's Oratorio *Jephte*", in *The Music Review*, 34, 1973; "The Composer Speaks: JB on *Cross Currents and Reflections* 1981–2", in *Stretto*, 4 (1), 1984; "James Durrant: Violinist Extraordinary", in *Stretto*, 6 (1), 1986.

On Beat: John Purser, "Scottish Women Composers", in *Chapman*, 6 (3–4), Summer 1980; P. Adkins Chiti, "Musiciste Famose: compositrici d'oggi", in *Strumenti e Musica*, April 1986; Anne Mackay, "Soundstrata", in *Music Current*, April 1990.

Janet Beat comments:

My interests are diverse and range from the scientific through a study of ancient civilisations, to world cultures and comparative religions. All this is reflected in my music in the use of technology and the influence of oriental music with its quarter- and micro-tones, and the choice of text in the vocal works. I like to explore fully the timbral range of the instruments. Here, there is an influence from electronic music in my writing for conventional instruments, which has exploited "aural sculpture" to encompass all the latest performance techniques.

* * *

The British composer Janet Beat has long been a vigorous presence on the Scottish new music scene, and has composed the vast bulk of her work since moving to Glasgow two decades ago. Most of that work has been written for either small combinations of instruments, instruments and electronic sound, or purely electronically-generated sound, with the exception of two compositions for larger forces, *Iter Temporis* and *Synchronism*.

While her fascination with electronically-generated and synthesized sound has increasingly come to dominate her work, her interest in the medium goes back to the late 1950s, when she first began to experiment with *musique concrète*. Beat owned the first synthesizer to be made commercially available in the United Kingdom, and created all her early electronic pieces with it, although she has now withdrawn most of them on the grounds of inadequate technical standards.

She still permits *Apollo and Marsyas* for clarinet and tape to be performed, a work which neatly encapsulates her liking for setting instrument and electronics in a kind of contrasting dialogue, with colourful and expressive clarinet lines weaving through the deep electronic soundscape.

Much of her subsequent work made use of this combination of instrumental and electronic sound, although she also continued to write for instruments alone, usually in solo or duo format, and in a determinedly avant-garde musical language. As the quality of electronic sound generation improved in both studio and performance situations, however, Beat has focussed her concentration more and more on the possibilities inherent in the medium.

Hunting Horns Are Memories, in which a horn player (Beat's own instrument) performs against a tape made up of synthesised horn sounds, or *Cross Currents and Reflections* for piano, electric piano, mono synthesizer and tape (commissioned by Gustav Fenyo), are both good examples of her experiments with the technology as it existed a decade ago.

Her preoccupation with electronic music has consistently gone hand in hand with an imaginative and often highly colourful fascination with timbral explorations, and the way in which timbre can be manipulated electronically to produce a bewildering range and variation from a single instrument or sound.

She has combined that fascination with a powerful liking for the harmonic and rhythmic devices of a wide variety of oriental music, notably in pieces like *Piangam* for piano and tape, which draws on the kind of soundscape created by a gamelan orchestra, or *Echoes from Bali* for computer-controlled synthesizer.

Beat describes her work with sound, whether instrumental, electronic, or a combination of both, as an attempt at creating a kind of "aural sculpture", and has been both imaginative and daring in her willingness to draw on a wide variety of musical idioms (including popular music and improvisational elements as well as those from non-Western cultures), conventional and unconventional performance techniques, and technological developments in pursuit of that end.

While a number of her contemporaries on the Scottish music scene have used electronics for specific effects in their music, Beat has taken on the challenge which electronic (and now computer-generated) music presents with complete enthusiasm and no small success. The recent formation of her five-piece performing group Soundstrata suggests that her increasing emphasis on electronics in recent years will continue to shape her work for some time to come.

—Kenny Mathieson

BEATH, Betty (professional name of Elizabeth Margaret Beath Cox). Australian. Born in Bundaberg, Queensland, 19 November 1932. Educated at Sydney Conservatorium (under Frank Hutchens); Queensland Conservatorium of Music, music scholarship, 1950, Dip.Mus., 1965–9; Australian Music Examinations Board, T.Mus.A., A.Mus.A. (singing); Trinity College of Music, L.T.C.L. (piano); musical study in New Guinea, Indonesia, Java, Bali. Married (1) John Beath,

22 May 1953, 1 son and 1 daughter; (2) David Cox, 21 February 1976. Registered teacher, Queensland Department of Education; music specialist and later head of music department, St Margaret's Anglican Girls' School, since 1967; lecturer/accompanist, Queensland Conservatorium of Music, Brisbane, since 1969; examiner, Australian Music Examinations Board, since 1973; represented women composers of Australia, 3rd International Congress on Women in Music, Mexico City, 1984; composer in residence, North Adams State College, Massachusetts, 1987; member, executive board, International League of Women Composers, 1986–7, 1988–9. Recipient: many eisteddfod competition prizes; twice finalist, ABC Concerto Competition (as pianist); South East Asian Fellowship, Literature Board of Australia Council (held jointly with David Cox), 1974. Mailing address: 8 St James Street, Highgate Hill, 4101 Queensland, Australia.

Publishers: Australian Music Centre, P.O. Box 49 Broadway, Sydney 2007, Australia; J. Albert Pty Ltd, Sydney; Cockatoo Capers, Highgate Hill; Playlab Press, Ashgrove, Queensland; Boolarong Publications, Queensland.

Chamber/instrumental:

Piccolo Victory, Images of Colonial Australia (flute/piccolo, harpsichord or piano, cello, rhythm sticks) 1982; first performed Brisbane, 25 April 1982. Recorded Grevillea GRV1082.
Trio (flute, harpsichord, cello) 1982.
Black on White (piano, left hand and ruler) 1983. Recorded Cockatoo Capers cassette.
Brisbane Waters (bass clarinet, with optional didjeridu tape accompaniment) 1986; first performed Pasadena, California, 1986.
Music for Gillian (alto flute, piano) 1988. Recorded Cockatoo Capers cassette.
Asmaradana (piano) 1988; first performed London, 20 May 1989. Recording Chromattica.
Contrasts (piano) 1990; first performed Liverpool, 26 April 1990. Recording Chromattica.

Vocal/choral:

Francis (tenor, piano; Cox) 1973.
In This Garden (medium voice, chamber orchestra; Cox) 1973; first performed Brisbane, 1973.
Seawatcher (medium voice, piano; Cox) 1973.
Riddles (medium voice, chamber orchestra) 1974; first performed Brisbane, 1974.
The Cry (medium voice, piano; Amano, Guest) 1974. Recorded ABC.
Fire's Song (Cox) 1974.
Askesis (medium voice, piano; Grass, Middleton) 1975. Recorded ABC.
Three Cautionary Songs (medium voice; Cox) 1975; first performed Brisbane, 1975.
Indonesian Triptych (medium voice, piano; Mohamad, Aveling) 1977; ABC broadcast, 7 February 1977. Recorded ABC.
Given the Time (medium voice, piano; Holford) 1978. Recorded ABC.
Songs from the Beasts' Choir (medium voice, piano; Gasztold, Godden) 1978; first performed New York, 1981.
Poems from the Chinese (soprano, clarinet, cello; translated Rexroth) 1979; first performed Brisbane, 21 October 1979. Recorded ABC.
Nawang Wulan (medium voice, piano; Sastrowardojo) 1980. Recorded ABC cassette.
Walking in Sunshine (6 two-part vocalise, piano) 1981.
Little Song 1981.
Three Psalms (high voice, flute, harp, cello; Psalms 23, 121, 150) 1981; first performed Brisbane, 2 August 1981. Recorded Grevillea cassette.
Manusia Pertama di Angkasa Luar (First Man in Outer Space) (tenor, piano; Sastrowardojo) 1983.
Yungamurra (soprano, flute, cello; or soprano, piano; Wrightson) 1984; broadcast ABC, 20 May 1985. Recorded Grevillea cassette.
Ninya (soprano, choir, flute, bassoon, piano, cello, double bass, percussion; Wrightson) 1985.
The Sermon to the Birds (La Predica Agli Uccelli) (soprano and alto, or alto choir, piano; Pasacoli, Gransden) 1986; first performed Brisbane, 9 October 1986. Recorded Grevillea cassette.
In the Carnarvon Ranges (soprano, alto, flute, piano, rhythm sticks; Cox) 1987; broadcast ABC, 1 February 1988.
Points in a Journey (soprano, flute, piano; Traherne, Milne, anon., Woodhouse, St Francis) 1987; first performed North Adams, Massachusetts, 7 October 1987. Recorded Grevillea cassette.
The Bride of Byfield (medium voice, piano; Woodhouse) 1988. Recorded Cockatoo Capers.
An Excuse for Not Returning the Visit of a Friend (soprano, flute, unpitched drum; Ch'en, translated Rexroth) 1988. Recorded Cockatoo Capers.
River Songs 1990–1.

Opera:

The Strange Adventures of Marco Polo (voice and piano or chamber orchestra; Cox) 1972, revised 1976 as *Marco Polo*; first performed Queensland, 1973.
Francis (for children; Cox) 1974; first performed Brisbane, 17 October 1974.
Balyet (Wrightson) 1990.

Other:

Abigail and the Bushranger (music drama for children's voices, piano, percussion; Cox) 1974; first performed Brisbane, 17 October 1974.
Abigail and the Rainmaker (music drama for children, piano, percussion; Cox) 1974; first performed Brisbane, 15 October 1976.
The Raja Who Married an Angel (music drama for children's voices, instrumental ensemble, piano; Cox) 1978, revised 1982; first performed Brisbane, 21 October 1979.
Procession . . . a March of Celebration . . . the March of the Bunyip (environmental music, chiefly percussion for untrained musicians) 1983; first performed Queensland, 1983.
Abigail and the Mythical Beast (music drama for children, instrumental ensemble, piano; Cox) 1985; first performed Brisbane, 1985.

PUBLICATIONS

By Beath: "School Opera", in *Innovations in Australian Secondary Education*, Sydney, 1977; *Reflections from Bali: A Personal Encounter with the Land and Its People*, Sydney, 1981; *Spice and Magic* (travel; co-written with David Cox), Brisbane, 1983; "Outstanding Queensland Women in Music",

"Third International Congress on Women in Music" and "Concert Tour and Retreat", reports and article published by International League of Women Composers, Autumn/Winter 1984–5.

On Beath: entry in LePage, *Women Composers, Conductors, and Musicians of the Twentieth Century*, Metuchen, New Jersey, 1988.

Betty Beath comments:

Although I am moving in new directions, much of my work has been written for the voice with piano, instrumental or orchestral accompaniment. This is not simply because the voice is a favourite instrument but also because I love words and the meanings of words. The text is tremendously important to me. I sometimes take months to find the text which I know is just right to set. I will have a very definite, certain response when this happens. Sometimes I am lucky when the poems or texts seem to come to me. Of course, I have worked a great deal with my husband, David Cox, who has a great regard for words. He makes a search, sometimes a very long one, for the simple, right way to say something. Actually, what I believe he achieves with words is what I hope to do in the setting. I am very much aware that the quality of the text has a corresponding relationship to the quality of the music it provokes. During the period when I am thinking about a poem and again in the actual writing, I feel strongly linked with the intention and thought of the poet. To be satisfying, the end result—the song—must be faithful to the intention of the poet through the text. I have not consciously made a search for exotic material. The fact that the writers may be is probably coincidental in that my choice was to do with content, simplicity, communication. In the case of the Javanese poets there is a small qualification, for not only was I attracted by the beauty of their poetic expression, I have also made a significant response to their country which is a lively influence in my work and in my life. Though I know Indonesia or indeed Asia, to be an important influence, I believe my music to be essentially Australian in character. I believe that in creating a work we subconsciously draw on the experience of our lives and that we are very much influenced by the landscape, the depth and breadth of our horizons, the rhythm and tempo of our language. I am interested in "new" work and "new" sounds are a wonderful discovery, even though they may be ancient—like the gamelans in Java or the sounds of a corroboree.

* * *

From the time she was three and a half years old, Betty Beath was destined by her family and friends to be a pianist. The rather lonely lifestyle that this orientation entailed did little to develop her self-confidence in any area other than piano playing, and her compositional efforts were for a long time diffident, shy attempts. The easy-going but generous encouragement she received from composer Frank Hutchens, whom she often encountered as an eisteddfod adjudicator in her early years, was one of the few positive influences she experienced. When she returned to tertiary music studies in her mid-thirties, after a hiatus of many years, she was unable to study composition formally as it was not available as an area of specialisation. To this day, she remains self-taught as a composer.

Her experience as an accompanist in singing studios led Beath to write for the voice, and vocal music forms a large proportion of her output. Of great significance was her meeting in 1970 with writer and artist David Cox, whom she later married: she has composed many settings of his words. The collaboration began with two works: one, the song cycle for soprano and chamber orchestra *In This Garden*, was written for performance at the Queensland Conservatorium of Music where Beath was working. The other commenced as music for a puppet play, but was completed as both a one-act opera *The Strange Adventures of Marco Polo* and a scaled-down version, *Marco Polo*, for use in schools.

As virtually a "beginner" composer in her forties, Beath felt none of the pressure to follow current musical trends which a younger composer might have undergone. She listened with interest to new music, but always responded to the innovative feelings which it might engender rather than by writing in a specific style as such. Composing according to a felt response has been a consistent characteristic of her work. When setting words, her method has been to consider the poem for a long time, trying to put herself in the mind of the poet in order to set the words in a manner so as to enhance, rather than to detract from them. Thus, while her compositions are carefully planned with regard to form and duration, a strong intuitive response has often altered the plan. In the case of the song cycle *River Songs* a dream affected her perception of the poems, and her subsequent setting.

Since a study trip with her husband to Indonesia in 1975, the music of that region has been frequently reflected in Beath's work: sometimes as a direct quotation of traditional Indonesian material, as in *Asmaradana*, and sometimes merely by the employment of similar modes and rhythms, as in *Music For Gillian*. Another ethnic influence has been the music and culture of the Australian Aborigines, evidenced in her choice of texts and in musical style: both can be heard in *Ninya*, a work for voices and instruments including traditional Aboriginal sounds.

The song cycle *Songs From the Beasts' Choir* was an important work for Beath. Not only did the piece receive wide acclaim, being performed at the Carnegie Recital Hall and the Symphony Space in New York, at the Piccolo Spoleto Festival in Charleston, and the Hugh Lane Gallery in Dublin; but the composer felt personally satisfied that she had captured the essence of the poems in music as had the poet in words. Beath's later works have been more free and spontaneous, seeking to engage the listener's emotions through an appropriate use of idiom.

—Jenny Dawson

BEDFORD, David. British/English. Born in London, 4 August 1937. Educated at Trinity College, London and Royal Academy of Music, London (under Lennox Berkeley), 1958–61, L.T.C.L., A.R.A.M.; further study under Luigi Nono, Venice, and at RAI Electronic Music Studio, Milan, 1962. Married (1) Maureen Parsonage in 1958, 2 daughters; (2) Susan Pilgrim in 1969. Porter, Guy's Hospital, London, 1956; teacher, Whitefield School, Hendon, 1965; teacher, 1968–80, and composer in residence, 1969–81, Queen's College, London; associate visiting composer, Gordonstoun School, Scotland, since 1983. Mailing address: 30 Shakespeare Road, Mill Hill, London NW7 4BA, England.

Publishers: Universal Edition; Novello.

Symphonies/orchestral:

This One for You 1965.
Gastrula 1968.
Star's End (electric guitar, electric bass guitar, percussion, orchestra) 1974.
Alleluia timpanis (orchestra, organ and recorders ad lib) 1976.
Prelude for a Maritime Nation 1981.
Ocean Star a Dreaming Song (youth or amateur orchestra) 1981.
The Valley Sleeper, the Children, the Snakes and the Giant 1983.
Symphony No 1 1984.
Ronde for Isolde (also version for symphonic wind band) 1985; first performed Gordonstoun, Fife, 28 November 1985.
Symphony No 2 (symphonic wind band) 1985; first performed St Albans, Hertfordshire, 7 April 1986.
Sea and Sky and Golden Hill (symphonic wind band) 1985; first performed Bristol, 20 September 1985.
The Transfiguration: A Meditation 1988; first performed Northampton, 22 November 1988.

Chamber/instrumental:

Piece for Mo (percussion, vibraphone, accordion, 3 violins, cello, double bass) 1963.
Piano Piece 1 1966.
Five (2 violins, viola, cello) 1967.
18 Bricks Left on April 21st (3 electric guitars) 1967.
Trona for 12 (flute, oboe, clarinet, bassoon, 2 trumpets, 2 trombones, 2 violins, viola, cello) 1967.
Pentomino (wind quintet) 1968.
Piano Piece 2 1968.
A Garland for Dr K. (flute/piccolo/alto flute, clarinet/E♭ clarinet/bass clarinet, violin/viola, cello, piano/harpsichord) 1969.
You Asked for It (acoustic guitar) 1969.
The Garland of Love (flute, clarinet, horn, trumpet, double bass, pop group, 6 girls to dance and turn pages) 1970.
The Sword of Orion (flute, clarinet, violin, cello, 4 metronomes, 2 percussion/32 instruments) 1970.
With 100 Kazoos (flute, oboe, clarinet, bass clarinet, horn, trumpet, trombone, string quartet, 100 kazoos in audience) 1971.
Spillihpnerak (viola) 1972.
Jack of Shadows (viola, 4 flutes, 2 horns, trombone, tuba, 2 cellos, 2 double basses) 1973.
A Horse, His Name Was Hunry Fencewaver Walkins (acoustic guitar, flute, clarinet, piano, violin, cello, double bass) 1973.
Pancakes, with Butter, Maple Syrup and Bacon and the TV Weatherman (brass quintet) 1973.
Variations on a Rhythm by Mike Oldfield (3 percussion/84 instruments) 1973.
Circe Variations (clarinet, piano, violin, cello) 1976.
The Ones Who Walk Away from Omelas (flute, oboe, clarinet, bassoon, timpani, electric guitar, electric bass guitar, fuzz pedals, 2 violins, viola, cello) 1976.
Fridiof Kennings (saxophone quartet) 1980.
Symphony for 12 Musicians (flute, 2 oboes, clarinet, horn, bassoon, 2 violins, viola, cello, bass drum, percussion) 1981.
Elegy and Caprice (oboe, piano) 1981.
Toccata in D minor (piano) 1981.
Sonata in One Movement (piano) 1981.
Wind Sextet 1981.
String Quartet in A minor 1981.
Five Diversions (2 flutes) 1983.
♩ = *120* (bass clarinet, tape delay) 1984.
Pentaquin (flute/piccolo, clarinet, viola, harp, percussion) 1985.
In memoriam (piano) 1986.
Verses and choruses (2 acoustic guitar) 1986.
For Tess (brass quintet) 1985; first performed Cheltenham, Gloucestershire, 15 July 1987.
Hoquetus David (2 pianos) 1987; first performed London, 5 September 1987.
Ma non sempre (piano) 1987; first performed London, 17 December 1987.
Memories of Ullapool (flute, guitar) 1987.
Erkenne Mich (flute/alto flute, oboe/cor anglais, bass clarinet, vibraphone) 1988; first performed Bristol, 4 March 1988.

Vocal/choral:

Two Poems (unaccompanied chorus; Patchen) 1963.
A Dream of the Seven Lost Stars (SSATBB choir, chamber ensemble; Patchen) 1964–5.
Music for Albion Moonlight (soprano, flute, clarinet, melodica, piano, violin, cello; Patchen) 1965.
O Now the Drenched Land Awakes (baritone, piano) 1965.
Wide Wide in the Rose's Side (SSA or SSS chorus, 8 chime bars) 1966.
That White and Radiant Legend (soprano, speaker, flute, oboe, clarinet, bassoon, violin, viola, cello, double bass; Patchen) 1966.
Come in Here, Child (soprano, amplified piano) 1969.
The Tentacles of the Dark Nebula (tenor, 3 violins, 2 violas, 2 cellos, double bass; Clarke) 1969.
Star Clusters, Nebulae and Places in Devon (mixed double chorus, brass) 1971.
Some Stars Above Magnitude 2.9 (soprano, piano) 1971.
Nurse's Song with Elephants (10 acoustic guitars/1 singer; Blake) 1971.
Holy Thursday with Squeakers (soprano, electric piano, viola/organ, soprano saxophone/bassoon, percussion; Blake) 1972.
An Easy Decision (soprano, piano; Patchen) 1972.
When I Heard the Learn'd Astronomer (tenor, 2 flutes, 2 oboes, 2 clarinets, 2 bassoons, 3 horns, trombone, bass trombone, tuba; Whitman/Flammarion) 1972.
Twelve Hours of Sunset (SSSSATBB choir, orchestra; Harper) 1974.
Because He Liked to Be at Home (tenor voice/treble recorder, harp; Patchen) 1974.
The Golden Wine Is Drunk (16 solo voices; Dowson) 1974.
The Odyssey (chorus, orchestra, synthesizers and electric keyboards; Homer) 1976.
The Song of the White Horse (30 unbroken voices, ensemble, electronic keyboards, medical helium, tape of "The Blowing Stone"; Chesterton) 1977.
On the Beach at Night (2 tenors, piano, small organ, 4 hands; Whitman) 1977.
The Way of Truth (SATB chorus, electronics; Parmenides/Popper) 1977–8.
Of Beares, Foxes and Many, Many Wonders (SSAATTBB choir, flute, oboe, clarinet, trumpet, 3 percussion, strings; Hakluyt) 1979.
Requiem (soprano, chorus, orchestra) 1980.
Vocoder Sextet (flute, clarinet, violin, cello, vocalist, EMS recorder) 1981.

The Juniper Tree (soprano, recorder, harpsichord; Grimm/Bragg) 1982.
Of Stars, Dreams and Cymbals (unaccompanied SATB chorus; Browne) 1982.
An Island in the Moon (unaccompanied SATB chorus; Blake) 1985–6.
Seascapes (string quintet or piano, voices) 1986.
The Camlann Game (children's voices, piano) 1986.
Be Music, Night (soprano, piano) 1986.
Into Thy Wondrous House (soprano, children's choir, SATB chorus, orchestra) 1987; first performed London, 13 June 1987.
Gere curam mei finis (soprano, alto, tenor, bass, harmonizer) 1987; first performed Brussels, 11 November 1987.

Opera:

The Rime of the Ancient Mariner (school opera; after Coleridge) 1978.
The Death of Baldur (school opera; Bragg, after the Prose Edda) 1979.
Fridiof's Saga (school opera; Bragg, after Icelandic saga) 1980.
The Ragnarok (Bragg, after Elder Edda, Prose Edda) 1982.
Odysseus (voices, piano solo or duet, flute, oboe, clarinet, string quartet) 1988.

Other:

Film scores: *The Killing Fields*, 1984; *Absolute Beginners*, 1986; *The Mission*, 1986.

* * *

Summarising David Bedford's career in *Baker's*, Nicholas Slonimsky permits himself a small sniff. "Returning to England [Bedford] taught at Queen's College in London, and played the organ in pop groups". Bedford was returning from a stint as a pupil of Nono's, having been relieved of a persistent attachment to Schoenberg. He joined up with Kevin Ayers, one of the original members of the art-rock band Soft Machine, in a new touring group called the Whole World (it also featured the eccentric but gifted saxophonist Lol Coxhill). The fruits of this association lie in a number of works from the early 1970s, in which Bedford combines amplified rock instrumentation with acoustic instruments.

Such experiments were to become a music industry joke within a very few years, but for a time it was very fashionable to pit rock bands against symphony orchestras (Deep Purple, Procul Harum) but Bedford's work in this direction was more than an imaginative extension of a banal marketing ploy. *Star's End* is the best of his pieces in this vein; it is still a haunting piece, with a fine sense of drama and beautifully orchestrated.

It was to be 10 years before Bedford tried his hand—successfully—at a full-scale symphony, but most of his chamber and ensemble work of the 1970s seems to be heading in that direction. All the same, Bedford's writing is not properly symphonic in development, favouring either the broadly dramatic style that was to come out in the mythic opera he has written for Gordonstoun, the cold-bath school where Prince Charles was a pupil, or else the very textural and slightly static style that was to be identified with the progressive-rock, proto-New Wave composer Mike Oldfield, with whom Bedford has collaborated successfully.

Bedford's music draws from rock something of its volume and dynamics, an area that was being explored on the continent, in Poland and elsewhere, at around the same time. The two-guitar piece *18 Bricks Left on April 21* ends with a high-volume improvisation; in contrast, *You Asked for It* calls on the virtuosity of the player—rather than the National Grid—to achieve the kind of inventive texture Bedford is looking for.

Much of his very best music has been to texts by the American poet Kenneth Patchen, an inspired choice for a composer of Bedford's sensibilities. In *That White and Radiant Legend*, the scoring is varied extensively according to the demands of the text (which is rather extreme) and Bedford balances speaking and singing voices very effectively. Though he has a special rapport with Patchen's verse, Bedford has also made vocal pieces out of simple lists of names, in this case, the names of stars and nebulae. *Star Clusters, Nebulae and Places in Devon* uses names in a particularly abstract way—the syllables of words split up and divided among vocal parts, then sounded together, so that the word becomes an a semantic "chord"—but also with a recognition of the simultaneity of physical (the stars) and historical (the prehistoric settlements of Devon) simultaneity.

The work is written in a distinctive space-time notation intended to give, as his occasional recourse to graphic notation also may, a clearer sense of what is required at a particular moment. Bedford has been an adventurous composer from the outset; he mixes elements of improvisation, a special sensitivity to language and to certain modulations of volume and metre to create music of genuine originality and great intellectual and emotional depth; he has also written particularly imaginative music for children, a field not quite colonised by Sir Maxwell Davies. Playing in pop groups seems to have done him no harm after all.

—James Weir

BENJAMIN, George (William John). British/English. Born in London, 31 January 1960. Educated at Westminster School, London 1974–77 (private tuition with Peter Gellhorn); Paris Conservatoire (composition under Olivier Messiaen), 1976–78; King's College, Cambridge (composition under Alexander Goehr, additional study with Robin Holloway), 1978–82; further research, electronics, IRCAM, Paris, 1985–87. Visiting professor of composition, Royal College of Music, London, since 1988; conductor, working with orchestras in Europe and the United States, including London Sinfonietta, Ensemble Intercontemporain, Musique Oblique, Halle, London Philharmonic Orchestra, St. Paul Chamber Orchestra; pianist, performances in France, Italy, Hong Kong, U.S. and Great Britain. Recipient: Lili Boulanger Award, 1985; Koussevitsky International Critics Award, 1987; Grand Prix Charles Cros du disque, 1987. Mailing address: c/o Allied Artists, 42 Montpelier Square, London SW7 1JZ, England.

Publisher: Faber.

Symphonies/orchestral:

Altitude (brass band) 1977; first performed York 1979. Recorded Green Records 1001.

Ringed by the Flat Horizon 1979–80; first performed France, 1980. Recorded Nimbus CD NI 5075.
At First Light (chamber orchestra) 1982; first performed London, 1982. Recorded Nimnus CD NI 5075.
Jubilation (orchestra, mixed children's groups) 1985; first performed London, 1985.
Antara (16 players, electronics) 1987, revised 1988–9; first performed Paris 1987; revised version first performed London, May 1989. Recorded Nimbus CD 5167.
Cascade 1990; first performed London, 1990.

Chamber/instrumental:

Sonata (piano) 1977–8; first performed France, 1978. Recorded Nimbus 45009.
Octet 1978; first performed London, 1979.
Flight (flute) 1979; first performed France, 1980. Recorded Nimbus 45009.
Duo (cello, piano) 1980. Recorded Nimbus 45009.
Sortileges (piano) 1981; first performed Cheltenham, 1982.
Meditations on Haydn's Name (piano) 1982.
Three Studies (piano) 1982–5; first performed London, 1986.
Fanfare for Aquarius 1983; first performed London, 1983.
Relativity Rag (piano) 1984.

Vocal/choral:

A Mind of Winter (soprano, small orchestra; Stevens) 1981; first performed Aldeburgh, Suffolk, 1981. Recorded Nimbus CD NI 5075.

Other:

Panorama (tape) 1985; first performed Paris, 1985.

PUBLICATIONS

On Benjamin: Paul Griffiths, (interview) in *New Sounds, New Personalities: British Composers of the 1980s*, London, 1985; Brian Morton, (interview) "Young at Heart, Wise in Time", in *Wire*, March 1990.

* * *

It has taken George Benjamin's reputation some time to recover from two critical obsessions: his youthful "precocity", and his association with Olivier Messiaen. The truth is that Benjamin has not been unduly prolific, the quality usually associated with precociousness. Though he writes relatively quickly, ideas take some time to gestate and he composes with an attention to detail unusual in a young composer. Nor is his work deeply marked, after a couple of apprentice pieces, by the influence of Messiaen, with whom Benjamin studied in Paris. There are undoubtedly elements of Messiaen's harmonic processes in some of the "early" work—such as Benjamin's use of the second mode of limited transpositions—but most of these could just as easily be traced back to Debussy or explained by Benjamin's dogged examination of the colouristic and allusive properties of chords.

Messiaen was perhaps more important as an example and encouragement than as a direct influence, and certainly Benjamin's voice matured remarkably early. The Piano Sonata is vigorously conceived and contains some striking rhythmic and harmonic effects. Nonetheless, Benjamin's bent has always been for orchestral composition. He first came to public attention in 1980 when *Ringed by the Flat Horizon*, a piece inspired by some lines in *The Waste Land* and a photograph of a lightning strike in the desert, made him the youngest composer ever to have a piece performed at the London Proms; he was 20. Despite the work's dramatic and imagistic properties, the piece is relatively formal and its climaxes—presumably representing the lightning—part of the catalytic process which generates the long slow chords with which it ends.

Benjamin's next major work *A Mind of Winter*, was a setting for soprano and chamber ensemble of Wallace Stevens's "The Snow Man", a poem greatly concerned with the transformative power of the imagination, the "mind of winter", over material with which it is identical in substance, as a snowman is to the surrounding snow. In Benjamin's setting, his only published work for voice to date, the vocal line is not distinct from the instrumental setting, but emerges out of it. This is an important indication of the direction in which his work was to develop and the first sign of an impatience with a music entirely dependent on chords.

His next important work, though, marked the pinnacle of his chordal approach. *At First Light* was to date Benjamin's best work and is certainly the most performed; it has also been superbly recorded. A colouristic piece, suggested by J. M. W. Turner's painting "Norham Castle: Sunrise", it is also the last piece, significantly, with a direct external stimulus and point of reference. Turner's radiant colour and post-modern lack of "finish" or resolution are both reflected in Benjamin's carefully ambiguous orchestration of chords, though the oboe is there to register the thematic material in a more direct way, much as Turner allows identifiable glimpses of solid objects through the shimmer (and much as Benjamin deployed the soprano in *A Mind of Winter*).

Thereafter, Benjamin's work changes quite markedly. He had never been drawn to electronic music, disliking the sound. Nonetheless, he continued to experiment with new technology, acquiring a pair of electronic keyboards tuned in quarter-tones and working on the very powerful 4X computer at IRCAM in Paris. The tape piece *Panorama* is unremarkable but the piece that followed was a new departure. *Antara*, completed in 1987 after a relatively fallow period, is in most respects antithetical to the aesthetic of electronic music. It is melodic, rhythmic and fast. Whereas in much contemporary music micrototones add no more than a few post-modernist spangles to a relatively conventional exterior, the 4X allowed Benjamin to compose both microtonally *and* virtuosically. Leaving IRCAM each day, Benjamin had listened to the music of some Peruvian buskers, playing on native panpipes or *antara*. Intrigued by the sound (as was Louis Andriessen in *Hoketus*), he turned to the 4X and devised a meta-instrument, synthesised, but increasingly indistinguishable in the score from the "acoustic" piccolos, just as the 2 percussionists' bells and anvils blend seamlessly with electronically manipulated resonances from the metal pipes which entwine the Pompidou Centre (where IRCAM is based). As in Andriessen's piece, the thematic material "hockets" in medieval fashion from one instrument to another; there are climaxes reminiscent of *Ringed by the Flat Horizon* and a similar coda in the strings, but *Antara* is absolutely distinctive and original and redirects Benjamin's attention away from chordal writing and toward a more polyphonic style that recentres his whole approach on the earliest Western music. So expensive is *Antara* to programme that Benjamin has decided to make a tape version of the electronic part—reluctantly, since the whole rationale was to humanise and invigorate electronic resources.

Cascade for orchestra takes him even further beyond the

chordal and allusive style of *Ringed by the Flat Horizon*. Benjamin insists that the title refers not to any actual physical waterfall but to the way in which the work is constructed and received; it is nonetheless interesting that he should have picked a title with some resonance in English Romanticism, rather than something from the natural sciences. The basic material—as in a waterfall—is absolutely simple, but indistinguishable as such from the overall movement of parts and virtually undetectable in isolation. So free is the material from the usual harmonic functions that it can be deployed across the entire rhythmic spectrum, from the lowest to highest registers, varying in speed and duration, breaking bar lines, being shared by instruments (an echo of the "hocketing" approach), discriminated only by the very largest parameters of the music. It is an astonishing achievement—one is tempted to add: for so young a composer—and points the way forward for Benjamin. No longer easily categorised either as a disciple of Messiaen or an interesting prodigy, he is likely to be one of the most distinctive and representative composers of the 1990s.

—James Weir

BENNETT, Richard Rodney. British/English; resident in U.S.A. since 1979. Born in Broadstairs, Kent, 29 March 1936. Educated at Leighton Park School, Reading; Royal Academy of Music, London (under Lennox Berkeley and Howard Ferguson), 1953–6; studied in Paris (under Pierre Boulez), 1957–9. Pianist; professor of composition, Royal Academy of Music, London, 1963–5; composer in residence, Peabody Institute, Baltimore, Maryland, 1970–1. Member of general council, Performing Rights Society, since 1975; vice-president, Royal College of Music, London, since 1983. Recipient: Arnold Bax Society Prize, 1964; Ralph Vaughan Williams Award for composer of the year, 1965; SFTA Award (for *Murder on the Orient Express*), 1975; also Ivor Novello Award and Academy Award nomination (for same work), 1976; C.B.E., 1977. Mailing address: The Endicott, 101 West 81st Street, Apartment 204, New York, New York, 10024, U.S.A.

Publishers: Novello; Universal Edition.

Symphonies/orchestral:

Horn Concerto 1955–6; first performed London, 18 February 1967.
Five Pieces 1956; first performed Darmstadt, 13 July 1956.
Music for an Occasion 1959; first performed London, 4 June 1959.
Journal 1960; first performed Cheltenham, Gloucestershire, 13 July 1961.
Suite française (small orchestra) 1961; first performed Cardiff, Wales, 22 October 1961.
Nocturnes (chamber orchestra) 1962–3; first performed Vancouver, March 1963.
Aubade 1964; first performed London, 11 September 1964. Recorded Argo ZRG 907.
Symphony No 1 1965; first performed London, 10 February 1966. Recorded RCA Victor SB 6730.
Suite (small orchestra) 1965.
Symphony No 2 1967; first performed New York City, 18 January 1968.
Piano Concerto 1968; first performed Birmingham, 19 September 1968. Recorded Philips 6500 301.
Oboe Concerto (string orchestra) 1969–70; first performed Snape, Suffolk, 6 June 1971.
Guitar Concerto (chamber orchestra) 1970; first performed London, 18 November 1970. Recorded RCA SB 6876; RCA ARC 3 0997.
Intrada (collaborative piece for 70th birthday of Sir William Walton) 1970; first performed London 29 March 1972.
Viola Concerto (chamber orchestra) 1973; first performed York, 3 July 1977.
Concerto for Orchestra 1973; first performed Denver, Colorado, 25 February 1974.
Violin Concerto 1975; first performed Birmingham, 25 March, 1976.
Zodiac 1975–6; first performed Washington, D.C., 30 March 1976.
Serenade (small orchestra) 1976; first performed London, 24 April 1977.
Actaeon (horn, orchestra) 1977; first performed London, 12 August 1977.
Music for Strings 1977; first performed Cheltenham, Gloucestershire, 7 July 1978.
Double Bass Concert (chamber orchestra) 1978; first performed London, 15 October 1978.
Sonnets to Orpheus (cello, orchestra; inspired by Rilke) 1978–9; first performed Edinburgh, 3 September 1979.
Harpsichord Concerto 1980; first performed St Louis, Missouri, 4 December 1980.
Anniversaries 1982; first performed London, 9 September 1982.
Freda's Fandango (80th birthday present to Sir Lennox Berkeley) 1982; first performed Cheltenham, Gloucestershire, 2 July 1983.
Memento (flute, strings) 1983; first performed London, 10 November 1983.
Sinfonietta 1984; first performed St Ives, Cambridgeshire, 10 February 1985.
Moving into Aquarius (collaboration with Thea Musgrave, in celebration of Sir Michael Tippett's 80th birthday) 1984; first performed London, 23 January 1985.
Morning Music (symphonic wind ensemble) 1986; first performed Boston, 25 July 1986.
Symphony No 3 1987; first performed Worcester, 24 August 1987.
Clarinet Concerto (clarinet, string orchestra) 1987; first performed Keele, Staffordshire, 15 February 1988.
Saxophone Concerto (alto saxophone, string orchestra) 1988; first performed London, 14 October 1988. Recorded Hyperion, release 1991.
Marimba Concerto (chamber orchestra) 1988; first performed Allentown, Pennsylvania, 11 March 1988.

Chamber/instrumental:

String Quartet No 1 1951.
Variations (oboe) 1953; first performed London, 23 January 1953.
String Quartet No 2 1953; first performed London, 5 October 1954.
String Quartet No 3 1953; first performed London, 1 February 1955.
Sonata (piano) 1954; first performed London, 1954.
Sonatina (flute) 1954; first performed London, 1 March 1955.

Four Improvisations (violin) 1955; first performed London, 4 December 1956.
Sonata No 1 (violin) 1955, revised 1961; broadcast BBC 10 March 1963.
Sonata (cello) 1955.
Sonata (viola) 1955.
Parallels (trumpet, piano) 1955.
Cycle for Piano I–IX 1956–7; first performed Paris, 25 January 1958.
Studies for Five Instruments (flute, oboe, violin, clarinet, alto saxophone) 1957; first performed Dartington, 15 August 1957.
Study (trumpet, piano) 1957; first performed Aldeburgh, Suffolk, 21 June 1957.
Theme and Variations (violin, viola) 1957; lost.
Music for Two Pianos 1957–8; first performed London, 6 June 1957; (complete) Darmstadt, 7 September 1958.
Cycle II for Paul Jacobs (piano) 1958; first performed Paris, April 1958.
Stanzas (flute) 1959.
Calendar (flute/piccolo, clarinet, bassoon, trumpet, trombone, timpani, percussion, violin, viola, cello) 1960; first performed London, 24 November 1960. Recorded HMV ASD 640; Argo ZRG 704.
Stanzas (organ) 1960; first performed London, 13 December 1960.
Winter Music (flute, piano) 1960; first performed London, 8 January 1961. Recorded Delta SDEC 18005.
Sonata (oboe, piano) 1961; first performed London, 8 January 1962.
Quintet (clarinet, string trio, piano) 1961–2; first performed March 1962.
Fanfare (brass quintet) 1962; first performed Devizes, Wiltshire, 24 November 1963. Recorded Argo ZRG 851.
Fantasy (piano) 1962; first performed Coventry, Warwickshire, 7 June 1962.
Five Studies (piano) 1962–4; first performed London, 27 October 1964. Recorded Philips 4FM 10002.
Rondo (flute, bassoon, viola, harp; collaborative "Reflections on a Theme of Benjamin Britten") 1963; first performed London, 25 October 1963.
A Jazz Calendar (flute, alto saxophone, tenor saxophone, baritone saxophone, 2 trumpets, horn, trombone/bass trumpet, tuba, piano, bass, drums) 1964; broadcast BBC, 5 June 1964. Recorded Philips 6500 301.
Trio (3 violins; 2 violins, viola) 1964.
Sonata No 2 (violin) 1964; first performed London, 29 January 1965.
Trio (flute, oboe, clarinet) 1965; first performed Zagreb, 1965.
A Canon for Stravinsky (string trio) 1967; first performed Cheltenham, Gloucestershire, 15 July 1967.
Quintet (flute, oboe, clarinet, horn in F, bassoon) 1967–8; first performed London 17 March 1968.
Capriccio (piano, 4 hands) 1968; first performed London, 25 February 1969.
Impromptu (guitar) 1968; first performed Blythburgh, 11 June 1969. Recorded RCA RL 25419.
Impromptu (flute) 1969; first performed London, 22 April 1969. Recorded UE 15043.
Madrigals (2 pianos) 1970–1; first performed Baltimore, Maryland, 4 February 1971.
Commedia I (flute, bass clarinet, alto saxophone, trumpet, cello, percussion) 1972; first performed Oxford, 16 April 1972.
Commedia II (flute, cello, piano) 1972; first performed New York City, 5 April 1973.
Commedia III (flute/piccolo, oboe, cor anglais, clarinet, horn, trumpet, percussion, piano/celeste, violin, cello) 1973; first performed London, 25 February 1973.
Alba (organ) 1973; first performed Bradford, Yorkshire, 3 November 1973. Recorded Vista VPS 1034.
Scena I (piano) 1973; first performed Lancaster, 3 April 1974.
Scena II (cello) 1973; first performed Bangor, Wales, 25 April 1974.
Commedia IV (brass quintet) 1974; first performed London 27 April 1974. Recorded Argo ZRG 713.
Four Piece Suite (2 pianos) 1974; first performed London, 31 August 1974. Recorded EMI EC 749116.
Quartet (oboe, string trio) 1974–5; first performed King's Lynn, Norfolk, 28 July 1975.
Telegram (piano) 1976; first performed London, 9 July 1976. Recorded Pearl SHE 537.
Kandinsky Variations (2 pianos) 1977; first performed London, 1 December 1977.
Scena III (clarinet) 1977; first performed London, 13 January 1978.
Sonata (horn, piano) 1978; first performed Edinburgh, 8 September 1979.
Sonata (violin, piano) 1978; first performed London, 17 January 1979.
Metamorphoses (4 violins, 2 violas, 2 cellos; based on a theme from Thea Musgrave's *String Quartet*, 1958) 1980; first performed Fishguard, Wales, 21 July 1980.
Six Tunes for the Instruction of Singing Birds (flute) 1981; first performed Burnham Market, Norfolk, 15 August 1981.
Music for String Quartet 1981; first performed Portsmouth, Hampshire, 29 March 1982.
Impromptu on the Name of Haydn (piano) 1981; broadcast BBC, 31 March 1982.
Sonatina (clarinet) 1981; first performed Newcastle-upon-Tyne, 31 March 1983.
After Syrinx I (oboe, piano; based on Debussy) 1982; first performed Seaton, Devon, 13 October 1983.
Concerto (wind quintet) 1983; first performed London, 15 August 1984.
Memento (flute, string ensemble) 1983; first performed Windsor, Berkshire, 28 September 1983.
Sonata (guitar) 1983; first performed Cheltenham, Gloucestershire, 17 July 1985.
Serenade II (ondes martenot, piano) 1984; first performed Little Missenden, Buckinghamshire, 11 October 1984.
After Syrinx II (marimba; based on Debussy) 1984, revised 1985; first performed New York City, 21 May 1985.
Sounds and Sweet Airs (flute, oboe, piano) 1985; first performed Chapel Hill, North Carolina, 26 April 1986.
Sonata After Syrinx (flute, viola, harp) 1985; first performed London, 20 May 1986.
Duo Concertante (clarinet, piano) 1985; first performed Cheltenham, Gloucestershire, 17 July 1986.
Reflections on a Theme of William Walton (6 violins, 2 violas, 2 cellos, double bass) 1985; first performed London, 20 May 1985.
Romances (horn, piano) 1985; first performed London, 25 February 1986.
Tango after Syrinx (piano) 1985.
Tender Is the Night: Suite (ondes martenot, string quartet) 1985, arranged from incidental music to the television serial, 1986; first performed Little Missenden, Buckinghamshire, 18 October 1986.
Dream Dancing (flute, oboe/cor anglais, clarinet/bass clarinet, horn, trumpet, amplified harpsichord, piano/celeste, violin, viola, cello, double bass) 1985–6; first performed London, 23 May 1986.

Lamento d'Arianna (string quartet) 1986; first performed Bromsgrove, Worcestershire, 7 May 1986.
After Ariadne (viola, piano) 1986; first performed Cheltenham, Gloucestershire, 7 July 1987.
Sonata (soprano saxophone, piano) 1986; first performed London, 22 November 1988. Recorded Hyperion A66246.
Suite for Skip and Sadie (the composer's cats; piano) 1986; broadcast, in part, 17 May 1987.
Sonata (wind quintet, piano) 1986–7; first performed New York City, 21 April 1987.
Three Romantic Pieces (piano) 1988; first performed Birmingham, 28 October 1988.

Vocal/choral:

Put Away the Flutes (soprano, SATB chorus, orchestra; Rodgers) 1952.
Nocturnal upon St Lucie's Day (soprano, piano; Donne) 1954; first performed London, 19 October 1954.
The Tillaquils (unaccompanied SATB chorus; Riding) 1955; first performed London, 11 March 1956.
Three Songs (tenor; Villa) 1955; first performed London, 7 February 1959.
Ricercar (unaccompanied SATB chorus) 1956; first performed London, 1 May 1956.
Farewell to Arms (unaccompanied SSAATTBB chorus; Peele) 1959.
The Approaches of Sleep (soprano, alto, tenor, bass, flute, oboe, clarinet, bassoon, horn, trumpet, harp, violin, viola, cello) 1959–60; first performed London, 15 January 1961.
Lament (tenor, guitar; Tichbourne) 1960; first performed Ipswich, 21 June 1960.
This Worlde's Joie (soprano, piano; anon. 14th century) 1960; first performed London, 17 November 1960.
Tom O'Bedlam's Song (tenor, cello) 1961; first performed Edinburgh, 22 November 1961. Recorded Argo ZRG 5475.
Childe Rolande to the Dark Tower Came (speaker, piano; Browning) 1961; first performed 9 January 1962.
Three Madrigals (unaccompanied SATB chorus; Jonson, anon.) 1961; first performed London, 6 March 1962.
London Pastoral (tenor, chamber orchestra; Wordsworth, Lydgate, Binyon, Griffin) 1962; first performed London, 13 July 1962.
Three Elegies (unaccompanied SSAATTBB chorus; Webster) 1962.
Nowell, Nowell, Tidings True (unaccompanied SATB chorus; anon. 15th century) 1963.
Two Lullabies (unaccompanied SSA chorus; Wedderburns) 1963; first performed London, 1963. Recorded Abbey XMS 727; LPS 764.
The Sorrows of Mary (unaccompanied SSATB chorus; anon., 15th century) 1964; first performed London, December 1964. Recorded Argo ZRG 5499.
Verses (unaccompanied SATB chorus; Donne) 1964; first performed London, 1965. Recorded Abbey LPB 783.
One Evening (tenor, guitar; Auden) 1964. Recorded Jupiter JUR 0A10.
Epithalamion (SATB chorus, orchestra; Herrick) 1966; first performed Leeds, 15 April 1967.
Soliloquy (voice, alto saxophone, tenor saxophone, trumpet, trombone, piano, bass, drums; Mitchell) 1966–7; first performed London, 4 March 1967.
Five Carols (unaccompanied SATB chorus; anon. 16th and 17th century) 1967; first performed Northampton, 23 September 1967. Recorded Abbey LPB 655.
The Music That Her Echo Is (tenor, piano; Dyer, Campion, anon. 16th century) 1967; first performed London, 6 October 1967.
Two Carols (soprano, alto, tenor, bass, SATB chorus; Herrick, anon. 15th century) 1968; first performed London, 12 December 1968; Broadstairs, Kent, 22 December 1968.
Crazy Jane (soprano, clarinet, piano; Yeats) 1968; first performed London, 17 June 1969.
Jazz Pastoral (jazz singer, alto saxophone, tenor saxophone, baritone saxophone, 2 trumpets, horn, trombone, piano, double bass, drums; Herrick) 1969; first performed London, 15 June 1970.
A Garland for Marjory Fleming (soprano, piano) 1969; first performed Edinburgh, 2 December 1970.
Four Devotions (unaccompanied SATB chorus; Donne) 1971.
Funny Thing (soprano, piano) 1971.
The House of Sleepe (2 counter-tenors, tenor, 2 baritones, bass; Ovid/Golding) 1971; first performed London, 18 January 1971. Recorded EMI EMD 5521.
She Reminds Me of You (soprano, piano) ?1971.
Tenebrae (baritone, piano; various) 1971; first performed London, 10 August 1974.
Sonnet Sequence (tenor, string orchestra; Shakespeare) 1972; first performed London, 23 April 1972.
Nightpiece (soprano, tape; Baudelaire) 1972; broadcast BBC, 23 May 1972.
Quietly with Bright Eyes (voice, piano, tape; cummings) 1972; first performed Manchester, 16 November 1972.
Time's Whiter Scenes (counter-tenor, lute; various) 1974; first performed Aldeburgh, Suffolk, 6 June 1975.
Spells (soprano, SATB chorus, orchestra; Raine) 1974–5; first performed Worcester, 28 August 1975. Recorded Argo ZRG 907.
The Little Ghost Who Died for Love (soprano, piano; Sitwell) 1976; first performed London, 31 January 1977.
First Thing About Me (soprano, piano) 1977; first performed Bath, 1978.
Let's Go and Live in the Country (soprano, piano) 1978. Recorded CUBE Hifly 28.
Our Own Kind of Dancing (soprano, piano) 1979; first performed Edinburgh, September 1979.
Nonsense (SATB chorus, piano duet; Peake) 1979; first performed Chester, 18 July 1984.
Puer Nobis (unaccompanied SATB chorus; Meynell) 1980; first performed Aberdeen, 21 December 1980.
I Never Went Away (soprano, piano) 1980; first performed Bromsgrove, Worcestershire, May 1986.
Letters to Lindbergh (SA chorus, piano, 4 horns; compiled by Hall) 1981; first performed London, 16 May 1982.
Vocalise (soprano, piano; Hansen) 1981; first performed London, 1 March 1983.
Seachange (tenor, baritone, SATB chorus, 24 voices; Shakespeare, Spenser) 1981; first performed Worcester, 23 August 1984.
This Is the Garden (high voice, piano; cummings) 1984; first performed Brighton, Sussex, 14 May 1985.
Five Sonnets of Louise Labe (soprano, flute/piccolo, oboe, clarinet, bassoon, horn, harp, 2 violins, viola, cello, double bass) 1984; first performed Chester, 24 July 1984.
Lullaby Mine Liking (unaccompanied SATB chorus, optional soloists) 1984; first performed Broadstairs, Kent, 23 December 1984.
Love Songs (tenor, orchestra; cummings) 1984; first performed Manchester, 4 March 1986.
Nowel (unaccompanied SATB chorus; de la Mare) 1986; first performed Cambridge, 24 December 1986.
And Death Shall Have No Dominion (TTBB chorus, horn;

D. Thomas) 1986; first performed London, 7 July 1988.
Lullaby Baby (unaccompanied SATB chorus; Phillip) 1986.
Dream Songs (mezzo-soprano or unison voices, piano; de la Mare) 1986.
Ophelia (counter-tenor, ondes martenot, harp, 9 solo strings or string orchestra) 1987; first performed Cheltenham, Gloucestershire 17 July 1987.

Opera:

The Ledge (Mitchell) 1960–1; first performed London, 12 September 1961.
The Mines of Sulphur (Cross) 1963; first performed London, 24 September 1965.
Penny for a Song (Graham, after Whiting) 1966–7; first performed London, 31 October 1967.
Victory (Cross, after Conrad) 1968–9; first performed London, 13 April 1970.

Ballet:

Jazz Calendar (ballet; choreography by Ashton; flute, alto saxophone, tenor saxophone, baritone saxophone, 2 trumpets, horn, trombone, tuba, drums, piano, double bass) 1963–4.
Isadora (ballet; choreography by Macmillan) 1980; first performed London, 30 April 1981.
Noctuary (ballet; piano after Joplin; choreography by Macmillan) 1981; first performed Armidale, New South Wales, 3 June 1985.

Film, radio and television music:

Interpol/(U.S.)*Pickup Alley* (film score; Donen) 1956.
The World Accused (documentary film score) 1956.
A Face in the Night/(U.S.)*Menace in the Night* (film score; Comfort) 1956.
Song of the Clouds (documentary film score; Anstey) 1956.
The Safecracker (film score; Milland) 1957.
The Man Inside (film score; Gilling) 1958.
Indiscreet (film score; Donen) 1958.
The Angry Hills (film score; Aldrich) 1959.
The Man Who Could Cheat Death (film score) 1959.
Blind Date/(U.S.)*Chance Meeting* (film score; Losey) 1959.
Out of Harmony (documentary film score) 1960.
A Question of Springing (documentary film score) 1960.
The Devil Never Sleeps/(U.S.)*Satan Never Sleeps* (film score; McCray) 1961.
They Took Us to Sea (documentary film score) 1961.
The Purple Stream (documentary film score; Donner) 1961.
Only Two Can Play (film score; Gilliat) 1961.
The March (film score; Green) 1961.
African Awakening (documentary film score; Hopkinson) 1962.
Judith (music for theatre) 1962.
The Wrong Arm of the Law (film score; Owen) 1962.
The Long Distance Piano Player (music for radio play) 1962.
Billy Liar (film score; Schlesinger) 1963.
Heavens Above (film score; Boulting) 1963.
Stephen D (television soundtrack) 1963.
Hamlet at Elsinore (television soundtrack) 1963.
One Way Pendulum (film score; Yates) 1964.
Malatesta (television soundtrack) 1964.
The Engineers (film score; Armstrong) 1965.
Hereward the Wake (television soundtrack) 1965.
The Nanny (film score; Holt) 1965.
The Diary of Nijinsky (radio) 1965.
European Tapestry (film score; Gould) 1965.
Timon of Athens (incidental music to Shakespeare) 1965.
A Penny for Your Thoughts (film score) 1966.
The Order (television soundtrack) 1966.
The Witches/(U.S.)*The Devil's Own* (film score; Frankel) 1966.
Billion Dollar Brain (film score; Russell) 1967. Recorded UA ULP 1183.
Far from the Madding Crowd (film score; Schlesinger) 1967.
Dismissal Leading to Lustfulness (television soundtrack) 1967.
Secret Ceremony (film score; Losey) 1968.
Twenty Four Hours (television signature tune) 1969.
The Buttercup Chain (film score; Miller) 1970.
Figures in a Landscape (film score; Losey) 1970.
Nicholas and Alexandra (film score; Schaffner) 1971. Recorded Bell 202; Columbia TWO 388.
Lady Caroline Lamb (film score; Bolt) 1972. Recorded HMV CSD 3728; ASD 3797.
Of Jewels and Gold (documentary film score) 1973.
Murder on the Orient Express (film score; Lumet) 1974. Recorded EMI EMC 3054.
Permission to Kill (film score; Frankel) 1975.
Sherlock Holmes in New York (film score; Sagal) 1976.
Survival (television soundtrack) 1976.
Abide with Me (television soundtrack) 1976.
L'Imprécateur (film score; Bertuccelli) 1977.
Eustace and Hilda (television soundtrack) 1977.
The Christians (television soundtrack) 1977.
Equus (film score) 1977.
The Brinks Job (film score; Friedkin) 1978.
Yanks (film score; Schlesinger) 1979. Recorded HMV ASD 3797.
Arena: La Dame aux Gladiolas (television soundtrack) 1979.
The Return of the Soldier (film score; Bridge) 1982.
Poor Little Rich Girl (television soundtrack) 1982.
Knockback (television soundtrack) 1984.
The Ebony Tower (television soundtrack) 1984.
Tender Is the Night (television soundtrack) 1985. Recorded Hannibal 1331.
Murder with Mirrors (film score; Lowry) 1985.
The Entertainers (television soundtrack) 1986.
The Charmer (television soundtrack) 1987.
Strange Interlude (television soundtrack) 1987.
Talking Pictures (television signature tune) 1987–8.
The Attic: The Hiding of Anne Frank (television soundtrack) 1988.

For children:

A Week of Birthdays (piano) 1961. Recorded Jupiter jep OC 26.
The Midnight Thief (Mexican folk tale retold for young children by Ian Serraillier; music by Bennett) 1963; first performed London, 30 March 1963. Recorded HMV DLP 1216.
Oxford Nursery Song Book 1964. Recorded Jupiter jep OC 31.
Farnham Festival Overture (orchestra) 1964; first performed Farnham, Surrey, 18 May 1964. Recorded Waverley LLp 1039.
Diversions (piano; clarinet) 1964.
Conversations (2 flutes) 1965.
The Insect World (unison voices/solo voice, piano; Clare, Oldys, Marvell) 1965; first performed London, 17 January 1966. Recorded HMV 7EG 8943; Unicorn RHS 316.
Crosstalk (2 clarinets, 2 bassett horns) 1966; first performed

Dartington, August 1966. Recorded Discourses All About Music ABM 24.
The Aviary (voices, piano) 1966; first performed London, 17 January 1966. Recorded HMV 7EG 8943.
All the King's Men (opera) 1968; first performed Coventry, Warwickshire, 28 March 1969. Recorded Abbey XMS 703.
Party Piece (piano, small orchestra) 1970; first performed Farnham, Surrey, 15 May 1971.
The Bermudas (high voices, tenor, chorus, orchestra; Marvell) 1971; first performed Reading, 20 May 1972.
Travel Notes I (string quartet) 1975.
Travel Notes II (flute, oboe, clarinet, 4 saxophones) 1975.
Up Bow, Down Bow I & II (violin, piano) 1979.
Summer Music (flute, piano) 1982; first performed London, 23 November 1982.

PUBLICATIONS

By Bennett: "In Search of Boulez", in *Music and Musicians* 1962–3; translator of Boulez's *Penser La Musique Aujourd'hui*, as *Boulez on Music Today*, London, 1971.

On Bennett: Nicholas Maw, "RRB", in *Musical Times*, 103, 1962; Christopher Palmer and Lewis Foreman, "RRB", in *British Music Now*, London, 1975.

* * *

Despite the fact that he has chosen to express himself in a language developed from, though no longer hinging upon, the Schoenbergian twelve-note row, the general tenor of Richard Rodney Bennett's music owes at least as much to a turn-of-the-century Englishness as it does to any central European tradition.

Gifted with an exceptional facility, he could well have opted for the temptingly fashionable internationalism of the 1950s, but his flirtation with avant-garde techniques lasted no more than the couple of years he spent as a student of Boulez in Paris. It was nevertheless the enriching effect of this experience that enabled him to pick up the stylistic threads of his teenage *Sonata* for piano in a series of works in which the essentially melodic basis of the twelve-note row was expanded to include ideas on harmonic proliferation learnt from Boulez. Dating from the early 1960s, *Five Studies* for piano make for interesting comparison as early evidence both of a distinctly more personal approach to serialism and of a musical vocabulary that, in essence, was to serve his expressive needs for the next 20 years or so.

It was not until 1979 that the keyboard ballet, *Noctuary*, signalled a perceptible change of direction in Bennett's music—serving both as a landmark and as a prelude to the stylistic developments of the 1980s. Setting out to explore the harmonic relationships between the strictly tonal world of the Scott Joplin piece it takes as its starting point and the strictly serial one of Bennett's own music, the work is an extended transformation, a series of slow-moving harmonic dissolves that shape the course of the musical journey from one extreme to the other. But it was *After Syrinx I* that seems finally to have provided the spur for a more permanent loosening of harmonic controls: here, the tonality of Debussy's "Syrinx" is not so much transformed as effortlessly absorbed into what Bennett has called a "more-or-less" serial texture—thus paving the way for *Memento* for flute and strings, in which a freely-composed theme creates its own harmonic reflections, and for *Love Songs*, where, conversely, an initial chord sequence yields corresponding melodic images. While in each case the influence of serial relationships was (and remains) undiminished, Bennett's newly atonal harmony had freed itself once and for all from the constrictions imposed by the need to avoid pitch repetition.

Since then, he has continued to widen the bounds of his neo-serial writing, reintroducing previously exluded elements (such as octaves and tonal chords) and devising wholly new and increasingly more flexible ways of applying serial techniques to the freely-evolving harmony specific to the expressive purpose of each succeeding work. Many of his recent works include quotation, employed either as an integral strand in the musical development (as in *Noctuary*, but also in *Reflections on a Theme of William Walton*), or as a starting point (the two pieces based on a madrigal by Monteverdi, and the five on Debussy's "Syrinx"—including *Dream Dancing*, in which the same composer's "Masques" is used as the rhythmic skeleton of the second movement).

No other composer has done more to develop the stylistic middle ground of 20th-century music—an area widely ignored throughout the 1950s and 1960s—or, incidentally, to encourage its listeners. As an extremely able pianist, equally adept in a wide variety of styles, he enjoys communicating through performance. As a composer whose works span the whole spectrum of compositional endeavour without ever reaching for emotional bounds that exceed the limits of common experience, let alone striving to shock, or merely to astonish, his music fulfils a real need, attracting audiences (and, indeed, performers) world-wide—whether for his operas, his orchestral works and virtuoso concertos, his sensitive and eminently singable vocal music, his outstanding chamber music, educational music, and his many memorable film scores.

—Susan Bradshaw

BENTZON, Niels Viggo. Danish. Born in Copenhagen, 24 August 1919. Educated: private study with jazz pianist Leo Mathisen, and with Karen Bentzon; Copenhagen Conservatoire (under Christiansen for piano, Jeppesen for theory, and Bargert for organ) 1938–43. Concert pianist, debut 1943; teacher, Aarhus Conservatoire, 1945–9; journalist/critic, *Politiken*. Recipient: numerous awards and honours. Mailing address: Egernvej 39, 2000 Copenhagen, Denmark.

Publisher: Wilhelm Hansen/Chester Music.

[An opus number does not always indicate that a work has been completed or published.]

Symphonies/orchestral:

Overture Op 14 (chamber orchestra) 1942; first performed Copenhagen, 18 August 1942.
Divertimento Op 19 (string orchestra) 1942.
Symphony No 1 Op 22 1943.
Orchestral Sonata Op 27 (flute, strings) 1944.
Symphony No 2 Op 36 (piano, orchestra) 1945.
Symphony No 3 Op 46 1947.
Concerto for Piano and Orchestra Op 49 1947–8; first performed Danish Radio, 18 November 1948.

Symphony No 4 "Metamorphoses" Op 55 1948; first performed Danish Radio, 23 February 1950.
Prelude and Rondo Op 56 (small orchestra) 1949.
Metaphor Op 58 (ballet suite) 1949; first performed Copenhagen, 30 March 1950.
Little Suite Op 60 (string orchestra) 1950.
Symphony No 5 "Ellipsen" 1950; first performed Copenhagen, 19 October 1950.
Intrada Op 64 1950.
Symphony No 6 Op 66 1950.
Concerto No 1 for Violin and Orchestra Op 70 1951.
Oboe Concerto Op 74 (oboe, strings) 1951.
Symphony No 7 "De 3 Versioner" Op 83 1951–2; first performed Copenhagen, 14 April 1953.
Variazioni breve Op 75 1952.
Piano Concerto No 3 Op 87 1952.
Symphonic Variations Op 92 1952; first performed Copenhagen, 12 June 1953.
Triple Concerto Op 94 (oboe, clarinet, bassoon, strings) 1953.
Concerto No 4 for Piano and Orchestra Op 96 1954; broadcast Copenhagen, 7 October 1954.
Symphonic Suite Op 101 1955.
Sinfonia Concertante Op 100 (clarinet, violin, 4 violas, 4 cellos, brass, timpani) 1955–6.
Concerto No 1 for Cello and Orchestra Op 106 1956; broadcast Copenhagen 29 August 1957.
Brilliantes Konzertino—Hommage à Mozart Op 108 1956.
Pezzi Sinfonici Op 109 1956; first performed Louisville, Kentucky, 1957. Recorded Louisville LOU-58-6.
Symphony No 8 Op 113 1957; first performed Odense, 21 January 1958.
Concerto per Archi Op 114 (1–5 violins, 1–2 violas, 1–2 cellos, double bass) 1957; first performed Copenhagen, 11 February 1963.
Konzert for Sechs Janitscharer Op 115 1958; first performed Copenhagen, 15 August 1958.
Concerto for Two Pianos and Orchestra Op 119 1958–63; first performed Malmo, Sweden, 10 March 1964.
Mutations Op 123 1959–60; first performed Alborg, 27 April 1960.
Five Mobiles Op 125 1960; first performed Aarhus, 9 September 1960.
Symphony No 9 Op 236 1960; first performed Odense, 29 May 1961.
Two Monkton Blues Op 127 (2 clarinets, 2 bass clarinets, winds, percussion, piano, double bass) 1960.
Rhapsody Op 131 (piano, orchestra) 1961; first performed Copenhagen, 18 May 1961.
Ostinato Op 133 1961; first performed U.S.A., February 1962.
Violin Concerto No 2 Op 136 1961; broadcast Copenhagen, 14 November 1963.
Overture Op 137 (small orchestra) 1961; first performed Copenhagen, 16 February 1962.
Sinfonia da camera Op 139 1962.
Concerto for Accordion and Orchestra Op 146 1962–3; first performed Copenhagen, 12 September 1963.
Concerto for Flute and Orchestra Op 147 1963; first performed Siegen, Germany, 8 October 1963.
Concerto for Orchestra Op 148 1963; first performed Gladsaxe, 11 October 1964.
Piano Concerto No 5 Op 149 1963; first performed Gothenburg, 11 November 1964.
Hommage à Jean Baptiste Lully Op 151 (ballet suite) 1963.
Symphony No 10 Op 150 1964; first performed Aarhus, 26 October 1964.
Suite for Foreigners Op 154 (Series of popular music 2) 1964; first performed Salerno, 25 July 1964,
Overture to "De Lystige Koner i Windsor" Op 155 (Series of popular music 3) 1964; broadcast Copenhagen, 14 April 1964.
Symphony No 11 "Salzburg" Op 158 1964; first performed Hamburg, 6 December 1965.
Symphony No 12 "Tunis" Op 166 1964; first performed Aarhus, 31 January 1966.
Copenhagen Concerto No 1 (Bach Compendium No 4) Op 167 (flute, horn, bassoon, harpsichord, strings) 1964; first performed Copenhagen, 31 August 1967.
Copenhagen Concerto No 2 (Bach Compendium No 5) Op 168 (violin, oboe, cello, harpsichord, strings) 1964; first performed Copenhagen, 31 August 1967.
Copenhagen Concerto No 3 (Bach Compendium No 6) Op 169 (piano, bassoon, viola, harpsichord, string orchestra) 1964; first performed Copenhagen, 31 August 1967.
[Copenhagen Concertos Nos 4, 5 and 6, Opp 170–2, not composed]
Concerto for Fiddle, Piano, and Percussion Op 176 1965; first performed Malmo, Sweden, 19 April 1966.
Sinfonia Concertante Op 178 (accordion ensemble, symphony orchestra) 1965; first performed Flensborg, Germany, 11 January 1967.
Symphony No 13 "Military" Op 181 1965; first performed Alborg, 2 February 1966.
Piano Concerto No 6 Op 195 1965–6; first performed Copenhagen, 2 June 1966.
Manfred Overture (Schumann Compendium) Op 220 1967; first performed Aarhus, 6 November 1967.
Symphonic Paraphrase of "Sorens Far Har Penge" Op 229 1968; first performed Copenhagen, 4 July 1968.
Parafrase over Aarhus Tappenstreg Op 230 1968.
Mini Symphony Op 231 1968; first performed Askov, 1 August 1968.
Piano Concerto No 7 Op 243 1968–9; first performed Copenhagen, 22 August 1969.
Ostre Gasvaerk No 2 Op 244 1969; first performed Copenhagen, 7 September 1969.
Chorus Daniensis No 2 Piece for Virtuoso Piano and Large Orchestra in Dano-Brazilian Style Op 247 1969; first performed Alborg, 9 September 1969.
Uddrag Op 266 1969–70; first performed Aarhus, 29 August 1970.
Formula Op 261 1970; first performed Graz, October 1970.
Busonism Op 267 (audio-visual concert piece for piano and orchestra) 1970–1; first performed Malmo, 4 May 1971.
Concerto for Clarinet and Orchestra Op 269 1970–1; first performed Copenhagen, 13 April 1972.
Overture and Epilogue to "Jenny von Westphalen" Op 270 1971; first performed Gothenburg, March 1971.
Epitaph for Igor Stravinsky (Stravinsky Compendium No 1) Op 272 1971; first performed Malmo, 4 May 1971.
Violin Concerto No 3 "The Paganini Concerto" Op (275) 1971.
Saltholm Op 294 1971.
Concerto for Viola and Orchestra Op 303 1972.
Suite as Far as Jazz-music Is Concerned Op 306 (big band) 1972.
Second Concerto for Cello and Orchestra Op 311 1973; first performed Alborg, 17 September 1975.
Pupitre 14 Op 339 1974.
Kronik om Rene Descartes Op 357 1975; broadcast Copenhagen, 26 February 1976.
Sonata Populare Op 364 (organ, 4 flutes, chamber strings) 1975.
Stills Op 367 (piano, symphony orchestra, big band) 1975.
Jazz at a Conservatory Op 371 (big band) 1975; first

performed Copenhagen, 21 November 1975.
Concerto for Tuba and Orchestra Op 373 1975.
Concerto No 4 for Violin and Orchestra Op 374 1975; first performed Copenhagen, 25 April 1976.
Concerto for Clarinet and Orchestra Op 375 1975.
Sinfonietta Op 378 (brass band) 1976.
Leipzigertage Op 383 (small concerto for piano and string orchestra) 1976.
Three Marches Op 387 1976; first performed Copenhagen, 12 October 1976.
Concerto No 2 for Flute and Orchestra Op 388 1976; first performed Aarhus, 25 October 1978.
Sinfonia concertante No 2 Op 390 1976.
Capriccio Op 396 (tuba, small orchestra) 1977; first performed Copenhagen, 24 June 1977.
Sinfonia Op 402 1977; first performed Sweden, 22 October 1978.
Punktum Finale Op 411 1978.
Concerto Barocco Op 419 (oboe, strings) 1978.
Knaldperle Op 421 1978.
In an Atmosphere of Italian Futurism Op 430 1979.
Symphony No 15 Op 432 1980.
Fragment Op 434 1980.
Variazioni senza Thema Op 438 (piano, orchestra) 1980.
Cello Concerto NBo 3 Op 444 1981.
Concerto for Horn and Orchestra Op 445 1981.
Concerto No 8 for Piano and Orchestra Op 450 1981.
Concerto No 5 for Violin and Orchestra Op 453 1983.
DSB Overture Op 469 (versions for brass band, military band, piano) 1984.
Concerto for Two Pianos and Orchestra Op 482 1985.
Concertino Op 483 (piano, woodwinds, percussion) 1985.
Concerto for Reduced String Section Op 488 (string orchestra) 1986.
Logumkluster-suite Op 505 1986.
Symphony No 16 Op 509 1987.
Symphony No 17 Op 522 1988; first performed Copenhagen, 30 May 1989.
Symphony No 18 Op 523 1988; first performed Tonder, Denmark, 1 December 1989.
Symphony No 19 Op 524 1988.
Symphony No 20 Op 525 1988.
Symphony No 21 Op 526 1988.
Symphony No 22 Op 527 1988.
Bolero II Op 535 (big band) 1989; first performed Copenhagen, 16 July 1989.
Concerto for Dizzy Op 547 (trumpet, orchestra) 1990.

Chamber/instrumental:

Klaverfantasi Op 1 (piano) 1939.
Klavermusik No 2: Allegro for Klaver Op 2 (piano) 1939.
(Seven) Smaa Klaverstykker [Klavermusik No 3] Op 3 (piano) 1939–40.
Sonata Op 4 (violin, piano) 1939.
(Eight) Studievariationer over en Dansk Folkevise Op 5 (flute) 1940.
Trio No 1 Op 6 (violin, viola, cello) 1940.
Klavermusik No 4 Op 7a (piano) 1941.
Klavermusik No 5 Op 7b (piano) 1941.
String Quartet No 1 Op 9 1941.
Musik Op (9) (violin, cello) 1941.
Toccata Op 10 (piano) 1941; first performed Copenhagen, 16 January 1942. Recorded LPWH 3015; HMV Z 276.
Sonatina Op 11 (piano) 1941.
Quintet Op 12 (flute, oboe, clarinet, bassoon, piano) 1942.
Prelude, Intermezzo and Fugue Op 13 (organ) 1942.
Rhapsody Op 15 (piano) 1942.
Suite and Variations Op 18 (violin) 1942.
Six Variations Op 17 (flute, piano) 1943.
Trio No 2 Op 20 (flute, oboe, piano) 1943.
Variations Op 21 (wind quintet) 1943.
Four Bagatelles Op 23 (piano) 1943.
Sonata No 2 Op 24 (violin, piano) 1943.
Trio Op 25 (piano, violin, cello) 1943.
Quartet Op 26 (flute, oboe/cor anglais, horn, bassoon) 1943.
Wind Quintet No 3 Op 29 1944.
Capriccietta Op 28 (violin, piano) 1945. Recorded Metronome MCEP 3064.
Sonata No 3 Op 30 (violin, piano) 1945.
Passacaglia Op 31 (piano) 1945. Recorded Odeon MOAK 30008.
Study Op 34 (double bass) 1945.
Prelude and Fugue Op 37 (piano) 1945.
Partita Op 38 (piano) 1945. Recorded HMV Z 7013–15.
Bagatelles Op 32 (string quartet) 1946.
Music for Seven Instruments Op 33 1946.
Musik Op (33) (violin, clarinet, cello, piano, guitar} 1946.
Square Root of Three Op 35 (violin, piano) 1946. Recorded Metronome MCEP 3069.
String Quartet No 2 Op 39 1946.
Sonata No 3 Op 44 (piano) 1946; broadcast Danish Radio, 30 December 1959. Recorded LPWH 3015; HMV Z 7030–31; HMV BLPC 2.
Concert Etude Op 40 (piano) 1947. Recorded HMV 7013–15.
Sonata No 1 Op (40) (piano) 1947.
Sonata No 2 Op 42 (piano) 1947. Recorded Odeon MOAK 30014.
Sonata No 1 Op 43 (cello, piano) 1947.
Dance Pieces Nos 1–3 Op 45 (piano) 1947–50; first performed Copenhagen, 12 March 1948. Recorded (No 1 and 2 "Valse subtile" and "Polonaise") Metronome MCEP 3069.
Sonata Op 47 (French horn, piano) 1947.
Two Pieces Op 41 (oboe, piano) 1948.
Five Inventions Op 50 (piano) 1948.
Chamber Concerto Op 52 (2 trumpets, clarinet, basson, double bass, percussion, 3 pianos) 1948. Recorded Fona M/S 9; HMV Z 7036–37.
Sonatina Op 53 (violin) 1948.
Sonata No 4 Op 57 (piano) 1948–9. Recorded Fona TF 117.
Quintet No 4 Op 59 (wind quintet) 1949.
Concert Etudes Nos 1–3 Op 48 (piano) 1950.
Sonata Op 63 (clarinet, piano) 1950.
Metamorphose over "Rullende Henad de Stovede Veje" (no opus number; piano) 1950; first performed Copenhagen, 1950.
Jazzhieroglyf (no opus number; 2 pianos) 1950; broadcast Danish Radio, 14 December 1950. Recorded Metronome CL 3002.
Musical Mosaic Op 54 (flute, violin, cello, piano) 1951. Recorded Triola TDLP 207.
Traesnit/Woodcuts Op 65 (piano) 1951. Recorded LPWH 3015; Recorded HMV KBLP 8.
Two Nocturnes Op 68 (piano) 1951.
Piccolo-Concerto Op 69 (piano, 2 violins, viola, cello, double bass) 1951.
Sonata Op 71 (cor anglais, piano) 1951; broadcast Copenhagen, 10 September 1951.
String Quartet No 3 Op 72 1951.
Sonata No 5 Op 77 (piano) 1951. Recorded Fona TF 117; HMV KALP 13.
Prologue, Rondo, Epilogue Op 78 (piano, 4 hands) 1951.
Sonata Op 73 (trumpet, piano) 1951–2.
Hornbaekiana Op 67 (violin, piano) 1952.

Bop Quintet Op 80 (wind quintet) 1952.
Trio Op 82 (trumpet, horn, trombone) 1952.
Duo Op 84 (violin, cello) 1952.
Capriccio Op 85 (piano) 1952.
Kaleidoscope Op 86 (piano) 1952.
Sonata No 6 Op 90 (piano) 1952.
Quartet Op 91 (flute, oboe, bassoon, piano) 1952–3.
Variations Op 93 (flute) 1953; first performed Copenhagen, 8 December 1953. Recorded Metronome MCLP 85024.
Elegy Op 88 (violin, viola, cello, double bass, clarinet, bassoon) 1954.
String Quartet No 4 Op 95 1954.
Pentachord Op 97 (piano) 1954.
Theme with Variations Op 98 (violin, cor anglais, cello) 1954; first performed Copenhagen, 15 October 1954.
Pezza Op 99a (12 pianos) 1954.
Fantasy and Rondo Op 99b (flute, piano) 1955.
Variations Op 103 (organ) 1955; first performed Copenhagen, 22 February 1956. Recorded Fona TF 132.
Sonata Op 51 (2 pianos) 1956.
Sonata Op 110 (cello) 1956.
Twelve Preludes Op 112 (piano) 1956–7; first performed Copenhagen, 7 November 1957.
Nine Pieces Op 111 (violin, viola) 1958; broadcast Copenhagen, 18 June 1958.
Concert for Six Percussionists Op 115 1958; Copenhagen, 15 August 1958. Recorded Point P 5008.
Quintet No 5 Op 116 (flute, oboe/cor anglais, clarinet, horn in F, bassoon) 1958.
Sonata Op 117 (piano, 4 hands) 1958; first performed Louisiana, Humlebaek, 17 August 1958.
Trio Op 118 (violin, cello, piano) 1958; first performed Copenhagen, 13 October 1958.
Sonata No 7 Op 121 (piano) 1959.
Sonata No 4 Op 122 (violin, piano) 1959; first performed Paris, 1960.
String Quartet No 6 Op 124 1960; first performed New York, 14 October 1960. Recorded Fona TF 126.
Propostae Novae Op 129 (2 pianos) 1960; first performed Copenhagen, 21 November 1961. Recorded Louisiana LPLP 3007.
Quintet Op 130 (flute, violin, viola, cello, piano) 1960–1; first performed Copenhagen, 12 March 1961.
Trio Op 134 (clarinet, cello, piano) 1961; first performed Copenhagen, 4 May 1962.
Epitaph Op 140 (piano) 1962.
Papuanerdans Op 142 (2 pianos) 1962.
Sonatine Op 143 (2 pianos) 1962; first performed Copenhagen, 6 March 1963.
Three Choral Pieces Op 145 (organ) 1962; first performed Copenhagen, 27 February 1963.
Suite for Foreigners Op 154 (also version for 2 pianos) 1964.
Das Tempererede Klaver Op 157 (piano; Bach compendium No 1) 1964; first performed Copenhagen, 12 May 1965. Recorded Fona LPK 540–41.
Fifteen Two-Part Inventions (Bach compendium 2) Op 159 (piano) 1964; first performed Stockholm, 15 January 1965.
Fifteen Three-Part Inventions (Bach Compendium 3) Op 160 (piano) 1964; first performed Stockholm, 15 January 1965.
Dukkens Menuet and Other Piano Miniatures for Young People Op 161 1964.
Two Vignettes Op 162 (piano) 1964.
Three Spanish Genre Pieces Op 163 (piano) 1964.
In the Zoo Op 164 (accordion) 1964. Recorded Hohner LP 3004.
Quartet No 7 Op 165 (string quartet) 1964; first performed Leningrad, February 1965.
Two Frederiksberg Suites Op 173–4 (piano) 1965; first performed Copenhagen, 26 April 1966.
Ten Small Preludes (Bach compendium 12) Op 175 (piano) 1965.
Third Stream Music Op 179 (piano, alto saxophone, double bass, trumpet, percussion) 1965; first performed Copenhagen, 4 September 1965. Recorded Fona LPJ 542.
Montmartre Concerto Op (179) (piano) 1965; first performed Copenhagen, 16 May 1965.
Sonatina (Bach compendium 13) Op 180 (descant recorder, harpsichord) 1965; first performed Borssalen, 20 August 1967.
Henry Miller Suite Op 182 (cello) 1965.
Sonata No 5 Op 183 (violin, piano) 1965.
Mycelie: Mycological Suite Op 186 (organ) 1965; first performed Copenhagen, 1 December 1965.
Jern Op 187 (music for Robert Jacobsen's radio play; piano, prepared piano, harpsichord) 1965; broadcast 28 November 1965.
Trivielle Synonymer Op 188 (harmony instrument) 1965.
Tojmusik Op 189 ("happening" for harmony instrument) 1965.
Bevarede Monumenter Op 190 ("happening" for piano, prepared piano, harpsichord, lights, etc) 1965.
Glarmesterattituder Op 191 1965.
Sonata No 8 "Faust sonata" Op 193 (piano) 1965; first performed Copenhagen, 26 April 1966.
Sonata No 9 Op 194 (piano) 1965; first performed Copenhagen, 26 April 1966.
Quintet Op 196 (piano, string quartet) 1966.
Poetic Sonatina Op 200 (oboe) 1966.
Ecossaises Op 202 (piano) 1966.
Trio Op 203 (violin, viola, cello) 1966.
Sonata No 10 Op 204 (piano) 1966.
Meddelse og Landskab Op 205 (piano) 1966; first performed Charlottenborg, 6 November 1966.
Ballade (Chopin compendium 1) Op 210 (piano) 1967.
Fantasy-Impromptu Op 211 (flute) 1967; first performed Carlsberg, 5 March 1967.
Six Valses Nobles et Sentimentales (Chopin compendium 2) Op 212 (piano) 1967.
Cinq mazurkas Délicieuses (Chopin compendium 3) Op 213 (piano) 1967.
Huit Nocturnes en couleurs (Chopin compendium 4) Op 214 (piano) 1967.
Barcarole (Chopin compendium 5) Op 215 (piano) 1967.
Sept Etudes (Chopin compendium 6) Op 216 (piano) 1967.
Camp Duo Op 217 (flute, cello) 1967; first performed Louisiana, 15 July 1967.
Scherzo (Chopin compendium 7) Op 218 (piano) 1967.
Rondo amoroso (Chopin compendium 8) Op 219 (piano) 1967.
Columbus Eier "Salz und Pfeffer" Op 221 (accordion) 1967.
Europaeisk Form og Koda (Falla compendium 1) Op 222 (piano/Spanish guitar) 1967.
Sonata No 2 Op 223 (cello, piano) 1967.
Pièce héroique (Saint Saens compendium 1) Op 224 (3 pianos) 1967.
Explosions Op 227 (2 pianos) 1967; first performed Copenhagen, 13 March 1968.
String Quartet No 8 "Dartmouth Quartet" Op 228 1968. Recorded Caprice CAP 1100.
String Quartet No 9 Op 232 1968.
Toccata, Aria and Fugue Op 233 (organ) 1968; first performed Copenhagen, 18 August 1968.
Aria con variazioni Op 234 (spinet) 1968.
Maximilian I Op 235 (violin, piano) 1968.

Kanonfotografen Op 236 (viola, piano) 1968.
Duet Op 237 (viola, organ) 1968.
In the Forest Op 239 (horn) 1968.
Paganini Variations Op 241 (piano) 1968. Recorded LPWH 3015.
Mozart Variations Op 242 (2 pianos) 1969.
"Bonner" Sonata Op 245 (piano) 1969.
Vibrations Op 246 (prepared piano) 1969.
Hoffmann Sonata Op 248 (piano) 1969.
Chorus Daniensis Op 249 (suite in 5 movements for beat group) 1969.
Vibrations Op 250 (second version; prepared piano) 1969.
Psyko-biologisk Musikmateriale Op (251) (synthetic suite from other pieces by NVB) 1969.
Sange uden Ord I–IV Op 252 (piano) 1969.
Comédie Italienne I–III Op 253 (piano) 1969.
Serapionsbroderne I–VI Op 254 (piano) 1969.
Kukkassen / Eight Snapshots Op 256 (piano) 1969.
Klavermosaik (no opus number; piano) 1969–70.
Sonata Op 257 (oboe, flute, clarinet, bassoon, horn, trumpet, trombone, piano, violin, viola, cello, double bass) 1970; first performed Copenhagen, 10 September 1970.
Duarder Op 259 (accordion, percussion) 1970; first performed Aarhus, 1970.
Trio Op 260 (clarinet, cello, piano) 1970.
Napoleon Sonata Op 263 (piano) 1970.
Rossini Sonata Op 264 (piano) 1970.
Devrient Sonata Op 265 (piano) 1970.
Sonatina in B Op (266) (piano or harpsichord, 4 hands) 1970.
Sonata No 3 Op 268 (cello, piano) 1971; first performed Copenhagen, 11 May 1971.
Julienne Op 271 (cello, piano) 1971.
Pavane (Stravinsky compendium 2 Op 273 (piano) 1971.
Grosses Trio Op 274 (flute, cello, piano) 1971; first performed Skive, Denmark, 8 March 1972.
Tyrkiet Op 275 (cartographic sonatas for piano) 1971.
Sonata Op 277 (trombone, piano) 1971; first performed U.S.A., 1 March 1972.
Sextet Op 278 (flute, oboe, clarinet, horn in F, bassoon, piano) 1971; first performed Esbjerg, 31 March 1972.
Sonata No 6 Op 280 (violin, piano) 1971; first performed Copenhagen, 16 May 1972.
Hommage à Picasso Op 281 (piano) 1971.
Hommage à Cesar Franck Op 282 (flute, piano) 1971; first performed Copenhagen, 13 March 1972.
Tekstsonate Op 284 (piano) 1972.
Suite royale Op 286 (flute, oboe, clarinets, tuba/euphonium, horn, cornets, trumpets, tenor horn, trombone, tuba, 2 percussion) 1972; first performed Copenhagen, 12 December 1972.
Emil Kraepelin: Characterological Study Op 287 (violin) 1972; first performed Copenhagen, 16 May 1972.
Sonata No 4 Op 289 (cello, piano) 1972; first performed Berlin, 9 May 1972.
Statics Op 290 (cello) 1972; first performed Berlin, 9 May 1972.
Organon Phlenomegno Germanico Op 291 (piano) 1972; first performed Berlin, 9 May 1972.
Melodia e ritmica Op 292 (accordion) 1972.
Variazioni puristica Op 293 (piano) 1972; first performed Copenhagen, 16 May 1972.
Otto von Guericke Suite; A Naturalistic Portrait Op 295 (piano) 1972; first performed Copenhagen, 1 May 1972.
Referater Op 296 (piano) 1972.
Substans Op 297 (piano) 1972.
Benyttet Afslutning pa en Koncert Op 298 (piano) 1972.
Huegens Op 300 (organ) 1972; unfinished.
Trio Op 301 (flute, harpsichord, piano) 1972.
Charming Sound (organ, harmonium, vibraphone, celeste, piano, flute, saxophone, cello) 1972.
From My London Diary Op 312 (piano) 1972.
Sonata Op 314 (flute, piano) 1972.
Dokumenta 5 No 2 Op 315 (piano) 1972; first performed Gothenburg, Sweden, 23 October 1972.
Sonata Op 316 (bassoon, piano) 1972.
Sydsjaellandske Sonater Op 317 (piano) 1972.
Suite Op 318 (cello, piano) 1972; first performed Copenhagen, 27 March 1973.
Sonata Op 319 (fiddle, piano) 1972; first performed Copenhagen, 28 March 1973.
After-Dinner Concert Op 305 (piano) 1973.
Sonata Op 320 (alto saxophone, piano) 1973; first performed Copenhagen, 30 March 1974. Recorded KontraPunkt 32017.
Preludes 2 Op 321 (piano) 1973; first performed Copenhagen, 27 March 1973.
Suite Op 322 (violin, piano) 1973; first performed Copenhagen, 28 March 1973.
Micro-macro Op 323 (piano) 1973.
Study on the G String "Paganini" Op 324 (violin) 1973; first performed Copenhagen, 28 March 1973.
Soloelement Op 325 (piano) 1973.
Sonata "The Italian" Op 326 (piano) 1973.
Duo concertante Op 327 (violin, piano) 1973; first performed Copenhagen, 1 August 1973.
Wittgenstein Op 329 (violin, piano) 1973.
Three Sonatas and Three Partitas Op 330 (violin) 1973; first performed Copenhagen, 24 November 1974.
Dar Es Salem Op 331 (fiddle, heterophonic piano) 1973.
Sechs Beschreibungen Op 332 (cello) 1973; first performed Stockholm, 6 October 1974.
Observations: Psycho-Biological Suite Op 333 (flute, oboe, piano) 1973; first performed Copenhagen, 29 April 1974.
Bones and Flesh Op 334 (concerto for 2 pianos) 1973; first performed Copenhagen, 29 April 1974.
Sonata No 12 Op 336 (piano) 1973; first performed Copenhagen, 29 April 1974.
Hsaerfuglen Op 337 (flute, oboe, clarinet, horn, double bass, saxophone) 1974.
String Quartet No 10 Op 338 1974.
Quartetto Sonare Op 340 (recorder, oboe, viola da gamba, spinet) 1974; first performed Copenhagen, 14 October 1975.
Pianisten og Proteserne Op 341 (piano, electronics) 1974.
Duettino Op 343 (alto flute, cor anglais) 1974.
Happy Birth-Day Op 344 (piano) 1974.
Quartetto I Op 345 (4 flutes) 1974; first performed Fuglsang, Denmark, 22 September 1974. Recorded BASF RLP 5002.
Sonata No 13 Op 348 (piano) 1974.
Fuglsangsuite Op (348) (piano) 1974.
Organisazione populare No 1 Op 349 (organ) 1974; first performed Copenhagen, 26 February 1975.
Organisazione populare No 2 Op 350 (organ) 1974; first performed Copenhagen, 26 February 1975.
Organisazione populare No 3 Op 351 (organ) 1974; first performed Copenhagen, 26 February 1975.
Organisazione populare No 4 Op 352 (organ) 1974; first performed Copenhagen, 26 February 1975.
Dialektisme Op 353 (violin, accordion) 1974.
Variations on "The Volga Boatmen" Op 354 (cello) 1974. Recorded SRLP 1320–22.
Sonata da camera Op 356 (2 flutes, organ) 1974; first performed Tastrup, 13 June 1975.
Six Sonatas (Sonata 1) Op 358 (cello) 1974.

Six Sonatas (Sonata 2) Op 359 (cello) 1975.
Six Sonatas (Sonata 3) Op 360 (cello) 1975 (*Sonatas 4, 5, 6 Opp 361–3* not composed).
Dialogue til en Horst (Bornholm) Op 365 (flute, organ) 1975; first performed Copenhagen, 14 July 1975. Recorded RECA ROLP 5007.
Quartetto 2 Op 368 (4 flutes) 1975; first performed Fuglsang, 17 August 1975.
Chropiamonos for Chromonica and Piano Op 369 (mouth organ, piano) 1975.
Kreta: Variations Antiques Op 370 (piano) 1975; first performed Copenhagen, 21 April 1976.
Chamber Sonata No 2 Op 372 (2 flutes, organ) 1975; broadcast 15 October 1978.
Trio Op 376 (violin, cello, piano) 1975; first performed Helsinki, 1976.
Duet Op 377 (flute, bassoon) 1975; first performed Tastrup, 25 January 1976.
Det Tempererede Klaver 2 Op 379 (piano) 1975–6; first performed Copenhagen, 28 April 1976.
Quartet "Den Hellige Familie" Op 380 (2 flutes, bassoon, harpsichord) 1976.
Hommage à Hegel Op 381 (flute) 1976; first performed Copenhagen, 19 April 1976.
Konfirmationmusik Op 382 (organ) 1976.
Overture Op 384 (piano) 1976.
Quartetto 3 Op 385 (4 bass flutes) 1976.
Bitter Skiffle Op 389 (flute, bass flute, piano) 1976.
Sonata symmetrico Op 391 (sopranino/soprano/alto/tenor recorders) 1976; first performed Aarhus, 10 May 1978.
String Quartet No 11 Op 392 1976; first performed Ronne, 19 August 1977.
Sonata Op 393 (tuba, piano) 1976.
En God Gammeldags Julevals (2 violins, piano, text) 1976.
Five Hula-Hula Pieces Op 394 (flugelhorn, 2 trumpets, bass trombone/alto trombone/contrabass trombone, 2 trombones, 4 horns, percussion to include timpani, vibraphone, xylophone) 1977.
Two Hula-Hula Pieces Op 395 (3 flutes, 2 oboes, cor anglais, 3 clarinets, bassoon, contrabassoon, bongo) 1977.
Prelude Op 397 (2 pianos) 1977.
Studie Op 398 (7 electric pianos) 1977.
Det Tempererede Klaver No 3 Op 400 (piano) 1977; first performed Copenhagen, 22 June 1977.
Toleranza Op 401 (2 trumpets, horn, 2 tubas) 1977.
Et Juletrae med Lys (piano, text) 1977.
Hommage à Joseph Beuys Op 403 1977–8:
Wiesbaden (Hommage à Joseph Beuys) Op 403a (cello, trombone) 1977.
Margarine (Hommage à Joseph Beuys) Op 403b (double bass, piano) 1977.
Joseph Beuys und Coyote (Hommage à Joseph Beuys) Op 403c (horn, double bass, piano) 1977.
Fett und Filz (Hommage à Joseph Beuys) Op 403d (tuba, piano) 1977.
Gebratene Fischgrate (Hommage à Joseph Beuys) Op 403e (viola, cor anglais) 1977.
Hasen–Intermezzo (Hommage à Joseph Beuys) Op 403f (piccolo) 1977.
Jeder Mann ein Kunstler (Hommage à Joseph Beuys) Op 403g (piano) 1978.
Quintetto "Spaghetti" Op 405 (4 flutes, piano) 1977.
Sonata No 1 "Der Floh" Op 406 (flute, organ) 1978.
Notturno in Berlingske (B♭) Op 407 (violin, cello, accordion, piano, 4 hands, drum) 1978.
Sonata No 2 "Die Schildkrote" Op 408 (flute, organ) 1978; first performed Copenhagen, 7 April 1978.
Det Tempererede Klaver No 4 Op 409 (piano) 1978; first performed Copenhagen, 29 June 1978.
Vasco da Gama Op 410 (piano) 1978.
Sonata diatonica Op 412 (tuba, flute, oboe, clarinet in C, horn in C, bassoon) 1978.
Something for a Workshop Op 413 (2 violins, viola, cello, bass guitar, cor anglais, horn, 2 flutes, contrabassoon, trumpet, synthesizer, keyboard, electric guitar, harp, drums) 1978.
Adagio Op 414 (flute, organ) 1978.
Sarkamesque Op 415 (piccolo, organ) 1978.
Sonata Op 417 (violin, viola, cello, piano) 1978.
We All Have Some Delay Op 418 (2 trumpets, horn, trombone, tuba) 1978.
Joseph Beuys Sonata Op 420 (versions for piano and prepared piano) 1978.
Sonata Op 422 (viola, piano) 1978.
Ein Flotenstuck, das mit Klavier zusammen-fallen (Hommage à Man Ray) Op 423 (flute, piano) 1978.
Variationer over "Den Forsvundne Mus" Op 424 (piccolo) 1978.
Hans (Jean) Arp Sonata Op 425 ("fonetic sound and clash piano") 1978.
Ariadne Musica Nova Op 426 (organ) 1979.
George Maciunas in Memoriam Op (426) (piano, electric piano) 1979.
1½ Fuga Op 427 (cello, piano) 1979.
Det Tempererede Klaver No 5 Op 428 (piano) 1979.
Barraque Dull Odde Op 429 (piano) 1979.
Hyfer Op 431 (marimba) 1979.
Dances and Kontre-Dances 1-5 Op 433 (piano—4 hands) 1980.
Little Piano Pieces Op 435 1980.
Little Piano Pieces Op 436 1980.
Sonata No 1 Op 437 (organ) 1980.
Piano Piece Op 439 1980.
Piano Trilogi Op 440 1980.
Sonata No 14 Op 441 (piano) 1981.
Pariser-Suite Op 443 (piano) 1981.
Sonata No 2 Op 446 (2 pianos) 1981.
Sonata No 15 "Salzburg-Sonate" Op 447 (piano) 1981.
Sct. Annae-Piece Op 448 (cello, piano) 1981.
Tema con variazioni Op 449 (2 pianos) 1981.
Observations: Psycho-Biological Suite Op 451 (revised version of op 333; flute, oboe, piano) 1981.
Pezzo per televisione Op 452 (violin, cello, oboe, horn, piano) 1983.
Three Waltzes Op 454a/b/c (2 pianos) 1983.
Reflections Op 455 (organ) 1983.
Sonata No 16 Op 456 (piano) 1983.
Sonata No 17 Op 457 (piano) 1983.
Twenty-One Inventions Op 458 (organ) 1983.
Sonata No 18 Op 459 (piano) 1983.
Sonata No 19 Op 460 (piano) 1984.
Sonata No 20 Op 461 (piano) 1984.
Sonata No 21 Op 462 (piano) 1984.
Sixteen Etudes Op 464 (cello) 1984.
Mimosas Op 465 (organ) 1984.
Sonate Facile Op 466 (2 pianos) 1984.
Bokkenheuser–Elegy Op 467 (piano) 1984.
Sonata No 22 Op 468 (piano) 1984.
The Well-Tempered Piano Volume 6 Op 470 1984.
Emancipatio Op 471 (alto saxophone, piano) 1985. Recorded KontraPunkt 32017.
Note-Book Op 472 (33 ultrashort piano movements) 1985.
Sonatina chromatica Op 473 (piano) 1985.
Climatic Changes Op 474 (baritone saxophone, piano, chamber ensemble) 1985.
Hommage à Pierre Boulez Op 475 (2 pianos) 1985.

Homage for Aero Op 476 (piano) 1985.
Quartetto brioso Op 477 (flute, violin, viola, cello) 1985.
Sonata Op 478 (soprano saxophone, piano) 1985. Recorded KontraPunkt 32017.
Tema con variazioni Op 479 (piano, 4 hands) 1985.
Pezzo Op 480 (soprano saxophone) 1985.
Sonata Op 484 (tenor saxophone, piano) 1985.
Sonata Op 485 (baritone saxophone, piano) 1986.
Solistic Duo Op 486 (2 pianos) 1986.
Motivation Op 490 (church bells) 1986.
Pezzo I—Pezzo II Op 491 (piano) 1986.
Quasi una passacaglia Op 492 (organ) 1986.
Duettino Op 493 (flute, guitar) 1986.
Jubilee Prelude Op 494 (organ) 1986.
Forest Pieces 1–6 Op 495 (piano) 1986.
Amalgam Op 496 (2 pianos) 1986.
Music for Firebird Op 497 (piano) 1986.
Sonatina Op 498 (alto saxophone, piano) 1986. Recorded KontraPunkt 32017.
Spies–Composition Op 499 (2 trumpets, piano) 1986.
IHS–Composition Op 501 (2 flutes, piano) 1986.
Sonata Op 502 (flute, guitar) 1986.
Sonata Op 503 (harp) 1986.
Plankton Op 504 (2 pianos, chamber ensemble) 1986.
Goldberg Variations II (Bach compendium) Op 506 (piano) 1987.
String Quartet in One Movement Op 507 1987.
Ohm Op 508 (piano, 4 hands) 1987.
Sonata Op 510 (oboe, piano) 1987.
Surroundings Op 511 (string quartet) 1987.
Star Tour Hymn Op 512 (piano) 1987.
Airplane March Op 513 (piano) 1987.
DSB-Gavotte Op 514 (violin, cello, piano) 1987.
Sometimes OK Op 515 (jazz arrangements) 1987.
Spirit Level Op 518 (piano, 4 hands) 1987.
String Quartet No 14 1987.
The Wild Painters Op 520 (3 flutes) 1987.
Watermusic II Op 528 (chamber ensemble) 1988.
Hieroglyph II Op 529 (2 pianos) 1988.
Well-Tempered Piano Volume 7 Op 530 1988.
Duo Konzertante Op 531 (violin, double bass) 1988; first performed Hamburg, Germany, 14 July 1989.
Well-Tempered Piano Volume 8 Op 532 1988; first performed Humlebaek, Denmark, 6 September 1989.
Fantasy and Fugue on B-A-C-H Op 533 (2 pianos) 1988.
Connected Bassins Op 534 (flute, piano) 1989.
Ondine II Op 537 (piano) 1989.
Poetic Sonatina Op 538 (oboe) 1989.
Duo Op 539 (violin, viola) 1989; first performed Dronningholle, Denmark, 13 December 1989.
Sonata Op 540 (bass saxophone, piano) 1989.
Well-Tempered Piano Volume 9 Op 541 1989.
Well-Tempered Piano Volume 10 Op 542 1989.
Poetic Sonatina II / Burla Op 543 (oboe) 1990.
Hommage à Carl Nielsen Op 544 (2 pianos) 1990.
Panorama Op 545 (11 instruments) 1990.
Well-Tempered Piano Volume 11 Op 546 (piano) 1990.
Choro Daniensis Op 549 (sextet) 1990.
Quartet Op 550 (violin, viola, cello, double bass) 1990.
Cabaret Voltaire Op 551 (violin, guitar) 1990.
Aebeltoft-Fanfare Op 552 (trumpet) 1990.

Vocal/choral:

Three Ballads Op 76 (mezzo-soprano, piano) 1952.
Two Songs Op 79 (soprano, piano) 1952.
Elementi Aperti Op 120 (mezzo-soprano, strings) 1959; broadcast Copenhagen, 7 December 1959.
Torquilla: Oratorium 2 × 7 Billeder Op 132 (speaker, soprano, mezzo-soprano, baritone, bass, mixed choir, orchestra) 1960–1; first performed Aarhus, 23 October 1961.
Alleluja Op 135 (soprano, organ) 1961.
Bonjour Max Ernst Op 138 (mixed chorus, orchestra) 1961; first performed Aarhus, 22 October 1962.
Sagn Op 152 (male choir, winds, timpani; Knudsen) 1964; first performed Copenhagen, 5 September 1964. Recorded Fona TF 131.
Meet the Danes Op 153 (speaker, orchestra; Nystad) 1964; first performed Aarhus, 16 August 1964. Recorded RCA DLPM 6404.
An Arab in Cologne Op 156 (speaker, piano, viola, xylophone, vibraphone, flute, guitar; Middleton) 1964.
Memories of Lorca (no opus number; version for voice and beat group) 1965. Recorded Philips PF 355 350.
Biafra (no opus number; version for voice and beat group) 1965. Recorded Philips PF 355 350.
Mali Op 201 (soprano, 2 percussionists, piano) 1966.
Shelley Songs Op 240 (voice, piano) 1968.
Manerejsen Op 255 (children's choir) 1969.
Vinduesmusik Op 262 ("happening" for choir and orchestra) 1970.
Forureningsvise Op 270 (unaccompanied choir) 1971.
La Ménagerie Roullier aber auch Manchmals Fussnoten zur Charles Camille Saint-Saens genannt Op 283 (speaker, flute, contrabassoon, trumpet in C, tenor trombone, violin, double bass, 2 harps, piano — 4 hands) 1971.
Zeit 17—Interludio Instrumentale—Zeit 18 Op 285 (alto, string quartet; Pandula) 1972.
Two Lyrical Songs Op 288 (voice, piano) 1972; unfinished.
Joseph von Eichendorff-Cyklus Op 342 (baritone, piano) 1974; unfinished.
Four Activities Op 346 (choir, instruments) 1974; first performed Copenhagen, 9 November 1974.
Cathegoriae Sacrale No 1: Hommage à Guillaume Dufay Op 347 (8-part unaccompanied chorus) 1974.
Riffelskud i en Gard—til dem I Kasernen og de Andre (no opus number; song) 1975.
En Sorgmunter Nytarsvise (no opus number; voice, piano) 1975.
Danmarkskantate Op 366 (soprano, alto, tenor, bass, orchestra) 1975; first performed Copenhagen, 21 November 1975.
Hommage à Zurich (Dadaist suite) Op 416 (mezzo-soprano, flute/piccolo, viola, cello) 1978.
Anti-Skarpretter Sang (no opus number; song) 1978.
Decembervise (no opus number; song) 1978.
A Psalm and a Poem Op 442 (mixed chorus, orchestra) 1981.
Psalms 1–20 Op 463 (soprano, organ; or mixed chorus; Mollehave) 1984.
Termalen Op 481 (reciter, cello, piano) 1985.
Song-Cyle Op 489 (soprano, guitar) 1986.
Mini-Cantata Op 521 (reciter, violin, clarinet, piano) 1988.

Opera:

Faust Op 144 (NVB, Kromann, after Goethe, Joyce, Kafka) 1963; first performed Kiel, Germany, 21 June 1964.
Bankchefen Op 355 1979.
Savonarola Op 500 1986.

Other:

Kurtisanen Op 89 (ballet; orchestra) 1953.

Macbeth Op 128 (music after Shakespeare; orchestra) 1960.
Doren Op 141 (ballet; orchestra) 1962.
Stivnet Erfaring Op 184 (music-theatre collective work for wind ensemble 1965.
Bijouteri Op 197 (sociological oratorio; assorted voices and instruments) 1966.
Den Europaeiske Vitalitet Op 198 (sociological oratorio; assorted voices and instruments) 1966.
Pan on Defensive: An Open-Air Sketch Op 238 ("happening") 1968.
Chimes All over the World Op 399 (tape) 1977; first performed Copenhagen, 1 June 1977.
Duell Op 404 (ballet; orchestra) 1977; first performed Stockholm, 12 November 1977.
Gluck: *Alceste Overture Op 487* (arranged for 2 pianos) 1986.

PUBLICATIONS

By Bentzon: *Tovtoneteknik*, Copenhagen, 1953; *Beethoven: en skitse af et geni*, Copenhagen, 1970; also poetry and other writings; reviews in *Dansk Musiktidsskrift* and *Politiken*.

On Bentzon: L. Thybo, "NVBs Klavermusik", in *Dansk Musikstidsskrift*, 21, 1946; A. Thoor, "NVB", in *Musikrevy*, 1949–50; B. Johnsson, "NVBs Klavermusik", in *Ord och Bild*, 1954; Meyer, et al., in *Musikaliske selvportraetter*, 1966; H. Norgaare, "Dobbelportratt av Vagn Holmboe och NVB", in *Musikrevy*, 1970; Klaus Mollerhoj, *NVBs Kompositioner*, catalogues work up to 1980/Op 429, Copenhagen, 1980.

* * *

The first point to register about Niels Viggo Bentzon's music is also, given the foregoing, the most obvious. There is a very great deal of it. He has composed obsessively in virtually every genre and for almost every conceivable combination of instruments. There is no simple, single explanation for his rate of production, but rather a combination of biographical and aesthetic pressures.

Bentzon was brought up in a family with longstanding musical traditions. The composers Johann Ernst and Johann Peder Hartmann were among his forebears; Jorgen Bentzon (1897–1951) was a cousin on his father's side; his mother was an accomplished pianist, who gave him his first lessons. Almost inevitably, the young Bentzon reacted against such a lineage and his first voluntary explorations in music were in jazz, a background which reappears throughout his work, in the symphonic writing as well as in the small ensemble pieces.

Bentzon's first compositions were written in a generic neo-classical idiom that might have lent itself to almost infinite but unadventurous variation. Nonetheless, he quickly found this language unsatisfactory and began to work towards a "metamorphic" style, similar to that of his only slightly less prolific compatriot Vagn Holmboe, which depended on the extended variation of chordal cells. The method is promulgated in the superb *Symphony No 4 "Metamorphoses"* from 1948, a better than average example of Bentzon's sometimes chaotic structural logic and, along with the Seventh of 1951–2, subtitled *"De 3 Versioner"*, the finest of his symphonies. In a sense, "metamorphism" runs parallel to serialism, conscious of it, but only locally dependent on serial techniques. (Though in the 1970s, he moved increasingly towards a rapprochement with the serialist orthodoxy of the time and wrote an important monograph on twelve-tone composition, there is only one work unambiguously in that idiom and that is the highly untypical *Bonjour Max Ernst* for choir and orchestra from 1961.)

For the most part, Bentzon's work is tonal, with a strongly dissonant surface and an improvisatory quality that recalls his interest in jazz. It is also declamatory and highly programmatic. Though the title of the fourth symphony refers to its guiding principle rather than to Ovid, many of his works are influenced by the literary or visual arts, and there is a large number of homages to artists and thinkers in other spheres; there are notable works dedicated to Sartre, Descartes, Picasso, the American sculptor Alexander Calder, and a sequence of works inspired by the German "social sculptor" Josef Beuys, whose radical performance style affected Bentzon.

Though his fundamental style has remained remarkably stable, Bentzon is a man of enormous cultural awareness and seems almost barometrically conscious of new artistic developments, even those which might seem inimical to his undoubted preference for control. In the late 1960s and early 1970s, he experimented successively with graphic notation, with "audio visual concert pieces" like *Busonism*, and with a series of "happenings" which are perhaps the only part of his huge output which can be considered ephemeral.

"Third Stream" music—a self-conscious hybrid of jazz with canonical European forms and instrumentations—is now considered dated, no longer a viable idiom. Bentzon's work in this area recalls the experiments of Americans such as Gunther Schuller, George Russell and Ornette Coleman, all of whom registered a significant presence in Scandinavia. His *Bop Serenade*, the big band *Suite as Far as Jazz Music Is Concerned* and the two *Monkton Blues* for ensemble are remarkable in their confident appropriation of the procedures and general ethos of jazz, even when they seem a trifle gestural. Given Bentzon's enthusiasm for preterite instruments—the accordion most notably—and his jazz background, it is perhaps odd that he had not until the 1980s composed more enthusiastically for saxophone. Association with the young saxophonist Per Egholm then led him to write a series of works for sax which are among his most impressive instrumental compositions of recent years; typically, he did not limit himself to the E♭ alto instrument but produced convincing sonatas for soprano, tenor, baritone and even the unwieldy bass saxophone.

Bentzon is a fine pianist, with a sure attack which is reflected in his extensive catalogue of keyboard pieces. One of his major projects of the last decade has been an extensive exploration of Bach's *Das wohltempierte Clavier*, an enthusiasm that roots Bentzon's modernist and populist leanings firmly in the very nub of the classical tradition. He is, along with Holmboe, unquestionably the most important Danish composer since Nielsen, and a significantly unparochial presence in modern European music.

—James Weir

BERGMAN, Erik (Valdemar). Finnish. Born in Nykarleby, 24 November 1911. Educated at Helsinki University (musicology and literature), 1931–3; Helsinki Conservatoire (composition and piano) 1931–8, diploma in composition; Berlin Hochsschule für Musik (under Heinz Tiessen), 1937–9; further study with Wladimir Vogel, Switzerland; folk music studies in Balkans, Turkey, Egypt, Far East, Mexico, South America. Married Solveig von Schoultz, 7 July 1961. Conductor, Helsinki Catholic Church Choir, 1943–50; music critic, *Nya Pressen*, 1945–7; music critic, *Hufvudstadsbladet*, 1947–76; conductor, Akademiska Sangforeningen, 1950–69; conductor, Muntra Musikanter, 1951–78; professor of composition, Sibelius Academy, 1963–76. Recipient: Sibelius Prize, 1965; titular member, Academy of Finland, 1982; Commander of the Order of the White Rose of Finland; Commander of the Order of the Lion of Finland; Pro Finlandia Medal; honorary member, Society of Finnish Composers; foreign member, Royal Swedish Academy of Music. Mailing address: Berggatan 22 C 52, SF-00100 Helsinki, Finland.

Publisher: Edition Fazer/Edition Pan, P.O. Box 169, SF-02101 Espoo, Finland.

Symphonies/orchestral:

Burla Op 31 1948; first performed Helsinki, 1949.
Tre aspetti d'una serie dodecafonica Op 46 1957; first performed Helsinki, 8 November 1957.
Aubade Op 48 1958; first performed Helsinki, 20 November 1959. Recorded Finlandia FA 314.
Circulus Op 58 1965; first performed, Helsinki, 21 May 1965.
Colori ed improvvisazioni Op 72 1973; first performed Copenhagen, 23 January 1974. Recorded Finlandia FA 330.
Dualis Op 86 (cello, orchestra) 1978; first performed Helsinki, 19 September 1978.
Arctica Op 90 (reworking of *Lapponia Op 76*) 1979; first performed Utrecht, Netherlands, 2 November 1979.
Birds in the Morning Op 89 (flute, orchestra) 1979; first performed Warsaw, Poland, 18 September 1979. Recorded Finlandia FACD 385.
Piano Concerto Op 94 1981; first performed Helsinki, 16 September 1981.
Ananke Op 97 1982; first performed Helsinki, 6 October 1982.
Violin Concerto Op 99 1982; first performed Mainz, Germany, 11 May 1984. Recorded Bis CD 326.
Tutti e soli Op 113 1989; first performed Helsinki, 1990.

Chamber/instrumental:

Suite Op 32 (guitar) 1949; first performed Zurich, Switzerland, 1950.
Intervalles Op 34 (piano) 1949; first performed Zurich, Switzerland, 19 October 1951. Recorded Toshiba TA 60001/2.
Sonatina Op 36 (piano) 1950; first performed Finland, 11 October 1951. Recorded Konserttikeskus KKLP 174.
Espressivo Op 40 No 1 (piano) 1952; first performed Helsinki, 5 December 1952.
Three Fantasies Op 42 (clarinet, piano) 1954; first performed Helsinki, 14 May 1954.
Exsultate Op 43 (organ) 1954; first performed 1955. Recorded EMI 5E 063–34484.
Concertino da Camera Op 53 (flute, clarinet, bass clarinet, percussion, piano, violin, viola, cello) 1961; first performed Helsinki, 24 November 1961. Recorded Love Records LRLP 228.
Aspekter Op 63 (piano) 1963. Recorded EMI 5E063–34484; MILS 8179.
Energien Op 66 (harpsichord) 1970; first performed Helsinki, 26 November 1971. Recorded Bis LP 68; Finlandia FACD 367.
A propos de B-A-C-H Op 79 (piano) 1976; first performed Helsinki, 21 March 1977.
Soltafara Op 81 (alto saxophone, percussion) 1977; first performed Helsinki, 16 January 1978.
Dialogue Op 82 (flute, guitar) 1977; first performed Savonlinna, Finland, 22 July 1977.
Midnight Op 83 (guitar) 1977; first performed London, 9 December 1977. Recorded Bis LP 207.
Silence and Eruptions Op 91 (flute, oboe, clarinet, bassoon, percussion, piano, 2 violins, viola, cello) 1979; first performed Stockholm, 16 June 1980.
Janus Op 22 (violin, guitar) 1980; first performed Jyvaskyla, Finland, 2 July 1980.
Mipejupa Op 96 (flute, alto saxophone, guitar, percussion) 1981; first performed Helsinki, 20 June 1981.
String Quartet Op 98 1982; first performed Kuhmo, Finland, 21 July 1982. Recorded Finlandia FACD 348.
Borealis Op 101 (2 pianos, percussion) 1983; first performed Washington, D.C., 19 November 1983.
Quo Vadis Op 102 (cello, piano) 1983; first performed Helsinki, 31 August 1984. Recorded Finlandia FACD 362.
etwas rascher Op 108 (4 saxophones) 1985; first performed Savonlinna, Finland, 10 August 1986.

Vocal/choral:

Det kom ett brev/Came a Letter Op 12 No 2 (mixed chorus; Lagerkvist) 1944. Recorded Finlandia FACD 371.
Mitt trad ar pinjen/My Tree Is the Stone-Pine Op 12 No 5 (mixed chorus; Lagerkvist) 1944. Recorded Finlandia FACD 371.
Majnätter/May Nights Op 20 (soprano, orchestra; Hemmer) 1946; first performed Stockholm, 20 May 1946.
Tre mindre allvarliga sanger/Three Less Serious Songs: Set I Op 22b (male chorus; Fridegard) 1946; first performed Helsinki 1949. Recorded (part only) MM LP 3/4.
Nej, inte du Op 22b No 2 (male chorus; Fridegard) 1946.
Ensamhetens sånger/Yksinaisyyden lauluja/Songs of Solitude Op 27 (mezzo-soprano baritone, orchestra; Sodergran) 1947; first performed Helsinki, 1949.
Den enda stunden/The Single Moment Op 33 No 6 (mixed chorus; Runeberg) 1949. Recorded Finlandia FACD 371.
Tre sanger/Three Songs Op 21/35 (mezzo-soprano/baritone, piano; consisting of *Serenad Op 35a*, *Si drommaren kommer dar Op 21 No 1*, *Jantblig Op 21 No 3*, but now intended to be sung as a set) 1946, 1950. Recorded Bis LP 88.
Tre mindre allvarliga sanger/Three Less Serious Songs: Set II Op 35b (male chorus; Lowenhjelm) 1950; first performed Helsinki, 1951.
Arkaisk bild/Ancient Portrait Op 35c (male chorus; Edfelt) 1950; first performed Helsinki, 1951. Recorded Akademiska Sangforeningen AS LP 629–516.
Nordisk var/Northern Spring Op 37a (male chorus, tenor, clarinet; Sodergran) 1951; first performed Helsinki, 1952. Recorded Muntra Musikanter MM LP 3/4.
Kun on oikeen hulivililuonto/Anyone Who's a Proper Rascal or *If You Take Life as It Comes Op 37b No 1* (male chorus; folksong) 1951; first performed Helsinki, 1952. Recorded Finnlevy SFX 21; Finlandia FA 31; Muntra Musikanter MM LP 3/4; Finlandia FACD 368.
Tre mindre allvarliga sanger/Three Less Serious Songs: Set III Op 39 (male chorus; Froding) 1952; first performed Helsinki, 1952. Recorded, in part only, Muntra Musikanter MM LP 5/6.

Rubaiyat Op 41 (baritone, male chorus, orchestra; Omar Khayyam) 1953; first performed Finland, 10 May 1953.

Akvarel / Watercolour Op 44b No 1 (mixed chorus; Hemmer) 1956. Recorded Finnlevy SFLP 8584; Finlandia FACD 371.

Med dig / Mit Dir / With You Op 45 (mezzo-soprano / baritone, piano; Lindorm, Lagerkvist, Boye) 1956; first performed Finland, 14 June 1956.

Adagio Op 47a (male chorus, baritone, flute, vibraphone; Bergman) 1957; first performed Helsinki, 10 May 1958.

Lamento e Burletta (no opus number; mixed chorus vocalise) 1957; first performed Helsinki, 23 April 1986.

Svanbild / Sygnus Op 47b (baritone, solo quartet, male chorus; von Schoultz) 1958; first performed Helsinki, 15 April 1959. Recorded Finnlevy SFX 21; Fona TF 119; MM LP 3/4; Akademiska Sangforeningen AS LP 629–516; YL LP 2.

Aton Op 49 (baritone, speaker, mixed chorus, orchestra; Akhenaton) 1959; first performed Helsinki, 29 April 1960.

Psalm Op 50a (mixed chorus; von Schoultz) 1959; first performed Helsinki, 2 March 1980.

Junibastu / June Sauna Op 50b (male chorus; von Schoultz) 1959; first performed Helsinki, 7 April 1960. Recorded RCA VICS 1602; ARR LP-3; Finlandia FA 321.

Drei Galgenlieder Op 51a (baritone, 2 speakers, male chorus; Morgenstern) 1959; first performed Helsinki, 1960. Recorded Finlandia FACD 368; in part only, RCA VICS 1602; MM LP 3/4; EMI 9C 063-83042.

Vier Galgenlieder Op 51b (3 speakers, mixed speaking chorus; Morgenstern) 1960; first performed Zurich, 3 December 1961. Recorded EMI 5E 063-34484; Finlandia FACD 371.

Regn / Rain (no opus number; mixed chorus; Froding) 1961; first performed Helsinki, 30 November 1986. Recorded Finlandia FACD 371.

Bauta Op 54 (male chorus, baritone, percussion; Edda/ Ohlmarks) 1961; first performed Helsinki, 25 November 1961.

Sela Op 55 (baritone, mixed chorus, chamber orchestra; Psalms/Buber) 1962; first performed Helsinki, 18 November 1962.

Faglarna / Die Vogel / The Birds Op 56a (baritone, male chorus, percussion, celeste; von Schoultz) 1962; first performed Helsinki, 6 April 1963. Recorded RCA YSVL 1-559; Philips 839 705 LY; Akademiska Sangforeningen AS 629-516; Chandos CHAN 8478.

Barnets drom / The Child's Dream Op 56b (child speaker, 2 male speakers, male chorus, recorder; Diktonius) 1963; first performed Helsinki, 30 November 1963.

Ha Li Bomp Op 57a (speaker, tenor, male chorus; Huldén) 1964; first performed Helsinki, 10 April 1965.

Tuonelas hjordar / Herds of Hades Op 57b (male chorus; Martinson, in homage to Sibelius) 1964; first performed Helsinki, 10 April 1965.

En sådan Kväll / Such an Evening Op 59a (soprano, mixed chorus; von Schoultz) 1965; first performed Turku, 11 June 1966. Recorded Finlandia FACD 371.

Sno / Snow Op 59b (flute, tenor, male chorus; Sandelin) 1966; first performed Uppsala, 1967. Recorded, part only, RCA VICS 1602.

Springtime Op 60a (baritone, mixed chorus; von Schoultz) 1966; first performed London, 22 February 1967.

Jesurun Op 61 (baritone, male chorus, 2 trumpets, 2 trombones, 3 percussion; Isaiah) 1967; first performed Helsinki, 10 May 1968.

Annonssidan / Small Ads Op 64 (baritone, 3 tenors, 25 speakers, male chorus; newspaper advertisements) 1969; first performed Finland, 1970.

Nox Op 65 (baritone, mixed chorus, flute, cor anglais, percussion; Quasimodo, Arp, Eluard, Eliot) 1970; first performed Gothenburg, 20 April 1970. Recorded EMI 5E 063-34484; Chandos CHAN 8478.

Requiem över en död diktare / Requiem for a Dead Poet—Gunnar Ekelöf in memoriam Op 67 (baritone, mixed chorus, 2 trumpets, 2 trombones, 2 percussion, organ; Wall) 1970; first performed Stockholm, 19 May 1975.

Missa in honorem Sancti Henrici Op 68 (mixed chorus, soloists, organ) 1971; first performed Helsinki, 5 September 1971. Recorded EMI 9C 063–38214.

Hathor Suite Op 70 (soprano, baritone, mixed chorus, flute, cor anglais, harp, 2 percussion; Schott) 1971; first performed Helsinki, 27 November 1971. Recorded Chandos CHAN 8478; Finlandia FACD 371.

Miksi Ei? / Warum Nicht? / Why Not? Op 71a (male chorus, 2 voices; both vocalise) 1972; first performed Helsinki, 1972. Recorded Finlandia FACD 386.

Myos nain / Auch so / Something Else Op 71b (mixed chorus, 3 soloists vocalise) 1972; first performed Debrecen, Hungary, 1972. Recorded Finlandia FACD 371.

Vestenvinden Op 73a (mixed chorus; Jacobsen) 1973; first performed Finland 23 November 1981.

Tyttoset / The Lasses Op 73b (mixed chorus, 3 soloists; folk song) 1973; first performed Windermere, Northumberland, 30 July 1976. Recorded Finlandia FACD 371.

Kaksi karjalaista kansanlualua / Zwei Karelische Volkslieder / Two Karelian Folksongs Op 73c (male chorus) 1973; first performed Finland, 10 June 1972.

Bardo Thodol Op 74 (speaker, mezzo-soprano, baritone, mixed chorus, orchestra; Tibetan Book of the Dead) 1974; first performed Helsinki, 19 May 1975.

Lapponia Op 76 (mezzo-soprano, baritone, mixed chorus vocalise) 1975; first performed Cambridge, 30 November 1975.

Min ros och lilja / My Rose and Lily Op 77a (male chorus, voice) 1975; first performed Helsinki, 14 April 1978. Recorded Muntra Musikanter MM LP 7.

Bon Appetit! Op 77b (speaker, baritone, male chorus) 1975; first performed Finland, 24 May 1976. Recorded Muntra Musikanter MM LP 5/6.

Noa Op 78 (baritone, mixed chorus, orchestra; Hebrew) 1976; first performed Helsinki, 25 October 1977.

Bim Bam Bum Op 80 (speaker, tenor, male chorus, flute, percussion; Morgenstern) 1976; first performed Uppsala, 23 April 1977.

Voices in the Night Op 84 (baritone, male chorus vocalise) 1977; first performed Reykjavik, 9 May 1979.

Dreams Op 85 (children's or women's chorus vocalise) 1977; first performed Debrecen, Hungary, 29 March 1982.

Triumf att finnas till / Triumph of Being Here Op 87 (soprano, flute, percussion; Sodergran) 1978; first performed Cologne, 25 January 1979.

Gudarnas spar / Tracks of the Gods Op 88 (alto, baritone, mixed chorus; Sodergran) 1978; first performed Helsinki, 2 March 1980.

Tipitaka Suite Op 93 (baritone, male chorus; Buddhist *Sutta Nipata*/Johansson) 1980; first performed Turku, Finland, 3 April 1982.

Four Vocalises Op 100 (mezzo-soprano, male chorus vocalise) 1983; first performed Helsinki, 24 November 1986. Recorded Finlandia FACD 368.

Lemminkainen Op 103 (speaker, mezzo-soprano, baritone, mixed chorus; *Kalevala*) 1984; first performed Helsinki, 8 May 1985.

Svep / Sweep (no opus number; reciter, mezzo-soprano, baritone, mixed chorus, instrumental ensemble; Ahlfors,

Hulden) 1984; first performed Helsinki, 5 February 1985.

Svit ur kantaten Svep / Suite from the cantata Sweep Op 104 (mezzo-soprano, speaker, flute, 2 trumpets, cello, percussion; Hulden/Bosley) 1984; first performed Dublin, 19 May 1986.

Lament and Incantation Op 106 (soprano vocalise, piano) 1984; first performed Cologne, 24 May 1985.

Bygden / The Village Op 107 (reciter, soprano, baritone, mixed chorus, child soprano, children's chorus, flute, clarinet, violin, viola, cello, percussion, with pipes, recorders, piccolo flute, flexatone, raspers, cowbells, bottles, gongs, rattles, etc; Hulden) 1985.

Forsta maj / May Day Op 109 (tenor, male chorus; Satherberg, Bottinger) 1985; first performed Helsinki, 7 March 1988.

Tule armaani / Come, My Love Op 111 (baritone, male chorus; EB, Kailas, Viita, Saarikoski, folk poem) 1988; first performed Helsinki, 23 November 1989.

Careliana Op 112 (6 male voices, AATBarBarB; folk songs) 1988; first performed Joensuu, Finland, 11 June 1989.

Opera:

Samothrake Op 69 (speaker, mixed chorus, contrabassoon, 2 trumpets, 2 trombones, 2 percussion, dancers; Ekelof) 1971; first performed Stockholm, 19 May 1975. Recorded Finlandia FACD 371.

Det sjungande trädet / The Singing Tree Op 110 (Carpelan, after folk tale) 1988.

Other:

In Springtime Op 95 (electro-acoustic) 1981.

PUBLICATIONS

On Bergman: *EB: A 70th Birthday Tribute*, Helsinki, 1981.

* * *

Erik Bergman is often considered to be Finland's first important "Modernist" who writes serial works which avoid any Romantic or National feeling. After completing studies at the Sibelius Academy in 1939, Bergman used concise, athematic writing often without a regular metre. He became fully expressionist after further study under Vogel. Few of Bergman's pieces follow traditional forms, although the three-movement *Colori ed improvvisazioni* develops motives symphonically. He has also incorporated Gregorian chant (the *Mass* and *Quo Vadis*) and humour (*Galgenlieder*, and in *Bim Bam Bum* where the choir are used as extra percussionists).

Early works, such as *Intervalles* suite and *Sonatina*, both for piano, display Bartókian rhythms used as a destabilising element; inflected scales following over-stressed pitches, each movement concentrating on a single interval; and frequent counterpoint between the hands. Rhythmic complexity continued into *Rubaiyat*. Serial techniques were included in male-choir folk-arrangements in 1951. Then in *Tre aspetti* a single set is used. Later both rhythm and pitch are derived ("Aubade"), until finally both orchestration and dynamics are derived ("Simbolo") although intervallic colour always predominates. Two influences are apparent in *Med dig*: Frank Martin and Joonas Kokkonen. The accompaniment often follows Martin's *Neuf Préludes* and *Tempest* music both in its rhythm and its offsetting of successions of upper consonances with dissonant bass-lines and pedal-points. Kokkonen's five repeated notes followed by an upward leap to a strong beat is found in three of the four songs.

During the mid-1960s, Bergman turned from serialism to controlled improvisation, where timbre becomes all-important (especially in *Circulus* for orchestra). Starting with *Springtime*, he worked on the notation/sound relationship, culminating in *Samothrake* (which includes a dancer and reciter) and the unaccompanied *Lapponia*. Complexity continued in *Tyttöset*, with attention given to extremes of compass and to thickly voiced chords.

With *Silence and Eruptions*, Bergman alternates precise rhythms with improvisation, while exploiting many of the atmospherically delicate sounds available, which either disintegrate or suddenly erupt. As in his *Violin Concerto*, the opening's main motif creeps in around the violin's bottom G# which eventually rises a semitone. The solo piano exploits palm-rubbing of the strings while the violin glissandos. Later movements develop another favourite device from Kokkonen: a long note which crescendos before eventually resolving onto a brief but accented nearby note, often accompanied by quiet oscillations. While the first movement of the *Violin Concerto* includes controlled improvisation against precise rhythms, the second movement develops Polish field technique. In the same year, Bergman completed one of his few chamber works, *String Quartet*, where ideas are often preceded by tremolo-texture and followed by silent pauses before developing in an outburst. Longer linear writing is reserved for the third movement.

Three mid-1980s works were connected with the Kalevala: *Lemminkainen* (where a mixed chorus is given organum-like passages against modern singing techniques and intervallic leaps; "Loitsuja" (*Charms*, a six-movement suite for soloists and male chorus); and *Lament and Incantation*. The Lament, with its roots in Karelian mourning songs, is mostly textless—one or two held notes followed by an accented staccato note (this Kokkonen device was still favoured by Bergman). The Incantation starts with a hissing sound which eventually explodes into coloratura figures, culminating in shouts intended to drive out demons.

Borealis again uses Bergman's 1979 technique of controlled improvisation pitted against notated rhythm. Frequent pedal-points and impressionist sounds predominate (such as Piano II playing inside the instrument, sometimes producing string glissandi while Piano I improvises and the percussionist bows a tam-tam). Bergman's first fully staged opera, *Det sjungande trädet* was written at the age of 77.

—Malcolm J. Hill

BERIO, Luciano. Italian. Born in Oneglia, 24 October 1925. Early music lessons with Ernesto Berio; educated at Liceo Classico, Milan (studying law), 1944; Conservatorio G. Verdi, Milan (under Giorgio Ghedini, Carlo Maria Giulini and Giulio Cesare Paribeni), 1945–50; Berkshire Music Centre, Tanglewood, Massachusetts (under Luigi Dallapicolla), 1952; Ferienkurse für Neue Musik, Darmstadt, 1954. Married (1) soprano Cathy Berberian in 1950 (dissolved 1964); (2) psychologist Susan Oyama in 1965 (dissolved 1971), 1 daughter and 1 son; (3) musicologist Talia Packer in 1977, 1 son. Founder/co-director (with Bruno Maderna), Studio de fonologia musicale, RAI broadcasting, Milan, 1955–60; teacher, Berkshire Music Centre, Tanglewood, 1960; teacher of composition, Dartington Summer School, England, 1961–2; teacher, then professor of composition, Mills College, Oakland, California, 1962, 1963–4; teacher, Juilliard School of Music, New York, 1965–71; work on television series "C'e musica e musica", Rome, 1971; director, electro-acoustic section, IRCAM, Paris, 1974–80; artistic director, Israel Chamber Orchestra, 1975; artistic director, Accademia Filarmonica Romana, 1976; artistic director, Orchestra Regionale Toscana, 1982; artistic director, Maggio Musicale Fiorentino, 1984. Founder/director, Tempo Reale, Florence, since 1987. Recipient: 34th Premio Italia (for *Duo*), 1982; honorary D.Mus., City University, London, 1980. Mailing address: Il Colombaio, Radicondoli, Siena, Italy.

Publishers: Universal Edition; Edizioni Suvini Zerboni.

Symphonies/orchestral:

Preludio a una festa marina (strings) 1944.
Concertino (clarinet, violin, harp, celeste, strings) 1950, revised 1951, 1970; first performed Milan, 1950. Recorded RCA RL 12291.
Variazioni (chamber orchestra) 1953–4; broadcast Hamburg, 23 February 1955.
Nones 1954; broadcast Rome, 15 October 1955.
Mimusique No 2 1955.
Allelujah I (6 instrumental groups) 1955–6; first performed Cologne, 1957; subsequently withdrawn and revised as *Allelujah II*.
Variazioni "ein Madchen öder Weibchen" (2 basset horns, strings) 1956; first performed Donaueschingen, 1956.
Divertimento (collaboration with Bruno Maderna) 1957; broadcast Rome, 2 December 1957.
Allelujah II 1957–8; broadcast Rome, 17 May 1958.
Tempi concertati (flute, violin, 2 pianos, small orchestra) 1958; broadcast Hamburg, 1960.
Quaderni I (from *Epifanie*) 1959; first performed Cologne, 1960.
Quaderni II (from *Epifanie*) 1961; first performed Vienna, 1961.
Quaderni III (from *Epifanie*) 1962; first performed Los Angeles, 1963.
Chemins I (harp, orchestra; based on *Sequenza II*) 1965; first performed Donaueschingen, 1965.
Chemins III (viola, flute, clarinet, trombone, electric organ, harp, marimbaphone/tam-tam, vibraphone/side-drum, viola, cello, orchestra; based on *Chemins II*) 1968, revised 1973; first performed Paris, 1968. Recorded RCA RK 11530/1-2.
Chemins IIB (large ensemble) 1970; first performed Berlin, 1970.
Bewegung 1971; first performed Glasgow, 1971.
Still 1971–3; first performed Glasgow, 1973.
Chemins IIC (bass clarinet, orchestra) 1971; first performed Rotterdam, 1972.
Concerto (2 pianos, orchestra) 1972–3; first performed New York City, 1973. Recorded RL 1674.
Point on the Curve to Find . . . (piano, 23 instruments) 1973–4; first performed Donaueschingen, 1974. Recorded RCA RL 12291.
Eindrucke 1973–4; first performed Zurich, 1974. Recorded Erato ECD 88151.
Chemins IV (oboe, strings; based on *Sequenza VII*) 1975; first performed London, 1975. Recorded RCA RL 12291.
Il ritorno degli snovidenia (cello, 30 instruments) 1976–7; first performed Basle, 1977.
Encore (later incorporated into *La vera storia*) 1978; first performed Rotterdam, 1978.
Scene (part of *La vera storia*) 1978; first performed Brussels, 1978.
Pas de quoi (part of *La vera storia*) 1978; first performed Cologne, 1978.
Concerto for Piano and Orchestra 1979.
Entrata (part of *La vera storia*) 1980; first performed San Francisco, 1980.
Accordo (4 wind groups) 1980; first performed Assisi, 1980.
Corale (based on *Sequenza VIII*; violin, 2 horns, strings) 1981; first performed Zurich, 1982.
Fanfara (part of *La vera storia*) 1981; first performed Venice, 1982.
Requies 1983–4; first performance of incomplete version *Requies: Frammento (in memoriam Cathy)*, Lausanne, 1984; first complete performance Aspen, Colorado, 1985.
Voci (viola, 2 instrumental groups) 1984; first performed Basle, 1984.
Formazioni 1986, revised 1988; first performed Amsterdam, 1987; revised version first performed Amsterdam, 1988.
Concerto II: Echoing Curves (piano, 2 instrumental ensembles; includes reworking of parts of *Points on the Curve to Find . . .*) 1988; first performed Paris, 1988.
Continuo 1989.
Festum 1989; first performed Dallas, Texas, 1989.

Chamber/instrumental:

Pastorale (piano) 1937.
Toccata (piano duet) 1939.
Divertimento (violin, viola, cello) 1947, revised 1985.
Tre pezzi (3 clarinets) 1947; first performed Milan, 1947.
Petite Suite (piano; from *Family Album*) 1947; first performed Como, 1948.
Quintetto (wind quintet) 1948.
Quartetto (wind) 1950–1; revised 1951 for wind quintet; revised 1970 with text by Levine, and subsequently performed New York City, 1971.
Sonatina (flute, 2 clarinets, bassoon) 1951.
Due pezzi (violin, piano) 1951, revised 1966; first performed Tanglewood, Massachusetts, 1952.
Study (string quartet) 1952, revised 1985; first performed Tanglewood, Massachusetts, 1952.
Cinque variazioni (piano) 1952–3; first performed Milan, 1953.
Quartetto (string quartet) 1956; first performed Vienna, 12 May 1959.
Serenata (flute, oboe, cor anglais, 2 clarinets, bassoon, horn, trumpet, trombone, harp, piano, violin, viola, cello, double bass) 1957; first performed Paris, 1957.
Sequenza (flute) 1958; first performed Darmstadt, 1958.
Differences (flute, clarinet, harp, viola, cello, tape) 1958; first performed Paris, 1959.
Sequenza II (harp) 1963; first performed Darmstadt, 1963.
Sincronie (string quartet) 1963–4; first performed Grinnell, Iowa, 1964.
Rounds (harpsichord) 1965, transcribed for piano 1967; first performed Basle, 1965; piano version first performed New York City, 1968.
Wasserklavier (piano) 1965; first performed Brescia, 1970.
Sequenza IV (piano) 1965–6; first performed St Louis, Missouri, 1966.
Gesti (recorder) 1966; first performed Bruggen, 1966.
Sequenza V (trombone) 1966; first performed San Francisco, 1966. Recorded Bis CD 388.
Sequenza VI (viola) 1967, revised for cello, 1981; first

performed New York City, 1967. Recorded RCA RK 11530/1–2.

Chemins II (viola, flute, clarinet, trombone, 2 percussion, harp, electric organ, viola, cello; based on *Sequenza VI*) 1967; first performed Copenhagen, 1968. Recorded RCA RK 11530/1–2.

Erdenklavier (piano) 1969; first performed Bergamo, 1970.

Sequenza VII (oboe, sound source) 1969; first performed Basle, 1969.

Memory (electric piano, electric harpsichord) 1970; first performed New York City, 1972.

Autre Fois ("berceuse canonique" for Igor Stravinsky; flute, clarinet, harp) 1971.

Musica leggera, canone per moto contrario e al rovescio, con un brevio intermezzo) (flute, viola, accompanied by cello; for Goffredo Petrassi's 70th birthday) 1974.

Fa-Si (organ, registration assistants) 1975; first performed Rovereto, 1975.

Sequenza VIII (violin) 1976–7; first performed La Rochelle, 1977. Recorded ADDA 81042.

Les Mots sont allés (cello) 1978; first performed Basle, 1978.

Duetti (34 pieces for 2 violins) 1979–82; first performance (27 pieces) Fiesole, 1981; complete, Los Angeles, 1984.

Chemins V (clarinet, digital system) 1980; first performed Paris, 1980; withdrawn.

Sequenza IXa (clarinet; based on *Chemins V*) 1980; first performed Arrignon, 1980.

Sequenza IXb (based on *Chemins V*, transcribed for alto saxophone) 1981; first performed London, 1981. Recorded ADDA 581047.

Lied (clarinet) 1983; first performed Geneva, 1983.

Sequenza X (trumpet in C, piano resonance) 1985; first performed Los Angeles, 1984.

Luftklavier (piano) 1985; first performed Italy, 1985.

Naturale (viola, tam-tam, tape) 1985; first recorded Taormina, 1985.

Terre chaleureuse (wind quintet; for Pierre Boulez's 60th birthday; preliminary sketch for *Ricorrenze*) 1985; first performed Baden-Baden, 1985.

Call—St Louis Fanfare (2 trumpets, horn, trombone, tuba) 1985, revised 1987; first performed St Louis, Missouri, 1985.

Ricorrenze (wind quintet) 1986–7; first performed Darmstadt, 1987.

String Quartet 1986–90.

Duetti per due violini (arranged for 2 guitars) 1987.

Comma (E♭ clarinet) 1987.

Sequenza XI (guitar) 1987–8; first performed Rovereto, 1988.

Psy (double bass) 1989.

Feuerklavier (piano) 1989; first performed New York City, 1989.

Vocal/choral:

O bone Jesu (choir) 1946.

Tre canzoni popolari (female voice, piano) 1946–7.

Tre liriche greche (voice, piano) 1946–8.

Due canti siciliani (tenor, male chorus) 1948.

Ad Hermes (voice, piano) 1948; first performed Oneglia, 1948.

Du pezzi sacri (2 sopranos, piano, 2 harps, timpani, 12 bells) 1949.

Magnificat (2 sopranos, SSAATB chorus, orchestra) 1949; first performed Turin, 1971.

Opus Number Zoo (reciters, flute, oboe, clarinet, bassoon, horn; Berberian; Levine/Hofbauer/Ottolenghi) 1950–1; first performed Milan, 1952.

Deus meus (voice, 3 instruments) 1951; first performed Milan, 1952.

El Mar la Mar (soprano, mezzo-soprano, flute/piccolo, 2 clarinets or bass clarinets, harp, chromatic accordion, cello, double bass; reduction for 2 sopranos, piano; also arranged for soprano, mezzo-soprano, flute/piccolo, 2 clarinets/1 bass clarinet, harp, accordion, cello, double bass; Alberti) 1951; first performed Royan, 1969.

Quattro canzoni popolari (addition of "Avendo gran disio", text by Lentini, to work of 1946–7) 1952; first performed Milan, 1952.

Chamber Music (female voice, clarinet, cello, harp; Joyce) 1953; first performed Milan, 1953.

Epifanie (soprano or mezzo-soprano, orchestra; Proust, Joyce, Machado, Simon, Brecht, Sanguineti) 1959–62; first performed (incomplete) Donaueschingen, 1961. Recorded RCA RK 11530/1–2.

Circles (women's voice, harp, 2 percussion; cummings) 1960; first performed Tanglewood, Massachusetts, 1960.

Esposizione (mezzo-soprano, 2 children's voices, dancers, 14 instruments, tape; Sanguineti/Halprin) 1962–3; first performed Venice, 1963; subsequently withdrawn and became part of *Laborintus II*.

Traces (soprano, mezzo-soprano, 2 actors, 2 choruses, orchestra; Oyama) 1964; first performed Buffalo, New York, 1965; subsequently withdrawn.

Folk Songs (transcriptions for mezzo-soprano, flute/piccolo, clarinet, 2 percussion, harp, viola, cello; various languages) 1964, version for orchestra, 1973; first performed Zurich, 1973. Recorded RCA RK 11530/1–2; Virgin Classics VC 7 90704–1.

Laborintus II (voices, instruments, tape; Sanguineti) 1965; first performed Paris, 1965. Recorded Harmonia Mundi HM 764.

Sequenza III (voice) 1965; broadcast Bremen, 1966. Recorded Virgin Classics VC 7 90704–1.

O King (voice, flute, clarinet, piano, violin, viola) 1967; first performed Berea, Ohio, 1967.

Questo vuol dire che (3 female voices, small choir, tape) 1968; first performed (incomplete, as *Cela veut dire*) Royan; complete, Rome, 1970.

Sinfonia (8 "Singstimme", orchestra; Levi-Strauss, Beckett, Berio; incorporates *O King*) 1968–9; first performed Donaueschingen, 1969. Recorded Erato ECD 88151.

Air (from *Opera*; soprano, orchestra; arranged for soprano, piano, violin, viola, cello; or orchestra; Striggio) 1969; first performed Rovereto, 1971.

Melodrama (from *Opera*; tenor, flute, clarinet, percussion, piano, electric organ, violin, cello, double bass) 1969; first performed Siena, 1971.

Agnus (from *Opera*; 2 sopranos, 3 clarinets, electronic organ or other sound source) 1971; first performed Muncie, Indiana, 1971.

Bewegung II (baritone, orchestra; Vergil) 1971; first performed Rotterdam, 1972.

Recital I (mezzo-soprano, 2 oboes, 2 clarinets, 2 horns, trumpet, trombone, percussion, harp, 3 pianos, violin, viola, cello, double bass; Moretti/Sanguineti; incorporates *Memory*) 1971; first performed Lisbon, 1972. Recorded SER 5665.

Ora (soprano, mezzo-soprano, flute, cor anglais, small chorus, small instrumental ensemble, orchestra; Vergil, Berio, Essam) 1971; first performed Detroit, Michigan, 1971; subsequently withdrawn.

E Vo' (flute, oboe, 3 clarinets, trumpet, trombone, percussion, piano, electric organ, violin, viola, cello, double bass) 1972; first performed Rovereto, 1972.

Cries of London (6 voices; version for 8 voices) 1973–4, 1975; first performed Edinburgh, 1975; revised version first performed La Rochelle, 1977. Recorded Decca 425 620–2.

Calmo (in memoriam Bruno Maderna) (soprano, flute, oboe, 2 clarinets, bassoon, horn, trumpet, trombone; Homer) 1974, recomposed for chamber orchestra, 1988–9; first performed Milan, 1974; recomposed version first performed Paris, 1989.

Coro (40 voices, instruments; folk texts, Neruda) 1974–6, extended 1977; first performed Donaueschingen, 1976; complete version London, 1977. Recorded Deutsche Grammophon DG 423 902–2.

Diario immaginario (radio piece for voices; Sermonti, after Molière) 1975; broadcast Florence, 1975.

Scene from "La vera storia" (mezzo-soprano, bass, mixed choir, orchestra; Calvino) 1981.

Duo ("imaginary theatre" for radio, a study for *Un re in ascolto*; baritone, 2 violins, mixed choir, orchestra; Calvino) 1982; broadcast Rome, 1982.

Ecce: musica per musicologi (written for 14th Congress International Musicological Society; women's voices, men's voices, bells; d'Arezzo) 1987; first performed Bologna, 1987.

Ofanim (2 instrumental groups, children's choir, women's choir, real-time computer music system; or singer, children's choir or tape, orchestra or tape, group: 2 clarinets, 2 trombones, 2 horns; Hebrew text) 1988; first performed Prato, 1988.

Canticum novissimi testamenti (unaccompanied SATB choir; or soprano, alto, tenor, bass, 4 clarinets, saxophone quartet; Sanguineti) 1988, 1989; first performed Trent, 1988; version for soloists and instruments first performed Paris, 1989.

Opera:

Passaggio ("*messa in scena*" for soprano, 2 choruses, orchestra; Sanguineti) 1961–2; first performed Milan, 1963.

Opera (10 actors, 2 sopranos, tenor, baritone, SSAATTBB ensemble, orchestra; Berio, Colombo, Eco, Striggio, Yankowitz) 1969–70; first performed Santa Fe, New Mexico, 1970.

La vera storia (Calvino) 1977–81; first performed Milan, 1982; parts performed separately.

Un re in ascolto (Calvino, Auden, Gotter, Shakespeare) 1979–83; first performed Salzburg, 1984; concert version for 6 soloists and orchestra, 1985–6, subsequently withdrawn.

Wir Bauen eine Stadt (opera for children after Paul Hindemith; versions for 2 pianos or chamber orchestra by Berio; version for instruments by Flavio Scogna) 1987.

Other:

Allez Hop ("racconto mimico" for mezzo-soprano, 8 mimes, dancers, orchestra; Calvino) 1952–9, revised 1968; first performed Venice, 23 September 1959; first performance of revised version Bologna, 1968.

Mimusique No 1 (single-track tape) 1953.

Mutazioni (clectronic) 1954; first performed Milan, 1956.

Ritratto di citta (single-track tape; collaboration with Bruno Maderna) 1954; first performed Rome, 1955.

Mutazione (single-track tape) 1955; first performed Milan, 1956.

Musica di scena No 9 (electronic study; collaboration with Bruno Maderna) 1955–6; broadcast Milan, 1956.

Studio No 3 (electronic study; collaboration with Bruno Maderna) 1955–6; broadcast Milan, 1956.

Studio No 4 (electronic study; collaboration with Bruno Maderna) 1955–6; broadcast Milan, 1956.

Film Music (electronic study) 1955–6; broadcast Milan, 1956.

Perspectives (2-track tape) 1956; first performed Milan, 1956.

Thema (Omaggio a Joyce) (2-track tape, recorded voice/Cathy Berberian) 1958; first performed Milan, 1958.

Momenti (4-track tape) 1960; broadcast Hamburg, 1960.

Visage (2-track tape, recorded voice/Cathy Berberian) 1960–1; broadcast Milan, 1961.

Il combattimento di Tancredi e Clorinda (soprano, baritone, tenor, 3 violins, continuo; after Monteverdi/Tasso) 1966; first performed New York City, 1967.

Le Grand Lustucru (arranged for mezzo-soprano and instruments from *Marie Galante* by Weill/Deval) 1967; first performed Venice, 1967.

Surabaya Johnny (arranged for mezzo-soprano and instruments from *Happy End* by Weill/Brecht) 1967; first performed Venice, 1967.

Ballad von der Sexuellen Horigkeit (arranged for mezzo-soprano and instruments from *Die Dreigroschenoper* by Weill/Brecht) 1967; first performed Venice, 1967.

Prayer-Prière (text by Calvino, written instructions; in honour of Karlheinz Stockhausen's 40th birthday) 1968.

The Modification and Instrumentation of a Famous Hornpipe as a Merry and Altogether Sincere Homage to Uncle Alfred (after Purcell, dedicated to Alfred Kalmus; flute, percussion, viola, cello, harpsichord) 1969; first performed London, 1969.

Après Visage (dance; tape, orchestra) 1972; first performed The Hague, 1972.

Linea (music for dance; 2 pianos, vibraphone, marimbaphone) 1973; first performed Grenoble, 1974. Recorded RCA RL 12291.

Per la dolce memoria di quel giorno (ballet; voices, piano, orchestra on tape; Béjart, after Petrarch) 1974; first performed Florence, 1974.

A-Ronne (radiophonic documentary for five actors; concert version for 8 voices; Sanguineti) 1974–5; broadcast Hilversum, 1974; concert version Liège, 1975. Recorded Decca 425 620–2; HMV EL 270452–4.

Quattro versioni originali della Ritirata Notturna di Madrid di L. Boccherini Sovrapposte e Trascrite per orchestra 1975; first performed Milan, 1975.

Siete canciones populares espanolas (by Manuel de Falla; arranged for mezzo-soprano, orchestra) 1978; first performed Italy, 1978.

Mix (material from *Linea* and *Sequenza IX*) 1985; first performed Taormina, 1985.

Naturale (theatre piece/dance; viola, tam-tam, voices on tape; Sicilian work songs and melodies) 1985–6.

Brahms-Berio Op 120 No 1 (clarinet or viola, orchestra) 1986; first performed Los Angeles, 1986.

Rendering ("Restoration of Fragments from a Symphony by Franz Schubert"; orchestra) 1989; first performed Amsterdam, 1989.

Lennon/McCartney: *Michelle*, *Ticket to Ride*, *Yesterday* (arranged for voice and—respectively—2 flutes, harpsichord; or flute, clarinet, harp, violin, viola, cello, double bass; flute, oboe, trumpet, violin, viola, cello, double bass; flute, harpsichord) 1967; first performed Venice, 1967.

Gustav Mahler: *Funf Fruhe Lieder* (arranged for male voices and orchestra) 1986; first performed Dobbiacco, 1986.

Gustav Mahler: *Sechs Fruhe Lieder* (arranged for baritone and orchestra) 1987; first performed Vienna, 1988.

Franz Schubert: *An die Musik* (arranged for chorus, small orchestra) 1989; first performed Paris, 1989.

PUBLICATIONS

By Berio: "Aspetti di artigianato formale", in *Incontri musicale: quaderni internazionali di musica contemporanea*, 3, Milan, 1959, translated into French in *Contrechamps*, 1 (on Berio), Lausanne, 1983; "Poesia e musica—un' esperienza", in *Incontri musicali*, 3, Milan, 1959, translated into French in *Contrechamps*, 1, Lausanne, 1983; "Du geste et de Piazza Carita", in *La Musique et ses problèmes contemporains: Cahiers Renaud-Barrault*, 1, 1963; "Eco in Ascolto", in *Contemporary Music Review*, 5, 1989; see also Edoardo Sanguineti, *Laborintus*, Milan, 1965; Italo Calvino, "Un re in ascolto", in *Sotto il sole giagura*, Milan, 1986, translated into English as *Under the Jaguar Sun*, New York, 1988.

On Berio: Reginald Smith Brindle, "Maderna and B", in *The Listener*, 85, 1971; George Flynn, "Listening to B's music", in *Musical Quarterly*, 61, 1975; Peter Altmann, *Sinfonia von LB: eine analytische Studie*, Vienna, 1977; Rossante Dalmonte and Balint Andras Varga, *LB: Two Interviews*, London, 1985, translated and edited by David Osmond-Smith from *Intervista sulla musica*, Bari, 1981, and *Bszelgetesek LB*, Budapest, 1981; David Osmond-Smith, *Playing with Words: A Guide to LB's Sinfonia*, London, 1985; David Osmond-Smith, *B*, Oxford Studies of Composers No 20, Oxford, 1991.

* * *

Of the major composers in the second half of the 20th century, Luciano Berio more than any, perhaps, has succeeded in conveying the novelty of new creative experience through music which commands a broad, even popular audience. His music breathes humanity and expressive sensibility; its sound is haunting, often ravishing. One senses the sheer musicality of an imagination which, through times dominated by intellectual systems, and despite Berio's own deep involvement with external ideas, speaks nevertheless first and last through the music itself. Returning again to what are now classic pieces of the second half of the 20th century, the listener is increasingly impressed as much by their inevitability and rightness as pure music, as by the impact of new invention and discovery. Not that Berio has taken an easy course, allowed himself to become routine or, latterly, to subside into the fashionable comforts of neo-romanticism. Instead, he has contributed very considerably to the onward progress of artistic thought; his musical vision has repeatedly led the way in its concepts and techniques. But if it is a music of ideas, it is also about people—their mannerisms, affections, fears, obsessions and memories—and about their attempts to communicate.

Berio has cast the performer not just as technician or interpreter, but as a whole person, complete with emotions and mental states. His series of *Sequenzas*, each for a solo instrument, demands from the performer both virtuosity of technique and virtuosity of awareness—of the inherent tensions between player and instrument, player and audience and of a particular instrumental gesture and its history. The act of performance is highlighted in his *Sequenzas*, but still more in works like *Recital* (written for Berio's first wife, Cathy Berberian) and the third movement of the *Sinfonia*, both of which explore memory and language, and are in effect anthologies of different styles, references and techniques.

What makes Berio's music particularly accessible is its theatricality; but the drama is not necessarily something one has to see. *A-Ronne*, for instance, which Berio has called a sound-documentary, creates a sense of aural theatre whose imaginary scenario is all the more vivid for not being explicit. In *Circles* the drama is essentially acoustic, but enhanced by visual gesture and movement. But there are also major works of staged music-theatre, *Recital*, *Passaggio*, *Laborintus II* and the "operas" (although far removed from the traditional meaning of that term) *Opera*, *La vera storia* and *Un re in ascolto*. The original concepts of theatre which make these pieces so remarkable emerged from a vortex of intellectual propositioning which Berio was able to share with unusually congenial collaborators: Umberto Eco, Edoardo Sanguineti and Italo Calvino, none of them conventional librettists but rather writer-scholars whose ideas he has found continually fascinating.

From an early age Berio had felt drawn to the theatre, and was influenced by such writers as James Joyce and Samuel Beckett. *Recital*, therefore, is not only a tribute to a most remarkable vocal artist; it acts through a Joycean stream-of-consciousness during which the singer's schizophrenic monologue is overwhelmed by the debris of accumulated repertoire. *La vera storia* explores self-commentary, a sort of hall of mirrors in which the text is observed from a multitude of different angles. *Un re in ascolto* focuses on the nature of listening. In both its text and music, and in the device of a theatre within a theatre, there are cyclic echoes and reenactments. Throughout most of Berio's major works, as David Osmond-Smith has observed, are striking continuities of theme, the denunciation of political oppression through violence and, repeatedly, the more fundamental theme of death. "Such insistence", he suggests, "may seem disconcerting to those accustomed only to the energy and *joie de vivre* of Berio's shorter concert-hall works. Yet a theatre of vitalistic gesture played out in the imagination requires mortality as a sounding board if it is to develop its full resonance."

Vocal music is central to Berio's work. It is a vehicle for lyricism, a framework for psychological and emotional suggestion, an analytical labyrinth in which to seek out the acoustic and semantic properties of a text, and an invitation to reinterpret historic techniques, whether as aria, choral polyphony, simple folksong, dramatic monologue, or even (as in some of his music for the Swingle Singers) as a contemporary equivalent of the humorous ensembles of Verdi's *Falstaff*. He has been drawn frequently to folk music and spoken of his Utopian ideal of creating a unity between folk and art music, "a real, perceptible, understandable continuity between ancient, popular music-making which is so close to everyday work, and our music". Parts of *Epifanie* have a folk-like intonation. The well-known *Folk Songs* are uncomplicated but nonetheless characteristic Berio "arrangements" of genuine folk material. *Cries of London* consists of archetypes viewed, as it were, from a distance. The splendidly Ivesian *Accordo*, written for outdoor performance, provides "windows" in which four independent wind bands can contribute their own popular repertory. In *Voci*, for viola and chamber ensemble, Sicilian songs of work and love are refracted and absorbed by a complex texture which is sometimes directly evocative of folk sources, but is mostly a thoughtful, introverted discourse proceeding on its own terms. The most extended of Berio's folk-inspired compositions is *Coro*; indeed it has the largest dimensions of any of his compositions apart from the operas. In *Coro* the human voice becomes part of the orchestral sound: each of the 40 singers is paired with an orchestral player. In the grandeur of its subject-matter which touches the whole of humanity, the telling interaction of folk texts from different countries with the words of Pablo Neruda, the interplay between dense and complex texture with music of affecting simplicity, in the gradual rotation and transformation of all this material, and, above all, in its prevailing mood of celebration and tragedy, *Coro* is Berio's most impressive and powerful concert masterpiece.

In *Coro*, a profoundly expressive purpose is served by innovative techniques. It is an axiom that Berio has considerably influenced contemporary musical language and notation, and contributed significantly to electro-acoustic music. With Bruno Maderna, in the early 1950s, he set up the first Italian electronic music studio in Milan, where he composed *Thema* (*Omaggio a Joyce*), originally created for radio, and *Visage*, incorporating the voice of Cathy Berberian and one of the most successful and durable works from the first decade of electronic music. The period between 1974 and 1980 when, invited by Pierre Boulez, Berio directed the electro-acoustic section of IRCAM was less productive of actual compositions than of research into real-time synthesis and transformation of sound. But the experience of working with the 4X led, in 1987 after extended negotiations, to the foundation in Florence of Berio's own centre for research, training and composition aptly named Tempo Reale. His first major work utilising this system, *Ofanim* (another movingly beautiful and theatrical use of voices, here two children's choirs and a Hebrew singer-dancer) makes impressive use of the computer's ability to place and move spatially, with startling precision, discrete components of live sound across eight different trajectories.

Berio is an accomplished conductor, and (as demonstrated in various published interviews) an original and stimulating thinker. He has spoken of music, "not as a language, but a language of languages" working on a multiplicity of layers. Part of this plurality is the revisiting and direct quotation of other music—now such a fashionable pastime of contemporary composers—an area in which, again, he has been a pioneer. In the *Sinfonia*, one of his most popular works, Berio carries off with astonishing bravura the "rehearing" of the scherzo of Mahler's Second Symphony, which runs through the third movement, as a vehicle for wide-ranging quotation. Transcriptions, orchestrations and transformations of other composers from Boccherini and Schubert to Mahler and Weill have been an ongoing hobby as, earlier, was the reworking of his own pieces in the series of *Chemins*. With typical perception, he has disarmingly remarked, "maybe this desire to try and possess everything is a little Faustian".

—Richard Steinitz

BERKELEY, (Sir) Lennox (Randal Francis). British/English. Born at Boars Hill, Oxford, 12 May 1903. Educated at Gresham's School, Holt, 1914–18; St George's School, Harpenden, 1919–20; Merton College, Oxford, 1922–6, B.A.; studied in Paris (under Nadia Boulanger), 1926–32. Married Elizabeth Freda Bernstein in 1946; 3 sons, including Michael Berkeley, *q.v.* Orchestral programme builder, BBC Music Department, 1942–5; professor, Royal Academy of Music, London, 1945–68. Recipient: Collard Fellowship, 1946; Commander of the British Empire, 1957; Cobbett Medal, 1962; Ordre de Mérite Culturel, Monaco, 1967; Papal Knighthood of St Gregory, 1973; knighted, 1973. **Died 26 December 1990**.

Publishers: Boosey & Hawkes; Schott; Stainer & Bell; Berben; Novello.

Symphonies/orchestral:

Suite 1927; first performed Paris, February 1928.
Symphony for Strings 1930–1; first performed London, 14 December 1931, but now lost.
Ballet for Orchestra 1932.
Overture Op 8 1934; first performed London, 1935.
Mont Juic Op 9 (orchestral suite, collaboration with Benjamin Britten) 1937; broadcast January 1938.
Introduction and Allegro Op 11 (2 pianos, orchestra) 1938.
Serenade Op 12 (string orchestra) 1939; first performed London, February 1940. Recorded Lyrita SRCS 80.
Cello Concerto 1939; first performed Cheltenham, Gloucestershire, 1982.
Symphony No 1 Op 16 1940. Recorded Lyrita SRCS 80.
Divertimento in B♭ Op 18 1943.
Nocturne Op 25 1946.
Concerto in B♭ Op 29 (piano, orchestra) 1947.
Overture 1947.
Concerto Op 30 (2 pianos, orchestra) 1948. Recorded Lyrita SRCS 80.
Sinfonietta Op 34 1950.
Flute Concerto Op 36 1952.
Suite 1953.
Variations on Sellinger's Round (strings; no 3 of a collaboration) 1953.
Suite from "Nelson" Op 42 1955.
Symphony No 2 Op 51 1956–8.
Concerto Op 46 (piano, double string orchestra) 1958.
Overture for Light Orchestra 1959.
Suite: A Winter's Tale Op 54 1960.
Five Pieces Op 56 (violin, orchestra) 1961.
Concerto Op 59 (violin, chamber orchestra) 1961.
Partita Op 66 (chamber orchestra) 1964–5.
Symphony No 3 in One Movement Op 74 1969.
Windsor Variations Op 75 (chamber orchestra) 1969.
Dialogue Op 79 (cello, chamber orchestra) 1970.
Palm Court Waltz Op 81 No 2 1971.
Sinfonia Concertante Op 84 (oboe, orchestra) 1973.
Antiphon Op 85 (string orchestra) 1973.
Suite Op 87 (strings) 1973–4.
Voices of the Night Op 86 1973.
Guitar Concerto Op 88 1974.
Symphony No 4 Op 94 1976–8.
Elegy Op 33 No 2a (arranged for strings) 1978.

Chamber/instrumental:

Minuet (2 recorders) 1924.
March (piano) 1924.
Toccata (piano) 1925.
Mr Pilkington's Toye (piano) 1925.
For Vere (piano) 1927.
Petite Suite (oboe, cello) 1927.
Serenade (flute, oboe, violin, viola, cello) 1929.
Piece (flute, clarinet, piano) 1929.
Suite (harpsichord) 1930.
Suite (flute, oboe, violin, viola, cello) ?1930.
Sonata No 1 (violin, piano) 1931.
Three Pieces (clarinet) ?1932.
Sonata No 2 Op 1 (violin, piano) 1933.
Polka Op 5a (piano) 1934. Recorded Kingdom KCLCD 2012.
Three Pieces Op 5 (2 pianos) 1934–8.
Three Pieces Op 2 (piano) 1935.
Trio (flute, oboe, piano) 1935.
String Quartet No 1 Op 6 1935.
Three Impromptus Op 7 (piano) 1935.

Five Short Pieces Op 4 (piano) 1936. Recorded Kingdom KCLCD 2012.
Sonatina Op 13 (recorder or flute, piano) 1939.
Four Concert Studies Op 14 No 1 (piano) 1940.
Impromptu (organ) 1941.
Sonata Op 20 (piano) 1941–5. Recorded Pearl SHE 576; Kingdom KCLCD 2012.
String Quartet No 2 Op 15 1942.
String Trio Op 19 1943.
Paysage (piano) 1944.
Sonata in D minor Op 22 (viola, piano) 1945.
Six Preludes Op 23 (piano) 1945. Recorded Lyrita RCS 9; Kingdom KCLCD 2912.
Introduction and Allegro Op 24 (violin) 1946.
Three Mazurkas Op 32 No 1 (piano) 1949; first performed Paris, October 1949. Recorded Kingdom KCLCD 2012.
Scherzo Op 32 No 2 (piano) 1949.
Theme and Variations Op 33 No 1 (violin) 1950.
Elegy Op 33 No 2 (violin, piano) 1950.
Sonatina Op 39 (piano duet) 1954.
Trio Op 44 (violin, horn, piano) 1954.
Sextet Op 47 (clarinet, horn, string quartet) 1955.
Concert Study in E♭ Op 48 No 2 (piano) 1955.
Concertino Op 49 (recorder or flute, violin, cello, harpsichord or piano) 1955.
Allegro (2 treble recorders) 1955.
Andantino Op 21 No 2a (based on Herbert setting; cello, piano) 1955.
Sonatina Op 52 No 1 (guitar) 1957.
Sonatina Op 52 No 2 (2 pianos) 1959.
Improvisation on a Theme of Manuel de Falla Op 55 No 2 (piano) 1960. Recorded KCLCD 2012.
Prelude and Fugue Op 55 No 3 (clavichord) 1960.
Sonatina Op 61 (oboe, piano) 1961.
Diversions Op 63 (8 instruments) 1964.
Three Pieces Op 72 No 1 (organ) 1966–8.
Nocturne Op 67 No 2 (harp) 1967.
Quartet Op 70 (oboe, string trio) 1967.
Theme and Variations Op 73 (piano duet) 1968.
String Quartet No 3 Op 76 1970.
Theme and Variations Op 77 (guitar) 1970.
Introduction and Allegro Op 80 (double bass, piano) 1971.
Duo Op 81 No 1 (cello, piano) 1971.
Palm Court Waltz Op 81 No 2a (piano duet) 1971.
In Memoriam Igor Stravinsky (string quartet) 1971.
Four Studies Op 82 (piano) 1972.
Quintet Op 90 (wind, piano) 1974–5.
Fantasia Op 92 (organ) 1976.
Prelude and Capriccio Op 95 1978.
Sonata Op 97 (flute, piano) 1978.
Bagatelle Op 101 No 1 (2 pianos) 1981.
Andantino Op 21 No 2a (organ; arranged by Jennifer Bate from Herbert setting) 1981.
Mazurka Op 101 No 2 (piano) 1982. Recorded Kingdom KCLCD 2012.

Vocal/choral:

Pastourelle (voice, piano; 13th century) 1924; first performed Oxford, 16 June 1924.
Rondeau (voice, piano; Charles d'Orléans) 1924.
The Thresher/D'un Vanneur de bleg aux vents (voice, piano; du Bellay) 1925; first performed Oxford, 12 March 1925.
Trois Poèmes de Vildrac (voice, piano) 1929.
La poulette grise (children's voices, trumpet, 2 pianos) 1931.
Ode (SATB chorus, trumpet, strings) 1932.
Jonah Op 3 (oratorio) 1933–5; broadcast 19 June 1936.
How Love Came In (voice, piano; Herrick) 1935.
Deux poèmes de Pindar: Dithyramb and Hymn (SATB chorus, soloists, orchestra) 1936; first performed London, 11 November 1936.
Songs Op 14 No 2 (voice, piano; Auden, O'Malley, Lorca, Labe, Passerat) 1937–40.
Domini est Terra Op 10 (chorus, orchestra) 1938.
Five Housman Songs Op 14 No 3 (voice, piano) 1940.
The Midnight Murk (unaccompanied SATB chorus; Sagittarius) 1942.
Two Songs (voice, piano; Yeats, Day-Lewis) 1943.
Lord, When the Sense of Thy Sweet Grace Op 21 No 1 (SATB chorus, organ; Crashaw) 1944.
A Festival Anthem Op 21 No 2 (SATB chorus, organ; Herbert, Vaughan) 1945.
Five Songs Op 26 (voice, piano; de la Mare) 1946.
Four Poems of St Teresa of Avila Op 27 (contralto, strings) 1947. Recorded HMV 20 HQM 1069.
Stabat mater Op 28/28a (6 solo voices, 12 instruments) 1947, arranged for voices and small orchestra by Michael Berkeley, 1978.
The Low Lands of Holland (voice, piano; trad./O'Malley) 1947.
Colonus's Praise Op 31 (SATB chorus, orchestra; Yeats) 1948.
There Was Neither Grass nor Corn (unaccompanied SATB chorus; Cornford) 1949.
Variations on a Hymn by Orlando Gibbons Op 35 (tenor, SATB chorus, strings, organ) 1951.
Three Greek Songs Op 38 (voice, piano; Sappho, Antipater, Plato) 1951.
Ask Me No More Op 37 No 1 (TTBB chorus; Carew) 1952.
Five Ronsard Sonnets Set 1 Op 40 (2 tenors, piano) 1952.
Spring at This Hour Op 37 No 2 (SSATBB chorus; Dehn) 1953.
Crux fidelis Op 43 No 1 (tenor, SATB chorus) 1955.
Look Up, Sweet Babe Op 43 No 2 (treble, SATB chorus, organ; Crashaw) 1955.
Salve Regina Op 48 No 1 (unison voices, organ) 1955.
Five Poems Op 53 (voice, piano; Auden) 1958.
So Sweet Love Seemed (voice, piano; Bridges) 1959.
Thou Hast Made Me Op 55 No 1 (SATB chorus, organ; Donne) 1960.
Missa Brevis Op 57 (SATB chorus, organ) 1960.
Autumn's Legacy Op 58 (high voice, piano; Beddoes, Durrell, Tennyson, Hopkins, Davies, Hartley Coleridge) 1962.
Batter My Heart Op 60 No 1 (soprano, SATB chorus, organ, chamber orchestra; Donne) 1962.
Justorum Animae Op 60 No 2 (unaccompanied SATB chorus) 1963.
Autumne Op 60 No 3 (voice, piano; Apollinaire) 1963.
Counting the Beats Op 60 No 4 (voice, piano; Graves) 1963.
Four Ronsard Sonnets Set 2 Op 62/62a (tenor, orchestra or chamber orchestra) 1963.
Mass for Five Voices Op 64 (unaccompanied SSATB chorus) 1964.
Songs of the Half-Light Op 65 (voice, guitar; de la Mare) 1964.
Three Songs Op 67 No 1 (unaccompanied TTBB chorus; Herrick, Bridges) 1965.
Signs in the Dark Op 69 (SATB chorus, strings; Lee) 1967.
Magnificat Op 71 (SATB chorus, orchestra) 1968.
The Windhover Op 72 No 2 (unaccompanied SATB chorus; Hopkins) 1968.
Hail, Holy Queen (voices, organ or piano) 1970.
Chinese Songs Op 78 (voice, piano) 1971.

Three Latin Motets Op 83 No 1 (unaccompanied SSATB chorus) 1972.
Hymn for Shakespeare's Birthday Op 83 No 1 (SATB chorus, organ; Day-Lewis) 1972.
Five Herrick Poems Op 89 (voice, harp) 1973–4.
The Lord Is My Shepherd Op 91 No 1 (treble, SATB chorus, organ) 1975.
Grace (SATB chorus) 1975.
The Hill of the Graces Op 91 No 2 (unaccompanied SSAATTBB chorus; Spenser) 1975.
Four Score Years and Ten (voice, piano; Ellis) 1977.
Another Spring Op 93 No 1 (voice, piano; de la Mare) 1977.
Judica Me Op 96 No 1 (unaccompanied SSATBB chorus) 1978.
Una and the Lion Op 98 (soprano, recorder, viola da gamba, harpsichord; Spenser) 1978–9.
Ubi Caritas Op 96 No 2 (unaccompanied SSATB chorus) 1980.
Magnificat and Nunc Dimittis Op 99 (SATB chorus, organ) 1980.
Sonnet Op 102 (voice, piano; Labe) 1982.
In Wintertime Op 103 (unaccompanied SATB chorus) 1983.

Opera:

Nelson Op 41 (Pryce-Jones) 1949–54.
A Dinner Engagement Op 45 1954.
Ruth Op 50 1956.
Castaway Op 68 1967.

Other:

The Judgement of Paris (ballet; orchestra) 1938.
Sweet Was the Song Op 43 No 3 (ballet; SATB chorus, organ) 1957.
Christ Is the World's Redeemer (hymn tune) 1963.
Three Hymn Tunes in Cambridge Hymnal (nos 40 "Hear'st Thou, My Soul", 61 "Lord by Whose Breath", 152 "I Sing of a Maiden") 1967.
Fanfare for Royal Academy of Music Banquet (band) 1972.
The Tempest (incidental music to Shakespeare) 1946; first performed Stratford-upon-Avon, 1946.
A Winter's Tape (incidental music to Shakespeare) 1960; first performed Stratford-upon-Avon, 1960.

Francis Poulenc: *Flute Sonata Op 93 no 2* (arranged for orchestra) 1975.

Film scores: *The Sword of the Spirit*, 1942; *Out of Chaos*, 1944; *Hotel Reserve*, 1944; *The First Gentleman*, 1947–8; *Youth in Britain*, 1957.

PUBLICATIONS

By Berkeley: Reports from Paris for *The Monthly Musical Record*, June 1929–June 1934; "Nadia Boulanger as Teacher", in *The Monthly Musical Record*, January 1931; "Britten and His String Quartet", in *The Listener*, 27 May 1943; contribution to *Benjamin Britten: A Commentary on His Works from a Group of Specialists*, edited by Donald Mitchell and Hans Keller, London, 1952; "The Sound of Words", in *The Times*, 28 June 1962; "Francis Poulenc", obituary, in *The Musical Times*, March 1963; in *Frederic Chopin: Profiles of the Man and Musician*, London, 1966; "Truth in Music", in *The Times Literary Supplement*, 3 March 1966; "Lili Boulanger", in *The Listener*, 5 March 1970; "Alan Rawsthorne", in *Composer*, Winter 1971; "A Composer Speaks", in *Composer*, Spring 1972.

On Berkeley: G. Bryan, "The Younger English Composers, V: LB", in *The Monthly Musical Record*, June 1929; "Newcomers—LB", in *The Chesterian*, April 1934; R. Hull, "The Music of LB", in *The Listener*, 10 July 1947; Wilfred Mellers, "The Music of LB", in *The Listener*, 24 June 1954; W. Dean, "LB's Orchestral Music", in *The Listener*, 7 April 1955; M. Schaffer, in *British Composers in Interview*, London, 1963; Peter Dickinson, "The Music of LB", in *The Musical Times*, May 1963; John Tavener, "LB at 70", in *The Listener*, 10 May 1973; Peter Dickinson, *Twenty British Composers*, London, 1975; "B at 75 Talks to Peter Dickinson", in *The Musical Times*, May 1978; Roger Steptoe, "Contemporary Composer Series, Sir LB", in *The Music Teacher*, July 1986; Peter Dickinson, *The Music of LB*, London, 1988.

* * *

During hesitant musical studies in his undergraduate years at Oxford, Lennox Berkeley produced a number of compositions—mostly songs—which were indifferently received and have, in the main, been lost. Those pieces that have survived betray several influences: there are neo-baroque echoes and bitonal flourishes and, especially in the technically demanding *Toccata* for piano, figurations which clearly owe a good deal to Ravel. In fact, Berkeley showed some of his compositions to Ravel, who provided the introduction to Nadia Boulanger which led to Berkeley's crucial formative studies in Paris.

Berkeley's music has never enjoyed the general acclaim awarded to close English contemporaries like Walton and Britten. His work with Boulanger included a strict grounding in academic counterpoint; but, at the same time, he ingested various contemporary continental influences which, while helping to enhance his expressive range, undoubtedly focused the suspicion of a deeply conservative British musical establishment. Like several of Boulanger's other leading pupils, he was slow to shake off certain aspects of her somewhat domineering pedagogism.

The young Berkeley was hampered by a lack of self-confidence in his musical abilities, a dangerous disability for an exponent of such a public art-form, and one which he never entirely overcame. Numerous early pieces were lost or disowned and his acknowledged Opus 1, the Second Violin Sonata, did not appear until 1933. This work is clearly marked by the rhythmic mannerisms and determined unsentimentality of Stravinsky's Violin Concerto and *Duo concertant*; neo-classical Stravinsky continued to provide an important inspiration for works from the later 1930s; examples include the piquant bitonal touches of the First Symphony. However, he had yet to feel secure with his style: the oratorio, *Jonah*, though it contains some fine passages (including a few which are indebted to Walton's *Belshazzar's Feast*, as well as to Stravinsky) and won Britten's qualified admiration, was later withdrawn.

Maturity arrived, perhaps unexpectedly, with the *Serenade* for string orchestra, an economically-scored piece in which there are still traces of Stravinsky; the style, however, is more relaxed, with a less fragmented rhythmic approach indebted to J.S. Bach and an almost Mozartian clarity of scoring. The First Symphony is another fluent offering, though its strength is discursive communication, rather than dramatic tension. His next orchestral work, the *Divertimento in B♭* is much tauter, with a densely argued sonata form opening movement and a strikingly successful scherzo.

In the immediate post-war years, Berkeley's music seems to acquire a new optimism, which is mirrored by various new influences. An excellent example is the exuberent Piano

Concerto Op 29, where "blue notes" are encountered in a manner very reminiscent of Gershwin; in the main theme of the finale, this trait is incorporated most engagingly into a theme of Prokofiev-like vitality. Berkeley, though by no means a keyboard virtuoso, demonstrates here—and in his other main keyboard works, the *Sonata* for piano and *Concerto* for two pianos—an idiomatic understanding of advanced keyboard technique. This must derive in large measure from his early admiration for Ravel.

During the 1950s and 1960s, Berkeley's work lost some of its easy communicativeness, as the composer continually sought new directions. Part of his restlessness was undoubtedly due to the strain of writing opera—where he was, as he felt acutely, in direct competition with Britten—and he tried to adjust by developing a free-atonal harmonic approach. Similarities have been noted between the horn *Trio* and Schoenberg's first *Chamber Symphony*, in that both use perfect fourth intervals in a virtually atonal fashion. In Aria I from the *Concertino*, elements of serial technique are regularly employed, despite Berkeley's earlier-professed belief in the superiority of the "aural satisfaction" of tonal harmony over the "arbitrary" twelve-note system. It is interesting, nevertheless, that those serial works for which he expressed greatest admiration—particularly Berg's Violin Concerto—tend to combine the mathematical synthesis of the tone-row with potent tonal elements. Berkeley continued to flirt with serialism, as in the slow movement of his own Violin Concerto and in parts of the Third Symphony, without ever espousing it wholeheartedly. Berkeley's output is personal and exquisitely crafted but in the end he failed to capture a wide audience. Ultimately, this may be because, despite his brilliant absorption of many styles, he lacked the self-belief to meld them with convincing individuality.

—Paul Horner

BERKELEY, Michael (Fitzhardinge). British/English. Born in London, 29 May 1948; son of Sir Lennox Berkeley, *q.v.* Educated at Westminster Cathedral Choir School, London; Oratory School; Royal Academy of Music, London, A.R.A.M., 1984; private study with Sir Lennox Berkeley and with Richard Rodney Bennett. Married Deborah Jane Coltman-Rogers in 1979; 1 daughter. Played in rock groups; phlebotomist, St Bartholomew's Hospital, London, 1969–71; presentation assistant, London Weekend Television, 1973; compere, BBC Radio 3, 1974–9; associate composer, Scottish Chamber Orchestra, 1979; member, executive committee, Association of Professional Composers, 1982–4; member, new music sub-committee, 1984–6, and music panel adviser, since 1986, Arts Council of Great Britain; member, Central Music Advisory Committee, BBC, since 1986; radio and television music presenter; adviser on plagiarism. Recipient: Guinness Prize (for *Meditations*), 1977. Mailing address: 49 Blenheim Crescent, London W11 2EF, England.

Publisher: Oxford University Press.

Symphonies/orchestral:

Meditations (string orchestra) 1977; first performed London, 1977. Recorded Hyperion A 66213.

Concerto for Oboe and String Orchestra 1977; first performed Burnham Market, Norfolk, 20 August 1977. Recorded Pearl SHE 583.

Fantasia Concertante (small orchestra) 1978; first performed London, 5 March 1978.

Fanfare and National Anthem (3 trumpets, 3 trombones; orchestra, with optional SSATB or unison chorus) 1979; first performed London, 1979.

Primavera (with optional wordless chorus) 1979; first performed London, 18 May 1979.

Uprising: Symphony in One Movement 1980. Recorded Hyperion A 66097.

Flames 1980; first performed Liverpool, 10 January 1981.

Suite: The Vision of Piers the Ploughman (2 horns, piano, percussion, strings) 1981; first performed London, 13 June 1981.

Gregorian Variations 1982; first performed London, 22 April 1982.

The Romance of the Rose (small orchestra) 1982; first performed London, 5 November 1982. Recorded Hyperion A 66097.

Concerto for Cello and Small Orchestra 1983; first performed Bletchley, Buckinghamshire, 20 February 1983.

Concerto for Horn and String Orchestra 1984; first performed Cheltenham, Gloucestershire, 17 July 1984.

Daybreak and a Candle End 1985; first performed London, 17 June 1985.

Organ Concerto 1987; first performed Cambridge, 23 July 1987.

Coronach (string orchestra) 1988; first performed Presteigne, Wales, September 1988.

Chamber/instrumental:

Passacaglia (piano) 1978; first performed London, 1978.

Strange Meeting (piano) 1978; first performed Berlin, December 1978.

String Trio 1978; first performed Leicester, 9 November 1978. Recorded Hyperion A 66109.

Etude des Fleurs (cello, piano) 1979, revised 1979; first performed London, 27 May 1979; revised version, London, 20 July 1979.

Sonata (violin, piano) 1979; first performed Cardiff, 4 December 1979.

Sonata (organ) 1979; first performed Milstatt, Austria, 26 August 1979.

Three Moods (oboe) 1979; first performed Knighton, Wales, 1979. Recorded Hyperion A 66109.

American Suite (flute or recorder, cello or bassoon) 1980; first performed London, 28 March 1980.

Chamber Symphony (flute/alto flute/piccolo, oboe, clarinet/bass clarinet, horn, violin, viola, cello, double bass, piano) 1980; first performed King's Lynn, Norfolk, 1 August 1980. Recorded Hyperion A 66213.

Lament (guitar) 1980.

Iberian Notebook (cello) 1980; first performed London, 18 January 1980.

String Quartet No 1 1981; first performed Ellesmere, Lancashire, 17 July 1981. Recorded Hyperion A 66109.

Variations on Greek Folk Songs (viola) 1981; first performed London, 18 May 1981.

Worry Beads (guitar) 1981; first performed London, 21 May 1981.

Nocturne (flute, harp, violin, viola, cello) 1982; first performed London, 9 February 1982.

Piano Trio 1982; first performed Luton, Bedfordshire, 18 January 1982. Recorded Hyperion A 66213.

Sonata in One Movement (guitar) 1982; first performed Edinburgh, 23 August 1982.
Music for Chaucer (brass quintet) 1983; first performed London, 1983. Recorded Chandos ABRD 1190/CHAN 8490 CD.
Quintet for Clarinet and Strings (clarinet, string quartet) 1983; first performed Battle, Kent, 17 July 1983. Recorded Hyperion A 66213.
String Quartet No 2 1984; first performed Monmouth, Wales, 17 January 1984.
Fierce Tears (oboe, piano) 1984; first performed London, 30 January 1984. Recorded Hyperion A 66213.
Funerals and Fandangos (violin) 1984.
Pas de Deux (recorder, guitar) 1985.
Flighting (clarinet) 1985.
Impromptu (guitar) 1985; broadcast BBC, 1985.
For the Savage Messiah 1985; first performed London, 23 May 1985.
A Mosaic for Father Popieluszko (violin, guitar) 1985; first performed London, 17 March 1985.
Keening (saxophone) 1987; first performed London, November 1988. Recorded Hyperion.
Quartet Study (String Quartet No 3) 1987.
Wild Bells (organ) 1988.
The Snake (cor anglais) 1990; first performed London, 5 May 1990.
Fierce Tears II (oboe) 1990; first performed Aldeburgh, Suffolk, 21 June 1990.
Entertaining Master Punch (from an opera in progress; wind quartet, violin, cello, piano, percussion, harp) 1990; first performed London, 7 February 1991.
Brass Octet (4 trumpets, 4 trombones) n.d.

Vocal/choral:

The Wild Winds (soprano, small orchestra; Blake) 1978; first performed London, 19 December 1978.
Rain (tenor, violin, cello; Edward Thomas) 1979; first performed London, 20 July 1979.
At the Round Earth's Imagin'd Corners (double choir, organ, optional trumpet; Donne) 1980; first performed Chichester, 26 July 1980.
Wessex Graves (tenor, harp; Hardy) 1981; first performed Wavendon, Buckinghamshire, 19 July 1981.
The Crocodile and Father William (unaccompanied girls' choir; Carroll) 1982; first performed Welbeck, Nottinghamshire, 22 May 1982.
Easter (SATB choir, organ, optional brass; Herbert) 1982; first performed London, 12 July 1982.
As the Wind Doth Blow (unaccompanied choir; anon. 16th century) 1983; first performed London, 25 June 1983.
Or Shall We Die? (oratorio for soprano, baritone, chorus, orchestra; McEwan) 1983; first performed London, 6 February 1983. Recorded EMI ASD 2700581.
Hereford Communion Service (SATB choir, organ) 1985; first performed Hereford, 16 August 1985.
Pasce Oves Meas (SATB choir, optional organ) 1985.
Song of Awakening Love (soprano, orchestra; E.B. Browning, C. Rossetti) 1986; first performed Cheltenham, Gloucestershire, 15 July 1986.
Speaking Silence (baritone, piano; anon, C. Rossetti, Yeats) 1986; first performed Cricklade, Wiltshire, 28 September 1986.
Verbum caro factum est (baritone, SATB chorus, organ) 1987; first performed Birmingham, 7 January 1988.
Beati mortui (unaccompanied SATB choir) 1988.
Jubilate Deo (unaccompanied SATB choir) 1988.
Amen dico vobis (unaccompanied SATB choir) 1988.
Laetentur coeli (unaccompanied SATB choir) 1988.
The Red Macula (SATB choir, orchestra) 1989; first performed Leeds, 5 May 1989.
Three Christmas Carols (unison voices, piano) n.d.

Other:

The Mayfly (ballet for children; violin, cello, flute, clarinet, percussion, piano) 1984; first performed Nether Wallop, Hampshire, 30 September 1984.
Captive (film music) 1986.
Bastet (ballet; orchestra) 1988; first performed Birmingham, 24 June 1988.

* * *

Lennox Berkeley was, in the words of one of his pupils, "too kind" to be a very effective teacher (it will be noted that no memoir of Nadia Boulanger ever stresses kindness among her virtues). Nonetheless, Berkeley was an important and influential teacher, numbering composers Nicholas Maw, John Tavener, Richard Rodney Bennett and his own son Michael Berkeley among his more successful students.

If there is such a thing as "anxiety of influence", it is not evident in Michael Berkeley's work, either as a composer or as a finely discriminating broadcaster on music. He acquired a mature voice early, with little of the querulousness and self-doubt that afflicted his father at the same age. In 1977, still under 30, Berkeley was awarded the Guinness Prize for his *Meditations* for strings, a comparatively minor and unruffled work that demonstrated a fine sense of instrumental colour in a well-established English tradition, but with little sign in it of what was to follow. Its successor, written on commission, was the altogether more complex *Fantasia Concertante*, no less clear-sighted in conception but virtuosic in its argument and development and a clear step toward the more adventurous musical language of the *Chamber Symphony*, whose underlying serial idiom and single movement structure recalls Schoenberg.

Over the next few years, Berkeley experimented frequently with single-movement works, apparently attempting to sustain a coherent structure—whether programmatic or formal—under a widely ranging display of instrumental colour and dynamics. The *String Quartet No 1* recalls Arthur Schnabel's in its capaciousness and intensity of purpose, but the culmination of this particular line of approach comes in the 1980 symphony in one movement *Uprising*.

This, and the remarkable oratorio *Or Shall We Die?* which followed in 1983, show how far Berkeley has moved—unless the reason is that the world has moved faster—from mystical and certainly apolitical aestheticism that was so characteristic of his father. *Uprising* was inspired by the revolt of the *mujahedin* in Afghanistan, and by the first stirrings of industrial democracy in Poland (Berkeley was later to write *A Mosaic for Father Popieluszko* for the unusual combination of violin and guitar in memory of the murdered priest; the choice of instrumentation and the inescapable emotionalism of the piece are a surprising echo of his father's work). *Uprising* is a powerfully dramatic piece of orchestral writing. There is a basic tone-row but it is put to unashamedly dramatic uses and, as Berkeley has said, its inversion is intended to convey a sense of political transformation, just as the stabs of brass are intended to convey oppressive power.

Though the generic structure may be Schoenbergian, there is no question but that the chief influence is Stravinsky. This is evident in the insistent use of chords and a nagging ambiguity in the pulse. It remains perhaps Berkeley's finest non-vocal work.

Unquestionably his most influential work to date has been *Or Shall We Die?*, written to a powerful anti-war text by the controversial novelist Ian McEwan and given more exposure than most such works by a television film made for and broadcast by Britain's then-adventurous Channel 4. Here Berkeley was able, as he seems not to have been in earlier vocal works, to subordinate his increasingly complex musical imagination to urgent simplicities of McEwan's warnings of nuclear disaster. Remarkably, *Or Shall We Die?* has survived its moment rather well; in a slightly less apocalyptic political atmosphere, it emerges as a finely universalised account of passion and compassion, suffering and courage.

These are the qualities that Berkeley's work most often expresses. His *Fierce Tears* for oboe is related in spirit to the more complex *Keening* for alto saxophone and piano, a wonderfully expressive piece that exploits the saxophone's expressive properties—lachrymose, but also aggressive—to the maximum. The piano piece *Strange Meeting* echoes Wilfred Owen's anti-war poem but combines such sentiments with Owen's complex use of consonance and assonance and his unexpected affirmation and acceptance. Compare Berkeley's choral setting of John Donne's "At the Round Earth's Imagin'd Corners" with Geoffrey Burgon's earlier version for soprano, trumpet and organ (Berkeley leaves the trumpet an option) and you gain a sense of how much more of the *text* Berkeley has absorbed. He is a composer of rare intelligence and commitment. It will be interesting to hear how his imagination responds to the fresh challenges of the 1990s.

—James Weir

BERNARD, Pierre. French. Born in Marseille, 8 July 1946. Educated at Conservatoire National Supérieur de Musique, Paris (under Pierre Schaeffer), 1969–71; studied electro-acoustic composition with Groupe de Recherche Musical de l'INA-GRM, 1969–71; training in audiovisual techniques and (with Jerome Andrews) in dance; University of Paris VIII (1st year of doctorate in aesthetics), 1989. Married Roberta Mencaraglia, 29 November 1969; 3 children. Artistic director, Festival de Musiue Contemporain, Paris, 1980–3; artistic director, Festival and first Colloque d'Informatique Musical, Campus d'Orsay, 1983; director of training courses and conferences, CEMAMu/UPIC, Paris, 1982–90. Recipient: prize (for *Jérémie*), Festival International de Musique Electroacoustique, Bourges, 1974. Mailing address: 29 rue Meslay, 75003 Paris, France.

Publisher: none.

Electro-acoustic:

Ocre 1970; first performed Paris, 1970.
Organ 1971; first performed Paris, 1973.
Souffle 1972; first performed Paris, 1973.
Jérémie 1972; first performed Bourges, 1974.
Piano d'ombre (tape, sounding board of piano) 1974; first performed Paris, 1974.
Déroulement 1974; first performed Paris, 1974.
Les Fenêtres s'ouvrent de l'intérieur 1975; first performed Cannes, 1976.
Regarder au dedans (voice, tape) 1975; first performed Paris, 1976.
Traversée 1976; first performed Evry, 1976.
La Foire à la feraille 1976; first performed Paris, 1976.
Trois Instants qui se suivent (tape, percussion) 1977; first performed Evry, 1977.
Concret 1 1977; first performed Paris, 1980.
Pour se perdre (with films on 3 screens) 1978; first performed Paris, 1980.
Chant 1 1978; first performed Paris, 1980.
Trace (tape, clarinets) 1979; first performed Paris, 1980.
Deux Lacs l'un sur l'autre se reposent (with flute) 1979; first performed Paris, 1980.
Ouverture 1980; first performed Paris, 1980.
St Merri (2 harmoniums) 1980; first performed Paris, 1980.
Duo pour basse seule (double bass, film) 1980; first performed La Rochelle, 1980.
Cendres 1981; first performed Bourges, 1981.
Solar (UPIC system) 1981; first performed Paris, 1981.
Instantané 1981; first performed Paris, 1981.
Assis face au ciel je contemple 1982; first performed Bourges, 1982.
Racines (4 congas) 1982; first performed Paris, 1983.
Ham Sa (UPIC system) 1983; first performed Paris, 1983.
Danse des ombres attardées 1984; first performed Bourges, 1984.
Solstice 1984; first performed Massy, 1984.
Rumeur 1984; first performed Massy, 1984.
Vision d'Azur 1984; first performed Massy, 1984.
Kanaké (with saxophones) 1984; first performed Besançon, 1985.
Etude en écailles (UPIC system) 1985; first performed Besançon, 1985.
Cristal (UPIC system) 1985; first performed Besançon, 1985.
Les Sept Anneaux (UPIC system; percussion, strings, brass, choir) 1986; first performed Vitry/Seine, 1986.
Exil (text by St John Perse) 1987; first performed Paris, 1987.
Holos 1988; first performed Paris, 1988.
Temps réel (UPIC system) 1989; first performed Lyon, 1989.
Plein Soleil sur la mer (Syter system) 1990.
Alliage rituel (collaborative work for UPIC system) 1990; first performed Glasgow, 1990.

Other:

La Vie au féminin (documentary film) 1974.
Kanaké (theatre music to work by Dobbelaere and Tjibaou) 1975; first performed Caledonie, 1975.
Meltemie (dance by Jackie Marques) 1975; first performed Paris, 1975.
Ski (music to film by C. Hauvette) 1975.
Miroir (collaboration with M. Puig) 1976; first performed Orsay, 1976.
Pourrait faire mieux (documentary film) 1976.
Rêve, cauchemar, aurore (dance by Jackie Marques) 1976; first performed Brussels, 1976.
Inde du nord (audio-visual) 1976.
Piano d'ombre (dance by Jackie Marques) 1978; first performed Bagnolet, 1978.
Trois Instants qui se suivent (dance by Jackie Marques) 1978; first performed Bourges, 1978.
Derrière la cour (documentary film) 1978.
Soleil sous la neige (dance by Jackie Marques) 1979; first performed Bagnolet, 1979.

Siddha Yoga Meditation (documentary film) 1979.
Clair, obscur (dance by Jackie Marques) 1980; first performed Genes, 1980.
Matinée chez la Princesse de Guermantes (Proust, directed by Lonsdale) 1983; first performed Bures/Yvette, 1983.
La Croisade des enfants (Brecht, directed by Dobbelaere) 1983; first performed Munich, 1983.
L'Adoration perpetuelle (Proust, directed by Malric) 1984; first performed Bures/Yvette, 1984.
Au suivant (dance by Jackie Marques) 1984; first performed Lille, 1984.
Un Jour en Flandre/Arc-en-ciel (by G. Dobbelaere) 1985; first performed Florence, 1985.
Fleur de Snas (dance by Jackie Marques) 1985; first performed Lille, 1985.
Accident personnel (dance by Jackie Marques) 1986; first performed Genes, 1986.
Les Sypres sont si loin (dance by Jackie Marques) 1986; first performed Bordeaux, 1986.
Exil (St John Perse, directed by Lonsdale) 1987; first performed Paris, 1987.
Les Grandes Heures de Guillaume (by G. Dobbelaere) 1987; first performed Caen, 1987.
La Charte (video by Philippe Missotte) 1988.
Or sujet (dance by Jackie Marques) 1989; first performed Lausanne, 1989.
L'Héritage de la chouette (television film by Chris Marker) 1989.
Le Désert (Onfroy, directed by Lonsdale) 1990; first performed Avignon, 1990.
Développement (video by Philippe Missotte) 1990.

PUBLICATIONS

By Bernard: "L'UPIC comme instrument d'interprétation", in *Contemporary Music Review*, 1990.

Pierre Bernard comments:

Several concerns underlie these works:

composition by synthesis, using electronic sounds, since 1970 (*Ocre*, *Organ*, *Traversée*, *Les Fenêtres s'ouvrent de l'intérieur*), moving on after 1980 to technologies like UPIC (*Solar*, *Ham Sa*, *Temps réel*) or SYTER (*Plein Soleil sur la mer*);

the use of sounds of every conceivable kind and source, from instruments, from nature, from urban life, mixed with electronic sounds (*Trois Instants qui se suivent*, *Déroulement*);

borrowings from other musics (*Kanaké*);

recordings left intact, without transformation, preserving their anecdotal coherence, in order to create musical soundtracks (*Concret 1*, *Instantané*, *Quotidien*);

music combining tape and instruments played acoustically but with a specific interaction (*Duo pour basse seule*, *Regarder au dedans*, *Racines*, *Kanaké*);

environmental music, dance, light, film (*Quotidien*, *La Vie des oreilles*, *Eclipse*, *Temps réel*).

My composition is grounded on sustaining a certain level of attention as against sudden changes of direction, but which is based on an insistence, the very same dynamic logic by which an engine steers and propels the traveller.

In this enterprise, sound-mixing is fundamental. It is this which provides the tension necessary to maintain contact with the audience. Sound-mixing sustains the simultaneous presence–absence of sound; the listener can sustain within himself the vanished instants or else simply exist in a presence which it is not possible to define consciously.

Sound filters and reverberation allow a displacement of objects in space, making them float and disappear.

Synthesis of sound privileges the tactile, kinetic presence of sound. Sound must have a body, to be palpable, to breathe, dance, to be sufficiently vital to create a living presence.

Composition should define itself step by step by the dynamic logic by which sound evolves, allowing the listener time to hear, to savour each sound, and to absorb it into his very being.

* * *

Pierre Bernard is almost exclusively a composer of electronic and electroacoustic music who, throughout his career, has made use of the newest technological resources.

In the 1970s, in works such as *Traversée*, *Organ* and *Ocre*, Bernard composed for magnetic tape. He also prepared *musique concrète*, some of it built on untransformed sounds, such as *Concret I*, *Instantané* and others (*Déroulement*, *Trois Instants qui se suivent*) using instrumental, natural or urban sounds mixed with electronics.

Bernard's work in the 1980s increasingly made use of computer synthesis, and two systems in particular. One is SYTER, a sophisticated sound transformation system that allows the composer, in Bernard's words, to "open sounds, like one does a fruit, to bring to light its subtle, delicate, geometrical structures". In *Plein Soleil sur la mer*, Bernard employs the computer to diffract sounds in a manner analogous to the sunlight of the title.

The other computer system used by Bernard is the UPIC, a powerful system originated by Xenakis to which input is made by drawing; the drawing board can represent a huge range of pitch and duration, and is supplemented by a number of geometrical operations with a corresponding effect on sound. Bernard's *Ham Sa* and *Solar* are generally held to be two of the pieces which have best exploited its compositional resources, and with *Temps réel* (1989), Bernard became the first writer of real-time performance material for the UPIC.

He has also written electro-acoustic pieces with semi-improvised activity by the performers (*Duo pour basse seule*, *Regarder au dedans*, *Racines*, *Kanaké*) and mixed-media pieces such as *Quotidien*, *La Vie des oreilles*, *Eclipse* and *Temps réel*, which is intended as a sound and light spectacle. Bernard attempts to avoid the aridity or intellectualism that is the worst danger of computer music, believing his work "has always essentially been a poetic quest". Although he has enjoyed the support of composers such as Xenakis, Luc Ferrari and Maurice Fleuret, he has stayed unaffiliated to any compositional school. "In the dynamic of my creation", Bernard says, "I am not trying to astonish other people but, above all, to astonish myself".

He writes what he refers to as inductive music, in which each sound is savoured in its own right. He thus pays great attention to sound and sound complexes, and sets them in an expansive architecture rather than a subordinating form (particularly good examples are *Plein Soleil* and *Solar*). His especial skill in this respect is a fastidious approach to mixing, which gives it a gestural, almost tactile presence intended to nourish a specific, fragile view of musical time: an eternal present which can, with care, nurture the ripples of past and future. This compositional philosophy seems flavoured by his interest in Eastern thought, especially Hinduism, imbuing it with a sobriety, but not austerity, that characterises his work.

—David Revill

BERNSTEIN, Leonard. American. Born in Lawrence, Massachusetts, 25 August 1918. Educated at Latin School, Boston, graduated 1935; Harvard University, Cambridge, Massachusetts (under Edward Ballantine, Edward Burlinghame Hill, A. Tillman Merritt and Walter Piston), 1935–9, B.A.; Curtis Institute, Philadelphia (piano with Isabella Vengerova, score reading with Renée Longy, orchestration with Randall Thompson), winters 1939–40, 1940–1; Berkshire Music Center, Tanglewood, Massachusetts (conducting with Sergei Koussevitzky), summers 1940, 1941. Married Felicia Montealegre Cohn in 1951 (died 1978); 2 sons and 1 daughter. Composer, pianist, international conductor. Assistant to Koussevitzky, Berkshire Music Center, 1942; arranger/transcriber/notater, Harms-Remick, New York, 1942; member of Revuers show troupe, 1942; assistant conductor, New York Philharmonic Orchestra, 1943; music director, New York City Symphony Orchestra, 1945–7; member of faculty, 1948–55, and head, conducting department, 1951–5, Berkshire Music Center; first American to conduct at La Scala, Milan, 1953; musical adviser/conductor, Israel Philharmonic Orchestra, 1948–9; music director, Brandeis University, Waltham, Massachusetts, 1951–6; co-conducter (with Dmitri Mitropoulos), 1957–8, musical director, 1958–69, and laureate conductor, 1969–90, New York Philharmonic; director, New York Philharmonic Orchestra Young People's Concerts broadcasts, 1958–71; president, English Bach Festival, 1972; Charles Eliot Norton Professor of Poetry, Harvard University, 1972–3; honorary president, Santa Cecilia Orchestra, 1983–90; president, London Symphony Orchestra, 1987–90. Recipient: Medals of the Defense Forces, Israel, 1948; Plaque from the Defense Forces, Israel, 1957; Alice M. Ditson Award, Columbia University, 1958; Peabody Award, University of Georgia, 1959; Sigma Alpha Iota Television Award, 1959, 1960, 1975; Thomas Alva Edison Mass Media Award, 1958, 1959, 1961; Sylvania Television Award, 1959; John H. Finley Award, City College of New York, 1959; distinguished Artists Award, High School of Performing Arts, 1959; Page One Award, Newspaper Guild of New York, 1960; Einstein Commemorative Award, Albert Einstein College of Medicine, 1960; Television Producers' Guild Award, 1962; Order of Merit Bernardo O'Higgins, Chile, 1964; Diplome d'Honneur, Academy of Arts, Prague, 1964; Commander, Order of the Lion, Finland, 1965; Leonie Sonning Music Prize, Denmark, 1965; *Billboard* Top Classical Artist/Album, 1965, 1966, 1967, 1972; Man of the Year, Harvard University, 1966; National Association of Record Manufacturers citations, 1966, 1967, 1969, 1972; Creative Artist Award, Boston University, 1966; Frank L. Weill Award, National Jewish Welfare Board, 1966; Eleanor Roosevelt Humanities Award, State of Israel Bonds, 1966; Dag Hammarskjold International Prize, 1966; Most Popular Classical Artist, Schwann Record Catalogue, 1967; Nicolai Medal, Vienna Philharmonic, 1967; Gold Medal, Mahler Gesellschaft, 1967; Grand Prix du Disque Classique, 1967, 1968, 1981; Medal of Honor, National Arts Club, 1968; Chevalier, Legion of Honour, France, 1968, Officier, 1978, Commandeur, 1985; Cavaliere, Order of Merit, Italy, 1969; Commander's Cross, First Class, Austria, 1970; Creative Arts Award, Brandeis University, 1973; Grand Order Cross for Science and Art, Austria, 1976; Montreal Prix Mondial du Disque, 1976; Handel Medallion, New York City, 1977; Ring of Honor, Vienna Philharmonic, 1978; Beethoven Medal, 1979; UNESCO Sterling Silver Wand, 1979; Theatre Hall of Fame, Scroll of Honor, 1979; Distinguished Achievement award, Third Street Music School Settlement, 1980; Career Achievement citation, Kennedy Center, 1980; S. Y. Agnon Gold Medal, Friends of Hebrew University, 1981; Golden Camera Award, Berlin, 1981; Order of the Aztec Eagle, Mexico, 1982; Man of the Year, Boston Latin School, 1984; Gold Medal, American Academy of Arts and Letters, 1985; National Fellowship Award, Philadelphia, 1985; Karl Amadeus Hartmann Medal, Bavarian Radio Symphony Orchestra, 1986; Crystal Globe Award (CBS Records), 1986; Commander's Cross of the Order of Merit, West Germany, 1987; Edward MacDowell Gold Medal, 1987; Gold Medal, Royal Philharmonic Society, London, 1987; Albert Schweitzer Music Award, 1987; Ernst von Siemens Music Prize, Germany, 1987; Grand Order of Merit of the Italian Republic, 1988; Venice Award, 1988; Grand Prix Nationale du Disque, 1988; Ritmo Prize, Spain, 1988; "Grammy" awards (National Academy of Recording Arts and Sciences), 1961 (2), 1962, 1963 (2), 1964, 1967, 1973, 1977, 1980 (2), 1985 (Lifetime Achievement), 1990; "Emmy" awards (National Academy of Television Arts and Sciences), 1957, 1958, 1960, 1961, 1962 (2), 1964, 1965, 1972, 1976, 1987. Honorary degrees: Northwestern University (Doctor of Fine Arts), 1957; Hebrew Union College (Doctor of Humane Letters), 1959; Temple University (LL.D), 1959; Dartmouth University (D.Hum.Litt.), 1960; Ohio State University (D.Hum.Litt.), 1964; University of Michigan (D.Mus.), 1964; Brown University (D.Mus.), 1966; Rockford College, (D.Hum.Litt.), 1966; Westminster Choir College (D.Hum.), 1966; Yale University (D.Mus.), 1966; Harvard University (D.Mus.), 1967; Wesleyan University (Doctor of Fine Arts), 1968; Tel Aviv University (D.Phil.), 1973; University of Warwick (D.Hum.Litt.), 1974; Butler University (D.Hum. Litt.), 1976; Johns Hopkins University (D.Hum.Litt.), 1980; Hebrew University, Israel (D.Phil.), 1981; Cleveland State University (D.Hum.Litt.), 1982; Boston University (D.Hum. Litt.), 1983; Pine Manor College (D.A.), 1987; Fairfield University (D.Hum.Litt.), 1989. **Died 14 October 1990.**

Publishers: Boosey & Hawkes; Amberson; Harms; Jalni.

Symphonies/orchestral:

Symphony No 1: "Jeremiah" (mezzo-soprano, orchestra; Bible) 1942; first performed Pittsburgh, 28 January 1944. Recorded Deutsche Grammophon 415 964–2.

Fancy Free (suite from the ballet) 1944; first performed Pittsburgh, 14 January 1945. Recorded HMV CDC7 47522-2.

On the Town (3 dance episodes; based on the musical) 1945; first performed San Francisco, 13 March 1947. Recorded CBS MK 42263; Deutsche Grammophon 415 966-2; HMV CDC7 47522 2; Philips 416-360 2.

Facsimile (choreographic essay; based on ballet) 1946; first performed Poughkeepsie, New York, 5 March 1947. Recorded HMV CDC7 47522-2.

Symphony No 2: "The Age of Anxiety" (piano, orchestra; inspired by Auden) 1949; first performed Boston, 8 April 1949. Recorded Deutsche Grammophon 415 964-2.

Prelude, Fugue and Riffs (clarinet, jazz orchestra) 1949; broadcast, 16 October 1955. Recorded CBS MK 42227.

Serenade (violin, harp, percussion, strings; inspired by Plato) 1954; first performed Venice, Italy, 12 September 1954.

On the Waterfront (symphonic suite; based on film soundtrack) 1955; first performed Lenox, Massachusetts, 11 August 1955. Recorded CBS MK 42263; Deutsche Grammophon 419 828 4.

West Side Story (symphonic dances; based on musical) 1960; first performed New York City, 13 February 1961. Recorded Deutsche Grammophon 410 025 2; DG 419 625 2; CBS MK 42263.

Fanfare I (inauguration of President Kennedy) 1961; first performed Washington, D.C., 19 January 1961.
Fanfare II (25th anniverary of High School of Music and Art) 1961; first performed New York City, 24 March 1961.
Symphony No 3: "Kaddish" (soprano, speaker, chorus, boys' chorus, orchestra; Hebrew liturgy) 1963, revised 1977; first performed Tel Aviv, 10 December 1963; Mainz, Germany, 25 August 1977. Recorded Deutsche Grammophon 423 582 2.
Two Meditations from "Mass" 1971; first performed Austin, Texas, 31 October 1971.
Mediation III from "Mass" 1972; first performed Jerusalem, 21 May 1972; withdrawn.
Dybbuk Suite Nos 1 & 2 / Dybbuk Variations (based on ballet) 1974; no 1 first performed Auckland, New Zealand, 16 August 1974; no 2, New York City, 17 April 1977. No 2 recorded Deutsche Grammophon 423 582-2.
Three Meditations from "Mass" (cello, orchestra; arranged for cello, piano) 1977-8; first performed Washington, D.C., 11 October 1977. Recorded Deutsche Grammophon 419 828-4.
Slava! (overture) 1977; first performed Washington, D.C., 11 October 1977.
CBS Music 1977; broadcast 1 April 1978.
Divertimento 1980; first performed Boston, 25 September 1980. Recorded Philips 416 360-2; Hungaroton HCD 12631-2; Deutsche Grammophon 419 828-4.
A Musical Toast 1980; first performed New York City, 11 October 1980. Recorded Deutsche Grammophon 419 828-4.
Halil (nocturne; flute, percussion, strings) 1981; first performed Jerusalem, 23 May 1981. Recorded Deutsche Grammophon 415 966 2.
Jubilee Games 1988; first performed Tel Aviv, 1988.
Arias and Barcarolles 1988; first performed New York City, 1989.

Chamber / instrumental:

Piano Trio 1937.
Music for Two Pianos 1937; first performed Brookline, Massachusetts, 12 June 1938; included in *On the Town*.
Music for the Dance Nos 1 & 2 (piano) 1937; first performed Brookline, Massachusetts, 12 June 1938; included in *On the Town*.
Piano Sonata 1938.
Scenes from the City of Sin (piano — 4 hands) 1939.
Violin Sonata 1940.
Four Studies (2 clarinets, 2 bassoons, piano) ?1940; broadcast Philadelphia, 1940.
Clarinet Sonata 1941–2; first performed Boston, 21 April 1942.
Seven Anniversaries (piano) 1943; first performed Boston, 14 May 1944. Recorded Pro Arte CCD 109.
Four Anniversaries (piano) 1948; first performed Cleveland, Ohio, 1 October 1948. Recorded Pro Arte CCD 109.
Brass Music (trumpet, horn, tuba, trombone, piano) 1948; first performed New York, 8 April 1959.
Elegy I (horn, piano) 1950.
Elegy II (trombone) 1950.
Elegy III (tuba, piano) 1950.
Five Anniversaries (piano) 1954. Recorded Pro Arte CCD 109.
Shivaree (brass, percussion) 1969; first performed New York City, 28 September 1971; included in *Mass*.
Touches (piano) 1981. Recorded Pro Arte CCD 109.
Song Without Words (piano) 1982. Recorded Pro Arte CCD 109.
Moby Diptych (piano) 1982. Recorded Pro Arte CCD 109.
Two Anniversaries (piano) 1982. Recorded Pro Arte CCD 109.
Thirteen Anniversaries (piano) 1988.

Vocal / choral:

Psalm CXLVIII (voice, piano) 1932.
I Hate Music: Five Kid Songs (voice, piano; song cycle) 1943; first performed Tanglewood, Massachusetts, 24 August 1943. Recorded Etcetera KTC 1037.
Lamentations (voice, piano; arrangement of 3rd movement of *Symphony No 1: "Jeremiah"*) 1945.
Afterthought (voice, piano) 1945; first performed New York City, 24 October 1948; withdrawn.
Hashkivenu (tenor, chorus, organ; Hebrew liturgy) 1945; first performed New York City, 11 May 1954.
La Bonne Cuisine (voice, piano; 4 recipes) 1947; first performed New York City, 10 October 1948. Recorded Etcetera KTC 1037.
Simchu Na (SATB chorus, piano; Hebrew folksong arrangement) 1947.
Reena (chorus, orchestra; Hebrew folksong arrangement) 1947.
Two Love Songs (voice, piano; Rilke) 1949; first performed New York City, 13 March 1963. Recorded Etcetera KTC 1037.
Yidgal (chorus, piano; Hebrew liturgy) 1950.
Silhouette (Galilee) (voice, piano) 1951; first performed Washington, D.C., 13 February 1955. Recorded Etcetera KTC 1037.
On the Waterfront (voice, piano; La Touche) 1954; withdrawn.
Get Hep! (voice, piano) 1955; withdrawn.
Harvard Choruses (male choir; Lerner) 1957; first performed New York City, 7 March 1957.
Chichester Psalms (treble, chorus, orchestra; Bible) 1965; first performed New York City, 15 July 1965. Recorded ASV CDRPO 8004; Hyperion CDA 66219; Deutsche Grammophon 425 965-2.
So Pretty (voice, piano; Comden, Green) 1968; first performed New York, 21 January 1968. Recorded Etcetera KTC 1037.
Warm-Up (mixed chorus; included in *Mass*) 1970.
A Little Norton Lecture (male voices; cummings; later included in *Songfest*)) 1973; first performed Cambridge, Massachusetts, 1973.
Songfest (6 solo voices, orchestra; O'Hara, Ferlinghetti, de Burgos, Whitman, Hughes, Jordan, Bradstreet, Stein, cummings, Aiken, Corso, Millay, Poe) 1977; first performed Washington, D.C., 11 October 1977. Recorded Deutsche Grammophon 415 965-2.
Mad Woman of Central Park West / My New Friends / Up! Up! Up! (voice, piano) 1979; first performed Buffalo, New York, 6 April 1979.
Piccola Serenata (voice, piano) 1979; first performed Salzburg, Austria, 27 August 1979. Recorded Etcetera KTC 1037.
Olympic Hymns (SATB chorus, orchestra; Kunert) 1981; first performed Baden-Baden, 23 September 1981.
Jubilee Games / Opening Prayer (baritone, orchestra) 1986.
Sean Song (voice, strings) 1986.
Trial Song from The Race to Unga 1987.
Missa Brevis (unaccompanied chorus, incidental percussion) 1987.
My Twelve Tone Melody (voice, piano) 1988.
Arias and Barcarolles (mixed voices, piano — 4 hands) 1988.

Opera:

Trouble in Tahiti 1951; first performed Waltham, Massachusetts, 12 June 1952.

Candide (comic operetta; Hellman, Wilbur, La Touche, Parker, Bernstein, Voltaire; orchestrated Kay, Bernstein) 1956, revised 1973; first performed Boston, 29 October 1956; revised version first performed Brooklyn, New York, 20 December 1973. Overture recorded Deutsche Grammophon 413 324-2/DG 423 198-2/Philips 416 360-2/HMV CDC7 47522-2/CBS MK 42263; theatre version, New World NWCD 340/1.

A Quiet Place 1983; first performed Milan, 1984. Recorded Deutsche Grammophon 419 761-2.

Other:

The Birds (incidental music to Aristophanes; voices, chamber orchestra) 1938; first performed Cambridge, Massachusetts, 21 April 1939.

The Peace (incidental music to Aristophanes; chorus, instrumental ensemble) 1940; first performed Cambridge, Massachusetts, 23 May 1941.

Fancy Free (ballet; Robbins) 1944; first performed New York City, 18 April 1944.

On the Town (musical; Comden, Green, Bernstein; orchestrated Green, Bernstein) 1944; first performed Boston, 13 December 1944.

Facsimile (ballet; Robbins) 1946; first performed New York City, 24 October 1946.

Peter Pan (incidental music to J.M. Barrie) 1950; first performed New York City, 24 April 1950.

Wonderful Town (musical; Comden, Green; orchestrated Walker) 1953; first performed New Haven, Connecticut, 19 January 1953.

On the Waterfront (film score; Kazan) 1954; released 28 July 1954.

The Lark (incidental music to Hellman/Anouilh; 7 solo voices) 1955; first performed Boston, 28 October 1955.

Salome (incidental music to Wilde; voice, orchestra) 1955.

West Side Story (musical; Sondheim/Laurents; orchestrated Ramin, Kostal, Bernstein; choreographed Robbins) 1957; first performed Washington, D.C., 19 August 1957; also motion picture, Wise and Robbins, 1961. Recorded Deutsche Grammophon 415 253-2; also suite in DG 417 354–2.

The Firstborn (incidental music to Fry) 1958; first performed New York City, 20 April 1958.

Mass (theatre piece; orchestra, chorus, boy singers, dancers, dancer-singers; orchestrated Tunick, Kay, Bernstein) 1971; first performed Washington, D.C., 8 September 1971; arranged for chamber orchestra, Los Angeles, 26 December 1972.

Dybbuk (ballet) 1974; first performed New York City, 16 May 1974.

By Bernstein (revue; unpublished and withdrawn theatre songs) 1975; first performed New York City, 23 November 1975.

1600 Pennsylvania Avenue (musical; Lerner; orchestrated Ramin, Kay) 1976; first performed Philadelphia, 24 February 1976.

Aaron Copland: *El Salon Mexico* (arranged for piano/2 pianos) 1941; first performed Boston, 18 November 1941. Recorded Pro Arte CCD 109.

Publications

By Bernstein: "The Absorption of Race Elements into American Music", dissertation, Harvard University, 1939; *The Joy of Music*, New York, 1959; *Young People's Concerts for Reading and Listening*, New York, 1962, revised and enlarged 1970; *The Infinite Variety of Music*, New York, 1966; *The Unanswered Question*, Cambridge, Massachusetts, 1976; *Findings*, New York, 1982; *LB: Ausgrwahlte Texte*, Berlin, 1988; many articles, reviews, programme and liner notes.

On Bernstein: H. Stoddard, in *Symphony Conductors of the USA*, New York, 1957; J. Briggs, *LB: The Man, His Work, and His World*, Cleveland, Ohio, 1961; A. Holde, *LB*, Berlin, 1961; J. Gottlieb, "The Music of LB: A Study of Melodic Manipulations", dissertation, University of Illinois, 1964; W.W. Tromble, "The American Intellectual and Music: An Analysis of the Writings of Suzanne K. Langer, Paul Henry Lang, Jacques Barzun, John Dewey and LB—With Implications for Music Education", dissertation, University of Michigan, 1968; J. Gruen, *The Private World of LB*, New York, 1968; E. Ames, *A Wind from the West: LB and the New York Philharmonic Abroad*, Boston, 1970; M. Cone, *LB*, New York, 1970; J.W. Weber, *LB* (discography), Utica, New York, 1975; "LB in Conversation with Robert Chesterman", in *Conversations with Conductors*, Totowa, New Jersey, 1976; J. Gottlieb, *LB: A Complete Catalogue of His Works*, New York, 1978; P. Robinson, *Bernstein*, New York, 1982; H. Matheopoulos, in *Maestro: Encounters with Conductors of Today*, London, 1982; J. Peyser, authorised biography, 1991.

* * *

The untimely death of Leonard Bernstein only one week after announcing his retirement from conducting due to ill-health ended a highly successful—if often controversial—career as both eminent international conductor and respected composer.

At the time of his death, Bernstein's standing owed rather more to the immediacy of his work on the podium, marked by an animated, highly expressive style and provocative interpretations, than to his compositions. It remains to be seen whether posterity arrives at a different balance.

Bernstein's musical career was always conducted over a high flame, from the time of his famous baptism when replacing Bruno Walter at one day's notice for a televised concert. That triumph launched him on an irreversible path to conducting fame; a staunch supporter of new music in the first half of that career, he grew increasingly preoccupied with the standard repertoire in his later years, particularly Mahler.

His work as a composer ran in tandem with conducting throughout, and exemplified a similar breadth and range of influence. Arguably, it is that very eclecticism, with its consequent lack of a distinctive voice or developed style, which will ultimately prevent his compositions from being regarded as a genuinely major contribution to contemporary music.

Against that, however, stands the fact that his work gained immeasurably in vitality from his multifarious preoccupations, although that may be more relevant to the quality of his writing for Broadway and Hollywood than for the concert stage. Both these strands co-existed from the early 1940s, in which decade he composed two of his three symphonies, but also the jazz-flavoured ballet *Fancy Free* and the superbly vigorous *On the Town*.

Bernstein took both aspects of his composition equally seriously, and quickly established his willingness to experiment with whatever musical forms suited his expressive purposes. His earliest compositions, like the *Clarinet Sonata*, are in a neo-classical mode; his first symphony, *"Jeremiah"*, draws on elements of the Jewish liturgical tradition within a more overtly Romantic register; *Fancy Free* makes colourful use of the harmonic and rhythmic language of jazz.

Berstein's second symphony, *"The Age of Anxiety"*, a brooding reflection on the *Zeitgeist*, made an even more eclectic use of diverse idioms, but succeeded in forging its material into an artistically integrated whole. While continuing to write for the concert hall, as in *Five Anniversaries* for piano or *Serenade*, his most enduring music of the ensuing decade was written for the popular stage.

Like Aaron Copland, Bernstein made important contributions in film music, notably with his score for Elia Kazan's *On the Waterfront*, but the most acclaimed of his scores was written for the Broadway production of *West Side Story*, which immediately became a highly successful film.

He had already made his mark on stage with *Trouble in Tahiti*, a comic blend of operetta and musical which was subsequently absorbed into a larger and more ambitious opera, *A Quiet Place* (which the composer considered his most important work), *Wonderful Town*, and his comic operetta *Candide*, adapted from Voltaire's novel, the overture of which became one of his most frequently performed concert pieces.

West Side Story, however, was hailed as a radical extension of the conventions of the musical, and while Bernstein's score again drew on a wide-ranging series of styles and modes, from the melodic sweetness of popular song to a rebarbative rhythmic energy reminiscent of Stravinsky, he achieves a remarkable unity of purpose within that eclecticism. Both show and film were enormous hits, and while the subsequent sound recording of the score with operatic singers under the composer's baton proved equally popular, it is an uneasy and curiously diffident mixture of largely incompatible elements. Nevertheless, its success is a sharp reminder of the enduring appeal of the music.

The subsequent decade saw the composer concentrating rather more on concert music, beginning with his third symphony, *"Kaddish"*, completed in 1963 (and revised in 1977), although commissioned eight years before. The work uses an innovative vocal score, drawing on both the Jewish prayer of the title and Bernstein's own demotic text to set up an argument with God.

With typical unpredictability, not to say perversity, the composer eschewed the kind of musical borrowings from the Jewish tradition he had implemented in *"Jeremiah"* in favour of the twelve-tone row, then predominent in American music. He had experimented with twelve-tone music as early as *"The Age of Anxiety"*, but always seemed happier with the more conventional tonality and diatonicism which closes *"Kaddish"*.

After a sabbatical year in which he attempted to develop his writing in the twelve-note from (during which he admitted to throwing away more music than he had actually published up to then), Bernstein reverted to his natural inclinations with one of his most fully realised scores, the lushly tonal *Chichester Psalms* for chorus and orchestra.

His *Mass* for an unbelieving age was a stagey affair, drawing on rock and blues bands as well as orchestra and choir, and pushing his eclectism to unprecedented lengths, but without ultimately achieving that unity of structure and purpose which had drawn together the diverse idioms of his best works.

Bernstein continued to combine composition with conducting throughout his career, and produced more notable works, including his *Songfest*, a setting of 12 songs for six singers and orchestra which attempted to survey 300 years of American history. That preoccupation with social and historical questions, as with religion, runs through all of his work, although the light-hearted and highly enjoyable *Divertimento* emphasised a less portentuous side to his concert music.

Bernstein is likely to be most fondly remembered almost as two different artists, one the exuberant popular composer of classic American musicals, the other as the tortured interpreter of the profound, soul-wrenching late Romantic classics. One of his last major projects was to conduct Beethoven's Ninth Symphony in a newly-united Berlin, with the culminating Schiller text amended as an "Ode to Freedom". Others might have done it with finer judgement, but surely no one would have coaxed more sheer emotion from the occasion.

—Kenny Mathieson

BIBALO, Antonio. Norwegian. Born in Trieste, Italy, 18 January 1922. Educated at Trieste Music Conservatory Giuseppe Verdi (under Luciano Gante, piano, and Giulio Viozzi, composition) 1938–46; Trinity School of Music, London (under Elisabeth Lutyens) 1953–6. Emigrated to Norway, 1956; Norwegian citizen, 1968. Married Grete Lis, 9 November 1969. Recipient: 3rd prize (for *Fantasy*), Wieniawski Composers' Competition, Warsaw, 1954–5; 2nd prize, Bela Bartók International Composition Competition, University School of Music, Bloomington, Indiana, 1958; Westfold Culture Prize (for *Concerto Allegorico*), Norway, 1970; Norwegian Cultural Prize, 1976; Prix d'Italia, 1987. Mailing address: 28 Gon, 3260 Ostre Halsem, Norway.

Publisher: Wilhelm Hansen, Copenhagen.

Symphonies/orchestral:

Concerto for Piano and Orchestra 1953; first performed Oslo, 1 August 1972.

Concerto da camera (piano, strings) 1954; first performed Oslo, 1969.

Fantasy (violin, orchestra) 1954.

Four Balkan Dances 1956.

Concerto allegorico (violin, orchestra) 1957; first performed Oslo, 1964.

Pitture astratte 1958; first performed Oslo, 1963.

Sinfonia notturna 1969; first performed Oslo, 1969. Recorded Aurora Contemporary NCD B 1943.

Concerto da camera No 2 (violin, harpsichord, string orchestra) 1970; first performed Oslo, 1970. Recorded Nordisc NORLP 310.

Piano Concerto No 2 1971; first performed Bergen, 27 April 1972.

Margarita infante 1972.

Freithoff-Suite 1976; first performed Bergen, 1976.

Symphony No 2 1979; first performed Bergen, 1979.

Musica (oboe, orchestra) 1989; first performed Oslo, 1989.

Chamber/instrumental:

Sonatina (piano) 1953.
Three Homages (piano) 1953; first performed Oslo, 1970. Recorded Philips "Contemporary Music in Norway" 6507 022.
Toccata (piano) 1953; first performed Oslo, 1970. Recorded Philips "Contemporary Music in Norway" 6507 022.
Four Balkan Dances (piano) 1956; first performed London, 1960.
Twelve Miniatures (piano) 1956.
Autumnale (piano, flute, double bass, vibraphone) 1968; first performed Oslo, 1979. Recorded Aurora Contemporary NCD B 1913.
Sonatina-Astrale (wind quintet) 1971; first performed Oslo, 1971. Recorded NCD B 1913.
Sonatina No 2 (wind quintet) 1972. Recorded on Philips 6507 015.
String Quartet 1972; first performed Oslo, 1972. Recorded NCD 4915.
Sonata No 1 (piano) 1972; first performed Oslo, 1972. Recorded Philips "Contemporary Music in Norway" 6507 022.
Sonata (piano) 1974.
Games (trombone, flute) 1975.
La notte (Sonata No 2) (piano) 1977; first performed Oslo, 1977. Recorded CBS 76631.
Study in Blue (guitar) 1983; first performed Oslo, 1983. Recorded PWSC 1031 Simax; VEPSCD 012–89.
Racconto d'una stagione alta (cello, piano) 1986.
Sonata (violin) 1987; first performed Stavanger, 1987. Recorded Aurora Contemporary ACD 4963.

Vocal/choral:

Elegia per un'era spaziale / Cantata for a Space Age (soprano, baritone, orchestra) 1963.
Endless Longing (nocturne for baritone, piano) 1967.
Serenata (baritone, men's choir) 1971.
Cantico (mezzo-soprano, tape) 1984; first performed Oslo, 1984. Recorded Aurora Classical ARCD 1919.
Two Intermezzi (baritone, flute) 1984–5.

Opera:

The Smile at the Foot of the Ladder (after Henry Miller) 1965; first performed Hamburg, 6 April, 1965.
Miss Julie (after Strindberg) 1975; first performed Aarhus, 1975. Recorded Nordisc NORLP 501/2.
Askeladden (radio opera) 1977; broadcast 1977.
Gespemster / Ghosts (after Ibsen) 1981; first performed Kiel, 1981. Recorded NC 4907.
Macbeth 1986–90; first performed Oslo, 29 September 1990.

Other:

Overture to Goldoni's "The Servant and Two Masters" 1968; broadcast Norwegian radio, 1968.
Pinocchio (ballet) 1969; first performed Hamburg, 1969.
Nocturne (for Apollo) 1972; first performed Oslo, 1972.
Flammen / Flames (ballet for television) 1974; first performed Oslo, 1974.
Ashes (ballet for television) 1987; first performed Oslo, 1987.

PUBLICATIONS

On Bibalo: John H. Yoell, in *The Nordic Sound*, Boston, 1974; Nils Grinde, in *Contemporary Norwegian Music, 1920–80*, Oslo, 1981.

Antonio Bibalo comments:

To introduce my music—theoretically, philosophically, stylistically—is not my strong side. I have always despised long analyses when these are not required for some real, serious purpose. Analysing my own works would not improve them; they have to be heard.

I am what one may call a spontaneous composer. Naturally, I use all that is possible in music, because art is and should be free. I have never been an avant-garde or a conservative composer. I tried to be a composer of our days and advance with them. But I have always respected all kinds of experiment in music, because the art of music cannot stop with any kind of given system; it has to go on.

* * *

Antonio Bibalo's curriculum vitae makes for unusual reading. Though he is now firmly established in the Norwegian musical establishment—as one of its less establishmentarian representatives—he was born and educated in the "international city" of Trieste, and is of Slovak descent. His musical education began conventionally enough at the Trieste Conservatory, but the disruption of World War II set him off on a long *Wanderjahr* which included stints as a nightclub pianist and, less productively in musical terms, a sanitation worker.

In 1953, though, his studies with the renegade English composer Elisabeth Lutyens at Trinity College, London, set him on course for a career in music. The final element in the coding that makes a composer was added in the summer of 1956, when he spent a holiday in Norway. Within a year, he was to settle in Scandinavia, where his first job was to copy the parts of Arne Nordheim's recently finished String Quartet. Bibalo's development as a composer continued under the rather younger Nordheim's generous patronage and support. His international reputation was secured in 1965, when his operatic adaptation of a Henry Miller story, *The Smile at the Foot of the Ladder*, was premiered with great success in Hamburg. Though the source seems a dangerously unpromising one, *Smile* is a work of great and lasting power, marked by Bibalo's adventurous tonality, multi-layered melodic invention and rhythmic energy.

There is, it seems, an innate resistance to serialism in the Scandinavian. Despite his apprenticeship to Lutyens, he has reverted to a twelve-tone idiom only rather sparingly. Even in the non-dramatic work, there is a strong element of theatricality in Bibalo's musical language. The *String Quartet* of 1972, dedicated to Nordheim, has an introspective quality that is reminiscent of Bartók. That influence—if it is conscious at all—is also evident in elements of the first piano concerto and in the chamber concerti, which betray echoes of Bartók's celebrated "night music".

Programmatically, Bibalo has shown a marked interest in space flight and astronomy, and in what could be called (without any hint of knocked-down Freudianism) the "dark side" of human existence, a concern presumably heightened by his translation to the seasonal extremes of Scandinavia. The *Sinfonia notturna*, incidentally his finest essay in symphonic writing, the *Sonatina-Astrale* for winds, and the marvellous *Elegia per un'era spaziale* all bear witness to these concerns.

Where they are developed in a psychological context, Bibalo reveals himself as only a rather heterodox Scandinavian. His adaptation of Ibsen's *Ghosts* is far removed from the conventional reading of that play (though it may preserve more of Ibsen's much misunderstood humour than most non-Scandinavian interpretations). Similarly, Bibalo adapts Strindberg's *Miss Julie* quite ruthlessly to the demands of operatic writing; in the process, as with the Ibsen, he reveals unexpected elements. His most recent opera, *Macbeth*, though brilliantly staged, is less compelling as a spectacle.

Bibalo belongs to no school. He is neither markedly conservative nor an out-and-out experimentalist. His work is characterised by strongly personal elements which draw confidently on the whole range of contemporary idioms and by a philosophical approach which might be considered mystical were it not so firmly grounded in the everyday.

—Brian Morton

BIRTWISTLE, (Sir) Harrison. British/English. Born in Accrington, Lancashire, 15 July 1934. Educated at Royal Manchester College of Music (under Frederick Thurston for clarinet, Richard Hall for composition), from 1952; Royal Academy of Music, London (clarinet under Reginald Kell). Married to Sheila Birtwistle; 3 sons. Co-founder, New Manchester Music Group, 1953; director of music, Cranbourne Chase School, Dorset, 1962–5; visiting fellow (Harkness International Fellowship), Princeton University, New Jersey, 1966; co-founder (with Peter Maxwell Davies), Pierrot Players, 1967–70; co-founder (with Alan Hacker), Matrix, 1970; Cornell Visiting Professor, Music, Swarthmore College, Pennsylvania, 1973–4; Sell Visiting Professor, New York State University, Buffalo, 1975; music director, National Theatre, London, since 1975. Recipient: (London) *Evening Standard* Opera Award (for *The Mask of Orpheus*), 1986; Grawemeyer Award, University of Louisville, Kentucky, 1986; Knighted, 1988. Mailing address: c/o Allied Artists Agency, 42 Montpelier Square, London SW7 1JZ, England.

Publisher: Universal Edition.

Symphonies/orchestral:

Chorales 1960–3; first performed London, 14 February 1967.
Three Movements with Fanfares 1964; first performed London, 8 July 1964.
Nomos (amplified flute, amplified clarinet, amplified horn, amplified bassoon, orchestra) 1967–8; first performed London, 23 August 1968.
An Imaginary Landscape (4 trumpets, 4 horns, 3 trombones, tuba, 8 double basses, 4 percussion) 1971; first performed London, 2 June 1971.
The Triumph of Time 1971–2; first performed London, 1 June 1972. Recorded Argo ZRG 790.
Grimethorpe Aria (brass band) 1973; first performed Harrogate, Yorkshire, 15 August 1973. Recorded Decca HEAD 14.
Melancolia I (A clarinet, harp, 2 string orchestras) 1976; first performed Glasgow, 18 September 1976.
Earth Dances 1985–6; first performed London, 1986.
Endless Parade (trumpet, vibraphone, strings) 1986–7; first performed Zurich, 1 May 1987.
Machaut à ma manière (recomposition of 3 pieces by Machaut: *O Livoris Feritas*, *Hoquetus David*, *Amen*) 1988.

Chamber/instrumental:

Refrains and Choruses (flute, oboe, clarinet, horn, bassoon) 1957; first performed Cheltenham, Gloucestershire, 11 June 1959. Recorded Philips SAL 3669.
Three Sonatas for Nine Instruments 1960; never performed and now lost.
Precis (piano) 1960; first performed Dartington, Devon, August 1960. Recorded HMV ALP 2098/ASD 645.
The World Is Discovered (after Heinrich Isaac; 2 flutes, oboe, cor anglais, 2 clarinets/1 basset horn or bass clarinet, 2 horns, 2 bassoons, harp, guitar) 1961; first performed London, 6 March 1961.
Entr'actes (flute, viola, harp; later used in *Entr'actes and Sappho Fragments*) 1962; first performed Devon, Autumn 1962.
Tragoedia (flute, oboe, clarinet, horn, bassoon [all doubling on claves], 2 violins, viola, cello, harp) 1965; first performed Devon, 20 August 1965. Recorded HMV ASD 2333/Argo ZRG 759.
Verses (clarinet, piano) 1965; first performed London, October 1965.
Chorale from a Toy Shop (original version: flute, oboe or clarinet, clarinet or cor anglais, horn or trombone, bassoon or tuba) 1967; first performed Lewes, Sussex, 28 March 1979; second version: 2 trumpets, horn, trombone, tuba; first performed London, 19 May 1978.
Three Lessons in a Frame (piano, flute/piccolo, clarinet, violin, cello, percussion) 1967; first performed Cheltenham, Gloucestershire, 17 July 1967.
Linoi (original version: A clarinet, with extension down to C, piano) 1968; first performed London, 11 October 1968; second version: adds tape realised by Peter Zinovieff and dancer; first performed London, 22 April 1969; third version: clarinet, piano, cello; first performed Huddersfield, Yorkshire, 19 November 1981.
Four Interludes for a Tragedy (reworking of interludes in *Monodrama*: basset clarinet in A, tape realised by Peter Zinovieff) 1968; first performed, without tape, London, 18 October 1968; with tape, London, 10 February 1969.
Verses for Ensembles (piccolo/alto flute, oboe/cor anglais, clarinet/E♭ clarinet, clarinet/bass clarinet/bassoon/contrabassoon, 2 trumpets, horn, 2 trombones, 3 percussion) 1968–9; first performed London, 12 February 1969. Recorded Decca HEAD 7.
Some Petals from my Twickenham Herbarium (piccolo, clarinet, viola, cello, piano, bells) 1969; first performed London, 22 April 1969.
Medusa (original version: flute/piccolo, clarinet/A clarinet/soprano saxophone, viola, cello—all amplified—piano/celeste, percussion, tape of synthesized sound, tape of alto saxophone distorted, "shozyg") 1969; first performed Sheffield, 22 October 1969; second version, including parodies of Bach: flute/piccolo, clarinet/A clarinet/soprano saxophone, viola/violin, cello—all amplified—piano/celeste, percussion, 2 tapes, synthesizer; first performed London, 3 March 1970.
Eight Lessons for Keyboards ("8 musical objects with instructions on how they might be realised") 1970; first performed London, 13 January 1970.
Signals (clarinet, electronic sounds) 1970; first performed Edinburgh, August 1970.

Dinah and Nick's Love Song (3 melody instruments, harp) 1970; first performed Sheffield, 26 October 1972.

Tombeau in Memoriam Igor Stravinsky (flute, clarinet, harp, string quartet) 1971; first performed London, 17 June 1972.

Sad Song (piano; dedicated to Adam Birtwistle) 1971.

Chanson de Geste (amplified sustaining instrument, tape realised by Peter Zinovieff) 1973; first performed, on double bass, Perugia, Italy, July 1973.

For O, for O, the Hobby-Horse Is Forgot (6 percussionists) 1976; first performed Tokyo, 10 February 1978.

Silbury Air (flute/piccolo/alto flute, oboe/cor anglais, clarinet/bass clarinet, bassoon/contrabassoon, trumpet, horn, trombone, piano, harp, percussion, 2 violins, viola, cello, double bass; score prefaced by "Pulse Labyrinth") 1977; first performed London, 9 March 1977.

Carmen Arcadiae Mechanicae Perpetuum (flute/piccolo, oboe, clarinet/bass clarinet, bassoon/contrabassoon, trumpet, horn, trombone, marimbaphone, piano or electric piano, 2 violins, viola, cello, double bass) 1977; first performed London, 24 January 1978.

Untitled Piece (for Bill Colleran's 50th birthday; flute, clarinet, horn, bassoon) 1979.

Clarinet Quintet (clarinet, 2 violins, viola, cello) 1980; first performed Huddersfield, Yorkshire, 21 November 1981.

Pulse Sampler (oboe, claves) 1981; first performed Huddersfield, Yorkshire, 20 November 1981.

Duets for Storab (2 flutes) 1983; first performed London, 25 March 1984.

Secret Theatre (flute, oboe, clarinet, bassoon/contrabassoon, trumpet, horn, trombone, percussion, piano, 2 violins, viola, cello, double bass) 1984; first performed London, 18 October 1984.

Hector's Dawn (piano) 1987.

Fanfare for Will (3 trumpets, 4 horns, 3 trombones, tuba) 1987; first performed London, 10 July 1987.

Vocal/choral:

Monody for Corpus Christi (soprano, flute, horn, violin; old English carol, Wedderburns) 1959; first performed, London, 5 April 1960.

Narration: A Description of the Passing of a Year (unaccompanied chorus; *Sir Gawain and the Green Knight*) 1963; first performed London, 14 February 1964.

Entr'actes and Sappho Fragments (soprano, flute, oboe, violin, viola, harp, percussion; *The Greek Anthology*) 1964; first performed Cheltenham, Gloucestershire, 11 July 1964.

Ring a Dumb Carillon (soprano/also playing suspended cymbals, clarinet, percussion; Logue) 1964–5; first performed London, 19 March 1965. Recorded Mainstream MS 5001.

Carmen Paschale (SATB chorus, organ ad lib; Sedulus Scotus, Waddell) 1965; first performed Aldeburgh, Suffolk, 17 June 1965.

Monodrama (soprano, m speaker, flute/piccolo/alto flute, clarinet/A clarinet/E♭ clarinet/bass clarinet, violin, cello, 2 percussion; Pruslin) 1967; first performed London, 30 May 1967.

Cantata (soprano, flute/piccolo, clarinet/high B♭ clarinet, violin/viola, cello, piano/celeste/glockenspiel/small bongo; Sappho, *The Greek Anthology*) 1969; first performed London, 12 June 1969.

Nenia: The Death of Orpheus (soprano, 3 bass clarinets/1 B♭ clarinet, piano/prepared piano, crotales; Zinovieff) 1970; first performed London, 20 November 1970. Recorded Decca HEAD 7.

Meridian (mezzo-soprano, horn, cello, 2 3-part choirs of sopranos, 3 oboes/cors anglais, 3 clarinets/bass clarinets, 2 harps, piano, 2 percussion; Logue, Wyatt) 1970–1; first performed London, 26 February 1971.

Prologue (tenor, bassoon, horn, 2 trumpets, trombone, violin, double bass; Aeschylus/Vellacott) 1971; first performed London, 18 April 1971.

The Fields of Sorrow (2 sopranos, chorus, 3 flutes, 3 cors anglais, 3 bass clarinets, 3 bassoons, horn, vibraphone, 2 pianos; Ausonius, Waddell) 1971, revised 1972; first performed Dartington, Devon, 7 August 1971. Recorded Decca HEAD 7.

Epilogue (baritone, horn, 4 trombones, 6 tam-tams — 2 players; Shakespeare) 1972; first performed London, 23 April 1972.

La Plage: Eight Arias of Remembrance (soprano, 3 clarinets, piano, marimba; Robbe-Grillet) 1972; first performed Sheffield, 26 October 1972.

. . . agm . . . (16 voices/SSSSAAAATTTTBBBB, 3 instrumental groups: high—2 flutes/piccolos, 2 oboes, clarinet, 2 trumpets, horn, 2 violins, viola; low—bass clarinet, bassoon, contrabassoon, 2 trombones, tuba, 2 cellos, double bass; punctuating—piano, 2 harps, 3 percussion; Sappho, Harrison) 1978–9; first performed Paris, 9 April 1979. Recorded Erato STU 71543.

Choral Fragments from . . . agm . . . (16 voices) 1979; first performed London, 5 April 1979.

On the Sheer Threshold of the Night (soprano, counter-tenor, tenor, bass, 12-part chorus; Boethius, Waddell) 1980; first performed Mells, Somerset, 31 May 1981.

Songs by Myself (soprano, flute, violin, viola, cello, double bass, piano, vibraphone) 1984; first performed London, 18 October 1984.

Four Songs of Autumn (soprano, string quartet; anon.) 1987; first performed London, 24 January 1988.

An die Musik (soprano, flute, oboe, clarinet, bassoon, vibraphone, 2 violins, viola, cello, double bass; Rilke) 1988; first performed London, 4 May 1988.

Opera/music-theatre:

Punch and Judy (Pruslin) 1966–7; first performed Aldeburgh, Suffolk, 8 June 1968. Recorded Decca HEAD 24/25.

Down by the Greenwood Side (dramatic pastoral for soprano, actors, flute/piccolo/alto flute, clarinet/E♭ clarinet/bass clarinet, bassoon/contrabassoon, cornet, trombone, euphonium, percussion; Nyman) 1968–9; first performed Brighton, Sussex, 8 May 1969.

The Mask of Orpheus (Zinovieff) 1973–84; first performed London, 21 May 1986.

Bow Down (music theatre for 5 actors, bamboo flute, bamboo pipes, oboes, penny whistles, percussion; Harrison) 1977; first performed London, 5 July 1977.

Yan Tan Tethera (Harrison) 1984; first performed London, 7 August 1986.

Sir Gawain and the Green Knight 1989–91; first performed London, 1991.

Other:

Music for Sleep (children's voices, piano, 3 or more percussion) 1963; first performed Winter 1963.

The Visions of Francesco Petrarca (baritone, mime ensemble, flute, oboe, clarinet, horn, trumpet, trombone, 2 violins, cello, school orchestra; Spenser, after Petrarch) 1965–6; first performed York, 15 June 1966.

The Mark of the Goat (for young people: actors, singers, 2 chorus, 3 melody instruments, 1 piano — 3 players, large and small percussion ensemble; Crang) 1966; broadcast Spring 1966.

Chronometer (tape; realised by Peter Zinovieff) 1971–2; first performed London, 24 April 1972. Recorded Argo ZRG 790.
The Offence (electronic score to film by Sidney Lumet) 1973.
Five Chorale Preludes (arrangement of J. S. Bach's *Durch Adam's Fall is ganz verderbt, Wernur den liben Gott lasst Walten, Christus, der uns selig macht, Jesus, meine Zuversicht, Das alte Jahr vergangen ist* for soprano, clarinet, basset horn, bass clarinet) 1975; first performed London, 15 September 1975.
Pulse Field (Frames, Pulses and Interruptions) (ballet, in collaboration with Jaap Flier, for 6 dancers, 3 bass trombones, 2 amplified double basses, 4 percussion) 1977; first performed Snape, Suffolk, 25 June 1977.

Ockeghem: *Ut Heremita Solus* (arranged for flute/piccolo/alto flute, clarinet/bass clarinet, viola, cello, piano, glockenspiel) 1969; first performed London, 12 June 1969.
Machaut: *Hoquetus David* (arranged for flute/piccolo, clarinet in C, violin, cello, glockenspiel, bells) 1969; first performed Sheffield, 22 October 1969.
Satie: *Mercure—Poses Plastiques* (arrangement of the ballet for flute/piccolo/alto flute, oboe/cor anglais, clarinet/bass clarinet, bassoon/contrabassoon, trumpet, horn, trombone, piano, percussion, 2 violins, viola, cello, double bass) 1980; first performed London, 4 April 1980.

Incidental music: *Amadeus, As You Like It, The Cherry Orchard* (collaboration with Dominic Muldowney), *The Country Wife, The Double Dealer, Hamlet, Herod* (collaboration with Dominic Muldowney), *The Oresteia, Tamburlaine the Great, The Trojan War Will Not Take Place*, *Volpone*: all productions at National Theatre, London, 1976–83.

PUBLICATIONS

On Birtwistle: R. Henderson, "HB", in *Musical Times*, March 1964; Gordon Crosse, "B's Punch and Judy", in *Tempo*, 85, 1968; Michael Nyman, "HB", in *London Magazine*, 11 (4), 1971; Meirion Bowen, "HB", in *British Music Now*, London, 1975; Michael Hall, *HB*, London, 1984; Paul Griffiths, (interview) in *New Sounds, New Personalities: British Composers of the 1980s*, London, 1985.

* * *

Among European observers, Harrison Birtwistle is widely regarded as the leading British composer of the 1990s. Of the so-called "Manchester School" (which included his fellow students at the Royal Manchester College of Music composers Peter Maxwell Davis and Alexander Goehr, the late pianist John Ogdon, and trumpet player turned conductor Elgar Howarth), Birtwistle was the slowest to develop, the most reticent to assert leadership. But now, in his late fifties, he has become indisputably the most interesting and original of his generation. Far from conforming to any "school", Birtwistle has maintained an almost hermetic independence and, with the years, grown more rather than less radical. While others retreat from the heady, iconoclasm of the 1960s and 1970s, Birtwistle's imagination has continued to push forward. The underlying intellectual ideas, unique approach to structure, distinctive technical devices and mesmerising sound of his music—all these give it its own unique magic. There is nothing else quite like it.

Not surprisingly, every-day concert audiences can find Birtwistle's music "difficult", and much less palatable than the softer and, ironically, more conventional language of some younger British composers. This is partly a matter of unfamiliarity. He has written relatively little for the standard symphony orchestra. Indeed, many of his finest instrumental and vocal works—and there are numerous examples—have been to commissions from the London Sinfonietta (or, in one instance, its French counterpart the Ensemble Intercontemporain), heard perhaps quite frequently but by a relatively small specialist audience, ardently admired, but taken only rarely into general concert use in Britain.

Birtwistle's music has unmistakable characteristics. The listener is assaulted by gritty, abrasive textures and a cutting-edge as hard as steel. Rhythmic mechanisms whirr mysteriously or clatter noisily and unevenly but with demonic force. Melody unfolds assymetrically, eruptively, and in long paragraphs, perhaps to journey through a melancholy landscape whose features hypnotically reoccur. The tactile, sculptural quality of his music calls to mind the visual arts from which, particularly in the work of Paul Klee, Birtwistle has repeatedly found inspiration. His structures have great dignity—even elegance—as Birtwistle propels these seemingly rough and obdurate materials through stately processions, dance-like rituals, cycles and symmetries with the instinct of an accomplished choreographer. "Composition", he has said, "is seeing how things can be juxtaposed dramatically in a landscape of intuition." Certainly, his work at the National Theatre must have contributed to his sense of dramatic timing, rhythm and pace.

Strophic and mosaic forms occur frequently in Birtwistle's music. The dramatic model of classical Greek theatre has had a profound influence upon him, as in the symmetrical structure and separation of "protagonist" and "chorus" in *Tragoedia*. So has D'Arcy Thompson's *On Growth and Form* contributed to his concepts of organic growth, which is a crucial process in his music. An important organising principle is the superimposition upon the methodical and uniformity of things which are capricious and unpredictable. Decorated and extended aria forms, clock-like rhythmic mechanisms and pulse grids which define tempo relationships occur in a number of works. But with *Nenia: The Death of Orpheus*, and more emphatically in *Meridian* and *The Fields of Sorrow*, there is a significant change of expressive emphasis. The primary colours of the earlier works give way to more subtle and transparent textures. The tone is gentler, the pulse grids are slowed down and elongated. A new departure in these pieces is the creation of instrumental "mobiles" revolving like satellites around a central core, so that one experiences a three-dimensional texture from which tangential layers audibly recede into a mist of distant sonorities.

It is Birtwistle's dramatic music which has made the widest impact. No less daring or uncompromising, the expanded resources of the theatre, with its ancient and archetypal resonances, provide a potent and communicative medium for an extraordinary musical mind. But recognition didn't come at once. *Punch and Judy*, when first performed at Aldeburgh in 1968, appeared to be harsh and savage to the point of offensiveness. Only 11 years later, did its revival and recording achieve for the work a notable triumph. In *Punch and Judy*, Birtwistle and his librettist, Stephen Pruslin, counterpoint violence against haunting lyricism. Little toccatas, only a few bars long, are juxtaposed with outbursts of anguished aggression, but equally with brief moments of seductive, mysterious tranquillity. The structure, made up of dozens of contrasting tiny, self-contained musical units has wide ranging allusions, among which ancient Greek drama, the Bach passions and neoclassicism are the most obvious.

Subsequent dramatic works, *Down by the Greenwood Side, Bow Down*, and his scores for *The Oresteia* and other productions at the National Theatre, develop the ritualistic, stylised aspects of his music. But it is *The Mask of Orpheus*, eventually produced by English National Opera at the Coliseum after 15 years' gestation, that shows outstanding mastery both of continuity and of the expressive material. There is a compassion and elegance about *Orpheus*, although it still unleashes extraordinary elemental energies, and a new development of Birtwistle's always fascinating treatment of time, which he has explained in words relevant to a great deal of his music: "Essentially I'm concerned with repetition, with going over and over the same event from different angles so that a multi-dimensional object is created, an object which contains a number of contradictions as well as a number of perspectives. I don't create linear music, I move in circles; more precisely I move in concentric circles." With *Orpheus*, Birtwistle could draw on a myth known to everybody, but concerning which there are numerous versions, interpretations and ambiguities. In his most recent opera, *Sir Gawain and the Green Knight* premiered at Covent Garden in May 1991, a simple story, here told in more evidently linear narrative, lies at the centre of a dramatic web embracing folktales, legend, medieval art, cyclic recurrence and ritual. The originality and breadth of these powerful stage works assures Birtwistle a place, with Benjamin Britten and Sir Michael Tippett, among the handful of major British opera composers of the 20th century.

—Richard Steinitz

BLAKE, David (Leonard). British/English. Born in London, 2 September 1936. Educated at Latimer Upper School, Hammersmith, London, 1947–55; and Gonville Caius College, Cambridge 1957–60, B.A., M.A.; awarded Mendelssohn Scholarship and travelled to study (with Hanns Eisler) at Deutsche Akadamie der Kunste, Berlin, East Germany, 1960–1. Military service: National service Royal Air Force, Far East, 1955–7. Married Rita Muir, 24 September 1960; 2 sons and 1 daughter. Schoolteacher, Ealing Grammar School, 1961; schoolteacher, Northwood Secondary School, Middlesex 1961–3; Granada Arts Fellow, 1963–4, lecturer in music, 1964–71, senior lecturer, 1971–6, and Professor of music, since 1986, University of York. Pianist and accompanist; piano director of own group Lumina (now defunct); conductor of Northern Sinfonia and London Sinfonietta; University of York ensemble. Teaching centres on composition, both Viennese schools. Mailing address: Mill Gill, Askrigg, Near Leyborn, North Yorkshire DL8 3HR, England.

Publisher: Novello.

Symphonies/orchestral:

Symphony for Chamber Orchestra 1966; first performed York, June 1966.
Metamorphoses 1971; first performed York, March 1971.
Violin Concerto No 1 1976; first performed London, 19 August 1976. Recorded Argo ZRG 922.
Sonata alla Marcia (chamber orchestra) 1978; first performed London, 17 May 1978.
Violin Concerto No 2 1983.
Scherzi ed Intermezzi 1984; first performed Bedford, 17 November 1984.
Pastoral Paraphrase 1988; first performed York, 1989.

Chamber/instrumental:

Variations (piano) 1960; first performed Cheltenham, Gloucestershire, 1961. Recorded EMI ASD 2551.
String Quartet No 1 1962; first performed London, 1962.
Sequence (2 flutes) 1967.
Nonet (wind) 1971, revised 1978; first performed London, 21 June 1971.
Scenes (cello) 1972; first performed London, October 1972.
String Quartet No 2 1973; first performed York, June 1973.
Arias (clarinet) 1978; first performed Newcastle, 23 January 1979.
Cassation (wind octet) 1979; first performed Sheffield, 19 May 1979.
Capriccio (7 players: flute/piccolo/alto flute, clarinet/E♭ clarinet/bass clarinet, clarinet/bass clarinet/soprano saxophone, violin, viola, cello, piano) 1980; first performed York, 14 January 1981.
Clarinet Quintet (clarinet, string quartet) 1980; first performed Bradford, 29 January 1981.
Scherzo and Two Dances (7 players: flute/piccolo, clarinet/E♭ clarinet, clarinet/bass clarinet/soprano saxophone, violin, viola, cello, piano) 1981; first performed York, 16 January 1982.
String Quartet No 3 1982; first performed Cambridge, 18 April 1983.
Fantasia (violin) 1984; first performed York, 21 November 1984.
Seasonal Variants (flute/piccolo, clarinet/A clarinet, clarinet/bass clarinet, string trio, piano) 1985; first performed Norwich, 18 November 1985.

Vocal/choral:

Three Choruses to Poems by Robert Frost (SATB, unaccompanied) 1964; first performed London, May 1966.
On Christmas Day (SATB, unaccompanied) 1965; broadcast BBC, 1967.
Four Songs of Ben Jonson (SATB, unaccompanied) 1965; broadcast BBC, 1967.
Beata L'Alma (soprano, piano; Read) 1966; first performed Harrogate, August 1967.
What Is the Cause (6 unaccompanied voices: SSATBarB) 1967; first performed Harrogate, August 1967.
The Almanack (SATB, unaccompanied) 1968; first performed York, 1968. Recorded Yorkshire Arts YAA 2.
Lumina (soprano, baritone, choir, orchestra; Pound) 1969; first performed Leeds, 1970.
The Bones of Chuang Tzu (baritone, piano) 1972, revised 1973 for baritone and chamber orchestra; first performed Aldeburgh, Suffolk, 1972; revised version first performed Glasgow, 25 March 1975.
In Praise of Krishna (soprano, 9 players) 1973; first performed Leeds University, 7 March 1973. Recorded ARGO ZRG 922.
Toussaint Suite (mezzo-soprano, baritone, orchestra; suite from opera) 1977; first performed London, 17 November 1983.

Toussaint: Song of the Common Wind (mezzo-soprano, orchestra; "scena" from opera; also version for mezzo-soprano, piano) 1977.
From the Mattress Grave (soprano, 11 players) 1978; first performed Newcastle, 1979.
Nine Poems of Heine (high voice, piano: 9 songs arranged from the cycle *From the Mattress Grave*) 1978.
Change Is Going to Come (mezzo-soprano, baritone, chorus, 4 players—clarinet, trumpet, viola, piano) 1982; London, 14 November 1982.
The Spear (male speaker, mezzo-soprano, 4 players) 1982.
Rise, Dove (bass-baritone, orchestra) 1983; first performed Manchester, 21 December 1983.

Opera:

It's a Small War (musical) 1962; first performed London, 1962.
Toussaint (baritone, mezzo-soprano, tenor, 2 bass leading roles, 3 soprano, 4 tenor, 3 baritone, 2 bass subsidiary roles, minor roles, double chorus, orchestra) 1976, revised 1982; first performed London, 28 September 1977; revised version first performed London, 6 September 1983.
The Plumber's Gift 1989; first performed London, 1989.

PUBLICATIONS

On Blake: Malcolm MacDonald, in *British Music Now*, edited by Foreman, London, 1975.

* * *

The turning point in David Blake's development as a composer came in 1960 when a Mendelssohn Scholarship enabled him to study abroad for a year. Slightly surprisingly, he chose to go to East Berlin to work with Hanns Eisler, a pupil of Schoenberg's who combined an absolute mastery of the twelve-tone technique with a Marxist-inspired lyrical populism.

In Blake's own words, Eisler tried to change him "from a dilettante to a composer". He withdrew all the apprentice pieces he had written at Cambridge, which were tonal with a heavy dressing of Mahler, and began to work in an altogether more rugged style. It's immediately clear that Eisler's influence was not a direct stylistic one—though the early serial *Variations* for piano is closer to Eisler than to Schoenberg—but primarily as a catalyst and an example of independent committed composition.

Since the early 1960s, Blake has developed away from the metropolitan music scene. Though he became a resounding and controversial presence with the London premiere in 1989 of his remarkable opera *The Plumber's Gift*, which is among the most intriguingly individual operatic works of recent years, he has preferred to work steadily in his northern fastness. His declared hostility to what passes for "popular music" today suggests an academic/avant-garde sensibility which is in no way borne out by his work. Blake writes in a free-flowing way, with no single dogmatic method. He has devised a method to suit the project at hand, whether it is the complex exercises of the first *String Quartet*, the considerable demands of a poem by the 16th-century poet Thomas Traherne (which he set for an Oxford album of *Carols of Today*), or the *Scenes* for solo cello, which is startling largely for its brilliant synthesis of serial procedures and a decidedly tonal "feel".

Thematically, Blake seems to be drawn to metaphors of continuity within change, metamorphosis and transfiguration. He is a Schoenbergian with a little Mahler still showing. The powerful *Metamorphoses* for orchestra followed closely in the tracks of what was certainly Blake's breakthrough work, one that combined his Viennese schooling with a strong thread of orientalism. Blake served as an interpreter in the R.A.F. in Hong Kong and maintains a strong interest in Chinese verse. *Lumina* is based on Ezra Pound's *Cantos*, a poetic cycle with a strong Chinese, and a strong political, component. The ferocity of Blake's adaptation of the notorious "Usury" Cantos conveys a vision of Hell not unworthy of another Blake. In contrast, his ability to communicate the lonely anguish and almost epiphanic stoicism of the *Pisan Cantos* is achingly beautiful.

So central is *Lumina* to Blake's career—he named his own performance group after the piece—and to his belief in the transformative power of spirit and imagination, that it represents the benchmark for everything that precedes and follows. He has written more beautifully for voices; the cantata *Beata L'Alma* to a text by Herbert Read is superb. He has written more persuasively for orchestra, as in *Metamorphoses*. He has more thoroughly synthesised his Eastern and occidental influences, as in *The Bones of Chuang Tzu* (which features a Cagean prepared piano and chance elements) and *In Praise of Krishna*. And he has written more powerfully in a political/historical vein, as in the opera *Toussaint*. He has never, though, combined all the diverse elements more completely.

Toussaint, based on the Haitian rising of Toussaint L'Ouverture, is an intriguing work. Blake uses folk materials and pseudo-classical interpolations to deliver his message. There are strong thematic and musical links with *Fidelio* in the story of slavery and liberation, and a deeply ironic use of tonal resolutions, as when the rising has been suppressed and "normality" restored. Blake has elsewhere—in *The Plumber's Gift* notably—buried careful signposts in his score. "Returns to tonality" must always be treated with suspicion, as must any *outre* expressionism, such as that parodied by the solo clarinettist in *Arias*, where the "diva" goes completely over the top.

The Heine settings exactly echo the sardonic, satirical gestures of the original text, but with an element of warmth and humane humour missing in the poet. Blake's attraction to the light and to the transformative power of the imagination is too strong to succumb to anything remotely resembling cynicism.

—Eleanor Caldwell

BLAKE, Howard (David). British/English. Born in London, 28 October 1938. Educated at Royal Academy of Music, London (piano under Harold Craxton, composition under Howard Ferguson), 1957–60. Conductor, pianist, lyricist; director, P.R.S. Ltd, 1978–87. Mailing address: Studio Flat 6, 18 Kensington Court Place, London W8 5BJ, England.

Publisher: Faber.

Symphonies/orchestral:

Toccata: A Celebration of the Orchestra 1976, revised 1988; first performed Croydon, Surrey, September 1976.
Sinfonietta (brass band: 4 trumpets, 4 trombones, horn, tuba) 1981; first performed Brighton, Sussex, May 1981.
Heartbeat (tenor saxophone, rhythm section, strings) 1982; first performed Brighton, Sussex, June 1982.
Concert Dances (piano, orchestra) 1984.
Concerto for Clarinet and Orchestra 1984; first performed London, 30 May 1985.
Nursery Rhyme Overture 1984; first performed St Albans, Hertfordshire, 26 October 1984. Recorded CBS HB1.
Suite: The Up and Down Man 1985; first performed London, December 1985.
Divertimento (cello, orchestra) 1985.
Fusions (arrangement of *Sinfonietta* for brass band, percussion) 1986; first performed Manchester, September 1986.
The Conquest of Space 1988. Recorded CBS HB1.
Concert Dances (wind orchestra) 1988; first performed Buxton, Yorkshire, August 1988.
Diversions (cello, orchestra) 1989; first performed Croydon, Surrey, 29 March 1989.
Clarinet Concerto 1990. Recorded Hyperion A66215.
Piano Concerto 1990.

Chamber/instrumental:

Piano Quartet in A minor 1974; first performed London, June 1974. Recorded Watermill 2002.
Reflections (violin, viola, cello, piano) 1974; first performed London, June 1974.
Burlesque Suite: The Up and Down Man (piano trio) 1974; first performed Haywards Heath, Sussex, May 1976.
Penillion (violin/flute/oboe, harp/piano) 1975; first performed London, April 1975.
Dances for Two Pianos 1976; first performed Brighton, Sussex, May 1976. Recorded Watermill 2001.
Prelude (from *Benedictus*; viola) 1979.
Fusion (edited version of *Sinfonietta*) 1986; first performed Manchester, September 1986.
The Snowman (arrangements for flute, piano; violin, piano; clarinet/tenor saxophone, piano) 1986.
Walking in the Air (arrangements for recorder, piano; flute, piano; clarinet/tenor saxophone, piano; trumpet/cornet, piano; guitar; violin, piano; easy piano) 1986.

Vocal/choral:

Three Sussex Songs (mezzo-soprano, piano; Garrett) 1973; first performed London, June 1974.
The New National Songbook (SATBarB or SATB, piano or instrumental ensemble) 1976; first performed London, 23 May 1976.
Two Songs of the Nativity ("Holy Mary, Mother Mild" for tenor, string quartet; "Of a Rose Is All My Song" for bass, string quartet or piano) 1976; first performed London, December 1976.
The Song of St Francis (SATB chorus, orchestra or organ) 1976, revised 1990; first performed Worth Abbey, Sussex, May 1977.
A Toccata of Galuppi's (baritone, harpsichord; R. Browning) 1978; broadcast BBC Radio 3, January 1981.
Benedictus (tenor, optional speaker, SATB chorus, optional trebles, orchestra; Biblical, Latin and English) 1979, revised 1985; first performed Worth Abbey, Sussex, 10 May 1980.
The Snowman (narrator, boy soprano, orchestra; Blake, after Briggs) 1982; first performed London, December 1983.
Walking in the Air (theme from *The Snowman*; boy soprano, orchestra; also arranged for voice, piano) 1982.
Shakespeare Songs (tenor, string quartet or string orchestra) 1987; first performed Chester, 21 July 1987.
Festival Mass (double choir, optional organ) 1987; first performed 23 August 1987.
Granpa (male speaker/singer, young girl soloist, SATB quartet or semi-chorus, children's choir, orchestra; Blake, after Burningham) 1988; first performed London 9 July 1989. Recorded CBS HB1.
Jubilate Deo (Psalm 100) (SATB chorus, organ) 1990; first performed Abington, Pennyslvania, 17 June 1990.

Opera:

The Station (7 singers, piano or instrumental ensemble) 1987.

Other:

Reflections (ballet) 1976; first performed London, 1976.
The Court of Love (ballet) 1977; first performed London, 1977.
Meeting and Parting (ballet) 1977; first performed London, 1977.
Leda and the Swan (ballet) 1978; broadcast BBC, 1978.
The Annunciation (ballet; small orchestra) 1979; first performed London, December 1979.
The Snowman: Schools Version (flexible scoring: narrator, boy soprano, optional SATB chorus, piano duet; or any combination of flute, oboe or 2nd flute, 2 clarinets, bassoon, 2 saxophones, 2 horns, 2 trumpets, trombone, tuba, recorders, timpani, 2 percussion, classroom percussion, rhythm guitars, bass guitar, strings) 1982–6; first performed Hereford, 9 December 1986.
Henry the Fifth (incidental music to Shakespeare) 1984; first performed London, 1984.
As You Like It (incidental music to Shakespeare) 1985; first performed London, 1985.
The Master Builder (incidental music to Shakespeare) 1989; first performed London, 1989.

Film scores: *The Duellists*, 1977; *Blood Relatives*, 1978; *Agatha*, 1978; *The Riddle of the Sands*, 1978; *SOS Titanic*, 1979; *The Lords of Discipline*, 1983; *Amityville 3D*, 1983; *A Month in the Country*, 1986; *The Canterville Ghost*, 1988.

Music for television: *The Avengers*, 1968–9; *The Remarkable Rocket*, 1974; *Stronger than the Sun*, 1977; *The Moon Stallion*, 1978; *Gentle Folk*, 1979; *Mrs Reinhardt*, 1981; *Down at the Hydro*, 1982; *The Snowman*, 1982; *Granpa*, 1988–9.

PUBLICATIONS

By Blake: 12 volumes of unpublished essays, 1958–90.
On Blake: Christopher Palmer, *HB*, in preparation, 1991.

Howard Blake comments:

I believe that Schoenberg's intellectual crusade to abolish melody, harmony and rhythm dealt a near death-blow to the inspired creation of meaningful new music in the second half of the 20th century. I believe that all great music evolves firstly from the critical assimilation of all available tradition, and secondly by attention to the popular current tonal innovations of the day.

I believe in the alchemical transmutation of material of Jung, and not the ivory tower attempt at language-creation, which derives at secondhand from Wagner's view of the artist as ersatz-god. I believe, with Plato, that the composer's function is to try to balance and reconcile the conflicting elements of society within his music, and that by doing so in an accessible and comprehensible language, he may then hope to have the vision to uplift and inspire society at large. I believe that the composer can only achieve this function by working with humility as a craftsman, responding to the requirements of the day: that, as William Blake said, "Eternity is in love with the productions of time."

My own music is melodic, harmonic, contrapuntal, rhythmic; hopefully inspirational, and hopefully non-elitist.

* * *

Howard Blake is that rarity in the contemporary music scene, a genuinely popular composer. If he has a recent parallel, it is probably Leonard Bernstein, though he is an altogether more "natural", less troubled composer than Bernstein even at his gentlest.

Blake's reputation now rests very squarely on the success of *The Snowman*, adapted from a story by Raymond Briggs, and particularly on its haunting theme "Walking in the Air". Since its first performance in 1982, the piece has become a Christmas standby in its animated form on British television. It is ironic but also inevitable that the popular and commercial success of *The Snowman*, together with Blakes's background as a journeyman composer of film and television music, has tended to compromise his critical reputation. However, its merits, and those of its successor *Granpa* are the classical merits *par excellence* and are clearly audible in Blake's concert music.

The purity of line and lack of clutter that make "Walking in the Air" so utterly and immediately memorable, is also what animates the *Clarinet Concerto* and a remarkable overture *The Conquest of Space*, in which Blake's use of unusual sonorities (ondes Martenot or synthesizer, and a choir) complements his apparent conviction that imaginative composition is still feasible within a constantly renewing harmonic tradition. At the end of the 1970s, he retreated to the country to work again at the basic pillars of harmony and counterpoint, slowly refining a technique and language that have little in common with most contemporary academic music. Blake is hostile to avant-gardist gestures, and to serialism. His most obvious (distant) influence is Mozart, but there is also something of his one-time teacher Howard Ferguson's neo-classical idiom and a strong sense of music as a cultural adhesive, rebonding a society fractured by modernism and its discontents. His major work to date, *Benedictus*, is a powerful and humane expression of faith in the transcendent power of imagination.

Though undoubtedly conservative, Blake is no reactionary. His lyrics are often wryly ironic and his scoring subtly inflected. A background in jazz is evident in his firm, but not mechanical, rhythm; the 1984 *Concert Dances*, in both its piano concertante and wind band versions, is an unstuffy set of exercises in popular forms, ragtime, jump, boogie, rock, cha-cha, but if the names of movements unavoidably suggest the "rhythm selectors" attached to cheap electric keyboards, there is nothing mechanical about Blake's variations on basic signatures and pulses.

Not the least significant aspect of Blake's recent career has been a recording contract—and personalised "HB" index number!—with CBS Records, a company noted for occasional, but imaginative experiments of this sort. Blake is unembarrassed and unhindered by his popularity. It is, as it was with Mozart, simply a response to a spontaneous melodic gift underpinned with considerable technical skill.

—Pamela Collins

BOLCOM, William (Elden). American. Born in Seattle, Washington, 26 May 1938. Educated at University of Washington, Seattle (as special student, aged 11; piano under Berthe Ponsonby Jacobson, theory and composition under George McKay and John Verrall; later studied poetry under Theodore Roethke), 1949–58, B.A.; Mills College, Oakland (under Darius Milhaud), 1958–61, M.A.; Conservatoire National Supérieur de Musique, Paris (under Darius Milhaud, Jean Rivier and Oliver Messiaen), 1959–61; Ferienkurse für Neue Musik, Darmstadt, 1960; Stanford University, California (advanced composition under Leland Smith), 1961–4, D.M.A.; further piano study with George Rochberg, 1966. Married (1) Fay Levine (dissolved 1967); (2) Katherine Agee Ling (dissolved 1969); (3) soprano Joan Morris, 28 November 1975. Acting assistant professor, University of Washington, Seattle, 1965–6; lecturer, then assistant professor of music, Queens College, City University of New York, 1966–8; visiting critic, Music Theatre Drama School, Yale University, New Haven, Connecticut, 1968–9; composer in residence, Theatre Arts Program, New York University, 1969–71; assistant professor, School of Music, 1973–7, associate professor, 1977–83, and full professor of music, since 1983, University of Michigan, Ann Arbor; jury member, National Endowment for Arts, 1976–7, 1984–5; concert and recording pianist. Recipient: William and Norma Copley Award, 1960; Kurt Weill Award for composition, 1962; Guggenheim Fellowships, 1964–5, 1968–9; Marc Blitzstein Award for excellence in music, theatre, American Academy of Arts and Letters, 1965. Mailing address: 3080 Whitmore Lake Road, Ann Arbor, Michigan 48105, U.S.A.

Publishers: E.B. Marks; Presser.

Symphonies/orchestral:

Symphony 1957.
Concertante (violin, flute, oboe, orchestra) 1961.
Concerto Serenade (violin, string orchestra) 1964.
Symphony: Oracles 1965.
Five (violin, piano, 3 string groups) 1966.
Commedia (chamber orchestra) 1971.
Summer Divertimento 1973.
Piano Concerto 1976.
Humoresk (organ, orchestra) 1979.
Symphony (chamber orchestra) 1979.
Ragomania 1982.
Violin Concerto 1983.

Chamber/instrumental:

String Quartet No 1 1950; withdrawn.
String Quartet No 2 1953; withdrawn.

String Quartet No 3 1954; withdrawn.
String Quartet No 5 1957; withdrawn.
Concert Piece (clarinet, piano) 1958.
Romantic Pieces (piano) 1959.
String Quartet No 6 1959; withdrawn.
Twelve Etudes (piano) 1959–60.
Fantasy Sonata No 1 (piano) 1961.
String Quartet No 7 1961; withdrawn.
Decalage (cello, piano) 1961.
Pastorale (violin, piano) 1961.
Octet (flute, clarinet, bassoon, violin, viola, cello, double bass, piano) 1962.
Interlude (2 pianos) 1963.
Dream Music No 1 (piano) 1965.
Session I (septet) 1965.
String Quartet No 8 1965.
Dream Music No 2 (harpsichord, 3 percussion) 1966.
Phrygia (harp) 1966.
Session II (violin, viola) 1966.
Session III (clarinet, violin, cello, piano, percussion) 1967.
Black Host (organ, percussion, tape) 1967.
Session IV (nonet) 1967.
Brass Knuckles (piano) 1968.
Garden of Eden (piano) 1969.
Dark Music (cello, timpani) 1969.
Praeludium (organ, vibraphone) 1969.
Chorale and Prelude on Abide with Me (organ) 1970.
Seabiscuits Rag (piano) 1970.
The Graceful Ghost (piano) 1970.
Duets for Quintet (flute, clarinet, violin, cello, piano) 1971.
Fancy Tales (violin, piano) 1971.
Frescoes (piano/harpsichord, piano/harmonium) 1971.
Hydraulis (organ) 1971.
Whisper Moon (flute, clarinet, 2 violins, piano) 1971.
String Quartet No 9: Novella 1972.
Raggin' Rudi (piano) 1972.
Duo Fantasy (violin, piano) 1973.
Trauermarsch (flute, oboe, electric harpsichord, electric cello) 1973.
Seasons (guitar) 1974.
Piano Quartet 1976.
Mysteries (organ) 1976.
Revelation Studies (carillon, 2 players) 1976.
Short Lecture (clarinet) 1976.
Sonata (violin) 1978.
Fields of Flowers (piano) 1978.
Afternoon, Rag Suite of Joplin, Lamb, Scott and Bolcom (clarinet, violin, piano) 1979.
Three Gospel Preludes (organ) 1979.
Brass Quintet 1980.
Monsterpieces (and Others) (piano) 1980.
Aubade (oboe, piano) 1982.
Gospel Preludes: Books II and III (organ) 1982.
The Dead Moth Tango (piano) 1983–4.
Lilith (saxophone, piano) 1984.

Vocal/choral:

Songs of Innocence and Experience (9 solo voices, 3 choruses, children's chorus, orchestra; Blake) 1956–81; first performed Stuttgart, 8 January 1984.
Morning and Evening Poems (alto, tenor/counter-tenor, instrumental ensemble; Blake) 1966.
Satires (unaccompanied mixed chorus) 1970.
Open House (tenor, chamber orchestra; Roethke) 1975.
Vocalise from Songs of Experience (unaccompanied mixed chorus) 1977.
Six Cabaret Songs (voice, piano; Weinstein) 1978.
Three Donald Hall Songs (mezzo-soprano/baritone, instrumental ensemble) 1979.
Six New Cabaret Songs (voice, piano; Weinstein) 1984.

Opera:

Dynamite Tonight (cabaret opera for 2 actors; Weinstein) 1963.
Greatshot (cabaret opera for 2 actors; Weinstein) 1966.

Other:

Theatre of the Absurd (actor, taped voices, wind quintet, piano, tapes, mechanized eyeballs) 1960.

John Gay: *The Beggars' Opera* (completion of Darius Milhaud's adapted version of 1936–7) 1978.

PUBLICATIONS

By Bolcom: (with Robert Kimball), *Reminiscing with Sissle and Blake*, New York, 1973; editor, *The Aesthetics of Survival: A Composer's View of the 20th Century* [the collected essays of George Rochberg], Ann Arbor, Michigan, 1984.

On Bolcom: J. Hiemenz, "Musician of the Month: WB", in *High Fidelity / Musical America*, 26 (9), 1976.

* * *

Somewhat the older of "the two Bills" who work a fine double-act at the University of Michigan (William Albright is the younger partner), William Bolcom shows no signs of undue sententiousness of gravitas. His career has been largely dedicated to the elimination of any hard and fast distinction between "serious" and "popular" music. Perhaps his most striking achievement has been the archaeology of 19th- and early 20th-century American popular forms and he is perhaps better known as a performer than as a composer.

He met the soprano Joan Morris in 1971; four years later, she became his wife. Together they have produced concerts and recordings of American parlour and vaudeville music. Bolcom has also recorded piano pieces by Darius Milhaud (who was his teacher at Mills College and in Paris) and George Gershwin. By far his greatest influence, though, has been on the rehabilitation of ragtime, a much debased currency in American music, but, along with jazz, arguably North America's single most important contribution to the musical language of the 20th century.

Most revivalist ragtime has been conditioned by the hectic and somewhat unthoughtful intepretations associated with Joshua Rifkin's soundtrack to *The Sting*. Bolcom—and William Albright—have returned to a much more varied dynamic, which preserves most of Joplin's original features, syncopation (not invariably), duple and quadruple meter (but again not invariably) and a structure based on the tonic and subdominant. Keyboard works such as *The Graceful Ghost* and *Seabiscuits Rag*, and *Raggin' Rudi* are typical of Bolcom's somewhat more lighthearted vein, but he also blends in more postmodern elements—a late serialism, odd collage effects, chance and improvisatory procedures (which are typical of ragtime in any case)—as in the curiously disturbing *Black Host* for organ, percussion and tape, and another organ piece, *Mysteries*. (His interest in organ has been reinforced by

Albright's more extensive explorations in that medium.) Bolcom has also adapted ragtime to much larger structures with some effect; the orchestral *Ragomania* is generally successful, and there are rhythmic allusions in some of the later ensemble pieces.

Bolcom withdrew seven early string quartets before he satisfied himself in that genre. The 1972 *Novella*, which is also his Ninth String Quartet, is a powerful piece, reflecting some of the dynamic and dramatic qualities adumbrated a decade earlier in *Decalage* for cello and piano, and the Octet for winds and strings. Other pieces from that early period typically draw on popular song in a manner which is half parodic and satirical, half respectful and affectionate; *Whisper Moon* is a good example, and Bolcom has continued to explore the parameters of popular forms, as in *The Dead Moth Tango* (composing tangos is, it seems, all the rage again).

Without any question, Bolcom's most important work to date is his large-scale setting of William Blake's *Songs of Innocence and Experience*. Long in the writing, it is a work that concentrates most of Bolcom's aesthetic and spiritual concerns. Setting Blake, like Emily Dickinson, is difficult because of, not despite, the apparently simple rhythms of the lines and "naive" forms. Bolcom's version is triumphant, sustaining the simplicity of Blake's diction, but combining it with the numinous complexity and difficulty of his underlying sense. His settings of Theodore Roethke, his old teacher at the University of Washington, are true to Roethke's fine inner rhythm and quiet intensity of emotion.

While his "cabaret operas" are not dated and some of his more *outré* experiments a little stale and time-bound, Bolcom is a considerable presence as a composer and performer. Less concerned with the deep structures of pieces than William Albright, he is nonetheless a confident musical architect, with a fine and lasting body of music to his credit. *Songs of Innocence and Experience* alone raises him to the highest level.

—Eleanor Caldwell

BOULEZ, Pierre. French. Born in Montbrison, Loire, 26 March 1925. Educated at lycées in Saint-Etienne and Lyon (music and higher mathematics); Conservatoire National Supérieur de Musique, Paris (advanced harmony under Olivier Messiaen, counterpoint under Andrée Vaurabourg-Honegger and René Leibowitz), 1942–5. Director of music, Jean Barrault theatre company, Paris, 1948; toured U.S.A. with French Ballet, 1952; founder (sponsored by Jean Barrault and Madeleine Renaud Barrault), Concert Marigny, later Domaine Musical, 1954; director of Domaine Musical until 1967 (succeeded by Gilbert Amy—Domaine Musical disbanded in 1973); teacher, Ferienkurse für Neue Musik, Darmstadt, 1958; Horatio Appleton Lamb Guest Lecturer, Harvard University, Cambridge, Massachusetts, 1963; principal guest conductor, Cleveland Symphony Orchestra, Ohio, 1968; principal conductor, BBC Symphony Orchestra, 1971–5; musical director, New York Philharmonic, 1971–7; conductor, centenary production of Wagner's *Ring* cycle, Bayreuth, 1976–80. Director, Institut de Recherches et de Coordination Acoustique/Musique (IRCAM), since 1975; consultant for special events, Orchestre National de France, since 1987. Honorary degrees: University of Cambridge, D.Mus., 1980; University of Oxford, D.Mus., 1987; and from Universities of Bristol, Leeds and Southern California. Mailing address: IRCAM, 31 rue St Merri, 75004 Paris, France.

Publisher: Universal Edition.

Symphonies/orchestral:

Symphony 1947; now lost.
Doubles 1958; first performed Paris, 16 March 1958; expanded as *Figures-doubles-prismes*, first performed Strasbourg, 10 January 1964; subsequently revised 1968.
Domaines (clarinet, 6 instrumental groups) 1961, 1968–9; first performed Brussels, 20 December 1968.
Eclats / multiples (orchestra; revised version of *Eclats*) 1966–in progress; first performed London, 21 October 1970. Recorded Sony SK 45839.
Livre pour cordes (string orchestra) 1968–in progress; part Ia first performed London, 1 December 1968; part Ib first performed Brighton, Sussex, 8 December 1968.
Mémoriales 1973–5; first performed London, 2 April 1975.
Rituel in memoriam Bruno Maderna (orchestra in 8 groups) 1974–5.
Notations I-IV 1980; begun 1945.
Répons (2 pianos, harp, vibraphone, glockenspiel, cimbalom, chamber orchestra, electronics) 1983.

Chamber/instrumental:

Notations (piano) 1945; first performed Paris, 12 February 1945; withdrawn.
Trois Psalmodies (piano) 1945; first performed Paris, 1945; withdrawn.
Variations pour la main gauche (piano, left hand) 1945; withdrawn.
Quartet (4 ondes martenot) 1945–6; withdrawn.
Sonata No 1 (piano) 1946; first performed Paris, 1946.
Sonatina (flute, piano) 1946.
Sonata (2 pianos) 1948.
Sonata No 2 (piano) 1948; first performed Paris, 29 April 1950.
Livre pour quatuor (string quartet) 1948–9; parts Ia/b, II first performed Donaueschingen, October 1955; parts V and VI first performed Darmstadt, 29 August 1961; parts IIIa/b/c first performed Darmstadt, 8 July 1962; subsequently withdrawn for revision as *Livre pour cordes*, from 1968.
Polyphonie (18 instruments) 1951; first performed Donaueschingen, 6 October 1951; withdrawn.
Structures: livre I (2 pianos) 1952; part Ia first performed Paris, 4 May 1952; first complete performance Cologne, 13 November 1953.
Sonata No 3: antipohonie, trope, constellation / constellation-miroir, strophe, séquence (piano) 1955–7; first performed Darmstadt, September 1957.
Structures: livre II (2 pianos) 1956–61; first performed Donaueschingen, 21 October 1961.
Strophes (flute) 1957.
Domaines (clarinet) 1961–8.
Marges (percussion ensemble) 1962–4; first performed Brussels, December 1964; withdrawn.
Eclats (15 instruments; later version for orchestra) 1965; first performed Los Angeles, 26 March 1965.
Pour le Dr Kalmus (flute, clarinet, violin, cello, piano) 1969.
". . . *explosante fixe* . . ." (unspecified instrumentation) 1971,

(revised 1974; first performed (flute, clarinet, trumpet), London, 17 June 1972; first performed (trumpet, harp, vibraphone, violin, viola, cello, electronics), New York City, 5 January 1973; revised version first performed La Rochelle, 6 July 1974; new version for 3 flutes, ensemble, 4X computer (IRCAM), electronics, 1989–90.
Messagesquisse (7 cellos) 1977; first performed La Rochelle, 1977.
Dérivé (flute, clarinet, vibraphone, piano, violin, cello) 1984.
Mémoriale (. . . explosante-fixe . . . originel) (flute solo, 2 horns, 3 violins, 2 viola, cello) 1985.
Initiale (brass septet) 1987.

Vocal/choral:

Le Visage nuptial (soprano, contralto, chamber orchestra, 2 ondes martenot, piano, percussion; Char) 1946, revised for soprano, contralto, female chorus, large orchestra, 1951–2; revised version first performed Cologne, 4 December 1957; re-orchestrated 1988–9.
Le Soleil des eaux (radio play for voice, orchestra; Char) 1948; broadcast ORTF, April 1948; revised for soprano, tenor, bass, chamber orchestra; first performed Paris, 18 July 1950; revised for soprano, tenor, bass, STB chorus, orchestra, 1958; first performed Darmstadt, 9 September 1958; revised for soprano, SATB chorus, orchestra; first performed Berlin, October 1965.
Séquence (oubli, signal, lapide) (12 unaccompanied voices; Gatti) 1952; first performed Cologne, 3 October 1952; withdrawn.
Le Marteau sans maître (alto, alto flute, guitar, vibraphone, xylorimba, percussion, viola; Char) 1952–4, revised 1957; first performed Baden-Baden, 18 June 1955.
Improvisation sur Mallarmé II: une dentelle s'abolit (soprano, celeste, harp, piano, tubular bells, vibraphone, 4 percussion, harp) 1957, revised for soprano and orchestra, 1962; first performed Hamburg, 13 January 1958; revised version first performed Donaueschingen, 20 October 1962.
Improvisation sur Mallarmé II: une dentelle s'abolit (soprano, celesta, harp, piano, tubular bells, vibraphone, 4 percussion) 1957, revised in part, 1983–4; first performed Hamburg, 13 January 1958.
Poésie pour pouvoir (5-track tape, orchestra; Michaux) 1958; first performed Donaueschingen, 19 October 1958.
Improvisation sur Mallarmé III: à la nue accablante tu (soprano, orchestra) 1959; first performed 10 June 1959.
Tombeau (soprano, orchestra) 1959, revised 1962; first performed Donaueschingen, 17 October 1959; revised version first performed Donaueschingen, 20 October 1962.
Don (soprano, piano; Mallarmé) 1960, revised for piano and orchestra, 1962; first performed Cologne, 13 June 1960; revised version first performed Donaueschingen, 20 October 1962.
Pli selon pli (consists of *Don, Improvisations sur Mallarmé I-III, Tombeau*) 1962.
e. e. cummings ist der Dichter (16 solo voices, 24 instruments) 1970–in progress; first performed Stuttgart, 25 September 1970.

Other:

Etudes sur un son (tape) 1951–2.
Etude sur un accord de sept sons (tape) 1951–2.
Orestie (incidental music to Aeschylus) 1955; first performed Bordeaux, 1955.
Symphonie mécanique (music to film by Jean Mitry; 1-track tape) 1955.
Le Crépuscule de Yang Kouei-Fei (music for radio play by Fauré, after Leconte) 1957.
Mon Faust (incidental music to Valéry) 1962.
Ainsi parla Zarathoustra (incidental music to Barrault, after Nietzsche) 1974; first performed Paris, October 1974.

Claude Debussy: *Chansons de Bilitis* (speaker, 2 flutes, 2 harps, celeste; reconstruction of celeste part) 1963–4.

PUBLICATIONS

By Boulez: "Probabilités critiques du compositeur", in *Domaine musical*, 1, 1954; "Der Vogel Strauss im Labor", in *Melos*, 23, 1956; "Zu meiner III. Sonate", in *Darmstadter Beitrage zur neuen Musik*, 3, 1960; "Diszipline und Kommunikation", in *Darmstadter Beitrage zur neuen Musik*, 4, 1961; "Wie arbeitet die Avantgarde?", in *Melos*, 28, 1961; "L'Esthétique et les fétiches", in Samuel (ed), *Panorama de l'art contemporain*, Paris, 1962, German translation in *Melos*, 34, 1967; "Poésie—centre et absence", in *Melos*, 30, 1963; "Le Goût et la fonction", in *Tel quel*, 14–5, 1963; *Penser la musique aujourd'hui*, Paris, 1964, translated into English as *B on Music Today*, London, 1971; "Hommage à Varèse", in *Nouvel observateur*, 17 November 1965; *Relèves d'apprenti* (collected articles), Paris, 1966; "En marge de là, d'une disparition (th. w. adorno—6.8.1969)", in *Melos*, 36, 1969; "Chemins vers 'Parsifal'", Bayreuth Festival programme, 1970, reprinted as DGG 2720034; "Technology and the Composer", in *Times Literary Supplement*, 6 May 1977; *Points de repère* (articles and texts), Paris, 1981, translated into English as *Orientations*, London, 1986.

On Boulez: György Ligeti, "PB: Entscheidung und Automatik in der Structure Ia", in *Der Reihe*, 4, 1958; Susan Bradshaw and Richard Rodney Bennett, "In Search of Boulez", in *Music and Musicians*, 11, 1963; J.-P. Derrien, "Dossier: PB", in *Musique en jeu*, 1, 1970; *Par volonté et par hasard* (interviews with Christine Deliège), Paris, 1975, translated into English, 1977; many others.

* * *

One of the most commanding musical personalities of the present day, Pierre Boulez has made an indelible impact as composer, conductor and writer on music. Undoubtedly the most brilliant of Messiaen's pupils in the 1940s, he quickly rose to prominence as an outspoken polemicist on behalf of post-Webernian serialism, promoting a new orthodoxy which saw even Schoenberg as a betrayer of modernist values.

After the uncompromising constructivism of *Structures*, Book I, in which serial methods are applied to dynamic levels, modes of attack, dynamic levels and durations as well as to pitch, Boulez developed a style which combined a fierce rigour of theory and technique with a sensitivity to qualities of sonority and musical effect which was matched occasionally by Stockhausen and sporadically by Berio but scarcely at all by other adherents to the aesthetic of "total serialism". The centrepiece of his output in the 1950s was *Le Marteau sans maître*, an epoch-making work which spawned a whole genre of song cycles (by other composers) with an instrumental ensemble dominated by flute, percussion and plucked strings. While the vocal writing in *Le Marteau* often gives clear articulation to the images which collide surreally in Char's poetry, Boulez also chooses on occasion to treat the words as sonorous objects devoid of meaning. The most notable feature of his handling of the text, however, is his conception of "commentaries" on the poems—instrumental movements in which the poetry is not heard, but whose progress it is perceived to inform absolutely. Boulez developed these ideas on a larger scale in *Pli selon pli* before turning principally to instrumental composition.

While Stockhausen followed the strict path of avant-garde progressivism at an astounding pace, apparently inventing a new and more advanced musical language with every work he produced, Boulez appeared to develop more slowly. Pieces began to emerge unfinished or as provisional "works-in-progress"; his sense of direction seemed uncertain. Towards the end of the 1960s, as Stockhausen burned himself out, Boulez began to devote his energies primarily to conducting, forging a reputation for outstanding accuracy in modern music based on his phenomenal ear for detail in even the most complex textures. He was thus spared the difficulty, which Stockhausen had to face, of continuing his career as a composer against the very different aesthetic background of the 1970s: to the concert-going public he was, in effect, a conductor who composed rather than vice versa. This period saw the production of *Rituel* and *Messagesquisse*—occasional pieces which he could not have been expected to produce in his earlier years and which remain among his most accessible scores.

It was a measure of the new eminence which Boulez had won as a conductor that the French Establishment saw fit to lure him back to Paris by setting up for him the Institute for Research and Coordination in Acoustics and Music (IRCAM). This allowed him to explore the consequences of the post-serialist aesthetic for electroacoustic music on a far grander scale than Stockhausen had ever managed in the 1950s—during which period Boulez himself had in fact produced virtually nothing in this field. At the same time as he pursued this apparently anachronistic quest, Boulez also began a continuing series of major revisions to his earliest, pre-*Structures* compositions. These two very different strategies had the effect of drawing together his past and his present in a way which completely superseded the progressivism of his youth while remaining true to its prevailing technical concerns. Together with his undeniable artistic success on the podium, this gave Boulez an aura of integrity which complemented the always apparent power of his intellect.

In recomposing his works of the 1940s, Boulez gave them a sonorous sheen which one can hardly call neo-Romantic but which seems likely to give them strong claims on the repertoire. The orchestral version of *Notations* and the new version of *Le Visage nuptial* make these works sound at last, as one might reasonably expect, very much of a piece with the Messiaen of the *Turangalîla* period. Having taken inspiration from Mallarmé in the 1950s, Boulez now composed afresh into his old scores the purely musical links with French culture which he had often sought to make apparent through his writings: even Debussy could now be heard in the background. *Répons* also has something of this quality, but his time at IRCAM has been slow to bear fruit, and it remains to be seen whether these two sides of Boulez's creative work can be successfully united in his future compositions.

—Anthony Pople

BOYDELL, Brian (Patrick). Irish. Born in Dublin, 13 March 1917. Educated at Rugby School, 1930–5; Clare College, Cambridge (Choral Exhibition) B.A. (1st Class Nat. Science Tripos) 1935–8; Royal College of Music, London, 1938–9; Royal Irish Academy of Music, Dublin, L.R.I.A.M. (Singing), 1941, Mus. B., 1942, Mus.D., 1959. Married Mary Jones, 6 June 1944; 3 sons (1 deceased). Professor of Singing, Royal Irish Academy of Music, 1944–52; Professor of Music, Trinity College, Dublin, 1962–82. Lecturer, broadcaster, teacher and adjudicator; conductor, 1942–67, then president, Dublin Orchestral Players; conductor, RTE Symphony Orchestra and CBC Orchestra, Toronto; director, The Dowland Consort, chamber choir specialising in Renaissance music, 1958–69. Founder member of Music Association of Ireland, since 1948; member of Irish Arts Council, 1961–83. Recipient: Honorary Doctorate of Music, National University of Ireland, 1974; Commendatore della Repubblica Italiana (for services to Italian Renaissance music), 1983; member of Aosdana, 1984; Honorary Life member of the Royal Dublin Society, 1987. Address: 30 Westland Row, Trinity College, Dublin 2, Ireland.

Publishers: various.

Symphonies/orchestral:

Pregaria a la Verge del Remei, Op 14 (string orchestra) 1941, revised 1945; first performed Dublin, 1942.
Laish, Op 17 (tone poem for orchestra) 1942; first performed Dublin, 8 June 1943.
Satirical Suite, Op 18a (adapted from incidental music to *The House of Cards Op 18*) 1942; first performed Dublin, 23 May 1944.
Symphony for Strings, Op 26 1945, revised 1946; first performed Dublin, 30 October 1945.
Magh Sleacht, Op 29 1947; first performed Dublin, 1948.
In memoriam Mahatma Gandhi Op 30 1948; first performed Dublin, 29 July 1948.
Ballet Suite: The Buried Moon, Op 32a 1949; first performed Drogheda, 25 February 1950.
Violin Concerto, Op 36 1953, revised 1954; first performed Dublin, 1 October 1954.
The Wooing of Etain: Suite No 1 Op 37a 1954; first performed Carlow, 20 November 1954.
The Wooing of Etain: Suite No 2 Op 37b 1954; first performed Dublin, 31 October 1954.
Megalithic Ritual Dances, Op 39 1956; first performed Dublin, 20 January 1957.
Meditation and Fugue, Op 40 1956; first performed Dublin, 20 January 1957.
Elegy and Capriccio, Op 42 (clarinet solo and string orchestra) 1956; first performed Dublin, 1956.
Ceol Cas Corach, Op 46 1958; first performed Dublin, 18 January 1959.
Shieldmartin Suite, Op 47 1959; first performed London, 1 June 1960.
Richard's Riot, Op 51 (percussion solo and orchestra) 1961; first performed Dublin, 30 November 1961.
Symphonic Inscapes, Op 64 1968; first performed Dublin, 26 January 1969.
Jubilee Music, Op 73 1976; first performed Dublin, 3 October 1976.
Fred's Folic, Op 74 (brass and reed band) 1977; first performed 1978.
Partita Concertante, Op 75 (violin, harp, orchestra: adapted from *Five Mosaics Op 69* and *Impetuous Impromptu Op 75a*) 1978.

A Wild Dance for Ceol Chumann Na Nog Op 78 1982; first performed 11 November 1983.
Masai Mara, Op 87 1988; first performed 30 June 1989.

Chamber/instrumental:

Oboe Quintet, Op 11 1940; first performed Dublin, 10 January 1944.
String Trio, Op 21 1944; first performed Dublin, 30 January 1944.
Sonata for Cello and Piano, Op 24 1945; first performed Dublin, 19 September 1945.
String Quartet No 1, Op 31 1947; first performed Dublin, 17 February 1952.
Divertimento for Three Music Makers, Op 38 (oboe, clarinet and bassoon) 1954; first performed Dublin, 17 November 1954.
Elegy, Op 42a (two violins and piano; or violin, clarinet and piano) 1956; first performed 1957.
String Quartet No 2, Op 44 1957; first performed 14 February 1959.
Quintet for Flute, Harp and String Trio, Op 49 1960, revised 1966, 1980; first performed Dublin, 28 June 1960.
Four Sketches for Two Irish Harps, Op 42 1962; first performed Dublin, 11 May 1962.
String Quartet No 3, Op 65 1969; first performed Dublin, 20 September 1970.
Five Mosaics, Op 69 (violin and harp) 1972; first performed 17 March 1974.
Fred's Frolic, Op 74a (brass and reed band; also arranged for piano — four hands) 1977; first performed 1978.
Impetuous Impromptu, Op 75a (violin, piano) 1978.
Brass Quintet 1984; first performed October 1984.

Solo instrumental:

Variations on the Snowy Breasted Pearl, Op 2 (piano) 1935.
Berceuse for a Young Pianist, Op 20 (piano) 1943.
Suite: Naughty Children, Op 27 (piano) 1945.
Shielmartin, Op 45 (piano) 1958.
Dance for an Ancient Ritual, Op 39a (adapted from *Megalithic Ritual Dance, Op 39*, piano) 1959.
Capriccio, Op 48 (piano) 1959; first performed 7 November 1963.
Sarabande, Op 53 (piano) 1963; first performed 7 November 1963.
A Pack of Fancies for a Travelling Harper, Op 66 (harp) 1970; first performed Dublin, 13 January 1971.
Three Pieces for Guitar, Op 70 1973; first performed Dublin, 9 January 1974.
An Album of Pieces for the Irish Harp Op 88 1989.

Vocal/choral:

Wild Geese Op 1 (low voice, piano) 1935; first performed Cambridge, 1937.
Rushlights Op 3 (low voice, piano) 1935; first performed Cambridge, 1935.
Cathleen, the Daughter of Hoolihan Op 4 (low voice, piano) 1936.
Watching the Needleboats at San Sabba (low voice, piano) 1936.
She Weeps over Rahoon Op 5 (low voice, piano) 1936.
Cradle Song (low voice, piano) 1937.
Aurelia Op 7 (low voice, piano) 1939.
The Bargain (soprano, piano) 1940.
An Easter Carol Op 12 (soprano, tenor, baritone, unaccompanied SATB chorus) 1940; first performed Dublin, 22 March 1943.
Hearing of Harvests Op 13 (baritone, orchestra, SATB chorus) 1940.
Alone Op 15 (low voice, piano) 1941.
The Lamenting Op 19 (baritone, string orchestra) 1942.
Three Songs for Soprano and String Quartet Op 10 1943; first performed Dublin, 30 January 1944.
The Feather of Death Op 22 (baritone, flute, violin, viola, cello) 1943; first performed Dublin, 30 January 1944.
Sleep Now, Op 23 (soprano, oboe or violin, string orchestra) 1944; first performed Dublin, 1 March 1945.
Five Joyce Songs, Op 28 (baritone, piano) 1946; first performed Dublin, 28 October 1946.
Five Joyce Songs, Op 28a (baritone, orchestra) 1946; first performed Dublin, 1948.
Because Your Voice Was at My Side Op 25 (high voice, piano; or oboe d'amore, violin, viola, cello) 1948.
Shatter Me, Music, Op 33 (unaccompanied SSATB chorus) 1952; first performed Dublin, 7 January 1953.
The Owl and the Pussy Cat, Op 34 (unaccompanied SATB chorus) 1952; first performed 1953.
Timor Mortis, Op 35 (tenor, SATB chorus, organ; or flute, oboe, clarinet, bassoon) 1952; first performed Dublin, 19 February 1959.
Noel, Op 41 (two treble voices, two recorders, string orchestra, or organ) 1956; first performed Monktown, 1957.
The Deer's Cry, Op 43 (baritone, orchestra or chamber group) 1957; first performed Dublin, 10 November 1957.
Mors et Vita, Op 50 (cantata for soprano, tenor, baritone, orchestra and SATB chorus) 1961; first performed Dublin, 11 January 1963.
Two Madrigals, Op 54 (unaccompanied SSATBB, SATB chorus) 1964; first performed Cork, 23 May 1964.
Carmen in Honorem Artis Musicae, Op 55 (baritone, orchestra, SATB chorus) 1964; first performed November 1964.
Three Yeats Songs, Op 56a (soprano, Irish harp) 1965; first performed Dublin, 24 March 1966.
Musician's Songs, Op 56b (soprano, Irish harp) 1965.
Four Yeats Poems, Op 56 (soprano, orchestra: adapted from *Op 56a/b*) 1965; first performed Dublin, 25 February 1969.
A Terrible Beauty Is Born, Op 59 (cantata for soprano, alto, baritone, narrator, orchestra, SATB chorus) 1965; first performed Dublin, 11 April 1966.
In Memorial Thomas McDonagh, Op 59a (contralto, piano) 1966; first performed Dublin, 31 March 1968.
Three Madrigals, Op 60 (unaccompanied SATB, SSATB chorus) 1967; first performed Dublin, June 1968.
College Graces, Op 62 (baritone, unaccompanied SATB chorus) 1967.
How Butler! How, Op 67 (unaccompanied TTBB chorus) 1971; first performed Dublin, July 1971.
Mouth Music for Ten Voices, Op 72 (4 sopranos, 2 contraltos, 2 tenors, 2 baritones) 1974; first performed Cork, 27 April 1974.
Mouth Music for Eight Voices, Op 72a (2 sopranos, 2 contraltos, 2 tenors, 2 baritones) 1974.
The Small Bell, Op 76 (cantata for SATB chorus, flute, harp, 2 violins, viola, cello) 1980; first performed Dublin, 5 May 1981.
Three Geological Glees, Op 77 (unaccompanied SATB chorus) 1981; first performed Dublin, 12 January 1982.
Monks and Raisins Op 79 (unaccompanied ATBarB) 1983; first performed Autumn 1984.
The Carlow Cantata or The Female Friend Op 83 (soprano,

tenor, baritone, SATB chorus, accompanied by clarinet, string orchestra or full orchestra) 1985; first performed Carlow, 10 November 1985.

Under No Circumstances: An Historical Entertainment Op 85 (tenor, baritone, narrator, SATB chorus, full orchestra) 1987; first performed Dublin, 10 March 1988.

Anthem "I Will Hear What the Lord Will Speak" (Psalm 85) Op 86 (SATB, organ) 1988; first performed Dublin, 26 June 1988.

Other:

The Strings Are False, Op 16 (orchestral overture to the play by Paul Vincent Carroll) 1942; first performed Dublin, 1942.

The House of Cards, Op 18 (incidental music to the play by Frank Carney; 2 pianos) 1942; first performed Dublin, 1942.

The Buried Moon, Op 32 (incomplete ballet) 1949.

The Wooing of Etain, Op 37 (orchestral incidental music to the play by Padraig Fallon) 1954; first performed 28 October 1956.

Yeats Country, Op 57 (incidental music to the film by Patrick Carey; flute, oboe, clarinet, bassoon, percussion, harp) 1965; first performed Dublin, 2 April 1965.

Ireland, Op 58 (orchestral incidental music to the film by Vincent Corcoran) 1965; first performed 17 April 1967.

Mists of Time, Op 61 (orchestral incidental music to the film by Patrick Carey) 1967.

Errigal, Op 63 (orchestral incidental music to the film by Patrick Carey) 1968; first performed Dublin, July 1968.

King Herod Explains, Op 68 (incidental music to the play by Conor Cruise O'Brien; mezzo-soprano, harp, gong) 1971; first performed Dublin, 1971.

Miss Julie Music, Op 71 (incidental music to the play by August Strindberg; soprano, rebec, guitar, percussion) 1974; first performed Dublin, 13 March 1975.

Toccata and Chorale for a State Occasion Op 80 (brass ensemble, for the inauguration of Aosdána) 1983; first performed April 1983.

Ceremonial Music for the Sultan of Oman, Op 81 (brass ensemble) 1983.

PUBLICATIONS

By Boydell: "Orchestral and Chamber Music in Dublin", in *Music in Ireland*, edited by Aloys Fleischmann, Cork, 1952; "Venues for Music in 18th-Century Dublin", in *Dublin Historical Record*, December 1975; "The Dublin Musical Scene, 1749–50 and its Background", in *Proceedings of the Royal Musical Association*, 105, 1978–9; Editor, "Introduction", "Music in Eighteenth-Century Dublin", in *Four Centuries of Music in Ireland*, London, 1979; articles on Broadway, Bunting, Cogan, Colgan, Davis family, Dublin, Dubourg, Fleischmann, Geary, Hollister, Francis Ireland, Delamaine, Jackson, Lee, Manwaring, Moore, Ogilby, O'Hara, Thumoth, Viner, Walker, Wexford, Woffington, Woodward, in *The New Grove Dictionary of Music and Musicians*, London, 1980; entries on Egan, Hollister, Rother, Weber and Woffington, in *The New Grove Dictionary of Musical Instruments*, London, 1984; "Half a Century of Music in Dublin", in *Dublin Historical Record*, June–September 1984; "Georgian Lollipops, or The Lighter Side of Classical Music", in *Popular Music in Eighteenth-Century Dublin*, Dublin, 1985; "Music and Society up to 1850" (2 chapters), in *A New History of Ireland*, vol. 4, edited by T.W. Moody & W.E. Vaughan, Oxford, 1986; "Music", in *Publick Virtue, Publick Love: The Early Years of the Dublin Lying-In Hospital*, edited by Ian Cambell Ross, Dublin, 1986; "The Virgin Mary in Music", in *Milltown Studies*, Autumn 1988; *A Dublin Musical Calendar 1700–1760*, Blackrock, 1988; "Thomas Bateson and the Earliest Degrees in Music Awarded by the University of Dublin", in *Hermathena* Summer 1989.

On Boydell: C. Acton, "Interview with Brian Boydell", *Eire-Ireland*, 4, 1970; Seoirse Bodley, in *New Grove Dictionary of Music and Musicians*, London, 1980.

Brian Boydell comments:

My style has evolved through an amalgam of influences, beginning in the mid-1930s with Delius, Warlock and Vaughan Williams. Then came the different impacts of Sibelius, Berg, Bloch and Stravinsky, followed by Bartók and also the harmonic theories of Hindemith. Contact with medieval music and plainsong was influenced in the 1950s. I was never happy with Schoenberg's approach. Always self-critical of any tendency to strive for astonishing originality, I have always tried to create sounds which I honestly believe to be expressive or beautiful, rather than up-to-date or fashionable, or dictated by any "system". Much of the inspiration for my music originates in a love of landscape (particularly Irish) and the wonders of natural phenomena. Although eschewing any temptation to "write down" to a popular audience, I believe communication to be a fundamental motive. I take particular joy in writing music that presents the challenge of being performable by amateur enthusiasts.

* * *

In his early *Symphony for Strings* Brian Boydell shows resource in exploring the sonorities of string writing, with an expansiveness natural to the ardour of youth, which was soon to be drastically curbed. His *Five Joyce Songs*, produced a year later, rely, as with Joyce, on understatement for their effect. The range is considerable, from the lilting folk song style of "Oh! It was out by Donnycarney" to the dramatic incisiveness of "I hear an army charging on the land".

The death of Mahatma Gandhi in 1948 inspired one of the composer's major works, an *In memoriam* in which the eloquence of grief, though not expressed in terms of memorable thematic material, rises to an impressive climax, and ends brokenly, with a moving coda. The influence of Bartók, probably the chief formative element in his style, is clearly felt in the works produced around this time, and most of all in the first *String Quartet*, an accomplished piece of writing, with a boldly shaped first movement, a vigorous fleeting scherzo, and a finale in which the essence is distilled out of the material already heard. This quartet has been so successful that it tends to dwarf the two-movement second quartet, in which the style of the first is developed further, perhaps with an undue amount of fragmentation.

Of his orchestral output, the *Violin Concerto* is probably the best constructed—brittle, energic, with moments of quiet, lyrical beauty, as in the etherial coda of the Lento, with its descending harp figures "dropping like the veils of the morning" beneath the falling sixths of the solo violin. By contrast, the composer's ebullient side emerges in some of the swaggering outbursts of the Rondo finale, especially in the second episode with its arresting chain of sevenths, and in the brass mélange after the cadenza. In this concerto, and in the *Megalithic Ritual Dances*—an Irish *Rite of Spring*, evoking a fantastic world of primitive imagery—the composer achieves a range of expression which some of the more up-to-date adventurers in compositional techniques would find difficult to emulate. In the *Quintet for Flute, Harp and String Trio* the influence of Bartók has been largely shed, giving, strangely enough, a sense of liberation. The soft sheen of the texture and the freer and more flexible rhythms of the first movement, the scurrying figures and thudding pizzicatos of the scherzo and the pastoral finale, all combine to make this the most poetic of the composer's works.

His two sets of madrigals for the Cork Choral Festival of 1963 and 1967, might be described as neo-Elizabethan, in their curious and rather whimsical blend of 16th-century English procedures and modal chromaticism, a vein already touched on by E.J. Moeran. Some of the choral works, such as the austere, medieval-inspired *Mors et Vita*, might be felt to be too static, or indeed to hieratic. But in *A Terrible Beauty Is Born*, commissioned by Radio Eireann in 1966 for the 50th anniversary of the 1916 uprising, the composer met the challenge of the occasion, and in many telling passages captured the sense of poignancy, of high endeavour, the elation and the despair of the poems chosen to represent the event, whether in the bare, flowing lines of "Red Hanrahan's Song", the seething movement of "The wind has bundled up the clouds", or the intense quiet of "But purer than a tall candle before the Holy Rood/Is Cathleen, the daughter of Houlihan".

The poetry of Yeats has always seemed to fire the composer's imagination, and a number of Yeats settings written for the poet's daughter-in-law, Gráinne Yeats, are among his best work. The accompaniments for the *Three Yeats Songs* are for Irish harp. In these and other settings he has enriched the scanty literature for this instrument, especially in his *Four Sketches for Two Irish Harps*, in which each harp is tuned to a different chromatic series, so that the range of what is normally regarded as a diatonic instrument has been extended with new and stimulating sound effects, the fourth sketch being a veritable tour-de-force.

Preoccupation with such effects shows a disposition well-suited for radio and film music, and in four of the films for which he has provided a sound track, entirely appropriate results have been brought about by devices such as the action of brush or drum-stick on piano strings, and feather on the harp. All his film music is marked by economy of sound, and an unerring sense of what Gerard Manley Hopkins would call the "inscape" of the subject on the screen.

Mouth Music, an ingenious exploration of various types of vocal timbre, was written for the Cork International Choral Festival of 1974. When asked to commemorate the 150th anniversary of the Trinity College Choral Society in 1987, he produced *Under No Circumstances: An Historical Entertainment*, based on the records of early meetings of the Society's committee, and in this work demonstrates his ability to underline the pomposity of the Victorian era with appropriate wit and humour. Perhaps the most impressive of all this composer's works is his *Masai Mara*, with a deft use of the tenor recorder to simulate eerie and mysterious bird calls, and with thoroughly original effects of orchestral colour.

Though he himself has spoken of his style as "central European", there lie not far beneath the surface certain individual mannerisms—details of melodic curve, certain tonal progressions—which relate back to Irish folk song, and which stamp the composer's work as part of the Irish tradition, as clearly as that of James Joyce.

—Aloys Fleischmann

BRANCA, Glenn. American. Born in Harrisburg, Pennsylvania, 6 October 1948. Educated at Emerson College, Boston (dramatic arts), 1967–71. Performer/writer, Bastard Theatre group, New York City, since 1975. Founder/member (with Jeffrey Lohn), Theoretical Girls rock band, 1976; other groups, theatre work, New York City, 1970s. Composer, conductor, performer. Mailing address: c/o Blast First!/Mute Records, 429 Harrow Road, London W10 4RE, England.

Publisher: none.

Chamber/instrumental:

Instrumental (6 electric guitars) 1979.
Dissonance (electric guitars) 1979.
The Spectacular Commodity (electric guitars) 1979.
Lesson No 1 (electric guitar) 1979.
The Ascension (rock band) 1980. Recorded ROIR A125.
Symphony No 1: Tonal Plexus (11 electric guitars, brass, percussion) 1981. Recorded 99 Records 99 01.
Symphony No 2: The Peak of the Sacred (electric guitars, percussion, other instruments) 1982.
Symphony No 3: Gloria (electric guitars, percussion, other instruments) 1983.
Symphony No 4: Physics (electric guitars, percussion, other instruments) 1983.
Symphony No 5: Describing Planes of an Expanding Hypersphere (electric guitars, percussion, other instruments) 1984.
Symphony No 6: Devil Choirs at the Gates of Heaven (10 electric guitars/bass guitar/keyboards, percussion) 1986. Recorded Blast First! BFFP 39.
Symphony No 7 (conventional instrumentation) 1991.

Other:

Anthropophagoi (music-theatre) 1975; first performed Boston, 1975.
Bad Smells (ballet; Tharp) 1982.
The Belly of an Architect (contribution to film score; Greenaway) 1988.

PUBLICATIONS

On Branca: John Rockwell, (various references) in *All-American Music: Composition in the Late Twentieth Century*, New York, 1983; Mark Sinker, "I Hear a Symphony" (interview), in *Wire*, June 1989.

* * *

"Tonal plexus", the title of his first "symphony", exactly describes the point of impact of Glenn Branca's music. Repetitive and insistent, it is almost fantastically loud, and a Branca performance has, to some ears, an almost totalitarian edge; in 1982, John Cage considered it to be hypothetically fascist, in effect if not intention.

Branca has no formal training as a musician. He studied drama and theatre arts before moving to New York as a performer on the fringe theatre/art rock scene. Theoretical Girls was one of a number of performing bands in the then-fashionable "No-Wave" scene, placing heavy emphasis on aggressive volume, "total environment" and a somewhat gestural aesthetic.

Branca's experiments with "formal" music for electric guitar were not entirely without precedent. He is close in orientation to composer/performers like Rhys Chatham and Paul Dresher, and he has drawn from the so-called minimalism of such very different composers as Terry Riley and Philip Glass (Glass's work is rock-oriented in the sense that he now attracts a rock audience and uses rock amplification).

After the ground- and speaker-breaking experiments of *The Ascension*, an LP recording of genuine power, Branca turned to writing "symphonic" pieces. These require protective quotes because they have been scored for groups of highly amplified electric guitars (usually very cheap models), strummed in repetitive patterns with no semblance of normal symphonic development. The metre is extremely simple and the pieces work by a steady accretion of layers which form interruption patterns, often at very high harmonics. At moments in *Devil Choirs at the Gates of Heaven*, the most recent (and apparently last) of the guitar-only symphonies, a listener may hear what appear to be voices singing or shouting. This is an auditory illusion, but it is an extremely powerful one and a performance of *Symphony No 6* is always a very remarkable experience.

Whether Branca is able to sustain interest as he turns towards more conventional instrumentation remains to be seen. Doubts about the implications of his music—and that of similar, rock-based units like Laibach and Test Department, who similarly exploit sheer noise—will doubtless continue, but the Symphonies do make a wryly subversive comment on current musical practice and on the fetishism of canonical forms; Branca's robotic guitarists are, and are intended to be, wholly *un*virtuosic; there is no release in his music. It may be that he represents an absolute dead end; it may be that he points the way forward. Only the next few years will tell.

—James Weir

BRANT, Henry (Dreyfuss). Canadian; resident in United States. Born in Montreal, Quebec, 15 September 1913. Educated at McGill Conservatorium, Montreal, 1926–9; Institute of Musical Art, New York City (piano under James Friskin, composition under Leopold Mannes), 1929–34; Juilliard School, New York City (under Rubin Goldmark), 1932–4; also studied composition with Wallingford Riegger, 1930–1; George Antheil, 1934–5; conducting with Fritz Mahler, 1938–9. Married Patricia Gorman in 1948; 3 children. Professional composer and arranger, 1930s–40s; teacher of composition and orchestration, Columbia University, New York City, 1945–52; teacher, Juilliard School, 1947–54; professor, Bennington College, Vermont, 1957–80. Recipient: Guggenheim Fellowships, 1947, 1956; Prix Italia (1st American recipient), 1955; elected to American Academy and Institute of Arts and Letters, 1979.

Publisher: self.

[Works marked * employ elements of spatial separation of instrumental and orchestral groups; much of Brant's work has been recorded, chiefly on CRI label.]

Symphonies/orchestral:

Double Bass Concerto 1930s.
Symphony 1930s.
Clarinet Concerto 1938.
Fisherman's Overture 1938.
Whoopee in D 1938.
Fantasy and Caprice (violin, orchestra) 1940.
Rhapsody (viola, orchestra) 1940.
The Great American Goof (ballet suite) 1940.
Violin Concerto 1940.
An Adventure (final movement of withdrawn *Symphony*) 1942.
Dedication in Memory of Franklin D. Roosevelt 1945.
The 1930s (symphonic movements) 1945.
Statements in Jazz (clarinet, dance orchestra) 1945.
Jazz Clarinet Concerto (clarinet, big band) 1946.
The Promised Land (symphonic movements) 1947.
Street Music (wind orchestra) 1949.
Origins (symphonic movements for percussion orchestra, organ) 1950.
*Antiphony I** (5 orchestras) 1953, revised 1968–9.
Galaxy II (wind orchestra, timpani, glockenspiel) 1954.
*Ceremony** (oboe, violin, cello, wind orchestra, piano—4 hands, percussion, voices) 1954.
*Labyrinth I** (20 solo strings, string orchestra, women's voices ad lib) 1955.
*On the Nature of Things** (woodwind, strings, glockenspiel) 1956.
*Antiphonal Symphony: Atlantis** (orchestra, band, percussion, mezzo-soprano, speaker, chorus) 1960.
*Fire in Cities** (orchestral groups, 2 pianos, 8 timpani, choruses) 1961.
*Voyage Four** 1963.
*Odyssey—Why Not?** (flute, flute ad lib, 4 small orchestral groups) 1965.
*Kingdom Come** (circus band, organ, orchestra) 1970.
*The Immortal Combat** (2 bands) 1972.
*An American Requiem** (5 wind groups, bells, brass, organ, percussion, optional soprano) 1973.
*Spatial Concerto: Questions from Genesis** (piano, orchestral groups, 8 sopranos, 8 altos) 1976.
*Antiphonal Responses** (3 solo bassoons, piano, orchestra, 8 dispersed instruments) 1978.
*Curriculum II** (dispersed orchestral groups) 1978.
*Trinity of Spheres** (3 orchestral groups) 1978.
*The Secret Calendar** (orchestral groups, instruments, voice) 1980.
*Meteor Farm** (2 percussion groups, jazz orchestra, gamelan, African drums, voices, Indian instruments, orchestra, chorus, 2 sopranos) 1982.
*Desert Forest** (dispersed symphonic groups) 1983.
*Litany of Tides** (violin, 2 orchestra, voices) 1983.
*Bran(d)t ann de Amstel/Fire on the Amstel** (100 flutes, 3 orchestras, 4 hurdy-gurdies, choruses, optional carillon) 1984.
*Western Springs** (2 orchestras, 2 jazz combos, 2 choruses) 1984.

Chamber/instrumental:

Sonata (2 pianos) 1931.
Angels and Devils (solo flute, 3 piccolos, 5 flutes, 2 alto flutes) 1931, revised 1956, 1979.
Variations in Oblique Harmony (4 instruments) 1931.
Music for a Five-and-Dime Store (violin, piano, kitchen utensils) 1932.
Four Chorale Preludes (2 pianos) 1932.
Mobiles (flute) 1932.
Partita (flute, piano) 1932, revised 1954.
Double-Crank Hand Organ (2 pianos, percussion) 1933.

Prelude and Fugue (string octet, woodwinds) 1934.
Requiem in Summer (wind quintet; based on *Prelude and Fugue*) 1934, revised 1955.
Duo (cello, piano) 1937, revised 1962.
The Marx Brothers (tin whistle/fife/piccolo, flute, oboe, harp, piano, viola, cello) 1938.
Variations on a Theme by Robert Schumann (2 pianos, trumpet, timpani) 1940.
Concerto (saxophone/trumpet, flute, 6 clarinets, tuba, percussion) 1941, revised 1970.
Downtown Suite (ensemble) 1942.
Imaginary Ballet (piccolo, cello, piano) 1946.
Funeral March for the Mass Dead (2 bassoons, cello, double bass) 1947.
All Souls' Carnival (flute, piano, accordion, violin, cello) 1949, revised 1957.
Millennium I (8 trumpets, chimes, glockenspiel) 1950.
Signs and Alarms (piccolo, 2 clarinets, brass, percussion) 1953.
Stresses (trumpet, piano, strings, percussion) 1953.
Ice Age (ondes martenot/clarinet, piano, glockenspiel, xylophone) 1954.
Piri (flute, harp, piano, glockenspiel) 1954.
Galaxy I (clarinet, horn, chimes, vibraphone) 1954.
*Hieroglyphics I** (viola, timpani, celeste, chimes, harp, distant voices, organ) 1957.
*Millennium III** (6 brass, 6 percussion) 1957.
*Joquin** (piccolo, 6 instruments) 1958.
Conversations in an Unknown Tongue (violin, viola, tenor violin, cello) 1958.
*Quombex** (viola d'amore, organ, distant music boxes) 1960.
*Barricades** (oboe/soprano saxophone, clarinet, bassoon, trombone, piano, xylophone, string quartet, male voice) 1961.
*Concerto with Lights** (violin, 10 instruments, lights) 1961.
*Headhunt** (trombone, bass clarinet, bassoon, cello, percussion) 1962.
Jazz Fugue (accordion quartet) 1962.
*The Fourth Millennium** (2 trumpets, horn, euphonium, tuba) 1963.
*Underworld** (saxophone, small organ) 1963.
Consort for True Violins (8 4-stringed bowed instruments) 1965.
*Hieroglyphics II** (violin, celeste, percussion and piano ad lib) 1966.
*Verticals Ascending** (2 wind ensembles) 1967.
*Chanticleer** (clarinet, piano, percussion, string quartet) 1968.
*Windjammer** (horn, piccolo, oboe, bass clarinet, bassoon) 1969.
*Crossroads** (violin, piccolo violin, mezzo-violin, viola) 1970.
Machinations (E♭ flute, double flageolet, double ocarina, ceramic flute, steel harp, organ, chimes, timpani) 1970.
*Divinity: Dialogues in the Form of Secret Portraits** (harpsichord, 2 trumpets, 2 trombones, horn) 1973.
*Sixty** (3 wind groups) 1973, revised, as *60/70*, 1982.
*Prevailing Wind** (wind quintet) 1974.
*Six Grand Pianos Bash—Plus Friends** (6 pianos, percussion, piccolos, 2 brass) 1974.
*American Commencement** (2 brass groups, 2 percussion groups) 1975.
From Bach's Menagerie (4 saxophones) 1975.
*American Debate** (2 wind/percussion groups) 1976.
*Cerberus** (piccolo, double bass, mouth organ, female voice) 1978.
*The $1,000,000 Confessions** (2 trumpet, 3 trombone) 1978.
*Orbits** (80 trombones, organ, female voice) 1979.
Solar Moth (solo violin, flute, alto flute, bass flute, harp, piano, 4 violins, 4 violas, marimba, voice, timpani) 1979.
*The Glass Pyramid** (woodwind, 2 pianos, percussion, strings, woodwind trio, chimes) 1980.
*Inside Track** (piano, sopranino saxophone, 3 instrumental groups, organ, voice) 1980.
*Horizontals Extending** (2 small wind groups, jazz drums, karate artist) 1982.
*Voor onder Water** (woodwinds, strings, percussion, tape, voices) 1983.

Vocal/choral:

The Three-Way Canon Blues (unaccompanied voices) 1947.
Credo for Peace (voices, speaker, trumpet) 1948.
Country Fair (voices, ensemble) 1949.
Madrigal en casserole (voices, piano) 1949.
*Millennium** (soprano, brass, percussion) 1954.
*Conclave** (mezzo-soprano, baritone, trumpet, trombone, piano, harp, timpani, glockenspiel) 1955.
*December** (soprano, tenor, speakers, choruses, orchestral groups) 1955.
*Encephalograms** (soprano, 7 instruments) 1955.
*The Grand Universal Circus** (8 voices, 32-voice choir, instruments) 1956.
*The Children's Hour** (6 voices, chorus, 2 trumpets, 2 trombones, organ, percussion) 1958.
*In Praise of Learning** (16 sopranos, 16 percussion) 1958.
*Mythical Beasts** (soprano/mezzo-soprano, instruments) 1958.
*The Crossing** (tenor, oboe/soprano saxophone, glockenspiel, violin, cello) 1959.
*The Fire Garden** (tenor/soprano, small chorus, piccolo, harp, piano, percussion) 1960.
*Feuerwerk** (speaker, winds, harpsichord, chimes, timpani, 2 violins, 2 violas) 1961.
*Fire in Cities** (choruses, 2 pianos, orchestral groups, 8 timpani) 1961.
*Dialogue in the Jungle** (soprano, tenor, 5 woodwind, 5 brass) 1964.
*Sing O Heavens** (soprano, alto, tenor, baritone, chorus, trumpet, trombone, piano, percussion) 1964.
*Nomads** (voice, percussion, brass, orchestra or wind band) 1974.
*Solomon's Gardens** (7 voices, chorus, 24 handbells, 3 instruments) 1974.
*A Plan of the Air** (soprano, alto, tenor, bass, baroque organ, 10 wind and percussion groups) 1975.
*Curriculum** (baritone, bass flute, bass clarinet, piano, timpani, marimba, viola, cello, double bass) 1975.
*Homage to Ives** (baritone, flute obbligato, 3 orchestral groups) 1976.
*American Weather** (8 voices, chorus, trumpet, trombone, chimes, glockenspiel) 1976.

Other:

City Portrait (ballet; orchestra) 1940; first performed New York City, 1940.

Film scores: *Capitol Story*, 1944; *The Pale Horseman*, 1944; *Journey into Medicine*, 1946; *My Father's House*, 1947; *Outbreak*, 1949; *The Big Break*, 1951; *Ode to a Grecian Urn*, 1953; *The Secret Thief*, 1956; *Your Community*, 1956; *Doctor "B"*, 1957; *Endowing Our Future*, 1957; *United Nations Day*, 1959; *Early Birds*, 1961.

PUBLICATIONS

By Brant: "Space as an Essential Aspect of Musical Composition", in Schwartz and Childs, *Contemporary Composers on Contemporary Music*, New York, 1967; "Spatial Music Progress Report", in *Quadrille*, 12 (3), 1979.

On Brant: D. Drennan, "HB's Use of Ensemble Dispersion, as Found in the Analysis of Selected Compositions", dissertation, University of Miami, 1975; K. Brion and J.E. Brown, "The Spatial Wind Music of HB", in *The Instrumentalist*, 30 (6), 1976; T. Everett, (interview) in *The Composer*, 7, 1976–7; D. Drennan, "HB's Choral Music", in *Choral Journal*, 17 (5), 1977; C. Gagne and T. Caras, (interview) in *Soundpieces: Interviews with Contemporary American Composers*, Metuchen, New Jersey, 1982.

* * *

Lost in space? Not so Monteverdi, Berlioz, Mahler, Wagner, Ives—all composers who showed particular talent for using spatial factors as an integral part of their musical practice. Not so too the Canadian-American Henry Brant, dedicated specifically to the exploration of spatial music since 1951. Born in Montreal in 1913, Brant began composing at the age of eight, moved to New York in 1929, where he studied at Juillard, and later made his living as a commercial arranger in radio and films (and later still as a college teacher), all the while pursuing his own idiosyncratic ideas on the side.

One of the first American composers to incorporate elements of jazz and popular culture in concert music, Brant's earlier works include a *Clarinet Concerto* and a *Saxophone Concerto* while a very early (1931) piece for honky tonk piano, clarinet and kitchen hardware gives due warning of his love for burlesque and of his sometimes zany humour—which crops up again in a 1938 Marx Brothers tribute scored for small orchestra and solo tin whistle.

A fascination with unusual instrumentations/timbral combinations has long been a distinctive Brant trait, from the 1931 *Angels and Devils* for solo flute with flute orchestra to 1979's *Orbits* for 80 trombones, organ and sopranino voice. However, inspired chiefly by Ives, Brant's major focus since the early 1950s has been the development of spatial music, in which both the positioning of the musicians around the performance area and the independence (from each other) of the various participating ensembles were of particular concern. Early works in the genre include *Antiphony 1, December* (the first contemporary multi-spatial piece to be performed in Carnegie Hall) and *Millennium*; later pieces also make use of theatre (*The Grand Universal Circus*), lighting (*Concerto with Lights*) and the continuous movement of the performers (*Windjammer*).

Based in California since 1980, Brant's more recent spatial pieces are among his most ambitious: *Meteor Farm* calls for an expanded orchestra, two choirs, jazz band, gamelan ensemble, African drummers/singers and Indian musicians; *Fire on the Amstel* requires four boatloads of 25 flutes each, four jazz drummers, four church carillons, three brass bands, three choruses and four street-organs. Regrettably, if not surprisingly, these works have yet to be recorded: the majority of Brant vinyl is restricted to smaller-scale pieces, such as the two-orchestra *Western Springs* and various chamber works—for example, *Solar Moth* and *Voor onder Water*.

Wilfrid Mellor's comment (*Music in a New Found Land*) that Brant is "a composer inspired by the gimmick rather than by human experience" seems harsh, especially in view of Brant's own testimony to the essential seriousness of his interest in musical multiplicity: "By 1950 I had come to feel that single style music, no matter how experimental or full of variety, could no longer evoke the new stresses, layered insanities and multi-directional assaults of contemporary life on the spirit." Spatial music, he felt, would "speak more expressively of the human predicament".

Many modern composers, from Elliott Carter to Karlheinz Stockhausen and Iannis Xenakis, apparently agree and have followed Brant in exploring a variety of different spatial factors. However, as far as I know, the only person to specifically cite Brant as an influence is the leading U.S. composer and jazz multi-instrumentalist Anthony Braxton, whose best-known spatial piece is his four-orchestra *Composition 82* and whose visions of a music created by orchestras on different planets and in different galaxies is probably as spatial as music is likely to get.

—Graham Lock

BRAXTON, Anthony (Delano). American. Born in Chicago, 4 June 1945. Educated at Chicago School of Music (under Jack Gell), 1959–64; Chicago Music College, 1963–6; Roosevelt University, Chicago (philosophy), 1966–8. Served in U.S. Army, 1963–6. Married Nickie Ann Singer, 29 June 1975; 2 sons and 1 daughter; 1 other daughter. Improvising musician, multi-instrumentalist—saxophones, clarinets, flutes; performed and recorded with many jazz groups including Creative Construction Company, Musica Elettronica Viva, Anthony Braxton/Derek Bailey duo, Anthony Braxton Quartet, etc; faculty member, Association for the Advancement of Creative Musicians School of Music, Chicago, 1966–9; Darius Milhaud associate professor of music, Mills College, Oakland, California, 1985–90. Professor of music, Wesleyan University, Middletown, Connecticut, since 1990. Recipient: *Swing Journal* Gold Disc awards (for Circle: *The Paris Concert* and for *Town Hall '72*), 1972, 1973; Prix D'Oscar, French Jazz Academy (for *The Complete Braxton* and *Creative Orchestra Music*), 1973, 1976; *Stereo Review* Record of the Year (for *Circle*), 1975; *Jazz Journal* Record of the Year (for Max Roach/Braxton duets), 1979. Mailing address: 36 Mansfield Terrace, Middletown, Connecticut 06457, U.S.A.

Publisher: Synthesis Music (self).

[Listings give Braxton's notated music only, not those pieces primarily for improvisation; most pieces have numerical or graphic titles, most of which are not shown, in addition to composition numbers; for details, refer to *Composition Notes*, under PUBLICATIONS below.]

Symphonies/orchestral:

D-J-30
N
Composition No 7 1969.

LJ-84M
C
Composition No 24 1971.

LJ-800
C
Composition No 27 1972; first performed San Jose, California, 1975.

L-J-37
C
Composition No 41 (chamber orchestra) 1974; first performed New York, 1977.

Composition No 83 (graphic title) 1977–8; first performed San Jose, California, 1977.
Composition No 82 (graphic title; for four orchestras) 1978. Recorded Arista A3L 8900.
Composition No 96 (graphic title; orchestra, 4 slide projectors) 1980; first performed Seattle, Washington, 1981. Recorded Leo LR 169.
Composition No 102 (graphic title; orchestra, puppet theatre) 1982; first performed Houston, 1982.
Composition No 137 (graphic title) 1988; first performed Amsterdam, 1989.

Chamber/instrumental:

Piano Piece No 1 1968.

L-J-74
C
Composition No 2 (4 single-line instruments) 1968; first performed Chicago, 1968.

Composition No 3 (graphic title; 8 single line instruments, piano, 2 percussion) 1968; first performed Chicago, 1969.
Composition No 4 (graphic title; 5 tubas) 1968. Recorded Freedom 400 112/113.
Composition No 5 (graphic title; piano) 1968.
Composition No 10 (graphic title; piano) 1969.

W-306
(427)
Composition No 12 (woodwind quintet) 1969.

LJ-75
C
Composition No 13 (4 single-line instruments) 1970; first performed Paris, 1970.

Composition No 14 (graphic title; any solo instrument) 1970; first performed Chicago, 1970.

RKM-B6
MSO |
7
Composition No 15 (any 4 instruments) 1970.

GN6
(X'70B) . . . K
Composition 16 (4 pianos) 1971. Recorded Musica MUS 2004.

8KN-(B-12)
|
R
Composition No 17 (string quartet) 1971; first performed Paris, 1979. Recorded Sound Aspects SAS CD 009.

8KN-(J-6)
|
R
Composition No 18 (string quartet) 1971; first performed San Jose, California, 1975.

SBN-A12
66K
Composition No 20 (2 instruments) 1971; first performed Paris, 1971. Recorded Delmark DS 428.

Composition No 22 (4 soprano saxophones) 1971; early version performed Chicago, 1968; published version transcribed from recorded performance, London, 1971. Recorded Freedom 400 112/3.

P-JOK
S-D-12
|
4
Composition No 30 (piano) 1973; first performed San Jose, California, 1975. Recorded (extracts) Finnadar SR 9011.

P-JOK
S-D-37
|
4
Composition No 31 (piano) 1973; first performed San Jose, California, 1975. Recorded (extracts) Finnadar SR 9011.

P-JOK
S-D-31
|
4
Composition No 32 (piano) 1974; first performed San Jose, California, 1975. Recorded (extracts) Finnadar SR 9011.

P-JOK
S-D-22
|
4
Composition No 33 (piano) 1974; first performed San Jose, California, 1975. Recorded (extracts) Finnadar SR 9011.

Composition No 37 (graphic title; 4 saxophones) 1974. Recorded Arista AL4032; Black Saint 120 1261/2/4.

LQS-26
D
Composition No 46 (flute, oboe, cor anglais, clarinet, bass clarinet, horn, trumpet, trombone, bass trombone, tuba) 1975; first performed Berkeley, California, 1975.

Composition No 50 (graphic score; 2 instrumentalists, 2 synthesizer players) 1975; first performed San Jose, California, 1975.
Composition No 59 (graphic title; 2 soloists, 13 instrumentalists) 1976; first performed Michigan, 1977. Recorded RCA Bluebird ND86579.
Composition No 63 (graphic title; 2 soloists, chamber ensemble) 1976; first performed Berlin, 1976. Recorded Arista AL5002.
Composition No 64 (graphic title; 2 single-line wind instruments) 1976; first performed Moers, 1976. Recorded Moers Music NOMU01036.

Composition No 65 (graphic title; sopranino saxophone, trombone) 1976; first performed Moers, 1976. Recorded Moers Music NOMU01036.
Composition Nos 74 A-E (graphic title; 2 multi-instrumentalists on single-line instruments; *74B* for 2 flutes) 1976; first performed Toronto, 1976. Recorded (*74A / B*) Sackville 3016.
Composition No 75 (graphic title; 3 instrumentalists) 1976–7; first performed New York City, 1976 or 1977.
Composition No 73 (graphic title; 3 multi-instrumentalists) 1977.
Composition No 75 (graphic title; 3 instrumentalists) 1977. Recorded Arista AB4181.
Composition No 90 (graphic title; any instrumentation) 1979; first performed Sweden, 1979.
Composition No 94 (graphic title; 3 instrumentalists) 1980; first performed Berlin, 1980.
Composition No 95 (graphic title; 2 pianists) 1980; first performed Pisa, 1980. Recorded Arista AL9559.
Composition No 98 (graphic title; 4 winds, 2 brass, piano) 1981; first performed Paris, 1981. Recorded Hat Art CD 6062.
Composition No 100 (graphic title; 15 instruments) 1981; first performed Hartford, Connecticut, 1981 or 1982.
Composition No 101 (graphic title; 1 [wind or brass] multi-instrumentalists, piano) 1981; first performed Michigan, 1982. Recorded Dischi Della Quercia Q28015; Hat Art CD 6019; Black Saint BSR 0106.
Composition No 103 (graphic title; 7 trumpets, tape, costumes, props) 1983.
Composition No 107 (graphic title; 2 [wind or brass] multi-instrumentalists, piano) 1983; first performed Minneapolis, 1984. Recorded Hat Art CD 6019.
Composition No 121 (graphic title; piano, 2 single-line instruments, percussion) 1984; first performed New York City, 1985. Recorded Leo CD LR 200/201.
Composition No 123 ". . . Shala addresses the concerns of the guardsmen and redirects their energies" (graphic title; flute, slides, constructed environment) 1985.
Composition No 125 ". . . 'heh! Don't fear this guy—Bubba John Jack is one of us" (graphic title; tuba, light show, constructed environment) 1986.
Composition No 129 (graphic title; 5 woodwind instrumentalists) 1986; first performed Oakland, California, 1988. Recorded Sound Aspects SAS CD 023.
Composition No 130 (graphic title; 4 instruments) 1986; first performed Oakland, California, 1988.
Composition No 139 (graphic title; piano) 1989. Recorded Hat Art CD 6019.
Composition No 146: Moogee & Stetson (graphic title; 2 sousaphones, percussion, 12 flutes) 1989; first performed Memphis, Tennessee, 1989.
Composition No 147 (graphic title; 3 clarinets, chamber ensemble) 1989; first performed Paris, 1989.

Opera:

Trillium Dialogues A: . . . After a Period of Change Zaccko Returns to His Place of Birth . . . (6 soloists, 6 instrumentalists, dancers, choir, large orchestra, stage set) 1985; first performed San Diego, California, 1985.
Trillium Dialogues M: Joreo's Vision of Forward Motion (6 soloists, dancers, choir, piano, large orchestra) 1986.
Trillium Dialogues R: Shala Fears for the Poor 1988.

Other:

SH-G46
|
(337)
Composition No 9 (4 amplified shovels, 1 pile of coal, costumes, choreography) 1969.

Composition No 19 (graphic title; marching music for 100 tubas) 1971.

CK7(GN)
437
Composition No 21 (tape, with or without instruments) 1971; early version performed Chicago, 1968 or 1969; published version is based on Paris recording Delmark DS428.

LAYSA-4
Composition No 28 (6 musicians, 6 dancers) 1973; first performed Paris, 1973.

Composition No 49 (graphic title; 1–20 musicians with or without dancers 1975; first performed New York City, 1975.
Composition No 127 (graphic title; violin, E♭ saxophone, trombone, piano, dance ensemble) 1986; first performed Berkeley, California, 1986.
Composition No 128 (graphic title; single-line wind instrument, 2 dancers) 1986; first performed Berkeley, California, 1986.
Composition No 132: "The search for Ashmenton's loyalties" (graphic title; 2 dancers, 6 B♭ saxophones or 6 clarinets or 6 E♭ sopranino saxophones, 16 or 8 violins, 12 or 6 violas, 8 or 4 cellos, 6 or 2 double basses, percussion, cathedral organ) 1986; first performed San Francisco, 1986.

PUBLICATIONS

By Braxton: *Tri-Axium Writings: 1–3*, Oakland, California, 1985; *Catalogue of Works*, Oakland, California, 1986; *Composition Notes: A–E*, Oakland, California, 1988.

On Braxton: Graham Lock, *Forces in Motion: AB and the Meta-Reality of Creative Music*, London, 1988.

* * *

"The challenge of creativity," says Anthony Braxton, "is to move towards the highest thought that you can think of." For Braxton himself that thought, which now includes a vision of intergalactic concerts played by orchestras in different star systems, began some 25 years ago with the notion of creating a specific solo language for his main instrument, the alto saxophone.

Born in Chicago in 1945, his early musical loves were rooted in the African-American cultural heritage: first the R&B of Frankie Lymon and James Brown, later post-bebop and avant-garde jazz, notably the saxophone styles of John Coltrane, Paul Desmond and Warne Marsh and the restructuralist compositions of Ornette Coleman and Cecil Taylor. Then, in the mid-1960s, Braxton became aware of the European avant-garde (Schoenberg, Stockhausen) and its American counterpart (Ives, Cage). Add to these his involvement in Chicago's influential Association for the Advancement of Creative Musicians (AACM) plus a generous appreciation of various iconoclasts—from Evan

Parker and Sun Ra to Henry Brant and Harry Partch—and the major influences behind his extraordinary range of musical activities are all in place.

At first, Braxton's "jazz" and "notated" pieces evolved along relatively distinct lines, although both were based on the "language music" he had developed for his solo alto concerts, itself based on a pool of nearly 100 "sound classifications" he had drawn up (e.g., "smeared sounds", "staccato long sounds", "cluster formations", etc.), various combinations of which he "grafted" together to create new works. Early (i.e., 1966–75) notated pieces included works for orchestra (*Composition Nos 7, 24, 27*), chamber orchestra (*41*), string quartet (*17, 18*), woodwind quintet (*12*) and solo piano (*1, 10, 30–33*), as well as works for more unusual instrumentation—four pianos (*16*), four soprano saxophones (*22*), 100 tubas (*19*) and four amplified shovels (*9*).

That concert promoters and record companies neglected these pieces in favour of his jazz work Braxton attributed to cultural racism, particularly to what he called the "what makes you think you can play classical music, nigger" syndrome. However, a deal with Arista Records did enable him to smuggle a few notated works onto disc: *Composition No 63* (for two soloists and chamber orchestra), *82* (for four orchestras—part of a planned series of multi-orchestra works and the only recorded example to date of his Brant-inspired interest in spatial music) and *95* (for two pianos).

In the last decade, Braxton's longstanding fascination with structure has focused on various collage procedures, as evidenced in his "multiple line" pieces (for instance, *Composition No 96*), his introduction of "pulse track structures" into his jazz quartet concerts and his 1988 declaration that all of his compositions, and all the parts of his compositions, could be played either simultaneously, independently or in any combination. In practice, this has often meant the concurrent performance of "jazz" and "notated" pieces, further blurring a distinction he'd already subverted in such works as *Composition Nos 98* and *107*, which include improvisation only within a very tightly defined structural context.

Apparently having chromesthetic perception—he says he *sees* his music as "a three-dimensional painting"—Braxton has long used visual factors in his work. Not only do all of his compositions have diagrammatic titles (opus numbers were not assigned until the 1980s), he has often employed various kinds of symbolic and graphic notation. In recent years, his work has increasingly taken on mystical and theatrical aspects: astrology, numerology, costume and gesture are among the elements he has tried to integrate in his music, particularly in the "ritual and ceremonial" series which began with *Composition Nos 95* and *96* in the late 1970s and now includes a planned 12-opera cycle, *Trillium*, of which three parts—"A", "M" and "R"—had been completed by the end of 1990.

Though recordings of his notated pieces are still relatively rare, recent concert premieres have included pieces for San Francisco's Grace Cathedral, London's Almeida Festival and the Paris Autumn Festival. A virtuoso player, composer, intellectual and visionary, Braxton has to date completed around 360 compositions plus the three-volume, philosophical *Tri-Axium Writings* and five books of *Composition Notes*. Probably his most remarkable achievement has been to create a uniquely brilliant synthesis of the African-American and European traditions; a music that, however fiercely intense or complex or lighthearted, moves always with the grace and daring of a passionate intelligence.

—Graham Lock

BRESNICK, Martin. American. Born in New York City, 13 November, 1944. Educated at Hartt School of Music, University of Hartford, Connecticut, B.A., 1967; Stanford University, California (studied electronic music under John Chowning, and composition under Gyorgy Ligeti), M.A., 1968, D.M.A., 1972; Akademie (now Hochschule) für Musik, Vienna (studied composition under Gottfried von Einem and electronic music under Friedrich Cerha), 1969–70. Married Anna Barbara Broell, 21 June 1969; 1 daughter. Instructor, San Francisco Conservatory of Music, 1971–2; lecturer, Stanford University, 1972–5; Yale School of Music, associate professor, 1981–7, and professor of composition and co-ordinator of the composition department, since 1987, Yale School of Music, New Haven, Connecticut. Trained as conductor; founder and director of Sheep's Clothing, the Yale College Ensemble for Contemporary Music; presently director of Alea II; member, Koussevitzky Foundation Commission, 1986. Recipient: Fulbright Fellowship, 1969–70; Walter J. Gores Award for Excellence in Teaching, Stanford University, 1973; National Endowment for Arts composer grants, 1974, 1979; ASCAP Awards, from 1975; Rome Prize Fellowship, 1975–6; MacDowell Colony Fellowship, 1977; Morse Fellowship, Yale University, 1980–1; First Prize (for *Conspiracies*), Premio Ancona, Italy, 1980; First Prize (for *Wir Weben, Wir Weben*), International Sinfonia Musicale Competition, 1982; Connecticut Commission on the Arts grant (in support of *String Quartet No 2 "Bucephalus"*, with Chamber Music America), 1983; First Prize (for *"Bucephalus"*), Composers Inc. Competition, 1985; semi-finalist (with *Just Time*), Friedheim Awards, 1987; First Prize (for *Trio*), Composers Inc. Competition, 1989. Mailing address: Yale School of Music, 96 Wall Street, New Haven, Connecticut 06520, U.S.A.

Publishers: Common Muse Music Publisher, 73 Foster Street, New Haven, Connecticut 06511; Bote und Bock, Berlin.

Symphonies/orchestral:

Ocean of Storms 1969–70.
Wir Weben, Wir Weben (string orchestra; also arranged for sextet and large chamber ensemble) 1978.
One (small orchestra) 1986.
Little Suite (amateur string orchestra) 1987.
Pontoosuc 1989; first performed New York, 1989.

Chamber/instrumental:

Piano Sonata 1963.
Themes and Variations (oboe) 1964.
Four Short Piano Pieces 1964–8.
Trio (2 trumpets, percussion) 1966.
Woodwind Quintet 1967.
String Quartet No 1 1968.
Introit (2 flutes, 2 oboes, 2 clarinets, 2 bassoons, 4 horns, 2 trumpets, 2 trombones) 1969.
Three Intermezzi (cello) 1971. Recorded CRI 468.
Musica (flute, clarinet, bassoon, horn, trumpet, trombone, violin, viola, cello) 1972.
B.'s Garlands (8 cellos) 1973. Recorded CRI 336.
Wir Weben, Wir Weben (3 violins, viola, cello, double bass; also 3 1st, 3 2nd, 3 3rd violins 3 violas, 3 cellos, double bass) 1978.
Conspiracies (solo flute, 4 other flutes; also solo flute, tape) 1979. Recorded CRI 468.
High Art (piccolo, toy piano) 1983; first performed New York, 1984.

Bread and Salt (2 flutes, 2 oboes, 2 clarinets, 2 bassoons, 2 saxophones, 2 horns, cello, double bass) 1984.
String Quartet No 2 "Bucephalus" 1984; first performed Portsmouth, New Hampshire, 1984. Recorded CRI 536.
Tent of Miracles (solo baritone saxophone, 3 other baritone saxophones; also baritone saxophone, tape) 1984; first performed Hartford, Connecticut, 1984.
Bag O'Tells (mandolin) 1984.
Just Time (woodwind quintet) 1985; first performed Norfolk, Connecticut, 1985.
Trio (violin, cello, piano) 1988; first performed Charlottesville, Virginia, 1988.

Vocal/choral:

Alyosha (baritone, piano) 1964.
Where Is the Way (unaccompanied SATB choir) 1970.
Stoneground (actors/singers) 1974.
Der Signal (flute, clarinet, saxophone, cornet, trombone, viola, cello, double bass, soprano, alto, mezzo-soprano, narrator or tape) 1982.
Three Choral Songs (unaccompanied SATB choir; Amichai) 1986.

Other:

PCOMP (tape) 1968.
Pour (tape) 1969.
Arthur and Lillie (music for film by J. Else) 1976.
Ants (woodwind quintet, string quartet, double bass, percussion, harp, soprano, mezzo-soprano, tenor, baritone, 5 actor/mimes) 1978.
The Day After Trinity (music for film by J. Else) 1980.
Lady Neil's Dumpe (DX7 digital synthesizer, TX 816/ Macintosh computer) 1988. Recorded Centaur CRC 2039.

Scores for Center for Visual History film series on American poets: *William Carlos Williams*, 1986; *Wallace Stevens*, 1987.

PUBLICATIONS

By Bresnick: "Cage's Unexpected Offspring", in *Mosaic*, 8(1), 1973; "Content, Periodicity and Space: 'Harmonielehre' by Diether de la Motte', in *Yale Journal of Music Theory*, Spring 1979; "New Music", in *How Music Works*, Schuckburgh Reynolds, 1981; "A Composer Looks at Form and Content", in *Prism*, February 1987; "Convention and the Hermetic in Schumann's Frauenliebe und Leben", in *Festschrift for Dr Leonard Ratner*, Pendragon, 1990.

* * *

Martin Bresnick has composed music for a variety of media, but has concentrated primarily on instrumental pieces ranging from works for solo performer to those for orchestra. One of the outstanding characteristics of this music is Bresnick's fascination with timbre. His exploration of timbre intensified while at Stanford, where Bresnick assisted John Chowning with the development of FM synthesis. Perhaps paradoxically, this interest in timbre is most clearly represented in his works for collections of a single instrument, such as *B.'s Garlands* for eight cellos or *Conspiracies* for solo flute and four other flutes. Composing for groups of the same instrument, Bresnick is able to magnify many of the subtle timbral characteristics of that instrument without masking those subtleties with other timbres. This creates a sonority which is both relatively monochromatic and extremely rich. Understanding the exigencies of different perfomance situations, in both *Conspiracies* and *Tent of Miracles* Bresnick indicates that the pieces may be performed either by several instrumentalists or by a solo performer with a prerecorded tape of the other parts. More recently, however, Bresnick has tended to compose for standard ensembles, such as his Second String Quartet, wind quintet (*Just Time*), and piano trio (*Trio*), or for larger mixed ensembles.

Several of Bresnick's compositions feature extended techniques, particularly when he is writing for a performer adept at the realization of those techniques. *Conspiracies*, for example, makes elaborate use of the increased sonic possibilities of the flute that have been developed in the last 30 years. The early First String Quartet contains a rock-like scherzo in which the cellist becomes the drummer of the group by drumming on the body of the cello, rather than playing the strings.

Rhythmically, the music written after 1978 shows an aversion to "irrational" subdivisions of the beat, such as triplets or quintuplets. Bresnick achieves rhythmic variety through different, often overlapping, meters, displacement of accents, and different groupings of the basic pulse. *One* maintains a single pulse and a single meter, but the 7/8 meter ranges from prominent to indiscernible because of Bresnick's use of accents and different note groupings.

As a young man, Bresnick worked with several different ways of structuring pitch. The earliest piece in his catalogue, *Themes and Variations*, for solo oboe, consists of a personalized use of twelve tone. This piece is Bresnick's only twelve-tone composition. *Three Intermezzi* is structured upon a single group of intervals, three consecutive minor seconds followed by a major second. No melodic fourths or fifths appear; the entire piece consists solely of major and minor seconds and thirds and their inversions. Bresnick's earlier pieces also make use of other pitch structuring devices. Algorithmic procedures were used to derive and develop material in *Introit*, which features many pitches that are fixed at specific registers, and a computer was used to aid in the composition of *Musica*.

B.'s Garlands in many ways sums up Bresnick's earlier works, but there are also indications of what is to follow. In the piece, Bresnick begins to use pitch-centered material, although the harmony is in no way functional. Rather, specific pitches are emphasized by reiteration and positioning within a given scale, even though the scales used are not diatonic. From this point on, Bresnick's music makes use of different types of scales, often being harmonically focused upon one or two specific pitches. Many of the procedures he uses to control pitch are similar from piece to piece, although the harmonic world that one piece exists in may be radically different from that of another. This is because of the different scale types used. The harmony that would be generated by a scale of eight contiguous semitones is very different from that generated by a scale that consists primarily of major seconds and minor thirds. Consequently, *Lady Neil's Dumpe*, which is composed using the church modes, inhabits a less dissonant sound world than *Bread and Salt*, which uses a far more chromatic collection of pitches. Bresnick's recent music, such as the Second String Quartet, has shown an increasing sensitivity to the subtleties of harmonic directionality, and may be described as sounding as if it is residing on a particular pitch center, although it never sounds as if it is in a particular key. Over the course of his career, Bresnick has composed music that is marked by the richness of its harmonic, timbral, and motivic development, and by the high quality of his intellect and craftsmanship.

—R. Peter Mueller

BRINDLE, Reginald Smith. British/English. Born in Bamber Bridge, Preston, Lancashire, 5 January 1917. Educated at Hutton Grammar School, 1928–33; University College of North Wales, Bangor, 1946–9, B.Mus., later D.Mus.; Accademia de Santa Cecilia, Rome (under Pizzetti), 1949–51, diploma in composition; private musical study with Luigi Dallapiccola, 1949, 1952–3; also studied and practised architecture, 1933–9, intermediate R.I.B.A. examinations. Served as Captain, Royal Engineers, 1940–6. Married Giulia Borsi, 4 April 1947; 4 children. Freelance journalist, teacher, translator, import-export manager, composer of film music, 1952–7; collaborator, Radio Italiana, 1956–61; active, along with Bussotti and Bartolozzi, in Scuola Dodecafonica group, Florence; lecturer, then senior lecturer and reader in music, 1957–67, and professor, 1967–70, University College of North Wales, Bangor; professor of music, University of Surrey, Guildford, 1970–83. Recipient: Don Sturzo Award, 1950; Fellowship, University of Wales, 1950; Clements Memorial Prize, 1953. Mailing address: "Fiorenza", 219 Farleigh Road, Warlingham, Surrey CR6 9EL, England.

Publishers: Schott, London; Suvini Zerboni, Milan; and others.

Symphonies/orchestral:

Concertino (guitar, chamber orchestra) 1951.
Sinfonia 1954.
Variations on a Theme by Dallapiccola 1955; broadcast BBC Wales, 1966.
An Epitaph for Alban Berg 1955; first performed Florence, 1956.
Symphonic Variations 1957; broadcast BBC, 1959.
Cosmos 1959; first performed Cheltenham, Gloucestershire, 1960.
Via Crucis 1960; broadcast BBC Wales, 1961.
Homage to H.G. Wells 1960; broadcast BBC, 1962.
Clarinet Concerto 1962.
Creation Epic 1964; first performed London, 1964.
Apocalypse 1970; first performed Cheltenham, Gloucestershire 1971.
Fons Bonitatis II 1973; first performed Guildford, Surrey, 1973.
Guitar Concerto 1977.
Le Chant du Monde (guitar orchestra, electronic keyboard, percussion) 1984; first performed Sable, 1984.
Recordando el gran maestro (guitar orchestra) 1987; first performed Seville, 1987.

Chamber/instrumental:

Fantasia I (guitar) 1944.
Serenata I (guitar) 1944.
Variations on Three Subjects (guitar) 1944.
Fantasia II in D (guitar) 1945.
Corrente (guitar) 1945.
Chorale and Prelude (guitar) 1945.
Chittareo (guitar) 1945.
Counterpoint Study (guitar) 1945.
Exercise in Arpeggios (guitar) 1945.
Fantasia Passacaglia (guitar) 1945.
Serenata II (guitar) 1946.
Scherzo (guitar) 1946.
Nocturne (guitar) 1946.
Berceuse à Diana (guitar) 1948.
Fuego Fatuo (guitar) 1948.
Danza Pagana (guitar) 1948.
Sonatina Florentina (guitar) 1948.
Vita Senese (guitar) 1948.
Arabesca (guitar) 1948.
Serenata III (guitar) 1948.
Preludes I–IV (guitar) 1948.
Variations No 5 (guitar) 1948.
Prelude No 5 (guitar) 1948.
Berceuse II (guitar) 1949.
Guitar Duo 1949.
Villanella (guitar) 1949.
Concertino (4 guitars) 1949.
Omaggio a Manuel de Falla (guitar) 1949.
Etruscan Preludes (guitar) 1949.
Berceuse III (guitar) 1950.
Sonata Senese (guitar) 1950.
Prelude (guitar; for film *Il Serchio*) 1950.
Dodecafonic Study (guitar) 1952.
Saraband (guitar; later became *Memento*) 1953.
El Polifemo de Oro (guitar) 1956.
Three Pieces (guitar, piano) 1956.
Ten-String Music (guitar, cello) 1957; broadcast BBC, 1959.
Five Sketches (violin, guitar) 1957; broadcast BBC, 1959.
String Quartet Music 1958; first performed London, 1960.
Concerto (5 instruments, percussion) 1960; broadcast BBC, 1960.
Segments and Variants (wind quintet) 1965; broadcast BBC, 1976.
Andromeda (flute) 1966; broadcast BBC, 1968.
Orion M42 (percussion) 1967; first performed Munich, 1977.
Auriga (4 percussion) 1967; first performed Paris, 1970.
Variants (guitar) 1970.
Music for Three Guitars 1970.
Concerto Breve "Omnis Terra" (8 guitars, percussion) 1971.
Tubal Cain's Heritage (trombone, piano) 1973; first performed Washington, D.C., 1973.
Concerto de angelis (4 guitars) 1973.
Memento (guitar; revision of 1953 *Saraband*) 1973.
November Memories (guitar) 1974.
Concerto "CumJubilo" (3 guitars) 1974.
Do Not Go Gentle . . . (guitar) 1974.
The Walls of Jericho (tuba) 1975; first performed Guildford, Surrey, 1976.
Four Poems of Garcia Lorca (guitar) 1975.
Sonata Two—El Verbo (guitar) 1976.
Guitarcosmos: Volumes 1 & 2 1976.
Guitarcosmos: Volume 3 1977.
Sonata Three—The Valley of Esdralon (guitar) 1978.
Chaconne and Interludes (The Instruments of Peace III) (2 guitars) 1978.
Sonata Four—La Brève (guitar) 1978.
Ten Simple Preludes (guitar) 1978.
Organ Symphony (organ) 1979.
The Pillars of Karnak (4 guitars; version for 2 guitars) 1979.
Sonata Five (guitar) 1979.
Missa de spiritus flammis (organ) 1980.
Canzona (guitar) 1980.

Preludes and Fantasias (guitar) 1980.
Regina caeli (organ) 1986.
The Harmonies of Peace (organ) 1986.
Inner Refrains (organ) 1988.
Creator alme siderum (organ) 1988.
Expectabant caeli et terra (organ) 1988.
The Firmament Beyond (organ) 1988.
Las doces cuerdas (2 guitars) 1989.

Vocal/choral:

Grafico della Petenera (mezzo-soprano, choir, instruments) 1956; broadcast BBC, 1969.
Genesis Dream (mezzo-soprano, flute, 2 clarinets, trumpet, 3 percussion, piano; Thomas) 1960; first performed Paris, 1960.
Extremum Carmen (mezzo-soprano, choir, instruments) 1961.
Three Japanese Lyrics (mezzo-soprano, instruments) 1966; broadcast BBC, 1966.
Discoveries (mixed choir) 1967; first performed Bangor, Wales, 1970.
Amalgam (mezzo-soprano, instruments) 1968; first performed Cheltenham, Gloucestershire, 1968.
Windhover (mixed choir) 1970; broadcast BBC, 1971.
Worlds Without End (choir, speakers, instruments, tapes) 1973; first performed Guildford, Surrey, 1974.
A Mass in English (choir, organ) 1974; first performed Wonersh, Surrey, 1975.
Two Poems of Gerard Manley Hopkins (voice, guitar) 1979.
Journey Towards Infinity (baritone, instruments) 1987.

Opera:

The Death of Antigone 1969; first performed Oxford, 1971.

Other:

Intavolatura di liuto (transcription into modern notation of lute music by da Crema, 1546) 1954.
Canzone a 8 (transcription of 1599 piece for 4 lutes by G.B. Terzi) 1973.
Canzone a 4 (transcription of piece for 2 lutes by Merulo) 1973.
Intabolatura de leuto (transcription into modern notation of lute music by Casteliona, 1535) 1975.
Intavolatura di liuto (transcription into modern notation of lute music by Terzi, 1593) 1975.

PUBLICATIONS

By Brindle: *Serial Composition*, Oxford, 1966; *Contemporary Percussion*, Oxford, 1970; *The New Music*, Oxford, 1975; *Musical Composition*, Oxford, 1986; numerous journal articles in United Kingdom, United States, Italy.

Reginald Smith Brindle comments:

Most influences on my style came from my years in Italy, when my compositional technique and style were much influenced by my friends in the Florentine Dodecaphonic School (nominally under Dallapiccola). I wrote music in the technique of serialism until about 1970, but tended to vary the musical style considerably. I justify this as such eclecticism was also typical of such great figures as Picasso and Stravinsky who had such varied "periods". However, such variety in my case has tended to bewilder the public who cannot identify my works so easily, even though the compositional technique is fairly constant. I do not regret this, as it would be boring for me to keep on and on in only one style. I like change, and these are the consequences.

* * *

It is a matter for considerable regret that more people know Reginald Smith Brindle as a teacher and critic than as a composer in his own right. He has nonetheless been an eloquent ambassador for the "New Music", and his book of that title is one of the most influential of generally accessible accounts of the avant-garde. Typically, he finds room in it for figures who are not elsewhere widely discussed. He is himself an eclectic and very varied composer, whose work, from the early guitar works to more recent organ and vocal pieces, is frankly sensuous, richly coloured and always dramatic.

It may be arguing too much to suggest that these are the products of Smith Brindle's years in Italy, for he is also very much his own man and is quintessentially English in his refusal to be entrapped by systems. It is, however, deeply significant that he should have studied with Luigi Dallapiccola, a heterodox serialist who may have devised a twelve-tone technique independently of Schoenberg and who certainly pioneered the use of atonality in melodic structures by way of innovative triads. Something of this evident in Smith Brindle's pieces, such as the *Dodecafonic Study* for guitar of 1952. Whatever else Smith Brindle derived from Dallapiccola and from the younger Scuola Dodecafonica composers like Bussotti and Bartolozzi, it was a passionate commitment to individual response to musical problems and situations; the *Variations on a Theme by Dallapiccola* are both respectful and firmly independent. There is almost nothing in his work-list that seems merely generic or formulaic, and there is certainly nothing that sounds like a mere problem-solving exercise. His abandonment of serialism after about 1970 was not a major recantation, merely a recognition that his own eclectic method was already breaking the strict bounds of that method.

A background in jazz is evident in some of his mature pieces, notably in some of the large scale works for guitar orchestra or guitar and orchestra. The 1970 *Apocalypse*, written at a point of change in Smith Brindle's career, and perhaps reflecting that, is one of the finest orchestral pieces of the past 25 years. His interest in astronomy, futurology and science fiction is explicitly acknowledged in the homage to H.G. Wells, but also in the flute piece *Andromeda*, a delightfully sustained solo, and in the remarkable solo percussion piece *Orion M42*, named after a galactic nebula in that constellation. He is a fine composer of vocal music, and here the debt to Dallapiccola is unquestionable; the rhythms of *Windhover* are perfectly adjudged, and his *A Mass in English* (no Latinist he) is superb.

Smith Brindle retired his chair at the University of Surrey in the mid 1980s, and there is sign again of renewed activity on a non-academic front. At 74, he betrays no symptoms of intellectual or artistic exhaustion.

—James Weir

BROTT, Alexander. Canadian. Born in Montreal, 14 March 1915. Educated at McGill University, Montreal,

Lic.Mus., 1932; Quebec Academy of Music, Laureat degree, 1933; Juilliard School of Music, New York, 1933–8, graduated 1937, post-graduate study, 1938. Married Lotte Goetzel, 27 April 1933; 2 sons. Violinist, composer, conductor; concertmaster, assistant conductor, Montreal Symphony Orchestra; founder, musical director, McGill Chamber Orchestra; instructor in violin and orchestration, 1939–1955, associate professor, chairman of instrumental department, 1955–65, professor, 1965–1980, and conductor in residence, 1974, McGill University; conductor, Montreal Pops Concert, since 1960; conductor, musical director, Kingston Symphony Orchestra and Kingston Pops Concert, since 1963. Recipient: Elizabeth Sprague Coolidge Award for composition, 1937, 1938; Loeb Memorial Award for performance, 1938–9; Lord Strathcona Award, 1939; CAPAC Composition Award, 1941, 1942, 1943; Olympic Medals for composition, Helsinki, London, 1948, 1952; 1st prize, Pan American conductors competition, 1957; D.Mus., Chicago University, 1960; Sir Arnold Bax Society Prize, gold medal (for *The Composer of the Commonwealth*), 1961; Prix du Disque, 1969; elected honorary member, Zoltan Kodaly Academy and Institute, 1970; hon. LL.D., Queen's University, 1973; Gold Medal of International Who's Who, 1973; annual prize, Jewish People's Schools and Peretz Schools, 1974; medal and diploma, Academjia Brasileira de ciencias humanas, 1975; elected Fellow, International Biographical Association, 1975; elected "Notable American of the Centennial Era", 1976; Canadian Music Council medal, 1976; Queen's Anniversary Silver Jubilee Medal, 1977, Medal of the Order of Canada, 1979; hon. D.Mus., McGill University, 1980; Order of Saint John of Jerusalem, Knight of Malta, 1985; Fellow, Royal Society of Arts, London, 1988; National Order of Quebec, 1988. Mailing address: Faculty of Music, McGill University, 5459 Earnscliffe Avenue, Montreal, Quebec H3X 2P8, Canada.

Symphonies/orchestral:

Oracle 1938.
Lullaby and Procession of Toys (string orchestra) 1939.
Lament 1939.
Ritual (string orchestra) 1939.
War and Peace 1944.
Laurentian Idyll 1945.
From Sea to Sea 1946.
Concordia 1946; first performed Prague, 1946.
Concerto for Violin and Orchestra 1950.
Critics Corner (strings, percussion) 1950.
Delightful Delusions 1951.
Royal Tribute 1953; first performed London, 1953.
Fancy and Folly 1953.
Sept for Seven (strings, winds, narrator) 1955.
Arabesque (cello, orchestra) 1958.
Analogy in Anagram 1959.
Three Astral Visions (string orchestra) 1960.
Martlett's Muse 1962.
Circle, Triangle, Four Squares (strings) 1963.
Paraphrase in Poliphony 1967.
Le Corriveau 1967.
Mini-Minus (chamber orchestra) 1968.
The Emperor's New Clothes 1970.
Seven Minuets, Six Canons 1971.
The Young Prometheus (based on *Twelve Preludes and Fugues* by Beethoven) 1971.
Satie's Faction (chamber strings) 1973.
Cupid's Quandary (violin, string orchestra, percussion) 1975.
Evocative Provocations (cello, orchestra) 1975.
E Dai P Milo (strings) 1976.
Hymn II Her (flute, bassoon, strings) 1977.
My Mother—My Memorial 1978.
Curioso Furioso (strings) 1982.
Trivial Trifles (strings) 1984.

Chamber/instrumental:

Invocation and Dance (violin, piano) 1939.
Lullabys and Procession of Toys (string quartet) 1939.
String Quartet 1940.
Piano Suite 1941.
Vignettes (piano) 1952.
Rhapsody (cello, piano) 1958.
Three Acts. Four Sinners (saxophone quartet) 1961.
Three on a Spree (flute, oboe, harpsichord) 1962.
Mutual Salvation Orgy (brass quintet) 1962.
Pristine Prism (violin) 1967.
Centennial Colloquy (13 wind instruments) 1967.
L'Accent (piano) 1971.
Spasms for Six (6 percussionists) 1971.
Tout de suite (cello) 1971.
Saxi-Foni-Saties (saxophone quartet) 1973; first performed Toronto, August 1973.
Psalmody (cello) 1974; first performed Montreal, January 1974.
Shofar (cello) 1976.
Double Entente (string quartet) 1976; first performed Montreal, August 1976.
Prisms (flute, guitar) 1984.

Vocal/choral:

Songs of Contemplation (soprano, strings) 1940.
Canadiana (unaccompanied choir) 1955.
Israel (choir, strings) 1956.
Vision of the Dry Bones (baritone, strings) 1960.
The Prophet (tenor, soprano, strings) 1960.
World Sophisticate (soprano, brass quintet) 1962.
Profundum Praedictum (bass, string orchestra) 1966.
Centennial Celebration (strings, female choir, narrator, 2 solo voices) 1967.
Elie, Elie (female voices, piano) 1967.
Esperanto (female voices, piano) 1967.
Badinage (mixed voices, piano) 1968.
How Thunder and Lightning Came to Be (bass, percussion, piano, narrator; orchestral version with soprano, bass) 1973.
Three Eskimo Songs (soprano, bass, percussion) 1973.
Four Songs of the Central Eskimos (soprano, bass, percussion) 1973.
Two Songs (Haida) (soprano, bass, percussion) 1973.
Time's Trial Triumph (unaccompanied choir) 1976; first performed Bonn, 1976.

Other:

Ravel: *Gaspard de la nuit* (orchestration) 1971.
Brahms: *Three Intermezzi* (orchestration) 1972.
Schumann: *Kinderszenen* (orchestration) 1973.

* * *

The Brotts dominate musical life in Montreal, one of those awesomely gifted families in whom there seems to be no limit of ability and enthusiasm. Alexander Brott is probably as well known as an educator and conductor as a composer of—

mostly—orchestral music. This is a pity, for he has a fine, distinctive voice, quirkily original without being unduly self-conscious. Early and wartime pieces like *Oracle* and *Laurentian Idyll* employ a large orchestral palette with considerable dexterity and exactness. Brott's instincts as a conductor have always been towards precision without fussiness and his own scoring is admirably precise, particularly in the strings and his writing for string orchestra—*E Dai P Milo, Curioso Furioso, Cupid's Quandary*—is always particularly vital.

As these titles suggest, Brott sees no reason to exclude humour from his music (though it has a dark side as well and a general air of not suffering fools gladly); Brott has been instrumental in bringing "pops" concerts to the Canadian public and thus constantly widening the audience for classical music. His own increasingly punning and tongue-in-cheek titles introduce a music confidently in possession of a strong, Romantic language, punctuated with unexpected and effectively placed harmonic innovations, off-centre rhythms and occasional, unexpected modulations of key, which are both attractive and occasionally thought-provoking. Brott has no truck with avant-garde gestures, but he is not a reactionary, preferring to write music that people will listen to, rather than the often antagonistic theory-music of extreme modernism.

The chamber pieces are not, in general, as compelling as the orchestral compositions, but there are some outstanding works among them, notably the string quartet *Double Entente, Saxi-Foni-Saties* for saxophones, and the much earlier *Lullabys and Procession of Toys*, which relates to a distinctive orchestral piece of 1939. His solo instrumental works are always dramatically conceived; *Pristine Prism* for violin is not nearly as untouchable as it sounds, while *Shofar* movingly explores Levantine themes.

Brott has written less vocal music, but what he has done is refreshingly offbeat, whether in his "higher" style for religious and philosophically-oriented pieces, or in the lighter, cabaret-ish vein. The *Three Eskimo Songs* are distinctive, as are *World Sophisticate* and the glimpse into Ezekiel of *Vision of the Dry Bones*.

He has been remarkably consistent in quality, rarely allowing his standards to drop. That is how he has treated his orchestras down the years. It is good to see that he is not afraid to preach as well as practice; there have been few better ambassadors for modern music.

—Paul Boursin

BROWN, Christopher (Roland). British/English. Born in Tunbridge Wells, Kent, 17 June 1943. Educated at Westminster Abbey Choir School, London, 1952–7; Dean Close School, 1957–62; King's College, Cambridge, 1962—5, B.A., M.A., 1968; Royal Academy of Music, London, 1965–7; Hochsschule für Musik, Berlin, 1967–8. Married (1) Anne Smillie, 29 March 1969; (2) Fiona Caithness, 28 December 1985; 1 daughter and 1 son. Professorial staff, Royal Academy of Music, London, since 1969; musical director, Cambridge Players, 1978–85; musical director, Huntingdonshire Philharmonic, Cambridgeshire, since 1976; resident conductor, Dorset Bach Cantata Club, Dorset, since 1988; also examiner, Associated Examination Board; composer in residence, Nene College, Northampton. Freelance composer, since 1968. Recipient: Guinness Prize for Composition, 1974, 1976; Collard Scholarship, Musicians Company, 1974; Prince Pierre of Monaco Prize, 1976; Washington International Competition (for *String Quartet No 2*), 1976. Mailing address: 6 Station Road, Catworth, Huntingdon, Cambridgeshire PE18 0PE, England.

Publisher: Chester Music, London.

Symphonies/orchestral:

Sinfonia 1970; first performed London, 1970.
Sonata for Strings Op 42 1974; first performed London, 18 February 1975.
The Sun Rising: Threnody for Orchestra Op 45 1976; first performed London, 27 February 1977.
Triptych Op 47 1978; first performed Birmingham, 7 December 1978.
Organ Concerto Op 49 1979; first performed St Albans, Hertfordshire, 1979.
Festive Prelude Op 49 1979; first performed London, 1979.
Festival Variations Op 54 1981; first performed Cambridge, 1982.
Rustic Dances Op 58 1983.
Into the Sun Op 62 1985; first performed London, 1985.
Toy Symphony Op 69 1986; first performed St Ives, Cambridgeshire, 20 December 1986.
Ruscelli d'Oro 1989; first performed London, 1990.

Chamber/instrumental:

Divertimento (wind quintet) 1962; first performed Cambridge, 1963.
Sonata (violin, piano) 1966; first performed Cambridge, 1966.
Trio Op 36a/b (violin, cello, piano) 1967, revised version for flute, oboe, piano 1975; first performed Wilmslow, Cheshire, 28 October 1972.
String Quartet No 1 1969; first performed Keele, Staffordshire, 1970.
Trio (recorder, cello, harpsichord; or flute, bassoon, piano) 1971; first performed Wilmslow, Cheshire, 1972.
Chamber Music Op 40 (clarinet, horn, violin, cello, piano) 1975; first performed London, 13 March 1975.
String Quartet No 2 Op 43 1976; first performed Washington, D.C., 1977.
Festival Variations Op 54 (string quartet) 1981; first performed Cambridge, 29 July 1981.
Toccata Op 56 (organ) 1982; first performed Melton Mowbray, Leicestershire, 7 August 1982.
Gallery Prelude Op 61 (organ; based on hymn "Bridehead") 1984; first performed Dorchester, Dorset, 17 June 1984.
Caprice Op 68 (recorder, piano or harpsichord) 1986; first performed Manchester, 1986.
Sonatina Op 69a (piano duet; arrangement of *Toy Symphony*) 1986.
Images Op 70 (brass quintet) 1987; first performed Cambridge, 1987.

Vocal/choral:

A Hymn to the Holy Innocents (tenor, chorus, orchestra) 1964; first performed Cambridge, 1965.
Three Shakespeare Songs (unaccompanied chorus) 1965; first performed Cambridge, 1965.
Laudate Dominum (chorus, organ) 1965; first performed Cheltenham, Gloucestershire, 1966. Recorded Abbey ABY 817.

Elegy (unaccompanied chorus) 1967; first performed London, 1967.
Woefully Arrayed (tenor, chorus, orchestra) 1967; first performed London, 1967.
Missa Brevis (alto, tenor, bass, chorus, orchestra) 1967; first performed London, 1968.
Aubade Op 17 (unaccompanied SSAATTBB chorus, soloists) 1968; first performed London, 15 May 1968.
Wordsworth Songs (mezzo-soprano, piano) 1969; first performed London, 1969.
Point of Departure (tenor, piano) 1969; first performed Cheltenham, Gloucestershire, 1969.
David Op 21 (mezzo-soprano, bass, chorus, orchestra) 1969; first performed Hereford, 25 August 1970.
Four Madrigals (unaccompanied chorus) 1969; first performed London, 1971.
Four Motets (chorus, organ) 1969; first performed Edington, 1970.
Laus Creatorum (chorus, organ) 1969; first performed London, 1969.
Nocturnal (alto, violin, cello, double bass, harpsichord) 1970; first performed Nottingham, 1970.
The Snows of Winter (SSATBB chorus, ensemble) 1970; first performed London, 1971.
Lauds (SSATBB chorus, brass quintet) 1970; first performed Tewkesbury, Gloucestershire, 1971.
Hodie Salvator Apparuit Op 28 (unaccompanied SSAATTBB, soloists) 1970; first performed London, 9 December 1970.
Herrick Songs (unaccompanied chorus) 1971; first performed London, 1971.
Three Medieval Lyrics Op 37 (soprano, tenor, chorus, orchestra) 1972; first performed London, 1973.
Oundle Jubilate (chorus, organ) 1972; first performed Oundle, Northamptonshire, 1973.
A-Courting We Will Go (soprano, tenor, piano) 1973; first performed Cheltenham, Gloucestershire, 1973. Recorded Unicorn Kanchana UKCD 2009.
Three Medieval Carols (unaccompanied men's voices) 1973; first performed Carlisle, Northumberland, 1973.
Festival Te Deum (chorus, organ) 1973; first performed Chichester, Suffolk, 1974.
Soliloquy Op 35 (counter-tenor or baritone or contralto, orchestra) 1976; first performed Monte Carlo, 1977.
All Year Round (tenor, guitar) 1976; first performed St Ives, Cambridgeshire, 1976.
The Harper of Chao (2 altos, viola da gamba, harpsichord) 1976; first performed Wye, Kent, 1977.
Hexham Mass (chorus, organ) 1976; first performed St Ives, Cambridgeshire, 1977.
Festival Venite (chorus, organ) 1976; first performed Uppingham, Leicestershire, 1977.
Even Such Is Time (unaccompanied SSAATTBB chorus) 1977.
Chauntecleer Op 50 (soprano, tenor, bass, SA chorus, orchestra) 1979; first performed London, 1980.
Magnificat Op 52 (soprano, alto, tenor, bass, chorus, orchestra) 1980; first performed London, 1981.
Seascape Op 53 (soprano, bass, reciter, chorus, brass) 1981; first performed St Ives, Cornwall, 1981.
The Vision of Saul Op 59 (soprano, alto, tenor, bass, chorus, orchestra) 1983; first performed London, 1984.
I Sing of a Maiden (unaccompanied SATB chorus) 1983.
Tres Cantus Sacri Op 60 (SATB chorus, orchestra) 1984; first performed Bristol, 16 June 1984.
From the Doorways of the Dawn Op 64 (unaccompanied chorus) 1985; first performed Tokyo, 1986.
Fair and Feast (bass, chorus, orchestra) 1986; first performed Saffron Walden, Essex, 1986.
Landscapes Op 67 (soprano, SATB chorus, orchestra) 1986; St Ives, Cambridgeshire, 4 April 1987.
The Circling Year (chorus, orchestra) 1989; first performed London, 1990.

Opera:

The Split Goose Feather 1978; first performed Huntingdon, Cambridgeshire, 1979.
The Ram King Op 55 (opera for children) 1982; first performed Birmingham, 28 April 1982.
The Two Lockets 1987; first performed Northampton, 1988.
Die Schwindlerin 1989; first performed Hamburg, 1990.

Other:

The Merry Wives of Windsor (incidental music for Shakespeare; wind quintet) 1963; first performed Cambridge, 1963.
Romeo and Juliet (incidental music for Shakespeare; wind quintet) 1964; first performed Cambridge, 1964.
Twelfth Night (incidental music to Shakespeare; wind quintet) 1965; first performed Cambridge, 1965.
A Midsummer Night's Dream (incidental music to Shakespeare; ensemble) 1965; first performed Stratford-upon-Avon, 1965.
The Caucasian Chalk Circle (incidental music to Brecht; ensemble) 1972; first performed Huntingdon, Cambridgeshire, 1972.
'Tis Christmas Time (original and arranged carols) 1977–88.

PUBLICATIONS

On Brown: Philip Radcliffe, "CB", in *Musical Times*, August 1970.

Christopher Brown comments:

Music must communicate. Music must sing. Music must have coherent structure, beauty of line, clarity of texture. Above all, music must be concerned first with humanity, with human emotions, with our fears, hopes, love, humour, warmth. It is not primarily about intellectual statements, though these statements must play a part in the expression. I hope my music expresses some of these ideals in a language which is relevant but part of an ongoing tradition, which stretches back to the masters of the past but looks forward to a positive future as well.

* * *

Christopher Brown has been described in the press as "one of the most accomplished composers" of the Leighton-Howells-Britten generation.

Brown excels in his choral music. He inherited the grace and naturalness of his teacher Sir Lennox Berkeley. Brown's style is lyrical and vocal. The *Guardian* described his *Hodie Salvator Apparuit* as a "delightful Christmas sequence", in music which "headily whirls you from one tonal centre to another, in writing that is challenging but rewarding both to singers and listeners".

Brown made his name with sacred pieces including carols and Christmas music favouring medieval and Latin texts, and Elizabethan poetry. The end of *A Hymn to the Holy Innocents* builds up to a beautiful lamenting climax. *Three Medieval Carols* show a mature style and wider technical range. The third opens with dramatic bell-like exclamations, a device recurring like an incantation in the openings of many later works such as *Hodie Salvator Apparuit*.

In the first of *Three Medieval Carols*, "Out of Your Sleep", the voices sing "Ah" in measured timings and the pitches vary with slow glissandos, merging into "nowell, nowell". This aleatoric technique suits the musical purpose here and recurs in many later works. His work *David* approaches the dimensions of the English oratorio, ending with a triumphant paen and massive Alleluias. This dramatic style suggested a move towards music-theatre, hence the children's opera *The Split Goose Feather*.

He began setting secular English nature poems, with instrumental accompaniments (*The Snows of Winter*) which led to his purely instrumental music. Yet he showed an awareness of new trends in Christian worship in the 1960s and 1970s—the use of congregational parts in services as in his *Oundle Jubilate* and *Hexham Mass*.

He also wrote works for the increasingly popular combination of voice and guitar, such as *All Year Round*. Then Brown turned to many instrumental works—a *Trio, Chamber Music, Sonata for Strings* and *String Quartet No 2*.

The Sun Rising, a strongly impressive orchestral threnody, was reviewed as "very powerful and brilliantly orchestrated", his orchestral technique growing with each work. Similarly his orchestral *Triptych* was praised by the *Musical Times* as "richly inventive, colourful and complex."

Brown then wrote many choral works, *Chauntecleer* (for children), *Tres Cantus Sacri* and *Magnificat*. This is intended to be a companion to Bach's *Magnificat* and is scored for the same performers. The Bach influence is again heard in *The Vision of Saul* (which quotes from Bach's cantatas and *The St Matthew Passion*).

More recently Brown has written a major work *From the Doorways of the Dawn*, songs mirroring American Indian texts. He has collaborated with Bob Devereux in *Landscapes* on the subject of man's relationships with the environment, and *Seascape*, exploring man's relationship with the sea; similar themes are also found in the operas *The Ram King* and *The Two Lockets*. Brown continues to write instrumental works, and has written two works for string orchestra—*Festival Variations* and *Into the Sun*.

Brown's music is communicative and vivid. He is flexible in responding to commissions, to which he brings commitment and craftsmanship.

His is an independent voice. Brown rejects fashion and his achievements are already considerable. As *Music and* Musicians wrote, "His music generally radiates an ingenuous spirit of joy, which is to be welcomed".

—Michael Dawney

BROWN, Earle (Appleton), Jr. American. Born in Lunenburg, Massachusetts, 26 December 1926. Educated at Northeastern University, Boston (mathematics and engineering), 1944–5; Schillinger School (Schillinger techniques of composition and orchestration), New York City, 1946–50; studied composition with Roslyn Brogue Henning, 1947–50. Teacher of Schillinger technique, Denver, Colorado, 1950–2; associate composer (with John Cage and David Tudor), Project for Music for Magnetic Tape, New York City, 1952–5; recording engineer and editor, Capitol Records, 1955–60; artistic director, "Contemporary Sound Series", Time-Mainstream Records, since 1960; composer in residence, Peabody Conservatory of Music, Baltimore, Maryland, 1968–70, 1971–2; composer in residence, Kunstler Programm, Berlin, 1970–1, Rotterdam Conservatory, 1974, California Institute of the Arts, 1974–83; Aspen Music Festival, Colorado, 1975, 1981, and Basel Conservatory, 1975; visiting professor, State University of New York, Buffalo, 1975, University of California, Berkeley, 1976, and Yale University, New Haven, Connecticut, 1980–1; guest conductor, Saarbrücken Rundfunk orchestra, 1981. Recipient: Guggenheim Fellowship, 1965–6; award of National Institute of Arts and Letters, 1972; Brandeis University Creative Arts Award, 1977. Mailing address: c/o I.C.I., 799 Broadway, Suite 642, New York, New York 10003, U.S.A.

Publishers: Associated; Schott; Universal.

Symphonies/orchestral:

Indices (concert version of ballet suite; chamber orchestra) 1954.
Light Music (large orchestra, lights, electronics) 1961.
Available Forms I (small orchestra) 1961.
Available Forms II (large orchestra, 2 conductors) 1962.
Modules I–II 1966.
Module III 1969.
Sign Sounds (small orchestra) 1972.
Time Spans (large orchestra) 1972.
Centering (violin, chamber orchestra) 1973.
Cross Sections and Colour Fields 1975.
Sounder Rounds 1982; first performed Saarbrücken, Germany, 12 May 1983.

Chamber/instrumental:

Fugue (piano) 1949.
Home Burial (piano) 1949.
Trio (clarinet, bassoon, piano) 1949.
Passacaglia (piano) 1950.
Strata (2 pianos) 1950.
String Quartet 1950.
Three Pieces (piano) 1951.
Perspectives (piano) 1952.
Music for Violin, Cello and Piano 1952. Recorded Mainstream 5007.
Folio (consists of *October 1952, November 1952 (Synergy), December 1952, MM 87, MM 135, Music for Trio for Five Dancers*; unspecified instrumentation) 1953; arranged for chamber ensemble 1981.
Twenty-Five Pages (1–25 pianos) 1953; first performed New York City, 14 April 1954.
Four Systems (unspecified instrumentation) 1954, arranged for chamber ensemble 1981.
Music for Cello and Piano 1954–5.
Four More (piano) 1956.
Pentathis (flute, bass clarinet, trumpet, trombone, harp, piano quartet) 1957–8.
Hodograph I (flute, piano/celeste, bells/vibraphone/marimba) 1959.
Novara (flute, bass clarinet, trumpet, trombone, harp, piano quartet) 1962. Recorded CRI 330.
Times Five (flute, trombone, harp, violin, cello, 4-track tape) 1963. Recorded CRI 330.

Calder Piece (4 percussion; with sculptural mobile) 1963–6.
Corroboree (3/2 pianos) 1964. Recorded Mainstream 5000.
Nine Rarebits (1/2 pianos) 1965. Recorded Wergo.
String Quartet 1965 1965. Recorded Mainstream 5009.
Event; Synergy II (11 woodwind, 8 strings) 1967–8.
Syntagm III (flute, bass clarinet, vibraphone, marimba, harp, piano/celeste, violin, cello) 1970.
Folio II (unspecified instrumentation) 1981.
Tracer (flute, oboe, bassoon, violin, double bass, 4-track tape) 1984; first performed Berlin, 8 February 1985.

Vocal/choral:

Tender Buttons (speaker, flute, horn, harp; Stein) 1953.
From Here (4 sopranos, 4 altos, 4 tenors, 4 basses, small orchestra) 1963.
Small Pieces for Large Chorus 1969–70.
New Piece Loops (part of projected *Folio II*; choir, small orchestra) 1971–2.
Windsor Jamba (Transients) (mezzo-soprano vocalise, flute, clarinet, piano, percussion, violin, viola, cello) 1980.

Other:

Octet I (8 tapes) 1952–3.
Indices (ballet) 1954.
Octet II (8 tapes) 1957.

PUBLICATIONS

On Brown: John Cage, in *Silence*, Middletown, Connecticut, 1961, 1966, in *A Year from Monday*, New York, 1967, and in *Notations*, New York, 1969; interview in Chase, *The American Composer Speaks*, Baton Rouge, Louisiana, 1966; Michael Nyman, in *Experimental Music: Cage and Beyond*, London, 1974; Rosenberg and Rosenberg, "EB", in *The Music Makers*, New York City, 1979; P.L. Quist, "Indeterminate Form in the Works of EB", dissertation, Peabody Conservatory of Music, 1984.

* * *

Earle Brown, Jr is a rare example of a composer who uses extra-musical references without sacrificing the musicality or humanity of his work. He has employed visual metaphors relating to 20th-century art, the work of sculptor Alexander Calder and painter Jackson Pollock in particular.

What intrigued Brown in the work of Calder was the mobility of its form. The work has a unique identity, but never appears the same way twice; it exists as a determinate assembly of materials and as a set of limitations on their juxtapositions. "There are", as Brown said, "basic units subject to innumerable different relations or forms".

His first attempts at a musical equivalent, such as the *Music for Violin, Cello and Piano*, are conventionally notated, equivalent to mobiles frozen into one position, "one static version of compositionally mobile elements".

Various pieces of the *Folio*, written only a year later, take over the principle of mobility more literally, and with greater success. The *Twenty-Five Pages* for piano may be read either side up; the eponymous pages may be played in any order; the twin-stave systems can be read in treble or bass clef; and the duration of each system is decided by the performer.

Pollock was of interest to Brown because of the spontaneity and immediacy of his creation. As with the principle of mobility, Brown's investigation of musical spontaneity moved through different stages. Brown attempted in writing *MM87* and *MM135* to compose "very rapidly and spontaneously and . . . in that sense" they were "performances rather than compositions". He then attempted to transfer that spontaneity to the performance situation. In *From Here* for chorus and orchestra, the two conductors are provided with scored materials whose sequence is not predetermined, and the choices of the chorus conductor take into account those of his orchestra counterpart. "The performance conditions of these works", Brown remarks, "are similar to a painter working spontaneously with a given palette".

Although Brown relates mobile and open form to Calder and Pollock, his aim is not to give an effect identical to visual works, nor to depict them aurally. For example, there is a difference between mobility in music, when sections come up in sequence as a result of live decisions, as against visual mobility when the whole work is immediately visible in a position determined by air currents. Brown was simply inspired by his mentors' working processes. He comments: "Comparisons are extremely dangerous and I emphasise that it is to the nature of the working process and the 'mobility' of the formal possibilities that I refer, not to the quality or effect of the results". The only wryly literal exception to this caveat is his *Calder Piece*, which uses a Calder mobile with four percussionists surrounding it as both a mechanical conductor and a sound source.

Brown's other innovations include time, since called proportional, notation and graphic notation. Part of the *Folio* series, *December 1952*, is the first completely graphic score, unless one goes tenuously back to the staffless neumes of the Middle Ages. Its monochrome quadrilaterals, reminiscent of Mondrian, cite modern art quite directly. A folio is, after all, a graphic artist's as much as a musician's showcase.

Despite his visual metaphors and notational experiments, Brown's results are distinctly musical. If he departs from his role as composer he points it out emphatically. The *Folio* extends the definitions of composition "as far out of normal realms as I could . . . just short of producing nothing at all". *December 1952*, for instance, is not music, but becomes music in performance; it is "not my work (only my idea for a work)".

The material he writes takes into account its open form use. To work effectively, furthermore, open-form music requires musical acuity and a thorough knowledge of the score.

Brown's works avoid the automatism of post-Webernian serial music and the transcendental austerity of Cage to engage the human ambiguities of their performers. "I prefer that each 'final form', which each performance necessarily produces, be a collaborative adventure, and that the work and its conditions of human involvement remain a 'living' potential of engagement". It thus embodies the uncertainties of life itself. "To balance . . . somewhere between determinism and anarchy . . . is probably basic to the nature of man", suggests Brown. "What interests me is to find the degree of conditioning . . . which will balance the work between the points of control and noncontrol . . . There is no final solution to this paradox . . . which is why art is".

—David Revill

BRUMBY, Colin (James). Australian. Born in Melbourne, 18 June 1933. Educated at Melbourne Boys' High School;

Melbourne University Conservatorium of Music, 1954–6, B.Mus., diploma of education, 1957, D.Mus., 1971; course in advanced musical composition and choral conducting, Santiago de Compostela, Spain, 1962; studied advanced composition, London, 1962–4; studied orchestral conducting, 1963–4; studied advanced composition, Rome, 1972–3; studied computer music, Stanford University, California, 1974. Military service in 2nd Field Artillery (Reserve), 1954. Married Jennifer Rae Dawson, 3 December 1983. Organist and choir master, St Oswald's Church of England, Glen Iris, Victoria, 1950–3; musical director, Camerata Quartet, Melbourne, 1954–6; musical director, Victorian Chamber Players, 1956; musical director, South Melbourne Symphony Orchestra, 1957; musical director, Sunshine High School, Melbourne, 1957–9; head of music, Kelvin Grove Teacher's College, Brisbane, 1960–2, and Greenford Grammar School, Middlesex, England, 1963–4; lecturer in music, 1964–6, and associate professor, since 1977, University of Queensland, Brisbane; musical director, 1966–8, 1977–86, senior lecturer, 1966–77, and head of music department, 1975–80, Queensland University Musical Society; musical director, Vocal Arts Ensemble, Brisbane, 1968; musical director, Queensland Opera Company, 1969–71; also baritone soloist/accompanist/duettist with wife, soprano Jenny Dawson; guest broadcaster, Australian Broadcasting Corporation. Recipient: Albert Maggs Award for musical composition, 1968; Advance Australia Award for Services to Music, 1981; Don Banks Fellowship, 1990; Australian Performing Rights Association Award for Most Performed Australasian Serious Work (for *Oboe Concertino*), 1990. Mailing address: 9 Teague Street, Indooroopilly, Queensland 4068, Australia.

Publishers: J. Albert & Sons, Allans, Asmuse (all Australia); York Editions, Fentone, Cambridge University Press, Ricordi (all U.K.); Walton's, Jenson's, Aberdeen Music; Lyra Music (all U.S.A.).

Symphonies/orchestral:

Concerto for Viola and Strings 1960; first performed Brisbane, 1960.
Antipodea (2 movements for orchestra) 1962; first performed Adelaide, 1962. Recorded ABC 40528.
Partite (clarinet, strings) 1962; first performed Brisbane, 20 June 1962. Recorded ABC 40564.
Fibonacci Variations 1964; first performed Adelaide, 1964. Recorded ABC 40528.
Mediterranean Suite (folk song arrangements) 1964; first performed Queensland, 4 January 1965.
Violin Concerto No 1 1969; first performed Brisbane, 28 February 1970.
Litanies of the Sun 1970; first performed Brisbane, 28 May 1971. Recorded ABC 1470.
The Phoenix and the Turtle 1974; first performed Canberra, 6 October 1974. Recorded EMI (Aus) OASD 430003.
French Horn Concerto 1974; first performed Brisbane, 2 April 1975.
Flute Concerto 1976; first performed Brisbane, 23 February 1977. Recorded EMI (Aus) OASD 4300003.
Entradas (for Stravinsky's 86th birthday) 1978. Recorded ABC 40564.
Musagettes 1978; first performed Brisbane, 2 October 1978.
Festival Overture on Australian Themes 1981; first performed Adelaide, 17 February 1982. Recorded Festival L38547.
Symphony No 1 1982; first performed Brisbane, 7 April 1982.
Paean 1982; first performed Sydney, 3 July 1982.
Violin Concerto No 2 1983; first performed Brisbane, August 1983.
Bassoon Concerto 1983; first performed Adelaide, 16 November 1983.
South Bank Overture 1984; first performed Brisbane, 23 April 1985.
Guitar Concerto 1985; first performed Brisbane, 22 May 1985.
Piano Concerto 1985; first performed Perth, 17 September 1985.
Oboe Concertino 1987; first performed Brisbane, 29 June 1987. Recorded Australian Music Centre CD.
Clarinet Concerto 1988; first performed Brisbane, 21 July 1989.
Scena for Cor Anglais and Strings 1988.

Chamber/instrumental:

Declamations (flute, oboe, piano) 1960s.
Four Exotic Pieces (flute, harp) 1961; first performed Brisbane, 1961.
Four Miniatures (flute, piano) 1961; first performed Brisbane, 16 December 1961.
Quintette (wind instruments) 1964; first performed Brisbane, 13 September 1967.
Four Antiphons (organ) 1964; first performed Brisbane, 1964.
String Quartet 1969; first performed Adelaide, 1975. Recorded ABC AC 1051.
Doubles (piano) 1970–1; first performed London, 1972.
Player Chooses (3 instruments, keyboard) 1973; first performed Sydney, 1973.
Four Duos (2 clarinets) 1975.
Chiaroscuro (clarinet, cello, piano) 1977; first performed Brisbane, 1978.
Antistrophe (piano) 1978; first performed Adelaide, 12 June 1978.
Suite (4 double basses) 1978; first performed Aldeburgh, Suffolk, 1980. Recorded Musica Viva MV 30-1076.
Haydn Down Under (bassoon, string quartet) 1980; first performed Brisbane, 1980.
Demotica (piano) 1980; first performed Brisbane, 10 October 1980.
The Seven Ages of Man (wind quintet, optional narration) 1981; first performed Sydney, 16 February 1982.
Improvisation (organ) 1981; first performed Brisbane, 16 December 1981.
Sonatina (clarinet, piano) 1982; first performed Sydney, May 1983.
Sonata (bassoon, piano) 1984; first performed Adelaide, 31 March 1985.
Fair and Flexi (music for melody and bass instruments with chords) 1984.
Piano Quartet 1985; first performed Brisbane, 10 May 1985.
Sonatina (flute, piano) 1985; first performed Brisbane, September 1985.
Four Aphorisms (clarinet, piano) 1986.
Mundoolun (cor anglais, piano) 1988; first performed Manchester, 1989.
Borromeo Suite (flute, guitar) 1990.
Harlequinade (piano) n.d.

Vocal/choral:

The Cloths of Heaven (SSA choir, piano) 1958.
Bonnie George Campbell (SA choir, piano) 1959.
Five-Part Songs (male voices) 1961; first performed Brisbane, 1961. Recorded ABC 40564.

Magnificat and Nunc Dimittis (unaccompanied SATB choir) 1961; first performed Brisbane, 1961.
Three Pastorals (medium voice, flute, harp; Sitzky) 1961.
Nel mio orto (medium voice, piano) 1964.
Dormi Jesus (unaccompanied SATB choir) 1965.
Andy's Gone with Cattle (unaccompanied SATB/SA) 1966.
Three Italian Songs (high voice, string quartet) 1968; first performed Adelaide, 1968. Recorded Festival SFC 80024.
Gilgamesh (narrator, SATB choir, brass, percussion; Shapcott) 1968; first performed Adelaide, 1968. Recorded ABC 40564.
Charlie Bubble's Book of Hours (soprano, mezzo-soprano, tenor, baritone, SATB chorus, orchestra) 1969; first performed Brisbane, 1969. Recorded Festival SFC 80024.
Bring Out Your Christmas Masks (soprano, mezzo-soprano, tenor, baritone, SATB chorus, dancers, actors, orchestra, organ) 1969; first performed Brisbane, 10 December 1969.
Ballade for St Cecilia (soprano, mezzo-soprano, tenor, baritone, SATB chorus, orchestra) 1970; first performed Adelaide, 1971. Recorded ABC RRCS 1467.
The Virgin and the Child (unaccompanied SATB choir) 1970. Recorded ABC RRCS-1470A.
A Windy Beach (3 solo singers, 3 groups of speakers, 1st and 2nd descant recorders, piano duet, percussion; Shapcott) 1970.
Celebrations and Lamentations (4 SATB choirs, wind, brass, percussion) 1972; first performed Brisbane, 25 May 1972. Recorded 23rd Inter-varsity Choral Festival disc.
This Is the Vine (soprano, alto, tenor, baritone, SATB choir, orchestra; Shapcott) 1972; first performed Melbourne, 24 February 1973.
Bess Songs (soprano, flute, guitar, tape; Shapcott) 1973; first performed Sydney, 29 October 1973.
God Be in My Head (SA choir, organ) 1973.
I Tarocchi (SATB choir, 2 pianos, percussion; Shapcott) 1975; first performed Adelaide, 13 December 1975.
Five English Lyrics ("Balow", "Tune Thy Music", "The Nut-Brown Maid", "O My Deir Heart", "Love Is Soft"; SATB choir, piano) 1975.
Mass (unison voices, organ) 1975.
Richard de Castre's Prayer to Jesus (unaccompanied SATB choir) 1976. Recorded ABC RCCS-1470A.
Te Deum (unison choir, organ) 1976.
Flood Valley (choir; Shapcott) 1977; first performed Adelaide, 7 October 1977.
The Carol Book ("Lully, Lulley", "In Excelsis Gloria", "Behold a Silly Tender Babe", "Nowell, Nowell", "Adam Lay Ybounden", "Jesu, Son Most Sweet and Dear", "Lord When the Wise Men"; SATB choir, piano) 1977.
The Round Book (original and traditional texts; SATB choir, piano) 1977.
Orpheus Beach (soprano, baritone, orchestra; Shapcott) 1978; first performed Brisbane, 10 October 1978.
Victimae paschali (SATB choir, string orchestra) 1978; first performed Brisbane, 29 April 1979.
Christmas Carols (15 carols in English, French, Latin; SATB choir, piano/organ) from 1978.
Motet and Mass: O sacrum convivium (SATB choir) 1978.
The English Songs ("Goe and Catche a Falling Starre", "Threnos", "The Lark Now Leaves His Watery Nest", "Come, Come, What Do I Here?", "The Souldier Going to the Field"; medium voice, piano) 1979; first performed Sydney, 1979.
Three Baroque Angels (SATB choir, orchestra; Shapcott) 1979; first performed Brisbane, 1979.
Fresca rosa novella / Quel rosignuol / Di giugno (high voice, piano) 1980; first performed Brisbane, 11 September 1980.
Mare (soprano; Fyleman) 1980; first performed Brisbane, December 1980.
Pater's Bathe (voice; Parry) 1981.
Liebesliederbuchlein ("Wie schon blut uns", "Eine Dunkle Wolk", "Ich Gib mich"; medium voice, piano) 1982; first performed Brisbane, 19 April 1983.
Amarilli (SATB choir; arrangement of aria by Caccini) 1982.
Jock o'Dreams (baritone; Fyleman) 1982; first performed Brisbane, 1982.
Heinz von Stein (baritone, piano; Leland) 1982; first performed Brisbane, 1982.
Music, When Soft Voices Die (baritone, piano; Shelley) 1982; first performed Brisbane, 1982.
Three Songs from a Spanish Madrigal (high voice, piano) 1983; first performed Brisbane, 23 October 1983.
Four Romantic Choruses (unaccompanied SATB chorus) 1983.
Three Songs ("Arabia", "Tom-a-Bedlam's song", "The Music Makers"; baritone, guitar) 1983; first performed Brisbane, 1983.
Flexi Scores ("Can't You Dance the Polka?", "Brumby's Run", "Threnos", "The Sailor's Consolation", "Ah, How Can I Depart?", "O Shepherds Leave Your Sheep", "A Rosebud in June", "An Eriskay Love Lilt", "Andy's Gone with Cattle", "A Round of Mix-Ups", "Because the Rose") 1983.
Nine Canons ("Drop, Drop, Slow Tears", "He That Is Down", "Who Would True Valour See", "Litany to the Holy Spirit", "Lord, We Give Thanks", "From All That Dwell/Psalm 117", "Bless Us, Lord", "My Soul, There Is a Country", "God Be in My Head"; 2-part choir, piano) 1983.
Three Lenten Motets ("Priusque gallus cantet", "Tu es Christus?", "Crucifigi eum!"; SATB choir, piano/organ) 1983; first performed Brisbane, 28 March 1983.
Close Thine Eyes (SATB choir, organ) 1983.
Festival Mass (SATB choir, wind, brass, percussion) 1984; first performed Brisbane, 11 August 1984.
Eight Anthems ("Jerusalem", "Lift Up Your Voices", "The Love of Christ", "Litany to the Holy Spirit", "The Greatness of the Lord", "My Soul, There Is a Country", "This Is the Truth", "Let Christians Rejoice"; unaccompanied SATB choir) 1984.
Chanson de Berberine (high voice, piano) 1984; first performed Brisbane, 18 September 1984.
A Poor Young Shepherd (high voice, piano; Verlaine) 1984.
Songs of the Sea ("The Sailor's Consolation", "Ships of Old Renown", "Sea Fever", "To Sea! To Sea!", "A Song of Desire", "A Wet Sheet and a Flowing Sea", "Two Chronometers", "His Heart Was True to Poll", "El Capitan-General", "The Walloping Window Blind", "The Hag", "Sea Foam", "A Gray Day", "Lost and Given Over", "Break, Break, Break!", "The Port o'Heart's Desire"; solo, unison, 2-part song, piano) 1984. Recorded ABC 4053.
Folk Songs of Australia ("The Ballad of 1891", "Ben Hall", "Death of Ned Kelly", "Freedom on the Wallaby", "Gallant Peter Clarke", "The Journeyman Tailor", "Ladies of Brisbane", "The Lime Juice Tub", "Moreton Bay", "The Rambling Sailor", "Van Diemen's Land", "Wild Rover", "With My Swag All on My Shoulder") 1984.
The Vision and the Gap (soprano, alto, tenor, baritone; Shapcott) 1984.
Psalm 148 (choir, band) 1984; first performed Brisbane, 11 August 1984.
Great Is Truth and Mighty Above All Things (baritone, solo, SATB choir, orchestra) 1985; first performed Brisbane, 10 May 1985.

A Service of Rounds (SATB choir) 1985.
Christmas Bells (unaccompanied SATB choir) 1985; first performed Europe, 1985.
Stabater mater dolorosa (soprano, baritone, string trio) 1986; first performed Brisbane, 1986.
Four Australian Christmas Carols (SATB choir, piano; original texts) 1986.
Magnificat and Nunc Dimittis (SSA choir, piano/organ) 1987.
The Ballad of Sydney Hospital (soprano, baritone, SATB choir, orchestra; Shapcott) 1988; first performed Sydney, 15 November 1988. Recorded MBS 18 CD.
The Ballad of Charlie Blow (SAB/SSA choirs, orchestra) 1988; first performed Sydney, 1988.
Inheritance (cantata for 3 choirs, verse-speaking choir, orchestra; Shapcott) 1990.

Also: *Songs from the House at Pooh Corner* (soprano, piano; Milne); *Charm Me Asleep* (unaccompanied SATB choir); *Fugues Are Fun* (unaccompanied SABar choir); *Gold* (unaccompanied SATB canon); *Signs of Rain* (unaccompanied SATB choir); *A Receipt for Salad* (unaccompanied SATB choir); *Carmen* (unaccompanied SATB choir); *Five White Swans* (unaccompanied SATB choir); *The Wind Is Rising* (SATB choir, piano; Shapcott); *When Whispering Strains* (unaccompanied SATB choir); *Drink Today* (unaccompanied SATB choir); *The Part-Song Book* (unaccompanied SATB choir).

Opera:

The Seven Deadly Sins 1970; first performed Brisbane, 12 September 1970.
The Marriage Machine 1971; first performed Sydney, 28 January 1972.
La Donna (libretto by Goddard) 1986.
Lorenzaccio (after de Musset) 1986–7.
Fire on the Wind (after Coburn) 1990.
Summer Carol (Shapcott) 1990.

Other:

Bunyip (television ballet; symphony orchestra) 1966; first performed Brisbane, 1966.
Rita and Dita (operetta for children) 1968; first performed Brisbane, 1968.
The Wise Shoemaker (operetta for children) 1968; first performed Brisbane, 1968.
Rita and Dita and the Pirate (operetta for children) 1969; first performed Brisbane, 1969.
The Prince Who Couldn't Laugh (operetta for children) 1969; first performed Brisbane, 1969.
The Two Suitors (operetta for children) 1970; first performed Brisbane, 1970.
Rita and Dita in Toyland (operetta for children) 1970; first performed Brisbane, 1970.
Rita and Dita and the Jolly Swagman (operetta for children) 1971; first performed Brisbane, 1971.
Cinderella (ballet arrangements of Rossini) 1975; first performed Brisbane, 10 December 1975.
Those Who Are Compelled (radio; orchestra, 3 speakers, 2 baritones) 1979; first performed Brisbane, 1979.
The Phoenix and the Turtle (incidental music) 1984; first performed Brisbane, 1985.
Hippolytus (incidental music to Euripides; organ, percussion, guitars, flute, oboe, mixed chorus) 1980; first performed Clayton, Victoria, 25 June 1980.
Masques (ballet music) 1980; first performed Brisbane, 18 August 1980.
Alice in Wonderland (ballet) 1987.
Capital Canberra (film score; small orchestra).
Follow the Leader (film score; recorder, guitar, cello).

PUBLICATIONS

By Brumby: *The Art of Producing the Musical Tone*, Brisbane, 1968; "Touring in the Outback", in *Opera News*, 34 (11), 10 January 1970; "Australia—A Survey", in *Schriften des Instituts für Asienkunde in Hamburg*, 27, Wiesbaden, 1970; "Conference", in *Musical Times*, 114, January 1973.

On Brumby: P. Bracanin, "CB", in *Australian Composition in the Twentieth Century*, edited by Calloway and Tunley, Melbourne, 1976.

Colin Brumby comments:

My early training and musical experiences were of the traditional kind, and it was not until a student at the Conservatorium that I first heard and was seduced by the music of Schoenberg. My development as a composer was shaped by this experience and it was not until 1972 when spending a year in Rome that I found myself in a *cul de sac* beyond which lay silence. This was not to my liking and it meant rejoining the mainstream of music and having to forge at that late stage a style that took account of the very parameters that the method of composing with twelve notes failed to take into account. I found myself, therefore, (and *The Phoenix and the Turtle* was the work in which this occurred) reappraising tonality and since that time have happily embraced that style of writing. In view of this, it will not surprise anyone to notice that my works place great emphasis on melody as the principal means of expression, and a harmony in which the notes *do* matter.

* * *

The splendour of liturgical services attracted Colin Brumby into church choirs during his school days, and consequently early influences upon his music were the great choral masterpieces of both the Anglican and Catholic church repertoire. His experiences as performer and conductor with church and school choirs and orchestras gave him a tendency to consider the performer's point of view which has never left him. His earliest compositions are tonal with traditional harmonies, using voices and instruments in a conventional and idiomatic manner. Another early and enduring influence was music of the Mediterranean, often manifest in his use of modes: the *Mediterranean Suite* is an arrangement for string orchestra of traditional melodies.

Although Brumby experimented with serial techniques during his student days, it was not until the 1960s that he embarked seriously upon investigation and employment of the twelve-tone method. His first large-scale work in this style was *Partite* for clarinet and strings, followed by others including the orchestral *Fibonacci Variations*. He also explored aleatory composition in works such as *Player Chooses* and Sonnets and Sonnetti. However, during this period Brumby also wrote tonal music, including several one-act operas for children.

The Phoenix and the Turtle for strings and harpsichord signalled the composer's final disenchantment with atonality; he had come to believe that such music held little fulfilment for himself, the performer or the audience. The work marks a personal rejection of serial and aleatoric philosophies: later pieces have used these methods merely to achieve a particular effect. An example is the final movement of the wind quintet *The Seven Ages of Man*, based on the text from Shakespeare's *As You Like It*, where "second childishness and mere oblivion" are signified by twelve-tone writing.

Certain features are characteristic of Brumby's works, both tonal and atonal. His writing is strongly melodic, a property which can be discerned even in his dodecaphonic compositions; there is inventive use of polyphony, noticeably in the orchestral pieces. He espouses Schoenberg's principle of development through continuous motivic variation. Formal organisation is strong, with use of Baroque and Classical forms such as sonata, fugue, canon, rondo, theme and variation; rounds feature in the choral works. Two 1984 compositions are deliberately modelled, in form, upon existing works: the *Piano Concerto* is formally identical with Beethoven's *Piano Concerto No 5 ("Emperor")*, while the *Piano Quartet* derives its form from the *Piano Quintet in A Major* of Dvořák.

Any discussion of Brumby's music must mention his extraordinarily fruitful collaboration with the writer Thomas Shapcott, who has provided the libretti for two operas and some dozen major choral works.

While many of Brumby's compositions are commissioned, some were written to fill a perceived lacuna: either in the repertoire as a whole, or in the composer's own output. Typical of the former are the *Oboe Concertino* and *Scena for Cor Anglais and Strings*, and of the latter *Symphony No 1 ("The Sun")* and a host of smaller works, often written for relaxation during the composition of larger pieces. As the lacunae are filled, commissions form a greater proportion of Brumby's writing. Many of these are celebratory: *This Is the Vine* for the 40th International Eucharistic Congress, *Paean* for the Australian Broadcasting Corporation's 50th anniversary, *The Vision and the Gap* for the 75th anniversary of the University of Queensland, *South Bank Overture* for the opening of the Queensland Cultural Centre, *The Ballad of Sydney Hospital* for the hospital's bicentenary. Writing for very specific conditions and forces has given Brumby expertise in accommodating capabilities ranging from those of school choirs and beginner instrumentalists to those of virtuoso performers.

—Jenny Dawson

BRYARS, (Richard) Gavin. British/English. Born in Goole, Yorkshire, 16 January 1943. Educated at Goole Grammar School, 1954–61; University of Sheffield (philosophy), 1961–4, B.A.; Northern School of Music, 1964–6; studied composition privately with Cyril Ramsey, 1954–61, George Linstead, 1961–6, Benjamin Johnston, 1968. Married Angela Margaret Bigley, 22 January 1971 (dissolved); 2 daughters. Double bass player in various improvising groups, including Joseph Holbrooke; music teacher, Drax Grammar School, Yorkshire, 1965–6; lecturer in liberal studies, Northampton College of Technology, 1966–7; lecturer, Portsmouth College of Art, 1969–70; founder/member, Portsmouth Sinfonia, 1970; lecturer, 1970–83, principal lecturer, 1983—5, and professor of music, since 1985, Leicester Polytechnic. Recipient: British Ambassador for the Fondation Erik Satie; member, College 'Pataphysique, since 1974; member, Oulipopo, 1974. Mailing address: c/o Erica Bolton & Jane Quinn, 15 Prebend Gardens, London W4 1TN, England.

Publisher: self.

Symphonies/orchestral:

Second Suite from "Irma" (piano, string orchestra) 1978.
Three Studies on Medea (2 pianos, marimba, 2 vibraphones, bells, cymbal, clarinet, tenor horn, strings) 1983.
Eglisak (version for chamber orchestra) 1984–5; first performed Strasbourg, 10 October 1985.
By the Vaar (double bass, string orchestra, bass clarinet, percussion) 1987; first performed London, 6 April 1987.

Chamber/instrumental:

Mr Sunshine (any number of keyboards, including 1 prepared piano) 1968; first performed Kingston, Surrey, 13 December 1968.
The Sinking of the Titanic (indeterminate, but possible materials include 2 stereo tapes, 4-part string ensemble, percussion, 2 low brass, brass quintet, cassette tape of speech, piano, harmonium, slides, visible sound effects, music box) 1969; first performed London, 1972. Recorded Editions EG EGED21; Les Disques du Crépuscule TWI 027.
Pre-Medieval Metrics (unspecified ensemble) 1970; broadcast November 1970.
The Ride Cymbal and the Band That Caused the Fire in the Sycamore Trees (1 or 2 prepared pianos) 1970; first performed London, 9 October 1970.
1, 2, 1–2–3–4 (ensemble) 1971; first performed Liverpool, 1971. Recorded Editions EG EGED22.
The Squirrel and the Rickety Rackety Bridge (2 players each with 2 guitars) 1971; first performed London, December 1972. Recorded Incus 2; Editions EG EGED28.
Jesus' Blood Never Failed Me Yet (ensemble, tape) 1971; first performed London, December 1972. Recorded Editions EG EGED21.
A Place in the Country (53 or 24 similar instruments in large outdoor space) 1972.
Long Players (3 strings; piano) 1975; first performed Keele, Staffordshire, 16 November 1983.
Ponukelian Melody 1975; original version for tuba, harmonium, tubular bells, voice—first performed London, 15 May 1975; version for bells, marimba, timpani, violin, reed organ, piano, double bass—first performed Birmingham, 5 November 1981; version for 2 pianos—first performed Amsterdam, 26 January 1980; arrangement by Andrew Thomson for bells, marimba, tuba, string quartet, piano—first performed London, 21 June 1984.
White to Play (and Win) (percussion trio, music box) 1976; first performed Brussels, 1 February 1976.
Tra-La-La-Lira-Lira-Lay (ensemble; formerly entitled *Detective Fiction and Related Subjects*) 1976; first performed Antwerp, 15 May 1976.
The Perfect Crime (2 pianos, tape, percussion, optional slides) 1977; first performed Brussels, 1 April 1977.
First Suite from "Irma" (2 pianos) 1977; Brussels, 2 April 1977.
White's SS (2 pianos) 1977; first performed Amsterdam, 10 June 1977; version for 2 pianos—4 hands, 3 players at 1 marimba, optional tuba first performed Paris, 16 November 1979.

R + 7 (percussion duo) 1977; first performed Utrecht, Netherlands, 12 June 1977.

Poggioli in Zaleski's Gazebo (piano, tuba, tuned percussion) 1977; first performed London, 1 November 1977.

Out of Zaleski's Gazebo (2 pianos—6 or 8 hands) 1977; first performed Louvain, Belgium, 12 December 1977.

Danse Dieppoise 1978; original version for harmonium, tuba, piano, vibes—first performed Amsterdam, 15 April 1978; version for harmonium, tuba, flute, clarinet, harpsichord.

My First Homage 1978; original version for 2 pianos—first performed New York City, 10 November 1978; version for 2 pianos, vibraphone (solo—4 hands, or 2 vibraphones)—first performed Paris, 16 November 1979; version for 2 saxophones, 2 vibraphones, piano, tuba, double bass, percussion—first performed Birmingham, 5 November 1981. Recorded Crepuscule TWI 027.

Ramsey's Lamp (2 pianos, 6 hands) 1979; first performed London, 4 February 1979.

Epsom Downs (percussion quartet) 1979; first performed Scraptoft, Leicester, 20 June 1979.

Sforzesco Sforzando (4 pianos) 1979; first performed Castello Sforzesco, Milan, 23 June 1979.

Epsom Downs Mark 2 (percussion duo) 1979.

The Cross Channel Ferry (elastic scoring: piano; 1 or 2 marimbas, or 1 marimba and 1 bass marimba, or 1 marimba and 1 vibraphone; viola and/or violin and/or treble viol, optional clarinet and/or 2nd violin; violin and/or bass clarinet and/or tuba, or double bass, optional steel drums and shakers) 1979; first performed Paris, 16 November 1979.

The Vespertine Park (1 or 2 pianos, 2 vibraphones or 1 vibraphone and 1 marimba or bass marimba/bells, optional steel drums and sizzle cymbal) 1980; first performed Paris, 25 October 1980. Recorded Crépuscule TWI 027.

The English Mail Coach (percussion quartet) 1980; first performed London, 23 April 1980. Recorded Crépuscule TWI 027.

After Mendelssohn (2 pianos) 1980; first performed Paris, 26 October 1980.

Hi-Tremolo (vibraphone, marimba or 2nd vibraphone, 2 pianos) 1980; first performed 26 October 1980. Recorded Crépuscule TWI 027.

Prolegomenon to "Medea" (clarinet, bass clarinet, marimba, bass marimba, violin, double bass, 2 casios, timpani) 1981; first performed Birmingham, 5 November 1981.

Allegrasco (soprano saxophone or clarinet, piano) 1983; first performed Leicester, 7 December 1983. Recorded ECM, release 1991.

2B (percussion ensemble; section from incomplete operatic collaboration with Robert Wilson, *Civil WarS*) 1983.

Les Fiancailles (2 pianos, 8 hands, string quintet, optional 2 vibraphones and sizzle cymbal; section form incomplete operatic collaboration with Robert Wilson, *Civil WarS*) 1983.

Eglisak (2 pianos, 2 violins, percussion) 1984–5; first performed Zurich, 28 April 1985.

Homage to Vivier (flute, clarinet, vibraphone, piano) 1985; first performed London, 1 July 1985.

String Quartet No 1 (Between the National and the Bristol) 1985; first performed Vienna, 8 October 1985. Recorded ECM New Series 1323 829484.

Viennese Dance No 1 (M.H.) (harmonium, string trio or string quartet, 6 percussion) 1985. Recorded ECM New Series 1323 829484.

Sketch for Sub Rosa (2 pianos) 1986.

Sub Rosa (ensemble) 1986; first performed Ghent, Belgium, 10 November 1986.

Pavanne (horn, violin, 3 percussion, double bass) 1986; first performed Paris, 20 November 1986.

The Old Tower of Lobenicht (piano/horn, bass clarinet, violin, bass, 2 percussion) 1987; first performed London, 13 June 1987.

Alaric I or II (2 soprano saxophones, alto saxophone, baritone saxophone) 1989; first performed Leicester, 3 October 1989. Recorded ECM, release 1991.

After the Requiem (guitar, string trio) 1990. Recorded in Oslo, 17–18 September 1990 for ECM, release 1991.

String Quartet No 2 1990; first performed Huddersfield, Yorkshire, 1 December 1990.

String Duo 1990; first performed Huddersfield, Yorkshire, November 1990.

Vocal/choral:

Ouse (2 singers) 1970; first performed York, 30 November 1984.

Ars Photographica (SATB chorus, harmonium, piano; section from incomplete operatic collaboration with Robert Wilson, *Civil WarS*) 1983.

Arias (for Marie Curie, The Queen of the Sea, Captain Nemo, The Japanese Bride; section from incomplete operatic collaboration with Robert Wilson, *Civil WarS*) 1983.

Effarene (soprano, mezzo-soprano, 4 pianos, 6 percussion; Marie Curie, Etel Adnam, Leo XIII, Verne) 1984; first performed London, 23 March 1984.

Pico's Flight (soprano, 2 flutes, piccolo, 2 oboe/cor anglais, 2 clarinet, bassoon, contrabassoon, 2 percussion, timpani, strings; Pico della Mirandola) 1985–6; first performed Egham, Surrey, 25 February 1986.

Glorious Hill (male alto, 2 tenors, baritone; Pico della Mirandola) 1988; first performed Lewes, Sussex, August 1988.

Dr Ox's Experiment (Epilogue) (soprano, 2 pianos, string quartet, bass, bass clarinet, 2 percussion including electric keyboard; Morrison, after Verne) 1988; first performed Bristol, 11 November 1988.

Incipit Vita Nova (male alto, violin, viola, cello; Dante, della Mirandola) 1989; first performed Leicester, 1 April 1989.

Cadman Requiem (vocal ensemble; traditional, Caedmon) 1989.

Opera:

Irma (opera realisation of work by Tom Phillips) 1977.

Medea (libretto after Euripides; design and direction by Robert Wilson; no violins in orchestra) 1982–4; first performed Lyon, France, 23 October 1984.

Other:

Made in Hong Kong (indeterminate) 1968; first performed London, February 1969; withdrawn.

The Music Lover's Portfolio (tape, live sounds) 1968; recorded London, 29 August 1968; withdrawn.

Marvellous Aphorisms Are Scattered Richly Through These Pages (theatre piece) 1969; first performed Cardiff, 6 November 1969.

A Must for All Sibelians (tape) 1969; first performed Helsinki, 1970.

Some of the Interesting Things You'll See on a Long-Distance Flight 1969.

Private Music 1969; first performed Cardiff, 1969.

Golders(as) Green by Eps(ups)om('n) Downs (indeterminate) 1969.

The Harp That Once Through Tara's Halls (low fidelity recording) 1970; imperfectly realised London, Summer 1970.
Serenely Beaming and Leaning on a Five-Barred Gate (private piece) 1970; first performed Portsmouth, Hampshire, 14 January 1970.
To Gain the Affections of Miss Dwyer Even for One Short Minute Would Benefit Me No End (electronic) 1970; first performed (privately and incompletely) Portsmouth, Hampshire, November 1970.
A Game of Football (for large spaces) 1970.
The Chair of BlaBlaBla (composed but not realised) 1971.
The Heat of the Beat (indeterminate) 1972.
Far Away and Dimly Pealing (indeterminate) 1972.
Sidescraper (dance piece for piano duet; choreography Christine Juffs) 1980; first performed September 1980.
Sixteen (dance tape; choreography by Christine Juffs) 1981.
Grey Windows (dance tape; choreography by Tony Thatcher) 1983; first performed Leicester, April 1983.
Hymne à la Rrose (fanfare for French village band; commissioned for unveiling of statue of Rrose Selavy in Rouen) 1984.
Summer and Smoke (incidental music to play by Tennessee Williams) 1987; first performed Leicester, September 1987.
Timon of Athens (music to Shakespeare) 1988; first performed Leicester, February 1988.
Easter (music to play by Strindberg) 1988; first performed Leicester, April 1988.
The Bells (theatre music) 1988; first performed Leicester, April 1988.
Invention of Tradition (music for opening of Tate Gallery, Liverpool; 2 organs, female choir, jazz alto saxophone, clarinet, bass clarinet, 4 percussion, 5 trombone, 2 euphonium, 2 tuba) 1988; first performed Liverpool, 24–6 May 1988.
Murders in the Rue Morgue (theatre music) 1989; first performed Leicester, December 1989.
The Crucible (theatre music) 1989–90; first performed Leicester, January 1990.
Four Elements (music for dance; choreography by Lucinda Childs) 1990; first performed Oxford, 16 November 1990.
A Winter's Tale (theatre music) 1990–1; first performed Leicester, January 1991.

PUBLICATIONS

By Bryars: "Notes on Marcel Duchamp's Music", in *Studio International*, 1975; *The Sinking of the Titanic*, score/documentation/realisation notes, in *Soundings*, 1975; catalogue to exhibition on Lord Berners, Como, 1979.

On Bryars: Keith Potter, "GB", in *Contact*, 22, 1981; Paul Griffiths, (interview) in *New Sounds, New Personalities: British Composers of the 1980s*, London, 1985.

* * *

Gavin Bryars is a major figure in British music whose reputation abroad is now being matched by increasing recognition in his own country. The qualities of irony and meta-irony lend a consistency to his output, but, notwithstanding that fact, it is possible roughly to divide his compositional career into three phases: the experimental years up to 1972; 1974 up to the staging of his opera *Medea* in 1984; and the subsequent years up to the present.

Throughout the 1960s Bryars was an active participant in the experimental tradition which can be traced back through the work of John Cage (with whom Bryars worked) to Erik Satie. British experimentalists tended to be based in art schools and it was at Portsmouth College of Art that Bryars founded the notorious Portsmouth Sinfonia whose members' lack of instrumental ability in no way hindered the seriousness with which they tackled the popular classics, often with unintentionally hilarious results. It was this element of ironic humour that distanced Bryars from the roughly contemporary Scratch Orchestra, whose Maoist zeal was incompatible with Bryars's approach to art (although he remains close friends with many of the key figures from the Scratch Orchestra). Bryars's compositions from this period are characterised by a certain "conceptual" content, a tendency to privacy, free association of ideas, a use of found material and some examination of his past experience as a jazz bass-player. Probably the most celebrated work is *The Sinking of the Titanic*, an open-form, perpetually unfinished piece begun in 1969. A performance unites the sounding elements of the celebrated marine disaster, painstakingly researched by Bryars, in a hypothetical extension of the last tune famously played by the ship's band, into eternity and underwater. The sounding results of this collage vary from performance to performance, but have nonetheless stabilised to some extent around a hyper-euphonious "wash" of slowed-down hymn tunes, some actually recorded underwater. The collage can have considerable psychological impact upon audiences and the work has been re-recorded as recently as 1990.

This phase of Bryars's work culminated, in 1972, in a two-year period during which he wrote no music, instead devoting himself to a study of Marcel Duchamp, the artist whose conceptual work prefigured experimentalism.

When Bryars reappeared as a composer he was armed with a Duchampian interest in the artificial, creating works of which he could boast that "every note was justified". Working with composers such as John White and Dave Smith, he formed a number of small ad-hoc ensembles, one of which toured England in 1981 and became a model for a number of ensembles which are still active, in particular "George W. Welch". Despite such public manifestations, Bryars was reluctant to classify himself as a "composer" at this time, preferring to model himself on the entity that was Marcel Duchamp. This tendency led to the admission of a wide-ranging collection of conceptual sources, including detective fiction, jazz, football and, above all, a certain area of French literature and art. *The Sinking of the Titanic* had made clear the 'pataphysical nature of Bryars's work and he developed this throughout the 1970s from within the Collège de 'pataphysique.

Bryars's reluctance to produce large numbers of musical "dots" was set aside in the early 1980s with the commissioning of an opera, *Medea*, to be directed by the American Robert Wilson, and staged in 1984 at the Operas de Lyon and Paris. The music for *Medea* typifies much of Bryars's style: non-functional tonality, repetitive patterns, a strong vocal sense, careful pacing and, somewhat replacing the conceptual content of recent music, the use of text.

Medea was an enormous success in France, but received little attention and no performances in Britain. Bryars's attempts to create further operas have led to a series of concert works which *have* been performed widely here. Compositions such as *Dr Ox's Experiment* and *The Old Tower of Lobenicht*, both performed by the Gavin Bryars Ensemble, are conceived in the manner of Busoni as satellite works of a larger operatic venture. These pieces are characterised by a rich, harmonic language which seems to derive from Richard Strauss, early Schoenberg and from a re-admission of jazz into Bryars's new-found ease of expression. Repetition is still the major impetus within the music, but it has little to do with the driving pulses of Steve Reich or the endless arpeggios of Philip Glass. Rather, repetition is used to *pace* the music and to provide accompaniment for long and lyrical melodies. The harmony of these works is invariably subtle, making much use of enharmonic changes (musical re-spelling of individual notes) to create a feeling of ambiguity. There is also a concentration upon textural nuances, particularly through the use of extreme registers or effects such as that at the end of the *String Quartet No 1*, which combines *scordatura* de-tuning of the strings with multiple use of harmonics, both natural and artificial.

The years from 1984 to the present have seen Bryars becoming more prolific. He has produced works for some of the leading performers of the time, including the Hilliard Ensemble, the Arditti Quartet, and jazz musicians such as Bill Frisell and Evan Parker. This accession to the state of "composer" has been hard-won, not through any external factors, nor because of lack of native talent or ability, but because of the intellectual rigour which led him to experimentalism and a natural tendency to restraint and discretion. Bryars has described the process thus: "It's like learning to ride a bike—it takes a while to master the technique, but once you have learnt, you start to do things, like seeing how slow you can go, pedalling in a straight line, taking your hands off the handlebars, and so on." This image echoes an image of a struggling cyclist in a drawing by Marcel Duchamp, the enigmatic title of which perhaps sums up Bryars's career to date: *The Apprentice in the Sun*.

—Andrew Hugill

BUCHT, Gunnar. Swedish. Born in Stocksund, Sweden, 5 August 1927. Educated at Uppsala University, 1947–53, Fil.Lic.; piano study with Y. Flyckt, theory with E. Eppstein, composition lessons with Karl-Birger Blomdahl, 1947–51; studied in Germany with Carl Orff, 1954, in Italy with Goffredo Petrassi, 1954–5, and in Paris with Max Deutsch, 1961–2. Married Bergljot Krohn, 12 April 1958. Performing pianist; folk high school teacher, 1953–4; chair, concert organization Fylkingen, 1956–9, and Society of Swedish Composers, 1963—9; taught at Stockholm Citizens' School, subsequently at Stockholm University, 1965–9; vice-president, ISCM International Praesidium, 1969–72; Swedish Cultural Attaché, Bonn, Germany, 1970–3; professor of composition, State College of Music, Stockholm, 1975–85; lecturer in musicology, Stockholm University, 1984. Recipient: membership, Royal Academy of Music, 1964. Mailing address: (winter) Rådmansgatan 74, S-113 60 Stockholm; (summer) Burge Hablingbo, S-620 11 Havdhem, Sweden.

Publisher: Svensk Musik/Edition Suecia, Box 27327, S-102

Symphonies/orchestral:

Symphony No 1 1952; first performed Stockholm, 1953.
Cello Concerto No 1 1954; first performed Stockholm, 1955.
Symphony No 3 1955; first performed Stockholm, 1955.
Divertimento 1956; first performed Stockholm, 1957.
Symphony No 4 1958; first performed Stockholm, 1959.
Symphony No 5 1960; first performed Stockholm, 1962.
Couplets and Refrains 1960.
Symphony No 6 1961; first performed Stockholm, 1963.
Strangaspel (strings) 1965.
Symphony No 7 1971; first performed Norrkoping, 1972. Recorded Caprice 1075.
Winter Organ 1974; first performed Gothenberg, 1975.
Journées oubliées 1976; first performed Stockholm, 1976.
Au-delà 1978; first performed Stockholm, 1979.
Violin Concerto 1979; first performed Stockholm, 1980.
The Big Bang—and After 1980; first performed Stockholm, 1981.
En clair obscur 1982; first performed Stockholm, 1982.
Sinfonia Concertante (flute, viola, harp, orchestra) 1982; first performed Norrkoping, 1983.
Symphony No 8 1982; first performed Stockholm, 1984.
Georgica 1982; first performed Stockholm, 1983.
Fresques mobiles 1986; first performed Stockholm, 1989.
Tonend bewegte Formen 1987.
Concerto for Arnholma (strings) 1989; first performed Arnholma, 1990.
Symphony No 9 1989; first performed Stockholm, 1990.
En var gick jag ut i varlden / One Spring I Went out into the World: Novel for Orchestra in 16 Chapters 1989; first performed Stockholm, 1990.
Cello Concerto No 2 1990.

Chamber/instrumental:

Sonata No 1 (piano) 1950; first performed Lubeck, 1951.
Sonato No 2 (piano) 1959; first performed Stockholm, 1960.
Study (clarinet) 1959; first performed Stockholm, 1959.
A huit mains (flute, violin, cello, harpsichord) 1975; first performed Gothenberg, 1976.
A mon gré (flute, clarinet, harp, celeste, viola, cello, double bass) 1978; first performed Stockholm, 1979.
Blad fran mill gulsippe ange I (clarinet, piano) 1985; first performed Stockholm, 1986.
Quatre Pièces pour le pianiste 1985; first performed Astorp, 1986.
Blad fran mitt gulsippe ange II (harpsichord) 1987; first performed Stockholm, 1989.

Vocal/choral:

Five Italian Songs (mezzo-soprano, piano; Ungareti, Quasimodo) 1955; first performed Stockholm, 1956.
Hommage à Edith Södergran (unaccompanied mixed chorus) 1956; first performed Stockholm, 1957.
Dagen svalnar (soprano, piano; Södergran) 1956; first performed Stockholm, 1957.
Ein Wintermarchen (voice, 8 instruments; Dürrenmatt) 1959; first performed Stockholm, 1963.
Kattens oron (reciter, 3 instruments; Forssell) 1960; first performed Stockholm, 1960. Recorded Caprice CAP 1042.
Hund skenar glad (soprano, female choir, instruments; Björling) 1961; first performed Stockholm, 1962. Recorded Caprice CAP 1075.
La fine della diaspora (choir, orchestra; Quasimodo) 1962; first performed Stockholm, 1963.
Set artidssanger (soprano, piano; Björling) 1965; first performed New York City, 1966.
Eine Lutherische Messe (soloists, choir, children's choir, orchestra; Forte) 1973.
Musik for Lau (voices, wind, percussion, tape) 1974; first performed Lau, Gotland, 1975.

Opera:

Tronkravarna / The Pretenders (Ibsen) 1964–5; first performed Stockholm, 1966. Recorded (part) Caprice CAP 1075.

Other:

Symphonie pour la musique libérée (tape) 1969; first performed Stockholm, 1969.
The Walls of Jericho (tape; also oratorio version) 1970; first performed Stockholm, 1970.

PUBLICATIONS

By Bucht: "Hommage à Edith Södergran", in *Modern Nordisk Musik*, edited by Bergstrom, Stockholm, 1957; "Symphonie pour la musique libérée", in *Nutida Musik*, 13 (3), 1969–70; "Wagner och Lorenz", in *Swedish Journal of Musicology*, 1972; "Karl-Birger Blomdahl som musik-dramatiker", in *Prisma*, 1973; *Electronic Music in Sweden, Swedish Government Report, SOU 1977:30*, 1977; "Berlioz—det oförutseddes mästere, in *Jakobs stege*, 5–6, 1978; "Kunst und Wissenschaft—Konflikt oder Koexistenz?", in *Festschrift Hans Eppstein*, 1981; "Fylkingen och avantgardet", in *Fylkingen Bulletin*, 1, 1983.

On Bucht: G. Bergendal, "GB", in *Thirty Three Swedish Composers*, Stockholm, 1972; Hans-Gunnar Peterson, "Stor i friare form", in *Konsertnytt*, 1, 1984–5; Gerd Schönfelder, "The Big Bang and After", in *Prinzip Wahrheit—Prinzipo Schonheit*, Stockholm, 1984; Lennart Reimers, "Uppbrottets Komponist", in *Musikrevy*, February 1988.

Gunnar Bucht comments:

Paraphrasing the French 18th-century philosopher, my own artistic motto could be read as "Tradition, what do you want from me? Live up to me—if you can!" This means: my relationship to tradition is dialogical; tradition is seen as challenge, not as a pillow. This outlook is reflected in my double activities as a composer and musicologist. The historical and analytical perspectives are always present in my creative work. At the same time, when teaching music history and analysis the artistic dimension is always there, I hope. I teach not only facts but experiences.

This tension between emotionality and intellectuality is reflected in the often dramatic character of my music. There is an affinity with Berlioz's *l'imprévu*, the unexpected, as a formal principle. In my music, the architecture is nearly bursting from within and at the same time is being kept on a tight rein. Maliciously, my music could be characterized as a composition of intensely dramatic and poetic moments on one side and road-consuming sections on the other. In my novel for orchestra *One Spring I Went out into the World* I have tried to overcome this discrepancy by an expressive and formal satiation of each chapter. The contrasts are maximal but thanks to the shorter durations the architecture reinforces the expression, or so I believe. This novel is a typical example of the growing pictorial character of my music, also reflected in the orchestral work *Fresques mobiles*. Imagined, dreamt pictures.

Orchestral work dominates my output, much of it of long duration. It satisfies my need for emotional expansion and narration. Since the 1970s, the titles reveal a lot about the contents. Reading them you could reformulate my artistic belief as follows: I believe in an absolute music permeated with extramusical ideas of the world, with echoes of history, with inner pictures and visions, with wordless drama.

* * *

In 1990, Gunnar Bucht reached what since 1824 has been considered a climactic moment in the orchestral composer's career, the premiere of his Ninth Symphony. Ironically, it also coincided with what is considered the grand climacteric in a man's life, his 63rd birthday. There is little sign that Bucht intends to rest on his laurels; 1990 also witnessed first performances of two more, dramatically different orchestral works, a second Cello Concerto and the remarkable "novel for orchestra" *One Spring I Went out into the World*.

If Bucht is a traditionalist, as the critical convention has it, he is a traditionalist of a rather special sort. While it is true that he has not turned to the more extreme language of the continental avant-garde and that he maintains an outwardly regressive loyalty to the symphonic form in something like its 19th-century outline, he is nonetheless one of the more daring composers of the older generation in contemporary Sweden. He received a firm grounding at the hands of Karl-Birger Blomdahl, leader of the famous Monday Group which dominated Swedish music, and had some of the knobblier edges knocked off by Goffredo Petrassi (a man with his own special stance on modern and classical tradition) and Max Deutsch.

A veteran of the folk high school and Citizens School system, Bucht acted as Sweden's cultural attaché to what was then West Germany in the early 1970s, before returning to teach at the State College of Music in Stockholm. By that point, he was an established symphonist. His Seventh, written before his return, is ironically his most transcendently "Swedish", a big rhapsodic work, generously developed, bursting with big symphonic ideas, barely contained by its structure, but closer in overall effect to Nielsen than to Sibelius.

Since then, the music has become more obviously pictorial, but not programmatic. The lovely *Fresques mobiles* has a dream-like quality that echoes the "space" effects of Bucht's creation-fantasy *The Big Bang—and After*, but with a remarkable intensity and a new sense of structure—discontinuous elements, collage effects, something akin to narrative suspense—that was to become the essence of his innovative "novel for orchestra". It is one of the most striking orchestral works performed anywhere in the last 10 years.

Bucht's music is absolute in that it obeys the organic imperatives of the form rather than any strict programme. Nonetheless, it is opened out to external reference of a particular, non-naturalistic sort. One might almost say that it contains history without attempting to describe it. That is one of the sterling qualities of Edith Södergran's verse, of which Bucht has made some striking settings.

As if to underline his confrontational attitude to tradition, his *Lutheran Mass* remains unperformed; the composer believes it may be "too dangerous" to be acceptable to the Swedish establishment. Generally, though, he does not seek to alienate his audience with modernist gestures—the putative objection to the mass is a liturgical one—and continues to produce music which is both accessible and deeply challenging, national and universal, "contemporary" and absolutely timeless.

—Henk Maarten

BUDD, Harold (Montgomery). American. Born in Los Angeles, California, 24 May 1936. Educated at Los Angeles City College, 1957–9; San Fernando State College, 1961–3, B.A., 1963; University of Southern California, Los Angeles, 1963–6, M.M., 1966. United States Army service, 1959–61. Married Paula Katzman in 1960; 2 sons. Cowboy, Mojave, California, early 1950s; social worker, Los Angeles County Department of Social Services, Watts, California, 1964–6; teacher, California Institute for the Arts, Valencia, 1970–6. Mailing address: 5812 Lindenhurst Avenue, Los Angeles, California 90036, U.S.A.

Publisher: Opal Limited, 330 Harrow Road, London W9 2HP, England.

Notated music:

One Sound (string quartet) 1968.
Intermission Piece (indeterminate) 1968.
Magnus Colorado (several gongs) 1969.
The Candy-Apple Revision (D♭ major chord for any instrumentation) 1970.
Lirio (solo tam-tam) 1971.
[All other works from the period 1963—71 (orchestral, chamber, vocal) withdrawn]
The Dragonfly Cymbal (piano) 1972.
Madrigals of the Rose Angel (female voices, harp, celesta, electric piano, percussion) 1972. Recorded on *The Pavilion of Dreams*, Editions EG EGED 30.
Butterfly Sunday (mezzo-soprano, harp) 1973. Recorded Editions EG EGED 30.
In Delius' Sleep (clarinet, piano) 1974.
Let Us Go into the House of the Lord (mezzo-soprano, harp) 1974. Recorded Editions EG EGED 30.
Song of Paradise: 17 Illuminations on the Holy Koran (bass-baritone, harp, glockenspiel, vibraphone, percussion) 1974.
Bismillahi 'Rrahman 'Rrahim (alto saxophone, electric piano, celesta, vibraphone, marimba, percussion) 1974–5. Recorded Editions EG EGED 30.
Juno (percussion ensemble) 1975. Recorded Editions EG EGED 30.
October Dreams (unaccompanied SATB choir; Toomer, Rosetti, Bethsebe, cummings) 1977.
Basheva Songs (Rossetti, Bethsebe) 1978.
Blue Room with Flowers and Gong 1985; first performed California, 1985.

Other:

[Since 1980, Budd's composition has been studio-based; individual works are not notated.]

Coeur d'Or 1972. Recorded Advance FGR 16.
The Oak of the Golden Dream 1979. Recorded Advance FGR 16.
The Plateaux of Mirror (collaboration with Brian Eno) 1981. Recorded Editions EG EGED 18.
The Serpent (in Quicksilver) 1981. Recorded Cantil 181; re-released Opal/Warners.
Abandoned Cities 1984. Recorded Cantil 181; re-released Opal/Warners.
Dark Star 1984. Recorded Cantil 384.
The Pearl (collaboration with Brian Eno) 1984. Recorded Editions EG 37.
Wonder's Edge (collaboration with E. Bowen) 1984. Recorded Cold Blue L 10.
The Moon and the Melodies (collaboration with The Cocteau Twins) 1986. Recorded 4AD CAD 611.
Lovely Thunder 1986. Recorded Editions EG EGED 46.
The White Arcades 1988. Recorded Opal/Warners.

PUBLICATIONS

On Budd: J. Silberman, "Interview with HB", in *LA Reader*, 31 October 1981; B. Jackson, "HB", in *BAM Magazine*, 12 February 1982; Brian Morton, "This Budd's for You", in *Wire*, February 1988; Craig Lee, "HB", in *LA Style*, February 1989.

Harold Budd comments:
It's simple: I want it to be devastating.

* * *

Harold Budd is a composer who has worked consistently within a limited range of musical resources, of emotional climate, of instrumental colour and of dynamics—a self-imposition that can give, at its best, a conceptual consistency and strength to his work. More than most composers he has remained rooted in the poetic overtones of his native environment—the fringes of Los Angeles. He has often spoken of the importance of his experience of living in the Mojave Desert. He has absorbed salient features of many of the diverse musics that he heard: Mexican Mariachi bands; the more ruminative forms of free and semi-free jazz; the film music of Ennio Morricone. From these he has learned the improviser's sense of space and a kind of musical poise.

Like a number of Californian composers of his generation he has an interest in the more meditative forms of music, in the idea of a controlled musical environment, and in a sense of non-doctrinaire spirituality. Some works from the 1960s are concerned with the idea of installation, in the visual art sense. *Magnus Colorado*, for several gongs, asks for a "very soft coloured light" to flood the performance area. *Lirio* has the simple notation "under a blue light, roll very lightly on a large gong for a long duration". *Intermission Piece* is a verbal score that sets up conditions for an ambient performance in any intermission (concert, play etc.) in a way not unrelated to Satie's earliest essays in his *Musique d'ammeublement* (1920). Even *Madrigals of the Rose Angel*, a later work for female choir, has the note that it should be performed "with dark lighting, maybe blue, preferably from above. It would be nice if the chorus were topless". To my knowledge this piece still awaits an authentic performance. As late as 1985 he included a piece in the New Music America Festival, *Blue Room with Flowers and Gong* which continued this concern for a total experience of both music and space. He has often spoken of the impact of the paintings of Mark Rothko on him, and there is a clear connection between these works and minimal or colour-field painters from the 1950s onwards.

During his period of military service he played drums with Albert Ayler, and several jazz musicians find their way into his conventionally notated works of the 1970s. *Let Us Go into the House of the Lord* is based on the playing of Pharoah Saunders; *Butterfly Sunday* is a free transcription of John Coltrane's *After the Rain*; *Bismillahi 'Rrahman 'Rrahim* was written for alto saxophonist Marion Brown, and involves improvisation. These come from the 1970s, a period in which we find all his notated pieces. They are characterised by extremely slow tempi, a free approach to rhythm with considerable rubato, extreme consonance, and an interest in lush orchestration utilising tuned percussion (celeste, glockenspiel, vibraphone), harps, keyboards (acoustic and electric) and colouristic untuned percussion (wind-chimes, tam-tam, sleigh-bells), accompanying solo instruments or voices. Many pieces have mystical or semi-religious connotations (the Koran, the Old Testament). At the same time he is fond of the abstraction of vocalise and several works from this period feature vocalise, most notably *Madrigals of the Rose Angel*, arguably his strongest work from the 1970s. The voices maintain an extremely slow unison (occasionally octave) melodic line against harmonies that drift from one major seventh chord to another with a quiet inevitability that is completely captivating once the listener accepts the basic premise of stasis and relative uniformity of colour.

It was the recording of these ensemble works in 1978 for Brian Eno's Obscure label that brought Budd to Europe and set in motion a shift in his career where his work became based in the recording studio, utilising solo keyboards and electronic treatment, collaborating with musicians from popular music such as Brian Eno or the Cocteau Twins. Here the limitation of his method of making pieces through improvising at the keyboard—a method that is less obvious in his notated works—can be apparent. Clearly his interest in ambient forms of music finds an aesthetic response in producers such as Eno. The earliest examples of this work are the least successful, perhaps because of the dominance of collaborators, but by the late 1980s, with works such as *The White Arcades*, Budd asserts himself more forcibly and raises himself above the sloppy contemplative vacuity of most New Age music thanks, probably, to his roots in music of greater toughness and durability.

—Gavin Bryars

BULLER, John. British/English. Born in London, 7 February 1927. Musical training in childhood; chorister, St Matthew's, Westminster, London; University of London (composition under Anthony Milner), 1959–64, B.Mus. Married the actress Shirley Claridge, 8 October 1955; 3 sons and 1 daughter. Architectural surveyor, until 1974; member, 1965, and chair, 1971–2, MacNaghten Concerts Committee; composer in residence and Forman Fellow, University of Edinburgh, 1975–6; composer in residence, Queen's University, Belfast, 1985–6. Recipient: selections, International Rostrum of Composers, Paris (*Proenca* and *The Theatre of Money*), 1978, 1982. Mailing address: c/o Oxford University Press, 7/8 Hatherley Street, London SW1P 2QT, England.

Publisher: Oxford University Press.

Symphonies/orchestral:

Proenca (with mezzo-soprano solo) 1977; first performed London, 6 August 1977. Recorded Unicorn Kanchana DKP 9045.

Theatre of Memory 1980–1; first performed London, 7 September 1981. Recorded Unicorn Kanchana DKP 9045.

Chamber/instrumental:

The Cave (flute, clarinet, trombone, cello, tape) 1970; first performed London, November 1970.

Scribenery (cello) 1971; first performed London, December 1971.

Poor Jenny (flutes—1 player, 1 percussion) 1973; first performed Aldeburgh, Suffolk, 1973.

Le Terrazze (tape, flute/piccolo, oboe/cor anglais, clarinet/contrabass clarinet/soprano saxophone, bassoon, contrabassoon, 2 horns, trumpet, 2 trombones, percussion, violin, viola, cello, double bass) 1974; first performed London, October 1974.

Familiar (string quartet) 1976; first performed Edinburgh, May 1976.

Sette Spazzi (2 clarinets/1 soprano saxophone, violin, cello, piano) 1977; first performed April 1978.

Towards Aquarius (flute, oboe, clarinet, bassoon, 2 horns, trumpet, 2 trombones, percussion, string quintet, tape) 1983; first performed London, 1 November 1983.

Vocal/choral:

Two Night Pieces from Finnegans Wake (soprano, flute, clarinet, piano, cello; Joyce) 1970–1; first performed London, April 1971.

Finnegan's Floras (14 voices/SSSSAAATTTTBBB, hand percussion, piano; Joyce) 1971–2; broadcast BBC, May 1972.

The Melian Debate (tenor, baritone, flute, cor anglais, horn, trumpet, harp, cello; Thucydides, Warner) 1972; first performed London, April 1972.

The Mime of Mick, Nick and the Maggies (soprano, tenor, baritone, chorus of 13, flute/alto flute/piccolo, oboe/cor anglais, clarinet/contrabass clarinet, bassoon, 2 horns, trumpet, 2 trombones, celeste/organ/piano, cello, double bass, speaker or tape; Joyce) 1976; part one broadcast BBC, August 1976; first complete performance London, 6 February 1978.

Kommos (soprano, alto, tenor, bass, electronics; Aeschylus) 1982; first performed London, 21 June 1982.

A La Fontana del Vergier (counter-tenor, 2 tenors, baritone; Macabrun) 1984; first performed Lewes, Sussex, 22 July 1984.

Of Three Shakespeare Sonnets (mezzo-soprano, flute, clarinet, harp, 2 violins, viola, cello) 1985; first performed London, 12 June 1985.

* * *

Although John Buller's professional composing career spans little more than 20 years and just over a dozen works, the honesty and unselfconscious originality of this handful of pieces leaves a remarkably distinct impression of musical character. Always in search of a technical control that would be both absolute yet able to embrace certain freedoms, it is somehow typical of the man that he should choose to pit himself against remorselessly difficult odds, particularly in relation to word-setting. The intellectual solemnity of the prose argument chosen for *The Melian Debate* is aptly mirrored in a musical argument based entirely on two five-note groups, and although the speech-type rhythms employed here are set against a metrical pulse almost throughout, they seem already straining to be free of their enforced synchronisation.

This feeling of unnatural constraint, of a barely supressed rhythmic impatience, was to be resolved through Buller's discovery of James Joyce. It was Joyce who enabled him to realise the possibility of the free permutation of a limited number of ideas, as well as to understand that the material for these ideas could be found in the common currency of everyday life. *Two Night Pieces from Finnegans Wake* had already started to expand the strict motivic writing of *The Melian Debate* into longer, more flowing melodic lines, when Buller began on the first of his large-scale works: together with three associated pieces, *The Mime of Mick, Nick and the Maggies* was to occupy him for the next four years. It was an ambitious project. Buller set out to compose a work, on a selection of texts from Part 2 of *Finnegans Wake*, in which musical allusion was to reflect the verbal allusions of Joyce's prose: in *The Mime of Nick, Mick and the Maggies* the notion of childhood memories prolonged into (and distorted by) adult life is mirrored in musical memories common to us all. But, as with Joyce, so with Buller: meanings are not always immediately apparent. Nevertheless, the work has an extra-ordinarily evocative flavour, and its woven memories cast long shadows in the mind of the listener.

It was also to be prophetic for Buller's own future, giving him the confidence to embark on two masterly orchestral works, *Proenca* and *Theatre of Memory*, both of which call upon memory, whether actual or imagined. *Proenca*—for soprano, electric guitar and orchestra—is astonishing first and foremost for its sheer professionalism: this is a breathtakingly lavish piece, rich in decorative effects, yet centred on a slowly evolving melody that is shaped and propelled by means of its own reflections. Reinventing the long-forgotten language of the troubadours, these reflected melodic layers give *Proenca* a three-dimensional harmonic background that can more readily support and absorb Buller's unbarred rhythmic patterns by allowing them to sink their independence within a chorus of sound. The clear distinction between the different rates of movement set up by these melodically-defined rhythms creates a flexible landscape which of itself shapes the form of the work. In this respect *Theatre of Memory* is even more striking, since the structure is now entirely abstract: without a background of verbal imagery, the voices of seven solo instruments are used to focus attention on the many contrasting aspects of an orchestral fabric that expresses memory as a function of the collective subconscious.

Buller's visionary ability to complete his large scale designs without blurring the initial inspiration is exceptional; if he has retained even part of the vision that originally prompted him to cast the story of *The Baxxai* as a full-length opera, now six years in the writing and due for performance in the summer of 1992, it should indeed be worth waiting for.

—Susan Bradshaw

BURGESS, Anthony (John Anthony Burgess Wilson). British/English. Born in Manchester, Lancashire, 25 February 1917. Educated at Bishop Bilsborrow Memorial School, Manchester, 1923–8; Xaverian College, Manchester, 1928–35; University of Manchester, B.A. (hons), 1937–40. British Army Education Corps 1940–6: Sergeant Major. Married (1) Llewela Isherwood Jones in 1942 (died 1968); (2) Liliana Macellari in 1968; 1 son. Instructor, Western Command School of Instruction, Wolverhampton, 1946–9; lecturer, Bamber Bridge Training College, 1949–51; English Master, Banbury Grammar School, 1951–4; senior lecturer in English, Malayan Teachers Training College, Khata Baru, 1954–7; English-language specialist, Department of Education, Brunei, Borneo, 1958–9; writer in residence, University of North Carolina, Chapel Hill, 1969–70; visiting professor, Princeton University, New Jersey, and Columbia University, New York, 1970; distinguished professor, City College, New York 1972–3; literary adviser, Guthrie Theatre, Minneapolis, 1972–75. Also writer/author. Recipient: Doctorate, University of Manchester, 1978, and University of Birmingham, 1986; Commandeur des Arts et des Lettres, France, 1987. Mailing address: 44 rue Grimaldi, Monaco.

Publisher: none.

Symphonies/orchestral:

Symphony 1937.
Sinfonietta (jazz combo) 1941.
Gibraltar (symphonic poem) 1944.
Cello Concerto 1944.
Song of a Northern City (piano, orchestra) 1947.
Partita (string orchestra) 1951.
Ludus Multitonalis (recorder consort) 1951.
Concertino (piano, percussion) 1951.
Cantata for Malay College 1954.
Symphony—Sinfoni Melayu 1956.
Concerto (flute, strings) 1960.
Passacaglia (orchestra) 1961.
Symphony in C 1975; first performed Iowa, 1975.
Piano Concerto 1976.
Mrs WS (ballet suite) 1979; broadcast BBC, 1979.
A Glasgow Overture 1985; first performed Glasgow, 1985.
Mr Burgess's Almanack 1988; first performed Geneva, 1988.
Petite Symphonie pour Strasbourg 1988; first performed Strasbourg, 1989.
Concerto Gross (4 guitars, orchestra) 1988; first performed Cannes, 1989.
Marche pour une Révolution 1989; first performed Venice, 1989.

Chamber/instrumental:

Sonata (piano) 1946.
Sonata (piano) 1951.
Quartet No 1 (guitars) 1984; first performed Monaco, 1985.
Quartet No 2 (guitars) 1987; first performed Monaco, 1989. Recorded REM 311111.

Vocal/choral:

The Brides of Enderby (voice, flute, oboe, cello, piano) 1976; first performed New York, 1978.
Man Who Has Come Through (voice, flute, oboe, cello, piano) 1984; first performed Nottingham, 1985.
La Piaggia del Pineto (voice, piano) 1988; first performed Amsterdam, 1989.

Opera:

Blooms of Dublin 1981; broadcast 1982.

Other:

Ascent of F6 (dance band) 1947; first performed Bamber Bridge, Lancashire, 1949.
The Adding Machine (dance band) 1949; first performed Bamber Bridge, Lancashire, 1950.
Cyrano de Bergerac (flute, trumpet, cello, percussion, keyboard) 1970; first performed Minneapolis, 1970.

PUBLICATIONS

By Burgess: *This Man and Music*, London, 1982; *Homage to QWERTYUIOP*, London, 1986; *New Libretto for Oberon*, London, 1986; *Carmen* (as translator), London, 1987; also many novels, short stories, plays and criticism.

Anthony Burgess comments:

As a practising novelist and critic, I must relegate my music to a secondary role that is, as I grow older, becoming possibly primary. My work is hardly known in Britain, but this will soon be remedied. Style? Eclectic.

* * *

The American novelist and short story writer Paul Bowles is perhaps the only other modern figure who has managed to combine a literary career with a significant body of musical composition as Anthony Burgess has. But whereas Bowles has largely given up composing, Burgess has placed increasing emphasis on his music, his first love, in the last few years and has returned to composing.

It has to be said that, for all his high public profile in the United Kingdom, mostly as a journalist and broadcaster, and despite the plaudits heaped on his *magnum opus Earthly Powers*, Burgess is still surprisingly undervalued as a writer and is virtually unknown as a composer, not even meriting an entry in *New Grove*. Music has played a significant role in his fiction. His novel *The Napoleon Symphony* deploys that overworked fictional analogy with more than usual success. There is also a striking musical thread running through the film version of his controversial *A Clockwork Orange*. It might almost be argued that both works are organised along musical lines, *Earthly Powers* symphonically, with frequent use of leitmotif, transitions of mood and large-scale resolutions, *A Clockwork Orange* in a more abstract and improvisational way.

Burgess, a man of enormous general culture, was self-taught as a composer, working his way through the classical canon at the same time as he was playing piano in jazz groups. Some of the more striking effects in his orchestral compositions, notably harmonies based on fourths, or sudden shifts into unexpectedly atonal territory, can be explained by this background. Certainly, there is a strongly rhythmic quality to his music which makes it instantly appealing and, it must be said, carries it across patches where the conception is thin. There is, however, great vigour in his *A Glasgow Overture*, the *Cello Concerto*, and the deceptive *Symphony in C*, which is not nearly as blandly affirmative or triumphal as its title key may suggest. It is not surprising to find that Burgess is a confident vocal and dramatic composer. His *Blooms of Dublin*, based on Joyce, is well worth a revival and he has produced interesting settings for his own Mr Enderby. In addition, he has written accomplished incidental music in an identifiable idiom. However, this is not where his main talent lies. Burgess is a more than able symphonist. His architecture is altogether more sound than that of a great many professional composers, and he has a good melodic sense. He has not in general produced good chamber music (nor is he adept as a short story writer) though in more recent years he has been intrigued by the unusual, "orchestral" sonority of the guitar quartet and has produced two fine works for this underworked genre. If this is "late" work, it is also extremely fresh, with an unsententious logic and an entirely self-consistent disposition of mood. And if, as he suggests, he will turn increasingly to music in years to come, it bodes very well indeed.

—Brian Morton

BURGON, Geoffrey. British/English. Born in Hambleside, Hampshire, 15 July 1941. Educated at Pewley School, Guildford; Guildhall School of Music and Drama, London (studying composition with Peter Wishart, trumpet with Bernard Brown). Married Janice Elizabeth Garwood in 1963 (dissolved); 1 son and 1 daughter. Freelance trumpeter, 1964–71: with Royal Opera House, Northern Sinfonia, Philomusica, London Mozart Players, Jacques and Capriol Orchestras; also session work, theatre and jazz bands. Full-time composer and conductor, from 1971. Recipient: Prince Pierre of Monaco Award, 1969; Ivor Novello Award, 1979, 1981. Address: c/o Chester Music, 8/9 Frith Street, London W1V 5TZ, England.

Publisher: J & W Chester.

Symphonies/orchestral:

Concerto for String Orchestra 1963; first performed Bath, 6 June 1977.
Gendling 1968; first performed London, 11 July 1968.
Alleluia Nativitas 1970; first performed London, 17 February 1970.
Cantus Alleluia 1973; first performed London, 10 April 1974.
May Day Prelude 1977; first performed London, 1 May 1977.
Brideshead Variations 1982; first performed London, 21 March 1982. Also brass band and concert band versions.
The Trial of Prometheus 1988; first performed London, 20 October 1988.

Chamber/instrumental:

Fanfares and Variants (2 trumpets, 2 trombones) 1969.
Lullaby and Aubade (trumpet, piano) 1972.
Gloria (piccolo, oboe, clarinet, horn, piano, cello) 1973.
Three Nocturnes (harp) 1974.
Four Guitars 1977.
Four Horns 1977.
Six Studies (cello) 1980.
Chamber Dances (flute, clarinet, horn, violin, viola, cello) 1982.
Little Missenden Variation (clarinet, cor anglais, horn, bassoon) 1984; first performed Little Missenden, Buckinghamshire, 13 October 1984.
Fanfare (horns, trumpets, trombones, tuba) 1985; first performed London, 1 May 1985.

Vocal/choral:

Three Elegies (SATB choir) 1964.
Cantata on Medieval Latin Texts (counter-tenor, flute, oboe, bassoon) 1964.
Short Mass (SSATB choir) 1965. Recorded Hyperion CDA 66123.
Acquainted with Night (counter-tenor, strings; Fletcher, Frost, Surrey, E. Thomas, Church) 1965; first performed London, 5 April 1966. Recorded EMI EL 7 49762 1.
Farewell Earth's Bliss (6 solo voices) 1966.
Hymn to Venus (mezzo-soprano, piano) 1966.
Three Carols (SATB chorus) 1967.
Two Hymns to Mary (SATB chorus; 16th/15th century) 1967, 1969. Recorded Hyperion CDA 66123.
Five Sonnets of John Donne (soprano, mezzo-soprano, flute, oboe, clarinet, horn, piano, timpani, cello) 1967.
Think on Dreadful Domesday (soprano, chorus, orchestra) 1969.

Five Alleluias (6 solo voices, or brass) 1970.
Golden Eternity (SATB chorus, harp, piano) 1970.
Mai Hamama (6 solo voices) 1970.
Songs of Mary (mezzo-soprano, viola, piano) 1970.
At the Round Earth's Imagin'd Corners (soprano, trumpet, organ; Donne) 1971. Recorded Hyperion CDA 66123.
Worldes Blisse (counter-tenor, oboe; trad.) 1971. Recorded EMI EL 7 49762 1.
Threnody (tenor, piano, amplified harpsichord) 1971.
A Prayer to the Trinity (SATB chorus; 15th century) 1972.
This Endris Night (tenor, women's chorus, brass ensemble, timpani) 1972. Recorded EMI EL 7 49762 1.
Dira vi amores terror (counter-tenor solo) 1973.
Nosche Oscura (6 solo voices) 1974.
Dos Coros (12 solo voices) 1975.
Canciones del Alma (2 counter-tenors, strings; St Juan de la Cruz, Campbell) 1975; first performed London, 30 April 1975. Recorded EMI EL 7 49762 1.
Requiem (soprano, counter-tenor, tenor, chorus, orchestra) 1976; first performed Hereford, 26 August 1976.
This World From (SATB chorus, organ; 16th century) 1979. Recorded CDA 66123.
Laudate Dominum (SATB chorus, organ) 1980. Recorded CDA 66123.
Hymn to St Thomas of Hereford (chorus, orchestra) 1981; first performed Hereford, 22 August 1982.
But Have Been Found Again (soprano, alto, SAATTBB chorus; St Juan de la Cruz, Campbell) 1983. Recorded CDA 66123.
The World Again (soprano, orchestra) 1983; first performed London, 9 October 1984.
A God and Yet a Man (SSAATTBB chorus) 1984.
Revelations (soprano, tenor, baritone, chorus and orchestra) 1984; first performed London, 13 April 1985.
The Names of the Hare (SATB chorus) 1985; first performed Milton Keynes, Buckinghamshire, 14 June 1986.
Lunar Beauty (counter-tenor, lute; Auden, MacNiece) 1986; first performed Harrogate, Yorkshire, 9 August 1986. Recorded EMI EL 7 49762 1.
Title Divine (soprano, orchestra) 1986; first performed London, 22 April 1987.
The Song of the Creatures (SATB chorus, organ) 1987; first performed Northampton, 21 September 1987.
Prayer to St Richard (SATB chorus) 1989.
Songs of the Creation (SATB chorus, organ) 1989.
Nearing the Upper Air (counter-tenor, recorder, cello, harpsichord) 1989.

Opera/dramatic:

Epitaph to Sir Walter Raleigh (soprano, mezzo-soprano, baritone or tenor, bass, flute/piccolo, oboe, clarinet/bass clarinet, bassoon, horn) 1968; first performed London, 8 February 1969.
Joan of Arc (3 sopranos, tenor, baritone, narrator, flute, cello, harpsichord, percussion) 1970; first performed Little Missenden, Buckinghamshire, October 1970.
The Fall of Lucifer (counter-tenor, tenor, baritone, SATB chorus, flute/piccolo, harpsichord, organ, 2 violins, cello, double bass) 1977; first performed Tilford, Surrey, 13 May 1977.
Mirandola (2 sopranos, 2 tenors, baritone, bass-baritone, bass, SATB chorus, 2 flutes/piccolos, 2 oboes/1 cor anglais, 2 clarinets, 2 bassoons/1 contrabassoon, 4 horns, 2 trumpets, 3 trombones, tuba, timpani, 2 percussion, strings; stage band of courtviolinist, mandolinist, drummer) 1980–1.
Orpheus (soprano, tenor, bass, SATB chorus, flute/piccolo, clarinet/bass clarinet, trumpet, percussion, harpsichord, strings) 1982; first performed Wells, Somerset, 17 July 1982.
Blood Wedding (music for National Youth Theatre production; Lorca) 1988.
Murder in the Cathedral (music for National Youth Theatre production; Eliot) 1988.
Hard Times (after Dickens) 1990.

Other:

Divertimento (brass quartet; for children) 1964.
The Golden Fish (ballet) 1964.
Fun in the Insect World (piano solo; for children) 1965.
Five Studies (brass quartet; for children) 1965.
Now Welcome Summer (unison voices, piano; for children) 1966.
Songs As If for Children (unison voices, piano) 1967.
Trio (2 trumpets, trombone; for children) 1968.
Beginnings (harp solo; for children) 1969.
Tomorrow Shall Be My Dancing Day (children's voices, recorders, piano, percussion) 1970.
Songs of Night (children's voices, recorders, piano, percussion) 1970.
And There Was War in Heaven (boys' voices, organ) 1970.
The Calm (ballet) 1974; first performed Manchester, September 1974.
Running Figures/Goldberg's Dream (ballet) 1975; first performed Leeds, 25 March 1975.
Step at a Time (ballet) 1976; first performed London, 4 November 1976.
Songs, Lamentations and Praises (ballet) 1979; first performed Jerusalem, 7 August 1979.
Chamber Dances (ballet) 1982; first performed Southampton, 16 September 1982.
Mass (ballet) 1984; first performed London, 16 September 1985.

Film scores: *Sunflowers*, 1967; *Bank on IBM*, 1968; *Monty Python's Life of Brian*, 1979; *Turtle Diary*, 1985.

Music for television: *The Letter*, 1969; The Changeling, 1973; *The Treasure of Abbot Thomas*, 1974; *Dr Who and the Terror of the Zygons*, 1975; *Love's Labours Lost*, 1975; *As You Like It*, 1978; *The Archer's Tale*, 1979; *Tinker, Tailor, Soldier, Spy*, 1979; *Testament of Youth*, 1980; *The Dogs of War*, 1980; *Brideshead Revisited*, 1981; *How Many Miles to Babylon?* 1981; *Soft Targets*, 1982; *Marks*, 1982; *Rolling House*, 1982; *Bewitched*, 1983; *Z for Zachariah*, 1983; *Goodbye Days*, 1984; *Mass for Man*, 1984; *Bleak House*, 1985; *The Death of the Heart*, 1985; *Happy Valley*, 1986; *Sophia and Constance*, 1988; *Narnia: The Lion, the Witch and the Wardrobe*, 1988; *Narnia: the Dawn Treader*, 1989.

* * *

A glance through Geoffrey Burgon's now extensive work-list reveals an apparent inconsistency of manner and possibly also of belief. Though primarily a composer of church choral and vocal music of remarkable purity and emotional intensity, Burgon is also credited with a score for the satirical and irreverent Monty Python film *Life of Brian*. Commissioned to write theme music for a British television adaptation of John Le Carre's Cold War thriller *Tinker, Tailor, Soldier, Spy*, Burgon wrote a *Nunc Dimittis*, which further confounded normal expectations by registering a minor hit in the singles charts. Indeed, the composer of such works as *Farewell Earth's Bliss* and *Joan of Arc* largely financed his career as a freelance composer with the proceeds of a BBC television commission for incidental music to the science-fiction fantasy *Dr Who and the Terror of the Zygons*. To date, by far his best known piece of music is his theme to the 1981 Independent Television adaptation of Evelyn Waugh's *Brideshead Revisited*.

If it is naive to concentrate too hard on oppositions and dichotomies in an artist's career, it may be an even greater mistake to force resolutions between them. Most careers advance piecemeal and in accordance with economically enforced circumstance (commissions, teaching posts) rather than any master-plan. The same is true of Burgon, but his career does seem to be very much of a piece. He was brought up in no significant religious background and seems to have turned to liturgical music at least in part because of formal properties such as polyphony, together with the possibilities of extremes of resonance; it has certainly not seemed inappropriate to him to write in liturgical idiom for a spy thriller (and it may be that Cold War psychology is a late, secular version of medieval Christian teleology). Even so apparently carefree a piece as the *Life of Brian* score merits careful examination; pastiche and parody, if they are to be successful, still require a confident command of the original language and Burgon's score has an eery otherworldly quality (as does the *Dr Who* music) that belies its "commercial" origins.

As a final paradox, his introduction to music came via jazz and he remains a keen listener and player. There is a clear link between jazz trumpet (Burgon's instrument, which he studied under Bernard Brown at the Guildhall) and the declamatory brass of medieval church music; he uses trumpet to great effect in the chamber piece *Lullaby and Aubade* and, echoing medieval techniques, in his setting of John Donne's *At the Round Earth's Imagin'd Corners* with soprano and organ.

Donne, it might be said, is the perfect text for Burgon, with that very distinctive mixture of sacred and profane, mystical and pragmatic; it is no coincidence that his *Joan of Arc* should have been premiered at Little Missenden, Buckinghamshire, one of the focal points of Anglo-Catholicism, a further link with the ambience of *Brideshead Revisited*. Elsewhere, he has adapted W.H. Auden (of whom the same might be said) and also St John of the Cross, in Roy Campbell's luminous translation, but he is unmistakably an English composer, working in a tradition that links Tallis and Britten. There is a particular emphasis on the human voice, notably the higher tenor ranges, and Burgon has written very effectively (*Canciones del Alma, This Endris Night* and elsewhere) for counter-tenor.

His orchestral and purely instrumental writing is less immediately striking than his vocal and choral music. Nonetheless, even here he has produced strikingly beautiful music, most notably the early *Concerto for String Orchestra* perhaps his first mature work, and the *Brideshead Variations*. Burgon is an important, individual voice.

—Eleanor Caldwell

BURT, Francis. British and Austrian. Born in London, 28 April 1926; resident in Vienna since 1956. Educated at St Edward's School, Oxford, 1940–4; Royal Academy of Music, London, 1948–51, Associate, 1957; Hochsschule für Musik, Berlin, 1951–4; study in Rome, 1954–5. Military service (partly in Nigeria), 1944–8. Married Lina Burt, 30 October 1968. Professor-in-ordinary, Hochsschule für Musik und Darstellende Kunst, Vienna, since 1973. Recipient: Mendelssohn Scholarship, 1954; fellowship, Fondation Européene de la Culture, 1956; Forderungsdpreisder Theodor Korner-Stiftung, 1973; Wurdigungspreis für Musik, Bundesministerium für Unterricht, Kunst und Sport, Vienna, 1978; Preis der Stadt Wien, Vienna, 1981. Mailing address: Mayerhofgasse 12/20, A-1040 Vienna, Austria.

Publishers: Universal Edition, Vienna; Bote & Bock, Berlin; Barenreiter-Verlag, Kassel.

Symphonies/orchestral:

Iambics Op 5 1953; broadcast Germany, 1955.
Espressione Orchestrale Op 10 1958–9; first performed Vienna, 1959
Fantasmagoria Op 12 1963; first performed London, 1963.
Morgana (5 pieces for orchestra) 1983–6; first performed Vienna, 1986. Recorded Classic Amadeo 431 8532.

Chamber/instrumental:

String Quartet Op 2 1951–2; first performed Berlin, 1953.
Serenata Notturna Op 3 (oboe, clarinet, bassoon) 1952; first performed Cologne, 1954; withdrawn.
Music for Two Pianos Op 4 1952; first performed Berlin, 1953.
Duo Op 7 (clarinet, piano) 1954; first performed London, 1963.
For William (flute, clarinet, horn, trumpet, percussion, piano, violin, viola, cello) 1988; first performed London, 1988.
Echoes (flute, clarinet, horn, trumpet, percussion, piano, violin, viola, cello) 1988–9; first performed Vienna, 1989. Recorded Classic Amadeo 431 8532.

Vocal/choral:

Two Songs of David Op 1 (unaccompanied chorus) 1951; first performed London, 1951.
Hute (no 3 of the *Liederheft für Margot und H.H.S.*; medium voice, piano; Sandburg) 1952.
The Skull "Being the Meditation of a Courtier upon the Skull of his Poisoned Mistress" Op 6 (tenor, piano; Tourneur) 1953–4, revised version for tenor, orchestra, 1955.
Bavarian Gentians Op 8 (vocal quartet, piano; Lawrence) 1956; Dartington, Devon, 1956.
Unter der Blanken Hacke des Monds (baritone, orchestra; Huchel) 1974–6; first performed Munich, 1976. Recorded Classic Amadeo 431 8532.
Und Gott der Herr sprach (mezzo-soprano, baritone, bass, 2 mixed choirs, large orchestra; Luther) 1976–83; first performed Vienna, 1984.

Opera:

Volpone, or The Fox Op 9 (Jonson) 1952–8, revised 1960–1; first performed Oldenburg, 1963.
Barnstable, oder Jemand auf dem Dachboden Op 13 (Saunders, Spiel) 1967–9; first performed Kassel, 1969.

Other:

Der Golem Op 11 (ballet) 1959–63; first performed Hannover, 1965. Recorded Classic Amadeo 431 8532.

PUBLICATIONS

By Burt: "An Antithesis—I: The Technical Aspect", in *The Score*, December 1956; "An Antithesis—II", in *The Score*, 19, 1957; "Two Open Letters to Boris Blacher", in *Tempo*, 104, 1973; "*Der Golem*", in *Judische Echo*, 1 September 1984.

On Burt: Annabella Cloudsley, "*Volpone* in Stuttgart and London: Two Productions of FB's Opera", in *Theatre World*, 57 (439), 1961; Franz Endler, "Kopf und Herz im Gleichgewicht. Komponisten auf neuen Wegen (XVII): FB", in *Die Presse*, October 1965; Walter Szmolyan, "Wurdigungspreis für FB", in *OMZ*, 35, 1980, and "Geburtskalendarium: Artikel anlasslich Bs 60. Geburtstage", in *OMZ*, 41, 1986; Sigrid Wiesmann, "Neues Musiktheater in Osterreich", in *OMZ*, 35, 1980; Manfred Blumauer, "Das Portrait: FB", in *Opernwelt*, 1983; "Kompositionsunterricht bei FB; Zusammenfasung eines Gesprachs mit dem o. Professor der Hochsschule für Musik und Darstellende Kunst in Wien", in *OMZ*, 40, 1985; Franz Zauner, "Meditation uber buchstaben: der Komponist FB und die Bucher", in *Weiner Zeitung*, 27 October 1987; Hartmut Krones, "FB—eine Besamtdarstellung", in *Musikalische Dokumentation FB*, Vienna, 1990.

Francis Burt comments:

In 1946, while serving in the army, I was posted to Nigeria for 15 months. The stay there made a deep impression on me. The music, mainly drum-music, of the Ibo people of southeastern Nigeria, with all its rhythmic vitality and complexity, not only showed me that a quite different sort of music was possible from that which I had got to know at school, but it also awoke my interest in the kinaesthetic elements of music. There is no direct African influence to be found in my work. Nevertheless, the driving force of almost all my earlier music is without doubt rhythm and the dance.

It was thus quite natural that, when I began studying in 1948, Stravinsky should become a major influence for me and that I should later turn to Boris Blacher as a teacher. The dry, anti-romantic irony common to both these composers was also a very welcome antidote to the somewhat pallid lyricism then prevailing in most British music.

Later I discovered that I had a particular talent for dramatic music. Indeed, it gradually became apparent that my musical style developed mainly in response to the demands of the particular text or dramatic situation for which I was writing the music. Thus my first opera *Volpone* is full of irony and parody, of dance rhythms, jazz influence and rhythmic drive. Such a style was quite inappropriate for *The Golem*, which is an essentially religious ballet, based on old Jewish legends. It led me to write a much darker, more expressive sort of music than I had ever written before, with considerable use of rubato, which I had hitherto abhorred.

These new elements then became an integral element of my style, which has continued to develop in a similar way, until now, far from the clear pulse and rhythmic drive of my earlier works, I write in a style somewhat influenced by electronic music: floating, with little sense of pulse, but with "bands" of sound, "sonic areas" and an ever-increasing multiplication of lines to form a polylinear mesh.

One can of course rejoin that it is I who select my texts and thus I who determine my development. That is of course true—although it is surprising how far the composition of, say, an opera can lead one away from one's starting point. Nevertheless, despite all the emphasis I like to lay on musical *thinking*, abstract musical speculation is not a primary impulse in my music. Rather, I have tried to develop and broaden my style in response to the expressive requirements of the particular work in hand, while at the same time striving to remain true to myself in such a way that the next piece may seem to follow logically from the previous one and in some way to sum up all that has gone before. In our pluralistic society, at a time when all lines of musical development seem to have petered out, this is the only course that I at least can take.

* * *

Francis Burt's musical language originally developed as an extension of the late-Romantic style, but he was soon stimulated by the works of Igor Stravinsky, who provided him with material from which he derived his individual voice. Chance operations also held a special fascination and there was the additional influence of Nigerian drum music (Burt spent some time in West Africa in the armed forces). However, it was due to his Berlin teacher, Boris Blacher, that Burt became acquainted with the richness of expressive means and the great palette of possibilities which, through craftsmanship, lay at the disposal of the composer.

Burt, like Blacher, did not turn his back on tradition, and in particular, tonality, but adapted the achievements of the past to his personal vision. In developing traditional idiom, he maintained a basic expressiveness that guaranteed the accessibility of his work to a broad audience.

The dance, a basic gestural element of Burt's music, was already apparent in *Iambics*. As befits the title, a single rhythm becomes the germ-cell which appears at every stage of the development, forming the introduction and the main body of the work as a sort of constant genetic transformation. Similar characteristics are to be found in the cantata *The Skull*. Here the addition of voice is important, alternating between free recitatives, expressive melodies and moments of mounting ecstasy, all in a directly communicative way. Finally, there is the intensification brought about by dense formations of chords, a device which points to the extensive linearity of Burt's future work. His skill in deploying simultaneous rhythmic layers is particularly evident in the delightful *opera buffa Volpone*. Acting as leitmotifs, the rhythmic patterns are used to represent the characteristics of different people and different levels of action within the plot.

The principle of consolidated sounds emanating from a transparent opening and progressing stepwise from there runs through *Espressione Orchestrale* and also the ballet *Der Golem*. Here, small particles are superimposed in a gradual concentration of sound and dramatic action. These, however, never operate as independent clusters but always adhere to the principle of accumulation.

The ecstatic sound which is evident throughout *Der Golem* is also a feature of Burt's next few works and with his *Unter der Blanken Hacke des Monds*, the next stage of his development is heard. Again and again, whole areas of sound result from the binding together of individual instrumental lines. In terms of material, these areas of sound are assigned individual value, whose colourful pictorialism and vocal variety emphasizes a range of expression wholly befitting the text. The latent tonality suggests an almost impressionistic approach.

Burt's later works display an increasing interest in contrapuntal lines which come together into blocks of sound and take their profile from motoric and occasionally aleatoric rhythms. This also applies to the oratorio *Und Gott der Herr sprach*, as well as to the orchestral pictures of *Morgana* where sound and subject are in close accord.

A provisional final point of Burt's developing style is documented in *Echoes*, completed in 1989, which again is determined by its content and by a transposition of musical and dramatic ideas. The motif revealed at the beginning prevails throughout the entire work. Burt develops linear mini-clusters; two or three melodic strands create a polylinear network of generally contrapuntal orientation and thus provides an extremely dense sound. The technique is adapted for chamber forces with a refinement of dramatic condensation to suit solo playing. Burt's musical language has developed to such a point that his musical philosophy is not backward looking but subject to the most stringent compulsion.

—Hartmut Krones
(translated by John Abbey and Ortwin Reim)

BUSH, Alan (Dudley). British/English. Born in London, 22 December 1900. Educated privately; then at Highgate Grammar School, London, 1911–7; Royal Academy of Music, London (under Frederick Corder for composition, Tobias Matthay and Lily West for piano, and Reginald Steggall for organ), 1918–22; piano lessons from Benno Moiseiwitch, Mabel Lander, 1924–9; private lessons with John Ireland, 1927–32; study with Artur Schnabel, 1928; studied philosophy and musicology, Berlin University (under Johannes Wolf and Friedrich Blume), 1929–31. Military service, private, Royal Army Medical Corps, 1941–5. Married Nancy Rachel Head in 1931; 3 daughters (1 deceased). Conductor, pianist. Professor of composition, 1925–78, and fellow, 1934, Royal Academy of Music; music adviser/conductor, London Labour Choral Union, 1929–40; founder, 1936, and president, 1941–76, Workers' Music Association; chair, Composers Guild of Great Britain, 1947–8. Joined Independent Labour Party, 1924, resigned and joined Labour Party, 1929; joined Communist Party, 1935. Recipient: Thalberg Scholarship, 1920; Matthew Phillimore Prize for piano playing, 1920; Carnegie Award, for *String Quartet in A minor Op 4*, 1923; Arts Council Opera Competition winner, 1951; Handel Prize, Halle, 1962; corresponding member, East Germany Academy of Arts, 1965; University of London, D.Mus., 1968; University of Durham, D.Mus. Honoris Causa, 1971. Mailing address: 25 Christchurch Crescent, Radlett, Hertfordshire WD7 8AQ, England.

Publisher: Peters Edition; Novello; Stainer & Bell; Henschelverlag Berlin.

Symphonies/orchestral:

Symphonic Impressions Op 8 1927; first performed London, 11 November 1930.
Dance Overture Op 12 (military band) 1930; orchestrated 1935.
Concerto for Piano and Orchestra Op 18 (baritone solo, male voice chorus in last movement; Swingler) 1937.
Symphony No 1 in C Op 21 1941.
Meditation on a German Song of 1848 Op 22 (violin, string orchestra; also version for violin, piano) 1941.
Overture: Festal Day Op 23 (original title *Birthday Greeting in Honour of Vaughan Williams*) 1942.
Fantasia on Soviet Themes Op 24 1942.
English Suite Op 28 (string orchestra) 1945–6.
Overture "Resolution" Op 25 1946.
Homage to William Sterndale Bennett Op 27 (string orchestra) 1946.
Piers Plowman's Day Op 30 1946–7.
Concerto for Violin and Orchestra Op 33 1948. Recorded Hyperion.
Symphony No 2: The Nottingham Op 33 1949.
Concert Suite Op 37 (cello, orchestra) 1952.
Defender of Peace Op 39 1952.
Dorian Passacaglia and Fugue Op 52 1959.
Symphony No 3: The Byron Symphony Op 53 (with baritone solo, mixed chorus in last movement; Solomos) 1959–60.
For a Festal Occasion Op 58 (organ, orchestra; version of Op 56 no 2) 1961.
Variations, Nocturne and Finale on an English Sea-Song Op 60 (piano, orchestra) 1962. Recorded PRT Virtuoso PVCD 8372.
Partita Concertante Op 63 1965.
Time Remembered Op 67 (chamber orchestra) 1969.
Scherzo Op 68 (wind orchestra, percussion) 1969.
Africa Op 73 (piano, orchestra) 1972.
Concert Overture for an Occasion Op 74 1972.
The Liverpool Overture Op 76 1973.
Festival March for British Youth Op 78 1973.
Lascaux Symphony Op 98 1983.
Meditation in Memory of Anna Ambrose Op 107 1985.
Song Poem and Dance Poem Op 109 (piano, string orchestra) 1986.
Serenade and Duet Op 111 (piano, string orchestra) 1986.

Chamber/instrumental:

Three Pieces for Two Pianos Op 1 1921; first performed London, 2 March 1921.
Sonata in B minor Op 2 (piano) 1921.
Fantasy Op 3 (violin, piano) 1923.
String Quartet in A minor Op 4 1923; first performed London, 4 December 1924.
Quartet Op 5 (piano, violin, viola, cello) 1924.
Five Pieces Op 6 (violin, viola, cello, clarinet, horn) 1925.
Prelude and Fugue Op 9 (piano) 1927.
Relinquishment Op 11 (piano) 1928.
Dialectic Op 15 (string quartet) 1929; first performed London, 22 March 1935. Recorded Hyperion.
Concert Piece Op 17 (cello, piano) 1936; first performed London, January 1937.
Le Quatorze Juillet Op 38 (piano) 1943.
Lyric Interlude Op 26 (violin, piano) 1944.
Three Concert Studies Op 31 (piano, violin, cello) 1947. Recorded ASV CD DCA 646.
Trent's Broad Reaches Op 36 (horn, piano) 1951.
Three English Song Preludes Op 40 (organ) 1952.
Northumbrian Impressions Op 42 (Northumbrian small pipes; also version, Op 42a, for oboe, piano) 1953.
Autumn Poem Op 45 (horn, piano) 1954.
Nocturne Op 46 (piano) 1957.
Two Melodies Op 47 (viola, piano) 1957.
Mister Playford's Tunes Op 49 (little suite for piano) 1958.
Two Ballads of the Sea Op 50 (piano) 1957–8.
Suite Op 54 (harpsichord or piano) 1960.
Three African Sketches Op 55 (flute, piano) 1960.

Two Occasional Pieces Op 56 (organ) 1960.
Three Raga Melodies Op 59 (violin) 1961.
Prelude, Air, and Dance Op 61 (solo violin, string quartet, percussion) 1963–4.
Meditation on the Ballad Geordie Op 62 (double bass, piano) 1964.
Two Dances Op 64 (cimbalom) 1965.
Suite Op 65 (2 pianos) 1967.
Serenade Op 70 (string quartet) 1969.
Pianoforte Sonata in A♭ Op 71 1970.
Corentyne Kwe-Kwe Op 75 (piano) 1972. Recorded Altarus AIR 2 9004.
Letter Galliard Op 79 (piano) 1974. Recorded Altarus AIR 2 9004.
Suite of Six Op 81 (string quartet) 1975.
Sonatina Op 82 (recorders, piano) 1975.
Compass Points Op 83 (pipes) 1976.
Twenty-Four Preludes Op 86 (piano) 1977. Recorded Altarus AIR 2 9004.
Sonatina Op 88 (viola, piano) 1978.
Pro Pace et Felicitate Generis Humani Op 89 (cello, piano) 1979.
Souvenir d'une nuit d'été Op 90 (piano, after Sergei Liapunov) 1979.
Meditation and Scherzo Op 93 (double bass, piano) 1980.
Concertino Op 94 (2 violins, piano) 1981.
Scots Jigganspiel Op 95 (piano) 1982.
Six Short Pieces Op 99 (piano) 1983. Recorded Hyperion A 66138.
Summer Fields and Hedgerows Op 100 (clarinet, piano) 1984.
Piano Quintet Op 104 1984.
Octet Op 105 (flute, clarinet, horn, string quartet, piano) 1985.
Canzona Op 106 (flute, clarinet, violin, cello, piano) 1985.
Serenade and Duet Op 111 (violin, piano) 1986.
Distant Fields Op 112 (piano) 1986.
Sonata in G Op 114 (piano) 1986.
Two Pieces for Nancy Op 115 1986.
Prelude and Concert Piece Op 116 (organ) 1986.
Suite Op 117 (organ) 1986.
Three Five Beat First Year Pieces Op 118 (piano) 1987.

Vocal/choral:

Two Songs Op 7 (soprano, chamber orchestra; Monro) 1925.
Song to Labour (mixed chorus, piano; Gilman) 1926.
Song of the Doomed Op 14 (tenor, female chorus, piano; Boden) 1929.
Song to the Men of England (unaccompanied mixed chorus; Shelley) 1929.
The Road (unaccompanied mixed chorus; Friedlander) 1929.
Question and Answer (mixed chorus, piano; Atterbury) 1931.
Hunger Marchers' Song (mixed chorus, piano; Swingler) 1934.
Labour's Song of Challenge (mixed chorus, piano; Swingler) 1936.
Make Your Meaning Clear (mixed chorus, piano; Swingler) 1939.
Prison Cycle (collaboration with Alan Rawsthorne; baritone, piano; Toller) 1939.
Against the People's Enemies (mixed chorus, piano; Swingler) 1940.
March of the Workers (mixed chorus, piano; Morris) 1940.
The Ice Breaks (mixed chorus, piano; Swingler) 1940.
Truth on the March (mixed chorus, piano; Swingler) 1940.
Unite and Be Free (mixed chorus, piano; AB) 1941.
The Great Red Army (mixed chorus, piano; Swingler) 1942.
Toulon (mezzo-soprano, mixed chorus, piano; N. Bush) 1942.
Song of the Commons of England (mixed chorus, piano; Carpenter) 1942.
Britain's Part (mixed chorus, speaker, piano, percussion; AB) 1943.
The Winter Journey Op 29 (soprano, baritone, mixed chorus, string quintet, harp; Swingler) 1946.
A World for Living (mixed chorus, piano; Swingler) 1946.
Lidice (unaccompanied mixed chorus; N. Bush) 1947.
Our Song (mixed chorus, piano; N. Bush) 1948.
Song of Friendship Op 34 (bass, mixed chorus, orchestra; N. Bush) 1949.
The Dream of Llewelyn Ap Gruffydd Op 35 (male voice chorus, piano; Swingler) 1950.
Shining Vision (mixed chorus, piano; Slater) 1950.
Voices of the Prophets Op 41 (tenor, piano; Isaiah, Milton, Blake, Blackman) 1953. Recorded Argo RG 439.
The Ballad of Freedom's Soldier Op 44 (tenor, bass-baritone, mixed chorus, orchestra; Manifold) 1953.
Like Rivers Flowing (SSATB part-song; N. Bush) 1957.
Nicht Den Tod Aus Der Ferne (baritone, mixed unison chorus, clarinet, trumpet, percussion, piano; Mueller) 1958.
Ballade Vom Marsche Auf Aldermaston (speaker, mixed chorus, 2 horns, 2 trumpets, 2 guitars, percussion, double bass; Mueller, N. Bush) 1958.
The World Is His Song Op 51 (mezzo-soprano/baritone, mixed chorus, 2 horns, 2 trumpets, 3 trombones, tuba, guitar, percussion, piano; N. Bush) 1958.
Seafarers' Songs Op 57 (baritone, piano) 1961.
The Tide That Will Never Turn (2 speakers, bass/baritone, mixed chorus, strings, percussion, piano; MacDiarmid) 1961.
Song of the Cosmonaut (mixed chorus, piano; Tomalin) 1961.
During Music (SATB part-song; Rossetti) 1963.
The Alps and Andes of the Living World Op 66 (speaker, tenor, mixed chorus, orchestra; Shakespeare, Huxley, N. Bush) 1968.
The Freight of Harvest Op 69 (tenor, piano; Warner) 1969.
Men Of Feeling Op 72 (male choir, piano; N. Bush) 1971.
Earth Has Grain to Grow (unaccompanied mixed chorus; Day Lewis) 1972.
Carol: The Earth Awakening Op 74 (female choir, organ; N. Bush) 1972.
Life's Span Op 77 (mezzo-soprano, piano) 1972.
Song for Angela Davis (mixed chorus, optional piano; N. Bush) 1972.
Africa Is My Name Op 85 (mezzo-soprano, mixed chorus, piano or orchestra; N. Bush) 1976.
Three Songs Op 86 (baritone, piano) 1979.
Woman's Life Op 87 (soprano, piano) 1979.
Two Shakespeare Sonnets Op 91 (voice, piano) 1980.
Turkish Workers' Marching Song Op 101 (chorus, piano) 1982.
The Earth in Shadow Op 102 (mixed chorus, orchestra) 1982.
Mandela Speaking Op 110 (baritone, chorus, orchestra) 1985.

Opera:

The Press Gang: or The Escap'd Apprentice (children's opera; N. Bush) 1946.
Wat Tyler (N. Bush) 1948–51; first performed Leipzig, 1953. 1953.
The Spell Unbound (Elizabethan opera for girls) 1953.
Men of Blackmoor (N. Bush) 1954—5; first performed Weimar, 1956.

The Ferryman's Daughter (school opera) 1961.
The Sugar Reapers (N. Bush) 1961–3; first performed Leipzig, 1966.
Joe Hill: The Man Who Never Died 1966–8; first performed Berlin, 1970.

Other:

The Pageant of Labour (theatre music) 1934.
His War or Yours (ballet) 1935.
Mining (ballet) 1935.
The Pageant of Co-Operation (theatre music) 1938.
The Star Turns Red (theatre music) 1940.
The Duke in Darkness (theatre music) 1942.
Macbeth (incidental music to Shakespeare) 1947.
Communist Manifesto Centenary Pageant 1948.
Songs of Asian Struggle (arranged by AB) 1969.

PUBLICATIONS

By Bush: *Strict Counterpoint in the Palestrina Style*, London, 1948; *In My Seventh Decade*, London, 1970; *In My Eighth Decade*, London, 1980.

On Bush: *AB at 60*, essays published by Workers' Music Association, 1960; *AB—A Life*, (film) by Anna Ambrose, 1983.

* * *

"In 1934 I became convinced that the facts about life, including human life, and about the inorganic world from stellar galaxies to atoms and for that matter to other particles discovered by 20th-century nuclear physics, were convincingly explained or brilliantly foretold between the years 1844 and 1896 by Karl Marx and Friedrich Engels." These are the convictions by which Alan Bush has lived his intellectual life since the 1930s; though at time of writing, there is no indication what his attitude may be to recent changes, affirmative and negative, in the Soviet bloc, he has shown no sign in the past of wavering even at those cruces—the Nazi-Soviet Non-Aggression Pact, Hungary, Czechoslovakia, Afghanistan, the *glasnost* thaw—which have driven even committed Communists back into the liberal mainstream. In the same essay in the collection *In My Eighth Decade*, Bush claims to owe his life "to the glorious Red Army".

But what about Bush's life as a composer? How has his apparently overdetermining commitment to Marxism influenced his work? It is always easier to discuss the ideological component of a vocal work (for which there is a text) than an instrumental or orchestral one. At the height of Stalinish paranoia, there was, of course, a handbook of "acceptable" revolutionary strategies in composition: major keys, "affirmative" themes and melodies, four-square metres. Bush's music has nothing to do with such things; his essay in a collection on Shostakovitch reinforced the pre-*Testimony* image of an apostate returned to the fold, but what was interesting about that essay was Bush's location of Shostakovitch's career in the wider context of Russian history, Imperial as well as Soviet. His own music needs to be heard in such a context; he has never been a "mere" ideologue, less so, one might say in his music even than in his writings. His sense of history is passionately developed and not restricted—as the *Lascaux Symphony* of 1983, inspired by ancient cave paintings in southern France, shows—to modern social and political history.

Though he has occupied high academic position in the British musical establishment (significantly, the first appointee in music history at the Royal Academy of Music), Bush is something of an outsider figure. Virtually all his important operatic writing has only been staged behind what used to be the Iron Curtain (though some recordings were made by the BBC); there are only a handful of works on record; and, despite a flurry of respectful attention at the time of Bush's 85th birthday, he rarely appears on concert programmes. Nonetheless, he is an important figure.

There is a major shift of style at the centre of Bush's career, towards a more populist, tonal idiom, less elitist in implication than the advanced modernism of his earlier work. Typically, though, Bush did not undergo the kind of radical purgation self-prescribed by younger radicals like Cornelius Cardew, who in the 1970s violently eschewed modernism of any kind in favour of a rigorously straightforward, declamatory music which was usually reducible to the sentiments expressed in the text or programme. Bush's response to the "crisis in modern music"—to quote a 1946 essay—was to turn to a "thematic" style, in which every note carries an unhierarchical thematic significance.

It is a shift of style rather than a break, however. Bush's music betrays a remarkable inner consistency from the A minor Quartet of 1924 right through to the outwardly schematic, cycle-of-fifths exercises of *Twenty-Four Preludes*. His masterpiece is the 1929 string quartet *Dialectic*, written in a single dense movement that attempts to convey formally and without easy resolutions the thesis-antithesis-synthesis trajectory of historicist logic. It is a demanding work, but it is also unquestionably one of the most significant pieces in modern quartet literature, one whose example seems, none-theless, to have been ignored.

It is a cliché that while Linz and Paris, London and Leningrad are well-known symphonic cities, Bush's "Nottingham", his Symphony No 2 is virtually unknown. Written in 1949, it is the most robust of his symphonic scores, far removed from the pastoralism of most English music even of that time. The attractive *Variations, Nocturne and Finale on an English Sea-Song* (for a long time the only music of Bush's available on commercial recording) conveys the same impression of deep confidence with the orchestra. Bush is a strongly intellectual technician, a scholar of Palestrina, and has an instinctive feel for structure and appropriate instrumental colour; his work is far removed from the catch-all Soviet-symphonic manner.

The 1948 *Concerto for Violin* combines a "thematic" disposition of material (in what resembles a serialist tone-row) in a broadly tonal fashion, but replete with tensions and internal contradictions that are left not to the solo violin to sort out—the heroic Byronism of the Third Symphony is not in evidence here—nor to the "collectivity" of the orchestra, but to the two in a vigorous cooperation.

In his operas, Bush attempted to create much the same overall effect. Though because they are constrained by history, stories such as that of the judicially murdered American radical Joe Hill and of Wat Tyler, nominal head of the Peasants' Revolt inevitably end in the defeat of the hero. Bush's response is a radicalisation of the normative endings of Shakespearean tragedy. Though Hill and Tyler are dead, their influence transforms the choric or purely musical conclusion in such a way as to suggest not a bland resolution or transcendence but a new and significantly higher level of struggle. It is one of the great pities that Bush's operas have not been properly staged in Britain.

His early career as a conductor of workers' choirs gave him a great facility for setting unpromising material. One piece, though, stands out. *Lidice*, for unaccompanied chorus, was inspired by the elimination of a small Bohemian village by the Nazis in reprisal for resistance activities. The work was premiered, with Bush conducting, at the site of the murdered village, a poignant act of remembrance and intercession which further underlines Bush's desire to push music beyond the commercial concert-hall constraints of contemporary music.

Bush has continued to compose, mainly for piano, and to widen the range of his interests. Since the mid-1960s, he has taken an interest in what would be called Third World politics—aspects of the anti-colonial struggle were already evident in his opera *The Sugar Reapers*—and to expand his musical vocabulary accordingly. He will certainly be remembered for *Dialectic*, for the haunting *Winter Journey* and *Voices of the Prophets*. He is already remembered by those whom he taught and those working people for whom he was an unexpected and dedicated introduction to the power of music.

—Brian Morton

BUSH, Geoffrey. British/English. Born in London, 23 March 1920. Educated at Salisbury Cathedral Choir School, 1928–33; Lancing College, 1933–8; Balliol College, Oxford (Nettleship Scholar and Masefield Memorial Student), 1938–40, 1945–6, B.A., B.Mus, 1940, M.A., D.Mus, 1946. Wartime service as assistant warden, Hostel of the Good Shepherd, Tredegar, Wales, looking after unbilletable evacuee children, 1940–5. Married Julie Kathleen McKenna, 15 April 1950; 2 sons. Organist, St. Luke's Chelsea, London, 1946–7; lecturer in music, Extra-Mural Department, University of Oxford, 1947–52; staff tutor in music, Extra-Mural Department, 1952–64, senior staff tutor in music, 1964–80, and music consultant, 1984–87, University of London; visiting professor, Kings College, London, 1969–89. Chair, 1957, and council member, since 1960, Composers Guild of Great Britain; member, Arts Council Music Advisory Panel, 1963–9; music advisor, John Ireland Trust, since 1969; chair, Members Fund of Performing Rights Society, since 1987; pianist; regular contributor to BBC programmes "Music Magazine", "Music Weekly"; contributor to journals *Composer, Musical Times, Music and Letters*; editor of scholarly editions. Recipient: Royal Philharmonic Society's Prize (for overture *Yorick*), 1949; honorary fellow, University of Wales, Aberystwyth, 1986. Mailing address: 43 Corringham Road, London NW11 7BS, England.

Publishers: Novello; Stainer & Bell.

Symphonies/orchestral:

Natus est Immanuel (string orchestra) 1939.
Rhapsody (clarinet, string orchestra or quartet) 1940.
Overture: The Spanish Rivals 1941; first performed Cheltenham, Gloucestershire, 1952.
Divertimento (string orchestra) 1943.
Sinfonietta Concertante (cello, small orchestra) 1943; broadcast BBC, 28 September 1945.
In Praise of Salisbury 1944.
Overture: The Rehearsal 1945; first performed Cheltenham, Gloucestershire, 14 June 1953.
Concerto for Oboe and Strings 1948; first performed London, 1956.
Two Minatures (string orchestra) 1948.
Overture: Yorick 1949; first performed Cheltenham, Gloucestershire, 13 July 1954. Recorded NPO Lyrita SRCS 95.
Concertino No 1 (piano, orchestra) 1953; first performed London, 11 February 1961.
Symphony No 1 1954; first performed Cheltenham, Gloucestershire, 8 July 1954. Recorded LSO Lyrita SRCS 115.
Symphony No 2 "The Guildford" 1957.
Concerto for Light Orchestra 1958.
Songs of Wonder (high voice and strings) 1959.
Hornpipe for St Cecilia's Day (movement from collaborative *Suite for St Cecilia's Day*, co-written with Iain Hamilton, Alun Hoddinott and Thea Musgrave) 1960; first performed Birmingham, 22 November 1960.
Suite: Old London (concert band) 1961.
Concerto for Trumpet, Piano and Strings 1962; first performed London, 1963.
Finale for a Concert 1964.
Music 1967. Recorded LPO Lyrita SRCS 57.
Consort Music: Six Victorian Sketches (string orchestra) 1987.

Chamber/instrumental:

Rhapsody (clarinet, string quartet) 1940.
Epigrams (piano) 1941.
Sonata (violin, piano) 1945.
Four Pieces (piano) 1946.
Nocture and Toccata (piano) 1947.
An Oxford Scherzo (2 pianos) 1949.
Three Dance Variations (harpsichord or piano) 1951.
Trio (oboe, bassoon, piano) 1952. Recorded Chandos ABRD 1196.
Two Pieces (organ) 1955.
Dialogue (oboe, piano) 1960. Recorded Chandos ABRD 1196.
Whydah Variations on a Theme by Balfour Gardiner (2 pianos) 1961.
Homage to Matthew Locke (3 trumpets, 3 trombones) 1962.
Air and Round-O (wind quintet) 1963. Recorded Chandos ABRD 1196.
Wind Quintet 1963. Recorded Chandos ABRD 1196.
Sonatina No 1 (piano) 1965; first performed BBC, 1967. Recorded Chandos ABRD 2006.
Sonatina No 2 (piano) 1969; first performed BBC, 1970.
Concertino No 2 (piano, 12 players) 1976.
Trumpet March (organ) 1981; first performed London, 1981.
Tributes: Five Respectful Pieces (clarinet, piano) 1986.
Two Bagatelles (cello, wind quintet) 1987.

Vocal/choral:

Te Deum in C (mixed voices, organ) 1938.
Five Choral Dances (unaccompanied mixed voices) 1941.
Portraits: 5 Songs About Musicians (unaccompanied mixed voices) 1942.
Five Spring Songs (high voice, piano) 1944.
A Christmas Cantata (chorus, orchestra) 1947. Recorded Saydisc SDL 352.
A Summer Serenade (chorus, orchestra) 1948.
Three Elizabethan Songs (high voice, piano) 1948.

Four Songs from Herrick's Hesperides (baritone, piano) 1949.
Farewell, Earth's Bliss (baritone, string quartet or string orchestra) 1950.
Twelfth Night, an Entertainment (chorus, orchestra) 1950.
Three Songs of Ben Jonson (high voice, piano) 1952. Recorded Chandos ABRD 1053.
The End of Love (baritone, piano) 1954. Recorded Chandos ABRD 1053.
In Praise of Mary (chorus, orchestra) 1955; first performed Hereford, 1955. Recorded Unicorn Kanchana DKP 9057.
Two Anthems (mixed voices, organ) 1956; first performed London, 21 November 1956.
Songs of Wonder (high voice, piano) 1959. Recorded Chandos ABRD 1053.
A Lover's Progress (tenor, oboe, clarinet and bassoon) 1961.
The Sweet Season: 4 Simple Songs (unaccompanied mixed voices) 1961.
Two Latin Hymns (unaccompanied mixed voices) 1963.
Greek Love Songs (baritone, piano) 1964. Recorded Chandos ABRD 1053.
Cantata Piccola (baritone solo, SATB chorus, strings, harpsichord or piano) 1965.
Two Shelley Songs (unaccompanied mixed voices) 1967.
Magnificat and Nunc Dimittis, Collegium Magdalenae Oxioniense (mixed voices, organ) 1968. Recorded Argo ZRG 722.
Missa Brevis Salisburiensis (mixed voices, organ) 1968. Recorded Abbey ACA 502.
Seven Limericks (chorus, orchestra) 1968.
A Menagerie (unaccompanied mixed voices) 1969.
Psalm 24 (mixed voices, organ) 1969.
Two Choruses (unaccompanied mixed voices) 1969.
Five Mediaeval Lyrics (baritone, piano) 1970.
A Nice Derangement of Epitaphs (unaccompanied mixed voices) 1971.
Daffydd in Love (mixed voices, organ) 1974.
A Little Love Music (soprano, tenor) 1976. Recorded Chandos ABRD 1053.
Magnificat and Nunc Dimittis: St. Paul's Service (mixed voices, organ) 1976. Recorded Abbey ACA 502.
Two Carols (mixed voices, organ) 1977. Recorded Abbey ACA 502.
Two Christmas Carols (1) unison voices, piano, percussion; 2) unison voices, organ or piano duet, optional percussion) 1978.
Phantoms (chorus, orchestra) 1978.
A Stevie Smith Cycle (high voice, oboe, cello, piano) 1981.
Cuisine Provençale (medium voice, piano) 1982; first performed London, 1982.
Daystar in Winter (mixed voices, organ) 1982.
Two Legends (mixed voices, organ) 1984.
Two Love Lyrics (medium voice, piano) 1984.
Mirabile Misterium (A Great and Mighty Wonder) (high voice, piano; or string quartet, harpsichord) 1985; first performed London, 1988.
Love's Labours Lost (soprano, baritone, orchestra) 1986.
Four Chaucer Settings (baritone, oboe, piano) 1987; first performed London, 20 February 1990.
Old Rhymes Re-Set (high voice, piano) 1987.
Songs of the Zodiac (high voice, piano) 1989; first performed London, 20 March 1990.

Operas/stage works:

The Blind Beggar's Daughter (Bathurst) 1952, revised 1964.
If the Cap Fits (after Molière) 1956.
The Equation (after Drinkwater's *X=O*) 1967.
Lord Arthur Savile's Crime (after Wilde) 1972.
The Cat Who Went to Heaven (after Coatsworth) 1974.
Love's Labours Lost (after Shakespeare) 1988.

Other:

The Merchant of Venice (incidental music to Shakespeare) 1964.

Realisations/completions of: Thomas Arne: *Sinfonietta on* Themes by Arne, Sonata (2 pianos); Schubert: scherzos from *Piano Sonata in C* (unfinished) and *Symphony No 8 in B minor* (unfinished); Henry Bishop: *Overture: The Miller and His Men*; Mozart: *Sonata in F (K.497)* (2 pianos); Sterndale Bennett: *Sonata* (2 pianos); *Castle Gordon* (mixed voices unaccompanied).

Editions of John Ireland: Collected Piano Music; Collected Songs (4 volumes); *Two Symphonic Studies*; *Scherzo and Cortege: Julius Caesar*; *A Downland Suite* (strings); *Elegiac Mediation* (strings).

Scholarly editions of Sterndale Bennett, Parry, Stanford, English song 1800–1860.

PUBLICATIONS

By Bush: *Musical Creation and the Listener*, London, 1954, revised 1967; "Song" and "Chamber Music", in *The Athlone History of Music in Britain, V: The Romantic Age*, edited by Nicholas Temperley, London, 1981; *Left, Right and Centre: Reflections on Composers and Composing*, London, 1983; *An Unsentimental Education*, London, 1990.

On Bush: Special GB issue of *Musical Times*, edited by Jasper Rooper, December 1967; David Rayl, "The Choral Music of GB", *Choral Journal*, November 1980; Geoffrey Crankshaw, "GB", in *Music and Musicians*, May 1982.

Geoffrey Bush comments:

Composers do not usually make conscious choices about the music they write: they write in accordance with the talents given to them. For this reason I do not write complex or experimental music: I have no gift for such things. Instead, my music is lyrical, rhythmic, economical, clear cut in texture and, as far as I can make it, direct of utterance.

I believe in the continuity of the English musical tradition and only wish that colleagues and fellow countrymen were more aware of it. Borrowing from other countries is as dangerous in music as it is in high finance. As a composer I am happiest writing songs and operas: words—when I find the right ones—are an unfailing stimulus.

* * *

Geoffrey Bush's most formative early experience was as a chorister at Salisbury Cathedral, where his encounter with 400 years of English choral music and the formidable professionalism of Sir Walter Alcock (the Cathedral organist and choirmaster) stamped is style indelibly. His time at Lancing College, where he learnt with Jasper Rooper, and at Oxford as a Scholar at Balliol College also had a profound effect, as did his studying with John Ireland, which extended either side of his University years. From these early encounters he developed an acute ear for sung harmonies emerging from contrapuntal movement, rather than as played on the piano, and learned to write music that was challenging and rewarding to perform, and to use as few notes as possible to create his musical effects. Economy and understatement have remained hallmarks of his style, partly through his aversion to lengthy, emotionally charged, Germanic music, and partly through his admiration of Russian (especially Prokoviev and Shostakovich) and French music, with its wit, brevity, harmonic colour and dependence on melody as a prime feature.

Bush's most characteristic music is for voices: stage-works, choral pieces and solo songs. He has a natural affinity for a wide range of texts (from Chaucer to Stevie Smith via Jonson, Wilde and Virginia Woolf), and his music embellishes and illuminates rather than fights the words. This is as true for his earliest works, such as *Three Elizabethan Songs* for high voice and piano, *Four Songs from Herrick's Hesperides* for baritone and piano or the beautiful choral cantata *In Praise of Mary*, where the harmonic language owes much to Delius and Ireland and the melodic style to the prevailing English syllabic manner. It also applies to later works such as *Phantoms* for female voices, the song-cycle *Mirabile Misterium* or the *Magnificat and Nunc Dimittis*, where the melodic style is more angular, and full of cadenza-type figures, and the harmonic language more freely dissonant. In the later works the textures tend also to be leaner and the individual lines more exposed—an indication of Bush's perennial aim for ever-greater concision.

Bush's structures are rooted in neo-classicism. Consequently not only are most of his pieces relatively short, but even the longer ones, such as the symphonies, tend to fall into sections. He once said that if a composer felt he wanted to write one tune after another he could not see why he should not do so. Such a remark, however, while demonstrating his general attitude, should not be taken as a blueprint for his musical constructions, which are much more tightly organised than this would indicate. His *Symphony No 1*, for instance, contains two sonata-principle movements, the first of which is preceded by an evocative slow introduction whose repetition elsewhere in the movement, and in the work, forms a focus for the whole piece. Yet the slow movement is even more typical of Bush. Firstly, it is dedicated to the memory of someone he admired (Constant Lambert), secondly it uses a stylised blues idiom in a serious context (a characteristically Bushian irony), and thirdly it is built on a series of gestures rather than full-blown ideas, which culminate in a quotation from Lambert's *Rio Grande*. Bush's formal style is not unlike a stage-play whose characters may appear stereotyped at first but who gather depth and meaning in the course of the action.

Bush's music is as varied as his tastes and interests. Few works omit a serious side, but he prefers to approach this obliquely and never overstate it. Much of his music is witty, in every sense. Some of his music is funny, such as the "Explosives aria" in the marvellous, one-act opera *Lord Arthur Savile's Crime*; some of it is witty in the clever sense, such as the delightful *Tributes* for clarinet and piano, each of whose movements evokes the style of its dedicatee. This work also uses tunes, as does his *Consort Music* for strings, that originated as songs in the pantomimes he wrote with Ronald Mason for the University of London Summer School at Westonbirt. These songs show another passion of Bush's, the American musical.

Apart from composing, Bush has been an ardent champion of English music, editing neglected works for *Musica Britannica* and the forthcoming collected works of Elgar. He has also written widely on music and broadcast frequently. Outside writing music, most of his time has been taken up teaching adults. For 30 years he was the Staff Tutor in Music at the Extra-Mural Department of London University. Like his music, Bush's lectures are deeply informed, elegantly presented and economically expressed. Beneath a disciplined, sometimes even austere, exterior he conceals passionate involvement and a generous quantity of emotion.

—Roderick Swanston

BUSSOTTI, Sylvano. Italian. Born in Florence, 1 October 1931. Education: violin lessons with Margherita Castellano, 1936–40; Conservatory "Luigi Cherubini", Florence (piano under Luigi Dallapiccola, harmony and counterpoint under Roberto Lupi), 1940, interrupted by war; self-taught composition, 1949–56; private classes with Max Deutsch, Paris, 1956–8; Ferienkurse für Neue Musik, Darmstadt, 1958; Rockefeller Foundation grant to visit United States, 1964–5; studied in Berlin, DAAD award, 1972. Member, Gruppo 70, 1963; teacher of music history, Academy of Fine Arts, L'Aquila, 1971–4; artistic director, La Fenice Theatre, Venice, since 1975; artistic consultant, Puccini Festival, Torre del Lago, 1979–81, thereafter director; teacher of composition and musical analysis, Fiesole School of Music, since 1980. Recipient: ISCM (Italian Section) prizes, 1961, 1963, 1965; All'Amelia Prize, Venice Bienniale, 1967; Toscani d'Oggi/Golden Olive Branch, 1974; Psacaropulo Prize, Turin, 1979. Mailing address: c/o Ricordi, via Berchet 2, Milan, Italy.

Publishers: Ricordi; Bruzzichelli; Moeck; Universal.

Symphonies/orchestral:

. . . et due voci 1958–85; first performed Venice, 1985.
I semi di Gramsci (symphonic poem for string quartet, and orchestra) 1962–71; first performed Rome, 22 April 1972.
Lorenzaccio Symphony I (soprano, large orchestra) 1974; first performed Royan, 28 March 1974. Recorded Deutsche Grammophon DGG 2531 011.
Lorenzaccio Symphony II 1978; first performed Rome, 17 December 1978.
Il Catalogo e' questo—I (Opus Cygne) (symphonic/choreographic movements) 1976–81; first performed Donaueschingen, 20 October 1979. Recorded Fonit Cetra ITL 70085.
Il Catalogo e' questo—II (Raragramma) 1979; first performed Donaueschingen, 20 October 1979.
Danza di buffera (from *Nottetempo*) 1980; first performed Palermo, 28 September 1980.
Le bal Miró (anthology for orchestra) 1981.
Rosso (rosso sangue) (rosso vivo) (rosso bandiera) 1984; first performed Lugano, March 1984.
Timpani 1985; first performed Rome, 12 January 1986.
H III (from *Il catalogo e questo IV*) 1987; first performed Tokyo, 1987.
Il poemetto (from *Il catalogo e questo IV* [*I Poemi*] 1987.

Chamber/instrumental:

Les Petits Plaisirs (ondes martenot) 1946–57.
La Recherche de bal perdu (piano) 1953–7.

Musica per amici (piano) 1957, revised 1971; first performed Florence, 1971.
Pas de deux (ondes martenot) 1958.
Breve (ondes martenot) 1958–72; first performed Dusseldorf, 1972.
Piano Pieces for David Tudor 1959.
Setti fogli (various) 1959.
Phrase à trois (string trio) 1960.
Pour clavier (piano) 1961. Recorded EMI EMSP 551.
Tableaux vivants (2 pianos; from *La Passion selon Sade*) 1964; first performed Bremen, 1964.
Rara (eco sierologico) (guitar, string trio, double bass) 1964–7. Recorded Deutsche Grammophon EGG 2530 307; Fonit Cetra ITL 70038.
Rara (dolce) (flute, with mime; from *La Passion selon Sade*) 1966; first performed Karlsruhe, 1969.
Solo (flute, clarinet/bass clarinet, trombone, harp, piano, viola, cello, 2 percussion; or flute, clarinet, trumpet, trombone, viola, cello, harp, celeste, 2 percussion; or 2 flutes/piccolo, oboe, oboe d'amore, 2 clarinets, 2 bassoons, 2 horns, percussion, celeste, piano, harp, cello; from *La Passion selon Sade*) 1967; broadcast Danish Radio, 3 February 1968. Recorded Ictus 0200; Erato STU 70624.
Marbre pour cordes (11 strings) 1967; first performed London, 10 November 1967. Recorded Erato STU 70624.
Ultima rara (pop song) (guitar; or guitar, 3 speakers) 1969; first performed Berlin, 1970. Recorded Deutsche Grammophon DGG 2530 561/037.
Foglio d'album (piano) 1970; first performed Venice, 1970.
Quartetto Gramsci (string quartet) 1971; first performed Siena, 26 August 1974.
Novelette (piano) 1973; first performed New York City, 20 November 1973.
Rondo' di scena (4 flutes; from *Phaidra/Heliogabalus*) 1975.
Brillante (piano) 1975; first performed Florence, 10 June 1976.
Ripetente (piano, clarinet, bassoon, trumpet, trombone, violin, double bass, percussion) 1976; first performed Milan, 12 February 1976.
Gran duo (cello, piano) 1977–8; first performed Middelburg, 1978.
Passo d'uomo (piccolo, timpani, 2 percussion groups; from *Phaidra/Heliogabalus*) 1978.
Tramonto (flute, horn, clarinet; from *Phaidra/Heliogabalus*) 1978.
"Dai, Dimmi, Su!" (11 instruments; from *Phaidra/Heliogabalus*) 1978.
Passo d'uomo (piccolo, timpani, percussion) 1978; first performed Rome, 17 December 1978.
Tramonto (flute, horn, clarinet) 1978; first performed L'Aquila, 5 March 1979.
Three Lovers Ballet (violin, cello, piano) 1978; first performed Fiesole, 1978.
Rondo' di scena (flute) 1978; first performed Siena, 28 August 1978.
Brutto, ignudo (bass clarinet) 1979; first performed U.S.A., 1980.
Accademia (flute, piano; from *Phaidra/Heliogabalus*) 1980; first performed Fiesole, 22 June 1981.
Nudo disteso (viola) 1980; first performed Venice, 1980.
Naked Angel Face (double bass) 1982; first performed 13 November 1982.
La vergine ispirata (harpsichord, another harmony instrument) 1982; first performed Paris, 21 March 1983.
Due concertanti I (piccolo, double bass) 1983; first performed June 1983.
Qu'un corps défigure (viola, oboe, bassoon, trombone, percussion) 1986.
Concerto all'Aquila (9 instruments) 1986; first performed London, 6 July 1986.
Olof Palme (piano) 1987.

Vocal/choral:

Autunno (4 voices; Villanova, Joyce, Trakl) 1950–3.
Tre canti (voice, piano; Gide) 1951–2.
Poesia di depisis (soprano, 15 instruments; on a theme of Dallapiccola) 1954; first performed Siena, 27 August 1975.
Nottetempo con lo scherzo e una rosa (voice, chamber orchestra; Pisis) 1954–7.
El carbonero (5 voices; anon.) 1957.
Due voci (soprano, ondes martenot, orchestra; La Fontaine) 1958.
Pièces de chair II (piano, baritone, female voice, instruments) 1958–60; first performed Paris, 22 October 1970.
Pearson Piece (baritone, piano) 1960.
"Extraits de concert" (voice, ensemble; from *La passion selon Sade*) 1965; first performed Milan, 28 February 1966.
Cinque frammenti all'Italia (vocal sextet, chorus; consisting of "Amicoro Odono i Colli", 1967; first performed Rome, 1967; "Solo el Misterio", 1967; first performed Hamburg, 1968; "La curva dell'amore", 1968; first performed Venice, 14 September 1968; "Per 24 voci adulte o bianche", 1967; first performed Bordeaux, 1967; "Rar'ancora", 1968; first performed Venice, 14 September 1968) 1967–8. Recorded Wergo 60048.
Julio Organum Julii (reciter, organ; Braibanti) 1968; first performed Bremen, 1968.
The Rara Requiem (vocal group, choir, guitar, cello, wind orchestra, piano, harp, percussion) 1969–70; first performed Venice, 13 September 1969.
Aria di Mara (soprano, orchestra; from *Lorenzaccio*) 1973; first performed Milan, 9 July 1973.
Lachrimae (voices) 1978; first performed Naples, 1978.
Citazione con quartina per Maurice (baritone, piano) 1981; first performed 19 June 1982.
In memoriam (Cathy Berberian) (voice, flute, viola, piano) 1984; first performed Castello Colonna, 8 September 1984.
Pianino (boy's voice, piano) 1987.

Opera/dramatic:

Juvenilia (ballet) 1951–3; first performed Segromigno, 5 August 1983.
Nottetempolunapark, *Arlechinbatoceria*, *Tre mascare in gloria* (marionette shows) 1954–6; first performed Florence and Aix-en-Provence, 1954–6.
La Passion selon Sade (chamber mystery play; Loulie) 1965; first performed in part Palermo, Sicily, 1965; first complete performance Stockholm, 1969.
Tema-variazioni (géographie française) 1965; first performed Zagreb, 1965.
Raramente (choreographic mystery play) 1971; first performed Florence, 1971.
Lorenzaccio (romantic melodrama, after Musset) 1972; first performed Venice, 7 September 1972.
Bergkristall (ballet) 1974; first concert performance Hamburg, 15 May 1973; first staged performance Rome, 1974. Recorded Deutsche Grammophon DGG 2531 011.
S*yro*
adun
ettimino
(monodance; text by Maraini) from 1974; first performed Royan, March 1974.

Oggetto amato (Pièce de chair) (ballet) 1975; first performed Milan, 1976.
Nottetempo (lyrical drama; Amidei, SB) 1976; first performed Milan, 7 April 1976.
Le rarita' potente (lyric scene) 1976–8; first performed Treviso, 12 October 1979.
Autotono (indeterminate score) 1977; first performed Treviso, 12 October 1979. Recorded Edipan Pan PRC S20 08.
Le Racine (piano bar pour Phèdre) (opera) 1980; first performed Milan, 9 December 1980.
Phaidra / Heliogabalus (ballet) 1981; first performed Turin, 1981.
Miro, L'uccello luce (ballet; after Dupin) 1981; first performed Venice, 25 September 1981.
Cristallo di Rocca (ballet, after Stifter) 1982; first performed Milan, 10 June 1983.

PUBLICATIONS

By Bussotti: "Nuova musica", in *L'arc*, Aix-en-Provence, 1961; "Note sur 'Piano Pieces for David Tudor' ", in *Marcatre*, Genoa, 1964; "20 appunti discena per La passion selon Sade", in *Marcatre*, 1965; "Due testi rifutati", in *Marcatre*, 1966; "Il gioco e la musica", in *Almanacca leterario Bompiani 1966*, Milan, 1967; "Theodor W. Adorno, l'extra e la linea della vita", in *Marcatre*, 1967; "Extra: publichiamo il privato", regular column in *Discoteca*, 1966–9.

On Bussotti: M. Bortolotto, "New Music in Italy", in Lang and Broder, *Contemporary Music in Europe*, New York, 1965; interview in *Discoteca*, 8(66), 1967; M. Bortolotto, "Le cinque tentazioni di SB", in *Fase seconda*, Turin, 1969; G. La Face, "Eros, grafia e musica nell'opera di SB", dissertation, University of Messina, 1970–1; F. Degrada, *Bussottiopera-ballet: SB eil suo teatro*, Milan, 1976.

* * *

A man of remarkable extremes, Sylvano Bussotti is quite simply the most controversial composer of the last half-century. His music is wildly theatrical, often concerned with erotic and homoerotic themes, autobiographical or personal to his circle of friends and dizzyingly self-referential. Having abandoned both the dogmas of the avant-garde and the freedoms of complete indeterminacy, he has devised a style in which the musical past and his own, interpreted without a hint of historicist perspective, are taken to be identical and mutually penetrative. The precocious young Bussotti was exposed to serialist methods very early but soon came to reject them in their dogmatically strict form in favour of an exploration of indeterminacy, inspired by John Cage, with whom he had an encouraging encounter at Darmstadt in 1958. His music, then and since, espouses a profound anarchism, hostile to the collectivity of present-day society and media (Bussotti, interestingly, has never been attracted to electronics), advocating or expressing an absolutism of the senses and completely self-absorbed. It is remarkably difficult to find one's way around Bussotti's work list because titles are repeated in different combinations, works endlessly gloss themselves and there are almost no generic works in evidence at all; Bussotti's dependence on the past is not a matter of form or of politics, but of intellectual deep structure, an extreme aestheticism.

The very important *Due voci* of 1958 marks his final rejection of restrictive serialism. In the important cycle *Pièces de chair II* with all its many offshoots (like the important *Pour clavier*) Bussotti examines his identity as composer by juxtaposing and then fusing an impassioned text (homoerotic and to a degree sadistic) with a lapidary instrumental score that is among the most remarkable achievements of the post-war period. His friendship with Romano Amidei generated a string of works called *Rara* in which memory, as a principle, began to occupy the central dynamic creative role, allowing Bussotti to see almost anything and everything *sub specie* whatever work was at hand.

A painter like his uncle and brother, Bussotti has used both graphic scores and imagistic conceptions of composition and performance. By this means he sought to overdetermine large-scale stage works like *Lorenzaccio*, attempting to control *all* the elements (analogically, at least, this is what had been happening in serialism). In doing so, pieces such as *La Passion selon Sade*, misleadingly titled, come to resemble the overweening *auteurism* of Artaudian theatre, in which the composer is demiurge rather than craftsman.

Freed of all moral or social commitment, Bussotti is able to launch into a music—increasingly theatrically-oriented—of intense violence and great beauty. After about 1975, he was prepared to subsume almost everything he wrote under the portmanteau term "Bussottioperaballet". *Lorenzaccio* was a majestic achievement, incorporating wholesale reference to Italian culture, sustaining elements of speech, dance, singing, instrumental music and invisible (because offstage) action. The high-tide line of self-revelation is long past but Bussotti continues to produce a work in which music is instinct not with one specialised function of the mind, but with the body (which, of course, contains the mind) and in which music is no longer privileged (that is, listened to in silence) over other means of expression and self-realisation.

—Guido Scarpone

BUTLER, Martin (Claines). British/English. Born in Romsey, Hampshire, 1 March 1960. Educated at University of Manchester, 1978–81, B.Mus.; Royal Northern College of Music, Manchester (composition and piano), 1978–82, G.R.N.C.M., P.P.R.N.C.M; Berkshire Music Center, Tanglewood, Massachusetts, 1982; Princeton University, New Jersey, 1983–7, M.F.A., 1985. Tutor in composition, Royal Northern College of Music, Manchester, 1988; lecturer in music, University of Sussex, Brighton, since 1988. Recipient: Mendelssohn Scholarship, 1988; Fulbright Fellowship, 1983–5; BMI Award for Student Composers (for *The Flights of Col*), 1984. Mailing address: c/o Oxford University Press, 7/8 Hatherley Street, London SW1P 2QT, England.

Publisher: Oxford University Press.

Symphonies / orchestral:

Concertino (chamber orchestra) 1983; first performed Paris, 20 November 1983.
The Flights of Col 1983; first performed London, 31 January 1986.
Cavalcade 1985; first performed Blandford, Hampshire, 31 March 1986.
Fixed Doubles 1989; first performed Scandinavia, 1990.

Chamber/instrumental:

Sonata (piano) 1982; first performed Manchester, May 1982.
From an Antique Land (2 flutes, 2 oboes, 2 clarinets/alto saxophone, 2 bassoons, 2 horns, 2 trumpets, 2 trombones, tuba, 2 percussion, piano) 1982; first performed Manchester, May 1982.
Dance Fragments (clarinet, horn, percussion, harp, violin, cello) 1984; first performed Princeton, New Jersey, 8 December 1985.
Capistrano Song (clarinet, tape) 1984; first performed Princeton, New Jersey, 21 October 1984.
String Quartet 1984; first performed Cheltenham, Gloucestershire, 16 July 1984.
Spells and Chants (2 pianos) 1985; first performed Princeton, New Jersey, 18 May 1986.
Tin Pan Ballet (flute/piccolo/alto flute, trombone, cello, percussion, piano, DX7 synthesizer) 1986.
Ballet con salsa (rewritten version of *Tin Pan Ballet*; brass, percussion, synthesizer) 1987.
Bluegrass Variations (violin) 1988.
Songs and Dances from a Haunted Place (string quartet) 1988; first performed London, 30 June 1988.
Piano, Piano (2 pianos, video) 1989; first performed London, 18 April 1989.
Jazz Machines (flute, clarinet, viola, cello, vibraphone, piano) 1990.

Vocal/choral:

Three Emily Dickinson Songs (soprano, clarinet, piano) 1985; first performed Princeton, New Jersey, 31 March 1985.
To See the Beauties of the Earth (unaccompanied SATB chorus) 1987.
Dirty Beasts (speaker, 6 instruments; Dahl) 1988; first performed Canterbury, Kent, 15 October 1988. Recorded Collins Classics.

Opera:

The Sirens' Song (baritone, soprano, small male chorus, flute, oboe, clarinet, trumpet, horn, trombone, percussion, piano, violin, viola, cello, double bass, tape; Charles Butler) 1986; first performed Heraklion, Crete, 24 August 1986.

Other:

Night Machines (tape) 1987; first performed Tanglewood, Massachusetts, 1987. Recorded Harmonia Mundi.
Graffiti (tape) 1989.

Martin Butler comments:

People have said that my music lacks a consistent style, an individual "voice". That's a fair criticism, but not one that I take negatively. As a teacher of mine once said, "If you've got a voice, it'll come out eventually". More importantly, I've always tried to be faithful to both the music and the ideas that really excite me, and these can be quite diverse. In one sense, our world is becoming ever more culturally—and thus more stylistically—"rich", and the cultural and stylistic range of my influences seems to expand accordingly. Recent pieces of mine have drawn, more or less directly, on Irish and bluegrass fiddle music, Latin salsa and dance music, and various types of jazz, for example. For me, this isn't a question of imitation or parody; it's a question of finding correspondences between myself and the world and using them expressively. I think many composers working today, perhaps to a greater degree than ever before, no longer see the idea of musical progress as a more or less straight line stretching from 1600, or even from the avant-garde of the early 1950s. Music is an essentially simple language, but one with many dialects, sophisticated and crude, popular and rarified—and very few of them leave me *totally* cold.

One important factor in the *way* various styles filter in and out of my work is my experience with electronic music. I have produced a number of tape pieces and employed synthesizers within ensembles, but have found that the impact of electronic techniques on my "acoustic" music has been quite forceful, too. There are tricks one does with sequencers, for example, which would never occur to one sitting in front of a blank page: methods of repetition, texture-building, counterpoint and so on that can magnify, distort, or simply "mix" familiar musical objects. This experience has perhaps had a greater influence on my compositional *technique* than any other in recent years.

To put it all less fussily, I don't at the moment feel any need to "forge a personal style" from so many different musical enthusiasms; in the future either that need or a style will emerge despite itself (if, in truth, it hasn't emerged already) . . .

* * *

Like a number of composers of his generation, Martin Butler started by accepting modernist ideas, but has since widened his expressive scope. In his earliest years as a student, composition grew naturally out of performance: as an accomplished pianist, Butler sought opportunities to write for and perform alongside friends, and these blossomed at the Royal Northern College of Music. Already in 1982, Butler received critical attention when his ensemble piece, *From an Antique Land*, was given its premiere by the RNCM Contemporary Music Ensemble: and the fluency and cogency of the orchestral work, *The Flights of Col*—written for the National Centre for Orchestral Studies—were quickly noted.

It is one of the abiding strengths of Butler's music that much of it has been stimulated by notions of performance practice, sometimes in close harness with visual or literary ideas. An impressive example is his second essay for the string quartet medium, called *Songs and Dances from a Haunted Place*. The initial impetus for the piece was an image of a ghostly Irish fiddler sitting on a rock on a deserted moor, playing his haunted ethereal fiddle. Ingeniously, Butler transferred this idea to the quartet, conceiving it as a single larger-than-life instrument whose open-string sonorities are emphasised at the expense of conventional polyphony. The energy stored up in the fantasy-like first section finds release in the "unstoppable" jig that follows.

Again, in *Spells and Chants*, the ritualistic chanting of the names of medieval demons and wizards in Ezra Pound's poem "The Alchemist" suggested a musical structure built from the juxtaposition of sonic blocks entirely germane to the two-piano medium. Three musical "types" intermingle—the flamboyant rhetoric of "spells", the canonic "chants" based on a *cantus firmus*, and static, reflective "prayers"—until towards the end, the pianistic canons converge so that the two instruments are eventually playing in unison. In *Piano, Piano*, Butler collaborated with the artist Sasha Craddock to create an experience of sounds and visual images that would run in parallel, rather than integrate with each other: here, the expansion and distortion of ideas in Butler's score is complemented by taped "ghost" pianos on tape. Sometimes, in the course of writing a work, Butler has modified his earliest notions to pursue an entirely contrary idea of potential of his medium. For instance, when commissioned to write a piece for the Australian group Fledermann, Butler's original intention was to underline the differences of colour and gesture germane to the ensemble's mixed instrumental line-up. But as he progressed with the work—*Tin Pan Ballet*—he felt impelled in the opposite direction, treating the ensemble as if it had the cohesiveness of a string quartet.

While Butler's early works manifest the structural rigour he acquired under the tutelage of Anthony Gilbert at Manchester, his music reached a kind of turning-point while he was in the United States. For there he not only made contact with other influential composers, such as Milton Babbitt and Luciano Berio, but came into contact with a wide range of vernacular musics, which have since affected deeply not only his own musical idiom, but nurtured his desire to reach to a wider audience. Many of his abundant short compositions since then have crystallised around concepts of performance drawn from popular styles. His solo violin piece for the 1988 Carl Flesch competition, *Bluegrass Variations*, evokes the style of country and bluegrass music through melodic glissandi, pentatonic scales, open string drones and banjo imitations, and it even quotes from the Patsy Cline country-pop number "Crazy". The physical gestures in performance are, in such pieces as this, as important as the notes themselves. By contrast, *Jazz Machines*, teeming with references to numerous jazz styles, hinges on the irony of making a mechanical-sounding music out of spontaneous, improvisatory types of performance.

Butler's explorations of electronics, at Princeton and in Berio's studio in Florence, Tempo Reale, have been largely geared to extending concepts of harmony in live performance. The fruits of all this—in his orchestral work, *O Rio*—have yet to be assessed. Likewise, aside from a 20-minute chamber opera, *The Sirens' Song*, performed in Heraklion, Crete in 1986, Butler has yet to find theatrical outlets for the plethora of skills he has so far acquired. But the foundations for an individual compositional career have certainly been laid.

—Meirion Bowen

C

CAGE, John (Milton, Jr). American. Born in Los Angeles, California, 12 August 1912 [*Grove's* gives 5 September]. Educated at Los Angeles High School, graduated 1928; Pomona College, Claremont, California, 1928–30; study in Europe; private study with pianist Richard Buhlig, theory with Adolph Weiss, 1933, and under Henry Cowell at New School for Social Research, New York; studied counterpoint with Arnold Schoenberg, California, 1934, and at University of California, Los Angeles. Married Andreyevna (Xenia) Kashevaroff in 1935 (dissolved 1945). Dance accompanist (and first meeting with Merce Cunningham), Cornish School, Seattle, Washington, 1938; taught course in new music, Chicago Institute of Design, 1941; moved to New York permanently, 1943; taught occasional courses, New School for Social Research, 1956–60; fellow, Center for Advanced Studies, Wesleyan University, Middletown, Connecticut, 1960–1, 1970; composer in residence, University of Cincinnati, 1967; associate, Center for Advanced Study, University of Illinois, Urbana, 1968–9; artist in residence, University of California, Davis, 1969; Charles Eliot Norton Professor of Poetry, Harvard University, 1988–9. Recipient: Guggenheim Fellowship, 1949; American Academy of Arts and Letters award, 1949; membership, American Academy, 1968; Thorne Music Scholarship, 1969; fellow, American Academy, 1978; Karl Sczuka Prize, 1979; Mayor's Award of Honor for Arts and Culture, New York City, 1981; Commandeur de l'Ordre des Arts et des Lettres, 1982; Notable Achievement Award, Brandeis University, 1983; member, Percussive Arts Hall of Fame, 1983; Doctor of All Arts *honoris causa*, California Institute of the Arts, 1986; Kyoto Prize, 1989. Mailing address: 101 West 18th Street, New York, New York 10011, U.S.A.

Publisher: Peters.

Works:

Three Songs (voice, piano; G. Stein) 1932.
Solo with Obbligato Accompaniment of Two Voices in Canon and Six Short Inventions on the Subject of the Solo (any 3 or more instruments encompassing range g to g″) 1933.
Sonata (clarinet) 1933. Recorded Advance FGR-4.
Sonata for Two Voices (2 or more instruments of range C′ to c″; c to c′) 1933.
Composition for Three Voices (any 3 or more instruments) 1933.
Six Short Inventions (alto flute, clarinet, B♭ trumpet, violin, 2 violas, cello) 1934.
Music for Xenia (piano) 1934.
Quartet (4 percussion) 1935.
Quest (piano) 1935.
Three Pieces (Tosses as It Is Untroubled) (2 flutes) 1935.
Two Pieces (piano) 1935, revised 1974. Recorded Columbia MS 7416/M2S 819.
Trio (percussion) 1936.
Five Songs for Contralto (voice, piano; cummings) 1938. Recorded Nonesuch 9 79178-Z; Unicorn RHS 353.
Metamorphosis (piano) 1938. Recorded Columbia MS 7416/M2S 819.
Music for Wind Instruments (flute, clarinet, bassoon; or oboe, horn; or flute, oboe, clarinet, horn, bassoon) 1938.
First Construction (in Metal) (6 percussion) 1939. Recorded Ictus N00 22; MMG 105; Philips 6526 017/CD 420 233-2PH.
Imaginary Landscape No 1 (2 variable speed turntables, frequency recordings, muted piano, cymbal) 1939. Recorded EMI 1 C 165-28954/57Y.
Ho to AA (voice, piano; Tracy) 1939.
Living Room Music (4 percussion) 1940. Recorded Classical Records 180491.
Second Construction (4 percussion) 1940. Recorded Conifer BIS 232.
Bacchanale (prepared piano) 1940. Recorded Columbia MS 7416/M2S 819; Musical Heritage Society 4187.
Third Construction (4 percussion) 1941. Recorded Nexus Records; Ictus N0022.
Double Music (collaboration with Lou Harrison; 4 percussion) 1941. Recorded Time S8000; Mainstream MS/5011; Classical Records 180491.
And the Earth Shall Bear Again (prepared piano) 1942. Recorded Tomato 7016.
Credo In Us (4 percussion, including radio or phonograph, piano) 1942. Recorded EMI 1 C 165-28954/57Y.
Forever and Sunsmell (voice, 2 percussion; cummings) 1942. Recorded Obscure OBS 5-A; Antilles AN 7031.
Imaginary Landscape No 2 (March No 1) (5 percussion) 1942.
Imaginary Landscape No 3 (audio frequency oscillators, variable-speed turntables, electric buzzer, amplified wire, amplified marimba) 1942.
In the Name of the Holocaust (prepared piano) 1942. Recorded mode 15 CD.
Primitive (string piano) 1942. Recorded mode 15 CD.
The City Wears a Slouch Hat (music for play by Kenneth Patchen; 4 percussion) 1942.
The Wonderful Widow of Eighteen Springs (voice, closed piano; Joyce) 1942. Recorded TurnaboutTV 34727; Obscure OBS 5-A; Antilles 7031; Wergo 60054; Victor SJV 1513.
Amores (2 solos for prepared piano, 2 trios for 3 percussion) 1943. Recorded Disc 875; Time S8000; Mainstream MS/5011; Opus One 22; Philips 9500 920; Conifer BIS 272; Ictus N0022.
Our Spring Will Come (piano) 1943. Recorded Primus P-66763.
A Room (piano or prepared piano) 1943. Recorded Tomato 7016.
She Is Asleep (voice, prepared piano; or quartet playing 12 tom-toms) 1943. Recorded THO MTH 149; Tomato 7016.
Tossed as It Is Untroubled (Meditation) (prepared piano) 1943. Recorded Columbia MS 7417/M2S 819.
Totem Ancestor (prepared piano; also version for dance with Laban notation) 1943. Recorded Tomato 7016.
A Book of Music (2 prepared pianos) 1944. Recorded Tomato 2-1001.
Four Walls (piano, vocal interlude) 1944.

The Perilous Night (prepared piano) 1944. Recorded Columbia MS 7416/M2S 819; Avant AR 1008; Pan 130.032.
Prelude for Meditation (prepared piano) 1944. Recorded Columbia MS-7416; M2S 819.
Root of an Unfocus (prepared piano) 1944. Recorded Columbia MS-7417/M2S 819.
Spontaneous Earth (prepared piano) 1944.
The Unavailable Memory Of (prepared piano) 1944.
A Valentine out of Season (prepared piano) 1944. Recorded Columbia MS 7417/M2S 819; Philips 9500 920.
Daughters of the Lonesome Isle (prepared piano) 1945.
Experiences 1 (duo for 2 pianos; solo for voice on text by cummings) 1945. Recorded Obscure OBS 5-A; Antilles AN 7031.
Mysterious Adventure (prepared piano) 1945.
Three Dances (2 amplified prepared pianos) 1945. Recorded Disc 643; Angel S-36059; Folkways F-6160.
Party Pieces (Sonorous and Exquisite Corpses) (20 pieces by Cage, Cowell, Harrison, Thomson; arranged for flute, clarinet, bassoon, horn, piano) c.1945.
Ophelia (piano) 1946.
Two Pieces (piano) 1946. Recorded Columbia MS-7417/M2S 819.
Sonatas and Interludes (prepared piano) 1946–8. Recorded Dial 19/20; CRI 199; Fylkingen FYLPX 101-2; Denon OX 7059-ND/C37-7673; Tomato 2-1001; New World 203 (parts); Wergo 60074 (1 part); Decca Headline 9; Etcetera ETC 2001; Hung HCD 12569 (parts).
Music for Marcel Duchamp (prepared piano) 1947. Recorded Columbia MS-7417/M2S 819; Cramps CRSLP 6101 N.1; Wergo 60074; Philips 9500 920.
Nocturne (violin, piano) 1947. Recorded Desto DC 6435/37.
The Seasons (ballet for orchestra) 1947. Recorded CRI SD-410.
Dreams That Money Can Buy (film score) 1947.
Dream (piano; arranged for viola and viola ensemble) 1948. Recorded Columbia MS-7417/M2S 819.
In a Landscape (harp or piano) 1948. Recorded Obscure OBS 5-A; Antilles AN 7031; Arch S-1787.
Suite (toy piano or piano) 1948. Recorded Columbia MS-7417/M2S 819.
Experiences 2 (voice; cummings) 1948. Recorded Obscure OBS 5-A; Antilles AN 7031.
String Quartet in Four Parts 1949–50. Recorded Columbia MS-4495; Deutsche Grammophon 2530735/CD 423 245 2GC; Turnabout 34610/3-Vox SVBX 5306; mode 17.
A Flower (voice, closed piano) 1950. Recorded Wergo 60054.
Radio Mix 1950. Recorded Cramps CRS LP6101.
Six Melodies (violin, keyboard) 1950. Recorded Mainstream MS/5016; Philips 9500 920; Finnadar 90023-1.
Concerto for Prepared Piano and Chamber Orchestra 1951. Recorded Avakian JCS-1; Nonesuch H-71202; Victor SJX 1003.
Imaginary Landscape No 4 (12 radios, 24 players, conductor) 1951.
Music of Changes (piano) 1951. Recorded Wergo 60 099; New World 214 (parts).
Sixteen Dances (flute, trumpet, 4 percussion, violin, cello, piano) 1951. Recorded CP2/15.
Two Pastorales (prepared piano) 1951. Recorded Tomato 7016; Edigsa AZ 70/11.
For MC and DT (piano) 1952.
Imaginary Landscape No 5 (any 42 recordings, score to be realised as tape) 1952.
Music for Carillon (graph score; 2- or 3-octave versions) 1952. Recorded Hearn-EM 1 C 065 02 469.
Music for Piano 1 1952.
Seven Haiku (piano) 1952. Recorded Tomato 7016.
Waiting (piano) 1952.
Water Music (pianist, using radio, whistles, water containers, deck of cards; score mounted as large poster) 1952.
Williams Mix (8 single-track or 4-double track tapes) 1952.
4′33″ (*tacet*, any instrument or combination of instruments) 1952. Recorded Cramps CRSLP 6101.
Music for Piano 2 1953.
Music for Piano 3 1953.
Music for Piano 4–19 (piano solo or ensemble) 1953.
Music for Piano 20 1953.
Music for Carillon Nos 2 and 3 1953. Recorded Hearn-EM 1 C 065 02 469.
59½″ (any 4-stringed instrument) 1953.
34′46.776″ for a Pianist (prepared piano) 1954.
31′57.9864″ for a Pianist (prepared piano) 1954.
Music for Piano 21–36, 37–52 (piano solo or ensemble) 1955.
Speech (5 radios with news reader) 1955.
26′1.1499 for a String Player (any 4-stringed instrument) 1955. Recorded (double bass) Nonesuch H 71237.
Music for Piano 53–68 (piano solo or ensemble) 1956.
Music for Piano 69–84 (piano solo or ensemble) 1956.
Radio Music (1–8 performers each at 1 radio) 1956. Recorded Cramps CRSLP 6101 N.1.
27′10.554″ for a Percussionist 1956. Recorded Finnadar SR 9017.
For Paul Taylor and Anita Dencks (piano) 1957.
Winter Music (1–20 pianists) 1957. Recorded Finnadar P-6775; CP2 EAA-85013-15; DGG 137 009; mode 3/6.
Concert for Piano and Orchestra (63 pages, to be played, in whole or in part, in any sequence; 84 "types" of composition are involved) 1957–8. Recorded Carpice CAP 1071; EMI 1C 165-28954/57Y.
Aria (voice) 1958. Recorded Time 58003/MS 5005; Virgin VC7 90704.
Fontana Mix (tape or any instrument) 1958. Recorded Turnabout 34046 (tape version); Folkways FT 3704; Time 58003 (with *Aria*); Columbia Ms-7139; Aspen 5–6; Massart M-133.
Indeterminacy (reader) 1958. Recorded Folkways FT 3704.
Solo for Voice 1 (any range) 1958. Recorded EMI 1C 165-28954/57 Y.
TV Koln (piano) 1958. Recorded Avant Records AR 1008.
Variations I (any number of players, any sound producing means) 1958. Recorded Heliodor 2549009; Wergo 60033; Da Camera Magna 93237.
Water Walk (tape) 1959.
Sounds of Venice (television piece) 1959.
Cartridge Music (amplified "small sounds", amplified piano or cymbal; any number of players and loudspeakers) 1960. Recorded Time 58009; DGG 137 009.
Music for Amplified Toy Pianos (any number) 1960. Recorded Cramps CRSLP 6101 N.1; EMI 1 C 065 02 469.
Solo for Voice 2 (any range; to be performed alone or with *Concert, Fontana Mix*, or *Cartridge Music*) 1960. Recorded EMI 1 C 165-28954/57 Y; Odyssey 32160156.
Music for "The Marrying Maiden" (magnetic tape for the play by Jackson Mac Low) 1960.
Theatre Piece (1–8 performers) 1960.
WBAI (auxiliary score with lecture *Where Are We Going? and What Are We Doing*? or instrumental performance with tape, recordings, radios, etc) 1960. Recorded Folkways FT 3704.
Where Are We Going? and What Are We Doing? (4 single-track tapes to be used in whole or part to provide a single lecture, or used in any combination up to 4 to provide simultaneous lectures) 1960.

Atlas Eclipticalis (86 instrumental parts to be played in whole or part, any duration, any ensemble; with or without *Winter Music*; also electronic version using contact microphones) 1961. Recorded Deutsche Grammophon 137009/2536 018; 643 543; 643 541–46.
Music for Carillon No 4 #1 (3- or 2-octave version) 1961.
Variations II (any number of players, any sound producing means) 1961. Recorded Columbia MS-7051 (piano); ME-ME2 (2 pianos, tape, unusual instruments); Jourandos de Musica Experimental JME ME 1–2; CBS France S 3461064.
0′00″ (4′33″ No 2) (solo to be performed in any way by anyone) 1962.
Variations III (any number of people performing any actions) 1963. Recorded Deutsche Grammophon 139 442 (organ, percussion, wind instruments); Wergo 60057 (ensemble).
Variations IV (any number of players, any sounds or combinations of sounds, produced by any means, with or without other activities) 1964. Recorded Everest 6132/3132/3230.
Electronic Music for Piano 1965.
Rozart Mix (assemblage of magnetic tape) 1965. Recorded EMI 1C 165–28 954–57.
Variations V (37 remarks *re* an audio-visual performance) 1965.
Variations VI (plurality of sound systems) 1966.
Variations VII (various means) 1966.
Music for Carillon No 4 #2 1966.
Music for Carillon No 5 (4 octaves) 1967.
Musicircus (diverse performers) 1967.
Newport Mix (tape loops) 1967.
HPSCHD (collaboration with Lejaren Hiller, Jr; 1–7 amplified harpsichords, 1–51 tapes) 1967–9. Recorded Nonesuch H-71224.
Reunion (diverse performers, plurality of electronic musics gated by a game of chess on electronically-prepared board) 1968.
Cheap Imitations (piano) 1969. Recorded Cramps CRSLP 6117 N.17.
Not Wanting to Say Anything About Marcel (collaboration with C. Sumsion; graphic work) 1969.
Sound Anonymously Received (unsolicited instrument) 1969.
33 1/3 (records, gramophones, audience participation) 1969.
Song Books (solos for voice; may be used with *Atlas Eclipticalis*) 1970. Recorded Wergo 60074; Chiaroscuro CR 196.
Mureau (voice) 1970.
Les chants de Maldoror pulverisés par l'assistance même (200 pages for a French-speaking public or no more than 200 persons) 1971.
Sixty-Two Mesostics re Merce Cunningham (unaccompanied voice, microphone) 1971. Recorded Cramps CRSLP 6101 N.1; Arch Records S-1752.
WGBH-TV (composer, technicians) 1971.
Bird Cage (12 tapes to be distributed by a single performer in a space in which people are free to move and birds to fly) 1972.
Mushroom Book (collaboration with L. Long and A. Smith; graphic work) 1972.
Cheap Imitation (orchestra; 24, 59 or 95 players) 1972.
Etcetera (orchestra, 6 pianos, tape) 1973.
Scenes re Morris Graves (graphic work) 1974.
Score (40 drawings by Thoreau) and 23 parts (any instruments and/or voices) 1974.
Etudes Australes (Books I–IV) (piano) 1974–5. Recorded Tomato 2-1101.
Empty Words (reader) 1974–5; first performed (part 4) Florida, 1991. Recorded Wergo WER 60074; Edition Michael F. Bauer MFB 003–004.
Child of Tree (Improvisation I) (percussion solo using amplified plant materials) 1975.
Lecture on the Weather (12 speaker-vocalists, preferably American men who have become Canadian citizens, tape) 1975.
Apartment House 1776 (materials for a musicircus for any number of musicians, in observance of the bicentennial of the U.S.A., to which are to be added, live or recorded, Protestant, Sephardic and American Indian songs, and Negro calls and hollers; to be played with or without *Renga*) 1976.
Branches (percussion solo/duet/trio/orchestra using amplified plant materials) 1976.
Quartets I–VIII (orchestra of 24, 41 or 93 instruments) 1976.
Renga (78 parts to be played alone or with *Apartment House 1776* or some other musicircus appropriate to another occasion, such as the birth or death of another musically productive nation or person, or the birthday of a society concerned with some aspect of creation productive of sound) 1976.
Quartet (concert band, 12 amplified voices) 1976–8.
Cheap Imitation (violin) 1977. Recorded CP2 No 7.
Freeman Etudes (violin) 1977. Recorded CP2; Lovely V 2051–2.
Inlets (Improvisation II) (3 players of water-filled conch-shells and 1 conch-player using circular breathing and the sound of fire) 1977.
Telephones and Birds (3 performers, telephone announcements and recording of bird songs) 1977.
49 Waltzes for the Five Boroughs (performer(s) or listener(s) or record maker(s)) 1977. Recorded Nonesuch D-79011.
Chorals (violin) 1978. Recorded CP2 No 7.
A Dip in the Lake: Ten Quicksteps, Sixty-One Waltzes, and Fifty-Six Marches for Chicago and Vicinity (performer(s) or listener(s) or record maker(s); transcriptions may be made for other cities, or places, by assembling through chance operations a list of 427 addresses and then, also by chance operations, arranging these in 10 groups of 2, 61 groups of 3 and 56 groups of 4) 1978.
Some of "The Harmony of Music" (Supply Belcher) (organist, 3 assistants) 1978.
Seven Day Diary (Not Knowing) (graphic work) 1978.
Seventeen Drawings by Thoreau (graphic work) 1978.
Variations VIII (no music or recordings) 1978.
Letters to Erik Satie (voice, tape) 1978.
Pools (conch shells, tape) 1978.
Il treno (3 happenings for prepared trains) 1978.
Signals (graphic work) 1978.
Someday (10-hour radio event) 1978.
Etudes Boréales (piano/violin) 1978–9. Recorded mode 1/2.
, *Circus on* [sic] (means for translating a book into a performance without actors, a performance which is both literary and musical or one or the other) 1979.
Hymns and Variations (12 amplified voices) 1979.
Changes and Disappearances (graphic work) 1979–82.
Litany for the Whale (vocalise for 2 voices) 1980.
Improvisation III (duets) 1980.
On the Surface (graphic work) 1980–2.
Thirty Pieces for Five Orchestras 1981; first performed Metz, November 1981.
Composition in Retrospect (computer) 1981.
Instances of Silence (installation using cassette recordings) 1982.
A House Full of Music 1982.
Dance/Four Orchestras 1982; first performed Cabrillo, 22 August 1982.

ear for EAR (Antiphonies) (4 widely separated single voices, 1 visible, the other(s) not) 1983.
Improvisation IV (Fieldings sixes) (3 cassette players using machines equipped with a device designed by John Fullemann which allows change in playback speed) 1983.
Postcard from Heaven (1–20 harps) 1983.
Ryoanji (voices, flute, oboe, double bass, percussion, small orchestra) 1983–5. Recorded mode 1/2.
Souvenir (organ) 1984.
Thirty Pieces for String Quartet 1984. Recorded mode 17.
Eight Whiskus 1984.
A Collection of Rocks (orchestra with voices) 1985.
ASLSP (piano) 1985.
Mirakus2 (voices; text from Duchamp) 1985.
Music for (title to be completed by adding the number of players performing) 1985.
Nowth upon Nacht (voice, piano; Joyce) 1985.
Selkus2 (voice) 1985.
Sonnekus2 (voice) 1985.
But What About the Noise of Crumpling Paper . . . (percussion ensemble) 1986.
Etcetera 2/4 Orchestras (materials for orchestral performance with or without 4 conductors and a tape recording of the environment in which the materials were created) 1986.
Haikai (gamelan) 1986.
Hymnkus (14 parts for alto flute, clarinet, alto saxophone, tenor saxophone, bassoon, trombone, 2 percussion, accordion, violin, cello, voice) 1986.
Thirteen Harmonies (violin, keyboard instrument) 1986.
Europera I/II (opera for 19 soloists and orchestra) 1987.
Organ2/ASLSP (organ) 1987.
Essay (computer-generated tape; writings through the *Essay: On the Duty of Civil Disobedience*, by Thoreau) 1988.
Five (5 voices or instruments) 1988.
Four Solos for Voices 93–96 (soprano, mezzo-soprano, tenor, bass) 1988.
One (piano) 1988.
Two (flute, piano) 1988.
Seven (flute, clarinet, percussion, piano, violin, viola, cello) 1988.
101 (orchestra) 1989.
2squared (2 pianos, 4 hands) 1989.
Four (2 violins, viola, cello) 1989.
Swinging (piano) 1989.
Three (3 recorder players; sopranino, soprano, alto, tenor, bassett, bass, great bass) 1989.
Twenty-Three (15 violins, 5 violas, 3 cellos) 1989.
Europera III/IV 1989.
Sculptures Musicales (music to Merce Cunningham's *Inventions*) 1989.
Five Stone Solo (amplified clay pots) 1991; first performed Florida, 1991.

PUBLICATIONS

By Cage: *Virgil Thomson* (with Kathleen O'Donnell Hoover), New York, 1959; *Silence*, Middletown, Connecticut, 1961; *A Year from Monday*, Middletown, Connecticut, 1968; *To Describe the Process of Composition Used in Not Wanting to Say Anything About Marcel*, Cincinnati, Ohio, 1969; *Notations* (with Alison Knowles), New York, 1969; *M*, Middletown, Connecticut, 1973; *Writings Through Finnegans Wake*, New York, 1978; *Empty Words*, Middletown, Connecticut, 1979; *Another Song* (accompanying photographs by Susan Barron), New York, 1981; *For the Birds* (conversations with Daniel Charles), Salem, Massachusetts, 1981; *Mud Book* (with illustrations by Lois Long), New York, 1982; *Themes and Variations*, Barrytown, New York, 1982; *X*, Middletown, Connecticut, 1983, 1986; *I–VI* (the Charles Eliot Norton Lectures, Harvard University, 1988–9), Cambridge, Massachusetts, 1990.

On Cage: **Books**—R. Dunn (ed), *JC*, catalogue of work, New York, 1962; R. Dunn (ed), *JC*, New York, 1962; Calvin Tomkins, in *The Bride and the Bachelors*, New York, 1965; S. Jubota, *Marcel Duchamp and JC*, New York, 1968; Richard Kostelanetz (ed), *JC*, New York, 1970; E.J. Snyder, "JC and Music Since World War II: A Study in Applied Aesthetics", dissertation, University of Wisconsin, 1970; Michael Nyman, *Experimental Music: Cage and Beyond*, New York, 1974; Paul Griffiths, *C*, London, 1981; Peter Gena and Jonathan Brent, *A JC Reader*, New York, 1982; David Revill, *JC: A Biography*, London, 1992; **Articles**—S. Goldstein, "JC", in *Music Business*, April 1946; Peggy Glanville-Hicks, "JC", in *Musical America*, 68 (10), 1948; L.A. Hiller and L.M. Isaacson, in *Experimental Music*, New York, 1959; Virgil Thomson, "JC Late and Early", in *Saturday Review*, 30 January 1960; Toshi Ichiyanagi, "JC", in *Ongaku geijutsu*, 19 (1), 1961; Wilfred Mellers, in *Music in a New Found Land*, New York, 1965; L.B. Meyer, "The End of the Renaissance?", in *Music, the Arts and Ideas*, Chicago, 1967; Susan Sontag, "The Esthetics of Silence", in *Styles of Radical Will*, New York, 1969; Chou Wen-chung, "Asian Concepts and Twentieth-Century Western Composers", in *Music Quarterly*, 57, 1971; Cornelius Cardew, in *Stockhausen Serves Imperialism and Other Articles*, London, 1974; Simon Emmerson, "JC", in *Music and Musicians*, 27 (3), 1978; Stephen Montague, "Significant Silences of a Musical Anarchist", in *Classical Music*, 22 May 1982; J. Rockwell, "The American Experimental Tradition and its Godfather", in *All-American Music: Composition in the Late Twentieth Century*, New York, 1983; T. DeLio, *Circumscribing the Open Universe: Essays on Cage, Feldman, Wolff, Ashley and Lucier*, Washington, D.C., 1984; **Interviews**—M. Kirby and R. Schechner, "An Interview", in *Tulane Drama Review*, 10 (2), 1965; L.G. Bodin and B.E. Johnson, "Semikolon: Musical Pleasure", in *Dansk Musikstidskrift*, 41, 1966; D. Charles, "Soixante réponses à trente questions", in *Revue d'esthétique*, 21 (2–4), 1968; W. Zimmermann, "JC", in *Desert Plants: Conversations with 23 American Musicians*, Vancouver, 1976; A. Gillmor, "Intervju med JC", in *Nutida Musik*, 21, 1977–8; Roger Reynolds, "JC and Roger Reynolds: A Conversation" in *Music Quarterly*, 65, 1979; T. Everett, "10 Questions, 270 Answers", in *Composer*, 10–11, 1980; C. Gagne and T. Caras, in *Soundpieces: Interviews with American Composers*, Metuchen, New Jersey, 1982; Stephen Montague, "JC at Seventy: An Interview", in *American Music*, 3, 1985; *Conversing with Cage* (interviews with Richard Kostelanetz), New York, 1988.

* * *

John Cage has now been one of the leaders of experimental composition for half a century. His works, particularly the widely-discussed pieces from the 1950s, have been seen as questioning the reasons human beings make music, and also asking what constitutes music itself. Throughout his musical career he has been a relentless experimenter—initially the result of an innovative, restless mind, later anchored in a deeply focussed aesthetic philosophy.

Although extremely keen on music, Cage's first thought for

a vocation was writing; he also painted, and briefly studied architecture. However, on his own account, those whose opinions he respected spoke more highly of his music than of his other work.

His first studies were with Richard Buhlig, then with Adolph Weiss and, for two years, with Schoenberg. He felt able to promise the latter he would devote his life to music. Despite the direction of his studies, Cage was never a writer of serial music in any textbook sense. He employed 25 pitch sets, in which all the pitches were to be presented before any were to be repeated. Later he worked with twelve tones fragmented motivically. But when he asked Schoenberg about serialism, the latter replied, "That's none of your business".

By the mid-1930s Cage's structural focus was time, at the level both of rhythmical cells and, especially, large-scale durational form. It was at this point that *silence* became important in Cage's explanation of his work. In a music centred on time, the absence of sound is structurally as important as its presence.

This approach to musical organisation can be seen at its clearest in his percussion ensemble pieces of the 1930s and 1940s—among the earliest of the genre—such as *First Construction*. The duration of local details stand in the same proportion to one another as the larger structural sections have to the whole.

The percussion pieces revealed, too, his tendency towards timbral innovation—devising, for example, the water gong (where the pitch of a resonating gong is modified by lowering the instrument into the water), and making use of industrial readymades such as spring coils or brake drums. Cage also experimented with early electronic resources such as recordings of single frequencies played on variable-speed turntables. Again, this inventiveness is not attributable to Schoenberg's influence; it has more to do with his nationality, and his inventor father. It led Schoenberg to characterise him, as Cage has often recounted, as "an inventor—of genius".

One of Cage's best-known musical inventions is the prepared piano, which he devised and first wrote for within a week. It consists of a standard piano with various objects, such as rubber stripping, felt, or bolts, placed on or between the strings. From its first use in *Bacchanale* (1938), the prepared piano was one of Cage's favoured resources up to the mid-1950s, appearing in a score of his works on an ever-grander scale technically and musically, reaching a high point in the *Concerto for Prepared Piano* of 1951.

The 1940s were a time of rapid changes for Cage, which centre on three new relationships. The first was with Merce Cunningham, the choreographer, whom Cage first met in 1938. Cage first wrote music for him in 1942, and at the inception of Cunningham's own troupe became musical director and so remained until 1966, the central focus of a long-term involvement with dance. Another meeting, in 1950, was with pianist David Tudor, who became a vital adjunct to much of Cage's music, from the *Music of Changes* onwards.

The third meeting, and the one with deepest theoretical ramifications, was with the Zen master Daisetz T. Suzuki, whose Columbia University classes Cage attended from 1945 to 1947. Engagement with Zen marked the flowering of a nascent interest in Eastern philosophy. Cage was deeply impressed by the Zen approach to life, the unmediated experience which comes from the abandonment of one's likes and dislikes. Zen became the touchstone for his relentless experimentation.

Cage became interested in writing music to integrate people with the sounds which surround them. One result of this was that all sound became material for music, regardless of its supposed aesthetic quality. Zen gave mystical credence to his earlier interest in the industrial everyday. Art for Cage ceased to be the creation of an alternative, more aesthetically perfect world, or a discoursing about it, but a way to bring ourselves back to it. Works can be made which do not depend for their meaning on self-reference, but turn their users out to experience the world. "Art", Cage suggested, "is a sort of experimental station in which one tries out living".

In 1951, Cage visited the anechoic chamber of Harvard University. He expected to hear pure silence, but was startled to find that he carried with him the sounds of his body. This helped him recontextualise silence as the absence of intention to produce sound. "Whether I make them or not", Cage suggested, "there are always sounds to be heard and all of them are excellent". The single most significant statement of his concern with Zen was *4′33″*, a piece for any instrument or combination of instruments in three movements. No sound is to be intentionally produced.

Cage's compositional method made a similar inversion of general practice. He took the abandonment of intentionality quite literally and began writing music according to chance operations. Asking questions which will be answered by chance became a discipline for Cage, the active counterpart to the passive discipline of cross-legged meditation. Cage reasoned that if chance governs the musical materials, likes and dislikes would be bypassed. The first full example of this approach was the *Sixteen Dances* (1951).

Chance operations have been derived from star maps, the imperfections which accidentally appear on sheets of paper, and, initially, magic squares and tarot cards. Most important is the ancient Chinese oracle the I-Ching, to which he was introduced by Christian Wolff in the early 1950s. Cage began using the coin oracle, in which a number between 1 and 64 is generated by throwing three coins six times, though without consulting the accompanying texts when writing music. The first piece written this way was the *Music of Changes* (1951).

An associated compositional resource used by Cage for similar ends is indeterminacy—the setting up of a situation of which the specific outcome cannot be predicted. Indeterminancy takes several forms—in notation, graphic scores such as *27′10.554″* or more recently *Ryoanji*; or text scores such as *Telephones and Birds*. There are also scores which can be reassembled from different elements for each performance, and the graphics interpreted in a variety of ways, such as *Fontana Mix* or several of the *Variations* series.

Indeterminate situations may also be brought about using interactive electronic circuits, as in *Variations V*, in which the movement of dancers modifies the sound, or *Reunion*, where electronic music is gated by the game on a specially prepared chessboard.

Recently Cage has become interested in indeterminate improvisation, setting up music situations in which the improvisation will not be defined by the taste of the performer—pieces such as *Inlets*, where players tilt conch-shells whose gurgles they cannot control.

Cage's music seems difficult to approach and to appreciate. If one takes his explanation of his activities seriously one can understand how this comes about. Most Western art has appeared to communicate expressively. A view of life comes across through a system of conventions, such as those of harmony. In the late 1940s, for biographical and musical reasons, Cage became tired of expressive music, and began to attempt to write music that would exemplify his view on life rather than express it. He did not step out of the anechoic chamber and write a song describing the sound of silence; only one year later he presented *4′33″*—putting the silence he had heard as directly as possible into a concert situation and calling it art.

If one takes Cage's account seriously and extrapolates from it, paradox arises: we can approach and appreciate his music given an understanding of his aims, but his stated aim is to eschew theorising. Lengthy explanation lets us grasp Cage's concern simply to practice what he preaches; what is essentially an optimistic and accessible approach to life is embodied in work which for most people is incomprehensible and appears pretentious. One is also faced with the frequent assertion that Cage's personality and pronouncements are more interesting than his music.

Cage has always been more than a composer. Since 1978 he has made annual visits to the Crown Point Press in California, producing prints and lithographs. Furthermore, various of his scores have been exhibited as visual artworks, for example *Renga* at the Museum of Modern Art.

His published work has focussed less and less on music, and increasingly on the development of his idiosyncratic style of poetry. His interest in mycology is well known, as is his enthusiasm for chess (he was taught by Marcel Duchamp), and his practice and advocacy of the macrobiotic diet. Cage is an avowed anarchist, although he is not active politically, preferring, as he says, to offer positive action in art rather than be involved in criticism or protest.

Cage has distinguished himself by the originality of his music and his unusual aesthetic, by a prolific and energetic output, by a refusal of compromise and through charismatic self-presentation. It has been asked what Cage's long-term legacy will be; his own interest, with exceptional clarity as to the limits of his responsibility, is in what he does now and next. Cage has often said that his favourite piece is the one he has not yet written. Whatever one makes of it, this attitude is a model of living which again embodies Cage's intriguing ability to make musical work a pointer for life: "I am not interested in the result of my activity. I am interested in being alive".

—David Revill

CAMILLERI, Charles. Maltese/British. Born in Malta, 7 September 1931. Educated at government schools, Malta, 1943–7; Lyceum High School, Malta, 1947–51; University of Toronto (under John Weinzweig), 1959–63, Mus.B. (hons). Married Doris Vella, 22 September 1959; 1 daughter and 1 son. Freelance composer/conductor, 1954/8; composer/conductor, CBC Radio, Toronto, 1959–64; music consultant, Rediffusion, 1965–8; professor of composition, Toronto Conservatory of Music, 1977–8; music consultant, J.B. Kramer, London, 1979–81; head of music, music centre, UNESCO Foundation of International Studies, Malta, 1987; professor/head of music programme, University of Malta; visiting professor/lecturer, U.S.A., Canada, Soviet Union, Scandinavia, elsewhere in Europe. Mailing address: Villa l'Ghana, Ryan Street, San Pawl tat-Targa, Naxxar, Malta.

Publisher: A. Lengnick and Co. Ltd, 421 Brighton Road, South Croydon CR2 6YR, England.

Symphonies/orchestral:

Malta Suite 1946; first performed Malta, 1948. Recorded RPO Aerco 81; Enterprise 002.
Piano Concerto No 1: Mediterranean 1948; first performed London, 1977. Recorded RPO Aerco 81.
Ouverture Classique 1962; first performed Toronto, 1962. Recorded Enterprise 002.
Violin Concerto No 1 1963; first performed Toronto, 1963.
Maltese Dances 1965; first performed Malta, 1965. Recorded Enterprise 002.
Zeitgeist 1968.
Orpheus Contemporaneous (jazz quintet, strings, percussion) 1968.
Piano Concerto No 2: Maqam 1970; first performed Kyoto, Japan, 1970.
Cosmic Visions (42 strings) 1976.
Spaces for Strings 1980; first performed London, 1980.
Organ Concerto 1981.
GDSH (vibraphone, orchestra) 1984; first performed Malta, 1984.
Piano Concerto No 3: Leningrad 1985–6; first performed Leningrad, 1987.
The Elements (ballet suite) 1987; first performed France, 1988.

Chamber/instrumental:

Five Maltese Dances (piano) 1954; first performed London, 1954. Recorded Vista VPS 1003.
Six Arabesques (cello) 1955.
Six Sonatinas (piano) 1955–6.
Divertimento (clarinet, piano) 1957; first performed London, 1959. Recorded Golden Crest Re 7082.
Times of Day (piano) 1959.
Etudes (piano) 1960.
Hemda (piano) 1962.
Sonata (2 trumpets) 1964; first performed Toronto, 1964.
Sonata (cello) 1964; first performed Helsinki, 1964.
African Dreams (piano) 1965.
Taqsim (2 pianos) 1967; first performed London, 1968. Recorded Vista 1007.
Mantra (piano) 1969.
Ragamats (piano) 1970.
City of Brass (piano, brass) 1970; first performed Colchester, Essex, 1990.
Piano Trio 1971; first performed Cheltenham, Gloucestershire, 1972. Recorded Vista 1008.
Missa Mundi (organ) 1971; first performed London, 1971. Recorded Argo ZRG 812.
Fantasia Concertante (8 different instruments) 1972. Recorded Maxsound MSCB 71.
The Sound of Silence (flute, oboe, percussion, strings) 1972; first performed Malta, 1973.
String Quartet 1973; first performed Salzburg, 1974.
Requiem for the Massacred (4 trumpets, 4 percussion) 1976; first performed Buffalo, New York, 1977.
Concerto Americano (piano) 1977.
Noospheres (piano) 1977–8.
Brass Quintet 1982. Recorded Merlin 86041.
Morphogenesis (organ) 1982.
Sonata (violin) 1982; first performed London, 1983.
Effusions (piano) 1984.
Interchangeable Galaxies (flute, piano) 1987; first performed Paris, 1987.
Mimar (piano, percussion) 1988.

Vocal/choral:

Missa Brevis (unaccompanied SATB chorus) 1972; first performed Copenhagen, 1973. Recorded Classical Elegance LSC 126.
Unum Deum (unaccompanied SATB chorus) 1980; first performed Reading, Berkshire, 1980. Recorded Classical Elegance LSC 126.
Pacem in terribus (unaccompanied SATB chorus) 1985; first performed Malta, 1989.
This Holy Earth (song cycle; baritone, piano) 1985. Recorded Massound MCBS 71.
Stone Island Within (soprano, cello, flute, percussion) 1985. Recorded Maxsound MCBS 71.
Songs of an Infant Species (song cycle) 1987.

Opera:

Melita (chamber opera) 1966–7; first performed Belfast, 1968.
Il-Weghda 1980; first performed Malta, 1981.
Il-Fidwa tal-Bdiewa 1982; first performed Malta, 1983.

PUBLICATIONS

By Camilleri: *Mediterranean Music*, Foundation of International Studies, UNESCO, 1988.

On Camilleri: Christopher Palmer, *The Music of CM*, London, 1974; Edwige Sapienza, *Portrait of a Composer*, Malta, 1988; "CM—An Interview", in *Classical Guitar*, 6, June 1988; "CM's Clarinet Repertoire", in *Clarinet and Saxophone Magazine*, 14, September 1989; Michael Bonello, *The Piano Music of CM*, Malta, 1989.

Charles Camilleri comments:

What I find restrictive in the harmony I was taught is its presentation as the only possible code, as an absolute. I think it is much more wholesome to think of the "harmony of the spheres"—that is, of the whole universe—as a model. Apparently random small events, accumulating and coagulating, produced the trajectory of evolution; and now scientists can picture what looked like a chaos of fortuitous mini-happenings as a singular process by which the most complex and beautiful integration of motley elements has occurred (and, indeed, is still going on, in as yet hardly discernible ways). Music of the kind I believe in is the prophetic image of the next phase in the unfolding of this harmony; it is the foreseeing of the cosmic embedded in the seemingly chaotic.

* * *

It is fortunate for the island of Malta that musical gifts of unique character reside in Charles Camilleri. Reared in the musical traditions of the island, his need to compose was finally sparked to flame by a London Promenade Concert in 1948. Camilleri's early pieces were simple extensions of the folk material around him. To a lesser talent nothing more need have happened. To this major talent the improvisatory tradition in folk performance was compelling, drawing out endless ideas for development and thereby stretching his creativity. That widened his horizons as he became aware that Maltese folk music is a single strand in a Mediterranean tapestry of extraordinary variety and richness. It is woven from many traditions, particularly those of North Africa and the Arab inheritance. Camilleri has all this in his blood as well as in his mind.

By the early 1950s he was travelling extensively. His need and opportunity for worldwide musical experience had arrived. He wrote for film and television in Australia and England, and visited American and the Far East. His mind was constantly grappling with the crosscurrents of musical style on the international scene in relation to his own. Out of the elements undergoing transformation from Camilleri's folk experiments, that of rhythm was critical. To notate the innumerable subtleties emerging from an amalgam of Mediterranean traditions and his own creative urge demanded complex subdivisions which he finally termed as "atomisation of the beat".

A decade later Camilleri was in Toronto reading music at the University, and taking composition with John Weinzweig. He grappled with serialism, and several works of this period are the result. But his music quickly absorbed what was relevant, strengthened its purpose, and the refining process continued. Particular fruits of the real Camilleri at this time were two books of *Etudes* and *Hemda*, all for piano.

By the mid-1960s Camilleri was back in Europe. If it may suggest an artist in desperate search for identity, hindsight demonstrates that a composer born into a small island community needs generous contact with the world and its massive accumulation of musical experience. In this way Camilleri could remain loyal to his intuitive voice while gaining perception and perspective. A major hurdle was still the notation on paper of the music that he felt impulsively from within. Each successive work increased the rhythmic subtleties for which precise notational accuracy was essential. *African Dreams* (piano solo) and *Taqsim* (two pianos) chart milestones of the period, revealing more than integration of the Mediterranean and related traditions. There was now a rising sense of the mysteries upholding all art.

Camilleri's thoughts on such fundamentals have been widely chronicled from both his lecturing around the world and from interviews and writings. Characteristic is the following: "Hasn't music always felt to be, at its greatest depths and in some sense, a sort of interface or cross-cutting between time and eternity, between language and silence . . . ?"

For Camilleri the 1970s became a time for mastering new dimensions as his vision widened and the world shrank. From this period in particular come *Piano Concerto No 2: Maqam* for piano and orchestra blending ritual (Africa), meditation (Orient) and rationalization (Europe); and the first major organ work, *Missa Mundi*, both eclectic and personal in reaction to Teilhard de Chardin. (The philosopher Peter Serracino-Inglott has perceived in this work "a fulfilling of Teilhard's aspiration to express the universe as longing for convergence of the cosmos on a divine centre".)

Such voyaging continues for Camilleri, today, tomorrow, and perhaps the day following. Recent years have given us *Noospheres* for piano, *Piano Concerto No 3*, *Morphogenesis* for organ (taking up where *Missa Mundi* left off), a brass quintet, two song-cycles and more piano pieces. The piano often opens up new ideas for Camilleri. He has cast aside the traditional role for its range of colour and sound qualities, especially in extremes of register, which dot his musical landscapes.

Camilleri spends much time writing in his native Malta, tireless in endeavour and limitless in patience. He knows what he has to do, even if the world finds that kind of dedication bewildering.

—Basil Ramsey

CARR, Edwin (James Nairn). New Zealander. Born in Auckland, 10 August 1926. Educated at Otago Boys' High School, 1940–3; Universities of Otago and Auckland, 1944–7; Guildhall School of Music, London (under Benjamin Frankel), 1948–56; Conservatorio di Santa Cecilia, Rome (under Goffredo Petrassi), 1954–5; Hochschule für Musik, Munich (under Carl Orff), 1957–8. Part-time teacher and condutor, Suffolk Rural Music School, 1960–72; fellow/part-time lecturer, University of Otago, 1973–4; part-time lecturer, New South Wales Conservatorium of Music, Sydney, 1975–84; also at New Ipswich Civil College and at Victoria University, Wellington; retired 1987. Full-time freelance composer, since 1988. Recipient: Wainwright Memorial Prize, 1951; Harriet Cohen Medal for a Commonwealth Composer, 1967; Mozart Fellowship, University of Otago, 1973–4. Mailing address: P.O. Box 1207, Taupo, New Zealand.

Publisher: self.

Symphonies/orchestral:

Prelude and Allegro 1949; lost.
Mardi Gras Overture 1950; first performed London, 1953. Recorded Kiwi/Pacific SLD 70.
Symphony (string orchestra) 1953.
Viola Concerto 1953; lost.
Nightmusic/Scherzo 1958; first performed Auckland, 1958. Recorded Kiwi/Pacific SLD 55.
Piano Concerto No 1 1962; first performed Wellington, 1962. Recorded Kiwi/Pacific SLD 70.
Five Pieces for Orchestra (arrangement of piece for piano) 1966; first performed Wellington, 1966.
Four Pieces (arrangement of chamber piece; oboe d'amore or oboe, harp, strings) 1967.
Aubade (arrangement of chamber piece; clarinet, orchestra) 1970; first performed Wellington, 1970. Recorded Kiwi/Pacific SLD 76.
Three Tableaux (from abandoned ballet *The Ordeal*) 1971.
Six Studies (string orchestra) 1972; first performed Wellington, 1972.
The Twelve Signs (no strings) 1974; first performed Wellington, 1974. Recorded Kiwi/Pacific SLD 76.
Sinfonietta 1979; first performed Sydney, 1983.
Koanga (arranged from piano piece) 1980.
Symphony No 1 1981; first performed Wellington, 1983.
Raumati (arranged from piece for piano duet) 1981.
In Memoriam—Paraphrase on "Kiwi" (clarinet, strings; tribute to Larry Pruden based on his film score) 1984.
Symphony No 2: The Exile 1984; first performed Wellington, 1984.
Promenade (ballet suite) 1985.
Overture: Pacific Festival 1985; first performed Wellington, 1986.
Piano Concerto No 2 1985; first performed Wellington, 1988.
Symphony No 3 1987; first performed Auckland, 1988.
Poems (piano, orchestra) 1990; first performed Wellington, 1991.
Overture: Gaudeamus 1990.

Chamber/instrumental:

Variations on a Theme by Douglas Lilburn (piano) 1948.
Variations (flute) 1948; lost.
Sonatina (piano) 1948; lost.
String Quartet No 1 1954.
Sonata No 1 (piano) 1954; first performed Siena, 1955. Record Kiwi SLD 19.
Suite No 1 (2 pianos) 1955.
Piano Trio 1958; first performed Wellington, 1959.
Suite No 2 (2 pianos) 1959, revised for 2 pianos, percussion, 1970; first performed Auckland, 1976.
Sonata (organ) 1959.
Solo Sonata (violin) 1961; first performed London, 1963.
Prelude and Three Pieces (viola, piano) 1962.
Four Marches (piano duet) 1964.
Five Pieces (piano) 1966; first performed London, 1966.
Piano Quintet 1966; first performed London, 1967.
Four Pieces (oboe d'amore, piano) 1966; first performed London, 1967.
Three Pieces (cello, piano) 1968.
Aubade (clarinet, piano) 1970.
Suite No 3 (2 pianos) 1971; first performed Wellington, 1976.
Four Short Concert Studies (piano) 1973; first performed Dunedin, 1974.
Five Bagatelles (piano) 1975; first performed London, 1975.
Sonata No 2 (piano) 1976; first performed London, 1976.
Makariri—Koanga (Winter–Spring) (piano) 1976; first performed Wellington, 1976.
Raumati—Ngahuru (Summer–Autumn) (piano duet) 1976.
Concert (trumpet, percussion) 1976; first performed Sydney, 1976.
Sonatina (piano) 1977; first performed Wellington, 1983.
Sonata (violin, piano) 1978; first performed London, 1978.
String Quartet No 2 1979; first performed Sydney, 1983.
Horn Trio 1982; first performed Sydney, 1985.
Sonata No 3 (piano) 1985; first performed Taihape, New Zealand, 1986.
The Four Elements (2 mandolins, mandola, guitar) 1988; first performed Sydney, 1988.
Quartet (piano, oboe, clarinet, bassoon) 1989.
Wind Octet (2 oboes, 2 clarinet, 2 bassoons, 2 horns) 1989; first performed Brisbane, 1989.
The Four Elements (Suite No 4) (2 pianos) 1990.

Vocal/choral:

A Blake Cantata (SA choir) 1952; first performed London, 1952. Recorded Kiwi/Pacific SLC 72.
Death of Orpheus (madrigal) 1954; lost.
An Edith Sitwell Song Cycle (mezzo-soprano, oboe, piano) 1966; first performed London, 1966.
Three Shakespeare Songs (mezzo-soprano, piano) 1967, 1973; first performed (2 songs only) London, 1966.
Three Songs from Childhood (mezzo-soprano, violin; Horder) 1970.
Auckland '71 Ode (speaker, SATB chorus, orchestra; Campbell, Adams) 1971; first performed Auckland, 1971.
Out of Dark (song cycle for mezzo-soprano, piano; Shaw) 1973, orchestrated 1983; first performed Dunedin, 1973.
Seven Medieval Lyrics (SATB chorus, orchestra) 1974; first performed Cambridge, New Zealand, 1974.
Three Love Songs (soprano, piano; Fairburn) 1975; first performed Sydney, 1975.
Seven Elizabethan Lyrics (SATB chorus, orchestra) 1976; first performed Sydney, 1976.
Five Wolfskehl Songs (baritone, orchestra) 1977; first performed Brisbane, 1979. Recorded Kiwi Pacific SLD 55.
Alcheringa (unison choir, piano) 1978.
An Easter Cantata (girls' choir, organ) 1980.
Song of Solomon (mezzo-soprano, baritone, speaker, SATB chorus, orchestra) 1987; first performed Christchurch, 1989.

Waikato Song (choir, 2 pianos) 1987.
The Eye of the World (soprano, SATB chorus, orchestra) 1989.

Opera:

Nastasya (Hill, after *The Idiot* by Dostoevsky) 1972; broadcast Wellington, 1974.
Lord Arthur Savile's Crime (Hill, after Wilde) 1989–91.

Other:

Prelude, Three Dances and Epilogue (ballet music; 2 pianos) 1953.
Cacciati dal Paradiso (ballet music; 2 pianos) 1955.
Electra (ballet; orchestra/piano, percussion) 1955, 1956.
The Snowmaiden (ballet; piano) 1963, orchestrated 1970; broadcast TV NZ 1971. Recorded Kiwi/Pacific SLD 55.
Promenade (ballet; orchestra) 1985; broadcast Radio NZ 1986.
Nicholas Nickleby (music for animated film) 1985.
The Mayor's New Coat (ballet for children; piano or piano duet) 1986.
Poems (ballet for clarinet, cello, piano; later arranged for piano, orchestra) 1988.

Claude Debussy: *Children's Corner Suite* (orchestrated) n.d.

PUBLICATIONS

By Carr: *Elementary Harmony for Students*, Sydney.

On Carr: Roger Joyce, "A Chronological List of the Compositions of Edwin Carr", dissertation, Victoria University, Wellington, n.d.

Edwin Carr comments:

So-called serious music has lost or not been able to attract a good deal of its audience because so many composers are obsessed with intellectual experimentation the results of which fail to communicate directly. I too explore possibilities from time to time in my work but I am mostly preoccupied with bringing back the melodic side of music and never being too abstruse harmonically, rhythmically or formally. Apart from the important evocative element in music I like to make music which is never too far away from "song and dance".

* * *

Edwin Carr is a prolific composer with a seemingly effortless style. He resisted serialism until 1962, when he put himself to the test by writing an unaccompanied violin sonata to prove the possibilities of melodic invention within the discipline of the twelve-note row. Since then, serialism has not overwhelmed his work, but has become an important tool in the construction and organization of his music. A mellifluous, supple melody and a spare rhythmic texture are the hallmarks of his style.

As a child in New Zealand, he used to listen to the gramophone records his father had collected of jazz and popular music, "gems" from musical comedies and the classics. Orchestral promenade concerts in Wellington introduced him to the "live" orchestra, and induced a lifelong aversion to Wagner, after hearing a concert performance of *The Flying Dutchman*. He was fascinated by the spectacular brass and percussion and the Sousa marches played by the Coldstream Guards, who visited Auckland in 1933. An obsession with French music began with a hearing of Dukas's *L'Apprenti Sorcier* when he was in the standard six class. Radio signature tunes, the wonderful selection of sheet music in Dunedin's Public Library, Walt Disney's *Fantasia* in 1940, Workers' Educational Association lectures using the Carnegie set of records of great American Orchestras and world performers and the daring programmes of the New Zealand Broadcasting Commission, were all positive and lasting influences on him.

He is a fine pianist and broadcast some Debussy for the New Zealand Broadcasting Commission when he was 20. Encouragement for his composing came from established figures like Douglas Lilburn, Eugene Goossens and Benjamin Frankel. He studied with Goffredo Petrassi at the Conservatorio di Santa Cecilia in Rome, with Carl Orff at the Hochschule für Musik in Munich, and with Benjamin Frankel at the Guildhall School of Music in London. He has won New Zealand Government Bursaries, the Mozart Fellowship in Dunedin, and British Council Scholarships.

The work with Frankel was, by far, the most rewarding and beneficial. Through him, Carr was able to assimilate the classics, rather than reject them; he could adapt the severe style of serialism without negating tonality, and he could argue points of difference with him, such as on French music, which he loved and Frankel did not.

Carr wrote three ballets for Il Nuovo Balletto d'Italia in 1955, travelling around Italy as one of the duo pianists and as music director of that company. Much later, between 1984 and 1987, ballet again became important with the successful collaboration with the ex-Royal Ballet dancer, Paul Vlasic, and an eventually abhorted Youth Ballet in Taupo, New Zealand.

Carr's first commission of an orchestral piece was *Nightmusic* for the New Zealand Symphony Orchestra conducted by John Hopkins in 1958. Since then, many works have been performed and recorded by the New Zealand Broadcasting Corporation, including the opera *Nastasya*, from Edward Hill's libretto based on Dostoevsky's *The Idiot*, the symphonic-cantata, *Song of Solomon* and many orchestral, solo and chamber-music works.

There is a sophisticated simplicity in Carr's work which reveals his love of the earth and need for the sun. He works with a fierce concentration and is rejuvenated by a dip in the thermal waters of his native New Zealand. He was a stimulating teacher whether it be to non-vocational adults at the New South Wales State Conservatorium of Music in Sydney, or at the New Ipswich Civic College, or to the students at the Suffolk Rural Music School, or at the Victoria University in Wellington. He retired from teaching in 1987, and has devoted himself entirely to composition.

—Sally Mays

CARTER, Elliott (Cook, Jr). American. Born in New York City, 11 December 1908. Educated at Horace Mann School, graduated 1926; Harvard University, Cambridge, Massachusetts, 1926–32, B.A. (English), M.A. (music); music study at Longy School, Cambridge, Massachusetts; studied harmony and counterpoint under Walter Piston, orchestration under Edward Burlinghame; Ecole Normale de

Musique, Paris (under Nadia Boulanger) 1932–5; course at Harvard University (under Gustav Holst), 1932. Married sculptor Helen Frost-Jones in 1939; 1 son. Music director, George Balanchine's Ballet Caravan, 1936–40; critic, *Modern Music*, 1937–42; teacher (of music, physics, mathematics, philosophy, Greek), St John's College, Annapolis, Maryland, 1940–2; consultant, United States Office of War Information, 1943–4; professor of composition, Peabody Conservatory, Baltimore, 1946–8; director, 1946–52, and president, American Section, 1952, International Society for Contemporary Music; professor of composition, Columbia University, 1948–50; professor of composition, Queen's College, New York, 1955–6; teacher, Salzburg Seminars, 1958; professor of composition, Yale University, 1960–2; American delegate, East-West Encounter, Tokyo, 1962; composer in residence, American Academy in Rome, 1963, 1967, and American school, West Berlin, 1964; professor of composition, Juilliard School of Music, New York, 1967; Andrew D. White Professor-at-Large, Cornell University, Ithaca, New York, 1967–8; teacher at Dartington and Tanglewood summer schools, and at Massachusetts Institute of Technology, Boston, and Johns Hopkins University, Baltimore, Maryland. Recipient: Juilliard Publication Award (for *Pocahontas*), 1940; American Composers' Alliance Prize (for *Quartet for Four Saxophones*), 1943; BMI Publication Prize (for *Canonic Suite*), 1945; first prize (for *Holiday Overture*), Independent Music Publishers Contest, 1945; Guggenheim Fellowships, 1945, 1950; first prize (for *String Quartet No 1*), International Quartet Competition, Liège, Belgium, 1953; Prix de Rome, 1953; Naumburg Prize (for *Sonata*), 1956; Pulitzer Prize, Critics' Circle Award, UNESCO Award (for *String Quartet No 2*); Sibelius Medal, Critics' Circle Award (for *Double Concerto*), 1961; Brandeis University Creative Arts Award, 1965; Harvard Glee Club Medal, 1967; elected member, American Academy of Arts and Letters, 1969; Gold Medal, National Institute of Arts and Letters, 1971; Pulitzer Prize (for *String Quartet No 3*), 1973; Handel Medallion, 1978; Ernst von Siemens Musik-Preis, Munich, 1981; Commandeur de l'Ordre des Arts et des Lettres, France, 1981; MacDowell Medal, 1983; George Peabody Medal, 1984; National Medal of Arts, 1985; honorary doctorates from New England Conservatory of Music, 1961, Swarthmore College, 1965, Princeton University, 1967, Ripon College, 1968, Oberlin College, Boston University, Yale University, Harvard University, all 1970, and Peabody Conservatory, 1974, and Cambridge University, 1983. Mailing address: Mead Street, Waccabuc, New York 10597, U.S.A.

Publishers: Boosey & Hawkes; Associated.

Symphonies/orchestral:

Symphony 1937; withdrawn.
English Horn Concerto 1937; withdrawn.
Prelude, Fanfare and Polka (small orchestra) 1938.
Suite from Pocahontas 1939, revised 1960. Recorded Epic; CRI.
Symphony No 1 1942, revised 1954; first performed Rochester, New York, 27 April 1944. Recorded Louisville; CRI.
Holiday Overture 1944; first performed Frankfurt, 1946. Recorded CRI.
Suite, from the Minotaur 1947. Recorded Mercury.
Elegy (strings; arrangement of *Elegy* for cello, piano) 1952; first performed New York, 1 March 1953.
Variations for Orchestra 1954–5; first performed Louisville, Kentucky, 21 April 1956. Recorded Columbia/CBS; Louisville; New World.
Double Concerto (harpsichord, piano, 2 chamber orchestras) 1961; first performed New York, 6 September 1961. Recorded Columbia; CBS; Nonesuch; EMI.
Piano Concerto 1964–5; first performed Boston, 6 January 1967. Recorded RCA; New World Records.
Concerto for Orchestra 1968–9; first performed New York, 5 February 1970. Recorded Columbia; CRI.
A Symphony for Three Orchestras 1976; first performed New York, 17 February 1977. Recorded Columbia.
Penthode (5 instrumental quartets) 1984–5; first performed London, 26 July 1985.
A Celebration of Some 100 X 150 Notes 1986; first performed Houston, Texas, 10 April 1987.
Oboe Concerto 1988.
Remembrance 1988.
Violin Concerto 1990; first performed San Francisco, April 1990.

Chamber/instrumental:

Piano Sonata c.1927–8; withdrawn.
String Quartet c.1927–8; withdrawn.
Sonata (flute, piano) 1934.
String Quartet 1935; withdrawn.
String Quartet 1937; withdrawn.
Canonic Suite (4 alto saxophones) 1939; revised for 4 clarinets, 1955–6; revised for 4 saxophones, 1981.
Pastoral (cor anglais/viola/clarinet, piano) 1940. Recorded Grenadilla; Orion; GC; GM Records.
Elegy (cello, piano; also arranged for string quartet, 1946; string orchestra 1952; viola, piano) 1941. Recorded (quartet) Golden Crest & Etcetera KTC 1066; (string orchestra) Nonesuch.
Piano Sonata No 1 1945–6; first performed New York, 16 February 1947. Recorded Nonesuch; Valois; EMI/Epic/Etcetera; Orion; American Recording Society.
Woodwind Quintet 1948; first performed New York, 21 February 1949. Recorded RCA; CBS/Vox; Classic Editions.
Sonata (cello, piano) 1948; first performed New York, 27 February 1950. Recorded Nonesuch; American Recording Society; Golden Crest.
Eight Etudes and a Fantasy (flute, oboe, clarinet, bassoon) 1949–50; first performed New York, 28 October 1952. Recorded CNS; Candide/Musical Heritage; Vox; CRI.
Eight Pieces for Four Timpani/Recitative and Improvisation (1 player) 1950–66. Recorded (entire) Odyssey; Bis; (parts) Erato.
String Quartet No 1 1950–1; first performed New York, 26 February 1953. Recorded Nonesuch; Columbia; Etcetera KTC 1065.
Sonata (flute, oboe, cello, harpsichord) 1952; first performed New York, 19 November 1953. Recorded Decca; Columbia; Deutsche Grammophon; Nonesuch; Golden Crest.
String Quartet No 2 1959; first performed New York, 25 March 1960. Recorded Nonesuch; Columbia/RCA; Etcetera KTC 1066.
String Quartet No 3 1971; first performed New York, 23 January 1973. Recorded Columbia; RCA; Musical Heritage; Etcetera KTC 1066.
Canon for Three: In Memoriam Igor Stravinsky (3 equal instruments) 1971; first performed New York, 23 January 1972. Recorded Desto Records; Crystal Records.
Duo (violin, piano) 1973–4; first performed New York, 21 March 1975. Recorded Nonesuch.
Brass Quintet (2 trumpets, horn, 2 trombones) 1974; first

performed London, 20 October 1974. Recorded Odyssey Records.
A Fantasy About Purcell's "Fantasia upon One Note" (2 trumpets, horn, 2 trombones) 1974; first performed New York, 13 January 1975. Recorded Odyssey Records.
Birthday Fanfare for Sir William Glock's 70th (3 trumpets, vibraphone, glockenspiel) 1978; first performed London, 3 May 1978.
Night Fantasies (piano) 1980; first performed Bath, 2 June 1980. Recorded Nonesuch; Bridge; Etcetera.
Triple Duo (flute, clarinet; or violin, cello; or piano, percussion) 1982–3; first performed London, 23 April 1983. Recorded Wergo WER 60124.
Changes (guitar) 1983; first performed New York, 11 December 1983. Recorded Bridge Records.
Canon for Four: Homage to William (flute, bass clarinet, violin, cello) 1984; first performed Bath, 8 June 1984. Recorded New Albion Records; GM Records.
Esprit rude/esprit doux (flute, clarinet; dedicated to Boulez) 1984; first performed Baden-Baden, 31 March 1985. Recorded New Albion Records; GM Records.
Riconoscenza per Goffredo Petrassi (violin) 1984; first performed Pontino, Italy, 15 June 1984. Recorded New World.
String Quartet No 4 1986; first performed Miami, 17 September 1986. Recorded Etcetera KTC 1065.
Enchanted Preludes (flute, cello) 1988.

Vocal/choral:

My Love Is in a Light Attire (voice, piano; Joyce) 1928 (other Joyce settings from the period lost).
Tarantella (male chorus, piano—4 hands, or orchestra; Ovid) 1936. Recorded Carillon; GSS.
The Bridge (oratorio; Crane) 1937.
Harvest Home (unaccompanied choir; Herrick) 1937; first performed New York, Spring 1938.
Let's Be Gay (female chorus, 2 pianos; Gay) 1937; first performed Wells, Spring 1938.
To Music (unaccompanied choir; Herrick) 1937; first performed New York, Spring 1938. Recorded New World; GSS.
Twelve Madrigals (3 to 8 voices) 1937; withdrawn.
Heart Not So Heavy as Mine (unaccompanied choir; Dickinson) 1938; first performed New York, 31 March 1939. Recorded Nonesuch; SPAMH; GSS.
Tell Me Where Is Fancy Bred? (alto, guitar; Shakespeare) 1938. Recorded Columbia; Unicorn.
The Defence of Corinth (speaker, male voices, piano—4 hands; Rabelais) 1941; first performed Cambridge, Massachusetts, 12 March 1942. Recorded Harvard Glee Club Records; Vox.
Three Poems of Robert Frost (mezzo-soprano, baritone, piano; "Dust of Snow", "The Rose Family", "The Line Gang") 1943, arranged for soprano/tenor, chamber orchestra, 1975. Recorded Bridge BCD 9014.
Warble for Lilac-Time (soprano/tenor, piano/small orchestra; Whitman) 1943, revised 1954; first performed Saratoga Springs, New York, 14 September 1946.
Voyage (mezzo-soprano/baritone, piano; Crane) 1943; arranged for small orchestra 1975, revised 1979; first performed New York, 16 March 1947. Recorded Unicorn.
The Difference (soprano, baritone, piano; van Doren) 1944.
The Harmony of Morning (female voices, small orchestra; van Doren) 1944; first performed New York, 25 February 1945. Recorded Vox; GSS.
Musicians Wrestle Everywhere (mixed voices, strings *ad lib*) 1945; first performed New York, 12 February 1946. Recorded Nonesuch; Vox; Deutsche Grammophon.
Emblems (male voices, piano; Tate) 1947; first performed New York, 1952. Recorded GSS.
A Mirror on Which to Dwell (soprano, flute/piccolo/alto flute, oboe/cor anglais, clarinet/E♭ clarinet/bass clarinet, percussion, violin, viola, cello, double bass; Bishop) 1975; first performed New York, 24 February 1976. Recorded Columbia; Bridge BCD 9014; (excerpts) Radio France/IRCAM.
Syringa (mezzo-soprano, baritone, alto flute, cor anglais, bass clarinet, trombone, percussion, piano, violin, viola, cello, double bass; Ashbery, ancient Greek) 1978; first performed New York, 10 December 1978. Recorded Bridge BCD 9014; CRI.
In Sleep, In Thunder (tenor, 14 players; Lowell) 1981; first performed London, 27 October 1982. Recorded Bridge BCD 9014; Wergo WER 60124.

Opera:

Tom and Lily (comic opera; 4 soloists, mixed chorus, chamber orchestra) 1934; withdrawn.

Other:

Philoctetes (incidental music to Sophocles; tenor, baritone, male chorus, oboe, percussion) 1931; first performed Cambridge, Massachusetts, 15 March 1933.
Mostellaria (incidental music to Plautus; tenor, baritone, male chorus, chamber orchestra) 1936; first performed Cambridge, Massachusetts, 15 April 1936.
Pocahontas (ballet; piano) 1936; first performed Keene, New Hampshire, 17 August, 1936; piano version withdrawn; also for orchestra, New York, first performed 24 May 1939.
The Ball Room Guide (ballet) 1937.
Much Ado About Nothing (incidental music to Shakespeare) 1937; withdrawn.
The Minotaur (ballet) 1947; first performed New York, 26 March 1947.

PUBLICATIONS

On Carter: **Books**—A. Edwards, *Flawed Words and Stubborn Sounds: A Conversation with EC*, New York, 1971; R. Jackson, *EC: Sketches and Scores in Manuscript*, New York, 1973; *EC: A 70th birthday Tribute*, London, 1978; J. F. Weber, *Carter and Schuman* (discography), Utica, New York, 1978; D. Schiff, *The Music of EC*, New York, 1983; W.C. Pflugradt, "EC and the Variation Process", dissertation, University of Indiana, 1984; C. Rosen, *The Musical Language of EC*, Washington, D.C., 1984; **Articles**—R. Kostelanetz, "EC", in *Master Minds: Portraits of Contemporary American Artists and Intellectuals*, New York, 1969; C. Gagne and T. Caras, "EC", in *Soundpieces: Interviews with American Composers*, Metuchen, New Jersey, 1982; J. Rockwell, "American Intellectual Composers and the 'Ideal Public'", in *All-American Music*, New York, 1983; Richard Dufallo, interview, in *Trackings: Composers Speak with Richard Dufallo*, Oxford, 1990.

* * *

Regarded in some quarters as the most significant living American composer, Elliott Carter has not been as conspicuously prolific as many of his contemporaries. Instead, he has preferred to work slowly and meticulously on a comparatively small, but nonetheless wide-ranging, body of compositions.

Carter's early interest in avant-garde music was fostered by a friendship—while still at school—with Charles Ives, but, like so many other Americans before and since, much of his early serious work was composed under the formidable influence of Nadia Boulanger, and reflected her characteristic neo-Stravinskian modes. His compositions from the ballet music for *Pocahontas* through to the prize-winning *Holiday Overture* reveal a well-honed sense of linear counterpoint, but that influence is balanced with a much more distinctive rhythmic complexity.

The *Piano Sonata No 1* marked a significant change in Carter's music, and launched a sharp move away from these neo-classical verities, a development which carried on in the *Sonata* for cello and piano and his First String Quartet. His new musical language was more austere, but at the same time experimented with extended harmonic forms, building on material derived from the overtone series of the piano, and with what he called "metrical modulation", a frequent shifting of tempo, metre and rhythm which became a principal characteristic of his music.

These compositions were less immediately populist but more musically advanced than his earlier work, or that of many of his contemporaries. The independent but parallel structure of the First String Quartet placed an unconventional stress on the inter-relationships between the instruments, each of which was independent of the other three, a theme which he took to even greater lengths in the Second String Quartet, and developed on a wider scale in the *Variations for Orchestra*, which he described as "a series of character studies in various states of interaction with each other both within each variation and between one and the next."

His work at this time was characterised by its polyrhythmic complexity and the abundant fertility of the musical ideas which he evolved within his rigorous, structurally elegant musical vocabulary. In the Third String Quartet, Carter varied the idea of independent voices by pairing off the instruments into two duos, within which each instrument played both singly and together, an idea he returned to in the often comic *Triple Duo*.

The major orchestral works of the 1960s, notably the *Piano Concerto* and the *Concerto For Orchestra*, continued the process of evolution signalled in the compositions of the 1950s, while the *Symphony for Three Orchestras* subdivided the orchestra into three component parts in the manner of Mozart's multiple-orchestra works, allowing him even greater scope for a satisfyingly rich exploration of their musical inter-relationships. That investigation of the possibilities inherent in multiple structure carried on to even greater lengths in *Penthode*, which divides its 20 players into five quartets.

His *Night Fantasies* for piano is one of his most immediately attractive and consonant compositions, a stridently assertive recitative in the middle aside, and has justly become one of his most popular works. His critical stock, already high, rose again with his Fourth String Quartet, which returned to the four-way dialogue of the Second Quartet, albeit ameliorated by a slightly more convivial tone of agreement between the disparate partners.

The success of the String Quartets, certainly among the very greatest written in the post-1945 period, and the general strength of his chamber music, have led some admirers to value this part of his work above all else, but to do so does scant justice to the clarity of purpose and single-minded determination to expand his musical language evident in all of his work.

His vocal scores, notably *A Mirror on Which to Dwell* (six poems by Elizabeth Bishop) and the bleak but powerful *In Sleep, In Thunder* (six poems of Robert Lowell), are considerable works in themselves, while his orchestral compositions have consistently risen to the challenge of pushing forward the boundaries of our musical language, and have done much to redefine our understanding of rhythm and tempo. In doing so, he has set some profound challenges for both performers and listeners, but his own abilities have never been overwhelmed by the scale of his ambition.

—Kenny Mathieson

CASKEN, John. British/English. Born in Barnsley, Yorkshire, 15 July 1949. Educated at University of Birmingham (under John Joubert and Peter Dickinson), 1967–71; Warsaw (under Andrzej Dobrowolski and Witold Lutoslawski), 1971–3. Lecturer, University of Birmingham, 1973–9, Huddersfield Polytechnic, 1979–81, and University of Durham, since 1981. Mailing address: 6 Carlton Terrace, Low Fell, Tyne and Wear NE9 6DE, England.

Publisher: Schott.

Symphonies/orchestral:

Arenaria (flute, 13 players) 1976; first performed Manchester, May 1976.
Tableaux des Trois Ages 1976–7; first performed Birmingham, September 1977.
Concerto for Piano and Orchestra 1980–1; first performed Manchester, 24 January 1982.
Masque (oboe, 2 horns, strings) 1982; first performed Windsor, 9 October 1982.
Erin (double bass, small orchestra) 1982–3.
Orion over Farne 1984; first performed Glasgow, 17 September 1984.
Mabaral Dreaming 1989; first performed Darlington, County Durham, 12 May 1989.

Chamber/instrumental:

Kagura (2 flutes, 2 oboes, 2 clarinets, alto saxophone, 2 bassoons, 2 horns, 2 trumpets) 1972–3; first performed Birmingham, May 1973.
Music for the Crabbing Sun (flute, oboe, cello, harpsichord) 1974; first performed London, 30 October 1976.
Music for a Tawny-Gold Day (viola, alto saxophone, bass clarinet, piano) 1975–6; first performed Amsterdam, September 1976.
Thymehaze (alto recorder, piano) 1976; first performed Birmingham, October 1976.
Amarantos (flute/alto flute, oboe, clarinet/bass clarinet, horn, trumpet, percussion, piano, viola, cello) 1977–8; first performed London, 12 December 1978.
Ligatura (organ) 1978–80; broadcast Radio Hilversum, 25 March 1983.
Melanos (tuba, alto flute, horn, trombone, percussion, piano, harp, double bass) 1979; first performed Midlands, 14 December 1979.

A Belle Pavine (violin, tape) 1980; first performed York, 14 June 1980.
String Quartet 1981–2; first performed London, 2 February 1982. Recorded Wergo WER 60096.
Eructavit (flute, clarinet, horn, bassoon, marimba, drum, piano, drone, violin, cello) 1982; first performed Durham, 26 November 1982.
Fonteyn Fanfares (12 brass) 1982.
Taerset (clarinet, piano) 1982–3; first performed Stockton-on-Tees, 2 May 1983.
Piper's Linn (Northumbrian small pipes, tape) 1983–4; first performed Glasgow, 21 September 1984.
Clarion Sea (2 trumpets, horn, trombone, tuba) 1984–5; first performed Birmingham, 5 May 1985. Recorded Wergo WER 60096.
Vaganza (large ensemble) 1985; first performed St Albans, Hertfordshire, 12 July 1985.
Salamandra (fire-haunt for 2 pianos) 1986; first performed Huddersfield, Yorkshire, 20 November 1986.
Lights and Turning Arcs (organ; reworking of *Ligatura*) 1989; first performed London, 24 June 1989.
Piano Quartet 1989–90; first performed Birmingham, 24 November 1990.

Vocal/choral:

Ia Orana, Gauguin (soprano, piano) 1978; first performed Leicester, January 1979. Recorded Wergo WER 60096.
Firewhirl (soprano, flute, clarinet, bassoon, horn, violin, viola, cello) 1979–80; first performed Bath, 25 May 1980. Recorded Wergo 60096.
To Fields We Do Not Know (unaccompanied chorus) 1983–4; broadcast BBC, 24 October 1985; first concert performance Durham, 26 October 1985.
The Land of Spices (unaccompanied chorus) 1990; first performed Durham, 22 June 1990.

Opera:

Golem (chamber opera; libretto in collaboration with Pierre Audi) 1986–8; first performed London, 28 June 1989. Recorded Virgin Classics, release 1991.

Other:

Soul Catcher (electronic) n.d.

PUBLICATIONS

By Casken: article on his music in *Contact*, 12, 1975.

On Casken: Paul Griffiths, (interview) in *New Sounds, New Personalities: British Composers of the 80s*, London, 1985.

* * *

The music of John Casken has a vividness and uncynical approachability rare in contemporary music, fostered by a sensitive timbral palette, skilful accumulation of texture and carefully controlled architecture and pace.

Casken's writing is dramatically expressive and tailored to his chosen instrumentation. His opera *Golem* contains notable instances—the lachrymose microtones which accompany the Golem's death, the unexpected eeriness of spring coils and struck suspended flower-pots, and driving use of the hi-hat which, interestingly, circumvents its usual rock music associations.

The writing is not so much innovative as appropriate. The effect which ends *Orion over Farne*, for instance—a cymbal placed upside down on a timpanum and rolled as the pedal is moved—is not original, but is imaginatively judicious.

This ear for timbre is most evident in instrumental writing. Although his electronic work has great vitality (*Soul Catcher*, for example), it is not especially rich in colour, perhaps due to the limitations of available equipment. The tape to *Golem* is a noteworthy exception.

Casken's work is often constructed episodically, with strong dramatic contrast, frequently with a taste of traditional structure. The four sections of *Orion over Farne* cite symphonic structure—fast, slow, a brisk scherzo-like passage, and a slow ending. His *String Quartet* juxtaposes four main musical elements—chords, scurrying figurations, harmonics over a shimmering chordal backdrop, and ostinati—in mosaic fashion in an overall fast-slow-fast configuration. Casken nevertheless consciously attempts to guard against his formal schemes being uninterestingly assimilable: The danger is of their over-use, in making them too obvious—the thread has to be there, but the listener has got to work a little, too".

One feature of Casken's work is a limited aleatoricism which owes much to Lutoslawski, whom Casken consulted while studying in Poland in the 1970s. Aleatoric writing is most evident in scales for small forces. The cello duo *Jadu* is written in proportional notation with noteheads signifying approximate durational values (fairly regular, quite quickly, very quickly). In *Tableaux*, patterns of notes are to be repeated without reference to other players, until the signal for the next section. Pieces for larger forces, such as *Eructavit*, tend to be more fully notated. A score such as *Amarantos* lies somewhere between the two, in focus, in notational style, and consequently in gesture.

Casken frequently employs extra-musical references. One is literature; setting poems (*Firewhirl*, for example), depicting moods (as in *Music for the Crabbing Sun*), narrating (*Ia Orana, Gauguin*). Another is art; the *Tableaux des trois ages* employs a series of Moreau paintings as the frame for an exploration of childhood, adulthood and old age. Casken also uses landscape as a stimulus, sometimes with directly musical ramifications, such as the recourse to folk instrumentation in *Piper's Linn*—Northumbrian small-pipes with a tape derived from them.

Casken believes that with the beginning of the 1990s the expressive and evocative qualities of music are valued again. He prefers an eclectic to a sectarian style, selecting "from all that is available", he said in the third person, "those qualities which will guide the realisation of his music, regardless of style". When Casken wrote *Golem* he was unconcerned "whether it's the 1950s, the 1980s, or the year 2010. I am working on an archetypal legend and all I can do is use what musical experience I have to reflect that".

—David Revill

CERHA, Friedrich. Austrian. Born in Vienna, 17 February 1926. Educated at Akademie für Musik und Darstellende Kunst, Vienna (composition under Alfred Uhl, violin under Vasa Prihoda), 1946–51; courses in philosophy and musicology, University of Vienna, 1946–50, Doctor of Philosophy. Wartime activity in resistance to Nazi regime. Married Gertraud Moslinger, 15 December 1952; 2 daughters. Founder (with Kurt Schwertsik), of new music ensemble die Reihe, 1958; lecturer and director, electronic music studio, 1960—69, associate professor of music, 1969, and professor, since 1970, Vienna Academy. Recipient: Theodor Korner Prize, twice; Forderungspreis, Vienna, twice; Ministry for Education and Art Prize; 1st prize in composition competition, Institute for the Encouragement and Promotion of Art; Austrian State Prize, 1986. Mailing address: Kupelwiesergasse 14, 1130 Vienna, Austria.

Publishers: Universal Edition; Doblinger, Vienna; Edition Modern, Munich.

Symphonies/orchestral:

Symphonische Dichtung (fragment) 1944–5.
Concerto for String Orchestra 1947–9.
Sinfonie (only movements 1 and 3 orchestrated) 1947–50; first movement performed as *Sinfonia in un movimento*, Innsbruck, 1950.
Tryptichon (flute, oboe, clarinet, horn, string orchestra) 1948–51.
Konzertante Sinfonie (piano, orchestra) 1950–3.
Relazioni fragili (harpsichord, chamber orchestra) 1956–7; first performed Vienna, 1960.
Espressioni fondamentali 1957; first performed Berlin, 1960.
Intersecazioni (violin, large orchestra) 1959–73; first performed Graz, 1973.
Fasce 1959–75; first performed Graz, 1975.
Mouvements I–III (chamber orchestra) 1960; first performed Berlin, 1962.
Spiegel I (large orchestra) 1960–1; first performed Warsaw, 1968. Recorded Musikprotokoll Dokumentationsplatte ORF 0120050/1/IGNM.
Spiegel II (55 strings) 1960–1; first performed Donaueschingen, 1964. Recorded Musikprotokoll Dokumentationsplatte ORF 0120050/1/IGNM.
Spiegel III 1960–1; first performed Stockholm, 1965. Recorded Musikprotokoll Dokumentationsplatte ORF 0120050/1/IGNM.
Spiegel IV 1960–1; first performed Graz, 1971. Recorded Musikprotokoll Dokumentationsplatte ORF 0120050/1/IGNM.
Spiegel V 1960–1; first performed Munich, 1971. Recorded Musikprotokoll Dokumentionsplatte ORF 0120050/1/IGNM; Amadeo AVRS 6456.
Spiegel VI 1960–1; first performed Hamburg, 1963. Recorded Musikprotokoll Dokumentationsplatte ORF 0120050/1/IGNM.
Spiegel VII 1960–1; first performed Vienna, 1972. Recorded Fonit Cetra LMA 3002; Musikprotokoll Dokumentationsplatte ORF 0120050/1/IGNM.
Symphonien für Blaser und Pauken (wind orchestra, drums) 1964; first performed Baden-Baden, 1970.
Langegger Nachtmusik I 1969; first performed Berlin, 1970.
Langegger Nachtmusik II 1970; first performed Hamburg, 1971.
Sinfonie 1975; first performed Royan, 1976.
Doppelkonzert (double concerto for violin, cello, orchestra) 1975–6; first performed Vienna, 1976.
Doppelkonzert (double concerto for flute, bassoon, orchestra) 1982; first performed Graz, 1983.
Monumentum: für Karl Prantl 1987–8.

Chamber/instrumental:

Duo (2 violins) 1935, revised 1937.
Sonata No 1 (violin) 1936.
Sonata No 2 (violin) 1937.
Gschwandtner Tanze (2 violins, viola, double bass) 1938.
Sonata (viola) 1939.
Ballade (piano) 1946.
Sonatina (piano) 1946.
Marchenland (piano; to texts by Haustein) 1946.
Sonata (violin, piano) 1947.
Konzertante Tafelmusik (oboe, clarinet, bassoon, trumpet) 1947–8.
Zwei Stucke: Meditation, Altes Lied (violin, piano) 1947–8, expanded 1951.
Suite (piano) 1948.
String Quartet No 1 1948.
Divertimento (homage to Igor Stravinsky; version of *Konzertante Tafelmusik*; 2 oboes, 2 clarinets, 2 bassoons, 2 trumpets, 6 percussion) 1947–54; first performed Vienna, 1955.
Sechs kleine Klavierstucke (piano) 1948–56.
Capriccio (violin, piano) 1949.
Ballettsuite (violin, piano) 1949.
Aria und Fuge (8 winds; incorporating 2 movements from 1st *Violin Sonata*, 1936) 1949.
Vergnugliche Musik (violin, clarinet) 1949.
Toccata (piano) 1950.
Sonata (viola, lute/guitar) 1951.
Sonata (viola, piano) 1951.
Pastoral Sonata (viola, piano) 1951.
String Quartet No 2 1951.
String Trio 1952.
Sonata (horn, piano) 1952.
Klavierbuch für Roswitha (piano) 1952–3.
Ricercar, Toccata, Passacaglia (flute, viola d'amore, lute or harpsichord) 1953; arranged for flute, viola d'amore, harpsichord, 1954.
Sonata No 3 (violin, piano) 1955.
Deux éclats en réflexion (violin, piano) 1956; first performed Vienna, 1957.
Formation et solution (violin, piano) 1956–7; first performed Darmstadt, 1958.
Klavierstück 58 (piano) 1958.
Enjambements (flute/piccolo, trumpet, trombone, 2 percussion, violin, double bass) 1959; first performed Paris, 1961.
Fünf kleine Stücke (clarinet, piano) 1960–4.
Sieben Anekdoten (flute, piano) 1960–4.
Fantasien nach Cardew's Herbst 60 (7 instruments) 1962–3.
Phantasma 63 (chamber ensemble) 1963.
Elégie (piano) 1964.
Catalogue des objets trouvés (chamber orchestra) 1968–9; first performed Vienna, 1970.
Adaxl-Suite (piano) 1970.
Curriculum (2 oboes, 2 clarinets, 2 bassoons, 2 horns, 2 trumpets, 2 trombones, tuba) 1972–3; first performed New York City, 1973.
Fier musikalische Grafiken (any instrumentation) 1973.
Netzwerke-Phantasie (piano) 1988.

Vocal/choral:

Schliesse mir die Augen beide (voice, piano; Storm) 1942.
Rohtraut, schon Rohtraut (voice, piano; Morike) 1942.
Der Silberreiher (voice, piano; Litaipo) 1945.
Morgen (voice, piano; Haustein) 1946.

Der Himmel war heut voller sterne (voice, piano; Haustein) 1946.
Ein buch von der Minne (voice, piano) 1946–54.
Andenken (voice, piano; Eichendorff) 1947.
Jeder Tag verklingt (voice, piano; Haustein) 1947.
Sei nicht mude, mein Kind (voice, piano; Mitterer) 1947.
Sonnengesang des heiligen Franz von Assisi (soloists, choir, harp, string orchestra) 1947–9; first performed Vienna, 1949.
Rubaijat des Omar Khajjam (unaccompanied mixed chorus) 1949–54.
An die Herrscher der Welt (soloists, unaccompanied mixed choir; *Buch der Weisheit*) 1950–1.
Sechs Lieder nach Hugo von Hofmannsthal (voice, piano) 1950.
Fragment aus dem I-Ging (soloists, chorus, orchestra) 1952.
Drei Lieder (12 voices, piano; Ecclesiastes, Talmud) 1953.
Sieben Rubaijat des Omar Khajjam (soprano, piano) 1957.
Exercises (baritone, speakers, chamber orchestra) 1962–8; first performed Vienna, 1968.
Verzeichnis (4 sopranos, 4 altos, 4 tenors, 4 basses, unaccompanied) 1969; first performed Bremen, 1970. Recorded Wergo WER 60070.
Baal-Gesange (baritone, orchestra; Brecht) 1979; first performed Hamburg, 1982. Recorded Eterna VEB 827892.
Keintate I (medium voice, 2 clarinets, 2 horns, percussion, accordion, 2 violins, viola, cello, double bass; Kein) 1982; first performed Vienna, 1983.
Requiem for Hollensteiner (speaker, baritone, mixed choir, orchestra; Bernhard) 1983; first performed Hamburg, 1984.
Keintate II (medium voice, 2 clarinets, 2 horns, percussion, accordion, 2 violins, viola, cello, double bass; Kein) 1983–4; first performed Graz, 1986.
Nachtgesang (tenor, orchestra) 1984; first performed Stuttgart, 1986.
Requiem für Rikke (from *Der Rattenfanger*; tenor, orchestra; Zuckmayer) 1984–9.
Eine Art Chansons (amplified medium voice, piano, percussion, double bass; Achleitner, Jandl, Ruhm, Schwitters, others) 1985; first performed St Polten, 1988.

Opera:

Baal (Brecht, Cerha) 1974–81; first performed Salzburg, 1981. Recorded Amadeo 415 266.
Der Rattenfanger (Zuckmayer) 1984–6; first performed Graz, 1987.

Other:

Klavierstücke (for young and improving pianists) 1948–64.
Drei Stücke für fruhzetig alternde Jugendliche (piano) 1948–64.
Spiegel (music for theatre; large orchestra, tape, dancers, props, lights) 1960–1.
"Und du . . . " (radiophonic composition for tape; Anders, Cerha) 1963; first performed Vienna, 1963.
Kinderstucke für Irina (piano) 1964.
Netzwerk (music for theatre; baritone, 6 speakers, chamber orchestra, mimes; based on *Exercises*) 1974–81; first performed Vienna, 1981.

Khatchaturian: *Poème* (arranged for violin, piano) 1947.
G. Machault: *Messe, Kyrie* (arranged for chorus, instrumental ensemble) 1948.
Sylvano Bussotti: *Manifesto per Kalinowski* (arranged for chamber ensemble) 1960. first performed Vienna, 1961.
Alban Berg/Friedrich Cerha: *Lulu* (completion of the 3rd act of the unfinished opera) 1962–78; first performed Paris, 1979.
Erik Satie: *Embryons dessechées* (arranged for chamber ensemble) 1966; first performed Vienna, 1968.
Paul Kont: *Strohkoffer* (arranged for violin, chamber orchestra) 1979; first performed Vienna, 1979.

PUBLICATIONS

By Cerha: "Der Turandotstoff in der deutschen Literature", dissertation, Vienna, 1949; "Die Wiener Schule und die Gegenwart", in *Osterreischen Muskizeitschrift*, 16, 1961; "Zu meiner Musik und einigen Problemen des Komponieriens heute", in *Beitrage 68/69*, Kassel, 1969; "Argbeitsbericht zur Herstellung des 3. Akts der Oper Lulu von Alban Berg", notes, Vienna, 1979; "Zu meinem Musiktheater", in *Osterreich zum Beiuspiel*, Salzburg, Vienna, 1982.

On Cerha: Kurt Blaukopf, "FC", in *Die Musik in Geschichte und Gegenwart*, Kassel, 1973; Harald Goertz, in *Osterreichische Komponisten der Gegenwart*, Vienna, Munich, 1979; Klaus Ager, "FC: *Spiegel*", in *Melos*, 1986; Richard Duffalo, (interview) in *Trackings*, Oxford, 1990.

Friedrich Cerha comments:

Background: after exploring high Modernism, the works of the Vienna School and serial technique (1946–56), independent development of those techniques (*Relazioni fragili, Intersecazioni*) and free use of sonority within traditional forms (*Mouvements, Fasce, Spiegel*). Apart from sound phenomena, a fundamental interest in formal processes. To create complex, organic structures, since about 1962, incorporating the most heterogeneous musical materials. To strive for control and synthesis of a multiplicity of musical material in order to achieve terse rhythm, clear melodic lines and harmonic development. Everyday experience is always of primary importance in the shaping of music.

* * *

Since the 1950s, the Austrian composer Friedrich Cerha has been one of the foremost exponents of avant-garde music, with an international reputation. After early attempts at a post-romantic style and the analysis of Stravinsky's compositional techniques, he turned, under the clear influence of the Darmstadt circle, to dodecaphonic and serial structures. In doing so, he used only those permutations of serial variation which ensured that the most important tone-rows were formed in a recognizable way.

Among other innovations, he succeeded in splitting up the rhythmic elements so that they progressed without too much obscuring detail. However, with regard to the sound itself, he always maintained certain points of crystallization which communicate to the listener contours and landmarks—as in *Relazioni fragili* and *Intersecazioni*—which sound almost "traditional". Making increasingly small and detailed alterations and a virtually imperceptible progress from one type of material to the other, Cerha worked on his great seven-part cycle *Spiegel*. Here, an initial impulse determines a subsequent event which, for its part, broadens out further and further until a chain of linear processes, each of which is indispensible and inconceivable without the rest, are bound together. Nevertheless, even here Cerha used more distant events in order to be able to create large-scale formal references by means of a principle of "feedback".

Spiegel was subsequently produced as a theatrical work. Its main actions are illuminated on the stage much as they are in purely formal terms in that sound masses rely heavily upon one another. According to Cerha, the subject of his scenes is man's conduct and interrelations.

In the late 1960s, Cerha once again utilised a succession of more traditional elements in preference to post-serial structures. In both *Catalogue des objets trouvés* and *Curriculum* one can detect a return to melodic lines, to a basic harmony and clarity of form built on the traditional idea of reprise. In *Curriculum* Cerha uses in addition a series of quotations from Charles Ives. In the *Doppelkonzert*, composed in 1975–6, he went one stage further, incorporating compositional ideas from Erik Satie, a gesture which bound him nonetheless with an explicitly avant-gardist or experimental traditional rather than a conventional one.

Meanwhile, in *Netzwerke-Phantasie*, written for the theatre, Cerha turned, both dramatically and musically, to those relationships between individuals and structures which create order. The result is a dovetailing of the work's main action, with the shorter entr'actes, where individuals are able to express themselves in a way that suggests heterogeneity has become the principle of style and action. In the two later stage works *Baal-Gesange* and *Der Rattenfanger*, Cerha takes on board a more usual understanding of the idea of tradition in terms of individual expressivity. Here, under the influence of Alban Berg's *Lulu*, Cerha again employs intense singing lines and works up all dimensions of speech into fine cantabile vocalism. This allows intermediate stages to become effective, eventually uncovering a rich orchestral language, the immediacy of which is not compromised by breaks in the structure.

In spite of this expressionistic stance, the material still follows a free tone-row and is made up of clear thematic references. And so it can be seen that there is, in fact, a stylistic return to the very earliest of Cerha's works. However, a traditional musical vocabulary finds its way into some of the late instrumental works. Of special interest here are the two collections *Eine Art Chansons* and the two *Keintaten*, in which Cerha, following the content or text respectively, indulges in a kind of stylistic pluralism which even embraces elements of Viennese song and folklore. It goes as far as to arrogate a post-modernist licence to dispose freely of *any* idiom from either past or present.

—Hartmut Krones
(translated by John Abbey and Ortwin Reim)

CHADABE, Joel (A.). American. Born in New York City, 12 December 1938. Educated at University of North Carolina, Chapel Hill (under Will Mason), 1955–9, B.A.; Yale University, New Haven, Connecticut, (under Elliott Carter), 1959–62, M.M. Married Françoise Chadabe, 28 October, 1968; 1 son. Ford Foundation Artist in Residence Fellowship, West Berlin, 1964; member of faculty, since 1965, and founder of electronic music studio, 1966, State University of New York, Albany; consultant, Bennington College, Vermont, since 1971; visiting faculty, University of North Carolina, Chapel Hill, 1974; member, board of directors, 1975–8, and since 1987, and president 1978–87, Composers' Forum Inc, New York City; software designer/president, Intelligent Computer Music Systems Inc, since 1986; visiting faculty, Rensselaer Polytechnic Institute, Troy, New York, Autumn 1986, Spring 1989; member, advisory committee, Center for Electronic Music, New York City, since 1987; visiting faculty, International Summer School and Festival on Computers and Art, Lugano, Switzerland, Summer 1989; touring performer on computer/synthesizer. Recipient: CAPS Award, New York State Council on the Arts, 1971; New York Foundation for the Arts Award, 1985. Mailing address: P.O. Box 8748, Albany, New York 12208, U.S.A.

Publisher: C. Fischer.

Symphonies/orchestral:

Many Mornings, Many Moods (percussion solo, computer/synthesizer, orchestra) 1988; first performed Buffalo, New York, 10 March 1988.

Chamber/instrumental:

Prelude to Naples (4 instruments) 1965; first performed Rome, 16 June 1965.
Street Scene (cor anglais, tape, slides) 1967; first performed New York City, 25 March 1969.
Monomusic (8 instruments) 1969; withdrawn.
Map (instruments, tape) 1970, revised 1972 by Lukas Foss.
Echoes (instrument, electronics) 1972; first performed Oberlin, Ohio, 10 November 1964.
From the 14th On (cello) 1973; first performed Annandale-on-Hudson, New York, 14 April 1973.
Chamber Music (percussion, tape) 1974.
Flowers (string instrument, tape) 1974; first performed Albany, New York, 22 June 1975.
Rhythms: Variation VI (violin, flute, vibraphone, electronic sounds on tape) 1982; first performed Albany, New York, 22 March 1983.
Variation (piano) 1983; first performed New York City, 5 December 1983.
The Long Ago and Far Away Tango (piano) 1984; first performed New York City, 27 February 1985.
After Some Songs (solo instruments, computer/synthesizer) 1987–9; first performed Baltimore, Maryland, 8 March 1987. Recorded Intelligent Music cassette.

Vocal/choral:

Several Views of an Elusive Lady (soprano, electronic sounds on tape) 1985; first performed Geneva, New York, 14 November 1985.

Other (tape and computer):

Drift (tape; collaboration with Lukas Foss) 1970.
Ideas of Movement at Bolton Landing (tape) 1971; first performed Syracuse, New York, 1 May 1971.
Shadows and Lines (tape; collaboration with Lukas Foss) 1972; first performed Buffalo, New York, 13 February 1973.
Dancers (tape) 1975.
Settings for Spirituals (computer-generated sounds as accompaniment to singer) 1977; first performed New York City, 15 May 1977. Recorded Lovely Music.
Playthings (installation) 1978; first performed New York, 27 May 1978.
Solo (computer/synthesizer) 1978, revised 1981; first performed Aarhus, Denmark, 30 August 1978.

Scenes from Stevens (computer/synthesizer) 1979; first performed New York City, 11 November 1979.
Rhythms (computer/synthesizer, percussion) 1980; first performed Baltimore, Maryland, 25 May 1980. Recorded Lovely Music.
Follow Me Softly (computer/synthesizer, percussion) 1984; first performed 12 April 1984.
Bar Music (computer/synthesizer) 1985; first performed Troy, New York, 25 April 1985.

PUBLICATIONS

By Chadabe: "New Approaches to Analog Studio Design", in *Perspectives of New Music*, 6 (1), 1967; "Mona Lisa II", in *Electronic Music Review*, 2 (5), 1969; "Der Elektronische Studio von Albany", in *Melos*, May 1971; "Le Principe du voltage-controle et ses implications pour le compositeur", in *Musique en Jeu*, 8, 1972, republished as "Il Principio del 'Voltage-Controle' e le sue implicazionni per il compositore", in *La Musica Elettronica*, edited by Pousseur, Milan, 1976; "The Voltage-Controlled Synthesiser", in *The Development and Practice of Electronic Music*, edited by Appleton and Perera, Englewood Cliffs, New Jersey, 1975; "Some Reflections on the Nature of the Landscape Within Which Computer Music Systems Are Designed", in *Computer Music Journal*, 1 (3), 1977; "Paths to a Point in a Musical Landscape", in *Proceedings of International Music and Technology Conference*, Melbourne, 1981; "Interactive Composing", in *Computer Music Journal*, 8 (1), 1984, republished in *The Music Machine*, edited by Roads, Cambridge, Massachusetts, 1989.

On Chadabe: James Fulkerson, "What Defines a Piece of Music?", in *The Computer*, 5 (1), 1973; Tom Johnson, "New Music", in *HiFidelity/Musical America*, 25 (9), 1975; Keith Potter, (interview) in "Why Small Is Beautiful", in *Classical Music*, June 1984; Peter Rothbart, (interview) in "Interacting with JC: Composing by Process", in *Seamus*, 2 (1), February 1987.

Joel Chadabe comments:

Since 1977, I've been composing and performing with a portable computer-synthesizer system throughout the world, in concerts with Jan Williams, Bruno Spoerri, Jim Fulkerson and other musicians.

My idea in working with these systems is to use them as intelligent instruments, intelligent in the sense that they function by themselves, generating information of their own devising. As composer, I create the sounds and the processes by which the system composes. As performer, I'm a musical guide, or conductor, steering the system through a composition, making musical decisions while performing. In the concerts I do with other musicians, the music is improvisational rather than fixed and the music unfolds as a result of a conversational relationship between performers.

The merging of popular traditions with aristocratic traditions and technology has been an interest of mine for quite a while. *After Some Songs*, for example, is a series of short pieces, many of them based on jazz classics. The pieces will vary from performance to performance, and some of the songs are more recognizable than others, but they include "Stella by Starlight", "There'll Never Be Another You", "Corcovado", "In a Sentimental Mood" and "My Funny Valentine".

* * *

Though he works at the frontiers of musical and informational technology, Joel Chadabe is not a technocrat. Nor has his music lost any of its basic sense of humor. As "late" as 1984, he is still able to produce a piece as easygoing and evocative as *The Long Ago and Far Away Tango*, or the torchy transformation of *After Some Songs*. Chadabe's technological and scientific experiments are not intended to obfuscate, but to invigorate, musical language. He is, by instinct, a performer, touring the United States and elsewhere with a carefully designed mini-computer system that, in contrast to much of the heavy artillery associated with IRCAM, is engagingly user-friendly; one installation from the latc 1970s, *Playthings*, allows a musically unskilled audience to create music from a sensitive environment, merely by moving through it, pointing, touching, stroking.

If there is a single workable analogy for Chadabe's aesthetic, it is probably not another composer at all (though he shares a basic ethos, if not the means of its realisation, with William Bolcom), but a poet. Chadabe has made explicit use of Wallace Stevens in his work, notably in an unusually academic computer/synthesiser work of 1979, but there are echoes of Stevens in *Several Views of an Elusive Lady* and of Steven's title "Ideas of Order at Key West" in Chadabe's *Ideas of Movement at Bolton Landing*, an earlier tape piece, and there is a sense in which they share an aesthetic philosophy. Stevens was much concerned with the way in which the imagination shaped its environment, almost as if imagination constituted an actual force of nature, like magnetism, bending everything in proximity to its sphere of influence.

That is how *Playthings* is intended to operate. There is nothing aggressive about it. Chadabe's music is uniquely approachable in this rather chilling field. It is difficult to imagine an IRCAM or Darmstadt composer producing anything like the *Settings for Spirituals* or the partly instrumental *After Some Songs*, which is exactly that, a medley *après* such jazz classics as "My Funny Valentine" and "Stella by Starlight". Like Tod Machover, Chadabe learned a great deal from his teacher Elliott Carter, particularly about how to modulate rhythms. In the 1980 piece called *Rhythms* a percussionist duets with an "intelligent" computer that responds to changes in metre as it creates a friendly environment for the human participant.

In contrast to what the maddeningly unprolific John Chowning has produced at Stanford University, Chadabe seems to have limned a way forward for computer composition/performance.

—Eleanor Caldwell

CHAILLY, Luciano. Italian. Born in Ferrara, 19 January 1920. Educated at Liceo Musicale Frescobaldi (violin), diploma 1941; University of Bologna, graduated 1943; Milan Conservatory, diploma in composition, 1945. Served in Alpini Regiment. Married Anna Maria Motta, 25 September 1950; 2 daughters and 1 son. Musical director, RAI-TV, Milan and Rome, 1951–67; artistic director, 1968–71, and general director, since 1976, Teatro alla Scala, Milan; professor of composition, Conservatory of Milan "G. Verdi", since 1968; artistic director, Angelicum, Milan, 1973–5; artistic director, Ente Arena, Verona, 1975–7; artistic director, Teatro dell'Opera, Genoa, 1983–5; docent, Istitute Universitario di Paleografia, Cremona, 1986–9; artistic director, orchestra and choir of RAI, Turin, 1989–90. Recipient: Premio Le Muse, 1968; Premio Leonardo, 1977; Premio S. Giorgio, 1981; Premio Frescobaldi, 1983; Premio Una Vita per la Lirica, 1984; Premio Scuola Cultura ed Arte, 1984; Gold Medal of the President of the Republic, 1984. Mailing address: Viale Bianca Maria 17, 20122 Milan, Italy.

Publishers: Ricordi, Milan; Sonzogno, Milan; Suvini Zerboni, Milan; Zanibon, Padua; Curci, Milan; others.

Symphonies/orchestral:

Toccata (string orchestra) 1947; first performed Pavia, 1948.
Sonata tritematica No 2 1952.
Sonata tritematica No 3 (chamber orchestra) 1954.
Sonata tritematica No 4 1955; first performed Bologna, 1967.
Sonata tritematica No 7 (string orchestra) 1956; first performed Milan, 1957.
Sonata tritematica No 9 1957; first performed Florence, 1960.
Sequenze dell'artide 1960; first performed Zurich, 1962.
Improvvisazione No 1 (vibraphone, cello, small orchestra) 1961; first performed Berlin, 1962.
Fantasia 1964; first performed Rome, 1965.
Piccole serenate (string orchestra) 1966; first performed Perugia, 1968.
Tre episodi (fanfare, small orchestra) 1974; first performed Osnabruck, 1974.
Contrappunti a quattro dimensioni 1975; first performed Palermo, 1975.
Triplum (violin, piano, orchestra) 1975; first performed San Remo, 1976.
Newton-Variazioni (chamber orchestra) 1979; first performed London, 1981.
Es-Konzert 1984; first performed Berlin, 1984.

Chamber/instrumental:

Istantanee di Anna Maria (piano) 1949; first performed Hilversum, Netherlands, 1950.
Sonata tritematica No 1 (piano) 1951; first performed Milan, 1952. Recorded Disco Rusty-Record RRCL/606625.
Sonata tritematica No 5 (cello, piano) 1954; first performed Milan, 1955. Recorded Disco Rusty-Record RRCL/606625.
Sonata tritematica No 6 (piano) 1955; first performed Milan, 1955.
Sonata tritematica No 8 (violin, piano) 1956; first performed Milan, 1958. Recorded Disco Rusty-Record RRCL/606625.
Sonata tritematica No 10 (string quartet) 1960; first performed Milan, 1963. Recorded Disco Rusty-Record RRCL/606625.
Sonata tritematica No 11 (2 pianos) 1961; first performed Milan, 1962. Recorded Disco Rusty-Record RRCL/606625.
Sonata tritematica No 12 (mandolin, piano) 1962; first performed Montevideo, 1962.
Due instantanee (piano) 1962; first performed Berlin, 1962.
Improvvisazione No 2 (piano) 1962; first performed Prague, 1965.
Improvvisazione No 3 (flute, cello, piano) 1962; first performed Rome, 1963.
Improvvisazione No 4 (harp) 1962; first performed Toulon, 1966.
Improvvisazione No 5 (violin) 1962; first performed Milan, 1962.
Improvvisazione No 6 (organ) 1962; first performed Foligno, 1968.
Improvvisazione No 7 (flute) 1962; first performed Rome, 1963.
Improvvisazione No 8 (cello) 1962; first performed Rome, 1963.
Improvvisazione No 9 (mouth organ or flute, strings, percussion) 1962; first performed Rome, 1963.
Improvvisazione No 10 (saxophone) 1962; first performed Paris, 1967.
Improvvisazione No 11 (oboe) 1962; first performed Amsterdam, 1968.
Improvvisazione No 12 (guitar) 1962; first performed Milan, 1987.
Recitativo e fuga (violin, viola, cello, guitar) 1967; first performed Rome, 1968.
Variazioni nel sogno (piano) 1973; first performed Ferrara, 1974. Recorded Disco Angelicum STA 9046.
Parametri (piano trio) 1974; first performed Zurich, 1974.
Recitativo e ostinato (2 trumpets, 2 trombones, organ) 1974; first performed Ancona, 1974.
Ricami (2 violins, viola) 1974; first performed Como, 1974. Recorded Disco Angelicum STA 9046.
Strutture (double bass, piano) 1975; first performed Verona, 1976.
Disegni (piano quartet) 1976; first performed Palma de Majorca, 1977. Recorded Disco Angelicum STA 9046.
Preludio e doppio canone (organ) 1978; first performed Aosta, 1980.
Psicosi (percussion) 1980; first performed Venice, 1981.
Serenata a Mauthausen (mandolin, piano) 1980; first performed Sesto S. Giovanni, 1981.
Sonata (guitar) 1981; first performed Rome, 1982.
Psicogrammi (harp) 1981; first performed Siena, 1982.
Es-Kammerkonzert (small instrumental ensemble) 1983; first performed Ferrara, 1984.
Dicotomia (trumpet, organ) 1984; first performed Milan, 1984.
Studio-variazioni (flute) 1985; first performed Erice, 1986.
Largo e pizzicato—Folk (12 cellos) 1986; first performed Bergamo, 1986.
Recitativo e allegro (violin, piano) 1987; first performed Gorizia, 1987.

Vocal/choral:

Lamento di Danae (soprano, piano; Simonide-Quasimodo) 1960; first performed Trieste, 1961.
Picola messa (unaccompanied SA choir) 1960; first performed Perugia, 1961.
Tre liriche (bass, piano; Rossi Lemeni, Fedrigotti, Pedroni) 1962; first performed Milan, 1964.
Madre (baritone, chorus, harp; Ravegnani) 1963; first performed Milan, 1964.
Missa Papae Pauli (6-part choir, orchestra; Bacchelli) 1963; first performed Milan, 1964.
Tiadele-Mo (baritone, small chorus, instruments; Pygmy text) 1965; first performed Rome, 1967.
Salmo (baritone, chorus, orchestra; Savonarola) 1967; first performed Perugia, 1968.
Ode a ferrara (reciter, choir, orchestra; D'Annunzio, Carducci, Ravegnani) 1968; first performed Rome, 1969.
L'Appello (baritone, 17 instruments) 1970; first performed Milan, 1972.
Tre liriche latine (tenor, harp; Catullus) 1971; first performed Rovereto, 1972.
Che vuoi pastore d'aria? (bass, choir, horn; Quasimodo) 1971; first performed Rome, 1972.
Liriche della resistenza Vietnamita (baritone, 11 instruments;

Bach Lien, Mien Duc Thang, Le Anh Xuan) 1975; first performed Milan, 1976.
Kinder-Requiem (4 soloists, children's voices, light voices, orchestra) 1977; first performed Turin, 1979.
Due liriche spirituali (mezzo-soprano, piano; S. Di Candia, St Francis) 1978; broadcast Radio Jugoslavia, 1981.
Tre madrigali di Cefalonia (unaccompanied mixed chorus) 1979.
De profundis di Cefalonia (3 choirs, 3 organs, 16 timpani) 1981.

Opera:

Ferrovia soprelevata (Buzzati) 1955; first performed Bergamo, 1 October 1955.
Una domanda di matrimonio (Fino and Vertone, after Chekhov) 1957; first performed Milan, 22 May 1957.
Il canto del cigno (Chailly, after Chekhov) 1957; first performed Bologna, 16 November 1957.
La riva delle sirti (Prinzhofer, after Gracq) 1958; first performed Monte Carlo, 1 March 1957.
Procedura penale (Buzzati) 1959; first performed Como, 30 September 1959.
Il mantello (Buzzati) 1960; first performed Florence, 11 May 1960.
Era proibito (Buzzati) 1962; first performed Milan, 5 March 1963.
Vassiliev (Chailly, after Chekhov) 1966; first performed Genoa, 1967.
Markheim (Prinzhofer, after Stevenson) 1967; first performed Spoleto, 1967.
L'Idiota (Loverso, after Dostoyevsky) 1969; first performed Rome, 14 February 1970.
Sogno (ma forse no) (Prinzhofer, after Pirandello) 1974; first performed Trieste 1975.
Il libro dei reclami (Prinzhofer, after Chekhov) 1975; first performed Vienna, 1975.
La cantatrice calva (Chailly, after Ionesco) 1984; first performed Vienna, 1986.

Other:

Fantasmi al Grand-Hotel (ballet) 1960; first performed Milan, 1960.
Il Cappio (ballet) 1961; first performed Naples, 1962.
Mastro Don Gesualdo (television) 1963; broadcast Rome, 1963.
L'Urlo (ballet) 1966; first performed Palermo, 1967.
Shee (ballet) 1967; first performed Melbourne, 1967.
Anna Frank (ballet) 1980; first performed Verona, 1981.

PUBLICATIONS

By Chailly: *Il matrimonio segreto di Cimarosa*, Milan, 1949; *I Personaggi*, Florence, 1972; *Cronache di vita musicale*, Rome, 1973; *Taccuino segreto di un musicista*, Bologna, 1973; *Buzzati in musica*, Turin, 1987; *Le variazioni della fortuna*, Milan, 1989.

On Chailly: M. Mila, in *Cronache musicali*, Rome, 1959; F. D'amico, in *I casi della musica*, Rome, 1962; R. Bacchelli, in *Sagi musicali*, Milan, 1968; E. Montale, in *Prime alla scala*, Milan, 1981.

Luciano Chailly comments:

My aesthetic position can be stated clearly: eclecticism. Indeed, my output has to be divided into three distinct periods: one of free atonality in a neoclassical climate (with a certain influence by Hindemith, whose 1948 Salzburg Mozarteum masterclass I attended); then, beginning with the *Sonata tritematica No 10*) a period of orthodox dodecaphony; finally, a more personal approach to serial technique, modulated, as in the opera *Sogno (ma forse no)*, by a more alluring musical ambience.

My main theatrical collaborator has been the novelist Dino Buzzati, with whom I have composed operas and, in 1960, the ballet *Fantasmi al Grand-Hotel* for La Scala in Milan. My favourite composers are Gesualdo, Bach, Mozart, Chopin, Mussorgsky and Stravinsky. For sport, I play tennis and ski. Hobby: stamp collecting.

* * *

Luciano Chailly's varied career spans not just composition, but spells as musical director for La Scala, Milan and Verona at the end of the 1960s, and before that a period of two decades at Italian Radio, whose music department he headed, latterly based in Rome. He later ran the Royal Theatre in Turin and still resides and works in Milan.

Chailly's compositions suggest several inputs: the eclecticism of the Malipiero generation, who advised their pupils (like Maderna, born in the same year as Chailly, 1920) not to identify too closely with a single compositional school; the lure of stricter, post-Webern formalism, closely linked with Dallapiccola; the impact on Italy of rival Post-Romantic movements, including neo-classical or neo-Baroque idioms filtered through Paris and the Berlin of Busoni and Strauss; and above all, Hindemith (whose classes in Salzburg Chailly attended in the late 1940s).

He was born into a comfortably-off Ferrara family and after early violin studies progressed to the University of Bologna and then Milan Conservatory after the war. The interest in composition was soon stirred and by the early 1950s a steady stream of works began emerging. He soon began his innovative series of 12 *Sonate tritematica* spanning a decade, written for various-sized ensembles—piano or two pianos, string solo (violin, cello, mandolin) with piano, chamber or full orchestra—on a triple-theme structure. Disciplined and economical, they hover between a dry academism and considerable dramatic tension and power. Like the Italy-based Henze and others, Chailly fashioned his own mix of serial-related and contrasting techniques; further hints of Messiaen or Stravinsky peer through the sonatas' textures.

Drama has played an important part in his output. In the late 1950s and 1960s Chailly, like Menotti, championed the one-act chamber opera, producing eight in rapid succession, followed by three more, widely staged in Italy and also abroad (notably in Germany, Austria, France and South America).

Two influences proved overriding: Russian Literature—three of his operas, *Una domanda di matrimonio* ("A Marriage Proposal"—one of his most successful), *Vassiliev* and the later *Il libro dei reclami* he based on Chekhov, while the full-length opera *The Idiot*, premiered in 1970 at Rome Opera, is drawn from Dostoevsky.

His recent resort to Ionesco (*La cantatrice calva*, performed in Vienna in 1986) further confirms Chailly's other fascination, with the absurd or unexpected. He has absorbed equally into his operas the irony of Brecht and Beckett, Berg or Hindemith, stoked by the emotional neutralising of the 1930s and wartime that fired French writers like Camus. (Comparably, Dallapiccola set St Exupery's *Vol de Nuit* at about this time). In Chailly it generated a fondness for the paradox or volte-face, characteristic of the unpredictable period he grew up in.

It is this which gave his half-dozen stage collaborations with Dino Buzzatti, including three early operas, *Procedura penale, Il mantello* and *Era proibito*, their potency. Greek ideas of trial, denouement and nemesis are never far absent. In one, a son returned from the war turns out to be a grotesque, ghostly parody of a dead man; in another, a family occasion transforms unexpectedly into a grisly trial. Their dramatic effect, being sometimes over-concentrated, deliberately harsh and expressionistic, did not always go down smoothly at Italian first performances. Some scenes were perceived overtly not to work, the intention perceived as confused. Others achieved the notoriety of *causes célèbres*. But these three pieces, together with the three-act *La riva delle sirti* (after Julien Gracq), written for Montecarlo, create an identifiable unit in Chailly's output and, effectively or not, reflect a well-defined, albeit bizarre or pessimistic outlook that echoes Italian post-war film directors like Fellini. Later works such as *L'Idiota* are no less important.

His social commitment emerges in a number of works, including *Liriche della resistenza Vietnamita* for baritone and ll-instrument chamber ensemble; the *Serenata a Mauthausen* for mandolin and piano; and the most recent of his five ballets, *Anna Frank*, based on the famous Amsterdam wartime diaries. The part-serial *Newton Variations*, whose structure (refraction, convergence, etc.) imaginatively derives from the British scientist's optical researches, were successfully premiered in London. Sacred works include two Masses, one dedicated to Pope Paul VI, and the later *Children's Requiem*. Among his full orchestral pieces the early *Sequenze dell'artide* enjoyed considerable success, as did *Contrappunti a quattro dimensioni* some years later; while the more recent and significant *Es-Konzert* for Berlin he has also arranged for a smaller ensemble.

—Roderic Dunnett

CHAUSHIAN, Levon. Armenian. Born in Yerevan, Armenia, 10 May 1946. Educated at P. I. Tchaikovsky Music School (piano and composition), Yerevan, 1954–64; State Conservatory "Sogoman Komitas", Yerevan, 1964–70. Married Gohar Shakhazizian in 1971; 2 children. Teacher of piano, Music College "R. Melikian", Yerevan, since 1970; teacher of choral score reading, State Conservatory "Sogoman Komitas", since 1973; secretary of the board, 1979–85, and deputy chairman, since 1985, Armenian Composers' Union. Recipient: prize, Competition for Young Composers, Moscow, 1962; 2nd prize, Competition for Young Composers (for *Symphonic Poem*), 1969; Lenin Komsomol Prize, 1974; 1st prize, Republican Competition (for *To the Unknown Soldier*), 1985. Mailing address: Mashtotz's Prospekt N.11, Apt.6, 375002 Yerevan, Armenia.

Publishers: Sovetskii kompozitor, Moscow; Musika, Neglinnaya 14, 103001 Moscow, U.S.S.R.; Schirmer.

Symphonies/orchestral:

Concerto for Piano and Orchestra 1963; first performed Yerevan, 1964.
Theme with Variations (concerto for orchestra) 1965; first performed Yerevan, 1966.
Symphonic Poem 1967; first performed Moscow, 1969.
Symphonic Poem: Kajastan 1970; first performed Yerevan, 1971.
Concerto for Violin and Orchestra 1972; first performed Yerevan, 1973.
Concerto No 2 for Piano and Orchestra 1976; first performed Yerevan, 1977.
Overture: Festal Fanfares 1979; first performed Yerevan, 1979.
Concerto for Flute and Chamber Orchestra 1980; first performed Yerevan, 1980.
Symphony: To the Unknown Soldier 1984; first performed Yerevan, 1984.

Chamber/instrumental:

String Quartet No 1 1967; first performed Yerevan, 1968.
Sonata No 1 (cello) 1973; first performed Yerevan, 1974.
Sonata No 2 (cello) 1974; first performed Yerevan, 1974.
Seven Preludes (piano) 1974; first performed Yerevan, 1974.
String Quartet No 2 1981; first performed Yerevan, 1982.
Sonata (violin, piano) 1982; first performed Yerevan, 1983.
Sonata No 1 (piano) 1982; first performed Yerevan, 1983.
Five Sonatinas (piano) 1985–7; first performed Yerevan, 1985–7.
String Quartet No 3 1986; first performed Yerevan, 1986.
Sonata: Tiagmus (violin) 1989; first performed Yerevan, 1989.
Epicentre (piano) 1989; first performed Yerevan, 1990.
Sonata No 2 (piano) 1990; first performed Yerevan, 1990.
Trio (piano, violin, cello) 1990.

Vocal/choral:

Cycle of Romances (soprano, piano; Tsahakian) 1974; first performed Yerevan, 1975.
Small Triptych (unaccompanied chamber chorus) 1978; first performed Yerevan, 1978.
Cycle of Romances (baritone, piano; Tsahakian) 1980; first performed Yerevan, 1980.
Razmakotch (unaccompanied chorus) 1981; first performed Yerevan, 1981.
The Seasons of the Year (unaccompanied children's chorus; Carapetian) 1986; first performed Yerevan, 1986.
Ode to Armenia (chorus, orchestra) 1987; first performed Yerevan, 1987.

PUBLICATIONS

On Chaushian: A. Areoshatian, "LC", in *Music of the Transcaucasian Republics*, Tiflis, 1975; S. Sevoian, "Tradition, Search, Self-Strengthening" in *Spring* (Yerevan), 8, 1981; M. Diloian, "A Word About Composers" in *Soviet Art* (Yerevan), 4, 1987; K. Djagatspanian, "The Price of Creative Life", in *Armenia Today* (Yerevan), 2, 1987; M. Berco, "LC", in *Portraits of Armenian Composers*, Moscow, 1991.

Levon Chaushian comments:

Creation for me is a kind of autoexpression, the possibility of declaring my own attitude to the surrounding reality and its problems. In striving to imbue my sounds with everyday human ideas, I hope that my music expresses at the same time that kind of national thinking which is characteristic of the Armenian people, their history and destiny.

* * *

Armenia is the most "integral" of the constituent Soviet republics. Approximately 90 per cent of the population is Armenian, a figure which contrasts with an average of between 60 and 70 per cent native indigenous population in the other republics. There is, as a consequence, a much closer identity of nation and culture than elsewhere in the Soviet Union and this is reflected in much of the music coming out of the region.

Modern Armenian music virtually stems from the pioneering example and eventual (psychological) martyrdom of Sogoman Komitas. Orphaned in childhood, the boy was given the name Komitas on his graduation from seminary in honour of a 7th century writer of doxologies. Working in Berlin in the early years of the 20th century, he collected vast amounts of material on Armenian music, creating a conceptual reservoir on which Armenian musicians still draw. Horrified by the Turkish massacre of Armenians in World War I, his mind gave way and he died in Paris in 1935. He is buried in Erevan and lends his name to the conservatory where Levon Chaushian received his higher training.

Among Armenian composers there is still a tension between the "official" neo-classicism imbued by the Soviet-dominated conservatories and a more imaginative development into formal music of some of the characteristic procedures of Armenian folk music. Younger composers such as Stepan Rostomian, a full decade Chaushian's junior, have been beneficiaries of a more enlightened tolerance of non-standard musical forms. Chaushian has by and large been obliged to work within an existing syntax. There is in his work a greater emphasis on traditional sonata form and on conventional harmonic development (in the chamber work most notably) which runs counter to the musical and emotional tenor of much of it. At the same time, though, elements of traditional music and of Armenian church music (Armenia has the oldest established Christian church in the world, founded around 300 A.D.) are increasingly evident in his subtle use of melodic line extension and unorthodox metrical development.

The three string quartets are all conventionally developed from quite simple material, but there is a freedom to the distribution of metres which lifts them out of the ordinary. The same is true of two fine cello sonatas and the later *Tiagmus* violin sonata, though here the requirements of solo performance entail a shift of emphasis away from multivoiced part-writing towards a conception in which some of the underlying transitions remain tacit.

Tiagmus ranks with his finest work, but his masterpieces to date have been the two symphonic poems of the late 1960s, both of which look forward to his powerful *To the Unknown Soldier* symphony, a work which transcends the "official" orchestral style in which it is written, and the moving choral *Ode to Armenia*. Inevitably, Chaushian has been much affected by the most recent catastrophic earthquake that razed much of Armenia and cost thousands of lives. The piano piece *Epicentre* resembles nothing more than a more dynamically paced version of McCabe's transcription of Haydn's *Seven Last Words*; there are no banal *terremoto* effects, just a simple articulation of passion—in the original sense—and of grief, and a strong sense of survival and continuity shining through in the kind of resolution that is typical of Chaushian's work.

He is still little known in the West, but his work is universal, touching on themes and using a language that has no national boundaries.

—Paul Boursin

CHAYNES, Charles. French. Born in Toulouse, 11 July 1925. Educated at Music Conservatory, Toulouse (violin); Conservatoire National Supérieur de Musique, Paris (composition under Darius Milhaud and Jean Rivier, harmony and fugue under Noel and Jean Gallon, chamber music under Joseph Calvet, violin under Gabriel Bouillon), graduated 1951; French Academy in Rome, 1952–5. Married Odette Decaux, 24 April 1948; 1 son and 1 daughter. Radio producer, since 1956, and director of programming, France-Musique, 1965–75, O.R.T.F.; artistic director (recording) Club Français Disques, 1958–62; Chief of music service, Radio France, 1975–90. Recipient: Grand Prix de Rome (for *Et l'homme vit se rouvrir les portes*), 1951; Concours Prince Rainier, 1960; Grand Prix de la Ville de Paris, 1965; Prix du disques, 1968, 1970, 1975, 1981; Prix du disque lyrique (for *Quatre Poèmes de Sappho*), 1974; Prix de la Tribune Internationale de Compositeurs UNESCO (for *Pour un monde noir*), 1979; Grand Prix Académie Charles Gros (for *Erszebet*), 1984; Chevalier de la Légion d'Honneur; Chevalier de l'Ordre des Arts et Lettres; Chevalier de l'Ordre National du Mérite, 1977. Mailing address: 42 rue du Commandant Mouchotte, 94160 St Mande, France.

Publishers: Editions Leduc; Editions Durand; Editions Ricordi.

Symphonies/orchestral:

Divertissement (strings) 1949; broadcast ORTF, January 1952.

Danses symphoniques 1951; first performed Cannes, 1953.

Concerto pour orchestre à cordes (string orchestra) 1953; first performed Frankfurt, 1954.

Ode pour une mort tragique 1953–4; first performed Vichy, 25 June 1954.

Symphonie 1955; broadcast 13 May 1957; first concert performance Turin, 10 October 1958.

Concerto for Trumpet and Chamber Orchestra 1956; broadcast 13 May 1958. Recorded Erato STU 70227.

Concerto for Violin and Orchestra 1958; broadcast ORTF, 14 March 1961.

Deuxième Concerto (concerto for orchestra) 1960; first performed Monte Carlo, 25 November 1962.

Quatre Illustrations pour "La Flute de jade" (flute, orchestra) 1960; first performed Aix-en-Provence, 23 July 1960. Recorded Erato STU 70227.

Concerto for Piano and Orchestra (chamber orchestra) 1961; first performed Paris, 17 February 1966. Recorded Erato STU 70451.

Expressions contrastées 1965; first performed Strasbourg, 23 June 1966.
Concerto for Organ (organ, strings, timpani, percussion) 1966; first performed Bratislava, Yugoslavia, 24 April 1969. Recorded Erato STU 70451.
Irradiations (violin, cello, harpsichord, strings) 1968; first performed Bordeaux, 9 June 1969.
Transmutations 1969; first performed Besançon, 4 September 1971.
Lieu de lumière 1972; first performed Provence, 7 July 1972.
Mazapan (orchestration of 1969 piece for Bronte; Bronte, strings) 1973; first performed Paris, 7 June 1974.
Peintures noires 1974; first performed Paris, 27 April 1975.
Visions concertantes (guitar, strings) 1976; first performed Besançon, 11 September 1976. Recorded Pathé Marconi CO 69 16364.
Les Caractères illisibles (after the poem by Jean Tardieu; chamber orchestra) 1978; first performed Paris, 21 January 1980.
Concerto for Clarinet and Orchestra 1979; first performed Orléans, 2 December 1979; partial performance Toulon, 23 May 1979.
Visages Myceniens 1983; first performed Toulouse, 1986.
Litanies 1988; first performed Metz, 1989.

Chamber/instrumental:

Trois Séquences (piano) 1950; broadcst ORTF, 1951.
Sonatina (flute, piano) 1951.
Sonata (violin, piano) 1952; first performed Paris, 16 June 1954.
Capriccio (piano) 1954; broadcast 3 February 1957.
Serenade (wind quintet) 1954; first performed Brussels, 31 January 1958.
Quadretti Italiani (violin) 1956; first performed Paris, 6 April 1960.
Lied, Scherzando et Final (double bass, piano) 1957.
Variations sur Tanka (flute, piano) 1962; first performed 15 May 1963.
Réflexes (violin, piano) 1963; broadcast 10 February 1964.
Trois Etudes linéaires (13 instruments, timpani, percussion) 1963; first performed Bordeaux, 3 June 1964.
Commentaires concertants (violin, piano; or violin solo, piccolo, oboe, clarinet, bassoon, 2 horns, trumpet, timpani, 2 percussion, harpsichord, double bass) 1964; piano version first performed Paris, 24 April 1968.
Substances convergentes (piano) 1964; first performed Paris, 19 January 1966.
Prélude pour la flute de jade (flute) 1965.
Alternances (viola, piano) 1965.
Concordances (Bronte, percussion, piano) 1967; first performed Rouen, 17 October 1967. Recorded Guilde Internationale du Disque SMS 2693.
Mazapan (Bronte, strings) 1969.
Diagramme (organ) 1970; first performed Paris, 12 September 1970.
String Quartet 1970; first performed Paris, 1 April 1971.
Impulsions (trombone, piano) 1970.
Séquences pour l'Apocalypse (horn, 2 trumpets, trombone, tuba, organ) 1971–2; first performed Bordeaux, 2 June 1972.
M'zab (piano) 1971; first performed Paris, May 1973. Recorded Calioppe CAL9857.
Interférences (cello, piano) 1973.
Joutes (organ, harpsichord) 1973–4; first performed Royan, 28 April 1975.
Tarquinia (ondes martenot, piano, percussion) 1973. Recorded Calliope CAL 1847.
Lyre (celtic harp or concert harp) 1975; broadcast 13 April 1976. Recorded SFP 9.1054.
Points de rencontre (ondes martenot, piano) 1975; first performed Boulogne-Billancourt, 11 June 1976.
Emergences (harpsichord) 1976; first performed Paris, 23 June 1977.
Et si c'était une valse (2 pianos) 1977; first performed Paris, 16 December 1977.
Valeurs transposées (flute, oboe, clarinet, bassoon, horn, piano, harp, guitar, percussion, string quartet) 1979; first performed Amiens, Spring 1981.
Fatum (guitar) 1979.
Cloches en jeu (carillon) 1979; first performed 16 June 1979.
Onze Visages . . . ou l'antifugue (6 violins, 2 violas, 2 cellos, double bass) 1979; first performed U.S.A., 1980.
A la Recherche du sacre (organ) 1983.
Lorsque Cecile chantait (flute, clarinet, violin, cello, piano) 1983.
Dialogues (2 guitars) 1983. Recorded Calliope 1663.
Mazapan II (Bronte, synthesiser, electronic percussion) 1986.

Vocal/choral:

Et l'homme vit se rouvrir les portes (cantata) 1951; first performed Rome, 1951.
Par ces Chemins du coeur (6 prayers for soprano, orchestra/piano) 1953; broadcast 23 October 1957; piano version broadcast 8 January 1958.
Trois Poèmes chinois (tenor, piano) 1962; first performed 15 May 1963.
Joie aux âmes (soprano, mezzo-soprano, counter-tenor, baritone, bass, flute, oboe, viola, trombone, bassoon; Norge) 1962; first performed Paris, 28 October 1966.
Quatres Poèmes de Sappho (coloratura soprano, string trio) 1968; first performed Toulouse, 26 November 1968. Recorded Pathé Marconi CO 69.16364.
Pour un Monde noir (soprano, orchestra; Wabe, Diop, Bolamba, Césaire) 1976–8; broadcast 14 June 1978; first concert performance Aix-en-Provence, 1979. Recorded Calliope CAL9857.
Poèmes itinérants (soprano, 2 guitars; Lorca) 1986.
Oginoha (soprano, flute, celtic harp, percussion; Japanese poetry) 1986. Recorded ADDA.
Au delà de l'espérance (mezzo-soprano, piano) 1989; first performed Bremen, 1989. Recorded ADDA.

Opera:

Erzsebet 1983; first performed Paris, 28 March 1983. Recorded Harmonia Mundi 5136.
Noces de sang (Lorca) 1988; first performed Paris, March 1988. Recorded Cybelia.

Other:

Douze Etudes progressives (violin; educational music) 1954.
Quinze Etudes (horn; educational music) 1958.
Quinze Etudes (trumpet; educational music) 1958.
Etude en deux parties opposées (accordion; educational music) 1971.
Improvisation à deux (cello, piano; educational music) 1982.
Jeu de cordes (violin, piano; educational music) 1982.
Prélude pour Fatum (guitar; educational music) 1982.

* * *

Though he has a thoroughly individual voice, and a robust musical imagination, there is still in Charles Chaynes's mature work a discernible influence from his former composition teacher Darius Milhaud, to whom the very moving *Lieu de lumière* is dedicated in *hommage*. A less prolific (some might feel more careful) composer than Milhaud, Chaynes has developed a highly adaptive style dependent on free atonality and on the incorporation of polytonal elements from non-European cultures. Whereas Milhaud turned to the Americas, jazz and West Indian dance music predominantly, Chaynes has more closely followed his country's post-war, post-colonial agenda in assimilating the musics of East Asia and Africa.

This is seen first in the four "illustrations" to *La Flûte de jade* and in the settings of Chinese poems, in neither of which are the "imported" elements made entirely integral to the overall conception. Perhaps because of its firmer rhythmic nature, Chaynes has been more successful in his appropriation of African idiom, which is achieved without pastiche (an occasional vice of Milhaud's) or mere decoration.

The piano sequence *M'zab* is among his most important works. Premiered by the composer's wife Odette Chaynes-Decaux, it presents a sound-picture of the Saharan region with its contrasts of sun-bleached rock and sand, and fertile oases. The opening section, incorporating Arab themes in multiple variation, is extremely agitated and is intended to suggest the "culture-shock" of a western explorer entering an unknown and extravagantly coloured world. This gives way to a second section, entitled "Beni-Izgem", which is more quietly meditative in its response to the light-soaked landscape. There are colouristic and rhythmic elements here, as in the first section, which are strongly but perhaps deceptively reminiscent of Olivier Messiaen. The final part, "Zelfana", restores some of the insistent rhythm of the opening pages. *M'zab* is evocative without being overtly imagistic. Elsewhere, as in the Goya-inspired *Peintures noires*, Chaynes has turned to pictorial inspiration.

He has made striking use, as have many other composers, of the work of Federico García Lorca, using Lorca's intense *Blood Wedding* as the basis of his second opera *Noces de sang*. Here and elsewhere, he is interested in exploring a Mediterranean-cum-African conception of "blackness" and of black consciousness. In its clearest ideological form, this is the *négritude* espoused by francophone African poets such as Aimé Césaire and Leopold Senghor. Chaynes's *Pour un Monde noir* is an extended hymn to the "poetic richness" of *négritude* and to the "disturbing and mysterious beauty" of the black woman; if there is a danger this could be interpreted as a patronising reinforcement of existing stereotypes about Negro women, the work itself, created for and dedicated to the black soprano Christiane Eda-Pierre, carries no such implication. Its opening movement, a setting of "Le Chanson du vent" by Mustapha Wade, again expresses the "*sanglots sonores*" of Arab music, with additional material derived from Pygmy sources. Elsewhere in the piece, Chaynes uses music from Gabon, Burundi and elsewhere in central Africa. The final two movements are paeans to the black woman (a poem by David Diop) and liberations (Césaire) respectively.

Here, as in the earlier concertos, Chaynes's deployment of a solo voice and orchestra is extremely fluent. His instrumental writing, whether for orchestra or chamber forces, is less consciously "difficult" and virtuosic than Milhaud's, but does retain much of his former teacher's complex melodic sense, shorn of some of its more backward-looking qualities.

Chaynes has—like Jolivet before him—recognised the importance of radio in the dissemination of "world music" and has been an imaginative and progressive broadcasting executive, making full use of that most democratic of media.

—Eleanor Caldwell

CHEN Yi. Chinese. Born in Guangzhou, 4 April 1953. Education: piano and violin lessons from age 3 under Zheng Ri-hua and Li Su-xin; private study of Chinese traditional music, Western and Chinese music theory under Zheng Zhong, 1970–7; Central Conservatory of Music, Beijing (composition under Wu Zu-qiang and Alexander Goehr), 1978–86, B.A., 1983, M.A., 1986; doctoral candidate, Columbia University, New York City (under Chou Wen-chung and Mario Davidovsky), since 1986. Married Long Zhou, 20 July 1983. Concert master/composer, Beijing Opera Troupe, Guangzhou, 1970–8; professional violinist; guest composer, Overseas Project Authority of Illinois, 1989; resident composer, Yaddo Community, New York, 1991. Recipient: Composition Award (for *Xian Shi*), Central conservatory, Beijing, 1983; 1st prize (for *Duo Ye*), 4th Chinese National Music Composition Contest, 1985; commission award (for *Guessing*), Renee B. Fisher Competition, 1989. Mailing address: 500 West 122 Street, Apt 2G, New York, New York 10027, U.S.A.

Publisher: none.

Symphonies/orchestral:

Xian Shi (viola concerto) 1983; first performed Beijing, 1983. Recorded China Record Company AL-57.
Duo Ye (chamber orchestra) 1985; first performed Beijing, 1985. Recorded China Record Company AL-57.
Symphony No 1 1985–6; first performed Beijing, 1986. Recorded China Record Company AL-57.
Sprout (string orchestra) 1986; first performed Beijing, 1986. Recorded China Record Company AL-57.
Two Sets (wind, percussion) 1986; first performed Beijing, 1986. Recorded China Record Company AL-57.
Duo Ye No 2 1987; first performed New York City, 1987.
Overture (full Chinese orchestra) 1989; first performed Hong Kong, 1990.
Overture No 2 (full Chinese orchestra) 1990; first performed Hong Kong, 1990.
Piano Concerto 1991; first performed Bonn, Germany, 1992.

Chamber/instrumental:

String Quartet 1983; first performed Zagreb, Yugoslavia, 1985.
Variations on the Theme of Awariguli (piano) 1984; first performed Italy, 1984.
Duo Ye (piano) 1985; first performed Beijing, 1985.
Yu Diao (piano) 1985; first performed Beijing, 1985.
Woodwind Quintet 1986; first performed Massachusetts, 1987.
Near Distance (flute, clarinet, violin, cello, piano, percussion) 1987; first performed Illinois, 1988.
The Tide (Chinese instrumental ensemble) 1988; first performed New York City, 1988.

A Mixed Accent (Chinese instrumental ensemble) 1990; first performed New York City, 1991.
Pipa Solo (Chinese plucking instrument) 1990; first performed New York City, 1991.

Vocal/choral:

Three Poems from the Song Dynasty (unaccompanied SATB chorus) 1986; first performed Hong Kong, 1986.
As in a Dream (2 songs for soprano, violin, cello) 1988; first performed New York City, 1988.

Other:

The Tablet (synthesizer music for dance) 1990; first performed New York City, 1990.

PUBLICATIONS

On Chen: Zhen Sheng, "Compose with New Concept—Young Female Composer CY", in *Shenzhen Daily*, 31 May 1986; Zhu Shi-rui, "The Formation and Development of Polyphonic Thought in Chinese Music", dissertation, Central Conservatory of Music, Beijing, June 1986; Guo Qing-ye, "Her Music Blends East, West", in *China Daily*, 6 June 1986; Wang Zhen-ya, "A Young Composer CY", in *People's Music Monthly*, 7, 1986; Margot Eisenmann, "Chinas musikalsche Spitzenkrafte", in *Bild*, 2 February 1987; Genevieve Lee, "CY: A Study of a Young Composer", dissertation, Yale University, March 1990; Vai Meng Lei, "*Duo Ye* for piano solo", dissertation, University of Illinois, Urbana, 1990.

Chen Yi comments:

Modern society is a great network of complex latitudes and attitudes. Everything exists in equal rights under different cultures, environments and conditions and each interacts with the others, changing from moment to moment, so that each and every experience encountered can become both a source and medium of creativity. In the case of music composition, it reflects the precipitation of a composer's cultural and psychological construct. A serious composer should learn to choose and adjust the yardstick, and more importantly to establish some relatively stable principles on which he or she can ground creativity. I want to try my best to get the essence of both Eastern and Western cultures and write more compositions that embody my temperament and the spirit of this brave epoch.

* * *

Chen Yi was born into a family of doctors with a strong musical interest. She began to study violin and piano with Zheng Ri-hua and Li Su-xin when she was only three years old. When the political tragedy of the Cultural Revolution overtook China, she tried hard to continue her musical studies, practising violin at home (with the mute attached) and even taking her instrument with her into the countryside, where she was sent to work for two years. However, as a more positive aspect of this experience, she started getting to know the wider life of her motherland and people. When she was 17, she returned to Beijing, served as concert master and composer with the orchestra of the Beijing Opera Troupe, and began researching Chinese traditional music, Western and Chinese music theory under Zheng Zhong.

When the school system was restored in 1977, Chen enrolled in the Beijing Central Conservatory, where she studied composition under Wu Zu-qiang and the British guest professor Alexander Goehr; she also studied Chinese traditional music systematically for eight years. She composed the first Chinese viola concerto *Xian Shi* in 1983, and gave a whole evening concert of her orchestral works jointly presented by the Chinese Musicians Association, the Central Conservatory of Music, Radio Beijing, CCTV and the Central Philharmonic Orchestra of China; this took place in Beijing in 1986. Chen has received many prizes and awards from prestigious institutions and a collection of her orchestral works has been released on disc by the China Record Company.

Since 1986, Chen has been a doctoral candidate at Columbia University, studying composition under Chou Wen-chung and Mario Davidovsky. Her chamber music was featured in *Sound and Silence*, a series of 10 films on contemporary music, broadcast on the European TV network since 1989.

As to her compositional style, she seldom uses directly available materials, such as tunes and rhythms, from the Chinese and Western traditions, but tries to distil from those traditions their essential character and spirit, and to develop materials abstractly in accordance with new concepts. The brief *Duo Ye No 2* for full orchestra thoughtfully combines Western orchestral idiom with traditional Eastern pentatonic tonalities. As the startling brass opening to *Duo Ye No 2* underlines, she is a bold (and sometimes humorous) composer, who orchestrates intelligently and effectively.

Her chamber piece *Near Distance* is a meditation on ancient culture and modern civilization, very effectively drawing together the musics of East and West. That, and the desire to create "real music" for future generations, is her main goal.

—Zhou Long

CHILDS, Barney (Sanford). American. Born in Spokane, Washington, 13 February 1926. Educated at Deep Springs College, California, 1943–5; University of Nevada (English, music and mathematics), 1947–9, B.A.; Oxford University (English language and literature; Rhodes scholar), 1949–51, B.A. (hons); M.A., 1955; Stanford University, California, (English, music; creative writing fellow) 1951–4; Ph.D., 1959; composition study with Leonard Ratner, 1952–3; Carlos Chavez, 1953; Aaron Copland, 1954; Elliott Carter, 1954–5. Military service, U.S. Army infantry, August 1945—December 1946. Design draughtsman, U.S. Electric Motors, Los Angeles, 1955; instructor in English, 1956–61, and assistant professor of English, 1961–5, University of Arizona, Tucson; poetry editor, *Genesis West* magazine, 1962–5; co-founder, Advance Recordings, 1964–82; dean, Deep Springs College, California, 1965–9; composer in residence, 1969–71, and acting dean, 1971, Wisconsin College-Conservatory, Milwaukee; faculty fellow in music and literature, 1971–3, professor of composition and music literature, since 1973, and faculty research lecturer, 1979, University of Redlands, California; visiting lecturer, University of London, Goldsmiths' College, Spring 1989. Associate editor, *Perspectives of New Music*; member of music selection committee, Dorland Mountain Colony, Temecula, California; performing participant, "Music for Clarinet and Friend"; director of University of Redlands New

Music Ensemble, and other new music groups in Wisconsin and Arizona. Recipient: Crofts Fellowship, Berkshire Music Festival, 1953, 1954; Koussevitzky award in composition, Berkshire Music Festival, 1954; MacDowell Colony fellowships, 1963, 1968, 1970, 1974, 1978 (as Norlin Foundation Fellow); University of Redlands award for outstanding teaching, 1983. Mailing address: 864 Hartzell, Redlands, California 92374, or, School of Music, University of Redlands, Redlands, California 92374, U.S.A.

Publishers: Smith; Tritone; American Composers Alliance, 170 West 74th Street, New York, New York 10023, U.S.A.

Symphonies/orchestral:

Symphony No 1 1954.
Concerto (cor anglais, strings, harp, percussion) 1955; first performed Newport, Oregon, 1990.
Symphony No 2 1956; first performed New York City, 1956.
Music for Almost Everybody 1964.
Music (piano, string orchestra) 1965.
Six Events for Fifty-Eight Players (band) 1965; first performed Ithaca, New York, 1965.
Operation Flabby Sleep (any number of orchestral instruments) 1968; first performed Milwaukee, Wisconsin, 1969.
Variations on a Theme of Harold Budd (string orchestra) 1969.
Concerto for Clarinet 1970; first performed Milwaukee, Wisconsin, 1970.
Supposes: Imago Mundi (symphonic band) 1970; first performed Huntington, West Virginia, 1971.
Concert Piece (tuba, band) 1973; first performed Atlanta, Georgia, 1974.
The Golden Shore (symphonic band) 1974; first performed New Haven, Connecticut, 1974.
September with Band (band) 1978.
A Continuance, in Seven Parts (band) 1979; first performed Platteville, Wisconsin, 1979.
Orrery (band) 1980; first performed Missouri, 1986.
Concerto for Timpani 1989; first performed Redlands, California, 1990.

Chamber/instrumental:

Sonata (clarinet) 1951; first performed Stanford, California, 1952.
Quartet (clarinet, strings) 1953; first performed Stanford, California, 1953.
Sonata (bassoon, piano) 1953; first performed Stanford, California, 1954.
Brass Quintet 1954; first performed Stanford, California, 1954.
Third String Quartet 1954; first performed New York City, 1955.
Quartet (harp, strings) 1954; first performed Chicago, 1974.
Four Involutions (for anglais) 1955; first performed Washington, D.C., 1961.
Five Considerations (horn) 1955.
Second Sonata (violin, piano) 1956; first performed Dallas, Texas, 1977.
Quartet (4 bassoons) 1958; first performed Tucson, Arizona, 1964.
Sonatina (alto saxophone) 1958; first performed Tucson, Arizona, 1959.
Sonata (oboe) 1958; first performed Portland, Maine, 1966.
Changes (3 oboes) 1959; first performed Amsterdam, 1959.
Brass Trio 1959; first performed Denver, Colorado, 1959.
Five Little Soundpieces (oboe) 1959; first performed Tucson, Arizona, 1964.
Sonata (flute, piano) 1960; first performed New York City, 1960.
Fourth String Quartet 1960; first performed New York City, 1962.
Sonata for Bass Alone (double bass) 1960; first performed New York City, 1961.
Quintet (brass, piano) 1961; first performed San Diego, California, 1988.
Sonata (trombone) 1961; first performed Tucson, Arizona, 1962. Recorded Avant AV-1006.
Welcome to Whipperginny (9 percussionists) 1961; first performed New York City, 1963.
Interbalances II (viola and any other instrument) 1961; first performed New York, 1963.
Interbalances I (oboe/cor anglais, bass clarinet/alto saxophone, double bass) 1962; first performed New York City, 1964.
Second Brass Quintet 1962; first performed New York City, 1963.
Take 5 (any 5 instruments) 1962; first performed Tucson, Arizona, 1963.
Interbalances III (cello and any other instruments, up to 5) 1962; first performed Tucson, Arizona, 1963.
Wind Quintet 1962; first performed New York City, 1962.
Interbalances IV (trumpet, optional reader) 1962; first performed Tucson, Arizona, 1962.
Second Wind Quintet 1962.
Stances (flute, silence) 1962; first performed Massachusetts, 1963.
Variations sur une chanson de canotier (brass quintet) 1963; first performed New York City, 1964. Recorded Crystal S-203.
Music for Winds (13 solo winds) 1963; first performed Tucson, Arizona, 1964.
Duo (flute, bassoon) 1963; first performed Tucson, Arizona, 1963. Recorded CRI 253.
Oboe Piece for Jackson Mac Low 1963; first performed Tucson, 1964.
Music for Two Flute Players 1963; first performed New York City, 1963. Recorded CRI 253.
Variations for David Racusen (horn) 1963; first performed Tucson, Arizona, 1964.
Sixth String Quartet 1964; first performed Dallas, Texas, 1965.
Interbalances VI (horn, piano, 2 tapes) 1964; first performed Ann Arbor, Michigan, 1964.
Quartet (flute, oboe, double bass, percussion) 1964; first performed Illinois, 1964.
Music for Contrabass and Friend (double bass and any other instrument) 1964; first performed Westbrook, Connecticut, 1964.
Third Wind Quintet 1964; first performed Tucson, Arizona, 1964.
Music for Bass Drum (3 players—hands only) 1964; first performed Massachusetts, 1965.
Music for Cello 1964; first performed Cambridge, Massachusetts, 1965.
Third Brass Quintet 1965; first performed Huntington, West Virginia, 1970.
Horn and Oboe Music 1965.
October Music (2 trumpets) 1965; first performed Michigan, 1968.
Any Five (any 5 of the 8 parts provided) 1965; first performed Michigan, 1966.

Music for a Celebration [piccolo(s), bass drum(s)] 1965; first performed Milwaukee, Wisconsin, 1970.
Jack's New Bag (10 assorted players) 1966; first performed Illinois, 1966.
Music for Trombone and Piano 1966; first performed Deep Springs, California, 1966.
The Golden Bubble (E♭ contrabass sarrusophone, percussion) 1967.
Fourth Wind Quintet 1967; first performed California, 1967.
Mary's Idea (tuba, harpsichord) 1967; first performed New Hampshire, 1968.
Mr T. His Fancy (double bass) 1967; first performed Pomona, California, 1968. Recorded Ars Nova A 1001.
Nonet (9 varied instruments) 1967; first performed San Diego, California, 1968.
Lynn Valley (clarinet, viola, piano, reader) 1967; first performed Brunswick, Maine, 1968.
Seventh String Quartet 1968.
Four Feathers (percussion quartet, tape) 1968; first performed Bridgeport, Connecticut, 1968.
Barnard I (clarinet, piano) 1968; first performed Michigan, 1969.
Barnard II (oboe, bassoon) 1968; first performed California, 1978.
Organ Piece 1968; first performed Ann Arbor, Michigan.
Somewhere (3 cellos, oboe, chime) 1968; first performed Idaho, 1984.
The Location of Music (flute, double bass) 1968; first performed California, 1968.
The Bayonne Barrel and Drum Company (improvising solo wind instrument, 13 winds, piano, 2 percussion) 1968; first performed California, 1969.
To Tell You (double bass, tape) 1969; first performed San Diego, California, 1972.
Music for Tubas (6 tubas) 1969; first performed New Hampshire, 1972.
Fifth Wind Quintet 1969; first performed Michigan, 1969.
J.D. (piano, 2 tapes) 1969; first performed Hanover, New Hampshire, 1970.
Seaview (tuba, piano) 1969; first performed California, 1971.
Night River Music (E♭ alto horn) 1969.
Out Back of the Drum Shop (snare drum) from 1970, first performed Redlands, California, various dates for different parts.
37 Songs (piano) 1971; first performed Milwaukee, Wisconsin, 1971. Recorded Avant AV 1008.
Trio (clarinet, cello, piano) 1972; first performed Los Angeles, 1972. Recorded ABC AB 67013.
Of Place, As Altered (5 B♭ clarinets) 1972; first performed California, 1972. Recorded Brewster BR 1317.
Supposes: Cloud Busters (tuba) 1972.
A Music; That It Might Be . . . (2 clarinets) 1973; first performed Denver, Colorado, 1973. Recorded Zanja ZJR 2.
London Rice Wine (any solo wind instrument) 1973; first performed Redlands, California, 1977.
Quintet (winds, harp, percussion) 1974; first performed Providence, Rhode Island, 1974.
Eighth String Quartet 1974; first performed Missouri, 1976.
Fourth Brass Quintet 1975; first performed Atlantic City, 1976.
Bowling Again with the Champs (6 improvisers, tape) 1976. Redlands, California, 1976.
A Question of Summer (tuba, harp) 1976; first performed Chicago, 1978. Recorded CRI 556.
Four Pieces for Six Winds (wind quintet, soprano/alto saxophone) 1977; first performed Redlands, California, 1978.
The Big New Improved Everybody Play Summer Music Clinic Twelve Clarinet Fun Piece 1977; first performed Redlands, California, 1977.
Couriers of the Crimson Dawn (any instruments) 1977.
Quartet/Fantasy (4 tubas) 1978; first performed Bowling Green, Ohio, 1979.
A Cello Piece 1978; first performed Bartlesville, Oklahoma, 1979.
Featuring "Mighty" Joe Nowhere
und die
*Greater Wairopi All *Stars* (7 equal instruments) 1978; first performed Evanston, Illinois, 1979.
Overture to "Measuring a Meridian" (wind sextet, percussion) 1978; first performed Redlands, California, 1979.
Seven Quiet Studies (percussion) 1978; first performed Redlands, California, ?1979.
Six Gamut Studies (marimba) 1978; first performed Terre Haute, Indiana, 1979.
A Clarinet Piece 1978; first performed Redlands, California, 1979. Recorded Roncorp EMS-021.
The Word from Department R (clarinet, alto saxophone) 1979; first performed Redlands, California, 1979.
Mosaic on a Theme of Balakirev (alto saxophone) 1979; first performed Redlands, California, 1980.
"Heaven to clear when day did close" (piano) 1980; first performed Redlands, California, 1980.
Sky Visit (cello) 1980; first performed Alabama, 1980.
Clay Music (4 players, specially designed clay wind instruments) 1980; first performed Los Angeles, 1980. Recorded Cold Blue E-1.
Sleep, and Then Going On (clarinet/cymbals) 1980; first performed Redlands, California, 1981.
Thirteen Classical Studies (double bass) 1981; first performed (part) Mexico City, 1981.
The Edge of the World (bass clarinet, organ) 1981; first performed Redlands, California, 1981. Recorded Advance FGR 13.
Real Music (2 clarinets) 1981; first performed Redlands, California, 1981.
81 Licks (trombone) 1983; first performed Redlands, California, 1983.
Pastorale (bass clarinet, tape) 1983; first performed Idaho, 1984.
Horn Octet 1984; first performed Redlands, California, 1984.
Instant Winners (E♭ clarinet) 1986; first performed New Mexico, 1986.
Blazer (snare drum) 1987; first performed Redlands, California, 1988.
A Box of Views (wind quintet, piano) 1988; first performed Las Vegas, 1988. Recorded Cambria CD 1044.
Fantasia on Lines of Walt Whitman 1988; first performed Palm Springs, California, 1989.
Grande Fantasie de concert ("Masters of the Game") (clarinet) 1990.

Vocal/choral:

Mass (unaccompanied chorus) 1954.
Seven Epigrams (soprano, clarinet) 1955; first performed Kansas, 1960.
Septet (instruments, voices) 1958; first performed Massachusetts, 1959.
Three Carols on Old Texts (unaccompanied chorus) 1960; first performed Kansas, 1961.
"Heal Me, O Lord" (chorus, trombone, piano) 1964; first performed Des Moines, Iowa, 1965. Recorded Gregorian EL 50.

Music for Singer (voice, piano—4 hands; music lost) 1964; first performed Hamilton, Ontario, 1965.
"This Is the Praise of Created Things" (chorus, oboe) 1965; first performed Des Moines, Iowa, 1965. Recorded Gregorian EL 50.
Nine Choral Fragments (unaccompanied chorus) 1965; first performed Des Moines, Iowa, 1967.
Quodlibet (large high school chorus, tape, lights, projections) 1967; first performed Sac City, Iowa, 1968.
A Glasse of Truth (chorus, tapes; tapes now lost) 1968; first performed Des Moines, Iowa, 1968.
Variations (chorus, tape, bells) 1968.
Variations on Poems of John Newlove (chorus, tape; tape may be lost) 1970; first performed Wisconsin, 1970.
Keet Seel (unaccompanied chorus; Childs, Donne, Herbert, Shakespeare) 1970; first performed Illinois, 1970.
Virtue (high voice, piano; Herbert) 1970; first performed Milwaukee, Wisconsin, 1971.
Maine Scenes (baritone, piano) 1970; first performed Michigan, 1971.
When Lilacs Last in the Dooryard Bloom'd (soloists, chorus, band; Whitman) 1971; first performed (part) River Falls, Wisconsin, 1971.
Of place, As Particular (soprano, tape, chimes) 1973; first performed Milwaukee, Wisconsin 1973.
Lanterns and Candlelight (soprano, marimba; Gibbons) 1975; first performed Greencastle, Indiana, 1976.
As Endless Autumn (chorus, horn, oboe) 1978; first performed Peterborough, New Hampshire, 1979. Recorded Aurora Borealis SCS 003.
Since Then (reader/piano) 1979; first performed Memphis, Tennessee, 1979.
Sunshine Lunch & Like Matters (reader/percussion/electronic music machine, bass clarinet; Kipling, other texts chosen by reader) 1984; first performed Redlands, California, 1984.

Other:

The Roachville Project (theatre piece for 4–10 people) 1967; first performed Los Angeles, 1967.
!BANANA FLANNELBOARD!—The Historic First Album (3 readers, tape delay system; Childs, Newlove) 1980; first performed Chicago, 1980.

PUBLICATIONS

By Childs: "Young Performers and New Music", in *Music Educators Journal*, September–October 1964; "The Beginning of the Apocalypse?", in *Kulchur*, Autumn 1964; "Articulation in Sound Structures: Some Notes Toward an Analytic", in *Texas Studies in Literature and Language*, Autumn 1966; co-editor (with Elliott Schwartz), *Contemporary Composers on Contemporary Music*, 1967, 1979; "Indeterminacy and Theory: Some Notes", in *The Composer*, Summer 1969; "Musical Continuity", in *Proceedings of the American Society of University Composers*, 6, 1973; "Towards a Philosophy of Notation", in *Proceedings of ASUC*, 7/8, 1974; "Teaching Music Theory: The Experimental College", in *Journal of Music Theory*, Spring 1974; "Some Anniversaries", in *Proceedings of ASUC*, 9/10, 1975; "Directions in American Composition Since the Second World War" (part II, 1960–75), in *Music Educators Journal*, March 1975; "Time and Music: A Composer's View", reprinted from Spanish version in *Perspectives of New Music*, Spring/Summer 1977; "Poetic and Musical Rhythm: One More Time", in *Music Theory: Special Topics*, edited by Browne, New York, 1981; "The Teaching of Composition to the Non-Composer", paper from conference of American Society of University Composers, reprinted 1984; "Aporia as Parataxis, or I Had One of Them Once, But the Wheels Came Off", in *ex tempore*, 5, 1988.

Barney Childs comments:

I have written music for 40 years because, as I suppose the case to be with all of us, I like doing it. I enjoy putting together what appear to me to work in context as good sounds, especially for performers who have asked me for pieces. I use whatever compositional means seem suitable for the occasion. Almost anything may be drawn upon if I can make it work right, although I'm not at ease with much of the present-day concern for systems and philosophies. By the circumstances of having lived much of my life in non-metropolitan parts of the American West, by not studying composition formally until my early twenties, and, when I did study, by working with New World composers, I have had no interest in the international music scene and its directions and stances, and the attendant polemics seemingly required. I'm not trying to prove anything.

Dane Rudhyar says somewhere that music is either talking music or dancing music. Most of what I write is probably the former. I'm most at ease composing for solo instrument or small ensemble, despite the occasional "big" work. The music usually affirms declamatory and lyric lines, drawing upon whatever "stylistic" influences—if one can still talk about specifically bounded "styles" these days—as seem workable in terms of available resources: "new instrumentation" sonorities, Ayler-and-after jazz, assembling and disassembling motives, surprise silences and repetition, variable and often gestural textures and rhythms, performer speech, virtuoso passages. "Form", says poet Robert Creeley, "is what happens."

I have drawn upon indeterminacy (has it yet been certified as Common Practice?) since 1961 in various approaches for many works. I haven't yet been able to make computer-aided composition and sound synthesizers behave properly, so maybe this is a defence mechanism for thinking that I can still make better choices, both as means and ends, than can the equipment.

Sometimes I wonder about what we are doing: the writing of music hardly anyone wants to hear is pretty well the bottom of the list in terms of today's consumer-approved activities (although I concede there is something to be said for the preparation of a dictionary of pre-medieval Finno-Ugric). Anyway, there's the music; may those who wish use it as they may please.

* * *

Barney Childs writes and speaks perceptively about music, maintaining a healthy scepticism for the "jargon overload" often found in the critical and aesthetic outpourings of music journals. His own thoughts on (and composition of) music maintain a serious insight blended with wit, based on a pragmatic, empirical approach. In his compositions intellectualism never dominates but ideas infuse the content of his most successful works with a quality of purpose.

It is rather too easy to describe his music as eclectic. It is certainly true that his output shows a wide range of stylistic and compositional procedures reflecting many trends in recent American music—not so much derivative but rather many very effective compositions presenting thoughtful reflections. His formal compositional studies were somewhat sporadic and he has always been an individualist, not interested in the fashionable aspects of trends but the ideas behind them. These approaches seem to be reflected in the variety of styles and activities pursued by those who have studied with him.

The grittier works of Copland, early Carter, Chavez and Hindemith colour the range of Childs's earlier pieces. However the significant part of his output dates from 1961 with his first compositional use of indeterminacy. An extreme case in performance terms, *The Roachville Project* gives instructions and conditions to build the tools (i.e., instruments) for an improvisation and then the instruction to improvise for an equivalent length of time. More representative are the series of Interbalances which have one part fixed, either fully by the composer or by the performer (prior to performance) from material provided and then one or more parts with more freedom in terms of choice of material (and sometimes instrumentation) for the other performer(s) to work around the given part.

Regarding form, this idea is apparent in his notion of "self-generating structures". *Any Five* uses any five of eight given parts covering high strings, low wind, etc. Wide-ranging material is contained in "boxes", some requiring preparation from the player. The ordering is determined by the players in various ways in a version of "mobile form" that requires chamber music responses, i.e., players listening and responding to the activities of others, for the relative quality of each performance.

Fundamental to many pieces is an interest in sound qualities, exemplified in many different ways. Several pieces from the early 1970s are quite and slow-moving, using basically relatively simple sound blocks that create powerful soundscapes (e.g., *Eighth String Quartet* or *Of Place, As Altered*). Texts are generally as an additional sound source (as in *Interbalances IV* and the spoken parts of *Any Five*). This extends to an interest in unusual techniques for conventional instruments—the clarinet overblowing, multiphonics and improvisational instructions helping create the powerful gestures of *The Edge of the World*; unusual demands on players—singing and playing on the rim of the bell in the *Horn Octet*; the use of unusual instruments—various ceramic ones in *Clay Music* and the use of "found objects"—*The Roachville Project, Any Five*.

Humour is often an important element—found in some of his titles, aspects of notation such as the Ivesian organ registrations of *The Edge of the World* in addition to the music itself.

Some of Childs's more recent works include more fully melodic lines, including repeated patterns e.g. *A Cello Piece* and "complete" notation. Even with the use of some more conventional aspects he does not believe in a return to traditional methods or ideology. Instead his work is a continuing search for fresh expression, tied specifically to his desire to see American composers following their own development rather than glancing nervously at European tradition.

—Michael Newman

CHOU Wen-chung. Chinese; naturalised American. Born in Chefoo, China, 28 July 1923. Educated at National Chunking University (studying civil engineering), B.S., 1945; New England Conservatory of Music, Boston, 1946–9; Columbia University, New York, M.A., 1954; private studies with Edgar Varèse, 1949–54, and with Nicholas Slonimsky, Boston. Married Yi-an Chang, 23 June 1962; 2 sons. Research associate in music, University of Illinois, Urbana, 1958–9; lecturer in music, Brooklyn College, New York, 1961–2; lecturer in music, Hunter College, New York, 1963–4; assistant professor of music, 1964–8, associate professor, 1968–72, chair of composition committee, music department, 1969–74, chair of music division, School of the Arts, 1969–89, acting dean, 1973, associate dean, 1975–6, and vice-dean, 1976–87, full professor, 1972–84, and Fritz Reiner professor of musical composition, and director, since 1984, Fritz Reiner Center for Contemporary Music, School of the Arts, Columbia University, New York; president, 1970–5, and honorary board member, since 1980, Composers Recording Inc.; composer in residence, Koussevitzky Composer's Studio, Tanglewood, Massachusetts, summers 1970, 1971; director, Center for U.S.-China Arts Exchange, since 1978; artistic director, Pacific Composers Conference, Hokkaido, Japan, 1990. Recipient: Guggenheim Fellowships, 1955, 1956; National Institute of the Arts and Letters award, 1963; William and Noma Copley Foundation award, 1966; special citation, American International Music Fund, 1970; honorary life member, Asian Composers' League, 1981; member, American Academy and Institute of Arts and Letters, 1982; Qingyun (Blue Cloud) Award, China Institute, 1985. Mailing address: 423 West 118th Street, Apt. 1E, New York, New York 10027, U.S.A.

Publisher: C.F. Peters, New York.

Symphonies/orchestral:

Landscapes 1949; first performed San Francisco, 1953. Recorded CRI 122.
All in the Spring Wind 1952–3; first performed Louisville, Kentucky, 7 December 1961. Recorded LOU 614.
And the Fallen Petals 1954; first performed Louisville, Kentucky, 9 February 1955. Recorded LOU-56-1.
In the Mode of Shang 1956.
Metaphors (winds) 1960–1; first performed Pittsburgh, 25 June 1961.
Riding the Wind (winds) 1964.
Pien (piano, percussion, chamber wind orchestra) 1966. Recorded CRI SD 251.
Beijing in the Mist 1985; first performed New York City, May 1986.

Chamber/instrumental:

Suite (harp, wind quintet) 1950.
Two Chinese Folk Songs (harp) 1950.
Three Folk Songs (flute, harp) 1950; first performed New York City, 19 January 1952.
Two Miniatures from the T'ang Dynasty (10 instruments) 1957.
Valediction (keyboard) 1957.
The Willows Are New (piano) 1957.
Soliloquy of a Biksuni (trumpet, brass, percussion) 1958; first performed Illinois, 18 December 1958. Recorded Crystal Records Recital Series S361.
To a Wayfarer (clarinet, harp, percussion, strings) 1958.
Cursive (flute, piano) 1963; first performed 13 January 1964. Recorded CRI SD 251.
The Dark and the Light (piano, percussion, violin, viola, cello, double bass) 1964.

Yu ko (9 instruments) 1965.
Ceremonial (3 trumpets, 3 trombones) 1968.
Yun (2 pianos, 2 percussion, wind sextet) 1969.
Echoes from the Gorge (chamber group) 1989; first performed New York City, 27 April 1989.

Vocal/choral:

Seven Poems of the T'ang Dynasty (high voice, ensemble) 1951.
Poems of White Stone (chorus, ensemble) 1958–9.

Other:

Hong Kong (music for documentary film) 1960; broadcast CBS TV, 1960.
Tomorrow (music for documentary film) 1961.
White Paper of Red China (music for documentary film) 1962; broadcast NBS TV, 1962.
A Day at the Fair (music for documentary film) 1964.
Red China: Year of the Gun? (music for documentary film) 1966; broadcast ABC TV, 1966.

Edgar Varèse: *Nocturnal* (soprano, bass, 12 wind instruments, strings, piano, percussion; completed by Chou from Varèse's sketches) 1973.
Edgar Varèse: *Amériques* (edition) 1974.
Edgar Varèse: *Intégrales* (edition) 1980.
Edgar Varèse: *Octandre* (edition) 1980.

PUBLICATIONS

By Chou: "Varèse: A Sketch of the Man and His Music", in *The Musical Quarterly*, April 1966; "Open Rather than Bounded" and "A Varèse Chronology", in *Perspectives of New Music*, Autumn 1966; "Towards a Re-Merger in Music", in *Contemporary Composers on Contemporary Music*, edited by Schwartz and Childs, New York, 1967; "East and West, Old and New", in *Asian Music*, Autumn 1968; "Single Tones as Musical Entities: An Approach to Structured Deviations in Tonal Characteristics", proceedings, American Society of University Composers, 1970; "Asian Concepts and Twentieth-Century Western Composers", in *The Musical Quarterly*, April 1976; "*Ionisation*", in *Die Reihe Musik-Konzepte*, Munich, 1978; "*Ionisation*: The Function of Timbres in its Formal and Temporal Organization", monograph of the Institute of Studies in American Music, n.d.

On Chou: Nicholas Slonimsky, "CWC", in *American Composers' Alliance Bulletin*, 9 (4), 1961; Gilbert Chase, in *America's Music*, New York, 1966; A. Frankenstein, "The Sound World of CWC", in *High Fidelity*, 20 (7), 1970; E. Pulido, "CWC", in *Heterofonia*, 11(6), 1978; Francisco F. Felciano, *Four Asian Contemporary Composers*, Quezon City, Philippines, 1983.

Chou Wen-chung comments:

As an artist, I find the ancient Chinese tradition of *wenren* (men of the arts) irresistible. It regards composing or any other creative medium as an integral part of the arts—the ultimate expression of the oneness between the human spirit and nature. In *qinqu* (music for the zither) as in *caoshu* (cursive calligraphy), dotting lines, accentuating turns, fluctuating density and modulating texture join to reveal a mind in equilibrium—in knowledge, discipline, aspirations and intuition.

In recent times, while Eastern music remains quiescent, Western music has been progressing toward not only modernity but also universality by absorbing the concepts and practices of other traditions. Today, mid-century Western music has emerged as one of the two interacting forces in a yin-yang diagram of musical legacies. Fully understood in their own cultural contexts, these legacies will merge and beget music of our own time. This is how I believe music will evolve in the next half-century; this is what I have been striving toward in the past half century.

* * *

It is difficult to over-estimate Chou Wen-chung's importance. Though his compositional output is quite modest in quantity, it is of considerable significance in the slow rapprochement of Western and Eastern musics in the second half of the 20th century. Chou regards this development as the prelude to a new universalism in which the dynamism of a Western experimental tradition unites with the philosophical stasis of a much older and more settled Oriental tradition to produce a "world-music" with none of the commercial or imperial connotations that term has recently attracted. His own work, though surprisingly little known outside the United States, has been a determined and subtle exploration of that synthesis.

He is important for other reasons, too. Resident in the United States since 1946, he has been a professor and head of the Fritz Reiner Center for Contemporary Music at Columbia University since 1984. As director of the Center for U.S.-China Arts Exchange, he has been an influential figure in the new understanding between East and West. His tenure as president of the important, composer-led CRI (Composers' Recording Inc.) label coincided with an encouraging growth in the amount of new music being commercially recorded. He is a fine and perceptive critic, balancing musicological analysis with a clear sense of the broader social and cultural ramifications of creativity.

In more purely musical terms, he is important for his activity on behalf of the still poorly assimilated Franco-American composer Edgar Varèse. Chou was Varèse's pupil and became his musical executor in 1965, completing the extraordinarily difficult *Nocturnal* from Varèse's sketches and notes. Chou's interest in chance procedures based on the I Ching and other Eastern scientific-philosophical principles has had an incalculable—and barely acknowledged—impact on John Cage and the Californian composers.

In his own work, Chou draws from Varèse a concern with the manipulation of intervals and sonorities in place of conventional thematic development. Tied in works such as *Pien* (a concept allied to but rather more metaphoric than Greek ideas of change and flux) to I Ching operations, Chou was able to generate tremendously complex structures with a great deal of internal freedom. This kind of thinking was related to his interest in traditional *qin* music, in which timbre and instrumental colour seem almost limitlessly variable.

The early *Landscapes* for orchestra is still, precisely speaking, a naturalistic piece, marked by implicit parallelism and an almost calligraphic economy of gesture. The impact on Varèse over the next five years brought about a great change. *And the Fallen Petals*, written at the end of his time with Varèse, is perhaps the only work that could be read as a direct *hommage*. Chou's personal style developed steadily thereafter, exploring dissonance, "pure sound" and other adventurous transformations of traditional musical language. *Cursive*, a duo piece, contains a level of internal variation, along the lines of Varèse's "organization of sound", which is far beyond the earlier work, and there is no sign in recent compositions of that adventurousness being compromised by either academicism or a comfortable personal manner.

If the future of creative music really is a new "Pacific" synthesis which absorbs the best of the European emigre avant-garde, native American and Commonwealth musics, and the arts of South and East Asia, then Chou Wen-chung is already at the vanguard. He belongs with the *wenren*, the "engineer-pioneers in art".

—Brian Morton

CLEMENTI, Aldo. Italian. Born in Catania, 25 May 1925. Education: piano lessons with Giovanna Ferro, 1938; Universities of Catania and Rome (composition under Goffredo Petrassi and Alfredo Sangiorgi), 1943–8; Accademia di Sta Cecilia, diploma in piano, 1946, diploma in composition, 1954; further piano study, Accademia Chigiana, Siena (under Pietro Scarpini), 1947; Ferienkurse für Neue Musik, Darmstadt, 1955–62, composition classes with Karlheinz Stockhausen, 1961–2; studied electronic music, Phonological Studio, Milan, 1956–62. Teacher of composition, Milan Conservatory; teacher of music theory, University of Bologna, since 1971. Recipient: 1st prizes, ISCM Italian section, (for *Episodi* and *Sette scene*), 1958, 1963. Mailing address: c/o Edizioni Suvini Zerboni, via Quiltiliano 40, Milan, Italy.

Publisher: Suvini Zerboni.

Symphonies/orchestral:

Ouverture 1954.
Tre studi (chamber orchestra) 1956–7.
Episodi 1958, revised 1959.
Sete scene (arranged from *Collage* for chamber orchestra) 1961.
Informel No 3 1961–3.
Variante B 1964.
Variante C 1964.
Concerto (2 pianos, 40 winds) 1967.
Sinfonia da camera (small orchestra) 1974.
Piano Concerto (piano, carillons, small orchestra) 1975.
Double Bass Concerto (double bass, carillons, small orchestra) 1976.
Clessidra (chamber orchestra) 1976.
Violin Concerto (violin, carillons, small orchestra) 1977.
Capriccio (viola, 24 instruments) 1979–80.

Chamber/instrumental:

Tre piccoli pezzi (Omagio a Bartók) (piano—4 hands) 1950.
Piano Quintet 1953.
Sonata (piano, trumpet, guitar) 1955.
Tre piccoli pezzi (flute, oboe, clarinet) 1955.
Due studi (trumpet, violin, piano) 1956.
Concertino (nonet) 1956.
Concertino in forma di variazioni (9 instruments) 1956.
Composizione No 1 (piano) 1957.
Ideogrammi No 1 (16 instruments) 1959.
Ideogrammi No 2 (flute, 17 instruments) 1959.
Triplum (flute, oboe, clarinet) 1960.
Informel No 1 (percussion, 12 keyboard players) 1961.
Informel 2 (15 players) 1962.
Invenzione (Omaggio a Petrassi) (violin, mandolin, trumpet, accordion, bass drum) 1962.
Intavolatura (harpsichord) 1963.
Reticolo: 11 (11 instruments) 1966.
Reticolo: 4 (string quartet) 1968.
Concerto (piano, 7 instruments) 1970.
B.A.C.H. (piano) 1970.
Reticolo: 12 (12 strings) 1970.
Replica (harpsichord) 1972.
Manualiter (organ) 1973.
Esercizio (B.A.C.H.) (mezzo-violin, violin, viola) 1975.
Reticolo: 3 (B.A.C.H.) (3 guitars) 1975.
Clessidra (11 instruments) 1976.
Sigla (organ) 1977.
Quintetto (strings) 1978.
Sphinx (violin, viola, cello) 1978.
Fantasia (lute; on a fragment by Michelangelo Galilei) 1978.
GiAn(ca)rlo CArDini (prepared piano) 1978.
Berceuse (bass clarinet, viola, cello ad lib, prepared piano) 1979.
L'orologia di ARcevia (13 players) 1979.
Madrigale (prepared piano—4 hands) 1979.
Variazioni (viola) 1979.
Elegia (flute, 4 bassoons, 4 horns, 4 trombones) 1979–81.
Nun Komm, der Heiden Heiland (2 trumpets, 2 trombones) 1980.
Didici variazioni (guitar) 1980.
Fantasia su roBErto FAbriCiAni (flute) 1980–1.
Pastorale (2 violins, viola, harpsichord, 8 carillons) 1981.
Concerto "2e2m" (16 instruments) 1981–2.

Vocal/choral:

Due poesie (voice, piano; Rilke, Hugo) 1946; first performed Vienna, 1947.
Cantata (soprano, speaker, chorus, chamber orchestra; Calderon) 1954; broadcast Hamburg Radio, 1956.
Variante A (chorus, orchestra; Mass) 1963.
Silben (female voice, clarinet, violin, 2 pianos) 1966.
Silbenmerz [female voice(s), actress(es), baritone(s)] 1970.
Otto frammenti (soprano, counter-tenor, organ, lute, viola da gamba; Charles d'Orleans) 1978.
Im Frieden dein, o Herre Mein (motet for 8 voices) 1980.

Opera/dramatic:

Collage (musical action based on visual material by Achille Perilli) 1960; first performed Rome, 1961.
Blitz (musical action; 21 instruments) 1972–3.
ES (after Nello Saito; 3 sopranos, 3 mezzo-sopranos, 3 contraltos, orchestra, 9 offstage instruments) 1978–80.
Collage 4: Jesu meine Freude (music and mime for 8 voices, 8 brass, tape) 1979.

Other:

Collage 2 (tape) 1960.
Collage 3: Dies irae (tape) 1966–7.

PUBLICATIONS

By Clementi: "A proposito della 'Serenata' di Petrassi", in *Il verri*, 5 (1), 1961; "Teatro musicale oggi", in *Il verri*, 16, 1964;

"Prefazione a Varese", in *Spettatore musicale*, 3 (4/5), 1968; "Ricordo di Bruno Maderna", in *La Biennale di Venezia: Annuario 1975 Eventi del 1974*, Venice, 1975.

On Clementi: M. Bortolotto, "AC", in *Melos*, 30, 1964; M. Bortolotto, "New Music in Italy", in *Contemporary Music in Europe*, edited by Lang and Froder, New York, 1965; M. Bortolotto, (interview) in *Spettatore musicale*, 2 (5), 1967; M. Bortolotto, "Una poetica artigiana", in *Fase seconda*, Turin, 1969.

* * *

Aldo Clementi's stylistic trajectory since the late 1950s has been not dissimilar to that of his compatriot Donatoni: an initial contact with and interest in the "compositional research" being conducted by the luminaries of the "Darmstadt school" followed by an increasing lack of confidence in the validity of serial/dialectical thinking, leading in these two cases to a concentration on the impersonal, "mechanical" aspects of compositional craft. In the work of both composers, the dialectical status of the *note* is undermined, either by emphasising its arbitrariness (e.g., Donatoni's habit of excavating random fragments from his own pieces and constructing new works from them) or submerging it in a network of "alternatives" (i.e., canons) so that individual pitch-contours are no longer discernible. In Clementi's mature works, those pitch-contours derive from preexistent, tonal music (Bach and the Beatles have provided notable examples) whose emotive and structural potential is completely cancelled out by their tenuous position as "cadaverous microorganisms" (Clementi's phrase). But the fact of their presence is crucial: the flattening-out of *all* significant contour in Clementi's music (the overall form being typically just as featureless) is the result of his conviction that describing the gradual *end* of music is the only task left to a composer, and the pulverisation of a wide spectrum of past musics into broadly similar-sounding expanses of lugubrious texture lends the whole programme a certain poignancy. Also the use of tonal elements (though multiplied canonically to occupy continuously the entire chosen chromatic space) produces a very specific quality in this texture, a softness, even a seeming passivity very different from textures composed (e.g., by Ligeti or Lutoslawski) from more atonal, jagged units.

Paradoxically, the creation of such polyphonies in solo instruments (as opposed to ensembles) is almost bound to bring about "virtuosic" demands on a performer, which might seem to be at odds with Clementi's stated purpose especially as he has, beginning with a Concerto for prepared piano in 1970, produced a series of works involving the "traditional" confrontation between a soloist and a more or less large ensemble. However, both in these and in his theatre piece *ES*, expectations of some kind of formal discourse are immediately dashed by the composer's weirdly inventive sidestepping. In the *Violin Concerto* the soloist (playing a sequence of awkward, disconnected phrases), the ensemble and a group (which plays continuously) of clockwork carillons meander through their permutations without regard for potential interrelationships; in *ES* three characters, each played by three singers, portray a whole gamut of stereotyped operatic emotions *simultaneously*, all the while embedded in a middle-to-upper-register fabric of sound produced by six nine-piece instrumental groups.

Clementi's is not an aesthetic philosophy which would be shared or even accepted as valid by many; unflinching negativity is one thing, working through it with Clementi's own brand of bleak "logic" quite another. Its justification must eventually lie in the musical experience itself, and in many works his singleness of purpose and (contradictory?) ear for intriguing sonority unite to produce a sombre allure without parallel. Even for Clementi, the decay and dissolution of music is not yet quite complete.

—Richard Barrett

CLOETE, Johan(nes Nicolaas). South African. Born in Moorreesburg, Cape, 17 November 1957. Educated at Kroonstad High School, graduated 1975; University of Cape Town, B.Mus., 1980; M.Mus. (composition), 1985; University of Stellenbosch, D.Phil. research, in progress 1991. Music critic, Argus Group newspapers, Cape Town, since 1983; temporary lecturer, University of Cape Town, from 1986 (halted by serious accident). Recipient: special VITA Award for contribution to theatre in the Cape. Mailing address: 109 Chester House, Chester Road, Rondebosch 7700, Republic of South Africa.

Publisher: Amanuensis Quality Editions, 16 Heseldon Road, Rondebosch 7700, Republic of South Africa.

Symphonies/orchestral:

Celebration 1988; first performed Cape Town, 1989. Recorded GSE Claremont Records, to be released.
Festival 1989; first performed Cape Town, 1990.
Vigil: Eniwetok 1989; first performed Stellenbosch, 1990.
"En Reposen au Soleil" 1990; first performed Johannesburg, 1990.
Haima-Phoos 1990.
Mai-Phen 1990.

Chamber/instrumental:

Ehieh Asher Ehieh (string quartet) 1981; first performed Cape Town, 1982.
The Return of Ulysses (string quartet) 1982.
Nostalgia for Space (makondere horns, electric guitar, harmonium, tape, piano, percussion, finger piano) 1983; first performed Cape Town, 1984.
Sine amore nil est jucundum (piccolo, bass clarinet, trumpet, chamber organ, 2 percussion, cello) 1984; first performed Cape Town, 1985.
Apokalypsis: Vortex (flute, oboe, clarinet, guitar, 2 percussion, violin, cello) 1987; first performed Cape Town, 1988.

Vocal/choral:

Aria I (from forthcoming opera *Mpho*; soprano, piano) 1986; first performed Cape Town, 1987.
Nightfall over the Martian Canals (mezzo-soprano, piano) 1987; first performed Cape Town, 1979.
Missa brevis (SATB choir) 1987; first performed Cape Town, 1988.
Mysterium Magnum (2 altos, 2 tenors, bass) 1988; first performed Cape Town, 1990.
Armageddon (2 altos, 2 tenors, bass) 1989; first performed Cape Town, 1990.

De signatura rerum (speaking chorus, mixed chorus, tape, 4 instruments) 1988–9.
Eingang (counter-tenor, 2 recorders, glockenspiel) 1990.
Apokalypsis: Lux (children's choir, soloists, chamber orchestra) 1990.

Other:

Music for theatre: *Greek*, *Kvetch*, *A Midsummer Night's Dream*, *From My Point of View*, *Anatomie Titus: The Fall of Rome*, *The Glass Menagerie*.

PUBLICATIONS

On Cloete: Penny Clough, in "A Survey of the Younger Generation of South African Composers", in *Composers in South Africa*, edited by P. Klatzow, Cape Town, 1987.

Johan Cloete comments:

I echo my deeply spiritual/mystical beliefs in my music. That is why most of my pieces are concerned with the invisible world. As a composer, I simply "dictate" what comes through me; and that is why the intellectual slant of my pieces is limited. Basically I have absorbed what I have learnt and what I am still learning. That knowledge is automatically stored in my subconscious mind which then leaves more space for consciously feeling my way through uncharted territory.

* * *

Sound, as the source of ancient creation and of life itself, is his primary occupation. Sound, as the impulse to a new experience, is his obsession. And it was also sound that changed the total course of his life.

As avant-garde composer and music critic of *The Argus*, a Cape Town daily newspaper, Johan Cloete was well-known in the early 1980s in Cape music circles as the angry young man who took delight in upsetting establishment views and destroying bourgeois securities. A road accident changed his course. He was suddenly engaged in a struggle for life, spending almost two years in hospital, coming close to death, but discovering that sound was a healing force. The experience afforded him a new perspective on his life and work. His only way back to health was via sound; through music, and specifically his own music, he could embrace life and celebrate the joy of creation. This has been the basis of all his recent work with a powerful autobiographical reference.

Cloete has studied mythology in depth and quotes extensively from Greek, Egyptian and Indian cultures where sound is considered as life impulse. The Bible, too, is a continual source of fascination, and the source of similar insights. These theories and beliefs not only from the basis of his own creative drive, but are also the subject of his doctoral studies at the University of Stellenbosch.

Influences on his early work included Karlheinz Stockhausen, John Cage, Mauricio Kagel and Luciano Berio. His first work, *Nightfall over the Martian Canals*, betrays definite traces of Berio's example, while other titles and the flirtation with electronic music stems from Stockhausen.

Cloete's meeting with Paul Rommelaere first directed his attention to the spiritual quality of the inner landscape, an introduction that led him to the work of Carl Jung, where the theory of sucessive syntheses of the soul leading to an entire person fascinated him. During 1981, the focus of his work moved away from the influence of other composers and toward a closer examination of his own inner processes, an exploration of the self in confrontation and harmony with the self. This was a slow process which demanded an indepth study of a much wider spectrum of composers; Peter Maxwell Davies and Benjamin Britten made a great impact on him.

In 1985, he discovered the work of Philip Glass and Glass's repetitive rhythms and synthesis of disparate elements into wholeness impressed him. The last direct influence on his work, though, are Arvo Part's beautiful melodies. The South African composer Roelof Temmingh has made his mark on Cloete's recent work, as have the rhythms of Afrikaans (Boeremusiek) and African folk music. Increasingly, though, after 1986, as he has begun to inhabit his own inner and intellectual world, he has come into mature and individual voice.

—Amanda Botha

CONYNGHAM, Barry (Ernest). Australian. Born in Sydney, 27 August 1944. Educated: originally studied jurisprudence; private lessons with Richard Meale; New South Wales Conservatorium, from 1966; University of Sydney (under Peter Sculthorpe), M.A.; private study in Japan with Toru Takemitsu, 1970; University of California, San Diego, certificate of post-doctoral studies, 1972–3; University of Melbourne, D.Mus. Married to Deborah Conyngham; 2 children. Part-time lecturer and tutor, University of New South Wales, and National Institute of Dramatic Art, 1968–70; senior tutor, University of Western Australia, 1971; post doctoral fellow, University of California, San Diego, 1972–3; visiting fellow, Princeton University, New Jersey, 1973–4; composer and researcher in residence, University of Aix-Marseille, 1974–5; lecturer, 1975–9, senior lecturer, 1979–84, and reader, 1984–90, University of Melbourne; visiting scholar, University of Minnesota, Minneapolis, 1982; visiting fellow, Pennsylvania State University, State College, 1982; Ministry of Arts Advisory Panel, 1982–5; board member, 1982–5, and chair, 1985–7, Australia Council Music board; member of board, Playbox Theatre Company; professor and head of School of Creative Arts, University of Wollongong, New South Wales, since 1990. Recipient: Churchill Fellowship, 1970; Harkness Fellowship, 1972–4; Australia Council Fellowship, 1975; Fulbright Senior Fellowship, 1982; Achievement Award, Australia Day Committee, 1987; Sounds Australian Critics Awards (for *Bennelong*), 1989; Australian Record Industry Association award for best classical recording (of *Southern Cross* and *Ice Carving*), 1987. Mailing address: School of Creative Arts, University of Wollongong, Wollongong, New South Wales, Australia.

Publisher: Universal Edition.

Symphonies/orchestral:

Crisis: Thoughts in a City (2 string orchestras, 3 percussion) 1968. Recorded ABC RRCS 1402.
Five Windows 1969. Recorded ABC RRCS 1421.
Ice Carving (violin, 4 string orchestras) 1970. Recorded EMI OASD 270403.

Water . . . Footsteps . . . Time (tam-tam, electric guitar, harp, piano, all amplified, 2 orchestras) 1970–1. Recorded Festival FC 80027.
Six (6 percussion, orchestra) 1971.
Without Gesture (percussion, harp, piano, orchestra) 1973.
Sky (string orchestra) 1977.
Percussion Concerto 1977.
Concerto for Double Bass: Shadows of Noh 1978.
Mirages 1978.
Concerto for Orchestra: Horizons 1981.
Double Concerto: Southern Cross (violin, piano, orchestra) 1981. Recorded EMI OASD 270403; Koch International, 1990.
Dwellings (small orchestra) 1982.
Cello Concerto (cello, string orchestra) 1984.
Recurrences (organ, celeste, 2 pianos, electric piano, orchestra) 1986. Recorded ABC Polydor, 1990.
Vast I "The Sea" 1987.
Vast II "The Coast" 1987.
Vast III "The Centre" (violin, viola, cello, double bass, orchestra) 1987.
Vast IV "The Cities" 1987.
Glimpses of Bennelong (chamber orchestra) 1987.
Concerto for Piano; Monuments (piano, DX7 synthesizer, orchestra) 1989; first performed Albany, New York, 19 May 1989. Recorded Koch International, 1990.
Concerto for Viola: Waterways 1989.
Concerto for Harp; Cloudlines 1990; first performed U.S.A., 1991.

Chamber/instrumental:

Jazz Ballet (saxophone, double bass, drums, flute, piano) 1964.
Sonata (cello) 1965.
Sonata (piano) 1966–7.
Dialogue (string trio) 1967.
Lyric Dialogue (5 flutes, oboe, cello) 1967.
The Little Sheriff (piano) 1968.
Prisms (6 violins) 1968.
Three (2 percussion, string quartet) 1970. Recorded ANC RRCS 1468.
Ends (piano) 1970.
Five (wind quintet) 1970–1.
Snowflake (piano, harpsichord, electric piano, celeste: 1 player) 1973. Recorded RCA VRCI 0083.
Playback (double bass or cello, tape) 1973.
ppp (piano) 1979.
String Quartet 1979. Recorded Move LF 3037.
Viola (viola) 1981.
Journeys (reed player, tape) 1981.
Voicings (flute, trombone, percussion, piano, tape) 1983.
Preview (cello) 1984.
Streams (harp, flute, viola) 1988; first performed Tokyo, October 1988.

Vocal/choral:

Farben (choir) 1968.
From Voss (female voice, harp, percussion, all amplified; White) 1973.
Edward John Eyre (narrator, chorus; Oakes, after Eyre) 1973. Recorded EMI OASD 7582.
Bony Anderson (baritone, flute/alto flute/piccolo, clarinet/bass clarinet, trumpet or horn or trombone, percussion, keyboard, violin, cello; Copland) 1978.
Basho (soprano, flute/alto flute/piccolo, clarinet/bass clarinet, trombone, percussion, piano, violin, cello; Basho) 1981; first performed London, 13 October 1981.
Imaginary Letters (unaccompanied voices) 1981. Recorded Arika AR002.
Antipodes (soprano, tenor, baritone, didgeridoo, SATB choir, orchestra) 1984–5.
Matilda (soloists, chorus, orchestra) 1988; first performed Melbourne, September 1988.

Opera:

Ned (Seymour) 1975–8.
The Apology of Bony Anderson (Copland) 1978.
Fly (Copland) 1981–4; first performed Move MD 3076.
The Oath of Bad Brown Bill (children's opera; Copland, Axelson) 1985.

Other:

Horizon (film soundtrack; 10-track tape) 1970; first performed Osaka, Japan, 1970.
Through Clouds (tape) 1974.
Mirror Images (4 actors, alto saxophone, percussion, cello, double bass) 1974–5.
Diamentina Ghosts (music theatre for soprano, 2 baritones, flute/alto flute/piccolo, clarinet/bass clarinet, trumpet, percussion, piano, violin, cello; Copland) 1988.
Vast (ballet; choreography by Graeme Murphy) 1988; first performed Melbourne, March 1988. Recorded ABC Polydor, 1990.
Bennelong (music theatre with puppets; soprano, chamber orchestra) 1988; first performed Holland, April 1988.

PUBLICATIONS

By Conyngham: (with A. Mander-Jones) "Direct Synthesis of Music", in *ACS Bulletin*, 7, 1976; "Music V—Beginner's Handbook", in *Internal*, 1979; (with R.P. Harris) "Some Problems in Synthesis of String Timbre", AARC, 1980; "Icecarving", in *Cadenza*, 12 (1), March 1984; "Australian Music Today", in *Music Today Quarterly*, Autumn 1988; "Music with an Australian Accent", in *Australian Studies*, 1989.

* * *

Possibly because Barry Conyngham's primary musical experience lay in the area of jazz—he performed in a jazz group while still at school—as a young composer he slipped easily into contemporary musical trends, and his early works often reveal a preoccupation with texture and timbre traceable to Penderecki and Ligeti. This aspect was evident from his first choral piece, *Farben*, and the more obvious *Snowflake*, for a single performer playing four keyboards: piano, harpsichord, celeste and electric piano. His orchestral work *Crisis: Thoughts in a City* took the concept further by physically separating its two string orchestras and percussion ensemble. This device was repeated in *Three* for two groups of percussion instruments and string quartet. He subsequently developed the idea of the physical orientation of the performer—*Five*, for wind quintet, saw the players moving around the concert hall in a series of complex manoeuvres—and it may well have been a factor in his interest in theatre works. Of these he has written several, for various combinations of forces, culminating in the opera *Fly*.

An interest in Asian music, first seen clearly in works such as *Three*, was strongly encouraged by a visit to Japan in 1970. Conyngham had been commissioned to devise the score for a film, *Horizon*, to be shown in the Australian pavilion at the Osaka Expo '70 Festival. This fortuitously coincided with his receiving a Churchill Fellowship for six months' study with the Japanese composer Toru Takemitsu. Takemitsu helped to make the composer's stay in Japan an extremely fruitful one, not only in terms of his musical and personal development, but also by introducing him to some of the world's leading contemporary music figures who were there for the festival. A distinctly Japanese manner of thinking, as well as elements of Japanese culture, can be discerned in Conyngham's two works from this period, *Water . . . Footsteps . . . Time* for four amplified solo instruments and orchestra, and *Ice Carving*, a form of concerto for amplified violin and four string orchestras.

Electronic music has formed a significant proportion of Conyngham's output. His music for *Horizon* comprised a 10-track recording, while later works included *Playback* for solo double-bass with a four-channel sound mixer and tape, and *Voicings* for instrumental ensemble and computer-generated tape. In addition, several pieces use amplified solo instruments (not, however, electronically treated): besides the two works from his Japanese sojourn, there are *Five Windows*, which includes an amplified piano amongst its orchestral instruments, and his large-scale programmatic work *From Voss* based on the novel by Patrick White.

One of Conyngham's most prestigious commissions was for the ballet score *Vast*. Created especially for the Australian Bicentenary, the ballet was an ambitious project in which the choreographer Graeme Murphy hand-picked dancers from major Australian companies, welding them into a team with his own highly distinctive feeling for movement. Murphy chose Conyngham to write the score after having used other of the composer's existing works, *Sky*, *Five Windows*, *Ice Carving* and *Snowflake*, for his ballet *Rumours* in 1978.

A strong visual or mental concept is at the heart of much of the composer's work. Pieces such as *Ice Carving* are quite specifically programmatic in their sound descriptions of a visual image. Others express a thought or emotion, such as the romantic nationalism inherent in his double concerto *Southern Cross*, which was acclaimed at the 1985 International Rostrum of Composers in Paris.

—Jenny Dawson

COOKE, Arnold (Atkinson). British/English. Born in Gomersal, Yorkshire, 4 November 1906. Educated at Street Court, Westgate-on-Sea, Kent, 1916–21; Repton School, 1921–5; Caius College, Cambridge (under E.J. Dent), 1925–9, B.A., 1928, B.Mus., 1929, D.Mus., 1948; Staatlich Akademische Hochsschule für Musik, Berlin (under Paul Hindemith), 1929–32. Lieutenant in Royal Navy, 1941–6. Director, Festival Theatre, Cambridge, 1932; professor of harmony, counterpoint and composition, Royal Manchester College of Music, 1933–8; professor of harmony, counterpoint and composition, Trinity College of Music, London, 1947–77; chair of Composers Guild of Great Britain, 1953; governor, Dolmetsch Foundation; president, Tonbridge Music Club. Recipient: third prize (for *Concert Overture No 1*), *Daily Telegraph* Overture Competition, 1934. Mailing address: Phyllis Cottage, Whetsted Road, Five Oak Green, Tonbridge, Kent TN12 6RU, England.

Publishers: Oxford University Press; Novello; Schott; Anglo-American Music Publishers; Peters; Emerson, Windmill Farm, Ampleforth, Yorkshire, England; Moeck Verlag, Postfach 143, D-3100 Celle, Germany; Belwyn-Mills Music, Woodford Green, Essex, England; Forsyth Brothers, Ampleforth, Yorkshire, England; Ricordo, Josef Weinberger, 12–14 Mortimer Street, London, England.

Symphonies/orchestral:

Horn Concerto 1928–9; destroyed by composer.
Concert Overture No 1 1934; first performed London, Summer 1934.
Passacaglia, Scherzo and Finale (string orchestra; arranged from *Octet for Wind and Strings*) 1937.
Piano Concerto 1939–40.
Concert Overture No 2: "The Processional" 1946.
Symphony No 1 in B♭ 1946–7; first performed London, 26 February 1949.
Concerto in D (string orchestra) 1948.
Two Orchestral Interludes (from *Mary Barton*) 1952.
Concerto for Oboe and String Orchestra 1954; first performed Cambridge, 1954.
Sinfonietta (chamber orchestra) 1954.
Concerto for Clarinet and String Orchestra 1955; first performed Cheltenham, Gloucestershire, 1957. Recorded Hyperion A66031.
Concerto for Recorder and String Orchestra (or flute) 1956.
Concerto for Violin and Orchestra 1958; first performed Cheltenham, Gloucestershire, 1959.
Jabez and the Devil (suite from the ballet) 1962. Recorded Lyrita SRCS78.
Symphony No 2 in F 1963.
Concerto for Small Orchestra 1966; first performed Bath, 1966.
Variations on a Theme of Dufay 1966.
Symphony No 3 in D 1967; first performed London, 1967. Recorded Lyrita SRCS 78.
York Suite (recorders, string orchestra, timpani, percussion) 1972.
Concerto for Cello and Orchestra 1972–3; first performed London, 1975.
Symphony No 4 in E♭ 1974; first performed London, 1975.
Symphony No 5 in G 1978–9; first performed London, 17 July 1981.
Symphony No 6 in E♭ 1983–4.
Repton Fantasia 1984.
Concerto for Orchestra 1986.

Chamber/instrumental:

Piano Sonata 1921; destroyed by composer.
Sonata for Cello and Piano in D minor 1925–6.
Violin Sonata 1926–7; destroyed by composer.
String Quartet in C# minor 1927–8.
String Trio 1929; destroyed by composer.
Capriccio, Intermezzo, and Scherzo (piano) 1930.
Passacaglia, Scherzo and Finale: Octet for Wind and Strings 1931.
Suite: Sextet for Brass 1931.
Quintet (harp, flute, clarinet, violin, cello) 1932.
String Quartet No 1 1933.
Duo (violin, viola) 1935; lost.

Ostinato, Intermezzo, and Capriccio (piano) 1935.
Flute Quartet (flute, string trio) 1936.
Sonata for Viola and Piano 1936–7.
Sonata for Two Pianos 1936–7.
Sonata for Piano 1938.
Sonata No 1 in G for Violin and Piano 1939.
Sonata No 1 in B♭ for Cello and Piano 1941.
Suite in C for Piano 1943, revised 1943.
Piano Trio in C 1944.
Variations on an Original Theme (string quartet) 1945.
Alla Marcia (clarinet, piano) 1946.
String Quartet No 2 in F 1947.
Oboe Quartet (oboe, string trio) 1948; first performed Cambridge, December 1948.
Piano Quartet in A 1949.
String Trio in B♭ 1950; first performed Cambridge, 1951.
Sonata No 2 in A for Violin and Piano 1951.
Rondo in B♭ for Horn and Piano 1951.
Quintet (horn, violin, 2 violas, piano) 1955.
Sonatina (flute, piano) 1956.
Sonata for Oboe and Piano 1957; first performed London, 1958.
Little Suite (flute, viola) 1957.
Scherzo (piano) 1957.
Suite (3 clarinets) 1958.
Sonata in B♭ for Clarinet and Piano 1959; first performed Hampton, March 1959. Recorded Hyperion A66044.
Sonata for Oboe and Piano 1959.
Dance of the Puppets (piano) 1959.
Pastorale (piano) 1959.
Divertimento (treble recorder, string quartet) 1960.
Wind Quintet 1961.
Suite (recorder, piano) 1961.
Prelude, Intermezzo & Finale (organ) 1962.
Sonata for Oboe and Harpsichord (or piano) 1962.
Quintet (clarinet, string quartet) 1962.
Quartet (flute, clarinet, cello, piano) 1964.
Fantasia (organ) 1964.
Quartet-Sonata (recorder, violin, cello, harpsichord) 1964.
Suite (recorder quartet) 1965.
Trio in E♭ (clarinet, cello, piano) 1965.
Piano Sonata No 2 in B♭ 1965.
Serial Theme and Variations (recorder) 1966.
Impromptu (organ) 1966.
String Quartet No 3 1967.
Toccata and Aria (organ) 1967.
Fugal Adventures (organ) 1967.
Quintet (piano, string quartet) 1969.
Sonata for Violin 1969.
Pavane (flute, piano) 1969.
Quartet (recorders) 1970.
Trio (recorders) 1970.
Sonata for Harmonica and Piano 1970.
Sonata No 1 for Organ 1971.
Septet (7 clarinets) 1971.
Intermezzo and Capriccio (harpsichord) 1971.
Suite (3 recorders, harpsichord) 1971.
Sonatina (3 recorders) 1972.
Divertimento (flute, oboe, violin, cello, piano) 1974.
Divertimento (descant and treble recorders, violin, cello, harpsichord) 1975.
Suite No 2 (piano) 1975.
Variations on Two Christmas Carols (3 recorders) 1975.
String Quartet No 4 1976.
Quartet (4 clarinets) 1977.
Quartet No 2 (recorders) 1977.
String Quartet No 5 1978.
Suite for Viols 1978.
Prelude and Dance (clarinet, piano) 1979.
Inventions (treble recorder) 1979.
Sonata No 2 for Cello and Piano 1979–80.
Sonata No 2 for Organ 1980.
Suite No 3 (piano) 1982.
Trio for Oboe, Clarinet and Bassoon 1984.
Capriccio (recorder, piano/harpsichord; for William Alwyn's 80th birthday) 1985.
Sonata for Alto Flute and Piano 1985.
Arietta (piano; or recorder, piano) 1986.
Sonata for Bassoon and Piano 1987.
Little Suite (treble recorder) 1987.
Sonata for Flute and Harp 1988.
Suite for Organ 1989.

Vocal/choral:

Holderneth (cantata for mixed chorus, baritone, orchestra; Sweeney) 1933–4.
Bedtime Songs (for children; Rathkey) 1939.
Labrador (voice, piano; Crane) 1939.
Four Shakespeare Sonnets (soprano, string orchestra) 1941.
Song (tenor, small orchestra; Hölderlin) 1945.
Four Songs (high voice; Housman, de la Mare, Nash, Milton) 1946–7.
Two Songs (baritone; Whitman, Auden) 1946–7.
Rain (voice, piano; Morrison) 1949.
Motet: Lord, Thou Hast Been Our Refuge (unaccompanied chorus) 1952.
Nocturnes (soprano, horn, piano) 1956.
Three Songs of Innocence (soprano, clarinet, piano; Blake) 1957.
Three Songs (tenor, guitar) 1959.
Five Part-Songs (unaccompanied SATB choir; Ford, anon., Campion, E. Brontë, Fletcher) 1959.
Psalm: O Sing unto the Lord (SATB chorus, organ) 1961.
Two Carols: O Men from the Fields & Three Wise Kings (unaccompanied chorus) 1961.
The Lord at First Did Adam Make (SATB chorus, organ) 1963.
Ode on St Cecilia's Day (cantata for soloists, chorus, orchestra) 1964.
Anthem: Loving Shepherd (chorus, organ) 1964.
Kleiner Gedichtkreis (baritone, piano) 1966.
Song on May Morning (unaccompanied SATB chorus) 1966.
Country Songs (bass, piano) 1968.
A Jacobean Suite (unaccompanied chorus) 1976.
The Seamew (baritone, flute, oboe, string quartet) 1979–80; first performed Mayshurst, Sussex, 1 November 1981.
Anthem on Psalms 19 & 100 (chorus, organ) 1981.
Three Flower Songs (soprano, treble recorder) 1987.
Five Songs of William Blake (baritone, treble recorder, piano) 1987.

Opera:

Mary Barton (Rathkey) 1949–52.
The Invisible Duke 1975.

Other:

Peer Gynt (incidental music to Ibsen) 1932–3.
The Merchant of Venice (incidental music to Shakespeare) 1932–3.
The Death of Gunnar and Burnt Njall (incidental music to radio drama) 1947.

Colorado Beetle (music for film; 13 instruments) 1948.
Jabez and the Devil (ballet; based on story by Benet) 1962; first performed London, 1962.

PUBLICATIONS

By Cooke: "Paul Hindemith", in *Music Survey*, 2 (1–2), 1949.

On Cooke: John Clapham, "AC: The Achievement of 20 Years", in *Music Survey*, June 1951; Francis Loring, "AC at 75", 1981.

Arnold Cooke comments:

My music is mainly based on traditional classical procedures and principles, as I was brought up with classical music from my early youth. Of course, these are combined with modern styles and characteristics.

I was early introduced to chamber music. At school, I learnt the piano and later the cello, and at Cambridge I became the cellist in an amateur string quartet. My feeling for form and logic in music was strengthened by my study with Paul Hindemith in Berlin, and also my awareness and understanding of modern idioms and styles.

I do not have any particular theories of composition, just a natural inclination for it, and a desire to achieve something in music.

* * *

Arnold Cooke is unusual among British composers of his generation in that his final training was undertaken abroad and under a major figure. His studies with Hindemith from 1929–32, besides imparting a more cosmopolitan outlook than was then usual among British musicians, gave him a complete and secure technical orientation whose potentialities he spent the rest of his career developing in a quietly personal manner without regard to fashion.

Among his characteristics are clarity of line, texture and overall form, these being indicative of his music's unfailing practicality. The expected Hindemith legacy is plain enough in early works such as *String Quartet No 1*, but the *Sonata for Two Pianos*, prompted by hearing Stravinsky's great *Concerto for Two Pianos*, was Cooke's first substantial piece to attract attention, in 1938. This was deserved because the Sonata is mature and quite masterful, yet a more individual voice became apparent after World War II, as in his *Symphony No 1*.

A high proportion of Cooke's output is chamber music, for a considerable variety of combinations, thus reminding us that Hindemith's pupils were required to have a working knowledge of all orchestral instruments. Contrapuntal skill is particularly evident in scores such as the Clarinet Quintet though so is Cooke's rhythmic conservatism. He fully accepted tonality also, and thus had no need of fundamental structural innovations, although his use of classical procedures did not mean that he was ever a neo-classicist in the Stravinsky sense.

Cooke is one of the few significant contemporary British composers apart from Fricker to write notable pieces for the organ, for example his *Fantasia*, *Toccata and Aria* and *Sonata*. His contrapuntal mastery is again an important factor in the success of these works, as is his feeling for the instrument itself as it has developed in recent decades. While there is emotional reserve in much of Cooke's music, there is also a lyrical quality that persists even in his largest pieces. His approach is, indeed, essentially instrumental, and many of his major works are orchestral, including six symphonies and 10 concertos.

Not that he has avoided the theatre. There is music for Shakespeare and Ibsen plays, and a ballet, *Jabez and the Devil*, that was commissioned for the Royal Ballet and given its premiere at Covent Garden in 1961. Cooke has also produced a few large compositions with voices, notably a setting of Pope's *Ode on St Cecilia's Day*, shorter choral pieces, and above all two operas. These are *Mary Barton* and *The Invisible Duke*, the latter a comic work.

Of greater consequence is *Mary Barton*, with a libretto by W.A. Rathkey based on Mrs Gaskell's novel of the same name. The plot has to do with industrial unrest in the north of England at the time of the Chartist movement. This story is apt for operatic treatment because it brings forward well-defined and opposing characters, stark contrasts between the leisure of the idle rich and the hopelessness of the workers' situation. There are also dramatic events such as the fire at the mill with which the action starts.

All this is far removed from the usual fare of operas, which have not much concerned themselves with social questions, and *Mary Barton* is also the work upon which Cooke spent more time than any other. In a good performance it would give a fine impression of the expressive range of which his elsewhere sometimes undemonstrative style is capable. Unfortunately, like *The Invisible Duke*, it has up to the time of this book's publication not been staged. Some of the symphonies, too, still await their first performance.

—Max Harrison

COPLAND, Aaron. American. Born in Brooklyn, New York, 14 November 1900. Educated at Boys' High School, Brooklyn, graduated 1918; early piano study under Leonard Wolfsohn, Victor Wittgenstein, Clarence Adler; private composition study under Rubin Goldmark, 1915; American Conservatory, Fontainebleau, Paris (under Paul Vidal and Nadia Boulanger), 1920–4; further study in France, England, Belgium, Italy, and visits to Europe, 1926, 1927, 1929. Organizer (with Roger Sessions), Copland-Sessions Concerts, 1928–31; founder, Yaddo Festivals, 1932; teacher, modern music course, New School for Social Research, New York, 1927–37; founder, American Composers' Alliance, 1937; head of composition department, 1940–65, American cultural ambassador to Latin America, 1941, 1947, and chair of faculty, 1957–65, Berkshire Music Center, Tanglewood, Massachusetts; lecturer, 1944, and Charles Eliot Norton Lecturer, 1951–2, Harvard University, Cambridge, Massachusetts; also board member, League of Composers (and contributor to its journal *Modern Music*), Koussevitzky Foundation, Composers Forum, Cos Cob Press, Edward MacDowell Foundation, Charles Ives Society, Naumburg Foundation and others; broadcaster, 1959–72. Recipient: Guggenheim Fellowship, 1925–7; RCA Victor Award (for *Dance Symphony*); Pulitzer Prize, and New York Music Critics' Circle Award (for *Appalachian Spring*), 1945; New York Music Critics' Circle Award (for *Symphony No 3*), 1947; Academy Award (for film score to *The Heiress*), 1950; Gold Medal for Music, American Academy of Arts and Letters, 1956; Presidential Medal of Freedom, 1964; Howland

Memorial Prize, Yale University, 1970; Commander's Cross of the Order of Merit, Germany, 1970; honorary member, Accademia di Santa Cecilia, Rome. Honorary doctorates: Princeton University, 1956; Brandeis University, 1957; Wesleyan University, 1958; Temple University, 1959; Harvard University, 1961; Rutgers University, 1967; Ohio State University, 1970; New York University, 1970; Columbia University, 1971; University of York, 1971. **Died 2 December 1990**.

Publisher: Boosey & Hawkes.

Symphonies / orchestral:

Cortège Macabre (from the ballet *Grohg*) 1923; first performed Rochester, New York, 1 May 1925.
Symphony (organ, orchestra; later arranged without organ as *Symphony No 1*) 1924; first performed New York City, 11 January 1925.
Dance Symphony (from *Grohg*) 1925; first performed Philadelphia, 15 April 1931.
Music for the Theatre (orchestral suite) 1925; first performed Boston, 20 November 1925.
Concerto for Piano and Orchestra (Jazz Concerto) (also arranged for 2 pianos) 1926; first performed Boston, 28 January 1927.
Symphonic Ode 1927–9, revised 1935; first performed Boston, 19 February 1932; revised version first performed 8 February 1960.
Symphony No 1 1928; first performed Berlin, 9 December 1931.
Symphony No 2 (Short Symphony) (also arranged for string quartet, clarinet, piano) 1932–3; first performed Mexico City, 23 November 1934. Recorded Pro Arte CDD 140; Deutsche Grammophon DG 427 335–2.
Statements: Militant, Cryptic, Dogmatic, Subjective, Jingo, Prophetic 1932–5; partial performance New York City, 9 January 1936; first complete performance New York City, 7 January 1942.
El Salon Mexico 1933–6; first performed Mexico City, 27 August 1937. Recorded CBS MK 42429; HMV CDC7 47716–2.
Fantasia Mexicana (adapted from a film score; also arranged for piano) 1936.
Billy the Kid (symphonic suite from the ballet) 1938; first performed New York City, 9 November 1940. Recorded CBS MK 42431.
An Outdoor Overture (also arranged for band) 1938; first performed New York City, 16 December 1938; band version first performed New York City, June 1942. Recorded Telarc CD 80117.
Quiet City (cor anglais, trumpet, strings; also chamber version) 1939; first performed New York City, 28 January 1941. Recorded Deutsche Grammophon DG 419 170–2; Argo 417 818–2.
John Henry (Railroad Ballad) (small orchestra) 1940, revised 1952; broadcast CBS, 5 March 1940; revised version first performed Michigan, 1953. Recorded Telarc CD 80117.
Rodeo: Four Dance Episodes (suite from the ballet) 1942; first performed Boston, 28 May 1943. Recorded CBS MK 42430.
Music for Movies (small orchestra; suite from film scores for *The City*, *Of Mice and Men*, *Our Town*) 1942; first performed New York City, 17 February 1943.
Appalachian Spring (suite from the ballet) 1944; first performed New York City, 4 October 1945. Recorded CBS MK 42430; Telarc CD 80078; Pro Arte CDD 140; others.
Letter from Home 1944, revised 1962; first performed New York City, 17 October 1944.
Jubilee Variations (on a theme by Eugene Goossens) 1944; first performed Cincinnati, Ohio, 23 March 1945. Recorded Telarc CD 80117.
Symphony No 3 1944–6; first performed Boston, 18 October 1946. Recorded Deutsche Grammophon DG 419 170–2; Telarc CD 80201; CBS 40-61869.
Concerto for Clarinet and String Orchestra (with harp and piano) 1948; first performed New York, 6 November 1950. Recorded RCA RD 87762.
The Red Pony (suite from film score) 1948; first performed 30 October 1948.
The Heiress (suite from film score) 1949.
The Tender Land (orchestral suite from the opera) 1956; first performed Chicago, 10 April 1958.
Orchestral Variations (based on 1930 *Piano Variations*) 1957; first performed Louisville, Kentucky, 5 March 1958. Recorded VNC 7530.
Connotations 1962; first performed New York City, 23 September 1962.
Emblems (symphonic band) 1964; first performed Tempe, Arizona, 18 December 1964.
Music for a Great City (based on film score *Something Wild*) 1964; first performed London, 26 May 1964.
Down a Country Lane (school orchesta) 1964; first performed London, 20 November 1964.
Inscape 1967; first performed Ann Arbor, Michigan, 13 October 1967.
Variations on a Shaker Song (from *Appalachian Spring*; school orchestra) 1967.
Three Latin-American Sketches: Estribillo, Paisaje mexicana, Danza de Jalisco 1972, original material from 1959; first performed New York City, 7 June 1972. Recorded CBS MK 42429.

Chamber / instrumental:

String Quartet 1914; unfinished.
Capriccio (violin, piano) 1916.
Moment Musicale (piano) 1917.
Danse caractéristique (piano, 4—hands) 1918; unfinished; arranged for orchestra, 1919.
Poem (cello, piano) 1918.
Waltz Caprice (piano) 1919.
Lament (cello, piano) 1919.
The Cat and the Mouse: Humoristic Scherzo (piano) 1920; first performed Paris, 23 September 1921.
Three Sonnets (piano) 1920.
Petit Portrait (piano) 1921.
Prelude (Second) (violin, piano) 1921.
Sonata in G major (piano) 1921.
Three Moods: Embittered, Wistful, Jazzy (piano) 1921.
Passacaglia (piano) 1922; first performed Paris, January 1923.
Sentimental Melody (piano) 1926.
Two Pieces: Nocturne, Ukelele Serenade (violin, piano) 1926; first performed Paris, 5 May 1926.
Rondino (string quartet; part of *Two Pieces*) 1923; first performed Fontainebleau, France, 1924.
Lento espressivo (string quartet) 1923–4; first performed New York City, 18 October 1984.
Four Piano Blues 1926–48; no 4 first performed Montevideo, 2 May 1942; first performance of complete set New York City, 13 March 1950. Recorded Chandos ABT 1104.
Lento molto (string quartet; part of *Two Pieces*) 1928; first performed New York City, 6 May 1928.

Vitebsk (violin, cello, piano) 1929; first performed New York City, 16 February 1929.

Dance of the Adolescent (from the ballet *Grohg*; 2 pianos) c.1930.

Piano Variations (basis for *Orchestral Variations*) 1930; first performed New York City, 4 January 1931. Recorded Chandos ABT 1104.

Elegies (violin, viola) 1932; first performed New York City, 2 April 1933.

Two Children's Pieces: Sunday Afternoon Music, The Young Pioneers (piano) 1936; first performed New York City, 24 February 1936.

Sextet (string quartet, clarinet, piano; arrangement of *Short Symphony*) 1937; first performed New York City, 26 February 1939.

Quiet City (clarinet, saxophone, trumpet, piano) 1939; first performed Boston, 27 February 1939. Recorded Deutsche Grammophon DG 419 170-2; Argo 417 818-2.

Episode (organ) 1941; first performed New York City, 9 March 1941.

Sonata (piano) 1941; first performed Buenos Aires, 21 October 1941. Recorded Chandos ABT 1104.

Danzon Cubana (2 pianos or solo piano) 1942; first performed New York City, 17 December 1942.

Fanfare for the Common Man (brass, percussion) 1942; first performed Cincinnati, Ohio, 12 March 1943. Recorded CBS MK 42430.

Sonata (violin, piano) 1943, arranged for clarinet, piano, 1981; first performed New York City, 17 January 1944; clarinet version first performed Rochester, New York, 1983.

Billy the Kid (arranged for 2 pianos) 1946; first performed New York City, 17 October 1946.

Piano Quartet 1950; first performed Washington, D.C., 29 October 1950. Recorded Pro Arte CDD 120.

Piano Fantasy 1957; first performed New York City, 25 October 1957.

Nonet (3 violins, 3 violas, 3 cellos) 1960; first performed Washington, D.C., 25 April 1961.

Down a Country Lane (piano; later orchestrated for schools) 1962.

Ceremonial Fanfare (4 horns, 3 trumpets, 3 trombones, tuba) 1969.

Inaugural Fanfare (winds, brass, percussion) 1969, revised 1975.

Duo (flute, piano) 1971; first performed Philadelphia, 2 October 1971.

Threnody I: Igor Stravinsky in memoriam (flute, string trio) 1971; first performed London, April 1972.

Night Thoughts (Homage to Ives) (piano) 1972; first performed Fort Worth, Texas, 17 September 1973.

Vocalise (arrangement of vocal piece for flute, piano) 1972.

Threnody II: Beatrice Cunningham in memoriam (G flute, string trio) 1973; first performed Ojai, California, 1 June 1973.

Midsummer Nocturne (piano) 1977.

Vocal/choral:

Melancholy: A Song à la Debussy (voice, piano; Farnol) 1917; unfinished.

Spurned Love (voice, piano; Aldrich) 1917.

After Antwerp (voice, piano; Cammaerts) 1917.

Night (high voice, piano; Schaffer) 1918.

A Summer Vacation (voice, piano) 1918.

Simone (soprano, piano; Gourmont) 1919.

Music I Heard (soprano, piano; Aiken) 1920.

Old Poem (high voice, piano; Waley) 1920; first performed Paris, 10 January 1922.

Four Motets (unaccompanied SATB chorus; Biblical) 1921; first performed Fontainebleau, Autumn 1924. Recorded CBS MK 42140.

Pastorale (high voice, piano; Mathers) 1921; first performed Paris, 10 January 1927.

Alone (voice, piano; Mathers) 1922; first performed New York City, 4 December 1985.

As It Fell upon a Day (soprano, flute, clarinet; Barnefield) 1923; first performed Paris, 6 February 1924.

The House on the Hill (unaccompanied SSAA chorus; Robinson) 1925; first performed New York City, 24 April 1925.

An Immorality (soprano, SSA chorus, piano; Pound) 1925; first performed New York City, 24 April 1925.

Poet's Song (medium voice, piano; cummings) 1927; first performed New York City, 1927.

Vocalise (high voice, piano; also arranged for flute, piano) 1928; first performed New York City, 11 October 1935.

What Do We Want? (SA chorus, piano; Abbey) 1935.

Lark (baritone, unaccompanied SATB chorus; Taggard) 1938; first performed New York City, 13 April 1943.

Lincoln Portrait (speaker, orchestra) 1942; first performed Cincinnati, Ohio, 14 May 1942. Recorded CBS MK 42431.

Las agachadas (unaccompanied SSAATTBB chorus; Spanish traditional) 1942; first performed New York City, 25 May 1942.

Song of the Guerrillas (from the film score *North Star*; baritone, TTBB chorus, piano; I. Gershwin) 1943.

The Younger Generation (from the film score *North Star*; SATB chorus, piano; I. Gershwin) 1943.

Twelve Songs of Emily Dickinson (high voice, piano) 1944–50; first performed New York City, 18 May 1950; orchestrated (8 only)—first performed New York City, 14 November 1970.

In the Beginning (mezzo-soprano, unaccompanied SATB chorus; Genesis) 1947; first performed Cambridge, Massachusetts, 2 May 1947.

Parable for a Solemn Occasion (speaker, orchestra; also arranged for organ and for band) 1949; first performed New York City, 10 December 1949.

Old American Songs (Set 1) (medium voice, piano; mostly 1830s–1840s) 1950; first performed Aldeburgh, Suffolk, 17 July 1950; arranged for medium voice and orchestra, first performed Los Angeles, 7 January 1955. Recorded Telarc CD 80117; CBS MK 42140.

Old American Songs (Set 2) (voice, piano; various) 1952; first performed Ipswich, Massachusetts, 1953; arranged for medium voice and orchestra, first performed Ojai, California, 25 May 1958. Recorded CBS MK 42140.

Dirge in Woods (high voice, piano; Meredith) 1954; first performed New York City, 28 March 1955.

Canticle of Freedom (unaccompanied mixed chorus; Barbour) 1955, revised 1965; first performed Cambridge, Massachusetts, 8 May 1955; revised version first performed Atlanta, Georgia, 19 October 1967. Recorded CBS 42140.

Opera:

The Second Hurricane (school play-opera; Denby) 1936; first performed New York City, 21 April 1937.

The Tender Land (Everett, after Johns) 1952–4; first performed New York City, 1 April 1954, revised 1955; first performed in revised, 3-act version Oberlin, Ohio, 20 May 1955. Recorded Virgin VCD 791113–2.

Other:

Grohg (ballet) 1922–5; only extracts published or performed.
Miracle at Verdun (incidental music to play by Chlumberg) 1931; first performed New York City, 16 March 1931.
Hear Ye! Hear Ye! (ballet) 1934; first performed Chicago, 30 November 1934.
Saga of the Prairies/Prairie Journal (music for radio; orchestra) 1937; first performed New York, 25 July 1937.
Billy the Kid (ballet) 1938; first performed Chicago, 6 October 1938. Recorded EMI CDC7 47382–2.
The Five Kings (incidental music to Shakespeare's history plays; quintet) 1939; first performed Boston, 27 February 1939.
The City (film music; chamber orchestra) 1939; first performed New York City, 1939.
From Sorcery to Science (score for puppet show) 1939; first performed New York City, 12 May 1939.
Of Mice and Men (orchestra score for film of Steinbeck novel; directed by Milestone) 1939; first performed New York City, 16 February 1940.
Our Town (orchestral score for film of Thornton Wilder play; directed by Wood) 1940; broadcast CBS, 9 June 1940. Recorded CBS MK 42429.
Rodeo (ballet) 1942; first performed New York, 16 October 1942.
North Star (music for film by Lewis Milestone, after Lillian Hellman) 1943.
Appalachian Spring (ballet; flute, clarinet, bassoon, piano, 4 violins, 2 violas, 2 cellos, double bass) 1943–4; first performed Washington, D.C., 30 October 1944. Recorded CBS MK 42431.
The Cummington Story (music for documentary film) 1945.
The Red Pony (music for film of Steinbeck novel; directed by Milestone) 1948; first performed New York City, 8 March 1949. Recorded CBS MK 42429.
The Heiress (music for film of James novel; directed by Wyler) 1948.
The World of Nick Adams (television score for adaptation of Hemingway) 1957; broadcast 10 November 1957.
Dance Panels (ballet) 1959, revised 1962; first performed Munich, 3 December 1962. Recorded EMI CDC7 49095–2.
Something Wild (music for film by Garfine) 1961.
CBS (signature tune) 1967; first broadcast 29 January 1967.
Largetto, Pomposo, Marcantissimo (1-page melody for 40th anniversary of Music Library Association) 1970; first performed Washington, D.C., January 1971.

PUBLICATIONS

By Copland: *What to Listen for in Music*, New York, 1939, 1957; *Our New Music*, New York, 1941, revised 1968 as *The New Music: 1900–1960*; *Music and Imagination*, Cambridge, Massachusetts, 1952, 1959; *Copland on Music*, New York, 1960; (with Vivian Perlis) *C—1900 Through 1942* (autobiography), New York, 1984.

On Copland: Virgil Thomson, "AC" in *Modern Music*, 9, 1932; A. Berger, *AC*, New York, 1953; J. F. Smith, *AC: His Work and Contribution to American Music*, New York, 1955; Hugo Cole, "AC", in *Tempo*, 76, 1966; E.T. Cone, "Conversations with AC", in *Perspectives of New Music*, 6 (2), 1968; Leonard Bernstein, "AC: An Intimate Sketch", in *High Fidelity*, 20 (11), 1970; Peter Dickinson, "C at 75", in *Musical Times*, 116, 1975; H. Wiley Hitchcock and others, "AC and American music", in *Perspectives of New Music*, 19, 1980; C. Gagne and T. Caras, "AC", in *Soundpieces; Interviews with American Composers*, Metuchen, New Jersey, 1982; C. Oja, "AC", in *American Music Recordings*, New York, 1982; J. Skowronski, *AC: A Bio-Bibliography*, Westport, Connecticut, 1985; Richard Dufallo, (interview) in *Trackings*, Oxford, 1990.

* * *

Aaron Copland's career spanned the first 90 years of the century, although the music for which he will be best remembered was written in a 20-year period, beginning with *El Salon Mexico* in 1935, and culminating in *The Tender Land* in 1954. During that time, Copland established a genuinely American voice in his composition.

The lasting popularity of the music he wrote in those 20 years has tended to overshadow the other areas of musical development which the composer pursued with equal relish. Indeed, Copland's work is often described as though it consisted of nothing more than the adaptation of folk melodies, jazz rhythms or colourful ethnic material to a stage or orchestral context, usually of a programmatic nature.

In fact, Copland drew on folk melodies in only a small number of works, and on jazz in even fewer. The bright, dancing rhythms of *El Salon Mexico*, *Danzon Cubana* or the later *Three Latin-American Sketches*, were specific exercises in the musical idioms of another country, while American folk material is directly quoted only in a small number of works, notably his famous ballets *Billy The Kid, Rodeo*, and *Appalachian Spring*, the *Lincoln Portrait* for orchestra and narrator, and the opera *The Tender Land*, in addition to his two settings of *Old American Songs*.

His success in forging the melodies, harmonic particularities and rhythmic vitality of these idioms into a wholly distinctive register is evident in that tendency for it to dominate our impression of his music.

Copland was always something of a trail-blazer, emerging from a distinctly unmusical family in Brooklyn, and nonplussing his highly conservative teacher with his interest in contemporary French idioms, before becoming the first of many Americans to study with the formidable Nadia Boulanger in Paris.

Copland's early music simultaneously pursues several different routes, partly under the influence of Boulanger's celebrated neo-classicism and his exposure to the Modernist ferment of Paris, and partly from his interest in early jazz, which he saw as creating a new and bold language which was specifically American.

His attempts to integrate jazz into a large scale orchestral structure are largely contained in the orchestral suites *Music for the Theatre* and the *Concerto for Piano and Orchestra*, but its influence, and especially rhythmic influence, made a permanent impression on his work.

His Clarinet Concerto, written for jazz clarinettist Benny Goodman, uses a Brazilian melody for its basic theme, but is a perfect example of the way in which Copland's developing musical language was able to reflect material from a variety of idioms and, while not directly quoting or even adapting, construct a wholly original work which remained redolent of its distant sources, yet retained its integrity of structure and language, without the tokenist elements all too common in this kind of exercise.

After the *Symphonic Ode*, Copland turned to a register which employed distinctly sparser sonorities and textural effects, but grew increasingly dissatisfied with the restriction which it placed on the size and breadth of his audience, the spark which fanned that 20-year outburst of composition in a distinctly more populist style.

Apart from the works which have made him most famous, Copland also wrote a considerable amount in his *Gebrauchsmusik* (or "functional music") mode, including incidental music for theatre and radio, and the scores for five films, including *The Red Pony* and *The Heiress*, which won him an Academy Award in 1950. Later pieces in that style included the orchestral suite *Music for a Great City*, which grew out of his film music for *Something Wild*.

A number of these compositions, including *An Outdoor Overture* (written, as was his first opera *The Second Hurricane*, for school-children) and the theatre music *Quiet City*, have slipped into the orchestral repertoire, as has the expanded version of his most celebrated work, *Appalachian Spring*. Originally composed for the Martha Graham Ballet Company and scored for a chamber group of 13 instruments in 1944, it was subsequently re-scored in a shorter and now more widely known version for orchestra in 1945.

Its rhythmic vigour, originality of orchestration, and the poignant appeal of the variations on the beautiful Shaker hymn " 'Tis a Gift to Be Simple" (or "Simple Gifts") which ends the piece, have ensured its continuing popularity, although the Montreal Olympics arguably made his lesser *Fanfare for the Common Man* his most widely heard piece of music.

The *Fanfare* (the music, sadly, does not quite live up to the stirring and evocative title) is quoted in the composer's Third Symphony, another composition which provides an exemplary illustration of the way in which Copland had absorbed and transformed the harmonic and rhythmic possibilities of the folk and other popular sources into his more complex compositional language.

Copland would carry many of these preoccupations forward into his later work, but the main new development of his music after this crucial period lay in his inevitably less popular exploration of twelve-tone music, beginning with the Quartet for piano and strings. Other significant works which employed this method included his *Piano Fantasy*, and the orchestral works *Connotations* and *Inscape*, all fascinating compositions in their own right.

In the latter stages of his life, Copland wrote increasingly less, and contented himself with conducting, and with the mantle of Grand Old Man of American Music, which he wore easily and with distinction. If the popular ballets of the 1940s will continue to dominate the perception of his music, it should not cloud the fact that he wrote much more of lasting value at all stages of his lengthy career, including a number of fine and diverse works for piano.

An erudite musical interpreter, commentator and critic, his own music consistently revealed not only a bold and compelling musical imagination, but also a palpable ability to build impressive and even gripping structures from the most simple, economically-employed musical materials. That strength in simplicity lies at the heart of his best work.

—Kenny Mathieson

CORDERO, Roque. Panamanian. Born in Panama, Republic of Panama, 16 August 1917. Educated at University of Minnesota music school, Minneapolis, 1943–4 (conducting under Dimitri Mitropoulos); Hamline University, St. Paul, Minnesota (composition under Ernst Krenek), 1943–47, B.A.; Berkshire Music Center, Tanglewood, Lenox, Massachusetts (conducting under Stanley Chapple), 1946; study with Leon Barzin in New York. Married Elizabeth L. Johnson, 30 June 1947; 3 sons. Founder, National Orchestra of Panama, 1938; assistant director, National Conservatory of Music, Panama, 1950–3; director/professor, National Institute of Music, Panama, 1953–64; conductor, National Orchestra of Panama, 1964–6; associate professor/assistant director, Latin American Music Center, University of Indiana, Bloomington, 1966–9; music editor, Peer-Southern Organization, New York, 1969–72; distinguished professor of composition, Illinois State University, Normal, 1972–87, now emeritus; guest conductor in Argentina, Brazil, Colombia, Chile, Panama, United States; visiting lecturer on Latin American music in United States, Spain, Central and South America. Recipient: Dimitri Mitropoulos Scholarship, 1943–7; Honorable Mention (for *Symphony No 1*), Reichold Contest, Detroit, 1947; Guggenheim Fellowship, 1949; Caro de Boesi Award, Venezuela (for *Second Symphony*), 1957; Elizabeth Sprague Coolidge commission, 1959; Koussevitzky Commission, 1960; D.Litt.Hum., Hamline University, 1966; Koussevitzky International Recording Award (for *Violin Concerto*), 1974; National Endowment for the Arts commission, 1976; Chamber Music Award, Costa Rica (for *String Quartet No 3*), 1977; Grand Cross of Vasco Nunez de Balbao, Panama, 1982; Most Distinguished Professor in Fine Arts, Illinois State University, 1983. Mailing address: Department of Music, Illinois State University, Normal, Illinois 61761, U.S.A.

Publishers: Peer-Southern Concert Music, 810 Seventh Avenue, New York, New York 10019, U.S.A.; North/South Consonance Editions, Box 698, Cathedral Station, New York, New York 10025, U.S.A.; Editions Salabert, 22 rue Chauchat, 75009 Paris, France; Berberi Edizioni Musicali, Ancona, Italy.

Symphonies/orchestral:

Brisas marinas (band) 1933; first performed Panama, September 1933; withdrawn.

Fantasía crepúsculo (band) 1933; first performed Panama, 1934; withdrawn.

Poema sinfónico Napoleón 1936; first performed Panama, 14 July 1936; withdrawn.

Capricho interiorano: Panamanian Folk Ballet Suite 1939; first performed Panama, August 1942.

Panamanian Overture No 2 1944; first performed Minneapolis, 5 April 1946.

Piano Concerto 1944; first performed Panama, 1955.

Ocho miniaturas / Eight Miniatures 1944, revised 1948.

Symphony No 1 1945; first performed Panama, 14 September 1955.

Movimiento sinfónico (strings) 1946.

Introducción y allegro burlesco 1950.

Adagio tragico (strings) 1955; first performed Panama, 1955.

Symphony No 2 1956; first performed Caracas, Venezuela, 6 April 1957. Recorded Louisville Editions 765.

Five Short Messages for Orchestra 1959; first performed Minneapolis, 1959.

Mensaje funebre (clarinet, strings) 1961; first performed Bloomington, Indiana, 1967.

Violin Concerto 1962; first performed Washington, D.C., 1965. Recorded Columbia M-32784.

Symphony No 3, with Theme and Five Variations 1965; first performed Caracas, 1966.
Circumvolutions and Mobiles (57 instruments) 1967.
Concertino (viola, strings) 1968.
Elegy (strings) 1973; first performed Normal, Illinois, 1977.
Momentum jubilo (fanfare for strings) 1973.
Six Mobiles for Orchestra 1974; first performed Normal, Illinois, 1975.
Obertura de salutacion 1980; first performed Normal, Illinois, 1987.
Symphony No 4: "Panamanian" 1986; first performed Normal, Illinois, 1987.

Chamber/instrumental:

Sonatina rítmica (piano) 1943.
Cinco miniaturas (piano) 1955.
Dos piezas cortas (violin, piano) 1945.
Sonatina (violin, piano) 1946.
Quinteto (flute, clarinet, violin, cello, piano) 1949; first performed Uruguay, 1957. Recorded Turnabout/Vox 34505.
Duo 1954 (2 pianos) 1954; first performed Panama, 1954. Recorded InterAmerican Editions 003.
String Quartet No 1 1960; first performed Washington, D.C., 1961.
Sonata (cello, piano) 1963; first performed Caracas, 1966.
Sonata breve (piano) 1966; first performed St Paul, Minnesota, 1967.
Tres mensajes breves/Three Brief Messages (viola, piano) 1966.
Permutaciones 7 (clarinet, trumpet, timpani, piano, violin, viola, double bass) 1967; first performed Rio de Janeiro, 1969.
String Quartet No 2 1968; first performed Alabama, 1969.
Paz, Paix, Peace (harp and trios: flute, cor anglais, bass clarinet; alto flute, clarinet, bassoon; violin, viola, cello) 1969; first performed Argentina, 1970.
String Quartet No 3 1973; first performed Costa Rica, 1977.
Variations and Themes for Five (flute, oboe, clarinet, horn, bassoon) 1975; first performed Chicago, 1976.
Soliloquios No 1 (flute) 1975; first performed Normal, Illinois, 1976.
Soliloquios No 2 (alto saxophone) 1976; first performed London, 1976.
Soliloquios No 3 (clarinet) 1976; first performed Normal, Illinois, 1979.
Double Concerto (without orchestra; violin, piano) 1978; first performed Washington, D.C., 1979.
Tres piececillas para alina (piano) 1978.
Music for Five Brass (2 trumpets, horn, trombone, tuba) 1980; first performed Normal, Illinois, 1981.
Soliloquios No 4 (percussion) 1981; first performed Normal, Illinois, 1981.
Soliloquios No 5 (double bass) 1981; first performed Normal, Illinois, 1983.
Petites Mobiles (bassoon, trios) 1983; first performed Miami, 1984.
Five New Preludes (piano) 1983; first performed Chicago, 1984.
Cinco mensajes para quatro amigos (guitar) 1983; first performed San Juan, Puerto Rico, 1984.
String Quartet No 4 1983; first performed Normal, Illinois, 1987.
Three Permutations 3 (violin, cello, double bass) 1984; first performed Normal, Illinois, 1987.
Sonata for Piano 1985; first performed Chicago, 1986.
Serenatas (flute, clarinet, viola, harp) 1987; first performed Normal, Illinois, 1989.
Three Miniminiatures for Ernst (flute, clarinet) n.d.

Vocal/choral:

Patria (SAATB chorus, reciter) 1944; first performed Mexico City, 1958.
Dos pequenas piezas corales/Two Short Choral Pieces (SATB chorus) 1966; first performed St Paul, Minnesota, 1967.
Cantata para la paz/Cantata for Peace (bass-baritone solo, SATB chorus, orchestra; Lincoln, Gandhi, Kennedy, King) 1979.

PUBLICATIONS

By Cordero: "Dodecafonismo vs. Nacionalismo?", in *Clave*, 6(5), 1957; "Nacionalismo vs. Dodecafonismo?", in *Revista Musical Chilena*, 13(67), 1959; *Curso de Solfeo*, Buenos Aires and Mexico, 1963; "Música y Educación", in *Tierra y Dos Mares*, 20, 1964; "La Música en Centro América y Panamá", in *Journal of Interamerican Studies*, 8(3), 1966; "The Folk-music of Panama", in *The New Grove Dictionary of Music and Musicians*, London, 1973; "Vigencia del Músico Culto", in *América Latina en su Música*, Unesco, 1978; "Raquel Boldorini", in *Latin American Music Review*, 3(2), 1982; "Remembranzas de RC", in *Revista Lotería Panamá*, September–October 1987.

On Cordero: Gilbert Chase, "Composed by Cordero", in *Américas*, 10(6), 1958, "Música Nova en las Américas", in *Américas*, 13(8), 1961, and "RC", in *New Grove Dictionary of Music and Musicians*, London, 1980; J. Orrego-Salas, "RC, un músico de América", in *Zig-Zag*, 2879, 1960; Ronald R. Sider, "The Art Music of Central America", dissertation, University of Rochester, 1967; Kurt Pahlen, "RC", in *Riemann's Musik Lexikon*, 1972; Priscilla Filos, "El Piano en las obras de RC", Panama, 1985.

Roque Cordero comments:

As a Panamanian composer, I am proud to represent my country in the field of contemporary music. My music, however, is not nationalistic in the sense of being a conscious exploitation of the folk music of Panama, but is the voice of man with strong emotional roots in that small country in the middle of the Americas. As such, I use whatever technical elements of 20th-century music that suit my personal expression, without following the different and changing directions of many international figures.

* * *

Roque Cordero is the most important composer Panama has produced. In addition, Cordero has had an international career and has been widely recognized as a leading Latin American composer of the century. Since 1972 he has taught at Illinois State University, where he is currently an emeritus professor. These few biographical facts need to be kept in mind to understand fully the impact of Cordero's background on his music.

Cordero's Panamanian origins are already reflected in such early works as the *Sonatina rítmica* (1943) and still are a powerful influence on his Fourth Symphony ("Panamanian") (1986). The impact of Afro-American syncopations and the rhythmic peculiarities of such native Panamanian dances as the cumbia give Cordero's music a strong rhythmic thrust and energetic personality. Regardless of the complex harmonic and structural features of a work, one finds rhythmic continuities which help shape the listener's awareness of form. Accordingly, sections are highlighted and articulated by incisive rhythmic profiles and strong melodic gestures.

In 1943 Cordero came to the United States to study with Ernst Krenek, the distinguished disciple of Arnold Schoenberg. The extreme chromaticism of the *Sonatina rítmica* for piano would soon develop into full serialism, but a serialism always affirming expressive cantabile. Thus melodic ideas and phrases are inspired by musical rather than cerebral considerations. This emphasis on musical comprehensibility and elegance is one of the hallmarks of Cordero's style.

One of the major works of this early exploration of serialism is the *Sonatina* for violin and piano. Cordero showed the Sonatina to Edgar Varèse, who found it a refreshing example of serial technique, especially at a time when Varèse felt that dodecaphonic procedures had reached a cul de sac. An even more important work of the period is the Second Symphony, which won the Caro de Boesi award at the Caracas Festival of Contemporary Music in 1957. This symphony demonstrated to Cordero's Latin American contemporaries that serialism and a heartfelt nationalism could be blended into a satisfying artistic integrity. In this regard, Cordero has been much influenced by the music of Alban Berg, whose serialism often recalls tonal shapes.

The Second Symphony also illustrates Cordero's concept of large-scale forms, forms grounded in the traditions of the past. Cordero prefers clearly designed formal plans with strong articulations and carefully planned climaxes. In many works the design is underpinned by a return of key thematic material, usually highlighted by a sustained climax. Thus the general impression is one of broad structures and solid development—all this probably a result of Cordero's admiration for Beethoven.

Cordero not only writes on a large scale, he also has explored the possibilities of solo instruments and chamber groups. A major contribution is the series of four string quartets, of which the most recent was premiered in 1987. Although Cordero himself is not a pianist, he has written many compositions for this instrument, including the challenging *Sonata for Piano*. Also worthy of mention are the five *Soliloquios* for solo instruments written for different faculty of Illinois State University. Each is either in two or three movements and is inspired by the virtuosic capabilities of the performer, as in the most recent of the set for string bass.

Like many composers of our day, Cordero is deeply moved by human issues and has written compositions which reflect his concerns. The most imposing of these is the *Cantata para la paz*, which grows out of Cordero's sense of the need for world peace. The Fourth Symphony ("Panamanian"), premiered in 1987 at a special festival at Illinois State University in honor of the composer's 70th birthday, is similarly grand in conception. It is not only a nostalgic testament to his native country, as mirrored in the folkloric element, but also a tribute to the nobility of all mankind, as symbolized in the frequent quotations of the old Latin hymn, "Te Deum laudamus".

Through his writing and teaching, Cordero has been a stimulus to many younger composers. Like Alberto Ginastera, Cordero has explored the full range of modern techniques without losing his individuality. This means that there is consistency of style from the earliest to the most recent efforts allied with a constant exploration of new textures and ideas. Cordero's work as a composer, teacher and writer of influential articles is thus unified by his zeal as spokesman for the cause of Latin American music.

In summation, Cordero is neither a conservative nor avant-garde composer. As he himself says, he walks at his own pace, unconcerned with the changing fashions of style. In all his compositions he is identifiably Panamanian—well underscored by his characteristic signature, "Roque Cordero, Compositor Panameño".

—Enrique Alberto Arias

CORIGLIANO, John (Paul). American. Born in New York City, 16 February 1938. Educated at Columbia College, New York City (under Otto Luening), B.A., 1959; Manhattan School of Music, New York City (under Vittorio Giannini); privately with Paul Creston. Writer and programmer for radio station WQXR and music director for WBAI, 1959–64; rock music arranger for Kama Sutra and Mercury Records; commercial producer; assistant on CBS-TV "Young People's Concerts", 1961–72; music director, Morris Theatre, New Jersey, 1962–4; teacher of composition, College of Church Musicians, Washington, D.C., 1968–70; music faculty, Manhattan School of Music, since 1971; distinguished professor of music, Lehman College, City University of New York, since 1973; composer in residence, Chicago Symphony Orchestra, since 1986. Recipient: prize (for *Violin Sonata*), Festival of Two Worlds, Spoleto, Italy, 1964; Guggenheim Fellowship, 1968; Cine Golden Eagle Award (for *A Williamsburg Sampler*), 1974: Grammy and Academy award nominations (for *Altered States* soundtrack), 1981; British Film Institute Anthony Asquith Award (for *Revolution* soundtrack), 1985; Academy Institute Award, American Academy of Arts and Letters, 1989. Mailing address: c/o Michael Mace Associates, 315 West 57th Street, Suite 18E, New York, New York 10019, U.S.A.

Publisher: G. Schirmer Inc.

Symphonies/orchestral:

Tournaments Overture 1965; first performed Louisville, Kentucky, 11 January 1980. Recorded Louisville Records 771.

Elegy 1965; first performed San Francisco, 1 June 1966. Recorded CBC Enterprises SMCD 5050–2; Louisville Records 771.

Concerto for Piano and Orchestra (also arranged for piano—4 hands) 1968; first performed San Antonio, Texas, 7 April 1968. Recorded Mercury Golden Imports SRI 75118.

Gazebo Dances (also for concert band and for piano—4 hands) 1974; first performed Woodbury, New Jersey, 20 February 1981. Recorded Golden Crest Records ATH-5083.

Overture to the Imaginary Invalid (from *Gazebo Dances*) 1974.

Concerto for Oboe and Orchestra (also arranged for oboe and piano) 1975; first performed New York City, 9 November 1975. Recorded RCA ARL-1-2534; RCA AGL1-4926.

Aria (oboe, strings; fourth movement of *Concerto for Oboe*) 1975; first performed Connecticut, 6 January 1977.
Voyage for String Orchestra 1976; first performed Rockland County, New York, 22 April 1977.
Concerto for Clarinet and Orchestra 1977; first performed New York City, 6 December 1977. Recorded New World Records 7762-1-RC.
Pied Piper Fantasy (flute, orchestra) 1981; first performed Los Angeles, 4 February 1982. Recorded RCA 6602-2-RC.
Promenade Overture 1981; first performed Boston, 10 July 1981.
Ritual Dance (from the soundtrack *Altered States*) 1981.
Three Hallucinations (from the soundtrack *Altered States*) 1981; first performed Syracuse, New York, 22 January 1982.
Summer Fanfare 1982; first performed Miami, Florida, 21 June 1982.
Echoes of Forgotten Rites 1982.
Voyage for Flute and String Orchestra 1983; first performed London, 26 November 1983. Recorded RCA 6002–2-RC.
Fantasia on an Ostinato 1986; first performed New York City, 18 September 1986.
Campane di Ravello (celebration piece for Sir Georg Solti) 1987; first performed Chicago, 9 October 1987.

Chamber/instrumental:

Kaleidoscope (2 pianos) 1959; first performed Spoleto, Italy, 28 June 1961.
Sonata for Violin and Piano 1963; first performed Spoleto, Italy, 10 July 1964. Recorded CRI SD 215; Laurel Records LR-137; Newport Records.
Etude Fantasy (piano) 1976; first performed Washington, D.C., 9 October 1976.
Fantasia on an Ostinato (piano) 1985; first performed Fort Worth, Texas, 24 May 1985. Recorded Van Cliburn Foundation Recordings VCS 1186; Chandos (in preparation).
Aria (oboe, string quintet) 1985.
Scherzo (oboe, timpani, 3 percussion, harp, piano/celesta; expanded from 3rd movement of *Concerto for Oboe*) 1975.
Voyage for Flute and String Quintet 1988; first performed Grand Canyon, Arizona, 17 September 1988.

Vocal/choral:

Petit Fours (voice, piano; Herrick, Nash, Bertrand, Coleridge) 1959.
Fern Hill (4-part mixed chorus, mezzo-soprano, orchestra or piano; or string orchestra, piano, optional harp; first part of *A Dylan Thomas Trilogy*) 1960–1; first performed New York City, 29 December 1961.
What I Expected Was . . . (4-part mixed chorus, 4 trumpets, 2 horns, 2 trombones, tuba, timpani, 2 percussion) 1962; first performed Tanglewood, Massachusetts, 16 August 1962.
The Cloisters (voice, orchestra; or voice, piano; Hoffman) 1965; first performed Washington, D.C., 2 May 1976; piano version first performed New York City, 15 November 1965. Recorded New World Records NW-327.
Christmas at the Cloisters (4-part mixed chorus, piano; Hoffman) 1966; broadcast 25 December, 1967.
Poem in October (tenor, orchestra; or tenor, flute, oboe, clarinet, string quartet, harpsichord/piano; second part of *A Dylan Thomas Trilogy*) 1970; first performed Washington, D.C., 24 April 1976. Recorded RCA ARL-1-2534; RCA AGL1-4926.
L'Invitation au voyage (unaccompanied 4-part mixed chorus; Baudelaire, Wilbur) 1971; first performed San Antonio, Texas, 13 May 1972.
Wedding Song (medium voice, melody instrument, organ/piano/guitar; Hoffman) 1971.
Creations (narrator, orchestra; Genesis) 1972, revised 1984; first performed Milwaukee, 3 October 1984.
A Black November Turkey (unaccompanied 4-part mixed chorus; Wilbur) 1972; first performed San Antonio, Texas, 20 January 1973.
Poem on His Birthday (baritone, 4-part mixed chorus, orchestra; third part of *A Dylan Thomas Trilogy*) 1976; first performed Washington, D.C., 24 April 1976.
Psalm No 8 (4-part mixed chorus, organ) 1976; first performed San Antonio, Texas, 18 October 1976. Recorded Telarc 5026.
Three Irish Folk Song Settings (voice, flute; Yeats, Colum, anon.) 1988; first performed New York City, 18 June 1988.

Opera:

A Figaro for Antonia 1986; first performed New York City, 19 December 1991.

Other:

The Naked Carmen (rock transcriptions of Bizet) 1970. Recorded Mercury SRM-1-604.
A Williamsburg Sampler (soundtrack) 1974.
Altered States (soundtrack to Ken Russell movie) 1980. Recorded RCA ABL1-3983.
Revolution (soundtrack to Hugh Hudson film) 1985.

PUBLICATIONS

On Corigliano: W.M. Hoffman, "JC on Cracking the Establishment", in *Village Voice*, 21 February 1976; E.W. Jeter, "The Study, Analysis and Performance of Selected Original Two-Piano Music of Contemporary American Composers" [includes analysis of *Kaleidoscope*], dissertation, Columbia University, 1978; D. Cariaga, "JC: Composer Who Writes to Order", in *Los Angeles Times*, 4 February 1979; A. Kozinn, "The 'Unfashionably Romantic' Music of JC", in *New York Times*, 27 April 1980; B. Holland, "Highbrow Music to Hum", in *New York Times Magazine*, 31 January 1982; G. Plaskin, "JC: Composing for a Living", in *M Magazine*, September 1984; R. Matthew-Walker, "Young American Composers: JC", in *Music and Musicians*, March 1986.

John Corigliano comments:

It has been fashionable of late for the artist to be misunderstood. I think it is the job of the composer to reach out to his audience with every means at his disposal . . . Communication of his most important ideas should be the primary goal.

* * *

John Corigliano is, above all else, a communicator. His work is accessible, unstrained, and with few of the pseudo-romantic agonies associated with self-conscious avant-gardism. He has a fine grasp of melody and rhythm and though much of his work since 1975 depends on a finely dramatised dissonance, he sustains a basically tonal orientation.

Brought up in a thoroughly musical environment—his mother was a gifted pianist, and his father the concertmaster of the New York Philharmonic—Corigliano's first professional involvement with music was a programmer for the New York broadcasting station WQXR. From there, he became an associate producer on CBS-TV's strongly influential "Young People's Concerts".

He first came to attention as a composer, interestingly enough, in his ancestral country. His piano duet *Kaleidoscope* was performed to great acclaim at the 1961 Festival of Two Worlds in Spoleto, Italy. Three years later, Corigliano was to win the Spoleto Festival Competition for the Creative Arts with his vigorously sardonic *Sonata for Violin and Piano*. It is a work which, though palpably "early" in its occasional naivety, nonetheless establishes the very American, "clean"-lined sound—the term is the composer's own—which allies Corigliano to native American composers like Copland, Harris and Bernstein, rather than to the murky chromaticism that descended on European music after Brahms and Wagner and led inexorably to Schoenberg. Corigliano's need for dramatic—sometimes melodramatic effect—has led him just as inexorably to dabble in serialist methods—but these are largely used as estrangement effects and in later years, in such pieces as his remarkable score for Ken Russell's science-fiction shocker *Altered States*, he devised more satisfyingly integral methods of producing such effects.

The 1968 Piano Concerto is perhaps the culmination of Corigliano's earlier style. Tonal, but by no means orthodoxly so, it counterpoises and gradually synthesises two intriguingly different themes. The first is an aggressive tattoo of three notes, the second a more lyrical theme which slowly metamorphoses into a more angular rhythm; Corigliano's fine rhythmic sense is particularly evident in the interplay of piano and orchestra.

His skill as a composer of vocal work was evident in his choral adaptation of Baudelaire's drug-inspired *L'Invitation au voyage*, a work he has subsequently arranged for orchestra and for flute and orchestra. This work may be seen as a foretaste of some of the ideas explored in the *Altered States* score. Chief among these is an almost obsessive concern for new and distinctive sonorities and for extreme dynamics.

In the mid 1970s, Corigliano began to compose works which were conceived not linearly, but as specific *Gestalts*, determined or conditioned by the specific timbre of the instrument—the virtuosic Clarinet Concerto from 1977 is the first fully developed expression of this method—and the internal configuration of the piece; he thus abandoned the more conventionally generic work he had been doing hitherto. The Clarinet Concerto largely abandons sonata form in favour of an "architectural" concept most clearly realised in his distribution of instruments throughout the concert hall in the closing "Antiphonal toccata" (a movement that underscores his continuing interest in the procedures of early music and similar in intention to his *Promenade Overture* where the orchestral players reverse the ending of Haydn's "Farewell" Symphony and walk on stage already playing).

The Clarinet Concerto is a work of staggering virtuosity, demanding the utmost discipline from the soloist, but it is not without humour. Corgliano's lighter side was demonstrated in his setting of *A Black November Turkey*, by Richard Wilbur, and in the opening passages of the 1975 Oboe Concerto, which includes a parody of the oboe's role in tuning the orchestra to its own A natural. There is a strong hint of Corigliano's self-conception in the 1981 *Pied Piper Fantasy* for flute and orchestra, with its implication of movement; the orchestra are the children—not the rats!—tempted away by the beguilements of the flute.

Corigliano briefly worked for a rock label and acquired an interest in studio effects, electronics such as the Moog synthesizer and sonority as a fundamental element in music. In 1970, he used the Moog in a rock transcription of *Carmen*, one of the more successful and satisfying tranformations wrought on the too-pliant body of Bizet's heroine. Corigliano is currently working on an operatic trilogy that re-examines Figaro—Beaumarchais's Figaro, rather than Mozart's. It continues the line established in the massive *Dylan Thomas Trilogy*, which was written over a 15-year period and encapsulates most of Corigliano's concerns and obsessions.

One can almost hear the sniffs of disdain at headlines such as "John Corigliano: Composer Who Writes to Order", which appeared in the *Los Angeles Times*. The fact is that Corigliano makes no hard and fast distinctions between serious and popular music (it is all serious and all popular); commissions represent specific conceptual challenges, and it is arguable that his finest work since the Clarinet Concerto and the Dylan Thomas symphony is the score for Russell's *Altered States*. The music is most remarkable for its virtual abandonment of harmony as a structural principle. It is a haunting, threatening score, built up in great blocks of pure sound, using an orchestra augmented with heavy percussion and two pianos retuned in quarter tones; it features daring microtonal passages and agitated shifts which echo the remarkable piano *Etude Fantasy* and *Fantasia on an Ostinato*; the latter piece again reflects Corigliano's interest in heightened states of awareness: hypnosis, intoxication, reverie.

Corigliano is a true original. Those who hear traces of Bartók or Beethoven or Mozart in his work are only tripping across false or satirical clues, or else conscious manipulations of tradition (as in the *Fantasia*). He is an original.

—Eleanor Caldwell

COWIE, Edward. British; Australian nationality since 1988. Born in Birmingham, 17 August 1943. Educated at University of London, B.Ed., 1964; Trinity College of Music, London, L.T.C.L., 1968; University of Southampton, B.Mus., 1970, D.Mus., 1979; University of Lancaster, Ph.D., 1983; teachers include Witold Lutoslawski, Peter Racine Fricker and Alexander Goehr. Married Stephanie McGrath in 1986; 2 children and 3 step-children. Senior lecturer, University of Lancaster, 1974–83; visiting professor, University of Kassel, Germany, 1979; professor of creative arts, University of Wollongong, New South Wales, Australia, 1983–89; professor of creative arts, James Cook University, Queensland, Australia, 1989–90; artistic director and professor of arts fusion, Australian Arts Fusion Centre, Brisbane, Queensland, Australia, since 1991. Painter—over 40 individual exhibitions since 1975, works in international museums and private collections; made television programmes on Edward Lear (Granada, 1978), own work (BBC North, 1979), Leonardo da Vinci (BBC, 1985); delivered the Gertrude Langer Memorial Lecture, Brisbane, Queensland 1987; conductor: Royal Liverpool Philharmonic Orchestra,

Philomusica of London, BBC Singers, ABC Symphony Orchestras in Sydney, Adelaide, Tasmania, Queensland, Seymour Group and Australia Ensemble. Recipient: Radcliffe International Composers' Prize, 1970; Gulbenkian Dance Award, Royal Ballet, 1971; Chopin Fellowship, Warsaw, Poland, 1971; Granda Composer in Residence, RLPO, United Kingdom, 1983–86. Mailing address: c/o Schott & Co., 48 Great Marlborough Street, London W.1., England.

Publisher: Schott & Co.

Symphonies/orchestral:

Moon, Sea and Stars 1974; first performed London, 1974.
Leviathan 1975; first performed London, 1975.
Clarinet Concerto 1975; first performed Manchester, 1976.
Columbine 1976; first performed Cheltenham, Gloucestershire, 1978.
Piano Concerto 1977; first performed London, 1977.
Concerto for Orchestra 1981; first performed Liverpool, 1983.
Symphony No. 1 "American" 1982; first performed Liverpool, 1984.
Leonardo (strings) 1982; first performed London, 1983.
Harp Concerto (strings) 1983; first performed Newcastle-upon-Tyne, 1984.
Choral Symphony 1983; first performed Leeds, 1984.
Atlas for Orchestra 1984; first performed Liverpool, 1986.
15-Minute Australia (for youth orchestra) 1985; first performed Liverpool, 1986.

Chamber/instrumental:

Cathedral Music for Brass 1976; first performed Manchester, 1977.
String Quartet No 2 1976; first performed Durham, 1977.
Falls of Clyde (2 pianos) 1976; first performed London, 1977.
Harlequin (solo harp) 1977; first performed Bradford, Yorkshire, 1980.
Commedia Lazzis (solo guitar) 1977; first performed London, 1977.
String Quartet No 3 1980; first performed Adelaide, 1984.
String Quartet No 4 1981; first performed Frankfurt, 1986.
Kelly-Nolan-Kelly (solo clarinet) 1981; first performed London, 1981.
Cartoon Music (percussion, keyboard, violin, cello) 1984; first performed Liverpool, 1986.
Sonata (piano) 1985; first performed London, 1987.

Vocal/choral:

Dungeness Choruses (SSSAAATTTBBB) 1968; first performed Folkestone, Kent, 1969.
Magdelena's World (soprano, piano) 1969; first performed London, 1971.
Gesangbuch (14 solo instruments, 24 solo voices; also unaccompanied version) 1971; first performed Brighton, 1975; unaccompanied version first performed London, 1978.
A Charm of Finches (soprano, 3 flutes) 1974; first performed Bath, 1975.
Brighella's World (baritone, piano) 1981; first performed Dartington, 1981.
Missa Brevis (SATB, organ) 1982; first performed Liverpool, 1984.
Avium Concentus (SSSAAATTTBBB) 1988; first performed London, 1990.

Opera:

Commedia 1978; first performed Kassel, Germany, 1979.

PUBLICATIONS

By Cowie: Articles in *The Listener*, *Music and Musicians*, *Art Monthly*, *Art International*, *Art Education*, *Australia*, *Composer Magazine*.

On Cowie: Anthony Burton, "People, Places and Music", in *The Listener*, June 1979; 11 television films on EC's work.

Edward Cowie comments:

My music has enjoyed mixed reaction from the critical press. In general, critics have described my music as "complex-confused-derivative-highly original-colourful-masterly-dull-formally amorphous etc . . . " The music has always arisen as a result of inspiration from observations of nature, the works of other Artists (especially painters), and from the nature of form itself. I have always believed that all of the arts languages are derived from central theories of form. As a result, my music does sometimes sound unpredictable and without clear formal direction. If this is an impression gained from some critics, it is certainly not the intention of my own way of forming musical compositions.

I continue to assume that listeners to my music will love the "works" of nature, and that they will find in the sound of my works, "echoes" from the world around us. I am unashamedly equally interested in tonality and atonality, and still believe that a "line-point-block" approach to composition will create melody and harmony without regard for avant-garde fashion, or the preconceptions of inhibited individuals. In recent times my music has become more introspective, and probably much tighter in form. I am now interested in form in its own right, and more and more pieces are composed through a contemplation of the formulation of "information" and perception through sound.

I am very much concerned with the relationships of my paintings with my music while also retaining a deep regard for the forces of nature upon my imagination. I must still say that my music is for those who love the sensation, structure and SENSE of nature, and that an individual who denies the possibility of filtering the structure of the living world through a compositional process will remain outside the field of intellectual and sensual capture which I hope my music offers. Walking in spring woods with a well-known critic in 1979, that critic was annoyed at my constant stopping to draw and record the landscape and the things that moved through it. "I simply like to walk", he said. Maybe we rush through life with so much preconceived information about art history that we cannot all yet see the wood for the leaves. Better to wish to see both, and in music, to be able to accept the dimensions of a fantasy which seeks to encapsulate existence through the order of the natural world.

* * *

If Edward Cowie's music has not generally been favoured by the musical and critical establishment, that is because he has stubbornly refused to accept certain tacit prescriptions (and restrictions) regarding the way a "career" is shaped and a consistent body of work developed. Cowie's career has been an echo of E.M. Forster's plaint that critics are only interested in "development"—the logical and sequential refinement of a personal voice—rather than in "works". Read globally as an oeuvre, Cowie's output can seem chaotic and indefinable; taken work by work, it is clear that he has a fine musical imagination backed up by strong conviction and emotion. Nonetheless, critics have obstinately refused to listen to him work by work, still looking for a underlying unity that Cowie probably does not pursue. In recent years, he has taken Australian citizenship, and makes his home there as professor of art fusion (a decidedly unEnglish chair) at Brisbane.

Cowie is attracted by universal intellects such as Leonardo or Goethe. He looks to them less for any totalising system than as a permission to be eclectic. In addition to his music, Cowie is a very skilful painter and poet, who has generally preferred to write his own texts. His painting, which veers toward a kind of abstract impressionism, deeply influenced by the natural world, betrays all the characteristics of his music, which is open in form, obeys no logic other than Cowie's immediate expressive needs, and is often more pictorial than plastic.

There is now no absolute stricture against blending tonal and serial procedures in a single piece or in successive pieces. What disturbs many critics, though, is Cowie's naturalistic attraction to "found" sounds, handled not in the aggressive, transformative manner of *musique concrète* but inwardly and affectionately. Like Messiaen (though there the analogy stops), Cowie has been much attracted by bird song, which he has used the in works as different as *A Charm of Finches*, one of his best known pieces, and the more recent choral *Avium Concentus*. But whereas Messiaen patiently transcribes bird song as a source of basic harmonic and melodic material with an inbuilt spiritual dimension, Cowie, who is a good ornithologist, nevertheless prefers to confront that spirituality directly and pragmatically. There is nothing over-literal in his work.

He is a fine pianist, with a good grasp of instrumental colours. The String Quartets are appealingly structured and not too insistently argued. The two-piano tone poem *Falls of Clyde* is a good example of his response to the natural scene, while *Kelly-Nolan-Kelly*, inspired by the Australian painter Sir Sidney Nolan's series-portraits of the famous bandit, is intriguingly offbeat. Cowie's orchestral writing lacks a certain edge, but his concertos have powerful and very moving passages.

—Eleanor Caldwell

CRESSWELL, Lyell (Richard). New Zealander. Born in Wellington, 13 October 1944. Educated at Victoria University of Wellington, 1965–8, B.Mus.; Canadian Commonwealth Scholarship, University of Toronto, 1969–70, Mus.M.; University of Aberdeen, 1972–4, Ph.D.; Dutch Government Bursary, Institute of Sonology, State University of Utrecht, 1974–5. Married Catherine Mawson, 4 January 1972. Music organiser, Chapter Arts Centre, Cardiff, 1978–80; visiting lecturer, universities of Auckland, Wellington, Otago and Canterbury, 1979; Forman Fellow in Composition, University of Edinburgh, 1980–2; work in computers, Massachusetts Institute of Technology, Cambridge, Massachusetts, 1982; Cramb Fellow in Composition, University of Glasgow, 1982–5; visiting lecturer, universities of Auckland and Wellington, 1983; featured composer, Musica Nova Festival, Glasgow, 1984; featured composer, BBC Scottish Symphony Orchestra tour to Poland, 1984; featured composer, Sonorities Festival of Twentieth-Century Music, Belfast, 1985; visiting lecturer, University of Wellington, 1987; featured composer, BBC Scottish Symphony Orchestra tour of Canada, 1988; guest of Festival of Filipino and Asian Music, Manila, 1988. Freelance composer, resident in Edinburgh. Recipient: BBC Young Composers Forum, 1973; Ian Whyte Award, Scottish National Orchestra, 1978; Australasian Performing Rights Association Silver Scroll, for services to New Zealand Music, 1979; *Wa*, *Salm* and *Concerto for Cello and Orchestra* selected as outstanding works, UNESCO International Rostrum of Composers, 1979, 1981, 1988; Prix du Public (courts métrages), Festival International de Musique de Besançon et de Franche-Comte, France, 1986. Mailing address: 4 Leslie Place, Edinburgh EH4 1NQ, Scotland.

Publisher: c/o Scottish Music Information Centre.

Symphonies/orchestral:

Concerto for Violin and Orchestra 1970.
Music for Strings with [2] Horns 1974.
Drones (harp, strings) 1975.
Salm 1978.
Manhattan Beach 1983.
Concerto for Cello and Orchestra 1984.
Speak for Us, Great Sea 1985.
The Magical Wooden Head (brass, percussion, timpani, strings) 1985.
A Modern Ecstasy (symphonic, with mezzo-soprano, baritone) 1986; first performed Glasgow, 1989.
The Pumpkin Massacre (chamber orchestra) 1987.
Passacaglia (small orchestra) 1989.

Chamber/instrumental:

String Quartet No 1 1970.
Aria (8 percussion, harp, clarinet, 5 violins, 5 cellos) 1973.
In Memory of . . . (cello) 1973.
In memoriam Norman Kirk (horn) 1974.
Music for Skinheads (3 percussion) 1975.
Wagner Is a Fink (brass) 1975.
Catharsis (alto saxophone) 1976.
Drones III (trombone, tape) 1976.
Opuscule (double bass, tape) 1977.
String Quartet No 2 1977.
The Sun Beat upon the Head of Jonah (guiro) 1977.
Paganini Variations (violin) 1977.
Drones IV (tuba, tape) 1977.
The Twin Peaked Mountain of Mars (cello) 1978.
Variations (violin) 1978.
Wa (trombone, percussion, tape) 1978.
Prayer for the Cure of a Sprained Back 1979.
Soliloquy on a Lambent Tailpiece (clarinet, violin, double bass) 1980.
The Silver Pipes of Ur (flute, oboe, clarinet, horn, basoon) 1981.
String Quartet No 3 1981.
MacPherson's Rant (clarinet/bass clarinet, horn, violin, double bass, piano) 1981.
O! 1982.
The Kauri Tree and the Whale 1983.
Octaves of Radiation (flute/piccolo, oboe, cor anglais clarinet, bass clarinet, bassoon, contrabassoon) 1983.

Violin Piece for Heather 1984.
The Grammar of Solitude (piano) 1985.
The Urim and the Thummin (organ) 1986.
Fragments of Existence Withdrawn from Time (trumpet, violin, synthesizer) 1987.

Vocal/choral:

Threnody for Mrs S. (speaker, flute, oboe, cor anglais, 2 clarinets, bassoon, horn, trumpet, trombone, harp, percussion) 1972.
A Feather of the Bird (tenor, bass clarinet, trumpet, violin, double bass percussion) 1973.
Drones II (unaccompanied SATB chorus) 1975.
O Let the Fire Burn (unaccompanied SATB chorus) 1981. Recorded Kiwi/Pacific Records.
The Alternative Soldier's Tale (narrator, clarinet, bassoon, trumpet, trombone, percussion, violin, double bass) 1981.
Seven Shaker Songs (baritone, piano) 1982.
Six Haiku (voice, piano), 1983.
The Fallen Dog (baritone, orchestra) 1984.
Our Day Begins at Midnight (narrator, piano, alto saxophone, tape) 1985.
To Aspro pano sto aspro (SATB unaccompanied) 1986.
White on White (a capella choir) 1986.

* * *

New Zealand expatriate Lyell Cresswell's work has been distinguished by a willingness to seek out material—both as subject matter and musical form—in unexpected and highly inventive corners. The composer made his first major impact with *Salm*, an instrumental work based on the style of Scottish Gaelic psalm singing found in the northwest of his adopted country.

That openness to musical influences from the folk or ethnic tradition has been a significant element in his work; even before *Salm*, he had invoked Ghanian, Moorish and Indian themes, among others. Scottish sources have continued to feed his work, but only as part of a wide-ranging and genuinely international sensibility, recognised as early as 1979 when he received a UNESCO award for *Wa* for trombone, percussion and tape.

Cresswell's early work included experimentation with aleatoric methods and electronic means, but has grown increasingly preoccupied with a dense and often complex textural exploration, and a constantly developing sense of structural refinement.

His *Concerto for Cello and Orchestra* is a prime example, with its sheets of sonorous string sounds set against tougher, more strident brass parts, through which wind the beautiful lyrical solo passages for the cello. As in most of his work, the balance between tension and climax is subtle and precise, as is the rigorous but uncontrived structure.

If Scotland has provided inspiration, so too have the history and legends of his native New Zealand, in pieces like *The Kauri Tree and the Whale* or *The Pumpkin Massacre*, an intense, dramatic chamber work based in unprogrammatic fashion on inter-tribal Maori skullduggery.

Wit and humour are a regular and refreshing part of Cresswell's work, both in his titles (*Wagner Is a Fink* for brass or the percussion piece *Music for Skinheads* both from 1975, a year in which he presumably felt particularly jocular) and within the music itself, as in his glosses on Sousa marches, but he has been most impressive when taking on large-scale and highly serious challenges.

The gripping *Our Day Begins at Midnight*, a musical recreation of one of neurologist Oliver Sachs bizarre case-histories, uses only a narrator, piano, saxophone and tape, but takes its scale from its imposing 50-minute duration and the universal resonances compacted within its thematic ambition. *Octaves of Radiation* for chamber forces is fiercely expressive and often highly dense, developing slowly over its length in characteristic fashion.

His ability to build convincing musical materials from fragments of ideas, imposing a remarkable cohesion as he goes, is well illustrated in *White on White* for a capella choir, a series of settings of poems by the Greek writer Jannis Ritsos. Arguably the most impressive of all his recent works, however, is the symphonic piece *A Modern Ecstacy*, which received its first complete performance in Glasgow in 1989.

The work, which incorporates text for mezzo-soprano and baritone, takes its title from *Macbeth*, and invokes such issues as creation, war and nuclear destruction within its dense, colourful, lucidly argued textures.

—Kenny Mathieson

CROSSE, Gordon. British/English. Born in Bury, Lancashire, 1 December 1937. Educated at University of Oxford (music history under Egon Wellesz), graduated 1961; further research (under Frank Harrison), Oxford, 1961–2; Accademia di Santa Cecilia, Rome (under Goffredo Petrassi), 1962. Tutor organiser to industry, Workers Educational Association, 1963; senior music tutor, extra-mural department, University of Birmingham, 1964–6; Haywood fellow in music, University of Birmingham, 1966–9; fellow in music, University of Essex, 1969–76; composer in residence, King's College, Cambridge, 1973; visiting professor in composition, University of California, 1977. Full-time composer since 1976. Recipient: Cobbett Medal, 1976. Mailing address: c/o Brants Cottage, Blackheath, Wenhaston, Halesworth, Suffolk IP19 1EX, England.

Publisher: Oxford University Press.

Symphonies/orchestral:

Elegy Op 1 (small orchestra) 1959–61; first performed Manchester, April 1962. Recorded OUP 203.
Concerto da Camera (Violin Concerto No 1) Op 6 (violin, winds, percussion) 1962; broadcast BBC, 1966; first concert performance London, 18 February 1968. Recorded HMV ASD2333/Argo ZRG 759.
Concerto for Chamber Orchestra Op 8 1962; first performed Budapest, 3 July 1968.
Symphonies Op 11 (chamber orchestra) 1964; first performed Birmingham, 13 February 1965.
Sinfonia concertante Op 13 1965; first performed Cheltenham, Gloucestershire, 13 February 1965; revised 1975–6 as *Symphony No 1*.
Ceremony Op 19 (cello, orchestra) 1966; first performed London, 4 August 1966.
Violin Concerto No 2 Op 26 1969; first performed Oxford, 29 January 1970.
Ouvert: Clos Op 27 (chamber orchestra) 1969; first performed London, 15 September 1969.

Some Marches on a Ground Op 28 1970; first performed Norwich, 14 October 1970.
Ariadne Op 31 (oboe, small orchestra) 1971–2; first performed Cheltenham, Gloucestershire, 11 July 1972. Recorded Argo ZRG 842.
The Demon of Adachigahara Op 21b (orchestral suite from the children's opera) 1973; first performed Snape, Suffolk, 22 July 1973.
Symphony No 2 Op 37 1974–5; first performed London, 27 May 1975.
Thel Op 38 (flute, 2 horns, strings/double string septet) 1974–6; first performed Aldeburgh, Suffolk, 27 June 1978.
Symphony No 2 Op 37 1975; first performed London, 27 May 1975.
Epiphany Variations Op 39 (double variations; also known as *Mag and Nunc*) 1975; first performed U.S.A., 1976.
Symphony No 1 Op 13a (revised version of *Sinfonia concertante*) 1976; first performed 28 March 1979. Recorded OUP 203.
Suite No 1 Op 29a (from *The Story of Vasco Op 29*) 1977; first performed London, 1 June 1977.
Play Ground Op 41 (ballet suite; full or reduced orchestration) 1978; first performed Manchester, 2 March 1978.
Dreamsongs Op 43 (extended orchestral version of chamber piece) 1979; first performed Edinburgh, 20 August 1979. Recorded OUP 203.
Concerto for Violoncello and Orchestra: In Memoriam Luigi Dallapiccola Op 44 1979; first performed Cheltenham, Gloucestershire, 7 July 1979.
Elegy and Scherzo alla Marcia Op 47a (string orchestra; adapted from *String Quartet Op 47*) 1980; first performed Snape, Suffolk, 24 June 1981.
Array (trumpet, strings) 1986; first performed London, 9 August 1986.
Quiet! (wind band) 1987; first performed Ryedale, 1987.

Chamber/instrumental:

Villanelles Op 2 (wind quintet, violin, cello) 1959, revised 1974; first performed Cheltenham, Gloucestershire, 1962; revised version first performed London, 23 November 1974.
Three Inventions Op 3 (flute, clarinet) 1959; first performed London, January 1966.
Canto Op 4 (flute, oboe, clarinet, bassoon, horn, trombone) 1961, revised 1963.
Carol Op 7 (flute, piano) 1962.
Studies for String Quartet (Set 1) Op 34a 1972–3; first performed Colchester, Essex, 1973.
Dreamsongs Op 35 (clarinet, oboe, bassoon, piano) 1973; first performed Aldeburgh, Suffolk, 1973.
Studies for String Quartet (Set 2) Op 34b 1977; first performed Brighton, Sussex, 1977.
Variations: Little Epiphany Op 39a (oboe, cello) 1977; first performed Cheltenham, Gloucestershire, 2 July 1977.
Wildboy Op 42 (concertante for clarinet and cimbalom, with flute, bassoon, horn, violin, viola, cello, double bass) 1978; first performed 13 February 1978.
String Quartet Op 47 1979; first performed London, 24 November 1980.
A Year and a Day Op 48a (clarinet) 1979; first performed London, 10 January 1980.
Trio (Rhymes and Reasons) Op 52 (clarinet, cello, piano) 1980; first performed Huntingdon, 17 November 1982.
Peace for Brass (4 trumpets, 4 trombones, horn, tuba) 1980; first performed King's Lynn, Norfolk, 29 July 1981.
Fear No More (oboe, oboe d'amore, cor anglais) 1980; first performed London, 5 October 1981.
A Wake (flute, clarinet, cello, piano) 1982; first performed Aldeburgh, Suffolk, 16 June 1982.
Watermusic (treble/descant/sopranino recorders, piano; also arranged for recorder, strings) 1982; first performed Glasgow, 3 December 1982.
Wavesongs (cello, piano) 1983; first performed Oxford, 30 October 1983.
Chime (2 B♭ trumpets, trombone, horn in F, tuba) 1983; first performed Cheltenham, Gloucestershire, July 1983.
Trio (violin, cello, piano) 1985; first performed London, 4 April 1986.
Oboe Quintet (oboe, string quartet) 1988; first performed Birmingham, 3 December 1988.

Vocal/choral:

Corpus Christi Carol Op 5 (soprano/tenor, clarinet, string quartet; 16th century) 1961; first performed London, 18 December 1964.
For the Unfallen Op 9 (tenor, horn, strings; Hill) 1963; first performed Liverpool, 17 September 1968.
Epitaph (unaccompanied SSATBB chorus; Raleigh) 1964.
Medieval French Songs Op 14 (soprano/tenor, clarinet, piano, percussion; or mezzo-soprano/baritone, piano) 1965, revised as *Three Songs to Medieval French Texts Op 14b* (medium voice, piano) 1965; first performed London, March 1969.
O Blessed Lord Op 15 (SATB chorus, cello) 1965; first performed Aldeburgh, Suffolk, 1965.
Two Christmas Songs (unaccompanied chorus; 15th and 11th centuries) 1965.
Changes: A Nocturnal Cycle Op 17 (solo voices, orchestra; Browne, Blake, Herrick, Hawes, Davenant, anon.) 1965–6; first performed Worcester, 1966. Recorded Argo ZRG 656.
A May Song Op 22 (unaccompanied SSATBB chorus; Herrick) 1967; first performed London, 4 October 1967.
Night Wind Op 21 (unaccompanied SATB voices; adapted from *The Demon of Adachigahara*) 1968.
The Covenant of the Rainbow Op 24 (chorus, organ, piano—4 hands; Chester Miracle) 1968; first performed Northampton, 20 September 1968. Recorded ABCD Cantus/Harmonia Mundi CAN 301.
The New World Op 25 (mezzo-soprano/baritone, piano; Hughes) 1969; first performed Worcester, 1972.
Memories of Morning: Night Op 30 (mezzo-soprano, orchestra; Rhys) 1971; first performed London, 8 December 1971.
Celebration (unison voices, mixed chorus, orchestra; Blake) 1972; first performed London, 16 September 1974.
The Cool Web Op 36 (soprano/tenor, piano; Stevie Smith, Graves) 1973–4; first performed Snape, Suffolk, 16 June 1975.
World Within Op 40 (narrator, mezzo-soprano, 10 instruments; E. Brontë) 1976; first performed London, 17 April 1977.
Verses in Memoriam David Munrow (counter-tenor, recorder, cello, harpsichord) 1979; first performed 8 September 1979.
Voices from the Tomb Op 36a (medium voice, piano; Stevie Smith) 1979; first performed London, 21 October 1980.
Harvest Songs Op 46 (double choir, junior choir, orchestra; Hughes) 1980; first performed Manchester, 18 July 1980.
Dreamcanon 1 Op 49 (alto, chorus, piano, electric piano, percussion; Raine) 1981; first performed London, 11 November 1981.

Wintersong Op 51 (2 alto, 2 tenors, 2 basses, optional percussion; Hughes) 1982; first performed London, 26 November 1982.
A Wake Again (2 counter-tenors, 2 recorders, cello, harpsichord) 1985; first performed New York City, 13 April 1986.
Armada Echoes (2 counter-tenors, tenor, 2 baritones, bass; Davis) 1988; first performed Plymouth, 10 July 1988.

Opera:

Purgatory Op 18 (Yeats) 1966; first performed Cheltenham, Gloucestershire, 7 July 1966.
The Grace of Todd Op 20 (Rudkin) 1967–8; first performed Aldeburgh, Suffolk, 7 June 1969.
The Story of Vasco Op 29 (Hughes, after Schehade) 1968–73; first performed London, 13 March 1974.
Potter Thompson Op 3 (Garner) 1972–3; first performed London, 9 January 1975.

Other:

Meet My Folks! Op 10 (speaker, children's voices, 8 instruments; Hughes) 1964; first performed Aldeburgh, Suffolk, 1964. Recorded HMV CLP 1893/CSD 1616/XLP 4000.
Rats Away! Op 12 (children's voices, 2 treble instruments, xylophone, chimes, percussion, bass instrument; anon.) 1964.
Ahmet the Woodseller Op 16 (unison voices, percussion, 8 instruments ad lib; Serraillier) 1964–5. Recorded HMV CLP 1893/CSD 1616/XLP 40001.
The Demon of Adachigahara Op 21 (narrator, children's voices, orchestra; Hughes) 1967.
The History of the Flood Op 23 (children's voices, harp; Heath-Stubbs) 1970.
Wheel of the World Op 32 (entertainment; Cowan, after Chaucer) 1969–72; first performed Aldeburgh, Suffolk, 5 June 1972.
Matthew Mark Luke and John (children's chorus, harp; from *Changes Op 17*) 1970; first performed London, 6 December 1970.
Holly from the Bongs Op 35 (nativity; Garner) 1973; first performed Manchester, 9 December 1974.
Wildboy Op 42a (ballet; orchestra) 1980; first performed Washington, D.C., 12 December 1980.
Young Apollo (ballet; orchestra) 1984; first performed London, 17 November 1984.
Gertrude's Prayer (voice, keyboard; setting of Kipling as test song for BP/Peter Pears Singing Competition) 1989.

PUBLICATIONS

By Crosse: "A Setting of W.B. Yeats", in *Opera*, 17, 1966; "My Second Violin Concerto", in *The Listener*, 83, 1970; "*Potter Thompson*—An Introduction", in *Opera*, 26, 1975.

On Crosse: J.C.G. Waterhouse, "The Music of GC", in *Musical Times*, 106, 1965; L. East, "The Problem of Communication—Two Solutions: Thea Musgrave and GC", in *British Music Now*, edited by Foreman, London, 1975.

* * *

Gordon Crosse's synthesis of musics past and present belongs to the same post-romantic recognition that "history" is a dark presence in the everyday world which we find in the work of poets such as Ted Hughes, Kathleen Raine and Geoffrey Hill, novelists such as Jean Rhys, Ian Serraillier and Emily Brontë. Cross has set all these writers—Hughes most frequently—with considerable success. There is in his work a sombreness and occasionally a thread of violence usually associated, as in these writers, with the irruption of some unresolved drama from the past, but there is also a raw and sometimes macabre humour similar to Hughes's. Crosse's musicological and literary interests usefully intertwine; what early in his career seemed no more than a rather shambolic eclecticism has developed, particularly since he gave up teaching in favour of full-time composition, into a powerfully personal style; though by no means innovative in terms of technical advance, it is nonetheless impressively self-consistent and always communicative.

In contrast to his slightly older near-contemporary Peter Davies (whose experiments with early music techniques echo Crosse's own), he was a relatively slow developer. After graduating, he went on to do two further years of research into 15th-century music, and went to Rome to study (as Davies had five years before) with Goffredo Petrassi. The veteran teacher saw immediately the limitations of a style based on Webernian cells and undigested medievalism and directed him toward an altogether "spikier" (Crosse's own word) development. This had an impact on the *Concerto da Camera* which acquired a violently contrastive scherzo and later became Crosse's first Violin Concerto. The full impact was slow to emerge, and there is a certain prolixity about many of the earlier scores, as in the punning *Grace of Todd* and the top-heavy *Story of Vasco*, neither of which built significantly on the operatic promise of *Purgatory*, though even here it is possible to see Crosse working out many of his more successful procedures in set-pieces.

Purgatory drew heavily on the example of Britten's *The Turn of the Screw*, and it is clear that Britten made an important impact on Crosse's sense of colour and timbre. (Crosse had been much associated with Aldeburgh.) The sense of transitoriness that pervades *Changes*, a good example of Crosse's dark-side sensibility, is very Brittenesque, as is the combination of high male voice, horn and strings in the setting of Geoffrey Hill's sardonically elegiac poem "For the Unfallen".

Set this against the slightly zany *Meet My Folks!* and *The Demon of Adachigahara* (both ostensibly for children, as *Changes* was for amateur forces) and it is clear that there is a surreal quality to some of Crosse's transitions of mood which is a function at this early stage of his apparent lack of certainty as an orchestrator and instrumental writer.

Though vocal and dramatic writing seem to be his great strengths, many of his procedures seem to have been worked out in a second Violin Concerto, a work replete with contrasts along almost every musical parameter and a significant sophistication of the language of the concertante of *Ariadne*. For full orchestra, rather than the chamber forces of the first Violin Concerto, it is a very powerful piece of writing, strongly resonant of medieval part-writing, remarkably unvirtuosic in the solo part, but nonetheless very dramatic and strongly argued.

Crosse's adaptation of Jean Rhys's *Wide Sargasso Sea* for mezzo-soprano and orchestra brings the Brontë connection (*Jane Eyre* this time) full circle. The story of the first Mrs Rochester and her descent into madness is his most explicit account of the past breaking through into the present. Premiered by Meriel Dickinson, *Memories of Morning: Night*, together with *World Within*, is arguably Crosse's most successful score; each has a beautifully balanced structure, lyrical and abstract by turns; there is, as the titles suggest, an underlying concern with opposition and an infolding of musical development which resists purely generic comparison; the same is true of *Dreamcanon 1*, which marks the high tide of Crosse's distinctively pre-modern brand of romanticism.

In the 1980s Crosse continued to write persuasive instrumental music. Here, as in the vocal writing, there is a now-seamless synthesis of early and modern idiom which elevates Crosse above self-conscious technical innovators and places him at the forefront of British music.

—Pamela Collins

CRUMB, George Henry. American. Born in Charleston, West Virginia, 24 October 1929. Educated at Mason College of Music, Charleston, B.M., 1950; University of Illinois, Champaign-Urbana (under Eugene Weigel), M.Mus., 1952; Hochschule für Musik, Berlin (under Boris Blacher), 1954–5; University of Michigan, Ann Arbor (under Ross Lee Finney), D.M.A., 1959. Married Elizabeth May Brown, 21 May 1949; 1 daughter and 2 sons. Teacher of theory and analysis, Hollins College, Virginia, 1958–9; instructor and assistant professor (piano and composition), University of Colorado, Boulder, 1958–65; creative associate/composer in residence, Buffalo Center for the Creative and Performing Arts, State University of New York, Buffalo, 1964–5; assistant professor, then full professor, 1965–83, and Annenberg Professor of the Humanities, since 1983, University of Pennsylvania, Philadelphia. Recipient: Elizabeth Croft fellowship for study, Berkshire Music Centre, 1955; Fulbright Scholarship, 1955–6; BMI student award, 1956; Rockefeller grant, 1964; National Institute of Arts and Letters grant, 1967; Guggenheim grant, 1967, 1973; Pulitzer Prize (for *Echoes of Time and the River*), 1968; UNESCO International Rostrum of Composers Award, 1971; Koussevitzky Recording Award, 1971; Fromm grant, 1973; member, National Institute of Arts and Letters, 1975; Ford grant, 1976; Prince Pierre de Monaco Gold Medal, 1989; Brandeis University Creative Arts Award; honorary member, Deutsche Akademie der Kunste; honorary member, International Cultural Society of Korea; 6 honorary degrees. Mailing address: 240 Kirk Lane, Media, Pennsylvania 19063, U.S.A.

Publisher: C.F. Peters, New York.

Symphonies/orchestral:

Poem 1946.
Gethsemane (small orchestra) 1947.
Prelude and Toccata 1951.
Trio (strings) 1982.
Diptych 1955.
Variazioni 1959; first performed Cincinnati, Ohio, 8 May 1959. Recorded Louisville LS 774.
Echoes of Time and the River: Four Processionals for Orchestra (Echoes II) 1967; first performed Chicago, 26 May 1967. Recorded Louisville S-711.
A Haunted Landscape 1984; first performed New York, 7 June, 1984. Recorded New World Records NW 326.

Chamber/instrumental:

Two Duos (flute, clarinet) ?1944.
Four Pieces (violin, piano) 1945.
Sonata (piano) 1945.
Sonata (violin, piano) 1949.
Three Pastoral Pieces (oboe, piano) 1952.
String Trio 1952.
Sonata (viola, piano) 1953.
String Quartet 1954.
Sonata (cello) 1955; first performed Ann Arbor, Michigan, 15 March 1957. Recorded Gasparo GS101; Desto DC-7169; Bis LP-65.
Five Pieces for Piano 1962; first performed Boulder, Colorado, 12 February 1963. Recorded Advance FGR-3; BIS LP-261.
Four Nocturnes (Night Music II) (violin, piano) 1964; first performed Buffalo, New York, 3 February 1965. Recorded Mainstream MS/5016; Columbia Odyssey Y35201; Music Broadcasting Society of New South Wales MBS 5.
Eleven Echoes of Autumn (Echoes I) (violin, alto flute, clarinet, piano) 1965; first performed Brunswick, Maine, 10 August, 1966. Recorded CRI S-233; Music Broadcasting Society of New South Wales MBS 5.
Black Angels (Thirteen Images from the Dark Land) (electric string quartet) 1970; first performed Ann Arbor, Michigan, 23 October 1970. Recorded CRI SD283; Turnabout 34610; Vox SVBS-5306; Philips 6500 881.
Vox Balaenae (for three masked players; electric flute, electric cello, amplified piano) 1971; first performed Washington, D.C., 17 March, 1972. Recorded Columbia Masterworks M 32739; Cameo Classics GOCLP 9018 (D).
Makrokosmos, Volume I (Twelve Fantasy-Pieces After the Zodiac for Amplified Piano) 1972; first performed Colorado Springs, Colorado, 8 February 1973. Recorded Nonesuch H-71293; Attacca Babel d527-2.
Makrokosmos, Volume II (Twelve Fantasy-Pieces After the Zodiac for Amplified Piano) 1973; first performed New York, 12 November 1974; first performance of volumes I and II together, Wichita, Kansas, 4 February 1975. Recorded Columbia Odyssey Y 34135; Attacca Babel d527–2.
Music for a Summer Evening (Makrokosmos III) (2 amplified pianos, 2 percussionists) 1974 first performed Swarthmore, Pennsylvania, 30 March 1974. Recorded Nonesuch H-71311; Bis LP-262; AMU Records ETST 038.
Dream Sequence (Images II) (violin, cello, piano, percussion, offstage glass harmonica) 1976; first performed Brunswick, Maine, 17 October, 1976. Recorded Columbia Odyssey Y 35201; Merlin Records, forthcoming.
Celestial Mechanics (Makrokosmos IV) (amplified piano—4 hands) 1979; first performed New York City, 18 November 1979; first performance of complete *Makrokosmos* cycle Buffalo, New York, 12 June 1980.
A Little Suite for Christmas A.D. 1979 (piano) 1980; first performed Washington, D.C., 14 December 1980. Recorded Bridge BDG 2007.
Gnomic Variations (piano) 1981; first performed Washington, D.C., 12 December 1982. Recorded Orion ORS 84473.
Pastoral Drone (organ) 1982; first performed San Francisco, 27 June 1984.
Processional (piano) 1983; first performed Tanglewood, Massachusetts, 26 July 1984.
An Idyll for the Misbegotten (amplified flute, 3 percussionists) 1986; first performed Toronto, November 1986.

Vocal/choral:

Four Songs (voice, clarinet, piano; English texts) ?1945.
Seven Songs (voice, piano; English texts) 1946.
Alleluja (unaccompanied chorus) 1948.
A Cycle of Greek Lyrics (voice, piano) ?1950.
Night Music I (soprano, piano/celeste, 2 percussion; Lorca) 1963, revised 1976; first performed Paris, 30 January 1964. Recorded CRI SD 218; Candide CE 31113; CBC SM 148.
Madrigals, Book I (soprano, double bass, vibraphone; Lorca) 1965; first performed Washington, D.C., 11 March 1966. Recorded AR-Deutsche Grammophon 0654 085; Vox Turnabout TV-S 34523; Bis LP 261.
Madrigals, Book II (soprano, flute/piccolo/alto flute, percussion; Lorca) 1965; first performed Washington, D.C., 11 March 1966. Recorded AR-Deutsche Grammophon 0654 085, Vox Turnabout TV-S 34523; Bis LP 261.
Songs, Drones and Refrains of Death (baritone, electric guitar, electric contrabass, amplified piano/amplified harpsichord, 2 percussion) 1968; first performed Iowa City, 29 March 1969. Recorded Desto DC 7155.
Madrigals, Book III (soprano, harp, contrabass, percussion; Lorca) 1969; first performed Seattle, Washington, 6 March 1970. Recorded AR-Deutsche Grammophon 0654 085; Vox Turnabout TV-S 34523; Bis LP 261.
Madrigals, Book IV (soprano, flute/alto flute/piccolo, harp, contrabass, percussion) 1969; first performed Seattle, Washington, 6 March 1970. Recorded AR-Deutsche Grammophon 0654 085; Vox Turnabout TV-S 34523; Bis LP 261.
Night of the Four Moons (alto, alto flute/piccolo, banjo, electric cello, percussion; Lorca) 1969; first performed Springfield, Pennsylvania, 3 March 1970. Recorded Columbia Masterworks M 32739.
Ancient Voices of Children (soprano, boy soprano, oboe, mandolin, harp, electric piano/toy piano, 3 percussion; Lorca) 1970; first performed Washington, D.C., 31 October 1970; first performance of complete Lorca cycle, Oberlin, Ohio, 26 February 1972. Recorded Nonesuch H-71255; Melodiya (USSR), forthcoming.
Lux Aeterna (for five masked musicians; soprano, bass flute/soprano recorder, sitar, 2 percussion; Latin Requiem Mass) 1971; first performed Richmond, Virginia, 16 January 1972. Recorded Columbia Odyssey Y 35201.
Star-Child (soprano, antiphonal children's voices, male speaking choir, bell ringers, large orchestra; *Dies Irae/Massacre of the Innocents*) 1977; first performed New York, 5 May 1977.
Apparition (soprano, amplified piano; Whitman) 1979; first performed New York, 13 January 1981. Recorded Bridge BDG 2002.
The Sleeper (soprano, piano; Poe) 1984; first performed New York, 4 December 1984.

PUBLICATIONS

By Crumb: "Music: Does It Have a Future?", in *The Kenyon Review*, Summer 1980; "Percussion; The *Terra Nova* of Contemporary Music", in *Forum des Percussions*, Paris, 1986.

On Crumb: J.A. Alcarez, *GC—entrivista y comentarias*, Mexico City, 1977; D. Ott, "The Role of Texture and Timbre in the Music of GC", dissertation, University of Kentucky, 1983; Don Gillespie (editor), *GC: Profile of a Composer*, New York, 1985; Richard Dufallo, (interview) in *Trackings*, 1990.

George Crumb comments:

Music might be defined as a system of proportions in the service of a spiritual impulse. I believe that music surpasses even language in its power to mirror the innermost recesses of the human soul. I am optimistic about the future of music. I frequently hear our present period described as uncertain, confused, chaotic. Perhaps two million years ago the creatures of a planet in some remote galaxy faced a musical crisis similar to that which we earthly composers face today. Is it possible that those creatures have existed for two million years without *new* music? I doubt it.

* * *

George Crumb's standing as one of the most innovative and important composers in contemporary music has perhaps been clouded by the more eccentric aspects of that urge toward experiment, particularly in his ritualistic and semi-theatrical compositions of the 1970s. The composer's willingness to try new things inevitably meant that there would be failures, but they should not be allowed to obscure either the seriousness or merit of his best work.

His earliest published compositions, which included a *String Quartet* and a stringent *Sonata* for solo cello, reflected the influence of the more advanced developments in European music, including the work of Alban Berg, Anton Webern and Béla Bartók. One of his first orchestral compositions, the *Variazioni*, reflected his interest in serialism, but even then he was taking a distinctly personal view of the system.

Thereafter, he grew increasingly fascinated by the sonic and textural possibilities of unorthodox instruments and techniques, in a manner which placed him in a more direct lineage from Charles Ives. The *Five Pieces for Piano* first suggested this new direction in his work, but subsequent developments coincided with his discovery of the work of Spanish poet Frederic García Lorca.

To say that Lorca was an important influence on the composer hardly does justice to the relationship which Crumb formed with the work of the poet, who had been murdered by Nationalist soldiers in 1936, during the Spanish Civil War. Crumb saw his own artistic aims and need to constantly push forward the boundaries of his music reflected in Lorca's work, and drew both material and inspiration from it.

Night Music I set two of Lorca's poems amid a series of seven "nocturnes", the other five being instrumental, and emphasised Crumb's developing fascination with bizarre and unconventional percussive and timbral effects. The *Madrigals, Books I* and *II* also drew on settings of Lorca's poems, which required a mezzo-soprano to sing in a wide range of styles and vocal effects, accompanied by vibraphone and double bass in the first book, and percussion and flute in the second.

The late 1960s and early 1970s were a period of rich, but not always entirely successful, experiment for the composer, beginning with his Pulitzer Prize-winning *Echoes of Time and the River*, a philosophical but non-programmatic work which required some of the musicians to march across the stage while performing, in what Crumb called "processionals".

Lorca provided the source and inspiration for two of his best known compositions of the period, *Songs, Drones and Refrains of Death* and *Ancient Voices of Children*, both of which fully demonstrate the experimental bias of his work. *Black Angels*, a disturbing composition for amplified and augmented string quartet, was the composer's response to the horrors of the Vietnam War.

His work increasingly made unconventional and sometimes

untoward demands on the performers. Players must shout, chant or whistle; instruments like jew's harp or musical saw are employed, or non-musical objects are pressed into service for their sonic possibilities; instrumental and vocal sound is modified and distorted; and the ritualistic and theatrical elements, including the wearing of masks in *Lux Aeterna* and *Vox Balaenae*, are foregrounded.

As with his use of unconventional tonalities (including a fascination with the microtonal systems of Indian music), these unorthodox effects are harnessed in a fully integrated fashion within the music, rather than gratuitously employed for their novelty or shock value. Each effect has a carefully planned and highly specific role (sometimes inspired by the composer's fascination with numerology) within the unfolding piece in which it appears, and often one in which abstract sonorities are combined in a strangely lyrical, highly evocative manner.

Crumb's affiliation with Ives extends to a fondness for incorporating distorted snatches of other music within his compositions, from folk songs (including the hymn "Will There Be Any Stars in My Crown?" from his native West Virginia, which the pianist must whistle in *Makrokosmos II*) through to Schubert's *Death and the Maiden* and Saint-Saens's *Danse macabre* (both in *Black Angels*).

In *Star-Child*, Crumb's most ambitious large-scale score (so much so that it requires four conductors), the performers are placed in unorthodox configurations throughout the room, but the resulting parable of a journey from darkness into light is not his most memorable one.

Later works of note include the orchestral composition *A Haunted Landscape*, but his best known compositions are arguably the *Makrokosmos* (meaning "whole universe") series, consisting of *I* and *II* for amplified piano, *III* for two amplified pianos and percussion, and *IV* for amplified piano (four hands). They place extreme technical demands on both performers and instruments, but are among the most intriguing music written for piano in the post-war period.

—Kenny Mathieson

CURTIS-SMITH, Curtis O(tto) B(ismarck). American. Born in Walla Walla, Washington, 9 September 1941. Educated at Whitman College, Walla Walla, Washington (piano under David Burge), 1960–2; Northwestern University, Chicago (piano under Gui Mombaerts), 1962–5, B.Mus., M.Mus.; University of Illinois, Champagn-Urbana, 1965–6; studied composition (under Kenneth Gaburo and Bruno Maderna), Berkshire Music Center, Tanglewood, Massachusetts, 1966, 1972. Married Kathryn A. McCoy, 16 July 1977. Associate professor of music, 1968–76, and full professor, 1977–90, Western Michigan University, Kalamazoo; visiting professor, University of Michigan, 1976–7; concert pianist and recitalist. Recipient: Koussevitzky Prize (for *Comédie*), 1972; Gold Medal (for *Five Sonorous Inventions*), VII Concorso Internazionale de Composizione, 1974; Gold Medal (for *Rhapsodies*), Concorso Internazionale di Musica e Danza G.B. Viotti, 1975; Prix du Francis Salabert (for *Belle du Jour*), 1976; distinguished faculty scholar award, Western Michigan University, 1979; prizes for piano performance. Mailing address: 2412 Crest Drive, Kalamazoo, Michigan 49008, U.S.A.

Publishers: Editions Salabert; Elkan-Vogel; Mel Bay Productions.

Symphonies / orchestral:

Yu sareba (Rice Leaves) 1967–8.
Xanthie: Winter Pieces (chamber orchestra) 1974.
Bells (Belle du Jour) (piano, orchestra) 1974–5; first performed Kalamazoo, Michigan, 1975.
GAS! (The Great American Symphony) 1982; first performed Kalamazoo, Michigan, 1982.
Songs and Cantillations (guitar, orchestra) 1983; first performed Philadelphia, 1983.
Variations on Amazing Grace (arranged for large orchestra from piano original) 1983–4.
Chaconne à son gout (Chaconnes, Puns and Fantasies on Three Notes 1984–5; first performed Kalamazoo, Michigan, 1984.
Celebration 1985; first performed Detroit, 1985.
Float Wild Birds, Sleeping (Haiku settings) 1989.
Concerto for Piano Left-Hand and Orchestra 1990.
Concerto for Violin and Orchestra 1990.

Chamber / instrumental:

Flute Sonata 1963.
String Quartet No 1 1964.
String Quartet No 2 1965.
Sections (flute, cello, double bass) 1967.
Pianacaglia (piano) 1967.
Trajectories (piano) 1968.
Pièce du jour (piano) 1971.
Fanaffair for Fanny (9 trumpets, 4-track tape) 1971.
Fanfare for the Dark (9 instruments) 1972.
Mateus (flute, piano) 1972.
A Song of the Degrees (2 pianos, percussion) 1972–3.
Five Sonorous Inventions (violin, piano) 1973. Recorded CRI SD-346.
Rhapsodies (piano) 1973. Recorded CRI SD-345.
Suite in Four Movements (harpsichord) 1975.
Tristana Variations (piano) 1975–6.
Unisonics (alto saxophone, piano) 1976. Recorded CRI SD-388.
Three Pieces (harp) 1976.
Music for Handbells (10 performers) 1976–7. Recorded CRI SD-388.
Partita (flute, clarinet, piano, percussion, violin, viola, cello) 1976–7.
Ensembles / Solos (12 instruments) 1977; first performed Ann Arbor, Michigan, 1977.
Partita (flute, clarinet, piano, percussion, violin, viola, cello) 1977; first performed Boston, 1977.
Tonalities (clarinet, percussion) 1978; first performed Sioux Falls, South Dakota, 1978.
Gargoyles (organ) 1978.
Masquerades (organ) 1978; first performed Seattle, Washington, 1978. Recorded CRI SD-409.
Plays and Rimes (brass quintet) 1979.
Prelude and Blues (guitar) 1979.
Sundry Dances (flute, oboe, clarinet, bassoon, saxophone, trumpet, trombone, tuba, double bass) 1979–80.
Black and Blues (piano, brass quintet) 1980.

For Gatsby (Steinway #DG 1281, piano) 1980; first performed New York City, 1982.
The Barbershop String Quartet 1980; first performed Chicago, 1980.
Music for an Orangewench (guitar quartet) 1980–1.
GAGS! (The Great American Guitar Solo) 1982; first performed San Francisco, 1982.
The Sweetgrass Trio 1982; first performed New York City, 1982.
Ragmala (A Garland of Ragas) (guitar, string quartet) 1983.
Variations on Amazing Grace (organ) 1983.
More Southpaw Pitching (piano) 1984; first performed New York City, 1985.
Sardonic Sketches (woodwind quintet) 1986.
Five Pieces (piano, percussion) 1987; first performed Darmstadt, Germany, 1988.
Fantasy Pieces (violin, piano) 1987; first performed New York City, 1987.
Bagatelles (guitar) 1989; first performed Ashville, North Carolina.

Vocal/choral:

All Day I Hear (unaccompanied SATB choir; Joyce) 1965.
"Till Thousands Thee": A Secular Cantata Without (6 sopranos, 2 trumpets, percussion) 1969.
"Passant. Un. Nous passons. Deux. De notre somme passons. Trois" (19 voices, 9 instruments; Rilke, Joyce, Homer, others) 1970.
Canticum novum / Desideria (10 voices, 11 instruments) 1971.
Comédie (song cycle; Beckett, others) 1972; first performed Tanglewood, Massachusetts, 1972.
Invocation—Alap (solo voices, SATB choir; Raga Kedar) 1982.
Beastly Rhymes (unaccompanied SATB choir; Pacock, traditional) 1983–4; first performed New Jersey, 1984.
Chansons Innocentes (soprano, piano) 1986; first performed Grand Rapids, Michigan, 1987.
A Civil War Song Cycle (mezzo-soprano, piano) 1987; first performed Chicago, 1987.
The Shimmer of Evil (baritone, piano or chamber orchestra) 1987; first performed Fontana, 1989.
Songs of Theodore Roethke (soprano, piano) 1987–90.

Other:

Electronic Study / Gong Sounds (4-track tape) 1972.
Summerian Sunshine (musique concrète) 1973.

PUBLICATIONS

By Curtis-Smith: "Bowing the Piano Strings", in *Woodwind World, Brass and Percussion*, January 1976.

On Curtis-Smith: David Burge, "CC-S's *Rhapsodies*", in *Contemporary Keyboard*, 3 (5), 1977; David Cope, in *New Directions in Music*, William C. Brown, 1989.

Curtis O.B. Curtis-Smith comments:

Listeners often comment on the importance of *colour* and *humour* in my music. The colouristic aspect is probably best represented by the "piano-bowing" technique, which I first developed in 1972. This technique consists of threading long, loose bows made of monofilament fishing line—without the "wood"—underneath the piano strings, and "bowing" the selected strings. In the lowest register of the piano, a single pitch such as low A♭ is capable of producing, in addition to the fundamental, various partials up to and beyond the 64th harmonic. The resulting effects are often mistaken for electronic in origin, though they are in fact much richer and complex, and more difficult to control.

My underlying reason for using this technique was not merely to produce pretty sounds, but to bring the piano into a closer timbral proximity to other instruments, as in *Unisonics*, *Ensembles / Solos* and *Fantasy Pieces*. With the exception of the last piece, I have not used this technique since the late 1970s. Not wanting to repeat myself, I turned away from it, though in a general way, colouristic considerations have remained important in my music in terms of orchestration, etc. The piano-bowing technique has since been borrowed and used by other composers, such as Steven Scott and George Crumb.

Turning now to *humour*. This ranges from the gently humorous, as in "In dulci jubilo" from *Masquerades*, to the musically witty, as in some of *Float Wild Birds, Sleeping*, to the black humour of "Death Jig" in *Sundry Dances*, to the bitterly sarcastic, as in *The Great American Symphony (GAS!)*. Its playful surface notwithstanding, "Dido's Dance" (the last movement of *GAS!*) is psychologically complex. It is funny and fiendish at the same time. There are musical "jokes" but, like many practical jokes, they conceal sarcastic motives behind the laughing mask. Indeed, the mask is the most compelling metaphor here: like a circus clown concealed by his mask, apparently slap-happy on the surface, but revealing a disillusioned face beneath the slapstick. (Behind the comic mask smirks the Dies Irae!) The clown turns things topsy-turvy; "high" art becomes a joke (as in the sacrilegious mutations of the Purcell), while "low" art is canonized (as in the pop tunes). Thus, on one level the piece may be heard as mere entertainment, while one a deeper level it may (and should!) be heard as an ironic, bitter and even frightening commentary on the very tunes and styles it purports to trifle with.

* * *

Curtis O.B. Curtis-Smith first garnered widespread attention in American new music circles with his solo piano piece *Rhapsodies*, written for David Burge. *Rhapsodies* is characterized by a slowly evolving harmonic rhythm; the harmonies themselves frequently hint at more traditional tonal sonorities, but Curtis-Smith employs them in a highly individualistic manner. Within this larger harmonic framework in the first movement, individual notes in chords are frenetically reiterated, with rapidly fluctuating dynamics—the effect is a pianistic version of the heterophonic textures that preoccupy much of Curtis-Smith's chamber and orchestral music since then.

Rhapsodies is marked by its virtuosic handling of extended piano techniques; at a time when many composers allowed varying degrees of rhythmic and/or timbral indeterminacy in their notations for extended techniques, Curtis-Smith's scores were unusual for their highly precise specifications. The pianist is required to play upon the piano strings with picks, mallets, piano-tuner's mutes, a wine bottle (the composer recommends Mateus!) and "bows" made out of fishing line. This last technique, which produces eerily beautiful sustained tones, was invented in *Rhapsodies*; other composers such as George Crumb and Stephen Johnson have subsequently used bowed piano.

In chamber works from the 1970s such as *Rhapsodies, Unisonics*, and the *Five Sonorous Inventions*, Curtis-Smith reveals a talent for discovering new sonoroties and successfully integrating them into the musical rhetoric of his pieces. The saxophone multiphonics in *Unisonics* and the quadruple-stops performed on a violin with a flat bridge and a specially built mute (in the *Five Sonorous Inventions*) never appear to be gimmicks but rather to arise organically from the compositional issues addressed. In these three works, and in *Music for Handbells*, Curtis-Smith can now be seen as one of the most original American composers of his generation.

In the late 1970s, he began to introduce vernacular music into his compositions. At the same time, like many other composers throughout the world, his rhythmic vocabulary became—superficially at least—more simple; in other words, the underlying pulse was more readily perceptible. His works became less abstract, their forms often influenced by manneristic constructs (such as the different traditions and associations evoked by the organ in *Masquerades*—the Lutheran tradition reflected in the chorale-prelude textures of four of the movements; the composer's own association of the instrument with bagpipes and carousels in other movements) or stream-of-consciousness sorts of free musical association in which musical ideas unpredictably submerge and resurface. Having contact with the "two Bills from [the University of] Michigan", that is, William Albright and William Bolcom, no doubt played some role in Curtis-Smith's new musical concerns.

While more recent works continue to have forms that could be seen as stream-of-consciousness narratives, Curtis-Smith's use of American vernacular idioms reached its peak in his *GAS! (The Great American Symphony)*. The last movement of this tongue-in-cheek work is entitled "Dido's Dance" with the subtitle "Dido Dies (Irae)". In it, the American national anthem, the *Dies Irae*, Purcell's "Dido's Lament", heavy metal riffs and "I Got a Gal in Kalamazoo" (the work was composed for the Kalamazoo Symphony), among other identifiable fragments, are freely associated.

A sense of humour and playfulness emerges in the works from the late 1970s onward. This is evident not only aurally, but in drawings and instructions in the scores. The second movement of *GAS!* ends with the mysterious proclamation "The Chicken Speaks!" above the banjo part; Curtis-Smith's autograph manuscript is full of clip-art hands with index-fingers pointing to principal lines and important information, while bald eagles patriotically adorn the margins.

Curtis-Smith's recent music reflects a variety of musical influences, such as Indian classical music (*Invocation*), contemporary Japanese music (*Float Wild Birds*) and change-ringing (*Concerto for Piano Left-Hand and Orchestra*). But like his best-known works from the 1970s, his music still embraces slow large-scale harmonic rhythms and heterophonic textures.

—Christian Hertzog

D

DAVIES, (Sir) Peter Maxwell. British/English. Born in Salford, 8 September 1934. Educated at Leigh Grammar School; Royal Manchester College of Music, graduated 1952; Manchester University, Mus.B., 1956; studied in Rome with Goffredo Petrassi, 1957; Harkness Fellow, Princeton University, New Jersey (studied under Roger Sessions and Milton Babbitt), 1962–4. Head of music, Cirencester Grammer School, 1959–62; composer in residence, University of Adelaide, 1966; founder and co-director (with Harrison Birtwistle) of the contemporary chamber music ensemble, the Pierrot Players, 1967 (reformed as The Fires of London, 1970; artistic director to 1987). Moved to island of Hoy, Orkney, 1970; founder and artistic director, 1977, and president, from 1986, St Magnus Festival, Orkney; artistic director, Dartington Summer School of Music, 1979–84; associate composer/conductor, Scottish Chamber Orchestra, since 1985. President, Schools Music Association, since 1983, North of England Education Conference, 1985, Composer's Guild of Great Britain, since 1986, and National Federation of Music Societies, since 1989. Fellow, Royal Northern College of Music, 1978; honorary member, Royal Academy of Music, 1979; member, Accademica Filarmonica Romana, 1979; honorary member, Guildhall School of Music and Drama, 1981. Recipient; honorary DMus, University of Edinburgh, 1979; honorary LLD, University of Aberdeen, 1981; Commander of the British Empire, 1981; honorary DMus, University of Manchester, 1983; honorary DMus, University of Bristol, 1984; honorary DMus, Open University, 1986; honorary DLitt, University of Warwick, 1986; Knight Batchelor, 1987; L'officier dans l'Ordre des Arts et des Lettres (France), 1988. Address: c/o Mrs Judy Arnold, 50 Hogarth Road, London SW5 0PU, England.

Publishers: Boosey & Hawkes; Chester Music; Schott; Longman.

Symphonies/orchestral:

Prolation 1958; first performed Rome, July 1959.
First Fantasia on an In Nomine of John Taverner 1962; first performed London, 13 September 1962.
Sinfonia (chamber orchestra) 1962; first performed London, May 1962. Recorded Unicorn Kanchana 9026CD/DKP 9058.
Second Fantasia on John Taverner's In Nomine 1964; first performed London, 30 April 1965.
St Thomas Wake Foxtrot for Orchestra on a Pavan by John Bull 1969; first performed Dortmund, 2 June 1969. Recorded Louisville Orchestra Records LS 770.
Worldes Blis 1969; first performed London, 28 August 1969.
Suite: The Boy Friend (from the soundtrack to a Ken Russell film) 1971; first performed London, 11 December 1971. Recorded Collins Classics, in preparation.
Stone Litany—Runes from a House of the Dead (mezzo-soprano, orchestra) 1973; first performed Glasgow, 22 September 1973.
Symphony No 1 1976; first performed London, 2 February 1978. Recorded Decca Head 21.
Black Pentecost (baritone, mezzo-soprano, orchestra) 1979; first performed London, 11 May 1982.
Symphony No 2 1980; first performed Boston, 26 February 1981.
Sinfonia concertante (wind quintet, chamber orchestra) 1982; first performed London, 12 August 1983. Recorded Unicorn Kanchana UKCD 2022/DKP 9058.
Into the Labyrinth (tenor, chamber orchestra) 1983; first performed Kirkwall, Orkney, 22 June 1983. Recorded Unicorn Kanchana UKCD 2022/DKP 9038.
Sinfonietta accademica 1983; first performed Edinburgh, 6 October 1983. Recorded Unicorn Kanchana UKCD 2022/DKP 9038.
Symphony No 3 1984; first performed Manchester, 19 February 1985. Recorded BBC Records 560.
An Orkney Wedding, with Sunrise (bagpipes, orchestra) 1985; first performed Boston, 10 May 1985. Recorded Unicorn Kanchana DKP 9070.
Violin Concerto 1985; first performed Kirkwall, Orkney, 21 June 1986. Recorded CBS 42449.
Jimmack the Postie 1986; first performed Kirkwall, Orkney, 22 June 1986.
Strathclyde Concerto No 1 for Oboe and Orchestra 1987; first performed Glasgow, 29 April 1987. Recorded Unicorn Kanchana 9085.
Strathclyde Concerto No 2 for Cello and Orchestra 1988; first performed Glasgow, 1 February 1989. Recorded Unicorn Kanchana 9085.
Concerto for Trumpet and Orchestra 1988; first performed Hiroshima, 21 September 1988. Recorded Philips, in preparation.
Symphony No 4 1989; first performed London, 10 September 1989.
Strathclyde Concerto No 3 for Horn, Trumpet and Orchestra 1989; first performed Glasgow, 19 January 1990.
Strathclyde Concerto No 4 for Clarinet and Orchestra 1990.

Chamber/instrumental:

Quartet Movement (string quartet) 1952; first performed London, 23 May 1983.
Sonata for Trumpet and Piano 1955; first performed Manchester, 1955. Recorded Nonesuch H71275, BIS 287 & Crystal CD 665.
Five Pieces for Piano 1956; first performed Liverpool, December 1956.
Stedman Doubles (clarinet/percussion—1 player) 1956, revised 1968; first performed Cardiff, 23 April 1968.
Clarinet Sonata (clarinet, piano) 1956; first performed Darmstadt, 20 July 1957.
Alma redemptoris mater (flute, oboe, 2 clarinets, bassoon, horn) 1957; first performed Dartington, Devon, 7 August 1957.
St Michael 1957.
Sextet (flute, clarinet, harpsichord, percussion, viola, cello) 1958, revised as *Septet* with addition of guitar, 1972.
Ricercar and Doubles on "To Many a Well" (flute, oboe,

clarinet, bassoon, horn, harpsichord, viola, cello) 1959; first performed Dartmouth, New Hampshire, 1959.

String Quartet 1961; first performed London, November 1961.

Shakespeare Music (alto flute, oboe, clarinet, bass clarinet, bassoon, horn, trombone, guitar, viola, double bass, percussion) 1964; first performed London, 8 December 1964.

Five Little Piano Pieces 1964; first performed Wardour Castle, Wiltshire, August 1964.

Seven in Nomine (flute, oboe, clarinet, bassoon, horn, harp, 2 violins, viola, cello) 1965; first performed London, 3 December 1965. Recorded Collins Classics, in preparation.

Antechrist (piccolo, bass clarinet, three percussionists, violin, cello) 1967; first performed London, 30 May 1967.

Hymnos (clarinet, piano) 1967; first performed Cheltenham, Gloucestershire, 1967.

Missa super L'Homme Armé (parody mass for speaker/singer, 6 players) 1968; first performed London, 22 April 1969.

Stedman Caters (flute/piccolo, clarinet, harpsichord, viola, cello, percussion) 1968; first performed London, 30 May 1968.

Purcell: Fantasia and Two Pavans (realisations for piccolo/flute, clarinet, harpsichord/out of tune upright piano, violin, cello, percussion) 1968; first performed London, 13 January 1969. Recorded Unicorn Kanchana KP 8005.

Solita (flute, optional musical box) 1969; first performed York, 25 January 1969.

Gabrieli: Canzona (realisation for 10 players) 1969.

Eram quasi agnus (seven wind, handbells, harp) 1969; first performed London, 19 June 1969.

Sub tuam protectionem (piano) 1969; first performed London, 13 January 1970.

Ut re mi (piano) 1970; first performed London, 19 January 1971.

Suite: The Devils (11 players, plus soprano obbligato: from the soundtrack to a Ken Russell film) 1971; first performed London, 11 December 1971.

Turris campanarum sonantium (percussion solo) 1971. Recorded L'Oiseau Lyre DSLO 1.

Ara coeli: Lullaby for Ilian Rainbow (guitar) 1972; first performed London, 18 September 1972. Recorded L'Oiseau-Lyre DSLO 3.

Fool's Fanfare (male speaker 2 trumpets, 2 trombones, ukelele/mandolin, 2 percussionists) 1972; first performed London, 23 April 1972.

Canon in memoriam Igor Stravinsky (flute, clarinet, harp, string quartet) 1972; first performed London, 17 June 1972; broadcast 6 April, 1972.

Dunstable: Veni sancte—veni creator spiritus (alto flute, A clarinet, glockenspiel, harpsichord/piano, viola, cello) 1972; first performed London, 6 May 1972. Recorded Unicorn Kanchana KP 8005.

Hymn to St Magnus (flute, A clarinet, piano/harpsichord/celeste, viola, cello, percussion) 1972; first performed London, 13 October 1972.

Renaissance Scottish Dances (flute, clarinet, guitar, violin, cello, percussion) 1973; first performed Dartington, Devon, 29 July 1973. Recorded Unicorn Kanchana DKP 9070.

Si quis diligit Me (alto flute, clarinet, celeste, crotales, viola, cello) 1973; first performed Dartington, Devon, 29 July 1973. Recorded Unicorn Kanchana KP 8005.

Purcell: Fantasia upon One Note (alto, basset horn, harpsichord, percussion, violin, cello) 1973; first performed London, 24 July 1973. Recorded Unicorn Kanchana KP 8005.

All Sons of Adam (alto, flute, clarinet, celeste, guitar, marimba, viola, cello) 1974; first performed London, 20 February 1974. Recorded Unicorn Kanchana KP 8005.

Psalm 124 (flute, bass clarinet, glockenspiel, marimba, guitar, violin, cello) 1974; first performed Dartington, Devon, 28 July 1974. Recorded L'Oiseau Lyre DSLO 12.

J.S. Bach: Two Preludes and Fugues C# Major The "48" Book I (flute, clarinet, harpsichord, marimba, viola, cello) 1974; first performed London, 27 November 1974. Recorded Unicorn Kanchana KP 8005.

Yesterday (arranged for guitar; Lennon/McCartney) 1974. Recorded L'Oiseau Lyre DSLO 3.

Ave Marie stella (flute, clarinet, piano, marimba, viola, cello) 1975; first performed Bath, 27 May 1975. Recorded Unicorn Kanchana KP 8002.

The Door of the Sun (viola) 1975; first performed Guildford, Surrey, 9 March 1976. Recorded Composers Recordings ACS 6017.

The Kestrel Paced Round the Sun (flute) 1975; first performed Guildford, Surrey, 9 March 1976.

The Seven Brightnesses (clarinet) 1975; first performed Williamsburg, Virginia, 12 October 1975.

Three Studies for Percussion (11 players) 1975.

My Lady Lothian's Lilt (alto flute, bass clarinet, viola, cello, percussion, plus mezzo-soprano obbligato) 1975; first performed Dartington, Devon, 20 August 1975.

Three Organ Voluntaries 1976; first performed Vestervig Kirke, Denmark, 31 July 1979. Recorded Pro Arte PR 168.

Kinloche His Fantassie (flute, clarinet, harpsichord, glockenspiel, violin, cello) 1976; first performed Dartington, Devon, 19 August 1976. Recorded Unicorn Kanchana DKP 9070.

Runes from a Holy Island (alto flute, clarinet, celeste, percussion, viola, cello) 1977; first performed Edinburgh, 6 September 1978; broadcast 6 November 1977. Recorded Unicorn Kanchana DKP 9033.

A Mirror of Whitening Light (flute/piccolo, oboe/English horn, A clarinet, bassoon, horn, trumpet, trombone, celeste, 2 violins, viola, cello, double bass, percussion) 1977; first performed London, 23 March 1977.

Our Father Whiche in Heaven Art (arranged for flute, clarinet, celeste, marimba, violin, cello) 1977; first performed Dartington, Devon, 18 August 1977. Recorded Unicorn Kanchana KP 8005.

Little Quartet No 2 (string quartet) 1977, revised 1987; first performed Canton, New York, 12 November 1987.

Four Lessons (2 keyboards) 1978; first performed Dartington, Devon, 23 August 1978.

Dances from "The Two Fiddlers" (piccolo, bass clarinet, violin solo, cello, piano, percussion) 1978, revised for violin, piano, 1988; first performed London, 6 October 1978; revised version first performed Orkney, 19 June 1988.

Nocturne (alto flute) 1979; first performed London, 28 January 1983.

Farewell to Stromness (piano) 1980; first performed Orkney, 21 June 1980. Recorded Unicorn Kanchana DKP 9070.

Yesnaby Ground (piano) 1980; first performed Orkney, 21 June 1980. Recorded Unicorn Kanchana DKP 9070.

A Welcome to Orkney (flute, oboe, A clarinet, bassoon, horn, 2 string quartets, double bass) 1980; first performed Orkney, 20 June 1980.

Little Quartet No 1 (string quartet) 1980; first performed Dartington, Devon, 26 July 1982.

Piano Sonata (organ) 1981; first performed Bath, 23 May 1981. Recorded Auracle AUC 1005.

Hill Runes (guitar) 1981; first performed Dartington, Devon,

25 July 1981. RCA Red Seal RL 25419.

The Bairns of Brugh (piccolo, bass clarinet, piano, marimba, viola, cello) 1981; first performed Bergen, 30 May 1981. Recorded Unicorn Kanchana DKP 9033.

Brass Quintet (2 trumpets, horn, trombone, tuba) 1981; first performed Boston, 19 March 1982.

Sea Eagle (horn) 1982; first performed Dartington, Devon, 16 August 1982.

Image, Reflection, Shadow (flute/piccolo/alto flute, A clarinet/bass clarinet, cimbalom, piano, violin, cello) 1982; first performed Lucerne, 22 August 1982. Recorded Unicorn Kanchana DKP 9033.

Organ Sonata 1982; first performed Orkney, 23 June 1982. Recorded Musica Nova, in preparation.

Tallis: Four Voluntaries (arranged for 2 trumpets, horn, trombone, tuba) 1982; first performed New York, 9 December 1983.

Gesualdo: Two Motets (arranged for 2 trumpets, horn, trombone, tuba) 1982; first performed Dartington, Devon, 18 August 1983.

March: The Pole Star (2 trumpets, horn, trombone, tuba) 1982; first performed Dartington, Devon, 18 August 1983. Recorded Merlin MRF 86041.

Birthday Music for John (flute, viola, cello) 1983; first performed Swansea, 13 October 1983.

Sonatine (violin, cimbalom) 1984; first performed London, 8 June 1984.

Unbroken Circle (alto flute, bass clarinet, piano, viola, cello) 1984; first performed Bath, 1 June 1984.

Guitar Sonata 1984; first performed Orkney, 20 June 1987.

Dowland: Farewell—A Fancye (alto flute, bass clarinet, viola, cello, piano, marimba) 1986; first performed London, 20 January 1987.

Mishkenot (9 players) 1988; first performed London, 3 May 1988.

Vocal/choral:

Five Motets (soprano, alto, tenor, bass, double SATB chorus, 2 violins, viola, cello, double bass, 2 trumpets, 2 trombones, 2 chamber organs, flute, oboe, clarinet, bassoon, contrabassoon) 1959; first performed London, 1 March 1965.

O magnum mysterium (SATB chorus, organ, ensemble) 1960; first performed Cirencester, Gloucestershire, 8 December 1960. Recorded Argo RG 327; Argo 5-BBA 1015.

Ave Maria, Hail Blessed Flower (SATB chorus) 1961. Recorded Argo RG 446, HMV CLP 3588.

Te lucis ante terminum (SATB chorus, 2 flutes, oboe, 2 clarinets, 2 trumpets, 2 trombones, guitar, cello, glockenspiel) 1961; first performed Cirencester, Gloucestershire, 30 November 1961.

Four Carols (SATB chorus) 1962.

Leopardi Fragments (soprano, mezzo-soprano, flute/piccolo, oboe, clarinet, bassoon, trumpet, trombone, harp, cello) 1962; first performed London, July 1962. Recorded HMV ALP 2093; ASD 640; Angel 36387; Argo ZRG 758.

Veni sancte spiritus (soprano, alto, tenor, bass, SATB chorus, orchestra) 1963; first performed Cheltenham, Gloucestershire, 10 July 1964.

Ecce manus tradentis (soprano, alto, tenor, bass, SATB chorus, flute, oboe, 2 bassoons/contrabassoon, horn, 2 trombones, harp, handbells) 1965; first performed Wardour Castle, Wiltshire, 20 August 1965.

Revelation and Fall (soprano, flute/piccolo, oboe, A clarinet/bass clarinet, bassoon/contrabassoon, horn, trumpet, trombone, harp, 2 violins, viola, cello, double bass, 3 percussionists; text by Georg Trakl) 1965, revised 1980; first performed London, 26 February 1968. Recorded HMV ASD 2427; Angel S 36558.

Notre Dame des fleurs (soprano, mezzo-soprano, countertenor, flute, clarinet, piano, percussion, violin, cello) 1966; first performed London, 17 March 1973.

Buxtehude: Also Hat Gott Die Welt Geliebet (soprano, flute, keyboards, violin, cello) 1970; first performed Dartington, Devon, 10 August 1970.

From Stone to Thorn (mezzo-soprano, basset horn, guitar, harpsichord, percussion; text by George Mackay Brown) 1971; first performed Oxford, 30 June 1971. Recorded L'Oiseau Lyre DSLO 2.

Tenebrae super Gesualdo (soprano, guitar, alto flute, bass clarinet, violin/viola, cello, marimba/glockenspiel, keyboards; also version for SATB choir) 1972; first performed London, 28 January 1984. Recorded Unicorn KP 8002.

Fiddlers at the Wedding (mezzo-soprano, alto flute, mandolin, guitar, percussion; George Mackay Brown) 1973; first performed Paris, 3 May 1974.

Dark Angels (mezzo-soprano, guitar) 1974; first performed Dartington, Devon 31 July 1974. Recorded Nonesuch H71342.

Anakreontika (mezzo-soprano, alto flute, harpsichord, cello, percussion) 1976; first performed London, 17 September 1976.

The Blind Fiddler (mezzo-soprano, flue/piccolo/alto flute, A clarinet/bass clarinet, harpsichord/celeste, guitar, violin, cello) 1976; first performed Edinburgh, 20 February 1976.

Norn pater noster (SATB chorus, organ) 1977.

Westerlings (SATB chorus) 1977; first performed (incomplete) Uppsala, 25 May 1977; first complete performance London, 15 October 1977.

Solstice of Light (tenor, SATB chorus, organ) 1979; first performed Orkney, 18 June 1979.

Lullaby for Lucy (SATB chorus) 1981; first performed 19 June 1981.

One Star, At Last (SATB chorus for Service of Nine Lessons and Carols) 1984; first performed Cambridge, 24 December 1984.

Excuse Me (mezzo-soprano, flute, A/B♭ clarinet, violin, cello, percussion) 1985; first performed London, 26 February 1986.

House of Winter (chorus/AATBBB or SATBBB sextet) 1986; first performed Orkney, 23 June 1986.

Sea Runes (chorus/AATBBB or SATBBB sextet) 1986; first performed New York, 16 November 1986.

Winterfold (mezzo-soprano, alto flute, bass clarinet, guitar, piano, viola, cello, percussion; text by George Mackay Brown) 1986; first performed London, 20 January 1987.

Hallelujah! The Lord God Almichtie (SATB chorus, organ) 1989; first performed Edinburgh, 11 June 1989.

Opera:

Taverner (14 solo singers, chorus, stage band, offstage instruments, orchestra) 1970; first performed London, 12 July 1972.

The Martyrdom of St Magnus (five singers, flute/piccolo/alto flute, A clarinet/bass clarinet, horn, 2 trumpets, keyboards, guitar, viola, cello, percussion) 1976; first performed Orkney, 18 June 1977.

The Lighthouse (tenor, baritone, bass, flute/piccolo/alto flute, A clarinet/bass clarinet, horn, C trumpet, trombone, keyboards, guitar/banjo, violin, viola, cello, double bass, percussion) 1979; first performed Edinburgh, 2 September 1980.

Resurrection (8 solo singers, electronic vocal quartet, 5 dancers, rock group, Salvation Army band, orchestra) 1987; first performed Darmstadt, 18 September 1988.

Music-theatre:

Eight Songs for a Mad King (baritone, flute, clarinet, keyboards, percussion, violin, cello; Randolph Stow, George III) 1969; first performed London, 22 April 1969. Recorded Unicorn UNS 261; Nonesuch H 71285.
Vesalii Icones (dancer, cello, flute, clarinet, piano, percussion, viola) 1969; first performed London, 9 December 1969. Recorded Unicorn RHS 307; Nonesuch H 71295.
Blind Man's Buff (mime, soprano/treble, mezzo-soprano, small orchestra) 1972; first performed London, 29 May 1972.
Miss Donnithorne's Maggot (female singer, flute/piccolo/alto flute, A clarinet, violin, cello, piano, percussion, 4 mechanical metronomes) 1974; first performed Adelaide, 9 March 1974.
Salomé (ballet in 2 acts; versions for full and reduced [38] orchestras) 1978; first performed Copenhagen, 10 November 1978; concert suite first performed London, 16 March 1979. Recorded EMI 157-39270/2.
Le Jongleur de Notre Dame (mime/juggler, baritone, flute/piccolo/alto flute, A clarinet/bass clarinet, violin, cello, piano/celeste, percussion, children's band) 1978; first performed Orkney, 18 June 1978.
The Yellow-Cake Revue (anti-nuclear cabaret; singer/reciter, piano) 1980; first performed Orkney, 21 June 1980.
The Medium (monodrama for unaccompanied mezzo-soprano) 1981; first performed Orkney, 21 July 1981.
The No 11 Bus (mime, two dancers, mezzo-soprano, tenor, baritone, flute/piccolo, A/B♭/bass clarinet, violin, cello, piano/celesta, percussion) 1984; first performed London, 20 March 1984.

Music for children:

Five Klee Pictures (school orchestra) 1957, revised 1976; first performed London, 16 October 1976.
William Byrd: Three Dances (school orchestra) 1959.
Five Voluntaries (school orchestra) 1960.
The Shepherds' Calendar (youth chorus, ensemble) 1965; first performed Sydney, 20 May 1965.
Five Carols (SA chorus) 1966; first performed London, 11 December 1966.
Stevie's Ferry to Hoy (piano) 1975.
The Two Fiddlers (opera for children; 5 solo singers, children's chorus, orchestra) 1978; first performed Orkney, 16 June 1978.
Kirkwall Shopping Songs (young children's voices, recorders, tuned and untuned percussion, piano) 1979; first performed Orkney, 16 June 1979.
Cinderella (pantomime opera for children; 11 solo singers, children's chorus, orchestra) 1980; first performed Orkney, 21 June 1980.
Farewell to Stromness (arranged for guitar) 1980; first performed Orkney, 23 June 1980.
The Rainbow (music-theatre for young children; 5 solo singers, children's chorus, ensemble) 1981; first performed Orkney, 20 June 1981.
Sonatina for Trumpet 1981.
Seven Songs Home (chorus) 1981; first performed Budapest, 13 December 1982. Recorded Unicorn Kanchana DKP 9070.
Songs of Hoy (voices, piano, descant recorders, guitar, tuned and untuned percussion) 1981; first performed Orkney, 21 June 1982.
First Ferry to Hoy (youth chorus, children's band, ensemble) 1985; first performed London, 12 November 1985.
The Peat Cutters (cantata for children's chorus, youth chorus, brass band) 1985; first performed Edinburgh, 18 August 1985.
Six Songs for St Andrew's (children's chorus, orchestra) 1988; first performed Orkney, 18 June 1988.
The Great Bank Robbery (music-theatre for solo singers, children's chorus, orchestra) 1989; first performed Orkney, 16 June 1989.
Jupiter Landing (music-theatre for solo singers, children's chorus, orchestra) 1990.
Dinosaur at Large (music-theatre for solo singers, children's chorus, orchestra) 1990.
Dangerous Errand (music theatre for very young children; solo singers, children's chorus, orchestra) 1990.

PUBLICATIONS

By Davies: "The Young British Composer", in *The Score*, March 1956; "Problems of a British Composer", in *The Listener*, 9 October 1959; "Music Composition by Children", in *Music in Education*, edited by Willis Grant, London, 1963; "*Taverner*: Synopsis and Documentation", in *Tempo*, 101, 1972; "Pax Orcadiensis", in *Tempo*, 119, 1976; "Symphony", in *Tempo*, 124, 1978.

On Davies: Stephen Pruslin (ed), *PMD: Studies from Two Decades*, London, 1979; Judy Arnold (ed), *PMD: The Complete Catalogue of Published Works*, London, 1981; Paul Griffiths, *PMD*, London, 1982; Richard Dufallo, (interview) in *Trackings: Composers Speak with Richard Dufallo*, Oxford, 1990.

* * *

The *Sonata for Trumpet and Piano* and *Five Pieces for Piano*, Peter Maxwell Davies's first published works, already exhibit traces of important preoccupations of his subsequent career. The Piano Pieces, especially, indicate his enthusiasm for Schoenberg and Webern. The structuring of this densely organised polyphonic music extends to rhythmic durations which reflect also Davies's interest in Messiaen and Indian music.

Alma redemptoris mater is based upon the plainsong Marian antiphon and draws too upon Dunstable's eponymous motet. Davies's rethinking of such medieval and renaissance construction plans as a basis for post-tonal composition is, in part, a legacy of his study of the Second Viennese School composers, especially Webern. Written in the same year as *Alma redemptoris mater, St Michael* adopts a plainsong from the Requiem Mass and develops it through fragmentation and a quasi-serial elaboration. The title of the orchestral *Prolation* refers to the relationship between semitone and minim rhythmic durations in medieval music. Once more, Davies's methodology shows both an historical and a contemporary European awareness—the structures based upon five durational values and five pitch classes have parallels in Webern and, more contemporaneously, Nono; they also recall the experiments with limited row structures (i.e., those containing less than the full 12 chromatic tones) which characterise late Stravinsky.

Around 1960, when Davies worked at Cirencester Grammar

School, his music was both restricted and encouraged to develop in new ways by the need to produce technically accessible music for school performance. The Bartókian *Five Canons* and, especially, the *Five Klee Pictures* demonstrate his increasing ability to create music capable of functioning on several levels. The *Klee Pictures*, all written in the style of voluntaries, are arrangements from pre-classical composers, but also manage to evoke specific pictures by Paul Klee.

Davies's "theatre music" style of the 1960s was announced by the opera *Taverner*, which epitomises his love for pastiche as a basis for composition and as a means to explore, on various musical levels, his concern for concepts of sincerity and betrayal: Taverner, the Tudor composer, is hounded for his Catholic faith, but is eventually corrupted and himself persecutes Catholics. *Revelation and Fall*, written contemporaneously with the opera, shares its debt to early music—cantus firmus and complex decorative melismata are employed, as is parody technique (both in the "renaissance" sense of using the entire texture of one piece as the basis for another, and as an ironic commentary). This work's contrapuntal complexity, use of an untranslated text by the German *fin de siècle* poet Georg Trakl and reliance upon shock tactics (the singer, dressed in a scarlet nun's habit and equipped with a megaphone, deploys vocal techniques ranging from *Sprechstimme* to screaming) powerfully evokes Schoenberg's *Pierrot Lunaire*.

In *Missa super l'Homme Armé*, Davies reworks a popular song which had provided the "scaffolding" for dozens of Mass settings during the 15th and 16th centuries. The vocal soloist, if male, should be dressed as a nun, if female as a monk. Structurally, this work peppers the tripartite Mass "Agnus Dei" form with tangential allusions, after the manner of Joyce's *Ulysses* (Davies's own comparison).

The most consistently successful of Davies's exhibitionist "theatre pieces" are *Eight Songs for a Mad King* and *Vesalii Icones*. The *Eight Songs* were first staged with the chamber instrumental group playing inside giant bird cages, a symbol of the Mad King's incarceration. One song is printed upon staves laid out in the shape of a cage, thus intensifying the staging "conceit"; this notational device too crops up in early music, particularly during the short-lived *Ars subtilior* phase of the late 14th century. *Vesalii Icones* comprises 14 dances which fuse the Fourteen Stations of the Cross with Vesalius's anatomical engravings from *De humani corporis fabrica*. The musical quotations and parodies are evident once more—a solo cellist functions on one level as assorted characters from the Passion story (Pilate, a flagellator, etc.) or as the anatomical demonstrator, stripping away layers of musical sinew to reveal the skeleton of the Scherzo from Beethoven's Fifth Symphony, or the canonic basis of de la Rue's *Missa super l'Homme Armé* (itself based on the monody which had inspired Davies's Mass).

The "theatre" style appears fitfully in Davies's music from the early 1970s onward, though its most sustained recurrences, *in Miss Donnithorne's Maggot* and *The Medium*, lack the tortured immediacy and conviction of previous essays. Early music models are still evident in works dating from the composer's residence in the Orkneys (notably in *Hymn to St Magnus* and in the ballet *Salomé*); in *St Magnus*, the sometimes polarised, often perplexingly fused duality between persecutor and victim is explored again, though it is now viewed through a close cultural and naturalistic association with the Orkney Islands themselves.

In recent years, Davies has ventured increasingly into the "classical" symphonic form; his four symphonies to date delineate the traditional structure with increasing clarity (though classical sonata forms had occurred in a number of earlier works), albeit with moments of his highly Expressionist and abrasive harmonic and timbral style.

Davies has recently been working upon a series of 10 concertos, intended for performance with the Scottish Chamber Orchestra. His interest in the "baroque" concerto style is not surprising, when one considers the strong element of expressive virtuosity in works like *Vesalii Icones*. The *Violin Concerto* written for Isaac Stern, blends technical display with traces of Scottish folk music and evocations of the Orkneys. Elements of 19th-century concerto form are also clear—the composer has acknowledged this work's links with the Mendelssohn Violin Concerto. At the moment, it seems that Davies's music will continue to marry his highly individual and uncompromising style with reworkings of conventional forms.

—Paul Horner

DELLO JOIO, Norman. American. Born in New York City, 24 January 1913. Education: initial music lessons (organ, theory) with father Casimir Dello Joio and organist Pietro Yon; All Hallows Institute, 1926–30; College of the City of New York, 1932–4; Institute of Musical Art, 1933–8; graduate study, Juilliard School of Music, New York City (under Bernard Wagenaar), 1939–41; Yale School of Music, New Haven, Connecticut (under Paul Hindemith), 1941; Berkshire Music Cente, Tanglewood, Massachusetts (under Paul Hindemith), 1941. Organist, Star of the Sea Church, New York City, 1927 (age 14); music director, Dance Players, 1941–3; teacher of music, Sarah Lawrence College, Bronxville, New York, 1945–50; professor of composition, Mannes College, New York City, 1956–72; founder/chair of policy committee, Contemporary Music Project for Creativity in Music Education, 1959–72; State Department Cultural Program bursar, travel to Bulgaria, Romania, Soviet Union, 1964; professor of music/dean of School of Fine and Applied Arts, Boston University, 1972–8. Recipient: Elizabeth Sprague Coolidge Award (for *Piano Trio*), 1937; Town Hall Composition Award (for *Magnificat*), 1942; Guggenheim Fellowships, 1943, 1944; New York Music Critics' Circle Awards (for *Variations, Chaconne and Finale* and *The Triumph of St Joan*), 1948, 1962; Pulitzer Prize (for *Meditations on Ecclesiastes*), 1957; elected to National Institute of Arts and Letters, 1961; "Emmy" award (for television soundtrack *The Louvre*), 1965. Honorary doctorates: Lawrence College, Wisconsin, 1959; Colby College, Maine, 1963; University of Cincinnati, 1969. Address: c/o Schirmer Inc. 225 Park Avenue South, New York, New York 10003, U.S.A.

Publishers: G. Schirmer; C. Fisher; Associated; Marks.

Symphonies/orchestral:

Piano Concertino 1938; withdrawn.
Flute Concertino 1938; withdrawn.
Ballad (strings) 1940; withdrawn.
Concertino for Two Pianos and Orchestra 1941; withdrawn.
Sinfonietta 1941.

Harmonica Concertino 1942; withdrawn.
Magnificat 1942.
To a Lone Sentry (chamber orchestra) 1943.
Concert Music 1944; first performed Pittsburgh, 4 January 1946.
On Stage (arranged from the ballet) 1945; first performed Cleveland, Ohio, 23 November 1945.
Harp Concerto 1945; first performed New York City, 20 November 1947.
Three Ricercari (piano, orchestra) 1946; first performed New York, 19 December 1946.
Serenade 1947–8; first performed Cleveland, Ohio, 20 October 1949.
Variations, Chaconne and Finale (Three Symphonic Dances) 1947; first performed Pittsburgh, 30 January 1948.
Concertato (clarinet, orchestra) 1949; first performed Chautauqua, New York, 22 May 1949.
New York Profiles 1949; first performed La Jolla, California, 21 August 1949.
Epigraph 1951; first performed Denver, Colorado, 29 January 1952.
Symphony: The Triumph of St Joan (arranged from opera) 1951; first performed, with choreography by Martha Graham, Louisville, Kentucky, 5 December 1951.
Meditations on Ecclesiastes (strings) 1956; first performed Washington, D.C., 17 December 1957.
A Ballad of the Seven Lively Arts (piano, orchestra) 1957.
Air Power (symphonic suite arranged from music for CBS television series) 1957.
Here Is New York (suite arranged from music for CBS television series) 1959.
Fantasy and Variations (piano, orchestra) 1961; first performed Cincinnati, Ohio, 9 March 1962.
Variants on a Medieval Tune (band; arrangement of "In dulce jubilo") 1963.
Three Songs of Chopin (arranged for orchestra) 1964.
From Every Horizon (band) 1964.
Antiphonal Fantasy on a Theme of Vincenzo Albrici (organ, brass, strings) 1965.
The Louvre (arranged for band from music for NBC television film) 1965.
Air (strings) 1967.
Five Images: Cortège (arranged for orchestra from piano work) 1967.
Five Images: Promenade (arranged for orchestra from piano work) 1967.
Five Images: Day Dreams (arranged for orchestra from piano work) 1967.
Five Images: The Ballerina (arranged for orchestra from piano work) 1967.
Fantasies on a Theme by Haydn 1968; first performed Little Rock, Arkansas, 3 June 1969.
Homage to Haydn 1968–9.
Songs of Abelard (band; originally entitled *A Time of Snow*) 1969.
Choreography (strings) 1972.
Concertante (band) 1973.
Lyric Fantasies (viola, strings) 1973.
Satiric Dances (band) 1975.
Colonial Ballads (band) 1976.
Colonial Variants: Thirteen Profiles of the Original Colonies 1976; first performed Philadelphia, 27 May 1976.
Arietta (strings) 1978.
Caccia (band) 1978.
Ballabili 1981.
Aria and Roulade (band) 1984.
East Hampton Sketches (strings) 1984.

Chamber/instrumental:

Piano Trio 1937; withdrawn.
Quartet (4 bassoons) 1937; withdrawn.
Sonata (cello) 1937; withdrawn.
Sonata A (violin) 1937; withdrawn.
Colloquy (violin, piano) 1938; withdrawn.
Sonata (violin) 1938; withdrawn.
Quintet (woodwind) 1939; withdrawn.
Suite (piano) 1940.
Trio (woodwind) 1940; withdrawn.
Fantasia on a Gregorian Theme (violin, piano) 1942.
Sonata No 1 (piano) 1943.
Prelude to a Young Dancer (piano) 1943.
Prelude to a Young Musician (piano) 1943.
Sextet (3 recorders, string trio) 1943.
Trio (flute, cello, piano) 1944.
Sonata No 2 (piano) 1944.
Duo concertante (cello, piano; 2 pianos) 1945.
On Stage (piano; arranged from the ballet) 1945.
Nocturne in E (piano) 1946.
Nocturne in F# (piano) 1946.
Variations and Capriccio (violin, piano) 1948.
Sonata No 3 (piano) 1948.
Concertante (clarinet, piano; arranged from orchestral piece) 1949.
Aria and Toccata (2 pianos) 1952.
Family Album (piano—4 hands) 1962.
Fantasy and Variations (arranged for 2 pianos from orchestral work) 1962.
Colloquies (violin, piano) 1963.
Night Song (piano) 1963.
Suite for the Young (piano) 1964.
Laudation (organ) 1965.
Five Images: Cortège (piano—4 hands) 1967.
Five Images: Promenade (piano—4 hands) 1967.
Five Images: Day Dreams (piano—4 hands) 1967.
Five Images: The Ballerina (piano—4 hands) 1967.
Five Images: The Dancing Sergeant (piano—4 hands) 1967.
Capriccio on the Interval of a Second (piano) 1968.
Bagatelles (harp) 1968.
Lyric Pieces for the Young (piano) 1971.
The Developing Flutist (flute, piano) 1972.
Lyric Fantasies (arranged for viola, piano from orchestral work) 1973.
Three Essays (clarinet, piano) 1974.
Stage Parodies (piano—4 hands) 1974.
String Quartet 1974.
Diversions (piano) 1975.
Five Lyric Pieces for the Young Organist 1975.
Salute to Scarlatti (piano or harpsichord) 1979.
Sonata (trumpet) 1979.
Concert Variations (piano) 1980.
Reflections on a Christmas Tune (woodwind quintet) 1981.
Song at Springtide (piano—4 hands) 1984.

Vocal/choral:

Ballad of Thomas Jefferson (voice, piano) 1937.
Gone (voice, piano; Sandburg) 1939; withdrawn.
Joy (voice, piano; Sandburg) 1939; withdrawn.
Mill Doors (voice, piano; Sandburg) 1939; withdrawn.
Chicago (SATB chorus; Sandburg) 1939; withdrawn.
Vigil Strange (SATB chorus, piano—4 hands) 1941.
The Mystic Trumpeter (SATB chorus, horn; Whitman) 1943.
A Jubilant Song (SATB/women's voices, piano; Whitman) 1945.

Symphony for Voices (SATB chorus; S.V. Benet) 1945; withdrawn, later revised as *A Song of Affirmation*.
A Fable (tenor, SATB chorus, piano; Lindsay) 1946.
New Born (voice, piano; Marshall) 1946.
There Is a Lady Sweet and Kind (voice, piano; Elizabethan) 1946.
The Assassination: Two Fates Discuss a Human Problem (voice, piano; Hillyer) 1947.
Lament (voice, piano; Tichborne) 1947.
Madrigal (SATB, piano; Rossetti) 1947.
Six Love Songs (voice, piano; Symonds, Suckling, Browning, Young) 1948.
The Bluebird (SATB chorus, piano; Machlis) 1950.
A Psalm of David (SATB chorus, strings, brass, percussion) 1950.
Song of the Open Road (SATB chorus, trumpet, piano; Whitman) 1952.
Song of Affirmation (revised version of *Symphony for Voices*; soprano, narrator, SATB chorus, orchestra; Benet) 1953.
Adieu, Mignonne, When You Are Gone (women's voices, piano; Meredith) 1953.
Someone's Coming (SATB chorus, piano; arranged from music for *The Tall Kentuckian*) 1953.
Sweet Sonny (SATB chorus, piano; arranged from music for *The Tall Kentuckian*) 1953.
The Lamentation of Saul (baritone, orchestra or sextet; D.H. Lawrence) 1954.
The Listeners (voice, piano; de la Mare) 1955.
O Sing unto the Lord (Psalm 98) (men's voices, organ) 1958.
To St Cecilia (SATB chorus, piano/brass; Dryden) 1958.
Un sonetto di Petrarca (Songs of Adieu) (voice, piano; Petrarch) 1959.
A Christmas Carol (SATB chorus, piano—4 hands; also arranged for SSA chorus, piano; or medium voice, piano; Chesterton) 1960.
Prayers of Cardinal Newman (SATB chorus, organ) 1960.
The Holy Infant's Lullaby (unison voices, organ; also arranged for SATB chorus, optional organ; or voice, piano; Bennet) 1961.
Bright Star (voice, piano; Hoffman) 1962.
Three Songs of Adieu (voice, piano; Symonds, anon.) 1962.
Song's End (SAA chorus, piano; Payne) 1963.
Three Songs of Chopin: The Lovers/The Ring/The Wish (SATB chorus, orchestra; arranged for orchestra; or voice, piano; Koniec, Pierschien, Zyczenic) 1964.
Songs of Walt Whitman ("I Sit and Look Out upon the World", "The Dalliance of Eagles", "Tears", "Take Our Hand"; SATB chorus, orchestra) 1966.
Proud Music of the Storm (SATB chorus, brass, organ; Whitman) 1967.
Christmas Music ("Bright Star", "God Rest Ye, Merry Gentlemen", "Hark, the Herald Angels Sing", "Holy Infant's Lullaby", "O, Come All Ye Faithful", "Silent Night"; SATB chorus, orchestra; also arranged for piano—4 hands) 1968.
Years of the Modern (SATB chorus, brass, percussion; Whitman) 1968.
Mass (SATB chorus, brass, organ/piano) 1969.
Songs of Abelard (version for voice, band) 1969.
Evocations: Visitations at Night (SATB chorus, optional children's voices, orchestra or piano; Hillyer) 1970.
Evocations: Promise of Spring (SATB chorus, optional children's voices, orchestra or piano; Hovey) 1970.
Come to Me, My Love (SATB chorus, piano; Rossetti) 1972.
Psalm of Peace (SATB chorus, trumpet, horn, organ/piano) 1972.
The Poet's Song (SATB chorus, piano; Tennyson) 1973.
Mass in Honor of the Eucharist (SATB chorus, cantor, congregation, brass, organ) 1975.
Note Left on a Doorstep (voice, piano; Peter) 1975.
Notes from Tom Paine (SATB chorus, piano) 1975.
Songs of Remembrance (baritone, orchestra; Wheelock) 1977.
The Psalmist's Meditation (SATB chorus, organ or piano) 1979.
Hymns Without Words (SATB chorus, piano or orchestra) 1980.
Love Songs at Parting (SATB chorus, piano) 1981.
I Dreamed of an Invincible City (SATB chorus, piano or organ) 1984.

Opera:

The Triumph of Joan (Machlis) 1949; first performed Bronxville, New York, 9 May 1950; withdrawn.
The Ruby (Mass, after Dunsany) 1953; first performed Bloomington, Indiana, 13 May 1955.
The Trial at Rouen (Dello Joio) 1955; broadcast NBC, 8 April 1956; revised as *The Triumph of St Joan*, 1959; first performed New York City, 16 April 1959.
Blood Moon (Hoffman) 1961; first performed San Francisco, 18 September 1961.

Other:

Prairie (ballet; arranged from *Sinfonietta*, 1941) 1942.
The Duke of Sacramento (ballet; 2 pianos) 1942; first performed New Hope, Pennsylvania, 1942; withdrawn.
On Stage (ballet; orchestra) 1945; first performed Boston, 1945.
Three Symphonic Dances (ballet; choreographed from 1947 *Variations, Chaconne and Finale*) 1947.
Diversion of Angels (ballet; choreographed by Martha Graham from *Serenade*, 1947–8) 1948; first performed New London, Connecticut, 1948.
The Tall Kentuckian (incidental music to play by Anderson) 1953; first performed Louisville, Kentucky, 1953.
Seraphic Dialogue (ballet rechoreographed from *The Triumph of St Joan Symphony*) 1955; first performed New York City, 1955.
There Is a Time (ballet; arranged from *Meditations on Ecclesiastes*) 1956.
Air Power (music for CBS television series) 1956; first broadcast 11 November 1956.
Profile of a Composer (music for television film; includes *Ballad of the Seven Lively Arts*) 1958; broadcast 1958.
Here Is New York (music for television; includes excerpts from *New York Profiles*) 1959; broadcast 1959.
The Saintmaker's Christmas Eve (music for ABC television film) 1959; broadcast 1963.
Vanity Fair (incidental music to CBS film of Thackeray) 1959; broadcast 1961.
Women's Song (ballet; arranged from *Harp Concerto*, 1945) 1960.
Anthony and Cleopatra (incidental music to Shakespeare) 1960; first performed Stratford, Connecticut, 1960.
Time of Decision (music for television) 1962.
The Louvre (music for NBC television film) 1962; broadcast 1965.
The Glass Heart (ballet; arranged and choreographed from *Mediations on Ecclesiastes*) 1968.
Satiric Dances for a Comedy by Aristophanes (band) 1974; first performed Concord, Massachusetts, 17 July 1975.
As of a Dream (modern masque; solo voices, SATB chorus, narrator, dancers, orchestra; Whitman) 1978.

PUBLICATIONS

On Dello Joio: R. Sabin, "NDJ", in *Musical America*, 70 (12), 1950; E. Downes, "The Music of NDJ", in *Musical Quarterly*, 48, 1962; M. Hinson, "The Solo Piano Music of NDJ", in *American Music Teacher*, 19, 1970; T.A Bumgardner, "The Solo Vocal Works of NDJ", dissertation, University of Texas, Austin, 1973; N.J. Boston, "The Piano Sonatas and Suites of NDJ", dissertation, Peabody Conservatory, 1984; T.A. Bumgardner, *NDJ*, 1989.

* * *

There were several generations of church organists in Norman Dello Joio's Italian-American family, but he has responded to influences whose variety reflects the American racial and cultural melting-pot. Certainly his music usually dances to recognisably American rhythms, though at the same time many of his large and distinctive compositions are rooted in medieval ecclesiasticism. Such pieces manage to be liturgical in spirit yet unmistakeably modern in their neo-modal, fairly dissonant polyphony. Gregorian chant and a personal adaptation of jazz rhythm might come together. A typical pair of works could be the *Variations, Chaconne and Finale* for orchestra and *Sonata No 3* for piano. He is particularly happy with variation technique, and both open with variations on the *De Angelis* kyrie and have ingenious and elaborate development, and a formal design that accommodates both vivid contrasts and lyrical intensity.

The recipient of many awards, Dello Joio's works have had numerous performances, at least in the U.S. He has always written with impressive facility, producing large quantities of compositions in every form, including much choral music that is ingratiating in its immediate effect. Some of these pieces are not free of clichés, but only someone deeply familiar with liturgical music could have produced, for example, *A Psalm of David*, which was prompted by Josquin's setting of Psalm 50 (51 in the King James version), *Miserere mei, Deus*. This work also shows the influence of Giovanni Gabrieli. Dello Joio's Whitman settings are notable in a rather different way, reflecting the poet's singing exultation and visionary freedom. Another kind of outlet for his lyric vein is demonstrated by *The Lamentation of Saul*, a composition for baritone and small instrumental ensemble. Not unexpectedly, the most striking of his songs are strongly dramatic and declammatory, such as *The Assassination: Two Fates Discuss a Human Problem* on a text adapted from Robert Hillyer.

Dello Joio's dramatic imagination happily unites with his consistently rich vein of melody in his operas, even if his spontaneity and prolific inventiveness have actually prevented him from portraying characters with sufficient individuality and differentiating sharply enough between moods, feelings, atmospheres. St Joan has been a particular source of inspiration and *The Triumph of Joan* was Dello Joio's first opera. It was withdrawn, however, and much of the music was reworked as *The Triumph of St Joan* symphony, introduced as a ballet by Martha Graham, then rechoreographed as *Seraphic Dialogue*. A further opera on this subject was *The Trial at Rouen*, broadcast on television in 1956, then revised for the stage as, yet again, *The Triumph of St Joan*. The case might seem unusual yet it is not uncommon for this composer's works to go through transformations of this kind. His *Meditations on Ecclesiastes*, a piece for string orchestra that won a Pulitzer Prize, was adapted as a ballet, *There Is a Time* and later rechoreographed as *The Glass Heart*.

These St Joan pieces are united in having music that is in Dello Joio's telling quasi-liturgical manner, yet *Seraphic Dialogue* is probably the finest, its score blending perfectly with Graham's choreography in a classic of the modern theatre that presented a beautiful vision of the saint. Utterly different is *The Ruby*, an opera with a liberetto by William Mass based on Dunsany's *A Night at the Inn*. This has blood-and-thunder music that makes a sharper, or at least more immediate, impression than more refined and subtle works. Such pieces relate, however, to Dello Joio's affinity with jazz and pre-rock popular music. This emerges in the large gestures and strong contrasts of pieces like his *Fantasy and Variations* for piano and orchestra, and also in his television music such as the 22-programme *Air Power* series of 1956–7 from which, typically, Dello Joio at once arranged a symphonic suite.

—Max Harrison

DEL TREDICI, David (Walter). American. Born in Cloverdale, California, 16 March 1937. Educated: piano student of Bernhard Abramowitsch, Berkeley, California; University of California, Berkeley (under Arnold Elston and Seymour Shifrin), 1956–9, B.A., Phi Beta Kappa; summer study (piano), Aspen Festival, Colorado, meets Darius Milhaud, 1958; Princeton University, New Jersey (under Roger Sessions and Earl Kim), 1959–60, 1963–4, M.F.A.; private study with Robert Helps, New York City, 1960–2. Recital and symphony pianist; composer in residence, Tanglewood Music Festival, Massachusetts, 1964–5, 1985; faculty member, Harvard University, Cambridge, Massachusetts, 1966–72; composer in residence, Marlboro Music Festival, 1966–7; faculty/member of Creative Associates Group, State University of New York, Buffalo, 1973; faculty, Boston University, 1973–84; composer in residence, Aspen Music Festival, Colorado, 1975, 1984; composer in residence, Rockefeller Foundation, Bellagio, Italy, 1983; faculty member, City College and Graduate School, 1984–86, and distinguished professor of music, since 1986, City College of New York; composer in residence, American Academy in Rome, 1985, and New York Philharmonic Orchestra, since 1988. Recipient: Kimber Award for instrumental performance, 1955; Woodrow Wilson fellowship, 1959; Hertz Award, 1962; National Academy of Arts and Letters award, 1968; Naumberg recording award, 1972; Brandeis University Creative Arts Award, 1973; Pulitzer Prize (for *In Memory of a Summer Day*), 1980; Freidheim Award (for *Happy Voices*), 1982. Mailing address: 463 West Street, Apt G121, New York, New York 10014, U.S.A.

Publisher: Boosey & Hawkes.

"Alice" works (inspired by Lewis Carroll's *Alice's Adventures in Wonderland* and *Through the Looking Glass*):

Pop-Pourri (amplified soprano, rock group: soprano saxophone/tenor, soprano saxophone/2 electric guitars, orchestra; Carroll; Litany of Blessed Virgin Mary; Lutheran hymn) 1968, revised 1973; first performed La Jolla, California, 28 July 1968.

An Alice Symphony (I. Speak Roughly/Speak Gently, II. The Lobster Quadrille, III. 'Tis the Voice of the Sluggard,

IV. Who Stole the Tarts?, V. Dream-Conclusion; amplified soprano, folk group: 2 soprano saxophones/mandolin/tenor banjo/accordion, orchestra; additional text by Bates) 1969, revised 1976.

The Lobster Quadrille (from *An Alice Symphony*; amplified soprano [may be omitted], folk group: 2 soprano saxophones/mandolin/tenor banjo/accordion, orchestra) 1969; first performed London, 14 November 1969.

In Wonderland (scene with Lobsters from *An Alice Symphony*: The Lobster Quadrille, 'Tis the Voice of the Sluggard, Dream-Conclusion; amplified soprano, folk group: 2 soprano saxophones/mandolin/tenor banjo/accordion, orchestra) 1969, revised 1974; first performed Aspen, Colorado, 29 July 1975.

Illustrated Alice (2 scenes from Wonderland from *An Alice Symphony*: Speak Roughly/Speak Gently, Who Stole the Tarts?, Dream-Conclusion; amplified soprano, orchestra) 1969, revised 1976; first performed San Francisco, 8 August 1976.

Adventures Underground (soprano, folk group: 2 soprano saxophones/mandolin/tenor banjo/accordion, orchestra) 1971, revised 1977; first performed Buffalo, New York, 13 April 1975.

Vintage Alice ("fantascene" on A Mad Tea Party; amplified soprano, folk group: 2 soprano saxophones/mandolin/tenor banjo/accordion, chamber orchestra) 1972; first performed Saratoga, California, 5 August 1972.

Final Alice (amplified soprano[s], folk group: 2 soprano saxophones/mandolin/tenor banjo/accordion; additional texts by William Mee and anon.; arias and scenes—I. The Set of Verses, II. She's All My Fancy Painted Him, The King's Muses, III. Contradictory Evidence, IV. Still More Evidence, Arguments in the Jury Chamber, Alice's Awakening Remembrance, V. Apotheosis: Acrostic Song) 1974–5; first performed Chicago, 7 October 1976. Recorded London Records LFR-71018.

Child Alice (amplified soprano[s], orchestra; I. In Memory of a Summer Day, Intermission, II. Quaint Events, Happy Voices, All in the Golden Afternoon) 1977–81; first performed New York City, 27 April 1986.

In Memory of a Summer Day (from *Child Alice*, Part I: Introduction, Simple Alice, A Tale Is Told: Triumphant Alice, Interlude, Ecstatic Alice, Postlude; amplified soprano, orchestra) 1980; first performed St. Louis, Missouri, 23 February 1980. Recorded Nonesuch 79043.

Interlude and Ecstatic Alice (from *In Memory of a Summer Day* [*Child Alice*, Part I]; amplified soprano, orchestra) 1980; first performed Los Angeles, 13 March 1981.

Triumphant Alice (Marcia) (from *In Memory of a Summer Day* [*Child Alice*, Part I]; orchestra) 1980.

Happy Voices (from *Child Alice*, Part II) 1980, revised 1984; first performed San Francisco, 16 September 1980; with concert finale, Los Angeles, 21 February 1985.

Quaint Events (from *Child Alice*, Part II; amplified soprano, orchestra) 1981; first performed Buffalo, New York, 19 November 1981.

All in the Golden Afternoon (from *Child Alice* Part II; amplified soprano, orchestra) 1981; first performed Philadelphia, 8 May 1981.

Acrostic Song (arranged for guitar; also for flute, piano; from *Final Alice*) 1982. Recorded Bridge 2004; flute and piano, Nonesuch 79114 1.

Acrostic Paraphrase (harp; based on *Acrostic Song* from *Final Alice*) 1983; first performed Tempe, Arizona, 22 June 1983.

Virtuoso Alice (piano; grand fantasy on a theme from *Final Alice*) 1984.

Haddocks' Eyes (amplified soprano, flute/piccolo, clarinet, horn, trumpet, piano, 2 violins, viola, cello, double bass; Carroll, Moore) 1985; first performed New York City, 2 May 1986.

Other:

Soliloquy (piano) 1958; first performed Aspen, Colorado, August 1958.

Four Songs on Poems of James Joyce (voice, piano) 1958–60; first performed Berkeley, California, 1 March 1961.

String Trio 1959; first performed Berkeley, California, 21 May 1959.

Two Songs on Poems of James Joyce (voice, piano) 1959, revised 1978; first performed Washington, D.C., 11 February 1983.

Fantasy Pieces 1959–60; first performed San Francisco, 1960. Recorded Desto 7110.

Scherzo (piano—4 hands) 1960; first performed New Brunswick, New Jersey, 1960. Recorded CRI S-294.

I Hear an Army (soprano, string quintet; Joyce) 1964; first performed Tanglewood, Massachusetts, 12 August 1964. Recorded CRI S-294.

Night Conjure-Verse (soprano, mezzo-soprano/countertenor, chamber ensemble; Joyce) 1965; first performed San Francisco, 2 March 1966. Recorded CRI S-243.

Syzygy (soprano, horn, orchestra; Joyce) 1966; first performed New York City, 6 July 1968. Recorded CRI S-492/Columbia MS 7281.

The Last Gospel (female voice, rock group: soprano saxophone/tenor and soprano saxophone/2 electric guitars, orchestra; Bible) 1967, new version 1984; first performed San Francisco, 15 June 1968; new version first performed Milwaukee, Wisconsin, 3 October 1984.

March to Tonality 1985; first performed Chicago, 13 June 1985.

Tattoo 1986; first performed Amsterdam, 30 January 1987.

PUBLICATIONS

By Del Tredici: "Contemporary Music: Observations from Those Who Create It", remarks (with others) in *Music and Artists*, 5 (3), 1972.

On Del Tredici: Oliver Knussen, "David Del Tredici and 'Syzygy'", in *Tempo*, 118, 1976; John Rockwell, (interview) in *New York Times*, 26 October 1980; John Rockwell, "DDT: the Return of Tonality, the Orchestral Audience and the Danger of Success", in *All-American Music: Composition in the Late Twentieth Century*, New York, 1983; T. Page, "The New Romance with Tonality", in *New York Times Magazine*, 29 May 1983; L. Brunner, "DDT: An Alice Symphony", in *Notes*, 41, 1984–5; Richard Dufallo, (interview) in *Trackings: Composers Speak with Richard Dufallo*, Oxford, 1990.

* * *

It seems fitting, given his playfulness as a composer, that there is a pun in David Del Tredici's surname. Much of his career has been, in the words of a 1985 orchestral piece, a "march to tonality" and away from the strict serialism of his training. "Tredici" is Italian for 13 and much of Del Tredici's career has been a search for the "13th note" that represents a step beyond the strict twelve-tone techniques of the serialists. Though it is intended half-humorously, there is thus also a serious underlying message to Del Tredici's constant use of this "signature" in his work. It appears verbally at the end of *Final Alice*, where he instructs performers to count aloud (in Italian) to 13, with a heavy emphasis on "tredici"; but it is also detectable in 13/8 time signatures and other devices so complex and cerebral as to cast serious doubt on his reputation as a crowd-pleasing populist who has turned his back on "serious" music in pursuit of commercial success and in defiance of Milton Babbitt's famously restrictive "Who cares if you listen?".

Del Tredici's career is striking not just for the enormous popular success he has enjoyed, but also for the fact that since 1968, virtually all of his published work has been directly inspired by Lewis Carroll's "Alice" stories. On the face of it, this seemed a quite appropriate choice of textual matter for a gifted young composer with excellent promotion prospects in the serialist establishment who chose to go off and write tonal, even tuneful, music. The perversity of Carroll's stories fitted very well the cross-grained quality of Del Tredici's gesture.

Initially, in *Pop-Pourri* and the *Alice Symphony*, Del Tredici seemed to be torn between his academic training and his new instinct for melody. Though the basic structure is tonal, the surface is harsh and dissonant and the use of a rock group in an approximately concertante role (a device, alternating rock and folk groups, which has been part of his work ever since) is not entirely successful. This is not to suggest that in his finest work, *Final Alice*, Del Tredici has capitulated to a reactionary tendency in modern music and contented himself with an idiom no more progressive than Richard Strauss (who is unquestionably an influence). In fact, *Final Alice* is a work of considerable intellectual complexity, full of multiple ironies and shifting resolutions that bely its rather static harmonic profile. It is no less challenging, to performer and listener alike, than the earlier Joyce settings, an almost equally significant choice of text, betraying an invigorating tension between "difficult" and lyrical directness.

Del Tredici has admitted that in *Final Alice* he is divided between the utterly different languages of symphonic and operatic music; it could be argued that this is precisely the dilemma he has inherited from Strauss. It is clear that he has not, or not yet, satisfactorily resolved it. *Final Alice* was originally intended, as the title suggests, to bring the sequence to a close; it would be cynical to claim that its commercial success (including a wonderful recording by Barbara Hendricks) persuaded him not to kill a golden goose, for it is clear that Del Tredici still regards the turn to tonality as a daring strategy, entailing risk rather than complacency, a challenge rather than a retreat.

Part of that challenge is political, relative to the politics of the musical world. Del Tredici has thrown down a gauntlet that has increasingly been taken up by rather younger composers who have broken free of the self-regarding complexities of avant-garde music in order to write pieces which combine complexity with simple enjoyment. To that extent, though there is no single technical innovation associated with his name, Del Tredici has been a path-breaker. He is quite simply one of the most enjoyable composers working in orchestral music today. He is witty—the orchestral parts for "The Mouse's Tale" in *Adventures Underground* wiggle down the score page—intellectually generous, and a formidable technician.

—Brian Morton

DENISOV, Edison (Vassilievich). Russian. Born in Tomsk, Siberia, 6 April 1929. Educated at Music School of Tomsk (piano student), 1946–7; University of Tomsk (mathematics), 1946–51; Moscow Conservatory, under Vissarion Chebaline and N.I. Peiko (composition), Viktor Zukkerman (analysis), Semion Bogatyzev (analysis), Vladimir Belov (piano). Married Ekaterina Kuprovskaia in June 1987; 3 daughters and 1 son. Teacher of musical analysis and counterpoint, now professor of orchestration, Moscow Conservatory, since 1960; member, Union of Composers, Moscow, since 1956, and Union of Cineastes, since 1965; president, Association for Contemporary Music, Moscow, since 1990. Recipient: Officier de l'Ordre des Arts et des Lettres, France, March 1986; Mitglieder der Bayerischen Akademie der Schonen Kunste, Germany, July 1989. Mailing address: Studentscheskaia 44/28, kv.35, Moscow 1221165, U.S.S.R.

Publishers: Universal Edition; Sikorski, France; Johnsallee 23, 2000 Hamburg, 13, Germany; Leduc, 175 rue St Honoré, 75040 Paris, France; Boosey & Hawkes: VEB Deutscher Verlag, Karlstrasse 10, 7010 Leipzig, Germany; Peters (Leipzig).

Symphonies/orchestral:

Symphony in C 1955.
Sinfonietta on Tadzhik Themes 1957.
Peinture 1970; first performed Graz, 30 October 1970. Recorded Eterna 8 27333; Opus 9110 1448; Amadeo C VSTX 1408; Melodia C 10 18757 62.
Concerto for Cello and Orchestra 1972; first performed Leipzig, 22 September 1973. Recorded Melodia C10-13893–4.
Concerto for Piano and Orchestra 1974; first performed Leipzig, 5 September 1978. Recorded Eterna 8 27333.
Concerto for Flute and Orchestra 1975; first performed Dresden, 22 May 1976.
Aquarelle (24 strings) 1975; first performed Paris, 12 June 1975.
Concerto for Violin and Orchestra 1978; first performed Milan, 18 July 1978.
Concerto for Flute, Oboe and Orchestra 1979; first performed Cologne, 24 March 1979.
Partita (violin, orchestra) 1981; first performed Moscow, 23 March 1981.
Tod ist ein langer Schlaf (cello, orchestra; variations on a theme by Haydn) 1982; first performed Moscow, 30 May 1982. Recorded Melodia C10 24593 004.
Concerto for Bassoon, Cello and Orchestra 1982; first performed Como, 24 September 1984.
Chamber Symphony 1982; first performed Paris, 7 March 1983. Recorded Melodia C10 28753 008.
Epitaph (chamber orchestra) 1983; first performed Reggio Emilia, 11 September 1983.
Concerto for Two Violas, Harpsichord and String Orchestra 1984.
Suite from the Ballet "Confession" 1985.
Happy End (string orchestra) 1985.
Five Paganini Caprices (violin, string orchestra) 1985.
Concerto for Viola and Orchestra 1986; first performed Berlin, 2 September 1986.
Concerto for Oboe and Orchestra 1986; first performed Cologne, 4 March 1988.
Symphony 1987; first performed Paris, 2 March 1988.
Cloches dans le broyard 1988; first performed Moscow, 19 August 1988.

Concerto for Clarinet and Orchestra 1989; first performed Lubeck, 8 July 1989.

Chamber/instrumental:

Sonata (2 violins) 1958; first performed Moscow, 28 February 1960.
Bagatelles (piano) 1960.
Sonata (flute, piano) 1960.
Music for Eleven Wind Instruments and Timpani (flute, 2 oboes, 2 clarinets, 2 bassoons, trumpet, 2 trombones, tuba, timpani) 1961; first performed Leningrad, 15 November 1965.
String Quartet No 2 1961.
Variations for Piano 1961; first performed Copenhagen, 28 March 1965. Recorded Opus 9111 0342.
Sonata for Violin and Piano 1963; first performed Moscow, 1 April 1972. Recorded Le Chant du Monde CM 480 LDX 485; Melodia C 10 07283 4.
Crescendo e diminuendo (harpsichord, 12 strings) 1965; first performed Zagreb, 14 May 1967. Recorded Columbia MS 7052.
Three Pieces for Piano (4 hands) 1967; first performed London, 16 February 1968.
Three Pieces for Cello and Piano 1967; first performed Moscow, 11 May 1968. Recorded Melodia C 10 10168.
Concerto (flute, oboe, piano, percussion) 1967.
Ode (In Memory of Che Guevara) (clarinet, piano, percussion) 1968; first performed Moscow, 22 January 1968. Recorded Balkanton 11542; Egred LD3653; Fratelli Fabbri Editori mm 1110.
Musique romantique (oboe, harp, string trio) 1968; first performed Zagreb, 16 May 1969. Recorded Melodia C 10 10983 4.
String Trio 1969; first performed Paris, 23 October 1969.
D-S-C-H (clarinet, trombone, cello, piano) 1969; first performed Warsaw, 26 September 1969.
Wind Quintet (flute, oboe, clarinet, bassoon, horn) 1969; first performed Amsterdam, 10 October 1970.
Silhouettes (flute, 2 pianos, percussion) 1969; first performed Baden-Baden, 20 December 1969.
Chant des oiseaux (prepared piano, tape) 1969; first performed Dubna, 20 December 1970.
Sonata for Alto Saxophone and Piano 1970; first performed Chicago, 14 December 1972. Recorded EMI C 065–12805; Open Loop XPL 1059; Colosseum Colos SM 640; Coronet LPS 3044.
Trio (violin, cello, piano) 1971; first performed Moscow, 30 October 1972. Recorded Le Chant du Monde CM 480 LDX 685.
Sonata for Cello and Piano 1971; first performed Royan, 8 April 1971.
Solo for Flute 1971; first performed Witten, 29 April 1973.
Solo for Oboe 1971; first performed Helsinki, 1971. Recorded Denon OX 7031 ND.
Canon en mémoire d'Igor Stravinsky (flute, clarinet, harp) 1971; first performed London, 1971. Recorded Opus 9111 1277.
Sonata for Clarinet Solo 1972; first performed Moscow, 1974. Recorded BIS LP 62.
Three Pieces for Harpsichord and Percussion 1972; first performed Moscow, 8 October 1983.
Two Pieces for Alto Saxophone and Piano 1974; first performed Bordeaux, June 1974.
Signes en blanc (piano) 1974; first performed Warsaw, 26 September 1974. Recorded Le Chant du Monde CN 480 LDX 685.
Chorale with Variations (trombone, piano) 1975; first performed Venice, 27 August 1976.
Four Pieces for Flute and Piano 1977; first performed Paris, 21 April 1978.
Concerto Piccolo (4 saxophones—1 performer, 6 percussionists) 1977; first performed Bordeaux, 28 April 1979.
Sonata for Flute and Guitar 1977; first performed Moscow, 25 December 1978. Recorded Dabringhaus und Grimm MD + G 1249.
Sonata for Violin Solo 1978; first performed Hamburg, 19 October 1978.
Feuilles mortes (harpsichord) 1980.
Sonata for Guitar Solo 1981.
Trio (oboe, cello, harpsichord) 1981; first performed Donaueschingen, November 1981. Recorded Eterna 729 277.
Sonata for Bassoon Solo 1982; first performed Moscow, 1 November 1982.
Sonata for Violin and Organ 1982; first performed Leningrad, 26 March 1983.
Chamber Music (viola, harpsichord, strings) 1982; first performed Moscow, 7 May 1983.
Sonata for Flute Solo 1982.
Five Studies for Bassoon Solo 1983.
Sonata for Flute and Harp 1983; first performed Moscow, 7 January 1984.
Three Pieces for Three Instruments 1983.
Diane dans le vent d'automne (viola, piano, vibraphone, double bass) 1984.
Es ist genug (vibraphone, piano, double bass; or viola, piano; viola solo, flute, oboe, celeste, 2 violins, viola, cello, double bass; variations on a theme of Bach) 1984, 1986; first performed Lucerne, September 1989.
Nuages noires (vibraphone solo) 1984.
In Deo speravit cor meum (violin, guitar, organ) 1984.
Two Pieces (flute) 1984.
Moonlit Countryside (clarinet, piano) 1985.
Three Pictures After Paul Klee (viola, oboe, horn, vibraphone, piano, double bass) 1985.
Sextet (flute, oboe, clarinet, violin, viola, cello) 1985.
Variations on a Theme of Handel (piano) 1986.
Variations on a Theme of Schubert (cello, piano) 1986.
Emergences-Resurgences (2 percussion) 1986.
Winterlandschaft (harp) 1986.
Quintet (piano, string quartet) 1987; first performed Bristol, May 1987.
Quintet (clarinet, string quartet) 1987; first performed Saarbrucken, 30 May 1987.
Der Dampfer fahrt am Hafen vorbel (12 children, percussion instruments) 1987.
Punkte und Linien (2 pianos—8 hands) 1988.
Strahlen ferner Sterne im gewolbten Raum (3 percussion) 1989.
Quartet (flute, violin, viola, cello) 1989; first performed Trent, 7 November 1989.
Three Pieces (percussion) 1989; first performed Moscow, 14 April 1989.

Vocal/choral:

Canti di Catullo (bass, 3 trombones) 1962; first performed Moscow, 18 March 1982.
Le Soleil des Incas (soprano, flute, oboe, clarinet, horn, trumpet, percussion, 2 pianos, violin, cello; Mistral) 1964; first performed Leningrad, 30 November 1964. Recorded MFCD 869; Melodia C 10 18403 4.
Chansons italiennes (soprano, flute, horn, violin, harpsichord;

Blok) 1964; first performed Leningrad, 10 May 1966.
Les Pleurs (soprano, piano, percussion; Russian popular songs) 1966; first performed Brussels, 17 December 1968.
Fünf Geschichten von Herrn Keuner (tenor, soprano clarinet, alto saxophone, trumpet, trombone, percussion, piano, double bass; Brecht) 1966; first performed Berlin, 20 February 1968.
Automne (13 natural voices) 1968; first performed Royan, 30 March 1969.
Deux Chansons sur les poèmes d'Ivan Bounine (soprano, piano) 1970; first performed Halle, 3 April 1971. Recorded Caprice CAP 1112.
Chant d'automne (soprano, orchestra; Baudelaire) 1971; first performed Zagreb, 16 May 1971.
La Vie en rouge (voice, flute, clarinet, violin, cello, piano, percussion; Vian) 1973; first performed Zagreb, May 1973. Recorded Le Chant du Monde LDX 78 806 CM 460.
Blatter (soprano, string trio; Tanzer) 1978; first performed Moscow, 28 January 1980.
Douleur (mezzo-soprano, clarinet, viola, piano; Mandelstam) 1979.
Sur le tournant (soprano, piano; Mandelstam) 1979; first performed Moscow, 28 January 1980.
Five Poems by Baratynsky (voice, piano) 1979; first performed Moscow, 28 January 1980.
Ton Image charmante (voice, piano; Pushkin) 1980; first performed Moscow, 8 December 1980.
Pour Flore (voice, piano; Jozef) 1980; first performed Moscow, 1 November 1982.
Requiem (soprano, tenor, choir, orchestra; Tanzer, liturgy) 1980; first performed Hamburg, 30 October 1980. Recorded Melodia C 10 29277 007.
Sur le bucher du neige (voice, piano; Blok) 1981; first performed Moscow, 12 April 1982.
Colin et Chloë (soprano, mezzo-soprano, tenor, choir, orchestra; suite from the opera *L'Ecume des jours*) 1981; first performed Moscow, 17 October 1983.
Lumière et ombres (bass, piano; Soloviev) 1982; first performed Moscow, 31 October 1983.
Venue du printemps (unaccompanied chorus; Fat) 1984.
Das bleue Heft (speaker, soprano, violin, cello, 2 pianos; Wedenski, Charms) 1984.
Wishing Well (mezzo-soprano, clarinet, viola, piano; Tanzer) 1985.
Au plus haut des cieux (soprano, ensemble; Bataille) 1986; first performed Paris, 11 May 1987.
Ewiges Licht (unaccompanied mixed choir) 1988.

Opera:

L'Ecume des jours (Vian) 1981; first performed Paris, 15 March 1986.
Quatre Filles (after Picasso) 1986.

Other:

Le Confession (ballet) 1984; first performed Tallin, 30 November 1984.

Schubert: waltzes, Op 9a, 9b, 18a, 67, 91a, 127 (chamber orchestra) 1981–4; *Ave Maria* 1982; *Hommage aux belles Viennoises Op 67* 1983.
Mussorgsky: *Enfantines* (soprano, orchestra) 1976; *Chants et danses de la mort* (bass, orchestra; recorded Melodia A 10 00105 004) 1983; *Sans Soleil* (voice, orchestra; recorded Melodia A 10 00105 004) 1981.
Beethoven: *Turkish March* 1982.
Mosolov: *Les Annonces* (voices, chamber orchestra; recorded Melodia C 10 25177 003) 1981; *Trois Scènes enfantines* (voice, chamber orchestra; recorded Melodia C 10 25177 003).
Chopin: *Etude Op 10*.

PUBLICATIONS

By Denisov: "Le variazioni op 27 di Webern" in *Collage 9*, December 1970; "The Compositional Process", in *Tempo*, June 1973; "*Ode* für Klarinette, Klavier und Schlaginstrumente" (self-analysis), in *Arbeitshaft*, 35, 1982; "Alcuni cazatteni della melodia nella musica contemporanea", in *Musica / Realita*, December 1982; *Percussion Instruments in the Modern Orchestra*, Moscow, 1982; *Modern Music: Problems of the Evolution of Technique and Composition*, Moscow, 1986; "I Do Not Like Formal Art", (interview) in *Sovietskeia Musica*, December 1989.

On Denisov: Alfred Schnittke, "ED" in *Res Facta*, 6, 1972; Detlef Gogowy, "Kunst als Kategorischer Imperativ", in *Musica*, January—February 1975, and "Mehr Oper als Musiktheater", in *NZ*, December 1986; Walentina Cholopowa, "Rhythmische Organisation in der Musik ED", in *Arbeitshaft*, 37, 1984; Frank Mallet, "D on *L'Ecume des jours*", in *Diapason*, March 1986; Helene Piezzakos, "*L'Ecume des jours*", in *Opera*, March 1986; Susan Bradshaw, "ED", in *Tempo*, 1988; Ramon Barce, "ED", in *Ritmo*, December 1989.

Edison Denisov comments:

Music is not only the interplay of sounds capable of conveying meaningful information. It can also powerfully influence human souls. For me, the language of music is much richer and more eloquent than that of words. In its sublime manifestations, music touches upon spiritual spheres that words cannot penetrate. Music is a spiritual art. It shall bring light and good to people.

The artist's personality, irrespective of the will, leaves its mark upon any composition. The work can be more or less objective in its aim, but the creator's individuality, his frame of mind and even the peculiarities of his character are embodied in his music. Music shall not discharge a transient function, I believe. Genuine music speaks about eternal things. There are moments of enlightenment, when the artist sees a different world. This is a moment of mystery, and not everyone is destined to have and insight into it. It is here that the lofty art begins, the border of spirituality that few people are destined to step over.

Freedom is a major precondition for creative work. But freedom can be achieved only through perfection. Profoundly studying traditions and experimenting in various fields of modern musical art, the composer achieves a freedom that enables him to speak earnestly. Each composer, sooner or later, reveals his own style, creating a synthesis of various types of contemporary music-writing technique. As contemporary music-writing becomes filled with clichés, it is particularly important to reject them and form a unique form of expression.

A composer must not work for the market. Genuine art can be created only in silence and in solitude. A genuine artist feels the transience and senselessness of the fuss around him and is capable of creating something genuine and eternal.

Nowadays, people are up to their ears in daily chores. The artist must work in solitude and have a communion with God in the inner recesses of his soul. I salute Music as the Art and underline the responsibility of an artist before himself and before God.

* * *

The work Edison Denisov now acknowledges as his opus 1 dates from the end of the 1950s. Written at a time when he was avidly exploring a much wider range of music than had hitherto been available to him (not only that of the post-war European avant-garde, but also Debussy, Bartók, Schoenberg, Webern and Berg), it was the *Sonata* for two violins which seems initially to have given him the confidence to pursue his quest for a more individual style. Six years, later, *Sun of the Incas* not only brought him wide acclaim as a major new voice on the contemporary scene, but revealed an increasingly personal amalgam of avant-garde influences tied to a securely "Viennese" foundation: quasi-improvisatory passages—with boxes of freely repeating patterns and notes without rhythmic definition—here contrast with an almost Schoenbergian kind of motor-rhythmic development much favoured by Denisov throughout the 1960s.

By the end of the same decade he had already evolved a mainly linear expression that was beginning to be recognisably his own (as in *Crescendo e diminuendo* for harpsichord and strings and the first and last of the *Three Pieces for Piano* duet), even though it as yet owed much to the fractured rhythms and angular lines which were the trademark of the international avant-garde. At the beginning of the 1970s, however, a more characteristic type of contrapuntal writing was starting to make itself felt: based on small intervals allied to irregular rhythms, often set within a framework of florid grace-note decorations, this quasi-canonic style is exemplified by *Signes en blanc* for piano. Moreover, the contrast between conjunct and disjunct intervals was here beginning to evoke a parallel response in the expressive connotations of conjunct and disjunct rhythmic counterpoints, while at the same time chordal harmony—as opposed to the harmonic counterpoint of his still mainly linear style—was emerging as both a stabilizing element and a purposeful stylistic enrichment. Combined with elements of jazz (both ragtime and blues), this latter feature was used to dramatic and often moving effect in *La Vie en rouge*, just as it was later to pervade his opera, *L'Ecume des jours*.

The harmonic overtones of *La Vie en rouge* seemed for a time to suggest that tonal centres, even specific quotations of tonal excerpts (like that of the Schubert song at the end of his *Concerto for Violin*), might not be too remote a goal. However, unlike many of his generation, in the Soviet Union as elsewhere, Denisov has resisted the temptation to cast his stylistic net too wide or too often; direct quotations are rare in his music, and his borrowings from mannerisms of the past have been restricted to those which he can also claim as his own—like the *lingua franca* of 20th-century popular music cited above. Such influences of the present as he has absorbed over the years have been the mainly technical ones which he has adapted to his own purpose, successfully forging them into a language by now unmistakeably his own. If, with some of the slighter pieces in his significantly large output, he has occasionally seemed in danger of becoming a victim of this very success—allowing the language to dictate or even to become the expression of the music—he has elsewhere shown an astonishing capacity for musical rediscovery and imaginative renewal within the strictly chosen limits of his well-defined personal vocabulary.

This is nowhere heard to more exhilarating advantage than in his major achievement of the 1980s, the opera *L'Ecume des jours*. Based on a novel by Boris Vian, the work reflects a sort of world-weary, jazz-influenced tonality, filtered through and overlaid with elements of the composer's own harmonic character, so that each appears mirrored in terms of the other. Such vivid harmonic contrasts alternate with passages of equally expressive counterpoint—always in close position, like a tangled web of interlocked melodies—and with widespread flurries of more dissonant arpeggiated chords and chromatic scale formations. As always with Denisov, the texture—and with it the structural phrasing—remains supremely clear: he has an exceptionally acute ear for the balance between background and foreground perspective. And just as his melodic gifts enable him to contour his music by means of rhythmically loose-limbed, non-repeating shapes that can properly be described as athematic, so his harmony has acquired a range that is atonal in the best and most positive sense of being able freely to cross selected boundaries.

—Susan Bradshaw

---

de PABLO, Luís. Spanish. Born in Bilbao, 28 January 1930. Educated: initial musical study at Fuenterrabía (Guipuzcoa), 1938; study of law, University of Madrid, graduated 1952; private musical study; composition study in France with Max Deutsch; advanced courses, Darmstadt, 1958–9, 1969, 1961, 1962. Married Marta Cárdenas, 7 April 1975. Member, Nueva Música group, Madrid, 1958; founder, Tiempo y música group, 1959–63; member, Música Abierta group, Barcelona, 1959; president, Spanish Jeunesses Musicales, 1960–3; artistic organizer, First Madrid Biennial of Contemporary Music, 1964; founder of Alea, Spain's first electronic music studio, 1964–5; and Alea, Música electrónica libre group for live electronic music, 1968; visiting professor, Torquato di Tella Institute, Argentina, 1969; professor of contemporary techniques of composition, Madrid Conservatory, 1969, 1975–88; co-director (with J.L. Alexanco), Encuentros de Arte, Pamplona, 1972; visiting Slee Professor of composition, State University of New York, Buffalo, 1973–4; professor of composition, Ottawa University, 1974–6, and of University of Montreal, 1975; president, Spanish section, ISCM, 1981; artistic adviser, Lille Festival, 1982; head, Centre for the Propagation of Contemporary Music, Spain, 1983; also, courses in Berlin, Santa Fé, Stockholm, Havana, Prague, Warsaw, Granada, Paris, Albany, Las Vegas, Siena, Toronto, Bordeaux. Recipient: popularity prize for music, *Pueblo* newspaper, Madrid, 1967; Grand Prix du Disque de l'Académie Charles Cros, 1969; Chevalier de l'Ordre des Arts et des Lettres, 1973; Luigi Dallapiccola Prize, 1979; Médaille d'Officier de l'Ordre des Arts et des Lettres, 1986; King's Gold Medal of Fine Arts, 1986; academician of Academy of Fine Arts, Spain, 1989. Mailing address: Relatores 22/5, 28012 Madrid, Spain.

Publisher: Edizioni Suvini Zerboni, Milan.

Symphonies/orchestral:

Invenciones 1954–5.
Sinfonías (17 brass) 1954, 1960; first performed Paris, 1965.
Radial (24 instruments) 1960.
Tombeau 1962–3; first performed Brussels, 1963. Recorded Wergo WER 60037.

Iniciativas 1966; first performed Donaueschingen, 1966. Recorded Wergo WER 60037.
Módulos II (2 orchestras) 1966.
Imaginario II 1967–8; first performed Royan, 1969.
Heterogéneo (orchestra, Hammond organ, 2 speakers) 1967–8.
Paráfrasis (on 3 motets by da Victoria; chamber orchestra) 1968.
Quasi una fantasía (string sextet, orchestra) 1969; first performed Paris, 1969.
Oriotaldi 1971.
Je mange, tu manges (chamber orchestra, tape) 1972; first performed Royan, 1973.
Eléphants ivres I (orchestra) 1972; first performed Royan, 1973.
Eléphants ivres III & IV (orchestra) 1973; first performed Royan, 1973.
Latidos 1974–80; first performed Paris, 23 January 1981.
Tinieblas del agua 1977–8; first performed Metz, 18 November 1978.
Piano Concerto No 1 1979; first performed Madrid, 1 March 1980. Recorded HH 7634772). Chamber version for piano and 18 instruments, as *Concerto da camera* 1979; first performed Quebec, 11 December 1980.
Piano Concerto No 2 1979–80; first performed Santander, 4 August 1982. Version for harpsichord, string orchestra and 2 percussion, as *Concerto* 1983; first performed Naples, 16 December 1983.
Intermezzo (from opera *Kiu*) 1982–3.
Adagio 1983; first performed Hilversum, 2 March 1984. Recorded AA 1185-010/1.
Meditación Instrumental (no 13 of *Tarde de Poetas*) 1986.
Fiesta 1987; first performed Rennes, 1987.
Senderos del aire 1987; first performed Tokyo, 1987.
Une Couleur . . . 1988; first performed Paris, 1988.
Figura en el mar 1989; first performed Metz, 1990.

Chamber/instrumental:

Coral (7 wind instruments) 1953.
Sonata (piano) 1954.
Móvil I (2 pianos) 1957, first performed Heidelberg, 1959.
Móvil II (piano—4 hands) 1958–67.
Libro para el pianista (piano) 1961.
Polar (11 instruments) 1961; first performed Darmstadt, 1961. Recorded Erato STU 70385.
Prosodía (6 instruments) 1962.
Condicionado (flute in G) 1962.
Cesuras (6 instruments) 1963; first performed Madrid, 1963. Recorded RCA LSC LM 16329.
Recíproco (flute, piano, percussion) 1963.
Módulos I (11 instruments) 1964–5; first performed Darmstadt, 1965. Recorded Erato STU 70385.
Ejercicio/Módulos IV (string quartet) 1964–7.
Módulos III (17 instruments) 1967.
Imaginario I (3 instruments) 1967.
Módulos V (organ) 1967; first performed Bremen, 1968.
Comme d'habitude (piano) 1970.
La libertad sonrie (15 instruments ad lib) 1971.
Promenade sur le corps (flute, percussion) 1971.
Vielleicht (6 percussionists) 1972; first performed Royan, 27 March 1975.
Eléphants ivres II (ensemble) 1972; first performed Royan, 1973.
Le Prie-Dieu sur la terrasse (1 percussionist) 1973; first performed Barcelona, February 1974.
Affetuoso (piano) 1973.
Déjame hablar (11 string instruments) 1974; first performed Royan, 27 March 1975.
Visto de cerca (3 instrumentalists, tape) 1974.
A modo de concierto (percussion, instruments) 1976.
Invitación a la memoria (chamber ensemble) 1976–7; first performed Saintes, 18 July 1978. Recorded RCA RL 35357.
Credo (2 flutes, 2 oboes, 2 clarinets, 2 bassoons, 2 horns) 1976; first performed Madrid, 31 April 1977.
Lerro (flute) 1977.
Oculto (bass clarinet/clarinet) 1977; first performed Saintes, 18 July 1978.
Trio (violin, viola, cello) 1978; first performed Madrid, 3 November 1980.
Dibujos (flute, clarinet, violin, cello) 1979; first performed Ville d'Avray, 4 February 1980.
Ofrenda (cello) 1980–2.
Tornasol (2 flutes, 2 clarinets, violin, viola, cello, double bass, tape) 1980–1; first performed Creteil, 24 February 1982. Recorded GA-314.
Cuaderno (5 pieces for piano; II and IV become *Dos improvisaciones* for harpsichord) 1982.
Saturno (2 percussionists) 1983.
Cinco meditaciones (15 players) 1983–4; first performed San Sebastian, August 1984.
J.H. (clarinet, cello) 1984.
Cuatro fragmentos de "Kiu" (violin, piano; based on the opera) 1984.
Fragmento (string quartet) 1985–6; first performed London, 1986.
"Los Fuegos" de "Soledad Primera" de Luis de Gongora (from *Tarde de Poetas*; bassoon, 2 horns, harp, celeste, 2 percussion, 2 violins, 2 violas) 1985–6.
Cuatro fragmentos de "Kiu" (flute, piano) 1986.
Transición instrumental No 2 (no 7 of *Tarde de poetas*; 2 flutes, marimba, 2 violins, 2 violas, cello) 1986.
Transición instrumental No 3 (no 9 of *Tarde de poetas*; 2 flutes, oboe, bassoon, 2 horns, piano, 2 percussion, 2 violins, 2 violas) 1986.
Transición instrumental No 4 (no 11 of *Tarde de poetas*; 2 flutes, harp, piano, vibraphone) 1986.
Metáforas (string quartet, piano) 1990; first performed London, 1990.

Vocal/choral:

Comentarios a dos textos de G. Diego (soprano, 3 instruments) 1956; first performed Barcelona, 1959.
Glosa a un texto de la "Soledad Segunda" de Luís de Gongora (no 2 of *Tarde de poetas*; voice, 2 horns, piano, vibraphone) 1961–86.
Escena (mixed chorus, strings, percussion; de la Vega) 1964.
Yo Lo Ví (12 voices in SATB trios) 1970; first performed Paris, 1970.
Very Gentle (2 voices, 2 players) 1973; first performed Royan, 1974.
Al son que tocan (voice, 8 instruments, tape; homage to Machado) 1974; first performed Madrid, November 1975.
Portrait imaginé (12 voices, 18 instruments, tape) 1974–5; first performed Ottawa, 1 October 1975. Recorded RCA RL 35326.
Zurezko Olerkia (8 voices, 4 percussion, Basque txalaparta) 1975–6; first performed Bonn, 24 May 1976.
Bajo el sol (49 voices; Ecclesiastes, Aleman, Byron) 1977; first performed Hamburg, 1978.

Ederki (soprano, viola, 4 bongos; Robertet) 1977–8.

Pocket Zarzuela (mezzo-soprano, flutes, clarinet, violin, cello, piano; Ullan) 1978; first performed Bonn, 9 October 1979.

Canción (soprano, oboe, trumpet, harp, celeste; Gil-Albert) 1979; first performed Champigny, April 1980.

Retratos de la conquista (32 voices; del Castillo) 1980; first performed Lille, 15 November, 1980.

Sonida de la guerra (soprano, tenor, reciter, small female chorus, flute, harp, celeste, 2 percussionists, cello; Aleixandre) 1980.

Una cantata perdida (soprano, double bass, percussion; Pessoa) 1981; first performed New York City, November 1981.

Viatges i flors (soprano, speakers, 40-voice choir, orchestra; Rodoreda) 1981–3; first performed Brussels, 10 October 1985.

Manantial (soprano, 2 violins, celeste, harp, flute; Guillen) 1982; first performed Valladolid, 12 November 1982.

Malinche (soprano, piano, tape; also version for soprano, piano) 1983, 1985–6; first performed Rome, 25 April 1985.

Dos epigramas de Marcial (2 female voices) 1984; first performed Sermoneta, 16 June 1984.

Ocho epigramas de Marcial (no 5 of *Tarde de poetas*; 3 sopranos, 3 altos, 3 tenors, 3 basses) 1984–6.

Serenata (mixed choir, band) 1985.

Cuatro canciones de Ibn Gabirol (no 1 of *Tarde de poetas*; baritone, 2 horns, trombone, harp) 1985; first performed Siena, 23 August 1985.

"On Begliett" (no 10 of *Tarde de poetas*; baritone, trombone) 1985.

Como moises es el viejo (12 mixed voices; Aleixandre) 1985; first performed Paris, 9 December 1985.

Surcar vemos (no 8 of *Tarde de poetas*; soprano) 1985–6.

Tarde de poetas (soprano, baritone, 12 voices, 18 instruments) 1985–6; first performed Alicante, 1986.

Dos Poemas de Juan Larrea (no 2 of *Tarde de poetas*; soprano, 10 players) 1986.

Opera:

Kiu (libretto by Vallejo) 1982–3; first performed Madrid, 16 April 1983.

Il viajero indiscreto (libretto by Molina-Foix) 1990; first performed Madrid, 12 March 1990.

Other:

Protocolo (2 voices, 13 instruments, mute characters) begun 1968.

Por diversos motivos (piano, voices, actors) 1969.

Soledad interrumpida (collaboration with mime J.L. Alexanco) 1971.

Historia natural (collaboration with mime J.L. Alexanco) 1972.

138 (film; collaboration with J.L. Alexanco) 1972.

Berceuse (3 flutes, 2 percussion, Hammond organ, soprano, actor) 1974; first performed Buffalo, New York, 30 January 1975.

Solo un psaso (flute, actor) 1974.

Chaman (tape) 1976.

Mahler: *Zu Strassburg auf der Schanz* (orchestration) 1985.

PUBLICATIONS

By de Pablo: (translator) *Arnold Schoenberg*, by H.H. Stuckenschmidt, 1961; *Approximación a una estética de la música contemporánea*, Madrid, 1968; many articles and essays, published worldwide.

On de Pablo: Tomas Marco, *LdP*, Madrid, 1967; Jose Luís García del Busto, *LdP*, Madrid, 1978; *Escritos sobre LdP*, Madrid, 1984; many essays, reviews, articles in different languages.

Luís de Pablo comments:

Let me start by quoting an Aztec poem: "Flowers are budding, they are fresh, they grow, they open their petals. You, o poet, pour the flowers of singing, scattering them over the others." May I say that I feel like this old poet?

All of us are bearers of hidden orders and disorders. Some are capable of giving them a shape through a work and, if we are lucky, they remain, though nobody knows for how long (man, after all, is a newcomer in this world, even if a noisy one). All of us are also sorcerer's apprentices. We release forces the consequences of which we cannot know, and, alas, there is no master to put them all back in the right place.

My flowers, my music aim to catch flashes of orders and disorders that are as changeable and fallible as myself. Its value, if any, is to be a partial witnessing of our boundless, unpredictable variety.

Yet I am not sceptical. In my music there is always an effort to define valid technical criteria, even if only to be employed in a single work and nothing more. And, above all, there is an overwhelming joy (which doesn't exclude melancholy and fear) in face of a challenge to use that freedom to imagine new works of richness and efficacy.

* * *

The mere fact that as of Autumn 1990 75 out of over 100 works of Luís de Pablo have had their world première outside of Spain is no minor demonstration of the worldwide esteem that this Basque-Spanish composer enjoys, and has enjoyed from the very beginning of his career.

And the geographical/chronological range of these first performances abroad is equally impressive, from *Polar* (Darmstadt, 1961) or *Módulos I* (Darmstadt, 1965) to *Fragmento* (London, 1986) or *Senderos del aire* (Tokyo, 1987). De Pablo was a regular guest of the Festival de Royan, France, with eight works performed between 1968 and 1975.

One obvious reason for this range must be the very noticeable quality, and variety, of the music. The risk of stereotyping is admirably avoided not least through the "avant-garde" attitude to contemporary development. This is clear from a quick overview of stylistic phases.

There is in de Pablo's official work list a series of *opera zero* (too "bartókian/stravinskyan etc."), explaining a remarkable early grip of modern techniques and aesthetical conceptions. Thus, the wind septet *Coral* is de Pablo's only work written in "serialism". De Pablo stayed aloof from the contemporary extremes, giving new techniques his personal stamp.

The swift turn from one extreme, serialism, to its "opposite", aleatory, is shown in *Móvil I* for two pianos. And already *Polar* for 11 instrumentalists in three groups shows "a total dominion and knowledge of the European avant-garde music" and places de Pablo "in the foremost position of the international avant-garde" (Daniel-Michèle Tosi in *Escritos sobre Luis de Pablo*, 1987), i.e., demonstrated through its perfect "dialogue" between the then uppermost elements of lines vs. "points".

Already in *Cesuras* we are confronted with "the classical jewel of this *postserial* (my italics) phase" (*ibid.*). The family of five (actually six, *Paráfrasis* originally called *Módulos VI*) works in the "family" of *Módulos* offers an evident advantage as a summary. Tomás Marco (in the aforementioned book) admirably shows how this important element in de Pablo's *langage technique* involves actual and basic problems in a personal art form. These "modules" should "be understood as closed unities of autonomous expressive significance, capable of combining themselves in a macro-structure that can be fixed or mobile" (T. Marco in *Historia de la música española*, 6, 1983).

In his *Aproximación a una estética de la música contemporánea*, de Pablo demonstrates his intellectual capacities in problematizing and explaining aesthetical dimensions, at the time (1968) showing his models of micro/macro-structuring of musical elements.

In our motley world of post-serial music, de Pablo now moves with serene certitude. A phase of "violence" of means and contents (as in *Tombeau*) is replaced from *Oriotaldi* onwards by a "calmer ambience and a new concept of sonorous beauty" (Marco), a fascinating period of "quotes" such as Victoria in *Eléphants ivres*, Monteverdi and Morton Feldman(!) in *Very Gentle*, Beethoven's Bagatelle op 119 in *Vielleicht*, etc., gently phases out.

Another "family", of "espectáculos" (*Protocolo, Por diversos motivos*, and not least the sinister "comedy" *Pocket Zarzuela*) anticipate the two operas *Kiu* and *El viajero indiscreto*, certainly decisive later works. De Pablo seems to have postponed a theatrical penchant until time was ripe, and their success proves him right. Here all previous conquests and postures, the outstanding mastering of sounds and a sophisticated humour, focus on "eternal" aspects of human life and estrangements, and the many intellectual and artistic skills summon up *homo sapiens* as above all *homo ludens*, i.e., man being *all music*.

—Hans Åstrand

DIAMOND, David (Leo). American. Born in Rochester, New York, 9 July 1915. Educated at Rochester public schools; Cleveland Institute of Music, 1927–9; University of Rochester, New York; Eastman School of Music, Rochester, (under Bernard Rogers), 1930–4; New Music School and Dalcroze Institute, New York City (under Paul Boepple and Roger Sessions), 1934–6; American Conservatory, Fontainebleau, France, summers 1937, 1938; private lessons with Nadia Boulanger (Paris, 1936), André de Ribaupierre, Hermann Scherchen. Teacher of composition, Metropolitan Music School, New York City, 1950; Fulbright Professor, University of Rome, 1951–2; settled in Florence, 1953; visiting professor, Salzburg Seminar, Schloss Leopoldskron, 1949; also Harvard University Seminar in American Studies, Cambridge, Massachusetts; Slee Professor, State University of New York, Buffalo, 1961, 1963; returned to U.S., 1965; teacher, 1965–8, and chair of composition department, 1967–8, Manhattan School of Music, New York City; visiting professor, University of Colorado, Boulder, 1970; composer in residence, American Academy in Rome, 1971–2; professor of composition and lecturer in graduate studies, Juilliard School of Music, New York City, since 1973; visiting professor, Lamont School, University of Denver, Colorado, 1983. Recipient: Juilliard Publication Award (for *Psalm*), 1937; John S. Guggenheim Memorial Grant, 1938, 1941, 1958; Prix du Rome, 1941; American Academy in Rome Award, 1942; Rockefeller Foundation Grant; Paderewski Prize, 1942–3; Stravinsky-ASCAP Award; Ernest Bloch Award; elected to National Institute of Arts and Letters, 1966, vice-president, 1974; William Schumann Lifetime Achievement Award, 1985. Mailing address: 249 Edgerton Street, Rochester, New York 14607, U.S.A.

Publishers: Boosey & Hawkes; Associated; C. Fischer; G. Schirmer; Southern.

Symphonies/orchestral:

Hommage à Satie (chamber orchestra) 1934.
Ballade (chamber orchestra) 1935.
Divertimento (piano, small orchestra) 1935.
Threnody 1935.
Variations on a Theme by Erik Satie 1935–6.
Psalm 1936; first performed Rochester, New York, 10 December 1936.
Suite No 1 from Tom 1936.
Violin Concerto No 1 1936; first performed New York, 24 March 1937.
Aria and Hymn 1937.
Variations on an Original Theme (chamber orchestra) 1937; first performed Rochester, New York, 23 April 1940.
Overture 1937.
Cello Concerto 1938; first performed Rochester, New York, 30 April 1942.
Heroic Piece (chamber orchestra) 1938; first performed Zurich, 29 July 1938.
Elegy in Memory of Maurice Ravel (brass, harp, percussion; revised for strings, percussion) 1938–9; first performed Rochester, 28 April 1938. Recorded Nonesuch Records, 1990.
Music (double strings, brass, timpani) 1938–9, revised 1968.
Concert Piece 1939; first performed New York, 16 May 1940.
Concerto (chamber orchestra) 1940.
Symphony No 1 1940–1; first performed New York, 21 December 1941.
Symphony No 2 1942; first performed Boston, 13 October 1942. Recorded Delos 3093.
Rounds (strings) 1944; first performed Minneapolis, Minnesota, 24 November 1944.
Symphony No 3 1945; first performed Boston, 3 November 1950.
Symphony No 4 1945; first performed Boston, 23 January 1948. Recorded Delos 3093.
Violin Concerto No 2 1947; first performed Vancouver, British Columbia, 29 February 1948.
Symphony No 5 1947–51, revised 1964; first performed Boston, 23 January 1948.
The Enormous Room (after cummings) 1948; first performed Cincinnati, 19 November 1949.
Timon of Athens 1949; first performed Louisville, Kentucky, 1949.
Piano Concerto 1949–50; first performed New York, 28 April 1966.
Ceremonial Fanfare (brass, percussion) 1950.
Symphony No 6 1951-4; first performed Boston, 8 March 1957.

Sinfonia Concertante 1954–6; first performed Rochester, New York, 7 March 1957.
Diaphony (organ, brass, 2 pianos, timpani) 1955, revised for organ, orchestra, 1968; first performed New York, 22 February 1956.
The World of Paul Klee 1957; first performed Portland, Oregon, 15 February 1958.
Symphony No 7 1959; first performed New York, 26 January 1962.
Symphony No 8 1960; first performed New York, 26 October 1961.
Elegies (for William Faulkner and e.e. cummings; flute, cor anglais, strings) 1962–3.
Piano Concertino 1964–5.
Violin Concerto No 3 1967–8; first performed New York, 1 April 1976.
Music (chamber orchestra) 1969–70.
Overture No 2: "A Buoyant Music" 1970.
Symphony No 9 (baritone, orchestra; Buonarotti) 1985; first performed New York, 17 November 1985.
Sinfonietta 1989; first performed Koger, 20 July 1990.
Kaddish (cello, orchestra) 1989; first performed Seattle, Washington, 9 April 1990.

Chamber/instrumental:

Many early works withdrawn.
Eight Piano Pieces for Children 1935.
Sonatina (piano) 1935.
Six Pieces (string quartet) 1935.
Partita (oboe, bassoon, piano) 1935.
Chamber Symphony (clarinet, bassoon, trumpet, viola, piano) 1935–6.
Chamber Music for Young People (violin, piano) 1936.
Four Gymnopedies (piano) 1937.
Cello Sonata 1936, revised 1938.
Concerto (string quartet) 1936.
Quintet (flute, piano quartet) 1937.
String Trio 1937.
Violin Sonatina 1937.
Piano Quartet 1938.
Fifty-two Preludes and Fugues 1939–40.
String Quartet No 1 1940.
Concerto (2 pianos) 1942.
String Quartet No 2 1943–4.
Violin Sonata 1943–6.
The Tomb of Melville (piano) 1944–9.
String Quartet No 3 1946.
Album for the Young (piano) 1946.
Canticle (violin, piano) 1946.
Perpetual Motion (violin, piano) 1946.
Sonata (piano) 1947.
Chaconne (violin, piano) 1948.
Quintet (clarinet, 2 violas, 2 cellos) 1950.
String Quartet No 4 1951.
Piano Trio 1951.
Sonata (violin) 1954–9.
A Private World (piano) 1954–9.
Sonata (cello) 1956–9.
Wind Quintet 1958.
String Quartet No 5 1960.
Night Music (accordion, string quartet) 1961.
Nonet (3 violins, 3 violas, 3 cellos) 1961–2.
String Quartet No 6 1962.
Then and Now (piano) 1962.
Sonata (accordion) 1963.
String Quartet No 7 1963–4.
String Quartet No 8 1964.
String Quartet No 9 1966.
Introduction and Dance (accordion) 1966.
String Quartet No 10 1966–8.
Alone at the Piano (piano) 1967.
Piano Quartet 1972.
Piano Sonata No 2 1972.
Violin Sonata No 2 1981.
Prelude, Fantasy and Fugue (piano) 1983.

Vocal/choral:

Many early works withdrawn.
Two Elegies (voice, string quartet; C. Rossetti) 1935.
This Is the Garden (unaccompanied mixed chorus) 1935.
Four Ladies (song cycle; Pound) 1935, revised 1962.
Vocalises (voice, viola) 1935.
A Song for Shabouth (children's chorus, piano) 1935.
Paris This April Sunset (2-part female chorus, cello, double bass; cummings) 1937.
Three Madrigals (unaccompanied mixed chorus; Joyce) 1937.
The Mad Maid's Song (voice, flute, harpsichord; Herrick) 1937, revised 1953.
Somewhere I Have Never Travelled (voice, orchestra; cummings) 1938.
Three Epitaphs (song cycle; Warner) 1938.
Five Songs from The Tempest (song cycle; Shakespeare) 1944.
Young Joseph (women's chorus, string orchestra; Mann) 1944.
L'Ame de Claude (song cycle; Debussy letters) 1949.
The Martyr (male chorus, with or without orchestra; Melville) 1950, revised 1964.
Mizmor L'David (sacred service; tenor, chorus, organ) 1951.
The Midnight Meditation (song cycle; Olson) 1951.
Ahavah (symphonic eulogy for male narrator, orchestra) 1954.
Two Anthems (unaccompanied mixed chorus) 1955.
Prayer for Peace (mixed chorus) 1960.
This Sacred Ground (baritone, chorus, children's chorus, orchestra; Lincoln) 1962.
We Two (song cycle; Shakespeare) 1964.
To Music (choral symphony for tenor, bass baritone, chorus, orchestra; Masefield, Longfellow) 1967.
Hebrew Melodies (song cycle; Byron) 1967–8.
Love and Time (song cycle; Louchheim) 1968.
A Secular Cantata (tenor, baritone, chorus, small orchestra; Agee) 1976; first performed New York, 5 February 1977.
A Song for Hope (8 solo voices, orchestra; Weisel) 1978.

Opera:

David (D.H. Lawrence) 1935.
Twisting of the Rope (Yeats) 1940.
Mirandolina (musical play; Goldoni, Brown) 1958.
The Golden Slippers (musical play; Galdos, Citron) 1965; first performed New York, 5 December 1965.
The Noblest Game (Louchheim) 1971–5.

Other:

Myriologue (ballet; piano) 1935.
Formal Dance (Martha Graham ballet; piano, trumpet, percussion) 1935; first performed New York, 10 November 1935.
Dance of Liberation (ballet; piano) 1936; first performed New York, 23 January 1938.

Tom (ballet after cummings) 1936.
Duet (ballet; clarinet) 1937.
Icaro (dance drama after de Bossis; narrator, piano, flute, percussion) 1937.
Prelude (ballet; piano) 1937.
The Dream of Audubon (ballet by Westcott) 1941.
Hear It Now (radio score) 1942.
The Man Behind the Gun (radio score) 1942.
The Tempest (incidental music to Shakespeare) 1944, revised for large orchestra 1946; first performed New York, 25 January 1945.
Labyrinth (ballet by Marchovsky) 1946; first performed New York, 5 April 1946.
Romeo and Juliet (incidental music to Shakespeare) 1947, revised 1950; first performed New York, 10 March 1951.
The Rose Tattoo (incidental music to Tennessee Williams) 1950–1; first performed New York, 3 February 1951.

Orchestrations of Satie: *Chorale hypocrite, Messe des pauvres, Passacaille, Gymnopédies*; Roger Sessions: *Scherzino*.

Film scores: *A Place to Live*, 1941; *Dreams That Money Can Buy*, 1943; *Strange Victory*, 1948; *Lippold's the Sun*, 1965; *Life in the Balance*, 1966.

PUBLICATIONS

By Diamond: The *Alice and Frederick Slee Lectures*, Buffalo, New York, 1963; articles, lectures in *Musical Quarterly, New York Herald-Tribune, Notes*; *The Midnight Sleep* (unpublished autobiography in progress).

On Diamond: B. Lemmon, "A New American Symphonist", in *Etude*, 9, 1942; M. Goss, "DD", in *Modern Music Makers*, New York, 1952; R. Friday, "Analyses and Interpretations of Selected Songs of DD", dissertation, New York University, 1984; J. Peyser, "A Composer Who Defies Categorization", in *New York Times*, 6 July 1985; Victoria Kimberling, *DD*, Metuchen, New Jersey, 1987.

David Diamond comments:

At 75, with so vast a catalogue of pieces, one hopes the future will bring my music to a larger audience, one not interested in Trends and The Now, but music for All Time, for all humanity, to satisfy the emotions and the mind and reaffirm the strength of Beauty, even when harsh, but Beauty nonetheless.

* * *

Treading a path between the insistently American symphonies of Aaron Copland and Roy Harris and the harking back to European models of Howard Hanson and Samuel Barber, David Diamond was among several American composers who came to prominence during the 1940s, all as symphonists, the others including Peter Mennin, Robert Ward and Vincent Persichetti. Like Ward and Mennin, Diamond studied at the Eastman School of Music under either Hanson or, in his case, Bernard Rogers. But his crucial teachers were Roger Sessions at the Dalcroze Institute in New York and later privately, then Nadia Boulanger in Paris. While in the French capital Diamond had contacts with Stravinsky, Ravel, Milhaud and Roussel that considerably broadened his intellectual horizons.

Commissioned and given its first performance by Dmitri Mitropoulos, *Rounds* for string orchestra was long Diamond's most often heard work in the United States, and it is very effectively written for the medium. Yet the backbone of his output is a sequence of nine symphonies, the first eight of which appeared at fairly regular intervals between 1940 and 1960, followed by a gap of 25 years before No 9 came in 1985. The overall achievement here typifies Diamond's large production of orchestral and chamber music and vocal works, including five operas.

In the symphonies and other large-scale instrumental pieces Diamond, often using basic sonata allegro or contrapuntal processes, develops characteristically lucid forms in one- or two-movement structures. The harmony is quite personal, having evolved from a diatonic modality into something more chromatic or pandiatonic. This probably reached its fullest development in *Symphony No 4*, with the move towards greater chromaticism illustrated by Symphony No 5.

A revision of the latter plus the actual composing of *Symphonies Nos 6–8* was done in Europe, though all were premiered in America. Besides his period of study with Nadia Boulanger, Diamond spent considerable time in Europe, starting with a Fulbright professorship at the University of Rome. He also had a long residence in Florence, taught at Salzburg and again in Rome, all this naturally having a marked effect on his outlook, though he remained a distinctively American composer.

And the craftsmanship was always meticulous. There are moments of austerity in Diamond's music, yet a lyrical romanticism is more typical, this being quite individual and its effect heightened by his fine orchestration. The *Elegy in Memory of Maurice Ravel* is a good example of his lyrical side, but gradually he moved towards a highly emotional expressionism, although at best thought and feeling are in a nearly ideal balance.

Clearly the actual quantity of music he has composed militates against Diamond becoming as well-known as he merits. His operas, for instance, have usually been left unstaged, and it is barely possible to sample the huge vocal and chamber music outputs, which are tellingly written for their various media. The chamber works began diatonically enough, as in the *Quintet* for flute, piano and string trio, even if there are hints of polytonality in the finale's keyboard part. Composed in 1936 and revised in 1938, the *Cello Sonata* is splendidly concentrated, with the two instruments very independent, particularly in the first movement. Another *Quintet*, for clarinet, two violas and two cellos is intriguingly dark in mood and colour even at fast tempos. It is sometimes close to atonality, for example the angular motto theme first heard from the clarinet alone which reappears, slightly altered, in retrograde form at the close of the first movement. Such comments, however, offer merely the briefest glimpses of a production with which it will take us many years to become properly acquainted.

—Max Harrison

DICKINSON, Peter. British/English. Born in Lytham St Annes, Lancashire, 15 November 1934. Educated at The Leys School, Cambridge, 1948–53; Queens' College, Cambridge, 1953–7, B.A., M.A.; Juilliard School of Music, New York City, 1958–9. Married Bridget Jane Tomkinson, 29 July 1964; 2 sons. Lecturer, College of S. Mark & S. John,

London, 1962–6; staff tutor in music, extramural department, 1966–7, and lecturer in music, University of Birmingham, 1970–4; (first) professor of music, 1974–84, and Emeritus professor, since 1984, University of Keele; founder member, Association of Professional Composers, 1980; member of board, Trinity College of Music, since 1984; member, Royal Society of Musicians since 1985; fellow, King's College, University of London, since 1989. Recipient: Fellow, Royal Society of Arts, 1981. Mailing address: c/o Novello & Co, 8 Lower James Street, London W1R 4DN, England.

Publisher: Novello.

Symphonies/orchestral:

Vitalitas 1959; first performed Mexico City, 1960.
Monologue (strings) 1959; first performed New York City, 1959.
Five Diversions 1969; first performed Leamington, Staffordshire, November 1969.
Transformations 1970; first performed Cheltenham, Gloucestershire, 3 July 1970.
Organ Concerto 1971; first performed Gloucester, 22 August 1971. Recorded EMI CDC 7 47584 2.
Concerto for Strings, Percussion and Electronic Organ 1971; first performed Birmingham, January 1971.
A Birthday Surprise (3 variations on *Happy Birthday*) 1979; first performed Manchester, 30 June 1979.
Piano Concerto 1984; first performed Cheltenham, Gloucestershire, 22 July 1984. Recorded EMI CDC 7 47584 2.
Violin Concerto 1986; first performed Leeds, 31 January 1986.
Jigsaws 1988; first performed Derby, 1988.
Merseyside Echoes 1988; first performed Liverpool, 1988.

Chamber/instrumental:

A Cambridge Postlude (organ) 1953; first performed Lytham St Annes, Lancashire, 9 January 1954.
Postlude on "Adeste Fideles" (organ) 1954.
Toccata (organ) 1955; first performed Cambridge, 17 November 1955. Recorded Hyperion A66061.
Five Essays (piano) 1956; first performed Cambridge, 1 May 1957.
Fantasy (clarinet, piano) 1956.
Threnody (cello, piano) 1956.
Vitalitas Variations (piano) 1957; first performed Mexico, 1960.
Variations on a French Folk Tune (harpsichord) 1957.
Meditation on "Murder in the Cathedral" (organ) 1958; first performed Beirut, 1959. Recorded Hyperion A66061.
String Quartet No 1 1958; first performed New York City, January 1960; revised version first performed Birmingham, 21 February 1972.
Study in Pianissimo (organ) 1959; first performed London, 26 June 1979. Recorded Hyperion A66061.
Air (flute) 1959.
Juilliard Dances (flute, clarinet, bassoon, trumpet, trombone, percussion, piano, cello) 1959; first performed New York City, 13 May 1959.
Fantasia (violin) 1959; first performed New York City, 3 May 1959.
Sonata (violin, piano) 1961; first performed New York City, 23 March 1961.
Baroque Trio (flute, oboe, harpsichord) 1962.
Four Duos (flute or oboe, cello) 1962; first performed Cheltenham, Gloucestershire, 9 July 1984.
Music for Oboe and Chamber Organ 1962; first performed Cleveland, Humberside, 18 May 1962.
Dirge (organ) 1963.
Five Forgeries (piano—4 hands) 1963.
Five Diversions (clavichord, harpischord or piano, solo or duet; also orchestral version) 1963.
Carillon (organ) 1964; first performed Kingswood, Surrey, 8 August 1964.
Three Statements (organ) 1964.
Four Easy Pieces (piano) 1965.
Paraphrase I (organ) 1967; first performed Pershore, 8 October 1967. Recorded Hyperion A66061.
Paraphrase II (piano; based on motet *Mark*) 1967; first recorded Birmingham, 3 December 1968.
Fanfares and Elegies (3 trumpets, 3 trombones, organ) 1967; first performed Pershore, 1967.
*(*Three*) *Satie Transformations* (piano; taken from orchestral *Transformations*) 1970; broadcast 21 December 1986.
Translations (recorder, viola da gamba, harpsichord) 1971; first performed London, 20 February 1971.
Metamorphosis (flute) 1971.
Suite for the Centenary of Lord Berners (clavichord; from the film *A Great Day for Bonzo*) 1972; broadcast 12 May 1974; first performed London, 23 October 1986.
Recorder Music (recorder, tape; or 2 recorders) 1973; first performed London, 8 February 1973. Recorded EMI SLS 5022.
*(*Four*) *Piano Blues* 1973; first performed London, 6 December 1985. Recorded Conifer CFRA 134.
String Quartet No 2 (string quartet, tape or offstage piano) 1975; first performed Harlow, Essex, 30 January 1977.
**Quartet Rag* (piano; taken from *String Quartet No 2*) 1975. Recorded Conifer CFRA 134.
Solo for Baryton (baryton, tape, viola da gamba or second baryton) 1976; first performed Birmingham, 28 February 1983.
Aria (horn, oboe, clarinet, bassoon) 1977; first performed Cambridge, November 1977.
**Blue Rose* (piano) 1979; broadcast 14 July 1985. Recorded Conifer CFRA 134.
The Unicorns (brass band version) 1982–4; broadcast 12 February 1987.
Lullaby (arranged from *The Unicorns*; oboe or clarinet, piano) 1982, arranged 1986; first performed at sea, SS *Sea Princess*, Mediterranean, 29 September 1986.
**Concerto Rag* (piano) 1984; broadcast 14 July 1985. Recorded Conifer CFRA 134.
**Wild Rose Rag* (piano) 1985; broadcast 14 July 1985. Recorded Conifer CFRA 134.
**Hymn-Tune Rag* (piano) 1985; broadcast 14 July 1985. Recorded Conifer CFRA 134.
Blue Rose Variations (organ) 1985; first performed New York City, 2 April 1986. Recorded Priory PRC 239.
American Trio (Hymns, Rags and Blues) (clarinet, violin, piano) 1985; first performed East Lansing, Michigan, 1985.
**Patriotic Rag* (piano) 1986; broadcast 21 December 1986.
London Rags (2 trumpets, horn, trombone, tuba) 1986; broadcast 13 March 1988.
Sonatas (piano, 2-channel tape playback) 1987; first performed London, 26 June 1987.

*Marked works published collectively as *Rags, Blues and Parodies*, 1986.

Vocal/choral:

Jesus Christ Is Risen Today (unaccompanied SATB chorus) 1955.
Four W.H. Auden Songs (soprano, piano) 1956; first performed London, 5 February 1958. Recorded Conifer CDFC 154.
A Dylan Thomas Song Cycle (baritone, piano) 1959; first performed New York, 3 May 1959. Recorded Conifer CDFC 154.
Three Comic Songs (tenor, piano; Auden) 1960; broadcast 22 February 1977. Recorded Conifer CDFC 154.
Let the Florid Music (tenor, piano; Auden) 1960; first performed London, 12 February 1963. Recorded Conifer CDFC 154.
Four Hopkins Poems (soprano, baritone, chorus, organ) 1960–4; first performed Northampton, 1960.
Two Motets (unaccompanied ATB chorus, version for organ as *Paraphrase I* and for piano as *Paraphrase II*; Blackburn) 1963.
Magnificat and Nunc Dimittis (unison voices, organ) 1963. Recorded TRF 239.
Christmas Is Coming (unaccompanied SATB chorus; traditional, Rainbow) 1964.
When I Was a Sailor (voices, percussion, 2 unspecified instrumental lines) 1965.
Mass (unaccompanied SATB chorus) 1965.
The Judas Tree (5 actors, 2 tenors, SATB chorus, chamber orchestra, organ) 1965; first performed London, 1965.
An e.e. cummings Song Cycle (mezzo-soprano, piano) 1965; first performed Cheltenham, Gloucestershire, 13 July 1967. Recorded Conifer CDFC 154.
Elegy (counter-tenor, cello, harpsichord; Swinburne) 1966.
For the Nativity (unaccompanied SATB chorus; Heath-Stubbs) 1966.
Martin of Tours (tenor, baritone, chorus, chamber organ, piano—4 hands; Blackburn) 1966; broadcast 1968.
Three Complaints (unison voices, unspecified instrumental parts, percussion; Whybrow) 1966.
A Red, Red Rose (mezzo-soprano, piano; Burns) 1967. Recorded Conifer CFRA 134.
The Dry Heart (unaccompanied SATB chorus; A. Porter) 1967; first performed Birmingham, March 1968.
Four Poems of Alan Porter (counter-tenor, harpsichord) 1968; first performed London, 8 August 1968.
Communion Service (2-part choir, organ) 1968.
Extravaganzas (medium voice, piano; Corso) 1969; first performed London, 16 October 1969. Recorded Argo ZRG 788; Conifer CFRA 134.
Outcry (contralto, SATB chorus, orchestra; Blake, Hardy, Clare) 1969; first performed Conventry, Warwickshire, 10 May 1969. Recorded Conifer CDCF 167.
Winter Afternoons (6 solo voices AATTBB, double bass; Emily Dickinson) 1970; first performed London, 19 January 1971. Recorded EMI EMD 5521.
So We'll Go No More A Roving (mezzo-soprano, piano; Byron) 1971; first performed London, 6 December 1985. Recorded Conifer CFRA 134.
Surrealist Landscape (any voice, piano, tape; Berners) 1973; first performed London, 8 November 1973. Recorded UNS 268; DKP(CD) 9093.
Lust (6 voices AATTBB, optional tape) 1974; first performed Cheltenham, Gloucestershire, 8 July 1974.
Late Afternoon in November (multiples of 16 unaccompanied solo voices) 1975; first performed Keele, Staffordshire, 13 November 1975.
A Memory of David Munrow (2 counter-tenors, 2 recorders, viola da gamba, harpsichord; wordless) 1977; first performed Manchester, 7 May 1977.
Schubert in Blue (mezzo-soprano, piano; Shakespeare) 1977; first performed London, 19 February 1978.
Reminiscences (mezzo-soprano, saxophone, piano; Byron) 1978; first performed London, 18 March 1979.
The Unicorns (soprano, brass band; Heath-Stubbs) 1982; first performed Stockholm, 31 October 1982. Recorded Bluebell BEL 153; Conifer CFCD 154 (part); Conifer CDCF 167.
Stevie's Tunes (mezzo-soprano, piano; Smith) 1984; first performed London, 14 March 1985. Recorded Conifer CFRA 134.
A Mass of the Apocalypse (speaker, SATB chorus, piano, 2 percussion) 1984; first performed London, 15 July 1984. Recorded Conifer CDCF 167.
Larkin's Jazz (speaker-singer, chamber group) 1989; first performed Keele, Staffordshire, 1990.

Other:

Vitalitas (ballet; orchestra) 1959; first performed Mexico City, 1960.
Juilliard Dances (flute, clarinet, bassoon, trumpet, trombone, percussion, piano, cello) 1959; first performed with choreography New York City, 13 May 1959.

As Performer (with Meriel Dickinson, mezzo-soprano): *Songs by Berkeley, Cross, Dickinson* Argo ZRG 788; *Dreamscapes* (works by Panufnik, Harvey, Lutyens, Dickinson) Unicorn UNS 268; *American Anthology* (works by Gershwin, Carter, Copland, Cage, Thomson) Unicorn Kanchana RHS 353; *An Erik Satie Entertainment* Unicorn Kanchana RHS 338; *A Portrait of Lord Berners* Unicorn Kanchana RHS 355; *Music of Eugene Goossens* Unicorn Kanchana RHS 348; *The Essential Satie* Conifer CDCF 183; (with Sara Francis, oboe) *Oboe and Piano Music: Howells, Rubbra, Harty* Hyperion A66206.

PUBLICATIONS

By Dickinson: (as editor) *Twenty British Composers*, London, 1975; "Directions of a Decade", in *Musical Times*, January 1987; *The Music of Lennox Berkeley*, London, 1988; "The American Concerto", in Robert Layton, *A Companion to the Concerto*, London, 1988; "Ives and Copland", in *Heritage of Music: Music in the Twentieth Century*, Oxford, 1989; "The Concept of a Style Modulation" in *Musical Times*, April 1989; many articles and reviews in *Musical Times, Music and Letters, The Musical Quarterly, The Independent, The Times Literary Supplement, The Times Higher Education Supplement*.

On Dickinson: R. Norrington, "PD", in *Musical Times*, February 1965; A. Payne, "PD", in *The Musical Times*, August 1971; M. Dreyer, "Composer at a Crossroad", in *Classical Music*, July 1984; C. Palmer, "Profile of PD", BBC London Proms programme, 1986; M. Pacey, "In Memoriam", in *The Strad*, April 1987; J. Greenhalgh, "The Third Hat", in *Classical Music*, 20 February 1988; J. Greenhalgh, "A Family Affair", in *Classical Music*, March 1989.

Peter Dickinson comments:

Ever since hearing live performances of Charles Ives in New York in the late 1950s and first meeting John Cage there, I have been interested in the effect of hearing different types of music simultaneously. I admired the inclusiveness of both composers but had to work my way slowly to what I wanted myself. The orchestral *Transformations* brings together straight and jazzed versions of the same material, derived from Satie's *Gnossiennes*. The Organ Concerto, and later the Piano and Violin Concertos, have various, highly selective blues, ragtime and jazz involvements. Like a novel or film, these concertos can change direction unexpectedly, but always with a rigorous control of their materials—a process of style modulation (a term I have invented to cover this procedure).

Not all my works have this range—songs are already a partnership with a poet, which is another dimension—but some provide the alter ego through tape playback of material recorded by the performer in advance. This is ideal for broadcasts or recording such as *Surrealist Landscape*, recorded by my sister Meriel Dickinson with me, or *Sonatas for Piano*, played by Eric Parkin with two channels of tape playback. My involvement with ragtime increased in the mid-1980s—with the *Blue Rose Variations* for organ, the *American Trio* and *London Rags* for brass quintet. The early Beatles was the source for *Merseyside Echoes*, commissioned by the Liverpool Philharmonic Orchestra, and poet Philip Larkin's taste in jazz—King Oliver and Sidney Bechet—was the basis for *Larkin's Jazz* for speaker-singer and chamber group.

* * *

In 1958, Peter Dickinson went to the United States to study at the Juilliard School. He met John Cage, and listened to jazz and the American classics. American music was to have a profound—and surprisingly growing—impact on his work. Though he has never written anything as anarchic as Cage or Ives, he continually subverts in his work any rigid demarcation between serious and popular music. He has written effective blues and rags, and incorporates elements of these idioms into larger scale works. The first example of this is the orchestral piece *Transformations*, written in 1970, while Dickinson was teaching at the University of Birmingham; here themes and melodic cells derived from Erik Satie are deployed in direct and improvisatory ways. This has become a distinctive feature of his work. His *Organ Concerto*, from the following year, is as unsolemn as possible, and the later Piano and Violin Concertos contain significant jazz, blues and rag episodes; the 1984 *Concerto Rag* is part of the *Piano Concerto* of that same year, a big, warm-hearted work typical of Dickinson's characteristic "layering" of popular and serious styles and featuring a part for upright barroom "joanna" in addition to the solo instrument.

This "layering", or "style modulation" as Dickinson calls it, is achieved in a rather different manner to William Bolcom's sometimes aggressively parodic and deconstructive manner. Though Dickinson has written parodies, as in the marvellous piano and vocal set *Rags, Blues and Parodies*, all his work is characterised by a genuine warmth of enthusiasm for the material he is exploiting which suggests something closer to a homage. He is particularly close to Satie, with a remarkable facility for "open" melodies that seem to be "found" rather than composed and which are simultaneously attractive to and resistant of improvisation. Dickinson also has an impeccable harmonic ear, as witness his *Merseyside Echoes*, commissioned for the opening of the "Northern" Tate Gallery in Liverpool and influenced by the pre-Maharishi Beatles.

Perhaps the key to his success as a composer has been his double career as a performer. For nearly 25 years, Dickinson has toured and recorded as accompanist to his sister, Meriel Dickinson, one of the finest mezzo-sopranos Britain has produced since World War II. The Dickinsons effected a small revolution in public appreciation of Erik Satie with their album *An Erik Satie Entertainment*; they have done similar, though perhaps less pressing, duty for the English eccentric Gerald Tyrwhitt-Wilson, Lord Berners. Meriel Dickinson has a strong, projective voice, not ideally suited for lieder but perfect for a more adventurous and eclectic programme, encompassing Gershwin, Brecht/Weill and Dickinson. He has written marvellous scores for her, notably the e.e. cummings cycle (John McCabe played the piano part at the Cheltenham premiere), *Surrealist Landscape, Stevie's Tunes* to verses by Stevie Smith, and the "Green"-Romantic *Outcry*, which contains setting of John Clare far more obliquely and wryly moving than those of Clare's townsman Malcolm Arnold. A man of great general culture, particularly in literature, Dickinson's handling of relatively intractable texts such as cummings, Smith and his namesake Emily Dickinson, a notoriously difficult poet to set convincingly, is deeply impressive, done with fine feeling and without bathos. There are early and later settings of Auden, the former more fluent in their lyricism but lacking the ambiguities Dickinson buries in "Happy Ending" from the later "comic" set, which was only finished in 1972.

Perhaps the most haunting of his vocal works is the 1982 cycle *The Unicorns* written on commission to the Swedish mezzo Elisabeth Söderström and the Solna Brass, and to a text by the blind poet John Heath-Stubbs. The unusual sonority of the instrumental part brought out the best of Dickinson the melodist; "Lullaby" is a minor modern classic, and the cycle is well represented in good quality recordings. His major non-orchestral work of recent years is the impressive *Mass of the Apocalypse*, an outwardly unEnglish score which makes interesting use of piano and percussion in place of the more usual organ. Like *Outcry*, it is a work of considerable contemporary resonance and reinforces the utter absence of dilettantism in Dickinson's work. He is an impressive figure who merits greater international recognition.

—Brian Morton

DIEMER, Emma Lou. American. Born in Kansas City, Missouri, 24 November 1927. Educated at College High School, Warrensburg, Missouri, graduated 1945; Yale School of Music, New Haven, Connecticut (under Richard Donovan and Paul Hindemith), 1947–50, B.M., 1949, M.M. (composition), 1950; Berkshire Music Center, Tanglewood, Massachusetts, (composition), 1954, 1955; Eastman School of Music, Rochester, New York (under Ernst Toch, Roger Sessions, Bernard Rogers and Howard Hanson), 1957–9, Ph.D. (composition), 1960. Composer; keyboard performer (piano, organ, harpsichord, synthesizer); composer in residence, Ford Foundation Young Composers Project, Arlington, Virginia, 1959–61; composer-consultant, Contemporary Music Project of Music Educators National Conference, Arlington, Virginia, 1964–5; professor of theory and composition, University of Maryland, 1965–70; professor of theory and composition, University of California, Santa Barbara, since 1971; organist in churches of various denominations, 1940–84; organist, First Presbyterian Church, Santa Barbara, California, since 1984; composer in residence, Santa Barbara Symphony Orchestra, 1990–2. Recipient: Woods Chandler Prize, Yale University, 1950; Fulbright Scholarship (composition and piano), Brussels Conservatoire, 1952–3; Louisville Orchestra Student Award (for *Suite for Orchestra*), 1955; Arthur Benjamin Award for orchestra music, 1959; National Federation of Music Clubs/ASCAP award for choral and instrumental music for high school and college, 1969; Yale School of Music Alumni Association Certificate of Merit, 1977; National Endowment for the Arts Composer Fellowship (electronic music), 1980; prize (for *La Rag*), Symposium VII for New Band Music, 1982; semi-finalist, Kennedy Center Friedheim Awards, 1989. Mailing address: 2249 Vista del Campo, Santa Barbara, California 93101-4657, U.S.A.

Publishers: Carl Fischer, New York; Plymouth Music Co., 170 N.E. 33rd Street, Fort Lauderdale, Florida 33334; Seesaw Music Corp., 2067 Broadway, New York, New York 10023, U.S.A.

Symphonies/orchestral:

Symphony No 1 1952–3; first performed (2nd movement) Seattle, Washington, 1963.
Concerto for Piano and Orchestra 1953.
Suite for Orchestra 1954; first performed Louisville, Kentucky, 1955.
Concerto for Harpsichord and Chamber Orchestra 1958; first performed Rochester, New York, 1960.
Symphony No 2 on American Indian Themes 1959.
Youth Overture (youth orchestra) 1959; first performed Arlington, Virginia, 1960. Recorded OAS 007.
Pavane (youth string orchestra) 1959; first performed Yorktown, Virginia, 1960.
Suite: "Brass Menagerie" (symphonic band) 1960; first performed Arlington, Virginia, 1960.
Rondo Concertante (youth/community orchestra) 1960; first performed Arlington, Virginia, 1960.
Symphonie Antique 1961; first performed Arlington, Virginia, 1961.
Festival Overture 1961; first performed Arlington, Virginia, 1961.
Concerto for Flute 1963; first performed Omaha, Nebraska, 1964.
Fairfax Festival Overture (piano, orchestra) 1967; first performed Virginia, 1967.
Concert Piece for Organ and Orchestra 1977; first performed Oregon, 1985.
La Rag (symphonic band) 1981; first performed Virginia, 1982.
Winter Day 1982.
Concerto for Trumpet and Orchestra 1983, revised for violin, orchestra, 1983.
Suite of Homages 1985; first performed San Francisco, 1985.
Serenade for String Orchestra 1988; first performed Santa Barbara, California, 1988.
Concerto for Marimba and Orchestra 1990; first performed San Francisco, 21 March 1991.

Chamber/instrumental:

Preludes (piano) 1945.
Chromatic Fantasy (piano) 1946.
Piano Suite No 1 1947.
Second Suite for Piano 1948.
Suite (flute, piano) 1948; first performed New Haven, Connecticut, 1948.
Sonatina (2 violins) 1948; first performed New Haven, Connecticut, 1948.
Sonata (violin, piano) 1949; first performed New Haven, Connecticut, 1949.
Sonata (piano) 1949.
Suite (2 pianos) 1949.
Suite No 1 for Children 1952.
Suite No 2 for Children 1952.
Quartet (piano, violin, viola, cello) 1954; first performed Washington, D.C., 1960. Recorded Orion OC 693.
Serenade (flute, piano; originally violin, piano) 1954.
Piano Sonata No 2 1955.
Toccata (marimba) 1955.
Lauda Anima (organ) 1956.
Diademata (organ) 1956.
Festival Voluntary for Feast of St. Mark (organ) 1957.
Sonata (flute, piano or harpsichord) 1958; first performed Rochester, New York, 1959. Recorded Golden Crest RE 7074.
Fantasie (organ) 1958.
"He Leadeth Me" (hymn setting for organ) 1959.
Woodwind Quintet No 1 1960; first performed Arlington, Virginia, 1960.
Declamation (brass, percussion) 1960; first performed Arlington, Virginia, 1960.
Ten Hymn Preludes (organ) 1960.
Time Pictures (piano) 1961.
Sextet (piano, woodwind quintet) 1962; first performed Washington, D.C., 1963. Recorded Orion OC 693.
Toccata (organ) 1965.
Seven Hymn Preludes (organ) 1965.
Seven Etudes (piano) 1965.
Fantasy on "O Sacred Head" (organ) 1967.
Toccata (flute chorus) 1968. Recorded Golden Crest 4088.
Toccata and Fugue (organ) 1969. Recorded Capriccio Series of New American Music 1.
Celebration: Seven Hymn Settings (organ) 1970.
Three Fantasies on Advent/Christmas Hymns (organ) 1970.
Sound Pictures (piano) 1971.
Music for Woodwind Quartet 1972.
Trio (flute, oboe, harpsichord, tape) 1972; first performed Santa Barbara, California, 1972. Recorded Orion OC 693.
Three Pieces for Carillon 1972.
Seven Etudes (piano) 1972.
Declarations (organ) 1973. Recorded Capriccio Series of New American Music 1.
Quartet (flute, viola, cello, harpsichord, tape) 1974.
Movement (flute, oboe, organ) 1974; first performed Santa Barbara, California, 1974.
Pianoharpsichordorgan (1 performer or 3) 1974.
Movement (flute, oboe, clarinet, piano) 1976.
Jubilate (organ) 1976.
Contrasts (organ) 1976.
Quadralogue (flute quartet) 1978.
Little Toccata (organ) 1978.
Hymn Preludes and Free Accompaniments (organ) 1978.
With Praise and Love Vol 1 & 2 (organ settings of 19th-century hymn tunes) 1978–9.
Carols (organ) 1979.
Toccata (piano) 1979. Recorded Coronet—Music by Women Composers 1.
Solotrio (xylophone, vibraphone, marimba—1 player) 1980.
Echospace (guitar) 1980.
Homage to Cowell, Cage, Crumb and Czerny (piano) 1981. Recorded Contemporary Record Society CRS 8635.
Improvisation on a Drawing by Ann Skiold (organ) 1981.
Add One No 1 (electronic piano, tape) 1981.

Add One Nos 2 & 3 (synthesizer, tape) 1981.
Encore (piano) 1982. Recorded Vienna Modern Masters, 1990.
Seven Pieces for Marilyn (piano) 1982.
Suite 1982 (harpsichord) 1982.
Elegy (organ duo) 1982.
Summer of '82 (cello, piano) 1982; first performed Goettingen, Germany, 1982. Recorded Orion OC 693.
Romantic Suite (organ) 1983.
Bellsong (carillon; also arranged for guitar) 1983.
A Day in the Country (clarinet, tape) 1984.
Funfest (piano, tape) 1984.
Suite of Easter Hymns (organ) 1984.
Little Suite (organ) 1985.
Folk Hymn Sketches (organ) 1986.
Rite of Summer (piano, tape) 1986.
Church Rock (organ, tape) 1986.
Adventures in Sound (piano) 1987.
Variations (piano—4 hands) 1987. Recorded Contemporary Record Society CRS CD 8949.
String Quartet No 1 1987; first performed Maryland, 1988.
Catch-A-Turian Toccata (violin, piano) 1988; first performed Wichita, Kansas, 1989.
Space Suite (piano) 1988.
Laudate (trumpet, organ) 1989; first performed Santa Barbara, California, 1989.
Preludes to the Past (organ settings of 19th-century hymn tunes) 1989.
There's a Certain Slant of Light, Winter Afternoons (flute, guitar) 1989; first performed Santa Barbara, California, 1990.
Reflections from the Tower (carillon) 1990.

Vocal/choral:

St Chrysostom (cantata for soloists, choir, organ; Biblical text) 1956.
Psalm CXXI (soprano or tenor, organ) 1957.
Praise the Lord (unaccompanied mixed chorus) 1957.
As a Hart Longs (accompanied or unaccompanied mixed chorus) 1957.
How Majestic Is Thy Name (unison choir, piano) 1957.
Before the Paling of the Stars (mixed chorus, piano or organ) 1957.
Honor to Thee (mixed choir, piano, organ) 1958.
Noel: Rejoice and Be Merry (mixed choir, piano or organ) 1959.
The Shepherd to His Love (SSA/SA/SATB/SAB chorus, flute, piano; Marlowe) 1959.
The Magnificat (SA chorus, piano or organ) 1959.
Mary's Lullaby (SSA, piano; Barkley) 1959.
A Christmas Carol (SSA chorus, piano) 1959.
Alleluia (SSA chorus, piano) 1959.
I Will Give Thanks (mixed choir, piano or organ) 1959.
I Stand Beside the Manger Stall (unaccompanied mixed chorus) 1959.
Praise of Created Things (voice or mixed choir, piano or organ; St Francis) 1959.
The Bells (mixed chorus, piano—4 hands) 1959.
The Angel Gabriel (mixed choir, piano or organ) 1959.
O Shenandoah (arranged for TTBB chorus, piano) 1959.
At a Solemn Musick (unaccompanied mixed chorus; Milton) 1960.
Fragments from the Mass (SSAA chorus) 1960. Recorded Golden Crest 5063.
Your Friends Shall be the Tall Wind (SSA/SATB chorus, piano) 1960.
O Come, Let Us Sing unto the Lord (SATB chorus, piano; arranged for TTBB chorus, piano) 1960. Recorded Golden Crest 5063.
Four Carols (SSA chorus) 1960.
Three Poems of Ogden Nash (TTB chorus, piano) 1960.
Praise Ye the Lord (mixed chorus, piano—4 hands) 1960.
Three Madrigals (mixed chorus, piano or organ; Shakespeare) 1960.
A Spring Carol (voice, piano; Blake, Song of Songs) 1960.
O, Give Thanks to the Lord (mixed choir, piano or organ) 1960.
To Him All Glory Give (chorus, orchestra; Hendry) 1960.
Outburst of Praise (mixed choir, piano; Latin, translated Dryden) 1961.
Now the Spring Has Come Again (mixed chorus, piano) 1961.
Thine, O Lord (2-part chorus, piano) 1961.
Proclaim the Day (mixed chorus, brass quartet) 1962.
Come Hither, You That Love (SSA chorus, flute, piano) 1963.
Three Mystic Songs (soprano, baritone, piano; Hindu poetry) 1963.
Cantata for Palm Sunday (choir, organ; Vaughan) 1963.
Alleluia! Christ Is Risen (mixed chorus, trumpet) 1964.
A Little Song of Life (SA/SATB chorus, piano) 1964.
A Babe Is Born (mixed chorus, brass quartet, tambourine) 1965.
Spring (mixed chorus, piano) 1965.
Dance, Dance, My Heart (mixed chorus, organ, optional percussion) 1965.
Anthem of Faith (mixed chorus, piano or organ) 1966.
Winds of Spring (unison chorus, piano) 1966.
For Ye Shall Go Out with Joy (mixed chorus, piano) 1967.
A Service in Music and Poetry (congregation, choir, soloists, organ, piano, percussion; various poets) 1967.
Verses from the Rubaiyat (unaccompanied mixed chorus) 1967.
The Prophecy (SSAA chorus; Bible) 1968.
Blessed Are You (mixed chorus, optional guitar) 1969.
Anniversary Choruses (chorus, orchestra; Psalms, Timrod, Rutledge) 1970.
O, to Make the Most Jubilant Song (mixed chorus, piano; Whitman, Tennyson) 1970.
Why So Pale and Wan? (unaccompanied mixed chorus) 1971.
Madrigals Three (mixed chorus, piano; Campion, Donne, Shakespeare) 1972. Recorded Golden Crest 5063.
O, to Praise God Again (unaccompanied mixed chorus) 1972.
Psalm CXXXIV (unaccompanied mixed chorus) 1974. Recorded Golden Crest 5063.
Two Madrigals (2-part chorus, piano) 1974.
Weep You No More, Sad Fountains (SA/TB chorus) 1974.
Love Is a Sickness Full of Woes (SAB chorus) 1974.
Jesus, Lover of My Soul (2-part chorus, flute, piano) 1974.
So Have I Seen a Silver Swan (unaccompanied mixed chorus) 1974.
Men Are Fools That Wish to Die (unaccompanied mixed chorus) 1974.
Romance (mixed chorus, piano) 1974.
Laughing Song (mixed chorus, piano—4 hands; Blake) 1974. Recorded Golden Crest 5063.
Praise the Lord (mixed chorus, brass quintet, optional timpani) 1974.
Choruses on Freedom (mixed chorus, strings, piano, percussion) 1975.
Sing, O Heavens (unaccompanied mixed chorus) 1975.
Four Poems by Alice Meynell (soprano or tenor, 2 flutes/piccolo, 2 percussion, vibraphone, xylophone, harp, harpsichord, piano, strings) 1976.

California Madrigals (mixed chorus, piano) 1976.
Three Poems by Alice Meynell (mixed chorus, woodwind quintet, percussion, marimba, vibraphone, piano, organ) 1976. Recorded Golden Crest 5063.
The Call (mixed chorus, strings, optional percussion) 1976.
From This Hour, Freedom (mixed chorus, strings, optional percussion) 1976.
Strong Son of God (mixed chorus, piano or organ) 1976.
Awake, My Glory (mixed chorus, optional guitar) 1976.
When in Man's Music (mixed chorus, piano) 1976.
Joy to the World (mixed chorus, piano) 1976.
The Lord Is My Light (mixed choir, piano or organ) 1977.
Wild Nights! Wild Nights! (mixed chorus, piano; Dickinson) 1978. Recorded Golden Crest 5063.
The Lord Is Mindful (mixed choir, piano) 1979.
Away, Delights (TTBB chorus) 1979.
Weep No More (SSA chorus) 1979.
Tell Me, Dearest, What Is Love? (unaccompanied mixed chorus) 1979.
Three Hymn Anthems: "God of Love and God of Power", "The Church's One Foundation", "How Firm a Foundation" (mixed choir, 4 trumpets, 3 trombones, 4 horns, tuba, timpani, optional percussion, organ; or organ only) 1981.
God Is Love (SSAATBB chorus, tape) 1982.
A Service for the Lutheran Church of the Reformation (congregation, choir, narrators, organ) 1982.
Clap Your Hands (mixed chorus, piano) 1982.
Countin-Out Rhyme (SSAA chorus) 1983.
Prairie Song (SSAA chorus) 1983.
Three Poems by Oscar Wilde (mixed chorus, piano) 1984.
The Lord's Prayer (SATB choir, tape) 1985.
Invocation (chorus, orchestra; Sarton) 1985.
Caprice (mixed chorus, piano) 1986.
"I Will Give Thanks to the Lord", "Let Thy Steadfast Love", "Sing Praises to the Lord" (mixed chorus, piano or organ) 1986.
And in the Last Days (mixed chorus, piano or organ) 1986.
Peace Cantata (mixed chorus, narrators, organ, brass, timpani) 1986.
Christ the Lord Is Ris'n Today (mixed chorus, 3 trumpets, organ; or organ only) 1987.
The Sea (mixed chorus, flute, clarinet, percussion, piano, strings) 1987.
Glory to God (mixed chorus, piano or organ; Hendry) 1988.
Christmas Cantata (mixed chorus, children's choir, soloists, readers, organ, piano, optional guitar, optional synthesizer; Hendry) 1988.
I Will Extol You (mixed chorus, piano or organ; Psalms) 1988.
What Child Is This? (mixed chorus, piano or organ; Dix) 1989.
Choral Responses for Worship (accompanied or unaccompanied mixed chorus) 1989.
Reasons Briefly Set Downe by th'Auctor to Perswade Euery-one to Learne to Singe (TTBB, piano) 1989; first performed Santa Barbara, California, March 1990.

Other:

Patchworks (electronic tape) 1978.
Scherzo (electronic tape) 1980.
Presto Canon (electronic tape) 1980.
Harpsichord Quartet (tape) 1980.
Of the Past (electronic tape) 1980.
Lightly Stepped a Yellow Star (electronic tape) 1983.
Three Poems by Emily Dickinson (computer tape) 1984.
Bakersfield Serenade (electronic tape) 1989.

As Performer: *Oatlands Sketches* for organ, by Clara Shore, Contemporary Record Society CRS 8842; album of Baroque music for trumpet and organ, Water Lilly Acoustics, Santa Barbara, 1990.

PUBLICATIONS

By Diemer: "Rebel on the Organ Bench", in *Journal of Church Music*, April 1981; "Fantasies and Improvisations", in *Journal of Church Music*, September 1981; "Loneliness of the Long-Distance Organ Composer", in *The American Organist*, September 1982; "Writing for Mallet Percussion", in *Woodwind, Brass & Percussion*, April 1983; "My Life as a Composer", in *The Piano Quarterly*, Spring 1985; "Women Teachers of Composition in the U.S. and Abroad", in *The Musical Woman*, vol. 3, 1990.

On Diemer: C. Ammer, in *Unsung: A History of Women in American Music*, Westport, Connecticut, 1980; J.W. LePage, in *Women Composers, Conductors and Musicians of the Twentieth Century*, Metuchen, New Jersey, 1980–3; Cynthia Clark Brown, "ELD: Composer, Performer, Educator, Church Musician", dissertation, Southern Baptist Theological Seminary, 1985; "The Reason for Being", (interview) in *American Women Composers News / Forum*, April 1986; Joyanne Outland, "ELD: Solo and Chamber Works for Piano Through 1986", dissertation, Ball State University, 1987; Eileen McDaniel, "The Choral Music of ELD", dissertation, Arizona State University, 1987; James McCray, "American Choral Music with Organ: The Music of ELD", in *The American Organist*, November 1987.

Emma Lou Diemer comments:

On my reasons to compose: to express the musical influences and styles that affect one's output like a stone gathering moss; to reflect the changing patterns of the society and world conditions (or to counteract them, as the case may be); and in so doing, to offer some knowledge, philosophy, insight, emotional release, diversion, entertainment to those who hear or perform the music. I have little affinity with the composers who write only for their fellow composers. Some of history's dullest, most ephemeral music has been produced for that reason.

* * *

The shaping of a musical language, style and career is influenced by many factors—social, cultural, political, religious and musical. Forming a dialectic relationship, the compositions of Emma Lou Diemer bear witness to two dominant stylistic and philosophical components: a conservative style heavily reliant on music of the past with its emphasis on the traditional musical elements, i.e., melody, harmony, rhythm, texture and form; and an innovative style which has sought either to stretch and expand these traditional elements or completely break away from them in an effort to establish a totally new and daring musical style. This compositional philosophy is reflective of the influences which were brought to bear on Diemer during her educative years, particularly those at Yale University with Hindemith and his concept of *Gebrauchsmusik*. Equally important to Diemer's philosophy is the idea of expressive communication. She says of composing, "I am most interested in my subjective idea of expressive content, emotion, education, entertainment, and amusement; all for purposes of communication."

In harmony with this philosophy, Diemer's approach to

writing music has been one of balance: balance between the classical concepts of structure, rhythm, harmony and texture and the more progressive concepts of the latter half of the 20th century.

For Diemer, the process of composition is intrinsically aligned with improvisation. While this process is not restricted to any particular time or place, it is almost always associated with the piano, Diemer's primary performing instrument. This improvisational spirit, pervading both Diemer's compositional philosophy and procedure, is merely reflective of the significance she places on freedom, creativity, and communication in music.

Diemer's compositional output can largely be divided between three types of works: symphonies, concertos and concert pieces; music for the church and school; and electronic music. This division is indicative of Diemer's conscious continual investment in both the professional and the non-professional musician, in both complex and simple styles.

Any attempt to classify rigidly Diemer's compositional style would be antithetical to her own philosophy of composition as an evolving art concerned with expressive, individualistic communication. Yet, certain salient features can be discerned: her integration of the romantic ideal of expressive content with the classical need for structured form; an overall robust energy; a poignant, lyric quality; a sense of economy of material; and a continual sifting and assimilating of innovative styles for approaches germane to her own needs.

Diemer's use of the conventional elements of music is at once traditional, innovative and daring. Melodically, she shows a preference for diatonic and sequential writing, and displays a lyric quality which avoids any overt atonal implications. Harmonically adventurous, Diemer often employs modal or shifting tonal centers and shuns prolonged dissonance. Frequent use is made of quartal harmony, major-minor sonorities, added notes, parallel progressions, polytonality and chords in which intervals of the second, fourth and fifth are prominent; thus creating a bright, expressive sonority. Influenced greatly by jazz and utilizing elements such as ostinati, syncopation, hemiola and irregular groupings and meters, Diemer's rhythmic writing is persistent and vigorous. Chordal and contrapuntal textures are equally represented in her compositional style. Timbral contrasts are important in both textures. Classically achieved, the structure of her works is based on conventional forms, such as rondo, sonata-allegro, song form, sectional and free forms.

Believing that she has something unique to offer, Diemer is indefatigable in her efforts to contribute to contemporary American music. To each of these endeavors, she has brought a sense of unswerving dedication and artistic integrity.

—Cynthia Clark Brown

DILLON, James. British/Scottish. Born in Glasgow, 29 October 1950. Educated at Glasgow School of Art, 1967–8; Polytechnic of Central London, 1972–3; Polytechnic of North London (acoustics, music and linguistics), 1973–6. Self-taught freelance composer; guest composer, Ferienkurse für Neue Musik, Darmstadt, 1982, 1984, 1986; guest lecturer, State University of New York, Stony Brook, 1986; part-time lecturer in composition, Goldsmiths' College, University of London, 1986–7; also at universities of Keele, Nottingham, Oxford. Recipient: Kranichsteiner Musikpreis, Germany, 1982. Mailing address: 80 Harvist Road, Queen's Park, London NW6 6HL, England.

Publisher: Peters Edition.

Symphonies/orchestral:

Windows and Canopies 1985; first performed Paris, October 1985.
Uberschreiten 1986; first performed London, June 1986.
helle Nacht 1987; first performed Glasgow, September 1987.

Chamber/instrumental:

Dillug-Kefitsah (piano) 1978; first performed Huddersfield, Yorkshire, 1978.
Crossing Over (clarinet) 1979; first performed London, April 1983.
Ti're-Ti'ke-Dha (drums) 1980; first performed London, April 1982.
. . . Once upon a Time (alto flute/piccolo, oboe/cor anglais, clarinet, bassoon, horn, trumpet, trombone, double bass) 1980; first performed York, July 1980.
Spleen (piano) 1980; first performed London, December 1980. Recorded Musica Nova.
Who Do You Love (flute/piccolo/bass flute, clarinet, percussion, violin/viola, cello, female voice) 1980; first performed London, February 1981.
Parjanya-Vata (cello) 1981; first performed London, May 1981.
Come Live with Me (flute/piccolo/alto flute, oboe/oboe d'amore/cor anglais, mezzo-soprano, piano, percussion) 1981; first performed London, February 1982.
East 11th St NY 10003 (6 percussion; part 1 of *Nine Rivers*) 1982; first performed London, October 1982.
String Quartet 1983; first performed Huddersfield, Yorkshire, November 1983.
Zone (. . . de azul) (clarinet, horn, trumpet, trombone, piano, violin, viola, cello) 1984; first performed London, January 1986.
Le Rivage (wind quintet) 1984; first performed Bath, May 1984.
Sgothan (flute) 1984; first performed La Rochelle, July 1984. Recorded ICONS Antidogma AM-I 861–862.
Diffraction (piccolo) 1985; first performed Paris, November 1985.
Birl (harpsichord) 1986; first performed London, March 1987.
Shrouded Mirrors (guitar) 1988; first performed Milan, May 1988.
Del Cuarto Elemento (violin) 1988; first performed London, July 1988.
L'ECRAN parfum (6 violins, 3 percussion; part 2 of *Nine Rivers*) 1989; first performed Oslo, April 1989.
La femme invisible (woodwind octet, electronic keyboard, 2 percussion; part 4 of *Nine Rivers*) 1989; first performed London, June 1989.
La coupure (percussion, electronics; part 5 of *Nine Rivers*) in preparation 1991.
L'Oeuvre au noir (bass clarinet/contrabass clarinet, bassoon, trombone, tuba, 2 percussion, 2 cellos, 2 double basses, electronic keyboards, electronics; part 6 of *Nine Rivers*) 1990.

éileadh sguaibe (7 brass, 2 percussion, electronics; part 7 of *Nine Rivers*) 1990.
Introitus (12 strings, electronics; part 8 of *Nine Rivers*) 1990.

Vocal/choral:

Evening Rain (voice) 1980; first performed Birmingham, April 1981.
A Roaring Flame (female voice, double bass) 1982; first performed London, January 1983.
(Time Lag Zero) (female voice, viola) 1982; first performed Brighton, Sussex, May 1982.
Viriditas (16 voices; part 3 of *Nine Rivers*) in preparation.
Oceanos (16 voices, 8 woodwind, 7 brass, 6 percussion, 12 strings, electronics; part 9 of *Nine Rivers*) 1991–2.

PUBLICATIONS

By Dillon: "Speculative Instruments", in *Le timbre: métaphores pour la composition*, edited by Barrière, Paris, 1987.

On Dillon: R. Wright, "JD", in *Contact*, 24, 1982; A. Schaathun, "Mot en Kontinuerlig musikk", (interview) in *Ballade*, 3, 1986; R. Wright, "Breaking Boundaries", in *The Listener*, 115 (2962), 1986; Paul Griffiths, "Die-Cast Composer", in *Classical Music*, 331, London, 1987.

* * *

Although born and brought up in Glasgow, James Dillon has moved in a very different direction from any of his fellow Scottish composers. The listener will not find, for example, any of the strains of traditional music which many of his contemporaries have drawn on, but rather an imaginative and controversial sound world which owes more to the example of Varèse or Xenakis than any indigenous musical traits.

Perhaps partly as a consequence, he remains less admired at home than he is in continental Europe, where his challenging works have generally found a more enthusiastic welcome to date.

Dillon first attracted major attention when Lontano performed his brash and raucous chamber piece . . . *Once upon a Time* (the inversion of the ellipsis is a tiny point, but highly typical of the composer's constant drive to subvert both artistic and intellectual expectations), closely followed by the equally energetic *Who Do You Love*, for female voice and instruments.

Commentators increasingly bracketed his music with that of Brian Ferneyhough, hearing a relationship between their use of extreme musical languages, unconventional instrumental techniques, densely compacted structural devices and complex rhythms, as well as often elliptical programme notes and statements of intent couched in a language quite as dense and technically obtuse as the music.

Dillon's music, however, while doing all these things, ultimately sounds quite different from Ferneyhough's, and he remains an original if not always accessible voice in contemporary British music. The complexities of solo instrumental works like *Crossing Over* for clarinet, *Spleen* for piano or *Parjanya-Vata* for cello contained the seeds which would sprout in his larger-scale works during the decade, while placing huge demands on the capabilities of both performer and instrument.

The *String Quartet*, while no less dense than the earlier chamber pieces cited above, or the percussion work *East 11th St NY 10003*, hinted at a more restrained vocabulary bordering at times on an almost elegant lucidity of expression, but his subsequent orchestral works pushed that register to new extremes.

The writings of Jacobus Boehme and Georges Bataille were part of the stimulus for *Uberschreiten*, a work which explored Bataille's notion of transgressional thought as a means to progress through shock, using an extreme and often disturbing musical rhetoric which militates against closure and completeness.

Dillon took those processes a stage further in the orchestral work *helle Nacht*. A series of massive, slab-like, densely scored crescendos proceed remorselessly but without ultimate direction through the 28 minutes of the work, denying any finality or the release of a climax, and throwing the listener back once again upon the processes at work, rather than any desired or imagined conclusion of them.

That is a line of musical development which can ultimately seem simply directionless, and there are passages in *helle Nacht* which arouse that suspicion, but the work unfolds with an exuberant, overpowering energy. The sheer compacted complexity of the tightly woven textural and rhythmic mass is at once challenging and disturbing, which is doubtless just as the composer intended.

More recently, Dillon has been at work on a multi-faceted creation to be called *Nine Rivers*, which will incorporate electronics and lighting effects within its finished form, and is intended to last around three hours.

—Kenny Mathieson

DINESCU, Violeta (Violeta Dinescu-Lucaci). Romanian; German citizen since 1989. Born in Bucharest, 13 July 1953; resident in Germany since 1982. Educated at G. Lazar Lyceum, Bucharest, bachelor's degree (composition, piano, pedagogy), 1972; Ciprian Porumbescu Conservatory of Music, Bucharest, master's degree (composition, with distinction), 1978; doctoral study, Heidelberg, 1984. Special correspondent on music, *Romania Literara, Muzica, Scinteia Tineretului*, Bucharest, 1975–82; instructor in theory, piano, harmony, counterpoint, aesthetics, George Enescu Music School, Bucharest, 1978–82; instructor in harmony, theory and counterpoint, Conservatory for Church Music, Heidelberg, 1986–90; instructor in harmony, theory and counterpoint, Conservatory for Music, Frankfurt, since 1989, and Conservatory for Church Music, Bayreuth, since 1990, European correspondent, *Living Music*, California, and International League of Women Composers, New York City, since 1987. Recipient: Union of Composers of Romania Award, 1975, 1976, 1980, 1983; National Council of Pioneers Award, Romania, 1982; 2nd prize, GEDOK Composition Competition, Germany, 1982; *Anna Perenna* selected for performance, International Competition for Young Composers, Hilchenbach, Germany, 1982; 3rd prize, International Competition for Composers, Okanagan, Canada, 1983; 3rd prize, International Competition for Women Composers, Lincoln, Nebraska, 1983; Promotion Prize for Young Composers, Stuttgart, 1983; 1st prize, International Competition for Composers, New York City, 1983; *Memories* selected for performance, International Competition of the New Music Orchestra, Washington, D.C., 1983; 3rd prize, G.B. Viotti International Music and Dance Competition, Vercelli, Italy, 1983; 1st prize, Annual Search for New Music

Composition contest, International League of Women Composers, New York, 1983; Grand Prize, Composers Guild Contest, Salt Lake City, Utah, 1984; two prizes, Royal National Eisteddfod, Wales, 1984; distinction, Viotti-Valsesia International Music Competition, Vercelli, Italy, 1984; honourable mention, Annual Search for New Music Composition contest, International League of Women Composers, New York, 1984; distinction, International Composition Competition, Ibague, Colombia, 1985; Valentin Becker Composition Prize, Bad Bruckenau, Germany, 1985; 4 1st prizes, 2 2nd prizes, Trophy of the International Eisteddfod Festival, Roodepoort, South Africa, 1985; 3 mentions, Valentino Bucchi International Competition, Rome, 1985; Internationaler Arbeitskreis für Musik Prize, Kassel, Germany, 1985; *Terra Lonhdana* selected for performance, ISCM World Music Days, Budapest, Hungary, 1986; 2nd prize, International Musica Antiqua Europae Orientalis Competition, Bydgoscz, Poland, 1986; 2nd prize, Carl Maria von Weber Composition for Opera, Dresden, 1986; 2nd prize, International New Music Composers Competition, New York, 1987; 2 1st prizes, 3rd prize, International Eisteddfod Festival, Roodeport, South Africa, 1987; 2nd prize, International competition for Composers, Spittal, Austria, 1988; Baldreit Composition Prize, Baden-Baden, Germany, 1988; 1st prize, International Valentino Bucchi Competition, Rome, 1988; *Dialogo* and *Loc Maria* selected for exhibition, (H)Ear Art, New York, 1989; selection for performance, Baden-Wurttemberg Choir Composition Competition, 1989; mention and selection for performance, International Composer Competition for chamber music with guitar, Berlin, 1989; selection and performance, 1st Leonie Rothschild Composition contest, New Orleans, 1989; honourable mention, Marzena Composition Competition, Seattle, 1990. Mailing address: Buttenstrasse 15, 7570 Baden-Baden, Germany.

Publishers: self; Ricordi, Munich (opera only).

Symphonies/orchestral:

Transformations 1978; first performed Tirgu Mures, Romania, 30 April 1982.
Anna Perenna 1979; first performed Craiova, Romania, 17 April 1982.
Memories (string orchestra) 1980; first performed Bucharest, 13 June 1981.
Akrostichon 1983; first performed Wiblingen, Germany, 17 July 1983.
Map 67 (chamber orchestra) 1987; first performed Donaueschingen, 17 October 1987.
Fresco (youth orchestra) 1989; Leimen-Heidelberg, 1 October 1989.
L'Ora X 1990.
Joc n.d.

Chamber/instrumental:

Pieces (piano) 1970.
Sonata (woodwind, piano) 1973.
Story (piano) 1977.
Echos I (piano) 1979; first performed Bucharest, 5 March 1980.
Arabesques (flute, percussion) 1980; first performed Bucharest, 1 February 1982.
Dialogo (flute, viola) 1981; first performed Bucharest, 7 December 1981.
Elogium (trumpet, trombone) 1981; first performed Bucharest, 20 October 1981.
Satya I (violin) 1981; first performed Bucharest, 17 April 1982. Recorded CPO Live 999016–1.
Satya II (bassoon) 1981; first performed Bucharest, 22 February 1982. Recorded CPO Live 999016–1.
Satya III (double bass) 1981; first performed Angoulême, France, 16 November 1982.
Satya IV (clarinet) 1981; first performed Darmstadt, 23 July 1982.
Satya V (bassoon, clarinet, violin, double bass) 1981.
Immagini (flute) 1982; first performed Bucharest, 28 February 1982. Recorded CPO Live 999016–1.
Echos II (piano, percussion) 1982; first performed Bucharest, 26 June 1982.
Parra Quitarra (guitar) 1982; first performed Bucharest, 17 April 1982.
Alternances (wind quintet) 1982; first performed Bucharest, 18 May 1982. Recorded CPO Live 999016-1.
Echos III (organ) 1982; first performed Heidelberg, 7 August 1983.
Prelude (harpsichord) 1982; first performed Mannheim, 7 April 1984.
Three Miniatures (saxophone quartet) 1982; first performed Mannheim, 9 November 1983.
Aion (clarinet, bassoon, cello, 2 double basses, percussion) 1982.
Intarsien (cello) 1983; first performed Mainz, 25 February 1984.
In Search of Mozart (chamber ensemble) 1983; first performed Mannheim, 13 March 1983.
Din Cimpoiu (viola) 1984; first performed Bucharest, 31 March 1985.
Abendandacht (trumpet) 1985; first performed Mannheim, 17 May 1985.
Scherzo da Fantasia III (violin, cello) 1985; first performed Wiesbaden, 15 September 1985.
Nakris (saxophone quartet) 1985; first performed Munich, 27 June 1985.
Melismen (recorder quintet) 1985; first performed Heidelberg, 9 July 1985.
Meandre (bass clarinet, piano) 1985; first performed Mannheim, 9 September 1985.
Improvisation (bass clarinet) 1985; first performed Mannheim, 9 September 1985.
Quasaar Paal 2 (Mutabor computer-organ, cello) 1985; first performed Darmstadt, 26 September 1985.
Improvisation (saxophone) 1986; first performed Illinois, 22 October 1986.
Atreju (flute, guitar) 1986; first performed Altenkirchen, Germany, 9 November 1986.
Dies Diem Docet (piano) 1986; first performed Frankfurt, 5 April 1987.
New Rochelle (DX7 synthesizer) 1987; first performed Braunschweig, Germany, 13 May 1987.
Trio (oboe, clarinet, bassoon) 1987; first performed Baden-Baden, 9 August 1987.
Loc Maria (organ, percussion) 1987; first performed Heidelberg, 20 July 1987.
Ostrov I (viola quartet) 1987; first performed Kassel, 17 June 1988.
Stringquartet din Terra Lonhdana 1987; first performed Munich, 6 March 1988.
Aretusa (violin) 1988; first performed Kiel, Germany, 7 March 1989.
Ostrov II (clarinet quartet) 1988; first performed Merksem, Belgium, 9 April 1989.

Terra Lonhdana (chamber ensemble) 1988; first performed Wiesbaden, 14 March 1989. Recorded Frauenmusikvertrieb.
Figuren II (2 guitars) 1989; first performed Heidelberg, 8 March 1990.
Kata (flute, piano) 1989; first performed New York City, 27 February 1990.
Wenn der Freude thranen fliessen . . . (cello, piano) 1990; first performed Amsterdam, 16 September 1990.
Immaginabile (recorder) n.d.
Cime lointaine (clarinet) n.d.
Scherzo da Fantasia IV (violin, double bass) n.d.
Sonatina (double bass, piano) n.d.
Sleep Song (double bass, piano) n.d.
Toy (double bass, piano) n.d.
Fragment II (flute, harp) n.d.
Figuren (3 double basses) n.d.
Contraste (trombone quartet) n.d.
Festspielfanfare (2 horns, 3 trumpets) n.d.
Letitae (3 flutes, 3 violas) n.d.
Flutesplay (8 flutes) n.d.

Vocal/choral:

Stalactites (voice, piano) 1972.
Bewitch Me into a Silver Bird! (chorus, orchestra) 1975; first performed Arad, Romania, 23 February 1982.
Latin Sentences (chorus) 1977; first performed Bad Bruckenau, Germany, 7 July 1985.
The Play (children's chorus, orchestra or percussion) 1978; first performed Mannheim, 8 May 1982.
Country of Songs (chorus) 1978.
Flowers (chorus) 1979.
Tamina (chorus) 1979.
Euraculos (voice, clarinet) 1980; first performed Bucharest, 20 June 1981. Recorded Electrecord ST-CS 0217; CPO Live 999016-1.
Ballade (chorus) 1980.
Song Remained in a Flute (chorus) 1980.
Arpagic (chorus) 1981.
In My Garden (chorus) 1981.
Amont (voice, harpsichord) 1984; first performed Ettlingen, 17 April 1985.
Mondnacht (voice, organ) 1985, Heidelberg, 12 July 1985. Recorded CPO Live 999016-1.
Zebaoth (baritone, 2 organs) 1986; first performed Heidelberg, 18 October 1986.
Three Songs: Crystal, The Goblet, Autumn (voice, harpsichord) 1985; first performed Heidelberg, 27 January 1986.
Concerto (orchestra, voice) 1986; first performed Ulm, Germany, 5 March 1987.
Quatrain (voice) 1986; first performed Heidelberg, 29 September 1987.
Mondnachte (voice, saxophone, percussion) 1986; first performed Heidelberg, 13 June 1987. Recorded Electrecord ST-CS 0217.
Flower Song (chorus) 1987; first performed South Africa, 3 October 1987.
Dona Nobis Pacem (voice, percussion, cello) 1987; first performed Bonn, 11 December 1987.
Rondo About the Spring (children's choir, flute ensemble) 1988; first performed Seckach, Germany, 18 June 1988.
Spring Song (children's choir, flutes, percussion) 1988; first performed Seckach, Germany, 18 June 1988.
Concertino (voice, orchestra) 1988; Baden-Baden, 26 August 1988.
Country of Doina (chorus) n.d.

Opera:

Hunger and Thirst (chamber opera) 1985; first performed Freiburg, 1 February 1986.
Der 35. Mai (children's opera) 1986; first performed Dresden, 30 November 1986.

Other

Der Kreisel (ballet; orchestra) 1985; first performed Ulm, Germany, 26 May 1985.
Tabu (music to 1931 film by Murnau) 1988; first performed Frankfurt, 5 April 1988.

PUBLICATIONS

By Dinescu: contributor to *Counterpoint Studies—Palestrina Melody Analysis*, Bucharest, 1976–9; "Allgemeine Gedanken zum komponiern", in *Neuland*, 4, 1983–4; "Jeunes compositeurs de Romanie", in *Sonances*, 3(2), 1984; "Gedanken zum Thema 'Kompositionstechnik und Mathematik'", in *Musik und Mathematik*, Berlin, 1985; "Heidelberg 1987", in *Living Music*, 5(2), 1987; various journal articles, reports and reviews in Romanian press and elsewhere.

On Dinescu: Brunhilde Sonntag, "VD", in *Komponistinnen*, 1984; Gabor Halasz, "Magie der Zahlen und Klange: der musikalische Sprache der VD und ihr Kammeroper 'Hunger und Durst'", programme notes, Freiburg, February 1986; Beate Schmalbrock, "VD—Persönlichkeit, Werk, Analysen", in *Komponistinnen unserer Zeit*, Essen, 1986; Detlef Gojovy, "Die untypische Art zu singen—die Komponistin VD", in *Neue Zeitung für Musik*, 9, 1987; Joseph Hausler, "Laudatio auf VD", programme notes for *Hunger und Durst*, Bonn, November 1987; Antje Olivier, Karin Weingartz-Perschel, "VD", in *Komponistinnen von A–Z*, Dusseldorf, 1988.

Violeta Dinescu comments:

In the beginning of every composition I try to find a sphere, an imaginary space, where the flood of imagination can meet the rigour of thought. It is necessary to control the different dimensions of the musical language in the microstructure as well as in the macrostructure.

One must understand my composition from the point of view of not only the world of pure sound, but also the deep connections with the basic rules of an abstract universe of thought, the world of scientific and philosophical principles.

Numbers are used in the music in different ways—as different intervals, directions, proportions—but remain within the limits given by the order, appearance and importance of certain numbers. The music tries to dominate this strength of succession and priority of numeric symbols, discovering new spaces which have their origin in the same structures. My aesthetic necessity is at the same time to better know the infinite universe of sound and to discover new relations between thought and its multitude of spiritual projections.

* * *

Perhaps the most convincing explanation for the size and confidence of Violeta Dinescu's compositional output (by age 38, she had written well over 100 mature pieces) is her refusal to subordinate individual moments of inspiration to a "system". Each of her pieces—even in the *Satya* instrumental sequence, a very individual descendant of Berio's *Sequenze*—

is determined by its own sound-space. Throughout her career, she has been particularly interested in new and unusual ways of producing sound, exploiting multiphonics on instruments such as saxophone, or exploring new electronic instruments such as the Mutabor organ.

Her attitudes can partly be explained by her background. Before she moved to Germany in the 1980s, she was brought up and educated in a country in which the academic establishment was deeply suspicious of the Western avant-garde. Her research at the Kyprian Porombescu Conservatory in Bucharest was into Romanian folk musics; that influence survives in many places in her work, in the simplicity of melody that she likes to interweave with an extreme variation of sound (as in the *Dialogue* for flute and viola, the opera *Hunger and Thirst*, and in much of her writing for brass).

After completing her graduate studies in 1978, though, Dinescu was free to follow her own instincts. She became increasingly interested in mathematical procedures and, from the brilliant orchestral *Anna Perenna* onwards, used mathematical ratios and sequences as a means not only of directly generating the actual content of a piece, but of determining its parameters (or boundaries in mathematical language) quite precisely. Dinescu's compositions always have a firm spatial identity, with a firmly defined micro-structure or "grain" which remains absolutely consistent and which is organised around particular pitches, almost as iron filings range around a magnet's poles. The actual *sound* of a piece, though, is always paramount and nothing she writes ever sounds formulaic or excessively abstract. She brings from folk music a strongly emotional, rhapsodic style with a constantly varying pulse which is strongly reminiscent of the open rhythm of Balkan and Transylvanian folk-epic, where metre is always conditioned by semantics and context.

As part of this perspective, she has long been convinced that there is nothing new under the musical sun. Her orchestral piece *Akrostichon* was commissioned for a 1983 festival linking modern and Baroque music; Dinescu's counterpoint is firm and her grasp of the spatial disposition sound extremely subtle. Her music has the esperantist quality of always seeming to translate itself into other idioms, a sense of being a summation of large areas of European musical tradition, both "high" and "popular", blending melody, homophony and polyphony quite seamlessly, so that each seems to take on characteristics of the others. It is "utopian" music in the strict sense, occupying a space in which the only applicable rules are the rules of that particular space; the effect is much as when physicists and applied mathematicians postulate a 5- or 7-dimensional space and then hypothesize the conceptual parameters of such a space.

Her trajectory northwest across a rapidly changing Europe is inscribed in her work, taking in Viennese orthodoxies, Italian heterodoxy, and the restless experimentalism of her new home. Dinescu is now firmly established as one of the most important composers of her generation.

—Henk Maarten

DLUGOSZEWSKI, Lucia. American. Born in Detroit, 16 June 1934 [*Baker's* and *Greene's* give 1931; *International Encyclopedia of Women Composers* gives 1925]. Educated at Detroit Conservatory (piano under Agelageth Morrison), 1940–6; Wayne State University, Detroit (physics and pre-med), 1946–9; Mannes College, New York (music analysis with Felix Salzer), 1950–3; additional piano lessons with Grete Sultan, composition with Edgar Varèse. Occasional teacher, New York University, and New School for Social Research, New York, since 1960; teacher and composer, Foundation for Modern Dance, since 1960; music director, Erick Hawkins Dance Company. Composer, performer, instrument designer and maker. Recipient: Tompkins Prize for poetry, 1947; National Institute of Arts and Letters Award, 1966; BMI-Thorne Fellowship, 1972; Koussevitzky International Recording Award (for *Fire Fragile Flight*), 1977. Mailing address: 15 East 11th Street, New York, New York 10003, U.S.A.

Publisher: Margun.

Symphonies/orchestral:

Orchestra Structure for the Poetry of Everyday Sounds 1952.
Orchestral Radiant Ground 1955.
Arithmetic Points 1955.
Flower Music for Left Ear in a Small Room 1956.
Instants in Form and Movement (timbre piano, chamber orchestra) 1957.
Suchness Concert (orchestra of invented percussion orchestra) 1958–60.
Four Attention Spans 1964.
Beauty Music 2 (specially devised percussion, chamber orchestra) 1965.
Beauty Music 3 (timbre piano, chamber orchestra) 1965.
Quick Dichotomies (2 trumpets, clarinet, orchestra of invented percussion) 1965.
Naked Flight Nageire (chamber orchestra) 1966.
Hanging Bridges (also version for string quartet) 1968.
Kitetail Beauty Music (violin, timbre piano, orchestra of invented percussion) 1968.
Naked Swift Music (violin, timbre piano, orchestra of invented percussion) 1968.
Skylark Concert, An Evening of Music (chamber orchestra) 1969–70.
Kireji: Spring and Tender Speed 1972.
Tender Theatre Flight Nageire (brass quintet, percussion orchestra) 1972–9. Recorded CRI SD 388.
Abyss and Caress (trumpet, small orchestra) 1975.
Amor New Tilting Night (chamber orchestra) 1978.
Startle Transparent Terrible Freedom 1981.
Quidditas Sorrow Terrible Freedom 1983–4.
Duenda Amor 1983–4.

Chamber/instrumental:

Sonata No 1 (piano) 1949.
Sonata No 2 (piano) 1950.
Sonata No 3 (piano) 1950.
Melodic Sonata (piano) 1950.
Sonata (flute) 1950.
Transparencies 1 (harp) 1952.
Transparencies 2 (flute) 1952.
Transparencies 3 (harp, violin) 1952.
Transparencies 4 (string quartet) 1952.
Archaic Music (timbre piano) 1953–6.
Naked Wabin (flute, clarinet, percussion, violin, double bass, timbre piano) 1956.
Music for Small Centers (piano) 1958.
Music for Left Ear (piano) 1958.

Flower Music (string quartet) 1959.
Rates of Speed in Space (ladder harp, quintet) 1959.
Delicate Accidents in Space (unsheltered rattle quintet) 1959.
Concert of Man Rooms and Moving Space (flute, clarinet, timbre piano, 4 unsheltered rattles, dispersed) 1960.
White Interval Music (timbre piano) 1961.
Archaic Aggregates (timbre piano, ladder harps, tangent rattles, unsheltered rattles, gongs) 1961.
Beauty Music (clarinet, percussion, timbre piano) 1965.
Percussion Airplane Hetero 1965.
Percussion Flowers 1965.
Percussion Kitetails 1965.
Suchness with Radiant Ground (clarinet, percussion) 1965.
Music for Left Ear in a Small Room (violin or piano) 1965.
Balance Naked Flung (clarinet, trumpet, bass trombone, violin, percussion) 1966.
Naked Quintet (brass) 1967.
Leap and Fall, Quick Structures (2 trumpets, clarinet, 2 violins, percussion) 1968.
Space Is a Diamond (trumpet) 1970. Recorded Nonesuch H 71275.
Swift Diamond (timbre piano, trumpet, invented percussion) 1970.
Velocity Shells (timbre piano, trumpet, invented percussion) 1970.
Sabi Music (violin) 1970.
Pure Flight Air (string quartet) 1970.
Amor Elusive Empty August (woodwind quintet) 1979.
Cicada Terrible Freedom (flute, string quintet, bass trombone) 1980–1.
Wilderness Elegant Tilt (11 instruments) 1981–4.
Duende Newfallen (bass trombone, timbre piano) 1982–3.
Quidditas (string quartet) 1984–5.

Vocal/choral:

Silent Paper Spring and Summer Friends Songs 1953–70.
Fire Fragile Flight (voice, orchestra) 1973. Recorded Candid CE 31113.

Opera:

Tiny Opera 1953.
The Heidi Songs (Ashbery) 1970.

Other/dramatic:

Moving Space Theater Piece (everyday sounds) 1949.
Openings of the Eye (dance; flute, percussion, timbre piano) 1952.
Desire (theatre piece for voice, timbre piano; Picasso) 1952.
Ubu Roi (incidental music to play by Jarry, Living Theater; everyday sounds) 1952.
Variations on Noguchi (film score; voices, everyday sounds) 1953.
Here and Now with Watchers (dance; timbre piano) 1954–7.
Eight Clear Places (dance; 100-piece orchestra of invented percussion) 1958–60.
Women of Trachis (incidental music for play by Sophocles, Pound) 1960.
Guns for the Trees (film score; orchestra) 1961.
Cantilever (dance; piano, orchestra) 1964.
To Everyone Out There (dance; orchestra) 1964.
Geography of Noon (dance; orchestra of invented percussion) 1964.
Lords of Persia (dance; 2 trumpets, clarinet, orchestra of invented percussion) 1965.
Dazzle on a Knife's Edge (dance; timbre piano, orchestra) 1966.
Lords of Persia 2 (dance; chamber orchestra) 1968.
Tight Rope (dance; chamber orchestra) 1968.
Agatholon Algebra (dance; timbre piano, orchestra) 1968.
Black Lake (dance; timbre piano, invented percussion) 1969.
Lords of Persia 3 (dance; chamber orchestra) 1971.
A Zen in Ryoko-in (film score; orchestra of invented percussion) 1971.
Of Love . . . Or He Is a Cry, She Is His Ear (dance; brass quintet, orchestra of invented percussion) 1971.
Angels of the Inmost Heaven (dance; trumpets, trombones, horn) 1972. Recorded Folkways FTS 33902.
Avanti (dance) 1983.
This Woman Duende Amor (dance) 1984–5.

PUBLICATIONS

By Dlugoszewski: "Notes of New Music for the Dance", in *Dance Observer*, November 1957; "Is music sound?", in *Jubilee* 9 (10), 1962; (with Vivian Fine) "Composer/Choreographer, Choreographer/Composer", in *Dance, Perspectives*, 16, 1963; *A New Folder* (poetry), New York, 1969.

On Dlugoszewski: Allen Hughes, "And Miss D. Experiments—a Lot", in *Time Magazine*, 7 March 1971; T. Johnson, "LD", in *High Fidelity/Musical America*, 25(6), 1975; J. Highwater, "LD Ascending", in *New York Arts Journal*, 8 (3), 1981.

* * *

It is by no means accidental that Lucia Dlugoszewski was first discovered by painters and poets, rather than by the musical establishment. Her first concert, at the Five Spot Cafe in New York in 1958, was sponsored by the sculptor David Smith; the New York School poet Frank O'Hara was the first to give her work serious attention; and she enjoyed the generous support of poet John Ashbery, some of whose poems she has set, and whose enigmatic language she echoes in her titles.

Dlugoszewski showed remarkable music promise as a child and was sent to the Detroit Conservatory to study piano. However, she moved across to medicine and natural sciences for a time, taking up serious study of composition again when she came to New York. Here, like so many other young composers in the early 1950s, she came under the influence of Edgar Varèse, whose conceptions of music as "organized sound" made a profound impact on her thinking.

Dissatisfied with conventional means of music making—and partly impelled by a fascination for sculptural form—Dlugoszewski set about creating new instruments. In this, she resembles the maverick Californian Harry Partch, who devised an extraordinary array of (mostly) percussion instruments. Dlugoszewski's most significant "invention" was actually a customised conventional piano, not so very far in conception from John Cage's "prepared" instruments of the late 1940s. The timbre piano operates like a very large dulcimer; strings are struck with mallets, or bowed and picked; the sound is resonant and melodic, but also curiously alien. Other inventions built for her by the sculptor Ralph Dorazio include ladder harps, "unsheltered" rattles, and various friction instruments. She follows Cage in employing natural sound in her *Moving Space Theater Piece* and the Living Theater production of Alfred Jarry's *Ubu Roi*.

Dlugoszewski's music is mainly associated with the dance and she is one of the most important contemporary composers to have concentrated on that medium. However, she has also produced a large body of concert music, much of it for percussion ensembles, but also for conventional forces. Her pieces seem to be related conceptually, if not generically, by titles permutated from a few key words: "duende", "flight", "terrible", "freedom", "naked", "transparent", "sorrow" and others. The verbal effect is rather closer to cummings (whom she has also set) than to Ashbery, but the effect of the music is more closely related to Ashbery's rich estrangement than to cummings's whimsy. Her large-scale percussion ensembles were put to effective use in *Suchness Concert* and in scores for dance, theatre and concert (*Eight Clear Places, Lords of Persia* and *Kitetail Beauty Music*).

In the late 1960s she explored the possibilities of breakneck speed, "flinging" and "leaping" styles, surprise effects and extremes of articulation, as in *Balance Naked Flung*. In the later 1970s, this gave way to a gentler "tilt", as in the orchestral *Amor New Tilting Night* and the ensemble *Wilderness Elegant Tilt*. Though the early piano Sonatas are brightly and inventively conceived, the String Quartets original, and *Space Is a Diamond* a superbly inflected trumpet solo, which underlines Dlugoszewski's delicacy, even at her most hectic, most of her work has been a subversion of normal generic expectations and the dreadful complacency (on the part of both audience and composers) that overtakes formulaic work scored for conventional instruments. Like Partch, Dlugoszewski is a genuine original. Though she has received her fair due of critical attention, and was the first woman to win the Koussevitzky International Recording Award (as late as 1977), she is perhaps *too* original to receive more than occasional lip service and is still too little heard.

—Pamela Collins

DMITRIEV, Georgy (Petrovich). Russian. Born in Krasnodar, 29 October 1942. Educated at P.I. Tchaikovsky State Conservatoire, Moscow, 1961–66; postgraduate study, 1966–8. Married Valentina Yefimovna Zagrebalnaya, 5 September 1970; 1 son and 1 daughter. Composition teacher, Central Music School, Moscow, 1968–85; senior teacher of composition, instrumentation and polyphony, Gnessin State Music Pedagogical Institute, Moscow, 1969–82; deputy chair of the board, Moscow Organization of Composers, R.S.F.S.R., 1987–8; chair of the board, Moscow Composers' Union, since 1988; secretary of the board, since 1989, and first deputy chair of the board, since 1990, Soviet Composers Union. Recipient: 1st prize, 9th International Composers' Competition, Budapest, 1988. Mailing address: Apt. 30, Building 6, Ul. Fomicheva 16, Moscow 123481, U.S.S.R.

Publishers: Edition Peters, Frankfurt; VAAP, Moscow (& Boosey & Hawkes; Le Chant du Monde, Paris; Internationale Musikverlage Hans Sikorski, Hamburg; Musik Fazer, Helsinki; Real Musical, Madrid; Ricordi, Milan; Schirmer, New York; Universal Edition, Vienna; Zen-On, Tokyo).

Symphonies/orchestral:

Symphony No 2: "On the Kulikovo Field" 1979; first performed Moscow, 1980.
Concerto for Violin and Orchestra 1981; first performed Moscow, 1981.
Kiev: A Symphonic Chronicle 1982; first performed Kiev, 1982.
Sybil (flute, chamber orchestra) 1982; first performed Moscow, 1983.
Ledostav-Ledokhod (2 string orchestras, percussion ensemble) 1986; first performed Zwickau, 1986.
Scene (harpsichord, double bass, string quartet, chamber orchestra) 1987; first performed Moscow, 1987.
Symphony No 3: "Misterioso" 1988; first performed Moscow, 1989.

Chamber/instrumental:

Sonata No 1 (piano) 1964; first performed Moscow, 1964.
Rhapsody (piano) 1964; first performed Moscow, 1964.
String Quartet No 2 1970.
String Quartet No 3 1975; first performed Moscow, 1975.
Quartet (solo clarinet) 1978; first performed Moscow, 1978.
Faces of Movements (flute) 1980; first performed Moscow, 1980.
Percussionata (metal percussion—1 player) 1980; first performed Moscow, 1980.
Three Concert Pieces (2 pianos) 1980; first performed Moscow, 1981.
Stained Glass Windows (oboe, clarinet, saxophone, viola, bassoon) 1980; first performed Moscow, 1981.
Nicolo (violin, piano) 1982; first performed Minsk, 1982.
String Quartet No 4: In Twelve Parables 1983; first performed Moscow, 1984.
Sonata No 2 (piano) 1985; first performed Tashkent, 1986.
Warsaw Fantasy (violin, piano) 1986–7; first performed Boston, 1988.
In Hermann Hesse's Style (saxophone quartet) 1987; first performed Moscow, 1987.
The Obelisk (piano duet) 1989; first performed France, 1989.
And I Saw the New Sky and the New Earth (ensemble) 1989; first performed Paris, 1990.

Vocal/choral:

Three Poems by F.I. Tyutchev (soprano, piano) 1968; first performed Moscow, 1968.
From Bulgarian Folk Poetry (soprano, clarinet, piano) 1977; first performed Moscow, 1977.
Voices of Violins (tenor, violin, percussion; Blok) 1983; first performed Moscow, 1983.
Povest Vremennykh Let/Russian Chronicle (soloists, choir, chamber orchestra) 1984; first performed Moscow, 1984. Recorded Melodiya A1000327 002.
The Last Bumble Bee (voice, violin, viola, cello; Bunin) 1985; first performed Moscow, 1985.
Cosmic Russia (soloists, reciter, mixed choir, orchestra) 1985; first performed Moscow, 1986.
In Memory of A.S. Pushkin (soloists, instrumental ensemble) 1986; first performed Moscow, 1986.
Entre Elle et moi (tenor, instrumental ensemble) 1988; first performed Tours, France, 1988.

Stabat mater dolorosa (mezzo-soprano, 2 choirs, organ, guitar, percussion; Akhmatova) 1988; first performed Moscow, 1988.
Stenza Razin (mezzo-soprano, baritone, percussion ensemble, tape; Tsvetayeva) 1989; first performed Moscow, 1990.
Four Poems by I. Annensky (mixed choir) 1989; first performed New York City, 1989.
Night Service (mixed choir) 1990; first performed Moscow, 1991.

Opera:

The Beloved and Lost (chamber lyrical opera; Dmitriyev, after Morley Callaghan) 1985–8.

Other:

Georgy Sedev (film music) 1974; first performed Moscow, 1974.
One, Two, Soldiers Marched (film music) 1976; first performed Kiev, 1976.
38, Petrovka Street (film music) 1980; first performed Moscow, 1980.
Start Liquidating (film music) 1983; first performed Moscow, 1983.
On the Eve (incidental music) 1985; first performed Kiev, 1985.
The General Rehearsal (incidental music) 1988; first performed Kiev, 1988.
The Devil Has Tempted Him (incidental music) 1990; first performed Moscow, 1990.
Adagio (Upic electronics) 1990; first performed Priverno, Italy, 1990.

Also: *The Album of a Young Trumpeter* (36 easy pieces) and *Little Stones from a Shop* (50 easy pieces for piano and piano duet).

PUBLICATIONS

By Dmitriev: *Percussion Instruments: Interpretation and the Present State*, Moscow, 1973; *On Dramaturgic Expressiveness of Orchestration*, Moscow, 1981; "How to Teach Composition for Children", in *A Child Playing Piano*, Moscow, 1981; "Lettre de Moscou", in *Stock*, Paris, 1981; "Close Contacts with Life Are Needed", in *Sovetskaya Muzyka*, 9, 1987.

On Dmitriev: "GD: Images Evoked by History", in *Literature and Arts in the U.S.S.R.*, 2, 1984; T. Zhurbinskaya, "GD", in *Moscow Composers* (3rd edition), Moscow, 1988; M. Lobanova, "GD", in *Music in the U.S.S.R.*, 3, 1988; M. Pritsker, "Trusting Intuition to a Greater Extent?", in *Sovetskaya Muzyka*, 8, 1988; E. Tarakanova, "Making Music Speak", in *Muzykanlaya Zhizn*, 19, 1988; L. Rimsky, "The Sense of Time: GD's Sound Frescoes", in *Melodiya*, 4, 1988; M. Lobanova, "GD's Cantata-Oratorio Works", in *Music of Russia*, Moscow, 1990.

Georgy Dmitriev comments:

At present I am committed to the free use of a variety of compositional techniques and styles provided they are unifiably consistent with a specific artistic concept and with a personal vision. At different times, and for different artistic purposes, I have used many compositional techniques, but have always tried to see and invent them afresh.

I adhere to the principle that the structural principle of a musical form should be adequate to the dramaturgy of the work, which is a purely musical category based on the specific modelling of a process. *Multi-layer form*, the vertical assembly of several dramaturgically independent strata-processes, is the most indicative of these.

I attach great importance to the organization of timbres in a work; these can convey the intonation-thematic or even assign meaning to the colouring (emblem-sonorism).

The method of the Philosophy of Orchestral Voice Knowledge serves for me as an instrument of global organization which materialises the artistic idea at the moment of its crystallization in the fabric.

I value national (Russian) creative roots which, to my mind, are vividly displayed in the historical genesis of the Spirit. I take as read the ethical-cosmic superfunction of art. This is very close to the Russian way of thinking and feeling.

* * *

Georgy Dmitriev studied under one of the most vigorously conservative musicians of the Soviet old guard, Dmitri Kabalevsky. For 12 years he taught at the Gnessin Institute. Today he is one of the rising stars within the official apparatus of the Union of Soviet Composers, a man with power over the immediate fate of the music of others.

And yet these bare statements hide the fact that for a considerable period of time Dmitriev was one of the more talented of the experimental composers grouped around Edison Denisov. Together with his slightly younger contemporaries like Elena Firsova and Dmitri Smirnov, he absorbed not only the modernism of Denisov's general outlook, but also a good deal of Denisov's specific techniques and even mannerisms. During the 1970s this influence of Denisov led Dmitriev to write some of his most interesting and, paradoxically, most individual works.

Dmitriev's chamber works are on the whole his most successful. Many of these include a voice, of one kind or another. Like most Russian composers, when he sets verses by the older Russian poets Dmitriev gravitates towards the harmonic and melodic traditions of the Russian romance. This is in line with Denisov's own practice in his song-cycles on poets like Pushkin and Blok. In such works, Denisov has provided a popular precedent for combining the gadgets of modernism with melodies and cadences strangely evocative of Glinka. Dmitriev picks up this precedent more or less intact in his 1970 Bunin cycle for tenor and string trio, *The Last Bumble Bee*. By 1982, his four settings of Blok for tenor, violin and percussion, *Voices of Violins* (written for the talented tenor/violinist Alexei Martynov), are markedly simpler and plainer, but, it has to be said, at the same time more sentimental and less thoughtful.

The chamber works of Dmitriev, which show him at his best and most characteristic, are his string quartets. His Second Quartet, although it takes the well-worn idea of an homage to Bartók (and even uses a B♭, E, A, B♭, A cipher derived from Bartók's name), is an effective and energetic rethinking of some of the more familiar gestures of Bartók's quartet writing.

The short Third Quartet is already much more advanced in sophistication. The influence of Denisov's typical heterophonic string writing is much in evidence throughout, albeit galvanised by Dmitriev's personal fondness for down-to-earth rhythms. Here too there is a cipher, derived from the name of BEEtHovEn. This crystallises at the end of the first movement, which the composer calls "Genesis". The second movement, "Alternativa" (a name which, in the Soviet Union, carries a suggestion of political opposition) is a fragmented development of ideas from the first. Both movements, however short, are extremely fragmented and sectional, suggesting that Dmitriev is much happier working in the smaller characteristic forms than in the larger structural ones.

This tendency to sectional thought leads to further and notable success in Dmitriev's Fourth Quartet. Subtitled *In Twelve Parables*, the work is apparently a paraphrase of part of the writings of St Paul. The 12 little movements of which this work is made are firmly and imaginatively contrasted one with the next and yet the whole work holds together with vigour and interest. Each section is given a title too, which offers, no doubt, a clue as to the extra-musical content as well as to the manner in which the music is to be played.

In recent years Dmitriev has become openly disillusioned with the future of more complicated kinds of music. At the same time he has accepted increasingly responsible official positions within the Union of Composers and has become more and more critical of his erstwhile friends on what he himself refers to as the "unofficial" wing of Soviet new music. His own more recent music seems clearly designed to create the minimum offense. In the light of works like the Third and Fourth Quartets, this would seem to be a pity.

—Gerard McBurney

DÖHL, Friedhelm. German. Born in Göttingen, 7 July 1936. Educated at Freiburg Musik Hochschule (piano and music education under Wolfgang Fortner), 1956–64; concurrently, Freiburg/Göttingen University (musicology, Germanic philology, art history, philosophy), D.Phil. (dissertation on Anton Webern published in book form, 1976), 1966; Studienstiftung des Deutschen Folkes, 1957–64; German Academy scholar, Villa Massimo, Rome, 1967–8. Lecturer in composition and music theory, Robert Schumann Conservatory, Dusseldorf, 1965–8; chief lecturer in music, 1969–72, and professor, 1972–4, Musicological Institute, Free University of Berlin; director and founder of Studio for Electronic Music, for Music and Theatre, and for Non-European Music, Music Academy, Basle, 1974–82; professor of composition, Music Conservatory, Lübeck, since 1982. Recipient: Rome Prize Villa Massimo, 1967–8; Förderungpreis, North Rhine-Westphalia, 1968; Berlin Prize, 1971. Mailing address: Victoriastrasse 13, D-2400, Lübeck, Germany.

Publisher: Breitkopf & Hartel, Wiesbaden.

Symphonies/orchestral:

Sound Scene III "Zorch" (3 pianos, orchestra) 1972.
Symphony (cello, orchestra) 1981; first performed Saarbrucken, 1981.
Tombeau 1982–3; first performed Kiel, 1983.
Passion 1984; first performed Hannover, 1984.
Winterreise (string orchestra) 1986.

Chamber/instrumental:

Piano Sonata No 1 "Rondos" 1959.
Duo (violin, piano) 1960.
Piano Sonata No 2 "Szenen" 1960.
Piano Sonata No 3 "Spielungen" 1961.
Oktett "Varianti" (flute, oboe, clarinet, bassoon, 2 violins, viola, cello) 1961; first performed Cologne, 1973.
Canto W (flute) 1962.
Improvisation I (organ) 1962.
Klangfiguren (wind quintet) 1962; first performed Freiburg, 1962.
Kartenspiele (2 violins) 1962.
Oculapsis (flute, piano) 1962.
Piano Sonata No 4 "Passages" 1962; first performed Göttingen, 1962.
Albumblätter I & II (1–10 flutes) 1963.
Julianische Minuten (flute, piano) 1963.
Toccata (flute, trumpet, harpsichord, piano) 1963–4; first performed U.S.A., 1971.
Tappeto (After Ungaretti) (cello, harp) 1967; first performed Munich, 1969. Recorded VDMK/DGG 3/0654966.
Pas de deux (violin, guitar) 1968; first performed Graz, 1969.
Klang-Szene I (2 Hammond organs, live electronics, 4 loudspeaker groups, props, lights) 1970; first performed Dusseldorf, 1970.
Klang Szene II (5 different ensembles, live electronics, props and lights) 1971; first performed Berlin, 1971.
Klangmodelle I–II (piano) 1971.
Deviazione (1 player) 1971; first performed Bonn, 1971.
Textur I (flute) 1971; first performed Bonn, 1971. Recorded Duraphon HD 320.
Textur II (piano) 1971; first performed Baden-Baden, 1973.
Sound of Sleat (string quartet) 1971–2; first performed Witten, 1974.
Cadenza (from *Sound Scene III*) (1–3 open grand pianos) 1972; first performed Zagreb, 1975.
Sotto Voce (flute, cello, piano) 1973; first performed Reykjavik, 1973.
"Odradek" (2 open grand pianos) 1976; first performed Basle, 1976.
Acht Portraits (piano) 1977–8; first performed Cologne, 1980.
"Der Abend / Die Nacht" (after Trakl) 1977–9; first performed Witten, 1980.
Drei Traum-Stücke (piano) 1978; first performed Witten, 1980.
Sieben Haiku (piano) 1979; first performed Cologne, 1980.
Fragment (organ) 1980; first performed Munich, 1980.
Two Songs of Palamidi (flute, guitar) 1980; first performed Nauplion, Greece, 1980.
Fünf Stücke (flute) 1980; first performed Basle, 1981.
Conductus (4 percussion) 1980; first performed Basle, 1981.
Fiesta (2 pianos) 1982; first performed Bremen, 1982.
Ballet mécanique (chamber ensemble) 1984; first performed Witten, 1984.
Nachtfahrt (open piano, tape ad lib, percussion) 1984; first performed Lübeck, 1984.
Winterreise (string quintet) 1985; first performed Bremen, 1986.
Bruchststücke (from *Winterreise*; piano) 1985.
"Goria" Fragment II (organ) 1986.
Kadenz (cello) 1986–7; first performed Hamburg, 1987.
"und wenn die Stimme . . . " (piano) 1986; first performed Lübeck, 1986.
Missa (Medea-Intepolation) (from the opera; 2 trombones, 3 percussion) 1989; first performed Witten, 1989.

Vocal/choral:

Sternverdunkelung (baritone, chorus, organ, instruments; Joel, Sachs) 1963.

Sieben Haiku (soprano, flute, piano) 1963; first performed Freiburg, 1963.
Sieben Haiku (soprano, piano) 1963–79; first performed Braunwald, Switzerland, 1980.
Fragment "Sybille" (baritone, flute, viola, cello, piano; Holderlin) 1963; first performed Cologne, 1967.
Epitaph "Tick Yuang Tuc" (soprano, chamber ensemble) 1963; first performed Cologne, 1971.
"Melancolia"—magische Quadrate (sporano, chorus, orchestra) 1967–8; first performed Cologne, 1968.
". . . wenn aber . . . " (baritone, piano; Holderlin) 1969; first performed Cologne, 1971.
Klang Szene II (vocal ensemble, strings, free jazz group, mechanical orchestra, electronics, objects, lights) 1971.
Sull (Mikrodramen I) (speaker, flute, props) 1972.
A & O I (1 speaker/4 character masks, microphones, loudspeaker, props, tape ad lib) 1973.
Textur III (speaker) 1973.
Anna K. Informationen über einen Leichenfund (speaker, bass drum, cello, tape, apparatus) 1973–4; first performed Witten, 1974.
Szene über einen kleinen Tod (woman's voice, flute, alto/bass flute ad lib, cello, cymbal, tap ad lib) 1975; first performed Zurich, 1975.
"Auf schmalen Grat" (requiem for 6 voices—soloists or ensemble) 1978; first performed Basle, 1979.
"Unterwegs" (7 stations for soprano, piano) 1978; first performed Dusseldorf, 1982.
Medea (monologue for soprano, flute, clarinet, trumpet, trombone, cello, double bass, piano, 2 percussion) 1979–80; first performed Witten, 1980.

Opera:

Medea 1980.

Other:

Ikaros (ballet for orchestra after a poem by Erik Lindgreen) 1977–8; first performed Basle, 1980.

PUBLICATIONS

By Döhl: "Sinn und Unsinn musikalischer Form", in *Terminologie der neuen Musik*, Berlin, 1965; *Weberns Beitrag zur Stilwende der Neue Musik*, 1976; "Komponist—in der Provinz?", in *Neue Zeitschrift für Musik*, 4, 1980; "Fragment über Musik—über meine Musik", programme notes, Donauschinger Musiktage, 1980.

On Döhl: H. Osch, (interview) in *Melos*, 5, 1975, and "FD", in *Neue Zeitschrift für Musik*, 5, 1990; Lutz Lesle, "Fragment, Labyrinth, Mythos—FD und seine Medea-Oper", in *Neue Zeitschrift für Musik*, 5, 1990.

* * *

As with so many composers of his generation, the rhythm of Friedhelm Döhl's compositional career is marked by the stages of his engagement with the musical revolution wrought by Anton Webern. Döhl's brilliant doctoral thesis, submitted at the University of Göttingen and subsequently published in book form, was on Webern's work. Here, as throughout his work, Döhl shows great awareness of the wider parameters of musical culture.

His first works were written in a loosely Schoenbergian style, freely atonal and serial, but he soon began to extend the principle of non-repetition into Webernian territory, to include tone colour as well as pitch, breaking up the basic tone row into sub-units which could then be further subjected to transformation, reducing the music to very basic cells, often characterized by major sevenths and minor ninths. Dohl's exercises in this vein were generally successful; the piano sonatas are precise, but somewhat enigmatic, suggesting (as does the critical confidence of *Weberns Beitrag zur Stilwende der Neue Musik*) that he already felt somewhat distanced from the master's example.

After 1960, his music began to change to include elements of improvisation and of freely associative musical elements unbound either by harmonic hierarchies or the functional restrictions of dodecaphony. This "abstract expressionist" period did not last very long. From the later 1960s onward, Döhl has written in an altogether more controlled and meditative music. It retains something of the fragmentation of the Webernian method, but the basic orientation is once more romantic, as in the superb Holderlin settings " . . . *wenn aber* . . . " or the 1972 string quartet *Sound of Sleat*, named after a sea channel in the Scottish Hebrides. There is something of the same quality in his *Winterreise*, not a vocal work, but an equally Schubertian string quintet of great originality (which was later orchestrated). Many of Döhl's works have an oneiric quality, explicitly in the *Drei Traum-Stücke* of 1978, more obliquely in the mysterious "*Odradek*".

Dance and drama are consistent elements in his mature work, though they are almost implicit, in the way that Muller's words are implicit in *Winterreise*, part of its iconic cultural standing. Döhl has been much involved with the visual arts; *Ballet mécanique* is a dedication to Léger and there are frequent pictorial analogies in his titles. The same is true of dance; works such as *Pas de deux* are for dance without movement.

Döhl has been working for some time on a *Medea* opera. Some fragments already exist. A piece for trombones and percussion was premiered in 1989, almost a decade after the extraordinary *Medea* monologue, which, unlike the English composer Gavin Bryars's cool, static reworking of the myth-material, restores an almost hyperthyroid intensity which lifts the material up and away from mere narrative and toward something altogether more expressive. The same qualities are evident in the slightly earlier "*Unterwegs*", seven "stations" for female voice and piano.

Technically, Döhl is remarkable. He is one of the two or three most innovative composers for small ensemble working in Europe today, with an instinctive grasp of instrumental colour that allows him to experiment with opened pianos and unusual instrumentations. He has an orientation, notably in the vocal and chamber work, reminiscent of Elliott Carter, who links expression and form to the point of identification. However, whereas Carter's harmonic and rhythmic language are now more or less settled, Döhl continues to experiment intensely but with no sign of restlessness or uncertainty. He is a composer who knows his direction and takes it without hesitation.

—Henk Maarten

DONATONI, Franco. Italian. Born in Verona, 9 June 1927. Educated at Liceo Musicale, Verona (violin, composition under Piero Bottagisio), entered 1934, aged 7; graduated in accountancy and general studies; Milan

Conservatory (counterpoint and fugue under Ettore Desderi), 1946–8; Bologna Conservatory (composition, band and choral music under Zecchi and Liviabella), 1948–51; Accademia di Santa Cecilia, Rome (under Pizzetti), 1952–3; Ferienkurse für Neue Musik, Darmstadt, 1954, 1958, 1961. Married Susan Park in 1958; 2 sons. Professor of composition, Bologna Conservatory, 1953–5, Turin Conservatory, 1956–69, and Milan Conservatory, since 1969; teacher of advanced courses, Accademia Chigiana, and Bologna Conservatory. Recipient: Radio Luxembourg International Composition Competition, 1952, 1953; 1st prize, ISCM Italian Section (for *Puppenspiel*), 1961; Marzotto Prize (for *Puppenspiel II*), 1966. Mailing address: 1 Via Giovanni Milani, Milan, Italy.

Publishers: Ricordi; Schott.

Symphonies/orchestral:

Concertino (brass, timpani, strings) 1952.
Concerto for Bassoon and Strings 1952.
Ouverture (chamber orchestra) 1953.
Sinfonia (strings) 1953.
Divertimento (violin, chamber orchestra) 1954.
Musica (chamber orchestra) 1955.
Strophes 1959.
Sezioni 1960.
Puppenspiel 1961.
Per orchestra 1962, revised 1962.
Black and White (strings) 1964.
Divertimento II (strings) 1965.
Puppenspiel II (flute, orchestra) 1965.
Doubles II 1969–70.
To Earle (chamber orchestra) 1970.
To Earle Two (11 instruments, orchestra) 1971–2.
Voci 1972–3.
Espressivo (oboe, cor anglais, orchestra) 1973–4.
Duo per Bruno 1974–5.
Portrait (harpsichord, orchestra) 1976–7.
Le ruisseau sur l'escalier (cello, chamber orchestra) 1980; first performed Paris, 30 April 1981.
Sinfonia Op 63 "Anton Webern" 1983; first performed 13 May 1983, Webern's centenary.
Diario '83 (4 trumpets, 4 trombones, orchestra; from the opera *Atem*; orchestrated from *Diario '76*) 1983–4; first performed Milan, 16 February 1985.
Eco (chamber orchestra) 1985–6; first performed Lisbon, 8/9 May 1986.

Chamber/instrumental:

Quartetto I (string quartet) 1950.
Recitativo e allegro (violin, piano) 1951.
Sonata (viola) 1952.
Sonata (harp) 1953.
Cinque pezzi (2 pianos) 1954.
Composizione in quattro movimenti (piano) 1955.
Tre improvvisazioni (piano) 1957.
Quartetto II (string quartet) 1958.
Movimento (harpsichord, piano, 9 winds) 1959, orchestrated 1962.
For Grilly (flute, clarinet, bass clarinet, percussion, violin, viola, cello) 1960.
Doubles (harpsichord) 1961.
Quartetto IV: Zrcadlo (string quartet) 1963.
Asar (10 strings) 1964.
Babai (harpsichord) 1964.
Etwas ruhiger im Ausdruck (flute, clarinet, violin, cello, piano) 1967.
Souvenir (15 instruments) 1967.
Black and White No 2 (keyboards) 1968.
Souvenir No 2: Orts (14 instruments, speaker ad lib) 1968.
Estratto (piano) 1969.
Solo 10 strings) 1969.
Estratto II (piano, harpsichord, harp) 1970.
Lied (13 instruments) 1972.
Jeux pour deux (harpsichord, organ) 1973.
Quarto estratto (flute, piccolo, celeste, mandolin, harp, piano, harpsichord, violin) 1974.
Lumen (piccolo, clarinet, celeste, vibraphone, viola, cello) 1975.
Terzo estratto (piano, wind octet) 1975.
Duetto (harpsichord) 1975.
Ash (flute, oboe, clarinet, piano, harpsichord, string trio) 1976.
Diario '76 (4 trumpets, 4 trombones) 1977.
Ali (viola) 1978; first performed Paris, 26 January 1978.
Spiri (2 violins, viola, cello, flute, oboe, clarinet/bass clarinet, celeste, vibraphone) 1978; first performed 18 January 1978.
About . . . (violin, viola, guitar) 1979; first performed Siena, 25 August 1979.
Argot (violin) 1979; first performed Siena, 25 August 1979.
Marches (harp) 1979; first performed Berkeley, California, 25 November 1979.
Nidi (piccolo) 1979; first performed Venice, 26 September 1979.
Clair (clarinet) 1980; first performed Siena, 26 August 1980.
Fili (flute, piano) 1981; first performed Venice, 7 October 1981.
The Heart's Eye (string quartet) 1981; first performed Venice, 7 October 1981.
Tema (flute, oboe, clarinet, bassoon, 2 horns, 3 violins, 2 violas, cello) 1981; first performed 8 February 1982.
Small (piccolo, clarinet, harp) 1981; first performed Siena, 25 August 1981.
Lame (cello) 1982; first performed Siena, 26 August 1982.
Feria (5 flutes, 5 trumpets, organ) 1982; first performed Bologna, 24 September 1982.
Alamari (cello, double bass, piano) 1983; first performed Siena, 29 August 1983.
Lem (double bass) 1983; first performed Rondottanta, 31 March 1984.
Ala (cello, double bass) 1983; first performed Siena, 23 August 1985.
Françoise Variationen (piano) 1983; first performed Avignon, France, 6 December 1983.
Rima (piano) 1983; first performed Cortona, 9 July 1983.
Cadeau (2 oboes, 2 bassoons, 2 horns, trumpet, harp, xylorimba, vibraphone, glockenspiel) 1984; first performed Touraine, 7 July 1985.
Ronda (violin, viola, cello, piano) 1984; first performed La Rochelle, 24 June 1984.
Darkness (6 percussion) 1984; first performed Strasbourg, 18 September 1984.
Ombra (contrabass clarinet) 1984; first performed Certaldo, 26 July 1984.
Omar (vibraphone) 1985; first performed Siena, 23 August 1985.
Sestetto (2 violin, 2 violas, 2 cellos) 1985; first performed Cremona, 22 September 1985.
Arpège (flute, clarinet, violin, cello, vibraphone, piano) 1986; first performed Paris, 30 March 1987.

Refrain (piccolo, bass clarinet, viola, double bass, mandolin, guitar, harp, marimba) 1986; first performed Amsterdam, 7 June 1986.

Vocal/choral:

Il libro dei sette sigilli (soloists, chorus, orchestra; Bible) 1951.
Serenata (soprano, 16 instruments; Thomas) 1959.
. . . *ed insieme bussarono* (female voice, piano; Kabir) 1978; first performed Stockholm, 7 November 1978.
Arie (voice, orchestra) 1978; first performed Rome, 15 March 1980.
De Pres (female voice, 2 piccolos, 3 violins; Robertet) 1979; first performed Paris, 9 February 1980.
L'ultima sera (female voice, flute, clarinet, violin, cello, piano; Pessoa) 1980; first performed Paris, 18 June 1981.
She (3 sopranos, violin, viola, guitar, piccolo, clarinet, harp; Park) 1983; first performed Rome, 24 September 1983.
In cauda (chorus, orchestra; d'Adda) 1983; first performed Venice, 30 September 1983.
Abyss (low female voice, bass flute, cor anglais, bass clarinet, contrabassoon, horn, tenor trombone/bass trombone, piano, percussion, viola, cello, double bass) 1983; first performed Metz, 18 November 1983.
Still (high soprano, 2 flutes, 2 violins, celeste, piano) 1985; first performed Milan, 21 April 1985.

Opera:

Atem 1983–4.

Other:

La lampara (ballet) 1957; first performed Milan, 1957.
Quartetto III (4-track tape) 1961.
L.A. Senese (collaboration with students at Accademia Chigana; 9 strings) 1970.

PUBLICATIONS

By Donatoni: "La musica elettronica", in *Discoteca*, 2(14), 1961; "Teatro musicale oggi", in *Il Verri*, 16, 1964; "Bisogna continuare", in *Musica Minima*, 2 (5), 1967; "Le parole che seguono", in *Spettatore musicale*, 2 (5), 1967; "Sulle ottime ragioni", in *Spettatore musicale*, 4, 1969; *Questo*, Milan, 1970; "Frammento interanalitico di un futuro anteriore", in *Spettatore musicale*, 6 (3), 1971.

On Donatoni: "New Music in Italy", in Lang and Broder, *Contemporary Music in Europe*, New York, 1965; M. Bortolotto, "Le idee di FD", in *Fase seconda*, Turin, 1969; M. Baroni, "FD, 1960–70", in *Notizario Suvini Zerboni*, Milan, 1971, also (in German) in *Melos*, 40, 1973.

* * *

The critical encounters of Franco Donatoni's life were his meetings with Bruno Maderna in 1953, the visits to Darmstadt immediately thereafter, and his friendship with the critic Mario Bortolotto, who has been a collaborator, critic and proponent of Donatoni's work ever since.

Maderna and Darmstadt opened the 26-year-old's eyes to the language of post-Webernian serialism. He had, up until 1953, been composing in a sombre, essentially tonal idiom with a strong Bartók influence and something of his teacher Petrassi's echoing of Hindemith's dissonances. It was a sufficient and flexible style for what Donatoni wanted to say. The early religious cantata *Il libro dei sette sigilli*, based on the Seven Seals of the Book of Revelation, and written under Petrassi's tutelage, and the slightly later *Sinfonia* and concertos are accomplished if not dazzling, but there already signs of straying even within that flexibility. *Musica* (the blandly uninformative title is perhaps significant) is a work in search of a new language, not just another dialect of post-Romantic atonality.

Within a year of *Musica*, he was composing in the advanced serialist language of Pierre Boulez, whose early piano music was particularly influential at Darmstadt. There was a transitional glance at Webern in *Composizione in quattro movimenti* (a debt more fully acknowledged in the 1983 performance of *Sinfonia Op 63 "Anton Webern"*), but it was with the much more loosely structured *Tre improvvisazioni* that Donatoni was to approach his mature style. He also took from Boulez a restless compulsion to revise and recompose works, and to cannibalise finished work for musical material. This is the origin of the *Divertimento II*, a version of his own second string quartet, while *Puppenspiel II* is a refinement and maturation of the original "marionette show" *Puppenspiel*. He also continued to turn to the work of other composers, notably Stockhausen, whose impact was second only to Boulez's, and also Schoenberg, whose *Fünf Klavierstücke* yielded the basic material for *Etwas ruhiger im Ausdruck*, a brilliant ensemble piece in which the original source is both declared and disguised.

Donatoni proved to be an excellent orchestrator—*Sezioni* is a wonderful essay in instrumental grouping—and a good instrumental craftsman (as in the quintet *For Grilly*). However, it was clear that the Darmstadt style would not remain sufficient for long. In *Per orchestra* (a transitional, but fully achieved work, much as *Musica* was), he began to explore a developing American obsession (Cage, Tudor, Brown) with chance operations, to which Stockhausen also subscribed. Donatoni's third "string quartet" had been a tape piece; his fourth, subtitled *Zrcadlo*, was determined by the players' reading of newspaper headlines. This method was quite soon exhausted and by the time of *The Heart's Eye*, Donatoni's brilliant 1981 quartet, he has returned without equivocation to conventional notation, but with a dramatically increased range of sonorities, timbres and instrumental colour as a result of his aleatory experiments. Much of this process he has discussed in his book *Questo*, an indispensable guide to his compositional motives and methods, and a sharp contrast to his later reticence about his methods.

Donatoni's recent work has been remarkable for its in-reaches its culmination in a remarkable sequence (and the influence of Berio's *Sequenze* in not far away) of solo instrumental compositions of the late 1970s and early 1980s; this includes *Lem* for double bass (by now a favourite Donatoni instrument), *Ombra* for the similarly pitched contrabass clarinet, another throwback to his dark student sound, *Ali* for viola, *Clair* for clarinet, and *Nidi* for piccolo (extremes of pitch being an abiding concern).

Donatoni's recent work has been remarkable for its individuality, but as the Webern homage demonstrates, he has never lost sight of the past. There are fewer allusions and archaeologies now, nothing on the scale of *Voci*, which is a long meditation, as if via Berio, on the name and key letters of B-A-C-H, a common compositional device; nor are there references as explicit as the pre-classical devices of *Solo*. What there is instead is a thorough absorption of the European tradition—only Petrassi seems to have "read" more—and a body of work which rivals Berio's in both quantity and importance.

—Guido Scarpone

DREW, James (Mulcrone). American. Born in St Paul, Minnesota, 9 February 1929. Educated at New York School of Music, 1954–6; Tulane University, New Orleans, M.A., 1964; private composition study with Edgard Varèse, 1956, and Wallingford Riegger, 1956–69; doctoral study, Washington University, St Louis, Missouri, 1964–5. Married in 1960; 1 son and 1 daughter. Instructor, School of Music, Northwestern University, Chicago, 1965–7; assistant professor of composition and theory, Yale University, New Haven, Connecticut, 1967–73; editorial board/reviews editor, *Yale Journal of Music Theory*, 1969–71; composer in residence, Yale University, Summer 1973, Berkshire Music Center, Tanglewood, Massachusetts, 1973; composer in residence/director, American Music theater, 1974–6; distinguished lecturer, School of Arts, California State University, Fullerton, 1976–7; visiting composer, University of California, Los Angeles, 1977–8; composer in residence, School of Music and Art, Norfolk, 1979; director, MMT Theater, New York/New Orleans, since 1979; director, Mysterious Travelling Cabaret, since 1980; associate composer/director, Raniero Production Group, Amsterdam, since 1987; leader, Ensemble Drew. Recipient: Guggenheim Fellowship, 1972–3; Morse Fellowship, 1967–71; Panamericana Prize (for *West Indian Lights*), 1974. Mailing address: Cooke Associates (management), Nicolaistraat 17, 2517 SX Den Haag, Netherlands; or c/o Theodore Presser Company, Presser Place, Bryn Mawr, Pennsylvania 19010, U.S.A.

Publisher: Presser.

Symphonies/orchestral:

Passacaglia 1957.
Symphony No 1 1968.
Concerto for Violino Grande 1969.
October Lights 1969.
Symphony No 2 1971; first performed New Haven, Connecticut, 1971.
Concerto for Small Percussion Orchestra 1972.
West Indian Lights 1973.
Concerto for Viola 1973.
Chamber Symphony 1976.
Symphony No 3 1977.
Sinfonia (strings) 1980.
Concerto for Two Cellos 1981.
Open/Closed Forms (chamber orchestra) 1982.
Faustus (2 pianos, cello, orchestra) 1983.
Cantobosolo (percussion, orchestra) 1987.

Chamber/instrumental:

Indigo Suite (piano, double bass, percussion) 1959.
Divisions (6 percussion) 1962.
Piano Trio 1962.
Polifonica I (flute, clarinet, oboe, string quartet, piano) 1963.
Four Pieces (string quartet) 1964.
Polifonica II (flute, percussion) 1966.
Primero libro de referencia laberinto (piano) 1969.
The Maze Maker (cello, tape) 1970.
Almost Stationary (piano trio) 1971.
Gothic Light (brass) 1972.
String Quartet No 1: Lux incognita 1972.
String Quartet No 2 1975.
Sonata (cello, piano) 1980.
Sonata (violin, piano) 1981.
St Mark Triple concerto (string trio) 1981.
Sonata (viola) 1982.
Chamber Concerto (winds, piano, percussion) 1985.
Cantobosolo (double bass) 1987.

Vocal/choral:

The Fading of the Visible World (soprano, tenor, bass, 4 voices, orchestra) 1976.
Orangethorpe Aria (soprano, clarinet, piano trio) 1978. Recorded TR Records.

Opera:

Mysterium (television opera) 1974–5.
Suspense Opera 1975.
Dr Cincinnati 1977.

Other:

Toward Yellow (ballet) 1970.
Crucifixus Domini Christi (ballet) 1975.
Five O'Clock Ladies (ballet) 1981.
Blue in Atlantis (actors/electronics) 1988. Recorded Maximus 102.

Videotapes: *Last Dance*, *Whisper*, *"Live" from the Black Eagle*.

PUBLICATIONS

By Drew: "Sabe lo que estoy oyendo?", in *Sonda*, 2, February 1968; "Information, Space and a New Time-Dialectic", in *Yale Journal of Music Theory*, 1969.

On Drew: J.K. Cordes, "A New American Development in Music: Some Characteristic Features Extending from the Legacy of Charles Ives", dissertation, Louisiana State University, 1976; G. Clarke, in *Essays in American Music*, Westport, Connecticut, 1977.

* * *

It is said that all contemporary American music gathers, in the words of Lou Harrison's title, at the tomb of Charles Ives. But to what extent has Ives really been assimilated? To what extent is he merely an icon, a declaration of musical independence from Europe, of greater symbolic than musicological importance?

Of all the composers who have been associated with Ives's presumed legacy, James Drew seems the only convincing claimant. His work depends on the coincidence of a great many apparently inimical musical styles; like Ives, Drew makes no attempt to "normalise" popular or non-canonical forms—as a thousand modern composers have been doing to jazz and blues—but is quite content to let them remain visible, on the surface, existing in their own right and terms.

Drew was brought up in Minnesota, but moved to New York to study with Varèse and Wallingford Riegger, before completing his studies in New Orleans, a city which is intrinsically dramatic, and in which music is inherently synthetic, drawing together a bewildering variety of influences. Like a good gumbo, Drew's music allows its components to stew just long enough to release, but not to lose, their flavours. He is brilliantly eclectic, in the sense that he unerringly chooses the correct gesture. His work as a performer is an important aspect of his career. Performances by the Ensemble Drew are often puzzling, sometimes maddening, but always provocative and stimulating. Drew has taken music beyond the merely musical.

In that regard, his work is similar to Robert Ashley's. Both have produced television operas, but then so has Gian Carlo Menotti. What links them is a pressing need to push music out beyond the concert hall, onto the streets and into homes. Though Ashley is an altogether more intellectual figure, Drew is no lightweight, contributing well-argued essays on aspects of modern music, its techniques and technology to English- and Spanish-language journals. He espouses something like the deceptive advanced amateurism associated with Satie or Ives, that simultaneous temptation and refusal to let the ears lie back in their easy chair and merely *consume* what is being fed to them.

Drew has written impressively large-scaled works in apparently conventional idiom. The symphonies are only Ivesian in their scope and occasional daring. By far the most successful of the orchestral pieces is the prizewinning *West Indian Lights*, but the concertos are always interesting. Drew's chamber music is always beautifully textured—for example the two *Polifonicas* and the piano trio *Almost Stationary*—without ever losing sight of a more dynamic logic.

Drew is a genuine American original. He belongs in the same category as Partch, Nancarrow, Ruggles and, inevitably, Ives. It is a tradition that sits easily upon him, as he moves forward into a fourth decade of making innovative music.

—Eleanor Caldwell

DREYFUS, George. Australian. Born in Wuppertal, Germany, 22 July 1928; emigrated to Australia, 1939. Educated at Vienna Academy of Music, 1955–6. Married Frances Kay Dreyfus, 4 November 1968; 2 sons and 1 daughter. Orchestral bassoonist, J.C. Williamson Theatres, and with Australian Broadcasting Commission, 1948–64; founded New Music Ensemble, Melbourne, 1958; freelance composer since 1965; creative arts fellowship, Australian National University, Canberra, 1967–8; foundation member/musical director, ISCM, Melbourne, 1965; formed George Dreyfus Chamber Orchestra, Melbourne, 1970; composer in residence, Mishkenot Sha'ananim, Jerusalem, 1980; artist in residence, Conservatorium of Music, Tianjin, China, 1983, and Conservatorium of Music, Shanghai, China, 1987. Recipient: Louis Lavater Prize, 1959; UNESCO Travelling Scholarship, 1966; Henry Lawson Award for Outstanding Services to the Arts, 1972; A.H. Maggs Award, 1973; Best Australian Album (for *Sextet for Didjeridu and Wind Instruments*), 1973; international award for best documentary (for *A Steam Train Passes*), 1975; Prix de Rome, 1976; APRA Serious Music Award, 1986. Mailing address: 3 Grace Street, Camberwell, Victoria 3124, Australia.

Publisher: Allans Publishing, 165 Gladstone Street, South Melbourne, Victoria 3205, Australia.

Symphonies/orchestral:

Symphony No 1 1962; first performed Melbourne, 1968. Recorded EMI OASD 7547.
Jingles (5 pieces) 1967; first performed Melbourne, 1968. Recorded Festival SFC-80021.
. . . and More Jingles (5 pieces) 1972.
Rush 1974; first performed Melbourne, 1974. Recorded WRC R05228; ABC/Festival L 38417.
Symphony No 2 1976; first performed Melbourne, 1977. Recorded WRC R08459.
Mary Gilmore Goes to Paraguay 1978; first performed Melbourne, 1979. Recorded WRC R08459.
Symphonie Concertante (bassoon, violin, viola, cello, string orchestra) 1978; first performed Ballarat, 1979.
Grand Ridge Road 1979; first performed Traralgon, 1980.
Folk Music with Large Orchestra 1981; first performed Melbourne, 1982.
Water Front 1982; first performed Melbourne, 1983. Recorded ABC/Festival L 38417.
Symphonic Movement 1988.

Chamber/instrumental:

Trio (flute, clarinet, bassoon) 1955; first performed Perth, 1956. Recorded Move MD 3071.
The Seasons (flute, viola, percussion) 1963; first performed Melbourne, 1963. Recorded ABC PRX 5599.
Quintet After the Notebook of J.-G. Noverre (flute, oboe, clarinet, horn, bassoon) 1965; first performed Adelaide, 1968. Recorded RCA SL 16374; Anthology of Australian Music CSM 14.
The Adventures of Sebastian the Fox (various instrumentations) 1968. Recorded ABW 4001.
Theme Music for Expo 70 (arranged for piano) 1970.
Sextet (didjeridu, flute, oboe, clarinet, horn, bassoon) 1971; first performed Adelaide, 1971. Recorded EMI OASD 7565.
Old Melbourne (bassoon, guitar) 1972; first performed Melbourne, 1973. Recorded Move MD 3071.
Rush (various instrumentations) 1974. Recorded Three Feet TF 002.
Ein Kaffeekonzert (piano, violin, cello) 1976; first performed Melbourne, 1977.
For Four Bassoons 1983; first performed Melbourne, 1984.
Sonata (violin, viola) 1989; first performed London, 1990.
Larino, Safe Haven 1989; first performed Melbourne, 1990.

Vocal/choral:

Galgenlieder (baritone, flute, clarinet, bassoon, violin; Morgenstern) 1956; first performed Perth, 1957. Recorded Philips AY 842721.
Songs Comic and Curious (baritone, wind quintet) 1959; first performed Melbourne, 1959. Recorded EMI OASD 7558.
Wilhelm Busch Lieder (soprano, flute, clarinet, bassoon) 1959.
From Within, Looking Out (soprano, flute, viola, vibraphone, celeste) 1961; first performed Melbourne, 1962. Recorded WRC A/601.
Music in the Air (baritone, flute, viola, percussion; McCuaig) 1961.
Ned Kelly Ballads (4 horns, rhythm accompaniment; Burstall) 1963.

Homage to Stravinsky (chorus; 10 voices) 1968.
Under the Gumtrees at Sunrise (4 solo voices, 2 choruses) 1968.
Reflections in a Glass House: An Image of Captain James Cook (speaker, children's chorus, orchestra) 1969.
Mo (baritone, strings, basso continuo) 1972.
Terrigal (treble choir, keyboards) 1976; first performed Adelaide, 1977.
An Australian Folk Mass (unison chorus, orchestra) 1979; first performed Melbourne, 1979.
The Grand Aurora Australis Now Show Celebration (soloists, chorus, orchestra) 1980; first performed Melbourne, 1981.
The Ballad of Charles Rasp (pop singer, chorus, concert band) 1983; first performed Melbourne, 1984.
Box Hill Gloria (pop singer, chorus, concert band, brass band, pipe band, string orchestra) 1984; first performed Melbourne, 1985.
Life Style (unaccompanied treble choir) 1987; first performed Melbourne, 1988.

Opera:

Garni Sands (Kellaway) 1965–6; first performed Sydney, 1972.
The Takeover (children's opera) 1969; first performed Canberra, 1969.
The Gilt-Edged Kid (Strahan) 1970; first performed Melbourne, 1976.
The Lamentable Reign of Charles the Last (pantopera; Robertson) 1975.

Other:

The Illusionist (film ballet and suite) 1964.
The Sentimental Bloke (musical) 1984; first performed Melbourne, 1985.

Film scores: approximately 60 scores for feature and documentary films and television, including *Rush*, 1974; *A Steam Train Passes*, 1974; *This Day Tonight*, 1975; *Power Without Glory*, 1976; *Dimboola*, 1976; *Break of Day*, 1976; *Deep Throat*, 1978; *Waterfront*, 1984; *Great Expectations*, 1986—recorded *The Film Music of George Dreyfus* Volumes 1 & 2, WRC R05228/R08459.

PUBLICATIONS

By Dreyfus: *The Last Frivolous Book* (autobiography), Sydney, 1984.

On Dreyfus: R. Covell, in *Australia's Music*, Melbourne, 1967; P.G. Downs, "GD's First Symphony", in *Meanjin Quarterly*, Summer 1968; A.A. McCredie, in *Musical Composition in Australia*, Canberra, 1969, and in *Catalogue of 46 Australian Composers and their Works*, Canberra, 1969; K. Lucas, "GD", in *APRA Journal*, 5, 1971; J. Murdoch, in *Australia's Contemporary Composers*, Melbourne/Sydney, 1972; K. Lucas, "GD's *Garni Sands*: A Forward Step for Australian Opera", in *Studies in Music*, 7, 1973.

* * *

Emigrating to Australia when he was around 11 years old, George Dreyfus subsequently experienced the same problem as native-born composers: a time delay before hearing live performances of new developments in European music. While sound recordings and scores of this music soon became available, his widest acquaintance, as a young man, was with the standard concert and opera repertoire of the time—Brahms, Tchaikovsky, Verdi, Puccini—which he played as bassoonist in various orchestras and ensembles.

His European heritage can be detected in early works such as his *Trio* for flute, clarinet and bassoon and the song-cycle *Galgenlieder*, both of which displayed a quirkiness and dry sense of humour reminiscent of French composers such as Poulenc. The use of parody, and even of direct quotation, is a strong feature of Dreyfus's work. The *Trio* made reference to Mendelssohn's *Wedding March*, the *Galgenlieder* quoted almost verbatim from Rimsky-Korsakov's *Scheherazade*, while the *Symphony No 1* was a consciously eclectic work designed to appeal to the listener, rather than to impress with innovative insights. Similarly, *Jingles* was written for young people, and was a pastiche of styles from classical to jazz and rock. Its title was a deliberate provocation, chosen solely to deride a critic who had scorned Dreyfus's use of an advertising jingle (his own) in his Symphony: a typical example of the composer's sometimes outrageous display of humour.

In the early 1960s he flirted with serialism and the theories of the Second Viennese School. The style fitted his mood, angry and experimental like so many writers of the time. He abandoned his previous manner of writing in the middle of a work—the ballad opera *Casanova*—and wrote the twelve-tone *Music in the Air* for baritone, flute, viola and percussion. While the work was a good example of its kind, audiences were unresponsive, and Dreyfus himself was not satisfied with the sterility he perceived in the style. He dabbled in variations and adaptations of the genre. Typical of this period was *From Within, Looking Out* for soprano, flute, viola, celeste and vibraphone, in which the text inspired the mood of each phrase but the words were treated as a vocalise. The form varied from very tightly planned to quite free. Echoes of this attitude to word setting can be found in the opera *Garni Sands*, as if the composer were laying down a challenge to his listeners.

If occasional works from *Symphony No 1* to *Symphonic Movement* were deliberate attempts to appeal to a wider audience, Dreyfus's music for film and television has never deviated from that philosophy, which doubtless explains his success in this field. His music for television such as the series *Rush*, *This Day Tonight* and *Waterfront* won immediate and widespread popular acclaim, while his output of music for film—including the notorious *Deep Throat*—has been prodigious.

Attempts to blend aspects of music from Western European tradition with that of the indigenous Australian Aborigines have had little success: John Antill's *Corroboree* was probably the only work to have aroused any degree of public interest before Dreyfus's *Sextet* for didjeridu and wind instruments. Using a collage technique, Dreyfus tackled the problem by structuring a piece that comprised variations of tone colour and dynamics, and within that framework writing music that showed off each instrument's own peculiar strengths and capabilities. For that reason, while the parts for the Western instruments were meticulously notated, only the duration of the didjeridu episodes was indicated. The nature of the contribution of this instrument, essentially an improvisatory one, was left to the artistry of the player, thus avoiding constricting it into an alien frame.

—Jenny Dawson

DRUCKMAN, Jacob (Raphael). American. Born in Philadelphia, 26 June 1928. Education: studied theory, composition and violin under Louis Gessensway, 1938–40; self-taught trumpeter, jazz and dance bands; solfege and score reading under Renée Longy, 1945; Berkshire Music Centre, Tanglewood, Massachusetts (composition under Aaron Copland), Summer 1949; Juilliard School, New York City (under Vincent Persichetti, Peter Mennin and Bernard Wagenaar), 1949–56, B.S., 1954, M.S., 1956; further study, as Fulbright Fellow, Ecole Normale de Musique, Paris (under Tony Aubin), 1954–5; further research in electronics, Columbia-Princeton Electronic Music Center, 1965–6, and, as Guggenheim Fellow, at ORTF, Paris, 1968. Married dancer Muriel Topaz in June 1954. Teacher, Juilliard School, New York, 1957–72; (concurrently) part-time teacher, Bard College, Annandale-on-Hudson, New York, 1961–7; associate director, Columbia-Princeton Electronic Music Center, 1967; director, electronic music studio, 1971–2, and since 1977, and chair of music department, since 1977, Yale University, New Haven, Connecticut; guest teacher, Berkshire Music Centre, Tanglewood, Massachusetts, 1972, 1973, 1977; composer in residence, Aspen Festival, Colorado, 1972, 1976, 1983, 1985, 1987, 1988, and Tanglewood, 1974, 1978; associate professor of composition, Brooklyn College, City University of New York, 1972–6; member, Music Advisory Panel, New York State Council on the Arts, 1975–8; chair, Composer-Librettist Panel, National Endowment for Arts, 1980; president, Koussevitzky Foundation, 1980; resident in music, American Academy, Rome, 1982; composer in residence, New York Philharmonic Orchestra, 1982–6; artistic director NYPO "Horizons" concerts of new music, 1983, 1984; Phi Beta Kappa Scholar, 1987–8. Recipient: Guggenheim Fellowships, 1957, 1968; Pulitzer Prize (for *Windows*), 1972; Brandeis University Creative Arts Award, 1975; elected, American Institute of Arts and Letters, 1978. Mailing address: c/o Boosey & Hawkes, 24 East 21st Street, New York, New York 10010, U.S.A.

Publisher: Boosey & Hawkes.

Symphonies/orchestral:

Concerto (strings) 1951.
Overture: Volpone 1953.
Violin Concerto (violin, small orchestra) 1956.
Windows 1972; first performed Chicago, 16 May 1972. Recorded CRI SD 457.
Incenters (trumpet, horn, trombone, orchestra; arrangement of chamber work) 1973; first performed Minneapolis, 23 November 1973.
Mirage 1976; first performed St Louis, Missouri, 4 March 1976.
Chiaroscuro 1976; first performed Cleveland, Ohio, 14 March 1977.
Viola Concerto 1978; first performed New York City, 2 November 1978.
Aureole 1979; first performed New York City, 6 June 1979. Recorded New World Records NW 318.
Prism 1980; first performed Baltimore, Maryland, 21 May 1980. Recorded New World Records NW 335.
Engram (arrangement for band of 3rd movement of *Prism*) 1982; first performed Ann Arbor, Michigan, 13 November 1987.
A Birthday Bouquet 1986; first performed New York City, 29 April 1986.
Athanor 1986; first performed New York City, 8 May 1986.
Paean 1986; first performed Houston, Texas, 3 January 1987.
In Memoriam Vincent Persichetti (written on a cantus firmus taken from the opening bars of Persichetti's *Symphony for Strings Op 61*) 1987; first performed New York City, 6 December 1987.

Chamber/instrumental:

String Quartet No 1 1948.
Duo (violin, piano) 1949; first performed Tanglewood, Massachusetts, August 1950.
Divertimento (clarinet, horn, harp, violin, viola, cello) 1950; first performed New York City, March 1953.
The Seven Deadly Sins (piano) 1955; first performed Paris, 1955.
Animus I (trombone, tape) 1966; first performed Annandale-on-Hudson, New York, 23 May 1966. Recorded Turnabout TV 34177.
String Quartet No 2 1966; first performed New York City, 13 December 1966. Recorded Vox SVBX 5306.
Incenters (trumpet, horn, trombone, with flute, oboe, clarinet, bassoon, percussion, piano/electric organ, violin, viola, cello, double bass) 1968; first performed New Brunswick, New Jersey, 7 May 1968. Recorded Nonesuch H-71253.
Animus III (clarinet, tape) 1969; first performed Paris, 23 October 1969. Recorded Nonesuch H-71253.
Valentine (double bass) 1969; first performed New York City, 19 November 1969. Recorded Nonesuch H-71253.
Orison (organ, tape) 1970; first performed New York City, 19 January 1970.
Delizie contente che l'aime beate (after Cavali; wind quintet, tape) 1973; first performed New York City, 13 December 1973. Recorded Vox SVBX 5306.
Other Voices (brass quintet) 1976; first performed Aspen, Colorado, 20 July 1976.
String Quartet No 3 1981; first performed Milwaukee, Wisconsin, 17 November 1981.
Tromba Marina (4 double basses) 1981; first performed New York City, 29 December 1981.
Reflections on the Nature of Water (marimba) 1986; first performed Washington, D.C., 7 November 1986.

Vocal/choral:

Laude (baritone, flute, viola, cello; medieval) 1952.
The Simple Gifts (SATB chorus, piano; Shaker) 1954.
Four Madrigals (unaccompanied mixed chorus; Beaumont, Jonson, Donne, Herrick) 1958; first performed New York City, 6 March 1959. Recorded Vox SVBX 5354.
Dark upon the Harp (mezzo-soprano, brass quintet, percussion; Psalms) 1962; first performed New York City, 1962. Recorded CRI SD 167.
Antiphonies I, II, III (2 unaccompanied mixed choruses; Hopkins) 1963; first performed (I and II) New York City, 28 February 1964; III first performed Tanglewood, 30 July 1976. Recorded Deutsche Grammophon DG 2530 912.
The Sound of Time (soprano, piano or orchestra; Mailer) 1964, 1965; first performed New York City, 3 December 1964; orchestral version first performed Provincetown, Massachusetts, 25 July 1965.
Dance of the Maidens (SATB chorus, organ, percussion) 1965.
Hymnus referamus (SATB chorus, organ, percussion; Psalms) 1965.
Psalm 89 (SATB chorus, organ, percussion) 1965.
Shir Shel Yakov: Sabbath Eve Service (tenor, chorus, organ)

1967; first performed New York City, 21 April 1967.

Animus II (soprano, 2 percussionists, tape; International Phonetic Alphabet) 1968; first performed Paris, 2 February 1970. Recorded CRI SD 255.

Lamia (soprano, orchestra; Ovid, Wagner, trad.) 1974, revised 1975; first performed Albany, New York, 20 April 1974; revised version first performed New York City, 17 October 1975; version for soprano and small orchestra first performed St Paul, Minnesota, 7 November 1986. Recorded Louisville First Editions LS 764.

Animus IV (tenor, instrumental ensemble, tape; Chabrier, Liszt) 1977; first performed Paris, 29 September 1977.

Bo (marimba, harp, bass clarinet, 3 female voices; Mu-Hua) 1979; first performed New York City 3 March 1979.

Vox Humana (soprano, mezzo-soprano, tenor, bass, mixed chorus, orchestra; Biblical) 1982–3; first performed Washington, D.C., 25 October 1983.

Other:

Music for the Dance (orchestra) 1949.

Spell (ballet; 2 pianos) 1951.

Interlude (ballet; flute, clarinet, timpani) 1953.

Suite (ballet; orchestra) 1953.

The Seven Deadly Sins (piano) 1955.

Performance (ballet; orchestra) 1960.

Measure for Measure (incidental music to Shakespeare; orchestra) 1964.

Odds and Evens (a game for children's orchestra) 1966.

Look Park (film score; tape) 1970.

Traite du rossignol (film score, tape) 1970.

Synapse (tape) 1971. Recorded Nonesuch H-71253.

Cavalli: *Delizie contente che l'aime beate* (arranged by Druckman for concert to demonstrate origins of *Prism*) 1985; first performed Akron, Ohio, 20 April 1985.

Charpentier: *Suite from Medee* (arranged by Druckman for concert to demonstrate origins of *Prism*) 1985; first performed Akron, Ohio, 20 April 1985.

PUBLICATIONS

On Druckman: S. Fleming, "JD", in *High Fidelity / Musical America*, 22 (8), 1972; A. Porter, in *Music of Three Seasons 1974–77*, New York, 1978; N. Uscher, "Two Contemporary Violin Concerti: A Comparison", in *Tempo*, 147, 1983; C. Gagne and T. Caras, "JD", in *Soundpieces: Interviews with American Composers*, Metuchen, New Jersey, 1982; Richard Duffalo, "JD", (interview) in *Trackings*, Oxford, 1990.

* * *

From his first pieces to the most recent, Jacob Druckman's music is dramatic, allusive, lyrical, often virtuosic and brilliantly colored. In a career spanning over 40 years, Druckman has written for a variety of media including orchestra, voice, tape, film, chamber ensembles and solo instruments. Characteristically, tone and texture undergo transformations, whether gradual or instantaneous, that are important in defining the music's emotional and dramatic qualities. Druckman has noted that "There are many things—orchestral color is a good example—that I consider intrinsic and structural in a piece that others would consider decorative. The whole concern of orchestral coloring is as central to me as sonata allegro form was to Mozart." Indeed, Druckman's use of timbre is innovative, subtle, and richly varied. He is widely regarded as one of the finest contemporary composers of orchestral music.

Druckman's compositions reflect a rich and varied musical tradition. His earliest works, such as *Duo* for violin and piano, are influenced by Stravinsky, early Schoenberg and Debussy. Other important early influences include Mahler, Ravel and Prokofiev. All of these composers continue to color Druckman's sonic pallet, but more recent works engage overtly with the musical tradition through allusion or even direct quotation of music both past and present. The range of references extends from the early 17th century to the late 20th and encompasses composers as diverse as Cavalli, Cherubini, Moussorgsky, Wagner, Bernstein and even Druckman himself, as well as harmonic principles of 1940s jazz. Although Druckman is widely considered one of the leaders of the new romanticism, in his case this does not refer to a return to tonality, but rather a rejection of many, although certainly not all, of the aesthetics of structuralism.

Druckman has worked in a variety of 20th-century idioms from twelve tone and aleatoricism to electronic music and music theater, and, most recently his music has been setting trends in the postmodern genre, new romanticism. While at Juilliard, first as a student and later as faculty, Druckman became increasingly involved with mid-20th-century concepts of controlling pitch and rhythm, principally serialism and aleatoricism. Many of his pieces up until the mid 1960s use a personalized form of twelve tone as well as proportional rhythmic notation and other aleatoric devices. The Second String Quartet is Druckman's last and most elaborate twelve-tone composition. While working on this quartet, he realized that he was becoming less interested in its intellectual complexities and more concerned with its gestural and humanistic properties. This change in focus defines a crucial turning point in Druckman's compositional development.

The same year that Druckman completed the Second String Quartet, he began working on the first of six electronic compositions, *Animus I* for trombone and tape. This work, like the majority of his electronic compositions, is concerned with the dramatic relationship of a live performer and recorded sounds. Although the timbral relationship of the trombone and tape in *Animus I* is at times organic, because portions of the tape were created by manipulating pre-recorded trombone sounds and occasionally expanding them beyond the trombonist's scope, conflict is created between player and machine. Theatrical actions underscore the relationship of the work's two different forces. When the tape imitates the trombone's music and then expands beyond it, the trombonist leaves the stage in anger. This theatricality is integral to the piece. Although Druckman's other electronic pieces do not always include theatrical gestures, these compositions are invariably dramatic. The only piece for tape alone, excepting a few film scores, is *Synapse* which was conceived of as an optional prologue to the solo bass piece Valentine, which is in itself theatrical through its ferocious and, at times, violent virtuosity.

Druckman has succeeded in transferring many of the vast timbral resources available in the electronic studio to the acoustic instruments of the orchestra. The scope of his timbral creativity is all the more impressive, because his instrumental writing, which does not rely heavily upon extended techniques, is steadfastly idiomatic. His orchestral composition *Windows* juxtaposes 20th-century sonorities to earlier harmonies as openings occur in the dense instrumental texture revealing music that is reminiscent of past centuries. In the many major orchestral compositions that have followed this Pulitzer Prize-winning work, Druckman continues to explore and refine this technique of combining strong, richly colored gestures in a contemporary harmonic language with quotations of older music. The junction of the two is frequently disquieting and dramatically urgent.

—R. Peter Mueller and Rachel Myers

DUFOURT, Hugues. French. Born in Lyon, 28 September 1943. Educated at Geneva Conservatoire, Switzerland (under Louis Hiltbrand), 1961–8; concurrently studied philosophy, graduated 1967; studied analysis, scoring, composition, conducting under Jacques Guyonnet, 1965–70; studied electronic music, Studio de Musique Contemporaine, Geneva. Organiser, new music concerts, Théâtre de la Cité de Villeurbanne, 1968; *assistant*, later *Maître-Assistant* in philosophy, Université Jean Moulin, Lyon, 1968–73; member (with Tristan Murail and Michaël Levinas), Groupe de l'Itinéraire, 1973; researcher, Centre National de la Recherche Scientifique (CNRS), Paris, 1973; co-founder (with Alain Bancquart and Tristan Murail), Collectif de Recherche Instrumental et de Synthèse Sonore, 1977; founder, 1982, and currently director, Centre d'Information et de Documentation "Recherche Musicale", 1982; currently head of research, CNRS. Recipient: Grand Prix de l'Académie Charles Cros (for *Saturne* recording), 1980. Mailing address: c/o Editions Jobert, 76 rue Quincampoix, 75003 Paris, France.

Publishers: Editions Jobert; Editions Salabert.

Symphonies/orchestral:

Surgir (large orchestra) 1980–4; first performed Paris, 13/14 February 1985.

Chamber/instrumental:

Brisants (piano, flute, 2 clarinets/bass clarinets, 4 trumpets, 3 trombones/bass trombones, 6 percussion) 1968; first performed Geneva, 30 November 1968.

Mura Della Citta di Dite (flute, oboe, clarinet, bass clarinet, horn, trumpet, trombone, 2 percussion, harp, celeste, electronic organ, 2 violins, viola, cello, double bass) 1969; first performed Geneva, 19 October 1969.

Down to a Sunless Sea (16 strings) 1970; first performed Geneva, 20 August 1970.

Erewhon I–IV (6 percussionists, 150 percussion instruments) 1972–6; first performed Royan, 4 April 1977.

La Tempesta: d'après Giorgione (flute/bass flute/amplified contrabass flute, oboe/cor anglais, clarinet/bass clarinet/amplified contrabass clarinet, trombone, electronic organ, vibraphone, electric guitar) 1976–7.

Antiphysis (flute, chamber ensemble) 1978; first performed La Rochelle, 7 July 1978. Recorded Erato STU 71544.

Sombre Journée (6 percussion) 1979; first performed Paris, 30 March 1979.

Saturne (3 flutes, 2 oboes/cor anglais/heckelphone/oboe d'amore, 2 clarinets/basset horns, bassoon/contrabassoon, 2 horns, trumpet, trombone/bass trumpet, tuba/euphonium, 6 percussion, 2 ondes martenot/electronic organ/synthesizer, 2 electric guitars/synthesizer) 1979; first performed Paris, 3 December 1979. Recorded Sappho 004.

La Nuit face au ciel (6 percussion) 1984; first performed Aix-en-Provence, 3 July 1984.

L'Heure des traces (2 flutes/piccolo/bass flute, 2 oboes/cor anglais/oboe d'amore, 3 clarinets/E♭ clarinet/basset horn/bass clarinet, bassoon/contrabassoon, horn, trumpet, tenor trombone/bass trombone, 3 percussion, 2 violins, 2 violas, cello, 5-string double bass) 1986; first performed Milan, 19 May 1986.

Hommage à Charles Negre (flute/piccolo/bass flute, oboe/cor anglais/oboe d'amore, clarinet/E♭ clarinet/bass clarinet, bassoon/contrabassoon, vibraphone, electric guitar) 1986; first performed Paris, 2 December 1986.

Le Philosophe selon Rembrandt (ensemble) 1987; withheld for revision.

Vocal/choral:

Dusk Light (soprano, mezzo-soprano, tenor, baritone, flute, 3 clarinets/bass clarinet/contrabass clarinet, horn, trumpet, trombone, 2 percussion, harp, celeste, electronic organ, 2 violins, viola, cello) 1971; first performed Geneva, 10 October 1971.

La Mort de Procris (12 unaccompanied mixed voices; Shakespeare) 1986; first performed 26 September 1986.

* * *

Hugues Dufourt has chosen to pursue a dual career in philosophy and composition. He graduated in the former in 1967, while studying music at the Geneva Conservatoire with Jacques Guyonnet, who introduced him to the theories and aesthetic of his own teacher, Pierre Boulez. Dufourt's earliest published work, the Boulez-like *Brisants* for piano and ensemble, dates from this time.

Dufourt also studied electronic music at the Studio de Musique Contemporaine in Geneva, returning to France in 1968 to teach philosophy at the Université Jean Moulin, in Lyon, where he remained until 1973. The previous year, still little known as a composer, he had embarked on the composition of his first large piece, the four-movement "symphony" *Erewhon* for six percussionists, requiring 150 instruments and playing for 75 minutes; it took him five years to complete. The title refers to the novel by Samuel Butler, an anagrammatic reversal of the original meaning of utopia: Nowhere. Dufourt aimed to create a paradoxical musical syntax analogous to the reversals of reality in Butler's novel; he tried to derive the structure and musical substance of the work directly from the acoustical nature of the instruments employed, reversing what he sees as the usual practice in contemporary composition of using the instruments to articulate a pre-existing, independently conceived structure. The four movements are contrasted in mood and scoring; in the swift first movement, drums predominate; the second features untuned wooden and metal instruments; the third, the slow movement, is for tuned bells and gongs; the work concludes with a culminatory final movement uniting all these instruments.

In 1973, Dufourt began a close association with the Groupe de l'Itinéraire, a collective of composers and performers founded in 1973 by Tristal Murail and Michaël Levinas; for them he composed two works, *La Tempesta: d'après Giorgione* and *Saturne*, both exploiting the group's resources in live electronics. The unusual scoring of *La Tempesta* places emphasis on low wind instruments such as contrabass flute and contrabass clarinet, the strange and awkward timbre of which Dufourt sees as a source of musical tension. The music mirrors the uneasy calm of Giorgione's painting in a subdued study in shadings of harmony and tone-colour with subtle use of electric guitar and ondes martenot. The first performances of *La Tempesta* and *Erewhon* within two days of one another at the 1977 Royan Festival brought Dufourt immediate and wide recognition on the international new music scene.

It was Dufourt's second work for L'Itinéraire, *Saturne*, which assured his reputation. *Saturne* is scored for a large ensemble of wind, percussion and live electronics, with more extensive use of low instruments—bass flutes and contrabass clarinet are joined by a heckelphone (a baritone oboe) and two bass trumpets. Acoustical considerations are once again paramount; the scoring allows Dufourt a complete range of sound, fron sine tones (ondes martenots) to white noise (percussion, electronics), with every degree in between. The music falls into three sections, the outer two calm and uneasy in the manner of *La Tempesta*, the central one tense, violent and ultimately explosive. The work as a whole, and the slowly accumulating energy of its central section in particular, are perhaps the clearest realisation of Dufourt's stated aims: he has said that he wishes to explore "dimensions of discomfort and malaise"; his music is an "integration of deformity, a surpassing of ugliness by means of a new syntax of tensions and transitions."

Perhaps because he has never tried to earn his living from composition, Dufourt's output is selective and he works slowly, composing only large-scale works—there are no "minor" works written on the side, no solo pieces or quartets. Between *La Tempesta* and *Saturne* came the flute concerto *Antiphysis*, an exercise in "blurred symmetry" with a ternary formal plan and a brooding atmosphere similar to *Saturne*. Dufourt's next work was his first and so far only orchestral piece, *Surgir* an imposing half-hour structure of considerable power, continuing Dufourt's exploration of ebbing and flowing instrumental masses. Only two pieces have been heard since, both for chamber ensemble and dating from 1986: *L'Heure des traces* and *Hommage à Charles Negre* are in Dufourt's brooding manner; in mood and scoring they recall two earlier works, *Antiphysis* and *La Tempesta* respectively. Another work, *Le Philosophe selon Rembrandt*, also for chamber ensemble, was announced for performance in 1987, but has been withheld for revision.

—Julian Anderson

DURKO, Zsolt. Hungarian. Born in Szeged, Hungary, 10 April 1934. Educated at Budapest Academy of Music (under Ferenc Farkas), 1955–60; Accademia di Santa Cecilia, Rome (under Goffredo Petrassi), 1961–3. Married Riota Geremcser in 1970; 2 sons. Freelance composer, 1963–71; teacher of 20th-century music, Budapest Academy of Music, 1971–7; music reader, Hungarian Radio, since 1982. Recipient: d'Atri Prize, Rome (for *Episodi sul tema B-A-C-H*), 1963; Erkel Prize, 1965, 1972; 3rd prize (for *String Quartet No 1*), International Composers' Competition, Jeunesses Musicales, Montreal, 1967; 2nd prize (for *String Quartet No 2*), Bela Bartók International Composers' Competition, Budapest, 1970; Special Citation, International Koussevitzky Award (for recording of *Fioriture*), 1971; Distinguished Composer of the Year (for *Burial Prayer*), UNESCO Tribune Internationale des Compositeurs, Paris, 1975; Kossuth Prize, 1978; Bartók Pasztory Award, 1983; Merited Artist of the Hungarian People's Republic, 1983; Outstanding Artist, Hungarian People's Republic, 1987. Mailing address: Bimbo ut 193, 1026 Budapest II, Hungary.

Publishers: Editio Musica Budapest; Boosey & Hawkes; Chester Music.

Symphonies/orchestral:

Episode sul tema B-A-C-H 1962–3.
Organismi (violin, orchestra) 1964. Recorded LPX 1298.
Una rapsodia ungherese/Hungarian Rhapsody 1964–5. Recorded LPX 11363; LPX 11525.
Cantilene (piano, orchestra) 1968.
Ballad (youth or amateur orchestra) 1970.
Refrains (violin, chamber orchestra) 1978.
Fantasia es utojatek (Fantasy and Postlude) (youth or amateur orchestra) 1979.
Quattro dialoghi (2 percussion, orchestra) 1979.
Piano Concerto 1980.
Ornamenti No 1 1984.
Ornamenti No 2 1985.

Chamber/instrumental:

Undici pezzi per quartetto d'archi (string quartet) 1962.
Psicogramma (piano) 1964. Recorded LPX 11363; Duchesne DD 6064.
Improvvisazioni (wind quintet) 1965.
String Quartet No 1 1966. Recorded LPX 11363.
Symbols (horn, piano) 1968–9. Recorded LPX 11363.
String Quartet No 2 1969. Recorded LPX 11546.
Colloides (flute, chamber ensemble) 1969. Recorded SLPX 11982.
Quartetto d'ottoni 1970.
Fire Music (flute, clarinet, piano, string trio) 1971; first performed London, 1971. Recorded SLPX 11607.
Iconography No 1 (2 bass viols or cellos, harpsichord) 1971; first performed Basle, 1971. Recorded SLPX 11607.
Assonanze (organ) 1971.
Iconography No 2 (horn, chamber ensemble) 1972; first performed Prague, 1972. Recorded SLPX 11607.
Chamber Music (2 pianos, 11 strings) 1972–3. Recorded SLPX 11803.
Mikrostrukturak (piano) 1973.
Serenata (4 harps) 1973.
Chance (piano) 1973.
Varianti (viola, piano) 1974.
Torpek es oriasok (Dwarves and Giants) (piano) 1974.
Turner Illustrations (violin, oboe, clarinet, 3 trombones, 3 percussion, celeste/harpsichord, harp, piano/electric organ, violin, viola, cello) 1976. Recorded SLPX 11982.
Eight Duos (2 horns) 1977.
Five Pieces (tuba, piano) 1978.
Gyermekzene (Children's Music) (piano) 1978.
Solo Suite No 1 (cello) 1978.
Movements (tuba, piano) 1980.
Andromeda (organ or harpsichord) 1980.
A Midsummer Night's Dream 1981.
Son et lumière (piano) 1982.
Three Essays (clarinet, piano) 1983.
Quartina (piano) 1983.
Sinfonietta (10 brass) 1983; first performed London, 1983. Recorded Chandos ABRD 1190.
Impromptus in F (flute, chamber ensemble) 1983; first performed London, 1983.

Teli zene (Winter Music) (horn, flute, clarinet, percussion, piano/organ, string quartet) 1984; first performed London, 1984.
Harom rondo (Three Rondos) (piano) 1984.
Clair-obscur (organ, trumpet) 1984.
Sextet (5 clarinets, piano) 1987.
Laude (organ) 1987.
Octet (woodwinds) 1988.
Suoni tenebrosi e corale (organ, 2 violas, 5 cellos, 3 double basses, celeste, percussion, 5 altos vocalise) 1988.

Vocal/choral:

Fioriture (chamber choir, orchestra) 1966. Recorded LPX 11363.
Dartmouth Concerto (soprano, chamber ensemble; Masefield) 1966; first performed U.S.A., 1966.
Altamira (chamber choir, orchestra) 1967–8. Recorded SLPX 11607.
Halotti beszed (Burial Prayer) (tenor, baritone, mixed choir, orchestra; 12th-century Hungarian) 1967–72. Recorded SLPX 11803.
Hat tanulmany (Six Studies) (mixed choir, piano) 1970–2.
Cantata No 1 (baritone, mixed choir, orchestra; Ady) 1971.
Cantata No 2 (double mixed choir, orchestra; Ady) 1972.
Het dallamrajz (mixed choir, piano) 1972.
Szechenyi Oratorio (baritone, mixed choir, orchestra; Szechenyi) 1981–2.
Pillanatkepek a Kalevalabol (unaccompanied mixed choir; Finnish *Kalevala*/Racz) 1986.
Ilmarinen (unaccompanied mixed choir; Finnish *Kalevala*/Racz) 1986.

Opera:

Moses (Madach) 1972–7. Recorded (extracts) SLPX 11982.

* * *

Together with Kurtag, Zsolt Durko is the most internationally esteemed of contemporary Hungarian composers, apart from Ligeti. All three of these musicians spent part of their student years outside Hungary and have used the experience to avoid becoming overwhelmed by the tradition of Bartók and Kodaly. However, each of them underwent very diverse experiences as students and these have contributed to the development of their strongly contrasted musical personalities (though, fascinatingly, the composers' shared roots remain apparent to some extent).

Durko's time in Rome with Petrassi gave him a sound technical grounding and also a strong interest in early music. This has often been compared with the formative influences upon other Petrassi students, such as Peter Maxwell Davies, though Durko's absorption of pre-classical influences has been less all-embracing: he does not utilise, for example, the scaffolding devices of late medieval and renaissance polyphony—isorhythm and cantus firmus—with the obsessive involvement of Davies. Instead, Durko has chosen to borrow the surface trappings of such music (in particular, plainsong themes) as a thematic source. This was originally a Late Romantic approach, seen for example at times in the music of Liszt and Pfitzner, but it has also become a trait of numerous contemporary Italian composers, such as Petrassi himself.

In Durko's early compositions, the favoured medium is instrumental writing. Voices, where present at all, have no text, and could be said to be employed as an unorthodox instrumental colour (as Debussy had used a female chorus in *Sirènes*); this technique is prominent in several pieces dating from the mid-1960s, of which *Fioriture* is probably the best known.

Formally, the early works depend heavily upon strings of short motifs; these are constantly varied, and the shifts are more immediately recognisable than the tiny, subtle variants to obsessively repeated musical cells which crop up in some Ligeti pieces (and in the work of the American Minimalists). Cluster harmonies abound. Durko's first orchestral piece, *Episode sul tema B-A-C-H*, is a good illustration of his instinctive mastery of building coherent structures from small units; admiration for Durko's achievement here is scarcely lessened by the fact that the B-A-C-H motif lends itself particularly well to closely argued variation and chromatic elaboration.

Durko has found a way to combine his liking for medieval music with his characteristically motivic approach to composition: when the succession of motifs has been "pre-arranged", he calls the structure "organismo", though the result is not *organum* in the sense understood by 13th-century musicians. Passages which lack this imposed structure are called "psicogramme". These two styles are adopted in the nine sections of his single-movement Violin Concerto, which was entitled "Organismi".

The highpoint of Durko's re-enactment of ideas from medieval music is the *Hungarian Rhapsody*, in which the two solo clarinets are tellingly deployed as a foil to the main orchestra. The thematic material is a pastiche—as Durko concedes in his preface—ordered in the manner of a medieval codex, but the harmonic treatment is intensely chromatic and there is little evidence, on the whole, of the parallel perfect-interval progressions generally associated with *organum*, until the final section. The extravagent instrumental melismata of this piece recur a year later in *Fioriture*; the virtuosic extravagance of some of these passages seems, however, closer to Ligeti than to the music's obvious model, Liszt, since cellular elaboration still predominates and much of the harmonic underlay is rather static.

Durko's more recent compositions have moved away to some extent from cluster-chords to more differentiated harmonies; often, he will base a section upon a synthetic chord which contains a distinctive intervallic configuration. Rhythmic clarity is more apparent in some pieces (for example, *Altamira*), but in others metrical order is deliberately obscured as the composer experiments with short aleatoric passages. Generally, these *are* brief and have the character of textural events, in the tradition of Ligeti or Lutoslawski, rather than resembling the more systematic randomisings of Cage and his adherents. From a most unusually disparate set of models, Durko has succeeded in establishing a novel and convincing voice and has never allowed his art to suffer, as some contemporary Hungarian musicians have, through overdependence upon the powerful legacy of Bartók.

—Paul Horner

DUSAPIN, Pascal. French. Born in Nancy, 29 May 1955. Educated at University of Paris VIII (plastic arts), and in faculty of science of arts (aesthetics and science under Iannis Xenakis), 1974–8; further study in Italy and United States.

Married to Beatrice Sinet; 3 children. Freelance composer. Recipient: Prix de la Fondation de la Vocation, 1977; Prix SACEM Hervé Dujardin, 1980; Prix de Rome, Villa Medicis, 1981–3; bursary, Académie des Beaux Arts, 1984. Mailing address: 16 impasse Gaudelet, 75011 Paris, France.

Publisher: Salabert.

Symphonies/orchestral:

La Rivière 1979; first performed Metz, November 1979.
L'Aven (C flute, orchestra) 1980–1; first performed Metz, November 1983.
Tre scalini 1981–2; first performed Paris, 27 April 1983.
Assai 1985; first performed Venice, 22 September 1985.
Haro 1986–7; first performed Lyon, 20 September 1986.

Chamber/instrumental:

Inside (viola) 1980.
Musique captive (piccolo, oboe, soprano saxophone, bass clarinet, contrabass clarinet, contrabassoon, 2 trumpets, bass trombone) 1980; first performed La Rochelle, July 1981.
Musique fugitive (string trio) 1980; first performed Aix-en-Provence, June 1980. Recorded Harmonia Mundi HMC 5139.
Fist (cor anglais, clarinet/bass clarinet, bassoon, horn, trombone, viola, cello, double bass) 1982.
Incisa (cello) 1982; first performed Siena, August 1984.
String Quartet 1982–3; first performed La Rochelle, June 1983. Recorded HMC 5139.
Hop' (4 trios: viola, flute, bassoon; violin, bass clarinet, horn; oboe, trumpet, cello; horn, clarinet, double bass) 1983–4; first performed Paris, 18 February 1985.
La Conversation (suite in 10 pieces; 2 clarinets/bass clarinet, bassoon, horn, trombone, violin, viola, cello) 1984; first performed Orléans, March 1986.
If (clarinet) 1984; first performed La Rochelle, July 1984. Recorded Harmonic Records H/CD 8721.
Itou (bass clarinet) 1985; first performed Strasbourg, 26 September 1985. Recorded Harmonic Records H/CD 8721.
Ici (flute) 1986; first performed Orléans, 24 January 1986.
Poco a poco ("pedagogical music"; 2 flutes, 2 clarinets, 2 cellos) 1986; first performed Romainville, 1987.
Indeed (trombone) 1987. Recorded Harmonic Records H/CD 8721.
Iti (violin) 1987. Recorded Harmonic Records H/CD 8721.
Laps (clarinet, double bass) 1987. Recorded Harmonic Records H/CD 8721.
Sly (8 pieces for 4 trombones) 1987.
In & Out (double bass) 1989; first performed Paris, 10 May 1989.
Times Zones (string quartet) 1989; first performed Paris, 18 October 1989.
I Pesci (flute) 1989; first performed Bastia, September 1990.

Vocal/choral:

Igitur (female voices, instruments; Lucretius) 1977.
Lumen (female voices, instruments; Lucretius) 1977.
L'Homme aux liens (2 sopranos, 3 violins; Lucretius) 1978; first performed Paris, March 1980.
Shin'gyo (soprano, piccolo; Japanese sutra) 1981; first performed Paris, March 1982.
Niobe (ou le Rocher de Sypile) (soprano, 12 mixed voices, oboe/cor anglais, 2 clarinets/bass clarinets, 2 violins, viola, 2 cellos; Ovid, Juvenbal, Seneca, Propertius) 1982; first performed Paris, 16 June 1984.
Semino (6 voices; Parmenides) 1985.
To God (soprano, clarinet; Blake) 1985; first performed Strasbourg, 30 September, 1987.
Aks (mezzo-soprano, flute/piccolo, clarinet/bass clarinet, 2 trumpets, 2 trombones, cello) 1987; first performed Paris, 13 November 1987.
Mimi (2 women's voices, oboe, bass clarinet, trombone; Cadiot) 1987; broadcast Radio France, 21 January 1987. Recorded Harmonic Records H/CD 8721.
Li-li-ko (soprano; Cadiot) 1987–8; first performed Royaumont, 29 May 1987. Recorded Harmonic Records H/CD 8721.
Anacoluthes (female voice, contrabass clarinet, double bass; Cadiot) 1988.
For O. (2 female voices, 2 bass clarinets; Daniel) 1988; first performed Strasbourg, 17 September 1989.
So Full of Shape Is Fancy (soprano, bass clarinet) 1990.

Opera:

Romeo et Juliette (Cadiot) 1988; first performed Montpellier, 10 June 1989.

PUBLICATIONS

By Dusapin: (with Olivier Cadiot) libretto to *Romeo et Juliette*, Paris, 1989.

On Dusapin: "Poétique de la rupture/Equilibre de l'instable", (interview) with Medhi Idir, Toulouse, 1989; *Les Cahiers du Cirem* (special PD number), June/September 1989.

* * *

One of the most orginal young composers in France, Pascal Dusapin came to music relatively late. It was a chance visit to Xenakis's *Polytope de Cluny* in 1972 that provoked in Dusapin the desire to compose. He subsequently attended Xenakis's classes in aesthetics and science at the Sorbonne, which had a considerable effect on him. His first works show a Xenakis-like preference for dense textures teeming with inner life.

Dusapin's personal voice emerged with the trilogy of works setting texts from Lucretius. These are written in a taut, strained style of fiercely wrought counterpoint, replete with microtones and glissandi. The all-pervading tension of the music is constantly embattled with the extreme energy of the material, and results in an explosive rawness which, while owing something to Xenakis and Varèse, is nevertheless highly individual. The two extremes of Dusapin's idiom at this time—enclosing tensions and explosive flight—are given their clearest expression in a pair of works from 1980, *Musique captive* for nine winds, and *Musique fugitive* for string trio. In the former, the energy is wholly imprisoned and contained; the piece is thus very brief and compact, writhing between a few agonised gestures; whereas in the longer *Musique fugitive*, the lines are perpetually clambering over themselves in increasingly desperate attempts to break out of the music's constraints.

The more exuberant, violent side of Dusapin's style is unleashed in three orchestral works from this time, *La Rivière*, the flute concerto *L'Aven*, and *Tre scalini*. In all three, Dusapin eschews all superfluity of ornament or special effect (percussion is absent from *La Rivière* and *Tre scalini*, being limited to a pair of timpanists in *L'Aven*), preferring to achieve his expressive ends primarily through pitch-duration considerations. In this respect, as well as in his liking for the dark timbres of timpani with low wind and strings, Dusapin's music has a number of points in common with Sibelius, whose continuously evolving form he has also emulated. This phase of Dusapin's output is brought to an effective climax with his first work of larger duration, the cantata *Niobe (ou le Rocher de Sypile)* for soprano, mixed chorus and ensemble, setting a variety of Latin texts on the myth of the title. Here, Dusapin's considerable lyrical and dramatic gifts are exploited to the full, in a superbly paced succession of tableaux depicting the heroine's gradual transformation into stone; the vocal writing is impressively varied, ranging from radiant microtonal chords for the chorus to the soprano's dejectedly winding monody at the end of the work.

In Dusapin's next major work, *Hop'*, for four groups of 3 instruments, a more gentle, relaxed manner becomes apparent. The texture is less contrapuntally dense and rhythmically simpler; there is a certain degree of repetition, such as had been entirely absent from his previous music and, in conjunction with this, clearly audible cellular working is introduced—a basic iambic figure is constantly varied and developed by all the instruments through the piece. The form, too, is exceptionally eloquent in its drive towards the homophonic conclusion.

The tendency towards greater harmonic and melodic simplicity is continued in Dusapin's most recent works, such as *Aks* and the lengthy orchestral *Haro*; both the new-found lyricism and the ease with larger forms proved significant pointers to the composition of Dusapin's first opera *Romeo et Juliette*, written to a libretto by Olivier Cadiot and first performed as part of the French Revolution Bicentennial celebrations at the 1989 Montpellier Festival. Here, Dusapin's lyricism is allowed freer reign than in any other work; the anguished violence which characterised his first mature works has almost entirely disappeared, although not everyone at the first performances was entirely convinced by the work's dramatic pacing. In addition to these larger works, Dusapin has recently composed a substantial quantity of solo pieces, duos and trios, most of them the result of an extensive collaboration with the versatile French group Accroche-Note.

—Julian Anderson

DUTILLEUX, Henri. French. Born in Angers, Maine et Loire, 22 January 1916. Educated at Conservatoire National Supérieur de Musique, Paris (harmony, counterpoint, fugue, analysis, composition, history of music under Jean and Noel Gallon, Henri Busser, Maurice Emmanuel), 1933–8. Served in Bataillon de l'Air, 1939–40. Married Geneviève Joy, 17 September 1946. Chorus master, Paris Opera, 1942; chief conductor, musical wing, O.R.T.F, 1945–63; professor of composition, Ecole Normale de Musique, Paris, 1961–70; vice-president, Syndicate Nationale des Auteurs Compositeurs, since 1962; associate professor of composition, Conservatoire National Supérieur de Musique, Paris, 1970–1. Recipient: Grand Prix de Rome, 1938; Grand Prix National de la Musique, 1967; Koussevitzky International Recording Award, 1976; World Record Award, Montreux, 1983; Prix International Maurice Ravel, 1987; Prix UNESCO-International Music Council, 1987. Associate member, Royal Belgium Academy, 1973; honorary member, American Academy of Arts and Letters, 1981. Mailing address: 12 rue St Louis en l'Ile, 75004 Paris, France.

Publishers: Leduc/Heugel, 175 rue St Honore, 75001 Paris, France; Schott, Mainz.

Symphonies/orchestral:

Les Hauts de Hurle-Vent (symphonic suite) 1941.
Sarabande 1941.
Symphony No 1 1951; first performed Paris, 7 June 1951. Recorded Erato 2292–45287–2; harmonia mundi HMC 905159.
Sérénade (for *La Couronne de Margaret Long*) 1956.
Symphony No 2 "Le Double" 1959; first performed Boston, 11 December 1959. Recorded Erato 2292-45287-2.
Métaboles 1965; first performed Cleveland, Ohio, 14 January 1965. Recorded Erato STU 70840; STU 71516.
Tout un monde lointain . . . (concerto for cello, orchestra) 1970; first performed Aix-en-Provence, 25 July 1970. Recorded EMI CDC 7 493042.
Timbres, espace, mouvement, ou La Nuit étoilée 1978; first performed Washington, D.C., 10 January 1978. Recorded harmonia mundi HMC 905159.
Concerto for Violin and Orchestra: L'Arbre des songes 1985; first performed Paris, 5 November 1985. Recorded CBS MK 42 449.
Mystère de l'instant (24 strings, cimbalom, percussion) 1989.

Chamber/instrumental:

Sonatina (flute, piano) 1942; first performed Paris, 1943. Recorded Music Minus One 8107; Crystal Records S 312.
Sarabande et cortège (bassoon, piano) 1942.
Au gré des ondes (piano) 1946.
Sonata (piano) 1947; first performed Paris, 1948. Recorded BAM LD 5020; Orion ORS 7299; Solstice SOCD 18.
Sonata (oboe, piano) 1947.
Sonata (piano) 1948.
Chorale, cadence et fugato (trombone, piano) 1950.
Tous les chemins (piano) 1961.
Bergerie (piano) 1963.
Résonances (piano) 1965.
Figures de résonances (2 piano) 1970. Recorded Erato, 1991.
Deux préludes (piano) 1974.
Ainsi la nuit (string quartet) 1975–6; first performed Paris, 1977. Recorded Masters MCD 17; Erato STU 71546; QL 01.
Trois Strophes sur le nom de SACHER (cello) 1976; first performed 1982.
Préludes (piano) 1977–88.
Sur un même Accord (piano) 1985.
Le Jeu des contraires (piano) 1988.

Vocal/choral:

Fantasio (baritone, piano or orchestra) 1941–2; first performed Paris, 1942.
Pour une amie perdue (baritone, piano or orchestra) 1942; first performed Paris, 1942.
Regards sur l'infini (baritone, piano or orchestra) 1942; first performed Paris, 1942.

La Géole (baritone, piano or orchestra) 1944; first performed Paris, 1944.
Chanson de la déportée (soprano, piano) 1945; first performed Paris, 1945.
Trois Sonnets de Jean Cassou (baritone, orchestra) 1953; first performed Paris, 1954.
Chansons de bord (children's chorus) 1959; first performed Paris, 1959.
San Francisco Night (soprano, piano) 1964; first performed New York City, 1964.

Other:

L'anneau du roi (lyric scene) 1938.
Salamacis (ballet) 1941.
Symphonie de danses (ballet) 1941.
La Princesse d'Elide (incidental music to Molière) 1946.
Monsieur de Pourceaugnac (incidental music to Molière) 1948.
Le Loup (ballet) 1953; first performed Paris, 18 March 1953.
Albert Roussel: *Des fleurs font une broderie* (arranged for orchestra; originally for voice, piano) 1941; first performed Paris, 1941.
Johan Alain: *Prière pour nous autres charnels* (orchestra; originally for 2 male voices, organ) 1944; first performed Paris, 1944.

PUBLICATIONS

By Dutilleux: "Opinion d'un musicien sur le théâtre musical radiophonique", in *Polyphonie*, 1948; "Diversities in Contemporary French Music", in *The Modern Composer and His World*, Toronto, 1962; "Qui reste fidèle à la musique symphonique?", in *Nouvel Observateur*, 24 June 1965; "Sur Hector Berlioz" in *Le Journal Musical Français*, January 1969; "Liberté et l'artiste", in *Harmonie* 44, 1971; "Sur Nadia Boulanger", in *La Quinzaine Littéraire*, November 1979; "Les tambours de l'étoile (Vincent van Gogh)", in *Le Nouvel Observateur*, 15 February 1985; L'ombre d'un géant (Maurice Ravel)", in *Le Monde de la Musique*, 103, 1987; "Musique et création", in *Revue Contrechamps*, Paris, 1989.

On Dutilleux: R. Jacobs, *HD*, Paris, 1974; Antoine Golea, *La Musique, de la nuit, des temps aux aurores nouvelles*, Paris, 1977; Royal S. Brown, (interview) in *High Fidelity—Musical America*, September 1978; Eric Mason, "HD—A Constant Evolution", in London Philharmonic Orchestra Year Book, March 1981; Dom Angelice Surchamp, *HD*, 1983; Daniel Humbert, *HD: l'oeuvre et le style musical*, Paris, 1985; J.F. Antonioli, (interview) in *Revue Romande*, 1985; Stephane Goldet, *Quatuors du 20ème siècle*, Paris, 1986; Gladis Bourdain, "HD—Elder Statesman of Music in France", in *New York Times*, 23 March 1986; Jukka Isopuro, "Ymmarrettavia saveltajia", in *Helsingin Sanomat*, June 1988; Pierrette Mari, *HD*, Paris, 1988; Jouni Kapianinen, "Sur HD", in *Helsingin Sanomat*, May 1989; Claus Kuhnl, "Poet der Nacht—HD", in *Neue Zeitschrift für Musik*, 1989; Tatiano Zolozova, in *Musique instrumentale française après la guerre*, Kiev, 1989; Gerd Sannemuller, "Permanente Variation", in *Neue Zurcher Zeitung* 6/7 October 1990; Claude Glayman, *Entretiens* (interviews), Paris, 1991.

Henri Dutilleux comments:

It seems to me very hubristic for an artist to want to define his aesthetic. Building up a body of work is a long process, consisting largely of trial and error and many years must pass before one achieves the distance, the detachment, the perspective which allows one to distinguish the broader lines of development.

With hindsight, it seems clear to me that there are a number of constants which began to appear in my music with the First Symphony (and even more so in the Piano Sonata, which pre-dates it by three or four years). In particular, it's with the First Symphony that one begins to see the importance of "memory" with all that entails in terms of variation, prefiguration, premonition.

There we're touching on the question of *musical time*, a particular perception of time, almost in the Proustian sense (and Proust has influenced me greatly). One can see that that preoccupation hardly abates in later work: the Second Symphony—subtitled "Le Double"—*Métaboles, Tout un monde lointain . . .* , *Ainsi la nuit*, and *Timbres, espace, mouvement*. Each of these refers to a notion of time as cyclical.

I can't help but see there a direct relationship with the way in which I perceive nature, as expressed in the final lines of my introduction to *Métaboles*: "In the conception of this work, the composer never ceased to dream of the mysterious and compelling realm of eternal metamorphosis. The spirit and the form of this music find their origins in an intense contemplation of nature."

In the same way, I made the following remarks with regard to "Temps suspendu", the last of the seven sections of the string quartet *Ainsi la nuit*: "A kind of clockwork establishes itself on a harmonic base of distant bells. Time seems *frozen*".

All of this suggests to me that the process of making music (which is a necessity, if a utopian one) partakes of something over and above the everyday world of work and its demands, partakes of ceremony, something almost sacred, consisting in large part of mystery and magic.

That is why, throughout my career, I have given particular attention to the ideas expressed by contemporaries in Jeune France, ideas which were already formulated on the eve of the last war, and which without doubt benefit from being placed counter to the prevailing tendencies of French music in that period. Others among them had advocated a return to a conception of music as entertainment and I very soon felt myself ill at ease with a musical philosophy which, though it had some very talented exponents, was far removed from my own aspirations. If, later, I distanced myself from some of the compositions of my youth, that is the reason.

This preoccupation with musical time is detectable in the form of my scores. I believe that two powerful influences have affected me in the sense of broadening out my forms: that of Beethoven first and foremost (but somewhat freely construed) and that of the Viennese School, which has certainly marked my style. Under neither influence, though, did I forget the basic traditions of French music. From the Orient, I received a very particular perception of time; and it was from that direction, much more than in timbre or instrumental novelty that I felt the impact of Oriental art.

* * *

Henri Dutilleux's musical apprenticeship at the Paris Conservatoire followed a typically rigorous path. He was an able student, winning the Prix de Rome, but, unlike certain predecessors who rebelled against the (to some) stultifying academicism of conservatoire music, Dutilleux absorbed models almost too easily. Perhaps in consequence, his own originality was stifled for a time and he was to withdraw a number of "derivative" early compositions. Furthermore, he has voiced personal dissatisfaction with some of his published works from this period.

In his approach to composition, Dutilleux offers a fastidious musical craftsmanship and seems conspicuously detached from any prevailing trends, though he has always kept abreast of developments in musical thought. Because of his determined individuality and attention to detail, Dutilleux's published output is tiny—exceptionally small for an internationally-regarded contemporary musician—and his reputation is based upon the handful of major works which have appeared since World War II. He writes very slowly and seems, as his friend Jean Roy observed, "resigned to the masterpiece".

The Piano Sonata, first performed by his wife, was Dutilleux's first widely recognised work. It was closely followed (at least by Dutilleux's standards!) by the First Symphony, an impressive four-movement score, with an almost Brahmsian first movement passacaglia. The orchestration is basically classical, though there is triple wind and a much enlarged percussion section; harmonically, Dutilleux opts for a kind of modal tonality, which has led many commentators to assess him as a descendant of Fauré, Roussel, Debussy and Ravel, though his language is so flexible and individual as to resist being pigeonholed.

In his Second Symphony, Dutilleux expanded upon several techniques used in its predecessor, in which the orchestra had been separated at numerous points, with small, sometimes unorthodox groups (from which individual instruments could be deployed in a soloistic manner), pitted against the remainder of the ensemble. The "main" orchestral sounds in such passages could be very heavy-textured; but because virtuoso display in the smaller groups was avoided for the most part, the result was no amalgam of the 19th-century heroic concerto and the Bartókian "concerto for orchestra". The Second Symphony confronts a chamber orchestra of 12 players, arranged in a circle around the conductor, with a much larger "standard" orchestra. The two groups are in conflict at some points, but are also combined, superimposed upon each other, or used to mirror material first heard in the other group, so that novel rhythmic and harmonic effects abound and there is a sense of great space and instrumental colour.

Dutilleux's works have, in the main, stemmed from commissions from international organisations or artists. One of the most successful of these commissions, the Cello Concerto written for Rostropovich, demonstrates the composer's wide artistic culture and the remarkably unselfconscious way in which he is able to use it to enrich his work. The concerto, subtitled *Tout un monde lointain . . .*, is a product of an intensive restudy of Baudelaire. Each of the five movements is furnished with a Baudelaire quotation though, while the character of the extract (and, arguably, of the entire poem from which it is drawn) is reflected by that of the music, overt programmatic associations are avoided. The harmony is still founded upon a highly flexible modal tonality and instrumental subdivisions, so effective in the symphonies, reappear. The evolution of this technique is most evident in the opening movement, "Enigme", where full orchestra is used in a highly sectionalised manner which Dutilleux himself has called "pointilliste". Elsewhere, the instrumentation is very subtly graded according to the mood of the solo cello part; Dutilleux is most closely attuned to the audibility requirements of his soloist, reducing the scoring deftly on occasions.

Timbres, espace, mouvement, known alternatively as *La Nuit étoilée*, was intended as a backdrop to Van Gogh's painting *The Starry Night*. Once again, Dutilleux prescribes a theatrical layout for his orchestra: the cellos are arranged in a semicircle around the conductor. In the opening movement, *Timbres*, violins and violas are omitted, so that the instrumental palette is appreciably darkened (Stravinsky had used the same device in *Symphony of Psalms*).

In his more recent scores, Dutilleux's preoccupation with orchestral sonority has seemed undiminished and he continues to animate large-scale forms with the dynamism engendered by interlocking sections of pointillistic or monodic scoring. A good example is the Violin Concerto where, having once more rejected using the form as a vehicle for technical display, Dutilleux instead concentrates upon combining soloist and orchestra with originality and exquisite judgment.

—Paul Horner

EARL, David. British. Born in Stellenbosch, South Africa, 5 October 1951. Educated at Rondebosch Boys' High School, Cape Town, 1959–69; Trinity College of Music, London (under Jacob Kaletsky, Ilona Kabos and Peter Feuchtwanger), 1971–5, F.T.C.L. Concert pianist. Recipient: prizewinner, International Piano Competition, Barcelona, 1975; 1st prize, SABC Piano Competition, 1976. Mailing address: c/o Roger Hancock, Greener House, 66–68 Haymarket, London SW1Y 4AW, England.

Publisher: none.

Symphonies/orchestral:

Piano Concerto 1980; first performed Cape Town, 1980.
Piano Concerto No 2 (2 pianos) 1984; first performed Cape Town, 1985.
Choral Symphony: Trumpets from the Steep (soprano, SATB chorus, orchestra) 1987–90.
Violin Concerto 1990; first performed Leicester, 1990.

Chamber/instrumental:

Piano Suite No 1: Mosaics 1977; first performed London, 1977.
Piano Suite No 2: Gargoyles 1990; first performed Memphis, Tennessee, 1990.

Other:

Cheri (ballet) 1980; first performed Edinburgh, 1980.
P'Tang Yang Kipperbang (film music; orchestra) 1982; broadcast Channel 4 Television (U.K.), 1982.
The Return of the Soldier (ballet) 1982; first performed Cape Town, 1982.
Arthur's Hallowed Ground (film music; orchestra) 1983; broadcast Channel 4 Television (U.K.), 1983.
Keep off the Grass (film music; orchestra) 1983.
The Price (music for television series) 1985.
Abelard and Heloise (ballet) 1985; first performed Cape Town, 1985.

* * *

David Earl is a highly accomplished pianist, frequently performing works by Chopin, Rachmaninoff, Prokofiev and Ravel. Earl is the first to admit that the roots of his own compositional language are embedded in this repertoire. He is unashamedly conservative in terms of tonal language, rhythm and structure.

Earl writes tonal music mostly without key signature. Employing a highly chromatic vocabulary, he still structures from a tonal centre. Phrases, sections and movements end unambiguously, further defined by Earl's use of strong contrasts to aid the structure. His music is without the rhythmic complexities apparent in more avant-garde scores.

One could call Earl a Romantic in Neo-Classical clothing. His work is most akin to that of Prokofiev and Ravel. Like the former he utilises the classical forms of Suite, Concerto and Symphony. Like the latter, he derives much of his inspiration from theatre and the ballet. Indeed Earl is at his most expressive with music that has a programme, especially ballet and film music where narrative inspires musical development.

Earl's ballet music is eminently danceable. The scores have a strong rhythmic momentum, attractive melodies and vivid contrasts of mood. He has a fine ear for instrumental colour and characterisation. In *Cheri*, the composer deliberately drew on the music of Satie and Ravel in order to evoke the period of Colette's novel. *Cheri* is written in one 65-minute act for orchestra with piano solo. *Abelard and Heloise*, a shorter one-act ballet, begins evocatively with unaccompanied plainsong which Earl uses throughout to dramatic effect. After this atmospheric beginning, the orchestra makes a sweeping entrance, a striking change of mood and pace.

The two piano suites, *Mosaics* and *Gargoyles*, show how much Earl has developed as a composer. The latter work is more varied and intricate in terms of figuration, texture, rhythmic and harmonic invention. Here the composer is very much in command of his style. Neo-classical pastiche mixes with the ebullient rhythmic passagework and the contrasting languor of the expressive melodies.

Earl conceived *Gargoyles* as a ghoulish, malevolent piece depicting gargoyles dancing at midnight on the rooftop of some imaginary gothic chateau. This romantic notion imparts an ironical quality to the piece, which utilises the forms of the baroque dance suite: Prelude, Sarabande, Gavotte and Musette, Pavane, Gigue. In the Prelude, unresolving parallel chords succeed each other in a Debussy-like manner. They are interspersed with muscular passages, technically demanding but written well for the fingers. Again Earl shows himself adept at structuring from sharp contrasts.

The *Piano Concerto* and the *Violin Concerto* are classical in form. The *Piano Concerto* is reminiscent of Prokofiev, particularly the impressive last movement which has an exhilarating momentum generated by repeating triplet figures, and a reprise of the expressive first movement theme at the very end of the work.

The *Violin Concerto* has an air of melancholy nostalgia. Here as in the *Concerto No 2* for two pianos and orchestra, Earl derives the thematic material for the entire work from the initial theme. The melodies are lyrical and span the wide range of the violin.

Earl is unique among South African-born composers as a performer whose pianistic accomplishments match his achievement as a composer. He often performs his own piano music. He has written the music for several acclaimed films and the prestigious television series *The Price*. He has achieved an international reputation as a composer of expressive and danceable ballet music.

—Renée Reznek

EBEN, Petr. Czechoslovak. Born in Zamberk, Czechoslovakia, 22 January 1929. Educated at Gymnasium, Cesky Krumlov, 1939–43; Academy of Music, Prague (piano under Frantisek Rauch, composition under Pavel Borkovec), 1948–53. Married Sarka Hurnikova-(Ebenova), 27 June 1953; 3 sons. Teacher, department of history of music, philosophical faculty, Charles University, Prague, 1955–90; professor of composition, Royal Northern College of Music, Manchester, England, 1978–9; and Academy of Music, Prague, since 1990; also concert and recital pianist. Recipient: medal (for *Six Love Songs*), World Festival of Youth, Moscow, 1957; two appreciations (for *Laudes*), Kassel International Competition, 1965; gold medal (for *Pragensia*), international competition of television films, New York, 1981; Czechoslovak National Prize (for *Job*), 1989. Mailing address: Hamsikova 19, 150 00 Prague 5—Motol, Czechoslovakia.

Publishers: Supraphon, Prague; Panton, Prague; Barenreiter, Kassel; United Music Publishers, London; Universal Edition, Vienna; B. Schott's Sohne, Mainz.

Symphonies/orchestral:

First Concerto for Organ and Orchestra: Symphonia gregoriana 1954; first performed Prague, 1954.
Concerto for Piano and Orchestra 1961; first performed Prague, 1962. Recorded Supraphon DV 5988.
Vox clamantis (symphonic movement for 3 trumpets and orchestra) 1969; first performed Prague, 1970. Recorded Panton 01 0277/110300.
Night Hours (concertante symphony for wind quintet, tenor tuba, string orchestra, children's choir ad lib, piano, percussion) 1975; first performed Leipzig, 1976. Recorded Panton 8110 0037.
Second Concerto for Organ and Orchestra 1982; first performed Vienna, 1983. Recorded Panton 8110 0391.
Prague Nocturne: Hommage à W.A. Mozart 1983; first performed Salzburg, 1984. Recorded Panton 81 0827.

Chamber/instrumental:

Sonata (oboe, piano) 1950; first performed Prague, 1952. Recorded Peking M 360.
Sonata in D♭ (piano) 1951; first performed Prague, 1952.
Suita balladica (cello, piano) 1955; first performed Prague, 1956. Recorded Supraphon DV 5522.
Sonatina semplice (violin or flute, piano) 1955; first performed Prague, 1957. Recorded Panton 010719.
The Little Ones' World (20 instructive pieces for piano) 1955.
Duetti per due trombe (2 trumpets) 1956; first performed Prague, 1956. Recorded Panton 110410.
Sunday Music (organ) 1957–9; first performed Prague, 1959. Recorded Supraphon DN 5175; Mixtur MXT 2 005 B; CTS 801207; Supraphon 110564-1131; Crystal Records S 182; Pallas 120; CTS 810621; Audite 51004; Lyrinx 8204-031; Melodija 33D-030347-48; Christophorus Verlag LC 0612; Vista VPS 1062; Teldec 6622038-01.
Folk Songs and Carols (instructive pieces for piano) 1960.
Duettinos (soprano instrument, piano) 1963.
Green Green Grove (8 arrangements of folk songs for piano—4 hands) 1963–79.
Ordo modalis (oboe, harp) 1964; first performed Prague, 1964. Recorded Supraphon 0 11 0429.
Laudes (organ) 1964; first performed Prague, 1964. Recorded Supraphon 0 11 0470; Melodija 04409-10; Lyrinx 8204-031; EMI F 670384; Teldec 6623410-01; Delta DRS 86-637; Supraphon 110564-1131.
Quintetto per stromenti a fiato (wind quintet) 1965; first performed Prague, 1966. Recorded Supraphon 1 41 0119/SUA ST 50892.
Fantasia vespertina (trumpet, piano) 1967.
Small Portraits (piano) 1968.
Brass Quintet; Variations on Chorale 1968–9; first performed Prague, 1970. Recorded Supraphon 1 19 0946.
Differences and Contrasts (11 motion etudes for piano) 1969.
Music for Oboe, Bassoon and Piano 1970; first performed Stockholm, 1971. Recorded Supraphon 1 19 1054.
Ten Chorale Overtures (organ) 1971.
Two Chorale Fantasias (organ) 1972; first performed Helsinki, 1973. Recorded Panton 8111 0044; EMI F 670395; Delta DRS 86-637.
Little Manual of Renaissance Instruments (concert variations for 4 players, 14 instruments) 1974.
Windows (trumpet, organ; on the pictures of Marc Chagall) 1976; first performed Prague, 1977. Recorded Panton 11 0672; Supraphon 1111 3019; ABAKUS LC 6461; Lyrinx 8204-032; EMI F 670384; Mitra CD 16205; Suisa MKH 40289; VDE-Gallo CD-604.
Small Chorale Partita (organ) 1978; first performed Poissy Yvelines, France, 1979. Recorded Delta DRS 86-637; EMI F 670 395.
Sonata: "Wood and Wind" (flute, marimba) 1978; first performed Prague, 1980. Recorded Supraphon 1119 2766.
Tabulatura nova (guitar) 1979; first performed Prague, 1981. Recorded Supraphon 1119 2938.
Faust (9-part cycle for organ) 1979–80; first performed Brno, 1980. Recorded Mitra 16 167; Lyrinx 8204-33; Panton 8111 0295.
Mutationes: per organo grande e piccolo 1980; first performed Cardiff, 1980. Recorded Lyrinx 8204-032; Supraphon 1111 3375.
String Quartet 1981; first performed Prague, 1981. Recorded Supraphon 1111 3377.
Fantasia (viola, organ) 1982.
Versetti (organ) 1982.
Landscapes of Patmos (organ, percussion) 1984; first performed Heidelberg, 1985. Recorded Panton 81 0827; EMI F 670 395.
Opponents (clarinet, piano, percussion) 1985; first performed Volnograd, Bulgaria, 1986.
A Festive Voluntary: On Good King Wenceslas Carol (organ) 1986; first performed Chichester, Sussex, 1986.
Piano Trio 1986; first performed Prague, 1986. Recorded Panton 810850-1111.
Risonanza (harp) 1986.
Tres iubilationes (4 brasses, organ) 1987; first performed Cambridge, England, 1987.
Hommage à Dietrich Buxtehude (organ) 1987; first performed Bad Oldesloe, 1987. Recorded Supraphon 110564-1131.
Hiob/Job (8-part cycle for organ) 1987; first performed London, 1988. Recorded Panton 81 0924-1111.
Sonata (harpsichord) 1988; first performed Munich, 1990.
Nonet 1988.
Two Movements (trombone, organ) 1988.
Letters to Milena (piano) 1990; first performed Brighton, Sussex, 1990.

Vocal/choral:

Six Love Songs (medium voice, piano) 1951; first performed Prague, 1957. Recorded Supraphon DM 6157/SV 8275; Supraphon 04 109.
Songs to Lute (voice, lute or guitar) 1951; first performed Prague, 1960. Recorded Supraphon 1 12 1484.

The Most Secret Songs (low voice, piano) 1952; first performed Cesky Krumlov, 1952.
Missa adventus et quadragesimae (male choir, organ) 1952; first performed Prague, 1955. Recorded Priory PR 125.
Songs from Cieszyn Region (low voice, piano) 1952.
The Twig Is Showing Green (children's choir, piano or instrumental ensemble) 1953–9; first performed Prague, 1956. Recorded Supraphon DM 5638; Panton 01 0110.
Three Low-Voiced Songs (flute, soprano, piano; Halas) 1956.
The Lover's Magic Spell (female voice, mixed choir) 1957; first performed Prague, 1959. Recorded Supraphon 0 89 9988/DV 5755/SUA 18506; Panton 8112 0426; Azymuth AZ 1027.
Epitaph (male choir; Ovid) 1957.
Love and Death (mixed choir) 1957–8; first performed Jihlava, 1959. Recorded Supraphon DV 5755/SUA 18506; Panton 810755-1211; Azymuth AZ 1027.
Bitter Earth (baritone, mixed choir, organ) 1959; first performed Prague, 1960.
On Swallows and Girls (female choir) 1959–60; first performed Plzen, 1962. Recorded Panton 11 0358.
Liturgical Songs (solo or unison, organ; 10 proprios in form of antiphons and psalms) 1960.
Christmas Songs (4-part cycle of 2- and 3-voiced children's choruses, piano; Tumlir) 1960.
Spring Ditties (7 single-voiced children's choruses, piano) 1961.
Six Songs on Rainer Maria Rilke (low voice, piano) 1961; first performed Prague, 1962. Recorded Supraphon 1112 2455.
In the Grass (14 dance games for single-voiced children's choir, piano or wind quintet) 1961–3.
Staves of Love (male choir; Shtchipatchew) 1963.
Unkind Songs (alto, viola) 1963; first performed Prague, 1964. Recorded Supraphon DV 6194, SV 8308.
Ubi caritas et amor (mixed choir) 1964; first performed Berlin, 1965. Recorded Supraphon 1 12 0880; Panton 810794-1211; Azymuth AZ 1027.
The Merry Go Round and the Stars (10 single- to 3-voiced children's choruses, piano; Siktanc) 1964.
Poetic Duets (2-voiced children's choir, piano ad lib; Nezval) 1965.
Chad gadyoh (male choir) 1965; first performed Prague, 1966.
Poetic Duets (children's choir) 1965; first performed Jirkov, 1966.
Little Mournings (soprano, piano; Rencova) 1965.
Balance (unaccompanied male chorus; Queneau) 1966.
Apologia Socratus (alto, baritone, mixed and children's choirs, orchestra) 1967; first performed Jihlava, 1967. Recorded Supraphon 0 19 0558/1 12 0880.
Vesperae (boys' and male choir, congregation, organ) 1968; first performed Montserrat, Spain, 1968. Recorded Vergara 14013-SL.
Trouvere Mass (choir, guitar, recorders) 1968–9; first performed Prague, 1969. Recorded Azymuth AZ 1027.
Elce, pelce kotrmelce (50 motion songs for single-voiced children's choir, piano; Fischer) 1969–70.
Cantica Comeniana (mixed or female choir; Komensky) 1970; first performed Prague, 1970. Recorded Azymuth AZ 1027.
Song of Ruth (alto, organ or piano) 1970; first performed Prague, 1970.
The Little Nightingale of Paradise (3-voiced polyphonic girls' choruses; Bolzano) 1970.
Dialogues (tenor, piano; Florian) 1970.
The Veil and the Tears (4 female choruses, bass clarinet) 1971.
Pragensia (chamber mixed choir, Renaissance instruments; Rudolphine) 1972; first performed Prague, 1973. Recorded Supraphon 1 19 1397/1 12 1607.
Four Choruses (unaccompanied female choir—I–III; mixed choir—IV) 1973.
One Day's Experiences (10 songs for single-voiced children's choir with second voice ad lib, piano; Hurnik) 1973.
Salve Regina (mixed choir) 1973; first performed Neerpelt, 1974. Recorded Panton 810794-1211; Azymuth AZ 1027; Panton 810827.
Greek Dictionary (female choir, harp) 1974; first performed Prague, 1977. Recorded Supraphon 1 19 2408/1112 2455; Balkanton BXA 11728; Panton 8112 0416.
Curious Songs (4 songs for solo adult voice, children's choir, piano) 1974.
Katonis moralia / Proverbial Wisdom (children's choir) 1974–5; first performed Liberec, 1975. Recorded Supraphon 1 12 2315; Neerpelt 6851 173.
Unsinkable Ship (unaccompanied mixed chorus; Buric) 1977.
Unlucky War (folk song arrangements for unaccompanied male choir) 1978.
Honour to Charles IV (male choir, orchestra) 1978; first performed Prague, 1978.
Greeting to Marsyas (mixed choirs, small ensemble) 1980.
Message / Botschaft (concertante song with orchestra; Maurer) 1981.
Missa cum populo (mixed choir, congregation, 4 brasses, organ) 1981–2; first performed Avignon, 1983. Recorded Panton 81 0801-1212.
Desire of Ancient Things (mixed choir) 1984; first performed Westport, Connecticut, 1985. Recorded Panton 810794-1211; Azymuth AZ 1027.
Sempiternal Cosmetics (female choir; Ovid) 1985; first performed Prague, 1986.
Night (mixed chorus; Macha) 1986.
Cantico delle creature (Song to Brother Sun) (mixed choir) 1987; first performed Neerpelt, 1988. Recorded Azymuth AZ 1027; Panton 810827.
Episode with Mr Mozart (4-voiced children's chorus; Skacel) 1988.
Breath of Long Bygone Days (mixed choir; Symons) 1988.
Prague Te Deum (choir, brasses or organ) 1990; first performed Prague, 1990.

Other:

Faust (incidental music to play by Goethe) 1976; first performed Vienna, 1976.
Hamlet (incidental music to play by Shakespeare) 1977; first performed Dusseldorf, 1977.
Curses and Blessing (ballet for choir, orchestra) 1983; first performed The Hague, 1983. Recorded Panton 810740-1231.

PUBLICATIONS

By Eben: *Ctgeni a hra partitur / Score Reading and Score Playing*, Prague, 1960.

On Eben: C. Hermitte, "PE", dissertation, University of Paris IV, Sorbonne, 1970; S. Landale, "The Organ Music of PE", in *The American Organist*, 1979, reprinted in *L'Orgue; Revue trimestrelle*, 169, and in *Musik und Kirche*, 5, 1980; Ch. Verhelet, "PE—*Faust* für orgel", dissertation, Lemmens-Institut Leuven, Frankfurt, 1987–8; J. Fishell, "The Organ Music of PE", dissertation, Northwestern University, Evanston, Illinois, 1988; Ch. Gans, "PE—*Hiob.* für orgel", dissertation, Hochsschule für Musik und Darstellende Kunst, Frankfurt, 1989; K. Vondrovicova, *PE—seznam del, soupis provedeni, diskografie, prheled zahranicnich cest a dalsi dokumentace* (list of compositions, performances, discography, survey of journeys in other countries and further documentation), Prague, 1990.

Petr Eben comments:

I think that the best explanation of one's language is to reveal its sources. I grew up in Cesky Krumlov, a dreamy medieval town—hence my love for medieval poetry, fine arts and some archaic musical elements. Due to the lack of organists during the war, I was, at the age of 10, entrusted to play the big organ in the main church, hence my love for this instrument and the strong influence which the plainchant had on me and my music. As a reaction against the German occupation a strong interest arose in Czech folklore—another source of inspiration. Imprisonment by the Nazis and the imminent prospect of death turned me to humanistic and philosophical interests and to spiritual music. Living 40 years under the pressure of a communist government, I was aware of what our people expected of their artists: to tell, sometimes by a hint or a symbol, what never could be pronounced openly in public life, hence my conception of my output not as a progressive self-realisation but as a message, and composition as in the service of truth. My goal: to contribute an atom's worth to what Teilhard de Chardin calls the spiritualisation of the world.

* * *

Petr Eben's early exposure to church organ music has been of great importance to his development as a composer. His international reputation is largely based on his *Sunday Music* for organ, which has been performed and recorded in Czechoslovakia, Germany, the U.S.A. and the Soviet Union. Eben's reputation as a composer for organ was later acknowledged by the commission of his Second Concerto for the first public concert on the new instrument in the ORF-Sendesaal in Vienna in 1983. Among his other compositions for his own instrument, the cycles *Laudes*, the nine-part *Faust* (originally conceived as incidental music for a production of Goethe in the Burgtheater, Vienna, in 1976, and characterized by contrast between a conventional "classical" stylization and the trivial sound of orchestrion to express the polarity between good and evil), and the eight-part cycle *Job* are all now established in the international canon.

The emphasis on organ music relates closely to Eben's important contribution to liturgical music where he tries to introduce new means of expression (as in the *Trouvere Mass*) and to compose in a post-Conciliar spirit of congregation participation (as he does in *Missa cum populo*).

Thematically, Eben's song cycles incline to a dark mood, largely determined by his chosen texts. These are drawn predominantly from love poetry of a reflective sort. The prizewinning cycle of *Six Love Songs* on medieval poetry was almost as important as *Sunday Music* in establishing his international reputation. In the choral works, Eben frequently uses classical texts; his *Greek Dictionary* was an attempt to demonstrate that the enlightened values of antiquity were expressed in the very language of ancient Greece.

Eben employs an impressive range of vocal means. The *Apologia Socratus* is again based on a classical text, this time Plato. Less conventional, though, are the cantatas *Honour to Charles IV* and the chamber choir cycle *Pragensia*, which draws on a Rudolphine alchemist's recipe book.

The works for solo instruments demonstrate a mature lyric-dramatic expressivity with a similarly wide range of inspiration. The cycle *Windows* for trumpet and organ was inspired—as were so many modern works—by Marc Chagall's work in stained glass and symbolizes the window as "a direction of view from the reality of the surrounding world to the world of imagination"; Eben chooses a predominantly free rhythmical structure in both instrumental parts in an attempt to solve the long-standing problem of coordinating the organ with other instruments. Trying to express his ideas as distinctly as possible, he frequently turns to concertante technique; in the symphonic movement for three trumpets and orchestra *Vox clamantis*, the orchestra is set in contraposition—medieval style—to the three solo instruments, at opposite sides of the platform. In the concertante symphony *Night Hours*, Eben follows Ives in introducing urban night sounds; in the same piece, with its complex orchestration, there are also detectable elements of jazz and dance music.

The 1981 *String Quartet* and 1986 *Piano Trio* both have a significant place in Eben's development, suggesting a new stage of synthesis in technique and expression. Nevertheless, plainchant and folk music remain the constant source of inspiration; they are, in his own words, his "subjective solution and remedy" for the variety of sophisticated intonation demanded by contemporary music.

Besides such returns to his musical roots, Eben also tries to locate human belief "in a sense of artistic creation that must be connected to some humble recognition of its ancillary function. This means neither composing only on liturgical texts, nor a swift and obedient reaction to political events. What I am speaking of", he continues, "is the endowing consciousness that is to be found in Teilhard de Chardin's writings. The creation of the world is never finished, but continues in an ever more splendid way, and we can help it toward completion with every honest deed . . . "

—Jan Dehner

EDLUND, Mikael. Swedish. Born in Tranås, 19 January 1950. Educated at University of Uppsala (musicology), 1970–2; State College of Music, Stockholm (composition under Ingvar Lidholm and Arne Mellnäs), 1972–5; study visits to United States and elsewhere, 1977–8. Member of board, 1975–9, and producer, 1979, Fylkingen Concert Organization, Stockholm; member of board, ISCM Swedish Section, since 1978; founder-member, Chamber Music Group, since 1983; teacher of composition, State College of Music, Gothenburg, 1985–7. Mailing address: Backvagen 2, S-19145 Sollentuna, Sweden.

Publisher: Nordiska Musikforlaget.

Symphonies/orchestral:

Piece for Orchestra 1990; first performed Stockholm, 1991.

Chamber/instrumental:

Trio Sol/Trio Sun (clarinet, bassoon or cello piano) 1980; first performed Junsele, 1980. Recorded Phodo Suecia PSCD 20.

Brains and Dancin' (string quartet) 1981; first performed Bergen, Norway, 1981. Recorded Phono Suecia PSCD 20.

Fantasia over en Stad/Fantasia on a City (piano) 1981–6; first performed Stockholm, 1986.

Jord / Earth (5 percussion) 1982; first performed Stockholm, 1982.
Sma Fotter / Small Feet (guitar) 1982; first performed Södertälje, 1983. Recorded Phono Suecia PSCD 19.
Music for Double Wind Quintet 1983–4; first performed Stockholm, 1984.
Orchids in the Embers (piano) 1984; first performed Stockholm 1985. Recorded DACo 237; Phono Suecia PSCD 20.

Vocal / choral:

The Lost Jugglery (mezzo-soprano, cello, piano, 2 percussion) 1974–7; first performed Stockholm, 1978.
Leaves (8 female voices, piano, electric piano, harp, 7 percussion) 1977–81; first performed Stockholm, 1988. Recorded Phono Suecia PSCD 20.

PUBLICATIONS

On Edlund: Hans-Gunnar Peterson, "ME", in *Swedish Composers of the 20th Century*, Swedish Music Information Centre, 1988.

* * *

Born in 1950, Mikael Edlund belongs to a generation that listened to rock 'n' roll and jazz while carrying out the spirit of the new left. With such roots he began his conservatory education in the early 1970s looking for compositional tools that both permitted profound thinking and was consistent with the personal and physical presence essential for rock 'n' roll and jazz.

Edlund's efforts could be said to concern sensibility and time. From that point of view the string quartet *Brains and Dancin'* has a central position among his works. Here rhythmically differentiated micromovements were contrasted with organic pulse and modal pitch organization in a process that developed from intricate polyphony to intense dance rhythms. The contrasting elements not only presupposed each other, they also generated each other. The course of musical events illuminated the dialectic between the cerebral and the corporeal and exemplified an aesthetic attitude, founded on the conception that sensibility in human action makes material reality gain its meaning.

The Lost Jugglery for mezzo-soprano, cello, piano and two percussionists pleads for a revival of the medieval role of the musician as a jester and joker. Here theatrical and ritual elements are integrated within the music. This is also true with *Jord* (*Earth*) for percussion ensemble, which stages the aforementioned dialectics as a play between earthbound percussion sounds and constructivistic rhythmic and metric patterns. This surely resembles the "instrumental theatre" of Maurizio Kagel and his followers, but even more so the obvious dramatic of a rock or free form jazz concerto.

Edlund's compositions always set out from the musician's actual working situation and the physical touch of the instrument. This is evident in solo pieces as *Sma Fotter* (*Small Feet*) for guitar, where the universe of pitches, timbres and articulations of the instrument is played off against its intimacy. In the "tango" *Orchids in the Embers* for piano some basic tango gestures act together with instrumental peculiarities to a structure, where cantability is contrasted to metrical abruptness.

The Fantasia over en Stad (*Fantasia on a City*) for solo piano starts with the bright and glittering opening of a piano concerto, but takes quite another way after the grand opening gestures. Melodic developments and association into harmony and timbre are means to build up a series of impressive night thoughts, connected with a strong feeling of darkness and absence. Throughout the work reminiscences of *örjanslåten*, a melody associated with the bells of Stockholm's city hall, give hints of a skyline.

Both as an aspect of rhythmic and metric complexity and with regard to the dramatic course, time has a fundamental importance in all Edlund's works. In *Trio Sol* (*Trio Sun*) for clarinet, bassoon (or cello) and piano, the form is apparently simple. It consists of an organic development of two melodic lines in the woodwinds supported by a repetitive pattern of semiquavers in the piano. Twice the development resolves in a contrasting mechanical hammering, the last time together with some rigid melodic attempts before the whole structure finally fades away. Here time unites the organic and the mechanical.

The trio is closely related to *Leaves* for four sopranos, four mezzo-sopranos, piano, electric piano, harp and percussion ensemble. This work is also constructed on the basis of a repetitive pattern of semiquavers, and is reminiscent of American minimalism of the 1970s (in fact Edlund began composing the work as a farewell to Santa Barbara in California). However, the repetitive pattern, presented by the more or less percussive instruments, is constantly and organically changing. The voices project it to another dimension, with independent melodic developments. The whole action culminates by means of a rather elementary harmonic progression and fades out against a stable fifth-interval. As well as the very accurate partiture such a construction shows that *Leaves* hardly is a naturalistic process of the kind Steve Reich has described. On the contrary it points beyond its own material being—a meticulously elaborated tapestry, woven by sensibility over time.

—Sten Dahlstedt

EDWARDS, George (Harrison). American. Born in Boston, Massachusetts, 11 May 1943. Educated at Oberlin College, Ohio, 1961–5, B.A.; Princeton University, New Jersey, 1965–8, M.F.A., 1967. Married Rachel C. Hadas, 22 July 1978; 1 son. Member, theory faculty, New England Conservatory of Music, Boston, 1968–76; part-time lecturer, Massachusetts Institute of Technology, Cambridge, Massachusetts, 1971; assistant professor of music, 1976–85, and associate professor of music, since 1986, Columbia University, New York City. Recipient: Woodrow Wilson National Fellowship, 1965; Koussevitzky Composition Prize, Tanglewood, 1967; Prix de Rome Fellowship, American Academy in Rome, 1973; Naumburg Recording Award, 1974; Guggenheim Fellowships, 1980, 1985; Koussevitzky Music Foundation Award, 1981. Mailing address: 838 West End Avenue, Apt 3a, New York, New York 10025, U.S.A.

Publisher: Mobart Publications/Jerona Music, P.O. Box 5010, Hackensack, New Jersey 07606, U.S.A.

Symphonies / orchestral:

Monopoly 1972; first performed Boston, 1973.
Giro 1974.
Moneta's Mourn 1983; first performed New York City, 1983.
Heraclitean Fire 1987; first performed New York City, 1987.

Chamber/instrumental:

Bits (11 players) 1966; first performed Tanglewood, Massachusetts, 1967.
Two Piano Pieces 1967; first performed Princeton, New Jersey, 1967.
String Quartet 1967; first performed Boston, 1970. Recorded CRI 265.
Double Play (2 pianos) 1970; first performed Boston, 1970.
Kreuz und Quer (5 players) 1971; first performed Cambridge, Massachusetts, 1971. Recorded CRI 323.
Two Bagatelles (piano) 1972; first performed Berkeley, California, 1973.
Exchange-Misere (5 players) 1974; first performed Rome, 1975. Recorded CRI 336.
Sonda (flute, piano) 1975; first performed New York City, 1977.
Draconian Measures (piano) 1976; first performed New York City, 1980.
Northern Spy (9 players) 1980; first performed New York City, 1981.
String Quartet No 2 1982; first performed Madison, Wisconsin, 1984.
Suave Mari Magno (piano) 1984; first performed New York City, 1985.
Five Etudes (piano) 1985.
Trio (violin, horn, piano) 1987; first performed New York City, 1988.
Parallel Convergences (11 players) 1988; first performed New York City, 1989.

Vocal/choral:

The Captive (soprano, 14 players) 1970; first performed Boston, 1971.
Three Hopkins Songs (2 sopranos, 2 pianos) 1972; first performed Cambridge, Massachusetts, 1973.
Veined Variety (soprano, 4 players) 1978; first performed New York City, 1978. Recorded Opus One 62.
The Leaden Echo and the Golden Echo (3 singers, chamber ensemble) 1979.
A Mirth but Open'd (soprano, piano) 1986; first performed New York City, 1987.

PUBLICATIONS

By Edwards: "A Conversation with John Rockwell and Roger Sessions", in *Threepenny Review*, Spring 1990; "Involuntary Affinities: New Music and Performance in the Twentieth Century", in *The Southwest Review*, 1991. "The Pleasure of Its Being Over", in *Partisan Review*, 1991.

On Edwards: Robert Black, " . . . And Each Harmonical Has a Point of Its Own", in *Perspectives of New Music*, 17, Autumn/Winter 1978.

George Edwards comments:

My music revels in the quixotic attempt to reconcile the irreconcilable. How can the treatment of pitch and time become the primary organizational and expressive resources without throwing away most of the new resources the 20th century has placed at our disposal? How can I cram the most diverse kinds of pacing into a short piece (*Kreuz und Quer*)? Is it possible to write a symphonic poem (with near-quotes from Schubert, Wagner and Mahler) in a harmonic language akin to Webern and Carter (*Moneta's Mourn*)? Can I rehabilitate 19th-century virtuoso piano writing without falling into pastiche (*Suave Mari Magno*)? Can modernism support a dialectic between protest and utopia (*Parallel Convergences*)? Are tonality and atonality really opposites, as most current theory seems to suppose, or can they be treated as opposite ends of a continuum (*String Quartet No 2*)?

These are not the musings of a postmodernist, but of a composer who wants to help rescue modernism from its hermetically sealed self-referentiality.

* * *

George Edwards has produced a convincing body of work, too consistently conceived to be called "eclectic", too thought-out and achieved to be considered experimental, too well synthesised to fall into any of the prevailing and opposing modern tendencies. He has written compelling orchestral music (notably *Heraclitean Fire* and *Moneta's Mourn*), two fine string quartets and the intriguing quintet *Kreuz und Quer*, which compress seemingly antagonistic musical philosophies into remarkably small compass, and some beautiful vocal pieces (including settings of Hopkins and the lovely *The Leaden Echo and the Golden Echo*), but it is perhaps his unique and idiomatic music for piano that is paradigmatic of his general compositional thinking.

One of its salient features is Edwards's idiomatic use of rhythm. In his music it is very rare for a given unit of pulse to obtain for any length of time. These pulse units are continually changing (sometimes even within a given measure). This fluidity helps delineate different harmonic units and seems to be an almost grammatical gloss on what is occurring in the phrase. This is akin to a written-out continuation of the performance style of tonal music which uses rubato to highlight, underline and comment on the story of the phrase and its fate in the overall structure of the piece. The traditional use of rubato is the process of stretching and condensing the flow of the music measured against a steady pulse. In Edwards's music, this becomes the process of stretching and condensing the flows themselves. The steady pulse disappears.

This rhythmic usage is applied to the different contrapuntal voices and helps maximise the shapes and independence of the individual lines. This peculiar polyrhythmic usage often leads to passages in which one note is not played off against another, but one flow is played off against another flow. The result can be passages of daring contrapuntal complexity, in which no simultaneous attacks occur, or where, for example, the simultaneous attacks occur in unison and delineate some special voice leading function, such as a slow-moving line changing registers and providing a longer range motion or "spine" for the phrase. This lack of simultaneous attacks sometimes functions similarly to the rubato characteristic of pianists from the earlier part of the century, where for delineating various lines and expressive effect the left and right hands were not always played together though notated together.

Another trait of Edwards's style is the manipulation of contrapuntal lines to articulate harmonic units characteristic and pervasive enough in a given piece to project clear harmonic tension, release and stasis (and in recent music, occasional tonal moorings). For atonal music to project a sense of harmonic rhythm is a rare accomplishment. This harmonic treatment enables his piano music to sound resonant and satisfyingly pianistic while often articulating a number of single-note lines which would otherwise sound hollow.

Many of these features are in fact elements of tonal music

transformed and applied to atonal music. The focus on voice leading, shape of phrase, harmonic elements resulting from contrapuntal procedures, rhythm and metre as a gloss on harmonic motion, are the kinds of hierarchical grouping procedures characteristic of tonal music. The compatability of these tonal and atonal elements makes some very eloquent music indeed. It is contrapuntally rich, harmonically clear and possesses a naturalness of flow in how it builds, climaxes and resolves. Interestingly, people are often baffled that music that "sounds so natural and seamless" appears so complicated and daunting in notation.

Edwards's large piano works fit within the tradition of great keyboard composers like Beethoven, Chopin, Schubert and Brahms, in that they seem to be equal parts Apollo and Dionysus, forged with classical and romantic elements of style and structure.

—Alan Feinberg

EDWARDS, Ross. Australian. Born in Sydney, New South Wales, 23 December 1943. Educated at Sydney Grammar School, 1956–61; New South Wales Conservatorium, 1959–62; University of Sydney, 1963, 1988–90, D.Mus.; University of Adelaide, 1966–71, B.Mus., 1968, M.Mus., 1971. Married Helen Hopkins, 7 August 1974; 1 son and 1 daughter. Senior tutor, 1973–6, and lecturer in composition, 1976–80, University of Sydney. Recipient: John Bishop Memorial Award, 1974; Don Banks Fellowship, 1989; Australian Creative Fellowship, 1990–3. Mailing address: c/o Boosey & Hawkes (Australia) Pty Ltd, Unit 12/6 Campbell Street, Artarman, New South Wales 2064, Australia.

Publisher: Universal Edition, London.

Symphonies/orchestral:

Etude 1969.
Mboc (strings) 1972.
Chorus (piano, orchestra) 1972.
Mountain Village in a Clearing Mist 1973; first performed Adelaide, 1974. Recorded ABC Polygram, release 1991.
Concerto for Piano and Orchestra 1982; first performed Sydney, 1983. Recorded ABC Polygram 426483-2.
Maninyas (violin, orchestra) 1988; first performed Sydney, August 1988. Recorded ABC Polygram, release 1991.
Yarregeh (percussion, orchestra) 1988; first performed Sydney, 1989. Recorded ABC Polygram, release 1991.
Aria and Transcendental Dance 1989; first performed Melbourne, 1990.

Chamber/instrumental:

Sextet 1966.
Sonata (9 instruments) 1967.
String Quartet 1968.
String Quartet No 2 1969.
Monos I (cello) 1970; first performed Vienna, 1972.
Monos II (piano) 1970; first performed London, 1971. Recorded EMI OASD 7567.
Five Little Piano Pieces 1976; first performed Sydney, 1976.
Shadow D-Zone (flute, clarinet/bass clarinet, percussion, piano, violin, cello) 1977; first performed Sydney, 1978.
The Tower of Remoteness (clarinet, piano) 1978; first performed Sydney, 1978. Recorded MBS, release 1991.
Laikan (flute, clarinet, percussion, piano, violin, cello) 1979; first performed Perth, 1980.
Kumari (piano) 1980–1; first performed Melbourne, 1981.
Maninya II (string quartet) 1982; first performed Sydney, 1982.
Ten Little Duets (2 high instruments) 1982; first performed Sydney, 1983.
Marimba Dances (marimba) 1982; first performed Wollongong, 1983. Recorded Southern Cross Records SCCD 1021.
Etymalong (piano) 1984; first performed London, 1984. Recorded CSM:3.
Reflections (piano, 3 percussion) 1985; first performed Sydney, 1985. Recorded Anthology of Australian Music on Disc CSM:2.
Maninya III (wind quintet) 1985; first performed Springwood, New South Wales, 1986. Recorded CSM:14.
Maninya IV (clarinet or bass clarinet, marimba) 1985–6; first performed Wollongong, New South Wales, 1986.
Three Children's Pieces (piano) 1988.

Vocal/choral:

Fiva Carols from Quem Quaeritis (SSAA chorus, 8–16 voices) 1967; first performed Adelaide, 1967.
Antifon (large SATB chorus, brass sextet, organ, 2 percussion) 1973; first performed Adelaide, 1974.
The Hermit of Green Light (voice, piano; Dransfield) 1979; first performed Sydney, 1979. Recorded CSM:15; MBS 21 CD.
Ab Estasis Foribus (SATB chorus, 8–16 voices; medieval Latin) 1980; first performed Sydney, 1980. Recorded EMI OASD 7629.
Maninya I (voice, cello) 1981; first performed Ballarat, 1981. Recorded MBS 21 CD.
Maninya V (voice, piano) 1986; first performed Sydney, 1986. Recorded MBS 21 CD.
Flower Songs (SATB chorus, 16 voices, 2 percussionists) 1986–7; first performed Sydney, 1987.

Opera:

Christina's World (2 mezzo-sopranos, tenor, baritone, tape, ensemble) 1983; first performed Sydney, 1983. Recorded ABC Polygram, release 1991.

PUBLICATIONS

By Edwards: "Credo", in *Sounds Australian*, Spring 1989.

On Edwards: James Murdoch, in *Australia's Contemporary Composers*, London, 1972; Michael Hannan, "RE, a Unique Sound-World", in *Australian Performing Rights Association Journal*, Sydney, March 1986; Jonathan Mills, "The Voice and the Kingdom", Blue Mountains Festival Performing Notes, Sydney, 1988; Michael Noone and Robert Parker (editors), in *Anthology of Australian Music on Disc: Handbook*, Canberra, 1989.

* * *

In his search for an individual style, Ross Edwards has investigated many paths. Works such as *Sextet* for wind instruments and *String Quartet No 1* explored serialism;

indeterminacy was a feature of *Mboc* for three or more string players, having an intentionally uninformative title and generally known as his third string quartet. *Monos I* for cello and *Monos II* for piano displayed modernist tendencies. However, the composer was not happy with his musical idiom, feeling his work to be too dense and complex; he expressed this by deliberately giving *Monos II* a stylistically inappropriate ending. The period of a government grant to compose coincided with a period almost of compositional paralysis: one work, *Chorus* for piano and orchestra, remained unsettled and was not performed.

Mountain Village in a Clearing Mist pointed the next direction Edwards would take, being a transitional work leading to his "sacred" style. Inspired by the visual and aural aspects of nature, he evolved a style that was calm, static and esoteric. It employed a very limited number of musical ideas, each prolonged and meticulously worked out. With the emphasis upon subtleties of timbre and sonority rather than melody and harmonic movement, there was no sense of progression; rather, the works took on a meditational character, intended to focus the listener's attention upon each individual moment. This style was later properly exemplified in *Shadow D-Zone* and its very similar successor, *The Tower of Remoteness*.

A further experimental and exploratory period ensued, with Edwards's compositional development hindered by his teaching commitments. A chance encounter with a Madagascan folksong set him on his next phase: excited by its rhythms and energy, he worked elements of it into *Laikan*, and its character infuses his *Maninya* series, culminating in *Maninyas* for violin and orchestra. The chant-like effect of its repetitive, angular rhythms gave the "maninya" style a philosophical kinship with his "sacred" works, which he continued to write contemporaneously. In addition, painstaking manipulation of limited material—in the minimalist "maninya" series, a limited set of notes—is common to both styles. Both were inspired by and imbued with the sounds and silences of the natural landscape: it was the desolate Yorkshire countryside that awakened him to natural stimuli, and the Australian bush that furnished him with them.

The idea of limiting his source material was an early one in Edwards's works, as was the exercising of an agonising precision in determining and notating it. His *String Quartet No 2* introduced a penchant for reworking earlier material, in that case from his nativity play *Quem Quaeritis*. This characteristic was most fully exemplified in *Maninyas* for violin and orchestra, in which he reused vocal lines and their accompaniments from both *Maninya I* and *Maninya V*.

Unlike *Mountain Village in a Clearing Mist*, which took its title from the work of a Zen monk who also sought to reveal the inner form of nature by the simplest possible means, the titles of its two stylistic successors had no significance. This verbal meaninglessness has been a frequent feature of Edwards's music. Both his song-cycle *The Hermit of Green Light* and chamber opera *Christina's World* used an intelligible text, but in general he has preferred to use random syllables and fragmented words—*Maninya I* and *V*, *Flower Songs*—or archaic texts such as in *Antifon* and *Ab Estasis Foribus*. The use of such texts has been deliberate, in order to avoid the music being dictated and controlled by the words.

—Jenny Dawson

EINEM, Gottfried von. Austrian. Born in Berne, Switzerland, 24 January 1918. Educated at Plön Gymnasium, Holstein; further study in England and Satzeburg; composition study under Boris Blacher, Berlin, 1941–3. Married (1) Lianne von Bismarck (died 1962); (2) Lotte Ingrisch in 1964. Repetiteur, Berlin Staatsoper, 1938–44; conflict with Gestapo, arrest and imprisonment, 1938; coach, Bayreuth Opera, 1938–9; resident composer and music adviser, Dresden State Opera, 1944; board member, Salzburg Festival, 1947–51, subsequently chair of artistic advisory board; director, Vienna Festival, 1959–63; president, Society of Authors, Composers and Music Publishers, 1965–70; board member, Konzerthausgesellschaft, Vienna, since 1965; professor of composition, Hochschule für Musik, Vienna, 1965–72, now emeritus. Recipient: Grosse Österreichische Staatspreis; Preis der Stadt Wien; freeman of Vienna and Bad Gross. Mailing address: Kapuzmergang 86, A-1010 Vienna-Hofburg, Austria.

Publishers: Boosey & Hawkes, London; Bote & Böck, Doberlin; Universal Edition, Vienna; Doblinger, Vienna; Schirmer, New York; Edition Peters, Frankfurt.

Symphonies/orchestral:

Capriccio Op 2 1942–3; first performed Berlin, 3 March 1943.
Concerto for Orchestra Op 4 1943; first performed Berlin, 3 April 1944.
Dantons Tod Op 6a (orchestral suite from the opera) 1948.
Orchestermusik Op 9 1948; first performed Vienna, 21 June 1948.
Serenade Op 10 (double strings) 1949; first performed Berlin, 30 January 1950.
Meditations Op 18 1954; first performed Louisville, Kentucky, 6 November 1954.
Pas de coeur Op 16a (orchestra suite from the ballet) 1954.
Four Episodes Op la (from the ballet *Prinzessin Turandot*) 1954.
Piano Concerto Op 20 1955; first performed Berlin, 6 October 1956.
Wandlungen Op 21 1956.
Symphonic Scenes Op 22 1956; first performed Boston, 11 October 1957.
Ballade Op 23 1957; first performed Cleveland, Ohio, 20 March 1958.
Tanz-Rondo Op 27 1959; first performed Munich, 13 November 1959.
Philadelphia Symphony Op 28 1960; first performed Vienna, 11 November 1961.
Nachtstück Op 29 1960; first performed Kassel, 16 November 1962.
Violin Concerto Op 33 1966–7; first performed Vienna, 31 May 1970.
Hexameron Op 37 1969; first performed Los Angeles, 19 February 1970.
Bruckner Dialog Op 39 1971; first performed Linz, 23 March 1974.
Wiener Symphonie Op 49 1976; first performed Minneapolis, Minnesota, 16 November 1977.
Arietten Op 50 (piano, orchestra) 1977; first performed Berlin, 20 February 1978.
Ludi Leopoldini (variations on a theme of Emperor Leopold) 1980; first performed Berlin, 12 October 1980.

Chamber/instrumental:

Four Piano Pieces Op 3 1943.
Two Sonatinas Op 7 (piano) 1947.
Sonata Op 11 (violin, piano) 1947.
Four Studies Op 34 (guitar) 1967.
Two Capriccios Op 36 (harpsichord) 1969.
Reifliches Divertimento Op 35a (from *Der Besuch der alten Dame*; horn, violin, viola, piano) 1973.
String Quartet Op 45 1975. Recorded Deutsche Grammophon.
Sonata Op 45 (violin) 1975.
Wind Quintet Op 46 1976.
String Quartet No 2 1977.
String Quartet No 3 1980.
Sonata (viola) 1980.
Steinbeis Serenade (octet) 1981.
Sonata (double bass) 1982.

Vocal/choral:

Eight Hafiz Lieder Op 5 (soprano/tenor, piano) 1944.
Five Songs from the Chinese Op 8 (mezzo-soprano, baritone, piano) 1946–8.
Hymnus Op 12 (alto, chorus, orchestra; Lernet-Holenia) 1949; first performed Vienna, 31 March 1951.
Japanische Blätter Op 15 (voice, piano) 1951.
Seven Songs Op 19 (voice, piano) 1954–6.
Five Songs Op 25 (soprano, tenor, piano) 1958.
Das Stundenlied Op 26 (mixed chorus, orchestra; Brecht) 1958; first performed Hamburg, 1 March 1959.
Von der Liebe Op 30 (soprano/tenor, orchestra) 1961; first performed Vienna, 18 June 1961.
Kammergesänge Op 32 (mezzo-soprano, baritone, small orchestra) 1965.
Geistliche Sonata Op 38 (soprano, trumpet, organ) 1971–3.
Rosa mystica Op 40 (baritone, orchestra; Artmann) 1972; first performed Vienna, 4 June 1973.
Die träumenden Knaben Op 41 (mixed chorus, clarinet, bassoon; Kokoschka) 1973.
An die Nachgebornen Op 42 (alto, baritone, mixed chorus, orchestra) 1973–6; first performed New York City, 24 October 1975.
Leb wohl, Frau Welt Op 43 (mezzo-soprano/baritone, piano; Hesse) 1974.
Liebes- und Abendlieder Op 48 (tenor, piano) 1977.

Opera:

Dantons Tod Op 6 (after Büchner) 1944–6; first performed Salzburg, 6 August 1948. Recorded Orfeo.
Der Prozess Op 14 (after Kafka) 1950–2; first performed Salzburg, 17 August 1953. Recorded Orfeo.
Der Zerrissene Op 31 (after Nestroy) 1961–4; first performed Hamburg, 17 September 1964.
Der Besuch der alten Dame Op 35 (Dürrenmatt) 1970; first performed Vienna, 23 May 1971. Recorded Amadeo.
Kabale und Liebe Op 44 (after Schiller) 1975; first performed Vienna, 17 December 1976. Recorded Polygram.
Jesu Hochzeit/The Wedding of Jesus 1980; first performed Vienna, 18 May 1980.
Tulifant 1989–90; first performed Vienna, 1990.

Other:

Prinzessin Turandot Op 1 (ballet) 1942–3; first performed Dresden, 5 February 1944.
Rondo von goldenen Kalb Op 13 (ballet) 1950; first performed Hamburg, 1 February 1952.
Pas de coeur (Tod und Auferstehung einer Ballerina) Op 16 (ballet) 1952; first performed Munich, 22 July 1952.
Glück, Tod und Traum (Alpbacher Tanzserenade) Op 17 1953; first performed Alpbach, 23 August 1954.
Medusa Op 24 (ballet) 1957; first performed Vienna, 16 November 1957.

Also realisations of Modest Mussorgsky (new ending to *St. John's Night on the Bare Mountain*) and Franz Schubert.

PUBLICATIONS

By von Einem: *Das musikalische Selbstportrait von Komponisten, Dirigenten, Sängerinnen und Sänger unserer Zeit*, Hamburg, 1963; "Ein Komponist im Turm", in *Melos*, 31, 1964; "Die Freiheit des Komponisten", in *Österreichische Musikzeitung*, 20, 1965; *Komponist und Gesellschaft*, Karlsruhe, 1967.

On von Einem: K. Laux, "GvE", in *Musik und Musiker der Gegenwart*, Essen, 1949; D. Hartmann, *GvE*, Vienna, 1967; H.H. Stuckenschmidt, *Die Grossen Komponisten unsereres Jahrhunderts*, Munich, 1971.

Gottfried von Einem comments:
My music is based on tonality and is meant to be sung and played by professionals. Listeners should be led to feel and to think.

* * *

Gottfried von Einem is perhaps the best-known Austrian composer of our time, and, though he has been dismissively labelled a "conservative", is one of the acknowledged masters of 20th-century music, whose success is based on sheer originality, inexhaustible musical resources, and a traditional idiom which nonetheless refuses to make use of blandly euphonious sound. Einem enlivens his works with a breathtaking vivacity, considerable rhythmic variety and harmonic freedom, without ever stepping outside the bounds of extended tonality. In formal terms, he generally follows the schema of classical-romantic music.

He is a born dramatist. His Opus 1, the ballet *Princess Turandot*, underlined his talent for skilful juxtaposition of dramatic action and lyrical music. His first opera, *Danton's Death*, which created a sensation at the Salzburg Festival in 1947, dominates the stage, inspired by Caspar Neher's sets and Buchner's gripping text. Each scene is a formal unit, motivic and thematic processes are independent but support, amplify or interpret the plot. Rhythmic variation, counterpoint, key symbolism and interrelations of sound all are given dramatic functions, as are extensive cantilenas, leitmotivic elements and specially semanticized chords.

In cases of "psychological" opera, with little physical action, the need for compact form became pressing. Inner relations are conveyed symbolically. *Zerissenen* is pervaded by broad melodic lines and sensuous singing; *The Visit of an Old Lady* is characterized by associative themes and dramatic interrelations; *Kabals and Love* appears strongly leitmotivic in relation to basic motives; *The Wedding of Jesus* is again based on sound and melodic relations. Strictly speaking, all these elements emerge from von Einem's striving for inner musical logic and his ability to develop action at all levels simultaneously.

In a modified form, his operatic method applies to his other work as well: the ballet scores, choral works, songs and "programmatic" instrumental works all create symbolic relations between sound and meaning, and here we see another important feature of von Einem's music: its combination of full sound and transparency. Within almost all the works, individual instruments are deployed as soloists, or within small groups, creating a considerable plasticity but also making it much easier for the listeners to follow the structural logic. In this way, instrumentation is also the means to dramatic effect, symbolism and motivic tension.

Von Einem has assimilated a number of stylistic influences. In his early years, he was interested in jazz and this appears in such pieces as *Philadelphia Symphony* in the form of syncopation, fast, brief ostinati and free accentuation. In addition, a neoclassical sense of movement pervades his chamber music right up to the present, while a romantic miniaturism in the songs gives von Einem's micro-organisms an extraordinary, visionary quality that comprises sound and sense in a minimum span of time.

Von Einem is one of the great modern traditionalists, not only enriching the genres he turns to but all facets of musical expression, remaining intelligible at all times.

—Hartmut Krones

ELIAS, Brian (David). British. Born in Bombay, India, 30 August 1948. Educated at St. Christopher's School, Letchworth, Hertfordshire, 1961–66; Royal College of Music, London, 1966–67; private lessons with Elisabeth Lutyens; extra-mural composition workshop at Juilliard School, New York City. Freelance editor, arranger and copyist; clerk and statistician assistant, 1972–78; currently full-time composer and freelance teacher. Recipient: Joint 2nd Prize (for *Proverbs of Hell*), Radcliffe Music Award, 1977. Mailing address: c/o Chester Music, 8/9 Frith Street, London WIV 5TZ, England.

Publisher: Chester Music.

Symphonies/orchestral:

L'Eylah 1983; first performed London 1984.

Chamber/instrumental:

Rondo (piano) 1962.
Sonata (flute, piano) 1964.
Five Pieces (piano—right hand) 1969.
Piece (cello) 1970; first performed London, 1970.
Duo (violin, piano) 1970; first performed London, 1970.
Tzigane (violin) 1978; first performed London, 1980.
Of Elutropia (cello) 1982.
L'Eylah (two pianos) 1984; first performed Dartington, Devon, 19 August 1984.
Geranos (flute, clarinet, percussion, violin, cello) 1985; first performed London, 6 November 1985.
Fantasia (violin, piano) 1986; first performed London, 2 June 1986.
Variations (piano) 1987; first performed London, 8 August 1989.
But When I Sleep (solo viola) 1987.
Pythikos Nomos (alto saxophone, piano) 1987–8; first performed London, 1 July 1988.

Vocal/choral:

La Chevelure (soprano, orchestra) 1967; first performed London, 1976.
Elm (soprano, tenor, piano; Plath) 1969; first performed London, 1969.
Two Songs (soprano, piano; Verlaine) 1969.
Dirge and Hymneal (soprano, baritone, piano; Beddoes) 1969; first performed London, 1969.
Peroration (soprano; Browning) 1973; first performed Oxford, 1973.
Proverbs of Hell (unaccompanied SATB chorus; Blake) 1975; first performed London, 1975.
Somnia (tenor, orchestra; Petronius) 1979; first performed Manchester, 1983.
At the Edge of Time (tenor, piano; Peake) 1982; first performed Dartington, Devon, 1982.
Song (soprano, hurdy-gurdy or harmonium, organ etc.) 1986; first performed London, 14 July 1986.
Five Songs to Poems by Irina Ratushinskaya (mezzo-soprano, orchestra) 1989; first performed London, 23 April 1989.

Opera:

Lost Hearts (chamber opera; M.R. James) 1966; first performed Dartington, Devon, Spring 1967.

PUBLICATIONS

By Elias: articles in musical journals.

* * *

Brian Elias has never been a composer who seeks to produce occasional pieces on demand; he writes slowly, focusing all his energies on each and every piece, whether large or small, until it is finished and polished to the best of his ability. His ambitions are centred on quality, not on the quantity of performances enjoyed by those with longer work lists, and it is for this reason that he has until recently been somewhat overshadowed by his more productive contemporaries.

He opened his account with an impressive flourish. Written when he was only 19, *La Chevelure* is a wonderfully free-soaring evocation of Baudelaire's ecstatic verse, and Elias's handling of orchestral colour already shows an exhilarating confidence. Yet he was not to write anything further on such a scale, or for comparable forces, for another 12 years.

The eight short pieces which followed (most of them for just one or two performers) were nevertheless important staging posts on the journey towards a style more personal than that of the expressive, Webern-influenced serialism he had used so instinctively in *La Chevelure*. Concentrating at first on writing for voices with piano, he set words by Sylvia Plath, Verlaine and Thomas Lovell Beddoes. The tiny *Five Pieces* for piano right hand were evidently composed as an exercise in limitations, and it is this sense of a carefully defined framework that characterises the period as a whole. But while several of these pieces occupy a fleeting sound world of delicate-textured restraint, others set out to extend the harmonic range in directions that would eventually lead to the large-scale developments of the 1980s. Meanwhile, three solo pieces (for cello, for voice and for violin) were to develop the extended melodic flow so strikingly characteristic of

Somnia and the *Five Songs to Poems by Irina Ratushinskaya*. But it is the last of these, *Tzigane*, which most clearly foreshadows the richly exuberant inventiveness of the works to come.

Even so, it could hardly have prepared for the astonishing change of scale: within the space of a year, Elias had moved from the miniature to the quasi-symphonic. In *Somnia*, a 25-minute setting of words by Petronius, the melodic elegance of earlier pieces is allied to a harmonic luxuriance scarcely hinted at elsewhere. This is a passionate, emotionally daring work, its extended serialism now largely sublimated, while the valedictory intensity of *L'Eylah* seems to close another cycle of musical events—fanning outwards from the shorter, song-like statements of *Somnia* to form the arch of a single-movement rondo of vivid contrasts and symphonic proportions.

But it was his investigation of rhythmic structures established by the ancient Greeks that was to fire his imagination in wholly new directions: the rhythmic structure of *Geranos* absorbs often quite extreme contrasts between strict and free, between fast and slow in relation to metrical pulse; it also reflects an almost classical kind of motivic development. Doubtless aware of the fruitfulness of this foray into the past, Elias reached for a still more specific model: mirroring both the structure and, in particular, the harmonic pacing of Beethoven's Opus 32, his own *Variations* likewise set virtuoso decorations against a deliberately simplified harmonic background.

Armed with the rhythmic and motivic developments of *Geranos* and the ideas on long-term harmonic pacing explored in the *Variations*, Elias embarked on his major work to date: the *Five Songs to Poems by Irina Ratushinskaya* show the composer at full stretch, in authoritative command of a technique able here to express a truly remarkable range of controlled emotional power.

—Susan Bradshaw

ELIASSON, Anders. Swedish. Born in Borlänge, 3 April 1947. Educated at State Academy of Music, Stockholm (composition under Ingvar Lidholm, harmony and counterpoint under Valdemar Söderholm), 1966–72. Member, artistic committee, Electronic Music Studio Foundation, Stockholm, 1972–3. Recipient: City of Stockholm Artist's Fellowship, 1973; Christ Johnson Prize, 1974; Royal Academy of Music Prize, 1983. Mailing address: c/o Swedish Music Information Centre, Sandhamnsgatan 79, Box 27327, S-102 54 Stockholm, Sweden.

Publisher: Edition Reimers, Stockholm.

Symphonies/orchestral:

Canti in lontanza (chamber orchestra) 1977; first performed Stockholm, 1 October 1977. Recorded Caprice CAP 1324.
Impronta 1978; first performed Norrköping, 22 September 1979.
Turnings 1978; broadcast Swedish Radio, 13 June 1979.
Desert Point (strings) 1981; first performed Växjö, Sweden, 13 February 1982.
Concerto for Bassoon and Orchestra 1982; first performed Stockholm, 19 February 1983. Recorded Caprice CD, 1991.
Sinfonia da camera 1984; broadcast Swedish Radio, 16 November 1984.
Symphony No 1 1986; broadcast Swedish Radio, 6 February 1987. Recorded Caprice CD, 1991.
Ostacoli (strings) 1987; first performed 31 January 1988. Recorded Caprice CD, 1991.
Fantasia 1988; first performed Stockholm, 5 March 1985.
Intermezzi (chamber orchestra) 1988; first performed Stockholm, 14 February 1989.
Sinfonia concertante (Symphony No 3) (alto saxophone, orchestra) 1989; first performed Trondheim, Norway, 16 November 1989.

Chamber/instrumental:

In medias (violin) 1970.
Intro (organ) 1970; first performed Stockholm, 31 May 1970.
Melos (string quartet) 1970.
Picknick (wind quintet) 1972.
Versione (piano) 1973.
Disegno della pioggia (piano—4 hands, cello, xylophone) 1974; first performed Helsinki, 10 October 1974.
Disegno per quartetto d'archi (string quartet) 1975; first performed Stockholm, 23 March 1976.
Disegno per sestetto d'ottoni (2 trumpets, horn, 2 trombones, tuba) 1975; first performed Boston, 26 October 1976.
Disegno per violoncello (cello) 1977; first performed Stockholm, 8 June 1978. Recorded Caprice CAP 1190.
La Fièvre (wind quintet) 1978; first performed Bäckedal, 1 August 1979. Recorded Caprice CAP 1271.
Malaria (clarinet, trumpet, trombone, percussion, double bass) 1978; first performed Stockholm, 7 December 1978.
Ombra (clarinet, wind quartet) 1981; broadcast Swedish Radio, 23 April 1981.
Notturno (bass clarinet, cello, piano) 1981; first performed Stockholm, 22 March 1982. Recorded ARTE 7115.
Disegno per clarinetto (clarinet) 1982; first performed Stockholm, 1982. Recorded ARTE 7115.
Disegno per clavicembalo (harpsichord) 1982; first performed Norrköping, 10 October 1982.
Suolo (piano) 1983.
Senza risposte (flute, violin, cello, piano) 1983; first performed Harstad, Norway, 24 June 1984. Recorded ACCD 1010.
Dai commini misteriosi (2 oboes, bassoon, harpsichord, double bass) 1983; first performed Brunswick, Germany, 28 November 1985.
Disegno per trombone 1984; first performed Stockholm, February 1984. Recorded BIS CD 388.
Disegno per flauto (flute) 1984; first performed Harnosand, 25 February 1985. Recorded MAP R-8502.
Disegno per pianoforte (piano) 1984. Recorded Caprice CAP 2021.
Disegno per quartetto d'archi e clavicembalo (string quartet, harpsichord) 1984; first performed Stockholm, 6 October 1985.
Poem (alto saxophone, piano; instrumental version of *Längs radien*) 1986–8.
Disegno per pianoforte No 2 (piano) 1987; first performed Stockholm, 24 August 1988.
Sotti il segno del sole (5 percussion, 3 flutes, 3 oboes, 3 clarinets, 3 bassoons, 3 horns, double bass) 1987; first performed Helsinki, 3 February 1988.

Vocal/choral:

Hymn (6 male voices, winds, percussion; Latin) 1970; first performed Helsinki, 1971.
Kantillation (mezzo-soprano, organ; Pabbaj-Sutta) 1970.
Då sade man . . . och nu (soprano, bass clarinet, cello, vibraphone, tam-tam; Japanese verse, translated Wahlund) 1972. Recorded Caprice CAP 1183.
Memet (unaccompanied mixed chorus; Hikmet, Haggqvist) 1972; first performed Umeå, 8 April 1973.
Inför logos (soprano, alto, tenor, bass, tape; Kafka) 1973; first performed Stockholm, 14 February 1973.
Oktober (mixed chorus; Aspenström) 1973.
Den gröna rosen / The Green Rose (cantata for soprano, saxophone quartet, percussion; Rozewicz) 1976; first performed Stockholm, 7 March 1978.
Canto dei vagabondo in memoria de Carolus Linnaeus (boy soprano, female chorus, orchestra) 1979; first performed Stockholm, 28 November 1980.
Serenad (reciter, flute, horn, harp, violin, viola, cello; Noren) 1980; broadcast Swedish Radio, 21 March 1982.
Breathing Room (mixed chorus; Tranströmer, translated Swenson) 1984; first performed Sodertalje, 13 October 1984.
Ave maris stella (mixed chorus; Hymn to Mary) 1985; first performed Helsinki, 28 September 1985.
Längs radien (voice, piano; Tranströmer) 1986; first performed Stockholm, 30 March 1987.

Opera:

En av oss (church opera; narrator, speakers, dancers, chorus, orchestra) 1974.

Other:

Backanterna (incidental music to Euripides) 1982; broadcast Swedish Radio, 4 April 1982.

PUBLICATIONS

On Eliasson: Hans-Gunnar Peterson, in *Swedish Composers of the 20th Century*, Stockholm, 1988.

* * *

You will find no better illustration than Anders Eliasson of the often-repeated truth that a real creative imagination exists simultaneously on many levels of thought. It explains why we find in his output the sort of apparent discontinuity we meet in mid-period Stravinsky (though there are few other similarities): to the ear, two works of Eliasson may be as different from each other as they are from those of a totally different composer, apart from the unifying force of his own intellect and vision. To achieve a workable basis for understanding what he is about requires separating these levels of thought, and it requires familiarity with a considerable proportion of his work. It also probably explains why so much pretentious garbage has been written about him, mostly couched in nebulous, quasi-poetical language and signifying nothing except that the commentator is both impressed and baffled. To be fair, the composer's own statements don't help much unless applied with some care, and seem at one level to have little to do with the rather serious, sincere and disciplined nature of most of his music.

As a pupil of Lidholm, Eliasson is a sort of grandson of Rosenberg, and thus heir to the great symphonic tradition. By "tradition" I do not mean the one he looked back at over his shoulder, but the one he carried forward. It may seem an odd word to use of Eliasson, with his distinctly contemporary sound-world. It must be remembered that Scandinavia is one of the few areas of the world where the Symphony is still a live issue. Again, I don't imply a romantic, nationalist tradition; rather the symphony is the form to which a composer still turns naturally when committing his most important statements to music: a habit of thought rather than a prescribed structure. It is this essentially serious habit of thought that identifies Eliasson's music. How he goes about implementing it in actual approach and technique—how he organises himself and his material to address specific problems—owes something to his other main teacher, Ligeti. His forms, often original (sometimes not), are characterised by rigorous working and clear outlines. What he is aiming for is quite simple; the things he has to do to get there are often fairly complex.

Before we can see daylight, we must distinguish between the impetus that originates the concept of the work, and his compositional process. The concept of each piece, that gets the juices flowing, may be philosophical, nature derived, religiously inspired, poetic, the response to a text and so on. The treatment is always based on purely musical precepts. A number of his pieces are entitled "Disegno"—about a dozen between 1974 and 1987—and form a very important group. The word, carefully chosen, means "drawing" as in sketch. It implies black-and-white and has associations with the concept of design. The pieces show a concern for musical essentials that make Eliasson impervious to the sort of stylistic influences that beset composers in the 1960s: you will look in vain for unconventional methods of performance or the use of electronics, but you will find conventional techniques stretched to their utmost as he explores a particular aspect of music with absolute thoroughness. In his service of what he terms "Musikängeln" (the Angel of Music) he makes a conscious decision that his musical personality, still more the public's expectations, must take second place to the musical "truth" each work is concerned with. He is genuinely surprised when a piece meets with acclaim, but it makes no difference to the next work, whose expressive profile will be ordained by its purpose, which may be a concern for the organisation of acoustic densities, or exploring the relationship of metrical possibilities as opposed to pulse or rhythm, or the susceptibility of exploitation and development of a particular interval or texture. He has the sense to realise that such explorations—they are much more than exercises—are fairly meaningless if obscured by other areas of expression: you learn nothing from them, so he takes pains to keep them untramelled and the rest of his palette neutral. Each aspect thus determines its own parameters of sound, style and structure, resulting in an extremely varied range of expression, which has nothing to do with eclecticism. If you are a serious, conscientious, self-effacing composer, and none is more so than Eliasson, rather than an ego-tripper, the musical consideration will dominate to produce apparently unconnected works, each undertaking to resolve new problems, with the material, choice and number of instruments most appropriate to them, not him.

All of this has given Eliasson's music considerable fluency in the handling of material and precision in the application of basic elements to musical ideas, which he exploits in the larger works such as the First Symphony: there is indeed a direct correlation between the size and scoring of works with the proliferation of their complexities, but even in big scores where the minutiae of the working of an idea may take place over a microscopically short span—in a bar or less, say—the overall precept is always a simple one, and it is always clearly articulated, never ambiguous. While the small works are concerned with a single element, the large ones employ a number of these, different, elements complementarally, to prosecute a single argument.

Eliasson's catalogue is extensive, including contributions to almost every genre, from opera and orchestral pieces to songs, and embracing a major body of chamber and instrumental works of considerable range, diversity and importance. Styles vary considerably, likewise accessibility, seriousness of intent less so. The feeling that there is sometimes a dimension missing is built into the system, but occurs surprisingly seldom, and the emotional impact, which seems to be self-generating, is often very real, though unintended as such by the composer. The rather fanciful and sometimes simplistic philosophical notions with which he surrounds his works are seldom more than appendages to the score he describes, their influence stopping shortly after the programme book. Musically he's all integrity: where there's a conflict of interest between the music and the flummery, the music always wins.

—Giles Easterbrook

EMMERSON, Simon (Thomas). British/English. Born in Wolverhampton, Midlands, 15 September 1950. Educated at Clare College, Cambridge, 1968–72, B.A. in natural sciences and music education; postgraduate studentship in electronic music, City University, London, 1974–6, Ph.D., 1982. Teacher, Shephalbury School, Stevenage, 1972–4; composer in residence, Digswell Arts Trust, Welwyn Garden City, Hertfordshire, 1972–7; visiting lecturer, 1976–8, lecturer in music, 1978–87, and senior lecturer in music, since 1987, City University, London; founder/secretary, from 1979, later treasurer and chairman, Electro-Acoustic Music Association of Great Britain; honorary visiting fellow, Massachusetts Institute of Technology media laboratory, Cambridge, 1987. Recipient: shared 1st prize (for *Time Past IV*), Bourges Electro-acoustic Awards, 1985. Mailing address: 15 Holligrave Road, Bromley, Kent BR1 3PJ, England.

Publisher: self.

Chamber/instrumental (with or without electronics):

Piano Piece I (prepared piano; or piano with electronics) 1971; first performed Cambridge, 11 March 1971.
Piano Piece II (piano with electronics) 1971, revised 1972; first performed Cambridge, 26 November 1971.
Digswell Tapes II (percussion with electronics) 1973; first performed London, 16 November 1973.
Piano Piece III (piano, electronics—2 performers) 1974–5; first performed Welwyn Garden City, Hertfordshire, 28 February 1975.
Spirit of '76 (flute with electronics) 1976; first performed London, 3 October 1976.
Variations (tuba) 1976; broadcast BBC Radio 3, 14 June 1978; first concert performance London, 19 November 1978.
But the Harp Never Plays . . . (tin whistle or flute, amplified piano) 1977; first performed Welwyn Garden City, Hertfordshire, 7 May 1977.
Chimera (bass trombone, 12 strings, tape) 1980; first performed London, 7 October 1980.
Time Past I (double bass, electronics) 1981; first performed London, 31 October 1981.
Time Past II (flute, cello, piano, tape, electronics) 1982; first performed London, 11 December 1982.
Piano Piece IV (piano, tape) 1985; first performed Stockton-on-Tees, Teeside, 8 June 1985.
Windbreak (trumpet, tape) 1985; first performed Edinburgh, 7 November 1985.
Reflections (trumpet, cello, soprano saxophone, percussion, piano, electronics) 1987–8; first performed London, 12 February 1988.
Pathways (flute, cello, sitar, tablas, keyboard, electronics) 1988–9; first performed London, 30 April 1989.
Shades (of Night and Day) (piano, electronics) 1989; first performed Norwich, 5 February 1990.

Vocal/choral (with or without electronics):

Shakespeare Fragments (soprano, flute, tuba, piano, electronics) 1978; first performed Birmingham, 6 May 1979.
Ophelia's Dream I (soprano, mezzo-soprano, tenor, bass, electronics) 1978; first performed London, 17 December 1978.
Ophelia's Dream II (2 sopranos, mezzo-soprano, tenor, baritone, bass, electronics) 1979; first performed London, 9 October 1979. Recorded Hyperion A66060.
Time Past IV (soprano, tape) 1984; first performed Tarragona, Spain, 4 July 1984.
Recollections (tenor, tape) 1985–6; first performed London, 20 January 1986.
Songs from Time Regained (soprano, ensemble, electronics) 1988; first performed London, 15 November 1988.
Sentences (soprano, electronics; Shakespeare, Thoreau, Whitman) 1990–1.

Other/electronic):

Digswell Tapes I (short wave radio, electronics) 1973; first performed Birmingham, 4 June 1976.
Time Past III (electro-acoustic tape) 1983–4; first performed London, 16 December 1984.

PUBLICATIONS

By Emmerson: "Stockhausen's *Mikrophonie II*", in *Contact*, Autumn 1975; "Ring Modulation and Structure", in *Contact*, Summer 1977; "Stockhausen's *Stimmung*", in *Contact*, Autumn 1979; "Stockhausen's *Mikrophonie I*" in *Contact*, Summer 1981; "Electro-Acoustic Music", in Spence and Swayne, *How Music Works*, London, 1981; "The Relation of Language to Materials", also introduction and editor, *The Language of Electroacoustic Music*, London, 1986; "Composing Strategies and Pedagogy", in *Contemporary Music Review*, 3(1), 1989; "Live Electronic Music in Britain: Three Case Studies", in *Contemporary Music Review*, 1990.

Simon Emmerson comments:

My work aims to mediate between harmonies and harmonic fields (often quite consonant) and the new timbral possibilities opened up by electronics and computers. Most of my works combine live performers and tape or live electronic systems and the "natural theatre" that this interaction involves (I am not interested in "music theatre" as it is commonly understood). Music may be seen as one of the great humanisers of technology, and I tend to have little sympathy with musical approaches that do not allow this expression much play. I am optimistic about the future of "art" music only paradoxically if it will cease to see itself in this way and become part of a more open field of musical possibilities of all sorts. Technology may—if used properly—increase this possibility.

* * *

After entering Clare College, Cambridge, in 1968 to study natural sciences (he was taking courses in physics, chemistry, crystallography and the history and philosophy of science), Simon Emmerson soon found that he was spending most of his time with musicians, composing, performing and discussing the most recent developments—most especially with Roger Smalley and Tim Souster at King's College, whose live electronic ensemble Intermodulation was being established at the time, and for which Emmerson worked as technical assistant for several concerts. While being prevented from changing to the music degree course, Emmerson switched to the education department, completing his degree and gaining a teaching certificate in physics and music.

He went on to teach both subjects at secondary school level for two years, meanwhile becoming composer in residence at the Digswell Arts Trust in Welwyn Garden City, where he was responsible for presentations, concerts and compositions with performers, sculptors, painters and other artists in the community. In 1974, he resigned his teaching post to take up the first Worshipful Company of Musicians Studentship in Electronic Music at City University, London, where he subsequently joined the staff to establish and direct the Electro-acoustic Music Studio. At City he also gained a doctorate with a thesis on "Analysis and the Composition of Electroacoustic Music".

All but one of his works have involved electronics in one form or another, either as live electronic manipulation or tape. He first came to attention in 1976 with a work for flute and "accelerating tape delay system", *Spirit of '76*, written for the American flute player Kathryn Lukas in the Bicentennial year. In 1979, his work *Ophelia's Dream II*, commissioned by the British vocal ensemble Singcircle, exploited to the full the vocal, dramatic and electro-acoustic potential of the ensemble, tracing out a drama of disintegration with a haunting urgency.

Emmerson's encounter around 1980 with the writings of Marcel Proust led to a series of works with the collective title "Time Past", which sought to examine a variety of aspects of memory and its relationship to music. *Time Past I* for double bass and tape uses a vast tape delay system (similar to that employed in Stockhausen's *Solo*) built by the West Square Electronic Ensemble who commissioned the work for the double bassist Barry Guy. *Time Past II* for instruments, electronics and tape, and *Time Past III* for tape alone followed, both based on the ideas of the writer Philip Oxman on the relationship of *drone* to *events* and *memory*. The series culminated in *Time Past IV* for soprano and tape, commissioned by Jane Manning and based on Shakespeare's Sonnet XXX, "When to the sessions of sweet silent thought/I summon up remembrance of things past . . . ", which won first prize at the Bourges International Electro-acoustic Awards in 1985, praised for its skill, concision and sensitivity.

In the second half of the 1980s, Emmerson's works have included commissions for a number of soloists and ensembles, always combining vocal or instrumental sound with electronic procedures. In 1988–9 he worked with and composed a work for the Euroasian ensemble Shiva Nova. *Pathways* for flute, cello, tabla, sitar, keyboard and electronics seeks to link Indian and European traditions through electronic means.

Emmerson's music always stresses the performer, seeking to establish communication with the audience through human gesture extended and expanded through electro-acoustic means.

—Christiane ten Hoopen

ENGLUND, (Sven) Einar. Finnish. Born in Gotland, Sweden, 17 June 1916. Educated at Sibelius Academy, Helsinki (piano under Martti Paavola, composition under Bengt Carlson, orchestration under Leo Funtek), diploma 1941; further study at Berkshire Music Center, Tanglewood, Massachusetts (under Aaron Copland), 1949. Married Siren Smolander, 3 October 1958, 1 son; 1 son and 2 daughters by previous marriage. Music critic, *Hufvudstadsbladet*, Helsinki, 1956–76; lecturer/senior lecturer in composition and music theory, 1957–81, and honorary professorship, 1976, Sibelius Academy, Helsinki; concert pianist. Recipient: member, Royal Academy of Music, Sweden, 1976; honorary member, German-Scandinavian Music Society, Germany, 1987. Mailing address: Lallukan Taiteilijakoti, Apollogatan 13A 48, SF-0100 Helsinki 10, Finland.

Publisher: Edition Fazer.

Symphonies/orchestral:

Symphony No 1: The War Symphony 1946; first performed Helsinki, 17 January 1947. Recorded Finnlevy SFX 34; Finlandia FA 304.

Epinikia (symphonic poem) 1947; first performed Helsinki, 2 July 1947. Recorded Finnlevy SFX 34.

Symphony No 2: The Blackbird Symphony 1947; first performed Helsinki 8 October 1948. Recorded Finlandia FA 304; Finnlevy SFX 34.

The Wall of China (concert suite from music to Max Frisch's play) 1949; first performed Helsinki, 21 October 1949.

Valsuralia (concert suite from music to Chekhov's *The Cherry Orchard*) 1951; first performed Helsinki, 7 February 1951.

Four Dance Impressions 1954; first performed Helsinki, 16 February 1954.

Valkoinen peura/The White Hart (concert suite from film music) 1954; first performed Helsinki, 14 March 1955.

Concerto for Cello and Orchestra 1954; first performed Helsinki, 17 May 1955.

Concerto No 1 for Piano and Orchestra 1955; first performed 2 March 1956. Recorded EMI 7491052 CD; Fennica SS7; SALP 2.

Odysseus (concert suite from the ballet) 1959; first performed Helsinki, 18 November 1959.

Symphony No 3 1969–71; first performed Helsinki, 12 May 1972.

Concerto No 2 for Piano and Orchestra 1974; first performed Helsinki, 4 February 1975.

Symphony No 4: The Nostalgic (chamber symphony for strings and percussion) 1976; first performed Helsinki, 26 October 1976. Recorded Finlandia FA 329.

Symphony No 5: Fennica 1977; first performed Helsinki, 6 December 1977. Recorded URALP 101.

Concerto for Violin and Orchestra 1981; first performed Tampere, 26 March 1982. Recorded FACD 343.
Serenade for Strings 1983; first performed Kaustinen, 15 February 1984. Recorded FUGA 3054.
Concerto for Flute and Orchestra 1985; first performed Helsinki, 16 September 1986. Recorded FACD 385.
Lahti-fanfaari (brass) 1986; first performed Lahti, 28 August 1986.
Symphony No 6 (choir, orchestra; Heraclitus, Saarikosi) 1986; first performed Helsinki, 12 March 1986.
Juhlasoitto 1917 / Ceremonial Music (fanfare for symphony orchestra) 1986; first performed Turku, 12 November 1987.
Overture: Odeion 1987; first performed Mikkeli, 18 January 1988.
Symphony No 7 1988; first performed Tampere, 11 January 1991.
Ciacona: Hommage à Sibelius 1990; first performed Helsinki, 13 September 1990.

Chamber / instrumental:

Humoresque (piano) 1936; first performed Helsinki, 1938. Recorded BIS 277 CD.
Quintet (piano, strings) 1941; first performed Helsinki, 1941.
Introduzione e Toccata (piano) 1950; first performed Helsinki, 29 November 1950. Recorded BIS CD 277.
Sonatina in D (piano) 1966; first performed Helsinki, 1968. Recorded BIS CD 277.
Introduzione e Capriccio (violin, piano) 1970; first performed Helsinki, 17 September 1973. Recorded RCA PL 40058.
Passacaglia (organ) 1971; first performed Helsinki, 9 February 1973. Recorded FA 308; Teldec 66.21100.
Panorama (trombone) 1976.
Marcia Funebre (organ) 1976; first performed Helsinki, 1 July 1976.
Divertimento Upsaliensis (wind quintet, string quintet, piano) 1978; first performed Uppsala, 9 December 1979.
Sonata No 1 (piano) 1978; first performed Reykjavik, Iceland, 21 October 1978. Recorded BIS CD 277.
Sonata (violin, piano) 1979; first performed Helsinki, 5 May 1980. Recorded ODE 726–2.
Arioso Interrotto (violin) 1979; first performed Helsinki, 1980. Recorded SALP 1.
Serenata elegiaco (violin) 1979.
De Profundis (14 brass) 1980; first performed Lieksa, 1980.
Concerto for Twelve Cellos 1980–1; first performed Helsinki, 3 April 1981. Recorded FACD 376.
Sonata (cello, piano) 1982; first performed Helsinki, 4 September 1982. Recorded FACD 376.
Trio (piano, violin, cello) 1982; first performed Kuhmo, 17 July 1983. Recorded FACD 364.
Pavane (violin, piano) 1983; first performed Espoo, 1983.
Pavane e Toccata (piano) 1983; first performed Helsinki, 11 November 1983. Recorded BIS CD 277.
Sonatina No 2: The Parisian 1984; first performed Helsinki, 11 October 1987.
String Quartet 1985; first performed Jyvaskyla, 27 June 1986.
Preludium & Fughetta (piano) 1985.
Suite: Viimeinen saari / The Last Island (cello) 1986; broadcast Finnish Television, 26 May 1987; first concert performance Naantali, 27 June 1987. Recorded FACD 376.

Vocal / choral:

Tistel och Lavendel (songs; Aner) 1964. Recorded FL 7004.
Chaconne (mixed choir, optional trombone, double bass) 1969; first performed Helsinki, 1969.
Hymnus Sepulcralis (unaccompanied mixed choir; Prudentius) 1975; first performed London, 27 September 1975. Recorded SFX 52.
Med herrarna i hagen (unaccompanied women's choir; folk song) 1977. Recorded LYR LP 7801.
Rukkaset (unaccompanied women's choir; folk song) 1977. Recorded LYR LP 7801.
Valvokaa! / Watch! (unaccompanied mixed choir) 1980; first performed Helsinki, 16 November 1980. Recorded Finlandia FA 342.
Merkkituli / The Traffic Light (unaccompanied male choir; Lauri) 1983; first performed Helsinki, 14 April 1984.
Kanteletar-sarja (unaccompanied women's choir; folklore from *Kanteletar*) 1984; first performed Joensuu, 18 June 1985. Recorded LYR LP 8602.
Sokerileipuri / The Sugar Baker (voice, instruments). Recorded EMI 5E062-34960.
Issin tissin (voices, instruments). Recorded EMI 5E062-34960.
Songs to the Poems of Viola Renvall, Benedict Zilliacus and Gunvor Aner (voice, piano). Recorded Finnlevy 7004.

Other:

Sinuhe (ballet; piano) 1953; first performed Helsinki, 1953; orchestrated 1965.
Odysseus (ballet; orchestra) 1959; first performed United States, 1959.
Musica I: Ole, dole, doff / Piiri pieni pyorii (instrumental arrangements for teaching purposes) 1965.
Tie musiikkiin / The Road the Music (educational) 1967.
Vi gor musik / Let's Make Music (educational) 1970.

PUBLICATIONS

On Englund: Paavo Heininen, "EE", in *Musiiki*, 4, 1984; Mikko Heinio, "EE: Modernist and Traditionalist", in *Finnish Music Quarterly*, 1986; Harri Wesmann, "Composer's Profile: EE", in *Nordic Sounds*, 12, 1986.

* * *

For other Finnish composers, the importance of Einar Englund's compositions is the degree to which he assimilated many of the styles of Prokofiev and Shostakovich, together with the neo-classical rhythms and themes of Stravinsky. Englund was also a jazz-pianist, which perhaps assisted him in securing both a multifaceted idiom and a solid developmental technique. Further neo-classical tendencies are heard in Englund's treatment of counterpoint, traditional structures and even more of tonality—which accounts for his refusal to become involved with serialism. But he was no romantic nationalist. Rather than continue in the Sibelian tradition, Englund rejected any Finnish connection with his works, placing himself very firmly in the sometimes unpopular "international" camp.

Within three years of the end of the war, Englund produced his first two symphonies, which placed him to the fore in contemporary Finnish composition. The First, "War" Symphony, was proclaimed as "impressive an account of war as Shostakovich's *Leningrad*". Although not programmatic, the majority of the symphony evokes the pains of a lengthy campaign, with intermittent glimpses of hope during fanfare passages. It is a brooding work, where the first movement's second theme is similar to that of Shostakovich's Fifth Symphony of 1937. Englund's Second Symphony subtitled "The Blackbird" because of the birdsong link-passage between the last two movements, highlights the dichotomy between pastoral beauty and man's folly at betraying nature. This contrast provided enough material for a concentration upon the variety of possible orchestral colour. These two symphonies, together with the tone poem *Epinikia* (written for the London Olympics), were the most nationally influential of Englund's compositions before he visited Tanglewood in 1949 to study under Copland.

In the *Four Dance Impressions*, the Cello Concerto and the First Piano Concerto, Englund's mid-1950s style incorporated ideas from Bartók's late works (especially Bartók's Third Piano Concerto) and the instrument-doubling of Shostakovich. Typical of these is the blatantly tonal Piano Concerto where non-resolving added-notes and chromaticism act merely as foils against pedal-points, and where motives are based around perfect fourths (which become augmented fourths only when forming octatonic melodies). Surprisingly, the first movement's cadenza is mainly a single line. After a lyrical slow movement reminiscent of Shostakovich and Khachaturian, the fugal finale is again based on perfect fourths, which climax with the soloist Regeresquely blazoning major triads against the orchestra's rhythmic canons. Generally a lightweight but well-crafted composition, it produced a halt in Englund's composing activities (apart from a one-act ballet *Odysseus* and some background and educational music). While he patiently lived through the Darmstadt movement's new hegenomy in Finland, Englund busied himself as teacher and critic.

23 years after his Second Symphony, Englund produced a Third. Here, Englund preserves his characteristic use of motives, form-generating bass-lines, fugues and martial overtones, while being less obviously indebted to Russian music (apart from the thematic lines of Shostakovich). From this work onwards, Englund's slow movements are based on even longer-lined melodies, although the structure of many later compositions are still often new. While his wind-less Fourth Symphony is much like a suite, and the one-movement Fifth Symphony is constructed more around rhythmic than pitch relationships, in the Sixth Symphony ("Aphorisms") Englund takes texts from Heraclitus and sets them for chorus and orchestra without reference to their meaning. Although there has been little stylistic evolution in Englund's post-1970 works, his *Concerto for Twelve Cellos* demonstrates his mastery of the combination of the suite and concertante forms.

—Malcolm J. Hill

ERB, Donald (James). American. Born in Youngstown, Ohio, 17 January 1927. Educated at Kent State University, Ohio, 1947–50, B.Sc. in liberal arts; Cleveland Institute of Music, Ohio, (under Marcel Dick), 1950–2, M.Mus., 1953; further study in Paris (under Nadia Boulanger), 1953; Indiana University, Bloomington, 1961–2, 1963–4 (composition under Bernard Heiden), D.Mus. Served in the United States Navy. Married Lucille I. Hyman, 10 June 1950; 3 daughters and 1 son. Jazz trumpeter; composer in residence and Kulas Professor, later distinguished professor, joint music program, Cleveland Institute and Case Western Reserve University, Cleveland, 1953–61, 1966–81, and since 1987; visiting professor, Roosevelt University, Chicago, Illinois, Summer 1966; Rockefeller Foundation composer in residence, Dallas Symphony, 1968–9; professor of composition, Indiana University, Bloomington, 1975–6, 1984–7; visiting professor, California State University, Los Angeles, Spring 1977; chair, composer-librettist panel, National Endowment for the Arts, 1977–9; visiting professor, Peabody Conservatory, Baltimore, Maryland, Autumn 1979; Algur H. Meadows Professor of Composition, Southern Methodist University, Dallas, Texas, 1981–4; visiting professor, University of Melbourne, Australia, Spring 1984. Recipient: Guggenheim Fellowship, 1965–6; National Council of the Arts Fellowship, 1967–8; Naumburg Recording Award, 1974; National Endowment for the Arts Award, 1980, 1984; American Academy and Institute of Arts and Letters Award, 1985. Mailing address: 4073 Bluestone Road, Cleveland Heights, Ohio 44121, U.S.A.

Publisher: Merion Music/Theodore Presser.

Symphonies/orchestral:

Chamber Concerto (piano, strings) 1958.
Bakersfield Pieces (trumpet, percussion, piano, strings) 1962; first performed Bakersfield, California, 1963.
Compendium (band) 1962.
Symphony of Overtures 1964; first performed Seattle, Washington, 1964. Recorded Turnabout TV S34433.
Bulgarian Bop (jazz band) 1965; first performed Sacramento, California, 1966.
Reticulation (symphonic band) 1965; first performed Bowling Green, Ohio, 1965.
Concert Piece No 1 (alto saxophone, band) 1966; first performed Cleveland, Ohio, 1966.
Stargazing (symphonic band. tape) 1966; first performed Cleveland, Ohio, 1966.
Concerto for Solo Percussionist and Orchestra 1966; first performed Detroit, Michigan, 1966. Recorded Turnabout TV S34433.
Christmasmusic 1967; first performed Cleveland, Ohio, 1967. Recorded Louisville LS 772.
The Seventh Trumpet 1969; first performed Dallas, Texas, 1969. Recorded Turnabout TV S34433.
Klangfarbenfunk I (rock band, orchestra, tape) 1970; first performed Detroit, Michigan, 1970.
The Purple-Roofed Ethical Suicide Parlor (winds, tape) 1972; first performed Atlanta, Georgia, 1972.
Autumnmusic (orchestra, tape) 1973; first performed New Haven, Connecticut, 1973. Recorded Louisville LS 772.
Treasures of the Snow 1973; first performed Newark, New Jersey, 1974.
Music for a Festive Occasion (orchestra, electronics) 1976; first performed Cleveland, Ohio, 1976.
Concerto for Trombone and Orchestra 1976; first performed St Louis, Missouri, 1976. Recorded Louisville Orchestra LS 772.
Concerto for Cello and Orchestra 1976; first performed Rochester, New York, 1976.
Concerto for Keyboards and Orchestra 1978; first performed Akron, Ohio, 1981.
Cenotaph for E.V. (symphonic band) 1979; first performed Ann Arbor, Michigan, 1980.
Concerto for Trumpet and Orchestra 1980; first performed Baltimore, Maryland, 1981.
Sonneries for Orchestra 1981; first performed Rochester, New York, 1982.
Prismatic Variations 1983; first performed St Louis, Missouri, 1984. Recorded Nonesuch Records 79118-1 F.

Concerto for Clarinet and Orchestra 1984; first performed London, 1985.
Concerto for Contrabassoon and Orchestra 1984; first performed Houston, Texas, 1985. Recorded Leonarda Records.
The Dreamtime 1984; first performed Boston, 1985.
Concerto for Orchestra 1985; first performed Atlanta, Georgia, 1985.
Concerto for Brass and Orchestra 1986; first performed Chicago, 1987.
Solstice 1988; first performed Cleveland, Ohio, 1988.
Symphony for Winds 1989; first performed Chicago, 1990.

Chamber/instrumental:

Correlations (piano) 1958.
Dialogue (violin, piano) 1958.
Music for Brass Choir 1960.
Music for Violin and Piano 1960.
String Quartet No 1 1960.
Sonneries (brass) 1961.
Concertante (harpsichord, strings) 1962.
Dance Pieces (trumpet, piano, percussion, violin) 1962.
Hexagon (flute, alto saxophone, trumpet, trombone, piano, cello) 1962.
Quartet (flute, oboe, alto saxophone, double bass) 1962.
Four (percussion) 1963.
Sonata (harpsichord, string quartet) 1963. Recorded CRI 183.
VII Miscellaneous (flute, double bass) 1964.
Antipodes (string quartet, 4 percussion) 1965.
Phantasma (flute, oboe, harpsichord, double bass) 1965. Recorded Opus One No 1.
Andante (flute/piccolo/alto flute) 1966.
Diversion for Two (trumpet, percussion) 1966. Recorded Opus One No 1.
String Trio (violin, cello, electric guitar) 1966. Recorded Opus No 1.
Summer Music (piano) 1966.
Reconnaissance (violin, double bass, electronics) 1967; first performed Cleveland, Ohio, 1967. Recorded Nonesuch H71223.
In No Strange Land (trombone, double bass, tape) 1968; first performed San Diego, California, 1968. Recorded Nonesuch H 71223.
Three Pieces (brass quintet, piano) 1968; first performed River Falls, Wisconsin, 1968. Recorded CRI SD 323.
Trio for Two (alto flute/percussion, double bass) 1968; first performed Los Angeles, 1968. Recorded Finnadar SR 9015; Ars Nova/Ars Antiqua AN 1008.
Basspiece (double bass, 4-track tape) 1969; first performed Cleveland, Ohio, 1970. Recorded Desto DC7128.
Music for Mother Bear (alto flute) 1970.
And Then, Toward the End (trombone, 4-track tape) 1971.
Fanfare (3 trumpets, 2 horns, 2 trombones, tuba, timpani, percussion) 1971.
Z milosci do Warszawy/For Warsaw with Love (clarinet, trombone, piano, cello, tape) 1971; first performed Warsaw, 1972.
Harold's Trip to the Sky (viola, piano, percussion) 1972; first performed Cleveland, Ohio, 1974. Recorded Crystal S531.
The Towers of Silence (electronic quartet) 1974; first performed DeKalb, Illinois, 1975.
Quintet (violin, cello, flute, clarinet, piano/electric piano) 1976; first performed Brunswick, Maine, 1976. Recorded Redwood ES 28.
Mirage (flute, double bass, trumpet, trombone, percussion, electric piano, electric harpsichord, electric organ) 1977; first performed Las Vegas, Nevada, 1977.
Trio (violin, percussion, keyboards) 1977; first performed Cleveland, Ohio, 1977. Recorded Crystal S505.
The Hawk (jazz ensemble) 1979; first performed Kansas City, 1980.
Nightmusic II (piano) 1979.
Nebbiolina (organ, 8 bell ringers) 1980; first performed Minneapolis, Minnesota, 1980.
Sonata (clarinet, percussion) 1980; first performed Boston, 1980.
Déjà vu (double bass) 1981.
Three Pieces (harp, percussion) 1981; first performed Nashville, Tennessee, 1983.
Hair of the Wolf—full Moon (string quartet) 1981.
The Last Quintet (flute, oboe, clarinet, horn, bassoon) 1982; first performed Nashville, Tennessee, 1983. Recorded Redwood ES 28.
The St Valentine's Day Brass Quintet 1982; first performed Nashville, Tennessee, 1983. Recorded Pantheon PFN2241.
Aura (string quintet) 1982; first performed Nashville, Tennessee, 1983.
The Devil's Quickstep (flute, clarinet, violin, cello, percussion, keyboards, harp) 1982; first performed Dallas, Texas, 1982. Recorded Spectrum SR 195.
Fantasy for Cellist and Friends (cello, 2–4 harmonicas, 4–8 percussion) 1983; first performed New York City, 1982.
Rainbow Snake (trombone, percussion, keyboards, tape) 1984; first performed Nashville, Tennessee, 1985.
Views of Space and Time (violin, keyboards, harp, percussion, amplification) 1987; first performed Cleveland, Ohio, 1987.
Three Poems (violin, piano) 1988; first performed Washington, D.C., 1988.
Watchman Fantasy (amplified piano, digital delay, synthesizer) 1989; first performed Oberlin, Ohio, 1990.
String Quartet No 2 1989; first performed New York City, 1990.

Vocal/choral:

Cummings Cycle (chorus, orchestra) 1963.
Fallout (chorus, narrator, string quartet, piano) 1964.
Kyrie (chorus, piano, percussion, tape) 1965. Recorded Ars Nova/Ars Antiqua AN 1008.
N 1965 (chorus, viola, cello, double bass, piano) 1965.
God Love You Now (chorus, speaker, harmonica, hand percussion) 1971.
New England's Prospect (chorus, orchestra) 1974; first performed Cincinnati, Ohio, 1974.

Other:

Fission (alto saxophone, piano, tape, dancers, lighting) 1968.
Souvenir (dancers, lighting, electronic sounds, musicians) 1970; first performed Oberlin, Ohio, 1970.

PUBLICATIONS

By Erb: "Orchestration", in *Encyclopaedia Britannica*, 1991.

On Erb: David Cope, in *New Directions in Music*, Boston, 1971, 1976, 1981, 1989; R. Jackson, "DE", in *BMI: The Many Worlds of Music*, 1971; Reimer and Evans, in *The Experience of Music*, Boston, 1972; William Thompson, in *Music for Listeners*, Boston, 1978; D. Felder, "Nightmusic II", in *Piano Quarterly*, 107, 1979, and "Interview with DE", in *Composer*, 10, 1980; John Suess, "The Solo Concerti of DE", in *Studies in the Schoenbergian Movement in Vienna and the United States*, 1990.

* * *

Donald Erb has never considered himself part of any particular "school" of composition. Over the past three decades his musical language has maintained a remarkable consistency: while different American compositional trends have waxed and waned, Erb has been constant of purpose.

The most immediately apparent aspect of Erb's music is its concern for tone colours and textures. His music extensively calls for performance techniques which are not standard for most classical musicians; these are so-called "extended techniques". He also requires performers to double on additional instruments to which they are unaccustomed, such as harmonicas and crystal glasses. This demand for non-standard instruments reached its apogee in the *Prismatic Variations* for orchestra of 1983, in which a large number of extra musicians (usually a children's orchestra) surround the audience, playing small bells and soda pop bottles.

Erb's handling of large-ensemble textures as solitary masses of sound resembles, perhaps more than any other American composer, the textural school of composition favoured by Eastern European composers such as Ligeti, Penderecki and Xenakis in the 1960s. *The Seventh Trumpet*, a piece which has received over 200 orchestral performances (an unheard-of amount for a contemporary American composer), is perhaps Erb's closest piece to this type of compositional thinking. An earlier example of this style of writing may be seen in the Percussion Concerto; in this piece, as in *The Seventh Trumpet*, Erb works with textural gestures as "motives" instead of rhythmic/melodic ideas. For instance, the work begins with a snare drum roll which is then "imitated" by harp and piano tremolos, bowed string tremolos, and wind and brass trills. The second movement treats glissandi in a similar manner.

In both of these works, as well as in subsequent orchestral compositions, Erb frequently uses a notation which allows for spontaneous moment-to-moment activity while maintaining control over the general texture or phrase. Erb does not consider this notion "indeterminate" or "aleatoric": he knows the sounds that he wants to achieve and his notation is perfectly adequate for his needs. Nevertheless, the technique does bear similarities to the "controlled aleatoricism" of Lutoslawski, Penderecki and Druckman.

Erb's own experience as a jazz trumpeter has informed his brass writing, which features typical jazz pitch inflections (such as "rips" and "smears") and facility with all types of mutes. This is demonstrated in works such as *Sonneries* for brass, and *Diversion for Two* for trumpet and percussion. The Trombone Concerto has several direct evocations of jazz, including long, elegant phrases for the soloist performed with a vibrato-rich tone that is reminiscent of Tommy Dorsey; the use of cymbals played with brushes to "keep time" in the first movement; and a knowledgeable handling of a large variety of mutes in the second movement.

Erb's interest in tone colour does not preclude a concern for pitch and rhythm. Many of his pieces before and after the late 1960s develop melodic/rhythmic motives in a fairly straightforward manner, not based upon any pre-compositional systems, but rather relying on intuitive decisions instead.

Erb has composed many works for live performers and tape; by the mid-1960s, he was established in the United States as one of the most important American composers for this genre (along with Morton Subotnick and Mario Davidovsky). The better-known works for this medium include *In No Strange Land* for trombone, double bass and tape; *Basspiece* for double bass and tape; and *Autumnmusic* for orchestra and tape. *Reconnaissance* was an international historical landmark for its incorporation of Moog synthesizers into live, determinately notated chamber music; although many improvisatory groups used synthesizers, only John Eaton had previously explored the use of synthesizers in this context.

Erb's works frequently exhibit multi-movement structures which are emotionally and dramatically analogous to traditional tonal multi-movement forms such as symphony (*Symphony of Overtures*) and the concerto (among his many orchestral concertos, the Trombone Concerto is perhaps his most dramatic contemporary reading of the 19th-century vehicle). Erb's broad textural gestures, his clear sense of motivic development, and the emotional sweep of his large-scale forms which often parallel the emotional rhetoric of Romantic works (but in a thoroughly contemporary fashion), are all factors in the popularity of his work among both musicians and audiences.

—Christian Hertzog

ERÖD, Ivan. Austrian. Born in Budapest, Hungary, 2 January 1936; emigrated to Austria after Hungarian revolution, 1956. Educated at secondary school, Budapest, 1946–54; Academy of Music, Budapest (piano under Pál Kadosa; composition under Ferenc Szabó, 1951–6; Academy of Music and Dramatic Art, Vienna (piano with Richard Hauser; composition under Karl Schiske; twelve-tone seminar under Hanns Jelinek), 1957–61, diploma with distinction in piano and composition; also summer schools, Darmstadt (piano with Eduard Steuermann; composition with Luigi Nono); and Siena (piano with Guido Agosti). Married Marie-Luce Guy, April 1969; 3 sons and 2 daughters. Solo coach, Vienna State Opera, 1962–4; solo (later head) coach, Festival of Vienna, 1962–8; professor, 1967–71, assistant professor, 1971–5, and full professor, 1975–89, University (Hochsschule) of Music and Performing Arts, Graz; professor, University (Hochsschule) of Music, Vienna, since 1989; concert pianist; member of "die reihe" ensemble; visiting lecturer, Germany, Italy, Hungary, U.S.A., Brazil. Recipient: Austrian Rome Prize, 1961; Bosendorfer Prize, Vienna, 1961; Busoni Prize, Bolzano (piano), 1962; composition prize, Central Savings Bank, Vienna Municipality, 1964; Austrian State Prize for opera composition, 1970; composition prize, Theodor Korner Foundation, 1971; composition prize, City of Vienna, 1974; composition prize, City of Graz, 1978; "Würdigungspreis" for music, Republic of Austria, 1980; Joseph Marx music prize, province of Styria, 1981; composition prize, City of Vienna, 1986. Mailing address: Gumpendorfer Strasse 9/13, A-1060 Vienna, Austria.

Publishers: Doblinger, Dorotheergasse 10, 1011 Vienna, Austria; Boosey & Hawkes; Edition Modern, Munich; Theaterverlag Eirich, Vienna.

Symphonies/orchestral:

Symphony in C (2 movements only) 1948.
Dorottya-Ouverture (ballet suite) 1956.

Sonata No 1 Op 5 1957; first performed Innsbruck, 11 May 1958.
Three Movements Op 7 (cello, orchestra) 1958; first performed Vienna, 20 June 1958.
Four Pieces Op 6a (version of Op 6 for string quartet) 1965.
Violin Concerto Op 15 1973; first performed Graz, 14 March 1973.
Sonata No 2 Op 16 1974; first performed Kapfenberg, 10 May 1974.
Piano Concerto Op 19 (also version for 2 pianos) 1975; first performed Graz, 17 January 1977.
Divertimento Op 20 (brass orchestra, percussion) 1976; first performed Graz, 19 March 1976. Recorded Musikverlag F. Schulz, Freiburg 48129/30; Crest INC-81-3; da capo 7127 a/b.
Viola Concerto Op 30 (also version for viola, piano) 1979–80; first performed Vienna, 23 May 1980.
Studien Op 33 (string orchestra) 1980; first performed Murzzuschlag, 8 December 1980.
Konzertante Fantasie Op 35 (viola, string orchestra) 1980–1; first performed Bad Harzburg, Germany, 27 June 1981.
Soirées imaginaires Op 38 (large orchestra) 1981; first performed Salzburg, 18 August 1981.
Symphonic Scene: "Hommage à Franz Liszt" Op 46 (large orchestra) 1983–4; first performed Vienna, 28 April 1985.
Réjouissance Op 48 (large orchestra) 1984; first performed Graz, 12 January 1985.
Three Interludes Op 50a (organ, orchestra; movements 2, 4 and 6 of cantata *Das Sein ist ewig*) 1985.
Minnesota Sinfonietta Op 51 1985–6; first performed Minneapolis, Minnesota, 17 July 1986.

Chamber/instrumental:

Variations (for school ensemble; on a Hungarian folk song) 1948.
Piano Works Op 1 1951–6.
Chamber Music Op 2 (string trio; string quartet) 1951–6.
Woodwind Trio Op 4 (oboe, clarinet, basson) 1957, revised 1987; first performed Vienna, 16 May 1957.
Four Pieces Op 6 (string quartet; also version for string orchestra, above) 1957; first performed Vienna, 26 February 1958.
Four Little Piano Pieces Op 8 1959; first performed Alpbach, Summer 1959.
Ricercare ed Aria S.C.H.E. Op 11 (flute, oboe, horn, bass clarinet) 1965; first performed Vienna, 16 February 1966.
Fanfare (brass, percussion) 1969.
Sonata No 1 Op 14 (violin, piano) 1969–70; first performed Vienna, 25 November 1970. Recorded Preiser Records SPR 10043.
String Quartet No 1 Op 18 1974–5; first performed Vienna, 8 December 1975.
Trio (No 1) Op 21 (violin, cello, piano) 1976; first performed Vienna, 25 April 1977.
Capriccio Op 23 (2 flutes, 2 oboes, 2 clarinets, 2 horns, 2 bassoons) 1976–7; first performed Vienna, 13 March 1977.
Hommage à Beethoven Op 24 (rhapsody for cello on a theme of Op 102/1 by Beethoven) 1977; first performed Linz, 23 January 1978.
String Quartet No 2 Op 26 1978; first performed Vienna, 7 March 1980.
Three Pieces Op 27 (violin) 1979; first performed Vienna, 19 April 1979. Recorded Amadeo Polygram 419 071-1.
Enjoying Life Op 29 (trumpet, piano) 1979; first performed Oberschutzen, 13 March 1985.
Canonic Variations Op 31 ("on a very well-known children's song"; string quartet) 1980; first performed Vienna, 12 March 1987.
15 November 1980 B Op 34 (cello, piano) 1980.
Veränderung Op 37 (piano; on a waltz by Diabelli) 1981; first performed Graz, 22 October 1981.
Capriccio 81 Op 41 (4 flutes/3 piccolos/alto flute, 2 harps) 1981; first performed Münster, 11 December 1981.
Trio No 2 Op 42 (violin, cello, piano) 1981–2; first performed Vienna, 19 April 1982.
Serenade: "Kleine sinnliche Abendmusik" Op 45 (string sextet) 1983; first performed Vienna, 19 February 1984.
"Sonata Milanese" Op 47 (bassoon, piano) 1984; first performed Klosterneuburg, 27 February 1985.
Schnappschüsse Op 52 (flute, 2 oboes, 2 clarinets, 2 horns, 2 bassoons) 1986; first performed Murzzuschlag, 2 November 1986.
Quartet Op 54 (violin, viola, cello, piano) 1987; first performed Vienna, 26 May 1988.
Brahms Variations Op 57 (piano) 1989; first performed Vienna, 1990.

Vocal/choral:

Songs and Choruses Op 3 (voice, piano; unaccompanied choir; baritone, orchestra; folk songs, Petofi, Joszef, Ady, Nagy, Kolscey) 1951–6.
Three Twelve-Tone Choruses (unaccompanied mixed choir; Morgenstern) 1958.
Tutto Ho Perduto Op 12 (soprano, violin, Ungaretti) 1966.
Milchzahnlieder Op 17 (soprano/children's choir, chamber orchestra/instrumental ensemble; Bletschacher) 1973; first performed Graz, 13 December 1974.
Two Hungarian Madrigals Op 22 (unaccompanied women's choir; Weores, Illyes) 1976.
Three Poems from Goethe's "Der West-Ostliche Divan" Op 36 (unaccompanied mixed choir) 1976, revised 1981; nos 1 and 2 first performed Graz, 1 June 1984; no 3 first performed Graz, 17 July 1981.
Krokodilslieder Op 28 (baritone, chamber orchestra; Bletschacher) 1979; first performed Alpbach, Tirol, 29 August 1983. Recorded Amadeo-Polygram 419 071 1.
Never Close Your Eyes . . . Op 32 (epithalamion for 3 female voices, bass, piano) 1980.
15 November 1980 A Op 34 (baritone, piano) 1980.
Tao Te King, Nr. 78: Der Mensch tritt ins Leben Op 40 (unaccompanied mixed choir; Lao-Tse, von Strauss) 1981; first performed Innsbruck, 27 June 1982.
Viva La Musica! Op 43 (unaccompanied mixed choir) 1982; first performed Graz, 15 July 1983.
Four Songs Op 44 (deep voice, piano; Celan, after Mandelstam, Esenin) 1983; first performed Graz, 17 February 1986.
Schwarzerde Op 49 (baritone, large orchestra; Mandelstam, Dutli) 1984–5; first performed Graz, 29 September 1985.
Das Sein ist Ewig Op 50 (organ solo, choir, orchestra; Goethe, Hesse) 1985; first performed Oberschutzen, 3 November 1985.
Beim Jungen Wein Op 53 (unaccompanied mixed chorus; Trakl) 1987; first performed Graz, 17 July 1987.
Canti di Ungaretti Op 55 (baritone, flute, clarinet, vibraphone, viola, cello) 1987–8; first performed Hanover, New Hampshire, 14 May 1988.
Vox Lucis Op 56 (baritone, oboe, orchestra) 1989; first performed Graz, 1989.

Opera:

La Doncella, el Marinero y el Estudiante Op 9 (Lorca) 1960; first performed Innsbruck, 25 May 1960.
Die Seidenraupen Op 10 (Bletschacher) 1964–8; first performed Vienna, 20 May 1968.
Orpheus ex Machina Op 25 (Wolkfind) 1977–8; first performed Graz, 14 October 1978.

Other:

Ole, Mein Knecht Op 13 (shadow-play for television; Plavetz) 1970; broadcast 11 October 1970.
Yerma Op 39 (incidental music to play by Lorca; voices, bassoon, guitar, percussion) 1981; first performed Graz, 27 November 1981.

PUBLICATIONS

By Eröd: "Warum komische Oper?", programme note for Vienna Festival, 1968; "Eine neue Operbeim Steirischen Herbst, *Orpheus ex Machina*", in *Österreichische Musikzeitschrift*, 33, 1978; "Bach und Fux in Unterricht und Praxis", Barenreiter, 1985; "Betrachtungen zu meinem Opern *Orpheus ex Machina* und *Die Seidenraupen*", Vienna, 1985; "Komponiern lehren und lernen", in *Österreichische Musikzeitschrift*, 42, 1987.

On Eröd: Kurt Blaukopf, "Stilmittel, Formen und Techniken . . . ", programme note for Vienna Festival, 1968; Walter Szmolyan, *Komponistorische Tendenzen der Einfachheit ...*, Vienna, 1981.

Ivan Eröd comments:

My instincts are, above all, those of a musician. The primary source of all my creative activity is music itself, not some sort of political, ideological or aesthetic programme. My message is not the translation of something else into music; it is immanently musical.

Another characteristic of my work is its lack of ambition to renew musical language. I use existing "words" for what I want to tell and I thereby expect my compositions to have a more immediate impact on the listener. I feel reluctant to explain them.

For me, the quality of handicraft is prior and senior to the originality of style. Certainly, my personality is determined by origin, education and personal preferences. Hungarian tradition, the influence of Viennese classical—and to some degree—20th-century music and even my Jewishness might be heard in my works. Personally, I feel that I give my best in some of my vocal and chamber music.

* * *

Ivan Eröd is one of those Austrian composers who, having started out as a serialist, has since consciously rejected avant-garde aesthetics. For more than two decades, he has allowed traditional elements to find a place in his music, and also those of popular music and jazz. For Eröd, musical language has come to be a means of communication. Intelligibility is of the utmost importance to him, as he once expressed: "When I write music, it is with the intention that it should be heard by the greatest number of people . . . I declare myself on the side of melody and form . . . originality at all costs is the antithesis of communication. Language, and that includes musical language, is a coming to terms."

The typical constructive principles of Eröd's music are, therefore, tonality, motivic relations, accessible form. He once characterized his aesthetic viewpoint as "friendly" towards both interpreters and listeners. For a contemporary composer, Eröd has enjoyed unusual popularity.

Eröd's compositional energies have been directed mainly to vocal and chamber music, and a number of concertos; he has shown much less interest in symphonic writing. The word has exerted an almost magical fascination on him, stimulating some of his most congenial works. The incorporation of textual material lends the music an almost declamatory quality; nonetheless, his melodic lines are never crudely welded to his text, but form autonomous shapes. This is true of his great opera *Die Seidenraupen* and of *Orpheus ex Machina* as well as of his songs, choral works and cantatas. His cosmopolitanism is clearly manifested in his choice of librettists, which extends from Richard Bletschacher to Osip Mandelstam, from Goethe to Giuseppe Ungaretti, from Hermann Hesse to Lao-Tse. In the case of *Vox Lucis*, texts appear in *six* languages (German, Hungarian, French, English, Italian and Russian), deployed in accordance with their specific sound values.

Eröd's introduction to music was via Hungarian folk song. Even though he turned to dodecaphony before he emigrated to Austria, the influence of his Viennese teachers strengthened his commitment to serial structures. *Die Seidenraupen* marked the turning point in his break with this aesthetic. With it, he established a kind of "dodecaphonic tonality"; Eröd uses rows in such a way that they they result in tonal complexes and progressions. In addition, allusions to Greek vocal music and Byzantine hymns suggested a pluralism that, 20 years later, would have been called "postmodern" (and, indeed, it anticipates this aesthetic).

An emphasis on entertainment, in a tonal idiom, and using stylistic elements from a broad range of popular music all characterize Eröd's next creative period, most noticeably in the chamber music and concertos. Even so, Eröd's work remains deeply serious and structured, simultaneously metaphysical and humanistic. His deeply held convictions brought a profound spiritualization to the cantata *Das Sein ist Ewig*, to the songs after Mandelstam and to *Vox Lucis*.

Eröd's "serious" and "entertainment" works are additionally impressive because of his imperturbable calm, his unruffled humour and his deep musicianship. Even when he composes for a specific occasion, a particular performer or a commercial commission, he is always wholly himself, totally identified with the task at hand, never tempted to compromise.

—Hartmut Krones

EUBA, Akin. Nigerian. Born in Lagos, Nigeria, 28 April 1935. Educated at Trinity College of Music, London, F.T.C.L. (piano), 1957; University of California, Los Angeles, B.A., 1964; University of Ghana, Legon, Ph.D., 1974. Married Titi Euba in 1961; 3 children. Senior programme assistant, Radio Nigeria, 1957–60; head of music and music research, Radio Nigeria, 1960–5; lecturer, University of Lagos, Nigeria, 1966–8; senior research fellow, 1968–76, and senior lecturer and acting head, department of music, University of Ife, Nigeria, 1976–7; director, 1977–80, and professor, 1978–81, Centre for Cultural Studies, University of Lagos; research scholar and artist in residence, Iwalewa-Haus, Africa Centre of University of Bayreuth, West Germany, 1986–91; founder and director, Centre for Intercultural Music Arts, London, since 1988. Recipient: Rockefeller Foundation Fellowship, 1962–4; University of California Regents Fellowship, 1965–6. Mailing address: P.O. Box 27, University of Lagos Post Office, Akoka, Lagos, Nigeria.

Publisher: University of Ife Press, Ile-Ife, Nigeria.

Symphonies/orchestral:

Introduction and Allegro 1959; first performed Bournemouth, 1960.
Dance to the Rising Sun (symphonic wind band) 1962; first performed Pittsburgh, 1963.
Olurounbi 1967; first performed Portland, Maine, 1967.
Ice Cubes (strings) 1970; first performed Lagos, 1970.

Chamber/instrumental:

String Quartet 1958; broadcast BBC, 1958.
The Wanderer (cello, piano) 1959; broadcast Radio Nigeria, 1960.
Five Pieces (cor anglais, piano) 1963; first performed Washington, D.C., 1964.
Wind Quintet (flute, oboe, clarinet, bassoon, horn) 1967; first performed Nairobi, 1967.
Music for Violin, Horn, Piano and Percussion 1969; first performed Nairobi, 1970.
Scenes from Traditional Life (piano) 1970; first performed Legon, 1971. Recorded Elekoto Music Centre EMC LP 001.
Wakar Duru: Studies in African Pianism Nos 1–3 (piano) 1987; first performed Bayreuth, 1989. Recorded Elekoto Music Centre EMC LP 001.

Vocal/choral:

Six Yoruba Folk Songs (soprano, piano) 1958; first performed Ibadan, c. 1959.
Chaka (soloists, chorus, chanter, mixed ensemble of western and African instruments) 1970; first performed Ile-Ife, 1970.
Dirges (speakers, singers, dancers, Yoruba drummers, tapes) 1971; first performed Munich, 1972.
Time Passes By (soprano, piano) 1984; first performed London, 1985.

Opera:

Bethlehem 1983; first performed Lagos, 1984.

PUBLICATIONS

By Euba: *Essays on Music in Africa vol. 1*, Bayreuth, 1988; *Essays on Music in Africa vol. 2: Intercultural Perspectives*, Bayreuth, 1989; *Yoruba Drumming: The Dundun Tradition*, Bayreuth, 1990.

On Euba: Joshua Uzoigwe, "AE: An Introduction to the Life and Music of a Nigerian Composer", dissertation, Queen's University, Belfast, 1978; Anna Ogunnaike, "Contemporary Nigerian Art Music: The Works of Bankole, Euba and Ekwueme", dissertation, University of Lagos, 1986.

Akin Euba comments:

My creative idiom derives from my fluency in both the African and western musical cultures and many of my compositions are a combination of African and western elements. As a composer and musicologist, my creative effort is informed by my analytical work and I belong to an emergent school of creative ethnomusicologists. I am an ardent promoter of interculturalism in music. I believe that in coming decades intercultural activity in music will intensify and that we are likely to witness some radical developments in music during the 21st century. These developments will be pioneered by non-western musicians: composers, performers, theoreticians, critics, educationists, media experts and so forth, from non-western cultures will become increasingly influential in the world of music.

* * *

Like Chou Wen-chung in the United States, Akin Euba is a passionate advocate and proponent of interculturalism, a coming together of so-called "First" and "Third" World artistic philosophies and procedures that moves beyond mere syncretism and toward the creation of a genuine "world music".

Born in Nigeria, Euba was thoroughly schooled in the theories and principles of European modernism, a background that is clearly discernible in his earlier work, but also in a later, more consciously African piece like *Scenes from Traditional Life*, a piano work based on a tone-row arranged in rhythmic units which can be deployed in any combination of vertical and horizontal juxtapositions. The result is a work of some complexity which calls upon both a European tradition (there is a clear reference in the title, as Euba concedes, to Robert Schumann's *Scenes from Childhood*, and in the music, to Schoenberg) and an emergent African idiom. Euba denies any pictorial or programmatic content in the piece, stating that the only connection between title and music is theoretical.

Scenes from Traditional Life may be seen as part of Euba's search for what he has called an "African pianism", a system of articulation and organisation as distinctive as those available to the European masters. Inevitably, his essays in this method lay great stress on percussive qualities of the piano (somewhat like the great jazz pianist Cecil Taylor's description of the piano as "88 tuned drums"). *Wakar Duru*, another successfully recorded piano piece, takes for its material songs from the Gbari and Yoruba people, and from the popular highlife idiom of the Nigerian cities. Significantly, Euba contrasts past and present within the piece, pointing up a difference between the old, "laid back" highlife style and the tough, urban cadences of a newer style known as *ikwokirikwo*.

Wakar Duru is perhaps Euba's most successful work to date. He does, though, have an impressive body of compositions, including the finely made *Ice Cubes* for strings and the beautiful vocal *Time Passes By*, first performed in London, where Euba has established the Centre for Intercultural Music Arts. He is, perhaps, every bit as significant as an educator and theorist. The essays on African music are powerfully and persuasively argued. Combined with his own composition, they look forward to a day when Africa's composers will receive the same recognition accorded writers like Chinua Achebe and Wole Soyinka, and for a music which, like their fiction, enjoys congress rather than compromise with European models and traditions.

—Isaac Musa

F

FARQUHAR, David (Andross). New Zealander. Born in Cambridge, New Zealand, 5 April 1928. Educated at St Peter's School, Cambridge, New Zealand, 1936–41; Wanganbui Collegiate School, 1942–5; University of New Zealand, 1946–8, B.A., B.Mus.; also private study with Douglas Lilburn; Cambridge University, United Kingdom, 1949–51, M.A.; Guildhall School of Music, London (composition under Benjamin Frankel), 1951–2. Married Raydia Guy D'Elsa, 2 June 1954; 1 son and 1 daughter. Junior lecturer, 1953–6, lecturer, senior lecturer, reader, 1957–76, and professor of music, since 1976, Victoria University of Wellington; founding president, Composers Association of New Zealand, 1974. Recipient: APRA-NZBS prize (for *Partita*), 1957; 2nd prize, APRA-NZBS competition (for *Harlequin* overture), 1959; co-joint winner, composition competition, University of Western Australia (for *Concertino*), 1961; CANZ Citation for services to New Zealand music, 1984. Mailing address: 15 Nottingham Street, Karori, Wellington, New Zealand.

Publishers: Boosey & Hawkes (Australia); Edizioni Berben, via Redipuglia 30–65, 60100 Ancona, Italy; Novello and Co; Prince Milburn Music, P.O. Box 995, Wellington, New Zealand; Wai-te-ata Press, Wellington; Yorke Edition, 31 Thornhill Square, London N1 1BQ, England.

Symphonies/orchestral:

Overture: Epithalamion 1954; first performed Wellington, 1957. Recorded Kiwi Pacific SLD 77.
Ring around the Moon (dance suite) 1957; first performed Wellington, 1957. Recorded Kiwi Pacific SLD 73.
Symphony No 1 1959; first performed Wellington, 1960. Recorded Kiwi Pacific SLD 14.
Overture: Harlequin 1959; first performed Wellington, 1960.
Concertino (piano, strings) 1960; first performed Perth, Australia, 1961. Recorded Kiwi Pacific SLC 72.
Elegy (strings) 1961; first performed Wellington, 1961.
Anniversary Suite No 1 1961; first performed Wellington, 1961.
Anniversary Suite No 2 1965; first performed Auckland, 1965.
Echoes and Reflections 1974; first performed Christchurch, 1975.
Evocation (violins) 1975; first performed Wellington, 1975. Recorded Kiwi Pacific SLD 48.
Symphony No 2 1982; first performed Wellington, 1983.
March (clarinet, strings) 1984; first performed Wellington, 1986.

Chamber/instrumental:

Five Canons (2 clarinets) 1951; first performed Cambridge, United Kingdom, 1951.
Partita (piano) 1957; first performed Wellington, 1957. Recorded Kiwi Pacific SLD 19.
Anniversary Duets (First Set) (piano duet) 1961.
Three Improvisations (piano) 1961; first performed Wellington, 1961. Recorded Kiwi Pacific SLD 78.
Ode (piano) 1963; first performed Cambridge, New Zealand, 1964.
Anniversary Duets (Second Set) (piano duets) 1964.
Suite (guitar) 1965; first performed Wellington, 1978.
Concerto (wind quintet) 1967; first performed Wellington, 1980. Recorded Kiwi Pacific SLD 61.
Three Pieces (violin, piano) 1967; first performed Wellington, 1967. Recorded Kiwi Pacific SLD30.
. . . And One Makes Ten (piano) 1969; first performed Wellington, 1971.
Fives (flute, 2 trumpets, percussion, piano; 5 dancers) 1971; first performed Wellington, 1971.
Duet (guitar, sitar) 1972.
Scenes and Memories (violin, percussion, piano) 1972; first performed Wellington, 1972.
Ostinato (gamelan) 1975.
Three Pieces (double bass) 1976; first performed Wellington, 1980.
Telephonics (piano) 1977; first performed Wellington, 1977.
Palindrome (gamelan) 1979.
Exchanges (guitar quartet) 1979; first performed Wellington, 1979.
Three Echoes (piano) 1979.
Five Scenes (guitar) 1980; first performed Wellington, 1980.
From Heaven I Come (organ) 1984; first performed Huddersfield, Yorkshire, 1986.
Suite (harpsichord) 1985; first performed Wellington, 1988.
Homage to Stravinsky (brass quintet or wind octet) 1986; first performed Wellington, 1988.
Concerto for Six (flute, clarinet, violin, cello, vibraphone, piano) 1987; first performed Auckland, 1987.
String Quartet 1989; first performed Wellington, 1989.

Vocal/choral:

Six Songs of Women (soprano, piano) 1957; first performed Wellington, 1957.
In Despite of Death (baritone, piano) 1958; first performed Wellington, 1959.
Three Scots Ballads (baritone, piano) 1960, orchestrated 1964; first performed Wellington, 1961; orchestral version first performed Wellington, 1965. Recorded (piano version) Kiwi Pacific SLD 32.
Festival Te Deum (SATB chorus, organ) 1963; first performed Wellington, 1964.
Five Shakespeare Songs (SSA chorus) 1965; first performed Cambridge, New Zealand, 1966.
The Islands (unaccompanied SATB chorus) 1967; first performed Wellington, 1968.
Sing unto the Lord (narrator, SATB chorus) 1970; first performed Auckland, 1971.
Bells in Their Seasons (double choir, orchestra) 1974; first performed Christchurch, 1974.
Magpies and Other birds (unaccompanied ATBarB chorus) 1976; first performed Christchurch, 1976.
Swan Songs (baritone, guitar) 1983; first performed Wellington, 1984.
ABC (unaccompanied SATB chorus) 1985; first performed

Auckland, 1985.
Writing on the Sand (mezzo-soprano, violin) 1987; first performed Wellington, 1987.
Three Cilla McQueen Songs (mezzo-soprano, piano) 1987; first performed Wellington, 1988.
Concerto sul "la" (chamber choir) 1988; first performed Wellington, 1988.

Opera:

A Unicorn for Christmas 1962; first performed Wellington, 1962.
O Captain Cook 1969; first performed Wellington, 1969.
Shadow 1970; first performed Wellington, 1988.

Other:

On Your Own (easy pieces for piano) 1962.
The Score (album of school songs) 1969.

PUBLICATIONS

By Farquhar: "Applied Music", in *Canzona*, 3(10), 1981.

On Farquhar: J.M. Thompson, in *Dictionary of New Zealand Composers*, Wellington, 1990.

David Farquhar comments:

I enjoy writing music for a wide range of performers, from beginning pianists to professional orchestra players and soloists. Music for voice is an important part of my output, and I am particularly interested in ways of combining and balancing aspects of song and dance in my compositions.

* * *

David Farquhar has earned for his music a place in the forefront of New Zealand contemporary composition for its clarity and wit, and for the consistent high quality of his technical skill. In a large output he has written for a wide variety of forces and combinations, and for all levels of performing ability, from easy piano pieces and songs for children to demanding works for the professional.

Early influences included performances in 1947 of Schubert, Bartók and Britten; the music of Stravinsky and Copland appealed to his love of colourful, springing rhythms, often dance-derived. Indeed, an early work which remains one of the most popular is the *dance suite* from the incidental music to the 1953 production of Christopher Fry's *Ring Round the Moon*, a translation of Anouilh. His spare instrumentation and lively yet varying moods aptly portray an atmosphere of slightly unreal gaiety. From this and many other theatre works, he has been described as "New Zealand's finest composer of occasional music": his association with the theatre led in 1962 to the full-length opera *A Unicorn for Christmas*, to a libretto by Ngaio Marsh. A one-act opera to his own libretto, *Shadow*, followed in 1970, but waited till 1988 for its first performance. *Fives*, for 5 dancers and 5 instrumentalists, while described as a concert piece, blurs the threshold between concert and theatre.

While the lack of immediate performance opportunities may have discouraged Farquhar from producing another opera, he has nevertheless maintained a continual association with the voice. His song cycles with piano span his 40 years of writing: the settings often dramatically enhance the mood of the poem, while the most recent set also explores extended sonorities of both voice and piano. *The Score* is a collection of 20 school songs; notable among his choral works is *Bells in Their Seasons*, a choral symphony for double choir and orchestra.

His instrumental work likewise spans his entire writing career. Many though by no means all the solo works are for piano, from the prize-winning *Partita*, and the exuberant Piano Concertino (with strings), to the selective sostenutos in *Three Echoes*. Resonance effects also feature in his *Five Scenes* for guitar. Ensemble works cover a wide range of combinations, from traditional chamber groups with or without piano, to cross-cultural combinations such as the *Duet* for guitar and sitar of 1972.

Stylistically, Farquhar's earlier music is notable for its general adherence to fairly traditional tonal idioms, clear-cut scoring and a harmonic spacing which often gives the texture an open-air feel. A small motive or particular interval generates much of his melodic invention: this in turn is typically expressed in different rhythms, which may be closely related but are set in relief to one another, either as answer or as contrast. From around 1970 he has additionally explored the use of other sonorities, for instance in the Concerto for Wind Quintet, and the influence of other cultures—*Ostinato* and *Palindrome* for gamelan. This evolution in style is well illustrated by the two symphonies: the first, uses triadic harmonies and traditional forms, while in the second Farquhar aims to lead his listeners "through an experience that uses music's dramatic qualities of narrative (connections), conflict (oppositions) surprise and resolution . . . ", to quote the composer's own words, using the rhythmic idea of "metrical modulation".

The directness of Farquhar's language has no need of great length. He feels music should entertain: his does, with wit and sparkle in faster rhythmic movements, or with slower, lyrical ones. Yet thanks also to his deft and sure craftsmanship his music goes beyond the merely glib and charming, to invite repeated hearings and performances.

—Margaret Lion

FEDELE, Ivan (professional name of Rocco Fedele). Italian. Born in Lecce, Apulia, Italy, 6 May 1953. Educated at G. Verdi Conservatory, Milan (harmony, counterpoint, fugue under Renato Dionisi; choral music under Amerigo Bortone; electronic music under Angelo Paggagnini), diploma in piano (under Bruno Canino), 1972, diploma in composition (under Azio Corghi), 1981; further piano study (under Ilonka Deckers), 1973–5; Academy of St Cecilia, Rome (composition under Franco Donatoni), graduated 1982; studied computer music, CNUCE, Pisa, 1978; studied under Luciano Berio, IRCAM, Paris, 1979; graduate in philosophy, National University of Milan. Married Della Rosa Fiere, 27 April 1978. Teacher of piano, Civic School of Music, Milan, 1975–81; teacher of composition, Civic School of Music, Milan, since 1981; teacher of harmony and counterpoint, Milan Conservatory, 1981–4; teacher of composition, Bologna Conservatory, 1984–5; teacher of composition, Turin Conservatory, since 1985. Recipient: Italian Radio Scholarship, 1971; 1st prize, piano competition, La Spezia, 1971; three works (*Chiari*, *Per accordar* and *Passaggio*) selected for Gaudeamus Music Week, 1981, 1982; honourable mention (for *E poi . . .*), Okanagan Music Festival, Canada, 1983; 1st prize (for *Epos*),

Concorso Internationale G. Petrassi, Parma, 1989. Mailing address: via Masotto 19, 20133 Milan, Italy.

Publishers: Edizioni Suvini Zerboni, Milan; Edipan, Rome.

Symphonies/orchestral:

Chiari 1981; first performed Rotterdam, 13 September 1981.
Divertimento (string orchestra; or 10 string soloists) 1981; first performed Rome, 14 October 1981.
Ma viele (viola, orchestra) 1984; first performed Rome, 2 March 1991.
Concerto for Violin and Orchestra 1985; first performed Milan, 5 January 1986.
Epos 1988; first performed Parma, 13 September 1989.

Chamber/instrumental:

Per accordar: String Quartet No 1 1981; first performed Rotterdam, 13 September 1981.
Passaggio (oboe) 1981; first performed Amsterdam, 1982.
Sorpresa (Aiscrim II) (piano) 1983; first performed Rome, 1983.
Viaggiatori della notte (3 pieces for violin) 1983; first performed Ferrara, 1984.
Il giardino di Giada (oboe d'amore, violin, viola, cello) 1983; first performed Milan, 1985.
. . . Ma non troppo (string quartet) 1983.
Aiscrim (flute, clarinet, piano) 1983; first performed Turin, 1989.
Armoon ("armonie di luna") (4 pianos) 1983–4; first performed Groningen, Netherlands, 1984.
Electra Glide (2 violins, viola) 1985; first performed Rome, 1985.
Magic (4 saxophones) 1985; first performed Schloss-Brenz, Germany, 1985.
Latinamix (guitar, piano, flute ad lib) 1985; first performed Buenos Aires, 1987.
Windex (clarinet) 1985; first performed Castiglione del Lago, Italy, 1985.
Chord (10 players) 1985; first performed Turin, 1986.
Modus (bass clarinet, percussion) 1987; first performed Macerata, 1988.
Bias (guitar, oboe) 1988; first performed Como, 1988.
Allegoria dell'Indica (11 players) 1988; first performed Cremona, 1988.
Mixtim (7 players) 1989; first performed Bologna, 1990.
Etudes boréales (piano) 1990; first performed Middleburg, Netherlands, 1990.

Vocal/choral:

E poi . . . (soprano, flute, oboe, 2 clarinets, bassoon, horn, piano, vibraphone, 2 violins, viola, cello; Lucchini) 1982; first performed Cremona, 1984.
Naturae ("metaphysical madrigal"; counter-tenor, tenor, bass) 1984.
Maja (soprano, piano, electronics) 1987; first performed Milan, 1988.

Opera:

Oltre narciso 1982; first performed Milan, 20 September 1982.
Impermanestra 1984; first performed Ferrara, 13 June 1984.

Other:

Attraversando la notte (video) 1986; first performed Amsterdam, 1986.
Il viaggio di ritorno (video) 1988; first performed Milan, 1988.
Paesi bassi (video) 1990; first performed Berlin, 1990.

PUBLICATIONS

On Fedele: Renzo Cresti, in *Verso Il 2000*, 1990; Lidia Bramani, "IF", in *Nuova rivista musicale italiana*, 1990.

Ivan Fedele comments:

The premise of composition, to me an inescapable prerequisite, is the consideration of music as the "poetic portrayal of the subject", in which both his sensitivities and his world view are expressed. From this derives an "ethical necessity", a categorical imperative that I set as the basis of all my work and which drives me to seek an ever closer cohesion between my being and my manifestations. The two chief modalities whereby I think the music and I compose it are diametrically opposed: one modality is speculative, while the other is sensual. From this point of view, in all my compositions you can find the "story" of a psychological journey, constantly oscillating between a physical and a mental pole, between a dynamic and a contemplative aspect.

* * *

In September 1989, having already attracted attention with the performance of his pieces at important festivals and other events, Ivan Fedele won the prestigious Goffredo Petrassi International competition with *Epos* for orchestra. This was the work that enabled the young composer to enter fully into the musical world, tracing out as it does both his roots and his future development and throwing retrospective light on the richly imaginative and finely wrought qualities of earlier works such as *Chiari* for orchestra, *Chord* for 10 instruments, and *Allegoria dell'Indica* for 11 players.

If, indeed, the icy sonority with which *Allegoria* opens or its echoes of a transfigured night arouse in the listener a reflective attention and sensation of strong dramatic tension, it is actually in *Epos* that this poetic thrill is translated into overwhelming, expressive composition. Some elements of the synthetic style of *Allegoria* are heard again in *Epos*, as atmospheric resolutions, and there are also traces of *Chord* hidden in the interstices of the metric scheme.

By this means, one is made aware of an evocative overlapping of pieces of very different sorts, a species of personal memory that revives and reuses elements of past work in order to reinforce or vary them. What is striking about *Epos* is the impact of great blocks of tone-colour, the density and physicality of the sound. It is Fedele's imaginative manipulation of dynamics that moulds the sonorities and the "movements". Elaborate developmental passages are contrasted with quite static areas of sound, which are closed and comparplative. In the periodic returns that reveal a flexible, cyclical form, Fedele's structural geometry and great narative lucidity allow a layering of simple figures almost like bricks in a wall. Fedele's technical mastery allows him to control every event conceptually and at the same time to reveal their secret poetry, the hidden spirit that makes the expressive arrangement of phrases so effective, opening doors onto a mysterious, meditative and even hypnotic universe. Apparently static textures suddenly throb with excitement.

Figure and ground, continuity and discontinuity, stasis and

dynamism, all play a part in a richly vital structure which alludes to literary metaphor, and pictorial and cinematographic experiences. Regardless of the specific semiotic rules, the listener is drawn into an involving and fascinating oscillation between a logical-mathematical formula and a far more intuitive spirit.

Fedele's conception of musical development always springs from a dialectic ingrained in sound rather than in language; the figures are the "shape" of the sound and are born from an idea of tone-colour in movement. The sound itself is thus conceived as something that is disclosed and defined stage by stage. The forms are broad and luxuriant, with linguistic and structural complexity achieved by sedimentation and a kind of osmosis between levels.

In his concerto for viola *Ma viele*, Fedele transforms the different backgrounds which are in dialogue with the solo instrument, emphasizing the relationship between the top level and the depth of the field that makes up the main perceptual material. The actual shape of that material is generated by setting the viola above a number of lively polydimensional backgrounds, in which rhythms are transformed, and colours and densities constantly recast. The piece summarizes Fedele's career and points forward to his ability to dissolve his cultural and technical roots in an exquisite blend of sound that suggests a genuine poetic impulse, an ancient and indispensable gift of finely honed creative communication.

—Lidia Bramani

FELCIANO, Richard (James). American. Born in Santa Rosa, California, 7 December 1930. Educated at Mills College, Oakland, California (under Darius Milhaud), 1952–3, M.A., 1955; Conservatoire National Supérieur de Musique, Paris (under Milhaud and Simone Plé-Caussade), 1953–5, 2 diplomas, 1955; University of Iowa, Iowa City (under Philip Bezanson), 1955–6, Ph.D., 1959; private study with Luigi Dallapiccola, Florence, Italy, 1958–9. Served in the United States Army, 1956–8. Married Rita Baumgartner, 2 July 1959; 2 sons. Associate professor of music and department chair, San Francisco College for Women, 1959–67; Ford Foundation Composer to Detroit public schools, 1964–5; resident composer, National Center for Experiments in Television, KQED, San Francisco, 1967–8, 1970–1; professor of music, since 1967, and founding director, Center for New Music and Audio Technologies, since 1987, University of California, Berkeley; Ford Foundation Composer to City of Boston (Office of Mayor), 1971–2. Recipient: Ford Foundation Fellowship, 1964–5; Guggenheim Fellowship, 1969–70; National Endowment for the Arts Fellowship 1970–1, 1979–80; Bellagio Residency, Rockefeller Foundation, 1975. Mailing address: 1326 Masonic Avenue, San Francisco, California 94117, U.S.A.

Publishers: Schirmer; Belwin-Mills; World Library.

Symphonies/orchestral:

Mutations 1966; first performed Berkeley, California, 1966.
Galactic Rounds 1972; first performed Boston, 1973.
Orchestra 1980; first performed San Francisco, 1980.
Concerto for Organ and Orchestra 1986; first performed Berkeley, California, 1986. Recorded Opus One.

Chamber/instrumental:

Evolutions (clarinet, piano) 1962; first performed Iowa City, 1962.
Gravities (piano, 4 hands) 1965; first performed San Francisco, 1965. Recorded CRI SD-349.
Contractions (woodwind quintet) 1965; first performed Detroit, Michigan, 1965.
Aubade (string trio, harp, piano) 1966; first performed San Francisco, 1965.
Spectra (double bass, flute) 1967; first performed Portland, Maine, 1967. Recorded CRI SD 349; Ars Nova AN 1001.
Crasis (flute, clarinet, violin, cello, piano, percussion, harp, tape) 1967; first performed San Francisco, 1967. Recorded CRI SD 349.
Noosphere I (alto flute, electronic tape) 1967; first performed Detroit, Michigan, 1967.
On the Divine Presence (organ) 1968.
Background Music (harpist, sympathetic piano, 2-channel tape, FM tuner, pocket radio) 1969; first performed Oakland, California, 1970.
Vineyards Music (subsequently entitled *Frames and Gestures*; piano quintet) 1970; first performed Saratoga, California, 1970.
Litany (organ, tape) 1970.
Lamentations for Jani Christou (12 players, tape) 1970; first performed Tanglewood, Massachusetts, 1970.
God of the Expanding Universe (organ) 1971. Recorded Grosvenor Records GRS 1017.
Stops (organ) 1972.
Ekagrata (organ) 1972; first performed Hartford, Connecticut, 1972.
I Make My Own Soul from all the Elements of the Earth (organ) 1972.
Chod (violin, cello, double bass, piano, 2 percussion, live electronics) 1975; first performed Berkeley, California, 1975. Recorded CRI SD 349.
And from the Abyss (tuba, tape) 1975; first performed New York City, 1975. Recorded Opus One 29.
On the Heart of the Earth (organ, 2 assistants) 1976.
In Celebration of Golden Rain (gamelan, pipe organ) 1977; first performed Berkeley, California, 1977. Recorded Cambridge Records CRS 2560.
From and To, With (violin, piano) 1980; first performed San Francisco, 1980.
Crystal (string quartet) 1981.
A View from the Window (harpsichord) 1981; first performed Berkeley, California, 1981.
Of Things Remembered (harp, flute, viola) 1981; first performed San Francisco, 1982.
Salvador Allende (string quartet, clarinet, percussion) 1982; first performed Regio Emilia, Italy, 1983.
Volkan (5 flutes, 1 player) 1983; first performed Turin, Italy, 1984.
Come Away with Me: Kindertotenlieder 1984 (recorder, electronic sounds) 1984.
Alleluia to the Heart of Stone (reverberated recorder) 1984; first performed San Francisco, 1985.
Pieces of Eight (double bass, organ) 1984; first performed Berkeley, California, 1985.
Dark Landscape (cor anglais) 1985; first performed San Francisco, 1985.
Lontano (harp, piano) 1986; first performed Berkeley, California, 1987.

Five Short Piano Pieces 1986; first performed Los Angeles, 1986.
Shadows (flute, clarinet, cello, piano, percussion) 1987; first performed San Francisco, 1987.
Constellations (3 brass quintets, 8 horns, 1 or 2 organs, extended reverberation) 1987; first performed San Francisco, 1987.
The Hollow Woods (2 recorders, live electronics) 1989; first performed San Francisco, 1989.
Palladio (violin, piano, percussion) 1989; first performed Berkeley, California, 1990.

Vocal/choral:

Three Madrigals from William Shakespeare (unaccompanied mixed voices) 1955; first performed Oberlin, Ohio, 1975.
Communion Service (mixed voices, organ) 1961; first performed Santa Rosa, California, 1963.
Two Hymns to Howl By (rounds for equal voices; Ginsberg) 1962; first performed Detroit, Michigan, 1965.
A Christmas Madrigal (mixed voices, brass, piano, percussion; medieval) 1964; first performed Detroit, Michigan, 1964.
Pshelley's Psalm (unaccompanied mixed voices) 1964; first performed Detroit, Michigan, 1965.
Four Poems from the Japanese (women's voices, 5 harps, percussion; translated Rexroth) 1964; first performed Detroit, Michigan, 1964.
The Captives (chorus, orchestra; Merton) 1965; first performed Indianapolis, 1965.
Pentecost Sunday: Double Alleluia (male chorus, tape, organ) 1967; first performed Pittsburgh, 1967.
Glossolalia (ritual for baritone, tape, percussion, organ) 1967; first performed New York City, 1967. Recorded Cambridge Records CRS 2560.
Mass in Unison (chorus, organ) 1967.
Songs for Darkness and Light (equal voices, unaccompanied or with organ; Biblical) 1970.
Sic Transit (equal or mixed voices, light sources, tape sounds, organ; St Matthew, John F. Kennedy, Martin Luther King) 1970; first performed New York City, 1970.
3
in in
1 1
in in
3 (antiphonal chorus, tape, organ(s), optional instruments) 1971; first performed New York City, 1971.
Signs (mixed voices, multiple projections, tape, organ; Buckminster Fuller, Revel, St Luke, Teilhard de Chardin) 1971; first performed New York City, 1971.
Out of Sight (mixed voices, tape, organ) 1971; first performed New York City, 1971.
Two Public Pieces ("The Not Yet Flower"—St John, "Cosmic Festival"—E. Browning, Emerson, Whitman: unison voices, tape) 1972.
The Angels of Turtle Island (soprano, flute, violin, percussion, live electronics) 1972; first performed Rhode Island, 1972. Recorded Grenadilla Records GS 1064.
The Passing of Enkidu (mixed voices, piano, 4 percussion, tape; after H. Mason) 1973, revised 1975.
Hymn of the Universe (mixed voices, tape; Teilhard de Chardin) 1973; first performed Princeton, New Jersey, 1973.
Te Deum (soprano, alto, tenor, bass, SATB chorus, boys' voices, organ, piano, percussion, 3 antiphonal trumpets) 1974; first performed New York City, 1974.
Susani (mixed voices, tape, organ; 14th-century German) 1974; first performed Hartford, Connecticut, 1975.
Windows in the Sky (unison voices, tape, organ; traditional hymn "Lasst uns erfreuen) 1976; first performed Ontario, 1976.
Alleluia to the Heart of (the) Matter (2 equal voices, organ; after Teilhard de Chardin) 1976; first performed Los Angeles, 1976.
The Seasons (unaccompanied SATB chorus) 1978; first performed River Forest, Wisconsin, 1978.
Lumen (soprano, organ) 1980; first performed Washington, D.C., 1982.
Mad with Love (chorus, organ, handbells; Catherine of Siena) 1981.
Furies (3 sopranos, 3 flutes) 1988; first performed San Francisco, 1988.

Opera:

Sir Gawain and the Green Knight (soprano, tenor, bass, baritone, mezzo-soprano, SAB chorus, flute, trumpet, cello, piano, percussion, piano/percussion; medieval poem) 1964; first performed San Francisco, 1964.

Other:

Noosphere II (electronic sound) 1967; first performed New York City, 1971.
Instruments of Violence (video) 1968; first performed San Francisco, 1968.
Trio for Speaker, Screen and Viewer (audience-participation television) 1968; first performed San Francisco, 1968.
Linearity (television piece for harp, live electronics) 1968; first performed San Francisco, 1968.
The Architect and the Emperor of Abyssinia (music for Arrabal play) 1969; first performed San Francisco, 1969.
Six Electronic Dances (television score) 1970.
Point of Inflection (with Stephen Beck; television music) 1971; first performed New York City, 1972.
Mother Goose—A Parable of Man (television) 1971.
The Municipal Music Box (electronic sound environment with light sculptures) 1972; first performed Boston, 1972.
Islands of Sound (environmental music for 14 carillons) 1975; first performed Fort Worth/Dallas, Texas, 1976.
The Tuning of the Sky (carillon) 1979; first performed Berkeley, California, 1979.
Berliner Feuerwerksmusik (sound environment for 3 ambulant carillons at Templehof Airfield, Berlin) 1987; first performed Berlin, 1987.

PUBLICATIONS

By Felciano: "Space, Color and Silence", in *Harp News*, Autumn 1965.

On Felciano: J.R. Little, "Serial, Aleatoric and Electronic Techniques in American Organ Music Published Between 1960 and 1972", dissertation, University of Iowa, Iowa City, 1975; Sigurd Christiansen, "The Sacred Choral Music of RF", dissertation, University of Illinois, Urbana, 1977.

Richard Felciano comments:

The best introduction to my work I can conceive is for the listener to adopt the position of a child, awestruck at the richness and detail of the physical world around it. Strike any object and the sound which emanates represents the physical world speaking to us, bypassing words and telling our brains directly the nature of its physical composition. Whether blown, bowed, struck or plucked, I think of musical instruments in the same way, and the act of composition became for me the way to build architecture-like structures from the "voices" of physical objects.

From what is said above, it should not be surprising that I am fascinated by acoustics, attracted to the writing of the French philosopher Teilhard de Chardin (from whom some of my titles are taken), or that I resist musical ideas which do not take the consequences of timbral decisions seriously.

One other thing: the most consistent influence in my life, and one which has become increasingly manifest, is that of my childhood in a small northern California community with substantial immigrant populations from Japan and Portugal. From these groups I learned a sense of ritual (which most Americans, never having experienced it, unfortunately equate with "theatre"), of structure, of awe, and of music as a social function. Though I didn't realize it at the time, the reality of my childhood world was Asia and Europe, and so it has remained in adult life: I am a globalist concerned with East and West, stasis and dynamism, meditation and dialectics—and with California as the edge where the two meet.

* * *

Richard Felciano is an explorer. With sound as his vessel, he pursues the path upon which all profound thinkers must travel: into the social and scientific workings of the "everyday" world, through the perceptions and creations of the pysche, and, finally, into humanity's ultimate destiny in the unmapped realms of the spirit.

For all their variety, each of his pieces is born from a similar process, which molds sound around the core of some philosophical or intuitive insight. It is his particular gift that his keen intellect has never betrayed him into academicism, or his spiritual commitment sent him wandering into some formless maze. It is precisely his ability to balance between two worlds—the mundane and elemental, the scientific and artistic—that gives so strong a human "scale" to his works, such clarity to even his busiest textures, such powerful embodiments to even his most challenging ideas.

Although his style has continually deepened, its basic elements were already present in his early "modernist" works. *Crasis*, for example, composed for seven instruments and electronic tape, sparkles with the language of the brave new world: the coloristic use of instruments as a substantive element, a non-diatonic melodic palette and self-defining, non-tonal harmony, textural multiplicity, freely orbiting rhythmic structures unfettered by a regular beat, and the fusion of art and technology, which has provided one of the great underlying themes of his career.

One most striking aspects of *Crasis* lay in its surrender of complete control over certain areas of horizontal conjunctions. This approach—truly an act of faith, which trades omniscience for a rich complexity—assumed a central role in *Galactic Rounds*, Felciano's exploration of the time-space continuum. In this orchestral work, the orbiting, interlocking paths of celestial bodies provide a model for a series of circling canonic patterns distributed among the players. The result is a massive musical mobile composed of independently rotating elements, each with its own tempo and rhythmic pattern, "a work," writes the composer, "which—like the universe—is full of motion yet always the same." In *The Angels of Turtle Island* Felciano gave himself over completely to the concept of the process piece, for which a composer provides basic material and the parameters for its development, and then stands back to let his progeny follow its own evolutionary destiny. In *Angels*, sustained notes and repeated motives are picked up and reproduced through a system of electronic delay, while its three players freely develop their parts against the fabric of cycling sounds. Through this dramatic musical ritual, the simplest of materials is transformed into a powerful tapestry of natural rhythms: birth and passing, regeneration and decay.

Angels, with its surrender of control, its absence of dialectic and its meditative pace, showed the intensity of Felciano's indebtedness to oriental thought. His synthesis of East and West, however, found its most dramatic embodiment in *In Celebration of Golden Rain*, in which western organ and eastern gamelan orchestra become sound and symbol of the twin pillars upon which his music rests. For all the drama of this bi-cultural encounter, however, it is in its celebration of pure, unadorned sound that *Golden Rain* makes its greatest impact. Through its leisurely development of hypnotic patterns, its expanded framework that invites listeners to explore the interstices where organ and gamelan meet, and its overriding sense of static timelessness, it offers the fundamental message that music is, after all, about stopping and simply, deeply, listening.

The large meditative canvases no longer dominated in the 1980s, but Felciano still journeyed deeper into his beloved sound. There is something almost classical in the way he has recently turned his attention inward to focus on the psycho-acoustical implications of his own medium. *Shadows*, with its prismatic scampering of impish figurations, is a dramatic study of the kinetic forces released in music—ephemeral, evanescent resonances that surround their generative tones. In its companion chamber piece, *Palladio*, time and motion have given way to an exploration of the acoustic and dramatic imperatives inherent in the relationships between two pitches. Here, the stability and architectural symmetry of open fifths become the warp for an intricately woven mini-concerto for violin, piano and percussion.

Throughout his career Felciano has remained an authentic creative artist: no matter how compelling his ideas have been, it is always against sound that they have been measured. It is fitting that, in his maturity—like some scientist seeking the universe in sub-atomic particles—Felciano has chosen to focus on the most basic elements of his art.

—Howard Hersh

FELD, Jindřich. Czechoslovak. Born in Prague, 19 February 1925. Educated: violin/viola lessons with father; composition at Prague Conservatory, 1945–8; composition at Prague Academy of Music, 1948–52; musicology, aesthetics, philosophy at Charles University, Prague, Ph.D., 1952. Married Helena Feldova, 23 July 1955, 1 daughter. Viola player, Military Symphony Orchestra, 1952–4; freelance composer, 1954–1968; teacher of composition/composer in residence, University of Adelaide, South Australia, 1968–9; professor of composition, Prague Conservatory, 1972–86; guest lecturer, University of Indiana, Bloomington, 1981, 1984; also guest lecturer in Norway, Denmark, West Germany and elsewhere; active in Czech Association of Musicians, especially since democratic revolution of 1989. Recipient: State Prize of Czechoslovakia, 1968. Mailing address: Pocernicka 513/56, 108 00 Prague 10—Malesice, Czechoslovakia.

Publishers: Czech Music Fund/Panton, Prague; State Musical Publishing House/Edition Supraphon, Prague; Editions Leduc, Paris; Editions Salabert, Paris; Barenreiter, Kassel; Edition Modern, Vienna; Schott, Mainz; others.

Symphonies/orchestral:

Divertimento 1950.
Furiant 1950.
Concerto for Orchestra 1951, revised 1957; first performed Prague, 1952.
Comedy Overture 1953.
Concerto for Flute and Orchestra 1954; first performed Prague, 1957. Recorded Supraphon; Serenus.
Rhapsody (violin, orchestra) 1956.
Concerto in C (chamber orchestra) 1956–7.
Sonata (flute, string orchestra) 1957, orchestrated 1965.
Concerto for Cello and Orchestra 1958; first performed Prague, 1960. Recorded Supraphon.
Concerto for Bassoon and Orchestra 1958–9.
Dramatic Overture "May 1945" 1959–60.
Suite (string chamber orchestra) 1960–1.
Thuringian Overture 1961.
Three Frescoes 1963; first performed Prague, 1964. Recorded Supraphon.
Concert Music (oboe, bassoon, orchestra) 1964; first performed Stuttgart, 1965.
Serenata giocosa (chamber orchestra) 1966.
Concert Piece (horn, orchestra) 1966.
Symphony No 1 1966–7; first performed Prague, 1969. Recorded Supraphon; Serenus.
Dramatic Fantasy "The Days of August" 1968–9. Recorded Panton.
Concerto for Oboe and Orchestra 1970.
Chamber Sinfonietta (strings) 1971.
Concert Suite (bass clarinet, piano, strings, percussion) 1972.
Concerto for Piano and Orchestra 1973; first performed Zlin, 1975. Recorded Panton; Serenus.
Concerto for Trombone and Orchestra 1974–5.
Concerto for Accordion and Orchestra 1975; first performed Glasgow, 1976.
"Partita Piccola" (accordion orchestra) 1976.
Concerto for Violin and Orchestra 1976–7; first performed Ostrava, 1978.
Evocations (accordion orchestra, percussion) 1977–8; first performed Copenhagen, 1980.
Serenade (string chamber orchestra) 1979. Recorded Panton.
Concert Fantasy (flute, string orchestra, percussion) 1979–80; first performed Paris, 1980.
Concerto for Saxophone and Orchestra 1979–80; first performed Nuremberg, 1982.
Concert for Harp and Orchestra 1982; first performed Prague, 1984. Recorded Supraphon.
Symphony No 2 1983; first performed Prague, 1985. Recorded Panton.
Concert for Saxophone and Symphonic Wind Band 1983–4; first performed Washington, D.C., 1985.
H.C. Anderson's Fairy Tales (accordion orchestra) 1984.
Fresco (symphonic wind band) 1985; first performed Bloomington, Indiana, 1986.

Chamber/instrumental:

Suite (clarinet, piano) 1948–9.
String Quartet No 1 1949.
Wind Quintet No 1 1949.
Sonatina (2 violins) 1952–3; first performed Prague, 1954.
Four Pieces (flute) 1954. Recorded World Record Club.
Two Compositions (cello, piano) 1954–5. Recorded Supraphon.
Sonata (viola, piano) 1955; first performed Prague, 1956.
Suite of Seven Small Pieces (violin, piano) 1955.
Rhapsody (violin, piano) 1956; first performed Brussels, 1959.
Sonata (flute, piano) 1957; first performed Prague, 1959. Recorded Columbia; RCA Victor CD.
Prelude and Toccata (piano) 1958–9.
String Quartet No 2 1959.
Prelude and Toccata (2 pianos) 1960.
Chamber Suite (9 instruments) 1960; first performed Prague, 1962. Recorded Panton.
Canonical Duet (2 violins) 1960.
Instructive Suite (clarinet, piano) 1960.
Trio (violin, viola, cello) 1961; first performed Prague, 1962.
Duo (flute, bassoon or bass clarinet) 1962.
String Quartet No 3 1962; first performed Munich, 1963.
Merry Intermezzo (3 violins) 1962.
Rhapsody (organ) 1963.
Trio (flute, violin, cello) 1963; first performed Berne, 1964.
Intermezzo (trumpet, piano) 1963.
Caprices (wind quartet, guitar) 1964.
Burlesque (oboe, piano) 1964.
Scherzino (clarinet, piano) 1964.
Suite in Miniature (3 violins, cello ad lib, piano) 1964.
String Quartet No 4 1965; first performed Prague, 1967.
Suite (accordion) 1965.
Concert Piece (horn, piano) 1965.
Three Pieces (oboe or flute or clarinet, piano) 1966.
Four Intermezzos (accordion) 1967. Recorded Hohner; Eterna.
Miniatures (violin, guitar, accordion) 1967–8.
Wind Quintet No 2 1968; first performed Adelaide, 1969. Recorded Supraphon; Serenus.
Sonatina (bassoon, piano) 1969.
Quintet (brass instruments) 1969–70; first performed Prague, 1971. Recorded Panton; Crystal.
Duo (2 accordions) 1970. Recorded Hohner.
Sonatina (clarinet, piano) 1970.
Concert Suite (bass clarinet, piano) 1971; first performed Biberach, Germany, 1971.
Two Partitas (2 or 3 recorders or flutes or oboes) 1971.
Sonata (piano) 1971–2; first performed Moscow, 1973. Recorded Panton; Serenus.
String Quintet (with 2 violas) 1971–2; first performed Lucany, Czechoslovakia, 1973.
Sonata (cello, piano) 1972; first performed Ostrava, 1974.
Trio (violin or flute, cello, piano) 1972; first performed Prague, 1973.
Two-Part Partita (accordion) 1972.
Contrasts (flute) 1973.
Little Chamber Music (wind instrument, violin, cello, piano) 1973.
Sonata (guitar) 1974; first performed Paris, 1975.
Five Style Studies (string quartet, flute, harp) 1974.
Concert Piece (accordion) 1974. Recorded Panton.
Little Caprice (flute, piano) 1974.
Barbaric Dance (guitar) 1974.
Little Divertimento (3 flutes) 1974.
Little Sonatina (viola, piano) 1974.
Two Dances (flute, guitar) 1975.
Five Inventions (2 flutes) 1975.
Suite Rhapsodica (clarinet) 1975–6; first performed New York City, 1976.
Concert Suite (6 percussionists) 1976; first performed Copenhagen, 1977. Recorded Panton.
Little Divertimento (4 horns) 1976.
Toccata and Passacaglia (harp) 1976.
"Partita Canonica" (3 trumpet, 3 trombones) 1976–7.
Epigrams (piccolo flute, tuba, harp) 1977.
Little Prelude (accordion) 1977.
Serenade (4 violins) 1978.

String Quartet No 5 1978–9; first performed Prague, 1981. Recorded Supraphon.
Music for Two Accordions 1979; first performed Copenhagen, 1980.
Moment Musical (accordion) 1979.
Cassation (9 flutes) 1980. Recorded Peter Music CD.
Toys (accordion) 1980.
Concert Duo (2 flutes) 1981; first performed Tallinn, Estonia, 1981.
Elegy (soprano saxophone or oboe, piano) 1981; first performed New York City, 1982. Recorded Delos CD.
Saxophone Quartet 1981; first performed Paris, 1983.
Sonata (oboe or soprano saxophone, piano) 1981–2; first performed Adelaide, 1982. Recorded Move.
Prelude and Fugue (accordion) 1982.
Introduction and Allegro (accordion, percussion) 1983; first performed Bonn, 1984.
Concert Music (viola, piano) 1983; first performed Rheinberg, Germany, 1983.
Sonata (violin, piano) 1985; first performed Prague, 1987. Recorded Panton.
Quartettino (recorders) 1985.
Sonatina (flute, harp) 1986.
Ten Pieces (2 guitars) 1986.
Concerto da camera (2 string quartets) 1986; first performed Stuttgart, 1986.
Trio (oboe, clarinet, bassoon) 1987. Recorded Panton.
Duo (violin, cello) 1989.
Sonatina (horn, piano) 1989.
Sonata (alto saxophone, piano) 1989.

Vocal/choral:

The War (male choir; Sramek) 1954; first performed Prague, 1955.
Nine Ditties to the Children (voice, piano; Halas, Kainar) 1958, 1964. Recorded (selection) Supraphon.
Songs of Animals (children's choir, piano; Hrubin) 1965.
Three Inventions (mixed chorus) 1966; first performed Jihlava, 1966. Recorded Panton.
Nonsense Rhymes (women's chorus, small instrumental ensemble or piano; Czech folk-poetry/English text Jane May) 1973; first performed Jihlava, 1974.
Ditties of Twelve Months (children's chorus, soloists, piano, flute, 2 trumpets, or orchestra; Ctvrtek) 1977.
Gloria Cantus (mixed choir; Latin text) 1984; first performed Jihlava, 1984.
Laus Cantus (soprano, string quartet) 1985; first performed Stuttgart, 1986.
Fables (children's choir, piano, recorder; Sefl) 1986.
Zoological Garden: Epigrams (children's choir, piano, Sefl) 1987.
Chinese Folk Songs (soprano, string quartet) 1987.
Cosmae Chronica Boemorum 1988-9.

Opera:

Fairytale About Budirlinek (radio opera) 1955.
The Postman's Tale (children's opera; Capek) 1956; first performed Plzen, 1968.

Other:

Martinu: *Seven Arabesques* (transcribed for clarinet or flute, piano, percussion) 1987.

PUBLICATIONS

By Feld: "Problems of Metrorhythmical Notation in the Composer's Praxis", in *Cas v hudbe / Time in Music*, Prague, 1984; "Problems of Contemporary Music", in *Collegium Musicum*, Prague, 1986; articles and reviews in *Hudebni rozhledy / Musical Review*, Prague.

On Feld: Helmut C. Jacobs, "Komponist und Werk: JF", and Fritz Dobler, "Werkbetrachtung", both in *Das Akkordeon*, 9, December 1984; Kenneth Fischer, "Czechoslovakian Composer JF", in *Saxophone Journal*, Summer 1987.

Jindřich Feld comments:

I have always held to the conviction that music comprises far more than structures. Music, above all, is a language, a means of communication between and among people. The basic musical idea originates with the composer, is transmitted by the performer, and then perceived by the listener. When formulating his message the compser must first have in mind the capabilities of the performer and then the receptiveness of the listener. The performer must possess a thorough understanding of the composer and his composition, in addition to an interpretative mastery in order to transmit successfully the composer's message to the audience. And finally, the listener, if he is educated and musically sensitive, is then able to perform and appreciate both the composer's work and its realization by the performing artist.

When the three sides of this triangle are sufficiently aligned, the music achieves its function. When the music is not successful, where does the blame lie? poor composition, inadequate performance, or unreceptive audience? Obviously, the same music cannot touch every individual, but without question every human being can be enriched by art in general and by music in particular. It would not be an exaggeration to state that music is one of man's necessities. To this end, man also needs education, cultivation, refinement of taste. Only then can music fulfil its very important role in a cultured society: aesthetic beauty. This is also my aim.

* * *

Jindřich Feld's substantial, varied and high-quality catalogue of works ranks him among the most prominent of contemporary Czech composers. His compositional output may be divided into three periods. The first of these comprises works from the 1950s among which *Concerto for Orchestra*, *Concerto for Flute and Orchestra* and *Concerto for Cello and Orchestra* are the most important. These compositions are characterized by a link with traditional European and especially Czech music, tonally based harmonies, clarity of form, strong rhythmic pulsation and instrumental virtuosity.

Concerto for Orchestra, Feld's graduation piece from the Academy of Music, is the earliest representative work and was created during the era of "socialist realism." This work both complied with and defied this dogma by incorporating both Czech folk song and a twelve-tone theme in the first movement. The *Concerto for Flute and Orchestra* reveals further developments of the composer's attributes and a penchant for writing for specific performers, a practice which continues to the present.

The second period brought some exciting changes in Feld's works. He began to incorporate modern technical composition methods—dodecaphony, serial technique and aleatorics—into his own personal style. From this period *String Quartet No 4*, *Symphony No 1* and *Dramatic Fantasy "The Days of August"* are most significant. The Czechoslovak State Prize winning *String Quartet No 4* and the *Symphony No 1* represent a synthesis of the composer's style at that time. The Quartet is a dodecaphonic work which emphasizes rhythmic vitality, sound effects, clear formal structure and detailed dynamic changes, while the Symphony is filled with distinctive contrasts, dramatic content and abrupt rhythmic and orchestral sound swells.

The *Dramatic Fantasy* is important in Feld's output since it is a rare example of program music from a composer who prefers to write absolute music. Its inspiration, the composer's anger at the Soviet invasion of Czechoslovakia in 1968, is also unique and accounts for the unusual foray into the realm of programmatic works.

Feld's third compositional period began in the 1970s and continues to the present. Works from this phase are a synthesis of the composer's creative focus typified by continued strengthening of both expression and content. Among the notable compositions in this period are the Concertos for piano, violin, saxophone and harp; *String Quartet No 5*; *Saxophone Quartet*; and *Symphony No 2*.

The largest, most significant work to date is the oratorio-cantata *Cosmae Chronica Boemorum* for soloists, mixed chorus and orchestra. Based on a medieval text of the earliest Czech history, this opus is sung in Latin with a narrator explaining the story in the language of the audience.

Feld's compositions feature a style variability ranging from early works of a Romantic quality with Classical 20th-century harmony and rhythm to later dodecaphonic and serial opuses. He subjects all musical parameters of his compositions to intense study before making his final selections. His creations have distinctive rhythms and demanding rhythmic expression indicating a lifelong interest of the composer and his belief that time and rhythm must be organized or chaos results. Architectural forms in Feld's works are clear and precise, and he gives imaginative attention to orchestration. Consideration is given not only to the entire orchestral timbre but also to the timbral possibilities of individual instruments, especially when chamber groupings occur within a larger score. Feld's output is not the work of a radical musician but represents an ongoing thoughtful and intellectual approach by the composer to new compositional methods and experiments.

—Lana Kay Johns

FERGUSON, Howard. British. Born in Belfast, 21 October 1908. Educated at Westminster School, London, 1922–24; Royal College of Music, London (piano under Harold Samuel, conducting under Malcolm Sargent), 1924–28. Served in the Royal Air Force, 1940–42. Assistant organizer, National Gallery Concerts, London, 1939–46; professor of composition, Royal Academy of Music, London, 1948–63; music editor and writer. Recipient: honorary D.Mus, Queen's University, Belfast, 1959. Mailing address: 51 Barton Road, Cambridge, CB3 9LG, England.

Publisher: Boosey & Hawkes.

Symphonies/orchestral:

Partita Op 5a (also 2-piano version) 1935–6; broadcast BBC, 1937.
Four Diversions on Ulster Airs Op 7 1939–42.
Concerto for Piano and Strings Op 12 1950–1; first performed London, 29 May 1952.
Overture for an Occasion Op 16 1952–3; first performed Belfast, 1953.

Chamber/instrumental:

Five Irish Folktunes (cello or viola, piano) 1927.
Sonata No 1 Op 2 (violin, piano) 1931; first performed London, 1932. Recorded RCA Victor Red Seal LCS-2909.
Four Short Pieces Op 6 (clarinet, piano) 1932–6; first performed London, 1937. Recorded Hyperion A66014.
Three Sketches Op 14 (flute, piano) 1932–52.
Octet Op 4 (clarinet, bassoon, horn, string quartet, double bass) 1933. Recorded Hyperion A66192.
Five Pipe Pieces (3 bamboo pipes) 1934–5.
English Suite (3 recorders) 1935; first performed London, 1935.
Partita Op 5b (2 pianos) 1935–6. Recorded Hyperion A66130.
Sonata in F minor Op 8 (piano) 1938–9; first performed London, 1940. Recorded Hyperion A66130.
Sonata (flute, piano) 1938–40.
Five Bagatelles Op 9 (piano) 1944; first performed London, 1944. Recorded HMVC3423; Hyperion A66192.
Sonata Op 10 (violin, piano) 1946. Recorded Hyperion A66192.
Two Fanfares Op 15 (4 trumpets, 3 trombones) 1952.

Vocal/choral:

Two Ballads Op 1 (baritone, piano/orchestra) 1928–32; first performed Cheltenham, Gloucestershire, 1934.
Three Medieval Carols Op 3 (voice, piano) 1932–3; broadcast BBC, 1934. Recorded Litton SSLP 137.
Discovery Op 13 (voice, piano; Welch) 1951; first performed London, 1951. Recorded Hyperion A66103; Decca 6BB 197–8.
Five Irish Folksongs Op 17 (soprano, chorus, orchestra) 1954; broadcast BBC, 1955. Recorded Litton SSLP 1137.
Amore Langueo Op 18 (tenor, chorus, orchestra) 1955–6; first performed Gloucester, 1956. Recorded EMI EL7 49627.
The Dream of the Rood Op 19 (soprano, chorus, orchestra) 1958–9; first performed Gloucester, 1959.

Other:

Chauntecleer (ballet) 1948.

PUBLICATIONS

By Ferguson: (as editor) *W. Tisdall: Complete Keyboard Works*, London, 1958; *Style and Interpretation*, 4 vols, 1963–4; keyboard works by Blow, 1964, and Purcell, 1964; *Early French Keyboard Music*, 2 vols, 1966; *Early Italian Keyboard Music*, 2 vols, 1968; *Early German Keyboard Music*, 2 vols, 1970; *Early English Keyboard Music*, 1971; (with Christopher Hogwood), *W. Croft: Complete Harpsichord Works*, 2 vols, London, 1974; *Anne Cromwell's Virginal Book 1638*, London, 1974; *F. Schubert: Piano Sonatas*, London, 1979; *Keyboard Works of C.P.E. Bach*, 4 vols, London, 1983; (as author) *Keyboard Interpretation from 14th to 19th Century*, Oxford, 1973, 3rd edition 1987.

On Ferguson: Alan Rideout (ed.), *The Music of HF*, London, 1989.

Howard Ferguson comments:
I stopped composing in 1959, having said all I had to say.

* * *

Howard Ferguson's output was rather small in size, 19 opuses plus five unnumbered works, yet distinctive in tone. He first gained attention with his First Violin Sonata, premièred in 1932, and after *The Dream of the Rood*, an extended work for the Three Choirs Festival of 1959, he felt that he had no more to say as a composer and hence stopped writing. This is an example that certain others might with advantage have followed.

A pupil of Harold Samuel for the piano as well as R.O. Morris for composition, Ferguson remained active in other directions. A fine pianist, he maintained notable partnerships with Yfrah Neaman (violin), Denis Matthews (piano) and toured widely as a performer. He was also a musicologist and prepared editions of Purcell and Schubert among others besides writing a book, *Keyboard Interpretation from 14th to 19th Century*.

The favourable impression made with the First Violin Sonata was confirmed the following year by Ferguson's *Octet*, which, like parallel works by later composers such as Thea Musgrave (*Chamber Concerto No 3*) and Joubert, employs the same instrumentation as Schubert's *Octet*. The first movement is in sonata form, the second is a scherzo, the third a lyrical ternary form, the finale another sonata form though with considerable references to the chief theme of the first movement. In fact all the thematic ideas are clearly related and this cyclic unity changes the effect of the classical forms used. At the same time this music is dark and mellow, announcing the vein of romanticism that was to inform most of Ferguson's compositions.

Sensitive judgement is apparent in the close weaving of the Octet's textures, the expressive management of its colours, and this specific aspect was further explored in the *Partita* for orchestra. This is also effective in the version for two pianos made in 1935–6, and in either form it demonstrates how a modestly personal idiom can yield striking, indeed, eloquent, results. Such is particularly the case with Ferguson's subtle and more concise Piano Sonata, dedicated to Samuel and completed during World War II. The latter circumstance may account for this being a gloomy work yet it is also a consistently inspired one whose most intense expression is probably in the sombre turbulence of the opening movement.

Such exceptional moments notwithstanding, Ferguson early arrived at his basically diatonic style and later made only slight extensions. An instance is the *Discovery* song cycle of 1951 with a Denton Welch text, which includes harmony more dissonant than usual. Generally, however, this idiom served Ferguson well in the handling of large and small traditional forms. In fact the effect he desired was usually achieved quite decisively, as in *The Dream of the Rood*. This stands with Arnold Cooke's *Ode to St Cecilia's Day* (1964) and Peter Racine Fricker's *The Vision of Judgement* (1957–8) as one of the last vital works in oratorio form to be composed in England. Ferguson's contribution is a distinguished one, yet he is the sort of traditional figure who is all to easily overlooked when the histories are written.

—Max Harrison

FERNEYHOUGH, Brian (John Peter). British/English. Born in Coventry, Warwickshire, 16 January 1943. Educated at Birmingham School of Music, 1961–3; Royal Academy of Music, London (under Lennox Berkeley), 1966–7; Sweelinck Conservatory, Amsterdam (under Ton de Leeuw), 1968–9; Basle Academy (under Klaus Huber), 1969–71. Married (1) Barbara J. Pearson in 1967; (2) Elke Schaaf in 1980; (3) Carolyn Steinberg in 1984 (dissolved 1989). Lecturer, 1973–8, and professor, 1978–86, Freiburg Musikhochsschule; visiting artist, Berlin, 1976–7; lecturer, Ferienkurse für Neue Musik, Darmstadt, 1976, 1978, 1980, 1982, 1984, 1986, 1988, 1990; leader of master classes, Civica Scuola di Musica, Milan, since 1984; principal composition teacher, Royal Conservatoire, The Hague, since 1986; professor of music, University of California, San Diego, since 1986; guest professor, Musikhogskolan, Stockholm, 1980, 1981, 1982, 1985, and University of Chicago, 1986. Recipient: Mendelssohn Scholarship, 1968; prizes (for *Sonatas for String Quartet*, *Epicycle*, and *Missa Brevis*), Gaudeamus Composers' Competition, Holland, 1968, 1969, 1970; honourable mention (for *Firecycle Beta*), ISCM Italian Section, 1972; special prize (for *Time and Motion Study III*), ISCM Italian Section, 1974; Koussevitzky Award (for *Transit*), 1978; Grand Prix du Disque, 1978, 1984; Chevalier de l'Ordre des Arts et des Lettres, 1984. Mailing address: Department of Music, University of California at San Diego, La Jolla, California 92093, U.S.A.

Publisher: Edition Peters.

Symphonies/orchestral:

Epicycle (strings) 1968; first performed Munich, April 1974.
Firecycle Beta 1969–71; first performed Venice, October 1976.
La Terre est un homme (101 players) 1976–9; first performed Glasgow, September 1979.
Carceri d'invenzione I (chamber orchestra) 1982; first performed London, November 1982.
Carceri d'invenzione IIa (flute, chamber orchestra) 1984; first performed Milan, February 1985.
Allgebrah (oboe, strings) 1990.

Chamber/instrumental:

Sonatina (3 clarinets, bassoon) 1963; first performed Birmingham, 1963.
Four Miniatures (flute, piano) 1965; first performed Basle, 1971.
Coloratura (oboe, piano) 1966; first performed Wezikon, Switzerland, 1972.
Epigrams (piano) 1966; first performed London, February 1967.
Sonata (2 pianos) 1966; first performed London, October 1967.
Three Pieces (piano) 1967; first performed London, 1968.
Prometheus (flute/piccolo, oboe, cor anglais, clarinet/E♭ clarinet, horn, bassoon) 1967; first performed London, March 1967.
Sonatas for String Quartet 1967; first performed Royan, 1975. Recorded RCA Red Seal RL 70610.
Funérailles (string septet, harp) 1969–77; first performed Saintes, July 1977. Recorded IRCAM/Erato STU 71556.
Cassandra's Dream Song (flute) 1971; first performed Royan, March 1974. Recorded Musicaphon Stil 31085 83; Bauer, Frankfurt.
Sieben Sterne (organ, 2 assistants) 1971; first performed Royan, March 1974.

Time and Motion Study I (bass clarinet) 1971–7; first performed Royan, March 1977.
Time and Motion Study II (cello, delay tape, modulation, amplification—3 assistants) 1973–6; first performed Donaueschingen, October 1977. Recorded Musicaphon BM 30 SL 1715.
Unity Capsule (flute) 1975–6; first performed Royan, March 1976. Recorded Editions Stil 31085 83.
Second String Quartet 1980; first performed Germany, September 1980. Recorded RCA Red Seal RL 70883.
Lemma-Icon-Epigram (piano) 1981; first performed La Rochelle, June 1981. Recorded Frequenz.
Superscriptio (piccolo; part of *Carceri d'invenzione* cycle) 1981; first performed Venice, September 1982. Recorded Bauer, Frankfurt; Etcetera KTC 1070.
Adagissima (string quartet) 1983; first performed La Rochelle, June 1984.
Kurze Schatten II (guitar) 1985–9.
Carceri d'invenzione IIb (flute) 1985; first performed New York, November 1985.
Carceri d'invenzione III (18 winds, 3 percussion) 1986; first performed Donaueschingen, October 1986.
Intermedio alla ciaccona (violin; part of *Carceri d'invenzione* cycle) 1986; first performed Donaueschingen, October 1986. Recorded Etcetera KTC 1070.
Mnemosyne (bass flute, tape; part of *Carceri d'invenzione* cycle) 1986; first performed Donaueschingen, October 1986. Recorded Etcetera KTC 1070.
Third String Quartet 1987; first performed Paris, October 1987.
La Chute d'Icare (clarinet, 7 players) 1988; first performed Strasbourg, September 1988. Recorded Etcetera KTC 1070.

Vocal/choral:

Missa Brevis (12 voices) 1969; first performed Royan, 1974.
Transit (6 amplified voices, chamber orchestra) 1972–5; first performed Royan, March 1975. Recorded Decca Headline HEAD 18.
Time and Motion Study III (16 voices, percussion, tape) 1974. Recorded Wergo 60111.
Etudes Transcendentales/Intermedio II (flute/piccolo/alto flute, oboe/cor anglais, cello, harpischord, soprano; part of *Carceri d'invenzione* cycle) 1982–5; first performed Venice, September 1985. Recorded Etcetera KTC 1070.

PUBLICATIONS

By Ferneyhough: "Aspects of Notational and Compositional Practice", in *Scritture Musicali*, Rome, 1978; in Italian, in *La Musica, Le Idee, Le Cose*, Florence, 1981; in French, in *Consequences*, Paris, 1986; "Carl Ruggles and Dissonant Melody", in *Nutida Musik*, Stockholm, 1982; "Lightning Conductors and Dowsing Rods; Thoughts on Composition Teaching", in *Nutida Musik*, Stockholm 1983.

On Ferneyhough: A. Clements, "BF", in *Music and Musicians*, 16(3), 1977; S. Gottwald, "BF oder Von der Metaphysik der Positivismus", in *Melos*, July/August 1977; Jonathan Harvey, "BF", in *Musical Times*, 120(1639), 1979; Keith Potter, "BF/Introduction", in *Contact*, 20, 1979; D. Gulli, "Liberta estruttura nella musica di BF", in *Spirale*, 1982; J. Bons, "Intervista a BF", in *I Quaderni della Civica Scuola di Musica*, Milan, 1983, and "Ear Mail: BF in Conversation", in *Key Notes*, Amsterdam, 1984; Paul Griffiths, (interview) in *New Sounds, New Personalities; British Composers of the 1980s*, London, 1985; F. Nicolas, "BF, compositeur", in *Le Perroquet*, February 1985; R. Toop, (interview) in *Contact*, 29, 1985.

* * *

It often seems that either Brian Ferneyhough's music is talked about more than listened to or performed, or that his name embodies some kind of numinous idea with scant reference to the compositions with which it is presumably connected. To his critics he often represents all that is most esoteric and pointless in the compositional ivory tower; to many of his supporters he appears as the torch-carrier for the centuries-old mainstream of "progress" in musical thought. Ferneyhough has no doubt inadvertently supplied support for both arguments in the often impenetrable verbal apparatus with which he surrounds the music. To dispose of this aspect first, closer examination of almost any of his published statements reveals a coherence, and indeed reasonableness, of which the more woolly-minded among composers would do well to take notice. For performers and listeners alike, the "difficulties" presented by Ferneyhough's music are mainly to do with depth and span of attention. The music resists casual listening as surely as it does sight-reading, but there is a great difference between this and, on the one hand, lack of interest in the sound itself, or on the other hand lack of sensitivity to performing resources (Ferneyhough is assiduous in researching instrumental possibilities, as many players eventually agree).

Ferneyhough's music certainly has its roots in the tradition of serial thinking, or, to be more general, "parametric" thinking, where the different (and differently defined) aspects or dimensions of a sound or complex of sounds may be not only *organised*, but organised *independently*. The density of sound and notation in most of his music is a result of his applying such principles to many more and much subtler "parameters" than he had previously. An instrumental line will hardly ever be free of layer upon layer of superimposed articulations, ornamentations and so on, which almost function as "counterpoints" to each other and to the pitch-contour itself (if indeed the latter remains discernible). The finished score is the "sounding trace" of a vast and contradictory network of processes and permutations, a network constructed to draw together and solidify what Ferneyhough has called an "unformed mass of creative volition". The title of his seven-part cycle *Carceri d'invenzione* ("prisons of invention") not only recalls Piranesi's etchings of imaginary dungeons, but also the process by which a composer might set up more or less systematic restrictions in order to channel an initially inchoate compulsion or desire. Nevertheless, however abstractly formulated these restrictions, Ferneyhough's music possesses abundant stylistic "signatures". It would be over-simplifying to talk of a "Ferneyhough sound" when one of the music's most obvious features is a refusal to arrive at a point of unequivocal statement, but on a "microscopic" level there are any number of characteristic gestures which occasionally emerge from his typically hyperactive polyphony.

Ferneyhough's earliest mature works date from the mid-1960s, when in the *Sonatas for String Quartet*, for example, disparate compositional means (serial and non-serial) coexist without fusing. This work is also typical in its fragmentary overall form; nearly all of Ferneyhough's longer compositions are either made up of separate, shortish movements, or divided into at least notionally discrete sections (24 in the *Sonatas*). The following works brought about increasingly complex relationships between deterministic and empirical composition, which are paralleled in the diverse degrees of notational exactitude in *Transit*. At the same time, tendencies towards "parametric polyphony" in writing for solo instruments reached their apogee in *Unity Capsule*, where the superimposed layers of notation for parameters such as embouchure position and vocal activity threaten to marginalise the (traditionally paramount) pitch structures.

The most recent works, while retaining and even building upon these characteristics, also embody a new openness to formal clarity (relatively speaking), exemplified in the gradual disintegration of a sharply-defined initial situation in *La Chûte d'Icare*, the starkly juxtaposed textures towards the end of the *Third String Quartet* or the series of linked etude-like miniatures which constitutes *Kurze Schatten II*. In these pieces, a more important structural role is played by contrasts in overall texture, although an essential ambiguity is retained, that sense of an endless recursion of qualifications around every statement, which is at the same time one of the most frustrating and one of the most rewarding features of Ferneyhough's work.

—Richard Barrett

FERRARI, Luc. French. Born in Paris, 5 February 1929. Educated at Conservatoire de Versailles, 1946–8; Ecole Normale de Musique, Paris (piano under Alfred Cortot, composition under Arthur Honegger), 1948–50; further study under Olivier Messiaen, 1953–4. Member, Groupe de Musique Concrète, 1958–66; co-founder (with Pierre Schaeffer), 1958, head, 1959–60, in charge of research into new instruments, 1960–1, and research director, 1960–1, 1963, Groupe de Recherche Musicale; Paris; professor of composition, Rheinische Musikschule, Cologne, 1964–5; professor of experimental music, Radio Stockholm, 1966; head of music, Maison de la Culture, Amiens, 1968–9; founder, Billig electro-acoustic studio, 1972; professor of composition, Conservatoire de Pantin, from 1978; founder, electro-acoustic composition and radiophonic research studio La Muse en Circuit, 1982. Recipient: Prix de la Biennale de Paris (for *Visage IV*), 1962; Prix Karl Sczuka, 1972 (for *Portrait-Spiel*), 1988 (for *Je me suis perdu*); Prix Italia (for *Et si toute entière maintenant*), 1987; Grand Prix de la Musique, 1989. Mailing address: c/o Michel Dumont, La Muse en Circuit, 52 rue de la République, 92170 Vanves, France.

Publishers: Editions Moeck; Schott; Editions Transatlantique; La Muse en Circuit.

Symphonies/orchestral:

Huit petites faces (chamber orchestra) 1955.
Composé Composite (orchestra, tape) 1962–3; first performed Venice, 1963, and Zagreb, 1963. Recorded Philips 836 894.
Symphonie inachevée (large orchestra) 1963–6; first performed Rennes, 1968.
Société IV—Mécanique Collectivité Individú (large orchestra) 1967; first performed Havana, Cuba, 1968.
Histoire du plaisir et de la désolation 1979–81; first performed Paris, November 1982.
En un tournement d'amour (49 musicians) 1986; first performed Nice, 1987.

Chamber/instrumental:

Suite (piano) 1952; first performed Miami, Florida, 1954.
Antisonate (piano) 1953; first performed Paris, 1955.
Sonatine Elyb (piano) 1953–4; first performed Darmstadt, 1956.
Quartet (violin, viola, cello, piano) 1953–4.
Suite hétéroclite (piano) 1955; first performed Paris, 1959.
Lapidarium (piano) 1955; first performed Paris, 1956.
Visage I (piano) 1956; first performed Darmstadt, 1957.
Visage II (brass, percussion) 1956; first performed Vienna, 1961.
Visage IV—Profils (10 instruments) 1957–8; first performed Cologne, 1959.
Flashes (14 instruments) 1963; first performed Paris, 1964.
Bachiques (Bachet instruments) 1963.
Und So Weiter (piano, tape) 1965–6; first performed Bremen, 1966. Recorded Wergo 60046.
Société II: Et si le piano était un corps de femme (piano, 3 percussion, 16 instruments) 1967. Recorded Deutsche Grammophon.
Interrupteur (10 instruments) 1967; first performed Barcelona, 1968. Recorded EMI C.061-11133.
Société V—Participation or Not Participation (6 percussionists, actor, public) 1967–9; first performed St Paul de Vence, France, 1969.
Tautologos 3 ou Vous plaîrait-il de tautologuer avec moi? (unspecified instrumentation) 1969. Version recorded EMI C 061 11133.
Le Dispositif et son disnégatif (unspecified instrumentation) 1969–70.
Danse des ministres chez les Pompidou (piano, cello, trombone) 1972.
Musique socialiste? Programme commun pour clavecin et bande (amplified harpsichord, stereo tape) 1972. Recorded Erato STU 71010.
Bonjour, comment ça va? (piano, cello, bass clarinet) 1972–9.
Cellule 75, Force du rythme et cadence forcée (piano, percussion, tape) 1975. Recorded La Muse en Circuit MEC01; CD Adda 581010.
Et tournent les sons dans la garrigue (unspecified instrumentation, stereo tape) 1977.
Exercices d'improvisation (jazz or other instruments, stereo tape) 1977.
A la recherche du rythme perdu (piano, tape, other instruments optionally) 1978.
Ce qu'a vu le cerf (instruments, tape) 1978. Recorded Ventadorn VT 323; CD Adda 581088.
Apparition et disparition mystérieuses d'un accord (4 alto saxophones) 1978.
Entrée (15 instruments) 1978–9.
Préface (piano; introduction to *Journal Intime*) 1983.
Patajaslotcha (paso doble, tango, java, slow, cha-cha; 9 instruments) 1984.
Collections de petites pièces ou 36 enfilades (piano, magnetophone) 1985. Recorded La Muse en Circuit MEC 01; CD Adda 581010.
Les émois d'Aphrodite (piano, clarinet, percussion, tape) 1986.
Un Calypso pour Colette (2 saxophones, 2 pianos, 2 percussion) 1987.
Conversation intime (harpsichord, percussion) 1987–8; first performed Paris, 1989.

Vocal/choral:

Tête à terre (voice, piano; Weingarten) 1956.
Visage III (reciter, violin, cello, clarinet, percussion; Cendrars) 1957–8. Recorded Radio France, 1962.
J'ai tort, j'ai tort, j'ai mon très grand tort (mixed chorus) 1969.
Monologos (solo voice, 2 magnetophones) 1970.
Chanson du Larzac (from the film *Presque rien ou le désir de vivre*; singer, guitar or accordion) 1973–4.
Une Soirée avec Matricia Perséverse (consists of *Entrée*, *Scène du va et vient* and *Sexolidad*) 1978–84.
Journal intime (reciter, female singer, piano) 1980–2; first performed Paris, 1982.
Sexolidad (reciter, 15 instruments, stereo tape) 1982–3; first performed Lille, 1983.

Opera:

La Musique à l'envers (fragment of a collective opera; Schaeffer) 1965; first performed Zagreb, 1965.

Other:

Etude aux accidents (*musique concrète*) 1958; first performed Brussels, 1958. Recorded BAM LD 070.
Etude aux sons tendus (*musique concrète*) 1958; first performed Brussels, 1958. Recorded BAM LD 070.
Passage pour mimes (*musique concrète*) 1959; first performed Rome, 1959.
Visage V (*musique concrète*) 1959; first performed Paris, 1959. Recorded Philips 6526 003.
Tête et queue du dragon (*musique concrète*) 1959–60; first performed Paris, 1960. Recorded Candide CE 31025.
Egypte ô Egypte I (music to a short by Jacques Brissot) 1960.
J'ai été coupé (stereo tape) 1960–9. Recorded Philips 836.885 DSY.
Tautologos I (electronic music) 1961; first performed Paris, 1962.
Tautologos II (*musique concrète*) 1961; first performed Paris, 1962. Recorded BAM LD 071.
Forme Bleue (instrumental score to an abstract short by Piotr Kamler) 1961.
Etude (instrumental score to an abstract short by Piotr Kamler) 1961.
Spontané I (improvisation for 9 performers) 1962.
Spontané II (improvisation for 10 performers) 1962.
Spontané III (improvisation for 8 performers) 1962; filmed by Gerard Patris.
Spontané IV (improvisation for 11 performers) 1962; filmed by Gerard Patris, June 1962.
Chastel (film score) 1962.
Egypte ô Egypte II (*musique concrète*, instruments) 1962; filmed by Jacques Brissot.
6 pour 4 (4-track tape) 1962; first performed Paris, 1962.
Les Pèlerins (35mm short in colour on Bayreuth Festival, collaboration with Jacques Brissot) 1962–3.
Portrait d'une autre (music to 35mm short in colour by Marie-Claire Patris) 1963.
Hétérozygote (stereo tape; "anecdotal" use of realistic sound, concrete images conjoined with abstract sounds and structures; listeners supply their own "anecdotes") 1963–4. Recorded Philips 836.885 DSY.
Music Promenade (electro-acoustic music; tape or version for 4 magnetophones) 1964–9. Recorded Wergo 60064.
Dernier matin d'E. A. Poe (music to 35mm short by Jean Barral) 1964.
Les réalisables et le journal d'une autobiographie (score in the form of a book, accompanied by autobiographical reflections) 1964–72.
Société I (*réalisable* text for 7 performers and real life; a "social game") 1965.
Les Grandes Répétitions (5 16mm films for television) 1965–6: *Et exspecto resurrectionem mortuorum*, by Olivier Messiaen, filmed in Chartres Cathedral in the presence of Charles de Gaulle, broadcast 11 November 1965; *Hommage à Varèse*, broadcast 20 April 1966; *Momente*, Karlheinz Stockhausen in rehearsal, broadcast June 1966; *Quand un homme consacre sa vie à la musique*, portrait of Herman Scherchen, broadcast November 1966; *Cecil Taylor*, and the discovery of free jazz, broadcast November 1966.
So (*musique concrète* for the film *Elektronische Musik* by A. Riedl) 1967.
Tinguely (*musique concrète* for television) 1967.
Société III: Les Jeunes Filles (16mm film) 1967.
Société VI—Liberté, liberté chérie (solo for the public) 1969.
Presque rien ou le lever du jour au bord de la mer (stereo tape) 1970. Recorded Deutsche Grammophon avantgarde 2 561 041.
Portrait-Spiel (stereo tape) 1971.
Unheimlich Schoen (stereo tape) 1971.
Pornologos 2 1971; performance may prove awkward.
Allo, ici la terre (music by Ferrari, slides by Jean-Serge Breton) 1971–4; first performed Bonn, 1972.
Danses organiques (stereo tape) 1971–3.
Kennen sie Schoenberg? (16mm film) 1972.
Journal d'un journaliste amateur (stereo tape) 1972.
Presque rien ou le désir de vivre (16mm film) 1972–3.
Petite symphonie intuitive pour un paysage de printemps (stereo tape) 1973–4.
Ephémère (stereo tape) 1974.
Labyrinthe de violence (tape, 2 slide projectors) 1975.
Algérie 76 No 1. La révolution agraire (tape, or tape and slides) 1976.
Algérie 76 No 2. Belghimpouze: Village socialiste (tape, or tape and slides) 1976.
Tuchan, village no 11350 ("symphonic reportage"; tape, slide projectors) 1976–7.
Algérie No 4: Promenade symphonique dans un paysage musical (stereo tape, images) 1976–8. Recorded INA-GRM 9104 fe.
Place des abesses (music for film by Erika Magdalinski; tape) 1977.
Les Apprentis (music to 16mm film by Gerard Patris) 1977.
Loin de l'équilibre (music to scientific film by Alain Bedos) 1977.
Presque rien no 2: "Ainsi continue la nuit dans ma tête multiple" (tape) 1977. Recorded INA-GRM 9104 fe.
Algérie No 3: La Société nationale de Sidérurgié (stereo tape with or without slides) 1978.
Chantal, ou le portrait d'une villageoise (stereo tape; collaboration with Brunhild Ferrari) 1978.
Scène du va et vient (actress, piano) 1978–80.
Le Dernier Soleil (film score) 1980.
Le Petit Pommier (film score; collaboration with David Jisse) 1980.
Ateliers (music to 16mm film by Joel Farge) 1981.
Chronopolis (music to an experimental animated film by Piotr Kamler) 1981–2.
Yetz (maintenant) (radiophonic composition) 1981–2.
Leçon de composition (tape) 1984.
Dialogue ordinaire avec la machine, ou trois fables pour bande doucement philosophique (stereo tape) 1984.
Strathoven (stereo tape) 1985.
Et si toute entière maintenant (stereo tape; Felous) 1987.

Recorded CD Adda 581079.
Je me suis perdu ou Labyrinthe portrait (stereo tape) 1988.
Presque rien avec filles 1989.

PUBLICATIONS

By Ferrari: "Preface à . . . Réflexion sur . . . ", critical text on the role of artistic creativity in contemporary society, in *Action Musicale*, July 1977; text of *Société I*, in *Chemin de ronde*, 3, 1983.

Luc Ferrari comments:

I have created works which stand more or less aloof from purely musical preoccupations. Some of them attempt to bring together different branches of what may be the same tree. The challenge is to express, by means of quite different resources, a passing show of ideas, sensations and intuitions; to observe the everyday in all its little particularities, which may be social, psychological or even sentimental. All this to be done in texts, instrumental scores, electro-acoustic compositions, reportage, film, drama . . .

* * *

The earliest extant work of Luc Ferrari dates from the 1950s: instrumental pieces, often for piano, from the piano *Suite* to *Visage IV* for 10 instruments. Then he became involved with the *musique concrète* group in Paris, joining Pierre Schaeffer's Groupe de Recherche Musicale in 1958. From the outset, in compositions such as *Etude aux accidents* and *Visage V*, Ferrari sought to capitalise on the concrete nature of his sound sources, rather than denature them by treatment and manipulation. As he clarified and refined this aim, his work became simpler in the density of sounds and the extent to which they were modified. Simultaneously, it involved storytelling or scene-painting for which the listener's creative engagement is required. Ferrari's first attempt at this sort of "anecdotal" composition was *Hétérozygote*, an "imaginary musical tale", "concrete images added to traditional, abstract sounds and structures". *Presque rien ou le lever du jour au bord de la mer* is a "musical photograph" of a fishing village at dawn. "A Tuscan landscape, an Alsatian forest, girls passing from afar" is Ferrari's comment on *Presque rien avec filles*, "and the rest is my secret". Even the title is suggestive of painting, having the tone of "still life with fruit". "I emit images," states Ferrari, "but more in the form of an empty frame which has to be filled in by listening."

Et si toute entière maintenant is a "symphonic tale" using sounds recorded on an ice-breaking ship, an orchestral score by Ferrari, and a spoken text by Colette Fellous. Ferrari remained in Paris to write his orchestral materials. In the finished piece they are heard only in fragments, transformed electronically and woven into the recordings and the text.

What can be heard of the orchestra is revealing, for the writing is effective and highly reminiscent of his teachers Honegger and Messaien. Ferrari permits us, and himself, only glimpses of his traditional musical expertise. It can well be asked how far this is an affirmative aesthetic decision, and how far it is a poignant reflection of the modernist handicap—the difficulty in finding meaning; the reluctance to deal with the ambiguities of working abstractly yet with engagement, in ways which synthesise and integrate human passions, problems and uncertainties. There is something slightly hopeless about Ferrari's anecdotal approach to composition. Consider titles such as *Histoire du plaisir et de la désolation* (Tale of pleasure and desolation), *Je me suis perdu ou Labyrinthe portrait* (I lost myself, or, Labyrinth portrait) and *Presque rien* (Nearly nothing). We do not hear Ferrari recorded in his soundscapes. Consider, too, the sound content of *Strathoven*: passages from the *Firebird* by Stravinsky and the Beethoven Fifth Symphony, as if, Ferrari invites us to imagine, "two people, who have never met before, speak at the same moment". The effect is that of flicking channels on a remote-control television, in the manner of sampling in popular music (*Strathoven* lasts about as long as a seven-inch single). Skill does not inhere in the creation of musical material, but in determining their juxtaposition, and in the technical accuracy of editing and processing. Perhaps tellingly, for the last few seconds we hear neither Beethoven nor Stravinsky, but thudding, chugging and labourer's voices, in the telltale acoustic spaciousness of a demolition site.

In his work as a whole, Ferrari's choice of sounds and his comments make plain his involvement with sound and his love for it, especially the ambient evocation of the countryside, its surprising richness ("the way in which this landscape has surprised me") and the interesting complexity of natural sound ("I love the sound that betrays small uncertainties"). As a solution to the problems and limitations of modern music, the work of Ferrari is clearly delineated and, as he described *Et si toute entière maintenant*, "giving off a sensuous warmth, struggling to keep out the cold".

—David Revill

FINE, Vivian. American. Born in Chicago, 28 September 1913. Educated at Chicago Music College (scholarship), 1919–22; studied violin under Silvio Sconti, 1923–4; piano lessons with Djane Lavoie-Herz, 1924–6; American Conservatory, Chicago (harmony and composition under Ruth Crawford [Seeger], counterpoint with Adolf Weidig), 1926–8; moved to New York, 1931; studied composition, counterpoint and orchestration under Roger Sessions, 1934–2, piano under Abbey Whiteside, 1937–45, orchestration under George Szeil, 1943; Dalcroze School, New York City, 1935–6. Married the sculptor Benjamin Karp in 1935. Teacher, New York University, 1945–8; teacher, Juilliard School, New York City, 1948, and State University Teachers' College, Potsdam, New York, 1951; teacher, Connecticut College School of Dance, 1963; teacher of composition and piano, Bennington College, Vermont, 1964; founder, and chair, 1961–5, American Composers' Alliance; director, Rothschild Foundation, 1953–60; composer in residence, Panorama of the Arts, University of Wisconsin, Oshkosh, 1968, and Skidmore College, Saratoga, New York, 1976. Recipient: Dollard Prize, 1966; nomination, Pulitzer Prize (for *Drama*), 1983; Guggenheim Fellowship, for composition, 1980; member, American Academy and Institute of Arts and Letters, 1980. Address: c/o Margun/Gunmar Music Inc., 167 Dudley Road, Newton Centre, Massachusetts 02159, U.S.A.

Publishers: Catamount Facsimile Editions; ACA; Margun.

Symphonies/orchestral:

Race of Life 1937.
Prelude and Elegiac Song (orchestra of muted strings; also string quartet) 1937.

The Race of Life; Concert Suite (from the stage work) 1937; first performed New York City, 27 April 1956.
Dance Suite (from *The Race of Life*) 1938.
Concertante for Piano and Orchestra 1944.
Concerto for Piano, Strings and Percussion 1972.
Romantic Ode (violin, viola, cello, string orchestra) 1976; first performed Bennington, Vermont, 28 August 1976.
Drama 1982–3; first performed San Francisco, 5 January 1983.
Poetic Fires (piano, orchestra) 1984; first performed New York City, 21 February 1985.

Chamber/instrumental:

Solo (oboe) 1929.
String Trio 1930.
Four Pieces (2 flutes) 1930.
Four Polyphonic Pieces (piano) 1931–2.
Divertimento (oboe, clarinet, bassoon, trumpet, piano, percussion) 1933.
Lyric Piece (cello, piano) 1937.
Sonatina (oboe or violin or cello, piano) 1939.
Five Preludes (piano) 1939–41.
Three Pieces (violin, piano) 1940.
Suite in E♭ major 1940.
Suite (oboe, piano) 1943.
Rhapsody on a Russian Folk Song (piano) 1944.
Capriccio (oboe, string trio) 1946.
Second Solo (oboe) 1947.
Chaconne (piano) 1947.
Divertimento (cello, percussion) 1951.
Sonata (violin, piano) 1952.
Variations (piano) 1952.
Sinfonia and Fugato (piano) 1952.
Variations (harp) 1953.
Composition (string quartet) 1954.
String Quartet 1957.
Three Pieces (flute, bassoon, harp) 1961.
Duo (flute, viola) 1961.
Fantasy (cello, piano) 1962.
Small Sad Sparrow (piano) 1963.
Dreamscape (percussion ensemble, 3 flutes, cello, piano) 1964.
Melos (double bass) 1964.
The Song of Persephone (viola) 1964.
Concertino (piano, percussion ensemble) 1965.
Chamber Concerto (cello, sextet) 1966.
Four Pieces (piano) 1966.
Quintet (string trio, trumpet, harp) 1967.
Second Prophet-Bird (flute) 1972.
The Flicker (flute/piano, right hand) 1973.
Three Buddhist Evocations (violin, piano) 1977.
Quartet (brass) 1978.
Momenti (piano) 1978.
Nightingales (motets for flute, oboe, violin, 2 violas, double bass) 1979.
Music (flute, oboe, cello) 1980.
Lieder (viola, piano) 1980.
Piano Trio 1980.
Double Variations (piano) 1982.
Quintet (oboe, clarinet, violin, cello, piano) 1984.

Vocal/choral:

The Riddle (part of *Four Lyric Songs*; voice, piano; Dickinson) 1933.
A Flower Given to My Daughter (part of *Four Lyric Songs*; voice, piano; Joyce) 1935.
Spring's Welcome (part of *Four Elizabethan Songs*; voice, piano; Lyly) 1937.
Daybreak (part of *Four Elizabethan Songs*; voice, piano; Donne) 1938.
The Bargain (part of *Four Elizabethan Songs*; voice, piano; Sidney) 1938.
The Passionate Shepherd to His Love and Her Reply (unaccompanied SAA chorus; Marlowe, Raleigh) 1938.
Adios (part of *Four Lyric Songs*; voice, piano; anon.) 1939.
Sonnet (part of *Four Lyric Songs*; voice, piano; Keats) 1939.
Tragic Exodus (vocalise, piano) 1939.
Dirge (part of *Four Elizabethan Songs*; voice, piano; Shakespeare) 1941.
Epigram and Epitaph (voice, piano; Jones, Wootton) 1941.
Stabat Mater (part of *Songs of Our Time*; voice, piano; Wittlin) 1943.
And What Did She Get, the Soldier's Wife? (part of *Songs of Our Time*; voice, piano; Brecht) 1943.
The Great Wall of China (medium voice, 2 violins, viola, cello; Kafka) 1947.
Psalm 13 (baritone, SSA chorus, piano or organ) 1953.
A Guide to the Life Expectancy of a Rose (soprano, tenor, flute, clarinet, violin, cello, harp) 1956.
Valedictions (soprano, tenor, mixed chorus, 10 instruments; Donne) 1959.
Morning (narrator, mixed chorus, organ; Thoreau) 1962.
The Confession (soprano, flute, violin, viola, cello, piano; Racine) 1963.
Epitaph (mixed chorus, orchestra) 1967; first performed Bennington, Vermont, 5 November 1983.
Paean (narrator, women's chorus, brass; Keats) 1969.
Sounds of the Nightingale (soprano, women's chorus, nonet; Keats and others) 1971.
Tortuga (voice, piano; Neruda) 1971.
Oda al piano (voice, piano; Neruda) 1971.
Missa brevis (taped voice, 4 cellos) 1972.
Teisho (small chorus or vocal octet, string quartet; parts arranged for violin, piano) 1976.
Meeting for Equal Rights, 1866 (soprano, baritone, narrator, mixed chorus, orchestra; 19th-century American text) 1976; first performed New York City, 23 April 1976.
Three Sonnets (baritone, orchestra; Keats) 1976; first performed Bennington, Vermont, 12 December 1976.
For a Bust of Erik Satie (soprano, mezzo-soprano, narrator, flute, bassoon, trumpet, trombone, cello, double bass; Guy) 1979.
Odo a las ranas (women's chorus, flute, oboe, cello, percussion) 1980.
Ode to Purcell (medium voice, string quartet) 1984.
Canticles for Jerusalem (voice, piano) 1983.

Opera/stage:

The Women in the Garden (chamber opera; VF) 1977; first performed San Francisco, 1978.

Other:

The Race of Life (dance after Thurber; piano, percussion; later orchestrated) 1937; first performed New York City, 23 January 1938.
Opus 51 (dance; piano) 1938; first performed Bennington, Vermont, 6 August 1938.
Tragic Exodus (dance; voice, piano; Holm) 1939; first performed New York City, 16 February 1939.
They Too Are Exiles (dance; piano—4 hands, cello, percussion;

Holm) 1939; first performed New York City, 7 January 1940.
Dollars and Cents (incidental music) 1941.
Alcestis (Martha Graham dance; orchestra) 1960; first performed New York City, 29 April 1960.
My Son, My Enemy (dance; string quartet, piano, percussion) 1965; first performed New London, Connecticut, 15 August 1965.

PUBLICATIONS

By Fine: "VF: Composer/Choreographer, Choreographer/ Composer" (with Lucia Długoszewski), in *Dance Perspectives*, 16, 1963.

On Fine: Wallingford Riegger, "The Music of VF" in *ACA Bulletin*, 8(1), 1953.

* * *

Astonishingly precocious, Vivian Fine began her studies at Chicago Music College aged only 5. Before she was out of her teens, her first compositions—and notably a fine oboe solo—were being professionally performed in New York City, where she moved in 1931 to continue her studies. Her first music, though tonal and virtually untouched by the Vienna-inspired theories then circulating in New York, was dramatically dissonant, marked by her use of the tritone and other preterite intervals. This may have been the legacy of her piano teacher Djane Lavoie-Herz, a pupil of Scriabin's, or of a later teacher Ruth Crawford (later Ruth Seeger), who was strongly influenced by Scriabin's harmonic conception.

Fine's music is remarkably consistent. Though the 1944 *Concertante* for piano is milder, with clear hints of diatonicism, she has stuck fast to her original style, very successfully broadening its expressive and generic range, and suffusing it with a distinctive humour and considerable emotional force. Perhaps her best known work is *A Guide to the Life Expectancy of a Rose*, a vocal piece set to a text taken from a gardening page. It is typical of her wit—and her instinctive feminism—that she should have set not only the Passionate's Shepherd's call to his love but also her reply. When in the early 1970s she was commissioned to write an opera, she chose to bring together Isadora Duncan, Gertrude Stein (whose views on the nature of roses must have struck a chord with Fine), Emily Dickinson and Virginia Woolf; *The Women in the Garden* was a considerable artistic and critical success that merits a revival, its unstuffy programme and ironic wit perfectly in tune with contemporary feminism.

Much of Fine's most distinctive work has had a theatrical background, mostly in dance. *Alcestis*, for Martha Graham, is perhaps the most realised, but *The Race of Life*, inspired by James Thurber, remains the most interesting musically. Together with *Opus 51*, it provides the material for the excellent 1938 *Dance Suite*.

Fine's orchestral music is strongly articulated, with forceful melorhythms and considerable dramatic force. *Drama* was premiered in 1983 by the San Francisco Symphony; two years later, the 72-year-old Fine took the solo part herself in her Greek-inspired *Poetic Fires*. An able pianist, she writes particularly well for the instrument; the *Double Variations* of 1982 are convincing exercises, though without the instinctive structural sense of earlier work.

It is, though, her vocal work which deserves to stand alongside the theatre and dance pieces. Fine's choice of texts has always been bold and intuitive. Her wartime settings of Brecht and Wittlin and later of Neruda are particularly moving, but she has also tackled the intractable Kafka (it is interesting to compare her *Great Wall of China* with Alexander Goehr's *The Law of the Quadrille* also by Kafka). By complete contrast, she is drawn to Keats; the sonnet settings for baritone and orchestra of 1976, following on from a pre-war essay for voice and piano, are beautifully and maturely handled.

An important presence on the American scene, Fine is still too little known elsewhere. She is highly significant composer, original, unfailingly individual and wry, quite unlike anyone else.

—Bea Weir

FINNEY, Ross Lee. American. Born in Wells, Minnesota, 23 December 1906. Educated at University of Minnesota, Minneapolis; Carleton College, Northfield, Minnesota, 1925–7, B.A., L.H.D.; privately, with Nadia Boulanger, 1927–8, 1932; Harvard University, Cambridge, Massachusetts (under Edward Burlingame Hill), 1928–9; privately, with Alban Berg, 1931–2; privately, with Roger Sessions, 1935. Served in American forces, Office of Strategic Services: Purple Heart and Certificate of Merit, 1943–5. Married Gretchen Ludke in 1930; 2 sons. Instructor, then professor, Smith College, Northampton, Maine, 1929–49; professor of composition and composer in residence, University of Michigan, Ann Arbor, 1949–73, subsequently emeritus; endowed chair in music, University of Alabama, Tuscaloosa, 1982–3. Recipient: Pulitzer Scholarship, 1937; Guggenheim Fellowships, 1937, 1948; Rome Prize, 1960; elected, National Institute of Arts and Letters, 1962; Brandeis Gold Medal, 1967; Phi Beta Kappa. Mailing address: 2015 Geddes Avenue, Ann Arbor, Michigan 48104, U.S.A.

Publisher: C.F. Peters, New York.

Symphonies/orchestral:

Violin Concerto 1933, revised 1952; first performed Ann Arbor, Michigan, 1951.
Barbershop Ballad 1940; broadcast 6 February, 1940.
Slow Piece (string orchestra) 1940; first performed Minneapolis, Minnesota, 4 April 1941.
Serenade (wind orchestra) 1940–1.
Overture for a Drama 1941; first performed Rochester, New York, 28 October 1941.
Symphony No 1 (Communique 1943) 1942; first performed Louisville, Kentucky, 1962. Recorded Louisville LOU 652.
Hymn, Fuging and Holiday 1943; first performed New York City, 17 May 1947.
Piano Concerto No 1 in E 1948; first performed Berne, Switzerland, 1951.
Variations 1957; first performed Minneapolis, Minnesota, 30 December 1965.
Symphony No 2 1958; first performed Philadelphia, 13 November 1959. Recorded Louisville LOU 625.
Symphony No 3 1960; first performed Philadelphia, 6 March 1964. Recorded Louisville LOU 672.

Three Pieces (chamber orchestra, tape) 1962; first performed Toledo, Ohio, 23 February 1963.
Concerto for Percussion and Orchestra 1965; first performed Northfield, Minnesota, 17 November 1966.
Symphonie concertante 1967; first performed Kansas City, Missouri, 27 February 1968.
Piano Concerto No 2 1968; first performed Ann Arbor, Michigan, 1 November 1972.
Summer in Valley City (band) 1969; first performed Ann Arbor, Michigan, 1 April 1971.
Landscapes Remembered 1971; first performed Ithaca, New York, 5 November 1972.
Spaces 1972, transcribed for concert band, 1986; first performed Fargo, North Dakota, 26 May 1972.
Symphony No 4 (large orchestra) 1972; first performed Baltimore, Maryland, 9 May 1973.
Violin Concerto No 2 1973, revised 1977; first performed Dallas, Texas, 31 March 1976.
Alto Saxophone Concerto (alto saxophone, wind orchestra) 1974; first performed Ann Arbor, Michigan, 17 April 1975.
Narrative (cello, 14 instruments) 1976; first performed Urbana, Illinois, 5 March 1977.
Concerto for Strings 1977; first performed New York City, 5 December, 1977.
Skating on the Sheyenne (band) 1977; first performed Brooklyn, New York, 20 May 1978.

Chamber/instrumental:

Sonata in D (piano) 1933.
Sonata No 1 (violin) 1934.
String Quartet No 1 1935.
String Quartet No 2 in D minor 1937.
Viola Sonata No 1 in A minor 1937.
Piano Trio No 1 1938.
Cello Sonata late 1930s; withdrawn.
Fantasy (piano) 1939.
String Quartet No 3 in G 1940.
Sonata No 3 (piano) 1942.
Duo (violin, piano) 1944.
Sonata No 4 (Christmastime, 1945) (piano) 1945.
Fiddle-doodle-ad (violin, piano) 1945.
Nostalgic Waltzes (piano) 1947.
String Quartet No 4 in A min 1947.
Piano Quartet 1948.
String Quartet No 5 1949.
String Quartet No 6 in E 1950. Recorded CRI 116.
Cello Sonata No 2 in C (cello, piano) 1950. Recorded CRI SD 311.
Violin Sonata No 2 1951.
Variations on a Theme by Alban Berg (piano) 1952.
Piano Quintet No 1 1953. Recorded COL ML 5477.
Viola Sonata No 2 1953.
Piano Trio No 2 1954. Recorded CRI 447.
Elegy and March (trombone) 1954.
String Quartet No 7 1955.
Violin Sonata No 3 1955.
Inventions (25 children's piano pieces) 1956.
Chromatic Fantasy in E (cello) 1957. Recorded CRI SD 311.
Fantasy in Two Movements (violin) 1958; first performed Brussels, 1958.
String Quintet 1958.
String Quartet No 8 1960.
Piano Quintet No 2 1961.
Sonata quasi una fantasia (piano) 1961.
Divertimento (wind quintet) 1963.
Divertissement (piano, clarinet, violin, cello) 1964.
Three Studies in Fours (4 percussion) 1965.
Five Fantasies (organ) 1967.
Thirty-Two Piano Games 1968.
Twenty-Four Inventions (piano pieces for children) 1970.
Two Acts for Three Players (piano, clarinet, percussion) 1970.
Two Ballades (flute, piano) 1973.
Seven Easy Percussion Pieces (4 percussion) 1973.
Tubes I (1–5 trombones) 1974.
Variations on a Memory (10 instruments) 1975.
Waltz (piano) 1977.
Quartet (oboe, cello, percussion, piano) 1979.
Two Studies (saxophone, piano) 1980.
Lost Whale Calf (piano) 1980.
Youth's Companion (piano) 1980.
Sonata (saxophone, piano; transcription of 1937 *Sonata in A major* for viola and piano) 1981.
Narrative in Retrospect (piano) 1983.
Hexachord (harpsichord) 1983.

Vocal/choral:

A Stranger to Myself (men's voices, brass) ?1935.
Poems by Archibald MacLeish (voice, piano) 1935.
Bleheris (tenor, contralto, orchestra; MacLeish) 1937.
Three 17th-Century Lyrics (voice, piano; Vaughan, Shakespeare, Milton) 1938.
Pole Star for This Year (tenor, contralto, choir, orchestra; MacLeish) 1939.
Oh, Bury Me Not (choir) 1940.
When the Curtains of the Night (TTBB or SSAA choir; Ogle) 1940.
Trail to Mexico (male chorus) 1941.
Pilgrim Psalms (choir; Ainsworth Psalter) 1945.
Words to be Spoken: Modern Canons (choir; MacLeish) 1946.
Poor Richard (voice, piano; Franklin) 1946.
Spherical Madrigals (SATB choir; Herrick, Herbert, Crashaw, Dryden, Donne, Marvell) 1947. Recorded CRI.
Three Love Songs to Words by John Donne (voice, piano) 1948.
Chamber Music (36 songs for solo voice, piano; Joyce) 1951–2.
Immortal Autumn (tenor, chorus; Whitefield) 1952; first performed Pittsburgh, 25 November 1952.
The Express (voice, piano; Spender) 1955.
Edge of Shadow (chorus, instruments; MacLeish) 1959; first performed Grinnell, Iowa, 22 April 1960.
Immortal Autumn (tenor, choir; Whitefield) 1962.
Still Are New Worlds (narrator, tape, choir, orchestra; Kepler, Harvey, Marlowe, Donne, Milton, Fontenelle, More, Galileo, Akenside, Pindar, Camus; part 1 of trilogy) 1962; first performed Ann Arbor, Michigan, 10 May 1963.
The Nun's Priest's Tale (soloists, small chorus, chamber orchestra; Chaucer) 1965; first performed Hanover, New Hampshire, August 1965.
The Martyr's Elegy (high voice, chorus, orchestra; Shelley; part 2 of trilogy) 1967; first performed Ann Arbor, Michigan, 23 April 1967.
The Remorseless Rush of Time (choir, orchestra; Conrad) 1969; first performed River Falls, Wisconsin, 23 April 1970.
Earthrise (soloists, choir, orchestra; Chardin, Thomas; part 3 of trilogy) 1978; first performed Ann Arbor, Michigan, 11 December 1979.

Opera:

Weep Torn Land 1984.
Computer Marriage 1987.

Other:

Heyoka (Chamber Concerto) (dance; violin, flute/piccolo, clarinet/bass clarinet, trumpet, bass trombone, percussion, string bass) 1981; first performed New York City, 14 September 1981.
The Joshua Tree (dance; violin, flute/piccolo, clarinet/bass clarinet, trumpet, bass trombone, percussion, string bass) 1981; first performed New York City, 14 October 1984.
Ahab (dance; violin, flute/piccolo, clarinet/bass clarinet, trumpet, bass trombone, percussion, string bass) 1985.

PUBLICATIONS

By Finney: *The Game of Harmony*, New York City, 1947; *Making Music: Time Line*, New York City, 1974; *Thinking About Music: Collected Writings of RLF*, Alabama, 1990.

On Finney: P. Cooper, "The Music of RLF", in *Musical Quarterly*, 44, 1955; H. Onderdonk, "Aspects of Tonality in the Music of RLF", in *Perspectives on American Composers*, edited by Boretz and Cone, New York City, 1971; G.M. Hinson, "The Solo Keyboard Works of RLF", in *American Music Teacher*, 20(6), 1971; D. Amman, "The Choral Music of RLF", dissertation, University of Cincinnati, 1972; R.M. Manning, "The Published Songs of RLF", dissertation, University of Miami, 1981; "A Tribute to RLF", in *Music at Michigan*, 15(2), 1982; C. Gagne and T. Caras, "RLF" in *Soundpieces: Interviews with American Composers*, Metuchen, New Jersey, 1982; Edith Borroff, in *Three American Composers*, Lanham, Maryland, 1985.

Ross Lee Finney comments:

Two remarkable changes have taken place in America (and perhaps elsewhere) during my lifetime that affect composers: one is technological and the other is sociological. The first is an electronic way to produce and record sound and the second is the concentration in the United States of the education of the composer in the large universities.

The electronic development not only makes possible a library of performances and furnishes a source of new sounds that can be used in composing music, but it also involves the composer in a new industry that is sometimes very lucrative. The second makes obsolete many of the old established institutions such as conservatories of music and the apprentice system that trained artists in europe. The university became the umbrella under which the sciences and arts flourished side by side with the old traditional curriculum. Fortunately a few conservatories have survived, but most, because of the problems of the frontier, have been absorbed into larger, multi-purpose institutions.

Because I grew up in North Dakota and Minnesota and my father was a university professor, my entire career, first as a student and then as a teacher, has been associated with colleges and universities. Even so, I am often very critical of the university administration's failure to understand the educational needs of the young artist and the advantages of the apprentice relationship in education.

I was fortunate to start teaching in the 1930s at Smith College where I had colleagues who were professional performers and friends like Roger Sessions, Frederick Jacobi and Werner Joste who were professional composers. There was an unusual library of recordings and scores that gave focus to my teaching. It was not, however, until the late 1940s, after the war, that I began to feel the impact of electronics, not until I had joined the faculty of the University of Michigan where, through the radio station WUOM, there could be taped recordings made of my works.

During the next three decades electronic music studios became an accepted part of many university schools of music, using at first an analogue technique in which the composer controlled the sounds that he used in his composition. With the introduction of a digital technique many new instruments were introduced in which sounds were pre-packaged and available to the composer without the need of splicing.

This new electronic equipment was vital for the lucrative recording industry but detrimental to the originality of the creative artist. The computer was welcomed by the scientific and scholarly community in the university and was of enormous value to the composer in copying scores and parts, but just how it could fit into the education of the young artist bewildered the administration.

It is "the best of times and the worst of times" for the American composer. The university is on the threshold of great development for artists, or a period of mediocrity.

* * *

Ross Lee Finney occupies a special place in the musical life of the United States. In addition to his distinguished career as a composer, from 1949 to 1973 at the University of Michigan Finney developed some of the best composers to emerge in America during mid-century.

Finney's early works are imbued with the ideals of the Depression generation of composers, despite his study with Nadia Boulanger in Paris in 1927–28 and again in 1932, and with Alban Berg in Vienna in 1931–2. They are direct, expressive, diatonic, rhythmically supple, very much part of the movement that spawned Aaron Copland, Walter Piston, Virgil Thomson and others of their generation.

Among the most representative of those works are the *Spherical Madrigals*, settings for a cappella chorus of six texts by six English poets of the 17th century, and the song-cycle *Chamber Music* to poems of James Joyce. *Chamber Music*, although not published until 1985 was written in 1951–2 just as Finney's style was about to undergo a profound change. It undertakes the difficult task of forging Joyce's brief lyrics into a unified whole. By means of a refined vocal line, flexible rhythms and a piano style that exhausts the potentialities of the instrument Finney pulls together Joyce's 36 poems into a coherent work. In its wide range and grand scale *Chamber Music* exhibits affinities with Schubert's *Winterreise*.

The *Spherical Madrigals*, more modest in scope, show many of the same characteristics, in particular two features of Finney's music prominent throughout his career: careful attention to the force and significance of every note and a wide expressive range. The expansive choral style is well-anchored tonally, another persistent trait of Finney's music.

In the early 1950s, perhaps as a long-delayed reaction to his study of twelve-tone serialism with Berg and owing in part to memories of active duty during World War II, Finney sought to expand his musical vocabulary by a turn to chromatic serialism. Characteristically he did not embrace the dogmatism of its Teutonic roots, instead developing a method whereby total chromaticism is rendered compatible with a strong tonal center, a phenomenon he terms, with Stravinsky, "pitch polarity".

Finney's method of composing with symmetrical hexachords is simple but ingenious. The tones of the chromatic scale are arranged in order as in conventional twelve-tone serialism, but the first six tones, and the second six, are understood to constitute groups within each of which the order is flexible. This allows a high degree of melodic and harmonic freedom and something akin to harmonic rhythm between the groups while not prohibiting the establishment of tonal centers. It accommodates freedom within order and tonality within the context of total chromaticism. All of Finney's works of the past three decades employ it.

The *Fantasy in Two Movements* for solo violin and the monumental Fourth Symphony provide excellent examples. Several fundamental characteristics of Finney's style meet in the Symphony. These include great rhythmic and metric flexibility extending to numerous unmetered sections set off against passages based on a strong pulse, an echo of Finney's early interest in jazz performance; strong emphasis on a lyrical melodic line; adherence to a central pitch, here B♭; and sophisticated orchestration. The Fourth Symphony stands as one of a handful of significant works in the genre by Americans.

The *Fantasy* is Finney's first work fully exploiting symmetrical hexachords. It was commissioned by Yehudi Menuhin who introduced it in a recital at the Brussels World's Fair in 1958. Its two hexachords are divided into symmetrical trichords, the music firmly oriented to the pitch D. It is of virtuoso dimension comparable in scope and complexity to the Bartók *Solo Sonata*.

In the past 25 years Finney has turned to composing music based on memory. His *Divertissement* of 1964 in his first such work, projecting Finney's memories of student days in Paris. More characteristic is *Landscapes Remembered* for small orchestra from 1971. The memories are those of Finney's childhood in the small North Dakota town of Valley City. The music quotes hymns and American folksongs couched in an atmospheric texture suggesting the fade-ins and fade-outs of cinema. The hexachordal structure is cunningly designed so that folk materials can be quoted within it.

Over his lengthy career Finney developed along with, at times well ahead of, his contemporaries. His oeuvre is large, wide-ranging, masterly, and has placed its creator among the top rank of composers in the United States.

—Frederic Goossen

FINNISSY, Michael (Peter). British/English. Born in London, 17 March 1946. Educated at Royal College of Music, London (composition under Bernard Stevens and Humphrey Searle, piano under Edwin Benbow and Ian Lake); further study in Italy under Roman Vlad. Founder/director of music department, London School of Contemporary Dance, 1969–74; co-director, Expose ensemble; performing pianist; guest artist, Victorian College of the Arts, Melbourne, 1982–3; has also taught at Chelsea College, Chelsea School of Art, both London, Dartington Summer School, Devon and Winchester College; executive committee member, International Society of Contemporary Music, from 1990. Featured composer Bath Festival, 1979; Huddersfield Festival, 1985. Recipient: 1st prize, Radcliffe Award (for *Cipriano*), 1975. Mailing address: c/o United Music Publishers Ltd, 42 Rivington Street, London EC2A 3BN, England.

Publishers: Oxford University Press; Universal Edition; United Music Publishers.

Symphonies/orchestral:

Piano Concerto No 1 1975, revised 1983–4.
Offshore 1975–6.
Piano Concerto No 2 1975–6; first performed Saintes, France, 15 July 1977.
Pathways of Sun and Stars 1976; first performed London, 15 November 1976.
Alongside (small orchestra) 1979.
Sea and Sky 1979–80.
Red Earth (2 didjeridus, orchestra) 1988; first performed London, 2 August 1988.
Eph-Phatha 1988–9; first performed Northampton, 2 May 1989.

Chamber/instrumental:

Song 5, 7, 8, 9 (piano) 1963–8.
As When upon a Tranced Summer Night (piano, 3 cellos, percussion) 1966–8.
Song 2, 4, 6, 10 (chamber ensemble) 1967–8.
Transformation of the Vampire (clarinet, 3 percussion, violin, viola) 1968–71.
n (1–4 instruments specified only by range) 1969.
Alice I (double bass) 1970–5; first performed Royan, France, 26 March 1975.
Alice II (cello) 1970–5.
Alice III (cello, percussion or silent actor) 1970–5.
Snowdrift (piano) 1972; first performed London, 6 February 1973.
Wild Flowers (2 pianos) 1974; first performed Paris, 26 October 1975.
Evening (alto saxophone, horn, trumpet, percussion, harp, cello, double bass) 1974; first performed Donaueschingen, 22 October 1976.
Ives (piano) 1974; first performed 24 March 1976.
Piano Concerto No 2 (piano, ensemble) 1975–6.
Ru Tchou—The Ascent of the Sun (drummer) 1976.
Jazz (piano) 1976.
Lost Lands (E♭ clarinet, soprano saxophone, violin, guitar, piano) 1977; first performed Graz, Austria, 13 October 1977.
All. Fall. Down (piano) 1977.
All the Trees They Are So High (violin) 1977.
English Country-Tunes (piano) 1977; first performed London, 18 December 1979.
Piano Concerto No 3 (solo piano, oboe/cor anglais, clarinet/bass clarinet, 2 trombones, cello, double bass) 1978.
Runnin' Wild (oboe; or, alto/tenor/soprano saxophone; or, bass clarinet) 1978.
Fast Dances, Slow Dances (piano) 1978–9.
Piano Concerto No 4 (solo piano) 1978–80.
Kagami-Jishi (flute, harp) 1979.
Grainger (piano) 1979.
Sikangnuqa (flute) 1979.
Hinomi (percussion) 1979; first performed Nottingham, 9 June 1980.
Piano Concerto No 5 (solo piano, flute/alto flute, oboe/oboe d'amore, mezzo-soprano, vibraphone) 1980.
Nancarrow (piano) 1980.
Reels (piano) 1980–1; first performed Brighton, Sussex, 30 November 1981.
Andimironnai (cello) 1981; first performed London, 24 June 1982.
Banumbirr (flute, clarinet, violin, cello, piano) 1982; first performed Melbourne, 16 May 1982.
Dilok (oboe, percussion) 1982; first performed Melbourne, 21 June 1983.

String Quartet 1984.
" . . . *above earth's shadow*" (solo violin, flute/piccolo, clarinet, violin, viola, cello, double bass) 1985.
Contretanze (flute, oboe, clarinet, percussion, violin, cello) 1985.
String Trio 1986.
Verdi Transcriptions (piano) 1986.
Gershwin Arrangements 1988; first performed London, June 1988.
Obrecht Motetten I (flute, clarinet, bassoon, trumpet, trombone, percussion, violin, viola, cello) 1988; first performed Amsterdam, 19 March 1989.
Obrecht Motetten II (mandolin, guitar, harp) 1988; first performed Stowmarket, Suffolk, 12 March 1989.
Nowhere else to go (clarinet, trumpet, cello, synthesizer, percussion, electronics) 1989; first performed London, 29 March 1989.
Obrecht Motetten III (viola solo, flute, oboe, clarinet, bassoon, horn, trumpet, trombone, percussion, 2 violins, cello, double bass) 1989.
Strauss Waltzes (piano) 1989; first performed Cambridge, 9 December 1989.
More Gershwin (piano) 1989.
Enek (violin) 1990; first performed London, 11 July 1990.
Obrecht Motetten IV (brass quintet) 1990; first performed Cambridge, 17 July 1990.

Vocal/choral:

From the Revelations of St John the Divine (high soprano, flute, 2 violins, 2 violas, 2 cellos) 1965–70.
Jeanne d'Arc (high soprano, tenor, flute, oboe, clarinet, horn, trumpet, trombone, harp, 3 percussion, 2 violins, viola, cello, double bass) 1967–71.
World (high soprano, soprano, alto, tenor, baritone, bass, orchestra; Holderlin, Rimbaud, Blake, Tennyson, Hopkins, Dante) 1968–74; first performed Royan, France, 23 March 1975.
Songs 14 and 15 (soprano; Whitman) 1968–75; first performed Ghent, Belgium, 11 September 1974.
Folk Song Set (voice, cor anglais, clarinet, flugelhorn, percussion, 2 violins, viola, cello, double bass; or, voice, flute, clarinet, piano, violin, viola, cello; or, voice, flute, oboe/cor anglais, piano, percussion) 1969–70, revised 1975–6.
Babylon (mezzo-soprano, ensemble) 1971.
Cipriano (tenor solo, 3 sopranos, mezzo-soprano, alto, tenor, baritone, 2 basses, unaccompanied; Calderón) 1974; first performed London, 11 December 1975.
Sir Tristan (soprano, clarinet, piano, violin, viola, cello) 1978.
Mountainfall (mezzo-soprano) 1978.
Ohi! Ohi! Ohi! (voice) 1978.
Goro (tenor, alto flute, clarinet, harp, violin, viola, cello) 1978.
Talawva (mezzo-soprano, instruments) 1979.
. . . *Fairest Noonday* . . . (tenor, piano) 1979.
Lord Melbourne (soprano, clarinet, piano) 1980.
Piano Concerto No 5 (piano, mezzo-soprano, flute/alto flute, oboe/oboe d'amore, vibraphone) 1980.
Moon's Goin' Down (voice; also, oboe, or saxophone, or bass clarinet) 1980.
Green Bushes (contralto, piano) 1980.
Vaudeville (mezzo-soprano, baritone, 2 mimes, clarinet, bassoon, flugelhorn, trombone, percussion, violin, double bass) 1982–3; first performed South Glamorgan, Wales, 30 August 1983.
Australian Sea Shanties (2-part female/1 part male chorus, unaccompanied) 1983; first performed Copenhagen, 22 July 1984.
Câtana (flute, oboe, clarinet, harp, piano, percussion, violin, viola, cello) 1984; first performed Egremont, Cumbria, 8 March 1985.
Ngano (mezzo-soprano, tenor, SSAATTBB chorus, flute, 2 percussion; traditional African songs) 1984; first performed London, 12 June 1984.
Celi (2 sopranos, flute, oboe, bass trombone, double bass; Hildegard of Bingen) 1984.
Haiyim (SATB chorus, 2 cellos; Psalms 24, 23, 6, 133, 19, 122) 1984; first performed London, 15 March 1985.
A Beuk o'Newcassel Sangs (soprano, clarinet, piano) 1988; first performed Newcastle, 16 February 1989.
Unknown Ground (baritone, violin, cello, piano) 1990; first performed Brighton, Sussex, 15 May 1990.
Le Lay de la Fonteinne (based on Machaut; mezzo-soprano, flute/piccolo, oboe, vibraphone) 1990; first performed London, 9 June 1990.
The Battle of Malden (baritone, SSATB chorus, small ensemble) 1990–1.

Opera/stage:

Mysteries ("The Parting of Darkness", "The Earthly Paradise", "Noah and the Great Flood", "The Prophecy of Daniel", "The Parliament of Heaven", "The Annunciation", "The Betrayal and Crucifixion of Jesus of Nazareth", "The Deliverance of Souls") 1972–9.
Circle, Chorus, and Formal Act (soloists, choruses, percussionists, instruments, dancers, mimes) 1973.
Commedia dell' Incomprensibile Potere che Alcune Donne Hanno Sugli Uomini (music theatre for soprano, counter-tenor, cello, cimbalom) 1973–5.
Bouffe (music theatre; for one person alone on stage) 1975.
Tom Fool's Wooing (music theatre for high soprano, 3 sopranos, mezzo-soprano, 2 altos, counter-tenor, 2 tenors, 2 baritones, 2 basses; 3 singers also play drums) 1975–8.
Mr Punch (music theatre for voice, flute, clarinet or oboe, violin, cello, percussion, piano) 1976–7.
The Undivine Comedy (chamber opera) 1987–8; first performed Paris, 11 May 1988.

PUBLICATIONS

On Finnissy: Richard Toop, in "Four Facets of 'The New Complexity'", *Contact*, Spring 1988; "Repertoire Guide: MF", in *Classical Music*, 26 January 1991.

* * *

Michael Finnissy's stylistic development begins from an early and seemingly effortless assimilation of the lessons to be drawn from the postwar avant-garde, although characteristically concentrating on their expressive and sonorous possibilities rather than compositional techniques. Particularly obvious from his earlier works is a taste for opulent textures festering with microscopic detail, an extrapolation from the decadent world of Bussotti or the Boulez of *Pli selon pli* or *Eclat*. As Finnissy's own character filters out, so does his admiration for and influence from a far less "obvious" (in musical-historical terms) collection of forebears: Ives, Grainger (and the folksong-transcription tradition), Busoni, Godowsky, Gershwin, Verdi. Several of these are best-known for their piano music; and Finnissy, as a fascinatingly unconventional virtuoso of that instrument himself, has contributed as much as any living composer to redefining and expanding the limits of pianistic writing, especially in such massive explorations as *English Country-Tunes* and *Verdi Transcriptions*. The element of virtuosic display is also present in such works (and in Finnissy's writing for other instruments and for voices), although the effect, as with Ives, is of constant striving for the not-quite-impossible rather than flaunting a superficial technical mastery. In any case, this is only one aspect of Finnissy's expressive world, which encompasses the wildest extremes of violence and stillness, harshness and lyricism, often in vertiginous succession.

Another important catalyst for Finnissy's imagination has been the music and art of cultures other than Western Europe. Where other composers have shown an anthropological or even quasi-imperialistic interest in "foreign cultures", Finnissy's relationship, he has stated, is no more or less than fraternal. Although, for example, the pungent microtonal textures and insistent percussive accompaniments of *Câtana* (the name of a Romanian dance) are suffused with the strident harmonies and assymetrical rhythms of Eastern European folk music, there is no question of the appropriation of musical material for the purposes of "high art", only an emulation of the emotional directness of a music still integral to the life of its society. The encounter with another tradition is always, for Finnissy, on equal terms.

One of the most striking aspects to a listener is Finnissy's tireless inventiveness in the colouristic use of instruments, both solo and in combination. The combinations themselves are frequently unusual enough (and indeed are "composed" as much as anything else), but even in, for example, his *String Quartet* with its enforced instrumentation, the specific use of the instruments creates a fresh, even subversive, angle on a mainstream genre. For over a dozen pages at the opening, none of the instruments descends as far as the treble stave. Later, although their microtonal peregrinations all occupy the same tightly-defined register (almost a Finnissy trademark), they are playing not only as soloists but in different tempi, contradicting the generally assumed purpose of the quartet as a musical unit; the form of the work is not polyphonic and discursive but improvisational and episodic. Much of the individuality of the "Finnissy sound" arises from *restricting* the capabilities of instruments (e.g., in register or tone-colour), into clear if unusual areas, for relatively long stretches, contradicting the tendency to shortwindedness and rapid turnover of textures prevalent in much contemporary music. Finnissy's antagonism to any kind of orthodoxy (even his own, given his periodic changes of stylistic emphasis) is a constant and deeply-felt feature of his personality in all its manifestations, both as composer and performer: this feature marks him out certainly from most British composers of his generation, but also allies him with the aforementioned composers (and their ambiguous relationship to the "historical mainstream") whose example has been so fruitful in his own work.

—Richard Barrett

FIRSOVA, Elena (Olegovna). Russian. Born in Leningrad, 21 March 1950. Educated in Moscow schools, 1957–65; Moscow Conservatory (composition under Alexander Pizumov), 1970–5. Married Dmitri Smirnov, *q.v.*, 19 August 1972; 1 son and 1 daughter. Music technician, Moscow, 1966–70; member, Union of Soviet Composers, since 1974; member, Association for Contemporary Music, 1990. Mailing address: c/o Dartington College of Arts, Totnes, Devon TQ9 6JE, England.

Publishers: Boosey & Hawkes, London; Hans Sikorski, Hamburg; G. Schirmer, New York; VAAP, Moscow.

Symphonies/orchestral:

Five Pieces Op 6 1971.
Chamber Music Op 9 (string orchestra) 1973.
Cello Concerto No 1 Op 10 1973; first performed Moscow, 10 June 1975.
Stanzas Op 13 1975.
Violin Concerto No 1 Op 14 1976.
Postlude Op 18 (harp, orchestra) 1977; first performed Moscow, 22 February 1978.
Chamber Concerto No 1 Op 19 (flute, strings) 1978; first performed Moscow, 10 March 1980.
Chamber Concerto No 2 (Cello Concerto No 2) Op 26 1982; first performed Moscow, 17 October 1982.
Violin Concerto No 2 Op 29 1983.
Chamber Concerto No 3 Op 33 (piano, orchestra) 1985.

Chamber/instrumental:

Invention a Two (piano; no opus number) 1966.
Two Polyphonic Pieces (piano; no opus number) 1966.
Legend (horn, piano; no opus number) 1967.
Scherzo Op 1 (flute, oboe, clarinet, bassoon, piano) 1967; first performed Moscow, May 1967.
Suite Op 2 (viola) 1967; first performed Moscow, May 1968.
Two Pieces (violin, piano; no opus number) 1968.
String Quartet No 1 (Five Pieces) Op 4 1970; first performed Moscow, 17 May 1971.
Sonata Op 5 (cello, piano) 1971; first performed Leningrad, 8 April 1972.
Piano Trio Op 8 1972; first performed Moscow, March 1973.
String Quartet No 2 Op 11 1974; first performed Moscow, 10 December 1974.
Capriccio Op 15 (flute, saxophone quartet) 1976; first performed Moscow, 27 April 1977.
Sonata Op 16 (clarinet) 1976; first performed Moscow, 31 October 1977.
Two Inventions (flute; no opus number) 1977.
Three Pieces (xylophone; no opus number) 1978.
Elegy Op 21 (piano) 1979; first performed Moscow, 15 October 1980.
Misterioso (String Quartet No 3) Op 24 (in memoriam Igor Stravinsky) 1980; first performed Moscow, 14 April 1982.
Three Pieces (horn, piano; no opus number) 1980.
Sphinx (harp; no opus number) 1982.
Spring Sonata Op 27 (flute, piano) 1982; first performed Moscow, 29 February 1984.
Mysteria ("Tajinstvo") Op 30 (organ, 4 percussion) 1984; first performed Moscow, 4 November 1984.
Fantasie Op 32 (violin) 1985; first performed Hamburg, 1985.
Music for 12 Op 34 (oboe, flute, clarinet, bassoon, horn, trumpet, harp, celeste, 2 violins, viola, cello) 1986; first performed Berlin, 12 September 1986.
Sonata Op 35 (piano) 1986.

Vocal/choral:

Three Romances on Poems by Boris Pasternak (voice, piano) 1966–7.

Creation (high voice, piano; Akhmatova) 1967.
Three Romances on Poems by Vladimir Mayakovsky (voice, piano) 1969.
Three Poems by Osip Mandelstam Op 3 (mixed chamber chorus) 1970.
Autumn Songs Op 12 (voice, piano; Tsvetaeva) 1974; first performed Moscow, 13 June 1975.
Petrarca's Sonnets Op 17 (voice, flute, oboe, horn, harp, celeste, violin, viola, cello; Mandelstam) 1976; first performed Moscow, 9 January 1978.
The Bell (in collaboration with Dmitri Smirnov; mixed chorus; Yesenin) 1976.
Night Op 20 (voice, saxophone quartet; Pasternak) 1978; first performed Moscow, 14 February 1983.
Tristia Op 22 (voice, chamber orchestra; Mandelstam) 1979.
Three Poems by Osip Mandelstam Op 23 (voice, piano) 1980; first performed Moscow, 21 November 1981.
Shakespeare's Sonnets Op 25 (voice, organ) 1981; first performed Moscow, 10 March 1986.
The Stone ("Kamen") Op 28 (voice, orchestra, Mandelstam) 1983.
Earthly Life Op 31 (soprano, flute, percussion, harp, 3 violins, 2 violas, cello, double bass) 1984; first performed London, 10 November 1986.

Opera:

Feast in Plague Time ("Pir vo vrjemja chumy") Op 7 (chamber opera; Pushkin) 1972.
The Nightingale and the Rose (after Wilde) 1991.

Other:

Hermitage: The Art of Ancient Greece (music for television film; in collaboration with Dmitri Smirnov) 1979.
Hermitage: The Art of Ancient Rome (music for television film; in collaboration with Dmitri Smirnov) 1979.
Hermitage: The Art of the Middle Ages (music for television film; in collaboration with Dmitri Smirnov) 1979.
L'Ecume des jours (arrangement of vocal score of opera by Edison Denisov) 1980.
Intermède from "The Age of Gold" (arrangement for flute and piano after Shostakovich) 1987.

PUBLICATIONS

On Firsova: Malcolm Hayes, "On the Huddersfield Contemporary Music Festival", in *New Music*, November–December 1986; Michael John White, "A Soviet View of Eternal Life", in *The Independent*, 12 November 1986.

* * *

Elena Firsova is one of the most important of that group of younger composers based in Moscow, whose music shows clearly the influence of the style and aesthetic of Edison Denisov. Together with her husband, Dmitri Smirnov, she has made good use of Denisov's example in matters of lyrical spontaneity and delicacy of heterophonic decoration, while at the same time claiming for herself a quite personal harmonic territory. It is perhaps most of all this sense of harmony, at once recognisably expressive and very private, which has brought her music considerable attention and respect in the West in recent years.

Firsova is by nature a poet of confidences. Her music, including her instrumental works as much as her many vocal ones, has much of the quality of lyric verse, especially of the confessional variety. It is thus no surprise to learn that the majority of her music is connected in one way or another with the poetry of Osip Mandelstam, perhaps Russia's greatest lyric poet since Pushkin.

Mandelstam was—and is—an almost emblematic figure for the Russian intelligentsia. As people struggle to comprehend the scale of Stalin's crimes, the image Mandelstam's fate offers, of the great artist being blotted out by the tyrant, has taken on a quality almost of the sacred. For a composer of Firsova's generation. Mandelstam's words offer not only a heady mix in themselves of all those spiritual values that the Soviet Union has been most at pains to destroy (the privacy of the individual, respect for individual life, a feeling for the sweetness of the transitory moment), but also the quality of being in themselves rare things, physically hard to find, part of Russia's real life, secret (though now less secret) and in principle anti-Soviet.

Firsova's music in the strongest of her Mandelstam-inspired works at once mirrors and echoes the passionate intimacy of the words and at the same time decorates them in the manner of an icon painter, who surrounds a familiar image with reverential gold. It is the resulting tension in this music between its expressive immediacy and its decorative sensuality that conveys the composer's sense of urgency that we should understand the importance of this poetry as she does.

Formally Firsova's music is possessed of unity rather than variety. A great number of her works (and especially of her instrumental works) are cast in a single movement. Many of these single movements follow much the same ternary design, where the three sections are markedly similar in character, perhaps with a suggestion of "development" in the second section and "recapitulation" (sometimes in retrograde) in the third. Often the sense that one has passed from one section to the next is conveyed by a somewhat more violent outburst of pointilliste fragmentation, which itself feels not like the result of any directed process, but rather a kind of formal punctuation, marking the break between sentences or paragraphs.

When multi-movement works do occur in Firsova's output, they tend to be the result of her setting contrasted poems, as in her cantata *Earthly Life*, one of the finest children of her love affair with Mandelstam. Here four small-scale settings of the poet's early work, each establishing a different mood with bagatelle-like economy, precede an altogether longer movement, to one of the greatest of Mandelstam's middle period elegies: "Into the circling dance of shadows . . ."

In recent years Firsova has extended her range of colours by venturing into the world of the larger orchestra, and even, in her recent *Augury* (a setting of Blake as translated by her husband), of chorus and orchestra. But she has still retained the same time-scale and formal preoccupations already familiar in her chamber works. One still has a sense of private rather than public music.

What this composer had until recently avoided, however, was the dramatic. True, there was an early student setting of Pushkin's *Feast in Plague Time.* But recently Firsova has suddenly written a new opera. Here too, as one might have expected from her orchestral works, what she has done is to make a usually all-too-public medium serve a private and intimate purpose. Taking Oscar Wilde's story *The Nightingale and the Rose*, she has produced a *drama per musica* where the dramatic like the musical is a curious mixture of fabular formality and almost child-like sentiment. The result is unexpected, winning and memorable.

—Gerard McBurney

FONTYN, Jacqueline (professional name of Jacqueline Schmitt-Fontyn). Belgian. Born in Antwerp, 27 December 1930. Studied piano under Ignace Bolotine (from age 5) and Marcel Maas; harmony, counterpoint, fugue, orchestration and composition under Marcel Quintet, Brussels; composition under Max Deutsch, Paris; composition with Hans Swarowski; Academy for Music and Arts, Vienna; Royal Chapel of Queen Elizabeth, Belgium, graduated in composition. Married Camille Schmitt, 18 July 1961 (died 1976); 1 son and 1 daughter. Professor of counterpoint, Royal Conservatory, Antwerp, 1963–70; professor of composition, Royal Conservatory, Brussels, 1970–9; conductor of orchestral and chamber groups. Recipient: silver medal (for *Trio*), international composition concourse, Moscow, 1957; Grand Prix de Rome, 1959; 3rd prize/Prix Sabam (for *String Quartet* Op 21), international quartet competition, Liège, 1959; Prix Irene Fuerisson de l'Académie Royale de Belgique (for *Sonate*), 1961; Prix Koopal (for *Piedigrotta*), Ministry of Culture, 1961; 1st prize (for *Trio*), Gedok Composition Contest, Mannheim, 1961; Oscar Espla Prize, for *Psalmus Tertius*), Alicante, 1962; Queen Elisabeth Composition Prize, 1964; 1st prize, Delta Omicron International Music Fraternity, United States, 1965; 2nd prize (for *Six Ebauches*), Czechoslovakia Radio, Prague, 1966; 1st prize (for *Six Ebauches*), Gedok Composition Contest, Mannheim, 1966; Prix des Jeunesses Musicales (for *Musica a quattro*), Brussels, 1967; 1st prize (for *Six Climats*), Halifax Teachers' Association competition, Canada, 1973; Prix Camille Huysmans (for *Ballade*), Antwerp, 1974; Prix Koopal, 1979; Prix Arthur Honegger de la Fondation de France (for *Quatre Sites*), 1981. Mailing address: rue Leonard Dekaise 6, B-1342 Limelette, Belgium.

Publishers: Bote & Bock, Berlin; Peer Southern, New York; G. Schirmer, New York.

Symphonies/orchestral:

Petite Suite Op 5 (chamber orchestra) 1952; first performed Antwerp, 1953; withdrawn.
Variations sur une chanson populaire flamande Op 6 1953; broadcast 1954; withdrawn.
Danceries Op 14 (transcription of Op 7 for violin and piano) 1956.
Divertimento Op 16 (string orchestra) 1957.
Prélude et rondo Op 17 1957; first performed Antwerp, 9 June 1958.
Mouvements concertants Op 18 (2 pianos, strings) 1957; first performed Antwerp, 2 December 1957.
Suite Op 19B (from the ballet *Piedigrotta*) 1960; first performed Antwerp, 26 November 1962.
Deux Estampes Op 23 1961; first performed Liège, 28 November 1967.
Digressions Op 24 (cello, chamber orchestra) 1962; first performed Belgium, 30 November 1962.
Six Ebauches Op 26 1964; first performed Hilversum, 1964.
Digressions Op 24C (chamber orchestra) 1964.
Galaxie Op 28 (chamber orchestra, or 17 instrumentalists) 1965; first performed France, 20 May 1970.
Concerto Op 30 (piano, orchestra) 1967; first performed Romania, 4 June 1974.
Nonetto Op 32 (chamber orchestra) 1969; first performed Prague, 13 June 1972.
Colloque Op 32B (wind quintet, strings) 1970.
Pour Onze Archets Op 37 1971.
Evoluon Op 39 1972; first performed Belgium, 14 November 1973.
Per Archi Op 37B (large string orchestra) 1973; first performed Antwerp, 15 March 1973.
Concerto Op 43 (violin, orchestra) 1974.
Frises Op 45 (large harmony orchestra) 1975; first performed Belgium, 28 January 1976. Recorded Terpsichore 1982 060.
Frises II Op 45B 1976; first performed Belgium, 26 February 1978.
Quatre Sites Op 46 1977; first performed Ottignies, 19 November 1981.
Halo Op 48 (chamber orchestra; or for harp, 16 instruments) 1978; first performed Flanders, 20 June 1980. Recorded Terpsichore 1982 024.
Zones Op 50 (chamber orchestra) 1979; first performed Washington, D.C., 14 April 1980.
Rhumbs Op 54 (chamber orchestra) 1980; first performed San Francisco, 15 March 1985.
Créneaux Op 58 (young people's orchestra) 1982; first performed San Francisco, 14 November 1987.
Arachne Op 61 1983; first performed Belgium, 30 October 1985.
Créneaux Op 58B (harmony orchestra) 1983; first performed Rotterdam, 18 December 1983.
In the Green Shade 1988; first performed Antwerp, 17 June 1988.
Rêverie et turbulence (piano, orchestra) 1989.

Chamber/instrumental:

Impromptu Op 3 (piano) 1951; broadcast 1954.
Impromptu II (piano) 1951.
Impromptu III (piano) 1952.
Sonate Op 4 (flute, piano) 1952.
Danceries Op 7 (violin, piano) 1953; first performed Antwerp, 1954.
Quintet Op 9 (flute, oboe, clarinet, horn, bassoon) 1954; first performed Antwerp, 1955; withdrawn.
Capriccio Op 10 (piano) 1954; first performed Belgium, 29 March 1962. Recorded Terpsichore 1982 046; Duchesne CD 71482.
Trio Op 12 (violin, cello, piano) 1956.
Sept Petites Pièces Op 15 (bassoon, clarinet, oboe) 1956.
String Quartet Op 21 1958; first performed Liège, September 1959.
Ballade Op 25 (piano) 1963; first performed Belgium, 1964. Recorded Terpsichore 1982 046; Duchesne CD 71482.
Digressions Op 24B (cello, piano) 1964; first performed Antwerp, 1965.
Mosaici Op 27A (piano) 1964. Recorded Terpsichore 1982 046; Duchesne CD 71482.
Mosaïques Op 27B (clarinet, piano) 1964; first performed Francorchamps, 29 August 1971.
Mosaico Op 27C (clarinet quartet) 1965; first performed Bouillon, 5 February 1967.
Five Mosaics Op 27D (wind quartet) 1965.
Musica a quattro (violin, cello, clarinet or viola, piano) 1966; first performed Val-Dieu, 23 May, 1975.
Dialogues Op 33 (alto saxophone, piano) 1969; first performed France, 29 May 1970.
Filigrane Op 34 (flute, harp) 1969; first performed Netherlands, 27 August 1972. Recorded Terpsichore 1982 024.
Colloque Op 32B (wind and string quintet) 1970.
Strophes Op 35 (violin, piano) 1970; first performed Brussels, 14 April 1972.
Spirales Op 36 (2 pianos) 1971; first performed Brussels, 31 January 1972. Recorded Duchesne CD 71482.
Six Climats Op 40 (cello, piano) 1972; first performed Belgium, 28 January 1974.

Shadows Op 41 (harpsichord) 1973; first performed Cracow, Poland, 1977.
Intermezzo Op 42 (harp) 1973; first performed Rome, 13 February 1974. Recorded Terpischore 1982 024.
Agami Op 44 (trumpet, piano) 1974; first performed Belgium, 23 December 1975.
Horizons Op 47 (string quartet) 1977; first performed Tiegelez-Spa, 2 July 1978.
Halo Op 48 (harp, 16 instruments; or chamber orchestra) 1978; first performed Flanders, between 20 June and 23 October, 1980. Recorded Terpsichore 1982 024.
Mime I Op 51 (flute, piano) 1980; first performed Brussels, 15 July 1984.
Mime II Op 51A (clarinet, piano) 1980; first performed Antwerp, 11 May 1982.
Mime III Op 51B (saxophone, piano) 1980; first performed Paris, 26 April 1982.
Mime IV Op 51C (flute, harp) 1980; first performed Stichting, Netherlands, 30 October 1980. Recorded Terpsichore 1982 024.
Mime V Op 51D (clarinet, harp) 1980.
Mime VI Op 51E (saxophone, harp) 1980; first performed Profondval, 25 March 1987.
Le Gong Op 52 (piano) 1980; first performed Belgium, November 1981. Recorded Terpsichore 1982 046; Duchesne CD 71482.
Bulles Op 53 (piano) 1980. Recorded Terpsichore 1982 046; Duchesne CD 71482.
Analects Op 55 (2 violins) 1981; first performed Louvain-la-Neuve, 27 April 1982.
Fougères Op 56 (viola, harp) 1981. Recorded Terpsichore 1982 024.
Fougères Op 56B (alto saxophone, harp) 1981; first performed Aix-en-Provence, 24 June 1982.
Fougères Op 56C (saxophone, piano) 1981; first performed Paris, 26 April 1982.
Aura Op 59 (piano) 1982; first performed Dusseldorf, 28 October 1983. Recorded Terpsichore 1982 046; Duchesne CD 71482.
Controverse Op 60 (bass clarinet, percussion; or, clarinet, percussion; or tenor saxophone, percussion) 1983; first performed on bass clarinet, Amsterdam, 10 September 1983; on clarinet, Paris, 26 October 1984; on saxophone, Profondval, 25 March 1987.
Zephyr Op 62 (bassoon, piano) 1984; first performed Tokyo, 8 October 1986.
Either . . . Or . . . / Entweder . . . oder . . . Op 63 (string quintet; or string quartet, clarinet) 1984; first performed Stradsshouwburgzwolle, 22 January 1985.
Cheminement Op 66 (9 players) 1986; first performed Utrecht, 10 October 1986.
La Devinière (violin, piano) 1987–8; first performed Germany, 10 April 1989.
Scurochiaro (flute, clarinet, bassoon, piano, violin, cello, double bass) 1989; first performed Baltimore, Maryland, 1989.
Compagnon de la nuit (oboe, piano) 1989.

Vocal/choral:

Berce de la poupée / Le vieux piano Op 1 (unaccompanied choirs) 1948; withdrawn.
Automne Op 2 (voice, piano; Apollinaire) 1949; first performed Antwerp, 1950; withdrawn.
Un Chat perdu (soprano, piano; Careme) 1950; withdrawn.
Les cloches (soprano, piano, Apollinaire) 1950; withdrawn.
Le Trapéziste qui a perdu son coeur Op 8 (mezzo-soprano, chamber orchestra; Fournier) 1953.
Het was een Maghetwtvercoen / Or je vous dis bonne nouvelle Op 11 (unaccompanied choir; old carol) 1955.
Deux Rondeaux de Charles d'Orléans Op 13 (soprano, piano) 1956; first performed France, April 1956.
Quatre Rondeaux de Charles d'Orléans Op 20 (unaccompanied mixed choir) 1958; withdrawn.
Psalmus tertius Op 22 (baritone, choir, orchestra) 1959; first performed Madrid, December 1962.
Madrigale e canzone Op 31 (unaccompanied choir; Burchiello) 1968; first performed Flanders, 1969.
Ephémères Op 49 (mezzo-soprano, 10 instruments, percussion ad lib; Guiette) 1979; first performed Caen, 8 March 1987.
Ephémères Op 49B (mezzo-soprano, orchestra) 1979; first performed Belgium, 24 August 1979.
Alba Op 57 (soprano, clarinet, cello, harp, piano; Cardarelli) 1981; first performed Antwerp, 18 April 1983.
Pro et antiverbes Op 64 (soprano, cello) 1984; first performed Oslo, 2 December 1984.
Rosa-Rosae Op 67 (soprano, alto, clarinet, violin, harp, piano; Rilke) 1986; first performed Kassel, 20 February 1987.
Ku soko (soprano or mezzo-soprano, piano; version for baritone, piano) 1989; first performed Belgium, November 1989.

Other:

Piedigrotta Op 19 (ballet; women's choir) 1958; first performed Antwerp, 29 May 1962.

PUBLICATIONS

On Fontyn: Bettina Brandt, *JF*, Berlin, 1990.

Jacqueline Fontyn comments:

I am sometimes asked "Why do you compose?" My answer is that I started composing when I was six and I have never thought of doing anything else. I am grateful to music for having chosen me! When I stop composing for even a month or two, I get nervous and even sick.

My stylistic evolution started seriously in 1948–50 with Hindemith and Bartók, moving on to Schoenberg between 1954 and 1979; it is still developing as I try to keep my musical language fluid and to avoid repeating myself. This gets harder as the list of works gets longer, but the range of possibilities is unlimited!

The form of a piece is very important to me, a certain sense of proportions, and, generally, a great diversity and contrast in the writing. My experience taught me to search for the greatest simplicity possible, using new signs and notation so as not to scare away well-intentioned interpreters, while achieving the desired sonority.

Although I may say that the orchestra is my favourite "instrument", one of my aims over the last 20 years has been to try to make young performers familiar with some aspects of contemporary composition by writing pieces which are technically easy; for example, *Bulles* and *Aura* for piano, *La Devinière* for violin and piano, and works such as *Créneaux* for symphony orchestra or symphonic band. I believe it is very important to get students of music and enthusiastic amateurs interested in the music of our time, so that the teachers of tomorrow will be motivated to make their own performing arts students curious about events beyond Prokofiev or my dear Albert Roussel. Why should we compose second rate music for children or for those marvellous band musicians?

I feel sad that prejudice against contemporary music has driven away a large part of the concert-going public. The fact that this was already true for Beethoven, Chopin, Brahms and so many "Masters" (see Nicholas Slonimsky's *Dictionary of Musical Invective*) is only a slight consolation. But the joy of creating is wonderful! And the "active" listeners, like Lutoslawski says, who appreciate my modest art, are another reason to go on composing; it is for them—and for my performers—that I write.

* * *

In a musical period which was often desiccated and intellectualised to excess Jacqueline Fontyn appeared not as a reactionary or nostalgically backward-looking artist, but as the heir and perpetuator of an art whose technique is not merely personal and solipsistic. The compositional process is submissive to the broader imaginative gesture, always poetic or in direct rapport with human feelings, closely allied to nature and its unities and continuities. As is evident, she is aware of the tragic ramifications and anguished discoveries of an age of transition, but her music is essentially affirmative and optimistic, full of serenity and a certain *joie de vivre*.

Fontyn's parents quickly noticed her precocity and, at the age of five, started her on on piano lessons with the excellent teacher Ignace Bolotine, who encouraged her taste for improvisation and transcribed her first small-scale compositions. At 13, Fontyn decided that she would be a composer. She studied notation, orchestration and composition in private with Marcel Quintet, and continued her education in Paris under Max Deutsch, in Vienna, where she pursued courses in orchestral direction, and finally at the Chapelle Musicale Reine Elisabeth. It was around this time that she met the composer Camille Schmitt who had just become director of the Royal Conservatory in Brussels. By nature enthusiastic and generous, Schmitt, whom she married in 1961, encouraged his young wife ceaselessly, giving her the opportunity to devote much of her time to her own music. Following his example, she worked with even greater rigour, producing on average only one or two carefully articulated pieces per year, a work rate which did not prevent her accepting—and fulfilling—commissions, mostly from abroad.

Fontyn has brought about a kind of synthesis between the music of the past and more recent additions to musical language. In terms of construction, a broadened and responsive counterpoint, a knowledge of instrumentation heightened by careful research into instrumental possibilities, are her fundamental resources, combined in the service of a new compositional trajectory. Freedom and flexibility of rhythm, reinvention of forms, free and undogmatic use of serial procedures, invention of new forms, aleatory techniques constrained by the demands of a particular schema, clusters and other means of aggregation, all these belong to a thoroughly contemporary language.

The full orchestra is Fontyn's instrument of choice, in which she has wrought a refined and complex timbral alchemy. Her style is very immediate, placing her square in her era. Nonetheless, one may find in it a number of diverse influences: at the outset of her career, Bach, Mozart, Haydn, Schumann, Mendelssohn; later, Ravel, Roussel, Hindemith, Bartók; later still, thanks to Max Deutsch, Schoenberg and serialism; finally, Lutoslawski for his new rhythmic language, and Dutilleux for the exactness of his thought and formal rigour. Fontyn has never submitted to any one tendency or school. However uncomfortable a position that may be, it has nonetheless been deeply rewarding.

—Pierre Heureux

FOSS, Lukas (Lukas Fuchs). American. Born in Berlin, 15 August 1922; family moved to Paris, 1933; then emigrated to the United States, 1937; became American citizen, 1942. Educated: piano lessons under Julius Goldstein-Herford; in Paris, piano study under Lazare Levy, flute under Marcel Moyse, composition under Noel Gallon, orchestration under Felix Wolfes, 1934–7; Curtis Institute, Philadelphia (piano under Isabelle Vengerova, composition under Rosario Scalero and Randall Thompson, conducting under Fritz Reiner), 1937–9; Berkshire Music Center, Tanglewood, Massachusetts (conducting under Serge Koussevitzky), 1939–43; Yale University, New Haven, Connecticut (special student of Paul Hindemith), 1939–40. Married Cornelia Brendel in 1951; 1 son and 1 daughter. Pianist, Boston Symphony Orchestra, 1944–50; fellow, American Academy in Rome, 1950–1; professor of composition and conducting, University of California, Los Angeles, 1953–63; founder/pianist, Improvisation Chamber Ensemble, 1957; State Department-sponsored cultural exchange to Soviet Union, 1960; music director/conductor, Buffalo Philharmonic Orchestra, 1963–70; founder/director, Center for Creative and Performing Arts, State University of New York, Buffalo, from 1963; guest teacher, Harvard University, Cambridge, Massachusetts, Manhattan School of Music, New York City, University of Cincinnati, Ohio, from 1969; conductor, Brooklyn Philharmonic Orchestra/now Brooklyn PO, from 1971; conductor, Kol Israel Orchestra, Jerusalem, 1972–6; music director, Milwaukee Symphony Orchestra, 1981–6. Recipient: New York Music Critics Circle Awards, 1944 (for *The Prairie*), 1954 (for *Piano Concerto No 2*), 1961 (for *Time Cycle*); Guggenheim Fellowship (youngest ever composer), 1945; Fulbright Award, 1950–2; elected, American Academy and Institute of Arts and Letters, 1983. Mailing address: 1140 Fifth Avenue, New York, New York 10028, U.S.A.

Publishers: Schirmer; Salabert; Fischer.

Symphonies/orchestral:

Two Symphonic Pieces 1939–40; destroyed.
Dance Sketch 1941.
Allegro concertante 1941.
Clarinet Concerto 1941; revised as *Piano Concerto No 1*, 1944.
1944.
October 1943.
Symphony in G 1944; first perfomed, Pittsburgh, 4 February 1945.
Ode 1945, revised 1958; first performed New York City, 15 March 1945.
Pantomime (after ballet *Gift of the Magi*) 1946.
Recordare 1948; first performed Boston, 31 December 1948.
Oboe Concerto 1948; broadcast 6 February 1950.
Elegy (based on *Clarinet Concerto*; clarinet, orchestra) 1949.
Piano Concerto No 2 1949, revised 1953; first performed Venice, 7 October 1951.
Symphony of Chorales 1956–8; first performed Pittsburgh, 24 October 1958.
Stillscape (24 winds) 1966.
Baroque Variations 1967.
Phorion (harpsichord, electric organ, electric guitar, strings; part of *Baroque Variations*) 1967; first performed New York City, 27 April 1967.
Cello Concerto 1967; first performed New York City, 5 March 1967.
Geod (4 orchestral groups) 1969; first performed Hamburg, 6 December 1969.

Orpheus (string instrument, small orchestra) 1972.
Fanfare (chamber orchestra, 3 folk instruments) 1973; first performed Istanbul, 28 June 1973.
Percussion Concerto (percussion/magician, mechanical metronomic conductor, orchestra) 1974.
Folksong 1975; first performed Baltimore, Maryland, 21 January 1976.
Solomon Rossi Suite 1975.
Quintets for Orchestra (based on *Brass Quintet*) 1979; first performed Cleveland, Ohio, 2 May 1979.
Night Music for John Lennon (brass quintet, orchestra) 1979–80.
Exeunt 1982.
200 Cellos, a Celebration 1982.
Orpheus and Euridice (2 violins, orchestra; based on *Orpheus*) 1984.
Renaissance Concerto 1985.

Chamber/instrumental:

Sonata (violin, piano) 1937.
Four Two-Part Inventions (piano) 1938.
Grotesque Dance (piano) 1938.
Sonatina (piano) 1939.
Four Preludes (flute, clarinet, bassoon) 1940.
Set of Three Pieces (2 pianos) 1940.
Duo (cello, piano) 1941.
Passacaglia (piano) 1941.
Fantasy Rondo (piano) 1944.
Dedication (violin, piano) 1944.
Early Song (violin, piano) 1944.
Composer's Holiday (violin, piano) 1944.
String Quartet No 1 in G 1947.
Capriccio (cello, piano) 1948.
Prelude in D (piano) 1950.
Scherzo ricercato (piano) 1953.
Concerto (5 improvising instruments) 1960.
Echoi (clarinet, cello, piano, percussion) 1961–3; first performed New York City, 11 November 1963.
Elytres (flute, 2 violins, instrumental group) 1964; first performed Los Angeles, 8 December 1964.
Etudes (organ) 1967.
Non-Improvisation (4 instruments) 1967.
Paradigm (percussionist/conductor, electric guitar, trio) 1968; first performed Buffalo, New York, 1969.
Waves (ensemble) 1969; withdrawn.
The Cave of Winds (wind quintet) 1972.
Ni Bruit, ni vitesse (2 pianos, 2 percussion) 1972.
MAP (Musicians at Play) (game for 4 instruments) 1973.
Divertissement "pour Mica": String Quartet No 2 1973; first performed Ojai, California, 1973.
String Quartet No 3 1975.
Curriculum vitae (accordion) 1975.
Music for Six (sextet) 1977.
Quartet Plus (2 string quartets, speaker) 1977; first performed New York City, 29 April 1977.
Brass Quintet 1978.
Curriculum vitae with Time Bomb (accordion, percussion, cap-gun) 1980.
Solo (piano) 1981.
Solo Observed (piano, cello, electric organ, vibraphone) 1982.
Percussion Quartet 1983.
Trio (violin, horn, piano) 1984.

Vocal/choral:

Three Songs (voice, piano; Shakespeare) 1938.
Wanderers Gemutsruhe (voice, piano; Goethe) 1938.
Cantata dramatica (tenor, chorus, orchestra) 1940; withdrawn.
Where the Bee Sucks (voice, piano; Shakespeare) 1940.
Melodrama and Dramatic Song of Michelangelo (voice, piano; Meyer) 1940.
We Sing (children's chorus, piano, drums) 1941; withdrawn.
Cool Prayers (unaccompanied mixed chorus) 1944.
The Prairie (soprano, alto, tenor, bass, mixed chorus, orchestra; Sandburg) 1944.
Tell This Blood (unaccompanied mixed chorus) 1945; withdrawn.
Song of Anguish (baritone, orchestra; Isaiah) 1945; first performed Boston, 10 March 1950.
Song of Songs (soprano, orchestra) 1946; first performed Boston, 7 March 1947.
Behold, I Build a House (mixed chorus, organ or piano) 1950.
Adon olom (cantor, mixed chorus, organ) 1951.
A Parable of Death (narrator, tenor, SATB chorus, orchestra; Rilke/Hecht) 1952; first performed Louisville, Kentucky, 11 March 1953.
For Cornelia (voice, piano; Yeats) 1955.
Psalms (mixed chorus, orchestra or 2 pianos) 1955–6; first performed New York City, 9 May 1957.
Time Cycle (soprano, orchestra; Nietzsche, Auden, Housman, Kafka) 1959–60; version for soprano, clarinet, cello, celeste, percussion, 1960; first performed New York City, 21 October 1960.
Fragments of Archilochos (counter-tenor, male speaker, female speaker, 4 small choruses, large chorus ad lib, mandolin, guitar, 3 percussion) 1965.
Three Airs for Frank O'Hara's Angel (soprano, female chorus, flute, piano, 2 percussion) 1972.
Lamdeni mi / Teach Me (mixed chorus, sextet) 1973.
American Cantata (tenor, mixed chorus, orchestra) 1976; first performed New York City, 1 December 1977.
Thirteen Ways of Looking at a Blackbird (soprano, flute, piano, percussion; Stevens) 1978.
And Then the Rocks on the Mountain Began to Shout (unaccompanied mixed chorus; based on *Brass Quintet*) 1978.
Round a Common Center (mezzo-soprano ad lib, piano quartet or quintet) 1979; first performed Lake Placid, New York, 30 January 1980.
Measure for Measure (tenor, orchestra; after *Solomon Rossi Suite*) 1980.
De profundis (unaccompanied mixed chorus) 1982.

Opera:

The Jumping Frog of Calaveras County (Karsavina, after Twain) 1949; first performed Bloomington, Indiana, 18 May 1950.
Griffelkin (Reed, after H. Foss) 1955; broadcast NBC, 6 November 1956.
Introductions and Goodbyes (baritone, chorus; Menotti) 1959; first performed New York, 5 May 1960.

Other:

The Tempest (incidental music to Shakespeare) 1940; first performed New York City, 31 March 1940.
The Heart Remembers (ballet; piano) 1944.
Within These Walls (ballet; piano) 1944.
Gift of the Magi (ballet after O. Henry; orchestra) 1945; first performed Boston, 5 October 1945.

PUBLICATIONS

On Foss: Wilfred Mellers, "Today and Tomorrow: LF and the Younger Generation", in *Music in a New Found Land*, New York/London, 1965; E. Salzman, "The Many Lives of LF", in *Saturday Review*, 1(8), 1967; J. Waugh, "Chance, Choice and LF", in proceedings of *First American Music Conference*, University of Keele, Staffordshire, 1976–7; A. Satz, "LF, Musician of the Month", in *High Fidelity / Musical America*, 31(1), 1981; C. Gagne and T. Caras, (interview) in *Soundpieces: Interviews with American Composers*, Metuchen, New Jersey, 1982.

* * *

A versatile musician, Lukas Foss has succeeded in many endeavors—as performing pianist, orchestral conductor, composition professor and contemporary music entrepreneur. Versatility has also fueled a compositional career in a broad range of mediums and approaches. Each work is colorful, dramatic, rich in detail, unique in character and singular in focus.

As a composer, Foss is influenced by his other modes of music-making. The influence of a virtuoso pianist shows in a strong neo-classical interest, dense counterpoint and elaborate repeated arpeggiations. The influence of an orchestral *maestro* shows in a taste for rich sound color combinations and complex textures. The influence of an organizer of new music performances shows in a cultured awareness of social context, spotlighting group dynamics in performer ensembles.

Growing out of an artistic and intellectual background, Foss's music is often based on a fascination with language, its potential for imagery, argument, and metaphor. A scientific attitude of discovery through experiment is also evident.

As a professor of composition at the University of California at Los Angeles in the 1950s, Foss's desire to demonstrate an experimental attitude led him to improvisation as a stimulating mode of musical discovery. The improvisation group he formed and performed with internationally irrevocably changed his direction as a composer. It closed a period of tonal lyricism and traditional expression by opening an endless quest for new modes of musical architecture and new possibilities of musical form. While the older works before this watershed represent a large body of related works, many of the subsequent compositions form smaller sets, groups of several works centered on the exploration of similar structural schemes.

One of the first experimental works points in its title to a consistent fascination with the flow of musical time. *Time Cycle* is based on writings of four different poets and authors about the experience of time. It presents many of the rhythmic qualities prevalent in later works, such as *Echoi* and the *Percussion Quartet*: restlessness, clock-like metric regularity, surprise interruptions and suspensions of time flow, highly elastic speeds of constantly exploding and dissipating activity. Even in chamber works without conductor such as *Echoi*, there is the sense of an unseen hand forcefully directing and bending the flow of events in time.

Textures are invaribly dense, combining several strata in contrapuntal collage or spinning kaleidoscopically through facets of a single but complex structure of sounds. Colors of sound are often treated as musical objects, isolated and delicate or combined into vivid, exotic composites. Although never himself a practitioner in the electro-acoustic medium, Foss acknowledges its strong influence in forging a precedent for textures and timbers of sound as primary and even solitary elements of musical interest.

Open form, an inevitable outcome of improvisation, infuses most Foss pieces. *Elytres* was the first of a series of works (including *For 24 Winds* and *Fragments of Archilochos*) to pose a dense texture of events which is cyclically explored by repeatedly dismantling it into component parts in different combinations. Foss chose to enact such a form by notational innovation, scoring the total textures in massive blocks, then providing a map of specified options for permutation by selected *tacets*. Many other works, including *MAP* and *Paradigm*, develop notational innovations to express musical materials as individual molecules, giving over to performer improvisation the role of connecting ideas into a variety of possible continuities in time.

Permutation takes on a different, smoother surface in works which employ layers of continuous ostinato patterns. As in the modular counterpoint of *Elytres* and contrapuntal collage in the Bach finale of *Baroque Variations*, the result is rich in relationship and teeming with change, hardly fitting the popular descriptive term, *minimalism*. In each approach, form is cyclic and metamorphic.

Despite a sense of style adaptable to the chosen musical problem, Foss's music remains rooted in its musical heritage. Avant-garde works of the 1960s such as *Baroque Variations* and more recent, reflective works such as the *Renaissance Concerto* and *Solomon Rossi Suite* pay homage to master composers of the past, quoting and wholly assimilating their music.

In addition to classical tradition, elements of popular music culture—dance music, jazz, even rock music—are incorporated. Foss has often been described as an eclectic sampler of styles. But he makes his own persuasive argument that the diversity of techniques employed and characters achieved manifest a resourceful spirit of exploration. In *Symphony* magazine (June 1989), Foss explains, "When I compose, I explore. It is a kind of burning curiosity, dare I say divine fire. With every piece I write, I try to solve a new problem. That's why I so often change techniques—which are not what people call style because they mix up style and technique. Actually, I don't change style, because style is my personality. I make things my own, and the more things you make your own, the richer your vocabulary is and the more fascinating your style is."

An acclaimed conductor controversial in the orchestral world for his contemporary music advocacy and bold interpretations of traditional repertoire, Foss consistently challenges musicians with his ideas, stimulating their creative contribution to his music. For the listener, there is always a challenge to engage actively in a provocative process of discovery.

—Thomas Clark

FOWLER, Jennifer. Australian. Born in Bunbury, Western Australia, 14 April 1939. Educated at University of Western Australia, B.A. (hons) in music, 1960; Dip.Ed., 1961; B.Mus., 1967; University of Utrecht, electronic music course, 1968–9; composition study under John Exton. Married Bruce Paterson, 18 December 1971; 2 sons. Teacher, Bunbury High School, 1962–3, Bentley High School, Western Australia, 1964–5, Cannington High School, Western Australia, 1966–8, and, Wykeham Secondary School, London, 1969–72. Recipient: Convocation Prize in music, University of Western

Australia, 1967; International Composers Prize (for *Hours of the Day*), Akademie der Kunste, Berlin, 1970; Radcliffe Award of Great Britain, 1971; 1st prize (for *Ravelation*), chamber music section, International Competition for Women Composers, Mannheim, Germany, 1975. Mailing address: 21 Deodar Road, Putney, London SW15 2NP, England.

Publisher: Universal Edition (Australia).

Symphonies/orchestral:

Fanfare (brass, string orchestra) 1968.
Sculpture in Four Dimensions 1969; first performed Perth, 1970.
Look on This Oedipus 1973; first performed Perth, 1975.
Chant with Garlands (strings, bells) 1974; first performed Manchester, 1983.
Ring out the Changes 1978; first performed London, 1978.

Chamber/instrumental:

String Quartet 1967.
Ravelation (2 violins, viola, 2 cellos) 1970–1; first performed Oxford, 1971.
Chimes, Fractured (2 flutes, 2 oboes, 2 clarinets, 2 bassoons, organ, bagpipes, 6 percussion) 1971; first performed Sydney, 1972. Recorded Festival Records, Australian Festival of Music, vol. 10.
Piece for an Opera House (2 pianos; or piano, tape; or solo piano) 1973; first performed Sydney, 1973.
Music for Piano—Ascending and Descending 1980; first performed London, 1980.
Piece for E.L. (piano; dedicated to Elisabeth Lutyens) 1981; first performed London, 1981.
The Arrows of Saint Sebastian I (flute, oboe, clarinet, bassoon, horn, trumpet, trombone, tuba, piano, 2 violins, viola, cello) 1981.
The Arrows of Saint Sebastian II (bass clarinet, cello, tape) 1981; first performed London, 1981.
Invocation to the Veiled Mysteries (flute, clarinet, bassoon, violin, cello, piano) 1982; first performed Sydney, 1982.
Threaded Stars (harp) 1983; first performed London, 1990.
Line Spun with Stars (violin or flute, cello, piano) 1983; first performed London, 1987.
Echoes from an Antique Land (5 tuned percussion; version for flute, clarinet, piano, string bass or bass guitar; version for flexible ensemble of 5 or 10 instruments) 1983; first performed London, 1985.
. . . Between Silence and the Word (flute, oboe, clarinet, horn, bassoon) 1987; first performed London, 1988.
Blow Flute: Answer Echoes in Antique Lands Dying (flute) 1987; first performed London, 1987.
Lament (baroque oboe, bass viol) 1987; first performed London, 1988.
Restless Dust (cello, piano; or viola, cello, double bass) 1988.
We Call to You, Brother (flute, cor anglais, cello, percussion, 2 trombones, didjeridu) 1988; first performed Nottingham, 1988.

Vocal/choral:

Voice of the Shades (soprano, oboe/clarinet, violin) 1967; first performed Helsinki, 1978.
Hours of the Day (4 soprani, 2 oboes, 2 clarinets) 1968; first performed Berlin, 1970.
Veni Sancti Spiritus—Veni Creator (12 solo singers, or chamber choir) 1971; first performed Hilversum, Holland, 1972.
Tell Out, My Soul (soprano, cello, piano) 1980; first performed London, 1980.
When David Heard . . . (medium-sized choir, piano) 1982; first performed York, Western Australia, 1983.
Letter from Haworth (mezzo-soprano, clarinet, cello, piano) 1984; first performed London, 1984.
And Ever Shall Be (mezzo-soprano, oboe, clarinet, trombone, violin, viola, cello, percussion) 1989; first performed London, 1989.

PUBLICATIONS

By Fowler: "My Own Ears", in *New Music Articles*, 4, 1985; "Credo", in Sounds Australian Journal, Autumn 1990.

On Fowler: Keith Potter, "Antipodean Connections", in *Classical Music*, January 1983.

Jennifer Fowler comments:

I like to think that much of my music can be played by "ordinary" performers, not necessarily by virtuosos who specialise in contemporary music. However, it is very difficult to reach "ordinary" performers and "ordinary" listeners! There are not many people prepared to step off the edge of the known and familiar. Yet, as a composer, one has to venture off the edge. Every human mind is blessed towards travelling along known paths in known directions. Somehow one must stimulate the imagination into making a step—seeing a vision—having something to say. Then one can communicate the sense of excitement.

* * *

A year's study on a Dutch Government Scholarship at the Studio of Electronic Music at Utrecht University in 1968 left a lasting impression upon Jennifer Fowler. Although she has not written any electronic music since then—for the lack of opportunity rather than by preference—much of the thinking behind this kind of composition pervades her work. The pieces display a preoccupation with variations in timbre, texture and sonority, generally affected by unusual combinations of instruments and the manner in which their particular sounds interact with each other. The most extreme example of this is probably *Chimes, Fractured*, an amusing occasional piece inspired by personal experience, written for an ensemble which includes bagpipes, organ and bells as well as more usual orchestral instruments. It was first performed at a Promenade Concert in Sydney in 1972, and was taken to the UNESCO International Rostrum of Composers in Paris later that year: the first work by a West Australian-born composer to achieve selection for this event.

The influence of electronically-generated sound can also be heard in Fowler's use of repetitive wave-like scale shapes, from *Sculpture in Four Dimensions* for orchestra and *Piece for an Opera House* to *Music for Piano—Ascending and Descending*.

Despite having lived in London since 1969, the composer reveals occasional musical characteristics that indicate an affiliation with the country of her birth. The music of the Australian Aborigines is a sporadic but persistent influence upon her writing. In *Chant with Garlands* for orchestra, the rhythmic pulse characteristic of the didjeridu and accompanying vocal chant can be discerned; it can also be heard in two works from 1982, the instrumental *Invocation to the Veiled Mysteries* and the lament *When David Heard . . .* for choir and piano. *We Call to You, Brother* actually incorporates a didjeridu into the ensemble of otherwise conventional instruments.

In her music, Fowler is constantly looking for new sounds and new possibilities of texture: she investigates the shaping of sound, the spacing of pitches, the rhythms made by varying the density of note clusters, and the psychological effect upon the listener of using the extremes of an instrument's registers. Hers is a very cerebral and intellectually motivated compositional process, with a deeply considered philosophical basis.

Fowler's works have received a number of awards in international competitions. *Ravelation* for string ensemble is one such piece which has been featured at various festivals, as has *Voice of the Shades* for soprano, oboe or clarinet, and violin. *Veni Sancti Spiritus—Veni Creator*, a composition for chamber choir woven around the original plainsong melody, was performed at the Guadeamus International Music Week in 1972, the International Competition for Women Composers in 1975, and the ISCM World Music Days in Brussels in 1981. Several other works have been commissioned, such as *And Ever Shall Be*, a set of four songs for mezzo-soprano and instrumental septet, which shows some minimalist influence in its emphasis on repetitive rhythms.

The move from Australia, firstly to study in Holland and afterwards to teach and subsequently settle in London, has proven to be of great value to this composer. By putting her in touch with both contemporary and women's music festivals and competitions, it has enabled her to reach a much wider audience, and to gain wider recognition for her music, than she would have been likely to achieve in other circumstances.

—Jenny Dawson

FOX, Erika. Austrian/British. Born in Vienna, 3 October 1936; emigrated to England, 1939. Educated at the Royal College of Music, London (piano under Angus Morrison, composition under Bernard Stevens); further composition study under Jeremy Dale Roberts, 1967, and (at Dartington) Peter Maxwell Davies and Harrison Birtwistle, 1968. Married Manfred Fox, 3 September 1961; 1 son and 1 daughter. Private teacher and pianist; teacher at Menuhin School, at Centre for Young Musicians, Pimlico, London; currently teaches composition workshop, junior department, Guildhall School of Music, London. Recipient: Finzi Award (for *Kaleidoscope*), 1983. Agent: Elinor Kelly, Westbrook Farm Cottage, Boxford, Near Newbury, Berkshire RG16 8DL. Mailing address: 394 Goldhawk Road, London W6 05B, England.

Publisher: self.

Symphonies/orchestral:

Cocytus 1973.
Litany (strings) 1981.
Osen Shomaat (small orchestra) 1985.

Chamber/instrumental:

In Memoriam Martin Luther King (cello, oboe) 1969.
Directions (A clarinet) 1970.
Serenade (piano, tape) 1971.
In Memoriam Igor Stravinsky (wind quintet, piano, percussion) 1971.
Round (8 violins, 3 violas, 3 cellos, double bass) 1972.
Lamentations for Four (2 cellos, 2 percussion) 1973.
Exercise (2 pianos) 1974.
To Veronica (piano) 1976.
Octet for Two (cello, piano, tape) 1977.
Omega Serenade (4 guitars/2 Requintos, tape) 1978.
Douganescu (violin, piano) 1979.
Paths Where the Mourners Tread (flute/alto flute/piccolo, oboe, percussion, harp, violin, viola, cello, double bass) 1980.
Epitaph for Cathy (basset clarinet; doubling on 3 gongs, 3 drums) 1980.
SHHS in Perpetuum Mobile (piano, 2 flutes, 2 violins, 2 cellos, wood block or claves) 1981.
Pas de deux (violin, double bass) 1981.
Spirals (bassoon, contrabassoon) 1982.
Movement for String Sextet (2 violins, 2 violas, 2 cellos) 1982.
Shir (flute, oboe, clarinet, bassoon, horn, trumpet, trombone, percussion, piano, 2 violins, viola, cello, double bass) 1983.
Kaleidoscope (flute, harp, vibraphone, cello) 1983.
Quasi una cadenza (horn, clarinet, piano) 1983.
Nick's Lament (guitar) 1984.
Silver Homage (trumpet, cello, piano, percussion) 1986.
Rivka's Fiddle (viola) 1986.
Dreaming (alto flute/piccolo, guitar) 1987.
On Visiting Stravinsky's Grave at San Michele (piano) 1988.
"Hungarian" Rhapsody (flute/alto flute, cor anglais, A clarinet/E♭ clarinet/bass clarinet, trumpet, piano) 1989.

Vocal/choral:

Eight Songs from Cavafy (mezzo-soprano, flute, oboe, bassoon, violin) 1968.
Nine Lessons from Isaiah (bass voice, string quartet) 1970.
Improvisation on Six Notes (soprano, flute, guitar) 1971.
Voices (soprano, mezzo-soprano, counter-tenor, tenor, baritone; all doubling on percussion) 1976.
Jeder Engel ist schrecklich (soprano, baritone, clarinet/bass/clarinet, horn, tenor trombone, bass trombone, 2 violins, viola, cello, double bass) 1976.
The Waters of Separation (girls' choir) 1978.
Frühling ist wiedergekommen (mezzo-soprano, piano) 1988.

Opera/dramatic:

Directions (clarinet, mime) 1970; first performed Dartington, Devon, 1970.
The Slaughterer (chamber opera: soprano, mezzo-soprano, contralto, tenor, baritone, bass, clarinet, trumpet, trombone, viola/fiddle, percussion) 1975.
The Bet (theatre work for narrator and puppets; flute/alto flute/piccolo/bass flute, piano, double bass, percussion, male and female voices; Elaine Feinstein) 1990.

Erika Fox comments:

My music is preoccupied largely with melody. Jewish liturgical chant and the Chassidic folk music of Eastern Europe are the main sources of my inspiration. Varied repetition and ornamentation take the place of "development". Rhythmic ostinati play a significant part in my compositions.

Freely combined melodic strands produce an effect related to heterophony, rather than "harmony", as traditionally understood.

I am interested in ritual, theatre and the art of "performance" per se, and much of my music reflects these interests. Although my instrumental output exceeds the vocal, I imagine everything I write as coming, in a sense, from the human voice.

* * *

Millicent Silver recognised Erika Fox's early musical talent and she was admitted to the Royal College of Music on a scholarship; later she studied there with Angus Morrison (piano) and Bernard Stevens (composition). After leaving college she taught music in schools and played for ballet classes; the latter gave her valuable experience in improvising music to rhythmical, dramatic movement. She spent her early adult life running a home, then in 1967 went to study with Jeremy Dale Roberts, who was instrumental in initiating her serious work as a composer. At a Dartington Summer School in 1968 she met Harrison Birtwistle, and he too had a great effect on her attitude to composition.

Fox fuses serial techniques with other non-tonal idioms, deriving rows from the time-honoured device of allowing notes to represent letters of the alphabet (A=C, B=C#, etc.). Thus, a name can be declaimed repeatedly, ensuring an ever-present symbolism. Such a literal *Leitmotif* was particularly appropriate for her puppet-opera *The Bet*, whose rows are as *dramatis personae*: WIDOW, JOSHUA, SPIRIT OF UNHAPPINESS, etc.

Fox agrees with Stravinsky that music cannot represent anything in itself, but achieves meaning through the context in which it is placed. This may emerge in the minutiae of a work's melodic content as well as in its form: in *Exercise* for two pianos, for example, the roles of players one and two at pianos one and two go through a variety of constantly changing relationships, highlighting questions of context and meaning. She is also obsessed with the dualism of opposing extremes. This can manifest itself on the surface of the music: lyricism/angularity, density/sparseness, height/depth, though at other times it is clear through scoring: her pieces are often for duos or for two pairs of instruments which represent opposing forces—for instance, two cellos/two percussionists in *Lamentations for Four* or piano and percussion/trumpet and cello in *Silver Homage*. That she often requires players to double shows that duality can be present within a single part. Her music often contains "dual monologues" as well, where neither musician appears to "listen" to the other.

The concepts of "dualism" and "contextual meaning" meet in her technique of juxtaposing serial music with freely composed, "Chassidic-like" melodies. Possibly, this reflects her personal history. The outside, modern "daylight" world of 20th-century England (serial music?) into which her background of Eastern European Jewry was so uneasily transplanted contrasts with the enclosed, unearthly "inner-lit" existence of home ("Chassidic" music). Serial and "Chassidic" fragments are usually woven into the fabric of the music and cannot be disentangled. Occasionally, however, the juxtaposition is overt: in *Osen Shomaat*, *Kaleidoscope*, *Quasi una cadenza* and especially her masterpiece *Shir*, dense textures give way to "Chassidic" melodies, declaimed in heterophony. These last three works were written after a visit to Jerusalem; though they are very different in character, they seem to form three facets of the same idea.

Fox's interest in ritual emerges in some of her circular, repetitive motivic ideas. These do not expand in the developmental sense, endowing the music with an aura of mysticism. Also, stage directions in her scores may mention a "ritual context" or a "ritualistic frame". The percussionist often assumes a controlling role, and can perhaps be likened to the *shaman* (medicine-man) of some ancient cultures. Percussion-playing is often coupled with directions to move about the stage, and the spatial element of performance—the relative physical position of different sounds—is of prime importance to Fox. Thus, it is vital to experience her music (or "music-theatre"?) in the three dimensions of the concert-hall rather than through recordings. Generally, her works for larger forces—particularly the theatre works—have been more successful than those for smaller, perhaps because her multi-faceted way of thinking can be allowed the space it needs on a larger canvass.

—Nicola Losseff

FRANÇAIX, Jean. French. Born in Le Mans, 23 May 1912. Private study with parents from age 4; Conservatoire National Supérieur de Musique, Paris; further study under Nadia Boulanger. Concert pianist; freelance composer. Recipient: premier prix (piano), Conservatoire de Paris, 1930. Mailing address: 43 rue Turbigo, 75003 Paris, France.

Publisher: Schott.

Symphonies/orchestral:

Concertino (piano, orchestra) 1932; first performed Paris, 13 February 1934.
Divertissement (string trio, winds, harp, double bass) 1933; first performed Paris, 22 December 1935.
Suite (violin, orchestra) 1934; first performed Paris, 1934.
Sérénade (small orchestra) 1934; first performed Paris, 1934.
Le Roi Nu/The Emperor's New Clothes (suite from the ballet) 1935.
Piano Concerto 1935; first performed Berlin, 3 November 1936.
Quadruple Concerto (flute, oboe, clarinet, bassoon, orchestra) 1935; first performed Paris, 1936.
Au Musée Grévin 1936; first performed Paris, 1936.
Musique de cour (flute, violin, orchestra) 1937; first performed Paris, 1938.
Divertissement (bassoon, strings) 1942; first performed Schwetzingen, 5 May 1968.
Rhapsodie (viola, winds) 1946; first performed London, January 1946.
Les Bosquets de Cythère 1946; broadcast 8 July 1947.
La Douce France 1946; first performed Paris, 21 November 1946.
L'Heure du berger (piano, strings) 1947; first performed Paris, 1947.
Symphonie d'archets (string orchestra) 1948; broadcast BBC, 1948.
Variations de concert (cello, strings) 1950; first performed Saarbrücken, 1960.
Les Zigues de Mars (suite from the ballet) 1950; first performed Paris, 19 February 1950.

Sérénade B E A (game on three notes for strings) 1952.
Symphony 1953; first performed La Jolla, California, 9 August 1953.
Si Versailles m'était conté (suite after film score) 1953; broadcast 8 May 1954.
Violin Concertino 1953.
Fantaisie (cello, orchestra) 1955; first performed Saarbrücken, 1955.
Hymne solennel 1956.
Six Grandes Marches dans le style du premier Empire (also for piano) 1957; broadcast 25 June 1957.
Divertimento (horn, orchestra) 1959; broadcast 5 March 1968.
L'Horloge de Flore (oboe, orchestra) 1959; first performed Philadelphia, 1 April 1961.
Concerto (flute, harpsichord, strings) 1959; first performed Paris, 7 February 1960.
Le Dialogue des Carmélites (symphonic suite) 1960; broadcast 4 April 1969.
Sei preludi (chamber string orchestra) 1963; first performed Lucerne, 3 September 1964.
Double Piano Concerto 1965; first performed Maastricht, 26 November 1965.
Flute Concerto 1966; first performed Schwetzingen, 13 May 1967.
Clarinet Concerto 1967; first performed Nice, 30 July 1968.
Violin Concerto 1968, revised 1970; first performed Quebec, 26–27 January 1970; revised version first performed Paris, 22 November 1970.
Jeu poétique (harp, orchestra) 1969; first performed Dresden, 12–13 October 1972.
Thème et variations 1971; first performed Bochum, Switzerland, 12–13 December 1974.
Quinze Portraits d'enfants d'Auguste Renoir 1971; broadcast 25 May 1972.
La Ville mystérieuse (fantasy for orchestra after Jules Verne) 1973; first performed Nuremberg, 15 March 1974.
Cassazione (3 orchestras) 1973; first performed Salzburg, 12 August 1975.
Double Bass Concerto 1974; first performed Frankfurt am Main, 1 November 1974.
Divertimento (flute, chamber orchestra) 1974; first performed Braunschweig, Germany, 29 November 1974.
Le Gai Paris (trumpet, winds) 1974; first performed Wiesbaden, 6 April 1975.
Concerto grosso (wind quintet, string quintet, orchestra) 1976; first performed Mainz, 6 February 1977.
Chaconne (harp, strings) 1976; first performed Gargilesse, 1 September 1977.
Variations sur un thème plaisant (piano, wind ensemble) 1976; first performed Mainz, 9 May 1977.
Concerto (2 harps, strings) 1978; first performed Zurich, 11 May 1979.
Ouverture anacréontique 1978; first performed Recklinghausen, 22 February 1981.
Thema con variazioni (clarinet, string orchestra) 1978; first performed Florence, 14 September 1978.
Bassoon Concerto (bassoon, chamber strings, piano), 1979; first performed Frankfurt, 20 May 1980.
Concerto No 2 (violin, small orchestra) 1979.
Petite valse européene (tuba, winds) 1979; first performed Schwetzingen, 14 May 1980.

Chamber/instrumental:

Huit Bagatelles (piano) 1931.
Scherzo (piano) 1932; first performed Paris, 5 March 1932.
Trio (string trio) 1933; first performed Paris, 15 June 1934.
Quartet (flute, oboe, clarinet, bassoon) 1933; first performed Paris, 26 April 1936.
String Quartet 1934; first performed Paris, 8 March 1937.
Quintet (flute, string trio, harp) 1934; first performed Paris, 24 May 1935.
Sonatine (violin, piano) 1934; first performed Paris, 17 February 1936.
Petit Quatuor (saxophone quartet) 1935; first performed Paris, 1947.
Sept Danses (10 winds; from the ballet *Les Malheurs de Sophie*) 1935; first performed Zagreb, 25 May 1970.
Cinq Portraits de jeunes filles (piano) 1936; first performed Paris, 1937.
Mouvement perpetuel (cello, piano) 1944.
Eloge de la danse (piano; after Valéry) 1947; broadcast 1947.
L'Heure du berger (flute, oboe, clarinet, horn, piano; version for flute, oboe, 2 clarinets, 2 bassoons, horn, trombone, piano) 1947.
Divertissement (oboe, clarinet, bassoon) 1947; first performed Paris, 26 January 1947.
Quintet (flute, oboe, clarinet, bassoon, horn) 1948; first performed Paris, 2 December 1954.
Deux Pièces (guitar) 1950.
Sonatine (trumpet, piano) 1952; first performed Paris, 1952.
Canon à l'octave (horn, piano) 1953.
Divertimento (flute, piano) 1953; first performed Paris, 12 January 1955.
L'insectarium (harpsichord) 1953; first performed Royaumont, 14 July 1957.
Si Versailles m'était conté (piano; from the film score) 1954.
Napoléon (piano—4 hands; from the film score) 1954.
Danse des trois arlequins (piano) 1955.
Huit Danses exotiques (2 pianos) 1957; first performed Paris, 15 November 1957.
Marche solennelle (organ) 1957.
Divertimento (horn, piano) 1959.
Sonata (piano) 1960; first performed Paris, 1960.
Suite carmélite (organ) 1960.
Cinq Danses exotiques (alto saxophone, piano) 1961.
Suite (flute) 1962.
Cinq "Bis" (piano) 1965.
Quartet (cor anglais, string trio) 1971.
Trio (flute, cello, harp) 1971.
Octet (clarinet, bassoon, horn, string quintet) 1972; first performed Vienna, 7 November 1972.
Neuf pièces caracteristiques (2 flutes, 2 oboes, 2 clarinets, 2 bassoons, 2 horns) 1973; first performed Schwetzingen, 8 May 1974.
Aubade (12 cellos) 1974; first performed Berlin, 30 September 1975.
Quasi improvisando (11 winds) 1975.
Quintet (clarinet, string quartet) 1977; first performed Munich, 18 June 1978.
Sept Impromptus (flute, bassoon) 1977; first performed Seattle, Washington, 12 October 1978.
Huit Bagatelles (string quartet, piano) 1980.
Tema con otte variazioni (violin) 1980; first performed Paris, 18 March 1981.
Danses exotiques (11 winds, percussion) 1981.
Piano Trio 1987.
Cinque piccoli duetti (harp, flute) n.d.
Suite (harp) n.d.
Duo baroque (double bass, harp) n.d.
Passacaglia (guitar) n.d.

Vocal/choral:

Cinq Chansons (2 voices, children's chorus, orchestra) 1932.
Trois Duos (2 sopranos, string quartet; after Aristophanes) 1934.
Trois Epigrammes (4 voices, string quintet; Marot, d'Orléans, du Bellay) 1938; first performed Nantes, 30 November 1938.
L'Apocalypse selon St Jean (4 solo voices, chorus, 2 orchestras) 1939; first performed Paris, 11 June 1942.
Cantate en l'honneur de Sully (baritone, 4 trumpets, strings, organ) 1942.
L'Adolescence clémentine (voice, piano; Marot) 1942; first performed Paris, 5 June 1942.
Deux Motets (voice, organ) 1946.
Cinq Poésies (voice, piano; d'Orléans) 1946; first performed Paris, 1946.
Invocation à la volupté (baritone, small orchestra; La Fontaine) 1946; first performed Paris, 1947.
Juvenalia (4 voices, piano duet; Juvenal) 1947; first performed Paris, 1947.
Prière du soir (voice, piano or guitar; d'Aubigne) 1947; first performed Paris, 1947.
Chanson (voice, piano or guitar; Marot) 1947.
Huit Anecdotes de Chamfort (voice, piano) 1949; first performed Royaumont, 26 June 1949.
Scherzo-Impromptu (voice, piano; de Vilmorin) 1949.
La Cantate de Méphisto (bass, strings; Valéry) 1952; first performed New York City, 25 January 1953.
Déploration de Tonton, chien fidèle (mezzo-soprano, strings; Ravon) 1956; first performed Paris, 22 October 1956.
Naissance du poussin (voice, piano; Drouet) 1957.
Chatte blanche (voice, piano; d'Aulnoy) 1957; first performed Aix-en-Provence, 27 July 1957.
L'Homme entre deux âges (voice, flute, string quintet) 1958.
La Grenouille qui veut se faire aussi grosse que la boeuf (soprano/tenor/male chorus, piano; La Fontaine) 1963, revised for chorus or vocal quartet; first performed Paris, 1963.
Le Coq et le renard (2 tenors, 2 basses or men's chorus, piano) 1963.
Les Inestimables Chroniques du bon géant Gargantua (speaker, strings; Rabelais) 1970; first performed Paris, 17 May 1971.
La Promenade à Versailles (2 tenors, baritone, bass, strings) 1976.
La Cantate des vieillards (tenor, baritone, 11 strings) 1978.
Psyche (speaker, orchestra; La Fontaine) 1981.

Opera:

Le Diable boiteux (chamber opera; Le Sage) 1937; first performed Paris, 30 June 1938.
L'Apostrophe (after Balzac) 1940; first performed Amsterdam, 1 July 1951.
La Main de gloire (after de Nerval) 1945.
Paris à nous deux (Roche, JF) 1954; first performed Fontainebleau, 7 August 1954.
La Princesse de Clèves (Lanjean, JF, after de la Fayette) 1965; first performed Rouen, 11 December 1965.

Other:

Scuola di ballo (ballet; after Boccherini) 1933; first performed Monte Carlo, 1933.
Les Malheurs de Sophie (ballet; after de Segur) 1935; first performed Paris, 25 February 1948.
Le Roi nu/The Emperor's New Clothes (after Andersen) 1935; first performed Paris, 15 June 1936.
Le Jeu sentimental (ballet) 1936; first performed Brussels, 8 July 1936.
La Lutherie enchantée (ballet) 1936; first performed Antwerp, 21 March 1936.
Le Jugement d'un fou (ballet; after Rabelais) 1938; first performed London, 6 February 1939.
Verreries de Venise (ballet) 1938; first performed Paris, 22 June 1939.
Les Demoiselles de la nuit (ballet) 1948; first performed Paris, 20 May 1948.
Les Camélias (ballet) 1950; first performed Wiesbaden, 15 October 1950.
Les Zigues de Mars (ballet) 1950.
Le Roi Midas (ballet; after Ovid) 1952.
Si Versailles m'était conté (film score) 1953.
Napoléon (film score) 1954.
La Dame dans la lune (ballet) 1958; first performed Paris, 18 February 1958.
Pierrot, ou les secrets de la nuit (ballet; Tournier) 1980.

Transcriptions of Emanuel Chabrier: *Souvenir de Munich*; Frederic Chopin: *Introduction et polonaise brillante*, *Twenty-Four Preludes*; Domenico Scarlatti: *Cinq Sonates*; Franz Schubert: *Six Impromptus et moments musicaux*; Carl Maria von Weber: *Preludio et momento capriccioso*.

PUBLICATIONS

On Françaix: M. Lanjean, *JF*, Paris, 1961.

* * *

Jean Françaix had a good start, his father being director of LeMans Conservatoire, his mother a professional singer and teacher. He began composing at six and his father invited comments on some of his pieces from Ravel, who said the "most fruitful" of the gifts they displayed was that of curiosity. After instruction from his parents Françaix attended the Paris Conservatoire, where he won a premier prix for piano. Throughout much of his life he toured widely, and recorded, as a highly accomplished pianist, latterly with his daughter Claude in his *Double Piano Concerto* of 1965. After the Conservatoire Françaix pursued further studies in composition with Nadia Boulanger and all his music is sure of its aims and has a concise practicality. Hence selecting items for comment from a vast and, it often seems, easily achieved output must be a somewhat arbitrary process.

So much of his music is full of bustle and levity that it is hard to think of Françaix as a member of the same generation of French composers as Messiaen and Jolivet. Often he cheekily veers close to, while seldom quite reaching, the commonplace, and simple procedures are artfully disguised. In part a latter-day Saint-Saëns, in part allied with Ibert and Sauguet, he continued a vein in French music close to that of Satie, though with a far more extensive and secure technique than that estimable *farceur*. Whereas a very minor composer such as Auric might sprinkle his music with piquant dissonances that make no real sense (e.g., his *Phèdre*), Françaix uses all processes with understanding and in fact with real precision, a good example being his Piano Concertino. This is a student work dating from 1932 which is almost a masterpiece of simplicity and established a style he employed over several decades. An early instance is the 1935 *Quadruple Concerto* for woodwinds, a later one the gossamer-light Harpsichord Concerto of 1959, the first movement of which is even fuller of ostinato figuration than is usual with Françaix.

In some larger pieces such as the four-movement *Piano Concerto* of 1935, commissioned as a result of the Concertino's success, structural weaknesses are evident. This is particularly so in the finale in this instance, yet the music's gaiety has over the decades retained something more than mere charm. And there are later items, like the 1955 *Fantaisie* for cello and orchestra that do have a well-organised form. So do the beautiful *Symphonie d'archets* of 1948 and the *Violin Concerto* of 1968–70.

Something close to music-hall high spirits, however, get into much of Françaix's chamber production, as with the *Divertissement* for oboe, clarinet and bassoon of 1947 or the 1942 one—only performed in 1968—for bassoon and strings. That not all his chamber works are like this is suggested by the *Piano Trio* of 1987, whose four deft, witty and thematically related movements are a late echo of the Parisian world of Milhaud, Poulenc and similar composers between the two World Wars.

There is tenderness and irony in such music as well as humour, this being confirmed by the waltz sequence of *Les Bosquets de Cythère*, and indeed Françaix's range is wider than is generally supposed. This is best shown by his theatre music, particularly his several operas, of which the four-act *La Princesse de Clèves* is the most impressive. His sense of the theatre is also evident in the verve and wit of his numerous ballets, for instance *Le Jeu sentimental*, which has especially inventive orchestration, and *Les Demoiselles de la nuit*, which boasts a scenario by Anouilh and whose characters are all cats.

Far more serious is *L'Apocalypse selon St Jean*, an oratorio dating from 1939. We are far here from the green-fields-and-Pepsodent atmosphere of so many of the instrumental pieces and this conveys the visionary nature of the saint's religious experiences in a manner which is recognisably that of Françaix yet is undeniably different from most of his work. It is impossible not to wonder what more he might have done in this direction.

—Max Harrison

FRICKER, Peter Racine. British/English. Born in London, 5 September 1920. Educated at St Paul's School, London; Royal College of Music, London (under R.O. Morris and Ernest Bullock); further study under Mátyás Seiber. Served in Royal Air Force, England and Far East, 1940–6. Married Helen Clench, 17 April 1943. Music director, Morley College, London, 1952–64; concurrently, teacher of composition, Royal College of Music, London, 1955–64; visiting, then full professor of music, from 1964, chair of music department, from 1970, and Faculty Research Lecturer, 1980; University of California, Santa Barbara; vice-president, Composers' Guild of Great Britain, 1986. Recipient: Alfred Clements Prize (for *Wind Quintet*), 1948; Koussevitzky Award (for *Symphony No 1*), 1949; Festival of Britain Competition for Young Composers prize (for *Violin Concerto*), 1951; Collard Fellowship, 1955; Order of Merit, Federal Government of West Germany, 1965. Honorary degrees: D. Mus., University of Leeds, 1965; Fellow, Royal Academy of Music, 1966. **Died February 1990.**

Publisher: Schott.

Symphonies/orchestral:

Rondo scherzoso 1948.
Symphony No 1 Op 9 1948–9; first performed Cheltenham, Gloucestershire, 5 July 1950.
Prelude, Elegy and Finale Op 10 (string orchestra) 1949; first performed Darmstadt, July 1949.
Concerto for Violin and Small Orchestra Op 11 1951; first performed London, 1951.
Concertante No 1 Op 13 (cor anglais, string orchestra) 1951; first performed Hampton Court, Middlesex, July 1951.
Symphony No 2 Op 14 1951; first performed Liverpool, 26 July 1951.
Concertante No 2 Op 15 (3 pianos, strings, timpani) 1951; first performed Hovingham, Yorkshire, July 1951.
Concerto for Viola and Orchestra Op 18 1953; first performed Edinburgh, 3 September 1953.
Concerto for Piano and Small Orchestra Op 19 1953–4; first performed London, 21 March 1954.
Rapsodia concertante (Concerto No 2) Op 21 (violin, orchestra) 1954; first performed Rome, April 1954.
Dance Scene Op 22 1955; first performed Stuttgart, January 1955.
Litany Op 26 (double string orchestra) 1955; first performed Cheltenham, Gloucestershire, July 1956.
Fantasie (on a Theme of Mozart) 1956; first performed Donaueschingen, October 1956.
Comedy Overture Op 32 1958; first performed London, November 1958.
Waltz (restricted orchestra) 1958.
Toccata Op 33 (piano, orchestra) 1959; first performed Liverpool, May 1959.
Symphony No 3 Op 36 1960; first performed London, 8 November 1960.
Concertante No 4 (flute, oboe, violin, strings) 1964; first performed Santa Cruz, California, 25 February 1969.
Symphony No 4: In Memoriam Mátyás Seiber Op 43 1967; first performed Cheltenham, Gloucestershire, 14 February 1967.
Three Scenes Op 45 1967; first performed Santa Barbara, California, 26 February 1967.
Seven Counterpoints Op 47 1967; first performed Pasadena, California, 21 October 1967.
Nocturne Op 63 (chamber orchestra) 1971.
Introitus Op 66 1972; first performed Canterbury, Kent, 24 June 1972.
Symphony No 5 Op 74 (organ, orchestra) 1975; first performed London, May 1976.
Laudi concertati Op 80 (organ, orchestra) 1978–9.

Chamber/instrumental:

Three Preludes Op 1 (piano) 1941–4.
Four Fughettas Op 2 (2 pianos) 1946; first performed London, June 1948.
Sonata Op 3 (organ) 1947.
Wind Quintet Op 5 1947; first performed London, March 1949.
String Quartet in One Movement Op 8 1948; first performed London, October 1949.
Sonata Op 12 (violin, piano) 1950; first performed Switzerland, September 1950.
Aubade (alto saxophone, piano) 1951.
Four Impromptus Op 17 (piano) 1952; first performed London, April 1952.

String Quartet No 2 Op 20 1953; first performed Cheltenham, Gloucestershire, June 1953.
Pastorale (3 flutes) 1954.
Nocturne and Scherzo Op 23 (piano duet) 1954; first performed London, January 1955.
Sonata Op 24 (horn, piano) 1955; first performed London, March 1955.
Four Sonnets (piano) 1955.
Trio (2 clarinets, bassoon) 1955–6.
Suite for Recorders (2 treble recorders, tenor recorder) 1956.
Four Sonnets (piano) 1956; first performed Stockholm, February 1956.
Suite (harpsichord) 1956; first performed Dartington, Devon, August 1956.
Choral (organ) 1956; first performed London, March 1956.
Sonata Op 28 (cello, piano) 1956; first performed London, December 1957.
Fourteen Aubades (piano) 1958; broadcast BBC, March 1958.
Variations Op 31 (piano) 1957; first performed Leeds, February 1958.
Octet Op 30 (flute, clarinet, horn, bassoon, violin, viola, cello, double bass) 1958; first performed London, February 1958.
Serenade No 1 Op 34 (flute, clarinet, horn, bassoon, violin, viola, cello, double bass) 1959; first performed Vancouver, December 1959.
Pastorale (organ) 1959.
Trio (Serenade No 2) Op 35 (flute, oboe, piano) 1959; first performed London, January 1960.
Wedding Processional (organ) 1960; first performed Cambridge, April 1960.
Twelve Studies Op 38 (piano) 1961; first performed Cheltenham, Gloucestershire, July 1961.
Flourish (brass choir) 1965.
Ricercare Op 40 (organ) 1965; first performed Zwolle, Netherlands, June 1965.
Four Dialogues Op 41 (oboe, piano) 1965.
Five Canons (2 flutes, 2 oboes) 1966.
Fantasy Op 44 (viola, piano) 1966.
Refrains Op 49 (oboe) 1968.
Episodes I Op 51 (piano) 1968.
Trio (Canon-ostinato) (organ) 1968.
Six Short Pieces Op 53 (organ) 1968.
Toccata: Gladius Domini Op 55 (organ) 1968–9.
Serenade No 3 Op 57 (saxophone quartet) 1969.
Three Arguments Op 59 (bassoon, cello) 1969.
Praeludium Op 60 (organ) 1969.
Paseo Op 61 (guitar) 1969.
Carillon Music I & II 1969–70.
Concertante No 5 Op 65 (piano, string quartet) 1971; first performed Santa Barbara, California, 29 January 1972.
Sarabande: In Memoriam Igor Stravinsky (cello) 1971.
Intrada Op 64 (organ) 1971.
A Bourrée: For Sir Arthur Bliss on his 80th birthday (cello) 1971.
Ballade Op 68 (flute, piano) 1972.
The Groves of Dodona Op 70 (6 flutes) 1973.
Spirit Puck Op 71 (clarinet, percussion) 1974.
Trio-Sonata Op 72 (organ) 1974.
String Quartet No 3 Op 73 1975.
Invention (organ, manuals only) 1976.
Seachant Op 75 (flute, double bass) 1976.
Anniversary Op 77 (piano) 1977.
Sonata Op 78 (2 pianos) 1977; first performed February 1978.
Serenade No 4 Op 79 (3 clarinets, bass clarinet) 1977.
Serenade No 5 Op 81 (violin, cello) 1979.
Five Short Pieces Op 83 (organ) 1980.

Vocal/choral:

Two Carols: A Babe Is Born, The First Christmas (unaccompanied SATB chorus) 1938, 1962.
Two Madrigals Op 4 1947.
Night Landscape Op 6 (medium voice, string trio) 1947.
Three Sonnets of Cecco Angiolieri da Siena Op 7 (tenor, wind quintet, cello, double bass; translated Rossetti) 1947.
King o'Luv (voice, piano) 1949.
Rollant et Oliver (unaccompanied chorus; *Chanson de Roland*) 1952; first performed April 1952.
Roses et Muguets (soprano, piano) 1952.
Elegy: The Tomb of St Eulalia Op 25 (counter-tenor, viola da gamba, harpsichord; Prudentius) 1955; first performed London, September 1955.
Two Carols: Mary Is a Lady Bright, In Excelsis Gloria (unaccompanied SATB chorus) 1956.
Musick's Empire Op 27 (chorus, small orchestra; Marvell) 1956; first performed London, May 1956.
The Vision of Judgement Op 29 (soprano, tenor, chorus, orchestra; Cynewulf) 1957–8.
Cantata: Colet (soloists, chorus, orchestra) 1959.
O Mistress Mine (tenor, guitar; Shakespeare) 1961; first performed Dartingon, Devon, July 1962.
Cantata (tenor, flute, oboe, clarinet, bassoon, horn, 2 violins, viola, cello, double bass; Saroyan) 1962; first performed Aldeburgh, Suffolk, June 1962.
O Longs Desirs Op 39 (soprano, orchestra; Labe) 1963; first performed London, September 1963.
Commissary Report (men's chorus) 1965.
Vocalise (soprano, piano) 1965.
Four Songs Op 42/42a (high voice, piano/orchestra) 1965.
The Day and the Spirits Op 46 (soprano, harp) 1967.
Ave Maris Stella Op 48 (male voices, piano) 1967.
Cantilena and Cabaletta Op 54 (soprano) 1967–8.
Magnificat Op 50 (soloists, chorus, orchestra) 1968; first performed Santa Barbara, California, 27 May 1968.
Some Superior Nonsense Op 56 (tenor, flute, oboe, harpsichord) 1968; first performed Santa Barbara, California, 26 February 1969.
The Roofs Op 62 (coloratura soprano, percussion) 1970.
Ich will meine Seele tauchen (baritone, piano) 1970.
Come Sleep Op 67 (contralto, alto, bass clarinet) 1972.
Seven Little Songs Op 69 (unaccompanied mixed chorus) 1972.
Two Madrigals of Petrarch (unaccompanied SSATB chorus) 1974.
Carol: Mirabilem Misterium (unaccompanied mixed chorus) 1974.
A Wish for a Party (male voice choir) 1977.
In Commendation of Music Op 82 (soprano, recorder, viola da gamba, harpsichord) 1980.
Six Melodies de Francis Jammes Op 84 (tenor, violin, cello, piano) 1980.

Opera:

My Brother Died (radio opera) 1952–4.
The Death of Vivien (radio opera) 1955–6.

Other:

Canterbury Prologue Op 16 (ballet) 1951.
La Mort d'Arthur (radio music) 1952.
The Quest for the Holy Grail (radio music) 1953.
Clive of India (radio music) 1954.
Lemons and Hieroglyphs (radio music) 1959.

Film scores: *The White Continent*, 1951; *Inside the Atom*, 1951; *The Undying Heart*, 1952; *The Inquisitive Giant*, 1958; *Atomic Energy*, 1958; *Das Island*, 1958; *Looking at Churches*, 1959.

PUBLICATIONS

On Fricker: D. Stevens, "PRF", in *Music*, 1952; C. Mason, "F and His Generation", in *The Listener*, 51, 1954; P. Evans, "F and the English Symphony", in *The listener*, 64, 1960; M. Schafer, in *British Composers in Interview*, London, 1963; D. Peart, "PRF's Symphony No 4", in *The Listener*, 77, 1967; R. Hines, in *The Orchestral Composer's Point of View*, Oklahoma, 1970; Alun Hodinott, "PRF", in *Music and Musicians*, 18(12), 1970; Francis Routh, in *Contemporary British Music*, London, 1972.

* * *

Though closely followed by Hamilton and Searle, Peter Racine Fricker was the first British composer to establish a reputation entirely after World War II. Beginning with the *Four Fughettas* for two pianos of 1946, his fame grew rapidly and was international. Thus *Symphony No 1* received the Koussevitsky Foundation Award in 1949 and Scherchen conducted his *Prelude, Elegy and Finale* at the Darmstadt Festival of Music of the Young Generation the same year. In 1950 Fricker's First String Quartet was performed at the Brussels ISCM Festival and in 1951 he won the Festival of Britain Competition for Young Composers with his First Violin Concerto. That same year his *Symphony No 2* was commissioned for the Liverpool Festival and in 1952 the Edinburgh Festival commissioned his Viola Concerto.

Utterly removed from the pastoral vein that informed much British music between the wars, Fricker's models, like those of Hamilton and Searle, were Continental. In his case they were Bartók, Schoenberg, Hindemith and Berg—though he resembled none of them. Again like Hamilton, Fricker's emphasis was on instrumental rather than vocal pieces, and this too was rather new in British music. He possessed a strong and highly flexible sense of large-scale form and said that he always conceived a piece as a whole before putting a note on paper. At first he cast his works in traditional forms revitalised in a personal way, but there were always exceptions such as *Symphony No 2* (1950–1). One of his finest compositions, this has three movements in rather complicated versions of rondo form. Concentrated in a different way is the First String Quartet, which runs all four movements into one, closely integrating them with thematic transformations.

While there are plenty of passages of melody with accompaniment in Fricker's scores, it was from the start evident that he was a masterly contrapuntist, an early demonstration being provided by the *Wind Quintet* of 1947, especially the third movement, a theme with five canonic variations. *String Quartet No 2* amply confirmed this skill, as had the passage in seven real parts in the first movement of *Symphony No 1*. Fricker's melodic lines themselves are acutely expressive while also nearly always being susceptible to further growth. In fact he could develop melody as a crucial part of the unfolding of long-range forms so as to contribute with remarkable sureness to the dramatic effect both at local level and with regard to the impact of the whole. *Symphony No 2* provides excellent instances.

The feeling of tonality is rarely quite lost in Fricker, but although his music is basically diatonic it usually has a quite high level of dissonance with tritones, major sevenths, minor ninths as well as many less stringent sounds. The chromaticism meant that leanings towards serial technique were unsurprising, although there are only a few wholly twelve-tone works, such as the *Four Sonnets* for solo piano of 1955. Serial tendencies probably also arose from his allowing motivic development as much as normal functional considerations to give rise to chord progressions. Certainly much of the expressive force of Fricker's music comes from its harmony. He was inclined to use the serial method as one resource among many, perhaps extracting themes and a harmonic vocabulary from a tone-row and then developing them along more traditional lines. Often, as in the *Litany* for double string orchestra of 1955, there is less strict serially organised music than freely composed material.

His concern with structural logic and motivic growth seldom diluted the strongly emotional character of Fricker's output, and as the years passed he became more, not less, adventurous, though with a line of consistent stylistic development evident overall. *Symphony No 4* is a notable example of his continuing explorations, its mosaic-like single movement being in ten closely related sections. Typical of the increased concentration of his later music, this particularly original score is dedicated to the memory of Fricker's last teacher, Mátyás Seiber. It makes some use of the tone-row of the latter's *String Quartet No 3* and the harmonies of his *Permutazioni a cinque* (from which Fricker had also employed ideas in his song cycle *O Longs Desirs*).

Symphony No 4 was completed in the United States, where in 1964 he settled for the rest of his life. The works Fricker wrote there mark a further stage in his artistic growth and display leaner textures, still greater concentration. This thinning-out had been anticipated, however, in such pieces as the *Tableau and Dance* movement of *Symphony No 1* with its transparent orchestration and strong rhythmic life. The rhythmic animation of his music is, indeed, an important factor, the *Toccata* for piano and orchestra being a vivid instance. As examples of Fricker's latter-day concentration see the two sets of *Episodes* of 1967–9 for solo piano. These further the thoughts and keyboard inventions of his *Twelve Studies*, a 1961 group that is a mine of new pianistic ideas and stands with the 1957 *Variations* among the finest keyboard music of any period by a British composer. Along with such achievements as the oratorio *The Vision of Judgement* and the *Octet* they make the long neglect of Fricker in his native land inexcusable.

—Max Harrison

FULKERSON, James (Orville). American. Born in Streator, Illinois [American *Grove* gives place of birth as Manville, Illinois], 2 July 1945. Educated at Illinois Wesleyan University, Bloomington (trombone under John Silber, composition under Wilbur Ogdon and Abram Plum), 1963–6, B.Mus.; University of Illinois, Urbana (computer/electronic composition and acoustics under Lejaren Hiller, Salvatore Martirano and Herbert Brun), 1966–9, M.M., work towards D.M.A.; private study with Kenneth Gaburo, 1968. Married (1) Teresa Alton, August 1966; (2) dancer Mary Elizabeth O'Donnell, 5 June 1968; 1 son. Research assistant, contemporary music pedagogy, University of Illinois, 1967–9; musical adviser, dance department, University of Illinois, Urbana, 1968–9; lecturer/instructor, 1969–70, and creative associate, 1969–72,

State University of New York, Buffalo; artist in residence, Deutscher Akademischer Austauschdienst, Berlin, 1973, and Victorian College of the Arts, Melbourne, 1977–9; associate lecturer, Dartington College of Arts, Totnes, Devon, 1982–6; artist in residence, Museum of Modern Art, Stockholm, 1983; visiting composer (electronic studio), California Institute for the Arts, Valencia, 1985; composer in residence, Theatre School in Amsterdam, 1986; lecturer in composition, University of Nottingham, 1987–90; featured lecturer, English New Dance Theatre summer school, Newcastle, England, 1989; co-director, Gulbenkian International Summer School for Composers and Choreographers, Bretton Hall, Yorkshire, 1990. Mailing address: Dorpsstraat 68, 1454-AN Watergang, Netherlands.

Publishers: Edition Modern, Munich; Seesaw Music, New York.

Symphonies/orchestral:

Globs (4 orchestral groups, live electronics, tape) 1968.
Something About Mobiles 1969.
Planes, Pts (4 orchestral groups; also version for computer-generated tape) 1969.
Behind Closed Doors 1971.
Guitar Concerto 1972.
Patterns X (orchestra or wind ensemble) 1972.
. . . To See a Thing Clearly 1972.
, For We Don't See Anything Clearly 1972.
Trombone Concerto (also version with brass and percussion) 1973.
Orchestra Piece (bass clarinet, bass trombone, piano, strings) 1974.
Stations, Regions and Clouds II (bass trombone, chamber orchestra) 1977.
Concerto for Amplified Cello and Chamber Orchestra 1978.
Stations, Regions and Clouds IV (amplified trombone, orchestra) 1979.
Symphony 1980.
Concerto (. . . Fierce and Coming from Far Away) 1981.

Chamber/instrumental:

Woodwind Quintet No 1 1965.
Woodwind Quintet No 2 1966.
Quintet (tenor sax, double bass, percussion, bass trombone, harpsichord) 1967.
Quartet for Dancers, or: One Thing Leads to Another (bassoon, piano, violin, trombone) 1967.
Patterns I (flute; with or without tape *Structures*) 1967.
I Should've Called It Something . . . for STRING QUARTET (any 4 instruments) 1968.
String Quartet 1968.
Morphosis I (jazz ensemble) 1968.
Now II (sound modulator, amplified clavichord, trombone, trumpet) 1969.
Mobiles and Loops (4 percussion, tape) 1969.
Patterns III (tuba) 1969.
SDTQ (1–4 bass trombone(s), double bass(es), flute(s), optional percussion; composed with the aid of the IBM 360 computer) 1969.
About Time (wind ensemble) 1969.
Morphosis II (4 trombones) 1970.
Morphosis III (4 trombones) 1970.
Two Activities (any instrument(s)) 1970.
Space Music (pianists) 1970.
TRIAD (pianists) 1971.
Two Activities II (large ensemble) 1971.
Space Music II (9–88 pianists) 1971.
Patterns II (guitar) 1971. Recorded Folkways Records FTS 33902.
Patterns IV (double bass) 1971.
Patterns VI (percussion) 1971.
Patterns and Processes (A) (chamber ensemble; score on 35mm slides) 1971.
Patterns and Processes (B) (percussion; score on 35mm slides) 1971.
Line Studies (tuba, double bass, prepared piano) 1971.
Line Studies II (tuba, guitar, double bass) 1971.
Line Studies III (percussion) 1971.
Projections (chamber ensemble; score on 35mm slides) 1971.
Folio (pianist) 1971.
Co-Ordinative Systems No 1 (solos to ensemble) 1972.
Patterns VII (any solo instrument) 1972. Recorded Folkways Records FTS 33902.
Space Music III 1972.
Patterns IX (chamber ensemble of sustaining instruments) 1972.
Patterns X (wind ensemble; also for orchestra) 1972.
Two Activities III (large ensemble) 1972.
Chord (any instruments or voices) 1972.
Co-Ordinative Systems No 2 (string quartet) 1972.
Patterns VIII (trombone) 1972.
Co-Ordinative Systems No 3 (cello, bass clarinet, bass trombone, 2 double basses) 1973.
Co-Ordinative Systems No 4 (chamber ensemble) 1973.
Co-Ordinative Systems No 5 (4 double basses) 1973.
Co-Ordinative Systems No 7 (3–8 players) 1974.
Patterns V (bass flute, viola) 1974.
Patterns XI (bass trombone) 1975.
Music for Brass Instruments I (brass quintet, tape) 1975.
Music for Brass Instruments II (bass trombone, pre-recorded bass trombones) 1975. Recorded Irida Records 0017.
Stations, Regions and Clouds I (trombone, piano, tape) 1975.
Co-Ordinative Systems No 8 (ensemble) 1975.
Co-Ordinative Systems No 9 (trombone, synthesizer) 1975.
Chamber Musics I (tuba, guitar, bass, flute/viola, electric piano, percussion) 1975.
Chamber Musics II (chamber ensemble; as for No I) 1975.
Co-Ordinative Systems No 10 (trombone, tape delay) 1976. Recorded Irida Records 0017.
Chamber Musics III (chamber ensemble; as for No I) 1976.
Chamber Musics IV (chamber ensemble; as for No I) 1976.
Chamber Musics V (chamber ensemble) 1976.
Bombs (bass trombone, prepared piano) 1976.
Space Music IV 1976.
Chamber Musics VI (alto or bass flute, tape) 1976.
Chamber Musics VII (viola, tape) 1976.
Chamber Musics VIII (guitar, tape) 1976.
Patterns XII (any solo instrument) 1977.
Between the Lines (solo instrument, tape, film) 1977.
In Quest of a Silence (trombone, vibraphone, piano) 1977.
Music for Brass Instruments III (12 brass instruments) 1978. Recorded Move Records, Australia.
Music for Brass Instruments IV (12 brass, 3 percussion, piano) 1978.
Music for Brass Instruments V (4 trumpets) 1978.
Music for Brass Instruments VI (solo trumpet, 4 trumpets) 1978.
Stations, Regions and Clouds III (trombone, tape) 1978.
Antiphonies and Streams (amplified trombone, tape delay, ring modulator) 1978. Recorded Irida Records 0017.

Memoirs of . . . (bass clarinet, prepared piano) 1979.
From Eric Dolphy (bass clarinet, tape delay, electronics) 1979.
Stationary Fields . . . Moving Fields (amplified cello, amplified trombone, tape delay systems) 1979.
Suite (amplified cello) 1979. Recorded Irida 0017.
From the Last Few Pages (trombone, live electronics) 1979.
Fields and Traces (trombone, tape, live electronics) 1979.
Elective Affinities (amplified cello, amplified trombone, tape, live electronics ensemble) 1979–80.
Force Fields and Spaces (trombone, tape, tape delay; with or without dance) 1981.
String Quartet No 3 (amplified) 1982.
Sonata (A) (flute, clarinet, violin, cello, piano) 1982.
Sonata (B) (flute, clarinet, violin, cello, piano) 1982.
Louison (guitar, soprano saxophone, alto trombone, electric piano) 1982.
Track Follows (trumpet, tape, trombone, tape delay) 1983.
Suite (violin) 1983.
Mini-Concerto (solo trombone, 3 trumpet, horn, 2 trombones, tuba) 1984.
Interesting Actions, Objects and Texts (shakuhachi, with optional tape, film, slides, electronics or movement) 1985.
Music of Parts (piano, cello, clarinet, violin, computer-generated tape) 1986.
Elective Affinities III (trombone, live electronics) 1987.
Traces and Moments (trombone, tape, electronics) 1987.
For Morty (In Memory of Morton Feldman) (trombone, piano, tape, live electronics) 1987.
met dank aan . . . (trombone, tape; dance score) 1988–9.
Temenos II (trombone, tape) 1989.
Temenos IIa (trombone, tape) 1989.
String Quartet No 4 in progress.

Vocal/choral:

Passages (voice, bass clarinet) 1965.
. . . Whiteness . . . Specks of . . . (soprano, bass trumpet, viola, 2 pianos) 1967.
For Norma (soprano, horn, double bass, percussion, flute, piano) 1968.
Chord (any voices or instruments) 1972.
Empty Whispers (voice, electronics; dance score) 1972.
He Was Silent for a Space (mixed choir, percussion) 1978.
Antiphonies and Streams II (tenor, live electronics) 1979.

Other:

Six Studies (graphic score; lights, sounds, dancers) 1967.
Music for Queen Elizabeth I (5 shouters, 2 musicians, 7 dancers, tape delay, 2 channel tape, voice-guns, microphones) 1968.
Structures (2-channel tape) 1968.
Episodes (full evening concert, with sculptor, film-maker, choreographer) 1968.
Hallway Environment No 1 (10 electronic tapes) 1968.
Planes, Pts (4-channel computer generated tape; also version for 4 orchestral groups) 1969.
Bugaboos (electronic score with animated film) 1969.
Form and Movement (instrumental score for live presentation/performance by industrial designer John Hanna; also for film and television) 1969.
Sound Environment No 2 (photoelectric oscillators, switches, pre-recorded electronic sounds) 1969.
Five Pages for Petr K. (graphic score, any medium) 1970.
For Betty Johnston (graphic score, any medium) 1970.
Pathways (audience) 1970.
Connections, Directions and Drones (lights, photoelectric oscillators, audience, cylinders) 1970.
Music for Audience Movement, Movement for Musicians 1971.
A Second Look at Pathways 1971.
Kinetic Sculpture No 1 (theatre piece) 1971.
Performance Kit No 2 (mime, acoustician) 1971.
Eros and Psyche (incidental music for play by John Argue) 1972.
Kinetic Sculpture No 2 (tape; theatre without actors) 1972.
Kinetic Sculpture No 3 (radio play) 1973.
Film (FF) (16mm films for percussion solo) 1972–3.
Tape 1973.
"What Is Performance?" (trombone, tape, slides, films) 1973.
Travelling Companion (electronic score for dance) 1973.
Small Brown Shell (amplified bottle; dance) 1973.
Soft Verges (texts, pre-recorded instrumental sounds; dance) 1974.
Co-Ordinative Systems No 6 (1–6 dancers, 4 musicians, 2 stereo tapes) 1974.
Tangential Patterns I (electronic music) 1974.
Tangential Patterns II (electronic music) 1974.
Kinetic Sculpture No 4 (radio play, theatre piece) 1974.
Kinetic Sculpture No 5 (theatre, radio play) 1974.
Tangential Patterns III (electronic tape) 1974.
Raucasity and the Cisco Kid . . . or I Skate in the Sun (solo instrument, tape, collage, 16mm film, slides) 1977–8.
Vicarious Thrills (pornographic film, amplified trombone) 1978–9.
Cheap Imitations, Parts I–V (Madwomen) (soloist, tape, films) 1980.
Wind Song (tape) 1982.
Put Your Foot Down, Charlie (dance, electronic piano, electric guitar, amplified tenor saxophone, amplified trombone, speaker, text, choreography) 1982.
Rats (dance, speaker/trombone, guitar/banjo, tenor saxophone, text, choreography) 1982–3.
Music for Sybrig (dance; electronic tape) 1987.
Music for Mary (dance; electronic tape) 1988.
Rivers (dance; electronic score) 1988.
The Marionette Theatre (live instrumentalist, tape, choreography) 1989.
Stones (electronic tape) 1989.
Whose Wings Are Those? (dance; electronic tape) 1989.
Used, Abused & Cheap Imitations (dance) 1989.
D1 (dance; electronic score) 1989.
D2 (dance; incorporates *D1*, part of trilogy *D1-D2-D3*) 1990.
The Archaeology of Silence 1990.

As performer: recorded performances of works by Kenneth Gaburo, Phill Niblock, John Rimmer, Roger Dean, Elliott Schwartz, self.

PUBLICATIONS

By Fulkerson: "Morton Feldman Is Dead", in *A Compendium of Contemporary Musical Thought*, London, Autumn 1991.

On Fulkerson: Stephen Montague, "F at Length", in *Classical Music*, 19 May 1984; (interview) in *Something About the Music I*, edited by Nicola Walker and Geoff Smith, London/New York, 1990.

James Fulkerson comments:

My composition is considerably influenced by my experience as a performer. I am interested in the social act of music performance and by the personal insights which stem from the hours of practice which any serious performer must undertake. I believe that I have a respect for tradition without being encumbered by it. Sal Martirano asked me in a composition lesson whether I would rather be known as an avant-garde composer or as a fine composer—I felt then it was more important to be forward-looking in one's work and I do now as well. I would hope it is possible to be both.

I have worked a great deal with dance and with experimental film and have composed for most instrumental mediums. I think that in the age of post-modernism, that the greatest requisite is one's imagination. I think it is necessary to have the strength to dream, to attempt the epic. Few composers would attempt the equivalent of *War and Peace*, but that is probably the most important challenge to composers today.

* * *

James Fulkerson belongs to that generation of American experimental composer who, in the wake of John Cage, aimed to expand the boundaries of musical art by continual questioning and reappraisal of its social and conceptual basis. He has said of his formative experiences at the University of Illinois that "the most important thing was to experiment, to examine our assumptions about art", and his principal works from this period, many of which are textual, graphical or improvisational (such as *Two Activities I–III, For Betty* Johnston and *Co-Ordinative Systems*), explore the theatrical situation and social interaction of musical performance. Often they examine the process of collaborative exchange between composer and performer and, as a leading exponent of extended trombone techniques who has had some 160 works written specially for him, Fulkerson has much experience in approaching this exchange from both viewpoints.

Though his music has come to be less overtly conceptual, he has constantly maintained the idea of one's work being a result of the questions one poses. This philosophical basis has underpinned his compositional development toward ever-increasing clarity, both of creative vision and the means to realise that vision. In this sense, while he owes much to Cage for his social and political stance as an artist, the clarity, sensuousness and (wilful) expressiveness of his *music* (such as *He Was Silent for a Space* or *The Archaeology of Silence*) are more closely related to the work of Morton Feldman.

Throughout his career, he has also been deeply involved with new dance (which he regards as a far more liberated art form than music) and has produced a huge variety of collaborative works with many choreographers including Richard Alston, Rosemary Butcher and, most often, his wife, Mary Fulkerson. His work in this medium falls largely into two categories: one which deals with meaning and/or feeling through the use of texts, narrative or role-playing; and another which deals with sound and movement as pure, abstract entities.

Put Your Foot Down, Charlie is an example of the former in which Mary Fulkerson, dressed in leather and chains, talks coolly to an imaginary Charlie against a background of laid-back rock music played on electric guitar, electric piano, amplified trombone and amplified saxophone. The result is a surreal and complex work of many levels and references which are "simultaneously real and complete fantasy" and it is in pieces such as this that Fulkerson is able to use materials drawn from modern culture, so that his music if often "both itself and referential at the same time".

Elective Affinities III was written for the dance duo *Glasshouses* and, by contrast, deals with sound and movement in more abstract terms. The score is for amplified trombone with live electronics which add low octave transpositions and huge reverberation (up to 99 seconds) to a handful of sustained trombone notes to produce a beautifully rich and expansive texture.

Electronics, like dance, have been a liberating force in Fulkerson's development and his work in this medium also often displays two approaches: namely, using tapes and samplers as means of capturing (like the camera and the photocopier) elements of our modern cultural and physical environments as material for new work (such as *Raucasity and the Cisco Kid . . . or I Skate in the Sun*); and, secondly, using electronics to produce new and abstract sounds "that just make my pulse race" (such as *D1-D2-D3*).

While Fulkerson's work continues to move toward ever-greater clarity, the ideas that he deals with become no less complex and this duality of approach has been a feature of his music since the early 1970s when he produced several extended single-pitch compositions (such as *, . . . For We Don't See Anything Clearly*) which use minimal material to explore the internal harmonic structure of sound. His aim now (as then) is to be consistent in his artistic vision, to find the clearest means for the realization of that vision, and to have the strength and integrity always to make that vision epic.

—Nicola Walker Smith and Geoff Smith

G

GALINDO (Dimas), Blas. Mexican. Born in San Gabriel [now known as Ciudad Venustiano Carranza], Jalisco, 3 February 1910. Education: music study from age 7 under Antonio Velasco; singer, organist, clarinettist in local bands; then at Conservatorio Nacional de Música de México, Mexico City (harmony, counterpoint and fugue under José Rolón, musical analysis and orchestration under Candelario Huizar, composition under César Chávez, piano under Rodríguez Vizcarra) 1931–43, Maestro en Composición, 1944; further composition study (under Aaron Copland), Berkshire Music Centre, Tanglewood, Massachusetts, summers 1941, 1942. Married Ernestina Mendoza-Vega, 3 October 1952; 2 sons. Co-founder (with Daniel Ayala, Salvador Contreras, and José Pablo Moncayo), El Grupo de los Cuatro modern music group, 1935–40; director, Conservatorio Nacional de Música, Mexico City, 1947–61; founding fellow (with Carlos Chávez, Rodolfo Halffter, José Pablo Moncayo, Jesús Bal and Luís Sandi), Ediciones Mexicanas de Música, 1947; conductor, Orchestra of the Institute of Social Security, Mexico, from 1955; founder member, Mexican National Academy of the Arts, 1966; founding member, Britannica Society, 1984. Recipient: 1st prize (for *Cantata a la Patria*), composition competition of the Public Education Secretary of Mexico, 1947; medal of the Order of the Restituted Poland, 1949; José Angel Llamas Award (for *Symphony No 2*), 2nd Latin American Festival, Caracas, Venezuela, 1957; 1st prize (for *Cantata Homenaje a Juárez*), State Government of Jalisco composition competition, 1957; 1st prize, (for *Cantata a la Independencia*), composition competition of the Public Education Secretary of Mexico, 1960; National Award of Arts and Sciences, Government of Mexico, 1964; nominal member, Academy of Arts, Mexico, 1968; State Government of Jalisco Award, 1983. Mailing address: Sur 71-A, No. 328, Col. Banjidal, Del. Iztapalapa, 09450 Ciudad de México, DF, Mexico.

Publishers: Ediciones Mexicanas de Música AC, Avenida Juárez 18, Desp. 206, Ciudad de México, DF, Mexico; C. F. Peters, New York.

Symphonies/orchestral:

Obra para orquesta mexicana 1938; first performed Mexico City, 1938.
Sones de mariachi (small orchestra) 1940; first performed New York City, 1940. Recorded Columbia Masterworks M-414.
Sones de mariachi (large orchestra) 1941; first performed Mexico City, 1941. Recorded Musart EMCD-3307.
Concerto No 1 for Piano and Orchestra 1942; first performed Mexico City, 1942.
Nocturno 1945; first performed Mexico City, 1945.
Arrullo (string orchestra) 1945.
Don Quijote 1947.
Homenaje a Cervantes (suite for orchestra) 1947; first performed Mexico City, 1948.
Poema de Neruda (string orchestra) 1948; first performed Mexico City, 1956.
Pequeñas variaciones 1951; first performed Mexico City, 1965.
Sinfonía breve (string orchestra; also known as *Pequeña sinfonía*) 1952; first performed Mexico City, 1952. Recorded RCA Victor MRL/S-002.
Obertura mexicana 1953; first performed Mexico City, 1953.
Symphony No 2 1957; first performed Caracas, Venezuela, 1957. Recorded Louisville Orchestra LS 761.
Concerto for Flute and Orchestra 1960; first performed New Orleans, 1965.
Concerto No 2 for Piano and Orchestra 1961; first performed Mexico City, 1962. Recorded UNAM VVMN-3.
Symphony No 3 1961; first performed Washington, D.C., 1961.
Four Pieces for Orchestra 1961; first performed Mexico City, 1963.
Concerto for Violin and Orchestra 1962; first performed Mexico City, 1970.
Three Pieces (clarinet, orchestra) 1962.
Overture (organ, orchestra) 1963.
Three Pieces (horn, orchestra) 1963.
Concertino (electric guitar, orchestra) 1973; first performed Mexico City, 1977.
Tríptico (string orchestra) 1974; first performed Mexico City, 1976.
Concertino (violin, strings) 1978; first performed Mexico City, 1979.
Concerto for Flute and Symphonic Band 1979; first performed Pittsburgh, 1980.
Homenaje a Juan Rulfo 1980; first performed Mexico City, 1980.
Obertura mexicana No 2 1981; first performed Guadalajara, Mexico, 1983.
Obertura mexicana No 3 1982.
Concerto for Cello and Orchestra 1984.
Suite (chamber orchestra) 1985.
Concerto for Guitar and Symphonic Band 1988.
Homenaje a Rodolfo Halffter 1989.

Chamber/instrumental:

Suite (violin, cello) 1933; first performed Mexico City, 1933.
La lagartija (piano) 1935; first performed Mexico City, 1935.
Quartet for Cellos 1936; first performed Mexico City, 1936.
Suite No 2 (piano) 1936.
Caricatura de vals (piano) 1936.
Jaliscience (piano) 1936; first performed Mexico City, 1936. Recorded Musart MCD-3012.
Preludio (piano) 1937; first performed Mexico City, 1937.
Bosquejos (oboe, clarinet, horn, bassoon) 1937; first performed Mexico City, 1937.
Concertino (2 pianos) 1938; first performed Mexico City, 1938.
Dos preludios (oboe, cor anglais, piano) 1938; first performed Mexico City, 1938.
Llano alegre (piano) 1938; first performed Mexico City, 1938.
Sexteto de alientos (flute, clarinet, bassoon, horn, trumpet, trombone) 1941; first performed Tanglewood, Massachusetts, 1941.

Arrullo (guitar) 1945.
Cinco preludios (piano) 1945; first performed Mexico City, 1947. Recorded Musart MCD-3028.
Sonata (violin, piano) 1945; first performed Mexico City, 1947.
Sonata (cello, piano) 1948; first performed Washington, D.C., 1953. Recorded Musart.
Pequeñas variaciones (organ) 1951; first performed Mexico City, 1952.
Siete piezas (piano) 1952; first performed Mexico City, 1952. Recorded—nos I, II, IV—Peerless LD-784; II–VI Angel SAN-35037; I, II UNAM MN-17.
Suite (violin, piano) 1957; first performed Mexico City, 1957. Recorded Musart MCD-3067.
Quintet for Bow Instruments and Piano 1957; first performed Washington, D.C., 1961. Recorded UNAM VVMN 13.
Los soldaditos de barro (piano) 1964; first performed Mexico City, 1972.
Cinco más cinco (piano) 1965; first performed Mexico City, 1965.
Tres sonsonetes (wind quintet, tape) 1967.
Muy serio (piano) 1968.
El gato mimas (piano) 1968; first performed Mexico City, 1971.
Los muñecos bailan (piano) 1969.
Quartet for Bow Instruments 1970; first performed Mexico City, 1970.
Estudio (organ) 1971; first performed Barcelona, 1972.
Titoco-tico (native percussion) 1971. Recorded UNAM VV MN-21.
Casi triste (piano) 1972.
Movimiento perpetuo (piano) 1972.
Pieza simple (piano) 1973.
Cancioncita (piano) 1973.
El juguete roto (piano) 1973.
Pequeña fantasia (piano) 1973.
Sonata (piano) 1976; first performed Mexico City, 1976. Recorded UNAM MN-17.
Invenciones (brass quintet) 1977.
Three Pieces (percussion) 1980.
Sonata (cello) 1981; first performed Mexico City, 1981.
Wind Quintet 1982.
Sin título (organ) 1983.
Duo (violin, cello) 1984.
Andante y alegro (guitar) 1986; first performed Mexico City, 1986.

Vocal/choral:

Caporal (mixed chorus) 1935; first performed Mexico City, 1935.
Alerta compañeros de trabajo (chorus) 1936; first performed Mexico City, 1936.
Mi querer pasaba el rio (voice, piano) 1939; first performed Mexico City, 1939. Recorded UNAM VVM-6.
La luna esta encarcelada (voice, piano) 1939; first performed Mexico City, 1939.
Poema de amor (voice, piano) 1939; first performed Mexico City, 1939.
Paloma blanca (voice, piano) 1939; first performed Mexico City, 1939. Recorded Musart MC 3002.
Páginas verdes (voice, piano) 1939; first performed Mexico City, 1939.
Jicarita (voice, piano/orchestra; del Rio) 1939; piano version first performed Mexico City, 1939. Recorded Musart MC 3002.
Aguilita mexicana (single voice) 1942; first performed Mexico City, 1942.
Canción escolar (3 equal voices) 1943; first performed Mexico City, 1943.
Pajarito corpulento (3 equal voices) 1943; first performed Mexico City, 1943.
Madre mia (2 equal voices; or voice, flute, oboe, clarinet, bassoon; or voice, piano; or voice, orchestra; Campos) 1943; piano version first performed Mexico City, 1946. Recorded Musart MC 3002.
Primavera (children's chorus, band/piano; del Rio) 1944; band version first performed Mexico City, 1944.
Hilitos de agua (voice) 1944.
Arullo (voice; 4 mixed voices; voice, orchestra; del Rio) 1945; piano version first performed Mexico City, 1946. Recorded Musart MC 3002; UNAM MN-18.
La Montana (mixed chorus) 1945; first performed Mexico City, 1945.
Uno es mi fruto (2 equal voices, chorus) 1945; first performed Mexico City, 1945.
A la patria (mixed chorus, orchestra; Lopez Velarde) 1946; first performed Mexico City, 1949.
Voz mía, canta, canta (3 equal voices) 1946.
Pasan los heroes (3 equal voices) 1946.
Canto al maestro justo sierra (voice, piano; chorus, orchestra; Martinez) 1947; choral version first performed Mexico City, 1947.
Soy una sombra (voice, piano) 1947; first performed Mexico City, 1947.
Tres canciones (voice, small orchestra) 1947.
Para mi corazón basta tu pecho (4 mixed voices) 1948.
Poema de Neruda (4 mixed voices) 1948.
Dos corazones heridos (4 mixed voices) 1948. Recorded RCA Victor PCS-4837-A.
Poema del corazón disperso (4 male voices) 1950; first performed Mexico City, 1950.
En ti la tierra canta (mixed chorus) 1950; first performed Mexico City, 1950.
Fuensanta (voice, piano; voice, flute, oboe, clarinet, bassoon) 1957; piano version first performed Mexico City, 1959. Recorded UNAM VVMN-6.
Homenaje a Juárez (soprano, tenor, bass, reciter, mixed chorus, orchestra) 1957; first performed Guadalajara, Jalisco, 1959.
La Paz (4 mixed voices) 1958.
A la independencia (soprano, alto, tenor, bass, mixed chorus, strings) 1960; first performed Mexico City, 1960.
Quetzalcoatl (narrator, orchestra; Novo) 1963.
Tríptico Teotihuacan (soprano, baritone, chorus, band, native instruments) 1964; first performed Teotihuacan, Mexico, 1964.
Corrido a Emiliano Zapata (chorus, band) 1964; first performed Yautepec, Morelos, Mexico, 1963.
Letanía erótica para La Paz (narrator, alto, tenor, bass, chorus, organ, orchestra, tape) 1965; first performed Mexico City, 1965.
La ciudad de los dioses (choir, narrators, orchestra; Novo) 1965.
Homenaje a Ruben Darío (reciter, string orchestra) 1966; first performed Managua, Nicaragua, 1967.
Cinco canciones a la madre muerta (voice, piano) 1971; first performed Mexico City, 1974.
Ma ye ya nican (mixed chorus; Nahuatl text) 1974.
Te canta mi esperanza (voice, piano) 1981.
Pajarito traidor (canon for 5 voices, unaccompanied mixed chorus) 1985.
Homenaje a Rufino Tamayo (tenor, orchestra) 1987; first performed Mexico City, 1987.
Popocatepetl (symphonic poem for soprano, tenor, orchestra) 1990.

Other:

Entre sombras anda el fuego (ballet; also known as *Three Preludes for Ballet*) 1940; first performed Mexico City, 1940.
Danza de las fuerzas nuevas (ballet) 1940; first performed Mexico City, 1941.
El zánate (ballet) 1947; first performed Mexico City, 1947.
Astucia (theatre music) 1948; first performed Mexico City, 1948.
La manda (ballet) 1951; first performed Mexico City, 1951. Recorded Forlane UM-3701.
El sueño y la presencia (ballet) 1951; first performed Mexico City, 1951.
Los signos del zodiaco (theatre music) 1951; first performed Mexico City, 1951.
La hija del yori (ballet) 1952; first performed Mexico City, 1952.
El maleficio (ballet) 1954; first performed Mexico City, 1954.
El tuerto (film music) 1954.
Canción de cuna (folk song arrangement for 3 equal voices) 1958.
Rosa de castilla en rama (folk song arrangement for 3 equal voices) 1958.
El abandonado (folk song arrangement for 4 equal voices) 1958.
Hermosa flor de pitaya (folk song arrangement for 3 equal voices) 1958.
La chinita maderista (folk song arrangement for 4 mixed voices) 1958.
Son los ojitos (folk song arrangement) 1958.
Y déjame llorar (folk song arrangement for 4 mixed voices) 1958.
Epido rey (theatre music) 1961; first performed Mexico City, 1961.

PUBLICATIONS

On Galindo: Robert Stevenson, *Music in Mexico*, New York, 1952; S. Kahn, *Fascinación de la música*, Mexico City, 1964; Coral Alvarez, *Compositores mexicanos*, Mexico City, 1971; Dan. Malmstrom, *Introduction to Twentieth-Century Mexican Music*, Uppsala, 1974; R.P. Conant, "The Vocal Music of BG: A Study", dissertation, University of Texas, Austin, 1977; Isabel Aretz (ed.), *América Latina en su música*, Mexico City, 1977; G. Behague, *Music in Latin America*, New York, 1979; A. Carpentier, *Ese músico que lleve dentro*, 1980; Julio Estrada (ed.), *La música de Mexico*, Mexico City, 1984; A. Navarro, *BG: semblanza y profiles de un compositor*, Mexico City, 1990.

Blas Galindo comments:

People often ask what "inspiration" means to me. I always answer that I do not believe in such a thing. They say that an artist is somehow inspired by a kind of spark. If this were true, I would already be charcoal. I do believe that "inspiration" is nothing else than the product of the organized work of man, by which I mean that work—that is, *organized* work—is the only way in which an artist can acquire the capacity for artistic creation.

They also ask me what does it mean to be a composer in Mexico. I think that being a composer in any country means the same thing: a complete dedication to the task. One has to invest very many hours a day, many days a week, all the weeks of the month, and very, very many years of one's life. If you do not do this, you will certainly not satisfy your needs. That is my case. If I don't work on my music, I am not happy. To be happy, I need to have my music in front of me, and creating it is a genuine pleasure. This is the way I explain it to my pupils and friends. They have to do music if they want to become composers.

They say that my music sounds "Mexican". Quite sincerely, I don't try to achieve this. My music is like that because I am like that. I am Mexican so my music has to be that way. When I finished by Second Concerto for piano, I thought about it as a universal work, without any folk theme. But when it is played in the United States, and most particularly in New York and Los Angeles, critics say that "it sounds very Mexican". That was not my intention. Mexicanness is implied deep in the scores, deep in my music.

* * *

Born in what was then San Gabriel, Jalisco, Blas Galindo comes partially of Huichol descent. Until he was 21, he lived in his small natal village, where he organized a band, played guitar and clarinet, and acted as church organist and choir director. In 1931, he entered the National Conservatory in Mexico City, where he studied under Manuel Rodríguez Vizcarra, Candelario Huizar, José Rolón and César Chávez. He graduated in 1944 with the Conservatory's highest distinction, the title of *Maestro en Composición*, having in the interim studied composition under Aaron Copland at the Berkshire Music Center, Lenox, Massachusetts, in the summers of 1941 and 1942.

He taught several months at a village school in 1934. From 1935 to 1940 he was a member of the so-called "Group of the Four"—El Grupo de los cuatros—with Daniel Ayala, Salvador Contreras and Pablo Moncayo. This group was nurtured by conservatory director Chávez who conducted the premiere of Galindo's *Sones de mariachi* (a medley of traditional Mexican street tunes which is perhaps his best-known work) at the Museum of Modern Art in New York City in May 1940. Beginning in 1944, he taught musical analysis, harmony, counterpoint and composition at the Mexico City National Conservatory, serving as director from 1947 to his retirement in 1961; a government pension allowed him to devote most of his time subsequently to composition. In 1966, along with Chávez and Rodolfo Halffter, he was a founding member of the Mexican National Academy of the Arts.

Starting from a highly successful folkloric stance (it is sometimes difficult to distinguish Galindo's music from actual, traditional folk melodies), he embraced pandiatonicism in 1945 with his *Cinco preludios* for piano, moving in his second and third symphonies to an energetic dissonance of a mid-period Hindemith variety. However great the amount of unresolved dissonance, at every stage in his long career, Galindo showed his concern for solid musical architecture, his thoroughly unreactionary respect for traditional forms and an unapologetic desire to speak to Mexican audiences rather than to trendsetters and doctrinaire critics abroad.

His choral works from the mid-1950s until the middle of the next decade followed the Brobdinagian proportions of the cantata *Primavera* of 1944, which featured a chorus of 1000 voices. These works have much in common with Heitor Villa-Lobos's large choral works written during the presidency of Getulio Varga.

—Robert Stevenson

GARDNER, John (Linton). British/English. Born in Manchester, 2 March 1917. Educated at Eagle House, Sandhurst, 1925–30; Wellington College, Berkshire, 1930–5; Exeter College, Oxford (organ under Sir Hugh Allen, Ernest Walker and Thomas Armstrong), 1935–9, B.Mus. Served in Royal Air Force, 1940–6. Married Jane Abercrombie, 19 March 1955; 1 son and 2 daughters. Chief music master, Repton School, 1939–40; repetiteur, Royal Opera House, Covent Garden, London, 1946–52; tutor, 1952–76, and director of music, 1965–9, Morley College, London; member of teaching faculty, Royal Academy of Music, London, 1956–86; director of music, St Paul's Girls' School, London, 1962–75. Director, since 1965, and deputy chair, 1983–8, Performing Rights Society. Recipient: Gold Medal, Bax Society, 1958; honorary R.A.M., 1958; C.B.E., 1976. Mailing address: 20 Firstwood Avenue, Epsom, Surrey KT19 0PR, England.

Publisher: Oxford University Press.

Symphonies/orchestral:

Serenade (oboe, piano, strings) 1937.
A Scots Overture (military band) 1941.
Prelude on "Das alte Jahr vergangen ist" (strings) 1944.
Symphony No 1 in D minor Op 2 1950; first performed Cheltenham, Gloucestershire, 5 July 1951.
Variations on a Waltz of Carl Nielsen Op 13 1951; first performed Cheltenham, Gloucestershire, 1952.
Suite from "Reflection" Op 14a 1953.
A Scots Overture Op 25 orchestrated 1954; first performed London, 16 August 1954.
Piano Concerto No 1 in B♭ Op 34 1957; first performed Cheltenham, Gloucestershire, 1957.
Suite of Five Rhythms Op 45 1960.
Sinfonia piccola Op 47 (strings) 1960.
Overture: Half Holiday Op 52 1963.
Concerto for Trumpet and Strings Op 53 1963.
Overture: Midsummer Ale Op 73 1965.
Blues in G Op 78 (school orchestra) 1966.
Occasional Suite Op 95 (3 clarinets, 3 recorders, harpsichord, strings) 1968.
An English Ballad Op 99 1969.
Three Ridings Suite Op 107i–iii 1970.
The Volunteer Op 113 (military band) 1972.
The Volunteer Mark 2 Op 114 1972.
Sonatina for Strings Op 124 1974.
Four Pieces for School Orchestra Op 88i–iv 1976.
English Suite Op 139 (concert band) 1977.
Divertimento Op 140 1977.
Symphony No 2 in E♭ Op 166 1985; first performed Croydon, Surrey, 1985.
Symphony No 3 in E minor 1989; first performed London, 1990.
Oboe Concerto Op 193 (string orchestra) 1990.

Chamber/instrumental:

Sonata No 2 (piano) 1934.
Rhapsody (oboe, string quartet) 1935.
String Quartet No 1 in G minor 1938; first performed Paris, 1939.
Theme and Variations Op 7 (2 trumpets, horn, trombone) 1950; broadcast BBC, 1951.
Romance Op 8 (trombone, piano) 1952.
A Wedding March Op 17 (organ) 1952.
Sonata Op 18 (oboe, piano) 1953.
Sonatina Op 28 (piano) 1954.
Fantasy on "Non, nobis Domine" Op 30 (organ) 1955.
Guitar solo for BBC TV *Julius Caesar* Op 43 1959.
Five Hymn-Tune Preludes Op 44 (organ) 1959.
Little Suite Op 60 (recorder, harpsichord) 1964.
Concerto da camera Op 91 (recorder, violin, cello, harpsichord) 1967.
Ein Albumblatt für Tom Op 94 (piano) 1968.
Prelude in G minor Op 96 (organ) 1968.
Partita Op 98 (cello) 1968.
Chamber Concerto Op 102 (organ, 11 instruments) 1969.
Duet for One Prince Op 106 (piano) 1970.
English Suite Op 110 (harpsichord) 1970.
Sonata secolare Op 117 (organ, brass quintet) 1973.
Pavan Op 123 (guitar) 1974.
Prelude on "Dominus regit me" Op 127 (organ) 1975.
Variations and Fugue on "Sine nomine" Op 128 (organ) 1975.
Two Variants on Bicclescombe Op 134 (piano) 1976.
Sonata da chiesa Op 136 (2 trumpets, organ) 1977.
Interlude Op 143 (organ) 1978.
Nocturno Op 144 (guitar) 1978.
String Quartet No 2: Twenty-five Preludes Op 148 1979; first performed Ambleside, Yorkshire, 1980.
Nocturno Op 144 (guitar) 1978.
High Heaven Fantasy Op 151 (organ) 1980.
Study Op 155 (flute) 1982.
Sonatina lirica Op 161 (brass quintet) 1983.
Flourish for a Wedding Op 162 (organ, brass quintet) 1983.
Furiant Op 163 (guitar) 1984.
Adam Op 164 (piano) 1984.
Four Piano Pieces Op 167i–iv 1985.
Saxophone Quartet Op 168 1985.
Tetrad Op 170 (lute) 1986.
Sonata No 2 in C Op 172 (oboe, piano) 1986.
Trifle for Tom (piano) 1986.
Pentad Op 173 (recorder octet) 1986.
French Suite Op 174 (saxophone quartet) 1986.
String Quartet No 3 in D Op 176 1986; first performed York, 1987.
Tombe en enfance (piano) 1987.
Five Dances Op 179 (organ) 1988.
Sonata No 3 in B♭ Op 183 (piano) 1988.
Dance Heptad Op 184 (recorder) 1988.
Fantasy and Fugue on a Prelude of Anton Bruckner Op 185 (organ) 1988.
Le Triton obsessionel Op 187 (piano) 1988.
Chanson triste Op 192 (oboe, piano) 1989.

Vocal/choral:

The Holy Son of God Most High (unaccompanied mixed chorus; More) 1938.
Wild Geese (voice, piano; Shen Yo) 1939.
A Widow Bird (voice, piano; Shelley) 1939.
Three Songs Op 1 (women's/boys' chorus, piano; Suckling, Breton, anon.) 1946.
A Slumber Did My Spirit Seal (voice, piano; Wordsworth) 1948.
And When the Day of Pentecost Was Come Op 4 (unaccompanied mixed chorus) 1950.
O Sing unto My Roundelay Op 5 (unaccompanied mixed chorus; Chatterton) 1950.
And Did Those Feet Op 6 (voice, piano; Blake) 1951.
Fair Daffodils Op 9 (unaccompanied mixed chorus; Herrick) 1951.
The Argument of His Book Op 10 (mixed chorus, orchestra; Herrick) 1951.

Cantiones Sacrae Op 12 (soprano, chorus, orchestra; Biblical) 1952; first performed Hereford, 1952.
O Clap Your Hands Op 15 (mixed chorus, organ) 1952.
The Turning Year Op 19 (unaccompanied mixed chorus; Scaife) 1953, revised 1966.
Hail the Day That Sees Him Rise Op 24 (mixed chorus, organ) 1954.
Love Came to Me One Sweet Spring Day Op 26 (unaccompanied mixed chorus; Broadwood) 1954.
A Fair Maid All Walking in Her Garden Op 27 (unaccompanied mixed chorus; folk song) 1954.
Two Carol Settings: The Holly and the Ivy, Good King Wenceslas Op 29i–ii (unaccompanied mixed chorus) 1954.
Salute to George Goetch Op 31 (unaccompanied mixed chorus; anon. German) 1955.
Tell Me Where Is Fancy Bred Op 33 (unaccompanied mixed chorus; Shakespeare) 1956.
Spring the Sweet Spring Op 35 (unaccompanied mixed chorus; Nashe) 1956.
Seven Songs Op 36 (mixed chorus, orchestra) 1957; first performed Birmingham, 1957.
Blessed Are All They That Fear the Lord Op 37i (unaccompanied mixed chorus) 1957.
Jubilate Deo Op 37ii (unaccompanied mixed chorus) 1957.
Motet: Veni Sancte Spiritus Op 38 (unaccompanied mixed chorus) 1958.
The Ballad of the White Horse Op 40 (mixed chorus, orchestra; Chesterton) 1958; first performed Bournemouth, 1959.
Carmen Heroidum Op 42 (mixed chorus, piano) 1959.
Herrick Cantata Op 49 (tenor, chorus, orchestra) 1960; first performed Birmingham, 1961.
A Latter Day Athenian Speaks Op 51 (unaccompanied mixed chorus) 1961.
Five Hymns in Popular Style Op 54i–v (mixed chorus, orchestra) 1962.
When Christ was Born of Mary Free Op 55 (equal voices) 1962.
Psalm 46 Op 56 (unaccompanied mixed chorus) 1963.
Two Tunes: Milly, Jemima Op 57i–ii (unaccompanied mixed chorus; Abercrombie, JG, after Maugham) 1963.
Angels from the Realms Op 58i (equal voices) 1963.
The Holly and the Ivy Op 58ii (mixed chorus, orchestra) 1963.
Dives & Lazarus Op 58iii (voice, piano) 1963.
The Noble Heart Op 59 (soprano, bass, mixed chorus, orchestra; Shakespeare/Greenwood) 1964; first performed Stratford-upon-Avon, 1964.
The Mystery of the Child Op 61 (mixed chorus, orchestra; Happold) 1964.
We Have a Strong City Op 62 (mixed chorus, organ) 1964.
I Will Lift up Mine Eyes Op 63 (unaccompanied boys'/women's chorus) 1964.
Danny Op 64 (equal voices) 1964.
We Wish You a Merry Christmas (mixed chorus) 1964.
O How Amiable Are Thy Tents Op 65 (mixed chorus, organ) 1964.
A Shakespeare Sequence Op 66i–viii (women's/boys' chorus, piano, 4 hands, percussion) 1964.
The Shout Op 67 (unaccompanied mixed chorus; Fox) 1964.
Cantor popularis vocis Op 68 (unaccompanied mixed chorus; Vellacott) 1964.
Fifteen Million Plastic Bags Op 69 (tenor, guitar; Mitchell) 1965.
Mass in C Op 70 (unaccompanied mixed chorus) 1965.
Fear No More: In memoriam Eric Newton Op 71 (unaccompanied mixed chorus) 1965.
Magnificat and Nunc Dimittis Op 72i (mixed chorus, organ) 1965.
Versicles and Responses Op 72ii (unaccompanied mixed chorus) 1965.
Our Captain Calls All Hands Op 74 (mixed chorus, piano) 1965.
Good King Wenceslas Op 75i (mixed chorus, orchestra) 1965.
Tomorrow Shall Be My Dancing Day Op 75ii (mixed chorus, piano, percussion) 1965.
Robin Adair Op 76i (unaccompanied mixed chorus; trad.) 1965.
Ver the Spring Op 76ii (unaccompanied mixed chorus; Shakespeare) 1965.
Viva la musica Op 77 (massed voices, instruments) 1966.
Ascendit Deus Op 79 (unaccompanied women's/boys' chorus) 1966.
As the Tree Falls (canon for equal voices) 1966.
Amen Canon (equal voices) 1966.
Alleluia Canon (equal voices) 1966.
O Waly, Waly Op 80 (women's/boys' chorus, piano) 1966.
Four Wanton Ballads Op 81i–iv (unaccompanied mixed chorus; Burns, anon.) 1966.
Cantata for Christmas Op 82 (mixed choir, small orchestra) 1966.
Bethlehem Op 83 (unaccompanied mixed chorus; French trad.) 1967.
The End Is the Beginning Op 84 (unaccompanied mixed chorus; Julian of Norwich) 1967.
Proverbs of Hell Op 85 (unaccompanied mixed chorus; Blake) 1967.
Rejoice in the Lord Always Op 86 (unaccompanied women's/boys' chorus) 1967.
Man That Is Born of Woman Op 87 (unaccompanied male chorus) 1967.
I Saw Three Ships Op 89 (quodlibet for massed voices, instruments) 1967.
Good Ale Op 90 (unaccompanied mixed chorus) 1967.
Te Deum in C Op 92 (mixed chorus, organ) 1968.
Wassail Op 97 (mixed chorus, orchestra) 1968.
Psalm 23 Op 93 (unaccompanied mixed chorus) 1969.
Jesu, dulcis memoria Op 100 (unaccompanied women's/boys' chorus) 1969.
Four Hymn Tunes Op 101 (unaccompanied male voices) 1969.
The Twelve Days of Christmas Op 103 (massed voices, instruments) 1969.
Three Amorous Airs Op 104i–iii (women's/boys' chorus, piano) 1970.
Cantata for Easter Op 105 (mixed chorus, organ, percussion) 1970.
Four Sailor Songs Op 108 (unaccompanied mixed chorus) 1970.
Four Carols and Christmas Hymn Op 109i–v (mixed chorus, organ, percussion; Austin, Wedderburn, Ravenscroft, anon.) 1970.
Te Deum for Tiffins Op 112 (mixed chorus, organ, percussion) 1972.
Solstice Carol Op 115 (mixed chorus, orchestra) 1973.
Magnificat and Nunc Dimittis in F Op 116 (mixed chorus, organ) 1973.
Five Encounters for Six Voices Op 118 (unaccompanied male voices) 1973.
A Song for St Cecilia's Day 1973 Op 119 (mixed chorus, organ) 1973.
Tennyson Trip Op 122 (unaccompanied mixed chorus) 1974.
Five Philanderers Op 125 (unaccompanied mixed voices) 1975.
Salute to A.C.F. (unaccompanied mixed voices) 1975.
Seven Songs to Poems by Stevie Smith Op 126 (mixed chorus, wind quintet) 1975, revised 1976.

Psalm 150 Op 129 (unaccompanied mixed voices) 1975.
The Gipsy Davey Op 130 (unaccompanied mixed chorus) 1975.
Lullaby My Liking Op 131 (mixed chorus, audience, orchestra) 1975.
Open Air Suite Op 132 (mixed chorus, brass band) 1976.
Ca' the Yowes Op 135 (unaccompanied mixed chorus) 1976.
Four Rounds Op 133 (equal voices) 1976.
Nine Poems from the Notebooks of William Blake Op 138 (unaccompanied mixed chorus) 1976.
Sunny Bank Carol Op 141 (unaccompanied mixed chorus) 1977.
Five Partsongs to Poems by Wallace Stevens Op 142 (unaccompanied mixed chorus) 1977.
Two Seasonal Songs Op 145 (mixed chorus, brass, percussion; Ewart) 1978.
Lone Dog Op 146 (women's/boys' chorus, piano) 1978.
Six American Hymns in Free Style Op 147i–vi (mixed chorus, piano) 1979.
O Little Town of Bethlehem Op 149 (mixed chorus, orchestra) 1980.
Hebdomade Op 150 (soprano, oboe, piano) 1980.
Room in the Inn Op 152 (mixed chorus, audience, flute, piano, bass, drums) 1981.
Te Deum for Pigotts Op 153 (mixed chorus, orchestra) 1981.
The Bell and Pipes Op 154 (mixed chorus, flute, celeste, vibraphone) 1981.
Grace for Dinner Op 156 (unaccompanied male chorus) 1982.
Mass in D Op 159 (mezzo-soprano, chorus, orchestra) 1983; first performed Dorking, Surrey, 1984.
Praise Him! Op 160 (mixed chorus, piano) 1983.
Triad Op 165i–iii (counter-tenor, lute; Breton, Greene, Robinson) 1984.
Three Carols Op 169i–iii (mixed chorus, brass quintet) 1985.
Let Us with a Gladsome Mind Op 171i (mixed chorus, organ; Milton) 1986.
To Music Bent Is My Retired Mind Op 171ii (mixed chorus, organ; Campion) 1986.
Ave Maria Op 175 (unaccompanied mixed chorus) 1987.
Octad Op 177 (soprano, baritone, 2 trumpets, organ) 1987.
Four Rounds Op 178i–iv (equal voices) 1987.
Everybody Sing Op 178v (mixed chorus, organ) 1987.
Mater Dolorosa Op 180 (unaccompanied mixed chorus; Barnes) 1988.
Six by Four Op 181/a (counter-tenor. recorder, harpsichord, cello, optional additional recorder) 1988.
Quodlibet Op 182 (unaccompanied mixed chorus) 1988.
Cantantibus Organis Op 186 (8-part mixed chorus) 1989.
Eternal Power Op 188 (boys' voices, organ; Wesley) 1989.
A House Not Made with Hands Op 190 (6-part mixed chorus) 1989.
Six Songs to Poems by Philip Larkin Op 191 (tenor, string quartet, piano) 1989.

Opera:

A Nativity Opera Op 3 (Tyrone Guthrie) 1950.
The Moon and Sixpence Op 32 (Terry, Jennings after Maugham) 1956; first performed London, 24 May 1957.
Vile Bodies Op 48 (musical; Terry, Jennings, after Waugh), 1960.
The Visitors Op 111 (Greenwood) 1971; first performed Aldeburgh, Suffolk, 10 June 1972.
Bel and the Dragon Op 120 1973; first performed London, 1973.
The Entertainment of the Senses Op 121 (masque) 1973; first performed London, 2 February 1974.
Tobermory Op 137 (Ewart, after Saki) 1976; first performed London, 1977.

Other:

Tamburlaine the Great Op 11 (incidental music to Marlowe) 1951; first performed London, 1951.
The Legacy (incidental music) 1951.
Reflection Op 14 (ballet) 1952; first performed Edinburgh, 1952.
Coronation Ceremony Op 16 (film music) 1952.
The Tower Op 20 (film music) 1953.
King Lear Op 21 (incidental music to Shakespeare) 1953; first performed Stratford-upon-Avon, 1953.
Hamlet Op 22 1953; first performed London, 1953.
King John Op 23 (incidental music to Shakespeare) 1953; first performed London, 1953.
Dress Rehearsal Op 39 (ballet) 1958.
All's Well That Ends Well Op 41 (incidental music to Shakespeare) 1959; first performed Stratford-upon-Avon, 1959.
The Finsbury Story Op 46 (incidental music) 1960; first performed London, 1960.

PUBLICATIONS

By Gardner: contributor to A. Walker (ed.), *Schumann*, London, 1973; and to Bacharach and Pearce (eds), *The Musical Companion*, London, 1977; also to magazines and periodicals.

John Gardner comments:

When I look back at all the music I've written, I despair of finding a persistent purpose, a connecting thread, an emergent evolution in it. I seem to have reacted to the circumstances in which I found myself to the best of my ability with varying success in a variety of styles and idioms from the conservatively contrapuntal (my *Fantasy and Fugue on a Prelude of Anton Bruckner* for organ) to the mid-century popular (my musical *Vile Bodies*, alas, never staged); from a watered-down dodecaphony (my opera *The Moon and Sixpence*) to an attempt to recreate late 15th-century polyphony (the "Sanctus" of my *Mass in D*). I have written a lot of bad music (my masque *The Entertainment of the Senses*), quite a bit of moderately good, though flawed music (my three symphonies) and, every now and then—perhaps once in a decade—something as good as my second oboe sonata.

As I've got older my dissonance threshold—that is, my tolerance of ugly sounds—has grown more immediate, so that my more recent music is sweeter to the ear than that I wrote 40 years ago. I think the medium for which I write with greatest ease and fluency is that of unaccompanied voices. Certainly the greatest masters in this field—guys like Josquin and Morely—appeal to me greatly. I like the way they put all the strength of their music in the notes themselves rather than in the way the notes are sung (and by this I don't mean that they don't have to be sung well). But their written scores are quite other than those of, say, Debussy, which depend greatly on the physical colour of sound rather than what one might term an argument on the musical staves.

Other composers I like include Sibelius, Shostakovich, Chopin, Tchaikovsky, Haydn. Baroque music is not a strong suit of mine—hectares of Bach repel me deeply, though I love some of the keyboard dances and many of the fugues (especially *The Art of Fugue*), and I live happily without Handel. Schubert I love—is there anything better than the B♭ piano trio?

Jazz is an especial interest and hobby of mine, though I'm a poor player. Once—ask Malcolm Arnold—I could make a tolerable attempt at playing like Teddy Wilson; now, with stiffening fingers and a slowing-down of the mental processes, I can't get near sounding like the players I really admire: Bill Evans, Horace Silver, Jimmy Rowles, Sir Charles Thompson. But I get a great kick out of listening cooperatively to them and could, if pressed, make a case for jazz's being the greatest 20th-century contribution to the art of music, seeing as how it is *really* new in so many respects, has revealed the formal bullshit in concert-music by its own unspoken example, and is as often euphorically happy and relaxed as it is overpoweringly sad.

* * *

After a conventional English education at Wellington College and Oxford University, John Gardner's career was interrupted by the outbreak of the 1939–45 war in which he served first as a Royal Air Force musician and then as a flight navigator. Since the war he has played a prominent role in British music not just as a prolific composer but also through his teaching at the Royal Academy of Music and elsewhere and through his tenure of various offices in the Composer's Guild of Great Britain, the Performing Right Society and the Arts Council Music Panel. On resumption of his musical career (as a repetiteur with the Covent Garden Opera) he suppressed a formidable body of precocious works and, in his own words, "made a fresh start as a composer". He has composed works in most of the familiar forms and adapted them to an unusually wide range of vocal and instrumental resources. Inevitably described as eclectic, his style can best be defined by attempting to isolate those features which are common to his work in diverse mediums. These would include an unswerving commitment to tonality, a predilection for logical but seldom extreme diatonic dissonance, a fertile contrapuntal ingenuity and a natural feeling for instrumental timbre and vocal inflection. The extrovert exuberance and directness of utterance which characterise much of his work sometimes lend it a certain "popular" character but always it exhibits a high degree of professional craftsmanship which often conceals a remarkable sophistication of technique. Although his first major success, the *Symphony No 1* (championed by Sir John Barbirolli), shows that his pre-war apprenticeship was not unaffected by the so-called English pastoral school, he has generally avoided the polymodal idioms and folk sources of Vaughan Williams and his disciples in favour of the more pungent harmony and sharper textures associated with Walton and Britten. His undeniable Englishness, though, can be more especially discerned in his awareness of Elizabethan speech rhythms and in his enrichment of the English choral tradition, albeit in an often idiosyncratic manner. He has spoken of himself as 'perhaps a primarily vocal composer' and, indeed, the *Jubilate Deo* with its objective, cool and at times medievally inspired clarity, the *Mass in C* and the secular cantata *A Latter Day Athenian Speaks* display a remarkably skilful and imaginative gift for unaccompanied choral writing. But several of his finest choral works involve instrumental forces and his handling of these is no less assured. Some of these are of almost symphonic dimensions, due in part to a tendency to divide the works into set-pieces or movements. *Cantiones Sacrae*, *The Ballad of the White Horse*, the *Herrick Cantata* and *The Noble Heart* are important works in this category. The weightiest of Gardner's five operas, *The Moon and Sixpence*, to a libretto by Patrick Terry after Somerset Maugham's novel, has a neurotic and violent intensity not often associated with this composer but which accords with the lurid scenario. Some critics discerned the influence of Berg and Britten here, largely on account of its use of dramatic orchestral interludes to further the narrative between scenes, but also because of its quite extensive use of dodecaphony.

Gardner has also composed a lot of 'light' and occasional pieces which are not easy to categorise with their highly individual blend of pastiche and erudite compositional skill. The dazzling fugue from the *Occasional Suite*, commissioned by the Aldeburgh Festival for the available forces of three clarinets, three recorders, harpsichord and strings is a case in point and the full scale *Symphony No 2* composed in an unashamedly 19th-century idiom for an accomplished youth orchestra is hardly a trifle. Gardner has also made increasing use of jazz and commercial sources over the years and this certainly accounts for the buoyant sales of miniatures like *Tomorrow Shall Be My Dancing Day* but the rousing rock finale to the children's opera *Bel and the Dragon* is entirely apposite dramatically and there is telling use of jazz and showbiz elements in the one act opera *Tobermory*. Gardner's enthusiasm for these idioms enables him to deploy them with far greater conviction than is often the case with the occasional flirtations of some composers. The prominent solo part for alto sax in the *Mass in D* is by no means a frivolity but as much an integral and unifying part of the structure as is the 17th-century canon by Adam Gumpelzhaimer which threads its way through *The Ballad of the White Horse*.

An assessment of a composer must take into account his avowed aims in so far as they are known and John Gardner is on record as saying that he aims to 'divert, to delight' but that he also recognises music's more exalted purpose 'to console and to heal' which is most eloquently expressed in the moving chorus "To Music, to Becalm His Fever" from the *Herrick Cantata*. The various influences and affectionate references to be observed in his music may be taken to reflect the breadth of his knowledge of music from Josquin to Bill Evans but, if one seeks the personal core of his language, it may be found (and he would not be the first composer to have revealed himself thus) in his latter day chamber works such as the *Saxophone Quartet*, the Second Oboe Sonata or the Third Piano Sonata where an unforced mastery of the traditional crafts of the composer enable him to express purely musical thought with the utmost lucidity.

—Hamish Milne

GE Gan-ru. Chinese. Born in Shanghai, 8 July 1954. Educated at Shanghai Conservatory of Music, string and wind department (violin), 1974–7; and in composition department, 1977–81; Columbia University, New York, composition department, since 1983. Married to Ge Wan-he. Assistant professor of composition, Shanghai Conservatory of Music, 1981–3. Mailing address: 300 Winston Drive, Apt 1423, Cliffside Park, New Jersey 07010, U.S.A.

Symphonies/orchestral:

Violin Concerto 1976; first performed Shanghai, 1976.
Chamber Symphony 1982; first performed New York, 1982.

Wu (piano, chamber orchestra) 1986; first performed Pittsburgh, 1986.
Questioning the Sky (koto, Chinese orchestra) 1987.
Gu Zheng Concerto (koto, orchestra) 1988.

Chamber/instrumental:

Twelve Preludes for Piano 1979; first performed (part only) Shanghai, 1979.
Moment of Time (piano) 1981; first performed Shanghai, 1981.
Yi Feng (cello) 1982; first performed Shanghai, 1982.
Fu (string quartet) 1984; first performed New York, 1984.
Capriccio (flute, piano) 1984; first performed New York, 1984.
Double Bass Quartet 1985; first performed New Jersey, 1985.
Gu Yue (Ancient Music) (piano) 1986; first performed New York, 1986. Recorded Mode Records 15.
Ingrain (flute, bass clarinet, piano) 1987; first performed Netherlands, 1987.
Dao (string quartet) 1987; first performed San Francisco, 1987.
Hao (flute, piano) 1988; first performed New York, 1988.
Yiin (flute, oboe, clarinet, piano, violin, cello, percussion) 1990; first performed Pittsburgh, 1990.

Vocal/choral:

Trio (soprano, flute, clarinet) 1981; first performed Shanghai, 1981.
Ji (symphonic requiem for mixed chorus, orchestra) 1989; first performed Florida, 1989.
Xiang Zhan (solo soprano) 1989; first performed Switzerland, 1989.

Other:

Today with Dragon (dance score; flute, clarinet, trumpet, trombone, percussion, violin, double bass) 1986; first performed New York, 1986.
A Great Wall (film soundtrack; synthesizer, piano, percussion) 1986; first performed New York, 1986.
Who Killed Vincent Chin? (documentary film soundtrack; synthesizer) 1987; first performed New York, 1987.
Color Schemes (television documentary; piano) 1988; first performed New York, 1988.
Resonance (dance score; flute, cello, Tibetan cymbals) 1988; first performed Massachusetts, 1988.
Tang Dynasty (television documentary; ancient zheng, percussion) 1990; broadcast PBS, 1990/1.

PUBLICATIONS

On Ge: Russ Jennings, "Chinese Avant-Gardist GG-r", in *Option* magazine, January/February 1988.

Ge Gan-ru comments:

I have been trying to focus on two issues which I think will be important for my composing.

On the one hand, I found that in Chinese music each of the so-called four basic elements—pitch, rhythm, timbre and duration—is different from the same element in Western music. For example, in Western music, composers are deeply concerned with the relationships between pitches. But in Chinese music what is important is the particular pitch and its microtonal and timbral characters. Pitch relationships are important, of course, but not to the extent that Western composers have made these relationships paramount.

The concept of meter and tempo differs also. In Chinese music (particularly in opera) we can often feel the tempo changing, from fast to slow or slow to fast. The relative consistency of accentuation found in Western music (dictated by meter) is not always present in Chinese music, although this is not as evident today as in early 20th-and particularly 19th-century music. Differences in timbre are due to the type of instruments used and the many and varied instrumental techniques employed during performance.

On the other hand, with the continuing exploitation of contemporary Western techniques, I find that there is much greater possibility of combining Chinese materials and Western techniques in my writing.

No matter whether you are a musician or non-musician, everyone has at certain times some musical imagination. The best composers are able to transfer their feelings 100% onto the music sheet. What I have been trying to do is increase the percentage of my imagination which I am able to convey. I believe this is the essence of being a real composer.

* * *

The course of music worldwide since World War II has been moulded by a growth in contacts and of a shared musical language, and by parallel developments in technical resources, particularly those of electronic music studios and new instruments. There has inevitably grown up a common aesthetic and international style (as has so depressingly occurred in urban architecture) which has made new music from different countries often far too much alike. From the post-war resurgence of artistic activity there emerged, for the first time in history, Asian composers of world stature, like Toru Takemitsu, Cho Wen-chung and Isang Yun. But these major personalities have inclined towards self-oriented modes of utterance typical of post-Renaissance Europe, and towards its most developed medium, the symphony orchestra; it was left to John Cage to assert the primacy of Eastern philosophies with their doctrines of acceptance and self-denial and to embrace the sounds of oriental in preference to European music.

Ge Gan-ru belongs to a younger generation of oriental composers. Influenced by Cage and George Crumb, as well as by Takemitsu, his music has discarded less of its Chinese ancestry and aesthetics, and offers us one of the more interesting and effective examples of the now fashionable synthesis of East and West. Its Chinese qualities include microtonal variation and folk-like melody, prosaic rhythm, timbral subtlety taking precedence over pitch relationships, a certain primitive and natural beauty, and an intuitive approach to structure derived more from inherited Chinese feeling and experience than from any calculated, analytical logic. Its Western features are its gestural shapes, its instrumentation and its adoption of the language and new playing techniques of post-Webernian European music. One senses the spiritual background and, even, the allegorical character of ancient Chinese music; at the same time, Ge's music is extrovert, flamboyant and sonically futuristic, as befits his adopted city New York.

Ge would appear to be the first avant-garde composer to have emerged from Communist China. He was fortunate in being able to benefit from the reopening of the Shanghai Conservatory which he entered in 1974, and from influential contacts with a handful of visiting Westerners. Nevertheless, his earlier, secretive study of music during the unsympathetic and hostile period of the Cultural Revolution is as remarkable a story of determination in the face of adverse circumstances as is that of his arrival, virtually penniless, in New York in 1983 to study with Chow Wen-chung. A quiet self-reliance and purposefulness are concealed beneath a warm, gentle and generous personality. He has industriously made a living writing music for TV and film productions, including the first joint Chinese-American feature film *A Great Wall*. Meanwhile, his instrumental music has had an increasing impact in the U.S. in performances by artists of the calibre of the Kronos Quartet, Pittsburgh New Music Ensemble, the New York Philharmonic and other orchestras. In Britain it has been played in Glasgow and featured at the Huddersfield Contemporary Music Festival.

Yi Feng for solo cello, composed in 1982 while Ge was still in Shanghai, already reveals strikingly avant-garde methods of sound production and notation. There is no hint of lyrical, Western melody and no significant pitch structure; rather, the percussive sounds, fluctuating tremolos, sliding tones and variable vibrato of traditional Chinese music. *Gu Yue (Ancient Music)* is particularly interesting since it applies these ancient instrumental techniques to that most Western of modern instruments, the grand piano. The extended use of the piano by Cowell, Cage and Crumb readily comes to mind yet, one feels, the piece would sit easily and naturally in a concert of indigenous Chinese music; the musical style and the titles of the four movements refer to traditional Chinese instruments, "Gong, Qin" (7-stringed zither), "Pipa" (lute) and "Drum". *Hao* for flute and piano comes closer to the evocative poetry of George Crumb's music.

These various musical influences are brought together with flair and energy in *Wu*, originally for piano and chamber orchestra but now rewritten for full symphony orchestra, which is one of Ge's most played works. Yet, writing for symphony orchestra also endangers artistic integrity; expansive gesture being at odds with an essentially intimate Chinese art, the sheer scale of the medium threatening to overwhelm the vibrant character of the individual note and decorated single line which, one feels, are at the heart of Ge's music. *Ji*, a symphonic requiem, which also uses chorus, in coming closest among Ge's works to Western tradition, doesn't entirely reconcile these problems. His most recent scores, *Questioning the Sky* and *Gu Zheng Concerto*, are both concertos for the Chinese koto, the first with traditional Chinese orchestra, the other with Western symphony orchestra. In these pieces, from different angles and, perhaps, more successfully he has addressed these fundamental issues again.

—Richard Steinitz

GEDDES, John Maxwell. British/Scottish. Born in Glasgow, 26 May 1941. Educated at Royal Scottish Academy of Music, Glasgow (under Gordon Cameron and Frank Spedding), 1959–62, R.S.A.M.D.; teaching qualification, Jordanhill College of Education, Glasgow, 1962–3; Royal Danish Conservatory, Copenhagen (under Niels Viggo Bentzon), 1967. Married Lily Grant Blain; 3 August 1964; 2 sons and 1 daughter. Assistant teacher of music, later head of music, secondary school, Glasgow, 1963–70; lecturer in music, physical education college, Edinburgh, 1970–3; lecturer in music, Notre Dame College, Glasgow, 1973–9; associate professor of music education, Oregon State University, Corvallis, 1979–80; director of music diploma, St Andrew's College, Glasgow, since 1980. Member, BBC Scottish Music Advisory Panel, 1970–75; chair, Scottish branch, Composers' Guild of Great Britain, 1976–8; national committee member, Scottish Society of Composers, 1980–4, 1987–91, and Scottish Arts Council, 1984–6; member, score reading pool, Society for Promotion of New Music, 1972–88. Recipient: composition prize, Royal Scottish Academy of Music, 1961; guest of honour, Warsaw Autumn Festival, 1987; guest of honour, Don Spring Festival, U.S.S.R., 1989; guest of honour, Sholokov Spring Festival, U.S.S.R., 1990. Mailing address: 21 Cleveden Road, Glasgow G12, Scotland.

Publisher: Scottish Music Information Centre.

Symphonies/orchestral:

Three Orchestral Pieces Op 6 1965.
Fanfare Op 8 (brass) 1966.
Fiddlers' Folly Op 12 (string orchestra) 1968.
Portrait of a City 1971.
Symphony 1974–5.
Lacuna 1977.
Ombre 1984.
Voyager 1985.
A Galloway Bouquet (concert band) 1987.
A Young Person's Guide to the Galaxy (string orchestra) 1987.

Chamber/instrumental:

Three Antique Pieces (piano) 1964.
Four Basilican Pieces (3 trumpets) 1964.
Sonata Op 9 (flute, piano) 1966.
Sonata Op 10a (piano) 1967.
Scherzo (oboe, piano) 1967.
Quaderno a quattro (2 pianos, percussion) 1970.
Sonata (oboe, piano) 1972.
Solos (oboe or cor anglais) 1974.
Coronach (horn, tape) 1974.
Fanfare on EABEH (4 trumpets, 3 trombones, tuba, timpani) 1977.
Callanish IV (cello) 1978.
Apt (viola) 1978.
Winter (clarinet) 1978.
Wolf of Badenoch (4 trumpets, horn, 3 trombones) 1979.
Viola! (12 violas) 1981.
Diversions (flute/alto flute, oboe/cor anglais, clarinet, bass clarinet, guitar, violin, viola, cello) 1983.
Prelude on BHS (brass) 1985.
Callanish V (guitar) 1985.
Callanish III (flute, guitar) 1986.
Callanish I (flute) 1986.
Dances of the Scottish Court (2 trumpets, horn, trombone, tuba, optional percussion) 1988.
Leo Dreaming . . . (trombone, tape) 1988.
Muzyka Kameralna (clarinet, string quartet, tape) 1988.
Gallery Fanfare (brass quintet) 1989.
Dances of the Scottish Court (arranged for flute, viola, guitar) 1990.
Trio (flute, viola, guitar) 1990.
Sonata cello, piano) 1990.

Vocal/choral:

Scottish Folk Songs (voice, orchestra) 1971.
Cantica nova (chorus, organ, piano, percussion) 1971.
Come, Holy Spirit (SSSSAAAA chorus, piano, percussion) 1972.
Rune (soprano, alto, tenor, bass, bass speaker, SATB chorus, tape, piano) 1972–3.
Four Burns Songs (mezzo-soprano, tenor, piano) 1977.
The Queen's Brangil (tenor, baritone, flute, clarinet, trumpet, trombone, percussion, piano, guitar, violin, viola, cello, double bass) 1977.
Seven Scots Songs (mezzo-soprano, piano) 1989.
A Burns Collection (mezzo-soprano, flute, viola, guitar) 1990.
In Tempore Belli (mixed chorus) 1991.

Other:

Altamira (electronics) 1974.
Maria Regina (ballet; small orchestra) 1977.
Nite Shift (computer) 1980.
Starscapes (computer) 1980.
Nite on the Calapooia (computer) 1980.
Faustusmusik (electronics) 1982.
Glass Castle (electronics) 1989.

Film scores: *Beyond the Grampians*, 1963; *Deeside*, 1969; *Islands of the West*, 1971; *A Point in Time*, 1973; *The Living Land*, 1975; *Highland Winter*, 1978.

PUBLICATIONS

By Geddes: "Thomas Wilson", in *Composer*, Winter 1984.

* * *

Glaswegian composer John Maxwell Geddes is essentially a composer in the symphonic tradition, and his most impressive work has been written for orchestral forces, although not necessarily in symphonic form or length. His early work revealed a rather tense, almost nervous undercurrent, but he has subsequently grown considerably more expansive, while his latest works foretell a growing suggestion of a near-mystical sense of serenity.

Geddes demonstrated his acute understanding of, and ability to harness and utilise, the potential of the orchestra in formative works like the *Three Orchestral Pieces* or *Portrait of a City*, which drew on a powerful and distinctly urban sensibility and musical language.

They served as launching pads for a major milestone, his First Symphony, a work which underlined the controlled clarity of his orchestration and tightly-knit musical argument. The opening movement gradually builds on a series of fragmentary ideas, moving towards a resolution of their relationships which is ultimately saved for the third and final movement, which draws these disparate strands together around the slow central movement, with its poignant Hebridean melody and carefully controlled aleatoric elements.

The symphony is notable for the unconventional richness of its textures and its often exotic colouration and tempos, all contained within a convincingly argued and fully integrated symphonic structure. The strain of Celtic romanticism implicit in the middle movement, and his interest in both the myths and the landscapes of ancient Celtic and Nordic cultures are taken up in subsequent works, notably the series of numbered *Callanish* pieces, which take their name from the famous stone circle on Lewis.

Callanish IV, for solo cello, is a fine example of the way in which Geddes is able to combine a musical register derived from the tradition of Gaelic psalm singing (the haunting dissonance of which has attracted many contemporary Scottish composers) with an individual, highly contemporary musical idiom which replicates, in a very different fashion, the rhythmic freedom and bold expression of that form.

Geddes has been much praised for three more recent short orchestral works, which some commentators have felt formed an informal triptych. The finely-wrought *Lacuna* combined the idea of the pattern formed by a tiny spiral shell with that of a spiral galaxy, and the music reflects a highly complex dialogue between theses extremes of minute specificity and universal grandeur. Compelling and dramatic, and without a single excess note, it remains one of his finest scores.

That precise attention to detail is repeated in *Ombre*, a work of fastidiously realised, brooding textures and remarkable timbral shifts, evolving slowly over the length of the piece, a characteristic of much of the work of a composer who has declared his impatience with being taken "on a forced march to the coda". That highly individual approach to time is one of the most distinctive elements of his music.

The most impressive of this trio, though, is also the shortest. At only seven minutes, *Voyager* is a masterly example of how to say much in a short compass. Its complex, shifting structure, subtle colouration, tightly defined interwoven textures and sheer sonic beauty all deepen the sense of awe, mystery and excitement which the title and the composer's allusion to Halley's Comet infallibly generate.

—Kenny Mathieson

GEHLHAAR, Rolf (Rainer). German; American citizen. Born in Breslau, Germany [now Wroclaw, Poland], 31 December 1943; emigrated to United States, 1953, citizenship, 1958. Educated at Yale University, New Haven, Connecticut, 1961–5, B.A.; University of California, Berkeley, 1965–7; acoustics research, IRCAM, Paris, 1979, 1981. Married Nouritza Matossian; 6 June 1976; 2 sons. Personal assistant to Karlheinz Stockhausen, 1967–70; co-founder/director, Feedback Studio, Cologne, 1970–6; director, composition course, Darmstadt Summer Courses for New Music, 1976, 1978; lecturer, Dartington College of Art, Devon, 1976–7; composer in residence, New South Wales Conservatorium of Music, Sydney, 1977; adviser on contemporary music, Arts Council of Great Britain, 1983; technical director, Music at Mill House Festival, Aynho, Oxfordshire, 1988, 1989; technical director, Sydney Spring International Festival of New Music and Visual Arts, 1990. Recipient: music prize of the State of North Rhine-Westphalia, 1973. Mailing address: 12 Glenilla Road, London NW3 4AS, England.

Publisher: Feedback Studio Verlag, Genterstrasse 23, D-5000 Cologne 1, Germany.

Symphonies/orchestral:

Phase (orchestra, tape delay) 1972; first performed Saarbrücken, 1972.
Prototypen (4 orchestral groups) 1973; first performed Saarbrücken, 1973.
Resonanzen (8 orchestral groups) 1976; first performed Cologne, 1976.
Lamina (trombone, orchestra) 1977; first performed Saarbrücken, 1977.
Tokamak (piano, orchestra) 1982; first performed Donaueschingen, 1982.

Chamber/instrumental:

Cello Solo 1966.
Beckenstück (6 amplified cymbals) 1969; first performed Darmstadt, 1970.
Klavierstück 2-2 (2 pianos) 1970; first performed Lucerne, 1970.
Klavierstück 1-2 (piano, electronics) 1971; first performed Saarbrucken, 1971.
Wege (2 amplified strings, amplified piano) 1971; first performed Cologne, 1971.
Musi-Ken (string quartet) 1971; first performed Essen, 1971.
Spektra (4 trumpets, 4 trombones) 1971; first performed Essen, 1975.
Solipse (cello, tape delay) 1974; first performed Bremen, 1975.
Rondell (trombone, tape delay) 1975; first performed Cologne, 1975.
Particles (10 instruments, soprano, tape delay) 1977; first performed London, 1978.
Polymorph (bass clarinet, tape delay) 1978; first performed Amsterdam, 1978.
Linear A (marimbaphone) 1978; first performed Darmstadt, 1978.
Camera oscura (brass quintet) 1978; first performed Saarbrucken, 1978.
Strangeness, Charm and Colour (piano, 3 brass) 1978; first performed London, 1978.
Fluid (piano, violin/clarinet) 1979; first performed Paris, 1979.
Pixels (8 wind instruments) 1980; first performed Paris, 1980.
Nairi (amplified violin/viola) 1983; first performed London, 1988.
Cusps, Swallowtails, and Butterflies (piano) 1983; first performed Oxford, 1984.
Infra (10 amplified instruments) 1985; first performed Bath, Avon, 1989.
Origo (5 amplified instruments) 1986; first performed London, 1987.

Vocal/choral:

Liebeslied (alto, orchestra; Mellor) 1974; first performed Graz, 1974.
Isotrope (mixed choir, 32 voices) 1977; first performed London, 1977.
Worldline (SATB choir, live electronics) 1980; first performed London, 1980.
Das Mädchen aus der Ferne (soprano, flute, piano) 1982; first performed Brussels, 1983.

Other:

Five German Dances (4-channel tape) 1975; first performed Darmstadt, 1976.
Sub Rosa (4-channel tape) 1980; first performed Lille, 1980.
Pas à pas . . . Music for Ears in Motion (16-channel computer music) 1981; first performed Paris, 1981.
Sound=Space (interactive electronic musical environment) 1985; first performed Paris, 1985.
Copernic Opera (15 dancers in a *Sound=Space*) 1986; first performed Montpellier, 1986.
Singularity (3 instruments in a *Sound=Space*) 1986; first performed Bremen, 1986.
Sudden Adventures (2 dancers in a *Sound=Space*) 1988; first performed London, 1988.
Head Pieces (2 heads in a *Sound=Space*) 1988; first performed London, 1988.
Diagonal Flying (piano, *Sound=Space* system) 1989; first performed Geneva, 1989.

PUBLICATIONS

By Gehlhaar: "Kompositionsstudio", in *Darmstaedter Beitraege zur Neuen Musik*, Mainz, 1974; "Kompositionsstudio", in *Darmstaedter Beitraege zur Neuen Musik*, Mainz, 1976; "*Fünf Deutsche Taenze*", in *Darmstaedter Beitraege zur Neuen Musik*, Mainz, 1976; "Zur Komposition Ensemble", in *Darmstaedter Beitraege zur Neuen Musik*, Mainz, 1976; "Sound=Space", in *Contemporary Music Review*, London, 1990.

On Gehlhaar: F. Ritzel, "Musik für ein Haus", in *Darmstaedter Beitraege zur Neuen Musik*, Mainz, 1968; H. Bachmann, "Die gespielte Mitbestimmung", in *Revue Musicale Suisse*, 1, 1978; B. Schiffer, "RG", in *Revue Musicale Suisse*, 6, 1978; D. and J.Y. Bosseur, "Revolutions musicales", in *Le Sycamore*, Paris, 1979.

Rolf Gehlhaar comments:

I have always considered music to be an architecture of time articulated by sound. Personal observation of natural phenomena and their theoretical explanation have been and are still my main sources of inspiration. My particular interests are perceptible organic structure, beautiful sound and finding ways to make one the consequence of the other.

The structural origin of many of my works may be traced to a fundamental "genetic" set of relationships which are derived in two ways: either in a process of acoustic analysis of the sounds which are to be employed, later to be shaped and reconstructed in the process of composition, or from a totally abstract geometry of proportions, usually drawn from some area of theoretical physics or mathematics.

This genetic kernel serves as the font for processes of growth and decay, genesis, mutation, equilibrium and catastrophe. In the process of interpolating between the "kernel" and the musical result, many different techniques of interpretation and transformation are explored, including immediate, intuitive as well as systematic ones, calculated on a computer: algorithms, number sets, fractal geometries, chaos theory, stochastic evolutions, statistical distributions and permutations with varying degrees of randomness.

In many instances, I have been able to express most of the structural ideas of a piece in the form of algorithms and numerical relationships, which are then captured in a computer programme. The programme, when executed, provides an output in the form of notes (more often only numbers) which are then translated into a traditional musical score. A few of the programmes I have developed actually produce a musical output in real time, made audible via synthesizers under control of the computer.

* * *

The main characteristics of Rolf Gehlhaar's music are diversity of form, universality of techniques and variety of expression. The broad scope of his activities during the past 20 years has encompassed composing, performing, music education and therapy, acoustic research, sound engineering, technical development and computer systems design and programming.

Gehlhaar was personal assistant to Karlheinz Stockhausen and performing member of the Stockhausen Ensemble from 1967 to 1970. He soon became recognised as one of Germany's promising young composers of the post-serialist 1970s and 1980s. Gehlhaar's instrumental works, many of them also employing electro-acoustic resources, display a firm architectural structure and a clear harmonic evolution concentrating on the interrelationship between timbre and rhythm. The music arises as much from the elegant interaction of finely articulated layers of sound as from their lyrical juxtaposition.

Three solo pieces, *Solipse* for cello, *Rondell* for trombone and *Polymorph* for bass clarinet, are excellent examples in which innovative instrumental writing, complemented by the eloquent employment of a time-delay system, gives rise to an almost orchestral range of colours and force of expression.

The works for small mixed ensembles, *Particles*, *Infra* and *Origo* achieve a similar range through clear harmonic control, incisive polyphony and the use of amplification to create a balanced dynamic among all the instruments.

His large instrumental works, in particular *Phase* for orchestra and time delay, *Liebeslied* for orchestra and alto and *Tokamak* for orchestra and piano, are each remarkable in their almost fierce concentration upon the establishment of a unique harmonic context. Each achieves this end in a different fashion. *Phase* bases all harmonic relationships on progressions of difference tones. *Liebeslied* derives the harmonic structure of the whole from the formants of the poem sung by the alto. *Tokamak* unfolds its harmonic order from a temporal polyphony generated by a specially designed computer programme based on catastrophe theory.

Gehlhaar's electronic music ranges in scope from tape pieces to live computer controlled performances, to interactive environments. It displays a similar concentration on the musical exploitation of the physical structure of sound and, in particular, its spatialisation. The pieces have a marked investigative character, almost as if each represents a set of solutions to a particular set of questions: "How can you make . . . ?" or "What happens when you . . . ?". Several of these works, for example *Five German Dances* and *Sub Rosa*, both for 4-channel tape, *Pas à pas . . . Music for Ears in Motion*, a real-time computer-generated sound environment and *Diagonal Flying* for piano and computer conrolled synthesizers, have postulated novel theoretical, technological and musical questions, developed unique methods and formulated many elegant solutions.

Gehlhaar, the son of the eminent rocket scientist Heinz Gehlhaar, has made outstanding contributions to the challenge of space in music. In his work *Five German Dances* for 4-channel tape, realised in 1975 in the Electronic Studio of the WDR in Cologne, he created a fantastic planetarium of sounds travelling in orbits around the listeners. These sounds behave exactly as if they were real objects emitting sound, changing pitch with changing velocity, changing colour with changing proximity, etc. Occasionally they collide and fracture or they pass through the listener's head, exploding at that very moment. At IRCAM in Paris, in 1981, in the environment *Pas à pas . . . Music for Ears in Motion*, he created for the first time ever, an acoustic analogue to a hologram. This real-time computer generated musical environment, based upon the phenomenon of acoustic interference patterning, allowed perambulating listeners to hear private sequences of pitches while walking about within a single common sound.

Even more innovative and revolutionary is his SOUND=SPACE, an interactive environment which he invented and developed. Persons within the SPACE are able to create and control their own music merely by moving about. SOUND=SPACE was designed to be extremely flexible, so that it has been possible to employ it in a great variety of ways: as a creative musical entertainment for the general public (Centre Pompidou, Paris), as a technological display for a science museum (La Villette, Paris), as a tool for therapy (Gulbenkian Foundation, Lisbon), as a creative resource for the mentally or physically handicapped (Almeida Festival, London), as a musical environment for dancers (France) and as an instrument for Gehlhaar's own numerous live performances. This system promises further applications in many fields in the future. It is a perfect example of Gehlhaar's proven musical talents and his expertise in scientific and computer techniques.

—Nouritza Matossian

GIELEN, Michael (Andreas). Austrian. Born in Dresden, 20 July 1927. Educated: 3 semesters of philosophy, Buenos Aires; also private piano and composition study under Erwin Leuchter; returned to Vienna, 1951, further study under Josef Polnauer. Married Helga Augsten, 20 May 1957; 1 daughter and 1 son. Repetiteur, Teatro Colon, Buenos Aires, 1947–50; conducting debut, 1952; conductor, Vienna State Opera, 1954–60; chief conductor, Royal Opera, Stockholm, 1960–5; conductor, Cologne Radio Symphony Orchestra, 1965–9; music director, Belgian National Orchestra, 1968–73; music director, Netherlands Opera, Amsterdam, 1973–5; music/artistic director, Frankfurt Opera, 1977–87; chief guest conductor, BBC Symphony Orchestra, 1978; music director, Cincinnati Symphony Orchestra, Ohio, 1980–6; chief conductor, South West German Radio Symphony Orchestra, Baden-Baden, since 1986; professor of conducting, Mozarteum, Salzburg, since 1987. Recipient: Hessischer Staatspreis, 1984; Adorno-Preis, City of Frankfurt, 1986. Mailing address: Kapuzinerstrasse 3, D-7570 Baden-Baden, Germany.

Publishers: Universal Edition, Vienna; Breitkopf & Hartel, Weisbaden.

Symphonies/orchestral:

Variations (40 instruments) 1959; first performed Vienna, 1959.

Mitbestimmungsmodell (orchestral musicians, 3 conductors) 1971; first performed Saarbrücken, 1972.

Einige Schwierigkeiten bei der Uberwindung der Angst 1972.
"Pflicht und Neigung" (small orchestra) 1988; first performed Bremen, 1989.

Chamber/instrumental:

Sonata (violin) 1946.
Variations (string quartet) 1947; first performed Buenos Aires, 1947.
Trio (clarinet, viola, bassoon) 1948.
String Quartet: "Un Vieux Souvenir" 1983; first performed Cincinnati, Ohio, 1985. Recorded Deutsche Grammophon DG 423 109 2.
Ruckblick (serenade for 3 cellos) 1989; first performed Linz, 1990.

Vocal/choral:

Music (baritone, trombone, percussion, piano, strings) 1954.
Vier Gedichte von Stefan George (chorus, 19 instruments) 1955–8.
Six Songs (bass, viola, clarinet, piano) 1958; first performed Vienna, 1958.
Die glocken sind auf falscher spur (soprano, speaker, cello, percussion, piano, electric guitar, tapes; Arp) 1967–9; first performed Saarbrücken, 1970.
Pentaphonie: Ein Tag tritt hervor / Una dia sobresale (piano obligato, vibraphone, marimba, electric guitar, harmonium, ondes martenot, 4 singers, 1 speaker, 4 instrumental quintets; Neruda) 1961–4; first performed Stockholm, 1965. Recorded Intercord 830 871.

PUBLICATIONS

On Gielen: R. Luck, "Dirigentem als Spezialisten?", in *Werkstattgesprache mit Interpreten neuer Musik*, Cologne, 1971.

* * *

Michael Gielen belongs to a small class of composer-conductors whose own compositional output is inseparable from their interpretations of others' work. In Gielen's case, the vital presences are the composers of the Second Viennese School and in particular Schoenberg. The mid-1950s settings of Stefan George, a poet to whom Schoenberg was particularly drawn, are done in orthodox serialist style and are strongly reminiscent of Schoenberg's Op 22 *Four Songs* of 1916. Later in his career, as his perspective on the modern tradition deepened and grew more autonomous, Gielen abandoned orthodox serialism in favour of a highly personal concatenation of modern styles in which he refers frequently and much more openly to the modernist classics.

In his brilliant and ironically titled 1983 string quartet *Un Vieux Souvenir*, the second violin comes onstage playing a motive that makes indirect reference to Alban Berg's *Lyric Suite* by alluding to the *Lyric Symphony* of Schoenberg's brother-in-law Zemlinsky. If this is the "old memory" of the title, it acts as a complex Proustian trigger for a highly deconstructive reverie that concentrates on images of decay and destruction. Gielen had been reading Walter Benjamin's essays on the Paris arcades and on Charles Baudelaire. In the quartet he uses two poems by Baudelaire—"Carrion" and "The Swan"—as ur-texts and as the thematic background to the second and fourth movements; neither is recited in its entirety, but the players are instructed to call out key phrases from each (in a language of choice), whose metaphoric content is also conveyed in the score. In a brief opening movement, Gielen introduces images of decay (sweeping glissandos from the viola) and of a dying swan escaped from the menagerie and helplessly flapping its wings in the dust of the boulevard (percussive *col legno* patterns from the cello). Behind them, the Zemlinsky melody is heard faintly. The whole pattern is interrupted by an eldritch sawing from the whole quartet which powerfully recalls air-raid sirens. Gielen has not made his programmatic intentions entirely clear, but it seems probable that the piece is an attempt to come to terms with the savage disruptions of World War II. There is a Hebraic quality to the Zemlinsky motives and the proliferating images of carrion, with its *"seltsame Musik"*, may be seen as a reference to the Holocaust. In the face of such destruction, the imagination of the artist is only apparently liberated by the "new language" of modernism, which reveals itself to be either a symptom or a contributary cause of the totalitarian destruction of the proud Germanic tradition of four-part writing that runs from Haydn to Webern.

Gielen is searching for a way out of that historical cul-de-sac. The quartet is an extraordinarily complex work, built on remarkably simple materials. The massive third and central movement deploys five *topoi* or cruces interspersed with silences; durations are determined by the Fibonacci sequence, and the movement works complex variations and intersections of all preceding material, together with a new, hymnic theme which ironically inverts the hymn of liberation in *Fidelio*, a detail that underlines the work's verbally-stated dedication "to the vanquished" and "to the captives". The final movements are both nihilistic and extraordinarily stoic; the performers face away from one another, the materials break down, but there is an underlying unity, even in the most fractured material, one that does not rely on the "old memory" of tradition, but does not reject it either.

That has been the trajectory of Gielen's career to date. His background (nephew of the great Polish–American pianist and composer Eduard Steuermann, an education in Latin America) gave him a literally eccentric perspective on the European tradition. His conducting and his own music reveal a powerfully analytical mind, which has sometimes led to dry and cerebral work (the early violin sonata is a brilliant exercise, but makes no great appeal to the emotions), and just as often to performances of considerable power and range. In 1949 Gielen performed Schoenberg's entire (but admittedly attenuated) piano output and in 1974 made the first recording of the massive, unfinished opera *Moses und Aron*. His first major conducting credits were of Stravinsky's ever-popular *Histoire d'un Soldat* and Honegger's *Joan of Arc at the Stake* and he participated in the first performance of Stockhausen's massive four-orchestra *Carré* in 1959 (Mauricio Kagel, Andrzej Markowski and the composer were the other conductors), a work that made a marked but altogether original impact on his own *Mitbestimmungsmodell* and the very brilliant *Pentaphonie*, after a text by Neruda. Gielen's chamber music includes the intriguingly voiced 1948 *Trio* for clarinet, bassoon and viola and the more recent *Ruckblick* for three cellos, another "look back" into the tainted wellsprings of tradition.

—Richard Stein

GIFFORD, Helen (Margaret). Australian. Born in Hawthorn, Victoria, 5 September 1935. Educated at Tintern Church of England Girls Grammar School, 1941–6; Melbourne Church of England Girls Grammar School, 1947–52; Commonwealth Scholarship, Melbourne University Conservatorium of Music (piano under Roy Shepherd, harmony under Dorian La Gallienne), 1953–7, Mus.Bac., 1958. Composer, Melbourne Theatre Company, 1970–82; composer in residence, Australian Opera, 1974; chair, Composers' Guild of Australia, 1978. Recipient: 1st Dorian La Gallienne Award, 1965; senior composer's fellowship, Australian Council for the Arts, 1974. Mailing address: 27 Smart Street, Hawthorn, Victoria 3122, Australia.

Publisher: Sounds Australian/formerly Australian Music Centre, P.O. Box 49, Broadway, New South Wales 2007, Australia.

Symphonies/orchestral:

Phantasma (strings) 1963.
Chimaera (large orchestra, harpsichord, 7 percussion) 1967; first performed Adelaide, 1967. Recorded Australian Composers ANC RRCS386.
Canzone: Hommage to Stravinsky (chamber orchestra) 1968.
Imperium (large orchestra, piano) 1969; first performed Melbourne, 1969. Recorded Australian Composers ABC RRCS 387.
On Reflection (2 violins, string orchestra) 1972.

Chamber/instrumental:

Fantasy (flute, piano) 1958; first performed Utrecht, Netherlands, 1960.
Sonata (piano) 1960; first performed Melbourne, 1960. Recorded Move MCDO42.
Septet (flute, oboe, bassoon, harpsichord, violin, viola, cello) 1962.
Skiagram (flute, viola, vibraphone) 1963; first performed Melbourne, 1963.
Catalysis (piano) 1964; first performed Melbourne, 1964. Recorded Anthology of Australian Music on Disc CSM:3 Mays.
Lyric (flute, clarinet, cello) 1964; first performed Melbourne, 1964.
String Quartet 1965; first performed Melbourne, 1965.
Cantillation (piano) 1966; first performed Melbourne, 1985. Recorded Move MD 3066.
The Spell (piano) 1966; first performed Melbourne, 1985. Recorded Move MD 3066.
Waltz (piano) 1966.
Fable (harp) 1966; first performed Melbourne, 1966.
Sonnet (flute, guitar, harpsichord) 1969; first performed Melbourne, 1969.
Of Old Angkor (horn, marimba) 1970; first performed Melbourne, 1970.
Company of Brass (3 trumpets, horn, 2 tenor trombones, bass trombone, euphonium, tuba) 1972; first performed Melbourne, 1973.
Souvenence (piano) 1973.
Play (piccolo, flute, clarinet, horn, trumpet, bass trombone, 4 percussion) 1979.
Time and Time Again (flute, clarinet, 2 percussion, piano, cello) 1981; first performed Sydney, 1981.
Going South (2 trumpets, horn, 2 trombones) 1987.
Toccata attacco (piano) 1990; first performed Melbourne, 1990.

Vocal/choral:

As Dew in Aprille (soprano, harp or piano or guitar) 1955; first performed Melbourne, 1955.
The Wanderer (male speaker, ensemble) 1962; first performed Melbourne, 1963.
Red Autumn in Valvins (mezzo-soprano, piano) 1964; first performed Melbourne, 1964.
The Glass Castle (soprano, 5-part female choir) 1968; first performed Melbourne, 1968.
Bird Calls from an Old Land (5 sopranos, 5-part female choir) 1971; first performed Melbourne, 1971.
Images for Christmas (speaker, ensemble) 1973; first performed Melbourne, 1973.
Foretold at Delphi (soprano, piccolo, oboe, Arab drum, prerecorded krumhorn; ancient Greek) 1978.

Opera/theatre:

Jo Being (4 soloists, chorus, orchestra) 1974.
Regarding Faustus (tenor, chorus, 14 instruments; Marlowe) 1983; first performed Adelaide, 1988.
Iphigenia in Exile (soprano, chorus, ensemble; Euripides) 1985; excerpts broadcast ABC/FM, October 1990.

Other:

The Caucasian Chalk Circle (incidental music to Brecht) 1970; first performed Melbourne, 1970.
All's Well That Ends Well (incidental music to Shakespeare) 1970; first performed Melbourne, 1970.
The Life of Galileo (incidental music to Brecht) 1971; first performed Melbourne, 1971.
Equus (incidental music to Shaffer) 1974; first performed Melbourne, 1974.
Pericles, Prince of Tyre (incidental music to Shakespeare) 1974; first performed Melbourne, 1974.
The Double Dealer (incidental music to Congreve) 1975; first performed Melbourne, 1975.
The Revenger's Tragedy (incidental music to Tourneur) 1975; first performed Melbourne, 1975.
Much Ado About Nothing (incidental music to Shakespeare) 1975; first performed Melbourne, 1975.
Othello (incidental music to Shakespeare) 1976; first performed Melbourne, 1976.
Ring Round the Moon (incidental music to Anouilh) 1977; first performed Melbourne, 1977.
The Merchant of Venice (incidental music to Shakespeare) 1977; first performed Melbourne, 1977.
Electra (incidental music to Sophocles) 1978; first performed Melbourne, 1978.
Macbeth (incidental music to Shakespeare) 1979; first performed Melbourne, 1979.
Rosencrantz and Guildenstern Are Dead (incidental music to Stoppard) 1980; first performed Melbourne, 1980.

PUBLICATIONS

By Gifford: "*Raison d'être*", in Grimshaw and Strahan, *The Half-Open Door*, Sydney, 1982; "Subliminal Coordinates: Drawing Threads", in *New Music Articles*, 7, 1989.

Helen Gifford comments:
My compositions are highly wrought but have no allegiance to any system of organisation.

* * *

Helen Gifford's characteristic tautly worked-out yet meditative response to the formal demands of creating a personal compositional style is evident from the beginning of her career as a composer in the mid 1950s.

Though the influence of her teacher, the English-born composer Dorian Le Gallienne, is apparent in the cool detachment and suppressed emotional currents of the only work to survive the student years, *As Dew in Aprille*, the more lasting influence came from her piano professor, Roy Shepherd, whose infectious love of French musical styles can be traced in all Gifford's subsequent piano works, tempered as this may be by the atonal fashions that finally permeated modernist Australian musical circles in the 1950s and 1960s. From the Piano Sonata through *Catalysis* and *Souvenence*, to the recent works for the pianist Sally May, there is an accelerating interest in edge timbre and the employment of the more explosive percussive effects which the instrument provides.

The English period, in the early 1960s, and her continued involvement with new music groups in Melbourne, alerted the composer to seminal creative events of the period. The central orchestral and chamber works of this time reflect the prevailing interest in fragmented tonal references and anti-melodic, pro-rhythmic/plosive progression.

Throughout the 1970s Gifford's association with the Melbourne Theatre Company produced incidental music, lamentably under-exploited by the group. Excerpts appeared in productions, but the full scores were neither understood as the original and separate works they are, nor recorded with any archival intent. The economic use of exotic sound for effect in these essays (the piercing magic of the Tibetan trumpet for *Pericles*, the body beating used to produce choric effects in *Equus*, or the hair-raising use of aluminum rods in *The Revenger's Tragedy*, for example) remains unmatched in the Australian theatre.

Gifford's lifelong interest in Asian music has also drawn her to write for percussion as frequently as commissions could be angled that way. In recent times she has shifted towards a more gap-closed, tonally centralised melodic line, though the highly crafted rhythmic plan and its attendant elegance of style remain as before.

Incidental music for the theatre inevitably led to the operatic works where the progression from wide-spaced to close-worked melodic lines is most noticeable and where the percussive element of the ensemble is very much in evidence. Though organic development of an initial theme triggers most of her instrumental work, she is also textually aware and insists on having a large input as far as her librettos are concerned.

The music for the (to date) three short operas—*Jo Being*, *Regarding Faustus* and *Iphigenia in Exile* (which, like *Foretold at Delphi*, were once designated as music-theatre) is close-worked, dense with reflections from the text, dramatically weighted, vocally demanding and acutely judged. Written for particular singers, (Robert Gard for *Regarding Faustus*, Barbara Sambell for *Iphigenia in Exile*), Gifford tailors her mono-operas to display specialist vocal strengths and to engage with classic themes; nothing in her oeuvre claims an Australian basis. Of the operas only *Regarding Faustus* has received a full production. Personally selected by Lord Harewood for the Bicentennial Adelaide Festival of 1988 and performed by the Victoria State Opera with unimpressive staging, it awaits a full realisation.

With her place in Australian music long established, and as adverse to publicity as ever, Gifford is currently deepening her involvement in writing for particular performers, instrumentalists as well as singers, and remains both aloof from current stylistic fashions and wary of attempts to intrude on her creative integrity. Hers is a memorably vivid impress, inviting contemplation rather than involvement, and admiration for her spartan wholeness.

—Thérèse Radic

GILBERT, Anthony (John). British/English. Born in London, 26 July 1934. Educated at Gunnersbury Grammar School; Lycée français de Londres; Collège libre de Juilly, France; qualified, Fellow of the Institute of Linguists, 1954; Trinity College of Music, London (piano under Denis Holloway, theory under Denis Lever), 1954–7; privately, Morley College, London (history of music, harmony, counterpoint and composition under Anthony Milner, orchestration, analysis and composition under Alexander Goehr, composition under Mátyás Seiber), 1957–63 (conducting under Lawrence Leonard and Norman Del Mar), 1967; Dartington Summer School, Devon (composition under Luigi Nono and Luciano Berio), 1961–2; Tanglewood, Massachusetts (as Margaret Lee Crofts Fellow, composition under Gunther Schuller, Elliott Carter and Roger Sessions), 1967; University of Leeds, 1982–4, M.A., D.Mus. pending. Translator, copyist, music editor, music library assistant, 1955–68; tutor in composition, 1968–71, and acting director of music, 1971–3, department of adult studies, Goldsmiths' College, London; composer in residence, University of Lancaster, 1970; visiting lecturer in composition, University of Liverpool, 1970; senior tutor in composition, 1973–9, and principal lecturer in composition, from 1979, Royal Northern College of Music, Manchester, senior lecturer in composition, New South Wales State Conservatorium of Music, Sydney, 1978–9; composer in the community, city of Bendigo, Victoria, Australia, 1981; member, BBC New Music Panel, since 1982. Recipient: Fricker Composition Prize, Morley College, 1981; honorary fellow, Royal Northern College of Music, 1981. Mailing address: Magpies, Teuthill, Alvanley, Cheshire WA6 9AL, England.

Publisher: Schott.

Symphonies/orchestral:

Sinfonia (chamber orchestra) 1965; first performed London, 30 March 1965.
Regions (2 orchestras) 1966; first performed London, March 1969.
Peal II (jazz or school orchestra) 1968.
Symphony 1973; first performed Cheltenham, Gloucestershire, 1973.
Ghost and Dream Dancing: Studies for Orchestra 1 1974; first performed Birmingham, September 1974.
Crow-Cry (chamber orchestra) 1976; first performed London, 16 March 1977.
Welkin (school or amateur orchestra) 1976; first performed Manchester, 18 February 1977.
Towards Asavari (piano, chamber orchestra) 1978; first performed Manchester, 27 January 1979.
Koonapippi (youth orchestra) 1981; first performed Kangaroo Flat, Victoria, 1981.
Bendigo Match (wind band) 1981; first performed Kangaroo Flat, Victoria, 1981.
Little Fantasia on Gold-Digger Tunes (chamber orchestra) 1981; first performed Kangaroo Flat, Victoria, 1981.

Dream Carousels (wind band) 1988; first performed London, 1989.
Tree of Singing Names (chamber orchestra) 1989; first performed Manchester, 1990.

Chamber/instrumental:

Sonata No 1 (piano) 1962; first performed Cheltenham, Gloucestershire, July 1962.
Duo (violin, viola) 1963; first performed London, 1963.
Serenade (oboe, horn, violin, viola, guitar, double bass) 1963; first performed London, November 1963.
Sonata No 2 (piano—4 hands) 1966, revised 1967; first performed London, May 1967; enlarged version first performed Tanglewood, Massachusetts, August 1967.
Brighton Piece (clarinet, horn, trumpet, trombone, cello, 3 percussion) 1967; first performed Brighton, Sussex, May 1967.
Nine or Ten Osannas (clarinet, horn, violin, cello, piano) 1967; first performed Dore Abbey, 11 October 1967.
The Incredible Flute Music (flute, piano) 1968; first performed London, July 1970.
Spell Respell (electric basset horn, piano) 1968; first performed Santa Monica, California, 30 January 1970.
Mother (solo cello, piccolo/flute, clarinet, violin/viola, keyboard, percussion) 1969; first performed York, 25 June 1969.
Treatment of Silence (violin, tape) 1969; first performed Lancaster, February 1974.
O'Grady Music (clarinet, cello, toy instruments) 1971; first performed Los Angeles, January 1972.
String Quartet with Piano Pieces 1972; first performed (quartet only) Lancaster, January 1972; first performance with piano pieces, Lancaster, November 1972.
Canticle I: Rock-Song (2 clarinets, bass clarinet, 2 horn, 2 trumpets, trombone) 1973; first performed London, June 1974.
Crow Undersongs (viola) 1979; first performed Sydney, 11 August 1979.
Begindigendigo (recorder ensemble) 1981; first performed Shepparton, Victoria, 1981.
Vasanta with Dancing (flute/alto flute, oboe/cor anglais, violin, viola, harp, percussion, harp, voice ad lib, optional dancer) 1981.
Gymnorhina (viola, piano) 1981; first performed Manchester, September 1981.
Sunrising (oboe, piano) 1981.
Little Dance of Barrenjoey (chamber ensemble) 1981; first performed London, 1981.
Two Birds by Kuring-Gai (horn, piano) 1982; first performed Manchester, 1982.
Moonfaring (cello, percussion) 1983; first performed Manchester, 1984.
Dawnfaring (viola, piano) 1984; first performed Hexham, 1986
Quartet of Beasts (flute, oboe, bassoon, piano) 1984; first performed Manchester, 1984.
Six of the Bestiary (saxophone quartet) 1985; first performed London, 1985.
Funtoons (children's pieces for piano) 1985.
Fanfarings (6/8 brass) 1986.
String Quartet No 2 1987; first performed Cheltenham, Gloucestershire, 1987.
String Quartet No 3: Super Hoqueto David 1987; first performed London, 1987.
Peal III (piano) 1988; first performed Manchester, 1988.
Peal IV (organ) 1988.
Four Small Farings (sopranino recorder/piccolo, piano) 1988.

Vocal/choral:

Missa Brevis (unaccompanied mixed chorus) 1965; first performed Cheltenham, Gloucestershire, July 1968.
Three War Poems (unaccompanied mixed chorus) 1966.
Shepherd Masque (young voices) 1968.
Love Poems (soprano, clarinet or bass clarinet, cello, accordion or chamber organ) 1970; first performed London, July 1970.
Canticle II: Anger (6 male voices) 1974; first performed Cheltenham, Gloucestershire, July 1974.
Inscapes (soprano, speaking voice, 2 clarinets/1 soprano saxophone/2 bass clarinets, percussion, harmonica) 1975.
Long White Moonlight (soprano, electric double bass) 1980; first performed Huddersfield, Yorkshire, 25 October 1980.
Chant of Cockeye Bob (children's voices, instruments) 1981; first performed Eppalock, Victoria, 1981.
Beastly Jingles (soprano, flute, mandolin, viola, guitar, double bass, percussion) 1984; first performed Utrecht, 1985.
Certain Lights Reflecting (soprano, orchestra; Sarah Day) 1989; first performed Cheltenham, Gloucestershire, 1989.

Opera:

The Scene-Machine (George MacBeth) 1970; first performed Kassel, 4 April 1971.
The Chakravaka-Bird (radio opera; Ramanujan, Ingalls, Gilbert) 1977.

PUBLICATIONS

By Gilbert: "Music for Serpents", in *The Listener*, July 1978; "Calling the Tune", in *Musical Times*, April 1980; "Birdsong: Some Technical Points for the Composer", dissertation, University of Leeds, 1984; "Michael Tippett, Magician of Our Time", in *Halle Magazine*, January 1985; "Dialogues with David Lumsdaine", *Festschrift* for Lumsdaine's 60th birthday, 1991.

On Gilbert: G.W. Hopkins, "The Music of AG", in *Musical Times*, December 1967; Leslie East, "A Survey of AG's Music", London (Schott), 1974; Priti Paintal, "A Comparative Study of the Integration of Eastern and Western Music in Two Compositions", dissertation, University of Manchester, September 1985.

Anthony Gilbert comments:
I have tried to avoid association with stylistic groups and doctrinaire attitudes; the penalty is that ready-made means of identifying my music do not exist. The spirit and the technique of my music, but not the notes, have over the years been very strongly influenced by non-European cultures, particularly Indian and, to a lesser extent, Indonesian. Instrumental colour plays an important role, as does rhythm of all kinds—pulsed rhythm, rhythmic cycles, large-scale structural rhythms, the growth, development transformation and decay of cellular rhythms.

This is the essence of it all: I strive after a music which not only dances, and sometimes sings, but also grows and breathes like a living organism.

* * *

Though Anthony Gilbert has written a number of works reflecting an interest in the art and mythology of India, he is a composer who remains thoroughly Western in his dogged pursuit of music as an evolving language and medium for the communication of personal experience.

A certain uncompromising spirit has been typical of Gilbert's endeavours from the very beginning. Born in 1934, he approached composition as a late-starter, enrolling at Morley College in 1957 at the age of 23. With characteristic pertinacity he worked first with Mátyás Seiber and then Anthony Milner. But the most important influence was three years of study with Alexander Goehr, from whom he readily absorbed the changed musical sensibility of the period, and the new awareness of continental developments already pioneered by the Manchester School.

The result can be heard both in the *Brighton Piece* and *The Incredible Flute Music*, reminiscent of Birtwistle in their angular lines and surprising discontinuities, but typical of Gilbert in their sonorous wholes. In the orchestral piece *Regions*, as in the Second Piano Sonata, for two pianos of the same year, another Gilbertian preoccupation became apparent in the use of timbre and tessitura to define musical form. And the deliberate contrasts of freedom and strictness within the String Quartet with Piano Pieces and *Nine or Ten Osannas* reflect an interest not only in the controlled indeterminacy of Boulez, but also the radical attitude to time and chance proposed by Cage.

Nine or Ten Osannas also revealed an unexpected talent for tone-painting and inspired whimsy that has reappeared from time to time within the interstices of Gilbert's larger works. *Inscapes* celebrates the beauty of nature through the sonorous prose of Gerard Manley Hopkins. Gilbert controls his tiny ensemble of soprano, reader, two readers and percussion with the imaginative skill of a true aphorist. More recently, this capricious vein has re-emerged in the three bestiary pieces inspired by the fantastic imagery of Jorge Luis Borges, *Quartet of Beasts* for flute, oboe, bassoon and piano, *Beastly Jingles* for soprano and ensemble, and *Six of the Bestiary* for saxophone quartet.

A fascination with the picturesque may also have been the inspiration for Gilbert's first major excursion into the world of Indian music: the BBC radio opera *The Chakravaka-Bird*. A previous opera *The Scene-Machine*, to a libretto by George MacBeth, had been produced at Kassel in 1971, and was followed by a Symphony for the Cheltenham Festival in 1973. With the exception of two string quartets, his list of works contains no further examples of music relating specifically to 19th-century forms. Nevertheless, the composer has continued to experiment with the parameters of the standard Western instrumental ensemble, both in *Towards Asavari* for piano and small orchestra and the Lontano commission *Vasanta with Dancing*.

Deeply committed to the cause of new music, Gilbert has been an active supporter both of the ICA and SPNM. He has also written a number of highly effective educational works. An inspiring teacher, he now divides his time between the Royal Northern College of Music, where he is Head of Composition, and several major universities in Australia. The history and landscape of that country have inspired recent works including the orchestral song-cycle *Certain Lights Reflecting*, to poems by the Tasmanian poet Sarah Day.

—Nicholas Williams

GITECK, Janice. American. Born in Brooklyn, New York, 27 June 1946. Educated at Mills College, Oakland, California (composition under Darius Milhaud), 1964–9, B.A., M.A. (composition); Conservatoire National Supérieur de Musique, Paris (composition under Olivier Messiaen), 1969–70; composition study under Barney Childs, Lowell Cross, Charles Jones, Leonard Klein, Morton Subotnick; piano study under Bernhardt Abramowitch, Morton Estrin, Russell Sherman, Rebecca Weinstock; studied Indonesian gamelan under Daniel Schmidt and Ghanaian percussion under Obo Addy; Antioch University, Seattle, Washington, M.A. (psychology), 1986. Composer, various dance companies, from 1964; director/coordinator, various musical groups, 1973–9; lecturer, piano and theory, Frankfurt American community, Germany, 1970–1; founder member, Port Costa Players; music director, Oakland Museum, California; music director, KPFA Radio; guest lecturer in composition, theory and analysis of twelve-tone music, California State University, Hayward, 1974; teacher of music and women's studies, Cornish Institute, Seattle, Washington. Recipient: Copley Fellowship, Aspen Music School, 1964; Francis J. Hellman Talent Award, Mills College, Oakland, 1964–8; 1st prize in composition, Mills College, Oakland, 1968, 1969; 1st prize (for *L' Ange Heurtebise*), Concorso Internazionale di Musica e Danza, Vercelli, 1973; Norman Fromm Composers Award (for *Thunder, Like a White Bear Dancing*), 1977. Mailing address: c/o Mode Records, P.O. Box 375, Kew Gardens, New York 11415, U.S.A.

Publisher: self.

Symphonies/orchestral:

TREE (chamber symphony) 1981; first performed San Francisco, 1981.
Loo-Wit (viola, orchestra) 1982.

Chamber/instrumental:

Trio (oboe, violin, cello) 1964.
Piano Quintet 1965.
String Quartet 1967.
Trey (3 piano pieces) 1968.
Variations (viola, piano) 1968.
Helixes (flute, trombone, violin, cello, guitar, piano, percussion) 1974.
Primaries (flute, percussion) 1977.
Breathing Songs from a Turning Sky (flute, clarinet, bassoon, cello, piano, percussion) 1979–80, revised 1984; first performed San Francisco, 1980. Recorded Mode Records mode 14; excerpt, Mills Records MC 01.
When the Crones Stop Counting (60 flutes) 1980.
Ah Ah Sh! Listen (gamelan, cellos, bassoons, drums, storyteller, dancer) 1981.
Tapasya (viola, percussion) 1987; first performed New York City, 1988.

Vocal/choral:

Anew (medium voice, piano; Zukofsky) 1969.
How to Invoke a Garden (SATB voices, 10 instruments; Jones) 1969.
Sun of the Center (medium voice, flute, clarinet, violin, piano; Kelley) 1970.
L'Ange Heurtebise (medium voice, piano; Cocteau) 1971.
Magic Words (tenor, soprano, piano; Native American texts) 1973.

Magic Words to Feel Better (unaccompanied mixed chorus) 1974.
Eight Sandbars on the Takano River (5 female voices, flute, bassoon, guitar; Snyder) 1976.
Matinée d'ivresse (soprano/tenor; Rimbaud) 1976.
Far North Beast Ghosts the Clearing (chorus; Cree text, translated Norman) 1978.
Callin' Home Coyote: A Burlesque (tenor, steel drums, double bass; MacAdams) 1978; first performed Amsterdam, 1978. Recorded Mode Records mode 14.
Om Shanti (soprano, sextet; part of *Music and Healing* series) 1986.
Pictures of the Floating World (chorus, 10 instruments) 1987; first performed Seattle, Washington, 1987.

Opera:

Messalina (mini-opera for medium voice, cello, piano) 1973.
A'Agipta (ceremonial opera for 3 singer/actors, dancer, 8 actor/instrumentalists; Pima and Papago Indian texts) 1976.

Other:

Study I (tape) 1969.
Study II (tape) 1969.
Traffic Acts (4-channel tape) 1969.
A Picture of Dorian Gray (theatre/dance after Wilde) 1974.
Thunder, Like a White Bear Dancing (performance ritual for soprano, flute, percussion, piano, chanters; Ojibwa picture songs) 1977. Recorded Mode Records mode 14.
Peter and the Wolves (actor, trombone, tape) 1978.

Film scores: *Hopi: Songs of the Fourth World*, 1983; *Hearts and Hands*, 1987.

PUBLICATIONS

On Giteck: Mildred Hamilton, "Old Sources for New Music", in *San Francisco Examiner*, November 1977; Marilyn Tucker, "JG's Mysterious Themes Lovingly Set to Music", in *San Francisco Chronicle*, 30 November 1977.

* * *

Almost all of Janice Giteck's music is concerned in some degree with ritual. In that sense, she has written very little "pure" or abstract music; an early string quartet, though unmistakably by her hand, is by no means representative of her mature work. Giteck's most recent sources have been explicitly concerned with the healing and transformative power of music, an interest which has led her back into academic study of psychology, not in the technical, neurological direction implied by psycho-acoustics, but in a more anthropological and folkloric way that suggests a feminisation—and Americanisation—of the theories of Carl Jung and Rudolf Steiner.

Giteck's most accessible work to date is *Breathing Songs from a Turning Sky*, a set of 10 meditations for chamber ensemble that draws on kabbalistic philosophy (perhaps mediated by Steiner) and on the conviction that all creativity (and her conception of it would seem to embrace the natural world as well as art and artefacts) is instinctive with the rhythm of breath. A further instance of this belief can be detected in her use of texts by Gary Snyder as background to the "burlesque" *Callin' Home Coyote* (its actual texts are by Louis MacAdams), in which the rhythm of the pace is dictated by breath-groups.

Breathing Songs is built on "non-Western" five-note scales (which are in fact a basic component of Native American musics) organized somewhat schematically in lateral pairs from which all the tonal material is derived. Far from sounding schematic, though, the whole work "breathes" round its silent seventh section, a half-minute of meditation in which the listener's breath is the only sound. The work is closely associated with the New Performance Group, which is also known for its work with John Cage.

If Giteck's use of silence carries implications radically different from Cage's, her basic aesthetic is still very much conditioned by the West Coast ethos to which Cage contributed so much. Her use of Native American materials, with their presumed transcultural links to other Pacific cultures, is highly assured and imaginative. The ritual *Thunder, Like a White Bear Dancing* draws on Ojibwa (perhaps better known as Chippewa) myth, a culture significantly punctuated by ritual dances: the Dream Dance, the Grass Dance, the Women's Dance. Its opening passage sets the quiet meditative calm of the traditional love-flute against a relentless drum pattern; when this lapses into silence, the main body of the work emerges, in an idiom that represents a powerful synthesis of European and American modernism (echoes of vocal music from Mahler and Schoenberg right through to Cage's "The Wonderful Widow of Sixteen Springs").

Giteck's most fully realised exploration of ritual is the opera *A'Agipta*, an immensely powerful work that met with considerable critical acclaim at its first performance, and which has pointed the way forward for "operatic" writing in a non-canonical tradition. Though Giteck's musical philosophy has something in common with that of Philip Glass (she is a very different species of minimalist, though), her most immediate associations are with the avant-garde performance music of such figures as Laurie Anderson and Meredith Monk. It is clear that Giteck's use of Native American resources is far more completely assimilated that Glass's; his very popular film score for Godfrey Reggio's *Koyaanisqatsi* (based on Hopi legend) is as disruptive and pessimistic as Giteck's music seems to be redemptive and restorative. It is not, however, blandly affirmative. Her interest in the Trickster legend—as developed in *Callin' Home Coyote*—gives a wry humour to her work that keeps it on a human scale, well within reach of audiences and performers alike.

—Bea Weir

GLASS, Philip. American. Born in Baltimore, Maryland, 31 January 1937. Educated at Peabody Conservatory, Baltimore (flute lessons), 1949–52; University of Chicago, 1952–6, B.A.; Juilliard School, New York City (composition under Bergsma and Vincent Persichetti), B.A., 1959, M.A., 1961; Aspen, Colorado (under Darius Milhaud), Summer 1960; composition study under Nadia Boulanger, Paris, 1963–5; collaboration and further study with Ravi Shankar and Allah Rakha (tabla), 1965; study travel in India, North Africa, Central Asia, 1965–6. Married (1) actress JoAnne Akalaitis (marriage dissolved); (2) doctor Luba Burtyk in 1980. Composer in residence, Pittsburgh public schools, 1961–3; formed Philip Glass Ensemble, 1968; co-founder (with Klaus Kertess), Chatham Square Productions (record company),

1971; signed exclusive recording contract with CBS, 1982. Recipient: Fulbright Scholarship, 1963; Rockefeller Foundation grant, 1978; *Musical America* Musician of the Year, 1985. Mailing address: International Production Associates, 853 Broadway, Room 2120, New York, New York 10003, U.S.A.

Publishers: Peters; Dunvagen/Presser; Chester Music.

Symphonies/orchestral:

Company (orchestrated from string quartet) 1983.
Music from The Civil Wars (Cologne) (optional mixed chorus) 1984.
Dance from Akhnaten 1984.
Concerto for Violin and Orchestra 1987.
The Light (symphony) 1987.
The Canyon 1988.

Chamber/instrumental:

[Though players have changed, the Philip Glass Ensemble has usually consisted of 2 or 3 saxophones/flutes, 2 keyboards, soprano, sound diffusion.]

String Quartet 1966.
In Again Out Again (2 pianos) 1967.
Pieces in the Shape of a Square (2 flutes) 1967; first performed New York City, 19 May 1968.
Strung Out (amplified violin) 1967. Recorded Music Observations CP2.
Gradus (soprano saxophone) 1969.
How Now (piano or ensemble) 1968.
Two Pages (electric keyboards) 1968.
Music in Contrary Motion (for Philip Glass Ensemble) 1969.
Music in Eight Parts (for Philip Glass Ensemble) 1969.
Music in Fifths (for Philip Glass Ensemble) 1969; first performed New York City, 16 January 1970. Recorded Chatham Square 1003.
Music in Similar Motion (for Philip Glass Ensemble) 1969, orchestrated 1981. Recorded Chatham Square 1003.
Music with Changing Parts (for Philip Glass Ensemble) 1970; first performed New York City, 10 November 1972. Recorded Chatham Square 1001/2.
Music in Twelve Parts (for Philip Glass Ensemble) 1971–4; first complete performance New York City, 1 June 1974. Recorded, parts 1 and 2, Caroline CA 2010.
Another Look at Harmony (for Philip Glass Ensemble) 1975.
Modern Love Waltz (flute, clarinet, 2 keyboards, optional harp and vibraphone; also for piano) 1977.
Music for a Performance/Reading by C. DeJong: Fourth Series Part II (flute, harmonica) 1978.
Mad Rush: Fourth Series Part III (organ) 1979.
Dance No 2 (Fourth Series: Part II) (organ) 1979.
Dance No 4 (Fourth Series: Part IV) (organ) 1979.
Facades (2 soprano saxophones, 2 violins, viola, cello, double bass) 1981.
Glassworks (for Philip Glass Ensemble) 1981. Recorded CBS FM 37265.
Floe (flute, soprano saxophone, tenor saxophone, 2 horns, piano/DX7) 1983. Recorded CBS FM 37265.
String Quartet No 2: Company 1983.
String Quartet No 3: Mishima 1985.
String Quartet No 4: Boczak 1989.

Vocal/choral:

Knee Play No 3 (unaccompanied SATB chorus; from *Einstein on the Beach*) 1976.
Fourth Series Part I (chorus, organ) 1978.
Vessels (2 sopranos, mezzo-soprano, tenor, baritone, bass, keyboard; from *Koyaanisqatsi*) 1981.
Habeve Song (soprano, clarinet, bassoon) 1982.
Hymn to the Sun (counter-tenor, orchestra; from *Akhnaten*) 1984.
Civil Wars (Rome Section) (soprano, alto, tenor, baritone, bass, SATB chorus, orchestra) 1984.
Three Songs (unaccompanied mixed chorus) 1986.
Itaipu (chorus, orchestra) 1988.
Hydrogen Jukebox (6 vocalists, 2 synthesizers, soprano saxophone/flute, alto saxophone/soprano saxophone, 2 percussion; Ginsberg) 1990.

Opera:

Einstein on the Beach (collaboration with Robert Wilson) 1975; first performed Avignon, France, 25 July 1976. Recorded CBS Masterworks M4 388 75; Tomato 4-2901; excerpts Tom 101.
The Panther (madrigal opera) 1980.
Satyagraha (DeJong, after *Bhagavad-Gita*) 1980; first performed Rotterdam, Netherlands, 5 September 1980. Recorded CBS M3K 39672.
The Photographer (chamber opera) 1982; first performed Amsterdam, Netherlands, June 1982. Recorded CBS.
Akhnaten 1983; first performed Stuttgart, Germany, 24 March 1984. Recorded CBS M2K 42457.
The Civil Wars: "A Tree Is Best Measured When It Is Down" (music-theatre, acts 1 and 5; with Robert Wilson) 1983; first performed Rome, 22 March 1984; first concert performance, Los Angeles, November 1984.
The Juniper Tree (after Grimm) 1986.
The Making of the Representative for Planet 8 (Lessing) 1987.
The Fall of the House of Usher (Yorinks, after Poe) 1988.
1000 Airplanes on the Roof (science fiction opera; Hwang) 1988; first performed Vienna, July 1988.
The Voyage (Hwang) 1991–2; first performed New York City, 1992.

Other:

Play (incidental music to Beckett) 1965.
Red Horse Animation (incidental music) 1968.
Music for Voices (incidental music) 1972.
The Lost Ones (incidental music) 1975.
The Saint and the Football Player (incidental music) 1975.
Dressed like an Egg (incidental music) 1977. Recorded Soho News 9H001.
North Star (film score) 1977. Recorded Virgin V2085/V2141.
Cascando (incidental music) 1979.
Mercier and Camier (incidental music) 1979.
Geometry of a Circle (film score) 1979.
Dance Nos 1–5 (choreography by Lucinda Childs) 1979. Recorded, nos 1 & 3, Tomato Tom 8029.
Dead End Kids (incidental music) 1980.
Koyaanisqatsi (film score; Reggio) 1981. Recorded Antilles ASTA 1.
Glasspieces (dance pieces from *Glassworks* and *Akhnaten*; Robbins) 1983.
Company (incidental music to Beckett; string quartet) 1983, orchestrated 1983.
Pages from Cold Harbor (incidental music) 1983.

Opening and closing music, Summer Olympics, Los Angeles, 1984.
Endgame (incidental music to Beckett) 1984; first performed New York City, 4 December 1984.
Mishima (film score; string quartet) 1985.
A Descent into the Maelstrom (dance-theatre; Molissa Fenley and Matthew Maguire, after Poe) 1986.
Songs from Liquid Days (album of collaborative pop songs) 1986.
Powaqqatsi (film score) 1987.
In the Upper Room (dance consisting of *Dance Pieces 1, 2, 5, 8 and 9*; Twyla Tharp) 1987; first performed New York City, 1987. Recorded CBS MK 39539.
The Thin Blue Line (film score; docudrama by Morris) 1988.

PUBLICATIONS

By Glass: with C. DeJong, *Satyagraha: M. K. Gandhi in South Africa, 1893–1914: The Historical Material and Libretto Comprising the Opera's Book*, New York, 1980.

On Glass: Michael Nyman, "Steve Reich, PG" in *Musical Times*, 112, 1971; D. Smith, "The Music of PG", in *Contact*, 11, 1975; Keith Potter, (interview) in *Contact*, 12, 1976; Walter Zimmerman, (interview) in *Desert Plants: Conversations with Twenty-Three American Musicians*, Vancouver, 1976; D. Bither, "PG: An Avant-Garde Composer for the '80s", in *Horizon*, 23(3), 1980; Wim Mertens, in *Amerikaanse repitieve muziek*, Bierbeek, 1980, translated as *American Minimal Music: LaMonte Young, Terry Riley, Steve Reich, PG*, New York, 1983; W. York, "Form and Process in *Two Pages* of PG", in *Sonus*, 1(2), 1981; C. Gagne and T. Caras, (interview) in *Soundpieces: Interviews with American Composers*, Metuchen, New Jersey, 1982; John Rockwell, "The Orient, the Visual Arts and the Evolution of Minimalism: PG", in *All-American Music: Composition in the Late 20th Century*, New York, 1983; many press articles, reviews and interviews.

* * *

Philip Glass has always been viewed with a degree of suspicion by the classical music establishment, and even more so by the operatic one, but the composer has found a level of popular acceptance for his work arguably unmatched by any other serious contemporary composer.

The roots of his repetitive, minimalist style were laid in Paris in 1965, where Glass had gone, as many American composers before him, to study with Nadia Boulanger. There, he had the opportunity to work with the Indian musicians Ravi Shankar and Allah Rahka, and learned seminal lessons about the possibilities of structuring music not through traditional Western harmonic methods, but by rhythmic cycles.

Although some early music in more conventional style was published, Glass later withdrew everything which pre-dated his conversion to what came to be known as Minimalism. The first period of this style extended until *Einstein on the Beach* in 1975, and is characterised by a series of works which apply this principle of structure-by-rhythm, often at considerable length.

The overlapping and interweaving of these rhythmic structures, and the almost total lack of harmonic development, lend the music a slow, curiously hypnotic effect, but can also produce passages of great drama, a factor which the composer has put to use in film soundtrack music. *Koyaanisqatsi* and *Mishima* are his best works in that genre.

If Glass's musical preoccupations, shared though they were by the likes of La Monte Young, Terry Riley and Steve Reich, were unorthodox, his formation of the Philip Glass Ensemble in 1968 to perform his music was equally so. That unorthodoxy increased when the composer added sound engineer Kurt Munkasci as part of the onstage performance in 1970.

It is not the least of the composer's achievements that he has succeeded not only in setting up a working band (he himself is a member) along the lines of a rock group, but has arranged both performance and publishing rights in a similar fashion, so that promotors found themselves paying a licensing fee to the Ensemble for the right to have his compositions, which he had licensed to the group, performed in their concerts.

Although he has written a fair amount of concert music, Glass has arguably won most recognition for his work in dance, film, music theatre and opera. His towering, cyclic scores lend themselves particularly well to the gradual unfolding of music theatre and opera, and his works in those categories are already winning the unusual distinction of entering the repertory.

The first of these major works, *Einstein on the Beach*, a mixed-media piece written with Robert Wilson, also signalled what was to become the main thrust of Glass's subsequent work. Up until then, the composer concentrated almost entirely on musical development through gradual changes in rhythmic structures, but subsequently he has paid much more attention to harmonic development, and on combining harmonic and rhythmic structure into a unified whole.

If *Einstein*, like *1000 Airplanes on the Roof*, is essentially a music theatre piece, both *Satyagraha*, based on the life of Gandhi, and the ancient Egyptian epic *Akhnaten* are genuine operas. By the time of their composition, Glass was heavily involved in exploring a return to tonality, but through the development of a polytonal music, in which the music implies a tonal centre, one which suggests more than a single possible tonal reading at any given time.

Other operas include *The Fall of the House of Usher* and an adaptation of Doris Lessing's *The Making of the Representative for Planet 8*. A new opera, *The Voyage*, was scheduled to be the Metropolitan Opera House's contribution to the 1992 celebrations of Columbus's voyage to America.

Unusually for a composer, Glass has a long-established policy of working in collaboration with artists from the visual arts and writing as well as theatre and music, a tendency which the composer himself feels has had a profound effect on his approach to music. He is, too, very much the kind of composer who works from subject matter rather than abstract musical ideas.

Glass successfully circumvented another frustration common to contemporary composers by signing a contract to record exclusively for Columbia Records. This example of his rock-oriented business acumen ensured his work would be copiously recorded and widely available, including a less than wholly successful album of pop songs, *Songs from Liquid Days*, which featured lyrics by such luminaries as Paul Simon, David Byrne and Laurie Anderson.

Ironically, his final album for the label, *Solo Piano*, has been widely regarded as a contractual filler, but is actually one of his most pleasing recordings, and makes a fine first taste of his work. Glass's music is certain to remain the subject of artistic controversy, but he is undoubtedly one of the best-known of all current composers, and has taken his music to audiences well beyond the reach of most of his contemporaries.

—Kenny Mathieson

GLOBOKAR, Vinko. French and Yugoslav. Born in Anderny, France, 7 July 1934. Educated at Ljubljana Conservatoire (trombone), 1949–54; Conservatoire National Supérieur de Musique, Paris, 1955–9; studied composition privately under René Leibowitz, 1959–63, and under Luciano Berio, 1965. Married Tatjana Kristan, 27 June 1964; 2 sons. Professor, Kölner Musik Hochschule, Cologne, 1968–76; head of department for vocal and instrumental research, IRCAM, Paris, 1976–80; professor, Scuola di Musica di Fiesole Florence, 1984–1990. Recipient: 1st prize for trombone and chamber music, Conservatoire National Supérieur de Musique, Paris, 1959; DAAD Fellowship, Berlin, 1964/65; 1st prize in radio competition, Belgrade, Yugoslavia, 1968; 1st prize Gaudeamus (composition) in Holland, 1968. Mailing address: 2 rue Pierre et Marie Curie, 75005 Paris, France.

Publishers: C.F. Peters; Ricordi.

Symphonies/orchestral:

Etude pour Folklora II (orchestra doubling folk instruments) 1968; first performed Frankfurt, 26 August 1968. Recorded Deutsche Grammophon avant garde 2561 108.

Concerto grosso (5 solo instruments—woodwind/brass/percussion/keyboard/string, amplified recorder, oboe, 2 clarinets, saxophone, bassoon, horn, trumpet, flugelhorn, 2 trombones, tuba, 3 percussion, electric guitar, harp, violin, viola, 2 cellos, double bass, tapes) 1969–75; first performed Cologne, 6 November 1970.

La tromba e mobile (1 or more wind orchestras, percussion) 1970; first performed Zagreb, 17 May 1979.

Ausstrahlungen (oboe or clarinet or bassoon or saxophone, small orchestra) 1971; first performed Royan, 8 April 1971. Recorded BASF EA 291 812.

Das Orchester 1974; first performed Bonn, 1 December 1974.

Der Käfig (chamber orchestra, improvising soloist) 1980; first performed Lugano, 7 February 1980.

Chamber/instrumental:

Plan (zarb, bass clarinet, tenor saxophone, flugelhorn, trombone) 1965; first performed Berlin, 16 June 1965.

Fluide (3 horns, 2 trumpets, flugelhorn, 2 trombones, tuba, 3 percussion) 1967; first performed Paris, 24 April 1967. Recorded BASF EA 291 812.

Discours I (trombone, 4 percussion) 1967; withdrawn.

Discours II (5 trombones or trombone and tape) 1967–8; first performed Cologne, 5 February 1968. Recorded Aulos 53532.

Etude pour folklora I (2 flutes/dvojnice; oboe/dvojnice, 3 clarinets/1 dvojnice, horn, trumpet, flugelhorn, trombone, tuba, 3 percussion, electric guitar/tambura, electric organ, viola/gusli, double bass) 1968; first performed Royan, 9 April 1968.

Discours III (5 oboes or oboe and tape) 1969; first performed Darmstadt, 29 August 1969. Recorded Aulos-Preciosa PRE 68517 AUL.

Correspondences (4 soloists: percussion and woodwind, brass or harmony instruments) 1969; first performed Berlin, 18 April 1969. Recorded BASF DC 218 031.

La Ronde (any number of melody instruments) 1970; first performed Berlin, 25 April 1970. Recorded Free Music Production, 1978.

Drama (piano, percussion, electronics) 1971; first performed Graz, 25 October 1971. Recorded BASF DC 218 031.

Atemstudie (oboe) 1972; first performed Stuttgart, 3 March 1972. Recorded BASF EA 291 812.

Vendre le vent (flute, oboe, clarinet, bassoon, saxophone, horn, trumpet, trombone, tuba, percussion, piano) 1972; first performed La Rochelle, 13 April 1973.

Notes (pianist) 1972; first performed Toronto, 22 May 1973.

Echanges (brass solo) 1973; first performed La Rochelle, 20 April 1973. Recorded Harmonia mundi Electrola 1C 065 99712.

Discours IV (3 clarinets) 1973–4; first performed Bremen, 4 May 1974. Recorded Harmonia mundi Electrola 1C 065 99712.

Limites (violin or viola) 1973; first performed Darmstadt, 30 July 1974. Recorded Thorofon MTH 180 66.21778.

Res/As/Ex/Ins-pirer (solo brass) 1973; first performed Tokyo, 6 March 1974. Recorded Harmonia mundi Electrola 1C 065 99712.

Toucher (percussionist/speaker) 1973; first performed Neheim-Husten, 23 November 1973. Recorded Aulos Preciosa PRE 68517 AUL.

Voix instrumentalisée (bass clarinet) 1973; first performed Neheim-Husten, 23 November 1973.

Laboratorium (incorporates *Toucher*, *Limites*, *?Corporel*, *Voix instrumentalisée*, *Echanges*, *Res/As/Ex/Ins-pirer*) 1973–85; first version performed Donaueschingen, 19 October 1973.

Dédoublement (clarinet) 1975; first performed Witten, 27 April 1975.

Monolith (flute) 1976; first performed Warsaw, 20 October 1976.

Koexistenz (1 or 2 cellos) 1976; first performed New York City, 30 October 1982.

Vorstellung (solo instrumentalist: string/woodwind/brass, film) 1976.

Pre-Occupation (organ, tape) 1980; first performed Munich, 16 May 1980.

Tribadabum extensif sur rythme fantôme (3 percussionists or percussion trio and unspecified number of additional percussionists) 1981; first performed Romans, 7 July 1981.

Discours V (4 saxophones) 1981; first performed London, 12 September 1981.

Discours VI (string quartet) 1982; first performed Witten, 23 April 1982. Recorded Aulos Preciosa PRE 685 17 Aul.

?Corporel (percussionist's own body) 1983; first performed Paris, 14 November 1984.

Introspection d'un tubiste (tuba, electronic diffusion, tape, lights, scenery) 1983; first performed Avignon, France, 25 July 1983.

Cri des Alpes (alphorn) 1986; first performed Helsinki, 4 December 1986.

Discours VII (brass quintet) 1987; first performed Florence, 14 November 1988.

Freu(n)de (6 cellos) 1987; first performed Graz, 22 October 1987.

Dos à dos (2 players) 1988; first performed Cologne, 24 January 1988.

Discours VIII (wind quintet) 1989; first performed Witten, 22 April 1989.

Ombre (percussionist, rhythm machine) 1989; first performed Tokyo, 27 May 1989.

Kvadrat (percussion quartet) 1989; first performed Lerchenborg, 28 July 1989.

Vocal/choral:

Accord (soprano, flute, trombone, cello, electric organ, percussion) 1966; first performed Berlin, 1 October 1966. Recorded Wergo WER 329.

Voie (3 choirs, orchestra, speaker) 1966; first performed

Zagreb, 16 May 1967. Recorded Aulos Preciosa PRE 68517 AUL; RTV LD 0803.
Traumdeutung (4 choirs, celeste, harp, vibraphone, guitar; version for 48 voices) 1967; first performed Rotterdam, 7 October 1968.
Airs de voyages vers l'intérieur (8 voices, clarinet, trombone, electronics) 1972; first performed Stuttgart, 3 November 1972. Recorded RTV LD 0803; Aulos 53577.
Un Jour comme un autre (soprano, cello, contrabass clarinet, percussion, tuba, electric guitar) 1975–85; first performed Metz, 21 November 1975.
Carrousel (4 singers, flute, 2 clarinets, saxophone, bassoon, horn, tuba, harp, guitar, accordion, electric organ, violin, viola, 2 cellos, double bass) 1976; first performed Zagreb, 11 May 1977.
Standpunkte (soloists, instrumental ensemble, choir, orchestra) 1977; first performed Donaueschingen, 22 October 1977.
Jenseits der Sicherheit (voice) 1981; first performed Bourges, 9 June 1981.
Miserere (orchestra, 5 narrators, jazz trio) 1982; first performed Cologne, 27 November 1982.
Les Emigrés (triptych consisting of *Miserere*, *Realities*, *Sternbild der Grenze*) 1982–7; first complete performance Bonn, 27 October 1987.
Realities (Augenblicke) (5 singers, tape, film, slide projection) 1984; first performed Paris, 4 June 1984.
Sternbild der Grenze (orchestra, baritone, alto, 5 singers, puppet show; Handke) 1985; first performed Metz, 21 November 1985.
Hallo, Do You Hear Me? (choir, symphony orchestra, jazz quintet) 1986; first performed simultaneously in Helsinki, Stockholm and Oslo, 9 March 1987.
Kolo (choir, trombone) 1988; first performed Cologne, 27 November 1988.

PUBLICATIONS

By Globokar: "Vom Reagieren", in *Melos*, February 1971; "Ils improvisent, improvisez, improvisons" in *Musique en jeu*, 6; "Der kreative Interpret", in *Melos*, February 1976; "Engagement Statt Schonheit", in *Noema*, 1, 1984; "Introspection eines Tubisten", in *Zeitschrift für experimentelle Musik*, January 1986; *VDIH <–> IZDIH*, Ljubljana, 1987; "Anti-Babadum", in *Neue Zeitschrift*, 3 March 1989; "Om det individuelle eller det kollektiev", in *Dansk Tidsskrift*, 5, 1989–90.

On Globokar: Klaus Henning Bachmann, "Eine Ahnung des *Morgen*", Wiesbaden, 1971; Wolfgang König, "Komposition und Improvisation", Wiesbaden, 1977; Marc Leman, "Niewe Techniken, Niewe Geluiden", dissertation, Rijksuniversitat Gent, 1980; Berthold Kloss, "Gesellschaftliches Engagement Kompositorischen VG", dissertation, Justus-Liebig Universität Giessen, 1982; John-Joseph Bingham, "The Innovative Uses of the Trombone in Selected Compositions of VG", dissertation, University of Illinois, Urbana, 1984.

* * *

Vinko Globokar seemed to emerge from nowhere as a composer. The 32-year-old trombone soloist's first published work had all the hallmarks of a fully mature compositional style and his later work represented a germination of elements already visible in *Voie*: the use of political references and texts (here, Mayakovsky's "October" poem); the synchronised use of alternative translations of a text; extraordinary treatment of voices and instruments; division and recombination of choir and orchestra; and finally an ambiguous title. "Voie" means path or track, but the homonym "voix" indicates voice or an expression of surprise.

As an experienced instrumentalist and magnificent improviser, Globokar seemed predestined to contribute to the musical development of the 1960s, notably the broadening of performance techniques and forms. His contribution, which could almost be regarded as acoustic research and which, as such, probably derives from Varèse, could most accurately be described as "conversion". For instance, in the course of performance a clarinet is broken down into its constituent sections, turning into a child's whistle, and an alpine horn with a trumpet mouthpiece. A wind player is instructed to play so continuously and without pausing for breath as to give the effect of strings. This all occurs in individual pieces of the appropriately named cycle *Laboratorium*. However, the overturning of technical performance conventions forms only one part of a radical process of thought that pushes back all musical, aesthetic and mental boundaries.

In addition to a short period with Luciano Berio, Globokar studied principally with René Leibowitz. In the Paris of the 1950s, he became involved with the intellectual set which included such figures as Jacques Lacan, Michel Leiris, Lévi-Strauss, Maurice Merleau-Ponty and Jean-Paul Sartre. Globokar's integration of ethnology, mythology, psychology and philosophy into his compositional thinking dates back to that time, leading to a concept of performance which absorbs the totality of experience. There is evidence of this in pieces such as *Traumdeutung*, a psychodrama for four choirs and four instrumentalists, *Concerto grosso*, a hybrid concerto/cantata in which, among other things, the players have to "translate" animal noises and transform them into music, *Das Orchester*, which deals with the mechanism of the supremacy of music, *Un Jour comme un autre*, a piece about torture, or a large triptych on emigration called *Les Emigrés* consisting of prose montage parts set to music and an accompanied slide montage and stage play. Globokar's communicative and deeply psychological main themes are evident throughout his 55 individual pieces, while the variously casted chamber ensembles that comprise the *Discours* cycle suggest something of his range.

In keeping with his extraordinarily free thinking, Globokar has used all conceivable means in his works, according to their particular conception: orchestral and folk instruments, tools, computers or children's toys, television sets and welding equipment—nothing is excluded out of hand. As with "happenings", performance instructions are sometimes not set out in detail. For the most part, though, Globokar's works are thoroughly "composed" on the basis of serial technique in a strict, sometimes rigid systematic manner (in *Miserere* the orchestra approximates the unchanging, fettered life of the emigré), but with echoes of an almost Ives-like freedom.

Globokar, however, has never set great store by "works of art". In Brechtian tradition, only the utility value of a pieces is important to him. His status is therefore due not only to that set of ensemble pieces which by virtue of their ingenious tone and uncompromising place in contemporary music approach canonical status, but also to his modern, rational, anti-regressive clarity. He is the great outsider in contemporary music, lying beyond all schools and fashions. From that position, though, he has recognized all the more keenly that music as art is interwoven with all aspects of human existence and that its roots lie elsewhere than in the conservatory.

—Werner Klüppelholz
(translated by Eleanor Caldwell)

GOEHR, (Peter) Alexander. British/English. Born in Berlin, 10 August 1932. Educated at Royal Manchester College of Music (under Hall), 1952–5; further study with Oliver Messiaen and Yvonne Loriod, Paris, 1955–6. Lecturer, Morley College, London, 1955–7; music assistant, BBC, 1960–8; Winston Churchill Trust Fellow, 1968; composer in residence, New England Conservatory, Boston, 1968–9; associate professor of music, Yale University, New Haven, Connecticut, 1969–70; West Riding professor of music, University of Leeds, 1971–6; artistic director, Leeds Festival, 1975; professor of music, University of Cambridge, since 1976; visiting profesor, Peking Conservatoire of Music, 1980; member, board of directors, Royal Opera House, 1982–7. Recipient: honorary fellow, Royal Academy of Music, 1975, Royal Northern College of Music, 1980, and Royal College of Music, 1981; honorary D.Mus., University of Southampton, 1973. Mailing address: The Gables, Swaffham Prior, Cambridge, Cambridgeshire, England.

Publisher: Schott.

Symphonies/orchestral:

Fantasia Op 4 1954, revised 1959; first performed Darmstadt, Summer 1956.
Hecuba's Lament Op 12 1959–61; first performed London, August 1961.
Violin Concerto Op 13 1961–2; first performed Cheltenham, Gloucestershire, 1962. Recorded HMV ASD 2810.
Little Symphony Op 15 1963; first performed York, 1963. Recorded Philips SAL 3497.
Little Music for Strings Op 16 1963; first performed Lucerne, 1963.
Pastorals Op 19 1965; first performed Donaueschingen, 1965.
Three Pieces from Arden Must Die Op 21a (wind band, harp, percussion) 1967; broadcast BBC Radio 3, 12 January 1979; first concert performance London, 16 January 1969.
Romanza Op 24 (cello, orchestra) 1968; first performed Brighton, Sussex, 1968. Recorded Unicorn DKP 9017; UKCD 2039.
Konzertstück Op 26 (piano, small orchestra) 1969; first performed Sydney, April 1969.
Symphony in One Movement Op 29 1969, revised 1981; first performed London, 19 May 1970.
Piano Concerto Op 33 1972; first performed Brighton, Sussex, 14 May 1972.
Metamorphosis/Dance Op 36 1973–4; first performed London, 17 November 1974. Recorded Unicorn DKP 9017; UKCD 2039.
Fugue on the Notes of the Fourth Psalm Op 38b (string orchestra) 1976; first performed London, 8 July 1976.
Romanza on the Notes of the Fourth Psalm Op 38c (2 violins, 2 violas, string orchestra) 1977; first performed Glasgow, February 1978.
Sinfonia Op 42 (chamber orchestra) 1979; first performed London, 20 November 1980. Recorded Unicorn Kanchana DKPCD 9012.
Deux Etudes Op 43 1980–1; first performed Glasgow, 17 September 1981.
Symphony with Chaconne Op 48 1985–6; first performed Manchester, 13 January 1987.
Still Lands (3 pieces for small orchestra; based on "Summer Is Icumen In", Schubert's "Ins Stille Land", Schumann's "Freundliche Landschaft") 1988–90.

Chamber/instrumental:

Sonata Op 2 (piano) 1951–2; first performed London, 1952. Recorded HMV ASD 645.
Fantasias Op 3 (A clarinet, piano) 1954; first performed London, January 1956.
String Quartet No 1 Op 5 1956–7, revised 1988; first performed Dartingon, Devon, 1959; first performance of revised version, London, 15 June 1988.
Capriccio Op 6 (piano) 1957; first performed Cologne, April 1958. Recorded Auracle Records AUC 1005.
Variations Op 8 (flute, piano) 1959; first performed Hovingham, Yorkshire, June 1959.
Suite Op 11 (flute, clarinet, horn, harp, violin/viola, cello) 1961; first performed Aldeburgh, Suffolk, 1961.
Three Pieces Op 18 (piano) 1964; first performed London, 11 April 1965. Recorded HMV ASD 2551.
Piano Trio Op 20 (violin, cello, piano) 1966; first performed Bath, Avon, June 1966. Recorded Argo ZRG 748.
String Quartet No 2 Op 23 1967; first performed Bristol, October 1967.
Nonomiya Op 27 (piano) 1969; first performed Macclesfield, Yorkshire, 12 May 1969. Recorded Auracle Records AUC 1005.
Paraphrase on the Dramatic Madrigal "Il Combattimento di Tancredi e Clorinda" by Monteverdi Op 28 (clarinet) 1969; first performed Edinburgh, 1969. Recorded L'Oiseau Lyre DSLO 1.
Concerto for Eleven Op 32 (flute, 2 oboes, 2 trumpets, tuba, percussion, 2 violins, viola, double bass) 1970; broadcast Belgium, 25 January 1971.
Chaconne for Wind Op 34 (2 flutes, 2 oboes, cor anglais, 2 clarinets/1 E♭, 2 bassoons, contrabassoon, 2 horns, 3 trumpets, 3 trombones) 1974; first performed Leeds, 3 November 1974.
Lyric Pieces Op 35 (flute, oboe, clarinet, bassoon, horn, trumpet, trombone, double bass) 1974; first performed London, 15 November 1974. Recorded Unicorn Kanchana DKPCD 9102.
String Quartet No 3 Op 37 1975–6; first performed London, 28 June 1976. Recorded Wergo WER 60093.
Prelude and Fugue Op 39 (3 clarinets) 1978; first performed Edinburgh, September 1978.
Chaconne for Organ Op 34a (organ; transcription of *Chaconne for Wind*) 1979; first performed Edinburgh, 1979.
Sonata Op 45 (cello, piano) 1984; broadcast BBC, 1986.
. . . A Musical Offering (J.S.B. 1985) . . . Op 46 (flute, 2 clarinets/bass clarinet, horn, trumpet in C, trombone, percussion, piano, 3 violins, 2 violas, double bass) 1985; first performed Edinburgh, 19 August 1985. Recorded Unicorn Kanchana DKPCD 9102.
. . . In Real Time Op 50 (piano cycle) 1989—in progress; first performed, in part, New York City, 11 November 1989; further pieces to be performed Southampton, 1992.
String Quartet No 4 Op 52 1990; first performed Iowa, 8 October 1990.
Variations on Bach's Sarabande from the English Suite in E minor (2 clarinets, 2 alto saxophones, 2 bassoons, 2 trumpets, trombone, timpani) 1990.

Vocal/choral:

Songs of Babel Op 1 (voice, piano) 1951.
The Deluge Op 7 (soprano, contralto, flute, horn, trumpet, harp, violin, viola, cello, double bass; Da Vinci) 1957–8; first performed London, February 1959.
Four Songs from the Japanese Op 9 (high voice, piano or

orchestra; from Lafcadio Hearn) 1959; orchestral version first performed Cheltenham, Gloucestershire, 1960. Recorded Pye GSGC 14105.

Sutter's Gold Op 10 (bass, mixed chorus, orchestra; after Eisenstein) 1959–60; first performed Leeds, Yorkshire, 1961.

Two Choruses Op 14 (unaccompanied mixed chorus; Milton, Shakespeare) 1962; first performed London, November 1962. Recorded HMV ASD 640.

A Little Cantata of Proverbs 1962.

Virtutes (9 songs and melodramas for speaker, mixed chorus, 2 clarinets ad lib, timpani, percussion, 2 pianos, organ, cello ad lib) 1963; first performed Whitley, Surrey, May 1963.

Five Poems and an Epigram of William Blake Op 17 (mixed chorus, trumpet) 1964; first performed London, 1964.

Warngedichte Op 22 (low voice, piano; Fried) 1966–7; first performed New York City, 1967.

Psalm 4 Op 38a (soprano, alto, female chorus, viola, organ) 1976; first performed London, 8 July 1976.

Babylon the Great Is Fallen Op 40 (chorus, orchestra) 1979; first performed London, 12 December 1979.

Das Gesetz der Quadrille / The Law of the Quadrille Op 41 (low voice, piano; Kafka) 1979; first performed Norwich, Norfolk, 18 October 1979. Recorded Wergo WER 60093.

Behold the Sun Op 44a (concert aria from the opera; soprano, instrumental ensemble) 1981. Recorded Unicorn Kanchana DKPCD 9102.

Two Imitations of Baudelaire Op 47 (unaccompanied mixed chorus; Lowell) 1985; first performed (part only), Southampton, 1985; first complete performance London, 29 June 1987.

Eve Dreams in Paradise Op 49 (mezzo-soprano, tenor, orchestra) 1987–8; first performed Birmingham, 14 March 1989.

Carol for St Steven (mixed chorus) 1989; first performed Cambridge, 24 December 1989.

Sing, Ariel Op 51 (principal mezzo-soprano, 2 sopranos, tenor saxophone / bass clarinet, trumpet, piano, violin / viola, double bass; Kermode) 1989–90; first performed Aldeburgh, Suffolk, 23 June 1990. Recorded Unicorn Kanchana, 1992.

Opera / dramatic:

Arden Muss Sterben / Arden Must Die Op 21 (Fried, after *Arden of Faversham*) 1966; first performance Hamburg, 5 March 1967.

Naboth's Vineyard Op 25 (1st part of *Music Theatre Triptych*; mezzo-soprano, tenor, bass, flute / piccolo, clarinet / bass clarinet, bass trombone, piano, 4 hands—violin, double bass; after I Kings XXI) 1968; first performed London, 16 July 1968.

Shadowplay Op 30 (2nd part of *Music Theatre Triptych*; tenor, speaker, alto flute, alto saxophone, horn, piano, cello; Cavander, after Plato) 1970; first performed London, 8 July 1970.

Sonata About Jerusalem Op 31 (bass, soprano, female chorus or soprano and 2 contraltos, boy's voice, flute / piccolo, clarinet / bass clarinet, horn, trumpet, bass trombone, piano, violin, cello, double bass, oriental or Indian bells played by singers; Obadiah the Proselyte, Samuel de Yahya ben al Maghribi, adapted by AG and Recha Freier) 1970; first performed Tel Aviv, January 1971.

Behold the Sun / Die Wiedertaufer Op 44 (opera in 3 acts; McGrath, AG) 1981–4; first performed Duisburg, Germany, 19 April 1985.

Other:

La Belle Dame sans merci (ballet; large or small orchestra) 1958; first performed Edinburgh, 1958.

PUBLICATIONS

On Goehr: Bayan Northcott (ed.), *The Music of AG: Interviews and Articles*, London, 1980; Paul Griffiths, (interview) in *New Sounds, New Personalities: British Composers of the 1980s*, London, 1985.

* * *

While the oeuvres of some composers show distinct breaks and stylistic shifts, Alexander Goehr's music has evolved in a slow, continuous metamorphosis beginning with what some have called the anonymous international style of the early 1950s and eventually shifting toward the increasingly harmonic simplicity of modally influenced music.

Goehr is widely recognised as one of the most prominent of the older generation of British post-war composers. Several published interviews provide valuable insight into his music and compositional processes. Goehr looks upon his own career as a gradual evolution, emphasizing continuity in the midst of change: "I never liked calling myself a serialist when I worked with twelve-tone technique and I would not wish to call myself a tonal composer now. I think this very terminology distorts things. I have not 'seen the light' as far as I know. I think there is a step by step continuity between what one has done and what one does now."

A member of the Manchester group and a student of Messiaen, Goehr acknowledges Schoenberg as his most pervasive influence. "I've admired other composers, especially my teacher Messiaen, but I really felt I belonged to the Schoenbergian family, as if I were a relative (a poor one perhaps). I perpetually walk on tracks. I read books, something catches my interest and suddenly I come across a reference to the fact that Schoenberg had been interested in the same thing. Consequently, there can be for me no thought of throwing off this powerful love and influence upon my life."

If Goehr feels part of the Schoenbergian family, Schoenberg was certainly part of Goehr's family. His father, the conductor Walter Goehr, was a composition student of Schoenberg's, who passed this legacy on to his son. Alexander Goehr's early music, for example the piano *Sonata Op 2*, displays the strong influence of the second Viennese school. His studies of medieval music and his work with Messaien resulted in an interest in modifying, but not abandoning, twelve-tone technique. In the mid-1960s, he developed a modal twelve-tone method that can be heard in such pieces as *Metamorphosis / Dance* and *Romanza* for cello and orchestra. More recent works such as the opera *Behold the Sun* incorporate modal, tonal and serial areas, thus creating dramatic tension through the juxtaposition of the characteristic sounds of each of these harmonic techniques. Goehr has related this compositional concept to the late works of Debussy, but not without a nod to Schoenberg: "[O]ne of the legacies of my father and of his Schoenbergian world was to use music of the past and present as a direct inspiration."

Goehr consciously appropriates and transforms formal strategies, procedures and conventions. Aptly describing himself as "a kind of musical thief [who does] the analysis for the plunder", he uses the past as a model, as an inspiration, and as a foil for his own harmonic and formal explorations.

One of his principal concerns is clarity of formal procedure. Unlike many of his contemporaries, Goehr does not shy away from using literal repeats of larger sections. This can be heard in the second movement of the third string quartet. He has also written themes and variations such as the Op 20 piano trio. Many of his pieces rely upon a dialectic created by the statement of a musical idea, variations upon it, then the statement of its antithesis. This dialectic strategy does not invariably result in the anticipated synthesis. For example, *Concerto for Eleven* alludes to Beethoven's *Piano Sonata in A major* by creating the expectation of a climactic finale, then foils this expectation through the placement of a reprise of the opening material in its stead.

Metamorphosis / Dance inverts the temporal structure of Beethoven's *Sonata Op 111*. Beethoven produces the accelerating pace in the beginning of this sonata by decreasing the length of the note values used while the underlying tempo remains the same, then reversing the procedure in the second half. Goehr reverses this technique. He decelerates the pace in the beginning of *Metamorphosis / Dance* by increasing the length of the note values, then accelerates in the second half.

The kind of play with anticipation and the thwarting of expectations that is found in the structure of Goehr's music is also a theme in many of the texts that he has set. Works such as *Behold the Sun*, *Shadowplay* and *Sonata About Jerusalem* focus on shattered hopes and human illusion—the cruelty and indifference that is part of the existential condition and the pain and pleasure provoked by the survival of hope against all odds.

While Goehr's work is grounded in tradition, he avoids the pitfalls of self-conscious pastiche or neo-academicism. He explains that his interest in the "common material" of the musical tradition involves "refinding methods of composing such materials from the past, such as figured bass techniques—though not . . . in any historical or stylistic sense. Ultimately the same rule applies to every artist; he has got to find something new."

—R. Peter Mueller and Rachel Myers

GÓRECKI, Henryk (Mikołaj). Polish. Born in Czernica, near Rybnik, Silesia, 6 December 1933. Primary school teacher, from 1951; student, Intermediate School of Music, Rybnik, 1953–4; State Higher School of Music, Katowice (composition under Boleslaw Szabelski), 1955–60; further study in Paris. Married Jadwiga Górecki in 1959; 2 children. Serious illness, 1973–4; recurs 1984–5. Docent, faculty of composition, and rector, from 1975, resigns in protest, 1979, and extraordinary professor, since 1977, State Higher School of Music, Katowice. Recipient: 1st prize (for *Monologhi*), Youth Competition, Polish Composers' Union, 1960; 1st prize (for *Symphony "1959"*), Youth Biennale, Paris, 1961; award of the Ministry of Culture and Fine Arts, Poland, 1965, 1969, 1973; 1st prize (for *Cantata*), Szczecin Composers' Competition, 1968; award of the Polish Composers' Union, 1970; 1st prize (for *Ad Matrem*), UNESCO International Composers' Rostrum, Paris, 1973; State Award of the First Degree (for *Ad matrem* and *Copernican Symphony*), 1976. Mailing address: Ul Feliksa Kona 4, m.1, 40–133 Katowice, Poland.

Publisher: Boosey & Hawkes.

Symphonies / orchestral:

Songs of Joy and Rhythm Op 7 (2 pianos, chamber orchestra) 1956–60; first performed Katowice, 27 February 1958.
Symphony No 1 "1959" Op 14 (string orchestra, percussion) 1959; first performed (minus "Antifonia" section) Warsaw, 1959.
Scontri / Collisions Op 17 1960; first performed Warsaw, 1960.
Three Pieces in the Old Style (string orchestra) 1963. Recorded Schwann 11615.
Choros I Op 20 (strings) 1964.
Refrain Op 21 1965; first performed Geneva, 1965.
Old Polish Music Op 24 (brass, strings) 1969.
Canticum graduum Op 27 1969; first performed Dusseldorf, 1967.
Symphony No 2 "Copernican" Op 31 (soprano, baritone, mixed choir, large orchestra; Psalms 145, 135, Copernicus) 1972; first performed Warsaw, 1973.
Three Dances Op 34 1973.
Symphony No 3: Symphony of Lamentation Songs Op 36 (soprano, large orchestra; old Polish religious and folk texts, translated Lisowski and Szewczyk) 1976; first performed Royan, France, 1977. Recorded Schwann 11615; Erato MCE 9275.
Harpsichord Concerto Op 40 (harpsichord or piano, string orchestra) 1980.

Chamber / instrumental:

Four Preludes Op 1 (piano) 1955.
Toccata Op 2 (2 pianos) 1955.
Variations Op 4 (violin, piano) 1956.
Quartettino Op 5 (2 flutes, oboe, violin) 1956.
Sonata No 1 Op 6 (piano) 1956, revised 1990.
Sonatina in One Movement Op 8 (violin, piano) 1956.
Lullaby Op 9 (piano) 1956.
From the Bird's Nest Op 9a (5 little preludes for piano) 1956.
Sundry Pieces Op 52 (piano) 1956–90.
Sonata Op 10 (2 violins) 1957.
Concerto for Five Instruments and String Quartet Op 11 (flute, clarinet, xylophone, mandolin, string quartet) 1957.
Five Pieces Op 13 (2 pianos) 1959.
Three Diagrams Op 15 (flute) 1959.
Diagram IV Op 18 (flute) 1961.
Genesis I: Elementi Op 19 No 1 (string trio) 1962.
Genesis II: Canti strumentali Op 19 No 2 (piccolo, flute, trumpet, mandolin, guitar, piano—4 hands, 2 percussion, 3 violins, 3 violas) 1962.
Muzyczka II / La Musiquette 2ème Op 23 (4 trumpets, 4 trombones, 2 pianos, percussion) 1967.
Muzyczka III / La Musiquette 3ème Op 25 (violas, any number, divided equally among parts) 1967.
Cantata (organ) 1968.
Muzyczka IV / La Musiquette 4ème Op 28 (clarinet, trombone, cello, piano) 1970.
Three Little Pieces Op 37 (violin, piano) 1977.
Mazurkas Op 41 (piano) 1980.
Lullabies and Dances Op 47 (violin, piano) 1982.
Recitatives and Ariosos—Lerchenmusik Op 53 (clarinet, cello, piano) 1984–6.
For You, Anne-Lill Op 58 (flute, piano) 1986–90.
Aria Op 59 (tuba, piano, tam-tam, bass drum) 1987.
Already It Is Dusk (String Quartet No 1) Op 62 1988.

Vocal / choral:

Three Songs Op 3 (medium voice, piano) 1956.

Epitafium/Epitaph Op 12 (mixed choir, piccolo, trumpet in D, 5 percussion, viola; Tuwin) 1958.
Monologhi Op 16 (soprano, 3 instrumental groups: 2 harps, glockenspiel, vibraphone, marimba; 6 suspended cymbals/ 3 players; 3 tam-tams, 3 gongs/2 players) 1960.
Genesis III: Monodrama Op 19 No 3 (soprano, metal percussion, 6 double basses) 1963.
Ad matrem Op 29 (soprano, mixed choir, orchestra; Latin) 1971.
Two Sacred Songs Op 30 (baritone, orchestra; Skwarnicki) 1971.
Euntes ibant et flebant Op 32 (unaccompanied mixed choir; Psalms 125, 94) 1971.
Two Little Songs Op 33 (4 equal voices; Tuwim) 1972.
Amen Op 35 (unaccompanied mixed choir) 1975.
Beatus vir Op 38 (baritone, mixed choir, large orchestra; Psalms 142, 30, 37, 66, 33) 1979; first performed Krakow 1979, in the presence of Pope John Paul II.
Broad Waters Op 39 (5 folksongs for unaccompanied mixed choir) 1979.
Two Songs of Lorca Op 42 (medium voice, piano) 1980.
Blessed Raspberry Songs Op 43 (voice, piano) 1980.
Miserere Op 44 (unaccompanied mixed choir) 1981.
Dark Evening Is Falling Op 45 (unaccompanied mixed choir) 1981.
My Vistula, Grey Vistula Op 46 (folksong for unaccompanied mixed choir) 1981.
Two Songs of Slowacki Op 48 (voice, piano) 1983.
Three Lullabies Op 49 (mixed choir) 1984.
O My Little Garland of Lavender Op 50 (folksong for mixed choir) 1984.
Cloud Comes, Rain Falls Op 50 (folksong for unaccompanied mixed choir) 1984.
Five Marian Songs Op 54 (mixed choir) 1985.
O domina nostra Op 55 (soprano, organ) 1985–90; first performed London, 7 July 1990.
Under Your Protection Op 56 (mixed choir) 1985.
Angelus Domini Op 57 (mixed choir) 1985.
Totus Tuus Op 60 (unaccompanied chorus) 1987.
Come, Holy Spirit Op 61 (mixed chorus) 1988.
Good Night Op 63 (soprano, alto flute, piano, 3 tam-tams) 1990.

PUBLICATIONS

On Górecki: Adrian Thomas, "The Music of HG: The First Decade", in *Contact*, 27, Autumn 1983, and "A Pole Apart: The Music of HG since 1965", in *Contact*, 28, Autumn 1984.

* * *

The emergence of Henryk Górecki on the international scene during the 1970s was one of the most welcome developments in contemporary music as well as in post-1945 Polish cultural life. His rugged individual voice is forged from diverse sources, and includes elements of avant-garde adventurousness, religious contemplation and "mountain top" capaciousness, coupled with a deep love of the folklore and customs of his native country. Górecki is highly regarded at home and has become internationally known through a handful of carefully crafted and cogently argued works.

Górecki was born in 1933 in the coal-mining region of Silesia, not far from the Czech border. He was a late developer in music and did not begin formal instruction in the subject until he enrolled as a composition student at the State Higher School of Music in Katowice, when he was nearly 22. Before this, he had worked as a primary school teacher. At Katowice he studied with the influential Boleslaw Szabelski, a former student of Szymanowski.

After graduating in 1960, Górecki studied in Paris (though not under Messiaen, as is sometimes suggested) where contact with the avant-garde affected him significantly, perhaps on a purely technical rather than emotional level. The horrific realities of war-time Poland were deeply rooted in the childhood memories of many of Górecki's generation but like Penderecki, to quote just one example, he was able to take full advantage of the cultural "thaw" that occurred during the late 1950s. This is not to suggest that Górecki was unaffected by Nazi oppression and Stalinist dictates. Such crucial aspects of Polish history may well have cemented the composer's sense of spiritual well-being and love for his native land and they represent a central component in any deeper understanding of his music.

Górecki has remained rooted to his native southern Poland. In 1975, he became rector of his old school at Katowice. From this base, he produced a number of award-winning compositions: the orchestral *Monologhi*, the *Symphony No 1 "1959"*, the *Cantata* for organ, and the vocal *Ad matrem*. Górecki's "rootedness" gives his music an unswerving sense of direction and a unique emotional impact. His first composition to win wider acceptance was *Scontri/Collisions*—the title is a play on Luigi Nono's *Incontri* (or "Meetings")—written in 1959. This colourful score eschews the greater avant-gardisms of many of his contemporaries. In many ways, *Scontri* is a musical collision between the music of Górecki's own generation and that of older figures, betwen prevailing trends and fierce independence. It was followed by works that radically reappraise Górecki's attitude towards composition. *Genesis* is tough and unyielding and displays his readiness to maximise the use of a minimum of compositional material. *Three Pieces in the Old Style* uses modal melodies and whole tone harmony moving in very slow tempos that reflect a heightened awareness of ritual and revelation. Górecki has also used quotations from other composers from time to time, notably in the powerfully expressive *Lerchenmusik* for clarinet, cello and piano, where Beethoven is quoted to great effect.

Górecki's reputation was greatly enhanced by three remarkable works from around the end of the 1970s: the *Symphony No 3*, *Beatus vir* and the *Harpsichord Concerto*. The 55-minute symphony makes innovative use of three slow movements, the first of them almost 25 minutes long; in it the soprano sings a text from the 15th-century "Holy Cross Lament". The canonic melodic outpouring is derived from a fusion of folk melodies and funeral songs. It is the music of one who has himself suffered appalling physical ailments but whose strength of character carries all with him. He also possesses a muscular sense of humour. Any image of the composer as a mountain recluse is offset in works such as the *Harpsichord Concerto*. The fast, flamboyant movements that make up this work utilize a web of interrelated thematic material which creates a compelling chain reaction effect; the earthiness of the Tatra highlanders is made evident in a short and concise musical utterance. In America the concerto has been hailed as a masterpiece of minimalism. Górecki, however, is no follower of trends. That he is one of the most innovative on contemporary composers is not disputed. He is also one of the most significant Polish creative artists in any field of creative endeavour from the death of Chopin to the birth of Solidarity.

—Lyn Davies

GOULD, Morton. American. Born in Richmond Hill, New York, 10 December 1913. Educated at Richmond Hill High School; Institute of Musical Art, New York; studied theory, harmony and composition under Vincent Jones, piano under Abby Whiteside. Married twice; 4 children. Concert, recital pianist, since 1920s; freelance composer and conductor (with New York Philharmonic, Philadelphia, Cleveland, Chicago, Pittsburgh, etc; also Australia, 1977; Japan, 1979; Mexico, 1980; Israel, 1981); staff pianist, Radio City Music Hall, 1931–2; composer, arranger, conductor, in charge of "Music for Today" broadcasts, Mutual Radio Network, New York, 1935–42; composer, arranger, conductor, CBS sponsored broadcasts, 1942–5; president, ASCAP, since 1986. Recipient: Grammy Award (for recording of Charles Ives works with Chicago Symphony Orchestra), 1966; American Symphony Orchestra League Gold Baton Award, 1983; other Grammy nominations; elected to American Academy of Arts and Letters and National Arts Club. Mailing address: 231 Shoreward Drive, Great Neck, New York, New York 11021, U.S.A.

Publishers: G. Schirmer, New York; Theodore Presser, Philadelphia.

Symphonies/orchestral:

(First) American Symphonette 1933.
Chorale and Fugue in Jazz (2 pianos, orchestra) 1934; first performed Philadelphia, 2 January 1936.
Second American Symphonette (with *Pavanne*) 1935; first performed New York City, 1938.
Third American Symphonette 1937.
Piano Concerto 1937; first performed New York City, 16 June 1938.
Violin Concerto 1938.
Stephen Foster Gallery 1939; first performed Pittsburgh, 12 January 1940.
A Homespun Overture 1939.
Foster Gallery Suite (from *Stephen Foster Gallery*) 1939.
Latin American Symphonette 1941; first performed New York City, 8 April 1941.
Spirituals for Orchestra 1941; first performed New York City, 9 February 1941. Recorded Columbia; RCA Victor; Mercury; Everest.
Cowboy Rhapsody 1942.
Lincoln Legend 1942; first performed Washington, D.C., 1 November 1942.
Symphony No 1 1942; first performed Pittsburgh, 5 March 1943.
American Salute 1942.
Interplay/formerly *American Concertette* (piano, orchestra; also ballet version) 1943; broadcast 25 August 1943. Recorded RCA Victor.
Fanfare for Freedom (brass, timpani, percussion) 1943.
Viola Concerto 1943; broadcast, Washington, D.C., 1943.
Concertette (viola, brass band) 1943.
Symphony No 2; Symphony on Marching Tunes 1944; first performed New York City, 2 June 1944.
Concerto for Orchestra 1945; first performed Cleveland, Ohio, 1 February 1945.
Harvest (harp, vibraphone, strings) 1945; first performed St Louis, 27 October 1945.
Ballad (symphonic band) 1946.
Minstrel Show 1946; first performed Indianapolis, 21 December 1946.
Symphony No 3 1946–7, revised 1948; first performed Dallas, Texas, 16 February 1947; revised version first performed New York City, 28 October 1948.
Holiday Music 1947.
Easter Morning (from *Holiday Music*) 1947.
First Thanksgiving (from *Holiday Music*) 1947.
Fourth of July (from *Holiday Music*) 1947.
Halloween (from *Holiday Music*) 1947.
Home for Christmas (from *Holiday Music*) 1947.
Philharmonic Waltzes 1948; first performed New York City, 16 November 1948. Recorded Columbia; Varese Sarabande.
First Noel (orchestra or band) 1948.
Good King Wenceslas 1948.
Adeste Fideles 1948.
It Came upon a Midnight Clear 1948.
Jingle Bells 1948.
Silent Night 1948.
Serenade of Carols 1949.
Fall River Legend: Suite (based on the ballet) 1949; first performed San Francisco, 6 January 1949. Recorded RCA Victor; Columbia; Mercury; Capitol.
Battle Hymn of the Republic 1950.
Big City Blues 1950.
Buckaroo Blues (band) 1950.
Family Album Suite 1951.
Symphony for Band 1952; first performed West Point, New York, 13 April 1952. Recorded Golden Crest.
Tap Dance Concerto 1952; first performed Rochester, New York, 16 November 1952. Recorded Columbia.
Dance Variations (2 pianos, orchestra) 1953; first performed New York City, 24 October 1953. Recorded RCA Victor; Koch International Classics.
Inventions (4 pianos, brass, percussion) 1953; first performed New York City, 19 October 1953.
Showpiece 1954; first performed Philadelphia, 7 May 1954.
Cinerama Holiday Suite 1955.
Skier's Waltz (from *Cinerama Holiday*) 1955.
Santa Fe Saga (symphonic band) 1956. Recorded Everest.
Hoofer Suite ("hoofer"/tap dancer, orchestra) 1956.
Derivations (clarinet, band) 1956; first performed Washington, D.C., 14–17 July 1956. Recorded Columbia.
Declaration: Suite (based on *Declarations*) 1957; first performed Washington, D.C., 22–23 January 1957.
Jekyll and Hyde Variations 1957; first performed New York City, 2 February 1957. Recorded RCA Victor.
St Lawrence Suite 1958; first performed Massena, New York, 5 September 1958. Recorded RCA Victor.
Cafe Rio (band) 1958.
Windjammer Main Theme: "The Ship" 1958.
Dialogues (piano, string orchestra) 1958; first performed New York City, 3 November 1958.
Rhythm Gallery (exposition of musical rhythm for orchestra and guide) 1958.
Spirituals (string orchestra, harp) 1961.
Prisms (symphonic band) 1962.
Festive Music 1964; first performed New York City, 16 January 1965. Recorded Varese Sarabande.
Dramatic Fanfares (band) 1964.
Formations (symphonic band) 1964.
World War I (selections from the CBS TV series) 1964.
Sarajevo Suite (from the CBS TV series) 1964.
Mini Suite (band) 1964.
Venice (2 orchestras, brass choirs) 1966; first performed Seattle, Washington, 2 May 1967. Recorded RCA Victor.
Columbia 1967.
Columbia: Broadsides for Orchestra 1967; first performed Washington, D.C., 14 July 1967. Recorded Louisville.
Columbian Fanfare (brass) 1967.
Vivaldi Gallery 1967; first performed Seattle, Washington, 25 March 1968. Recorded RCA Victor.

Troubadour Music (4 guitars, orchestra) 1968; first performed San Diego, California, March 1969.
Soundings 1969; first performed Atlanta, Georgia, 18 September 1969.
Concerto Grosso (4 violins, orchestra) 1969; first performed New York City, 4 December 1988.
Fanfare for Freedom 1971.
Symphony of Spirituals 1976; first performed Detroit, Michigan, 1 April 1976. Recorded Louisville.
American Ballads (settings of American tunes) 1976; first performed New York City, 24 April 1976.
Elegy (suite from television music to *Holocaust*) 1978.
Holocaust: Suite 1979, revised for band 1980.
Cheers: Celebration March 1979; first performed Boston, 1 May 1979.
Burchfield Gallery 1979; first performed Cleveland, Ohio, 9 and 11 April 1981. Recorded RCA.
Celebration 81 1981; first performed New York City, 27 April 1981.
Cello Suite (cellos, chamber orchestra) 1982; first performed Miami, Florida, Spring 1982.
Housewarming 1982; first performed Baltimore, Maryland, 16 September 1982. Recorded Louisville.
Gala for Band 1983.
Centennial Symphony (band) 1983; first performed Austin, Texas, Spring 1983.
Flourishes and Galop 1983; first performed Louisville, Kentucky, 1983. Recorded Louisville.
Cellos (orchestra of cellos) 1984; first performed Arizona, 1 June 1984. Recorded Musical Heritage.
Flute Concerto 1984; first performed Chicago, April 1985.
Classical Variations on Colonial Themes 1985; first performed Pittsburgh, 11 September 1986.
Notes of Remembrance 1989; first performed Washington, D.C., 14 June 1990.
Minute and Waltz Rag 1990.
Diversions (tenor saxophone, orchestra) 1990.

Chamber/instrumental:

Boogie Woogie Etude (piano) 1943.
Suite (violin, piano) 1945.
Dance Gallery (piano) 1945.
Abby Variations (piano) 1962.
At the Piano (Books 1 & 2) 1964.
Ten for Deborah (piano) 1965.
Tuba Suite 1971.
Suite (cello, piano) 1981.
Concerto Concertante (piano, violin, woodwind quintet) 1983; first performed Washington, D.C., 29 October 1983. Recorded Musical Heritage.
Patterns (piano) 1984.
Pieces of China (piano) 1985.
Two Pianos 1987.

Vocal/choral:

Of Time and the River (unaccompanied chorus) 1946.
Declarations (symphonic narrative for 2 solo speakers, speaking male chorus, orchestra; Declaration of Independence) 1956.
Come Up from the Valley, Children (4-part mixed chorus, piano) 1964.
Dancing Days (4-part mixed chorus, piano; version for stage band) 1964.
Hello Song (4-part mixed chorus, piano) 1964.
Two for Chorus: Sing/Tropical Lullaby (children's chorus) 1966.
Something to Do (cantata; Leigh) 1976; first performed Washington, D.C., September 1976.
Quotations (chorus, orchestra) 1983.
American Sing (vocal quartet, orchestra) 1984.
A capella (double chorus) 1987.

Other:

Interplay (ballet by Robbins) 1945; first performed New York City, 17 October 1945.
Billion Dollar Baby (musical; Comden, Green) 1945; first performed New York City, 1945.
Delightfully Dangerous (film score) 1945.
Fall River Legend (ballet by De Mille) 1947; first performed New York City, 22 April 1947.
Arms and the Girl (musical; Fields) 1952.
Cinerama Holiday (film score) 1955.
Windjammer (film score) 1958.
Clarinade (ballet; Balanchine) 1964.
Apple Waltzes (ballet; Balanchine) 1969.
Chorales and Rags (ballet; Balanchine) 1969.
Concerto Grosso (ballet; Balanchine) 1969.
Something to Do (cantata-musical; Leigh) 1976; first performed Washington, D.C., September 1976.
Music for Holocaust (television series) 1978; first broadcast April 1978. Recorded RCA Victor.
Apple Waltzes (ballet by Balanchine) 1982. Recorded RCA.
I'm Old Fashioned: Astaire Variations (ballet by Robbins) 1983; first performed Washington, D.C., June 1983.

Edvard Grieg: *Ich Diebe Dich* (orchestration) 1947.
Edvard Grieg: *Wedding Day at Troldhaugen* (orchestration) 1947.

PUBLICATIONS

On Gould: L. Evans, "MG: His Life and Music", dissertation, Columbia University Teachers' College, 1978; K. LaFave, "Interplay: MG Talks About Collaborating with Choreographers", in *Ballet News*, 5(6), 1983.

Morton Gould comments:

I am what I am and there is not much I can do about it except to try and improve. I am not a purist and espouse no dogma but am curious and fascinated by the infinite variety of all kinds of musical sounds.

* * *

Morton Gould started composing at six and the first concert of his works took place when he was 16. In Nicolas Slonimsky's phrase, "he played the piano for silent films and in loud jazz bands" and did all kinds of other musical work from his teens onwards. Radio in particular led to many opportunities for composing music of the more approachable kind, typical being his various symphonettes and concertettes. One of these contained the highly melodious *Pavanne*, which for some years was a light orchestral "hit" in the U.S. Gould also wrote more serious works including symphonies and concertos, some of the latter using procedures adapted from the baroque yet also including a concerto for tap dancer and orchestra.

Of particular interest is *Venice*, for double orchestra and brass choirs, echoing the kind of music composed for St Mark's in earlier centuries. Some of his music has also been employed for ballet, the *American Concertette* for piano and orchestra, for example, being choreographed by Jerome Robbins in 1945 as *Interplay*. Another of his ballets is *Fall River Legend*, choreographed by Agnes De Mille and telling of the redoubtable Lizzie Borden. Gould has also done much conducting of weightier scores, and with the Chicago Symphony Orchestra made the pioneer recording of Ives's *Symphony No 1*, receiving a Grammy Award for this in 1966. He also has appeared on television as a musical commentator.

Characteristic of his more popular works are the *American Symphonette No 1* of 1933 and, from a year later, the *Chorale and Fugue in Jazz*, performed in 1936 by Stokowski. In his teenage piano recitals Gould often improvised on themes submitted by the audience, and this ability made him especially sympathetic to jazz. Among several scores of interest in this connection is *Derivations* for clarinet and band, written for Benny Goodman. Gould said that in composing this he was "putting types of familiar jazz vernacular to more classical, formalistic use" and that he attempted "through a manipulation of patterns to give the whole a feeling of improvisation". In fact Gould has been more successful than some more renowned figures in applying classical procedures to jazz, folk and pre-rock popular idioms. This is partly a matter of breaking down the given material into short motives that are more susceptible to developmental and related processes than whole melodies of a traditional kind. Another sort of flexibility arises from his harmony, which is marked by frequent modulations and relationships between the keys which are out of the ordinary. There is also great rhythmic freedom in his music, fluent counterpoint and highly effective orchestration.

Among other Gould scores of popular origin there is in particular a lot of Americana, notably the *Cowboy Rhapsody*, placing such melodies as *Home on the Range* in symphonic circumstances, *American Ballads*, *Classical Variations on Colonial Themes* and *Spirituals for Orchestra*, a thoroughly effective 1941 piece not to be confused with the *Symphony of Spirituals* written for the 1976 American Bicentennial. Among the composers who use traditional and popular material in this way Gould has been more often performed, at least in the U.S., by eminent conductors and leading orchestras. And items like the *American Salute* and *Cowboy Rhapsody* are almost classics with American high school orchestras and bands.

Predictably enough, Gould has also written a considerable quantity of music for television, including *Holocaust*, duly arranged as suites for band and symphony orchestra, and for films, even appearing in one of the latter, *Delightfully Dangerous*. He has also composed Broadway musical shows, including *Arms and the Girl* and most notably *Billion Dollar Baby*. Another stage work is the ballet *Clarinade*, choreographed by George Balanchine in 1964 and employing the *Derivations* score.

—Max Harrison

GRAHN, Ulf (Åke Wilhelm). Swedish; resident in United States. Born in Solna, 17 January 1942. Sang in St Jacob's Boy's Choir, 1956–61. Educated at Stockholms Borgarskolas Musiklinje/Stockholm Citizens Music School, Westrell (violin, piano and composition under Hans Eklund), 1960–9; Stockholms Musikpedagogische Institut, State Academy of Music (piano under Herbert Westrell, composition with Gunnar Johanson, violin under Rudolf Forsberg) 1965–8, diploma in violin; School of Music, Catholic University of America, Washington, D.C., 1972–4, M.M. 1973; studied business administration and development, Uppsala University, 1986. Married pianist Barbro E. M. Dahlman, 15 August 1969; 1 son. Instructor, Stockholm school board, 1960–4, 1969–72; instructor, Lidingo Music School, 1964–70; teaching assistant/lecturer, Catholic University of America, Washington, D.C., 1972–6; founder/music director, Contemporary Music Forum, Washington, D.C., 1973–85; lecturer, Northern Virginia Community College, 1975–9; founder/artistic director, Aurora Players, since 1983; lecturer, then associate professor, since 1983, George Washington University, Washington D.C.; publisher/owner, Edition Nglani, since 1985; artistic and managing director, Musik vid Siljan, 1988–9; consultant in cultural economics; artist in residence, Wolf Trap Farm Park, Virginia, 1976, 1977, and at Centre Culturel Suédois, Paris, Swedish Institute, Athens, University of North Dakota, Grand Forks, James Madison University, Virginia, Chicago Musical College, and Roosevelt University, Illinois; freelance reporter on American music, Swedish Radio Network. Recipient: State Composer's Scholarship, Sweden, 1971; prize, Stockholm International Organ Days, 1973; special commendation, ISCM U.S. Section international composition contest, 1976; Composers' Conference Fellowship, Vermont, 1980. Mailing address: Langbackav. 1, S-61900 Trosa, Sweden; or, 7407 Holly Avenue, Takoma Park, Maryland 10912, U.S.A.

Publishers: Seesaw Music, 2067 Broadway, New York, New York 10023, U.S.A.; Edition Suecia, Box 27327, S-10254 Stockholm, Sweden; Edition Nglani, P. O. Box 871, Merrifield, Virginia 22116, U.S.A.

Symphonies/orchestral:

Musica da camera (chamber orchestra) 1964.
Fancy (Romantic orchestra) 1965.
Symphony No 1 (large orchestra) 1966–7.
Lamento (strings) 1967; first performed Norrkoping, Sweden, 1 June 1972.
Hommage à Charles Ives (strings) 1968; first performed Trondheim, Norway, 13 February 1969.
Chamber Concerto for Double Bass (double bass, small orchestra) 1968; first performed Santa Barbara, California, 7 February 1973.
Joy (symphonic band) 1969; first performed Stockholm, 2 February 1970.
Ancient Music (piano, chamber orchestra) 1970; broadcast Danish Radio, 20 March 1972.
A Dream of a Lost Century (chamber orchestra) 1971; first performed Stockholm, 1 June 1972.
The Wind of Dawn (orchestra, tape) 1973; first performed Sterling, Virginia, 15 April 1978.
Concerto (orchestra, SATB vocalise) 1973; first performed Cincinnati, Ohio, 10 April 1981.
Concerto for Viola d'Amore (small orchestra) 1976; first performed Washington, D.C., 17 January 1977.
Concertino (piano, strings) 1979; first performed Reston, Virginia, 28 February 1981.
Symphony No 2 1984; first performed Stockholm, 20 June 1984.

Concerto for Guitar and Orchestra 1985; first performed Reston, Virginia, 15 June 1985.

Chamber/instrumental:

Quattro pezzi (violin, cello) 1964.
Opus III per quintetto di fiati (woodwind quintet) 1965.
Liten Serenad (2 oboes) 1965; first performed Lunevad, July 1967.
Four Pieces (guitar) 1966.
Tre Miniatyrer (viola, piano) 1966.
Elegi (oboe, horn, cello) 1967.
Trio (flute, oboe, clarinet) 1967; first performed Louisiana, 10 March 1975.
Suite (2 violins, viola) 1967.
To Barbro (piano) 1967; first performed Kristinehamn, 18 April 1969.
Pezzo per organo (organ) 1968; first performed Stockholm, 29 April 1968.
Pan (alto recorder, guitar) 1968; first performed Copenhagen, 20 February 1970.
Intermezzo (2 violins, viola, 2 cellos, 2 pianos, harpsichord) 1968.
Music for Four (violin, clarinet, cello, piano) 1968.
Tre Skisser (2 trumpets, horn, trombone) 1968; first performed Norrkoping, 9 June 1971.
Musik für Oboe Solo 1968; broadcast Swedish Radio, 28 August 1973.
Kadenza (flute) 1968; first performed Washington, D.C., 16 April 1979.
For Two English Horns 1968.
Dialog (flute, clarinet) 1969.
Chanson (flute, clarinet) 1969.
Beautiful Thoughts for the Voice of a Violoncello (cello) 1969; first performed Paris, February 1970.
Mist (flute, violin, viola) 1969; broadcast Swedish Broadcasting Corporation, 19 September 1971.
Rondo (variable ensemble) 1969; first performed Stockholm, 1969.
Tale (organ) 1969; first performed Stockholm, 10 June 1971.
Two pieces (piano) 1969; first performed Stockholm, 2 October 1969.
Thoughts on the Modern World (chamber ensemble) 1970.
Halloween (clarinet) 1970; first performed Leksand, Sweden, 8 July 1971.
Cinq Préludes (piano) 1970; first performed Helsinki, 12 February 1971. Recorded Opus One Records 33.
Sounding (piano, tape) 1970–1; first performed Stockholm, 25 April 1971.
Snapshots (piano) 1971; first performed Swenen, 8 January 1974. Recorded Opus One Records 38.
Signaler (2 trumpets, 2 trombones) 1971; first performed Ingesund, August 1968.
Två Pieces for Eric (guitar) 1971.
Lockrop (clay flute) 1971; broadcast Swedish Radio, 12 September 1971.
Tensta Emotions (clarinet, trombone, piano) 1971; first performed New York City, 16 October 1971.
Mosaik (Orff instruments) 1971.
Cermoni (variable instruments, action/movement) 1971.
Looking Forward to . . . (organ) 1972; first performed Stockholm, 5 March 1973.
Mirrors (organ) 1972; first performed Stockholm, 5 March 1973.
Alone (flute) 1972; broadcast Swedish Radio, 10 June 1974.
Sine Nomine (variable instrumentation; based on *Mosaik*) 1972; first performed Lundsberg, Sweden, 16 July 1972.
This Reminds Me of . . . (flute, clarinet, horn, trombone, percussion) 1972; first performed Washington, D.C., 15 December 1975.
Pace (flute, tape) 1973; first performed Washington, D.C., 15 July 1975.
Two Dances: Dance of the Shapes, Dance of the Island (large chamber ensemble) 1973; first performed Washington, D.C., 28 January 1974.
Soundscape I (flute, bass clarinet, cor anglais, percussion) 1973; first performed Washington, D.C., 28 October 1973.
Soundscape II (10 players) 1974; first performed Memphis, Tennessee, 13 February 1981.
Order-Fragments-Mirrors (for Contemporary Music Forum and Fusion Jazz Quartet) 1974; first performed Washington, D.C., 19 May 1975.
Pieces for the Nieces (piano) 1975; first performed Washington, D.C., 6 November 1977.
Outside the Window (trumpet) 1976.
Magnolias in Snow (flute, piano) 1976.
Sonata (piano, flute, percussion) 1976; first performed Washington, D.C., 5 November 1976. Recorded Opus One 40.
Returning (flute, clarinet, violin, cello, piano, percussion, tape delay) 1976; first performed Washington, D.C., 17 May 1976.
Trombone Unaccompanied?! (trombone) 1977; first performed Washington, D.C., 19 December 1977.
From the Past (recorder, hand drum) 1977.
In the Shade (5 percussionists) 1977; first performed Washington, D.C., 31 March 1978. Recorded Caprice 1265.
Divertimento (2 oboes, bass clarinet, trumpet, harp, piano) 1977–8.
Où allez-vous? (flute, clarinet, violin, piano) 1978; first performed Washington, D.C., 10 March 1978.
L'Arbre de Noël (piano) 1978; first performed Washington, D.C., 18 December 1978.
Interlude (flute, viola, piano, 4 hands) 1978.
String Quartet No 2 1979; first performed Washington, D.C., 16 November 1979.
Floating Landscape (2 piccolos, 2 flutes, 2 alto flutes, 2 bass flutes) 1979.
Etude pour la salle de Corcoran (audience/chorus, flute, clarinet, violin, piano, percussion) 1979.
Sonata (piano) 1980; first performed Washington, D.C., 8 June 1980. Recorded Orion 85 483.
Piano Quartet 1980; first performed Washington, D.C., 19 April 1982.
Rondeau (flute, bass clarinet, viola, guitar, percussion) 1980; first performed Stockholm, 9 May 1982.
Summer Deviation (flute, violin, viola, cello, piano) 1981; first performed Sala, Sweden, 14 September 1982.
Images (bass clarinet, marimba) 1981.
Fantasia (organ) 1982.
Through the Passage of Time (alto Renaissance recorder, low tuning) 1982; first performed Washington, D.C., 23 January 1983.
Sonata (violin, piano) 1983; first performed Washington D.C., 20 May 1983.
Christmas Mosaic (any number of instruments) 1983.
Preludes Book II (1–3) (piano) 1984; first performed Washington, D.C., 16 May 1984.
A due (piano, 4 hands) 1985; first performed Washington, D.C., 16 June 1985.
Ballad (alto saxophone) 1985; first performed East Lansing, Michigan, 10 April 1986.
Fantasia (guitar) 1985; first performed New York, 1 February 1986.

Barcaroll (flute, piano) 1985.

Scherzo (piano, 6 hands) 1986; first performed Washington, D.C., 16 October 1986.

Preludes Book II (4–5) (piano) 1987.

Encore (piano) 1988; first performed Washington, D.C., 28 April 1988.

Nocturne (violin, cello, piano, tape) 1988; first performed Washington, D.C., 7 March 1988.

Celebration (marimba) 1988.

Nocturne (piano, 6 hands) 1989; first performed Sweden, 5 July 1989.

Music Box Music (any 3 instruments) 1989.

Three Aspects of the River (piano) 1989; first performed Kil, Sweden, 1989.

Three Dances with Interludes (6 percussion) 1990; first performed Stockholm, 3 April 1990.

The Enchanted Forest (woodwind quintet) 1990; first performed Sweden, February 1991.

Vocal/choral:

Blott en Dag (chorus; Ahnfeldt) 1960; broadcast Swedish Television, 1 January 1961.

Ensam (26 songs for voice and piano; Hallquist, others) 1961–4; first performed Stockholm, 21 April 1965.

Bön I Svaghet (voice, piano or organ; Stavert) 1961; first performed Stockholm, 1 January 1962.

Herre du Vet (voice, piano or organ; Olofsson) 1962.

Ett Enda Litet Ord (voice, piano or organ; Nyquist) 1963; first performed Lidingo, 29 September 1963.

Stilla Hav Ro (voice, piano or organ; Persson) 1963; first performed Lidingo, 4 August 1963.

Jag Beder Ej (voice, piano or organ; Malmberg) 1963.

Det Kan Handa (voice, piano or organ; Lund) 1963.

Iakttagelse (unaccompanied SATB chorus; Jonsson) 1963.

Afton Psalm (unaccompanied SATB chorus; Runeberg) 1963.

Nattvakten Visa (unaccompanied SATB chours; Swedish verse) 1963.

Den Doda Fragar (voice, piano; Asplund) 1964; first performed Stockholm, 10 February 1972.

Veronica (voice, piano; Asplund) 1964; first performed Stockholm, 10 February 1972.

Visa (voice, piano; Asplund) 1964; first performed Stockholm, 10 February 1972.

Att Äga (voice, piano or organ; Essen) 1964; first performed Lidingo, 31 May 1964.

Ar Icke Ljuset (voice, piano; Blomberg) 1964.

Jag Horde (voice, piano; Fredin) 1964.

Rakneramsa (unaccompanied SATB chorus; Swedish verse) 1964.

Narmare (voice, piano; Jandel) 1964.

Uppenbarelse (voice, piano or organ; Bohlin) 1965.

Manniskosonen (voice, piano or organ; Renvall) 1965; first performed Lidingo, 21 March 1965.

Hopp (voice, piano or organ; Martinson) 1965; first performed Lidingo, Spring 1966.

Jag Ville Saga Nagot (voice, piano; Malmberg) 1965.

Vandraren (voice, guitar or piano; Gustavsson) 1965.

Det Blir Nagot Att Fa (voice, guitar orpiano; Gustavsson) 1965.

Den Smala Vagen (voice, guitar or piano; Gustavsson) 1966.

Grund (voice, guitar or piano; Gustavsson) 1966.

Riket (voice, guitar or piano; Gustavsson) 1966.

Kidrons Dal (voice, guitar or piano; Gustavsson) 1966.

Morgones Rost (unaccompanied SATB chorus; Backlund) 1966.

Kraksonat (unaccompanied SATB chorus) 1966.

Fan och Herr Luther (unaccompanied SATB chorus) 1966.

Pour Quatre (alto, flute, trombone, double bass; Saigyo/Wahlund) 1966; broadcast Swedish Broadcasting Corporation, 21 May 1967.

Arabesk (baritone, 4 percussionists) 1966.

Det Ar Ny Afton (voice, piano or guitar; Martinson) 1967.

Ute Pa Havet (voice, piano or guitar; Martinson) 1967.

Det Ar Ny Afton (unaccompanied SAB chorus; Martinson) 1967; first performed Lidingo, December 1967.

Ute Pa Havet (unaccompanied SAB chorus; Martinson) 1967; first performed Lidingo, 20 May 1969.

Scen (soprano, chorus, piano, rock group; Jorgensen) 1968.

Ur Ker-Men (soprano, piano; Wistrand) 1969.

I Vasterland (unaccompanied male chorus; Wistrand) 1969.

Drommarnas Vag (unaccompanied SATB chorus; Fujiwara no Motoshi/Wahlund) 1969.

I Bokskogen (voice, piano; Ossiannilsson) 1970.

Tva Dagsedlar (voice, guitar) 1971.

Det Ar Nagon I Narheten (soprano, flute, guitar; Wistrand) 1971; first performed Washington, D.C., 20 February 1976.

Maskrosen (unaccompanied SATB chorus; Setterlind) 1972.

Till Vagorna (unaccompanied SATB chorus; Setterlind) 1972.

Du Behover Intet Saga (unaccompanied SATB chorus; Setterlind) 1972.

Picnic in the Jungle (SATB chorus, tape) 1973; first performed Gothenburg, Sweden, 17 March 1974.

Soundscape IV (voice, flute, bass clarinet, piano, percussion) 1975; first performed Washington, D.C., 28 February 1977.

Soundscape III (soprano, flute, clarinet, violin, cello, piano, percussion; Whitman) 1975–7; first performed Washington, D.C., 19 September 1977.

Vaggvisa (voice, piano; Setterlind) 1977.

Sonata: Regions of Time (high soprano, piano; wordless) 1978; first performed Stockholm, 1 August 1978.

Du Silence (soprano, bass clarinet; Rodenbach) 1979; first performed Washington, D.C., 28 June 1979.

Aftermath (unaccompanied SATB chorus) 1979.

I'm Nobody (voice, piano) 1979.

Vad Sorg över Stranden (voice, piano) 1979.

Stormar (voice, piano) 1979.

Jutta Kommer Till (voice, piano) 1979.

A Clear Midnight (soprano, clarinet; Whitman) 1980; first performed Washington, D.C., 15 October 1984.

Paret (voice, piano) 1980.

Three Songs (soprano, orchestra; Asplund) 1981.

Try Smiling (soprano, flute, piano) 1982; first performed Washington, D.C., 19 January 1983.

Eldorado (baritone, flute, clarinet, violin, piano; Poe) 1982; first performed Washington, D.C., 15 January 1983.

Matthew 10:43–45 (unaccompanied SATB chorus) 1983.

John 14:6, 9 (unaccompanied SAB chorus) 1983.

Try Smiling (voice, piano) 1984; first performed Washington, D.C., 26 February 1984.

Always Finish (voice, piano) 1984.

Do It Now (voice, piano) 1984.

Afton Port till Evigheten (voice, piano) 1984.

The Red Queen's Lullaby (voice, piano; Carroll) 1984.

Morgon (unaccompanied male chorus) 1984.

Three German Folksongs (alto, violin, cello, piano) 1985.

The King-Fisher Song (voice, piano) 1985.

Psalms 36:8, 10 (SATB chorus, trombone, organ) 1986.

Lady Muriel's Song (voice, piano; Carroll) 1987.

A Thorn (voice, piano) 1989.

The Duchess's Lullaby (voice, piano; Carroll) 1989.

Other:

Calling (electro-acoustic) 1970; first performed Stockholm, 25 April 1971.
Coco Sherry (electro-acoustic) 1970.
The Vagabond (electro-acoustic) 1971; first performed Davis, California, 5 April 1972.
The Visit (electro-acoustic) 1971; first performed Stockholm, 8 November 1971.
Land of the Silver Bird (electro-acoustic) 1971; first performed New York City, 27 April 1972.
Landskapsmusik I (materials for improvisation) 1971; first performed Sweden, Summer 1971.
Landskapsmusik II (materials for improvisation) 1972; first performed Sweden, Summer 1972.
Once upon a Time (electro-acoustic) 1972; first performed Davis, California, 5 April 1972.
Milky Way on My Mind (electro-acoustic) 1972; first performed Davis, California, 5 April 1972.
Per Gynt's Farewell to Norway (electro-acoustic) 1972; first performed Albany, New York, 5 April 1973.
Lux (ballet; adapted from *The Visit*, with new ending) 1972; first performed Sweden, 6 April 1972.
Music for The Tempest (electro-acoustic theatre music) 1973; first performed Washington, D.C., 8 December 1973.
Skugglek (ballet) 1973; first performed Stockholm, Autumn 1973.
Picnic in the Jungle I (electro-acoustic) 1973.
Picnic in the Jungle II (electro-acoustic) 1973.
Picnic in the Jungle III (dance, tape) 1973; first performed Arlington, Virginia, 4 April 1975.
Creation (ballet; electro-acoustic) 1974; first performed Maryland, 1 March 1974.
Music to One Flew over the Cuckoo's Nest (electro-acoustic theatre music) 1974; first performed Washington, D.C., 1 March 1974.
Hommage to the Soap Opera (ballet; electro-acoustic) 1975; first performed Rockville, Maryland, 1 March 1975.

PUBLICATIONS

On Grahn: Gran Bergendahl, "UG", in *Nutida Musik*, 8, 1967.

Ulf Grahn comments:

A composer needs to communicate with people of his own time. It is for his own time he composes, shares ideas and non-verbal events. Music can only be articulated at the actual moment of its making, by real instruments, not carried through speakers and amplifiers. A meeting of minds . . .

* * *

Baker's says rather sniffily of Ulf Grahn that he "maintains the golden mean of contemporary idioms, without doctrinaire deviations, scrupulously serving the tastes of the general audience". While it is true that Grahn adheres to no particular faction in contemporary music—serialism, minimalism, neo-tonality—and while it is perfectly clear that he intends his music to be entertaining and approachable, this is not to say that it is unsophisticated or banal. Grahn's populism masks a deceptive complexity, particularly of rhythm, in the way that David Del Tredici's music is deceptively complex beneath its beguiling surface (the two composers also share an enthusiasm for Lewis Carroll, Grahn setting a number of the poem in recent years).

Tremendously prolific, Grahn has a substantial body of work in all genres except opera. His music is tonal and melodic in a fairly traditional way, but it deploys rhythm and instrumental colour imaginatively and in a way that challenges performers. His most dedicated interpreter has been his wife, the pianist Barbro Dahlman, who has premiered and recorded a number of his works, notably *Snapshots*, a mini-suite of eight loosely connected images which exploit a whole range of piano techniques, including playing on open strings.

Something of the same rhythmic energy is communicated in a piece for percussion ensemble *In the Shade*. This is a bravura work, with a strong theatrical component. It relates to Grahn's interest in improvisatory music which is evident not just in pieces like *Order-Fragments-Mirrors* but in the widest spectrum of his work. The 1980 Piano Sonata is a free-ranging, 20-minute work in a single movement with an associative quality that draws together even apparently unrelated ideas and themes into a convincing whole.

Though much of Grahn's instrumental work is brightly and lushly scored, some of his orchestral pieces are notably austere and even forbidding. *A Dream of a Lost Century*, written around the time of his emigration to the United States, is a finely modulated but stark piece for chamber orchestra which does offer of being undiscovered music from an unknown civilization in the past. In this regard, it is in line with the very beautiful *Ancient Music* for piano and orchestra, and with Grahn's first and more satisfactory essay in symphonic writing. Finished in 1967, the *Symphony No 1* is a strongly rhythmic work, with beautifully balanced orchestration, and a simple, solid thematic drive that could be otiose were it not so well handled. The slightly later *Hommage à Charles Ives* bears comparison with Lou Harrison's similarly inspired work, but is more limber and ironic with a more widely arrayed instrumentation.

Perhaps the underlying thematic interest in Grahn's work is his very Scandinavian insistence that clear, limpid surfaces only mask dark and troubled waters. There is a disturbing quality to some of his music that has been called "convulsive", and which recalls the disturbed cadences of 19th-century Spasmodic poetry. It is nonetheless very beautiful, with a restorative calm and strong harmonic or melodic resolutions.

Grahn is a hyperactive musician. In addition to composing, he is a university teacher and publisher, reports on American music for the Swedish broadcasting service, and acts as a consultant on cultural economics, a field of growing importance in the U.S. A passionate believer in live music (his electro-acoustic compositions are much more firmly voiced than was usual for their time) he recognises in a firmly practical way the economic and social jeopardies that confront new music performance.

—Henk Maarten

GRISEY, Gérard. French. Born in Belfort, 17 June 1946. Educated at Trossingen Conservatory, Germany, 1963–5; Conservatoire National Supérieur de Musique, Paris (composition under Olivier Messiaen), 1965–7, 1968–72; l'Ecole Normale Supérieure de Musique, Paris (composition under Henri Dutilleux), 1968; Conservatoire de Paris further composition study (under Karlheinz Stockhausen, Iannis

Xenakis, György Ligeti), 1972; studied electro-acoustic music under Jean-Etienne Marie, 1969; Faculté des Sciences, Paris (acoustics under Emile Leipp), 1974; further study at IRCAM, Paris. Freelance composer; co-founder of performing ensemble and musicians' collective L'Itinéraire; teacher of composition, Ferienkurse für Neue Musik Darmstadt, summers 1976–82; teacher of composition, University of California, Berkeley, 1982–5; professor of orchestration and composition, Conservatoire de Paris, since 1987. Recipient: prizes for harmony, fugue, piano accompaniment, composition, Conservatoire de Paris; Prix de la Fondation de la Vocation; Prix de Rome, 1972–4; Prix de composition, Biennale Internationale de Paris; Prix Hervé Dugardin, 1975; DAAD Fellowship, Berlin, 1980. Mailing address: c/o Editions Salabert/Ricordi, 22 rue Chauchat, 75009 Paris, France.

Publisher: Salabert/Ricordi.

Symphonies/orchestral:

Vagues, chemins, le souffle (clarinet, orchestra) 1970–2; first performed Paris, 1975.
Dérives (2 orchestral groups) 1973–4; first performed Paris, 31 October 1974. Recorded Erato.
Modulations (part of cycle *Les Espaces acoustiques*; 1976–7; first performed Paris, 9 March 1978.
Manifestations (student orchestra) 1976; first performed Gennevilliers, November 1978.
Transitoires (part of cycle *Les Espaces acoustiques*) 1980; first performed Venice, 1981.
Epilogue (concluding part of cycle *Les Espaces acoustiques*) 1985; first performed Venice, 1985.
Le Temps et l'écume 1989.

Chamber/instrumental:

Echanges (prepared piano, double bass) 1968; first performed Paris, 1969.
Mégalithes (15 brass) 1969.
Perichoresis (3 instrumental groups: viola, bass clarinet, tenor trombone, piano, 4 hands; flute/piccolo, clarinet, tuba, harp; trumpet, cor anglais, double bass, percussion) 1969–70; first performed Paris, 1970.
D'Eau et de pierre (2 instrumental groups: flute/piccolo, clarinet, bassoon, horn, 2 violins, viola, cello, double bass; piccolo clarinet, oboe/cor anglais, trumpet, trombone/tenor trombone/bass trombone, bass tuba, 2 percussion) 1972; first performed Metz, 1972.
Périodes (part of cycle *Les Espaces acoustiques*; flute, clarinet, trombone, violin, viola, cello, double bass) 1974; first performed Rome, 11 June 1974.
Partiels (part of cycle *Les Espaces acoustiques*; 2 flutes/piccolos/1 alto flute, oboe/cor anglais, 2 clarinets/A clarinet, bass clarinet/contrabass clarinet, 1 or 2 horns, trombone/tenor trombone/bass trombone, 1 or 2 percussion, accordion with chromatic stops, 2 violins, 2 violas, cello, double bass) 1975; first performed Paris, 4 March 1976. Recorded Erato.
Prologue (viola with or without electro-acoustic environment) 1976; first performed 16 January 1978.
Sortie vers la lumière du jour (electric organ with ring modulator and phase shift, 2 flutes/1 piccolo/1 alto flute, 2 clarinets/1 bass clarinet, horn, trumpette, bass trombone, 2 percussion, 2 violins, viola, cello, double bass) 1978.
Jour, contre-jour (electric organ with ring modulator and phase shift, 2 flutes/1 picolo/1 alto flute, 2 clarinets/bass clarinets, horn, trumpet, bass trombone, percussion, 2 violins, viola, cello, double bass, tape) 1978–9; first performed Paris, 9 March 1979.
Tempus ex machina I (6 percussion) 1979.
Tempus ex machina II (3 percussion) 1980; in progress.
Solo pour deux (clarinet, trombone) 1981; first performed Venice, 1982.
Anubis-nout (bass clarinet) 1983; first performed Pontieno, Italy, 1984.
Quintette–Talea (violin, cello, flute, clarinet, piano) 1986; first performed Paris, 1987.
Cinq Miniatures (2 horns) 1989.

Vocal/choral:

Initiation (baritone, trombone, double bass) 1970; first performed Paris, 1981. Recorded Point Radiant.
Les Chants de l'amour (12 mixed voices, tape) 1982–4; first performed Paris, 1985.

PUBLICATIONS

By Grisey: "Zur Entstehung des Klanges", in *Darmstadter Beiträge*, Mainz, 1978; "La Synthèse instrumentale", in *Siècle*, 1986; "Tempus ex machina: réflexions sur le temps musical", in *Neuland*, 3, 1986; *D*, in *Contemporary Music Review*, 1986; *Musique et Psychologie*, Paris, 1986; "Structuration des timbres dans la musique instrumentale", Paris, 1989.

On Grisey: Anne le Baron and Denys Bouliane, "Darmstadt 1980", in *Perspectives of New Music*, Autumn 1981; Guy Lelong, "Les dérives sonorés de GG", in *Art Press*, March 1988.

* * *

Gérard Grisey's first mature work dates from the early 1970s, when he turned away from the serial style then dominant in France and began to explore the acoustic properties of sound as the basis of his music. The first major piece of this sort was *Dérives* for two orchestral groups, in which a recurring harmonic spectrumon E♭ is used as a point of maximum stability and consonance, a reference mark by which the listener may gauge the rate and extent of change the music undergoes. Encouraged by the possibilities of this new, non-tonal use of consonance, Grisey immediately began a large-scale project using this idea in a more complex manner.

Périodes for seven instruments was the first completed part of the cycle *Les Espaces acoustiques* which was to occupy Grisey for the next 11 years. The entire cycle is based upon the pattern inhalation-exhalation-rest; the moments of rest are marked by regular, periodic patterns and a part of a harmonic spectrum on E (= 41.2 Hz, the "tonic" of the cycle); the inhalations develop these repetitive figures and push them into a state of maximum disorder and instability; the exhalations proceed from the resulting disorder back towards a new point of rest on E. In *Périodes* the influence of the Italian composer Giacinto Scelsi, whose music Grisey encountered while on a Prix de Rome bursary at the Villa Medici, is clearly felt. The extreme slowness of much of the music, the microtonal string writing and the fine timbral shadings are all similar to Scelsi's music, even though the context of these phenomena is radically different in its developmental character.

The next work in the *Espaces acoustiques* cycle, *Partiels* for 18 instruments, expands the basic formal pattern established in *Périodes* into different areas; here Grisey began to blur the distinction between harmony and timbre (a feature already implicit in *Périodes*). The opening point of rest consists of a low E on trombone followed by a chord on the other instruments which is an instrumental simulation of the trombone's timbre—the result is a hybrid of "chord" and "timbre". Long stretches of *Partiels* are also generated by ring-modulation—combinations of sum and difference tones—producing harmony with an unreal, almost electronic character (although the piece is purely instrumental). Both of these forms of "instrumental synthesis", as Grisey terms it, are found in the following two works, *Modulations* for 33 instruments and *Transitoires* for large orchestra. In the former, several types of brass mute are instrumentally synthesised, while in the latter an entire orchestra "dissects" the timbre of a double bass. The opening *Prologue* for solo viola is a study in various types of bowing pressure and position and its opening theme forms the basis of the *Epilogue*, again for large orchestra, that brings the cycle to a close on an unsettling note of maximum disorder.

Two major pieces from the 1970s do not belong to the *Espaces acoustiques* project; *Sortie vers la lumière du jour*, with its sibling *Jour, contre-jour*, both for ensemble with electronics, is a study in gradually drifting harmony and timbre around a central harmonic spectrum; the six-percussion work *Tempus ex machina* explores streams of superimposed pulses and tempos, again within carefully controlled processes of transformation. The title of this last work refers to an important treatise Grisey worked on throughout the decade, "Tempus ex machina—A Composer's Reflections on Musical Time", in which Grisey ponders the psychological and phenomenological properties of time, pulse and sound, including detailed examination of accelerating and decelerating patterns and their conceptual significance; this treatise has been highly influential on other composers, notably Tristan Murail, as well as many composers of the following generation. Grisey has also had considerable influence through his teaching at Darmstadt, at the University of California, Berkeley, and, since 1987, at the Paris Conservatoire.

Since 1982, Grisey has sought to evolve a more flexible style with greater elements of unpredictability and volatility, while remaining faithful to his precept that "music is made with sounds, not with notes". In *Les Chants de l'amour*, an IRCAM commission for voices and tape, and in the piano quintet *Talea*, the processes have become more elusive, the music more discontinuous, with greater dramatic impact, a feature shared with his most recent work, *Le Temps et l'écume* for orchestra. In this last piece, indeed, Grisey has attempted to make the very notion of continuity or lack of it a structural force: three types of "time"—extremely slow, extremely compressed and "normal"—are superimposed and contrasted, with varying degrees of transition between them. The degree of abruptness between one passage of time and the next is the music's focus. Grisey is a founder-member of the ensemble and musicians' collective L'Itinéraire, who have been one of the main advocates of his music and for whom many of his works were especially composed.

—Julian Anderson

GROSS, Eric. British; Austrian born; now resident in Australia. Born in Vienna, 16 September 1926. Educated at Trinity College of Music, London, licentiate, 1958, fellow, 1963; University of Aberdeen, M.A., 1957, M.Litt., 1970, D.Mus., 1975. Married Pamela Margaret Mary Davies, 22 February 1955. Freelance pianist/arranger/conductor, United Kingdom, Ceylon and elsewhere, 1941–58; lecturer, New South Wales Conservatorium, Sydney, 1959–60; lecturer in music 1960–71, senior lecturer 1971–4, and associate professor, since 1974, University of Sydney; visiting professor of music, University of Guyana, Georgetown, 1989; past president, now vice-president, Fellowship of Australian Composers; treasurer, Asian Composers' League. Recipient: DAAD Scholar, Berlin, 1974, 1981; Albert H. Maggs Composition Award, University of Melbourne, 1976. Mailing address: Unit 54, 84 St George's Crescent, Drummoyne, New South Wales 2047, Australia.

Publishers: Australian Music Centre/Sounds Australian, P.O. Box 49, Broadway, New South Wales 2007, Australia; MCA/Leeds Music, G.P.O. Box 4917, Sydney 2001, Australia.

[Dates given are for first performance, not completion or publication.]

Symphonies/orchestral:

Sinfonietta Op 9 first performed Sydney, 1961. Recorded ABC PRX-5586.
Variations Op 7 first performed Sydney, 1965.
Symphony No 1 Op 20 first performed Aberdeen, 1967. Recorded ABC AC 1006.
Of Strings and Things Op 50 first performed Adelaide, 1970.
Antubconseas Op 11 first performed Sydney, 1972.
Moonscape Op 32 (string quartet, string orchestra) first performed Brisbane, 1972. Recorded ABC AC 1006; Jade CD.
Fanfopus Op 13 first performed Sydney, 1973.
Dusekiana No 1 Op 55 (violin, orchestra) first performed Sydney, 1975.
Duskeiana No 2 Op 56 (violin, orchestra) first performed Sydney, 1975.
Dusekiana No 3 Op 58 (violin, orchestra) first performed Sydney, 1975.
Overture and Incidental Music to Cymbeline Op 90 first performed Sydney, 1976.
Na Shledanou v Praze Op 94 first performed Olomouc, Czechoslovakia, 1976.
Prelude to Paradise Op 100/2 first performed Adelaide, 1977.
Bravura Op 116 (brass, percussion) first performed Sydney, 1979.
Concertino for Orchestra Op 108 first performed Sydney, 1979.
Trilogy Op 112 first performed Hobart, Tasmania, 1979.
Symphony No 2 Op 123 first performed Hamelyn, 1981.
Concert Movement Op 134 (plectrum orchestra) first performed Sydney, 1983. Recorded HR 001 AMCOS.
Piano Concerto Op 135 first performed Melbourne, 1983.
Violin Concerto No 1 Op 137 first performed Olomouc, Czechoslovakia, 1983.
Concerto for Mandolin Orchestra Op 140 first performed Sydney, 1984.
Concerto No 1 for Mandolin and Chamber Orchestra Op 141 first performed Sydney, 1984.
First Suite for Plectrum Orchestra Op 143 first performed Sydney, 1985.

Brassophony Op 146 (brass band) first performed Sydney, 1987.
Golden Jubilee Fantasy Op 158 first performed Sydney, 1987.
Fanfare Technological Op 162 (brass band) first performed Sydney, 1987.
Concerto for Oboe and Strings Op 152 first performed Olomouc, Czechoslovakia, 1988.
Violin Concerto No 2 Op 144 first performed 1989.
Concerto No 2 for Mandolin and Chamber Orchestra Op 151 first performed Sydney, 1991.
Swing One of Three Op 171 (big band) first performed Sydney, 1991.

Chamber / instrumental:

Classical Interlude Op 29 (string quartet or string orchestra) first performed Aberdeen, 1957.
The Merry Peasant Band Op 30 (flute, oboe, clarinet, horn, trumpet) first performed Sydney, 1959.
Habanera-Serenade Op 31 (violin, piano) first performed Sydney, 1960. Recorded ABC O/N 40453; Jugoton ULP 2476.
Academic Fanfare Op 59 (3 trumpets, 3 trombones) first performed Sydney, 1960.
Fanfare for a Queen Op 60 (3 trumpets, 3 trombones) first performed Aberdeen, 1967.
Rondino pastorale Op 33 (flute or violin, harp or piano; versions for string quartet and string orchestra) first performed Sydney, 1962.
Rondino tranquillo Op 34 (string quartet; version for string orchestra) first performed Sydney, 1962.
Rondino tranquillo Op 34/1 (harp) first performed Sydney, 1962.
Trio Op 10 (flute, oboe, clarinet) first performed Sydney, 1962. Recorded HMV OASD 7565.
Rondo tranquillo Op 34/2 (piano) first performed Sydney, 1962.
Quartet Op 12 (flute, violin, cello, harpsichord) first performed Orange, New South Wales, 1964.
Interlude Op 36 (6 horns in F) first performed Sydney, 1965.
Three Bagatelles Op 37 (flute) first performed Sydney, 1965.
Statement and Retraction Op 38 (carillon) first performed Sydney, 1966.
Wedding March Op 39 (organ) first performed Sydney, 1967.
Wedding March for Pamela and Michael Op 61 (organ) first performed Pittsburgh, 1971.
Moods in Miniature Op 40 (piano) first performed Sydney, 1972.
Two Pieces Op 42 (organ) first performed Sydney, 1972.
Duet: Eugel and Marmaduke Op 62 (2 cellos) first performed Newcastle, New South Wales, 1973.
Occasional Music Op 21 (brass, percussion) first performed Newcastle, New South Wales, 1973. Recorded ABC AC 1009.
Psalmody Op 57 (wind quintet) first performed Adelaide, 1975.
Prelude on the Shepherd of Bethlehem Op 95 (organ) first performed Sydney, 1976.
Bassetereo Op 91 (trumpet, horn, trombone, tuba, harp, basset horn) first performed Sydney, 1977.
Three Bagatelles Op 96 (alto saxophone) first performed Melbourne, 1977.
Prelude to Paradise Op 100/1 (organ) first performed Sydney, 1977. Recorded Jade CD 1013.
Quintet Op 102 (alto saxophone, string quartet) first performed Hobart, Tasmania, 1977. Recorded Move MS 3058.
Silas Pilgrim Trio Op 97 (flute, clarinet, bassoon) first performed Sydney, 1977.
Six Miniatures Op 103 (trumpet, trombone, tuba) first performed Melbourne, 1978.
Bridal March Op 104 (organ) first performed Sydney, 1978.
Duet: Bill and Bowmore Op 114 (2 cellos) first performed Newcastle, New South Wales, 1978.
Three Inventions Op 111 (trombone, cello) first performed Canberra, 1978.
Song 424/50 Op 113 (flute, cello, trombone, 2 percussion) first performed Sydney, 1979.
Suite for Double Reeds Op 115 (large double reeds) first performed Sydney, 1979.
Quartet Op 118 (2 flutes, 2 oboes) first performed Sydney, 1979.
Klavierstücke I Op 120 first performed Sydney, 1980. Recorded CSM CD 3.
Three Sketches Op 121a (trumpet, piano) first performed Sydney, 1980.
Four Dialogues Op 121 (flute, clarinet) first performed Berlin, 1981.
Trio Op 124 (oboe, clarinet, horn) first performed Berlin, 1981.
Septaphony Op 125 (flute, oboe, clarinet, horn, violin, double bass, piano) first performed Berlin, 1981.
Recessional Op 126 (organ) first performed Sydney, 1981.
Klavierstücke II (piano) first performed Sydney, 1982. Recorded CSM CD 3.
Flute Quartet Op 128 (flute, violin, viola, cello) first performed Perth, Western Australia, 1982.
Study for Misha Op 130 (violin, piano) first performed Prague, 1982.
Brian David Hess Op 131 (guitar) first performed Sydney, 1982.
Three Pieces for Five Fingers or One Hand Op 133 (piano) first performed Sydney, 1982.
Quartettsatz Op 132 (oboe, horn, guitar, percussion) first performed Berlin, 1983.
Centormedique Op 136 (organ) first performed Sydney, 1983.
Ian's Shenanigan No 1 Op 142 (recorder) first performed Sydney, 1985.
Geburtstagsgruss for J.S.B. Op 145 (organ) first performed Sydney, 1985. Recorded Jade CD 1013.
Classical Interlude Op 29/2 (plectrum quartet) first performed Sydney, 1986.
Mandolin Quartet Op 148 (mandolin, violin, viola, cello) first performed Sydney, 1986.
Thanksgiving Op 149 (piano) first performed Sydney, 1986.
Klavierstücke III Op 150 (piano) first performed Sydney, 1986. Recorded CSM CD 3.
Cadenza I Op 153/1 (mandolin) first performed Sydney, 1986.
Cadenza II Op 153/2 (mandolin) first performed Sydney, 1986.
Rondino pastorale Op 33/4 (plectrum quartet) first performed Sydney, 1987.
Six Moods in Miniature Op 40/2 (plectrum quartet) first performed Sydney, 1987.
Three Miniplectra Op 155 (plectrum quartet or orchestra) first performed Sydney, 1987.
Mandigar I Op 156 (plectrum ensemble) first performed Sydney, 1987.
Saxophone Quartet No 1 Op 155a first performed Bad Seegeberg, Germany, 1988.
Austral Scots Op 158/2 (violin, piano, optional clarinet) first performed Sydney, 1988.
Plectrum Trio (or Quartet) No 1 Op 159 first performed Sydney, 1988.

Plectrum Trio (or Quartet) No 2 Op 160 first performed Sydney, 1988.
Euphonism I Op 161 (euphonium, piano) first performed Sydney, 1988.
Plectrum-Pizzicato Op 164/1 (plectrum quartet) first performed Sydney, 1989.
Anna's Plectrum Op 164/2 (plectrum quartet) first performed Sydney, 1989.
Three Fragments Op 133A/1–3 (guitar) first performed London, 1989.
Ian's Shenanigan No 2 Op 142/2 (recorder) first performed Sydney, 1989.
Paul and Adrian Op 165 (2 mandolins) first performed Sydney, 1989.
Moon Interlude Op 41/2 (guitar) first performed Sydney, 1989.
Habanera-Guitarserenad Op 31/2 first performed Sydney, 1989.
Five Simple Pieces Op 169/1–5 (piano) first performed Sydney, 1989.
Trio Op 170 (oboe, 2 cors anglais) first performed Melbourne, 1990.
Cadenza III Op 153/3 (mandolin) first performed Sydney, 1990.
Thoughts of Sunraysia Op 171/1 (tuba, piano) first performed Sydney, 1990.
Tubism Op 171/2 (tuba, piano) first performed Sydney, 1990.
Barbara and Deborah Op 175 (5 mandolin duets) first performed Sydney, 1990.
Plectrabrass Op 176 (brass, plectrum quartet) first performed Sydney, 1990.
Three Pieces Op 172/1–3 (recorder) first performed Sydney, 1991.
Three Inventions Op 177 (mandolin/organ) first performed Sydney, 1991.
Songs of Australia Op 178 (oboe, 2 cors anglais) first performed Melbourne, 1991.
Two Pieces Op 167 (violin, organ) first performed Lund, Sweden, 1991.
Concertino for Mandolin and Wind Quintet Op 179 first performed Sydney, 1991.
First Trio for Saxophones OP 180 first performed Berlin, 1991.
Hooperisms Op 181 (6 mandolin duets) first performed Sydney, 1991.
Study for the Left Hand Op 182 (free bass accordion) first performed Sydney, 1991.

Vocal/choral:

Four Psalms Op 3 (unaccompanied SATB chorus) first performed Aberdeen, 1957. Recorded ABC RRC-71/PRX 5600/RRC 67.
Labyrinth of Love Op 4 (cycle for tenor, piano) first performed Sydney, 1958. Recorded RCA VRL 1–0124.
Ding, Dong, Bell Op 8/1 (unaccompanied SSA chorus) first performed Sydney, 1959.
A Ditty Op 8/2 (unaccompanied SSA chorus) first performed Sydney, 1959. Recorded ABC RRC 67.
Sonnet 35 Op 43 (tenor, piano) first performed Sydney, 1957.
Two Songs: Love's Philosophy and The Maid's Lament Op 45 (soprano, piano) first performed Sydney, 1958. Recorded ABC O/N 40453.
Songs for "The Winter's Tale" Op 46 (bass) first performed Sydney, 1964.
A Time to Every Purpose Op 17 (cantata for soprano, tenor, chorus, flute, violin, cello, bass clarinet) first performed Sydney, 1965.
Pacem in Terris Op 15 (soprano, bass-baritone, chorus, flute, violin, cello, bass clarinet, 2 trombones, tuba) first performed Sydney, 1966.
Bring Us Good Ale Op 22 (SATB chorus, piano) first performed Aberdeen, 1967.
Three Burns Settings Op 47 (soprano, piano) first performed Aberdeen, 1967. Recorded RCA VRL 1-0124.
The Shepherd of Bethlehem Op 16 (bass-baritone, SATB Chorus, girls' choir, boys' choir, organ, optional military band) first performed Sydney, 1968.
The Snow Gum Op 23 (SSA chorus, optional baritone, piano, optional percussion) first performed Sydney, 1968.
Three Burns Settings Op 48 (soprano, instrumental group) first performed Sydney, 1968.
Wedding Responses (Anglican) Op 24 (unaccompanied SATB chorus) first performed Sydney, 1969.
Sing with a Spirit Op 25 (canticle for St Cecilia's Day; SSA chorus, instrumental ensemble) first performed Sydney, 1969.
Cantata for a Centenary Op 14 (SATB chorus, organ, carillon) first performed Sydney, 1970.
I Was Glad (Psalm 122) Op 26 (SATB chorus, organ) first performed Sydney, 1970.
Psalm 122 Op 27 (unaccompanied SATB chorus) first performed Sydney, 1970. Recorded ABC RRCS 1470.
Psalm 130 Op 28 (unaccompanied SATB chorus) first performed Sydney, 1970. Recorded ABC RRCS 1470.
Wait for Tomorrow Op 85 (baritone) first performed Sydney, 1970. Recorded Fable FB 019.
Five Burns Settings Op 49 (bass-baritone, piano) first performed Sydney, 1970. Recorded RCA VRL 1-0124.
Two Australian Folk Songs Op 6 (soprano, orchestra) first performed Sydney, 1959
The Austral Moths Op 50 (baritone, piano) first performed Newcastle, New South Wales, 1972.
Sunset, Moon, Dreams Op 18 (SATB choir, string orchestra or piano) first performed Perth, Western Australia, 1972. Recorded ABC AC 10009.
Hark, Hark, the Lark Op 92/1–2 (soprano, guitar or harp; also version for soprano, piano) first performed Sydney, 1975; piano version first performed Sydney, 1976.
Lullaby Op 52/2 (soprano, harp or piano) first performed Sydney, 1976.
May in Italy Op 89 (counter-tenor, Renaissance ensemble) first performed Sydney, 1976.
Hymn Tune: Plymouth Op 98 (unaccompanied SATB chorus) first performed Sydney, 1977.
Hymn Tune: Drummoyne Op 99 (unaccompanied SATB chorus) first performed Sydney, 1977.
Six Henry Lawson Settings Op 105 (bass-baritone, double bass, orchestra) first performed Sydney, 1978.
Holy Communion Service (Anglican) Op 110 (unison voices, keyboard) first performed Perth, Western Australia, 1978.
Five Burns Songs Orchestral Op 49/2 (bass-baritone, orchestra) first performed Sydney, 1979.
Three Irish Contrasts Op 119 (unaccompanied SATB chorus) first performed Sydney, 1980.
Ferial Responses (Anglican) Op 138 (unaccompanied SATB chorus) first performed Sydney, 1983.
An Australian Symphony Op 163 (unaccompanied male voice choir) 1984.
Three Songs Op 139 (soprano, clarinet, piano) first performed Sydney, 1984.
Six Songs Op 147 (soprano, string quartet) first performed Perth, Western Australia, 1986.
Five Christmas Carols Op 168/1–5 (SA chorus, keyboards) first performed Sydney, 1987.

Opera:

The Amorous Judge Op 51 first performed Sydney, 1965.

Other:

Canberra Today and Tomorrow Op 63 (music for documentary film) first performed Sydney, 1959.
Australian Weekend Op 64 (music for documentary film) first performed Sydney, 1960.
Calling Sydney Harbour Op 65 (music for documentary film) first performed Sydney, 1960.
Another Sunny Day Op 66 (music for documentary film) first performed Sydney, 1961.
Festival in Adelaide Op 67 (music for documentary film) first performed Sydney, 1962.
Course Set for Tomorrow Op 68 (music for documentary film) first performed Sydney, 1963.
From the Tropics to the Snow Op 69 (music for documentary film) first performed Sydney, 1964.
Tobruk to Tarakan Op 70 (music for documentary film) first performed Sydney, 1964.
The Ugly Duckling Op 52 (pantomime) first performed Sydney, 1965.
Wide Pastures Op 71 (music for documentary film) first performed Sydney, 1965.
Tree Business Op 72 (music for documentary film) first performed Sydney, 1965.
Hobart Op 73 (music for documentary film) first performed Sydney, 1966.
Adventures of the Seaspray Op 87 (television music) first performed Sydney, 1966. Recorded HMV EA 4816.
Dream Concerto Op 93 (ballet; piano, orchestra) first performed Aberdeen, 1967.
Forest Without Spears Op 74 (music for documentary film) first performed Sydney, 1968.
New Guinea Election Story Op 75 (music for documentary film) first performed Sydney, 1968.
In One Lifetime Op 76 (music for documentary film) first performed Sydney, 1968.
The Big Nine Op 86 (television music) first performed Melbourne, 1969.
Rooftopics Op 77 (music for documentary film) first performed Sydney, 1971.
Hector and Millie Save Uncle Tom Op 78a (music for documentary film) first performed Sydney, 1973.
Silas Pilgrim Op 97a (music for documentary film) first performed Sydney, 1977.
The Grand Adventure Op 101 (music for marionettes) first performed Sydney, 1977.
Harvest of Melody (arrangement) first performed Sydney, 1977. Recorded Move MS 3029.
African Suite Op 106 (television music) first performed Sydney, 1978.
Alan Light sings Great Bass Ballads first performed Sydney, 1980. Recorded Move MS 3029.

PUBLICATIONS

By Gross: "The Contemporary Australian Composer and Society", Perth, 1971; "Backgrounds and Problems for an Historical and Critical Edition of the String Quartets of F.X. Dusek", Adelaide, 1972; "Music Manuscripts in the Library of St Bonifaz, Munich—A Preliminary Catalogue", Adelaide, 1975; "Some Thoughts on Composing a Saxophone Quartet", in *Clarinet Scene*, New South Wales, 15 (1), November 1990.

On Gross: Roger Covell, in *Australia's Music*, Melbourne, 1967; Andrew D. McCredie, *Catalogue of Forty-Six Australian Composers*, Canberra, 1969; James Murdoch, in *Australia's Contemporary Composers*, Melbourne, 1975; Margaret Seares, "EG", in Callaway and Tunley, *Australian Music*, Melbourne, 1978; Ian Shanahan, "Anthology of Australian Music on Disc", in Noone and Parker, *Handbook . . .* , Canberra, 1989.

Eric Gross comments:

Virtually all of my music has been composed for immediate performance or recording purposes. A number of my compositions resulted also from my association, as conductor, with choral or orchestral organizations. I believe that my first duty as a composer, apart from the maintenance of artistic integrity, is to my performers/interpreters because it is they who must work and expend time and energy in order to bring my music to life and to place it before an audience. Music must convince its performers before it can convince its audience. My aim is to communicate with the audience by stating musical ideas which the audience, present or future, may find to have some relevance to its own musical ideas or needs. If I write music for a specific occasion, I try to make it appropriate to that happening and if such an "occasional" composition has sufficient intrinsic merit, it may perhaps survive and be given further performances. There were times when I have made political statements in music either by implication, as in my orchestral work *Na Shledanou v Praze*—its first performance took place in Olomouc, a Czech city with a Russian garrison on its outskirts and I therefore used the Czech national anthem as my main theme—or by the use of pertinent philosophical or political texts, as in my cantata *Pacem in Terris*. This uses extracts from an encyclical of the same name by Pope John XXIII. I wrote this in 1962 when Khruschev foreshadowed the beginning of the end of Stalinism in the USSR and the Kennedy presidence gave hope to the Western world. In addition to a predilection for jazz idioms, my world-wide travels tend to give my music a cosmopolitan flavour with some traces of Asian or South American influences emerging.

Although musically I tend to be somewhat conservative, I enjoy experimentation expecially when I have sympathetic virtuosi available, as for example in some of my mandolin, recorder or trombone pieces, and I enjoy using unusual combinations wherever posible, as in my first symphony, where I have three counter-tenors seated within the woodwind section.

* * *

Eric Gross is virtually unique among Australian composers in that, although he is not a member of the avant-garde, he has succeeded in carving a quite personal stylistic niche for himself by founding his musical language upon a rich mélange of traditional, mid-20th-century idioms. Few composers anywhere have achieved true originality while their music has been overtly steeped in the conventional. But Gross's music transcends mere pastiche, and is dignified to the point that it is immediately and unmistakably recognizable as his own. Yet within Australia, his music seems to be underrated (whereas his younger, more conservative colleagues often find undeserved favour). Fortunately, this situation is offset to some extent by the significant degree of respect and attention his music has received within Europe: Gross's compositions are regularly performed in Czechoslovakia, in particular. Gross, nevertheless, is rarely commissioned in the formal sense (through government funding instrumentalities), so that he invariably writes, when requested, for specific performers and circumstances. His professionalism dictates a very close, collaborative working relationship with the players throughout each stage of the compositional process.

In terms of his style and development, Gross has maintained from the start of his career a remarkable consistency within his prodigious musical output, which can be bifurcated into two distinct regions. His lighter, more commercially oriented music is exemplified by numerous forays into film music. The title track to *Adventures of the Seaspray* is typical. His oeuvre of serious art-music compositions, on the other hand, is intended for consumption in the context of the concert hall. They embrace a highly diverse array of performance media—with the notable exception of the electronic music genre—including large-scale theatrical forms such as opera (*The Amorous Judge*). The orchestral works, characteristically brilliant in their orchestration, include several concertos (for piano, violin, oboe and mandolin) as well as symphonies, overtures and other important pieces (*Sinfonietta, Variations* for orchestra, *Concertino* for orchestra).

Gross's choral and vocal compositions comprise various song cycles, cantatas, art songs and Psalm settings. One can loosely trace their stylistic lineage, through the use of parallel harmonic motion and *organum*-like 4ths, to the English choral tradition dominated during this century by Vaughan Williams, Holst and Britten, and at the same time (in some regards) to the rhythmic vitality and harmonic spice of Walton. In many ways, they form a microcosm of his work as a whole. It is possible, within his *Three Burns Settings* for instance, to discern a stylistic remnant of his sojourn in Scotland, a folk-like jauntiness which permeates much of his output.

Gross's collection of chamber compositions covers almost every conceivable instrumental combination, from a single player right up to those which fall into the brass/military band repertoire. Perhaps central to this corpus are his works involving the mandolin, which arose from a long and fruitful relationship with mandolinists Paul and Adrian Hooper and their ensemble, *The Sydney Mandolins*. A recent piece for mandolin and string trio is, arguably, a masterpiece that exhibits the musical density of Schoenberg's *String Trio* or Stravinsky's *Orchestra Variations*.

Gross's early experience as a jazz pianist entailed considerable amounts of improvisation in a wide variety of idioms with idiosyncratic harmonic, rhythmic and textural devices. Many of the procedures of jazz have left their technical and aesthetic mark in works such as the *Klavierstücke*: Gross always prefers to compose in a rather free and intuitive manner, without resorting to the openly cerebral, "pre-compositional" grand designs or material-generating and ordering processes commonly found in post-1945 serialism. Moreover, the temporal facet of his music derives its rhythmic zest from Bartók and Hindemith, to whom one can also attribute Gross's single-minded pursuit to create an organic, thematic unity at every architectonic level of the music.

Throughout much of Gross's compositional output, one can find characteristic pitch structures and mannerisms that seemingly stem from his encounter with the jazz world: "altered" jazz chords and parallel chordal progressions—often moving by semitones—are abundant, and the interval of the perfect 4th is ubiquitous. (The 4th is actually Gross's fundamental building block, from which a multitude of other intervals and sonorities are derived. Superimposed 4ths yield minor 7ths, and, by inversion within the octave, minor 7ths give major 2nds; the perfect 4th when similarly inverted gives the perfect 5th. Tritones are also common. These intervals may then be combined and/or stacked upon each other in various ways—synchronously [vertical chords] or linearly [melody].) We therefore frequently observe, in this composer's harmonic vocabulary, superimposed perfect 4ths or 5ths, quasi-pentatonic harmonies, as well as complex and dissonant pitch constructions that can be synthesized from sets of perfect 4ths and/or tritones.

Gross's overriding formal preoccupations are based upon the ancient transformational principle of *variation*, set within contrasting sectional structures that involve, between relatively clearcut (sub)sections, the cyclical development, recurrence and progressive metamorphosis of different themes and motives themselves generated in a quasi-serial fashion from elementary intervallic cells. A modular or lattice-type structure often manifests itself, whereby predominantly self-contained musical fragments of various lengths reappear in a modified, expanded or truncated form within a musical context quite disparate from their initial statement. Such fragments are usually well-defined, being separated by a caesura or a ritardando (deceleration), or even a sudden change in dynamic level.

The fundamental principle of *variation*, as a generator of musical material, is, of course, firmly rooted within the jazz tradition (even though Gross's resultant mosaic approach to form is generally quite alien to that genre). Furthermore, although a clearly audible "musical logic" is exhibited, the feeling of discontinuity caused by a mosaic variation structure, where there is a constant and obvious interplay of contrasting ideas and styles, tends to negate any sense of the classical dialectical notions of climax and repose (except perhaps as localized phenomena) in Gross's music.

Gross is undoubtedly a composer of some creative significance, whose individual contribution to Australian musical culture is singularly impressive both in its qualitative and quantitative aspects. In the light of this assertion, it is to be hoped that the Australian musical establishment will soon come to reassess the output of this talented composer, and give him due positive support—like their European counterparts—by redressing the current scandalous situation of local neglect.

—Ian Shanahan

GRUBER, HK (professional name of Heinz Karl "Nali" Gruber). Austrian. Born in Vienna, 3 January 1943. Member of Vienna Boys' Choir, 1953–7. Educated at Vienna Hochsschule für Musik (double bass under Alfred Pianyavsky and Ludwig Streicher, composition with Alfred Uhi and Erwin Ratz, serial method with Hanns Jelinek, also horn, electronic music, film music and dance), 1957–63; masterclass in composition under Gottfried von Einem, 1963–4. Double bass player, *Die Reihe* ensemble, 1961; principal double bass, Tonkunstler Orchestra, 1963–9; co-founder, with Kurt Schwertsik and Otto M. Zykan, *MOB art & tone ART* ensemble, 1968–71; double bass player/actor, Austrian Radio Symphony Orchestra, since 1969. Recipient: prize (for *Concerto for Orchestra*), Österreichische Jugendkulturwoche, Innsbruck, 1966; Music Prize, Austrian Ministry of Culture and Education, 1979. Mailing address: c/o Theater-Verlag Eirich GmbH, Lothringerstrasse 20, 1030 Vienna, Austria.

Publisher: Boosey & Hawkes.

Symphonies/orchestral:

Concerto for Orchestra 1960–4.
Manhattan Broadcasts (light orchestra) 1962–4; first performed Vienna, 1964.
Fürbass (double bass, orchestra) 1965.
Revue (chamber orchestra) 1968.
Arien (violin, orchestra) 1974–5; withdrawn.
Vergrösserung / Magnification 1970.
Violin Concerto " . . . aus Schattenduft gewebt" / " . . . of shadow fragrance woven" 1977–8; first performed Berlin, 29 September 1979.
Demilitarized Zones / Entmilitarisierte Zonen (march paraphrases for brass band) 1979; first performed Zagreb, 17 May 1979.
Charivari: Austrian Journal 1981.
Rough Music (percussion, orchestra) from 1982.
Nebelsteinmusik (Violin Concerto No 2) (violin, strings) 1988; first performed Austria, 19 July 1988.
Cello Concerto (cello, small orchestra) 1989; first performed Tanglewood, Massachusetts, 3 August 1989.

Chamber / instrumental:

Suite (2 pianos, winds, percussion) 1960.
Improvisationen (wind quintet) 1961.
Episoden (2 pianos) 1961.
Concerto No 1 (flute, vibraphone, xylophone, percussion) 1961.
Concerto No 2 (tenor saxophone, double bass, percussion) 1961.
Four Pieces (violin) 1963; first performed Vienna, 20 May 1966.
Gioco a tre (violin, cello, piano) 1963.
Two Rhapsodies (cello, piano) 1964.
Six Episodes from a Discontinued Chronicle / Sechs Episoden aus einer unterbrochenen Chronik (piano) 1967; first performed Vienna, 20 February 1968.
Spiel (wind quintet) 1967.
Bossa Nova (ensemble) 1968.
3 MOB Pieces (7 interchangeable instruments with percussion; flute or oboe, violin, clarinet; clarinet or violin, trumpet; trumpet or clarinet; trombone or horn, bassoon, cello; guitar or keyboard; violin or clarinet; cello or bassoon, double bass) 1968, revised 1977; first performed Graz, 14 October 1979.
Die wirkliche Wut über den verlorenen Groschen (5 players) 1972.
Festmusik (chamber ensemble) 1972.
Phantom bilder auf der spur eines verdächtigten Themas / Photo-Fit Pictures on the Track of a Suspected Theme (flute/piccolo, oboe, clarinet, trumpet, trombone, percussion, classical guitar, piano, string quartet, double bass ad lib) 1977; first performed London, 7 March 1979.
Luftschlösser / Castles in the Air (piano) 1981; first performed Schloss Grafenegg, Austria, 9 May 1981.

Vocal / choral:

Mass (mixed chorus, 2 trumpets, cor anglais, double bass, percussion) 1960.
Drei Lieder (baritone, ensemble, tape; Tagore) 1961.
Vier Lieder (soprano, piano; Bletschacher) 1964.
Fünf Kinderlieder (unaccompanied SSAA choir; Bletschacher) 1965, revised 1980.
Die Vertreibung aus dem Paradies / The Expulsion from Paradise (1 male, 1 female or 3 male, 1 female speakers, flute, alto saxophone, horn, percussion, piano, double bass) 1966, revised 1979; first performed Vienna, 11 February 1969.
Der Kastengeist (song; Bletschacher) 1968.
Gomorrah (musical spectacle; Bletschacher) 1970–2.
3 Mai (song; Schwertsik, Schwertsik, Unger, after Gruber) 1973. Recorded with band accompaniment Jeunesses Musicales 1011.
Marihuana-Song (Bletschacher) 1973.
Die Wette (Beletschacher) 1973.
Die oete Leier (song; Schwertsik, Schwertsik, Unger) 1974. Recorded with band accompaniment Jeunesses Musicales 1011.
Hobby Song (Schwertsik, Schwertsik, Unger) 1974. Recorded with band accompaniment Jeunesses Musicales 1011.
Wenn der Tango erwacht (song; Schwertsik, Schwertsik, Unger) 1974. Recorded with band accompaniment Jeunesses Musicales 1011.
Reportage aus Gomorrah (5 singers, 8 players; Bletschacher) 1975–6. *Rauchlied* (song; Bletschacher) 1976.
Frankenstein!! (baritone chansonnier, orchestra; after children's rhymes by H. C. Artmann) 1976–7; first performed Liverpool, 25 November 1978; ensemble version for baritone chansonnier, flute/piccolo, clarinet, bassoon, horn, trumpet, percussion, piano, string quintet, 1979; first performed Berlin, 30 September 1979.
Der Hausdrache (song; Bletschacher) 1980.

Other:

Konjugationen (tape) 1963.

Cadenzas for Domenico Puccini: *Piano Concerto in B♭*, 1965; Dittersdorf: *Sinfonia Concertante* (viola, double bass), 1968, and *Concerto in D* (double bass), 1968.

* * *

Two of HK Gruber's earliest works dating from 1960, the *Suite* and the *Mass*, illustrate the contradictory tensions which have persisted in his music between the idea of art as iconoclastic and subversive (as in the former piece) and as a disciplined, orderly activity (the *Mass*). This contradiction is confirmed in the much more impressive *Concerto for Orchestra* because it co-exists within a single work. Although he studied twelve-note techniques and was involved in performances of avant-garde works as a double bass player in the *Die Reihe* ensemble, Gruber's reputation rests on a highly individualistic voice, which is esentially tonal. The serial works of the mid-1960s, like the *Four Pieces* for solo violin, the *Gioco a tre* and the *Two Rhapsodies* for cello and piano, were produced side by side with, for instance, *Manhattan Broadcasts* for light orchestra. And in the *Konjugationen* of 1963, an electronic piece that includes jazz, we see a further attempt at integrating opposing strands.

This characteristic has been pervasive and has infused Gruber's developing relationship to the Viennese heritage from Mahler through Berg (notably in both of Gruber's violin concertos) to Eisler and beyond.

How to forge a coherent personal style from disparate material was an abiding concern during the mid-1960s. One way ahead was seen in the melodrama *Die Vertreibung aus dem Paradies* of 1966, in which collage, quotations and the conventions of cabaret and music theatre are interspersed within an adventurous and exploratory tonal language. In 1968, he became a co-founder (with Kurt Schwertsik and Otto M. Zykan) of the *MOB art & tone ART* ensemble, with the aim of livening up the stiff academicism prevalent in Vienna at the time. Thereafter, he produced many works of wit and irony, the most outstanding of which is the satire-cum-cabaret *Frankenstein!!* which brought him to international prominence. This setting of children's rhymes by H.C. Artmann takes an ironic view of contemporary super-heroes and other elements of popular culture (including references to Batman and Superman). It is written for "chansonnier"—most memorably Gruber himself—and an orchestra that includes real and toy instruments. Its melodic appeal and harmonic clarity, coloured with a virtuoso orchestrator's touch, gives a great lucidity to a work that was described formally as a "pan-demonium for baritone and orchestra", and informally as "a maddeningly memorable 30 minutes of inspired and carefully calculated lunacy". The serious aspect of Gruber's *Frankenstein!!* and his other fun-pieces lies in his iconoclastic view of the Viennese tradition. Musically, too, Gruber, draws from the potentially serious reservoirs of serialism even in his lightest pieces, but if the shadow of *Pierrot Lunaire* lurks in the background of *Frankenstein!!* its particular brand of Expressionism is distilled and indeed subverted by Gruber's easygoing and deliciously suggestive idiocy.

Some years previously, between 1971 and 1974, Gruber experienced a compositional block exacerbated by his inability to finish his first Violin Concerto. This important work was eventually completed in 1977–8, and in it Gruber's profound allegiance to Stravinsky is seen side by side with, perhaps inevitably, resonances of Berg's Violin Concerto. Gruber finds a polarity between the two, and in this intensely expressive work he confirms a necessary balance between a rather fragile, post-Weill lyricism and the anarchy of *Frankenstein!!*.

The second violin concerto, entitled *Nebelsteinmusik*, also has allusions to Viennese forebears, Alban Berg of the *Lyric Suite* this time, and one of Gruber's mentors, Gottfried von Einem. Gruber's pluralism is again very apparent in this work which explores a series of moods, mellow, whimsical, soulful, witty and dancing by turns, before a final gloriously self-indulgent burlesque.

The Cello Concerto of 1989 provides a recent focus on Gruber's original and, to some, rather unsettling split personality. Here again the skill with which he confronts the surface sweetness of Viennese music is evident in the sardonic, cabaret-derived undercurrents which, with the manically high cello writing, often creates a sense of unease. The work ends with lilting, beseeching rhythms of great beauty, but one is left asking, yet again, whether the music's smile is really what it appears to be.

—Richard Elfyn Jones

GUBAIDULINA, Sofia (Asgatovna). Russian. Born in Chsistopol, Tatar S.S.R., 24 October 1931. Educated at Kazan Music Academy (theory under Nazib Zhiganov, piano under Maria Piatnitskaya), 1946–9; Kazan Conservatory (piano under Leopold Lukomsky and Grigory Kogan, composition under Albert Leman), 1949–54; Moscow Conservatory (composition under Nikolai Peiko and Vissarion Shebalin), 1954–63; further research, Electronic Music Studio, Moscow, from 1968. Accompanist, Moscow Theatre Institute, 1963–4; Composer, Studio of Documentary Films, 1963–7; composer, Studio of Art Films, Odessa, 1964–9; composer, Taganka Theatre, Moscow, 1966; composer, Studio of Animated Cartoons, from 1968; composer, Moscow Soviet Theatre, from 1970; co-founder, with Viktor Suslin and Vyacheslav Artyomov, improvisation group Astraea, 1975. Recipient: 1st prize (for *Stufen / Steps*), 7th International Composers' Competition, Rome, 1975; composition prize, Prince Pierre de Monaco Foundation, 1987. Mailing address: 2aya Pugachovskaya ulitsa, dom 8, korp. 5, kv. 130, 107061 Moscow, U.S.S.R.

Publisher: Sikorski.

Symphonies / orchestral:

Symphony 1958.
Piano Concerto 1959.
Adagio and Fugue (violin, string orchestra) 1960.
Overture: Triumph 1963.
Fairy Tale Poem 1971; first performed Moscow, March 1971.
Detto II (cello, orchestra) 1972; first performed Moscow, 5 May 1973. Recorded Melodia C-10-10167-68.
Concerto (bassoon, low strings) 1975; first performed Moscow, 6 May 1976. Recorded Melodia C-10-12749-50.
Concerto (symphony orchestra, jazz band) 1976; first performed Moscow, 16 January 1978.
Te salutant (cappriccio for large light orchestra) 1978; first performed Moscow, 1978.
Introitus (piano, chamber orchestra) 1978; first performed Moscow, 22 February 1978.
Offertorium (violin, orchestra) 3 versions—1980, 1982, 1986; original version first performed Vienna, 30 May 1981; revised version first performed Berlin (F.D.R.), 24 September 1982; final version first performed London, 2 November 1986. Recorded Deutsche Grammophon.
(Last) Seven Words (cello, bayan, strings) 1982; first performed Moscow, 20 October 1982.
Stimmen . . . Verstummen . . . (symphony in 12 movements) 1986; first performed Berlin, 4 September 1986.
Antwort ohne Frage (3 orchestras) 1988.

Chamber / instrumental:

Sonatina (piano) 1952.
Eight Preludes (piano) 1955.
Variations (string quartet) 1956.
Piano Quintet 1957; first performed Moscow, 1958.
Intermezzo (8 trumpets, 16 harps, percussion) 1961.
Chaconne (piano) 1962; first performed Moscow, 13 March 1966. Recorded Melodia D-021555.
Allegro rustico (flute, piano) 1963; first performed Riga, 1963.
Sonata (piano) 1965; first performed Moscow, 1967.
Five Etudes (harp, double bass, percussion) 1965; first performed Moscow, 25 February 1967.
Sonata (percussion) 1966.
Pantomime (double bass, piano) 1966; first performed Moscow, 17 May 1981.
Musical Toys (14 piano pieces for children) 1969. Recorded (3 parts only) Melodia C-50-09933-34.
Toccata-troncata (piano) 1971.
Concordanza (flute, oboe, clarinet, bassoon, horn, percussion, violin, viola, cello, double bass) 1971; first performed Prague, 23 May 1971. Recorded Melodia C-10-18403-4; Panton 11-0342-3.

String Quartet No 1 1971; first performed Cologne, 24 March 1979.
Music for Harpsichord and Percussion Instruments (instruments from the Mark Pekarsky collection) 1972; first performed Leningrad, 5 April 1972.
Ten Preludes (cello) 1974; first performed Moscow, 12 December 1977.
Quattro (2 trumpets, 2 trombones) 1974; first performed Moscow, 22 November 1974.
Rumore e silenzio (percussion, harpsichord/celeste) 1974; first performed Leningrad, 16 April 1975.
Invention (piano) 1974.
Sonata (double bass, piano) 1975; first performed Moscow, April 1978.
Two Ballads (2 trumpets, piano) 1976.
Light and Darkness (organ) 1976; first performed Leningrad, 21 May 1979.
Trio (3 trumpets) 1976.
Dots, Line and Zigzag (bass clarinet, piano) 1976; first performed Berlin, 22 February 1977.
On Tatar Folk Themes (soprano/alto/bass domra, piano) 1977.
Duo-sonata (2 bassoons) 1977; first performed Moscow, 17 May 1978.
Misterioso (7 percussion) 1977; first performed Moscow, 5 April 1977.
Quartet (4 flutes) 1977.
Lamento (tuba, piano) 1977.
Muzika (harpsichord, percussion) 1977.
Song Without Words (trumpet, piano) 1977.
Detto I (organ, percussion) 1978; first performed Moscow, 14 October 1979.
Sounds of the Forest (flute, piano) 1978.
Sonatina (flute) 1978.
De Profundis (bayan) 1978; first performed Moscow, 8 April 1980. Recorded Melodia C-20-16633-4.
Two Pieces (horn, piano) 1979.
Jubilatio (4 percussion) 1979; first performed Moscow, 13 January 1979.
In croce (cello, organ) 1979; first performed Kazan, 27 March 1979. Recorded Opus 9111 1277.
Garten von Freuden und Traurigkeiten / The Garden of Joys and Sorrows (flute, harp, viola, speaker ad lib; Tanzer) 1980; first performed Moscow, 9 February 1981.
Sonata: Rejoice! (violin, cello) 1981.
Descensio (3 trombones, 3 percussion, harp, harpsichord/celeste, celeste/piano) 1981; first performed Paris, 30 April 1981.
Quasi Hoquetus (viola, bassoon, piano) 1984; first performed Moscow, 16 January 1985.
Sonata (bayan) 1985.
String Quartet No 2 1987; first performed Kuhmo, Finland, 23 July 1987.
String Quartet No 3 1987; first performed Edinburgh, 22 August 1987.

Vocal/choral:

Fatseliya (soprano, symphony orchestra; Prishvin) 1956; first performed Moscow, 1957.
Night in Memphis (mezzo-soprano, male choir, orchestra; ancient Egyptian, translated by Akhmatova and Potapova) 1968; first performed Prague, December 1970.
Rubayat (baritone, chamber orchestra; Omar Khayyam, Hafiz, Khakani) 1969; first performed Moscow, 24 December 1976. Recorded Melodia C-10-15059-60.
Stufen / Steps (orchestra with speaking choir; Rilke) 1972.
Roses (soprano, piano; Aygi) 1972; first performed 15 January 1974.
Counting Rhymes (voice, piano; Satunovsky) 1973.
Hour of the Soul (revised version of *Percussio di Pekarski*; mezzo-soprano, percussion, large orchestra; Tsvetayeva) 1974, 1976–88.
Laudatio Pacis (collaboration with Marek Kopelent of Czechoslovakia and Paul-Heinz Dittrich of the German Democratic Republic; soprano, alto, tenor, bass, speaker, 2 mixed choirs, large orchestra; Comenius) 1975.
Perception (soprano, baritone, 2 violins, 2 violas, 3 cellos, double bass, tape; Tanzer, Psalms) 1983; first performed Lockenhaus, 11 June 1986.
Hommage à Marina Tsvetayeva (unaccompanied mixed choir) 1984.
Hommage à T.S. Eliot (soprano, clarinet, bassoon, horn, 2 violins, viola, cello, double bass) 1987; first performed Cologne, 25 March 1987. Recorded Deutsche Grammophon.
Witty Waltzing in the Style of Johann Strauss (soprano, clarinet, bassoon, horn, 2 violins, viola, cello, double bass) 1987; first performed Cologne, 25 March 1987.
Two Songs from German Folk-poetry (soprano, flute, harpsichord, cello) 1988.
Jauchzt vor Gott (mixed choir, organ) 1989.

Other:

Volshebnaya svirel (ballet) 1960.
Flute of Tania (ballet) 1961.
Begushchaya po volnam (ballet) 1962.
Vivente–non vivente (tape) 1969–70.

Film scores: *The Scarecrow* (Bykov); *The University Chair*; *The Circus Tent* (Garanima, after Lorca); *Veliki Samoyed* (Kordon).

PUBLICATIONS

On Gubaidulina: V. Gibelli, in *Storia della musica sovietica: compositoriu ecomposizioni della Russia europeas e asiatica*, Pavia, 1964–5; in *Muzykalnaya literatura iz SSR*, Moscow, 1976; G.B. Bernndt and I.M. Yampolski, in *Sovietske Kompozitory i Muzykoviedy*, Moscow, 1978; Judith Lang Zaimont, in *The Musical Woman*, Westport, Connecticut, 1984.

* * *

All of Sofia Gubaidulina's works breathe an air of spirituality. Her music radiates a sense of religious mystery, and of contemplative, ecstatic fervour whose intensity transcends any outward appearance of asceticism and frugality. Its roots lie in a mixture of the Muslim, Orthodox, Jewish and Roman Catholic faiths. Gubaidulina's father was a Tartar and his father a mullah, while her mother came from Russian, Polish and Jewish stock. Oriental influences are evident both in her philosophical outlook and in her musical technique; in the twisting cello monody of *In croce*, for example, and the singular atmosphere of *The Garden of Joys and Sorrows*. She has said of herself, "I am the place where East meets West". But the mystical philosophy and ritual are tempered by a love of poetry and literature, particularly the work of Westerners like T.S. Eliot. Time passing, slowly unfolding rhythmic arcs, proportion and temporal balance are her constant concerns.

The sound of her music is particularly distinctive. Gubaidulina is preoccupied with the intrinsic character of single notes, vibrant, trembling and fragile as if audibly blown into life by their creator. Often the music is spun from threads so slender as to attenuate almost to vanishing point. Its beauty springs from the fluctuating, improvisatory lines with their subtlety of decoration, and from the profound dignity of timeless chant. Her original timbral palette, fondness for untempered tunings, surrealistic sound world and unorthodox playing techniques are the metaphors of a deeper psychological drama played out, as often as not, through a powerful confrontation of opposites. On the one hand there are the introspective quicksands of a volatile, unstable chromaticism; on the other the reassuring radiance of soaring melody and triadic harmony.

Gubaidulina's remarkable *(Last) Seven Words* for cello, bayan (button accordion) and strings is archetypal. Its religious subject matter (although suppressed at the Moscow premiere) unmistakably underpins a structure drawing on quotation—here a fragment of Heinrich Schütz's *Seven Words*—and numerous devices of musical symbolism. The soloists' music uses novel and unique means of sound production in an expressive dialogue between the "human" breathing of the accordion and the "spiritual" domain of the cello. The *tutti* strings evoke, through the overlayering of simple chant-like phrases, the spirit of old Slavic church music. Inexorably the texture grows denser and the soloists' lament more declamatory and impassioned, moving to an almost violent dramatic climax from which the music dies away in insubstantial, disembodied fragments.

Many of Gubaidulina's works are for such unusual combinations of instruments and written for the artistry of particular players, revealing an exceptional unity between the composer's conception, the personality of the interpreter and the essential character of the instrument. She has worked closely with the brilliant Moscow percussionist Mark Pekarsky; in the 1970s she founded an improvisation group with two other composers using rare Russian, Caucasian and Central Asian folk instruments; and her forays into jazz include a score backing the scat singing of the gypsy Valentina Ponomareva. During her early career she earned a livelihood writing music for films. Her later, large-scale concert works include the symphony *Stimmen . . . Verstummen . . .* in 12 movements, one of them for conductor alone, which caused a sensation at the Berlin Festival in 1986, and the violin concerto *Offertorium*. In this impressive single movement, a strange, surreal landscape of ruminating gestures and colouristic sound effects gives way, at length, to a profoundly beautiful melody whose sustained and eloquent sorrow taps that vein of Russian melancholy familiar in the music of Tchaikovsky and Shostakovitch. The work is freely derived from the Royal Theme of Bach's *Musical Offering* to which it pays a sort of homage; in this and in other pieces, Gubaidulina skillfully unites the past with the avant-garde, reassuring the ordinary listener that conventional expression can still be meaningful in a contemporary context.

A shrewd appraisal of Gubaidulina's music comes from her friend and colleague, Alfred Schnittke: "From her first pieces, Sofia Gubaidulina revealed in her music an unusual stylistic unity, a highly original spiritual world and an unbending composer's will. The stylistic evolution she has undergone since then has merely enhanced the expressiveness of her music without in the least affecting its character. Her extreme self-criticism compels her to spend much time on polishing the most minute details—which, however, leads not to superficial elegance but to strict asceticism. Her music is well integrated and devoid of all compromise. Such is the composer herself. The strictest demands she imposes on herself are combined in her with kindliness and benevolence, broadmindedness and tolerance for other peoples' musical thinking and styles."

—Richard Steinitz

GUDMUNDSEN-HOLMGREEN, Pelle. Danish. Born in Copenhagen, 21 November 1932. Educated: violin lessons from 1948; private lessons in theory and composition under Finn Høffding, 1951–3; at Royal Danish Conservatory of Music, Copenhagen (theory, composition and history of music under Finn Høffding and Svend Westergaard, instrumentation under Vagn Holmboe), 1953–8. Married Gunvor Kaarsberg, 21 November 1959; 1 son and 1 daughter. Technical assistant, Royal Theatre, Copenhagen, 1959–64; Teacher of composition, Jutland Conservatory of Music, Aarhus, 1967–72. Recipient: Lange-Muller Stipend, 1965; Herman Sandbergen Prize, 1971; Carl Nielsen Prize, 1973; Music Prize of the Nordic Council (for *Symphony, Antiphony*), 1980. Mailing address: Eggersvej 29, 2900 Hellerup, Denmark.

Publishers: Edition Wilhelm Hansen, Copenhagen; Society for the Publication of Danish Music, Copenhagen.

Symphonies/orchestral:

Overture for Strings 1955.
Lamento (strings, percussion) 1957.
Symphony 1962–5.
Chronos (chamber orchestra) 1962. Recorded EMI 6C 063-38100.
Collegium Musicum Koncert (chamber orchestra) 1964.
Mester Jakob / Frère Jacques (chamber orchestra) 1964.
Five Pieces 1966.
Symphony: Pa Rygmarven 1966.
Tricolore I 1966.
Segnali (wind orchestra) 1966.
Tricolore II 1967.
Tricolore III 1967.
Variations on "Moster Rix" (chamber orchestra) 1968.
Three Movements (strings, percussion) 1968.
Piece by Piece (chamber orchestra) 1968.
Kadence (wind orchestra) 1969.
Tricolore IV 1969. Recorded DG DMA 018.
Prelude and Fugue (brass band, electric guitar, percussion) 1969.
Catalogue and Coda (wind orchestra) 1969.
Quartet for Eighteen (wind orchestra) 1970.
Mirror II 1973.
Symphony, Antiphony 1974–7.
Triptych (percussion, orchestra) 1985.
Concerto Grosso (string quartet, orchestra) 1990.

Chamber/instrumental:

Variations (cello) 1954.
Nonet (woodwind quintet, 3 percussion, piano) 1958.
String Quartet No 1 1959.
Quartetto facile: String Quartet No 2 1959.
Five Little Studies: String Quartet No 3 1959. Recorded SUDM 012.

Variations (piano) 1959.
Lilleforspil (piano, 2 violins, cello) 1960.
Two improvisations (flute, clarinet, horn, trumpet, trombone, 2 percussion, vibraphone, piano, double bass) 1960.
In terra pax (clarinet, 2 percussion, piano) 1961.
Recapitulations (chamber ensemble) 1965.
Til Far (clarinet, bassoon, 2 trombone, percussion, piano, cello, double bass) 1965.
Re-recapitulations (chamber ensemble) 1967. Recorded SUDM 012.
Canon (any 9 instruments) 1967.
String Quartet No 4 1967. Recorded SUDM 012.
Udstillingsbilleder / Pictures at an Exhibition (piano) 1968. Recorded CBS 73870.
Infantile Music (6–100 players) 1968.
Horizontale Born; To and from Terry Riley (5 pianos, 20 instruments ad lib) 1968.
Plateaux pour deux (percussion, cello) 1970. Recorded Paula 24.
I midten og ud (alto saxophone, percussion, guitar, piano, vibraphone, double bass) 1970.
Terrace in Five Stages (wind quintet) 1970. Recorded Philips 6578007.
Solo (electric guitar) 1971–2. Recorded SUDM 012.
So Long (electric guitar) 1972.
Kong Kristian stod i et yndigt land (soprano saxophone, tuba, 2 percussion, piano, string quartet) 1973.
Mirror III (organ) 1974.
Re-Cycling (2 flutes, trumpet, 2 cellos, 2 double basses) 1975. Recorded EMI 065-39331.
Den gamle mand (2 flutes, harp, viola, cello) 1976.
October (piccolo, 2 flutes, 2 oboes, cor anglais, 2 clarinets, contrabass clarinet/bass clarinet, bassoon, contrabassoon) 1977.
Passacaglia (clarinet, piano, tabla, violin, cello) 1977. Recorded Paula 24.
Duo I–II ("dramatic incident" for bassoon, cello) 1978.
Praeludium til din tavshed / Prelude to Your Silence (flute, bass clarinet, piano, guitar, 2 percussion, viola, cello) 1978. Recorded Paula 24.
Mosaik (various combinations of: clarinet, horn, 2 accordions, 2 violins, 2 cellos, piano, 2 flutes, 2 bassoons, percussion) 1979.
Mirror Pieces (clarinet, cello, piano) 1980. Recorded SUDM 012; Paula PACD 57.
Step by Step: String Quartet No 5 1982.
Parting: String Quartet No 6 1983.
Parted: String Quartet No 7 1984.
Ground: String Quartet No 8 1986.
reTurning (flute, clarinet, percussion, harp, piano) 1987.
Naer og fjern (wind quintet, string quartet, double bass) 1987.
Concord (flute, oboe, clarinet, bassoon, trumpet, 2 horns, trombone, percussion, piano, 2 violins, viola, cello, double bass) 1988.
Octopus (organ, 4 hands) 1989.

Vocal/choral:

Vandringen / Wandering (mixed chorus; Knudsen) 1954, version for soloist, chorus, orchestra, 1957.
Five Songs (soprano/tenor, flute, violin, cello) 1958.
Den hvide hejre (children's choir, female choir) 1960.
Nar solen stiger (children's choir, female choir) 1960.
En sod digter (mixed chorus) 1960.
Ebbe Skammelsen (mixed chorus, orchestra) 1961.
Je ne me tairai jamais. Jamais (narrator, mixed chorus or 12 mixed voices, oboe, bassoon, 2 trombones, piano, electric organ, mandolin, viola, double bass; Beckett) 1966.
Three Songs to Texts from "Politiken" (alto, percussion, guitar, violin, viola, cello) 1967.
Three Statements (children's choir, equal voices; Nielsen) 1969.
Examples (mixed chorus; Nielsen, Strandgaard, Nordbrandt) 1970. Recorded LPWH 3019.
Yes–No (double chorus; G-H, Holm) 1973.
Songs Without (mezzo-soprano, piano; anon., Herrick, Wordsworth, Beckett) 1976. Recorded Danica DLP 8056.
Lys / Light (SATTB choir, organ; Bible) 1976.
Din tavshed / Your Silence (soprano, flute, clarinet, piano, guitar, percussion, viola, cello) 1978. Recorded Paula 24.
Jubilemus (male choir, 2 trombones, contrabassoon) 1981.
Born (mixed choir, children's choir, clarinet, contrabassoon, trombone, 5 percussion, electric guitar, electric bass, electric organ, violin) 1981.
Born pa langs (til og fra Terry Riley) (children's choir, instruments) 1984.
Tilfaeldigheden og nodvendigheden / Le Hasard et la nécessité (2 choirs, orchestra; Suneson) 1985.
Mordet i Finderup / The Murder in Finderup (mixed choir, 2 trombones ad lib) 1986. Recorded Danica DLP 8083.

Other:

Mirror I (tape) 1971–3.
Den gamle mand (television ballet; 2 flutes, harp, viola, cello) 1976.
Rituelle danse (ballet; 2 versions—5 percussion, electric guitar; 6 percussion) 1976.
Trio (music to ballet *Moder*; violin, horn, percussion) 1979.
Flight (ballet; flute, clarinet, horn, 6 percussion) 1981.

PUBLICATIONS

By Gudmundsen-Holmgreen: "Omkring *Repriser*", in *Dansk Musiktidsskrift*, 41, 1966; "Om *Tricolore* for orkester", in *Ta*, 1(3), 1967; "Jantenatur", in *Dansk Musiktidsskrift*, 48, 1974; "Om *Spejl* for orkester", in *Dansk Musiktidsskrift*, 49, 1974.

On Gudmundsen-Holmgreen: P. Nielsen, "Omkring den ny enhelted", in *Dansk Musiktidsskrift*, 41, 1966; P. Nielsen, "Den demokratische daemon" in *Nutida Musik*, 11(1), 1968–9; P. Nielsen, "Kunst en state natur", in *Dansk Musiktidsskrift*, 46, 1971; Jan Andersen, "Dagens Portraet", in *Politiken*, 30 October 1990.

Pelle Gudmundsen-Holmgreen comments:
Small pieces of EVERYTHING seeming to be NOTHING—AGAIN and AGAIN.

* * *

No matter whether one is familiar with 20th-century New Music or not, the experience of listening to a piece by Pelle Gudmundsen-Holmgreen is something quite remarkable.

Samuel Beckett's world is close to the heart of what Gudmundsen-Holmgreen has done. They share a taste for near-silence—and long passages in works by Gudmundsen-Holmgreen are disconcertingly subdued and muttering. No less characteristically, however, his music can be alarmingly (or refreshingly) violent in expression and in the actual quantities of sound. Here a stubborn (and mischievous) refusal to be good and behave may induce him to explore the limits of what things will take—not for the sake of being extreme, but as a means to making an impression that goes beyond the veneer of convenience and tradition and probes the deeper layers of the musical self, while he as a composer may well have been engaged in a more sophisticated dialogue with the music of other times and other cultures. The Romantic heritage has never been quite his cup of tea, however—by nature and upbringing he is more open to the joys of jazz, Baroque music, African rhythms, Asian rites and early Nordic modernist classics such as Sibelius and (notably) Nielsen. Stravinsky is another venerated guiding star.

Not that Gudmundsen-Holmgreen's music sounds much like anything else, or anyone else's. Nor does it seem at first particularly "interesting" by any "advanced" 20th-century standard. Basically he makes do with the simplest materials, and more often than not the aesthetic perplexity of the listener is provoked by the indeceptive simplicity. Gudmunsen-Holmgreen is a master of achieving effects by abstaining from effects. On the other hand, what the listener may take to be moments of collage and/or persiflage will turn out to be the implementation of dramaturgical decisions in the architectural context of the unfolding musical structure, or maybe the composer's ironic sense of humour was just tickled by possibilities offered to him by the System.

Gudmundsen-Holmgreen has always been a meticulous and exacting composer, although his laconic programme notes tend to well-nigh disown his efforts and the final result. By nature he is a sceptic and quite incapable of any sentimental or coy adherence to preconceived patterns of style and idea(l)s. How, then, has he managed to take arms against the sea of aesthetic and technical troubles confronting anyone who aims at meaningfully writing non-traditionalist new scores for an age of anxiety with all kinds of music in the air, night and day?

The fairly high degree of stylistic unity within the main body of Gudmundsen-Holmgreen's production masks the fact that a change in his working conditions has been taking place during the last couple of decades. In earlier years he would go to his collection of materials, his *objets trouvés*, and then painstakingly bring some of them together in forms governed by *ad hoc* laws of construction—drawing on his considerable fund of knowledge, of course, but essentially playing it by ear. How could he escape from this typically 20th-century hole without falling into all the well-known 20th-century traps? Luckily he detected the makings of a system for constructional choice and procedure, or rather, a system which pre-organizes the parameters of material and form by establishing a network of symmetrical structures spreading out from a number of fixed points and forming sets of patterns that mirror each other. The system constantly surprises him by proving to be more useful (and more fun!) than anticipated, but it would be wrong to imagine that it has made things easier: What matters to the composer is that it offers him a different kind of freedom of choice than he had before. What matters to the listener is that Gudmundsen-Holmgreen's trust of the workings of this special system seems to make his highly individual kind of music increasingly accessible to the common man as well as the mandarins of Art, notwithstanding the complexity of engineering behind the scene.

One should be wary of linking any two prominent composers of exactly the same age, writing much the same kind of music within the same geographical and cultural framework. Gudmundsen-Holmgreen and Per Nørgård are no identical twins, though they are exact contemporaries, share the same background as composers, and for obvious reasons have become eminent and integral parts of the same New Music environment in Denmark and Scandinavia. Both are master craftsmen exerting a deep and lasting influence on composers around them—albeit in very different ways, according to personal and artistic characteristics. For the benefit of listeners unfamiliar with their work, one might venture to sum up the difference between the two very Scandinavian Danish composers as follows. Indirectly first: If Per Nørgård were a painter also modelling in soft materials, then Gudmundsen-Holmgreen would be the draughtsman also sculpting in metal and stone. More directly—if the key words for the music of Nørgård are melody, soul and vision, then for Gudmundsen-Holmgreen they are rhythm, body and form.

—Svend Ravnkilde

GUGEL, Alexander. Lithuanian/Soviet. Born in Vilnius, 24 January 1961. Educated at Kharkov Art Institute (composition). 1979–84. Flautist in regimental orchestra. Kharkov, 1984–6; teacher of composition, Children's Music School, Kharkov, since 1986, and Music College, Kharkov, since 1988. Mailing address: Pr. Traktorostroiteley 138–A, k–12, 310121 Kharkov, Ukraine.

Publisher: none.

Symphonies/orchestral:

Symphony 1984–7.
March (wind orchestra) 1985.
Dedication to Arvo Pärt 1989; first performed Kiev, 1990.

Chamber/instrumental:

Music for Piano 1980; first performed London, 1989.
Trio (piano, violin, cello) 1980.
Elegy (piano, clarinet) 1981–7; first performed Lvov, 1989.
Sonata No 1 (piano) 1982–9.
Capriccio (piano) 1988; first performed Moscow, 1989.
Sonata No 2 (piano) 1989.
Moment musical (piano) 1989.
Three Lithuanian Songs (piano, tinkling instruments) 1989; first performed Omsk, 1990.
To Geometry (piano) 1989; first performed Omsk, 1990.
For Flying Away Birds (piano) 1989; first performed London, 16 June 1990.
Eleven Exercises (piano) 1990; first performed London, 1990.
Two Chorale Postludes (violin, cello, double bass) 1990; first performed London, 1990.
For Elise I (piano) 1990; first performed London, 1990.
For Elise II (piano) 1990; first performed London, 1990.

Vocal/choral:

Five Songs on Verses by Aleksandr Blok (soprano, piano) 1986; first performed Kiev, 1986.
Liturgy Fantasia (mixed chorus, organ) 1986–8.
Duet on a Poem by Osip Mandelstam (tenor, cello) 1986; first performed Kiev, 1987.
Three Poems of M, Martinaitis (tenor, flute; version for chamber choir) 1988.
Three Catholic Songs (women's or children's chorus, organ) 1988.

Alexander Gugel comments:

I regard my musical activities as more of a hobby, which I would find even more difficult to give up than to pursue (obviously I am well aware that this particular hobby demands professionalism and great commitment).

I have always been bothered by two particular aspects of music: its capacity to appear before one's eyes as a row of unfolding visual images and to be itself born from visual images; and secondly, music's tendency sometimes only partially to embody the composer's idea, inserting in its place something of its own, something the composer does not expect; as a result, it seems that music "knows" more than its composer and is correcting its evolution by itself.

While working on pieces, I have always felt the desire to reproduce rather than create, to follow rather than lead. For me, following means listening. That is what I always hope to do.

I feel that in my music I am not focusing on that which I possess, but on that which I lack in real life. Consonance and tonality are the things closest to me in music, and latterly also the absence of inner conflict (conflicts can remain "outside the brackets", since music itself often seems to me to be a sort of antithesis to many things we encounter in life).

At the moment I am drawn in the direction of seeking to write music which has no need of any inner interaction and metamorphosis, and in which the initial material is also its conclusion. My piano compositions of the last one and a half years have been dedicated to these goals in varying degrees, but they are evident in earlier work as well.

* * *

At just a fraction over 30, Alexander Gugel still has to be accounted promising rather than yet in possession of a completely fledged and mature style. Though his work shows signs of marked individuality and imagination, the single biggest influence on his career so far has been the music of the Estonian-born Arvo Pärt; Gugel is from the neighbouring Baltic republic of Lithuania, though he is now based in Kharkov. In an important sense, Pärt underwent on Gugel's behalf the conventional enchantment-disenchantment with serial modernism which has become in turn the conventional dialectic of the contemporary composer.

There are few signs in Gugel's work that he has sought to assimilate many of the sanctified procedures of the modernist tradition, though titles like *Moment musical* and *For Elise* suggest strongly that his awareness of tradition is at a different focal length. His compositions are tonal, consonant and minimal, though their minimalism is utterly different from that of any of the currently prominent American Minimalists (except, perhaps LaMonte Young) who generally prefer to work paratactically with much larger units of musical material. Nor is Gugel's work so intense rhythmically, though there are signs in the most recent piano compositions that he has refined his sense of metre and duration, and done so organically, rather than by chance procedures or Fibonacci sequences or any other fashionable timetable.

Gugel's work is marked by an absence of conflict. His static harmonies give no sense of forward motion and, whether or not one claims a metaphoric equivalence between music, authorial psychology and social conditions, gives no hint of responsiveness to political and cultural developments. To that degree, its underlying philosophy is eidetic, bracketing off music from any representational significance, normative or redemptive purpose. His music is, quite simply, a realm apart.

The fledgeling minimalism of the *Dedication to Arvo Pärt*, Gugel's first major piece (though there is a symphony still in manuscript, unperformed), is meditative and sombre. It takes wing in a moment of remarkable frozen movement in the superb 1990 piece *For Flying Away Birds*, a short solo piano work in the same mysterious C# minor as Beethoven's so-called "Moonlight" sonata, in which the basic chord is subjected to a wide variety of transformations, none of which fundamentally affect its substance. It is perhaps too easy to decode the piece's symbolism in whatever direction suits: the birds may fly, but certainly cannot fly away (a parable of artistic life as the Soviet cultural weather changes); alternatively the "cage" of tonality may very well be the key to ultimate freedom as opposed to the illusory freedoms of modernism. Gugel appears to contemplate these and related themes in other works, few of them with quite such a degree of compression. *To Geometry* has an ironic edge and a set of axes that are more Zen than Euclidean. The two generic piano sonatas have not yet been heard but the early *Music for Piano* suggests that Gugel is trying to invest classical forms with a new contemporary significance.

His vocal works are powerfully conceived, most notably the Mandelstam setting of *Duet*, one of the finest modern Soviet works for voice, but they are typically undramatic and inward and the idea of an opera from Gugel is for the time being inconceivable along conventional lines. He is nonetheless an exciting talent, with some reputation already in the West.

—Richard Stein

H

HALFFTER, Cristobal (professional name of Cristobal Halffter Jiménez-Encina). Spanish. Born in Madrid, 24 March 1930. Educated at Royal Conservatory of Music, Madrid (composition under Conrado del Campo), 1947–51, diploma; further study under Alexandre Tansman, Paris. Married Maria Manuela Caro, 25 May 1950; 3 children. Teacher of composition and musical form, 1961–6, and director of institute, 1964–6, Royal Conservatory of Music, Madrid; lecturer, University of Navarra, 1970–8; occasional lecturer, Ferienkurse für Neue Musik, Darmstadt; president, ISCM, Spanish section, 1976–8; artistic director, studio for electronic music, Heinrich Strobel-Stiftung, Freiburg, 1979; principal guest conductor, National Orchestra, Madrid, 1989–90. Recipient: honorary member, European Academy of Science, Arts and Humanities, Paris, 1980; Gold Medal for the Fine Arts, Spain, 1981; honorary member, Royal Academy of the Fine Arts San Fernando, Madrid, 1983. Mailing address: c/o Universal Edition, Bösendorferstrasse 12, Postfach 3, A-1015 Vienna, Austria.

Publisher: Universal Edition.

Symphonies/orchestral:

Scherzo 1951.
Piano Concerto 1953; first performed Madrid, 13 March 1954.
Two Movements (strings, timpani) 1956; first performed Madrid, 26 June 1957.
Concertino (string orchestra; expanded version of *String Quartet No 1*) 1956.
Cinque microformas 1960.
Rhapsodia española de Albeniz (piano, orchestra) 1960.
Sinfonia (3 instrumental groups) 1963.
Secuencias 1964; first performed Madrid, 16 June 1954.
Lineas y puntos (winds, tape) 1967; first performed Donaueschingen, 22 October 1967.
Anillos (see also ballet) 1967–8.
Fibonacciana (flute, string orchestra) 1970; first performed Lisbon, 30 May 1970.
Planto por las victimas de la violencia (chamber orchestra, tape) 1971; first performed Donaueschingen, 17 October 1971.
Requiem por la libertad imaginada 1971.
Pinturas negras (orchestra, concertante organ) 1972.
Processional (2 pianos, winds, percussion) 1973; first performed Strasbourg, 8 June 1974.
Cello Concerto 1974; first performed Granada, 24 June 1975.
Elegias a la muerte de tres poetas españoles 1974–5.
Lineas y puntos (winds, electronics) 1976.
Officium defunctorum 1979; first performed Paris, 1979.
Violin Concerto 1979.
Cello Concerto No 1 1979.
Tiento 1980.
Fantasia über einen Klang von G.F. Handel (4, 8 or 12 cellos, strings) 1981.
Sinfonia Ricercata (organ, orchestra) 1982.
Versus (large orchestra) 1983.
Parafrasia (on Handel's *Fantasia on One Note*) 1984.
Double Concerto in Two Movements (violin, viola, orchestra) 1984.
Cello Concerto No 2: "No queda mas que el silencio" 1985.
Tiento del primer tono y batalla imperial 1986.
Dortmunder Variationen 1986–7.
Piano Concerto 1987–8.
Concerto for Saxophone Quartet and Orchestra 1989.

Chamber/instrumental:

Sonata (piano) 1951.
Three Pieces: String Quartet No 1 1955.
Three Pieces (flute) 1959.
Sonata (violin) 1959.
Formantes (2 pianos) 1961.
Codex (guitar) 1963.
Espejos/Mirrors (4 percussion, tape) 1963.
Antiphonismoi (7 players) 1967.
Oda para felicitar a un amigo (flute in G, bass clarinet, viola, cello, percussion) 1969.
Studie II (flute cadenza from *Fibonaciana*) 1969.
Memories, 1970: String Quartet No 2 1970.
Noche activa del espiritu (2 pianos, ring modulators) 1973.
Tiempo para espacios (harpsichord, 6 violins, 3 violas, 2 cellos, double bass) 1974.
Pourquoi (6 violins, 3 violas, 2 cellos, double bass) 1974–5.
Variations über das Thema eSACHERe (cello) 1975.
Variaciones sobre la resonancia de un grito (3 clarinets, 3 trombones, 3 cellos, piano/ring modulator, harpsichord/ring modulator/electric organ) 1976–7.
String Quartet No 3 1978.
Adieu (harpsichord) 1978.
Mizar (2 flutes, electronic ensemble) 1979; first performed Basle, Switzerland, 1 June 1980.
Mizar II (2 flutes, electronics) 1979.
Debla (flute) 1980.
Ricercare (organ) 1981.
Concierto (flute, 2 violins, 2 violas, 2 cellos) 1982.
Cadencia (piano) 1983.
Slava da Budjet Mir S Toboj (6 horns, 4 trumpets, 4 trombones, tuba) 1986.
El ser humano muere solamente quando lo olvidan (piano; page in memory of Arthur Rubinstein) 1987.
Cancion callada in memoriam Federico Mompou (violin, cello, piano) 1988.
Fandango (8 cellos) 1988–9.

Vocal/choral:

Antifonia pascual a la virgen (Regina coeli) (soprano, contralto, orchestra) 1951.
Misa ducal (chorus, orchestra) 1955; first performed Madrid, 14 May 1956.
In exspectione resurrectionis Domini (cantata) 1962.
Brecht-Lieder (voice, orchestra) 1967.
In memoriam Anaick (child narrator, children's chorus, instruments ad lib) 1967.

Symposion (baritone, chorus, orchestra) 1968.
Yes Speak Out (cantata; Corwin) 1968; first performed New York City, 12 December 1968.
Noche pasiva del sentido (soprano, 2 percussion, tapes) 1971.
Gaudium et Spes (Beunza) (32 voices, 4-track tape, 2 2-track tapes) 1972.
Oración a platero (narrator, chorus, children's chorus, 5 percussion) 1975.
Jarchas de dolor de Ausencia (3 sopranos, 3 altos, 3 tenors, 3 basses; 14th-century Spanish Jewish poetry) 1979.
Noche pasiva del sentido (soprano, 2 percussion, 4 tape recorders, 2 tape delays; San Juan de la Cruz) 1979.
Leyendo a Jorge Guillen (speaker, viola, cello) 1982.
Dona nobis pacem (4-part mixed choir, 4 horns, 4 trumpets, 4 trombones, 3 percussion) 1984.
Tres poemas de la lirica española (baritone, orchestra) 1984–6.
Canciones de al Andalus (mezzo-soprano, string quartet; el-Katib, anon., ibn Ezra) 1987–8.
Dos motetes (unaccompanied mixed choir) 1988.
Muerte, mudanza y locura (live voices, electronic tape; Cervantes) 1989.

Opera:

Don Quichotte 1969; first performed Dusseldorf, 1970.

Other:

Saeta (ballet) 1955; first performed Madrid, 28 October 1955.
Anillos (ballet) 1967–8; first performed Lyon, 13 April 1971.
La musica callada (audio visual environment) 1982–3; realised in Baden-Baden, Germany.

Johann Strauss: *Annen-Polka* (arranged for flute, oboe, clarinet, bassoon, string quartet) 1982.

PUBLICATIONS

By Halffter: "Elegien zum Tode dreier spanischer Dichter", in *Darmstadter Beitrage zur Neuen Musik*, Mainz, 1976; "Variationen über das Echo eines Schreis—eine Analyse", in *Teilton*, 4, 1985.

On Halffter: Hubert Daschner, "Tonende Einsamkeit—Schweigende Musik. Zum geistlichen Werk von CH", in *MusikTexte*, 32, 1989.

* * *

The best-known Spanish composer of recent times, Cristobal Halffter (or, more properly, Cristobal Halffter Jiménez-Encina) was born in Madrid, the descendant of German immigrants. Two of his uncles, Rodolfo Halffter (born 1900) and Ernesto Halffter (born 1905), were also composers. Cristobal quickly followed their example. At the Royal Conservatory in Madrid he studied composition under Conrado del Campo. Later he went to Paris and took private lessons under Alexandre Tansman. From 1961 he taught composition and analysis at the Madrid Conservatory, directing the institute between 1964 and 1966. He also taught at the University of Navarra and at the Darmstadt summer courses. As director of arts at the Electronic Studio belonging to the Heinrich Strobel Foundation in 1979, he made a close study of the most recent technical innovations. He made his conducting debut with the Orchestra Manuel de Falla in 1953 and conducted frequently thereafter.

Bartók and Stravinsky were his earliest influences, but so too was Spanish music and particularly that of de Falla. Though Halffter never identified with any one tendency, he was to sample many of the philosophies of the avant-garde: dodecaphony (as in the 1959 *Sonata* for violin), serialism (as in *Cinque microformas* for orchestra), and "open" and aleatory concepts (in *Formantes* for two pianos). In addition, he experimented with live electronics in the 1976–7 *Variaciones sobre la resonancia de un grito*.

However, innovation is always subordinated to communication, and any resulting structure is directed to the revelation of the work's content. In *Noche pasiva del sentido* the soprano varies phonemes and sequences of phonemes from a text by Spanish mystic San Juan de la Cruz, while percussion and tape attempt to mediate the semantics on a different, non-verbal level. Only when all the compositional parameters coincide is a sufficient communicative, semantic and expressive level attained. In this respect, the avant-garde of the 1950s and 1960s held only passing interest for Halffter, its ideas seamlessly integrated into a much broader whole.

The musical material often consists of very simple sound-gestures (semitones, repetitive sound-groups and descending cadences in *Elegias a la muerte de tres poetas españoles*). Electronic transformation affords a versatile, multi-faceted constructive device, building up from a base of quite scant material (as in *Variaciones sobre la resonancia de un grito*). Halffter's use of electronics is formal but always expressive; as he has said, new means offer a way into mystical areas which can only be grasped with great difficulty by traditional instrumentation.

In the *Variaciones*, a new technique helps to convey the cries for freedom of those who suffer under despotism. Halffter's emotional and intellectual world is fundamentally religious. Under the Franco dictatorship, the social and political circumstances of his compatriots forced him to comment. His is a music of engagement and religious sensibility, urging humanitarian values. Nonetheless, a change in political circumstances does not render it obsolete. The *Officium defunctorum*, which numbers among Halffter's masterpieces for its exemplary synthesis of compositional devices (though not in this case electronics), is a modern requiem dedicated to all those who gave their lives for others. The slightly naive and "unconscious joy" of his early works has been transformed—in his own words—into a "conscious hope".

—Joachim Noller

HALLGRIMSSON, Haflidi. Icelandic. Born in Akureyri, 18 September 1941. Educated at the Music School of Reykjavik, 1958–62; Accademia Sancta Cecilia, Rome, 1962–3, diploma; Royal Academy of Music, London, 1964–67, recital medal; private studies in composition with Alan Bush and Peter Maxwell Davies. Married Ragnheidur Arnadottir, 31 August 1975; 3 children. Cellist, English Chamber Orchestra, London, 1968–74; principal cellist, Scottish Chamber Orchestra, Edinburgh, 1977–83; cello teacher, Royal Scottish Academy of Music and Drama, Glasgow, 1983; founder/member, Mondrian Piano Trio, Edinburgh, 1983–88; principal cellist, London Festival Orchestra, London, since 1984. Recipient: Madam Suggia

Prize (for cello), 1966; first prize, Viotti International Competition for Composers, 1975; second prize, Wieniavski International Competition for Composers, 1985; Nordic Council Prize, 1986. Mailing address: 10 Warrender Park Crescent, Edinburgh EH9 1DX, Scotland.

Publishers: Chester Music, London; Ricordi.

Symphonies/orchestral:

Poemi (violin, strings) 1984; first performed Reykjavik, 1985. Recorded ITM CD 6-02.
Mystery Play (string orchestra) 1985; in progress.
Daydreams in Numbers (string orchestra) 1986; in progress. Recorded MRFD CD 88101.
Vetrarvers / Words in Winter (soprano, orchestra) 1987; first performed Reykjavik, 1987.

Chamber/instrumental:

Venetian Quartet 1963; first performed Reykjavik, 1963.
Solitaire (cello) 1969, revised 1979; first performed Reykjavik, 1970.
Five Pieces for Piano 1971; first performed Reykjavik, 1971.
Hoa-Haka-Hana-Ia (clarinet, marimba, harp, strings, percussion) 1972, revised 1976; first performed Paris, 1977; withdrawn for revision.
Duo (viola, cello) 1972; first performed Reykjavik, 1973.
Seven Icelandic Folksongs (arrangements for cello, piano) 1973; first performed Reykjavik, 1974.
Divertimento (harpsichord, string trio) 1974.
Verse I (flute, cello) 1975; first performed London, 1976. Recorded MRFD CD 88101.
Verse II (flute, amplified clavichord, cello, piano) 1975; first performed London, 1975.
Fimma (cello, piano) 1976; first performed London, 1976.
Origami (piano trio) 1977; first performed Bergen, 1977.
Polar (ensemble) 1978.
Jacob's Ladder (guitar) 1984; first performed Edinburgh, 1984. Recorded MRFD CD 88101.
Tristia (guitar, cello) 1984; first performed Reykjavik, 1984. Recorded MRFD CD 88101.
Seven Folksongs from Iceland (cello, piano; arranged for young performers) 1985.
Four Icelandic Folksongs (piano) 1985; first performed London, 1986.
Scenes of Poland (piano solo, for young performers) 1988.
Strond (harpsichord) 1988. Recorded MRFD CD 88101.
String Quartet: From Memory 1989.
Four Pieces: In memoriam Bryn Turley (string quartet) 1990.
The Flight of Icarus (flute) 1990.
The Flight of Time (violin) 1990.
Wind Quintet 1991.

Vocal/choral:

Elegy (mezzo-soprano, flute, 2 cellos, piano, celeste; Quasimodo) 1971; first performed Copenhagen, 1972.
Songs for Children 1976; first performed London, 1976.
You Will Hear Thunder (soprano, cello; Akhmatova) 1982; first performed Reykjavik, 1982.
Triptych (unaccompanied voices; Quasimodo) 1986; first performed Aberdeen, 1986.
Four Icelandic Folksongs 1988; first performed Hamrahlidar-korinn, Norway, 1989.

* * *

Since the mid-1980s the music of the Icelandic composer Haflidi Hallgrimsson has begun to reach a wide audience in Great Britain and Scandinavia. Probably the most performed work to date is *Poemi*, a 20-minute concerto for violin and string orchestra which has received several awards, including the coveted Nordic Council Prize. It was commissioned by the Scottish Chamber Orchestra in Edinburgh, where Hallgrimsson and his family have made their home (he was the orchestra's principal cellist from 1977 to 1983). The first performance was given by the Icelandic Symphony Orchestra under the composer's direction in Reykjavik during January 1985; the soloist was Jaime Laredo.

Each of *Poemi*'s three movements seeks to "recreate in music the poetic essence" of an allegorical painting by Marc Chagall depicting a biblical text. The first, "The Dream of Jacob", is still and visionary, while the second and third, "The Sacrifice of Isaac" and "Jacob in Combat with the Angel" are startling and increasingly violent. The virtuoso solo part veers between sinuous, singing chromaticism and jagged chordal exclamation. The orchestral texture is at first aleatoric, and hesitant, but becomes powerfully direct, generating enormous tension.

Painting, poetry, dream, virtuosity—all are important for Hallgrimsson. As a composer, he can be styled a late developer, someone who began to compose as a child, but whose stringent self-criticism led him to destroy or withdraw almost everything produced before the age of 40. (*Verse I* of 1975, a vivid, almost Brittenesque sea-and-cloudscape for flute and cello is one of the few survivors). Only then did he find his own musical language.

His public career had at first been that of a virtuoso cellist, who had studied in his native Iceland, then in Rome (with Mainardi), and London, and who had subsequently travelled the world. Composition studies in London with Alan Bush provided solid and traditional technical grounding, and generated an interest in Icelandic folk-song. Further study with Peter Maxwell Davies brought Hallgrimsson face-to-face with himself as a highly disciplined late 20th-century artist. These studies all focused and furthered Hallgrimsson's fascination with the music of Debussy, Janăćek, Berg and Lutosławski.

In Rome, Hallgrimsson had become interested in painting. Since that time, he has been known as a fastidious and humorous draughtsman and colourist, influenced by Klee, Mondrian and Chagall. His children's pieces for cello and piano are published with his own illustrations.

All of Hallgrimsson's music has a dazzling clarity of texture. Considerable complexity and depth are created by the superimposition/juxtaposition of very simple elements. His work has a refined, dreamlike fluidity which can be disconcerting: in much of it the element of large-scale repetition is absent. Small-scale repetition and ostinatos do appear in his simpler works, such as *Jacob's Ladder* for guitar, or the ongoing series of string orchestra miniatures *Daydreams in Numbers*, or the *Tristia* sequence for cello and guitar. Here the literary reference is to Ovid's poems of exile and to Mandelstam: the seven short movements are painfully evocative tone pictures of Icelandic scenes remembered from the composer's childhood. Childhood memories, again, provided the source for the pithy, complex 25-minute first string quartet *From Memory* of 1989, commissioned by the Carl Nielsen Quartet of Copenhagen.

Hallgrimsson's work is mainly instrumental, but there are three important vocal works. *Triptych*, for mixed voices a cappella, creates complex harmonic structures from poems by Salvatore Quasimodo. *You Will Hear Thunder* for soprano and cello, which sets Anna Akhmatova's tragic texts in an often austere, almost onomatopoeic fashion, was written for Jane Manning, as was *Vetrarvers/Words in Winter* of 1987. The first of these two orchestral songs, settings of the composer's own texts, exploits the highest registers, the second the lowest, of a virtuoso soprano voice.

Both of these songs powerfully place man in nature, and create a "luminous dream" landscape of glaciers and lava fields under the aurora borealis. Along with the first string quartet, they are perhaps Hallgrimsson's most substantial and provocative works to date. They "assemble reminders", and seek to give man back his dignity. They constitute a manifesto against the confusion, ugliness and brutality of late 20th-century urban civilisation.

—Neil Mackay

HAMBRAEUS, Bengt. Swedish. Born in Stockholm, 29 January 1928. Educated: organ lessons under Alf Linder, 1944–8; Uppsala University, 1947–56, M.A., 1950, Fil.Lic., 1956, musicology; further study, Ferienkurse für Neue Musik, Darmstadt, 1951–3. Married Enid Odenaes, 21 March 1960; 1 son and 1 daughter. Organist; musicologist; amanuensis and librarian, Institute for Musicology, Uppsala University, 1948–56; music staff, from 1957, head of chamber music section 1965–8, and production manager 1968–72, Swedish Broadcasting Corporation; emigrated to Canada, 1972; professor of music, McGill University, Montreal, from 1972. Recipient: member, Royal Academy of Music, Sweden, 1967. Mailing address: Faculty of Music, McGill University, 555 Sherbrooke Street West, Montreal, Quebec H3A 1E3, Canada.

Publishers: AB Nordiska Forlaget, Stockholm; Ed. Jacques Ostiguy, 12790 rue Yamasak, Saint-Hyacinthe, Quebec J2T 1B3, Canada; Svensk Musik; Centre de Musique Canadienne.

Symphonies/orchestral:

Concerto for Organ and String Orchestra Op 16 1948.
Kleine Musik Op 18 1b (oboe, strings, timpani) 1949.
Rota (3 orchestral groups, percussion, tape) 1956–62; first performed Stockholm, 27 May 1964.
Transfiguration 1962–3; broadcast Swedish Radio, 20 February 1965. Recorded SWS SLT 33181.
Rencontres 1968–71; broadcast Swedish Radio, 8 September 1971. Recorded Caprice CAP 1032.
Pianissimo in due tempi (20 strings) 1970–2; first performed Uppsala, 16 April 1972.
Invocation 1971; first performed Ames, Ohio, 11 November 1971.
Continuo a partire de Pachelbel (organ, orchestra) 1974–5; first performed Nuremburg, 15 June 1976.
Ricordanza 1975–6; first performed Norrkoping, 29 April 1977. Recorded Caprice CAP 1137.
Parade (wind orchestra) 1977; first performed Stockholm, 1979.
That Harmony (brass band) 1983.
Quodlibet re BACH 1984; first performed Toronto, 15 March 1985.
Litanies 1988–9; first performed Stockholm, 13 May 1990.

Chamber/instrumental:
Toccata Op 7/1 (piano) 1947–9.
Concerto (organ, harpsichord) 1947–51.
Koralforspel Op 4 (organ) 1948.
Cercles (piano) 1948.
Toccata pro tempore pentecostes Op 12/2 (organ) 1948.
Music for Ancient Strings Op 15/3 (string ensemble, harpsichord) 1948.
Musique pour trompette Op 18/2 1949.
Introitus et Triptychon Op 19 (organ) 1949–50.
String Quartet No 2 Op 21: A Fancy in Homage to Henry Purcell 1949.
Musik für orgel Op 24/2 (organ) 1950.
Kammarmusik Op 28 (flute, oboe, clarinet, alto saxophone, viola, harpsichord) 1950.
Recitativ och Koral (violin, piano) 1950.
Liturgia Op 24/3 (organ) 1951–2.
Giuco del Cambio/Vaxelspel Op 33 (flute, cor anglais, bass clarinet, vibraphone, harpsichord, piano, 3 percussion) 1952–4; first performed Stockholm, 29 January 1955.
Permutations and hymn: Nocte surgentes Op 36 (organ) 1953.
Komposition for Studio II (vibraphone, chimes, 3 percussion, piano, harpsichord, organ) 1955.
Constellations I (organ) 1958; broadcast Swedish Radio, 2 September 1959.
Introduzione—Sequenze—Coda (3 flutes, 6 percussion) 1958–9; first performed Stockholm, 11 December 1959.
Constellations II (organ, tape) 1959; broadcast Danish Radio, 13 January 1960.
Segnali (electric guitar, harp, violin, viola, cello, double bass) 1959–60; broadcast Swedish Radio, 8 April 1962.
Constellations III (organ, tape) 1961; broadcast Danish Radio, 30 October 1961.
Mikrogram; Seven Aphorisms (alto flute, viola, vibraphone, harp) 1961; first performed Stockholm, 4 December 1961. Recorded Caprice CAP 1176.
Notazioni (harpsichord, 3 flutes, cor anglais, bass clarinet, 3 trumpets, 3 trombones, celeste/glockenspiel, 6 percussion) 1961; first performed Stockholm, 17 March 1965.
Interferenzen (organ) 1961–2; first performed Bremen, 4 May 1962.
Notturno de vecchi strumenti (soprano recorder, krumhorn, alto bassoon, viola d'amore, bass gamba, clavichord, 2 glockenspiels, tambourine) 1961; first performed Stockholm, 17 November 1963.
Transit II (horn, trombone, electric guitar, piano) 1963; first performed Malmo, 30 November 1963.
Invenzione 1 (Quartetto III) (string quartet) 1964–7; first performed Jonkoping, 12 February 1967.
Tre pezzi (organ) 1966–7. Recorded Caprice CAP 1108.
Klockspel/Musical Box/Glockenspiel (piano) 1968.
Nebulosa (organ) 1969; first performed Falkenberg, 10 July 1969.
Carillon: Le Recital oublié (2 pianos) 1972–4; first performed Toronto, 7 December 1974. Recorded Caprice CAP 21331.
Toccata pro organo: Monumentum per Max Reger (organ) 1973; first performed Nuremburg, 7 June 1973.
Ricercare (organ) 1974; first performed Stockholm, 15 February 1975.
Icons (organ) 1974–5; first performed Toronto, 29 September 1975. Recorded RCI 481.
Advent: Veni redemptor gentium (organ, 4 trumpets, 4 trombones, percussion) 1975.
Extempore (organ) 1975; first performed Vancouver, 9 November 1975.
Jeu de cinq (wind quintet) 1976; first performed Toronto, 24 February 1977.

Antiphonie (organ) 1977.
Parade (wind ensemble, percussion) 1977; first performed Stockholm, 12 October 1978.
Constellations IV (organ, percussion) 1978; first performed Nuremburg, 24 October 1974.
Relief—haut et bas (2 flutes, 3 horns, trombone, 2 percussion, 2 double basses) 1979; first performed Montreal, 10 April 1980.
Strata (2 oboes, 2 clarinets, 2 basset horns/alto clarinet, 2 bassoons, 2 horns, double bass) 1979–80; first performed Stockholm, 20 September 1980.
Capriccio I (harpsichord) 1980; first performed Stockholm, 31 January 1983.
Livre d'orgue (organ; 4 volumes) 1981; first performed (7 parts of volume 1) Rochester, Minnesota, 18 October 1981; volume 4 first performed Montreal, 9 May 1982.
Voluntary on a Swedish Hymn Tune from Dalecarlia (organ) 1981; first performed Rock Islands, 9 November 1981.
Sheng (oboe, organ) 1983; first performed Toronto, 12 September 1984. Recorded MAP R 8606.
Monologo (flute) 1984.
Tre intermezzi (piano) 1984; first performed Toronto, 29 May 1984. Recorded Caprice CAP 2021.
Variations sur un thème de Gilles Vigneault (organ) 1984; first performed Montreal, 28 October 1984.
La Passacaille errante—autour Haendel 1985 (organ) 1984; first performed Stockholm, 24 August 1985.
Pedalexercitium (organ) 1985.
Trio sonata (free bass accordion, trombone, prepared piano) 1985; first performed Vancouver, October 1985.
Vortex (2 pianos) 1986; first performed Montreal, 22 March 1987.
Mirrors (oboe sounds; tape, 1 or more oboist) 1986–7; first performed Montreal, 27 April 1987.
Après-Sheng (organ) 1988.
Night-Music (guitar, percussion) 1988.
Cadenza (organ) 1988.
Dos recercadas (guitar, cello) 1988.
Cinque studi canonici (2 flutes) 1988.
Nazdar M J (3 trumpets, 4 horns, 3 trombones, tuba, timpani, chimes) 1989.

Vocal/choral:

Cantigas de Santa Maria Op 17 (soprano, alto, baritone, 3 instrumental groups) 1949; first performed Stockholm, 17 December 1949.
Cantigas de Santa Maria Op 17b (chorus, organ) 1950.
Triptychon Op 26 (unaccompanied mixed chorus; Latin) 1950.
Spectrogram Op 34 (soprano, flute, vibraphone, percussion; anon.) 1953.
Antiphonies en rondes Op 35 (soprano vocalise, orchestra) 1953.
Psalmus CXXI (soprano, organ) 1953.
Psalmus CXXII (soprano, organ) 1953.
Gacelas y casidas de F. García Lorca Op 37 (tenor, flute, cor anglais, bass clarinet, vibraphone, bells, percussion; translated Lundkvist) 1953; first performed Stockholm, 23 January 1953.
Crystal Sequence Op 38 (soprano chorus, 2 trumpets, vibraphone, bells, percussion, 12 violins) 1954.
Responsorier (tenor, mixed chorus, congregation, 2 organs; Psalms) 1964; first performed Uppsala, 16 June 1966.
Tre Hopi-Sanger (choir, xylophone, 3 tom-toms; trad., Fredenholm) 1965.
Praeludium, Kyrie, Sanctus (2 choirs, soloist, 2 organs, congregation) 1966; first performed Stockholm, 13 August 1966.
Motetum archangeli Michaelis (mixed chours, organ) 1967; first performed Stockholm, 15 October 1967. Recorded HEJ LP 010; PSC 1034.
Nonsens (mixed chorus) 1970.
Inductio (soprano, alto mixed chorus, 3 trumpets, 3 trombones; biblical) 1979; first performed Montreal, 8 February 1980.
Alpha—Omega (mixed choir, organ; biblical) 1982.
Constellations V (2 amplified sopranos, mixed choir, organ; Corinthians) 1982–3; first performed Nuremburg, 16 September 1983.
Symphonia sacra in tempore passionis (soloists, mixed chorus, winds, percussion; anon.) 1986; first performed Montreal, 6 March 1987.
Apocalipsis cum figuris secundum Duerer 1498 (bass, chorus, organ; Biblical) 1987; first performed Nuremburg, 7 October 1988.
Five Psalms (unaccompanied mixed choir) 1987.
Echoes of Loneliness (4 choirs; J.G. Brown) 1988; first performed Canada, 7 May 1988.

Opera:

Experiment X (church opera for soloists, orchestra; Wall) 1968–9; first performed Stockholm, 9 March 1971.
Se människen (church opera; Wall) 1970; first performed Stockholm, 15 May 1972.
Sagan (radio opera; Runsten, Bergman) 1978–9; broadcast Swedish Radio, 31 August 1980.
L'Oui-dire 1984–6.

Other:

Doppelrohr (electronic music) 1955; first performed Cologne, 30 May 1956. Recorded PS CD 41.
Fresque sonore (electronic music) 1956–7. Recorded SWS SLT 33181.
Visioner over en svensk folkvisa (electronic music) 1959; broadcast Swedish Radio, 13 November 1959.
Othello (incidental music; voice, flute, piccolo, horn, viola, harp, timpani, percussion) 1961; first performed Stockholm, 19 January 1961.
Backaskog (incidental music; Aberg) 1962.
Sergeant Musgrave's Dance (incidental music to play by Arden; trumpet, trombone, percussion) 1962; first performed Stockholm, 25 January 1962.
Intrada (electronic music) 1976.

PUBLICATIONS

By Hambraeus: *Codex Carminum Gallicorum*, Uppsala, 1961; *Portrait av Bach* (with others), Stockholm, 1968; *Om Notskrifter*, Stockholm, 1970.

On Hambraeus: Rolf Haglund, "BH—den harmoniske musikern", in *Musikrevy*, 37, 1982; Fred Steltzfaus, "The Choral Music of BH", Association of Canadian Choral Conductors, 2(3), 1983; Antony Hodgson, in *Scandinavian Music: Finland and Sweden*, Cranbury, New Jersey/London, 1984; Hans-Gunnar Peterson, "BH", in *Swedish Composers of the 20th Century*, Stockholm, 1988.

Bengt Hambraeus comments:
Any research and creative work may need an ivory tower.

But if there are no windows or doors, or even an emergency exit from such a tower, the scholar and artist may forget our most important responsibility and function in community and environment: to share experience and knowledge; and to be ready to assist those who may need our help. I believe in pluralism and interdisciplinary thinking; narrow specialization often lacks global views and perspectives. Music must be seen as a marvellous adventure, as a living organism, and not as a commercialized business with standard routines. As a composer, I feel as an explorer—my music reflects many impulses from Western or "non-Western" cultures in East, North or South. 40 professorial years as a composer, musicologist, broadcast music administrator and academic teacher gave me the opportunity to learn from past and present and to become aware of the vibrant powerfield between the regional and the international. But I also discovered the real genetic code to my music: the universal sound of wind, water, thunder, snowstorms, and animal calls in the wilderness which I first experienced in my early childhood. Only quite recently did I become aware that such sounds had served as a control signal to almost everything I have composed, for voices, instruments, or in various electronic studios; nature helped me to create organic musical structures more than any teacher would have been able to do.

* * *

Bengt Hambraeus first made an impact in the mid-to-late 1950s as the heir of the pioneering and progressive movement that had electrified and revolutionised Swedish music after World War II. His multi-disciplined career as virtuoso organist (he was the first to introduce Messiaen's music to Swedish audiences) and musicologist (researching particularly into medieval and non-European musics) gave his own works a distinctive patina, while his participation from 1951 in the courses at Darmstadt ensured a full knowledge of all the latest avant-garde trends current at the time. Hambraeus was one of the very first composers in Scandinavia (let alone Sweden) to investigate electronic music, composing *Doppelrohr* (albeit realised in Cologne) for tape in 1955, three years before Blomdahl set about the electronic interludes for his opera *Aniara*. Further electronic works have continued to appear, sometimes in combination with natural instruments, as in the five *Constellations*. *Rota*, scored for three orchestras, percussion and tape, was completed in 1962, and is the synthesis of this initial breakthrough phase in his output.

The *Constellations* series is perhaps the most important of his early works, and the most influential. The First is for organ alone; it is an exposition of Hambraeus's pioneering organ techniques and novel sound world that were the fruits of his unique brand of scholarly expertise, complete instrumental command and Darmstadt-derived cerebration. The Second is for tape alone, while in the Third he progressed his instrumental procedures in conjunction with electronics in a highly ingenious development based on *Constellations I*. Two further works in the series appeared, with added vocal elements. His influence on the next generation of Swedish composers, Bo Nilsson for example, has been of prime importance; elsewhere György Ligeti has acknowledged that Hambraeus provided the spur for his own organ work, *Volumina* (1961), written for the Swedish organist-composer, Karl-Erik Welin. A comparison of Ligeti's two Studies, *Harmonie* (1967) and *Coulée* (1969), with a contemporary work of Hambraeus's such as *Nebulosa* (1969) shows just how far apart they had become. *Nebulosa* is a fine example of Hambraeus's mature style: firmly controlled continuous variation enlivened by an acute colouristic sense, laid out in a most idiomatic fashion for the console, often creating a static or slow-moving dissonant harmony, more tonally based but without a firm pulse, yet which is also capable of considerable cumulative power.

If Hambraeus has written many works for his own instrument, he has also composed choral and chamber music, pieces for ensembles of ancient instruments plus three operas. The intriguing, aptly titled *Experiment X* is a chamber opera, while the succeeding *Se människen* is for church performance, and *Sagan* for radio. Dating from 1972 is an orchestral collage, *Rencontres*, a curious study in sonority subjecting elements from mainly 19th-century composers (plus Varèse!) to an idiosyncratic treatment within his equally idiosyncratic sound world. *Ricordanza* bears witness to Hambraeus's acute interest in non-European musics (in this case the ritualistic music of Tibet). His representation on disc has not been extensive; *Fresque sonore*, for organ, harpsichord, percussion and ring modulator was coupled with the orchestral *Transfiguration*; *Rencontres*, *Ricordanza* and a few electronic pieces have appeared, but seemingly none of the important organ or choral works.

If his scholarly reputation and the continued performance of several works, particularly his organ concertos, kept Hambraeus's name alive at home, the works premiered during the Stockholm New Music Festival in 1990 consolidated his position still further and confirmed the continuity of vision within his output. *That Harmony* for brass reflects the influence of his North American sojourn in its rather Ivesian treatment of American and Swedish hymnody. *Après-Sheng* utilises his own researches into sound production on the organ to evoke (rather than emulate) the Chinese musical instrument, and attracted comment for the integral treatment of the pedals. *Litanies*, with its homage to Jehan Alain, is again a synthesis of Hambraeus's musical outlook, fully demonstrating that there has been no slackening of his inspiration or invention. One Swedish critic was led to remark after the festival "perhaps there should be a music festival just for Bengt Hambraeus".

—Guy Rickards

HAMILTON, Iain (Ellis). British/Scottish. Born in Glasgow, 6 June 1922. Educated at Mill Hill School, London; engineering apprentice; Royal Academy of Music (under Harold Craxton and William Alwyn), 1947–50; concurrently at University of London, B.Mus. 1950. Engineer, 1939–47; lecturer, Morley College, London, 1951–60, and University of London, 1952–60; secretary, Institute of Contemporary Arts, London, 1958–60; chair, Composers Guild of Great Britain, 1958; Mary Duke Biddle Professor of Music, Duke University, Durham, North Carolina, 1961–81; composer in residence, Tanglewood, Massachusetts, 1962; member, Music Advisory Panel, BBC, and National Music Council. Recipient: Dove Prize, Royal Academy of Music, 1950; Koussevitzky Foundation Award (for *Symphony No 2*), 1951; Royal Philharmonic Society Prize (for *Clarinet Concerto*), 1951; Clements Memorial Prize (for *String Quartet No 1*);

Edwin Evans Memorial Prize (for *Three Nocturnes*), 1951; Arnold Bax Gold Medal, 1957; Vaughan Williams Award, 1974; Butterworth Medal. Honorary D.Mus., University of Glasgow, 1970. Mailing address: 1 King Street, London WC2E 8HN, England.

Publishers: Schott; Theodore Presser.

Symphonies/orchestral:

Variations on an Original Theme Op 1 (string orchestra) 1948; first performed Edinburgh, February 1952.
Symphony No 1 Op 3 1948; first performed Edinburgh, December 1952.
Clarinet Concerto Op 7 1950; first performed London, April 1952.
Sinfonia Concertante (violin, viola, chamber orchestra) 1950.
Symphony No 2 Op 10 1951; first performed Cheltenham, Gloucestershire, June 1953.
Violin Concerto Op 15 1952; first performed London, January 1956.
Overture: Bartholomew Fair Op 17 1952; first performed Manchester, January 1956.
Symphonic Variations Op 19 1953; first performed Cheltenham, Gloucestershire, 1956.
Scottish Dances Op 32 1956; first performed London, November 1956. Recorded Louisville LOU 625.
Sonata Op 34 (chamber orchestra) 1957; first performed Liverpool, September 1958.
Concerto for Jazz Trumpet and Orchestra Op 37 1957; first performed London, 1958.
Overture: 1912 Op 38 1957; first performed London, December 1958.
Sinfonia (2 orchestras) 1958; first performed Edinburgh, September 1959.
Ecossaise 1959; first performed Edinburgh, September 1959.
Piano Concerto 1960, revised 1967; first performed Edinburgh, February 1961; revised version first performed London, November 1970.
Arias (small orchestra) 1962; first performed Cheltenham, Gloucestershire, 1963.
The Chaining of Prometheus (winds, percussion) 1963.
Cantos 1964; first performed London, August 1965.
Concerto for Organ and Small Orchestra 1964; first performed North Carolina, May 1965.
Circus (2 trumpets, orchestra) 1969.
Alastor 1970.
Voyage (horn, chamber orchestra) 1970. Recorded CRI SD 280.
Amphion: Violin Concerto No 2 1971.
Commedia (concerto for orchestra) 1972; first performed London, 4 May 1973.
Aurora 1975; first performed New York City, 21 November 1975.
The Alexandrian Sequence (chamber orchestra) 1976.
Symphony No 3 in G "Spring" 1981.
Symphony No 4 in B 1981.

Chamber/instrumental:

Quintet No 1 (clarinet, string quartet) 1948.
String Quartet No 1 Op 5 1950; first performed London, May 1950.
Quartet (flute, string trio) 1951.
Variations (violin) 1951.
Three Nocturnes Op 6 (clarinet, piano) 1951.
Sonata Op 9 (viola, piano) 1951.
Capriccio (trumpet, piano) 1951.
Sonata No 1 Op 13 (piano) 1951, revised 1971; first performed London, February 1952. Recorded Lyrita RCS 5.
Sonata (clarinet, piano) 1954.
Octet (strings) 1954.
Serenata (violin, clarinet) 1955.
Piano Trio Op 25 1955; first performed Dartington, Devon, 1956.
Three Pieces Op 30 (piano) 1956. Recorded Argo ZRG 5425.
Sonata No 1 (cello, piano) 1959; first performed Glasgow, April 1959. Recorded Argo ZRG 5425.
Fanfares and Variants (organ) 1961; first performed London, November 1961.
Sextet (flute, 2 clarinets, violin, cello, piano) 1962; first performed North Carolina, February 1963. Recorded CRI 205.
Sonatas and Variants (10 winds) 1963; first performed North Carolina, February 1963.
Nocturnes with Cadenzas (piano) 1963; first performed New York City, February 1964. Recorded CRI 205.
Quintet (brass) 1964; first performed New Jersey, November 1964.
Aubade (organ) 1965.
Sonata notturna (horn, piano) 1965; first performed London, November 1965. Recorded Argo ZRG 5475.
String Quartet No 2 1965; first performed Baltimore, Maryland, March 1966.
Sonata for Five (wind quintet) 1966.
Three Scenes (trumpet, piano) 1966. Recorded Avant AV 1003.
Sonata (flute) 1966.
Threnos—In Time of War (organ) 1966. Recorded Crystal S180.
Paraphrase (of music for organs in *Epitaph for This World and Time*) 1970.
Sea Music: Quintet No 2 (clarinet, string quartet) 1971.
Palinodes (piano) 1972. Recorded CRI S-407.
Roman Music (organ) 1973.
Sonata No 2 (piano) 1973.
Sonata (violin) 1974.
Sonata No 2 (cello, piano) 1974.
A Vision of Canopus (organ) 1975.
Hyperion (clarinet, horn, violin, cello, piano) 1977.
Spirits of the Air (bass trombone) 1977.
Sonata No 3 (piano) 1978.
String Quartet No 3 1984.
String Quartet No 4 1984.
Le Tombeau de Bach (organ) 1986.
Le Jardin de Monet (piano) 1986.
Windflowers (harp, flute, cor anglais, clarinet, horn, trumpet, percussion, violin, viola, cello) 1987.

Vocal/choral:

Songs of Summer (soprano, clarinet, cello, piano) 1954.
The Fray of Support Op 21 (mixed chorus; ancient Border gathering song) 1954; first performed Dartington, Devon, 1954.
The Bermudas Op 33 (baritone, chorus, orchestra; IH, Jourdain, Marvell) 1956; first performed London, October 1957.
Cantata No 1 (tenor, piano; Burns) 1957.
Five Love Songs Op 36 (high voice, orchestra) 1957; first performed Cheltenham, Gloucestershire, 1961.
Nocturnal (11 solo voices; Donne) 1959; first performed London, February 1960.

A Testament of War (baritone, small ensemble; Lucan) 1961; first performed London, April 1961.
Dialogues (coloratura soprano, small ensemble; Chateaubriand) 1965; first performed Buffalo, New York, April 1965.
Epitaph for This World and Time (3 choruses, 3 organs) 1970. Recorded CRI SD 280.
Te Deum (mixed chorus, winds, percussion) 1972.
Five Lyrics of Torquato Tasso (baritone, piano) 1973.
The Golden Sequence (unaccompanied SATB chorus) 1973.
To Columbus (mixed chorus, 3 trumpets, 3 trombones, percussion; Whitman) 1976.
The Spirit of Delight (soprano, baritone, piano; Shelley) 1978.
Requiem (unaccompanied SATB chorus) 1979.
Mass in A (unaccompanied SSATTB chorus) 1980.
Vespers (mixed chorus, 2 pianos, harp, percussion; includes "Cradle Song" and "A Hymn to the Virgin") 1980.
Ricordanza (high voice, piano; Herbert) 1981.
The Morning Watch (mixed chorus, 2 oboes, cor anglais, 2 bassoons, 2 trumpets, 3 trombones) 1981.
The Passion of Our Lord According to Saint Mark (soprano, alto, tenor, bass, chorus) 1982.
Love Is Life's Spring (soprano, piano; Clare) 1982.
The Bright Heavens Sounding (soprano, alto, tenor, bass, chorus, flute, 2 oboes, bassoon, 2 horns, 2 trumpets, strings; Spenser) 1985.
The Convergence of the Twain (SATB chorus, piano; Hardy) 1985.
Prometheus (soprano, mezzo-soprano, tenor, baritone, SATB chorus, orchestra) 1986.
Paris de crépuscle à l'aube (settings of Baudelaire) 1987.
The Summer Fields (unaccompanied SATB chorus; Clare) 1987.

Opera:

The Royal Hunt of the Sun (after Shaffer) 1966–8, orchestrated 1975; first performed London, 2 February 1977.
Agamemnon (after Aeschylus, translated Vellacott) 1967–9.
Pharsalia (after Lucan) 1968.
The Catiline Conspiracy (after Ben Jonson) 1973; first performed Stirling, Scotland, 16 March 1974.
Tamburlaine (after Marlowe) 1976; broadcast BBC, 14 February 1977.
Anna Karenina (after Tolstoy) 1977–8; first performed London, 7 May 1981.
Dick Whittington (after Tracey) 1980–1.
Lancelot 1982–3.
Raleigh's Dream 1983.

PUBLICATIONS

On Hamilton: A. Milner, "IH", in *Musical Times*, 97, 1956; G. Mason, "The Recent Music of IH", in *The Listener*, 58, 1957; W. Mann, "IH's Road to Serialism", in *The Times*, 5 October 1959; Christopher Grier, "Serialism Too Soon", in *Music and Musicians*, 17(12), 1968–9, and "Composing and Teaching in the United States", in *Music and Musicians*, 18(5), 1969–70.

* * *

Iain Hamilton initially trained as an engineer and said this had an effect on his musical thought in that it instilled a sense of design and proportion, leading to structural considerations always being of prime importance to him. This is confirmed by the way his music developed overall. From the start of his career a preference for large, serious works—symphonic in breadth, romantic, even passionate, in tone and already mature technically—was evident. Examples include the Clarinet Quintet and above all his *Symphony No 1* of 1948, a score full of intense emotion unerringly expressed.

The influences, aside from Britten in a few very early pieces such as the *Variations on an Original Theme* for strings, were from abroad, specifically Bartók, Stravinsky and Copland, and in this as in his early emphasis on instrumental music Hamilton resembled his contemporary Fricker. The swift acceptance of their work in the immediate post-World War II years signalled a desire to rejoin the international mainstream after the insularity of much British music during the 1920s and 1930s. And Hamilton received recognition abroad with his *Symphony No 2* receiving a Koussevitsky Foundation Award in 1951. His reputation was secured with several further prizes around this time, for example from the Royal Philharmonic Society for his *Clarinet Concerto* and the Clements Memorial Prize for *String Quartet No 1*.

Whatever the influences apparent at this stage, the energy of these and other works of this period was entirely Hamilton's own. He conveyed it chiefly through long, wide-arching melodies and pungent rhythms with quite frequent ostinatos. Sometimes there is too much activity and the gestures become over-emphatic, the textures crowded. But there are no such faults in Hamilton's two finest scores of this time, the *Violin Concerto Op 15* and *Symphonic Variations*, both full of music of great and perfectly convincing intensity unfolded in lucid forms of some originality. This is especially true of the *Variations*, a set of a dozen variations making up a dark-coloured three-movement symphony. Virtuoso performance is often demanded by the works of this period, for example the Viola Sonata, whose gestures are passionate and sometimes much syncopated. The strong dramatic sense evident in many of these pieces later emerged in its fullest form in Hamilton's stage works.

Meanwhile a second phase began with shorter compositions, some indicating a new interest in vocal writing, others the beginnings of serialism. The language of the earlier pieces, while essentially diatonic, had shown an increasing use of chromatic and even bitonal elements. But now a simpler diatonic vocabulary reappears, both in the vocal works, for instance the Burns Cantata, and in some of the chamber music of this time. Simultaneously there emerged Hamilton's first ventures into 12-note technique, for example the *Three Pieces* for piano of 1956. These and comparable items were still tonal, however. This period came to an end with another large work, *The Bermudas*, which took further the type of word-setting found in the smaller choral pieces, much of it in rhythmic unison. This is an outstanding score, quite vividly suggestive, especially at the beginning, of the far, wide perspectives of the open sea.

In a third period the use of serial methods became far more extensive, this partly a result of a study of Webern. It changed drastically the outward character of Hamilton's music although his energetic artistic personality remained fully recognisable. In fact the impetus for his new direction had come from within, underlined by the serial pieces having a wider range of expression. From the first substantial work of this new phase, the Sonata for Chamber Orchestra of 1957, it is obvious that we already are far beyond the high romance of, for instance, *Violin Concerto Op 15*, and that Hamilton is employing a new kind of gesture. This is confirmed by the Cello Sonata and especially the Sinfonia for Two Orchestras, the latter causing a gratifying uproar when premiered at the 1959 Edinburgh

Festival. It consists of brief, interconnected sections alternating with cadenza-like "tessituras" for different groups of instruments. There is further structural originality in the Cello Sonata, whose continuous discourse runs through four cadenzas and three movements of decreasing speed. Some remarkable effects are drawn from both instruments, and a complex dissonant harmonic language is combined with post-Webernian textures of an entirely personal kind. A comparable plan underlies the highly ingenious, not to say kaleidoscopic, *Sonatas and Variants* for 10 wind instruments, in which three sonatas are framed by five variants.

A degree of exoticism further broadened Hamilton's idiom, apparently as a result of visits to the West Indies during the 1960s. Examples are the 1965 *String Quartet No 2* and *Dialogues*, settings of Chateaubriand for soprano and instrumental ensemble. His longstanding concern with the theatre also began at last to find expression—first in incidental music, then in a magnificent series of operas which add major new aspects to his achievement. This large corpus of work has had only a small fraction of the attention it deserves. A still further development was an increasing number of scores that were the result of extra-musical promptings, usually literary. Instances are the exceptional *Palinodes* for piano and *Commedia*, a concerto for orchestra that relates to *The Divine Comedy*.

—Max Harrison

HARBISON, John. American. Born in Orange, New Jersey, 20 December 1938. Educated at Harvard University, Cambridge, Massachusetts (under Walter Piston), B.A., 1960; Hochsschule für Musik, Berlin (under Boris Blacher), 1961; Princeton University, New Jersey (under Roger Sessions and Earl Kim), M.F.A., 1963. Married Rose Mary Pedersen in 1963. Conductor, Princeton University Orchestra, Brandeis Contemporary Chamber Players, and Da Capo Chamber Players; Junior Fellow, Harvard University, 1963–9; Rockefeller Composer in Residence, Reed College, Portland, Oregon, 1968–9; Class of 1949 Professor of Music, Massachusetts Institute of Technology, Cambridge, Massachusetts, since 1969; music director, Cantata Singers, 1969–74; composer in residence, Pittsburgh Symphony Orchestra, 1982–4, Berkshire Music Center, Tanglewood, Massachusetts, Summer 1984, and Los Angeles Philharmonic Orchestra, 1985–8; music director, Collage New Music, 1985–8; guest conductor with Los Angeles Philharmonic, Speculum Musicae, Los Angeles Chamber Orchestra, St Paul Chamber Orchestra, and Utah Symphony Orchestra. Recipient: Guggenheim Fellowship, 1978; Kennedy Center-Friedheim Award, 1980; Pulitzer Prize (for *The Flight into Egypt*), 1988; MacArthur Fellowship, 1989. Mailing address: 449 Franklin Street, Cambridge, Massachusetts 02139, U.S.A.

Publisher: G. Schirmer.

Symphonies/orchestral:

Sinfonia (violin, double orchestra) 1963; first performed Cambridge, Massachusetts, March 1964.
Diotima 1976; first performed Boston, 10 March 1977.
Descant-Nocturne (on a lullaby by Seymour Shifrin) 1976; first performed New Hampshire, 14 July 1980.
Piano Concerto 1978; first performed New York City, 12 May 1980. Recorded CRI S440.
Violin Concerto 1978–80, revised 1987; first performed Boston, 24 January 1981.
Snow Country (oboe, strings) 1979; first performed Boston, March 1981.
Symphony No 1 1981; first performed Boston, 22 March 1984. Recorded New World NW 331.
Deep Potomac Bells (250 tubas) 1983.
Concerto for Clarinet, Oboe, and Strings 1985; first performed Sarasota, Florida, 14 June 1985.
Remembering Gatsby: A Foxtrot for Orchestra 1986; first performed Atlanta, Georgia, 1986.
Symphony No 2 1987; first performed San Francisco, 13 May 1987.
Concerto for Double Brass Choir and Orchestra 1988; first performed Los Angeles, 26 April 1990.
Concerto for Viola and Orchestra 1989; first performed New Jersey, 18 May 1990.
Symphony No 3 1990; first performed Baltimore, Maryland, 26 February 1991.

Chamber/instrumental:

Duo (flute, piano) 1961; first performed New York City, 1961.
Verses (violin) 1964; withdrawn.
Confinement (flute, oboe/cor anglais, clarinet/bass clarinet, alto saxophone, trumpet, trombone, percussion, piano, violin, viola, cello, double bass) 1965; first performed New York City, February 1967. Recorded Nonesuch H-71221.
Four Preludes (3 oboes; or flute, clarinet, violin; or flute, oboe, clarinet) 1967; first performed Cambridge, Massachusetts, April 1969.
Serenade (flute, clarinet, bass clarinet, violin, viola, cello) 1968; first performed Portland, Oregon, May 1969.
Parody-Fantasia (piano) 1968; first performed New York City, December 1969.
Piano Trio 1969; first performed Cambridge, Massachusetts, April 1969.
Bermuda Triangle (amplified cello, tenor saxophone, electric organ) 1970; first performed New York City, April 1973. Recorded CRI S-313.
Die Kurze (piano, flute, clarinet, violin, cello) 1970; first performed New York City, February 1970.
Amazing Grace (oboe) 1972; first performed New York City, January 1973.
Quintet for Woodwinds 1979; first performed Boston, 15 April 1979. Recorded CRI S-436.
Organum for Paul Fromm (piano, marimba, vibraphone, cello, harp) 1981; first performed Chicago, January 1982.
Piano Quintet 1981; first performed Santa Fe, New Mexico, 7 August 1981. Recorded Nonesuch.
Variations (clarinet, violin, piano) 1982; first performed Santa Fe, New Mexico, 23 July 1982. Recorded Northeastern NR230.
Exequiem for Calvin Simmons (alto flute, bass clarinet, 2 violas, cello, vibraphone, piano) 1982; first performed Boston, 15 February 1983.
Overture: Michael Kohlhaas (brass ensemble) 1982; first performed Madison, Wisconsin, November 1982.
String Quartet No 1 1985; first performed Washington, D.C., 11 October 1985.
Twilight Music (horn, violin, piano) 1985; first performed New York City, 22 March 1985.
Four Songs of Solitude (violin) 1985; first performed

Cambridge, Massachusetts, 11 December 1985.
Music for Eighteen Winds (2 flutes/piccolo, 2 oboes, 2 clarinets, 2 bassoons/contrabassoon, alto saxophone, 4 horns, 2 trumpets in C, 2 trombones/bass trombone, tuba) 1986; first performed Cambridge, Massachusetts, 18 April 1986.
Christmas Concerto (brass quintet) 1987; first performed 24 December 1987.
String Quartet No 2 1987; first performed Boston, November 1987.
Piano Sonata 1987; first performed Grand Tetons, Wyoming, 2 August 1988.
Magnum mysterium (brass quintet) 1988; first performed New York City, December 1988.
Two Choral Preludes (brass quintet) 1988.
Fantasy Duo (violin, piano) 1988; first performed Washington, D.C., 2 December 1988.
November 19, 1828 (violin, viola, cello, piano) 1989; first performed Atlanta, Georgia, 30 November 1989.

Vocal/choral:

Autumnal (mezzo-soprano, piano; Dickinson, Baudelaire, Rilke) 1965; first performed Waltham, Massachusetts, March 1966.
Shakespeare Series (sonnets for mezzo-soprano, piano) 1965; first performed Cambridge, Massachusetts, November 1965.
Music (unaccompanied SATB chorus; Shelley) 1966; first performed Cambridge, Massachusetts, 1971.
Five Songs of Experience on Poems of William Blake (SATB chorus, string quartet, 2 percussion) 1971; first performed Cambridge, Massachusetts, February 1973. Recorded CRI S-313.
Elegiac Songs (mezzo-soprano, chamber orchestra; Dickinson) 1974; first performed New York City, 1974.
Book of Hours and Seasons (mezzo-soprano or tenor; flute, cello, piano; Goethe) 1975; first performed Cambridge, Massachusetts, March 1976.
Moments of Vision (soprano, tenor/also playing handbells, alto recorder/sopranino recorder/bass recorder/alto crumhorn, viola da gamba, lute/hurdy-gurdy/dulcimer; Hardy) 1975; first performed Amherst, Massachusetts, 1989.
Three Harp Songs (tenor, harp; Snyder, Fried, Hamilton) 1975; first performed March 1976.
The Flower-Fed Buffaloes (baritone, SSATBB chorus, clarinet, tenor saxophone, violin, cello, double bass, vibraphone, percussion; Lindsay, Crane, Fried, Snyder) 1976; first performed Boston, 27 February 1978. Recorded Nonesuch 71366.
Samuel Chapter (soprano/tenor, flute, clarinet, viola, cello, piano, percussion; Bible) 1978; first performed Cambridge, Massachusetts, October 1978. Recorded Nonesuch 79129.
Nunc dimittis (TB chorus, piano; Bible) 1980; first performed Cambridge, Massachusetts, 12 December 1981.
Motetti di Montale (mezzo-soprano, piano; Montale) 1980; first performed Santa Fe, New Mexico, 4 August 1981.
Mirabai Songs (soprano, piano; second version for soprano, alto flute, bass clarinet, percussion, harp, violin, viola, cello, double bass; Mirabai, Bly) 1982; first performed Boston, 9 September 1983; second version first performed, 1 February 1984. Recorded Northeastern N230; Nonesuch.
The Flight into Egypt (soprano, tenor, SATB chorus, 2 oboes, cor anglais, bassoon, 3 trombones/bass trombone, chamber organ, strings; Bible) 1986; first performed 21 November 1986.
The Natural World (soprano, flute, clarinet, violin, cello, piano; Bly, Stevens, Wright) 1987; first performed Los Angeles, 1989. Recorded New World.
The Three Wise Men (reader, brass quintet; Bible) 1988.
Simple Daylight (soprano, piano) 1988; first performed San Francisco, 1990.
Words from Paterson (baritone, flute/alto flute, oboe/cor anglais, viola, cello, piano, harp; Williams) 1989; first performed Washington, D.C., 1990.

Opera:

Winter's Tale (after Shakespeare; 8 male, 3 female voices, SATB chorus, orchestra) 1974; first performed San Francisco, 20 August 1979.
Full Moon in March (after Yeats; soprano, tenor, mezzo-soprano, baritone, dancer, flute, oboe, bass clarinet, percussion, prepared piano, string trio) 1977; first performed Boston, 30 April 1979. Recorded CRI 454.

Other:

The Merchant of Venice (incidental music to Shakespeare; string orchestra; or string quartet, double bass) 1971; first performed Jaffrey, New Hampshire, August 1973.
Ulysses' Bow (ballet) 1983; first performed Pittsburgh, 11 May 1984. Recorded Nonesuch 79129.
Ulysses' Raft (ballet) 1983; first performed New Haven, Connecticut, 6 March 1984.

PUBLICATIONS

By Harbison: "Six Tanglewood Talks", in *Perspectives of New Music*, 1985; "Facing Rock Reality", in *Contemporary Music Review*, 1990.

On Harbison: M. Hallowell, "Textural Notes", in *Boston Phoenix*, 23 October 1979; B. Zakariasen, "His Music Smacks of Old Masters", in *New York Daily News*, 2 September 1981; A. Ulrich, "The Trials of a Hot Composer", in *San Francisco Examiner*, 20 October 1981; Lloyd Schwartz, "Music: Hard-Won Directness", in *Atlantic Monthly*, 253(3), 1984; J. Tassel, "A Homecoming for JH", in *Boston Globe Magazine*, 26 February 1984; Barbara Isenberg, "Courting the Muse", in *Los Angeles Times* 1990.

John Harbison comments:

What we compose must be larger than our personalities, more dangerous than merely "expressing ourselves". It must create something the hearer wants to hear before he or she knows they want to hear it.

We no longer can think of concert music surviving our time. It must survive first to the next performance and sound more necessary.

"Compose" means to take the sonic impulses darting about like ions in the air and place them in time and space such that they arrest the ears of each sympathetic listener—the populist naturalness of the troubadour, the speculative transport of the monk.

* * *

An extremely lyrical strain runs through all of John Harbison's music. A look at the listing of his output shows a large number of vocal, choral and operatic works, and his interest in singing can be heard even in his instrumental and orchestral music, which always seems to return to the lyrical, even after passages of great density and complexity. This lyrical impulse, combined with a remarkable feel for atmosphere and color, gives Harbison's music its individuality and its impact.

One can hear a broad range of influences in Harbison's music, but the composer blends these elements into a unified whole. For example, in *The Flower-Fed Buffaloes*, a work for baritone, chorus and chamber ensemble, Harbison sets poems of Vachel Lindsay, Hart Crane and other American poets. This work is a good example of Harbison's eclectic style—a combination of French impressionism, American jazz and swing, and occasional touches of the austerity of some of his teachers (Blacher and Sessions). The very first song in this cycle has the gentle, rocking motion and melodic curve of 1930s American swing. Then suddenly, in the second song, we encounter wider melodic leaps, more dissonant harmonies, and a generally severe atmosphere. And so it goes throughout—a different character for each poem, but Harbison throughout.

One unifying factor is that lyrical bent noted above. Even in music that cannot be said to "sing" in the traditional sense, Harbison's melodic profile can be found in a phrase here or there. Another is the strong rhythmic profile that all of his music exhibits. Also omni-present is the polyphonic style of his writing. No matter how richly scored any moment, you can always hear each strand. The climactic passages of his First Symphony, for example, have a massive sonority equalling that of Shostakovich, but the music never thickens into a solid block of sound. In general, his style is that of a delicate painter interweaving strands of light and shade, all of which retain their individual character. A genuine strength of Harbison is his ability to match the color and effect of his vocal music to the text he is setting. Words and music genuinely interact and amplify each other. He also exhibits a trait rare in composers of the present era—humor.

Harbison has carried on a fairly important career as a conductor, and has been associated with many ensembles and orchestras in that capacity. That, plus his residency with two major American orchestras (Pittsburgh and Los Angeles) have given him an indepth working knowledge of the orchestral musician, and players (often a very conservative lot to be sure) often comment on the fact that his music suits their instruments better than that of most composers of the post-World War II era.

At present Harbison already has an impressive output. In recent years, though, his music has been performed with increasing frequency and his popularity seems to have grown. His relatively conservative style was out of fashion in the 1960s and 1970s, but in the 1980s began making a comeback. One would have to guess that his best work and greatest acceptance is yet to come.

—Henry Fogel

HARPER, Edward (James). British/English. Born in Taunton, Somerset, 1941. Educated at Christ Church College, Oxford; Royal College of Music, London; further study under Franco Donatoni, Milan. Lecturer and subsequently reader, Faculty of Music, University of Edinburgh, since 1964, pianist/conductor; director, New Music Group of Scotland, from 1973. Mailing address: 7 Morningside Park, Edinburgh EH10 5HD, Scotland.

Publisher: Oxford University Press.

Symphonies/orchestral:

Piano Concerto 1969; first performed Edinburgh, 29 January 1970.
Bartók Games 1972; first performed Edinburgh, 26 November 1982.
Sonata (chamber orchestra) 1972; first performed Edinburgh, 25 February 1973.
Fantasia I 1976; first performed Edinburgh, 27 March 1976.
Fern Hill (chamber orchestra) 1976; first performed St Andrews, Fife, 23 February 1977.
Symphony 1978–9; first performed Edinburgh, March 1979.
Fantasia IV (violin, piano, small orchestra) 1980; first performed St Andrews, Fife, 26 February 1981.
Clarinet Concerto 1982; first performed Llandaff, Wales, 3 June 1982.
Intrada After Monteverdi (transcription of chamber work) 1982; first performed Edinburgh, 6 October 1983.
Fantasia V (passacaglia for chamber orchestra) 1985; first performed Orkney, 24 June 1985.
Double Variations (oboe, bassoon, winds) 1989; first performed Manchester, 12 August 1989.

Chamber/instrumental:

Quintet (flute, clarinet, violin, cello, piano) 1974; first performed Glasgow, May 1974.
Ricercari in memoriam Luigi Dallapiccola (flute, clarinet, bass clarinet, horn, trumpet, piano, harp, percussion, violin, viola, double bass) 1975; first performed Edinburgh, 30 August 1975.
Fantasia II (11 solo strings) 1976; first performed Dundee, 21 April 1976.
Fantasia III (brass quintet) 1977; first performed Edinburgh, 3 November 1977.
Intrada After Monteverdi (flute/piccolo, clarinet, bass clarinet, horn, trumpet, percussion, harp, piano, violin, viola, cello, double bass) 1982; first performed Edinburgh, 10 September 1982.
String Quartet No 2 1986; first performed Edinburgh, 17 December 1986.
In memoriam (Kenneth Leighton) (cello, piano) 1990; first performed Edinburgh, 8 May 1990.

Vocal/choral:

Seven Poems by e.e. cummings (soprano, orchestra) 1977; first performed Glasgow, 1 November 1977.
Chester Mass (mixed chorus) 1979; first performed Chester, 20 October 1979.
The Universe (unaccompanied SSATB chorus; de la Mare) 1979.
Mass: Qui creavit coelum 1986; first performed Oxford, 28 May 1987.
Caterwaul (soprano, double bass; Savage) 1986; first performed London, 12 June 1986.
Homage to Thomas Hardy (baritone, chamber orchestra) 1989; first performed Cheltenham, Gloucestershire, 1990.
The Lamb (soprano, chorus, orchestra) 1990; first performed Glasgow, 9 December 1990.

Other:

Fanny Robin (after Hardy, additional material by Savage) 1974; first performed Edinburgh, February 1975.
Hedda Gabler (after Ibsen) 1984–5; first performed Glasgow, 5 June 1985.
The Mellstock Quire (chamber opera) 1987–8; first performed Edinburgh, 10 February 1988.

William Byrd: *Three Motets* (arranged for 2 trumpets, horn, tenor, bass trombone or tuba) n.d.

* * *

Although born in Somerset, Edward Harper's musical life has been conducted in Scotland, through his long association with the University of Edinburgh. The composer was also instrumental in setting up the now sadly defunct New Music Group of Scotland in 1973, and that ensemble gave the premiere performance of several of his works.

Harper is probably best known for his operas *Fanny Robin*, based on episodes from his beloved fellow-West Countryman Thomas Hardy's *Far from the Madding Crowd*, and his adaptation of Henrick Ibsen's *Hedda Gabler*. Composed as a kind of companion piece-cum-riposte to Purcell's *Dido and Aeneas*, the brief, highly economical score of *Fanny Robin* is one of his best, incorporating humour and an imaginative use of English folk material within its 13 episodic passages.

Harper has returned to Hardy as a source of inspiration on more than one occasion, including the less successful opera *The Mellstock Quire*, and *Homage to Thomas Hardy* for baritone and chamber orchestra. He has drawn on such literary material on a number of occasions, as in the lovely but distinctly muscular quasi-sinfonietta setting *Fern Hill*, inspired by a Dylan Thomas poem, or the rather more assertive *Seven Poems by e.e. cummings* for soprano and orchestra.

Apart from a short *Piano Concerto*, the vibrant and exciting *Bartók Games* is the earliest work listed in Harper's current catalogue, and it marked the onset of a greater reliance on a more tonally based development in his music. The richness of colouration and texture which would mark his subsequent work is already fully present here.

Harper has a highly developed capacity for paying tribute to earlier composers, but in a manner which is both original and fully integrated within his own music, even where he uses direct quotation (although the second movement of his *String Quartet No 2*, which pays overt homage to Beethoven, is a not entirely successful exception).

Symphony, for example, a spacious and finely-wrought meditation, opens with a lengthy slow theme which is identical in the sequence of notes to the equivalent theme in Elgar's *First Symphony*, but takes on an entirely different character from its distinct rhythm.

His *Intrada After Monteverdi* is an exhuberant example of the humour and sense of fun which pervades his music, while the moving *Ricercari in memoriam Luigi Dallapiccola* has been performed to great effect as a continuous extension of that composer's *Quaderno musicale di Annalibera*, with the ensemble picking up the theme from the dying notes of the piano to make a seamless fusion of the two works.

His series of *Fantasia* pieces (the third of which has a companion brass setting of *Three Motets* by William Byrd) for a variety of chamber and orchestral forces are among his most accomplished works. Other major compositions include the *Chester Mass*, commissioned to mark the 1900th anniversary of the founding of the city, and the *Clarinet Concerto*, along with a rich vein of chamber music, including the powerful *In memoriam (Kenneth Leighton)* for cello and piano.

Whatever idiom he chooses, Harper always gives off a strong sense of having something worthwhile to say in it, and his presence on the Scottish music scene has been hugely beneficial.

—Kenny Mathieson

HARRISON, Lou (Silver). American. Born in Portland, Oregon, 14 May 1917. Educated at San Francisco State College (composition under Henry Cowell), 1934–5; Mills College, Oakland, California, 1936–9; University of California, Los Angeles (composition under Arnold Schoenberg), 1941. Moved to New York, 1943; music critic, New York *Herald Tribune*, 1945–8; teacher, Greenwich House School, New York City; dance accompanist; florist; instrument maker; editor of New Music Edition/promoter of music by Charles Ives, Carl Ruggles; edited/premiered, Ives's *Symphony No 3*, 1947; teacher of music, Portland, Oregon, 1947–8; teacher, Black Mountain College, North Carolina, 1948–9; settled in Aptos, California; visited Rome, 1954; worked in animal hospital, composing at night, 1957–60; visited Far East, 1961; senior scholar, East-West Center, University of Hawaii, Honolulu, 1963; research in Oaxaca de Juarez, Mexico, 1965; teacher of music, San Jose State College, California, 1967–80; musical director, Red Gate Shadow Players, 1970; constructed gamelan Si Darius, 1972; visiting professor, Stanford University, California, 1974, Centre for World Music, University of California, Berkeley, 1975, and University of Southern California, Los Angeles, 1977; Darius Milhaud Professor of Music, Mills College, Oakland, California, 1980–5, now emeritus; Senior Fulbright Scholar, New Zealand universities, 1983. Recipient: Guggenheim Fellowship, 1952, 1954; From Award, 1955; Phoebe Katchum Thorne Award, 1965. Mailing address: 7121 Viewpoint Road, Aptos, California 95003, U.S.A.

Publishers: New Music Edition; Peters; Peer Southern.

Symphonies/orchestral:

Suite for Symphonic Strings 1936–60; first performed Louisville, Kentucky, 1960.
Symphony No 3 1937–82; first performed Aptos, California, Summer 1982.
Concerto for Violin and Percussion Orchestra 1940–59.
Elegiac Symphony 1941–75; first performed Oakland, California, 1975.
Alleluia 1944; first performed New York City, 1944.
Suite No 1 (string orchestra) 1947.
Suite No 2 (string orchestra) 1948; first performed New York City, 1948.
Symphony on G 1948–54, finale revised 1966; first performed Aptos, California, Summer 1964.
The Marriage at the Eiffel Tower (orchestral suite from the dance) 1949.
Suite (violin, piano, small orchestra) 1951; first performed

New York City, 1951. Recorded New World Records NW 366-2; CRI SD 114.
Praises for Hummingbirds and Hawks (suite for small orchestra from the dance) 1951.
Moogunkwha, se tang ak (Korean court orchestra) 1961; first performed Seoul, 1961.
Pacifika rondo (chamber orchestra, Western and Oriental instruments) 1963; first performed Honolulu, Hawaii, Spring 1963.
Concerto for Organ, Percussion and Orchestra 1972–3; first performed San Jose, California, Spring 1973.
Simfony in Free Style (17 flutes—3 or 4 players, and trombone, bells, drums, 5 harps, celeste/vibraphone, tack piano, 8 viols) 1980.
Double Concerto (violin, cello, large Javanese gamelan) 1981–2.
Piano Concerto 1985. Recorded New World Records NW 366-2.

Chamber/instrumental (including gamelan):

Six Sonatas for Cembalo (harpsichord) 1936–40; published *New Music Editions* 1943. Recorded (no 2) Mills Records 001.
Prelude and Sarabande (piano) 1937.
Three Sonatas (piano) 1938.
Concerto No 1 (flute, percussion) 1939.
Canticle No 1 (5 percussion) 1940.
Song of Queztecoatl (percussion quartet) 1940.
Canticle No 3 (flute/ocarina, guitar, percussion) 1941.
Double Music (collaboration with John Cage; percussion quartet) 1941. Recorded New World NW 330.
Fugue (percussion quartet) 1941.
Labyrinth (91 percussion instruments—11 players) 1941.
Suite (piano) 1943.
Schoenbergiana (6 woodwinds; arranged by R. Hughes) 1945.
Siciliana (wind quintet) 1945.
Motet for the Day of Ascension (7 strings) 1946.
Air (flute) 1946.
Praises for Michael the Archangel (piano) 1946.
String Trio 1946. Recorded New World NW 319.
Suite (cello, harp) 1949. Recorded New World NW 281.
Little Suite (piano) 1949.
Suite No 2 (string quartet) 1949–50.
Seven Pastorales (4 woodwinds, harp, strings) 1952.
Serenade (guitar/harp) 1952.
Koncherto (violin, 5 percussion) 1959.
Concerto in slendro (violin, celeste, 2 tack pianos, strings) 1961.
Quintal taryung (2 flutes, changgo) 1961.
Sonat per psaltero (psaltery) 1961.
Prelude (p'iri, harmonium) 1962.
Wesak Sonata (psaltery) 1963.
Majestic Fanfare (trumpets, percussion) 1963.
At the Tomb of Charles Ives (chamber ensemble) 1964.
Avalokiteshvara (harp, jaltarang) 1965.
Music for Violin (duos with other instruments) 1967–9.
Bevereley's Troubadour Piece (harp, 2 percussion) 1968.
In Memory of Victor Jowers (clarinet, piano) 1968.
Harp Solo 1968.
The Garden at One at a Quarter Moon (psaltery) 1969.
Suite (collaboration with Richard Dee; violin, American gamelan) 1972–3. Recorded New Albion NA 015.
Arion's Leap (justly tuned instruments, percussion) 1974.
Gending Pak Chakro (Javanese gamelan) 1976.
Lagu sociseknum (Javanese gamelan) 1976.
Lancaran Daniel (Javanese gamelan) 1976.
Main bersama-sama (horn, Sundanese gamelan degung) 1978.
Serenade for Betty Freeman and Franco Asseto (Sundanese gamelan degung, suling) 1978.
String Quartet Set 1978–9. Recorded CRI ACS-6006.
Suite (guitar, percussion) 1978–9.
Threnody for Carlos Chavez (Sundanese gamelan degung, violin) 1979.
Bubaran Robert (Javanese gamelan) 1981.
Gending Alexander (Javanese gamelan) 1981.
Gending Demeter (Javanese gamelan) 1981.
Gending Hermes (Javanese gamelan) 1981.
Gending Haephaestus (Javanese gamelan) 1981.
Lancaran Samuel (Javanese gamelan) 1981.
Ladrang Epikuros (Javanese gamelan) 1981.
Ladrang Samuel (Javanese gamelan) 1981.
Gending Claude (Javanese gamelan) 1982.
Gending Dennis (Javanese gamelan) 1982.
Gending Palladio (Javanese gamelan) 1982.
Gending Pindar (Javanese gamelan) 1982.
Lancaran Molly (Javanese gamelan) 1982.
For the Pleasure of Ovid's Changes (Javanese gamelan) 1983.
Gending James and Joel (Javanese gamelan) 1983.
Gending Sinan (Javanese gamelan) 1983.
Ketawang Wellington (Javanese gamelan) 1983.
Lagu lagu Thomasan (Cirebon gamelan pelog) 1983.
Lagu Victoria (Cirebon gamelan) 1983.
Gending William Colvig (Javanese gamelan) 1983.
Ladrang Pak Daliyo (Javanese gamelan) 1984.
Lagu Elang Yusuf (Cirebon gamelan slendro) 1984.

Vocal/choral:

Mass (SATB chorus, trumpet, harp, strings) 1939–54.
May Rain (voice, tack piano, tam-tam) 1941.
Pied Beauty (voice, trombone/cello, flute, percussion) 1941.
Easter Cantata (soloists, chorus, orchestra) 1943–6.
Fragment from Calmus (alto/baritone, piano) 1946.
Sanctus (voice) 1946.
Alma redemptoris mater (baritone, violin, trombone, tack piano) 1949.
A Political Primer (soloists, chorus, orchestra) 1951.
Holly and Ivy (voice, harp, strings; Snyder) 1951.
Peace Piece Three (voice, violin, harp, strings) 1953.
Four Strict Songs (8 baritones, orchestra) 1955.
A Joyous Procession and a Solemn Procession (chorus, trombones, percussion) 1962.
Nova odo (chorus, orchestra) 1962.
Haiku (unison voices, xiao, harp, percussion; Davis) 1968.
Peace Piece Two (tenor, 3 percussion, 2 harps, string quintet) 1968.
Peace Piece One (unison voices, trombone, 3 percussion, 2 harps, organ, string quintet; Metta Sutra, translated Conze) 1968.
La koro sutro (mixed chorus, American gamelan, percussion orchestra; Heart Sutra, translated into Esperanto) 1972. Recorded New Albion NA 015.
Scenes from Cavafy (baritone, male voices, large Javanese gamelan) 1979–80.
The Foreman's Song Tune (chorus, gamelan) 1983.

Opera:

Rapunzel (Morris) 1954; first performed Rome, 1954.
Young Caesar (puppet opera; Gordon) 1971.

Other:

Peter Pan (incidental music to Barrie) 1934.
Changing World (dance) 1936; first performed San Francisco, 1936.
Choephore (incidental music to Aeschylus) 1937.
Elektra (incidental music to Euripides) 1938.
The Trojan Women (incidental music to Euripides) 1938.
The Winter's Tale (incidental music to Shakespeare) 1938.
Green Mansions (dance by Beals) 1939; first performed San Francisco, Summer 1939.
Something to Please Everybody (dance by Horton) 1939; first performed Redlands, California, 1939.
Johnny Appleseed (dance by Beals) 1940; first performed San Francisco, 1940.
Omnipotent Chair (dance by Klepper) 1940; first performed Oakland, California, Summer 1940.
Jeptha's Daughter (theatre piece; narrator, dancers, 2 flutes, percussion, other musicians; biblical) 1940–63.
The Beautiful People (incidental music to play by Saroyan) 1941.
Orpheus (dance by Zenor; voices, chorus, percussion orchestra) 1941–69; first performed San Jose, California, 1969.
Party Pieces (Sonorous and Exquisite Corpses) (collaborative game of 20 musical *cadavres exquises*/"Consequences" by LH, John Cage, Virgil Thomson, Henry Cowell; arranged by R. Hughes for flute, clarinet, bassoon, horn, piano) 1945–6.
Perilous Chapel (dance by Erdman) 1948; first performed New York City, 1948.
Western Dance (dance by Cunningham; piano) 1948; first performed New York City, 1948.
The Marriage at the Eiffel Tower (dance by Bird) 1949; first performed Portland, Oregon, Summer 1949.
The Only Jealousy of Emer (dance-drama after Yeats; small orchestra) 1949.
Solstice (dance by Erdman; flute, oboe, trumpet, celeste, tack piano, 2 cellos, double bass) 1949; first performed New York, 1949.
Almanac of the Seasons (dance by Bird) 1950; first performed Portland, Oregon, 1950.
Io and Prometheus (dance by Erdman) 1951; first performed New York City, 1951.
Praises for Hummingbirds and Hawks (dance by Broughton) 1951.
Cinna (incidental music to Corneille) 1957.

John Cage: *Suite for Toy Piano* (orchestration).
Dee: *Suite for Cheng* (orchestration).
Dee: *Spring in Loyang* (orchestration).

Film scores: *Nuptiae*, 1973; *Discovering Korean Art*, 1979; *Beyond the Far Blue Mountains*, 1981–2; *Devotions*, 1983.

PUBLICATIONS

By Harrison: *About Carl Ruggles*, New York, 1946; *Music Primer: Various Items About Music to 1970*, New York, 1971; contributor to *Soundings: Ives, Ruggles, Varèse*, Santa Fe, New Mexico, 1974.

On Harrison: E. Turrell, "LH", in *American Harp Journal*, 3(1), 1971; W. Colvig, "A Western Gamelan", in Grayson (ed), *Sound Sculpture: A Collection of Essays by Artists*, Vancouver, 1975; V. Rathbun, "LH and His Music", dissertation, San Jose State University, California, 1976; S. Barrouyer, "L'Anniversaire de LH, mai 1977", in *Musique en jeu*, 30, 1978; W. Siegel, (interview) in *Dansk musiktidsskrift*, 53(1), 1978; C. Crawford, (interview) in *Musicworks*, 9, 1979; P. Garland, "LH: A Quick Glance Across the Years", in *Americas: Essays on American Music and Culture, 1973–80*, Santa Fe, New Mexico, 1982; C. Rutman, "The Solo Piano Works of LH", dissertation, Peabody Conservatory, Baltimore, Maryland, 1983.

* * *

Lou Harrison is one of those rare composers who can embrace eclecticism and create a unique style of music. The philosophical foundation of his music is the assimilation of divergent musical sources, such as the European Baroque and the Indonesian gamelan traditions, into a new musical tradition. The assimilation is always democratic in that one tradition never dominates another; each contributes equally. Harrison is much more than an adept musical craftsman. He is a musical philosopher, poet and practitioner whose lifestyle and beliefs are aspects of his art. Consequently, in order to know the art, one must know the man, and vice versa.

Harrison's views on music reflect, in part, the views of his teachers, Arnold Schoenberg and Henry Cowell. While both were musical innovators, their innovations were very different. Schoenberg's music continued and expanded the European tradition, while Cowell's music is influenced by his explorations into the music of Asian cultures, indigenous western American music and the foundations of musical expression. By fusing Cowell's and Schoenberg's approaches with compositional innovations of his own, such as experimental tunings, Harrison has created an immensely diverse, original and cogent body of work. Each composition, from the *String Trio*, which is firmly rooted in the Second Viennese School, to the *Suite* for violin, piano and small orchestra, which combines elements of gamelan and the Baroque suite, is a reflection of Harrison's belief that a composer is free to use any sound in the environment. His compositions also reflect his sense of place geographically, as a Pacific Rim composer, and historically, as a composer who has available the entire corpus of Western art music.

Other influences on Harrison's music include another student of Cowell's, John Cage, and in a more limited way, Harry Partch, who perhaps inspired Harrison's own experiments with non-traditional tunings and instrument building. In 1941 Cage and Harrison collaborated on *Double Music* for four percussionists. The title reflects the complementary nature of their relationship in writing the music, since each composer wrote two of its four sections. In spite of its transparent sectional demarcation by composer, *Double Music* does not sound disjointed or discontinuous. The organic development of the music is due in part to the ease with which Harrison's and Cage's musical personalities blended and to *Double Music*'s simple compositional premise. The piece is composed entirely of eighth notes grouped by twos and threes.

The collaborative impulse is another aspect of Harrison's unique approach to composition. Although it has never been a big part of the European tradition, collaborative composition is a very important feature of many Asian cultures. Harrison's continued interest in collaborative composition produced *Suite* for violin with an American gamelan, written in 1974 with Richard Dee. The suite consists of a Threnody, Estampie, Air, Three Jahlas and a Chaconne. Unlike *Double Music*, the various sections of the suite were not alternately composed by Harrison and Dee. According to the composers, the work was cooperatively planned and integrated with their collaborative ideas at every level.

Besides the direct influence of his teachers and colleagues, the music of Ives, Ruggles and Varèse have been an important part of Harrison's development. During his years in New York, he championed their music by presenting it in concerts. Perhaps his most important achievement as impresario and performing musician was to conduct the premiere of Ives's Third Symphony.

Although Harrison has described his musical output in terms like his "San Francisco period" or "mission period (1930–42)", these labels are indications more of philosophical transition than of stylistic change. The music follows a non-linear path of development that is reflected in the dates he attaches to his compositions. The *Suite for Symphonic Strings*, for instance, is dated 1936–60, because the work consists of music composed or sketched over a 24-year period. Works like the Suite illustrate many of the general characteristics defining Harrison's music, such as love of the melodic line, polyphonic textures, dance forms and rhythms, and progressive harmonic relationships.

Although it contains new as well as older material, and its nine movements represent a variety of compositional styles, the *Suite for Symphonic Strings* is a unified work. The cohesive elements of his style coupled with his eclectic approach to composition allow the integration of otherwise diverse musical styles into a natural and organic sound. The Suite successfully integrates the ninth movement, a slow and romantically expressive "Nocturne" written in the Locrian mode, the second movement, a chromatic chorale titled "Et in Arcadia Ego," and the first movement, "Estampie," based on a medieval dance. Another element enrichening the sound of the music is Harrison's instruction to use "just" intonation in the diatonic movements, 1, 4, 6 and 9.

The *Concerto for Violin and Percussion Orchestra* exemplifies the mixture of Western and Eastern traditions characteristic of much of Harrison's music. Following the Western tradition, the three movements of the work are Allegro, maestoso; Largo, cantabile; and Allegro, vigoroso, poco presto. The percussion orchestra consists of traditional instruments, such as tam-tams, triangles, snare drum and bass drum, and instruments constructed from flower pots, coffee cans, brake drums and pipe lengths. While the violin maintains its role as soloist, the percussion orchestra is more than just accompaniment or a foil for the violin. It creates a textured sound mass that shimmers with coloristic orchestrations. In this capacity, the percussion ensemble captures and recreates the spirit of the gamelan.

Harrison has also composed works for larger ensembles. Most notable are the *Symphony on G* and the *Piano Concerto*. Although the symphony was composed using twelve-tone techniques, it is tonally centered. Some of the more interesting aspects of this work include the use of a prepared piano and the "Scherzo," which is a dance suite that contains a polka. The *Piano Concerto* combines the perpetual energy of the gamelan with the polyphonic playfulness of the Baroque composers. In this work, the piano's black keys are tuned to mathematically precise 4ths and 5ths, while the white keys resemble "just" intonation. By tuning each section of the orchestra to a different aspect of this tuning, Harrison creates complex harmonic relations from simple materials.

Harrison's music is a joyful celebration of the diversity that makes up our world. Perhaps his success is due in part to the sincerity with which he embraces the musical traditions of the world. Nevertheless, his music is more than the sum of its traditions; it is the expression of an acute musical personality.

—Ciro G. Scotto

HARVEY, Jonathan (Dean). British. Born in Sutton Coldfield, Warwickshire, 3 May 1939. Educated at St Michael's College, Tenbury, 1948–52; Repton, 1952–57; St John's College, Cambridge (and composition study under Erwin Stein and Hans Keller), M.A., D.Mus.; Glasgow University, Ph.D., 1964; Harkness Fellowship, Princeton University, New Jersey (under Milton Babbitt), 1969–70. Married Rosaleen Marie Barry in 1960; 1 son and 1 daughter. Lecturer, University of Southampton, 1964–77; reader, University of Sussex, Brighton, 1977–80. Recipient: Mus.D., Cambridge University, 1972; honorary D.Mus., University of Southampton, 1990; member, Academia Europaea, 1989. Mailing address: 35 Houndean Rise, Lewes, Sussex BN7 1BQ, England.

Publishers: Novello; Faber.

Symphonies/orchestral:

Symphony (formerly called *Three Pieces for Orchestra*) 1966.
Chaconne on "Iam Dulcis Amica" 1967.
Benedictus 1970.
Persephone Dream 1972.
Inner Light III 1975.
Whom Ye Adore 1981; first performed Scotland, 19 September 1981.
Bhakti (short and long version: chamber orchestra, quadraphonic tape) 1982; first performed Paris, 3, 4, 6, 7 December 1982. Recorded NMCD001.
Easter Orisons (chamber orchestra) 1983; first performed Newcastle, 15 January 1984.
Gong-Ring (chamber ensemble, electronics) 1984; first performed Edinburgh, 1 September 1984.
Madonna of Winter and Spring (orchestra, synthesizers, electronics) 1986; first performed London, 27 August 1986.
Lightness and Weight (solo tuba, orchestra) 1987; first performed Poole, Dorset, 18 February 1987.
Timepieces (orchestra, 2 conductors) 1987; first performed Saarbrücken, Germany, 23 September 1988.
Cello Concerto 1990.

Chamber/instrumental:

Dialogue (cello, piano) 1965.
Variations (violin, piano) 1965.
Transformation of "Love Bade Me Welcome" (clarinet, piano) 1968.
Four Images After Yeats (piano) 1969.
Laus Deo (organ) 1969.
Studies (two clarinets in B♭) 1970.
Piano Trio (violin, cello, piano) 1971.
Quantumplation (flute, clarinet, violin, cello, percussion, piano) 1973.
Inner Light I (flute/piccolo, clarinet, violin, viola, cello, percussion, piano, tape) 1973.
Round the Star and Back (piano, other instruments capable of a reasonable blend) 1974.
Smiling Immortal (chamber ensemble, tape) 1977; first performed London, 11 July 1977.
String Quartet 1977; first performed Southampton, Hampshire, 6 March 1979. Recorded RCA RL 70883.
Album (seven miniatures for flute/piccolo, oboe/oboe d'amore/cor anglais, clarinet/E♭ clarinet/bass clarinet, bassoon/contrabassoon, horn) 1978; first performed Durham, 27 October 1979.
Concelebration (chamber ensemble—flute, clarinet, cello,

piano, percussion) 1979, revised 1981; first performed London, 1 June 1980.
Be(com)ing (clarinet, piano) 1979; first performed London, 22 October 1981.
Toccata (organ, pre-recorded tape) 1980.
Modernsky Music (2 oboes, bassoon, harpsichord) 1981; first performed Scunthorpe, 18 September 1981.
Curve with Plateaux (cello) 1982; first performed Brighton, Sussex, 21 February 1982.
Nataraja (flute, piano) 1983; first performed Lewes, Sussex, 20 January 1984.
Flight-Elegy (violin, piano) 1984; first performed Brighton, Sussex, 8 May 1984.
Ricercare una melodie (trumpet, tape delay; also versions for pre-recorded tape; or flute, tape delay; or oboe, tape delay) 1985; first performed London, 10 January 1985.
Tendril (flute/piccolo, cor anglais/oboe, clarinet, bassoon, horn, piano, single strings) 1987; first performed London, 10 June 1987.
String Quartet No 2 1988; first performed Brussels, 17 March 1989.
The Valley of Aosta (flute/piccolo, cor anglais/oboe, soprano saxophone, trumpet, 2 violins, viola, cello, 2 harps, piano, percussion, synthesizer) 1988; broadcast Radio France, 7 March 1989.

Vocal/choral:

Four Songs of Yeats (bass, piano) 1965.
Cantata I (soprano and baritone solo, SATB chorus, organ, strings, orchestra; anon., Yeats) 1965.
Iam dulcis amica (2 sopranos, 2 tenors, 2 basses; or chorus; Turner) 1967.
Cantata II: Three Lovescapes (soprano, piano; Prince, San Juan de la Cruz) 1967.
Carol (unaccompanied SATB or AATB or TTBB chorus) 1968.
Cantata III (soprano, flute, clarinet, piano, electronic organ, percussion, violin, cello; biblical) 1968.
Cantata IV: Ludus amoris (soprano, tenor, speaker, large mixed chorus, orchestra; 16th-century Spanish mystics, Gascoigne, Seferis) 1969.
In memoriam (soprano, flute, clarinet, violin, cello; Ginsberg) 1969.
Cantata V: Black Sonnet (soprano, mezzo-soprano, baritone, bass solo, wind quintet; G.M. Hopkins, JH) 1970.
Cantata VI (small SATB chorus, small string orchestra; Kierkegaard) 1970.
Cantata VII: On Vision (soprano and tenor solo, large mixed chorus, chamber group; San Juan de la Cruz, Virginia Woolf, Enoch, JH) 1972.
Angel Eros (high voice, string quartet) 1973.
Correspondences (mezzo-soprano, piano; Baudelaire) 1975.
Sobre un éxtasis de alta contemplación (SATB choir; San Juan de la Cruz) 1975.
Spirit Music (soprano, 3 clarinets, piano; Rudolph Steiner) 1975.
The Dove Descending (SATB choir; T.S. Eliot) 1975.
Inner Light 2 (2 sopranos, alto, tenor, bass, tape, horn, trumpet, trombone, harp, piano, electric organ, percussion, string quartet, synthesizer, tape) 1977; first performed Cheltenham, Gloucestershire, 8 July 1977.
Magnificat and Nunc dimittis (SSATB chorus, organ) 1978; first performed Winchester, Hampshire, 29 July 1978.
Hymn (SATB chorus, orchestra) 1979; first performed Winchester, Hampshire, 12 July 1979; Cheltenham, Gloucestershire, 13 July 1979.
O Jesu nomen dulce (unaccompanied SATB chorus) 1980; first performed Winchester, Hampshire, 29 November 1979.
Resurrection (double SATB chorus, organ) 1981; first performed Worcester, 28 August 1981.
Lullaby for the Unsleeping (medium voice, piano; J.V. Taylor) 1982; first performed London, 22 November 1985.
The Path of Devotion (SATB chorus, small orchestra) 1983; first performed London, 16 February 1985.
Come, Holy Ghost (unaccompanied double SATB chorus) 1984; first performed Winchester, Hampshire, 26 July 1984. Recorded Libra LRS150.
Nachtlied (soprano, piano, pre-recorded tape; Goethe, Rudolph Steiner) 1984; first performed Harrogate, Yorkshire, 11 August 1984.
Song Offerings (soprano, flute, clarinet, 2 violins, cello, double bass, cornet, piano) 1985; first performed London, 22 March 1985. Recorded Nimbus NI 5167.
Forms of Emptiness (unaccompanied SATB choir; e.e. cummings) 1986; first performed London, 15 April 1986.
God Is Our Refuge (SATB, organ; Psalm 46) 1986; first performed Chichester, Sussex, 5 June 1986.
Lauds (SATB choir, cello; J.V. Taylor) 1987; first performed Winchester, Hampshire, 23 July 1987.
From Silence (soprano, violin, viola, percussion, 3 synthesizers, tape with 3 technicians) 1988; first performed Massachusetts, 2 February 1989.

Opera:

Passion and Resurrection (church opera in 12 scenes; soloists, chorus, horn in F, trumpet, tenor trombone, bass trombone, tuba, 2 percussion, 7 violins, viola, 2 cellos, 2 double basses, large organ, chamber organ ad lib) 1981; first performed Winchester, Hampshire, 21/22 March 1981.

Electronic/tape:

Time-points (2 channel tape) 1970.
Mortuos plango, vivos voco (computer-manipulated concrete sounds—pre-recorded tape) 1980; first performed Lille, 30 November 1980. Recorded Erato STU 71544; EMI TCESD 178319.
Ritual Melodies (tape) 1990.

PUBLICATIONS

By Harvey: *The Music of Stockhausen*, London, 1975; articles in *Tempo* and *Contemporary Music Review*.

On Harvey: D. Brown, "JH", in *Musical Times*, 1, 1968; P. Evans, "JH", in *Musical Times*, 116, 1975; Paul Griffiths, (interview) in *New Sounds, New Personalities: British Composers in the 1980s*, London, 1985.

* * *

A remarkable feature of Jonathan Harvey's music is the way it attempts to prehend the numinous. From childhood he has been aware the the visionary power of music and recognised it in the pieces written by his father (a gifted amateur composer) as well as more formally in the daily rituals of a chorister's life at St Michael's Church, Tenbury. At Cambridge, he was preoccupied with mystical ideas while becoming acquainted with procedures in medieval and renaissance music that were later to influence his own compositions. During the 1960s, he composed freely, responding to a wide variety of musical and religious experiences in his settings of medieval texts, St John of the Cross, Milton, Kierkegaard and Virginia Woolf.

Schoenberg, Berg, Messiaen and Britten were early influences and a broader base was achieved through the guidance of Hans Keller. In 1966 came what Harvey has described as his "Stockhausen conversion". The power of Stockhausen's new rhythms, dislocated counterpoints and long silences had a profound effect on Harvey and inspired him to develop, somewhat systematically, a complex and personal language.

His studies with Milton Babbitt in 1969–70 taught him the value of a strong intellectual framework and he became fascinated by Babbitt's cerebral control and depth of structure. While Stockhausen helped to focus Harvey's quest for a spiritual music, Babbitt's serialism was a rather different, more technical liberating influence.

Since the early 1970s, Harvey has developed as a composer of intense individuality. In particular, he has succeeded in integrating extra-musical connotations, from nature and the other arts, and above all from visionary experiences of various kinds. The resulting inclusive nature of his musical expression is presented without sacrificing technical control, and in this respect Harvey's formal discipline may be attributed to his careful study of Schenker's analytical methods.

His skill as an orchestrator has been apparent in a number of works since *Persephone Dream*, written in 1972 and hailed as the most imaginative and lucid work produced by an English composer of his generation. Other works which show a sure command of the orchestra are *Whom Ye Adore*, *Easter Orisons* and *Madonna of Winter and Spring*. The latter work combines the orchestra with synthesizers and electronics, and Harvey's work in this mixed medium has generally won him much admiration. But pure electronic music has a limited appeal for him and is usually directed towards that continuum which links electronic with acoustic sound, timbre with harmony. His first venture into taped music was at IRCAM in 1980, when he composed *Mortuos plango, vivos voco*. In this work, recordings of Harvey's chorister son and of the great bell of Winchester Cathedral were subjected to computer engineering with great effect. The interaction of the immaterial world of the human voice and the bell with the material technology of the electronic studio was a formidable synthesis, and the work has become a classic of its genre.

Bhakti for instrumental ensemble and quadrophonic tape was also composed at IRCAM and is notable for balancing strict organisation of pitch and timbre with freely exuberant dramatic gestures which relate to Eastern and medieval arts. Its basic thematic material, a twelve-note idea, illustrates a novel procedure which Harvey has adapted from Renaissance music. The twelve notes are balanced symmetrically with an axis in the middle of the musical space acting as a pivot for successive sounds to mirror each other on either side, therefore contradicting that tonal basis (whose chords are read from the bass upwards) which have governed Western music since 1600.

The transcendental quality of Harvey's music does not lose its force when he turns to the more intimate genre of chamber music. His two string quartets both take on a spiritual dimension. He has also produced a large and varied output of choral music, often in a modal style and suited to church performance, and of these perhaps the most substantial is his church opera *Passion and Resurrection*.

—Richard Elfyn Jones

HAYS, Sorrel (Doris Ernestine Hays). American. Born in Memphis, Tennessee, 6 August 1941. Educated at the University of Chattanooga, Tennessee (under Harold Cadek), 1959–63, B.M.; Munich Hochschule für Musik (under Frederik Wuehrer), 1963–6, artist's diploma; University of Wisconsin, Madison, 1967–8 (under Paul Badura-Skoda), M.M.; composition study, University of Iowa (under Richard Hervig and Robert Schallenberg), Summer 1969; private new music study under Hilde Some, 1975–7. Concert pianist, 1971–85; teacher/resident composer, University of Wisconsin, Madison, 1967–8, Cornell University, Ithaca, New York, 1969, Queen's College, New York City, 1975–6, and at Ithaca College, New York, Georgia State University, Atlanta, San Francisco State University, Converse College, Spartanburg, South Carolina, Appalachian State University, Boone, North Carolina, University of Heidelberg, and University of South Carolina, Charleston; consultant in new music, text series *Music*, Silver Burdett, 1974–82; resident artist, Georgia Arts Council, 1976; assistant chair, International League of Women Composers, 1979–84; consultant for artist grants, CAPS, New York State Arts Council, 1980–2. Recipient: performance award, Wisconsin State Composition contest, 1968; 1st prize, Competition for Interpreters of New Music, Rotterdam, 1971; citation of merit, 1976; 1st prize, American Film Festival (for *Southern Voices: A Composer's Exploration*). Mailing address: 697 West End Avenue, Penthouse B, New York, New York 10025, U.S.A.

Publishers: Henmar/C.F. Peters Corp., New York; Tallapoosa Music (self).

Symphonies/orchestral:

Pieces from Last Year (chamber orchestra, ocarina, piano) 1975; first performed Albany, Georgia, 1976.
Harmony (In der bleierne Zeit) (string orchestra) 1985; first performed Baltimore, Maryland, 1986.

Chamber/instrumental:

If (piano, 4 tapes) 1970.
Scheveningen Beach (flute quintet) 1972.
Chartres Red (piano) 1972.
Pipsissewa, Trailing Arbutus (buchla, piano) 1973.
PAMP (amplified piano, tape, bird calls) 1973.
Translations and Comments (piano, tape, improvising instruments) 1974.
Juncture Dance (7 percussionists) 1974.
For My Brother's Wedding (organ) 1974.
Breathless (bass flute) 1976.
Sunday Nights 1976; first performed New York City, 1976. Recorded Finnadar/Atlantic SR 2–720.
Sensevents for Lenox Square (5 chamber instruments, tape) 1976.
Sensevents for Lincoln Center (violin, viola, cello, flute, oboe, horn) 1977.
Sunday Mornings (piano) 1977.
For A.B. (clarinet, piano) 1977.
Winded (piccolo) 1978.
Passion Flower, Sunflowers, Orange Butterfly Weed (buchla, piano) 1978.
Characters (harpsichord, string quartet, 3 winds) 1978.
Tunings (double bass) 1978.
Certain; Change (bass flute, piccolo, tape) 1978.
Segments/Junctures (viola, clarinet, piano) 1978.
Tommy's Trumpet (trumpet duo) 1979.
Etude Base Basses (piano) 1979.

Past Present (piano) 1979. Recorded Opus One Records *Soundbridge*.
City Cedar, Pink Turtlehead (buchla, tape) 1979.
Tunings (bassoon, clarinet, flute) 1979.
Fanfare Study (trumpet, trombone, horn) 1980.
Saturday Nights (piano, tape) 1980.
Tunings (viola) 1980.
Homing (violin, piano) 1981.
Tunings (string quartet) 1982; first performed New York City, November 1981.
Rocking (flute, violin, piano) 1982; first performed New York City, March 1983.
M.O.M. 'N P.O.P. (3 pianos, film, tape) 1983; first performed Bremen, 1984.
Rocking (flute, violin, viola, optional light effects) 1983.
After Glass (10 percussion) 1983; first performed Weston, Massachusetts, April 1984.
Bits (piano, DX7 synthesizer) 1987. Recorded Opus One 135CD.
Juncture Dance III (7 percussion) 1988.
90's: A Calendar Bracelet (MIDI grand piano) 1989; first performed New York City, 6 April 1990. Recorded Opus One Records *Soundbridge*.

Vocal/choral:

Duet (audience, piano) 1970.
Four Against Three (4-part spoken chorus) 1973.
Make a Melody, Make a Song (voice, piano) 1973.
Song for Bringing a Child into the World 1973.
You, Where You Have Fallen From 1973.
Just by Sitting 1973.
Song of the Sky 1973.
Brian Walkin' Talkin' Blues (voice, optional double bass) 1973.
Lookout (3-part children's chorus) 1974.
Star Music (chorus, tape, bells) 1974.
The High and the Low of It and the Long and Short of It (tape for dance) 1974.
Hands Full (women's choir, tam-tams, tape) 1975.
For Women (5 songs for soprano) 1976.
Set of Cheeky Tongues (soprano, piano) 1976.
Tunings (soprano, violin, clarinet, flute) 1979.
In-de-pen-dance (chanter, nylon strings) 1979.
Delta Dad (voice, piano) 1979.
Did Sid and Busy Lizzie (children's voices) 1979.
Hush (soprano, reco-reco, sand block) 1981. Recorded Finnadar/Atlantic 902661.
Tunings (soprano, violin, piano, cello) 1981.
Exploitation (soprano, tape) 1981.
The Gorilla and the Girl (tape for dance) 1981.
Brian Swan's Versions of American Indian Ritual Songs (baritone, piano) 1981.
Blues Fragments (soprano, piano) 1981; first performed Chattanooga, Tennessee, February 1982. Recorded Folkways 37476.
Southern Voices for Orchestra (soprano, orchestra) 1981; first performed Chattanooga, Tennessee, 1982.
Circling Around (baritone, flute, piano) 1982.
Ex-, Rock-, In-, Re- (chant, tape) 1982.
Rest Song (mixed chorus) 1982.
Lullago (baritone, scat singer) 1982.
Celebration of No (women's voices on tape; or tape, violin, cello, prepared piano, film, slides, chanters) 1983. Recorded Folkways 1983.
Searching Song (soprano, piano) 1989; first performed New York City, 1 April 1990.

Opera:

Love in Space 1986; first performed Cologne, June 1986.
The Glass Woman 1989; in progress.

Other:

Arabella Rag and Twenty-One Other Electronic Music Shorts 1971.
Hands and Lights (piano, photocells, flashlights) 1971.
Syn Rock (electronic) 1971.
Bleep M (electronic) 1971.
Creepy Street (electronic) 1971.
13th Street Beat (electronic) 1971.
Giraffe Round Around (electronic) 1971.
Merry Grate Round (electronic) 1971.
Grim Carnival (electronic) 1971.
Carnibell (electronic) 1971.
Somersault Beat (electronic) 1971.
Round Around (plastic sculptures, lights, tape) 1974.
Spectrum (graph piece) 1974.
The Invasion of the Love Drones (film music) 1975.
Sensevents (sculptures, dancers, lights, 6 musicians, tape) 1977; first performed New York City, August 1977.
Awakening Poem (tape) 1979.
Reading Richie's Paintings (synthesizer, flute, slides) 1979.
Southern Voices (tape) 1980.
Only (piano, 2 tapes, slides, film) 1981.
Water Music (soprano, tape, water pump, slides) 1981.
Flowing Quilt, Creeks and Bathtubs, Waterfalls (soprano, violin, tape, slides, film, water pool and pump) 1982.
Peace Camps (tape) 1983.
Something (to Do) Doing (14 actors, scat singer, effects music) 1984–90; first performed New York City, April 1990.
Echo: Watcha Say/Wie Bitte? (Hoerspiel, recorded sound) 1987.
Sound Shadows (2 synthesizers, drum machine, oboe, didjeridu, dancer, percussionist, video, tape) 1989; first performed New York City, 27 April 1990.
The Hub (soundscape of city of Atlanta with text, poetry, music) 1990.

PUBLICATIONS

By Hays: *Sound Symbol Structures: An Introduction to New Keyboard Notation*, n.d.; "Something (to Do) Doing" and other poems and articles, in *Ear* (New York), 1978–84; "Celebration of No", in *EMMA* (Germany), November 1983; "The Woman in My Music", in *Neuland* (Germany), 4, 1983–4.

On Hays: Helen Smith, "She Creates Art Form with Sights, Sounds", in *Atlanta Constitution*, 10 January 1976; Mary Campbell, "[S]H: Artist with a Mission", in *Pittsburgh Post-Gazette*, 10 October 1977; Allan Kozinn, "Spoleto", in *News and Courier* (Charleston, South Carolina), 30 May 1981; Allann Kozinn, "Electronic Music", in *New York Times*, 5 June 1983; Andrea Richter, "Frau und Musik", dissertation, Hochsschule für Musik Westfalen Lippe, February 1985; Kyle Gann, "Opera Glasses", in *Village Voice*, 22 August 1989.

Sorrel Hays comments:

My music divides itself into two areas: the more traditional instrumentations, orchestral and chamber; and various-media ensembles which often include electronic keyboards and audio processors, as well as dance and film/video, actors and tape collage. Much of my work in the 1980s was generated by commissions from Westdeutscher Rundfunk Köln, and was postproduced with all the electronic richness which is possible in multi-track studios. In both areas of composition, I have sometimes drawn on my rural childhood for elements of folk and rhythm and melody of dialect for musical impressions of the southern United States—where-I-come-from pieces. Uppermost to solve in the acoustic challenges I choose is the emotional impact of lyrical fragments, set in an acoustical space which can transcend the seeming sequential nature of music. The subtext of human intercourse is for musical lines in space.

* * *

With a virtuosic command of new technologies, Sorrel Hays's music recalls and reinvents sound shapes of the past in distinctive and personal ways. Southern Sacred Harp and hymn singing, jazz, fife and drum bands, the accents and rhythms of everyday speech heard in childhood, are evoked in *Sunday Mornings* and *Sunday Nights* for piano, a series of chamber works called *Tunings*, and in *Southern Voices* scored both for tape and orchestra with soprano. The latter was the subject of an award-winning video documentary by George Stoney. Acclaimed initially for her interpretations of piano works of Henry Cowell, Hays then turned to creating her own innovative music for piano, both solo, and in combination with instrumental ensembles, tape and synthesizer. *Bits* for amplified piano and Yamaha DX7 synthesizer tuned a quartertone higher, drum machine and tape, explores sliding microtonal pitches and reverberation techniques.

Hays has produced a large body of activist art. She believes that knowledge of history can be used for political change in the present. Such works include *Celebration of No*, which uses women's voices in 21 languages; and *Sleepers*, a Finnadar recording of lull music by herself and other composers. Her activism grew out of her personal history as granddaughter of a circuit-riding Methodist minister.

For a 1991 compact disc recording, Hays describes *Past Present* as a "distillation of sound memories" of piano pieces by Chopin, Ravel, Debussy and Messiaen which she has played and loved. Trills, runs and clusters exploit the piano's color and resonance in curtailed gestures which place the work's language clearly in the 20th century. Subliminal hints of jazz rhythms in the processions of clustered secundal harmony give *Past Present* an American presence despite the European past celebrated.

Also on the Soundbridge cd is her *90's: A Calendar Bracelet* for Yamaha MIDI Grand Piano. The pieces are inscribed in a birthday book of scores named for women who have touched and changed her life, such as composers Ethyl Smyth and Ruth Crawford Seeger. The pieces may be listened to in any sequence. To the sounds scored for acoustic piano are fitted like a many-colored overcoat one of four assemblages of electronic pitches, timbres and touches preset as MIDI information to tone generators and processors. The electronic presets which include eerie echoing effects of electronic portamento provide structural cross references with the harmonic and thematic linkages among pieces.

Hays periodically has used improvisatory forms within highly organized notated instrumentations. Her *Sensevents* for moving sculptures, patterned light sequences, dancers, tape and musicians, is scored in cyclical lyrical lines, for three strings and three winds playing asynchronously. The musicians played when dancers activated sculptures or lights with foot switches. The piece was performed at Lincoln Center Festival Out-of-Doors, and in other versions at a large shopping mall in Atlanta, in a small art museum, and at Queens College, New York City.

Hays's facile ability to compose for extremely varied media and venues has allowed her to produce a large body of contrasting works. Some of her chamber works such as *Rocking* for flute, violin and viola, recall late 20th-century romantic lyricism. Others, such as her radio Hoerspiel *Something (to Do) Doing* in collage mixture of scat singer, Gertrude Stein quoting herself and hundreds of sound effects punctuated by footsteps in mud, in snow, on concrete, place her among the post-Cageian composers who freely include any acoustic material in their musical organizations.

Sound Shadows, a major theater work, arose out of Hays's explorations into echo sound in outdoor locations such as caves, canyons and coves. Commissioned by Westdeutscher Rundfunk Cologne to produce a Hoerspiel called *Echo: Whatcha Say / Wie Bitte?*, she recorded or solicited location recordings from 11 countries, in places as varied as a sandstone cove on Lake Powell at the Grand Canyon and the Three Echo Steps at the Temple of Heaven in Beijing. From these sounds, she moved to the symbolic aspects of echo—as repetition, in memory and the visual shadows or echo of an idea. *Sound Shadows* used aural gestures by a dancer-percussionist, video of an Aleut singer in a purification ritual for the dwelling of someone who has died, with echo sound as the signature of the departing spirit. In *Sound Shadows* Hays used oboe, saxophone, tape and sampler keyboard in an hour-long lyrical exploration of reverberation and its connotations.

The lyrical bent is never far in Hays's music. Her occasional use of dense collage textures as in *Southern Voices for Orchestra* always shows a preference for contrapuntal line layering. In her brief forays into gestural abstraction, such as *Segments / Junctures* for clarinet, piano and viola, the aura is of quiet expressionism.

New York Times critic Allan Kozinn describes Hays's music as "complex and dense in texture, but much of it also shows a winningly humorous and human side. Though sometimes harsh, it's rarely severe."

—Loretta Goldberg

HE Lu-ting. Chinese. Born in Hunan, 20 July 1903. Educated at Changsha Arts School, Hunan Province; Shanghai National Music School. Married Jiang Rui-zhi in 1932; 2 daughters. President, Central Philharmonic Orchestra, Ya'nan, 1946–9; president, Shanghai Conservatory of Music, Shanghai, 1949–84, now emeritus; president, Shanghai Branch, Chinese Musicians Association, 1949–84, now emeritus; vice-president, Chinese Federation of Literature and Art, since 1979; honorary member, International Musicians' Council. Recipient: Alexander Tcherepnin Chinese Style Work Competition, 1st prize, 1934, 2nd honorary prize, 1934. Mailing address: Shanghai Conservatory of Music, 20 Fen Yang Lu, Shanghai 200031, People's Republic of China.

Publisher: Shanghai Conservatory of Music.

Symphonies/orchestral:

Wan Hui/Evening Party (arranged from piano work) 1935; broadcast Central Broadcasting Station, 1935. Recorded China Record 69982.
Senjidema 1945; first performed Yan'an, 1945. Recorded China Record—People 50128A.

Chamber/instrumental:

Mu Tong Duan Di/The Shepherd Boy's Recorder (piano) 1934; first performed Shanghai, 1934.
Lullaby (piano) 1934; first performed Shanghai, 1934.
Evening Party (piano) 1935.

Vocal/choral:

Song of the Troop (voice or chorus) 1937; first performed 1938.
Protecting Home Village 1937.
Spring Ploughing 1939.
On the Jia Ling River 1939.

Other:

Film scores: *Young People in War Years*; *Crossroad*; *Mission on Streets*.

PUBLICATIONS

By He: translator, *Harmony—Its Theory and Practice*, 1936, and *Selected Papers on Music*, 1981, both by Ebenezer Prout.

* * *

Now an influential theorist, composer and educator, He Lu-ting was born to a peasant family in Hunan Province. As a child he was fond of music, particularly folk music, and learned to play the harmonica as well as Chinese bamboo flute at an early age. After studying piano, violin, Chinese traditional instruments and music theory, he taught music and fine art and edited children's books. In 1931 He entered the Shanghai National Music School to study Western music composition formally.

Three years later, he won a prestigious composition competition for Chinese-style piano works with his solo piano piece *Mu Tong Duan Di/The Shepherd Boy's Recorder*, which was published in China, Japan, Germany, Austria, France and the United States by Alexander Tcherepnin, the White Russian emigré composer who was instrumental in introducing Western contemporary music to China in the 1930s. He Lu-ting uses diatonicism in constructing pentatonic tunes in the style of Chinese folk music. *The Shepherd Boy's Recorder* captured the spirit, simplicity and colour of Chinese folk music and has become an important piece in the Chinese piano repertoire.

Since 1934, He has composed many influential songs and music for the film industry in Shanghai. After serving as a music administrator and teacher during World War II, he went to Yan'an, the area governed by the Communist Party from 1935 to 1949, and became the president of the Central Philharmonic Orchestra in 1946. He has written two major works for orchestra: *Wan Hui/Evening Party* was originally entitled "Celebrating the New Year", and *Senjidema*, the name of a pretty Mongolian girl, draws its theme from a folk song.

As president of the Shanghai Conservatory of Music and president of the Shanghai branch of the Chinese Musicians' Association from 1949 to 1984, He has been an influential administrator and educator. The policies developed during his tenure of office have enabled a new generation of musicians to flourish. He is in addition a significant theorist. Recognizing the importance of Ebenezer Prout's *Harmony—Its Theory and Practice*, he translated it into Chinese. A selection of his papers on music were published in 1981.

—Chen Yi

HEDSTRØM, Åse. Norwegian. Born in Moss, 17 April 1950. Educated at Norwegian State Academy of Music, Oslo (composition under Finn Mortensen), degree in instrumental pedagogics, 1975, diploma in composition, 1980; Institute of Sonology, Utrecht (composition and electronic music under Werner Kaegi and Gottfried Michael Koenig), 1975–9. President, Ny Musik [Norwegian Section of ISCM], Norway, 1975–9; part-time music coordinator, Hoevikodden Art Centre, Oslo, 1983–7; full-time composer, since 1987. Recipient: Norwegian Composers' Association "Work of the Year" (for *Right After*), 1987; UNESCO Rostrum of Composers recommended work (for *Nenia*), Paris, 1988. Mailing address: c/o Norsk Musikforlag, P.O. Box 1499, Vika, N-0116 Oslo 1, Norway.

Publisher: Norsk Musikforlag.

Symphonies/orchestral:

Faser/Phases 1980.
Anima 1983–4.
Nenia 1985–6.
Saisir/Grasp (chamber orchestra) 1987–8.
Sug (percussion quartet, symphonic wind orchestra) 1990.

Chamber/instrumental:

Close By (flute, clarinet/bass clarinet, violin, cello) 1980.
Chain (piano) 1983. Recorded NCD 4923.
Right After (flute, clarinet, violin, cello, piano) 1984.
Grata (flute, violin, viola, cello, harp, piano) 1986.
Sorti (string quartet) 1987.
Signs and Pictures (piano) 1988; first performed London, 16 June 1990.
. . . *Di tanto in tanto* . . . (marimba) 1990.

Vocal/choral:

Distances (percussion, tape) 1981.
Krets (tenor, flute, percussion, tape) 1982–3.
Through (mezzo-soprano, percussion, tape) 1983.
Krets (mezzo-soprano, trombone, percussion, tape) 1983–5.

PUBLICATIONS

On Hedstrøm: Geir Johnson, "History and Intuition", (interview) in *Ballade*, 1, 1988; Erling E. Gulbrandsen, "I'd

Rather Hear with My Own Ears", (interview) in *Prisma-Nytt*, September–November 1988.

* * *

Åse Hedstrøm came to international notice with the success of her orchestral piece *Nenia* at the UNESCO Composers' Rostrum in 1988. Named after the "sad song" that accompanies the death of Orpheus (Harrison Birtwistle has composed a similarly-titled work), it gives an excellent account of Hedstrøm's brilliantly classical and poised synthesis of the personal and the mythical. All of her music seems to be wrested from a kind of primitive chaos, its often mournful calm masking considerable energy and a spirit of resistance. The recent solo piano *Signs and Pictures* is, like much of her work, only implicitly and incidentally programmatic, drawing on a huge range of musical and metaphorical associations for its effects. Yvar Mikhashoff, who commissioned and premiered the piece in London in 1990, has described its effect as that of a mysterious, indecipherable language, a hieroglyphic whose semiology is vastly different from our everyday, linear language but to which it bears a fragmentary, almost dream-like kinship; Hedstrøm's music often communicates in this way, either interstitially or by recourse to a vast, buried collective unconscious (the parallels with Birtwistle are again evident).

Hedstrøm studied composition with the late Finn Mortensen, one of the finest Norwegian composers of his generation, and there are signs of his influence on her orchestral writing, though not in her much more personal chamber work. The "early" *Phases* is identifiably Norwegian and to that degree untypical of the cool "international" style that has become Hedstrøm's distinctive style; the brilliant *Grasp* for small orchestra provides a perfect contrast. After graduating in composition she then moved on to the influential Institute of Sonology at Utrecht in the Netherlands, where she studied composition and electronic music under Gottfried Michael Koenig, an experience that helped foster her superbly intuitive feel for instrumental texture and sonority. Her vocal works are particularly impressive in this regard; her use of electro-acoustic elements in the imaginatively scored *Through* is virtuosic.

Widely respected as an organizer of new music events—she was president of the Norwegian branch of ISCM and sat on the programme committee for the 1990 World Music Days in Oslo—she has an increasing international reputation as a composer in her own right, creating work which, while making little overt reference to contemporary events and issues, seems to strike deep at the fundamental questions of our time, and which represents an impressively personal response to the shifting environment of contemporary music.

—Henk Maarten

HEININEN, Paavo. Finnish. Born in Helsinki, 13 January 1938. Educated: private music study under Usko Merilainen; Sibelius Academy, Helsinki (theory and composition under Aare Merikanto, Einojuhani Rautavaara, Einar Englund and Joonas Kokkonen), 1956–60, diploma; Helsinki University; further composition study under Bernd Alois Zimmerman, Cologne, 1961; Juilliard School of Music, New York City (composition under Vincent Persichetti and Eduard Steuermann), 1962; further composition with Witold Lutosławski, Poland, 1965–6. Teacher of theory and composition, Turku Institute of Music, Finland, 1962–5, and Sibelius Academy, Helsinki, since 1966. Mailing address: Pöytäalhoutie 81, SF-04400 Järvenpää, Finland.

Publishers: Fazer; Edition Pan.

Symphonies/orchestral:

Symphony No 1 Op 3 1958, revised 1960; 1st and 3rd movements first performed Oslo, 1959; revised version first performed Helsinki, 24 March 1964.
Tripartita Op 5 1959; first performed Helsinki, 11 November 1960.
Adagietto (Second Movement) 1959–60; first performed Turku, 24 March 1960.
Concerto for String Orchestra Op 6 1959, revised 1963; first performed Helsinki, 19 April 1960; revised version first performed Turku, 30 May 1963.
Symphony No 2: Petite Symphonie joyeuse d'après vieux cahiers Op 9 1962; first performed Helsinki, 7 December 1962. Recorded Finlandia FACD 373.
Soggetto Op 10 1963; first performed Helsinki, 12 January 1965.
Adagio . . . Concerto per orchestra in forma di variazioni Op 12 1963, revised 1966; first performed Helsinki, 24 January 1964; revised version first performed London, 19 February 1967. Recorded Philips 802 854 LY.
Concerto for Piano and Orchestra Op 13 1964; first performed Turku, 23 January 1965.
Concerto for Piano and Orchestra No 2 Op 15 1966; first performed Turku, 1 December 1966. Recorded Finlandia FACD 373.
Arioso Op 16 (strings) 1967; first performed Helsinki, 21 May 1967. Recorded Da Camera Magna SM 91022; Finlandia FACD 373.
Symphony No 3 Op 20 1969, revised 1977; revised version first performed Helsinki, 24 January 1978. Recorded Fuga 3047.
Symphony No 4 Op 27 1971; first performed Oslo, 4 September 1972.
Tritopos Op 38 1977; first performed Helsinki, 7 March 1978.
Dia Op 36 1979; first performed Helsinki, 12 September 1979.
Attitude Op 44 1980; first performed Helsinki, 10 December 1980.
Concerto for Piano and Orchestra No 3 Op 46 1981; first performed Helsinki, 13 March 1982.
. . . Floral View with Maidens Singing . . . Op 47 1982; first performed Kokkola, 8 April 1983. Recorded Fuga 3045; Ondine ODE 722-2.
Saxophone Concerto Op 50 1983; first performed Helsinki, 29 August 1983.
KauToKei Op 52 (double string orchestra) 1985; first performed Helsinki, 12 February 1986.
Cello Concerto Op 53 1985; first performed Helsinki, 26 February 1986.

Chamber/instrumental:

Toccata Op 1 (piano) 1956; first performed Jyväskylä, 1957.
Sonatine Op 2 (piano) 1957; first performed Helsinki, 1958. Recorded Toshiba TA 600001/4.
Quintet Op 7 (flute, saxophone, piano, vibraphone, per-

cussion) 1961; first performed Helsinki, 16 October 1963.

Musique d'été Op 11 (flute, clarinet, violin, cello, harpsichord, vibraphone, percussion) 1963, revised 1969; first performed Tampere, 11 October 1967. Recorded Finlandia FACD 365.

Discantus I Op 14 (alto flute) 1965; first performed Darmstadt, 24 August 1966. Recorded Cipango/Asia Rec CC 5002; Sibelius-Akatemia SALP 1; Ondine ODE 734-2.

Oculus aquilae—trittico per organo Op 18 (organ) 1968; first performed Glasgow, 23 October 1978.

Discantus II Op 21 (clarinet) 1969; first performed Helsinki, 28 January 1970.

Poésies des pensées Op 23 (cello) 1970.

Cantilena I Op 24a/b/c (violin/viola/cello) 1970; first performed Hyvinkää, 7 April 1972.

Sonata Op 25 (violin, piano) 1970; first performed Helsinki, 18 February 1973. Recorded Ondine ODE 726-2.

Cantilena II Op 26 (cello) 1970; first performed London, 4 April 1979.

Libretto della primavera Op 28 (piano; consists of Op 24a *Sonatina*, Op 24b *Due Danze*, Op 28c *Piccola poesia*) 1971; first performed Helsinki, 5 November 1972. Recorded (Op 28a only) Konserttikeskus KKLP 174.

. . . irdisch gewesen zu sein . . . Op 29a (organ) 1972; first performed Lahti, 9 August 1976.

. . . des Saglichen Zeit . . . Op 29b (organ) 1972; first performed Helsinki, 9 December 1973.

Deux Chansons Op 31 (cello, piano; or cello, orchestra) 1974, revised for orchestra 1976; first performed Helsinki, 4 September 1975; orchestral version first performed Tampere, 25 February 1977. Recorded ("Serenade" only—orchestral version) Finlandia FACD 362.

Poesia squillante ed incandescente—Sonata per pianoforte Op 32a 1974; first performed Helsinki, 14 February 1979. Recorded Tactus TA 8010.

Préludes—études—poèmes Op 32b (piano) 1974; first performed Pieksamaki, 3 October 1976.

String Quartet Op 32c 1974; first performed Helsinki, 21 January 1976. Recorded Ondine ODE 733-2.

Poésies-périphrases Op 32d (piano) 1975; first performed Viitasaari, 8 June 1986.

Discantus III Op 33 (alto saxophone) 1976; first performed Helsinki, 11 May 1977.

Cantilena III Op 34 (violin) 1976; first performed 1982.

Gymel Op 39 (bassoon, tape) 1978; first performed Hameenlinna, 3 July 1979.

Touching Op 40 (guitar) 1978; first performed Helsingborg, 22 February 1979. Recorded BIS LP 207.

Jeu I Op 42 (flute, piano) 1980; first performed Helsinki, 23 May 1980. Recorded Ondine ODE 734-2.

Jeu II Op 43 (violin, piano) 1980; first performed Helsinki, 27 January 1981.

Beateth Op 48 (percussion) 1982; first performed Tampere, 17 April 1984.

Dicta (Nonette avec milieu) Op 49 (9 onstage players, 14 distributed among audience) 1983; first performed Helsinki, 25 March 1983.

Triple Aperçu d'une amie qui fut (piano; for young players) 1984.

Cinq Moments du jour Op 51 (piano) 1984.

Vocal/choral:

Canto di Natale Op 8 (soprano, piano; Jacopone da Todi) 1961; broadcast Finnish Radio, December 1961.

Cantico della creature Op 17 (baritone, piano or organ or orchestra; Francis of Assisi) 1968; first performed Helsinki, 4 December 1972.

Love's Philosophy Op 19 (tenor, piano; Yeats, Shelley, Shakespeare) 1968, 1973; first performed London, 4 April 1979.

The Autumns Op 22 (unaccompanied mixed chorus; Basho, other *haiku*, translated Blyth) 1970; first performed Helsinki, 29 January 1971. Recorded Fennica Nova FENO 1.

Schatten der Erde Op 30 (mezzo-soprano, piano; Gryphius, Rilke, Hölderlin) 1973; first performed Helsinki, 16 November 1975.

. . . cor meum . . . Op 35 1976–9; broadcast BBC, 14 November 1979; first concert performance Helsinki, 25 April 1980.

Reality Op 41 (soprano, flute, oboe, clarinet, bassoon, horn, percussion, piano, violin, viola, cello; Montale, Jouve, Nin) 1978; first performed Edinburgh, 18 October 1978.

Virsi '81/Hymn '81 (mixed chorus, organ) 1981; first performed Laulu, 5 April 1981.

Four Lullabies Op 56a (male voices; Schoultz, Linjama, PH, wordless) 1986.

Opera:

Silkkirumpu/The Damask Drum Op 45 (concerto for singers, players, words, images, movements; PH, after Zeami Motokiyo, translated Eeva-Liisa Manner, James Kirkup) 1981–3; first performed Helsinki, 5 April 1984. Recorded Finlandia FACD 106.

Veitsi/The Knife Op 55 (Meri) 1985–8; first performed Savonlinna, 3 July 1989.

Other:

Maiandros Op 37 (electro-acoustic) 1977; broadcast Finnish Radio, 23 March 1977. Recorded Fennica Nova FENO 5.

Aarre Merikanto: *Symphonic Study* (reconstruction of fragmentary 1928 score) 1981; first performed Helsinki, 3 March 1982. Recorded Finlandia FACD 349.

PUBLICATIONS

On Heininen, "PH", Finnish Music Information Centre, 1989.

* * *

Beginning in the 1980s, Paavo Heininen has been seen to occupy an increasingly important position in the musical life of Finland, as composer, teacher and musicologist. As a teacher, Heininen's role has been evident from the subsequent international success of several former pupils, Jouni Kaipainen, Magnus Lindberg and Kaija Saariaho not least among them. As a musicologist, his work on the music of his own teacher, Aare Merikanto, has been of incalculable importance in that composer's recent re-evaluation, particularly of the mutilated *Symphonic Study* (1928) which Heininen painstakingly reconstructed. As a composer, though, Heininen was somewhat undervalued until his first opera, *The Damask Drum*, burst onto the Savonlinna stage in 1984. The emotional range it displayed, from ferocity to exquisite beauty to raging madness, is extraordinary in a first opera, and the innately theatrical adaptation of the Japanese Nō play within a totally convincing musical framework proved utterly compelling. Its immediate success catapulted Heininen into the forefront of public attention and his serial, expressionistic style with its colourful and dynamic instrumentation established him as a substantial alternative to Kokkonen and Sallinen.

Performances and recordings of his music increased in the wake of the opera's production: even the ultra-conservative Helsinki Philharmonic Orchestra recorded (in 1988) a CD of three accessible early works, *Arioso* (1967), *Piano Concerto No 2* (1966) and *Symphony No 2* (1962). *Arioso* is scored for string orchestra and was one of the few pieces by Heininen that had managed to maintain a fingerhold in the repertoire during the 1970s, even being recorded. The orchestral *Concerto in the Form of Variations: Adagio* (1963–6) is generally accepted as the masterpiece of his early career, and reflects Heininen's high regard for the music of Karl Amadeus Hartmann (the title recalls that of Hartmann's Second Symphony).

While engaged in the composition of *The Damask Drum*, Heininen took time off to compose another short string orchestral piece, . . . *Floral View with Maidens Singing* . . . , a beautiful and highly inventive miniature tone poem based on a folktune popular in Finland in a saccharine arrangement by Karl Ekman.

Heininen has tackled most of the major forms, often in characteristically ingenious ways: witness the complex integral relationship between his Piano Sonata (Op 32a) and String Quartet (Op 32c). Both works date from 1974 and were grouped in a collection of four works published as Opus 32. The Sonata is descriptively titled *Poesia squillante ed incandescente* and bears eloquent testimony to both his personal knowledge of the keyboard (as do the Preludes, Studies and Poems of the same collection) and intensity of expression. The String Quartet, like the Violin Sonata of four years earlier, is not as forward-looking as so much of his mature music. The Quartet is less relaxed than the Violin Sonata, but both of these are lyrical, even nostalgic in tone, as if looking back over their creator's shoulder. The Quartet is certainly worthy of comparison with those of Berg and Schoenberg. Critics of Heininen have accused him at times of being motivated more by the idea of being a composer than by a purely musical impulse; however, the Violin Sonata, String Quartet and *The Damask Drum* all provide incontestable evidence of the imaginative power, beauty and sheer musicianship of his music. His second opera, *The Knife*, won the competition for a new Finnish opera for Savonlinna in 1990 (beating entries by Rautavaara—*Vincent*—and Kalevi Aho). Although being well-received musically the premiere production was less than satisfactory.

His career as a symphonist has been rather chequered. The serial First Symphony was only premiered in truncated form and has still not been played in full. The Second, *Petite Symphonie joyeuse d'après vieux cahiers*, dates from his period of study with Persichetti in the United States, and stands in a similar position within Heininen's output as the *Simple Symphony* does within Britten's. It is an engaging light piece despite the advanced idiom and fully lives up to its epithet. The expansive Third Symphony is in a most original design that can be viewed with equal validity as being in one, two, three or four movements, and inhabits a more serious world than either the Second or Fourth Symphonies. Heininen's orchestral style is well-exemplified by the symphonies with their cogency of thought and brilliant orchestration, which can be powerful and evocative by turns. He is also, like Einar Englund, a considerable pianist and his piano writing exhibits graphically his good working knowledge of the keyboard (he recorded his Second Concerto, issued in a coupling with Englund playing his own First). The concerto form, as with opera, has increasingly been attracting his attention with a Third Piano Concerto appearing in 1981, followed by others for saxophone and cello. A string of chamber works for various enterprising combinations (e.g., *Gymel*, the *Jeu* and *Discantus* series, *Touching* for guitar) serve to illustrate further his continuing concern with and intuitive grasp of instrumental resource. In the field of electronic music, his *Maiandros* created a considerable impression even if attention has shifted more to the works of his pupils (Saariaho, for instance). Hopefully, Heininen will return to the larger abstract instrumental forms to synthesize those elements of his style most recently displayed in the operas and concertos with his previous developments. A Fifth Symphony or Second String Quartet would both be formidable achievements indeed.

—Guy Rickards

HENKEMANS, Hans. Dutch. Born in The Hague, 23 December 1913. Educated: studied piano and composition with Bernard van den Sigtenhorst Meyer, 1926–31; studied composition with Willem Pijper, 1933–8; studied medicine, University of Utrecht, from 1931; University of Amsterdam, doctorate, 1981. Concert pianist, debut 1945, retired 1969; practising physician and psychiatrist; teacher of composition and instrumentation, Gröningen Conservatory, and Amsterdam Muzieklyceum. Mailing address: c/o Donemus, Paulus Poterstraat 14, 1071 CZ Amsterdam, The Netherlands.

Publisher: Donemus.

Symphonies/orchestral:

Concerto for Piano and String Orchestra 1932.
Passacaglia en gigue (piano, orchestra) 1941–2.
Primavera (brass, strings) 1944, revised 1959.
Concerto for Flute and Orchestra 1946.
Concerto for Violin and Orchestra 1948–50.
Concerto for Viola and Orchestra 1954.
Concerto for Harp and Orchestra 1955.
Partita 1960.
Barcarola fantastica 1962.
Dona Montana 1964.
Elegies (4 flutes, orchestra) 1967.
Concerto for Horn and Orchestra 1981.
Villanelle (horn, orchestra; after Paul Dukas) 1984.
Riflessioni (string orchestra) 1985–6.
Concerto for Cello and Orchestra 1988.

Chamber/instrumental:

Sonata (cello, piano) 1936.
Etude (piano) 1937.
Sonata (2 pianos) 1943.
Sonata (piano) 1958.
Quintet (flute, oboe, clarinet, fagot, horn) 1962.
Quattro pezzi (harp, flute) 1963.
Voor de wind (carillon) 1963.
Aere festivo (3 trumpets, 2 trombones) 1965.

Vocal/choral:

Driehonderd waren wij (mixed chorus, orchestra) 1933.
Ballade d'Orléans (alto, small orchestra) 1936.
De Tooverfluit (tenor, piano) 1946.
Drie liederen (medium voice, piano) 1964.
Bericht aan de levenden (chorus, orchestra, reciter) 1965.

Villonerie (baritone, orchestra) 1965.
Tre aspetti d'amore (mixed chorus, orchestra) 1968.
Canzoni amorose del Duecento (soprano, baritone, piano, orchestra) 1972–3.

Opera:

Winter Cruise (8 soloists, orchestra) 1977.

Other:

Claude Debussy: *Twenty four Preludes* (orchestration).

PUBLICATIONS

By Henkemans: articles in *Netherlands Medical Review* and *Mens in Melodie*; *Daar zit je dan*, 1961; *Sublimation Problems with Artists and Their Therapy*, Amsterdam, 1981.

* * *

To an outside observer, a striking feature of the music scene in The Netherlands is its discontinuity. The first two decades of the century are well-represented, and performances of contemporary music (scores from 10 years ago to the present) are extremely well-supported, but between them there is an almost total void. While this has stimulated a vigorous and varied culture, it has considerably eroded anything in the nature of a national voice. In this context, Hans Henkemans stands as a rather special figure, not quite unique, but the most substantial composer to straddle the generations still living, and the most consistent creative voice to carry forward the authentic Dutch musical language with genuine originality. It is this balance of originality and tradition that gives his work its unique blend of freshness and familiarity.

He first attracted attention, still in his teens, with a Concerto for piano and strings (1932), before he had begun his studies with Pijper but already showing some of his influences. His career thus began at a time when Pijper was not only extremely active, but rather controversial, and if it was Pijper who met the best Europeans as their equal and created a viable Dutch equivalent, it was Henkemans who developed it in its least diluted form.

Henkemans freely acknowledges a number of other influences on his developing language and technique—Ravel, Franck, Debussy, even Grieg, though perhaps some more at secondhand via one of his other careers: until the late 1960s he was an active and very successful concert pianist. Yet a third career has run in tandem, that of doctor and psychiatrist. This side of his life has had a major effect on his creative side, and not merely the analytical: I can detect distinct stylistic parallels with the only other psychiatrist I can think of who approaches the front rank of composers—Robert Still—of translating intellect into sensitivity and making accessible certain modern music techniques. The symbiosis of performing and composing is both subtle and pervasive in Henkemans's case. At an immediate level it has resulted in several important pieces for his instrument: the concerto mentioned, another (1936), the sonatas for piano (1968) and for two pianos (1944) and the *Passacaglia and Gigue* (1942). As a familiar and acquired means of expression he also finds it an invaluable adjunct to composing: not writing "at the keyboard" but using it to mould and shape an idea into a piece. Strangely it has also encouraged rather than suppressed variety of expression, for just as different piano works require different techniques—arm pieces, wrist pieces, finger pieces or shoulder pieces—so performing has stimulated in him the awareness that a technique or language suitable to one piece is wrong for another. It has also taught him the value of effective writing for instruments, and where difficulties exist they are never gratuitous and are always tempered by practicality. For a composer who makes extensive use in orchestral works of solo instruments, and constructing translucent textures out of melodic lines, this is important.

Henkemans has always been loyal to his musical vision, which is a blend of emotion (albeit restrained emotion) and impressionism, and it is the consistency of his working method that has made the emergence of his unmistakable style continuous rather than dramatic, and allowed him entirely to absorb various influences into a highly personal language. Pijper's qualities and standards of self-criticism rather than his mannerisms had the greatest effect, and Henkemans's studies with the great man taught him to emphasise elements personal to himself. In a slightly crude form, his own qualities were already in place, needing only refinement, from the early 1930s. There is a sort of post-Pijper "Dutchness" which underpins his whole output, up to the opera *Winter Cruise* and the Cello Concerto of 1988. He has always built up structures from the expansion of germ-cells, and employs them in combination with free sonata forms. His melodic and harmonic forms stem from a fairly systematic use of the octotonic scale to produce major/minor key centres. The resulting introspective sound-world is moderated in turn by very sensitive scoring and delicacy of texture even at moments of great power.

The mood that pervades Henkemans's music up to the late 1950s is predominantly lyrical, often intensely nostalgic but never simply self-indulgent. Indeed it is the self-discipline that makes the emotion so potent, as in the concertos for viola and, even more marked, violin. By the Piano Sonata of 1958 he is moving towards altogether grimmer matters, and with the *Partita* for orchestra (1960) the feeling of menace is rather more than a suggestion. He seems to shrink back from the brink of the macabre by revising *Primavera*—one of his most open and genial works—and taking refuge in complex polyphony in the *Quintet* (1962). In these and subsequent scores he adds a dimension of instrumental virtuosity (if not exactly flamboyance), enhancing what Kees van Baaren called "die krankhaft moralische Schönheit" (the morbid beauty) with echoes of Mahlerian grotesquery. In time, these too become absorbed and transformed into a more resigned, subtle expression of works like *Elegies* (1967) and *Riflessioni* (1986), and the overtly backward-looking *Canzoni amorose del Duecento* (1973).

Aided by the enlightened Dutch arts-funding policy, and his own highly successful careers, Henkemans has been liberated from the commission treadmill. Since the prolificacy of his early period his output has been comparatively small (often interspersed with periods away from composition), and remarkably consistent. He permits himself to write only such pieces as he pleases, when he wants to tackle them, and without feelings of pressure to compromise his integrity or style except from within. It is true that the second of the *Tre aspetti d'amore* uses a serial them, but the heart of the work is still an impressionist, emotional one, He will take a technique when it suits his own purpose, but he is never hijacked by it. Indeed, it is probably his imperviousness to influences outside the world of his own musical vision that guarantees not only his individuality of personality but the probable enduring survival of his scores.

—Giles Easterbrook

HENZE, Hans Werner. German. Born in Gütersloh, Westphalia, 1 July 1926. Educated at Staatsmusikschule, Braunschweig, 1942; Kirchenmusikalischen Institut, Heidelberg, under Wolfgang Fortner, 1946. Military service making propaganda films, 1944; British prisoner of war, 1945. Repetiteur, Stadttheater, Bielefeld, 1945; musical director, Heinz Hilpert's Deutsches Theater, Constance, 1948; artistic director, Ballet of Hessian State Theatre, 1950. Emigrated to Forio d'Ischia, Italy, 1953. Professor of composition, 1961, and teacher of masterclass in composition, 1962–7, Mozarteum, Salzburg; teaching and research in Havana, Cuba, 1969–70; professor of composition, Staalichen Hochschule für Musik, Cologne, 1980; artistic director, Accademica Filarmonia Romana, 1982. Member of Akademie der Künste, Berlin, 1960–8, and Bayerische Akademie der Schönen Künste, Munich. Recipient: Robert Schumann Prize, 1952; Prix d'Italia, 1954; Sibelius Gold Medal, 1956; North Rhine-Westphalia Art Prize, 1956; Music Critics' Prize, Buenos Aires, 1958; Kunstpreis, Berlin, Niedersachsischer Kunstpreis, 1962; University of Edinburgh, D.Mus., 1971; Ludwig-Spohr Preis, 1976. Mailing address: 00047 Marino, Rome, Italy.

Publisher: Schott.

Symphonies / orchestral:

Kammerkonzert (piano, flute, strings) 1946; first performed Darmstadt, 27 September 1946.
Symphony No 1 1947, revised for chamber orchestra, 1963; first performed Darmstadt, 1947; revised version first performed Berlin, 9 April 1964. Recorded Deutsche Grammophon; Harmonia Mundi.
Concertino (piano, wind orchestra, percussion) 1947; first performed Baden-Baden, 5 October 1947.
Violin Concerto No 1 1947; first performed Baden-Baden, 12 December 1948.
Symphony No 2 1949; first performed Stuttgart, 1 December 1949. Recorded Deutsche Grammophon.
Symphony No 3 1949–50; first performed Donaueschingen, 7 October 1951. Recorded Deutsche Grammophon.
Piano Concerto No 1 1950; first performed Düsseldorf, 14 September 1952.
Sinfonische Variationen (chamber orchestra) 1950; first performed Wiesbaden, 1950.
Boulevard Solitude (symphonic suite) 1953; first performed Aachen, 7 June 1952.
Ode an den Westwind (cello, orchestra) 1953; first performed Beilefeld, 30 April 1954.
Quattro poemi 1955; first performed Frankfurt, 31 May 1955.
Drei sinfonische Etuden für Orchester 1955–64; first performed Hamburg, 14 February 1956.
Symphony No 4 1955; first performed Berlin, 9 October 1963. Recorded Deutsche Grammophon.
Jeux des Tritons (piano, orchestra; from the ballet *Undine*) 1956–7, revised 1967; first performed Zurich, 28 March 1960.
Sonata per Archi (chamber orchestra) 1957–8; first performed Zurich, 21 March 1958.
Drei Dithyramben (chamber orchestra) 1958; first performed Cologne, 27 November 1958.
Antifone 1960; first performed Berlin, 20 January 1962.
Symphony No 5 1962; first performed New York, 16 May 1963. Recorded Deutsche Grammophon.
Los Caprichos 1963; first performed Duisburg, 6 April 1967.
Zwischenspiele für Orchester / Symphonic Interludes from "Der junge Lord" 1964; first performed Berlin, 12 October 1965.
Manadenjagd / The Hunt of the Menads (from the opera *Die Bissariden*) 1965.
Fantasia für Streicher (strings; for the Schlondorff film *Der junge Torless*) 1966; first performed Berlin, 1 April 1967. Recorded Deutsche Grammophon.
Concerto per contrabbasso (double bass, orchestra) 1966; first performed Chicago, 2 November 1967. Recorded Deutsche Grammophon.
Doppio Concerto (oboe, harp, strings) 1966; first performed Zurich, 2 December 1966. Recorded Deutsche Grammophon.
Telemanniana 1967; first performed Berlin, 4 April 1967. Recorded Schwann.
Piano Concerto No 2 1967; first performed Bielefeld, 29 September 1968. Recorded Deutsche Grammophon.
Symphony No 6 (2 chamber orchestras) 1969; first performed Havana, Cuba, 26 November 1969. Recorded Deutsche Grammophon.
Compases para preguntas ensimismadas (viola, 22 instrumentalists) 1969–70; first performed Basle, 11 February 1971. Recorded Decca.
Violin Concerto No 2 1971; first performed Basle, 2 November 1972. Recorded Decca.
Heliogabalus Imperator 1971–2; first performed Chicago, 16 November 1972.
Tristan (piano, orchestra, tape) 1973; first performed London, 20 October 1974. Recorded Deutsche Grammophon.
Concert Suite "Katharina Blum" (chamber orchestra) 1975; first performed Brighton, Sussex, 6 May 1976.
Ragtimes and Habaneras (brass) 1975; first performed London, 13 September 1975. Recorded Decca.
Aria de la folia espãnola (chamber orchestra) 1977; first performed St Paul, Minnesota, 17 September 1977.
Il vitalino raddopiato (violin, chamber orchestra) 1977; first performed Salzburg, 2 August 1978.
Konzertstück (violin, small orchestra) 1977–85; first performed Frankfurt, 29 August 1986.
Dramatische Szenen aus "Orpheus" I & II 1979; first performed Zurich, 6 January 1981; Frankfurt, 12–13 September 1982.
Arien des Orpheus (guitar, harp, harpsichord, strings; version for strings only) 1979; first performed Chicago, 16 November 1980; string version first performed Chicago, 25 November 1981.
Barcarola 1979; first performed Zurich, 22 April 1980. Recorded NDR-Schallplatte.
Cinque piccoli concerti 1980–2; first performed Cabrillo, 26 August 1983.
Le Miracle de la rose (clarinet, 13 players) 1981; first performed London, 26 May 1982.
I Sentimenti di Carl Philipp Emanuel Bach (flute, harp, strings) 1982; first performed Rome, 14 April 1982.
Symphony No 7 1983–4; first performed Berlin, 1 December 1984.
Deutschlandsberger Mohrentanz I & II (4 recorders, guitars, percussion, string quartet, string orchestra) 1984–5; first performed Deutschlandsberg, Austria, 14 October 1984, 19 October 1985.
Sieben Liebeslieder (cello, orchestra) 1984–85; first performed Cologne, 12 December 1986.
Fandango 1985; first performed Paris, 5 February 1986.
An eine Aolsharfe (guitar, 15 instruments) 1985–6; first performed Lucerne, 27 August 1986.
Zwölf Kleine Elegien (Renaissance instruments) 1986.

Chamber/instrumental:

Sonata (violin, piano) 1946.
Sonatinae (flute, piano) 1947. Recorded CBS.
String Quartet No 1 1947; first performed Heidelberg, 1947. Recorded Wergo.
Kammer-Sonate (piano, violin, cello) 1948, revised 1963; first performed Cologne, 16 March 1950. Recorded Harmonia Mundi.
Variationen für Klavier (piano) 1949; first performed Frankfurt, 17 June 1949. Recorded Advance.
Serenade (cello; also version for double bass) 1949. Recorded Da Camera.
String Quartet No 2 1952; first performed Baden-Baden, 16 December 1952. Recorded Wergo.
Quintet (flute, oboe, clarinet, F horn, bassoon) 1952; first performed Radio Bremen, 15 February 1953. Recorded Candide Voc; Philips.
Concerto per il marigny (piano, clarinet, bass clarinet, F horn, C trumpet, trombone, viola, cello) 1956; first performed Paris, 9 March 1956. Recorded Vega.
Drei Tentos (guitar: from *Kammermusik*) 1958. Recorded RCA; Le Connaisseur; EMI.
Sonata (piano) 1959; first performed Berlin, 26 September 1959.
Six Absences (harpsichord) 1961. Recorded Philips.
Lucy Escott Variations (piano; version for harpsichord) 1963; first performed Berlin, 21 March 1965. Recorded Philips.
Adagoi (clarinet, horn, bassoon, string quintet) 1963; first performed SFB Berlin, December 1963.
Divertimenti (2 pianos) 1964; first performed New York, 30 November 1964.
In memoriam: Die weisse Rose (flute, cor anglais, bass clarinet, bassoon, horn, trumpet, trombone, string quintet) 1965; first performed Bologna, 16 March 1965. Recorded Decca.
Memorias de "El Cimarron" (guitar) 1970; first performed Aldeburgh, Suffolk, 22 June 1970. Recorded Deutsche Grammophon.
Prison Song (percussion, tape; Ho Chi Minh) 1971. Recorded Decca.
Carillon Récitatif Masque (mandolin, guitar, harp) 1974. Recorded 2001.
Royal Winter Music (guitar; first sonata on Shakespeare characters) 1975–6; first performed Berlin, 20 December 1976. Recorded RCA; Dabringhaus & Grimm; Paula.
String Quartet No 3 1975–6; first performed Berlin, 12 September 1976. Recorded Wergo.
Amicizia (A clarinet, trombone, cello, percussion, marimba, vibraphone, piano) 1976; first performed Montepulciano, 6 August 1976.
String Quartet No 4 1976; first performed Schwetzingen, 25 May 1977. Recorded Wergo.
Sonatina (trumpet) 1976. Recorded Vega.
String Quartet No 5 1976; first performed Schwetzingen, 25 May 1977. Recorded Wergo.
Charakterstücke (2 guitars; arranged from *Don Chisciote della Mancia*) 1976.
Sonata (violin) 1976–7; first performed Montepulciano, 10 August 1977. Recorded Le Connaisseur.
S. Biagio 9 Agosto ore 1207 (double bass) 1977.
L'Autunno (flute/piccolo/alto flute, oboe/oboe d'amore, B♭ clarinet/A clarinet/bass clarinet, horn, bassoon/contrabassoon) 1977; first performed London, 28 February 1979.
Five Scenes from the Snow Country (marimba) 1978. Recorded Wergo.
Sonata (viola, piano) 1979; first performed Witten, 20 April 1980.
Royal Winter Music (guitar; second sonata on Shakespeare characters) 1979; first performed Brussels, 25 November 1980. Recorded Musikproduktion; Dabringhaus & Grimm; Paula.
Sonatina (violin, piano) 1979; first performed London, 2 December 1980.
Etude Philharmonique (violin) 1979.
Toccata senza Fuga (organ) 1979.
Drei Märchenbilder (guitar; arranged from *Pollicino*) 1979–80.
Sechs Stücke für junge Pianisten (piano) 1980; first performed Stuttgart, 13 October 1982.
Cherubino (piano) 1981; first performed Berlin, 23 August 1981.
Euridice (harpsichord) 1981.
Canzona (oboe, 3 violas, cello, piano, harp) 1982; first performed Stuttgart, 6 June 1982.
Sonata per otto ottoni (trumpets in G and B, flugelhorn, bass trumpet, 2 trombones, bass trombone) 1983; first performed Berlin, 17 September 1983.
Capriccio (cello) 1983; first performed Linz, 24 September 1983.
Sonate für sechs Spieler (flute/alto flute, clarinet, violin, viola, percussion, marimba, piano) 1984; first performed London, 26 September 1984. Recorded Milan.
Selbst– und Zweigespräche (viola, guitar, chamber organ) 1984–5; first performed Bruhl, 29 September 1985.
Serenade (violin) 1986; first performed Bad Godesburg, 1 June 1986.

Vocal/choral:

Fünf Madgrigale/Five Madrigals (small mixed choir, ensemble) 1947; first performed Frankfurt, 25 April 1950.
Der Vorwurf/The Reproach (baritone, trumpet, trombone, string orchestra; Werfel) 1948; first performed Darmstadt, 29 July 1948.
Chor gefangener Trojer/Chorus of the Captured Trojans (mixed choir, large orchestra; Goethe) 1948, revised 1964; first performed Bielefeld, 6 February 1949.
Wiegenlied der Mutter Gottes/Lullaby of the Blessed Virgin (choir, bass flute, clarinet, F horn, C trumpet, trombone, harp, viola, cello, bass; Vega) 1948; first performed Duisburg, 27 June 1954. Recorded Decca.
Whispers from Heavenly Death (soprano or tenor, C trumpet, celesta, harp, cello, percussion; also arranged for piano accompaniment; Whitman) 1948; first performed Frankfurt, 1950. Recorded Deutsche Grammophon.
Apollo et Hyazinthus (improvisations for harpsichord, alto voice, flute, clarinet, F horn, harpsichord, 2 violins, viola, cello; Trakl) 1949; first performed Frankfurt, 26 June 1949. Recorded Decca.
Ein Landarzt/A Country Doctor (baritone, orchestra; Kafka) 1951–64; first performed Berlin, 13 October 1965.
Fünf neapolitanische Lieder/Five Neapolitan Songs (medium voice, chamber orchestra) 1956; first performed Frankfurt, 26 May 1956. Recorded Deutsche Grammophon.
Nachtstücke und Arien/Nocturnes and Arias (soprano, large orchestra; Bachmann) 1957; first performed Donaueschingen, 20 October 1957. Recorded Harmonia Mundi.
Kammermusik (tenor, guitar, clarinet, F horn, bassoon, guitar or harp, string quintet; Hölderlin) 1958; first performed Hamburg, 26 November 1958. Recorded Decca.
Drie Fragmente nach Hölderlin (voice, guitar) 1958.

Judische Chronik 1960. Recorded Wergo.
Novae de Infinito Laudes (four soloists, mixed choir, ensemble; Bruno) 1962; first performed Venice, 24 April 1963.
Being Beauteous (coloratura soprano, harp, 4 cellos; Rimbaud) 1963; first performed Berlin, 12 April 1964. Recorded Harmonia Mundi.
Cantata della Fiaba Estrema (soprano, small choir, ensemble; Morante) 1963; first performed Zurich, 26 February 1965.
Ariosi (soprano, violin, orchestra; also arranged for piano accompaniment—4 hands; Tasso) 1963; first performed Edinburgh, 23 August 1964.
Chorfantasie (chamber choir, trombone, 2 cellos, bass, small organ, percussion) 1964; first performed Selb, 23 January 1967.
Musen Siziliens / Muses of Sicily (choir, 2 pianos, 2 flutes, 2 oboes, 2 clarinets, 2 bassoons, 4 horns, 2 trumpets, 2 trombones, drums; Vergil) 1966; first performed Berlin, 20 September 1966. Recorded Deutsche Grammophon.
Das Floss der "Medusa" / The Raft of the "Medusa" (soprano, baritone, sprechstimme, mixed choir, orchestra; Guevara) 1968; first performed Hamburg, 9 December 1968. Recorded Deutsche Grammophon.
Versuch über Schweine / Essay on Pigs (baritone sprechstimme, chamber orchestra; Salvatore) 1968; first performed London, 14 February 1969. Recorded Deutsche Grammophon; Harmonia Mundi.
El Cimarron (voice, flute, guitar, percussion; Barnet) 1969–70; first performed Aldeburgh, Suffolk, 22 June 1970. Recorded Deutsche Grammophon.
Voices / Stimmen (2 singers, instrumental ensemble; various) 1973; first performed London, 4 January 1974. Recorded Decca; Harmonia Mundi.
Jephte (oratorio by Carissimi, realised by HWH; 7 soloists, choir, ensemble) 1976; first performed London, 14 July 1976.
El Rey de Harlem (singer, small instrumental ensemble; Lorca) 1979; first performed Witten, 20 April 1980.
Orpheus Behind the Wire / Orpheus hinter Stacheldraht (unaccompanied choir; Bond) 1981–3; first performed Southampton, Hampshire, 10 September 1985.
Drei Lieder (tenor, piano; Auden) 1983; first performed Aldeburgh, Suffolk 15 June 1983.

Opera / theatre:

Das Wunderschaft / The Magic Theatre (versions for speakers and singers; Cervantes) 1948, revised 1964; first performed Heidelberg, 7 May 1949; revised version first performed Frankfurt, 30 November 1965.
Ein Landzart / A Country Doctor (radio and stage versions; Kafka) 1951, revised 1965; first performed Hamburg, 19 November 1951; revised version first performed 30 November 1965. Recorded Deutsche Grammophon.
Boulevard Solitude (Weil, Jokisch) 1951; first performed Hannover, 17 February 1952.
König Hirsch / King Stag (Cramer) 1952–5; first performed Berlin, 23 September 1956; original version restored, Stuttgart, 5 May 1985.
Der Prinz von Hamburg (Kleist) 1958; first performed Hamburg, 22 May 1960.
Elegy for Young Lovers / Elegie für junge Liebende (Auden, Kallman) 1959–61; first performed Munich, 20 May 1961. Recorded Deutsche Grammophon; Harmonia Mundi.
Il Re Corvo oder Die Irrfahrten der Wahrheit / The Vagrancies of the Truth (reduced version of *King Stag*) 1962; first performed Kassel, 10 March 1963.
Der junge Lord / The Young Lord (Bachmann, Hauff) 1964; first performed Berlin, 7 April 1965. Recorded Deutsche Grammophon.
Das Ende einer Welt / The End of a World (stage version; Hildesheimer) 1964; first performed Frankfurt, 30 November 1965.
The Bassarids / Die Bassariden (Euripides, Auden, Kallman; also concert suite) 1965; first performed Salzburg, 6 August 1966.
Moralities / Moralitäten (Aesop, Auden) 1967; first performed Cincinnati, Ohio, 18 May 1968. Recorded Deutsche Grammophon.
Der langwierige Weg in die Wohnung der Natascha Ungeheuer / The Tedious Way to the Place of Natascha Ungeheuer (Salvatore) 1971; first performed Rome, 17 May 1971. Recorded Deutsche Grammophon.
La Cubana oder Ein Leben für die Kunst / A Life for the Arts (Enzensberger, Barnet) 1973; first performed Munich, 28 May 1975.
Streik bei Mannesmann 1973. Recorded Plane.
We Come to the River / Wir erreichen den Fluss (Bond) 1974–6; first performed London, 12 June 1976.
Don Chischiotte della Mancia (Lorenzi, Paisiello) 1976; first performed Montepulciano, 1 August 1976.
Pollicino (Leva) 1979–80; first performed Montepulciano, 2 August 1980.
The English Cat / Die englische Katze (Bond) 1980–3; first performed Stuttgart, 2 June 1983.
Odipus der Tyrann oder Der Vater vertreibt seinen Sohn und schickt die Tochter in die Küche (Hollmuller) 1983; first performed Kindberg, 30 October 1983.
Das verratene Meer 1989; first performed Berlin, 5 May 1990.

Other:

Ballett-Variationen (ballet; orchestra; also concert version) 1949; first performed Wuppertal, 21 December 1958; concert version first performed Dusseldorf, 3 October 1949.
Jack Pudding (ballet; orchestra; also concert version) 1949; first performed Wiesbaden, 1 January 1951; concert version first performed Heidelberg, 23 June 1950.
Rosa Silber (ballet scenes for orchestra) 1950; first performed Berlin, 8 May 1951.
Die schlafende Prinzessin / The Sleeping Princess (ballet; orchestra) 1951; first performed Essen, 5 June 1954.
Labyrinth (ballet; oboe, tenor saxophone, bass clarinet, F horn, C trumpet, trombone, 3 percussionists, strings) 1951; concert version first performed Darmstadt, 29 May 1952. Recorded Decca.
Der Idiot (ballet after Dostoyevsky; orchestra) 1952; first performed Berlin, 1 September 1952.
Maratona (ballet by Visconti; orchestra; also concert version for flute, alto saxophone, tenor saxophone, B jazz trumpet, jazz trombone, 3 percussionists, piano) 1956; first performed Berlin, 24 September 1957; concert version first performed 8 February 1957.
Undine (ballet; orchestra; also four concert versions) 1956–7; first performed London, 27 October 1958; *Erste Suite* first performed Stuttgart, 1959; *Zweite Suite* first performed Mannheim, 3 March 1958; *Trois Pas des Tritons* first performed Rome, 10 January 1959; *Hochzeitsmusik / Wedding Music* first performed 1957. Recorded Columbia.
Der Kaisers Nachtigall / L'Usignolo dell'Imperatore (ballet by Majo; flute, bass clarinet, celeste, marimba, piano, 4 percussionists, viola, cello; also concert version) 1959; first performed Venice, 16 September 1959; concert version

first performed Berlin, 26 September 1959. Recorded Decca.
Muriel (musical fragments from a film score) 1963. Recorded Milan.
Tancredi (ballet by Csobadi, based on the withdrawn *Pas d'action*, 1952; orchestra; also concert version) 1964; first performed Vienna, 14 May 1966; concert version first performed Hamburg, 15 January 1953.
Katharina Blum (concert suite from film score) 1976. Recorded Milan.
Orpheus (ballet by Bond; orchestra) 1978; first performed Stuttgart, 17 March 1979.
Une Petite Phrase (piano; from the film *Un Amour de Swann*) 1984. Recorded Milan.

Richard Wagner: *Wesendonk-Lieder* (orchestration for alto, chamber orchestra) 1976; first performed Cologne, 25 March 1977.
Claudio Monteverdi: *Il ritorno d'Ulisse in patria* (free reconstruction of 1641 opera) 1981; first performed Salzburg, 16 August 1985.

PUBLICATIONS

By Henze: *Eine Sammlung von Vorträgen und Aufsätzen aus den Jahren 1952–62*, Mainz, 1964; *Neue Aspekte der musikalischen Asthetik I, II, III*, Frankfurt, 1979, 1986; *Schriften und Gespräche*, East Berlin, 1981; *Musik und Politik: Schriften und Gespräche von 1955–1984*, Munich, 1984 (in English as *Music and Politics: Collected Writings 1953–81*, London and Ithaca, New York, 1982).

On Henze: Everett Helm, "Six Modern German Composers", in *The Anglo-German Review*, 1956–7; Klaus Geitel, *HWH*, Berlin, 1968; Peter Heyworth, "H and the Revolution", in *Music and Musicians*, September 1970, and conversation with HWH, "I Can Imagine a Future", in *The Observer*, 23 August 1970; Jean-Christophe, "Musiques d'aujourd'hui", in *Scherzo*, 1972; Bernard Jacobson, "H—Light and Dark Forces Held in Balance", in *Classical Music*, July 1977; Dieter Rexroth, *Der Komponist HWH*, Mainz, 1986; Peter Petersen, *HWH*, Hamburg, 1988.

* * *

Cicero would have had a hard time, faced with the music of Hans Werner Henze, making the distinctions he so loved to make. For in Henze the traditional category-pairs like the good and the useful, or beauty and duty, have always been inextricably mixed.

The best German composer of our time—if Henze, who has lived in Italy since 1953, can still be counted as German—has also given the best proof that music can be politically committed without degenerating into propaganda or poster-art. To suggest that any one piece can provide a key to every facet of his extraordinarily copious output would be foolish. But there are highly characteristic works that seem to bring the major strands of Henze's mind into particularly clear relief. Such a work is *Voices*, a "collection of songs for two vocalists and instrumental groups", written in 1973, that exemplifies Henze's sheer breadth of style, emotional range and intellectual sympathy.

At one extreme, *Voices* interprets the classically-turned lines of a poem like Heinrich Heine's "Heimkehr", with its evocation of the world of the German Lied. At the other extreme, it embraces the splashy vernacular vigour of radical black poets like Victor Hernandez Cruz and Walton Smith. Coexisting with these two elements, and characterizing Henze just as surely, is a strain of pure hedonism, celebrating beauty for its own sake, and celebrating beauty also as a musical manifestation of sensuous delight. Running like an unbreakable thread through the verses of the Cuban revolutionary poets Miguel Barnet and Heberto Padilla (neither of whom feels the need to thumb his nose at linguistic tradition in the manner of their North American brothers) and of the Italian Resistance writers also included, this penchant for luxury of sound and image culminates, at the end of *Voices*, in a rapturous setting of Hans Magnus Enzensberger's "Das Blumenfest." And all this is accomplished with a chameleon-like facility for varied idioms, from crisp ballad textures à la Weill or Eisler to a chromatic expressionistic intensity descended from the Second Viennese School and a motoric drive reminiscent of Stravinsky, that never compromises the clarity of Henze's individual voice.

It would be easy, tracing the line of continuity back from the Henze of 1973 (and of later dramatic works like the ballet *Orpheus*) to the equally unequivocal hedonism of his work in the 1940s and 1950s, to point out how firmly the sensuous preoccupation is rooted in the early Henze's love of subjects drawn from classical Greek mythology, how natural such a leaning must have been for a composer schooled in Goethe, Hölderlin, and the other pillars of German literature, and how doubly natural it now seems in a German composer who at the age of 27 adopted Italy as his homeland. But to concentrate on the line of spiritual descent might be to miss the point that is salient about this sensuous predilection. In a period when most composers took refuge either in systematization or in an equally extreme mystical rejection of all logical rules—when Stockhausen concentrated in one phase on totally organized parameters and in another on the pursuit of the state of trance, and when even a musician as accomplished as Xenakis spoke of musical phenomena only as "interesting," reserving the word "beautiful" for mathematical formulae—it was precisely his continued dedication to that old concept beauty, and to a beauty apprehended in clearly human and humanistic terms, that shaped Henze into the rare and treasurable creator he was and is.

It is, again, Henze's unflagging humanity that makes the question of where his inspiration will lead him now, in the wake of the collapse of international communism, a positive and intriguing question rather than a negative and depressing one. His artistic sympathy for left-wing causes has always been focused on individual values, not on the generalistic cant of the class war; and consequently his credibility is likely to survive the darkest eclipse of any or all leftist political systems. Like Beethoven (who, Sir Donald Tovey observed, knew that "the sublimest artistic treatment [of a generally heroic subject] would consist in taking a single case"), Henze has framed even the most ideologically inclined of his dozen or so operas in individual terms. Thus all of them, from quirky satires like *The Young Lord* to a supreme masterpiece like *The Bassarids*, make their impact in vivid human terms, leaving the party manifestos of lesser composers to languish in the limbo of a "universality" bereft of individual reference.

Henze's humanism does not inform his explicitly narrative works only. He told me in an interview back in 1976: "In every phrase you write you can hear your grandfathers—you can hear Josquin, and Verdi, and Monteverdi, and Mozart. And if you try to deny all this, what you produce will be something inhuman—a kind of Fascist art." The words suggest an inner unity of human and musical concerns that helps to explain how it is that even his supposedly "abstract" works, such as the Fifth String Quartet and the Seventh

Symphony, can come close to emulating respectively the visionary individualism and the dramatic dynamism of late and middle Beethoven, and how a teeming operatic fresco like *We Come to the River* can combine a veritably Wagnerian physical scale with a no less Wagnerian humanity and expressive daring.

—Bernard Jacobson

HILLBORG, Anders. Swedish. Born in Stockholm, 31 May 1954. Educated at State College of Music, Stockholm (composition under Gunnar Bucht), 1976–82; further study in United States (including lessons under Morton Feldman at Buffalo, New York), 1980. Music teacher, Orebro, early 1980s; collaborator, Teater Modern performance group; board member, Fylkingen, Stockholm, since 1980, and Swedish Composers Society, since 1989; programming board member, Stockholm Philharmonic, since 1989; professor of composition, Malmo Music Academy, since 1989. Recipient: 2nd prize, International Composers Rostrum, 1990. Mailing address: Katarina Vāstra Kyrkogata 6c, S-116 25 Stockholm, Sweden.

Publisher: Nordislka Musikförlaget, Nybrog. 3, S-1143 34 Stockholm, Sweden.

Symphonies/orchestral:

Worlds 1979; first performed Helsinki, 1980.
Celestial Mechanics 1985; first performed Stockholm, 1986. Recorded Phono Suecia PSCD 52.
Clang and Fury 1988; first performed Stockholm, 1989. Recorded Phono Suecia, 1989.
Violin Concerto 1991.

Chamber/instrumental:

Lamento (clarinet, strings) 1982; first performed Stockholm, 1982. Recorded Phono Suecia PSCD 52.
Music for Ten (10 cellos) 1986; first performed Stockholm, 1987.
Haut Posaune (trombone, drum machine) 1989; first performed Stockholm, 1990. Recorded Phono Suecia PSCD 52.
U-Tangia-Na (trombone, organ) 1990; first performed Stockholm, 1991.
Close Ups (flute) 1991.
Hyacintrummet (harp) 1991.

Vocal/choral:

Lilla Sus Grav (16-part mixed choir) 1978; first performed Stockholm, 1979.
Stella Maris (mixed choir) 1983; first performed Stockholm, 1983.
Se Jag vill skapa . . . (mixed choir) 1983; first performed Stockholm, 1983.
mouɔaaəyiywɔoum (16-part mixed choir) 1983; first performed Stockholm, 1983. Recorded Phono Suecia PSCD 44.

Other:

Mental Hygien II (electronic) 1979; first performed Stockholm, 1979.
Rite of Passage (electronic) 1981; first performed Stockholm, 1981. Recorded Fylkingen Records FYLP 1027.
Kama Loka (electronic) 1981; first performed Stockholm, 1981.
Ghost Sonata (electronic) 1982; first performed Stockholm, 1982.
Living Room (electronic) 1983; first performed Stockholm, 1983.
Rap-Ode (electronic) 1988; first performed Stockholm, 1988.
Friends (mixed media) 1988; first performed Stockholm and Tokyo, 1988.
Broken Necklace (rock ballad; extract from *Friends*) 1988. Recorded Mercury 870 138 7.
The Give Away (synthesizer music for film *Pass*) 1989.

PUBLICATIONS

On Hillborg: essays on *Celestial Mechanics* in *Nutida Musik*, 1, 1986–7, and in *Artes*, 2, 1986–7; Hans-Gunnar Peterson, "AH", in *Swedish Composers of the 20th Century*, Stockholm, 1988.

Anders Hillborg comments:

My origins in rock music probably influenced my musical thinking a great deal; my compositions range from conventional rock music to wild experiments with microtonal structures, and, as opposed to previous generations of composers, maybe, I see no conflict in working with musical concepts so far apart. Experiment and tradition are not separate, but are constantly intertwined in the process of composing. Maybe a Stravinskian attitude.

Perhaps *Clang and Fury* for orchestra and *Haut Posaune* for trombone and drum machine would give a true picture of my musical landscape.

* * *

Artistic influences is a complex and sometimes baffling process, rarely reducible to clear, one-on-one relationships. If the spirit of Stravinsky oversees Anders Hillborg's work, influencing its bold syncretism and rapid imaginative transitions, his more specific debts seem almost bafflingly various. Schooled at the State College of Music in Stockholm under Gunnar Bucht, a "conservative" whose traditionalism sometimes masks a powerful musical imagination, Hillborg's precociously mature style combines a confident grasp of orchestration and instrumental colour with something of the rock musician's subordination of traditional musical parameters to sheer dynamics and sonority. After a study visit to the United States in 1980, he was briefly attracted to the static harmonies and relentless rhythmic drive of the so-called Minimalist composers, Americans like LaMonte Young, Steve Reich and Philip Glass, all of whom drew some of their procedures from rock and jazz. However, he found this tendency too limiting. Far more significant in his development were his meetings with the British composer Brian Ferneyhough, a leading light of the "New Complexity", and with the senior American composer Morton Feldman, with whom he briefly but fruitfully studied composition.

Both encounters gave Hillborg the confidence to synthesise apparently contradictory musical procedures within a single piece. The recent *Haut Posaune* (which utilises an electronic rhythm machine) is a powerful statement of his method on a relatively small scale. Like the *Music for Ten* (cellos) and *U-Tangia-Na* for the traditional combination of trombone and organ, it creates a fabric of microtonal responses which can be developed in an apparently improvisatory way or foreclosed quite abruptly, as if according to the dictates of a rigidly determinant matrix.

Far more impressive are the earlier orchestral *Celestial Mechanics* and *Clang and Fury*, both which combine enormous amounts of barely contained energy with a fine structural sense. In comparison with other young composers—Steve Martland in the United Kingdom, Glenn Branca in the United States—Hillborg is subtle and instinctively romantic, layering themes and textures, much as a studio producer might overdub and superimpose tracks in rock music, in order to create a sound texture which is both aesthetically rich and intellectually complex.

Hillborg's most immediate source for this technique and for his abiding interest in microtones is his work in the electronic music studio, and the important electro-acoustic pieces of the early 1980s. Of these, the *Ghost Sonata*, based not on Beethoven but on Strindberg's trance-like play, is the most significant. His vocal music is absolutely of a piece with the rest of his work: the phonetic *muoɔaaəyiywɔoum*, like the earlier *Lilla Sus Grav*, is a masterly treatment of multi-part chorus.

Hillborg's music is physical, immediate and absolutely self-consistent. He has combined a basically "experimental" orientation with an identifiable voice. Not yet 40, he must still be considered promising, but without much of the ironic hesitation that normally accompanies that rather ambiguous compliment.

—Henk Maarten

HILLER, Lejaren A(rthur), Jr. American. Born in New York City, 23 February 1924. Educated at Princeton University, New Jersey (chemistry), B.A., 1944, M.A., 1946, Ph.D., 1947; also composition study with Roger Sessions and Milton Babbitt; University of Illinois, M.Mus., 1958. Married; 1 son and 1 daughter. Member of chemistry faculty, 1952–8, and music faculty, 1958–68, University of Illinois, Urbana; Slee Professor of Composition, since 1968, and co-director (with Lukas Foss), Center for the Creative and Performing Arts, 1968–74, State University of New York, Buffalo; Fulbright Lecturer, Warsaw, 1973–4, and Bahia, Brazil, 1980. Mailing address: Department of Music, State University of New York, Buffalo, New York 14260, U.S.A.

Publishers: Theodore Presser; Edition Peters.

Symphonies/orchestral:

Piano Concerto 1949.
Suite (chamber orchestra) 1951.
Symphony No 1 1953.
Symphony No 2 1960.
Time of the Heathen (chamber orchestra) 1961.
A Preview of Coming Attractions 1975.

Chamber/instrumental:

Sonata No 1 (piano) 1946, revised 1968.
Sonata No 2 (piano) 1947.
Piano Trio 1947.
Seven Artifacts (piano) 1948, revised 1972–3.
Children's Suite (piano) 1949.
Sonata No 1 (violin, piano) 1949.
String Quartet No 1 1949.
Sonata No 3 (piano) 1950.
Sonata No 4 (piano) 1950; first performed Buffalo, New York, May 1950. Recorded Orion ORS 75176.
Fantasy (3 pianos) 1951.
String Quartet No 2 1951.
String Quartet No 3 1953.
Twelve-Tone Variations (piano) 1954.
String Quartet No 4: Illiac Suite (collaboration with Leonard Isaacson) 1955–6.
Sonata No 2 (violin or cello, piano) 1955.
Two Theater Pieces (piano) 1956.
Scherzo (piano) 1958.
Divertimento (chamber ensemble) 1959.
Sonata No 5 (piano) 1961. Recorded Orion ORS 75176.
String Quartet No 5: In Quarter Tones 1962.
Amplification (jazz group, tape) 1962.
Machine Music (piano, percussion, tape) 1964.
Suite (2 pianos, tape) 1966.
HPSCHD (collaboration with John Cage; 1–7 amplified harpsichords, 1–51 tapes) 1967–9.
Three Algorithms (collaboration with R. Kumra; instruments, tape) 1968–72.
Computer Music (collaboration with G.A. O'Conner; percussion, tape) 1968.
A Cenotaph (2 pianos) 1971.
Sonata No 6 (piano) 1972.
String Quartet No 6 1972. Recorded 1974.
A Portfolio (unspecified instruments, tape) 1974.
Six Easy Pieces (violin, piano) 1974.
Malta (tuba, tape) 1975. Recorded.
Persiflage (flute, oboe, percussion) 1977.
Diabelskie Skrzypce (fiddle, harpsichord) 1978.
String Quartet No 7 1979.
An Apotheosis of Archaeopterix (piccolo, berimbau) 1979. Recorded 1981.
Minuet and Trio (sextet) 1980.
Quadrilateral (piano, tape) 1981. Recorded 1984.
Tetrahedron (harpsichord) 1982.
Tango (piano) 1984.
Expo '85 (synthesizers, tapes) 1985. Recorded 1986.

Vocal/choral:

Jesse James (4 voices, piano; Benet) 1950.
Five Appalachian Ballads (voice, guitar or piano) 1958. Recorded 1977.
Spoon River (2 narrators, instruments; Masters) 1962.
Computer Cantata (collaboration with Robert Baker; soprano, chamber orchestra, tape) 1963. Recorded 1967.

Theatre:

Blue Is the Antecedent of It (electronic theatre fantasy; Leckel) 1959.
Cuthbert Bound (4 actors, tape; Newton) 1960.
A Triptych for Hieronymus (actors, dancers, orchestra, tape, slides, film; Smalley) 1966.
An Avalanche (prima donna, pitchman, pianola, percussion,

tape; Parman) 1968. Recorded.
Three Rituals (2–4 percussion, film, lights) 1969.
Rage over the Lost Beethoven (piano music from *Sonata No 6* or ad lib; Parman) 1976.
Ponteach (narrator, piano) 1977.

Other:

A Dream Play (incidental music to Strindberg) 1957.
The Birds (incidental music to Aristophanes) 1958.
Nightmare Music (tape) 1961.
Man with the Oboe (incidental music to Smalley) 1962.
Seven Electronic Studies (tape) 1963. Recorded 1965.
Electronic Sonata (tape) 1976.
Midnight Carnival (tapes, environments, loudspeakers) 1976; first performed St Louis, Missouri, 1976.
Chang Fu, the Witch of Moon Mountain (incidental music to Smalley) 1982.
Three Compositions (tape; text by Emily Dickinson) 1983.

PUBLICATIONS

By Hiller: *Experimental Music*, New York, 1959; many technical articles in *Perspectives of New Music* and *Journal of Music Theory*.

On Hiller: C. Gagne and T. Caras, (interview) in *Soundpieces: Interviews with American Composers*, Metuchen, New Jersey, 1982; S. Husarick, "John Cage and LH: *HPSCHD*, 1969", in *American Music*, 1(2), 1983.

* * *

Lejaren A. Hiller, Jr. is best known as a pioneer of computer applications in music, and as a composer of electronic and theatrical works.

One characteristic embodied in his output is a tension between music and science. At Princeton University in the late 1940s, he studied chemistry to doctoral level, while being taught theory and counterpoint by Milton Babbitt and Roger Sessions. For the next 11 years he earned his living as a scientist. During that time he began, and in 1956 presented, the *Illiac Suite* of four movements for string quartet, in collaboration with Leonard Isaacson. It was the first computer-generated score, written using the Illiac digital machine of the University of Illinois.

The first movement was generated by relating randomly derived integers to a two-octave diatonic C-major scale. The succession of notes was determined by inputting the rules of 16th-century counterpoint, which were then used to set the ensuing melodies in two voices. The second movement deploys all 14 rules of strict first-species counterpoint. The third is a study in rhythmic and dynamic variety, and the last an essay in twelve-tone technique.

Suite was a technological breakthrough, but as Hiller admits, was a group of experiments, albeit one reflecting the personality of its programmers. His claims for computer composition in general were correspondingly modest. "My objective", he recalled some years later, ". . . is not the immediate realization of an aesthetic unity, but the providing and evaluating of techniques whereby this goal can eventually be realized", and furthering understanding of the source and principles of the aesthetic qualities of music. In subsequent years he further refined his computer techniques, in, for example, the *Computer Cantata* for soprano, tape and ensemble, written with Robert Baker using an IBM 7090 machine. Between 1967 and 1969 he collaborated with John Cage on the composition and subsequent recording of *HPSCHD* for up to seven harpsichords and up to 51 tapes, an interesting conjunction of Hiller's use of mathematical probability in information technology and Cage's interest in chance as a mystical discipline.

The burgeoning research in information technology throughout the 1950s, which provided the foundation for computer composition, was also used by Hiller as an analytic resource. In the early 1960s he prepared information theory analyses of Webern's opus 21 Symphonie (with Ramon Fuller) and of sonata expositions by Beethoven, Berg, Hindemith and Mozart (with Calvert Bean).

Much of Hiller's music, from *Blue Is the Antecedent of It* (1959) onwards, has been for tape or for tape with instruments, though of course the computer was initially a compositional resource and was not used for synthesis. He has composed a great deal of incidental music for films and plays, including *Blue* . . . , and theatre pieces of his own such as *An Avalanche* or *A Triptych for Hieronymus* for actors, dancers, projections and tape.

In 1976, Hiller took over a dozen blocks of St Louis, Missouri, for his spectacle *Midnight Carnival*. Speakers lined the streets, distributing 46 channels of sound for some four or five hours to upwards of 20,000 participants.

Hiller's compositional resources are varied. Although in no sense a revivalist, he writes tonal as readily as serial music. He deploys the most traditional musical forms, yet understands them through information theory; he calls for microtones, not only in his electronic pieces, but in instrumental scores such as the Fifth String Quartet. Hiller composes for electronic resources, yet also for folk instruments, such as the devil's fiddle (*Diabelskie Skrzypce*) or the duet of piccolo and berimbau in *An Apotheosis of Archaeopterix*.

"My general approach", Hiller told Cole Gagne and Tracy Caras, "is empirical and eclectic". The unifying factor is not rigid pre-compositional recipes but a constant balancing of spontaneity and rationality which seems expressive of his character.

—David Revill

HOBBS, Christopher. British/English. Born in Hillingdon, Middlesex, 9 September 1950. Educated at St Nicholas Grammar School, Northwood, 1961–7; Trinity College of Music, London, 1963–6; Royal Academy of Music, London (composition under Cornelius Cardew, percussion under Patricia Brady), 1967–9. Married Margaret Coldiron, 7 July 1984. Performer, Scratch Orchestra, AMM Music, 1969–71, Promenade Theatre Orchestra, 1970–3, Hobbs-White Duo (with John White), 1973–6, and Live Batts!, from 1987; founder/editor, *Experimental Music Catalogue*, 1969–74; lecturer in liberal studies, Epsom Art College, Surrey, 1970–1; lecturer in fine arts, Croydon Art College, Surrey, 1971–2; director of music, Drama Centre, London, since 1973; lecturer in music, literature and piano, Leicester Polytechnic, since 1986. Mailing address: 21 Chippendale Street, London E5 OBB, England.

Publishers: Needham Publications, Needham, Massachusetts; Forward Contemporary Music, 32 Knights Par, Kingston on Thames, Surrey, England.

Chamber/instrumental:

Harp Star Pieces (harp) 1967.
Christmas Pieces: Two Volumes (organ duet) 1967–8, 1969.
Trio (2 violins, 3 violas, 2 cellos) 1968.
Music for the Crumbling Cookie 1 & 2 (unspecified ensemble) 1968.
Working Notes (3 toy pianos, reed organ) 1969.
The Remorseless Lamb (piano duet or 2 pianos) 1970.
Out of Exercise 3 (piano) 1970.
12-Bar Blues Machine (4 toy pianos) 1970.
Czerny's 100 Royal Bouquet Waltzes for the Piano by Lanner and Strauss, Arranged for Such as Cannot Reach an Octave (unspecified number of pianos) 1970.
Sad Lost-F Mantra (3 toy pianos, percussion) 1970.
Aran (percussion, toy piano, reed organ; revised for percussion and keyboard ensemble) 1970–3.
Mastery of the Beat (4 reed organs) 1971.
Trio (3 percussion) 1971.
Two 15th-Century Roll-Offs (4 toy pianos, 4 reed organs) 1971.
Two Doomsday Machines (4 reed organs) 1971.
55 Endings from 66 Choral Improvisations in 8 Major Keys (ensemble) 1971.
Out of Exercise 2 (ensemble) 1971.
Piobaireachd Exercise (ensemble) 1971.
Oxford Street Walk (oboe, clarinet, trombone, drum) 1972.
Pretty Tough Cookie (2 pianos) 1972.
Dufay Accompli (4 toy pianos, 4 reed organs) 1972.
Scriabin Readymade (4 toy pianos) 1972.
With the Ascending Modulation, His Fame May Rise (3 reed organs) 1972.
Imitation Roll-Off (oboe, clarinet, trombone, percussion) 1973.
G Major Machine (4 reed organs) 1973.
Straight Off the Top (oboe, bass clarinet, trombone) 1973.
Piano Piece 1–12 1973.
The Back Gate of Kiev (4 reed organs) 1973.
Rhythm Walk (4 percussion) 1973.
Out of Exercise (4 toy pianos, 4 reed organs) 1973.
Festival Machine (2 reed organs, percussion, metronomes) 1973.
Climax Hit-Off (4 toy pianos, 4 reed organs) 1973.
Number Piece 1 (2 percussion) 1973.
Exercise for Percussionists (percussion ensemble) 1973.
Daughter of Luna (2 toy pianos, 2 reed organs, percussion) 1973.
Heavy Viking Systems (2 percussion) 1973.
Number Piece 2 (2 percussion) 1973.
A Fair Lick (2 percussion) 1973.
Lincoln E. Moses Comes Down from the Mountain (2 percussion) 1973.
Steady Pace Journey (2 percussion) 1974.
First Duet Set (piano) 1974.
Village Organist Roll-Off (2 toy pianos, 2 reed organs) 1974.
Slow Swing (toy piano, reed organ, tuba) 1974.
Timpani Studies (2 percussion) 1974.
Soft Saxon Systems (percussion ensemble) 1974.
Rondo-Fantasia (ensemble) 1974.
Another Exercise (2 percussion) 1975.
Systemic Mettle (2 percussion) 1975.
Second Duet Set (piano) 1975.
Knight's System (2 percussion) 1975.
Sonatina (piano) 1975.
Six Preludes and Five Chorales (3 clarinets, bass clarinet) 1975.
Symphonic Dances (reed organ, percussion, toy piano) 1975.
Sonatina (tuba, piano) 1975.
Preludes (tuba, piano) 1975.
Prelude alla Reminiscenza (toy piano, reed organ, bassoon) 1975.
Symphonic Dances 2 (tuba, piano, reed organ/percussion) 1975.
A Mother's Son (2 percussion) 1975.
Number Piece 3 (2 percussion) 1975.
Intermezzo 1 (2 toy pianos, percussion) 1976.
Intermezzo 2 (2 toy pianos, percussion) 1976.
Mummers Are Coming (2 toy pianos, 2 reed organs) 1976.
Sonatina (piano) 1976.
Twelve Sketches (tuba, piano) 1976.
Sonatina (bassoon, piano) 1976.
Study for Solo Percussion 1977.
Orangerearrangement (flute, percussion) 1977.
Alleluia (2 pianos) 1977.
Two Sonatinas (piano) 1977.
Recitative (bass clarinet, vibes, celeste, percussion) 1979.
Three for Redlands (ensemble) 1979.
Sonatina (piano) 1979.
Seventeen One-Minute Pieces (string quartet) 1980.
Sextet (saxophone, wind quintet) 1980.
Sonatina (piano) 1980.
The Wide Open Spaces (ensemble) 1981.
Swiftly to Virginia (E♭ clarinet, piano) 1982.
Rites of Passage (clarinet, piano/percussion) 1982.
Foottight and Fancy Bound (alto saxophone, vibraphone, tape) 1984.
Four Studies in Shadow (bass flute, bass clarinet, bassoon) 1984.
Four Pieces (ensemble) 1985.
A Short Set (ensemble) 1986.
Sonatina (piano) 1986.
Four Pieces (tuba, electric keyboard) 1986.
Second String Quartet 1987.
A Turn Around the Old Gothic Swing (ensemble) 1987.
Fanfares (2 E♭ clarinets) 1987.
Another Part of the Forest (ensemble) 1988.
In Other Parts of the Forest (2 pianos, harmonium) 1989.

Vocal/choral:

Two Watt Settings (male voice quartet) 1970.
The Castle Keep (amplified speaking voices) 1970.
He's My Guy (speaking voices, 4 reed organs) 1971.
Woman Has Naught to Do with Fame (speaking voices, 4 reed organs) 1971.
Four Morgenstern Songs (baritone, piano) 1975.
In the Silent Void (baritone, viola, piano/percussion) 1981.
Five Morgenstern Songs (baritone, piano) 1984.
Conspicuous Consumer (mezzo-soprano, ensemble) 1988.
Drei Lieder aus "Der Struwwelpeter" (baritone, piano) 1990.

Opera:

The Mountebanks (operetta; libretto by W. S. Gilbert) 1976.

Other:

[Indeterminate pieces use verbal notation and are for unspecified numbers of performers.]

One Note (indeterminate) 1966.
To All Who Live in Simple Unpretentious Houses (indeterminate) 1967.
Measuring Means (indeterminate) 1967.

Song 1 (indeterminate) 1967.
Song 2 (indeterminate) 1967.
The Glory of Highland Scotland (Tour 47) (indeterminate) 1968.
Too Soft to Touch But Too Lovely Not to Try (indeterminate) 1968.
Walk Event (indeterminate) 1968.
Higgins' Eternal Ink (indeterminate) 1968.
125 Questions for Pianists (indeterminate) 1969.
Two Compositions, 21 May 1969 (indeterminate) 1969.
Voicepiece (indeterminate) 1969.
The Friesian Cow (indeterminate) 1969.
Shortly Before Midnight (indeterminate) 1969.
Can You Hear Me, Mother? (indeterminate) 1969.
Home (tape) 1970.
McCrimmon Will Never Return (indeterminate) 1970. Recorded Obscure Records.
The Loves, Lives and Murders of Lancelot Barabbas Quail (theatre music) 1977.
The Measures Taken (theatre music) 1978.
Still Life, and Moving (electric keyboards, tape) 1979.
A Chaste Maid in Cheapside (theatre music) 1979.
The Storm (theatre music) 1979; first performed Israel, 1979.
Still Life, and Moving (Detail) (electric keyboards, tape) 1979.
Bloomers from Bash Street (theatre music) 1980; first performed London, 1980.
Pericles (incidental music to Shakespeare) 1980; first performed Northampton, 1980.
The Broken Heart (theatre music) 1981; first performed London, 1981.
An Italian Straw Hat (theatre music) 1981; first performed London, 1981.
The Only Game in Town (electric keyboards) 1982.
Berenice (theatre music) 1982; first performed London, 1982.
Uncle Vanya (incidental music to Chekhov) 1982; first performed London, 1982.
Britannicus (theatre music) 1982; first performed London, 1982.
The Mother-in-Law (theatre music) 1982; first performed London, 1982.
Hamlet (incidental music to Shakespeare) 1983.
Exit the King (theatre music) 1983; first performed London, 1983.
Twelfth Night (incidental music to Shakespeare) 1983; first performed Oxford, 1983.
The Rime of the Ancient Mariner (theatre music) 1985; first performed Oxford, 1985.
Alice in Wonderland (theatre music) 1985; first performed Oxford, 1985.
Life Is a Dream (theatre music) 1986; first performed London, 1986.
Back Seat Album (electric keyboard, tape) 1987.
Come On, Get It Together Chaps! (computer) 1988.
Changes 1 (computer) 1988.
Changes 2 (computer) 1988.
Batt Jogg (electric keyboards, 2 players) 1990.
Amphitryon (theatre music) 1990; first performed London, 1990.
House (electric keyboards, solo) 1990.
The Exception and the Rule (theatre music) 1990; first performed London, 1990.
The Batts of the Delectable Mountains (electric keyboards, 2 players) 1990.
Miyama (electric keyboard, solo) 1990.
Cathedral (electric keyboard, solo) 1990.
Batt Scrapps (electric keyboards, 2 players) 1990.
Batt Flapp (electric keyboards, 2 players) 1990.
Batt Fancie (electric keyboards, 2 players) 1990.
Ethnic Rock (electric keyboard, solo) 1991.
Slow Rock 1 (electric keyboard, solo) 1991.

PUBLICATIONS

By Hobbs: "Listen, Act", in *The Musical Times*, July 1968; "Cornelius Cardew", in *Dictionary of Contemporary Music*, New York, 1974; "Cardew as Teacher", in *Perspectives of New Music*, 20 (1), 1981; co-editor, improvisation issues, *Perspectives of New Music*, 1985.

On Hobbs: Peter West and Peter Evans, "Interview with CH", in *Contact*, 3, 1971; Michael Nyman, in *Experimental Music: Cage and Beyond*, New York, 1974; Virginia Anderson, "British Experimental Music: Cornelius Cardew and his Contemporaries", dissertation, University of Redlands, California, 1983; Gavin Bryars, "Satie and the British", in *Contact*, 25, 1983; Virginia Anderson, "CH: The Enfant Terrible at 40", in *Contemporary Music Review*, 1991.

Christopher Hobbs comments:

I write more in response to specific circumstances than *in abstracto*: an interesting group of instruments, a pending concert (to paraphrase Doctor Johnson, the knowledge that one is to play a concert in two weeks time focusses the mind wonderfully), or just a casual request for a piece, is sufficient. I am concerned less with producing definitive statements than with being useful: fulfilling a need, plugging a gap. To exist as I do in a kind of musical underground in England is a great help—one has the liberty to be gently subversive, there are no pressures to create masterpieces. The composers whom I respect the most—Alkan, Busoni, Satie, Cardew, White—are all mavericks, and I rejoice in their company, whether philosophical, musical or personal. My references? Busoni to the darker side, jazz and cheap forms of music making to the lighter, Satie as a kind of fulcrum in between. Add the influence of the West Coast of the United States (its sunshine, people, music) and you have the general picture. Nervous about being trapped in classification, I resist peering too intently. I welcome the future with considerable delight.

* * *

Christopher Hobbs's early mature music (1966–9) is indeterminate. Most of these works are text pieces, and exhibit the influence of his teacher at the Royal Academy of Music, Cornelius Cardew. *One Note* (1966), Hobbs's earliest existing piece, originally was designed to be determinate as to performance, the random elements having been used in composition. On Cardew's advice, however, Hobbs produced the work in text, so that performers could realise the piece themselves by using telephone books to produce the random elements.

Other early works use different methods of deriving indeterminacy. *Walk Event* lets the performer think of a number to determine the structure of the motion. A found system of indeterminate performance occurs in *The Island Game Rite*, a piece published in the Scratch Orchestra's *Nature Study Notes*. Hobbs applied a pop psychology game of moral relativity which appeared in the *Evening Standard* to direct improvisation. There are five characters in the game, and performers determine such aspects as dynamics, duration, reactions to other performers, etc., in proportion to their assessment of the characters' relative moral value.

Once Hobbs began performing with what would become

the Promenade Theatre Orchestra rather than the mixed group of musicians and non-musicians in the Scratch Orchestra, he adapted random procedure to the manipulation of existing works to form (*à la* Duchamp) readymades, such as *The Remorseless Lamb*. Hobbs took a piano-duet version of Bach's *Sheep May Safely Graze*, and reorganised the placement of measures using random means. His work for the PTO branched out into other systems of composition. *Working Notes* is a traditional repetitive piece, while *The Back Gate of Kiev*, in its use of a pitch system, heralds later durational systems of the Hobbs-White Duo. *Aran*, for percussion and toy pianos, uses a knitting pattern for an Aran sweater to determine its structure. *McCrimmon Will Never Return* is a simultaneous exposition of variants of a Scottish bagpipe tune slowed down so that the skirls become melodic lines.

When the PTO broke up, Hobbs and John White, in their work as the Hobbs-White Duo, turned almost exclusively to percussion in their first few years. The loss of pitch considerations allowed both composers to explore durational systems. Hobbs found the work of British systems artists such as Jeffrey Steele, and Samuel Beckett's permutational book *Watt*, influences for his percussion music. A simple system, such as Beckett's three frogs croaking at intervals of eight, five and three, not only indicates placement of each part, but also its eventual duration, as when the separate parts arrive on the same beat the piece is over. This structure is evident in several of Hobbs's percussion works, such as *Number Piece 1*.

Hobbs and White returned to pitch-based instruments, first through their secondary instruments of bassoon and tuba, later as a piano duo, and as Hobbs found that pitches were less readily controlled by systems, his work became more empirically based, more grounded in traditional music models. Much of Hobbs's music of this period is influenced by the work of White, because of their close collaboration, and exhibits an interest in music by Busoni, Alkan, Liszt and other giants of 19th-century piano literature. Hobbs followed White's miniature sonatas with his own, more massive sonatinas, and at the end of the Duo, Hobbs entered into his only complete essay in pastiche, in *The Mountebanks*, in which he set a W.S. Gilbert libretto.

Since 1976, Hobbs has used more jazz and popular dance elements in his works. *Swiftly to Virginia* includes a tossed-off reference to *An American in Paris*; *A Turn Around the Old Gothic Swing* has a cocktail piano solo and a modern jazz vibes break at structural points; *Another Part of the Forest* uses an altered theme by Carla Bley as a motivic element. Much of Hobbs's later music, from his *Sonatina* (1975) through his string quartet music, to the E♭ clarinet and viola ensemble pieces for the Hartzell Hilton Band, has waltz-like sections.

Ethnic sources such as Scottish bagpipe tunes and Sumatran folk music occur in a piano sonatina of 1977 and *Rites of Passage*, respectively. Because of avant-garde performers in America for whom he writes, some of Hobbs's music in the 1980s, like his Wind Sextet, has occasionally exhibited a grittier, less accessible surface. Recently, Hobbs has returned to work with John White in a live electronics group called Live Batts! In music for this group, and in his solo electronic music, one can detect a kind of generic homage to rock. Hobbs has also returned to systems as a generating process for some of his electronic pieces.

—Virginia Anderson

HODDINOTT, Alun. British/Welsh. Born in Bargoed, Glamorganshire [now Mid Glamorgan], Wales, 1 August 1929. Educated at University College of Wales, Cardiff, B.A., 1949, doctorate, 1960; studied piano under Arthur Benjamin, London. Married Beti Rhiannon Huws in 1953; 1 son. Faculty member, Cardiff College of Music and Drama, 1951–9; lecturer, 1959–65, reader, 1965–7, and professor, 1967–87, University College, Cardiff; artistic director, Cardiff Festival of Twentieth-Century Music, from 1966. Recipient: Walford Davis Prize, 1954; Bax Medal, 1957; Fellow, University College of Wales, Cardiff, 1981; John Edwards Memorial Award; Hopkins Medal, St David's Society of New York. Mailing address: Maesawelon, Mill Road, Lisvane, Cardiff, Wales.

Publisher: Oxford University Press.

Symphonies/orchestral:

Concerto for Clarinet and String Orchestra Op 3 1950; broadcast BBC, 15 March 1951; first concert performance Cheltenham, Gloucestershire, 16 July 1954. Recorded Decca SXL 6513.

Fugal Overture Op 4/2 1952; broadcast BBC, 20 April 1953.

Nocturne Op 5 1952; broadcast BBC, 22 September 1953.

Symphony No 1 Op 7 1954–5; first performed Pwllheli, Caernarvonshire, 5 August 1955.

Concerto for Oboe and Strings Op 8 1955; first performed Sheffield, 13 October 1971.

Concerto for Harp and Orchestra Op 11 1957; first performed Cheltenham, Gloucestershire, 16 July 1958. Recorded Decca SXL 6513.

Concertino Op 14 (viola, small orchestra) 1958; first performed Llandaff, Glamorgan, 25 June 1958.

Four Welsh Dances Op 15 1958; first performed London, 28 June 1958. Recorded HMV ASD 2739.

Two Welsh Nursery Tunes (no opus number) 1959; broadcast BBC, 22 January 1961.

Nocturne and Dance Op 16/2 (harp, orchestra) 1959; first performed 20 June 1959.

Concerto for Piano, Winds and Percussion Op 19 1960; first performed London, 22 February 1960.

Concerto for Piano and Orchestra No 2 Op 21 1960; first performed Cardiff, 5 August 1960. Recorded Decca SXL 6606.

Entry (no opus number) 1960; first performed London, 22 November 1960.

Concerto for Violin and Orchestra Op 22 1961; first performed Birmingham, 30 March 1961.

Folksong Suite (no opus number) 1962; first performed 29 April 1962.

Symphony No 2 Op 29 1962; first performed Cheltenham, Gloucestershire, 1962. Recorded Pye TPLS 13013.

Variations Op 31 1963, revised 1964; first performed Newtown, 4 August 1963.

Sinfonia Op 34 1964; first performed Birmingham, 19 April 1964.

Overture: Jack Straw Op 35 1964; first performed Aberystwyth, Cardiganshire, 1 May 1964.

Concerto Grosso No 1 Op 41 1965; first performed Caerphilly, Glamorgan, 11 June 1965.

Aubade and Scherzo Op 42 (horn, strings) 1965; first performed Cardiff, 24 October 1966.

Concerto for Piano and Orchestra No 3 Op 44 1966; first performed Cheltenham, Gloucestershire, 12 July 1966.

Overture: Pantomime Op 45 1966; first performed Croydon, Surrey, 16 July 1966.

Concerto Grosso No 2 Op 46 1966; first performed Ammanford, Carmarthenshire, 28 July 1966.
Variants Op 47 1966; first performed London, 2 November 1966.
Night Music Op 48 1966; first performed Aberystwyth, Cardiganshire, 30 January 1967.
Concerto for Organ and Orchestra Op 51 1967; first performed Llandaff, Glamorgan, 19 June 1967.
Sinfonietta I Op 56 1968; first performed Cardiff, 29 April 1968.
Fioriture Op 60 1968; first performed Aberdeen, 24 November 1968.
Symphony No 3 Op 61 1968; first performed Manchester, 5 December 1968. Recorded Decca SXL 6570.
Nocturnes and Cadenzas Op 62 (cello, orchestra) 1969; first performed Cardiff, 27 February 1969.
Welsh Dances: Second Suite Op 64 1969; first performed Merthyr, 16 April 1969. Recorded MFP 2129.
Concerto for Horn and Orchestra Op 65 1969; first performed Llandaff, Glamorgan, 3 June 1969. Recorded Decca SXL 6606.
Investiture Dances Op 66 1969; first performed London, 22 June 1969.
Sinfonietta II Op 67 1969; first performed Cheltenham, Gloucestershire, 1969.
Divertimento Op 69 (small orchestra) 1969; first performed Llandaff, Glamorgan, 15 November 1969.
Symphony No 4 Op 70 1969; first performed Manchester, 4 December 1969.
Sinfonietta III Op 71 1970; first performed Swansea, 10 March 1970. Recorded Decca SXL 6570.
Suite Op 72/1 1970; first performed Southampton, Hampshire, 16 April 1970.
The Sun, the Great Luminary of the Universe Op 76 1970; first performed Swansea, 8 October 1970. Recorded Decca SXL 6570.
Concertino for Trumpet, Horn and Orchestra Op 72/2 1971; first performed Llangefni, Gwynedd, 8 April 1971.
Sinfonietta IV Op 72/3 1971; first performed Rhos, 30 July 1971.
The Hawk Is Set Free Op 72/4 1972; first performed Abergavenny, Gwent, 21 September 1972.
The Floore of Heav'n Op 72/5 1973; first performed London, 30 April 1973.
Symphony No 5 Op 81 1973; first performed London, 6 March 1972. Recorded Decca SXL 6606.
Landscapes Op 86 1975, revised 1975–6; first performed Criccieth, Gwynedd, 8 August 1975; revised version first performed Cardiff, 8 August 1975.
Welsh Airs and Dances (no opus number; symphonic wind band) 1975; first performed Cardiff, 21 August 1975.
French Suite Op 91 (small orchestra) 1977; first performed Cardiff, 13 March 1977.
Passaggio Op 94 1977; first performed Cheltenham, Gloucestershire, 6 July 1977.
The Heaventree of Stars Op 102 1980; broadcast BBC, 5 March 1980.
Lanterne des morts Op 105/2 1981; first performed Cardiff, 21 September 1981.
Quodlibet on Welsh Nursery Tunes (no opus number) 1982; first performed Cardiff, 9 January 1983. Recorded Phoenix DGS 1040.
Hommage à Chopin Op 107/2 1984.
Scenes and Interludes Op 115 (concertante for trumpet, harpsichord, string orchestra) 1984; first performed St Davids, Dyfed, 2 June 1984.
Symphony No 6 Op 116 1984; first performed Cardiff, 15 June 1984.
Welsh Dances: Third Suite Op 123 1985.
Concerto for Violin, Cello, Piano, and Orchestra Op 124 1986; first performed Cheltenham, Gloucestershire, 5 July 1986.
Divisions Op 126 (concertante for horn, harpsichord, string orchestra) 1986; first performed Cardiff, 2 July 1986.
Concerto for Orchestra Op 127 1986; first performed Cardiff, 22 July 1986.
Concerto for Clarinet and Orchestra No 2 Op 128 1987; first performed Manchester, 20 February 1987.

Chamber/instrumental:

String Trio Op 1 1949; first performed Cardiff, 20 March 1950.
Quartet Op 6 (clarinet, violin, viola, cello) 1953–4.
Nocturne No 1 Op 9 (piano) 1956; first performed Swansea, 22 February 1956. Recorded Lyrita RCS 27 m.
Septet Op 10 (clarinet, horn, bassoon, piano, violin, viola, cello) 1956, revised 1973; broadcast BBC, 8 December 1956.
Rondo scherzoso Op 12/1 (trumpet, piano) 1957; first performed Cardiff, 4 July 1957.
Rondo scherzoso Op 12/2 (trombone, piano) 1957; first performed Cardiff, 3 February 1958.
Nocturne No 2 Op 16/1 (piano) 1959; first performed London, 13 March 1959. Recorded Lyrita RCS 27 m.
Sonata No 1 Op 17 (piano) 1959; first performed Cheltenham, Gloucestershire, 12 July 1959. Recorded Lyrita RCS 27 m.
Sonatina Op 18 (clavichord) 1959–63; first performed Bangor, Caernarvonshire, 11 March 1964. Recorded Lyrita RCS 27 m.
Sextet Op 20 (flute, clarinet, bassoon, string trio) 1960; first performed Llandaff, Glamorgan, 28 April 1960.
Sonata No 2 Op 27 (piano) 1962; first performed London, 16 February 1962. Recorded Lyrita RCS 27 m.
Variations Op 28 (flute, harp, clarinet, string quartet) 1962; first performed Anglesey, 7 April 1962.
Fanfare (no opus number; 3 trumpets, 3 trombones, drums) 1963; first performed Cardiff, 14 November 1963.
Divertimento Op 32 (oboe, clarinet, horn, bassoon) 1963; first performed Cardiff, 26 November 1963.
Sonata Op 36 (harp) 1964; first performed Cheltenham, Gloucestershire, 1964.
Toccata alla giga Op 37/1 (organ) 1964; first performed Walsingham, Norfolk, 12 August 1964.
Sonata No 3 Op 40 (piano) 1965; first performed Bangor, Caernarvonshire, 8 March 1965.
String Quartet Op 43 1965; first performed Dynevor, 10 September 1966. Recorded Pye GSGC 14107.
Arabesque (no opus number; violin, piano) 1966.
Intrada Op 37/2 (organ) 1966; first performed Cambridge, 15 July 1967.
Sonata No 4 Op 49 (piano) 1966; first performed Aberystwyth, Cardiganshire, 30 January 1967.
Sonata Op 50 (clarinet, piano) 1967; first performed London, 14 December 1967. Recorded Pye GSGC 14107.
Suite Op 52 (harp) 1967; first performed Dynevor, 7 July 1967.
Nocturnes and Cadenzas Op 53 (clarinet, violin, cello) 1968; first performed Newport, 8 February 1968.
Sonata No 5 Op 57 (piano) 1968; first performed Cardiff, 27 April 1968.
Divertimenti Op 58 (8 instruments) 1968; first performed Cheltenham, Gloucestershire, 11 July 1968.
Sonata No 1 Op 63 (violin, piano) 1969; first performed Cardiff, 8 March 1969.
Sarum Fanfare Op 37/3 (organ) 1970; first performed

Salisbury, Wiltshire, 2 May 1970.
Fantasy Op 68/2 (harp) 1970; first performed London, 14 May 1970.
Sonata No 2 Op 73/1 (violin, piano) 1970; first performed Birmingham, 9 May 1970.
Sonata No 2 Op 73/2 (cello, piano) 1970; first performed London, 15 May 1970.
Piano Trio Op 77 1970; first performed Cardiff, 31 December 1970. Recorded Argo ZRG 691.
Sonata No 3 Op 78/1 (violin, piano) 1971; first performed Cardiff, 2 March 1971. Recorded Argo ZRG 761.
Sonata Op 78/2 (horn, piano) 1971; first performed St Donats, Glamorgan, 28 August 1971.
Sonata No 6 Op 78/3 (piano) 1972; first performed London, 10 March 1972.
Piano Quintet Op 78/4 1972; first performed Lancaster, 2 March 1972.
Ritornelli Op 85/1 (trombone, ensemble) 1974; first performed London, 3 May 1974.
Sonata No 4 Op 89 (violin, piano) 1976; broadcast BBC, 3 March 1976.
Italian Suite Op 92 (recorder, guitar) 1977; first performed London, 4 March 1977.
Sonata No 2 Op 96 (cello, piano) 1977; first performed London, 27 November 1977.
Sonatina Op 98/1 (guitar) 1978.
Sonatina Op 98/2 (2 pianos) 1978; first performed London, 4 October 1978.
Scena Op 100/1 (string quartet) 1979; first performed Portsmouth, May 1979.
Ritornelli Op 100/2 (brass) 1979; first performed Cheltenham, Gloucestershire, June 1979.
Nocturnes and Cadenzas Op 101/2 (flute) 1981; first performed Manchester, 1 April 1981.
Ritornelli Op 104 1981; first performed Bracknell, Berkshire, 26 June 1981.
Quodlibert on Welsh Nursery Tunes (no opus number; brass quintet) 1983; first performed Kimbolton, 22 May 1983.
Masks (no opus number; oboe, bassoon, piano) 1983; first performed Epsom, Surrey, 23 November 1983.
Piano Trio No 2 Op 111 (violin, cello, piano) 1983; first performed Cardiff, 13 March 1984.
Bagatelles (no opus number; oboe, harp) 1984; first performed London, 7 March 1984.
String Quartet No 2 Op 113 1984.
Sonata No 7 Op 114 (piano) 1984.
Sonata (4 clarinets) 1985; first performed Cardiff, 21 January 1986.
Passacaglia and Fugue Op 122 (organ) 1985; first performed Cardiff, 2 June 1985.

Vocal/choral:

Two Songs Op 2 (bass, piano; Fletcher) 1950; first performed Cardiff, 25 November 1955.
Lullaby Op 4/1 (medium voice, piano; anon.) 1950; first performed Cardiff, 15 November 1951.
Carol (no opus number; 2 voices, piano) 1952; first performed Cardiff, 7 December 1953.
Codiad Llaer (no opus number; part song for 2 tenors, 2 basses; Glyn Jones) 1958; first performed Rheinfelden, September 1972.
The Race of Adam Op 23 (masque for soloists, chorus, boys' voices, orchestra, organ) 1961; first performed Llandaff, Glamorgan, 23 June 1961.
Great Art Thou (no opus number; SATB chorus, organ) 1961; first performed Llandaff, Glamorgan, 30 September 1961.
Carol Op 25 (unaccompanied SSA chorus) 1961; first performed Cardiff, 3 December 1961.
Rebecca Op 26 (ballad for unaccompanied SATB chorus) 1961; first performed London, 21 June 1962.
Job Op 24 (bass, mixed chorus, orchestra) 1962, revised 1977; first performed Swansea, 18 May 1962.
Three Medieval Songs Op 30 (unaccompanied SSA chorus) 1963; first performed Farnham, Surrey, 1963.
Every Man's Work (no opus number; SATB chorus, organ) 1964; first performed Llanishen, Glamorgan, 15 March 1964.
Introit (unaccompanied SATB chorus) 1964; broadcast BBC, 27 May 1964.
Danegeld Op 33 (6 episodes for mixed chorus) 1964; first performed Cork, 22 May 1964.
What Tidings Op 38/1 (carol for unaccompanied SATB chorus) 1964; first performed London, 18 December 1964.
Four Welsh Songs (no opus number; unison voices, piano or orchestra) 1964; first performed Newtown, 3 August 1965.
Medieval Carol Op 38/2 (voice, piano) 1965; first performed Cowbridge, Glamorgan, 27 October 1965.
Dives and Lazarus Op 39 (cantata for soloists, chorus) 1965; first performed Farnham, Surrey, 20 May 1965.
Roman Dream Op 54 (soprano, ensemble) 1968; first performed Paris, 16 February 1968.
An Apple Tree and a Pig Op 55 (unaccompanied mixed voices) 1968; first performed London, 17 March 1968.
Barti Ddu Op 59 (chorus, orchestra) 1968; first performed Caernarvon, 24 July 1969.
Eryri (no opus number; soloists, chorus, orchestra) 1969; first performed Caernarvon, 1 July 1969.
Out of the Deep Op 74 (motet for SATB chorus) 1970; first performed Cardiff, 9 March 1971.
Voyagers Op 75 (baritone, male voices, orchestra; White) 1970.
The Tree of Life Op 79 (oratorio for soprano, tenor, chorus, orchestra) 1971; first performed Gloucester, 25 August 1971.
Four Welsh Songs (no opus number; male voices, piano) 1971; first performed San Francisco, 8 October 1971.
St Paul at Malta Op 80 (cantata for tenor, chorus, orchestra) 1971; first performed Stroud, Gloucestershire, 14 October 1971.
Puer Natus (no opus number; carol for voices, organ) 1971; first performed Cardiff, 16 December 1971.
Ieunctid y Dydd (no opus number; mixed voices, organ) 1972; first performed Llandaff, Glamorgan, 5 June 1972.
Ancestor Worship Op 82 (high voice, piano; Humphreys) 1972; first performed Glamorgan, 19 September 1977.
The Silver Swimmer Op 84 (mixed voices, piano duet; White) 1973; first performed Austin, Texas, 10 July 1973.
Five Landscapes—Ynys Mon Op 87 (tenor, piano) 1975; first performed Cardiff, 27 May 1975.
Two Welsh Folk Songs (no opus number; SATB chorus, piano) 1975.
A Contemplation upon Flowers Op 90 1976; first performed Fishguard, Dyfed, 1976.
Sinfonia fidei Op 95 (soprano, tenor, chorus, orchestra) 1977; first performed Llandaff, Glamorgan, 18 June 1977.
Dulcia iuventutis Op 97/1 (male chorus, organ) 1978; first performed Cardiff, 13 January 1978.
Hymnus ante somnum Op 97/2 (male chorus, organ) 1979; first performed Aldeburgh, Suffolk, 23 June 1979.
Great Is the Lord (no opus number; SATB chorus, organ) 1979; first performed Cardiff, 26 November 1979.
Survivors (no opus number; unaccompanied mixed voices) 1979; first performed Dublin, 9 January 1980.
Te Deum Op 105/1 (mixed voices, organ) 1981; first

performed Fishguard, Dyfed, 29 July 1981.
Six Welsh Folksongs (no opus number; arranged for high voice, orchestra) 1981; first performed Vienna, 10 May 1982.
In parasceve Domini III; Nocturno (no opus number; motet for female voices, piano) 1982; first performed Llangollen, Clwyd, July 1982.
Ingravescentem Aetatem Op 108 (mixed chorus, piano duet) 1983; first performed Kansas, 10 April 1983.
Bells of Paradise Op 117 (Christmas cantata for baritone, mixed chorus, orchestra) 1984.
The Silver Hound (opus number; tenor, piano) 1985; first performed London, 6 January 1986.

Opera:

The Beach of Falesa (Jones; after Robert Louis Stevenson) 1973; first performed Cardiff, 26 March 1974.
The Magician Op 88 (Morgan) 1975; broadcast Independent Television, United Kingdom, 11 February 1976.
What the Old Man Does Is Always Right Op 93 (Myfanwy Piper) 1977; first performed Fishguard, Dyfed, July 1977.
The Rajah's Diamond Op 99 1979; broadcast (television) 24 November 1979.
The Trumpet Major Op 103 (Myfanwy Piper; after Hardy) 1981; first performed 1 April 1981.

PUBLICATIONS

On Hoddinott: A.F. Leighton Thomas, "AH", in *Musical Times*, October 1955; B. Hesford, "The Piano Works of AH", in *Musical Opinion*, April 1966; M. Boyd, "*The Beach of Falesa*", in *Musical Times*, March 1974; C. Powell, "H's First Opera", in *Music and Musicians*, March 1974.

* * *

Alun Hoddinott's musical language has remained basically tonal, though his harmony is often complex, using intense chromaticism or artificial chord structures. Although he has spent most of his life in South Wales, his influences are cosmopolitan: specifically Welsh themes seem to appeal little to him and overt references to his Celtic heritage are found mostly in his Suites of Welsh Dances and in a few other miscellaneous occasional pieces. Of course, the fact that several of these pieces stand among Hoddinott's most popular works, together with his preeminence in the Welsh musical establishment, has misled some analysts to categorise him as a nationalist.

Several student works, dating from the period of Hoddinott's undergraduate studies with Arthur Benjamin, were subsequently withdrawn; but these undoubtedly helped him to develop the confident tonal idiom and pellucid instrumentation found in the Clarinet Concerto of 1950. Two years later, in the *Nocturne* for orchestra, Hoddinott paints in richer colours, for which the principal models have been identified as Chopin, Debussy and Bartók. Certainly, the device of developing the melodic argument through constant motivic alterations is typical of Chopin, whereas the fastidious orchestral gradations suggest a deep study of Debussy. However, the most striking feature of this piece is its use of modified ternacy, or palindromic arch structure, a form which has become inextricably linked with Bartók and which was retained by Hoddinott in numerous subsequent compositions.

Hoddinott is not an early music specialist; neither does he appear to have made a self-conscious study of pre-classical works, as a significant number of his peers did, in order to reappraise his own musical vocabulary. Nevertheless, from the mid 1950s onwards, his music features some very real pre-classical traits. One of the most important of these is his tendency to subordinate recognised harmonic structures to contrapuntal considerations.

The coherent marriage of diatonic harmony and closely argued imitative counterpoint is one of the crowning achievements of late Baroque music; above all, of J.S. Bach. Hoddinott's approach in pieces like the "Nottorno" from his 1955 Oboe Concerto is closer to High Renaissance music in its insistence that counterpoint is supreme, (even if—in Hoddinott's case—this leads to empirical or, to modern ears at least, awkward harmonies). His melodies are usually of short span, featuring very recognisable intervallic shapes, which provide an invaluable signpost within his sometimes ornate contrapuntal discourses. This liking for distinctive intervals, not surprisingly, led to a desire to base pieces upon artificial chord structures. An obvious precedent for this latter practice is Skriabin and in at least one piece—*The Sun, The Great Luminary of the Universe*—Hoddinott has achieved a potent update of the Skriabinesque "tone poem" where the colouristic properties of (largely synthetic) harmony on which the work is based obviously complements its extra-musical message. One distinctive interval which Hoddinott particularly favours is the tritone; like Bartók (who had developed procedures used by Liszt and Wagner), tensions inherent in this interval are expanded into conflicts between tonal centres separated by a tritone, leading in turn to struggles for supremacy on a large scale, which can sustain the harmonic argument on a "macro" level.

Hoddinott's prolific output has spanned all the standard categories and shows fluency and self-confidence; he has freely absorbed many styles, including Debussian Impressionism, Bartók, serialism and even aleatoric elements. His instrumental writing is colourful and assured and the rhythmic drive of much of his work produces a great immediacy, which has contributed to his popularity as a commissioned artist—Hoddinott has an impressive catalogue of commissions from prominent virtuosi and orchestras, as well as from international music festivals, radio and television. Now in his 60s and freed from the routines of teaching and administration, he is composing with undiminished vigour.

—Paul Horner

HÖLLER, York. German. Born in Leverkusen, 11 January 1944. Initially self-taught; piano, harmony and ear-training from 1956; Cologne Musikhochschule (composition under Bernd Alois Zimmermann, electronic composition under Herbert Eimert, piano under Alfons Kontarsky and E. Schmitz-Göhr, orchestral conducting under W. van der Nahmer), 1963–70, state degree in music education, 1967; concurrently studied philosophy and musicology, University of Cologne; Ferienkurse für Neue Musik, Darmstadt (under Pierre Boulez), 1965; research (under Karlheinz Stockhausen), electronic studio, West Germany Radio. Pianist, debut 1960; solo coach (under Hans Zender), Theatre of the City of Bonn, 1968–9; half-year residence, Cité

Internationale des Arts, Paris, 1974–5; teacher of analysis and music theory, Cologne Musikhochschule, 1976–89; residency, Villa Massimo, Rome, 1984–5, and IRCAM, Paris, 1986; composition seminar, Freiburg Conservatory of Music, 1988; director, WDR Electronic Music Studio, Cologne, since 1990. Recipient: Bernd Alois Zimmermann Prize, City of Cologne, 1979; Music Promotion Prize (Forder-Preis), City of Cologne, 1979; Chevalier de l'Ordre des Arts et des Lettres, France, 1986; UNESCO International Composers' Rostrum Prize (for *Piano Concerto*), Paris, 1987; Association of French Theatre and Music Critics prize (for *Der Meister und Margarita*), 1989; Rolf Liebermann Prize for best European opera premiered between 1987 and 1990 (for *Der Meister und Margarita*), 1990. Mailing address: c/o Boosey & Hawkes GmbH, Prinz Albert Strasse 26, W-5300 Bonn 1, Germany.

Publishers: Breitkopf & Hartel; Boosey & Hawkes.

Symphonies/orchestral:

Topic (large orchestra) 1967; first performed Darmstadt, 1970.
Concerto for Piano and Orchestra 1970; in progress.
Chroma (orchestra, electronically processed organ) 1972–4; first performed Berlin, 1978.
Arcus (chamber orchestra, electronically processed instruments on tape) 1978.
Umbra (orchestra, tape) 1979–80; first performed Saarbrücken, 1980.
Mythos (chamber orchestra, electronically processed sound) 1979–80; first performed Cologne, 1981.
Résonance (orchestra, computer sounds on tape) 1981.
Schwarze Halbinsein (large orchestra, electronic tape) 1982.
Piano Concerto 1983–4; first performed London, 3 December 1985.
Magische Klangestalt (large orchestra) 1984; first performed Hamburg, 16 March 1986.
Improvisation sur le nom de Pierre Boulez (17 instruments) 1984–5; first performed Baden-Baden, 31 March 1985.
Fanal (trumpet, orchestra) 1989–90; first performed Paris, 17 June 1991.
Pensées (piano, large orchestra, electronics) 1990–1; first performed Cologne, 1993.
Aura (large orchestra) 1991–2; first performed Chicago, 1993.

Chamber/instrumental:

Fünf Klavierstücke (piano) 1964.
Diaphonie: Hommage à Béla Bartók (2 pianos) 1965, revised 1974; first performed Berlin, 1965; revised version first performed Cologne, 26 February 1984.
Drei Stücke (string quartet) 1966.
Sonate informelle (Sonata No 1) (piano) 1968.
Sonata (cello) 1969.
Epitaph (for Jan Palach) (violin, piano) 1969.
Tangens (cello, electric guitar, electric organ/piano, 2 synthesizers) 1973.
Klanggitter (cello, piano, synthesizer, tape) 1976.
Antiphon (string quartet, tape) 1977.
Moments musicaux (flute, piano) 1979.
Pas de trois (violin, cello, double bass) 1982.
Sonata No 2: Hommage à Franz Liszt (piano) 1987; first performed Frankfurt, 7 January 1989.

Vocal/choral:

Herr, es ist Zeit (soprano, 8 instruments; Rilke) 1966.
Traumspiel (soprano, large orchestra, tape; after Strindberg) 1983; first performed Metz, 18 November 1983.

Opera:

Der Meister und Margarita (after Bulgakov) 1985–9; first performed Paris, 20 May 1989.

Other:

Horizont (4-track electronics) 1972.
Klanggitter (electronic) 1976.

PUBLICATIONS

By Höller: "Kritisch Untersuchung der seriellen Kompositionstechnik", dissertation, Cologne, 1967; "Zufall und Notwendigkeit", in *Horizont*, 1972; "Resonance: Composition Today" and "Composition of the Gestalt, or the Making of an Organism", in *Contemporary Music Review*, 1 (1), 1984.

* * *

York Höller is one of the most individual and personal of composers working today. His development has been largely free of the fashionable and ephemeral. He instead pursues an independent course with a rigour and single-mindedness that is as rare among composers as it is striking.

In this he resembles his teacher Bernd Alois Zimmermann who, while a leading figure of the post-war avant-garde and always a radical in his compositional method, remained aloof from the merely dogmatic. Zimmermann was happy to use conventional forms such as the concerto and opera, and within these adopted a more dynamic and directly expressive musical language than that of most of his contemporaries. A similar immediacy, combined with a clear technical control, is characteristic of Höller's own music. His use of musical quotation is another inheritance from Zimmermann, whose music he continues to admire and whose *Die Soldaten* (1970) Höller counts as one of the greatest operatic works of the century.

Quite apart from his own (to date only) opera *Der Meister und Margarita*, Höller's work is often dramatic at root. Some works such as *Schwarze Halbinsein* and *Traumspiel*, although intended for concert performance and calling on substantial orchestral resources, are in effect miniature operas. *Traumspiel* sets for soprano and orchestra sections of Strindberg's *Dreamplay*. These settings are separated from each other by explosive and highly colourful orchestral interludes. Höller has also shown increasing interest in the abstract drama of the concerto and concertante-like forms. His *Piano Concerto* is a masterpiece, Lisztian in its full-blown opposition of piano and orchestra. Moreover, the interplay between the different worlds of live and electronic or electronically transformed sound that features in much of his output is often conceived in dramatic terms, as in the electronic "shadowing" of the live orchestral sound in *Umbra* and in the warping of natural instrumental colour in *Arcus*.

In *Der Meister und Margarita* these different worlds are echoed in the contradictory realities of Bulgakov's multilayered novel on which it is closely based. The results of the Devil's visit to Stalinist Moscow of the 1930s provide Höller with the opportunity to explore his various compositional preoccupations to the fullest extent yet. It is an enthralling work on a grand scale and contains some of the richest and most compelling music he has yet written.

In Wagnerian fashion the centre of gravity of the opera's musical argument lies with the orchestra (together with the tape when used). At no time does it have a role subsidiary to that of the voices; rather it comments on and informs the stage action. In fact, at a number of crucial points it leaves the stage behind, in the vivid interludes between the various scenes and in the ballet at the heart of the second act depicting Satan's Ball.

Alongside this use of the orchestra is an important lyrical element which in part derives from the composer's "Gestalt" method of composition. "Gestalt" is not a word that translates easily into English, meaning at the same time form, shape and whole. Höller uses it to label a method in which a single melody, or more precisely a melodic formula, is made to govern all aspects of a work's construction, from the large-scale formal design to the smallest detail of pitch, harmony and rhythm. Stockhausen does something similar in works from *Mantra* onwards. But for Stockhausen, given that every element of the piece is defined in advance, the working out of this formula can become little more than a process, no matter how absorbing. While no less disciplined, Höller is a much more intuitive musician for whom method is the means, not the end.

—William Mival

HOLLIGER, Heinz. Swiss. Born at Langenthal, 21 May 1939. Educated at Bern, Paris and Basle, under Emile Cassagnaud (oboe), Yvonne Lefebure (piano), Sandor Veress and Pierre Boulez (composition). Married to harpist Ursula Hanggi Holliger. Professor of oboe, Freiburg Music Academy, since 1965. International concert and recording soloist. Recipient: Sonning-Preis, Copenhagen; Musikpreis der Stadt Frankfurt; Komponistpries des Schweizerischen Tonkünstlervereins. Mailing address: c/o B. Schott's Söhne, Musikverlag, Postfach, D-6500 Mainz, Germany.

Publisher: B. Schott's Söhne, Musikverlag, Postfach, D-6500 Mainz, Germany.

Symphonies/orchestral:

Elis—Drei Nachtstücke (arranged from piano version) 1963, revised 1973; first performed Basle, 3 May 1973.

Siebengesang (oboe, orchestra, singers, loudspeakers) 1966–7; first performed Rotterdam, 17 June 1968.

Pneuma (large wind ensemble, percussion, organ, radios; also version for small wind ensemble) 1970; first performed Donaueschingen, 18 October 1970; small ensemble version first performed Amsterdam, 4 July 1971.

Atembogen 1974–5; first performed Basle, 6 June 1975.

Ubungen zu Scardanelli (small orchestra, tape; part of *Scardanelli-Zyklus*) 1978–85; first performed Donaueschingen, 18 October 1985.

Ad marginem (chamber orchestra, tape) 1983; first performed Baden-Baden, 8 March 1985.

Engführung (chamber orchestra; part of *Ubungen ze Scardanelli* cycle) 1983–4; first performed Donaueschingen, 18 October 1985.

Der ferne Klang (chamber orchestra, tape; part of *Ubungen zu Scardanelli* cycle) 1983–4; first performed Donaueschingen, 18 October 1985.

Schaufelrad (chamber orchestra, 4 or 5 female singers ad lib; part of *Ubungen ze Scardanelli* cycle) 1983–4; first performed Donaueschingen, 18 October 1985.

Turm-Musik (flute/alto flute/bass flute, small orchestra, tape) 1984; first performed Basle, 17 January 1985.

Tonscherben 1985; first performed Geneva, 26 September 1985.

Zwei Liszt-Transkriptionen (large orchestra) 1986; first performed Basle, 12 February 1987.

Chamber/instrumental:

Sonata (oboe) 1956.

Elis: Drei Nachtstücke für Klavier (piano) 1961, revised 1966; first performed Basle, 18 January 1962.

Sequenzen über Johannes I, 32 (harp) 1962; first performed Celerina, 7 August 1962.

Mobile (oboe, harp) 1962; first performed Paris, 13 February 1963.

Trio (oboe/cor anglais, viola, harp) 1966; first performed Paris, 15 February 1967.

"h" (string quintet) 1968; first performed Darmstadt, 29 August 1969.

Cardiophonie (oboe, 3 magnetophones) 1971; first performed Zagreb, 8 May 1971.

Studie über Mehrklänge (oboe) 1971; first performed Tokyo, 20 November 1974.

Lied (flute or alto flute or bass flute) 1971; first performed Basle, 4 December 1972.

Kreis (4–7 wind instruments; or 3–6 wind instruments and 1 string instrument; or tape) 1971–2; first performed Graz, 14 October 1972.

String Quartet 1973; first performed Royan, 23 March 1975. Recorded Wergo 60084.

Chaconne (cello) 1975; first performed Zurich, 2 May 1976. Recorded Wergo 60084.

Come and Go (versions for 3 violas; or 3 flutes/alto flutes/bass flutes; or 3 clarinets/bass clarinets) 1976–7; first performed flutes, Tokyo, 1 March 1983; clarinets, Zurich, 2 March 1987.

Sommerkanon IV (chamber group; part of *Ubungen zu Scardanelli* cycle) 1978; first performed Donaueschingen, 18 October 1985.

Fünf Stücke (organ, tape) 1980; first performed Donaueschingen, 18 October 1980.

"(t)air(e)" (flute; part of *Scardanelli-Zyklus*) 1980–3; first performed Strasbourg, 1 October 1983.

Studie II (oboe) 1981; first performed Geneva, September 1982.

Trema (viola; versions for cello and violin) 1981, 1983; first performed (viola) Paris, 1 July 1981; (cello) Baden-Baden, 10 May 1983; (violin) Paris, 19 March 1984.

Duo (violin, cello) 1982; first performed Baden-Baden, 10 May 1983.

Vier Lieder ohne Worte (violin, piano) 1982–3; first performed Saarbrücken, 17 May 1985.

Choral a 4 (2 violins, 2 violas, 2 cellos; or alto flute, clarinet, 2 horns, viola, cello; or cor anglais, clarinet, horn, trombone, 2 cellos; part of *Ubungen zu Scardanelli* cycle) 1983; first performed Donaueschingen, 18 October 1985.

Choral a 8 (chamber group; part of *Ubungen zu Scardanelli* cycle) 1983; first performed Donaueschingen, 18 October 1985.

Eisblumen (2 violins, 2 violas, 2 cellos, double bass; part of *Ubungen zu Scardanelli* cycle) 1985; first performed Donaueschingen, 18 October 1985.

Quodlibet pour Aurèle (sur fond familial) (flute, with flute, 2 violins, horn) 1986; first performed Basle, 2 February 1986.

Praeludium, Arioso und Passacaglia (harp) 1987; first performed Saarbrucken, 12 May 1988.

Felicity's Shake-Wag (violin, cello) 1988; first performed Berne, 17 December 1988.

Quintett für Klavier und vier Bläser (piano, wind quartet) 1989; first performed Vienna, 25 March 1990.

Vocal/choral:

Drei Liebeslieder (alto, orchestra; Trakl) 1960; first performed Geneva, 12 May 1962.

Erde und Himmel (tenor, flute, violin, viola, cello, harp; Gwerder) 1961; first performed Amsterdam, 10 June 1963.

Schwarzgewobene Trauer (soprano, oboe, cello, harpsichord; Weder) 1961–2, revised 1966; first performed Basle, 5 December 1962.

Vier Miniaturen (soprano, oboe d'amore, celeste, harp; Magdeburg, anon.) 1962–3; first performed Berne, 21 March 1965.

Glühende Rätsel (9 altos, ensemble; Sachs) 1964; first performed Basle, 14 January 1982.

Dona nobis pacem (12 unaccompanied singers) 1968–9; first performed Graz, 21 October 1971. Recorded Wergo 60070.

Psalm (unaccompanied mixed choir; Celan) 1971; first performed Stuttgart, 10 June 1972.

Die Jahreszeiten (unaccompanied mixed choir, with instruments ad lib; Scardanelli, Hölderlin; part of *Scardanelli–Zyklus*) 1975, 1978, 1979; first performed (Spring, Summer Autumn, Winter I) Donaueschingen, 21 October 1977; Spring, Summer, Autumn II, Stuttgart, 19 June 1982; Spring, Summer, Autumn, Winter III, Graz, 17 October 1983; Winter II, Donaueschingen, 19 October 1985. Recorded Wergo 60084.

Not I (soprano, tape; Beckett) 1978–80; first performed Basle, 14 January 1982.

Gesänge der Frühe (choir, orchestra, tape; Schumann, Hölderlin) 1987; first performed Cologne, 4 March 1988.

Jisei (counter tenor or alto, 2 tenors, bass, Japanese temple chimes ad lib; Basho, Fuso, Saimaro, Saimu, Meister) 1988; first performed Fribourg, 9 July 1988.

Variazioni su nulla (counter tenor or alto, 2 tenors, bass; Ungaretti) 1988; first performed Fribourg, 9 July 1988.

Opera/theatre:

Der magische Tänzer (2 singers, 2 dancers, 2 mimes, choir, orchestra, tape; Sachs) 1963–5; first performed Basle, 26 April 1970.

Come and Go (chamber opera, 3 flutes [or flute, alto flute, bass flute], 3 clarinets [or clarinet, bass clarinet, contrabass clarinet] 3 violins; Beckett; also concert version) 1976–7; first performed Hamburg, 16 February 1978.

Not I (monodrama, soprano, tape; Beckett) 1979–80; first performed Avignon, 15 July 1980.

What Where (baritone, 3 bass-baritones, 4 trombones, 2 percussionists; Beckett) 1988; first performed Frankfurt, 19 May 1989.

* * *

In the early years of Heinz Holliger's compositional career, the period of *Glühende Rätsel* and *Der magische Tänzer*, his adherence to the conventions of late serialism gave away little enough of the much more individual music which was to follow. Even so, his keen literary sensitivity, and preference for florid and unusual tone-colours, raised these works above the modish eclecticism of much mid-1960s composition. Experience as a uniquely gifted and versatile oboist, and originator of new performing techniques (for example in collaboration with Luciano Berio and Vinko Globokar), probably encouraged his transition from the cautiously extended traditional virtuosity of *Siebengesang* (which could still almost be called an "oboe concerto") to the systematic exploitation of extreme performing situations.

In the intentionally exhausting *Cardiophonie*, for example, the oboist's heartbeat is amplified, gradually accelerating as the music accumulates physical stress; the *Studie über Mehrklänge* consists almost entirely of an uninterrupted chordal flux in which the oboe completely loses its traditional character. Holliger's interest in denatured vocal and instrumental practices, in contrast to Kagel's superficially similar experiments, has a more serious, even tragic, intention behind it. His *Psalm* (on a bleakly blasphemous text by Paul Celan, who had taken his own life shortly before) retreats painfully from an unbearably literal "text setting" to atomise the poem in a stream of unprecedented vocal behaviour; his *String Quartet* describes a long downward curve from hysterical activity to impoverished, detuned whisperings, with hardly a recognisable "note" at any stage.

In Holliger's work, deformed and rarefied sonorities take on a poetic, almost lyrical function; it is hardly surprising that he has chosen to set no less than three of Samuel Beckett's plays as music-theatre compositions—with, it must be said, mixed results. *Come and Go*, the most sophisticated of the three, expands Beckett's "dramaticule" into a sequence of gradually disintegrating refractions of itself in several languages, achieving memorability through its meticulously cavalier attitude to the text. In contrast *Not I*, a more "straightforward" setting, does little apart from slowing down and obscuring a piece of drama which depends crucially on breathless speed and absolute clarity.

Another writer with whom Holliger has shown profound sympathies is Friedrich Hölderlin, whose late poems provide the textual framework and atmosphere for the *Scardanelli-Zyklus*. The cumulative power of this evening-long cycle of interlinked vocal and instrumental pieces has scarcely been approached in recent years, with its absolutely assured handling of a wide but carefully-chosen variety of resources, its exquisitely poised melancholia and its refusal to employ anything resembling received expressive means.

—Richard Barrett

HOLLOWAY, Robin (Greville). British/English. Born in Leamington Spa, 19 October 1943. Educated at St Paul's Cathedral Choir School, London; King's College School, London; King's College, Cambridge, 1961–4, M.A.; New College, Oxford, 1965–7, Ph.D., D.Mus. Research fellow, Caius College, Cambridge, 1969–75; lecturer in music, University of Cambridge, since 1975. Mailing address: Gonville and Caius College, Cambridge CB2 1TA, England.

Publisher: Boosey & Hawkes.

Symphonies/orchestral:

Concertino No 1 Op 2 (small orchestra) 1964, revised 1968–9; first performed Blackpool, Lancashire, 1964; revised version first performed London, 14 March 1969.
Concerto Op 6 (organ, wind) 1965–6; first performed St Albans, Hertfordshire, 1 July 1967.
First Concerto for Orchestra Op 8 1966–9; first performed Glasgow, 25 April 1973.
Concertino No 2 Op 10 (small orchestra) 1967, 1974; first performed London, 8 January 1975.
Divertimento No 1 Op 11 (amateur orchestra, piano obbligato) 1968; first performed Cambridge, 9 June 1968.
Scenes from Schumann Op 13 1970; first performed Cheltenham, Gloucestershire, 10 July 1970.
Domination of Black Op 23 1973–4; first performed London, 8 August 1974.
Romanza Op 31 (violin, small orchestra) 1976; first performed London, 1978. Recorded Chandos ABRD 1056.
Second Concerto for Orchestra Op 40 1978–9; first performed Glasgow, 22 September 1979.
Idyll Op 42 (small orchestra) 1979–80; first performed Cheltenham, Gloucestershire, 17 July 1981.
Horn Concerto Op 43 1979–80; divided for practical reasons into two smaller works:
Sonata Op 43a (horn, orchestra) 1979–80; first performed London, 1988.
Adagio and Rondo Op 43b (horn, orchestra) 1979–80; first performed Cambridge, 31 July 1987.
Diptych Op 23a (from *Domination of Black*) 1980; first performed Munich, 2 December 1983.
Ode Op 45 (wind quartet, strings) 1980; first performed London, 4 June 1980.
Men Marching Op 50 No 1 (brass band) 1981–2; first performed Leeds, Yorkshire, 26 September 1982.
From Hills and Valleys Op 50 No 2 (brass band) 1981–2; first performed London, 19 February 1984.
Serenata notturna Op 52 (4 horns, small orchestra) 1982; first performed London, 9 December 1984.
Second Idyll Op 54 (small orchestra) 1982–3; first performed London, 10 October 1983.
Seascape and Harvest Op 55 1983–4; first performed Birmingham, 29 April 1986.
Viola Concerto Op 56 1983–4; first performed London, 7 September 1985.
Romanza Op 59 (oboe, strings) 1984; first performed Peterborough, Northamptonshire, 30 August 1986.
Ballad Op 61 (harp, orchestra) 1984–5; first performed Cheltenham, Gloucestershire, 28 July 1985.
Bassoon Concerto Op 63 1984; first performed Newcastle-upon-Tyne, 8 January 1986.
Serenade in G Op 64 (strings) 1986.
Inquietus Op 66 1986; first performed London, 3 April 1987.
Panorama (for the 40th birthday of Prince Charles) 1988; first performed London, 28 March 1989.
Double Concerto for Clarinet and Saxophone Op 68 1988; first performed London, 1989.
Concerto for Violin Op 70 1990; first performed Manchester, 1991.
Entrance; Carousing; Embarkation Op 71 (symphonic wind band) 1990.
Serenade in E (strings) 1990.

Chamber/instrumental:

Garden Music Op 1 (flute, oboe, clarinet, bassoon, horn, percussion, piano, violin, cello) 1962; first performed Cambridge, 1962.
Music for Eliot's "Sweeney Agonistes" Op 4 (quintet) 1965.
Fantasy Pieces (on the Heine "Leiderkreis" of Schumann) Op 16 (piano, 2 flutes/piccolos, oboe, clarinet, bassoon, horn, trumpet, 2 violins, viola, cello, double bass) 1971; first performed Oxford, 11 December 1971.
Evening with Angels Op 17 (2 flutes/piccolos, oboe/cor anglais, 2 clarinets/1 E♭ clarinet/1 bass clarinet, bassoon, horn, trumpet, trombone, tuba, celeste, 2 violins, viola, cello, double bass) 1972; first performed London, 1973.
Divertimento No 2 Op 18 (flute/piccolo, 2 oboes/1 cor anglais, 2 clarinets, 2 bassoons, 2 horns) 1972.
Concertino No 3 (Homage to Weill) Op 29 (flute, clarinet, alto saxophone, bassoon, horn, trumpet, trombone, 2 percussion, 2 violins) 1975; first performed Farnham, Surrey, 23 January 1977.
Clarissa Symphony Op 30a (from the opera; tenor, soprano, orchestra; Richardson) 1976, 1979, 1982; first performed Birmingham, 9 December 1982.
The Rivers of Hell Op 34 (flute/piccolo/alto flute, oboe/cor anglais, clarinet/E♭ clarinet/bass clarinet, percussion, piano, viola, cello) 1977; first performed London, 1 November 1977.
Three Slithy Toves (2 clarinets) 1978.
Serenade in C Op 41 (clarinet, bassoon, horn, 2 violins, viola, cello, double bass) 1978–9; first performed London, 18 March 1979.
Aria Op 44 (flute/alto flute/piccolo, oboe/cor anglais, clarinet, bassoon, horn, trumpet, trombone, percussion, 2 violins, viola, cello, double bass) 1979–80; first performed London, 1980.
Sonata Op 47 (violin) 1981; first performed Linz, Austria, 29 September 1981.
Tune en rondeau (oboe) 1981.
Suite (saxophone) 1982.
Showpiece (Concertino No 4) Op 53 (flute/piccolo, oboe, clarinet, bassoon, horn, trumpet, trombone, percussion, piano, 2 violins, viola, cello, double bass) 1982–3; first performed London, 23 May 1983.
Serenade in E♭ Op 57 (wind quintet, string quintet) 1983–4; first performed London, 26 June 1985.
First Partita (horn) 1985.
Second Partita (horn) 1985.
Serenade in G Op 64 (2 violins, 2 violas, 2 cellos, double bass) 1986; first performed Keele, Staffordshire, 14 May 1987.
Organ Fantasy Op 65 1986; first performed Windsor, Berkshire, 2 May 1987.
Brass Quintet (Divertimento No 5) Op 67 1986–7; first performed Warwick, 5 July 1988.
The Spacious Firmament Op 69 (chorus, orchestra; Blake) 1990.
Hymn to the Senses Op 70 (unaccompanied chorus; J. Fuller) 1990.
Lord, What Is Man? (unaccompanied SATB chorus; Crashaw) 1991.

Vocal/choral:

Three Poems of William Empson Op 3 (mezzo-soprano, flute/piccolo/alto flute, clarinet/bass clarinet/alto saxophone, percussion, harpsichord, double bass) 1964–5.
Music for Eliot's "Sweeney Agonistes" Op 4 (6 players and speakers: flute/piccolo, clarinet/alto saxophone/soprano

saxophone, cornet, trombone, percussion) 1965; concert version first performed Oxford, 13 June 1967.
In Chymich Art Op 5 (soprano, baritone, nonet) 1965–6.
Four Housman Fragments Op 7 (soprano, piano) 1965–6; first performed Oxford, 22 May 1966.
Melodrama Op 9 (speaker, male chorus, ensemble) 1967.
Tender Only to One Op 12 (soprano; Stevie Smith) 1968–9; first performed Bingley, Yorkshire, February 1976.
The Wind Shifts Op 14 (high voice, strings; Stevens) 1970; first performed Tenbury Wells, 22 May 1971.
Banal Sojourn Op 15 (high voice, piano; Stevens) 1971; first performed (incomplete) Wangford, Suffolk, 12 July 1971; complete version first performed London, 23 October 1973.
Georgian Songs Op 19 (baritone, piano) 1972; first performed (incomplete) Cambridge, 1972; complete version first performed London, 1978.
Cantata on the Death of God Op 20 (soloists, chorus, orchestra; Nietzsche) 1972–3.
Five Little Songs About Death Op 21 (soprano; Stevie Smith) 1972–3; first performed Sunderland, November 1974.
Five Madrigals Op 22 (unaccompanied chorus; Joyce, Eliot) 1973; first performed London, 1 May 1975.
Lights Out Op 24 (baritone, piano; Edward Thomas) 1974; first performed London, 10 April 1975.
In the Thirtieth Year Op 25 (tenor, piano; Cunningham) 1974; first performed London, 10 April 1975.
Author of Light Op 26 (alto, piano; Jacobean texts) 1974; first performed London, 10 April 1975.
The Leaves Cry Op 27 (soprano, piano; Stevens, Christina Rossetti) 1974; first performed London, 10 April 1975.
Sea Surface Full of Clouds Op 28 (soloists, small chorus, chamber orchestra; Stevens) 1974–5; first performed London, 1975. Recorded Chandos ABRD 1056.
This Is Just to Say Op 32 (tenor, piano; W.C. Williams) 1977; first performed Aldeburgh, Suffolk, 16 June 1977.
Nursery Rhymes (Divertimento No 3) Op 33a (soprano, wind quintet; trad.) 1977; first performed London, 19 June 1982.
Conundrums (Divertimento No 4) Op 33b (soprano, wind quintet; trad.) 1977–9; first performed Glasgow, 23 January 1983.
The Blue Doom of Summer Op 35 No 1 (voice, harp; Firbank) 1977; first performed London, 27 September 1984.
Willow Cycle Op 35 No 2 (voice, harp; Shakespeare, Raleigh, trad.) 1977; first performed Aldeburgh, Suffolk, 23 June 1978.
Hymn for Voices Op 36 (unaccompanied chorus) 1977; first performed Bath, 28 May 1978.
From High Windows Op 37 (baritone, piano; Larkin) 1977; first performed Huntingdon, 8 March 1978.
The Consolation of Music Op 38 No 1 (unaccompanied chorus; Herrick, Strode) 1977; first performed London, 22 January 1979.
He-She-Together Op 38 No 2 (unaccompanied chorus; Joyce) 1978; first performed London, 21 June 1980.
Killing Time (soprano; Auden. Stevie Smith, Raleigh) 1978.
The Noon's Repose Op 39 (tenor, harp; T.S. Eliot, Stevens, Marvell) 1978–9; first performed (incomplete) Aldeburgh, Suffolk, 9 June 1979; complete version first performed London, 8 July 1985.
Divertimento No 4 Op 33b (soprano, wind quintet) 1979.
A Medley of Nursery Rhymes and Conundrums Op 33c (arranged for mezzo-soprano, piano; trad.) 1979; first performed Cambridge, 22 February, 1979.
Wherever We May Be Op 46 (soprano, piano; Graves) 1980–1; first performed St Ives, Cornwall, 9 September 1982.
Brand Op 48 (dramatic ballad for soloists, chorus, orchestra; after Ibsen) 1981.
The Lover's Well Op 49 (bass-baritone, piano; Hill) 1981; first performed Cambridge, 26 April 1984.
Women in War Op 51 (4 voices, piano) 1982.
Anthem (unaccompanied chorus; Bridges) 1982.
Moments of Vision Op 58 (speaker, quartet) 1984.
On Hope (soprano, mezzo-soprano, string quartet) 1984.
The Spacious Firmament Op 69 1990; first performed Birmingham, 1991.

Opera:

Clarissa Op 30 1976; first performed London, 1990.

PUBLICATIONS

By Holloway: *Debussy and Wagner*, Eulenberg Books, 1978; chapters on Wagner and Berg in *Opera on Record*, London, 1979–1983; in *The Music of Alexander Goehr*, London, 1980; in *The Britten Companion*, London, 1984; on Schubert and Wolf in *Lieder on Record*, Cambridge, 1986; in *Salome*, Cambridge, 1990; in *Elektra*, Cambridge, 1991.

On Holloway: special issue of *Tempo*, 129, 1979; Paul Griffiths (interview) in *New Voices, New Personalities: British Composers in the 1980s*, London, 1985.

Robin Holloway comments:

I am trying to write music which, though conversant with most of the revolutionary technical innovations of the last 80 years or so, and by no means turning its back on them, nonetheless keeps a continuity of language and expressive intention with the classics and romantics of the past.

* * *

Robin Holloway studied at King's College, Cambridge, then New College Oxford (where he began his thesis which became the book *Debussy and Wagner*), finally obtaining a research fellowship at Gonville and Caius College, Cambridge where he completed his thesis. In 1975, he was appointed lecturer for the Music Faculty at Cambridge University, where he has remained ever since.

Holloway's principal composition teacher was Alexander Goehr, and Holloway's first works were tautly composed serial pieces written in an uncompromisingly modernist idiom under the influence of his teacher as well as of serial Stravinsky, Boulez and the later Tippett. A large quantity of smaller pieces in this style, such as the *Concertino No 1* and the *Concerto* for organ and wind were followed by Holloway's first large-scale work, the *First Concerto for Orchestra*, completed in 1969. This features a rich and fluently handled orchestral palette; there are already signs of breaking free from the constraints of the modernist aesthetic—a Brahms song is quoted at the work's climax.

Holloway's next work, *Scenes from Schumann*, did indeed depart radically from the accepted canons of modernism. Each movement is based upon a Schumann song, subjected to many types of rearrangement, decoration, reharmonisation and rhythmic dislocation, as well as incorporating discrete quotes from other works of German Romanticism (as suggested by the texts or titles).

The movements trace a progressive distancing from the

originals, the final movement "Spring-Night-Rounds" being a very free fantasy around material from Schumann. Holloway has stated that his attention was to "get inside the Schumann songs and send them out in different directions", but in fact the work marked the beginning of his own compositional maturity, for in it he discovered and came to terms with his preference for richly chromatic harmony with a strongly tonal, often late-Romantic flavour.

There immediately followed a number of works pursuing the same line of thought; some, such as the *Fantasy Pieces* were again directly based upon Schumann (in this case the *Liederkreis* cycle), while others pay homage to the whole German Romantic ethos, as is the case with the huge orchestral work *Domination of Black*. The harmony in the latter, while still strongly tonal in parts (some sections are very distantly based on the Schumann *Kerner-Lieder*), begins to develop along more idiosyncratic non-tonal paths (as in the movement entitled "Summer Rain"), and the cantata *Sea Surface Full of Clouds* (on Wallace Stevens texts) makes further inroads in this direction. Here, for the first time in several years, Holloway eschews all quotes or referentially tonal material, employing instead a non-tonal but richly consonant harmonic language, at once transparently consistent and highly atmospheric, with a delicate orchestral colouring to match. The vocal writing is supple, expressive and utterly natural. The following year saw the composition of Holloway's first and so far only opera, *Clarissa*, completed within an extraordinary compositional burst of some three weeks. Holloway cunningly distilled Richardson's mammoth novel into a compact, two-act libretto, exposing the main outlines of the story and focusing as much as the drama as possible onto Clarissa and her suitor, later violator, Lovelace. The music mirrors the claustrophobic obsessiveness of the plot in cloying harmony of almost Bergian intensity, finally breaking out into quotes from a Hugo Wolf song and a Bach chorale as the heroine undergoes her *Liebestod*; as usual with Holloway, these quotes are not merely flights of fancy but have been carefully woven into the texture of the opera before making their presence explicit. Being uncommissioned, *Clarissa* had to wait 14 years for its first stage production, at the English National Opera, on which occasion it was revealed to be one of the most powerful British operas since Britten.

Holloway's next works returned increasingly to the constructivist techniques with which he began his career, but the experience gained since *Scenes from Schumann* gave the music far greater harmonic control and aural coherence. The two most ambitious such pieces, the chamber work *Aria* and the *Second Concerto for Orchestra* display an exuberant abandon in polyrhythmic layering and stylistic cross-cutting reminiscent of Ives, Grainger and Carter. The *Second Concerto*, arguably Holloway's finest orchestral work to date, unites within its three movements wildly disparate material (including scraps of Neopolitain songs, Chopin, Wagner and the English Hymnal) through a carefully worked-out intervallic scheme, allowing even the densest passages, such as the nightmarish central barcarolle, to be audibly related to the whole.

Since this watershed, Holloway has pursued a quirky, unpredictable path through the entire history of Western music, regarding any material as possible fodder for the quasi-cubist dissection he had previously applied to German Romanticism. In the *Serenade in C*, Mozartian clichés are bizarrely distorted and transformed; some pieces treat neo-Baroque figuration in a similar manner (the organ interlude in *Brand*, the *Romanza* for oboe and strings), while others, such as the *Ballad* for harp and orchestra, seem to deal with the English "pastoral" idiom of Finzi or Vaughan Williams. Sometimes Holloway fashions idiosyncratic connections between diverse styles: the slow movement of the *Serenade in E* for strings, mysteriously weaves together passages from Purcell's *Dido and Aeneas*, Brahms's *Horn Trio*, a Wagner leitmotif from the *Ring* and Tchaikovsky's *Pathétique Symphony*, exposing their common rhythmic and melodic contours.

The more recent orchestral works such as *Seascape and Harvest* and *Panorama* return to late Romantic territory with a new-found lack of inhibition which has infuriated some critics but whose originality is never in doubt, most especially in the former, a luxuriantly orchestrated two-movement structure made to measure for its dedicatees, Simon Rattle and his City of Birmingham Symphony Orchestra.

Always a prolific composer, Holloway has continued to provide a stream of smaller or more occasional pieces which vividly illustrate his compositional versatility, such as the two *Idylls* for chamber orchestra, the concertos for bassoon, viola, and the *Ballad* for harp and small orchestra, and the "revue" *Women in War*, as well as a large quantity of songs. However, much of his output has been composed out of sheer inner necessity, without commission. To the previously mentioned example of *Clarissa* should be added the oratorio *Brand* (after Ibsen), the *Cantata on the Death of God* (after Nietzsche) and the concert opera *Peer Gynt* (still in progress, begun in 1984); all are scored for soloists, chorus and large orchestra. Until these works, clearly central to Holloway's imagination, are performed in full it will not be possible to form a balanced view of Holloway's work as a whole.

—Julian Anderson

HOLMBOE, Vagn. Danish. Born at Horsens, Jutland, 20 December 1909. Educated at Copenhagen Conservatory (under Finn Høffding and Knud Jeppesen), 1925–9; Berlin Hochsschule für Musik (under Ernst Toch), 1930; ethnomusicological study in Romania, 1933–4. Married pianist Meta Graf in 1934. Private teacher, 1930s; teacher, Institute for the Blind, Copenhagen, 1940–9; teacher, 1950–5, and professor of theory and composition, 1955–65, Copenhagen Conservatory. Music reviewer, *Politiken*, Copenhagen, 1947–55. Recipient: first prize, Royal Danish Orchestra Scandinavian Competition, 1939; many other awards and honours. Mailing address: c/o Danish Music Information Centre, Vimmelskaftet 48, DK 1161 Copenhagen K, Denmark.

Publisher: Wilhelm Hansen, Copenhagen/Chester Music, London.

Symphonies/orchestral:

Symphony No "A" in F 1927; withdrawn.
Symphony No "B" in D 1928; withdrawn.
Concerto for Orchestra 1929.
Concerto for Chamber Orchestra 1931; first performed Copenhagen, 3 April 1933.
Chamber Music No 1 (small orchestra) 1931.
Chamber Music No 2 (string orchestra) 1932.
Suite for Chamber Orchestra No "A" 1932, revised 1933; subsequently withdrawn.
Overture No "A" 1932; withdrawn.
Overture No "B" 1932; withdrawn.

Music I (school orchestra) 1932.
Divertimento No 1 1933; first performed Copenhagen, 29 March 1933.
Divertimento No 2 (strings) 1933; first performed Copenhagen, 31 January 1944.
Concerto for Strings 1933.
Suite for Chamber Orchestra No 1 Op 1 1935; first performed Copenhagen, 30 March 1936.
Overture No "C" 1935; withdrawn.
Chamber Sonata No 1 1935.
Symphony No 1 Op 4 1935; first performed Aarhus, 21 February 1938.
Romanian Suite (piano, chamber orchestra) 1935.
Rhapsody Op 5 (flute, chamber orchestra) 1935; first performed Copenhagen, 1939.
Suite for Chamber Orchestra No 2 Op 6 1935–6; first performed Copenhagen, 20 April 1939.
Little Overture 1936; first performed Copenhagen, 16 March 1938.
Serenade Op 3 1936; first performed Copenhagen, 21 October 1939.
Suite for Chamber Orchestra No 3 Op 11 1936; first performed Copenhagen, 23 November 1938.
Concerto Symphony Op 13b (violin, orchestra) 1937.
Concerto for Violin and Orchestra Op 14 1938.
Symphony No 2 Op 15 1938–9; first performed Copenhagen, 5 December 1939.
Concertino 1938; first performed Copenhagen, 6 June 1941.
Romanian Suite (chamber orchestra) 1938.
Chamber Concerto No 1 Op 17 1939; first performed Copenhagen, 5 March 1941.
Chamber Concerto No 2 Op 20 1940; first performed Copenhagen, 21 April 1942.
Chamber Concerto No 3 Op 21 1940.
Concertino No 1 Op 22 (violin, viola, strings) 1940; first performed Copenhagen, 16 September 1963.
Concertino No 2 Op 24 (violin, strings) 1940; first performed Copenhagen, 12 June 1948.
Symphony No 3: "Sinfonia Rustica" Op 25 1941; first performed Copenhagen, 12 June 1948.
Symphonic Overture Op 28 1941; first performed Copenhagen, 13 April 1943.
Symphony No 4: "Sinfonia Sacra" Op 29 1941, revised 1945; first performed Copenhagen, 11 September 1945.
Chamber Concerto No 4 Op 30 (piano, violin, cello, chamber orchestra) 1942; first performed Copenhagen, 22 March 1943.
Chamber Concerto No 5 Op 31 (viola, orchestra) 1943; first performed Copenhagen, 14 February 1946.
Chamber Concerto No 6 Op 33 (violin, orchestra) 1943; first performed Copenhagen, 12 December 1944.
Symphony No 5 Op 35 1944; first performed Copenhagen, 16 June 1945.
Chamber Concerto No 7 Op 37 (oboe, orchestra) 1944–5; first performed Copenhagen, 29 January 1948.
Chamber Concerto No 8: "Sinfonia Concertante" Op 38 1945; first performed Copenhagen, 26 July 1947.
Chamber Concerto No 9 Op 39 (violin, viola, orchestra) 1945–6; first performed Copenhagen, 26 October 1954.
Chamber Concerto No 10: "Trae-messing-tarm" Op 40 1945–6; first performed Randers, 26 April 1946.
Symphony No 6 Op 43 1947; first performed Copenhagen, 8 January 1948.
Chamber Concerto No 11 Op 44 (trumpet, orchestra) 1948; first performed Copenhagen, 8 April 1949. Recorded MGM E3557.
Symphony No 7 Op 50 1950; first performed Copenhagen, 18 October 1951.
Chamber Concerto no 12 Op 52 (trombone, orchestra) 1951; first performed Copenhagen, 23 May 1952.
Chamber Symphony No 1 Op 53 1951; first performed Copenhagen, 9 March 1951.
Symphony No 8: "Sinfonia Boreale" Op 56 1951–2; first performed Copenhagen, 5 March 1953. Recorded Fona M7; Turnabout TV 341685.
Sinfonia in memoriam Op 65 1954–5; first performed Copenhagen, 5 May 1955.
Chamber Concerto No 13 Op 67 (oboe, viola, orchestra) 1955–6; first performed Randers, 6 November 1958.
Epitaph: Symphonic Metamorphosis Op 68 1956; first performed London, 28 December 1956.
Sinfonia I Op 73a (strings) 1957; first performed Copenhagen, 3 July 1958.
Sinfonia II Op 73b (strings) 1957; first performed Aarhus, 20 November 1958.
Concertino 1957; first performed Copenhagen, 28 September 1958.
Sinfonia III Op 73c (strings) 1958–9; first performed Aarhus, 22 January 1962.
Skoven Op 74 1960; first performed Randers, 2 May 1961.
Monolith: Symphonic Metamorphosis Op 76 1960; first performed Aarhus, 9 September 1960.
Epilogue: Symphonic Metamorphosis Op 80 1961–2; first performed Gothenberg, 23 November 1962.
Sinfonia IV Op 73d (strings) 1962; first performed Aarhus, 27 January 1964.
Sinfonia Sielariana 1964.
Symphony No 9 Op 95 1968; first performed Copenhagen, 19 December 1968.
Chamber Symphony No 2 Op 100 1968; first performed Copenhagen, 20 January 1969.
Den Galsindede Tyrk Op 32b 1968; first performed Copenhagen, 30 August 1970.
Chamber Symphony No 3 Op 103a 1969–70; first performed Aalborg, 14 October 1970.
Symphony No 10 Op 105 1970–1, revised 1972; first performed Detroit, Michigan, 27 January 1972.
Tempo Variable: Symphonic Metamorphosis Op 108 1971–2; first performed Bergen, Norway, 24 May 1972.
Concerto for Orchestra and Cello Op 120 1974.
Recorder Concerto Op 122 1974.
Flute Concerto Op 126 1975.
Tuba Concerto Op 127 1976.
Violin Concerto Op 139 1979.
Symphony No 11 Op 144 1980.
Flute Concerto No 2 Op 147 1981.
Concerto for Brass Op 157 1984.
Intermezzo Concertante Op 171 (tuba, string orchestra) 1987.
Symphony No 12 Op 175 1988; first performed Cardiff, Wales, 21 October 1989.
Prelude: To the Victoria Embankment Op 184 (chamber orchestra) 1990.

Chamber/instrumental:

Duo (2 violins) 1926.
Trio (flute, 2 violins; or 3 violins) 1926.
Quartet for Strings No "A" in C 1927; withdrawn.
Quartet for Strings No "B" in E 1927; withdrawn.
Scherzo (piano) 1928.
Piece for Three Violins 1928.
Bagatelle Arabesque (violin, piano) 1928.
Quintet for Strings in E♭ 1928.
Twelve Little Pieces (piano) 1928–9.

Molto allegro scherzande (violin) 1929.
Chorale Fantasy in E (piano) 1929.
Quartet for Strings No "D" in D 1929; withdrawn.
Quartet for Strings No "E" 1929–30; withdrawn.
Sonata for Piano No "A" 1929.
Sonata for Violin and Piano No "A" 1929; withdrawn.
Prelude (piano) 1930.
Suite for Piano No "A" 1930; withdrawn.
Trio for Strings No "A" 1930; withdrawn.
Sonata for Piano No "B" 1930; withdrawn.
Four Pieces (piano) 1930.
Quintet (strings?) 1930.
Quartet (flute, oboe, viola, cello) 1930.
Quartet for Strings No "F" 1930; withdrawn.
Symphony for Piano 1930.
Five Pieces (piano) 1930.
Five One- and Two-Part pieces (piano) 1930.
Allegro affetuoso (piano) 1931.
Little Pieces (piano or recorders) 1931.
Suite for Piano No "B" 1931; withdrawn.
Pieces for Piano 1931.
One-, Two-, and Three-Part Pieces (piano) 1931.
Allegro sostenuto (piano, violin) 1931; first performed Copenhagen, 1 November 1931.
Trio for Strings No "B" 1931; first performed Copenhagen, 2 November 1932; subsequently withdrawn.
Julen (piano) 1931.
Trio for Strings No "C" 1931; withdrawn.
Suite for Piano No "C" 1931; withdrawn.
Concerto for Piano 1931.
Suites and Dances (piano) 1931.
Seven Preludes (piano) 1932.
Quartet for Strings No "G" 1932; withdrawn.
Five Duets (flute, viola) 1932; first performed Copenhagen, 6 November 1932.
Trio (oboe, bassoon, horn) 1932, 1939; first performed Copenhagen, 1 February 1939.
Capriccio (piano) 1932; first performed Copenhagen, 6 November 1932.
Seven Duos (flute, horn) 1932.
Four Duos (flute, trombone) 1932; first performed Copenhagen, 11 November 1933.
Trio for Strings No "D" 1932; withdrawn.
Chamber Music No 3 (percussion, piano) 1932.
Six Pieces (piano) 1933.
Suite for Piano No "D" 1933; withdrawn.
Quartet for Strings No "H" 1933; first performed Copenhagen, 26 October 1934; subsequently withdrawn.
Quintet for Winds (flute, oboe, clarinet, bassoon, horn) 1933; first performed Copenhagen, 30 October 1933.
Divertimento No 3 (2 oboes, 2 trumpets, 2 trombones) 1933.
Six Sketches (piano) 1934.
Chamber Music No 4 (oboe, violin, cello) 1934.
Ten Romanian Dances (piano) 1934.
Sonata for Violin and Piano No 1 Op 2 1935; first performed Lund, 13 November 1935.
Serenade (flute, clarinet, bassoon) 1935.
Rhapsody (clarinet, violin) 1936.
Quartet Op 9 (flute, violin, cello, piano) 1936; first performed Paris, July 1937.
Quintet Op 10 (flute, oboe, clarinet, violin, viola) 1936; first performed Copenhagen, 24 July 1939.
Suite Op 12a (piano) 1937; first performed Copenhagen, 16 January 1944.
New Pieces (piano) 1937.
Danish Suite Op 12b (piano; also orchestrated) 1937.
Rhapsodic Interlude Op 8 (clarinet, piano, violin) 1938; first performed Copenhagen, 22 October 1938.
Music for Violin Choir 1938.
Sonata for Violin and Piano No 2 Op 16 1939; first performed Copenhagen, 16 January 1942.
Six Pieces (piano) 1939.
Etude (piano) 1939.
Serenade Op 18 (flute, piano, violin, cello) 1940; first performed Vienna, 25 March 1949. Recorded HMV DB 5297.
Notturno Op 19 (flute, oboe, clarinet, bassoon, horn) 1940; first performed Copenhagen, 2 November 1940. Recorded HMV DA 525859.
String Quartet No 1 Op 26 1941, 1944, revised 1949.
Sonatina briosa Op 27a (piano) 1941; first performed Copenhagen, 30 October 1942.
Sonatina capricciosa Op 27b (flute, piano) 1942.
Five Epigrams (piano) 1942.
Quartet for Strings No "J" 1944; withdrawn.
String Quartet No 2 Op 47 1948–9; first performed Copenhagen, 31 January 1950. Recorded HMV DB 20137/8/9; Fona LPK 538; Fona TF 109.
String Quartet No 3 Op 48 1949–50; first performed Copenhagen, 18 November 1950. Recorded Fona TF 110.
Suona da bardo (Symphonic Suite) Op 49 (piano) 1949–50; first performed Copenhagen, 3 April 1951.
Isomeric duo concertante Op 51 (2 violins, piano) 1950; first performed Copenhagen, 20 July 1950.
Primavera Op 55 (flute, piano, violin, cello) 1951; first performed Copenhagen, 24 October 1952. Recorded Triola TDCP 207.
Sonata (violin) 1953.
String Quartet No 4 Op 63 1953–4, revised 1956; first performed Copenhagen, 8 January 1955. Recorded Fona LPK 538; Fona TF 109.
Trio Op 64 (piano, violin, cello) 1954; first performed Copenhagen, 24 October 1956.
String Quartet No 5 Op 66 1955; first performed Kolding, 20 February 1956. Recorded Fona TF 110.
Quartetto medico Op 70 (flute, oboe, clarinet, piano) 1956.
Sonata Op 71 (flute) 1957; first performed Copenhagen, 2 April 1957. Recorded Fona TF 123.
Aspekter Op 72 (flute, oboe, clarinet, bassoon, horn) 1957; first performed Copenhagen, 9 April 1958.
Tropos Op 75 (2 violins, 2 violas, cello) 1960; first performed Kongens Lyngby, 9 October 1960.
String Quartet No 6 Op 78 1961; first performed Hindsgavl, August 1962. Recorded Fona LPK 543; Fona TF 108.
Quintet for Brass Op 79 (horn, 2 trumpets, trombone, tuba) 1961. Recorded TF 125.
Sonata Op 82 (double bass) 1962.
Sonata Op 83 (violin, viola) 1963.
String Quartet No 7 Op 86 1964–5; first performed Birkerod, 27 September 1965.
String Quartet No 8 Op 87 1965; first performed Frederiksberg, 14 December 1965. Recorded Fona LPK 543; Fona TF 108.
Moto austero Op 88a (piano) 1965; first performed Copenhagen, 29 April 1967.
Sonata No 3 Op 89 (violin, piano) 1965; first performed Brussels, 4 May 1965.
String Quartet No 9 Op 92 1965–6, revised 1969; first performed Horsens, 23 August 1967. Recorded Fona TF 133.
Quartet Op 90 (flute, violin, viola, cello) 1966; first performed Hindsgavl, 15 July 1966.
Sonatina Op 93 (oboe, piano) 1966; first performed Copenhagen, 21 November 1966.
Trio Op 97 (flute, cello, percussion) 1968; first performed

Kongens Lyngby, 8 October 1968.
Sonata Op 101 (cello) 1968–9; first performed Berlin, April 1969.
String Quartet No 10 Op 102 1969; first performed Gothenburg, 7 April 1970. Recorded Fona TF 133.
Musik til Morten Op 104 (oboe, string quartet) 1970; first performed Humlebaek, 17 November 1970. Recorded Philips 6578 006.
Fanden los i vildmosen Op 106a (clarinet, 2 violins, double bass) 1971; first performed Vra, 30 July 1971.
Musik for fugle og groer Op 106b (2 flutes, 16 bassoons) 1971.
Ondata Op 109 (tuned gongs) 1972; first performed Malmo, 2 December 1973.
Moto austero Op 88b (piano) 1972.
I venti Op 99b (piano) 1972.
String Quartet No 11 "Quartetto rustico" Op 111 1972; first performed Soro, 8 March 1972.
Fabula I Op 112 (organ) 1972; first performed Copenhagen, 26 March 1973.
Contrasti Op 113 (organ) 1972; first performed Skovshoven, 28 November 1973.
Sextet Op 114 (flute, clarinet, bassoon, violin, viola, cello) 1972–3; first performed Odense, 13 November 1973.
Fabula II Op 115 (organ) 1973; first performed Ortona, Italy, July 1973.
String Quartet No 12 Op 116 1973; first performed Hillerod, 19 November 1973.
Diafora Op 118 (4 strings) 1973.
Fanfare Op 121 (3 trumpets, timpani) 1974.
String Quartet No 13 1975.
String Quartet No 14 1975.
Nuigen Op 129 (piano, violin, cello) 1976.
Firefir Op 130 (4 flutes) 1976–7.
String Quartet No 15 1976–7.
Trio Op 137 (clarinet, cello, piano) 1978.
Notes Op 140 (3 trombones, tuba) 1979.
Sonata No 1 Op 141 (guitar) 1979.
Sonata No 2 Op 142 (guitar) 1979.
Sonata Op 143a (accordion) 1979.
Sonata Op 145 (recorder, harpsichord) 1980.
String Quartet No 16 Op 146 1981.
Music with Horn Op 148 (violin, horn, piano) 1981.
Five Intermezzi Op 149 (guitar) 1981.
String Quartet No 17 "Mattinata" Op 152 1982.
String Quartet No 18 "Giornata" Op 153 1982.
Gioco Op 155 (violin, viola, cello) 1983.
Ballata Op 159 (violin, viola, cello, piano) 1984.
String Quartet No 19 "Serata" Op 156 1985.
String Quartet No 20 "Notturno" Op 160 1985.
Sonata Op 162 (tuba, piano) 1986.
Prelude: To a Pine Tree Op 164 (chamber ensemble) 1986.
Quintet Op 165 (2 violins, viola, cello, double bass) 1986.
Prelude: To a Dolphin Op 166 (chamber ensemble) 1986.
Duo concertante Op 167 (violin, guitar) 1986.
Prelude: To a Maple Tree Op 168 (chamber ensemble) 1986.
Prelude: To a Willow Tree Op 170 (chamber ensemble) 1987.
Sonata Op 172 (trombone, piano) 1987.
Translation Op 172a/b (violin, viola, cello, double bass, piano) 1987, revised 1989.
Parlare del piu e del meno Op 176 (guitar) 1988.
Capriccio Op 177 (clarinet, piano) 1988; first performed Horsens, 11 March 1989.
Sonata Op 178 (viola) 1988.
Burlesco Op 179a (accordion) 1989.
Prelude: To the Pollution of Nature Op 180 (chamber ensemble) 1989.
Epos Op 182 (2 pianos, percussion) 1990.

Vocal/choral:

Stjerner (voice, piano; Stuckenberg) 1928.
Requiem (soloists, choir, orchestra; Hebbel) 1931.
Three Songs (children's voices; Claudius, Rilke, VH) 1931.
Provinsen (soloists, choir, flute, oboe, violin, cello; Bergstedt) 1931.
Weg im Dezember (voice, piano; Seitz) 1933.
De Danske taalte ikke tvang (choir; Jensen) 1934.
Tre Lyriske Sange Op 7a (soprano, piano; Petersen) 1936.
Stilfaerdige sange Op 7b (mezzo-soprano, piano; Kolbenhoff) 1936.
Den dovne trillebor (mixed choir; Kristensen) 1936.
Psalm 62 Op 13a (choir) 1937.
Two Songs (men's voices; Herdal, Garff); first performed 1 December 1940.
Jeg har sortnende og hvitende sande (mixed choir; Hallar) 1940.
Eight Canons (voices) 1941.
Twelve Canons (voices) 1941.
Cantata No 2 (choir, orchestra) 1941; first performed Horsens, 19 December 1941.
Cantata No 3 (voices, strings) 1942; first performed Horsens, 28 June 1942.
Cantata No 4 (voices, orchestra) 1942–5; first performed Copenhagen, 26 November 1945.
Two Songs (mezzo-soprano, piano; Bjornson, Ibsen) 1942.
Jeg ved enurt sa dejlig Op 36 (mixed choir) 1943; first performed Copenhagen, 12 May 1944.
Five Songs Op 34 (men's and mixed choirs; Lagerkvist) 1943. Recorded Fona TF 119.
Sonatina Op 41 (soprano, alto, tenor; Mistral, Jorgensen) 1946.
Arhundredstjernen (baritone, choir, orchestra; Ingemann) 1946; first performed Copenhagen, 18 March 1947.
Cantata No 6 (choir, orchestra; Thisted) 1947; first performed 27 January 1948.
Ikke forlig (men's voices; Munk) 1948; first performed Copenhagen, 10 December 1952.
Tolv danske skaemteviser Op 45a (mezzo-soprano, piano; trad.) 1948.
Traeer og vaekster Op 45b (mezzo-soprano, piano; La Cour) 1949.
Bjergenes sang (mezzo-soprano, piano) 1949–52.
Cantata No 7 (sopranos, women's voices, orchestra or 2 pianos) 1949; first performed Copenhagen, 27 October 1949.
Cantata No 8 (baritones, bass, reader, string orchestra; Garff) 1951; first performed Falster, 1 May 1952.
Liber canticorum I Op 54 (mixed voices; biblical) 1951–2; first performed Copenhagen, 14 November 1953.
Moya—Seven Japanese Songs Op 57 (mezzo-soprano, piano; Yakamoshi, Komashi, Yorikito, Fukayubu, Kawayi, Yosano, Motokato) 1952; first performed Copenhagen, 24 January 1961.
Sendebunde Op 58 (baritone, piano; La Cour) 1952.
Liber canticorum III Op 60 (mixed voices; biblical) 1953; first performed Stockholm, 25 May 1954.
Liber canticorum IV Op 61 (mixed voices; biblical) 1953; first performed Copenhagen, 5 July 1953.
Liber canticorum IV Op 61 (mixed voices; Bible) 1953; first performed Copenhagen, 5 July 1953.
Traeet Op 62 (choir, chamber orchestra; La Cour) 1953.
Cantata No 9 (women's voices, violin, cello, flute, 2 pianos) 1955; first performed Randers, 28 April 1955.
Three Inuit Songs—Set No 1 Op 69 (baritone, men's voices, timpani) 1956; first performed Copenhagen, 26 May 1956.

Cantata No 10 (mixed voices) 1957; first performed Copenhagen, 2 July 1958.
Cantata No 11 (baritone, mezzo-soprano, mixed choir, wind orchestra) 1958; first performed 4 September 1958.
Simeons lovsang (mixed voices; biblical) 1958.
Cantata No 12 (mezzo-soprano, contralto, baritone, mixed choir, orchestra) 1958–9; first performed Aarhus, 11 September 1959.
Three Songs (equal voices) 1959; first performed Copenhagen, 14 October 1959.
Three Songs (mixed voices, piano; Schade, Rasmussen) 1960.
Five Songs (equal voices; Hagerup, Rasmussen, Jensen, Andersen) 1961.
Hevjie i homru, haremaelta kvaedie Op 81 (mixed voices; Djurhuus) 1962–4.
Glemselshejren (mixed voices; Havamal, Icelandic) 1963; first performed Copenhagen, 8 December 1963.
Requiem for Nietzsche Op 84 (alto, tenor, baritone, choir, orchestra; Bjornvig) 1963; first performed Copenhagen, 26 November 1964.
Evangeliesprak (women's voices, baritones ad lib; biblical) 1964.
Sange modf vardybet/sol og kavi Op 85 (voices; Heinsesen, Djurhuus) 1964–5, 1968; first performed Copenhagen, 17 April 1974.
Kibarjuk: Three Inuit Songs—Set No 2 Op 91 (translated Rasmussen) 1966.
Three Jaeger Songs Op 98 (mixed voices) 1966–8.
Zeit Op 94 (alto, string quartet; Pandula) 1966; first performed Holsteboro, 14 January 1968.
En tosset verden (voice, piano; or children's voices, 2 recorders, Orff instruments) 1966.
Beatus Vir (Liber canticorum V) Op 96 (mixed voices; biblical) 1968; first performed Copenhagen, 27 May 1968.
De vilde hvide/Nikke nikke nambo (mixed voices, percussion; Anderson) 1968.
Funf spate Lieder (mezzo-soprano, piano; Graf) 1969.
Solsort (mixed voices; Rasmussen) 1970.
Cantata profana Frise Op 103b (mixed voices) 1970.
Edward Op 107a (baritone, orchestra; trad.) 1971.
The Wee, Wee Man Op 107b/110b (tenor, orchestra; or mixed voices) 1971, 1972; first performed Aldeburgh, Suffolk, 9 June 1972.
A Lyke-Wake Dirge Op 110a (mixed voices) 1972; first performed Copenhagen, 9 May 1973.
Hyld (equal voices; Jaeger) 1972.
Two Songs (mixed voices; Kristensen) 1972.
Beatus parvo Op 117 (mixed voices, orchestra) 1973.
A hellu eg stoe Op 119 (mixed voices; Matras) 1974.
Song at Sunset Op 138 (mixed voices) 1978.
Biblical Cantata Op 150 (soloists, chorus, orchestra) 1982.
Brugvar Op 151 (soprano, baritone, mixed voices) 1982.
Two Sarvig Psalms Op 154 (mixed voices) 1983.
Laudate Dominum Op 158b (mixed voices) 1984.
Ode to the Soul Op 161 (mixed chorus, brass) 1985.
Psalm 84 Op 163 (mixed voices) 1985.
Rejsende Op 169 (mixed chorus; Sorensen) 1986.
Psalm 65 Op 173 (mixed chorus) 1987.
Winter Op 181 (soprano, mixed chorus; Brown) 1989.
Die Erfullung Op 183 (soprano, baritone, 2 choruses, 9 winds; Novalis) 1990.

Opera:

Lave og Jon (Thorbjornsen) 1946–8.
Kniven 1960; first performed Copenhagen, 2 December 1963.

Other:

Music I (school orchestra) 1932.
Piano Music for Children 1938.
Fanden og Bergemestern (symphonic fairy play) 1940.
Den galsindede tyrk Op 32a (ballet) 1942–4.
Flojten Op 42 (music for radio play; orchestra) 1946.
J.F. Willumsen (music for film) 1951; first performed 28 September 1951.
Gnavpotten (incidental music to Menander) 1959; first performed Copenhagen, 8 September 1959.
Julius Caesar (incidental music to Shakespeare) 1963; first performed Copenhagen, 14 March 1964.
Multityder (music for film; chanter, clarinet, percussion, violin, cello) 1969; first performed Copenhagen, 6 July 1970.

PUBLICATIONS

By Holmboe: *Mellemspil (Interlude)*, 3 essays, Copenhagen, 1961.

On Holmboe: Paul Rapoport, *VH: A Catalogue of His Music* (including discography, bibliography, essays; issued in honour of the composer's 70th birthday), 2nd edition, Copenhagen, 1979.

* * *

Vagn Holmboe has produced an extensive portfolio of music, including substantial groups of work in a number of conventional forms, which has assured him pre-eminence among contemporary Danish composers (if not among all contemporary Scandinavian musicians). Inevitably, he has been compared with Nielsen, and there are numerous points of contact between the two: a shared love of classical forms, an interest in counterpoint and a great, yet highly personalised mastery of instrumentation.

Holmboe has never been an avant-gardist. His musical education was excellent, though solidly conventional, and his early works owe less to his research into Romanian folk music (a field which had opened up wide new vistas of musical language for Bartók some 30 years earlier—though Holmboe also discovered Bartók's music at the time he was undertaking the folk music studies) than to his admiration for the idea of "neo-classicism" in music, whose most prominent advocates at that time were Hindemith and Stravinsky. His harmonic language has remained tonal (though contrapuntal logic is usually stressed more heavily) and his style has not been subsumed into any school or trend.

Among the cornerstones of Holmboe's achievement is his symphonic output. Besides his group of full-scale symphonies, this category includes the 12 Chamber Concertos he produced during the late 1930s and 1940s. They are scored for a variety of solo instruments; the orchestration of the first three concertos is restricted to strings; Holmboe had developed his skill with scaled-down orchestral forces in a number of previous works, including the First Symphony, and he built upon this experience with almost Brahmsian thoroughness before proceeding to use more elaborate orchestras. Another interesting feature of the Chamber Concertos is that they tend to stress Neo-Classicism—especially motoric or highly patterned or stylised rhythms—in a manner which has obvious links with Stravinsky.

The Fifth Symphony, one of Holmboe's first pieces to be widely appreciated outside Denmark, persists with the stock-in-trades of neo-classicism, but this approach is broadened by a much more overt reliance upon stylistic traits which may be derived from the composer's folk music studies; in particular, the harmonic and melodic structure of certain passages features a decidedly modal inflection. The Sixth Symphony, like its predecessor, is in two movements and is neo-classical in orientation, though here Holmboe gives prominence to the idea of transformation of themes (while preserving their essential identity) as an important principle of symphonic construction. This device, initially popularised in the 19th century by Berlioz and Liszt (and Wagner—his *Leitmotif* concept is closely related to thematic transformation), was developed in the 20th century by numerous composers, notably Mahler, Strauss and Sibelius. After World War II, Holmboe was to promote this approach as "the form of our time".

During the early 1950s, Holmboe began to publish *a capella* motets; these show his uncluttered mastery of counterpoint to excellent effect; the simple yet telling choral settings are a reminder that much of Holmboe's training in counterpoint came from the great Palestrina scholar, Knud Jeppesen, who did much to modernise the study of Late Renaissance polyphony by basing his approach upon careful and comprehensive study of a composer's oeuvre.

Holmboe had written several string quartets before the piece which he called "Number 1", but those have remained unpublished. Subsequently, he published quartets regularly and they have some claim to be regarded as the kernel of his output, by virtue of their closely argued textures and dramatic involvement. Their preoccupations differ in no essential respect from those of the composer's other works: there is fluent manipulation and transformation of thematic ideas, which is used on occasion to unify separate movements. There are also neo-classical traits, such as the Chaconne movement from the Third Quartet (which also suggests parallels with Nielsen). The later symphonies and concertos continue to explore these concerns. Holmboe has created a large body of high-quality music which, while not of startling modernity, is unusual in its coherence and fidelity to its creator's ideals.

—Paul Horner

HOLT, Simon. British/English. Born in Bolton, Lancashire, 21 February 1958. Educated at Bolton School, until 1976; Bolton Art College, 1976–7; Royal Northern College of Music, Manchester (composition under Anthony Gilbert), 1978–82. Featured composer, Bath Festival, 1985; visiting tutor, music department, City University, London, from 1989; composer in residence, Aldeburgh Festival, Summer 1991. Recipient: finalist (with *Wyrdchanging*), Politis Prize, Boston University, 1981; Royal Philharmonic Society Award, Performing Rights Society Award, Gemini Fellowship (all for *Capriccio Spettrale*), 1989; selection (*Danger of the Disappearance of Things)*, ISCM World Music Days, Oslo, 1990. Mailing address: c/o Universal Edition, 2–3 Fareham Street, London W1V 4DU, England.

Publisher: Universal Edition.

Symphonies/orchestral:

Syrensong 1987.
Viola Concerto 1990–1.

Chamber/instrumental:

Palace at 4 a.m. (flute, oboe, clarinet, cello) 1980; first performed Cardiff, 2 December 1981.
Mirrormaze (3 flutes/1 piccolo/1 alto flute, 2 oboes/1 cor anglais, E♭ clarinet, A clarinet, 2 horns, 2 percussion, double bass) 1981; first performed Manchester, 9 March 1981.
Maiastra (flute/alto flute) 1981; first performed Manchester, 22 January 1982.
Kites (flute/piccolo, oboe/cor anglais, clarinet, bassoon, horn, string quartet) 1983; first performed London, 13 April 1983.
Shadow Realm (clarinet, cello, harp) 1983; first performed London, 30 June 1983.
. . . era madrugada (piccolo/flute, A clarinet/bass clarinet, horn, piano, viola, cello, double bass) 1984; first performed London, 24 May 1984.
Piano Piece (for Harrison Birtwistle's 50th birthday) 1984; first performed London, 4 October 1984.
Burlesca Oscura (clarinet/bass clarinet, string quartet) 1985; first performed Bath, 1 June 1985.
Tauromaquia (piano) 1985; first performed London, 12 January 1987.
Capriccio spettrale (flute/alto flute, clarinet/bass clarinet, horn, trumpet/piccolo trumpet, 2 violins, 2 violas, cello, double bass) 1988; first performed Stuttgart, 9 September 1988.
Duendicitos (piano) 1988; first performed London, 1988.
Danger of the Disappearance of Things (string quartet) 1989; first performed Leeds, Yorkshire, 2 July 1990.
Sparrow Night (solo oboe, flute/piccolo, A clarinet/E♭ clarinet/bass clarinet, horn, harp, piano, violin, viola, cello, double bass) 1989; first performed London, 24 March 1990.

Vocal/choral:

Lunas Zauberschein (mezzo-soprano, bass flute) 1979; first performed Manchester, 20 March 1979.
Wyrdchanging (mezzo-soprano, 2 flutes/1 piccolo/1 alto flute, oboe, A clarinet, bass clarinet, horn, percussion, 3 violins, viola, 2 cellos, double bass; Old English "The Ruin", translated Alexander) 1980; first performed Manchester, 7 April 1981.
Canciones (mezzo-soprano, flute/alto flute/piccolo, oboe, horn, harp, string quintet; Lorca) 1986.
Ballad of the Black Sorrow (2 sopranos, mezzo-soprano, tenor, baritone, bass, flute/piccolo, oboe, E♭ clarinet/bass clarinet, A clarinet/bass clarinet, bassoon/contrabassoon, horn, 2 trumpets, trombone, harp, 4 violins, 2 violas, 2 cellos, 2 double basses; Lorca) 1988; first performed London, 24 January 1988.
A Song of Crocuses and Lightning (soprano, horn, harp, viola, double bass; Carver) 1989; broadcast London Weekend Television, 29 December 1989.

* * *

Simon Holt's music is the strangest and most attractive mixture of two fundamentally opposed characteristics. On the one hand he is clearly an aesthete. Much of his music revels in the sweetness of the moment, in the pleasures of experience revealed without apparent order and in an abundance of colours and rich harmonies. It can seem music written very much for sensation and almost without regard to form or to perceptible logic.

But at the same time, this feeling of decadence, sensuality and spontaneous abundance is under constant assault in Holt's works by another kind of music of quite the opposite character—violent, destructive and verging on the starkly expressionist. There is a tendency at such moments to extremes of register, to chords and instrumental combinations suggestive of sighs and screams, and to rhythmic gestures which offer a menacing sense of pulse that may well seem quite at odds with the rest of the composition.

The result of this memorable and often alarming confrontation between, as it were, two polarised worlds in Holt's imagination is the feeling that we are listening to the working out of some private myth, whose personal significance may appear to elude us, but whose emotional drama is impressively plain. And this myth is not accidental, as is clear from the musical alertness with which this confrontation is described in the pieces themselves, the poeticisms of Holt's titles (*Mirrormaze*, *Syrensong*), and his fondness for texts which reflect preoccupations parallel to those we feel in the music.

In a way, Holt's music reflects something of the same sense of conflict found in the work of some of the writers and painters of the past—the English poets of the 1890s or Viennese painters of the kind that Schoenberg knew. Underneath the apparently visceral and sensual surface of this conflict a clear moral sensibility is at work. It is not just the musical images in themselves that appeal to Holt, but their suggestive power, their implication of consequences. Indeed behind the confrontation in this music of violence and pleasure, there is often a strong interest in the meaning of feelings like guilt and regret; it takes a considerable composer to make music carry this kind of resonant implication.

The forms of Holt's music can seem at first hearing almost irritatingly arbitrary and improvisational. It is always clear from the first note that here are no number series, no Fibonacci-based proportions, no motivic development—none, in short, of the fashionable or traditional devices of integrity. And as each piece proceeds we may be bothered too by its complete lack of what even the French call "la grande ligne".

Only when we understand what Holt is doing instead do we hear another kind of logic at work in this music, a logic not imposed from outside but which springs from within the imagery itself. Then too we hear that the behaviour of each idea is dependent precisely on the role of that idea within the ebb and flow of the overriding conflict. In other words, the ideas are not dependent on the conflict but rather, vice versa.

Nowhere in Holt's music is this better expressed than in his orchestral work *Syrensong*. The ritornello-like collection of themes that opens and closes and divides the work's three main sections seems at each of its returns to be not in fact a return at all but a rediscovery of another kind of music that we had not known before.

—Gerard McBurney

HOLTEN, Bo. Danish. Born in Copenhagen, 22 October 1948. Educated at University of Copenhagen; largely self-taught as composer. Director, vocal group Ars Nova; music critic and editor, *Dansk Musiktidsskrift*; principal guest conductor, BBC Singers, from 1991. Mailing address: Marstrandsgade 28, 2100 Copenhagen O, Denmark.

Publisher: Wilhelm Hansen, Copenhagen/Chester Music, London.

Symphonies/orchestral:

Mahler-Impromptu 1972–3.
Venetian Rhapsody (chamber orchestra) 1974.
Caccia 1979.
Symphony (with chorus; vocalise, Blake) 1981–2.
Plainsongs (trumpet, orchestra) 1989; first performed Haarlev, 31 October 1989.

Chamber/instrumental:

Cut (6 percussion) 1980.
Puder og Skar/Pillows and Fragments (2 trumpets, horn, trombone, tuba) 1981.
Czerny Goes Mad (6 percussion) 1983.
Ancher Erectum (2 percussion) 1984.
Valsevaerk/Waltz-Ache (vibraphone) 1984.
Sarabande à trois (oboe, cello, harpsichord) 1984.

Vocal/choral:

Liden Kirstin pa Balet/Little Kirstin at the Stake (soprano solo, mixed chorus) 1972.
Pavane-Fantasia (2 sopranos, alto, tenor, bass, mixed chorus) 1974.
Sonata (soprano, violin, cello) 1976.
Tallis Variations (mixed chorus, 4 violins, 2 violas, 2 cellos, double bass) 1976.
La Douce Nuit (mixed chorus, bells; Baudelaire) 1976.
The Garden of Love (tenor, oboe, clarinet, string quartet; Blake) 1979.
Bolge og Hak/Wave and Cut (mixed chorus, 6 percussion) 1979.
Hexeskud/Lumbago (mixed chorus, flute, 4 saxophones, trumpet, electric guitar, synthesizer, electric bass, keyboard, 4 percussion, 2 conductors) 1981.
The Clod and the Pebble (2 mixed choruses, wind quintet, 2 saxophones, electric guitar, electric bass, keyboard, 2 percussion) 1982.
Flammen og Kullet/The Flame and the Coal (medium voice, flute, violin, viola, cello, piano; Claussen) 1983.
Isaac and Ivan and Innsbruck (2 unaccompanied mixed choruses) 1983.
Five Motets (unaccompanied mixed chorus; Grundtvig) 1983.
Imperia (mixed chorus, orchestra; Claussen) 1983.
Psallite (mixed chorus, 2 clarinets, bass clarinet, 2 percussion) 1983.
The Hours of Folly (medium/high voice, flute, clarinet, string quartet) 1984.
Tertia Die (mixed chorus, orchestra) 1985.
Waltz-Ache II (mixed chorus, vibraphone) 1985.
Nordic Suite (unaccompanied mixed chorus) 1989; first performed Copenhagen, 30 August 1989.

Opera:

The Bond (soprano, baritone, tenor, mixed chorus, orchestra; Blixen) 1978–9.

Other:

Whale Waves (tape) 1981.

Film scores: *Zappa*; *The Element of Crime*; *Faith, Hope and Charity*.

PUBLICATIONS

On Holten: Jorgen I. Jensen, "BH", Wilhelm Hansen, Copenhagen, 1986.

* * *

At the time when Bo Holten was studying at the University of Copenhagen, in the late 1960s and early 1970s, the musical climate in Denmark was characterised by a receptivity to new ideas: experiments with the "new simplicity", musique concrète, together with the hierarchical style developed by Per Nørgård created an environment from which Holten emerged with no perceived opinion of what a modern composer is "supposed" to do. Consequently Holten could see no disparity between the structure of modern music and the spontaneity of jazz or earlier musics, nor did he ever feel the need to conceal what might, in other circumstances at that time, have been regarded as an unfashionable interest in the music of the late romantics or impressionists. He also believed that composition should never be divorced from practical music-making and has most tellingly demonstrated this over the last decade as director of the renowned vocal ensemble Ars Nova. Holten has enjoyed writing music for both amateurs and students to perform and has also pioneered the programming of many concerts with unusual juxtapositions of music: classical music with jazz, contemporary music with the music of the Middle Ages and Renaissance, Eastern and Western musical traditions together in one programme. The influence of these different musics often permeates his own compositions, but no one influence has become a dominant force.

The vast majority of his works for all genres include the human voice in some way and it is Holten's understanding of the enormous possibilities of vocal writing that is one of the principal hallmarks of his diverse music style. Indeed, it is perhaps significant that his first large-scale work was an opera, *The Bond*, based on a short story by Karen Blixen (the story was actually entitled "The Ring"—it needs no great leap of the imagination to work out why Holten changed the title!). In this work Holten has fused a quasi-symphonic development of thematic material with the immediacy of music drama. Much of the material is derived from a six-note tone row which he used again a number of times over the years, and the orchestral textures are enhanced not only by the solo voices, but also by a wordless chorus which appears at crisis points in the drama and acts as a bridge within the action. Holten obviously enjoyed the fluidity of sound allowed him by the use of the wordless chorus, and he employed the device again in the first movement of his next major work, the *Symphony* which was commissioned by Danish Radio for the 50th jubilee of the Radio Choir.

The voice is, of course, not always used wordlessly in Holten's work—in the second movement of the Symphony, for example, the chorus sings a text by one of his favourite poets, William Blake. Further analysis of his sources shows that he chooses texts from a variety of European languages: Blake again in the frequently performed *The Garden of Love* for tenor and chamber ensemble, Baudelaire in *La Douce Nuit* for a cappella choir, Sophus Claussen in the song cycle *Flammen og Kullet* (*The Flame and the Coal*) and in *Imperia*, a work for full orchestra and choir from the same year.

Apart from his love of vocal writing, contrapuntalism is another thread that can be traced throughout Holten's diverse output. He is attracted to the polyphony of the Middle Ages, Renaissance and Baroque, and its influence can be seen in such works as the *Pavane-Fantasia* for solo voices and a cappella choir which is based on the famous *Pavane, Lord Salisbury* of Orlando Gibbons, the *Tallis Variations* for mixed chorus and strings, and in his most performed work, *Caccia* for orchestra. "Caccia" is a term for a popular 2-part canonic form of the 14th and 15th centuries and Holten's piece is an experimental maze of canons of his own invention, often heard simultaneously. Indeed it is not until the finale movement that he employs an original 14th-century caccia.

Contrapuntalism is not, however, solely the province of earlier musics, and it is perhaps this same facet which has drawn Holten to contemporary jazz. His most recent concerto, for trumpet and orchestra written for the Danish jazz trumpeter, Palle Mikkelborg, demonstrates this most successfully through its fusion of improvisatory and notated material.

Holten is not ashamed of accessibility. The impact of his music is felt by both audiences and players alike and it would seem likely that during the 1990s his reputation as both conductor and composer will grow in tandem outside his native Denmark.

—Rosemary Johnson

HOSOKAWA, Toshio. Japanese. Born in Hiroshima, 23 October 1955. Educated at Hochschule der Kunste, Berlin, 1976–82; Staatliche Hochschule der Musik, Freiburg, 1983–6. Married Yoko Hosokawa, 1 November 1985. Recipient: 1st prize, Valentino Bucchi composition competition, Rome, 1980; 1st prize, Berlin Philharmonic Orchestra centenary awards, 1982; Arion Music Prize, Tokyo, 1985; Otaka Prize, Tokyo, 1989; Kyoto Music Prize, 1989. Mailing address: 2-4-5, 101 Shibakubo, Tanashi-shi, Tokyo, Japan.

Publisher: Scott (Japan), 301, 3-4-3 Iidabashi, Chiyoda-ku, Tokyo 102, Japan.

Symphonies/orchestral:

Preludio 1982; first performed Berlin, 1982.
Pass into Silence 1983; first performed Tokyo, 1983.
Tokyo 1985 (Japanese *gagaku* orchestra, shōmyō) 1985; first performed Tokyo, 1985.
Seeds of Contemplation (Japanese *gagaku* orchestra, shōmyō) 1986; first performed Rimini, 1986. Recorded Fontec FOCD 3259.
Jenseitz der Zeit / Beyond Time (violin, string orchestra) 1987; first performed Osaka, 1987. Recorded Camerata C32 CM 87.
Ferne-Landschaft / Far Landscape I 1987; first performed Kyoto, 1987. Recorded Denon 33CD 2545; Fontec FOCD 3225.
Per sonare (flute, orchestra) 1988; first performed Tokyo, 1988. Recorded Fontec FOCD 3225.

Chamber/instrumental:

Winter Bird (violin) 1978; first performed Lübeck, Germany, 1978. Recorded ALM Records AL 28.
Melodia (accordion) 1979; first performed Hannover, Germany, 1979. Recorded ALM Records AL 28.
String Quartet: Urbilder 1980; first performed Tokyo, 1981. Recorded ALM Records AL 28; Fontec FOCD 3108.
By the River (harp) 1982.
Dan-So (violin, cello, piano) 1984; first performed Cologne, 1985.
Sen I (flute) 1984; first performed Tokyo, 1985. Recorded Fontec FOCD 3211.
Sen II (cello) 1986; first performed Tokyo, 1987. Recorded Fontec FOCD 3225.
Utsurohi (shō, harp) 1986; first performed Tokyo, 1986. Recorded Fontec FOCD 3211.
Im Tal der Zeit / In the Valley of Time (string quartet, piano) 1986; first performed Kusatsu, 1986. Recorded Fontec FOCD 3225.
Fragmente I (shakuhachi, koto, samisen) 1988; first performed Tokyo, 1988. Recorded Fontec FOCD 3259.
Fragmente II (alto flute, string quartet) 1989; first performed Kuhmo, 1989.
Fragmente III (wind quintet) 1989; first performed Cairo, 1989.

Vocal/choral:

Ren-Ka I (soprano, guitar) 1985; first performed Freiburg. Recorded Fontec FOCD 3211.
Ren-Ka II (soprano, chamber ensemble) 1987; first performed Geneva, 1987.
Ren-Ka III (soprano, violin, viola da gamba, harp) 1989; first performed Geneva, 1990.
Hiroshima Requiem 1989.
Birds Fragments I (mezzo-soprano, flute, harp) 1990; first performed Milan, 1990.

Other:

Shi no toge / The Sting of Death (film score; harp, percussion, string orchestra) 1990; first performed Shochiku, 1990.

* * *

The geographical isolation of the Japanese archipelago from the centres of modern music in Europe and America has greatly influenced its native musical development. At the end of World War II, half a century after adopting Western instruments, Japanese composers were still inevitably absorbed in catching up with the Occidental avant-garde. At the same time, though, the need to reconsider Japanese traditional music became more urgent, and since the 1960s experiments combining Japanese and Western instruments have been increasingly common.

Compared to an older generation of composers—Toshi Ichiyanagi, Toru Takemitsu, Jyoji Yuasa and Maki Ishii—who had to grope for a language at the intersection of East and West, the post-war generation of composers born in the 1950s and after is free of any conflict between Eastern and Western values and can express their synthesis very naturally. Toshio Hosokawa's music is in this regard symbolic of the Japanese younger generation. He has researched deeply into the European music tradition during his years of study in Berlin and Freiburg, and has consequently mastered a universal musical language. His fundamental musical thought is inseparable from ancient Oriental thinking and his creation is based on the raising of barriers between East and West.

This attitude is already clearly seen in early works such as *Melodia* for accordion and *By the River* for harp. Among his notes of the time, there is a passage from Hermann Hesse's *Siddhartha*. On a riverbank, Siddhartha is taught to "listen" by a ferryman and by "listening" transcends his self and enters the sphere of unity. To transcend mere listening to actual sound, to listen to silence: this is an Oriental concept which has influenced both Takemitsu and John Cage (who has studied Zen). Hosokawa's creation begins from this need to listen, and by that means effects a rapprochement of East and West; in his music art is no longer an expression of the self, but the mirror of the cosmos (in its etymological sense of order) focussing on human deeds. This is recognizable in the methods used in the String Quartet "Urbilder" and in *In the Valley of Time*, beginning with a single note as if silence were suddenly resounding and then spreading fanwise into a harmony to five, and after much meandering, its final breath in a single note.

But it is the works written for solo instrument and orchestra which best indicate the passive relationship between human beings and the cosmos. In *Beyond Time* for violin and string orchestra and the flute concerto *Per sonare*, the fundamental characteristic of the concerto genre—solo instrument opposed to orchestra—is completely lost. In both works, the orchestra symbolises the cosmos and the solo instrument the human player who is wrapped in the huge maternal body and emerges in the form of a musical schema. If one thinks of Takemitsu's *November Steps*, whose principal object was the opposition of East and West, it is clear that though both begin with Oriental thought, the two composers are creating totally different kinds of music.

Japanese instruments do play an important role in Hosokawa's creation, especially the shō, which exerted a very important influence on his musical thought. The shō resounds continuously to the in-and-out motion of the breath. In ancient gagaku, the shō's *aitake* (harmonies) gradually escape direct listening and consciousness, becoming the background on which the schema woven by the hichiriki and the ryūteki unfolds. Hosokawa calls this "background" musical possibility, the possibility of unlistened sonority, "womb sounds". *Utsurohi* for shō and harp is an example; the shō symbolizes a celestial body, and the harp human beings. Just as people breathe the cosmic rhythm, the uninterrupted harmonies of the shō form the womb from which the harp's pitches are chosen and transposed. The central position of the shō player in *Seeds of Contemplation*, based on the motif of mandala, is also related to this concept.

Hosokawa calls the space symbolically formed by the "womb sounds" the "womb space". This space is full of the (silent) reverberation of still unheard and already heard sounds. Human breath (voiceless sound) is momentarily vocalized and then returns to silence; the existence of the "womb space" is indicated by this motion. Its repetition transmits the pulse of the womb. Hosokawa has written a series of works for solo instrument entitled *Sen* ("line") which stands in this case for the line traced by the Japanese calligraphy brush, representing thereby the dynamism of the Zen monk who starts from a point in the primitive chaos, moves across the white paper and returns to the initial point. Accordingly, in the first part of *Tokyo 1985*, the Zen monks singing the shōmyō in an unusual breath-voiceless sound incarnate the existence of the womb space in the depths of Tokyo, while in *Far Landscape* for orchestra, brass instruments are set in the rear of the audience in order to draw it into the midst of the womb space.

Finally, a few words need to be said about the "alienation" method used in Hosokawa's recent works. This method is most obvious in such large-scale works as *Tokyo 1985* and *Seeds of Contemplation* in which Hosokawa experiments with the transposition of traditional melodies into alien contexts (in the former, the fourth movement of Beethoven's Ninth Suymphony, in the latter, the Tendai Shōmyō. In the *Fragmente* series for small ensembles, complete alienation is attempted by directing the instruments away from their traditional performance. "Alienation" for Hosokawa means a strategy for evading convention. One by one, he questions all the possibilities of self-expression that European music has fostered in order to render the reverberation that is beyond human knowledge.

Hosokawa's creation, consecrated to the principle of non-action, is analogous to prayer. To this aspect of his work the *Hiroshima Requiem* attests most directly. What we hear from the chaotic music space in its second movement "Death and Resurrection", is a longing for resurrection. The notion of music-as-prayer—as in the work of Arvo Pärt of Sofia Gubaidulina—is now exerting a deep influence on the Western world, and the secret power of Hosokawa's music stems from that same source.

—Miyuki Shiraishi

HOVANESSIAN, Simon. Armenian. Born in Yerevan, 16 January 1940. Educated in primary and secondary schools, Yerevan, 1949–58; Music College, 1952–8; Music Institute, 1958–61; University, 1958–63; Conservatory, 1961–6. Married Mariana Makichian, 5 August 1961; 1 son (deceased). Factory worker, Factory Wi3, Yerevan, 1957–63; music editor/publisher, 1963–76, and art director, musical community, choral conductor/conductor of folk instrument orchestra, since 1976, Armenian Blind Society. Recipient: diploma (for *Symphonic Poem on the Memory of Komitas*), Union Festival of Young Composers, 1961; 3rd level diploma, International Composers' Competition, Czechoslovakia, 1985; 1st prize (for *Armenian Miniatures*), 4th International Composers' Competition, 1988; Honoured Worker of Art of Armenia. Mailing address: Demirchian Str 27, Apt la, Yerevan 2, 375002, Armenia.

Publishers: Sovetaban Grokh, Terian Str G 1, Yerevan 9, 375005, Armenia; Sovestskii kompozitor, Moscow.

Symphonies/orchestral:

Symphonic Poem on the Memory of Komitas 1969; first performed Yerevan, 1969.
A Poem to the Soldier of Freedom 1973.
Symphony for Strings 1975.
Sinfonietta on the Memory of A. Isahakian 1976; first performed Yerevan, 1976. Recorded Melodia C10 18525 6.
Symphony (orchestra, choir) 1989–90.

Chamber/instrumental:

Rondo (violin, piano) 1962; first performed Yerevan, 1963.
Toccatina (piano) 1963; first performed Yerevan, 1963.
String Quartet No 1 1967; first performed Yerevan, 1967.
String Quartet No 2 1971; first performed Yerevan 1971. Recorded Melodia C10 18525 6.
Poem (piano) 1973; first performed Yerevan, 1974. Recorded Melodia C10 18525 6.
Sonata (viola) 1978; first performed Yerevan, 1979. Recorded Melodia C10 18525 6.
Three Pieces (oboe, piano) 1982.
A Cycle of Pieces (flute, oboe) 1983; first performed Yerevan, 1984.
Armenian Miniatures (piano) 1986; first performed Yerevan, 1986.
String Quartet No 3 1987; first performed Yerevan, 1988.
Sonata (bassoon) 1988.
Children's Games (piano) 1989.

Vocal/choral:

Requiem on the Memory of Komitas (voices, orchestra; Charenz) 1966; first performed Yerevan, 1972.
A Cycle of Songs (voice, piano) 1967; first performed Yerevan, 1968.
Ayastan (unaccompanied mixed chorus) 1979; first performed Yerevan, 1980.
My Motherland (mixed chorus, piano) 1980; first performed Yerevan, 1980.
My Great Motherland (unaccompanied mixed chorus) 1982; first performed Yerevan, 1983.
Autumn (chorus, piano) 1983; first performed Yerevan, 1983.
Don't Cross the Road (unaccompanied mixed chorus) 1983; first performed Yerevan, 1983.
Armenia, You Are a Wonder (unaccompanied mixed chorus) 1983; first performed Yerevan, 1983.
I Am Your Son, Armenia (unaccompanied mixed chorus) 1985; first performed Yerevan, 1986.
Kele, Lao (unaccompanied mixed chorus) 1986; first performed Yerevan, 1986.

PUBLICATIONS

On Hovanessian: Joan Zurabian, "Music Is His Life", in *Musu Jodis*, 11, 1974; George Geodakian, "Unexpected or Inevitable", in *Sovetakan Arvest*, 8, 1976; Armenui Ashkhanian, "To Behold the Melody", in *Sovetakan Hayastan*, 8, 1988.

Simon Hovanessian comments:

I believe that the highest purpose of the artist is devotion to nation. The stronger the ties between a nation's history and its artist, the more sincere and natural its art. The source of my work is the national culture of Armenia, its religion and its folklore. I would never deny the importance of new tendencies in art, provided they are not merely today's fashion. To be earnest and sincere at all times: this is my living and artistic credo. Perhaps I am conservative.

* * *

Fate has dealt Simon Hovanessian more than one unkind blow; in childhood, he lost his eyesight; later, his own son was to die young. However, he has maintained a proud and always generous independence, never allowing his disability or misfortunes to become the basis for judgement of his work or his personality. His attitude to his situation is evident from his treatment of the "Dies Irae" theme and his thematic handling of Fate. More practically, he has been since 1976 organiser and artistic director of the choir and folk-instrument orchestra of the Armenian Blind Society. These were the first groups to perform and popularize the work of contemporary Armenian composers. His work with the choir has included the composition of lyrical and patriotic songs for it.

National spirit is conveyed in Hovanessian's work not just by his use of folkloristic images but also in the thematicism of the music itself, which is deeply penetrated by the "semantics" of his native musical language. With its particular national colouring and individual solution to artistic and aesthetic problems, Hovanessian's music is increasingly known outside the borders of Armenia.

He belongs to the generation of Armenian composers which emerged in the second half of the 1960s and which was remarkably quick to work out its own aesthetic principles. Even so, Hovanessian's first works suggest a highly individual creative intelligence and personality. His attempts to communicate transcendent ideas and to incarnate his patriotic feelings are almost palpable.

The image of Sogomon Komitas, founder of the modern school of Armenian music and a power symbol of the spiritual image of the Armenian people, stands over Hovanessian's work, most explicitly in the *Requiem* and the later *Symphonic Poem*, written in 1969 to commemorate the centenary of his great predecessor's birth. The fact that Hovanessian read history in parallel with his musical studies helped him to absorb the historical and cultural legacy of his people and to embody longstanding national values in contemporary artistic forms.

His 25-year career as a composer is dominated by the epic and the lyrical, images which transfer into deeply rooted psychic images. His perception and reflection of reality has steadily deepened. Of his orchestral work the most substantial are the *Symphony for Strings* and the *Sinfonietta* which follows a programme based on the history of the Armenian people. Each movement reflects a particular event and the piece deploys two folk elements which gradually converge and become a *leitmotiv* based on seconds, fourths and sevenths, a device characteristic of Hovanessian's music.

Of the chamber works, the *Sonata* for viola exposes the subtle expressive nature of his music. The first of two contrasting movements is based on an improvisation which uses the medieval melody "Yor Jam"/"That Hour". It develops into a dramatic monologue with fatal intonations of the "Dies Irae". The second movement, with its vital thematic dynamism and dancing rhythm, leads to a mood of bright optimism. Here, as in *Three Pieces* for oboe and piano and the prize-winning piano cycle *Armenian Miniatures*, one can detect Hovanessian's characteristic combination of lyricism, strong-willed epic and dance, and a laconic, reserved style. He is strongly disposed toward sonata form, but with a freedom of development and of thematic interrelation that is highly distinctive. Here more than elsewhere it is possible to detect Hovanessian's ability to combine an acutely modern musical language with a profound loyalty to his roots.

His string quartets were quick to attract recognition. The second is full of dramatic incident. A tune based on seconds generates the melodic material which underlines his typical monothematism. Once again, the piece grows out of an opposition of two contrastive movements: an opening largo, passionate and psychologically profound, then—without a break—a bright, dancing conclusion.

It was 16 years before he wrote another string quartet, this time dedicated to the memory of his violinist son, a student at the Conservatory in Yerevan. The first movement is based on Armenian liturgical singing and on a *leitmotiv* drawn from his son's initials (G-A-G-Es-H) and is further penetrated by "Dies Irae" intonations. The piece is full of both grief and courage, its mourning intonation slowly and dramatically superseded by the optimistic claims of the Spirit.

—Jean Zurabian

HOVHANESS, Alan (Alan Vaness Chakmakjian). American. Born in Somerville, Maine, March 8 1911. Educated at Tufts University, Boston, 1929–32; New England Conservatory, Boston (composition under Frederick Converse), 1932–4; studied with Bohuslav Martinu at Tanglewood, Massachusetts, 1942. Married Elizabeth Whittington in 1959. Organist, Armenian Church of St James, Boston, 1940s; faculty member, New England Conservatory, 1948–51; composer in residence, University of Hawaii, Honolulu, 1962. Recipient: Guggenheim Fellowship, 1952, 1954, 1958; Fulbright Fellowship, 1959; Rockefeller Fellowship, 1962; member, American Institute of Arts and Letters, 1977. Address: c/o Peters Edition, 373 Park Avenue South, New York, New York 10016, U.S.A.

Publishers: Associated; Peer; Peters.

Symphonies/orchestral:

Storm on Mt Wildcat 1931, revised as *Boreas and Mt Wildcat Op 2a* 1936.
Celestial Fantasy Op 44 1935, orchestrated 1944.
Monadnock Op 2 1935, revised 1936.
Prelude and Quadruple Fugue Op 128 1936, orchestrated 1954.
Symphony No 1 "Exile" Op 17 1937; first performed London, 26 May 1939.
Suite No 1 Op 26 1937.
Concerto for Cello and Orchestra Op 27 (Op 17/2) (string orchestra) 1937.
Hymn to Shasta Op 31 1938.
Psalm and Fugue Op 40a 1941.
Alleluia and Fugue Op 40b 1941.
Three Armenian Rhapsodies Opp 45, 51, 189 1944.
Lousadzak "The Coming of Light" Op 48 (piano, orchestra) 1944; first performed Boston, 4 February 1945. Recorded Music Masters MMD 60204K.
Khrimian Hairig Op 49 (trumpet, strings) 1944.
Elibris, God of Dawn Op 50 (flute, orchestra) 1944; first performed San Francisco, 26 January 1950.
Symphony No 10 Op 184 (chamber orchestra) 1944, revised 1965.
Return and Rebuild the Desolate Places Op 213 (trumpet, wind orchestra) 1944, revised 1965.
Tzaikerk "Evening Song" Op 53 (chamber orchestra) 1945.
Anahid Op 57 (flute, cor anglais, trumpet, timpani, percussion, strings) 1945.
Vosdan 1945, revised 1948.
Prayer of St Gregory Op 62b (trumpet, orchestra) 1946.
Kohar Op 66 1946.
Agori (first version) 1946.

Symphony No 8 "Arjuna" Op 179 (piano, chamber orchestra) 1947; first performed Madras, 1 February 1960.
Overture (trombone, strings) 1948.
Haroutian Op 71 (trumpet, orchestra) 1948.
Sosi (The Forest of Prophetic Sound) Op 75 (violin, piano, horn, timpani, giant tam-tam, strings) 1948.
Tapor Op 14 (wind band) 1949.
Suite Op 15 (wind band) 1949.
Is There Survival? (King Vahaken) Op 59 1949.
Zartik Parkim Op 77 (piano, chamber orchestra) 1949.
Artik Op 78 (horn, orchestra) 1949.
Diran Op 94 (baritone horn/trombone, orchestra) 1949.
Symphony No 9 "Vartan" Op 80 (Op 180) (chamber orchestra) 1950; first performed New York, 11 March 1951.
Janabar Op 81 (violin, piano, trumpet, strings) 1950; first performed New York, 11 March 1951.
Agori (second version, 2 chamber orchestras) 1950.
Concerto No 1 "Arevakal, Season of the Sun" Op 88 1951; first performed New York, 18 February 1952.
Concerto No 2 Op 89a (violin, orchestra) 1951.
Khaldis Op 91 (piano, 4 trumpets, percussion) 1951.
Three Improvisations of Folk Tunes (wind band) 1951.
Talin Op 93 (viola, orchestra) 1952.
Harmonica Concerto Op 114 1952.
Concerto No 4 Op 89b 1953.
Concerto No 5 1953.
Concerto No 6 1953.
Partita Op 98 (piano, orchestra) 1953.
Symphony No 5 "Short Symphony" Op 170 1953, revised 1963.
Concerto No 7 Op 116 1953.
Tower Music Op 129 (large wind ensemble) 1954.
Symphony No 13 Op 190 1954, revised 1960.
Vision from High Rock Op 123 1954.
Symphony No 2 "Mysterious Mountain" Op 132 1955; first performed Houston, Texas, 31 October 1955. Recorded Music Masters MMD 60204K.
Symphony No 3 Op 148 1956; first performed New York, 14 October 1956.
Concerto No 8 Op 117 1957.
Meditation on Orpheus Op 155 1957. Recorded CRI 134/BCD 1004.
In Memory of an Artist Op 163 1958.
Symphony No 4 Op 165 (wind orchestra) 1958; first performed Pittsburgh, 28 June 1959.
Symphony No 6 "Celestial Gate" Op 173 (chamber orchestra) 1959, revised 1960.
Accordion Concerto Op 174 1959.
Symphony No 7 "Nanga Parvat" Op 175 (band) 1959.
Symphony No 11 "All Men Are Brothers" Op 186 1960, revised 1970; first performed New Orleans, 21 March 1960; revised version first performed New Orleans, 31 March 1970.
Symphony No 12 Op 188 (with SATB chorus) 1960.
Symphony No 14 "Ararat" Op 194 (wind orchestra) 1961.
Mountain of Prophecy Op 195 1961.
Symphony No 15 "Silver Pilgrimage" Op 199 1962; first performed New York, 28 March 1963.
Symphony No 16 "Korean Kayageum" Op 202 (strings, Korean percussion) 1962; first performed Seoul, 26 January 1963.
Symphony No 17 "Symphony for Metal Orchestra" Op 203 (6 flutes, 3 trombones, percussion) 1963; first performed Cleveland, Ohio, 23 October 1963.
Symphony No 18 "Circe" Op 204a 1963.
Variations and Fugue Op 18 1964.
Meditation on Zeami Op 207 1964.
Floating World "Ukiyo" Op 209 1964; first performed Salt Lake City, Utah, 30 January 1965.
Fantasy on Japanese Woodprints Op 211 (xylophone, orchestra) 1964; first performed Chicago, 4 July 1964.
Island Sunrise Op 107 1965.
The Holy City Op 218 1965; first performed Portland, Oregon, 11 April 1967.
Symphony No 19 "Vishnu" Op 217 1966; first performed New York, 2 June 1967.
Ode to the Temple of Sound Op 216 1966.
Fra Angelico Op 220 1967; first performed Detroit, Michigan, 21 March 1968.
Requiem and Resurrection Op 224 (brass, percussion) 1968.
Symphony No 20 "Three Journeys to a Holy Mountain" Op 223 (band) 1968.
Vibration Painting Op 226 (13 strings) 1968.
Shambala Op 228 (violin, sitar, orchestra) 1968.
Hymn to Yerevan Op 83 (wind orchestra) 1969.
Symphony No 21 "Etchmiadzin" Op 234 (2 trumpets, strings) 1970.
And God Created Great Whales Op 229/1 (orchestra, with tape of hump-back whale voices) 1970; first performed New York, 11 June 1970.
Symphony No 22 "City of Light" Op 236 1971.
Symphony No 23 "Ani" Op 249 (band) 1972.
Overture to Pericles Op 261 1973.
Harp Concerto Op 267 (harp, strings) 1973.
Symphony No 24 "Majnun" Op 273 (tenor, chorus, trumpet, strings) 1973; first performed Lubbock, Texas, 25 January 1974.
Symphony No 25 "Odysseus" Op 275 1973; first performed London, 10 April 1974.
Dawn at Mount Tahoma Op 272 1973.
Ode to the Cascade Mountains Op 279 1974.
Symphony No 26 "Consolation" Op 280 (strings) 1975; first performed San Jose, California, 24 October 1975.
Rubaiyat Op 308 (speaker, accordion, orchestra) 1975; first performed New York, 20 March 1977.
Fanfare to the New Atlantis 1975.
Ode to Freedom Op 284 (violin, orchestra) 1976; first performed Vienna, Virginia, 3 July 1976.
Symphony No 27 Op 285 1976.
Symphony No 28 Op 286 1976.
Symphony No 29 Op 289 (horn, orchestra) 1976; first performed Minneapolis, Minnesota, 4 May 1977.
Symphony No 30 Op 293 (small orchestra) 1976.
Symphony No 31 Op 294 (strings) 1976; first performed Seattle, Washington, 7 December 1977.
Symphony No 32 "The Broken Wings" Op 296 (chamber orchestra) 1977.
Symphony No 33 Op 307 (chamber orchestra) 1977.
Symphony No 34 Op 310 1977.
Symphony No 35 Op 311 (Korean instruments) 1978; first performed Seoul, 9 June 1978.
Symphony No 36 Op 312 (flute, orchestra) 1978; first performed Washington, D.C., 16 January 1979.
Symphony No 37 Op 313 1978.
Symphony No 38 Op 314 (soprano, small orchestra) 1978.
Symphony No 39 Op 321 (guitar, orchestra) 1978.
Symphony No 40 Op 324 (brass, timpani, orchestra) 1979; first performed Interlochen, Michigan, 9 April 1982.
Guitar Concerto Op 325 1979.
Symphony No 41 "Mountain Sunset" Op 330 1979.
Guitar Concerto Op 331 1979.
Symphony No 42 Op 332 1979.
Symphony No 43 Op 334 (oboe, trumpet, timpani, orchestra) 1979; first performed Aptos, California, 20 August 1981.

Symphony No 45 Op 342 (2 pianos, large orchestra) 1979.
Copernicus Op 338 1980.
Symphony No 44 Op 339 1980.
Saxophone Concerto Op 344 (soprano saxophone, strings) 1980.
Greek Rhapsody No 2 Op 341 1980.
Symphony No 46 "To the Green Mountains" 1980–1; first performed Burlington, Vermont, 2 May 1981.
Symphony No 47 "Walla Walla, Land of Many Waters" (soprano, orchestra) 1981; first performed Walla Walla, Washington, 24 November 1981.
Symphony No 49 "Christmas Symphony" Op 356 (strings) 1981.
Symphony No 48 "Vision of Andromeda" Op 355 1982; first performed Miami, Florida, 21 June 1982.
Symphony No 50 "Mount St Helens" Op 360 1982.
Symphony No 51 Op 364 (trumpet, strings) 1982.
Ode to Mount Hood Op 370 (band) 1982.
Symphony No 52 "Voyage to Vega" Op 372 1982.
Star Dawn Op 377 (band) 1982.
Symphony No 53 Op 378 1982.
Symphony No 54 Op 379 1982.
Symphony No 55 Op 380 1982.
Symphony No 56 "Cold Mountain" Op 381 (tenor, soprano, clarinet, strings) 1982.

Chamber/instrumental:

Oror (Lullaby) Op 1 (violin, piano) 1927.
Suite Op 193 (cello, piano) 1927, revised 1961.
Suite Op 1 (string quartet, piano) 1928, revised 1934.
Piano Quintet No 1 Op 9 1927, revised 1962.
Piano Trio Op 3 1935.
Three Preludes and Fugues Op 5 (Op 10) (piano) 1935.
Toccata and Fugue Op 6 (piano) 1935, *Toccata* revised 1970.
Sonata Ricercare Op 12 (piano) 1935.
Prelude and Fugue Op 13 (oboe, bassoon) 1935, revised 1937, 1967.
Suite Op 21 (cor anglais, bassoon) 1935, revised 1937, 1967.
Lament Op 25 (clarinet) 1935.
String Quartet No 1 Op 8 1936.
Two Suites Opp 9, 14 (piano) 1936.
Fantasy Op 15 (piano) 1936.
Prelude and Fugue Op 10 (flute, clarinet) 1936.
Lament Op 20b (piano) 1937.
Mystic Flute Op 22 (piano) 1937.
Violin Sonata Op 11 (violin, piano) 1938.
Nocturne Op 20 (harp) 1938.
Ghazal Op 36 (piano) 1938.
Slumber Song Op 52/2 (piano) 1938.
Sandra's Dance Op 58 (piano) 1941.
Dance Ghazal (piano) 1941.
October Mountain Op 135 (6 percussion) 1942.
Five Fantasies Op 70 (brass choir) 1943, revised 1967.
Twelve Armenian Folk Songs Op 43 (piano) 1943.
Arshalouis Op 47b (violin, piano) 1943.
Lousnag Kisher Op 52/1 (piano) 1943.
Siris Dance Op 52/3 (piano) 1943.
Canzona and Fugue Op 72 (horn, 2 trumpets, trombone/tuba) 1943, revised 1967.
Mazert nman rehani (Thy Hair Is Like Basil Leaf) Op 38 (piano) 1944.
Varak Op 47 (violin, piano) 1944.
Artinis Op 39 (piano) 1945.
Invocations to Vahaken Op 54 (piano, percussion) 1945.
Sonata "Hakhpat" Op 54/2 (piano, percussion) 1945.
Two Pieces Op 55 (piano) 1945.
Chahagir Op 56/1 (viola) 1945.
Yeraz Op 56/2 (violin) 1945.
Mihr Op 60/1 (2 pianos) 1945.
Greek Rhapsody No 1 (piano) 1946.
Vijag Op 37 (2 pianos) 1946.
Saris Op 67 (violin, piano) 1946.
Lake of Van Sonata Op 175 (piano) 1946, revised 1959.
Madras Sonata Op 176 (piano) 1946, revised 1960.
Yenovk (The Troubadour) Op 176/2 (piano) 1948, revised 1951, 1958.
O World Op 32b (trombone, piano) 1948.
Shatakh Op 63 (violin, piano) 1948.
Achtamar Op 64/1 (piano) 1948.
Suite Op 23 (oboe, bassoon) 1949, revised 1967.
Sharagan and Fugue Op 58 (brass choir) 1949.
Divertimento Op 61/5 (wind quartet/4 clarinets) 1949.
Shalimar Op 177 (piano) 1949, revised 1960. Recorded Fortuna Records 17062 2.
Toccata and Fugue on a Kabardin Tune Op 6/2 (piano) 1951.
Lullaby Op 52/7 (piano) 1951.
Sanahin Op 69 (organ) 1951, revised 1968.
Kirghiz Suite Op 73 (violin, piano) 1951.
Fantasy on an Ossetin Tune Op 85 (piano) 1951.
Upon Enchanted Ground Op 90/1 (flute, harp, tam-tam, cello) 1951.
Gamelan and Jhala Op 106 (carillon) 1951.
String Quartet No 2 Op 147 1951.
Allegro on a Pakistan Lute Tune Op 104/6 (piano) 1951.
Orbit No 1 Op 90/2 (flute harp, celeste, tam-tam) 1952.
Quartet No 1 Op 97 (flute, oboe, harpsichord, cello) 1952.
Suite Op 99 (violin, piano, percussion) 1952.
Hanna Op 101 (2 clarinets, 2 pianos) 1952.
Orbit No 2 Op 102 (piano) 1952.
Jhala Op 103 (piano) 1952.
Pastoral No 1 Op 111/1 (piano) 1952.
Hymn to a Celestial Musician Op 111/2 (piano) 1952.
Quartet No 2 Op 112 (flute, oboe, harpsichord, cello) 1952.
Mountain Idylls Opp 52/4, 5, 6 (piano) 1953, 1949, 1932.
Piano Quintet No 2 Op 103 1953, revised 1963.
Sonata Op 121 (ryuteki, shō; or flute, organ) 1953.
Suite Op 96 (piano) 1954, revised 1967.
Duet Op 122 (violin, harpsichord) 1954.
The Flowering Peach Op 125 (clarinet, sax, harp, percussion) 1954.
Harp Sonata Op 127 1954.
Dawn Hymn Op 138 (organ) 1954.
Koke no niwa (Moss Garden) Op 181 (cor anglais, harp, percussion) 1954, revised 1960.
Nocturne Op 20/2 (flute, harp) 1956.
Sonata Op 145 (piano) 1956.
Seven Greek Folk Dances Op 150 (harmonica, piano) 1956.
Do You Remember the Last Silence? Op 152 (piano) 1957.
Poseidon Sonata Op 191 (piano) 1957.
Suite Op 166 (accordion) 1958.
Sextet Op 164 (recorder, percussion, string quartet) 1958.
Child in the Garden Op 168 (piano) 1958.
Sonata Op 171 (hichiriki, shō, oboe, organ) 1959.
Bardo Sonata Op 192 (piano) 1959, revised 1960.
Wind Quartet Op 159 1960, revised 1965.
Two Sonatas Op 110 (koto/harp) 1962.
Sonatina Op 120 (piano) 1962.
Ko-Ula-U Op 136 (2 pianos) 1962.
Two Macedonian Mountain Dances Op 144 (piano) 1962.
String Trio Op 201 1962.
Nagooran (South Indian instruments) 1962.
Sonata Op 119 (ch'in) 1962.
Three Visions of St Mesrob Op 198 (violin, piano) 1962.

Sonata Op 200 (trumpet, organ) 1962.
Two Ghazals Op 36a/b (piano) 1963. Recorded (a) Fortuna Records 17062 2.
Sonata Op 130 (2 oboes, organ) 1963, revised 1964.
Mysterious Horse Before the Gate Op 205 (trombone, percussion) 1963.
Three Haiku Op 113 (piano) 1964.
Sonata Op 118 (flute) 1964.
String Quartets Nos 3 and 4 Op 208/1–2 1964.
Fantasy on Japanese Wood Prints Op 211 (xylophone, piano) 1964.
Six Bagatelles Op 30 (string quartet) 1964.
The World Beneath the Sea No 1 Op 133 (saxophone, harp, 3 percussion) 1965.
The World Beneath the Sea No 2 Op 133/2 (clarinet, harp, percussion, double bass) 1965.
Yakamochi Op 193/2 (cello, piano) 1965.
Bare November Day Op 210 (piano/harpsichord/organ/clavichord) 1965.
Dark River and Distant Bell Op 212 (piano/harpsichord) 1965.
Five Visionary Landscapes Op 214 (piano) 1965.
Six Dances Op 79 (brass quintet) 1967.
Sextet Op 108 (violin, percussion) 1967.
Bacchanale Op 203a (5 percussion) 1967.
Mountains and Rivers Without End Op 225 (10 instruments) 1968.
Spirit of Ink Op 230 (3 flutes) 1968.
All the World's a Dance of Snobbery Op 233 (piano) 1970.
St Nerses the Graceful Op 235 (3 clarinets) 1970.
Nagooran Op 237 (double bass, percussion) 1971.
Komachi Op 240 (piano) 1971.
Tsamico and Fugue Op 241 (piano) 1971.
Island of Mysterious Bells Op 244 (4 harps) 1971.
The Garden of Adonis Op 245 (flute, harp/piano) 1971.
Hermes Stella Op 247 (piano, tam-tam) 1971.
Dawn on the Mountain of Initiation Op 248 (piano) 1972.
Ruins of Ani Op 250 (4 clarinets) 1972.
Khorhoot Nahadagatz Op 251 (oudh, string quartet) 1972.
Firdausi Op 252 (clarinet, harp, percussion) 1972.
Shah-Nameh Op 252/1 (flute, oboe, 2 shawms, oriental instruments) 1972.
Seven Love Songs of Saris Op 252/3 (violin/flute, piano) 1972.
Cello Sonata Op 255 1972.
Clarinet Quartet Op 262 1973.
Night of a White Cat Op 263 (clarinet, piano) 1973.
Tumburu Op 264/1 (piano trio) 1973.
Varuna Op 264/2 (piano trio) 1973.
Adagio and Fugue Op 265 (string quartet) 1973.
Sonata Op 266 (2 bassoons) 1973.
Suite Op 270 (harp) 1973.
Pastoral and Fugue Op 271 (2 flutes) 1973.
O Lord, Bless Thy Mountains Op 276 (2 pianos tuned ¼-tone apart) 1974.
Fantasy Op 277 (double bass, piano) 1974.
Psalm to St Alban Op 282/2 (4 brass) 1974.
String Quartet No 5 Op 287 1976.
Suite Op 290 (4 trumpets, trombone) 1976.
Suite Op 291 (saxophone, guitar) 1976.
Septet Op 295 (flute, clarinet, bass clarinet, trumpet, trombone, double bass, percussion) 1976.
Sonata Op 322 (clarinet, harpsichord) 1976.
Sonata Op 297 (2 clarinets) 1977.
Three Sonatas Op 299 (piano) 1977.
Suite Op 300 (flute, guitar) 1977.
Sonata "Fred the Cat" Op 301 (piano) 1977.
Sonata Op 302 (oboe, bassoon) 1977.
Sonata "Ananda" Op 303 (piano) 1977.
Five Sonatas Opp 306, 318, 337, 357, 361 (harpischord) 1977–81.
Sketchbook of Mr Purple Poverty Op 309 (piano) 1977.
Starry Night Op 288 (flute, harp, xylophone) 1978.
Two Sonatas Opp 316, 329 (guitar) 1978–9.
Sonata Op 317 (alto flute/bass flute) 1978.
Sunset on Mt Tahoma Op 319 (horn, 2 trumpets, trombone, organ) 1978.
Two Sonatas Opp 326, 328 (3 trumpets, 2 trombones) both 1979.
Love Songs Vanishing into Sounds of Crickets Op 327 (piano) 1979. Recorded Fortuna Records 17062 2.
Trio Op 331 (alto saxophone, tenor saxophone, baritone saxophone) 1979.
Four Nocturnes Op 334 (soprano saxophone, piano) 1979.
Sonata "Mount Chocorua" Op 335 (piano) 1979.
Sonata "Blue Job Mountain" Op 340 (piano) 1979.
Sonata "Catamount" Op 345 (piano) 1980.
Sonata "Prospect Hill" Op 346 (piano) 1980. Recorded Fortuna Records 17062 2.
Pleiades Op 350/2 (gamelan) 1981.
Corruption in Office Op 351 (piano) 1981.
Sonata Op 352 (organ) 1981.
Sonata "Journey to Arcturus" Op 354 (piano) 1981.
Psalm Op 358 (brass quartet) 1981.
Cascade Mt Dances Op 362 (piano) 1981.
Lake Winnipesaukee Op 363 (flute, oboe, cello, 2 percussion, piano) 1982.
Sonata "Hiroshige's Cat Bathing" Op 366 (piano) 1982. Recorded Fortuna Records 17062 2.
Sonata "On the Long Total Eclipse of the Moon, July 6, 1982" Op 367 (piano) 1982.
Sonata "Tsugoharu Fujita's Cat" Op 368 (piano) 1982.
Sonata "Lake Sammamish" Op 369 (piano) 1982.
Campuan Sonata Op 371 (viola, piano) 1982.
Prelude and Fugue Op 373 (brass quartet) 1982.
Sonata "Spirit of Trees" Op 374 (guitar, harp) 1982.
Clarinet Sonata Op 375 1982.
Sonatina Op 382 (organ) 1983.
Killer of Enemies Op 383 (flute, clarinet, trumpet, trombone, percussion, violin, double bass) 1983.
Music Op 384 (flute, harp, xylophone) 1984.
Organ Sonata No 2 "Invisible Sun" Op 386 1985.

Vocal/choral:

Christmas Song (Watchman, Tell Us of the Night) Op 34 (bass, SATB choir, organ/small orchestra) 1927, revised 1962.
The Moon Has a Face Op 156 (voice, piano; Stevenson) 1930.
Missa brevis Op 4 (SATB choir, organ, strings) 1935.
Three Odes of Solomon Op 5 (Op 30) (voice, piano) 1935, revised 1937.
Hear My Prayer, O Lord Opp 16, 149 (SATB choir) 1935, revised 1960.
Layla Op 29 (voice, piano) 1935, revised 1937.
Love Songs of Hafiz Op 33 (voice, piano) version 1, 1935, revised 1938; version 2, 1957.
The God of Glory Thundereth Op 140 (tenor, SATB choir, organ) 1935, revised 1960.
Alleluia Op 158/11 (SATB choir, organ/piano) 1935, revised 1957.
How I Adore Thee Op 7 (voice, piano) 1936.
Two Motets Op 12 (soprano, flute) 1936.
Three Songs Op 19 (voice, piano) 1936.

Lament Op 20a (voice, piano) 1936.
Easter Anthem Op 18 (soprano, SATB choir, organ) 1937.
O Lord Our Lord Op 23 (bass, SATB choir, organ) 1937.
Why Has Thou Forsaken Me? Op 24 (soprano, SATB choir, organ) 1937.
The Voice of the Lord Op 25 (tenor, SATB choir, organ) 1937.
I Will Extol Thee Op 27 (voice, piano) 1937.
O Lord, Rebuke Me Not Op 28 (SATB choir, organ) 1937.
To the Blessed There Is Joy Op 32 (soprano, female voices) 1937.
Out of the Depths Op 142/3a (solo voice, SATB choir, organ) 1937, revised 1960.
Four Songs Op 35 (voice, piano) 1938.
Two Songs Op 42 (voice, piano) 1938.
Yar Nazani Op 24 (voice, piano) 1939.
Behold, God Is My Help Op 26 (SATB; revised SATB, organ/piano) 1940, revised 1967.
O Lord God of Hosts Op 27 (SATB; revised SATB, organ/piano, optional brass) 1940, revised 1967.
Two Songs Op 32 (voice, piano) 1941.
Protest and Prayer Op 41 (tenor, TTBB choir, piano) 1941, revised 1968.
I Will Rejoice in the Lord Op 42 (SATB choir, organ) 1941.
Let Us Love One Another Op 46 (tenor/baritone, SATB choir) 1941, revised 1968.
Two Shakespeare Sonnets Op 31 (voice, piano) 1942.
Avak the Healer Op 64 (soprano, trumpet, strings) 1945, revised 1946.
The Flute Player of the Armenian Mountains Op 239 (voice, piano) 1946, revised 1971.
Angelic Song Op 19 (soprano, horn, strings) 1948.
Pagan Saint Op 74/1 (voice, piano; Cloos) 1948.
Lullaby of the Lake Op 74/4 (voice, piano; Cloos) 1948.
Raven River Op 74/8 (voice, piano; Cloos) 1948.
30th Ode of Solomon Op 76 (baritone, SATB choir, small orchestra) 1948.
Songs with Armenian Words Op 238 (voice, piano) 1948.
Black Pool of Cat Op 84/1 (voice, piano; Harper) 1949.
Innisfallen Op 84/2 (voice, piano; Harper) 1949.
Three Songs Op 95 (voice, piano; Harper) 1949.
Transfiguration Op 82 (tenor, SATB choir) 1950.
And as They Came Down from the Mountain Op 82/13–16 (tenor, SATB choir) 1950.
Sing Aloud Op 68 (SATB choir) 1951.
Make Haste Op 86 (SATB choir) 1951.
Four Motets Op 87 (SATB choir) 1951.
Shepherd of Israel Op 192 (solo voice, orchestra) 1951.
Ave Maria Op 100/1a (SSAA choir, 2 oboes, 2 horns, harp) 1952.
As on the Night (Christmas Ode) Op 100/1b (soprano, celeste, strings) 1952.
From the End of the Earth Op 177 (SATB choir, organ) 1952.
Easter Cantata Op 100/3 (soprano, SATB choir, small orchestra) 1953.
Canticle Op 115 (soprano, small orchestra) 1953.
Anabasis Op 141 (narrator, soprano, bass, SATB choir, organ) 1953.
Glory to God Op 124 (soprano, alto, SATB choir, brass, percussion) 1954.
The Stars Op 126 (soprano, SATB choir, small orchestra) 1954.
The Brightness of Our Noon Op 131 (SATB choir) 1954.
Live in the Sun Op 169 (solo voice, celeste) 1954, revised 1960.
The Beatitudes Op 100/2 (SATB choir, small orchestra) 1955.
O Lady Moon Op 139 (solo voice, clarinet, piano) 1955.
Ad Lyram Op 143 (solo voices, SSAATTBB choir, orchestra) 1955; first performed Houston, Texas, 12 March 1957.
Hercules Op 56/4 (soprano, violin) 1956.
To the God Who Is in the Fire Op 146 (tenor, TTBB, percussion) 1956, revised 1965; first performed Urbana, Illinois, 13 April 1957.
O Goddess of the Sea Op 151 (voice, piano) 1957.
Dawn at Laona Op 153 (voice, piano) 1957.
Persephone Op 154 (voice, piano) 1957.
Magnificat Op 157 (solo voices, SATB choir, orchestra) 1957.
Look Toward the Sea Op 158 (baritone, SATB choir, trombone, organ) 1957.
The Lord's Prayer Op 35 (SATB choir, organ) 1958.
Psalm CXLVIII Op 160 (bass, SATB choir, organ) 1958.
O for a Shout of Sacred Joy Op 161 (SATB choir, organ) 1958.
Psalm XXVIII Op 162 (SATB choir, organ) 1958.
Glory to Man Op 167 (SAB choir, organ) 1958.
Immortality Op 134 (soprano, SATB) 1960.
Fuji Op 182 (female voice, small orchestra) 1960.
Wind Drum Op 183 (unison voices, small orchestra) 1962.
Jesus, Lover of My Soul Op 53 (solo voice, SATB choir, organ) 1963.
I Have Seen the Lord Op 80 (SATB choir, trumpet, organ) 1963.
O God Our Help in Ages Past Op 137 (SATB choir, organ) 1963.
In the Beginning Was the Word Op 206 (solo voices, SATB choir, orchestra) 1963.
Make a Joyful Noise Op 105 (SATB choir, brass, organ) 1967.
Adoration Op 221 (soprano, alto solo, female voices or tenor, bass solo, male voices, orchestra) 1968.
Praise the Lord with Psaltery Op 222 (SATB choir, orchestra) 1968.
I Will Lift Up Mine Eyes Op 93 (SATB choir, organ) 1969.
Four Songs Op 242 (voice, piano) 1971.
Saturn Op 243 (solo voice, clarinet, piano) 1971.
Four Motets Op 246 (SATB choir) 1971, revised 1972.
Spirit Cat Op 253 (voice, piano) 1971.
Two Songs Op 254 (voice, piano) 1972.
The Hermit Bell-Ringer of the Tower Op 256 (male voices, flute, chimes) 1972.
Three Madrigals Op 258 (SATB choir) 1972.
Three Motets Op 259 (SATB choir) 1972.
For the Waters Are Come Op 257 (male voices) 1973.
Four Motets Op 268 (SATB) 1973.
Three Motets Op 269 (SATB choir) 1973.
Three Sasa Songs Op 274 (voice, piano) 1973.
The Way of Jesus Op 278 (folk mass for SATB choir, unison voices, 3 guitars, orchestra) 1974; first performed New York, 23 February 1975.
A Simple Mass Op 282 (solo voices, chorus, organ) 1975.
Glory Sings the Setting Sun Op 292 (soprano, clarinet, piano) 1977.
How I Love Thy Law Op 298 (soprano, clarinet, piano) 1977.
A Presentiment Op 304 (voice, piano) 1977.
Celestial Canticle Op 305 (voice, piano) 1977.
Adoration Op 221 (solo voice orchestra; version of accompanied choral work) 1978.
Songs Op 315 (high soprano) 1978.
Teach Me Thy Way Op 320 (female voices) 1978.
On Christmas Eve a Child Cried Out Op 337 (chorus, flute, harp) 1979.
Revelations of St Paul Op 343 (oratorio for soprano, tenor, baritone, SATB choir) 1981.
Stars Sing Bell Songs Op 350/1 (soprano, gamelan) 1981.
Lazelar Op 353 (bass, orchestra) 1981.

God Is Our Refuge and Strength Op 359 (SATB choir, orchestra) 1981.
Shigure Op 365 (voice, piano) 1982.
The Waves Unbuild the Wasting Shore Op 376 (tenor, SATB choir, organ) 1983.
Cantate domine Op 385 (SATB choir, organ) 1984.

Opera:

Etchmiadtin Op 62 1946.
Blue Flame Op 172 (chamber opera) 1959.
The Burning House Op 185 (chamber opera) 1960.
Spirit of the Avalanche Op 197 (chamber opera) 1962.
Pilate Op 196 (chamber opera) 1963.
Travellers Op 215 (chamber opera) 1965.
The Leper-King Op 219 (dance drama) 1965.
Lady of Light Op 227 (opera/oratorio) 1969.
Pericles Op 283 1975.
Tale of the Sun Goddess Going into the Stone House Op 323 1978.

Other:

Ardent Song (ballet; Graham) 1954.
A Rose for Miss Emily Op 229/2 (ballet; after Faulkner) 1969.
Dream of a Myth Op 257 (ballet) 1973.
Plains Daybreak (ballet; Hawkins) 1977.

PUBLICATIONS

On Hovhaness: Arnold Rosner, "An Analytical Survey of the Works of AH", dissertation, State University of New York, Buffalo, 1972; B. Silver, "Henry Cowell and AH: Responses to the Music of India", in *Contributions to Asian Studies*, 12, 1978.

* * *

Alan Hovhaness is perhaps one of the most prolific American composers alive today with over 400 works in his catalog. His compositions include operas, chamber works for many different ensembles, symphonies, choral works, orchestral concertos and works for solo instruments. Besides his compositional activities, Hovhaness has conducted or played piano in many of his works, written the librettos for his operas and composed many poems for his vocal compositions. Although his oeuvre resembles the output of many 19th-century European composers, because of the ensembles he has chosen to compose for, the compositions reflect many 20th-century avant-garde sensibilities. Another aspect of his work, its essentially "tonal" language, gives Hovhaness the appearance of being a neo-classicist or neo-romantic. However, his use of scalar and harmonic resources transcends neoism. One 20th-century aesthetic, eclecticism, is evident in all of Hovhaness's work. His borrowings from the Western tradition include modal techniques from the Renaissance and contrapuntal techniques from the Baroque. His borrowings from non-Western cultures include Armenian folk melodies, the creation of original *ragas* in the Indian tradition and from the Japanese Gagaku tradition he acquired a non-European harmonic and melodic vocabulary. For instance, the influence of the shō, a mouth organ that plays chord clusters used in a Gagaku ensemble, is heard in the *Duet* for violin and harpsichord.

While many 20th-century composers have made the development of a new musical syntax the central feature of their work, Hovhaness has concentrated on the mystical and religious aspects of musical expression. Of course, his metaphysical interests are most obvious in his texted compositions, but even his instrumental works bear subtitles that reveal their religious or philosophical underpinnings. For example, about the orchestral composition *Floating World*, Hovhaness says the music is an abstraction of a Japanese idea in which the "Floating World" either represents the Buddhist concept of uncertainty, unpredictability and the insubstantial qualities of the material world, or it represents the concepts of pleasure and delight from the Edo period of Japan. The possible conflict that exists between the interpretations provides a scenario for the contrasting sections of the work. In its essence, Hovhaness's music is programatic. Consequently, form, imitative counterpoint, the movement from one scale or mode to another, the creation of *raga* type melodic fragments, and harmonic coloration, serve a narrative function.

Hovhaness's work also exhibits a 20th-century concern with the exploration of new timbral resources. In the *Suite* for violin, piano and percussion the inside of the piano is used to create gong-like sounds. Perhaps the most dramatic exploration of timbre occurs in the composition *And God Created Great Whales*. In this work, four sections using taped whale sounds alternate with orchestral passages. The timbre and intervallic structure of the whale songs directly and indirectly influence the timbral colors used by the acoustic instruments. The trombones and violins, for instance, imitate the whale sounds through the use of glissandos, while unmeasured passages of repeated melodic figures with various types of articulations sound as if they are providing an abstract timbral commentary on the whale sounds. He has also experimented with microtonality.

Hovhaness's earlier works, numbering well over a thousand, were destroyed by the composer in the early 1940s. The compositions written after 1943 show the influence of his studies of the seventh-century Armenian religious music (a return to his own Armenian roots), Asian music and the music of South India. The *Armenian Rhapsody No 3* for string orchestra dates from this period, and is representative of the compositional strategies that have interested Hovhaness throughout his career.

In the preface to the score, Hovhaness says that the work is based on two melodies: a Maundy Thursday tune *Sird Im Sasani* (My Heart Is Shattered) and the folk song *Bagh Aghpiuri Mod* (By the Cold Fountain). He goes on to say that "the music is a miniature spiritual history of Armenia in three arcs of sound: 1) Cry of the soul of the Armenian people; 2) Harp of exile whispers, sofly touched in a distant land; 3) Dream of village fountain, fleeting, dissolving into nothingness."

The first section opens with the cellos answered by the violins and violas. The imitative texture continues, producing a responsorial effect. Although the opening measures suggest a dorian mode (a true dorian since the central pitch is D), by the third measure the modal centre is destabilized with the introduction of the pitch F#. Two measures later, B♭ and E♭ are introduced, but the tonal center remains D. The B♭ might be expected in the Dorian mode, however, the E♭ and F# give the scale an exotic quality. After exploring the D pitch area, the tonal center shifts to G minor-major, a move facilitated by the introduction of the E♭ and F#. At the close of the first section, the tonal center shifts back to D, thereby creating an ABA form.

Hovhaness's music, like much Asian and Indian music, is melodic in nature, but his music combines exotic scales and raga-like melodies with the formalism of Baroque counterpoint. Canons, imitative counterpoint and fugues of all types have been a ubiquitous feature in his works. He often does not develop melodies in the Western sense, but he constantly presents them in new contexts. When compositions employ a traditional European mode or a collection of pitches, such as the seven note collection C, G, A♭, B♭, D#, E and F# in the first movement of *Symphony No 15: Silver Pilgrimage*, the pitch material tends to be limited to that mode or collection. However, one instrument, such as the celeste in the *Mysterious Mountain, Symphony No 2*, will introduce the notes that are not members of the mode or collection in order to produce a quasi-mysterioso effect.

While Hovhaness's music is essentially melodic, harmonic structures also play an important role. However, his harmonies are often non-triadic. Tone clusters are frequently juxtaposed to or combined with contrapuntal writing. This technique is especially evident in the *Poseidon Sonata* for solo piano. Hovhaness also uses traditional Western harmonic structuers, such as major and minor chords, but in non-functional contexts. The works after the 1970s appear to emphasize chordal sonorities. The *Symphony No 22, City of Light*, is an excellent example of Hovhaness's chordal style.

A particularly important feature of his compositional style is the use of rhythmically free sections (*Senza misura*) that alternate or are combined with meterically notated ones. The *Symphony No 25* titled *Odysseus Symphony*, is representative of this technique. While the strings play unmeasured tremelo, the winds repeat short melodic phrases that are articulated by means of crescendo and decrescendo. The effect produced is waves of quasi-chaotic sound coalescing into order when the winds begin to play in a meter. This technique is reminiscent of the *alapana* or *alap* introductions that begin many Indian compositions. Hovhaness, however, makes the *senza misura* sections of his works essential aspects of their form.

Hovhaness has managed create a musical path all his own. He has produced and continues to produce an outstanding body of work. He is one of the most frequently performed and commissioned American composers, and his works are well received by audiences.

—Ciro G. Scotto

HOVLAND, Egil. Norwegian. Born at Mysen, Eidsberg, 18 October 1924. Educated at Oslo Musikkonservatorium (organ scholar under Arild Sandvold and Per Steenberg), 1946–9; studied composition in Oslo (under Bjarne Brustad), Copenhagen (under Vagn Holmboe), Tanglewood, Massachusetts (under Aaron Copland), and Florence (under Luigi Dallapiccola). Married Synnove Hovland, 11 January 1947; 3 children. Organist of Glemmen Church, Frederikstad, since 1949; commissioned to revise hymnal and liturgical books for Church of Norway, since 1957. Recipient: various awards and honours; prize (for *Jotuslatt*) in Musicians' Association of Oslo Composers' Contest, 1953; Knight of the Royal Order of Saint Olav, 1983. Mailing address: Labrahen 14c, N-1600 Frederikstad, Norway.

Publisher: Norsk Musikforlag, Box 1499 Vika, N-0116 Oslo 1, Norway.

Symphonies/orchestral:

Passacaglia and Fugue Op 12 (string orchestra; based on traditional Norwegian tune) 1949.
Jotuslatt Op 17 1951; first performed Oslo, 1953.
Symphonia Veris Op 20 1952–3; first performed Oslo, 10 December 1954.
Concertino for Three Trumpets and Strings Op 23 1954–5; first performed Oslo, 25 January 1957.
Symphony No 2 Op 24 1954–5; first performed Bergen, 8 November 1956.
Suite for Flute and Strings Op 31 1959; first performed Oslo, 28 April 1960.
Festival Overture No 2 Op 39a (symphonic band) 1962; first performed Bergen, 1962. Recorded RCA L4352.
Festival Overture No 2 Op 39b 1962; first performed Bergen, 15 October 1962.
Lamenti per orchestra Op 43 1963; first performed Oslo, 24 April 1964. Recorded Philips 6507 010; Aurora Contemporary NCD-B 4944.
Fanfare and Chorale Op 54a (symphonic band) 1966; first performed Norway, June 1966.
Fanfare and Chorale Op 54b 1967; first performed Bergen, 6 June 1967. Recorded Philips 6507 040; Aurora Contemporary NCD-B 4944.
Third Symphony Op 30 (recitation, SATB choir, orchestra; Bible, Medboe) 1969–70; first performed Oslo, 9 April 1970.
Rhapsody 69 Op 65 1969; first performed Oslo, 3 October 1970.
Concerto for Trombone and Orchestra Op 76 1972; first performed Bergen, 7 September 1972. Recorded NC 6009.
Concerto for Violin and Orchestra Op 81 1974; first performed Frederikstad, 5 November 1974.
Noel Variations Op 84 (orchestral version of op 83 no 1) 1975; first performed Stavanger, 18 June 1975.
Concerto for Piano and Orchestra Op 91 1976–7; first performed Oslo, 1 December 1977.
Tombeau de Bach Op 95 1977–8; first performed Oslo, 18 August 1978.
Concerto for Piccolo Flute and String Orchestra Op 117 (amplified piccolo) 1986; first performed Oslo, 20 April 1989.

Chamber/instrumental:

Five Chorale Preludes for Organ Op 4 1945.
Chorale Partita No 1 Op 7 (organ; based on hymn "Gjor doren hoy") 1947.
Orgel—Te Deum Op 8 (organ; based on Te Deum of Early Church) 1947. Recorded Varese VS 85 022; Callisto CS 85022.
Improvisata Op 9 (organ; based on 13th-century Norwegian terce hymn to St Magnus, Earl of the Orkneys) 1948.
Chorale Partita No 2 Op 10 (organ; 7 variations on the hymn "Hvo ene lader Herred rade") 1948–55.
Three Choral Preludes for Organ 1950s.
Suite for Flute and Piano Op 15 1950; first performed Copenhagen, 21 October 1951. Recorded NC 3820.
Nu la oss takke Gud (organ toccata) 1953.
Suite No 1 Op 21 (organ) 1954–6.
Music for Ten Instruments Op 28 (flute, oboe, clarinet, bassoon, horn, 2 violins, viola, cello, double bass) 1957; first performed Oslo, 28 March 1958. Recorded Forum FORLP 6100.
Klaverstykker Op 29 (piano) 1958–67, 1983.
Chorale Partita No 3 Op 32 (organ; 6 variations on hymn "Klippe, du som brast for meg") 1959.

Motus per flauto solo Op 36 (flute) 1960; first performed Oslo, 4 December 1961.

Cantus I Op 45 (flute, harpsichord) 1964. Recorded BIS LP 68.

Varianti per due pianoforti Op 47 (2 pianos) 1964; first performed Stockholm, 15 August 1964.

Trio for Violin, Cello and Piano Op 48 1965; first performed Trondheim, 6 January 1977.

Quintet for Winds Op 50 1965; broadcast Danish Radio, 7 September 1965. Recorded Philips 839 248 AY; Aurora Contemporary NCD-B 4944.

Elementa pro organo Op 52 (organist, 2 assistants) 1965; first performed Oslo, 22 June 1965. Recorded Philips 853 000 AY.

Lord God, Thy Glorious Name and Honour Op 56 (organ; chorale partita no 5) 1967; first performed Coventry, Warwickshire, 1967. Recorded Simax PN 2013.

Variations for Oboe and Piano Op 64 1968–9; first performed Oslo, Spring 1970. Recorded Philips 6507 053.

Four Interludes to "Missa Vigilate" Op 67 (organ) 1969; first performed Stockholm, 24 October 1969. Recorded Polyhymnia PRC 7811; NC 3846; Aurora Contemporary NCD-B4944.

Interludium (organ; from the opera *Brennen / The Well Op 77*) 1971–2.

Job: Suite No 2 for Organ Op 79 1973; first performed Gjovik, 8 May 1973. Recorded Simax PN 2003; Polyhymnia PRC 7811.

Cantus II Op 83 No 1 (descant recorder, piano) 1974–5; first performed Oslo, 13 April 1975. Recorded BIS LP 202.

Gelobt sei Gott im Hochsten Thron Op 90 (organ; chorale partita no 6) 1975; first performed Valer, Ostfold, 5 October 1975.

Crux Ave—Jerusalem, du hochgebaute Stadt Op 102 (organ; chorale partita no 7) 1978–9; first performed Tromborg, 16 September 1979.

Cantus III Op 103 (violin, piano) 1979–80; first performed Stavanger, 8 May 1980.

Cantus IV Op 97 (brass quintet) 1979; first performed Bergen, September 1979.

Second Quintet for Winds Op 110 1980; first performed Oslo, 15 October 1980.

Il Canto del Mare Op 114 (organ) 1980; first performed Strasbourg, 20 May 1981. Recorded Simax PN 2013.

String Quartet No 1 Op 116 1981; first performed Oslo, 20 October 1981.

Cantus V Op 120 (trombone, organ) 1982; first performed Stockholm, 19 April 1983.

Cantus VI (Ved haandarbeit) Op 118 (bass/treble/descant/sopranino recorder, flute in G/flute in C/piccolo, piano) 1982; first performed Oslo, 1983.

Cantus VII (il Maestro) Op 132 (organ, 3 trumpets, 2 horns, 3 trombones, tuba, timpani) 1985; first performed Trondheim, 21 June 1985.

Cantus VIII Op 129 (oboe, string quartet) 1985–6; first performed Oslo, 15 May 1986.

Cantus IX Op 133 (organ, percussion) 1986; first performed Oslo, 15 November 1986.

Vocal / choral:

6 Koraler Op 1 (voice, piano; no 6 for SATB chorus; Eriksen, Bonnevie, Johnson, Blix) 1944.

8 Sanger for Solostemme og Klaver Op 2 (voice, piano; Hovden, Orheim, Blix, Walton, Eriksen, Landstad, Hognestad) 1944–5.

2 Motetter for 4st. blandet kor Op 5 (motets for mixed choir) 1946.

4 Koral-Bearbeidelser for 5st. blandet kor a cappella Op 6 (four hymns arranged for unaccompanied 5-part choir) 1947.

To Gammeltestamentlige Singer for Sopran, Floyte og Orgel Op 16 (soprano, flute, organ; Old Testament) 1950; first performed Copenhagen, 21 October 1951.

Kristus er her Op 26 (narrator, solo voices, choir, organ; Hovda) 1955–6; first performed Oslo, 5 July 1956.

Solokantate for Bass og Orgel Op 27 (solo cantata, bass, organ; Jeremiah) 1956; first performed Oslo, 11 April 1956.

Vexilla Regis Op 33 (chorale partita no 4 for organ and unison choir) 1959.

Sanger for Solostemme og Klaver Op 34 (voice, piano; Sande, Overland, Tul, Handagard, Hovden) 1959–64.

Solokantate No 2—Opploft Ditt Syn, Du Kristensjel Op 35 (soprano, bass, flute, violin, organ; Landstad) 1960; first performed Frederikstad, 26 June 1960.

Velt alle dine veie Op 37 (cantata for solo voices, congregation, choir, flute, oboe, violin, organ) 1961; first performed Oslo, 26 June 1961.

Gloria Op 40a / b (original version for mixed choir, 7 brass; second version for mixed choir, organ) 1962; first performed Stavanger, 22 September 1963.

Et Norsk Te Deum / A Norwegian Te Deum Op 41a / b (original version for mixed choir, 3 trumpets, 3 trombones, tuba, 2 oboes, 2 bassoons, organ and congregation; second version for mixed choir, organ) 1962; first performed Stavanger, 22 September 1963.

The Song of Songs Op 42 (soprano, violin, percussion, piano; Solomon) 1963; first performed Stockholm, 30 March 1963.

Magnificat Op 44 (contralto, recorder, harp) 1964; first performed Oslo, 8 March 1964. Recorded NC 3846; Aurora Contemporary NCD-B 4944.

Du vaere lovet, Jesus Krist Op 46 (choral cantata for mixed choir, 3 trumpets, strings, organ and congregation ad lib) 1964.

Jule-Litani / Litania i Jultid / Christmas Litany Op 49 (narrator, soprano, SATB choir, orchestra, organ) 1965; first performed Trondheim, 26–7 June 1965.

Rorate Op 55 (solo organ, flute, oboe, 4 percussion, strings, 5 soprano voices, tape) 1966–7; broadcast Norwegian Radio, 25 December 1974. Recorded NC 4906.

Guds Sonn steg ned a tjene Op 57 (choral cantata for mixed choir, string orchestra; Dahl) 1967.

How Long, O Lord? Op 58 (motet for unaccompanied mixed choir; Psalm 13) 1967; first performed Bergen, 24 May 1968. Recorded NKLP 15; Philips 854 000 AY.

Missa vigilate Op 59 (choir, baritone, soprano, 2–5 dancers, organ, tape) 1967; first performed Oslo, 14 October 1967.

Lilja—ord om kjaerlik fra hogsongen (The Lily) Op 61 (female narrator, orchestra; Song of Solomon) 1968; first performed Norwegian Radio, 6 April 1969. Recorded Philips 6507 046; NC 3846.

Regn—en barnevise med musikk Op 62 (unison children's choir, 2 violins, piano, percussion; Obstfjelder) 1968.

Den Vakreste Rosen (The Loveliest Rose in the World) Op 71 (narrator, 4 soprano voices, organ, orchestra; Andersen, trad.) 1970; first performed Norwegian television, 24 December 1970. Recorded Proprius PROP 7755.

Saul Op 74 (motet for narrator, mixed choir, organ) 1971; first performed Alesund, 26 September 1971. Recorded Proprius PROP 7770; NC 3846.

Missae Misericordiae Op 80 (unaccompanied mixed choir) 1973; first performed Frederikstad, 13 October 1974. Recorded NKLP 15.

Kyrkans eviga Lovsang Op 82 (triple choir, 2 horns,

2 trombones, tuba, tubular bells, organ) 1974; first performed Karlstad, 15 June 1975. Recorded Kyrkoton LP 156.
Motets Op 87:
1. "Se, dager kommer" (SSSSSAA choir) 1975; first performed Molde, 22 June 1975.
2. "Laudate dominum" (SSA choir) 1976; first performed Bergen, 29 May 1976. Recorded NKLP 15; ProMus PP 9003.
3. "Bli hos oss" (4–5 part mixed choir, organ) 1978. Recorded Simax PSC 1034.
4. "O Come, Let Us Sing" (SSAA choir; Psalm 95).
5. "Rcturn, My Soul" (SATB choir, soprano solo; Psalm 116) 1986.

Nyttarsklokkene / Ring Out, Wild Bells Op 100 (3 female voices, narrator, organ, harp, double bass; Tennyson, Grythe) 1979; first performed Norwegian television, 31 December 1979.
Intrada: Navnet Jesus Op 105 (SATB choir, congregation, 2 brass groups: 3 trumpets, 3 horns, tuba, or 6 trombones, tuba, orchestra; Welander) 1980; first performed Oslo, 23 November 1980.
Djuren i stallet Op 106 (narrator, SSAA choir, 2 clarinets, 2 cellos, double bass, celeste, harp; Hallqvist) 1980; first performed Oslo, 18 December 1980.
Meditasjon Op 115 (narrator, SSATB chorus, congregation, organ, orchestra; Bjorlykke) 1980; first performed Oslo, 23 November 1980.
Profane Choir Songs Op 108 (I—male chorus; Kvalstad; II and III—SSA choir; Catullus, Eggen, Hallqvist) 1982.

Opera:

Brunnen / The Well Op 77 (church opera for flute, organ, percussion, solo singers, speaking choir, dancers, tape; Wall) 1971–2; first performed Oslo, 17 March 1982.

Other / liturgical:

100 Salmeforspill (from Opp 3 and 13) (organ or harmonium; 100 chorale preludes for use during service).
Orgelmusik til Bruk ved Gudstjenesten Op 14 (organ music in six books for use during service).
Motetter til Kirkearet / Motets for the Liturgical Year Op 25 1957:
"Se, din Konge kommer til deg" (4-part choir).
"Spenn beltet om livet" (3-part choir).
"Rydd vei for Herren" (2-part choir, organ).
"Hor pa meg, mitt folk!" (solo voice, organ).
"Fikentreet uten frukt" (solo voice, organ).
"Jesus Kristus er den samme" (4-part choir).
"Go ogsa dere til min vingard" "(2-part choir, organ).
"Salige er de somhorer Guds ord" (4 or 5-part choir).
"Sennepskornet" (4-part choir).
"Frelsens dag" (4-part choir).
"Vaer tro" (4-part choir).
"Og ordet ble Kjod" (4-part choir).
"Hosianna i det hoyeste" (4-part choir).
"Improperiene: Mitt folk, mitt folk" (4-part choir, solo voice).
"Hvofor soker dereden levende blandt de dode" (3-part choir, organ).
"Fred vaere med dere" (4-part choir).
"Jeg er veien, sannheten og livet" (solo voice).
"Den somber, han far" (4-part choir, organ).
"Talsmannen, den Hellige And" (2-part choir, organ).
"Sa hoyt har Gud elsket verden" (solo voice).
"Herre, var Herre" (4-part choir).
"Hva gagner det er menneske" (solo voice). Recorded NKLP 15.
"Kom for na erdet ferdig" (2-part choir, organ).
"Dom ikke" (4-6 part choir). Recorded Lynor LYLP 505.
"Frykt ikke" (4-part choir).
"Den kongelege lov" (2-part choir).
"Til bords i Guds rike" (4-part choir).
"Loven og profetene" (4-6 part choir). Recorded NKLP 15.
"Jerusalem" (4-8 part choir). Recorded NKLP 15; NC 6108.
"Han har gjort alle ting vel" (2-part choir, organ).
"Sok forst Guds rike" (4-part choir).
"De ydmyke" (4-part choir).
"Du skal elske Herren din Gud" (2-part choir).
"Loft troens skjold" (4-part choir). Recorded Philips 839 235 NY.
"De salige" (4-5 part choir).
"Dette er min Fars vilje" (solo voice).
"Ver miskunnsame" (3-part choir).
"Himmel og jord" (solo voice).
"Velsignet vaere kongen" (solo voice).
"Herren er minhyrde" (4-part choir, organ).
"Marias lovsang" (4-part choir, solo group, organ).
"Til Himmels upp var Frelsar for" (unison choir, organ).
"Lovad vare Herren, Israels Gud" (3-part choir, organ).
"I klentrogna, varfor radens" (3-part choir, organ).
"Frukta icke, Maria" (3-part choir, organ).
"Hjalparen, den Heliga Ande" (3-part choir, organ).
"Se, vi ga nu upp til Jerusalem" (3-part choir).
"Fruckta icke; harefter" (4-part choir).
"Van hjalper det en manniska" (unison choir, organ).
"Kommen, ty nu ar allt redo" (2-part choir, organ).
"Jag ar vagen och sanningen och livet" (unison choir, organ).
"Himmel och jord" (unison choir, organ).

Introitus Op 38 (A—arrangement of ancient introits; B—newly composed introits) 1961.
Salmemelodier for Menighetssang / Hymn Tunes for Congregation Op 51 (words by various hands, but chiefly by Hallqvist) 1965.
21 Inngangssanger / 21 Introit Hymns Op 53 (congregation, choir, organ) 1968–9.
Uppstandelsemassa / Resurrection Mass Op 60 (choir, 3 trumpets, 3 trombones, 2 organs, congregation; trad., Hartman) 1968; first performed Uppsala, Easter 1968.
Se, jeg gjor all ting nye Op 63a (liturgical drama; narrators, soprano, unison children's choir, oboe, organ, congregation) 1968.
Tacksamhetens Massa Op 66a (thanksgiving mass) 1969. Recorded Proprius PROP 7755.
Bibelske sanger for kor, orgel og menighetssang Op 107 (17 psalms) 1970–84.
Et barn er off fodt Op 63b (liturgical drama; narrators, soprano, choir, organ, congregation) 1971.
Introitus-Sanger Op 68 (13 introits commissioned by church committee). Nos 1, 3, 4, 5, 6, 10 recorded Kyrkoton LP 156.
Allhelgensmesse / All Saints Mass Op 70 (soprano, choir, 3 trumpets, 3 bassoons, tuba, congregation) 1970. Recorded NKLP 5.
Ordinarie-Sanger Op 72 (commissioned by church committee) 1971.
Missa Brevis Op 73 (choir, organ, congregation) 1971; first performed Glemmen, 1971. Recorded Lumi LU 200/64.
Langfredag / Good Friday Op 75 (choir, organ, congregation) 1972; first performed Grefsen, 30 March 1972.

Missa Verbi Op 78 (3 trumpets, 2 horns, 3 trombones, tuba, organ, congregation) 1973; first performed Frederikstad, 22 September 1973. Recorded NKLP 6.

Familjegudst janstens Laudamus Op 66b (commissioned by church committee) 1974.

I Dag/Today Op 85 (choir, instruments, etc.) 1974; first performed Ransater, 5–11 August 1974. Recorded FXLP 5.

Diskanter: Hefte 1 Op 86 (16 descants). Recorded Lumi LU 200/64; Lynor LYLP 504.

Liturgisk Musikk for Menighet og Orgel Op 88 (liturgical music for congregation and organ) 1975.

I Soluppgangen/At Daybreak Op 89 (choir, instruments, etc.) 1975; first performed Ransater, 4-10 August 1975. Recorded NKLP 9.

Diskanter: Hefte 2 Op 92 (21 descants) 1976.

Nagon/Someone Op 93 (choir, instruments, etc.) 1976; first performed Ransater, 2–8 August 1976.

Diskanter: Hefte 3 Op 98 (15 descants) 1977.

Hosianna Op 99 (for choir, instruments, etc.) 1977; first performed Ransater, 2–7 August 1977.

Koralboker/Melodisamlinger Op 125 (most arranged for piano or organ) 1977–83.

Gud synes om Deg Op 101 No 1 (SA children's choir, organ, congregation; Hallqvist) 1978; first performed Trondheim, 10-11 June 1978.

Diskanter: Hefte 4 Op 104 (19 descants) 1978.

Han lever idag Op 101 No 2 (SA children's choir, organ, congregation; Hallqvist) 1979; first performed Stavanger, 27 May 1979.

Gutten som englene sang om Op 101 No 3 (SA children's choir, organ, piano, flute, percussion, congregation; Hallqvist) 1979; first performed Glemmen, 23 December 1979.

Diskanter: Hefte 5 Op 109 (21 descants).

Diskanter: Hefte 6 Op 112 (15 descants).

Syn mitt hjerte Op 113 No 1 (biblical play for SA choir, baritone, flute, organ, congregation; Hallqvist) 1980; first performed Eidsvoll, 7 September 1980.

Mannen i treet Op 113 No 2 (biblical play for SA choir, solo voices, organ, piano, flute, speaking parts, congregation; Hallqvist) 1980–1; first performed Glemmen, 6 March 1981.

Baer langtmin sang Op 113 no 3 (missionary scene for choir and congregation; Skeie) 1981; first performed Hamar, 1981.

Sa lenge vi vandrer pa Jorden Op 113 No 4 (biblical play for SA choir, solo voice, piano, speaking parts, congregation; Hallqvist) 1981.

Pilgrimsmesse Op 111 (SATB choir, organ, 3 flugelhorns, 2 horns, 3 trombones, tuba, congregation) 1981–2; first performed Hamar, 31 October 1982.

Op 94 (choral adaptations and arrangements) 1982:
- "Syng ut i fryd" (3 equal voices).
- "Lover Gud i Himmelkor" (unison voices, organ, recorders).
- "Pa jorden fred og glede" (unison voices, 2 descant recorders, organ).
- "A, kom, la oss folge stjernen/Adeste, fideles" (mixed choir).
- "Nu la oss takke Gud" (4-part choir, brass, organ).
- "Av hoyheten opprunnen er" (4-part choir, 2 oboes, organ).
- "I Himmelen" (solo voice, 2-part children's or female choir, organ).
- "Kling no klokka" (3 female voices). Recorded FXLP 10.
- "Vi vil ga ut" (4-part chorus, flute, guitar, organ, piano, double bass, percussion).

Josef og brodrene Hans—I. Josef, Drommeren Op 113 No 5 (biblical play for SA choir, solo voices, piano, speaking parts, congregation; Hallqvist, Skeie) 1982; first performed Glemmen, 19 December 1982.

Dona nobis pacem Op 124 No 1 (ballet; SATB choir, organ, flute, trombone, drum, narrator, dancers) 1982; first performed Glemmen, 21 March 1982.

Den heliga dansen / The Sacred Dance Op 124 no 2 (ballet; choir, spoken voice, dancers with organ, vibraphone, percussion) 1982.

Josef og brodrene Hans II. Josef i Egypt Op 113 no 6 (biblical play for SA choir, solo voices, piano, speaking parts, congregation; Hallqvist, Skeie) 1982; first performed Glemmen, 19 December 1982.

Danse de la mort Op 127 (ballet; orchestra, dancers) 1983; first performed Bergen, 8 June 1983.

Mor Maria Op 113 No 7 (biblical play for SA choir, solo voices, piano, organ, speaking parts, congregation; Hallqvist, Skeie) 1984; first performed Glemmen, 1984.

Veni creator spiritus Op 124 No 3 (ballet; choir, narrator, dancers with organ, piano, timpani, percussion) 1984.

Diskanter: Hefte 9 Op 131 (9 descants); first performed Frederikstad, 22 June 1985.

Diskanter: Hefte 8 Op 132 (16 descants).

14 Preludier och satser till inngangspalmer Op 130 (instruments, choir; in 2 sets).

Preludier og satser til inngangssalmer (further set of 5).

Skapelsen Op 113 No 8 (biblical play for unison children's choir, piano, percussion, speaking parts, congregation; Hallqvist, Skeie) 1985; first performed Glemmen, 1985.

Den rike mann og Lasarus Op 113 No 9 (biblical play for SA choir, soprano, piano, organ, flute, double bass, percussion, leader, congregation; Hallqvist, Skeie) 1986; first performed Molde, 19–21 June 1987.

Noa gar i land Op 113 No 10 (biblical play for SA choir, solo voices, piano, organ, percussion, congregation) 1987; first performed Glemmen, 20 March 1988.

Diskanter: Hefte 7 Op 119 (14 descants).

PUBLICATIONS

On Hovland: Tor Brevig, "EH", in *Nutida Musik*, 5, 1963/4; Nils Grinde, in *Festskrift til EH pa 50-arsdagen*, Frederikstad, 1974; *Contemporary Norwegian Music 1920–80*, Oslo, 1981; Raymond Arnold Olien, "EH: Four Selected Works", thesis, University of Illinois, Urbana, 1982; Constance Marie Jaeger, "A Survey of Notable Composers of Organ Music in Norway, with Particular Emphasis upon EH", thesis, University of Washington, Seattle, 1984; Eva Valebrokk, in *Ni norske Kunstnere*, Oslo, 1988.

* * *

The works of Egil Hovland cover a wide range of styles and genres, a variety which is probably unique in Norway. However, church music makes up the largest part of his output. In fact, the different phases of his development reflect that of Norwegian music in general. With national Romanticism as his point of departure, Hovland composed in a neo-classical style in the 1950s, and, having explored dodecaphony, aleatorics and aspects of timbre during the 1960s, he eventually returned to a period of neo-romantic simplicity with elements of style-synthesis in the 1970s and 1980s.

The aesthetics of "Art pour l'art" seem quite alien to Hovland. The techniques he uses are always subordinate to the possibilities of an adequate subjective expression. However, balancing expression and technique in the live concert situation is equally important. A satisfying communication between composer-musician-listener is essential for Hovland.

Characteristic features of the works from the 1950s, for example *Symphonia Veris* are the divertimento-like idiomatic way of writing together with the use of lively rhythms. Impulses from Stravinsky, Bartók and Copland are evident.

As a direct result of studying with Dallapiccola in Italy, Hovland began radical experiments with form and sound during the 1960s. *Lamenti per orchestra* marks an important milestone, not only in Hovland's output, but also in Norwegian music at the time. The work is built on a twelve-tone row which is symmetrical around an axis of a tritone. Aleatorics and electronics also feature, and sonorous effects and a richness of colours come to the fore in the work. The texture shows possible influences of Penderecki, but the overall impression is that of a "Nordic expressionism".

Lamenti is, in spite of its modernisms, still rooted in tradition. The new techniques employed did not cause a radical change of style. Stylistic consolidation, rather than innovation, is significant for Hovland. He has always followed the musical developments of the continental precursors with great interest and curiosity, but never took up a leading position of exploring new techniques and concepts for their own sake.

The *Quintet for Winds* takes a central place among chamber works from the 1960s. Consisting of seven short movements, the piece contains a variety of techniques and means of expression—clusters, static passages of sound, repetitive ostinatos, punctual-textures and melodic progressions of tone-colours. The concentration and stringency of these aphorisms makes the Quintet one of Hovland's most prominent works.

Looked upon as church music, *Elementa pro organo* is a progressive work, but it was *Missa vigilate* that caused one of the biggest music scandals in Norway since the post-war period. It was not the music as such that made the work so controversial, but the fact that Hovland had inserted a choreographed scene, which provoked the conservative Norwegian church. His striving for renewal and his flexible attitude towards sacred music makes Hovland the foremost radical of church music in Norway.

The typical stylistic writing, sometimes virtuoso and light in character, reappears in an uncomplicated, accessible style from the 1970s onwards.

In the *Concerto for Piccolo Flute and String Orchestra* disparate elements are mixed, e.g., a choral melody, which seems totally out of place, unexpectedly appears—an indication of the way Hovland lets his intuition determine the working out of the compositions, thus allowing his music to be "less pretentious and serious".

Being an organist and a participant in the musical activities of the congregation, Hovland has produced a great deal of *Gebrauchsmusik*. For Hovland it is both natural and important to create music in the traditional classical idiom as well as in its popular form. Hovland then, is a creative composer–musician in practice.

—Björn Billing

HOYLAND, Vic. British/English. Born in Wombwell, Yorkshire, 11 December 1945. Educated at University of Hull; University of York (composition under Robert Sherlaw Johnson and Bernard Rands), D. Phil. Hayward Fellow in Music, University of Birmingham, 1980–3; visiting lecturer in music, University of York, from 1983; lecturer, Barber Institute for Fine Arts, Birmingham, from 1985; founder, now artistic director and co-director, Northern Music Theatre. Mailing address: c/o Universal Edition, 2–3 Fareham Street, London W1V 4DU, England.

Publisher: Universal Edition.

Symphonies/orchestral:

In Transit 1987; first performed London, 4 August 1987.

Chamber/instrumental:

Esem (double bass, 2 flutes/alto flute, 2 clarinets/bass clarinet, vibraphone, celeste, cello, electric organ) 1975.
Serenade (2 flutes/piccolos, 2 clarinets, trumpet, trombone, harp, piano/celeste, vibraphone, glockenspiel, 3 cellos, 2 double basses) 1979.
Andacht zum Kleinem (flute/alto flute, clarinet/bass clarinet, trumpet/trumpet in C, trombone, harp, vibraphone/glockenspiel, violin, viola, cello) 1980.
Reel (3 oboes, 3 cors anglais, 2 bassoons, contrabassoon) 1980.
Quartet Movement (string quartet) 1982.
Fox (2 alto flutes/flute/piccolo, clarinet/bass clarinet, vibraphone/glockenspiel, 2 violins, viola, cello, double bass, piano, harp) 1983.
Quintet of Brass 1985.
String Quartet 1985.
Hoquetus David (flute, clarinet, trombone, harp, violin/mandolin, viola, double bass) 1987; first performed London, 1 September 1987.
Work-Out (trombone) 1987; first performed London, 1 September 1987.
Work Out for Marimba (marimba, kat) 1988.
Of Fantasy, Of Dreams and Ceremonies (13 solo strings: 7 violins, 3 violas, 2 cellos, double bass) 1989; first performed Birmingham, 5 March 1989.
Trio (piano, violin, cello) 1989; first performed Huddersfield, Yorkshire, 23 November 1990.
Quintet (piano, string quartet) 1990; first performed London, 3 July 1990.

Vocal/choral:

Em (24 voices SATB; Anglo-Saxon poem *The Ruin*) 1970.
Es (3 speakers, 12 voices SATB, flute, alto flute, 2 percussion, vibraphone, harp, violin, viola, cello, double bass; Satie) 1971.
Jeux-Thème (mezzo-soprano, 2 flutes, 2 clarinets, 2 trumpets, 2 trombones, 4 percussion, vibraphone, marimba, harp, celeste, piano, organ, 4 cellos, 2 double basses; Verlaine) 1972; first performed York, 1973.
Ariel (voice, solo flute, 2 flutes, 2 harps, 2 vibraphones, 2 marimbas, 4 percussion; Plath) 1974–5.
Michelagniolo (baritone, chorus, large ensemble) 1981; first performed 11 May 1984.
Head and Two Tails (consisting of *Bitch* for solo male voice, *Dumb Show* for male and female participant, percussion and amplified voice, *Foxed* for 8 voices [3 solo, 5 chorus],

4 percussion, 2 amplified pianos; Old and Middle English texts) 1984.
Seneca / Medea (soprano, alto, tenor, bass, alto flute, clarinet, piano, vibraphone, percussion, marimba, violin, cello; Seneca) 1985.
Crazy Rosa—La madre (mezzo-soprano, flute/alto flute, clarinet/bass clarinet, 2 percussion, piano, harp, viola, cello; Fo, translated Hirst) 1988; first performed London, January 1990.

Other:

Xingu (music theatre for orchestra and 3 groups of children, 25+ in each) 1979.

* * *

Even in his instrumental and orchestral music (two categories which have so far been much overshadowed by his vocal writing) there is no mistaking Vic Hoyland's fundamentally dramatic emphasis. His sole purely orchestral work to date is the 1987 London Proms commission *In Transit*, a work of powerfully muted harmonies and no less paradoxical narrative development. Though its climaxes are more than adequately prepared for, the overall impression is episodic and suggests nothing more strongly than a Wim Wenders road movie in which gestures and signs are of far greater significance than destinations or resolutions.

There is, though, nothing haphazard about Hoyland's music, which usually depends on a forceful rhythmic argument; *In Transit* features five percussionists ranged in a dominating half-circle around the perimeter of the orchestra, and the superb music theatre piece *Xingu* grows almost entirely out of the rhythms of the opening movement. *Xingu*'s subject matter, the organic and untroubled existence of an Amazonian tribe, is reflected in the music without banality. It is also, of course, a magnificent *coup de théâtre*, with young chorus members popping up all over the auditorium.

Hoyland introduces them with an untypical and so probably ironic quote from Wagner's *Siegfried*. It may be that he is making a point about heroism, for a good deal of his vocal work has a quietly tortured and almost apocalyptic intensity that relocates heroism at the borders of endurance and annihilation. His dramatic *Michelagniolo*, written for his own Northern Music Theatre, uses an unfamiliar but impeccable version of Michelangelo's name to estrange the subject slightly in the manner of Berio (who is perhaps the only living composer to whom Hoyland appears to carry a debt) but with a strongly individual voice. This was evident from his earliest experiments in setting Anglo-Saxon texts, right down to the heartbreaking *Crazy Rosa—La madre* in which Dario Fo's surreal transvaluation of emotions is supplied with an utterly convincing musical correlative. Hoyland has also set Verlaine, a text by Satie and Sylvia Plath, always with an intuitive feel for the cadence of the original.

This comes at least in part from his background in theatre but also less obviously from his lifelong interest in the plastic arts, calligraphy and architecture in particular; his chamber piece *Fox* is based on a Braque graphic. Much of his instrumental writing has the broad, gestural solidity of a calligraphic character, and an outwardly diffident title like *Work-Out*, used for a trombone and a marimba piece, may also punningly relate to his liking for structures that decipher themselves, work themselves out in ways that conceal rather than reveal any programmatic or purely referential intent. His first fully fashioned string quartet (there is an intriguing single movement piece from 1981) was written astonishingly quickly in the summer of 1985 and has an impressive architecture centred on a slow third movement that contains his finest melodic writing. This is a piece of music which obstinately refuses to reveal its own mechanisms.

Hoyland gives no sign of being interested in systems for their own sake. He is generously undogmatic and writes with the freehanded confidence of a good draughtsman, in whose individual pencil strokes there is almost as much interest as in the finished outline. If he has not yet tackled work on the very largest scale, that may be because he has been able to invest smaller structures with so much energy and intensity, but it is also because he is a fundamentally practical man, committed to an art of the feasible. His commitment is to music as a dramatic and not an intellectual art. He is also absolutely humane, and in the Shakespearean meditation for strings *Of Fantasy, Of Dreams and Ceremonies* there is a hint of how far his imagination can range within the limited compass of the "wooden O".

—Russell Kane

HRABOVSKY, Leonid (Leonid Grabovsky). Ukrainian. Born in Kiev, 28 January 1935. Educated at University of Kiev, 1951–6; Kiev Conservatory (composition under Lev Revutzky and Boris Liatoschinsky), 1954–62, diploma, 1962. Teacher, Kiev Conservatory, 1961–3, 1966–8; freelance composer, 1969–81; settled in Moscow, 1982; translator, researcher, editor of journal *Sovietskaya muzyka*, from 1982. Mailing address: ulitsa Sussanina, dom 2, korp. 1, kv. 64, 127486 Moscow, U.S.S.R.

Publishers: Muzyka Moskau; Musytschna Ukraina, Kiev; Hans Sikorski, Hamburg.

Symphonies / orchestral:

Symphonic Frescoes on a Theme of Boris Prorokov Op 10 1961.
Four Inventions (transcription of Op 11a for chamber orchestra) 1965.
Little Chamber Music No 1 (chamber strings, 16 players) 1966.
Homöomorphie IV 1970.
Little Chamber Music No 2 (oboe, harp, 12 strings) 1971.
Meditation and Pathetic Recitative (string orchestra) 1972.
Five Character Studies (transcription of Op 11b for orchestra) 1975.
On St John's Eve (symphonic legend after Gogol) 1976.

Chamber / instrumental:

Sonata Op 8 (violin) 1959.
Four Two-Part Inventions Op 11a (piano) 1962.
Five Character Studies Op 11b (piano) 1962.
Trio (violin, double bass, piano) 1964, revised 1975.
Microstructures (oboe) 1964, revised 1975.
Constants (solo violin, 4 pianos, 6 percussion groups) 1964.
Homöomorphie I–III (piano; III, 2 pianos) 1968–9.
Ornament (oboe, harp or guitar, viola; variable duration) 1969.

Bucolic Strophes (organ) 1976.
Concorsuono (horn) 1977.
Concerto misterioso (flute, clarinet, bassoon, antique cymbals, harpsichord, harp, violin, viola, cello) 1977.
Für Elise (piano) 1988.

Vocal/choral:

Four Ukrainian Songs Op 6 (mixed chorus, orchestra; folk texts) 1959.
Five Poems by Vladimir Mayakovsky Op 9 (baritone, piano) 1962.
Pastelle (mezzo-soprano, violin, viola, cello, double bass; Tylschina) 1964, revised 1975.
Two A Cappella Choruses (Mayakovsky, Asseyev) 1964.
On Japanese Haiku (tenor, piccolo, bassoon, xylophone) 1964, revised 1975.
An Epitaph for Rainer Maria Rilke (soprano, harp, celeste, guitar, bells) 1965, revised 1975.
La Mer/The Sea (speaker, chorus, organ, orchestra; St John Perse) 1966–70.
Marginalia on Heisenbuttel (speaker, 2 trumpets, trombone, percussion) 1967, revised 1975.
Kogda (soprano, violin, clarinet, piano, strings ad lib; Khlebnikov) 1987.

Opera:

The Bear (chamber opera after Chekhov; piano score) 1963.
The Marriage Proposal (chamber opera after Chekhov; piano score) 1964.

PUBLICATIONS

By Hrabovsky: "Über meinen Lehrer", (memoir of Boris Liatoschinsky) in *Sovetskaya Muzyka*, 2, 1969; "Glanzend und zugleich etwas armlich", in *Sovetskaya Muzyka*, 10, 1988; "Zauber der ukrainischen Musik", in *Die Musik*, 1, 1989.

On Hrabovsky: Grigori Golowinski, "Kuhn und originell", in *Sovetskaya Muzyka*, 10, 1962; Julli Malischev, "Die sinfonischen Fresken von LH", in *Ukrainische Musikwissenschaft*, Kiev, 1968; "Die Avantgarde von Kiew. Eine Retrospektive auf halbem Weg", in *Melos* 4, 1976; Hannelore Gerlach, "Portrat—LG", in *MuG*, 12, 1977.

* * *

Leonid Hrabovsky is one of a number of interesting and influential composers to emerge in Kiev during the 1950s under the tutelage of the distinguished composer–teacher Boris Liatoschinsky. Others in the same group include the then ultra-modernist Vitalii Hodziatsky and the now neo-Slavophile Valentin Silvestrov.

These Kievan composers, by comparison with their Moscow counterparts, have been developing until recently a much stronger and more Western inclination towards rigour and system in their compositional techniques and their various aesthetic stances. Perhaps this reflects something of the way in which the Ukraine has always felt itself more a part of Europe than Russia ever has.

And out of these, Hrabovsky is undoubtedly the one who has thought most deeply about the painful ambiguity underlying the geographical and historical position of all Soviet composers of his generation. He is rare among these composers for the depth of his knowledge and understanding of 20th-century music in the West; indeed his articles over the last few years in *Sovietsakaya muzyka* have proved him to be probably the most informed and cultivated critic in that country at the moment. At the same time, as his music itself makes clear, he has thought deeply about the peculiar roots of the native tradition, which he sees as not just Russian but Slavic and Siberian.

Hrabovsky's earliest mature compositions show him grappling in an individual manner with the expressive problems left behind in the aftermath of Darmstadt. It is obvious from these works that the rigours of serial thought held tremendous appeal for him, but that at the same time he harboured colouristic and rhetorical ambitions of a different kind, probably owing more to Viennese expressionism.

The culmination of this early period and, indeed, one of this composer's very finest works is his large-scale setting of texts by St John Perse for speaker, chorus, organ and orchestra, *La Mer* or *L'amer* (much of Perse's meaning depends on this particular word play). This work was performed with some success in Western Europe, but, as so often, success abroad led to difficulties at home.

In the later 1960s Hrabovsky began to move towards a position which he himself describes as minimalist ("I believe", he says, "that I wrote the first Soviet minimalist music."). Actually this overworked term gives little hint of the range and subtlety of the music he was to produce in this style. Chief among his pieces belonging to this period are the *Concerto misterioso* and the great cycle of works he has called *Homöomorphie*. The wealth of invention in this music and the frequent sense (to borrow from his own title) of mystery both stem from a quality which was already present in his earlier works and which has continued to be important to this day: an overriding concern with the power of number and numerical proportion as a means towards fundamental unity.

It is perhaps this quality that best illustrates Hrabovsky's sense of himself as balanced between Europe and Asia. For while part of this composer's concern with number can certainly be traced to a European tradition running back through Stockhausen, Debussy and Bach to the Middle Ages, the way in which Hrabovsky makes his numbers expressive, the way in which he defines the kind of underlying unity that he is seeking in his music, owes most, by intention and effect, to the spiritual and ritual traditions of Asia and in particular to the Shamanic influences that, according to Hrabovsky, Igor Stravinsky was among the first to exploit.

In more recent years unhappy circumstances have, for a time, prevented Hrabovsky from writing at all. But within the last five or six years he has at last begun composing again, reemerging with a language of compressed violence and extreme refinement of sound, a language that unites the leading strengths of both his earlier periods.

—Gerard McBurney

HSU Tsang-houei. Taiwanese. Born in Chang-hua, 9 June 1929. Educated at National Taiwan Normal University, Taipei, B.A.; Institut de Musicologie, University of Paris, Sorbonne, Certificat d'Etude Supérieure in history of music. Married Li Chi-Huei in 1979; 2 children. General secretary, Chinese Folk Arts Foundation, Taipei, since 1969; vice chair,

Asian Composers' League, Taipei, 1972–90; professor, Graduate Institute of Music, National Taiwan Normal University, since 1980; chair, Chinese Composers' Association in Taiwan, since 1988; director, Chinese Traditional Music Center, Council for Cultural Planning and Development, Taipei, 1990. Recipient: Golden Hand Prize, Taiwan International Junior Chamber of Commerce, 1965; Wu San Lien Literature and Arts Prize, 1979; Chevalier de l'Ordre des Arts et des Lettres, France, 1985. Mailing address: 7 Fl., No. 6, Lane 122, Sec. IV, Jen-Ai Road, Taipei, Taiwan.

Publisher: Chinese Music Book Store, 26 Ai-Kuo E. Road, Taipei, Taiwan.

Symphonies/orchestral:

Ode to Fatherland Op 11 (with children's chorus) 1963–5.
Chinese Festival Overture Op 18 1965–80.
Two Movements Op 26 (string orchestra) 1970.
Symphony: White Sand Bay Op 29 1974.
Spring for All Op 36 (piano, traditional Chinese orchestra) 1981.

Chamber/instrumental:

Sonatina Op 3 (violin, piano) 1957.
Sonata Op 6 (violin, piano) 1958–9.
Nostalgia: Three Tunes Op 7 (violin, cello, piano) 1959.
One Night at Lena's Op 9 (piano) 1960–2.
Quintet Op 10 (flute, clarinet, violin, cello, piano) 1960–87.
Five Preludes Op 16 (violin) 1965–6.
The Blind Op 17 (flute) 1966–76.
The Reminiscence of Childhood Op 19 (Chinese ocarina) 1967.
Sonata Op 27 (clarinet, piano) 1973–83.
Taiwan Op 28 (violin, clarinet, piano) 1973.
Five Episodes Op 30 (piano) 1975–6.
Three Pieces Op 21 (huqin) 1977.
Grand Harp Op 21 (pipa) 1977.
Twenty Pieces for Children Op 34 (piano pieces based on folk melodies) 1980.
Twenty Pieces for the Young Op 35 (piano pieces based on folk melodies) 1981.
Dou-o's Lament Op 43 (cello or viola, piano) 1988.

Vocal/choral:

Four Songs Op 1 (voice, piano; Guo Moruo, Xu Zhimo, Monique Manim, HT-h) 1956.
Two Songs Op 2 (soprano, piano) 1957–8.
Four Poems by Bai Qiu Op 4 (baritone, piano) 1958–9.
Two Poems Op 5 (soprano, chamber group) 1958.
Military Wagons Marching Op 8 (cantata; Du Fu) 1958.
Five Poems by Bai Qiu Op 12 (solo voice) 1961.
Song of Burying Flowers Op 13 (cantata; Cao Chan) 1962.
Nyuguanzi Op 14 (soprano, strings percussion) 1963.
Ode to the National Father Op 15 (cantata; Huang Jiayian) 1965.
Twelve Poems by Yang Huan Op 23 (voice, piano) 1969–73.
Children's Songs Op 24 (voice, piano; Yang Huan) 1970.
Poetry of the Forest Op 25 (cantata; Yang Huan) 1970–81.
Friendship Op 32 (voice, piano; Chen Tingshi, Ya Xian, Yu Guangzhong, Chen Xuxi, Zhao Erdai, Zhu Wei-min) 1978–9.
Children of Lion Mountain Op 37 (children's cantata; Deverge) 1983.
The Bridge Op 42 (soprano, orchestra; Deverge) 1986.

Opera:

The Legend of White Snake Op 33 (Da Huang) 1979–87.

Other:

Chang-o Flies to the Moon Op 22 (modern ballet) 1968.
The Peach Blossom Op 33 (modern ballet) 1977.
Peach Blossom Girl Op 38 (folk ballet) 1983.
Chen San and the Fifth Madame Op 39 (folk ballet) 1985.

PUBLICATIONS

By Hsu: *A Study of Debussy*, Taiwan, 1961, 1983; *Musical Journal of a Chinese in Paris*, Taiwan, 1962, 1982; *Whither Does Chinese Music Go?*, Taiwan, 1964, 1983; translator of Igor Stravinsky, *Seven Lectures on Music*, Taiwan, 1965, 1985; *National Music*, Taiwan, 1967; *A Study of Occidental Music*, Taiwan, 1969; *The Research of Taiwanese Folk Songs at Present Stage*, Taiwan, 1969, 1986; *Encyclopaedic Handbook of Music*, Taiwan, 1969; *Stories from the History of New Chinese Music*, Taiwan, 1970, 1986; *Debussy*, Taiwan, 1971; translator of Charles Koechlin, *Counter Point*, Taiwan, 1972; *Tidbits of Music*, Taiwan, 1975, 1983; *In Search for the Root of Our Folk Music*, Taiwan, 1979, 1986; *The Folk Songs of Taiwan Fok-lau People*, Taiwan, 1982; *An Introduction to Chinese Ethnomusicology*, Taiwan, 1985; *The Colourful Folk Music of Taiwan*, Taiwan, 1985; *Essays on Folk Music*, 2 vols, Taiwan, 1987–8.

On Hsu: Mao Gi-tseng, "Sentiment Connects to China—An Interview with HT-h, Taiwan Celebrity", in *People's Music* (Beijing), April 1989; Chen Pei-Chi, "HT-h", in *Taiwan Veracity* (Taipei), July 1989; Wu Jia-yu, "HT-h and the Asian Composers' League", in *Music and Audio*, April 1990; "HT-h in the Eyes of his students", in *Central Daily News* (Taipei), 29 May 1990; Tseng Yuan-yi, "The Path to Chinese Music", in *United Daily News* (Taipei), 24 May 1990.

* * *

Hsu Tsang-houei was among the very first composers to introduce the techniques of Western contemporary music to Taiwan and to promote cultural exchanges of composers and performing artists throughout the Asian countries.

After his return from studying in Paris, Hsu became deeply involved in promoting new music, training music professionals and carrying out research into Chinese traditional music. His achievement lies mainly in the creation of music that reflects the spirit of Chinese tradition. In it, he recognizes that cultural exchange, which has been an integral part of Asia's cultural history, contributes more than incidentally to the uniqueness of Asian music. Hsu sees the need for musicians in the Asian nations to foster and continue this exchange—most particularly in the field of new music. With this aim in view, he joined with a number of other Asian composers to found the Asian Composers' League in 1972.

The influences on Hsu's musical technique and materials are derived from Chinese traditions and fall into three main bands: traditional melody with minor changes that still preserve the original melodic structure (this is seen most clearly in vocal works, and works for amateurs and children); fragments quoted from traditional music serving as themes for Hsu's own compositions; and finally, the adoption of melodic and rhythmic patterns in his avant-garde compositions.

Hsu is the foremost ethnomusicologist and leading

composer working in Taiwan today. His career has been an untiring search for ways to combine traditional musical elements with modern Western techniques, and this he has done with remarkable success.

—Chew Shyh-ji

HUBER, Nicolaus A. German. Born in Passau, Bavaria, 15 December 1939. Educated at Passau Gymnasium, 1950–8; Musikhochsschule, Munich (piano under Oskar Koebel, composition under Franz Xaver Lehner and Gunther Bialas, electronic music under Josef Anton Riedl), 1958–67; Ferienkurse für Neue Musik, Darmstadt (composition under Karlheinz Stockhausen), 1967; composition study with Luigi Nono, Venice, 1967–8. Organist. Junior teacher, 1962–4; lecturer in theory and analysis, since 1969, and professor of composition, since 1974, Folkwang-Hochsschule, Essen; member of Josef Anton Riedl's Ensemble, 1969–71; vice president, German Section, International Society of Contemporary Music, 1971–4; collaboration with P. Maiwald's free/political theatre group, 1975–80; guest lecturer, Cursos Latinamericanos de Musica Contemporanea, Venezuela, 1985; lecturer, Ferienkurse für Neue Musik, Darmstadt, 1988; guest lecturer, Conservatorio Nacional Quito, Ecuador, 1990. Recipient: Cultural Prize for Music, City of Munich, 1969; composition prize, Darmstadt (for *Versuch über Sprache*), 1970; fellowship, Cité Internationale des Arts (Paris), 1971; Förderungs-Preis, Berlin, 1988. Mailing address: Waldsamm 72, D-4300 Essen 1, Germany.

Publishers: Barenreiter; Breitkopf & Hartel; "plane", Dortmund.

Symphonies/orchestral:

Parusie—Annäherung und Entfernung (orchestra, tape) 1967; first performed Frankfurt, 1968. Recorded harmonia mundi DMR 1016 18.
Epigenesis III (strings, 2 percussion) 1968–9; first performed Hannover, 1970.
Harakiri (small orchestra, tape) 1971; first performed Darmstadt, 1972.
Lernen von 1977; first performed Hannover, 1979.
Morgenlied 1980; first performed Saarbrücken, 1981.
Sphärenmusik 1981; first performed Berlin, 1982.
Nocturnes 1984; first performed Donaueschingen, 1985.
Vier Stücke/Four Pieces (orchestra, tape) 1986; first performed Saarbrücken, 1988.
Go Ahead 1987–8; first performed Cologne, 1989.
Annäherung an ein Wollknäuel 1990–1; first performed Stuttgart, 1992.

Chamber/instrumental:

Spektrale (piano) 1964; first performed Darmstadt, 1965.
Sonata (violin) 1965; first performed Munich, 1966.
Mimus (2 horns, 2 trumpets, 2 trombones, bass tuba, 2 percussion, piano) 1965; first performed Hannover, 1967.
Rituale (organ) 1965; first performed Munich, 1968.
Informationen über die Töne E-F/Information About the Notes E and F (string quartet) 1965–6; first performed Munich, 1967.
Chronogramm (clarinet, violin, cello, piano) 1966; first performed Madrid, 1968.
von . . . bis . . . (viola, harmonium, piano, percussion) 1966; first performed Munich, 1968. Recorded Deutsche Grammophon.
Traummechanik (percussion, piano) 1967; first performed Hannover, 1968.
Epigenesis I (4 recorder players) 1967–8. Recorded Teldec.
Epigenesis II (recorder player, tape) 1967–9; first performed Witten, 1969.
Versuch zu "Versuch über Sprache" (improvising musicians, tape) 1970; first performed Bonn, 1970.
Darabukka (piano) 1976; first performed Paris, 1977.
Dasselbe ist nicht dasselbe (small drum) 1978; first performed Witten, 1978. Recorded harmonia mundi DMR 1022–24; Edition V, Verlag "plane" 88504.
Presente (trombone) 1979; first performed Darmstadt, 1980.
Solo für einen Solisten (violin) 1980–1; first performed Witten, 1983.
Vor und Zurück (oboe) 1981; first performed Montepulciano, 1982.
Sechs Bagatellen (flute/piccolo/bamboo flute, oboe, clarinet/bass clarinet/contrabass clarinet, bassoon/contrabassoon, percussion, harp, bass guitar ad lib, violin, viola, cello, double bass, tape) 1981; first performed Cologne, 1982. Recorded harmonia mundi HM 713 D.
Aus Schmerz und Trauer (alto saxophone or clarinet) 1982; first performed Nuremburg, 1982.
Turmgewasche (harp) 1982–3; first performed Witten, 1983.
Trio mit Stabpandeira (viola, cello, double bass) 1983; first performed Bonn, 1984.
Der Ausrufer steigt ins Innere (cello) 1984; first performed Stuttgart, 1985.
La Force du vertige (flute, clarinet, violin, cello, piano/percussion) 1985; first performed Nice, 1986.
Auf Flügeln der Harfe (accordion) 1985; first performed Tokyo, 1986. Recorded Gaudeamus CD 1; Edition V "plane" 88663.
Demijour (oboe, cello, piano) 1985–6; first performed Leipzig, 1987.
Doubles, mit einem beweglichen Ton (string quartet) 1987; first performed Cologne, 1988.
Air mit Sphinxes (flute, oboe, clarinet, bassoon, horn, trumpet, trombone, 2 percussion, harp, 2 violins, viola, cello, double bass) 1987; first performed Paris, 1988.
Töne suchen einen Autor (unspecified instrumentation, wind machine) 1988; first performed Witten, 1988.
Clashmusic (cymbals) 1988; first performed Cologne, 1988.
Herbstfestival (4 percussion) 1989; first performed Freiburg, 1989.
Seifenoper (oboe, cor anglais, trombone, viola, cello, double bass, piano, percussion) 1989–90; first performed Salzan, 1990.
Statement (Zu einen Faustschlag Nonos) (piano) 1990–1; first performed Hannover, 1990.
Beds and Brackets (piano, tape) 1990; first performed Munich, 1991.

Vocal/choral:

Versuch über Sprache (16 solo voices, Chinese cymbals, Hammond organ, double bass, 2-track tape) 1969; first performed Darmstadt, 1970. Recorded Deutsche Grammophon avantgarde 4.
Banlieue ("Sprechchor"—8 voices in 3 groups; "Augen

Musik"—2 performers, headphones, 2 tape machines, 2 loudspeakers, guitar, drum; "Schauplatze der Revolution") 1972–3; "Sprechchor" and "Augen Musik" first performed Bonn, 1974; "Schauplatze der Revolution" first performed Witten, 1974.

Gespenster (large orchestra, tape, reciter/singer; Brecht) 1976; first performed Bonn, 1977.

Tote Metren (bass baritone, clarinet/bass clarinet/contrabass clarinet, bassoon/contrabassoon, horn, piano, percussion, 2 violins, cello, double bass) 1989; first performed Frankfurt, 1989.

Tenebrae (4-part choir) 1990; first performed Hannover, 1990.

Zwei Chöre (Celan) n.d.

Other:

Aion (4-track tape, fragrance) 1968–72; first performed Cologne, 1972.

Anerkennung und Aufbehung (4 films, 3 2-track tapes, improvisation; Lukacs) 1971–2; first performed Munich, 1972.

Four *Politrevuen* 1976, 1977, 1978–9, 1980. Recorded "plane" 88184.

PUBLICATIONS

By Huber: contribution on Ensemble, in Rolf Gehlhaar, "Zur Komposition Ensemble", *Darmstädter Beiträge zur Neuen Musik*, 11, 1968; "Die Komponisitionstechnik Bachs in seinen Sonaten und Partiten für Violine solo und ihre Anwendung in Weberns op 27/2", in *Zeitschrift für Musiktheorie*, 1 (2), 1970; "Apropos 'Viel Lärm um nichts' ", in *Melos*, 39, 1972; "Der Komponist Gunter Bialas. Zum 65. Geburtstag meines Lehrers", in *Musica*, 26, 1972; in "Uber der Kompositiontechnik einiger Lieder der 1. Politrevue 1976", in *Eiserne Lerche*, Dortmund, 1976; "Zu Fritz Buchtger", in *Neue Musik in der Bundesrepublik Deutschland. Dokumentation 1975–6 1976–7*, Bonn, 1979; "Ist Komponieren lehrbar/lernbar?", in *Musica*, 35, 1981; "Einige Anmerkungen zum Problem Komponist und Gesellschaft", in *Interface*, 12(1/2), 1983; "Über komnzeptionelle Rhythmuskomposition", in *MusikTexte*, 2, 1983; "Gedanken zum Umfeldder Tonalität", in *MusikTexte*, 6, 1984; "Reflexion über Rhythmus", in *Programmheft Rheinisches Musikfest 1987*, Cologne, 1987.

On Huber: Ulrich Dibelius, "Gesellschaft als Partner und Modell. Zum Komponieren von NAH", in *Musica*, 26, 1972; Reinhard Oehlschlagel and others, "Chronologie eines Kompositionsauftrages", in *Melos*, 39, 1972; Monika Tibbe, "NAH", in *Neue Zeitschrift für Musik*, 135, 1974; Friedrich Dudda, "NH's 'Darabukka' ", in *Feedback Papers*, 15, 1978; Hanns Werner Heister, "Konspiration und Agitation. Ein Versuch über die 'Sechs Bagatellen' für Kammerensemble von NAH", in *Melos*, 46, 1984; Helmut Lachenmann, "Magier und Chirurg. Uber NAH", in *MusikTexte*, 20, 1987.

Nicolaus A. Huber comments:

Around 1976 (with *Darabukka*) my experience as a composer led me in the direction of a special technique which I have called "rhythm composition".

For the most part this is defined by the duration of a piece, the number of beats and proportion of beats and rests. The variability of these components turns form into a continuous process. Because of the mutuality of time relative to a dialectical understanding of montage, new material is always assimilable and comprehensible. Montage remains open to the most varied areas of expression, genres and intonations from worker's music, agitprop music and others. This is not simply a matter of psychic variation in which what the composer defines as music at a given moment can be experienced whole. It is rather a question of form defined as "detailed argumentation" in which what is meant by a certain piece is only known when it ends. Similar to Eisenstein's "pathetic construction"—"the seated man jumps up", "the mute shouts"—no one thing exists independent of its opposite; this facilitates composing according to extremes and developing a multiplicity of dialectical relationships from a single unity, a procedure noted by Bloch.

The bourgeois legacy of subjectivity, expressivity and lyricism can thus be appropriated. It is not without good reason that the first chapter of the *Communist Manifesto* is a long hymn to the achievements of the bourgeoisie.

Crises can do us no harm.

Glasnost and *perestroika* confirm: our way is the right one.

Even our sorrow is puffed up and ostentatious; our moderation never goes hungry.

In South America a guitarist can be murdered. What he has to say is taken seriously.

However, I am well! I thrive on the affluence of action.

The political, the fragmentary, the absurd, entertainment music, mass industry, rhythm composition, the opera, post-modern, the iconoclastic, the non-reflective, New Age, anything goes: because no one listens to us.

The obligation to communicate leaves motivation to rot.

"Anything goes" doesn't ask what doesn't.

Pluralism does not ask what we need.

In a time of disorientation, there is only one reliable certainty: pursue insecurity with all one's strength.

That was Arnold Schoenberg's spirit.

I want him for us all, enquiring about the new sources of our judgement.

* * *

Nicolaus A. Huber's work to date can be divided into three stages criss-crossed by dialectical cohenrences. After an initial period marked by small-scale perceptions rendered ever more concrete and intense, there began in 1969 a period characterised by critical composition and political engagement, which persisted until the mid 1980s when Huber began to reflect anew on musical material within a dramatically altered (geo)political situation.

After some early pieces—there is a score for solo violin from 1959 whose six movements each consist of just one sound event—Huber enrolled as a composition student under Franz Xaver Lehner at Munich. If this was little more than a continuation of his studentship in music education and a brief probationary period as a teacher, his work with Gunter Bialas between 1964–7 marked the beginning of a determination to dedicate himself to composition.

Huber's urgent inquiry at this period concerns the purification of musical language in such a way that the listener will be induced to listen intensively again. Such a question is implicitly critical of music organized serially without reference to comprehensibility. Huber's response is to proceed from "principles" rather than from "series". According to this reasoning, coherence is dependent on just one parameter responding to the underlying principle. Meaning and content are then generated by an independent treatment of all other parameters. In the string quartet piece *Information About the Notes E and F*, Huber restricts the sound material to just these two notes, but provides a constant flow of new "information" about them by changing durations, sound-colours, dynamics and registers. Other notes occur only incidentally in the aura around the basic material. In 10 minutes, E and F are purified, rescued from their "phrygian disposition".

Huber's understanding of the material constraints on performance had largely been inculcated by Stockhausen; from Nono he learned that styles, settings and new techniques are not only available but ought to be understood against the background of a particular historical context. (Huber's analysis and composition classes at Essen have until recently strongly featured such a recognition.) He had made use of Marxist models long before his time in Venice, but from then on Marxism largely determined his conception of musical material and his practice as a composer in general. In *Harakiri*, Huber notes and subverts the use of crescendo and alternation as being connected with certain expressive characteristics of bourgeois 19th-century music; accumulation followed by an eruptive climax (a "certain sphere of ballyhoo") on one note. In *Harakiri*, the eruption anticipated after one minute of steady crescendo is replaced by a recorded peal of thunder over the loudspeakers. This is what Huber called "critical composition"; not only is the musical material purified, the listener's attitudes are intended to develop in a "progressive" direction.

There is a touch of deconstruction here. By contrast, Huber's "rhythm composition", which begins with *Darabukka* in 1976, turns out to be a technique which inherits and incorporates the positive aspects of the past. Rhythmic patterns, tested in communicative contexts, serve as generators for all levels of the composition. *Morgenlied* for orchestra is based on a rhythmic model from Cuba, *guaracha*, which is 16 semiquavers [sixteenth notes] long and consists of 11 attacks. With it corresponds not only 16 sections of 11 units each but also an internal rhythm of the first four groups of 11 (3 5 3/6 5/5 6/3 3 5) which again dictates possible changes of harmony, texture, dynamics and sound colour. Besides a differentiated tempo-structure, reflecting bodily rhythms, he includes martial rhythms, a song from the French Resistance, and an anti-Vietnam song in German. In this way, Huber is not only able to show solidarity for Third World countries within a broader discussion of world policy, but integrates folkloristic elements into a tradition of working class and liberationist music.

This phase coincided with Huber's collaboration with Peter Maiwold and an independent theatre group. Drawing on his experiences with Josef Anton Riedl's multimedia Ensemble, Huber created a form of political revue and also performances at mass rallies, in local pubs and tents.

In the 1983 *Trio mit Stabpandeira* for viola, cello and double bass, a "rhythm composition" based on a Fibonacci sequence and thus apparently abstract and "aesthetic", the political virtually lies in ambush, capturing the trio towards the end in the tones of an alarm siren. In the new political climate initiated in the Soviet bloc in the late 1980s, all possibility of communist revolution seemed to run out, not only in Latin America but also in Europe where there was no longer a working class audience attuned to "progressive" elements in music. (Significantly, the Cursos Latinamericanos de Musica Contemporanea, on which Huber taught in 1985, took place for the last time in 1989.) Huber reacted to these changes in the political wind with a new examination of musical material. Not only did his resources broaden (in his orchestral pieces, there are now parts for brasses, which he had previously considered ideologically incriminated and also simpler intervals, such as octaves), he also explores whole new areas of musical terrain now that there is no longer any need to cleanse musical expression of its "bourgeois" associations.

The orchestral piece *Go Ahead*, first performed in 1989, is a melody of 14 notes, consisting of seconds and thirds, whose six repeats successively omit the previous outer notes. In addition, the third repeat exactly joins up with the second. By using this extremely rational procedure, Huber achieves the irrational: the listener loses all sense of orientation; Huber has, in his own term, introduced a "shrug" into the listening experience. Repetition destroys coherence in *Go Ahead*; change is not variation, but an entirely new quality for which desubjectivised listening is the requisite perception, a will not to interpret, but to leave the music as it is.

For all the changes he has gone through, especially in the most recent phase of his career, Huber has retained his identity within contemporary composition. His *Four Pieces* for orchestra and tape, written in 1986 after a symposium on postmodern music in Patras, Greece, can be understood as a set of "cartoons" on the "talented but uncreative" practices of postmodern composition. It is "second-hand" music whose diffuse material and sound is inherently pleasurable, like the passage for three tam-tams in the second piece "Olympic Operation". On the other hand, Huber quotes "Monoritmica" from Alban Berg's *Lulu* and destroys that pleasure by ending the work with Lulu's "death fifths", which Berg had already related to Marie's death in *Wozzeck*, when the painter commits suicide after Dr Schon reveals Lulu's past. In the same way, Huber's "Olympic Operation" deprives postmodern composers of their innocence by means of a conscious "prostitution of composing" and by demonstrating the descent of their material as well as of their traditions of expression, implying that they must give it up or at very least reconsider it.

—Stefan Orgass

HUMBLE, Keith. Australian. Born in Geelong, Victoria, 6 September 1927. Educated at University Conservatorium of Music, Melbourne, 1947–9, Dip.Mus.; Royal Academy of Music, London, 1950–1, L.R.A.M; Ecole Normale de Musique, Paris, 1951–2, 6ème degré perfectionnement; further study, Paris (composition and conducting under René Leibowitz), 1952–4. Conductor and pianist; teacher of piano, accompaniment, theory and orchestration, 1956, senior lecturer in composition, and founder of Electronic Music Studio, Grainger Centre, 1966–9, University Conservatorium of Music, Melbourne, 1956; assistant to René Leibowitz, Paris, 1957–9; founder, musical director, Le Centre de Musique, Paris, 1959–68, 1966–7, 1968; teacher of composition to pre-teen pupils, 1959–68; Regent's Lecturer, 1969, visiting professor, 1970, and professor, 1971–74, University of California, San Diego; Music Committee member and member, Special Projects Committee, Australian Council for the Arts, 1969–70; visiting lecturer, Boston University and University of New York, Albany, 1970; foundation professor, music department, La Trobe University, Victoria, 1974–89, emeritus since 1989; music director, Australia Contemporary Music Ensemble (ACME), 1975–8; conductor, soloist, Ensemble Sonor, 1982–90; music consultant, Victoria College for the Arts, 1990. Recipient: Critics' Award (Australia),

1976, 1977 (as pianist), 1977 (as conductor); member, Order of Australia, 1982. Address: c/o Universal Edition (Australia), 2 Fareham Street, London W1V 4DU, England.

Publishers: Universal Edition (Australia); Allans Music; La Trobe University Press; Australia Music Centre.

Symphonies/orchestral:

Arcade V 1969; first performed Melbourne, 1969.
Après la Légende (piano, orchestra) 1969; first performed Perth, Western Australia, 1970. Recorded ABC RRCS/386.
Statico III 1972–3; first performed Melbourne, 1974.
A Festival Fanfare for a City (version for band and orchestra) 1984; first performed Melbourne, 1984.

Chamber/instrumental:

Sonata (violin, piano) 1951.
String Trio 1953; first performed Cheltenham, Gloucestershire, 1958. Recorded ABC RRCS/382.
Folio No 1 (3 pieces for piano) 1953–9.
Folio No 2 (3 pieces for piano) 1954.
Sonata No 1 (piano) 1959; first performed Melbourne, 1965. Recorded Move Records.
Ainsi s'achève (3–6 instruments, harp, 3 percussion, piano) 1967; first performed Paris, 1967.
Five Pieces (violin, piano) 1967; first performed Melbourne, 1967.
Three Statements (piano) 1967.
Music for Monuments (instruments, tape; or version with voices) 1967; first performed Paris, 1968.
Materials for Larountala (22 solo strings) 1968; first performed Melbourne, 1968. Recorded ABC RRCS/382.
Solfège I (diverse instruments, electronics ad lib) 1968; first performed San Diego, California, 1968.
Arcade Ia (organ, percussion, tapes) 1969. Recorded NMA Tapes 7.
Arcade II (piano) 1969; first performed Melbourne, 1969.
Arcade IIIa (flute) 1969.
Arcade IIIb (flute, electronics) 1969; first performed Melbourne, 1970.
Arcade IV (guitar, percussion) 1969; first performed Melbourne, 1970.
Statico I (organ, 2 synthesizers) 1971; first performed Melbourne, 1971.
A Music for Baroque Ensemble (harpsichord, flute, oboe, double bass) 1971. Recorded ABC AC1011.
Kadenz (flute) 1972.
Sounds for/and/or (cello, electronics) 1972.
Sounds for/and/or (bass, electronics) 1973.
Prime Riff (percussion ensemble, tape) 1974; first performed Melbourne, 1974.
Sonata No 2 (piano) 1977, revised 1980; first performed Melbourne, 1977.
Trio No 2 (violin, clarinet, piano) 1982; first performed La Jolla, California, 1989.
Five Pieces in Two Parts (cello, piano) 1982; first performed Melbourne, 1982.
Ways, By-Ways (chamber ensemble) 1983; first performed Sydney, December 1983. Recorded Larikan Records LRF 156.
Treatments No 2 (extended for flute, cello, piano, tape) 1984.
Sonata No 3 (piano) 1985; first performed Melbourne, 29 November 1985.
Trio No 3 (flute, percussion, piano) 1985; first performed Melbourne, 1985.
Trio No 4 (transcription of Liszt's "Orpheus"; violin, cello, piano) 1986; first performed Melbourne, 25 July 1986.
Kal Ida's Cope (trombone, tape; or piano, trombone; or trombone, piano, tape; or piano, tape; or trombone, keyboard percussion; part 1 extended for trombone, piano, percussion) 1986–7; extended version first performed Melbourne, 21 March 1987.
Module No 1 (percussion) 1986; first performed Sydney, 1987.
Sonata No 1 (percussion) 1986.
Landscapes (instrumental ensemble, tape) 1987.
Etchings (percussion quartet) 1988.
Four All Seasons (string quartet/string orchestra) 1989.
Sonata No 4 (piano) 1990.

Vocal/choral:

Songs of Depression (soprano, piano) 1955.
Fragments of War Poems (soprano, instruments; Mathews) 1959; first performed Paris, 1964.
A Book of Songs of Love and Death (tenor, piano; Greek) 1966; first performed United States, 1966.
Trois Poèmes à crier et à danser (choir) 1968; first performed Melbourne, 1968.
Trois Poèmes d'amour (tenor, piano) 1970; first performed San Diego, California, 1970.
La Légende (cantata for voice, choir, electronics, instruments) 1970; first performed Melbourne, 1971.
The Seasons (7 haiku for 4 choirs) 1971.
ACCJ (large choir) 1979; first performed Melbourne, 1979.
Three Choral Pieces for Children 1982; first performed Melbourne, 1985.
Five Cabaret Songs 1985; first performed La Jolla, California, 1985; included in *A Set of Cabaret Songs*, 1990.
Soundscapes (double choir, instrumental ensemble) 1987; first performed Melbourne, 24 July 1987.
Two Cabaret Songs 1987; first performed Melbourne, 1988; included in *A Set of Cabaret Songs*, 1990.
Nocturnes (choir, piano or chamber orchestra) 1988–90.
Cabaret Song: O Tell Me the Truth About Love (Auden) 1990; included in *A Set of Cabaret Songs*, 1990.
In Pace (introits, chorales and chorale preludes for choir, harp, percussion) 1990.
A Set of Cabaret Songs (includes *Five Cabaret Songs*, *Two Cabaret Songs*, *O Tell Me the Truth About Love*) 1990.

Opera:

Now V 1971.

Other:

Pièce méchante I-III (number and nature of performers indeterminate) 1965.
Musique limitées (number and nature of performers indeterminate) 1966.
Solfège II (performer, electronics) 1969.
Nunique I (number and nature of performers indeterminate) 1968.
Nunique IIa (number and nature of performers indeterminate) 1968.
Nunique IIb (number and nature of performers indeterminate) 1968.
Nunique III (number and nature of performers indeterminate) 1969.

Arcade Ib (tape) 1969.
Nunique IV (number and nature of performers indeterminate) 1971.
Treatments No 1 (for Me) (number and nature of performers indeterminate) 1971.
Nunique VI (number and nature of performers indeterminate) 1971.
Nunique VII for Brisbane (number and nature of performers indeterminate) 1972.
Parodie: Time Piece; Bird Songs at Even-Time; Ground; Mass (electronic) 1972.
And Tomorrow (electronic) 1972; first performed La Jolla, California, 1972.
Paris: Bar Suite (electronic) 1972.
Four Studies for 201 (number and nature of performers indeterminate) 1972.
In Five (number and nature of performers indeterminate) 1972.
Paraphrase in Five plus Mass = Statico II (number and nature of performers indeterminate) 1972. Recorded Move MS 3006.
Nunique VIII (A Festival of the Arts) 1973; first performed Melbourne, 1973.
Treatments 1–20 (tape) 1973–4.
Prime ONE (electronic) 1974.
Prime TOO (electronic) 1975.
Prime One Too (electronic; synthesis of *Prime ONE* and *Prime TOO*) 1976.
Ceremonial Music (tape) 1976.
Polysaccharides (number and nature of performers indeterminate) 1977; first performed Sydney, 1977.
Molly's Lament (number and nature of performers indeterminate) 1978; first performed Adelaide, 1978.
Songs Sadly (number and nature of performers indeterminate) 1979; first performed Zagreb, 1979.
Extension of Treatments No 1 (number and nature of performers indeterminate) 1979; first performed Monash, Victoria, 1979.
A Festival Fanfare for a City (number and nature of performers unspecified) 1981; first performed Geelong, 1981.
Nunique IX 1984; first performed San Diego, California, May 1984.
Kal Ida's Cope (tape version) 1986.
The Improvisation Project No 1 1986.
Sound Landscapes (electronic) 1987.

PUBLICATIONS

On Humble: A. Payne, "Flair and Sensibility", in *Music and Musicians*, December 1963; Roger Covell, in *Australia's Music: Themes of a New Society*, Melbourne, 1967; Andrew McCredie, *Musical Composition in Australia*, Canberra, 1969; John McCaughey, "Notes on Contemporary Music", in *Melbourne University Magazine*, 1970; James Murdoch, in *Australia's Contemporary Composers*, Melbourne, 1972; Laughton Harris, "KH", in Callaway and Tunley, editors, *Australian Composition in the Twentieth Century*, Melbourne, 1975; John Whiteoak, (interview) in *New Music Articles*, 14(21), 1989.

Keith Humble comments:

I've always looked upon music, or composition, as being a *creative* process, as distinct from a *product*. If I have criticism of a lot of the composers today, it's because they make products and I don't think of composition as being a product. I think of composition as being a process, an exchange of concepts, and an exchange of ideas—we're talking about improvisation, and improvisation is really composition. A lot of the music I hear today, a lot of so-called compositions, I look on as products—they're for sale.

* * *

Keith Humble's musical activities have developed in a multitude of ways, for he is at once a "straight" serial composer, an experimental improvisor, a virtuoso pianist, a conductor and a music educator, and has pursued each of these activities with a remarkable degree of achievement. Humble received his early musical training in Melbourne, then left for Europe where he further developed his pianistic skills and began serious composition studies. In the 1950s he came under the spell of the second Viennese school which, in post-war Paris, was represented by René Leibowitz, whose writings on twelve-tone music attracted a flock of young composers. Following studies with Leibowitz, Humble evolved individual techniques of serial composition which continue in his mature style to form the basic approach to this aspect of his output. However, in Humble, the rigorous serial approach coexists with other, more specifically experimental, compositional activities.

After several years in Europe, Humble returned to Australia, but his inability to relate to the essentially conservative musical forces in Melbourne at that time provoked his early return to Paris—a fortuitous event as, in reaction to the negative Australian experience, his energies became strongly directed into new musical endeavours. Principal among these was the founding and directing of Le Centre de Musique, a platform for the presentation of contemporary music involving the participation of performers, composers and postgraduate students from throughout the world. Humble himself conducted most of the concerts and performed as pianist in them. He also became interested in the group improvisation or "interactive workshop" methods of the French playwright Marc'O, and later transported this approach into his *Nunique* format. Humble's nine Nuniques are large-scale collective works in which disparate events, or projects, are evolved within a single context. Performers of all kinds, musicians, actors, dancers and others, are presided over by the composer (or director) to participate individually and in groups in order to develop, through controlled improvisation, the overall structure of the work. Projects can be, and are, freely transplanted from one Nunique to another so that one could justifiably speak of a single Nunique with varied interpretations or performances. In the catalogue of Humble's works, these and other improvised compositions have no instrumental designations since each realisation depends on the forces available at any given time and place.

In recent times Humble's essays in the realm of improvisation involve his participation in KIVA, a research-performance ensemble dedicated to the performance of notationless music, which saw its beginnings in the early 1970s and has since toured extensively in the United States, Australia and Europe. The playing nucleus of KIVA comprises Jean-Charles François (percussion), John Silber (trombone) and Humble himself on keyboards.

From the late 1960s until the present time, Humble's activities have continued in many countries and, following playing, conducting and lecture tours in the U.S., he was appointed Professor in the Music Department of the University of California at San Diego in the early 1970s. During the same period Humble was also active in promoting contemporary music in Australia, forming the ISCM and the

Society for the Private Performance of New Music (SPPNM). Later, he helped form the Australian Contemporary Music Ensemble (ACME) of which he was the musical director. In 1974 he was appointed Foundation Professor at La Trobe University in Victoria for the forming of the Music Department. He now had *carte blanche* to give full rein to his ideas on music education and lost no time in impregnating this new environment with electronic and improvisation laboratories wedded to a traditional theory and analysis core programme, an approach developed from his music education experience in Paris and San Diego. On retiring from La Trobe, Humble was nominated Emeritus Professor, and has resumed his activities in the U.S. and in France, where he is involved as consultant in the formation of music education projects for the European Community.

Humble's musical philosophy is based on the belief that the Western tradition of change and evolution can only be maintained by dissent; the opposite breeds complacency resulting in the preservation and continuation of dead practices. For this reason the language of his serial composition is uncompromising as is that of his experimental works, which are more often intended to stimulate hostile reaction than they are designed to please. Some of Humble's major composition), the string quartet *Four All Seasons, Etchings,' Statico III* and *Polysaccharides* (large orchestra), *Nocturnes* (choir and chamber orchestra), *Treatments 1–20* (tape composition), the string quartet *Four All Seasons, Etchings,'* (percussion quartet) and 60 songs contained within various song cycles.

—Lawrence Whiffin

HURD, Michael (John). British/English. Born in Gloucester, 19 December 1928. Educated at Crypt Grammar School, Gloucester, 1939–47; Pembroke College, Oxford (under Sir Thomas Armstrong, Edward Rubbra and Bernard Rose), 1950–3, M.A.; also composition lessons with Sir Lennox Berkeley. Military service in Intelligence Corps, 1947–9. Professor of theory, Royal Marines School of Music, Deal, Kent, 1953–9; thereafter, freelance composer; also, at various times, conductor of Petersfield Operatic Society, Alton Choral Society, Chichester Symphony Orchestra; chair, Petersfield Music Festival. Mailing address: 4 Church Street, West Liss, Hampshire GU33 6JX, England.

Publisher: Novello & Co.

Symphonies/orchestral:

Overture to an Unwritten Comedy 1970; first performed Radnor, Montgomeryshire, 31 October 1970.
Dance Diversions 1972; first performed Havant, Hampshire, July 1972.
Sinfonia Concertante (violin, string orchestra) 1973; first performed Petersfield, Hampshire, 22 June 1973.
Concerto da Camera (oboe, small orchestra) 1979; first performed Havant, Hampshire, 16 June 1979.
Little Suite (strings) 1985–6.

Chamber/instrumental:

Sonatina (flute, piano) 1964; first performed Bristol, 1964.
Harlequin Suite (2 trumpets, horn, trombone, tuba) 1971, revised 1982; first performed Farnham, Surrey, 11 May 1971.
Bagatelles (piano) 1986; first performed Melbourne, 1986.
Five Preludes (piano) 1989; first performed Melbourne, 1989.
Sonata (violin, piano) 1989; first performed Melbourne, 1989.

Vocal/choral:

Canticles of the Virgin Mary (SSA choir, orchestra or piano; 15th-century English carols) 1965; first performed Farnham, Surrey, 19 May 1965.
A Song for St Cecilia (SATB choir, orchestra with strings or piano; Dryden) 1966; first performed Havant, Hampshire 1967.
Missa brevis (SSA choir, strings/organ) 1966; first performed Farnham, Surrey, 1967.
Jonah-man Jazz (pop cantata for unison voices, flute/piccolo, oboe, bass clarinet, alto saxophone, trumpet, double bass; or piano) 1966; first performed London, December 1966.
Praise Ye the Lord (SATB, organ) 1966.
O Saving Victim (SATB choir, organ) 1966.
A Song for St Cecilia (SATB choir, organ) 1966.
Shore Leave (baritone, strings or piano; Causley) 1967; first performed Haslemere, Surrey, 1967.
Music's Praise (SATB choir, strings or piano; Pope, Strode, Shakespeare, Herrick) 1968; first performed Stroud, Gloucestershire, 30 October 1968.
Charms and Ceremonies (unison voices, SSA choir, orchestra or piano; Herrick) 1969; first performed Malvern, Hereford and Worcester, 1969.
Five Epitaphs (unaccompanied SSA choir) 1969; first performed Ayr, Scotland, 5 February 1970.
Carmina amoris (baritone, piano) 1970; first performed Westonbirt, Gloucestershire, 19 May 1970.
Diversions (unison voices, recorder[s], percussion, piano; Keats, Elder, anon. 17th century) 1970; first performed Petersfield, Hampshire March 1970.
Sea and Shore Songs (unison voices, piano; de la Mare) 1970.
O Come Let Us Sing unto the Lord (SATB choir, organ) 1972.
Swingin' Samson (pop cantata for unison voices, piano, optional drum and double bass) 1972; first performed Southend, Argyll, 1972.
Flower Songs (SSA choir, orchestra or piano; Herrick) 1973; first performed Southampton, Hampshire, 23 May 1974.
The Phoenix and the Turtle (mezzo-soprano, SATB choir, strings, timpani; also piano reduction; Shakespeare) 1974; first performed Canterbury, Kent, 16 June 1974.
Hip-Hip Horatio (pop cantata for tenor/narrator, unison voices, piano; Blom) 1974; first performed London, 15 March 1975.
This Day to Man (SATB choir, orchestra or piano; Kindlemarch, Southwell, Austin, Pestel, Wither) 1974, revised 1979; first performed Chichester, Sussex, 14 December 1974; revised version first performed 8 December 1979.
Shepherd's Calendar (baritone, SATB choir, orchestra or piano; Clare) 1975; first performed Southampton, Hampshire, 10 October 1975.
Rooster Rag (pop cantata for unison voices, piano) 1975; first performed Cookham, Berkshire, 2 May 1975.
Merciles Beaute (unaccompanied SATB choir; Chaucer) 1977.
Round the Town (unison voices, piano; Causley) 1978.

Pilgrim (pop cantata for narrator, unison voices, piano) 1978; first performed Bedfordshire, 10 March 1978.
Nine of Anon (unison/2-part voices, piano) 1981.
Adam-in-Eden (pop cantata for narrator, unison voices, piano) 1981; first performed Margate, Kent, 24 March 1981.
Mrs Beeton's Book (pop cantata for unison, 2- and 3-part voices, piano) 1982; first performed Petersfield, Hampshire, March 1984.
A New Nowell (pop cantata) 1986; first performed London, 1987.
Captain Coram's Kids (pop cantata) 1988; first performed London, 1988.
Prodigal (pop cantata) 1988; first performed Adelaide, 1989.
The Liberty Tree (pop cantata) 1989; first performed Northampton, 1989.
King and Conscience (pop cantata) 1990; first performed Canterbury, Kent, 1990.

Opera:

Little Billy (nautical opera for children; 5 characters/1 spoken, chorus, piano) 1964; first performed Newham-on-Severn, Gloucestershire, March 1964.
Mr Punch (operatic entertainment for young people; 8 characters, optional chorus, piano, ad lib percussion) 1970; first performed Gothenburg, Sweden, 3 April 1970.
The Widow of Ephesus (alto, soprano, baritone, orchestra; David Hughes) 1971; first performed Stroud, Gloucestershire, 23 October 1971.

Other:

Cider with Rosie (incidental music to play directed by James Roose-Evans) 1963; first performed King's Lynn, Norfolk, 1963.
Flickorna (film score for Mai Zetterling, Sweden) 1968.
Playthings (incidental music to play directed by Mai Zetterling) 1980; first performed Vienna, 1980.
Scrubbers (film score for Mai Zetterling, Sweden) 1982.

PUBLICATIONS

By Hurd: *Immortal Hour: The Life and Times of Rutland Boughton*, London, 1962; *Sailors' Songs and Shanties*, London, 1965; *Soldiers' Songs and Marches*, London, 1966; *The Composer*, Oxford, 1968; *An Outline History of European Music*, Sevenoaks, Kent, 1968; *Elgar*, London, 1969; *Vaughan Williams*, London, 1970; *Mendelssohn*, London, 1970; *The Ordeal of Ivor Gurney*, Oxford, 1978; *Oxford Junior Companion to Music*, Oxford, 1979; *Vincent Novello & Company*, London, 1981; *The Orchestra*, London, 1981.

Michael Hurd comments:

My music is accessible and, in the traditional sense, very tuneful. It is, however, not entirely predictable: certain rhythmic and harmonic subtleties lifting it, I hope, somewhat out of the ordinary. I have written a great deal for adventurous amateurs, and for children. And I enjoy this, as I believe that a composer's primary duty is to be useful to the community he finds himself in. I am greatly influenced by literature—hence all the choral music—and in this respect, as in my basic musical style, I suppose I belong very firmly in the Parry-Elgar-Vaughan Williams-Finzi-Britten tradition—though necessarily a minor member of that illustrious order!

* * *

Michael Hurd is accomplished as both composer and biographer. After postwar harmony and counterpoint studies at Oxford under Bernard Rose and Edmund Rubbra (both also successful composers), he turned to Lennox Berkeley. Since then, French influence has remained strong in his work—the attraction not so much the lushness of Ravel or weightier demands of Messiaen and Boulez as the lightness and wit of Les Six, together with the freshness and lyricism their imitators brought to English music of the inter-war years.

Approachability characterises his output. The tuneful *Concerto da Camera* for oboe and his Flute Sonatina both pay tribute to Poulenc. Like Françaix and others, Hurd has a way of capturing that outdoor, "champêtre" feel Poulenc achieves in his chamber or small orchestral works. Often in Hurd's music essentially tonal (though by no means always predictable) harmonies support a naturally flowing, faintly or overtly modal solo line, offset by gently syncopated rhythms that preserve an overall atmosphere of ease and well-being. A similar lyrical quality and mood characterises his gently jazzy *Harlequin Suite* for brass and the more recent *Little Suite* for strings.

Hurd's fondness for singable tunes, rhythmic vibrance and approachability reflects his own musical origins and a profound dislike of unduly complex scores for amateurs. Urging that such music be as practical and manageable as possible, Hurd carefully limits the scope and performance demands of his instrumental and vocal pieces to the capabilities of the numerous amateur or semi-professional groups, notably in his native Hampshire, who have continued to turn to him for commissions.

His particular success has been in the vocal and choral fields. His chamber opera *The Widow of Ephesus* is a three-part, chorusless one-act *Divertissement*, to a text by David Hughes and himself based on the well-known Greco-Roman tale: its neat, economical scoring for single wind, string quintet with double bass and piano recalls Walton's 1960s pastiche *The Bear*, which wittily employs a related textual theme.

Hurd's attractive choice of texts reflects his fondness for secular word-setting, something he shares with several of those he admires or has written about, including Britten, Tippett and Finzi. While drawing on the Elizabethans, Herrick (*Five Epitaphs, Charms and Ceremonies, Flower Songs*) and Dryden (*A Song for St Cecilia*), he has also composed unison songs in lighter vein to words by de la Mare and Charles Causley.

Shepherd's Calendar, his extended setting of John Clare for baritone, SATB and orchestra, is one of his most impressive achievements: a modal, almost ecclesiastical, French underlay is evident early in the work and increasingly inventive, vigorous canonic writing for voices and instruments follows as the four contrasting movements are unveiled. In *Shore Leave*, a cycle for baritone and strings, he offers the clearest evidence of his special affection for the unusually gifted English song composer, Ivor Gurney, of whom he has written the still definitive biography. An acknowledged debt to Britten (compare the latter's own *Flower Songs* and *Hymn to St Cecilia*) can be sensed in the counterpoint, invention and musical textures.

Other important SATB works include his early cycle, *Music's Praise*, which incorporate settings (with strings) of Shakespeare and Pope, the three brief unaccompanied Chaucer rondels entitled *Merciles Beaute* and the Elizabethan/Shakespearian threnody *The Phoenix and the Turtle*, into which he introduces a highly effective mezzo-soprano solo line.

Hurd writes especially well for equal voices: his delightful early work *Charms and Ceremonies* and the later *Nine of Anon* each have optional unison or SSA parts. Of the Herrick pieces, *Flower Songs* are for SSA with strings, whereas *Five Epitaphs* sets the poetry unaccompanied. He has also used SSA forces effectively in his church music: *Canticles of the Virgin Mary* or the *Missa brevis*, with its implicit tribute to not just Britten but the plainsong-influenced French school (Duruflé or Langlais), like much of his equal-voice output works equally well with boys' or girls' voices, the continental debt immediately apparent in the tender *berceuse* and accompanying organ of the Mass's *Sanctus*.

Hurd's entertaining pop cantatas—the first (*Jonah-man Jazz*) something of a trail-blazer back in the mid 1960s—are too widely known and performed to need elaboration. Since the bestselling *Jonah* and *Swingin' Samson*, more than a dozen have emerged, their punchy, wittily anachronistic libretti (usually by the composer) offset by neat pastiches of jazz, blues and other idioms Hurd admires or likes to share with his young singers, whom he always stretches sufficiently (he refuses to compromise young voices by "writing down" for them). Those on biblical themes include *Adam-in-Eden* and *Prodigal*, while among his longer efforts *Hip-Hip Horatio*, recalling a sea theme which surfaces often in his work, *Mrs Beeton's Book* and *Mr Punch*, a small-scale opera or "entertainment" for youngsters given its first performance in Sweden, all enjoy continuing success both at home and abroad.

—Roderic Dunnett

HUSA, Karel. Czech/American. Born in Prague, 7 August 1921. Educated at Prague Conservatory of Music (composition under Jaroslav Ridky, conducting under Pavel Dedecek and Vaclav Tilich), 1941–5; Academy of Music, Prague (composition under Ridky), 1945–7; Ecole Normale de Musique, Paris (composition under Arthur Honegger, conducting under Jean Fournet); Conservatoire National de Musique Supérieure, Paris (conducting under Eugène Bigot), 1948–9; also privately in Paris under Nadia Boulanger (composition) and Andre Cluytens (conducting), 1946–9. Emigrated to the United States, 1954; American citizenship, 1959. Secretary of Czech section, International Society for Contemporary Music, 1946; guest conductor, Radio Prague, 1945–6; jury member, Paris National Conservatory, 1952–3, and Fontainebleau School of Music and Arts, 1953; conductor, Cento Soli Orchestra, Paris, 1953–4; assistant professor, 1954–6, associate professor, 1957–60, professor, 1961–72, and Kappa Alpha Professor of Music (composition, theory, conducting, orchestration), since 1973, Cornell University, Ithaca, New York; director, Cornell University Orchestra, 1956–75, Ithaca Chamber Orchestra, 1957–63, and Cayuga Chamber Orchestra, 1978–84; guest conductor with Orchestre National de France, Orchestre des Cento Soli, Hamburg Radio Orchestra, and in Prague, Paris, Stockholm, Oslo, Geneva, Brussels, London, Manchester, Munich, Basle, Lausanne, New York, Boston, Buffalo, Rochester, Baltimore, Cincinnati, Denver, San Diego, Syracuse, Hong Kong, Puerto Rico, Singapore and Tokyo. Recipient: Czech Academy of Arts and Sciences Prize (for *Sinfonietta*), 1948; Lili Boulanger Foundation Prize (for *String Quartet No 1*), 1950; prize at Bilthoven Contemporary Music Festival (for *String Quartet No 1*), 1951; Guggenheim Fellowships, 1964, 1965; Pulitzer Prize in Composition (for *String Quartet No 3*), 1969; Orpheus Award, Phi Mu Alpha Musical Fraternity, 1972, 1974, 1980; D.Mus., Coe College, 1976; Friedheim Award, (for Recollections), 1983; Sudler International Award (for *Concerto for Wind Ensemble*), 1984; Sterling Silver Bicentennial Medallion, University of Georgia, 1984; Sousa Order of Merit, J.F. Kennedy Center, Washington, D.C., 1985; D.Mus., Cleveland Institute of Music, 1985; D.Mus., Ithaca College, 1986; honorary membership, Association of French Saxophonists, 1986; Karel Husa Professorship in composition established, Ithaca College, 1986; honorary membership, ARDESA/Society of German Saxophonists, 1988; Master Teacher Award, Music Teachers National Association, 1988; American Academy and Institute of Arts and Letters Award, 1989. Mailing address: 1032 Hanshaw Road, Ithaca, New York 14850, U.S.A.

Publishers: AMP/G. Schirmer; Schott.

Symphonies/orchestral:

Overture Op 3 (large orchestra) 1946; first performed Prague, 18 June 1946.

Sinfonietta Op 4 1947; first performed Prague, 25 April 1947.

Trois Fresques 1947, revised 1963; first performed Prague, 27 April 1949; revised version first performed Syracuse, New York, 5 May 1963.

Divertimento (string orchestra) 1948; first performed Paris, 30 October 1949.

Concertino (piano, orchestra) 1949; first performed Brussels, 6 June 1952.

Musique d'amateurs (4 easy pieces for oboe, trumpet, percussion, strings) 1953; first performed Germany, 1954.

Portrait (string orchestra) 1953; first performed Donaueschingen, 10 October 1953.

Symphony No 1 1953; first performed Brussels, 4 March 1954. Recorded CRI SD 261.

Four Little Pieces (strings) 1956; first performed Furstenbeck, Germany, 17 March 1957.

Fantasies 1956; first performed Ithaca, New York, 28 April 1957. Recorded GR GS 1054; EDUL ED 023.

Divertimento (brass, percussion) 1958; first performed Ithaca, New York, 17 February 1960.

Poem (viola, chamber orchestra/piano) 1959; first performed Cologne, 12 June 1960.

Elégie et rondeau (alto saxophone, orchestra) 1961; first performed Ithaca, New York, 6 May 1962. Recorded BR 1295; BR 12216; BR 1203.

Mosaiques 1961; first performed Hamburg, 7 November 1961. Recorded CRI SD 221.

Serenade (woodwind quintet, strings, harp, xylophone; expansion and orchestration of *Evocations of Slovakia*) 1963; first performed Baltimore, Maryland, 7 January 1964. Recorded CRI SD 261.

Concerto for Brass Quintet and String Orchestra 1965; first performed Buffalo, New York, 15 February 1970.

Concerto for Alto Saxophone and Concert Band 1967; first performed Ithaca, New York, 17 March 1968. Recorded GC ATH 5066; BR 1216; BR 1203.

Music for Prague 1968 (original version for concert band) 1968; first performed (band version) Washington, D.C., 31 January 1969; orchestral version first performed Munich, 31 January 1970. Recorded Louisville LS 722; Golden Crest CRS 4134; CBS Masterworks MK 44916.

Apotheosis of This Earth (original version for concert band) 1970; first performed Ann Arbor, Michigan, 1 April 1972. Recorded Golden Crest CRS 4134.
Concert for Percussion and Wind Instruments 1971; first performed Waco, Texas, 7 February 1972. Recorded Golden Crest ATH 5066.
Two Sonnets from Michelangelo 1971; first performed Evanston, Illinois, 28 April 1972. Recorded Louisville LS 7.
Concerto for Trumpet and Wind Orchestra 1973; first performed Storrs, Connecticut, 9 August 1974.
Al Fresco (concert band) 1973; first performed Ithaca, New York, 19 April 1975. Recorded Golden Crest ATH-5066.
The Steadfast Tin Soldier (narrator, orchestra) 1974; first performed Boulder, Colorado, 10 May 1975.
Fanfare (brass, percussion) 1980; first performed Portland, Oregon, 20 March 1980.
Pastoral (string orchestra) 1980; first performed Miami Beach, Florida, 12 April 1980.
Concerto for Wind Ensemble 1982; first performed Michigan, 3 December 1982. Recorded Mark PC-23700.
Symphony No 2: "Reflections" 1983; first performed 16 July 1983.
Concertino for Piano and Wind Ensemble (revision of 1949 *Concertino*) 1984; first performed Florida, 27 January 1984.
Smetana Fanfare 1984; first performed San Diego, California, 3 April 1984.
Symphonic Suite 1984; first performed Georgia, 1 October 1984.
Concerto for Orchestra 1986; first performed New York City, 25 September 1986.
Concerto for Organ and Orchestra 1987; first performed Cleveland, Ohio, 28 October 1987.
Concerto for Trumpet and Orchestra 1987; first performed Chicago, 11 February 1988.
Concerto for Cello and Orchestra 1988; first performed Los Angeles, 2 March 1989.

Chamber/instrumental:

String Quartet Op 2 1942–3.
Sonatina (piano) 1943; first performed Prague, 20 April 1945. Recorded GR CRS-4175.
Suite Op 5 (viola, piano) 1945; first performed 26 November 1946.
Sonatina Op 6 (violin, piano) 1945; first performed 27 September 1945.
String Quartet No 1 1948; first performed Prague, 23 May 1948. Recorded LPI PLI-117.
Piano Sonata No 1 1949; first performed 19 April 1950.
Evocations of Slovakia (clarinet, viola, cello) 1951; first performed Paris, 4 May 1952. Recorded GR GS-1008.
String Quartet No 2 1953; first performed Paris, 23 October 1954. Recorded ER 3290.
Four Little Pieces for Strings 1955; first performed Furstenbeck, Germany, 17 March 1957.
Eight Czech Duets (piano—4 hands) 1955; first performed 28 April 1956. Recorded Orion 81412.
Elégie (piano) 1957; first performed 15 November 1967. Recorded Grenadilla CRS-4175.
Two Preludes (flute, clarinet, bassoon) 1966; first performed Ithaca, New York, 21 April 1966. Recorded Vox SVBX-5307.
String Quartet No 3 1968; first performed Chicago, 14 October 1968. Recorded EDR 3290.
Divertimento for Brass Quintet (expansion of movements from *Eight Czech Duets*) 1968; first performed Ithaca, New York, 20 November 1968. Recorded Golden Crest CRS-4114.
Studies for Percussion 1968.
Sonata for Violin and Piano 1973; first performed New York City, 31 March 1974. Recorded Grenadilla GS-1032.
Piano Sonata No 2 1975; first performed 4 October 1975. Recorded Grenadilla CRS-4175.
Landscapes (brass quintet) 1977; first performed Kalamazoo, Michigan, 17 October 1977. Recorded CRI SD 192.
Three Dance Sketches (percussion) 1979; first performed Miami Beach, Florida, 12 April 1980.
Intradas and Interludes (7 trumpets, percussion) 1980; first performed Columbus, Ohio, 20 June 1989.
Sonata a tre (violin, clarinet, piano) 1982; first performed Hong Kong, 23 March 1982. Recorded CRS-648.
Recollections (woodwind quintet, piano) 1982; first performed Washington, D.C., 28 October 1982.
Variations (violin, viola, cello, piano) 1984; first performed Atlanta, Georgia, 20 May 1984. Recorded Orion ORP-86498.
Intrada (brass quintet) 1984; first performed 15 November 1984.
Frammenti (organ) 1987; first performed 6 November 1987.
String Quartet No 4 "Poems" 1990.

Vocal/choral:

Twelve Moravian Songs (voice, piano; folk texts) 1956; first performed April 1968. Recorded Redwood ES 12; GR GSC-1073.
Festive Ode (chorus, orchestra; Blackall) 1964; first performed 9 October 1964.
Apotheosis of This Earth (version for chorus, orchestra) 1973; first performed Ithaca, New York, 2 April 1973.
An American Te Deum (baritone, chorus, wind ensemble; also version for baritone, chorus, orchestra; Thoreau, Rolvaag, Reezina, folk texts) 1976, 1978; first performed Cedar Rapids, Iowa, 4 December 1976; orchestral version first performed Washington, D.C., 10 May 1978.
Three Moravian Songs (unaccompanied mixed chorus) 1981; first performed 14 March 1981.
Every Day (unaccompanied mixed chorus; Thoreau) 1981; first performed Ithaca, New York, 14 November 1981.
Cantata (male chorus, brass quintet; Robinson, Dickinson, Whitman) 1983; first performed Wabash, 20 April 1983.

Other:

Monodrama (ballet for orchestra) 1976; first performed Indianapolis, 26 March 1976.
The Trojan Women (ballet for orchestra) 1981; first performed Louisville, Kentucky, 28 March 1981. Recorded Louisville LS 775.

William Herschel: *Sinfonia No XIV in D major* (1762) (arranged for orchestra); first performed Ithaca, New York, 28 August 1962.
Jean-Baptiste Lully: *Carnaval, a Masquerade* (arranged for orchestra); first performed Ithaca, New York, 24 November 1963.
Michel Delalande: *Cantemus domino* (arranged for soli, chorus, orchestra); first performed Ithaca, New York, 5 March 1967.
Le Ballet des muses (arranged for orchestra); first performed Ithaca, New York, 13 May 1979.

PUBLICATIONS

By Husa: Four articles on musical life in Paris, in *Tempo* (Prague), 19 January 1947, May–June 1947, 20 January 1948, and November–December 1948 (in Czech); "Problemy dnesniho skladatele", in *Perspektivy* (New York), February 1963; "Disturbed Music Lover vs. Contemporary Composer", in *Instrumentalist*, October 1970; "Vzpominky na Bohuslava Martinu" (reminiscences), in *Promeny* (New York), April 1972; "The Acceptance of Contemporary Music", in American Symphony Orchestra League *Newsletter*, April 1972; "Thoughts on Czech Composers", in *Music Journal*, 30, 1972; "Meet the Composer: KH—Apotheosis of This Earth", in *Instrumentalist*, August 1973; "Some Thoughts on Percussion", in *Woodwind World—Brass and Percussion*, 14(3), 1975; "Why a New Trumpet Concerto?", in *Getzen Gazette* (Elkhorn, Wisconsin), August 1975; "Music for Prague 1968", in *The College and University Band*, edited by Johnson, MENC, 1977.

On Husa: Arthur Hegvik, "KH Talks About His Life and Work", in *Instrumentalist*, May 1975; Lawrence W. Hartzell, "KH: The Man and the Music", in *The Musical Quarterly*, January 1976; Kjellrun Kristine Hestekin, "Structural elements in KH's *Apotheosis of This Earth*, dissertation, University of Wisconsin, Madison, 1976; Crystal Impola, "An Analysis of the *Concerto for Alto Saxophone and Concert Band* by KH", dissertation, Eastern Michigan University, Ypsilanti, 1978; Mallory B. Thompson, "KH: *Concerto for Wind Ensemble*", dissertation, Eastman School of Music, Rochester, New York, 1985; Donald Mclaurin, "The Music of KH", dissertation, Florida State University, Tallahassee, 1985; Byron Adams, "A Catalogue of the Compositions of KH", Cornell University, Ithaca, New York, 1986; Thomas Iannaccone, "KH: A Composer for His Time and Beyond", in *Cross-Currents: A Yearbook of Central European Culture*, Ann Arbor, Michigan, 1988.

Karel Husa comments:

Music to me mirrors life; it reflects the time in which it is written. When we hear a work by Monteverdi, the Renaissance comes to our mind; with Bach, it is the religion and philosophy of the 18th century; with Beethoven, the revolutionary movement in Europe; with Debussy, the sophisticated impressions as seen by a master of French colours; and with Bartók, the energy as well as anguish of the 20th-century man.

I have been mostly concerned with giving my musical ideas the right proportions, contrasts and colours within forms such as modern sonatas and symphonies, concertos, variations, and leaving to the listener the freedom of understanding the content. Naturally, I use today's language and am trying to find in every work some new paths, forms, orchestration, sounds or new techniques on any given instrument. There have been times, though, when I feel the need to communicate to the audience my specific views and feelings on certain human values, for instance, freedom. This is why I have given one of my compositions the title *Music for Prague 1968* instead of *Symphony No* . . . As a composer, I can fight with notes and sounds.

Another work, *Apotheosis of This Earth*, written in 1970, deals with our problems of reckless living and destruction which could lead us to a dangerous future. And the last of my "manifestoes" is the ballet *The Trojan Women*, on the eternal subject of barbarism, based on the play of Euripides; not much has changed since 415 B.C.

The rest of my works do not wish to control listeners, but on the contrary to give them a freedom to choose what they feel in and about my music.

* * *

The music of Karel Husa represents an important continuation of the Czech musical tradition in the 20th century as exemplified by such composers as Janáček and Martinů. Although Husa has spent the greater part of his creative life in the United States, he has continued to look to the Czech tradition while addressing an international audience of performers and listeners. While Husa has only occasionally used Czech and Slovak folk music, in such scores as the *Evocations of Slovakia* for clarinet, viola and cello and the *Eight Czech Duets* for piano, his musical heritage proclaims itself just as surely in a series of works that combine instrumental brilliance and rhythmic propulsion with a remarkable intensity of expression.

In the early scores written between 1946 and 1953, Husa experimented with various compositional techniques and aesthetic ideologies. The influence of contemporary French music, especially that of Husa's teacher Honegger, is evident in the neoclassic *Divertimento* for string orchestra and the witty *Concertino* for piano and orchestra. During this period Husa was also attracted to both *Debrauchsmusik* and the use of folk materials. Husa later became interested in dodecaphonic procedures: his ingenious adaptations of serial techniques led to such disparate scores as the tenebrous, lyrical *Poem* for viola and chamber orchestra and the colourful, extrovert *Mosaiques* for orchestra.

By the middle of the 1960s, Husa had used these various tools to forge a style all his own. Husa composed two works in 1968 that brought his name before a wide audience: the Third String Quartet, which was awarded the 1969 Pulitzer Prize in music, and *Music for Prague 1968* for wind orchestra (also for full orchestra), which has received over 10,000 performances since its premiere in 1969. Inspired by the Soviet invasion of Czechoslovakia, *Music for Prague 1968* is the first of a triptych of scores which address contemporary global problems, a triptych which includes *Apotheosis of This Earth* for wind orchestra (also full orchestra and chorus) and the ballet *The Trojan Women*. In addition, Husa investigated many different genres throughout the 1970s and early 1980s, composing chamber and orchestra music, concertos for percussion and wind ensemble, and trumpet and wind orchestra, the ballet *Monodrama* and *An American Te Deum* for baritone, chorus and wind orchestra (also for full orchestra).

With the completion in 1986 of the massive *Concerto for Orchestra*. Husa entered into a period of intensified lyricism and increasing introspection. Husa further explored these expressive resources in the three concertos that followed: the exuberant *Concerto* for trumpet and orchestra; the radiant *Concerto* for organ and small orchestra; and the dramatic *Concerto* for cello and orchestra. An intimate example of this late style is found in the luminous Fourth String Quartet (*"Poems"*).

Husa's music is first and foremost an intensely compassionate response to a world that is often turbulent and tragic. In order to articulate his musical reactions, Husa feels free to employ any stylistically appropriate means available: all the techniques and theories he adopts are subject to his aesthetic aims. While he often uses serial elements, such as twelve-note aggregates, to provide motivic coherence and directional logic to a work, invariably Husa adapts serialism to the empirical necessities of his artistic vision, never allowing any theory undue influence over his expressive intent. From this interplay between formal control and uninhibited emotion, Husa creates scores which engage the listener on both the visceral and intellectual levels, while providing a searching critique of the excesses and injustice of late 20th-century society.

—Byron Adams

HVOSLEF, Ketil (originally Ketil Saeverud). Norwegian. Born in Bergen in 1939. Educated at Music Conservatory, Bergen (viola and organ), graduated 1962; further composition study under Karl-Birger Blomdahl and Ingvar Lidholm, Stockholm, and Thomas Rajna and Henri Lazarof, London. Teacher of ear-training and theory, Music Conservatory, Bergen, 1964–80; full-time composer from 1980; resident part of each year in Rome. Mailing address: c/o Norwegian Music Information Centre, Tordenskioldsgt. 6B, N-0160 Oslo 1, Norway.

Publisher: Norsk Musikforlag.

Symphonies/orchestral:

Concertino for Piano and Orchestra 1964.
Concerto for Trumpet and Orchestra 1969.
Miniett (violin, amateur string orchestra) 1971.
Mi-Fi-Li (symphonic poem) 1971. Recorded Bis LP 129.
Concerto for Double Bass and Orchestra 1973. Recorded Philips 6529 041.
Variations (chamber orchestra) 1976.
Concerto per Cello 1976, 1987.
Double Concerto (flute, guitar, strings) 1977. Recorded Bis LP 129.
Concertino 1979.
Concerto for Bassoon and Strings 1979.
Suite (school orchestra) 1980.
Antigone (symphonic variations) 1981–2.
Air 1983.
Vind (flute, winds, percussion) 1983.
Il compleanno (symphony orchestra, 2 sextets — flute, oboe, 2 violins, 2 cellos/double bass) 1985.
Concerto for Violin and Orchestra 1988–9.
Concerto per violoncello ed orchestra Nr 2 1990–1.

Chamber/instrumental:

Wind Quintet 1964. Recorded Philips 6507 044.
Ariseturo (percussion, 8 winds) 1966.
Duetti per fagotti (2 bassoons) 1966.
Suite: Six Pieces for Six Strings (guitar) 1966.
String Quartet No 1 1969.
Rondo con variazioni (piano) 1970. Recorded Philips 6507 054.
Flauto Solo (flute) 1970. Recorded Philips 6507 044.
Tromba Solo (trumpet) 1971. Recorded Varèse International VS 81 019.
Sextet (oboe, bassoon, trumpet, trombone, violin, cello) 1972.
Organ Variations 1972.
String Quartet No 2 (1st violin = Hardanger fiddle) 1973.
Organo Solo (organ) 1974. Recorded Philips 6507 055.
Nordic Counterpoint (2 fiddles, 6 bottles) 1974.
Kim (4 crumhorns SATB, 4 recorders, bass gamba, percussion) 1975. Recorded Philips 6529 109.
Trio (oboe, viola, percussion) 1978.
Ludium (7 flutes) 1978.
Octet (8 flutes) 1978. Recorded Philips 6529 041.
Brass (4 trumpets, 4 trombones, 4 horns, tuba) 1978.
Duo: What to Make Out of Seven Feathers (2 accordions) 1979.
Concerto for Violin and Pop Band (solo violin, piano/electric piano/electric organ, electric guitar, electric bass, percussion) 1979.
Violino Solo (violin) 1980.
Sextet: Post (flute, clarinet, horn, piano, guitar, violin) 1980.
Miniboogietriowoogie (piccolo, flute, piano) 1981.
Duodu (violin, viola) 1982.
Beethoven Fantasy (piano) 1982.
Erkejubel (2 trumpets, 2 trombones, polyphonic synthesizer, percussion) 1982.
Quintet (clarinet, string quartet) 1983.
Chitarra Solo (guitar) 1983.
Acanthus (accordion) 1984.
Fanfare (3 trumpets, 3 percussion) 1984.
Rikstrio (flute, violin, synthesizer) 1984.
Paskevariasjoner / Easter Variations (organ) 1986.
Scheherazade forteller videre / Scheherazade Carries on with Her Story (violin, harp) 1986.
Sextet (flute, 5 percussion) 1986.
Toccata; Fontana dell 'Organo, Villa d'Este (organ) 1988.
Framenti di Roma (oboe, clarinet, bassoon) 1988.
Kirkeduo (guitar, organ) 1988.

Vocal/choral:

So Einsam is der Mensch (unaccompanied mixed chorus or vocal quartet; Sachs) 1970.
Or Havamal / Sayings of the High One (SATB chorus, orchestra) 1971, revised 1974.
Kvartoni (soprano, soprano recorder/tenor recorder, guitar, piano) 1974. Recorded Bis LP 129.
Trio (soprano, alto, piano) 1974. Recorded Philips 6529 041.
Collage i Svart / Hvitt med Rodt / Collage in Black / White with Red (baritone speaker, violin, guitar, clarinet/bass clarinet, percussion; Monsen) 1975.
Concerto for Choir and Chamber Orchestra (SATB chorus, flute, clarinet, viola, piano, percussion) 1977. Recorded Philips 6529 021.
Spillemaend / Fiddlers (SATB chorus, Hardanger fiddle, organ; Ibsen) 1980.
Nattlig Madonna / Nocturnal Madonna (unaccompanied male chorus; Sodergran) 1984.
Dano Tiore (soprano, 3 strings, harpsichord) 1985.
Entrata Bergensis (buekorps, SATB chorus, tape, orchestra) 1989.

Opera:

The Ballad of Narcissus and Echo (unaccompanied choral opera; Andersson) 1981.
Dode Sardiner ("mimic criminalopera" with slides; Stalesen) 1986–7.
Trio for Tretten; Acotral (soprano, mezzo-soprano, tenor, bass, 2 violins, viola, cello, flute, oboe, clarinet, bassoon, percussion) 1987.

Other:

Hjallarbrui (incidental music) 1973.
The Flies (incidental music to play by Sartre) 1974.
Og Vegine Falle So Vide (incidental music) 1974.
A Dream Play (incidental music to Strindberg) 1975.
Miss Julie (incidental music to play by Strindberg) 1975.
Faust (incidental music to play by Goethe) 1977.
King Lear (incidental music to play by Shakespeare) 1978.
Antigone (incidental music to play by Sophocles) 1980.
Barabbas (incidental music to play by Ghelderode) 1981.
Richard III (incidental music to play by Shakespeare) 1982.
Lutzen (incidental music to play by Orlander) 1983.
King John (incidental music to play by Shakespeare) 1983.
Richard II (incidental music to play by Shakespeare) 1983.
Johannes Apenbaring 12. Kap. (recitation, organ, dancer) 1984.
Faust (new music to play by Goethe) 1985.
Pantagleize (incidental music to play by Gleize) 1986.
Lykke pers Reise (incidental music to play by Strindberg) 1987.

Music for television: *Fisketorget i Bergen*, 1970; *Vigd til Kampen*, 1973; *Fader Per*, 1974; *Oberosterreich*, 1975; *Historien om Digteren Lin Pe og Hans Hamme Trane / The Story of the Poet Lin Pe and His Tame Crane*, 1975; *Svalbard*, 1979; *Menmenneske / Fellow Man*, 1980; *Det Gode Menneske fra Sezuan*, 1984; *Av Manneskinn Gror det Ingenting*, 1987.

PUBLICATIONS

On Hvoslef: Nils Grinde, in *Contemporary Norwegian Music, 1920–80*, Oslo, 1981.

* * *

Ketil Hvoslef is the son of the veteran Norwegian composer Harald Saeverud. In 1980, when he resigned from his teaching post at the Bergen Conservatory to become a full-time composer, he adopted his mother's name. This had nothing whatever to do with a desire, common among Norwegians of his generation, to dissociate himself from any parental flirtation with the Nazi-dominated puppet Quisling regime of the war years (Saeverud, on the contrary, regarded his work of the early 1940s as a "personal war" against Hitler), but rather to protect his compositional output from inevitable and largely meaningless comparison with his father's.

There are signs already that Hvoslef may be nearly as prolific. He is certainly harder to categorize, working in an area of free tonality that allows him to adapt his means and methods according to the particular piece on which he is working. His style thus modulates between a latter-day neo-classicism, which is by no means insensitive to the original product, and a kind of gentle avant-gardism laced with considerable humour. Hvoslef studied twelve-tone technique with Henri Lazarof and in 1969 wrote a serial string quartet and a number of other works in relatively orthodox Viennese manner, but with a distinctive approach to variation retained from the earlier neo-classicism. His remarkable symphonic *Mi-Fi-Li* introduces the concept of "motivic assimilation" which has lain behind most of his work for the ensuing two decades. This technique, which has clear similarities with serial procedures, allows an entire piece to be generated from a single and relatively simple motif, which is subject to any number of transformations and inversions, and which can be distributed freely across the rhythmic or timbral range; compare the blandly serial *Flauto Solo* of 1970, with the remarkable *Ludium* for seven flutes and *Octet* for eight flutes, written eight years later. The method has proved a far more congenial technique for Hvoslef than orthodox serialism and has allowed him to preserve a particular balance of old and new in his work.

He had a relatively conventional musical education, but the influence of his best knowm composition teachers Karl-Birger Blomdahl and Ingvar Lidholm doubtless pushed him in the direction of a modernity that takes full account of the music of the past. Hvoslef has written a number of more or less standard concertos, notably for trumpet and for double bass; there is also a fine double concerto for flute, guitar and strings, and the altogether more original (if in the second instance now slightly dated) concertos for choir and chamber forces, and for violin and rock group. A fine and adventurous instrumentator, Hvoslef has not been seduced by electronics (though he accepts the resources of polyphonic keyboard synthesizers in some works) and prefers to explore the potential of existing but often neglected instruments and instrumental combinations. He has written effective music for crumhorns and recorders, for accordions, for the unlikely combination of guitar and organ, and oboe, viola and percussion; the first violin part of his second string quartet is scored for Hardanger fiddle, a Norwegian folk instrument with sympathetic drone strings, and the effect is every bit as distinctive and unsettling as any modernist *scordatura*.

He has written some vocal music, though this is not his forte, and operatic writing is clearly inconsistent with the non-narrative character of his most characteristic work. Highly regarded in his native country, Hvoslef is winning a growing reputation overseas (he now lives in Rome for part of each year). He has been well-represented on commercial records and is an accessible and stimulating voice. It may well be that outside Norway, Harald Saeverud will one day have to be identified as Ketil Hvoslef's father.

—Brian Morton

HWANG Byung-ki (Hwang Pyŏnggi). Korean. Born in Seoul, 31 May 1936. Educated at College of Law, Seoul National University, 1955–9, B.A.; study of *kayagŭm* zither, Korean Traditional Performing Arts Centre, 1952–9. Married Han Malsuk, 27 May 1962; 2 sons and 2 daughters. Instructor, College of Music, Seoul National University, 1959–63; instructor, Korean Traditional Performing Arts Centre, 1962–6; visiting lecturer, University of Washington, Seattle, Summer 1965; guest artist, University of Hawaii, Honolulu, Summer 1965; instructor 1976–74, and professor, since 1974; College of Music, Ehwa Women's University; member of board, Cultural Properties Management Committee, Seoul, since 1973, International Society of Contemporary Music, Korean section, since 1978; visiting scholar, Harvard University, Cambridge, Massachusetts, 1985–6. Recipient: 1st prize, Korean Broadcasting System Traditional Music Concours, 1957; Ministry of Information Traditional Music Prize, 1965; drama music prize, *Han'guk ilbo / Korean Daily News*, 1974. Mailing address: 1–316 Puk Ahyŏn-dong, Sŏdaemun-ku, Seoul, Korea.

Publisher: Sumandung, 349–1 Ŭlchiro 3-ga, Chung-ku, Seoul, Korea.

Symphonies/orchestral:

Mandaeyŏp haet'an 1974.
Unhak / Crane in the Clouds 1978.

Chamber/instrumental:

Sup / The Forest (kayagŭm zither) 1963. Recorded RS 069.
Kaŭl / Fall (kayagŭm zither) 1963. Recorded RS 069.
Sŏngnyujip / The Pomegranate House (kayagŭm zither) 1964; first performed Honolulu, Hawaii, 1965. Recorded RS 069.
Pom / Spring (kayagŭm zither) 1967. Recorded RS 069.
Karado / Kara Town (kayagŭm zither) 1967. Recorded RS 069.
Mansangman hwanip / Slow-Fast-Slow (horizontal flute, taegum) 1971.
P'ungyo / Song of the Wind (oboe) 1972.
Ch'imhyangmu / Dance to an Indian Perfume (kayagŭm zither) 1973; first performed Amsterdam, 1974. Recorded RS 069.
Pidan'gil / The Silk Road (kayagŭm zither) 1977. Recorded RS 104.
Aibogae / Children's Games (2 kayagŭm zithers, horizontal flute, drum) 1978. Recorded RS 104.
Chashi / Early Night (horizontal flute) 1978.
Chŏnsŏl / The Legend (kayagŭm zither) 1979. Recorded RS 104.
Yongmok / The Haunted Tree (kayagŭm zither) 1979. Recorded RS 104.
Harimsŏng (horizontal flute) 1982.
Pam ŭi sori / Sounds of the Night 1984; first performed Tokyo, 1985.
Sanun / Mountain Rhyme (komun'go zither, horizontal flute) 1984. Recorded RS 143.
Namdo hwansanggok / Southern Fantasy (kayagŭm zither) 1988.
Soyŏp sanbang / The Hermit's Pavilion (komun'go zither, drum) 1990.

Vocal/choral:

Kukhwa yŏp'esŏ / Beside a Chrysanthemum Tree (voice, zither, flute, drum) 1962.
Ch'ŏngsando (chorus) 1974.
Kanggsangsullae (chorus; arrangement of women's folksong) 1974.
Chŏnyŏk songju / Evening Chant (chorus) 1983.
Pyŏgŭl nŏmŏsŏ / Beyond All Barriers (song for opening of Seoul Olympiad) 1988.
Kohyang ui tal / Moon of My Hometown (voice, zither, drum) 1990.

Other:

Migung / The Labyrinth (dance; female voice, zither) 1975. Recorded RS 143.
Pari kongju (dance; legend of first Korean shaman) 1978.
Yŏne pult'a olla / Raising Buddha's Lotus (dance) 1983.

Film scores: *Taewon'gun and the Empress Min*, 1957; *Phoenix*, 1962; *Kayagum*, 1964; *Sujŏl / Faithfulness*, 1973.

PUBLICATIONS

By Hwang: "Kayagŭm chakkokpobe taehan yon'gu" [Composing for the Zither], in *Yesul nonmunjip*, 17, 1975; "The Aesthetic Characteristics of Korean Music in Theory and Practice", in *Asian Music*, 9 (2); "Chont'ong ŭmakkwa hyŏndae ŭmak" [Traditional and Contemporary Music], in *Han'guk ŭi minjok munhaw* [Popular Culture in Korea], Songnam, Korea, 1979; "Umakchŏk shigan'gwa ridŭm" [Time and Rhythm in Music], in *Wŏlgan ŭmak* [Monthly Music], 3, 1983; "Some Notes on Korean Music and Aspects of Its Aesthetics", in *World of Music*, 27 (2), 1985; "The Influence of Asian Music on Western Composition", in *Nonch'ong*, 57, 1987.

On Hwang: Alan C. Heyman, "Korean Music: New Faces and New Music—*Kayagŭm* Virtuoso HB-k", in *Korea Journal*, 5 (2), and "HB-k *Kayagŭm* Masterpieces", in *Korea Journal*, 25 (5); Yun Chunggang, "Sup'eso chŏnsŏlkkaji: kayagŭmgogŭl t'onghae pon HB-k ui umakkwa sasang" [The Music and Influence of HB-k from *The Forest* to *The Legend*], in *Kaeksok* [Auditorium], 3, 1985; Pak Yonggu, "Ojik han saram: HB-k" [Only One Man: Hb-k], in *Onŭl ŭi ch'osang*, Seoul, 1989; Andrew Killick, "New Music for Korean Instruments", dissertation, University of Hawaii, Honolulu, 1990.

Hwang Byung-ki comments:

I have been concerned for many years with the aesthetics of Korean music. My motivation, both as performer and composer, has been to increase our awareness of Korean culture and arts. When I graduated, there was no modern Korean music. We have no heroes like Beethoven or Bach in the West. We celebrate the king under whom a piece originated, or the piece itself, but not an individual composer. After researching some rules—for in Korea we had been only concerned with imitating the West—I composed *Sup / The Forest.* Thus, then, was the first contemporary piece of Korean music. My development of new music works from the knowledge that we must learn and keep traditional languages. If I forget the traditions of Korea, my music means nothing: my inspiration comes from the past and the new floats on the old.

* * *

Hwang Byung-ki claims, with some justification, to have composed the first contemporary Korean music: *Sup / The Forest* back in 1963. Before this, musicians such as Kim Kisu (1917–1986) who had composed music had restricted themselves to traditional instruments played in traditional ways. (The same can be said of Hwang's first acknowledged piece, *Kukhwa yŏp'esŏ / Beside a Chrysanthemum Tree*. "Contemporary" implies to Hwang music with new ideas but close links to the past. The four movements of *Sup*—"Green Shade", "Cuckoo", "Rain", "Moonlight"—thus have much in common with Edward MacDowell's sketches (pieces which Hwang knew), yet differ because of their allegiances. "Green Shade" is a long court-inspired melody (that reappears in his 1974 choral piece, *Ch'ŏngsando*); "Cuckoo" strictly follows a folk rhythmic cycle—*chungjungmori* (in 12/8 time) but is far more descriptive than old music; "Rain" is inspired by the last movement of the folk genre *sanjo*, but extends way beyond octave alternations to new and intricate ostinato-plus-melody patterning.

Hwang studied the 12-string plucked long zither, *kayagŭm*, for seven years under Kim Yŏngyun, Kim Yundŏk and Shim

Sanggon. This has become the instrument for which the bulk of his pieces are written. *Ch'imhyangmu* is perhaps his most successful piece for the instrument to date, deriving its title from *mu* [dance] and the name of an Indian perfume. Hwang claims that the piece explores the Buddhist art of the Korean Shilla kingdom (to 935 AD), hence chooses a special tuning derived from sacred chants. The score of *Ch'imhyangmu* is divided into three sections linked through common tonal centres of A and E. The first is closest to the old, with both melody and rhythm reminiscent of *sanjo* (three folk rhythmic cycles are marked: *chungmori* [12/4 time], *ŏtchungmori* [6/4 time] and *chungjungmori* [12/8 time]). The second, a ternary slow-fast-slow, introduces new ideas: arpeggios, "microtonal shading" where the same pitch is produced on adjacent strings, lefthand melody (traditionally only the right hand plucked the strings), and flicked repeating tones. The drum is also struck on its wooden body. The third movement lets off fireworks. Starting with a folksy *hwimori* compound meter, ascending triplets in the right hand are underwritten by left hand arpeggiated chords. Settling through a 4/4 passage, triadic arpeggios both ascending and descending give way to a falling cadence played by the left hand against "microtonal" double-strikes of the right hand. A graphic representation of a dynamic build and fall precedes simultaneous left and right hand arpeggios. A single, quickly damped A marks the end.

Hwang has rarely moved from this comfortable blend of old and new. Critics thus argue he has lapsed into a style which cannot develop. Two things argue for this perspective: his devotional piece commissioned for the 1988 Olympics, *Pyŏgŭl nŏmŏsŏ / Beyond All Barriers*, was rejected for being too plain, too simple for the martial arts demonstration it was meant to accompany; and in the 1980s, Hwang has been unable to compose many pieces. One piece argues to the contrary; this is *Migung / The Labyrinth*. Adventurous and progressive, *Migung* was considered so shocking that for several years the government effectively black-listed it. Alan Heyman relates that this followed a performance which "sent a woman screaming from the concert hall", adding that he hopes it will remain Hwang's only venture into modern "abstract madness". *Migung* is essentially a dance piece, and the score comprises just a single sheet of graphic notation supplemented by a table of explanations. In seven sections, the third ("Groaning") provides most ammunition for his critics, while two offer verbal texts. One, "Reading a Newspaper Article", increases in pitch and volume until the words disappear; the other, "Chant", takes a simple mantra that allows for gradual dissipation of energy. The vocal line is left relatively flexible, but new techniques for the zither are closely prescribed. The player uses bows and plectrums, at one point striking a bamboo drum beater that has been threaded between strings. Hwang, in a 1979 article, acknowledged some familiarity with Henry Cowell's earlier experiments and claimed that *Migung* could not be classified as either Korean or Western music. Yet, even if this indicates influence from the West, Hwang remains adament that he should continue to produce compositions that blend old and new Korean elements.

—Keith Howard

I

ICHIYANAGI, Toshi. Japanese. Born in Kobe, Hyogo, 4 February 1933. Educated: studied composition with Kishio Hirao and John Cage, piano with Chieko Hara, Beveridge Webster and Bernhard Weiser; Juilliard School of Music and New School for Social Research, New York City, 1954–8; returned to Japan, 1961. Married Yoko Ono in 1957 (dissolved 1963). Rockefeller Foundation composer in residence, New York, 1967; DAAD composer in residence, Berlin, 1976; artistic director, Interlink Festival, Tokyo, and Tokyo International Music Ensemble; advisor, National Theatre, Tokyo; adviser, Orchestra Ensemble, Kanazawa. Recipient: 1st prize, Mainichi/NHK Composition Contest, 1949, 1951; Elizabeth A. Coolidge Prize, New York; Koussevitzky Prize, Berkshire Music Center, Tanglewood, Massachusetts; Otaka Prize (for *Reminiscences of Spaces*), 1981, (*Circulating Scenery*), 1984; Nakajima Prize, 1984; Record Academy Award (Japan) for *Cosmos of Toshi Ichiyanagi*, 1984; Ordre des Arts et des Lettres (France), May 1985; Mainichi Newspaper Art Prize, 1989; Kyoto Music Prize, 1989; Otaka Prize (for *Winter Portrait*), 1989, (for *Symphony "Berlin Renshi"*) 1990. Mailing address: 6-11-1017 Udagawacho, Shibuyako, Tokyo 150, Japan.

Publisher: Schott.

Symphonies/orchestral:

Life Music (orchestra, tape) 1962. Recorded Victor SJB 1501; EMI C165-28-954/47.
The Field 1966.
Activities (electric ensemble, orchestra) 1967.
Up-to-Date Applause (pop group, orchestra, tape) 1968.
In the Reflection of Lighting Image (percussion, orchestra) 1980; first performed Osaka, July 1980.
Piano Concerto No 1 "Reminiscence of Space" 1981; first performed Tokyo, March 1981. Recorded CBS Sony 00AC1432-5.
Engen (koto, orchestra) 1982; first performed Tokyo, March 1982.
Violin Concerto "Circulating Scenery" 1983; first performed Tokyo, May 1983. Recorded Camerata CMT 3024; CBS Sony 32DC350.
Time Surrounding 1984; first performed Tokyo, March 1984.
Paganini Personal (marimba, orchestra; also versions for marimba, piano; marimba, piano, chorus) 1984–6; first performed Sapporo, July 1984.
Symphony "Time Current" (chamber orchestra) 1986; first performed Paris, February 1987.
Interspace (string orchestra) 1987; first performed Sapporo, March 1987.
Reingaku Symphony "The Shadows Appearing Through the Darkness" (ancient instruments, gagaku orchestra with Shōmyō Buddhist chanting) 1987; first performed Tokyo, September 1987.
Piano Concerto No 2 "Winter Portrait" 1987; first performed Paris, January 1988.
Symphony "Berlin Renshi" (soprano, tenor, orchestra) 1988; first performed Tokyo, November 1988.
Existence (organ, orchestra) 1989; first performed Tokyo, June 1989.
Voices from the Environment 1989; first performed Tokyo, September 1989.
Concerto "The Origin" (koto, chamber orchestra) 1989; first performed Brussels, October 1989.
Reigaku Symphony No 2 "Kokai" (gagaku, reigaku-orchestra, shōmyō) 1989; first performed Tokyo, September 1989.
Symphonic Movement "Kyoto" 1989; first performed Kyoto, December 1989.

Chamber/instrumental:

Sonata (violin, piano) 1954; first performed New York City, December 1954.
String Quartet 1957; first performed New York City, 1957.
Music for Piano No 2 1959.
Music for Piano No 3 1960. Recorded Denon OW784OND.
Music for Electronic Metronome (3–7 players) 1960.
Music for Piano No 4 for David Tudor 1960.
Music for Piano No 5 1961. Recorded Denon OW784OND.
Music for Piano No 6 1961; first performed New York City, February 1961.
Music for Piano No 7 1961.
Duetto (string instrument, piano) 1961.
Sapporo (any number of players, conductor) 1962. Recorded EMI C165-28-954/57.
Pratyahara Event (music event for 3–7 players) 1963–73; first performed Tokyo, May 1973.
String Quartet No 1 "Nagaoka" (graphic score) 1964; first performed Tokyo, May 1966.
Appearance (3 instruments, 2 oscillators, 2 ring modulators) 1967.
Arrangements (percussion) 1972; first performed Berlin, October 1976. Recorded RCA RDC9 JRL1-1333.
Piano Media 1972; first performed Tokyo, May 1972. Recorded Angel EAC 60153.
Vine of Sounds (harp) 1972.
Music for Living Process (ensemble, 2 dancers) 1973. Recorded Victor SJX 7359.
Trichrome (ensemble) 1975.
Multiple Space (organ) 1976; first performed Bremen, Germany, May 1976.
Time Sequence (piano) 1976; first performed Tokyo, October 1976.
Scenes I (violin, piano) 1978; first performed Tokyo, January 1978. Recorded Victor SJX 9541.
Scenes II (violin) 1979; first performed Tokyo, January 1979. Recorded Camerata CMT 4016.
Recurrence (flute, clarinet, percussion, harp, piano, violin, cello) 1979; first performed Middleburg, Netherlands, July 1979.
Distance (Noh-flute, flute, clarinet, 2 percussion, piano, cello) 1979; first performed Cologne, 1979.
Scenes III (violin) 1980; first performed Tokyo, January 1980. Recorded Camerata CMT 4026.
Two Existence (2 pianos) 1980; first performed Tokyo, June 1980. Recorded Camerata CMT 4016.

Kaze no Iroai (flute) 1980; first performed Tokyo, July 1980.
Ogenraku (gagaku ensemble) 1980; first performed Tokyo, October 1980.
Scenes IV (violin, piano) 1981; first performed Tokyo, January 1981.
Wa (13-stringed koto, 17-stringed koto, piano, percussion) 1981; first performed Berlin, September 1981.
Before Darkness Appears (accordion, piano) 1981; first performed Tokyo, December 1981.
Time in Tree, Time in Water (percussion, piano) 1981; first performed Cologne, September 1981. Recorded CBS Sony 32DC1009.
Paganini Personal (marimba, piano) 1982; first performed Karuisawa, August 1982.
Flowers Blooming in Summer (harp, piano) 1982; first performed Tokyo, October 1982. Recorded Camerata CMT 4016.
Enenraku (gagaku ensemble) 1982; first performed Tokyo, October 1982.
Scenes V (violin, piano) 1982; first performed Tokyo, October 1982.
Hoshi no Wa (shō) 1983; first performed Tokyo, February 1983. Recorded Camerata CMT 4026; CBS Sony 32DG60.
Rinkaiiki (sangen) 1983; first performed Tokyo, February 1983.
Hikari-nagi (ryuteki, percussion) 1983; first performed Tokyo, May 1983.
Portrait of Forest (marimba) 1983; first performed Tokyo, September 1983.
Wind Trace (marimba, vibraphone, antique cymbal) 1984; first performed Tokyo, June 1984.
Cloud Shore, Wind Roots (ancient instruments, gagaku ensemble) 1984; first performed Tokyo, September 1984.
Accumulation (shakuhachi, 2 kotos, sangen) 1984; first performed Tokyo, March 1984.
Cloud Figures (oboe) 1984; first performed Tokyo, November 1984. Recorded Camerata CMT 4026.
Cloud Atlas I, II, & III (piano) 1985; first performed Tokyo, June 1985.
Yami o Irodoru Mono (2 violins, piano) 1985; first performed Kusatsu, August 1985.
Piano Quintet "Prana" 1985; first performed Paris, January 1986.
Still Time I (shō) 1986; first performed Tokyo, July 1986.
Still Time II (kugo) 1986; first performed Tokyo, March 1986.
Perspectives (violin) 1986; first performed Tokyo, December 1986.
String Quartet No 2 "Interspace" 1986.
Presage (6 ondes martenot) 1986; first performed Marseille, February 1987.
Winter Portrait II (koto) 1987; first performed Tokyo, March 1987.
Katachi naki Mugen no Yoha (koto) 1987; first performed Sapporo, October 1987.
Inter Konzert (piano) 1987; first performed Tokyo, April 1987.
Still Time III (harp) 1987; first performed Lerchenborg, Denmark, August 1987.
Cloud Atlas IV, V & VI (piano) 1987; first performed Tokyo, December 1987.
Transstream (18 percussionists) 1987.
Water Relativity (hitsu, kin) 1989; first performed Tokyo, March 1989.
Wind Gradation (ryuteki, piano) 1989; first performed Los Angeles, April 1989.
Piano Nature (piano) 1989; first performed Tokyo, May 1989.
Wind Stream (flute) 1989; first performed Sapporo, June 1989.
Cloud Atlas VII, VIII & IX (piano) 1989; first performed Tokyo, November 1989.
The Source (marimba) 1989; first performed Tokyo, June 1990.
Inexhaustible Fountain (piano) 1990; first performed Osaka, January 1990.
The Way (2 shō, u, 2 hichiriki, o-hichiriki, shakuhachi, koto, biwa, 2 percussion) 1990; first performed New York, February 1990.

Vocal/choral:

Extended Voices (chorus) 1967.
Music Project No 1 (voice, electronics) 1969.
Music for Living Space (chorus, computer) 1970; first performed Osaka, 1970.
Voice Field (children's chorus; Tanikawa) 1973; first performed Tokyo, January 1974. Recorded King SKM(H) 2224-7.
Mizu no Seiri [Physiology of Water] (voice, piano) 1976.
Aru Toki (soprano, piano; Santoka) 1981; first performed Tokyo, November 1981.
Kodomo no Jujigun (mixed chorus; Brecht, Hasegawa) 1983; first performed Tokyo, September 1983.
Heso no Uta (children's chorus; Muchaku) 1984; first performed Tokyo, October 1984.
Requiem (male chorus; Kihara) 1985.
Paganini Personal (marimba, piano, mixed chorus; Iwaki) 1986; first performed Tokyo, March 1986.
Music for Art Kites (soprano, flute) 1989; first performed Shizuoka, August 1989.

Other:

Parallel Music (electronic) 1962; broadcast October 1962.
Life Music (electronic music) 1964.
Shiki soku ze ku, ku soku ze shiki [Lust Is Emptiness and Emptiness Lust] (electronic) 1965.
Tinguely Mixture No 2 (electro-acoustic) 1965.
Funkakushi (electro-acoustic) 1966.
Shikisokuzeku-Kusokuzeshiki (electro-acoustic) 1967.
The Third Fashion (electronic) 1968.
Music Project 1–2 (electronic) 1968.
Tokyo 1969 (electronic) 1969; broadcast January 1969.
Theatre Music (electronic) 1969.
Environmental Music 1–3 (electronic) 1970.
Mandarama (electronic) 1970.
Piano Media (electronic) 1972.
Improvisation, September 1975 (Toshi Ichiyanagi, Michael Ranta, Takehisa Kosugi) 1975. Recorded Iskra 002.

PUBLICATIONS

On Ichiyanagi: Karlheinz Stockhausen, in *Texte*, 3, 1971.

* * *

An introductory anecdote could best sum up the approach of Toshi Ichiyanagi. One day in class, John Cage was commenting on the work of his pupils. When he began to make suggestions to Ichiyanagi, the latter stared icily into space and said, icily, "I am not you". Individualism is the guiding thread of Ichiyanagi's work, manifested in a flamboyant but carefully nurtured spontaneity.

Although of Japanese birth, Ichiyanagi studied in America from the age of 19, and he based his work in the polymorphous resources offered by experimental music in the

New World. He has produced works and performances involving chance elements, graphic notations, unconventional performance techniques and electronic resources. The string quartet *Nagaoka* requires the players to finger at the soundhole and bow over the fingerboard. *Music for Piano No 4 for David Tudor* calls for any number of pianists and consists of a terse text, "use sustaining sound(s) and silence(s) only. No attack should be made".

Sapporo, for up to 15 players plus conductor, may be played on any sound sources which can meet the requirements of the score—signs which identify sustaining sounds, chords, attacked and sliding sounds. Where more than two signs are present, a selection of the elements may be made and sounds produced accordingly.

In the mid-1960s, Ichiyanagi returned to Japan for extensive work in the NHK radio electronic music studio, producing works such as the *Tinguely Mixture No 2*, *Funkakushi* and *Shikisokuzeku-Kusokuzeshiki*. Electro-acoustic pieces include his earlier *Appearance* for three players and sound projectionist. The performers work through their parts at their own pace, so it is impossible to predict which sounds will be transformed and which ring modulated. *Life Music* for orchestra and tape is written in the form of graphic suggestions for imitative and transformative processes, on seven sheets, each of two minute's duration, which may be played in any order.

Ichiyanagi has occasionally made reference to the sound-world of modern popular music; one rather unlikely page of *Life Music* instructs the percussionists on cue to improvise patterns in the style of jazz or rock, and *Up-to-Date Applause* is scored for pop group, tape and orchestra.

Certain pieces seem to fall as much within the ambit of conceptual art or theatre as of music. *Music for Electronic Metronome* for three or more performers consists of a chart with variable starting points and various routes to the end; it predates Ligeti's *Poème symphonique* of 1962. *Distance* requires sounds to be set off from a point at least three metres from their point of issue. Another piece calls for darts to be thrown at a piano from the wings.

Experimental Music is written for four people sitting on upright chairs. As slowly as possible, each player leans sideways. Within perhaps four minutes, they overbalance, at which point each should silently but ferociously struggle with his or her chair. The players freeze, and then begin to tilt their chairs again as the curtain falls. Contact microphones on the floor amplify the proceedings.

Ichiyanagi's music has individuality, sensitivity and expansiveness. His scores tend to leave a great deal of latitude to the performer. In conducted pieces, the conductor functions as coordinator rather than controller. In *Life Music*, he or she beats time to synchronise the relation between instruments and tape, and in *Sapporo* acts as a focal point, given priority only because he or she starts off the piece, and because one of the piece's instructions explicitly requires other players to watch the conductor. As with other music taking this approach, this requires a sensitive rapport between players (indeed, *Sapporo* has a sign which tells the performer to listen to what others are playing).

Ichiyanagi's music also gives the impression of expansiveness, whether in the spatial separation of the performers (*Sapporo*), the delicate spacing of the notes, or the resultant stretching of the listener's perception of time. "It does not", as John Cage said elsewhere, "make the air any heavier than it was before".

—David Revill

IMBRIE, Andrew (Welsh). American. Born in New York City, 6 April 1921. Educated: piano lessons from age 4 with Ann Abajian, later Pauline and Leo Ornstein; Princeton Day School, New Jersey, graduated 1935; studied composition with Nadia Boulanger, Paris, 1937; Lawrenceville School, New Jersey, graduated 1938; studied piano with Robert Casadesus, Summer 1941; Princeton University (under Roger Sessions), B.A., 1942; University of California, Berkeley (again under Sessions), M.A., 1947. Served in the U.S. Army Signal Corps, 1942–6: 2nd lieutenant. Married Barbara Cushing in 1953; 2 sons (1 deceased). Fellow, American Academy in Rome, 1947–49; professor of music, since 1949, holder, Jerry and Evelyn Hemmings Chambers Chair, 1989–91, and faculty research lecturer, 1990–1, University of California, Berkeley; also on faculty of San Francisco Conservatory of Music; composer in residence, American Academy in Rome, 1967–8; Jacob Siskind Visiting Professor, Brandeis University, Waltham, Massachusetts. 1982; Recipient: New York Music Critics' Award, 1944; Alice M. Ditson Award, Columbia University, 1947; Merit Award, Boston Symphony, 1950; Guggenheim Fellowship, 1953–4 (Rome), 1959–60 (Tokyo); Brandeis University Creative Arts Award, 1957; Naumburg Recording Award, 1960; elected to National Institute of Arts and Letters, 1969; Hinrichsen Award, 1971; elected to American Academy of Arts and Sciences, 1980. Mailing address: 2625 Rose Street, Berkeley, California 94708, U.S.A.

Publishers: Malcolm Music, Delaware Water Gap, Pennsylvania; Shawnee/Schirmer.

Symphonies/orchestral:

Ballad 1947; first performed Rome, June 1949.
Violin Concerto 1954; first performed Berkeley, California, 22 April 1958. Recorded Columbia CSP 6597.
Little Concerto (piano—4 hands, orchestra) 1956; first performed Oakland, California, 14 November 1961.
Legend 1959; first performed San Francisco, 9 December 1959. Recorded CRI 152.
Symphony No 1 1965; first performed San Francisco, 11 May 1966.
Chamber Symphony 1968; first performed Hanover, New Hampshire, 11 August 1968.
Symphony No 2 1970; first performed San Francisco, 20 May 1970.
Symphony No 3 1970; first performed Manchester, England, 4 December 1970.
Cello Concerto 1972; first performed Oakland, California, 24 April 1973.
Piano Concerto No 1 1973; first performed Saratoga, California, 4 August 1973.
Piano Concerto No 2 1974; first performed Indianapolis, 29 January 1976.
Flute Concerto 1977; first performed New York City, 13 October 1977.

Chamber/instrumental:

String Quartet No 1 1942; first performed New York City, 1944. Recorded Columbia ML 4844.
Trio No 1 (violin, cello, piano) 1946; first performed Princeton, New Jersey, 1947.
Piano Sonata 1947; first performed Rome, 1947.
Divertimento (flute, bassoon, trumpet, violin, cello, piano) 1949; first performed Rome, 1949.

Serenade (flute, viola, piano) 1952; first performed San Francisco, 1953. Recorded Desto DC 7150.
String Quartet No 2 1953; first performed Cambridge, Massachusetts, 1953. Recorded Contemporary S 7022.
String Quartet No 3 1957; first performed Urbana, Illinois, 1957. Recorded Contemporary S 7022.
Impromptu (violin, piano) 1960; first performed New York City, 1960. Recorded Orion ORS 73107.
Cello Sonata (cello, piano) 1966; first performed San Francisco, 1967. Recorded Desto DC 7150.
Three Sketches (trombone, piano) 1967; first performed San Francisco, 1967. Recorded New World Records NW 254.
Dandelion Wine (oboe, clarinet, string quartet) 1967; first performed Milwaukee, Wisconsin, 1968. Recorded Turnabout TV 5 34520.
Here We Stand (fanfare; double brass ensemble) 1969.
String Quartet No 4 1969; first performed Madison, Wisconsin, 1969. Recorded New World Records NW 212.
A Hawk for Peace (fanfare; brass) 1970.
To a Traveler (clarinet, violin, piano) 1971; first performed San Francisco, 1972.
Fancy for Five (5 trombones) 1972.
Short Story (piano) 1982; first performed New York City, 1983.
Pilgrimage (flute, clarinet, violin, cello, piano, percussion) 1983; first performed Boston, 1984. Recorded GM 2019CD.
Dream Sequence (flute, oboe, clarinet, violin, viola, cello, piano, percussion) 1986; first performed New York City, 1986.
Daedalus (piano) 1986; first performed New York City, 1987.
Organ Prelude 1987; first performed Berkeley, California, 1987.
String Quartet No 5 1987; first performed Madison, Wisconsin, October, 1989.
Three Piece Suite (harp, piano) 1987; first performed San Francisco, 1988.
Trio No 2 (violin, cello, piano) 1989; first performed San Francisco, 1990.

Vocal/choral:

On the Beach at Night (mixed chorus, string orchestra; Whitman) 1949; first performed Berkeley, California, 1950. Recorded Vox SVBX-5354.
Three Songs (soprano, piano/orchestra; Frost, Masters, Ransom) 1949; first performed Lucca, Italy, 1949.
Two Christmas Carols (male voices, piano) 1955.
Introit, Gradual and Alleluia for All Saint's Day (chorus, organ) 1956.
Drum Taps (mixed chorus, orchestra; Whitman) 1960; first performed New York City, 1961.
Psalm XLII (TBB choir, organ) 1962.
Tell Me, Where Is Fancy Bred (soprano, clarinet, guitar; Shakespeare) 1964.
Three Songs (mixed chorus; cummings, Euripides, Roethke) 1965.
Let All the World (SATB choir, brass, percussion, organ; Herbert) 1971.
Prometheus Bound (3 soloists, double chorus, orchestra, dance; Aeschylus) 1979; first performed Berkeley, California, 1980.
Five Roethke Songs (soprano, piano) 1980; first performed San Francisco, 1981.
Three Campion Songs (soprano, alto, tenor, bass, piano) 1981; first performed New York City, 1984.
Song for St Cecilia's Day (mixed chorus, brasses, percussion, 2 pianos, flute, 2 violins; Dryden) 1981; first performed Hayward, California, 1981.
Requiem: In memoriam John Imbrie (soprano solo, mixed chorus, orchestra) 1984; first performed San Francisco, 1985.

Opera:

Three Against Christmas or, Christmas in Peebles Town (Wincor) 1960; first performed Berkeley, California, 3 December 1964.
Angle of Repose (O. Hall, after Wallace Stegner) 1976; first performed San Francisco, 6 November 1976.

PUBLICATIONS

By Imbrie: "Roger Sessions, in Honor of His 65th Birthday", in *Perspectives of New Music*, 1(1), 1962; "Our Measure of Eternity" (analysis of the end of Stravinsky's *Les Noces*), in *Perspectives of New Music*, 9(2) and 10(1), 1971; "The Symphonies of Roger Sessions", in *Tempo*, 103, 1972; "'Extra' Measures and Metrical Ambiguity in Beethoven", *Beethoven Studies*, edited by Alan Taylor, New York, 1973.

On Imbrie: Martin Boykan, "AI: *Third Quartet*", in *Perspectives of New Music*, 3(1), 1964; Douglas Durant, "AI: Analysis and Speculations" (dissertation), Brandeis University, Waltham, Massachusetts, 1988.

Andrew Imbrie comments:

Composing for me is a matter of drawing out the consequences (as I perceive them) of an initial idea. The idea may present itself as contour, rhythm, gesture or some combination of these; and the first step for me is to pin it down, to give it more definite shape and character. Once the idea has become specific enough, it begins to generate its own continuation. This is possible because every idea worthy of the name is fraught with potential energy; its components interact so as to create an expectation of forward movement. If this does not happen, it is always because the idea has been imperfectly realised and must be tinkered with until its various aspects are brought into effective cooperation.

The energies released by the first forward impulse eventually expend themselves to a point where they create a demand for contrast; yet the character of the new material is very much conditioned by that of the old. Thus the original idea generates not only its own continuation but the nature of its own opposite as well. In composing, I must ultimately reconcile the various opposing forces by finding a dramatically convincing resolution of their conflicts. The sense of the larger structure becomes increasingly clear as the work progresses.

I am not one of those composers who work by scenario, though I often sketch ahead for considerable distances before filling in details. Choices are determined by my sense of the rightness of events in context. Yet "contextual" does not seem a satisfying description. For me, no piece of music, however internally consistent, can be a law unto itself. Comprehensibility presupposes certain assumptions common to composer and listener—assumptions not stated but shared through much listening to music of all kinds. The composer relies on some of these, stretches others, defies still others. His style is the result of a fusion of countless predilections and habits, choices both conscious and unconscious.

These shared assumptions ensure not only comprehensibility but confidence. The listener must be somehow able to recognize the exercise of craft on the composer's part—to sense that the musical ideas, through the toughness of their own identity, create a resistance to the will of the composer who thought them up. The composer exerts his will on the material, but in terms not contradictory to the nature of that material. The listener's confidence is bestowed only if he can follow the trail of that encounter.

It is evident, then, that the unfolding of the musical drama is important to me: I do not regard my compositions as spatial or static. They move through time, and on a human scale. Music is sometimes characterized as "process". Although, of course, music does, by definition, proceed, the term carries with it the unpleasant connotation of a manufacturing method (the pigs go in here, the sausages come out there). I prefer to think of music as discourse. The energies just described—the contrasts, the proportions and resolutions—are deployed in time in such a way as to attempt to meet the listener's requirements as he reacts to what is happening, and to engage him in the drama. The listener's requirements are assessed by a composer in the following way: he must, while composing, try to hear his own piece as if he were someone else.

* * *

Although his music has won consistent popular and critical acclaim and numerous prizes, Andrew Imbrie has often been categorized as an "academic composer". True, he has had a long association with the University of California at Berkeley, where beyond a role as composition professor, he has involved himself in the whole of academic life. He has been a musical mentor to countless composers, working to help them find their own path of thought and expression rather than prescribing an "academically correct" method. The results show in the success and strikingly contrasting styles of two of his better-known students, the experimentalist Larry Austin and the more traditional David Del Tredici.

Choosing to characterize his approach to his own work not as that of an experimenter nor a traditionalist, Imbrie is in fact the quintessential American individualist, employing his intellect in the expression of an intuitive sense of musical drama.

Imbrie's own early study of piano and theory obviously provided him with a strong grasp of counterpoint. His own compositional mentor, Roger Sessions, helped instill the intuitive quest for clarity of expression.

Imbrie's music evidences an educated awareness and understanding of the early modern masters. Stravinsky's pulsing rhythmic energy and striking dissonances, Bartók's complex counterpoint of twisting lines, Schoenberg's exploration of complex new sonorities of pitch and color, Ives's bold collages—all of these qualities are assimilated as influences in Imbrie's own distinctive style.

Adept at a full range of musical genres, his string quartets and other chamber music are masterful, his symphonies and other orchestral works are colorful, and his operatic and other dramatic vocal works are powerful. While each work poses a challenging richness and dynamism, he acknowledges listeners' likely interests and ability to comprehend complex musical ideas.

Especially in the chamber music, Imbrie writes for the performers as well as for listeners. Lines capitalize on the natural character and idioms of the instrument being written for, and vocal writing incorporates the natural speaking rhythm of words.

Although sensitive to the varying requirements and potentials of different musical mediums and genres, all his works share three fundamental traits: they are intensely contrapuntal in texture, energetic in rhythmic vitality, and dramatic in gesture and form. These features are evident in the intense initial impetus at the beginning of each work, the point at which Imbrie himself claims to start the conceptual building of a composition. "I always start at the beginning and let the ideas shape themselves as they must; the direction they will pursue and the changes in character they will undergo become increasingly clear as I go on. I find that an initial musical statement, once made, raises obligations that the composer must have the wit to recognize and to fulfill."

Gestures are mostly angular but with a strong sense of direction. Distinct lines, each charged with rhythmic energy and developmental potential, are contrapuntally combined. Colorations of musical presentation, although skillfully orchestrated, do not become primary objects of attention but serve to detail the fundamental structures. Harmonies are intense and complex, presenting a variety of intervals without employing any rigid system of selection. Bold dissonance in both tight and broad spacings is often tempered by combination with more stable, rooted intervals.

The result is a coherence found not on the elastic surface but deeper at the music's exploratory core. Although in this "through-composed" approach, form is a discovered outcome of initially chosen ideas and their potentials, there is a taste for symmetry. Sections of music seem to balance naturally in proportion and weight; ideas and moods return, altered as in a reminiscence to bring the musical experience full circle. In many works, such as *Symphony No 3*, one comes upon a tranquil lyricism in the middle of the work which feels like the calm center of this swirling circle. Such exquisite passages seem to glimpse beneath the assertive arguments of a powerful musical discourse into the very soul of a sensitive musician.

—Thomas Clark

ISRAELYAN, Martin. Armenian. Born in Leninakan [now Kymairy], 25 March 1938. Educated at secondary school, 1945–55; Leninakan Music College, 1959–64; Yerevan State Conservatory "Sogomon Komitas", 1964–9. Married Nojemsar Israelyan in 1966; 2 daughters. Teacher of music, Music College, Yerevan, 1969–81; professor, Yerevan State Conservatory "Sogomon Komitas", 1970–3; teacher of music, Music School, Yerevan, 1981. Member of Composers' Union, since 1969. Recipient: prize, Moscow All-Union Young Composers Arts Festival (for *Music*), 1969. Mailing address: Bushindgakhyan 198, 57, Yerevan 375078, Armenia.

Publisher: none.

Symphonies/orchestral:

Contrasts 1966–7; first performed Yerevan, 1967.
Music (symphony orchestra) 1969; first performed Yerevan, 1969.
Symphony 1980–1; first performed Yerevan, 1984.
Capriccio (chamber orchestra) 1982. Recorded Melodia C10 25255006.
Concerto for Cello and String Orchestra 1982; first performed Yerevan, 1983.
Concerto for Chamber Orchestra 1983; first performed Yerevan, 1983. Recorded Melodia C10 28619000.

Concerto for Violin and Chamber Orchestra 1985; first performed Yerevan, 1985. Recorded Melodia C10 28619000.

Chamber/instrumental:

Sonata (piano) 1965; first performed Yerevan, 1965.
String Quartet No 1 1966; first performed Yerevan, 1966.
Three Duets (cello, piano) 1972; first performed Yerevan, 1974.
Septet (woodwind, strings, piano) 1973; first performed Yerevan, 1974.
Sonata No 1 (cello, piano) 1976; first performed Yerevan, 1977. Recorded Melodia C10 1006364.
Sonata No 2 (cello, piano) 1987; first performed Yerevan, 1988.
Hymns: Fiat Lux (flute, oboe, clarinet, bassoon, horn, trumpet, trombone, 2 violins, viola, cello, double bass, percussion, piano) 1989; first performed Metz, France, 1989.
String Quartet No 2 1990.

Vocal/choral:

First Book of Tags (mezzo-soprano, flute, clarinet, percussion; Narekatsi) 1971.
Second Book of Tags (soprano, piano; Metzarents) 1974.
Sonnets (soprano, chamber orchestra; Edoyan) 1980; first performed Yerevan, 1981.
Evening Songs (soprano, piano; Metzarents) 1982; first performed Yerevan, 1983.
Song of Bread (soprano, tenor, chorus, orchestra; Varudzan) 1985; first performed Yerevan, 1986.
Autumn Songs (soprano, orchestra) 1985.

PUBLICATIONS

On Israelyan: Svetlana Sarkisyan, "Musyka ormianka", in *Ruch muzyczny* (Poland) 1980, and in *Music in the USSR*, Moscow, 1985; Marina Berko, "Lyric Monologues by MI", in *Sovietskaya Musyka*, 6, 1985; Tatyana Porwoll, "Musik in Armenien", in *MusikTexte*, 32, 1989; Svetlana Sarkisyan, "MI", in *Neue Zeitschrift für Musik*, 1991.

* * *

Raised in Leninakan (now known as Kymairy) in Armenia, Martin Israelyan began his musical education in the local music college, where he learned to play *kjamancha*, the national instrument of Armenia. In 1964 he moved to Yerevan, where he studied composition at the Sogomon Komitas Conservatory under Grigor Yekhiazaryan. His graduate piece *Music* for symphony orchestra won a prestigious prize at an All-Union Arts Festival for young composers in Moscow, and his subsequent work has attracted wide recognition in Armenia and abroad. Chamber pieces have been performed in Paris, Buenos Aires and elsewhere, and were strongly featured in the Soviet Music Festival "New Beginnings" in 1989, in Prague during the "Days of Armenian Music" and in Metz during the "Rencontres Internationales de Musique Contemporaine". He has collaborated with such performers as the cellist Medeya Abramyan, the singer Valery Georgiev, Aleksandr Lazariev and Paul Mefano, writing *Hymns: Fiat Lux* to Mefano's commission for the ensemble 2E2M.

Israelyan's early work was strong influenced by the Second Viennese School, in particular Webern's serialism, and by Boulez's aesthetic. At the same time, though, his work gives clear expression to some of the basic constructions of medieval Armenian music. As a result, he came to use pentatonic scales based on whole tones, a device which he has maintained up to the present. This formula, which offers the possibility of transforming a series of distinct fifths, became more developed in the direction of pentatonality and diatonality based on simple initial melodies. In each case, the development of the music depends on rhythmic modification, the significance of which is particularly heightened in conditions where the music texture is particularly homogenous, and that is the case with much of Israelyan's work.

Israelyan's stylistic evolution falls into two periods. In the first, from the mid-1960s, serial procedures predominate: the *Septet*, the first Cello Sonata, the cello/piano duets, and the two *Books of Tags*; the second, from the late 1970s, includes the *Symphony*, the cantata *Song of Bread*, the concertos for instruments and orchestra, the *Hymns* and *Autumn Songs*. These later works played a part in mitigating the sternness of the early period and introducing a new expressive emphasis in which the synthesis of elements predominantly literary in origin is subordinated to the overall musical conception. The periods are united by Israelyan's pantheistic attitude which excludes from his music all hint of tragic tension.

—Svetlana Sarkisyan

J

JIMÉNEZ-MABARAK, Carlos. Mexican. Born in Tacuba, Mexico, 31 January 1916. Educated: studied piano under Jesús Castillo, Guatemala, 1923–7; Escuela Salvador Sanfuentes; piano lessons at Conservatorio Nacional de Música, Santiago, Chile, 1928–9; Liceo de Aplicacion, Santiago, Chile, 1930–3; moved to Europe with family, 1932; Institute of Advanced Studies in Music and Drama, Brussels (piano under Madame Jacobi, harmony under Nellie Jones), from 1933; student, Professional School of Radiotelegraphy and Radiotelephonics, diploma; Choral Society of Brussels (choral singing under Gaston Peellaert), Royal Conservatory, Brussels (harmony, counterpoint, musical analysis under Marguerite Wouters), and Royal University, Brussels (musicology under Charles Van den Borren), all 1933–6; returned to Mexico, 1937; Conservatorio Nacional de Música, Mexico City (orchestration under Silvestre Revueltas), 1938; further study in Europe—Accademia de Sancta Cecilia, Rome (composition under Guido Turchi), Paris (twelve-tone music under René Leibowitz), 1953–6. Professor of musical education, harmony and composition, National Conservatory of Music, Mexico City, 1942–65; professor, Villahermosa School of Arts, Tabasco, 1965–8; cultural attaché, Mexican Embassy, Vienna, Austria, 1972–4. Recipient: diploma (in recognition of contributions to children's theatre), Institute Nacional de Bellas Artes, Mexico, 1959; honorary diploma (for services to Mexican music), Conservatorio Nacional de Música, 1965; gold medal (for *Fanfarria Olímpica*), Asociación Nacional de Interpretes, Mexico, 1968; Distinguished Visitor, Municipal Union of Puebla, 1985. Mailing address: Bucareli No. 181, privada Ideal No. 8, colonia Juárez, delegación Cuauhtemoc, 06600 D.F. Mexico.

Publishers: Verlag Dr Alfred Hiller, Vienna; Editions J. Buyst, 76 avenue du midi, Brussels, Belgium; Schott, Brussels; Ricordi Americana, Buenos Aires; Ediciones Mexicanas de Musica.

Symphonies/orchestral:

Symphony in E♭ 1945; first performed Mexico City, 6 July 1945.
Concerto in C (piano, chamber orchestra) 1945; first performed Mexico City, 8 November 1946.
Symphony in One Movement 1962; first performed Mexico City, August 1962.
Obertura para orquesta de arcos (strings) 1963; first performed Mexico City, 2 September 1963.
Sinfonía concertante (piano, orchestra; also version for 2 pianos) 1968; first performed Mexico City, 11 March 1977.

Chamber/instrumental:

Allegro romántico (piano) 1935.
Pequeño preludio (piano) 1935.
Danza española I (piano) 1936.
Danza española II (piano) 1936.
Sonata del majo enamorado (piano) 1936.
Preludio y fuga (clarinet, piano) 1937.
Concierto del abuelo (piano, string quartet) 1938.
Quartet in D (Homenaje a Sor Juana) 1947.
Retrato de Mariana Sánchez (piano) 1952.
Variaciones sobre la alegría (2 pianos) 1952.
El retrato de lupe (violin, piano) 1953.
La fuente armoniosa (piano) 1957.
Concierto (piano, timpani, bells, xylophone, percussion) 1961; first performed Mexico City, 17 June 1962.
Five Pieces (flute, piano) 1965; first performed Mexico City, 8 August 1966.
La ronda junto a la fuente (flute, oboe, violin, viola, cello) 1965; first performed Mexico City, 1966.
Two Pieces (cello, piano) 1966.
Invention (clarinet, trumpet) 1970.
Invention (oboe, tenor trombone, piano) 1971.

Vocal/choral:

Tres pequeños poemas de Amado Nervo (voice, piano) 1937.
Dos españoladas (voice, piano; Lorca) 1939.
Tres canciones breves (voice, piano) 1941.
Poema del rio (voice, piano; Nandino) 1942.
Dos cantos con texto de F. Garcia Lorca (unaccompanied 4-part chorus) 1944.
Dos cantos (unaccompanied 4-part chorus; Durán) 1944.
Un pastorcito solo (unaccompanied 3-part chorus; San Juan de la Cruz) 1944–62.
Ven conmigo al bosque ameno (unaccompanied 3-part chorus; Polo) 1944–62.
Zarzamora (unaccompanied 3-part chorus; Lorca) 1944–62.
Jugaba en la mañana (unaccompanied 3-part chorus; Nuño) 1944–62.
Toque de Alba (unaccompanied 3-part chorus; Góngora) 1944–62.
Este niño se lleva la flor (unaccompanied 3-part chorus; Lope de Vega) 1944–62.
Nunca le temi al espanto (unaccompanied 3-part chorus; Leon) 1944–62.
La novia (unaccompanied 3-part chorus; Alberti) 1944–62.
Agua ¿Dónde vas? (unaccompanied 3-part chorus; Lorca) 1944–62.
Pastoral (unaccompanied 3-part chorus; Jímenez) 1944–62.
Nana (unaccompanied 3-part chorus; Alberti) 1944–62.
Canciones con texto de Carlos Luis Saénz (unaccompanied 3-part chorus) 1944–62.
Dos canciones arcaicas (voice, piano; Enzina, Santillana) 1946.
Soneto de González Durán (unaccompanied 4-part chorus) 1946.
La canción de la pilmana (voice, piano; Cravioto) 1947.
Homenaje a Gil Vicente (unaccompanied 4-part chorus) 1947.
¡Ay! (voice, piano; Lorca) 1947.
Los niños heroes (mixed chorus, orchestra; Nervo) 1947.
Muerto se quedó en la calle (unaccompanied 4-part chorus; Lorca) 1948.
Cinco nanas (unaccompanied 4-part chorus; Alberti) 1949.
Tres poemas de Jorge Gonzalez Durán (voice, piano) 1950.

Canción banal (voice, piano; Anacreonte) 1951.
Estancias nocturnas (voice, piano; Villaurrutia) 1952.
Dos cantos (unaccompanied 4-part chorus; Alberti) 1954.
El pescador sin dinero (unaccompanied 4-part chorus; Alberti) 1955.
Dos lieder sobre una serie dodecafónica (voice, piano; Solana, Prados) 1956.
Canción rústica (unaccompanied 4-part chorus) 1957.
Traspié entre dos estrellas (reciter, trumpet, percussion, piano, 2 violins, double bass; Vallejo) 1957; first performed Mexico City, 6 June 1957.
Te doy mi amistad rendida (unaccompanied 4-part chorus; Léon) 1958.
Seis canciones para cantar a los niños (voice, piano; Saénz) 1958.
Homenaje a Juarez (soloists, chorus, orchestra; Nuño) 1958.
Pregón (unaccompanied 4-part chorus; Alberti) 1959.
Rosa del mar (unaccompanied 4-part chorus; Saénz) 1960.
Dos Poemas de Nicolás Guillén (voice, piano) 1963.
Simón Bolivar (soloists, chorus, orchestra; Pellicer) 1983; first performed Mexico City, 2 December 1983.
Estudio para voz de bajo (voice, piano; Pellicer) 1987.
Epitafio (voice, piano; Nandino) 1987.
Décimas mortales (voice, piano; Nandino) 1989.
Canto de muerte (unaccompanied 4-part chorus; Nandino) 1990.

Opera:

Misa de seis (Carballido) 1960; first performed Mexico City, 21 June 1962.
La guerra (Alejandro) 1980; first performed Mexico City, 26 September 1982.

Other:

El sastrecillo y el duende (incidental music and songs to play by Amador) 1939; first performed Mexico City, 24 October 1945.
La muñeca pastillita (music to children's play by Lira; orchestra) 1942; first performed Mexico City, 11 June 1942.
Pirrimplín en la luna (music to children's play by Gómez; orchestra) 1942; first performed Mexico City, 5 November 1942.
Los empeños de una casa (incidental music to comedy by Sor Juana Ines de la Cruz) 1944; first performed Mexico City, July 1944.
El hombre que casó con mujer muda (incidental music to play by Anatole France; flute, clarinet, bassoon, 2 violins, cello) 1944; first performed Mexico City, 19 December 1944.
El amor del agua (ballet; trumpet, percussion, piano, double bass) 1945.
Marujilla (incidental music and songs to play by Gutierrez; orchestra) 1946; first performed Mexico City, 1946.
Cáligula (incidental music to play by Camus; flute, clarinet, horn, trumpet, percussion, harp) 1947; first performed Mexico City, 1947.
Balada del pájaro y las doncellas (ballet) 1947; first performed Mexico City, November 1948.
Balada del venado y la luna (ballet) 1948; first performed Mexico City, 7 December 1949.
Danza fúnebre (ballet; orchestra) 1949; first performed Mexico City, 10 December 1949.
Una viuda difícil (incidental music to comedy by Roxlo) 1950; first performed Mexico City, 29 March 1950.
Recuerdo a zapata (ballet-cantata; soloists, chorus, orchestra) 1950; first performed Mexico City, 1951.
Balada mágica o danza de las cuatro estaciones (ballet) 1951; first performed Mexico City, 24 April 1952.
Pastillata (children's ballet; orchestra) 1951; first performed Mexico City, 1951.
Retablo de la annunciación (ballet; string orchestra) 1951; first performed Mexico City, 3 November 1952.
Volpone (overture and 2 dances to play by Jonson; flute, bassoon, harpsichord) 1951; first performed Caracol, 1951.
El nanual herido (ballet) 1952; first performed Mexico City, 22 January 1954.
Nerón (incidental music; orchestra) 1952.
La maestra rural (ballet) 1952; first performed Mexico City, 1952.
Balada de los quetzales (ballet) 1953; first performed Antigua, Guatemala, 16 March 1956.
El ratón pérez (children's ballet; soprano, baritone, clarinet, trumpet, percussion, piano, 2 violins, double bass) 1955.
La llorona (incidental music, songs and dances to play by Toscano) 1958; first performed Mexico City, 18 April 1958.
La leña está verde (incidental music to play by Gorostiza) 1958; first performed Mexico City, 30 October 1958.
El paraíso de los Ahogados (ballet based on *Tlalocan* mural) 1960; first performed Mexico City, 11 October 1960.
La llorona (ballet after Toscano; orchestra) 1961; first performed Mexico City, 1961.
La portentosa vida de la muerte (ballet after Cuéllar; tape) 1964; first performed Mexico City, 20 July 1964.
Pitágoras dijo . . . (ballet after Pythagoras; baritone, 2 clarinets, 2 trombones, bells, xylophone, timpani, gong, percussion, piano, double bass) 1966; first performed Mexico City, 11 August 1966.
Balada de los ríos de Tabasco (ballet) 1990.

Film scores: *Deseada* (with E. Hernandez Moncada), 1950; *Pito perez*, 1953; *El Cristo negro*, 1954; *Paraíso escondido*, 1959; *El tejedor de Milagros*, 1961; *Los signos del zodíaco*, 1962; *Tiempo de morir*, 1965; *Recuerdos del porvenir*, 1968; *Rosario*, 1970; *La virgenes locas*, 1971; *Triángulo*, 1972; *El pacto*, 1976; *Las mariposas disecadas*, 1979.

* * *

Few living composers are so comprehensively grounded in contemporary musical philosophies and at the same time so thoroughly untendentious as Carlos Jiménez-Mabarak. He has worked in virtually all the canonical genres—symphonic, chamber and instrumental music, choral and vocal writing, opera, dance and drama—but manages throughout to retain an absolutely distinctive "voice" which is never reducible to its constituent components and influences.

These are themselves very wide-ranging. Jiménez-Mabarak pursued a doggedly eclectic path in his younger days. In addition to his piano and composition studies, he received a broad humanities education in Santiago de Chile, before moving for a period in the mid-1930s to Belgium where he studied musicology, theory and radiophonics, and experienced at first hand the upheavals of musical modernism. His first works were tonal and neo-classical, with a strong flavour of Maurice Ravel and something of Sergei Prokofiev's ability to see the orchestra as a palette of instrumental colour-groups to be deployed in carefully modulated or dramatically contrastive ways. The early pieces are always identifiably Mexican in their use of folk themes but are by no means blandly nationalistic and have much in common with the work of Jiménez-Mabarak's great predecessor Silvestre Revueltas (with whom he studied orchestration).

Never content to treat his musical language as a fixed set of syntactical rules, Jiménez-Mabarak returned to Europe for a second significant period of study under the sponsorship of UNESCO. Working in Paris with René Liebowitz, he had his first experience of twelve-tone composition, a procedure that (duly personalised and stripped of all dogmatic associations) has informed his work ever since, occupying a spectrum marked out by Schoenberg's free atonality and a more strictly serial demarcation of tonal parameters.

It is clear that Jiménez-Mabarak did not merely stumble across dodecaphony; he went out consciously to look for it. There is sufficient indication in his early compositions that he was aware of the blind alleys and ambiguities confronting tonal composition in the 20th century. The still-magnificent First Symphony, premiered in 1945 by the great Mexican composer/conductor Carlos Chávez, moves in a heroic and almost pianistic E♭, but with much of the ambiguity that permeates Beethoven's similarly keyed *Eroica* symphony. The same is true of the Piano Concerto from the same year, scored for an intriguingly pitched chamber orchestra and far from as blandly affirmative as the opening Allegretto would suggest.

Jiménez-Mabarak's chamber and instrumental music shows the same awareness of the dramatic potential of near-dissonance and timbral juxtaposition. The two *Invenciones* of 1970 and 1971 are scored for clarinet and trumpet, and for oboe, tenor trombone and piano respectively. Powerfully written, they belong to no readily identifiable or categorisable "school" and convey a weight of musical information and dramatic force worthy of a much larger ensemble. The same is true of the rather earlier chamber concerto for piano and percussion, which is predictably rhythmical in conception, but far more unexpectedly tuneful; along with the earlier quartet in homage to Sor Juana Ines de la Cruz, it is Jiménez-Mabarak's most impressive small-group work.

Perhaps the heart of his output lies in his dramatic music. He has had a lifelong association with the theatre and has written opera, theatre and ballet scores. *Misa de seis*, first performed in 1962, is small in scale but full of musical incident, a more satisfactory work than its successor *La guerra*. Unusually, though, much of Jiménez-Mabarak's very finest work has been written as incidental music to theatrical works by others. Particularly fine is his 1947 score for Albert Camus's *Cáligula*; once again the instrumental coloration is distinctive and on this occasion provides a perfect subtext to Camus's preoccupation with the ambivalences and unbalances of the "heroic" personality; the problem seems to appeal to Jiménez-Mabarak and his scores for *Volpone* and *Nero* are distinctively voiced.

He has made important settings of Lorca, Alberti and Nandino, and his *Traspié entre dos estrellas* after César Vallejo, though spoken rather than sung, is one of the finest vocal works to emerge from modern Latin America. A profound rhythmic sense underlies his work for the ballet. Jiménez-Mabarak has a particular gift for counterbalancing melodies which seem to contradict the basic pulse of a passage, but which provide an additional dynamic. He is particularly noted for his work in children's theatre, and has contributed several significantly unpatronising scores for young performers. A tireless innovator, he was the first composer to introduce electronic music into Mexican culture; the avant/retro gestures of the electronic score for *El paraíso de los Ahogados* underline his equal commitment to tradition and change. He is without doubt Mexico's most important living composer and his work lives in the most profound sense: growing, breathing, complex and straightforward, individual and universal at once.

—Guido Scarpone

JOLAS, Betsy (Elizabeth Illouz). French and American. Born in Paris, 5 August 1926. Educated at a French lycée; moved to the United States in 1940 to complete schooling and to study with Helen Schnabel (piano), Carl Weinrich (organ) and Paul Boepple (composition); Bennington College, Vermont, B.A., 1946; Conservatoire National de Musique Supérieure, Paris (under Darius Milhaud, Olivier Messiaen, and Simone Plé-Caussade), from 1946. Married Gabriel Illouz, 27 August 1949; 2 sons and 1 daughter. Replacement for Olivier Messiaen, 1971–74, and professor of advanced analysis, since 1975, Conservatoire National de Musique Supérieure, Paris; visiting professor at Tanglewood, Massachusetts, Yale University, New Haven, Connecticut, universities of California, Berkeley and San Diego, and Boston University; Darius Milhaud Professor, Mills College, Oakland, California. Recipient: Laureate du Concours International de Direction d'Orchestre, Besançon, 1953; Copley Foundation prize, Chicago, 1954; ORTF prize, France, 1961; American Academy of Arts prize, 1973; Koussevitzky Foundation prize, 1974; Grand Prix National de la Musique, 1974; Grand Prix de la Ville de Paris, 1981; Grand Prix de la Sacem, 1982; member of American Institute of Arts and Letters, 1983; Chevalier de l'Ordre National du Mérite; Commandeur des Arts et Lettres. Mailing address: 12 rue Bonaparte, 75006 Paris, France.

Publishers: Alphonse Leduc, 175 rue St Honoré, 75040 Paris; Salabert/Ricordi, 22 rue Chauchat, 75009 Paris, France.

Symphonies/orchestral:

Symphony (light orchestra) 1957.
Quatre Plages (string orchestra) 1967; first performed Paris, 1968.
Musique d'hiver (organ, small orchestra) 1971; first performed Baden-Baden, 1971.
Trois Rencontres (string trio, large orchestra) 1973; first performed Strasbourg, June 1974.
Tales of a Summer Sea 1977; first performed Tanglewood, Massachusetts, August 1977.
Onze Lieder (trumpet, chamber orchestra) 1977; first performed Paris, October 1977.
Stances (piano, orchestra) 1978; first performed Paris, April 1978. Recorded Ades 14.1013.
Cinq Pièces pour Boulogne (small orchestra) 1982; first performed Boulogne, 7 June 1983.
Préledes-Fanfares-Interludes-Sonneries (wind orchestra, percussion) 1983; first performed Paris, 28 January 1984.
Concerto for Viola 1990–1.

Chamber/instrumental:

Trifolium (flute, piano) 1947.
Sonate à trois (string trio) 1955.
Sonata (viola) 1955.
Figures (flute, oboe, clarinet, horn, trumpet, 2 violins, viola, piano) 1956–65; first performed Evreux, 20 March 1984.
String Quartet No 1 1956.
Episode 1 (flute) 1964.
Le Chant de l'amour triomphant (instrumental ensemble) 1964.
J.D.E. (flute, oboe, clarinet, bass clarinet, bassoon, horn, trumpet, trombone, harp, 2 violins, viola, cello, double bass) 1966; first performed La Chaux de Fonds, February 1966. Recorded Ades 14.1013.
D'un Opéra de voyage (2 flutes, cor anglais, 3 clarinets, bass clarinet, horn, trumpet, trombone, harp, percussion,

violin, viola, cello, double bass) 1967; first performed Royan, April 1967. Recorded Ades.
Tranche (harp) 1967; first performed Zagreb, 1967.
Points d'Aube (viola, 13 wind instruments) 1968; first performed Le Havre, February 1968. Recorded Ades 14.1013.
Etats (violin, 6 percussionists) 1969; first performed Persepolis, September 1969.
Lassus Ricercare (2 trumpets, 3 trombones, 2 pianos/piano and celeste, harp, percussion) 1970; first performed Paris, 1971.
Remember (cor anglais or viola, cello) 1971; first performed Royan, April 1971.
Fusain (piccolo/bass flute) 1971; first performed Rennes, January 1972.
Chanson d'approche (piano) 1972; first performed London, January 1973.
Autour (harpsichord) 1972; first performed Royan, April 1973.
Quatuor III (string quartet) 1973; first performed Washington, D.C., January 1974. Recorded CRI 332.
B for Sonata (piano) 1973; first performed New York, January 1974.
Scion (cello) 1973.
How Now (clarinet, horn, bassoon, 2 violins, viola, cello, double bass) 1973; first performed Paris, June 1974.
Well Met (7 violins, 2 violas, 2 cellos, double bass) 1973; first performed Paris, May 1976.
O Wall (wind quintet) 1976; first performed New York, November 1976.
Musique de jour (organ) 1976; first performed Royan, March 1976.
Episode Second: Ohne Worte (flute) 1977; first performed Paris, 1977.
Quatre Duos (viola, piano) 1979; first performed Paris, April 1980.
Trois Etudes campanaires (piano or carillon) 1980; first performed Paris, 6 June 1980.
Auprès (harpsichord) 1980.
Pièce pour Saint Germain (piano) 1981.
Episode troisième (trumpet) 1982; first performed Paris, 1982.
Calling E.C. (piano) 1982; first performed Le Havre, 21 September 1983.
D'un Opéra de poupée en sept musiques (flute, clarinet, horn, percussion, electric guitar, piano, 2 ondes martenot, 4 electric pianos, violin, cello, sound diffusion) 1982; first performed Paris, 1984.
Points d'or (saxophone, 15 instruments) 1982.
Une journée de Gadad (piano) 1983; first performed Le Havre, 21 September 1983.
Episode quatrième (tenor saxophone) 1983; first performed Budapest, December 1983. Recorded Polyart PAR 5303.
Trois Duos (tuba, piano) 1983; first performed Lugano, 23 March 1984.
Episode cinquième (cello) 1983; first performed Paris, 17 January 1985.
Quatre Pièces en marge (cello, piano) 1983.
Petite Pièce sérieuse pour concert de famille (piano) 1983.
Tango Si (piano) 1984; first performed Toronto, 25 September 1984.
Episode sixième (viola) 1984; first performed Paris, 10 June 1985.
Episode septième (electric guitar) 1984; first performed Bourges, 1985.
Episode huitième (double bass) 1984; first performed Nice, February 1985. Recorded ADDA 581043.
Signets (piano; hommage à Maurice Ravel) 1987; first performed Montpellier, 1987.
Music for Joan (vibraphone, piano) 1988; first performed Buffalo, New York, 1988.
Trio (violin, cello, piano) 1988; first performed New York, 1989.

Vocal/choral:

Mass 1946.
Plupart du temps (mezzo-soprano, piano; Reverdy) 1949.
Chansons pour Paule (soprano, piano) 1951.
Arbres (unaccompanied choir) 1954.
Pantagruel (mixed choir) 1954.
Enfantillages (unaccompanied women's choir) 1954.
Et le Reste à l'avenant (unaccompanied choir) 1954.
Orca (unaccompanied choir) 1955.
Everysom sings (double women's choir, brass) 1955.
Cinq Poèmes de Jacques Dupin (soprano, piano or orchestra) 1959.
L'oeil égare dans les plis de l'obéissance du vent (soprano, alto, bass, mixed choir, orchestra; Hugo) 1961.
Mots (soprano, mezzo-soprano, alto, tenor, bass, flute, oboe/cor anglais, clarinet, bassoon, harpsichord, harp, percussion) 1963; first performed Geneva, March 1964.
Quatuor II (coloratura soprano, violin, viola, cello) 1964; first performed Paris, March 1966. Recorded CDC 7 499042.
Motet II (mixed choir, 36 voices; Dupin) 1965; first performed Angers, October 1986.
Diurnes (unaccompanied mixed choir, 12–72 voices) 1970; first performed Romans, July 1979.
Sonate à 12 (3 sopranos, 3 altos, 3 tenors, 3 basses) 1970; first performed Royan, April 1971. Recorded Cassette Radio-France INE 290.
Caprice à une voix (male or female voice) 1975; first performed La Rochelle, July 1975.
Caprice à deux voix (soprano, counter-tenor or alto) 1978; first performed Paris, March 1979.

Opera:

Le Pavillon au bord de la rivière (chamber opera; 2 flutes, 1 cor anglais, 3 trombones, percussion, soprano, 6 singers; Kua Han Chin) 1975; first performed Avignon, July 1975.
Le Cyclope (chamber opera; 3 trombones, 1 electric guitar, 1 bass guitar, percussion, 9 singers; Euripides) 1986; first performed Avignon, July 1986.
Schliemann (orchestra, sound diffusion; Bayen) 1987; first performed Lyon, 1991.

Other:

Ajax (incidental music to Sophocles) 1960.
The Trojans (incidental music to Euripides) 1961.
La Dernière Existence au camp de Tatenberg (incidental music to Gattis) 1962.
Iphigénie (incidental music to Racine) 1964.
Code génétique (film soundtrack) 1964.
La Tempête (incidental music to Shakespeare; vocal and instrumental ensemble) 1966.
Voix premières (radio play) 1974.

PUBLICATIONS

By Jolas: "Il fallait voter sériel meme si", in *Preuves*, 170, 1969; "Sur Ives: The Unanswered Question", in *Musique en jeu*, 1, 1970; "Réponse à l'enquête: L'éducation musicale et les compositeurs", in *Interéducation*, 1970; "Voix et musique", in *Bulletin de la Société Française de Philosophie*, 2, 1972; "Des Deux Côtes de l'Atlantique", in Papiers, editor, *20 Images de la musique française*, 1985; "Un choc très doux . . ." (about Webern), in *Le Monde* 1983; "L'Analyse, pourquoi faire", in *Analyse Musicale*, 1990.

On Jolas: Maurice Fleuret, "La Musique au féminin", in *Nouvel Observateur*, 1966; "Entretien avec BJ" (interview), in *Les Lettres françaises*, 1968; "Entretien avec BJ" (interview), in *Courrier musical de France*, 1969; Esperanza Pulido, "Con BJ en Paris", in *Heterofonia*, 11 (6).

Betsy Jolas comments:

The whole idea of creation was deeply etched into my childhood milieu. I was surrounded by poets, men of letters. When I was little, I wanted to write and paint, was always organising little productions. I was a child who didn't have to be kept busy or entertained, and out of that came my preference for a solitary, self-contained existence.

My attraction as a composer to the human voice I put down to my mother, who had wanted a career as a singer and accompanied herself on the guitar. She was always busy; I saw and talked with her very little, but her words were every bit as important as her laughter and singing.

Like all girls, I learned piano, and very soon was taking as much pleasure in reading music as in reading a book. At 13 or 14, I wanted to be Mozart; I wrote an opera. Around 16 or 17, I had doubts about my instrumental ability. Piano practice weighed heavily on me. I had no natural gifts and that saved me. It seemed to me that composition was the one thing I could do well.

I know when a work of mine comes into being. It is when I can listen to it within myself and repeatedly from one end to another. In that way, I take a bearing on the main lines of its development, its raison d'être and occasion. That overall perspective, a kind of aerial view of the piece, from which I can already identify hills and valleys, fields, woods and rivers, both precedes and conditions any elaboration of detail. Things which barely signify at the outset, once reassessed in the light of necessary means, force me to accept often important modifications, which may be quite radical in view of the original form; yet its outline remains to some extent right through the process of composition.

Each of my works has its own structure. I can detect between them, however, certain constant characteristics, notably a progression from simple to complex, and vice versa, a rejection of internal boundaries and false continuities. My goal is vast and ambitious but can be summarised in a few words: a music permanently reborn.

* * *

The music of Betsy Jolas has been influenced by a unique European-American background. Her mother, Maria MacDonald, was an American writer and translator; her father, Eugène Jolas, a noted French literary figure, who worked with James Joyce on the editing and publication of his books, particularly *Ulysses*. Betsy Jolas's unusual name, a combination of the quintessential American "Betsy" (not Elizabeth) with the French Jolas, is an immediate clue to the composer's Franco-American ancestry. She has retained dual citizenship: her permanent home is in France, yet she maintains close contact with America, where she spent several formative years during World War II in secondary school followed by Bennington College. Growing up in a literary milieu, Jolas has been particularly drawn to vocal music and to opera, although her oeuvre includes large symphonic pieces and instrumental works for a wide range of combinations.

Following World War II, music became international in style, rather than nationalistic. Jolas's work is a good example: her strict compositional methods based on a kind of individualized serialism are derived from European sources; and interest in unusual colors and combinations reflects the teachings of her French mentors. Darius Milhaud and Olivier Messiaen; and other qualities, such as an active imagination, a direct approach, and forthright sense of humor, may be traced to her American heritage. Although Jolas's music blends elements from her Franco-American background, it bears a recognizable and characteristic personal stamp.

Jolas's concern with the relationships between words and music resulted in the song cycle of 1949, *Plupart du temps,* her first major work to reflect this interest, which can be traced in subsequent pieces and finally in her three operas composed since 1975. Each is different from the other, yet all pay careful attention to the text and to the dramatic blending of words with music. The first, a chamber opera, *Le Pavillon au bord de la rivière,* was commissioned by the French government for the U.S. Bicentennial in 1976 for performance at the Avignon Festival and in several midwest American cities. It is a chamber opera using a 13th-century Chinese text in which the seven instrumentalists are required to use their instruments in unusual ways. The singing style is non-traditional with an emphasis on the spoken word. Jolas's second opera, *Le Cyclope*, makes use of the original text of Euripides and calls for the use of actors rather than professional singers. *Schliemann,* Jolas's third opera, is scheduled for production by the Lyon Opera. It is also experimental in nature.

Teaching is an important element in Jolas's life and career. She combines a thorough knowledge of her craft with a dynamic and strong personality, and has made a substantial mark on composition students in France and America. She first taught at the Paris Conservatoire as a substitute for Messiaen in 1971 at his request, and since 1975, has been a regular member of the Conservatoire faculty. She frequently divides her time between France and the U.S., effectively teaching as a guest at various schools, among them Tanglewood Music Center, Yale University and Boston University.

Without ever making a special point of being a "woman" in a field that has been almost exclusively male, Jolas is one of a few women composers to make an important contribution in her field, and to be recognized, performed, recorded and honored by her two countries and by the international world of music.

—Vivian Perlis

JONES, Daniel (Jenkyn). British/Welsh. Born in Pembroke, South Wales, 7 December 1912. Educated University College of Wales, Swansea, B.A in English literature, 1934, M.A., 1939, D.Mus., 1951; Royal Academy of Music, London (composition under Harry Farjeon, conducting under Sir Henry Wood, also viola and horn), 1935–8; further study under Mendelssohn Scholarship in Rome, Vienna and elsewhere. Married (1) Penelope Eunice

Bedford, 8 July 1937, 3 daughters; (2) Irene Pearl Goodchild, 13 March 1944, 1 son and 1 daughter. Served in British Army Intelligence Corps, 1940–6. Composer; editor of Dylan Thomas's collected verse, published 1971. Recipient: Olive Prescott Prize, 1936; Royal Philharmonic Society prize, 1950; Prix Italia, 1954; honorary fellow, Institute of Arts and Letters, 1963; D.Litt., 1970, and honorary fellow, 1988, University of Wales; Fellow, Royal Academy of Music, 1981. Mailing address: 53 Southwood Lane, Newton, Swansea SA3 4QD, Wales.

Publishers: Hinrichsen Edition, Ltd; Lienau; Novello; University of Wales Press.

Symphonies/orchestral:

Symphonic Prologue 1938; withdrawn.
Five Pieces 1939; withdrawn.
The Flute Player (after Kalidasa) 1942.
Comedy Overture 1942.
Cloud Messenger (after *The Tale of Genji*) 1945.
Miscellany (20 short pieces) 1946.
Symphony No 1 1947; first performed Liverpool, 6 August 1948.
Symphony No 2 1950.
Symphony No 3 1951; first performed June 1952.
Symphony No 4: In memoriam Dylan Thomas 1954. Recorded Oriel ORM 1002.
Suite: Dobra Niva 1956.
Overture: Ieuenctid / Youth 1956.
Salute to Dylan Thomas 1956.
Symphony No 5 1958; first performed 18 February 1959.
The Knife: Introduction to Act II (from the opera) 1961.
Symphony No 6 1964. Recorded Oriel ORM 1004.
Capriccio (flute, harp, strings) 1965.
Violin Concerto 1966.
Investiture Processional Music (for the investiture of HRH the Prince of Wales) 1969.
Dark Presentiment (from the cantata *The Witnesses*) 1971.
Sinfonietta No 1 1972.
Symphony No 7 1972. Recorded ASD 2855; Oriel ORM 1002.
Symphony No 8 1972. Recorded BBC Artium REGL 359.
Symphony No 9 1974. Recorded BBC Artium REGL 359.
Dance Fantasy 1976. Recorded BBC Artium REGL 359.
Symphony No 10 1981.
Oboe Concerto 1982.
Symphony No 11 1983.
Symphony No 12 1985.
Cello Concerto 1986; first performed Swansea, 4 October 1986.
Fantasia: Whither, O Whither Art Thou Fled? (orchestral interlude from the cantata *Come My Way, My Truth, My Life*) 1987.
Overture: Orpheus and Bacchus 1989; first performed Guildford, Surrey, 24 September 1989.
Sinfonietta No 2 1991; first performed Canford, 16 August 1991.

Chamber/instrumental:

Three Fugues (piano) 1941.
Twenty-four Bagatelles (piano) 1943–55; withdrawn.
String Trio No 1 1946.
Sonata (3 kettle drums) 1947; withdrawn.
String Quartet No 1 1948.
Eight Pieces (violin, viola) 1948; withdrawn.
Wind Septet 1949; withdrawn.
Wind Nonet 1950; withdrawn.
Sonata (4 trombones) 1955; withdrawn.
String Quartet No 2 1957. Recorded Argo ZRG 772.
String Trio No 2 1970. Recorded Argo ZRG 772.
Toccata (organ) 1972.
Sonata (cello, piano) 1973.
String Quartet No 3 1975. Recorded Chandos ABRD 1043.
Prelude: "A Refusal to Mourn" (organ) 1978.
String Quartet No 4 1978; first performed Bishopton, 1978. Recorded Chandos ABRD 1043.
Suite (flute, harpsichord) 1979.
String Quartet No 5 1980; first performed Manchester, 10 November 1980. Recorded Chandos ABRD 1043.
String Quartet No 6 1982.
String Quartet No 7 1988.
Divertimento (wind quintet) 1990.

Vocal/choral:

Kyrie (8-part chorus) 1949.
The Country Beyond the Stars (cantata for chorus, orchestra; Vaughan) 1958; withdrawn.
O Lord, Have Thou Respect (chorus) 1960; withdrawn.
Virginia's Aria (from *The Knife*; soprano, orchestra) 1961.
St Peter (oratorio for soprano, tenor, bass; Bible) 1962; withdrawn.
The Three Hermits (SATB chorus, piano or organ; after Tolstoy) 1969.
Triptych (SATB chorus, piano; Blake, Donne) 1969.
Ballad of the Standard Bearer (tenor, piano; Rilke) 1969; first performed Cheltenham, Gloucestershire, 1969.
The Witnesses (TTBB chorus, orchestra; St Francis, Blake, Psalms, DJ) 1971.
Mor (chorus, piano; G. Thomas) 1971; withdrawn.
Hear the Voice of the Ancient Bard (SATB chorus, orchestra; Blake) 1977; first performed Swansea, 9 December 1977.
To Night (SATB chorus, piano; Shelley) 1978; first performed Cardiff, 8 February 1979.
Come My Way, My Truth, My Life (tenor, SATB chorus, orchestra; Herbert) 1987; first performed Swansea, 10 October 1987.

Opera:

The Knife (5 soloists, chorus, orchestra) 1961; first performed London, 1963.
Orestes (after Aeschylus; mezzo-soprano, tenor, small chorus, orchestra) 1968.

Other:

Under Milk Wood (radio score to Dylan Thomas dramatic poem) 1954.

PUBLICATIONS

By Jones: "Elizabethan Lyric Poetry and Its Relations with Elizabethan Music", dissertation, University College of Wales, Swansea, 1939; "The Elizabethan Lyric", in *The Score*, 2, 1950; "Some Metrical Experiments", in *The Score*, 3, 1950; "An Attempt to Formulate General Aesthetic Principles Through Music Aesthetics", in *The Score*, 11, 1955; contribution to *Artists in Wales*, Llandysul, 1971; (editor) *Complete Poems of Dylan Thomas*, London, 1971; *My Friend Dylan Thomas*, 1973.

On Jones: A. Stewart, "DJ's Opera", in *Musical Times*, 114, 1963; Francis Routh, in *Contemporary British Music*, London, 1972.

* * *

Throughout his long career, Daniel Jones's allegience to traditional compositional forms and to tonality has remained undiminished. Like his two outstanding younger colleagues, Alun Hoddinott and William James Mathias, Jones has spent almost all of his artistic life within Wales. While all three of these musicians maintain a distinctly unparochial approach to their Celtic heritage, Jones's attitudes are notably cosmopolitan and he absolutely refuses to submit to narrow "folksong-inspired" idioms, whether ersatz or otherwise.

In the 1930s, Jones became deeply interested in oriental art forms, when in British music this was a fringe interest, shared mainly by cultish figures such as Sorabji, and international popularity for musical exotica, fuelled above all by Messiaen, still lay more than a decade ahead. These interests did not leave a lasting imprint upon Jones's compositions; but the technique of "complex metres", first encountered in his work in 1936, was of permanent value. It involves basing the metric underlay of a section upon an aggrandation of irregular groups (for example, 9 + 2 + 3 quavers [eighth notes] to a bar), in a manner reminiscent of some of Bartók's metrical structures, notably the "Six Dances in Bulgarian Rhythm" from *Mikrocosmos, Book VI*. This technique helps to imbue many of his compositions with an attractively rough-hewn rhythmic vitality while preserving their overall coherence. The possibilities of this system are most graphically portrayed in the *Sonata* for three unaccompanied kettledrums, a four-movement composition in which the composer's rhythmic ingenuity is put to the severest test, since kettledrums are non-chromatic and therefore only three different pitches are capable of being played in each movement. While accepting that the complex-metres system requires that difficult and irregular time signatures be used for extended passages, Jones insists that the basis of the system is aesthetic rather than purely mathematical, because the unifying presence of a fixed pattern creates both large-scale order and the prospect of improved flexibility.

Some of Jones's outstanding achievements have been in the orchestral field, where the backbone of his output comprises the 12 symphonies. The symphonies show characteristics which emerge also in his other major works (e.g., operas, chamber music): one of the most significant of these is "through-composition", in which the important thematic and harmonic procedures of a piece are outlined during its opening pages. This helps to impose unity upon a work comprising many sections and/or several discrete movements. Often—as in the Seventh Symphony, a work which makes extensive use of the "complex-metres" system—the practice makes the structure of the whole readily apparent.

Jones has said that with the completion of his Twelfth Symphony, his cycle is completed, but he continues to compose and to accept commissions, although he is now approaching 80. His symphonies and operas have sometimes been criticised for attempting to sustain grandiose structures which are not invariably warranted by the quality of the thematic material. However, the best of the symphonies do have a clarity, sureness of touch and individuality which should ensure their future. Moreover, in the *Dance Fantasy* for full orchestra, written with many of his most characteristic technical devices to the fore, Jones has created a truly delightful miniature, one of the most outstanding short pieces of post-War British music.

—Paul Horner

JOSEPHS, Wilfred. British. Born in Newcastle-upon-Tyne, 24 July 1927. Educated at Rutherford Grammar School, 1939–45; University of Durham Sutherland Dental School 1945–51, B.D.S.; musical studies under Arthur Milner, 1947; Guildhall School of Music and Drama, London (Wainwright Scholarship under Alfred Nieman), 1954–56; studied with Max Deutsch, Paris under Leverhulme Scholarship. Served in Royal Army as Dental Officer, 1951–53. Married Valerie Gloria Wisbey, 2 September 1956; 2 daughters. Visiting composer in residence, University of Wisconsin, Milwaukee, 1970; visiting composer in residence and visiting professor, Roosevelt University, Chicago, 1972; music consultant, London International Film School, since 1988. Recipient: competition prize (for *String Quartet No 1*), Liège, Belgium, 1956; Cobbett Prize, 1956; Hurlestone Trophy, 1957; Harriett Cohen Medal, 1957; 1st prize (for *The Ants*), Jeunesses Musicales, 1962; 1st International Composing Competition of City of Milan and La Scala, Italy (for *Requiem*), 1963; Guardian/Arts Council Prize (for *The King of the Coast*), 1969. Mailing address: 15 Douglas Court, Quex Road, London NW6 4PT, England.

Publishers: Novello & Co.; Basil Ramsey, 609 Rayleigh Road, Eastwood, Leigh-on-Sea, Essex SS9 5HU, England.

Symphonies/orchestral:

Sinfonietta 1950s; withdrawn.

Comedy-Overture: The Ants Op 7 1955; broadcast BBC, 6 February 1961.

Symphony No 1 Op 9 (one movement) 1955, revised, 1955, 1957–8, 1974–5; first performed London, 17 December 1955.

Elegy for Strings Op 13 1957; first performed London, 25 May 1957.

Concerto a Dodici Op 21 1959; broadcast BBC, 18 March 1967.

A Tyneside Overture Op 26 1960; first performed Newcastle-upon-Tyne, 1960.

Concerto da Camera Op 25 (solo violin and piano/strings) 1959–60; first performed Maastricht, Holland, 20 December 1961.

Meditatio de Beornmundo Op 30 (solo viola, strings) 1960–1; first performed Birmingham, 7 May 1961.

Aelian Dances Op 35 1961; broadcast BBC, 1 December 1962.

Monkchester Dances Op 37 1961.

Cello Concerto Cantus natalis Op 34 1961–2; broadcast BBC, 16 January 1971.

Symphony No 2 Op 42 1963–4; first performed Cheltenhem, Gloucestershire, 5 July 1965.

The Great War: Theme & March Glorious 1964; first performed BBC television, 1964.

Canzonas on a Theme of Rameau Op 49 (strings) 1965; first performed London, 13 February 1966.
Piano Concerto No 1 Op 48 1965; first performed London, 5 March 1967.
Concerto for Light Orchestra Op 51 1966; first performed Munich, 1 October 1967.
Polemic Op 56 (strings) 1967; first performed Harrogate, Yorkshire, 14 August 1967.
Spirit of the Waltz 1967.
Symphony No 3 Philadelphia Op 59 (small orchestra) 1967; first performed London, 15 April 1969.
Symphony No 4 Op 72 1967–70; broadcast BBC, 26 May 1983.
Rail Op 57 (symphonic picture for string orchestra) 1967; first performed Newcastle-upon-Tyne, 15 June 1967.
Oboe Concerto Op 58 1967, revised 1968; first performed Hemel Hempstead, Hertfordshire, 25 September 1967.
Serenade for Small Orchestra Op 67 1968.
Variations on a Theme of Beethoven Op 68 1969; first performed New York, 23 January 1970. Recorded Unicorn-Kanchana DKP 9026.
Double Violin Concerto Op 69 (2 solo violins, string orchestra) 1969; first performed London, 19 September 1969.
Symphony No 5 Pastoral Op 75 1970–1; first performed Kingston-upon-Hull, Humberside, 25 November 1971. Recorded Unicorn-Kanchana DKP 9026.
The Last Last Post Op 79 1971.
Piano Concerto No 2 Op 77 1971; first performed Dudley, Lancashire, 19 May 1972.
Saratoga Concerto Op 82a (triple concerto for guitar, harp, harpsichord solo, chamber orchestra) 1972; first performed Manchester, 16 April 1978.
Encore (on a Theme of Scott Joplin) ("Maple Leaf Rag") Op 82b (guitar, harp, harpsichord solo with or without orchestra) 1972, orchestrated 1978.
Concerto for Brass Op 88 (brass band) 1972–3; first performed Hanley, Staffordshire, 9 August 1974. Recorded Trax Classique—TRXCD 114 and TRXC 114.
Overture: The Four Horsemen of the Apocalypse Op 86 1973–4; first performed Gloucester, 18 August 1974.
Symphony No 6 Op 83 (lyric soprano, baritone solo, chorus SATB) 1974.
Clarinet Concerto Op 95 1975; first performed Edinburgh, 12 June 1976.
Symphony No 8: The Four Elements Op 98 (wind orchestra or symphonic band) 1975–7; first performed Harrogate, Yorkshire, 13 August 1977.
Symphony No 7: Winter Op 96 (small orchestra) 1976; first performed Bournemouth, 14 December 1978.
Symphonic Poem Eve (d'après Rodin) Op 100 1977–8.
Concerto for 4 Pianos (& 6 Percussion, Without Orchestra) 1978; first performed Manchester, 15 March 1979.
Symphony No 9: Sinfonia Concertante Op 112 (small orchestra) 1979–80; first performed Warrington, 11 February 1981.
Concerto d'Amore Op 113 (violin[s] and orchestra) 1979; first performed Hertogenbosch, Holland, 12 February 1980. Recorded Decca 425 401–2.
Consort Music Op 117 (5 trumpets, 4 horns, 2 tenor trombones, bass trombone, tuba, 2 percussion, timpani) 1980; first performed London, 21 December 1980.
Double Bass Concerto Op 119 1980; first performed Chester, 1 August 1981.
Overture: The Brontës Op 121 1981; first performed Halifax, Yorkshire, 1 May 1982.
Overture: High Spirits Op 129 1981–2; first performed Sevenoaks, Kent, 2 April 1983.
Percussion Concerto Op 130 (solo percussion, brass ensemble) 1982; first performed London, 15 January 1983.
Concerto for Viola and Small Orchestra Op 131 1983; first performed Adelaide, Australia, 21 February 1987.
Overture: The Heaving Bagpipe Op 133 1984. Recorded Decca 425 401–2.
Feu de joie Op 134 1984; first performed London, 18 June 1984.
Symphony No 10 Circadian Rhythms Op 137 1985; first performed Norwich, Norfolk, 19 October 1985.
A Celebratratory Overture "Caen Wood" Op 136 1985; first performed London, 8 June 1985.
Disconcerto Op 138 (solo piano and orchestra) 1985; first performed Freiburg, Germany, 25–26 May 1986. Recorded Decca 425 401–2.
Fanfare (on the Notes C, D) (4 horns, 3 trumpets, 3 trombones, tuba, double bassoon) 1986; first performed London.
Fanfare Prelude Op 140 (2 piccolos, 2 A cornets, 2 bass clarinets, timpani, 2 percussion, strings) 1986; first performed London, 30 October 1986.
Festival Overture (on Brabant Themes) Op 145 (band and orchestra) 1987; first performed Holland, 28 November 1987.
Battle of Britain Suite Op 157 1989–90.
In the North—Hommage à Sibelius Op 158 1990.
Wordless Song Op 160 (string orchestra) 1990.

Chamber/instrumental:

String Quartet No 1 Op 6 1954; first performed London, 17 December 1955.
Siesta Op 8 (violin, piano) 1955; first performed London, 1955–56.
Solo Violin Sonata Op 15 1957; first performed London, 1 April 1958.
Wry Rumba Op 12 (wind quintet) 1957–60.
String Quartet No 2 Op 17 1957–8, revised 1960; broadcast Belgian radio, September 1959.
An Old English Suite Op 31 (E♭ clarinet, 2 B♭ clarinets, basset horn, 2 bass clarinets) 1961; first performed London, 1964.
String Quintet Op 32 "Requiescant pro defunctis fundaeis" (2 violins, viola, 2 cellos) 1961; first performed London, 24 September 1965.
Five Fictitious Folksongs Op 36 (flute, oboe/2 clarinets, clarinet, bassoon) 1962.
Chacony Op 38 1962–3; first performed New York, 23 October 1963. Recorded Orion Records ORS 78292.
Piano Sonata No 2 Op 40 1963; first performed Nova Scotia, 16 August 1963.
Octet Op 43 (clarinet, horn, bassoon, string quartet, double bass) 1964; first performed London, 18 March 1966.
Violin Sonata No 1 Op 46 1965; first performed New York, 22 October 1965.
Flute Trio Op 50 (flute, violin, cello) 1965–6; first performed London, 11 May 1969.
String Trio Op 55 1966; first performed Birmingham, 15 April 1967.
14 Studies Op 53 (piano) 1966; first performed Cheltenham, Gloucestershire, 18 July 1967. Recorded Novello Records LP NVL 104; MC NVLC 104; CD NVLCD 104.
Toccata Op 66 (guitar) 1968.
29 Preludes Op 70 (piano) 1969; first performed London, 13 March 1970.
Solo Cello Sonata Op 73 1970; broadcast BBC, 17 December 1971.

Doubles Op 85 1970–3; first performed Turnhout, 23 March 1977. Recorded Novello Records LP NVL 104; MC NVLC 104; CD NVLCD 104.
Horn Trio Op 76 (horn, violin, piano) 1971, revised 1971; first performed Newport, Wales, 7 November 1971.
String Quartet No 3 Op 78 1971; first performed Milwaukee, Wisconsin, 3 March 1974.
Solo Oboe Piece Op 84 1973; first performed London, 1 April 1974.
Piano Trio Op 93 1974, revised 1981; first performed Newcastle-upon-Tyne, 21 February 1979.
Sonata for Brass Quintet Op 92 (2 trumpets, tenor trombone, horn, tuba) 1974, revised 1981; first performed Nottingham, 16 November 1981.
Piano Quintet Op 91 1974–6; first performed Newcastle-upon-Tyne, 15 September 1978.
Violin Sonata No 2 Op 90 1975; broadcast BBC, 29 November 1976.
Sonata Duo Op 97 (piano duet) 1976; first performed Washington, County Durham, 29 December 1978.
Flute Sonata Op 99 1976–7; first performed London, 3 March 1977.
Fantasia on Three Notes Op 105 (organ) 1978; first performed London, 10 July 1980.
Wind Quintet Op 102 1978; first performed London, 5 March 1978.
Byrdsong Op 104 1978; first performed London, 30 September 1981.
Thoughts on a Spanish Guitar Op 111 1979; first performed London, 9 April 1980. Recorded Bedivere Records BVR 316.
Oboe Quartet Op 110 (oboe, violin, viola, cello) 1979; first performed London, 18 March 1966.
Tombeaux Op 115 (organ) 1980; first performed Edinburgh, 27 August 1980.
Double Bass Sonata Op 119 1980; first performed Leeds, 29 May 1981.
Piano Piece Op 114 (clarinet, piano) 1980; first performed London, 1 March 1980.
Quartet Prelude in Honour of Joseph Haydn Op 124 No 1 (string quartet) 1981; first performed Harrow, Essex, 17 July 1986.
String Quartet No 4 Op 124 No 2 1981; first performed London, 8 September 1982.
Eight Aphorisms for Trombone Octet Op 125 (2 alto, 4 tenor, 2 bass trombones) 1981; first performed Bristol, 26 July 1982.
Testimony Op 122 (toccata for organ) 1981; first performed Leeds, 1 December 1981. Recorded Trax Classique—CD/ Cassette TX 131.
Two Flute Studies (for Simon Hunt) Op 127 (solo flute) 1982.
Arcadian Rhapsody Op 132 (flute, string trio, harp) 1984; first performed Newcastle-upon-Tyne, 7 October 1984.
Clarinet Quintet Op 135 (A clarinet, string quartet) 1984–5; first performed Arundel, Sussex, 25 August 1985.
Arabesques Op 150 (piano) 1985–8.
Northumbrian Dances Op 139 (soprano saxophone, piano; 5 dances based on Northumbrian tunes) 1986; first performed Hexham, Northumberland, 11 July 1986.
Serenade to the Moon Op 141 (3 clarinets, bass clarinet/4 saxophones/woodwind quartet/string quartet/orchestra) 1986; first performed Ciudad Real, Spain, 1 April 1987.
William's Fancye Op 143 (5 players, variable instrumentation) 1986.
Violin Sonata No 3 Op 147 1986–7.
Prelude for Leon Goossens's 90th Birthday Op 110A (oboe, piano) 1987; first performed 12 June 1987.
Clarinet Sonata No 1 Op 148 (A clarinet, piano) 1987–8; first performed London, 27 April 1988.
Oboe Sonata Op 152 (oboe, piano) 1988.
Papageno Variations Op 153 (wind sextet—flute/piccolo, oboe, clarinet, horn, bass clarinet, bassoon) 1989; first performed Letchworth, Hertfordshire, 3 February 1990.
Second Sonata for Brass Quintet Op 154 (2 trumpets, tenor trombone, horn, tuba) 1989.

Vocal/choral:

The Little Dog's Day Op 151 (soprano, 2 clarinets, viola, cello, bass; Brooke) 1951–88.
Twelve Letters—An Entertainment Op 16 (narrator, B♭ clarinet, string trio, piano, version for narrator, piano; Belloc) 1957; first performed London, 19 January 1964. Recorded Unicorn Records KPM 7014.
Requiem Op 39 (solo bass, baritone or bass-baritone, solo string quintet [2 cellos], double chorus; Kaddish) 1962–3; first performed Milan, 28 October 1965. Recorded Unicorn-Kanchana DKP 9032.
4 Chinese Lyrics Op 41 (2 or more voices, piano or guitar) 1963; first performed London, 13 November 1963.
Protégez-moi Op 44 (children/women's voices [min. 4], piano, optional recorders, percussion, school orchestra) 1964; first performed London, 11 March 1968.
Four Japanese Lyrics Op 47 (high voice, piano, optional clarinet, oboe, cor anglais, violin, viola or cello; Shigeji, Iku, anon., translated Thwaite, Bownes) 1965.
So She Went into the Garden Op 45 (3-part equal voices, piano, optional recorders) 1965.
Two Cat Songs Op 54 (unaccompanied SATB chorus; Ewart Milne, Kops) 1966.
This Is the Key of Kingdom Op 52 (children's or women's voices) 1966.
Mortales Op 62 (SATB, optional baritone soloists, adult SATB, children's choruses) 1967–9; first performed Cincinnati, Ohio, 23 May 1970.
Adam & Eve—An Entertainment Op 61 (narrator, flute, oboe/English horn, clarinet/bass clarinet, bassoon, horn, trumpet, trombone, tuba, 1 percussion, piano, violin, viola, cello, double bass; also narrator with solo piano or various intermediate forces) 1967–8; first performed London, 4 February 1968.
Nightmusic for Voice and Orchestra Op 71 1969–70; first performed Liverpool, 23 October 1974.
Death of a Young Man Op 74A/B (song cycle for baritone, piano; or baritone, chamber orchestra; Jacobson) 1970; piano version first performed, Harrogate, Yorkshire, 5 August 1971.
Happitaphs (12 Happy Epitaphs) Op 81 (children's or adult voices, piano) 1971.
Aeroplanes & Angels Op 103 (SATB chorus, piano duet; Gunter Grass) 1977–8; first performed London, 12 April 1978.
Songbook Op 107 (voice, piano) 1978–9.
Spring Songs Op 120 (SATB chorus; Marlowe, *Song of Songs*, Cornish, Lyly, Herrick) 1981; first performed Cork, Ireland, 30 April 1981.
"Aria" from "Quasimodo and Giulietta" Act 9. Sc. 4 by "Giacomo Scarlatina" 1987; first performed Dusseldorf, 1 January 1988. Recorded Decca 425 401–2.
Two A Cappella Choruses to Words by Christina Rossetti Op 146 ([a] SATB chorus; [b] TTBB chorus) 1987.
Tenebrae Op 156 (chorus SATB, piano duet, optional flute/ alto flute, optional percussion and strings) 1989.

Opera/theatre:

The Magical Being (ballet in 1 act; Walter Gore scenario; 4 solo dancers, flute, clarinet, bassoon, trumpet, percussion, piano duet) 1961; first performed Newcastle-upon-Tyne, 31 May 1963.
The Nottingham Captain (music-theatre to libretto by Arnold Wesker; narrator, voices, 7 instruments) 1962; first performed Wellingborough, Northamptonshire, 11 September 1962.
The King of the Coast (children's musical in 3 acts; book and lyrics by Gwen March) 1962–7.
Pathelin (libretto by Edward Marsh; 1 soprano, 4 tenors, 1 bass-baritone, 1 bass, harp, 1 percussion, strings) 1963.
The Tempest—4 Songs and Incidental Music (high voice, oboe/cor anglais, harp, 1 percussion) 1963.
La Répétition de Phèdre (1-act ballet, scenario Norman McDowell, choreography Janine Charrat; ensemble, medium orchestral, full orchestral versions) 1964, orchestral version 1965; first performed Newcastle-upon-Tyne, 22 June 1964.
Henry IV (Parts 1 and 2)—Incidental Music 1964.
Samson Agonistes—Incidental Music 1965.
The Appointment Op 63 (television opera; Kops) 1968.
A Child of the Universe Op 80 (narrator, alto, tenor, baritone, bass, 7 actors, dancers, mimes, corps de ballet, choruses, orchestra) 1971.
Through the Looking Glass and What Alice Found There Op 101 (children's opera, libretto adapted from Lewis Carroll) 1977–8; first performed Harrogate, Yorkshire, 3 August 1978.
Equus Op 116 (ballet based on Peter Shaffer Play) 1980; first performed Baltimore, Maryland, 21 March 1980.
Rebecca Op 126 (opera in 3 acts based on Daphne du Maurier novel, libretto by Edward Marsh; 2 sopranos, 1 alto/mezzo, 1 mezzo, 1 alto, 1 tenor, 2 baritones, 1 bass-baritone, 2 basses [11 singers]) 1981–3; first performed Leeds, Yorkshire, 15 October 1983.
Alice in Wonderland Op 144 (children's opera) 1985–8.

Other (mostly educational):

Pièces pour ma belle-mère Op 18 (piano) 1958–9.
Little Venice Serenade Op 23 (percussion, strings, violas optional) 1960; first performed Essex, 22 March 1963.
Cadenzas for Mozart's E flat Piano Concerto K.482 1967.
Fourteen Caprices for Two Cellos (for pupil and teacher) 1969.
A Trio of Trios (Variations on Well-Known French Tunes) Op 87 (piano trio) 1974.
Philippa Variations Op 89 1974; first performed Manchester, 24 May 1975.
The Montgolfiers' Famous Flying Glove Op 128 (operetta for schools) 1982; broadcast BBC, 1983.

Film and television music: *My Three Brothers*, and *Oxford*, both 1958; *Hotel Imperial Series*, *The Man*, *The Skeleton Clock*, *The Boer War*, *Answered Prayers*, *The Substitute*, *Lies My Father Told Me*, *The Webster Boy*, *Cash on Demand*, *Two-Letter Alibi*, *Sixty Years of Fashion*, *Keeping the Peace*, *Land of Britain*, *The Heart of the Matter*, *They Chose the Sea*, and *700,000,000*, all 1960 or 1961; *The Trouble with Women*, *The Lark*, *The Father*, *The Widowing of Mrs Holroyd*, *Doomsday at Eleven*, *Night Without Pity*, *More Dustbins Get the Sack*, *University of London*, and *Brilliant Fire*, all 1962; *Ever Since Paradise*, *Fruit at the Bottom of the Bowl*, *The Quails*, *Orpheus Three*, *Bomb in the High Street*, *The Controllers*, *Meet the Midland*, *Mindover Metal*, *Portrait Series*, *Most Precious Gift*, and *The Forth Road Bridge*, all 1963; *The Great War*, *Aspidistra in Babylon*, and *Crime and Punishment*, all 1964; *The Navigators*, *Nightmare on Instalments*, *Goodbye Johnnie*, *D.H. Lawrence* (series), *Nineteen Eighty Four*, *Fanatic ("Die, Die My Darling")*, *Twenty-Four Hours to Kill*, and *School Is Everywhere*, all 1965; *Wesker Trilogy*, *Weaver's Green*, *Talking to a Stranger (Hopkins Quartet)*, *Solo for the Banker*, *The Deadly Bees*, *City in the Kingdom Rail ("Journey to Tomorrow")*, and *Engineers in Steel*, all 1966; *The Prisoner*, *D.H. Lawrence* (2nd series) , *Retreat*, *The Lost Years of Brian Hooper*, *Pitch-Poi*, *Jamie on Flying Visit*, *Hostile Witness*, *Indus Waters*, and *The Ladder*, all 1967; *The Making of Music*, *The Appointment*, *Birthday*, *The Exiles*, *My Side of the Mountain*, and *Waterloo*, all 1968; *The Beast in the Jungle*, *The Fosters*, *Somerset Maugham Series*, *A Voyage Round My Father*, *Sweeney Todd*, *Horizon*, *The Warmonger*, *Grasshopper Island*, and *'42:6 Ben Gurion Biography*, all 1969; *Shadow of Progress*, 1970; *Suspicion*, *The Guardians*, *Somerset Maugham*, *The British Empire*, and *Cider with Rosie*, all 1971; *Lady Glencora's Waltz (The Pallisers)*, *Pollyanna*, *Love Story*, *The Brontës*, *Dark Places*, and *Swallows and Amazons*, all 1973; *A Provincial Lady*, *Robinson Crusoe*, *Cheri*, *A Place in Europe*, *Callan*, *All Creatures Great and Small*, and *A Heritage to Build On*, all 1974; *Making Faces*, *The Inventing of America*, *The Ghosts of Motley Hall* (1st series), and *Sea Area Forties*, all 1975; *The House of Bernarda Alba*, *The Hunchback of Notre Dame*, *I, Claudius*, *Motley Hall* (2nd series), *The Parenthood Game*, and *Noah*, all 1976; *Gammon & Spinach*, *The Norman Conquests*, *Sister Dora*, *People Like Us*, *Enemy at the Door*, *Motley Hall* (3rd series), *Disraeli*, *The Uncanny*, *Black Sun ("The Lorry")*, and *The Flame Moves East*, all 1977; *Diary of Britain*, *Fanfare for Young Musicians*, *The Voyage of Charles Darwin*, *The Atom Spies*, *A Case of Cruelty to Prawns*, *Churchill and the Generals*, *Quest of Eagles*, *Pride and Prejudice*, *Cocoa*, and *Project North Sea*, all 1978 or 1979; *The Human Race*, *Carpathian Eagle*, *Miss Morrison's Ghosts*, *Strangled*, *A Gift of Tongues*, *A Walk in the Dark*, *Dear Enemy*, and *The Tartan Xmas Tree*, all 1980 or 1981; *The Moles*, *Weekend Playhouse*, *The Home Front*, *The Making of Britain* (series), *The Brief*, *A Married Man*, *The Gay Lord Quex*, and *Pope John Paul II*, all 1982 or 1983; *A Crack in the Ice*, *The Making of Britain* (series), *Martin's Day*, *Mata Hari*, and *The Inheritance*, all 1984; *Return of the "Antelope"*, *The Making of Britain* (series), *Drummonds* (series), and *Redrick*, all 1985 or 1986; *Evil*, *Making of Britain* (series), *Art of the Western World*, *Horizon: "Wasting the Alp"*, and *Horizon: "The Company of Ants and Bees"*, all 1987, 1988, or 1989.

Wilfred Josephs comments:

Trying to teach young composers, I am struck particularly by the problem all of them seem to carry like a millstone on their backs—the problem of identity.

We are all conscious of it: most of us must have been told by our teachers not to *strive* to be original—just to be ourselves and this originality (if we possess the seeds of it) will come of its own accord. But it is difficult to follow such sound advice: some of us strive at any cost to add our own ten cents' worth of "new" something-or-other—be it timbre, nomenclature, anti-heroics, or whatever. Young composers seem to be in despair at being able to co-exist with such *widely* dissimilar figures as Stockhausen, Shostakovich, Henze, Copland, Cage, Xenakis, Messiaen, Britten, Carter.

But was this any different for Brahms, born six years after the death of Beethoven? For Berlioz, writing along with Beethoven, Meyerbeer, Donizetti, Schubert, Rossini,

Smetana and Strauss the elder? Or for Gershwin whose *Rhapsody in Blue* and *Concerto in F* appeared simultaneously with *Wozzeck*, Nielsen's Sixth Symphony, Ravel's *L'Enfant et les sortilèges*, Janǎček's *Makropoulos Affair*, Vaughan Williams's *Pastoral Symphony*, Schoenberg's Opus 25 *Piano Suite?*

The answer must lie within each of us himself: only a constantly refreshed determination to be faithful to one's own musical destiny, regardless of others, can result in anything other than painful posturing—painful to oneself as well as to others. Sincerity is apt to be derided nowadays, but only self-sincerity can help to produce anything worth considering in the musical sweepstakes which exist now, and which have always existed. Fashion is only for boutiques.

* * *

Trained in music initially part-time while he qualified as a dentist, Wilfred Josephs studied with Arthur Milner in Newcastle-upon-Tyne, Alfred Nieman in London and Max Deutsch in Paris, emerging from student status in 1959. Four years later he won the First International Composing Competition of La Scala and the City of Milan with his *Requiem*, a 55-minute setting of the Hebrew Kaddish, which Carlo Maria Giulini, performing it with the Chicago Symphony Orchestra in 1972, described as "the most important work by a living composer". Coming as it did after a number of other prizes, the success of the *Requiem* relieved Josephs from the need to earn a living from dentistry. He has since devoted himself entirely to composition, and he has built up an impressive catalogue of works in all genres, including 10 symphonies, concertos for various instruments, chamber music and an opera based on Daphne du Maurier's *Rebecca* that has been played before full houses by the British company Opera North.

In these three decades, Josephs has established himself as one of England's most liberally gifted composers. At the same time he has consistently pointed the way towards creative developments that have subsequently been adopted by numbers of colleagues and have thus taken on the nature of trends, such as the music-theatre explorations of the late 1960s and 1970s, anticipated in his *Nottingham Captain* as early as 1962.

Josephs's music showed a recognizable personality from the start, but works of the early 1950s like the now-withdrawn *Sinfonietta* were still clearly a product of the familiar English historical-pastoral tradition. Max Deutsch, however, was a distinguished Schoenberg pupil, and his teaching clearly helped the young composer to assimilate the lessons of the Second Viennese School and to come out, as it were, on the other side. Beginning with the *Cello Concerto Cantus natalis* of 1961–2, Josephs's music displays an arrestingly individual use of techniques derived from serialism while emancipating itself with increasing sureness from the grip of twelve-note chromaticism. In the gradual shift of contemporary music back to practices once regarded as seditious—the expressive use of tonal harmony, and particularly the writing of real tunes—it was natural that a composer blessed with Josephs's outstanding melodic gift should have found himself consistently in the vanguard.

Other stylistic explorations have further diversified his range. Works like the choral and orchestral *Mortales*, *29 Preludes* for piano and the masterly Fourth Symphony began to integrate stringently controlled aleatoric elements into a musical language that otherwise remained fully determinate. But the development of a new creative relationship with the music of the past has for Josephs, as for many of his contemporaries, proved to be a still more fertile resource. *Canzonas on a Theme of Rameau* became only the first of a series of works to derive a world of illuminating and touching allusiveness from their retrospective evocations of various pre-existing musics. In following through on this and his other creative concepts, Josephs has never lost what is perhaps the most striking of his talents: the ability to impart to every piece in a large output, and to each movement within a given piece, the character of a *trouvaille*. The stroke of inspiration may be a structural device, like the brilliant foreshortening of sonata form in the Second Symphony, or a memorable tune, like the one that dominates the last movement of *Mortales*, or a textural/metric/thematic idea such as informs the Tenth Symphony, *Circadian Rhythms*, of 1985; but in each case it results in a profile as personal and unmistakable as any parent's or child's within the family resemblance that unites the Josephs oeuvre.

—Bernard Jacobson

JOUBERT, John (Pierre Herman). South African/British. Born in Cape Town, 20 March 1927; settled in United Kingdom, 1946. Educated at Diocesan college, Cape Town, 1934–44; Royal Academy of Music, London (under Theodore Holland and Howard Ferguson), 1946–50, B.Mus. Married Florence Mary Litherland in 1951; 1 son and 1 daughter. Lecturer in music, University of Hull, 1950–62; reader in music, University of Birmingham, 1962–86; visiting professor, University of Otago, New Zealand, 1979. Recipient: Royal Philharmonic Society Prize, 1949; winner (with *O Lorde, the Maker of Al Thing*), Novello Anthem Competition, 1952. Mailing address: 63 School Road, Moseley, Birmingham B13 9TF, England.

Publisher: Novello, London.

Symphonies/orchestral:

Overture Op 3 1951; first performed Cheltenham, Gloucestershire, 1953.
Symphonic Prelude Op 9 1953; first performed Durban, 1954.
Violin Concerto Op 13 1954; first performed York, June 1954.
Symphony No 1 Op 20 1955; first performed Hull, April 1956.
Piano Concerto Op 25 1958; first performed Manchester, January 1959.
A North Country Overture Op 28 1958; first performed Manchester, 1958.
Sinfonietta Op 38 1962; first performed Birmingham, April 1962.
In Memoriam 1820 Op 39 1962; first performed Johannesburg, 1962.
Three Interludes (from Op 51 *Under Western Eyes*) 1968.
Symphony No 2 Op 68 1970; first performed London, 24 March 1971.
Bassoon Concerto Op 77 1974; first performed Carlisle, 12 March 1975.
Threnos Op 79 (harpsichord, 12 solo strings) 1974; first performed London, 30 March 1974.

Deploration Op 92 1978; first performed Birmingham, 28 December 1978.
Temps perdu Op 99 1984; first performed London, 1 October 1984.

Chamber/instrumental:

String Quartet No 1 Op 1 1950; first performed London, 1951.
Divertimento Op 2 (2 pianos) 1950; first broadcast 1952.
Sonata Op 6 (viola, piano) 1951; first performed Johannesburg, 1952.
Miniature String Quartet Op 10 1953.
Dance Suite Op 21 (piano) 1956. Recorded MSCB 33.
Sonata in One Movement (Sonata No 1) Op 24 (piano) 1957. Recorded MSCB 33.
Trio Op 30 (violin, viola, cello) 1958; first performed Birmingham, January 1960.
Octet Op 33 (clarinet, bassoon, horn, string quartet, double bass) 1961; first performed Hull, June 1961.
Passacaglia and Fugue Op 35 (organ) 1961. Recorded RAC Victrola VICS 1642.
Sonata a cinque Op 43 (recorder or flute, 2 violins, cello, harpsichord) 1963; first performed Cheltenham, Gloucestershire, 1963.
Duo Op 65 (violin, cello) 1971; first performed London, 29 January 1970.
Kontaktion Op 69 (cello, piano) 1971; first performed Birmingham, 27 September 1971.
Sonata No 2 Op 71 (piano) 1972; first performed Birmingham, 1 March 1976.
String Quartet No 2 Op 91 1977; first performed Birmingham, 18 February 1978.
Chamber Music Op 104 (brass quintet) 1985; first performed Hereford, 22 August 1985. Recorded Merlin MRF 86041.
String Quartet No 3 Op 112 1986; first performed Birmingham, 13 March 1987.
Piano Trio Op 113 1986; first performed Hereford, 19 March 1987.
Improvisation Op 120 (treble recorder, piano) 1988; broadcast 21 October 1988.
String Quartet No 4 "Quartetto Classico" Op 121 1988; first performed Birmingham, 19 October 1989.
Six Short Preludes on English Hymn Tunes Op 125 (chamber organ) 1990; first performed Peterborough, 4 July 1990.

Vocal/choral:

Five Songs Op 5 (tenor, piano; Chapman, Donne, anon.) 1951.
Torches Op 7a (SATB choir, orchestra; also for SATB, organ; unison or 2-part choir, piano; traditional Spanish, Trend) 1951. Recorded (organ version) Argo ZRG 5333.
O Lorde, the Maker of Al Thing Op 7b (SATB chorus, organ; Henry VIII) 1952. Recorded Pilgrim JLP 154.
The Burghers of Calais Op 12 (soprano, counter-tenor, 2 tenors, baritone, bass, SATB chorus, chamber orchestra; Hunter) 1953; first performed London, March 1954.
There Is No Rose of Such Virtue Op 14 (unaccompanied SATB choir; old English) 1954. Recorded HMV CSD 3636; Argo ZRG 5446.
Great Lord of Lords Op 16 (SATB choir, organ; anon.) 1954.
The God Pan Op 18 (SSA choir, piano; Fletcher) 1955.
Libera plebem Op 19 (unaccompanied SATB choir with divisions; first part of *Pro Pace*) 1955; complete cycle first performed, London, 1 November 1960. Recorded Pearl SHE 534.
Incantation Op 22 (soprano, alto, tenor, bass; or soprano, SATB choir; Yeats) 1956.
Welcome Yule Op 27 (unaccompanied SATB choir; old English) 1956. Recorded Argo ZRG 5446.
Two Invocations Op 26 (tenor, piano; Blake) 1958.
Solus ad victumam Op 29 (unaccompanied SATB choir with divisions; third part of *Pro Pace*) 1958; complete cycle first performed, London, 1 November 1960. Recorded Pearl SHE 534.
O tristia secla priora Op 32 (unaccompanied SATB choir with divisions; second part of *Pro Pace*) 1959; complete cycle first performed, London, 1 November 1960. Recorded Pearl SHE 534.
Christ Is Risen Op 36 (SATB choir, organ; Corinthians) 1960.
Missa Beatis Ioannis Op 37 (SATB choir, organ) 1961.
Sweet Content Op 40 (unaccompanied SATB choir; Dekker) 1962; first performed Birmingham, 1963.
Leaves of Life Op 41 (ballad cantata for school choir SATB, piano; medieval English) 1962; first performed Farnham, Surrey, 1963.
Urbs beata Op 42 (tenor, baritone, SATB chorus, orchestra; Genesis, Philippians) 1963; first performed Cape Town, November 1963.
The Holy Mountain Op 44 (SATB choir, 2 pianos; Isaiah) 1963; first performed Birmingham, March 1964. Recorded Argo ZRG 5426.
O Lord Our God Op 45 (SATB choir, organ; Psalm 8) 1963.
God Rest You Merry, Gentlemen (no opus number; SATB choir, organ) 1963.
Communion Service in D Op 46 (unison voices, SATB choir, organ) 1964.
The Beatitudes Op 47 (soprano, tenor, unaccompanied SATB choir; St Matthew) 1964.
Te Deum Op 49 (soprano solo, SATB choir, organ; also unison part for congregation) 1964.
Here We Come A-Wassailing (no opus number; unaccompanied SATB choir) 1964.
Hymn-Tune ("For the Beauty of the Earth") (no opus number; SATB choir, piano) 1965.
O Praise God in His Holiness Op 52 (SATB choir, organ; Psalm 150) 1967.
Lord, Thou Hast Been Our Refuge Op 53 (SATB choir, organ; Psalm 90) 1967. Recorded Abbey LPB 663.
Two Hymn Tunes ("To Mercy, Pity, Peace and Love", and "He That Is Down Need Fear No Fall") (no opus number; SATB choir, piano) 1967.
The Choir Invisible Op 54 (baritone, SATB chorus, orchestra; Ecclesiasticus, Spender, George Eliot) 1968; first performed Halifax, Yorkshire, 1968.
Let There Be Light Op 56 (unaccompanied SSS AAA TTT BBB choir) 1968.
Magnificat and Nunc dimittis (in A) Op 57 (SATB choir, organ) 1968.
Nowell Op 58 (SATB choir, organ; old English) 1968.
The Martyrdom of St Alban Op 59 (speaker, tenor, bass, SATB chorus, chamber orchestra; Tunnicliffe) 1968; first performed St Albans, Hertfordshire, June 1969.
How Are My Foes Increased, Lord! Op 61 (SATB choir, organ; Psalm 3, Herbert) 1969; first performed London, July 1969.
All Wisdom Cometh from the Lord Op 62a (SA choir, organ; Ecclesiasticus) 1969.
I Will Lift up Mine Eyes unto the Hills Op 62b (SSAA choir, piano; Psalm 121) 1969.
Six Poems of Emily Brontë Op 63 (high voice, piano) 1969; first performed Manchester, 1969.
Dialogue Op 64 (soprano, counter-tenor, harpsichord; Marvell) 1969; first performed London, January 1970.
African Sketchbook Op 66 (soprano, alto, 2 basses, flute,

oboe, clarinet, horn, bassoon; Hottentot animal poems) 1970; first performed London, April 1970.

The Raising of Lazarus Op 67 (mezzo-soprano, tenor, SATB chorus, orchestra; Tunnicliffe) 1970; first performed Birmingham, 1971.

Behold, the Tabernacle of God Op 70 (SATB choir with divisions, organ) 1972; first performed Belfast, 1973.

Four Stations on the Road to Freedom Op 73 (2 sopranos, 2 altos, 2 tenors, 2 basses; Bonhoeffer) 1972; first performed London, 16 May 1972.

Three Hymns to St Oswald Op 74 (SATB choir, organ; anon. medieval Latin) 1972, revised 1974; first performed Worcester, 29 August 1972; Cheltenham, Gloucestershire, April 1976. Recorded MSCB 34.

Coverdale's Carol Op 75 (unaccompanied SATB choir) 1972.

Five Carols for Five Voices Op 78 (soprano, alto, tenor, 2 basses; old English) 1973; first performed London, 16 December 1973.

Two Antiphons Op 80 (6 solo male voices; Herbert) 1974; first performed Cleobury Mortimer, 14 September 1974.

Sleep Canticle Op 81 (unaccompanied SATB choir with divisions; Browne, Julian of Norwich) 1974; first performed Norwich, Norfolk, 2 November 1974.

Crabbed Age and Youth Op 82 (counter-tenor, recorder, viola da gamba, harpsichord) 1974; first performed London, 9 November 1974.

The Magus Op 83 (tenor, 2 baritones, SATB chorus, orchestra; Acts, Tunnicliffe) 1976; first performed Sheffield, Yorkshire, 29 October 1977.

Lines from "The Youth of Man" Op 90 (unaccompanied SATB choir with divisions; Arnold) 1977; first performed Birmingham, 2 March 1977.

Herefordshire Canticles Op 93 (soprano, baritone, mixed and boys' choruses, orchestra; Latin, Hopkins, T.S. Eliot) 1979; first performed Hereford, 23 August 1979.

The Turning Wheel Op 95 (soprano, piano; Dallas) 1979; first performed Otago, New Zealand, 1 October 1980.

Gong-Tormented Sea Op 96 (baritone, SATB chorus, orchestra; Whitman, Campbell, Yeats) 1981; first performed Birmingham, 29 April 1982.

Three Portraits Op 97 (unaccompanied SATB choir; Skelton) 1983; first performed Cork, April 1983.

The Phoenix and the Turtle Op 100 (2 sopranos, string trio, harpsichord; Shakespeare) 1984; first performed Stratford-on-Avon, 23 August 1984.

The Hour Hand Op 101 (soprano, recorder; Lowbury) 1984; first performed Birmingham, 1 September 1984.

Three Carols Op 102 (unaccompanied SATB choir with divisions) 1984; first performed Sheffield, Yorkshire, 24 November 1984.

Magnificat and Nunc dimittis in C Op 103 (SATrB choir, organ) 1984; first performed Dundee, 20 October 1985.

Autumn Rain Op 105 (SSAA choir, piano; Lawrence) 1985; first performed London, 14 September 1985.

Glory and Honour Op 106 (SATB choir, organ) 1985; first performed Exeter, Devon, 14 June 1986.

Rorate coeli Op 107 (unaccompanied SATB choir; Liber Usualis) 1985; first performed Newcastle-upon-Tyne, 30 November 1985. Recorded Ear 002.

Music for a Pied Piper Op 108 (AATBB, recorder, 2 violins, bass viol, violone, 2 lutes; Browning) 1985; first performed London, 21 January 1986.

South of the Line Op 109 (soprano, baritone, chorus, 2 pianos, timpani, percussion; Hardy) 1985; first performed Birmingham, 1 March 1986. Recorded EAR 002.

The Instant Moment Op 110 (baritone, string orchestra; Lawrence) 1986; first performed Birmingham, 21 March 1987.

Vision and Prayer Op 111 (SATB choir, piano—4 hands; Micah, Scottish Psalter) 1986; first performed Cheltenham, Gloucestershire, 8 November 1986.

A Hymne to God the Father Op 114 (unaccompanied SATB choir; Donne) 1987; first performed Radley, Oxfordshire, 19 November 1987.

Introit: Lord, in the Strength of Grace Op 115 (unaccompanied SATB choir; Wesley) 1987.

Whitsun Carol Op 115(b) (unaccompanied SATB choir; St Ambrose) 1987; broadcast BBC, 7 June 1987.

Roundelay Op 116 (soprano, bass viol, lute) 1987; first performed Birmingham, 30 June 1987.

Jolly Good Ale Op 117 (2 altos, tenor, 3 basses) 1987; first performed Birmingham, 19 September 1987.

Tristia Op 118 (soprano, baritone, clarinet, piano; Mandelstam) 1987; first performed London, 13 June 1988.

They Are Happy Op 119 (SATB choir, organ; Psalm 36) 1988; first performed Birmingham, 30 July 1988.

Missa brevis Op 122 (soprano, alto, tenor, bass, chorus, chamber orchestra) 1988; first performed Birmingham, 16 October 1988.

Sonnet Op 123 (unaccompanied SATB choir; Swinburne) 1989.

For the Beauty of the Earth Op 124 (soprano, baritone, chorus, orchestra; Hopkins, Psalms, hymn) 1989; first performed Birmingham, 25 November 1989.

Opera:

Antigone Op 11 (radio opera; Trickett, Sophocles) 1954; broadcast BBC, 21 July 1954.

In the Drought Op 17 (Wood) 1955; first performed London, 13 December 1959.

Silas Marner Op 31 (Trickett, George Eliot) 1961; first performed Cape Town, 20 May 1961.

The Quarry Op 50 (for young players; Holbrook) 1964; first performed London, 25 March 1965.

Under Western Eyes Op 51 (Cliffe, Conrad) 1968; first performed London, 29 May 1969.

The Prisoner Op 76 (opera for schools; Tunnicliffe, Tolstoy) 1973; first performed London, 16 March 1973.

The Wayfarers Op 98 (opera for young people; Tunnicliffe, Chaucer) 1983; first performed Huntingdon, 4 April 1984.

PUBLICATIONS

By Joubert: "The Choir Invisible", in *Musical Times*, 109, 1968; (interview in 2 parts) in *Composer*, 31–32, 1969; "Under Western Eyes", in *Musical Times*, 110, 1969; "Composing Music for Poetry", in *Composer*, 72, 1981; "On Setting Yeats's *Byzantium*", in *Musical Times*, 122, 1982.

On Joubert: Wilfred Mellers, "JJ and the Blessed City", in *Musical Times*, 105, 1964; Peter Dickinson, "JJ Today", in *Musical Times*, 112, 1971; E. Bradbury, "JJ", in *The New Grove Dictionary of Music*, 9, 1980; Kenneth Birkin, "JJ at 60", in *Musical Times*, 128, 1987.

John Joubert comments:

Any introduction to my life and work would have to take account of the fact that I was born and spent the first 19 years of my life in South Africa, with all that implies in terms of the political and racial tensions which have always prevailed there. Though descended from the early French and Dutch settlers at the Cape, my first language was English and I was educated at an Anglican church school where I was introduced to the riches of English music and the Anglican choral tradition. This perhaps explains why so much of my output has been either vocal or choral.

Though I have lived in England continuously since first coming here to study, the influence on my music of my early background can still be felt, not only in its clarity of outline—a result, perhaps, of early exposure to African sun and sky—but also in the choice of some of its subject-matter, notably in the Second Symphony of 1970, dedicated to the victims of Sharpeville, or in the more recent *South of the Line*, which sets poems by Thomas Hardy on the subject of the Anglo-Boer War.

Despite having received my early training at the Royal Academy of Music, I have spent a large part of my life working in universities as a lecturer in all aspects of music and this has also had its effect on the way my music has developed. It has taught me to look analytically and critically at the great European musical tradition, to appraise it and get on intimate terms with it in a way which would never have been possible otherwise. Far from being stifled or overwhelmed by the sheer magnitude of the historical past, I have been inspired and energized by it to the extent that I can begin to see myself as a part—however insignificant—of a tradition which is not only still alive, but which provides me with the material and subject-matter of my art. Hence my symphonies, my concertos, my operas, my chamber music. Hence, too, my sense of the abiding importance of craftsmanship, the only means whereby traditional forms can be revitalized and bent to personal expressive ends.

Any composer coming to maturity during the post-war period has had to come to some sort of accommodation with serialism, whether or not he accepts it wholly. I have never felt that a system of thought originally designed to suppress a phenomenon so fundamental as tonality could lead to anything but a crisis in communication, and so it has proved. I have never used serialism even in a modified way, and it is perhaps a sign of the times that whereas before I may have been embarrassed by such an admission, I can now proclaim it openly and even with some pride—though an artist can never take the credit for factors which operate from below (or above?) the level of conscious volition.

* * *

John Joubert's journey to England in 1946 was virtually a pilgrimage and London the Mecca where, in direct contrast to the musical isolation of South Africa, he was able to deepen his knowledge of, and to participate in, the European Tradition. Initially, he was influenced by the Elizabethan musical heritage (*Five Songs Op 5*), early study of which reflected a need to come to terms with the cultural roots of his adopted homeland. The subtle rhythmic counterpoints, so distinctive a feature of the English Madrigal School, contributed significantly to his vocal/rhythmic style as did the music of Walton, Stravinsky and Benjamin Britten, the latter a composer Joubert deeply admired and whose literary discrimination and expressive sensibility finds a counterpart in his own work.

The immediate post-student years brought recognition; *O Lorde, the Maker of Al Thing* which won a Novello prize and the popular *Torches* was followed by *There Is No Rose of Such Virtue*. Such success inevitably brought categorisation but although Joubert has never ceased to be active in the vocal field and is, perhaps, the most significant composer on the English cathedral and church music scene, his output extends far beyond the purely liturgical. Indeed, he might claim to have given a new, symphonic dimension to vocal ensemble writing in the imaginative *Pro Pace* motets and their counterpart, the superb *Rorate coeli*.

The 1960s saw outstanding influences, including Sibelius and Shostakovitch, gradually absorbed into a personal style which communicates with increasing authority and power. Developed unashamedly from a representative tradition, Joubert's music is characterised by an underlying diatonicism, lyricism and architectural coherence which achieves a communicative impact rare in our times. Nevertheless, it would be erroneous to regard him as a musical conservative. His retention of tonal parameters is symptomatic of a nature that scorns to abandon a vital, dramatic, expressive and structural resource. Within the broader concept of "key" a flexible and far from traditional harmonic language has evolved through which he conveys his ideas in a thoroughly individualistic manner.

In the 1970s a new, authoritatively Joubertian voice is apparent. *Six Poems of Emily Brontë*, born of established mastery in practically every genre, are clearly of catalystic import. The inherent dramatic instinct that had already drawn him to opera (on his own admission a preferred art form) with *Silas Marner* and *Under Western Eyes* acquires here fresh impetus. These songs, imaginative settings whose technical means define an artistic vision of deep compassion and concern for the human condition, patently crystallise the mature elements of his style. They demonstrate characteristic melodic major/minor third alternations, striking intervallic extensions and a tonality often obscured by composite and bitonal harmonies—the whole, underpinned by consummate musical craftsmanship.

Joubert's is music of conviction, operating within a clearly defined social context. Commissions, satisfying a self-expressed need to play an intelligible musical role in the community, act as inspiration and spur to achievement. His attitude to his roots is ambivalent. Though manifestly under the spell of his homeland, he took British nationality after the Sharpeville massacre, to whose victims the Second Symphony is dedicated. South Africa has inspired other works, outstandingly the *African Sketchbook* songs and the cantata *South of the Line* whose shared material—conscious self-quotation—reveals a tendency which also contributes to coherence of compositional style.

This style has become more sharply defined in the last decade; the musical materials subjected to ever more stringent intellectual control and technical refinement. This is evidenced, not only in chamber works, such as the Second String Quartet, *Temps perdu* and the *Piano Trio Op 113*, but also on a larger scale in the *Herefordshire Canticles, Gong-Tormented Sea* and the choral symphony *For the Beauty of the Earth*. These, together with the superb D.H. Lawrence cycle *The Instant Moment* testify to an underlying integrity manifest in music that asserts a moral, even a prophetic power. This inherently lyrical oeuvre speaks directly and with conviction, breathing a contemporary spirit and communicating on the highest artistic and intellectual plane. The 1980s have witnessed an upsurge of creative energy in which Joubert's instinctive, fluent musicality is tempered by a formidable concentrative power. One looks forward to a new initiative in the form closest to his heart, in the opera *Jane Eyre* with which he is currently occupied.

—Kenneth Birkin

K

KAGEL, Mauricio. Argentinian. Born in Buenos Aires, 24 December 1931. Education: failed entrance to Buenos Aires Conservatory of Music; thereafter largely self-taught, but also studied music theory under Juan Carlos Paz and piano, cello, organ, voice and conducting under Alfredo Schiuma and others; also philosophy and literary history, University of Buenos Aires. Artistic consultant, Agrupacion Nueva Musica, from 1949; pianist, Teatro Colon, Buenos Aires, 1949–56; film and photography critic, *Gente de Cine* and *Nueva Vision*, Buenos Aires, 1952–6; emigrated to Cologne, Germany, 1957; faculty, Ferienkurse für Neue Musik, Darmstadt, from 1960; founder, Kölner Ensemble für Neue Musik, 1961; Slee Professor of Composition, State University of New York, Buffalo, 1964–5; visiting lecturer, Film and Television Academy, Berlin, 1967; director, Scandinavian Contemporary Music Course, Gothenburg, 1968; head, Cologne Contemporary Music Courses, 1969–75; professor of contemporary music theatre, Musikhochsschule, Cologne, since 1974. Recipient: Mozart Medal, City of Frankfurt, 1983; Commandeur de L'Ordre des Arts et des Lettres, France, 1985. Mailing address: c/o Universal Edition, Bosendorferstrasse 12, Postfach 3, A-1015 Vienna, Austria.

Publishers: Universal Edition; Edition Peters.

Symphonies/orchestral:

Hétérophonie (orchestra; indeterminate elements, oboe gives A# for tuning) 1959–61; first performed Cologne, 22 May 1962.
Sonant (electric guitar, harp, double bass, small orchestra) 1961.
Diaphonie II (orchestra, 2 slide projectors) 1964.
Music for Renaissance Instruments (chamber orchestra) 1966.
Klangwehr (I & II) (military marching band, 40 minimum; II includes chorus) 1969–70.
Musi (string orchestra: 6 + 6 mandolins, 6 mandolas, 6 + 6 guitars, cello, 2 double basses) 1971.
Variationen ohne Fuge (based on Brahms's *Variationen und Fuge* on a theme of Handel) 1972.
Finale (chamber orchestra) 1981.
Szenario (strings, tape) 1988.
Musik für Tasteninstrumente und Orchester (2 pianos, 2 electric organs, orchestra) 1989.
Osten (chamber orchestra) 1989.

Chamber/instrumental:

String Sextet 1953, revised 1957.
Traummusik (instruments, *musique concrète*) 1954.
Transicion II (piano, percussion, 2 magnetic tapes) 1959.
Pandora's Box (bandoneon) 1960.
Sonant (guitar, harp, double bass, 2 percussion/membrane instruments) 1960.
Mimetics (Metapiece) (piano; may be played simultaneously with another work, by Kagel or another living composer) 1961.
Musik aus Tremens (electric guitar, bass guitar, amplified double bass, Hammond organ, percussion, tapes) 1963, revised 1965.
Schlag auf Schlag (4 music saws, percussion) 1963–4.
Match (2 cellos, percussion) 1964.
Mirum (tuba) 1965.
Pas de cinq (5 percussionists) 1965.
Chamber Music for Renaissance Instruments (2–22 players) 1965, revised 1966.
String Quartet 1965–7.
Phantasie (organist, assistants, 2 tape machines) 1967.
Freifahrt (from *Staatstheater*; variable instrumentation, 18–36 players in any equal groups, minimum 6, of brass, percussion, strings) 1967–70.
Spielplan (from *Staatstheater*; 5–7 players) 1967–70.
Der Schall (5 players in 5 different instrumental configurations, including toy instruments, winds, percussion, guitars, etc.) 1968.
Acustica (III) (2–5 instrumentalists, wind, plucked, percussion instruments; other sound sources) 1968–70.
Morceau de concours (trumpet) 1968, 1971.
Unter Strom (3 players: Spanish guitar, electric guitar, electric bass guitar, guitar strings, coffee grinder, walkie-talkies, electric fans, etc.) 1969.
Atem (1 wind instrument) 1970.
Tactil (3 pianos, string instruments, tone generators) 1970.
Charakterstück (zither quartet) 1971.
Siegfriedp' (cello) 1971.
Exotica ("non-European instruments"; 6 players and up to 60 instruments) 1971–2. Recorded Deutsche Grammophon DG 2530 251.
General Bass (instruments capable of producing continuous sound) 1971–2.
Aus Zungen Stimmen (accordion quintet) 1972.
Unguis Incarnatus Est (piano and ". . ."; any other instrument within range C–c") 1972.
An Tasten (piano) 1977.
Variété (clarinet/bass clarinet/alto saxophone, trumpet, accordion, piano/electric organ, percussion, cello) 1977.
MM 51 (piano) 1977.
Die Rhythmusmaschinen (drum machines or tapes, 2 percussion) 1978.
Dressur (trio for wooden percussion) 1978.
Zehn Marsch um den Sieg zu verfehlen / Ten Marches to Miss the Victory (woodwind, brass, percussion) 1978–9. Recorded Preciosa Aulos PRE 66004 AUL.
Blue's Blue ("ethnomusicological reconstruction" for clarinet, trumpet, guitar, double bass) 1979.
Klangwölfe (violin, piano) 1979.
Rrrrrrr . . . (radio fantasy in 41 pieces, all titles begin with "r": 11 pieces for winds, double bass, percussion; 7 pieces for mixed choir; 8 pieces for organ; 6 percussion duos; 4 pieces for soprano orbaritone; 5 pieces for jazz group) 1982. Recorded (organ pieces) Preciosa Aulos PRE 66004 AUL.
Aus dem Nachlass (viola, cello, double bass) 1983.
Der Eid des Hippokrates (piano—3 hands) 1984.
Trio (violin, cello, piano) 1984–5.
Pan (piccolo, string quartet) 1985.

String Quartet No 3 1988.
Phantasiestück (flute, piano, clarinet, bass clarinet, violin, viola, cello) 1989.
Zwei Akten (saxophone, harp) 1989.

Vocal/choral:

Palimpsestos (unaccompanied chorus) 1950.
Anagrama (speaking chorus, coloratura soprano, alto, baritone, bass, flute, clarinet, bass clarinet, 3 percussion, celeste, 2 harps, 2 pianos) 1957–8.
Improvisation ajoutée (choir, organ) 1961–2.
Phonophonie (4 melodramas for 2 voices, sound sources) 1963.
Diaphonie I (chorus, orchestra, slide projectors) 1964.
Diaphonie III (chorus, 2 or more slide projectors) 1964.
Musik aus Diaphonie (6–10 singers and/or unspecified instruments) 1964.
Hallelujah (sopranos, altos, tenors, basses; 4 or 8 of each) 1967–8.
Debut (from *Staatstheater*; 60 voices—15 sopranos, 15 altos, 15 tenors, 15 basses) 1967–70.
Ensemble (from *Staatstheater*; 16 voices) 1967–70.
Saison (from *Staatstheater*; singing game in 65 parts) 1967–70.
Die Mutation (male choir, piano obligatto) 1971.
Recitativarie (singing harpsichordist) 1971–2.
Abend (double vocal quartet, trombone quintet, electric organ, piano) 1972.
Gegenstimmen (children's choir, harpsichord obligatto) 1972.
1898 (20–25 children's voices, piano, percussion; other instrumentation unspecified) 1972–3.
Kantrimusik (pastoral for singers, B♭ clarinet, C trumpet, bass tuba in F/C, violin, upright piano, 2 guitars/octave guitar/Spanish guitar/ukulele/mandolin/tenor banjo; instrumentalists double on percussion) 1975.
Chorbuch (vocal group, piano, harmonium/electric organ) 1978.
Tango Aleman (voice, violin, bandoneon/accordion, piano) 1978.
Ex-Position (consists of *Chorbuch* and *Die Rhythmusmaschinen*; vocal ensemble, harmony instruments) 1978.
Vox humana? (women's voices, loudspeaker, orchestra) 1979.
Mitternachtsstück (solo voices, speaking choir, flute, bass clarinet, tuba, 2 percussion, harp, celeste, harmonium, violin) 1981.
Rrrrrrr . . . (radio fantasy in 41 pieces; includes 7 pieces for mixed choir; 4 pieces for soprano or baritone) 1982.
Fürst Igor, Strawinsky (bass voice, cor anglais, horn, tuba, viola, 2 percussion) 1982.
Intermezzo (solo speaker, mixed chorus, flute, clarinet, horn, tuba, piano percussion, strings) 1983.
Der Erschöpfung der Welt (concert version; 3 speakers, soprano, alto, tenor, baritone, bass, mixed chorus, orchestra) 1984.
Sankt-Bach-Passion (mezzo-soprano, tenor, baritone, speaker, double chorus, boys chorus, large orchestra) 1985.
Ein Brief (mezzo-soprano, orchestra) 1986.
Quodlibet (female voice, orchestra) 1988.
Fragende Ode (double choir, instruments, percussion) 1989.

Opera/theatre:

Antithèse (1 or 2 performers with electronics) 1962.
Sur Scène (6 participants: musicians instructed to interfere with actors and singers) 1962; first performed Bremen, 6 May 1962.
Composition and Decomposition (reader) 1963.
Tremens (dramatic montage) 1963–5.
Die Himmelsmechanik (compositon with scenery) 1965.
Pas de cinq (variable scene for 5 performers) 1965.
Parkett (from *Staatstheater*; 10–76 participants) 1967–70.
Repertoire (from *Staatstheater*; dramatic concert piece) 1967–70.
Staatstheater (scenic composition: ballet for non-dancers, sounds produced by household utensils including chamber pot and enema equipment) 1970–1; first performed Hamburg, 25 April 1971.
Con voce (3 mimes, instruments ad lib) 1972–3.
Mare nostrum (scenic composition) 1975.
Variété (artists, musicians) 1977; first performed Metz, France, 1977.
Umzug (mime) 1977.
Der Erschöpfung der Welt (opera) 1979; first performed Stuttgart, 8 February 1980.
Aus Deutschland (*lieder* opera) 1981.
Der Tribun (political orator, marching band, loudspeaker) 1981.
La Trahison orale / Der mündliche Verrat (musical epic on the Devil; 1 female performer, 2 male singers, tuba, viola/violin, double bass, piano/electric organ, 3 percussion, tape) 1983.
"*. . . nach einer Lektüre von Orwell*" (dramatic environment/*Horspiel*) 1984.
Tantz-Schul (dance drama) 1988.

Other:

Transicion I (electronic sound) 1958.
Pandora's Box (tape) 1961.
Prima vista (slides, sound sources) 1962–4.
Camera oscura (chromatic game for light sources, loudspeakers, tape machines, actors) 1965.
Kommentar + Extempore (speech, mime) 1966–7.
Montage (variety of sound sources) 1967.
Einspielungen (from *Staatstheater*; loudspeaker, with voices and instruments ad lib) 1967–70.
Kontra > Danse (from *Staatstheater*; ballet for non-dancers) 1967–70.
Ornithologica multiplicata (exotic birds) 1968.
Privat (solitary listener: tape recorder, telephone, radio, coffee machine, shower, typewriter, etc.) 1968.
Synchronstudie (film projection, noise maker, performer) 1968–9.
Acustica (I) (loudspeaker, tape) 1968–70.
Acustica (II) (experimental tone generator, loudspeaker) 1968–70.
Ludwig van (film-collage of Beethoven pieces) 1970.
Probe (collective improvisation) 1971.
Programm (includes *Abend, Aus Zungen Stimmen, Charakterstück, Gegenstimmen, General Bass, Die Mutation, Musi, Recitativarie, Siegfriedp', Unguis Incarnatus Est, Von Horensagen*) 1971–2.
Zwei-Mann-Orchester (2 one-man-bands) 1971–3.

Guillaume de Machault: *Two Ballads* (realised for solo voice and/or mixed choir, and flute, cor anglais, bass clarinet, horn, tuba, viola, harp, celeste, piano) 1984.

* * *

Even as a young man, Mauricio Kagel cultivated a diversity of pursuits: in addition to his first compositions, he wrote on Argentinian photography and film, studied literature (above all, the work of Jorge Luis Borges) and philosophy (in which his principal interest was Spinoza) and worked as répétiteur in the opera house. His versatility alone makes Kagel's achievement unique; he has produced orchestral, chamber, instrumental and vocal work, and a remarkable body of dramatic pieces. In addition, he has scored a number of films and radio plays.

With the absurdist cantata *Anagrama* musical theatre—and the theatricalisation of music—became Kagel's firm domain. Around 1960, for example, he established a genre "instrumental theatre", in which he directed the musicians' performance, as in the string quartets, or in *Match*, a piece for two cellos and percussion to which is added such unusual activities as a game of dice, or as when he interprets the rhythms of a percussion quintet scenically, or in *Die Himmelsmechanik*, where he creates stage decor for a silent theatre. The process culminates in the epochal *Staatstheater* in which opera itself (with all its artifice and illusion) becomes the actual subject-matter. In "instrumental theatre", as in his work for radio and film, Kagel extended the philosophy of musical composition to include "non-harmonious materials".

Since the early 1970s and the Beethoven film *Ludwig van*, music once again predominates, but into the tradition that runs from Bach to Brahms, Kagel incorporates popular musical elements. In the *Variationen ohne Fuge*, he takes Brahms's Handel variations with apparent fidelity to the original and translates them atonally; likewise with 49 out of 371 four-part Bach chorales in *Chorbuch*. Kagel's most effective and distinctive compositional principle is collage. This is the method used in the *lieder* opera *Aus Deutschland* in which a range of piano-accompanied art songs are cut up, recomposed and staged with Schubert as a character.

With the *Sankt-Bach-Passion*, a musical biography of the composer, Kagel turns historian. He remains a universal composer even when working within the tradition in what may seem a sideline but which is part of the "acoustic theology" which informs his work from the less than pious *Der Erschöpfung der Welt* to *La Trahison orale*, the latter a collage of devil stories.

Since the early 1980s, Kagel has turned with renewed vigour to canonical and traditional forms. In *Rrrrrrr . . .* , a collection of 41 pieces, all beginning with the letter R (as in "Rhinelander", "Rhapsody", "Rejouissance") or in the Third String Quartet, to date the high point of this new direction. Kagel was examining the past with a view to its potential usefulness to the present, while in no way abandoning his fundamental commitment to producing ambiguous results from unambiguous means. It might be said that one of Kagel's fundamental principles vis-à-vis tradition is the dialectic of familiarisation and distraction. He frequently adds familiar patterns which are quickly alienated by the unfamiliar context. Alternatively, he creates the expectation of rhythmic regularity and predictability, only to confound it with a constantly shifting pattern. The use of historical motifs and patterns which have helped condition a listener's responses to music allows Kagel to unsettle even the most conditioned tastes. All allusions to the past in Kagel's work combine familiarity with jarring strangeness. Kagel's music demands to be heard and insists: nothing is certain, be alert.

Alongside Cage and Stockhausen, Kagel is arguably one of the most distinguished of contemporary composers and is certainly the most sceptical, dialectical and paradoxical.

—Werner Klüppelholz
(translated by Eleanor Caldwell)

KAIPAINEN, Jouni (Ilari). Finnish. Born in Helsinki, 24 November 1956. Educated at Sibelius Academy, Helsinki (composition under Aulis Sallinen and Pavo Heininen), 1975–81. Married Sari-Anne Liljendahl, 9 September 1977; 1 son. Freelance composer, since 1981. Recipient: Best Work of the Year, UNESCO International Composers Rostrum, 1981; Spurs of Criticism, Finnish Critics' Circle (for most promising debut of the year), 1982. Mailing address: Onkiniemenkatu 9 D 30, SF-33230 Tampere, Finland.

Publisher: Wilhelm Hansen, Copenhagen.

Symphonies / orchestral:

Symphony Op 20 1980–5; first performed Helsinki, 1985.
Carpe diem (chamber orchestra) 1990.

Chamber / instrumental:

String Quartet No 1 1973.
String Quartet No 2 1974.
Sonatina Op 9 (piano) 1976.
" . . . La Chimère de l'humidité de la nuit?" Op 12b (alto saxophone) 1978.
Ladders to Fire Op 14 (2 grand pianos) 1979.
Trois Morceaux de l'aube Op 15 (cello, piano) 1980–1.
Je chante la chaleur désespérée Op 16 (piano) 1981.
Far from Home Op 17 (flute, alto saxophone, guitar, percussion) 1981.
Altaforte Op 18 (electric trumpet, piano) 1982.
Trio I Op 21 (clarinet, cello, piano) 1983.
Elegia Op 22 (cello, piano) 1983.
Parcours Op 23 (flute, harpsichord) 1983.
Titus-Elegy Op 24b (flute, string quartet) 1983.
Quartetto III Op 25 (string quartet) 1984.
Piping Down the Valleys Wild Op 26 (bass clarinet, piano) 1984.
Conte Op 27 (piano) 1985.
Andamento (Trio II) Op 28 (flute, bassoon, piano) 1986.
Trio III Op 29 (violin, cello, piano) 1986–8.
Gena Op 31 (accordion) 1987.
L'annello di Aurora (violin) 1988.

Vocal / choral:

Yolaujuja / Nocturnal Songs Op 11 (soprano, chamber ensemble; Po Chu-i) 1978.
Cinq Poèmes de René Char Op 12a (soprano, orchestra) 1978–80.
Pitkan Kesan Poikki Iltaan / The Summer's Journey Towards Night Op 13 (soprano, flute, horn, percussion, cello; Ronimus) 1979.
Muunlaisten Musiikkia / Music of Persons of Another Kind Op 19 (mezzo-soprano, piano; Salminitty) 1982.
Stjarnenatten / Star Night (soprano, ensemble) 1989.
Lachrymosa (double chorus) 1989.

Opera / theatre:

Konstanzen Ihme / The Miracle of Konstanz Op 30 (television opera; Siltanen) 1987–8.

Other:

Titus Andronicus Op 24a (incidental music to Shakespeare; flute, brass quartet) 1983.

PUBLICATIONS

By Kaipainen: essay in Nieminen and Hako, *Ammatti: saveltaja* [Profession: composer], Helsinki, 1981; essays in *Finnish Music Quarterly*.

* * *

Perhaps the most gifted of the younger Finns, Jouni Kaipainen was one of a circle of promising composers to gather round the influential Paavo Heininen in Helsinki. Heininen's absolute meticulousness and encyclopaedic understanding of all phases of modern music has rubbed off on his pupil. Even so, it is difficult to pin Kaipainen down to any single "influence"; he has much in common with Berio, not least in the vocal works (and shared a platform with the Italian master at the 1985 Helsinki Biennale, when Kaipainen's only non-vocal work to date for full orchestra was premiered); he owes something to Messiaen's handling of instrumental colour, and even more so in the symphony to another brilliant French orchestrator, Henri Dutilleux. There are already signs, though, that Kaipainen is transcending all external influences and forging a personal style of considerable individuality.

Its underlying philosophy is one Kaipainen shares with the French Dadaist/Surrealist poet René Char, five of whose poems he set while still a student as his opus 12a. At the heart of his thinking is the conviction that there is no restrictively "proper" material for music; this has not meant a turn to *musique concrète* or to an exploration of sheer noise, but it has led him to widen his palette in keeping with the requirements of each individual piece, and to be willing to bring or force together (in a manner consistent with the Dadaist conception of beauty, but with an impact not dissimilar to English Metaphysical poetry) elements which in isolation would seem to belong to quite different areas of musical discourse.

Deeply versed in modern music, Kaipainen draws on its methodologies and styles with considerable freedom, and frequently embroiders quotations and explicit allusions to other composers into his work. His first mature work, the extraordinary *Ladders to Fire*, inspired by the novelist Anaïs Nin, is largely built of allusive material, as is the surreal *Trois Morceaux de l'aube*, which interweaves fragments of Mahler and Wagner into strikingly dissonant passages in such a way as to suggest the curious distortions of recollection. This is the basic emphasis of the *Symphony*, a work that eschews conventional development and recapitulation in favour of a dream-like, shuttering repetition. In much the same way, the 1984 *Quartetto III*, effectively the first mature work in that form, disrupts the normal progression and ends with an outwardly uncharacteristic slow movement which further illuminates his Gielen-like handling of string textures.

Though he appears to be more at home with strings than with winds, his chamber compositions for ensembles and duos featuring flute, saxophone, bass clarinet and in one striking instance, for electric trumpet, reveal a composer with an insatiable appetite for fresh instrumental textures and for the developmental logic required to convert these into actual music. The use of quotes from Char as titles to non-vocal music is again characteristic. The most recent work, *Carpe diem*, extends his technique further and suggests a reviving interesting in larger-scale structures.

Much has been made of the rapid change of style in approach in Kaipainen's first full decade as a professional composer. Outwardly, these changes are quite dramatic, but virtually all his work, from the lush vocal pieces of 1978 to 1980 (a vein temporarily set aside) to the nervous brilliance of instrumental pieces of the next few years, has a deep underlying consistency of purpose which is highly impressive. Kaipainen's is a voice that can only gain in authority.

—Signe Maarten

KALABIS, Viktor. Czechoslovak. Born in Červený Kostelec. Educated at Prague Conservatory (under Emil Hlobil and Jaroslav Řídký), 1945–8; Academy of Arts and Music, Prague, 1948–52; Charles University, Prague (philosophy, music theory, psychology, aesthetics), 1948–52. Married harpsichordist Zuzana Růžičková, 8 December 1952. Editor and musical producer, Czech Radio, Prague, 1951–71; full-time composer, since 1972; choirmaster, 1973–5; occasional conductor. Recipient: Czechoslovak Music Critics Prize, 1967; Clement Gottwald State Prize, 1969; Artist of Merit, 1983. Mailing address: V. K. Slezska 107, 130 00 Prague 3, Czechoslovakia.

Publishers: Panton; Supraphon.

Symphonies/orchestral:

Hommage à Stravinski Op 3 (concerto for chamber orchestra) 1948.
Overture Op 7 1950.
Concerto for Cello and Orchestra Op 8 1951.
Straznice Suite Op 9 1953.
Concerto for Piano and Orchestra Op 12 1954. Recorded Supraphon SU 1101680.
Symphony No 1 Op 14 1957.
Concerto for Violin and Orchestra Op 17 1959. Recorded Supraphon 18502.
Symphony No 2 "Sinfonia pacis" Op 18 1961. Recorded Supraphon SU 58592.
Chamber Music for Strings Op 21 1963. Recorded Supraphon SU 8355.
Symphonic Variations to an Original Theme Op 24 1964. Recorded Supraphon SU 1101512.
Concerto for Large Orchestra Op 25 1966. Recorded Supraphon SU 1101412.
Symphony No 3 Op 33 1971. Recorded Panton PA 110349.
Symphony No 4 Op 34 1972. Recorded Supraphon SU 1101784.
Concerto for Trumpet and Orchestra Op 36 1973. Recorded Supraphon SU 1192035.
Concerto for Harpsichord and String Orchestra Op 42 1975. Recorded Supraphon SU 14102755.
Symphony No 5 Op 43 1976. Recorded Panton PA 8110126.
Concerto No 2 for Violin and Orchestra Op 49 1978. Recorded Supraphon SU 1103035.
Two Worlds Op 54 (ballet suite) 1980. Recorded Supraphon SU 11193210.
Tristium Op 56 (concertant fantasy; viola, string orchestra) 1981.
Fable Op 59 (chamber orchestra) 1983.
Concertino Op 61 (bassoon, winds) 1983.
Concerto No 2 for Piano and Winds Op 64 1985.
Diptych Op 66 (strings) 1987.

Chamber/instrumental:

Sonata No 1 Op 2 (piano) 1947.
Sonata No 2 Op 4 (piano) 1948.
String Quartet No 1 Op 6 1949.
Divertimento Op 10 (wind quintet) 1952. Recorded Supraphon SU 5484.
Bagpiper Suite Op 11 (oboe, piano) 1953.
Nonet No 1 "Classical" Op 13 1956.
String Quartet No 2 Op 19 1962. Recorded Supraphon SU 58855.
Six Two-Voice Canon Inventions Op 20 (harpsichord) 1962. Recorded Supraphon SU 11121706.
Symphonic Fresco Op 22 (organ) 1963.
Accents Op 25 (cycle of piano expression etudes) 1967. Recorded Supraphon SU 0190557.
Small Chamber Music Op 27 (wind quintet) 1967. Recorded Supraphon SU 11111426.
Sonata Op 28 (violin, harpsichord) 1967. Recorded Supraphon SU 11121706.
Sonata Op 29 (cello, piano) 1968. Recorded Panton PA 110490.
Sonata Op 30 (clarinet, piano) 1969. Recorded Panton PA 110231.
Variations Op 31 (horn, piano) 1969. Recorded Supraphon SU 1191053.
Sonata Op 32 (trombone, piano) 1970. Recorded Supraphon SU 1191398.
Three Pieces Op 33 (flute) 1973. Recorded Panton PA 110439.
Trio Op 35 (violin, cello, piano) 1974. Recorded Supraphon SU 11121706.
Intrata, Aria e Toccata Op 41 (piano) 1975.
Nonet No 2 "Homage to Nature" Op 44 1975. Recorded Supraphon SU 81110097.
Reminiscences Op 46 (guitar) 1977.
String Quartet No 3 Op 48 1977.
Spring Whistles Op 50 (wind octet) 1979. Recorded Panton PA 11192736.
Three Polkas Op 52 (piano) 1979. Recorded Supraphon SU 11192934.
Aquarelles Op 53 (harpsichord) 1979.
Suite Op 55 (clarinet, piano) 1981.
Sonata No 3 Op 57 (piano) 1982. Recorded Supraphon SU 11193549.
Sonata Op 58 (violin, piano) 1982.
String Quartet No 4 "Ad Honorem J.S.B." Op 62 1984.
String Quartet No 5 Op 63 1984.
Duettino Op 67 (violin, cello) 1987.
String Quartet No 6 Op 68 1987.

Vocal/choral:

Birds' Marriages Op 5 (high voice, piano; folk verse) 1949.
Five Romantic Songs to Words by R.M. Rilke Op 38 (high voice, strings) 1973. Recorded Supraphon SU 11122455.
Singing a Song Op 40 (2- and 3-part canon choruses for children; Hrubín) 1974.
The War Op 45 (chamber cantata for mixed chorus, dulcimer, flute; folk verse) 1977.
Three Children's Choruses Op 47 (with piano) 1978.
The Dawn Op 51 (unaccompanied mixed chorus; Sefl) 1979. Recorded Panton PA 81120190.
The Autumn Op 60 (unaccompanied mixed chorus; Halas) 1984.
Canticum canticorum Op 65 (contralto, tenor, mixed chorus, chamber orchestra; Vulgate) 1986.

Other:

Two Worlds Op 54 (ballet to Lewis Carroll's *Alice in Wonderland*) 1980–1. Recorded Supraphon SU 11193210.

* * *

In assessments of his achievement, the perfect craftsmanship of Viktor Kalabis's work is usually emphasised, a view that is confirmed by the predominance of classical forms and genres in his mainly instrumental output. His technical perfection is bound up with his initial training. At conservatory, he was strongly influenced by Igor Stravinsky.

His acceptance and transformation of Stravinsky's neo-classicism is clearly perceptible in the Op 2 *Sonata No 1* for piano, in which a rhythmical beat and motoric motion combine to create a structure on which is constructed a broadly vaulted melody of almost romantic proportions. His immediately subsequent work, the Op 3 Concerto for chamber orchestra, written in homage to the Russian, definitively absorbs his example. It is the second part of this piece, built on the melodic tradition formed by the Czech modification of Stravinsky's style but imaginatively distinct and expressing Kalabis's own ideas, that breaks the bounds of rigorous neo-classicism. Other composers whose influence is evident in Kalabis's development are the late Beethoven and the Bartók of the string quartets. The acknowledgement of Janáček in the Op 27 *Small Chamber Music* for wind quintet is particularly interesting; while the middle Andante is based on pure lines and their colouring by instrumental ornamentation, Janáček's repercussions and instigations are developed in quick outer movements.

While Kalabis found his idiom in neo-classicism and in folklore, the innovations of the Second Viennese School intensified his emphasis on precise technique (especially in counterpoint). His extraordinary technical abilities enabled him to master large-scale forms in a way that assured accessibility as well as gaining the respect of outstanding orchestras and soloists (the Czech Philharmonic, the Staatskapelle Dresden, the violinist Josef Suk and the French trumpeter Maurice André all responded strongly to his work). The Fifth Symphony was composed for and performed on the occasion of the 50th anniversary of the Czechoslovak Radio Symphony Orchestra; its concise, one-movement form, internally differentiated and highly communicative, represents Kalabis's response to the deep impression that Michelangelo's best works have made on him.

A significant body of Kalabis's work is constituted by his compositions for harpsichord, dedicated to his wife Zuzana Růžičková; the instrument suits his neo-classical orientation and his writing for it represents significant progress in formulating a new stylistics.

The quality of Kalabis's vocal compositions (which are by no means numerous) is suggested by the interest outstanding singers and choirs have shown in his work; the *Five Romantic Love Songs*, set after Rilke, was recorded by Ernst Häfliger, while the well-known Gachlinger Kantorei led by Helmuth Rilling commissioned the *Canticum canticorum* for alto, tenor, mixed chorus and chamber orchestra. In his ballet *Two Worlds*, based on Lewis Carroll's *Alice in Wonderland*, Kalabis wanted to express the book's universal, allegoric significance: the difficulty of establishing relations between individuals and between individuals and the world.

What is distinctive about Kalabis's music is his ability to arrange musical material objectively in space and time and to charge it with almost romantic emotional force. The two sides of his creative nature influence and correct one another and it is this polarity which forms the basis of his individuality.

—Jan Dehner

KANCHELI, Giya. Georgian. Born in Tbilisi, 10 August 1935. Educated at Georgian State Conservatory, Tbilisi (composition under I.I. Tuskiya), 1959–63. Married Jikia Valentina, October 1967; 1 son and 1 daughter. Teacher of music, Georgian State Conservatory, from 1970; musical consultant, Rustaveli Theatre, Tbilisi, since 1971; first secretary, Care Union of Georgian Composers, Tbilisi, 1984–90; secretary, Care Union of Soviet Composers, Moscow, since 1986. Recipient: State Prize, Soviet Union, 1976; State Prize, Georgia, 1981. Mailing address: 26th of May Street 6, 380064 Tbilisi, Georgia.

Publishers: Hans Sikorski, Hamburg; Sovetskii kompozitor, Moscow; G. Schirmer, New York.

Symphonies/orchestral:

Concerto for Orchestra 1962; first performed Tbilisi, 1963.
Largo and Allegro (string orchestra, piano, kettledrums) 1963; first performed Tbilisi, 1963.
Symphony No 1 1967; first performed Tbilisi, 1968. Recorded Melodia C10 05979-80.
Symphony No 2: Chants 1970; first performed Tbilisi, 1970.
Symphony No 3 1973; first performed Tbilisi, 1973. Recorded Melodia C10 01084 3000; Olympia OCD401.
Symphony No 4 1975; first performed Tbilisi, 1975. Recorded Melodia 33C10 12551; Panton 110582.
Symphony No 5 1977; first performed Tbilisi, 1978. Recorded Melodia 33C10 12552; MFCD 896.
Symphony No 6 1979, revised 1980; first performed Tbilisi, 1980; revised version first performed Leipzig, 1981. Recorded Melodia C10 20843 000; Olympia OCD 401.
Symphony No 7: Epilogue 1985; first performed Prague, 1986.
Liturgy (viola, large orchestra) 1989; first performed Berlin, 1990.
Morning Prayers (chamber orchestra; part I of cycle *Life Without Christmas*) 1990; first performed London, 1990.
Midday Prayers (clarinet, chamber orchestra; part II of cycle *Life Without Christmas*) 1990.

Vocal/choral:

Bright Sorrow (2 boy soloists, boys' chorus, symphony orchestra; Shakespeare, Goethe, Tabizde, Pushkin) 1985; first performed Leipzig, 1985. Recorded col legno 0647286; Melodia C10 26605 006.

Opera/dramatic:

The Pranks of Hanum (musical comedy) 1973.
Music for the Living (pageant opera in collaboration with Robert Strua) 1984; first performed Tbilisi, 1984.

Other:

Khanuma (theatre music to play by Tsagareli) 1968; first performed Tbilisi, 1968.
The Caucasian Chalk Circle (incidental music to Brecht) 1975; first performed Tbilisi, 1975.
Easy Money (incidental music to Ostrovsky) 1979; first performed Dusseldorf, 1979.
Richard III (incidental music to Shakespeare) 1979; first performed Tbilisi, 1979.
As You Like It (incidental music to Shakespeare) 1980; first performed Dusseldorf, 1980.
King Lear (incidental music to Shakespeare) 1987; first performed Tbilisi, 1987.

Film scores: *Don't Grieve*, 1969; *The Cranks*, 1974; *Mimino*, 1977; *The Passport*, 1990.

PUBLICATIONS

On Kancheli: Givi Ordzonikidze, "Formation", in *Sovetskaia Muzika*, 10, 1976; Inna Barsaova, "Musical Dramaturgy in GK's *Symphony No 4*", in *Musikalni Sovremennik*, 5, 1984; Nona Shakhnazarova and Grigori Golovinski, (interview) in *New Life and Traditions in Soviet Music*, Moscow, 1989; Natalia Zeifas, "Chants About the Music of GK", Moscow, 1991.

* * *

Giya Kancheli is undoubtedly the most important living Georgian composer. His distinctive music has won a wide following in recent years, often far from his native land. This fact is the odder because it is founded on a fairly small output of pieces written over a long period of time (although, recently, this composer has been forced to step up his rate of production to meet a large number of commissions from Western performers).

At the heart of Kancheli's output lies his series of seven symphonies. These, the composer tells us, had from long ago been intended to be a series of six. Pressure from supporters of his music abroad persuaded him to add a seventh to the canon.

Kancheli's symphonies are certainly not symphonies in the ordinary sense of that word. Nor indeed do they fit easily into the standard forms favoured by the Union of Composers. For the most part they are one-movement works, often with unusual elements in the orchestration and cast in forms which have almost nothing to do with familiar traditions. They are also filled with images, intonational and ritual, that are clearly designed to provoke strong feelings of association in the minds of a native Georgian audience. To those less familiar with the amazing richness of Georgian folk music (and, in particular, with the music of the high mountain region of Svaneti) as well as with the sonorous Byzantine music of the Georgian church, all these characteristics and associations in Kancheli's music must run the risk of remaining on the level of alluring exoticism.

Kancheli's path to his highly recognisable style has not been quite the same as that of other Soviet composers of his generation. Others have, like him, arrived at a state of great simplicity, a state which depends heavily on the evocative power of certain tonal procedures closely associated with various musics of the past. One need only think of Arvo Part, Valentin Silvestrov or even, in certain works, Alfred Schnittke. But these men all arrived at their new styles after an early baptism in the long suppressed fire of modernism—

they proceeded from complexity to simplicity, as it were. Kancheli never really went through that phase of interest in the devices and desires of Western modernism. After a conventional education in the rhetoric and techniques of official Soviet music, he passed directly to what he wanted to say, to a language which is, paradoxically, at once eclectic and pared down.

No doubt part of Kancheli's advantage lay in his being a Georgian. Georgia, proud and independent for centuries, still preserves a certain isolation within the Russian Empire; now at this time, of course, it is once again seeking complete freedom from Russia. In Kancheli's music one may feel much the same attitude towards the Russian and indeed the wider European musical tradition as one may find in the political history of the composer's country. The stylistic and technical contexts and developments that define the meaning of European music for Europeans, and which, for Russians, carry another meaning as of something from which they have been brutally shut out, are, for a Georgian, almost irrelevant. Shut within Georgia's obsessional passion to define itself in terms of itself, a Georgian composer almost inevitably must come to see the available imagery of Europe, whether northern or southern, old or new, as simply that, available for use, regardless of what it may have meant originally.

It is a tribute to the strength of Kancheli's imagination that from the hotch-potch of sources from which he derives his music—the operatic cadences of middle-period Verdi, the ornaments of Bach, the magic effects of Rimsky-Korsakov, as well as a whole host of native Georgian idioms nearer to him—he has created a language of his own, unified, processional and, above all, movingly affirmative.

Perhaps part of the key to his success lies in the sheer simplicity of his invented forms, and of the bright clear imagery with which he defines and dramatises them. This imagery often takes the form almost of a choric quotation, itself defined not only by pitch and rhythm and instrumentation, but also by style. In the Third Symphony, for example, this takes the form of an imitation Svaneti funeral lament, sung by a solo voice, and usually quite separate from the orchestra. In the Fifth, we hear a fragment of pseudo-18th-century harpsichord music performing much the same function, while in the Sixth Symphony it is four solo violas who take on this role, at once standing outside the sudden violence of the orchestra and at the same time holding that violence together in a greater atmosphere of calm.

Calm is perhaps this composer's most distinctive attitude. It is one that finds powerful expression in two recent works. One is the pageant-opera Kancheli wrote with the famous theatre director, Robert Strua, *Music for the Living*. This tells a tale of the aftermath of war and is written in four languages including ancient Sumerian. The other work is the oratorio in memory of the victims of World War II, *Bright Sorrow*. The simplicity and emotional directness of this music is, maybe, deeply Georgian, but there is no doubt that it can make a powerful appeal also to those who live far from the Caucasus.

—Gerard McBurney

KANG Sukhi (Kang Sŏkhŭi). Korean. Born in Seoul, 22 October 1934. Educated at Seoul National University College of Music, 1955–60; Stadtliche Hochschule für Musik, Berlin, 1970–1; Technische Universitat für Musik, Berlin, 1971–5. Served in Korean land forces, 1957–9. Married (1) Cho Pyŏngok, 9 December 1961, 2 sons; (2) Han Okhŭi, 21 August 1976, 1 son. Artistic director, Pan Music Festival, Seoul, since 1969; president, International Society for Contemporary Music, Korean section, since 1972; editor, *Konggan* [Space] magazine, Seoul, since 1976; artistic member, electronic studio, Technische Universitat, Berlin, 1980–2; professor of composition, since 1982, and chair, Department of Composition, 1987–91, Seoul National University College of Music; co-organizer, Inventionen experimental music festival, Berlin, 1982–3; vice-president, International Society of Contemporary Music, Unesco, Paris, 1984–90; music editor, *Arts and Criticism* magazine, Seoul, 1987–8; music director, closing ceremony of 24th Olympiad, Seoul, 1988; board member, Kim Sugŭn Culture Foundation, since 1988, and Wookyung Culture Foundation, since 1989; honorary adviser, Alban Berg Association, Japan, since 1989. Recipient: Unesco International Rostrum of Composers selection, 1976; Korean National Ministry of Culture composer's prize, 1978; Korean National Presidential composer's prize, 1979; film music prize of *Korea Daily News* film and theatre competition, 1979; Ministry of Culture Daejong Movie Competition, film music prize, 1979; *Nong* (for flute and piano) selected "Work of Exceptional Merit between 1960–80 in the world", American Flute Association, 1980; Music Pen Club of Korea "Best Musician of the Month", 1984; Music Association of Korea "Best Musician of the Year", 1989. Mailing address: 19–302 Un-ma Apt, Daechi-dong, Kangman-ku, Seoul; or College of Music, Seoul National University, Kwanak-ku, Seoul, Korea.

Publishers: Edition Modern, Munich; Breitkopf und Hartel, Wiesbaden; Edition Sonoton, Munich; Edition Gravis, Waldschwalbach.

Symphonies/orchestral:

Generation '69 1969; first performed Seoul, 24 March 1969.
Reflexionen 1975; first performed Seoul, 9 October 1975. Recorded WDR Production.
Catena 1975; first performed Solingen, 31 May 1975.
Dalha 1978; first performed Seoul, 14 September 1978. Recorded Seoul Record.
Mega-Melos 1980; first performed Berlin, 19 September 1980. Recorded SFB Production radio.
Mutation Perpetua (24 players, tape) 1982; first performed Vienna, 5 November 1982.
Symphonic Requiem 1983; first performed Seoul, 7 November 1983. Recorded KBS Production.
Successions 1985; first performed Berlin, 15 June 1985.
Ch'uit'ahyang (Korean traditional orchestra) 1987; first performed Seoul, 23 June 1987.
Prelude "Gala" 1989; first performed Seoul, 31 March 1989.

Chamber/instrumental:

Piano Sketch No 2 1966; first performed Seoul, 9 December 1966.
Nirmanakaya (cello, piano, percussion) 1969; first performed Seoul, 5 September 1969.
Roundtone (flute, oboe, clarinet, viola, cello, vibraphone, percussion) 1969; first performed Seoul, 9 September 1969.
Apex (piano) 1972; first performed Bremen, 1 July 1972.
Parodie (flute, organ) 1972; first performed Berlin, 13 December 1972.
Nong (flute, piano) 1973; first performed Berlin, 1 March

1973. Recorded SFB Production.
Kleines Stück (oboe, cello, harp) 1973; first performed Berlin, 6 March 1973.
Strukturen (4 cellos) 1973; first performed Berlin, 19 June 1973.
Banya (flute, oboe, clarinet, tuba, violin, cello, piano, percussion) 1974; first performed Berlin, 6 March 1974.
Metamorphosen (flute, string quartet) 1974; first performed Tokyo, 17 July 1974. Recorded Da Camera Magna.
Dialog (viola, piano) 1976; first performed Berlin, 23 February 1976. Recorded SKC.
Myung (4 huns, taekum, kayagŭm, tam-tam) 1976; first performed Seoul, May 1976.
Dala (Parodie Waltz) (clarinet, trombone, cello, piano, tape) 1980; first performed Warsaw, 22 September 1980.
Bronzenzeit / The Bronze Age (percussionist, tape) 1980; first performed Cologne, 5 August 1980.
Aniri Ia / Ib (guitar) 1981; first performed 1 April 1981.
Manpa (flute, flute orchestra) 1982; first performed Berlin, 31 March 1982. Recorded Sonoton LC 6542.
Thal (contrabass flute) 1983; first performed Berlin, 8 April 1983. Recorded Sonoton LC 6542.
Inventio (piano, tape) 1984; first performed Berlin, 18 February 1984. Recorded Edition RZ LC 8864.
String Quartet No 1 1986; first performed Saarbrucken, 29 May 1986.
Sonatebach (piano) 1986; first performed Seoul, 28 November 1986.
Aniri IV (harp) 1987; first performed Vienna, 23 May 1987.

Vocal / choral:

Lyebul (male voice, male chorus, 30 percussionists) 1969; first performed Seoul, 20 November 1969.
Buru (female voice, flute, clarinet, piano, 2 percussionists) 1976; first performed Berlin, 7 October 1976. Recorded Jigu Records.
Cantata "Yong-bi" (3 soloists, 2 mixed choirs, orchestra) 1978; first performed Seoul, 21 April 1978.
Vision (female voice, guitar, tape) 1978; first performed Seoul, 21 April 1978.
Aniri II (female voice, tape) 1983; first performed Berlin, 13 February 1983.
Aniri III (female voice) 1984; first performed Berlin, February 1984.
Cantata "The Rite of Sun" (soloists, mixed choir, orchestra) 1985; first performed Seoul, 3 October 1985.

Other:

The Feast of 'id (electronic) 1966; first performed Seoul, 9 December 1966.
Mosaico (electronic) 1981; first performed Berlin, 7 April 1981. Recorded Sonoton LC 6542.
Klangspuren (electronic) 1981; first performed Berlin, 7 April 1981. Recorded Sonoton LC 6542.
Odysse (musique concrète) 1984; first performed Berlin, 5 September 1984.
Penthesilea (music theatre) 1986; first performed Berlin, 2 March 1986. Recorded WDR Cologne.
Lung (Dragon) (animated film with soundtrack) 1986; first performed Seoul, 15 October 1986.
Feng-hwang (Phoenix) (animated film with computer soundtrack) 1988; first performed Berlin, 21 August 1988.
Prometheus's Arrival (torch music for 24th Olympiad) 1988; first performed Seoul, 15 September 1988. Recorded on cassette, 24th Olympic Games Committee, Korea.

PUBLICATIONS

By Kang: "Ŏje onŭl maeil ŭmakhaenbgsawa han'guk ŭi ŭmak p'ungt'o", in *Konggan / Space*, December 1975; "T'ŭkchip ŭmak ŭi makp'ajie sŏn hyŏndae ŭmak", in *Konggan / Space*, October 1976; "Kim Chŏngja tŏkch'anghoe", in *Wŏlgan*, 1976–7; *In Search of the Music of the World*, Seoul, 1979; "Ch'angjo ŭi yurinŭl kobalhanda", in *Ŭmak Pang / Music Room*, December 1979; "Pak tonguk t'aakki tokchuhoe", in *Piano ŭmak / Piano Music*, 6(9), 1982; "Ttajigo karigo che 10 hoe p'an ŭmakche", in *Madang / Performance Space*, November 1982; "Chŏnt'onggwa hyŏndaerul innŭn p'ungt'-ogidae", in *Kaeksŏk / Auditorium*, January 1985; "Munhwa ollimp'ik hyanghan toyak ŭi hae", in *Ŭmak tonga / East Asian Music*, 1, 1987; "Chujebalp'yo", in *Ch'angakhoe / Vocal Music*, May 1988; also articles in *Konggan*, *Umak Pang*, *Kaeksok*, *Ch'angakhoe*, 1975–88.

On Kang: Pak Yonggu, "Chakkaron—KS", in *Konggan / Space*, November 1984; Sŏn Kwangju, "Berlin segye yesulje han'guk ch'amga ŭi chuyŏk—KS", in *Ŭmak tonga*, July 1985; Yi Kangsuk, "KS—wa 4 myŏng", in *Han'guk ilbo / Korean Daily News*, 18 December 1986; "Pan Music Leader—KS", in *Koreana*, February 1988; "Composer's Portrait—KS", Perspective Composer's Group, Seoul, 1990.

Kang Sukhi comments:

Recently I have heard the sounds of stone. One day I was visiting Haein temple. While walking along a stream in a nearby valley, I heard something totally new. It was not the sound of flowing and shimmering water, but came glistening from the stream bed. It was the sound of variously shaped large and small pebbles. This mysterious—perhaps imagined—sound spread around me, being modulated by everything it came into contact with. It was one with my heartbeat.

Beside the path I was walking along was red cherry blossom. The blossom shone in a rainbow of colours as it reflected the sun. Stones in the blossom's shade resonated dark and gloomy deep in the earth. Stones lit in the patches of sunlight filtered through the blossom and gave metallic clangs: *chaeng*.

Since then I have listened to all objects. Around Haen temple few loud sounds disturb the peace. At a great temple in Kyongju, the capital of the ancient Shilla kingdom, there are two pagodas. One resounds like a fairy. The other remains silent, like an expressionless old monk. The nearby stone Buddha who looks out to sea towards Japan gives off sound, but never mutters a word. I have been attracted to a story in which an old monk preached to stones. What could the story mean?

In Spring 1980, I was commissioned by WDR Cologne to write a piece for percussion and electronic sounds. I concentrated on metallic sounds and chose *The Bronze Age (Bronzenzeit)* as my title. From then on, all metallic things—from tiny bells to large gongs—seem to generate imaginary sound worlds for me. In the bronze instruments excavated in China, for example, I hear the delicate sounds produced during manufacture; pressing, beating and polishing.

Yet again, when I look at paintings, new sound worlds open up. One painting generated the sound of a river flowing; another offered a mysterious world of clouds that echoed as they floated away.

Too many fantastic, mysterious sounds came to me. I could bear it no longer, so began to work through them one by one in my subsequent compositions.

* * *

Kang Sukhi's sheer energy is amazing. Since 1969 he has directed the Pan Music Festival, the Korean showcase for contemporary music. Since moving to Germany for a time beginning in 1970—a result of studying informally under Isang Yun as the latter recovered in a Seoul hospital from imprisonment—he has regularly visited Europe, composing at the electronic studios of Berlin Technical University and WDR Cologne. In 1968 he was given two years to live, but in 1990 completed five years as vice-president of the International Society for Contemporary Music.

Kang's music, like the Pan Music Festival, is in many ways eclectic. He started to compose in a newly industrializing Korea where few had studied abroad or knew much about contemporary music. He helped organize the first concerts of the music of Messiaen and Cage, and composed the first Korean electronic music (on primitive equipment), *The Feast of 'id*. Prior to 1970 his output appears to be slightly imitative, experimenting with others' styles rather than developing his own. He left for Germany with a reputation for being reactionary, established not least because of the scandal of Paik Nam June's *Sex Music*, written for Kang's first Pan Festival and performed in a country which upheld Victorian morality.

Five years' European study, initially under Boris Blacher, was crowned with the "rationalistic", highly-structured orchestral piece *Catena*. From Europe Kang learned much about musical construction; indeed many of his forms are virtually architectural (for a good example, see *Mosaico*), and it is no surprise to learn that for 15 years he has been music editor for an architectural magazine, *Konggan* [Space]. In Europe, however, he also learned to be Korean, as demonstrated by *Nong*, for example. Written for flute and piano, the piece takes its title from the Korean term for ornamentation, *nonghyŏn*. In traditional Korean music, ornaments decorate slow monodic lines; in ensembles, ornaments create heterophony. In *Nong*, Kang seeks to move melodic tones into the background until only fragments of ornaments remain. Starting from an initial high A played monotonously by the two instruments, the effect is of fleeting glissandi, of short "foamy" decorations.

Nong gave rise to a sequence of chamber pieces, including three specifically for flute: *Metamorphosen, Manpa* and *Thal*. What starts as an exercise in *Metamorphosen*—harsh breathing moving towards smooth musical tones—becomes integral to the plot of *Manpa*. The latter interprets an ancient legend about the invention of the Korean bamboo flute, as the *Manp'ashik chŏt*, the "flute to calm 10,000 waves". As the solo flute speaks, so the waves and wind (represented by an ensemble of 14 flutes) are calm; as the solo pauses, so the ensemble increases in intensity; flutter-tonguing, harmonics and breath tones litter the texture as *Manpa* builds to complex chords that echo the Asian mouth-organ. Tension rises until the soloist proclaims his authority.

In 1976 the Berlin Meta Musik Festival commissioned from Kang a piece that was to be both Eastern and Western. Kang, in *Buru*, consequently turned to Korean Buddhist philosophy and shamanism, finally crafting a 25-measure tune in the southwestern tritonic folksong mode of *kyemyŏnjo*. A singer intones the melody—A, C, E, with semitone acciaccaturas. When the first percussionist joins, it is with an image of a shaman's bell tree; when the second percussionist is added, we hear a gong pattern redolent of shaman rituals. Yet the rhythm comes from Buddhist chanting. *Dalha*, an American commission for an orchestral piece based on Korean music, continues in the same vein. Kang chose the court piece *Sujech'ŏn* as his basis and, in struggling to accommodate the old with the new, favoured strident sound blocks and high ornamentation that clearly echoed court ensembles.

It would be a mistake to label Kang as Korean or Western, for the distinction hardly concerns him. His pieces are not stylistically consistent, not least since he approaches each as a new challenge. Yet Kang as the rationalist remains, as was apparent most recently in his computer music for the 1988 Olympics—music which, in keeping with his reputation, was almost rejected. And Kang as the Korean remains strong, witnessed by titles as much as fleeting lines which once derived from traditional ornamentation patterns.

—Keith Howard

KAPYRIN, Dmitri. Russian. Born in Moscow, 28 February 1960. Educated at Musical School, Moscow, 1970–5; Music College, Moscow (composition under Viktor Egorov), 1975–9; Lvov Conservatory, Western Ukraine (composition under Leshek Mazepa), 1979–84. Married Lidia Volitowitch, 1 November 1986; 1 son. Military band arranger during national service, 1984–6; teacher at music studio, Junost House of Culture, Moscow, since 1986. Mailing address: Angazskaya st.37/18, kv.79, Moscow 127412, U.S.S.R.

Publisher: Sovetskii kompozitor, Moscow.

Symphonies/orchestral:

Symphony Op 3 1984; first performed Lvov, 1984.
Music for Harp, String Orchestra and Bells Op 5 1986.
Dreams Op 12 1990.

Chamber/instrumental:

Sonata Op 1 (viola, piano) 1983; first performed Lvov, 1983.
Music for String Quartet Op 2 1983; first performed Lvov, 1983.
Three Pieces Op 4 (harp) 1985.
Conditions Op 6 (piano) 1987; first performed London, 1989.
Evening Music Op 7 (guitar) 1987; first performed Lvov, 1989.
An Approach to Jupiter Op 9 (violin, viola, cello, piano) 1988; first performed Lvov, 1989.
Sonata Op 10 (clarinet, piano) 1988; first performed Vozonezh, 1989.
And a Light Through Foliage Op 11 (flute, cello, piano) 1989.
Sounds and Voices Op 13 (flute, clarinet, violin, vibraphone, harp, piano) 1990.
Sotto voce Op 14 (piano) 1991.

Vocal/choral:

Three Songs by F. Tyutchev Op 8 (baritone, piano) 1987.

Dmitri Kapyrin comments:

I believe that with the pieces written after 1986, I have reached a new aesthetic and stylistic stage in my work. The basic structure of these pieces is created as a rule by the interaction of harmonies of limited transposition (usually three transpositions of the harmony of tone–semi-tone, with certain modifications); apparently tonal formations, which are treated as modes (which is what they are in essence); and free twelve-tone writing, which is also treated as harmony.

The employment of "microthematism" has played an important role in certain recent compositions. The number of microthemes has varied between five and 10 (sometimes even more) in each piece. Some of them—those in the foreground—contain the basic intonational load of the piece, while others play a more subordinate role. But both constitute an important unifying means, and permit the attainment of greater structural and intonational wholeness, pervading the entire musical fabric on horizontal and vertical planes and endlessly modifying and replacing each other.

* * *

It is tempting to attach more than incidental significance to the fact that Dmitri Kapyrin's first acknowledged works date from the end of his military service in 1986, a moment which coincides with a marked liberalisation in Soviet culture. Most of the pieces written before that time he now considers to have been withdrawn, though he has assigned his first three opus numbers to earlier work (a viola sonata, a non-canonical string quartet and a symphony) which he considers worth preserving. Though a Muscovite, Kapyrin's musical education was carried out in relative isolation at the Lvov Conservatory in the Western Ukraine, and though he is not self-consciously an outsider, he has kept somewhat apart from the debates and fashions which have divided younger composers in Moscow and Leningrad.

His technique veers towards minimalism and his compositions resemble a densely worked tapestry in which threads of strikingly different hue and tension are interwoven, sometimes dominating the foreground, sometimes disappearing for substantial periods into a supporting background. The technique is most obvious in the microthematicism that has emerged in his work since about 1988. By this means, Kapyrin is able to organize a freely determined group of themes into a viable and self-supporting musical fabric which is remarkably difficult to identify stylistically. If the warp of the music is essentially harmonic and tonal, with a strong modal component and a particular emphasis on modes of limited transposition, the weft is unmistakably derived from twelve-tone writing (in which Kapyrin had a thorough if unorthodox grounding). Typically, though, Kapyrin does not use serial passages merely for contrast or for intonational emphasis; nor does his work ever suggest a irresoluble conflict between tonal and non-tonal elements. Like his near-contemporary Aleksandr Gugel, a composer who has embraced harmony and melody wholeheartedly, Kapyrin is not interested in dramatising conflict. As such, his work is remarkably static and "cool". The orchestral piece *Dreams* has an attractive oneiric logic that precisely depends on its not resolving any of its constituent juxtapositions; these do genuinely reflect the simultaneous logic/illogic of dream imagery and they are intended to be accepted on their own terms.

Kapyrin's structural skill is supported by his talent as an instrumentator. The fine orchestral *Music* for harp, bells and strings is a remarkable exercise in sonority and one of the finest orchestral works by a young Russian. Among his chamber works *An Approach to Jupiter*, though to some extent intended as a programme piece, is also a brilliant exercise in instrumental colour. Rather more densely worked, *Sounds and Voices* is perhaps his finest ensemble work to date, bringing together a tremendous amount of thematic material and managing to make it sound coherent and highly unified rather than merely discursive or experimental; again, the tone colours are brilliantly handled, transcending all risk of superficial prettiness.

By his own accounting, Kapyrin has only just entered the second half of his first decade as a professional composer. It is a more than auspicious debut.

—Ivan Shearer

KARAYEV, Faraj. Azerbaijani. Born in Baku, U.S.S.R., 19 December 1943. Educated at Baku State Conservatory, 1961–6, 1969–71, M.A., 1966, Ph.D., 1971. Married Inna Karayev in 1970; 2 children. Teacher of music theory, Music School, Baku, 1961–6; assistant professor, 1966–80, and professor, since 1980, Baku State Conservatory. Recipient: Honoured Artist, 1982. Mailing address: Triokhprudny per. 11/13, Apt. 114, Moscow 103001, U.S.S.R.

Publishers: Sovetskii kompozitor, Moscow; Sikorsky, Hamburg; Schirmer.

Symphonies/orchestral:

Concerto grosso 1967; first performed Baku, 1967.
Tristessa II (symphonic and chamber orchestra) 1980.
Tristessa I (chamber orchestra) 1982; first performed Baku, 8 February 1982. Recorded Melodia N C10 28337 002.
I Said Farewell to Mozart on Carl's Bridge in Prague 1983; first performed Erevan, May 1983.
1791 (serenade for symphony orchestra) 1984; first performed Moscow, April 1984. Recorded Melodia N C10 22547.
Four Postludes 1989.
The (Moz)art of Elite 1990.

Chamber/instrumental:

Sonata for Two Performers (3 pianos, bells, vibraphone, tape) 1976; first performed Baku, February 1977. Recorded Melodia N C10 15175 76.
In memoriam (string quartet) 1987; first performed Moscow, December 1988.
A Crumb of Music for George Crumb (flute, oboe, clarinet, bassoon, horn, trumpet, trombone) 1987; first performed Lugano, Switzerland, October 1987.
TERMINUS (cello) 1988; first performed Bonn, September 1989.
Chamber Concerto (wind quintet) 1988.
Small Music of the Sad Night (flute, clarinet, guitar, mandolin/guitar, harp, violin, viola, double bass) 1989; first performed Amsterdam, June 1989.
Alla nostalgia (flute, clarinet, horn, violin, viola, cello) 1989; first performed Bern, Switzerland, January 1990.
Postludio (piano) 1990.
Waiting for Godot (bassoon, trombone, cello, double bass soloists, with ensemble or chamber orchestra) 1990.

Vocal/choral:

Journey to Love (soprano, flute, clarinet, bells, vibraphone, piano, prepared piano, jazz quartet [electric piano, electric guitar, bass guitar, drums], tape, strings) 1987–8.

Other:

The Shadows of Kobystan (ballet) 1969; first performed Baku, 1969. Recorded Melodia 33D 027272.
Kaleidoscope (ballet) 1970; first performed Baku, 1970.

PUBLICATIONS

By Karayev: collaboration on "Kara Karayev: Soviet Composer", Moscow, 1978.

On Karayev: R. Fakhradova, "FK", in *Music of the Transcaucasus*, Baku, 1975; Oleg Felzer and A. Bretanitskaya, "FK", in *Composers of the Soviet Republics*, 5, 1986; Alexander Ivashkin, "FK", in *Music in the USSR*, 10–12, 1987; Hannelore Gerlach, "Kara Karayev: Festival Music of XX Century", in *Musik und Gesellschaft*, 4, 1988; Tatyana Porwoll, "New Music in Azerbaijan", in *MusikTexte*, 26, 1988.

Faraj Karayev comments:

All art, and thus all music, is a form of autobiography. Music is written by those who cannot bear to see it written by another. A composer is not capable of being content with his own music. Music is unending: the composer must just keep on going.

The only true criterion for the criticism of music is a desire to be its creator. Happy is the man able to beat out his own time.

One can never keep one's own creation in perspective: the only people who compose are those with enough strength of mind to leave this pointless activity alone.

All music is beautifully written.

* * *

Faraj Karayev is the son and disciple of the renowned composer Kara Karayev, the founder of the Azerbaijan school of composers.

Faraj Karayev first became known after the appearance of the ballets *The Shadows of Kobystan*, his first composition performed in Europe, and *Kaleidoscope*. However, the genesis of Karayev's artistic personality occurred a few years later and is marked by the composition of the *Sonata for Two Performers*.

His early works reflect a diligent effort to assimilate the technique of the musical titans of the 20th century, especially Stravinsky and Webern. In his mature compositions the traces of influence of Ligeti and Lutosławski are detectable.

Karayev's music appeals, to a large extent, to the listener's musical knowledge. The composer uses complex "secondary" signs-allusions—hints being more frequent than direct quotations—derived from the musical sources that in one way or another stimulated the evolution of his own style. Such allusions, being perfectly fused into the text, expand the composition's associative gamut, its socio-cultural scope, registering symbolic-emotional parallels to the "original" pattern.

Karayev consistently avoids any established forms and genre generalizations associated with classical music. However, despite the variety of the titles and the multiplicity of the performing staves of his works, most of them are, in essence, symphonies.

His music is devoid of any novelistic "narrativity"; the composer shuns contrasts within a movement. Rather, each movement is a reflection of a facet of the protagonist's inner world, an image of his spiritual condition.

The basis of the fabric of Karayev's compositions is formed by meticulously selected, extended complexes, occasionally consisting of one or two chords, or even one or two notes (e.g., the string quartet *In memoriam*). These complexes are arranged, as a rule, by a limited and controlled aleatory.

Karayev's music is replete with the dynamic marks PP, PPP, PPPP, niente, quasi niente. This dearth of sound is dualistic: it is the serene silence of repose, contemplation, light and love, but it is also the silence of intensive inner tension, very gradually, almost imperceptibly giving rise to the sensation of the tragic. The tragic mode suffuses all of the composer's mature compositions; their predominant themes are sadness, sorrow, *Weltschmertz*. This is reflected in the choice of subjects and in the titles of the compositions: *Tristessa* (Farewell Symphony to the Father's Memory), *Small Music of the Sad Night, I Said Farewell to Mozart . . .*, *A Crumb of Music for George Crumb*, inspired by Emily Dickinson's poem "If I shouldn't be alive".

The *moto* of his symphonic conceptions emphasize the meaninglessness of motion, which is usually perceived by us as "vanitas vanitorum" and acquires a negative connotation.

One of the hallmarks of Karayev's style is the concretization of the compositional idea by adding taped extra or para-musical components. They are represented by concrete natural sounds: sea sounds, cries of seagulls, city at night, child's crying, authentic sounds of Azerbaijani folk instruments. "Connatural" to this aspect is another distinguishing feature of his style: pre-imposed theatricalization of performance of his score. In Karayev's instrumental theatre acting personae-instrumentalists (frequently dispersed throughout the hall) whisper, chat and shout, mime, walk about. Such diverse effects, coexisting on a par with purely musical fabric, are synthesized by the composer with astounding naturalness, and help the listener to find orientation in the complex system of musical intonations.

Karayev's ethnic ancestry manifests itself in deep ties to the principles of the Azerbaijani musical thinking, to the aesthetics of folk music, which have been perfectly expressed in the folk professional genre "mugam." The time-dispersed emotional message whose nucleus is the basic modal-characteristic melodic turn (it goes through constant variant transformations, but is always recognizable) is represented in mugam by an extensive type of development. Its predominant characteristic is an immersion into a variety of sound shades in prolonged emotional states. Karayev's music is in many respects similar; developing slowly, without didacticism or declamation, it penetrates, "infects". And just the way in mugam concretization is realized in the text, since Azerbaijani mugam is a vocal-instrumental genre, Karayev's music creates an associative structure of extramusical—visual, concrete, and "secondary-musical"—collage-allusionary signs.

Karayev's music is inspired by a wide range of artistic phenomena: Paleolithic drawings, 19th- and 20th-century poetry, Samuel Beckett's theatre of the absurd, and the music of both Mozart and our contemporaries.

—Oleg Felzer

KARETNIKOV, Nikolai. Russian. Born in Moscow, 28 June 1930. Educated at Central Music School, Moscow, from 1948; Moscow Conservatoire, from 1953. Married Olga

Negkina in 1969; 2 sons. Works banned in Soviet Union and only rarely performed, 1962–84; member, Union of Composers, from 1956; member, Union of Cinematographers, from 1966. Mailing address: Sadovotriumfal'naya, dom 14-12, kv. 37, 103006 Moscow, U.S.S.R.

Publishers: Peters; Sovetskii kompozitor, Moscow.

Symphonies/orchestral:

[2 early symphonies withdrawn]
Symphony No 3 Op 10 1959.
Symphony No 4 Op 17 1964; first performed Prague, 1968.
Concerto for Thirty-Two Winds Op 19 1967.
Chamber Symphony Op 21 1968.

Chamber/instrumental:

Lento Variations Op 11 (piano) 1961.
Sonata Op 16 (violin, piano) 1962; first performed 1982.
String Quartet Op 18 1963.
Two Pieces Op 23 (piano) 1969.
From Shalom Aleikhem Op 27 (concert suite for chamber ensemble) 1986.
Piano Quintet Op 29 1990.

Vocal/choral:

Eight Psalms in Memory of Boris Pasternak Op 24 (male chorus) 1969–89; first performed Moscow, 1989.

Opera:

Till Eulenspiegel Op 26 (Lungia and NK, after de Coster) 1985.
Misteriya apostola Pavla/The Mystery of St Paul Op 28 (Lungin) 1987.

Other:

Vanino Vanina Op 13 (ballet by Vasilev and Kasatkina, after Stendhal) 1961; first performed Moscow 1962.
Kronika Tsakhes po prozvaniyu Tsinnober/The Chornicle of Zaches, Called Zinnobel Op 20 (ballet by Vasilev and Kasatkina, after Hoffmann) 1968; first performed Hannover, 1970.

Film scores: *Beg/Run*; *Skvernyi anekdot/A Rotten Tale* (after Dostoevsky); *Pervossiyane/First Russians*; over 50 others.

Incidental music: *King Lear*; *A Man for All Seasons*; *Macbeth*; *Ten Days Which Shook the World*; over 30 others.

PUBLICATIONS

By Karetnikov: *Temy s variatsiayami/Themes and Variations*, Moscow, 1990, Paris, 1991.

On Karetnikov: Mikhail Tarakanov, "Apologiya nepriznannaya", in *Sovetskaya Muzyka*, 7, 1990.

Nikolai Karetnikov comments:

I am an orthodox Christian. I consider the work of J. S. Bach as the most important to me, as well as the Viennese school (including Wagner) and the "New Viennese School".

* * *

Nikolai Karetnikov was already a well-established young composer in a recognisably orthodox Soviet style when, in the late 1950s, he was swept away by his first encounters with the music of the Second Viennese School. Nearly all his music since then has reflected his unshakeable faith in the central significance of the great Austro-German tradition, from Bach to Webern. In particular much of it reflects the clear influence of Schoenberg, whose early twelve-note works demonstrated the fundamental principle Karetnikov felt he had been looking for. The sense, in a number of these pieces, of their being almost an act of belated Russian homage to the Viennese master, is sharpened by the Schoenbergian opus numbers (Opp 11, 23 and 25) which are assigned to his three strong sets of piano pieces.

Undoubtedly the most impressive of the first fruits of Karetnikov's engagement with dodecaphony was his Fourth Symphony of 1964 (Karetnikov's first two symphonies were student efforts which he now disowns). This five-movement piece powerfully demonstrates the way Karetnikov synthesised the unifying rigour of Schoenberg and a capacity for sparse, but sonorous orchestral writing in the best Soviet traditions. It also illustrates a highly thematic approach to large-scale form, which probably owes most to the mentor of Karetnikov's early years, Shostakovich. This is open-hearted, almost open-air music, worlds away from either the socialist kitsch or the nationalist introspection that were (and still are) the staple of most Soviet orchestral music.

After the vigour and élan of those years, Karetnikov appeared to his contemporaries to fall silent. An enormous output of film music was all that most people heard from him. Partly, this was a result of exterior disapproval of his "Western" interests and loyalties. But it was also because, far from falling silent, Karetnikov had actually embarked on no less than two quite different compositions, both conceived on the largest scale. What both works have in common however is a vigorous moral content, obviously anti-Soviet, as well as several episodes of choral music, liturgical in style, which appear almost identically, except for their words, at critical moments in both works.

One of these compositions is *Till Eulenspiegel*, which the composer has designated a *singspiel*, on account of the separation of the individual musical numbers by speech. Unlike Strauss, whose version of this famous story emphasises the strip-cartoon comedy, Karetnikov has focussed on the most serious and even terrifying aspects of this tale of Flemish resistance against the Spanish, the poverty of Till, the ubiquity of the secret police and their informers, the horror of being burnt at the stake. In other words, Karetnikov has chosen by all the means at his power to stress parallels with the history of the U.S.S.R. in our own time.

Musically *Till Eulenspiegel* is in a multitude of different styles (though all the material is ultimately derived from one twelve-note row), all of which are violently contrasted with one another in such a way as to reflect the equally violent moral and historical confusions of the story. It is worth adding that this opera was embarked upon before Schnittke began his experiments with "polystylistics". Recently, by means so miraculous as to defy belief, Karetnikov has contrived to make a secret underground recording of the entire work, a fact which makes *Till Eulenspiegel* the first *samizdat* opera.

Its companion work, *The Mystery of St Paul*, is an opera-oratorio in the tradition of *Moses und Aron*. Here there are fewer stylistic variations. The music is continuous and grows naturally out of the language of the Fourth Symphony; it is in Karetnikov's "own" style. Again the composer has aimed for the clearest possible political message, seeing in the confrontation of the Emperor Nero and St Paul an obvious parallel with the many tragic confrontations between Stalin (and later his successors) and figures such as Shostakovich, Pasternak and Solzhenitsyn.

Neither *The Mystery of St. Paul* nor *Till Eulenspiegel* has yet been heard in public. *St Paul* has yet indeed to be heard in any form. This is a pity. Both works are remarkable monuments to the moral resistance of the last three decades as well as being in themselves eloquent and richly beautiful pieces of music theatre.

Since finishing these two operas Karetnikov, in his 60th year, has returned to chamber music and completed a powerful new Piano Quintet. It is hoped that he will now find time to add other works of this kind, which may stand a better chance of bringing his name before a wider audience.

—Gerard McBurney

KARKOFF, Maurice (Ingvar). Swedish. Born in Stockholm, 17 March 1927. Educated: studied music theory privately under Karl-Birger Blomdahl, 1944–7; studied piano, Royal College of Music, Stockholm, 1945–51, teaching diploma; studied composition under Lars-Erik Larsson, 1948–53; further composition study under Erland von Koch, Hans Holewa (Stockholm), Vagn Holmboe (Copenhagen), Nadia Boulanger and André Jolivet (Paris, 1957), Wladimir Vogel (Switzerland, 1959–61), Alexander Boscovitch (Tel Aviv, 1963), and orchestration under Jorgen Jersild. Married; 1 son, the composer Ingvar Karkoff. Music critic, *Stockholms Tidingen*, 1962–6; teacher of theory and composition, Stockholms Kommunala Musikinstitut, from 1965. Recipient: Broadcasting Symphony Orchestra Prize, 1962; Christ Johnson Music Prize, 1964; City of Stockholm Prize of Honour, 1976; member, Royal Swedish Academy of Music, 1977; Atterberg Prize, 1983. Mailing address: Stramaljvaegen 4, 161 50 Bromma, Sweden.

Publishers: Gehrmann, Box 6005, 102 31 Stockholm, Sweden; Swedish Music, Box 27327, 102 54 Stockholm, Sweden.

Symphonies/orchestral:

Serenade Op 6 (string orchestra) 1953.
Short Variations Op 9b (version for string orchestra) 1954–6; first performed Malmo, 21 January 1964.
Sinfonietta 1954.
Saxophone Concertino 1955.
Symphony No 1 Op 17 1955–6; first performed Bergen, Norway, 22 October 1956.
Concerto for Violin and Orchestra 1956, revised 1959.
Symphony No 2 Op 25 1957; broadcast Swedish Radio, 5 January 1959.
Concerto for Piano and Orchestra 1957, revised 1960.
Concerto for Cello and Orchestra 1957–8. Recorded Caprice, 1983.
Lyric Suite No 1 (small orchestra) 1958.
Concerto for Trombone and Orchestra 1958.
Lyric Suite No 2 (small orchestra) 1958.
Symphony No 3: Sinfonia breve Op 83 1958–9; first performed Gavle, 10 January 1960.
Nine Aphoristic Variations 1959.
Concerto for Horn and Orchestra 1959.
Concerto for Clarinet and String Orchestra 1959.
Festmarsch Op 49a 1960; first performed Sweden, 16 May 1960.
Concerto da camera (winds, percussion, double basses) 1961, revised 1965.
Variazioni 1961.
Serenata Op 61b (chamber orchestra) 1961; first performed Stockholm, 28 February 1963.
Sete pezzi (large orchestra) 1962.
Concerto da camera (balalaika, orchestra) 1962–3.
Suite per archi e cembalo (strings, harpsichord) 1962.
Concerto for Orchestra 1963.
Symphony No 4 Op 69 1963–4; first performed Stockholm, 4 April 1964. Recorded SCD 1023.
Symphony No 5: Sinfonia da camera Op 72 1964–5; first performed Gavle, 11 November 1965.
Figure transformate Op 78 1965–6; broadcast Swedish Radio, 27 January 1967.
Oriental Pictures 1965–6.
Vision 1965–6.
Transfigurate mutate 1966.
Tripartita (orchestra) 1966–7.
Textum (string orchestra) 1967.
Metamorphoses 1967.
Quattro parti (brass, percussion) 1968.
Epitafium (chamber orchestra; also for nonet) 1968.
Sinfonietta grave 1968–9.
Five Summer Scenes Op 98 1969; first performed Gavleborg, 1 March 1970.
Partes caracteris 1971.
Symphonic Reflections 1971. Recorded Caprice, 1983.
Symphony No 6 Op 116 1972–4; first performed Stockholm, 12 October 1974.
Chamber Concerto No 2: "from 803" (winds, 2 percussion) 1974. Recorded Caprice CAP 3009.
Concertino for Oboe, String Orchestra and Percussion 1974–5.
Symphony No 7: Sinfonia da camera Op 128 1975; first performed 9 November 1976.
Concerto for Trumpet and Orchestra 1976.
Ceremony Music (30 winds, 3–5 percussion) 1977.
Concerto for Bass Flute and Chamber Orchestra 1977.
Tre colori (string orchestra) 1978. Recorded Caprice, 1983.
Textur 1978.
Tre schizzi da Capri (small orchestra) 1979–80.
Symphony No 8 Op 145 1979–80.
Musica seria (flute, harpsichord, strings) 1980.
A Short Symphony (symphonic band) 1980–1; first performed Stockholm, 27 September 1982.
Notturno (clarinet/bass clarinet, strings; orchestration of chamber piece) 1981.
Dolorous Symphony (string orchestra) 1981–2.
Symphony No 10 Op 158 1984–5; first performed Norrkoping, 9 June 1988.
Little Symphony Op 162 1987.
Fantasia Op 166 1988.
Sinfonietta No 5 1990.
Four Sketches Op 171 (string orchestra) 1990.

Chamber/instrumental:

Sonatina Op 2 (piano) 1950.
Duo Op 3 (clarinet, bassoon) 1951.
Elva pianostycken Op 5b (piano) 1951.
Sonata (flute) 1953.
Sonatina Op 7 (violin) 1953.

Rapsodisk fantasi Op 8a (alto saxophone, piano) 1953.
Zoologiske Bilder (violin, viola, guitar) 1953–66.
Short Variations Op 9 (string quartet) 1954; first performed Stockholm, 19 March 1955.
Sonata No 1 (cello, piano) 1954–5.
Sonata (piano) 1956. Recorded Caprice, 1983.
Sonata (violin, piano) 1956.
Quintet (flute, oboe, clarinet, horn, bassoon) 1956–7.
Liten romans (Oriental Nocturne) (violin, viola, cello, piano) 1956–9.
Litet kaleidoskop (piano) 1956–67. Recorded Prop 9952.
String Quartet No 1 Op 26 1957; broadcast Swedish Radio, 14 April 1959.
Divertimento (flute, oboe, horn, bassoon) 1957.
Quartet Op 33 (2 trumpets, horn, trombone) 1958; broadcast Swedish Radio, 6 December 1958.
Partita piccola (piano) 1958.
Two Impressions (flute, harp) 1958.
Miniature Suite (piano) 1958–9.
Drei Klavierstücke für die linke hand (piano—left hand) 1959.
Serenata piccola Op 34c (wind quintet) 1959; first performed Stockholm, 19 April 1961.
Little Suite Op 42 (flute) 1959; broadcast Swedish Radio, 24 December 1959.
Trio (violin, viola, cello) 1960.
Quartetto piccola (flute, violin, cello, piano) 1960–1.
Suite (guitar) 1960–1.
Suite Op 54 (guitar) 1961–79.
Serenata Op 61a (flute, violin, viola, guitar) 1961.
Trio (violin, viola, guitar) 1961. Recorded AGLP S 2.
Three Poems (piano) 1961.
Capriccio over fotboll (piano) 1961.
Serenata (flute, violin, viola) 1961.
Adagio doloroso (violin or viola or cello, organ or piano) 1962.
Festfanfar 1962 til KFUM's 75-arsdag (2 trumpets) 1962.
Fem sma skisser Op 66 (piano) 1963–4.
Duo Op 71 (violin, viola) 1963–4.
Petite musique Op 74 (4 clarinets) 1965.
Notturno (clarinet/bass clarinet, piano) 1966. Recorded Ferm FLPS 2.
Scitatio Op 80 (double bass) 1966.
Metamorphoses (4 horns) 1966.
Five Aphorisms Op 81a (1–4 clarinets) 1966–84. Recorded HOMLP 1001.
Oriental Pictures (violin or viola, piano; or piano—2 or 4 hands) 1966–7. Recorded Ferm FLPS 6; SWS SLT 33184.
Terzetto (flute, cello, piano) 1967–8.
Tre episodi (clarinet, cello, piano) 1968.
Epitafium Op 93 (flute, oboe, clarinet, bassoon, horn, string quartet) 1968; first performed Norrkoping, 9 October 1979. Recorded Caprice CAP 1189.
Quattro parti Op 94 (13 brass, percussion) 1968; first performed Stockholm, 26 November 1969.
Aspects (guitar) 1968.
Poema del sole (organ) 1969.
Monopartita (piano) 1969. Recorded SWS SLT 3340.
Inno a San Michele (organ) 1969.
Vid Hangers kalla / The Spring at Hanger (flute or alto flute) 1970.
Sonata (6 brass) 1970.
Quattro momenti (violin, piano) 1970.
Epitafium Op 192 (accordion, electric guitar, percussion) 1970; first performed Oslo, 15 April 1970.
Tre espressioni (2 pianos) 1971. Recorded Caprice CAP 1227.
Sei pezzi brevi Op 113 (oboe) 1972.
Characters (wind quintet, trombone, euphonium, percussion) 1973–4. Recorded Caprice CAP 1074.
Prelude and Dance (oboe, piano) 1974.
Three Nocturnes (piano) 1974.
Quasi una marcia Op 123 (2 wind quintets, percussion) 1974.
Miniature Suite (violin) 1975.
Suite Op 127 (bassoon) 1975.
Riflessioni Op 130 (organ) 1975.
Serenata Op 131 (flute or alto flute, guitar) 1975–6; first performed Norrkoping, 28 February 1963.
Sonata Op 137 (violin) 1977–8.
Sonata (violin) 1977–8.
Cinque caratteri (flute, clarinet) 1978.
Divertimento (2 clarinets, 2 bassoons) 1978.
Contrasts Op 150 (horn) 1982.
Fanfarfantisi Op 154 (trumpet) 1984.
String Quartet No 2 Op 154 1984.
Ernst & Spass Op 156 (saxophone quartet) 1984; first performed Brno, 6 November 1986. Recorded Caprice CAP 21349.
Sonata piccola Op 159 (clarinet, piano) 1985–6.
Sonatina Op 159 (alto saxophone, piano) 1985–6; first performed Amsterdam, 21 September 1986.
Reflexionen Op 160 (saxophone quartet) 1986; first performed Ulriksdal, 6 July 1987.
Drommeri / Poem Op 165 (clarinet, viola, alto saxophone, piano) 1988.
Femton albumblad Op 167 (piano) 1988–9.
Suite Op 168 (bass flute) 1989; first performed Stockholm, 24 September 1989.
Two Pieces (tuba) 1990.

Vocal/choral:

Fifteen Romances (voice, piano) 1951–3.
Kvall i inlandet Op 4d/3 (voice, piano; Martinson) 1953.
Akallan (unaccompanied male chorus) 1953.
Four Romances (high voice, piano) 1954.
Varnatten i hagen (unaccompanied 3-part mixed chorus; Ekelund) 1954.
Seven Songs (voice, piano) 1954.
Det ar om aftonen Op 10/5 (voice, piano; Lagerkvist) 1954–5. Recorded Caprice 1189.
Sov tills jag kommer Op 11b (4 soloists, piano; unaccompanied mixed chorus; unaccompanied female chorus; Forss) 1954–72.
Six Serious Songs (low voice, orchestra) 1955.
Six Allvarliga Songs (high voice, orchestra) 1955.
Nocturnernas samtal / Dialogue of the Nocturnes (unaccompanied mixed chorus) 1955.
En vantans visa (unaccompanied 3-part mixed chorus; Hagstrom) 1955.
Fran kvall till soluppgang / From Evening to Sunrise (high voice, 5 instruments) 1956.
Sakta som en laga Op 20/1 (unaccompanied mixed chorus; Englund) 1956. Recorded Caprice CAP 1189.
Du ar helig (unaccompanied men's or mixed chorus) 1956.
Det Svenska Landet Op 28 (cantata for baritone, male chorus, orchestra; Osterling) 1956; first performed Karlskoga, 20 April 1959.
Lek (unaccompanied mixed chorus; Setterlind) 1957.
Fran Elegi til Silversang / From Elegy to Silver Song (mixed chorus, 8 instruments) 1957–60.
En sagosang (solo voice; Setterlind) 1959.
Livet / Life Op 41 (alto, orchestra) 1959.
Ten Japanese Songs (high voice, piano or orchestra) 1959.
Gesang des Abgeschiedenen (5 romances for baritone, piano or orchestra) 1960.
Du skall komma (unaccompanied men's, women's or mixed

chorus; Toron) 1960.
Himmel och Jord (cantata) 1960.
Ten Japanese Pictures (baritone or mezzo-soprano, piano) 1961, 1969.
Scherzo Op 60/3 (mixed speaking chorus; Rohlfs, Krause) 1961; first performed Stockholm, 7 April 1962. Recorded Bell 181.
Der en dod alsharinna Op 62/1 (bass, piano, Otomo) 1961–2.
Karlekens vandring/Love Wandering (5 Indian love songs for tenor, piano; or female voices; or male chorus; Tagore) 1962. Recorded Caprice CAP 1189.
Da korsbarsblommorna blommar Op 62/2 (bass, piano; Minamoto) 1962.
Regn (2-part mixed chorus, piano; Setterlind) 1962.
Lill-Dum (unaccompanied 2-part female choir; Setterlind) 1962.
Six Nocturnes (soprano, flute, violin, viola, guitar) 1963.
Sju rosor senare/Seven Roses Later (reciter, speaking chorus, mixed chorus, orchestra; Celan) 1964.
De rasade murarnas frid/Peace on Broken Walls Op 65a (unaccompanied mixed chorus; Lagerkvist) 1964.
Jeremiah 46 (reciter, baritone, speaking chorus, men's chorus, orchestra; Luther, Buber) 1965.
Das ist sein Erlauten (cantata) 1965.
Septemberljus (unaccompanied mixed chorus; Hagström) 1965.
Ser Spinozaforscher. Grabenschrift in die Luft geschrieben (unaccompanied male chorus) 1966; first performed Stockholm, 10 December 1966.
The Rainy Day Op 85 (unaccompanied mixed chorus; Longfellow) 1967.
Landschaft aus Schreien/Landscape of Cries Op 86 (soprano, reciter, oboe/oboe d'amore/cor anglais, 2 clarinets, double bass, harp; Sachs) 1967. Recorded SUEC PS 2.
Four Sacred Songs (unaccompanied mixed chorus) 1967.
Ingen vet vagen/Nobody Knows the Way (5 songs for alto, piano) 1969–70.
In the Beginning (soloists, mixed chorus) 1970–1.
Karleken (voice, piano; or children's chorus) 1971.
Dygnets skiftningar/Shades of Night and Day Op 122 (voice, piano) 1972–4; first performed Stockholm, 21 February 1975. Recorded Bell 128.
Efter varje natt (unaccompanied mixed chorus; Henmark) 1973.
Six Chinese Impressions (soprano, flute, oboe, clarinet, cello, percussion) 1973.
Dar dricka konjak (unaccompanied mixed chorus; Henmark) 1974.
Varsel och aningar/Forebodings and Presentiments (high voice, wind instruments, percussion) 1975.
Four Indian Love Songs (high voice, flutes) 1976.
Sex Katter/Six Cats (high voice, flute, clarinet, percussion) 1977.
Luce e dolore (high voice, piano) 1978.
Drei Gesange zu Traklgedichten (high voice, 4 instruments; Trakl) 1978.
Var alsklings vagga (unaccompanied male choir) 1978; first performed Stockholm, 10 December 1978.
Voices from the Past: Songs to Seven Korean Poems (contralto or baritone, small string orchestra) 1981.
Den alsakde i seggelblaten Op 161 (voice, alto, flute, bass clarinet, guitar, vibraphone; Hitomaro) 1986.
Karlak och var i japan Op 161 (5 female voices, flute/alto flute/piccolo, clarinet/bass clarinet, guitar, 2 percussion) 1986–7; first performed San Francisco, 13 March 1988.
Blicken an 1juv (unaccompanied mixed chorus) 1989.
Five Songs Op 174 (bass baritone, piano) 1990.
Ten Chinese Songs Op 177 (mezzo-soprano or baritone, piano) 1990.
Gluhende Ratsel Op 177 (alto/dramatic mezzo-soprano, piano; Sachs) 1990.
Three Chinese Songs Op 178 (high voice, piano) 1990.

Opera:

Granskibbutzen/The Frontier Kibbutz (chamber opera) 1971–2.

PUBLICATIONS

On Karkoff: Anthony Hodgson, in *Scandinavian Music: Finland & Sweden*, London, 1984; Hans-Gunnar Peterson, "MK", in *Swedish Composers of the 20th Century*, Stockholm, 1988.

* * *

Maurice Karkoff is a prolific and flexible composer, as is evident from his extensive opus list and his heterogeneous background. This is also mirrored in the variety and multiplicity of his musical language. His is an impulsive, emotional personality, and he seeks to put into his music the sum of private thoughts and external impressions. "To create music involves an affirmation of one's inner oppositions, and making them fruitful. For me, composition is a form of expression resulting in the experiences of pain, grief, affection, or joy."

This restlessness and perpetual searching is reflected in a music full of nuances, and there have been several turning points in Karkoff's development. In an article in 1958 he mentions three main sources of inspiration: the inhuman cruelty and oppression during World War II, his love for Swedish nature, and his contact with Swedish poets of the 1940s and 1950s. During the 1960s, a fourth theme developed with Karkoff's discovery of Jewish-Oriental cultures and their musics.

The years 1956–58 were an intense creative period, when Karkoff felt comfortable in a post-romantic linear-symphonic way of writing. In 1959 he made contact with Wladimir Vogel, with whom he pursued strict studies in dodecaphony. The doctrines of this technique seem diametrically opposed to Karkoff's aesthetics, but caused, paradoxically, a revolution in his composing. For Karkoff the conflict is necessary, since it both stimulates and restrains his vivid imagination and intuition, from which his music is generated.

These studies resulted in a sharpening of intellectual concentration and a greater technical coherence. Orthodox twelve-tone technique is used in Karkoff's breakthrough, *Variazioni* for orchestra. The music takes up a position between classical variation and modern metamorphosis. One of his most prominent works is *7 Pazzi*, whose exquisite orchestral texture communicates his *Weltschmertz* in what he calls an "expressionistic impressionism".

It would be alien to Karkoff's nature to confess and conform to the one single -ism alone. In 1963 he made a journey to Israel, and was profoundly moved by the sufferings of the Jewish people. He was also affected by their music—asiatic scales, asymmetric rhythms and the long-woven melismas of religious incantation. His *Symphony No 4* marks a new phase. The music speaks of desperation and devastation in a chaotic, claustrophobic mass of sounds. But gradually the light of hope rises, and an optimistic conclusion prevails. The symphony offers a glimpse of Karkoff's creative paradox—that conflict generates life and annihilation presupposes creation. *Symphony No 6* may be seen as a summary and intensification of Karkoff's expressionistic powers. In the

1980s he made his way towards a new kind of classicism.

In spite of the impression of pluralism, there are notable threads and unifying characteristics: a free tonal lyrical expressionism, with pronounced undertones of both Nordic Romanticism and Eastern exoticism, and the dominating use of the elegiac mode. Karkoff's personal engagement in the political–social world of ours is a frequently recurring theme. His strength lies in the combination of a receptive attitude and thorough craftmanship.

Some of Karkoff's choral and piano music, together with several orchestral pieces—*Vision* and *Tre colori*—were written for amateur musicians. With these he aims at an integration in society: "They are often performed, and through them I feel contact with people."

There is still room in Karkoff's turbulent commitment to countervailing forces for irony and humor, as in the piano piece *Capriccio for Football*.

—Björn Billing

KASPAROV, Yuri. Armenian. Born in Moscow, 8 June 1955. Educated at Moscow Institute, 1972–8; Moscow Conservatoire, 1980–4. Married Tatiana Kudriavteeva, 6 June 1987. Music editor in chief, Central Documentary Film Studio, Moscow, 1984–9; artistic director, ACU Ensemble, Moscow, from 1989. Recipient: laureate, All-Union Composers Competition, 1985; laureate, Guido d'Arezzo International Competition, Italy, 1989. Mailing address: naberzhne Taras Shevchenko, dom 1/2, kv.121, 121059 Moscow, U.S.S.R.

Publisher: VAAP/Boosey & Hawkes.

Symphonies/orchestral:

Symphony No 1: Guernica 1983; first performed Moscow, 1984.
Symphony No 2: Kreuzer Symphony 1985; first performed Yaroslavl, 1987.
Linkos 1988; first performed Norrkoping, Sweden, 1990.
Genesis (triptych for orchestra) 1989.
Chamber Symphony: Sileneium (14 players) 1989; first performed Moscow, 1990.
Concerto for Oboe and Orchestra 1990.

Chamber/instrumental:

Diffusion (3 ensembles) 1987; first performed Tcheljabinsk, 1989.
Postludio (harp) 1987–8.
Devil's Trills (variations on a theme by Tartini; 16 performers) 1988; first performed Moscow, 1990.
Variations (clarinet, piano) 1988.
Sketch with Collage (violin, trumpet, piano) 1988.
Epitaph: In memoriam Alban Berg (violin, oboe, harp, percussion) 1989; first performed Moscow 1989.
Sonata-infernale (bassoon) 1989.
Notturno (violin, clarinet, piano) 1989; first performed Moscow, 1990.
Credo (organ) 1989.
Invention (string quartet) 1989; first performed Leningrad, 1989.
Cantus Firmus (violin) 1989–90; first performed Pontino, Italy, 1990.

Vocal/choral:

Ave Maria (12 soloists, violin, organ, vibraphone) 1989; first performed Moscow, 1990.

Other:

Scores for 35 Soviet films.

PUBLICATIONS

By Kasparov: articles in *Sovetskaya muzyka*, other music journals, and newspapers.

On Kasparov: Elena Dmitrakova, "YK", in *Sovetskaya muzyka*, 1991.

Yuri Kasparov comments:

Unlike many of my colleagues, I don't consider the reflection of reality in sound as the main mission of musical art. No doubt it is necessary for individuals and societies to understand the complicated political situations and crises they undergo, but these cannot represent the main subject matter of music.

When a house is built, it has to be safe and stable. Decorative style and curlicues are secondary. If maximum stability coincides with minimum outlay, then we may say that such a structure is a work of art. We might even call such a structure a masterpiece if its technical and aesthetic dimensions are tightly interlocked in a complicated, multi-dimensional system of coordinates.

Unfortunately, like so many poorly constructed houses, musical compositions are inclined to collapse and reach our ears as brick fragments and mortar dust. With a house, it is quite easy—you can *see* that it is unsound. With music, you have to train your ear and develop your instincts rather highly. This is not so easy in countries where (as in the Soviet Union) music education is better geared to the production of musical hacks than of composers.

The main mission of any composer and the basis of his creativity is the ability to understand and to follow the deeply specific laws of music that hold true for all times and all peoples.

In my works, I try to shape all the coordinates of the music into a certain geometrically consistent form, much as happens to the coordinates of mathematical functions in n-dimensional space. These coordinates are the sound level, rhythm, metre, timbre, and so on. At the same time, I try to use any available possibility to develop my thinking along the path of each musical coordinate. For me, timbre has always been pre-eminent. Here the most important thing is to search for interesting sonorous accords, to study their functionality, to find the logic by which one is transformed into another . . .

I do not presently believe that musical sound represents a kind of ideal real beyond human understanding, the kind of abstraction often imputed to Webern for one. To my mind, sound with a specific level, timbre and duration must always be the basis of any composition. The laws of acoustics are the basis of functionality; if the laws of functionality are allied to a genuine creative urge, then real musical art may emerge.

* * *

Yuri Kasparov is one of the most interesting of the younger generation of composers in Moscow today. As yet, we have heard little of his music outside Russia. This situation, although it will no doubt change in time, is partly a result of the fact that many of his strongest pieces are written for large orchestral forces of a kind that are expensive to promote.

So far two quite distinct sides to Kasparov's imagination have emerged. In his largest works, including *Linkos* for orchestra and the Oboe Concerto, he has favoured a broad, violent and even vulgar heterophonic style that owes much to the techniques of certain Polish composers and especially to Lutosławski.

To describe this music as "vulgar" may seem like a criticism, but it is in fact this vulgarity that is Kasparov's distinctive strength, that makes it sound so unlike such a refined figure indeed as Lutosławski. In a piece like *Linkos*, for example, well-crafted waves of heterophonic textures not only contain splashes of vulgar instrumentation within themselves (note-rows on swanee whistles, corny parallel thirds on the trumpets using wa-wa mutes, horror-film cluster effects), but are built overall into a series of climaxes that at first strike one as shockingly obvious and belonging to the cinema; however, as the piece progresses, these same climaxes turn out to have a curious internal and relative logic whose cumulative effect is impressive and unconventional.

The other side to Kasparov's work is seen in smaller-scale works like *Diffusion* and *Genesis* and even a rare chamber work, the miniature *In memoriam Alban Berg*. Here the dominant influence is the middle-period works of the Second Viennese School. Kasparov seeks a fluent and precise pantonal counterpoint designed to make one very aware of the motivic unity and development of a fundamental idea, conceived in the first place in terms of pitch relationships, rather than as colour or effect as in his larger works. These more intimate pieces have a sense of airy lyricism about them that is certainly respectful and sensitive, but hardly as curious as the vulgarity of the larger heterophonic works.

In recent years Kasparov has become more isolated from his contemporaries in Moscow. This has at least in part to do with his strongly expressed views about the state of Russian music today. He has frequently argued, in public and private, that the whole tradition of Russian music is too dependent on extra-musical symbolism and association (whether religious, political or nationalistic) and that Russian music of our time would benefit from becoming "purer", more concerned with itself for its own sake, as, in Kasparov's opinion, Western music is. This, Kasparov argues, would lead to Soviet musicians being less isolated.

Kasparov's position is of course itself part of the old tradition of Russian Westernising and dependent on a mass of very local assumptions. But something of the energy of his argument certainly carries over into his music, giving it a certain directness and strength. And this is certainly an attractive feature of a composer who comes from a culture where many young composers do indeed rely lazily on religious and nationalist formulae to give their music a sometimes spurious meaningfulness. Kasparov knows his mind and his music is the fresher for it.

—Gerard McBurney

KAYN, Roland. German. Born in Reutlingen, Württemberg, 3 September 1933. Educated at Staatliche Hochsschule für Musik, Stuttgart, and Kirchenmusikschule, Esslingen, 1952–5; first experiments with electro-acoustic music, WDR electronic music studio, Cologne, 1953; Technische Hochsschule, Stuttgart (social theory under Max Bense); Staatliche Hochsschule für Musik, Berlin (composition under Boris Blacher, analysis under Josef Rufer), 1956–8. Married Lydia Onrust, August 1971. New music editor, Norddeutscher Rundfunk radio station, Hamburg, 1964–9; programme consultant, Goethe Institute, Amsterdam, since 1970; has worked at the Institute of Sonology, University of Utrecht, since 1970; founder, Gruppo Internazionale d'Improvisazione Nuovo Consonana, Rome, 1979; member, artistic committee, Donaueschinger Musiktage, 1979–82; Recipient: 1st prize (for *Kammerkonzert*), "Music of the 20th Century", Tokyo, 1958; Rome Prize, 1960; prize, Concorso Internazionale Nuova Musica, Rome, 1962, 1964; music prize, 4th Biennale, Paris, 1965. Mailing address: Zuidereind 124, NL-1243 Graveland, The Netherlands.

Publishers: Suvini Zerboni, Milan; Moeck, Celle.

Symphonies/orchestral:

Orchesterstück (organ, large orchestra) 1950.
Sequenzen 1957; first performed Hannover, 1969.
Aggregate (winds, strings, percussion) 1958; first performed Darmstadt, 1959.
Aggregates Sonores 1959–71.
Vectors I 1960; first performed Venice, 1961.
Vectors II (4 ensembles, orchestra) 1960, 1967.
Vectors III (2 orchestras) 1972–7.
Chreodes 1980–2.
Supra 1984–6.

Chamber/instrumental:

Fünf kleine Klavierstücke (piano) 1951.
Divertimento (2 pianos) 1953.
Meditationen (organ) 1953.
Kammerkonzert (6 winds, percussion) 1953.
Spektren (string quartet) 1956; first performed Darmstadt, 1957.
Quanten (piano) 1957; first performed Darmstadt, 1958.
Schwingungen / Oscillations (5 sound ensembles) 1961–2; first performed Palermo, 1963.
Galaxis ("multiple sound structure" for variable ensemble) 1962; first performed Rome, 1964.
Allotropie (various instrumental groupings) 1962–4.
Inerziali (5–20 players) 1963; first performed Donaueschingen, 1965.
Signals (7 instrumental groups) 1964–6; first performed Hamburg, 1966.
Diffusions (1–4 electronic organs) 1965; first performed Stockholm, 1968.
Engramme (15–60 instruments) 1971–3.
Circuits intégrés (1–4 pianos, 1–6 percussionists, tape) 1972; first performed Amsterdam, 1973.
Gyron (1–4 ensembles) 1975–6.

Vocal/choral:

Phasen (voices, 4 percussion groups) 1961; first performed Venice, 1962.
Cybernetics II (7 choral groups, tone generators, electronics, tape) 1968.
Ektropie (1–4 choirs, 1–4 orchestras) 1973.
Syn (2 choirs, orchestra) 1977–8.

Other:

Impulse (electronic) 1959–60.
Cybernetics I (electro-acoustic) 1966–8; first performed Hamburg, 1969.
Entropy PE 31 (electro-acoustic) 1967–70; first performed Hamburg, 1970.
Cybernetics III (electro-acoustic) 1969; first performed Venice, 1969.
Simultan (electro-acoustic composition for 1–5 rooms) 1970–2; first performed Bremen, 1974.
Monades (electro-acoustic) 1971; first performed Hamburg, 1972.
Eon (electro-acoustic) 1975; first performed Bonn, 1975.
Makro (electro-acoustic) 1977.
Infra (electro-acoustic) 1978–9; first performed Utrecht, 1980. Recorded Colosseum 1477.
Tektra (electro-acoustic) 1980–2; first performed Utrecht, 1984. Recorded Colosseum 1479.
Ready Made I & II (electro-acoustic) 1982; first performed Linz, 1984.
Scanning (electro-acoustic) 1982–4.
Collage / Décollage (electro-acoustic) 1983.
Assemblage (electro-acoustic) 1984.
Sybernetic Serendipity (electro-acoustic) 1985.
An Artificial Acoustic Environment (electro-acoustic) 1986.
Transfluxion (electro-acoustic) 1987.
Zygyzi Dynamical Units (electro-acoustic) 1988.

PUBLICATIONS

By Kayn: "Struktur und Klangin der Elektronischen Musik", in *La Biennale de Venezia*, 44/55, 1961; "Selbstportrait", in *Begegnung* (programme notes), Donaueschingen, 1965; "Random or Not Random", in *Horyzonty Muzycky*, 1966; "Erweiterungen und Grenzen des Instrumentalklangs", in *Horyzonty Muzycky*, 1966; "Diffusions", in *Nutida Musik*, 1967; "Kybernetische Prozesse in instrumentaler und elektronischer Musik", in *Collage*, 1971; "Aspekte der Generierung ästhetischer Information im akustischen Signalraum", in *Duitse Kroniek*, 1971; "Komponiern zwischen Computer und Kybernetik", in *Melos / NZ*, 1977.

On Kayn: "RK", *Collage*, 7, 1967; H. Krellmann, "Gespräch mit RK", in *Die Welt*, 12 November 1968; L. Kupper, "Musique cybernétique", in *Tendances Actuelles de l'Art Musical*, 1971.

* * *

Roland Kayn started his compositional career at the age of 17 with *Orchesterstück* for large orchestra and organ, a piece characterized by free atonality. Written three years later, *Kammerkonzert* for six wind instruments and percussion utilized an extended twelve-note technique, and won first prize at the Festival of the 20th-century Music in Karuizawa, Japan in 1958. In the first half of the 1950s Kayn's basic aesthetic was opposed to the serially organized music of his contemporaries. He composed several works exploring different styles, for example *Fünf kleine Klavierstücke*, which restricted the sound material to the five notes of the pentatonic scale, using only the black keys of the piano. The *Meditationen* for organ combined chorale, twelve-note technique and polytonality.

As early as 1953 Kayn had contacted the Cologne electronic studio of West German Radio, but he was discouraged by its directors who told him to study the music of Webern and to change his technique of composition toward serialism. Among his teachers were Boris Blacher and Max Bense, one of the founders of information aesthetics (the application of information theory on art). Their influence directed Kayn to a statistical type of composition, first reflected in *Spektren* for string quartet and *Sequenzen* for orchestra. These works employ statistical frequency distributions within the parameters of pitch, duration and density.

Kayn's subsequent works (*Quanten, Aggregate, Impulse*) explored another aspect of sound both in the instrumental and electronic spheres: the use of micro intervals allowed the production of tone mixtures outside the traditional tempered system and the construction of simultaneously employed temperatures of different kind. In the case of the electronic piece *Impulse*, however, these complexities render actual realization impracticable because the conventional equipment at the studios in Warsaw (1960) and Cologne (1962) were inadequate to produce the work within a reasonable time.

At the beginning of the 1960s Kayn began to abrogate all elements of order in his music. In orchestral works like *Vectors, Schwingungen / Oscillations* and *Galaxis* the combination of virtually chaotic sound events leads to the production of acoustical super signals (a term token from information theory meaning the perception of higher level signals composed of many lower level signals).

With *Phasen* for voices and percussion orchestra Kayn began to introduce regulation processes which influence the actual shape of the piece on the basis of interactions between the performers. Other examples are *Allotropie* for orchestra, *Signals* for seven instrumental groups, which almost eliminates any determined pitch constellations, and *Cybernetics II* for voices, orchestra and electro-acoustic devices.

Kayn, who since 1970 has worked at the University of Utrecht's Instituut voor Sonologie, transferred his cybernetic principles to the realm of electro-acoustic music in *Cybernetics I* and *III*. Based on human and animal vocal material chains of acoustical signals trigger new processes of sound themselves. *Ektropie* for chorus and orchestra is characterized by the evolution of slowly changing sound modulations. Together with *Circuits Intégrés* for 1–4 pianos, *Engramme* for 15–60 disposable instruments and the electro-acoustic *Eon*, it belongs to the project *Rot* (random organized time), the components of which may be performed simultaneously. *Engramme* comprises a complex repertory of signals from which the performers may select in a free or determined way. Kayn realized several purely electro-acoustic works at the Instituut voor Sonologie which were all produced by means of highly complex cybernetic processes of control and regulation, among them *Monades*, *Makro* and *Infra*.

—Rolf Klein

KELEMEN, Milko. Yugoslavian. Born in Podravska Slatina, Croatia, 30 March 1924. Educated at Academy of Music, Zagreb (under Stjepan Šulek), 1945–60; Conservatoire National de Musique Supérieure, Paris (under Olivier Messiaen); Musikhochsschule Freiburg im Breisgau (under Wolfgang Fortner). Married Miro Slava, 10 July 1965.

Assistant professor, Academy of Music, Zagreb, 1954–7; participant, Ferienkurse für Neue Musik, Darmstadt, since 1955; organiser, 1959, and president, since 1961, Zagreb Biennale of New Music; worked at Munich Studio for Electronic music, 1966–8; professor of composition, R. Schumann Institut, Dusseldorf, 1971–3, and Hochsschule für Musik, Stuttgart, 1973–91. Recipient: Beethoven Prize, City of Bonn, 1958; prize of Italian Section, SIMC, 1959; 3 times prizewinner, music prize, City of Zagreb; Brasilia Prize, 1974; Vladimir Nazor Prize, 1984; Grosses Bundes Verdienst-Kreuz, Germany; Chevalier de l'Ordre des Arts et des Lettres, France. Mailing address: Bergstrasse 62/2, 7 Stuttgart 1, Germany.

Publisher: Peters, Frankfurt.

Symphonies/orchestral:

Little Music for Strings 1947; first performed Zagreb, 12 December 1947.
Preludio, Aria e Finale (strings) 1948; first performed Zagreb, 20 May 1948.
Sinfonietta (chamber orchestra) 1950; first performed Zagreb, 4 May 1950.
Sinfonie (large orchestra) 1952; first performed Zagreb, 18 February 1952.
Piano Concerto 1953; first performed Zagreb, 22 February 1953.
Violin Concerto 1954; first performed Zagreb, 20 June 1957.
Improvisations concertantes (strings) 1955; first performed Zagreb, 10 October 1955. Recorded Vanguard Amadeo AVRS 5032; Jugoton LSY 61189.
Adagio ed Allegro (strings) 1955; first performed Zagreb, 16 February 1956.
Three Dances (viola, orchestra) 1956; first performed Zagreb, 20 December 1957.
Bassoon Concerto 1956; first performed Zagreb, 13 May 1957.
Concerto giocoso (chamber orchestra) 1956; first performed Zagreb, 10 January 1957.
Concertino (double bass or cello, orchestra) 1957; first performed Zagreb, 20 April 1957.
Sinfonische Musik 57 1957; first performed Zagreb, 4 April 1958.
Konstellationen (chamber orchestra) 1958; first performed Cracow, 20 April 1960.
Five Essays (strings) 1959; first performed Lucerne, 31 August 1961.
Skolion 1960; first performed Cologne, 12 June 1960. Recorded Jugoton LPYV 84.
Transfigurationen (piano, orchestra) 1960; first performed Hamburg, 6 April 1962. Recorded Jugoton ULPSV 29.
Der Spiegel (suite from the ballet; orchestra) 1960.
Equilibres (2 orchestras) 1962; first performed Bonn, 19 March 1962.
Sub Rosa 1965; first performed Zagreb, 12 May 1965.
Surprise (strings) 1966; first performed Zagreb, 12 May 1967. Recorded Philips 6500314; Jugoton LSY 61189.
Compose (2 pianos, orchestra) 1967; first performed Donaueschingen, 23 October 1967. Recorded Philips 6500314.
Changeant (cello, orchestra) 1969; first performed Cologne, 8 November 1968. Recorded Philips 6500314.
Floreal 1970; first performed Washington, D.C., 30 October 1970. Recorded Philips 6500314.
Olifant (trombone/alphorn/Bali-flute/zurla/etc., 2 orchestral groups) 1971; first performed Royan, 8 April 1971.
Passionato (flute, 3 orchestral groups) 1971; first performed Berlin, 18 October 1972. Recorded Studio 74 KL002.
Abecedarium (strings) 1973; first performed Graz, 13 October 1974. Recorded Jugoton LSY 61189.
Mirabilia (piano, ring modulator ad lib, 2 orchestral groups) 1974; first performed Paris, 21 April 1975. Recorded Yugoton 66012.
Tantana (improvisation for 10–20 players) 1974; first performed Opatija, 12 November 1975.
Mageia 1978; first performed Augsburg, 12 June 1978. Recorded AG 511 01 87 A.
Infinity 1979; first performed Zagreb, 18 May 1979. Recorded AG 511 01 87 A.
Grand Jeu classique (apparently also listed as *Silverline*; violin, orchestra) 1981; first performed Metz, 21 November 1982.
Archetypon 1982; first performed Hannover, 13 January 1986.
Love Song (strings) 1983; first performed Zagreb, 5 January 1984.
Fanfare (brass) 1983; first performed Zagreb, 9 February 1984.
Phantasmen (viola, orchestra) 1984; first performed Stuttgart, 16 December 1985.
Drammatico (cello, orchestra) 1984; first performed Stuttgart, 3 March 1985.
Fantasia 1985; first performed Mainz, 8 October 1988.
Antiphonie (organ, orchestra) 1986; first performed Zagreb, 8 April 1987.

Chamber/instrumental:

Thema mit Variationen (piano) 1948; first performed Zagreb, 4 May 1949.
Sonata (piano) 1954; first performed Siena, 20 August 1954. Recorded Vega Paris C30A70; Jugoton LY 66031.
Music for Violin 1957; first performed Zagreb, 4 April 1958. Recorded Jugoton LPYV 639.
Etudes contrapuntiques (wind quintet) 1959; first performed Paris, 14 November 1959. Recorded Time Records New York 58006.
Study (flute) 1959; first performed Darmstadt, 5 September 1959.
Sonata (oboe, piano) 1960; first performed Darmstadt, 7 July 1960. Recorded Jugoton LY 66052.
Der Esel geht am Meer spazieren (9 little pieces for piano) 1961. Recorded Studio 74 ST742.
Radiant (flute, viola, piano/celeste, harp, percussion) 1963; first performed Darmstadt, 16 July 1963. Recorded Jugoton LY 66052.
Dessin commenté (piano) 1964; first performed Bremen, 6 May 1964.
Entrances (wind quintet) 1966; first performed Hanover, New Hampshire, 10 June 1966.
Musik für Judith (electronically processed and acoustic instrumental sounds) 1966; first performed Munich, 10 April 1966.
Motion (string quartet) 1968; first performed Madrid, 4 March 1969.
Fabliau I (flute) 1972; first performed Stockholm, 20 October 1972. Recorded Schwann Musica Mundi VMS 483.
Varia Melodia (string quartet) 1972; first performed Dusseldorf, 21 September 1972. Recorded Studio 74 KL002; col legno 0647 237.
Fabliau II (organ, microphone) 1972; first performed Dusseldorf, 10 May 1972. Recorded Studio 74 KL002.
Splintery (string quartet) 1977; first performed Paris,

5 December 1977. Recorded Jugoton LY 66052; col legno 0647 237.
Rontondo I (wind trio) 1977; first performed Witten, 27 April 1977. Recorded Jugoton LY 66052.
Zehn Fabeln (soprano/alto recorders) 1979.
Fabliau III (flute, harpsichord) 1980; first performed Siena, 10 August 1980.
Rontondo II (harmonica, wind trio) 1980; first performed Stuttgart, 3 October 1980.
Zehn Fabeln (piano) 1985.
Love Song (saxophone quartet) 1985; first performed Stuttgart, 6 September 1985.
Säulen des Himmels (piano) 1986; first performed Stuttgart, 8 October 1986.
Memories (string trio) 1986; first performed Zagreb, 30 January 1987.
Sonette (string quartet) 1987; first performed Bomberg, 22 May 1987.

Vocal/choral:

Drei Impressionen (mixed choir, 4 cellos, piano; Ujevic) 1955; first performed Zagreb, 16 April 1956.
Die Spiele (baritone, strings; Popa) 1957; first performed Strasbourg, 13 May 1958.
Inserate (mixed choir) 1959; first performed Paris, 29 February 1961.
Epitaph (mezzo-soprano, viola, percussion; Vitez) 1961; first performed Darmstadt, 8 September 1961.
Der neue Mieter (tenor, mezzo-soprano, 2 baritones, orchestra; Ionesco) 1962; first performed Münster, 15 September 1964.
Hommage à Heinrich Schutz (unaccompanied mixed choir, solo voices; biblical) 1964; first performed Berlin, 12 May 1965.
O Primavera (tenor, strings; 17th-century Italian) 1965; first performed Zagreb, 19 May 1965.
Die Wörter (mezzo-soprano, orchestra; Sartre) 1966, 2 versions; first performed Lubeck, 9 May 1966.
Musik für Heissenbuttel (mezzo-soprano, violin, cello, clarinet; Heissenbuttel) 1967; first performed Rome, 24 February 1968.
Passionato (flute/alto flute/piccolo, 3 choral groups) 1972.
Gasho (4 choral groups) 1973; first performed Tokyo, 20 April 1974.
Die sieben Plagen (mezzo-soprano; Arrabal) 1974; first performed Vienna, 19 November 1975.
Monogatari (12 solo voices; version of *Gasho*) 1974; first performed Paris, 12 December 1978.
Die Richter (from the ballet-opera *Apocalyptica*) 1977; first performed Zagreb, 9 May 1977.
Drei irische Volkslieder (mixed choir; Irish folk songs) 1979; first performed Cork, 10 May 1980.
Landschaftbilder (mezzo-soprano, string quartet; Schutting) 1985; first performed Graz, 24 October 1986.

Opera:

Der Belagerungszustand (after Camus) 1968–9; first performed Hamburg, 13 January 1970. Recorded Electrola 1 C 195–29107/09.

Other:

Der Spiegel/Le Héros et son miroir (ballet; orchestra) 1960; first performed Paris, 18 August 1960.
Abbandonate (ballet; orchestra) 1964; first performed Lübeck, 1 September 1964.
Yebell (action for singer, mime, dancer, with orchestra) 1972; first performed Munich, 1 September 1972.
Apocalyptica (multi-media ballet-opera; Arrabal) 1977; concert version first performed, 10 October 1979.

PUBLICATIONS

By Kelemen: *Klanglabyrinthe: Reflexionen eines Komponisten über die Neue Musik* (with an interview with Joachim Kaiser), Munich, 1981. in Serbo-Croat, 1982, in French, 1985.

On Kelemen: Kresimir Kovacevic, "Drei kroatischen Komponisten und ihre Werke", in *Nakladni zavod Hrvatske*, 1957; Everett Helm, "MK, Yugoslav Avantgardist", in *Musical America*, 1962; Martine Cadieu, "Sartre chantant, Ionesco dansant par MK", in *Nouvels littéraires*, 1965; Ulrich Dibelius, in *Moderne Musik 1945–65*, Munich, 1966; Josef Hausler, in *Musik im 20, Jahrhundert*, Bremen, 1969; Hanspeter Krellmann, "Pladoyer für MK", in *Musica*, 1971; Eva Sedak, "MK, oder das Spiel der Flucht vor ältern und neuen Dogmenin der Musik", in *Nakladni zavod Hrvatske*, Zagreb, 1972; Fred Prieberg, "Zwanzig Fragen an MK", in *Melos*, 1974; Irmgard Scharbeth, in *Musiktheater mit Rolf Liebermann*, Hamburg, 1975; Niksa Gligo, "Passionato für Flöte und gemischten Chor von MK", in *Zeitschrift für Musiktheorie*, 1975; Alison Browning, "Une Conversation avec MK", in *Cadmos*, 1979.

Milko Kelemen comments:

In time it became clear to me that the unconscious sphere in music is just as important as the conscious—and even if the principle of equalization alone is not a "conditio sine qua non", it is certainly a principle that both spheres must be contained within the music. In order to come closer to the root of these problems, I experimented in this field with my own compositions. I tried composing a very rational sort of music based on mathematical constructions and for a while I enjoyed it. But even after producing a few minutes of music I felt that something was missing: the unconscious sphere which cannot easily be explained by the conscious mind.

Imagination is another phenomenon without which it is impossible to compose. It is the ability to visualize something which is not yet "present". To be more exact, it is the talent of allowing new ideas to enter into the consciousness and to combine them with already existing conscious experiences.

The origins of creativity are hard to describe and it is practically impossible to give information about the first moments in the creation of a composition, partly because every composer produces ideas in a different way. But one thing is certain: a composer should never be satisfied with doubtful results in the first creative moments, for these manifestations of the imagination have the greatest influence on the further development of the composition.

* * *

It is impossible to get an objective insight into Milko Kelemen's music without knowing about his unusual relation to Croatian music after World War II and the exceptional role he has played in its development. Kelemen comes from the highly esteemed school of Stjepan Šulek (1914–1986), the composer who gave Croatian music an international identity, ignoring the folkloristic background of his predecessors. However, Šulek's creative beliefs ignored 20th-century tendencies in favour of neo-romantic, eclectic expression. It is quite predictable that young composers would react to this aesthetic attitude (and all of Šulek's students did), but Kelemen was the first one who made opposition his creative credo. From the 1950s onward he violently polemicized in his work not only against the aesthetic views of his teacher but also against any narrow-minded and provincial view which considered the newest tendencies in the development of contemporary music as blasphemous and non-musical. Kelemen also realized that contemporary music in its real sense should be somehow brought into Croatian musical culture. At the end of the 1950s he began thinking about founding an international festival of contemporary music; Music Biennale Zagreb started in 1961.

Kelemen's polemics against the views of his first teacher and his older colleagues were not based on the presumption of exclusiveness. In fact he did not attack their views but their ignorance, the provincial self-satisfaction which was the source of their contempt towards something that they essentially did not know. And this proves not only Kelemen's tolerance but also his open-mindedness and his conceptual candour.

In discussing the problem of defining music today, Kelemen has always avoided giving any categorical answer from the composer's point of view. "For me music is always what I am composing in this very moment. If it were not music, I would not compose it! And I know that this 'music' can be something entirely different in my next piece." When presented with the notion that the composer's point of view should be the basis for any contemporary definition of music because the composer is still the only one who makes it and is responsible for it, he used to answer: "You can start from this point if you want. You can generalize my view as a composer's view on the philosophical or aesthetical basis. I will maybe accept your generalized definition. But if you ask me again what music is, instead of trying to define it with the words I will again have to show you some notes I have just written down!" This kind of belief in the rightness of his own music somehow vindicates Kelemen's tolerance, understandable only through his permanent creative curiosity, the necessity to create always something entirely new but nevertheless confidently musical. It is difficult to reduce his immense opus to any common denominator. It is useless to look at the traditional genre criteria: his pieces for string quartet differ one from the next; his vocal pieces are again highly dependent on the choice of the text and its treatment; his orchestra never sounds quite the same way. And it is entirely impossible to trace any of his possible models or ideals. Kelemen is indeed one of the most outstanding composers today because his creative profile is so paradigmatic for today's contemporary music.

—Nikša Gligo

KELTERBORN, Rudolf. Swiss. Born in Basle, 3 September 1931. Educated at Basle Music Academy (under Walther Geiser); Basle University (under Jacques Handschin), 1950–3; further composition studies under Willy Burkhard and Boris Blacher; Nordwestdeutscher Musikakademie, Detmold (under Gunter Bialas and Wolfgang Fortner), 1955. Married Erika Salathe, 6 July 1957; 1 daughter and 1 son. Teacher and conductor in Basle, 1955–60; teacher of theory and composition, 1960–8, and professor, 1963, Nordwestdeutscher Musikakademie, Detmold; teacher, Conservatory and Musikhochschule, Zurich, 1968–75; editor in chief, *Schweizerische Musikzeitung*, 1969–74; guest lecturer in United States, 1970; head of music department, Radio of German and Raetoromanic Switzerland, 1974–80; professor, Staatliche Hochschule für Musik, Karlsruhe, 1980–3; guest lecturer in United States, 1980, England, 1981, and Japan and South Korea, 1986; director, Music Academy, Basle, since 1983. Recipient: Bernhard Sprengel Prize of German industry, 1962; Conrad Ferdinand Meyer Prize, 1970; Zurich Radio Prize for series on "Understanding Music by Listening Consciously", 1973; composition prize of the Schweizerischer Tonkünstlerverein, 1984. Mailing address: Pilgerstrasse 31, CH-4055 Basle, Switzerland.

Publishers: Barenreiter, Heinrich Schutz Allee D-3500 Kassel, Switzerland; Bote und Bock, Hardenbergstrasse 9a, D-1000 Berlin, Germany; Edition Modern, Munich; Universal-Edition, Vienna; Breitkopf & Hartel, Wiesbaden; Verlag Hug & Co., Zurich; Selbstverlag Rudolf Kelterborn.

Symphonies/orchestral:

Suite (brass, percussion, string orchestra) 1955; first performed Stockholm, 1956.
Sonata für 16 solo-streicher (strings) 1955.
Mouvements 1957; first performed Winterthur, 23 May 1959.
Canto appassionato 1958; first performed Darmstadt, 6 July 1960.
Concertino (piano, 2 percussion, strings) 1958–9; first performed Lausanne, 3 September 1960.
Kammersinfonie 1 (violin, 10 winds, percussion, harp, strings) 1960; first performed Kassel, 9 October 1960.
Variationen (oboe, strings) 1960; first performed Lissabon, 2 March 1961.
Metamorphosen 1960; first performed Basle, 7 November 1960.
Lamentationes (string orchestra) 1961; first performed Stuttgart, 1 April 1962.
Scènes fugitives (alto and sopranino recorders, orchestra) 1961; first performed Braunschweig, 9 November 1962.
Vier Nachtstücke (chamber orchestra) 1963; first performed Zurich, 11 December 1963. Recorded Musicaphon BM 30 SL 1716.
Kammersinfonie II (string orchestra) 1964; first performed Zurich, 21 August 1964.
Zwei Szenen (from the opera *Kaiser Jovian*) 1964–5; first performed Bielefeld, 6 January 1967.
Musik für Klarinette und Streicher 1965–6; first performed Lucerne, 28 August 1966. Recorded Musicaphon BM 30 SL 1533.
Phantasmen 1965–6; first performed Hannover, 28 January 1967. Recorded Musicaphon BM 30 SL 1716.
Sonata sacra (brass) 1965–6; first performed Basle, 18–19 January 1968.
Sinfonie 1 1966–7; first performed Zurich, 5 January 1968.
Miroirs 1966; first performed Detmold, 3 May 1968.
Sinfonie 2 1969–70; first performed Munich, 22 October 1970.
Traummusik (small orchestra) 1971; first performed Zurich, 28 January 1972.
Kommunikationen (6 instrumental groups) 1971–2; first performed Lucerne, 15 August 1973.
Changements 1972–3; first performed Montreux, 19 September 1973.
Nuovi canti (flute, chamber orchestra) 1973; first performed Munich, 24 April 1974. Recorded EL 17010/CD 6069.
Tableaux encadrés (13 solo strings) 1974; first performed Zurich, 15 June 1975.

Espansioni (symphony no 3, for large orchestra, baritone, tape; Ungaretti) 1974–5; first performed Basle, 29–30 September 1976. Recorded Musicaphon BM 30 SL 1716.
Szene (12 solo cellos) 1977; first performed Lucerne, 30 August 1980.
Erinnerungen an Orpheus 1977–8; first performed Berne, 18 January 1979.
Visions sonorés (6 percussion groups, with flute/piccolo, clarinet/brass clarinet, brass, strings) 1979; first performed Basle, 4 June 1980. Recorded Jecklin Disco 599.
Chiaroscuro: Canzoni per orchestra 1979–80; first performed Salzburg, 29 August 1980.
Musica luminosa per orchestra 1983–4; first performed Locarno, 13 September 1985.
Sinfonie 4 1985–6; first performed Bamberg, 3 February 1987.
Sonatas for Winds 1986; first performed Zurich, 24 February 1987.
Musik für Kontrabass und Orchester 1986–7; first performed 3–4 March, 1988.

Chamber/instrumental:

Sonata (2 pianos) 1955; first performed Amriswil, 3 June 1956.
Streichquartett 2 1956; first performed Munich, 27 October 1959. Recorded Musicaphon BM 30 SL 1942.
Metamorphosen (piano) 1956. Recorded Musicaphon BM 30 SL 1533.
Kammermusik für Flöte, Violine und Klavier 1957.
Fünf Fantasien (transverse flute, cello, harpsichord) 1958; first performed Basle, 1959.
Sieben Bagatellen (wind quintet) 1958.
Lyrische Kammermusik (clarinet, violin, viola) 1959; first performed Basle, May 1960. Recorded Musicaphon BM 30 SL 1537.
Varianti (6 instruments) 1959.
Ritornelli (harpsichord) 1960.
Sonata (oboe, harpsichord) 1960.
Streichquartett 3 1962; first performed Hannover, 23 October 1963. Recorded Musicaphon BM 30 SL 1537.
Esquisses (harpsichord, percussion) 1962.
Meditationen (6 wind instruments) 1963.
Musik für Violine und Gitarre 1964.
Vier Miniaturen (oboe, violin) 1964.
Monosonata (piano) 1965; first performed Geneva, 5 May 1966. Recorded BM 30 SL 1533.
Fantasia a tre (piano trio) 1967; first performed Braunschweig, 21 November 1967.
Moments musicaux (bassoon, piano) 1967.
Incontri brevi (flute, clarinet) 1967; first performed Braunwald, 24 July 1968. Recorded Musicaphon BM 30 SL 1533.
Zwei Sonaten (organ; from *Musica spei*) 1968; first performed Lausanne, 28 November 1969.
Streichquartett 4 1968–70; first performed Zagreb, 12 May 1971. Recorded EL CD 6066.
Oktett (clarinet, horn, bassoon, 2 violins, viola, cello, double bass) 1969; first performed Zurich, 29 January 1970.
Vier Stücke (clarinet, piano) 1969; first performed Witten, 26 April 1970.
Inventionen und Intermezzi (2 gambens, harpsichord) 1969.
Musik für Klavier und Kleines Orchester (piano, small orchestra) 1970, revised 1985.
Monumentum (organ) 1971; first performed Berlin, 19 September 1971.
Neun Momente (viola, piano) 1973; first performed Berlin, 26 September 1973.
Reaktionen (violin, piano) 1973–4; first performed Mannheim, 22 November 1974.
Kammermusik für fünf Bläser (flute/piccolo, oboe, clarinet, horn, bassoon) 1974; first performed Zurich, 21 June 1975. Recorded Musicaphon BM 30 SL 1716.
Consort-Music (flute/piccolo/alto flute, clarinet/bass clarinet, trumpet, string quartet) 1975; first performed Hamburg, 15 June 1976.
Sevenminute-Play (flute, piano) 1976; first performed New York, 20 February 1977.
Monodie I (flute, harp) 1977.
Fünf Monologe (guitar) 1977.
Trio (flute, oboe, bassoon) 1980; first performed Lucerne, 30 August 1981.
Notturni (cello, double bass) 1981; first performed Munich, 6 December 1982.
Musik für sechs Schlagzeuger (6 percussionists) 1983–4; first performed Basle, 24 September 1984.
Six Short Pieces (flute, viola, guitar) 1984; first performed San Francisco, 10 February 1985.
Sonate in einem Satz (cello, piano) 1985; first performed Bruchsal, 22 September 1985. Recorded EL 17010/CD 6069.
Escursioni (flute, cello, harpsichord) 1988–9; first performed Berne, 16 May 1989.
Streichquartett 5 1989; first performed Basle, 25 October 1989.
Streichquartett 5 1989; first performed Basle, 25 October 1989.

Vocal/choral:

Elegie (alto, oboe, viola, percussion, harpsichord) 1955.
Missa (soprano, tenor, SATB choir, orchestra) 1958; first performed Basle, 1 December 1961.
Canta profana (baritone, choir, 13 instruments) 1959–60.
Die Flut (speaker, soprano, alto, tenor, baritone, double SATB choir, orchestra; Buber) 1963–4; first performed Basle, 14 May 1965.
Kana / Auferstehung (baritone, 2 violins, organ; Meier) 1964; first performed Berlin, 7 May 1965.
Der Traum meines Lebens verdämmert (mezzo-soprano, flute, 2 clarinets/bass clarinet, harp, string quartet; Hausmann) 1964; first performed Basle, 8 June 1965.
Tres cantiones sacrae (double SATB choir; Augustine) 1967; first performed Kassel, 12 April 1969. Recorded CAN 658 225.
Fünf Madrigale (soprano, tenor, orchestra; Ramuz, Shakespeare, Labe, Trakl, Petrarch) 1967–8; first performed Lucerne, 20 August 1969.
Dies unus (soprano, male voice choir, orchestra; Moses) 1971–2; first performed Zurich, 26 May 1973.
Drei Fragmente (SATB choir; Trakl, Browning, Petrarch) 1973; first performed Stuttgart, 10 February 1974. Recorded Jecklin Disco 599.
Gesänge zur Nacht (soprano, chamber orchestra; Bachmann, Burkart) 1978; first performed Zurich, 2 March 1979.
Fünf Gesänge (SATB choir, clarinet, horn, trumpet, trombone; Meier) 1980–1; first performed Basle, 5 February 1982.
Schlag an mit deiner Sichel (4 voices, renaissance instruments) 1981–2. Recorded Jecklin Disco 599.
Monolog der Ophelia (from scene 5 of the opera *Ophelia*; soprano, orchestra; Meier) 1985; first performed Basle, 11–12 December 1986.
Lux et tenebrae (soprano, baritone, men's choir, orchestra; based on *Dies unus*) 1986–7; first performed Basle, Autumn 1989.

Gesänge der Liebe (baritone, orchestra; Salomonis) 1987–8; first performed Lucerne, 1988.

Opera:

Die Erretung Thebens 1960–2; first performed Zurich, 23 June 1963.
Kaiser Jovian (Meier) 1964–6; first performed Karlsruhe, 4 March 1967.
Ein Engel kommt nach Babylon (Dürrenmatt) 1975–6; first performed Zurich, 5 June 1977.
Der Kirschgarten (Chekhov, Duwel) 1979–81; first performed Zurich, 4 December 1981.
Ophelia (Meier) 1982–3; first performed Schwetzingen, 2 May 1984.

Other:

Relations (ballet) 1973–4; first performed Berne, 16 February 1975.
Die Schwarze Spinne (music based on Gotthelf) 1982.

PUBLICATIONS

By Kelterborn: "Aufsatz zu einem atonalen harmonischen Ordnungsprinzip", in *Schweizerische Musik Zeitung*, 1954; *Etuden zur Harmonielehre*, n.d.; *Zum Beispiel Mozart*, n.d.; *Musik im Brennpunkt*, 1988.

On Kelterborn: in *New Grove Dictionary of Music and Musicians*; Ernst Mohr, "Zur Kompositions-Technik RK", in *Musica*, 24, 1970; Wolf Eberhard von Lewinski, "Schwierige Musik zum Verstehen. Der Komponist RK" in *Musica*, 24, 1970; Dino Larese and Franzpeter Coebels, *RK*, Amriswil, 1970; Martin S. Weber, "Die Orchesterwerke RK", in *Schwäbische Sängerzeitung*, April 1975; "RK", in *Die Musik in Geschichte und Gegenwart*, Kassel, 1979; Kurt von Fischer, "RK", in *Dissonanz*, 4, 1985.

Rudolf Kelterborn comments:

A number of techniques from serial procedures to limited aleatoric methods are important in my music. In several works the expressive domain is already alluded to in the title: *Nachtstücke / Night Pieces*, *Phantasmen*, *Traummusik / Dream Music*, *Erinnerungen an Orpheus / Recognitions of Orpheus*, *Chiaroscuro*. Its language ranges from meditative and lyrical restraint to dramatic forcefulness, from emotional distance—partly determined by constructive principles—to elementary directness. The "contents" of my music are characterized by the often simply unbearable tension between the wonders of the world and the tremendous possibilities of life on the one hand, and the fears, terrors and misery of our times on the other.

* * *

All of Rudolf Kelterborn's teachers—Walther Geiser in Basle, Willy Burkhard in Zurich, and Boris Blacher in Salzburg—left distinct traces in his early works. In his composition studies at the North West German Academy of Music at Detmold, the young Kelterborn was influenced by Gunther Bialas and Wolfgang Fortner. Significantly, at that time Fortner composed dodecaphonically, while Bialas employed an extended tonality. Kelterborn, who in his numerous studies has proved himself an undogmatic theoretician, understands that philosophical principles in music are only ever part of an ever more extensive range of possibilities.

He had already uncovered versatile solutions and new creative principles during the 1950s, receiving international recognition for works such as the *Suite* for brass, percussion, and string orchestra premiered in Stockholm in 1956. With him, as with Stravinsky, there is always a trade-off between structural considerations and innovative sonorities. Early pieces such as the *Sonata* for 16 solo strings, in which high and low strings create a dispersed double choir, or the Second String Quartet which consists of two outer movements of experimental sound and a middle movement of impervious texture, already indicate a very personal aesthetic insight within the contemporary avant-garde.

In the years that followed Kelterborn developed at a remarkable rate, though he shied away from any illusion of "accelerated stylistic development", a notion which Heinz-Klaus Metzger adhered to (their dispute took place in the journal *Weltwoche* in April 1967). The *Lyrische Kammermusik* for clarinet, violin and viola had already shown how Kelterborn sought to develop the basic serialist methodology with both intellectual lucidity and a kind of playfulness. The later *Variations* for oboe and orchestra uses a dodecaphonic cell thematically; variations 5 and 7 are assigned to string soloists but throughout the work the oboe part, conceived for Heinz Holliger, remains central whatever its register.

In the mid-1950s, Kelterborn began to recognize the dangers (to both the music and its audience) inherent in interpreting dodecaphony dogmatically and statically. The titles alone of three orchestral pieces, *Mouvements* from 1957, *Metamorphosen* from 1960, and *Changements* from 1973, give notice of a commitment to motion and change, and this became the distinguishing characteristic of Kelterborn's work. A title like *Vier Nachstücke*, a chamber orchestra work from 1963, is either deceptive or ironic, for every allusion to "night music" is ripped to pieces by sudden expressionistic outbursts, and dynamically articulated processes begin to emerge which are continued throughout the next three decades, culminating subtly in *Chiaroscuro: Canzoni per orchestra* and the *Visions sonores* for six percussion groups and six obbligato instruments. Even so, the 1988 *Gesänge der Liebe* surpasses even these for variety.

Kelterborn once admitted: "When I feel I have reached a certain stage in my work, I write a new string quartet". This is particularly true in the case of the third, written in 1963. The two outer movements, subtitled "Scena I" and "Scena II" are based on a "principle of dramatic form". In the first of these, a cantabile idea is opposed to a "vehemently disgruntled motive". The latter more and more begins to dominate as the movement progresses, gradually overpowering the cantabile and finally destroying it. The process is rather different in "Scena II". In between, the middle movement, "Fantasia notturno", creates a mood of lunar irrationality, in which—as in some of his other works—Kelterborn avoids the imputation of bland rationality by setting out from the secure ground of his own conception, and assimilating "classical" as well as "romantic" features without losing the actuality of his own musical language.

Kelterborn's outstanding quality, whatever the genre, is a firm confidence in both the external influences bearing on a work and its internal potentialities. A wide education allows him to draw from a wide range of biblical texts (the Vulgate in *Musica spei*, Martin Buber's translation in *Die Flut*), and from Augustine's *Confessions* in *Tres cantiones sacrae*. He has a barometric instinct for dramatic subject-matter in his operas, and has collaborated with contemporaries like Meier and Dürrenmatt (the latter arranged the libretto of *An Angel Comes to Babylon* for him).

In *Fünf Madrigalen*, Kelterborn integrated fragments of texts by five different poets in such a way that they throw extra light upon an instrumental setting which was composed first. The colour values of his music and its motion enabled works like *Miroirs* and *Metamorphosen* to appear in dance versions. His only ballet to date, *Relations*, reveals ideas about human nature which demand to be enlarged upon not only in an acoustic, but also in a visual way.

I had to sum up Kelterborn's compositional merits in 1984 for a prize awarded by the Schweizerische Tonkunstlerverein. I wrote: "Rudolf Kelterborn's compositions communicate equally well with amateurs as with specialists. By fruitfully pursuing the problem of musical 'communication', not only in the orchestral work bearing that name, but in all his works, he has managed to create a body of work of unusual breadth and integrity. His artistic intelligence has enabled him to combine his inner imperatives seamlessly with the external demands of composition. As fantasy and realism harmonize in his personality, they also prove to be the basic poles of work of universal resonance. Rudolf Kelterborn has not only enriched Swiss culture, but also the music of our time."

—Andres Briner
(translated by C. Nielinger)

KENNAN, Kent (Wheeler). American. Born in Milwaukee, Wisconsin, 18 April 1913. Educated: private keyboard study; University of Michigan, Ann Arbor, 1930–2; Eastman School of Music, Rochester, New York, 1932–4, 1935–6, B.M. (composition and theory), 1934, M.M. (composition), 1936; study in Rome (under Ildebranda Pizzetti), 1937. Served in U.S. Army Air Corps as bandsman, warrant officer bandleader, 1942–5. Instructor in theory and piano, Kent State University, Ohio, 1939–40; professor, Ohio State University, Columbus, 1947–9; teacher of orchestration and composition, Eastman School of Music, summers 1954, 1956; instructor, 1940–2, and professor of theory and composition, 1946–7, 1949–83, now emeritus, University of Texas, Austin. Recipient: Prix de Rome, 1936. Mailing address: 1513 Westover Road, Austin, Texas 78703, U.S.A.

Publishers: Carl Fischer, New York; Warner/Chappell Music, 265 Secaucus Road, Secaucus, New Jersey 07094, U.S.A.; G. Schirmer, New York.

Symphonies/orchestral:

Night Soliloquy (flute, piano, strings; or flute, wind ensemble; also arranged for flute, piano) 1936; first performed Rochester, New York, 1938. Recorded RCA Victor; Mercury; Columbia; Grand Awards.
Il campo dei fiori (trumpet, orchestra) 1937; first performed Rochester, New York, 1939. Recorded Mercury.
Nocturne (viola, orchestra) 1937; first performed Rochester, New York, 1939. Recorded Mercury.
Promenade 1938; first performed Rochester, New York, 1939. Recorded Mercury.
Symphony 1938; first performed Rochester, New York, 1938.
Dance Divertimento (arranged for 2 pianos) 1938; first performed Rochester, New York, 1939.
Andante (oboe, orchestra) 1939.
Concertino (piano, orchestra; arranged for piano, wind) 1946.

Chamber/instrumental:

Sonata (piano) 1936 (incomplete).
Night Soliloquy (flute, piano/guitar/harp/vibraphone) 1936; first performed Rochester, New York, 1939. Recorded Carlston Records 101.
Three Preludes (piano) 1939.
Sea Sonata (violin, piano) 1939.
Sonata (piano) 1942 (incomplete).
Sonatina (piano) 1945.
Scherzo, Aria and Fugato (oboe, piano) 1948.
Two Preludes (piano) 1951.
Sonata (trumpet, piano) 1956; first performed St Louis, Missouri, 1956. Recorded Crystal S368; Trumpeter; Golden Crest; Telarc 5032.

Vocal/choral:

A Clear Midnight (voice, piano; or chorus, piano) 1938; first performed Rome, 1939.
I Saw the White Daisies (voice, piano) 1938; first performed Rome, 1939.
I Shall Not Care (voice, piano) 1938; first performed Rome, 1939.
Blessed Are They That Mourn (chorus, orchestra) 1939; first performed Kent, Ohio, 1940.
The Unknown Warrior Speaks (unaccompanied male chorus) 1944; first performed Washington, D.C., 1944.
A John Donne Prayer (chorus, piano, glockenspiel) 1946; first performed Austin, Texas, 1980.

Other:

Prokofiev: *Sonata Op 94 for Flute or Violin and Piano* arranged for clarinet, piano or orchestra) 1984; first performed Oberlin, Ohio, 1985.
Brahms: *Sonata Op 100 for Violin and Piano* (arranged for clarinet, piano) 1988; first performed Chicago, 1988.
Brahms: *Intermezzo Op 118 No 2 for Piano* (arranged for cello, piano) 1988; first performed Austin, Texas, 1989.

PUBLICATIONS

By Kennan: *The Technique of Orchestration*, Englewood Cliffs, New Jersey, 1952, 1979, 1990; *Counterpoint*, Englewood Cliffs, New Jersey, 1959, 1972, 1987.

On Kennan: J. A. Wyss, "The Art Songs of KK", dissertation, University of Texas, Austin, 1981.

* * *

Though his output is rather small and the bulk of his important work was written before he was 40, Kent Kennan is a significant presence in American music, enjoying a status not dissimilar to that of Howard Ferguson in England, another composer whose recent silence has not diminished his overall importance. Kennan's manuals on orchestration and counterpoint are both still in print and have been of considerable significance to three generations of American music students. He is known as a fine teacher.

His early orchestral work is marked by elements of impressionism, with a constant Romantic undercurrent which gives a strong emotional charge to such pieces as *Night Soliloquy*, the *Andante* for oboe and orchestra, and the beautiful *Nocturne* for viola and orchestra. The 1938 *Symphony* demonstrates impressive technical skills (of a sort adumbrated in the textbooks mentioned above) and a finely dramatic edge. It is, perhaps, one of the forgotten masterworks of the American symphonic canon and deserves to be revived. Not the least of Kennan's influences in the early part of his career, before he took a marked and permanent turn toward neo-classicism of a not entirely Stravinskian sort, was jazz. There are echoes of it in the rhythmic awareness, though not the specific metres, of *Dance Divertimento* (which usefully stands comparison with some of Aaron Copland's early dance scores) and in the exuberant *Il campo dei fiori*, where the distinctive valving of the jazz soloist combines with the strongly evocative middle-register trumpet sound associated with Italian concert bands; Kennan studied under Ildebranda Pizzetti as a Prix de Rome laureate in 1936–7. There is also a fine trumpet sonata, extensively recorded. Kennan's experience as an army bandmaster in the years that followed cannot be adduced as an influence, but does seem to confirm his facility in this direction.

Perhaps the high-tide line of Kennan's career as a composer was the premiere of his moving unaccompanied choral piece *The Unknown Warrior Speaks*, which was given in the presence of the then First Lady, Eleanor Roosevelt. It is, perhaps, his finest single work, and one of the significant American choral works of its period. Kennan's imaginative skills as a setter of texts are further evident in *A John Donne Prayer* with its ringing glockenspiel part, and in the lovely *A Clear Midnight*.

In recent years, Kennan has made impressive transcriptions and arrangements of works by Prokofiev, whose asymmetric metres he has occasionally adopted, and by Brahms. Typical of the whole range of his work they are intelligently conceived and impressively crafted.

—Russell Kane

KERNIS, Aaron Jay. American. Born in Philadelphia, 15 January 1960. Educated at San Francisco Conservatory of Music (under John Adams), 1977–8; Manhattan School of Music, New York City (under Charles Wuorinen and Elias Tanenbaum), 1978–81, B.Mus.; Yale School of Music, New Haven, Connecticut (under Jacob Druckman, Gilbert Amy, Bernard Rands and Morton Subotnick), 1981–3, M.Mus. Freelance composer; sometime conductor. Recipient: BMI Student Composer Awards, 1976, 1983, 1984; Rome Prize, American Academy in Rome, 1984–5; Joseph N. Bearns Prize, Columbia University, 1985; Guggenheim Fellowship, 1985–6; New York Foundation for the Arts Fellowship, 1988; Tippett Award; National Endowment for the Arts grant. Mailing address: c/o G. Schirmer/Music Sales Corp., 225 Park Avenue South, 18th floor, New York, New York 10003, U.S.A.

Publishers: Schirmer; Wilhelm Hansen/Chester, London.

Symphonies/orchestral:

Mirror of Heat and Light (Cycle V—Part 2) (large orchestra) 1984–5; first performed New York City, 1985.
Invisible Mosaic III (large orchestra) 1988; first performed New York City, 1989.
Symphony in Waves 1989; first performed St Paul, Minnesota, 1989.

Chamber/instrumental:

Four Miniatures (2 alto saxophones) 1977.
Cycle II (2 pianos—4 or 8 hands) 1979; first performed New York City, 1980.
Morning (viola, guitar) 1980.
Meditation (in Memory of John Lennon) (cello, piano) 1981; first performed New York City, 1983.
Suite in Three Parts (guitar) 1981; first performed New Haven, Connecticut, 1984.
Music for Trio (Cycle IV) (flute, cello, piano) 1982; first performed New Haven, Connecticut, 1982.
Suite in Three Parts (organ) 1982; first performed New Haven, Connecticut, 1982.
Passacaglia-Variations (viola, piano) 1985; first performed San Francisco, 1986.
Invisible Mosaic I (clarinet, violin, cello, piano) 1985–6; first performed (partial) New York City, 1988.
Phantom Polka (accordion) 1987; first performed New York City, 1988.
Poisoned Nocturnes (piano) 1987.
Before Sleep and Dreams (piano) 1987–90; first performed Washington, D.C., 1990.
Delicate Songs (flute, violin, cello) 1988; first performed New York City, 1989.
Invisible Mosaic II (flute, oboe, clarinet, bassoon, trumpet, horn, trombone, tuba, piano, harp, 2 percussion, 2 violins, viola, cello, double bass) 1988; first performed Paris, 1988.
String Quartet ("musica celestis") 1990; first performed New York City, 1990.

Vocal/choral:

Six Fragments of Gertrude Stein (soprano, flute) 1979; first performed New York City, 1980.
Stein Times Seven (SSATB choir, piano) 1980; first performed New York City, 1981. Recorded CRI, release 1991; no 6 on Nonesuch "Songs of America".
Death Fugue (bass-baritone, double bass, percussion) 1981; first performed New Haven, Connecticut, 1982.
Cycle III (soprano, baritone, flute, oboe, piano, harp, guitar, viola, 2 percussion) 1981; first performed New York City, 1982.
Nocturne (soprano, trumpet, 2 pianos, 2 percussion) 1982; first performed New Haven, Connecticut, 1982.
Teach Me Thy Way, O Lord (SATB choir, organ) 1982; first performed New Haven, Connecticut, 1982.
Morningsongs (baritone, flute, 2 clarinets, bassoon, horn, harp, percussion, violin, viola, cello) 1982–3; first performed Tanglewood, Massachusetts, 1983. Recorded CRI, release 1991.
Dream of the Morning Sky (Cycle V—Part 1) (soprano, large orchestra; Momaday) 1982–3; first performed New York City, 1983.
America(n) (Day)Dreams (mezzo-soprano, flute, clarinet, trumpet, horn, percussion, harp, piano, violin, viola, cello, double bass) 1984; first performed New York City, 1984.
Praise Ye the Lord (unaccompanied SATB choir) 1984; first

performed New Haven, Connecticut, 1984.

I Will Lie Down (SATB choir, piano) 1985.

Love Scenes (soprano, cello) 1986–7; first performed New York City, 1987. Recorded CRI, release 1991.

Songs of Innocence (Books I and II) (high voice, piano; Blake) 1988–9; first performed New York City, 1989.

Brilliant Sky, Infinite Sky (baritone, violin, percussion, piano) 1990; first performed St Paul, Minnesota, 1990. Recorded CRI, release 1991.

Aaron Jay Kernis comments:

My work has often been an amalgam of many different styles and influences, the most important being that of 19th-century music, minimalism and impressionism. My musical development accelerated after discovering minimal music in my late teens. I began to compose music that dealt with rhythm, time, pitch and form in a highly organized way; more often than not this music was exceedingly lush, lyrical and dramatic and used these elements to establish tight formal unity and coherence. Later I decided to leave the notion of such conscious control behind, preferring instead to allow myself more freedom in my range of choices while still retaining the sense of the organic whole that I had developed through the strictly controlled earlier work. At this time in my life (having recently turned 30) I feel I have reached a crucial juncture. Now the search for freedom and greater access to my unconscious, so difficult and painful through my late 20s, seems to have led me to a place where the diverse influences in my work are converging and unifying into a distinct, personal identity once more. Of great importance along the way has been my love of composing for the voice and for the orchestra.

I find myself more comfortable with music that is consistently beautiful (or pretty) than dissonant or tense like most modernist music. (On the other hand, I regard Morton Subotnick, Harrison Birtwistle and Ralph Shapey as three of the strongest musical visionaries of our time. In the end the vision is often more important in my estimation than the specific nature of the musical language used to elucidate it.) Mostly, I'm impatient with music that is all one thing or the other. I wish to compose music that speaks to all the emotions—music that has beauty, melody (an element that has been especially neglected in recent music), tension and relaxation, conflict and resolution. I feel a greater kinship with music of past centuries than with that of our century, but at the same time feel vehemently that we cannot return to the past musically (as some neo-romantics and neo-modernists have tried to do) but must carry the present, past and future with us at all times.

I hope to create music that has the potential to transmit emotions and experiences felt during the compositional process—music that speaks and sings in fresh ways and ultimately moves the listener.

* * *

A measure of instant fame befell the diminutive, soft-spoken Aaron Jay Kernis in June 1983. At the age of 23 he was invited to submit his orchestral work *Dream of the Morning Sky* for a public sight-reading session by Zubin Mehta and the New York Philharmonic. At a certain juncture, Mehta stopped the orchestra and complained of some obscurity in the score. "Just read what's there," the composer snapped back, earning a round of applause from the mostly young, new-music-oriented audience. The press was also in attendance; within a week the young composer had achieved national recognition.

Kernis had, by that time, already obviously achieved some fame on his own, or Mehta wouldn't have had that score on his podium. Born in Philadelphia, Kernis claims not to have had any leanings toward music until age 12. After that, he taught himself piano and, later, composition. He studied at the San Francisco Conservatory, Manhattan School of Music, Yale School of Music and—as laureale of the coveted Rome Prize—the American Academy in Rome; his teachers included influences as diverse as the romantic-minimalist John Adams and the strict atonalist Charles Wuorinen.

Barely past 30, Kernis has already demonstrated a remarkable diversity of styles, and his music has been taken up by an impressive number of orchestras and other performing groups. *Dream of the Morning Sky*, the work that gave Mehta some difficulty (but was described by the critic Andrew Porter as "rich and imaginative") is full of a young man's exuberance. A large orchestra is called for; the harmony is full of glitter, an almost blinding and original summoning of the forces of latter-day diatonicism. At the end a soprano, much amplified, sings the verses of a pantheistic poem by N. Scott Momaday. Reminiscences in the score of some of David Del Tredici's *Alice* works do it no discredit.

The quality of eclecticism is evident in most of Kernis's music, but among the many voices heard his own is predominant. There is a genial intermix in for example his *America(n) (Day)Dreams* between a light-textured but somewhat abrasive dissonant counterpoint in some of the sections, interspersed with sudden and often droll plunges into a corny and old-fashioned pop-song style. On the other hand, in his quiet, haunting *Love Scenes* for voice and cello alone, the kinship to the soaring lyricism of Mahler comes occasionally to the fore.

At his young age Kernis has fared remarkably well among his contemporary composers in securing distinguished performances. His most ambitious orchestral work to date, the 30-minute *Symphony in Waves*, was commissioned and performed by the St Paul Chamber Orchestra under John Adams. *Love Scenes* was introduced by the marvellous young American soprano Dawn Upshaw; the song-cycle *Brilliant Sky Infinite Sky* was first sung by Sanford Sylvan; *Invisible Mosaic III* had its acclaimed premiere by Stanislaw Skrowacewski and the New York-based American Composers Orchestra.

The Mosaic series is one of Kernis's most noted creations to date. Stemming, he claims, from his first viewings of the famous medieval mosaics at Ravenna, the three works are meant to be the reflection of Kernis's own reactions to these ancient stones, and to a series of personal visions they inspired in him. The first two in the series are for chamber ensemble; the third, composed in 1988, calls for full orchestra.

It is a remarkable work, lasting some 15 minutes and traversing in that time an impressively broad orchestral vocabulary. Wisps of Stravinsky surface from time to time; this is the outside influence most readily identified. For the rest, *Invisible Mosaic III* is one of the bravest works by a young composer—"brave" in the sense that anyone of less than "star" stature would dare to compose for large orchestra in a dense and difficult style that must conductors—and most boards of directors of orchestras—would shy away from. The element of bravery in Kernis's music has always been readily detectable.

—Alan Rich

KETTING, Otto. Dutch. Born in Amsterdam, 3 September 1935. Educated at Royal Conservatory, The Hague (trumpet, composition under Piet Ketting), 1952–8; further composition study under Karl Amadeus Hartmann, Munich. Trumpeter, The Hague Philharmonic Orchestra and with other orchestras, 1955–61; teacher of composition, Rotterdam Conservatory, 1967–71; teacher of composition, Royal Conservatory, The Hague, 1971–4; director, Rotterdam Conservatory contemporary music ensemble, from 1978; artistic adviser, Utrecht Symphony Orchestra, from 1983. Recipient: Gaudeamus Composition Prize (for *Due canzoni*), 1958. Mailing address: c/o Donemus, Paulus Potterstraat 14, 1971 CZ Amsterdam, The Netherlands.

Publishers: Donemus; Edition Basart; Orpheus Edtie.

Symphonies/orchestral:

Sinfonietta (wind, percussion, strings) 1954.
Fanfares (brass, percussion) 1956.
Passacaglia 1957.
Due canzoni 1957. Recorded Vierhonderd Jaar Nederlandse Muziek, vol.2.
Concertino (2 trumpets, orchestra) 1958.
Symphony No 1 1959.
Divertimento festivo (brass) 1960. Recorded Eurosound ES 46.344.
Concertino (jazz quintet, orchestra) 1960.
Fanfare et cortège 1960.
Intrada festiva 1960.
Variazioni 1960.
Pas de deux 1961.
Premiere (big band) 1961.
Alleman (suite from the film by Haanstra) 1963.
Collage No 9 (22 players) 1963; first performed Amsterdam, 26 January 1966.
Collage No 6 (free-jazz group, orchestra) 1967.
In memoriam Igor Stravinsky 1971.
Time Machine (winds, percussion) 1972; first performed Rotterdam, 5 May 1972.
For Moonlight Nights (flute, 26 instruments) 1973; first performed Hilversum, 17 April 1975.
Adagio (chamber orchestra) 1977.
Symphony for Saxophones and Orchestra 1978. Recorded Composers' Voice CVH 1.
Monumentum (brass, piano, percussion) 1983.
Capriccio (violin, chamber orchestra) 1987.
Adagio 1989. Recorded Composers' Voice CVS 1984/2.
Symphony No 3 1990.

Chamber/instrumental:

Prelude and Fugue 1952 (piano) 1952.
Fuga 1953 a tre voci (piano) 1953.
Concerto per organo (organ) 1953.
Drie fanfares (brass sextet) 1954.
Sonata (brass quartet) 1955.
Komposition mit zwolf Tonen (piano) 1956.
Sonatina I (piano) 1956.
Kleine Suite (3 trumpets) 1957.
Serenade (cello, piano) 1957.
Intrada (horn or trumpet) 1958.
Thema en variaties (clarinet, bassoon, piano) 1958.
Collage No 8 (bass clarinet or flute, piano) 1958.
Four Pieces for Jazz Ensemble (septet) 1964.
A Set of Pieces (jazz quartet) 1964.
A Set of Pieces (flute, piano) 1967. Recorded Composers' Voice CV 8102.
A Set of Pieces (wind quintet) 1968.
Minimal Music (5 players) 1970.
Collage No 5 (piano) 1976. Recorded Attacca Babel 8421–6.
Mars (4 clarinets, 4 saxophones) 1979.
Quodlibet (2 percussion, piano, bass clarinet, string quartet) 1979.
Autumn (horn, piano) 1980.
Musik zu einem Tonfilm (2 saxophones, trumpet, trombone, percussion, piano, 2 violas) 1982.
Summer (bass clarinet, flute, piano) 1985. Recorded Attacca Babel 8531–6.
Trio (violin, cello, piano) 1988.
Winter (alto flute, harp, violin, cello) 1988.
Preludium (12 saxophones) 1989.

Vocal/choral:

Kerstliederen (chorus, orchestra) 1953.
Bim en Bom (children's chorus, piano) 1958.
Alabama (*sprechstimme*, flute, double bass) 1966.
Four Negro Spirituals (voice, 5 instruments) 1968.
Song Without Words (soprano, piano) 1968.
The Light of the Sun (soprano, orchestra) 1978. Recorded Composers' Voice CVH 8504.

Opera:

Dummies (soprano, tenor, baritone, instrumental ensemble; Schierbeek) 1974; first performed The Hague, 14 November 1974.
O, Gij, Rhinoceros (4 voices, instrumental ensemble) 1977; first performed 2 June 1977.
Ithaka (soloists, chorus, orchestra; Hin, OK) 1986. Recorded Composers' Voice CVS 1986/4.

Other:

Het Laatste Bericht (ballet by Harkarvy; orchestra) 1962.
Cymbeline (incidental music to Shakespeare; octet) 1962.
Intérieur (ballet by Flier; orchestra) 1963.
Barrière (ballet by Flier; tape) 1963.
De Gouden Sleutel (ballet by Glasstone; flute, clarinet, harp, piano, percussion) 1964.
Faust (incidental music to Goethe; tape) 1964.
De wolken voorbij (incidental music to Billetdoux; quartet) 1965.
Antigone (incidental music to Sophocles; male choir, sextet) 1966.
Hamlet (incidental music to Shakespeare; tape) 1966.
Collage No 7 (ballet by Sanders; orchestra) 1967.
Luther (incidental music to Osborne; tape) 1967.
Zoveel vragen (incidental music to Brecht; voice, 2 instruments) 1968.
Hippolytus (incidental music to Euripides; chorus, quintet) 1969.
Eduard II (incidental music to Brecht; voice, septet) 1970.
Fata banana (incidental music to Lucebert; voice, 10 instruments) 1971.
Hippe vogels van Bikini (incidental music to van Houweningen; tape) 1971.
Theatre Piece (ballet by Sanders; tape) 1973.
Romance in Rotterdam (incidental music to de Boer; voice, orchestra) 1976.

J.S. Bach: *Vor Deinen Thron* (arranged for small orchestra) 1957.

V. Haussmann: *Pavane* (arranged for string orchestra) 1958.
Maurice Ravel: *Manteau de Fleurs* (arranged for mezzo-soprano, orchestra) 1990.

Film scores: *Chemie*, 1962; *Presenting IHC Holland*, 1963; *Alleman*, 1963 (recorded BV Haast 023); *Scheepsbouw*, 1963; *Co Westerik*, 1965; *Slochteren aan de lijn*, 1965; *The River Must Live*, 1966; *The Land Must Provide*, 1967; *Bloemkamp*, 1969; *Gas voor Muggenbeet*, 1970; *Air Is for Breathing*, 1970; *Er zijn nog Zeeuwen*, 1971; *Bij de beesten af*, 1972 (recorded BV Haast 023); *Den Biesbos*, 1973; *Doktor Pulder zaait papavers*, 1975 (recorded BV Haast 023); *Uit het gezichtspunt van de eeuwigheid*, 1977; *Het Archief*, 1979; *Grootstad*, 1980; *Het theater van het geheugen*, 1982; *De Anna*, 1983; *The Color of Holland*, 1988.

* * *

Any composer's personality is formed by the influence on his creative imagination and impulse of his background, training and total experiences: his art is a product of the interaction of this personality with the aesthetic, social and political circumstances in which he is placed by chance and chronology. This is worth repeating, because the musical situation in Holland is only imperfectly grasped outside its boundaries. For reasons of political history and the many changes in these boundaries, Holland as we know it is a fairly young nation, and while composers of the "low countries" have been at the forefront of European culture since the Renaissance, a specifically "Dutch" tradition of composition, while distinct and recognisable, has shallow roots. While (with Scandinavia) it flourishes more than anywhere else in Europe currently, the Dutch composition school has been relatively brief, historically, unlike its performing tradition.

Otto Ketting was born in Amsterdam in 1935, and like many composers of his generation—Schat, Lovendie, Louis Andriessen, Kox, for instance—reached early maturity in the mid 1950s. Holland had lost more self-respect than most nations during World War II, and musically the nation was holding its breath. Diepenbrock was no more than a dim memory. Pijper was dead, Badings discredited, Hendrik Andriessen seemed to breath the air of another age and the one really major original voice, Vermeulen, who might have acted as a rallying point, lived quite apart from the centre stage, an Achilles brooding in his tent, unperformed, almost an embarrassment. The establishment was in the hands of a few minor if worthy figures like Flothuis, Landré, van Lier, Esher. If not actually a vacuum, Holland was certainly an area of low pressure. Out of this emerged the two characters of Henkermans, last link with the old pre-war tradition, and Ton de Leeuw, a sort of John the Baptist figure—pioneer and guru, opening a dozen doors but entering none of them. Unshackled by a strong Nationalist tradition, the new generation took on board influences from a vast range of sources in a breezy, undogmatic way to establish a rich proliferation and variety of musical voices, and a development quite different from the mainstream of the European post-war avant-garde: fresh, characteristic and unique.

Ketting graduated (in trumpet and composition) from the Royal Conservatory in The Hague, where he later taught composition for a number of years. He continued his studies with Karl Amadeus Hartmann, whose qualities of clarity, force and integrity left an indelible mark on the young Dutchman. The influences most clearly seen on Ketting's first mature works—the *Passacaglia* and *Due canzoni* for instance—are of early Webern in the intellectual precision of structure, notation, organisation of material, removal of gesture and padding, formal layout and concentration, and of Schoenberg expressionism in the late romantic sound world and strict, if undogmatic response to serialism. A distinct personality is nevertheless clearly in evidence, and its increasing emergence in *Symphony No 1* is as much a feature of his stylistic development as his growing confidence in the deployment of large forces. Also noticeable early, and throughout his compositional career, is a characteristic use of wind instruments, both in separate ensemble and as an individual section within the orchestra. This, coupled with certain rhythmic patterns and particular combinations with other instruments, has caused at least one commentator to think of Stravinsky.

No genuine creative imagination exists on only one level of thought, however; it continually finds new sets of problems to solve and does so with new material—exactly the position in which Ketting found himself in the 1960s, with his self-constructed musical world, complete, perfect, freestanding but basically becalmed. He needed opening up. The winds that filled his sails were the same subversive ones that blew many less resolute composers off course in that remarkable decade—jazz, improvisation, minimalism, the "discovery" of Varèse—but which Ketting with his firm ideals integrated into his own voice. He was also invited to compose film music, and the combination served rapidly to loosen his style and enrich his palette, his early fragility and concern for minutiae being replaced with greater vigour and range of force. We see a number of scores involving jazz instruments—*Concertino* or *Collage No 6*, for instance. Drama *per se*—albeit musical drama—became an integral part of his work, with a confidence to allow instruments to advance a musical argument rather than be dominated by it. An atmosphere or mood was perceived as an element in music, in its own right, related, and not a side issue to be avoided. This is seen clearly in perhaps his best-known score, *Time Machine* for wind instruments and percussion, and reaches its most extreme form in *For Moonlight Nights* for flute and 26 players.

Ketting's development can most obviously be seen approaching a new phase in the late 1970s, for instance in his second Symphony for saxophone quartet and orchestra, a work of great power, challenging, striking, and essentially of transition. The stunning explosion of sound at the opening looks backward, while the constantly unfolding melody which binds the work together and into which everything eventually integrates points the way forward. On the other side of the watershed comes *The Light of the Sun* for soprano and orchestra, originally written in 1978, but which he felt sufficiently pleased and at the same time dissatisfied with to revise five years later for an important musical occasion.

It is this reassertion of his earlier concern with restraint and understatement, the attention to detail and a search for musical "purity", but in the light of his wilder experiences, that mark out his most recent work, a synthesis of a new lyricism, sureness of instrumentation and sensitive concern for colouration and harmony. The intellectual has largely been replaced by an emotional base, but emotion seen at a distance—described rather than wallowed in. These are evident in the Piano Trio, *Symphony for Saxophones*, and, most of all, in the opera *Ithaka*—a work of real drama (as opposed to melodrama) of personality and situation, but where we feel we are eavesdropping on a series of private conversations and monologues rather than attending the usual theatrical bull-fight. It is a new way of expressing emotion. We leave the theatre feeling reflective rather than shaken, and wonder, for at least the third time in his composing career, where Ketting can possibly go from here.

However, he's done it before, and I dare say he'll do it again, solving new problems, with new material, in his own way.

—Giles Easterbrook

KEURIS, Tristan. Dutch. Born in Amersfoort, 3 October 1946. Educated at Utrecht Conservatory (composition under Ton de Leeuw). Married to Marianne Keuris; 2 children. Teacher, Sweelinck Conservatory, Amsterdam; head of composition, Utrecht Conservatory. Recipient: Composition Prize, Utrecht Conservatory; Matthijs Vermeulen Prize (for *Sinfonia*), 1975; Cultural Award, Hilversum, 1982. Mailing address: Tesselschadelaan 23, 1217 LG Hilversum, The Netherlands.

Publishers: Novello; Donemus.

Symphonies/orchestral:

Kwartet 1967.
Choral Music 1969.
Concerto for Alto Saxophone and Orchestra 1971.
Sinfonia 1974.
Serenade (oboe, orchestra) 1976.
Piano Concerto 1980.
Movements 1981.
Violin Concerto 1984.
Variations (strings) 1985.
Concerto for Saxophone Quartet and Orchestra 1986; first performed Amsterdam, 21 June 1987.
Aria (flute, orchestra) 1987; first performed Scheveningen, The Netherlands, 21 April 1988.
Symphonic Transformations 1987; first performed Houston, Texas, 18 September 1987.
Catena: Refrains and Variations (31 winds, percussion, celeste) 1988; first performed London, 2 November 1989. Recorded Tele-Ac CD, 1990.
Three Sonnets (alto saxophone, orchestra) 1989; first performed Amsterdam, 8 September 1989.

Chamber/instrumental:

Play (clarinet, piano) 1967.
Sonata (piano) 1970.
Saxophone Quartet No 1 1970.
Concertante Muziek (clarinet, horn, bassoon, piano, string quartet) 1973.
Muziek (clarinet, violin, piano) 1973.
Fantasia (flute) 1976.
Concertino (bass clarinet, string quartet) 1977, revised 1979.
Capriccio (2 oboes/1 cor anglais, 4 clarinets/2 bass clarinets, 2 bassoons, 4 horns, double bass) 1978.
Sonata (violin) 1979.
Eight Miniatures (clarinet, mandolin, guitar, marimba, violin, double bass) 1980.
Divertimento (wind quintet, violin, double bass, piano) 1982.
String Quartet No 1 1982.
Quartet for Clarinets 1983.
String Quartet No 2 1985; first performed The Netherlands, 1986. Recorded Attacca Babel 8948–5.
Music for Saxophones (saxophone quartet) 1986; first performed London, 3 March 1987.
Aria (flute, piano; reduction of orchestral piece) 1987; first performed Scheveningen, The Netherlands, April 1988.
Five Pieces (brass quintet) 1988; first performed Rotterdam, 1 April 1989.
Clarinet Quintet 1988; first performed Amsterdam, 20 January 1989.
Intermezzi (flute, 2 oboes, 2 clarinets 2 bassoons/1 contra-bassoon, 2 horns) 1989; first performed Manchester, 5 November 1989.
Canzone (clarinet) 1990.

Vocal/choral:

To Brooklyn Bridge (24 voices—6 each SATB, 4 clarinets, 4 saxophones, 2 pianos, 2 harps, 3 double basses; Hart Crane) 1988; first performed Utrecht, 17 December 1989.
Three Michelangelo Songs (mezzo-soprano, orchestra) 1989; first performed Arnheim, 21 March 1990.
L'infinito (vocal quintet, instrumental ensemble) 1990–1; first performed Utrecht, 28 February 1991.

* * *

Except where they actually *create* them, important composers seldom have much to do with national schools of composition: originality defines its own boundaries and creates followers rather than acknowledges leaders. In recent years, Holland has produced two dominant composers: Louis Andriessen is the major national figure, whose work has (rightly) found favour and performances throughout the world, and carried the banner of Dutch music overseas. Tristan Keuris is undeniably an international figure, standing quite apart from the mainstream of Dutch musical life, almost in isolation, though in the last few years the establishment—the press and his fellow composers—have come to recognize him as a fairly exceptional talent, and something to be proud of.

I say "almost" in isolation not because it is a small, overcrowded country, but because he has developed his own circle of current and ex-pupils, all devoted to him and his work. It tells us something about the man: it has happened not because he has wooed his students, but because he is an inspiring teacher, and he inspires because he is utterly in command of his material and able to communicate his love and respect for music as clearly in the conservatory as he can in the concert hall. He argues with fellow pedagogues because he wants the best deal he can get for his students; he does not argue with other composers because largely he keeps out of their way. In his life, as in his music, he is a mixture of the passionate and the objective, the strictly demanding and the indulgent. He requires of others no more than he gives of himself—his best—but settles for nothing less.

Musically, Keuris settled upon a certain course of action very early on. It was almost as if he had in mind that one day he would produce the perfect, definitive work, which would combine all the skills, bring inspiration, technique, vision, craft and hard work together into a complete statement leaving nothing out. In this light, everything can be seen as preparatory work, a step on the way. Earliest pieces are overtly exploratory, investigating sheer sound, sometimes bizarre combinations of instruments. Gradually discipline of a sort is imposed on them, but not much: that is not what they were for. Nor did a lot of himself go in—he was astute enough to realise that his personality was not formed, that it would come in time. He also had no compunction about withdrawing these pieces. By nature he looks forward. There are, of course, several failures along the road, but no culs-de-sac. In fact they proved much to the public's liking, with the result that he received his commission for *Sinfonia*, his first real international success. It is for huge orchestra, dexterously employed, full of striking musical imagery, sharp edged and focussed yet good to listen to. At a superficial level it is more "original" than some later pieces, but in other respects not.

Keuris's development has been steady and continuous, as one aspect of technique after another is perfected in an appropriate work, the knowledge stored away and then given full rein later. It is fascinating to see him systematically addressing questions of orchestral texture (*Sinfonia*, *Movements*), string writing (*Variations*), wind writing (*Catena*, *Intermezzi*), brass (*Five Pieces*), part-writing and quartet texture (*No 1* is the exercise, *No 2* the masterpiece), rhythmic, harmonic refinement, lyrical content, the voice (*Three Michelangelo Songs*), choral texture (*To Brooklyn Bridge*), intractible forces (*Eight Miniatures*), and see the individual personality emerging, perhaps not coincidentally. Even pieces that don't really "belong" in the schedule, like the *Three Sonnets*, *Quartet for Clarinets* or *Passeggiate* solve some little structural nicety or problem of voicing. This is not saying that he deliberately "holds back" in any work or short-changes a commissionee: rather the opposite—he gives each piece everything he's got, just selects rather carefully those commissions that will allow him to move a step closer to his firmly envisaged goal, and test out what he has learned before.

Perhaps more important is Keuris's growing mastery of form and structure, in parallel with the technical assurance. The orchestral sound is almost coincidental, certainly subservient to other considerations. Basically it is now traditional/accessible in effect, but with that exhilarating strength and sense of regeneration you get only when everything is there to serve a purpose—the advancement of a musical argument in the most lucid and appropriate way possible. What is striking in a piece like *Movements* is the appropriateness of everything—the material to the forces, the treatment to the material and the duration of both episodes to sections, and sections to each other, and to the treatment. *Symphonic Transformations* or the *Concerto for Saxophone Quartet and Orchestra* is striking in the juxtaposition and organic development of complementary lines of thematic material through the medium of pure orchestral writing in the context of abstract thought. Both, together with *Catena*, explore single-movement forms combining exposition of several thematic cells by motivic development and rigorous working, of successive tension and relaxation, the interweaving of apparently disparate elements and voices, providing the *fact* of development within a manageable time-scale. This requires minute organisation of material and produces the effect of balance of colour to structure, of instinct to intellect, and gives a clear formal outline: they are thus symphonic in content but not shape, while *Movements* is symphonic in shape but not content. In all we can see the tesserae of the epigrammatic early chamber pieces in their true perspective, part of a composite mosaic.

Recently a strong sensual streak has appeared in Keuris's music, and new pieces like *Three Michelangelo Songs* and *L'infinito* display a sheer ravishing beauty of sound, almost unique in the serious contemporary repertoire.

—Giles Easterbrook

KIM, Earl. American. Born in Dinuba, California, 6 January 1920. Educated at Los Angeles City College, 1937–9; University of California, Los Angeles (under Arnold Schoenberg), 1939–40; University of California, Berkeley (under Roger Sessions and Marc Bloch), 1946–7, 1949–50, B.A., 1951–2, M.A.; Harvard University, Cambridge, Massachusetts, M.A., 1967. Served in the U.S. Army Air Force Intelligence, 1942–6: Captain. Married (1) Nora Philipsborn in 1947; (2) Miriam Kagan in 1956; (3) Martha Potter in 1977. Lecturer, University of California, Berkeley, 1950–1; instructor, later associate professor, Princeton University, New Jersey, 1952–67; composer in residence, Princeton Seminar in Advanced Musical Studies, 1963, Marlboro Music Festival, 1965, Dartmouth Festival for the Arts, 1971, Tanglewood, Massachusetts, 1972, and Aspen Center for Compositional Studies, Colorado, 1986, 1987, 1989; professor, 1967–71, and James Edward Ditson Professor, 1971–90, emeritus, since 1990, Harvard University, Cambridge, Massachusetts. Recital pianist; co-founder and president, Musicians Against Nuclear Arms, 1981–4. Recipient: Prix de Paris, 1947–9; Guggenheim Foundation Fellowship, 1956; Brandeis University Creative Arts Award, 1971; honorary member, Phi Beta Kappa, 1990. Mailing address: 57 Francis Avenue, Cambridge, Massachusetts 02138, U.S.A.

Publisher: self.

Symphonies/orchestral:

Dialogues (piano, orchestra) 1959; first performed Princeton, New Jersey, 1959.

Violin Concerto 1979; first performed New York City, 1979. Recorded EMI Angel.

Chamber/instrumental:

Four Bagatelles (piano) 1950; first performed Berkeley, California, 1950.

Two Bagatelles (piano) 1950. Recorded RCA Victor LM 7042.

Act Without Words (from *Narratives*; trombone, cello) 1976; first performed Cambridge, Massachusetts, 1979.

Monologues (from *Narratives*; violin, cello, piano) 1976; first performed Washington, D.C., 1977.

Twelve Caprices (violin) 1980; first performed New York City, 1982.

Scenes from Childhood, August 1945 (brass quintet) 1984; first performed Boston, 1984.

Vocal/choral:

Letters Found near a Suicide (baritone, piano; Horne) 1954; first performed Princeton, New Jersey, 1954.

. . . Dead Calm . . . (from *Exercises en Route*; soprano, flute/piccolo, oboe, violin, cello, 2 percussion; Beckett) 1961; first performed Princeton, New Jersey, 1961.

They Are Far Out (from *Exercises en Route*; soprano, violin, cello, 2 percussion; Beckett) 1966; first performed Princeton, New Jersey, 1966.

—Gooseberries, She Said (from *Exercises en Route*; soprano, flute, oboe, clarinet, violin, cello, 2 percussion; Beckett) 1967; first performed Waltham, Massachusetts, 1967.

. . . Rattling On . . . (from *Exercises en Route*; soprano, flute, oboe, clarinet, violin, cello, percussion; Beckett) 1970; first performed Cambridge, Massachusetts, 1970.

Exercises en Route (concert version) 1971; first performed (complete) Marlboro, Vermont, 1982.

Earthlight (from *Narratives*; high soprano, muted violin, piano, lights; Beckett) 1973. Recorded New World NW 237.
Melodrama 1 (from *Narratives*; woman's voice, piano; Beckett) 1973; first performed Cambridge, Massachusetts, 1979.
Eh Joe (from *Narratives*; woman's voice, 2 violins, cello, 2 trumpets, alto trombone; Beckett) 1974; first performed Cambridge, Massachusetts, 1975.
Lines from Lessness (from *Narratives*; high soprano; Beckett) 1975; first performed Cambridge, Massachusetts, 1979.
Melodrama 2 (from *Narratives*; woman's voice, 2 violins, piano; Beckett) 1975; first performed Cambridge, Massachusetts, 1979.
Now and Then (soprano, flute, harp, viola; Chekhov, Beckett, Yeats) 1981; first performed Chicago, 1982.
Where Grief Slumbers (soprano, harp, string orchestra or string octet; Rimbaud, Apollinaire) 1982, revised 1989; first performed Cincinnati, Ohio, 1986; chamber version first performed Cambridge, Massachusetts, 1990.
Cornet (narrator, orchestra; Rilke) 1983; first performed Hartford, Connecticut, 1984.
The Seventh Dream (from *Scenes from a Movie*; soprano, baritone, violin, cello, piano; Rilke) 1986; first performed Cambridge, Massachusetts, 1987.
The Eleventh Dream (from *Scenes from a Movie*; soprano, baritone, violin, cello, piano; Rilke) 1988; first performed Cambridge, Massachusetts, 1990.
Three Poems in French (soprano, string quartet; Verlaine, Baudelaire) 1989.
Four Lines from Mallarmé (voice, flute, vibraphone, 4 percussion) 1989; first performed Massachusetts, 1990.
Some Thoughts on Keats and Coleridge (unaccompanied SATB voices) 1990.

Opera/music-theatre:

Exercises en Route (music theatre version; soprano, flute/piccolo, oboe, clarinet, violin, cello, 2 percussion, dance, narrator; Beckett) 1971; first performed Cambridge, Massachusetts, 1971.
Narratives (music theatre version; woman's voice, high soprano, teleprojected actor, 2 violins, cello, 2 trumpets, trombone/alto trombone, piano, lights; Beckett) 1979; first performed Cambridge, Massachusetts, 1979.
Footfalls (soprano, mezzo-soprano, 2 pianos, harpsichord) 1981; first performed Cincinnati, Ohio, 1985.

PUBLICATIONS

On Kim: Elaine Barkin, "EK's *Earthlight*", in *Perspectives of New Music*, 19, 1980–1; G.L. Jeffers, "Non-Narrative Drama: Settings by Virgil Thomson, Ned Rorem and EK of Plays by Gertrude Stein and Samuel Beckett", dissertation, University of California, Los Angeles, 1983; J. Tassell, "Golden Silences: The Flowering of EK", in *Boston Globe Magazine*, 27 February 1983.

Earl Kim comments:

Music is the most direct and unobstructed pathway to feelings and how difficult it is to express them—really, truthfully express them—without indirection of willful obstruction.

Would that one could translate oneself—literally, leaving no space for intervention between the imagined and reality.

* * *

Earl Kim, a Korean-American, chooses to express himself through miniatures that are finely-chiselled and breathtakingly intimate. This miniaturist tendency is revealed also in large-scale works, which are conceived as a conglomerate of "vignettes". His music shuns easy exuberance and contrived brilliance, instead favoring leisurely events and sparse textures. The music's economy is conveyed by a sparing use of notes and frequent silences, which imbue the music with a sense of hesitancy and incompleteness on the one hand, and expectancy on the other. The music's message thus lies only partly in what is revealed, and partly in what is unexpressed, a message pervasive of melancholy and deep contemplation. But the focus on emotion is not undercut by an indulgent subjectivity. Rather, he captures emotions in a direct yet disinterested manner. Although a student of Schoenberg, he is not a serialist and has never written an entirely serial work. The aesthetic bent for terseness and understatement makes Kim a closer "ally" to Webern than to Schoenberg. Although Kim and Webern share a penchant for brevity, Kim prefers to convey his music through the most direct means that often include tonal harmony, unambiguous structures and the repetition of clear rhythmic and melodic patterns. However, the apparent brevity and disjointedness of the music do not diminish its innate lyricism, which is a function of its vocal tendencies.

The bond of word and music underpins Kim's work. To him, words evoke images as no other medium can. Thus vocal compositions constitute the bulk of his output, often with instrumental works such as his *Violin Concerto* containing programmatic literary allusions. The importance of this marriage of word and music is evidenced by his long and close identification with the works of Samuel Beckett, a wellspring of inspiration for Kim. (Other literary sources include Yeats, Chekov, Verlaine, Baudelaire and Rilke.) Like Beckett's art, Kim's is about probing the meaning and essence of human existence and the true nature of the self. His music is concerned with stripping away non-essentials in a single-minded pursuit of the essentials so that no barrier may obstruct a direct reflection of innermost feelings. In his involvement with multimedia theater works that combine music, speech and visual images, Kim again follows Beckett's lead, for example in *Exercises en Route* and *Narratives*.

Adding to the Western literary elements that inform Kim's work, it also displays a general oriental air that is indebted to Asian cultures. For example, he acknowledges an unconscious use in his music, for over a decade, of an underlying tempo (M.M. ♪ = 40) that is characteristic of Korean court music. His fondness for heterophonic doubling of the voice by an instrument bespeaks another Asian trait. The concept of *Dead Calm*, part of *Exercises en Route*, draws on the aesthetics of the Japanese rock garden. In it, protruding large rocks form isolated island groups against a sea of white crushed stones. One can experience varying grouping of some but not all of the large rocks from different vantage points. These discrete rock images are translated into music as palindromes flanked by silences and reinterpreted continually by a technique of rotating, rearranging and displacing a limited number of pitches, rests and rhythmic values.

The composer's aesthetic outlook, which is inspired by divergent sources both Eastern or Western, is on the surface the mere sum of many eclectic separatenesses, yet on a deeper level a synthesis with recurrent themes of alienation, a search for life's essential meaning and a yearning for an inner peace. His music is an intensely personal spiritual journey predicated on a self-effacing attitude. The listener is an outsider who "eavesdrops" on a hermit in quiet contemplation.

Kim's approach to music thus reflects a quintessentially Asian perspective.

—David Tsang

KIM Young Dong (Kim Yŏngdong). Korean. Born in Seoul, 29 January 1951. Educated at Korean Traditional Music School, Seoul 1965–71; Seoul National University, 1971–5, B.A.; Göttingen University, Germany, 1984–6; Free University of Berlin, 1987–8. Married Chŏng Okcho, 1 August 1987; 1 child. *Taegŭm* performer, Korean Traditional Performing Arts Centre, Seoul, 1978–81; lecturer, department of traditional music, Ehwa Women's University, Seoul, 1981–3; guest conductor, Korean Broadcasting System Traditional Music Orchestra, 1990; conductor and music supervisor, Pusan Municipal Traditional Music Orchestra, since 1990; director of *Han'guk chŏngagwŏn*/Korean Court Music Institute, since 1990; announcer/presenter, Buddhist Broadcasting Service, since 1990. Recipient: drama music prize, *Han'guk ilbo / Korea Daily News*, 1975; national prize for dance music, 1980; national prize for composition, 1981; Korean Broadcasting System traditional music composition prize, 1983; film music prize, 1985; popular music prize, 1986; Belgian film festival film music prize, 1986. Mailing address; Sŏgang Apartment 2-1107, 186-25 Hongun 3-dong, Sodeamun-gu, Seoul, Korea.

Publisher: Seorabul Record Company, Seoul.

Symphonies/orchestral:

Wech'ŏn / The Esteemed Place 1981.
Maegut / Shaman Ritual to a Falcon 1981. Recorded SRB 0091.
Tan'gun shinhwa / The Spirit of Korea's Mythical Founder 1983. Recorded SRB 0091.

Chamber/instrumental:

P'amun / Ripples (ensemble) 1983.

Vocal/choral:

Myŏngsŏk ŭmak / Meditation Music 1989. Recorded SRB 3013.

Two albums of original songs and folksong arrangements. Recorded SPEC 057; SRB 0219.

Other:

Hanne ŭi sŭngch'ŏn / The Life of Hanne (drama) 1974.
Mul t'oridung / The Sound of Water (drama) 1978.
Ch'um sori / Dance Song (traditional Korean dance) 1980.
T'aejon (dance music) 1980.
Ttang kut / Earth Ritual (dance music) 1980.
Abae ŭi kajok / The Family of Abae (television music) 1980.
Salp'o kanŭn kil / The Road to Sal Port (television music) 1981.
Ŏdum ŭi chashiktŭl / Children of Darkness (film music) 1981.
Pŏngŏri Samnyong / Dumb Samnyong (television music) 1982.
Ttanengbyŏt / The Ribbon of Sunshine (film music) 1984.
Han ture / One Team (music for contemporary dance) 1986.
Changsaengdo / Picture of Long Life (dance music) 1988.
Adada (film music) 1988.
Ttang ŭi Sori / Song of the Earth (dance music) 1989.
Kuro arirang / The Song of Kuro (dance music) 1989.
Noksaek ŭi pulkil / Green Fire (dance music) 1989.
Sujech'ŏn (arrangement of ancient court music) 1990.
Chŏlmŭn nal ŭi ch'osang / Portrait of the Young Day (film music) 1990.
Sangnyŏngsan (arrangement of one movement from court suite *Yŏngsan hoesang*) 1990.

PUBLICATIONS

By Kim: "Who Is Isang Yun?", in *Shin Tonga*, May 1989; contributor to "Symposium on Traditional Music", in *Minjok ŭmak hakchi / Folk Music Scholarship*, 1989; regular column in newspaper *Han'gyŏre shinmun*, from 1989.

On Kim: articles by No Tongun and others in magazines *Kaeksŏk / Auditorium* and *Ŭmak Tonga / East Asian Music*.

Kim Young Dong comments:

In each composition I write there are special things. Each piece explores the notion of tradition, just as every composer in Korea who uses Korean instruments claims to write music that stems from "the tradition". In folk music there are many different winds blowing. In court music, too, there are many different winds. A composer's style reflects his background and training and, since I trained within a court music institute, I utilize this experience in my compositions. But I also use folk music, trying to combine the two worlds, bringing in colours from many different places. As a contemporary music composer, I am meant to create new pieces, not just copy the old tradition.

Music reflects local dialects. It is because of the rhythm of language that we respond to music, saying "Where have I heard that before?" It is my job as a composer to bring out the feeling that what is heard is something East Asian. I must, through my music, offer connections to the past for those who will listen.

* * *

When Kim Young Dong won his first award, a prize for drama music from the *Han'guk ilbo* (Korean Daily News), he heralded the arrival of a new generation of composers. Yet his career has followed the well-trodden paths of many composer-performers: schooling at the Korean Traditional Music School, further study at Seoul National, the nation's most prestigious university, and four years work as a *taegŭm* (horizontal flute) player with the Korean Traditional Performing Arts Centre. Thus his background is entirely in traditional music. Only in the 1980s did he try to broaden his musical background; for four years he studied ethnomusicology at the German universities of Göttingen and Berlin. But he returned to Korea without any diploma, complaining that German academics wouldn't dirty their fingers with music itself.

Much of Kim's reputation has been built on the fact that he has kept well ahead of his compatriots. He has rarely been satisfied with imitating old music, though his fascination for music performed outside the concert environment stems primarily from distrust of the establishment (until the mid 1980s, Korean academics and performers urged composers to remain faithful to the "tradition"). Thus, four of Kim's awards have been for music to accompany dance, theatre and film. An individual style was already present in his first drama, *Hanne ŭi sŭngch'ŏn* (The Life of Hanne), but only with 1980s pieces does that style extend to compositions for traditional ensembles, such as *Maegut* (Shaman Ritual to a Falcon). In the first movement of *Maegut* a solo male singer starts by intoning stable pitches within standard modes, but then suddenly glides upwards to a thin falsetto: the falcon rises into the air. Later, a similar portamento marks the time when the falcon's spirit—the bird having been accidentally killed—departs. *Tan'gun shinhwa*, a piece depicting the legendary founder of Korea, matches the old (e.g., the echoes of traditional percussive punctuation at the opening) with the new (mysterious chords held on groups of ocarina, empty but resonant gong clashes, and so on).

Kim is a popular composer. Perhaps, though, he has achieved much by default. His more accessible songs were taken up by university students in the early 1980s who, as they sought to protest against a military dictatorship, abandoned Western pop and looked for songs they could regard as "traditional." Kim's songs, issued on two albums, were never traditional, however, for in them he sought to develop a new musical language that combined Western melodies with Korean percussion. In the same vein, his music to the film *Ŏdum ŭi chashiktŭl* (Children of Darkness) remains widely admired, arguably, less because of the music than the film's depiction of poverty. And, again, his most successful album to date is *Myŏngsŏk ŭmak* (Meditation Music) which, although filled out with flute solos and synthesized chorus prepared by Kim, is mainly a recording of Buddhist chants and calls.

At a time when Western music reigns supreme in Korea, Kim professes that he would like more people to listen to indigenous music. In effect, his taste for popular music stems from this desire—the world of Korean instruments may be strange and austere, so Kim adds melodies and harmonic constructs played on Western instruments and introduces great timbral colour. Court music may be redolent of a past age, so Kim has recently composed and performed new versions of *Sujech'ŏn* and *Sangnyŏngsan*, pieces played in the court throughout the Chosŏn [Yi] dynasty (1392–1910). Court and folk music may have no appeal to the youth of today; Kim therefore writes descriptive ensemble music (*Wech'ŏn* and *Maegut* are examples) and songs designed specifically for children. Behind all Kim's actions lies a simple philosophy: Kim is a Korean composer dedicated to compose new Korean music that grows from indigenous genres and respects its ancient workmanship.

—Keith Howard

KIRCHNER, Leon. American. Born in Brooklyn, New York, 24 January 1919. Educated: piano lessons under Richard Buhlig; Los Angeles City College; University of California, Los Angeles (composition study under Arnold Schoenberg); University of California, Berkeley (music theory under Albert Elkus and Edward Strickland, graduate study under Ernest Bloch), 1938–42, B.A., 1940, M.A., 1948; private study under Roger Sessions, 1942. Military service, 1943–6. Married Gertrude Schoenberg (no relation to the composer) in 1949. Teacher, San Francisco Conservatory, from 1946; lecturer in theory, University of California, Berkeley, 1949; lecturer/assistant professor/associate professor, University of Southern California, Los Angeles, 1950–4; Luther Brusie Marchant Professor, Mills College, Oakland, California, 1954–61; member of faculty, from 1961, and Walter Bigelow Rosen Professor, 1966–89, Harvard University, Cambridge, Massachusetts; guest professor, University of California, Los Angeles, 1970–1; director, Harvard Players, from 1973; director, Harvard Chamber Orchestra, from 1978; also Slee Professor, State University of New York, Buffalo, and professorships at Yale University, New Haven, Connecticut and Juilliard School of Music, New York City; composer in residence, Santa Fe Chamber Music Festival, 1983; composer in residence, Tanglewood, Massachusetts, 1985; also at Aspen, Marlboro, Charleston and Spoleto Festivals; fellow, Stanford Center for Advanced Study in the Behavioural Sciences, California. Recipient: New York Music Critics Award (for *String Quartet No 1*), 1950, (for *String Quartet No 2*), 1960; Naumburg Recording Award (for *Piano Concerto No 1*), 1953; Pulitzer Prize (for *String Quartet No 3*), 1967. Mailing address: Department of Music, Faculty of Arts and Sciences, Harvard University, Cambridge, Massachusetts 02138, U.S.A.

Publishers: Associated/Schirmer; Mercury.

Symphonies/orchestral:

Piece (piano, orchestra) 1946.
Sinfonia 1951; first performed New York City, January 1952.
Piano Concerto No 1 1953; first performed New York City, 23 February 1956. Recorded New World NW 286.
Toccata (strings, solo winds, percussion) 1955; first performed San Francisco, 16 February 1956. Recorded Louisville First Orchestra First Edition LS 68 3.
Concerto (violin, cello, 10 winds, percussion) 1960; first performed Baltimore, Maryland, 1960. Recorded Epic LC 3830/BC 1157.
Piano Concerto No 2 1963; first performed Seattle, Washington, 28 October 1963.
Music for Orchestra 1969; first performed New York City, 16 October 1969.
Music for Flute and Orchestra 1978; first performed Indianapolis, 20 October 1978.

Chamber/instrumental:

Duo (violin, piano) 1947; first performed Berkeley, California, 1947. Recorded Medea MCLP 1002.
Sonata (piano) 1948; first performed New York City, March 1949. Recorded Epic LC 3862/BC 1262; Educo 3081; CRI 461.
Little Suite (piano) 1949.
String Quartet No 1 1949; first performed New York City, March 1950. Recorded CRI 395.
Sonata concertante (violin, piano) 1952; first performed New York City, 30 March 1952. Recorded Desto DC 7151; Epic LC 3306.
Trio (violin, cello, piano) 1954; first performed Pasadena, California, 30 November 1954. Recorded Epic LC 3306; Centaur 1004.
String Quartet No 2 1958. Recorded CBS MQ 32740.
Fanfare (brass trio) 1965; first performed Marlboro, Vermont, 1965.

String Quartet No 3 (with tape) 1966; first performed New York City, 27 January 1967. Recorded CBS MS 7284; Vox SVBX 5306.
Flutings for Paula (from the opera *Lily*; flute, optional percussion) 1973, 1977.
A Moment for Rogers (piano) 1978.
Five Pieces (piano) 1984.
Fanfare (7 brass) 1985.
Music for Twelve 1985.
For Cello Solo 1986; first performed Charleston, South Carolina, 20 May 1988.
For Violin Solo 1987; first performed Indianapolis, 13 September 1986.
Five Pieces (piano) 1987; first performed Boston, 7 March 1987.
Two Duos (violin, cello) 1988.
For Solo Violin II 1988; first performed Washington, D.C., 22 January 1989.
Triptych (consists of *For Solo Cello*, *Two Duos*; violin, cello) 1988; first performed Tanglewood, Massachusetts, 17 August 1988.

Vocal/choral:

Letters (soprano, piano; Alexander) 1943; first performed Berkeley, California, 1946.
The Times Are Nightfall (soprano, piano; G.M. Hopkins) 1943; first performed Berkeley, California, 1946.
Dawn (chorus, organ; Lorca) 1943–6; first performed New York City, February 1949.
Of Obedience (soprano, piano; Whitman) 1950; first performed Los Angeles, 1950.
Words from Wordsworth (unaccompanied chorus) 1968.
Lily (from the opera; soprano, flute, oboe, clarinet, horn, bassoon, celeste, percussion, piano, violin, viola, cello) 1973.
The Twilight Stood (soprano, piano; Dickinson) 1983; first performed Charleston, South Carolina, 1 June 1983.

Opera:

Lily (after Saul Bellow: *Henderson the Rain King*) 1973–6; first performed New York City, 14 April 1977.

PUBLICATIONS

On Kirchner: A.L. Ringer, "LK", in *Musical Quarterly*, 43, 1957.

* * *

The two main threads in Leon Kirchner's catalogue of compositions are orchestral works (with or without a solo instrument) and chamber music. The principal exception is his opera *Lily* based on Saul Bellow's novel *Henderson the Rain King*. Of the instrumental music most, for example the two piano concertos and three string quartets, is written for ensembles that have a long history in the classical tradition, a history which for the most part involves abstract formal structures and an avoidance of programmatic ideas. But while Kirchner's music may not tell stories, it always tends towards the dramatic, mixing tempos and characters from moment to moment.

Since studying with Arnold Schoenberg in the late 1930s Kirchner has crafted his own personal style. Undoubtedly the influence of the second Viennese school is there, yet this is not dry, academic music. Rather it is characterised by a linear chromaticism, asymmetrical rhythms, sensuous lyricism and in his own words, the quest for "loveliness in verticality". His pieces are conceived as essential wholes, often in linked movements and using repetitive materials; but despite the tight structures, the overall impression is one of spontaneity. In listening to Kirchner's music one never feels one is very far from the man himself. To quote Aaron Copland: "Kirchner's pages prove that he reacts strongly to (today's unsettled) world; they are charged with an emotional impact and explosive power that is almost frightening in intensity. . . . No wonder his listeners have been convinced".

His early works (those from the late 1940s) clearly demonstrate the allegiance to Schoenberg. The *String Quartet No 1* for example is constructed from a series of pitches which appear in many different permutations, but already the clear design, rhythmic vitality and extremes of colour and mood look forward to Kirchner's own mature style. *String Quartet No 2*, written nine years later, is structured from recurring materials, but is thinner in texture, finely proportioned and extremely sensitive to the capabilities of each instrument. *String Quartet No 3* (for String quartet and tape) shows the results of Kirchner's growing fascination with electronics and his success, in typical Kirchneresque fashion, of exploiting the expressive capabilities of seemingly rigid materials. Rather than functioning as a contrasting sound source the tape is used to enlarge the more flexible instrumental qualities of the quartet.

A key work compositionally was the *Concerto* for violin, cello, 10 winds and percussion. Unlike his previous pieces the structure of this piece derives from the shifting relationship between soloists and ensemble rather than from thematic development. The end result is more spontaneous and improvisatory.

Similar compositional development can be seen in the orchestral music from the same period: *Sinfonia*, *Toccata* and the two Piano Concertos. By 1969 *Music for Orchestra*, commissioned by the New York Philharmonic, shows Kirchner embracing a strongly tonal style and orchestrating brilliantly with the use of many exotic colours as well as controlled improvisation. The structure of the work is determined through the building and release of tension and the flow of musical events and the piece was hailed by the New York *Post* as "impressionism heard through a twentieth-century prism".

Kirchner's search for compositional completeness culminates in his opera *Lily*. In this work he demonstrates a natural capability for the pacing and matching of musical and dramatic events and heightens the drama of the piece by his use of a wide range of effects, from the electronic transmission of speech, choral chant and conventional opera singing to quasi-pop music.

Of his most recent works, *Music for Twelve* stands out for its dramatic expression. In scale and ensemble of diverse instruments, this work might call to mind Schoenberg's opus 9 *Chamber Symphony*; but if Kirchner still identifies with the aesthetics of his master, the improvisatory sensuality in the constantly shifting pace and timbres of *Music for Twelve* shows his complete freedom of compositional procedures.

—Rosemary Johnson

KLATZOW, Peter (James Leonard). South African. Born in Springs, Transvaal, 14 July 1945. Educated at St Martin's

School, Rosettenville, Johannesburg; private music study to 1964; Royal College of Music, London (piano under Kathleen Long and Angus Morrison, composition under Bernard Stevens, orchestration under Gordon Jacobs); further study with Nadia Boulanger, Paris, 1965–6. Teacher, Rhodesian College of Music, Salisbury (now Harare), Rhodesia (now Zimbabwe), 1966–8; music producer, South African Broadcasting Corporation, Johannesburg, 1969–72; Professor, University of Cape Town, since 1973; founder of publishing company Musications, 1981. Recipient: Royal Philharmonic Prize (for *Variations*; youngest ever recipient), 1965; Ashberg Hopwood and Crewe Prize, Royal College of Music, London, 1965; Pablo Casals Memorial Prize (for *The Temptation of St Anthony*), 1977; Stroud Festival Prize, 1977. Mailing address: 22 Miller Road, Claremont 7700, South Africa.

Publisher: Musications, P.O. Box 23475, Claremont 7735, South Africa.

Symphonies/orchestral:

Variations 1964.
Interactions (piano, percussion, chamber orchestra) 1971; first performed Johannesburg, 1973.
Symphony: "Phoenix" 1972; first performed Johannesburg, 1973.
Time Structure 2 1974; first performed Johannesburg, 1977.
Still Life with Moonbeams 1975; first performed Johannesburg, 1975.
The Temptation of St Anthony after Hieronymus Bosch (cello, orchestra) 1972; first performed Barcelona, 1977.
Concerto for Horn and Orchestra 1978; first performed Johannesburg, 1979.
Concerto for Organ and Orchestra 1981; first performed Johannesburg, 1981.
Incantations 1984; first performed Grahamstown, South Africa, 1984.
Concerto for Marimba and String Orchestra 1985. Recorded Etcetera CD KTC 1085.
Figures in a Landscape 1985; first performed Durban, 1986.
Citiscape 1986; first performed Johannesburg, 1987.
A Chrysalis in Flames 1988; first performed Grahamstown, South Africa, 1989.
Concerto for Clarinet and Chamber Orchestra 1989; first performed Cape Town, 1991.

Chamber/instrumental:

Moments of Night (piano) 1969; first performed Pretoria, 1969.
Piano Piece I 1970.
Time Structure I (piano) 1973; first performed Johannesburg, 1973.
The Garden of Memories and Discoveries (2 pianos, 2 guitars, 2 percussion, harpsichord, electric organ) 1975; first performed Cape Town, 1975.
The World of Paul Klee (flute, piano) 1977; first performed Cape Town, 1978.
Ach Bach (organ) 1977.
Night Magic (violin, horn, piano) 1978; first performed Stroud, Gloucestershire, 1978.
Chamber Concerto for Seven (flute, clarinet, horn, guitar, percussion, electric organ) 1979; first performed Cape Town, 1979.
Three Movements (piano) 1980; first performed Johannesburg, 1981.
Murmurs of Tiger and Flame (piano) 1982; first performed Cape Town, 1982.
Cythera Among the Lynxes (flute, harp) 1982; first performed Johannesburg, 1983.
Figures in a Landscape I (flute, marimba) 1985; first performed Cape Town, 1986. Recorded Claremont Records.
A Branch of Dreams (piano) 1986; first performed Cape Town, 1987.
String Quartet 1987; first performed Magaliesberg, South Africa, 1988.

Vocal/choral:

In Memoriam N.P. van Wyk Louw (soprano, strings) 1970; first performed Cape Town, 1970.
Charms and Incantations (soprano, tenor, horn, guitar) 1979; first performed Cape Town, 1980.
Mass (choir, horn, marimba, strings; or choir, organ) 1988, revised 1990; first performed Cape Town, 1989; revised version first performed Cambridge, 1990.
Congregational Eucharist (choir, organ) 1990; first performed Cape Town, 1990.
Praise the Lord, O My Soul (choir, organ) 1990; first performed Cape Town, 1990.

Opera:

The Beggar's Opera (flute, horn, violin, double bass, harpsichord) 1986; first performed Grahamstown, South Africa, 1986.

Other:

Drie Diere (ballet; orchestra) 1980; first performed Cape Town, 1980.
Vespers (ballet; orchestra) 1986; first performed Cape Town, 1986.

PUBLICATIONS

By Klatzow: (editor), *Composers in South Africa Today*, Cape Town, 1987.

On Klatzow: Avril Herber, in *Conversations*, Johannesburg, 1979; James May, "PK", in Klatzow, *Composers in South Africa Today*, Cape Town, 1987.

* * *

Peter Klatzow's early compositions—primarily piano works—were tonal. At the Royal College of Music, Bernard Stevens introduced him to the works of Janaček, Stravinsky and Hindemith. He also became acquainted with the work of Alban Berg. The influence of all of these composers is evident in the *Variations* for orchestra.

While he was studying with Nadia Boulanger, Klatzow's style changed dramatically; he became acquainted with the works of the European avant-garde and for the next number of years the influence of composers such as Boulez and Stockhausen can be detected in his work.

Years of deliberate experimentation led to a rather eclectic style; the mature style that emerged from this consists of a synthesis of its most important elements. In his later works, small intervallic cells act as the main referential material which controls both melody and harmony. The latter is also largely determined by a logical approach to voice leading. Further features include a careful juxtaposition of tonal and atonal material, the exploration of modal and octatonic pitch material and a carefully controlled overall structure. The *Mass* of 1988 can be regarded as a definitive return to tonality, enriched and extended as that may be.

Klatzow completed a number of serial works in the 1960s, but most of these have been lost. *Piano Piece I* is the only remaining twelve-tone work. It is not serial; the twelve notes of the chromatic scale are unordered. The piece consists of 28 statements of the chromatic complex; it is like a set of variations from which certain textural, rhythmic and harmonic ideas gradually emerge. Even though rarely implied in the title, the variation principle perhaps forms the backbone of most of Klatzow's formal structures.

Although Klatzow wrote some aleatoric works in the 1970s, he always retained control over the basic material. *The Garden of Memories and Discoveries*, a broadcast work written for the South African Broadcasting Corporation, contains aleatoric sections as well as a *musique concrète* tape. The organ piece *Ach Bach* is perhaps his best-known aleatoric work. Here interaction is created between brief, graphically notated sections and chord sequences taken from a Bach chorale of the performer's choice.

Although Klatzow has written for most mediums, in later years orchestral works have predominated. These include two ballets, *Drie Diere* and *Vespers*, based on poems by N.P. van Wyk Louw. At present he is completing a ballet on *Hamlet*.

He has composed five works for a solo instrument and orchestra: concertos for horn, organ, marimba and clarinet, and *The Temptation of St Anthony After Hieronymus Bosch* for cello and orchestra. The *Concerto for Organ and Orchestra* is an important addition to this genre. It has an ingenious formal structure of three movements played without a break which incorporates the three sections of a traditional sonata-form movement. The third movement—the recapitulation—is a passacaglia, the theme of which is based on the first subject from the exposition. Tonality functions in an obvious way in the *Concerto for Marimba and String Orchestra*, which has become one of Klatzow's most frequently performed works.

In *Symphony: "Phoenix"* his first major symphonic work, Klatzow introduced a motive B♭-D-E. This has become a hallmark of almost every work Klatzow has written since then, and is stated in one of his most successful orchestral works, *Incantations*, which illustrates almost all the traits of his mature style. He uses two scales, the octatonic and the lydian. The two principal germ cells are A-B♭-D♭ (minor intervals derived from the octatonic scale) and B♭-D-E (major intervals derived from the lydian mode). The main thematic source, a two-part chant in the bassoons, appears three times. Melodically the octatonic (minor) motive is present in the chant; harmonically it outlines the tritone from the lydian (major) motive by moving from F major to B major. The piece also contains elaborate tritonal passages and some indeterminate material. The latter is strictly controlled in an overall form which again largely relies on the variation principle.

—James W. May

KNAIFEL, Alexander. Russian. Born in Tashkent, Uzbekistan, 28 November 1943. Educated at Leningrad Conservatoire special musical school, 1950–61; Moscow Conservatoire, 1961–3; Leningrad Conservatoire, 1963–7. Married to Tat'yana Melent'eva; 1 daughter. Member, Union of Composers, from 1968; member, Union of Cinematographers, from 1987; independent composer. Mailing address: Sverdlovsky Prospekt, dom 25, kv.130, 194214 St Petersberg, U.S.S.R.

Publishers: Sovietskii kompozitor, St Petersberg; Muzyka, St Petersberg; Hans Sikorski, Hamburg.

Symphonies / orchestral:

Burleska (trombone, string orchestra) 1963.
Mechta / Dream (fantasia for chamber orchestra) 1963.
131 (viola, double bass, winds, percussion) 1964.
Onrush (ballet symphony) 1964.
Gryadushchego grada vzyskuyushchie / Seekers of the Future City (2 fragments for large string orchestra, percussion, organ) 1965.
Magdalene Repentant (choreographic scene inspired by Rodin and Titian) 1967.
Medea (Kolkhidskaya volshebnitsa / Kolkhida Enchantress) (choreographic symphony in 2 parts) 1968; first performed Leningrad, 1984.
Zhanna / Joan (passion for 13 groups of instruments) 1970–8.
Rannie zhuravli / Early Cranes (valedictory music in 12 minor tonalities) 1979.
Vera (variations and stanza of dedication for string orchestra) 1980; first performed Riga, 1986.
Bezumie / Madness (blank music for chamber orchestra on themes by Korney Chukovsky, Mahler, Tyutchev and Akhmatova) 1987.
Litania 1988.

Chamber / instrumental:

Small Suite (piano) 1961.
Two Pieces: Dyad (flute, viola, piano, percussion) 1963; first performed Leningrad, 1964.
Klassicheskaya syuita / Classical Suite (piano) 1963; first performed Leningrad, 1964.
Ostinati (violin, cello) 1964; first performed Baku, 1988.
Musique militaire (piano) 1964; first performed Leningrad, 1971.
Passakalia (organ) 1965; first performed Leningrad, 1967.
Razoruzhenie / Disarmament (choreographical strip-tease for ensemble; after cartoons by Herluf Bidstrup) 1966.
Lamento (cello) 1967; first performed Warsaw, 1983.
Tuyrnirnaya muzyka / Tournament Music (horn, piano) 1967; first performed Leningrad, 1975.
Tertium non datur (harpsichord) 1967.
A Prima Vista (4 performers/5 groups of percussion) 1972; first performed Cologne, 1979.
Rafferti (jazz ensemble) 1980.
Solaris: fragment canticum eternum (35 Javanese gongs) 1980.
Da / Yes (soloist, ensemble) 1980; first performed Moscow, 1981.
Nika (72 fragments for 17 performers on bass instruments) 1983–4.
Agnus Dei (4 instrumentalists: keyboard, percussion, electronic instruments, saxophone, double bass) 1987; first performed Leningrad, 1987.

Vocal / choral:

Shvyrni ego v moi sad / Chuck It into My Garden (fugato for

mixed chorus, orchestra; Bazen, translated Kudinov) 1962.
Ispoved / Confession (reader, percussion ensemble) 1963.
Pesnya Roberta Bernsa / Song of Robert Burns (baritone, piano; Burns, translated Marshak) 1963; first performed Moscow, 1987.
Pyat' stikhotvoreniya M.Y. Lermontova / Five Poems of Lermontov (unaccompanied mixed chorus) 1964; first performed Leningrad, 1984.
Angel (unaccompanied mixed chorus; Lermontov) 1964.
O gluposti / About Stupidity (choral fugue) 1964.
Pamyati S.Y. Marshaka / In Memory of S.Y. Marshak (6 lyric epigrams for baritone, piano) 1964; first performed Leningrad, 1966.
Kentervil'skoe prividenie / The Canterville Ghost (romantic scenes for bass, soprano, chamber orchestra; Kramarova, after Wilde) 1965; first performed Leningrad, 1974.
Petrogradskie vorob'i / Petrograd Sparrows (suite-phantasmagoria for boys' chorus, chamber orchestra) 1967; first performed Leningrad, 1978.
Tuyrnirnaya muzyka / Tournament Music (voice, ensemble) 1967.
150 000 000 (dithyramb for mixed chorus, 6 piccolos, 6 trumpets, 6 trombones, 12 double basses, 3 groups of kettledrums; Mayakovsky) 1968.
Monodia (female voice; Latin version of Buchanan's Psalm 22) 1968; first performed Leningrad, 1968. Recorded Chant du Monde LDC 278 972/73.
Lenin. Pis'mo chlenam Ts. K / Lenin's Letter to the Members of the Central Committee (fatum in unison for bass chorus, 11-voice symphonic orchestra) 1969.
Anna Akhmatova's Midnight Verses (commentary for 4 performers; duration depends on size of auditorium) 1972–3.
Status Nascendi (3 groups of performers) 1975; first performed Leningrad, 1975.
Ainana (17 variations on a name for chamber chorus, percussion, tape recorder) 1978; first performed Zurich, 1989.
Glupaya loshad / Stupid Horse (15 tales for singer, piano; Levin, English version by Solasko) 1981; first performed Leningrad, 1981. Recorded Melodiya A 10 00377 004.
Sluchainoe / Accidental (girl soloist, mixed chorus, string orchestra, organ) 1982.
Yazicheskii rok / Pagan Rock (bass chorus, percussion, rock group) 1982.
Protivostoyanie / Opposition (suite for bass chorus, large orchestra) 1984; first performed Leningrad, 1987.
Bog / God (2 choruses; Derzhavin) 1985.
Kryl'ya Kholopa / The Wings of a Lackey (vocal/choreographic fresco; Samoilov) 1986.
Skvoz' radugu nevol'nykh slyoz / Through the Rainbow of Unwilling Tears (trio for singer, cello; Akhmatova, Ttutchev) 1988; first performed London, 1989.

Opera:

Kentervil'skoe prividenie / The Canterville Ghost (prologue and 3 acts for bass, soprano, chamber orchestra; Kramarova, after Wilde) 1965; first performed Leningrad, 1974.

Other:

Shagi na snegu (instrumentation of Debussy's *Prelude No 6* for orchestra) 1970.
Appelli (instrumentation of 6 pieces by T. Voronina for chamber orchestra) 1972; first performed Leningrad, 1981.

Film scores: *Sled rosomakhi / The Wolverine's Trail*, 1978; *Rannie zhuravli / Early Cranes*, 1979; *Rafferti*, 1980; *Ya—aktrisa / I Am an Actress*, 1980; *Trebuyutsya muzhchini / Men Are Required*, 1982; *Torpedonostsy / Torpedo Carriers*, 1983; *Protivostoyanie / Opposition*, 1984–5; *O tom, chego ne bylo / About That Which Did Not Happen*, 1986; *Mif / Myth*, 1986; *Petrogradskie gavroshi / Petrograd Street Urchins*, 1987; *Bol'shaya igra / The Big Game*, 1988; *Kriminal'nyi talent / Criminal Talent*, 1988; *C.P. raionnogo masshtaba / Party Member of Regional Scale*, 1988; *Etyo bylo u morya / It Was by the Sea*, 1989.

PUBLICATIONS

By Knaifel: "I pravda, kak zvezda v nochi otkrylas" [Subjective reflections on Shostakovitch's 15th String Quartet], in *Sovetskaya muzyka*, 11, 1975.

On Knaifel: Tat'yaba Voronina and Boris Kats, "Eskizy k portreta", in *Sovetskaya muzyka*, 4, 1975; Hannelore Gerlach, "Funfzig sowjetische Komponisten", Dresden, 1984; Hubert Meister, "AK: ja", in *Melos*, 8, 1984, and *AK: catalogue général*, Paris, 1987; Tat'yana Baranova, "The Music of Numbers of AK", in *Music in the USSR*, April–June 1989; Tat'yana Egorova, "Chuvtsvo garmonii", (joint interview with film director Semyon Aronovich) in *Muzykal'naya zhizn*, 12, 1990; Larisa Kirillina, "O muzyke zhivoi i . . .", (round table discussion on *Agnus Dei*) in *Sovetskaya muzyka*, 8, 1990.

* * *

In the Soviet present, as in the Russian past, there have been two distinct traditions within cultural life, one Western-looking and determined that Soviet culture should be part of the European tradition, the other nationalistic and isolationist, intent on purifying Russia from corrupting foreignness.

Into the noise of the struggle of these two opposed camps, the music of Alexander Knaifel comes like a quiet and cooling wind. It is music apparently unruffled by the passions and loyalties that so inflame other people.

Perhaps the nearest comparison one might attempt could invoke the names of Feldman, say, or Cage. But Knaifel's music is one which owes nothing to chance and the vast and transcendental spaces it inhabits do not suggest the arbitrary will or fancy. Instead this is a composer who seems to have returned music to the primal simplicities of Pythagorean speculation.

Of course, in one sense, what Knaifel is doing fits well with the Russian tradition. For the Russians, as the works of Dostoyevsky, Solovyov and Scriabin make clear, have always had a feeling for metaphysical speculation. At the same time, deeply rooted in that same tradition lies also the idea of art as expression. And *express* is precisely what Knaifel's music does not do. The enormous length of many of his major works (often a single movement may last two hours or more) allows him to make structures in sound which are almost things, buildings in acoustic space inside which we may live for a period of time.

The difference, of course, is that in a building we may choose our own speed to wander round. In a musical work the speed of our apprehension is chosen for us—usually extremely slow in a Knaifel work. Nor do the walls and roofs of that building include any familiar features of melody, harmony or rhythm. Usually it confronts us with the single note, pitch and duration united as one thing, naked material.

And yet, however abstract may be the composer's overall

conception, the strength of this music lies in Knaifel's remarkable awareness of the physical excitement of his raw material. He is a composer who bathes in the sensuality of sound, even when at first hearing that sound may appear sparse in the extreme.

A number of Knaifel's more recent works include texts, but texts which, although they are performed, are not heard. In his *Agnus Dei*, for example, he includes words from the liturgy as well as extracts from a diary of a young girl who died of starvation in the siege of Leningrad. The performers see these texts in their copies, but they are instructed to "perform" them silently. In the more recent *Through the Rainbow of Unwilling Tears* the same thing is done using poems by Tiutchev and Akhmatova. Here the audience is asked to listen to the poems first, so that they may have some idea of what is going on in the performers' minds.

There is another side to Knaifel's talent which is worth noting. In some pieces he shows an almost dada-ist sense of humour, the flip side perhaps of the extreme solemnity of some of his other works. His early opera, *The Canterville Ghost*, a delightfully ridiculous work, is one of the few Soviet operas to pick up on the wild excitement and disruption of Shostakovich's *The Nose*. And in the enormous song-cycle *Stupid Horse*, written for his daughter, Knaifel makes virtuosic play with clapping games, the pianist playing notes higher than the keyboard actually goes, the singer whistling and so on. Indeed this is perhaps his most accessible piece.

—Gerard McBurney

KNUSSEN, (Stuart) Oliver. British/Scottish. Born in Glasgow, 12 June 1952. Educated at Purcell School of Music; private composition study under John Lambert, 1963–8; further study with Gunther Schuller, 1970–3. Married Susan Freedman in 1972; 1 daughter. Conductor, debut with own *Symphony No 1*, 1968; composer in residence, Aspen Festival, Colorado, 1976; composer in residence, Arnolfini Gallery, Bristol, 1978; instructor in composition, Royal College of Music, London, 1977–82; guest conductor, London Sinfonietta, Philharmonia Orchestra, and others, from 1981; guest teacher, Berkshire Music Center, Tanglewood, Massachusetts, 1981; co-artistic director, Aldeburgh Festival, Suffolk, since 1983; composer in residence, Philharmonia Orchestra, from 1984. Recipient: Countess of Munster Award, 1964, 1965, 1967; Peter Stuyvesant Foundation Award, 1965; Watney Sargent Award for young conductors, 1969; Margaret Grant Composition Prize, Tanglewood (for *Symphony No 2*), 1971; winner, 1st Park Lane Group composer award, 1982. Mailing address: Flat 3, 167 West End Lane, London NW6 2LG, England.

Publisher: Faber.

Symphonies/orchestral:

Symphony No 1 Op 1 1966–7; first performed London, April 1968; withdrawn.
Concerto for Orchestra Op 5 1968, revised 1974.
Symphony No 2 Op 7 (soprano, small orchestra) 1970–1; preliminary version first performed Windsor, 3 October 1970; final version first performed Tanglewood, Massachusetts, 18 August 1971. Recorded Unicorn Kanchana DKP 9027.
Choral Op 8 1970–2; first performed New York City, 30 March 1975.
Music for a Puppet Court Op 11 (2 chamber orchestras; after John Lloyd, 16th century) 1972, 1983; first performed London, 23 August 1983.
Symphony No 3 Op 18 1973–9; first performed London, 6 September 1979. Recorded Unicorn RHD 400.
Coursing Op 19 (chamber orchestra) 1979. Recorded Unicorn Kanchana DKP 9027.
The Wild Rumpus Op 20b (from the opera *Where the Wild Things Are*) 1983; first performed London, 21 July 1987.
Fanfares for Tanglewood (brass, percussion) 1986; first performed Tanglewood, Massachusetts, 2 August 1986.

Chamber/instrumental:

Processionals Op 2 (wind quintet, string quartet) 1968, 1978; first performed Bristol, 15 December 1978.
Masks Op 3 (flute) 1969.
Three Little Fantasies Op 6a (wind quintet) 1970, revised 1983; first performed Kingston-upon-Thames, 1 June 1983. Recorded Arabesque 6535.
Turba (double bass) 1971.
Ophelia Dances, Book 1 (Op 13) (flute, cor anglais, clarinet, horn, piano, celeste, violin, viola, cello) 1975; first performed New York City, 9 May 1975. Recorded Unicorn RHD 400.
Autumnal Op 14 (Triptych, Part 1) (violin, piano) 1976–7; first performed London, 10 July 1980.
Cantata Op 15 (Triptych, Part 3) (oboe, string trio) 1977; first performed Athens, Greece, 17 September 1979. Recorded Unicorn Kanchana DKP 9027.
Sonya's Lullaby Op 16 (Triptych, Part 2) (piano) 1977–8; first performed Amsterdam, 6 January 1979. Recorded Electric Candle ECR 001.

Vocal/choral:

Hums and Songs of Winnie-the-Pooh Op 6 (high soprano, flute, cor anglais, clarinet/contrabass clarinet, percussion, cello; Milne) 1970, 1983; first performed Aldeburgh, Suffolk, 14 June 1983.
Rosary Songs Op 9 (soprano, clarinet, viola, piano; Trakl) 1972; first performed London, 21 August 1972.
Océan de terre Op 10 (soprano, flute/alto flute, clarinet/bass clarinet, percussion, piano/celeste, violin, cello, double bass; Apollinaire) 1972–3, revised 1976; first performed London, 29 July 1976.
Trumpets Op 12 (soprano, 3 clarinets; Trakl) 1975; first performed London, 27 February 1975. Recorded Unicorn Kanchana DKP 9027.
Frammenti da "Chiara" Op 19a (2 unaccompanied female choruses, 24 voices minimum) 1975, 1986; first performed London, 23 June 1986.
Songs and a Sea Interlude Op 20a (soprano, orchestra; from the opera *Where the Wild Things Are*; Sendak) 1979–81; broadcast BBC, 14 February 1981.

Opera:

Where the Wild Things Are Op 20 (OK, Sendak) 1979–83; original version first performed Brussels, 28 November 1980; final version first performed London, 9 January 1984. Recorded Unicorn Kanchana DKP 9044; Thorn EMI TVT 90 3449 2 (video).

Higglety Pigglety Pop! Op 21 (OK, Sendak) 1983–5; first performed Glyndebourne, Sussex, 5 August 1985. Video Thorn EMI TVT 90 3449 2.

Other:

Perotin: Alleluya nativitas (arranged for wind quintet) 1987; first performed London, 1 September 1987.

Mussorgsky: *Marriage* (orchestrated by OK and Colin Matthews) 1981.

PUBLICATIONS

On Knussen: Paul Griffiths, (interview) in *New Sounds, New Personalities: British Composers of the 1980s*, London, 1985.

* * *

Oliver Knussen's trajectory through contemporary British music has been a slightly strange one. Although born in Glasgow, Knussen emerged as a composer very much in an English tradition, albeit augmented by a strong American influence fueled by his time under Gunther Schuller at Tanglewood, and an ear for the harmonic richness of early 20th-century French music.

He was hailed as something of a prodigy when his *Symphony No 1* was performed in London when the composer was only 15 years old. Inevitably derivative, it was nonetheless a finely crafted and well-constructed composition. Knussen, though, has withdrawn it from the list of his published works, although he has spoken of perhaps issuing a revised version for youth orchestras.

If the burden of being identified as the great white hope of English music has lain heavily on him, it was not apparent in the next few years, when he produced a stream of works at a pace which he has never come close to emulating since.

More importantly, though, a distinctive voice began to emerge in these works, notably in the *Concerto for Orchestra*, the flute piece *Masks* and the *Symphony No 2*. The complex but highly-defined textural detail emerging in these works has remained a crucial element in his music, but he has been less inclined to develop a monolithic compositional style alongside it.

That restless predeliction for stylistic experiment has been construed as a weakness in some quarters, but it has kept Knussen's music from falling into overly predictable forms. Throughout the 1970s, the composer produced a series of chamber works which permitted him the freedom to indulge in more radical variations than were generally evident in the more public pronouncements of his large orchestral works, including a *Symphony No 3*.

The most compelling of these compositions are *Music for a Puppet Court*, the masterly Apollinaire setting *Océan de terre* and the complexly layered *Coursing*, but his music of this period is consistently fascinating. By the end of the decade, his compulsion to tinker and revise was well established; Knussen himself has said that he sometimes feels that he never really finishes a work. Much of that continual rewriting is generated by his need to ensure that the highly detailed, scrupulously constructed textures and rhythms of his work are articulated with the maximum possible clarity and finesse.

In the second half of the 1970s, Knussen's output slowed down considerably, although the developments in his music throughout the decade were focussed in the first of what he called his fantasy operas, *Where the Wild Things Are*. Based on Maurice Sendak's best-selling book, *Where the Wild Things Are* took up a preoccupation with children's literature which has been evident in such earlier Knussen works as *Hums and Songs of Winnie-the-Pooh* or *The Cheshire Cat*. A work of great colour and vigour, it refused any temptation to be condescending to a young audience.

His subsequent work in the genre, *Higglety Pigglety Pop!*, fell short of emulating the strengths of *Where the Wild Things Are*, perhaps in part because the source material was not as strong.

Knussen's output has slowed to a trickle in the 1980s, with only an orchestral suite drawn from *Where the Wild Things Are, Higglety Pigglety Pop!* itself, and *Fanfares for Tanglewood* to add to his list of works, while much of his time has been given over to conducting. Given his increasingly meticulous and protracted compositional practices, though, that need not be interpreted as a premature drying-up of inspiration.

—Kenny Mathieson

KOENIG, Gottfried Michael. German. Born in Magdeburg, 5 October 1926. Educated at Wilhelm Gymnasium, Braunschweig, 1936–44; Staatsmusikschule Braunschweig, 1946–7; Nordwestdeutsche Musikakademie Detmold, 1947–50; Staatliche Hochschule für Musik, Cologne, 1953–4; Bonn University, 1963–4. Military service, 1944–5. Married Ruth Cardew (née Aaronberg) in 1960; 1 daughter and 1 son. Assistant, Electronic Music Studio, Cologne Radio, 1954–64; lecturer in electronic music, composition and analysis, Staatliche Hochschule für Musik, Cologne, 1963–4; artistic director, Institute of Sonology, University of Utrecht, 1964–86. Recipient: Incentive prize, Federal State of North Rhine-Westphalia, 1961; Matthijs Vermeulen Prize, City of Amsterdam, 1987. Mailing address: E. Meysterlaan 89, CL-3533 Utrecht, The Netherlands.

Publishers: TONOS International Editions, Ahastrasse 9, 6100 Darmstadt, Germany; Edition Peters, London.

Symphonies/orchestral:

Harpsichord Concerto (harpsichord, 2 flutes, string orchestra) 1948–9; first performed Detmold, 1949.
Horae (3 ballet scenes) 1951; first performed Darmstadt, 1951.
Beitrag 1985–6; first performed The Hague, 1986.

Chamber/instrumental:

Two Pieces (piano) 1957; first performed Cologne, 1959.
Woodwind Quintet (flute, oboe, cor anglais, clarinet, bassoon) 1958–9; first performed Cologne, 1960.
String Quartet 1959 1959; first performed Cincinnati, Ohio, 1960.
Project 1—Version 1 (flute, oboe, cor anglais, clarinet, bass clarinet, saxophone, bassoon, horn, trumpet, trombone, violin, viola, cello, double bass) 1965–6; first performed Utrecht, 1968.
Project 1—Version 3 (flute, clarinet, horn, marimba, vibraphone, 2 pianos, violin, cello) 1967; first performed Vienna, 1969.

Übung für Klavier (piano) 1969–70; first performed Bremen, 1979.
Segmente 1–7 (piano) 1982; first performed Amsterdam, 1982.
Segmente 99–105 (violin, piano) 1982; first performed Venice, 1982.
Drei ASKO Stücke (flute, 2 clarinets, saxophone, bassoon, 2 trombones, marimba, piano, 2 violins, viola, cello, double bass) 1982; first performed Amsterdam, 1982. Recorded Wergo CD WER 2022–50.
Segmente 92–98 (violin, cello) 1983; first performed Vancouver, 1985.
Segmente 85–91 (flute/piccolo, bass clarinet, cello) 1984; first performed Priverno, 1987.
Intermezzo (flute/piccolo/bass flute, bass clarinet/E♭ clarinet, piano) 1987; first performed Ghent, 1989.
String Quartet 1987 1987–8; first performed Sermoneta, Italy, 1988.

Other:

Klangfiguren I (electronic sounds) 1955; first performed Cologne, 1955.
Klangfiguren II (electronic sounds) 1955–6; first performed Cologne, 1956. Recorded harmonia mundi 1008 DMR/hm; BV HAAST 9001/9002.
Essay (electronic sounds) 1957–8; first performed Cologne, 1958. Recorded BV HAAST 9001/9002.
Materialien zu einem Ballett (electronic sounds) 1961.
Suite (electronic sounds) 1961; first performed Cologne, 1961.
Terminus 1 (electronic sounds) 1962; first performed Cologne, 1963. Recorded BV HAAST 9001/9002.
Terminus 2 (electronic sounds) 1966–7; first performed Utrecht, 1967. Recorded LP DGG 643 545; BV HAAST 9001/9002.
Terminus X (electronic sounds) 1967; first performed Maastricht, 1967. Recorded Philips 863.933 DSY.
Funktion Grün (electronic sounds) 1967; first performed Bremen, 1968. Recorded LP DGG 643 545.
Funktion Gelb (electronic sounds) 1968; first performed Berlin, 1968. Recorded Wergo WER 324.
Funktion Orange (electronic sounds) 1968; broadcast Cambridge, Massachusetts, 1969.
Funktion Rot (electronic sounds) 1968; first performed Utrecht, 1968. Recorded BV HAAST 9001/9002.
Funktion Blau (electronic sounds) 1969; first performed Prague, 1969. Recorded Philips 6526 004; BV HAAST 9001/9002.
Funktion Indigo (electronic sounds) 1969; first performed Utrecht, 1969. Recorded BV HAAST 9001/9002.
Funktion Violett (electronic sounds) 1969; first performed Utrecht, 1970. Recorded BV HAAST 9001/9002.
Funktion Grau (electronic sounds) 1969; first performed Stockholm, 1970. Recorded BV HAAST 9001/9002.
Output (computer-generated sounds) 1979; first performed Essen, 1979. Recorded BV HAAST 9001/9002.

PUBLICATIONS

By Koenig: "Studio Technique", in *die Reihe*, 1, 1958; "Henri Pousseur" and "Bo Nilsson", in *die Reihe*, 4, 1960; "Via electronica", in *Movens*, 1960; "Notizen zur musikalischen Ökonomie", in *Neue Musik*, 2, 1960; "Studium in Studio", in *die Reihe*, 5, 1961; "Neue Notationsformen", in *Musikhandel*, 13(1), 1962; "Über einige Aspekte gegenwärtiger Instrumentalmusik", in *Musik im Unterricht*, 53(10), 1962; "Preludier til min stråkkkvartett", in *Nutida Musik*, 6(6), 1962; *Musik in ihrer technischen Rationalität*, Bilthoven, 1963; "Einführung in die elektronische Musik", in *Musik im Unterricht*, 55(5), 1964; "Serielle und aleatorische Verfahren in der elektronischen Musik", in *Die Sonde*, 5(1), 1965; "The Second Phase of Electronic Music", in *VISION 65*, International Center for Typographic Arts, 1966; "Notes on the Computer in Music", in *The World of Music*, 9(3), 1967; "Commentary", in *die Reihe*, 8, 1968; "Project 1", in *Electronic Music Reports*, 2, 1970; "The Use of Computer Programmes in Creating Music", in *Music and Technology*, 1970; "Composition Processes", in *Computer Music*, Canadian Commission for UNESCO, 1980; "Musica elettronica—gli inizi, appunti per una interpretazione", in *Di franco evangelisti e di alcuni storici del tempo*, 1980; "Aesthetic Integration of Computer-Composed Scores", in *Computer Music Journal*, 7(4), 1983; "Some Observations on the Impact of Technology on Music", in *Art and Reality: a Casebook of Concern*, Vancouver, 1986; "Genesis of Form in Technically Conditioned Environments", in *Interface*, 16, 1987; "Ligeti und die elektronische Musik", in *Studien zur Wertungsforschung*, 19, 1987; "Tabellen, Graphiken, Klänge", in *MusikTexte*, 30, 1989; "Musik und Zahl", in *Musik-Konzepte*, 66, 1989; *The Complete Theoretical Texts*, Saarbrücken, 1991.

On Koenig: Ulrich Dibelius, "GMK", in *Moderne Musik 1945–65*, 1966; Konrad Boehmer, "Indetermination und neue Perspektiven der Formbildung", in *Zur Theorie der offenem Form in der Neuen Musik*, 1967; Rudolf Frisius, "Zum Notationsproblem in der elektronischen Musik", in *Interface*, 7(2/3), 1978; Otto E. Laske, "Composition Theory in K's Project One and Project Two", in *Computer Music Journal*, 5(4), 1981; Konrad Boehmer, "GMK", in *MusikTexte*, 17, 1986; Patrick Fleury, "GMK, Un pionnier de la musique électronique", in *Kanal*, 40, 1988; Heinz-Klaus Metzger, "Der Musik GMK an dem Rand geschrieben", and Wolf Frobenius, "GMK als Theoretiker der seriellen Musik", both in *Musik-Konzepte*, 66, 1989.

* * *

From 1954 to 1964 Gottfried Michael Koenig worked in the Cologne electronic music studio of West German Radio. The studio's main aesthetic objective was to pursue the consequences of serial composition by electronic means. In this position he produced electronic works by composers like Bengt Hambraeus, Mauricio Kagel, György Ligeti and Henri Pousseur and assisted Karlheinz Stockhausen with *Gesang der Jünglinge* and *Kontakte*. In 1955 Koenig entered the main area of his activities as a composer with his first electronic pieces *Klangfiguren I* and *Klangfiguren II*. The latter piece was criticized because of its radical use of noise leading to an "ugliness" of sound not attempted in electronic music until then. It can be looked at as a counterpart to Stockhausen's *Studie II*, the goal of which was the integration of pitch and timbre. *Klangfiguren II* explored the whole repertory of electronic sound possibilities with the basic categories sine wave (a single frequency), white noise (all audible frequencies) and impulse (a click without audible pitch). In 1957 he realized a piece (*Essay*) involving the transition from micro-time (the temporal realm of frequencies, i.e., microseconds) to macro-time (durations, i.e., larger fractions of a second). Two years later this became the basic principle of Stockhausen's *Kontakte*.

Koenig's instrumental pieces of the same period, mainly

chamber music, represent, while serially organized in contrapuntal strata of parameters, a remarkably free style including independence of serial schemes and openness to subjective control. His various writings reveal him also to be one of the most important theorists of serial music. His *Musik in ihrer technischen Rationalität* (Music in Its Technical Rationality) contains several articles on the fundamentals of serial and aleatory composition, which go far beyond similar articles by more famous composers. An earlier article "Musik und Zahl" (Music and Number) envisioned the concept of computer music for the first time in Europe. At that time Koenig's theoretical thinking had left behind the technical limitations of the Cologne studio. He came to the insight that true serial music could only be achieved by starting at the final element of sound, which is not a single wave period as imagined by Stockhausen, but a single elongation (amplitude of a wave at a point of time, today more commonly known as "sample").

As a consequence Koenig left Cologne in 1964 and became artistic and scientific director of the Institute of Sonology at the University of Utrecht. There electronic music was transformed into a scientific subject dealing with the complex aspects of sound, thus conducting basic research necessary for the production of musical works. The most important instrument of this research is the computer for which Koenig has developed several programs concerning both the production of sound and the structure of composition.

After the completion of a large number of electronic pieces grouped by their titles—*Funktion Grün*, *Funktion Rot* (Function Green, Function Red)—Koenig's interest shifted more and more to the application of the computer in composition for traditional instruments. In 1965 *Projekt 1* marked the beginning of a series of computer programs serving this purpose. He is currently at work on *Projekt III*, a program dealing with general characteristics of the act of composing such as compositional strategies. Koenig has become sceptical of the term "computer music", which nowadays normally connotes the use of MIDI instruments (sampling machines controlled by computers in order to replace acoustical instruments). To him this is simply electronic music, whereas in *his* computer music the computer is involved in the act of composition.

—Rolf Klein

KOKKONEN, Joonas. Finnish. Born in Iisalmi, central Finland, 13 November 1921. Educated at Sibelius Academy, Helsinki (harmony and piano under Selm Palmgren), 1940–1, 1945–9, diploma in piano, 1949; Helsinki University, 1940–8, M.A. in musicology. Military service as sergeant, 1939–44. Married Anita Kokkonen, 3 August 1980; 5 children. Concert pianist, debut 1950; music instructor 1948–9, professor of composition 1959–63, and governor 1966–80, Sibelius Academy, Helsinki; chair, Society of Finnish Composers, 1965–70, and board of Finnish Copyright Bureau (TEOSTO), from 1968. Recipient: elected to Finnish Academy, 1963; Nordic Council Music Prize (for *Symphony No 3*), 1968; Wihuri International Sibelius Prize, 1973; *doctor honoris causa*, Jyvaskyla, 1976, and Helsinki University, 1990. Mailing address: Tuulimyllyutie 5, SF-04400 Järvenpää, Finland.

Publishers: Fazer; Schirmer; Muntra Musikanter.

Symphonies/orchestral:

Musiikkia Jousiorkesterille/Music for Strings 1956–7; first performed Helsinki, 1957. Recorded Finlandia FA 329; Bis CD 485.
Symphony No 1 1958–60; first performed Helsinki, 1960. Recorded Bis CD 485.
Symphony No 2 1961; first performed Helsinki, 1962. Recorded BIS LP 189.
Sinfonia da camera (12 strings) 1962; first performed Lucerne, 1962. Recorded Finlandia FACD 014.
Opus sonorum 1964; first performed Helsinki, 1964.
Symphony No 3 1967; first performed Helsinki, 12 September 1967. Recorded Finlandia FA 310.
Symphonic Sketches 1968; first performed Helsinki, 1968. Recorded Bis CD 468.
Concerto for Cello and Orchestra 1969. Recorded Finlandia FA 310.
Symphony No 4 1971; first performed Helsinki, 7 November 1971. Recorded BIS LP 189.
Inauguratio 1971.
". . . durch einen Spiegel . . ." (metamorphoses for strings, harpsichord) 1976–7; first performed Lucerne, 1977. Recorded Finlandia FA 323/FACD 014.
Interludes from "The Last Temptations" (from the opera) 1977; first performed Helsinki, 1977.
Symphony No 5 1982; first performed Helsinki, 12 January 1983.
Il Paesaggio (chamber orchestra) 1986–7; first performed Järvenpää, 1987.

Chamber/instrumental:

Trio (violin, cello, piano) 1948; first performed Oslo, 1948. Recorded Finlandia FACD 364.
Quintet (piano, string quartet) 1953; first performed Helsinki, 1953. Recorded HMV 5E063 34330.
Sonatina (piano) 1953; first performed Helsinki, 1953. Recorded MHS 3596.
Duo (violin, piano) 1955; first performed Helsinki, 1955. Recorded SALP 1.
String Quartet No 1 1958–9; first performed Helsinki, 1959. Recorded Finlandia FACD 355.
String Quartet No 2 1964–6; first performed Helsinki, 1966. Recorded Phillips 802 855LY.
Haasoito/Wedding March (organ) 1968.
Five Bagatelles (piano) 1968–9; first performed Gothenburg, 1969. Recorded EMI HMV 5E063 34483; Finnlevy SFX 45.
Surusoitto/Funeral March 1969.
Wind Quintet 1973; first performed Oslo 1974. Recorded (3rd movement only) JAVKLP-0184.
Lux aeterna (organ) 1974; first performed Helsinki, 1974. Recorded Finlandia FA 308.
Sonata (cello, piano) 1976; first performed Zurich, 1976. Recorded EMI HMV 5E063 34330.
String Quartet No 3 1976; first performed Helsinki, 1976. Recorded Fuga 3012.
Iuxta crucem (organ) 1979; first performed Lahti, 1979. Recorded Lahti Organ Festival LOF 80/3.
Improvvisazione (violin, piano) 1982; first performed Indianapolis, 1982.

Vocal/choral:

Ikivihrea/Evergreen (school cantata for mixed chorus, boys' and girls' choruses, boy or girl soprano, piano) 1953.
Illat/Evenings (voice, piano; Vala) 1955; first performed Helsinki, 1957.
Lintujen Tuonela/Hades of the Birds (voice, orchestra; Mustapaa) 1958–9.
Missa a cappella (unaccompanied mixed chorus) 1963; first performed Helsinki, 1963. Recorded EMI 5E 063 34483.
Sammakon virsi sateen aikana/Psalm of the Frog in the Rain (unaccompanied male chorus; Mustapaa) 1963.
Laudatio domini (soprano, mixed chorus) 1966; first performed London, 1966. Recorded Finngospel FGCD 1057.
Erekhteion (soloists, mixed chorus, orchestra; Kivimaa) 1969–70.
Sub rosa (voice, piano; Manner) 1973; first performed Helsinki, 1973.
Requiem (soprano, baritone, mixed chorus, orchestra) 1981; first performed Helsinki, 1981.
Sormin soitti Vainamoinen/Vainamoinen Plucked the Strings (unaccompanied male chorus; *Kalevala*) 1985; first performed Helsinki, 1985.

Opera:

Viimeiset kiusaukset/The Last Temptations (Lauri Kokkonen) 1973–5; first performed Helsinki, 2 September 1975. Recorded Finlandia FA 104 LP3.

Other:

Religioso (piano piece for young players; published in *Koskettimet kertovat/Fun on the Keys*) 1956.
Christmas Songs for Children (texts by Suomalainen, Ahokainen, Paloheimo, Havvaio) 1956–66.

PUBLICATIONS

By Kokkonen: many press articles and reviews, from 1950; "The Road to Mental Music", in *Finnish Music Quarterly*, 4, 1988.

On Kokkonen: E. Salmenhaara, "JK romantisoituua klassikko", in *Suomen Musiikin Vuosikirja*, 1967–8; Paavo Heininen, "JK", in *Musiiki*, 3/4, 1972; E. Tawaststjerna, "Viimieset kiusaukest suurtapaus" [premiere of *The Last Temptations*], in *Esseita ja arvostelvja*, Helsinki, 1976; Glenn Norman Koponen, *A Study of the Symphony in Finland from 1945–75 with an Analysis of Representative Compositions* [includes analysis of JK's *Symphony No 3*], University Microfilms, 1980; Timo Makinen, "The Vital Importance of Technique", in *Finnish Music Quarterly*, 4, 1986; Seppo Murto, "Great Religious Works", in *Finnish Music Quarterly*, 2, 1987.

Joonas Kokkonen comments:

A composition is a biological entity as well. It begins from a mystery, from some unfathomable silence. It grows like a tree from a seed. The germ possesses a fantastic capacity for growth. Many people think that the growing power of the initial motive is its most important feature.

However, the gist of the matter is the extent of its growth. This is the most important concern in creating a large form.

* * *

Joonas Kokkonen's return in 1967 from free twelve-tone to tonal style, plus his development of the non-Sibelian Finnish symphony, were the strongest influences upon his students Sallinen and Heininen. Many of Kokkonen's works emanate from cells based on a major third or a perfect fourth, while his works often incorporate accompanimental ostinato. The neo-renaissance *Missa a cappella* is built around a single cell; the later multi-motived *Laudatio domini* includes spoken passages. His main church work, *Requiem*, continues to exploit contrapuntal/linear writing while only subtly varying tension. Kokkonen's greatest work, the opera *The Last Temptations*, contains numerous contrapuntal devices and motives which pervade all his writings (up to the Third String Quartet.

In his early *Piano Sonatina*, octatonic light dissonances accompany neo-baroque lines. *Musiikkia Jousiorkesterille* (four movements for strings) introduces one of Kokkonen's favourite melodic devices: a sustained pitch which momentarily swerves by a semitone at its accented mid-point. Kokkonen's first important composition, the First String Quartet, grows from a few highly organised cells which combine to produce a thematic yet linear work. In *Symphony No 1*, pedal points create tonal centres, while a twelve-note row is based mainly on intervals of seconds and thirds. The expressionist *Symphony No 2* and *String Quartet No 2* were followed by two further symphonies which embody a more relaxed sense of freedom and space. While his earlier symphonies emphasized logical development of twelve-tone material, Kokkonen now concentrated on strong tonal centres and interesting orchestral tone-colour.

Rhythmic sequences associated with altered transpositions characteristically abound in *Five Bagatelles* for piano. Local tonicity is highlighted by exploiting pedal-like basses. The Cello Concerto is exceedingly kind to the soloist: difficult passages are left unaccompanied and liberamente so that pulse-keeping is not imperative at points of possible stress; the soloist often sets a new episode's pace; the cadenza reworks earlier material without adding new fussy details—short bravura sequences are interpolated between statements of earlier phrases. Lines and voicing in the first two movements recall Hindemith in presentation and Shostakovich in figuration. Unexpectedly, the third movement is an Adagio in which the major-to-minor third is foremost. An essentially slow cadenza precedes a brief vivace where quasi-Shostakovich finale cross-string arpeggios and scales are skilfully presented. The *Wind Quintet*'s motivic pitches, be they highly elongated or rhythmic and brief, are taken from a varied ordering of the chromatic scale of a perfect fourth, one of the central pitches being made into the tonic.

The Last Temptations was Kokkonen's most influential work, in its effect upon his later writing and in its redefinition of modern Finnish opera. When a particular pitch has served its purpose as local tonic, rather than go through a process of modulation, it either sidesteps or fuses the harmonic system by drastically altering the orchestral colour on a suddenly held cluster. Exceedingly well-crafted orchestration produces much of the local interest. Memorable themes are used for fast passages (e.g., two dotted rhythms followed by three descending staccato notes, found in the opera's dancing section and in the finale of *Wind Quintet*). Many of the slower melodies found in the opera are constructed from a horizontalised small cluster of semitones, finishing with a descending tone followed by an ascending perfect fifth. In these works, as in the *Requiem* and *Musiikkia Jousiorkesterille*, Kokkonen uses an unpredictable order of unconnected open-spaced primary triads devoid of vertical dissonance. The resulting idiom also provides many non-passing-note harmonisations of the chorale which binds the opera's scenes together.

—Malcolm J. Hill

KOLB, Barbara. American. Born in Hartford, Connecticut, 10 February 1939. Educated: clarinet lessons under William Goldstein, from 1950; Hartt School of Music, University of Hartford, Connecticut (clarinet under Louis Speyer, postgraduate composition study under Arnold Franchetti), 1957–64, B.Mus., 1961, M.Mus., 1965; Fulbright Scholar, Vienna, 1966; Berkshire Music Center, Tanglewood, Massachusetts (under Gunther Schuller and Lukas Foss), 1964, 1968; Mills College, Oakland, California (Ford Foundation studentship in electronic music), 1973. E♭ clarinettist, Hartford Symphony Orchestra, 1960–6; instructor in clarinet and music theory, Hartt School of Music, University of Hartford, 1962–4; music copyist, New York City, 1965; resident in Rome, 1969–71; trustee, American Academy in Rome, 1972–5; composer in residence, Marlboro Music Festival, 1973; assistant professor of music theory, Brooklyn College, New York, 1973–5; composer in residence, American Academy in Rome, 1974–5; resident in Paris, 1976–7; visiting professor, Temple University, Philadelphia, 1978; director, "Music New to New York" series, Third Street Music School Settlement, New York City, from 1979; 9-month residency, IRCAM, Paris, 1983–4; visiting professor of composition, Eastman School of Music, Rochester, New York, 1984–5. Recipient: MacDowell Colony Fellowship, 1968, 1969, 1971, 1972, 1980, 1983, 1987–9; Prix de Rome, 1970; Alumna of the Year, Hartt School of Music, 1978; Kennedy Center Friedheim Award (for *Millefoglie*), 1987; Ford Prize. Mailing address: 41 West 72nd Street, New York City, New York 10023, U.S.A.

Publishers: Boosey & Hawkes; Fischer; Peters.

Symphonies/orchestral:

Soundings (2 conductors) 1971–2, revised 1975, 1978; orchestral version first performed New York City, 11 December 1975.
Grisaille 1978–9; first performed Portland, Maine, 13 February 1979.
Yet That Things Go Round (chamber orchestra) 1986–7, revised 1988; first performed New York City, 2 May 1987.
The Enchanted Loom 1988–9; first performed Atlanta, Georgia, 15 February 1990.
Voyants (piano, orchestra) 1989; first performed Paris, 1990.

Chamber/instrumental:

Rebuttal (2 clarinets) 1965. Recorded Opus One 14.
Figments (flute, piano) 1967, revised 1969. Recorded Desto DC 7143.
Crosswinds (1 flutes, 2 cors anglais, 2 bass clarinets, alto saxophone, 2 bassoons, 2 horns, 2 trumpets, 2 trombones, 4 percussion) 1969; first performed Rome, 24 September 1970. Recorded Galaxia GAL 004.
Trobar Clus (flute/alto flute, trumpet, 2 trombones, 2 percussion, amplified harpsichord, guitar, violin, 2 violas, cello) 1970; first performed Tanglewood, Massachusetts, 17 August 1970. Recorded Turnabout TV 34487.
Toccata (harpsichord, tape) 1971.
Solitaire (piano, tape) 1971. Recorded Turnabout TV 34487.
Soundings (flute, oboe, clarinet, bassoon, horn, percussion, harp, string quartet, tape) 1971–2, revised 1975, 1978; first performed New York City, 27 October 1972.
Spring River Flowers Moon Night (2 pianos, tape) 1974–5; first performed New York City, 12 January 1976. Recorded CRI SD 361/572.
Looking for Claudio (guitar, tape) 1975; first performed Brussels, 22 May 1975. Recorded CRI SD 361/527.
Appello (piano) 1976; first performed Washington, D.C., 20 October 1976. Recorded CRI SD 537/572.
Homage to Keith Jarrett and Gary Burton (flute, vibraphone) 1976, revised 1977; first performed Dallas, Texas, 31 March 1976. Recorded Leonarda LPI 121; CRS 8245.
Musique pour un vernissage (flute, guitar, violin, viola) 1976–7; first performed Paris, 1977; concert version performed Washington, D.C., 3 February 1979; withdrawn.
Related Characters (B♭ clarinet or trumpet or viola or alto saxophone, piano) 1980; first performed Los Angeles, 7 November 1982.
Three Lullabies (guitar) 1980; first performed Paris, 27 March 1980. Recorded Bridge BDG 2001.
Cavatina (violin or viola) 1983, revised 1985; first performed Washington, D.C., 21 May 1983.
Millefoglie (flute, oboe, clarinet, bass clarinet, trombone, 2 percussion, amplified harp, cello, computer-generated tape) 1984–5, revised 1987; first performed Paris, 5 June 1985.
Time . . . and Again (oboe, string quartet, tape) 1985; first performed Washington, D.C., 22 November 1985.
Umbrian Colors (violin, guitar) 1986; first performed Marlboro, Vermont, 13 August 1986.
Molto allegra (guitar) 1988.
Extremes (flute, cello) 1989; first performed New York City, 15 March 1989.

Vocal/choral:

Chansons bas (soprano, harp, percussion; Mallarmé's "Le Cantonnier", "La Femme de l'ouvrier", "Le Marchand d'ail et d'oignons", "Le Vitrier", "Le Crieur d'imprimés", Interlude, "La Marchande d'habits) 1966. Recorded Desto DC 7143.
Three Place Settings (narrator, clarinet, violin, double bass, percussion; Diamond's "I Think I'll Have . . . on a Plate", Brown and Brown's "Roast Peacock", Costa's "Automort") 1968. Recorded Desto DC 7143.
Songs Before an Adieu (soprano, flute/alto flute, guitar; Pinsky's "The Sentences", cummings's "Now I Lay", Stern's "Cantata", Popa's "Gluttonous Smoke", Apollinaire's "L'Adieu") 1976–9; first performed Chicago, 23 May 1979. Recorded Bridge BDG 2004; "Sentences" recorded Turnabout TV S 34727.
Chromatic Fantasy (amplified narrator, amplified alto flute, oboe, soprano saxophone, trumpet, vibraphone, amplified vibraphone, electric guitar or electric harpsichord or electric piano; Stern) 1979; first performed River Falls, Wisconsin, 4 November 1979.
The Point That Divides the Wind (3 male voices, organ, 4 percussion; Franciscan/Gregorian chant) 1981–2; first performed New York City, 7 March 1983.
The Sundays of My Life (jazz song) 1982.

Other:

Cantico (tape collage score for film on life of Francis of Assisi by James Herbert) 1982; first shown New York City, 5 December 1982.

PUBLICATIONS

On Kolb: C.Gagne and T. Caras, (interview) in *Soundpieces: Interviews with American Composers*, Metuchen, New Jersey, 1982.

* * *

Supremely talented, Barbara Kolb is one of the most distinctive and individual American composers to emerge since World War II. She was the first American woman to win the Ford Prize, and has been widely recognized by European composers and conductors as well as by those in the United States.

Her work is strongly evocative and heterodox, adapting serial techniques to a highly personal vision often inspired by the visual arts (as in *Grisaille*) and by literature. The abiding impression—and "impression" may give away at least some of her sources—is a highly textural music based on repeated thematic gestures and careful rhythmic modulation, from which emerge powerful climaxes which are sometimes profoundly alienating, sometimes highly ambiguous. Her carefully assimilated influences include Claude Debussy (notably in works such as *Millefoglie*, which employs the same overlapping brushwork as *Grisaille*, to even greater effect), Chopin (as in *Solitaire*), Satie (as in the "*musique d'ammeublement*" for a Paris gallery opening) and American jazz. Her homage to jazz musicians Keith Jarrett and vibraphonist Gary Burton pairs vibes with flute, rather than with Jarrett's instrument, the piano, but it does capture something of Jarrett's intensely articulated solo style, as well as his notorious alternation between rigidly structured melodic passages and episodes of apparent freedom.

This is already evident in her first acknowledge work, *Rebuttal*, in which precisely metered passages are opposed to those which (though strictly notated) allow the two clarinettists considerable freedom. *Solitaire* makes similar use of a degree of indeterminacy, allowing the pianist to structure the material within certain parameters of choice. The piece also alternates between atonality and a species of diatonicism, quoting Chopin almost ironically.

The same device was employed even more successfully in the solo piano *Appello* which takes its tone-row from Pierre Boulez's 1951 *Structures*, but transforms his lockstep abstraction into a work which strongly suggests an improvisatory "development". Which in fact goes nowhere, because Kolb's work resists traditional harmonic resolutions. She nonetheless gives a strong impression of tonal centring, without mono-directional impulse and movement. It is very much like the movement of natural forces, the sea (Debussy again) or the accumulation of rain or thunder, and Kolb's climaxes emerge in a way that recalls the dramatic inversions and collapses of catastrophe theory. *Soundings*, her best-known work, accumulates material in progressively stratified melorhythms, but constantly plumbs a thematic centre which in *Grisaille* is gradually, then suddenly submerged in a furious cross-hatching.

Her recent *The Enchanted Loom* for full orchestra draws together many of the threads laid out in subsequent versions of *Soundings* (Kolb is a dedicated and painstaking reviser of her work). A full-voiced and complex work, certainly her best for larger forces, it suggests an aural gloss on Remedios Varo's great painting *Bordando el manto terrestre* (used to great effect by Thomas Pynchon in his novel *The Crying of Lot 49*), in which women trapped in a tower weave the fabric of the physical world, pushing it out through narrow slots that stand for the birth canal and for a prison-door judas. It is a creative gesture that visually links childbirth and imprisonment, for the women are guarded by a masked figure associated with an alchemical crucible or alembic. Like Varo's, Kolb's work is *sui generis* and intensely personal. Whether it typifies a distinctively female sensibility is always debatable, and pointlessly so, but it is clear that Kolb has taken possession of the formulas and crucibles of modern composition and has worked her own alchemy, as she indicates in Boulez's direction, without enslavement to any of the prevailing ideologies or schools.

—Bea Weir

KONDO, Jo. Japanese. Born in Tokyo, 28 October 1947. Educated at Tokyo National University of Fine Arts, 1968–72, B.Mus. Married Masako Kondo, 25 February 1972. Lecturer, Tokyo Gakugei University, 1976–9; visiting lecturer, University of Victoria, British Columbia, 1979; artistic director, Musica Practica Ensemble, Tokyo, since 1980; lecturer, Ochanomizu University, Tokyo, 1983–8; composer in residence, Hartt School of Music, University of Hartford, and Real Art Way, both Hartford, Connecticut, 1986; lecturer, Tokyo University of Arts, since 1986; professor, Elizabeth University of Music, Hiroshima, since 1988; associate editor, *Contemporary Music Review*, since 1989. Recipient: Rockefeller Fund grant, New York City, 1977–8; British Council senior fellowship, 1986. Mailing address: 210–92 Jomyoji, Kamakura-shi, 248 Japan.

Publishers: C.F. Peters, New York; Zen-On, Tokyo.

Symphonies/orchestral:

Birdphone Functions 1974; first performed Tokyo, 1975.
A Shape of Time (piano, orchestra) 1979; first performed Tokyo, 1980. Recorded ALM AL-27.
Pastoral 1989; first performed Tokyo, 1989.
In the Woods 1989; first performed Osaka, 1990.

Chamber/instrumental:

Monologue and Five Fragments (flute, piano) 1968; first performed Tokyo, 1969.
String Quartet 1969; first performed Tokyo, 1972.
Breeze (2 flutes, 2 clarinets, cello, double bass, 3 percussion) 1969; first performed Osaka, 1970.
Summer Days (clarinet, tape) 1970; first performed Tokyo, 1970. Recorded ALM AL-13.
Modulation (double bass, koto, prepared piano, percussion) 1970; first performed Tokyo, 1970.
For Piano Players (any number of instruments) 1971; first performed Tokyo, 1971.
Air No 1 (piano, trumpet) 1971; first performed Tokyo, 1972. Recorded EMI Japan EAA 85014.

Her (trombone, double bass, 2 banjos, prepared piano, harp) 1972; first performed Tokyo, 1973.
Mr Bloomfield, His Spacing (string quartet) 1973; first performed Tokyo, 1973. Recorded ALM AL-13.
Orient Orientation (any 2 instruments of the same kind) 1973; first performed Tokyo, 1973. Recorded ALM AL-1.
Standing (any 3 instruments of different families) 1973; first performed Tokyo, 1973. Recorded ALM AL-1; CP2 USA 11.
Wait (5 percussion) 1973; first performed Tokyo, 1973. Recorded RCI 652.
Falling (2 violas, double bass, electric piano) 1974; first performed Tokyo, 1974. Recorded ALM AL-1.
Click Crack (piano) 1974; first performed Tokyo, 1974. Recorded ALM AL-1.
Pass (banjo, 2 guitars, harp, harmonica, taisho-koto) 1974; first performed Tokyo, 1974. Recorded ALM AL-1.
Sight Rhythmics (violin, banjo, tuba, electric piano, steel drum) 1975; first performed Tokyo, 1975. Recorded ALM AL-12.
Sight Rhythmics (piano) 1975; first performed Tokyo, 1975. Recorded ALM AL-13; CP2 11.
The Shape That Follows Its Shadow (2 pianos) 1975; first performed Tokyo, 1976.
Walk (flute, piano) 1976; first performed Tokyo, 1976. Recorded ALM AL-13.
Under the Umbrella (5 percussion) 1976; first performed Tokyo, 1976. Recorded CP2 11.
Luster Gave Her Hat and He and Ben Went Across the Backyard (3 marimbas) 1976; first performed Tokyo, 1977.
Knots (2 guitars, electric piano, percussion) 1977; first performed Tokyo, 1977. Recorded ALM AL-12.
Retard (violin) 1977; first performed Tokyo, 1978. Recorded Victor SJX 9541.
Strands I (flute, cor anglais, viola, double bass, banjo, electric piano, percussion) 1978; first performed Tokyo, 1978.
A Crow (sopranino saxophone) 1978; first performed Tokyo, 1978.
Walk (piano) 1979; first performed Tokyo, 1979.
When Wind Blew (12 instruments) 1979; first performed Middleburg, Holland, 1979.
Threadbare Unlimited (8 strings) 1979; first performed Tokyo, 1979.
An Insular Style (flute, clarinet, harp, percussion) 1979; first performed Tokyo, 1980.
Strands II (2 or 3 pianos) 1980; first performed Tokyo, 1980.
An Elder's Hocket (flute, clarinet, piano, marimba) 1980; first performed Tokyo, 1981.
Left Bank (14 instruments) 1981; first performed Tokyo, 1981.
Duo (harp, guitar) 1981; first performed Tokyo, 1982. Recorded ALM AL-27.
Still Life (8 violins) 1981; first performed Tokyo, 1982. Recorded ALM AL-27.
Strands III (violin, piano) 1982; first performed Tokyo, 1982. Recorded ALM AL-27.
Forme semée (trombone, piano) 1982; first performed Tokyo, 1982.
Trio (Moor) (viola, bassoon, piano) 1982; first performed Tokyo, 1983.
Diptych (violin, horn, trombone, piano, glockenspiel) 1983; first performed Tokyo, 1983.
Dance(s) (3 shō) 1983; first performed Tokyo, 1984.
Hunisuccle (14 instruments) 1984; first performed Tokyo, 1984.
Antilogue (oboe, string quartet) 1984; first performed Tokyo, 1984.
Theatre (3 clarinets, bass clarinet) 1984; first performed Tokyo, 1985.
Bonjin (alto flute, double bass, female voice) 1985; first performed Sermoneta, Italy, 1985. Recorded ALM ALCD-36.
Isthmus (7 instruments) 1985; first performed Tokyo, 1985.
A Scribe (flute, trombone, piano, percussion) 1985; first performed New York City, 1986.
Words (flute, clarinet, harp, piano, percussion) 1986; first performed Tokyo, 1986.
The Serotinous (piano, 9 instruments) 1986; first performed Kamo, Niigata-ken, Japan, 1986. Recorded ALM ALCD-36.
Dance(s) (organ) 1986; first performed Tokyo, 1986.
A Volcano Mouth (3 marimbas) 1986; first performed Tokyo, 1987.
Res sonorae (oboe, viola, 12 instruments) 1986; first performed London, 1988. Recorded ALM ALCD-36.
Beginning, Middle and End (flute, string quartet) 1987; first performed Geneva, 1987.
High Song (soprano flute, shakuhachi) 1987; first performed Dartington, 1987.
Untitled (violin, 8 trombones, 2 horns) 1987; first performed Tokyo, 1987.
Vox humana (organ) 1988; first performed Tokyo, 1988.
Ars brevis (mandolin) 1988; first performed Kyoto, 1988. Recorded ALM ALCD-36.
Hypsotony (string quartet) 1989; first performed London, 1989.
Yokohama (2 violins, bass flute, piano) 1989; first performed Yokohama, 1990. Recorded ALM ALCD-36.
Pendulums (percussion) 1990; first performed Tokyo, 1990.

Vocal/choral:

Kekai-Sekai (mixed chorus) 1976; first performed Tokyo, 1977.
Two Pieces (mixed chorus) 1980; first performed Tokyo, 1982.
New Buds on the Elderberry Tree (soprano) 1982; first performed Middleburg, Netherlands, 1983.
Jo-Ka (Buddhistic chanting chorus, 20 Japanese Gagaku instruments) 1985; first performed Tokyo, 1986.

Other:

Never Return (tape) 1970; first performed Tokyo, 1971.
Riverrun (tape) 1977; first performed Tokyo, 1977.
Tokyo Bay 1986; first performed Tokyo, 1987.

PUBLICATIONS

By Kondo: *Sen no Ongaku (Linear Music)*, Tokyo, 1979; *Ongaku no Shuji (Seed of Music)*, Tokyo, 1983; *Mimi no Shiko (Thinking Ear)*, Tokyo, 1985; "The Art of Being Ambiguous", in *Contemporary Music Review*, 2 (2), 1988.

Jo Kondo comments:

Each sound must have its own entity and life. What I am doing in my compositions is to create a web of intertonal relationships, while trying to safeguard the possibility of aurally perceiving the individual entity and life of every single tone in that relationship.

* * *

As a student of the Tokyo National University of Fine Arts in the late 1960s. Jo Kondo delivered a piece at the end of each of the four academic years for examination purposes. The first piece, *Monologue and Five Fragments*, had to be converted to a different instrumentation (flute, piano) as the first version employed too many "unusual" techniques of sound production on the piano. One of the main characteristics of Kondo's later style, the preference for calm and reserved sounds can already be recognized in this piece.

After *String Quartet*, which showed influences by Penderecki and Lutosławski, he achieved his first mature piece with *Breeze* for nine instruments, performed on the Expo at Osaka 1970. *Breeze*, with its graphical notation and around 3000 instructions, demands the highest efforts of the performers, especially concerning their mutual interdependence. Kondo says that he had wanted to create something like the Japanese tea ceremony in music. John Cage's thoughts about interpenetration of both musical sounds and the sounds of everyday-life, which were inspired by the study of Zen Buddhism, are brought home to their original environment. But Kondo shared only the affinity to calmness and long silences with Cage, there were no chance operations or indeterminacy. Several other pieces explored that new look at Cage's aesthetics. Although sounds of everyday-life are used, Kondo always cared for transparency and the absolute quality of the sounds.

In the following years Kondo developed a new musical concept called "Sen No Ongaku" which can be roughly translated as "Linear Music". It refers to the impression of the listener who perceives music as an uninterrupted stream of tones. Notes are not separated or grouped in order to enable equal attention to each of them. This contributes to the primary purpose to write music which excludes anthropocentricisms like expressivity and speech-likeness. Kondo turned away from complexity at the surface of music by using conventional instrumental timbres—usually a chamber ensemble—and lightening the compositional structures. Dynamic and melodic ranges are reduced, and gamuts of sounds are limited to carefully selected notes. Harmonically and melodically Kondo's music of the 1970s is close to make an almost tonal impression but remains always ambiguous. *Sight Rhythmics* exists in two versions for piano and for chamber ensemble. It extends the tendency of reduction and abstractness into the realm of musical form. Its six movements remain almost identical to each other, changing only in details which at first might not easily be perceived. Kondo calls this "pseudo-repetition" since it lies somewhere in between repetition and variation. Using the above-mentioned techniques he achieves an emotionless, abstract kind of music giving the impression of a "dynamic stasis", an attitude towards music which is not far from Morton Feldman's. His way of composing does not take on any mathematical procedures as it might seem if one considers earlier attempts for abstractness in music. He composes mainly by listening to the relationships between sounds in order to achieve a calculated ambiguity concerning their functions in tonal, rhythmical aspects as well as structurally viewed.

The strictly linear concept of "Sen No Ongaku" was evolved toward one giving equal attention to the harmonic relationships between sounds in works like *Still Life* for eight violins. During the 1980s the tonal ambiguity of earlier works gave way to a more atonal type of harmony (e.g., in *Res sonorae* for 14 instruments) without changing the general identity of Kondo's style.

—Rolf Klein

KONSHINA, Elena (Sergeevna). Russian. Born in Kirovgrad, Sverdlovsk region, 9 January 1950. Educated at Music School, Vladimir, 1964–9; Leningrad Conservatoire, 1970–5. Piano soloist, Vladimir Philharmonia, 1969–70; teacher and soloist, Music School, Vladimir, since 1975; member, Union of Composers, from 1980. Mailing address: Ulits Feigina, dom 1, kv. 19, 600009 Vladimir 9, U.S.S.R.

Publisher: Union of Composers, Moscow.

Symphonies/orchestral:

Concerto for Piano and Orchestra 1975; first performed (on 2 pianos) Vladimir, March 1976.

Chamber/instrumental:

Sonata (piano, cello) 1973; first performed Leningrad, 1974.
Trio (oboe, bassoon, cello) 1977; first performed Moscow, 1981. Recorded Melodiya CIO 231761000.
Sonata (piano) 1979.
Three Preludes (piano) 1985.

Vocal/choral:

About 40 unaccompanied choral works, 1975–90.

Other:

Netochka Nezvanova (incidental music to play after Dostoevsky) 1983; first performed Smolensk, 1983.
Nakhlebnik (incidental music to play after Turgenev) 1983; first performed Vladimir, 1983.

PUBLICATIONS

By Konshina: series of popular articles on church music, local press, Vladimir, 1990.

Elena Konshina comments:

I have tried several times to write about my music. Each time, I either exaggerated, or the opposite, or came up with illusory ideas about what I had already written or should have written.

So I must limit myself to the words of St Efrem Sirin which best describe what my creative energies and my life are directed to: "*O Silence—the stairway to the heavens!*"

* * *

Elena Konshina is a quietist, living in the ancient town of Vladimir far away from the larger centres of Soviet cultural activity. Her music is almost completely unknown even a few hours away in Moscow.

In one sense her music might hardly seem to merit our attention at all, so deeply and traditionally Russian does it at first seem. Her unaccompanied choruses on texts of Rubtsov for example might as well be the work of one who had lived no later than Taneyev and, moreover, one who had heard no other music than that written within the closed borders of the Russian Empire.

And yet, in the extreme modesty and privacy of the mostly miniature works of this composer, in the apparent conservatism of its style, there is contained a fierce and beautiful individuality. Somehow, even in these choral works, the harmony never moves quite the way we think it will, the conventional resolutions are never quite as formulaic or as reassuring as they ought to be. Something is disturbing about this music, not allowing too quick judgement. Konshina has succeeded where many Soviet composers have failed, in the attempt to revive the older Russian traditions and make them anew and of our own time.

One of Konshina's finest pieces is her *Three Preludes* for piano: "Morning Silences", "Quietness and Stillness" and "Evening Song". Typically these pieces strike us at first as the merest minimal retelling of certain very well-worn pianistic effects and tonal devices. But as we open our ears to their carefully thought out inner structures, to the composer's extreme sensitivity to register and texture, we are admitted to another world beyond the surface sounds.

We are not surprised to learn that this composer is deeply religious, nor indeed that she, in her own words, is "not afraid of being provincial". Konshina has evidently grasped her isolated situation in Vladimir, not as deprivation, but as a gift, allowing her to concentrate her vision, to purify it of the alien. And if we are, rightly, suspicious of the aggressive primitivism of nationalism, in Konshina's music we hear the other side of loyalty to the tribe, an almost ecstatic transcendance from the individual consciousness to the common experience.

In some ways Konshina's music is at its most appealing where there is a sense of tension between the chosen medium and the native language. In the piano pieces, for example, there is a constant striving towards a sound-world beyond the reach of that particular instrument. And in the beautifully simple *Trio* for oboe, bassoon and cello, we hear almost an imagined religious ritual—private prayer rather than public ceremony—that is charmingly at odds with the gaucheness of the instrumental combination.

—Gerard McBurney

KOPELENT, Marek. Czechoslovak. Born in Prague, 28 April 1932. Educated at Prague Academy of Arts (composition under Jaroslav Ridký), 1951–5. Music director, Musica Viva Pragensis ensemble, since 1965; visiting scholar, German Academy, Berlin, 1969; guest lecturer, Kazimierz Summer School, Poland, 1985; guest teacher, Paris Conservatoire; competition jury member, Rio de Janeiro, 1970, Biennale de Paris, 1971, ISCM Festival, Bonn, 1976, Alte Kirche Boswil, 1980, Kazimierz Serocki Competition, Warsaw, 1984. Mailing address: Czech Music Information Centre, Besedni 3, 118 00 Prague 1, Czechoslovakia.

Publishers: Panton; Editio Supraphon; Breitkopf & Härtel, Wiesbaden; Barenreiter, Kassel; Universal Edition, Vienna; Edition Modern, Munich.

Symphonies/orchestral:

Satanela (based on the poem by Jaroslav Vrchlický) 1954–5.
Contemplation (chamber orchestra) 1966. Recorded Supraphon.
Accords et désaccords (12 instruments concertante, orchestra) 1968.
Appassionata (piano, orchestra) 1970–1.
A Few Minutes with an Oboist (concerto galante for oboe, chamber orchestra) 1972.
Games (alto saxophone, orchestra) 1974–5.
Likeable Music with a Folk Motif (dulcimer, orchestra) 1976.
Symphony 1982.
Greetings 1984.
Concertino (cor anglais, chamber orchestra) 1984.

Chamber/instrumental:

Some early works withdrawn.
String Quartet No 3 1963. Recorded Supraphon.
Canto intimo (flute, vibraphone) 1963.
Music for Five (oboe, clarinet, bassoon, viola, piano) 1964–5.
A Tribute to Vladimír Holan (nonet) 1965.
For Arnŏst Wilde (piano) 1966.
String Quartet No 4 1967. Recorded Supraphon.
Hallelujah (organ) 1967. Recorded Supraphon.
Bijou de Bohème (harpsichord) 1967.
Still Life (chamber ensemble) 1968. Recorded Supraphon.
Musique piquante (violin, dulcimer or piano) 1971.
Brass Quintet 1972.
Sonata (11 strings) 1972–3.
Rondo: Before the Arrival of the Charming Executioner, or Three Bows to Hope (5 percussion) 1973.
Tukata (harp, harpsichord, dulcimer or electric guitar) 1974.
Ballad (piano) 1976.
Capriccio (trumpet) 1976.
Triste e Consolante (wind quintet; new or early instruments) 1977.
In Praise of Dawn (organ) 1978.
Tocata (viola, piano) 1978.
Musica lirica (flute, violin, piano) 1978–9.
Furiant (piano trio) 1979.
String Quartet No 5 1979–80.

Vocal/choral:

Angry Songs (baritone, piano; Petrarch) 1956.
Bread and Birds (contralto, reciter, mixed chorus, orchestra; Skacel) 1957–62.
Miniature Songs (baritone, piano; ancient Japanese) 1960–1.
Nenie for the late Hana Hlavsova (flute, 9 female voices, chamber ensemble) 1960–1. Recorded Supraphon.
Matka / Mother (frescoes for mixed chorus, flute) 1964. Recorded Supraphon; Deutsche Grammophon.
Cantus Suplex (12 unaccompanied voices; medieval Latin) 1966.
Stone Prayer (reciter, 2 mixed chamber choruses, 3 tom-toms; Holan) 1967.
Snehah (soprano, jazz contralto on tape, tape, chamber ensemble) 1967. Recorded Supraphon.
Plants (mixed chorus, trumpet, timpani ad lib) 1969.
Black and White Tears (voice) 1972.
Syllables mouvementées (unaccompanied chamber chorus) 1972.
Vacillat pes meus (unaccompanied mixed chorus; Psalms) 1972.
Laudatio pacis (oratorio co-written with Sofia Gubaidulina [USSR] and P. H. Dittrich [Germany]; soprano, contralto, tenor, bass, reciter, chamber chorus, mixed chorus, orchestra; Comenius) 1975.
Il canto di li augei (soprano, orchestra; Italian Renaissance verse) 1977–8.
The Casting of Dice (4 reciters, tape of Mallarmé poem) 1980.
Legend de passione St Adalberti Martyris (reciter, mixed chorus, orchestra; Bohemian legend) 1981.

Amusing Song (unaccompanied mixed chorus; Volný) 1982.
Excited Song (baritone, brass quintet; Hora) 1982–3.
Agnus Dei (soprano, chamber ensemble; Luther) 1983.
Regina Lucis (unaccompanied mixed chorus; Franus Hymnal) 1985.
Ona Skutecne Jest/She Really Exists (tenor, bass, reciter, mixed chorus, children's chorus, orchestra; Holan) 1985–6.

Theatre:

Errant Voice (actress, tape, chamber ensemble, 16 or 35mm film, lights ad lib) 1969.
Musica, or A Story of Long Long Ago That Angels Pass on from Age to Age (singspiel for soprano, 2 actors, flute, oboe, harpsichord; Sobotka) 1978–9.
A Woman's Lament (melodrama for actress, 7 brass, 14 female voices, children's chorus; Procházková) 1980.

Other (mainly for children):

Four songs to Verses by Vítězslav Nezval (children's chorus, piano) 1960.
Abbreviations (piano, 4 hands) 1962.
Four Pieces (trombone, piano) 1963.
Little Suite (trumpet, piano) 1963.
Dotty Ditties (children's chorus) 1967.
Daybreak (large children's chorus) 1967.
The Universe's Secret Signals (piano—6 hands) 1972.
Two (piano—4 hands) 1973.
Rondo (piano—for the left hand when the right one happens to be in a plaster cast) 1975.
A Strange Dance: Podpantoflicek (piano—4 hands) 1980.
Good Morning (piano—4 hands) 1980.
A Fond Farewell (flute, piano) 1981.
Cantus simplex (children's chorus) 1983.

George Gershwin: *Prelude for Piano* (arranged for 4 hands) 1980.

Incidental music to radio drama: *Hamlet; Richard III*; Vrchlický's *Sarka*; Madakhov's *Tragedy of Man*; Dostoevsky's *White Nights*; Šalda's *Crowds*.

Music for poetry readings at Viola Theatre: Nezval: *Poems of the Night* (recorded Supraphon); Holan's *Night with Hamlet*; Mácha's *May*.

* * *

Marek Kopelent was one of the composers who helped re-establish contacts between Czech music and the contemporary European mainstream in the 1960s. He turned very soon from his initial late-Romanticism to the style and techniques of the Second Viennese School, especially those of Webern, who represents his most important single influence. However, Kopelent has not applied serialist procedures dogmatically; he uses the system to build his own style which remains flexibly responsive to contemporary musical language.

Looking for an underlying principle in his work, the fundamental recognition is Kopelent's vision of musical activity as some spatio-temporal entity (much like the unities of drama) which exists latently and is reinvented with each new work. The definition of such begins at a tone-point at the start of the melody, or at a tone-field (often of modal character) whose main characteristic is its timbre. To charge his music with significance, he sometimes uses quotations or stylistically variant fragments.

The structural principles of classical drama are used in the third string quartet, which is written in serial idiom. The *Brass Quintet* draws attention to a taped fragment of choral singing. In the *Sonata* for 11 Strings, the means of defining musical space and endowing it with meaning is particularly significant: modally constructed chords are dynamized by quarter-tone shifts and changes in timbre, while the whole movement points (by means of the choral fragments) to the mighty C major chord which symbolizes positive spiritual value.

In his concertante compositions, Kopelent sometimes treats the solo instrument as a narrative "protagonist" (as in *Games* for alto saxophone and orchestra); in *Likeable Music with a Folk Motif*, the choice of instrument—in this case, dulcimer—dictates the type of musical material; at other times (as in *Il canto de li augei*) he creates an illusion of latter-day Mozart. To express his views on contemporary issues, he turns to historical themes: the collaborative oratorio *Laudatio pacis* and the *Legend de Passione St Adalberti Martyris*.

The large 1982 *Symphony* marks the culmination of Kopelent's creative development so far; in it instruments are deployed solistically or in small chamber groupings. Its musical material is formulated in two contrasting ways: a melodic motif is opposed to aggressively stylized blocks of sound. As in other of Kopelent's works, this motif is an "alien" fragment, in this case a funeral march; after its gradual deconstruction, its idiom recurs, signalizing the re-introduction of a main theme which is clearly defined in the extended tonality. In spite of a prevailingly depressive, almost Mahleresque mood, the Symphony ends on a positive note.

—Jan Dehner

KORNDORF, Nikolai. Russian. Born in Moscow, 23 January 1947. Educated at Moscow Conservatoire, 1965–70, 1975–9. Married Averina Galina in 1970; 2 sons. Professor of instrumentation, Moscow Conservatoire, since 1972. Recipient: City Prize of Duisburg, Germany, 1990. Mailing address: Novie Cheremushki kvartal 32-A, korp. 4, kv. 100, 113461 Moscow, U.S.S.R.

Publisher: none.

Symphonies/orchestral:

Symphony No 1 1975; first performed Moscow, 16 December 1977.
Symphony No 2 1980; first performed Moscow, 25 October 1982.
Concerto capriccioso (cello, large string orchestra, keyboard instruments, percussion) 1986.
Hymn I: Sempre tutti 1987; first performed Moscow, 27 May 1988. Recorded Art and Electronics AED 68017.
Hymn II 1987; first performed Moscow, 18 March 1989.

Chamber/instrumental:

Confessiones: Chamber Symphony No 1 (flute, oboe, clarinet, bassoon, horn, trumpet, trombone, piano, 2 percussion, violin, viola, cello, double bass) 1979; first performed Moscow, 15 December 1979. Recorded Melodiya C10 15169–70.
Yarilo (piano) 1981; first performed Moscow, 8 June 1981.

Recorded Melodiya C10-21917.
Primitive Music (12 saxophones) 1981; first performed Moscow, 25 April 1984.
Movements (12 percussionists) 1982; first performed Moscow, 30 November 1981.
Lullaby (2 pianos) 1983; first performed Moscow, 8 October 1984.
Con sordino (16 solo strings, harpsichord) 1984; first performed Moscow, 19 October 1985.
Brass Quintet 1985.
Amoroso: Chamber Symphony No 2 (flute, oboe, clarinet, 2 horns, harp, viola, cello, double bass, 2 percussion) 1986; first performed Moscow, 22 December 1986.
Trio (violin, viola, cello) 1986.

Vocal/choral:

Da!/Yes! (rite for soprano, 2 tenors, cor anglais, clarinet, bassoon, horn, trumpet, trombone, organ, bass guitar, 2 percussion, tape) 1982; first performed Moscow, 17 December 1984.
Chant (mezzo-soprano, tape) 1982; first performed Moscow, 14 March 1983.
Laments (cantata for chamber chorus, percussion) 1983.

PUBLICATIONS

By Korndorf: new translation and edition of Adam Carse: *The History of Orchestration* (1925), with introduction and commentary, 1990.

* * *

Nikolai Korndorf occupies a most interesting position in the field of contemporary Soviet music. Almost alone among his peers he has shown practically no interest in the traditional rhetorical and expressive manners of Soviet music (i.e., those derived from the symphonic works of Prokofiev and Shostakovich), although he is certainly a nationalist. Instead, his music looks back to another Russian tradition dating from before the 1917 Revolution: the primitivism that was so fashionable in the circles of *The World of Art* and exemplified most powerfully in music like Stravinsky's *Rite of Spring* and Prokofiev's *Scythian Suite.* To listen to works like Korndorf's *Sempre tutti*, *Yarilo* and *Da!* is to be transported to an earlier Slavic world, one of intoxicating tribal loyalties and a close religious connection to nature.

This tradition to which Korndorf belongs is one that has had a valuable part to play in all the arts in Russia in our century. It is also closely linked with the so-called Slavophile movement, the tendency that aspires to a greater independence from European styles and ways of thinking. Immense problems face all Russians seeking to trace the roots of their culture; so often those roots have already been torn up by the hands of a violent oppressor. For those such as Kordorf it seems an important task to establish or restore that sense of historical and mythological background without which there can be little sense of communal identity.

Typically Korndorf favours religious and ritualistic forms. Even his dynamic forms are processional rather than dialectical. He often uses themes and ideas that remind one of the music of worship of the dances and songs of the peasant village. Like the nationalist composers of a century and a half ago, he sometimes seems, especially in his works of the early 1980s, to be deliberately avoiding anything which could suggest a link with the recognisable preoccupations of the most well-known Western composers, as though such links might be heard as a weakness or a dilution of the essential Russian idea.

And yet there is a sense in which Korndorf seems to have been deeply impressed by certain Western tendencies of recent times and that is in his use of repetitive patterns and phrasing of a variety of different kinds. His music tends to be built out of whole webs of sequences of small and often rather basic ideas which cannot but strike a European ear as having at least something in common with the procedures of various American minimalists.

And yet it would be wrong to describe this composer's music as in itself minimalist, whatever the principles by which it is made. For from his earliest works Korndorf has favoured sumptuous textures, loud climaxes and an overall awareness of drama that prevents one from hearing the elaborate patterns of repetition and phrasing that he favours as things in themselves. When we hear a piece by Steve Reich, for example, we are asked to find meaning within the pattern. When we listen to Korndorf, we are asked to imagine that the pattern is simply part of a greater primarily extra-musical event, some ancient Siberian animist rite perhaps or, in more recent works, some psychic or even sexual upheaval. In other words, Korndorf remains squarely within fundamentally romantic and Russian and Soviet assumptions about the significance of symbol and metaphor.

Korndorf's works so far fall into two quite distinct periods. In his earlier works, leading up to the mid-1980s, the various elements in his music were more distinct. His *Symphony No 2*, for example, is a severe essay in the processional style, replete with homophonic hints of early orthodox hymnody. His chamber symphony *Confessiones*, from the same time, is more evocative of folk music. It is also more loose texturally, for it contains a great deal of free repetition of parts for long stretches of time. Here there is also some sense of spacial drama, with instruments moving their positions.

Perhaps the strongest work of Korndorf's earliest period is his remarkable *Yarilo* for piano and tape. This work, named after the Sun God of pre-Christian Russia, was written for the remarkable playing talents of the composer's friend and colleague, Vassili Lobanov. In Lobanov's hands the piece makes an extremely powerful, not to say violent, impression.

All these earlier works are held together by a fondness for plain single-movement forms which, almost invariably, build towards substantial climaxes. In more recent years, beginning with the remarkable transitional work *Da!*, Korndorf has set out towards a new kind of language, where the relationships of the parts to the whole—and especially to the climaxes, which are more varied and unconventional in their placing—are somewhat more complex. Much of the music's detail is considerably simplified.

The results, in works like the *Lullaby* for two pianos, and the chamber orchestral *Amoroso*, reveal a new and softer side to Korndorf's character. At the same time Korndorf has continued to produce works which continue his earlier fascination with the seismology of erupting violence. Indeed, the aptly named *Sempre tutti* must count as one of the most physically aggressive orchestral scores by any young composer of today.

In the late 1980s Korndorf has worked on an opera based on the unusual subject of the friendship by letter between the poets Rilke, Tsvetaeva and Pasternak. Korndorf's music has always been dramatic in the looser sense of that word and it may well be that he has more work to do in the theatre in the future.

—Gerard McBurney

KOTIK, Petr. Czechoslovak; United States resident. Born in Prague, 27 January 1942. Educated at Prague Conservatory and Academy of Music (flute under Frantisek Cech), 1956–63, 1966–9, B.A., M.A.; private composition study under Jan Rychlik, Prague, 1960–4; Music Academy, Vienna (composition under Karl Schieske, Hans Jelinek, Friederich Cerha), 1963–6, B.A. Married Charlotta Kotik, 30 September 1966; 2 sons. Performing flautist, Europe, 1961–9; founder and director, Musica Viva Pragensis, 1961–4; founder and director, QUAX Ensemble, 1966–9; teacher of flute and composition, Center of the Creative and Performing Arts, State University of New York, Buffalo, 1969–74; founder, S.E.M. Ensemble, 1970; organized Chocorua '73: New Music in New Hampshire, 1973; research/realisation, musical works of Marcel Duchamp, 1974; teacher of composition, York University, Toronto, 1975–6; visiting lecturer/performer, Symposium of Composers, University of São Paulo, Brazil, and elsewhere in Latin America, 1978–86; first return to Czechoslovakia, 1978; residency in Hungary, 1986; lecturer/performer, art galleries throughout America and Europe. Recipient: special prize for flute, Gaudeamus Competition, 1965. Mailing address: c/o S.E.M. Ensemble, P.O. Box 37, Brooklyn, New York 11215, U.S.A.

Publishers: Srajer; Universal Edition.

Orchestral:

Six Plums 1965–8.

Chamber/instrumental:

Congo (flute, oboe, clarinet, bassoon, viola, cello, double bass) 1962.
Kontrapunkt (alto flute, cor anglais, clarinet, bassoon, viola, cello) 1962–3.
Music for Three (viola, cello, double bass) 1964.
Spontano (piano, 10 winds) 1964.
Alley (instrumental ensemble) 1969–70.
How Empty Is My Wilderness (solo instrument, tape) 1971.
Drums (2–6 percussion) 1977.
August/October (viola/cello, instrumental ensemble) 1981.
Music for Winds 1981–2.
Apparent Orbit (solo instrument, ensemble) 1981–5.
Solos and Incidental Harmonies (flute, violin, 2 percussion) 1983, revised 1984; first performed New York City, August 1987.
Wilsie Bridge (instrument, ensemble) 1986–7; first performed New York City, February 1989.

Vocal/choral:

There Is Singularly Nothing (21 instrumental and vocal solos, capable of being performed separately; Stein) 1971–3.
Variations (collage of vocal and instrumental pieces; Stein, Fuller) from 1972.
Observing with Variations (collage of vocal works; Stein) 1973.
John Mary (2 solo voices, 3 instruments, percussion; Stein) 1973–4.
If I Told Him (voice, instruments; Stein) 1974–5.
Many Many Women (2, 4 or 6 voices, 2, 4 or 6 instruments; Stein) 1975, revised 1978. Recorded Labor Records, 1980.
Explorations in the Geometry of Thinking (6 or more voices; Fuller) 1978–82.
Commencement (2 solo voices) 1981.

Other:

Contraband (live electronics, 2–6 performers) 1967.
Piup (4-track tape) 1967.
Aria (tape/theatre) 1969.

* * *

Although Petr Kotik has not developed a major following as a composer, his compositional development reflects the important aesthetic struggle between the compositional control associated with the new tonality and post-Cagean chance operations. In doing so, Kotik has developed an unique compositional voice, blending the sounds of the Middle Ages with the sounds of rock and the compositional techniques of Cage and the computer. In addition, Kotik's work as a flutist/ensemble leader has given him not only an outlet for his own compositions, but has also enabled him to present the works of important but infrequently performed composers, such as Jackson Mac Low, John Cage, Pauline Oliveros, Jon Gibson, Cornelius Cardew, Christian Wolff and others.

While Kotik's compositional process has been based on chance operations since the 1960s, the degree of indeterminacy has decreased as the composer attempts to exercise more control over the foreground counterpoint of his works. The compositions of the 1960s involved graphs which, although they determined all musical parameters, were drawn by Kotik without relation to the actual sounding work.

From 1971 to 1982, Kotik used graphic material derived from physiological tests performed on rats at the State University of New York at Buffalo's Medical School to determine pitch and rhythm of the individual parts. Since each part could begin at any point as determined by the performers, and since the parts were composed without any relation to one another, counterpoint was left by the composer to chance. It was during this time period, when Kotik composed his most important and best-known works with texts (*Many Many Women*—text by Gertrude Stein and *Explorations in the Geometry of Thinking*—text by R. Buckminster Fuller), that he developed a distinctive sound. Some of the individual parts are doubled at the perfect fourth or fifth, recreating the sound of parallel organum. The counterpoint resulting from the interplay of these individual parts doubled in fourths or fifths has been compared to a combination of Machaut, Stravinsky and Cage. Another feature of this repertoire is the generally slow-moving nature of the melodic lines, with a feeling of duple subdivision of a basic pulse.

In an attempt to exercise more control over his compositions, Kotik, with the assistance of composer/programmer Charles Ames, developed a computer program in 1982 for controlled chance operations based on Markov chain processes. These two-step processes, in which each choice is influenced by the next previous result, are used to determine various musical parameters. Concurrent with Ames and Kotik's development of the Markov chain program, Kotik made the following three other significant changes which have affected the structure of his works from 1983 to the present: (1) the frequent use of a quadruple subdivision of the pulse; (2) the use of a fully-realized score; and (3) the use of unpitched percussion instruments.

Solos and Incidental Harmonies represents a transition from the sound of the *Many Many Women*-era works and the works of the late 1980s. *Solos* . . . uses the quadruple subdivision of the pulse primarily in the solo sections and the percussion part. Kotik continues to make significant use of the Machaut-like free counterpoint of the 1970s, with each part still composed separately. The performers, however, are not given the freedom to begin and end their sections of material at will. Rather, *Solos and Incidental Harmonies* represents a single realization of the *Many Many Women*-type possibilities of counterpoint.

Both *Solos and Incidental Harmonies* and *Wilsie Bridge* make significant use of drums and cymbals, generally playing heavily syncopated figures within a quadruple subdivision of the beat. The percussion effect suggests a combination of tribal drumming and the heavily syncopated beat of jazz-rock ensembles such as Weather Report, and represents a fundamental change in foreground style from the slower-paced, less "beat-oriented" works of the 1960s and 1970s.

—James E. Perone

KRENEK, Ernst (originally Křenek). Austrian; naturalized American. Born in Caslav, Vienna, 23 August 1900. Educated at Institut der Christlichen Schulbrüder, 1906–10; Gymnasium Wien-Wahring, 1911–16; Wiener Musikakademie (under Franz Schreker), 1916–18; Wiener Universität, 1918; classes with Schreker, Berlin, 1920. Military service, 1918. Married (1) Anna Mahler, January 1924 (dissolved 1924); (2) Berta Hermann; (3) Gladys Nordenstrom in 1950. Teacher, Staatliche Hochschule für Musik und Darstellende Kunst, 1920; visited Paris, 1924; assistant director, Kassel Opera, June 1925; assistant director, Weisbaden Opera, 1927; returned to Vienna, 1928; founder/contributor, music journal *23*, 1932–7; chair, Austrian Association of Playwrights and Stage Composers, 1933; declared a "degenerate" artist by Nazis, 1933; promoter of new music concerts, 1934–5; lectures, *Über Neue Musik*, 1936; tours America, 1937; emigrated to U.S. (via London, Brussels, Zurich, Scandinavia), 1938; lecturer, Vassar College, Poughkeepsie, New York, 1939; head of music, dean of fine arts, Hamline University, St Paul, Minnesota, 1942; American citizen, 1945; guest lecturer, University of New Mexico, Albuquerque, 1947; settles in California as freelance composer and teacher, 1947; visiting professor, Brandeis University, Waltham, Massachusetts, 1965; settles in Palm Springs, California, 1966; visiting professor, Peabody Institute, Baltimore, Maryland, 1967, and University of Hawaii, Honolulu, 1967; Regents Lecturer, University of California, San Diego, 1970; established American archive, 1978. Festivals of music by Krenek at: Raleigh, North Carolina, 1967; Minneapolis, 1965, 1975; Graz, Austria, 1969; Northridge, California, 1974; universities of California, Santa Barbara, 1979, and San Diego, 1985. Recipient: extraordinary member Berlin Academy of Art, 1960; Great Silver Medal for Service to Austrian Republic, 1960; member, National Institute of Arts and Letters, 1960; honorary doctorate, University of New Mexico, 1960; Grand Austrian State Prize, 1963; Grand Medallion of Merit, Federal Republic of Germany, 1965; Bach Prize, Hamburg, 1966; honorary fellow, University of California, San Diego, 1966; Music Prize, Brandeis University, 1969; Ring of Honour, City of Vienna, 1970; honorary citation for arts and sciences, Austria, 1975; honorary doctorate, Philadelphia Musical Association, 1977; honorary citizenship, Vienna, 1982. Mailing address: c/o BMI, 320 West 57th Street, New York, New York 10019, U.S.A.

Publishers: Barenreiter; Schott; Universal.

Symphonies/orchestral:

Symphony No 1 1921; first performed Berlin, 17 March 1922. Recorded Amadeo 415 8251.

Concerto Grosso No 1 (flute, clarinet, bassoon, violin, viola, cello, string orchestra) 1922; first performed Weimar, 19 August 1922.

Symphonic Music 1922; first performed Donaueschingen, 30 July 1922.

Symphony No 2 1922; first performed Kassel, 11 June 1923. Recorded Amadeo 415 8251.

Symphony No 3 1922; first performed Berlin, 1922. Recorded Amadeo 415 8251.

Piano Concerto No 1 in F# major 1923; first performed Winterthur, 19 December 1923.

Symphonische Musik No 2 (chamber orchestra) 1923; first performed Berlin, 1 February 1924.

Concerto Grosso No 2 (violin, viola, cello, orchestra) 1924; first performed Zurich, 14 October 1924.

Concertino (flute, violin, harpsichord, string orchestra) 1924; first performed Winterthur, 18 February 1925.

Violin Concerto No 1 1924; first performed Dessau, 5 January 1925.

Stücke 1924; first performed Winterthur, 4 November 1926.

Symphony 1924–5; first performed Leipzig, February 1926. Recorded Torofon Capella ETHK 34/4.

Potpourri 1927, revised 1954; first performed Cologne, 5 November 1927; revised version first performed Stuttgart, 22 October 1957.

Kleine Symphonie (chamber orchestra) 1928; first performed Berlin, 3 November 1928.

Theme and 13 Variations 1931; first performed New York, 29 October 1931.

Piano Concerto No 2 1937; first performed Boston, 4 November 1938.

Symphonic Piece (string orchestra) 1939; first performed Basle, 11 June 1940.

Little Concerto (piano and organ or second piano, orchestra) 1939–40; first performed Poughkeepsie, New York, 23 May 1940.

I Wonder as I Wander 1942; first performed Minneapolis, 11 December 1942.

Tricks and Trifles/Hurricane Variations (arranged for orchestra from 2 piano version) 1946; first performed Minneapolis, 27 March 1946.

Symphonic Elegy (string orchestra) 1946; first performed Saratoga Springs, New York, 3 September 1946. Recorded Columbia ML 4524.

Piano Concerto No 3 1946; first performed Minneapolis, 22 November 1946.

Symphony No 4 1947; first performed New York, 27 November 1947.

Symphony No 5 1947–9; first performed Albuquerque, New Mexico, 16 March 1950.

Piano Concerto No 4 1950; first performed Cologne, 22 October 1951. Recorded Contemporary Records AP123.

Double Concerto (violin, piano, orchestra) 1950; first performed Donaueschingen, 6 October 1951. Recording MGM E3218.

Harp Concerto (chamber orchestra) 1951; first performed Philadelphia, 12 December 1952.

Concerto for Two Pianos 1951; first performed New York, 24 October 1953.

Sinfonietta a Brasiliera (string orchestra) 1952; first performed Besançon, 6 September 1953.

Cello Concerto No 1 1952–3; first performed Los Angeles, 4 March 1954.
Violin Concerto No 2 1953–4; first performed Cologne, 18 February 1955.
Symphony Pallas Athene 1954; first performed Hamburg, 11 October 1954.
Eleven Transparencies 1954; first performed Louisville, Kentucky, 12 February 1955. Recorded Louisville Orchestra LOU 56–3.
Capriccio (cello, orchestra) 1955; first performed Darmstadt, 31 May 1955. Recorded Orion ORS 79362.
Sieben leichte Stücke (string orchestra) 1955; first performed Mainz, 1955. Recorded Preiserrecords SPR 10049.
Divertimento 1956; first performed Ossiach, Austria, 23 August 1986.
Kette, Kreis und Spiegel, sinfonische Zeichnung 1956–6; first performed Basle, 23 January 1958.
Hexahedron (small orchestra) 1958; first performed Darmstadt, 7 September 1958.
Quaestio temporis 1959; first performed Hamburg, 30 September 1960.
From Three Make Seven 1960–1, revised 1968; first performed Berlin, 3 March 1965; revised version first performed Baden-Baden, 16 February 1968. Recorded Orion ORS 78290.
Six Profiles 1965–8; first performed Fargo, North Dakota, 14 March 1970.
Horizon Circled 1967; first performed Rochester, Michigan, 12 August 1967. Recorded Orion ORS 78290.
Perspektiven 1967; first performed Ravinia, Illinois, 6 July 1968.
Exercises of a Late Hour 1967, revised 1969; first performed San Diego, California, 19 January 1968.
Fivefold Enfoldment 1969; first performed Bonn, 5 January 1970. Recorded ORF 120 423.
Kitharaulos (oboe/cor anglais/oboe d'amore, harp, piano, percussion, strings) 1971; first performed The Hague, 20 June 1972. Recorded Varese Sarabande VR 81200.
Statisch und Ekstatisch 1972; first performed Zurich, 23 March 1973. Recorded Varese Sarabande VR 81200.
Von vorn herein (small orchestra, piano, celeste) 1974; first performed Salzburg, 21 August 1974. Recorded Orion ORS 78290.
Aug-und Ablehnung 1975; first performed Nuremburg, 13 June 1975. Recorded ORF 120 423.
Dream Sequence (symphonic band) 1975–6; first performed Maryland, 11 March 1977. Recorded Crest CBDNA 77-6.
Concerto (organ, strings) 1978–9; first performed Ossiach, Austria, 22 July 1979.
Im Tal der Zeit (chamber orchestra) 1979; first performed Graz, 26 October 1980.
Arc of Life (chamber orchestra) 1981; first performed Palm Springs, Florida, 24 February 1982.
Organ Concerto 1982; first performed Melbourne, 17 May 1983.
Cello Concerto No 2 1982; first performed Salzburg, 9 August 1983.

Chamber/instrumental:

Double Fugue (piano) 1917; first performed Vienna, 14 May 1918.
Sonata for Piano No 1 in E♭ major 1919; first performed Salzburg, 3 May 1920.
Sonata for Violin and Piano in F# minor 1919–20; first performed Berlin, 21 June 1921.
Serenade (clarinet, viola, cello) 1919; first performed Berlin, 8 February 1921.
Piano Sonatinas 1920.
Tanzstudie (piano) 1920.
String Quartet No 1 1921; first performed Nuremberg, 16 June 1921.
String Quartet No 2 1921; first performed Berlin, 24 April 1922. Recorded Musikproduktion Dabringhaus und Grimm L3280.
Toccata und Chaconne über den Choral Ja, Ich Glaub an Jesum Christum (piano) 1922; first performed Berlin, 16 October 1922.
Eine kleine Suite von Stücken über denselbigen Choral, versichiedenen Charakters/Little Suite (piano) 1922; first performed Berlin, 16 October 1922. Recorded RCA Victor 15862.
String Quartet No 3 1923; first performed Salzburg, 3 August 1923. Recorded Polydor 66101; Deutsche Grammophon 66201; Musikproduktion Dabringhaus und Grimm MD+GL 3281.
String Quartet No 4 1923–4; first performed Salzburg, 5 August 1924.
Piano Sonata 1924; first performed Berlin, 12 December 1924.
Kleine Suite (clarinet, piano) 1924; first performed Bamberg, 7 January 1967.
Violin Sonata No 1 1924; first performed Darmstadt, 28 November 1960.
Klavierstücke (piano) 1925; first performed Kassel, 18 November 1925. Recorded Society of Participating Artists SPA 4.
Intrada (clarinet, bassoon, trumpet, 2 horns, trombone, timpani) 1927; first performed Kassel, 1 June 1927.
Piano Sonata No 2 1928; first performed Berlin, 27 March 1929. Recorded Melodia CM 031134.
Triophantasie (violin, cello, piano) 1929; first performed Berlin, 15 May 1930.
String Quartet No 5 1930; first performed Copenhagen, 29 September 1930. Recorded Composers Recordings CRI SD 522.
Vier Bagatellen (piano—4 hands) 1931; first performed Vienna, 25 April 1937. Recorded Music Library MLR 7014.
String Quartet No 6 1936; first performed Darmstadt, 16 January 1936.
Zwölf Variationen in drei Sätzen (piano) 1937; first performed Los Angeles, 16 December 1937.
Twelve Short Piano Pieces Written in the Twelve-Tone Technique 1938; first performed Washington, D.C., 3 January 1939. Recorded Columbia X171; Paraclete Music Disc 51B.
School Music (wind and piano pieces) 1938–9; first performed Ann Arbor, Michigan, 27 July 1939.
Cello Suite 1939; first performed Poughkeepsie, New York, 16 November 1939.
Organ Sonata No 1 1941; first performed Poughkeepsie, New York, 3 May 1942. Recorded Musica Viva MV 50–1090; Psallite 66/27 768 PES.
Sonatina for Flute and Viola (also arranged for flute and clarinet) 1942; first performed Buenos Aires, 30 October 1944.
Viola Sonata 1942; first performed Chicago, 11 April 1947.
Piano Sonata No 3 1942–3; first performed Minneapolis, 1 December 1943. Recorded Columbia ML 5336; Le Chant du Monde LDX 78799; includes talk by Krenek.
String Quartet No 7 1943–4; first performed Indianapolis, 15 November 1944. Recorded Musikproduktion Dabringhaus und Grimm MD+GL 3281.
Sonata for Violin and Piano 1944–5; first performed Minneapolis, 21 October 1945. Recorded Preiserrecords SPR 10049.

Trio for violin, clarinet and piano 1946; first performed St Paul, Minnesota, 27 November 1946. Recorded Crystal S645; Supraphon 111 2147.
Piano Pieces 1946; first performed St Paul, Minnesota, 9 February 1947. Recorded Society of Participating Artists SPA 4.
Piano Sonata No 4 1948; first performed San Francisco, 5 November 1948. Recorded Music Library MLR 7014; Music Heritage Society MHS 3874.
Violin Sonata No 2 1948; first performed Washington, D.C., 19 December 1948. Recorded Orion ORS 73107.
Short Pieces (string quartet, or string orchestra) 1948; first performed Basle, 17 January 1955.
Sonata for Violin and Piano 1948; first performed San Francisco, March 1949. Recorded Deutsche Grammophon DG 36005.
String Trio 1948; first performed Los Angeles, 4 April 1949. Recorded Calig CAL 50 861.
George Washington Variations (piano) 1950; first performed Los Angeles, 24 September 1950.
Piano Sonata No 5 1950; first performed Cologne, 1950. Recorded Music Library MLR 7029.
Parvula corona musicalis (string trio) 1950; first performed Rome, 15 January 1951. Recorded Philips 411 062–1.
Invention (flute, clarinet) 1951; first performed Bamberg, 7 January 1967.
Piano Sonata No 6 1951; first performed Donaueschingen, October 1951.
Quintet (flute, clarinet, oboe, bassoon, horn) 1952; taped at WDR, Cologne, 1952.
Fantasy (cello, piano) 1953; first performed Lucerne, April 6 1954.
Miniature (piano) 1953; published in *New Mexico Quarterly* 1953.
Twenty Miniatures (piano) 1953–4; first performed St Gallen, 21 September 1954.
Six for Two (two pianos; arranged from *20 Miniatures*) 1954; first performed Chicago, 18 October 1959.
Suite (flute, piano/string orchestra) 1954; first performed Santiago, Chile, 5 July 1956.
Suite (clarinet, piano/string orchestra) 1955; first performed Miami, 29 November 1962. Recorded Mark MMF 3355.
Harp Sonata 1955; first performed New York, 27 January 1958. Recorded Klavier KS 507.
Oboe Sonatina 1956; first performed New York, 9 May 1960.
Monologue (clarinet) 1956; first performed New York, 9 May 1960. Recorded Advance FGR4; MRS 32640; others.
Marginal Sounds (violin, piano, celeste, vibraphone, xylophone, percussion) 1957; first performed New York, 22 February 1960.
Pentagramm (flute, oboe, clarinet, bassoon, horn) 1957; first performed Los Angeles, 31 March 1958. Recorded Lyrichord LC 158.
Guitar Suite 1957; first performed Los Angeles, 16 February 1959. Recorded Orion ORS 78323.
Echoes from Austria (piano arrangements) 1958. Recorded Orion ORS 76246.
Sechs Vermessene (piano) 1958; first performed Kassel, 9 October 1960. Recorded Candide CE 31015.
Flötenstücke neunphasig (flute, piano) 1959; first performed Venice, 27 September 1960. Recorded Orion ORS 78295.
Hausmusik (cycle for days of week: piano—4 hands; soprano recorder, guitar; 2 recorders, violin; violin, guitar; soprano recorder, violin; violin, piano; piano, soprano recorder, violin, guitar) 1959; first performed Berlin, 22 November 1959.
Basler Massarbeit (2 pianos) 1960; first performed Basle, 19 January 1961.
Organologia (organ) 1962; first performed Mulheim 24 November 1968.
Toccata (accordion) 1962. Recorded Orion ORS 75204.
Cello Studien / Vorkehrungen zur Rückkehr sind getroffen (1 and 4 cellos) 1963; first performed Riehen, Switzerland, 23 April 1968.
Fibonacci Mobile (string quartet, piano—4 hands) 1964; first performed Hanover, New Hampshire, 7 July 1965.
Stücke (oboe, piano) 1966; first performed Zagreb, 21 May 1967. Recorded Philips 6500 202; Orion ORS 78288.
Piano Piece in Eleven Parts 1967; first performed Chicago, 4 December 1970.
Pieces (trombone, piano) 1967; first performed Buffalo, New York, 5 November 1967. Recorded Orion ORS 78295.
Doppelt beflügeltes Band (2 pianos, tape) 1970; first performed Graz, 26 October 1970. Recorded Orion ORS 75204.
Duo (flute, double bass, tape) 1970; first performed Palm Desert, California, 24 January 1971.
10 Choralvorspiel (organ) 1971.
Orga-nastro (organ, tape) 1971; first performed Ann Arbor, Michigan, 18 October 1971. Recorded Musica Viva MV 501090.
Aulokithara (oboe/cor anglais, harp, tape; arrangement of *Kitharaulos* for orchestra) 1971; first performed Mainz, 11 October 1972. Recorded Orion ORS 76246.
Four Winds Suite (organ) 1975; first performed Düsseldorf. Recorded Musica Viva MV 501090.
Acco-music (accordion) 1976. Recorded Melbourne Records SMLP 4034.
Opus 231 (violin, organ) 1979; first performed Vienna, 10 March 1980. Recorded Musica Viva MV 501090; EMI Electrola ASD 308 531 D.
String Quartet No 8 1980–1; first performed New York, 7 June 1981.
Streichtrio in zwolf Stationen (string trio) 1985; first performed Pasadena, California 16 February 1988.

Vocal/choral:

Lieder (voice, piano; Goering) 1921–2.
Lieder (voice, piano; Kraus) 1922.
Der Zwingburg (scenic cantata) 1922; first performed Berlin, 20 October 1924.
Lieder (voice, piano; Werfel, Gezelle) 1922.
Lieder (voice, piano; Krzyzanowski, Klopstock) 1923; first performed Berlin, 26 March 1926. Recorded EMI Electrola; Preiserrecords SPR 3338.
Gemischte a cappella-Chöre (SSAATTBB; Claudius) 1923.
Lieder (voice, piano; Goering, Reinhart) 1924.
Lieder (voice, piano; Verhaeren) 1924; first performed Los Angeles, 28 May 1950. Recorded Orion ORS 79348.
Vier kleine Männerchöre (alto solo, TTBB; Hölderlin) 1924; first performed Vienna, 25 March 1935.
Die Jahreszeiten (SATB chorus; Hölderlin) 1925; first performed Donaueschingen, July 1925. Recorded Orion ORS 80377.
Vier a cappella-Chöre (SATB; Goethe) 1926; first performed Vienna, 7 December 1927.
O Lacrymosa (high/medium voice, piano; Rilke; also version with 2 flutes, 2 clarinets, 2 bassoons, harp) 1926; first performed Cologne, 29 January 1927. Recorded Orion ORS 75204.
Gesänge nach alten Gedichten (mezzo-soprano, piano; Gunther, Weckherlin, Fleming; also arranged for woodwinds) 1927; first performed Berlin, 21 November 1929.
Gesänge (baritone, piano; Goethe) 1927; first performed Dresden, 5 November 1928. Recorded Orion ORS 78298.
Konzert-Arie (soprano, piano, orchestra; Goethe) 1928; first

performed Berlin, June 1928.

Gemischte Chöre (SATB; Keller) 1929; first performed Vienna, 27 November 1932. Recorded Orion ORS 80377.

Reisebuch aus den Österreichischen Alpen (voice, piano) 1929; first performed Leipzig, 17 January 1930. Recorded Telefunken BLE 14113; Philips 6747061.

Fiedellieder (medium voice, piano; Storm, Mommsen) 1930; first performed Dresden, 11 April 1930.

Durch die Nacht (soprano, piano; Kraus; also arranged for orchestra) 1930–1; first performed Dresden, 10 April 1931; orchestral version first performed Vienna, 19 June 1932.

Die Nachtigall (soprano, piano; Kraus; also arranged for 2 flutes, strings) 1931; first performed Frankfurt, 26 November 1931; orchestral version first performed Berne, 27 October 1931.

Gesänge des späten Jahres (voice, piano) 1931; first performed Dresden, 25 March 1932. Recorded Edition Rhodos ERS 1202–3.

Kantate von der Vergänglichkeit des Indischen (soprano, chorus, piano; 17th-century German texts) 1932; first performed Vienna, 16 April 1932.

Fragmente aus den Bühnenwerke Karl V (soprano, orchestra) 1932; first performed Barcelona, 19 April 1936. Recorded Preiserrecords SPR 10049.

Das Schweigen (bass, piano; Gemminger) 1933; first performed Winterthur, 24 January 1934.

Während der Trennung (mezzo-soprano, baritone, piano; Fleming) 1933; first performed Winterthur, 24 January 1934.

Austrian Folk Songs (arranged for SATB, soprano solo) 1934; first performed Vienna, 25 February 1935.

Italian Ballads (voice, piano) 1934.

Lieder nach Worten von Franz Kafka (voice, piano) 1937–8; first performed Poughkeepsie, New York, 1 March 1942. Recorded Carolina Records 712C-1463.

Two Choruses on Elizabethan/Jacobean Poems (SSAA chorus; Drummond, Raleigh) 1939; first performed Poughkeepsie, New York, 7 December 1940.

Proprium missae in festo SS Innocentium martyrum (die 28 Decembris) (SSAA chorus) 1940; first performed Poughkeepsie, New York, 15 December 1940.

La Corona (cantata for mezzo-soprano, baritone, organ, percussion; Donne) 1941; first performed Copenhagen, 1958.

The Holy Ghost's Ark (mezzo-soprano, oboe, clarinet, viola, cello; Donne) 1941; first performed Madison, Wisconsin, 24 July 1941.

Lamentatio Jeremiae Prophetae (SSAATTBB) 1941–2; first performed Kassel, 5 October 1958. Recorded Barenreiter Musicaphon 30L 1303–4.

Cantata for Wartime (women's chorus, orchestra; Melville) 1943; first performed Minneapolis, 24 March 1944.

Five Prayers for Women's Voices over the Pater Noster as cantus firmus (SSAA chorus; Donne) 1944; first performed St Paul, Minnesota, 3 June 1945. Recorded Audio Engineer Associates AEA 1094.

The Ballad of the Railroads (medium voice, piano) 1944; first performed New York, 5 April 1950. Recorded Edition Rhodos ERS 1201–3.

Santa Fe Timetable (SSAATB; railroad timetable) 1945; first performed Los Angeles, 20 February 1961.

Aegrotavit Ezechias (SSA chorus, piano: Isaiah) 1945; first performed St Paul, Minnesota, 12 March 1947.

Etude (coloratura soprano, alto) 1945; first performed St Paul, Minnesota, 1946.

In paradisum (soprano, mezzo-soprano, alto) 1946; first performed 10 May 1946.

Songs on Poems by Gerard Manley Hopkins (tenor, piano) 1946–7; first performed Waco, Texas, 25 April 1947. Recorded Orion ORS 79348.

Remember Now (motet for soprano, mezzo-soprano, alto, piano; Ecclesiastes) 1947; first performed St Paul, Minnesota, 1947.

Medea (mezzo-soprano, orchestra; Jeffers/Euripides) 1951; first performed Philadelphia, 13 March 1953.

Sacred Songs (medium voice, piano) 1952; first performed New York, 4 January 1953. Recorded Barenreiter Musicaphon 30L 1534.

Choruses (SATB, organ/piano) 1953; first performed Pasadena, California, May 1955.

Motette zur Opferung für das ganze Kirchenjahr (SABar) 1954; first performed Vienna, 27 September 1954.

Proprium missae in domenica tertia in quadragesima (SABar) 1955.

Psalmenverse zur Kommunion für das ganze Kirchenjahr (chorus) 1955.

Ich singe wieder, wenn es tagt (SATB, string orchestra/string quartet; Vogelweide) 1955; first performed Linz, 14 May 1956.

Spiritus intelligentiae, Sanctus (2 singers, speaker, electronics) 1955–6; first performed Cologne, 30 May 1956.

Guten Morgen, Amerika (SATB; Sandburg) 1956.

Sestina (soprano, flute, clarinet, trumpet, 2 percussionists, guitar, piano, violin) 1957; first performed New York, 9 March 1958. Recorded Epic LC 3509.

Missa duodecim tonorum (SSA or TTB, organ) 1957; first performed Vienna, 1958.

Sechs Motetten nach Worten von Franz Kafka (SATB) 1959; first performed Berlin, 29 September 1959.

Children's Songs: Three Madrigals (SSA; Shakespeare, Herrick, Tennyson) 1960.

Children's Songs: Three Motets (SSA) 1960.

The Flea (tenor/soprano, piano; Donne) 1960; first performed Raleigh, North Carolina, 1968.

Kanon Igor Strawinsky zum 80. Geburtstag (2-voice chorus) 1962; first performed Los Angeles, 2 March 1962.

Nach Wie vor der Reihe nach (2 speakers, orchestra) 1962; first performed Stuttgart, 25 October 1962.

O Holy Ghost (SATB) 1964; first performed Berlin, 3 May 1965. Recorded Orion ORS 80377.

Wechselrahmen (soprano, piano; Barth) 1964–5; first performed Dusseldorf, 9 September 1965. Recorded Orion ORS 76246.

Quintina über die fünf Vokale (soprano, recorder, vibraphone, xylophone, guitar, viola, percussion, tape) 1965; first performed Copenhagen, 3 October 1965. Recorded Orion ORS 80380.

Glauben und Wissen (chorus, 4 speakers, orchestra) 1966; first performed Hamburg, 21 December 1966.

Proprium für das Dreifaltigkeitsfest (soprano, SATB, 2 trumpets, timpani, organ) 1966–7; first performed Basle, 2 July 1967.

Instant Remembered (soprano, orchestra; Plato, Kierkegaard, Goethe, Rilke, Seneca, Hopkins, Kraus) 1967–8; first performed Hanover, New Hampshire, 1 August 1968.

Proprium Missae per a la festa de la nativitat de la Mare de Deu (8 de septembre) (chorus, instruments, organ; in Catalan) 1968; first performed Montserrat, Abadia, 22 August 1968.

Deutsche Messe (Ordinarium) (SATB, clarinet, trumpet, 2 trombones, timpani, percussion) 1968; first performed Lucerne, October 1969.

Messe "Gib uns den Frieden" (solo voices, SATB, instruments) 1970; first performed Hamburg, 12 October 1971.

Three Sacred Pieces (SATB) 1971; first performed Ann Arbor, Michigan, 18 October 1971. Recorded Orion ORS 76246.
Three Lessons (SATB) 1971; first performed Ann Arbor, Michigan, 18 October 1971. Recorded Orion ORS 80377.
Lieder (soprano, piano; Sauter) 1972; first performed Vienna, 22 September 1975. Recorded Educo 4049.
Spätlese (baritone, piano) 1972; first performed Munich, 22 July 1974. Recorded Orion ORS 78298.
Zeitlieder (mezzo-soprano, string quartet; Pandula) 1974; first performed Augsburg, 15 May 1974.
Feiertags-Kantate (speaker, mezzo-soprano, baritone, SATB, orchestra) 1974–5; first performed Berlin, 12 September 1975.
Two Silent Watchers (voice, piano; Rudulph) 1975; first performed Palm Springs, Florida, 1976.
Settings of Poems by William Blake (SATB) 1976; first performed Honolulu, Hawaii, May 1977. Recorded Orion ORS 80377.
They Knew What They Wanted (narrator; oboe, piano, percussion, tape; Boccaccio, Genesis) 1977; first performed New York, 6 November 1978. Recorded ORF 120 423; Orion ORS 80380.
The Dissembler (baritone, ensemble) 1978–9; first performed Baltimore, Maryland, 11 March 1979. Recorded Orion ORS 79362.
For Myself, at Eighty-Five (4-voice canon) 1985; published in *Perspectives in New Music*, 1985.
Opus Sine Momine (soprano, mezzo-soprano, baritone, narrator, chorus, orchestra) 1986–8.

Opera/theatre:

Der Sprung über der Schatten (comic opera) 1923; first performed Frankfurt, 9 June 1924.
Orpheus und Eurydike 1923; first performed Kassel, 27 November 1926.
Bluff (operetta) 1924–5; withdrawn.
Jonny Spielt Auf 1927; first performed Leipzig, 10 February 1927. Recorded Amadeo AURS 5038; extracts on Parlophone E 10698; Deutsche Grammophon AM 953; Polydor 19808.
Der Diktator 1926; first performed Wiesbaden, 6 May 1928.
Das geheime Königreich (fairytale opera) 1926–7; first performed Wiesbaden, 6 May 1928.
Schwergewicht, oder Die Ehre der Nation (operetta) 1927; first performed Wiesbaden, 6 May 1928.
Leben des Orest 1930; first performed Leipzig, 19 January 1930.
Kehraus um St Stephen 1930; first performed Hamburg, 1987; unauthorised performance of first scene.
Karl V 1932–3; first performed Prague, 22 June 1938. Recorded Amadeo AURS 305.
Cefalo e Procri 1933–4; first performed Venice, 15 September 1934.
Tarquin 1940; first performed Poughkeepsie, New York, 13 May 1941.
What Price Confidence? (chamber opera) 1945; first performed Saarbrücken, 22 May 1962.
Dark Waters 1950; first performed Los Angeles, 2 May 1951.
Pallas Athene weint 1952–3; first performed Hamburg, 17 October 1955.
The Belltower (Melville) 1955–6; first performed Urbana, Illinois, 17 March 1957. Recorded University of Illinois CRS 5.
Ausgerechnet und verspielt (television opera) 1960–2; first performed Vienna, 25 July 1962; entr'acte, (*Roulette Sestina*) first performed Mannheim, 15 October 1964.
Der goldene Bock 1962–3; first performed Hamburg, 16 June 1964. Recorded (part) EMI Electrola 1C 195-299 107/9.
Der Zauberspiegel (television opera) 1965–6; first performed Munich, 6 September 1967.
Sardakai 1968–9; first performed Hamburg, 27 June 1970. Recorded (part) EMI Electrola 1C 195-29 107/9.
Flaschenpost von Paradies: oder der Englischer Ausflug (television play; tenor, bass, dancers mimes, speakers, electronic tape, percussion, piano) 1972–3; first performed Vienna, 8 March 1974.

Other:

Mammon (ballet; orchestra) 1925; first performed Munich, 1 October 1927.
Der Vertauschte Cupido (ballet) 1925; first performed Kassel, 25 October 1925.
Vom Lieben Augustin (incidental music to play by Anton Schmidt; accordion, guitar, clarinet) 1925; first performed Kassel, 28 November 1925.
Die Rahe des verlohnten Liebhabers (puppet play, voice, violin, piano) 1925; first performed Zurich, 1926.
Das Gotteskind (incidental music to radio play) 1925; first performed Radio Kassel, 1925.
Der Triumph der Empfindsamkeit (incidental music to play by Goethe; orchestra) 1925; first performed Kassel, 9 May 1926; concert version, Hamburg, 28 November 1927.
Lustige Marsche (band) 1926; first performed Baden-Baden, July 1926. Recorded Louisville Orchestra LS 756; Crest CBDNA 77-4.
Ein Sommernacthstraum (incidental music to Shakespeare) 1926; first performed Heidelberg, July 1926.
Marlborough s'en va-t-en guerre (incidental music to play by Archand; piano, percussion) 1927; first performed Kassel, 11 May 1927.
Kleine Blasmusik (concert band) 1931; first performed Frankfurt am Main, 16 June 1932. Recorded Louisville Orchestra LS 756.
Simeon der Stylit 1935–7; first performed Salzburg, 22 July 1988.
L'Incoronazione di Poppea (orchestration and translation of Monteverdi's opera) 1936; first performed Vienna, 25 September 1937; concert suite, Los Angeles, 21 January 1963.
Eight Column Line (ballet; flute, clarinet, bass clarinet, trumpet, piano, string quartet) 1939; first performed Hartford, Connecticut, 19 May 1939.
Sargasso (ballet version of *Symphonic Elegy*) 1946; first performed New York, 24 March 1965.
Jedermann (incidental music to play by Hofmannsthal; 2 voices, orchestra) 1960; first performed Salzburg, 30 July 1962; also film score, 1968.
Jest of Cards (ballet, arranged from *Marginal Sounds*) 1962; first performed San Francisco, 17 April 1967.
Alpbach Quintet (ballet; flute, oboe, clarinet, horn, bassoon, percussion) 1962; first performed Alpbach, 25 August 1963.
San Fernando Sequence (electronic tape) 1963; first performed San Francisco, 15 March 1963.
Konig Oedipus (incidental music to play by Sophocles) 1964; first performed Salzburg, 27 July 1965.
Quintona (electronic tape) 1965; first performed San Fernando, 1965.
Franz Schubert: completion of *Piano Sonata in C minor D. 840* 1921; first performed Berlin, 5 January 1922. Recorded Concert Hall Society B-3.

Gustav Mahler: edition of first and third movements of *Symphony No 10* 1924; first performed Vienna, 12 October 1924. Recorded Epic BC 1024; SPA 31; Columbia M2 31313.

PUBLICATIONS

By Krenek: autobiographical manuscript, held in Library of Congress, Washington, D.C., until 15 years after EK's death; *Uber neue Musik: sechs Vorlesungen zur Einführung in die theoretischen Grundlagen* Vienna, 1937, translated as *Music Here and Now*, New York, 1939; *Studies in Counterpoint, Based on the Twelvetone Technique* New York, 1940; *Selbstdarstellung*, Zurich, 1948, translated as "Self Analysis", in *New Mexico Quarterly*, 1953; *Musik im Goldenen Westen*, Vienna, 1949; *Johannes Okeghem*, New York, 1953; *Zur Sprache gebracht*, Munich, 1958, translated as *Exploring Music*, London, 1966; *Tonal Counterpoint in the Style of the 18th Century*, New York, 1958; *Modal Counterpoint in the Style of the 16th Century*, New York, 1959; *Prosa, Drama, Verse*, Munich, 1965; *Horizons Circled: Reflections on My Music*, Berkeley, California, 1974; *Im Zweifelsfälle: Aufsätze über Musik*, Vienna, 1984; many others.

On Krenek: W.L. Ogdon, "Series and Structure: An Investigation into the Purpose of the Twelve Note Row in Selected Works of Schoenberg, Webern, Krenek and Leibowitz", dissertation, Indiana University, Bloomington, 1955; F. Saathen, *EK*, Munich, 1959; T.W. Adorno, "Zur Physiognomik EK", in *Moments Musicaux*, 1964, and *Theodor W. Adorno und EK: Briefwechsel*, Frankfurt, 1974; L. Knessel, *EK*, Vienna, 1967; C. Mauer-Zenck, *EK: ein Komponist im Exil*, Vienna, 1980; O. Kollitsch (ed), *EK: Studien zur Wertungsforchung*, Vienna, 1982; J. Rockwell, "The Rise of American Art Music and the Impact of the Immigrant Wave of the late 1930s: EK", in *All American Music: Composition in the Late Twentieth Century*, New York, 1983; EK issue of *Musik-Konzepte*, 39/40, 1984; Garrett H. Bowles, *EK: A Bio-Bibliography*, London, 1986.

* * *

"What I really would like, is to become someone else and, fifteen years after my death, walk to the Library of Congress and look up what I have written. This, however, will not be granted. Yet I may hope that I then will be in a position of having all insight and knowledge that a human being can desire, without consulting any terrestrial papers." In 1950, by then an American citizen, Ernst Krenek deposited a hefty autobiographical manuscript in the Library of Congress with instructions that it was not to be examined until 15 years had elapsed since his death. Whatever revelations it contains, students of Krenek's work may experience the same feelings as its author in the remarks above from his essay "On Writing My Memoirs". The terrestrial papers, both music scores and published writings, are so extensive and heterogeneous that critics may despair of ever achieving any overview of Krenek's work other than *sub specie aeternitatis*, which is, of course, too late for a Ph.D. or a published book.

Krenek has continued to compose into his ninth decade, adding to a body of work remarkable in range and diversity. If he is still more highly regarded in his native Europe (which he left over half a century ago) than in his adoptive home, that is because, as John Rockwell and others have noted, Krenek's is a thoroughly European sensibility, only incidentally and occasionally touched by American aesthetic values. In the late 1950s, he began to take an interest in the then fashionable question of indeterminacy; however, the main work to result, *Sestina*, is a philosophical essay on the theme, rather than an embodiment of it. Similarly, his most self-consciously "American" work, the *Santa Fe Timetable*, written as if in anticipation or celebration of his taking American citizenship in 1945 and consisting of a simple choral listing of railroad destinations, is curiously ersatz. Much the same charge is often levelled at his earlier "jazz" opera *Jonny Spielt Auf*, written in 1926 and immediately and internationally successful. The piece, which was revived in London in the early 1980s (and quickly revealed as a piece of ephemera) had in fact very little to do with jazz at all. Far from prefiguring any supposed Americanism, *Jonny* confirms his thoroughgoing Europeanism (symbolically, in a career laden with symbolic moments, its American premiere starred not a Negro as in the original production, but a white actor/singer in blackface). *Jonny* is of only period interest now, but it does help suggest Krenek's almost barometric responsiveness to musical fashion.

It is significant that the most important revelation of Krenek's first years in the United States was his discovery at Vassar College, where he became a professor, of a collection of work by the 15th-century composer Joannes de Ockeghem, whose diversity of surnames—Okchem, Ockenheim, HoqQueham—suggests something of Krenek's own protean nature, and whose work was to have a strong impact on Krenek's own highly individual adaptation of the modern idiom.

A student of Franz Schreker, Krenek grew up in an atmosphere of late Romanticism, an affiliation symbolized by his marriage to Anna Mahler (and even more so by its brevity) and best represented by the Schubertian *Resisebuch aus den Österreichischen Alpen*. Already a radical—his Second Symphony caused the first of many uproars—he matured quickly into a style which developed in the direction of polytonality and atonality. His First and Second String Quartets were both written under the palpable influence of Bartók, with nods in the complex contrapuntal direction of late Beethoven. The second demonstrated Krenek's liking for long thematic sequences based on identical intervals, a device that resurfaces after his turn to twelve-tone and serial procedures.

Jonny was part of an effort to write more accessible music, an urge doubtless encouraged practically by his stint as répétiteur at Kassel, and ideologically by his contact with the neo-classicists. The Third and Fourth String Quartets mark a turn away from hard-core dissonance and towards a more ironic and personable music; the Third contains a Viennese waltz and the Fourth elements of jazz altogether more authentic than those that were to inform his opera.

After considerable heart-searching, Krenek turned to twelve-tone composition in 1933. The first and most doctrinaire work in this style was the highly political opera *Karl V*, which was suppressed, as its predecessor *Kehraus um St Stephan* had been, not because it was "offensive" but because it was patently directed at the Nazis's aggressive pan-Germanism. A composer who could apotheosise a black fiddler sitting on top of a stylized globe and then extol the virtues of the Habsburg Charles V was unlikely to receive much favour from Austria's quasi-fascist establishment, even then preparing for *Anschluss*, and Krenek's exile became inevitable.

In the United States, he developed a modified serialism which resembled Milton Babbitt's mathematical structures; the piano quintet *Fibonacci Mobile* from 1964 was a particularly successful example. He was never a strict serialist, but used tone-rows to generate thematic material which he then manipulated according to his multifarious needs. His Eighth String Quartet, written three and a half decades after the dense, single-movement Seventh, is a freely atonal piece which seems to generate its own rows—rather than vice versa—and which has an almost improvisatory and occasionally discursive feeling that is typical of Krenek's American period. His study of Ockeghem provided further impetus to his notion of "rotating" series, a device that gives even some of his stiffer scores a polyponic freedom that is tremendously engaging.

In the 1950s, he encountered electronic music at Darmstadt. Though he has produced little in the way of "pure" electronic compositions—the *San Fernando Sequence* of 1963 attracts the same misgivings as *Santa Fe Timetable*—it became an important element in his musical thinking, stimulating an interest in purely textural sonorities which is evident in the magnificent *Horizon Circled* and the smaller-scale *Arc of Life*, two works that run counter to the received view of Krenek as a rather cerebral ultra-modernist. In the same way, his vocal music is often wry and ironic, veering between toughly philosophical texts and such lighter—but no less thoughtful—settings as Donne's "The Flea" and, in *They Knew What They Wanted*, Boccaccio.

No final verdict on Krenek is possible, not least because he remains such a potent presence on the Californian music scene. However, it is clear that in his life and work, he has embodied much of the history of 20th-century music. His legacy is a complex gloss on its triumphs and failings.

—Richard Stein

KUPKOVIČ, Ladislav (Karol). Slovak. Born in Bratislava, 17 March 1936. Educated at the State Conservatory, Bratislava, 1950–5; Academy of Music, Bratislava, 1955–61. Married three times, 1960, 1976, 1988; 2 daughters. Conductor, Hungarian Folk Ensemble, Bratislava, 1959–60; violinist, Slovak Philharmonic Orchestra, 1961–5; freelance conductor and composer; founder/director, Hubda Dneska (Music of Today) Ensemble, 1963–70; co-founder of "New Music Days", Smolenice, Bratislava, 1968; emigrated to West Berlin, 1970; conducted first performance of Stockhausen's *Mixtur*, Cologne, 1971; teacher, from 1973, and professor of composition, since 1976, Hannover Musikhochschule. Recipient: prize for best film music of the year in Czechoslovakia, 1966; scholarship from Deutscher Akademischer Austauschdienst/German Academic Exchange Service, 1969–71; first prize for church music, Neuss, West Germany, 1980. Mailing address: Hochschule für Musik und Theater Hannover, Emmichplatz 1, 3000 Hannover, Germany; or Ruhmkarffstrasse 17, 3000 Hannover 1, Germany.

Publishers: Universal Edition, Vienna; Barenreiter, Kassel; Klaus Werner Verlag, Hannover; Moeck Verlag, Celle.

Symphonies/orchestral:

Ozveny 1965.
Dioe 1968.
Morceau de genre (nach E. Elgar) (version for violin, trumpet, timpani, strings) 1968. Recorded EMI Victrola.
Praparierter Text 4 (chamber orchestra; version for full orchestra) 1968, 1970.
Etude (nach J. Offenbach) (strings, trumpet, timpani, glockenspiel; in the style of J. Offenbach) 1968.
B.-Erinnerungen (orchestra, electronic sounds) 1970.
Notausgang (orchestra, microphones for verbal conducting) 1970.
Stimmen (strings, microphones for verbal conducting) 1970.
Staccato (winds, percussion, keyboard instruments, plucked instruments, strings) 1970.
Monolith (48 strings) 1971.
Souvenir (orchestra/string orchestra; original version for violin, piano; version for accordion) 1971. Recorded EMI Electrola; Ariola; Classic Aid.
Serandalusia (nach P. de Sarasate) (violin, string orchestra, with trumpet, timpani, percussion; in the style of Sarasate) 1971.
Ein Serenade mit dem Beckenschlag (string orchestra, percussion) 1971.
Ein Gesprach mit Gott 1972.
Das Gebet (strings, 2 or 3 percussionists on vibraphone, glockenspiel, other chiming instruments) 1972–3.
Serenata 1976.
Postillion-Cornet (trumpet, orchestra) 1977.
Chaconne No 1 (large wind ensemble) 1977.
Marsch (violin, orchestra) 1978.
K. and K. Musik 1978.
Cassation 1979.
Violin Concerto in D major 1980.
Schwetzinger Divertimento (strings) 1980.
Concerto in D major (accordion, orchestra) 1980.
Concerto in C major (cello, orchestra) 1980.
Concerto in A major (piano, orchestra) 1980.
Small Rococo Symphony 1981.
Great Symphony in D major 1981.
Concerto in E major (violin, orchestra) 1981.
Orchestral Variations on a Slovak Hymn-Tune 1981.
Rococo Symphony No 2 in C major 1982.
Rococo Symphony No 3 in C minor 1982.
Concertante (violin, cello, piano, orchestra) 1982.
Chaconne (strings) 1984.
Concerto in G major (violin, orchestra) 1984.
Cassation in C major (youth orchestra) 1984.
Eine Kleine Promenade durch die Musikgeschichte (7 variations on song "Storyboard") 1985.
Symphony in G major 1987.
Concerto in D♭ major (piano, orchestra) 1989.
B-A-C-H Variations 1989.

Chamber/instrumental:

Das Fleisch des Kreuzes: Impression auf das bild von M. Medek (trombone, 10 percussionists) 1961–2.
"..." (bass clarinet; version for cello) 1962.
Praparierter Text 2 (flute, trumpet, tympani, violin, cello, double bass, tape; based on Mozart: *Jupiter Symphony*, 1st movement) 1968.
Morceau de genre (piano; versions for accordion; violin, piano) 1968.
Praparierter Text 1 (violin, tape; based on Brahms: *Symphony No 1*, 2nd movement) 1968.
Praparierter Text 3 (cymbals, bass drum, tape; based on Beethoven: *Symphony No 9 "Choral"*, 4th movement) 1968.
Weniger und Mehr (6 instruments covering 6 instrumental groups) 1968.

Interpretation einer Kritik (variable ensemble, tape) 1970.
Treffpunkt (variable wind ensemble) 1970.
Intrada (brass ensemble) 1970.
klanginv-AS'-ion (trumpet solo, 12 trumpets, 4 horns, 4 trombones, 4 tubas, percussion) 1971.
Bahnhofsangriff (brass and woodwinds ad lib) 1971.
Souvenir (violin, piano) 1971.
312-SL / 723 (2 accordions) 1975.
Happy-End (4 pianos) 1976.
Rrrondo (cello, piano) 1977.
Chaconne No 1 (large wind ensemble) 1977.
Clavierubung (4 pianos) 1977. Recorded EMI Victrola.
Sankt-Vincent-Variationen (piano) 1977. Recorded EMI Victrola.
Marsch B-dur (violin, piano; or accordion) 1978. Recorded Ariola.
Requiem für "Meine" Selbstmorder (2 pianos) 1978.
Three Piano Pieces 1978.
Scherzo (viola, piano) 1978.
Das Kleine Souvenir (violin, piano) 1978.
Der Juwelierladen / The Jewellery Shop (violin, piano) 1978.
Romance (accordion) 1978.
String Quintet in D♭ major 1978.
String Quartet in D major 1978.
Sonatina in G major (violin, piano) 1979.
Sonatina in F major (violin, piano) 1979.
Sonatina in D major (violin, piano) 1979.
Sonata in F major 1979.
Chaconne No 3 in G minor (organ) 1979.
Four Minuets (recorder, basso continuo) 1979.
Quartet in E major (flute, violin, viola, cello) 1980.
Quartet in A major (oboe, violin, viola, cello) 1980.
Kleine Partita (accordion, violin, vibraphone/marimba) 1980.
March in F major (violin, piano) 1980.
Sonata in A major (violin, piano) 1980.
Quintet in A major (harp, string quartet) 1980.
Harfenwalzer (variable instrumentation) 1980.
Theme and Five Variations (with Fugue) (4 violins) 1980.
Partita (recorder, piano; also for flute or oboe, or violin, with piano) 1980.
Little Suite in D major (violin, cello, piano) 1980.
Sonata in D major (cello, piano) 1980.
Fugue in C major (5 accordions) 1981.
Six Little Pieces (6–7 recorders) 1981.
Wind Serenade in E major (2 flutes, 2 oboes, 2 clarinets, 2 bassoons, 2 horns, 2 trumpets) 1981.
Thirty-Three Variations on an Original Theme (piano) 1981.
Sonata in G major (piano) 1981.
Theme and Variations (violin, piano) 1981.
Sonata in B major (piano) 1981.
Polka in C minor (2 pianos) 1981.
Waltz (2 pianos) 1981.
Suite (string quartet) 1981.
Sonatina in G major (double bass, piano) 1981.
Variations on an Icelandic Song (accordion) 1982.
Variations on "I Kiss Your Hand, Madame" (flute, oboe, clarinet, bassoon, horn, trumpet, trombone, piano, harp, 2 percussion, string quintet) 1982.
Variations on a Slovak Folk Song (accordion, high instrument, low instrument) 1983.
Hommage à Marschner (oboe, clarinet, bassoon, piano, string quintet) 1983.
Sonatina in G major (flute, cymbal) 1984.
Tanze aus Pannonien (cello or violin or viola, piano) 1984.
Sonata in B major (violin, piano) 1984.
Serenade in G major (4 violins, 4 violas, 4 cellos, double bass) 1984.
Sonata Movement in D major (flute, accordion) 1984.
Quintet in A major (2 violins, viola, cello, piano) 1984.
String Quartet in D minor 1984.
Quintet in B♭ major (2 violins, 2 violas, cello) 1984.
Theme, Variations and Fugue in E major (2 pianos) 1984.
Miniatur (string quartet) 1985.
Partita No 2 (alto recorder, piano) 1985.
Trio in B♭ major (violin, cello, piano) 1985.
Octet in G major (clarinet, bassoon, horn, 2 violins, viola, cello, double bass) 1986.
Quartet in A major (violin, viola, cello, piano) 1986.
Quartet in B♭ major (violin, viola, cello, piano) 1986.
Theme and Variations on an English Song (2 violins) 1986.
Trio in B major (violin, cello, piano) 1987.
Trio in D major (flute, bassoon or cello, piano) 1987.
Three Little Pieces (young musicians, any instrumentation) 1987.
String Quartet in B♭ major 1987.
String Quartet in G major 1988.
Trio No 1 in B♭ major (oboe, clarinet, bassoon) 1988.
Trio No 2 in B♭ major (oboe, clarinet, bassoon) 1988.
Suite in G major (2 cellos) 1988.
Octet in D major (2 oboes, 2 clarinets, 2 horns, 2 bassoons) 1988.
Two Capriccios (Polka, Chaconne) (violin) 1988.
Quintet in C major: Reincarnation (oboe, clarinet, horn, bassoon, piano) 1989.
Armenian Song (violin, piano) 1989.
Quartet in F major (violin, viola, cello, piano) 1989.
Variation für die Drude-Variationen (violin, clarinet, cello, piano) 1989.
Twenty-Four Caprices (violin) 1990.

Vocal / choral:

Pismena—Buchstaben (8 vocalists—4 male, 4 female) 1967.
Dreiklang (mixed choir or women's choir) 1972.
Chaconne No 2 (5 voices ad lib) 1977.
Missa Papae Ioannis Pauli Secundi (mixed choir, orchestra) 1979.
Cantata (soloists, mixed chorus, orchestra) 1981.
Eight Lieder (2 tenors, 2 basses, piano; Fischer, Lorm, Eichendorff, Liliencron, Storm, von der Vogelwiede) 1986.

Opera / dramatic:

The Mask (10 soloists, orchestra, choir, ballet; Hoffmann) 1986.
Das Hundepferd (opera for children; Lenzen) 1987.

Other:

Prolify (open performance) 1968; performed Smolenice, 1968.
R-Musik (tape) 1968–73.
K.-Rhapsodie with *K.-Intermezzi* (collective title for *Etude, Morceau de genre, Souvenir, Serandalusia, Eine Serenade mit dem Beckenschlag*) 1968–71.
Musikalische Ausstellung (open performance) 1970; performed Berlin, 1970.
Musik für das Ruhrfestspielhaus (*Wandelkonzert*) 1970; first performed Recklinghausen, 2 July 1970.
Musikatlas (open performance) 1971; first performed Hannover, 1971.
Klanginvasion auf Bonn (150 musicians, city) 1971.
E-Musik (electronic music) 1971.

PUBLICATIONS

By Kupkovič: "The Role of Tonality", in *Tempo*, 135, 1980.

On Kupkovič: E. Frandsen, (interview) in *Kolner Rundschau*, 4 September 1971; M. Lichtenfeld, "A Meeting with LK", in *Melos*, 41, 1974; L. Bauche, "Radikalkurmusik: LK und das Populare in der Musik", in *Frankfurter Allgemeine Zeitung*, 13 June 1980; Sarah Elizabeth Davies, "LK", dissertation, Leicester Polytechnic, 1989.

* * *

Ladislav Kupkovič worked until 1970 in Czechoslovakia as a conductor, violinist and as a composer for film and television. His commitment to new music led him to found the Hubda Dneska Ensemble (Music of Today) and his own music away from the professional demands of film and television was strongly related to the music of the European avant-garde centred around Stockhausen. Indeed Kupkovič conducted the first performance of Stockhausen's *Mixtur* and is the work's dedicatee. In 1969 he spent some time in Berlin on a DAAD fellowship and settled in Germany shortly after. Ironically his work moved in a direction completely at odds with the musical climate of his adopted country reaching a point where his music is baffling to many of his contemporaries. This is because his music became not only tonal but tonal in a startling way.

Several of his earlier works had involved experimental forms of performance similar in concept to the environmental works of John Cage (pieces such as Cage's *Music Circus*, *HPSCHD*, or the indeterminate works of the 1950s where pieces could be played simultaneously). These "Wandelkonzert" involved programming pieces of varying lengths for different times and spaces within an overall time-scheme. *Music für das Ruhrfestspielhaus* involved 40 players who took over the Ruhr Festival Playhouse for three hours, while *Klanginvasion auf Bonn* used 150 musicians who were located in different parts of the city, playing a range of music—much of it by Kupkovič—within a 12-hour period.

Some of the items within these performances were what Kupkovič calls Präparieté Texte where he isolated parts of existing works (by Brahms, Mozart, Beethoven, Bach) which are barely audible in the original music, for example the second violin or viola. This was an early example of an interest in deconstruction and reconstitution that was to prove important for him in making the transition from being an atonal composer, to being the most "emphatically tonal" composer active today. In 1968 he wrote a short piece for violin and accordion, *Morceau de genre*, in which he subjected short extracts from a violin piece by Elgar to obsessive repetition of short phrases to make an extremely witty and occasionally (for the unsympathetic listener) irritating work. From this point onwards there was an immense shift in his music. For a time his tonal works coexisted with atonal works, but by the mid-1970s all his work was tonal and he became extraordinarily prolific. His work became not only tonal but tonal within the confines of particular classical models and, indeed, it can frequently be difficult to know whether a work is by Kupkovič or, for example, Mozart. The earliest works in this new style often had a satirical edge but little by little this defence mechanism was dropped to reveal himself not only as a superb craftsman, but also as a composer who believed in tonal approaches from previous eras, while inhabiting the present.

In 1979 he gave a talk at the Music Symposium, Graz Musikprotokoll on the given them of "New Simplicity". He began his talk by outlining his own evolved position. For him two things seemed to be wrong with the assumption behind the symposium: "1. Present-day music is not evolving from the complex to the simple, but from the atonal to the tonal. 2. Atonal does not mean complicated, and tonal does not mean simple." What Kupkovič does, in essence, is to get rid of the concept of "avant-garde". As he points out, neither Bach nor Mozart were avant-gardist and he wishes to remove the adjective completely. His own music is both brilliantly well-written curiously disturbing, and it is not merely anachronistic. There is a sense of peering into the past through a distorting lens that manages to reveal a clear picture, but a picture that never existed until the lens was put in place. The closest equivalent in literature would be Borges's imaginary author Pierre Menard who singlehandedly rewrites the *Don Quixote* of Cervantes, but not by copying, nor by pastiche or mimicry, but entirely as a new and original piece of writing.

—Gavin Bryars

KURTÁG, György. Hungarian. Born in Lugos [Lugoj], Romania, 19 February 1926. Educated: studied piano under Magda Kardos, composition under Max Eisikovits, Timisoara, from 1940; Budapest Academy of Music (composition under Sandor Veress and Ferenc Farkas, piano under Pál Kadosa, chamber music under Leo Weiner), 1946–53; further study in Paris (under Marianne Stein, Olivier Messiaen and Darius Milhaud), 1957–8. Married to Maria Kurtág; 1 son. Teacher, later professor of chamber music, Budapest Academy of Music; now retired. Recipient: Erkel Prize, 1954, 1956, 1969; Kossuth Prize, 1973; Merited Artist, 1980; Outstanding Artist, 1984; Bartók-Pasztory Award, 1984; Officier de l'Ordre des Arts et des Lettres, France, 1985; corresponding member, Bavarian Akademie der Schonen Künste, 1987; member, Akademie der Künste, Berlin, 1987. Mailing address: 2621 Veroce, Lihego utca 3, Liszt Ferenc ter 9 1 6, 1061 Budapest, Hungary.

Publisher: Editio Musica Budapest, P.O.B. 322, 1370 Budapest, Hungary.

Symphonies/orchestral:

Viola Concerto 1954.
Movement (viola, orchestra; first movement of *Viola Concerto* which can be played separately) 1954.

Chamber/instrumental:

Suite (piano duet) 1950.
Suite (piano) 1951.
String Quartet Op 1 1959. Recorded SLPX 11 846.
Wind Quintet Op 2 1959. Recorded SLPX 11 846.
Eight Piano Pieces Op 3 1960. Recorded SLPX 11 846.
Eight Duos Op 4 (violin, cimbalom) 1961. Recorded SLPX 11 686/11 846.
Jelek/Signs Op 5 (viola) 1961.
Szalkak/Splinters Op 6b (cimbalom) 1973.
Szalkak/Splinters Op 6c (piano) 1973. Recorded SLPX 11 686.

Games / Jatekok (no opus number; 4 books for piano) 1973–6. Recorded (parts only) SLPX 11 846.
Guitar Pieces Op 15 1975.
Hommage à András Mihály Op 13 (12 microludes for string quartet) 1977.
The Little Predicament Op 15b (piccolo, trombone, guitar) 1979.
Bagatelles Op 14d (flute, piano, double bass) 1981.

Vocal / choral:

Cantata 1953; withdrawn.
Bornemissza Peter mondasai / The Sayings of Peter Bornemisza Op 7 (soprano, piano) 1963–8. Recorded SLPX 11 845.
In Memory of a Winter Sunset Op 8 (4 fragments for soprano, violin, cimbalom; Gulyas) 1969. Recorded SLPX 11 686.
Four Capriccios Op 9 (soprano, flute/piccolo, oboe, clarinet, bassoon, horn, percussion, cimbalom, harp, piano/celeste, string quintet; Bálint) 1972.
Four Songs to Poems by János Pilinsky Op 11 (bass or bass-baritone, clarinet, horn, violin, viola, cello, 2 cimbaloms, bass zither or viola da gamba or double bass, Bozay zither) 1975. Recorded SLPX 11 845.
S.K. Remembrance Noise Op 12 (soprano, violin; Tandori) 1975.
Messages of the Late Miss R.V. Troussova Op 17 (soprano, oboe, clarinet, horn, mandolin, cimbalom, harp, piano, celeste, vibraphone, percussion, violin, viola, double bass; Dalos) 1976–80; first performed Paris, 14 January 1981. Recorded Erato STU 71 543; SLPX 12 776.
Herdecker Eurythmie Op 14 (speaking voice, lyre, flute, violin; Lösch) 1978.
Omaggio a Luigi Nono Op 16 (chorus; Akhmatova, Dalos) 1979; first performed London, 3 February 1981.
Scenes from a Novel Op 19 (soprano, violin, double bass, cimbalom; Dalos) 1981–2. Recorded SLPX 12 776.
Fragments to Poems by Attila Jószef Op 20 (20 movements for soprano) 1981.
Seven Songs Op 22 (soprano, cimbalom; Károlyi, Kobayashi Issa/Tandori) 1981.
Eight Choruses Op 23 (mixed choir; Tandori) 1981–2, 1984.
Kafka Fragments Op 24 (soprano, violin) 1985–6.
Three Old Inscriptions Op 25 (soprano, piano) 1986.
Requiem po drugu Op 26 (soprano, piano; Dalos) 1986–7.

* * *

The main Hungarian composer to emerge after the country's problems of the 1940s and early 1950s was György Kurtág. By the late 1950s Kurtág had acquired a thorough understanding of many earlier schools of composition from outside Hungary, and he gradually integrated them into a personal style. In addition to the influence of Schumann, Stravinsky, Bartók and Webern, he became obsessed with ostinato technique.

After disowning his earlier works, Kurtág designated the arch-form *String Quartet* his "Op.1", thereby affirming a new style and a new technique. The Quartet excels in quickly changing, highly contrasting textures, but is practically all homophonic; the only real counterpoint comes either as fast close-knit canon or in brief quiet high four-part glissandi. The six-movement structure of the Quartet influenced Kurtág's works of the next few years: they are all microform suites, where movements are associated either in the manner of their development, or in the character of their rhythms or tempos. After the *Wind Quintet*, where a chain of slow movements is surrounded by briefer fast movements, *Eight Piano Pieces* contains numerous colouristic effects (quickly repeated notes, trills, tremolo, glissandi and playing using fore-arms) while employing ostinato, dodecaphony and free atonal techniques. *Eight Duos* for violin and cimbalom groups its eight movements into 3+3+2, while showing the rhythmic inflections of Bartók and the rhythmic treatment of Messiaen.

The Sayings of Peter Bornemisza is an extended work for solo voice and piano, on texts by the 16th-century Hungarian writer. 24 microforms combine into four large sections, with effective word-setting and quasi-impressionist mood-enhancement throughout. Rather than dwelling on a single syllable, the text is only interrupted by an occasional outburst on the piano. An enormous three-octave compass is required by the singer: the piano part although difficult is seldom obtrusive. Motives are simple to recognize, with much imitation between the three staves. The *Cantata* includes fugues and canons in five parts but the rhythm is never complex. Kurtág's virtuoso piece for cimbalom, *Splinters*, exploits the procession from staccato diads to a single line contrasted with brief flurries over a repeated pedal. Meanwhile, dynamics provide variety.

While continuing to write microform works, often as song cycles, many of Kurtág's compositions are designated "Hommage-pieces". These instrumental forms are heard in *Hommage à András Mihály* (12 microludiums for string quartet), but his text-related Hommage-works prove to be his greatest achievement. The choral cycle *Omaggio a Luigi Nono* was first performed by the BBC Singers and his famous song cycle *Messages of the Late Miss R.V. Troussova* was commissioned by I.R.C.A.M. *Omaggio* and *Messages* both set three-line poetry by Rimma Dalos, who writes in Russian. In these works, Kurtág exploits a large volume of sound with a multicolored polyphonic compositional style. *Omaggio* comprises thick brief phrases interspersed by breaks in the overall sound, written in free rhythm set by the conductor (the score gives only white or black notation without rhythmic stems). A vast dynamic range is exploited but never suddenly changed. There is some antiphonal writing, producing chromatic clusters when soft, or (more frequently) producing one voice far-distanced from the others. Kurtág makes great vocal demands of intonation, dramatic, lyrical and coloratura techniques, bel canto operatic and song styles, declamation and speech (somewhat simpler demands were present in the *Cantata*). Ever since *Omaggio*, Kurtág has obliterated the difference between instrumental and vocal parts mainly by reducing the range of dramatic variety while treating instruments as though they were voices.

—Malcolm J. Hill

KVANDAL, Johan. Norwegian. Born in Oslo, 8 September 1919. Educated at Music Conservatory, Oslo (organ and conducting; composition and counterpoint under Per Steenberg, piano under Ingebjorg Gresvig, organ under Arild Sandvold, composition under Geirr Tveitt); further composition study under Joseph Marx, Vienna, Nadia Boulanger, Paris, 1952–4, and Boris Blacher, Berlin, 1970. Organist, Valerengen Church, Oslo, 1959–74. Mailing address: c/o Norwegian Music Information Centre, Tordenskiodoldsgt. 6B, N-0160 Oslo 1, Norway.

Publisher: Norsk Musikforlag.

Symphonies/orchestral:

Divertimento Op 3 (5 solo strings) 1941.
Norwegian Overture Op 7 1951.
Variations and Fugue Op 14 1954.
Symphony No 1 Op 18 1959.
Symphonic Epos Op 21 1962.
Concerto for Flute and Strings Op 22 1963. Recorded Philips 6507 013.
Skipper Worse Suite Op 28b (from television music) 1968.
Sinfonia concertante Op 29 1968.
Antagonia Op 38 (concerto for 2 string orchestras and percussion) 1973. Recorded Philips 6507 060.
Concerto for Oboe and String Orchestra Op 46 1977. Recorded Philips 4081-1.
Concerto for Violin and Orchestra Op 52 1979. Recorded NOP 1828.
Truptychon Op 53 1979.
Concerto for Chamber Orchestra Op 55 1980.
Legende Op 61 (bassoon, string orchestra; also chamber version) 1983.
Concerto for Organ and String Orchestra Op 62 1984.
Poem Op 66b (violin, string orchestra) 1985.
Visions Norvegiennes/Norske Utsyn-Orkesterfantasi Op 67 1985.

Chamber/instrumental:

Five Small Pieces Op 1 (piano) 1940.
Sonatina Op 2 (piano) 1941.
Divertimento Op 3 (5 solo strings) 1941.
Rondo Op 16 No 1 (violin, piano) 1941.
Rondo grazioso Op 5 No 1 (piano) 1942.
Lyric Pieces Op 5 Nos 4–7 (piano) 1942, 1946.
Fugue (no opus number; string quartet) 1946.
Octet 1946 Op 54 (2 oboes, 2 clarinets, 2 bassoons, 2 horns, double bass ad lib) 1946, revised 1980. Recorded Simax PSC 1037.
Fantasy Op 8 (piano) 1947.
Three Norwegian Folk Tunes Op 5 No 2 (piano) 1948.
String Trio Op 12 1950.
String Quarter No 1 Op 11 1954.
Capriccio Op 16 No 2 (violin, piano) 1955.
Choral Prelude on "Ljoset Yver Landet Dagna" (no opus number; organ) 1956.
Toccata Op 5 No 3 (organ or piano) 1958.
Duo Op 19 (violin, cello) 1959. Recorded Philips 6507 008.
Meditation and Choral Prelude (no opus number; organ) 1961.
Three Hymn Tunes Op 23b (wind quintet) 1963.
Romance Op 16 No 3 (violin, piano) 1964.
Romance Op 16 No 4 (flute, piano) 1964.
Aria, Cadenza e Finale Op 24 (violin, piano) 1964. Recorded TT Studio Classic TTLP 102.
Miniatures Op 43 a/b (4 violins or string quartet) 1965–6.
String Quartet No 2 Op 27 1966. Recorded Philips 6507 060.
Glockenspiel Minuet (from television play *Skipper Worse*; piano) 1968.
Introduction and Allegro Op 30 (horn, piano) 1969. Recorded BIS LP 171; Varèse International VS-810-16; Aime Lainesse 001/2.
Fantasies on Three Country Dances Op 31 (piano) 1969. Recorded Philips 6507 012.
Da Lontano Op 32 (alto flute or clarinet, piano) 1970. Recorded Philips 6507 020; Varèse International VS-85019.
Quintet Op 34 (winds) 1971. Recorded Philips 6507 043.
Partita on the Folk Tune "Hvor er det Godt a Lande" Op 36 (organ) 1971.
Duo concertante Op 41 (2 pianos) 1974.
Quartet Op 42 (flute, violin, viola, cello) 1975–6. Recorded Varèse International VS-85019.
Two Norwegian Dances Op 44 (based on *Halling* and *Springdans* from Grieg's *Peer Gynt*; string quartet) 1976.
Sonata Op 45 (violin) 1976. Recording Philips 6507 060.
Elegy and Capriccio Op 47 (viola) 1977.
Prelude (no opus number; organ) 1977.
Quintet Op 50 (Hardanger fiddle, string quartet) 1978.
Nocturne: The Dream Op 56 (alto flute or clarinet, piano) 1980.
Jew's Harp Waltz (no opus number; piano) 1980. Recorded NC 4903.
Night Music Op 57 (2 oboes, 2 clarinets, 2 bassoons, 2 horns, double bass) 1981. Recorded Simax PSC 1037.
Overture-Fantasy Op 59 (3 horns, 2 trumpets, 2 trombones, tuba) 1982.
String Quartet No 3 Op 60 1983.
Legende Op 61 (bassoon, 5 solo strings) 1983.
Sonata: The Heming Ballad Op 63 (harp) 1984.
Skjemtevise og Gjeterlokk Op 64 (for schools; descant recorder, clarinet, 2 violins, double bass, piano, celeste, percussion) 1984.
Sonata Op 65 (guitar) 1984. Recorded Simax PSC 1031; WEPS 1012.
Poem Op 66a (violin, piano or organ) 1985.
Hymn Tune Op 68 (horn) 1986.
Norwegian Folktunes Op 70 Nos 1–8 (piano) 1986–7.
Sonata Op 71 (accordion) 1987.
Horn Quartet Op 73 1988.

Vocal/choral:

Songs Op 9 Nos 1–10 (voice, piano) 1939–83.
Seven Songs Op 4 (voice, piano) 1940–1.
Three Christmas Hymns (no opus number; voice, piano or organ) 1946.
Barneviser/Nursery Rhymes (no opus number; voice, piano) 1946–7.
Two Froding Songs Op 9 Nos 11 & 12 (high voice, piano) 1948.
Vakn Op du som sover/Thou Who Sleepest Awake Op 13 (motet for mixed chorus; Landstad) 1950. Recorded Philips 839 235 NY.
Drikkevise/Drinking Song (no opus number; unaccompanied men's chorus; Wergeland) 1950.
Sang til Stella/Song for Stella Op 6 (soprano, string orchestra or piano; Wergeland) 1951.
Solo Cantata No 1 Op 10 (high voice, orchestra) 1953. Recorded Orpheum 8404.
Draumkvaede Melodies Op 15 (soprano, mixed chorus, piano or organ) 1955.
Seven Religious Folk Songs Op 23a (voice, piano) 1955.
Benedicam dominum Op 17 (soprano, organ; Psalms) 1957.
Three Songs Op 20 (SSA chorus; Wergeland, Holberg, Skjaeraasen) 1960.
Three Motets Op 35 (unaccompanied mixed chorus) 1963, 1971. Recorded (no 1 only) Philips 6578 108.
Jer er kommet som et Lys til Verden/I Am Come a Light unto the World Op 35 (mixed chorus; soprano, organ; biblical) 1963.
Pleiadene ved Midnatt/The Pleiades at Midnight Op 25 (men's chorus, speaking chorus; Hauch) 1965.
Kristus, Du er alt hitt Hap/Christ, You Are My Only Hope (no opus number; voice, organ; Ellingsen) 1965.
Allmakts Gud/Almighty God (no opus number; voice, organ; Smemo) 1965.

Two Asen Hymns (no opus number; piano or organ accompaniment) 1965.
O Domine Deus Op 26 No 2 (soprano organ; Maria Stuart) 1966. Recorded Philips 854 000 AY.
For Trykkefriheten / For Freedom of the Press (no opus number; unaccompanied mixed chorus; Wergeland) 1966.
Efter Tidens Leilighed (no opus number; unaccompanied men's chorus; Wergeland) 1966.
Til Dig Herre / To Thee, O Lord: Solo Cantata No 2 Op 26 No 1 (soprano, organ) 1966.
Skapningen Lenges / The Expectation of the Creature: Solo Cantata No 3 Op 33 (low voice, organ; Romans) 1970.
Nature Op 37 (baritone, violin, piano; Aukrust) 1972.
O Dyp av Rikdom Hos Gud / Oh, the Depth of the Riches Op 39 (SATB chorus, organ; biblical) 1973.
Norske Stevtoner Op 40 (voice, piano) 1974.
Two Songs Op 48 (unaccompanied mixed chorus; Rysstad, traditional) 1978.
Michelangelo-Poem Op 49 (soprano, piano or orchestra) 1978.
Ibsen Cantata Op 51 (soprano, baritone, mixed chorus, orchestra) 1978.
Two Love Songs Op 58 (voice, piano; Overland) 1982.
Underet / The Miracle Op 69 (unaccompanied mixed chorus; Eidslott / Sateren) 1986.
Ballade om Freden Op 72 (unaccompanied mixed chorus; Charles d'Orléans, translated Gundelach) 1987.

Other:

Skipper Worse (music to television play by Kielland) 1968.

PUBLICATIONS

On Kvandal: Bjarne Kortsen, "JK", in *Norsk Musiktidsskrift*, 1, 1968; Conrad Baden, "JK", in *Norsk Musiktidsskrift*, 4, 1979; Nils Grinde, in *Contemporary Norwegian Music, 1920–1980*, Oslo, 1981.

* * *

One of the most frequently performed of modern Norwegian composers, Johan Kvandal works in an accessibly neo-classical vein, with references back and forth to Bartók, to the Norwegian folk music that was his first discernible influence, and to the Baroque *sonata da chiesa*. Kvandal's earliest pieces up to his Opus 7 *Norwegian Overture* were based on "*slatt*" or country themes and are sufficiently conventional to have been written at any point in the previous two decades. The watershed in his early career was a period of study with the "gentle tyrant" Nadia Boulanger in Paris in the early 1950s. In addition to opening Kvandal's mind to the broader parameters of contemporary European music, it helped dissociate him from the narrow parochialism of his teacher Geir Tveitt (the 10-minute egg of hard-boiled Norwegian nationalism) and from his composer father David Monrad Johansen, whose nationalist sensibilities had led him, in common with too many Norwegians of that generation, into a profoundly unfortunate enthusiasm for the less-than-gentle tyranny of the Nazi-sponsored Quisling government.

In Paris, Kvandal became aware of the work of Stravinsky and Messiaen, and of the less literal, Bartókian potential of folk themes within a broadly neo-classical aesthetic. The most significant product of this period of development is the superb *Symphonic Epos* of 1962, perhaps Kvandal's greatest single work, with an almost perfect internal balance and a complex narrative line. Works like the three "*slatt*" fantasies and the powerful *Antagonia*, written in the early 1970s and scored for two string orchestras, dramatise his lifelong effort to assimilate folk and international elements without surrendering to either; there are still elements of folk themes in the profoundly beautiful concerto for oboe and strings and, even more explicitly, in the Opus 50 *Quintet* for string quartet and Hardanger fiddle (a violin fitted with sympathetic drone strings, somewhat in the manner of a sitar), which is among his finest chamber works. Elsewhere, he has used "*stev*" elements, reminiscent of Scottish "flyting". The recent Opus 70 piano arrangements of folk materials are both strongly individual and absolutely true to source.

The second string quartet is the most explicitly Bartókian piece (though there are subliminal hints of Bartók's treatment of rhythm in the 1979 Violin Concerto), with a highly unified, almost palindromic structure that is characteristic of Kvandal's intuitive grasp of form. It is a highly powerful work, much more nakedly emotional in development (even within its highly schematised single-movement structure) than is typical of this somewhat reserved composer. Much of Kvandal's emotional force has gone into his vocal and religious music, and his organ pieces—he played the full-voiced instrument in the Valerengen Church, Oslo, for nearly 15 years—have something of Messiaen's charged intensity.

Kvandal's use of elements of Baroque music is perhaps his most significant "innovation". These are not intended as pastiche, nor are they conservative in effect. Though his work remains fundamentally tonal, there is a greater emphasis on melody than on larger-scale harmonic progression, lending even his symphonic writing a quality of open-ended polyphony which is highly striking.

In distancing himself from his father's nationalism, Kvandal in no way turned his back on Norway. The 1985 orchestral fantasy is triumphant summation which makes little use of blandly folkloristic elements. Kvandal has been an important presence on the music scene there for more than 40 years, and if the inherited guilt of the war years weighed on him at all, his response has been profoundly healthy and realistic, rescuing the best of the native Norwegian tradition and paring it of its associated complacent bombast. There is a gentle strength and a muscular spirituality to Kvandal's music that appeals to audiences not least for its absolute irreducibility.

—Brian Morton

KVĚCH, Otomar. Czech. Born in Prague, 25 May 1950. Educated at Prague Conservatory (composition under M. Raichl, F. Kovaříček, J.Z. Bartoš), 1965–9; organ study with J. Kuban; Prague Academy of Arts and Music (composition under J. Pauer), 1969–74. Military service in the V. Nejedly Army Artistic Ensemble, 1975–6. Married Miluska Wagnerova, 30 March 1972; 2 daughters. Coach, National Theatre Opera Ensemble, Prague, 1973–6; musical producer, Czechoslovak Radio, Prague, 1976–80; creative secretary, Union of Czech Composers, 1980–9; dramaturge, Czechoslovak Radio, since 1990. Recipient: Czech Ministry of Culture Young Composers Competition prizes (for *When the Road Ended*), 1974, second prize (for *Sonata of Love for*

Life), 1976, first prize (for *Transformation*), 1978, first prize (for *String Quartet No 4*), 1982, first prize (for *Symphony in E♭ major*), 1983; SCSKU prizes, 1977, 1986; first prize, Llangollen (for song "Kitchen Band"). Mailing address: Korunni 67, 130 00 Praha 3, Czechoslovakia.

Publishers: Czech Music Fund, Hire Library of Music Materials, Parizska 13, Prague 1; Panton Publishers, Ricni 12, Prague 1, Czechoslovakia.

Symphonies/orchestral:

Homage to J.S. Bach (Suite) 1971; first performed Prague, 1972. Recorded Radio Plzen.
Symphony for Organ and Orchestra 1973–4; first performed Prague, 1974. Recorded Radio Prague.
Transformation (violin, strings) 1976; first performed Prague, 1978. Recorded Supraphon 1110 2853.
Overture 1979.
Symphony in E♭ major No 1 1980; first performed Prague, 1983. Recorded Panton 8110 0517.
Carnival of the World (overture for symphony orchestra) 1983; first performed Prague, 1985. Recorded Panton 8110 0539.
Symphony in D major No 2 1984; first performed Prague, 1985. Recorded Panton 81 0745-1031.
RUR (passacaglia for orchestra, based on the play by Josef and Karel Čapek) 1986; first performed Prague, 1987. Recorded Panton 81 0838–1011.
Capriccio (piano trio, orchestra) 1987; first performed Teplice, 1988.
Symphony for String Quartet and Orchestra 1987; first performed Prague, 1989.

Chamber/instrumental:

Sonata for Violin and Piano No 2 1970.
String Quartet No 1 1972.
String Quartet No 2 1973; first performed Prague, 1974.
String Quartet No 3 1974; first performed Tanvald, 1976.
Sonata for Violin and Piano No 1 1974.
Competition Music (bassoon, piano) 1974.
Quintetery (wind quintet) 1976; first performed Prague, 1976.
Trio (violin, cello, piano) 1977; first performed Prague, 1977. Recorded Supraphon 1 19 2237.
Sonata for Piano 1977; first performed Karlovy Vary, 1979.
Furioso (oboe, piano) 1977.
String Quartet No 4 1979; first performed Prague, 1981. Recorded Panton 81111 0380.
Adagio and Allegro (tuba, piano) 1980.
Sonata for Violin and Piano No 3 1982; first performed Prague, 1983.
Prague Panorama (organ) 1982.
Six Preludes (flute) 1983; first performed Marianske Lazne, 1984.
Duo (oboe, bassoon) 1984; first performed Boulder, Colorado, 1985.
Sonata for Cello and Piano 1985; first performed Karlovy Vary, 1986.
String Quartet No 5 1985; first performed Prague, 1987.
Portrait (Sonata-fantasy) (organ) 1986; first performed Avignon, 1987.
Dance Fantasy (4 guitars) 1987; first performed Prague, 1988.
Sonata for Viola and Piano 1989.
Album (piano cycle) 1989.
Quintet (piano, string quartet) 1990.

Vocal/choral:

When the Road Ended (soprano, piano) 1972; first performed Prague, 1972. Recorded Panton 22 0484.
Tales of the Spruce (children's choir, narrator, orchestra; Kralik) 1975.
What Do You Hide (bass-baritone, piano) 1976; first performed Prague, 1976.
In the Country of Memories (higher voice, piano) 1977; first performed Prague, 1978. Recorded Panton 81 0680-1211.
Sonata of Love for Life (baritone, string orchestra; Hrubin) 1975; first performed Prague, 1976.
The Way Through the Parlour (bass-baritone, male choir, orchestra; Hrubin) 1978; first performed Prague, 1979. Recorded Supraphon 11 19 2598.
Lullaby for Martin (chamber male choir; Branislav) 1978.
Three Male Choruses (to Lada's Pictures) (bugle-horn, choir; Bednar) 1982; first performed Olomouc, 1987.
Drinking Songs (baritone, piano) 1983; first performed Svetla, near Sazavou, 1988.
From Sci-Fi Notes (female chorus; Janovic) 1985.
String Motifs (mixed choruses; Neruda) 1987.

Opera:

Spring Is Here (children's radio opera; Kralik) 1975.
Before Christmas (children's radio opera; Kralik) 1978.
When Autumn Came (children's radio opera; Kralik) 1980.
It Is Holidays Time (children's radio opera; Kralik) 1983.

Other:

Three Shots for Accordion (instructional) 1973.
Sonatina (instructional piece for 2 trumpets, trombone) 1974.
Introduction, Fugue and Coda (accordion; instructional) 1978.

PUBLICATIONS

On Kvech: Eva Pensdorfova, "Sanskrtu nerozumim", in *Hubedni rozhledy*, 1987.

* * *

Perhaps the most gifted of the younger generation of Czechoslovak composers, Otomar Kvěch came of age musically at a moment of maximum disruption in Czech cultural and political life. The "Prague Spring" and subsequent Warsaw Pact invasion coincided with his latter years at the Prague Conservatory, where he studied under Bartoš and Raichl. Nonetheless, Kvěch seems remarkably untouched by these upheavals; his music has a calm concentration that is undisturbed by any overt programmatic intention other than an un-complacent affirmation of Czech culture.

His first acknowledged works date from the very early 1970s and are already astonishingly mature. The orchestral suite dedicated in *Homage to J.S. Bach* has a sure contrapuntal grasp and a fine awareness of instrumental values. The three early string quartets are equally assured but show little signs of the remarkable development Kvech was to undergo in the mid-1970s.

Whatever the catalyst, Kvěch began to re-examine his work in the wake of *Sonata of Love for Life*, a subtle and uplifting vocal work to a text by Hrubin. His harmony deepened in resonance to accommodate a more detailed and extensive melodic line, and his rhythm relaxed noticeably, to a point where pieces seem to be structured according to an underlying pulse rather than to any key or series. The first major piece to embody these changes was the remarkable *Transformation*. Though brief in comparison to his earlier symphonic pieces and the masterly symphonic work to come, it is charged with musical information and drama, and has a beguiling part for solo violin which can be read as Kvech's personal odyssey through his own music. The Fourth String Quartet echoes some of these changes, developing instrumental syntax and sonority very considerably and evolving a far more sophisticated structure than its predecessors. Along with *Prague Panorama* and *Portrait*, both for organ, and the marvellous *Dance Fantasy*, it is his finest chamber work.

In 1983, Kvěch's First Symphony was premiered in his native city to considerable acclaim. It is a powerful objective statement of symphonic values and language, in the same affirmative E♭ major as Beethoven's *Eroica* and with something of the same tensions and ambiguities built into its most positive elements. The orchestration is very powerful and the conclusion completely apt. It is in most respects a finer and more questing work than its successor. Premiered two years later, and written in a clear and vigorous D major, the Second Symphony features the kind of superb scoring for open strings that resurfaces in the recent *Symphony for String Quartet and Orchestra*, but it is a more academic piece that lacks the underlying personal vision of its predecessor.

That vision is also evident in the vocal works, and particularly in the two settings of Hrubin. *The Way Through the Parlour* is a virtual companion piece to the *Sonata*, a darker and more complex view of life which mirrors the change in compositional philosophy represented by *Transformation* and the orchestral passacaglia *RUR*, after the Čapeks. Kvěch balances voice and orchestra superbly well and gives the verse a new richness of suggestion. His status as one of Czechoslovakia's most significant post-war composers seems assured.

—Richard Stein

L

LA BARBARA, Joan (professional name of Joan Linda Lotz La Barbara Subotnick). American. Born in Philadelphia, Pennsylvania, 8 June 1947. Educated at Abington High School, Pennsylvania, diploma, June 1965; Syracuse University, New York (voice under Helen Boatwright), 1965–8; New York University (composition), 1968–70, B.S. in music education; additional voice tuition at Berkshire Music Center, Massachusetts (under Phyllis Curtin) and at Juilliard School of Music, New York City (under Marion Szekely Freschl). Married Morton Subotnick, 18 December 1979; 1 son. Vocalist, Steve Reich & Musicians, 1971–4; co-founder, New Wilderness Preservation Band, 1973; vocalist, Philip Glass Ensemble, 1973–6; contributing editor, *High Fidelity / Musical America*, 1977–87; Artist in Residence, DAAD Kunstlerprogram, Berlin, 1979; teacher of composition and singing, California Institute of the Arts, Valencia, since 1981; vice-president, American Music Center, New York City, since 1982; co-artistic director, New America Music Festival, Los Angeles, 1984–5; co-president, New Music Alliance, 1986–7; also residencies as Visiting Slee Composer at the Center for Creative and Performing Arts, State University of New York, Buffalo; visiting artist in residence, Kutztown College of Art, Pennsylvania, Crane University School of Music, University of Illinois, Urbana, California Institute of the Arts, University of Minnesota and Minneapolis Augsburg College, both Mills College and California College of Arts and Crafts, Oakland, California, San Francisco Conservatory of Music, Royal Conservatory of Music, Den Haag, The Netherlands, Gettysburg College, Pennsylvania, Hochschule der Kunst, Berlin, and Musik Akademie der Stadt, Basle, Switzerland; workshops on traditional and extended vocal techniques at Fêtes Musicale de la Sainte Baume, 1977, Los Angeles Institute of Contemporary Art, 1978–9, Lutzowstrasse Project, Insel Musik 2, Hochschule der Kunst, Berlin, 1979, American Center for Students and Artists, Paris, 1979, 1980, California Institute of the Arts, 1978–85, and Royal Conservatory of Music, Den Haag, 1988. Recipient: ISCM League of Composers International Jury Prize (for sound sculpture/environment *Cyclone*), 1977; National Endowment for the Arts fellowships, 1980 (visual arts), 1981 (music composition), 1984–5 (solo recitalist), 1985 (interarts), 1988 (opera/music theatre), 1988 (recording). Mailing address: 121 Coronado Lane, Santa Fe, New Mexico 87501, U.S.A.

Publisher: self.

Voice (with orchestra):

Chandra (solo voice, male chorus, orchestra) 1975, revised 1983; first performed Bremen, Germany, May 1978.
The Solar Wind III (solo voice, orchestra) 1984; first performed San Francisco, June 1984.

Voice (amplified voice/extended technique; with instruments):

Thunder (voice, 6 timpani, electronics) 1975.
Ides of March I–VIII (voice, instruments) 1975–7.
Chords and Gongs (voice, cimbalom, gongs) 1976.
Loisada (voice, kalimba, cimbalom, steel drum) 1977.
Silent Scroll (voice, flute, clarinet/double bass, percussion, gong, zoomoozophone) 1982; first performed New York, 1982. Recorded Finnadar.
Vlissingen Harbor (voice, flute/piccolo, trumpet, clarinet, harp, piano/celeste, cello, percussion) 1982; first performed Los Angeles, 6 December 1982. Recorded Nonesuch 78029.
The Solar Wind I (voice [1 or 2], flute/piccolo, cor anglais, clarinet, horn, 2 percussion, harp, viola, cello, double bass, piano) 1982; first performed Los Angeles, 7 February 1983. Recorded Nonesuch 78029.
The Solar Wind II (mixed chorus, flute/piccolo, keyboard synthesizer, 2 percussion) 1983; first performed Copenhagen, 14 November 1983.
A Rothko Study (voice, bass flute, bass clarinet, bowed vibraphone, bowed piano, viola, cello, double bass, synthesizer) 1985; first performed Los Angeles, 3 November 1985.
Helga's Lied (voice, wind quintet, string quintet) 1986; first performed Aarhus, Denmark, 10 October 1986.
Urban Tropics (voice, percussion, concrete recordings; also version for vox, tape) 1988; first broadcast 2–12 December 1988.

Voice (extended technique; with electronics):

Vocal Extensions (voice, electronics) 1975.
An Exaltation of Larks (voice, electronics) 1976.
Cathing (voice, tape) 1977.
Twelvesong (voice, tape; version for 12 voices) 1977.
Klee alee (voice, tape; also version for 16 voices) 1979.
Shadowsong (voice, tape; also version for 16 voices) 1979.
Erin (voice, tape; version for 16 voices) 1980.
October Music: Star Showers and Extraterrestrials (voice, tape; also version for 16 voices) 1980; first performed Paris, October 1980. Recorded Nonesuch 78029.
Winds of the Canyon (voice, tape) 1982, revised 1986; first performed San Francisco, 12 November 1983; revised version first performed Los Angeles, 3 March 1986.
Berline Traume (voice, tape; also version for multi-tracked tape) 1983; first performed Minneapolis, 18 February 1984.
Time(d) Trials and Unscheduled Events (voice, tape; also 8 voices on multi-track tape; also version for 8 live voices) 1984, 1987.
After "Obervogelsang" (voice, tape) 1984.
ROTHKO (amplified voice, 16 voices, 2 bowed pianos on tape) 1985; first performed Houston, Texas, 5 April 1986.
Loose Tongues (8 voices, tape) 1985.
Urban Tropics (voice, tape) 1988; first performed Ventura, California, 30 March 1989.

Voice (amplified/extended technique):

Hear What I Feel 1974.
Performance Piece 1974, revised 1979; first performed Berkeley, California, 1979.

Voice Piece: One-Note Internal Resonance Investigation 1974.
Circular Song 1975.
Les Oiseaux qui chantent dans ma tête 1976.
Space Testing (acoustic voice) 1976.
Twelvesong (12 voices) 1977; first performed Radio Bremen, 1977. Recorded Wizard 2283.
Klee alee (16 voices) 1979; first performed Paris, 1979. Recorded Wizard 2279; Lovely 3001.
Shadowsong (16 voices) 1979; first performed Paris, 1979. Recorded Wizard 2279; Lovely 3001.
Twelve for Five in Eight (5 or more voices) 1979; first performed Valencia, California, 1979.
"Quatre Petites Bêtes" (8 voices; also version for tape) 1979; first performed Cologne, 1979. Recorded Wizard 2283.
Erin (16 voices) 1980; first performed Hilversum, The Netherlands, 1980. Recorded Wizard 2283.
October Music: Star Showers and Extraterrestrials (16 voices) 1980; first performed Paris, 1980. Recorded Nonesuch 78029.
Time(d) Trials and Unscheduled Events (8 live voices) 1987; first performed Los Angeles, July 1987.
Conversations 1988; first performed Rome, 3 August 1988.

Opera:

Prologue to The Book of Knowing . . . (and) of Overthrowing (solo aria for voice and tape with visual environments and costume by Judy Chicago; to be developed as full-scale opera) 1988; first performed New York City, 6 July 1988.
Events in the Elsewhere (interactive media opera; computer systems/software allowing voice to control all aspects of the stage environment including theatrical lighting, video and music sequence cueing and camera action; inspired by Stephen Hawking) 1989–90; first performed Santa Fe, New Mexico, 24–6 August 1990.

Other:

Hunters (video) 1975.
Vermont II (video) 1975.
Cyclone (amplified voice, tape, light-panning activating device; revised as installation, 16-track tape) 1976, revised 1979.
She Is Always Alone (video) 1979.
The Executioner's Bracelet (tape) 1979.
"Quatre Petites Bêtes" (tape) 1979.
Responsive Resonance with Feathers (piano, tape) 1979.
As Lightning Comes, in Flashes (2–6 amplified voices, dancers, video) 1982. Recorded Wizard 2283.
Autumn Signal (tape) 1982.
3 Space Trio/Lament for the Wizard (video; collaboration with E. Emshwiller) 1982.
Voice Windows (voice, interactive video systems) 1986; first performed Los Angeles, 3 March 1986.
L'albero dalle foglie azzurre/Tree of Blue Leaves (oboe, tape) 1989; first performed St Louis, Missouri, 20 March 1989.
Klangbild: Köln (sounds and impressions of Cologne collected for a "sound painting of the city") 1989–90.
"A Self-Portrait in Sound" (aural portrait combining 12 years of soundworks) 1990; broadcast West Deutscher Rundfunk, 1990.
In the Dreamtime (sonic self-portrait) 1990.

Performer: recordings of works by Steve Reich, Philip Glass, Lou Harrison, John Cage, Don Sebesky, Jim Hall, Bruce Ditmas, Garrett List, Hugh Romney/Living Theatre, Stanley Silverman and Richard Foreman, Charles Dodge, Morton Subotnick, and Morton Feldman.

PUBLICATIONS

By La Barbara: music reviews for *SoHo Weekly News*, 1973–6, and *Los Angeles Times*, 1977–9; monthly articles on new music as contributing editor to *Musical America/High Fidelity* magazine, 1977–87; articles for *Data Arte* (Milan) and *Liberation* (Paris).

On La Barbara: W. Zimmerman, "JLaB", in *Desert Plants: Conversations with 23 American Musicians*, Vancouver, 1976; D. Sofer, "JLaB: Voice Is the Original Instrument", in *Synapse*, 1(6), 1977; K. Jensen, "JLaB", in *Contact*, 22, 1981.

Joan La Barbara comments:

Much of my recent work has involved the creation of "sound paintings", sonic impressions of places or visual experiences, which I render onto tape much as a painter renders on canvas. I have done both abstract sound paintings, such as *Twelvesong*, commissioned by Radio Bremen in 1977, and "translations" of specific paintings, such as *Klee alee*, commissioned by RIAS-Berlin, after Paul Klee's *Hauptstrasse und Nebenstrasse*, and *ROTHKO*, commissioned by New Music America for the 1986 Houston Festival, after the magnificent murals in the Rothko Chapel. I have also created sound paintings of places: *Urban Tropics*, commissioned by New Music America, is a portrait of Miami, for the 1988 Miami Festival; *Berline Traume*, commissioned for the Airworks radio series in 1983, represents memories of Berlin. More recently, I have been working on a portrait of Cologne (*Klangbild: Köln*).

My work generally involves my signature "extended vocal techniques".

* * *

Joan La Barbara's compositions are closely connected with her work as a performer. La Barbara trained as a classical soprano, but in the course of her studies came to feel that the field required a destructive conformity. She instead began to sing in jazz and avant-garde settings, performing at the beginning of the 1970s in the ensembles of Steve Reich and later Philip Glass. Seeking the freedom of repertoire and experimental range enjoyed by instrumentalists, La Barbara began investigating extended vocal techniques such as multiple stops, circular breathing (singing on the in- as well as the out-breath), clicks and vocal fry; as one reviewer put it, her music sounded like "the whole of the Mormon Tabernacle Choir on hallucinogens".

La Barbara began to compose for extended voice—in practice, her own—and it has remained the trademark of her music, even after she also began to score for traditional instruments. Since this main resource is grounded in her performance experience, she brings to it a feel for what is practical and practically experimental. When in *Twelve for Five in Eight* high vocal flutters give way to easy descending glissandos, the relaxation is for the performer both musical and physical.

"I rarely, if ever, compose music from a system or a musical theory," La Barbara has said. She begins from the discoveries of improvisation and examines them and her responses to them. While leading to musicianly discovery, this leaves La Barbara's work in constant danger of being diffuse and formally weak.

Her earliest pieces take the form of simple analytical studies. The *Voice Piece: One-Note Internal Resonance Investigation* takes a vocal pitch and modifies it by directing it to different resonating spaces, thickening it with multiphonics, and singing with open or closed mouth. *Circular Song* consists of a cycle of increasingly complex glissandos as a means of exploring the circular breathing technique. Other works of the 1970s are studies in the relation of singer to environment. *Space Testing* uses the range of vocal effects to determine and highlight the unique resonating frequency of the performance space—reminiscent of Alvin Lucier's live electronic exploration of room resonance, *I Am Sitting in a Room*. *Hear What I Feel* is an experiment in translating into vocal sound the tactile experience of the blindfolded performer after an hour of sensory deprivation.

The *Ides of March* series explores microtonal pitch relations and their associated beat frequencies. In one section, for instance, each of three vocalists sings in unison with a string player, then over several minutes makes a glissando up a minor second. As string and voice pitches separate, the beats accelerate; for example, from zero to 35 beats per second from A to A#. Alongside this concern with the analytical exploration of the inner life of sounds, typical of the avant-garde, La Barbara explores the interface of spontaneity by calling for a third player to elaborate the impulses and passions implied by but not audible in the tuning duo.

La Barbara has increasingly inclined towards programmatic inspiration: creation mythology in the *Prologue to The Book of Knowing . . . (and) of Overthrowing*, a filler paragraph describing *The Solar Wind*, the sights and sounds of *Vlissingen Harbor*, and images of Olympic athletes in her commission for the Los Angeles Olympiad, *Time(d) Trials and Unscheduled Events*. In her "sound paintings" she has translated images into music (*Klee alee* and *ROTHKO*), and composed portraits of Berlin (*Berline Traume*) Miami (*Urban Tropics*) and Cologne (*Klangbild: Köln*). In the latter, she attempts to convey in musical time an archaeology of the city. "I want to get this sense of layers", she writes, "so that it's not just a snapshot of today. I'm trying to really create a sense of the background of the city."

In some respects, La Barbara understands her improvisation as the enunciation of unconscious processes. "I let the sound come out as a clue to a place in memory where the information is stored", she writes. Neither predicting nor analyzing, she vocalizes what she is "touching", and thereby "I get to information which is locked". For her sonic self-portrait *In the Dreamtime*, "I'm thinking about the way we order things in dreams". In this respect, La Barbara becomes concerned with the imaginary, with a theatrical, arguably superficial depiction of inner life. "You know that wonderful movie, *Forbidden Planet*, monsters from the Id?" she asks when characterizing *October Music: Star Showers and Extraterrestrials*. "I'm trying to create monsters from the Id." This tendency is evinced most strongly, as musical inspiration and performance psychology, in *Shadowsong*, "the interplay between the conscious daily activities of the mind and the shadow or memories that sometimes invade our thoughts".

—David Revill

LACHENMANN, Helmut (Friedrich). German. Born in Stuttgart, 27 November 1935. Educated at Staatliche Hochschule für Musik, Stuttgart (piano with Jurgen Uhde, theory and counterpoint with Johann Nepomuk David), 1955–8; studied composition with Luigi Nono, Venice, 1958–60. Guest professor, Hochschule für Gestaltung, Ulm, 1961–73; first public appearance as composer, Venice Biennale, and Internalionale Ferienkurse für Neue Musik, Darmstadt, 1962; research, electronic studio, University of Ghent, 1965; theory teacher, Musikhochschule, Stuttgart, 1966–70; lecturer, Pädagogische Hochschule, Ludwigsburg, 1970–2; coordinator, composition studio, Internationale Ferienkurse, Darmstadt, 1972; professor of music, Padagogische Hochschule, Ludwigsburg, 1972–6; composition master class, University of Basle, 1972–3; professor of composition, Musikhochschule, Hannover, 1976–81; instructor, Ferienkurse, Darmstadt, 1978, 1982; instructor, Cursos Latinamericanos de musica contemporaranea, Brazil, 1978, and Dominican Republic, 1982; professor of composition, Musikhochschule, Stuttgart, since 1981; appointment to Hochschule der Kunste, Berlin (turns down offer to succeed Isang Yun as professor of composition); composition seminars in Toronto, 1982, Buenos Aires, Santiago, Chile, and Tokyo, all 1984, Villafranca, 1986, and Oslo and Paris, both 1989. Member, Akademie der Kunste, Berlin, Akademie der Schonen Kunste, Munich, and Freie Akademie dere Kunste, Mannheim. Recipient: cultural prize of music, City of Munich, 1965; composition prize, City of Stuttgart, 1968; Bach Prize, City of Hamburg, 1972. Mailing address: Hans-Thoma-Weg 20, D-7250 Leonberg 6 (Hofingen), Germany.

Publisher: Breitkopf & Hartel, Walkmuhlstrasse 52, Postfach 1707, D-6200 Wiesbaden 1, Germany.

Symphonies/orchestral:

Souvenir 1959; first performed Cologne, 1979.

Notturno (Musik für Julia) (cello, orchestra) 1966–8; first performed Brussels, 25 April 1969.

Air (percussion, orchestra) 1968–9; first performed Frankfurt, 1 September 1969. Recorded Harmonia Mundi DMR 1015.

Kontrakadenz 1970–1; first performed Stuttgart, 23 April 1971. Recorded Wergo Wer 60122.

Klangschatten—mein Saitenspiel (strings, 3 pianos) 1972; first performed Hamburg, 20 December 1972.

Fassade (orchestra, tape) 1973; first performed Bonn, 22 September 1973.

Schwankungen am Rand 1974–5; first performed Donaueschingen, 17 October 1975.

Accanto (clarinet, orchestra) 1975–6; first performed Saarbrücken, 30 May 1976. Recorded Wergo 60122.

Tanzsuite mit Deutschlandlied (string quarter, orchestra) 1979–80; first performed Donaueschingen, 18 October 1980. Recorded Harmonia Mundi DMR 1015.

Harmonika (tuba, orchestra) 1981–3; first performed Saarbrücken, 15 May 1983.

Ausklang (piano, orchestra) 1984–5; first performed Cologne, 18 April 1986.

Staub 1985–7; first performed Saarbrücken, 19 December 1987.

Tableau 1988–9; first performed Hamburg, 4 June 1989.

Chamber/instrumental:

Füf Variationen über ein Thema von Franz Schubert (piano) 1956; first performed Stuttgart, 1957. Recorded Harmonia Mundi DMR 2011; Col Legno 429356 2.

Rondo (2 pianos) 1957; first performed Stuttgart, 12 March 1958.

Fünf Strophen (9 instruments) 1961; first performed Venice, 13 April 1962.
Echo Andanate (piano) 1962; first performed Darmstadt, 18 July 1962. Recorded Col Legno 429356 2.
Wiegenmusik (piano) 1963; first performed Darmstadt, 1 April 1964.
Introversion I (6 instruments) 1964; first performed Darmstadt, 19 July 1964.
Introversion II (6 instruments) 1965; first performed Munich, 22 February 1965.
Streichtrio (violin, viola, cello) 1965; first performed Ghent, 29 March 1966.
Interieur (percussion) 1966; first performed Santa Fe, New Mexico, 14 August 1967.
Trio Fluido (clarinet, viola, percussion) 1966; first performed Munich, 5 March 1968.
temA (flute, mezzo-soprano, cello) 1968; first performed Stuttgart, 19 February 1969.
Pression (cello) 1969; first performed Como, 30 September 1970.
Guero (piano) 1970; first performed Hamburg, 1 December 1970. Recoded Col Legno 429356 2.
Dal Niente (Interieur III) (clarinet) 1970; first performed Nuremberg, 4 June 1970. Recorded Aktive Musik.
Gran Torso (string quarter) 1971; first performed Bremen, 6 May 1972. Recorded Col Legno 0647277.
Salut für Caudwell (2 guitars) 1977; first performed Baden-Baden, 3 December 1977. Recorded Col Legno 0647277.
Ein Kinderspiel (piano) 1980; first performed Toronto, 17 February 1982.
Mouvement (—vor der Erstarrung) 1982–4; first performed Paris, 12 November 1984. Recorded Harmonia Mundi HM 713D.
Toccatina (violin) 1986; first performed Stuttgart, 20 May 1988.
Allegro sostenuto (B♭ clarinet/bass clarinet, cello, piano) 1986–8; first performed Cologne, 3 December 1989.
"Reigen seliger Geister" (string quartet no 2) 1989; first performed Geneva, 28 September 1989.

Vocal/choral:

Consolation I (12 singers, 4 percussionists; Toller) 1967; first performed Bremen, 3 May 1968. Recorded Wergo Wer 60122.
Les Consolations (16 singers, orchestra; Andersen, Toller, Gebet) 1967–8, 1977–8; first performed Darmstadt, 10 August 1978.
Consolation II (16 singers; Gebet) 1968; first performed Basle, 15 June 1969.

Other:

Szenario (electronic tape) 1965; first performed Belgium, 20 June 1965.

PUBLICATIONS

By Lachenmann: "Gitteerstabe am Himmel der Freiheit", in *Melos*, 27 (3), 1960; *The Score*, 27, 1960; "Klangtypen der Neuen Misik", in *Zeitschurift für Musiktheorie*, 1 (1), 1970; "Zur Analyse neurer Misik", in *Die Weltprobelmatik in der Musikdidaktik*, edited by Werner Krutzfeld, Dusseldorf, 1973; "Selbstportrait 1975", in *Programmheft der Donaueschinger Musiktage*, Donaueschingen, 1975; "Uber das Komponiern", in *MusikTexte*, October 1986; "Bremer Resolution. Zur Situation der Neuen Musik in den Horfunkprogrammen der ARD", in *MusikTexte*, February 1987; "Zur Situation der Musik in Deutschland nach 'Darmstadt'", in *Musique pure dans un siècle sale: New Music Darmstadt, 1950–60*, edited by Friedrich Hommel and Wilhelm Schluter, Darmstadt, 1988.

On Lachenmann: Herbert Henck, "Literatur zur HL", in *Ansatze zur Musik der Gegenwart*, edited by Neuland, Cologne, 1980; Clytus Gottwald, "HL", in *The New Grove Dictionary of Music and Musicians*, London, 1980; Klaus-Michel Hinz, "Zur Tradition der Jungen Avantgarde", in *Neue Zeitschrift für Musik*, September/October 1980; Marc Vignal, "L", in *Larousse de la musique*, Paris, 1982; Martin Kaltenecker, "Le Rêve instrumental: à propos de HL", in *Entretemps*, April 1986; special issue of *Musik-Konzepte*, October 1988.

Helmut Lachenmann comments:

If the act of composing is meant to go beyond the tautological use of pre-existing expressive forms and—as a creative act—to recall that human potential which grants man the dignity of a cognisant being, able to act on the basis of this cognition, then composition is by no means a "putting together" but rather a "taking apart" and more: a confrontation with the interconnections and necessities of the musical substance. Whichever way this process is effectuated, be it rationally or intuitively, it alone can make good Schoenberg's unsurpassable observation: the artist's goal—to express himself.

Since *temA* and *Air* my music has been concerned with rigidly constructed denial, with the exclusion of what appears to me as listening expectations preformed by society. The aesthetic offer, the intensity—if one wants—the beauty, of music is for me inseparably bound to the efforts with which the composer opposes such pre-determinations in his materials; this is a confrontation with the social reality implicit therein, which he depicts, thereby expressing himself.

* * *

Helmut Lachenmann himself has set out the theory and practice of his idiosyncratic aesthetic programme in a forthright and eloquent manner elsewhere. His is a profoundly humanistic attitude to the responsibility of the composer, ultimately grounded in Marxist dialectics like that of his teacher Luigi Nono (whose interpretation of their aesthetic implications was very different). On the other hand, his insistence upon *denial* of received musical norms rather than *affirmation* of an alternative seems to sit uneasily with a revolutionary perspective. Moreover, Lachenmann's "received norms", being those of the European classical tradition , may well not correspond to those of his audience: a work such as *Gran Torso* may exist for its composer in a dialogue with the history and assumptions of the string quarter medium, but listeners might be more struck by its apparent relationship to the more exploratory regions of free improvisation. This of course is not necessarily a criticism of the music in itself: Lachenmann's painstakingly-evolved mode of expression remains but a starting point for the listener to generate his/her own experience. The point is that the intellectual rigour of Lachenmann's methods should not be interpreted as implying a "command" that the music be apprehended in a certain way.

Even so, Lachenmann's music usually presents a forbidding face to the world, thanks to his avoidance of any kind of formal continuity or cross-referencing and his endless inventiveness in producing any sound from an instrument except that which it was intended to produce (another aspect of denying expectations and exposing, rather than concealing, the effort and means of sound production). Much of *Gran Torso*, for example, hovers on the brink of audibility, as the bows are applied to virtually every part of the instruments; in *Kingerspiel* for piano the "musical material", largely consisting of dense and loud chords at the top end of the keyboard, serves only to draw attention to the action of the instrument as hammers clunk noisily against strings; in *Salut für Caudwell* the only "harmony" produced by the two guitars (and then only fleetingly) is that of the open strings. Even the huge *Ausklang* for piano and orchestra, lasting almost an hour, resolutely refuses to link its disjointed and tenuous gestures into any recognisable pattern other than a constant annihilation of "development". The pianist spends as much time scraping the (amplified) keyboard as if it were a guiro as he/she does in "normal" playing. The idea of a "piano concerto" is exhaustively negated. But this is of course not "enough" to constitute a significant musical experience. What is ultimately impressive is that Lachenmann, despite or because of his tortuous rationale, has developed a memorable compositional idiom whose expressive impact can often be powerful. The impression of individuality, of a strong continuity of *personality* in Lachenmann's music, is everpresent. What appears in theory to be denial is indeed transformed in practice into affirmation.

—Richard Barrett

LADERMAN, Ezra. American. Born in Brooklyn, New York, 29 June 1924. Educated at High School of Music and Art, New York City; composition study under Stefan Wolpe, from 1946; Brooklyn College, City University of New York (composition under Miriam Gideon), 1946–9, B.A.; Columbia University, New York City (composition under Otto Luening and Douglas Moore, musicology under Paul Henry Lang), 1949–2, M.A. Served in U.S. Army, 1942–5. Married to Aimée Davis; 3 children. Freelance composer of film and broadcast music, 1950s; teacher of music, Sarah Lawrence College, Bronxville, New York, 1960–1, 1965–6; residency, Bennington Composers Conference, Vermont, 1967, 1968; composer in residence and professor of music, State University of New York, Binghamton, 1971–82; chair, Composer-Librettist programme, 1972, and director of music section, 1979–82, National Endowment for the Arts; president, National Music Council, since 1982; composer in residence, American Academy in Rome, 1982–3. Recipient: Guggenheim Fellowships, 1955, 1958, 1964; Prix de Rome, 1963; Academy Award (for score to *The Eleanor Roosevelt Story*), 1966. Mailing address: c/o National Music Council, 45 West 34th Street, Suite 1010, New York, New York 10001, U.S.A.

Publishers: Oxford University Press; G. Schirmer.

Symphonies/orchestral:

Piano Concerto 1939; first performed New York City, June 1939.
Leipzig Symphony 1945; first performed Wiesbaden, May 1945.
Concerto for Bassoon and Strings 1948.
Concerto for Violin and Chamber Orchestra: Chai ivri 1951, revised 1960; broadcast CBS Television, 10 November 1963.
Organization 1952.
Sinfonia 1956; first performed New York City, 1956.
Piano Concerto 1957.
Identity 1959.
Stanzas (21 solo instruments) 1959.
Symphony No 1 1964; first performed Rome, 2 July 1964.
Concerto for Orchestra: Satire 1968; first performed Minneapolis, Minnesota, 24 October 1968.
Flute Concerto: Celestial Bodies (flute, strings) 1968; first performed Milwaukee, Wisconsin, 1968.
Priorities (jazz band, rock band, string quartet) 1969; first performed Binghamton, New York, 1969.
Symphony No 2: Luther 1969.
Symphony No 3: Jerusalem 1973; first performed Jerusalem, 7 November 1976.
Concerto for Viola and Chamber Orchestra 1977; first performed St Paul, Minnesota, 13 April 1978.
Violin Concerto 1978; first performed Philadelphia, 11 December 1980.
Piano Concerto No 1 1978; first performed Washington, D.C., 12 March 1979.
Symphony No 4 1980; first performed Los Angeles, 22 October 1981.
Summer Solstice 1980; first performed Philadelphia, 5 August 1980.
Concerto for String Quartet and Orchestra 1981; first performed Pittsburgh, 6 February 1981.
Symphony No 5: Isaiah (soprano, orchestra) 1982; first performed Washington, D.C., 15 March 1983.
Concerto for Flute, Bassoon and Orchestra 1982; first performed Philadelphia, 27 January 1983.
Sonore 1983; first performed Denver, 10 November 1983.
Symphony No 6 1983; first performed Houston, Texas, 28 September 1985.
Symphony No 7 1984.
Cello Concerto 1984–5.

Chamber/instrumental:

Prelude in the Form of a Passacaglia (piano) 1947–8.
Sonata (cello, piano) 1948.
Prelude (organ) 1950.
Sonata (flute, piano) 1951.
Piano Quintet 1951.
Sonata No 1 (piano) 1952.
String Quartet 1953.
Themes and Variations (violin, piano) 1954.
Woodwind Quintet 1954.
Duo (violin, cello) 1955.
Music for Winds, Strings and Harpsichord 1955.
Sonata No 2 (piano) 1955.
Piano Trio 1955, revised 1959.
Duet (flute, dancer) 1956.
Serenade (clarinet) 1956.
Three Pieces (clarinet, cello, piano) 1956.
Three Pieces (piano) 1956.
Sonata (violin, piano) 1956.
Dance Quartet (flute, clarinet, cello, dancer) 1957.
Sonata (flute, piano) 1957.
Partita (cello) 1957.
Theme, Variations and Finale (wind quartet, string quartet) 1957.
Wind Octet 1957.

Sonata (clarinet, piano) 1958.
Portraits (violin) 1959.
Sextet (wind quintet, double bass) 1959.
String Quartet No 1 1959.
Oboe Quartet 1960.
String Quartet No 2 1962.
Duo No 2 (violin, cello) 1963.
String Quartet No 3 1966.
A Single Volice (oboe, string quartet) 1967.
Double Helix (flute, oboe, string quartet) 1968.
Nonette (brass, winds, piano, strings) 1968.
Duo (violin, piano) 1970.
Five Trios and Fantasy (woodwind quintet) 1972.
Partita: Meditation on Isaiah) (cello) 1972.
Elegy (viola) 1973.
Momenti (piano) 1974.
String Quartet No 4 1974.
Echoes in Anticipation (concerto for oboe and septet) 1975.
Twenty-Five Preludes in Different Forms (organ) 1975.
Others Voices (viola, tape) 1976.
String Quartet No 5 1976.
Cadence (2 flutes, 9 strings) 1978.
String Quartet No 6 1980.
Partita (violin) 1982.
String Quartet No 7 1983.
Duo (cello, piano) 1984.
String Quartet No 8 1985–6.

Vocal/choral:

Esther (speaker, oboe, strings) 1960.
Song of Songs (soprano, piano; biblical) 1960.
Solos and Chorale (SATB soloists) 1960.
The Eagle Stirred (soloists, mixed chorus, orchestra; Roskam) 1961.
Songs for Eve (soprano, piano; MacLeish) 1966.
Magic Prison (after film score; 2 narrators, orchestra; Dickinson, Higginson) 1967; first performed New York City, 12 June 1967.
The Trials of Galileo (soloists, mixed chorus, orchestra; Darion) 1967.
Songs from Michelangelo (baritone, piano) 1968.
From the Psalms (soprano, piano) 1970.
Thrive upon the Rock (mixed chorus, piano; Rosten) 1973.
A Handful of Souls (soloists, mixed chorus, organ; Darion) 1975.
Columbus (bass baritone, orchestra; Kazantzakis) 1975.
Worship (soprano, tenor, piano; Rosten) 1976.
Song of Songs (soprano, flute, clarinet, violin, cello, piano) 1977.
A Mass for Cain (soloists, mixed chorus, orchestra; Darion) 1983.

Opera/dramatic:

Jacob and the Indians (Kinoy, after Benet) 1954; first performed Woodstock, New York, 24 July 1957.
Goodbye to the Clowns (Kinoy) 1956.
The Hunting of the Snark (after Lewis Carroll) 1958; concert version first performed New York City, 25 March 1961; stage version first performed New York City, 13 April 1978.
Sarah (Roskam) 1959; broadcast CBS Television, 29 November 1959.
Dominique (musical comedy; Darion, after Kinoy) 1962.
Air Raid (MacLeish) 1965.
Shadows Among Us (Rosten) 1967.
And David Wept (operatic cantata; Darion) 1970; broadcast CBS Television, 11 April 1971; stage version first performed New York City, 31 May 1980.
The Questions of Abraham (operatic cantata; Darion) 1973; broadcast CBS Television, 30 September 1973.
Galileo Galilei (Darion; after *The Trials of Galileo*) 1978; first performed Binghamton, New York, 3 February 1979.

Other:

Duet (dancer, flute) 1956.
Dance Quartet (dancer, flute, clarinet, cello) 1957.
Machinal (incidental music) 1960; first performed New York city, 7 April 1960.
Esther (ballet; scored for speaker, oboe, strings) 1960.
Song of Songs (ballet; scored for soprano, piano) 1960.
Solos and Chorale (ballet; scored for SATB soloists) 1960.

Film scores: *The Charter*, 1958; *The Invisible Atom*, 1958; *The Question Tree*, 1962; *Odyssey*, 1964; *The Eleanor Roosevelt Story*, 1965; *The Black Fox*, 1965; *Magic Prison*, 1966; *The Meaning of Modern Art*, 1967; *Confrontation*, 1968; *Image of Love*, 1968; *The Bible as Literature*, 1972; *Burden of Mystery*, 1972.

Television music: *Herschel*, 1959; *The Invisible City*, 1961; *The Voice of the Desert*, 1962; *Eltanin*, 1962; *Grand Canyon*, 1964; *The Forgotten Peninsula*, 1967; *Our Endangered Wildlife*, 1967; *California the Most*, 1968; *Before Cortez*, 1970; *In the Fall of 1844*, 1971; *Cave People of the Philippines*, 1972; *Lamp unto My Feet*, 1978.

PUBLICATIONS

On Laderman: S. Fleming, "Musician of the Month: EL", *High Fidelity / Musical America*, 30 (3), 1980.

* * *

It is difficult to see why Ezra Laderman has been so adhesively labelled a conservative. It may be that he shares the fate of Archibald MacLeish (a poet Laderman has set to great effect), who despite impeccable leftist credentials was consigned to the side of reaction as soon as he became Librarian of Congress in Washington. Laderman's career as an administrator, first at the National Endowment for the Arts, more recently at the National Music Council, has been highly influential, but it has not dimmed (and has barely slowed) his compositional output, which remains bold, distinctive and often startlingly radical.

Perhaps the most powerful symbol of Laderman's work as a whole is the single-movement *String Quartet No 7*, written in 1983. Here Laderman develops six quite different musical ideas in such a way as to suggest classical developmental procedures and, simultaneously, their disruption. Only at the very end does a recognizable melody emerge, and it has the tragic cadence of Laderman's finest symphonic writing inspired by the Judaeo-Christian tradition.

The device had been used before, most notably in the Fourth String Quartet. Here, Laderman assigned specific dramatic characteristics to each of the four players, allowed them to interact in paired relationships, culminating in a brief climax in which differences are subordinated to a common humanity. It is possible to read the contrary and dialectical relationships of the individual voices—neo-classical and expressionistic, "quixotic", "satiric", "compassionate" and "destructive"—as qualities embodied in Laderman's own musical personality.

Military service in Germany at the end of World War II allowed him to see the contradictions of the European tradition and its nemesis at first hand. Laderman's *Leipzig Symphony* was performed in Occupied Germany in 1945. As with his piano concertos and string quartets, he did not begin to number his symphonies until somewhat later; whether this implies dissatisfaction or not is unclear, for the *Leipzig Symphony* is a superb piece of writing, satiric, compassionate, destructive of slavish convention and utterly quixotic in its determination to preserve tonality in the mid-stream of atonal and chance-ridden modernity. Thoughout his career, and most notably in the fine mid-period symphonies, the "Luther" and the "Jerusalem", he has shown an awareness of the philosophical underpinnings of twelve-tone technique which has allowed him to use it freely and very convincingly without ever losing touch with its dialectical tonal foil. The tension between the two, as the third and fifth symphonies suggest, is historical as much as musical. Something of the same opposition underlies his interest in Galileo Galilei's heroic defence of Copernican over Ptolemaic astronomy.

In the Fifth String Quartet Laderman gives colour elements and bowing devices the status of pitch in a tone row; the piece also manipulates a trio of generic devices—sonata, dance, theme-with-variations—in a way that further breaks down the distinction between tonal and non-tonal music. If there is a slightly unadventurous approach to instrumental colour and form in some of Laderman's instrumental music, it is more than made up for with works such as these.

Formal experiment is a basic instinct with him, as is an unembarrassed programmatic intent. The 1968 *Double Helix*, which has some of the same qualities of miniature concertante as the later *Echoes in Anticipation*, sets oboe and flute in spiralling lines over a string quartet in an effort to reduplicate the molecular form of DNA. The intention is not merely pictorial (or micro-pictorial!) but technical too, for the spin of melodic atoms away from their tonal "bonding" is part of the drama of the piece, as it is in the First (by number, third by actual count) Piano Concerto. In that work Laderman sets a warmly tonal melody in counterpoint to a strictly twelve-tone theme and does so without obvious strain. The constant symbolic signification is the ability to travel some distance from the fundamental values of Western or Hebraic tradition, but to stay bound in the same gravitational orbit by the pull of common humanity (of which DNA is the basic stuff); there is a certain ironic correctness in the fact that Laderman's most publicly successful work was the Oscar-winning score to *The Eleanor Roosevelt Story*!

The imagination and the conventions by which it is channelled are to Laderman a "magic prison" (the title of his superb narration for orchestra based on the lives of the poet Emily Dickinson and her confidant Higginson) in which incarceration is a form of higher liberty.

—Russell Kane

LANDOWSKI, Marcel (François Paul). French. Born in Pont L'Abbé, Finistère, 18 February 1915. Studied under Henri-Paul Busser, Philippe Gaubert and Charles Munch. Married the pianist Jacqueline Potier, 1 July 1941; 3 children. Director, Conservatoire de Boulogne sur Seine, 1959–61; director of music, Comédie-Française, 1961–5; inspector-general, l'Enseignement Musical, Ministry of Cultural Affairs, 1964; director of music, lyrical arts and dance, Ministry of Cultural Affairs, 1970–5; director of cultural affairs, City of Paris, 1977; vice-president, Théâtre Musical de Paris-Châtelet, since 1979; permanent secretary, Académie des Beaux-Arts, Institut de France, from 1986. Recipient: Prix Maurice Ravel, SACEM, 1973; elected member, Institut de France, Académie des Beaux Arts, 1975; doctor honoris causa, Federal University of Brazil, Rio de Janeiro, 1980; Commandeur de la Légion d'Honneur, France, 1987. Mailing address: Académie des Beaux Arts, 23 quai de Conti, Paris 75006, France.

Publishers: Editions Salabert; Editions Choudens, 38 rue Jean Mermoz, Paris 75008, France.

Symphonies/orchestral:

Clairs-obscurs (suite for orchestra) 1938; first performed Paris, 1938.
Piano Concerto No 1 1941; first performed Paris, 1 March 1942.
Concerto for Cello and Orchestra 1944–5; first performed Paris, 1946.
Edina (symphonic poem for large orchestra) 1946.
Le Petit Poucet (symphonic suite) 1947; first performed Paris, 1947.
Symphony No 1: Jean de la peur 1948; first performed Paris, 1949. Recorded Philips 6505 060; Erato MusiFrance 245 018 2.
Concerto for Ondes Martenot, Strings and Percussion (also arranged for piano, and 2 percussion) 1954. Recorded Erato CDE 3354.
Concerto for Bassoon and Orchestra 1957.
Mouvement (strings) 1960.
L'Orage (symphonic poem) 1961.
Concerto for Piano and Orchestra No 2 1963; first performed Paris, 28 February 1964. Recorded Erato STV 70560.
Symphony No 3: Des Espaces 1964–5. Recorded Philips 6505 060; Erato MusiFrance 245 018 2.
Symphony No 2 1965; first performed Strasbourg, 24 June 1965. Recorded Erato STV 70560.
Ballet des jeux du monde (large orchestra) 1965.
Concerto for Flute and Strings 1967.
"Au bout de chagrin, une fenêtre ouverte" (concerto for trumpet, orchestra, tape) 1976; first performed Paris, 24 June 1977.
Le Fantôme de l'Opéra (symphonic suite; from the ballet) 1979. Recorded Erato STU 71490.
Improvisation (trombone, orchestra) 1983; first performed Toulon, May 1983.
Pour les orchestrades 1985; first performed St Liberal, 31 August 1985.
Symphony No 4 1988; first performed Paris, 15 October 1988. Recorded Erato MusiFrance 245 018 2.
Quatre Préludes pour L'Opéra des Bastilles 1989. Recorded PV 789121.

Chamber/instrumental:

Sonatina (piano) 1940; first performed Paris, 10 May 1941.
Concerto for Ondes Martenot (transcribed for piano, 2 percussion) 1954. Recorded CCV 1022.
Quatre Préludes (percussion, piano) 1963.

Etude de sonorité (violin, piano) 1974; first performed Paris, 10 June 1974.
Cahier pour quatres jours (trumpet, organ) 1977; first performed Munich, February 1978. Recorded Erato STU 71082.
Souvenir d'un jardin d'enfance (oboe, piano) 1977; first performed Paris, 1 June 1977.
Improvisation (trombone, piano) 1983.
Sonate brève (cello) 1985.
Blanc et feu (horn, 2 trumpets, trombone, tuba) 1986.
Petite Chanson de l'amitié (4 cellos) 1987; first performed Paris, 31 March 1987.

Vocal/choral:

Rythmes du monde (oratorio) 1941.
Cantata: Jesus, là es-tu (contralto, female chorus, piano or strings) 1948. Recorded Edici 004 101; CCV 1022.
Chants d'innocence (4 unaccompanied choruses, equal voices) 1952.
Les Notes de nuit (reciter, chamber orchestra) 1961. Recorded Auvidis AV 4278.
Cantata: "Aux Mendiants du ciel" (soprano, small orchestra) 1966.
Messe de l'aurore (soloists, mixed chorus, orchestra; Emmanuel) 1977; first performed Paris, 14 November 1977.
Un Enfant appelle (soprano, cello, orchestra; Noël) 1978; first performed Washington, D.C., 9 January 1979. Recorded Erato STU 71515.
Le Pont de l'espérance (soloists, mixed chorus, orchestra; Lamartine) 1980; first performed Vaison-la-Romaine, 8 August 1980.
La Prison (soprano, cello, flute, trumpet, percussion, piano, optional string orchestra) 1981; first performed Aix-en-Provence, 18 July 1983. Recorded Erato 71515.
Chant de paix "Ecoute ma voix . . . " (soprano, child's voice, baritone, children's chorus or mixed chorus, orchestra or organ; Carol Woytyla/Pope Jean Paul II, translated Emmanuel) 1985; first performed Bercy, 4 July 1985. Recorded Auvidis AV 4832.
Les Deux Soeurs (vocal quartet; Noël) 1986; first performed Rome, 17 June 1986.
La Symphonie de Montsegur (soprano, baritone, orchestra) 1987; first performed Paris, 18 October 1987.

Opera:

Le Fou 1948–55. Recorded Erato STU 71249.
Le Ventriloque 1955–6. Recorded Pathe Marconi DTX 346.
L'Opéra de poussière 1958–62; first performed Avignon, 25 October 1962.
Les Adieux 1959; first performed Paris, 8 October 1960. Recorded Guilde Française du Disque.
La Sorcière du placard aux balais / The Witch of the Broom Cupboard (mini-opera for children after Gripari; translated Drake) 1983; first performed Sevres, 2 May 1983. Recorded Auvidis AV 4278; Salabert SC010.
Montsegur (Caillet, Sainderichin, ML) 1985; first performed Toulouse, 1 February 1985. Recorded Cybelia CY 850/851.
La Vieille Maison (child, soprano, tenor, baritone, 3 male roles, children's choir, orchestra) 1987; first performed Nantes, 23 February 1988. Recorded Erato ECD 75535.

Other:

Le Rire de Nils Halerius (ballet; large orchestra) 1944–8; first performed Mulhouse, 19 January 1951.
Le Fantôme de l'Opéra (ballet after Leroux; orchestra) 1979; first performed Paris, 22 February 1980.
Les Hauts de hurlement / Wuthering Heights (ballet after E. Brontë; orchestra) 1982; first performed London, 28 December 1982. Recorded Pathe Marconi C 0697340.

PUBLICATIONS

By Landowski: *Batailles pour la musique*, Paris, 1979; *La Musique n'adoucit pas les moeurs*, Belfond, 1990.

On Landowski: "La Musician de l'espérance", in *La Revue Musicale*, 372–4; *ML*, in "Musiciens de tous les temps" series, Paris.

* * *

Marcel Landowski was born into an artistic and musical family; his father was a sculptor of some reputation and his paternal grandmother a daughter of the composer Henri Vieuxtemps. The Landowskis were used to personal upheaval. His grandfather was Polish (hence the family name) and had escaped to France from a Czarist prison. When the Germans, armed with the Schlieffen Plan, swept through Belgium and northern France in Autumn 1914, the family uprooted and resettled at the southwestern tip of Brittany, where Marcel was born.

Native environment can explain anything and nothing. There is nothing in Landowski's music of the passionate Bretonism that informed much of Jean Langlais's output, but there is an independent, autodidactic quality to even his most mature work that hints at a youth spent out of earshot of the buzz of new fashion and theory. He initially rebelled against the disciplines of the conservatory but was encouraged by Noël Gallon, younger of the influential brothers who taught solfege and counterpoint at France's premier school, and developed rapidly, particularly in the direction of vocal and dramatic music, though his early symphonic and concertante writing is extremely impressive.

Much of his adult life has been divided between composition and administration. Landowski deserves enormous credit for his efforts at restructuring post-war French music and putting it on a footing that could rival German and American models. He is currently permanent secretary of the Académie des Beaux Arts, but devotes much of his time again to composition; his latest work is a remarkable "late" flowering of qualities evident from the outset.

An eclectic in the strictest sense of the word, Landowski has drawn freely from most of the significant developments of 20th-century music, mixing atonal elements with a dramatic polytonality, incorporating electronic and electro-acoustic elements where he deems them valid, never falling into the pit of dogmatism. His primary virtue is accessibility, and he has laid particular emphasis on making his work approachable for young listeners.

Landowski's music, from the first symphony *Jean de la peur* to the *Chant de paix* of 1985, is always broadly spiritual in intent and expresses a belief in the power of love—*caritas* and *agape*—in the face of the totalising structures of science, politics and theory. The *Chant de paix*, based on texts by the present Pope, is a remarkable affirmation, not just of peace in a concrete and particular sense, but of music as the one realm that escapes absolutely the snares of reason (for which, read "rationality"). Landowski has been much drawn to mystery, and his experiments in electro-acoustic effects have largely been directed to broadening the timbral and thematic possibilities of conventional scoring; this is most clearly seen in his ballet *Wuthering Heights*, but also in the remarkable *Concerto for Ondes Martenot*, a work that raises the instrument from merely colouristic duties and places it at the head of a procession of technological innovations—synthesizers, tone generators and so on—which have revolutionised the tonality of modern music.

Not primarily known as a composer of chamber and instrumental works (though there are a fine piano sonatina and striking pieces for trumpet and organ, and trombone and piano), Landowski is a master of dramatic orchestration with a powerful emotional undertow. His range of interests is probably best sampled in *Le Rire de Nils Halerius*, a work which includes elements (one act each) of opera, ballet and oratorio. Less well-known in Britain and the United States than in his native country, he is without question one of the masters of modern French music.

—Russell Kane

LANGLAIS, Jean(-François-Hyacinthe). French. Born at La Fontenelle, Illeet-Vilaine, Brittany, 15 February 1907. Blind from birth. Educated at the National Institute for the Young Blind, Paris (under André Marchal), 1917–30; Conservatoire National Supérieur de Musique, Paris (organ classes under Marcel Dupré, 1st prize, 1930; composition classes with Paul Dukas, 2nd prize, 1935). Married (1) Jeanne Sartre in 1931; 1 son and 1 daughter; (2) Marie Louise Jaquet in 1979; 1 daughter. Professor, National Institute for the Young Blind, Paris, 1930–68; professor of organ and composition, Schola Cantorum, Paris, 1961–76. Organist at Notre-Dame de la Croix and at Saint-Pierre de Montrouge, 1935–45, and Sainte-Clotilde Basilica, Paris, 1945–77. International recital organist: United States debut, 1952; final professional recital, Royal Festival Hall, London, 1988. Recipient: Grand Prix du Disque, 1956; Prix Madam René Coty, 1956; Bronze Medal of the City of Paris; Prix Rossini; Prix d'Auberville; Commandeur des Arts et Lettres; Officier de la Légion d'Honneur, et des Palmes Académiques; Chevalier de l'Ordre de Saint-Grégoire-le-Grand; Doctor Honoris Causa: Texas Christian University, Forth Worth, and Duquesne University, Pittsburgh, 1976, and Catholic University, Washington, D.C., 1981; Fellow of the Royal College of Organists. **Died 8 May 1991.**

Publishers: Leduc, Paris; F. Bock-Tarzana, California; Novello; Combre, Paris; Universal Editions; Bornemann.

Symphonies/orchestral:

Cloches 1935.
Essai sur L'évangile de Noël 1935; first performed Lyon, February 1936.
Hymne d'action des grâces 1935; first performed Lyon, February 1936.
Piece in Free Form (orchestra and organ, or string quartet) 1935; first performed Paris, 28 January 1936.
Suite concertante (cello, orchestra; also piano—4 hands) 1936.
Symphonie concertante (piano, orchestra; arrangement of 2 movements of *Suite Concertante*) 1936.
Pièce symphonique (variant of parts of *Quintette*, *Piece in Free Form*, *Theme, Variation and Final*, *Deuxième Concerto*) 1937.
Theme, Variation and Final 1937; revised as *Theme and Variations for Organ, Brass and Strings*; first performed Paris, June 1938; revised version first performed New York, 21 April 1978.
Le Diable qui n'est à personne (orchestra, ondes martenot) 1946; first performed Paris, 14 February 1947.
Légende de St Julien l'hospitalier 1947; first performed Paris, 8 March 1948.
Premier Concerto (organ/harpsichord, orchestra) 1949.
Le Soleil se lève sur Assise 1950; first performed Paris, 30 December 1950.
Deuxième Concerto (organ, orchestra) 1961; first performed Cleveland Heights, Ohio, 11 May 1962. Recorded Proprius PROP 7784.
Troisième Concerto: Réaction 1971; first performed Potsdam, New York, 2 March 1978. Recorded ABC ABCL 8103.
Réminiscences 1980; first performed Quimper, 6 August 1980.

Works for organ:

Prélude et fugue 1927; first performed Paris, July 1927.
Adoration des bergers (only surviving item of *Six Preludes*) 1929; first performed Paris, 1930. Recorded Musical Heritage Society 7275.
Trois Poèmes évangéliques 1932; first performed Paris, 29 May 1932. Recorded Musical Heritage Society; Delos DEL 25443.
Trois Paraphrases grégoriennes 1933–4; first performed Paris, 28 June 1934. Recorded Musical Heritage Society; Erato LDE 3045/3024; Solstice SOL 1; Coronata COR 001; many others.
Vingt-Quartre Pièces pour orgue ou harmonium 1933–9; first performed Paris, 1939. Recorded Musical Heritage Society; Solstice SOL 1; Erato LDE 3045, parts.
Légende de Saint Nicolas (later incorporated in *Folkloric Suite*) 1937.
Première Symphonie 1941–2; first performed Paris, June 1943. Recorded Alpha ALA 521.
Neuf Pièces 1942–3; first performed Paris, 1944. Recorded Musical Heritage Society; parts on SOL 1; Alpha ALA 548; Motette 1003; Decca SDD-R404.
Deux Offertoires pour tous les temps 1943; first performed Paris, 24 June 1943. Recorded Musical Heritage Society; Erato CDE 3049.
Fête (first American commission) 1946; published in *Modern Anthology*, 1949. Recorded Bridge 2241; Unicorn Kanchana DKP 9007.
Suite brève 1947; first performed Paris, 1947. Recorded Musical Heritage Society; Phillips 65 28 001; Priory PR 116/148; Centaur CRC 2042.
Suite médiévale en forme de messe basse 1947; first performed Paris, 1948. Recorded Musical Heritage Society; Erato LDE 3024; Priory PR 173; Cameo C 4020.
Suite française 1948; first performed Radio-Lorraine, 8 May 1949. Recorded Musical Heritage Society.
Incantation pour un jour saint 1949; first performed Paris, 1950. Recorded Musical Heritage Society; Erato LDE 3049; Deutsche Grammophon DGM 19091.
Hommage à Frescobaldi 1951; first performed Paris, 1952. Recorded CBS 51236.
Suite folklorique 1952; first performed United States, 1954. Recorded Musical Heritage Society.
Dominica in Palmis 1954; first performed Paris, 1955. Recorded Musical Heritage Society.

Huit Pièces modales 1956; first performed Paris, 1956. Recorded Connaisseur Epsilon EPS 4514; Citadel 116.001.
Organ Book 1956. Recorded Musical Heritage Society.
Triptyque 1956–7; first performed London or Leeds, February 1958. Recorded Musical Heritage Society; Vista VPS 1029.
Office pour la Sainte Famille 1957; first performed Paris, 1958.
Three Characteristic Pieces (written as alternative to *Tryptyque* for Novello's Organ Music Club) 1957. Recorded Musical Heritage Society; Centaur 2042.
Office de la fête de la Sainte Trinité 1958; first performed Paris, 1959.
Miniature 1958; first performed New York, 30 December 1958. Recorded Mirrosonic CS 7145.
Troisième Symphonie 1959, revised 1979; first performed Paris, 31 May 1982. Recorded Festivo 097.
American Suite (in 7 movements) 1959–60; no record of first complete performance, New York, 1970. Recorded Austin CM 7245, parts.
Rhapsodie savoyarde 1960; first performed Megève, August 1960.
Trois Méditations sur la Sainte Trinité 1962; first performed Paris, 1962. Recorded Musical Heritage Society.
Douze Petites Pièces (organ or harmonium) 1962. Recorded Musical Heritage Society.
Essai (Trial) (for examination of advanced organ students) 1962; first performed Paris, May 1962.
Homage to J. Ph. Rameau 1962–4; first performed New York, 20 July 1965. Recorded Motette M 11170.
Prelude on Coronation 1963; first performed Paris, 1963.
Poem of Life 1965; first performed Paris 1965. Recorded Musical Heritage Society.
Poem of Peace 1965; first performed Washington, D.C., 16 January 1967. Recorded Musical Heritage Society; Avant Quart 3001.
Poem of Happiness 1966; first performed Paris, 17 May 1969. Recorded Musical Heritage Society; Avant Quart 3001.
Sonate en trio 1967; first performed Paris, May 1968.
Adoration 1968; first performed Mulhouse, March 1969. Recorded Weilden WS 109.
Livre oecumènique 1968; first performed Paris, 19 June 1968. Recorded Motette M1003; Citadel 116.001.
Prélude dans le style ancien 1968; first performed Mulhouse, 1969.
Three Voluntaries 1969; first performed Paris, 9 November 1971. Recorded Musical Heritage Society.
Trois Implorations 1970; first performed Paris, March 1971. Recorded Cantilena MC 1821 and Solstice SOL 1, parts only.
Chants des bergers, prière des mages 1971, 1981.
Cinq Chorals 1971.
Offrande à Marie 1971; first performed Washington, D.C., 20 August 1972. Recorded Musical Heritage Society; Tempo FR 760310.
Cinq Méditations sur l'Apocalypse 1973; first performed Paris, 11 April 1974. Recorded Arion ARN 38 312.
Suite baroque 1973; first performed Mulhouse, 2 December 1973. Recorded Musical Heritage Society; Coranata COR 4001.
Huit Chants de Bretagne 1974; first performed Notre-Dame, Paris, 20 November 1975. Recorded Musical Heritage Society; Arion ARN 34 331.
Trois Esquisses romanes (for 2 organs) 1974; first performed Angoulême, 1974. Recorded March MC 8651; Motette Ursina M1016 33.
Célébration (a tribute to Frank Cunkle) 1975.
Trois Esquisses gothiques (for 2 organs) 1975; first performed Washington, D.C., 29 October 1976. Recorded Arion ARN 38 486; Motette Ursina M10166 33.
Four Preludes 1975; first performed The Netherlands, 24 October 1975.
Mosaïque I 1959, 1976; first performed Pittsburgh, 21 October 1976. Recorded Disque Syrinx LX 301; FSM 68 203 EB.
Mosaïque II 1976; first performed Pittsburgh, 15 September 1977. Recorded Alpha ACA 548.
Mosaïque III 1977; first performed Pittsburgh, 25 April 1978.
Choral, Ave Maris Stella 1977. Recorded Coronata COR 001; Erato LDE 3049.
Deuxième Symphonie: alla Webern 1977; first performed Elsah, Illinois, 3 April 1977.
Progression 1978; first performed Paris, 21 May 1979. Recorded Musical Heritage Society; Alpha ACA 548.
Triptych grégorien 1978; first performed Pittsburgh, 14 September 1978. Recorded Musical Heritage Society.
Prélude grégorien 1979; first performed Washington, D.C., 19 September 1979.
Trois Noëls avec variations 1979; first performed Paris, 30 December 1979. Recorded Musical Heritage Society.
Diptych, Offrande à une âme 1979; first performed Paris, 29 March 1980. Recorded Musical Heritage Society.
Rosace 1980; first performed Paris, 7 June 1982.
Marienstatt Chorals 1980; first performed Marienstatt, 1980.
Prélude et allegro 1982; first performed Cardiff, 28 May 1983.
Cinq Soleils 1983; first performed Comminges, 13 August 1983.
Sept Etudes de concert (for solo pedals) 1983; first performed Ingolstadt, 14 August 1985.
Brèves 1 & 2 1983; for examinations and competitions.
Méthode d'orgue (in collaboration with Marie Louise Jaquet-Langlais) 1984; published 1984.
Huit Préludes 1984; first performed Pittsburgh, 9 September 1984. Recorded Musical Heritage Society.
Miniature II 1984; first performed Kirchhundem, 13 May 1984.
B.A.C.H. (six pieces for the tricentennial of J.S. Bach) 1985; first performed Paris, 21 December 1985. Recorded Priory PR 214.
Talitha Koum (Résurrection) 1985; first performed Paris, 18 November 1985.
Drei Leichte Stücke für Orgel 1985; first performed Berlin, 14 March 1987.
American Folk Hymn Settings 1986; first performed St Louis, Missouri, 8 June 1986.
Fantasy on Two Scottish Themes 1986; first performed Edinburgh, 10 June 1987.
In Memoriam 1986; first performed Bonn-Beuel, Germany, 13 February 1987.
Trumpet Tune 1987; first performed New York, 1987.

Chamber/instrumental:

Ave Marie Stella (organ, French horn) 1934. Recorded Medias MEM 007.
Suite (piano—4 hands) 1934, revised 1947.
Fantaisie / Pièce en forme libre (piano, string quartet) 1935.
Trio pour flûte, violon, alto (flute, violin, viola) 1935; first performed Paris, 9 February 1935.
Messe pour deux voix (and harmonium) 1935; first performed Escalquens, September 1935.
Mouvement perpétuel (piano, or piano and organ) 1936; first performed Paris, 3 May 1938.
Prelude and Fugue (piano) 1936; first performed Paris, 1937.
Ligne (cello) 1937; first performed Nantes, 1937.

Suite armoricaine (piano) 1938; first performed Paris, 3 May 1938.
Suite bretonne (string ensemble) 1938; first performed Paris, 21 December 1938.
Histoire vraie pour une mon (piano, or flute and piano) 1941.
Deux Pièces (flute, piano) 1942.
Duo pour violon et violoncelle / Suite concertante 1943; first performed Paris, 1943.
Suite pour clavecin (harpsichord) 1944; first performed Munich, 28 June 1986.
Pièces (violin, piano) 1951; first performed Paris, 1951.
Sonnerie (4 trumpets, 4 trombones) 1961; first performed Paris, 1961.
Elégie (flute, oboe, clarinet, French horn, bassoon, string quintet) 1965; first performed Rennes, 21 March 1966.
Carillons (handbells) 1967; first performed Denver, 30 June 1968.
Pieće (trumpet, organ) 1971; first performed Pittsburg, 26 April 1972.
Sept Chorals (trumpet, organ) 1972; first performed Paris, 21 and 28 February 1974. Recorded Erato 71272; Solstice SOL 14.
Diptyque (piano, organ) 1974; first performed Radio ORTF, 11 February 1974.
Cinq Pièces (flute or violin, piano or organ) 1974, based on 1954 *Cinq Melodies*; first performed Fort Worth, Texas, 9 February 1975. Recorded REM 00847; RLP 5011.
Sonatine (trumpet, organ) 1976; first performed Pittsburgh, 25 April 1978. Recorded Crystal S661; Erato STU 71272; Vista UPS 1107.
Pastorale et rondo (2 trumpets, organ) 1982; first performed Altenberg, Germany, 30 September 1982. Recorded Ursina M 2011.
Petite Rapsodie (flute, piano) 1983.
Petite Suite (piano) 1986; first performed Paris, June 1986.
Noël breton (piano) 1987; first performed Paris, 3 June 1987.
Mouvement pour flûte (or oboe, or violin) 1987; first performed Pittsburgh, 6 October 1987.
Vitrail: Pièce pour clarinet et piano 1987; first performed Roumazieres, 1988.

Vocal/choral:

Tantum ergo (3 mixed voices, organ) 1930.
Deux Chansons de Clement Marot (4 mixed voices, unaccompanied) 1931; first performed Paris, 10 June 1931.
Cinq Motets (2 equal voices, organ) 1932, revised 1942; first performed Paris, 29 May 1933. Recorded Studio SM45–87, complete; Coronata COR 5001, parts.
Une Dentelle s'abolit (voice and piano) 1934.
Humilis (voice, piano) 1935; first performed Paris, 5 December 1935.
Deux Psaumes (4 mixed voices, orchestra or piano or organ) 1937; first performed Paris, 19 March 1938.
Psaume solennel I (choirs, organ, brass, timpani) 1937; first performed Boys Town, Nebraska, 30 August 1963.
Mélodies (voice, piano) 1938.
Parfums (voice, piano) 1938.
Tantum ergo (8 mixed voices) 1940; first performed Paris, 25 June 1940.
Quatre Mélodies (voice, piano) 1940.
Mystère du vendredi saint (choir, orchestra, organ) 1943; first performed Montrouge, Good Friday 1943.
Pie Jésu (soprano or tenor, 2 violins, cello, organ, harpsichord; or choir, soloists) 1943.
Trois Motets (voice, orchestra or organ) 1943; first performed Cologne, 1944.
La Ville d'Ys (choir, solo soprano, orchestra; Breton folksong harmonised for 4 mixed voices) 1945; first performed Paris, 19 December 1948. Recorded Erato CDE 1012 A.
Cantate à St Vincent de Paul (choir, with string orchestra, or organ) 1946; first performed Rennes, 1946.
Pour Cecile (voice, piano) 1946.
Paroles (voice, piano) 1946; first performed Paris, 10 May 1946.
Cantate en honneur de Saint Louis de Montfort (3 trebles, organ, 3 trumpets) 1947; first performed Nantes, 1947.
Au Pied de Clavaire (voice, piano) 1947.
Libera Me, Domine (3 mixed voices, organ) 1948; first performed Paris, 7 December 1948. Recorded Coronata COR 5001.
Cantique dans gloire à Seigneur (voice and organ; parts by Langlais) 1948–52. Recorded Studio SM 33–74.
Messe solennelle (4 mixed voices, congregation, 2 organs, or brass and 1 organ) 1949; first performed Paris, 15 October 1950. Recorded Argo ZRG 662; BIS LP 289; Cambridge CRS 407.
Trois Pièces (medium voice/choir, organ/harpsichord) 1949. Recorded Coronata COR 5001; Erato STU 70358; Musical Heritage Society 3745.
Trois Mélodies (voice, piano) 1949.
Cantate de Noël (soloists, choirs, with flute, oboe, 2 clarinets, bassoon, trumpets, 2 horns, percussion, piano, celeste, harpsichord) 1951; first performed Paris, 25 December 1951.
Passe-temps de l'homme et des oiseaux (voice, piano) 1951; first performed Paris, 4 October 1951.
Advent the Promise (4 mixed voices) 1952.
My Heart's in the Highlands 1952; first performed Paris, 22 June 1952.
Missa "In Simplicitate" (voice, organ or strings) 1952. Recorded Musical Heritage Society 3748; Eurosound 313–20; Erato STU 70358.
Mass in Ancient Style (4 mixed voices, optional organ) 1952; first performed Cambridge, Massachusetts, 1952. Recorded Cambridge Records CAS 407.
Armor (voice, piano) 1952.
Hommage à Louis Braille (voice, piano) 1952; first performed Paris, 29 January 1952. Recorded FY P1.
Caritas Christi (4 mixed voices, organ) 1953; lost.
Chants pour la messe / Messe "joie sur terre" (voice, organ or harmonium) 1953–61. Recorded Studio SM 33–74.
Missa Salve Regina (3 part men's choir, congregation, trumpets, trombones, organs; also reduction for one organ, no brass) 1954; first performed Paris, Christmas 1954. Recorded Argo 596 017; Erato CDE 3023; Solstice SOL 14.
Cinq Mélodies sur des pièces de Ronsard (voice, piano) 1954. Recorded FY P1.
Trois Chansons populaires bretonnes (4 equal voices, or 3 trebles, 1 tenor) 1954.
Saint Clement (voice, piano) 1954.
Laudamus Jerusalem Dominum (4 mixed voices, congregation, organ, optional trumpets, trombones) 1955; first performed Rennes, July 1956.
Antiennes (4 mixed voices) 1955. Recorded (part only) Studio SM 45-24, 33-09.
Prélude, fugue et chaconne (4 mixed vocalises) 1956.
Dieu, nous avons vu ta gloire (4 mixed voices, with organ or harmonium) 1956.
Cantique eucharistique (voice, organ) 1956; first performed Rennes, July 1956. Recorded Studio SM 33–74.
La Passion (8 soloists, narrator, choirs, orchestra) 1957; first performed Paris, March 27 1958.

Le Mystère du Christ (narrator, soloists, choir, orchestra) 1957; first performed Paris, 1958.
Psalm 150 "Praise Ye the Lord" (TTB, organ) 1958; first performed Boston, 10 January 1959.
Cantate "en ovale comme un jet d'eau" 1958; first performed Paris, 1959.
Regina coeli (2 trebles, organ) 1958.
Missa misericordia domini (3 mixed voices, organ) 1958; first performed Boys Town, Nebraska, 1959.
Vanité et audité (4 mixed voices) 1958. Recorded Coronata COR 5001.
L'Errante (voice, piano) 1959.
Sacerdos et Pontifex "Tu es Pontifex" (choir, organ, trumpets) 1959; first performed Boys Town, Nebraska, August 1959. Recorded Coranata, 1988.
Noëls populaires anciens (youth choir) 1960. Recorded Erato LDEV 2024; Studio SM 3011.
Neuf Chansons folkloriques françaises (choir, piano) 1960. Recorded Erato STE 60011; Studio SM 3011.
Motet pour un temps de pénitence (4 mixed voices) 1961; first performed Paris, 15 February 1961.
Europa (voice) 1961.
Nouveaux Chants français pour la messe (choir) 1961; first performed Paris, March 1961.
A La Claire Fontaine (6 mixed voices) 1961.
Ave Marie Stella (3 equal voices) 1961.
Deux Chansons populaires de Haute Bretagne (4 or 6 mixed voices) 1961.
Offertoire pour l'office de Sainte Claire (3 equal voices) 1962.
Mackenzie (voice, piano) 1962.
Missa Dona Nobis Pacem (voice, organ) 1962.
Douze Cantiques bibliques (4 mixed voices, various accompaniments) 1962. Recorded Disques Pastorale et Musique PM 17038.
Chants pour la Pentecôte (voice, organ, harmonium) 1963.
Deux Mélodies (voice, piano) 1963; first performed Paris, 13 June 1965.
Psaume solennel II (choirs, organ, optional brass) 1963; first performed Providence, Rhode Island, 7 March 1965.
Chants pour les dimanches de l'Avent (voice, organ or harmonium) 1964.
Mass "God Have Mercy" (choir, congregation, organ) 1964.
Psaume solennel III (choirs, organ, optional brass) 1964; first performed Hartford, Connecticut, 7 March 1965. Recorded Solstice SOL 14.
Mass "On Earth Peace" (voice, organ) 1965.
Messe: "Dieu, prends pitie" (4 part or unison choir, congregation, organ) 1965. Recorded Disques Pastorale et Musique PM 17053 M.
Canticle of the Sun (3 trebles, various accompaniments) 1965; first performed Philadelphia, 7 March 1967.
Chant d'entrée pour la fête de St Vincent (unison choir with 4 mixed voices) 1965.
Répons pour une messe de funérailles (3 mixed voices, organ or harmonium) 1967.
Psaume 120 (4 mixed voices, organ) 1968; first performed Paris, Christmas 1968.
Festival alleluia (4 mixed voices, organ) 1969; first performed Mulhouse, October 1970.
Solemn Mass (4 mixed voices, congregation, organ, brass) 1969; first performed Washington, D.C., 1 November 1969.
Cantate: Le Prince de la paix (4 mixed voices, organ) 1970; first performed Paris, 24 December 1970.
Hymn of Praise "Te Deum Laudamus" (4 mixed voices, congregation, organ, trumpets, percussion) 1973; first performed Pittsburgh, 1974. Recorded Coronata, 1988.
Trois Oraisons (voice or choir, organ, flute or violin) 1973; first performed Cancale, 13 August 1973. Recorded (part) Abbey APR 301.
Répons liturgiques protestants (with organ accompaniment) 1974.
Vocalise (voice, piano) 1974; first performed Paris, 1975.
Psaume 116 "Laudate Dominum Omnes Gentes" (6 mixed voices, 3 trumpets, organ) 1976.
Cantique en honneur d'Anne de Bretagne (voice, organ) 1976; first performed Nantes, 1 December 1977.
Psaume 111 "Beatus Via Qui Timet Dominum" (4 mixed voices, organ) 1977; first performed Cambridge, Massachusetts, 21 April 1978. Recorded Coronata 5001.
Three Short Anthems (4 mixed voices) 1979; first performed Burlington, North Carolina, 17 June 1979.
Mass: "Grant Us Thy Peace" (4 mixed voices) 1979; first performed Worcester, 24 March 1981. Recorded Alpha ACA 533.
Corpus Christi (SSAA, organ) 1979; first performed Wormbach, Germany, 25 August 1982. Recorded Coronata COR 5001.
A la Vièrge Marie (solo voice, organ or piano) 1981; first performed Cleveland, Ohio, 13 December 1981.
Alleluia, amen (voice, organ) 1982; first performed Paris, 27 March 1983.
Hymne de soir (TTBB) 1984; first performed Paris, 14 May 1984.
A Morning Hymn (4 mixed voices, organ or piano) 1985; first performed San Francisco, 12 January 1986.
The Threefold Truth (distributed in computer form) 1985; first performed San Francisco, Easter Day 1986.
Ubi caritas (4 mixed voices, organ) 1986; first performed Boston, 12 October 1986. Recorded Coronata, 1988.
Mort et résurrection: In memoriam Jehan Alain 1990.
Ave Maria (voice, organ, violin, cello) n.d.

Other:

Organ improvisations recorded by Langlais: *The Lourdes Hymn*, 1969, Vantage SLBB 1015; *Veni Creator/Ein Feste Burg*, 1969, Avant Quart AQ 3001; *Adoromp Holl*, 1976, Arion ARN 36 331; *Conditor Alma Siderum*, 1979, Motette Ursina 1023; *Salve Regina*, 1979, Motette Ursina 1023, and 1986, Media MEM 009F; *Choralfantasie über "Aus Tiefer Not"*, 1981, Motette Ursina M 1037; *Fantasie uber B.A.C.H.*, 1981, Motette Ursina M 1037; *The Chorale "Herr Gott: Dich Loden Alls Wir"*, 1983, Coronata 4001; *Kyrie "Orbis Factor"*, 1983, Coronata 4001, and 1985, Cantilena MC 1820; *Puer Natus Est*, 1983, Motette Ursina M 5004; *Louange à Dieu*, 1985, Cantilena MC 1820; *Seigneur Jesus, ne pas rebuke*, 1985, Cantilena MC 1820; *Veni Creator*, 1985, Cantilena MC 1820; *Ce que le Dieu veut ce soit fait toujours*, 1985, Cantilena MC 1820; *Alleluia, Messe du très saint sacrament/Confitebor Tibi*, 1986, Medias MEM 0009; *Breton Thèmes*, 1987, GAIF 387; also recordings of work by other composers: J.S. Bach; C.P.E. Bach; Jacques Boyvin; Antoine Calvière; François Coûperin; Louis Couperin; Pierre de Muge; Gabriel Fauré; César Franck; Olivier Messiaen; Johann Pachelbel; Henry Purcell; Charles Tournemire; Louis Vierne.

PUBLICATIONS

On Langlais: P. Giraud, "Le Thème grégorien dans les oeuvres pour orgue de JL", *Orgue*, 122–3, 1967; R.T. Nyquist, "The Use of Gregorian Chant in the Organ Music of JL", dissertation, Indiana University, Bloomington, 1968;

JL, "Quelques Souvenirs d'un organiste d'église", in *Orgue*, 137, 1971; *JL: A Bio-Bibliography* (contains two interviews with JL), edited by Kathleen Thomerson, Westport, Connecticut, 1988.

Jean Langlais commented (1991):

I like everything that is beautiful. I believe in God and in the Blessed Virgin Mary. I am first a Breton.

* * *

Jean Langlais's first piece for organ, *Prelude and Fugue* in A♭ (written when he was 20), demonstrates the attractions to harmonic color and to contrast which remained basic to his style throughout his life. The rich impressionistic harmonies of the simple prelude contrast with the complex but clear counterpoint of the virtuostic fugue. Langlais deliberately alternated between writing simple and complex pieces, textures and forms. His frequent key changes and the sectional nature of his writing reflect his love of contrast. His harmonies reveal a strong influence of the impressionistic school's color chords (often ninth chords), the use of Gregorian modality, combined with chromaticism, and the medieval sounds of parallel fourths and fifths.

The beauty of Gregorian chant melodies and the inspired improvisations of Charles Tournemire shaped the musical, rhythmical and metrical freedom of the young Langlais. Although he wrote only a few fugues, counterpoint is very evident throughout the span of his works, and themes often appear in canon.

Langlais drew his thematic material from Gregorian chant, folksong melodies and original themes. His love of Breton folklore is reflected in many works such as the *Suite folklorique, Huit Chants de Bretagne, La Ville d'Ys, Suite bretonne*, and *Suite armoricaine* (originally titled *Suite celtique pour piano*). His most frequently performed works are evenly divided among those based on original themes, those based on folk melodies, borrowed themes, or hymn tunes, and those based on Gregorian themes.

During World War II Langlais's style became more dissonant, rhythmically intricate and metrically flexible, as seen in *Première Symphonie* for organ. His use of frequently changing, asymmetrical meters led him to omit any time signature on some works, or to use a circle to indicate a constantly varying measure length.

After the war he wrote three large ensemble works (commissioned by Radiodiffusion Française as stage music for drama programs), cantatas with orchestra, works for string ensembles and concertos. These compositions did not find publishers or many performances; instead demand grew for his vocal and organ music.

Forms, ideas and sounds of the past attracted Langlais, who sought to combine the past and the future. His deliberate intent to recreate a "mood" of the past, to combine musical history with his own sounds, is reflected in the titles of many of his pieces. Langlais often constructed abstract-sounding themes by assigning pitches to the letters spelling a name.

Other sources for inspiration include Langlais's strong Catholic faith, with many works dedicated to the Virgin Mary and settings of Marian hymns; the Christian Church (*Te Deum, Incantation, Livre oecumènique, Trois Implorations*); and the theme of death and eternal life (*Mors et resurrectio, In Paradisum, Chant de peine, Chant héroïque, Diptych, Offrande à une âme, In memoriam*, and *Mort et résurrection: In memoriam Jehan Alain*).

During the 1950s and 1960s Langlais's works were more frequently performed in America than in Europe, but in the 1970s and 1980s performances and recordings increased in England, Germany, Scandinavia and Australia. His later style is characterized by motive themes and rhythms developed by repetition, and his most important piece of the last decade is *Vitrail* for clarinet and piano, written for his son Claude.

—Kathleen Thomerson

LANSKY, Paul. American. Born in New York City, 18 June 1944. Educated at Queens College, New York City (under George Perle and Hugo Weisgall), 1961–5, B.A.; Princeton University, New Jersey (under Milton Babbitt, Earl Kim and Edward Cone), M.F.A., 1969, Ph.D., 1973. Married Hannah MacKay, 26 August 1968; 2 sons. Teacher, preparatory department, Mannes College of Music, 1963–8; horn player, Dorian Wind Quintet, 1965–7; instructor, Swarthmore College, Pennsylvania, 1968–9; professor of music, Princeton University, since 1969; composer in residence, New South Wales Conservatorium of Music, Sydney, 1982, 1988, Aspen Music Festival, Colorado, 1986–7, and California Institute of the Arts, Valencia, 1987; visiting professor, State University of New York, Buffalo, 1988; Branscombe Distinguished Visiting Artist in Residence, Rensselaer Polytechnic Institute, Troy, New York, 1989; composer faculty, June in Buffalo Festival, New York, 1989. Former member, executive committee, American Society of University Composers; former co-editor, *Proceedings of the American Society of University Composers*; former associate editor, *Perspectives of New Music*; principal investigator for grants, Centers for New Music Resources, 1979, 1982, 1984, 1986, and 1989, and panellist (services to composers, composers' fellowships, overview, special projects), 1987–9, National Endowment for the Arts; principal investigator, New Jersey Department of Higher Education, Computers in Curriculum, 1986. Recipient: Bearns Prize, 1965; Woodrow Wilson Fellowship, 1966; Oliver Ellsworth Bicentennial Preceptorship, 1974–7; League of Composers, ISCM Electronic Music Award, 1975; American Society of Composers, Authors and Publishers awards, from 1976; American Academy/Institute of Arts and Letters, Princeton University, 1977; Jerome Foundation Award, 1981; commission from Koussevitsky Foundation at Library of Congress, 1981; National Endowment for the Arts, composers fellowship, 1981; Columbia-Princeton Electronic Music Center commission, 1982; Fromm Foundation for Contemporary Music commission, 1985; Australian-American Bicentennial Foundation award, 1988; National Endowment for the Arts composer's fellowship, 1988; Guggenheim Fellowship, 1990; Queens College Choral Society Award, 1990. Mailing address: 3 Ziff Lane, Princeton Junction, New Jersey 08550, U.S.A.

Publishers: Boelke Bomart, Box 5010, Hackensack, New Jersey 07606, U.S.A.; GrimTim Music (self), 3 Ziff Lane, Princeton Junction, New Jersey 08550, U.S.A.; Semar Editore, 2 Via S. Agata de Goti, 0018 Rome, Italy.

Chamber/instrumental:

Verse and Refrain for Solo Flute 1966; first performed Princeton, New Jersey, 1966.

String Quartet No 1 1967; first performed Princeton, New Jersey, 1967.
Piano Piece in Three Parts 1968.
Modal Fantasy (piano) 1970. Recorded CRI SD-342.
String Quartet No 2 1971, revised 1977. Recorded CRI SD-402.
Affine Study (piano) 1972.
Fanfare (2 horns) 1976.
Dance Suite (piano) 1977; first performed New York, 1978.
Serenade (violin, viola, piano) 1978.
Crossworks (piano, flute, clarinet, violin, cello) 1978. Recorded Nonesuch H-71351.
As If (string trio with computer-synthesized tape) 1981–2; first performed Princeton, New Jersey, 1983.
Values of Time (string quartet, wind quartet, tape) 1987; first performed Aspen, Colorado, 1987.
Stroll (piano, flute, cello, marimba, tape) 1988; first performed Sydney, 24 June 1988.

Electronic/computer:

mild und leise (computer-synthesized tape) 1973. Recorded Columbia-Odyssey Y34149.
Artifice (on Ferdinand's Reflection) (computer-synthesized tape) 1975–6.
Six Fantasies on a Poem by Thomas Campion (computer-synthesized tape) 1978–9. Recorded CRI SD-456.
Folk-Images (computer-synthesized tape) 1980–1.
As It Grew Dark (computer-synthesized tape) 1983. Recorded Wergo 2013–50.
Guy's Harp (computer-synthesized tape) 1984. Recorded New Albion Records.
Idle Chatter (computer-synthesized tape) 1985. Recorded Wergo CD 2010–50.
Wasting (with Brad Garton and Andrew Milburn; computer-synthesized tape) 1985. Recorded Centaur CD CRC 2076.
Just More Idle Chatter (computer-synthesized tape) 1987. Recorded Centaur CD CRC 2076.
Notjustmoreidlechatter (computer-synthesized tape) 1988. Recorded in *Tellus: The Audiocassette Magazine, #22 False Phonemes*; Neuma CD 450–73.
Smalltalk (computer-synthesized tape) 1988. Recorded New Albion Records.
The Lesson (computer-synthesized tape) 1989.
Talkshow (real-time performance system) 1989.
Not So Heavy Metal (with Steve Mackey; computer-processed performance) 1989. Recorded New Albion Records.
Late August (computer-synthesized tape) 1989. Recorded New Albion Records.
QuakerBridge (computer-synthesized tape) 1990.

PUBLICATIONS

By Lansky: addition to *Serial Composition and Atonality* by George Perle, 3rd ed., Berkeley/Los Angeles, 1972; "The Music of Claudio Spies: An Introduction", in *Tempo*, 103, 1972; "Texture", in *Dictionary of Contemporary Music*, edited by John Vinton, New York, 1974; "Pitch-Class Consciousness", in *Perspectives of New Music*, 13(2), 1975; *"Musikmaschinen"*, in *Osterreichische Musickzeitschrift*, 13(10), 1976 (translated as "Music-Making Machines" in special American issue, October 1976); (with Carlton Gamer) "Fanfares for the Common Tone", in *Perspectives of New Music*, 14(2), 1976; (with R. Cann, K. Steiglitz, M. Zuckerman) "Practical Considerations in the Application of Linear Prediction to Music Synthesis", in *Proceedings of the First International Conference on Computer Music*, 1976; "Acoustics of Music", in *American Academic Encyclopaedia*, vol. 13, 1980; "Atonality", "George Perle", "Set" and (with George Perle) "Twelve-Note Composition", in *The New Grove Dictionary of Music and Musicians*, vols 1, 14, 17 and 19, 1980; *Mix: A Program for Digital Signal-Processing, Editing and Synthesis*, Princeton, New Jersey, 1983; "Computers and Musical Expression: A Conversation with PL and Steve Birchall", in *Softside*, February 1984; "Computers and Society", in *Technology and Society*, 44(1) 1985; "The Sound of Software: Computer-Made Music", in *Perspectives in Computing*, 5(3–4) 1985; "It's About Time; Some Next Perspectives—Parts 1 and 2", in *Perspectives of New Music* 27(2), 28(1), 1989–90; "A View from the Bus: When Machines Make Music", in *Perspectives of New Music*, 28(2), 1990.

On Lansky: Curtis Roads, "Interview with PL", in *Computer Music Journal*, 7(3), 1983; Charles Dodge and Thomas Jerse, in *Computer Music*, New York, 1985; David L. Code, "Observations in the Art of Speech: PL's Six Fantasies", in *Perspectives of New Music*, 28(1), 1990; Denise Ondishko, "Music of PL", PhD dissertation, Eastman School of Music, Rochester, New York, 1990.

Paul Lansky comments:

I am very interested in finding the implicit music in the world around me. To this end, I have adopted computer music technology as a kind of aural microscope on the sounds of the world. My pieces concern themselves with the way people speak, formally and informally (*Six Fantasies on a Poem by Thomas Campion*, *Smalltalk*, *Idle Chatter*), the way they play musical instruments, formally and informally (*Guy's Harp*, *As It Grew Dark . . .*), the sounds of urban scenes (*QuakerBridge*, *Stroll*), and anything else whose odd shape and contour has the potential to make interesting music.

The music I have tended to make using these means has not been extreme or unusual, but rather fairly straightforward. I have noticed an interesting cross-fertilization of contexts in this respect: taking something explicitly non-musical, such as two people chatting casually *(Smalltalk)*, and highlighting the contours and inflections using relatively simple tonal means provides a new insight into the nature of tonality as well as into the implicit music of language.

In these senses I regard myself as an "experimental" composer. My goals are not mainly to achieve relative mastery of one form or another (aside from intransigent computers!), as they are to explore and experiment. Some of my pieces are successful experiments, others not so successful. My reasons for choosing a project thus have more to do with its promise as a means of exploration and experimentation than with its promise of success. For me, success means creating new ways of listening and hearing, and making exciting music in the process.

* * *

Paul Lansky has emerged as one of the most prominent figures in the computer music field, being a pioneer in digital sound synthesis techniques, particularly the technique known as linear prediction (LPC). His articles, editorial contributions and book reviews in *Perspectives of New Music* have brought him recognition as a theorist, author and critic as well as a composer. Recently Lansky has received recognition for the computer software programs (CMIX) he initially developed for his own work.

It is difficult to characterize Lansky's musical compositions as a whole because he is not tied to any particular method or approach. His work covers a wide range of musical stances, from eclectic references (*Folk-Images*) to twelve-tone structure (*String Quartet*) to stochastic processes (*Idle Chatter*). Not only does he organize each piece in different ways, he also orients each work differently with regard to the traditional modes of listening found in popular and classical music.

Lansky's early compositions were written for chamber ensemble, solo instrument or computer-synthesized tape. During his student years he was influenced by the music and ideas of Milton Babbitt and George Perle. His collaboration with Perle on the development of the twelve-tone modal system between 1969 and 1971 brought his ideas and music compositions to the attention of a wide audience. With *mild und leise* Lansky began exploring a new approach to music composition. Here, he experiments with timbre as a structural concept, and with pitch configurations such as the "Tristan chord," rather than abstract pitch class combinations. This orientation toward music composition is described by Lansky as "confronting objects already laden with musical implications" and is also adopted in *Artifice (on Ferdinand's Reflection)*. His later works continue his interest in music embedded in tradition by containing clear references to popular, jazz and folk song.

Since 1979, the year he completed *Six Fantasies on a Poem by Thomas Campion*, he has preferred writing for computer-synthesized tape alone. *Fantasies* is pivotal to Lansky's compositional development; it was written as a deliberate break from some of his previous approaches to composition and makes extensive use of LPC synthesis techniques. LPC involves analyzing an existing sound in order simply to reproduce that sound, or to create new sounds by modifying the properties defined by the analysis. In *Fantasies*, *Folk-Images*, *Guy's Harp* and *Not So Heavy Metal*, Lansky captures and cultivates the natural beauty and complexity of sounds made by humans—whether deliberately or implicitly musical. (All of his music written after *Fantasies* makes use of sound material first generated acoustically by humans.) *Guy's Harp* and *Not So Heavy Metal* explicitly make use of live performances in a photographic sense; they are collaborative works in that the final product relies heavily on the original musical material of the performer. Another interest introduced in *Fantasies* is his fascination for the manner by which people listen to music. This interest pervades all of his later works, and becomes a major focus in *As If*.

In *Idle Chatter* and its two follow-up works Lansky broadened his compositional approach as he began to rely more heavily on computer-assisted composition. Here he sets up conditions under which the computer is called upon to help define and create complex textures and procedures. This approach is developed further in his later computer-synthesized works, and culminates in *Smalltalk*. His ideas on the direction of computer music have been expressed recently in several articles published in *Perspectives of New Music* and are a good source of information for his views on computer music in general.

—Denise Ondishko

LARSEN, Libby (professional name of Elizabeth Brown Reece). American. Born in Wilmington, Delaware, 24 December 1950. Educated at University of Minnesota, Minneapolis (composition under Dominick Argento, Eric Stokes and Paul Fetler), B.A., 1971, M.M., 1975, Ph.D. in theory and composition, 1978. Married James Reece, 6 September 1975; 1 daughter. Teaching assistant, University of Minnesota, since 1973; co-founder (with Stephen Paulus), from 1973, and manager-composer, 1985, Minnesota Composers Forum; composer in residence, Minnesota Orchestra, 1983–5. Recipient: National Opera Institute Fellowship, 1980; Minnesota Woman of the Year in Arts, 1981; National Endowment for the Arts Fellowships, 1982, 1984; American Express Woman to Watch, 1984; Outstanding Achievement Award, University of Minnesota, 1987. Mailing address: 2205 Kenwood Parkway, Minneapolis, Minnesota 55405, U.S.A.

Publisher: E.C. Schirmer.

Symphonies/orchestral:

Weaver's Song and Jig (string band, orchestra) 1978.
Three Cartoons 1980.
Pinions (violin, chamber orchestra) 1982.
Deep Summer Music (trumpet, orchestra) 1982–3.
Overture: Parachute Dancing 1984.
Symphony: Water Music 1984; first performed New York City, 30 January 1985.
Coriolis 1985.
Fanfare 1985.
What the Monster Saw 1987.
Collage: Boogie 1988.
Concerto for Trumpet and Orchestra 1988.
Concerto: Cold, Silent Snow (flute, orchestra) 1989.
Grand Rondo (concert band) 1989.
Sun Song (concert band) 1990.
Tambourines 1990.
Ghosts of an Old Ceremony (orchestra with dancers) 1991.
Symphony: The Lyric 1991–2.

Chamber/instrumental:

Theme and Deviations (harp) 1972.
Black Roller (flute, clarinet, bassoon, oboe, violin, viola, cello, piano) 1975.
Istar Fantasia (guitar) 1976.
Cajun Set (guitar, violin, viola, cello) 1976.
Air and Jig (clarinet quartet) 1976.
Suite (piano) 1976.
Four on the Floor (violin, cello, double bass, piano) 1977.
Argyle Sketches (guitar) 1979.
Bronze Veils (trombone, percussion) 1979.
Impromptu (flute, oboe, bassoon) 1979.
Ulloa's Ring (flute, piano) 1980. Recorded Pro Arte 1086.
Scudding (cello) 1980.
Triage (harp) 1981.
Circular rondo (flute, guitar) 1981.
Aubade (flutes) 1982. Recorded Pro Arte 1086.
Canti Breve (flute, guitar) 1982.
Theme and Deviations (harp) 1982.
Sonata in One Movement on Kalenda Maya (organ) 1983.
Jazz Variations (bassoon) 1984.
Northern Star Fanfare (chamber ensemble) 1985.
Song Without Words (chamber ensemble) 1985.
Alauda (flute) 1986.
The Astonishing Flight of the Gump (chamber ensemble) 1986.
Juba (cello, piano) 1986.
Love and Hisses (double woodwing quintet) 1986.

Up, Where the Air Gets Thin (cello, double bass) 1986.
Vive (flute quartet) 1988.
Kathleen, As She Was (oboe, harpsichord) 1989.
Aspects of Glory (organ) 1990.
Hindsight (flute, live and pre-recorded video) 1990.
Quartet Schoenberg, Schenker, Schillinger (string quartet) 1991.
Schoenberg, Schenker, Schillinger (flute, oboe, violin, viola, sampler) 1991.

Vocal/choral:

Soft Pieces (chorus) 1974.
Lacrimae Christi (soloists, chorus, orchestra) 1974.
The Art of Love (soprano, tenor, harp, oboe, percussion, dance) 1974–5.
Tom Twist (narrator, mime, orchestra; Butler) 1975.
Saints Without Tears (soprano, flute, bassoon; McGinley) 1976.
Three Rilke Songs (soprano, harp, flute, guitar) 1977.
Cowboy Songs (soprano, piano) 1978.
Eurydice (soprano, string quartet; H.D.) 1978.
Ringeltanze (mixed chorus, piano, handbells) 1979.
Dance Set (SATB chorus, clarinet, cello, percussion, piano) 1980.
Double Joy (double mixed chorus, orchestra, handbells) 1980.
In a Winter Garden (soprano, tenor, SATB chorus, chamber orchestra; Hampl) 1982. Recorded Pro Arte 151.
A Creeley Collection (tenor, SATB chorus, flute, percussion) 1984.
Clair de lune (unaccompanied TTBB chorus) 1985.
Coming Forth into Day (soprano, baritone, SATB chorus, orchestra) 1985.
I Love the Lord (anthem for chorus) 1985.
Moon Door (solo voice) 1985.
Clair de lune in Blue (unaccompanied SATB chorus) 1986.
Peace, Perfect Peace (unaccompanied SATB chorus) 1986.
Pied Glory (SATB chorus, organ) 1986.
Black Birds, Red Hills (solo voice) 1987.
Canticle of the Sun (unaccompanied chorus) 1987.
Garden Wall (unaccompanied chorus) 1987.
ME (Brend Ueland) (soprano, piano) 1987.
Ringeltanze (TTBB chorus, handbells, orchestra) 1987.
Songs of Youth and Pleasure (unaccompanied SATB chorus) 1987.
The Settling Years (SATB chorus, woodwind quintet, piano) 1988.
Stepping Westward (SSA chorus, handbells, oboe, marimba) 1988.
Three Summer Scenes (SATB chorus, orchestra) 1988.
Sonnets from the Portuguese (solo voice; Browning) 1989.
Songs from Letters (unaccompanied chorus) 1989.
Everyone Sang (unaccompanied TTBB chorus) 1991.

Opera:

Some Pig 1973.
The Words upon the Windowpane (after Yeats) 1978; first performed Minneapolis, Minnesota, 1978.
The Silver Fox (opera for children) 1979; first performed St Paul, Minnesota, 1979.
Tumbledown Dick (after Sutton) 1980; first performed St Paul, Minnesota, 1980.
Psyke and the Psyskraper 1982.
Clair de lune (after Hampl) 1984; first performed Little Rock, Arkansas, 1984.
Beauty and the Beast 1989.
Frankenstein, the Modern Prometheus 1990.
A Wrinkle in Time 1991–2.

* * *

At a little over 40, Libby Larsen is already a distinctive voice in contemporary American music. Like Dominick Argento, her teacher at the University of Minnesota, she is possessed of extraordinary melodic facility and harmonic flair, and combines apparently disparate elements with consummate ease. Underlying her work is a strong interest in American popular musics, an interest she combines with elements of freely deployed atonal harmony and the kinds of repetitive structure often associated with so-called minimalism but which in her work have an altogether more folkish and less doctrinaire quality.

Larsen's orchestral pieces are constructed with a careful eye to the harmonic architecture, built up out of pitch clusters that have an almost physical impact. The violin concerto *Pinions* is perhaps the best of the orchestral works, though the Symphony has a freshness that lifts its rather static, non-narrative quality out of the ordinary; the concertos for flute and trumpet are freshly conceived, and demanding without being unapproachable. The deceptively hard-edged contours of *Three Cartoons* fit the ostensible subject matter very well, but it seems clear that Larsen also means the word to be construed in its original sense of a rough sketch or draft, and there are echoes of it in the later and very fine *Symphony: Water Music* first performed in New York in 1985.

Larsen's instrumental pieces bear a much more direct imprint of popular music drawing on country themes and parlour songs in a highly original way. She has a particular affinity for flute, played with a deliberately roughened edge that again recalls folk and popular music. There is a strong improvisational element—or at least the impression of one—in her scores, fostered by an interest in jazz and its open-ended resolutions, yet all of her work betrays a tight formal control that belies its almost casually textured surface. A fine song-setter, Larsen has made superb versions of a set of Robert Creeley lyrics and of three beautiful Rilke poems. The latter balance text and music exactly in ways that recall the confidence of the operas.

Perhaps her most significant single work to date is the opera *Frankenstein, the Modern Prometheus*, a work which restores not just Mary Shelley's very important subtitle, but some of the emphases of Shelley's novel which have been lost in more recent film and other popular adaptations. *Frankenstein* and the ritualised orchestral choreography of *Ghosts of an Old Ceremony* underline Larsen's inherently dramatic sense; like the recent flute piece *Hindsight*, the opera features highly imaginative use of electronic and video resources. With Stephen Paulus, another very confident young operatic composer, albeit a more conservative one, Larsen co-founded the influential Minnesota Composers Forum, and as one of its managing composers, Larsen has wielded some influence over the development of music in the Twin Cities. Less well-known in America as a whole than she should be, her work bespeaks very considerable promise. She combines technical rigour with humour and a fine instinct for the telling moment; conscious of tradition, she is not burdened by it, preferring to interpret the term in a liberal plural; by the same token, her attraction to new technology and performing techniques never becomes doctrinaire.

—Pamela Collins

LASOŃ, Alexander. Polish. Born in Siemianowice Slaskie in 1951. Educated at State Higher School of Music, Katowice (under Józef Swider); International Courses for Composers, Burgas, Bulgaria (under Ton de Leeuw, Marin Goleminov and Andrei Eshpai), 1979; Ferienkurse für Neue Musik, Darmstadt, 1984; scholarship from Witold Lutosławski, 1987–9. Lecturer, Silesian University (Cieszyn branch); vice-chair, Polish Society for Contemporary Music, Warsaw, since 1986. Recipient: prizewinner, All-Poland Piano Improvisation Competition, Gdansk, 1972; 2nd prize (for *Symphony No 1*), G. Fitelberg Competition for composers, Katowice, 1976; composition competition, "Young Composers for the Young Town" Festival, Stalowa Wola, 1978; 2nd prize (for *The Mountains*), youth branch, Polish Composers' Union, 1980; 1st prize (for *Symphony No 1*), young composers category, UNESCO Composers' Rostrum, Paris, 1980; Beethoven Prize, Bonn (for *Symphony No 2*), 1980; Silesian Polyhymnia Award (for *Chamber Music* and *Three Songs*), 1985; Wyspianski Award, first degree (for overall achievement), 1986; 5th place (for *String Quartet No 2*), UNESCO Composers' Rostrum, Paris, 1988. Mailing address: c/o Ars Polona, Krakowskie Przedmiescie 7, P.O. Box 1001, 00-068 Warsaw, Poland.

Publishers: PWM Edition; Edition Tonos, Darmstadt.

Symphonies/orchestral:

Impressions (piano, orchestra) 1974.
Symphony No 1 (winds, percussion, 2 pianos) 1975. Recorded Polskie Nagrania SX 2076.
Symphony No 2: Concertante (piano, orchestra) 1977–9. Recorded Polskie Nagrania SX 2458.
Gory / The Mountains 1979–80. Recorded Polskie Nagrania SX 2173.
Concerto in memoriam Pablo Casals (cello, orchestra) 1985.
Chamber Concerto (oboe, chamber orchestra) 1986.
Katedra / The Cathedral 1988.

Chamber/instrumental:

Sonata (violin, piano) 1970–1.
Chamber Music No 1: of Stalowa Wola (piano, string quartet) 1974–8.
Sonata No 1 (violin) 1975.
Chamber Music No 2 (piano, 2 horns, trumpet, 2 trombones, tuba) 1976.
Concerto (piano, 3 tapes) 1976.
Music in Four Movements (double bass, piano) 1977.
Chamber Music No 3 (2 oboes, 2 horns, 2 trumpets, tuba, percussion, piano) 1978, revised 1989–90. Recorded Polskie Nagrania SX 2434.
String Quartet No 1 1980.
Spring (wind quintet) 1980–1.
Chamber Music No 5: Cztery Pory Roku / Four Seasons of the Year (clarinet, trombone, piano, 5 violins, 3 violas, 2 cellos) 1981–4.
Sonata No 2: "Hebrew" (violin) 1983–4.
Concertino (violin, piano) 1986.
String Quartet No 2 1987. Recorded Polskie Nagrania SX 2577.

Vocal/choral:

Songs (soprano, piano; Teresa Snopkowska) 1973.
Muzyka u Szekspira (baritone, tape; Shakespeare) 1975.
Three Songs (alto, oboe, violin, cello, piano; Iłłakówicz) 1983.

Other:

Music (tape) 1975.

PUBLICATIONS

On Lasoń: Eugenia Wybraniec, "The Romantics of 1951", in *Trybuna Robotnicza*, 25–26 August 1979; Krzysztof Baculewski, "Summer Music at 'Warsaw Autumn'", in *Ruch Muzyczny*, 18 November 1979, and "'The Mountains', 'Lamia', Penderecki", in *Ruch Muzyczny*, 30 October 1983.

* * *

Aleksander Lasoń's *Symphony No 1* is scored for 33 woodwinds and brass, nine percussionists and two pianos. A controlled aleatoricism pervades the work's two substantial movements with the composer retaining control but allowing the players freedom to synchronize the numerous ostinato figures. The work opens with ostinatos for pianos and bells which are to be freely repeated *presto possibile* (meaning "in the chosen, possibly fast, tempo"). Later variants of this direction are simply flexible and marked *tempo libero* (meaning "in the chosen, slightly slower, tempo). Some of the wind instruments are directed to play "the highest note possible", others "the lowest note possible". Dramatic rhythmic alternations of all these features make for a tense opening in which temporal control is achieved by counting in seconds rather than in beats and bars. In contrast, a more conventional, surging passage follows whose harmonic clusters and regular crotchet [quarter note] tread have a ritualistically monumental power. The dramatic opposition of these two contrasting ideas provides the formal basis for this opening movement.

The second movement is an exhilarating scherzo. It is fast and furious and, as is usual in Lasoń's music, it has great formal clarity. Clearly defined and memorable blocks of textures are presented in juxtaposition, then played off against each other (with a variety of interactive procedures) to make a capacious and substantial symphonic argument.

The orchestral tone poem *Gory* ("Mountains") illustrates similar techniques (many of which are typical of a number of recent Polish compositions). This work is sectional in form and constructed from different types of complex ostinatos which contrast with or complement each other. The work opens with low, cavernous string sounds which gradually become active by means of nervous, chromatic twists, subtle portamentos and clusters. Other sections are more overtly nervous, and different forms of agitation occur, varying from dramatic reiterations of semi-quavers [sixteenth notes] to chromatic embellishments around a single central note. As in *Symphony No 1*, a striking contrast to the generally rich ornamental progress is seen in the form of a simple, song-like declamation in a tonally clear Lydian A. This appears twice during the work with a telling effect and it confirms Lasoń's fondness for tempering textural proliferation with simpler gestures which help to clarify the form and deepen the expressive impact.

In contrast to these two major works by Lasoń's are the *Three Songs* for contralto, oboe, violin, cello and piano. These are setting of poems by Kazimiera Iłłakówicz and are among Lasoń's most beguiling achievements. The first song "Creatures Complain" shows a rhythmic exploration of whole tones as a prelude to expressive triadic (Lydian) gestures at an emotional climax—and all shaped within a homogenous but volatile contrapuntal texture. For "Evil

Spirit", Lasoń produces a wry, ironic effect by means of simple passages in extended diatonic harmony (at times white notes only). Then he uses poignant minor ninth chords to characterize them further (and in a rather threatening manner). The third song "Lady Bewitcher" maintains the tonal equilibrium in an expanded C# major. Here, radiant temolandos and triadic inflexions integrate well within a complex four-part counterpoint.

Lasoń's creative imagination, perceptive grasp of form, well-judged handling of complex textures and sure dramatic sense make him one of the most self-assured and technically proficient of his generation of Polish composers. Above all, his control of aleatoricism in order to simplify rhythmic problems is achieved without loss of thematic and melodic substance, a feature which is characteristic of many of the strongest pieces of the so-called "Polish school".

—Richard Elfyn Jones

LeBARON, (Alice) Anne. American. Born in Baton Rouge, Louisiana, 30 May 1953. Educated at University of Alabama, University, B.A., 1974; Salzedo Harp Colony (private study under Alice Chalifoux), 1974, 1976; Hochschule für Musik, Cologne (under György Ligeti), 1975, 1980–1; State University of New York, Stony Brook, M.A., 1978; private study, National Institute of Classical Music, Seoul, 1983; Columbia University, New York City (composition under Bulent Arel and Chou Wen-chung), D.M.A., 1989. Married Edward Eadon, 6 July 1982. Assistant to the directors, Electronic Music Studios, State University of New York, Stony Brook, 1977–8; instructor of music theory, University of Alabama, University, 1978; artist in residence, Decatur, Alabama, 1979–80; teacher of theory and composition, State University of New York, Stony Brook, 1981–2; teacher of survey courses in classical music and jazz, Columbia University, New York City, 1984–5; producer, contemporary music series, Washington, D.C., 1986–7. Performing harpist, zither player. Recipient: Arnold Salop Memorial Award and Mu Phi Epsilon Award (for *Three Motion Atmospheres*), 1974; Bearns Prize (for *Metamorphosis*), 1978; IBM Student Composer Award (for *Light Breaks Where No Sun Shines*), 1979; GEDOK Prize (for *Rite of the Black Sun*), 1980; Fulbright Scholarship, 1981; New Music consort prize (for *Lamentation / Invocation*), 1984; Guggenheim Fellow, 1991. Mailing address: 322 East 70th Street, #207, New York, New York 10021, U.S.A.

Publishers: MMB Music Inc.; APR Publishers Inc.

Symphonies/orchestral:

Three Movements (string orchestra) 1973.
Strange Attractors 1987; first performed New York City, 19 January 1990.

Chamber/instrumental:

Resonances (piano, harp, timpani) 1971.
Giuoco piano (piccolo, flute, 2 trumpets, 2 trombones, double bass) 1971.
Passacaglia (violin, flute, oboe, clarinet, bassoon, cello) 1971.
Fertility (marimba, 2 bongos, double bass) 1971.
Spicebox of Strings (violin, piano) 1972.
Music for Peyote Cactus (viola, oboe, tenor saxophone, large gong, temple-blocks, tam-tam, wind chimes, percussion, viola, bass clarinet, vibes) 1973.
Three Motion Atmospheres (brass quintet) 1974; first performed Georgia, 22 February 1975.
Memnon (6 harps) 1976; first performed 22 June 1979.
Extensions (3 movements for harp, piano, large percussion ensemble) 1977.
Metamorphosis (piccolo, flute, oboe, clarinet, horn, tenor trombone, harp, large percussion ensemble) 1977; first performed Fresno, California, 28 March 1979.
Rite of the Black Sun (percussion quartet; after Antonin Artaud) 1980; first performed New York City, 11 December 1980.
After a Dammit to Hell (bassoon) 1982; first performed New York City, 13 November 1982.
Planxty Bowerbird (harp, electronics) 1982; first performed San Francisco, 19 May 1984.
Noh Reflections (string trio) 1986; first performed Philadelphia, 8 May 1987.
I Am an American . . . My Government Will Reward You (harp, tape) 1988; first performed Toronto, 13 February 1988.
Telluris Theoria Sacra (flute, clarinet, violin, viola, cello, piano, percussion) 1989; first performed 31 March 1990.
Waltz for Quintet (flute, violin, viola, cello, piano) 1989; first performed Atlanta, Georgia, 12 April 1989.

Vocal/choral:

I Saw a Man Pursuing the Horizon (baritone, piano, harp; Crane) 1972.
In the Desert (soprano, flute, marimba, temple blocks; Crane) 1973.
Concerto for Active Frogs (bass/baritone, small mixed chorus, violin, viola, cello, oboe, tenor saxophone, bassoon, trombone, tuba or double bass, percussion, tape) 1974; first performed Alabama, 12 May 1976.
Her Cardboard Bathroom (narrator, 2 flutes, oboe, clarinet, contrabass clarinet) 1976.
Light Breaks Where No Sun Shines (soprano, alto, tenor, mixed chorus, 2 percussion, 2 bass drums, Chinese bell tree, tam-tam, percussion; Thomas) 1977.
The Sea and the Honeycomb (soprano, flute, clarinet, 2 percussion, piano) 1979; first performed Vermont, 1 August 1979.
Umi (mezzo-soprano, orchestra) 1982.
Lamentation / Invocation (baritone, clarinet, harp, cello) 1984; first performed New York City, 7 November 1984.
Dish (soprano, electric violin, percussion, electric bass, violin) 1990; first performed 8 October 1990.

Opera:

Orpheus Lives (chamber opera for 4 soloists, 2 choruses, 12 instruments, tape) 1980.
The E & O Line (electronic blues opera for 4 principals, 6-part mixed chorus, 3-part female chorus, keyboards, electric guitar, saxophones, horn, harp, percussion, tape) 1989.

Other:

Quadratura circuli (electronic tape) 1978; first performed New York City, 24 June 1978.

The Moonbeam Wishbook (film score; organ, piano, harp) 1980.
Cumuline (dance; tape) 1982.
Eurydice Is Dead (dance; tape) 1983; first performed 14 April 1983.
Bouquet of a Phantom Orchestra (for the Anne LeBaron Quintet: trumpet, tuba, electric guitar, percussion, harp) 1990; first performed Washington, D.C., 15 March 1990.
Top Hat on a Locomotive (for the Anne LeBaron Quintet) 1990; first performed Washington, D.C., 15 March 1990.
Superstrings and Curved Space (for the Anne LeBaron Quintet) 1990; first performed Washington, D.C., 15 March 1990.
Bottom Wash (for the Anne LeBaron Quintet) 1990.
The Celluloid Doll (for the Anne LeBaron Quintet; electric guitar, harp, tuba) 1990; first performed Hartford, Connecticut, 4 August 1990.

Chamber improvisations: *Butterfly Collection*, *Drunk Underwater Koto*, *Jewels*, *Rare Sea Wolves*, *Siesta*, *Sudden Noticing of Trees*, *Transparent Zebra*, *Ukrainian Ice Eggs*, 1970s–1980s.

* * *

Of all the "hyphenate" composer-performers at work in contemporary music, Anne LeBaron is the one who has perhaps most seamlessly joined the two halves of her musical personality. A harp and zither player of quite extraordinary facility, she has also written an impressive body of vocal and chamber music, two impressive orchestral works, and is currently preparing her opera *The E. & O. Line*, an "electronic blues" reading of the Orpheus and Eurydice legend for production in 1992.

LeBaron's imagination and performance ethos are haunted by the Orphean myth. She has transformed contemporary harp playing, restoring it from its 19th-century role as a colour instrument, providing soft arpeggiations at the fringes of a symphonic score or else bland programmatic effects (heaven, angels, running water, first fine careless raptures of love) in movie scores, into a solo instrument of considerable and sometimes disturbing power. LeBaron is currently contemplating a harp concerto (a rare item in the orchestral repertoire), building significantly on her relatively small output for larger forces.

The bulk of her mature work (there are a large number of early and improvisational pieces which she no longer acknowledges) is for small instrumental groups, with or without voice. These very frequently but not inevitably include a part for harp. Her playing technique, refined during periods of study at the Salzedo Harp Colony and at the National Institute of Classical Music in Seoul, is very extended and frequently involves electronic transformation of instrumental sound, as in her remarkable and very bitter solo piece *I Am an American . . . My Government Will Reward You.*

This, and the slightly earlier *Planxty Bowerbird* are the key instances of LeBaron's work for her own instrument. She is no less impressive with other instrumental combinations. The solo bassoon piece *After a Dammit to Hell* opens up the range of this slightly diffident instrument; the relatively unfamiliar sonority is employed to great effect in a series of dramatic descents and rapid articulations. *Rite of the Black Sun* for percussion quartet is inspired by Antonin Artaud and is a work of studied complexity, entirely *sui generis*; it develops relatively simple materials in a way that is almost incantatory. In her vocal music, LeBaron is drawn to deceptively simple lyrics (novelist Stephen Crane's much underrated verse is a perfect example) which carry a deep undercurrent of often disturbing significance.

LeBaron is as interested in contemporary physics as in ancient myth, though neither element is allowed to dominate. Just as her use of electronics is patiently woven into the acoustic fabric of a piece, so any compositional systems she might use are not discernible in the final piece and are, in any case, drawn from that end of quantifiable logic that is closest to magic and incantation. *Rite* might just as well have been inspired by Richard Feynman or Stephen Hawking as by Artaud, and the recent orchestral *Strange Attractors* reveals the same perfect blend of mystery and firm structural logic.

The latter quality at least is all too rare in contemporary improvised music, much of which is marred by cynical or merely naive obfuscation. LeBaron has collaborated with some of the leading improvising musicians of Europe—notably Tristan Honsinger, Evan Parker, Paul Lovens and Derek Bailey (with whose improvising collective Company she made a distinguished appearance in 1982)—and has performed with a number of American groups playing innovative improvisational music. These include The LSD Trio, Jewels, and her own Quintet, which affords her a regular outlet for new compositions.

The E. & O. Line and the prospective concerto for harp and orchestra will help establish LeBaron as one of the most significant compositional voices of her generation. The world rarely tears contemporary Orpheuses to bits, but it has an uneasy habit of consigning them to the critical underworld. If the world decides to "discover" her, it will do well to remind itself that she has been playing and composing brilliantly for some considerable time.

—Bea Weir

LEDENYOV, Roman (Semyonovich). Russian. Born in Moscow, 4 December 1930. Educated at Central Musical School of Moscow Conservatoire, 1942–8; Moscow Conservatoire (composition under A.N. Alexandrov), 1948–58. Married Elvira Eduardovna Ledenyova in 1955; 1 son. Teacher of music theory, Moscow Conservatoire, 1956–64; member, Composers' Union of U.S.S.R., since 1956; secretary of board, Composers' Union of the R.S.F.S.R., 1970–3; member, Union of Cinematographists, since 1972. Recipient: Merited Artist of R.S.F.S.R., 1982. Mailing address: ul. Studentcheskaya d.44/28, kv. 118, 121165 Moscow, U.S.S.R.

Publishers: Sovetskaya kompozitor, Moscow; Moscow-Music; Ricordi, Milan; Peters, Leipzig; Associated Music Publishers.

Symphonies/orchestral:

Violin Concerto Op 12 1966; first performed Moscow, 1972.
Concerto-Poem Op 13 (viola, orchestra) 1967; first performed Moscow, 1973. Recorded Melodiya 33A 025045.
Tales of Green Balloons Op 15 (orchestral suite from the ballet) 1967; first performed Moscow, 1980. Recorded Melodiya C10 21703 004.
Concerto-Nocturne Op 14 (flute, orchestra) 1967–8.
Nocturnes Op 19 (version for chamber orchestra) 1968.

Concerto-Elegy Op 28 (cello, orchestra) 1980; first performed Moscow, 1980. Recorded Melodiya C10 17373.
Concerto-Romance Op 29 (piano, orchestra) 1980; first performed Moscow, 1981. Recorded Melodiya C10 21704.

Chamber/instrumental:

Sonata Op 1 (clarinet, piano) 1956; first performed Moscow, 1956.
Sonata: In Memory of Sergei Prokofiev Op 4 (piano) 1957; first performed Moscow, 1958.
String Quartet Op 7 1963; first performed Moscow, 1964. Recorded Melodiya 33A-025118.
Six Pieces Op 16 (string quartet, harp) 1967; first performed Prague, 1967. Recorded Panton 110342-366; Melodiya C10 06186.
Ten Sketches Op 17 (chamber ensemble) 1967; first performed Moscow, 1967.
Seven Moods Op 18 (chamber ensemble) 1967; first performed Moscow, 1970.
Nocturnes Op 19 (version for chamber ensemble) 1968; first performed Moscow, 1970.
Mini-Suite Op 20 (organ) 1968; first performed Moscow, 1968.
Brief Tunes Op 21 (string quartet) 1968; first performed Moscow, 1970. Recorded Melodiya C10 06186.
I Play the Clarinet Op 22 (clarinet, piano) 1969; first performed Poland, 1976.
Four Drawings Op 23 (chamber ensemble) 1969; first performed Moscow, 1973.
Elegiac Sextet Op 30 (2 violins, 2 violas, 2 cellos) 1980; first performed Moscow, 1984.
Reminiscences Op 31 (clarinet, E♭ clarinet, basset horn, bass clarinet) 1982; first performed Moscow, 1987.

Vocal/choral:

Nekrasov's Books Op 24 (bass, piano) 1970–1; first performed Moscow, 1974. Recorded Melodiya C10 15360/20867 002.
The Seasons Op 39/1 (unaccompanied chorus) 1979; first performed Moscow, 1979.
Three Poems Op 34 (bass, symphony orchestra; Rubtsov) 1982; first performed Moscow, 1989.
The Winter Etudes Op 39/2 (chorus, vibraphone, crotales) 1983; first performed Tallinn, 1983.

PUBLICATIONS

By Ledenyov: (ed) *Georgi Sviridov*, Moscow, 1979; "Na tsene—*Loengrin*", in *Sovetskii artist*, 19 June 1983; "O V.Y. Shebaline", in *Pamyati V. Y. Shebaline*, Moscow, 1984; "Georgi Sviridov", in *Muzyka v SSSR*, 1, 1984; "Shtrikhi k portretu Aleksandra Vedernikova", in *A. Vedernikov*, Moscow, 1985; "Andrei Eshpai i ego muzyka", in *A. Eshpai*, Moscow, 1988; "Podlinnost" [on V. Fedoseev], Moscow, 1989; "Shtrikhi k portretu A. N. Alexandrovna—kompozitora i pedagoga", in *A.N. Aleksandrov*, Moscow, 1990.

On Ledenyov: Alfred Schnittke, "Navstrechu slushatelyu", in *Sovertskaya muzyka*, 1, 1962; Dmitri Blagoi, "Chtob vsyudu byla tol'ko schast'e", in *Sovertskaya muzyka*, 6, 1967; Janos Breuer, "Zene; kronika", in *Nepszabadsag* (Budapest), 15 October 1974; Svetlana Savenko, "O tvorchesve RL" in *Muzyka i sovremennost/Muzyka*, 10, 1976; ; Aleksandr Medvedev, "RL: epos i lirika", in *Kniga i iskusstvo v SSSR*, 34 (3) 1982; Hannelore Gerlach, in *Funfzig sowjetische Komponisten*, Leipzig, 1984; Svetlana Savenko, "Estestvennost' tvorcheskoi evolyutsii", in *Muzyka Rossii*, Moscow, 1984; Margarita Katunyan, "Grani krasoty i smysla" in *Muzyka v SSSR*, 2, 1986; Kimmo Lilja, "RL kehottaa saveltajia saveltamaan", in *Turun sanomat*, Turku, Finland, 1989.

Roman Ledenyov comments:

In the art of the 20th century, particularities of style have in my opinion started to play a more important role than inner contest. The presence of original technological apparatus and signs of eccentric fantasy can no longer guarantee the quality of the creative persona.

The most notable recent trend in music—minimalism—represents an interesting reaction to the excessive complexities of the 1960s avant-garde, but, like other movements, it has become not so much the expression of the individuality of major talents, as a tendency dictated by fashion. Having arisen as a polemical stance against previous styles, it now suffers from a certain extremism and oversimplification.

At the beginning of my creative career, the music of Sergei Prokofiev served as my artistic model. In the 1960s I was influenced, like many others at the time, by the New Viennese School and by Webern in particular. But from then on I felt an urge to write in a simpler idiom which was linked to the traditions of the Russian school and in particular its inclination towards drawn-out melodies. A great exponent of this trend here is Georgi Sviridov, who some consider to be an innovator, others a reactionary.

Many young composers—the students I see at the Conservatoire—are striving to write music which is uncomplicated, clear and harmonious. Some see this as backward-looking, but there are others who manage to write music that is fresh, modern and natural.

Tendencies towards refined and rational composition will probably become less prominent. But experimental art is vital, as are searches for new means and a new expressive language.

* * *

Roman Ledenyov is one of that same generation of composers to which such composers as Alfred Schnittke and Edison Denisov belong. Like them, he grew up in the Stalinist era, cut off from most Western music from Wagner onwards. Like his friends and contemporaries, he was mightily stimulated by the comparative freedoms of the Khrushchev Thaw and the new contacts with the West that came about that time.

There are a number of closer parallels too between Alfred Schnittke and Ledenyov. Both were clearly impressed by their discovery of the music of Schoenberg and the Second Viennese School. And both wrote works in the early 1960s that show them grappling to integrate what was new to them with the musical language which they already knew.

But there are differences too. To listen to a work like Schnitte's First Violin Sonata is to hear a young composer trying to make a twelve-note row—constructed of a chain of thirds—throw up melodies and expressive gestures more reminiscent of, say, Shostakovich. Schnittke is moving from Schoenberg to Shostakovich.

Ledenyov on the other hand in a work like his *Violin Concerto* seems to be moving in the opposite direction, from Shostakovich (and indeed Prokofiev) towards Schoenberg. The piece begins as a typical concerto in a recognisably mid-century Soviet idiom, but from the end of the exposition onwards (the concerto is in a single large movement) it enters an increasingly anguished and fractured musical territory, in the course of which the basic thematic material is made to encounter a whole series of twelve-tone ideas. The feeling of chromatic saturation eventually crystalises into a colossal statement of one fundamental row.

The *Violin Concerto* is evidently Ledenyov's attempt to grapple with what is new. As such, not surprisingly, it is shot through with the inflections of expressionism. This style did not remain characteristic of his language, for almost immediately after finishing this work, the composer embarked on two other concertos (for flute and viola) which both show a radical pruning and toning down. The *Concerto-Nocturne* for flute is particularly remarkable, not least in its bizarre scoring for an assortment of keyboard instruments, harps, guitars and percussion, as well as a section of violins. It opens with an eleven-note row, articulated by the "orchestra" in a Webernian pointiliste manner. But the flute line that grows out of this is by contrast, soft, linear and nostalgic. The resulting synthesis between these two quite opposite styles is beautifully handled to create an intimate, unusual music.

The tendency towards the miniature that was initiated by the viola and flute concertos becomes even more marked in the works that Ledenyov produced over the following few years. In collections such as his *Six Pieces* for string quartet and harp, and the *Ten Sketches* and *Seven Moods* for a variety of mixed ensembles, he pursued the ideal of Webernian compression without ever allowing his music to sound quite like Webern. Listening to this music one has almost the impression that Ledenyov is determined to show that the "intonations" of Russian music are just as capable of being expressed within the shortest time-span as any German motive or principle of voice-leading.

But there is more than mere intention at work in these pieces. Ledenyov here speaks with a special tone of voice, a quiet precision of vision, an atmosphere of humility and and absence of self-promotion, that is certainly a most unusual and stimulating quality to find in the normally theatrical and often noisily complaining world of Soviet music. It is certainly through his miniatures that Ledenyov has made his most remarkable contribution to contemporary music.

In later years, perhaps not surprisingly, Ledenyov has turned away from miniature expression as well as from any interest in the musical values of the Second Viennese School. After a bleak period of silence he re-emerged under the influence of the conservative Slavophile Georgy Sviridov as a neo-Russianist. Works such as the *Concerto-Romance* for piano and orchestra and the *Concerto-Elegy* for cello and orchestra show him writing in a language whose melody and harmony owes most to figures like Tchaikovsky and Rachmaninov, albeit with a fluidity and a feeling for general outlines rather than precise detail that mark the music out as still of our own time rather than of that of those masters.

And, although at first glance, it may seem that Ledenyov has abandoned precisely those qualities that made his earlier work so interesting, even his newer "Russian" music is controlled by a sense of tact, gentleness and distinction that still make this composer one of the more attractive figures working in the Soviet Union today.

—Gerard McBurney

LEE, Noel. American; resident in France. Born in Nanking, China, 25 December 1924. Educated at Harvard University, Cambridge, Massachusetts (under Walter Piston, Irving Fine and Tillman Merritt), 1942–3, 1946–8, B.A.; New England Conservatory of Music, Boston, 1946–8, artist's diploma; further composition under Nadia Boulanger, Paris. Served in U.S. Army, 1943–45. Performing and recording pianist; visiting professor, Brandeis University, Waltham, Massachusetts, summers 1958–9; visiting professor, Dartmouth College, Hanover, New Hampshire, summers 1968–9; visiting professor, Cornell University, Ithaca, New York, springs 1967, 1972, 1986. Recipient: Prix Lili Boulanger, 1953; Young Composers' Contest Prize, Louisville Orchestra, 1954; American Academy of Arts and Letters Award, 1959; 1st prize (for *Five Songs on Lorca*), Arthur Shepherd Composition Contest, 1961; 2nd prize (for *Four Etudes Set II*), Arthur Honegger Composition Contest, 1986. Mailing address: 4 villa Laugier, 75017 Paris, France.

Publishers: Schott, Mainz; Editions Billaudot, Paris; Oxford University Press; Theodore Presser, U.S.A.; Southern Music, U.S.A.; MMB Music, St Louis.

Symphonies/orchestral:

Capriccio: On the Return of Beloved Friends 1952; first performed Louisville, Kentucky, 1954.
Fantaisie-Ballet 1953; first performed Nancy, France, 1954.
Overtures and Litanies (string orchestra) 1954; first performed Paris, 1957.
Diversions (chamber orchestra) 1958; first performed Moscow, 1963.
Profile 1958.
Elegies and Variations 1960.
Errances (symphonic band) 1972; first performed Ithaca, New York, 1973.
Caprices on Name Schoenberg (piano, orchestra) 1975; first performed Paris, 1976. Recorded CRI 408.
Triptyque (violin, piano, orchestra) 1986.

Chamber/instrumental:

Sonata Mostly in minor (violin) 1951; first performed Copenhagen, 1973.
Three Preludes: Mobiles, Ink drawing, Dry Points (piano) 1951; first performed Bryanston, 1951.
Pavane (2 flutes, piano—3 hands; or 2 harps) 1951; first performed Château d'Artigny, 1984.
Fantasy Around C (2 pianos) 1952; first performed Paris, 1954.
Capriccio scherzoso (piano—4 hands) 1952; first performed Bamberg, 1952.
Partita (oboe, clarinet, horn, bassoon, piano) 1952, revised 1987; first performed Paris, 1957.
Variations (harpsichord, flute, violin, cello) 1953; first performed Paris, 1953. Recorded Fona TF 130.
Fantaisie—Ballet (3 pianos) 1953, revised 1987.
Sonata in One Movement (piano) 1955; first performed Paris, 1955. Recorded Fona TF 122; Circe 87114 LD.
Two Movements (string quartet) 1956; first performed Paris, 1957.
Dialogues (violin, piano) 1958; first performed Boston, 1958. Recorded Fona TF 130; CRI 408.
Diversions: Parade, Cavorting, Encounter, White Heat (piano—4 hands) 1958, revised 1984.
Sonatine (piano) 1959; first performed Paris, 1960. Recorded Fona TF 122; Circe 87114 LD.
Two Movements for Trio (violin, cello, piano) 1960; first

performed La Rochelle, 1960. Recorded Fona TF 130.

Four Etudes Set I (on a Rhythm from Béla Bartók with Varied Sonorities for High Notes and for Low Notes) (piano) 1961; first performed Paris, 1962. Recorded Fona TF 122; Circe 87114 LD.

Commentaries on a Theme from Aaron Copland (trumpet, clarinet, piano) 1966; first performed Ada, U.S.A, 1971.

Four Etudes Set II (for Legato Playing with Sonorous Effects for Velocity on Chords from Charles Ives) (piano) 1967; first performed Berlin, 1967. Recorded Fona TF 122; Circe 87114 LD.

L'Ami, l'adoré (violin, cello, horn, piano) 1969; first performed Amsterdam, 1972.

Convergences (flute, harpsichord) 1972; first performed Ithaca, New York, 1972. Recorded Fona TF 130; CRI 408.

Errances (2 pianos—8 hands, some percussion) 1972, revised 1980; first performed Amsterdam, 1983.

Chroniques (piano) 1977; first performed Estoril, Portugal, 1979. Recorded Estoril 87114 LD.

Triedre (violin, piano) 1980; first performed London, 1981.

Variations antiques (flute, piano) 1981.

Intervalle (piano) 1982.

Multiples (harpsichord) 1985; first performed Washington, D.C., 1986.

Mosaïques (organ) 1989; first performed St Bernard de Comminges, 1989.

Vocal/choral:

The Song of Songs (soprano, piano; biblical) 1949; first performed Paris 1950.

Rhapsodies from the Unknown Prophet (soloists, reciter, SATB chorus, orchestra or 2 pianos; Old Testament) 1952, revised 1979.

Four Songs from Hamlet (unaccompanied soprano: "How Should I Your True Love Know?", "Tomorrow Is St Valentine's Day", "They Bore Him Bare-Faced"; unaccompanied baritone: "The Grave Digger's Song") 1953; first performed Paris, 1954.

Paraboles (tenor, SMsATBarB chorus, orchestra, transcribed for organ, flute, oboe, bassoon, harp, percussion; Valéry) 1954.

Five Songs on Lorca (soprano, flute, guitar) 1955; first performed Paris 1956. Recorded CRI 147.

Three Intimate Songs (tenor, piano; Makanowitzky) 1955; first performed Paris 1956.

Four Ballades (dramatic soprano, orchestra; Pozzi) 1956; first performed Paris, 1958.

Sonnets of Summer and Sorrow (bass-baritone, horn, piano; Shakespeare) 1957; first performed Paris, 1959.

Devouring Time (SATB chorus, piano concertante; Shakespeare, Sonnet 19) 1957, revised 1975.

Seis canciones amarillas (soprano or baritone, piano; Lorca) 1959; first performed New York, 1960.

Luna de tarde (mezzo-soprano or baritone, piano; Lorca) 1959.

Four Songs on Baudelaire (mezzo-soprano, or baritone, piano) 1971; first performed Lyon, 1973.

Songs of Calamus (tenor or soprano, clarinet, cello, small percussion, piano; Whitman) 1976; first performed Paris, 1976.

Duo—Ut ou Do? (dramatic soprano, baritone, piano) 1978; first performed Nancy, France, 1978.

Three Songs from Shakespeare ("Take, O Take Those Lips Away", "Orpheus", "The Grave Digger's Song"; baritone, guitar) 1979.

Three Songs from Shakespeare ("Take, O Take Those Lips Away", "Orpheus", "Who Is Sylvia?"; tenor, clarinet, cello, vibraphone) 1982; first performed Paris, 1982.

Deux Chants en trio (high soprano, violin, piano) 1985; first performed Maisons-Lafitte, 1985.

Azurs (mezzo-soprano or baritone, piano—4 hands; Rimbaud) 1986.

Stand on the Highest Pavement (mezzo-soprano, piano; Eliot) 1988.

Two Songs from Shakespeare's Plays ("Take, O Take Those Lips Away", "Orpheus with His Lute"; mezzo-soprano or baritone, cello, piano) 1989; first performed St Bernard de Comminges, 1989.

Other:

Our Drawings (documentary film score; flute, clarinet, piano, percussion) 1953; first performed Paris, 1953.

Lorraine-Escaut (documentary film score; chamber orchestra) 1957; first performed Paris, 1957.

Profondeur 4000 (documentary film score; chamber orchestra) 1957; first performed Paris, 1957.

Vingt Minutes à Sollac (documentary film score; chamber orchestra) 1961; first performed Paris, 1961.

Cadenzas and organ points to the following piano concertos: Mozart—K.242, K.271, K.288, K.365, K.414, K.415, K.449, K.450, K.453, K.466, K.467, K.482, K.491, K.503. K.595; Beethoven—Piano Concerto No 1.

Completion of piano works by Schubert: *Sonata in C* D.346, *Sonata in F# minor* D.571 and 570, *Sonata in C* D.613 and 612, *Sonata in F minor* D.625 and 506, *Sonata in C* D.840, *Impromptu in C minor D.916C, Sonata Movement in E minor* D.994.

Recordings by Lee: piano works by Claude Debussy, Antonin Dvořák, Jules Massenet, Maurice Ravel, Franz Schubert, Camille Saint-Saens, Igor Stravinsky.

PUBLICATIONS

On Lee: Art Lange, in *Fugue*, February 1980; Edward Tatnall Canby, in *Audio*, August 1980.

Noel Lee comments:

The principal influences of my earlier years were Igor Stravinsky and Aaron Copland—rhythm is extremely important in all my works—and in later years the orchestra of Henri Dutilleux.

Music is made to be heard (the composer is not a visual artist) and, more important, it should be made to communicate, not *only* to other musicians, but nevertheless and incidentally *also* to other musicians. The compositional technique employed is the composer's private affair and to expose, explain, dissect it for cult worship is really of no interest.

The *sound* first of all—not only timbre, but particularly the choice of notes and of their relationships to each other. As a performer, I would always prefer, insist even, that the composer assume fully his own profession, leaving nothing of importance—nothing structural in any case—to the whims of "mere" performers.

* * *

"Lee is neither a slave to dodecaphonic methodology nor a free-wheeling Neo-Romantic reactionary; he uses all twelve tones when they suit a particular score, but he is often able to manipulate them in such a way as to create definite tonal effects." This comment, by the American music and record critic Art Lange concerning a recording of Noel Lee's *Caprices on the Name Schoenberg* could probably apply to the harmonic language of the major part of Lee's works. His first influence at Harvard University were the New England symphonists, of which Walter Piston is perhaps the best example. During his studies in Paris with Nadia Boulanger, it was inevitable that Stravinsky's influence should predominate. Later contact with serial music, particularly during the festivals at Dartington Hall in Devon during the 1950s, incited the composer to invent his own serial technique, lightened, tightened, retaining the structural value of tonal centres, however subtle or flexible they may become. (Webern was perhaps a temporary influence here; Schoenberg never was.) Finally, the orchestra and the music of Dutilleux were to make a profound impression.

In general, Lee, who pursues a simultaneous career as concert pianist, is not interested in how his work may look on paper or in fashion, but only in how it sounds. This may confuse those who like to categorize and his critics have been quick to draw unhelpful analogies: "full of Berio-like woodwind colours", "making the outcome sound rather like a French Elliott Carter."

One evident structural element in Lee's work, found also in his playing, is rhythmic drive—a direct, frank, often irregular, always choreographic one. (This is a frequent characteristic of American composers and stems undoubtedly from their contact, if not directly, with jazz musicians.) Nadia Boulanger spoke admiringly of his combination of strength and delicacy. In *Chroniques*, the pianist is asked to pluck and strum the strings; in *Caprices*, he uses the same device and asks the pianist to drum on the wood of the instrument as well. Further evidence of his interest in sound-colour comes in *Convergences* where the flute and harpsichord fall into rhythmic patterns in which they imitate one another, before veering off once again in pursuit of their own instrumental nature. Other than the use of twelve-tone techniques in such a manner as to suggest tonal pivots, mention should be made of Lee's use of dialoguing, not simply between individual instruments or sections of the orchestra, but between motivic elements themselves.

The vocal music is passionate, sometimes violent, dissonant, hallucinogenic and mysterious, perfectly in keeping with texts by Rimbaud, Baudelaire and Lorca.

—Patrick Gillis

LEES, Benjamin (Benjamin Lisniatsky). American. Born in Harbin, Manchuria, 8 January 1924; came to United States in infancy. Educated: piano study, Los Angeles and San Francisco; University of Southern California, Los Angeles (composition under Halsey Stevens, Ingolf Dahl and Ernst Kanitz), 1945–8; private study under George Antheil, 1948–53; further study, Longpont-sur-Orge, France, 1954–5, 1957–61, Vienna, 1955–6, and Helsinki (Fulbright scholar), 1956–7; returned to U.S.A., 1961. Served in U.S. Army, 1942–5. Married Leatrice Banks in 1949. Accompanist, composer of movie scores, early 1950s; teacher of composition, Peabody Conservatory, Baltimore, Maryland, 1962–4, 1966–8, Queen's College, New York, 1964–6, Manhattan School of Music, New York City, 1972–4, and Juilliard School, New York City, 1976–7. Recipient: Guggenheim Fellowship, 1955. Lives in Great Neck, New York. Mailing address: c/o Boosey & Hawkes, 24 West 57th Street, New York, New York 10019, U.S.A.

Publisher: Boosey & Hawkes.

Symphonies/orchestral:

Profile 1952; broadcast NBC Radio, 1952; first concert performance New York City, 18 April 1954.
Declamations (piano, strings) 1953; first performed Oklahoma City, 15 February 1956.
Symphony No 1 1953.
Piano Concerto No 1 1955; first performed Vienna, 26 April 1956.
Divertimento-Burlesca (chamber orchestra) 1957.
Interlude (strings) 1957.
Symphony No 2 1958; first performed Louisville, Kentucky, 3 December 1958. Recorded.
Violin Concerto 1958; first performed Boston, 8 February 1963. Recorded.
Concertante breve 1959.
Concerto for Orchestra 1959; first performed Rochester, New York, 22 February 1962. Recorded.
Interlude (strings) 1960.
Prologue, Capriccio and Epilogue 1961. Recorded.
Oboe Concerto 1963.
Concerto for String Quartet and Orchestra 1964; first performed Kansas City, 19 January 1965. Recorded.
Spectrum 1964.
Concerto for Chamber Orchestra 1966.
Fanfare for a Centennial (brass, percussion) 1966.
Piano Concerto No 2 1966; first performed Boston, 15 March 1968.
Silhouettes 1967.
Symphony No 3 1969. Recorded.
Etudes (piano, orchestra) 1974; first performed Houston, Texas, 28 October 1974.
Passacaglia 1975; first performed Washington, D.C., 13 April 1976.
Labyrinths (wind band) 1975; first performed Bloomington, Indiana, 18 November 1975.
Concerto for Woodwind Quintet and Orchestra 1976; first performed Detroit, Michigan, 7 October 1976.
Variations (piano, orchestra) 1976; first performed Dallas, Texas, 31 March 1976.
Mobiles 1979; first performed New York City, 13 April 1979.
Double Concerto (piano, cello, orchestra) 1982; first performed New York City, 7 November 1982.
Concerto for Brass Choir and Orchestra 1983; first performed Dallas, Texas, 18 March 1983.
Portrait of Rodin 1984.
Symphony No 4: Memorial Candles (mezzo-soprano, violin, orchestra; Sachs) 1985.
Symphony No 5 1986.

Chamber/instrumental:

Sonata No 1 (piano) 1949.
Sonata No 2 (piano) 1950.
Sonata (horn, piano) 1951.
Sonata (2 pianos) 1951.
String Quartet No 1 1952. Recorded.

Evocation (flute) 1953.
Toccata (piano) 1953.
Sonata No 1 (violin, piano) 1953.
Movemente da camera (flute, clarinet, piano, cello) 1954.
Fantasia (piano) 1954.
Ten Pieces (piano) 1954.
Three Variables (oboe, clarinet, bassoon, horn, piano) 1955.
String Quartet No 2 1955. Recorded.
Sonata No 3: Sonata breve (piano) 1956.
Six Ornamental Etudes (piano) 1957.
Kaleidoscopes (piano) 1959.
Epigrams (piano) 1960; withdrawn.
Three Preludes (piano) 1962.
Sonata No 4 (piano) 1963. Recorded.
Invenzione (violin) 1965.
Duo (flute, clarinet) 1967.
Study No 1 (cello) 1969.
Odyssey (piano) 1970.
Sonata No 2 (violin, piano) 1973. Recorded.
Collage (string quartet, wind quintet, percussion) 1973; first performed Milwaukee, Wisconsin, 8 May 1973.
Dialogue (cello, piano) 1977; first performed New York City, 2 March 1977.
Sonata (cello, piano) 1981. Recorded.
String Quartet No 3 1981.
Fantasy Variations (piano) 1983.
Piano Trio 1983.

Vocal/choral:

Four Songs of the Night (soprano, flute, oboe, clarinet, bassoon, horn, trumpet, timpani, celeste, 2 violins, viola, cello, double bass; Nickson) 1955.
Three Songs (alto, piano; Nickson, Blake) 1959.
Cyprian Songs (baritone, piano; Nickson) 1960.
Visions of Poets (soprano, tenor, chorus, orchestra; Whitman) 1961; first performed Seattle, Washington, 15 May 1962.
The Trumpet of the Swan (narrator, orchestra; White) 1972; first performed Philadelphia, 13 May 1972.
Staves (soprano, piano; Nickson) 1979.
Omen (soprano, piano; Nickson) 1980.
Paumanok (mezzo-soprano, piano; Whitman) 1980.

Opera:

The Oracle 1956.
Medea in Corinth (soprano, mezzo-soprano, baritone, bass, wind quintet, optional timpani; after Jeffers) 1970; first performed London, 10 January 1971.
The Gilded Cage (Reid) 1970–2; withdrawn.

Other:

Soliloquy Music for King Lear (flute) 1975.
Scarlatti Portfolio (ballet; orchestra) 1979; first performed San Francisco, 15 March 1979.

PUBLICATIONS

On Lees: D. Cooke, "The Music of BL", in *Tempo*, 51, 1959, and "The Recent Music of BL", in *Tempo*, 64, 1963; Niall O'Loughlin, "BL'S String Quartet Concerto", in *Tempo*, 82, 1967, and "Two Works by BL", in *Tempo*, 93, 1970; Nicholas Slonimsky, "BL in Excelsis", in *Tempo*, 113, 1975.

* * *

It is always dangerous to read programmatic intentions into perfectly rational and conventional technical devices, but there is something curiously symbolic about the solo instrumental passages with which Noel Lees characteristically opens his symphonies and concertos. However traditional in orientation Lees's music has been—and he has shown little sign of submission to the blandishments of the avant-garde—he is nevertheless highly individual, as befits a man who learned his craft with the maverick George Antheil, and cleaves to a rather solitary furrow. Though the basic architecture of his orchestral work is classical, its exact configurations are unusual, as seen in his preference for concertos with multiple soloists and for devices like the slow climaxes to the very fine Second and Third symphonies.

Though double and occasional triple concertos are well attested in the classical canon, Lees has produced convincing works for string quartet and orchestra, woodwind quintet and orchestra, and, more recently, brass and orchestra, in which he shows a confident grasp of complex orchestral forms. He has also written a fine *Double Concerto*, and a *Concerto for Orchestra* which strongly reflects his early interest in Bartók's elegant dissonances. His other main influence was Prokofiev, from whose work he learned how to deploy effectively asymmetric rhythms, how to assimilate unusual semitonal intervals within a basically tonal structure, and how to orchestrate in such a way that instrumental groups assume as well-defined a voice as in chamber music.

Lees's symphonies are infinitely more interesting than those of his teacher Antheil, an unapologetic ultra-modernist, who later apologised and returned to rather drearily accessible scores of a thoroughly regressive sort. Lees, by contrast, has remained remarkably true to his original conception. His distinctive voice was established early with the well-received *Profile*, a work of great freshness. Its subtle ironies have deepened into something like tragic expressiveness by the time of the Fourth Symphony, which features a part for mezzo-soprano and a setting of verse by Nelly Sachs. Lees has by no means exhausted the seam; he has since written a further symphony of great power and his orchestral music of the 1980s shows no sign of tiredness.

Of his instrumental works, the most impressive are the two early string quartets. Set alongside exactly contemporary American quartets by George Rochberg and Milton Babbitt, it is again clear that Lees is no doctrinaire modernist but an independent musical thinker who has gone back to fundamentals with a finely developed sense of instrumental values and an impressive stock of informing ideas.

Lees's vocal and dramatic work is less well-known, though the two fine Whitman settings are highly regarded. Perhaps his finest vocal piece, *Visions of Poets* rises to the challenge of Whitman's long lines with an uncluttered orchestral score that combines the concision and elisions of piano accompaniment with the richness of full scoring. His dramatic *Medea of Corinth*, based on a text by Robinson Jeffers, is *sui generis*, an experiment that does not quite come off. Elsewhere, Lees has turned to J.R. Nickson for tersely lyrical texts that perfectly suit his style.

The piano music is richly varied, with the same emphasis on angular rhythms and unusual chord resolutions, all within a reassuringly tonal framework. The two-piano Sonata of 1951 is a bravura masterpiece. Lees gives no sign of pandering to any lowest common denominator. Nonetheless, he has produced a body of music which is utterly approachable and inexhaustibly rich. As he enters his fifth decade as an active composer, he deserves the widest and closest attention.

—Russell Kane

LEEUW, Ton de. Dutch. Born in Rotterdam, 16 November 1926. Educated: Studied piano and theory under Louis Toebosch, Breda, and composition under Henk Badings, Amsterdam, 1947–9; composition under Olivier Messiaen and Thomas de Hartmann, Paris, 1949–50; further study in ethnomusicology under Jaap de Kunst, Amsterdam, 1950–4; study trips to India, Iran, Japan and the Philippines, 1961. Married Arlette Reboul in 1952; 3 daughters and 1 son. Elder brother of pianist/composer Reinbert de Leeuw, born 1938. Director of sound, 1954–9, and programme director, contemporary and non-Western music, from 1956, Dutch National Radio, Hilversum; professor of composition, Amsterdam and Utrecht conservatories, since 1959; lecturer in contemporary music, University of Amsterdam, 1962–84; director of Amsterdam Conservatory, since 1972. Recipient: Prix Italia (for *Hiob*), 1956; Prix des Jeunesses Musicales (for *String Quartet No 1*), 1961; Mathijs Vermeulen Prize (for *Car Nos Vignes sont en fleur*), 1982; Johan Wagenaar Prize, 1983. Mailing address: Costeruslaan 4, Hilversum, The Netherlands.

Publisher: Donemus.

Symphonies/orchestral:

Concerto grosso (string orchestra) 1946.
Treuermuziek in memoriam Willem Pijper 1948.
Symphony (strings, percussion) 1950.
Symphony for Strings 1951.
Pluto Suite 1952.
Concerto for Violin and Orchestra 1953.
Suite (youth orchestra) 1954.
Mouvements rétrogrades 1957. Recorded BFO/CVCD 10; Radio Nederland RN 1965 109 531; Polygram BV 6814.781/786.
Nritta (orchestral dance) 1961. Recorded Radio Nederland RN Opus 65.
Concerto for Violin and Orchestra No 2 1961.
Ombres 1961. Recorded DAVS 6301.
Symphony of Winds 1963. Recorded DAVS 66/4.
De Bijen 1964.
Syntaxis II 1966; first performed Utrecht, 16 May 1966.
Spatial Music I (variable orchestra, 32–48 players) 1966. Recorded DAVS 7001; Radio Nederland RN Opus 68.
Spatial Music III (4 orchestral groups) 1967.
Spatial Music IV: Homage to Igor Stravinsky (chamber orchestra) 1968.
Music for Strings 1970. Recorded DAVS 7273/4; Radio Nederland RN 6808.047.
Gending (gamelan orchestra) 1975; first performed Hilversum, 11 October 1975. Recorded CV 7602.
Alba (chamber concerto) 1982, revised 1985.
Resonances 1984–5.
Concerto for Two Guitars and Chamber String Orchestra 1987–8.
Piano Concerto: Danses sacrées 1990.

Chamber/instrumental:

Scherzo (piano) 1948.
Trio (violin, viola, cello) 1948.
Introduzione e passacaglia (organ) 1949.
Sonatina (piano) 1949.
Sonata (flute, piano) 1949.
Sonata (2 pianos) 1950.
Four Preludes (piano) 1950.
Variations on a French Popular Song (piano) 1950.
Five Etudes (piano) 1951.
Sonata (violin, piano) 1951.
Vier Ritmische etudes (piano) 1952.
Trio (flute, clarinet, piano) 1952.
Vijf schetsen (oboe, clarinet, bassoon, violin, viola, cello) 1952.
Drie Afrikaanse etudes (piano) 1954.
Lydische Suite ((piano) 1954.
Zes Dansen (piano) 1955.
Andante en Vivace (flute, piano) 1955.
Sonatina (violin, piano) 1955.
String Quartet No 1 1957–8. Recorded Omega 145.543–45; Columbia 33 CHX 8.
Antiphonie (wind quintet, electronics) 1960. Recorded CV 7803.
String Quartet No 2 1964. Recorded CV 8302; Philips 6500881.
Schelp (flute, viola, guitar) 1964.
The Four Seasons (harp) 1964.
Men Go Their Ways (piano) 1964. Recorded CV 7904.
Night Music (flute) 1966. Recorded Radio Nederland RN Opus 72.
Music for Violin 1967. Recorded CV 7602.
Music for Oboe 1969.
Music for Organ and Twelve Players 1970–1.
Reversed Night (flute) 1971.
Spatial Music II (percussion) 1971.
Midare (marimba) 1972. Recorded CV 7602; Moers Music 0 1068—LC 6059.
Sweelinck Variations (organ) 1972–3.
Music for Trombone 1973–4.
Mo-do (harpsichord or clavichord) 1974.
Rime (flute, harp) 1974.
Linkerhand en rechterhand (piano) 1976. Recorded Attacca Babel 8421–6.
Mountains (bass clarinet, tape) 1977.
Modal Music (accordion) 1978–9.
Interlude (guitar) 1984. Recorded CVS 1986/6; Radio Nederland RN Opus 85.
Apparences I (cello) 1987.
Apparences II (clarinet quartet) 1987.
Les Adieux (piano) 1988.
Hommage à Henri (clarinet, piano) 1989.
Trio (flute, bass clarinet, piano) 1990.

Vocal/choral:

Berceuse presque nègre (medium voice, piano) 1948.
Diablerie (soprano, piano) 1948.
Goden en zangers (soprano, piano) 1948.
Die Weise von Liebe und Tod (voice, piano) 1948.
De ueren van de bittere pasasie Jesu Christi (voice, piano) 1949.
Vijf Liederen (voice, piano; García Lorca) 1952. Recorded Eurosound 46 675.
Twee Liederen (soprano, piano; Mistral) 1953.
De Toverfluit (4 songs for soprano, flute, cello, piano) 1954.
Acht Europese liederen (voice, piano) 1954.
Vier liederen (voice, 3 recorders) 1955.
Hiob / Job (soloists, chorus, orchestra, tape) 1956.
Brabant (medium voice, orchestra) 1959.
Haiku (songs and interludes, voice, piano) 1963.
Psalm 118 (3-part chorus, 2 trombones or organ) 1966.
Haiku II (soprano, orchestra) 1968.
Vocalise (alto) 1968.
Lamento Pacis (mixed chorus, instruments) 1969.
Cloudy Forms (4-part male chorus) 1970.

The Magic of Music (2-part chorus) 1970.
The Birth of Music (2-part chorus) 1975.
The Birth of Music II (voices, speaker, tape) 1978.
And They Shall Reign For Ever (mezzo-soprano, clarinet, piano, percussion) 1981. Recorded CV 8502.
Car Nos Vignes sont en fleur (12-part mixed chorus) 1981. Recorded CV 8502.
Invocations (chorus, mezzo-soprano, instrumental ensemble) 1983. Recorded CV 8502.
Chimères (2 counter tenors, tenor, 2 baritones, bass) 1984.
Les Chants de kabir (6 voices) 1985.
Transparence (18-part chorus, 3 trumpets, 3 trombones) 1986.
Cinq Hymnes (chorus, 2 pianos, percussion) 1987–8.

Opera:

Alceste (television opera) 1963; broadcast 13 March 1963.
De Droom / The Dream (soprano, alto, baritone, mixed chorus, orchestra; haiku) 1963; first performed The Netherlands, 16 June 1965. Recorded Radio Nederland RN 518/519/520.

Other:

Electronic Suite (tape) 1958.
De Bijen / The Bees (ballet; orchestra) 1964; first performed Arnheim, 15 September 1965.
Krishna en Radha (ballet; flute, harp, percussion) 1964.
Syntaxis I (tape) 1966.
Litany of Our Time (television play; soprano, flute, harp, piano, double bass, 2 percussion, 3-part chorus, tape, live electronics) 1969–70; broadcast, 1 January 1971. Recorded CVS 1986/6.
Chronos (4 sound tracks) 1980.
Clair-Obscur (electronic) 1981–2. Recorded CVS 1986/6.

PUBLICATIONS

By de Leeuw: *Muziek van de twintigate eeuw / Music of the Twentieth Century*, Utrecht, 1964; also *Key Notes 3*, 1976, and *Key Notes 9*, 1979.

* * *

In the late 1940s Ton de Leeuw studied composition with Henk Badings, and then moved to Paris for a year to study composition with Olivier Messiaen and orchestration with Thomas de Hartmann. Already at that time de Leeuw had developed a vital interest in non-Western music, sensing the need to go beyond the boundaries of European music: " . . . it was no longer possible for me to project my musical development against the sole background of a few centuries of European music. My interests rapidly widened: the twentieth century, the Renaissance, the Middle Ages, all music outside of Europe." His encounter with non-Western cultures provides not only a key to his music, it also reveals much about his socio-philosophical thinking and view on life, fully aware that "there are other people who live, think and feel in terms totally different from ours". Exploring this embracing of many cultures, he undertook further studies in ethnomusicology with Jaap de Kunst in Amsterdam from 1950–4.

He first gained international attention in 1956 with his radiophonic oratorio *Job*, which was awarded the Prix Italia. But it is his subsequent work for orchestra, *Mouvements rétrogrades* that embodies certain basic features which will recur throughout his large compositional output, and marks the beginning of his mature development. Such factors include his search for a static style, purposefully reducing expressive and emotional elements, the balanced and quiet atmosphere in his music which provides it with a sort of stillness, but above all his application of modality. This main feature should not be understood in the Western sense of the term (which emphasizes the scalar aspects of a mode), but rather in its original meaning stressing additional features such as pitch succession, pitch hierarchy and ornamentation which constitute the individuality of a particular mode (for example the Indian *raga*).

After his first trip to Asia in 1961, where he spent several months in India and Iran, de Leeuw's pieces from the 1960s to the mid 1970s are dominated by the encounter of Western and Oriental traditions. Most notable are *Symphony of Winds*, a homage to Stravinsky, *Haiku II* and *Lamento Pacis*. *Gending*, a work for gamelan, epitomizes his "individual acculturation", as he summarizes in a note to the piece: "At both the conscious and the subconscious levels East and West constitute one vast source of human action. The 'other culture' is no longer something whose individuality can be approached from outside, but is a living factor in the creative perception of the individual."

Along with his interest in non-Western musics, de Leeuw has always been involved with the more experimental developments of the post-World War II era, such as the exploration of "space" in the cycle *Spatial Music* or new systems of notation as in *Midare*. De Leeuw has also been involved with the electro-acoustic medium, directing for some years the Sweelinck studio in Amsterdam. After early works such as *Antiphonie* and *Syntaxis I* he did little work in this medium, but a revived interest starts with *Mountains* and continues with works such as *The Birth of Music II*, *Chronos* and *Clair-Obscur*.

From the late 1970s onwards de Leeuw's modal thinking becomes more diatonic. *Car Nos Vignes sont en fleur*, which won the Matthijs Vermeulen Prize, is the first composition of a triptych of pieces on biblical texts and its primary modal feature is centricity of pitch. *And They Shall Reign For Ever* and *Invocations* complete the triptych.

In 1983 he was awarded the Johan Wagenaar Prize, in recognition of his entire oeuvre to date and as a tribute to a composer who occupies a central position in post-War Dutch composition. De Leeuw has been very successful in developing a genuine personal style in which elements from other cultures have been absorbed and integrated to expand and enrich his own world.

—Christiane ten Hoopen

LeFANU, Nicola (Frances). British/English. Born in Essex, 28 April 1947; daughter of Dame Elizabeth Maconchy. Educated at St Mary's School, Calne, Wiltshire, 1958–64; early composition study under Jeremy Dale Roberts; St Hilda's College, Oxford, 1965–8, B.A., 1968, M.A., 1971; Royal College of Music, London, 1968–9; Harvard University, Cambridge, Massachusetts, and Brandeis University, Waltham, Massachusetts (composition under Earl Kim and Seymour

Shifrin; as Harkness Fellow), 1973–4. Married David Lumsdaine, *q.v.*, 16 March 1979; 1 son. Director of music, Francis Holland School, London, 1969–72, and St Paul's Girls School, London, 1975–7; senior lecturer, King's College, London, since 1977 (post shared with David Lumsdaine); composer in residence, New South Wales Conservatorium, Sydney, 1979 (post shared with David Lumsdaine). Recipient: Cobbett Prize (for *Variations* for oboe quartet), 1969; BBC Composers Prize (for *Variations* for oboe quartet), 1972; Mendelssohn Scholarship, 1973; Harkness Fellowship, 1973; Honorary D.Mus., University of London, 1988; Leverhulme Award, 1989. Mailing address: 9 Kempe Road, London NW6 6SP, England.

Publisher: Novello.

Symphonies/orchestral:

Preludio I (chamber orchestra) 1967; first performed London, 1969.
The Hidden Landscape 1973; first performed London, 1973.
Columbia Falls 1975; first performed Birmingham, 1976.
Preludio II (chamber orchestra) 1976; first performed London, 1977.
Farne 1980; first performed London, 1980.
Variations (piano, orchestra) 1982; first performed London, 31 December 1982.
Concerto for Alto Saxophone and String Orchestra 1990; first performed Kanstinen, Finland, January 1990.

Chamber/instrumental:

Soliloquy (oboe) 1966; first performed Oxford, March 1967.
Variations (oboe, violin, viola, cello) 1968; first performed London, 1969.
Chiaroscuro (piano) 1969; first performed London, February 1970.
Abstracts and a Frame (violin, piano) 1971; first performed London, October 1971.
Songs and Sketches (6 or more cellos) 1971; first performed Farnham, Surrey, May 1972.
Omega (organ) 1971, revised 1984; first performed London, 1972.
Clarinet Quintet 1971; withdrawn.
Collana (solo percussion, flute/alto flute, clarinet/bass clarinet, violin, cello, double bass) 1976; first performed Boston, 25 April 1976.
Deva (solo cello, alto flute, clarinet, bassoon, horn, violin, viola, double bass) 1979; first performed London, 23 March 1979. Recorded Chandos ABR 1017.
Trio I (flute/piccolo, cello, percussion) 1980; first performed London, 15 June 1981.
SPNM Birthday Fanfare (2 trumpets) 1983; first performed London, 1983.
Moon over Western Ridge, Mootwingee (saxophone quartet) 1985; first performed Stuttgart, 6 November 1985. Recorded col legno BN 30 SL 6.5503.
Invisible Places (clarinet, 2 violins, viola, cello) 1986; first performed Southampton, Hampshire, 4 June 1986.
Lament 1988 (oboe/cor anglais, clarinet/bass clarinet, viola, cello) 1988; first performed London, 30 March 1988.
String Quartet 1988; first performed Bedford, 13 October 1988.
Lullaby (A clarinet, piano) 1988.
Nocturne (cello, piano) 1988; first performed London, 20 October 1988.

Vocal/choral:

Il Cantio dei Cantici II (soprano; Song of Songs) 1968; first performed London, March 1969.
But Stars Remaining (soprano; Day Lewis) 1970; first performed London, February 1971. Recorded Chandos ABR 1017.
Christ Calls Man Home (2 sopranos, 3 unaccompanied SATB choruses) 1971; first performed Cheltenham, Gloucestershire, 4 July 1971.
Rondeaux (tenor, horn; medieval French) 1972; first performed London, November 1972.
The Valleys Shall Sing (SATB chorus, 2 bassoons, 2 trumpets, 3 trombones; Psalms) 1973; first performed Norwich, Norfolk, October 1973.
Paysage (baritone; Apollinaire) 1973; first performed Aldeburgh, Suffolk, 21 June 1973.
The Same Day Dawns (soprano, flute/alto flute, clarinet/bass clarinet, violin, cello, percussion; Tamil, Chinese, Japanese, Kannada, Akkadian) 1974; first performed Boston, 4 November 1974. Recorded Chandos ABR 1017.
The Little Valleys (adapted from *The Valleys Shall Sing* for unaccompanied female chorus; Psalm 65) 1975; published as supplement to *Musical Times*.
For We Are the Stars (16 solo voices SATB; American Indian) 1978; broadcast BBC, 30 September 1982.
Verses from Psalm 90 (soprano, 2 unaccompanied mixed choruses) 1978; first performed London, 5 December 1978.
Like a Wave of the Sea (mixed chorus, ensemble of early instruments; Hindi, Lewis Carroll, Bible) 1981; first performed Nottingham, 1 March 1981.
The Old Woman of Beare (amplified soprano, flute, oboe, clarinet, bassoon, horn, trumpet, trombone, 2 percussion, harp, violin, viola, cello; 9th/10th-century Irish) 1981; first performed London, 3 November 1981.
A Penny for a Song (soprano, piano; early Irish, de la Mare) 1981; first performed Dublin, 8 January 1982.
Rory's Rounds (for young singers; nursery rhymes, riddles) 1983.
Trio 2: Song for Peter (soprano, clarinet, piano; Dickinson, Hughes, Chekhov) 1983; first performed London, 3 March 1983.
Stranded on My Heart (tenor, SATB chorus, string orchestra; traditional, Tagore, John Fuller, Sutton, Hindi) 1984; first performed St Albans, Hertfordshire, 16 June 1984.
Wind Among the Pines: Five Images of Norfolk (soprano, orchestra) 1987; first performed Snape, Suffolk, 1987.
I Am Bread (soprano, piano; Kennelly) 1987; first performed Brighton, Sussex, 21 May 1987.

Opera/dramatic:

Anti-World (music theatre for dancer, soprano, baritone, alto flute, clarinet, percussion; Russian) 1972; first performed June 1972.
The Last Laugh (ballet; soprano, tape, flute, cor anglais, clarinet, percussion, viola, double bass) 1972; first performed London, April 1973.
Dawnpath (chamber opera; baritone, soprano, male dancer, flute/alto flute, clarinet/bass clarinet, horn, cello, percussion; American Indian) 1977; first performed London, 29 September 1977.
The Story of Mary O'Neill (radiophonic opera for soprano, 16 solo voices SATB) 1986; broadcast BBC, 4 January 1989.
The Green Children (children's opera; Crossley-Holland) 1990; first performed King's Lynn, Norfolk, 1990.
Blood Wedding 1991–2; first performed London, 1992.

Other:

Wild Ride to Heaven (radiophonic adventure playground; collaboration with David Lumsdaine) 1980; broadcast BBC, 1980.

PUBLICATIONS

By LeFanu: "Master Musician: An Impregnable Taboo?", in *Contact*, 31, September 1987.

On LeFanu: Valerie O'Brien, "Living British Women Composers", in *The Musical Woman*, 1983; Jane Weiner LePage, in *Women Composers of the Twentieth Century*, vol. 3, 1988.

Nicola LeFanu comments:

In 1985, Jane LePage asked me for a personal statement, and I have expanded and updated it here, since I don't think I can better what I wrote then.

If I look back and consider my life so far (over 25 years of composing), I would say that the two formative influences in my life are two composers: my mother Elizabeth Maconchy, and my husband David Lumsdaine. What I owe them is inestimable.

Beyond that I would look back at my education, and remember the years of musical discovery in my late teens: studying with Jeremy Dale Roberts, friendships begun at Oxford and the Royal College of Music which still continue, and then later the inspiration of working with Earl Kim at Harvard.

If I were to single out particular events, then I think the premiere performances of *Columbia Falls* in 1975, and the experience of raising an infant (my son Peter was born in 1982) would stand out above all else for me. Next after that would come my predilection for opera: working with the BBC Singers on my radio opera *The Story of Mary O'Neill* or working in Norfolk in 1990, rehearsing *The Green Children*, the children's opera I wrote with the poet Kevin Crossley-Holland.

If I had to choose one work to represent me, it would be *The Old Woman of Beare*. I think it encompasses both the lyric and the dramatic aspects of my work, and it could only have been written by a woman.

* * *

Growing up in a cultured household (her mother is the distinguished composer Elizabeth Maconchy, her father William a noted medical historian—and descendant of Sheridan LeFanu) Nicola LeFanu found herself in an ideal environment for a budding composer. Music was as natural a part of life as eating; early on, she attended concerts with her mother and experienced a great deal of modern music at first hand, at an impressionable age.

When LeFanu reached her early composing years—the late 1960s and early 1970s—she had reason to suppose that all that women composers of her mother's generation and later had struggled for was finally bearing fruit. But LeFanu came to recognise an inescapable truth: discrimination—conscious or otherwise—against women composers remains a fact of life. Early on, she saw that for no good reason music by her mother's male contemporaries was more often heard than music by her mother. Reactionaries may argue their corner, but LeFanu has repeatedly made the point that whatever she does as a composer, her music "is written out of the wholeness of myself, and I happen to be a woman". Most people believe that it is impossible to tell if a piece of music is by a man or a woman; this is true only up to a point, and the point is symphonic composition. For whatever reasons, women composers very rarely, if at all, write symphonies.

In this regard, perhaps her mother's example counted (Elizabeth Maconchy wrote one symphony—and that for double string orchestra); but more importantly for LeFanu's development were the encouragement from her mother (recognising in her daughter a genuine creative talent, and not the fascination of childish mimicry) and the aesthetic milieu of London in the late 1960s. For that was notably an age of change: pop music began to be taken very seriously; Pierre Boulez—then chief conductor of the BBC Symphony in collaboration with the Corporation's Music Controller, Sir William Glock—was giving challenging programmes; the spectacularly-gifted 1930s generation of British composers (notably Peter Maxwell Davies, Harrison Birtwistle and Richard Rodney Bennett) was making a big impact on the country's musical life. No wonder the young LeFanu found herself "intoxicated by the diversity of opportunities".

Her music is very much that of her generation: a fluent technique is taken for granted; she adopts a personal approach—not a blind adherence—to serialism; nothing is consciously avoided as a prerequisite or has to be included as a *sine qua non*. Her development shows her growing predelictions rather than early on striking a compositional pose and sticking to it. Unlike her contemporaries who have slid into a miasmic lingua franca, LeFanu's individuality has been apparent from the start. However, she may have been influenced in passing by her mother, by later teachers Jeremy Dale Roberts, Anthony Gilbert, Earl Kim, by Messiaen, Dallapiccola and early Harrison Birtwistle, by the works of her husband David Lumsdaine. Through her work shines the spirit of an artist whose creativity is fully responsive to extra-musical stimuli, especially words, and whose responses have generally taken one of two points of departure: the lyrical, small-scale form and the dramatic, large-scale structure. The former is best found in *Soliloquy* for solo oboe (her first acknowledged work), perhaps also in *Deva* (cello and chamber ensemble), *Invisible Places* (clarinet quintet) and *The Same Day Dawns*; the latter in the orchestral *Columbia Falls* and *The Hidden Landscape*. When they combine in *The Old Woman of Beare* (a work which seems much longer than its 20 minutes), *The Story of Mary O'Neill* (an astonishing radio opera for 17 voices without instruments) and the community opera *The Green Children* the result is arguably the most compelling of her work, free from rhetoric.

The best of LeFanu's music exhibits such characteristics as sensitivity, practicality, colour (through her fastidiously-chosen instrumental combinations) and perseverance. Her deep-seated Celtic lyricism (both her parents are Irish) has—unselfconsciously—produced some of the finest music of her generation.

—Robert Matthew-Walker

LEVINAS, Michaël. French. Born in Paris, 18 April 1949. Educated at Conservatoire National Supérieur de Musique, Paris (composition under Olivier Messiaen, piano under Yvonne Lefébure and Yvonne Loriod, also notation, chamber music, conducting, electro-acoustic music), 1961–74. Married

Danielle Cohen, 2 September 1985. Concert pianist; co-founder (with Gérard Grisey and Tristan Murail), Groupe de l'Itinéraire, 1973; teacher, Ferienkurse für Neue Musik, Darmstadt, 1982, 1986; professor, Conservatoire National Supérieur de Musique, Paris, since 1988. Recipient: Prix de Rome 1975. Mailing address: c/o Salabert, 22 rue Chauchat, 75009 Paris, France.

Publisher: Salabert.

Symphonies/orchestral:

L'orateur muet 1970; first performed Paris, October 1970.
Orchestre 1973; first performed Paris, March 1973.
Ouverture pour une petite fête étrange (2 orchestras, tape) 1979; first performed Metz, 18 November 1979. Recorded Ades 14.072-2.
Reminiscence d'un jardin féerique 1987; first performed Montpellier, 15 July 1987.
La Cloche felée 1988; first performed Paris, 18 February 1990.

Chamber/instrumental:

Arsis et Thesis, ou la chanson du souffle (amplified bass flute) 1971; broadcast Radio France, 1971. Recorded INA-AM 821.10.
Clov et Hamm (trombone, amplified tuba, percussion, 2 tapes) 1973; first performed Paris, 1973. Recorded Ades 14.072-2.
Appels (flute, oboe, clarinet/A clarinet, bassoon, horn, cornet, trombone, piano, double bass—all amplified; 2 percussion) 1974; first performed La Rochelle, 1974. Recorded INA-AM 821.10.
Concerto pour un piano espace (piano, flute, 2 trumpets, 3 trombones, viola, cello) 1976; first performed Paris, 1977.
Pièce sur des thèmes de boîte à musique (piano, harpsichord) 1977; first performed Paris, 1977.
Etude sur un piano espace (piano) 1977; first performed Paris, 1977.
Strettes tournantes-migrations (flute, bass clarinet, bassoon, 2 horns, viola, cello, double bass) 1978; first performed Paris, October 1978.
Contrepoints irréels III—Rencontres (4 flutes; version for 6 flutes, lute, ondes martenot, electric organ, percussion, tape, sound diffusion) 1980; first performed Lille, 1980; revised version first performed Paris, 1981. Original version recorded Ades 14.072-2.
Concerto pour un piano espace No 2 (flute, horn, trumpet, percussion, piano, cello, electronics) 1980; first performed Lyon, 1980.
Les Rires du Gilles (pan flute, clarinet, horn, trumpet, percussion; also version for saxophones) 1981; first performed Metz, 1981. Recorded Ades 14.072-2; saxophone version recorded Poly-Art Records PAR 5301.
Arcades (viola, piano) 1982; first performed Paris, 1982.
Arcades II (viola solo, piano, timbale, 4 violas, 4 cellos, 2 double basses) 1982; first performed Milan, 1982.
Troisième Arcade: Le Choeur des Arches (piano percussion, percussion, 4 violas, 4 cellos, 2 double basses, tape) 1984; first performed Paris, January 1984. Recorded Salabert Actuels SCD 8801.
Quatrième Arcade (arrangement of *Arcade III* for 2 violas, 2 cellos, tape) 1984; first performed Cannes, 1984.
Spirale d'oiseaux (horn, tape, sound diffusion) 1984; first performed Brême, 1984. Recorded Salabert Actuels, 1991.
La Voix des voix (flute/piccolo/alto flute, bass clarinet, bassoon, horn, trumpet, trombone, tuba, 2 percussion, double bass, electronics, echo chamber) 1984.
Cadence pour un lever de rideau (piano percussion, flute, horn) 1984.
Résonances polyphoniques ou la montée des oiseaux (double bass, sound diffusion) 1985; first performed Paris, 1985.
Variation sur un ut clair (piano, electronics) 1986; first performed La Rocque d'Antheron, 6 August 1986.
Voûtes (6 percussion) 1988; first performed Strasbourg, 27 September 1988.
Préfixes (17 musicians) 1990; first performed Paris, 7 March 1991.

Vocal/choral:

Voix dans un vaisseau d'Airain "Chant en escalier" (voice, flute, horn, piano, tape) 1977; first performed Paris, March 1978. Recorded INA-AM 821.10.
La Romance d'Ariel (after Debussy's *Chansons*; soprano, flute, 2 clarinets/bass clarinet, horn, percussion, piano, celeste, violin, cello) 1983; first performed Aix-en-Provence, 1983.
Villanelle (after Berlioz's *Nuits d'été*; soprano or tenor, small orchestra) 1984; first performed France, 1984.
Barberine (after Lekeu, text by Apollinaire; soprano, small orchestra) 1986.
Les Réciproques (3 sopranos, 3 altos, 3 tenors, 3 basses—unaccompanied) 1986; first performed Metz, November 1986.

Opera:

La Conférence des oiseaux (narrator, 2 comic sopranos, flute, saxophones, horn, piano, electric organ, 2 percussion, double bass, tape; Attar/Carrière) 1985; first performed Paris, 11–12 May 1985. Recorded Ades 14.104–2.

PUBLICATIONS

By Levinas: "Qu'est-ce que l'instrumental?", in *Darmstadter Beitrage*, 18, 1982.

* * *

Michaël Levinas has pursued two careers in music, as a composer and as a pianist. Although he has performed many contemporary pieces, many written specially for him, he has specialised in 19th-century music, notably Beethoven, whose complete piano sonatas he has frequently performed and has recorded. Levinas has also specialised in the works of Chopin and Schumann.

While in Messiaen's class at the Conservatoire, he met his gifted contemporaries Gérard Grisey and Tristan Murail; in 1973, they founded the Group de l'Itinéraire, a composers' collective and ensemble which has played a significant role in revitalising contemporary French music. As well as continuing to administer L'Itinéraire, Levinas has become increasingly active as a teacher and lecturer.

His distinctive style arises from his conviction that "all instrumental music tends towards opera"; for him, the act of making music is essentially theatrical, even mimetic. While sharing with his French contemporaries a concern for the acoustic properties of sounds, Levinas is equally fascinated by the psychological associations of instruments. His early bass flute piece *Arsis et Thesis, ou la chanson du souffle* is a study in patterns of inhalation and exhalation; the noise of the performer's breath plays as important a role as the sound of the flute, and the speed and lengths of the musical phrases are determined by breath speed.

This liking for dirty, noisy timbres is developed in *Clov et Hamm* for trombone, tuba, percussion and tape, in which the spirit of two characters from Samuel Beckett's *Endgame* is evoked by a variety of unconventional playing techniques such as speaking and crying into the instruments, to the accompaniment of taped sounds from a building site. *Appels*, for horn and ensemble, extends the timbres of the wind instruments by having a snare drum placed directly in front of each of them; the result is a complex mixture of the instruments' timbre with the sympathetic rattling of the snares. The work is a typically extrovert study in wild, untempered calls initiated by the solo horn, inspired by those moments in 19th-century music where the music freezes to reveal offstage instruments; Levinas cites Beethoven's *Leonora Overtures*, and moments from Berlioz, Wagner and Mahler as examples.

This conception of space as a psychological and theatrical dimension in music has played a crucial part in all Levinas's subsequent works. In the two *Concertos pour un piano espace*, a piano is given a variety of artificial acoustics by means of digital reverberation, while similar treatment is given to the voice in *Voix dans un vaisseau d'Airain*. In both cases, the purpose is not merely to distort the instrument but to suggest a variety of physical—and hence psychological—spaces surrounding it in the imagination of the listener.

Levinas exploited all of these techniques in a massive work for two full orchestra and tape *Ouverture pour une petite fête étrange*. Here all the brass instruments are provided with sympathetically rattling snare drums, while the orchestras are complemented by several contingents of offstage brass; the tape provides a distorted complement of the orchestral sonorities, also pre-recorded material from several of Levinas's earlier works. The full force of the two orchestras is selectively employed; much of the piece uses small, self-contained groups of instruments whose music return in irregular counterpoint to one another.

After so many pieces of "imaginary" theatre, Levinas finally composed a real opera in 1985. *La Conférence des oiseaux* is based on an old Persian tale by Attar. The main character, a virtuoso singing and speaking role written for Martine Viard, is a fanatical hoopoe who convinces her fellow birds to go in search of their supposed king, Simorg; the search turns out to be illusory and most of the birds die in its course. The vocal style employed requires the artificial prolongation of certain consonants and vowels, incorrectly placed stresses and frequent swoops or leaps; the result is a mixture of normal speech and bird-like cries. The work is written for chamber forces, all the roles being taken by three voices, with a small ensemble and live electronics; reverberation is once again abundantly used to suggest different scenic environments.

The tragic outcome serves to emphasize the fundamental sadness at the heart of Levinas's music. His obsession with distorted timbres and the extremes of instrumental articulation or lack of it show a *commedia dell'arte* penchant for laughter of a basically pessimistic kind.

—Julian Anderson

LIDHOLM, Ingvar. Swedish. Born in Jonkoping, 24 February 1921. Educated at high school, Sodertalje (violin lessons under Hermann Gramms, orchestration under Natanael Berg); State Academy of Music, Stockholm (under Charles Barkel, violin under Axel Runnqvist, conducting under Tor Mann), 1940–5; private composition study under Hilding Rosenberg, 1943–5; further study in France, Switzerland, Italy, 1946–7; Ferienkurse für Neue Musik, Darmstadt, 1949. Viola player, Stockholm Opera, 1943–7; deputy board member, Society of Swedish Composers, 1947–51, 1963–5; director of music, municipality of Orebro, 1947–56; director of chamber music, Swedish Broadcasting Company, 1956–65; professor of composition, Stage Academy of Music, Stockholm, 1962–75; vice-president, Royal Academy of Music, 1963–9; editor, *Nutida Musik*, 1967; director of planning, music department, Swedish Radio, since 1975. Recipient: Jenny Lind Foundation Fellowship, 1946–7; Christ Johnson Prize, 1958; Koussevitzky International Recording Award, 1965; Salzburg Opera Prize (for *Hollandarn*), 1968. Mailing address: Uttringe Hages Vag 33, 14400 Ronninge, Sweden.

Publishers: Nordiska Musikforlaget; Phono Suecia; Wilhelm Hansen, Copenhagen; Edition Suecia; Edition Modern, Munich; Donemus, Amsterdam; Edition NGLANI, Merrifield, Virginia; Edition Reimers, Bromma; Ethos, Oswego, New York; Breitkopf & Hartel, Weisbaden; Walton; others.

Symphonies/orchestral:

Toccata e canto (small orchestra) 1944.
Concerto for Strings 1945. Recorded ABCD 019.
Nocturne (from incidental music to *Cyrano de Bergerac*) 1947.
Music for Strings 1952. Recorded ACCD 1008; Caprice CAP 1167/CAP 21366; BIS LP 285.
Ritornello 1955; first performed Stockholm, 17 February 1956. Recorded SR LP 1339; SCD 1027.
Mutanza 1959–65; first performed Orebro, 15 November 1959.
Motus—Colores 1960; first performed Cologne, 13 June 1960.
Poesis 1963; first performed Stockholm, 14 January 1964. Recorded SCD 1027; SWS SLT 33160.
Greetings from an Old World 1976; first performed New York City, 10 November 1976. Recorded Caprice CAP 1167/ CAP 21366.
Kontaktion (hymn for orchestra) 1978; first performed Moscow, 6 February 1979. Recorded Caprice CAP 1167/ CAP 21366.

Chamber/instrumental:

Rosettas visa (piano) 1942. Recorded Bell 183.
String Quartet 1945; first performed Stockholm, 9 March 1946.
Sonata (flute) 1946. Recorded Caprice CAP 1119; BIS LP 150.
Sonata (piano) 1947; first performed Stockholm, 25 October 1947. Recorded Bell 183; Caprice CAP 1025.
Sonatina No 1 (piano) 1947. Recorded Bell 139.
Ten Miniatures (nos 1–8 for piano; nos 9–10 for piano—4 hands) 1948.
Klavierstück 1949 (piano) 1949. Recorded Bell 139; MAP R-8609; Sonet SLP 2032.
Sonatina No 2 (piano) 1950. Recorded Bell 139.
Little String Trio 1953.
Concertino (flute, oboe, cor anglais, cello) 1954; first

performed Stockholm, 16 October 1954.

Invention (clarinet, bass clarinet; or viola, cello; or piano) 1954. Recorded BIS LP 62.

Quattro pezzi (cello, piano) 1955; first performed Stockholm, 16 May 1955.

Fanfare (for ISCM's World Music Days, Stockholm; 2 trumpets, 2–4 horns, 2 percussion) 1956; first performed Stockholm, June 1956.

Fantasia sopra Laudi (cello) 1977; broadcast Swedish Radio, 21 June 1977. Recorded ACLP 104.

Amicizia (clarinet) 1980; first performed Hasselby, 7 March 1980.

Variazioni sopra Laudi (organ; with Karl-Erik Welin) 1982; first performed Stockholm, 27 October 1982.

Tre elegier—Epilog (string quartet) 1982–6; first performed Stockholm, 23 October 1986.

Vocal/choral:

Three Songs (voices, string orchestra; various) 1940–5.

Six Songs (voice, piano; Gullberg, de Vega/translated Hagberg, others) 1940–5. Recorded (in parts) Bell 128/193.

Rosettas visa (voice, piano; Büchner) 1943.

Saga—Jungfrulin (2 songs for voice or women's chorus or men's chorus, piano; Harninge) 1945–55.

Laudi (unaccompanied mixed chorus; Biblical) 1947. Recorded PS CD 35; BIS LP 14.

Cantata (baritone, orchestra; Dante, Lagerkvist, Boye) 1949–50.

Fyra korer (unaccompanied mixed chorus; Nilsson) 1953; first performed Stockholm, 25 May 1954. Recorded Caprice CAP 1037.

Three Ekelof Songs (soprano, oboe, clarinet, viola, cello) 1954.

Canto LXXXI (unaccompanied mixed chorus; Pound) 1956; first performed Stockholm, 24 February 1957. Recorded ARR LPS 4; ART ALP 103; PS CD 35.

Skaldens natt (soprano, chorus, orchestra; Almqvist) 1958–81; original version broadcast Norddeutscher Rundfunk, 6 April 1959; revised version broadcast Swedish Radio, 23 October 1981.

Motto (unaccompanied mixed chorus; Ovid) 1959; first performed Stockholm, 15 November 1959.

Three Strindberg Songs ("Ballad"—baritone solo or unison mixed chorus; "Sommarafton"/"Summer Evening"—unaccompanied mixed chorus; "Valkommen ater snalla sol"/ "Welcome, Gentle Sun"—unaccompanied mixed chorus) 1959.

Two Greek Epigrams ("Kort ar rosornas tid"—3-part male chorus, "Phrasikleia"—soprano solo, 4-part female chorus) 1959; first performed Stockholm, 15 November 1959. Recorded Caprice CAP 1230.

Nausikaa einsam (scene for soprano, mixed chorus, orchestra; Eyvind Johnson) 1963; first performed Ingesund, 2 June 1963. Recorded Caprice CAP 1022/CAP 1110/CAP 21366.

Stamp Music I (soprano, tam-tam; score printed on Swedish postage stamp) 1971. Recorded CAP 1112.

Stamp Music II (unaccompanied mixed chorus; piano; score printed on Swedish postage stamp) 1971. Recorded PROP 7802.

A riveder le stelle (unaccompanied mixed chorus; Dante) 1971–3; first performed Stockholm, 20 January 1974. Recorded PS CD 35; Opus 3 8111.

Och inga trad skall vacka dig (dramatic scene for soprano, mixed chorus, string quartet, electronics) 1973–4; broadcast Swedish Television, 12 March 1974.

Perserna (dramatic scene for tenor, baritone, narrator, large male chorus; Zilliacus, after Aeschylus) 1978. Recorded OD 8004.

Two Madrigals (unaccompanied mixed chorus; Strindberg) 1981; first performed Minneapolis, Minnesota, 12 September 1982.

De profundis (unaccompanied mixed chorus; Psalms, Strindberg) 1983; first performed Stockholm, 23 October 1983.

Opera:

Hollandarn/The Dutchman (television opera; Grevenius, after Strindberg) 1967; broadcast Swedish Television, 10 December 1967.

Ett dromspel (after Strindberg) 1990.

Other:

Cyrano de Bergerac (incidental music; orchestra) 1947.

Riter (ballet; orchestra) 1959; first performed Stockholm, 1 November 1961. Recorded SCD 1027; Decca SXL 6180.

PUBLICATIONS

By Lidholm: "*Poesis* for Orchestra", in *Three Aspects of New Music*, Stockholm, 1968.

On Lidholm: Bruce Edward Brolsma, "The Music of IL", dissertation, Northwestern University, Evanston, Illinois, 1979; Harald Herresthal, G.G. Mayer and N. Wallin, "Drei analysen von *Greetings from an Old World*", Stockholm, 1980; Anthony Hodgson, in *Scandinavian Music: Finland & Sweden*, Rutherford, New Jersey, 1984; Stig Jacobsson, "IL", in *Swedish Composers of the 20th Century*, Stockholm, 1988.

* * *

Ingvar Lidholm studied primarily under Hilding Rosenberg and later became a member of the Monday Group. Lidholm was the first of his generation in Sweden to accept the idiom of Webern. The mid-1950s saw the final traces of Hindemith and Nielsen disappear from his style. Within a few years, his acceptance of "hard-line serialism" had developed into the adoption of Polish "sound-block sonorities", which Lidholm discusses in *Three Aspects of New Music*. The greatest influences of Lutosławski and Penderecki are found in *Poesis* for orchestra.

The early Piano Sonata exploits changes of colour and texture rather than of development or dialogue. In some sections the rhythm has vitality, while pitches create short-lived dissonances (which are subsumed into the linear movement). In other sections a wide-compassed melodic line predominates, whose inevitable if seldom predictable pitch-progression is surrounded by tranquillo sonorities. *Music for Strings* consists of long Rosenberg-like phrases which are suddenly interrupted by drastic changes of dynamic. The employment of textural contrast as the main unifier of a work continues in the cantata *Skaldens natt*, where two descriptive orchestral movements offset four expressionist vocal movements.

Laudi established Lidholm as a choral composer, and after the Piano Sonata, his last fully-tonal work, he returned to choral works. These culminated in an unaccompanied suite "A Capella Bok" which becomes increasingly difficult as it progresses and ends with a setting of Ezra Pound's *Canto LXXXI*, where pitch-entries, close-harmony, precise intonation and voicing are all thoroughly tested. Lidholm's television opera *The Dutchman*, incorporating orchestra, tape-collage and electronics, was structured around commercial breaks. Contrast is created by having music which is purposely antagonistic to the visual aspect of television.

Three works provide points of style central to Lidholm's work. *Ritornello* for orchestra brought Lidholm more fame than any other piece. It uses "gestures" such as brief string glissandos, frequent string unison passages, slow repeated notes and chromatic movement followed by sevenths or ninths, with effective use of percussion in nearly every bar. Harmonies are often presented in an order designed to be appreciated from the top downwards. *Mutanza* for orchestra, orchestrated mostly as chamber music, has post-Webern textures which are interspersed with longer passages where playing characteristics change frequently. The ballet *Riter* incorporates taped electronic music in Part Three after a string-less *Pesante* movement of mostly block brass-writing.

Like many Monday Group composers, Lidholm's final bars of a piece return to the work's opening. *Ritornello* starts softly with a percussion crescendo and ends, after very loud semiquaver chords, with solitary unpitched percussion trilling into silence. *Riter* opens with percussion crescendo but adds a single treble line to the dying percussion at the close. *Mutanza*'s opening percussion is extended into a whole introductory section, and the piece finishes with bass drum accompanying increasingly quiet flute harmonics. Lidholm also uses acciaccaturas placed, like Stravinsky's *Les Noces*, some distance from their "resolution". In *Mutanza*, acciaccaturas are often positioned at the beginning of a phrase; by *Riter* they also occur as slides towards the end of a phrase. The interval of a third predominates all three works; rhythm is simplistic unless pitted, as in *Riter*, against a tape. Many pieces, from *Mutanza* onwards, quote his earlier works; even the central climax of *Mutanza* comes from a prominently repeated chord near the end of *Ritornello*.

—Malcolm J. Hill

LIEBERMANN, Rolf. Swiss. Born in Zurich, 14 September 1910. Educated at University of Zurich (law); composition lessons under Hermann Scherchen and Wladimir Vogel. Worked as assistant to Scherchen, Prague, Budapest, Vienna; assistant to Scherchen, then director of radio orchestra, orchestral department, Beromunster German-Swiss Radio, 1945–7; musical director, North German Broadcasting System, Hamburg, 1957–9; general manager, Hamburg Opera, 1959–73, and since 1985; director, Théâtre National de l'Opéra, Paris, 1974–80; guest professor, Mozarteum, Salzburg, 1982. Mailing address: c/o Universal Edition, Bosendorferstrasse 12, Postfach 3, A-1015 Vienna, Austria.

Publishers: Universal Edition, Vienna; Ars Viva Verlag, Weihergarten, Postfach 3640, D-6500 Mainz, Germany.

Symphonies/orchestral:

Furioso 1947; first performed Dallas, Texas, 9 December 1950.
Suite on Six Swiss Folksongs 1947; broadcast BBC, 10 January 1947.
Symphony 1949 1949.
Suite: Leonore 40/45 (from the opera) 1952.
Concerto for Jazz Band and Symphony Orchestra 1954; first performed Donaueschingen, 17 October 1954.
Geigy Festival Concerto (drum, large orchestra) 1958.
Liaison (cello, piano, orchestra) 1983.

Chamber/instrumental:

Sonata (piano) 1951.
Boogie Woogie (piano; from *Concerto for Jazz Band and Symphony Orchestra*) 1954.
Musique pour clavecin (harpsichord) 1966.
Essai 81 (cello, piano) 1981.

Vocal/choral:

Giraudoux-Cantata: Une des fins du monde (medium voice, orchestra) 1944.
Chinesische Liebeslieder (high voice, harp, string orchestra) 1945.
Musik (symphonic scene for speaker, orchestra; Verlaine, Baudelaire) 1949.
Streitlied Zwischen Leben und Tod (soprano, mezzo-soprano, tenor, bass, mixed chorus, orchestra; Kothe) 1950.
Lied der Yvette (from the opera *Leonore 40/45*; soprano, orchestra; Ströbel) 1952.
Arie und Grosse Szene der Penelope (from the opera; soprano, orchestra; Strobel) 1954.
Capriccio (soprano, violin, orchestra) 1959.
Ferdinand (speaker, piccolo, flute, clarinet, bass clarinet, 8 percussion, piano, mandolin, violin, viola, cello; Leaf) 1984.

Opera/dramatic:

Leonore 40/45 (Strobel) 1951–2; first performed Basle, 25 March 1952.
Penelope (Strobel) 1953–4; first performed Salzburg, 17 August 1954.
The School for Wives (Strobel; after Molière) 1954–5, revised in 3 acts as *Der Schule der Frauen*; first performed Louisville, Kentucky, 1955; revised version first performed Salzburg, 1957.
La Foret/Der Wald 1985–6; first performed Geneva, 1987.

Other:

Symphony: Les Echanges (156 machines recorded on tape) 1964; first performed Lausanne, 24 April 1964.

PUBLICATIONS

On Liebermann: *Festschrift in Honour of RL on His 60th Birthday*, Hamburg, 1970.

* * *

Rolf Liebermann's compositional career is curiously attenuated. Though he has begun to compose again in the 1980s after one (purely nominal) retirement from a career in music administration, most of his music was composed in the 1950s. Then, it created quite a stir, and Liebermann was widely considered to be the coming man, attracting international interest and significant performances of his work in the United States.

Liebermann's academic career was in legal studies, but music rapidly became his avocation and he benefited from private lessons with the Russo-German Wladimir Vogel and the intuitive and brilliant conductor Hermann Scherchen, whose assistant Liebermann became. In keeping with Vogel's combination of modernist—chiefly serial—procedures and a thoroughgoing mysticism, Liebermann's work had a strongly theatrical emphasis; there is an element of theatre in all his work, even in such offbeat pieces as the symphonic *Les Echanges*, a tape track of industrial machines intended as background music for an exposition in Lausanne in 1964. He drew eclectically on a wide range of modern styles and methods. Much like Ernst Křenek, whom he resembles in all but size of output, he was attracted both to the high mandarin style of the Second Viennese School and to its apparent antithesis, jazz and popular music. Liebermann's *Concerto for Jazz Band and Symphony Orchestra*, like Křenek's "jazz" opera *Jonny Spielt Auf*, had very little authentic jazz in it, but it was a brave attempt to assimilate high and popular styles and it enjoyed a brief *succès de fou*.

Of far more lasting significance are Liebermann's operas *Leonore 40/45* and *Penelope*, works of considerable imaginative verve and ambitiously constructed. Liebermann's adaptation of Molière's *School for Wives* is a lighter work. His chamber music is modestly proportioned, but there is a fine early piano sonata.

Liebermann had virtually given up composing by the early 1960s. Thereafter, he concentrated on a remarkable career as an operatic impresario, re-establishing the Hamburg Opera as a company of international stature, and reviving the moribund Paris Opera. Such was his reputation and personal charisma that after his "retirement" in 1980, Liebermann was tempted back to administer the faltering Hamburg company for a second tenure. At the same time, he began to compose again, most successfully in the orchestrial *Liaison* for his favoured cello and in the opera *Der Wald*. A unique figure in contemporary music, Liebermann's reputation does hang heavily on a tacit "might have been", but his extant music is powerfully imagined and stands comfortably alongside some of the outstanding works of his generation.

—Dieter Schoof

LIGETI, György (Sandor). Hungarian; naturalised Austrian citizen. Born in Dicsöszentmárton [now Tîrnăveni], Transylvania, 28 May 1923. Educated at secondary school in Klausenberg [or Kolozsvár, now Cluj], Transylvania, until 1941; Klausenberg Conservatory (composition under Ferenc Farkas) 1941–3; composition study with Pál Kadosa, Budapest, 1942–3; Budapest Academy of Music (composition with Sandor Veress, Pál Járdányi, Ferenc Farkas, Lajos Bárdos), 1945–9. Married Vera Spitz in 1957; 1 son. Lecturer, Budapest Academy of Music, 1950–6; fled Hungary after suppression of uprising, 1956; freelance work, electronic music studio, West German Radio, Cologne, 1957–8; settled in Vienna, 1959–69, Austrian citizen from 1967; lecturer, Ferienkurse für Neue Musik, Darmstadt, 1959–72; visiting professor, Stockholm Music Academy, 1961–71; composition teacher in Madrid, 1961, Bilthoven, The Netherlands, 1962–3, Essen, 1963, Jyväskylä, Finland, 1964–5, Tanglewood, Massachusetts, 1973, Siena, 1974, and Aix-en-Provence, 1979; composer in residence, Stanford University, California, 1972; professor, Hochschule für Musik und darstellende Künste, Hamburg, since 1973; serious illness hampered work, late 1970s. Recipient: 1st prize (for *Apparitions* and for *Requiem*), ISCM Composition Competition, Rome, 1964, 1966; elected to Swedish Academy of Music, Stockholm, 1964; Koussevitzky Foundation Prize, 1965; Beethoven Prize, Bonn (for *Requiem*), 1967; Medal of Honour, University of Helsinki, 1967; elected to Akademie der Kunste, Berlin, 1968; honorary member, Musikverein für die Steiermark, 1969; 1st prize (for *Lontano*), International UNESCO Competition, 1969; elected member, Freie Akademie der Künste, Hamburg, 1971; Berliner Kunstpreis, 1972; member, Orden pour le Merite, Bonn, 1975; Bach Prize, Hamburg, 1975; member, Bayerische Akademie der Schönen Künste, Munich, 1978; elected, American Academy and Institute of Arts and Letters, 1984; Prix Ravel, Paris, 1984; Béla Bartók-Ditta Pasztory Prize, Budapest, 1984; honorary member, International Society for New Music, 1984; Prix Arthur Honegger, 1985; Grawemeyer Award, Louisville, Kentucky (for *Etudes pour piano*), 1986; Ehrenzeichen zur Wissenschaft und Kunst, Austria, 1987; Ehrening, Vienna, 1987; honorary doctorate, University of Hamburg, 1988; commandeur, Ordre National des Arts et des Lettres, Paris, 1988; composition prize, Fondation Prince Pierre de Monaco. Mailing address: Movenstrasse 3, D-2000 Hamburg 60, Germany.

Publishers: Schott, Mainz; Peters, Frankfurt; Universal Edition, Vienna; Edition Musica, Budapest.

Symphonies/orchestral:

Ballad and Dance on Romanian Folksongs (small school orchestra) 1949–50.

Romanian Concerto 1951.

Apparitions 1958–9; first performed Cologne, 19 June 1960.

Atmosphères (large orchestra) 1961; first performed Donaueschingen, Germany, 22 October 1961. Recorded Wergo WER 60022/60162 50.

Fragment (chamber orchestra) 1961; first performed Munich, April 1962.

Concerto for Cello and Orchestra 1966; first performed Berlin, 19 April 1967. Recorded Wergo WER 60036/60163 50.

Lontano (large orchestra) 1967; first performed Donaueschingen, 22 October 1967. Recorded Wergo WER 60036/60163 50.

Ramifications (string orchestra or 12 solo strings) 1968–9; first performed Berlin, 23 April 1969; solo string version first performed Saarbrücken, 10 October 1969. Recorded Wergo WER 60059/60162 50.

Chamber Concerto (13 instruments) 1969–70; first performed Berlin, 1 October 1970. Recorded Wergo WER 60059.

Melodien 1971; first performed Nuremburg, 1971.

Double Concerto (flute, oboe, orchestra) 1972; first performed Berlin, 16 September 1972. Recorded Wergo WER 60076/60156 50.

San Francisco Polyphony 1973–4. Recorded Wergo WER 60076/60163 50.

Concerto for Piano and Orchestra 1985–8; first 3 movements performed Graz, Austria, 23 October 1986; movements 4 and 5 first performed Vienna, 29 February 1988.

Concerto for Violin and Orchestra 1990; first performed Cologne, 3 November 1990.

Chamber/instrumental:

Sonata (cello) 1948–53; first performed Paris, 24 October 1983.
Musica ricercata (11 piano pieces) 1951–3; first performed Sundsvall, Sweden, 18 November 1969.
Ricercare: Ommaggio a Girolamo Frescobaldi 1953.
String Quartet No 1: Metamorphoses nocturnes 1953–4; first performed Vienna, 8 May 1958. Recorded Wergo WER 60079.
Six Bagatelles (wind quintet) 1953; first performed Sodertalje, Sweden, 6 October 1969.
Volumina (organ) 1961–2; broadcast Radio Bremen, 4 May 1962. Recorded Wergo WER 60022.
Poème symphonique (100 metronomes) 1962; first performed Hilversum, 13 September 1963.
Harmonies: Etude No 1 (organ) 1967; first performed Hamburg, 14 October 1967. Recorded Wergo WER 60076/60161 50.
String Quartet No 2 1968; first performed Baden-Baden, 14 December 1969. Recorded Wergo WER 60079.
Continuum (harpsichord) 1968; first performed Basle, 1968. Recorded Wergo WER 60045/60100.
Ten Pieces (wind quintet) 1968; first performed Malmo, Sweden, 20 January 1969. Recorded Wergo WER 60059.
Coulée: Etude No 2 (organ) 1969; first performed Basilika Seckau, Austria, 19 October 1969. Recorded Wergo WER 60076.
Monument–Selbstportrait–Bewegung (3 pieces for 2 pianos) 1976; first performed Cologne, 15 May 1976. Recorded Wergo WER 60100.
Passacaglia ungherese (harpsichord) 1978; first performed Lund, Sweden, 5 February 1979. Recorded Wergo WER 60100.
Hungarian Rock (chaconne for harpsichord) 1978; first performed Cologne, 20 May 1978. Recorded Wergo WER 60100.
Trio (violin, horn, piano) 1982; first performed Hamburg, 7 August 1982.
Etudes pour piano: Book 1 (consisting of I "Désordre", II "Cordes vides", III "Touches bloquées", IV "Fanfares", V "Arc en ciel", VI "Automne à Varsovie") 1985; I first performed Bratislava, 15 April 1986; II, III, VI first performed Warsaw, 24 September 1985; IV, V first performed Hamburg, 1 November 1985. Recorded Wergo WER 60134.

Vocal/choral:

Idegen Földön/Far from Home (unaccompanied 3-part female chorus; Balassa, trad.) 1945–6; first performed Stockholm, 17 April 1971.
Magany/Solitude (unaccompanied 3-part chorus) 1946; first performed Stuttgart, 18 May 1983.
Papaine/Widow Papai (unaccompanied mixed chorus; trad.) 1953; first performed Stockholm, 16 May 1967.
Matraszentimrei Dalok (2- and 3-part children's or women's chorus, unaccompanied; trad.) 1955; first performed Saarbrücken, 9 June 1984.
Ejszaka/Night (unaccompanied mixed chorus; Weöres) 1955; first performed Stockholm, 16 March 1968.
Reggel/Morning (unaccompanied mixed chorus; Weöres) 1955; first performed Stockholm, 16 March 1968.
Aventures (coloratura soprano, alto, baritone, flute, horn, percussion, harpsichord, piano/celeste, cello, double bass) 1962; first performed Hamburg, 4 April 1963. Recorded Wergo WER 60022/60045 50.
Nouvelles Aventures (coloratura soprano, alto, baritone, flute/piccolo, horn, percussion, harpsichord, piano/celeste, cello, double bass) 1962–5; first performed Hamburg, 26 May 1966. Recorded Wergo WER 60022/60045 50.
Requiem (soprano, mezzo-soprano, 2 mixed choruses, orchestra) 1963–5; first performed Stockholm, 14 March 1965. Recorded Wergo WER 60045.
Lux aeterna (unaccompanied 16-part mixed chorus) 1966; first performed Stuttgart, 2 November 1966. Recorded Wergo WER 60026.
Clocks and Clouds (SMsA chorus, 12 soloists ad lib, orchestra) 1972–3; first performed Graz, 15 October 1973.
Scenes and Entr'actes (from *Le Grand Macabre*; soprano, mezzo-soprano, buffo tenor, character baritone, mixed chorus ad lib, orchestra) 1978; first performed Berlin, 21 December 1978. Recorded Wergo WER 60085.
Three Phantasies after Friedrich Hölderlin (unaccompanied 16-part mixed chorus) 1982; first performed Stockholm, 26 September 1983.
Magyar Etudok/Hungarian Studies (unaccompanied 8-, 12- and 16-part mixed chorus) 1983; nos 1 and 2 first performed Stuttgart, 18 May 1983; no 3 first performed Metz, 17 November 1983. Recorded Wergo WER 60111.
Nonsense Madrigals (6 unaccompanied voices) 1988.

Opera/dramatic:

Aventures & Nouvelles Aventures (coloratura soprano, alto, baritone, flute/piccolo, horn, percussion, harpsichord, piano/celeste, cello, double bass) 1966; first performed Stuttgart, 19 October 1966.
Le Grand Macabre (after Michel de Ghelderode; freely adapted by Michael Meschke, GL) 1974–7; first performed Stockholm, 12 April 1978.
Rondeau (actor, tape) 1976; first performed Stuttgart, 26 February 1977.

Other:

Alte ungarische Gesellschaftstänze/Regi magyar tarsas tancok (18th-and 19th-century themes after Bihari, Lavotta, Csermak, Rozsavolgyi; flute ad lib, clarinet ad lib, string orchestra) 1949.
Six Miniatures (co-written with Friedrich K. Wanek; 2 flutes/piccolos, 2 oboes/cors anglais, 2 clarinets, 2 bassoons, 2 horns) 1953–75; first performed Schwetzinger, 16 May 1976.
Glissandi (electronic) 1957. Recorded Wergo WER 60076/60161 50.
Artikulation (electronic) 1958; first performed Cologne, 25 March 1958. Recorded Wergo WER 60059/60161 50.

PUBLICATIONS

By Ligeti: "Die Funktion des Raumesin der Musik", in *Forum*, 76, 1960; "Wandlungen der musikalischen Form", in *Die Reihe*, 7, 1960; "Kompositorische Tendenzen heute", in *Neue Musik*, 1, Munich, 1961; "Metamorphoses of Musical Form" in *Die Reihe*, 7, 1965; "Neue Notation—Kommunikationsmittel oder Selbstzweck?", in *Darmstadter Beitrage zur Neuen Musik IX*, 1965; "Form in der Neuen Musik", in *Darmstadter Beitrage zur Neuen Musik X*, 1966; "Weberns Melodik", in *Melos*, 33, 1966; "Sustande, Ereignisse, Wandlungen", in *Melos*, 5, 1967; "Fragen und Antworten von mir selbst", in *Melos*, 12, 1971; "Apropos Musik und Politik", in *Darmstadter Beitrage zur Neuen Musik XIII*, 1972; "Mein

Judentum", in *Mein Judentum*, Berlin/Stuttgart, 1978; "Musik und Technik", in Batel, Kleinen, Gunter and Salbert (eds), *Computermusik*, Laaber, 1987.

On Ligeti: Ulrich Dibelius, "GL", in *Moderne Musik I 1945–65*, Munich, 1966; Ove Nordwall, *L-dokument*, Stockholm, 1968, and *GL: Eine Monographie*, Mainz, 1971; Yehuda Yannay, "Towards an Open-Ended Method of Analysis of Contemporary Music", dissertation, University of Illinois, Urbana, 1974; Ove Nordwall, "GL. Dokumentation", in *Nutida Musik*, 19, 1975–6; Paul Griffiths, *GL*, London, 1983; Janet Owen Thomas, "L's Organ Music", in *Musical Times*, 124, 1983; Gianmario Borio, (interview) in *Musica/Realta*, 13, 1984; Denys Bouliane, (interview) in *Neuland*, 5, 1984–5; Enzo Restagno, *GL*, Turin, 1985; Hans-Joachim Erwe, (interview) in *Zeitschrift für Musikpadagogisk*, 37 (11), 1986; Antoine Bonnet, "Sur L", in *Entretemps*, 1, 1986; Clytus Gottwald, (interview) in *In Harmoniques*, May 1987; Otto Kolleritsch, *GL: Personalstil–Avantgardismus–Popularitat*, Vienna/Graz, 1987; Herman Sabbe, *GL*, Munich, 1987; also special GL numbers of: *Musik und Bildung*, 7, 1975, and 15, 1983; *Nutida Musik*, 19, 1975; *Sonus*, 9, 1988.

* * *

Like many central European composers whose musical education spanned the immediate Post-war years, György Ligeti's apprenticeship was heavily influenced by Bartók. Nevertheless, from quite early on, other echoes—renaissance polyphony and the Western avant-garde, for example—are discernible. Ligeti began experimenting with electronic composition around the time of his escape from the Hungarian uprising: two tape-pieces, *Artikulation* and *Glissandi*, present in somewhat rudimentary form an approach in which feverish chromatic detail overlays a static harmonic foundation. This is developed in the two orchestral pieces, *Apparitions* and *Atmosphères*, which first brought him widespread attention.

In *Volumina*, Ligeti developed a pictorial "chord-cluster" notation used already in *Atmosphères*. The system is far less labour-intensive to write down (improvisatory, meandering passages are indicated by a mass of wavy lines, heavily scored "clusters" by means of thick black lines, etc.—no detailed representation of pitch or durational values is required). Moreover, because rhythmic movement (as opposed to small-scale motion and passagework, which are almost ubiquitous) has been virtually quenched by judicious overlapping of entries, and the chord clusters prevent any coherent harmonic development, *Volumina* is projected to the listener as a "sound continuum"—the music fades out as a sustained cluster is supressed, when the performer switches off the motor of the organ.

A number of pieces dating from roughly the same period as *Volumina*—*Poème symphonique* for 100 metronomes, *Aventures* and *Nouvelles Aventures*—mark a more sterile phase in Ligeti's career, during which technical virtuosity or, in the case of the *Poème symphonique*, somewhat puerile humour, overcame the serious possibilities broached in *Volumina*. However, from 1963–5, Ligeti was also working on his *Requiem*, a project which he had already attempted twice during the 1950s, without progressing very far. The "Kyrie" movement is among the most convincing products of the composer's "cluster" style; the choir is separated into 20 narrow-ranged vocal parts, each of which maintains an intricate, though by no means integrated, texture. Comparisons with the chaotic effect of various renaissance contrapuntal extravaganzas (for example, by Ockeghem and Tallis) have often been made.

Ligeti followed up the Requiem with an unaccompanied choral work, *Lux aeterna*, which both distils and builds upon the myriad counterpoints of the *Requiem*'s "Kyrie". 16 solo voices interlock in ornate canonic style, but at times the music focuses upon its simple harmonic background, a chord consisting of a major second overlaid by a minor third.

Lontano, written for a large orchestra, also weaves dense textures from a mass of independent contrapuntal voices in which the sheer complexity of the argument causes harmonic progression to vanish for long periods. Occasionally harmonic clarity reigns, only to be obscured anew by fascinatingly detailed small-scale movement. This is probably the most immediately striking facet of Ligeti's style; it is summed up by the title of his vocal work *Clocks and Clouds* (taken from an essay by Karl Popper).

Continuum displays Ligeti's usual concern for macro-stasis: his method here of building upon a basic chordal structure gradually to "fill in" the intervening chromatic tones is a stock-in-trade. But he also exploits brilliantly the harpsichord's individuality: its dry, monochrome sonority is emphasised through extremely rapid passage work. The music develops through ascending registers, so that the repetitive patterns and lack of harmonic progression, and the inevitable extraneous sounds of the keyboard mechanism, combine in a nightmarish approximation of pounding insect wings.

Ramifications, written for a 12-part string orchestra, explores quarter-tone harmony (a device utilised also by Bartók). Ligeti divides his forces, with six players tuning to normal pitch and the remainder employing *scordantura*—their instruments are tuned a quarter tone sharp. Interaction of the groups produces some grating dissonances. *Scordantura* recurs in the *Double Concerto* for flute and oboe, where the quarter tone effects are introduced as a refinement of Ligeti's typical ploy of adding unused elements from the chromatic series to his static harmonies.

The second part of *Monument–Selbstportrait–Bewegung* emphasises Ligeti's sense of affinity with contemporary American "minimalist" composers, whose work is based largely upon static harmony and develops through gradual shifts in repeated rhythmic patterns. This movement's full title is "Self-portrait with Reich and Riley (and with Chopin in the background)". The acutely-observed, mildly ironic impression of Ligeti and the Minimalists given in the first section opens out via a reiterated tritone figure into what is, in effect, a recreation of the *moto-perpetuo* finale of Chopin's B♭ minor Piano Sonata. Ligeti avoids literal quotation here (he had borrowed from a wide range of composers elsewhere, notably in works from the late 1960s such as the Second String Quartet—at about the same time, similar pastiche was being practised by Berio and others), but the spirit of Chopin's movement, especially its desperate opaqueness and violent dynamic contrasts, is unerringly captured.

Ligeti's first opera *Le Grand Macabre* is set in the fantasy world of "Breughelland", replete with the blended realism and phantasmagoria which Ligeti admires in the paintings of Breughel and Bosch. *Le Grand Macabre*, primarily a work about waning human powers and death, has enjoyed a degree of international attention almost unparalleled for a modern opera.

For a time after completing *Le Grand Macabre*, Ligeti's output was slight, partly because of his poor health, but perhaps also as a reaction to the opera's sombre conclusion. During the 1980s, however, he has moved into a new career phase, launched by the Horn Trio, in which the piano features prominently. This work was intended as a homage to Brahms, though his influence is not especially pervasive. Ligeti's recent music tends to cultivate, rather than expand upon, the rhythmic density and harmonic intensification apparent in his work since about the mid 1960s. It remains to be seen whether he will stay comfortable within the parameters of this style.

—Paul Horner

LILBURN, Douglas. New Zealander. Born in Wanganui, 2 November 1915. Educated at University of Canterbury, Christchurch; Royal College of Music, London (under Ralph Vaughan Williams). Freelance composer, guest conductor, teacher, press critic, Christchurch, 1940–6; composer in residence, Cambridge Summer Music Schools, 1946–9, 1951; part-time tutor in music, 1947–9, lecturer 1949–55, senior lecturer 1955–63, and professor 1970–9, Victoria University, Wellington; founder, Wai-te-ata Press Music Editions, 1967; founder director, Electronic Music Studio, Victoria University, 1966–79. Recipient: Percy Grainger Prize, 1936; Cobbett Prize, 1939; Hubert Parry Prize, 1939; 3 prizes, New Zealand Centennial Music Competitions, 1940; Philip Neill Memorial Prize, 1944; honorary doctorate, University of Otago, 1969; citation for services to New Zealand music, Composers Association of New Zealand; Order of New Zealand, 1988: Mailing address: 22 Ascot Terrace, Thorndon, Wellington, New Zealand.

Publishers: Price Milburn Music Ltd, P.O. Box 995, Wellington, New Zealand; Wai-te-ata Press Music Editions, c/o Music Department, Victoria University of Wellington, P.O. Box 600, Wellington, New Zealand.

Symphonies/orchestral:

Forest (symphonic poem) 1936.
Drysdale Overture 1937, revised 1940, 1986; first performed London, 1938. Recorded Kiwi Pacific SLD 86.
Festival Overture 1939; first performed London, 1939. Recorded HMV MALP 6008/ASDM 5001; Kiwi Pacific SLD 75.
Overture Aotearoa 1940; first performed London, 16 April 1940. Recorded Kiwi Pacific SLD 14/SLD 79; Oryx 1900; Kiwi Pacific/Jerusalem SCD 8004.
Introduction and Allegro (strings) 1942; first performed Auckland, 1942. Recorded (*Allegro* only) Kiwi Pacific SLD 37.
Four Canzonas (strings) 1943–50, arranged from incidental, 1980. Recorded Kiwi Pacific SLD 67.
A Song of Islands (also cited as *Song of the Antipodes*) 1946; first performed Wellington, 20 August 1947. Recorded Kiwi Pacific SLD 79.
Cambridge Overture 1946. Recorded Kiwi Pacific SLD 77.
Diversions (string orchestra) 1947; first performed Wellington, 1947. Recorded Kiwi Pacific SLD 37; Jeru ATD 8203; Kiwi Pacific/Jerusalem SCD 8004.
Symphony No 1 1949; first performed Wellington, 1951. Recorded Kiwi Pacific SLD 75.
Symphony No 2 1951, revised 1974; first performed Wellington, 1953. Recorded Kiwi Pacific SLD 48; Jeru ATD 8203; Kiwi/Jerusalem SCD 8004.
Suite 1955, revised 1956; first performed Auckland, 1955. Recorded Kiwi Pacific SLD 75.
A Birthday Offering 1956; first performed Wellington, 1956. Recorded Kiwi Pacific SLD 86.
Symphony No 3 1961; first performed Wellington, 1962. Recorded Kiwi Pacific SLD 14.

Chamber/instrumental:

Allegro concertante (violin, piano) 1944, revised 1945; first performed Wellington, 1988.
Prelude and Fugue in G minor (organ) 1944; first performed Dunedin, 1944.
Three Sea Changes (piano) 1945–72, revised 1981. Recorded Kiwi Pacific SLD 78.
String Trio (violin, viola, cello) 1945; first performed Christchurch, 1945. Recorded Kiwi Pacific SLD 57/58.
Chaconne (piano) 1946; first performed London, 1954. Recorded Pye GSGC 14110.
String Quartet in E minor 1946, revised 1981; first performed Wellington, 1950. Recorded Kiwi Pacific SLD 57/58.
Sonatina (piano) 1946; first performed Auckland, 1946. Recorded Kiwi Pacific SLD 78.
Sonatina (clarinet, piano) 1948; first performed Auckland, 1948. Recorded Kiwi Pacific SLD 57/58.
Sonata (piano) 1949; first performed Wellington, 1949. Recorded Kiwi Pacific SLD 57/58.
Sonata in One Movement (violin, piano) 1950; first performed London, 1950. Recorded Kiwi Pacific SLD 32.
Duos (2 violins) 1954; first performed Wellington, 1954. Recorded Kiwi Pacific SLD 57/58.
Quartet (2 trumpets, horn, trombone) 1957; first performed Wellington, 1980. Recorded Kiwi Pacific SLD 72.
Wind Quintet 1957; first performed Wellington, 1957. Recorded Kiwi Pacific SLD 57/58.
Sonatina No 2 (piano) 1962; first performed Wellington, 1962. Recorded Kiwi Pacific SLD 32.
Seventeen Pieces (guitar) 1962–70. Recorded Kiwi Pacific SLD 47.
Nine Short Pieces (piano) 1965–6, revised 1967. Recorded Kiwi Pacific SLD 19.

Vocal/choral:

Prodigal Country (baritone, mixed chorus, orchestra; Curnow, Whitman) 1939; first performed Wellington, 1940. Recorded Kiwi Pacific SLFD 86.
Elegy: In memoriam Noel Newson (2 voices, strings; Herrick, Blake, Herbert, Shakespeare) 1945; first performed Christchurch, 1945. Recorded Kiwi Pacific SLD 67.
Three Songs (voice, piano; Dallas, Dowling) 1947–54.
Elegy (baritone, piano; Campbell) 1951; first performed Wellington, 1951. Recorded Kiwi Pacific SLD 13/68.
Sings Harry (baritone, piano; or tenor, guitar; Glover) 1953; first performed Wellington, 1954. Recorded Kiwi Pacific SLD 47/EC 26.
Three Songs (baritone, viola; Bethell, Mason, Baxter) 1958; first performed Wellington, 1958. Recorded Kiwi Pacific SLD 30.

Other:

Landfall in Unknown Seas (incidental music for narrator, string orchestra; Curnow) 1942; first performed Wellington, 1942. Recorded Kiwi Pacific SLD 2/79.
Three Poems of the Sea (narrator, string orchestra; trad., Shakespeare, Curnow) 1958; first performed Wellington, 1959. Recorded Kiwi Pacific SLD 67.
The Return (electronic sound image of poem by Alistair

Campbell) 1965. Recorded SLD 13/68.
Poem in Time of War (electro-acoustic) 1967. Recorded Kiwi Pacific SLD 44/46.
Summer Voices (electro-acoustic) 1969. Recorded Kiwi Pacific SLD 44/46.
Expo '70 Dance Sequence (electro-acoustic) 1970. Recorded SLD 44/46.
Three Inscapes (electro-acoustic) 1972. Recorded Kiwi Pacific SLD 44/46.
Carousel (electro-acoustic) 1976. Recorded Kiwi Pacific SLD 54.
Winterset (electro-acoustic) 1976. Recorded Kiwi Pacific SLD 59.
Of Time and Nostalgia (electro-acoustic) 1977. Recorded Kiwi Pacific SLD 59.
Triptych (electro-acoustic) 1977. Recorded Kiwi Pacific SLD 59.
Soundscape with Lake and River (electro-acoustic) 1979; first performed Kiwi Pacific SLD 59.

PUBLICATIONS

By Lilburn: "A Search for Tradition", 1984, and "A Search for a Language", 1985, both University of Otago Open Lecture, Alexander Turnbull Library, Wellington.

On Lilburn: Valerie Harris and Philip Norman (eds), *DL: A Festschrift for DL on His Retirment from the Victoria University of Wellington*, Wellington, 1980; Jill Palmer, *The Collection of DL: MSS in the Alexander Turnbull Library*, Wellington, 1980; Philip Norman, "The Beginnings and Development of a New Zealand Music: the Life and Work of Douglas Lilburn, 1940–65", dissertation, University of Canterbury, Christchurch, 1983; John Mansfield Thomson, *A Biographical Dictionary of New Zealand Composers*, Wellington, 1990, and *The Oxford History of New Zealand Music*, Auckland, 1991.

* * *

General agreement gives Douglas Lilburn the accolade of being New Zealand's first recognised composer. His life and work is of singular significance, and has already left an indelible mark. All through his composing career he has lived out his belief that music must reflect the ideals and aspirations of its own culture if it is to communicate fully in an international sense. His is a New Zealand perspective, yet his music touches the universal, so strong is his identification with his immediate environment and so authentic the voice that expresses that interaction. He has written theatre, film, orchestral, chamber, solo and electronic music of evocative power, in a highly articulate and immediately recognisable personal style.

Alongside his own career he has taught another generation of composers, some of whom have also gained international recognition; he also pioneered the writing and appreciation of electronic music in New Zealand, and founded the Wai-te-ata Press Music Editions, now a major publisher of New Zealand works. In 1960 he successfully campaigned for composers' rights in the face of planned retrogressive copyright laws, and his Lilburn Trust now supports a wide range of musical endeavours. Articulate with words as well as with sounds, in 1946 and 1969 he gave two open lectures: subsequently published, these remain basic reading for anyone wishing to understand New Zealand music, not to mention Lilburn's own considerable personal evolution.

Analysts have divided his work into three distinct phases. The first encompasses his student years, from the overture *Forest* (1936) which won the Percy Grainger prize and enabled him to travel to London, through the *Overture Aotearoa* (1940), to his return to New Zealand in 1941, and six "fruitful, formative years" in Christchurch where deep and lasting associations were established with leading New Zealand artists, poets and literary figures of his generation. Other works from this phase include *Landfall in Unknown Seas*, a setting of Allen Curnow's poem for narrator and strings, itself a landfall in a new-found "composition territory"; several piano and chamber works, a song cycle, and incidental music for Ngaio Marsh's dramatic productions; and two symphonies, the first somewhat meditative, and the second more expansive. Taken together the works of these early years show remarkable breadth as well as depth, inspired by the contours, and even the psyche, of the New Zealand landscape. Two composers influential at this time were Vaughan Williams and Sibelius—both popular and both nationalist in outlook and style. To this Lilburn added his own practicality, doubtless influenced by his family farming background.

After the Second Symphony Lilburn explored the work of Bartók, Stravinsky, contemporary Americans (especially Copland) and composers of the Second Viennese School: this second phase of his composition has been termed "eclectic". Works from these years range from the song cycle *Sings Harry* (1953), based on a back-country character celebrated in a series of poems by Denis Glover, through various chamber and orchestral works, to the terse, single-movement Third Symphony of 1961.

Thereafter Lilburn's search for validity of expression led him away from instrumental music, into the electronic sound world, a medium through which he believed he could find a means of expression more direct than anything he had known before. His sensitivity to other art forms remained: characteristically for his first work in this genre he realised a "sound image" to Alistair Campbell's poem *The Return*. Subsequent electronic works moved beyond mere imagery, from the powerful *Poem in Time of War* and *Summer Voices*—"impressions of half-heard sounds in the summer air"—to *Three Inscapes*, showing complete mastery of pure electronic sound. The last work of this phase, *Soundscape with Lake and River* (1979), takes its inspiration from the waters and moods of Lake Taupo, and fuses literal with electronic sound. Perhaps in so doing, it almost brings Lilburn's compositional development full circle.

Thus the three phases, though distinct, are nevertheless a continuing evolution, with inspirational and stylistic elements traceable throughout. It is an evolution not only of Lilburn's own music, but also of his response to changing international trends. He has above all shown himself to be a composer with the integrity and courage to search for and follow his own path, within his own environment and using his own experience, regardless of where that may lead. For that vision reflected in his music he takes his place not only in contemporary New Zealand but in the world at large.

—Margaret Lion

LINDBERG, Magnus. Finnish. Born in Helsinki, 1958. Educated at Sibelius Academy, Helsinki (composition under Einojuhani Rautavaara and Paavo Heininen), 1973–81; private composition study with Gérard Grisey and Vinko

Globokar (Paris), Franco Donatoni (Siena) and Brian Ferneyhough (Darmstadt); further study in electronic music under Osmo Lindeman (Helsinki) and at EMS Studio (Stockholm). Concert and recording pianist; co-founder (with Esa-Pekka Salonen), instrumental ensemble Toimii. Recipient: selected work (*Kraft*), International Rostrum of Composers, 1986; Prix Italia (for *Faust*), 1986; Nordic Music Prize (for *Kraft*), 1987. Mailing address: Rauhankatu 7, SF-00170 Helsinki, Finland.

Publishers: Ricordi, Milan; Hansen, Copenhagen; Edition Pan.

Symphonies/orchestral:

Ritratto (small orchestra) 1979–83; first performed Milan, 27 February 1983. Recorded FACD 365.
Drama 1980–1; first performed Helsinki, 8 February 1981.
Sculpture II 1981; first performed Helsinki, 13 October 1982.
Tendenza (chamber orchestra) 1982; first performed Paris, 27 January 1983.
Kraft 1983–5; first performed Helsinki, 4 September 1985. Recorded FACD 372.
Trois Sculptures 1988–9; first performed Helsinki, 13 March 1989.
Kinetics 1988–9.
Marea 1990.

Chamber/instrumental:

Musik for tva pianon (2 pianos) 1976.
Tre stycken/Three Pieces (horn, violin, viola, cello) 1976; first performed Helsinki, 25 May 1977. Recorded SAOLP 101.
Klavierstück (piano) 1977; first performed Helsinki, 14 June 1977.
Arabesques (wind quintet) 1978; first performed Helsinki, 5 October 1980.
Espressione I (cello) 1978.
Tre sma pianostycken (piano) 1978. Recorded FUGA 3038.
Play I (2 pianos) 1979; first performed Helsinki, 9 September 1980.
Espressione II (violin) 1979; first performed Viitasaari, 1982.
Quintetto dell 'estate (flute, clarinet, violin, cello, piano) 1979; first performed Helsinki, 24 May 1980.
Sonatas (violin, piano) 1979; first performed Helsinki, 7 May 1980.
Layers (unspecified ensemble) 1979, in progress; first performed Helsinki, 3 April 1981.
. . . de Tartuffe, je crois (string quartet, piano) 1981; first performed Kuhmo, 27 July 1981. Recorded FACD 361.
Linea d'ombra (flute, saxophone, guitar, percussion) 1981; first performed Milan, 17 March 1983.
Action—Situation—Signification (horn or clarinets, piano, percussion, cello, tape) 1982; first performed Jyväskylä, 6 July 1982. Recorded FACD 372.
Ablauf (clarinet, 2 percussion ad lib) 1983; first performed Helsinki, 15 April 1983.
Ground (harpsichord) 1983; first performed Viitasaari, 6 August 1985.
Zona (cello solo, alto flute, clarinet, percussion, harp, piano, violin, double bass) 1983; first performed Hilversum, The Netherlands, 2 December 1983.
Metal Work (accordion, percussion) 1984.
Stroke (cello) 1984; first performed Helsinki, 30 December 1984.
UR (clarinet, violin, cello, double bass, piano) 1986; first performed Paris, 11 October 1986.
Twine (piano) 1988; first performed Bremen, 19 May 1988.

Vocal/choral:

Jag vill breda vingar ut (mezzo-soprano, piano; Björling) 1977–8.
Untitled (20 singers; wordless) 1978.

Other:

Etwas zarter (tape) 1977.
Ohne Ausdruck (tape) 1978; first performed Helsinki, 15 April 1983.
Molière or The Conspiracy of Pietists (incidental music to the play by Bulgakov) 1980; first performed Helsinki, 1980.
Faust (radiophonic composition; text by Juha Siltanen) 1985–6; broadcast Finnish Broadcasting Company, 17 August 1986.

PUBLICATIONS

By Lindberg: "Retrospektiivinen katsaus savellystohoni", in Ammatti, *Saveltaja, Synkooppi ry*, Helsinki, 1981; "Rapport 1984", in *Musikrevy*, 2, 1984; "Thoughts on Being a Composer", in *Finnish Music Quarterly*, 3–4, 1987.

On Lindberg: Risto Neiminen, "The Calculation of Processes Is a Source of Inspiration", in *Finnish Music Quarterly*, 3, 1986, German version in *MusikTexte*, 18 February 1987, Finnish version in *Rondo*, 1, 1987; Jouni Kaipainen, "Muotokuvasta veistokseen, draamasta voimaan", in *Kultuurivihkot*, 5, 1986; Risto Nieminen, "ML pa jakt efter urkraft", in *Nutida music*, 3, 1986–7; Asbjørn Schaathun, "ML: den talefore modernist", in *Ballade*, 1, 1987.

* * *

Magnus Lindberg is one of the remarkable generation of young Finnish composers born in the mid-to late 1950s, all of whom studied at the Sibelius Academy in Helskini with Paavo Heininen. The others include, most notably, Kaija Saariaho, Esa-Pekka Salonen and Jouni Kaipainen. Of these four, Lindberg is the complexicist—continually fascinated by the intricacies of how things work (he is particularly obsessed by rhythm and the properties of time)—and a practical experimenter, ever trying to extend compositional boundaries. Together with Esa-Pekka Salonen he formed the instrumental ensemble Toimii as a working laboratory for his compositional ideas.

Study outside Finland in the early 1980s, principally with Vinko Globokar and Gérard Grisey in Paris, broadened his musical outlook, and Globokar's uncompromising view of the composer's responsibility to remain true to his ideals moved Lindberg to declare his creed: "Only the extreme is interesting. Striving for a balanced totality is nowadays an impossibility." The practical demonstration of this creed is nowhere more clearly demonstrated than in *Action—Situation—Signification*, a substantial chamber work, written for members of Toimii. Two books formed an important starting point: Pierre Schaffer's *Traite des objets musicaux* and Elias Canetti's *Masse und Macht*. The former provided a model for classifying sounds and sound sources; from Canetti Lindberg took the analogies between the behaviour of certain natural phenomena and crowds, attempting to translate them into sound by furnishing each of the basic elements (the four movements are Sea, Rain, Fire and Wind) and his chosen sound sources with a different numerical value. The end results are treated with comprehensive serial organisation, and this work demonstrates Lindberg's most extreme use of sound to regulate the construction of the work.

During the composition of *Zona*, a highly virtuosic piece for solo cello and ensemble, Lindberg found himself more and more preoccupied with the complexity of rhythmic calculation. By the time he moved to *Kraft* for solo ensemble and orchestra, he felt the need to devise a computer programme to take over the calculation, and spent a year working on this compositional tool. The programme was to have consequences beyond *Kraft*, marking Lindberg's move away from precise serialism and liberating him into taking a more simple approach, softening the block-like entities he had previously favoured into continuums. The sonority of *Kraft* is harsh, metallic and intense and involves the solo ensemble (Toimii again) percussively playing a number of sound-producing objects such as car springs, chair legs and stones which Lindberg collected, as well as their ordinary instruments, while the sound is spatially diffused both by loud-speakers and by the physical movement of the members of Toimii around the hall.

In his next two orchestral works, *Kinetics* and *Marea*, Lindberg investigates the properties of textural motion and experiments with the possibilities of composing a harmonic foreground over a carefully orchestrated background of chords. *Marea* is, in fact, based on a repeated sequence of twelve-tone chords, the fundamentals of which form a ground bass. The paring down process begun in *Kraft* has continued and the overall harmonies have a new richness which give one just the faintest reminder that Lindberg is a successor to the Sibelian tradition. If this appears to be a new, mellow Lindberg, it is probably as well to remember that the composer has not forgotten the world of *Action—Situation—Signification*, and that he cites one of the ideas he found in Canetti, the endless motion of the sea, as being fundamental to the world of *Marea*. It seems likely that given the restless questing of his mind, Lindberg's compositional approach will also continue in *moto perpetuum*.

—Rosemary Johnson

LLOYD, George (Walter Selwyn). British/English. Born in St Ives, Cornwall, 28 June 1913. Ill health interrupted education; studied violin privately under Albert Sammons, counterpoint under C.H. Kitson and composition under Harry Farjeon. Married Nancy Kathleen Juvet in 1937. Served in Royal Marines band on Arctic convoys, 1939–42, invalided out with severe shell shock following sinking of H.M.S. *Trinidad*; severe health problems; moved to Switzerland, 1945–8; further breakdown of health, 1951; mushroom and carnation farming, only intermittent composition, 1951–73. Recipient: O.B.E. (Order of British Empire), 1970. Mailing address: 199 Clarence Gate Gardens, Glentworth Street, London NW1 6AU, England.

Publisher: none.

Symphonies/orchestral:

Symphony in A No 1 1932. Recorded Albany Troy 032.
Symphony No 2 1933. Recorded Conifer 139.
Symphony No 3 1933.
Symphony No 4 1946. Recorded Albany AR 002; Lyrita 129.
Overture: The Serf 1947.
Symphony No 5 in B♭ 1948. Recorded Albany Troy 022; Lyrita 124.
Overture: John Socman 1951. Recorded Albany Troy 015.
Symphony No 6 1956. Recorded Albany Troy 015.
Symphony No 7 1959. Recorded Conifer 143.
Symphony No 8 1961. Recorded Lyrita 113.
Piano Concerto No 1: Scapegoat 1963. Recorded Albany Troy 037.
Piano Concerto No 2 1964. Recorded Albany Troy 037.
Piano Concerto No 3 1968. Recorded Albany Troy 019.
Symphony No 9 1969. Recorded Conifer 139.
Suite: Charade 1969.
Violin Concerto No 1 1970.
Piano Concerto No 4 1970. Recorded Albany AR 004.
Violin Concerto No 2 (strings) 1977.
Symphony No 10: November Journeys (brass) 1982.
Royal Parks (brass band) 1984. Recorded Chandos 8483.
Symphony No 11 1985. Recorded Conifer 144.
Forest of Arden (wind band) 1987. Recorded LDR Records 001.
Symphony No 12 1989. Recorded Albany Troy 032.
English Heritage (brass band) 1989.

Chamber/instrumental:

An African Shrine (piano) 1966. Recorded Albany AR 003.
Aubade (2 pianos) 1971.
St Antony and the Bogside Beggar (piano) 1972. Recorded Albany AR 003.
The Lily Leaf and the Grasshopper (piano) 1972. Recorded Albany AR 044.
The Transformation of the Naked Ape (piano) 1972. Recorded Albany AR 044.
The Aggressive Fishes (piano) 1972. Recorded Albany AR 003.
The Road Through Samarkand (piano) 1972. Recorded Albany AR 003.
Lament, Air and Dance (violin, piano) 1975. Recorded Troy 029.
Sonata (violin, piano) 1976. Recorded Troy 029.
Intercom Baby (violin; arranged for piano) 1977. Recorded Albany AR 003.
A Miniature Triptych (2 trumpets, horn, trombone, tuba) 1981.

Vocal/choral:

Extracts from the Serf (soloists, chorus, orchestra) 1974.
Per vigilium Veneris/The Vigil of Venus (large chorus, orchestra) 1980.

Opera:

Iernin 1934; first performed Penzance, Cornwall, 6 November 1934.
The Serf 1938; first performed London, 20 October 1938.
John Socman 1951; first performed Bristol, 15 May 1951.

* * *

When George Lloyd showed the score of his hard-won Sixth Symphony to a musical friend, he was told that the work had "no contemporary significance". If this was to say that Lloyd was not a modernist, then that remains largely true. His work is essentially tonal and constructed on the two traditional pillars of harmony and melody. However, even given the relatively lightweight score of the Sixth, it seems odd to dismiss him as a reactionary. The (admittedly few) critics who do are confounded by Lloyd's considerable popularity and it requires no extensive biographical notes to hear the dark side of his work.

In 1942, the Royal Navy ship on which he was serving as a Royal Marine was sunk while on Arctic convoy duty. Lloyd's health broke down, compounding difficulties he had already suffered in childhood. A highly promising musical career, signalled by the production of two operas before he was 25, looked blighted. Lloyd moved with his wife to her native Switzerland, where he attempted to come to terms with his appalling wartime experiences in his Fourth and Fifth Symphonies. (If the Sixth seems blandly affirmative, it is perhaps only in contrast to the more complex psychological seascapes of its two predecessors.) Though the Fifth makes no direct programmatic reference to the War, the Fourth is as direct a confrontation with that experience that Lloyd was to attempt, except perhaps in the first three piano concertos.

There is in Lloyd's work an intriguing dialectic between brasses and strings. His orchestration is distinctive by the extent to which he opposes these major instrumental groups, with what must be programmatic as well as technical intent. His First Violin Concerto is for string orchestra, a device which presents unusual problems of dynamics and sonority. Later in his career, his Eleventh Symphony, an accounting of visits to English cathedrals, is for brasses alone. The opposition is most dramatic in the opening movements of the Fourth Symphony, which begins in pastoral mode with no brass or timpani, a colour palette which is both identifiably "English" and curiously alien. In the second movement, huge militaristic brass chords give way to a long, rather lugubrious chorale with no scoring for the higher strings; the climax, after a lament of almost Mahleresque pessimism, is brightly affirmative. Musically, as well as psychologically, it is a triumph.

Similar thematic ground is covered in the First Piano Concerto, whose unusual subtitle "Scapegoat" underlines Lloyd's striking combination of biblical reference and very considerable "contemporary significance". Much as the Fourth Symphony seemed to establish a restorative musical syntax, the three piano concertos represent a clear attempt to re-establish relations between "protagonist" and "scene". The opening Furioso of the Third is perhaps his darkest music, but it contains the seeds of a rather more ambiguous redemption in its solo passages and conclusion.

The ritual goat of Judea and the Jews of Auschwitz were linked in the First Piano Concerto in an example of the historical syncretism that is so typical of Lloyd's imagination. Basically an orchestral composer, and one of the finest orchestrators since Vaughan Williams, he has also written intriguing chamber works, including a remarkable sequence of piano pieces, mostly done in 1972, but signalled by the long *An African Shrine*, which was written for the late John Ogdon (another brilliant musician dogged by health problems) in 1966 and which contrasts the stillness of the religious object with the violence surrounding it. Musically, it is one of the most completely satisfying piano works in the contemporary literature. There is a quieter alienation at play in *Intercom Baby*, an ironic lullaby for a mother whose "closeness" to her child is dependent on a radio alarm; though doubtless partly tongue-in-cheek, it is a curiously disturbing image. *The Road Through Samarkand* was inspired by the sight of Buddhists chanting on London's Oxford Street, in pursuit of a meretricious and illusory transcendence that is nonetheless hopeful in its very lack of realism. (One of the striking features of the "dark" piano concertos is the amount of light they absorb: at their heart, as in all of Lloyd's work, is a simple, basic humanity.) *St Antony and the Bogside Beggar* explores similar material in contemporary Northern Ireland. A passage in Konrad Lorenz describing the anomalous viciousness of Siamese fighting fish inspired one of Lloyd's liveliest works; bright and sinuous melodies suddenly erupt into violence.

Nervous problems limited Lloyd's ability to finger the violin. Most of his music was written in isolation, with none of the contact with performers (John Ogdon was the sole exception) on which most practising composers thrive and depend. Lloyd's decision to practise on his violin again led to the bittersweet *Lament, Air and Dance*, one of the finest violin and piano pieces by an Englishman since the death of Delius. In contrast, the *Sonata* that followed is slightly colourless.

Lloyd's vocal music is less well-known—and his operatic career seems to be in abeyance. However he has scored considerable critical success in recent years with his *Per vigilium Veneris*. Its reception underlines his return to full-time composition and a growing interest in his work. The "years of silence" proved to be deceptively fruitful and Lloyd has built up a body of work that is both distinctive, accessible and genuinely inspiring. Given his life and circumstances, what is of greatest contemporary significance is that he should have continued to compose at all.

—Richard Stein

LLOYD, Jonathan. British/English. Born in London, 30 September 1948. Educated: studied composition with Emile Spira, 1963–5; Royal College of Music, London (under Edwin Roxburgh), Junior Exhibitioner, 1965–6, full-time student (composition under Roxburgh and John Lambert, and electronic music under Tristram Cary), 1966–9; Mendelssohn Scholarship, Paris, 1969–70; further study with Henri Pousseur, and at Tanglewood, Massachusetts (under György Ligeti), 1969–73. Worked with Contemporary Music Group, 1965–6, and Twentieth-Century Ensemble, 1966–9; occasional work as performer, busker, street musician, 1974–7; composer in residence, theatre department, Dartington College, Devon, 1978–9. Freelance composer. Recipient: Koussevitzky Prize (for *Scattered Ruins*), 1973. Mailing address. c/o Boosey & Hawkes, 295 Regent Street, London W1R 8JH, England.

Publisher: Boosey & Hawkes.

Symphonies/orchestral:

Cantique (small orchestra) 1968, revised 1970; first performed in open rehearsal London, January 1970; first complete public performance London, February 1973.
Time Caught by the Tail (strings, percussion) 1969.
Coming into Gone (large orchestra, chanters) 1974.
Viola Concerto (viola, small orchestra) 1979–80; first performed London, 10 November 1981.

Fantasy (violin, orchestra) 1980.
Rhapsody (cello, orchestra) 1982.
Symphony No 1 1983; first performed Birmingham, 19 January 1989.
Symphony No 2 1983–4; first performed Baden-Baden, 12 February 1988.
Symphony No 3 (chamber orchestra) 1987; first performed Bracknell, Berkshire, 27 June 1987.
Symphony No 4 1988; first performed London, 26 July 1988.
Symphony No 5 1989.

Chamber/instrumental:

Will It Always Be Morning (ensemble) 1970.
Won't It Ever Be Morning (alto flute/piccolo, oboe/cor anglais, E♭ clarinet/bass clarinet, alto saxophone, bassoon, 2 horns, trumpet, trombone, percussion, piano/harmonium, electric guitar, 2 violins, viola, cello) 1980.
John's Journal (alto saxophone/soprano saxophone, piano) 1980; first performed London, 4 March 1981.
Waiting for Gozo (alto flute/piccolo, oboe/cor anglais, clarinet/E♭ clarinet/bass clarinet, bassoon/contrabassoon, horn, trumpet, trombone, 2 violins, viola, cello, double bass) 1981; first performed London, 15 January 1982.
Three Dances (consisting of *Keir's Kick* for string quartet or string orchestra, double bass ad lib; *Ben's Boogie* for wind quintet; *Fancy Three* for ensemble: flute, cor anglais, clarinet, bassoon, horn, 2 violins, viola, cello; or orchestra) 1981–2; first performed Reykjavik, Iceland, 18 June 1982.
Brass Quintet 1982.
Wind Quintet (flute, oboe, clarinet, bassoon, horn) 1982; first performed London, 5 January 1984.
String Quintet No 1 (2 violins, 2 violas, cello) 1982.
String Quintet No 2 (mandolin, lute, guitar, harp, double bass) 1982.
Don't Mention the War (oboe, cor anglais, trombone, percussion, piano/electric organ, viola, cello, double bass) 1982; first performed Montepulciano, Italy, 2 August 1983.
Just Another Day (soprano saxophone, piano) 1983.
The Shorelines of Certainty (from *Songs from the Other Shore*; flute, clarinet, 2 percussion, piano, harp, violin, viola, cello) 1984; first performed Aldeburgh, Suffolk, 17 June 1984.
Time Between Trains (alto flute/clarinet, soprano saxophone/alto saxophone, percussion, piano, violin, viola, double bass) 1984; first performed Bracknell, Berkshire, 30 June 1984.
It's All Sauce to Me (from *Songs from the Other Shore*; violin, piano) 1984; first performed Brighton, Sussex, 14 May 1984.
String Quartet No 1: Of Time and Motion 1984; first performed London, 25 June 1986.
Songs from the Other Shore (consisting of *It's All Sauce to Me* for violin, piano; *The Mill of Memories* for clarinet, cello; *Like Fallen Angels* for flute, viola, harp; *The Shorelines of Certainty* for flute, clarinet, 2 percussion, piano, harp, violin, viola, cello) 1984–6; first performed London, 11 May 1986.
The Five Senses (flute, guitar) 1985; first performed Brisbane, 7 September 1985.
True Refuge (clarinet, piano) 1985; first performed Huddersfield, Yorkshire, 21 November 1985.
Sonata (oboe, piano) 1985.
The New Ear (sonata for winds; 4 clarinets/1 doubling on E♭ clarinet and alto and soprano saxophones/1 doubling on alto flute/1 doubling on bass clarinet and bassoon and contrabassoon, horn, 2 trumpets, trombone, tuba, percussion) 1985; first performed Colchester, Essex, 28 September 1985.
Feuding Fiddles (2 violins) 1986; first performed London, 25 June 1986.
One Step More (flute/piccolo, oboe d'amore, cello, harpsichord) 1986; first performed Bracknell, Berkshire, 5 December 1986.
Almeida Dances (clarinet/alto saxophone, percussion, piano, 2 violins, viola, cello) 1986; first performed London, 25 June 1986.
Airs and Graces (violin) 1987; first performed London, 28 February 1987.
Dancing in the Ruins (sextet) 1990.

Vocal/choral:

Till the Wind Blows (soprano) 1969.
The Other Shore (chorus, orchestra) 1975.
Everything Returns (soprano vocalise, orchestra) 1977–8; first performed BBC recording, 4 October 1979.
Three Songs ("The Bird of Paradise", "The River", "Why Am I Here?"; voice, viola, piano) 1980; first performed Douglas, Isle of Man, August 1980.
Towards the Whitening Dawn (chorus, chamber orchestra; Scejes, after Rasmussen) 1980; first performed London, 4 March 1981.
If I Could Turn You On (high soprano, chamber orchestra; Laing) 1981.
No Man's Land (chorus, orchestra) 1982.
Mass (6 solo voices; Latin) 1983; first performed London, 10 April 1984.
Missa brevis (unaccompanied double chorus; Latin) 1984.
Revelation (unaccompanied chorus) 1990.
Marching to a Different Song (soprano, chamber orchestra) 1991.

Opera/dramatic:

Scattered Ruins (music theatre piece; soprano, flute/alto flute/piccolo, clarinet/bass clarinet, 2 trumpets, 2 trombones, percussion, harp, electric organ/harpsichord/celeste, mandolin/bass guitar; Latin text) 1973; first performed Tanglewood, Massachusetts, August 1973.
Musices genus (masque for soprano, piano, ensemble: soprano/also plays upright piano, alto flute/piccolo, clarinet/bass clarinet, violin/viola, viola, cello, guitar/electric guitar/banjo, electric organ/celeste, percussion—all players doubling on crotales; 2 buskers: ukulele, clarinet, bass drum, cymbals; medieval woodcuts and Flemish paintings) 1974.
The Adjudicator (community opera; Michael John White) 1985; first performed Blewbury, Oxfordshire, 15 April 1986.

Other:

Baal (incidental music to Brecht play) 1979.

* * *

Jonathan Lloyd is one of the most individual and imaginative British composers of his generation. After preliminary studies with the Webern pupil Emile Spira, he studied composition at the Royal College of Music with John Lambert from 1966–9, during which period he composed the first piece he still acknowledges, *Cantique*, for small orchestra. This already contains elements which were to remain typical of Lloyd's music: an episodic, volatile form full of unpredictable changes of direction, and great diversity of material including, at one point, a brief hint of jazz. After a succession of scholarships and awards (including a Mendolssohn Scholarship in 1969, and a Tanglewood Fellowship in 1973, where he attended Ligeti's classes and where *Scattered Ruins* won the Koussevitzky Prize), Lloyd temporarily abandoned composition; between the years 1974–7, he worked as an occasional performer, busker and street musician. In 1977 he began his first major work, *Everything Returns*, for wordless soprano and orchestra, completed the following year. As the title indicates, this work contains a high degree of repetition; essentially, a single gesture is endlessly reworked and varied, expanded, contracted, developed. The material is a bizzare mixture of Ligeti-like floating textures overlaid with fragments of jazz, big band and popular music, while the soprano is restricted to the occasional hysterical laugh before launching into a passage of scat-singing near the end of the work.

Lloyd's *Viola Concerto*, from the following year, is a more extended example of the same type of stylistic mix. The three movements follow the traditional concerto format (fast-slow-fast), including a central fast episode within the slow movement so that the whole piece contains a degree of Barlók-like symmetry. The orchestration for the ensemble is rich and virtuosic, creating the illusion of a large orchestral sonority; the writing for the viola is thoroughly idiomatic, ranging from long flowing melodies to bravura passages of great energy. A pastiche waltz is woven in and out of the texture, and the orchestration also features a jazz kit (like many of Lloyd's works) which reinforces the moments of big band-like exuberance in the last movement. As before, a large amount of inexact repetition is included, with the same music being obessively reworked and revised, a characteristic shared with the ensemble piece *Won't It Ever Be Morning* composed in 1980. Here, the jazz element found in so much of Lloyd's music comes to the fore; the work opens with a lethargic piano solo, with lush harmonies suggesting Gershwin and Messiaen, and then retreats into furtive, elusive scurryings for the different instrumental groups; over the next 15 minutes, these gradually accumulate energy and direction, before the work lapses again into vague nightclub musings without ever having fulfilled any evident goal. Lloyd has diversified his output in recent years to include a wide variety of solos and smaller works, often with quasi-humorous titles and exploiting the resources of the instruments with great imagination (*It's All Sauce to Me*, for violin and piano, *True Refuge*, for clarinet and piano, *The New Ear*, for winds, brass and percussion). He has also embarked upon an impressive sequence of symphonies (five so far, written between 1983 and 1989). These show Lloyd evolving a more flexible and fluid syntax, less immediately dependant on pastiche and stylistic allusion. The most elaborate and ambitious of these is the Fourth Symphony, a BBC commission for the London Promenade Concerts in 1988. The work is based upon the simplest and most obvious melodic fragment, the C-major scale, which is invested with all manner of expression and mood; the work does include episodes of jazz, rock and such, but these are now very smoothly integrated into the texture as just another transformation of the basic material. Rather than conforming to any preconceived sonata-like form, the work evolves freely out of repeated gestures and fragments (as by now customary with Lloyd) which evolve in subtly different ways on each recurrence. The tone of the work is decidedly tense and uneasy, with a new-found seriousness which throws the more obviously "popular" elements into a more threatening context. The large orchestra, which includes a quartet of saxophones as well as Lloyd's beloved electric guitar, mandolin and jazz kit, is deployed selectively and delicately, often focussing upon chamber-music size ensembles within the forces available—the tutti is exploited only at a few climactic passages. Lloyd's large output also includes concertos for violin (*Fantasy*) and cello (*Rhapsody*), as well as a "community opera" *The Adjudicator*; apart from which, there is little vocal music—only the *Mass*, a typically idiosyncratic and unusual approach to the traditional Latin text.

Lloyd's persistent use of "found material", of popular idioms in unexpected contexts, has led some to accuse him of frivolity and superficiality; but there is more to his music than the craziness which is its most obvious trait. His dexterity in scoring, the clarity and practicality with which he notates his complex superimpositions of tempo and metre, are exceptional in themselves. His chief qualities, however, lie in the ease with which he synthesizes his wildly disparate materials into hauntingly original landscapes whose intent and effect, far from being frivolous, are frequently profoundly disquieting.

—Julian Anderson

LOBANOV, Vassily. Russian. Born in Moscow, 1947. Educated at Tchaikovsky Conservatoire, Moscow (piano under Leo Naumov, composition under Sergei Balasanyan and Alfred Schnittke), 1963–71. Independent composer, since 1971; concert pianist, major debut 1976. Mailing address: ulitsa Gottwalda, dom 10, kv. 20, 125047 Moscow, U.S.S.R.

Publisher: Fazer, Espoo, Finland.

Symphonies/orchestral:

Symphony No 1 Op 22 (chamber orchestra: 4 flutes, trumpet, harpsichord, strings) 1977; first performed Moscow, 1979.
Concerto for Piano and Chamber Orchestra Op 35 1981; first performed Moscow, 1981.
Concerto for Cello and Orchestra Op 42 1984; first performed Moscow, 1985.
Arias (violin, strings) 1985; first performed Moscow, 1986.
Sinfonietta Op 47 (chamber orchestra) 1986; first performed Moscow, 1986.
Concerto for Viola and String Orchestra Op 52 1989.

Chamber/instrumental:

Four Pieces on Three Notes (in Imitation of Stravinsky) Op 1 (piano) 1963; first performed Moscow, 1963.
Two Pieces: A Mood, Bas-Relief Op 2 (violin, piano) 1963; first performed Moscow, 1963.
String Quartet No 1 Op 4 1965; first performed Moscow, 1966.
Twelve Preludes Op 5 (piano) 1965; first performed Moscow, 1965.
Sonatina Op 6 (piano) 1966; first performed Moscow, 1966.
Partita Op 9 (piano) 1967; first performed Moscow, 1967.
Pieces for Children Op 10 (piano) 1968.
String Quartet No 2 Op 11 1968; first performed Moscow, 1968.
Five Preludes Op 12 1969; first performed (3 only) Moscow, 1979.

Suite No 2 Op 13 (piano) 1971.
Sonata No 1 Op 14 (cello, piano) 1971; first performed Moscow, 1971.
Sonata No 2 Op 17 (piano) 1973.
Suite No 3 Op 19 (piano) 1974; first performed Moscow, 1975.
Sonata Op 20 (flute) 1974.
Prelude, Aria and Jib Op 23 (violin, piano) 1977; first performed Moscow, 1977.
Two Pieces: Modulation, Solfeggio Op 24 (flute) 1978.
Seven Pieces Op 25 (cello, piano) 1978.
String Quartet No 3 Op 26 1978.
Three Pieces: Mirage, Invention, Chorale Op 28 (xylophone) 1978.
Seven Slow Pieces Op 34 (piano) 1978–80.
Trio Op 29 (flute, clarinet, bassoon) 1979; first performed Moscow, 1979.
Variations Op 30 (2 trumpets) 1979.
Adagio Op 32 (violin, cello, piano) 1980; first performed Moscow, 1980.
Sonata No 2 Op 33 (piano) 1980; first performed Moscow, 1980. Recorded Melodiya C10 21917 000.
Oda Trave / Ode to Grass Op 37 1982; first performed Moscow, 1982.
Sonata Op 38 (flute) 1983; first performed Moscow, 1983.
Ode to the Wind Op 41 (violin, piano) 1984; first performed Pultava, 1984.
Four Pieces in a Strict Style Op 43 (clarinet, piano) 1984.
Four Diatonic Preludes Op 44 (piano) 1984; first performed Tsita, 1984.
Sonata Op 45 (clarinet, piano) 1985; first performed Munich, 1986.
Two Preludes Op 46 (piano) 1986; first performed Moscow, 1986.
Fantasia Op 48 (cello) 1987; first performed Munich, 1987.
String Quartet No 4 Op 49 1987; first performed Moscow, 1988.
String Quartet No 5 Op 50 1988; first performed Kuhmo, 1988.
Sonata No 2 Op 53 (cello, piano) 1989; first performed London, 1989.
Three Fragments Op 54 (piano) 1989; first performed London, 1989.
Sonata in Five Fragments Op 55 (violin, piano) 1989; first performed Glasgow, 1989.

Vocal / choral:

Three Haikus Op 3 (low voice, piano; Basho) 1963.
Three Romances (bass, piano; Blok—"The Thief", "The Dwarf", "The Storm Angel") 1965.
Five Romances Op 15 (low voice, piano; Chutsev—"Shadows", "Madness", "The Flow", "Earth", "Ocean") 1971.
Lieutenant Schmidt Op 31 (oratorio for soprano, bass, chorus, orchestra; Pasternak) 1979.
Four Poems Op 39 (bass, piano; Parin—"A Walk", "Petals", "Darkness", "Archetype") 1984; first performed Moscow, 1984.
Golos / The Voice Op 40 (soprano, piano; Karpelan—"And the Word", "Listen", "The Drop", "And They Fall", "Morning Is Late", "The Tree", "Crows", "No Sound Is Heard") 1984; first performed Moscow, 1984.

Opera:

Antigone Op 51 (Parin, after Sophocles) 1985–8; first performed Swezdlovsk, 1988.

Other:

Johannes Brahms: piano transcriptions of 3 songs, *Op 8* ("Juchne!", "In der Gasse", "So stehen wir") 1967; first performed Moscow, 1968.
Peter Tchaikovsky: *Pas d'action* from *Swan Lake* (transcribed for violin, cello, string orchestra) 1980; first performed Moscow, 1980.
Igor Stravinsky: *Italian Suite* (transcribed for cello, chamber orchestra) 1985; first performed Riga, 1986.

* * *

Vassily Lobanov is not only a composer but an extremely fine pianist, whose performing career has led to his working with musicians as distinguished as Sviatoslav Richter, Natalia Gutman and the late Oleg Kagan. This career has had a great effect on Lobanov's music, both in terms of the artists for whom he has written and in the very way that his musical language has developed. "Whenever I begin a piece of music", Lobanov has commented, "I first of all imagine the performer in front of the audience. From that experience come the opening notes."

Lobanov is one of the younger generation of Moscow composers for whom such figures as Alfred Schnittke and Edison Denisov have been crucial as artistic examples. As a student at the Tchaikovsky Conservatoire in Moscow Lobanov showed the clear influence of Denisov's distinctive aesthetic; works such as the *Adagio* for piano trio and the *Seven Pieces* for cello and piano reveal several characteristic Denisov fingerprints, including a fondness for sinewy chromatic heterophony and a loosely post-Darmstadt style of pointillisme.

It was rather later that Lobanov began to come under the influence of Schnittke, and this was to lead to a much more productive discovery of his own identity. He has said that Schnittke helped him to find the confidence to write the way he really wanted to. In particular Schnittke encouraged Lobanov to confront the question of his talents as an improviser and the way in which these might enable him to find paths and points of connection between performance and composition.

The first quality to note about Lobanov's more mature style is his fondness for repeated arpeggio patterns and even something of the effect of Reichian phasing, built of the common materials of Western music. Some of his works, like the lovely Second Piano Sonata, can even sound obviously minimalist in character, and some of his more recent compositions like his opera *Antigone* almost touch the world of pop music.

But the repeated patterns in Lobanov's music do not really serve the speculative conceptual purposes of a Steve Reich or the architectural ones of a John Adams. Instead they seem to be there in order to allow the player (that is, by implication, the composer) maximum freedom and looseness in performance. To hear Lobanov playing his own piano music is to ride on a beguiling wave of spontaneity, and to sense the constant possibility that the music might perpetuate its state of flux and transformation for ever, or, on the other hand, die in a moment's time.

Another side of Lobanov's character is a fondness for extremely bleak but evocative melodic writing, often sounding to English ears not unlike the later works of Britten, but presumably really more closely related to Shostakovich. Lobanov's song-cycle *The Voice* to poems by Bu Karpelan is perhaps the finest example of this vein in his music, a work which finds an exquisite laconic balance between the opposed senses of expressive deliberation and improvisational freedom.

Here, where the notes are so few, the improvisation seems at its most meaningful, at once easy and extremely difficult.

In some more recent compositions, Lobanov has seemed to be trying to integrate his style within the rather obvious formal traditions of Soviet music. This has led to several sonatas for instrument and piano. A recent sonata for cello and piano, was written in memory of the victims of the Armenian earthquake; another, for clarinet and piano, was written out of Lobanov's experience of playing with the Swiss clarinettist Edward Brunner. At the same time, in his recent Viola Concerto for Yuri Bashmet, Lobanov has included some surprising elements of rather brash vulgarity.

Lobanov's is a brave path, one that presupposes a certain proportion of less successful works, precisely because of the nakedness of the improvised experience and the freedom from the kinds of controlling techniques that are important to most other composers. At its worst his music can retreat to a mere background of mood. At its best, in his Cello Concerto for his friend Natalia Gutman perhaps, he offers an experience of high refinement.

—Gerard McBurney

LOCKWOOD, Annea [Anna] (Ferguson). New Zealander. Born in Christchurch, New Zealand, 29 July 1939. Educated at Canterbury University, Christchurch, 1958–61, B.Mus.; Royal College of Music, London (piano under E. Kendall Taylor, composition under Peter Racine Fricker), diploma, 1963; Ferienkurse für Neue Musik, Darmstadt, 1961–2; Staatliche Hochschule für Musik, Cologne (under Gottfried Michael Koenig), 1963; Electronic Music Centre, Bilthoven, The Netherlands (under Gottfried Michael Koenig), 1963–4; University of Southampton, Hampshire (psycho-acoustics under Peter Grogono), 1969–71; Electronic Music Studios, London, 1970. Married to Harvey Matusow. Non-lecturer, Anti-University of London, 1968; teacher of music, Hunter College, City University of New York, from 1973; visiting professor at various American campuses, including Queens College, City University of New York, and at Bedford Women's Correctional Facility, Bedford, New York; professor of music, Vassar College, Poughkeepsie, New York, since 1983. Mailing address: Baron de Hirsch Road, Crompond, New York 10517, U.S.A.

Publishers: Schirmer; Source; Morrow.

Symphonies/orchestral:

Violin Concerto 1962.

Chamber/instrumental:

Deep Dream Dive (double bass, electronics) 1973.
Consulting Musician (1 instrument, live electronics) 1975.

Vocal/choral:

Serenade No 1 (soprano, flute; Anakreon) 1962.
A Abelard, Heloise (chamber cantata for mezzo-soprano, 10 instruments) 1963.
Aspekte einer Parabel (baritone, 10 instruments; Kafka) 1964.
Serenade No 2 (soprano, orchestra, tape; Perse) 1965.
Humming (mixed chorus/70+) 1972.
Malaman (1–4 voices) 1974. Recorded New Wilderness Audiographics 7704.
Spirit Catchers (4 amplified voices) 1974.
Malolo (lullaby for 3 women's voices) 1982. Recorded Finnadar 90226 1.

Other:

Love Field (tape) 1964.
Glass Concert I (amplified glass instruments/2 players) 1966.
Shone (mixed media) 1966.
Piano Transplants (sound sculptures/recorded placements) 1968–71; "Piano Burning" performed London, 3 October 1968; "Piano Drowning" performed Amarillo, Texas, 27 December 1972; also "Piano Garden".
Sound Her, Sound Umbrella (sound sculptures) 1969.
Glass Concert II (amplified glass instruments) 1969.
Glass Water (electronic) 1969.
Gentle Grass (rite for 6 players) 1970.
End (electronic; collaboration with H.M. Matusow) 1970. Recorded Sveriges Radio RELP 1102.
Dark Touch (aural and tactile materials) 1970.
Tiger Balm (tape) 1970. Recorded New Wilderness Audiographics 7704; Opus One 70; Source 9.
Bus Trip (journey with food, free love and electronic score) 1971.
Windhover (tape) 1972.
Glade (wine glasses) 1972. Recorded New Wilderness Audiographics 7704.
Eye/Ear (mixed media) 1972.
Cloud Music (tape) 1973. Recorded New Wilderness Audiographics 7704.
And Sound Flew Like a Bird (tape) 1973. Recorded New Wilderness Audiographics 7704.
The River Archive; Play the Ganges Backwards One More Time, Sam (installation for mixed media) 1973–4.
World Rhythms (10-track tape, gong) 1975. Recorded New Wilderness Audiographics 7704; Arch S 1765.
Singing to Earth, Singing the Air (electronic) 1976.
Woman Murder (tape) 1977. Recorded New Wilderness Audiographics 7704.
Spirit Songs Unfolding (tapes, slides) 1977.
Conversations with the Ancestors (installation/mixed media) 1979.
Pillow Talk, Love Stories and Comedies (tape, pillow) 1981.
Delta Run (tapes, slides, choreography) 1981; first performed Chicago, 1982.
The River Archive; Sound Map of the Hudson (installation for mixed media) 1982. Recorded Audio Arts 6.

PUBLICATIONS

By Lockwood: *Tiger Balm*, in *Source Magazine*, 9, 1971; *River Archive*, in *Source Magazine*, 10, 1973; *Consulting Musician* and *Spirit Catchers*, in *Ear Magazine*, 1(5), 1975; (with Alison Knowles), *Women's Work*, 1980.

* * *

To describe Annea Lockwood as "avant-garde" is a little like describing Pope John Paul II as "a Catholic". For 30 years, Lockwood has been exploring the boundaries of musical imagination with a dogged resistance to convention.

While she has occasionally fallen foul of mere fashion, most notably in her conceptual/performance works of the late 1960s, she has also produced work of remarkable, evanescent beauty.

Her training was reasonably conventional, including periods of study with Peter Racine Fricker in London, and the electronics expert Gottfried Michael Koenig at Bilthoven. She did further research into psycho-acoustics at the University of Southampton. Her earliest works were in a routinely atonal idiom. The *Violin Concerto*—her sole finished orchestral piece—suggests a good technical grounding rather than genuine imaginative force, but the chamber settings of Kafka and of Heloise, Abbess of Paraclete, are considerably more robust.

Drawing on her training with Koenig, Lockwood thereafter threw herself into electronic and mixed media composition. In view of the later *Bus Trip*—perhaps the only modern score to offer "free love", but not intriguingly the only one to throw in food—the early tape piece *Love Field* is susceptible to a certain prejudice as to subject matter. It is, in fact, a threnody to John F. Kennedy, named after the Dallas airfield where the Presidential jet landed before the fatal motorcade. Lockwood's experiments with ambient sound developed more fully later. In the mid 1960s, much of her attention was devoted to scoring for a multiplicity of glass objects and instruments—light bulbs, bottles and jars, fluorescent tubes, mobiles, glass mobiles constructed for the nonce—which could be tapped, bowed, and in some cases, snapped or shattered. It may be worth noting that Benjamin Franklin (who represents the pragmatic, technics-obsessed branch of early Americanism) invented the glass harmonium; later experimenters with the medium include the great instrument-builder Harry Partch and the singer–choreographer Meredith Monk, who accompanies vocal pieces with rubbed wine glasses. It is typical of Lockwood, though, that she should take an existing line of inquiry and stretch it to its limits, or *ad absurdum*. It has been the acceptance of absurdity that has sustained her career.

In that she is closely allied to John Cage. Taking her cue directly from Cage's "preparation" of the piano, Lockwood set about testing the most canonical—but also, since she used upright models, the most populist—of all modern instruments to (literal) destruction. The *Piano Transplants* were an attempt to expose a series of pianos to air, earth, fire and water. One was more or less conventionally prepared and subjected to Aeolian inspiration; one was buried to form a "piano garden"; a third was drowned in a lake in Amarillo; and a fourth burned following a seance to summon up the ghost of Ludwig van Beethoven. All of these events were scrupulously taped (though there was a certain coyness about what the German composer may have dictated from beyond the grave).

Since the early 1970s, Lockwood has been largely concerned with performance and with environmental sound. Her *River Archive* is an ambitious attempt—related to Joan La Barbara's city portraits—to compress actual ambiences into a highly metaphoric aural structure. *World Rhythms*, a 1975 piece whose title is more redolent of late 1980s "World Music" obsessions, requires a large gong to be beaten ritualistically at very slow intervals, the decay of each tone being transformed by the resonance of a multi-tracked ambient tape.

Though many of her most extreme pieces, some of them devised in collaboration with her husband Harvey Matusow, seem unfeasibly time-bound, the more radical artistic experiments of the 1960s are currently the subject of renewed interest and serious attention. In that light, and in view of the rigour which underlies their deceptively casual and capricious externals, Lockwood's works may yet be considered some of the most significant conceptual developments of the last three decades.

—Brian Morton

LOEVENDIE, Theo. Dutch. Born in Amsterdam, 17 September 1930. Educated at Amsterdam Conservatory (clarinet, and composition under Leon Orthel). Originally active in jazz as clarinettist and with own ensemble; began writing concert music in earnest, 1968; professor of composition, Rotterdam Conservatory, 1970–88; composition seminar, Hameenlinna, Finland, 1979; composer in residence, Lerchenborg Music Days, Denmark, 1982; composition seminar, University of New Mexico, Albuquerque, 1984; lecturer, Ferienkurse für Neue Musik, Darmstadt, 1986; other lectures worldwide, 1986; professor of composition, Royal Conservatory, The Hague, since 1988. Recipient: Edison Award (for jazz recording), 1969; Wessel Ilcken prize (for jazz activities), 1979; Edison Award (for *De Nachtegaal*), 1982; Koussevitzky International Record Award (for *Flexio*), 1984, shared with Pierre Boulez; Matthijs Vermeulen Prize, City of Amsterdam (for *Naima*), 1986; £M Music Award (for lifetime achievement), 1988. Mailing address: Donemus, Paulus Potterstraat 14, 1071 CZ Amsterdam, The Netherlands.

Publishers: Donemus; Peer, Hamburg.

Symphonies/orchestral:

Confluxus (jazz orchestra, symphony orchestra) 1966.
Scaramuccia Op 1 (clarinet, orchestra) 1969. Recorded Donemus DAVS 7374/4.
Orbits (horn solo, 4 obligatto horns, orchestra) 1972–6.
Incantations (bass clarinet, symphony orchestra) 1975. Recorded Donemus CV 7802.
Flexio 1979. Recorded Donemus CV 8301.
In Prison (orchestral fragment from *Naima*) 1983.
Music for a Strange Wedding (from *Naima*) 1983.
Intermezzo (from *Naima*) 1986.
Naima Suite 1986.

Chamber/instrumental:

String Quartet 1961.
Three Pieces (youth ensemble; 2 flutes, oboe, 2 clarinets, piano) 1964.
Toccata (piano) 1965.
Tre pezzi (3 clarinets) 1968.
Ten Easy Sketches (clarinet, piano) 1970.
Music (bass clarinet, piano) 1971. Recorded Gaudeamus 72001.
Aulos (1 or more wind and/or string instruments) 1972.
Two Trios (small percussion ensemble) 1973.
Prelude (6 conga players) 1974. Recorded Classic Records CRC 180491.
Timbo (6 percussionists) 1974. Recorded Donemus CV 7802.
Two Short Pieces (piano) 1976; published in *Neue Niederländische Klaviermusik* I.

Strides (piano) 1976. Recorded Donemus CV 7802; Etcetera KTC 1097.
Two East Pieces (piano) 1977. Recorded Golf 001; Attacca Babel 8241–6.
Music (flute, piano) 1979. Recorded Donemus CV 81092; Gaudeamus Perspectives 1989.
Voor Jan, Piet en Klaas (2 pianos—8 hands) 1979.
Nonet (piccolo/flute, clarinet, bassoon, horn, trumpet, trombone, piano, harpsichord, percussion) 1980. Recorded Donemus CVS 1984/2; BFOA-17.
Venus and Adonis (bass clarinet, mandolin, guitar, violin, percussion) 1980. Recorded Etcetera KTC 1097.
Walk (piano) 1985.
Dance (violin) 1986.
Back Bay Bicinium (7 instruments) 1986.
Duo (bass clarinet) 1987. Recorded Attacca Babel 8945 1.
Plus One (flute, bass clarinet, piano) 1988.

Vocal/choral:

The Nightingale (narrator, 7 instruments) 1974–9. Recorded Donemus CVS 1981/1.
Six Turkish Folkpoems (soprano, flute, clarinet, harp, piano, percussion, violin, cello) 1977. Recorded Donemus CV 7802; RO 400 Years of Dutch Music 1; Etcetera KTC 1097.
All the Flowers of the Spring (from *Naima*; mezzo-soprano, piano) 1985.
Two Songs (from *Naima*; mezzo-soprano, 8 instruments or piano) 1985. Recorded Etcetera KTC 1097.
As Fast as Thou Shat Wane (from *Naima*; soprano, piano) 1985.
Oh oor o hoor (baritone, orchestra) 1987.
Scene Two (from *Esmee*; soprano, tenor, orchestra) 1988.
Een Nachtegaal uit Echternach / A Nightingale from Echternach (soprano or mezzo-soprano, piano) 1989.

Opera/dramatic:

De Nachtegaal/The Nightingale (music theatre for narrator, orchestra) 1981. Recorded R O Sprookjes.
Naima (soloists, mixed chorus, orchestra) 1982–5; first performed Amsterdam, 1985. Recorded Donemus CVS 1986/5.
Esmee 1988–91; first performed Amsterdam, 1992.
Gassir, the Hero (chamber opera) 1990; first performed Boston, 1991.

* * *

To understand Theo Loevendie's rather unique situation, it is necessary to probe his cultural background a little. At a national level, The Netherland's enlightened commissioning, performing and publishing policy which encouraged and supported living composers was in itself a dramatic remedy for the disarray—cultural as well as social—in which the country found itself (even more than the rest of contemporary Europe) after the end of World War II. At a personal level, composers found themselves in something of a stylistic crisis. Forced by the humiliating circumstances of The Netherland's occupation and the new feeling of Europeanness to reject any association with the old pre-war nationalism, without a composer of international standing living in the country to act as a sort of rallying point, yet given every encouragement to write and get performed, the younger composers moved almost wholesale to serialism in the decade-and-a-half following liberation. Against such a setting Loevendie developed, in his twenties a student of Leon Orthel (who, together with Hans Henkermans, represented the link with the authentic "Dutch" school of pre-war composers), in a music scene dominated by serialism, a style for which he had absolutely no sympathy. He found an outlet for his enormous creativity instead in the fields of jazz, and was already a professional jazz musician when he entered the Amsterdam Conservatory at 25. Accordingly he found himself, equipped with the full technique necessary for "serious" composition, effectively isolated from the contemporary music scene.

The consequences were numerous. The most obvious is that, apart from a handful of student works, he composed exclusively in the jazz field until he was nearly 40. Another is that, while holding a prominent position among living Dutch composers, Loevendie has always been active and extensively performed outside of The Netherlands. It was one of these overseas engagements—a visit to Turkey, playing clarinet with his ensemble—that provided one of the most potent experiences to influence his later style. It stimulated in him a love of the underlying features of Middle-Eastern music, where melody, rhythm and timbre replace harmony as the driving force in his mature output. A less obvious, but even more important consequence, is the resulting resiliance and integrity of his style and language.

It must be stressed that Loevendie is not a late developer, still less a late starter: he both started and developed at the same rate as his colleagues, but did not find the impulse to put it into formal scores. There are simply no "early" works (just as, with Mendelssohn, there are no late works). If, at the age of 39, possessing the skills associated with composition for the concert hall but keeping them unemployed for over a decade while swimming against the tide, you suddenly find both the will and confidence to write, it probably means that your language is fully in place, your influences fully absorbed and your style worked out. If, moreover, you do it in an intrinsically alien atmosphere, you must be relatively sure not only of what you are going to say, but of your ability to say it clearly and unambiguously. Loevendie's "Op 1" (*Scaramuccia* for clarinet and orchestra) is a thoroughly mature, fluent and characteristic work, and the advances displayed by subsequent scores—structural and organisational for the most part—are no more nor less than you would expect to find in any composer's *mature* output: they are differences of degree, not direction.

The influence of jazz on Loevendie's music is not straightforward. He is not a "cross-over" composer in the normal sense, and he will say that there is no direct link between his jazz playing and his concert music. Certainly jazz mannerisms do not invade his scores (with the single possible exception of *strides* for piano)—the influences take place below the surface, and are both subtle and pervasive, and he may be largely unconscious of them himself. He is clearly aware of the importance of making an immediate impact in the sound of a piece: the ear is gripped from the outset. Melodic shapes are muscular, purposeful and show the hand of the practical performer in the way important material is both clearly to be heard and also written for the instruments so that they sound to best advantage in their tessitura. While he may justify them by citing the processes involved, forms and structures are intuitive, extensions of essentially musical possibilities of cellular expansion which give the scores a linear cohesion and make dogma quite unnecessary. The pacing is likewise instinctive and usually appropriate. Moreover, melodies and rhythms interact to combine a sense of improvised freedom and a feeling of inevitability—the sign of a seasoned jazz performer.

Similarly, Loevendie's interest in Turkish music is not merely on the surface, even in the deservedly well-known *Six*

Turkish Folkpoems: no cheap travelogue these, but a pungently austere cycle, the music completely original, recreating the substance of ethnic material rather than simply imitating the mannerisms. Like much of his work it is sharply rather than luxuriously coloured, rhythmically vital, direct though complex, and tightly and sparingly constructed. It shares with pieces like the *Nonet* and *The Nightingale* a use of melodic lines that are highly ornamented while retaining complete clarity, and finds its rhythmic counterpoint in scores like *Timbo* for six percussion players, and the modestly titled *Prelude* for congas. This elaboration of rhythmic and melodic patterns is very clearly seen in the *Music* for flute and piano—perhaps his most extreme use of isorhythms, ostinatos and hererophony—but has its most significant application in works for the theatre, a medium with no prescribed forms. In the opera *Naima*, perversely, Loevendie actually employs a classic formula—the Passacaglia—but by desynchronising the theme (16 notes) and the rhythmic pattern (20 notes) he gives himself scope for considerable freedom without losing cohesion, and exploits his lyrical gift and fondness for unexpected shifts.

Since the late 1970s Loevendie has begun using a device he calls "curve technique", a thematic treatment with structural implications. An extended melody has both an overall shape (curve) and may be regarded as a succession of intervals. These intervals are then expanded or contracted, but by adjusting the compensation of their juxtaposition, the curve can be left (more or less) intact, affording freedom, organic growth and above all forward movement. By devising the thematic element carefully and exploiting its harmonic implications, he is able to retain the tensions and frictions of a tonal system of harmony while liberating himself from the tyranny of major/minor relationships. His discovery of this device has been quite natural, and has nothing to do with bloodless thought. Like all original composers, Loevendie, if he thinks about it at all, knows that form is nothing more than the most appropriate way of expressing a musical idea—it is what turns an idea into a piece. Form develops to assist musical expression: music doesn't exist to flesh out forms. With Loevendie expressive force is the music's function—the forms just help it along.

—Giles Easterbrook

LOGOTHETIS, Anestis. Greco-Bulgarian; Austrian citizen. Born in Pyrgos [now Burgas], Bulgaria, 27 October 1921; emigrated to Thessaloniki, Greece, in 1934. Educated at Classical Gymnasium, Thessaloniki, 1935–41; studied mechanical engineering at Technische Hochschule, Vienna, from 1942; Musikhochschule, Vienna (composition under Alfred Uhl), 1946–51. Married Maria Stahlich in 1952; 1 daughter. Freelance composer. Recipient: Theodor Korner Prize, 1960, 1963; 1st prize, New Music Competition, Athens, 1962; Special State Prize, Vienna, 1985; Gold Medal of Honour, Vienna, 1986; Special Prize of the Austrian Ministry of Education, Arts and Sport, 1989. Mailing address: Hegergasse 4/9, A-1030 Vienna, Austria.

Publishers: Universal Edition, Vienna; Breitkopf & Hartel, Wiesbaden; Edition Modern, Munich; Ricordi Verlag, Munich.

Symphonies/orchestral:

Polynom 1957–8.
Koordination (5 orchestral groups) 1960.
Maandros 1963; first performed Berlin, 1965.
Dynapolis 1964; first performed Athens, 1978.
Labyrinthos 1965.
Enoseis 1965.
Diffusion 1965; first performed Athens, 1967.
Enklaven 1966; first performed Saarbrücken, 1972.
Konvektionsströme 1968.
Styx 1968; first performed Hannover, 1969. Recorded Amadeo Verlag 419 074 1; Thorofon CTH 2026.
Zonen 1969; first performed Munich, 1969.
Wellen 1974.
Rondo 1979.
Sinfonie Zyklischer Kontrapunkte 1987.

Chamber/instrumental (mainly for unspecified instrumentation):

Integration (violin, cello, piano) 1953.
Peritonen (horn, piano) 1954.
Struktur-Textur-Spiegel-Spiel 1959; first performed Vienna, 1962.
Cycloide 1960.
Parallaxe 1960.
Expansion-Kontraktion 1960.
Verkettungen 1960.
Reflexe I 1960.
Kulmination I, II 1961; first performed Athens, 1962.
Sieben Kooptationen 1961; first performed Wiesbaden, 1970.
Kleine Parallaxe 1962.
Odysse 1963; first performed Stuttgart, 1967.
Kentra 1964; first performed Zagreb, 1965.
Dispersion 1964; first performed Zagreb, 1965.
Seismographie I 1964; first performed Athens, 1967.
Seismographie II 1964; first performed Frankfurt, 1967.
Linienmodulationen 1965; first performed Vienna, 1989.
Integration 1966; first performed Zagreb, 1967.
Diptychon 1966; first performed Amsterdam, 1973.
Rondo 1967.
Grafische Notationen (collection of graphic pieces) 1967.
Mensuren 1969; first performed Ossiach, 1969.
Kollisionen 1970; first performed Vienna, 1970.
Komplementares 1970; first performed Athens, 1975.
Fusion 1971; first performed Rotterdam, 1972.
Klangraume I, II 1972; first performed London, 1975.
Volant 1972; first performed Athens, 1975.
Musikfontane 1972; first performed London, 1973.
Emanation 1973; first performed Warsaw, 1974.
Apollonion 1975; first performed Dortmund, 1976.
Geomusik 1976; first performed Graz, 1981.
Doppelspirale 1985; first performed Voralb, 1987.
Paysage de Temps 1986.

Vocal/choral:

Chor der Puppen / Chor I (4 female, 4 male voices) 1967; first performed Vienna, 1989.
Pataphysik (mixed chorus) 1967.
Styxische Flusse (chorus, orchestra) 1970; first performed Athens, 1971.
Chor II (mixed chorus) 1979; first performed Karnten, 1979.
Chor III: Ach wie schon . . . (mixed chorus) 1984.

Dramatic:

Anastasis 1961, 1969. Recorded Amadeo 419 074 1.
Mantratellurium (*Horspiel*) 1961, 1970; broadcast 1971.
karmadharmadrama 1967.
? or *Knotenschrift* 1967; first performed Weiz, 1972.
Kybernetikon (*Horspiel*) 1971–2; broadcast 1973.
Kerbtieparty (*Horspiel*) 1972–3; broadcast 1974.
Menetekel 1974–5; first performed Stuttgart, 1975.
Im Gespint 1976; first performed (in part) Vienna, 1977; broadcast 1978.
Daidalia or *Das Leben einer Theorie* 1976–8; first performed Athens, 1979.
Woraus is der Stein von Sisyphos? 1982–4.

Other:

Eine Legende aus Schottland (electro-acoustic film score) 1970; first performed Vienna, 1971.
Meomsa (electro-acoustic score to film by Linda Christanell) 1988; first performed Vienna, 1988.

PUBLICATIONS

By Logothetis: *Notation mit graphischen Elementen*, Salzburg, 1967; "Kurze Musikalische Spurenkunde", in *Wort und Wahrheit*, 2, 1969; "Eine Darstellung des Klanges", in *Melos*, 2, 1970; "*karmadharmadrama*: Oper ingraphische Notation", in *Osterreichische Musikzeitschrift*, 10, 1972; "Impulse", in *UE rote reihe*, 34, 1973; *Zeichen als Aggregatzustand der Musik*, Munich, 1974; "Komponiern für die Jugend", in *Osterreichische Musikzeitschrift*, 6, 1975; "Von der Bedeutung der Dinge", in *Osterreichische Musikzeitschrift*, 6, 1980; "Scherzophren", in *Ars electronica*, 1988.

On Logothetis: H. Hoachim, "Die Partitur von morgen", in *Die Welt*, 26 October 1963; Karlheinz Roschitz, *Al und die Musikalische Graphik*, Vienna, 1969; Sigrid Wiesmann, "Prophets in Their Own Country", in *Austria Today*, 4, 1975; Alexander Puhringer, "Sprache und Musik in AL", in *Neuma*, 1, 1984; Hartmut Krones, "Wurdigungspreis 1989 für Musik an AL", in *Osterreichische Musikzeitschrift*, 6, 1990.

Anestis Logothetis comments:

Working on *Polynom* for orchestra which I conceived as a diagram and tried to transcribe into standard stave notation, I realised that the traditional system with the punctuated infrastructure of its pure-tone notation interfered with visualization of sound quality, and consequently alienated it and was incapable of expressing it.

This fact revealed to me the double function of any notation. It conveys not only the contents of a composition, but also imposes its own mechanism on the compositional process. A notation is simultaneously innovative in its explorations of all the latent possibilities of sound, and restorative in its conventional use of the already established. Therefore, a body of notation is guiding consciousness and imposing a sound-aesthetic at the same time.

I tried to prove my observations of the reciprocal relationship between musical thinking and scores by investigating musical history, namely the replacement of Byzantine *neumes* (with their implicit recognition of sliding tones) by Guido DiArezzo's five-line system; I also observed the same relationship in my own work.

Out of these investigations I developed around 1958 a desire to develop a notation consisting of symbols which are informative about the inter-relationship and affinity of sounds, and which encourage ways of reading and interpreting, as well as the innovative handling of instruments, but which moves away from the conventional well-tempered tuning which the five-lines stave support and without which it would collapse. The creation of new instruments which apply the principles of non-temperament is thus encouraged.

I realised that graphic elements can be expressed in three ways for the purpose of musical interpretation. They can symbolize a situation by representing it, they can trigger an associative relation, and finally they can signal commands.

From these three types of reaction to graphic elements I developed a flexible but nevertheless binding script of sound characters which can be combined to form new images depending on compositional intentions, and which reveal the control of the sound-flow and structures in return. The notation on a single sheet of paper guarantees an overview of the larger form. Details are created spontaneously moment by moment and counterpoint themselves in a multiplicity of ways. They are dependent on the process of transfer from their graphically fixed state to that of fluid sound. In this way, my scores not only make sound-happenings visible, they also enable modifying interventions.

The concept of "polymorphy", as a formal principle of my works, or rather as a creative derivative of their realisation, was first applied to my work in 1960.

* * *

While the graphic scores of Anestis Logothetis owe a debt to the work of Morton Feldman, John Cage and others in the 1950s, they represent an unique middleground approach to graphic notation and the balance of indeterminacy and predictability. In addition, Logothetis's graphic scores possess a classic proportion of visual balance and contrast absent from many such works of other composers, giving them an aesthetic integrity beyond their role as musical scores.

Many of Logothetis's works of the 1950s, such as *Integration* for violin, cello and piano and *Peritonen* for horn and piano, show at least some degree of influence of the composer's teacher Alfred Uhl, and are generally written for specified instrumentations. As the decade of the 1960s approached, however, Logothetis turned increasingly to graphic notation and open instrumentation and developed a clear, three-fold system of symbology, which reached maturity in such works as *Sieben Kooptation*. The composer has used three types of functional icons since the early 1960s: (1) action symbols, which indicate lines of motion and constellations of points which are to be simulated by the performer; (2) associative symbols, which indicate specific types of intensity and timbral changes; and (3) note symbols, which indicate specific pitch-classes. The best introduction to the range of possibilities presented by Logothetis's system of notation is his *Grafische Notationen* which is a collection of pieces composed between 1960 and 1967.

The mixture of indeterminacy and specificity inherent in Logothetis's approach represents a middleground among proponents of graphic notation. The composer's works are consistently more determinate than works such as Cage's *Fontana Mix* (1959) or Sylvano Bussotti's *Five Piano Pieces for David Tudor* (1959). Logothetis does not, however, go as far as composers such as Robert Moran in the latter's *Four Visions* (1963), in which possible realizations of the graphic materials are presented. Logothetis typically allows for performer choice of instrumentation (sound sources) and the mapping of event orders and direction, but insists that the performer attempts strictly to interpret the symbols in an appropriate manner, not merely using the score as a vehicle for improvisation.

Logothetis's scores generally have a classic visual form or motion which gives them a life beyond that of the concert hall. In particular, a classic golden section focal point can be found in works such as *Cycloide*, *Parallaxe*, *Kleine Parallaxe* and *Labyrinthos*, while other works, such as *Expansion-Kontraktion*, *Verkettungen* and *Reflexe I* exhibit a strong visual pull on the diagonal (considered a strong motion not only in the visual arts, but also in theatrical and dance staging). Contrast in line, shape and texture from piece to piece provide a visual (and aural) range of diversity to Logothetis's scores missing from those of some of his contemporaries. That some of the composer's scores were successfully exhibited in Viennese galleries also attests to their validity as purely visual works of art.

Given the indeterminacy of several aspects of the body of work produced by Logothetis since 1960, it is virtually impossible to describe the sound of one of the composer's works. Each performance of *Labyrinthos*, for example, will sound different in many respects. The individual gestures will (or should if the composer's admonishment to avoid improvisation is followed) sound similar, but their temporal placement, exact duration and instrumentation are all subject to change. This type of music, then, is a rich source for aesthetic debate—this is especially true in the case of Logothetis's composition, with its high level of visual artistry.

—James E. Perone

LOPES-GRAÇA, Fernando. Portuguese. Born in Tomar, 17 December 1906. Educated at High School, Lisbon, 1919–26; Lisbon Conservatory of Music (piano, composition and theory), 1923–31; University of Lisbon, and University of Coímbra, 1928–34; Sorbonne, Paris (musicology), 1938–9. Teacher of piano, Lisbon Conservatory, 1931 (not authorized by government); teacher of music, Coímbra Institute, 1932–6; teacher of composition, Academia de Amadores de Música, Lisbon, 1941–54, 1973–87; conductor, AAM Chorus, 1950–90; artistic director, Academia de Amadores de Música, 1973–90. Recipient: prizes of the Círculo de Cultura Musical, 1940, 1942, 1944, 1952; Prince Rainier III of Monaco Prize, 1965; APY GA HAPOAOB (Soviet Union), 1976; Grande Officiel da Orden Militar de Santiago de Espada, Portugal, 1980; Ordem do Infante D. Henrique, Portugal, 1986; Doctor honoris causa, University of Aveiro, 1986. Mailing address: Mi Paraiso 2, Avenida da República, 2775 Parede, Portugal.

Publishers: Schott, Germany; Suvini Zerboni, Milan; Novello, London; Carvalho, Portugal.

Symphonies/orchestral:

Poemeto (strings) 1928.
Preludio, pastoral e dança 1929.
Piano Concerto No 1 1940; first performed Lisbon, 1941.
Três danças portuguesas 1941; first performed Marseille, 1941. Recorded Decca SLPDB 1018.
Piano Concerto No 2 1942, revised 1954; first performed Lisbon, 1953. Recorded Columbia PMX 5008.
Sinfonia 1944; first performed Oporto, 1953.
Cinco estrelas funerarias 1948; first performed Oporto, 1948. Recorded Decca SLPDB 1018.
Scherzo heroico 1949.
Suite rústica No 1 1950–1.
Marcha festiva 1954.
Cinco velhos romances portugueses (chamber orchestra) 1954–5.
Concertino (piano, brass, strings, percussion) 1956; first performed Lisbon, 1962. Recorded Melodia 364.
Divertimento (wind, timpani, celli, double basses) 1957.
Gabriela, cravo e canela (overture) 1960–3.
Canto de amor e de morte 1961; first performed Lisbon, 1964. Recorded A Voz de Dono 8E 063/40345.
Poema de dezembro 1961; first performed Oporto, 1962. Recorded Decca SLPDB 1018.
Para una criança que vai nascer (strings) 1961.
Concertino (viola, orchestra) 1962; first performed Lisbon, 1963. Recorded Melodia 36.4.
Concerto de câmera (cello, orchestra) 1965; first performed Moscow, 6 October 1967.
Quatro bosquejos (strings) 1965; first performed Lisbon, 1966. Recorded A Voz de Dono 8E 063/40345.
Viagens na minha terra (2 suites) 1969–70; first performed Lisbon, 1970. Recorded Ad Nova 6015/0.
Fantasia (piano, orchestra) 1974.
Sinfonietta (Homenagem a Haydn) 1980; first performed Lisbon, 1981. Recorded Portugal Som 860017/PS.
In Praise of Peace 1986; first performed Cracow, 1986.

Chamber/instrumental:

Variaçoês sobre um tema popular português (piano) 1927.
Prelúdio, cançáo e dança (piano) 1927.
Três epitáfios (piano) 1930.
Sonatina No 1 (violin, piano) 1931, revised 1951.
Sonatina No 2 (violin, piano) 1931.
Sonata No 1 (piano) 1934.
Nove danças breves (piano) 1938–48.
Sonata No 2 (piano) 1939, revised 1956.
Seis bagatelas (piano) 1939–48.
Piano Quartet 1939, revised 1963.
Prelúdio, capricho e galope (violin, piano) 1941, revised 1951.
Onze glosas (piano) 1949–50.
Pranto à memória de Manuela Porto (piano) 1950.
Sonata No 3 (piano) 1952.
Twenty-Four Preludes (piano) 1952–8.
Viagens na minha terra (piano) 1953.
Elegia a memória de Herculano de Carvalho (piano) 1953.
Três velhos fandangos portugueses (piano) 1953.
Três canções populares portuguesas (cello, piano) 1953.
Página esquecida (cello, piano) 1953.
Epitalamio (piano) 1953.
Album do jovem pianista (piano) 1953–63.
Natais portugueses (piano) 1954.
Dos embalos (piano) 1955.
Melodias rústicas portuguesas (piano) 1957.
Três peças (violin, piano) 1959.
Prelúdio e dança burlesca (2 pianos) 1959.
In memoriam Béla Bartók (8 suites for piano) 1959–64.
Pequeña triptico (violin, piano) 1960.
Dos sonatinas recuperadas (piano) 1960.
Sonata No 4 (piano) 1961.
Prelúdio e fuga (violin) 1961.
Canto de amor e de morte (piano quintet) 1961.
Para uma criança que vai nascer (ensemble) 1961.
Quatro improvisos (piano) 1961.
Quatro invenções (cello) 1961.
Músicas festivas (piano) 1962–72.
Cosmorama (piano) 1963.

String Quartet No 1 1964; first performed Madrid, 1972.
Adagio alla danza (cello, piano) 1965.
Suite rústica No 2 (string quartet) 1965; first performed Oporto, 1966. Recorded Imavox IM 40005.
Catorze Anotações (string quartet) 1966; first performed Equaria, Portugal, 1967. Recorded Imavox IM 40005.
Natais portugueses (piano) 1966.
Sete lembranças (wind quintet) 1966.
Prelúdio e Baileto (guitar) 1968.
Paris, 1937 (2 pianos) 1968.
O túmulo de Villa Lobos (wind quintet) 1970.
Partita (guitar) 1970–1.
Four Pieces (harpsichord) 1971.
Sonata No 5 (piano) 1977.
Sete apotegemas (oboe, viola, double bass, piano) 1981.
Sonata No 6 (piano) 1981.
String Quartet No 2 1982.
Tre equali (double bass) 1986.

Vocal/choral:

Primeira anteriana (voice, piano; Quental) 1928.
Três poemas em prosa (voice, piano; Tagore) 1929.
Três poemas (voice, piano; Monteira) 1931.
Duas canções (voice, piano; Pessoa) 1934.
Três canções ao gosto popular (voice, piano; Botto) 1934.
Seis canções sobre quadras populares portuguesas (voice, piano) 1934.
Ícaro (voice, piano; Regio) 1935.
Marcha quase funebre (voice, piano; Queiroz) 1935.
Pastoral (voice, piano; Duarte) 1935.
As três canções de Olívia (voice, piano) 1935.
O menino da sua mare (voice, piano; Pessoa) 1936, orchestrated 1959.
Pequeño cancioneiro do menino Jesus (female voices, 2 flutes, string quartet, celeste, harp; traditional) 1936–59.
Três sonetas de Camões (voice, piano) 1939.
Vinte e quatro canções populares portuguesas I (voice, piano) 1939–42.
Três sonetilhas (voice, piano; Fereira) 1942.
Vinte e quatro canções populares portuguesas II (voice, piano) 1942–6.
História trágico-marítima (baritone, orchestra; baritone, alto, female chorus, orchestra) 1943–60; first performed Lisbon, 1960. Recorded Diapasao 25001.
Cantos tradicionais portugueses da Natividade (Cantata do Noel I) (mixed choir) 1945–50.
Três cantos da terra (mixed choir; Carvalho, Monte, Silva Santos) 1946.
Cantares (voice, piano; Oliveira) 1946.
Três canções corais (mixed choir; Ferreira, Cochofel, Oliveira) 1946.
Trovas (voice, piano) 1947.
Six Vieilles Chansons françaises (voice, piano) 1948.
Nove canções populares portuguesas (voice, orchestra) 1948–9.
Seis velhos romances portugueses (mezzo-soprano, 12 instruments) 1949, revised as *Sete fragmentos de . . .* (voice, chamber orchestra) 1965.
Six Old English Songs (voice, piano) 1949.
Sept vieilles chansons grecques (voice, piano) 1950.
Três canções (voice, piano; Pessoa) 1950, orchestrated 1960.
Canção do embalo (voice, piano; Sousa) 1950.
Duas canções do Finis patriae (voice, piano; Junqueiro) 1950–1.
Duas canções (voice, piano; Pascoal) 1950–1.
Dix Chansons populaires tcheques et slovaques (voice, piano) 1950–1.
Cinq Chansons populaires russes (voice, piano) 1950–1.
Nove encomendações das almas (mixed choir) 1950–3.
Quatro redondilhas de Camões (mixed choir) 1950–3.
Cinco canções de Os dias íntimos (voice, piano; Cochofel) 1950–66.
Para as raparaigas de coimbra (mixed choir; Nobre) 1951.
Dos sonetos (voice, piano; Nobre) 1951.
Inscrição para o túmulo de uma donzela (voice, piano; Castro) 1951.
Duas trovas tristes e duas alegres (mixed choir; traditional) 1951.
Dez sonetos (mixed choir; Barros) 1951.
Vinte e quatro canções populares portuguesas IV (voice, piano) 1951–9.
Balada de uma heroina (mixed choir; Ferreira) 1953.
Seven Negro-American Folksongs (voice, piano) 1953.
Primavera (voice, piano; Duarte) 1953.
Terra e céu (voice, piano; Oliveira) 1953.
Cuatro canciones de Federico García Lorca (baritone, chamber instrumental ensemble) 1954.
Três líricas espirituais (4 solo voices; Vicente) 1953–63.
Dez canções populares brasileiras (voice, piano) 1954.
Dos canções castelhano portuguesa de Rio de Oro (voice, piano) 1954.
Canções regionais portuguesas I (mixed choir) 1954.
Balada da Coimbra (voice, piano; Regio) 1955.
Três líricas castelhanas de Camões (mixed choir) 1955.
Canções regionais portuguesas II (mixed choir) 1955.
Dos romancas viejos (mixed choir) 1956.
Psalm 120 (mixed choir) 1956.
Em louvor do sol (mixed choir; Duarte) 1956.
Três esconjuros (choir; traditonal) 1956.
Desafio (voice, piano; Baudeira) 1957.
Barca bela (voice, piano; Garrett) 1957.
Canções regionais portuguesas III (choir) 1957.
Nana, nana (choir; Andrade) 1957.
O rouxinal do Calvário (choir) 1957.
Dois cantos religiosas tradicionales de Galicia (choir) 1958.
Canções regionais portuguesas IV (choir) 1958.
Cantos de Natal (female voices, chamber orchestra) 1958.
Rondes et complaintes des provinces de France (choir) 1958–9.
As cançoezinhas de Tila (voice, piano; Araujo) 1958–9.
Canções regionais portuguesas V (choir) 1959.
Cantiga (voice, piano; Duarte) 1959.
As maõs e os frutos (voice, piano; Andrade) 1959.
Dois canções (voice, piano; Vasconcelos) 1959.
Dois romances (voice, piano; Rodrigues) 1959.
Aquela triste e leda madrugada (voice, piano; Camões) 1959.
Divindade da terra (voice, piano; Duarte) 1959.
Duas cantigas de embalar (voice, piano; Bolto) 1959.
Sol algueres la fora (choir; Cochofel) 1960.
Cuatro liricas castelhanos (voice, piano) 1960.
Canção VI (voice, piano; Camões) 1960.
La vem o touro vermelho (voice, piano; Araujo) 1960.
Tomanos a vila depois de um bombardamento (voice, piano; Pessoa) 1960.
O sol é grande (voice, piano) 1960.
Seguias tu pela estrada (voice, piano; Lacerda) 1960.
Nove cantigas de amigo (voice, piano) 1960, orchestrated 1964.
Nove cantigas de terreiro (voice, piano; Nemesio) 1960.
Cantata de Noel No 2 (choir) 1960–1.
Canções tradicionais brasileiras (choir) 1960–1.
Trovas de Coimbra (choir; Sousa) 1961.
Para o túmulo de Manuel de Falla (choir) 1961.
Duas canções (voice, piano; Nascimento) 1961.
Guirlanda para Federico García Lorca (voice, piano) 1961.

Três sonetos a noite (4 solo voices; Bocage) 1961–6.
Mar de Septembro (voice, piano) 1962.
Fragmento da uma carta (voice, piano; Camões) 1962.
Canções regionais portuguesas VI (choir) 1963.
Aquela por quem padeço (voice, piano; Durco) 1963.
Immortalis dede (voice, piano; Regio) 1963.
Quatre Sonnets (voice, piano; Ronsard) 1964.
Canções regionais portuguesas VII (choir) 1965.
Canções regionais portuguesas VIII (choir) 1966.
D. Duardos e Flerida (cantata-melodrama in 2 parts for narrator, mezzo-soprano, alto, tenor, chorus, orchestra) 1966–9.
Quatro poemas (voice, piano; Passache) 1967.
Diptico das viagens apogadas (voice, piano; Nobre) 1967.
Lírico de F.P. (soprano, alto, tenor) 1968.
Quatro cantos de Sophia (voice, piano; Andrade) 1968–9.
Segunda anteriana (voice, piano; Quental) 1968–9.
Cantos sefardis (voice, piano) 1969, nos 2, 3, 6, 10, 11, 12 orchestrated as *Seis cantos sefardis* 1971.
Avisamente (choir; Camões) 1972.
Canções regionais portuguesas IX (choir) 1972.
Canções regionais portuguesas X (choir) 1973.
Réquiem pelas vitimas do fascismo em Portugal (soloists, chorus, orchestra) 1978; first performed Lisbon, 1981. Recorded Portugal Som 86004/PS.
Sete predicações d'Os Lusiades (tenor, bass, male chorus, 12 wind instruments; Camões) 1980; first performed Estoril, 1980.
Dez novos sonetos de Camões (voice, piano) 1984.
Cantos de mágoa e desalento (voice, piano) 1987.
Nove ordes de Ricardo Reis (voice, piano) 1987.
Quatro momentos de Alvaro de Campo (voice, piano) 1987.
Dez novos sonetos de Camões (tenor, piano) 1987; first performed Macao, 1987.
Canciones de tierras altas (tenor, piano; Machado) 1989; first performed Turin, 1990.

Opera:

Don Duardos e Flerida (narrator, mezzo-soprano, alto, tenor, chorus, orchestra; Vicente) 1964–9; first performed Lisbon, 1970.

Other:

La Fièvre du temps (ballet) 1938; first performed Paris, 1938.
Dancares (ballet) 1984.

PUBLICATIONS

By Lopes-Graça: *Breve enscaio a evolucáo das formas musicais*, Lisbon, 1940, 1959, 1984; *Reflexoes sobre a música*, Lisbon, 1941, 1978; *Introdução à música moderna*, Lisbon, 1943, 1946; *Música e músicos modernos*, Oporto, 1943; *A música portuguesa e os seus problemas*, I, Oporto, 1944, II, Coimbra, 1959, III, Lisbon, 1974; *Dicionário de música*, vol. 1, 1944, vol. 2, 1959; *Talia, euterpe e terpsichore*, Lisbon, 1945; *Pequeña historia de música de piano*, Lisbon, 1945; *Viana da mota*, Lisbon, 1949; *Canção populare portuguesa*, Lisbon, 1953; *Igor Stravinsky and Béla Bartók*, 1959; *Musicalia*, Lisbon, 1960; *Lieder de Welt: Portugal*, Hamburg, 1961; *Nossa companheira música*, Lisbon, 1964; *Páginas escolhidas de crítica e estética musical*, Lisbon, 1966; *Disto e daquilo*, Lisbon, 1973; *Um artista intervem / Cartas com alguma moral*, Lisbon, 1974; *Escrito musicológicos*, Lisbon, 1977; many others, including translations of Rousseau, Mann, Percy Buck, Alan Bush, Romain Rolland, Balzac.

On Lopes-Graça: *FL-G 75o aniversário*, Coimbra, 1981; J.M. Bettencourt de Câmara, *Comemoração do 80o aniversário de FL-G*, Lisbon, 1986; Mário Vieria de Carvalho, *O essencial sobre FL-G*, Lisbon, 1989.

* * *

Fernando Lopes-Graça's music is suffused with Portuguese national character on three distinct levels. There is his deep knowledge of peasant and folk music, from which he has abstracted and combined elements with his own individual musical language; there is his deep familiarity with and research into the whole development of Portuguese culture, its myths and history, language and literature (and Lopes-Graça has made settings of nearly all the major Portuguese poets); there is, finally, a critique of a certain view of "folk music" which took root and spread during Salazar's dictatorship as an arm of nationalist propaganda.

Lopes-Graça's works based on folk materials are not conventional arrangements, aiming no higher than local colour or the picturesque; they rather regard folkloristic material in a reflective and sometimes subversive way, creating on occasion a kind of "alienation effect", which reflects not only the folkloristic material, but also its historical, sociological and cultural background.

Criticism is for Lopes-Graça a valid underpinning of communication. This is the upshot of his conviction that music is "a product of an equation between the artist and his milieu". Since the early 1940s, he has tried to develop alternative communicative structures, in opposition to the established music forms he has criticised in frequent press articles and essays. By founding the "Sonata" concert company, he was able to combine his own (mainly vocal and chamber) work with a commitment to other contemporary composers; this was done in the interests more of a cultural engagement with the democratic resistance movement, than of an engagement with a "pure" musical avant-garde. Thanks to this choir of amateur singers, which he has now directed for over 40 years, he reaches a broad spectrum of society (labour, farmers, students, folk-associations) with a repertoire which consists very largely of his own brilliant, courageous folk-song arrangements. Before the restoration of democracy with the April Revolution of 1974, he had created numerous revolutionary and labour songs, intended for circulation as a "music of social intercourse" in democratic demonstrations and assemblies (and among political prisoners).

In general, vocal music takes up a far larger share of his total output than any other genre. Until the 1960s, orchestras were only very seldom permitted to perform his work. This meant that for much of his development, Lopes-Graça was only able to write for the forces he had at hand. This was not merely a matter of survival, however, but prompted by a strong will to affect directly his milieu. His activity as a choral director brought few rewards, either material or of status, and he was forced to make a living translating great works of literature.

His own greatest works were only created after the cultural-political developments of the period 1968–74 which allowed their commission and performance. The consequence of building an oeuvre for "alternative" structures of communication is that the aesthetic demands of modernity in his work are never in conflict with his socio-political activity. Simplification, in the interests of easier consumption, or a need to be liked and appreciated, are not valid conceptions for him. His music represents a challenge and a call to thought.

Lopes-Graça's modernity is based on a compositional technique which developed from his acquaintance with important 20th-century stylistic developments: Debussy's extension of—rather than break with—the principles of harmony; Ravel's subtle sound-coloration, pianism and humour; Falla as a proof of Iberian consanguinity; Bartók (especially admired) as a precursor in integrating ethnic elements; Stravinsky as rhythmic, harmonic and coloristic technician; Schoenberg and Alban Berg as the starting point of a "dramatic expressionism" that leads to the atonality noticeable in Lopes-Graça's work after 1961. From these, and from his native resource, Lopes-Graça has constructed a creative synthesis, a highly individual musical language, which both reveals and builds on his inner conflicts and those of his nation.

—Mário Vieria de Carvalho

LORENTZEN, Bent. Danish. Born in Stenvad, 11 February 1935. Educated at University of Aarhus (under Knud Jeppesen); Royal Danish Academy of Music, Copenhagen (under Vagn Holmboe, Jørgen Jersild and Finn Høffding), diploma in music theory, 1960. Married Edith Kaerulff Moeller, 2 August 1958; 1 son and 3 daughters. Assistant professor, Royal Academy of Music, Aarhus, 1962–71; work in electronic music, Stockholm EMS, 1967–8; independent composer, since 1971; "Composer of the Year" for Danish choirs, 1990. Recipient: Prix Italia (for *Euridice*), 1970; Danish state grant for life, since 1982; 1st prize, Serocki Competition, Poland (for *Paradiesvogel*), 1984; 1st prize, Spittal, Austria (for *Olof Palme*), 1987; 2nd prize, Messiaen competition, Bergamo (for *Luna*), 1988; 2nd prize, Competition Leuven, Belgium (for *Prozession*), 1989. Mailing address: Soefoften 37, DK-2820 Gentofte, Denmark.

Publishers: Wilhelm Hansen, Copenhagen; Engstrom & Sodring; Copenhagen; Samfundet, Copenhagen.

Symphonies/orchestral:

Deep 1967, revised 1981; first performed Aarhus, 1983.
Tide 1971; first performed Copenhagen, 1971.
Partita Popolare (string orchestra) 1976; first performed Radio Denmark, 1979.
Oboe Concerto 1980; first performed Radio Denmark, 1982.
Cello Concerto 1984; first performed Radio Denmark, 1984.
Piano Concerto 1984; first performed Odense, 1984.
Latin Suite No 1 1984; first performed Gillelje, 1984.
Saxophone Concerto (orchestra without strings) 1987; first performed Radio Denmark, 1987.
Latin Suite No 2 (symphonic band) 1988; first performed Odense, 1988.
Venezia (symphonic band) 1989; first performed Aarhus, 1989.
Latin Suite No 3 (symphonic band) 1990.

Chamber/instrumental:

Cyclus I (violin, cello, double bass) 1966; first performed Copenhagen, 1967.
Cyclus II (2 percussion, harp) 1966; first performed Copenhagen, 1967.
Cyclus III (cello, tape) 1966, 1981; first performed Copenhagen, 1967. Recorded SUDM 026 MC.
Quadrata (string quartet) 1963; first performed Aarhus, 1969.
Intersection (organ) 1970; first performed Aarhus, 1971. Recorded DCCD 9009.
Syncretism (clarinet, cello, trombone, piano; with conductor) 1970; first performed Aarhus, 1970.
Five Easy Pieces (piano) 1971; first performed Aarhus, 1971.
Quartetto barbaro (string quartet) 1971.
Quartz (violin) 1971; first performed Aarhus, 1976.
Granite (cello) 1971; first performed Aarhus, 1976. Recorded SUDM 006.
Quartetto rustico (string quartet) 1972.
Puncti (organ) 1973; first performed Neppel, The Netherlands, 1973. Recorded DCCD 9009.
Triplex (organ) 1974; first performed Norden, Germany, 1974. Recorded DCCD 9009.
Groppo (organ) 1975; first performed Soroe, 1975. Recorded DCCD 9009.
Nimbus (organ) 1977; first performed Soroe, 1978. Recorded DCCD 9009.
Cruor (organ) 1977; first performed Aarhus, 1978. Recorded DCCD 9009.
Contorni (violin, cello, piano) 1978; first performed Copenhagen, 1980. Recorded Pauk PACD 57.
Colori (piano) 1978; first performed Copenhagen, 1978. Recorded DMAMC 050.
Samba (clarinet, cello, trombone, piano; with conductor) 1980; first performed Warsaw, 1980. (Recorded SUDM 007.
Round (alto saxophone) 1981; first performed Salzburg, 1981. Recorded SUDM 026 MC.
Mambo (clarinet, cello, piano) 1982; first performed Odense, 1982.
Sol (organ) 1982; first performed Soroe, 1982.
Wunderblumen (flute, oboe, clarinet, bassoon, horn, percussion, piano, string quartet, double bass; with conductor) 1982; first performed Aarhus, 1985. Recorded Point PLP 5061.
Warszawa (bass clarinet/alto saxophone, piano) 1983; first performed Aarhus, 1983.
Paesaggio (flute, oboe, clarinet, horn, bassoon, violin, viola; with conductor) 1983; first performed Radio Denmark, 1983. Recorded SUDM 026 MC.
Paradiesvogel (flute, clarinet, violin, cello, percussion, piano; with conductor) 1983; first performed Warsaw, 1984. Recorded Point PLP 5061.
Diamond (clarinet) 1983; first performed Aarhus, 1984.
Luna (organ) 1984; first performed Soroe, 1984.
Mars (organ) 1985; first performed Assens, 1985. Recorded SUDM 026 MC.
Dunkelblau (alto flute, viola, harp) 1985; first performed Copenhagen, 1985. Recorded SUDM 026 MC.
Goldranken (piano) 1987; first performed Aalborg, 1987.
Nachtigall (piano, live electronics) 1988; first performed Aarhus, 1988.
Intrada (brass quintet) 1990; first performed Aarhus, 1990.
Alpha and Omega (basset horn, organ) 1990; first performed Copenhagen, 1990.
Farbentiegel (alto saxophone, piano) 1990.
Three Carillons (carillon) 1990; first performed Ebeltoft, 1990.

Vocal/choral:

New Choral Dramatics (unaccompanied choir) 1968, 1982; version printed, 1971.

Choral Songs to Mao Zedong (equal voices, mixed chorus) 1970–2; broadcast Radio Denmark, 1970–2. Recorded RSK 12, 14 20.
My Bride Is Like a Garden (soprano, 2 flutes, 4 horns, 2 keyboards, 3 percussion) 1972.
Purgatorio (mixed chorus; Enzensberger) 1975; broadcast Norddeutsche Rundfunk, 1978.
Carnaval (soprano/3 voices, tape) 1976; broadcast Westdeutsche Rundfunk, 1979.
Three Madrigals (mixed chorus) 1977; first performed Aarhus, 1980.
Ammen Dammen Des (equal voices) 1981; first performed Copenhagen, 1982.
Five Motets to Isajah (mixed chorus) 1982–3; first performed Copenhagen, 1983–5.
Graffiti (mixed chorus) 1984; first performed Copenhagen, 1984.
Genesis (mixed chorus, orchestra) 1984; first performed Aarhus, 1985.
Auschwitz (unaccompanied choir) 1986; first performed Copenhagen, 14 April 1989.
Olof Palme (unaccompanied choir) 1987; first performed Spittal, Austria, 1987.
Comics (unaccompanied choir) 1988; first performed Aarhus, 1988.
De kaekke nonner / The Cheerful Nuns (mixed chorus) 1988; first performed Copenhagen, 16 April 1989.
Septimus Angelus 1988; first performed Aarhus, 5 March 1989.
Ich bin eine Rose 1988; broadcast Radio Denmark, 20 February 1989.
Tordenskiold (unaccompanied choir) 1990; first performed Ebeltoft, 1990.
Prozession (unaccompanied choir) 1990; first performed Leuven, Belgium, 1990.
Middle Class Blues (unaccompanied choir) 1990; first performed Copenhagen, 1990.
Mund (unaccompanied choir) 1990; first performed Copenhagen, 1990.
Alskens Dansk (unaccompanied choir) 1990; first performed Aalborg, 1990.

Opera:

Statten Mette 1963, 1980; first performed Danish television, 1981.
The Snake / Die Schlange 1964, 1974; first performed Braunschweig, Germany, 1975.
Euridice 1965; broadcast Radio Denmark, 1969.
Die Musik kommt mir ausserst bekannt vor / Do You Know the Tune They're Playing 1974; first performed Kiel, 1974.
Eine wundersame Liebegeschichte (Leinert, BL) 1979; first performed Munich, 1979.
Toto, the Clown 1985; first performed Copenhagen, 1985.
Fackeltanz 1990.

Other:

Studies for Two (instrumental theatre: cello/guitar, percussion) 1967; first performed Aarhus, 1967.
The End!? (instrumental theatre; cello) 1969; first performed Aarhus, 1969.
Friisholm (for 16mm film; cello) 1971; first performed Copenhagen, 1971.
The Bottomless Pit (electronic music) 1972; first performed Oslo, 1972. Recorded Point PLP 5072.
Nubes / Cloud Drift (electronic music) 1973; first performed Aarhus, 1973. Recorded Point PLP 5072.
Visions (electronic music) 1978; broadcast Radio Denmark, 1979. Recorded Point PLP 5072.
Three Mobiles (instrumental theatre; flute, cello, piano) 1990; first performed Odense, 1990.
Seven Children's Songs. Recorded 45 WH 1713; RS MC 5021; FACK 7601.

PUBLICATIONS

By Lorentzen: "Musikens Material och Form 3", 1968, "Musikens AHC", 1969, and Mer og Musiken", 1972, all Swedish Radio; "The Listener in the Centre", in *Danish Music Magazine*, 6, 1968; "Creative Music Theory", Edition Egtved, 1973; "Electronic Music Means Switched-On Creativity", in *Music Educators Journal*, 6, 1981–2; "Paradise Lost", in *Danish Music Magazine*, 4, 1981–2.

On Lorentzen: Frank Pooler, "In Quest of Answers", in *The Choral Journal*, October 1973; Carl Bergstrom-Nielsen, "Portrait of the Composer", in *Danish Music Magazine*, 1976; Michael Bonnesen, "Stalten Metre", in *Danish Music Magazine*, 6, 1981–2; Jens Bruno Hansen, "I anledning af Lorentzen Organ Music I", in *Organistbladet*, May 1988; K.A. Rasmussen, *Noteworthy Danish Composers*, Copenhagen, 1990.

* * *

Bent Lorentzen has composed music since earliest childhood. At the University of Aarhus, he studied with the great counterpoint specialist Knud Jeppesen, later transferring to the Royal Danish Academy of Music in the capital, where he worked with Holmboe, Høffding and Jersild. After completing his degree in 1960, he undertook supplementary training in music pedagogy and became a state accredited teacher of music theory and history. Afterwards, he accepted a position at the Royal Danish Academy in Aarhus, and taught theory and instrumentation there until 1971, since when he has been a full-time composer. In the late 1960s, he worked at the newly formed electronic music studio in Stockholm, where he produced a record mainly for students of and about electronic music.

The basis of Lorentzen's production is what he himself terms "sonic thinking", or composition based on sound colour itself, the components of which are ordered and categorized in universal patterns. He found the foundation of this in orthodox serial technique as he experienced it through the Second Viennese School (and most particularly in the work of Alban Berg), and this accounts for his ties to expressionism and the Central European avant-garde represented by Stockhausen.

At the same time, he was strongly inspired by contemporary Polish music (first and foremost Witold Lutosławski) and his music has been particularly well-received in both Germany and Poland, where his instrumental *Paradiesvogel* was awarded first prize in an international competition honouring Kazimiers Serocki.

Lorentzen's work spans a wind range of genres: works for large orchestra, pieces for mixed ensemble, a noteworthy series of solo instrumental works, a string of organ works, vocal and choral music, operas, instrumental theatre and, of course, electronic music; since 1980, he has written effective solo concertos for oboe, cello, piano and saxophone.

Throughout Lorentzen's work one finds realistic material extended beyond itself into a kind of super-realism kept in restraint by a strict, almost ecstatic intellectual procedure, and the resulting expression can be highly provocative. His works are always rich in associations. For example, *Tide* from 1971 refers not only to tidal waters but also implies "something incessantly expanding". The title *Quartz* is not merely pictorial; the piece is based on careful observation of the mineral's atomic structure.

The operas are a story in themselves, each imbued with the composer's enthusiastic involvement in the given subject, through which he views contemporary structures and phenomena. He utilizes powerfully expressive formulations, frequently with the inclusion of extra-musical—often very grotesque—effects. Here, as elsewhere in his work, one finds quotations from old masters used as music-dramatic effects, an ironic and affectionate greeting to and from the present and past.

In 1977, Lorentzen visited Brazil, and was greatly inspired by the attitude towards music which he encountered. Works like *Samba*, *Mambo*, and the Latin Suites ensued. Such surprising approaches, and the sharply profiled creations that result, invite the suggestion—only half joking—that Lorentzen is the unicorn of contemporary Danish music.

—Helmer Norgaard

LOUDOVÁ, Ivana. Czech. Born in Chlumec nad Cidlinou, 8 March 1941. Educated at grammar school (leaving examination, 1958); studied piano with her mother, Bozena Loudová; Prague Conservatory (composition under Professor Miroslav Kabeláč), 1958–61; Prague Academy of Arts and Music (first woman student of composition, under Professor Emil Hlobil), 1961–6; summer courses at Darmstadt, 1967–9; postgraduate study under kabeláč, 1968–72; French government scholarship (studying with Olivier Messiaen and André Jolivet), Experimental Studio, Bourdan, ORTF, 1971. Married Miloš Haase, 16 August 1973; 1 son. Freelance composer, since 1972; composer in residence, American Wind Symphony Orchestra, Pittsburgh, 1980. Recipient: honourable mention (for *Rhapsody in Black*), GEDOK-Mannheim Competition, 1966; first prize (for *Meeting with Love*), Jihlava Vocal Competition, 1966; second prize (for *Merry Counterpoints*), Jirkov vocal composition competition; several other prizes for children's choruses in Jirkov and Olomouc Competitions; second prize (for *Concerto*), Young Czech Composer Competition, 1975; first prize (for *Sonetto*) in Guido d'Arezzo International Competition, 1978; second prize (for *Little Christmas Cantata*), OIRT Competition, Moscow, 1978; first prize (for *Canonical Songs*), Jirkov choral competition, 1978; first prize (for *The Look Back*), Jihlava Vocal Competition, 1981; second prize (for *Songs About Roses*), Olomouc composition competition, 1983); first prize (for *Occhi lucenti e belli*), XIth Guido d'Arezzo international composers' competition, 1984. Mailing address: Aubrechtové 3100, 106 00 Prague 10, Czechoslovakia.

Publishers: Supraphon, Palackeho 1, 112 99 Prague 1, Czechoslovakia; Panton, Ricni 12, 118 00 Prague, Czechoslovakia; CHF, Czech Music Foundation, Parizska 13, 11000 Prague, Czechoslovakia; C.F. Peters, New York; Schirmer, New York; Joshua Corp., New York; Suvini-Zerboni, Milan.

Symphonies/orchestral:

Fantasy 1961; first performed Prague, 12 June 1961.
Concerto (chamber orchestra) 1962; first performed Prague, 24 April 1963.
Symphony No 1 1964; first performed Prague, 1965.
Symphony No 2 (alto solo, choir, large orchestra) 1965; first performed Prague, 1966.
Spleen (homage to Baudelaire for symphonic orchestra) 1971; first performed Prague, 1972. Recorded Panton 11 0490.
Hymnos (wind instruments, percussion, orchestra) 1972.
Chorale 1974; first performed Prague, 1975. Recorded Panton 11 0490.
Concerto (6 percussion, organ, wind orchestra) 1974; first performed Pittsburgh, 1975. Recorded Panton 810438 1 011.
Cadenza (violin, flute, string orchestra) 1975.
Nocturno (viola, string orchestra) 1975; first performed Prague, 1976. Recorded Panton 810678 1011.
Partita in D (flute, harpsichord, string orchestra) 1975; first performed Bern, 1977.
Magic Concerto (xylophone, marimba, vibraphone, wind orchestra) 1976.
Concerto breve (flute or violin, orchestra) 1979; first performed Pardubice, Czechoslovakia, 1979.
Olympic Overture (wind orchestra) 1979.
Dramatic Concerto (solo percussion, wind orchestra) 1979; first performed Pittsburgh, 1980. Recorded Panton 810754 1-031.
Luminous Voice (cor anglais, wind orchestra) 1985; first performed Pittsburgh, 1986.
Double Concerto (violin, percussion, strings) 1989; first performed Prague, 1989.

Chamber/instrumental:

Suite (flute) 1959; first performed Novy Bydžov, Czechoslovakia, 1973.
Sonata for Violin and Piano 1961; first performed Prague, 1961.
Preludes (piano) 1961; first performed Prague, 1961.
Sonata (clarinet, piano) 1963–4.
String Quartet No 1 1964; first performed Prague, 1964.
Sonatine (oboe, piano) 1965.
Ballata Antica (trombone, piano) 1966.
Solo for King David (harp) 1972; first performed Kralupy, 1974.
Air a due boemi (bass clarinet, piano) 1972; first performed Biberach, West Germany, 1972. Recorded Panton 110 369.
Ritornello (2 trumpets, horn, tuba, percussion) 1973.
Agamemnón (percussion solo) 1973; first performed Prague, 1974.
Per Tromba (5 studies for trumpet) 1974; first performed Prague, 1974.
Romeo and Juliet (Renaissance suite for flute, violin, viola, cello, harp or lute) 1974.
String Quartet No 2 (in memory of Bedřich Smetana) 1976; first performed Prague, 1978. Recorded Panton 8111 0030.
Aulos (bass clarinet) 1976.
Soli e tutti (flute, oboe, violin, viola, cello, harps) 1976; first performed Holice, 1976.
Ballata eroica (violin, piano) 1976; first performed Prague, 1977.
Meditations (flute, bass clarinet, piano, percussion) 1977; first performed Prague, 1979.
Mattinata (clarinet, trombone, cello) 1978.

Con umore in F (bassoon) 1978.
Quintetto giubiloso (2 trumpets, horn, trumbone, tuba) 1979; first performed Prague, 1980. Recorded Panton 8111 0227.
Musica festiva (3 trumpets, 3 trombones) 1981; first performed Prague, 1981. Recorded Panton 8111 0282.
Flower for Emanuel (in memory of C.P.E. Bach; jazz quintet) 1981.
Duo concertante (bass clarinet, marimba) 1982; first performed Biberach, West Germany, 1982.
Two Eclogues (in memory of Vergil; flute, harp) 1982; first performed Prague, 1982.
Variations for Cat (violin) 1982.
Four Pieces (clarinet) 1983; first performed Lázně Bělohrad, 1983.
Hukvaldy Suite (in memory of Leos Janaček; string quartet) 1984; first performed Slanec, 1984.
Tango Music (piano) 1984; first performed Oslo, 1985.
Monumento (organ) 1985; first performed Prague, 1986.
Trio in B♭ (violin, cello, piano) 1987; first performed Prague, 1987.
Italian Trio (clarinet, bassoon, piano) 1987; first performed Karlovy Vary, 1988.
Don Giovanni's Dream (wind octet) 1988; first performed Prague, 1989.
Variations on a Stamic Theme (string quartet) 1989; first performed Prague, 1990.

Vocal/choral:

Heavenly Guilt (single voice, piano) 1965.
Meeting with Love (male choirs, flute, piano; Italian Renaissance poetry) 1966; first performed Jihlava, 1966. Recorded Supraphon 20424.
Stabat Mater (unaccompanied male chorus) 1966; first performed Prague, 1968.
Good Night Songs (unaccompanied single voice or children's chorus) 1966.
Riddles (2-part children's choir, piano) 1966.
Mummy (cycle for 3-part unaccompanied children's choir) 1966.
The Little Prince (children's cantata; soprano, alto, reciter, children's choir, ensemble; Saint Exupéry) 1967; first performed Prague, 1967.
Kuroshio (soprano, large mixed choir) 1969; first performed Prague, 1969. Recorded Panton 110358.
Ego Sapientia (unaccompanied male chorus; Book of Proverbs) 1969; first performed Jihlava, 1970.
Gnómai (soprano, flute, harp) 1970.
Ten Minutes' Silence (children's choir, instruments) 1974.
Canonical Songs (children's choir) 1977.
Sonetto per voci bianche (unaccompanied women's and children's choirs) 1978; first performed Arezzo, 1979.
The Look Around (unaccompanied women's chorus) 1981.
Merry Counterpoints (3 unaccompanied children's choirs) 1981.
Amor (unaccompanied mixed choir) 1981.
Trefoil (children's choir, tam-tam, triangle) 1981.
Italian Triptych (unaccompanied mixed choir) 1982; first performed Prague, 1982.
Fortune (cantata for unaccompanied mixed and children's choirs) 1983; first performed Prague, 1983.
Little Evening Music (mixed choir, oboe) 1983.
Songs About Roses (2-part unaccompanied children's choir) 1983.
Occhi lucenti e belli (unaccompanied women's choir) 1984.

Other:

Rhapsody in Black (ballet; orchestra) 1966; first performed Prague, 1967.

Ivana Loudová comments:

In each new work I wish to bring something new: compositional solutions, new forms, expressions or timbres. I also transform traditional elements in my own way, combining them with modal systems, elements of chance, timbral techniques. I don't orientate myself exclusively to any one tendency, but conform above all to the mission and content of each work. Technique has to be understood functionally. Behind most of my compositions are humanistic ideas such as love, fortune, joy, beauty and belief.

* * *

Ivana Loudová's work up to the present suggests a personality in which a powerful rationality plays a significant role in the creative process. This obviously inborn disposition was positively encouraged by her teachers in Prague—Emil Hlobil and, above all, Miroslav Kabeláč—and in Paris, where she worked under Olivier Messiaen and André Jolivet. Educated in traditional as well as contemporary techniques, she uses both according to the dictates of the specific piece on which she is working. Her willingness to modify and transform existing technical means is evident as early as her student years in the *Sonata for Violin and Piano*.

Her technical virtuosity is always accompanied by deep feeling and an intense emotion is another outstanding component of her artistic personality; by means of it, she tries to address her audience, to evoke a resonance. She fulfils this purpose most fully in her vocal compositions, in which she often turns to Italian Renaissance poetry (as in *Meeting with Love* and the *Italian Triptych*); elsewhere, she has turned to newer Czech poetry (*The Look Around*, *Little Evening Music*, *Amor* and others); or she writes her own texts, most notably in her works for children. Loudová quite evidently understands the child's psyche.

Her instrumental compositions form a no less significant part of her output and are often inspired by the soloist for whom she is writing. That is why her compositions are so demandingly stylized. She has written a significant body of work for percussion, often in combinations with winds (for example, *Agamemnón* or the *Magic Concerto*, *Luminous Voice* and the earlier *Hymnos*.

She has been influenced equally by literature and by her surroundings, and in her symphonic writing concentrates on the colour of the orchestral sound. She began work on *Spleen*, her homage to Charles Baudelaire, at the time of her stay in Paris, which coincided with the 150th anniversary of the poet's birth. As if by contrast, her homage to Bedřich Smetana—the Second String Quartet—is written in a distinct and bright line. This single movement composition reflects in an unusual way Smetana's own first quartet "From My Life". Loudová made use of the poet's name as a cipher: B♭ in the first dramatic part and E♭ (in Czech usage, *Es*) in the second, lyrical section.

Loudová has taken part in several composition competitions and has won a number of prestigious prizes. Her work is much performed in Czechoslovakia and is increasingly known abroad.

—Jan Dehner

LUCIER, Alvin (Augustus, Jr). American. Born in Nashua, New Hampshire, 14 May 1931. Educated at Portsmouth Abbey School, graduated 1950; Yale University, New Haven, Connecticut (under Howard Boatwright, Richard Donovan, David Kraehenbuhl and Quincy Porter), B.A., 1954; Brandeis University, Waltham, Massachusetts (composition under Arthur Berger, Irving Fine and Harold Shapero), M.F.A., 1960; Berkshire Music Center, Tanglewood, Massachusetts (composition under Lukas Foss, orchestration under Aaron Copland), summers 1958, 1959; further study, Rome, 1960–2. Married Wendy Wallbank Stokes in 1979; 1 daughter. Assistant professor, Brandeis University, 1962–9; co-founder (with Robert Ashley, Gordon Mumma and David Behrman), Sonic Arts Union, 1966; John Spencer Camp Professor, since 1969, and chair, world music department, since 1979, Wesleyan University, Middletown, Connecticut; musical director, Viola Farber Dance company, 1972–7; guest composer, Aspen Music Festival, Colorado, 1984, 1987; Master Artist, Atlantic Center for the Arts, New Smyrna Beach, Florida, 1985; Branscomb Distinguished Lecturer, Rensselaer Polytechnic Institute, Troy, New York, January 1990; composer in residence, DAAD Kunstler Program, Berlin, 1990–1. Recipient: Samuel Wechsler Prize in Composition, 1959; Jack E. Lund Prize, 1959. Mailing address: 42 Pinewood Terrace, Middletown, Connecticut 06457, U.S.A.

Publishers: Lovely Music, 105 Hudson Street, Room 200, New York, New York 10013, U.S.A.; Berandol; CPE; Criss-Cross Art Communications.

Symphonies/orchestral:

Partita (flute, harpsichord, strings) 1954; first performed New Haven, Connecticut, 1954.
Concerto for Trumpet and Chamber Orchestra 1959; first performed New York City, 1959.
Music for Bassoon and Strings 1959.
Hartford Memory Space 1970; first performed Hartford, Connecticut, 1970.
Crossings (small orchestra, slow sweep/pure wave oscillator) 1980; first performed Chicago, 6 July 1982. Recorded Lovely Music LCD 1018.
Serenade (winds, pulse wave oscillators) 1984; first performed Aspen, Colorado, 1985.

Chamber/instrumental:

Sonata da camera (brass, percussion) 1956.
Festival Music (wind quintet) 1960.
Fragments for Strings (string quartet) 1961.
Action Music (piano) 1962; first performed Rome, 1962.
Composition for Pianist and Mother 1964.
Shapes of the Sounds from the Board (piano) 1979; first performed New York City, 1979.
In Memoriam Jon Higgins (clarinet, oscillator) 1984; first performed Hartford, Connecticut, 1984. Recorded Lovely Music LCD 1018.
Septet (3 winds, 4 strings, oscillator) 1985; first performed Middletown, Connecticut, 1985. Recorded Lovely Music LCD 1018.
Tribute to James Tenney (double bass, 2 oscillators) 1987; first performed New York City, 1989.
Kettles (5 timpani, 2 oscillators) 1987; first performed Philadelphia, 1987.
Fidelio Trio (viola, cello, piano) 1988; first performed Hartford, Connecticut, 1988.
Silver Streetcar for the Orchestra (triangle) 1988; first performed Miami, Florida, 1988.
Music for Piano and Amplified Sonorous Vessels 1990; first performed Berlin, 1991.

Vocal/choral:

Song for Soprano 1963; first performed Waltham, Massachusetts, 1984.
North American Time Capsule (voices, vocoder) 1967. Recorded CBS Odyssey 32 16 0258.
I Am Sitting in a Room (voice on tape) 1970; first performed New York City, Spring 1970. Recorded Lovely Music LCD 1013.
The Duke of York (voices, synthesizers) 1971.
Still and Moving Lines of Silence in Families of Hyperbolas (singers, players, snare drums, dancers) 1973–4, revised for soprano, instruments, oscillators, 1982–4; first performed Paris, 1974. Recorded Lovely Music VR 1014/5.
Lullaby (solo voice) 1980.
Intervals (chorus, sound-sensitive lights) 1983; first performed Middletown, Connecticut, 1983.

Electronic/environmental:

Music for Solo Performer (enormously amplified brain waves, percussion) 1965; first performed Waltham, Massachusetts, 5 May 1965. Recorded Lovely Music VR 1014.
Whistlers (electronic) 1967.
Chambers (sounds in large and small resonant environments) 1968; first performed New York City, June 1968.
Vespers (4 pulse wave oscillators) 1969; first performed Ann Arbor, Michigan, 1967. Recorded Mainstream 5010.
Hymn (amplified performers) 1970.
The Queen of the South (players, responsive surfaces, strewn materials, closed-circuit television) 1972; first performed Providence, Rhode Island, 3 December 1972.
The Fires in the Minds of the Dancers (4-track playback environment) 1974.
Bird and Person Dyning (performer, electric bird call) 1975; first performed Buffalo, New York, 1975. Recorded Cramps Records.
Music on a Long Thin Wire (audio oscillators, electric monochord) 1977; first performed Potsdam, New York, 1977. Recorded Lovely Music VR 1011/2.
Direction of Sounds from the Bridge (string, oscillator, lights) 1978.
Clocker (performer with galvanic skin response sensor, digital delay system) 1978; first performed New York City, 1978.
Ghosts (performer, lights, oscillator, loudspeakers) 1978.
Job's Coffin (amplified chest of drawers) 1979.
Solar Sounder I (solar electronic music system) 1979.
Music for Pure Waves, Bass Drums and Acoustic Pendulums 1980; first performed New York City, 1980. Recorded Lovely Music VR 1017.
Reflections of Sounds from the Wall (electronic) 1981; first performed Buffalo, New York, 1981.
Sferics (acoustic disturbances in the ionosphere) 1981; first performed New York City, 1982.
Seesaw (sound installation) 1983; first performed New York City, 18 December 1983 to 21 January 1984.
Spinner (sound installation) 1984; first performed Hartford, Connecticut, July 1984.
Sound on Paper 1985; first performed Islip, New York, 8 September to 20 October 1985.
Amplifiers and Reflectors (work in progress) 1990.

Other:

Shelter 1967.
Nothing Is Real (arrangement of The Beatles's "Strawberry Fields"; piano, teapot, miniature sound system) n.d. Recorded Toshiba EMI.

PUBLICATIONS

By Lucier: "The Making of *North American Time Capsule*", in *Electronic Music Review*, 1968; "Program Proposal: Pepsi Pavilion—Expo 70", in *Pavilion*, New York, 1972; score and photos to *The Queen of the South*, in D. Reck, *Music of the Whole Earth*, New York, 1977; "The Tools of My Trade", in *Contiguous Lines: Issues and Ideas/SONUS*, 2 (1), 1981; "Still and Moving Lines of Silence", in *Individuals: Post-Movement Art*, New York, 1982; "Chambers", Chicago, 1980; "*Seesaw*: Essay with Graphics", in *Words and Spaces*, New York, 1989.

On Lucier: Gordon Mumma, "AL's *Music for Solo Performer*", in *Source*, 2, 1968; Michael Nyman, "Private Environmental Systems of AL", in *Experimental Music*, London, 1972, New York, 1974; Stuart Marshall, "AL's Music of Sounds in Space", in *Studio International*, London, 1976; W. Zimmermann, (interview) in *Desert Plants: Conversations with Twenty-Three American Musicians*, Vancouver, 1976; Thomas DeLio, "The Shape of Sound", in *Circumscribing the Open Universe: Essays on Cage, Feldman, Wolff, Ashley and AL*, Washington, D.C., 1984; Reinhard Oehlschlagel, "The Space Acts as a Filter", in *MusikTexte*, October 1987; James Tenney, "About AL", in *Alvin Lucier: Catalogue*, Chicago, 1988; Geoff Smith and Nicola Walker, (interview) in *Something About the Music: Interviews with Seventeen Experimental Composers*, London/New York, 1990.

Alvin Lucier comments:

Although I am trained in Western classical music, my compositional activity for the past 30 years has been almost wholly in the American experimental music tradition. Rather than continuing to write in one of the 20th-century music languages, I have spent my time exploring the natural characteristics of sound and its actions in space. This often requires the rejection of any kind of musical grammar in favour of more single-minded testing processes.

Certain works of the late 1960s and early 1970s actually use rooms and concert halls as musical instruments. By filling a space with certain kinds of sounds, the acoustical signature of the space may be heard. Subsequent pieces seek to reveal the hidden sonic and visible identities of, for example, extended wires, flat plates, pieces of paper, and the heads of bass drums. When certain physical objects are excited by sound waves, their modes of vibration may be perceived in surprising and often chaotic ways. Other pieces endeavour to make vivid for listeners the spatial characteristics of sound. By means of very close tunings, sound waves can be heard to spin through space in various directions and different speeds. I am now imagining a new form of music in which the harmony, melody and rhythm take place in three-dimensional space, a music in which one's attention is focussed more on where the sound goes after it has left its source, rather than how it looks when read from left to right on a page or played from high to low on a musical instrument.

Often a work may exist as a sound installation as well as a live performance piece. Since many of my pieces are explorations of the physical characteristics of sound, the presence of purposeful human activators is not of primary importance. Therefore, many of my works are exhibited in art galleries rather than performed in concert halls.

Recently, however, I have returned to composing pieces for classical music instruments. There are two reasons for this: one, I feel a nostalgia for the sounds of those instruments and the manner in which they are played; and two, more and more players are asking for pieces. I am delighted to accept the challenge of making works for instrumentalists in the same spirit and with the same poetry as my earlier, electronic works.

In general, I try to make my pieces as simple and as economical as possible. Most of my compositional time is spent in getting to the core of the idea of the work rather than designing complex embellishments or making attractive surfaces. This attribute, along with certain recycling procedures in some works, fragile ecologies in others, is my way of addressing some important issues of our time.

* * *

Alvin Lucier has eschewed conventional musical instrumentation and notation in favour of electronic systems which generate sound by interaction with their environment. A Lucier piece is like aural research, setting up an open process to discover the characteristics in sound of sometimes unlikely sources.

One variable which Lucier has exploited is the nature of the performance environment. In *Shelter*, Lucier explores its spatial dimensions, using high-gain vibration pickups which sense movement. *Vespers* exploits space in a more dynamic—and more theatrical—fashion. Blindfolded performers are equipped with hand-held echo-location devices known as sondols. Each performer attempts to orient him or herself in space with the aim of timing the echo to fall on the off-beat of the outgoing pulse, taking "slow sound photographs of his surroundings".

I Am Sitting in a Room investigates the acoustic dimensions of the performance space. A reader describes what he or she is doing: sitting in a room recording the sound of his or her own voice. The recording is played back, the playback re-recorded and played back. The result, however, is not simple repetition. The resonant frequencies of the room gradually reinforce themselves and within some 20 minutes to half an hour all trace of speech is obliterated, leaving a field of shimmering, faintly pulsing tones.

Lucier pioneered bio-music, in which the physical processes of living beings are made audible. In *Music for Solo Performer*, electrodes are attached to the performer's scalp to pick up alpha waves from the brain. These currents are amplified, routed through a low-pass filter and played over speakers, which set off resonance in a number of percussion instruments. The piece is highly theatrical; donning the electrodes and calibrating the equipment tends to fascinate the audience. The performer must learn to control consciously what is otherwise an automatic brain function. As Gordon Mumma has commented, the complex requirements of the piece have meant that knowledge necessary for successful performance has been transmitted by word of mouth in a kind of oral tradition.

The Queen of the South also requires the assimilation of new skills. Granules (iron filings, for example) are placed on resonant surfaces such as drumheads or metal plates. Sounds are directed at the surfaces and the aim is to produce certain patterns by creating the appropriate vibrations. Here the visual result is at least as important as, and indeed determines, the aural.

Whistlers resembles the *Music for Solo Performer* in that it draws on naturally occurring electrical signals, but on a much grander scale. Here, Lucier's apparatus processes the electronic disturbances in the ionosphere which give the work its title.

None of these pieces requires specifically musical skills of the performers involved. It is the task of the performer which is central, and taste or preference is irrelevant; in *Vespers*, for example, the goal is dispassionate echo-location. The key to Lucier's success in what we call music is the quality of his aural results, however unlikely their conditions or starting-points.

—David Revill

LUENING, Otto (Clarence). American. Born in Milwaukee, Wisconsin, 15 June 1900. Educated at State Academy of Music, Munich (under Anton Beer-Walbrunn), 1915–7; Municipal Conservatory of Music, Zurich, 1917–20; University of Zurich, 1919–20, D.Mus.; also privately with Philip Jarnach and Ferruccio Busoni; Wesleyan University, Chicago (under Wilhelm Middleschulte). Married (1) Ethel Codd, 19 April 1927 (dissolved); (2) Catherine Brunson, 5 September 1959. Flautist, conductor of opera and symphony orchestras, Munich and Zurich, 1915–20; conductor, first all-American opera performance, Chicago, 1922; coach and executive director, opera department, Eastman School of Music, Rochester, New York, 1925–8; assistant conductor, later conductor, Rochester American Opera company, New York; associate professor, University of Arizona, Tucson, 1932–4; chair, music department, Bennington College, Vermont, 1934–44; founder member, 1938, and president 1945–51, American composers Alliance; director of music, Bennington School of the Arts, Vermont, 1940–1; associate conductor, New York Philharmonic Symphony Chamber Orchestra, 1936–7; associate professor, chair of music department, 1944–8, professor, 1948–64, and professor of Joline Foundation, 1944–64, Barnard College, New York City; music director, Brander Matthews Theatre, 1944–59, professor of music, 1949–68, professor emeritus, since 1968, and music chair, School of the Arts, 1968–70, Columbia University, New York City; co-founder, 1954, president 1968–70, chair of the board, 1970–5, and co-president 1975–7, Composers Recordings Inc.; visiting composer and trustee, American Academy in Rome, 1958, 1961, 1965; co-director, Columbia-Princeton Electronic Music Center, 1959–80; member, composition faculty, Juilliard School of Music, New York City, 1971–3; Distinguished Hadley Fellow, 1975, and visiting composer 1977–9, Bennington College; visiting composer, 1977, and composer in residence, Peabody Conservatory, Baltimore, Maryland, 1977–8; visiting composer, University of Southern California, Los Angeles, 1978; guest conductor, Vermont Symphony Orchestra, 1978, 1985; visiting composer, New York University, 1979; visiting composer, University of Wisconsin, Kenosha-Parkside, 1979–82; guest conductor, Res Musica, Baltimore, 1984, International Festival of the Americas, Miami, 1984, and National Orchestra of New York, 1986. Recipient: David Bispham Medal for American opera, 1933; National Institute of Arts and Letters award, 1946, elected 1952, vice-president 1953; citation for outstanding achievements and contributions to education and music, Wisconsin Senate and House of Representatives, 1965, 1976; citation, National Association of Composers and Conductors, 1966; honorary member and visiting scholar, Phi Beta Kappa, 1966; American Composers Alliance Laurel Leaf Award, 1970, and Laurel Wreath Award, 1985; Thorne Music Fund Foundation award, 1972; National Endowment for the Arts award, 1974, 1977; medallion and citation, Wisconsin Academy of Sciences, Arts and Letters, 1977; Creative Arts Award, Brandeis University, 1981; American Eagle Award, National Music Council, 1985; citation, Broadcast Music Inc., 1985; citation, League-ISCM, 1986. Mailing address: 460 Riverside Drive, Apt 71, New York, New York 10027, U.S.A.

Publishers: ACA; Boosey & Hawkes; Highgate Press.

Symphonies/orchestral:

Music for Orchestra 1923; first performed New York City, 26 May 1978.
Concertino (flute, chamber orchestra) 1923; first performed Philadelphia, 1935.
Symphonic Fantasia No 1 1924; first performed Rochester, New York, 25 November 1925. Recorded CRI 103/CRI ACS 6011.
Serenade (3 horns, strings) 1927; first performed Rochester, New York, 12 January 1928.
Short Symphony 1929–80.
Two Symphonic Interludes 1935; first performed New York City, 11 April 1936.
Prelude to a Hymn Tune by William Billings 1937; first performed New York City, 1 February 1937. Recorded Desto D-429/DST-6429.
Suite (strings) 1937; first performed Saratoga Springs, New York, 12 September 1937.
Elegy for the Lonesome Ones (Short Ballad) (2 clarinets/2nd clarinet ad lib or muted trumpets or violins or violas, strings) 1937.
Serenade (flute, strings) 1939–40; first performed New York City, 19 October 1956.
Symphonic Fantasia No 2 1939–49; first performed New York City, 13 October 1957.
Prelude (chamber orchestra) 1946; first performed Saratoga Springs, New York, 14 September 1946.
Kentucky Concerto (originally entitled *Louisville Concerto*) 1951; first performed Louisville, Kentucky, 5 March 1951. Recorded (*Rondo* only) CRI 103/CRI ACS 6011.
Legend (oboe, strings) 1951; first performed New York City, 1 July 1951. Recorded Desto DC-6466/X-46466.
Wisconsin Suite of Childhood Tunes Remembered 1954; first performed New York City, 28 March 1954.
Song, Poem and Dance (flute, strings) 1958.
Lyric Scene (flute, strings) 1958; first performed Arlington, Virginia, 25 October 1964. Recorded Desto DC 6466/X-46466.
Fantasia (string quartet, orchestra) 1959; first performed New York City, 18 April 1959.
Synthesis (orchestra, tape) 1962; first performed Erie, Pennsylvania, 22 October 1963. Recorded CRI 219.
Broekman Fantasia (strings) 1966; first performed Munich, 1979.
Symphonic Fantasia No 3 1969–81; first performed New York City, 26 January 1982.
Symphonic Fantasia No 4 1969–81; first performed New York City, 14 May 1984.
Sonority Forms 1973; first performed Bennington, Vermont, 14 October 1973.

Elegy for the Lonesome Ones (2 clarinets, strings) 1974.
Symphonic Interlude No 3 1975.
A Wisconsin Symphony 1975; first performed Milwaukee, Wisconsin, 3 January 1976.
Potawatomi Legends (small orchestra) 1980; first performed Parkside, Wisconsin, 13 April 1980.
Sonority Forms II 1983; first performed Bennington, Vermont, 4 June 1983.
Symphonic Fantasia No 5 1985, begun 1948.
Symphonic Fantasia No 6 1985.
Symphonic Interlude No 4 1985.
Symphonic Fantasia No 7 1986.
Symphonic Interlude No 5 1986.
Symphonic Fantasia No 8 1986.
Symphonic Fantasia No 9 1989.
Symphonic Fantasia No 10 1990.

Chamber/instrumental:

Little Miniature Pieces (piano) 1906.
Theme with Variations (piano) 1907.
Piece (piano) 1913.
Waltz (piano) 1913.
Piece (string quartet) 1914.
Fantasie Stücke (piano) 1915.
Four Short Pieces (piano) 1915.
Piece (organ) 1916.
Fugue (piano) 1917.
Gavotte (piano) 1917.
One Step (piano) 1917.
Piece (piano) 1917.
Thema con variazione (piano) 1917.
Gavotte (cello, piano) 1917.
Sonata No 1 (violin, piano) 1917.
Sextet (flute, clarinet, horn, violin, viola, cello) 1918.
Choral Vorspiel zu "Christus der is mein Leben" (organ) 1918.
Fuga a tre voci (piano) 1918.
Slumbersong (piano) 1918.
Variations on Christus is mein Leben (4 horns) 1918.
Fugue (string quartet) 1919.
Sontina (flute, piano) 1919.
String Quartet No 1 1919–20.
Contrapuntal Study (piano) 1921.
Trio (violin, cello, piano) 1921.
Chorale Fantasy (organ) 1922.
Variations on "Yankee Doodle" (piccolo, piano) 1922.
Sonata No 2 (violin, piano) 1922.
Coal Scuttle Blues (piano; version for 2 pianos) 1922, also 1929.
String Quartet No 2 1923. Recorded CRI 303.
Legend (violin, piano) 1923–4.
Sonata No 1 (cello) 1924.
Two Bagatelles (piano) 1924.
Hymn to Bacchus (piano) 1926.
Dance Sonata (piano) 1928.
Eight Pieces (piano) 1928.
Intermezzo III (piano) 1928.
Six Short and Easy Pieces (piano) 1928.
String Quartet No 3 1928. Recorded CRI 303.
Fantasia (organ) 1929. Recorded CRI 219.
Fantasia brevis (flute, piano) 1929.
Short Fantasy (violin, horn) 1930.
Three Pieces: Birds, Swans, Stars (piano) 1932–3.
Intermezzi (piano) 1932–6.
Fantasia No 2 (piano) 1933.
Mañana (violin, piano) 1933.
Phantasy (piano) 1935.
Waltz (piano) 1935.
Six Preludes (piano) 1935–51.
Fantasia Brevis (violin, viola, cello) 1936.
Andante (piano) 1936.
Eight Preludes (piano) 1936.
Fantasia brevis (clarinet, piano) 1936. Recorded Grenadilla GSC 1059.
Five Short Sonatas (flute, piano or harpsichord) 1937.
Variations on a Theme Song for a Silent Movie (cor anglais, piano) 1937.
Short Fantasy (violin, piano) 1938.
Two Inventions (piano) 1938.
Fuguing Tune (flute, oboe, clarinet, bassoon, horn) 1938.
Six Inventions (piano) 1938–9.
Fuga a tre voci No 2 (piano) 1939.
The Bass with the Delicate Air (flute, oboe, clarinet, bassoon) 1940.
Short Sonata No 1 (piano) 1940. Recorded Serenus SRS 12091.
Variations (piano or harpsichord) 1940.
Canonical Study (piano) 1941.
Canons (harpsichord or piano) 1941.
Easy Canons (piano) 1941.
Andante and Variations (Sonata No 3) (violin, piano) 1942.
Variations on Bach's Chorale Prelude "Liebster Jesu wir sind hier" (cello, piano) 1942.
Fantasia (harpsichord or piano) 1942.
Canon in the Octave (piano) 1945.
Suite (cello or viola, piano) 1946.
Ten Pieces for Five Fingers (piano, left hand) 1946.
Suite No 1 (flute) 1947.
Easy March (recorder, flute, oboe, piano) 1950.
Three Nocturnes (oboe, piano) 1951.
Legend (oboe, string quartet) 1951. Recorded CRI SD-501.
Trio (flute, violin, piano) 1952.
Sonata (bassoon, piano) 1952.
Suite (double bass, piano) 1953.
Sonata (trombone, piano) 1953. Recorded Crystal S-388.
Sonata in memoriam Ferruccio Busoni (piano) 1955–66. Recorded CRI 334/CRI ACS 6011.
Sonata (viola) 1958.
Gay Picture (piano) 1957.
Short Sonata No 2 (piano) 1958. Recorded Serenus SRS 12091.
Short Sonata No 3 (piano) 1958. Recorded Serenus SRS 12091.
Sonata (double bass) 1958.
Sonata Composed in Two Dayturns (Sonata No 2) (cello) 1958.
Sonata No 1 (violin) 1958.
Suite No 2 (flute) 1959. Recorded CRI CD 561.
Three Fantasies (guitar) 1960.
Gargoyles (violin, synthesized sound) 1960. Recorded Columbia ML-5966/6566.
Suite No 3 (flute) 1961. Recorded CRI 400.
A Day in the Country (violin, tape) 1961.
A Study in Synthesized Sounds (tape) 1961.
Trio (flute, cello, piano) 1962. Recorded CRI 303.
Sonority Canon (2–37 flutes) 1962.
Three Duets (2 flutes) 1962.
Elegy (violin) 1963.
Suite No 4 (flute) 1963. Recorded CRI 400.
Duo (violin, viola) 1963.
March for High and Low Instruments (any combination) 1963.
Suite for High and Low Instruments (any combination) 1963.

Entrance and Exit Music (3 trumpets, 3 trombones, cymbal) 1964.
Short Sonata (Sonata No 3) (flute, piano) 1966.
Fantasia (cello) 1966.
Trio (3 flutes) 1966.
Sonata No 3 (violin, piano) 1966.
Meditation (violin) 1967.
The Bells of Bellagio (piano—4 or 6 hands) 1967.
Rondo (accordion) 1967. Recorded Finnadar 7 90234–1.
Short Sonata No 4 (piano) 1967. Recorded Serenus SRS 12091.
Fourteen Easy Duets (2 recorders) 1967.
Sonata No 2 (violin) 1968.
Suite No 5 (flute) 1969. Recorded CRI 400.
Trio (trumpet, horn, trombone) 1969.
Sonata No 3 (violin) 1970. Recorded CRI 303.
Introduction and Allegro (trumpet, piano) 1970.
Eight Tone Poems (2 violas) 1971.
Fugue (organ) 1971.
Short Sonata No 2 (flute, piano) 1971.
Chorale Fantasy and Fugue (organ) 1971.
Variations on "Fugue and Chorale Fantasy" (organ, electronic doubles) 1973. Recorded CRI 334.
Prelude (flute, clarinet, bassoon) 1974. Recorded Golden Crest CRS 4140.
Fugue (flute, clarinet, bassoon) 1974. Recorded Golden Crest CRS 4140.
Mexican Serenades (double bass, wind, percussion) 1974.
Short Suite (Four Cartoons) (flute, clarinet, bassoon) 1974. Recorded Golden Crest CRS 4140.
Suite (2 flutes, piano, cello ad lib) 1976.
Triadic Canons (2 violins, flute) 1976.
Canons (2 flutes) 1979.
Short Sonata No 5 (piano) 1979. Recorded Serenus SRS 12091.
Short Sonata No 6 (piano) 1979. Recorded Serenus SRS 12091.
Short Sonata No 7 (piano) 1979.
Divertimento (oboe, string trio) 1981.
Divertimento (brass) 1981.
Duet (flute, viola) 1981.
Fantasia and Dance (violin) 1982.
Fantasia (piano trio) 1982.
Fantasia (clarinet) 1982.
Sonority Forms I (piano) 1982–3.
Sonority Forms II: The Right-Hand Path (piano, right hand) 1984.
Fugue and Choral Fantasy (organ, electronic tape) 1984.
Green Mountain Evening (ensemble) 1984.
Opera Fantasia (violin, piano) 1985.
Tango (piano) 1985.
Serenade and Dialogue (violin, piano) 1985.
Serenade (violin, cello, piano) 1985.
Three Fantasias (Baroque flute) 1985.
Three Fantasias (guitar) 1985.
Suite (horn) 1985.
Three Canons (2 flutes) 1985. Recorded CRI CD 561.
Duo (flute, viola) 1985.

Vocal/choral:

Trio (soprano, mezzo-soprano, alto) 1914.
An den Traume (soprano, piano; Cornelius) 1915.
Der Eichwald (soprano, piano; Lenan) 1915.
Septembermorgen (soprano, piano; Morike) 1915.
Wir wandeln alle den Weg (soprano, piano; Bodenstedt) 1915.
Two Songs (soprano, piano; German sacred texts) 1916–7.
In Weihnachstszeiten (soprano, piano; Hesse) 1917.
Cum spiritus sancto (unaccompanied SATB chorus) 1917.
Three Swiss Folksongs (unaccompanied SATB chorus) 1917.
Mysterium (soprano, piano; Frey) 1917.
Requiescat (soprano, piano; Wilde) 1917.
Three Songs: At Christmas, Noon silence, Venilia (soprano, piano; Hesse, Sharpe) 1917–22, orchestrated 1927.
Frühling (soprano, piano; Hesse) 1918.
Vater unser in Himmelreich (unaccompanied SATB chorus) 1918.
Wie sind die Tage (soprano, piano; Hesse) 1918.
Transience (soprano, piano; Naidu) 1922.
Enigma Canon (after Bach; unaccompanied SSAATB chorus) 1922.
The Soundless Song (soprano, flute, clarinet, 2 violins, viola, cello, dancers, light; also for soprano, piano) 1923.
Trio (soprano, flute, violin) 1924.
Gliding O'er All (soprano, piano; Whitman) 1927.
If That High World (unaccompanied SSA chorus) 1927.
Sun of the Sleepless (unaccompanied SSA chorus; Byron) 1927.
A Roman's Chamber (soprano, piano; Shelley) 1928.
Auguries of Innocence (soprano, piano; Blake) 1928.
Infant Joy (soprano, piano; Blake) 1928.
Locations and Times (soprano, piano; Whitman) 1928.
To Morning (soprano, piano; Blake) 1928.
Visored (soprano, piano; Whitman) 1928.
Wake the Serpent Not (soprano, piano; Shelley) 1928.
Young Love (soprano, piano; Blake) 1928.
A Farm Picture (soprano, piano; Whitman) 1929.
Here the Frailest Leaves of Me (soprano, piano; Whitman) 1929.
I Faint, I Perish (soprano, piano; Shelley) 1929.
The Dawn (soprano, piano; anon.) 1930.
Behold the Tabernacle of God (soprano, SATB chorus, piano or organ) 1931.
Anthem (SATB chorus, organ) 1932.
When in the Languor of Evening (soprano, chorus, string quartet or woodwind quintet, piano) 1932.
Hast Never Come to Thee (soprano, flute) 1936.
At the Last (soprano, piano; Whitman) 1936.
Forever Lost (soprano, piano; Taggard) 1936.
Only Themselves Understand Themselves (soprano, piano) 1936.
Swing, Swing and Swoon (soprano, piano; Taggard) 1936.
Suite (soprano, flute) 1936.
Christ Is Arisen (SSAATB chorus, piano or organ, strings, flute ad lib, clarinet ad lib, bassoon ad lib) 1940.
Ic denke Dein (unaccompanied SSAA chorus) 1942.
Nine Songs to Emily Dickinson Texts (soprano, piano) 1942–51.
Alleluia (unaccompanied SATB chorus) 1944.
Pilgrim's Hymn (SA chorus, piano or orchestra) 1946.
Love's Secret (soprano, piano; Blake) 1949. Recorded Desto D 411-12/DST 6411–12.
The Maidens of Shang-ti (unaccompanied SSA chorus) 1949.
Vocalise (unaccompanied SSAA chorus) 1949.
Divine Image (soprano, piano; Blake) 1949. Recorded Desto D 411–12.
The Tiger's Ghost (unaccompanied TTBB chorus; Swenson) 1951.
She Walks in Beauty (soprano, piano; Byron) 1951.
The Harp the Monarch Minstrel Swept (soprano, piano; Byron) 1951.
Lines from a Song for Occupations (unaccompanied SATB chorus; Whitman) 1964. Recorded Finnadar 90850–1.
Psalm 146 (unaccompanied SATB chorus) 1970.

Six Proverbs (alto, piano) 1973.
The Little Vagabond (soprano, piano; Blake) 1980.
Silent, Silent Night (soprano, piano; Blake) 1980.
No Jerusalem But This (voices, mixed chorus, 15 instruments; Menashe) 1982.
Lines from The First Book of Urizen and Vala; or a Dream of Nine Nights (voices, chorus; Blake) 1983.
Ah! Sunflower (soprano, piano; Blake) 1984.
The Lily (soprano, piano; Blake) 1984.
Laughing Song (tenor, baritone/counter-tenor; Blake) 1984.

Opera:

Evangeline (after Longfellow) 1930–2, revised 1947–8; first performed New York City, 5 May 1948.

Other:

Sister Beatrice (incidental music to Maeterlinck) 1926; first performed Rochester, New York, 15 January 1926.
Blood Wedding (incidental music to Lorca) 1940; first performed Bennington, Vermont, 1 December 1940.
Fantasy in Space (tape) 1952; first performed New York City, 28 October 1952. Recorded Desto DC 6466/X-46466.
Invention in Twelve Notes (tape) 1952; first performed New York City, 28 October 1952. Recorded Desto DC 6466/X-46466.
Low Speed (tape) 1952; first performed New York City, 28 October 1952. Recorded Desto DC 6466/X-46466.
Incantation (collaboration with Vladimir Ussachevsky) 1953. Recorded Desto DC 6466/X-46466.
Rhapsodic Variations (orchestra, tape; collaboration with Vladimir Ussachevsky) 1953–4; first performed Louisville, Kentucky, 20 March 1954. Recorded Louisville LOU 545-5.
A Poem in Cycles and Bells (orchestra, tape; collaboration with Vladimir Ussachevsky) 1954; first performed Los Angeles, 15 November 1954. Recorded CRI 112/CRI ACS 6011.
Of Identity (ballet) 1954; first performed New York City, 9 February 1955.
Carlsbad Caverns (television score; collaboration with Vladimir Ussachevsky) 1955.
Theatre Piece No 2 (ballet for voice, instruments, tape) 1956; first performed New York City, 20 April 1956. Recorded CRI 268.
King Lear (incidental music to Shakespeare; tape collaboration with Vladimir Ussachevsky) 1956. Recorded CRI 112.
Dynamophonic Tape 1958.
Concerted Piece (orchestra, tape; collaboration with Vladimir Ussachevsky) 1960; first performed New York City, 10 March 1960. Recorded CRI 227.
Back to Methusaleh (incidental music to Shaw; collaboration with Vladimir Ussachevsky) 1960.
Diffusion of Bells (collaborationwith H. El-Dabh) 1962–5.
Electronic Fanfare (collaboration with H. El-Dabh) 1962–5.
Moonflight (tape) 1968. Recorded Desto DC 6466/X-46466.
Incredible Voyage (television score; collaboration with Vladimir Ussachevsky and others) 1968.
In the Beginning (tape) 1970.

Recorded anthologies of Luening's music: *The Music of OL*—CRI ACS 6011; *A Tribute to OL*—CRI CD 561.

Publications

By Luening: *The Odyssey of an American Composer* (autobiography), New York, 1980; many articles and reviews.

On Luening: Charles Wuorinen, "Conversation with OL", in *Perspectives of New Music*, 10 (1), 1971; D.W. Moore, "Composers Recordings: At the Quartet-Century Mark, Carter Harmon and OL Talk About CRI's Past, Present and Future", in *American Record Guide*, 43 (4), 1980; John Rockwell, "An Influential Musician at 80", in *New York Times*, 15 June 1980; Robert Moog, "The Columbia-Princeton Electronic Music Center: Thirty Years of Explorations in Sound", in *Contemporary Keyboard*, 7 (5), 1981; J. Krutz, "OL: An 85-Year Investment in American Music", in *The Sinfonian*, 35 (1), 1985; B. Wentz, "OL at 85", (interview) in *High Fidelity/Musical America*, 35 (11), 1985; Severine Neff, "OL, Barnard and Electronic Music", in *Barnard Alumnae Magazine*, Spring 1988.

* * *

Otto Luening's motto is from the poetry of William Blake:

To see a World in a Grain of Sand
And Heaven in a Wild Flower
Hold Infinity in the palm of your hand
And Eternity in an hour.

Even in the large forms of opera and symphony, Luening's music is never grandiose but in his words, "simple and poetic". It aims to maximize the presence and power of the single pitch, however complex the musical texture. Luening's study of Haydn and Mozart has led to concerns for clarity of form and texture, precision of pitch choice, careful use of resonance and concern for practicality. The result is a style featuring lyricism and humor.

Luening has written over 350 works in every medium including his pioneering achievements in tape and electronic music; moreover, he has displayed the virtually unheard-of ability to collaborate with other composers such as his student and colleague, Vladimir Ussachevsky and friend Ernst Bacon. Luening's work parallels the primary historical and aesthetic movements of the 20th century starting from German late 19th-century chromaticism (for example *Symphonic Fantasia No 1*, *Sextet*, *The Soundless Song*), moving into the modal language of North American regionalism (*Coal Scuttle Blues*, *Evangeline*), and into a non-tonal language built from varied, resonant harmonic combinations in the overtone row (*Symphonic Fantasia No 2*, *Symphonic Fantasia No 5*) and finally after 1950 into atonal electronics (*Fantasy in Space*, *Gargoyles*). Luening, however, wrote triadic atonal music in the neo-tonal 1930s, humorous tonal music in the humorless, twelve-tone 1950s, predominantly acoustic music in the electronic 1960s, everything but minimalism in the 1970s. In the 1980s Luening has focused on small chamber works (*Opera Fantasia* for violin and piano, *Suite* for horn) and five orchestral works always entitled *Symphonic Fantasia*. Together the series of Symphonic Fantasias span Luening's long compositional career: the First Symphonic Fantasia was completed in 1924, the tenth, in 1990. Taken as a group, the fantasias display a compendium of lifetime compositional concerns, not the least of which is a sharp comprehension of instrumental craft and the performer's capabilities, whether modest or advanced.

If Luening has a mentor besides Haydn or Mozart, it is his teacher, the pianist-composer Ferruccio Busoni. From his several years of work with Busoni and his colleague Philipp Jarnach Luening acquired his preoccupation with originality and clarity of form as well as his interest in electronic music, the field in which he was to become a pioneer. As he described in 1988,

> My personal preoccupation with electronic music goes back to my connection with Busoni. He had heard about a demonstration by an American engineer, Thaddeus Cahill, and in 1907 he wrote a little booklet called *Sketch of a New Aesthetic of Music*. In it he wrote that the orchestral palette was getting too restricted, but that now, with a new means of electric sound production, there would be new horizons.

Luening's interest in electronics from *Fantasy in Space* to *Moonflight* was always the aural impact, never mere technology. He has quoted Busoni's remark about the electronic medium: "only conscientious and long periods of experimentation and continuing ear training will make this uncommon material plastic and useful for artistic purposes".

Busoni also introduced Luening to the ideas of the German American theorist Bernhard Ziehn. Ziehn was an eminent contrapuntist who gave Busoni the solution to the quadruple counterpoint in Bach's last fugue in *Die Kunst der Fuge* which Busoni ultimately used in his *Fantasia Contrapunttistica*. Luening has exploited Ziehn's concepts of canon, plurisignificance of tones, and symmetrical inversion in many works including *Symphonic Fantasia No 1* and the *Sonata in memoriam Ferruccio Busoni*. Ziehn's theories are not centered in timbral concerns; Luening, however, has incorporated Ziehn's ideas into his own theory of "acoustic harmony"—the manipulation and reinforcement of overtones within musical textures. As a result of "acoustic harmony," particular voicings arise which allow every tone to project even in a complex texture; in combination such tones produce a rich orchestral texture not unlike the beginning of Busoni's *Doktor Faust*. Thus through "acoustic harmony" Luening's crystalline textures take shape, allowing simple elegance of form and articulation: "a World in a Grain of Sand."

—Severine Neff

LUMSDAINE, David. Australian. Born in Sydney, 31 October 1931. Educated at Sydney University and New South Wales Conservatorium, graduated 1952; further study in England under Matyas Seiber and Lennox Berkeley. Married Nicola LeFanu, *q.v.*, 16 March 1979; 1 son. Founder, Manson Room for study of new music, Royal Academy of Music, London, 1964; lecturer in music, and founder of electronic music studio, University of Durham, 1970–81; brief return to Australia, 1973; visiting professor, University of Adelaide, 1976; further visits to Australia, 1978–9; composer in residence, Sydney Conservatorium (post shared with Nicola LeFanu), 1979; joint senior lectureship (with Nicola LeFanu), King's College, University of London, from 1981. Mailing address: 9 Kempe Road, London NW6 6SP, England.

Publisher: Australian Music Centre Ltd, P.O. Box N690, Grosvenor Place, Sydney, New South Wales, Australia.

Symphonies/orchestral:

Variations for Orchestra 1960; first performed London, 1960; withdrawn.
Short Symphony 1961; first performed London, 1961; withdrawn.
Bach Music (based on Fugue VIII of *Der Kunst der Fuge*) 1965; withdrawn.
Episodes (orchestra) 1968–9; first performed London, 1972.
Salvation Creek with Eagle (chamber orchestra) 1974; first performed Durham, 1974; first public performance London, 1976.
Sunflower (to the Memory of Luigi Dallapiccola) 1975; first performed Middlesbrough, Yorkshire, January 1976.
Evensong (brass band) 1975; first performed Bristol, 1975.
Hagoromo (large orchestra) 1977; first performed Paris, December 1977.
Shoalhaven (small orchestra) 1982; first performed Nowra, New South Wales, December 1983.
Mandala V (symphony orchestra) 1988; first performed Sydney, May 1989.
The Arc of Stars (string orchestra) 1990–1.

Chamber/instrumental:

Ruhe Sanfte, Sanfte Ruh' (piano) 1964; first performed Reading, Berkshire, 1978.
Kelly Ground (piano) 1966; first performed London, 1966.
Flights (2 pianos) 1967; first performed London, 1967.
Mandala I (wind quartet) 1967; first performed London, 1970.
Mandala II (flute, clarinet, viola, cello, percussion) 1969; first performed London, 1969.
Looking Glass Music (brass quintet, prerecorded tape) 1970; first performed London, 1971.
Kangaroo Hunt (piano, percussion) 1971; first performed Oxford, 1971.
Caliban Trio (piano trio, prerecorded tape, live electronics) 1972; first performed Cheltenham, Gloucestershire, 1972.
Mandala III (transcription of last Chorus of Bach's *St Matthew Passion*, followed by instrumental sonata and *Ruhe Sanfte, Sanfte Ruh*"; piano, flute, clarinet, viola, cello, Chinese bell) 1978; first performed Bristol, 1978.
Cambewarra (piano) 1980; first performed Manchester, 1981.
Mandala IV (string quartet) 1983.
Bagatelles (flute, clarinet, piano, violin, viola, cello) 1985; first performed New South Wales, 1985.
Empty Sky, Mootwingee (flute, trombone or horn, cello, pitched percussion, 2 pianos) 1986; first performed Sydney, September 1986.
A Dance and a Hymn for Alexander Maconochie (flute, A clarinet, percussion, mandolin, guitar, violin, double bass) 1988; first performed Melbourne, August 1988.
Round Dance (sitar, tabla, flute, cello, keyboard) 1989; first performed London, March 1989.
Sine nomine (an album of pieces for alto saxophone/clarinet, pitched percussion) 1990.

Vocal/choral:

The Ballad of Perse O'Reilly (tenor, male chorus, 2 pianos; Joyce) 1953–81.
Missa brevis (SATB chorus, organ) 1964; first performed London, 1966.
Annotations of Auschwitz (soprano, flute/trumpet, horn, violin, cello, piano; Porter, Bible) 1964; first performed London, 1965.

Dum medium silentium (introit for unaccompanied SATB chorus) 1964–75.
Easter Fresco (soprano, flute, horn, harp, piano; St John) 1966; first performed London, 1970.
Aria for Edward John Eyre (soprano, double bass, chamber ensemble, narrators, prerecorded tape, live electronics; Eyre's journal) 1972; first performed Liverpool, 1973.
My Sister's Song (soprano; Tamil) 1974; first performed London, 1975.
Tides (narrator, 12 singers, percussion; Wittgenstein, Boehme, Plotinus, Boethius, *Rig Veda*, Maori and Indian creation myths) 1979; radiophonic version broadcast Sydney, 1979.
What Shall I Sing? (soprano, 2 clarinets) 1982; first performed Helmsley, Yorkshire, 1983.
Where the Lilies Grow (unaccompanied 8-part chamber choir; Border ballad) 1985; first performed Sydney, June 1985.
Just So Stories (narrator, dancers, computer generated tape; Kipling) 1990; first performed London, August 1990.
A Tree Telling of Orpheus (soprano, flute, clarinet, violin, viola, cello; Levertov) 1990.

Other:

Big Meeting (quadrophonic tape; electronic fantasy based on Durham Miners Gala, 1971) realised 1978.
Wild Ride to Heaven (radiophonic adventure playground; collaboration with Nicola LeFanu) 1980; broadcast BBC, 1980.
Four Soundscapes (consisting of *Lake Emu*, *Meunga Creek*, *River Red Gums & Black Box*, *Butcher Birds at Spirey Creek*; field recordings for broadcast) 1990; broadcast ABC radio, May 1990.
Soundscape 5: Cambewarra 1991.

David Lumsdaine comments:

So what's the special nature of composing for me? In silence, listening. Listening for what arises of its own accord. Listening to this sound, discrete and particular, letting it grow in its own way. Transcribing the sound, following its shape with a pencil, is not a separate thing. Composition *is* the activity of listening. Listening, not before, not after. Now.

No separate thought of audience, of players. The listener is players and audience.

Too often, we think of music as a score that a composer presents to a player, saying "Here's my music. Take it (the music) away, learn it (the music) and play it (the music)". But music is an activity, not a piece of paper.

In his introduction to *The Raw and the Cooked*, Lévi-Strauss wrote "Music becomes actual . . . through and by the listener . . . Music has its being in me, and I listen to myself through it."

I could say "Music has its being in me and I perform myself through it" or "Music has its being in me and I compose myself through it".

The vision I'm listening to might have become a poem. The sound I see might have become a painting. Inside the activity of composing, I see and feel the sounds around me. Everything is tangible, everything is fluid, dynamic. Yet everything is also *itself*. And everything is myself.

The quiet in which I compose is not a different part of my world, set apart in contrast to noise, bustle and contradictions of the rest. The quiet is the focal point in which everything stills, becomes transparent; and I can listen, not only to what I know, but also to what I don't know I know.

* * *

David Lumsdaine's music reveals a restless curiosity and readiness to take on board new developments that make it difficult to pin down his style. Pursuing a sequence of works, one has the impression that just as things are settling into a pattern, he is off on another tack, even in another idiom, only to recover his original thread several works later, refreshed by the change.

Surveying the output, two consistent key features emerge from the titles (always, with Lumsdaine, what a work is called being highly pertinent to its inner nature): the recurrence both of works with a specific Australian territorial connection; and (five times), of pieces called *Mandala*. Mandala, for Lumsdaine, is not merely a representation of the flat, circular diagram used as a focus for meditation by some Buddhists; his are solid, and transparent, seeming to rotate on any axis (as, indeed, do the matrices generating their main pitch-material), giving constantly changing perspectives of a central core.

There is a progression discernible through both series, from metaphor in the earlier works to near-representation—embodiment, almost—in the later ones. *Kelly Ground*, the first of the "Australian" works, consists of a beautifully poised cycle of piano variations, entirely self-referring musically, but having the atmosphere of a northern Victorian landscape. The listener is left with an impression of rolling hills and broad horizons, of the stillness of a night sky with stars, of the magpie's fluting before dawn, and of choruses of small birds. Even so there is no attempt in Kelly Ground, at direct representation, whereas in *Cambewarra*, Lumsdaine's most recent piano work, there is an out-and-out celebration of the changing light and birdsong on a mountainside in southern New South Wales: one can virtually identify the species. These pieces, along with two others, are major contributions to the 20th-century piano repertoire; all are virtuoso works, written with complete understanding of the piano's capabilities.

The first two Mandalas, by the same token, have structures inspired by observations of natural phenomena—mostly circlings, like the flight patterns made by flocks of waders on an estuary, perhaps—but without the slightest attempt at portrayal. These are structural models only. *Mandala V*, on the other hand, is a big orchestral canvas celebrating, and indeed literally reproducing, birdsong in the Australian bush. Here one can catch a glimpse of the essential Lumsdaine in the slow rotation of the expansive soundscapes, the dance and flicker of myriad details, the inexorable logic of the underlying structure, and the sense of perspective with which he deploys his orchestral forces. *Mandala V* is not only a summation of all the composer's main preoccupations of the preceding 25 years: the soundscapes, the mechanisms for structural control, and the integrative harmonic thought; but also, effortlessly, without any sense of compromise, it is very obviously a warm and "public" work.

Yet "going public" has not been one of Lumsdaine's main concerns. He has a hearty contempt for those composers who court popularity, either in their attitudes or in their music. All the same, from time to time he has written works which are straightforwardly entertaining. He sees no reason to downrate these in relation to the rest of his output, and in the wheeling rhythms of *Round Dance*, say, or the startling juxtapositions and associations of material in *Bagatelles*, or the dancing counterpoint of *What Shall I Sing?*, it is easy to perceive Lumsdaine's preoccupations in another guise.

Lumsdaine has a passion to record, untransformed, the sounds of nature, not only for purposes of documentation, but also for others to enjoy, believing that these rhythms and changing patterns of sound, captured over time-spans of an hour or more, have an elegance of form all their own. The microphone has been an important composing tool for him since the beginning, and the series of electro-acoustic works is impressive. Here again, we find a progression from transformation and "metaphor" in the early works (now, alas, mostly withdrawn), through *Big Meeting*'s sound-treatment and semi-representation of the sounds of the 1971 Durham Miner's Gala, and on through the near-literal presentation and collage of *Wild Ride to Heaven* (1980), to the straightforward natural soundscapes of 1989 which, with titles such as *Lake Emu* and *Butcher Birds at Spirey Creek*, are barely edited field recordings. Curiously, they sound more like Lumsdaine than any of the other works for tape.

The main body of Lumsdaine's work is inner and contemplative, conveying powerful messages for those who are prepared to accompany him on these journeys of the imagination. The most significant works are all quite long in clock time, and the going can sometimes be rugged, but no one who travels through the 57 minutes of *Aria for Edward John Eyre* and experiences, through Lumsdaine, the visions, sufferings and discoveries of this explorer, or who shares the half-hour of changing lights and colours, and the slow swell and wild dancing of *Hagoromo*, can fail to be struck by the visionary quality, and the sheer originality, of the music.

—Anthony Gilbert

LUND, Gudrun. Danish; American citizen. Born in Aalborg, 22 April 1930.Educated at Royal Danish Conservatory, Copenhagen, B.A. (piano), 1953; University of Copenhagen, M.A. (musicology), 1955; resident in United States, 1956–66 (naturalised 1963); returned to Denmark (further composition study under Svend S. Schultz and M. Winkel Holm), from 1966; further study in United States, 1983. Composer, pianist, violinist, teacher, musicologist. Mailing address: 31 Svalevej, DK-2900 Hellerup, Denmark.

Publisher: Samfundet, 3 Valkendorfsgade, DK-1151 Copenhagen K, Denmark.

Symphonies/orchestral:

Scherzo Op 2 1976.
A Festive Overture Op 15 1977.
Chamber Concerto Op 18 (oboe, viola, orchestra) 1977.
Variations and Theme Op 24 (clarinet, strings) 1978.
Concerto for Alto Trombone and Chamber Orchestra Op 26 1978.
Consequences Op 32 1979.
Divertimento Op 37 (2 trumpets, chamber orchestra) 1979.
Concerto for Oboe and Strings Op 55 1981.
Patchwork: A Symphony in Four Colours Op 63 1982.
Negotiations Op 76 (wind band) 1983.
Walking Along Op 86 (clarinet, orchestra) 1984.
Chase Op 97 1986.
Celebration Op 100 (military band) 1986.

Chamber/instrumental:

A Woman's Mind Op 4 (piano) 1976.
String Quartet No 1 Op 8 1976.
Trio Op 10 (flute, violin, viola) 1976.
Quartet Op 13 (oboe, violin, viola, cello) 1977.
Duet Op 17 (2 oboes) 1977.
String Quartet No 2 Op 20 1978.
Trio Sonata 1978 Op 21 (trumpet, trombone, organ) 1978.
Music for Seven Players Op 22 (harpsichord, flute, oboe, string quartet) 1978.
Trio Op 23 (flute, viola, piano) 1978.
Trio Op 25 (clarinet, viola, piano) 1978.
Sonata for Two Musicians Op 28 (recorder, violin) 1978.
Patterns Op 29 (wind quintet) 1978.
Variations in Four Movements Op 30 (piano, violin, cello) 1978.
Quintetto di bassetto Op 34 (flute, oboe, basset horn, horn, bassoon) 1979.
Sonata Op 38 (viola) 1979.
Relations Op 39 (trombone, wind quintet) 1979.
Six Duets Op 40 (2 trumpets) 1979.
Serenata seriosa Op 42 (string trio) 1980.
Seven Facets Op 43 (organ) 1980.
Quintet Op 44 (piano, string quartet) 1980.
Reflections Op 47 (trombone, organ) 1980.
Variations on an Innocent Theme Op 49 (wind quintet) 1980.
Sonatina Op 50 (oboe, piano) 1981.
Sonatina Op 50a (flute, piano) 1981.
Quartet Op 52 (clarinet, violin, viola, cello) 1981.
Five Boys I Know Op 53 (bass trombone) 1981. Recorded SUDM 007.
Sonata con forza Op 54 (cello) 1981.
Three Melodic Studies Op 56 (4 cellos) 1981.
Uneven Partners Op 58 (flute, double bass) 1981.
Sonata Op 61 (piano) 1981.
Goddag mand, okseskaft Op 62 (oboe, horn, violin, cello) 1882.
Lonely Souls Op 64 (oboe, alto saxophone, organ) 1982.
Abstract Op 66 (accordion) 1982.
Piano Trio Op 67 1982.
Three Subjects Op 68 (alto trombone, tenor trombone, bass trombone) 1982.
String Quartet No 4 Op 70 1983.
Abstract, Too Op 71 (flute, clarinet, bassoon, viola, cello, double bass) 1983.
Clarinet Quartet Op 72 (4 clarinets) 1983.
Con Anima Op 73 (flute, violin, viola, cello) 1983. Recorded SUDM 022.
Break Op 74 (oboe) 1983.
A Suite in 3½ Movements Op 75 (flute, viola) 1983.
String Quartet No 5 Op 77 1984.
Three Canons and a Row Op 80 (2 clarinets) 1984.
Rainbow Op 81 (flute, violin, viola, cello, piano, harp) 1984.
Continuous Op 82 (tuba) 1984.
Co-Existence Op 83 (double bass, piano) 1984.
Klip Op 85 (15 instruments; adults or children) 1984.
Flip-Flop Op 87 (viola) 1985.
Three Canons and a Row Op 80a (viola, cello) 1985.
Diversions Op 88 (flute, oboe, clarinet, horn, bassoon, 2 violins, viola, cello, double bass) 1985.
Lydbillede Op 91 (piano, violin, cello) 1985.
Match Op 92 (piano) 1985.
Up and Down Op 93 (mandolin ensemble) 1986.
Five Duos Op 99 (wind quintet) 1986.
Ten Together Op 101 (flute, oboe, clarinet, bassoon, horn, 2 violins, viola, cello, double bass) 1987.
Games With—Op 102 (guitar) 1987.
Two Moving Op 103 (violin, cello) 1987.
Little Suite Op 106 (3 flutes) 1987.
Five Pieces for Grand Piano Op 109 1988.
Eleven Variations Op 110 (2 violins, bassoon) 1988.

Two Movements and a Pause Op 113 (violin, viola, cello) 1988.
Five Girls I Know Op 114 (trumpet, trombone) 1988.
Lullaby Op 115 (double bass, tape) 1988.
Moving Around Op 116 (flute, clarinet, violin, cello, piano) 1988.
Ten Pictures Op 118 (piano) 1988.
Trio basso Op 119 (viola, cello, double bass) 1989.

Vocal/choral:

Elegy Op 3 (tenor, mixed voices, orchestra: Thomas, "Do Not Go Gentle into That Good Night") 1976.
Two Songs Op 6 (voice, piano, cello; Ditlevsen) 1976.
Four Songs About the Seasons Op 7 (voice, piano) 1976.
Four Songs for Mixed Voices Op 12 (Schade) 1977.
Skisma Op 14 (soprano, orchestra; Ditlevsen) 1977.
The Flute Op 16 (soprano, flute, piano; Meyer) 1977.
Two Worldly Hymns Op 19 (soprano, violin, strings; Ditlevsen) 1977.
Thoughts in the Dark Op 35 (male voices; Ditlevsen) 1979.
Three Songs About Life and Death Op 36 (soprano, trombone, organ; Risbjerg Thomsen) 1979.
The Princess and the Pea Op 41 (musical fairy-tale after Andersen) 1980.
Three on a Line Op 45 (3 male voices) 1980.
About Life and Nature Op 46 (voice, violin; Housman) 1980.
Winter Sonata Op 51 (soprano, cello, double bass) 1981.
Eight Danish Songs Op 57 (voice, piano) 1981.
A Prayer of Pain Op 60 (boys' chorus, organ) 1981.
Sorrow Op 65 (soprano, mixed voices, oboe, piano) 1982.
Destruction Op 69 (soprano, accordion, hammer) 1983.
Why Don't They Listen? Op 78 (soprano, tenor, clarinet, organ) 1984.
Round of the Seasons Op 79 (mixed voices) 1984.
Driving in the Fog Op 84 (mezzo-soprano, piano) 1984.
Drama in Four Acts Op 89 (tenor, string quartet) 1985.
Questions Op 94 (soprano, violin, accordion) 1986.
My Relation to the Seasons Op 95 (soprano, flute, oboe, clarinet, harpsichord) 1986.
The Organist Op 96 (soprano, violin, organ) 1986.
A Woman's Nature Op 98 (soprano, flute, oboe, clarinet, bassoon, horn, harpsichord) 1986.
Summer Op 104 (soprano or tenor, piano, tape) 1987.
Yes-No Op 105 (soprano, contralto, alto, harpsichord) 1987.
Six Lives Op 107 (soprano, girls' choir, 2 women's choirs, flute, clarinet, violin, viola, cello) 1987.
Ditlevsen songs Op 108 (soprano, cello) 1988.
Sounds in the Park Op 111 (soprano, flute, bassoon, trumpet, trombone, violin, viola, cello, double bass) 1988.
Rehearsal Op 112 (soprano, flute, bassoon, trumpet, trombone, violin, viola, cello, double bass) 1988.
Jungle Music Op 117 (soprano, violin, percussion, tape) 1988.
Snake Op 120 (mixed chorus, tenor, piano; Lawrence) 1989.

* * *

It was the late 1970s before Gudrun Lund attached opus numbers to her works; Opus 1 is still tantalisingly absent. Though by no means as prolific as her notoriously hyperactive fellow-countrymen Niels Viggo Bentzon and Vagn Holmboe, she has nonetheless amassed an impressive body of work which, like Bentzon's in particular, encompasses a wide spectrum of both familiar and unexpected instrumental combinations. She has, for instance, written very effective solo pieces for accordion and bass trombone, while her *Destruction* from 1983 is rather menacingly scored for soprano, accordion and hammer.

Lund's music has grown simpler in style as its structures have gained in complexity. This has as little to do with the New Simplicity which played such a major role in modern Danish music, as it has with the so-called New Complexity associated with such composers as Brian Ferneyhough. Lund's style is entirely original and personal, though it draws eclectically on the full range of modern techniques and procedures, and her scores are marked by an imaginative use of serialism, graphic notation, *musique concrète*, and so on. Lund abandoned instrumental virtuosity along with her original metrically conservative and completely tonal style. Her more recent pieces have depended on a subtle interplay of relatively simple materials, a device which may draw some of its theoretical underpinning from American minimalism. Her use of tone-rows is carefully restricted and shows little of the ramifying complexity that has come to be associated with latter-day serialism; nor, though, are her rows used to suggest a tonal centre or as rather cosmetic alienation effects. Her recent music has been indisputably modern, related not so much to Bentzon's and Holmboe's inherently conservative "metamorphism" but rather to more radical American developments.

Patchwork draws on a very limited orchestral palette and builds into a work of very serviceable imagination, cleverly varied. It also hints, in its reference to a non-canonical art or craft, at a distinctively female sensibility, and this becomes an explicit theme in Lund's work of the 1980s. The chamber piece *Co-Existence* is the most radically structured of her works; the piano part is divided into four movements, but the double bass plays five, so the two performers overlap, breaking in the middle of each other's movements. She has also written a flute and viola duo in three and a half movements and there are elements of the same procedure in the *Five Duos* for wind quintet. The vocal piece *Driving in the Fog* distributes rhythmic patterns in much the same way, breaking down any sense of voice-plus-accompaniment in favour of a much more disorientated and improvisational grasping after meaning that becomes typical of Lund's vocal "setting". A similar, but timbral, opposition is used in the aptly titled *Uneven Partners* for flute and double bass, a work of decidedly American accent. Lund's abilities as a highly evocative colourist are evident in *Lonely Souls*, a gorgeously cadenced work for oboe, alto saxophone and organ. In all of these pieces, there is a basic lack of symmetry that lends even relatively abecedarian themes and motives a tremendous depth of association.

In the later 1980s, Lund has produced a series of self-written vocal pieces—*My Relation to the Seasons*, *A Woman's Nature*, *Summer* and *Yes-No*—that are among her most personal works. Her handling of voice is absolutely assured and always humane, with a strong leavening of humour. Titles like *Walking Along*, *Chase*, *Celebration* (for military band) and, especially, *Fun* underline her lack of interest in the grand attitudinizing that goes along with a great deal of orchestral writing even in the 1980s. If there is a single defining characteristic of a "female sensibility", then it is, perhaps, this faintly ironic refusal to be drawn into an aggressive and competitive intellectualism, a willingness to make statements quietly, with no universalising intent and with a calm disregard for aesthetic or generic convention. Lund is an important figure. She also makes music that is deeply enjoyable.

—Bea Weir

LUTOSŁAWSKI, Witold. Polish. Born in Warsaw, 25 January 1913. Educated: studied piano privately under J. Smidowicz, 1924–5; studied violin under Lidia Kmitowa, 1926–32; studied mathematics, Warsaw University, 1931–3; Warsaw Conservatory (piano under Jerzy Lefeld, composition under Witold Maliszewski), 1932–6, diplomas in piano and composition, 1936, 1937. Married Maria-Danuta Dygat in 1946. Performing pianist, 1932–5; served in Polish Army, from 1939, briefly captured by Nazis; clandestine performances in private houses, Warsaw, 1939–45; worked as piano duo with Andrezej Panufnik, Warsaw, 1940–4; worked with Polish Radio, 1945; conductor, debut 1952; member, programme committee, Warsaw Autumn Festival, 1956, from 1958; chair of programme council, Polish Music Publications; member, presidential committee, International Society for Contemporary Music, 1959–65; composition teacher, Berkshire Music Center, Tanglewood, Massachusetts, 1962; composition teacher, Dartington Hall, Devon, 1963, 1964; composer in residence, Dartmouth College, Hanover, New Hampshire, 1966; composition teacher, Aarhus Conservatory, Denmark, 1968; also taught composition at Stockholm Academy, Folkwang Hochschule für Musik, Essen, and Texas State University; vice-president, Polish Composers' Union, 1973–9. Recipient: City of Warsaw Music Prize, 1948; Polish Music Festival Prize, 1951; State Prizes, Poland, 1952, 1955, 1964, 1978; Prime Minister's Prize for Children's Music, 1954; prizes, Polish Composers' Union, 1959, 1973; 1st prizes, UNESCO Composers' Rostrum, Paris, 1959, 1964, 1968; prize, 1st class, Polish Ministry of Culture and Art, 1962; membership, Swedish Royal Academy of Music, 1962; 1st prize, Gesellschaft der Musikfreunde, Vienna, 1963; 1st prize, International Music Committee, 1963; National Prize, 1st class, 1964; International Koussevitzky Prize, 1964; Grand Prix du Disque, Paris, 1965; plaque, Freie Akademie der Kunste, Hamburg, 1966; honorary member, Free Academy of Arts, Hamburg, 1966; Herder Prize, 1967; Sonning Prize, 1967; extraordinary member, Academy of Arts, West Berlin, 1970; associate member, Germany Academy of Arts, East Germany, 1970; Prix *ad honorem*, President of France, 1971; Ravel Prize, 1971; Sibelius Prize, Wihuri, 1973; member, Bayerische Akademie der Schonen Kunste, Munich, 1973; corresponding member, American Academy of Arts and Letters, 1975, and Royal Academy of Music, London, 1976; City of Warsaw Prize, 1977; Order of Builders of People's Poland, 1977; honorary member, Guildhall School of Music, London, 1978; foreign associate, Académie des Beaux Arts, Paris, 1979; award of Polish Central European Society of Culture, 1979; member, European Academy of Arts, Sciences and Humanities, from 1980; honorary member, Wiener Konzertgesellschaft, from 1980; Commandeur de l'Ordre des Arts et des Lettres, France, 1982; Ernst von Siemens Musikpreis, 1983; Solidarity Award, 1984; University of Louisville Grawe Meyer Award for music composition (for *Symphony No 3*), 1985; UNESCO/International Music Council Award, 1985; Prize of Queen Sophia of Spain, 1985; Gold Medal, Royal Philharmonic Society, 1985; International Record Critics' Award (for *Symphony No 3*), 1986; *High Fidelity*/Grammy award, 1987; member, Académie Royale des Sciences, des Lettres et des Beaux Arts, Brussels, 1987; honorary member, Accademia Nazionale de Santa Cecilia, Rome, 1987. Honorary doctorates: Cleveland Institute of Music, 1971; University of Chicago, 1973; University of Warsaw, 1973; Northwestern University, Evanston, Illinois, 1974; University of Lancaster, 1975; University of Glasgow, 1977; Copernicus University, Torun, 1980; University of Durham, 1983; Jagiellonian University, Cracow, 1984; Royal Northern College of Music, Manchester, 1987; Queen's University, Belfast, 1987; Baldwin Wallace University, Berea, Ohio, 1987; University of Cambridge, 1987. Mailing address: UL Smiala 39, 01-523 Warsaw, Poland; or PAGART (Polish Artists Agency), Plac Zwyciestwa 9, 00-078 Warsaw, Poland.

Publishers: Polskie Wydawnictwo Muzycne, Warsaw; Chester Music, London.

Symphonies/orchestral:

Symphonic Variations 1938; broadcast Polish Radio, April 1939; first concert performance, Cracow, 17 June 1939. Recorded EMI ED 29 1172-1/1172-4.

Symphony No 1 1941–7; first performed Katowice, 6 April 1948.

Overture (strings) 1949; first performed Prague, 9 November 1949.

Mala suita/Little Suite (chamber orchestra) 1950, arranged for full orchestra 1951; first performed Warsaw, 20 April 1951.

Concerto for Orchestra 1950–4; first performed Warsaw, 26 November 1954. Recorded Philips 412 377 1PSP/4PSP.

Preludia taneczne/Dance Preludes (clarinet, harp, piano, percussion, strings; arranged from chamber piece) 1955; broadcast Polish Radio, 1955; first performed Aldeburgh, Suffolk, June 1963. Recorded Philips 416 817 1PH/4PH; Hyperion A66 215; Unicorn Kanchana DKPC 9066.

Muzyka zalobna/Funeral Music (string orchestra) 1958; first performed Katowice, 26 March 1958. Recorded Philips 412 377 1PSP/4PSP.

Three Postludes I—1958–63; II-III—1960; I first performed Geneva, 1 September 1963; first complete performance Cracow, 8 October 1965. Recorded (I only) EMI ED 29 1172-1/1172-4.

Gry weneckie/Venetian Games (chamber orchestra) 1961. Recorded Polski Nagrania PNCD 041.

Symphony No 2 1967; 2nd movement first performed Hamburg, 15 October 1966; first complete performance, Cracow, 8 October 1965. Recorded Polski Nagrania PNCD 041.

Livres pour orchestra 1968; first performed Hagen, Germany, 18 November 1968. Recorded Polski Nagrania PNCD 042.

Cello Concerto 1969–70; first performed London, 14 October 1970. Recorded Philips 416 817 1PH/4PH.

Preludes and Fugue (chamber string orchestra) 1972; first performed Graz, Austria, 12 October 1972. Recorded Polski Nagrania PNCD 043.

Mi-parti 1976; first performed Amsterdam, 22 October 1976. Recorded Polski Nagrania PNCD PNCD 043.

Variations on a Theme of Paganini (piano, orchestra) 1978; first performed Miami, Florida, 18 November 1979.

Novelette 1978–9; first performed Washington, D.C., 29 January 1980. Recorded Polski Nagrania PNCD 043.

Double Concerto (oboe, harp, orchestra) 1979–80. Recorded Philips 416 817 1PH/4PH.

Grave (cello, chamber strings) 1981, orchestrated 1982; first performed Paris, 26 August 1982.

Symphony No 3 1981–3; first performed Chicago, 29 September 1983. Recorded Philips 416 387-1PH/4PH.

Chain 1 (chamber orchestra) 1983; first performed London, 4 October 1983. Recorded Polski Nagrania PNCD 044.

Chain 2 (violin, orchestra) 1985; first performed Zurich, 31 January 1986. Recorded Polski Nagrania PNCD 044; Deutsche Grammophon DG 423 696 2.

Chain 3 1986; first performed San Francisco, 10 December 1986. Recorded Polski Nagrania PNCD 044.

Fanfare for Louisville (winds) 1986; first performed Louisville, Kentucky, 19 September 1986.
Piano Concerto 1988; first performed Salzburg, 19 August 1988.
Partita (violin, orchestra) 1988, orchestrated from chamber piece; first performed London, 17 October 1990.
Interlude 1989; first performed London, 17 October 1990.

Chamber/instrumental:

Sonata (piano) 1934; withdrawn.
Variations on a Theme of Paganini (2 pianos) 1941; first performed Warsaw, 1941. Recorded Philips 411 034 2; Polski Nagrania PNCD 045.
Bukoliki (piano) 1952.
Preludia taneczne/Dance Preludes (1st version; clarinet, piano) 1954; first performed Warsaw, 15 February 1955.
Dance Preludes (3rd version; flute, oboe, clarinet, bassoon, horn, solo strings) 1959; first performed Louny, 10 November 1959.
String Quartet 1964; first performed Stockholm, 12 March 1965. Recorded Pavane ADW7 149; Olympia OCD 328.
Sacher Variations (cello) 1975; first performed Zurich, 2 May 1976.
Epitaph (oboe, piano) 1979; first performed London, 3 January 1980. Recorded Polski Nagrania PNCD 045.
Grave (cello, piano) 1981; first performed Warsaw, 22 April 1981. Recorded Polski Nagrania PNCD 045.
Mini Overture (horn, 2 trumpets, trombone, tuba) 1982; first performed Lucerne, 11 March 1982. Recorded Chandos ABRD 1190.
Partita (violin, piano) 1984. Recorded Polski Nagrania PNCD 045.
Slides (flute, oboe, clarinet, bassoon, horn, percussion, piano, guitar, string quartet) 1988; first performed New York City, 1 December 1988.

Vocal/choral:

Twenty Polish Christmas Carols (voice, piano) 1946, revised 1984.
Two Nightingales (for children; SA chorus, piano; Tuwim) 1947; first performed Cracow, 26 January 1978.
About Mr Tralalinski (SSA chorus, piano; Tuwim) 1947; first performed Cracow, 26 January 1948.
Strawchain and Other Songs (SA chorus, flute, oboe, 2 clarinets, bassoon; or piano) 1950–1; broadcast Polish Radio, 1951.
Three Children's Songs (SSA chorus, piano; Krzemieniecka, Barto) 1951; broadcast Warsaw 1951.
Tryptyk slaski/Silesian Triptych (soprano, orchestra) 1951; first performed Warsaw, 2 December 1951.
Five Songs (female voice, piano or 30 instruments; Illakowicz) 1956–8. Recorded Polski Nagrania PNCD 045.
Trzy poematy Henri Michaux/Three Poems of Henri Michaux (20-part SATB chorus, orchestra) 1962–3; first performed Zagreb, 9 May 1963. Recorded Polski Nagrania 041.
Paroles tissées (tenor, orchestra; Chabrun) 1965; first performed Aldeburgh, Suffolk, 20 June 1965. Recorded Polski Nagrania PNCD 042.
Les Espaces du sommeil (baritone, orchestra) 1975; first performed Berlin, 12 April 1978. Recorded Philips 416 387 1PH/4PH.
Seventeen Polish Christmas Carols (soprano, small female chorus) 1984; first performed London, 5 December 1985.
Chantefleurs et chantefables (soprano, orchestra) 1991; first performed London, 8 August 1991.

Publications

By Lutosławski, "Nowy utwor na orkiestre symfoniczna" [on *Symphony No 2*], in *Res facta*, 4 (6), 1970.

On Lutosławski: Ove Nordwall (ed), *WL*, Stockholm, 1968; Z. Zielinski, "Droga tworczosci WL" ["The Development of WL's work"], in *Ruch muzyczny*, 9, 1968; M. Piotrowska, "Aleatoryzm WL na tle genezy tego kierunku w muzyce wspolczesnej" ["WL's Use of Aleatory Technique in Relation to Contemporary Musical Developments in That Field"], in *Muzyka* 14(3), 1969; Tadeusz Kaczynski, *Conversations with WL*, Cracow, 1972, London, 1984; L.G. Rappoport, *Vitol'd Luitoslavsky*, Moscow, 1972; B. Pociej, *WL a wartosc muzyki* ["Assessing WL's Music"], Cracow, 1976; Balint Andras Vargas, *WL Profile*, London, 1976; Richard Duffalo, (interview) in *Trackings*, Oxford, 1989.

* * *

Along with Krzszytof Penderecki, 20 years his junior, Witold Lutosławski is the best-known and most highly valued of the composers to benefit from the loosening of artistic restrictions after the 1956 uprising in Poland, an event which set the stage for a remarkable upsurge in genuinely creative composition in that country.

Lutosławski spent the war years arranging songs and playing piano in a cafe in Warsaw with fellow composer Andrzej Panufnik, although his transcriptions were ultimately destroyed. His pre-war compositions, like the *Symphonic Variations*, reflect the influence of Karol Szymanowski, a dominant figure in pre-war Polish music.

The immediate post-war liberation, in which he finished the densely argued and almost atonal First Symphony he had worked on since 1941, was short-lived, and Zhadanov's decree that "Dissonance is the enemy of the people" put paid to any early development of that compositional style.

Instead, he turned to an economical and highly lucid use of material derived from folk songs, which he recast in a vigorous, distinctly Bartókian vein. The most celebrated work of this period is the attractive *Concerto for Orchestra*, evidence in itself that the composer did not allow imposed necessity to compromise the quality of the work he was able to produce. His five *Dance Preludes* for clarinet and orchestra from this period are now enjoying a more recent but no less deserved popularity.

Lutosławski returned to atonality in the first major work under the new freedom from artistic repression, his *Funeral Music* for string orchestra, dedicated to the memory of Bartók. The four-movement work employs serial techniques, and makes much use of subdivisions within the orchestra, but remains a highly expressive and intensely personal document.

A hearing of John Cage's *Concerto for Prepared Piano and Orchestra* sharpened Lutosławski's appetite for experiment, this time with aleatory procedures, albeit within a strictly controlled framework. The orchestral work *Venetian Games* is the first composition in which he utilises limited chance procedures in the tempos.

The composer followed this work with further such experiments in *Three Poems of Henri Michaux* for chorus and orchestra and the *String Quartet*, and they have remained a recurring feature of his work since.

The Second Symphony, closely followed by the *Livres pour orchèstre* and a gripping *Cello Concerto* commissioned by Mstislav Rostropovich, initiated a period in which he has combined both closely and loosely notated music within his scores, concentrating on creating a finely crafted, even luxuriant harmonic and textural whole from the combination.

His developing love for delicate textures and an almost exotically interweaved tonal colouration (often ascribed to the influence of Debussy and Ravel) are evident in the Third Symphony and other works of the period, such as *Les Espaces du sommeil* for baritone and orchestra, the charming and witty *Double Concerto* for oboe, harp and chamber orchestra or the orchestral works *Mi-parti*, *Chain 1* and *Chain 2*.

The Third Symphony, one of his most closely argued and expressive scores, is completely notated, but calls for passages of "aleatory counterpoint", in which individual instruments (or small groupings) are directed by the composer to play thematically derived and related notes against the main progression of the two-movement work. Lutosławski prefers that his elements of chance actually leave little to chance, but remain under the close control of the composer, rather than be handed over to the whims of the performers in the prescribed Cagean manner.

The structure of the continuous two-movement work, in which the first movement sketches in thematic and motivic material which engages the listener without permitting the satisfaction of release, a culmination reserved for the second movement, is a kind of allusive compacting of sonata form, and a compelling study not only in a highly distinctive musical language, but also in refined musical architecture.

Lutosławski has not been the most prolific of composers, but has characteristically worked on pieces over extended periods of time, which may in part account for the highly refined sense of structure and meticulously imaginative orchestration which his compositions unfailingly reveal.

—Kenny Mathieson

M

MA Shui-long. Republican Chinese/Taiwanese. Born in Keelung, Taiwan, 17 July 1939. Educated at National Taiwan Academy of the Arts, Taipei, 1959–64, diploma; Regensburg Kirchenmusik, Germany, 1972–5, diploma. Married Hau Zi-Chen, 29 March 1969; 2 children. Professor, department of music, Seechow University, Taipei, 1975–81; chair, music department, National Taiwan Academy of the Arts, 1981–2; chair, department of music, 1982–7, and dean of academic affairs, since 1987, National Institute of the Arts, Taipei; member of board of trustees, Council for Cultural Planning Development of the Executive Yuan, since 1988; chair, Republic of China committee, Asian Composers' League, since 1990. Recipient: Chung-Shan Liberal Arts Award, National Liberal Arts Foundation, 1977; Wu San-Lien Liberal Arts Composition Award; Fulbright Scholarship, 1986–7. Mailing address: 5F, No. 11, Ln 20, Ta-Chih Street, Taipei, Taiwan 10497, Republic of China.

Publisher: Republic of China Committee, Asian Composers' League, 3F, No. 10, Ln. 11, King-Men Street, Taipei, Taiwan, Republic of China.

Symphonies/orchestral:

Fantasia (flute, orchestra) 1974; first performed Regensburg, 1975.
The Peacock Flies Southeast (symphonic poem) 1977; first performed T'ai-Chung, Taiwan, 1977.
Playing with Lights 1977; first performed Taipei, 1977.
Aurora (symphonic band) 1979; first performed Taipei, 1979.
Bamboo Flute Concerto 1980; first performed Taipei, 1981.

Chamber/instrumental:

Classical Suite (piano) 1962; first performed Taipei, 1962.
Sonata (piano) 1963; first performed Taipei, 1963.
Sonata (violin, piano) 1963; first performed Taipei, 1964.
Trio (flute, cello, piano) 1967; first performed Taipei, 1967.
Taiwan Suite (piano) 1967; first performed Taipei, 1968.
A Sketch of the Rainy Port (piano) 1969; first performed Taipei, 1969.
String Quartet No 1 1970; first performed Taipei, 1971.
Sonata (piano) 1975; first performed Regensburg, 1975.
Flute Fantasia (solo flute) 1975; first performed Regensburg, 1975.
Dialogue (violin, piano) 1975; first performed Regensburg, 1975.
Toccata and Fugue (organ) 1975; first performed Regensburg, 1975.
Expectation (10 traditional Chinese instruments) 1976; first performed Taipei, 1976.
Capriccio (cello, piano) 1978; first performed Taipei, 1978.
Shui Long Yin (pipa) 1979; first performed Taipei, 1979.
String Quartet No 2 1982; first performed Taipei, 1983.
Image & Idea (hsiao/shakuhachi, 4 cellos) 1988; first performed Taipei, 1989.

Vocal/choral:

Dusk (soprano, bass, piano) 1963; first performed Taipei, 1963.
Five Poems from the Tang Dynasty (voice, piano) 1964; first performed Taipei, 1965.
Nostalgic Melody (soprano, piano) 1970; first performed Tainan, 1971.
Suona and Voice (suona, voice, piano) 1978; first performed Taipei, 1976.
The Blue Brook (unaccompanied chorus) 1978; first performed Taipei, 1978.
Four Songs (voice, piano) 1979; first performed Taipei, 1979.
Ching Ming (mixed chorus, bamboo flute, feng-lou) 1979; first performed Taipei, 1979.
Lament of Tou O (voice, suona, percussion) 1980, revised 1987; first performed Taipei, 1980; revised version first performed New York City, 1987.
I Am (soprano, hsiao, 9 percussion) 1985; first performed Taipei, 1985.

Other:

Collection of Chinese Folk Songs (4 volumes; unaccompanied mixed chorus) 1976–8; first performed Taipei, 1978.
Collection of Chinese Folk Songs (3 volumes; chorus) 1976–8; first performed Taipei, 1978.
Liao Tien-Ting (ballet; orchestra) 1979; first performed Taipei, 1979.
Thirty-Two Piano Pieces from Chinese Folk Songs (for young players) 1979–80; first performed Taipei, 1980.

PUBLICATIONS

By Ma: *Counterpoint*, Taipei, 1972; *Introduction to Twelve Tone*, Taipei, 1976.

* * *

Ma Shui-Long is considered to be perhaps the most influential figure in contemporary Taiwanese music. He has had a twofold impact, both as a distinguished composer and as an educator.

His music reveals his consistent search for a means of musical expression that combines traditional Chinese idioms and materials with the contemporary Western techniques to which he was exposed as a student in West Germany. He has made a particular study of such elements of traditional music as instrumental timbre, vocal technique and the concept of time. His use of traditional instruments—such as pipa, shuona, feng-lou and shakuhachi—and his understanding of traditional methods and techniques make him one of the few composers able to integrate Eastern and Western elements within the compass of a single composition, and without strain or special pleading.

Ma's musical aesthetic is fundamentally concerned with the relationship between man and society. He is neither a purist nor an academic abstractionist, but believes that music is a means to express human emotion in all its forms and moods. His music is deeply rooted in the traditions and cultural values of present-day Taiwan, and conveys much of his country's distinctive and sometimes highly complex historical role, sitting off-shore of Communist China and looking largely to the West for political and cultural support. Nonetheless, Ma finds most of his material in the daily life of Taiwan and in its regional musical traditions, particularly the "nanquan". In search of a personal style, Ma explains that "I looked into Chinese language to find my musical language and rhythm". The results are impressively crafted, self-consistent and absolutely individual in manner.

Ma's concerns as an educator are related to his musical ones. Long convinced of the need to offer artistic professionals a grounding in both oriental and occidental techniques, he was at last able to give these demands institutional shape when in 1982 he established the first such curriculum in Taiwan at the National Institute of the Arts music department.

An influential and much respected figure, Ma is an important figure whose reputation in the West seems likely to grow as his work becomes better known.

—Chew Shyh-Ji

MACEDA, Jose. Filipino. Born in Manila, 31 January 1917. Educated at Ecole Normale de Musique, Paris (piano under Alfred Cortot), 1937–41, diplome de virtuosité; Queen's College, New York City, 1950–2, A.B.; Columbia University, New York City, 1952; Northwestern University, Evanston, Illinois, University of Chicago, Indiana University, Bloomington, 1957–8; studied *musique concrète* under Pierre Schaeffer, Radio Télévision Française, 1958; University of California (under E. Robert Schmitz), 1961–3, Ph.D. Married Madelyn Clifford, 21 April 1954; 4 daughters. Professional pianist, 1937–57; professor, 1946–88, and professor emeritus, since 1988, University of the Philippines, Quezon City; member, editorial board, *Acta Musicologica*, 1978–86, and *International Review of Aesthetics and Sociology of Music* (Yugoslavia), since 1980. Recipient: Guggenheim Award, 1957–8; Rockefeller Grant, 1961–3; Republic Cultural Award, Philippines, 1968; Ordre des Palmes Académiques, 1978; Outstanding Research Award, University of the Philippines, 1985; University of the Philippines, composer's award, 1985; John D. Rockefeller Award, Asian Cultural Council, New York, 1988; Tanglaw ng Lahi, Atteneo University, 1988; Gawad sa Sining (art prize), Cultural Centre of the Philippines, 1989. Mailing address: Department of Music Research, College of Music, University of the Philippines, Quezon City 1101, Philippines.

Publisher: none.

Compositions (which do not fall into conventional Western categories or genres):

Ugma-Ugma (native instruments and chorus; "blocks of sound alternate with tense-high voices") 1963; first performed Los Angeles, 1963.

Agungan (families of gongs; "decays, densities, colours, gongs struck with sticks, hands, sliding palms") 1965; first performed Quezon City, 1965.

Kubing (bamboo instruments, men's voices) 1966; first performed Quezon City, 1966.

Pagsamba (ritual music for a circular auditorium; 100 voices, 116 instrumentalists, chorus of 25 men; Tagalog text of Catholic Mass) 1968; first performed Quezon City, 1968.

Cassettes 100 (100 participants with cassette recorders play together a music with a simple choreography) 1970; first performed Manila, 1971.

Ugnayan (music for 20 radio stations; thousands of people within a radius of 100 kilometres of Manila played with their transistor radios in parks and listened to a meditative music) 1974; first performed Manila, 1974; taped version, Bonn, 1980.

Udlot-Udlot (drone, mixed instruments, voices; 1000 performers in open-air ritual) 1975; first performed Manila and Quezon City, 1975.

Ading (200 performers; 100 instrumentalists, 100 voices, and the public; "drones, melodic cells") 1978; first performed Quezon City, 1978.

Aroding (40 mouth harps, men's voices) 1983; first performed Quezon City, 1983.

Siasid (bamboo percussion, 5 blown bamboo tubes, 5 violins) 1983; first performed Quezon City, 1983.

Suling-Suling (10 flutes, 10 buzzers, 10 flat gongs) 1985; first performed Manila, 1985.

Strata (10 buzzers, 10 sticks, 5 tam-tams, 5 flutes, 5 cellos, 5 guitars) 1988; first performed Quezon City, 1988.

Dissemination (5 flutes, 5 violins, 5 oboes, 5 horns, 3 cellos, 2 double basses, gong, 2 whistles) 1990; first performed Manila, 1990.

PUBLICATIONS

By Maceda: "A Search for an Old and a New Music in South East Asia", in *Acta Musicologica*, 51(1), 1979; "Maschine, Bordun und Bevolkerung, Bausteine für eine neue Musik in Asien", in *NZ Zeitschrift für Musik*, 5, 1980; "Philippines", in *New Grove's Dictionary of Music*, 1980; *A Manual of a Field of Music Research with Special Reference to South East Asia*, UNESCO/University of the Philippines, 1981; "Xenakis, l'architecture, la musique", in *Regards sur Iannis Xenakis*, Paris, 1981; "A Cure of the Sick *bpagipat* in Dulawan, Cotobato (Philippines)", in *Acta Musicologica*, 56(1), 1984; "A Concept of Time in a Music of South East Asia", in *Ethnomusicology* 30(1), 1986; "In Search of a Source of Hemitonic and Anhemitonic Scales in South East Asia", in *Acta Musicologica*, 2, 1990; many technical and (ethno)-musicological publications.

On Maceda: Hans von Schurmann, (interview) in *Bonner Stadtanzeiger*, 1980; Felipe M. De Leon, Jr, "He Introduced Us to New Music But JM Remains Unknown to Many", in *Malaya*, 17 March 1988; Vernon Go, "*Dissemination*—Redefining That Which Is Rhythm and Melody", in *Starweek*, 22 July 1990; Armando Manalo, "JM: Avant-Garde", in *Philippines Journal*, 26 July 1990.

Jose Maceda comments:

I started music composition after I began studies on the musics of South East Asia and ethnomusicology in general. My first works in the 1960s employed native musical instruments, bamboo and gongs in blocks of sound, densities, colours and linguistic effects, the vocabulary of that period. In the 1970s, I prepared a music for hundreds of performers—

carrying cassette tape-recorders or transistor radios—deployed in open space, moving inside buildings, with choreography. The vast numbers distribute music in space: the more the participants the more the space. Radio transmitters, receivers and recorders become musical instruments. *Udlot-Udlot* (1975) probes into basic musical elements—a pulse, mixed sounds, one-tone melody—written for simple instruments that anyone can play. The music has an economic symbolism—a division of labour for many, rather than a special task for a few.

The early 1980s mark a more moderate number of performers still employing native instruments. In *Aroding* (1983), a juxtaposition of the twanging of 40 bamboo jaw harps with closely related pitch-intervals form a gauze-like screen, a sheer curtain to a network of fixed intervals of seven male voices. *Siasid* (1983) and *Suling-Suling* (1985) employ blown tubes, violins and flutes which work in groups, thus obscuring their melodic lines. In *Strata* (1988), five flutes, five cellos and five guitars form separate layers with crisscrossing pitches blurring each other, approaching the opaque colours of bamboo, wood and bronze instruments.

Dissemination (1990) divides 25 orchestral instruments into five groups of colours and ranges—flutes, violins, oboes, horns, cellos/double basses. Every group is a unit spectrum which when superimposed one on top of the other builds a tall edifice sometimes viewed from the first floor, sometimes the third floor, sometimes all the floors sounding together. *Dissemination* has in mind its transformation into very narrow or very wide spectra that only computers can assemble.

It seems apparent that ethnomusicology and a slow but ever-increasing change in electro-magnetic engineering influence my works. Audiences say that my music evokes an atmosphere of ritual; it is grave and serious.

Music composition is an exploration of the world. At the time of the Renaissance, the prevailing view was the individuality of man, a quest for his spirit now including all music cultures, a most enriching musical experience which, however, does not necessarily identify a concept of life that befits the modern world.

It is technology rather than notions of past cultures that appears to shape a new music. Indeed, individual cultural concepts and use of all kinds of instruments affect musical character, especially if they can be integrated with technology. Technology heeds not the particularities of pentatonic scales, equal temperament, improvisation, chance or rhythm. It forces us into another musical dimension, in tests of perception of maximum densities, speeds, heights, a discernment of colour-blends compressed into very narrow or very wide spectra—all of which may be applied to the computer whose hidden qualities may be revealed less through extremes of technique impossible with existing instruments, and more in a discovery of an organization or language of such extremes.

* * *

The first truly Asian composer of the 20th century, by common consent, is Jose Maceda. While Asian avant-garde composers emulated their Western colleagues, Maceda remained true to the Philippine spirit.

As the foremost ethnomusicologist on Southeast Asian music in the Philippines and the leading composer in the country, his music reveals his efforts to find a force of musical expression which is new and yet rooted in the Philippine culture. His employment of native instruments, his preference for open-air spaces, his use of massive human forces and performance/audience duality—all these demonstrate the influence of the music and musical thoughts of Southeast Asian rural traditions. Maceda's understanding of the dimensions of native tradition and his ability to integrate these elements into his music have made him a genuinely *Asian* avant-garde composer.

Maceda's musical aesthetic lies in the relationship between man and society. Music as ritual is one of the important aspects in understanding Asian music; Maceda explains further, "It is in ritual that music becomes an integral part of the ritual where all members of the society are participants—performers, dancers, and the whole audience made up the whole musical event."

Maceda is concerned with man's relationship to his natural environment, and aims to recreate in his works the richness of the sounds that abound in it. He says that "the sound they (villagers) produced are sounds heard frequently . . . These sounds may be heard in the open air, almost anywhere, and even played within places of abode, their sounds travel beyond their confines . . . There is less interest in refining or perfecting the make of a few musical instruments. A musical interest lies in a diversity of sounds which allow for a freer use of musical elements." It is not difficult then to understand the open-air spaces in place of auditoriums and the employment of native instruments (such as bamboo instruments and gongs) over Western instruments. (He rarely requires Western instruments except in *Cassettes 100* where he uses a contrabass and a violin.)

As an avant-garde composer, Maceda examined the musical elements (such as the concept of time, instrumental timbre, vocal techniques, drone and melody, and density of sound found in nature) exhibited in village music and searched for an ultimate solution in using these elements in his music. Maceda defined drone as a periodic reiteration or a continuous playing of one or more tones which form a block upon which a melody circulates, and melody as consisting of a permutation, combination or an arrangement of two or more tones with or without pitch. Maceda classified further six forms of combining drone and melody—"drone alone; two or more drones sound simultaneously; drone and melody are consecutive, not simultaneous; drone accompanies melody; several drones and one melody; and several people each play a drone to make a melody." Combinations of these can easily be found in his music, for example, *Udlot-Udlot*, *Ading*, and *Ugnayan*. Like his avant-garde contemporaries, Maceda also explored the rich vocal qualities in native Philippine singing styles. *Kubing*, for example, is a result of such studies where vocal plosives, stops, clicks, vowel colors, glissando trill, uncertain pitches, and speech-like phones are the essential musical elements of the work.

Massive human forces, drones as repetitive patterns and melody as permutation result in a unique manner of orchestration where a large ensemble is required. The notation resulting from such orchestration is a complex one of layers involving independent rhythmic and melodic patterns where no two layers contain the same pattern. Moreover, the patterns in each layer undergo constant transformation. This concept of orchestration is typical of Southeast Asian ensemble composing.

In his music, Maceda has successfully transformed the rich treasure of folk material and has demonstrated the plausibility of writing truly "Asian music".

—Chew Shyh-Ji

MÂCHE, François-Bernard. French. Born in Clermont-Ferrand, 4 April 1935. Educated at Ecole Normale Supérieure, 1955–8, diploma in Greek archaeology, 1957, *agrégation* in classical literature, 1958; Conservatoire National Supérieur de Musique, Paris (composition under Olivier Messiaen), 1959–61. Lieutenant de réserve, French Army. Married Marie-Luce Staib, 25 May 1973; 1 daughter. Lecturer in Greek archaeology, 1958–9, and professor of classical philology, University of Paris, 1962–83; director of Groupe de Recherche Musicales, 1962; professor of ancient Greek, Sarah Lawrence College in Paris, 1968; president of French Section of I.S.C.M., 1978–81; professor of musicology, University of Strasbourg, since 1983. Recipient: Prix Italia, 1977; national doctorate, 1980; Prix Chartier de l'Académie Française, 1984; Grand Prix National de la Musique, 1988; commandeur de l'Ordre des Arts et des Lettres, 1990. Mailing address: 83 rue Vieille du Temple, 75003 Paris, France.

Publisher: Durand.

Symphonies/orchestral:

La Peau du silence 1962, version for large orchestra, 1966; another version, 1970; first performed Tokyo, 24 October 1986; large orchestra version first performed Warsaw, 24 September 1968; revised version first performed Strasbourg, 12 January 1971. Recorded Radio-France SRF 1001.

Synergies 1963; first performed Paris, 18 March 1963. Recorded Philips 836894 DSY.

Le Son d'une voix (chamber orchestra) 1964; first performed Warsaw, 23 September 1966.

Rituel d'oubli (wind, percussion, tape) 1969; first performed Strasbourg, 11 June 1970.

Répliques 1969; first performed Royan, 3 April 1969.

Rambaramb (orchestra, tape) 1972; broadcast Radio France, 8 May 1973.

Le Jonc à trois glumes 1974; first performed Seillans, 8 July, 1974.

Andromède (large orchestra; with 3 pianos, 2 choirs: 12/60 voices) 1979; broadcast Radio France, 4 June 1980.

Chamber/instrumental:

Duo (violin, piano) 1956; first performed Bilthoven, The Netherlands, 3 September 1957.

Canzone I (trumpet, cornet/2nd trumpet, horn, trombone, tuba) 1957, film version 1960; first performed Paris, 16 June 1960.

Volumes (7 trombones/4 horns and 3 trombones, 2 percussion, 2 pianos, 12/4/2-track tape) 1960; first performed Paris, 30 June 1960. Recorded BAM-AZ LD 071.

Canzone II (trumpet, cornet/2nd trumpet, horn, trombone, tuba) 1963; first performed Paris, 15 February 1963. Recorded Erato STU 70860.

Sporanges (harpsichord, violin) 1965.

Canzone III (3 trumpets, 4 trombones) 1967; broadcast Radio France, 13 February 1969.

Canzone V (violin, 3 double basses, theatrical set) 1969; first performed Blanc-Mesnil, 20 March 1988.

Kemit (darboukka or zarb) 1970; first performed Royan, 16 April 1973. Recorded Erato STU 70860/9109 GU.

Korwar (modern harpsichord, tape) 1972; first performed Bourges, 30 June 1972. Recorded Erato STU 70860/9109 GU.

Temes Nevinbur (2 pianos, 2 percussion, tape) 1973; first performed Royan, 16 April 1973. Recorded Erato STU 70860.

Naluan (flute, clarinet, 1/2 percussion, piano, violin, viola, cello, double bass, tape) 1974; first performed Baden-Baden, 8 July 1974.

Marae (6 amplified percussion, tape) 1974; first performed Royan, 25 March 1975.

Solstice (modern harpsichord, organ) 1975; first performed Royan, 28 March 1975. Recorded Erato STU 71266.

Parthenocissus Peverelliana (string quartet) 1976; first performed Paris, 5 May 1976.

Kassandraa (2 oboes/1 cor anglais, clarinet, bass clarinet, bassoon, contrabassoon, trumpet, 2 trombones, 3 percussion, 2 pianos, tape) 1977; broadcast Radio France, 16 October 1977. Recorded INA-GRM 9107.

Areg (piano—4 hands) 1977; broadcast Radio France, 9 December 1977.

Octuor Op 35 (clarinet, bassoon, horn, 2 violins, viola, cello, double bassoon) 1977; first performed Paris, 20 June 1977.

Aera (xylophone, 2 marimbas, 3 vibraphones, 19 Thai gongs, timbales, tubular bells; 6 players) 1978; first performed Paris, 30 March 1979.

Amorgos (2 bassoons, 2 trombones, 2 percussion/electric organ, piano, 2 violins, viola, cello, double bass, tape) 1979; first performed Metz, 16 November 1979. Recorded INA-GRM 9107.

Toin Theoin (2 clarinets) 1979; first performed Blanc-Mesnil, 27 February 1980.

Sopiana (flute, piano, tape ad lib) 1980; first performed Pecs, Hungary, 12 July 1980. Recorded INA-GRM 9107; RCI 650.

Nocturne (piano/preferably Bosendorfer Imperial, tape/realised on Upic) 1981; first performed Middleburg, The Netherlands, 4 July 1981.

Anaphores (modern harpsichord, percussion/1 player: vibraphone, marimba, chimes, 12 Thai gongs, 9 tam-tams, gong) 1981; broadcast Radio France, 1 March 1982. Recorded Erato NUM 5034.

Autonomie (piano—4 hands; or 2 harpsichords; or marimba—4 hands; or 2 marimbas) 1981; first performed Boulogne-Billancourt, 22 March 1982.

Phénix (vibraphone, 9 tam-tams; 1 player) 1982; first performed Peking, 28 September 1982.

Aulodie (oboe, tape; versions for soprano saxophone and for piccolo clarinet) 1983; first performed Amsterdam, 25 June 1983. Recorded Polyart ADDA 5304/581047.

Styx (2 pianos—8 hands) 1984; first performed Aix-en-Provence, 3 July 1984.

Lethe (2 pianos—8 hands) 1985; first performed Warsaw, 22 September 1985.

Iter Memor (cello, Kurzweil 250 piano/Midi piano with Akai S900) 1985; broadcast Radio France, 12 November 1985.

Heol an Ankou (organ, 3 trombones) 1985; first performed Rennes, 28 November 1985.

Uncas (flute, clarinet, percussion, 2 Mirages/2 Midi pianos with 2 Akai S900, Voicetracker, 2 violins, viola, cello, tape) 1986; first performed Paris, 9 June 1986.

Eridan Op 57 (string quartet) 1986; broadcast Radio France, 17 January 1987.

Mesarthin (2 pianos) 1987; first performed Blanc-Mesnil, 20 March 1988.

Aliunde (clarinet/contrabass clarinet, soprano, percussion/including Indian tablas, Midi piano with sequencer and Akai S900) 1988; first performed London, 4 July 1988.

Tempora (3 claviers échantilloneurs Akai S900, sequencer) 1988; first performed Paris, 27 February 1989.

Figures (bass clarinet, vibraphone) 1989.

Guntur Madu (modern harpsichord) 1990.
Khnoum (échantilloneur Akai S1000, 5 percussion) 1990.
Guntur Sari (organ) 1990.

Vocal/choral:

Safous mêlé (alto solo, 4 sopranos, 4 altos, 2 flutes, 2 oboes, 4 percussion, harp) 1959; first performed Paris, 5 October 1963.
Nuit blanche (reciter, tape; Artaud) 1966; first performed Warsaw, 1966.
Canzone IV (2 sopranos, alto, tenor, bass) 1968; first performed Paris, 1 April 1968.
Danäe (3 sopranos, 3 altos, 3 tenors, 3 basses, percussion; 12 damarus for the singers) 1970; first performed Persepolis, 3 September 1970. Recorded Barclay 995013.
Rituel (pour Les Mangeurs d'ombre) (3 sopranos, 3 altos, 3 tenors, 3 basses; percussion/1 player: 4 gongs, 4 temple blocks, maracas, whips) 1979; first performed Bordeaux, 16 May 1979.
Temboctou (2 sopranos, 2 mezzo-sopranos, 3 baritones, tenor, bass, 2 trombones, guitar, percussion, 2 medieval reeds, clarinet, electronics, tape) 1982; first performed Colmar, 16 June 1982.
Rasna (No 2 of the *Trois Chants sacrés*; solo voice) 1982; first performed Paris, 5 December 1984.
Muwatalli (No 1 of the *Trois Chants sacrés*; mezzo-soprano/ baritone, percussion) 1984; first performed Paris, 5 December 1984.
Cassiopée (SATB choir, percussion/2 players: 6 timbales, gong, 2 cymbals) 1988; broadcast Radio France, 20 March 1989.
Maponos (No 3 of the *Trois Chants sacrés*; solo voice; low-pitched drum) 1990.

Other:

Prélude (tape) 1959; first performed Paris, 1 June 1959. Recorded Philips 836894 DSY.
Lanterne magique (tape) 1959; first performed Paris, 23 June 1959.
Terre de feu (tape) 1963; first performed Warsaw, 22 September 1966. Recorded BAM-AZ 30 LD 072; Candide-Vox CE 31025.
Soleil rugueux (tape) 1965; first performed Viitasaari, Finland, 29 July 1987. Recorded Scherchen EPML 48 17.
Nuit (tape; as for *Nuit blanche*) 1966, 1971; first performed Royan, 16 April 1973.
Agiba (tape) 1971; broadcast Radio France, 8 May 1973.
Da Capo (organ, 2 percussion, 3 medieval reed-players, 10 jesters, sound environment, tape) 1976; first performed Avignon, 15 July 1976.
Regimen (tape; No 1 of the *Quatre Phonographies de l'eau*) 1980; first performed Avignon, 12 July 1980.
Ianassa (tape; No 2 of the *Quatre Phonographies de l'eau*) 1980; first performed Avignon, 12 July 1980.
Proteus (tape; No 3 of the *Quatres Phonographies de l'eau*) 1980; first performed Avignon, 12 July 1980.
Speio (tape; No 4 of the *Quatre Phonographies de l'eau*) 1980; first performed Avignon, 12 July 1980.
Hyperion (tape; realised on Upic) 1981; first performed Paris, 19 June 1981.
La Traversée de l'Afrique (tape, realised on Kurzweil 250) 1985; first performed Buenos Aires, 28 August 1985.
Tithon (tape; realised on Upic) 1989; first performed Lille, 19 October 1989.

PUBLICATIONS

By Mâche: "Connaissance des structures sonores", in *Revue Musicale*, May 1959; "Synthèse experimentale" (concert programme), *Groupe de Recherches Musicales*, 30 June 1960; "Le Réalisme en musique", in *Cahiers d'Etudes de Radio-Télévision*, Paris, September/December 1960; "Le Son et la musique", in *Mercure de France*, November 1963; "Musique et logique formelle", in *Mercure de France*, February 1964; "L'Art d'aujourd'hui", in *Revue d'Esthétique*, August–December 1964; "La Couleur grecque chez Xenakis", in *Encyclopédie des Musiques Sacrées*, Paris, 1968; "La Domaine Musicale, in *Nouvelle Revue Française*, March 1969; "Les Musiques artificielles", in *Diagrammes du Monde*, April 1969; "Neuf Journées de musique contemporaine", in *Nouvelle Revue Française*, December 1969; "Une Ville sonore", catalogue to *Mutations* exhibition, Ceret, 1971; "The Nonesuch Guide to Electronic Music", in *World of Music*, Kassel/ Basle/Paris/London, 1971; "La Musique a-t-elle la parole? Méthodes linguistiques et musicologie", in *Musique en Jeu*, November 1971; "La Création musicale d'aujourd'hui", in *Cultures* (Unesco), 1973; "Surréalisme et musique", in *Nouvelle Revue Française*, December 1974; "Le Concert acousmatique a-t-il un avenir", in *Cahiers Recherche-Musique*, October 1977; "Les Mal entendus; compositeurs des années 70", in *Revue Musicale*, November 1978; "L'Age Freudien de la musique", in *Panorama de la Musique*, January 1980; "Situation de la création musicale", in *Colloque SIMV/* Festival de Lille, November 1980; "Considérations biomusicologiques", in *Interface*, 11(1), 1982; contribution to Rio and Rostain, *L' Opéra mort ou vif*, Paris, 1982; "La Musique égale du mythe", in *Silences*, 1, 1985; "L'Analyse mélodique", in *International Review of the Aesthetics and Sociology of Music*, Zagreb, 1986; "La Musique au naturel", in *Les Cahiers du CREM*, March 1987; "L'Ellenismo di Xenakis", in *Xenakis*, Turin, 1988; "Le Mythe avant la lettre", in *Art, Mythe et Création*, Dijon, 1988.

On Mâche: Maurice Fauré, "Dans le laboratoire de la musique concrète", in *Les Lettres Nouvelles*, June 1959; Martine Cadieu, (interview) in *Les Lettres Françaises*, July 1968; Edith Walter, "Dialogue avec FBM", in *Harmonie*, 87, 1973; G.J. Faccarello, "FBM, mouvement purement logique et pure logique du mouvement", in *Musique de Tous les Temps*, 16, 1974; Jean-Jacques Nattiez, *Fondements d'une Sémiologie de la Musique*, 1975; Domitille Roy, "FBM, le plaisir du son", in *Culture & Communication*, 9, 1978; Jean-Michel De Montremy, (interview) in *La Croix*, 1980; Brigitte Massin, "FBM: l'âge freudien de la musique", in *Panorama de la musique*, 1980; Miriam Rovsing Olsen, (interview) in *Dansk Musik Tidsskrift*, 5, 1980; Daniel Charles, "Le Musicien et ses modèles", liner to disc INA-GRM 9107; Francis Bayer, "Sous le signe du réel, autour de l'oeuvre de FBM", in *Revue d'esthétique*, 4, 1982; Jacques Adam, *FBM*, Musique et culture series, 29 (4), 1984; Bernard Thomas, "Nature et musique dans l'oeuvre de FBM", dissertation, University of Paris, 1986; Dany Genoud, "FBM: Musique et philosophie dans *Kassandra*", dissertation, University of Lyon, 1988.

* * *

The compositional approach of François-Bernard Mâche centres on nature—imitating, ordering or transforming the given in a dialectical relationship. His theory uses a complementary set of precise comparisons to structural linguistics.

Mâche describes himself as having a compositional attitude rather than a system. Music exists in nature, and nature constitutes the ultimate source of all artistic creation. Nature here must be understood in the characteristically French sense which goes back at least as far as Rousseau. Any sound can be the starting point for music; there is a continuum rather than a frontier between music and noise, and the anecdotal associations of the later need not rule out its musical use.

Composing is not an act of pure imagination, but a dialogue between the composer's thoughts and what nature offers. The sound-material is the starting point, which imposes a style, and through that the composer may discover the music latent in the sounds.

Mâche thereby seeks to establish a "sonorous relation of people to their environment". "Making music", he says, "is not to monologue in accordance with conventional language, nor to remain speechless amidst the marvellous sounds of the world, but to pursue a dialogue with them".

Mâche's pursuit of these ideas has involved various imitative or transliterative techniques. In *Volumes*, the tape is derived from manipulation and filtering of the tone-colours of the ensemble, leading to close timbral associations. *Rambaramb* employs a tape of non-manipulated sounds, which are transcribed imitatively in orchestral parts in terms of pitch and rhythm. *La Peau du silence* and *Safous mêlé* extend the transliterative idea somewhat; both involve transcription of modern Greek poems into orchestral music by tabling a system of phonetic equivalences. In other pieces, Mâche has transformed the source material. His main essay in this technique, *Terre de feu*, is principally derived from the sounds of struck metal instruments, sped up to produce sounds reminiscent of water and slowed to resemble struck gongs. In a recent work realised at Les Ateliers Upic in Paris, he worked similarly with the sounds of crickets.

Mâche bases his theory of music on linguistics. Music according to him is certainly not a language, but the way each operates is analogous. Since language has been clearly theorised, especially in the structural linguistics which were having such broad influence in the 1960s, music and language can be usefully related.

Mâche bases his theory of music on linguistics. Music system. The minimal musical element is not the sound object, although that remains a prerequisite; it is the relation between sounds. Each sound object is defined in relation to its place in the whole. Although Stockhausen, for example, put similar emphasis on patterns of relationship rather than discrete pitches when theorising serialism in the 1950s, Mâche arrived at his views primarily by a linguistic route ("Webern and Schoenberg left me cold", he said of twelve-tone music).

Mâche has made further use of this in his critical work, attempting in papers such as *Méthodes linguistiques et musicologie*, a rigorous semiology of music comparable to Roland Barthes's formalisation of the signs of fashion in *Système de la Mode* (1967).

For Mâche, music exemplifies the place of human beings in the universe and their interrelations with it. "The real purview of music", he proposes, "is a deep and intense affirmation of the whole of reality, a microcosm of the world in sound—a world where man holds a place which, even if primary, is nevertheless miniscule".

—David Revill

MACHOVER, Tod. American. Born in New York City, 24 November 1953. Educated at University of California, Santa Cruz, 1971–3; Columbia University, New York City, 1973–4; Juilliard School, New York City, B.M., 1975, M.M., 1977; further study in computer music, Massachusetts Institute of Technology, Boston, and Stanford University, California, studied composition under Luigi Dallapiccola, Roger Sessions and Elliott Carter. Married Anne Marie Stein, 31 December 1984. Principal cellist, National Opera of Canada, Toronto, 1975–6; composer in residence, 1978–9, and director of musical research 1980–4, IRCAM, Paris; music/electronic music faculty member, Massachusetts Institute of Technology, since 1985. Recipient: Marion Freschl composition Prize, 1974; George Gershwin Prize, 1975; MacDowell Colony Fellow, 1975; East-West International Composition Prize, 1975; Charles Ives Fellowship, National Institute of Arts and Letters, 1976. Mailing address: Media Laboratory, E 15-487, Massachusetts Institute of Technology, Cambridge, Massachusetts, 02139, U.S.A.

Publisher: Ricordi.

Symphonies/orchestral:

Desires (large orchestra) 1983–4.

Spectres Parisiens (flute, horn, cello, synthesizer, computer, chamber orchestra) 1983–4; first performed Paris, 18 May 1984.

Chamber/instrumental:

Sun (piano) 1974.

Yoku Mireba (flute, cello, piano) 1977; first performed Princeton, New Jersey, 14 October 1977.

With Dadaji in Paradise (cello) 1977–8, revised 1983; first performed New York City, 15 May 1978.

Concerto for Amplified Guitar and Chamber Ensemble (guitar, flute/piccolo, oboe/cor anglais, clarinet/bass clarinet, bassoon, horn, trombone, piano, 2 violins, viola, cello, double bass, 2 percussion) 1978; first performed New York City, 22 May 1979.

Light (flute, oboe, horn, bassoon, trumpet, trombone, piano, 2 percussion, string quartet, harp) 1979; first performed Metz, 15 November 1979.

Deplacements (guitar, tape) 1979, revised 1983–4; first performed London, 3 May 1979; new version first performed New York City, 29 March 1984.

String Quartet No 1 1981; first performed New York City, 11 May 1984.

Winter Variations (flute, oboe, B♭ clarinet, bassoon, piano, violin, viola, cello, double bass) 1981; first performed New York City, 10 April 1981.

Chansons d'amour (piano) 1982; first performed Paris, 8 December 1983.

Electric Etudes (cello, tape, electronics) 1983; first performed Paris, 6 December 1983.

Hidden Sparks (viola) 1984; first performed 1985.

Nature's Breath (flute, oboe, clarinet, bassoon, horn, harp, vibraphone, marimba, 2 violins, viola, cello, double bass, tape) 1985.

Towards the Centre (6 instruments, live electronics) 1987; first performed New York City, 28 April 1989.

Bug-Mudra (2 guitars, percussion, live computer) 1989.

Vocal/choral:

Ye gentle birds (soprano, mezzo-soprano, 2 flutes, oboe, horn, bassoon/contrabassoon; Spenser) 1976; first performed Amsterdam, 7 September 1977.
Fresh Spring (baritone, flute, oboe, clarinet, horn, trombone, violin, viola, 2 percussion; Spenser) 1977; first performed New York City, 10 April 1977.
Two Songs (soprano, flute, clarinet, harp, viola, double bass; Moss) 1978; first performed New York City, 22 May 1979.
Soft Morning, City! (soprano, double bass, computer tape; Joyce) 1980; first performed London, 20 May 1980.

Opera:

Valis (after Philip K. Dick) 1985–7.

Other:

Fusione Fugace (4-track tape/computer) 1982; first performed Venice, 28 September 1982.

PUBLICATIONS

By Machover: "Le Compositeur et l'ordinateur", Paris, 1981; "Le Concepte de recherche en musique", Paris, 1984; "Some Thoughts on Computer Music", New York, 1984; "A View of Music at IRCAM" and "Computer Music with and Without Instruments", *Contemporary Music Review*, 1(1), 1984; "A Stubborn Search for Artistic Unity", New York, 1986.

On Machover: P. de Lara, "Un Nouveau Mode de composer", in *Dialectiques*, 1980; F. Lewis, "Boulez, Computers and Music", in *New York Times*, 7 January 1980; S. McBride, "IRCAM in Paris: Where Composers Go to Play with Sound", in *Christian Science Monitor*, 11 February 1982; D. Jameux, "Qui cherche trouve: Un colloque international à Paris", in *Art Press*, 69, 1983; J. Peyser, "American Technology Thrives in Paris", (interview) in *New York Times*, 6 May 1984.

* * *

"We are quickly moving towards a time when the entire electronic instrument range will simply become part of the orchestral resources available to the composer." Though no utopian, Tod Machover's compositional work looks steadily forward to a time when there will be no meaningful distinction between electronic and instrumental sound, merely a vastly enlarged continuum of timbral possibilities from which the composer may draw at will. Machover's work is organised not according to pitch, thematic or rhythmic centres, but according to complex spectral effects generated from a basic sonority (such as the low open C on cello from which *Electric Etudes* is derived) and developed by recourse to a shifting range of harmonic and inharmonic partials which are increasingly difficult to limit.

Machover's early experiments with electronics were in such "mixed" works as *Deplacements* and the marvellous *Light* for large ensemble. There then followed a period in which he returned to purely instrumental composition, notably the piano *Chansons d'amour* and a string quartet in which his old teacher Elliott Carter is briefly but powerfully discernible. In 1982, Machover composed *Fusione Fugace*. The intention was to use electronic means to create a piece of genuine chamber music that was intimate, virtuosic, humanised. Using the 4X computer at IRCAM Machover built a harmonic series over a single pitch. Generating a chord (quite freely), he derives new timbral groups without simple internal harmonic relationships, but which generate a basic spectrum, from which new "harmonic" structures can be inferred. Though conceived on the massive, powerful 4X, the piece is intended for live performance and the published score contains sufficient detailed information to render it feasible for a range of existing performance technology.

Essentially a transitional work, *Fusione Fugace*, which was premiered in Venice in 1982, represented a turning point in Machover's career. His next pieces were a synthesis of both electronic and instrumental means and took him a step closer to the seamless assimilation of the one to the other that was and remains his underlying goal. The *Electric Etudes* for his own instrument, the cello, are profound and generously polyphonic, developing a language already adumbrated in the solo cello piece *With Dadaji in Paradise*. Undoubtedly the culmination of this period in Machover's career, though, is the superb orchestral *Spectres Parisiens*. This is perhaps his most important single work to date (though Machover is always more interesting in relation to processes and groups of works than for single pieces) in that it generously extends his concept of spectral variation and the disposition of "pseudo spectra" (a notion he asks us to understand metaphorically) as the basis of all timbral and ultimately pitch material.

It will clearly take some time and an even more complex synthesis than he has yet achieved for Machover's spectral transitions and timbral reifications to attain the same mnemonic structural function as pitch and pulse in more conventionally organised music. However, it is clear that Machover is working a half-step ahead rather than more conventionally in the wake of the available performing technology. With bases at IRCAM and the Massachusetts Institute of Technology, he is uniquely placed to explore the interplay between a rapidly developing technology and a music in search of a new, non-totalising logic. Perhaps only when intelligent machines take their place alongside living performers on the concert platform will his considerable imagination be freed of the residues of the modernist tradition. It may very well then transpire that Machover is the first truly post-modern composer.

—Russell Kane

MacMILLAN, James. British/Scottish. Born in Kilwinning, Ayrshire, 16 July 1959. Educated at Cumnock Academy; University of Edinburgh, B.Mus., 1981; University of Durham, Ph.D., 1987. Married Lynne Frew, 9 July 1983. Lecturer, University of Manchester, 1986–8; part-time lecturer, University of Edinburgh, 1988, Royal Scottish Academy of Music and Drama, Glasgow, since 1989; artistic director, Edinburgh Contemporary Arts Trust, since 1989; affiliate composer, Scottish Chamber Orchestra, Edinburgh, since 1990. Mailing address: c/o Universal Edition, 2/3 Fareham Street, London W1V 4DU, England.

Publisher: Universal Edition.

Symphonies/orchestral:

The Keening 1986.
Festival Fanfares (brass band) 1986; first performed Kilmarnock, Ayrshire, May 1986.
Into the Ferment 1988; first performed 19 December 1988.
Tryst 1989; first performed Kirkwall, Orkney, 17 June 1989.
The Berserking—Piano Concerto 1990; first performed Glasgow, 22 September 1990.

Chamber/instrumental:

Study on Two Planes (cello, piano) 1981; first performed Edinburgh, 4 March 1984.
The Road to Ardtalla (flute/piccolo, clarinet/bass clarinet, horn, violin, cello, piano) 1983; first performed Manchester, November 1987.
Three Dawn Rituals (flute/piccolo, clarinet/E♭ clarinet, horn, bassoon, violin, cello, vibraphone, prepared piano) 1983; first performed London, 2 November 1985.
Sonata for Piano 1985; first performed London, 26 February 1989.
Two Visions of Hoy (oboe, flute, clarinet, horn, bassoon, cello, percussion) 1986; first performed Manchester, June 1986.
Untold (flute/piccolo, oboe/cor anglais, clarinet, bassoon, horn) 1987; first performed Ayr, 13 September 1988.
Litanies of Iron and Stone (clarinet, soprano saxophone, trombone, tape) 1987; first performed Glasgow, 14 September 1987.
Visions of a November Spring (string quartet) 1988; first performed Glasgow, 3 May 1989.
After the Tryst (violin, piano) 1988.
The Cumnock Orcadian (oboe, 4 clarinets, 2 trumpets, trombone, piano, 3 violins/2 violins and viola, cello; or multiples of these) 1989; first performed Kirkwall, Orkney, 16 June 1989.
The Exorcism of Rio Sumpul (chamber ensemble, 14 players) 1989; first performed Glasgow, 28 January 1990.
. . . As Others See Us . . . (flute, clarinet, bassoon, trumpet, percussion, violin, viola, cello, double bass) 1990; first performed London, 5 April 1990.
Sowetan Spring (chamber ensemble) 1990.

Vocal/choral:

Beatus Vir (SSATBB chorus, organ) 1983; first performed Norwich, Norfolk, 2 July 1983.
Songs of a Just War (soprano, flute/piccolo, oboe/cor anglais, clarinet/bass clarinet, harp, viola, cello; Neruda, Soutar, Tsou Ti-fan) 1986; first performed Edinburgh, May 1986.
Comet New-Born, Arising at Morning (cabaret singer, alto saxophone, tenor saxophone, flugelhorn, trombone, drum machine/drummer, electronic keyboard, double bass/bass guitar; Shakespeare, Bovshover, Henderson) 1987; first performed Edinburgh, November 1987.
Variation on Johnny Faa' (soprano, flute/piccolo, cello, harp) 1988; first performed Edinburgh, August 1988.
Ruin (SSATB chorus) 1989; first performed Ayr, 8 June 1989.
Cantos Sagrados (SATB chorus, organ) 1989; first performed Edinburgh, 10 February 1990.
The Confession of Isobel Gowdie (soprano, orchestra) 1990; first performed London, 22 August 1990.

Music-theatre:

Busqueda (flute, clarinet, 3 trumpets, 3 trombones, 2 percussion, 2 harps, 2 cellos, double bass, 8 actors, soprano, speaker; Mothers of the Disappeared, Argentina) 1988; first performed Edinburgh, 6 December 1988.

PUBLICATIONS

On MacMillan: Keith Potter, "JM: A New Celtic Dawn?", in *The Musical Times*, January 1990.

James MacMillan comments:

My recent music (works from 1988–90) have come to maturity at a time when there is a general renaissance of the arts in Scotland, and at a time when there is increasing interest in the work of Scotland's composers. Significantly, there are strong Scottish traits in these works, but also an aggressive and forthright tendency with a strong rhythmic physicality, showing the influence of Stravinsky, Messiaen, and some minimalist composers. To use this latter description would, however, be misleading, as the apparent "Celtic" nature of the music displays a latent lyricism combined with a "primitive" forcefulness in the handling of pulse and harmony.

My philosophy of composition looks beyond the introversion of the New Music "ghetto" and seeks a wider communication while in no way promoting a compromising populism. I attempt to look out from the narrow confines of contemporary music's orthodoxies. Composers should offer more, and consequently deserve more than their island of non-communication, abandoned by their contemporaries as purveyors of the "inconceivable" and salesmen of the unimaginable.

The "modernist" zeal of the post-war generation of composers who attempted to eschew any continuation of tradition is anathema to me. I respect tradition in many forms, whether cultural, political or historical, and in keeping up a continuous, delicate scrutiny of old forms, ancient traditions, enduring beliefs and lasting values one is strengthened in one's constant, restless search for new avenues of expression. The existence of the influence of the old alongside the experiments of the new should not appear incongruous. Therefore, in ideological terms my works express the timeless truths of Roman Catholicism alongside a fierce socialist commitment. And musically one can hopefully sense the depths of times past integrating with attempts at innovation.

* * *

James MacMillan's music underwent a significant metamorphosis in the middle of the 1980s, and specifically from the time of his electro-acoustic composition *Litanies of Iron and Stone* in 1987. The stylistic shift which this piece signalled represents MacMillan's abandonment of his more conventionally academic earlier style, represented by works like the exotic *Three Dawn Rituals*, *The Road to Ardtalla*, or *Two Visions of Hoy*.

The textural density and urgent rhythmic outbursts of *Litanies* pointed the way to a new determination to incorporate the exuberant drive of rock music, a late discovery for a composer whose background lay in the folk and classical traditions, into a register which was not afraid to resort to either tonality or emotional directness in communicating his always explicit intentions.

Each of the major works that followed *Litanies* has taken an external subject—usually political or religious, and often both—as its starting point, although he has generally tried to avoid a too specific programmatic identification within the music itself.

The vibrant energy and rhythmic dynamism of these works is manifest in a series of compositions around violent themes, as in *The Exorcism of Rio Sumpul*, inspired by a helicopter attack on a village in El Salvador, or the music theatre piece *Busqueda*, which mixes the letters of mothers to their disappeared relatives in Argentina with excerpts from the Latin Mass.

The most significant work of the period, the orchestral composition *The Confession of Isobel Gowdie*, reflects his interest in a wide variety of Scottish traditional musics, notably in the opening section. Just as he attempts to avoid overt programmatic content, however, so he transforms that original source material in a fresh and highly appealing fashion, absorbing these diverse strands into a compelling contemporary idiom which is both complex and robust.

His *Piano Concerto* is often more properly a composition for piano and orchestra than a formal concerto, but, while it lacks quite the same degree of clarity of shape and purpose evident in *Isobel Gowdie*, it reveals the same preoccupation with developing a register that is vibrant, accessible and bursting with rhythmic energy.

The composer's fascination with rhythmic and textural qualities of music from outside his indigenous musical tradition is evident in *Three Dawn Rituals*, based on the Indonesian gamelan tradition but scored for western instruments, and continues in his *Sowetan Spring*, adding a further characteristic colouration to an already diverse palette.

It seems entirely likely that MacMillan's determination to communicate as directly as a complex musical idiom will allow, together with his articulate advocacy of both his work and the extra-musical intent behind them, will find favour with both orchestras and audiences in a way which remains rare in contemporary music.

His list of commissions is already lengthy, including a chamber opera to add to his writing for voice, which includes *Busqueda* (scored for the same forces as Berio's *Laborintus*) and devotional choral works like *Beatus Vir* and *Ruin*. It would seem impossible, though, for MacMillan to sustain the creative outpouring of the years 1987–90, during which time he composed 10 major pieces, often working on two simultaneously.

—Kenny Mathieson

MACONCHY, (Dame) Elizabeth. British. Born in Broxbourne, Hertfordshire, 19 March 1907. Grew up in Ireland. Educated at Royal College of Music, London (composition under Charles Wood and Ralph Vaughan Williams, counterpoint under C.H. Kitson, piano under Arthur Alexander), 1923–27; further study in Prague under Karel Jirák, 1929–30. Married William LeFanu in 1930; 2 daughters, including Nicola LeFanu, *q.v.* Independent composer; chair, Composers Guild, 1959–60; president, Society for Promotion of New Music, from 1977. Recipient: Octavia Blumenthal Travelling Scholarship, 1929; *Daily Telegraph* Prize (for *Oboe Quintet*), 1933; Edwin Evans Prize, 1948, 1969; LCC Prize, 1953; Radcliffe Award, 1969; Gedok International Prize, 1961; medal for services to chamber music, Worshipful Company of Musicians, 1970; Commander, Order of the British Empire (C.B.E.), 1977; Fellow, Royal College of Music; Honorary Fellow, St Hilda's College, Oxford, 1987; Dame of the British Empire (D.B.E.), 1987; Cobbett Medal for services to chamber music; vice-president, Society of Women Composers and Workers Music Association. Mailing address: Shottesbrook, Boreham, Chelmsford, Essex.

Publishers: Alfred Lengnick; Oxford University Press; Ricordi; Boosey & Hawkes; Chappell; Faber; York Edition; British & Continental; Hinrichsen.

Symphonies/orchestral:

Concerto for Piano and Chamber Orchestra 1928.
Concertino (piano, string orchestra) 1928; first performed London, 1930.
Suite: The Land 1929; first performed London, 1930.
Suite (chamber orchestra) 1930.
Viola Concerto 1937.
Dialogue (piano, orchestra) 1940; first performed London, 1942.
Puck Fair (ballet suite) 1940; broadcast BBC, 1944.
Theme and Variations (string orchestra) 1942; broadcast BBC, 1947.
Variations on a Well-Known Theme 1942.
Concertino (clarinet, string orchestra) 1945; first performed Copenhagen, 2 June 1947.
Symphony (double string orchestra) 1948.
Two Dances from "Puck Fair" (from the ballet) 1950; broadcast BBC Wales, 1950.
Double Concerto (oboe, bassoon, string orchestra) 1950; first performed London, 1950.
Concerto for Bassoon and String Orchestra 1950; first performed London, 1952.
Nocturne 1951; first performed London, 1951.
Symphony for Double String Orchestra 1952–3; first performed 1954.
Overture: Proud Thames 1953; first performed London, 1953.
Serenata concertante (violin, orchestra) 1962; first performed Birmingham, 1963.
Variazioni concertante (oboe, clarinet, bassoon, horn, strings) 1964–5; first performed London, 1965.
An Essex Overture 1966; first performed Essex, 1968.
Music for Woodwind and Brass 1966; first performed Thaxted, Essex, midsummer 1966.
Three Cloudscapes 1968; first performed Cheltenham, Gloucestershire, 1968.
Epyllion (cello, 14 strings) 1975; first performed Cheltenham, Gloucestershire, 1975.
Sinfonietta 1975–6; first performed Chelmsford, Essex, 1976.
Romanza (viola, chamber orchestra) 1978; first performed London, 12 March 1979.
Little Symphony 1980; first performed Norwich, Norfolk, 28 July 1981.
Music for Strings 1983; first performed London, 26 July 1983.

Chamber/instrumental:

Quintet (oboe, string quartet) 1932; broadcast BBC, 1933.
String Quartet No 1 1933; first performed London, 1933. Recorded Unicorn Kanchana DKPCD 9080.
Duo (2 violins) 1934.
Prelude, Interlude and Fugue (2 violins) 1935; first performed Prague, 4 September 1935.
String Quartet No 2 1936; first performed Paris, 1937. Recorded Unicorn Kanchana DKPCD 9080.

String Quartet No 3 1938; broadcast BBC, 1938. Recorded Unicorn Kanchana DKPCD 9080.
Sonata (violin, piano) 1938.
Viola Sonata 1938.
A Country Town (piano) 1939; first performed London, 1944.
Contrapuntal Pieces (piano) 1941.
String Quartet No 4 1943; first performed London, 1944. Recorded Unicorn Kanchana DKPCD 9080.
Serenade (cello, piano) 1944.
Sonata (violin, piano) 1944.
Divertimento (piano, cello) 1944; broadcast BBC, 1948.
String Quartet No 5 1948; first performed London, 1949. Recorded Argo RG 329; Unicorn Kanchana DKPCD 9081.
String Quartet No 6 1950; first performed London, 1951. Recorded Unicorn Kanchana DKPCD 9081.
Duo, Theme and Variations (violin, cello) 1951; first performed London, 1951.
String Quartet No 7 1955–6; broadcast 1958. Recorded DKPCD 9081.
Three Pieces (2 clarinets) 1956.
Trios (strings) 1957.
Variations on a Theme from Vaughan Williams's "Job" (cello) 1957; first performed London, 1957.
Reflections (oboe, clarinet, viola, harp) 1960; broadcast BBC, 1961.
The Yaffle (piano) 1962; first performed 1963.
Mill Race (piano) 1962; first performed 1963.
Quintet (clarinet, strings) 1963; broadcast BBC, 1964.
Sonatina (string quartet) 1963; first performed London, 1963.
Sonatina (piano) 1965.
Variazoni concertanti (oboe, clarinet, horn, strings) 1965.
Sonatina (harpsichord) 1965–6; first performed Birmingham, 1965.
Notebook (harpsichord) 1965–6; first performed London, 1974.
Music for Woodwinds and Brass 1966.
String Quartet No 8 1966; first performed London, 1966.
Six Pieces (violin) 1966; first performed Edinburgh, 1966.
Preludio, Fugue and Finale (piano—4 hands) 1967; first performed London, 1968.
Conversations (clarinet, viola) 1967–8; first performed London, 1969.
String Quartet No 9 1968–9; first performed London, 1970. Recorded Argo ZRG 672.
Music (double bass, piano) 1970; first performed London, 1971.
String Quartet No 10 1971–2; first performed Cheltenham, Gloucestershire, 1972.
Three Bagatelles (oboe, harpsichord or piano) 1972; first performed London, 1972.
Oboe Quartet 1972; first performed London, 1972. Recorded HMV HQS 1298.
Three Preludes (violin, piano) 1972; broadcast Radio Telefis Eireann, 1972.
Five Sketches (viola) 1972–3.
Morning, Noon and Night (harp) 1976; first performed Aldeburgh, Suffolk, 1977.
String Quartet No 11 1976; first performed London, November 1977.
Three Pieces (harpsichord) 1977.
Sonatina (harpsichord) 1977.
Contemplation (cello, piano) 1978.
Colloquy (flute, piano) 1978–9.
String Quartet No 12 1979.
Romanza (viola, string quintet) 1979; first performed London, 12 March 1979.
Fantasia (clarinet, piano) 1979; first performed Summer 1980.
String Trio (violin, viola, cello) 1980.
Trittico (2 oboes, bassoon, harpsichord) 1981.
Piccola musica (string trio) 1981; first performed Cheltenham, Gloucestershire, 13 July 1981.
Tribute (violin, 8 winds) 1983.
String Quartet No 13: Quartetto Corto 1983.
String Quartet No 14 1984.
Narration (cello) 1985.
Excursion (bassoon) 1985.

Vocal/choral:

Ophelia's Song (soprano, piano; Shakespeare) 1929; first performed London, 1929.
The Garland (song cycle for soprano, piano; *Anacreontica*, translated William LeFanu) 1938; first performed London, 1938.
The Voice of the City (unaccompanied women's voices; Jacqueline Morris) 1943.
Stalingrad (unaccompanied women's chorus) 1946.
Sonnet Sequence (soprano, string orchestra; Gee) 1946.
A Winter's Tale (soprano, string quartet) 1949; broadcast BBC, 1959.
Six Yeats Settings (soprano, SSA chorus, clarinet, 2 horns, harp) 1951; first performed Ipswich, Essex, 1952.
Christmas Morning (women's voices, piano; or small ensemble of recorders/other winds, percussion, piano; biblical, traditional) 1962; first performed London, 1963.
The Armado (SATB chorus, piano) 1962; first performed London, 1964.
Samson and the Gates of Gaza (SATB chorus, orchestra; Lindsay) 1963–4; first performed Chelmsford, Essex, 1964.
The Starlight Night (high voice, orchestra; Hopkins) 1964; first performed London, 1970.
Nocturnal (unaccompanied SATB chorus; Barnes, Edward Thomas, Shelley) 1965; first performed Cork, 1965.
Propheta Mendax (3-part boys' or women's chorus; medieval Latin) 1965; first performed London, 1968.
Four Shakespeare Songs (soprano/tenor, piano) 1965; broadcast BBC, 1966.
Hymn to God the Father (tenor, piano; Donne) 1965; broadcast BBC, 1966.
Hymn to Christ (tenor, piano; Donne) 1965; broadcast BBC, 1966.
The Sun Rising (tenor, piano; Donne) 1966; broadcast BBC, 1966.
Three Donne Songs (tenor, piano) 1966.
I Sing of a Maiden (4-part chorus) 1966; first performed 1967.
This Day (3-part high voices) 1966.
Peace (high voice, orchestra; Hopkins) 1966; first performed London, 1970.
And Death Shall Have No Dominion (SATB or TrATB chorus, 2 horns, 3 trumpets, 3 trombones; Dylan Thomas) 1968–9; first performed Worcester, 1969.
May Magnificat (high voice, orchestra; Hopkins) 1970; first performed London, 1970.
Ariadne (soprano, orchestra) 1970; first performed King's Lynn, Norfolk, 1971. Recorded on L'Oiseau Lyre SOL 331.
Prayer Before Birth (4-part women's voices; MacNeice) 1971; first performed Cork, 1971.
Faustus (tenor, piano; Marlowe) 1971; first performed London, 1972.
Fly-by-Nights (treble voices, harp; anon.) 1973; first performed London, 1974.
Three Songs (tenor, harp; Byron, Shelley, Campbell) 1973–4; first performed Aldeburgh, Suffolk, 1974.

Sirens' Song (unaccompanied SATB chorus; William Browne) 1974; first performed London, 1974.
Two Epitaphs (unaccompanied SSA chorus; Quarles, anon.) 1975; first performed 1976.
Pied Beauty (chorus, brass; Hopkins) 1975; first performed Salisbury, Wiltshire, 1976.
Heavenhaven (chorus, brass; Hopkins) 1975; first performed Salisbury, Wiltshire, 1976.
Sun, Moon and Stars (song cycle for soprano, piano; Traherne) 1978.
The Leaden Echo and the Golden Echo (SATB chorus, alto flute, viola, harp; Hopkins) 1978.
Heloise et Abelard (dramatic cantata for soprano, tenor, bass, SATB chorus, orchestra) 1978; first performed Croydon, Surrey, March 1979.
Four Miniatures (unaccompanied SATB chorus) 1978.
Creatures (unaccompanied SATB chorus) 1979; first performed Summer 1980.
My Dark Heart (soprano, instrumental ensemble; Petrarch) 1982.
L'Horloge (soprano, clarinet, piano) 1983.
Still Falls the Rain (double chorus; Edith Sitwell) 1984.
The Bellman (unaccompanied SAATBB chorus) 1985.
Butterflies (voice, harp) 1986.

Opera:

Trilogy (may be performed separately):
The Sofa (6 soloists, SATB chorus, chamber orchestra; Ursula Vaughan Williams) 1956–7; first performed London, 13 December 1959.
The Three Strangers (5 soloists, SATB chorus, chamber orchestra; after Hardy) 1958–67; first performed Bishop's Stortford, Hertfordshire, 1968; London, 5 June 1968.
The Departure (2 soloists, offstage SATB chorus, chamber orchestra; Anne Ridler) 1960–61; first performed London, 16 December 1962.
The Birds (extravaganza after Aristophanes; 4 soloists, speakers, SATB chorus, orchestra) 1967–8; first performed Bishop's Stortford, Hertfordshire, 1968.
Johnny and the Mohawks (opera for young children; unison voices, recorders, percussion) 1969; first performed London, 1971.
The Jesse Tree (church opera; 4 soloists, actors, chorus, mimes, dancers, 12 instrumentalists; Anne Ridler) 1969–70; first performed Dorchester, Dorset, 1970.
The King of the Golden River (children's opera for 5 soloists, children's chorus, 13 instrumentalists; Anne Ridler, after Ruskin) 1975; first performed Oxford, 1975.

Other:

Great Agrippa (ballet) 1933.
The Little Red Shoes (ballet) 1935.
Puck Fair (ballet) 1940; first performed Dublin, 1940.
Shoheen Sho Lullaby (arrangement of traditional Irish lullaby; soprano, piano; translated William LeFanu) 1954.
Witnesses (incidental music to play by Anne Ridler; 2 sopranos, flute, oboe, clarinet, horn, cello, percussion, ukelele or banjo) 1966.

Publications

By Maconchy: "A Composer Speaks", in *Composer*, Winter 1971–2; "On Writing String Quartets", liner note to Unicorn Kanchana DKPCD 9080/1.

On Maconchy: F. Howes, "EM", in *Monthly Music Records*, July–August 1939; A. Macnaghten, "EM", in *Musical Times*, 1955.

* * *

Elizabeth Maconchy's artistic development is one of the more remarkable of all 20th-century British composers, for three reasons: first, her background is that of an Irish girl, born before partition into a family with no identifiable interest in music yet being encouraged by her parents to pursue advanced study in London at the Royal College of Music; secondly, she had to make her way in an exclusively male sphere (Dame Ethel Smythe was her only role model); and last, the incontestable quality and worth of her music.

In 1920s Britain it was extremely difficult for a young woman to be seriously considered as a composer—and as a 16-year-old Dublin girl, having heard only one orchestral concert and one string quartet recital in Ireland, Maconchy had enormous additional drawbacks to overcome. At London's Royal College of Music she lost the Mendelssohn Scholarship by one vote; Sir Hugh Allen, the College's then Director, later supposed the panel thought she would marry and never write another note.

Within that environment, and doubtless spurred on by her disappointment, Maconchy showed a creative energy and artistic individuality which appear all the more surprising. But however interesting composers' lives may seem, ultimately they are judged by their music and nothing else—and from the beginning the prolific Maconchy's music has been (despite the vicissitudes of long periods of ill-health and the demands of bringing up a family) that of a practical composer in complete command of the tasks to hand, which have ranged from operas to solo piano pieces, from orchestral music to string quartets.

Of her impressive body of work, Maconchy's 14 quartet essays are central to her development, their composition ranging over 50 years from 1933 to 1984. These quartets fall into four periods which correspond to evolutionary aspects of her art, aspects which never deviate from her earliest and most profound characteristics. One of the more extraordinary features of Maconchy's creativity is the almost total absence of immediately identifiable influences: in spite of her College tutors there is little of the "English Pastoral School" in her early work, even in the 1928 *Concertino* for piano and chamber orchestra. This may be because she is essentially an Irish—more properly Celtic—artist, not an English one, and also because early on she experienced Czechoslovakian music at source, notably Janáček's operas, during extended post-graduate study in Prague during 1929–30 with several lessons from the admirable Karel Jirák.

1930 saw her orchestral suite *The Land* premiered at the Proms. Maconchy's command of orchestral and instrumental colour is another notable feature of her work, at the heart of which is its sheer musicality. Maconchy is a serious artist, never treating her listeners as fools or consciously wooing them with "gorgeous" sounds. Her music concentrates on the material at hand—tonally based, yet fluent and fluid, free-ranging yet always under control; her command of mood, her passion and vitality, the energy and intellectual rigour of her finest works ensure that if she can produce music in a lighter vein (The *Puck Fair* ballet—and the orchestral suite; *Johnny and the Mohawks*, a children's opera; *The Yaffle* and *Mill Race* for piano) the force of her artistic personality commands admiration. She has a marked flair for the dramatic, as the operas and ballets clearly show; and as the operas also demonstrate, her vocal writing is distinctive and entirely graceful. Occasionally, her beguilingly fastidious ear may trap the superficial listener into thinking her music is beautiful texture and precious little else, but the depth of utterance of such powerfully attractive works as the *Symphony* for double string orchestra, the Bassoon Concerto, the second Clarinet Concertino and the *Serenata concertante* for violin and orchestra, to say nothing of her masterly string quartets, reveals the rare integrity of this admirable and important artist.

—Robert Matthew-Walker

MAEGAARD, Jan (Carl Christian). Danish. Born in Copenhagen, 14 April 1926. Educated at Royal Conservatory of Music, Copenhagen (theory under Poul Schierbeck and B. Hjelbmorg, counterpoint under Knud Jeppesen, orchestration under J. Jersild, music history, composition, double bass, piano), 1945–50; University of Copenhagen (musicology under Jens Peter Larsen), 1951–7, music teaching qualification (theory and history), 1953, Mag.Art., 1957, Dr. Phil., 1972; University of California, Los Angeles (musicography under Robert Nelson), 1958–9. Served in Danish Royal Navy, 1950. Married Kirsten Offer Andersen, 14 August 1973 (dissolved 1989); 2 daughters. Freelance musician, 1949–56; board member, Danish section, International Society of Contemporary Music, 1949–67; music critic, various newspapers, 1952–60; teacher, Royal Conservatory, Copenhagen, 1953–8; assistant professor 1959–61; associate professor 1961–71, and professor since 1971, University of Copenhagen; consultant, 1962–78, and chief consultant, since 1983, music department, Danish State Radio; visiting professor, State University of New York, Stony Brook, 1975; professor of music, University of California, Los Angeles, 1978–81. Recipient: member, Royal Danish Academy of Sciences and Letters, 1986; member, Norwegian Academy of Sciences and Letters. Mailing address: Duevej 14.6, 2000 Frederiksberg, Denmark.

Publishers: Engstrom & Sodring, Palaegade 6, DK-1261 Copenhagen K, Denmark; Samfundet, Copenhagen; Wilhelm Hansen, Copenhagen.

Symphonies/orchestral:

Kammerkoncert No 1 Op 5 (flute, oboe, clarinet, bassoon, strings) 1949; first performed Copenhagen, 1950. Recorded Point PLP 5063.
March Op 29 (string orchestra) 1956.
Kammerconcert No 2 Op 38 (flute, oboe, bassoon, string orchestra, piano ad lib) 1961–2; first performed Copenhagen, 1961. Recorded Point PLP 5063.
Due tempi Op 39 1961; first performed Copenhagen, 1961.
Marineforeningens (jubilee march for military band) 1963.
Danmark trofast Op 56 (orchestration of Op 55) 1971.
De profundis Op 65 (orchestration of Op 64) 1976.
March Op 67 (military band) 1980.
Triptykon Op 72 (violin, string orchestra) 1984; first performed Elsinore, 1984.
Sinfonietta Op 76 (strings) 1986; first performed Elsinore, 1986.

Chamber/instrumental:

Koncertetude/Passacaglia Op 6 (piano) 1949.
Suite Op 9 (violin, piano) 1949.
Trio Op 10 (oboe, clarinet, bassoon) 1949; first performed Copenhagen, 1951.
Wind Quintet Op 11 1951.
Suite Op 12 (2 violins) 1951.
Quasi una sonata Op 14 (viola, piano) 1952.
Sonata Op 15 (bassoon, piano) 1952.
Variations impromptus Op 21 (violin, viola, cello, piano) 1953.
Fem orgelkoraler Op 26 (organ) 1954.
Sonata Op 27 (piano) 1955.
Fem praeludier Op 32 (violin) 1956; first performed Copenhagen, 1958.
Cinque pezzi Op 35 (piano) 1959; first performed Denmark, 1959. Recorded Philips DMAMC 050.
Trio Serenade: O alter Duft aus Marchenzeit Op 36 (violin, cello, piano) 1960; first performed Copenhagen, 1960. Recorded Tonart 23.
Octomeri Op 40 (violin, piano) 1962; first performed Copenhagen, 1962. Recorded PLP 5163.
ISCM-Fanfare Op 44 (4 trombones) 1964.
Aus tiefer Not Op 47 (organ) 1966.
Movimento Op 48 (clarinet, horn, string quartet, percussion, Hammond organ) 1967.
Tre orgelkoraler Op 51 (organ) 1969.
Musica riservata No 1 Op 52 (string quartet) 1970; first performed Odense, 1970. Recorded PLP 5063.
Tre orgelkoraler Op 58 (Op 51 arranged for 2 pianos) 1974.
Danse til Marina Op 59 (piano) 1975.
Musica riservata No 2 Op 61 (oboe, clarinet, bassoon, saxophone) 1976; first performed Copenhagen, 1976.
Pastorale Op 63 (piano) 1976; first performed Copenhagen, 1976.
Canon Op 68 (3 flutes) 1980; first performed Copenhagen, 1983.
Passacaglia-Fantasi-Choral Op 69 (organ) 1981; first performed Turo, 1983.
Musica riservata No 3 Op 70 (flute, oboe, cello, harpsichord) 1982.
Fantasi: Indsigter—udsigter Op 71 (organ) 1983; first performed Copenhagen, 1987.
Labirinto I Op 77 (viola) 1986; first performed Odense, 30 March, 1989.
Labirinto II Op 79 (guitar) 1987; first performed Mexico, 12 January, 1989.
Duo-Phantasy Op 81 (2 guitars) 1988.
Double Op 82 (cello) 1988.
Pierrot in the Ball Room Op 84 (waltz for 2 guitars) 1988.
Kinderblicke Op 86 (guitar) 1989.

Vocal/choral:

Pigens mode med Pan Op 1 (soprano, flute, clarinet, piano; Pedersen) 1947.
Blomsterdigte Op 2 (soprano, piano; Thomsen) 1948.
Fuglene Op 3 (unaccompanied mixed chorus; Tjung) 1948.
Legend Op 4 (soprano, violin, piano; Hellsing) 1949.
Tre sange til bibelske tekster Op 8 (unaccompanied mixed chorus; biblical) 1949; first performed Copenhagen, 1951.
Den gyldene harp Op 13 (song cycle for soprano, mezzo-soprano, oboe, cello, piano; Chinese verse) 1952.
Herre, hor min bon Op 17 (motet for unaccompanied mixed chorus) 1952.

Fem sange Op 18 (voice, piano; Thomsen) 1952.
To sange Op 19 (voice, piano; Petersen) 1952.
Tre sange Op 20 (unspecified instrumentation; Heltberg, Hoffmann) 1952.
Ga udemon sletterne Op 23 (mixed chorus, string orchestra; Jaeger) 1953; first performed Nordborg, 1954.
De fire dvaerge Op 24 (voice, piano; Pedersen) 1953.
Jaevdognseleg / Elegy of Equinox I Op 28 (soprano, cello, organ; Wivel) 1955.
To motetter Op 30 (unaccompanied mixed chorus; biblical) 1956.
Fem sange Op 31 (voice, piano; Petersen) 1956.
Asiatisk tanke Op 33 (voice, piano; Kristensen) 1957.
Lang eftermiddag Op 34 (unaccompanied mixed chorus; Schade) 1958.
To sange Op 37 (unaccompanied male choir; Brandt, Larsen) 1960.
Fem sange Op 41 (unspecified instrumentation; Thomsen) 1962.
Dagstromme Op 43 (unaccompanied male chorus; Sarvig) 1964.
Folkvisan Op 45 (unaccompanied female chorus; Svanström) 1965.
Sic enim amavit Op 49 (mixed chorus and/or soprano, trumpet, organ) 1967; first performed Aalborg, 1969.
Tre sange Op 50 (chorus, piano; Steen) 1969.
Tre nye sange Op 53 (chorus, piano; Hein, anon.) 1970.
Fem lyriske monologer Op 54 (soprano, piano; Thomsen) 1970; first performed Copenhagen, 1972.
Danmark trofast Op 55 (tenor, piano; Rifbjerg) 1970.
Tre korsange Op 57 (unaccompanied mixed chorus) 1971.
Bla drom Op 60 (unaccompanied male chorus) 1975.
De profundis Op 64 (male chorus, piano; Petersen) 1976; first performed Copenhagen, 1976.
Song of the Conch-Shell Op 74 (male chorus, piano) 1984; first performed Copenhagen, 1991.
A disse vinterveje Op 83 (voices, organ ad lib; Sarvig) 1988.
To sange Op 85 (voice, piano; Kristensen) 1988.
Liebeslied Op 87 (contralto, 2 guitars; Rilke) 1990.
Landet som icke ar Op 88 (unaccompanied mixed chorus; Södergran) 1990.

Other:

Don Quixote Op 7 (incidental music; violin, clarinet, horn, piano) 1949; first performed Copenhagen, 1949.
Den hvide souper Op 25 (music for radio play; flute, oboe, violin) 1954.
Antigone Op 46 (music for television production of Sophocles; tenor, bass, male chorus, orchestra) 1966; broadcast Danish Television, 1967.

J.C. Bach: *Sinfonia concertante in A major* (cadenza for violin celio; Op 16) 1952.
W.A. Mozart: *Horn Concerto No 3* (cadenza to 1st movement; Op 22) 1953.
Arnold Schoenberg: *Variations on a Recitative* (orchestration; Op 62) 1976; broadcast Danish Radio, 1978.
J.S. Bach: *Praeludium og fuga in F minor* (orchestration; Op 66) 1977.
P. Heise: *Skovensomhed* (arranged for unaccompanied male chorus; Op 73) 1984.
P. Heise: *Dyvekes Sange* (arranged for soprano, orchestra; Op 78) 1986; first performed Haderslev, 1988.
P. Schierbeck: *Sig naermer tiden* (arranged for tenor, male chorus; Op 80) 1987.

PUBLICATIONS

By Maegaard: *Musikalisk modernisme*, Copenhagen 1964, 1971, Swedish and Finnish editions, 1971; *Studien zur Entwicklung des dodekaphonen Satzes bei Arnold Schönberg*, Copenhagen, 1972; "Schönbergs Zwolftonreihen", in *Die Musikforschung*, 29 (4), 1976; *Praeludier til musik af Schönberg*, Copenhagen, 1976; *Indforing i Romantisk Harmonik I–II*, Copenhagen, 1981; "Weberns Zworftonreihen", in *Analytica*, Stockholm, 1985; "The Nomenclature of Pitch-Class Sets", in *Journal of Music Theory*, 29, 1985; "Zur harmonischen Analyse der Musik des 19. Jahrhunderts", in *Musikkulturgeschichte*, Wiesbaden, 1990; many other articles.

On Maegaard: Peter Brask, "Mennesket, musikken og metoderne" [The Man, the Music and the Means], in *Dansk Musiktidsskrift*, 63(3), 1988–9.

Jan Maegaard comments:

Composing is a way of life to me: I couldn't be without and still feel fulfilled. When composing I am able to express myself, my feelings and insights, more clearly and eloquently than would otherwise be possible. Still, the work of a composer is that of a craftsman. You must master the craft of composition, of counterpoint, of orchestration, and so on, and also be able to "think" music without the aid of words and pictures. A composer is, to me, a person who has accomplished all this and, in addition, has a vivid imagination and feels the urge to express himself.

My list of compositions since 1947—88 opus numbers by now—comprises several means of expression from the simplest song to the most sophisticated work of chamber music, and some of them may seem to have little in common. They do all stem, though, from an urge to express myself.

* * *

One of the key experiences in Jan Maegaard's early life must have been the moment in 1958 when he sat down at Arnold Schoenberg's desk in Brentwood Terrace, Los Angeles: "Please, make yourself comfortable, his pencils are still there . . . " He had, at last, won the confidence of Mrs Schoenberg, having passed her thorough examination of his ambition to study the manuscripts of the late master, and his qualifications to do so. The forces that had propelled the young scholar from distant Denmark to that Californian treasure chest had their origins some five years before, sparked by the exultation of his first looking into Schoenberg's *Serenade* Op 24—nothing less than a revelation for a composer well versed in the Nielsen tradition, and with 20 well-mannered works already behind him.

From now on Maegaard would conduct his musical education alone. His monumental Schoenbergian *Studies* . . . are, in fact, a by-product of this advanced self-education. Through these studies he gained a deep insight into Schoenberg's compositional process, as well as an understanding of the historical and structural development from late Romantic chromaticism to atonality and twelve-tone music. Undoubtedly, his stubborn will to get to the very bones of these matters has kept him safe from epigonality: What he learned from Schoenberg was first of all the ethos of workmanship, and then the importance of technical skills.

Earning his living as a university professor he has been able to pursue his own uncompromising course as a composer. This does not mean that he has avoided commissioned works (incidental music, some lyrical choruses and a couple of hilarious marches); nor has he been insensitive to the products of his contemporaries. As an attentive listener (and propagator) of new music, he has constantly been improving and enriching his own expressional vocabulary. In fact, *expression* (not Expressionism!) might well be seen as the core of his endeavours: the necessity of communicating the agitations and vacillations, the anguish and the dreaming freedom of the spirit in its own language, music. But, paradoxically perhaps, you have to listen carefully to catch the messages, as his spirit is a reticent one, its occasional brusqueness the proof of its shyness.

Some of Maegaard's most intimate music is characteristically found in the chamber works he labels *Musica riservata* (opera 52, 61, 70). The insights one gets here could be deepened by listening to the two *Labirinto* solo works (opus 77 for viola, opus 79 for guitar). The techniques of these works, which span almost 20 years, are rather different, from serialism based upon a systematically transposed ten-tone set combined with ametrical musical prose in the string quartet opus 52, to the free use of nine-tone scales in the solo works, where the order of the small sections is left to the performer's choice. The unusual combinations in opus 61 and opus 70 witness a keen ear for the minute nuances of sound colour. Emotionally differentiated also, these works leave no doubt as to their common origin; they bear the print and burden of the same personality, even if you would not call it a "style".

The bulk of Maegaard's output consists of small-scale works, but his skill in handling the orchestral forces was demonstrated already in the stark *Due tempi*, which sound as determinate as they actually were written, that is, as strictly predeterminated serial pieces. However, his orchestration skill was masterfully demonstrated in his reworking of Schoenberg's *Variations on a Recitative*, for organ, and was used with cunning economy in the Heise songs (*Dyvekes Sange*), where gradual changes in the instrumentation mirrors the emotional ripening of young Dyveke, the tragic heroine of the poems.

Technically speaking five periods are discernible in Maegaard's oeuvre to date: diatonic music in the style of Nielsen (*Trio Op 10* or *Sonata Op 15* for bassoon); twelve-tone music "following the row" (*Five Preludes Op 32* or *Trio Serenade Op 36*); total serialism (*Due tempi Op 39*), occasionally combined with freedom of choice of the order of sections, which neutralizes the epic element of the music (*Chamber Concerto Op 38*); music based on preconstructed cycles of trichords (the male chorus *Song of the Conch-Shell Op 74*), gradually giving way to a new orientation towards the use of tonal functions, including nine-tone scales (the violin concerto *Triptykon Op 72*). If it seems that his work has come full circle, this is only a semantic illusion: the tonality of the mature works is quite different from that of the early ones.

Maegaard's music has a distinctive profile, and deserves a prominent place in modern music; that it is relatively unknown even to the Danish public may be due to Maegaard's reluctance to promote his own work.

—Peter Brask

MAGEAU, Mary (Jane Magdalen). American; resident in Australia since 1974. Born in Milwaukee, Wisconsin, 4 September 1934. Educated at DePaul University, Chicago (under Leon Stein), B.Mus., 1963; University of Michigan, Ann Arbor (composition with Leslie Bassett and Ross Lee Finney, continuo harpsichord with Ellwood Derr), M.Mus. (composition), 1969; Berkshire Music Centre Composer Fellowship Programme, (under George Crumb), Tanglewood, Massachusetts, 1970; International Dance Course Composers/Choreographers, Melbourne, 1984; private harpsichord study with Audley Green and Anthony Jennings. Married Kenneth Luton White, 26 December, 1974; 2 sons. Harpsichordist, University of Michigan Collegium Musicum, Ann Arbor, and Contemporary Directions ensemble; lecturer, Scholastica College, Duluth, Minnesota, 1969–74; guest lecturer, University of Wisconsin, Superior, 1973; lecturer, Queensland University of Technology, Brisbane, 1974–86; harpsichordist, Brisbane Baroque Trio, 1977–88; lecturer, Queensland Conservatorium of Music, Brisbane, 1987–90. Recipient: silver medal, Gottschalk Centenary Composition Competition, 1970. Mailing address: 57 Ironside Street, St Lucia, Queensland 4067, Australia.

Publishers: G. Schirmer, New York; Loux Music Publishers, P.O. Box 34, Hannacroix, New York, U.S.A.; J. Albert & Son, Pty Ltd, 139 King Street, Sydney, New South Wales, Australia.

Symphonies/orchestral:

Variegations 1968; first performed Ann Arbor, Michigan, 22 March 1969.
Montage 1969; first performed Duluth, Minnesota, October 1970.
Celebration Music (symphonic band) 1971.
Indian Summer (youth orchestra) 1976; first performed Brisbane, 24 October 1977.
Concerto Grosso (flute, cello, harpsichord, timpani, percussion, string orchestra) 1982; first performed Brisbane, 12 March 1988.
Pacific Portfolio (youth orchestra) 1983; first performed Ascot, Queensland, 11 October 1983.
Concerto (harpsichord, strings) 1988; first performed Brisbane, 16 June 1989.
Dance Suite (cello, orchestra) 1988; first performed Wagga, New South Wales, 16 October 1989.
Triple Concerto (violin, cello, piano, orchestra) 1990.

Chamber/instrumental:

Three Movements (cello) 1968.
Three Pieces (organ) 1968; first performed Cincinnati, Ohio, 1968.
Fantasy Music (violin, piano) 1972; first performed Superior, Wisconsin, October 1972.
Arches (violin, clarinet, piano, tape) 1972.
Interaction (clarinet, tape) 1972.
Forensis (flute, oboe, clarinet, bassoon, 2 percussion) 1973.
Forecasts (piano) 1974.
Contrasts (cello) 1976. Recorded Grevillea Records GRV 1070.
Australia's Animals (piano) 1976.
Ragtime: Elite Syncopations (piano) 1977. Recorded Move Records MD 3066.
Dialogues (SATB recorder quartet) 1977.
Doubles (SATB recorder quartet) 1977.
Cityscapes (piano) 1978.
Statement and Variations (viola) 1979; first performed Lawrence, Kansas, 1981.
Pacific Ports (piano—4 hands) 1979.
Sonate Concertante (flute, cello, harpsichord) 1980; first performed Brisbane, June 1980. Recorded Grevillea Records GRV 1080.
March (piano—4 hands) 1980.

Cantilena (flute, percussion) 1981; first performed Brisbane, 2 August 1981.
Winter's Shadow (harpsichord, chimes) 1983.
Nach Bach (harpsichord) 1983.
Soliloquy (piano) 1984.
Concert Pieces (violin, cello, piano) 1985; first performed London, 21 January 1985.
Duo Concertant (violin, harpsichord) 1985; first performed Kelvin Grove, Queensland, 28 March 1985.
Scarborough Fair Variations (flute, cello, harpsichord) 1985. Recorded Grevillea Records GRV 1081.
Discorsi Musicale (treble recorder, viola da gamba, harpsichord) 1985; first performed Carseldine, Queensland, 6 September 1985.
Peace Suite (harpsichord) 1988; first performed Hartford, Connecticut, 1989.
Playback (2 treble, 1 bass instrument, piano) 1989.
Landscape (percussion ensemble) n.d.

Vocal/choral:

Mass for Our Lady of Victory (unison choir, organ) 1967.
A Chime of Windbells (mixed choir, flute, percussion) 1971.
I Never Saw Another Butterfly (5 songs for soprano, clarinet, viola, piano, 2-channel tape) 1972.
Lacrimae (SSAT chorus, percussion) 1972; first performed Duluth, Minnesota, 1972. Recorded Sound S80 1995.
A Community Mass (mixed choir, congregation, organ) 1978.
The Line Always There (SSAA chorus, flute, percussion, piano duet) 1981; first performed Queensland, 1981.
Time Pieces (SATB chorus, percussion) 1988; first performed Brisbane, 1988.

Other:

Sound and Space Adventures (incidental music) n.d.
Miniatures (music to accompany book *In Tune With Music*, no 2). Recorded Grevillea Records.

Editions of Corelli: *La Follia*; Albinoni: *Adagio*, for baroque trio. Recorded Grevillea GRV 1082.

PUBLICATIONS

By Mageau: "Baroque Performance Practice: The Essential Ornaments", in *Music Teachers Association of Queensland Journal*, April 1984.

On Mageau: entries in Aaron I. Cohen, *International Encyclopaedia of Women Composers*, New York and London, second edition, 1987; Jane Weiner LePage, *Women Composers, Conductors and Musicians of the Twentieth Century*, volume III, New Jersey and London, 1988.

Mary Mageau comments:
MUSIC—the art of sound in time.
For its creation:
a sensitive ear
an intuitive feeling for the wholeness of things
a developed craft
an elegant solution

* * *

Mary Mageau began composing relatively late in her musical life, and quite by chance: needing one unit to complete her Bachelor of Music degree, she took the only available option—composition—and discovered in herself a passion for it. Her earliest works followed contemporary trends, being very avant-garde. However, observing the alienating effect such works were having upon audiences, and experiencing considerable difficulty in persuading musicians to perform them, she underwent a philosophical change. Determining that these early works were not a true representation of how she felt about music, she destroyed most of them. *Montage* for symphony orchestra was the first major work to show the beginnings of her new more lyrical style.

A move to Australia in 1974 facilitated Mageau's stylistic development, as she then felt herself to be under much less pressure from musical fads and fashions. In 1977, she joined flautist Adelaide Brown and cellist Gary Williams to form the Brisbane Baroque Trio. Her compositional output from this time was curtailed by the exigencies of performance, and also by family obligations: while her two sons were young, she did not want to deprive them of her time. Although small, her musical production nevertheless remained consistent, comprising mainly chamber music, including several commissions for the Trio. One notable exception was a larger-scale orchestral work, *Indian Summer*, written to celebrate the American Bicentennial; it is a reflective and lyrical work, making use of American folk tunes.

Despite her wider experience in the chamber repertoire, Mageau found orchestral writing easier to handle, largely because of the greater subtlety of gesture required in chamber composition. A breakthrough in this respect came with *Sonate Concertante*, in which she achieved a much tighter form than she had previously; this is characteristic of subsequent chamber works.

The Trio ceased performing in 1988, which coincided with the commissioning of *Concerto* for harpsichord and strings. This work, a hybrid of chamber and orchestral music, was written in a flexible manner whereby the solo instrument generally alternates with the accompaniment. The piece can therefore be performed with forces ranging from a string quintet to full orchestral strings, without overwhelming the delicate solo instrument. It heralded a move by Mageau into larger forms and forces, typified by the *Triple Concerto* for violin, cello and piano with symphony orchestra. This commission resulted from an earlier work, *Concert Pieces* for violin, cello and piano, and signalled a new stylistic direction for the composer. In earlier pieces she had used large intervals in her scales, employing softer-edged harmonies. Her new writing included a sequence of alternate semitones and tones, with a more biting and aggressive harmonic foundation to her music; it became stronger and leaner, increasingly chromatic but still retaining its lyricism.

In her earlier works Mageau revised portions that dissatisfied her, taking great pains that only the preferred version remained extant. Later compositions have been planned much more carefully, with the larger design clear in her mind before commencement, reducing the need for revision and rewriting.

During the period in which she performed with the Trio, Mageau observed that her composition often tended to reflect the influence of the group's repertoire: she found herself writing in a neo-Baroque style. Aside from considerations of time, it was partly for this reason that she resolved to give up performing. Moreover, to increase the individuality of her style of composition, she has decided for the moment not only to cease performing other music, but also to avoid listening to much of it, so that she can explore her own ideas without outside musical influence.

—Jenny Dawson

MAIGUASHCA, Mesias. Ecuadorian; German citizen. Born in Quito, Ecuador, 24 December 1938. Educated at Conservatorio de Musica, Quito, to 1960, further study in piano and composition, 1965; Eastman School of Music, Rochester, New York, B.Mus., 1961, M.Mus., 1962; Instituto di Tella, Buenos Aires, 1963–5; resident in Germany from 1966; further study, Musikhochschule, Munich and Cologne, and WDR Electronic Music Studio, Cologne, 1966–72; study tours to North and South America, and Eastern Europe, 1969–72. Married Gabriele Schumacher in 1972; 1 son and 1 daughter. Sound engineer, Collegium Vocale Köln, and Ballet des 20. Jahrhundert, 1968–72; assistant to Karlheinz Stockhausen, German pavilion, Universal Exposition, Osaka, Japan, 1970; co-founder (with Peter Eotvos, Joachim First and Gaby Schumacher), Gruppe Oeldorf, 1972–8; docent, Cursos Latinamericanos, Buenos Aires, 1977; freelance composer, Baden-Baden, since 1977; researcher, Centre Européen pour la Recherche Musicale (CERM), Metz, 1978; researcher, Institute pour la Recherche et Coordination Acoustique/Musicale (IRCAM), Paris, 1981; teacher, Budapest Music Academy Summer School, Gyor, 1983, 1984; summer semester in electronic music, Basle Music Academy, 1985; visiting teacher in electronic music and composition, Electronic Music Studio, Institut für Neue Musik and Musikhochschule, Freiburg, 1985; summer semester, Electronic and Computer Music Studio, Conservatorio Nacional de Quito, Ecuador, 1987; professor of electronic music, Musikhochschule Freiburg, from 1990. Mailing address: Jaisbuhlstrasse 1, 7570 Baden-Baden, Germany.

Publishers: Feedback Studio Verlag, Justerstrasse 23, 5 Cologne 1, Germany; Edition Modern, Munich; Editions Salabert, Paris.

Symphonies/orchestral:

Per-Fiati (wind orchestra, 2 accordions) 1975; broadcast WDR Cologne, 1975.
Monodias e interludios (version for orchestra) 1984–7; first performed Metz, 1988.

Chamber/instrumental:

String Quartet 1964; first performed Buenos Aires, 1964.
Ubungen (violin, clarinet, cello; also version for violin, clarinet, cello, 3 synthesizers; further version for violin or cello, synthesizer) 1972–3; first performed Cologne, 1973; synthesizer version first performed Washington, D.C., 1974; cello version first performed Bogota, 1973.
Oldorf 8 (violin, clarinet, cello, organ, synthesizer, tape) 1972–4; first performed Darmstadt, 1974.
Agualarga (2 pianos, electronics) 1974; first performed Darmstadt, 1974.
Lindgren (low melody instrument, tape; versions for cello, trombone, saxophone) 1976.
Y ahora vamos por aquí . . . (8 instruments, tape) 1977; first performed Witten, 1978.
Intensidad y altura (6 percussion, tape) 1979; first performed Metz, 1980.
FMelodies I (instrumental ensemble, computer-generated sounds) 1980; first performed Paris, 1982.
Ecos (32 sound sources/36 players, electronically generated sounds) 1981–2; first performed Donaueschingen, 1982.
Impulse (4 quartets of children) 1983; first performed Gernsbach, 1983.
FMelodies II (cello, percussion, computer-generated sound) 1983–4; first performed Bremen, 1984.
Monodias e interludios (2 flutes, 2 clarinets, percussion, bass obligato) 1984; first performed Paris, 1984.
La Seconde Ajoutée (2 pianos) 1984–6; first performed Saarbrücken, 1986.
Barcarola bitística (2 microcomputers, video monitors) 1985; first performed Middleburg-Utrecht, 1986.
Vorwort zu Solaris (cello, trumpet, percussion, saxophone, tape; version for Baroque ensemble, tape) 1989; first performed Berlin, 29 January 1990.
Moments musicaux (string quartet, tape) 1989; first performed Alicante, 19 September 1989.
Video-Memorias (2 flutes, computer installation) 1989; first performed Quito, October 1989.
Labertintos (organ, tape) 1990; first performed Metz, 17 November 1990.

Vocal/choral:

A Mouth-Piece (6 vocalists, electronics) 1970; first performed Cologne, 1972.
Solitarium (6 vocalists, electronics; Jodorowski) 1976; first performed Witten, 1976.

Electronic/mixed media:

Dort wo wir leben (electronic/*musique concrète*) 1967; first performed Washington, D.C., 1968.
Hor-Zu (electronic/*musique concrète*) 1969; first performed Cologne, 1970.
AYAYAYAYAY (electronic/*musique concrète*) 1971; first performed Washington, D.C., 1972.
A Mandelbox (computer installation) 1987–8; first performed Donaueschingen, 1988.
Como (tape) 1988.

PUBLICATIONS

By Maiguashca: "Informationen zu *Ubungen*", in *Feedback Papers*, 9; "Zu *FMelodies II*, in *Neuland*, 5, 1981; "Spectrum-Harmony-Melody-Timbre", in *Timbre*, IRCAM, Paris, 1985; "To Hear a Picture, to See a Music", in *Systèmes Personnels*, IRCAM, Paris, 1986.

Mesias Maiguashca comments:
For me, music is:

expressive form
a private paradise
an ivory tower
introspection
extrospection
hobby
obsession
trade
but above all:
autiobiography, diary, SELF-PORTRAIT

* * *

A key work of Mesias Maiguashca's, *Y ahora vamos por aquí . . .*, begins with a huge gong-tone followed by a long silence, a process repeated and progressively modulated by a numerically determined grid of instrumental sounds. This gong sound, which sounds as if it echos down the ages, uncovers two essential dimensions of Maiguashca's musical universe: the ritual dimension of a sound which has acquired historically a religious, magical, social and communitarian dimension; and a technological dimension in the spectrum of sound made possible by recent developments in frequency modulation by computer. These two dimensions—ancient and ritual, present-day and technological—recur throughout Maiguascha's output.

Y ahora vamos por aquí . . . is written for eight instruments and tape. It served as a point of departure for a series of compositions based on the technique of modulations and on the FM wavelength spectrum, as well in his work on differential sound: *FMelodies I*, *Ecos*, the orchestral version of *Monodias et interludios* and more recently *A Mandelbox*, which uses a Mandelbrot algorithm to combine FM modulations with the transformation of sonically generated spectral forms.

Of these pieces, *FMelodies* is central. It is based on two spectral zones generated by the principle of FM modulation. A carrier frequency is modulated by a frequency that shifts over the 10 octaves of the audible range. At the same time, a fluctuating network of lateral frequencies is deployed round the axial frequencies, a process which lends the FM spectrum some of the qualities of an organic system, a complex acoustic substance. The electronic component is not restricted to simple tape material; Maiguashca interpolates a further layer between it and the spectra generated by the instruments, playing freely with spectral affinities, the affinities between the intrinsic frequencies of the FM spectrum and the extrinsic contributions of the instruments.

In the range of possibilities opened up by computer, what interests Maiguashca—over and above precise control of the acoustic material—is the possibility of concentration on complex spectra and non-tempered sounds (harmonic fractions, differential sounds) in such a way as to create quasi-organic transformations. Maiguashca works neither in contrasts nor in solid architectures. He operates with monodic textures, macro-spectral materials, with modulation of dis-harmonies and *non-harmonies*. He calls the slowly evolving architecture of his works "*Makro-Raum Zeit Form*" and expresses it in terms of proportions.

That tendency was already visible in *Y ahora vamos por aquí . . .* That piece inhabited a rather uncertain ground, its sound overdetermined by a "fuzzy logic" which unveils once again the composer's central method: an accumulation of sounds relevant to distant or ancient rituals, the fundamental spectrum of the gong-tone, and the new acoustic phenomena resulting from musical applications of vanguard information technology. From such densely stratified work one occasionally gains a sense of a much older modulation "*à la Bach*", or even a whiff of science fiction. Far from being revolutionary, Maiguascha gives off above all a sense of mythic tranquility which reflects his Indian roots.

His father, an Ecuadorian Indian and author of a book entitled *El Indo, cerebro y corazón de América* [Indians: Hearts and Minds of a Continent], analysed the process by which the indigenous population were enslaved in Ecuador and struggled for their educational rights. In 1970, Mesias Maiguashca spent six months in Osaka, as part of Stockhausen's circle, and seemed to rediscover there some long-lost aspect of his distant origins. This cannot of course stand in place of a more systematic argument in the story of Maiguashca's development, but the experience seems to belong there as an extension of that concern for far-away realms and an extra-European universe of discourse which plays such a part in his works. In particular the notion of extended, indeterminate, extratemporal space is intrinsic to his work; it may be possible to detect there a conceptual coincidence between an interest in acoustic phenomena directed by the techniques of FM modulation and the characteristic acoustic effects of the Gagaku of ancient China or the music of modern Japan.

Maiguashca has long had a preoccupation with electro-acoustic music. On his arrival in Germany in 1966, he was confronted by studio techniques, by electronic music, and by the montage and *musique concrète* experiments of the WDR Studio in Cologne. In 1970, he went to Japan with Stockhausen to complete an installation at the universal exposition in Osaka. In 1972, he founded the Oeldorf group with Peter Eotvos, Joachim First and Gaby Schumacher, and collaborated with the electro-acoustic Feedback Studio. Six years later, his interest was further developed by his collaboration with Peter Leunig at the Centre Européen pour la Recherche Musicale, in Metz. And then, in 1981, there was IRCAM.

Contact with the German school of electronic composition, and in particular with Stockhausen, played a significant role in Maiguashca's fascination with information theory, cybernetics, theorising about micro-and macro-forms, composing by ratios, and the quantification of musical material. In the late 1980s he began studying fractals, a line of inquiry enshrined in a series of recent works—*Barcarola bilística*, *A Mandelbox* (a computer installation), *Vorwort zu Solaris*, *Video-Memorias*—with a common theme, Stanisław Lem's novel *Solaris*. On the basis of this interest, he has collaborated in constructing an interactive environment in which visitors participate in the evolution of fractal-generated universes in real time.

However, Maiguashca continues to explore, extending his work in computer-assisted composition, applying his findings to instrumental and acoustic contexts; as he moves into virgin territory in electro-acoustic music, and beyond the conventional boundaries of instrumental language, he seems to be searching for an ancient, mythic musical terrain.

—Emmanuelle Loubet

MALEC, Ivo. Yugoslav. Born in Zagreb, 30 March 1925. Educated at University of Zagreb, and Music Academy, Zagreb, 1945–51, diploma in composition and conducting; further study under Pierre Schaeffer, Group de Musique Concrète, from 1955; settled in Paris, 1959. Director, Rijeka Opera, Fiume, 1952–3; administrator, Groupe de Recherche Musicale, from 1960; co-founder, Musique Plus; professor, Conservatoire National Supérieur de Musique, Paris, from 1972. Recipient: 1st prize in composition, Music Academy, Zagreb; music prize, City of Zagreb; Grand Prix de l'Académie Charles Cros; Grand Prix de l'Académie du Disque; Diapason d'Or. Mailing address: c/o Editions Salabert, 22 rue Chauchat, 75009 Paris, France.

Publishers: Salabert; Breitkopf & Hartel; Editions Françaises de Musique.

Symphonies/orchestral:

Mouvements en couleur 1959; first performed Paris, March 1960. Recorded Jugoton LPY V 84.

Tutti (orchestra, tape) 1962; first performed Paris, 1962. Recorded Philips 836 894 DSY.

Sigma (large orchestra) 1963; first performed Zagreb, May 1963. Recorded Philips 836 891 DSY; INA-GRM Gramme 9105ma.
Vocatif 1968; first performed Paris, 1968. Recorded INA-GRM Gramme 9105ma.
Lumina (chamber strings, tape) 1968; first performed Lucerne, September 1968. Recorded INA-GRM Gramme 9105ma; Philips 6521 017.
GAM(m)MES 1971; first performed Strasbourg, June 1971.
Tehrana 1975; first performed Tehran, October 1975.
Arco-22 (22 strings) 1976; first performed Chiraz-Persepolis, August 1976.
Ottava bassa (double bass, orchestra) 1983; first performed Paris, April 1984.
Ottava alta (violin, orchestra) 1986.

Chamber/instrumental:

Dialogues (harpsichord or piano) 1961; first performed on piano, Zagreb, 1963; first performed on harpsichord, Frankfurt, 1966.
Miniatures pour Lewis Carroll (violin, flute, harp, 2–3 percussion) 1964; first performed Opatija, Yugoslavia, 1964. Recorded Philips 836 891 DSY.
Kitica (violin, flute, clarinet, trombone) 1972; first performed Paris, 1972.
Actuor (6 percussion) 1973; first performed La Rochelle, April 1973. Recorded Harmonia Mundi HM 5134.
Arco-11 (11 solo strings) 1975; first performed Paris, June 1975.
Week-End (3 synthesizers, tape) 1982; first performed Paris, May 1982.
Pieris (2 harps) 1985; first performed Paris, August 1985.
Attacca (percussion, tape) 1985.
Forma (string trio, tape) 1986–7.
Arco-1 (cello) 1987.

Vocal/choral:

Les Douze Mois (voice, instrumental ensemble) 1960; broadcast Radio France, 1 January 1961.
Cantate pour elle (soprano, harp, 4-track stereo tape) 1966; first performed May 1966. Recorded Philips 836 891 DSY.
Oral (actor, large orchestra) 1967; first performed Zagreb, May 1967. Recorded Erato STU 70431.
Lied (18 voices SATB, 39 strings) 1969; first performed Dubrovnik, July 1970. Recorded Philips 6521 017.
Dodecameron (12 unaccompanied voices SATB) 1970; first performed Royal, April 1971. Recorded Barclay 995 013; INA-GRM Gramme 9105ma.
Victor Hugo—Un contre tous ("musical poster" for 2 actors, mixed chorus, orchestra, tape) 1971; first performed Avignon, August 1971.
Vox, vocis (2 sopranos, 1 mezzo-soprano, 2 violins, viola, cello, double bass, trumpet, harp, 2 percussion; or for small orchestra) 1979; first performed Metz, November 1979. Recorded INA-GRM Gramme 9105ma.

Other:

Dahovi I (stereo tape) 1961; first performed Paris, 1962. Recorded Philips 836 891 DSY.
Dahovi II (stereo tape) 1962; first performed Paris, 1962. Recorded Philips 67 40 001.
Luminétudes (stereo tape) 1968; first performed Bordeaux, November 1970. Recorded Philips 6521 017.
Bizarra (stereo tape) 1972; first performed Paris, 1972. Recorded Philips 6521 017.
Triola, ou La symphonie pour moi-même (stereo tape) 1978; first performed Metz, November 1978. Recorded INA GRM 830 11.
Recitativo (4-track stereo tape) 1980; first performed Paris, April 1980. Recorded INA-GRM Gramme 9105ma.
Carillon Choral (stereo tape) 1981; first performed Lyon, March 1982.

PUBLICATIONS

By Malec: "Regard jeté dans un passe-miroir", in *Bulletin-Programme*, 14, INA-GRM, Paris, 1975; "Texte et/ou Musique", in *Recherches*, Paris, January 1980.

On Malec: Peter Selem, *Novi zvuk* [New sounds], Zagreb; Pierre Schaeffer, *La Musique Concrète*, Paris; issues of *Harmonie*, 94, February 1974; *Harmonie-Opéra*, 20, May 1982; *Revue Musicale*, 314–5, 1978; "Atelier de musique", television series on IM, Belgrade Television/Sarajevo Television, October 1983; *L'Exposition IM*, catalogue, Belgrade, October 1985; double issue of *Revue-Musical*, 1986.

* * *

Ivo Malec is one of the few prominent members of the Groupe de Recherches Musicales in Paris to have composed extensively for live performance as well as on tape, which is a crucial factor in the evolution of his attitude towards every aspect of composition: the nature and manipulation of "raw" materials, the organisation of forms and processes, the dramatic and expressive aims of the music, and the interconnections between all of these. Through Pierre Schaeffer, the only composition teacher he acknowledges, he absorbed the importance of the connection between surrealism and *musique concrète*, and his vocal and instrumental music too is informed by an idiosyncratic sense of incongruous juxtaposition, of delirious extremes of tenderness and violence, of "convulsive beauty". The influence of *musique concrète* on his live-performance music is seen above all in the tactile way in which he treats compositional "objects", gestures, motifs or single internally complex sounds, almost as if they were *objets trouvés* (which in a sense of course they are), and incorporates them into forms which have much of the atmosphere of bizarre, oneiric narratives. It is hardly surprising that he has been drawn repeatedly to writing for voices and for stringed instruments, exploiting to the full the allusiveness of the former (although usually without words), the physicality of bow against string in the latter, and the enormous range between stridency and delicacy in both.

In *Lumina* (part of a cycle also containing *Luminétudes* and *Lied*, thus combining voices, strings and electro-acoustic music) the confrontation between the largely textural string music and the sparse, abrasive interjections of the tape produces a sequence of dramatic situations of a sophistication rarely found in attempts to combine live and prerecorded sounds. The later *Arco-11*, *Arco-22* and *Arco-1* continue the preoccupation with string instruments with undimmed inventiveness, as does the massive ("symphonic", in the composer's words) *Ottava bassa*. As preparation for the composition of the latter, Malec hired a double bass for a period of lone experimentation, rather than relying on received information, which again underlines a studio-influenced tendency to make the closest possible contact with the mechanism of sound production.

That Malec's vocal compositions stem from a similar standpoint is evidenced most strikingly by *Dodecameron*: while the human voice's unique capacity for expressive directness is deployed with startling virtuosity (not to mention that required by the singers), the performers are essentially treated as *sound generators* and their material assembled as if it were so many painstakingly-recorded samples. To a lesser extent, the same qualities are found in the works for orchestra, although the necessity to be somewhat less adventurous (in other words more pitch-centred) in the treatment of wind instruments exposes a certain relative lack of finesse in the handling of harmonic materials.

On the other hand, in *Triola* Malec has created one of the most powerful and fascinating works in the entire field of electro-acoustic music. Its sound-world, largely "artificial" in origin (which lends further weight to the sense of dislocation engendered by the occasional "natural" sounds), has few parallels even in Malec's own oeuvre, occupying the furthest possible extremes of barely articulated rage, introspective stillness and a Magritte-like friction between musical "images" in its three interlinked movements, with a combined duration of over half an hour.

It is a pity that Malec's extraordinary body of work has had negligible influence outside France; his music gives off a genuine sense of freedom and exhilaration with the immediacy and richness of sounds, which is never lost sight of or defused by theoretical speculation.

—Richard Barrett

MANSURIAN, Tigran. Armenian. Born in Beirut, Lebanon, 27 January 1939. Educated at Beirut Catholic School, 1945–7; secondary school, Artik, Armenia, 1947–54; Yerevan Music School, 1956–60; Yerevan State Conservatoire, 1960–7. Married Nora Aharonian in 1960; 1 son and 1 daughter. Teacher of contemporary music theory, 1967–76, and teacher of composition, since 1986, Yerevan State Conservatoire. Recipient: 1st prize, Young Composers Competition, Moscow (for *Partita*), 1967; Vilnius Film Festival Award (for film score *A Piece of Sky*), 1980; State Prize of Armenia (for *Cello Concerto No 2* and *Tovem*), 1981; State Prize of Armenia (for film score *The Tango of Our Childhood*), 1985. Mailing address: ul. Terian 56, dom. 14, Yerevan 9, Armenia, U.S.S.R.

Publishers: Ricordi, Milan; Hans Sikorski, Hamburg; Associated, U.S.A.

Symphonies/orchestral:

Partita 1967; first performed Yerevan, 1967.
Preludes 1975–6; first performed Yerevan.
Cello Concerto No 1 1977; first performed Yerevan, 1977.
Canonical Ode (2 string orchestras, 4 harps, organ) 1977; first performed Yerevan, 1977.
Cello Concerto No 2 1978; first performed Yerevan, 1978.
Double Concerto (violin, cello, string orchestra) 1978; first performed Riga, 1978.
Nachtmusik 1979–80; first performed Yerevan, 1980.
Concerto for Violin and String Orchestra 1982; first performed Moscow, 1983.
Choreographic Sketches after Andersen's "Ice Queen" (string orchestra) 1986; first performed Riga, 1987.
Cello Concerto No 3 1988–9.

Chamber/instrumental:

Sonata (piano) 1966; first performed Moscow, 1967.
Interior (string quartet) 1970; first performed Paris, 1972.
Sonata No 1 (cello, piano) 1973.
Sonata No 2 (cello, piano) 1974; first performed Moscow, 1974.
Quintet (flute, oboe, clarinet, bassoon, horn) 1974; first performed Yerevan, 1974.
The Rhetorician (harpsichord, flute, violin, double bass) 1978; first performed Moscow, 1979.
Tovem (15 soloists) 1979; first performed Moscow, 1979.
Commemorating Stravinsky (15 soloists) 1981; first performed Moscow, 1982.
String Quartet No 1 1983–4; first performed Yerevan, 1984.
String Quartet No 2 1984; first performed Yerevan, 1984.
Five Bagatelles (violin, cello, piano) 1985; first performed Telavi, Georgia, 1985.
Tombeau (cello, concussion instruments) 1988; first performed London, 1989.

Vocal/choral:

Three Songs After García Lorca (voice, piano) 1966; first performed Yerevan, 1966.
Four Hairens from Hanapet Kuchak (voice, piano) 1967; first performed Yerevan, 1967.
Three Nairian Songs (voice, orchestra) 1975; first performed Yerevan, 1976.
Three Madrigals (voice, flute, cello, piano) 1980; first performed Yerevan, 1981.
Sunset Songs (cycle for voice, piano) 1984–5; first performed Yerevan, 1985.
The Land of Nairi (cycle for voice, piano) 1986; first performed Yerevan, 1986.
Miserere (voice, string orchestra) 1988; first performed Lyon, 1989.

Other:

The Colour of Pomegranate (film score; Parajanov) 1969.
King John (incidental music to Shakespeare) 1979.
Coriolanus (incidental music to Shakespeare) 1979.
A Piece of Sky (film score; Malian) 1979.
The Ice Queen (ballet after Hans Christian Andersen, in memory of the children who died in the Armenian earthquake of December 1988) 1989–90; first performed Yerevan, 1990.

PUBLICATIONS

On Mansurian: M. Berko, in *The Music of the Transcaucasian Republics* [in Russian], 1975; Hannelore Gerlach, in *Funfzig sowjetische Komponisten*, 1984; M. Nestyeva, *Music in the USSR*, July/September 1987.

Tigran Mansurian comments:

An ideal music would be represented by a single super-radiant sound which would envelop all of us into itself, making all of us infinitely happy. This great sound does not exist. That is why music presents itself to us in a human image, in accordance with reality. And that is why it is important that composition must also possess the exactness, the precision of that reality.

My reality consists of the Armenian language as a phonetic system, of ancient Armenian music, spiritual and secular, and of a rich worldwide experience of musical composition which is true to the reality. The dream of a single, super-radiant sound makes definite the imperfection of human musics. Great musicians are trying to overcome that imperfection.

* * *

Tigran Mansurian is undoubtedly the most important living composer in Armenia. He is also a key figure in the emergence of a strongly modernist tendency in contemporary Soviet music in the years following the death of Stalin.

Both these facts are worth stressing precisely because they are somewhat contradictory. For the Armenian culture to which Mansurian belongs is highly nationalistic and certainly ill-disposed to the unifying ironed-out qualities of centralised Soviet culture. It is also not especially friendly to Western cultures. Mansurian's achievement is to have participated fully in the musical society that has given us such (basically Russian) composers as Valentin Silvestrov, Edison Denisov, Sofia Gubaidulina and Alfred Schnittke, to have stayed in touch against all the odds with all musical developments in the West—Mansurian is a Francophile with a particular regard for Debussy and Boulez—and, at the same time, to have remained profoundly loyal to his Armenian roots and branches and especially to the truths enshrined in the work of Komitas Keworkian, probably the greatest Armenian composer and scholar of all.

Mansurian's early start in life was extremely unpromising, impoverished and isolated, but out of his original lack of opportunities he developed an unflinching curiosity and openness. No doubt these qualities spurred him on to travel the more than a thousand miles to the Baltic during his summer holidays to visit the library where Luigi Nono had persuaded a sympathetic librarian to house scores by Schoenberg, Webern and the Darmstadt composers that he had brought from the West.

The first results of the young Armenian's contact with such music include some particularly fine piano works, of a distinctive refinement that owes much to Webern and Boulez, but at the same time is clearly expressed in a harmonic language all the composer's own.

The extreme delicacy of the early works was already by the early 1970s giving way to rather tougher and larger structures. The evolution of Mansurian's two splendid cello sonatas gives some idea of his search for the purest expression of what he has to say. The first sonata is almost suggestive of the world of expressionism, the music louder, more violent and tormented than the earlier piano music and cast in much larger forms. By the next year, the second sonata, on the same scale but with something of the delicacy of the earlier music, is beginning to admit distinct strains of early Armenian ecclesiastical music into the generally serial domain. The odd thing about this music is the gracefulness with which Mansurian mixes his two quite different sets of associations. There is nothing here of the torture of Schnittke's "polystylistics". What Mansurian is looking for is synthesis.

As the Armenian elements began to dominate Mansurian's music more and more, perhaps inevitably the serial elements began to retreat. Modal harmony became more and more of a feature in his works. And, perhaps most oddly in our day, Mansurian began to pay more attention to the harmonic idiom of Bartók. Bartók of all composers respected most the character of the folk material on which he drew, and by implication the cultural identity of the people on whose music he drew. Mansurian always admired the passive respect that comes from accepting music material for what it is and not trying to force it into unkind shapes. Such an attitude of mind was clear in his early serial works, with their quiet respect for the inevitability of natural proliferation of the idea itself. This too was what he admired in Debussy, who had the capacity to allow ideas simply to be. So in the more recent works inspired by Armenian musical materials of one sort or another, Mansurian has *appeared* to change style more than he actually has. All that he has done really is to allow the material once again to speak for itself.

One of the most powerful expressions of this attitude in Mansurian's recent music is his Third Cello Concerto, in which passive respect is seen at its most imaginative, and also at its most energetic. Passivity, we see, does not mean standing still. Thoroughly folk-inspired melodic ideas seem to generate from within themselves a constant stream of new ideas and associations, which fold in and out of one another with an enchanting sense of natural spontaneity.

In very recent years, Mansurian's search for an ever greater synthesis and natural simplicity has led him into the field of children's music. To this end he has completed a number of sonatinas for children to play. Technically and stylistically these might seem a long way from his earlier Webernian piano music. But there is much in the underlying spirit that has not changed.

—Gerard McBurney

MANZONI, Giacomo. Italian. Born in Milan, 26 September 1932. Educated at Liceo Musica Laudamo, Messina (composition under Gino Contilli), 1948–50; Conservatorio Giuseppe Verdi, Milan, 1950–6, degree in piano, 1954; concurrently Universita Commerciale Bocconi, Milan, degree in foreign languages (German), 1955; period of study in Germany, 1954–5; Ferienkurse für Neue Musik, Darmstadt, summers 1956, 1957. Married Eugenia Tretti in 1960; 1 son. Editor, *Il Diapason* music magazine, 1955–6; music critic, *L'Unita*, Milan, 1958–66; teacher of harmony and counterpoint, Conservatorio Giuseppe Verdi, 1962–4, 1968–9, and from 1974; teacher of harmony and counterpoint, 1965–8, and teacher of composition, 1969–74, Conservatorio G.B. Martini, Bologna; music editor, *Prisma*, 1968; resident in Berlin, Deutscher Akademischer Austaschdienst, 1982; master class in composition, Scuola di Musica, Fiesole, since 1988. Recipient: UNESCO Prize (for *Parole da Beckett*), 1973; Premio Abbati della Critica (for *Masse: Omaggio a Edgard Varèse*), 1986; prize for best music theatre work (*Dr Faustus*) in Italy, 1989. Mailing address: Viale Papinano 31, 20123 Milan, Italy.

Publishers: Ricordi; Suvini Zerboni.

Symphonies/orchestral:

Fantasia-recitativo-finale 1956; first performed Milan, 21 January 1957.
Studio per 24 (chamber orchestra) 1962; first performed Venice, 13 April 1962.
Studio No 2 1962–3; first performed Milan, 20 April 1963.

Insiemi 1967; first performed Milan, 30 October 1969.
Multipli (chamber orchestra) 1972–3; first performed Washington, D.C., 23 February 1973.
Variabili 1973; first performed Bolzano, 8 March 1973.
Masse: Omagio a Edgard Varèse (piano, orchestra) 1977; first performed Berlin, 6 October 1977.
Lessico (double string orchestra) 1978; first performed Piacenza, 23 May 1978.
Modulor (4 orchestras) 1979; first performed Venice, 7 October 1979.
Ode 1982; broadcast RAI, Milan, 11 March 1983.
Nuovo incontri (violin, strings) 1984; first performed Florence, 5 June 1984.

Chamber/instrumental:

Piccola suite (violin, piano) 1952–3.
Klavieralbum 1956 (piano) 1956; first performed Milan, 2 March 1956.
Seconda piccola suite (violin, piano) 1956; first performed Darmstadt, 21 July 1957.
Improvvisazione (viola, piano) 1958; first performed Milan, 26 May 1959.
Musica notturna (flute, 2 clarinets, bassoon, horn, percussion, piano) 1966; first performed Venice, 12 September 1967. Recorded Fonit Cetra ITL 70045.
Quadruplum (2 trumpets, 2 trombones) 1968; first performed L'Aquila, 30 March 1969. Recorded Desto DC 6477 A.
Spiel (11 strings) 1969; first performed London, 26 April 1969.
Parafrasi con finale (flute, clarinet, bassoon, horn, trumpet, trombone, harpsichord, double bass, percussion) 1969; first performed Nuremberg, 6 June 1969.
String Quartet 1971; first performed Como, 30 September 1972.
Percorso a otto (2 woodwind quartets: flute/alto flute/piccolo, oboe, cor anglais, clarinet, bass clarinet, 2 bassoons; or flute/alto flute/piccolo, bass flute/flute, cor anglais, heckelphone, clarinet, contrabass clarinet, bassoon, contrabassoon) 1975; first performed Utrecht, 3 September 1976.
Epodo (flute, oboe, clarinet, horn, bassoon) 1976; first performed Fiesole, 18 July 1977.
Sigla (2 trumpets, 2 trombones) 1976.
Percorso C2 (bassoon, 11 strings) 1976; first performed Graz, 15 October 1977.
Percorso F (double bass) 1976; first performed Royan, 26 March 1976.
Percorso GG (clarinet, tape) 1979; first performed Siena, 10 August 1979.
Hölderlin: Epilogo (cor anglais, horn, trumpet, trombone, percussion, 2 violins, viola, cello, double bass) 1980; first performed Paris, 12 June 1981.
D'improvviso (6 or 12 percussion) 1981; first performed Milan, 11 April 1983.
Echi (guitar) 1981; first performed Turin, 2 October 1982.
Incipit (piano) 1983; first performed Florence, 2 September 1984.
Incontro (violin, string quartet) 1983; first performed Naples, 22 November 1983.
Opus 50 (daunium) (flute/piccolo, oboe, clarinet, bassoon, horn, percussion, 2 violins, viola, cello, double bass) 1984; first performed Foggia, 14 November 1984.
"Der Strahlen der Sonne" (flute, piano, harp, glockenspiel, percussion, 2 violins, viola, cello) 1985; first performed Milan, 21 April 1985.
Percorso H (flute) 1987.
Frase (clarinet, piano) 1988.
To Planets and to Flowers (saxophone quartet) 1989; first performed Bonn, May 1989.

Vocal/choral:

Preludio–"Grave" di W. Cuney-Finale (female voice, clarinet, violin, viola, cello) 1956; broadcast RAI, Rome, 30 June 1958.
Cinque vicariote (mixed chorus, orchestra; popular Sicilian texts) 1958; broadcast RAI, Turin, 29 November 1968.
Tre liriche di Paul Eluard (female voice, flute, clarinet, trumpet, violin, cello) 1958; first performed Rome, 14 May 1958.
Due sonetti italiani (unaccompanied mixed chorus; Leopardi) 1961; first performed Siena, 5 August 1987.
Don Chisciotte (soprano, small chorus, chamber orchestra; Hikmet) 1961; first performed Venice, 14 September 1964.
Quattro poesie spagnole (baritone, clarinet, viola, guitar; Pacheco, Goytisolo, Alberti) 1962; first performed Florence, 21 March 1962.
Spass (female voice, piano; Schwitters) 1965; first performed Rome, 4 March 1966.
Ombre (alla memoria di Che Guevara) (choral voices, orchestra) 1968; first performed Bologna, 10 May 1968.
Parole da Beckett (2 choruses, 3 instrumental groups, tape) 1970–1; broadcast RAI, Rome, 21 May 1971.
Hölderlin: Frammento (mixed chorus, orchestra) 1972; first performed Venice, 17 September 1972.
Suite Robespierre (2 sopranos, mezzo-soprano, baritone, bass, 2 reciters, mixed chorus, orchestra) 1976; broadcast RAI, Turin, 19 November 1976.
Estremita (voice; Leonetti) 1983; first performed Reggio Emilia, 11 September 1983.
Scene Sinfoniche per il Doktor Faustus (mixed chorus ad lib, orchestra; Mann) 1984; first performed Milan, 3 October 1984.
Omaggio a Josquin (transcription of *Nymphes des bois*; soprano, horn, violin, 2 violas, cello; Molinet) 1985; first performed Rome, 24 February 1987.
Studio per il finale del Doktor Faustus (mixed chorus, orchestra; Mann) 1985; first performed Venice, 26 September 1985.
Dedica (flute, bass voice, mixed chorus, instrumental group ad lib, orchestra) 1985–6; first performed Parma, 9 May 1986.
"Uei prea la biele stele . . . " (unison male chorus, 1 or 2 bass drums; traditional) 1987.
Ten Poems by Emily Dickinson (soprano, 14 strings, 2 harps) 1988; first performed Venice, 1989.
An die Musik (soprano, flute; Rilke) 1989.

Opera/dramatic:

La legge 1955.
La sentenza (Jona) 1960; first performed Bergamo, 13 October 1960.
Atomtod (Jona) 1964; first performed Milan, 27 March 1965.
Per Massimiliano Robespierre 1974; first performed Bologna, 17 April 1975.
Doktor Faustus (after Mann) 1988; first performed Milan, 16 May 1989.

Other:

Studio No 3 (electronic) 1964; first performed Milan, 15 April 1966.

Malina (score to film by Bachmann/Schroter; soprano, string quartet, orchestra) 1990.

PUBLICATIONS

By Manzoni: "Bruno Maderna", interview in *der Reihe*, 4, 1958; "Lui e lei nel terzo millennio: la musica", in *Giornale pianeta*, 2, June–August 1965; *Guida all'ascolto della musica sinfonica*, Milan, 1967; "La passione elettronica di Luigi Nono", in *Prisma*, 1, 8–10, August–October 1968; *A. Schönberg: L'uomo, l'opera, i testi musicali*, Milan, 1975; translation of Arnold Schoenberg, *Manuale d'armonia*, Milan, 1963, *Elementi di composizione musicale*, Milan, 1969, *Esercizi preliminari de contrappunto*, Milan, 1970, and *Analisi e pratica musicale*, Turin, 1974; translations of T.W. Adorno, *Filosofia della musica moderna*, Turin, 1959, *If fido maestro sostituto*, Turin, 1969, and *Introduzione alla sociologia della musica*, Turin, 1971.

On Manzoni: Peter Paul Nash, "Textbook Avant-Garde", in *The Listener*, 17 February 1983; Joachim Noller, *Engagement und Form. GMs Werk in Kulturtheoritischen und musikhistorischen Zusammenhangen*, Frankfurt, 1987; Fabrizio Dorsi, *GM*, Milan, 1989.

* * *

Giacomo Manzoni began his musical studies in 1948 under Gino Cortilli, a pioneer of twelve-tone music in Italy. Two years later, deeply impressed by his contact with Cortilli, he moved to the conservatory in his native Milan, where he gained a diploma in piano in 1954, and concurrently studied German, graduating with a dissertation on "The Role of Music in the Work of Thomas Mann".

Manzoni had already produced work as a student, and in 1956 and 1957 attended the summer courses at Darmstadt, studying serialism intensively. His creative thought is based on an ideology committed to the traditions of the Enlightenment and highly politicised. From 1960 to 1986, he was a member of the Italian Communist Party (PCI) and in the 1970s took part in a number of political and cultural initiatives led by the PCI. His engagement, however, especially as reflected in his music, remained reserved and subtle; Manzoni has always regarded political engagement as an artistic stance and is impatient of extramusical gestures.

In the face of his teachers' classicism, Manzoni turned ever more confidently to the thought and techniques of the Second Viennese School and the Darmstadt circle. Needless to say, though, his acceptance of serialism was not uncritical; he learned much from outsiders like Bruno Maderna and Luigi Nono and from their example began to construct his own philosophy. To be relevant to social realities, the rational bases of serialism have to be connected to historical, cultural and individual factors. Serialism as a dogma is of minor importance to him; Manzoni's real interests lie in new possibilities of microstructure, which are in themselves secondary to the expressive phenomenology of the completed piece.

Having explored horizontal microstructures, Manzoni entered new terrain in the 1960s, increasingly occupied with the macrostructural architecture of sound (and taking Edgard Varèse as his model), discovering vertical sound-structures and structured sound as the basic material of musical construction. He paid special attention to the phonetic and musical values of language, as well as to the extended instrumental resources, such as multiphonics, opened up by new playing techniques. In several choral and orchestral works of the 1970s, Manzoni manages to integrate these elements into large-scale forms (see the settings for chorus in *Parole da Beckett* and *Hölderlin: Frammento*) as well as settings for orchestra in *Modulor* and the homage to Varèse *Masse*.

Manzoni's major works combine a whole range of past achievements and closely relate to the human existential situation. His compositions for music theatre seem to be the most appropriate outlet for his distinctive interaction of musical autonomy and engagement. In the 1980s, Manzoni strove for a new balance of vertical and horizontal structures, whereby certain constellations of intervals are emphasised in both dimensions. Structure, once understood as the organisation of parameters, is now a melting pot of accumulated sound material embodying a range of different (including tonal) resources. Personal style is equated with historical synthesis.

—Joachim Noller

MARCUS, Bunita. American. Born in Madison, Wisconsin, 5 May 1952. Educated: studied composition under Franz Loschnigg, 1968–73; University of Wisconsin, Madison, 1973–6, B.M. in music theory; State University of New York, Buffalo (under Morton Feldman), 1977–81, Ph.D. in composition. Teaching artist, Western New York Institute, and State College at Buffalo, 1982–3; teaching artist, Lincoln Center Institute, and Teachers College, Columbia University, both New York City, 1983–5; guest lecturer/artist, Yale Summer School of Music and Art, New Haven, Connecticut, 1984; assistant professor of composition, Brooklyn College, City University of New York, 1984–6; composer in residence, University of California, San Diego, 1986; independent composer, since 1986; writer on new music for *Elle* and other magazines; guest editor, *New Observations* art journal; producer (with Francesco Clemente), Salon Concert series; pianist and conductor. Recipient: ISCM 1st selection (*Two Pianos and Violin*) World Music Days, Graz, 1982; ISCM League of composers, National composers competition, 1983; Kranichsteiner Musikpreis, Darmstadt, 1986; National Endowment for the Arts Composer's Fellowship, 1988–90. Mailing address: 415 Ocean Parkway, #3D, Brooklyn, New York 11218, U.S.A.

Publisher: none.

Chamber/instrumental:

1975 (Arp 2500, synthesizer, alto saxophone, bass clarinet, guitar, steel drum) 1975; first performed Madison, Wisconsin, 1975.
Quintet (clarinet, bass clarinet, 3 percussion) 1976; first performed Madison, Wisconsin, 1976.
Apogee One (guitar) 1976.
Parent Terrain (clarinet, bass clarinet, cello, double bass, 2 percussion) 1977; first performed Buffalo, New York, 1977.
Apogee Two (double bass, percussion) 1977; first performed Buffalo, New York, 1977.

Apogee Three (clarinet) 1977; first performed Buffalo, New York, 1978.
Apogee Four (alto flute, percussion) 1978; first performed Buffalo, New York, 1978.
Oboe, Clarinet, Bass Clarinet, Trumpet, Trombone 1978; first performed Buffalo, New York, 1978.
Piano Piece 1979; first performed Buffalo, New York, 1979.
Untrammeled Thought (cello, piano) 1979; first performed Buffalo, New York, 1979.
Wolpe Variations (piano) 1980.
Two Pianos and Violin 1981; first performed Buffalo, New York, 1981.
Merry Christmas, Mrs Whiting (piano) 1981; first performed Buffalo, New York, 1983.
Solo (flute) 1982; first performed Berlin, 1982.
Music for Japan (flute, clarinet, harp, piano, percussion) 1983; first performed Tokyo, 1983.
Sleeping Woman (flute, violin, piano) 1984; first performed London, 1985.
Lecture for Jo Kondo (alto flute, violin, piano, percussion, optional speaking voice; Shapiro) 1985; first performed London, 1985.
The Rugmaker (string quartet) 1986; first performed Middleburg, The Netherlands, 1986.
Corpse and Mirror (violin, 16 gongs, 2 vibraphones, koto) 1986; first performed Darmstadt, 1986.
Adam and Eve (flute, violin, cello, piano, 2 percussion) 1987; first performed Middleburg, The Netherlands, 1987.
But to Fashion a Lullaby for You (piano) 1988; first performed New York City, 1988.
Julia (piano) 1989; first performed Tokyo, 1990.
Clear Ideas (percussion, piano, tape) 1990–1; first performed China, 1991.

Vocal/choral:

Valentine (voice) 1974; first performed Buffalo, New York, 1980.
Droum (soprano, mezzo-soprano, tenor, flute, bass clarinet, violin, double bass, guitar, percussion) 1975; first performed Madison, Wisconsin, 1975.
Untrammelled Thought (voice, piano) 1980.

Other:

The Sky Is Falling (tape) 1974.
Tape Piece 1975.
Perhaps a Woman Would Know (tape, dance, brass, percussion, actors, poetry) 1976.
Visa (tape, film, slides, classical guitar) 1976.
Readings of a Political Nature (speaker) 1990.
Knife Facts (2 martial artists, knives, props) 1990.
Women's Work (actress, props, tape) 1990.
Ice Falling (tape) 1990.
Imaginary Max (tape) 1990.

PUBLICATIONS

By Marcus: participant in "Conversation with Morton Feldman, John Cage", in *RES* 6, 1983, and in *MusikTexte*, 5, 1983; "Memorial Eulogy" [to Morton Feldman], in *MusikTexte*, 22, 1987; "A Conversation on Composition and Improvisation" (with LaMonte Young and Morton Feldman), in *RES*, 13, 1987; "Who's Afraid of New Music?", in *Elle*, March 1989; "Random Notes from Manuscripts: 1979–86", and as guest editor, *New Observations Art Journal*, May 1989; "The Listening Mind" (on conductor Catherine Comet), in *Elle*, October 1989; "Maestro Bravissimo" (on conductor Marcello Panni), in *Elle*, November 1989.

On Marcus: Jan Williams, "An Interview with Morton Feldman" (contains discussion of percussion writing in *Music for Japan*), in *Percussive Notes* 21(6), September 1983, and "Conversation with Morton Feldman, John Cage" (contains discussion of *Solo* for flute), in *RES*, 6, 1983, also in *MusikTexte*, 5, 1983; Barbara Monk Feldman, "All Things Being Unmeasured" (discussion of *Corpse and Mirror* and *Two Pianos and Violin*), in *New Observations Art Journal*, May 1989.

Bunita Marcus comments:

Listeners often mistakenly think that I am interested in beauty because I occasionally have passages of exquisitely beautiful music in my works. But I am only interested in beauty because it is "superficial", it is sometimes so "on the surface" and impersonal that it doesn't get in the way of what it is I'm *really* trying to express.

Recently there has been a great deal of repetition in my work, and each time something is repeated it is changed minutely. I am interested in finding the absolute smallest change I can make that will change the underlying experience of the music the *most*. This is what Morton Feldman and Chris Newman have both referred to as "non-developmental development" in my work—where nothing (in the music, that is) seems to be developing, yet the emotional experience of the piece is moving ahead at a relatively good pace.

My focus is 100% on subtext. I want to create a music where everything is internal and subconscious; where nothing seems to be happening at all, and you are changing inside.

* * *

Bunita Marcus played the piano and clarinet from an early age. A particularly fine clarinettist, she played every kind of music, from dixieland and dance band to orchestral music. With this rich and diverse musical background, she started composing at the age of 14, and commenced composition studies a few years later. As an undergraduate student at the University of Wisconsin in the mid 1970s, Marcus worked prolifically in both instrumental and electronic media, including multi-media pieces. She describes many of these as student exercises.

An important turning point in her music came when she began studying with Morton Feldman at Buffalo in 1976. Feldman was an important influence, especially on her early work, for example in her approach to form, in the pacing of the music, in her approach to the registration of individual pitches and the voicing of chords, and in the choice of such titles as *Oboe, Clarinet, Bass Clarinet, Trumpet, Trombone*. In this piece many of Marcus's own musical characteristics are already present: the permutation and rotation of tiny melodic fragments, repetition of chord sequences with slight rhythmic alterations, subtle displacement of beats and avoidance of a rigid metre, and different rhythmic proportions in several parts creating a kind of heterophony. This is one of a number of purely instrumental works written while at Buffalo; electronic composition ceased due to the absence of a studio there, though she has returned to this medium in the last few years.

Untrammeled Thought could be seen as a concentrated version of *Two Pianos and Violin*. Using just one piano together with a stringed instrument, and lasting about a fifth of the time, *Untrammeled Thought* does not repeat several fragments; rather there is just one repetition of the whole piece. And unlike the longer piece, where different metres exist for each instrument, creating mainly independent voices, here the two instruments are very much one voice. The registration of each note is an integral feature, as it was for Feldman. At 40 minutes, *Two Pianos and Violin* stands as the composer's longest piece to date, and ranges over a rich field of musical images. By using three different sets of metres simultaneously, Marcus is able to combine several musical images. About midway through the piece there is a section of counterpoint where all three instruments play similar material, but later the parts separate in style and direction, as instructed by the composer, and return shortly before the end of the piece playing three different "solos".

Patterning has featured greatly in Marcus's music since the mid 1980s. She compares this to the example of Kurdish rugs, both in the graphic pattern(s) of the design and in the overall placement of colour on the grid, or the work of Jasper Johns, in particular since 1970. She is concerned with patterns for the amusement of the listener, rather than patterns explained or discussed, as demonstrated in *Lecture for Jo Kondo*, *The Rugmaker* and *Adam and Eve*. Both in the visual analogies and in her own works, Marcus describes the ideas as "playful, but still thoughtful", and this is what leads one into the artist's own creative imagination. *Lecture for Jo Kondo*—Jo Kondo is a Japanese composer who shares a number of Marcus's own aesthetic preoccupations—alternates two types of musical phrase: those consisting of four simultaneous melodies—one for each instrument, where the shape and direction of the melodic line takes precedence over rhythmic precision—and those in which the four parts interweave to form a composite melody (Marcus calls this type "counterpoint"). This work may be performed with a spoken text (poems by David Shapiro), and may be prefaced by a shorter piece, *Sleeping Woman*, whose final section pre-echoes the opening material of *Lecture*.

The Rugmaker ranks as one of the finest string quartets by any living composer, and should really be in the repertoire of most quartets. An important aspect of this piece is the movement of sound, an obvious example being the four- and five-note rising figures about midway into the piece, which are passed from one instrument to another, or the ascending and descending scales which dominate the latter part of the piece. If the desired placing of the amplified instruments around the audience were always possible, this very physical projection of the patterning process could be perceived. There are, on the other hand, sections of total unanimity of sound, particularly striking in the repeated eight-part chords (all players double-stopping) which close the piece.

Although not programmatic, *Adam and Eve* is a piece about love. Marcus wanted to explore, through music, the human experience of love with all the tangents, diversions and complications that might arise. Much of the work consists of melodies and melodic fragments for flute and strings, floating almost freely over a texture of repetitive figures, mainly in the piano and tuned percussion. The arpeggiated figures in the piano, outlining minor triads, might suggest the world of Philip Glass, but Marcus imbues these repetitions with far greater meaning. For her, repetition *is* variation—"to repeat something is to change it". This work and its immediate predecessor, *The Rugmaker*, reveal a new sophistication in the parameter of dynamic gradation. The often continuously quiet dynamics of the earlier pieces have given way to a greater range of dynamics as well as constant subtle and expressive changes within even the shortest of phrases.

As well as continuing to write purely instrumental music, Marcus has been working recently in the electronic medium again, combining tape with instruments and producing tape pieces using concrete sounds. She has also worked in the medium of film, and presented a good deal of performance art. Marcus is undoubtedly one of the most important composers of her generation, and one of the most original working in America today. She has always eschewed the glamour of minimalism, and has little sympathy for overly complex music in which pitch is arbitrary. Describing herself as a "post-minimalist", and her music as consonant rather than tonal, reductive rather than minimal, she has struck out on her own path, creating music in which each note—with its attendant register, instrumentation and articulation—is significant, and in which the smallest rhythmic movement is an important musical event.

—Michael Blake

MARSH, Roger (Michael). British/English. Born in Bournemouth, 10 December 1949. Educated at William Ellis School, London; composition lessons under Ian Kellam; University of York (composition under Bernard Rands), B.A., 1971, D.Phil., 1975; University of California, San Diego (as Harkness Fellow), 1976. Married the harpist Christina Rhys, 24 July 1976; 2 sons and 1 daughter. Director, Clap music theatre ensemble, 1972–5; lecturer, 1978–85, and head of department, 1985–8, University of Keele, Staffordshire; member of music department, University of York, since 1988. Mailing address: 69 Marsh Lane, Nantwich, Cheshire CW5 5LH, England.

Publisher: Novello.

Symphonies/orchestral:

Dum's Dream (concert version) 1973; first performed York, 1973.
Still 1980, revised 1987; first performed Birmingham, 13 November 1981; revised version first performed Liverpool, 12 May 1987.
Stepping Out (orchestra, chamber orchestra, piano) 1990.

Chamber/instrumental:

Jesters—(for Sicks) (2 oboes, 2 clarinets, 2 bassoons) 1972; first performed York, June 1972.
Serenade (amplified double bass, 15 strings) 1974; first performed London, 16 July 1974.
Sweet and Short (clarinet, piano, double bass) 1974; first performed London, 10 September 1974.
Variations for Trombones (alto trombone, 2 tenor trombones, bass trombone; or alto trombone, tape) 1977; first performed Los Angeles, 5 February 1979.
Time Before (double bass, tape) 1977; first performed London, 19 January 1979.
Point to Point (2 oboes, 2 clarinets, 2 horns, 2 bassoons) 1979; first performed Sheffield, 19 May 1979.
Two Movements (2 flutes, 2 clarinets, harp, string quartet) 1979; first performed London, 9 October 1979.

Spit and Blow (tuba) 1981; first performed Birmingham, 27 February 1983.
Heaven Haven (harp; trio version forms part of *Song of Devotion*) 1982; first performed Isle of Man, August 1983.
Music for Piano and Instruments (piano, flute/piccolo, oboe, 2 clarinets/1 bass clarinet, bassoon, horn, trumpet, trombone, tuba, 2 percussion) 1986; first performed York, 17 March 1986.
Ferry Music (clarinet, cello, piano) 1988; first performed London, 6 October 1988.
Dying for It (flute, oboe, clarinet, bassoon, marimba, violin, viola, cello double bass) 1988.
Easy Steps (piano) 1989.

Vocal/choral:

PS (female voice, double bass, trombone; Beckett) 1971; first performed London, December 1972.
Streim (soprano, flute, clarinet, trumpet, double bass) 1972; first performed London, October 1972.
The Lover's Ghost (folk song for soprano, 2 flutes, 2 clarinets, cello) 1972, revised for high voice, harp, 1976; revised version first performed London, 5 January 1975.
Dum ("vocal-percussive fantasy" for male vocalist/actor; Emerson, Donne, Brooke, Christina Rossetti, anon., Lord's Prayer) 1973–7.
On and On (folk song for soprano, 2 clarinets, bass clarinet) 1975; first performed London, 27 February 1975.
Three Hale Maries (3 sopranos, flute, clarinets, trumpet, harp, piano, 2 percussion, viola, cello) 1976; first performed San Diego, California, 17 March 1977.
Another Silly Love Song (soprano, clarinet, piano) 1976; first performed St Albans, 12 January 1977.
Not a Soul But Ourselves . . . (2 female and 2 male voices, independent amplification; Joyce) 1977; first performed San Diego, California, 29 November 1977. Recorded Wergo WER 60094.
Bits and Scraps (soprano, alto, tenor, bass, technician/vocalist, light; also version for actor/vocalist, tape; Beckett) 1979; first performed London, 6 May 1979.
A Psalm and a Silly Love Song (soprano, mezzo-soprano, flute, clarinet, trumpet, viola, cello) 1979; first performed London, 25 April 1979.
The Wormwood and the Gall (mezzo-soprano, flute/alto flute, clarinet, percussion, harp, viola, cello; Jeremiah) 1981; first performed London, 6 July 1981.
Words of Love (baritone, 2 oboes, bassoon, harpsichord; Joyce) 1982; first performed Llantwit Major, South Glamorgan, 26 August 1982.
Deliah (soprano, alto saxophone or A clarinet; part of *Samson*) 1982; first performed Birmingham, 18 September 1982; first performance of clarinet version Cambridge, 18 July 1985.
Songs of Devotion (soprano, clarinet, guitar; includes vocal arrangement of *Heaven Haven*) 1983; first performed York, 10 March 1984.
Samson (baritone, 4 sopranos, 2 basses, alto saxophone/soprano saxophone, all with individual amplification) 1983; first performed London, 20 October 1984.
Three Biblical Songs (soprano, baritone, small female chorus, orchestra; Psalms 136, 92, 137; part of *The Big Bang (Part 1)*) 1985; first performed Norwich, Norfolk, 1 July 1989.
The Song of Abigail (soprano, flute, oboe, clarinet, trumpet, trombone, tuba, percussion, piano, violin, viola, cello) 1986; first performed London, 7 March 1986.
Love on the Rocks (4 amplified voices, 4 amplified flutes, tape, live electronics) 1989.

Other:

Cass (music theatre for female voice, flute, jug, 6 men; Aeschylus freely adapted) 1970; first performed York, March 1972.
Calypso (music theatre for soprano, flute, 2 male actors, prepared tape; Odyssey) 1973; first performed Bedford, March 1973.
Scènes de ballet (actor, 3 actor-singers, 1 singing actress, 2 pianos, percussion, Gene Kelly/Fokine) 1974; first performed London, 17 February 1974.
The Big Bang (Part 1) (music theatre for soprano, baritone, actor-singers, small chorus, orchestra; incorporating *Three Biblical Songs*, *A Song of Abigail*, "Love Song") 1989; first performed Norwich, Norfolk, 1 July 1989.

* * *

Roger Marsh's output divides into two categories: music theatre and concert works. The division, however, is more practical than aesthetic, since there is considerable cross-fertilization between the two and the key ideas of theatre and poetic myth pervade both. It is also worth noting that all his work is possessed of a keen sense of humour.

Music theatre may be defined as a genre in which theatrical presentation serves to emphasize the musical gestures. Marsh's influences in this area include Japanese Noh drama and Samuel Beckett. The focus is invariably upon heightened rhetorical gesture, stripped of peripheral or background detail and made without reference to the traditions of either Chekovian and Shakespearian theatre or "classical" music. An early example of such writing is a work for solo male performer entitled *Dum* in which a human fly trapped in a spider's web of poetry and the Lord's Prayer shouts, crashes and bangs his way into a confused, almost nihilistic state reminiscent of the Dada sound poems of Kurt Schwitters. More recently, the large-scale work *The Big Bang* takes up a Biblical theme by drawing parallels between the story of King David and Mario Puzo's *The Godfather*. This piece is really an assemblage of numerous shorter works, each following the story of a single biblical or mythical figure (Samson, Abigail, Delilah and so on). Marsh shares James Joyce's love of stories simply told and many of these works feature a protagonist whose narrative style appeals directly to the audience and sometimes draws upon a common experience such as cinema, the Anglican Church or punk rock.

Marsh's non-theatrical output includes orchestral and chamber music. All the music is characterised by a certain poetic fragility. In recent years, he has attempted to inject muscularity into the music, principally through a new-found interest in the piano, but even in a work full of bold gestures such as *Easy Steps* for solo piano the writing remains crystalline. He has an interest in taking performers into slightly dangerous or unexplored territory on their instruments, a risk which can result in a feeling or imminent peril during performance. He also shows a reluctance to make use of unifying devices such as drones, ostinatos and other conventional accompaniments. His orchestration tends towards a delicacy of tone, and in a recent work, *Stepping Out* he makes use of a spatial distribution of orchestra, chamber orchestra and piano solo, which allows for a layering of textures.

Marsh's most frequently heard work to date is *Not a Soul But Ourselves . . .*, scored for four voices. This was first written for the Extended Vocal Techniques Ensemble of California, then performed and recorded by Electric Phoenix, and finally made into a staged piece by the music theatre group Vocem. An extension of the Anna Livia Plurabelle chapter of Joyce's *Finnegans Wake*, the music comprises a delicate tracery of predominantly small vocal sounds, combined in carefully balanced and shifting aggregations of inflection, interspersed with silence. The piece shows clearly Marsh's feel for balance and timing and his sensitivity to rhetoric and its antithesis, muttering.

Marsh shares many of he attributes of a poet: he is something of an outsider, his language is condensed, heightened and loaded with meaning, there tends to be a "tone of voice" in his work. He dislikes the redundancy of musical and theatrical gesture and prefers not to be seen as a composer seeking an established position or a conventional celebrity.

—Andrew Hugill

MARTINO, Donald (James). American. Born in Plainfield, New Jersey, 16 May 1931. Educated at Syracuse University, New York, 1948–52, B.M.; Princeton University, New Jersey, 1952–4, M.F.A.; composition study with Roger Sessions and Milton Babbitt; studied in Florence under Luigi Dalapiccola, 1954–6. Served on Army Reserves, 98th Division Army Band, 1948–52. Married (1) Mari Rice in 1953 (dissolved 1968), 1 daughter; (2) Lora Harvey in 1969, 1 son. Instructor (theory and woodwind), Third Street Settlement School, New York, 1956–7; instructor of music, Princeton University, 1957–9; assistant professor 1959–66, and associate professor of music theory, 1966–9, Yale University, New Haven, Connecticut; teacher of composition, summers 1965–7, 1969, and composer in residence, 1973, Berkshire Music Center, Tanglewood, Massachusetts; chair of composition department, New England Conservatory, Boston, 1969–70; visiting lecturer, Harvard University, Cambridge, Massachusetts, 1971; Irving Fine Professor of Music, Brandeis University, Waltham, Massachusetts, 1980–3; professor of music, 1983–9, and Walter Bigelow Rosen Professor of Music, Harvard University, since 1989; member, American Academy of Arts and Sciences; member, National Institute of Arts and Letters, College Music Society, American Composers Alliance, American Music Center, International Society for Contemporary Music, American Society of Composers, International Clarinet Society, and Broadcast Music Inc.; professional clarinettist (jazz and concert music). Recipient: BMI Student Composer awards, 1952, 1953; Bonsall Fellowship, 1953–4; Kosciuszko scholar, 1953–4; National Federation of Music Clubs award, 1953; Kate Neal Kinley fellowship, University of Illinois, 1954–5; Fulbright grant, Florence, 1954–5, 1955–6; Pacifica Foundation award, 1961; creative arts citation, Brandeis University, 1963; Morse Academy fellowship, 1965; National Institute of Arts and Letters grant, 1967; Guggenheim Fellowship, 1967–8, 1973–4, 1982–3; National Endowment for the Arts grant, 1973, 1976, 1979, 1989; Mass Council on Arts grant, 1973, 1979, 1982; Pulitzer Prize for music (for *Notturno*), 1974; member, American Academy Institute of Arts and Letters, 1981; Harvard University, honorary M.A., 1983; first prize, Kennedy Center Friedheim Awards, 1985; Mark M. Horbilt award, Boston Symphony Orchestra, 1987; American Academy of Arts and Sciences fellowship, 1987. Mailing address: 11 Pembroke Street, Newton, Massachusetts 02158, U.S.A.

Publishers: Dentalian Inc (self); E.C. Schirmer; McGinnis and Marx; Ione Press Inc., Boston.

Symphonies/orchestral:

Sinfonia 1953; withdrawn.
Contemplations 1956; first performed Tanglewood, Massachusetts, 1965.
Concerto for Piano and Orchestra 1965; first performed New Haven, Connecticut, 1965.
Mosaic for Grand Orchestra 1967; first performed Chicago, 1967.
Cello Concerto 1972; first performed Cincinnati, Ohio, 1979.
Ritorno (also for concert band) 1975; first performed Plainfield, New Jersey, 1976.
Triple Concerto (clarinet, bass clarinet, contrabass clarinet, orchestra) 1977; first performed New York, 1979. Recorded Nonesuch H71372.
Divertissements 1981; first performed Groton, Massachusetts, 1981.
Saxophone Concerto (also piano reduction, commissioned 1988) 1987; first performed Monadnock, New Hampshire, 1987.

Chamber/instrumental:

String Quartet No 1 1950–1; withdrawn.
Sonata (clarinet, piano) 1951; first performed Syracuse, New York, 1952.
Suite of Variations on Medieval Melodies (cello) 1952, revised 1954; first performed Boston, 1980. Recorded CRI CD 564.
String Quartet No 2 1952; withdrawn.
A Set for Clarinet 1954; first performed Princeton, New Jersey, 1954. Recorded CRI 374; Crystal S335; Advance FGR4; Advance 15S.
Harmonica Piece 1954.
String Quartet No 3 1954; withdrawn.
Quodlibet (flute) 1954; first performed Syracuse, New York, 1954. Recorded CRI 212.
String Trio 1955; withdrawn.
Sette canoni enigmatici (various quartet ensembles: 2 violas, 2 cellos/bassoons; or string quartet; or 2 clarinets, alto clarinet/basset horn, bass clarinet) 1956; first performed Boston, 1971.
Quartet (clarinet, strings) 1957; first performed New York, 1957.
Piano Fantasy 1958; first performed New York, 1959.
Trio (violin, clarinet, piano) 1959; first performed New York, 1959. Recorded CRI 240.
Cinque frammenti (oboe, double bass) 1961; first performed Hartford, Connecticut, 1961. Recorded Advance FGR1.
Fantasy Variations (violin) 1962; first performed Tanglewood, Massachusetts, 1964. Recorded Advance FGR 66; CRI 240.
Concerto for Wind Quintet (flute, oboe, clarinet, bassoon, horn) 1964; first performed Tanglewood, Massachusetts, 1964. Recorded CRI 230.
Parisonatina al'dodecafonia (cello) 1964; first performed New Haven, Connecticut, 1964. Recorded CRI CD 564.
B,A,B,B.I.T.T (clarinet) 1966; first performed New Haven, Connecticut, 1966. Recorded Advance 17S.
Strata (bass clarinet) 1966; first performed Madison, Wisconsin, 1970. Recorded CRI 499.
Pianississimo (piano) 1970; first performed Boston, 1973.
Augenmusik: A Mixed Mediacritique (actress, danseuse, or uninhibited female percussionist) 1972; first performed Boston, 1972.
Notturno (flute, clarinet, violin, cello, percussion) 1973; first performed New York, 1973. Recorded Nonesuch H71300.
Impromptu for Roger (piano) 1977; first performed Princeton, New Jersey, 1977.

Quodlibets II (flute) 1980; first performed New York, 1981.
Fantasies and Impromptus (piano) 1981; first performed Washington, D.C., 1981. Recorded New World 320.
Suite in Old Form (piano) 1982; first performed Boston, 1987. Recorded Tonmeister CD UMKAPELL 89.
String Quartet 1983; first performed Washington, D.C., 1984. Recorded CRI CD 551.
Canzone e tarantella (clarinet, cello) 1984; first performed Pontino, Italy, 1984. Recorded Italia Fonitcetra Itl 70103.
From the Other Side (flute, cello, percussion, piano) 1988; first performed Sydney, 1988.

Vocal/choral:

Separate Songs (high voice, piano; Joyce, Housman) 1951; first performed Syracuse, New York, 1952.
The Bad Child's Book of Beasts (high voice, piano; Belloc) 1952; first performed Syracuse, New York, 1952.
Three Songs (high or low voice, piano; Joyce) 1955; first performed New York, 1957.
Portraits (mezzo soprano, bass baritone, mixed chorus, orchestra; Whitman, Millay, cummings) 1955.
anyone lived in a pretty how town (SATB chorus, piano; cummings) 1955; first performed Boston, 1970.
Two Rilke Songs (mezzo soprano, piano) 1961; first performed New Haven, Connecticut, 1964.
Seven Pious Pieces (SATB chorus, piano or organ) 1971; first performed Boston, 1973. Recorded New World 210.
Paradiso Choruses (12 soloists, mixed chorus, children's chorus, orchestra, tape; Dante) 1974; first performed Boston, 1975. Recorded Golden Crest NEC 114.
The White Island (chorus, orchestra; Herrick) 1985; first performed Boston, 1987.

Other:

The White Rooster (film soundtrack; chamber orchestra) 1953; first performed Princeton, 1953.
The Lonely Crime (film soundtrack; chamber orchestra) 1958; first performed Princeton, New Jersey, 1958.

PUBLICATIONS

By Martino: *String-O-Graph*, Newton, Massachusetts, 1979; *178 Chorale Harmonizations of J.S. Bach: A Comparative Edition for Study*, Newton, Massachusetts, 1984, revised 1985; "The Source Set and Its Aggregate Formations", in *Journal of Music Theory*, 5(2); "Claudio Spies: Tempi", in *Perspectives of New Music*, 2(2); "Notation in General—Articulation in Particular", in *Perspectives of New Music*, 4(2).

On Martino: Henry Weinberg, "DM: Trio", in *Perspectives of New Music* 2(1), 1963; B. Fennelly, "DM: 'Parisonatina al'Dodecafonia' ", in *Perspectives of New Music*, 8(1), 1969; William Rothstein, "Linear Structure in the 12-Tone System: An Analysis of DM's 'Pianississimo' ", in *Journal of Music Theory*, 14(2), 1980; J. Chute, "Publish or Perish", in *HiFi*, 32(1), 1982; special 60th birthday edition of *Perspectives of New Music*, to be published 1991.

Donald Martino comments:

My work has always been founded on the premise that only from the purest and most rigorous manipulation of the elements of my craft could I forge an expressive, dramatic, essentially romantic music which would be capable of presenting to the world the totality and speciality of my thoughts and feelings. Since the early 1950s the chromatic universe has provided the language; the grammar and syntax have always been my own personal translations of what I have inherited from the past. That past has never constrained or inhibited my vision; on the contrary, it has always been truly inspirational. And in its forms and vehicles of discourse I have found a fundamental geometry, infinite and universal in its capacity for transformation.

A unique property of my style, derived from my early training as a clarinettist, is its inclusion of virtuosity not just as a technical attribute but as an expressive component functioning as a metaphor for what might be called "the life struggle". I have been led to postulate a vital coalition in which the degree of difficulty of the music, both technically and interpretively, *is* its drama. Virtuosity is, therefore, a primal source of the conception itself.

No musical experience other than composition has been so stimulating to me as performing. Although over the years I have had to give up performing, I am compensated for that loss by the sense that as composer I am simply a performer whose instruments are themselves performers. It is as though through my compositions I were able to play upon an imaginary pipe organ whose stops are living beings, each of whom is me. Thanks to this fantasy, my career as performer continues still.

To those who either condemn or exalt the meticulousness of my notation, I respond that each of my scores issues forth charged with those markings which would signify that in the mind of its creator it has already received countless performances.

It follows then that the characteristics of acoustical instruments themselves have provided a rich source of inspiration. Each composition not only expresses my peculiar audition of these characteristics but derives its particular logical-spiritual unfolding from the sounds my instruments make. It is these sounds I imagine my instruments to be capable of producing that, in stimulating those improvisatory, analytical, deductive and speculative processes which are both simultaneous and continuous components of the creative process, in turn unlock from within me the network of sentiments and ideas known as a musical composition.

* * *

Donald Martino is one of a number of composers, also including Benjamin Boretz, Peter Westergaard, James K. Randall and Henry Weinberg, who studied with both Roger Sessions and Milton Babbitt and formed a kind of "Princeton School". In his own way, each followed Babbitt in his extension into other parameters of the twelve-tone method of composition and its consequent transformation into a system (something to which Schoenberg always objected). The result is music shaped by extremely complex networks of relationships, and Martino, who also studied with Luigi Dallapiccola, has in particular developed a quasi-mathematical way of composing using arithmetical permutations of rhythmic and tonal elements. However fiercely complicated in their organisation, though, his works are at the same time densely expressive, dramatic in much of their gesture, and even romantic in feeling.

Although most of his output has been chamber works (some of these withdrawn), vocal music or for solo instruments, there have been several orchestral pieces and at least one contribution to music theatre, *Augenmusik: A Mixed Media-critique* "for actress, danseuse or uninhibited female percussionist and electronic tape". Martino has also written songs in pre-rock popular style, jazz arrangements and some film scores.

In chamber pieces such as the *Concerto for Wind Quintet* or the remarkable *Notturno* of 1973 (for which Martino was awarded a Pulitzer Prize) there is often an interplay between ensemble passages that are very dense in both sound and serial organisation and sensitively shaped, cadenza-like solos. Following on from these pieces, he has taken a special interest in writing for unaccompanied instruments, among such pieces being *B,A,B,B.I.T.T* for clarinet with C extension (Martino is himself an excellent clarinettist).

For many of the solo pieces he indicates with notations of highly specific attacks, bowings, fingerings and so forth exactly how each note is to be produced while at the same time giving the player some freedom within the complex overall framework. He constantly seeks to extend the capabilities of each instrument.

Martino calls for a use of the sounds that is closely related to the articulation of the musical structure of each work. Thus such factors as specific methods of note production, dynamics and register are associated with particular pitch sets, and often serve to heighten the contrapuntal content of the piece. As much is exemplified by a score such as *Parisonatina al'dodecafonia* for solo cello. Again, in compositions like *Pianississimo* for piano aspects of the music's form are conveyed by differentiated articulation, dynamics or registral stratification. Beyond all such considerations, however, the great diversity of sounds and the sustained intensity with which they are used appear to be the most striking features of Martino's music.

—Max Harrison

MARTLAND, Steve. British/English. Born in Liverpool, August 1959. Educated at University of Liverpool, graduated 1981; Royal Conservatory, The Hague, (composition under Louis Andriessen), 1982–5; Tanglewood, Massachusetts (composition under Gunther Schuller), 1984. Full-time composer; leader, Steve Martland Band. Recipient: Mendelssohn Scholarship, 1981; joint winner (for *Babi Yar*), SPNM Orchestral Competition, 1983; Government Composition Prize, The Netherlands, 1985. Mailing address: c/o Schott & Co. Ltd, 48 Great Marlborough Street, London W1V 2BN, England.

Publisher: Schott.

Symphonies/orchestral:

Lotta continua (orchestra, jazz band: alto saxophone, flugelhorn, electric guitar with flanger pedal and volume control, drums) 1981, revised 1984; revised version first performed London, June 1984.

Babi Yar (large orchestra in 3 groups) 1983; first performed Liverpool, 22 November 1985. Recorded Factory Classical Facd 266.

Orc (horn, small orchestra) 1984; first performed Amsterdam, 14 January 1985.

Dividing the Lines (brass band) 1986.

Crossing the Border (string orchestra) 1990–1.

Chamber/instrumental:

Remembering Lennon (flute, A clarinet/wine glasses tuned to C# and A, percussion, piano/wine glasses tuned to G#/woodblock, violin/wine glass tuned to D#, viola, cello) 1981, revised 1985; first performed Glasgow, 1981; revised version first performed Keele, Staffordshire, 29 October 1985.

Duo (B♭ trumpet, piano) 1982; first performed Liverpool, 1982.

Kgakala (piano) 1982; first performed London, 1982. Recorded Factory Classical Facd 306.

American Invention (3 groups: flute, bass clarinet, piano, violin, viola; flute, bass clarinet, piano, violin, cello; horn in F, drums, bass guitar) 1985; first performed Aldeburgh, Suffolk, 10 June 1985.

Shoulder to Shoulder (flute/piccolo, alto saxophone, tenor saxophone, baritone saxophone, horn, 3 trumpets, 2 trombones, bass trombone, piano or synthesizer, bass guitar) 1986; first performed Amsterdam, 9 December 1986. Recorded Attaca Babel Volharding 007/Babel 8953 6DDD.

Remix (alto saxophone, tenor saxophone or bass clarinet, flugelhorn, trombone, percussion, synthesizer or electric harpsichord, amplified violin, amplified bass; larger version for soprano saxophone or B♭ clarinet, alto saxophone, tenor saxophone, flugelhorn, 2 trombones, drums, synthesizer, electric guitar or synthesizer, amplified violin, amplified viola, amplified bass) 1986; first performed Amsterdam, 6 November 1986. Recorded Hat Art CD 6056.

Big Mac I (bass clarinet, tenor saxophone or bass clarinet, drum machine/keyboard) 1987; first performed The Hague, 27 May 1987.

Big Mac II (alto saxophone, tenor saxophone, flugelhorn, trombone, synthesizer, vibraphone, electric violin, double bass) 1987.

Drill (2 pianos) 1987; first performed Rotterdam, 14 January 1988. Recorded Factory Classical Facd 256.

Principia (alto saxophone, tenor saxophone, trumpet/flugelhorn, trombone, drums ad lib, synthesizer or piano, electric violin, double bass) 1989; first performed Leeds, 7 March 1990.

Birthday Hocket (2 pianos; for Louis Andriessen at 50) 1989; first performed Amsterdam, 6 June 1989.

Vocal/choral:

Canto a la esperanza (soprano, electric guitar, chamber orchestra) 1982, in progress; first performed London, 1983.

El pueblo unido jamas sera vencido (voices, flute, alto saxophone, tenor saxophone, baritone saxophone, horn, 3 trumpets, 2 trombones, bass trombone, keyboard, double bass; traditional) 1987; first performed Amsterdam, 9 September 1987.

Glad Day (voice, alto saxophone, tenor saxophone, baritone saxophone, trumpet/flugelhorn, trombone, drums, synthesizer, bass guitar, 2 violins, viola, cello; Keane) 1988; first performed Amsterdam, 6 June 1988. Recorded Factory Classical Facd 306.

Terra firma (5 voices with amplification and video by Robert Katz; Keane) 1989; first performed London, 14 March 1989.

Skywalk (5 unaccompanied voices or unaccompanied mixed chorus) 1989; first performed Nantwich, 24 June 1989.

Principia (version for voice ad lib, alto saxophone, trombone, drums ad lib, synthesizer or piano, electric violin, double bass) 1989; first performed Amsterdam, 25 April 1990.

Other:

Divisions (electronic tape) 1986–7; first performed Welwyn Garden City, Hertfordshire, 25 September 1987.
Albion (audio-visual project) 1988; broadcast BBC Television, 18 December 1988.
Ghost Story (incidental music to television play by Julian Jarreld) 1989.
The Task (incidental music to play by Heiner Müller) 1989.
Home, Away from Home (incidental music to television play by Marjoleine Boonstra) 1989; broadcast Dutch Television, Autumn 1989.
Cult (sound-track to dance/theatre project by Julian Jarreld for television) 1990.
Wolf-gang (Mozart arrangements for wind band) 1991.

PUBLICATIONS

On Martland: Mark Sinker, "Notating the Class War", in *Wire*, 61, March 1989.

* * *

With few exceptions, post-war composition has ignored (or significantly misunderstood) the degree to which recording, broadcasting and amplification technology—mediated almost entirely through pop music—have transformed not just how people hear music, but what they hear as music. New hierarchies of form and structure have evolved, the palette of possible sounds (and concomitant public "ear") has expanded beyond easy summary, and the dominance of harmony and melody within notated development is forcefully challenged by a deliriously liberating imprecision of detail within overall sonic "production" ambience.

If nothing else, Steve Martland is young enough, as a British composer come to maturity during the late 1980s, to be acutely aware of this challenge. He wants to rise to it—it is certainly no accident that he is presently signed to Factory Records, a relatively small but provocatively inventive 1980s pop/avant-rock label.

In his early work—such as 1981's *Remembering Lennon* (which treats Lennon's "Imagine" as medieval music would a contemporary folk song, as a Cantus Firmus)—he has not found a way to get beyond pop content as callow homage (which is then misread as novelty gesture). Certainly he seems tired of its being brought up, and almost of having written it.

Studying in The Netherlands with Louis Andriessen Martland developed a taste for dirty minimalism and a resistance to various modernist orthodoxies (which he insists dominate British academic classicism). He also leans towards an intense socialist politics quite unlike most of his British contemporaries. In this context, the exhaustive piano duo *Drill* (with its block structures, hocketing rather than counterpoint, and at most fragmentary melodies), parody marches such as *Remix* and orchestral works like *American Invention* and *Babi Yar* explore the dynamics (the compromises and social significance) of musical performance itself.

Working in the U.K. with Test Dept, the metalbashing agitrock organisation, he's proceeded to elaborate a potent, almost mocking relationship with aspects of the British pastoral tradition: elements of semi-pastiche and found sound (for example folk songs) interweave with his own deliberately coarse writing, for standard and electric instrumentation, in *Albion*, to intensify and undercut a clutch of conflicting national nostalgias. Central to his style by now is a churning intensity which worries at an uncritical classical satisfaction at its own verities.

He may still believe that "classical" music offers a unique analytical rigour, as well as deep possibilities not yet exploited—though certainly latent—in overground pop (and underground rock), but he appears to allow himself to listen as if everything is already pop (or rock), or ought to be. At his best, even in extended pieces, he is working the way a great producer works on a single, not advancing the emotional logic of the all-round sound as if notated considerations no longer quite existed. He has taken to requesting that his records be played at "high volume"—and classical musicians have been known to inform him that they are "frightened" by his work, or (occasionally) his "fascism".

Andreissen has commended his work for posing problems, rather than for striving for obvious beauty. As a result, it is probable that no audience quite exists for Martland in his own country, where "serious" and "pop" listeners are still separated by absurd comprehension (and class) gulfs.

—Mark Sinker

MARTTINEN, Tauno (Olavi). Finnish. Born in Helsinki, 27 September 1912. Educated at Viipuri [Vyborg] Music Institute (conducting and composition), 1920–35; Sibelius Academy, Helsinki (under Peter Akimov, Ilmari Hannikainen and Selim Palmgren), 1935–7; further study under Wladimir Vogel, 1958. Married Ilmi Tellervo Tuomisto in 1944; 4 children. Conductor, Hämeenlinna City Orchestra, 1948–58; founder and director, Hämeenlinna Music Institute, 1952–75; chair, Hämeenlinna Arts Union, 1963–73. Recipient: Finnish Cultural Foundation Special Prize, 1956; honorary prize, Finnish Radio children's music competition, 1958, joint 1st prize (for *Symphony No 4*), Camden Festival of Finnish Music, London, 1967; 1st prize (for *Beatrice*), Finnish National Opera, 1970; honorary prize, Finnish Composers Union and Kalevala Society, 1982; Art Prize (for *The Pharaoh's Letter* and *Symphony No 7*), City of Tampere, 1983; first ever Sibelius Award, 1990. Mailing address: Lahdensivuntie 30, 13100 Hämeenlinna, Finland.

Publishers: Edition Fazer; Jasemusiikki; Naiskuoroliitto; Sulasol; Eres.

Symphonies/orchestral:

Symphony No 1 Op 2 1958.
Symphony No 2 Op 4 1959.
Linnunrata / The Milky Way Op 7 1960–1.
Symphony No 3 Op 18 1960–2.
Rembrandt Op 11 (cello, orchestra) 1962. Recorded Finnlevy SFX 37.
Concerto for Violin and Orchestra Op 13 1962.
Concerto for Piano and Orchestra No 1 Op 23 1964.
Symphony No 4 Op 31 1964.
Manalan linnut / Birds of the Underworld Op 38 1964.
Fauni Op 26 1965.
Panu, tulen jumala / Panu, God of Fire Op 28 1966.
Concerto for Cello and Orchestra "Dalai Lama" Op 30 1966, revised 1979.

Maailman synty / Creation of the Earth 1966.
Symphony No 5 "The Shaman" Op 35 1967–72.
Mont Saint Michel Op 42 1968.
Pentalia Op 50 1969.
Pohjola / The North Op 67 (wind orchestra; consists of *Pohjola, Pohjolaisten tanssi / Dance of the Northerners, Kaamos / The Long Gloom, Henkien tanssi / Dance of the Spirits*) 1970–7.
Concerto for Bassoon and Orchestra Op 40d 1971, revised 1983–4.
Concerto for Flute and Orchestra Op 72 1972.
Concerto for Piano and Orchestra No 2 Op 74 1972.
Concerto for Clarinet and Orchestra "Hirvenhiihto" / "On the Tracks of the Winter Moose" Op 89 1974.
Symphony No 6 Op 92 1974–5.
Symphony No 7 Op 136 1977.
Concerto espagnole Op 144 (flute, orchestra) 1978.
Yo linnakkeessa / Night on the Fortress Op 150 (wind orchestra) 1978.
Elegia Op 169 (harp, strings) 1979.
Voces polaris Op 173 1979.
Sirius Op 181 / 2 (wind orchestra) 1980.
Concerto for Piano and Orchestra No 3 Op 200 1981.
Concerto for Two Pianos and Orchestra Op 200 / 2 1981.
Vainamoisen synty / Vainamoisen's Birth Op 201 1981.
Adagio Op 212 1982.
Vainamoisen lahto Pohjolaan Op 213 / 2 1982.
Songs of the Great River (orchestral suite from the opera) 1982.
Concerto grosso Op 216/2 (violin, viola, cello, organ, orchestra) 1983.
Matka aamun maahan / A Trip to the Land of Dawn (Ommagio a Hermann Hesse) Op 301 (strings, but without violas) 1984. Recorded Fuga, 1990.
Concerto for Piano and Orchestra No 4 1984.
Symphony No 8 1986.
Symphony No 9 1988.

Chamber / instrumental:

Delta Op 9 (clarinet, piano) 1962. Recorded Ponsi PEALP 10.
Hahmoja / Silhouettes Op 14 (piano, percussion) 1962.
Loitsu / The Conjuration Op 15 (3 percussion) 1963.
Alfa Op 16 (flute, 7 cymbals) 1963.
Nonet No 1 Op 19 (flute, oboe, clarinet, bassoon, horn, violin, viola, cello, double bass) 1963.
Four Preludes Op 22 (piano) 1965.
Titisee Op 24 (piano) 1965.
Taara Op 34 (piano) 1967.
Intrada Op 36 (organ) 1967.
Adagio (organ) 1967.
Nonet No 2 Op 41 / 2 (flute, oboe, clarinet, bassoon, horn, violin, viola, cello, double bass) 1968.
Vipusessa kaynti / Visit to the Giant Sage Vipunen Op 44 (7 double basses) 1969.
String Quartet No 1 Op 50 1969.
Sonatina Op 52 (piano) 1970.
Notre Dame Op 59 (organ) 1970.
String Quartet No 2 Op 63 1971.
Kupoli / The Cupola Op 65 / 2 (organ) 1971.
Paasiainen / Easter Op 66 (piano) 1971.
Duo Op 66 / 2 (clarinet, percussion) 1971.
Larghetto (organ) 1972.
Orgelstück Op 70 (organ) 1972.
Nonet No 3 Op 79 (flute, oboe, clarinet, bassoon, horn, violin, viola, cello, double bass) 1973.
Ilmatar, ilman impi / Ilman, Virgin of the Air Op 88 (piccolo) 1974. Recorded BIS LP 100.
Sonata Op 90 (piano) 1975.
Alussa oli sana . . . / In the Beginning Was the Word . . . Op 95 (organ) 1975.
Septemalia Op 97 (7 double basses) 1975. Recorded Tactus TA 8002.
Three Preludes Op 99 / 1 (guitar) 1975.
Kukonaskel / Giant Stride Op 100 (2 pianos) 1975.
Pisaroita / Water Drops Op 109 (piano) 1976.
Varahtelyja / Vibrations Op 119 (piano) 1976.
Homage to Johann Sebastian Op 123 (guitar) 1977.
Divertimento Op 127 (oboe / cor anglais, percussion) 1977.
Kimalluksia / Glittering Op 134 (piano) 1977.
Intermezzo Op 149 (flute, guitar) 1977–8.
Impression Op 140 (cello) 1978.
Trio Op 141 (piano, violin, cello) 1978.
Kirinmyllyn tarinaa / The Old Mill Tells Its Tale Op 143 (clarinet) 1978.
Prelude Op 158 (organ) 1978.
Le Commencement Op 160 (flute, oboe, piano) 1978.
Quo vadis Op 168 (flute / piccolo / alto flute, oboe / cor anglais, bassoon / contrabassoon, harpsichord) 1979.
Largo religioso Op 187 (organ) 1980.
Maahinen / The Gnome Op 198 (bass clarinet) 1981.
Duo Op 205 (viola, piano) 1981.
Fantasia on the Theme B-A-C-H Op 84 (organ) 1982.
Illusio Op 214 (clarinet) 1982.
Trio Op 216 / 1 (violin, viola, cello) 1982.
String Quartet No 3 Op 228 1983.
Japanilaisessa puutarhassa / Japanese Garden Op 217 (piano) 1983. Recorded FUGA 3038.
Profeetta / Prophet Op 234b (organ) 1984.

Vocal / choral:

Kokko, ilman lintu / Eagle, Bird of the Air Op 1 (mezzo-soprano, orchestra; *Kalevala*) 1965.
Der Feurbogen / The Bow of Fire Op 43 (bass, piano trio; *Kalevala*) 1969.
Jeesus ja Pietari / Jesus and Peter Op 61 (baritone, organ) 1969–70.
Aania Nooan arkista / Sounds from Noah's Ark Op 65 (unaccompanied male chorus; de Gasztold, translated Turkia) 1971.
Liebeslieder der Antike / Love Songs from Olden Times Op 73 (song cycle for piano, orchestra) 1972.
Naktergalen / The Nightingale Op 94 (voice, piano; or voice, flute, cello, harp; Ullvinge) 1976.
Nain oli alussa / Thus Was the Beginning (suite for children's chorus, soloists, instruments; consisting of *Ensimmainen paiva / The First Day Op 122 / 1, Elaman synty / The Birth of Life Op 122 / 2*, and *Paratiisi / Paradise Op 190*) 1977–80.
Der Busenfreund / The Bosom Friend Op 129 (bass, wind quintet; Busch) 1977.
Cantate Jehovae canticum novum Op 139 (mixed or boys' chorus, organ, string orchestra; biblical) 1978.
Canticum canticorum Op 153 (mezzo-soprano, piano or harp; biblical) 1978.
Lapin lauluja Op 161 No 1 (voice, piano; Kumpuniemi) 1978.
Rohkea ratsastaja Op 178 (reciter, male chorus; Kivi) 1980.
Kaupunkini Op 183 (voice, orchestra; Heikkero) 1980.
Aapon tarina Hiidenkivella Op 184 (tenor, male chorus, reciter; Kivi) 1980.
Juudaksen suudelma / The Kiss of Judas (bass, 2 baritones, tenor, mixed chorus, male chorus, organ; biblical) 1981.
Offenbarung Johannes Op 137 (bass, male chorus, organ;

biblical) 1981.
Mullan uni Op 197 (voice, piano; Selja) 1981.
Eliabetin lauluja I IV (song cycles for piano and—III only—flute; Laurila) 1981.
Juhani Turun torilla (baritone, clarinet, cello, piano; Kivi) 1981.
Simeoni saapasnahkatornissa (baritone, clarinet, cello, piano; Kivi) 1981.
Timon harharetki (baritone, clarinet, cello, piano; Kivi) 1981.
Timon ryyppyreissu (baritone, clarinet, cello, piano; Kivi) 1981.
Kotiinpaluu (baritone, clarinet, cello, piano; Kivi) 1981.
Kalve impi (reciter, female chorus) 1981.
Vaeltajan laulu Op 201 (voice, piano; ancient Persian) 1981.
Missa choralis Op 203 (unaccompanied mixed chorus) 1981.
Maa jota ei ole Op 209 (female chorus, cello, double bass, percussion; Södergran) 1982.
Rakastavaiset ja linnanherra Op 210 (reciter, female chorus; Kivi) 1982.
Pohjolan neiti / The Maid of Pohjola Op 213 / 1 (recitation, orchestra) 1982.
Iku-turso Op 219 No 2 (unaccompanied male chorus; *Kalevala*) 1983.
Veljesten paluu Jukolaan (unaccompanied male chorus; Kivi) 1983.
On jouluilta (unaccompanied male chorus; Kivi) 1983.
Timon laulu (baritone, male chorus; Kivi) 1984.

Opera:

Neiti Gamardin talo / The House of Lady Gamard (after Balzac) 1960–71.
Paallysviitta / The Cloak Op 17 (after Gogol) 1962–3.
Kihlaus Op 20 (after Kivi) 1964.
Apotto ja ikaneito / The Abbot and the Old Maid (after Balzac) 1965.
Tulitikkuja lainaamassa / Borrowing Matches Op 25 (after Lassila) 1965–9.
Lea Op 33 (after Kivi) 1967.
Polettu oranssi / Burnt Orange Op 41 (after Manner) 1968.
Mestari Patelin / Master Patelin Op 69 (after anon. play) 1969–72.
Noitarumpu / Shaman's Drum Op 85 (after Outakoski) 1974–6.
Psykiatri / The Psychiatrist Op 93 1974.
Laestadiuksen saarna / Laestadius's Sermon 1974–6.
Meedio / The Medium Op 105 1975–9.
Jaarlin sisar / The Earl's Sister Op 126 (Isomäki) 1977.
Faaraon kirje / The Pharaoh's Letter Op 192 (Mutru) 1978–80.
Kullanmuru / The Golden Treasure Op 180 (musical; Pihlajamäki, after Andersen) 1980.
Suuren joen laulu / Song of the Great River (Yrjänä) 1982–4.
Wedding (after Chekhov) 1984.
Seven Brothers (after Kivi) 1991.

Other:

Tikkaat / The Ladder Op 21 (ballet; after Henry Miller) 1955.
Dorian Grayn muotokuva / The Picture of Dorian Gray Op 48 (ballet; after Wilde) 1969.
Lumikuningatar / The Snow Queen Op 54 (ballet; after Andersen) 1970.
Beatrice Op 57 (ballet; after Dante) 1970.
Paivanpaasto / The Sun out of the Moon Op 120 (ballet; after *Kalevala*) 1975–7.
Ruma ankanpoikanen / The Ugly Duckling Op 115 (ballet; after Andersen) 1976, 1982–3.

PUBLICATIONS

On Marttinen: Anthony Hodgson, in *Scandinavian Music: Finland and Sweden*, Cranbury, New Jersey and London, 1984.

* * *

After going through a late-romantic phase typical of many lesser Finnish composers of the time, Tauno Marttinen underwent dramatic stylistic changes in the 1950s. This was occasioned by the contemporary ideas reaching Finland, and as a result, like many Finns and Swedes at the time Marttinen undertook study in Switzerland under Wladimir Vogel. From this experience he came to terms with serialism. At first he used it strictly and rejected his earlier works. Later, by choosing which rules to bend, he started to develop a more personal idiom. These freer serial works can be viewed as a third period before, in the mid-1960s, Marttinen turned to the mysticism of Finnish folklore (e.g. using Kalevala themes), explorations into several religions, and free-tonality rather than serialism. The colour-contrast of contemporary Finnish art was here paralleled by a heightened interest in instrumental colour. A fifth period sees him coalescing and simplifying the ideas of earlier periods while incorporating both neo-baroque and neo-classical features.

Marttinen's first two symphonies display his strictest use of dodecaphonic procedures, but, like many works of the non-integral serialists, tonality is never totally abandoned. His Fourth Symphony represents an individual stylistic direction in the modern Finnish symphony, and has been described as "a kind of natural-mystic phase, with the composer giving more scope to unrestrained fantasy". Marttinen uses scales as the basic component in this work, and is able to create passages where tonal implications can be either fully exploited or merely hinted at. Because he avoids triadic constructions, a linear style of modal composition often results. The Fourth Symphony opens with a sound-mass built on a descending chromatic scale. Variations of this device are frequently heard later in the work. Then a dorian scale on B is used as the foundation for the development of scale motives in the first movement. The second movement uses synthetic-scale material (e.g., the dorian scale plus the augmented fourth) which is also found in the final movements in the form of motives. According to Marttinen, his mystical philosophies, being closely connected with his concept of meditation, strongly influenced his Fourth and Fifth Symphonies: neo-modal scales and mildly primitive sounds are used to convey apparently "exotic" philosophical ideas.

Marttinen regards his symphonies as highly personal works from a philosophical point of view, and suggests that, within his 20-year cycle of seven symphonies (1957–77), elements of Christianity, Buddhism, Kalevala, pantheism, reincarnation and Nordic heathen mysticism are manifested. In all but the Second Symphony, a prominent celeste is added to the normal orchestra; the ensemble is augmented in the seventh by a harpsichord.

Although he is known outside Finland primarily as an instrumental composer, Marttinen's music dramas and comic operas have achieved note among his fellow countrymen. This is especially true of his two television operas, *The Cloak* and *Burnt Orange*. Marttinen's musical show *The Golden Treasure* and all his 10 stage operas, apart from *Lea*, *The Psychiatrist* and *The Medium*, include dance (he also composed the music for six ballets between 1955 and 1983).

Marttinen's solo concerto series, which idiomatically feature such instruments as piano, cello, bassoon and flute, has also produced perhaps his greatest work, the Violin Concerto of 1962. In all, Marttinen is a highly prolific composer who achieved over 200 opus numbers before his 70th birthday.

—Malcolm J. Hill

MATHIAS, William (James). British/Welsh. Born in Whitland, Dyfed, 1 November 1934. Educated at University College of Wales, Aberystwyth (under Ian Parrott), B.Mus., 1956; Royal Academy of Music, London (composition under Lennox Berkeley, piano under Peter Katin), 1957. Lecturer in music, 1969, and professor and head of department of music, from 1970, University College of North Wales, Bangor; lecturer in music, University of Edinburgh, 1968–9; pianist and conductor; artistic director, North Wales Music Festival, St Asaph. Recipient: Fellow of the Royal Academy of Music, 1965; D.Mus., University of Wales, 1966; Bax Society Prize, 1968; John Edwards Memorial Award, 1981. Mailing address: Y Graigwen, Cadnant Road, Menai Bridge, Anglesey, Gwynedd LL59 5NG, Wales.

Publisher: Oxford University Press.

Symphonies/orchestral:

Piano Concerto No 1 Op 2 1955.
Berceuse Op 4 1956.
Divertimento Op 7 (string orchestra) 1958; first performed London, March 1958. Recorded Decca SXL 6468.
Piano Concerto No 2 Op 13 1960; first performed Llandaff, Glamorgan, 1961.
Music for Strings Op 14 1960; first performed London, 3 December 1961.
Dance Overture Op 16 1961; first performed Wales, 10 August 1962. Recorded Decca SXL 6607.
Invocation and Dance Op 17 1962; first performed Cardiff, 1 March 1962. Recorded Decca SXL 6607.
Serenade Op 18 (chamber orchestra) 1962; first performed 5 June 1962.
Prelude, Aria and Finale Op 25 (string orchestra) 1964; first performed Caerphilly, Glamorgan, 23 May 1964. Recorded Decca SXL 6468.
Concerto for Orchestra Op 27 1965–6; first performed Liverpool, 29 March 1966.
Symphony No 1 Op 31 1966; first performed Llandaff, Glamorgan, 23 June 1966. Recorded Oriel ORM 1004; Nimbus NI 5260.
Sinfonietta Op 34 1967; first performed Leicester, 1 May 1967. Recorded REC 222.
Litanies: Concertante Music for Orchestra Op 37 1968; first performed 28 February 1968.
Piano Concerto No 3 Op 40 1968; first performed Swansea, 15 October 1968. Recorded Decca SXL 6513.
Festival Overture Op 42 1970; first performed Gwynedd, June 1970.
Harp Concerto Op 50 1970; first performed Bournemouth, 1 June 1970. Recorded Decca SXL 6607.
Intrada Op 54 (small orchestra) 1970–1; first performed Aberystwyth, Dyfed, 8 April 1971.
Concerto for Harpsichord, Strings and Percussion Op 56 1971; first performed Fishguard, Dyfed, 26 August 1971.
Holiday Overture Op 57 1971; first performed Llandudno, Gwynedd, 30 September 1971.
Celtic Dances Op 60 1972; first performed August 1972. Recorded REC 222.
Laudi Op 62 1973; first performed Llandaff, Glamorgan, 11 June 1973. Recorded Argo ZRG 882.
Clarinet Concerto Op 68 1975; first performed Bangor, Gwynedd, 22 September 1975. Recorded Argo ZRG 882.
Vistas Op 69 1975; first performed Swansea, 25 October 1975. Recorded Argo ZRG 882.
Dance Variations Op 72 1977; first performed London, 1 July 1977.
Melos Op 73 (flute, harp, percussion, strings) 1977; first performed Abbotsham, Devon, 24 April 1977.
Vivat regina Op 75 (brass band) 1977; first performed London, 11 June 1977. Recorded RCA RL 25143.
Helios Op 76 1977; first performed Llandaff, Glamorgan, 16 June 1977.
Requiescat Op 79 1977; first performed Portmadoc, Gwynedd, 9 February 1978.
Reflections on a Theme of Tomkins Op 86 (flute, oboe, organ, harpsichord, strings) 1980; first performed St David's, Dyfed, 1981.
Symphony No 2: Summer Music Op 90 1983; first performed Liverpool, 14 May 1983. Recorded Nimbus NI 5260.
Organ Concerto Op 91 1984; first performed London, 12 September 1984
Horn Concerto Op 93 (horn, timpani, strings; arranged for horn, piano) 1984; first performed Llandaff, Glamorgan 9 June 1984.
Anniversary Dances Op 95 1984; first performed Bangor, Gwynedd, 16 February 1985.
Carnival of Wales (no opus number) 1987; first performed Cardiff, 24 July 1987.
Violin Concerto 1989–91.
Oboe Concerto (no opus number; string orchestra) 1990; first performed Llantilio Crossenny, Gwent, 6 May 1990.
Symphony No 3 1991.

Chamber/instrumental:

Divertimento Op 1 (violin, piano).
Sonatina Op 3 (clarinet, piano) 1956; first performed Cheltenham, Gloucestershire, 13 July 1957.
Sextet Op 8 (clarinet, string quartet, piano) 1958.
Improvisations Op 10 (harp) 1958; first performed London, 1958. Recorded L'Oiseau Lyre SOL 308.
Sonata Op 15 (violin, piano) 1961; first performed Cheltenham, Gloucestershire, 12 July 1962. Recorded Argo ZRG 771.
Toccata alla danza (no opus number; piano) 1961; first performed 1962.
Postlude (no opus number; organ) 1962. Recorded L'Oiseau Lyre SOL 342.
Partita Op 19 (organ) 1962; first performed London, 26 October 1962. Recorded L'Oiseau Lyre SOL 342; APR 306; Wealden WS 199.
Variations on a Hymn Tune ("Braint") Op 20 (organ) 1962; first performed Llandaff, Glamorgan, 7 December 1962. Recorded L'Oiseau Lyre SOL 342.
Quintet Op 22 (flute, oboe, clarinet, horn, bassoon) 1963; first performed Cheltenham, Gloucestershire, 4 July 1963. Recorded Argo ZRG 771.
Sonata Op 23 (piano) 1963; first performed Bangor, Gwynedd, 11 March 1964.
Divertimento Op 24 (flute, oboe, piano) 1963. Recorded Argo ZRG 771.

Processional (no opus number; organ) 1964. Recorded P5 100; Cassion LPB 738; Argo 807.
Piano Trio Op 30 1965; first performed Cheltenham, Gloucestershire, 9 July 1965.
Invocations Op 35 (organ) 1966; first performed Liverpool, 4 April 1967. Recorded L'Oiseau Lyre SOL 342; Decca SDD 236.
Toccata Giocosa Op 36/2 (organ) 1967. Recorded L'Oiseau Lyre SOL 342; Studio Two 338; Wealden WS 192.
String Quartet Op 38 1967; first performed Cardiff, 25 April 1968. Recorded Argo ZRG 771.
Concertino Op 65 (flute or recorder, oboe, bassoon, harpsichord or piano) 1974; first performed London, 6 March 1974.
Jubilate Op 67 No 2 1974; first performed Hereford, 1974. Recorded L'Oiseau Lyre SOL 342.
Zodiac Trio Op 70 (flute, viola, harp) 1976; first performed Glamorgan, 19 August 1976.
Fantasy Op 78 (organ) 1978; first performed Manchester, 7 September 1978.
Canzonetta Op 78 No 2 (organ) 1978.
Ceremonial Fanfare (2 trumpets in C) 1979; first performed Whitland, Dyfed, 20 October 1979.
String Quartet No 2 Op 84 1980; first performed St David's, Dyfed, 6 March 1981.
Antiphonies Op 88 No 2 (organ) 1982; first performed Cardiff, 13 May 1982. Recorded Alpha ACa 507.
Sonata No 2 Op 94 (violin, piano) 1984; first performed Swansea, October 1984.
Berceuse Op 95 No 3 (organ) 1985; first performed Newbury, Berkshire, 9 May 1985.
Sonatina (no opus number; flute, piano) 1986; first performed Beaumaris, Gwynedd, 12 June 1986.
String Quartet No 3 (no opus number) 1986; first performed Harrogate, Yorkshire, 7 August 1986.
Soundings (no opus number; brass quintet) 1988.
Santa Fe Suite (no opus number; harp) 1988; first performed London, September 1988.
Fenestra (no opus number; organ) 1989–90; first performed Keele, Staffordshire, 22 January 1990.
Carillon (organ) 1990–1.

Vocal/choral:

Seven Poems of R.S. Thomas Op 6 (tenor, harp, chamber orchestra) 1957.
In Praise of Love Op 11 (cantata) 1959.
Three Part Songs Op 12 (male voices, piano) 1959.
All Thy Works Shall Praise Thee Op 17b (SATB chorus, organ; Psalm 145) 1961; first performed Llandaff, Glamorgan, 28 February 1962.
St Teilo Op 21 (cantata/masque) 1962.
Wassail Carol Op 26/1 (SATB chorus, organ) 1964; first performed Cambridge, 24 December 1967. Recorded Argo ZRG 5450/5499.
Make a Joyful Noise unto the Lord Op 26/2 (SATB chorus, organ) 1964; first performed Brecon, Brecknockshire, 17 October 1964. Recorded Abbey LPB 663/APS 307.
Festival Te Deum Op 28 (SATB chorus, organ) 1964; first performed Manchester, 1965. Recorded Guild GRS 7005; Decca/Qualiton SQAD 102.
O Sing unto the Lord Op 29 (SATB chorus, organ) 1965; first performed Aldeburgh, Suffolk, 1965.
Three Medieval Lyrics Op 33 (SATB chorus, 2 trumpets, percussion, organ) 1966; broadcast ATV, 1 January 1967.
Invocations Op 35 (organ) 1967.
Communion Service in C Op 36 (unison voices, organ) 1967.
Four Welsh Folk Songs Op 39 (unaccompanied SATB chorus) 1968.
Psalm 150 Op 44 (mixed voices, orchestra and/or organ) 1969; first performed Worcester, 24 August 1969.
Lift Up Your Head O Ye Gates Op 44 No 2 (SATB chorus, organ) 1969.
Ave Rex Op 45 (mixed voices, organ or orchestra) 1969; first performed Llandaff, Glamorgan, December 1969. Recorded Decca SXL 6607.
Sir Christemas Op 45a (from *Ave Rex*; SATB chorus, organ, strings, piano/organ; or full orchestra) 1969. Recorded OUP 150; Abbey APS 313.
O salutaris hostia Op 48 (unaccompanied male voices) 1969. Recorded Polydor 2460 182.
Bless the Lord Op 51 (SATB chorus, organ) 1970.
Gloria Op 52 (male voices, organ) 1970; first performed Swansea, 5 December 1970.
Magnificat and Nunc Dimittis Op 53 (SATB chorus, organ) 1970; first performed Cambridge, 6 March 1971.
A Babe Is Born Op 55 (SATB, organ or piano duet) 1971; first performed Cardiff, 18 December 1971.
Alleluya Psallat Op 58 (SATB chorus, organ) 1972; first performed 25 October 1972.
Elegy for a Prince Op 59 (baritone, orchestra; Gruffudd ab yr Ynad Coch, translated Conran) 1972; first performed Llandaff, Glamorgan, 10 June 1972. Recorded Argo ZRG 882.
A Vision of Time and Eternity Op 61 (contralto, piano; Vaughan) 1972; first performed Bangor, Gwynedd, 27 September 1972.
Introit: The Law of the Lord Op 61 No 2 (unaccompanied SATB chorus) 1972; first performed Llandaff, Glamorgan, 8 October 1972. Recorded Abbey APS 307.
Ceremony After a Fire Raid Op 63 (SATB chorus, piano, percussion; Thomas) 1973; first performed London, 19 September 1973.
Missa brevis Op 64 (SATB chorus, organ) 1973; first performed Northampton, 1973.
This Worldes Joie Op 67 (soprano, tenor, bass, SATB chorus, orchestra) 1974; first performed Fishguard, Dyfed, 17 August 1974.
The Fields of Praise Op 74 (tenor, piano; Thomas) 1976; first performed Bangor, Gwynedd, 3 March 1977.
A Royal Garland Op 77 (unaccompanied SATB chorus) 1977; first performed Paris, September 1977.
Arise, Shine Op 77 No 2 (SATB chorus, organ) 1977; first performed 17 June 1985.
Nativity Carol Op 77 No 3 (SATB chorus, organ or piano duet or 3 trumpets, 3 trombones, tuba, percussion, organ) 1977; first performed London, 11 December 1977.
A May Magnificat Op 79 No 2 (double choir with chime bars) 1978; first performed Cork, 5 May 1978.
Shakespeare Songs Op 80 1979; first performed Cardiff, 8 February 1979.
Songs of William Blake Op 82 (mezzo-soprano, horn, piano, celeste, strings) 1979; first performed Fishguard, Dyfed, 29 July 1979.
Rex gloriae Op 83 (unaccompanied mixed voices) 1981; first performed Stuttgart, May 1981.
Te Deum Op 85 (soprano, mezzo-soprano, tenor, SATB chorus, orchestra) 1981; first performed Aberdeenshire, 10 October 1981.
Let the People Praise Thee O Lord Op 87 (SATB chorus, organ or orchestra; Psalm 67) 1981; first performed London, 29 July 1981.
Praise Ye the Lord Op 87 No 2 (SATB chorus, organ; Psalm 148) 1981; first performed St Woolos, 13 October 1981.

Lux aeterna Op 88 (soprano, mezzo-soprano, contralto, boys' chorus, SATB chorus, organ, orchestra) 1982; first performed Hereford, 26 August 1982.
All Wisdom Is from the Lord Op 88 No 2 (SATB chorus, organ; Ecclesiasticus) 1982; first performed Salisbury, Wiltshire, 23 July 1982.
Salvator mundi Op 89 (SSA chorus, piano duet, percussion, string orchestra) 1982; first performed Cheltenham, Gloucestershire, 10 December 1982.
Except the Lord Build the House Op 89 No 2 (SATB, organ and/or 3 trumpets, optional timpani and percussion) 1982; first performed Cambridge, Massachusetts, 11 November 1982.
A Grace Op 89 No 3 (unaccompanied SATB chorus) 1982; first performed London, 24 November 1982.
Hear O Thou Shepherd of Israel Op 89 No 4 (SATB chorus, organ; Psalm 80) 1982; first performed Bangor, Gwynedd, 8 January 1983.
O Be Joyful in the Lord Op 90 No 2 1983; first performed San Antonio, Texas, 26 April 1983.
Oh How Amiable Op 90 No 3 (SATB chorus, organ) 1983; first performed Llandaff, Glamorgan, 5 June 1983.
Tantum ergo Op 90 No 4 (SATB chorus, organ) 1983; first performed Fort Worth, Texas, 2 February 1983.
Let Us Now Praise Famous Men Op 91 No 2 (SATB chorus, organ or orchestra) 1984; first performed Worcester, 18 August 1984.
Alleluia, Christ Is Risen Op 91 No 3 (SATB chorus, organ, optional brass) 1984; first performed New York City, 20 May 1984.
Missa aedis Christi (in memoriam William Walton) Op 92 (SATB chorus, organ) 1984; first performed Oxford, 10 June 1984.
Angelus (no opus number; SSA chorus, piano) 1984.
Veni sancte spiritus Op 96 (SATB chorus, organ, 2 trumpets, percussion) 1985; first performed Hereford, 20 August 1985.
O aula nobilis Op 95 No 4 (SA chorus, 3 trumpets, timpani, 3 percussion, piano duet) 1985.
Gogoneddawg Arglwydd Op 95 No 5 (SATB chorus, brass, organ) 1985; first performed Rhyl, Clwyd, 1985.
Let All the World in Every Corner Sing Op 96 No 2 (SATB chorus, organ, optional brass) 1985; first performed London, 25 June 1987.
O Clap Your Hands Op 96 No 3 (SATB chorus, organ) 1985; first performed London, 28 February 1986.
Salve regina Op 96 No 5 (TTBB or SATB chorus) 1985; first performed 1986.
The Echoing Green (SSAA chorus, piano; Blake) 1985.
I Will Lift up Mine Eyes to the Hills (SATB chorus, organ) 1986; first performed Stockport, Cheshire, 15 January 1987.
Rejoice in the Lord Op 99 No 1 (SATB chorus, organ) 1987; first performed Springfield, Massachusetts, June 1987.
O Lord, Our Lord (no opus number; SATB chorus, organ, optional brass) 1987; first performed Princeton, New Jersey, 16 May 1987.
Cantate domino (no opus number; SATB chorus, organ) 1987; first performed Ludlow, Shropshire, June 1987.
As Truly as God Is Our Father (no opus number; SATB chorus, organ) 1987; first performed London, 30 June 1987.
Thus Saith God the Lord (An Orkney Anthem) (no opus number) 1987; first performed Kirkwall, Orkney, 21 June 1987.
Riddles (no opus number; 6 soloists, SATB chorus, piano, bells) 1987; first performed Vancouver, 6 February 1988.
Y nefoedd sydd yn datgan gogoniant Duw (no opus number; SATB chorus, organ) 1988; first performed St Asaph, Clwyd, 25 September 1988.
Sweet Was the Song (no opus number; SATB chorus, organ or piano) 1988; first performed Worthington, Ohio, 25 June 1988.
Learsongs (no opus number; SA chorus, piano duet; or clarinet, trumpet, piano duet, percussion, double bass) 1989; first performed Toronto, 1989.
World's Fire (no opus number; soloists, chorus, orchestra) 1989; first performed St Asaph, Clwyd, 30 September 1989.
Doctrine of Wisdom (no opus number; SATB chorus, organ) 1990; first performed London, 17 May 1990.

Opera:

The Servants Op 91 (Iris Murdoch) 1980; first performed Cardiff, 15 September 1980.
Jonah: A Musical Morality (no opus number; baritone, tenor, SA chorus, SATB chorus, orchestra; Causley) 1988; first performed Guildford, Surrey, 6 July 1988.

Other:

Culhwch and Olwen Op 32 (entertainment) 1966.
As You Like It (no opus number; incidental music to Shakespeare) 1967.

PUBLICATIONS

On Mathias: S. Walsh, "The Music of WM", in *Musical Times*, January 1969; Michael Dawney, "WM", in *Composer*, Summer 1974.

* * *

William Mathias is one of the most fluent and accessible of contemporary British composers. His gift for composition had been pronounced from an early age; fluency was advanced by his undergraduate experiences at University College, Aberystwyth, where students were encouraged to compose (and perform their own works) regularly. Few of these works are ever performed nowadays, though they are well-constructed and written in an easy, conversational idiom which betrays several influences; Bartók's style is of paramount importance, emerging in certain melodic and rhythmic fingerprints, as well as through the use of palindromic structures. Mathias first used a palindrome in *Berceuse*; it has also been a much-favoured structure in the work of his near contemporary, Alun Hoddinott.

Mathias has not chosen to pursue stylistic fashions in music; techniques like serialism and aleatoricism seem to hold little interest for him. There are a few passages in his works where precise notation is abandoned for a time, but these are purely colouristic; chance elements never obliterate basic harmonic and structural features and the aleatory sections are short-lived.

Before embarking on a large symphonic work for full orchestra, Mathias polished his craft with a number of less ambitious orchestral works, among which three pieces for string orchestra—*Divertimento, Music for Strings* and *Prelude, Aria and Finale*—are outstanding. The *Divertimento*, in particular, displays considerable technical mastery (of canonic writing, for instance) and was one of Mathias's first pieces to attract widespread attention.

For his first full-scale orchestral work, Mathias chose the

somewhat modish title of "Concerto for Orchestra"; but this piece is far less concerned with highlighting sectional virtuosity in the orchestra in the manner of earlier genre pieces by Bartók, Lutosławski and others; its main link with concerto form, in the usual sense, is that it is cast in three movements. The first of these is particularly significant as an example of Mathias's most individual treatment of sonata form: the expository melodic material is reduced to its essentials during the development and is recapitulated, as it were, in skeletal form.

Some 17 years separate the two symphonies which Mathias has so far completed (a third has been commissioned by the BBC for 1991). The Second Symphony can be appreciated on two distinct levels: as an abstract "pure-music" work in three movements, or as an atmospheric response to various Celtic sources, including Arthurian legend and poetry by Taliesin and Dylan Thomas. Mathias has spent most of his career in Wales and is often at his most impressive when writing in direct response to some aspect of this Celtic heritage. However, he is also cosmopolitan, able to absorb an enormous range of musical influences. These include the flirtations with Latin American music found in pieces dating from the late 1960s, such as the Third Piano Concerto; but there are also complex, sometimes quasi-baroque structures where instrumental virtuosity helps to underline some external drama; perhaps pre-eminent in this second category is the *Organ Concerto*, in which variation form is employed to underline the extra-musical theme of the 14 Stations of the Cross. Such ideas are scarcely new, but, as always with Mathias, they are treated with imagination and skill.

—Paul Horner

MATSUDAIRA, Yori-Aki [Yoriaki]. Japanese. Born in Tokyo, 27 March 1931; son of Yoritsune Matsudaira, *q.v.* Educated at Tokyo Metropolitan University (biology), 1948–57; self-taught as composer. Teacher of physics and biology, Rikkyo [St Paul's] University, Tokyo, from 1958; founder, composing collective Group 20.5. Secretary of Japanese Section, ISCM. Recipient: composition prize, ISCM Festival, 1958. Mailing address: 3-31-9 Kasuga-cho, Nerima-ku, Tokyo, Japan.

Publisher: Suvini Zerboni.

Symphonies/orchestral:

Configuration (chamber orchestra) 1963; first performed Tokyo, 29 March 1967.
The Symphony (chamber orchestra) 1971.
Messages (wind orchestra, tape) 1972.

Chamber/instrumental:

Variations (piano trio) 1957; first performed Tokyo, 15 November 1957.
Speed Co-Efficient (flute, piano, keyboard percussion) 1958.
Orbites I–III (flute, clarinet, piano) 1960.
Variations on a Noh Theme (flute, clarinet, 3 percussion, piano, violin, viola, cello; collaboratively composed by Group 20.5) 1960.
Instruction (piano) 1961.
Co-Action I & II (cello, piano) 1962.
Parallax (flute, oboe, clarinet, bassoon, saxophone) 1963.
Rhymes for Severino Gazzelloni (flute/percussion) 1965–6; first performed Venice, 10 September 1966.
Distributions (string quartet, ring modulator) 1966–7; first performed Tokyo, 16 March 1968.
Alternations (jazz group: trumpet, piano, double bass, drums, with ring modulator) 1967.
Allotropy (piano) 1970.
Gradations (violin, viola, oscillator) 1971.
Messages (wind players) 1972; first performed Tokyo, February 1973.
Trichromatic Form (harp) 1973.
Transient '74 (guitar, organ, harp, percussion) 1974.
Simulation (tuba) 1974.
Coherency for Ark (flute, clarinet, percussion, harp, keyboard) 1976.
Brilliancy (flute, piano) 1978.
Erixatone (electric piano) 1979.
Perspective (piano) 1988.
Gala (piano) 1990.

Vocal/choral:

What's Next? (soprano, 2 noise makers) 1967–71; first performed Graz, Austria, 12 October 1972.
Wand Waves (reciter, tape) 1970; first performed Tokyo, 15 March 1970.
Substitution (soprano, piano) 1972; first performed Freiburg, November 1972.

Opera:

Sara 1960; first performed Tokyo, 12 November 1960.

Other:

Ishikawa no iratsume (traditional dance drama) 1964; first performed Tokyo, July 1964.
Transient '64 (tape) 1964.
Assemblages (tape) 1968.
Why Not? 1970.
Where Now? (3 dancers, ensemble) 1973.
Shift (dance, tape) 1976.

PUBLICATIONS

By Matsudaira: *Conpyuta to ongaku* [Computers in Music], Tokyo, 1972.

* * *

In early chamber works like *Speed Co-Efficient* (1958) and *Orbites* (1960) Yori-Aki Matsudaira employed serial methods by totally organizing the parameters of pitch, duration, attack, intensity and timbre of sounds. However, he did not include the space of performance. For his aleatory pieces like *Instruction* for piano and *Co-Action I & II* for cello and piano Stockhausen's *Klavierstück XI* served as the model with respect to the performers' freedom to choose the actual order of formal sections. Chance operations were also involved in the composition of *Rhymes for Severino Gazzelloni* for flute and percussion and *Transient '64*. The pitch scale of the latter was based on the results of an experiment dealing with the perception of extreme pitches. The chance processes within vacuum tubes produced the indeterminate events of the composition and was then fixed on tape.

When Matsudaira stayed in the United States in the mid-1960s he was influenced not so much by its music, but rather by the American art scene, where he encountered Hyper-realism, Pop-Art and Op-Art. He became especially interested in the combining techniques of Robert Rauschenberg, who included heterogeneous materials in his paintings. This had an immediate impact on Matsudaira's method of composition in the decade until about 1976. He began incorporating materials found in contemporary or historical musical contexts in his works as quotations. *Alternations* for a jazz-like combo and ring modulator quoted Tekla Badarzewska–Baranowska; *Allotropy* for piano alluded to Chopin's *Prelude Op 28 No 15* with its tone repetitions; the tape composition *Assemblages* was put together from many pieces of different kinds of recorded sound. He also began using electronics, first in *Distributions* for string quartet with ring modulator (1966–7), a piece which was inspired by the tuning process before a concert. It employed typical elements from this process like glissandos, quarter tones and long silences.

Matsudaira explored the theatrical element of music in *Why Not?* and *Where Now?*. There are several versions (theatrical, electronic and instrumental) of *Why Not?* from which one has to be selected before being performed. The details of the events (such as their duration) must then be determined by the performers using decks of playing cards. *Where Now?*, an explicit theater piece for actress, male dancer and instrumentalists, concerns misunderstanding and loss of communication. The actions of the leading character are reflected by similar actions of the instrumentalists. A radical sonority was achieved in a similarly-named piece *What's Next?*. Besides a soprano voice and tape it employed two noise makers, including motorbikes.

From 1976–7 Matsudaira moved toward modality. *Coherency for Ark* for chamber ensemble paraphrases the row of Berg's *Lyric Suite*. His interest in the rhythms of morse code was reflected in *Erixatone* for electric piano, where a text generated the morse code on which the rhythms of the piece are based.

Only recently has Matsudaira's style become more chromatic and non-tonal again with *Perspective* for piano. *Gala* for piano returns to the quotation technique by intermodulating the quotation in different parameters. An enormous quantity of quotations from the history of music are connected by interludes based on morse code; a passage's harmony may be derived from Messiaen while its melody is derived from Mozart.

—Rolf Klein

MATSUDAIRA, Yoritsune. Japanese. Father of Yori-Aki Matsudaira, *q.v.* Born in Tokyo, 5 May 1907. Educated at Keio University (French literature); studied composition privately under Kosuke Komatsu; studied composition under Alexandre Tansman, and Alexander Tcherepnin, 1935–7. Joined Shinko Sakkyokuka Renmei, 1931; founder/co-director, from 1937, secretary, 1953–5, chair, 1956–60, Nihon Gendai Sakkyokuka Renmei, later Japanese Society for Contemporary Music. Recipient: Weingartner Prize (for *Nanbu min 'yo shu No 1*), 1937; ISCM Prize, 1952; Zerboni Prize (for *Metamorphosis on "Saibara"*), 1954; International Composition Competition Prize, Rome, 1962. Mailing address: 6-4-8 Nakomo, Nakano-ku, Tokyo, Japan.

Publisher: Suvini Zerboni, Milan.

Symphonies/orchestral:

Pastorale 1935.
Theme and Variations on a Folksong from the Nanbu District (piano, orchestra) 1939; first performed Tokyo, 17 December 1939.
Theme and Variations on Etenraku (piano, orchestra) 1951.
Ancient Japanese Dance 1952; first performed Berlin, 9 October 1953.
Figures sonores 1956; first performed Zurich, 1 June 1957.
Umai/Right Dance 1957; first performed Darmstadt, 11 September 1958.
Samai (chamber orchestra) 1958; first performed Rome, 15 June 1959.
Danse sacré 1959.
Danse finale 1959.
Bugaku kumikyoku/Dance Suite (3 orchestral groups) 1959; first performed Donaueschingen, 18 October 1959.
Bugaku (chamber orchestra) 1961; first performed Palermo, 6 October 1962.
Three Movements (piano, orchestra) 1962; first performed Stockholm, 20 March 1964.
Ritual Dance and Finale 1963.
Piano Concerto 1964; first performed Madrid, 20 March 1965.
Music for Seventeen Performers: Toei/Projection, Henkei/Metamorphosis (flute, oboe, clarinet, harp, piano, vibraphone, xylophone, 10 percussion) 1967.
Junkansuru gakusho/Rotating Movements (2 chamber orchestras) 1971; first performed Graz, Austria, 10 October 1972.
Prelude, Interlude and Aprèslude 1973.

Chamber/instrumental:

Komoriuta to orugoru/Lullaby and Music Box (piano) 1928–31.
Prelude in D (piano) 1934.
Sonatina (flute, piano) 1936.
Mittsu no den'en bukyoku/Six Pastoral Dances (piano) 1939–40.
Prelude in G (piano) 1940.
Sonatina (flute, clarinet) 1940.
Sonata (cello, piano) 1942, revised 1947.
Concertante (2 pianos) 1946.
Piano Trio 1948.
Sonatina (piano) 1948.
Sonata (violin, piano) 1948.
String Quartet No 1 1949.
Sonata (piano) 1949.
Suite (flute, horn, piano) 1950.
String Quartet No 2 1951.
Sonata (violin, piano) 1952.
Somakusha (flute; also for flute, oboe, harp, percussion, piano, strings) 1961, revised 1970.
Serenade (flute, oboe, percussion, strings) 1962.
Suite (10 instruments) 1963.
Concerto da camera (harpsichord, harp, instrumental ensemble) 1964.
Dialogue choréographique (wind quintet, harp, 2 pianos, percussion) 1966; first performed Royan, France, 3 April 1967.

Portrait (2 pianos) 1967.
Portrait (2 pianos, 2 percussion) 1967–8.
Pieces for Children (piano) 1968.
Lullabies (piano) 1969.
Pieces for Children from Nursery Rhymes and Folksongs (piano) 1969–70.
Etudes on Japanese Melodies (piano) 1970.
Bairo (chamber ensemble) 1983.

Vocal/choral:

Nanbu, min'yo shu/Folksongs from Nanbu District No 1 (voice, piano) 1928–36.
Nanbu, min'yo shu/Folksongs from Nanbu District No 2 (voice, piano) 1938.
Kokin-shu (soprano, piano) 1939–45, orchestrated 1950.
Metamorphosis on an old Japanese Melody "Saibara" (soprano, chamber orchestra) 1953; first performed Haifa, Israel, 3 June 1954.
Koromogae/Love Song (soprano, chamber orchestra) 1954; first performed Venice, 11 December 1968.
Katsura (soprano, guitar, harp, harpsichord, percussion) 1959.
Jisei, a roei/Two Stars in Vega (soprano, flute, oboe, harp, piano, vibraphone, percussion) 1967.
Kashin, a roei (female voices, orchestra) 1969.

PUBLICATIONS

By Matsudaira: *Kindai waseigaku/Harmony Today*, Tokyo, 1955, revised 1969–70; "The Origins of Gagaku", in *Japanese Music*, Tokyo, 1967.

On Matsudaira: K. Akiyama, "YM", in *Record geijutsu*, December 1971.

* * *

In 1930 Yoritsune Matsudaira joined a group of young Japanese composers devoted to neo-classicism. They represented an anti-romantic movement against the nationalistic style, then predominating Japanese music. In his *Prelude in D* for piano Matsudaira used modal melody shapes and bitonality. The second movement of the flute *Sonatina* already shows a melodic influence of gagaku, the ancient imperial court music of Japan, within a neo-classicist environment. He was also influenced by Alexandre Tansman and Alexander Tcherepnin, who both visited Japan during the 1930s. His *Theme and Variations on a Folksong from the Nanbu District* for piano and orchestra reveals a French harmonic style, with a special reference to Tansman in the way of resolving the tritone (Matsudaira's favorite interval), but is still Japanese in many other aspects.

Matsudaira employed the twelve-note technique for the first time in *Theme and Variations on Etenraku* for piano and orchestra. This work on a famous gagaku theme consists of six variations and a finale and combines heterogeneous styles such as the twelve-note technique in the third variation and jazz in the fifth variation, on a mainly polymodal basis. From *Metamorphosis on "Saibara"* on Matsudaira used the twelve-note technique more frequently. In this composition for soprano and chamber orchestra the twelve-note row is derived from the modes on which the old song "Saibara" is based. The vocal style includes the use of traditional techniques such as glissandos and portamentos.

In the 1950s Japanese composers of a younger generation considered Matsudaira's style old-fashioned because of his persistent use of traditional Japanese elements. But his style moved more and more toward the contemporary avant-garde language, and two of his works gained interest among these composers. *Umai* and *Samai* for orchestra impressed them not only by the extremely slow tempo at the beginning with subsequent acceleration, but also with the use of traditional percussion instruments. The major works of composers like Toshiro Mayuzumi and Toru Takemitsu cannot be imagined without the influence of these two pieces.

Since Matsudaira did not want to appear as a mere gagaku composer he utilized serialist methods or even aleatory, for instance in *Somakusha* for flute solo. This work clearly follows the example of Stockhausen's concept of "ambiguous form", which enables the performer to decide on the actual order of the parts of the work.

In the past 30 years Matsudaira has continued to refine the combination of gagaku elements with an avant-garde idiom. In his mainly instrumental compositions he uses formal concepts of gagaku, such as the division of a piece into a prelude and a main part, and the acceleration of tempos throughout a piece. He prefers instrumental timbres—mainly woodwind instruments like flutes and oboes—which resemble those of the original gagaku instruments at least in the manner of sound production. Sometimes an entire piece like *Bairo* for chamber ensemble is built upon the melodic and temporal structure of a piece from the gagaku repertoire. In other cases one of the highly standardized formal principles of gagaku music serves as a model for the construction of a composition. In his more recent works Matsudaira bases his harmonic and melodic constructions on sets of notes which are derived from gagaku modes.

Since serialism and other avant-garde idioms are historical phenomena and the younger generation of Japanese composers has turned toward post-modernism by now, it is refreshing to see how Matsudaira, who is still remarkably creative in his 80s, preserves a modern musical language in his compositions.

—Rolf Klein

MATSUMURA, Teizo. Japanese. Born in Kyoto, 15 January 1929. Educated at Daisan Kotogakko (preparatory course for Kyoto University), 1940–4; suffered tuberculosis; private piano lessons under Tsuneharu Takahashi, harmony lessons under Toshio Nagahiro; moved to Tokyo, 1949; private lessons in harmony, counterpoint and composition under Tomojiro Ikenouchi, composition under Akira Ifukube. Married Kusumi Matsumura, 1 April 1957; 1 daughter and 1 son. Committee member, Japanese Contemporary Music Society, from 1952; joined Shinshin Kai group, 1957; professor, Tokyo National University of Fine Arts and Music, 1975–87; director, Japanese Federation of Composers, from 1982, Japan-Soviet Music Association, from 1983, and Japan-China Cultural Exchange Association, from 1987. Recipient: 1st prize, NHK-Mainichi Music Competition (for *Introduction and Allegro concertante*), 1955; Otaka Prize (for *Prelude*), 1968, (for *Piano Concerto No 2*) 1978; Fukuyuma Prize (for *Piano Concerto No 1*), 1973; Suntory Music Prize (for *Piano Concerto No 2*), 1978; Grand Prix, National Art Festival (for *Piano Concerto No 1*), 1981; other prizes and awards. Mailing address: 2-36-5 Moto-Izumi Komae-shi, Tokyo 201, Japan.

Publishers: Zeno-On, Tokyo; Ongaku No Tomo, 30 Kagura-zaka-6, Shinjuku-ku, Tokyo 162, Japan.

Symphonies/orchestral:

Introduction et Allegro concertante 1955; first performed Tokyo, 22 October 1955.
Symphony 1965; first performed Tokyo, 15 June 1965. Recorded Victor VDC 5510; Columbia OS 10096-N; Victor SJX 1023/9560/1174.
Prelude 1968; broadcast NHK Radio, Japan, 7 November 1968; first concert performance Tokyo, 28 February 1969. Recorded Victor VX 60; Denon OW 7847-N; Victor VDC 5510.
Piano Concerto No 1 1973; broadcast NHK Radio, Japan, 4 November 1973; first public performance Tokyo, 28 February 1975. Recorded Victor SJX 9560/1175.
Piano Concerto No 2 1978; first performed Tokyo, 13 May 1978. Recorded Victor SJX 9560/1175.
Cello Concerto 1984; first performed Tokyo, 27 February 1984. Recorded Camerata 30 CM-85.
Pneuma (strings) 1987; first performed Tokyo, 19 September 1987.
Hommage à Akira Ifukube 1988.
Offrande orchestrale 1989; first performed Tokyo, 21 September 1989.

Chamber/instrumental:

Cryptogame (flute, oboe, clarinet, horn, trumpet, trombone, 2 percussion, piano, violin, cello, electric violin, musical saw) 1958; first performed Tokyo, 10 November 1958. Recorded King SKR 1019; GT9327; Victor SJX 9562.
Musique pour quatuor à cordes et piano (string quartet, piano) 1962; first performed Tokyo, 2 April 1962. Recorded Columbia OW 7850.
Deux Berceuses à la Grèce (piano) 1969; first performed Tokyo, 1969. Recorded Columbia ELS 3227; Toshiba EMI TCN 002; Victor SJX 9562; Victor VDC 1415.
Poem—I (shakuhachi, 13-string koto) 1969; first performed Osaka, 1969. Recorded Victor SJX 1026/9564; RCA RCL 8041; Victor CDMC 2019.
Courtyard of Asparas (flute, violin, piano) 1971; first performed Tokyo, 22 November 1971. Recorded RCA IRZ 2217; Victor SJX 9562.
Poem—II (shakuhachi) 1972; first performed Tokyo, 1972. Recorded Victor JRZ 2528/SJX 9564.
Poème (shinobue, biwa) 1979; broadcast NHK Radio, Japan, November 1979; first public performance Tokyo, 20 May 1980. Recorded Victor SJX 9564.
Fantasy (13-string koto) 1980; first performed Tokyo, 20 October 1980. Recorded Victor SJX 9564; Denon W8 7093; Camerata 32CM-92.
Poème (alto saxophone, biwa; transcribed from *Poème* for shinobue and biwa) 1980; first performed Tokyo, November 1980.
Air of Prayer (17-string koto) 1984; first performed Tokyo, 5 November 1984.
Air of Prayer (transcribed for cello) 1985; first performed Tokyo, 7 March 1985.
Spelmatica (cello) 1985.
Piano Trio 1987; broadcast NHK Radio, Japan, 1 April 1988; first public performance Tokyo, 30 June 1988.

Vocal/choral:

Achime (soprano, 2–3 percussion, flute, oboe, clarinet, alto saxophone, bassoon, horn, trumpet, trombone, cello, double bass; Kagura) 1957; first performed Tokyo, 23 October 1957. Recorded Victor SJX 9563.
Totem Ritual (soprano, mixed chorus, orchestra) 1969; first performed Tokyo, 1970.
Asparas (female voices, small orchestra) 1969.
Two Poems by the Prince of Karu (soprano, piano) 1973; broadcast NHK Radio, Japan, 12 March 1974; first public performance Tokyo, 18 February 1974. Recorded Victor SJX 9563.
Hymn to Aurora (mixed chorus, oboe d'amore, percussion, cello, harp, piano, organ; *Rig-Veda*, translated Hayashi) 1978; first performed Tokyo, 15 November 1978. Recorded Victor SJX 9563.

Also *Pastoral*, *Snow* (Miyoshi), *Snowing Like Petals* (Yanase)—all choral; *White Smoke* (Yanase), *A Book of Travels of an Earthworm* (Yanase)—solo vocal.

Opera/dramatic:

Flute of Devil's Passion (mini-opera; baritone, male chorus, ryuteki, orchestra; Koizumi) 1965; broadcast NHK Radio, Japan, 1965.
The Drifting Reed (musical fantasy for vocal, reflection, orchestra; Minakami) 1979; broadcast NHK television, Japan, July 1979.
The Patient Waters (lyric tragedy for reflection and orchestra) 1985; broadcast NHK television, Japan, 1985.

Other:

Akira Ifukube: Ujungajujana (orchestral transcription of piano part from *Ancient Minstrelsies of Gilyak Tribes* for voice and piano) 1984.

Theatre music: *Blood Sleeps on Standing* (Terayama), 1960; *God and the Devil* (Sartre), 1965; *Andromache* (Racine), 1966; *Orfeo ed Euridice* (Anouilh), 1967; *The Merchant of Venice* (Shakespeare), 1968; *Hamlet* (Shakespeare), 1968; *Marie Stuart* (Schiller), 1968; *Hail* (Minakami), 1969; *Kanoushougai* (Minakami), 1969; *Flower Mansion* (Shiba), 1970; *The Temple of a Wild Goose* (Minakami), 1971; *Hunger Strait* (Minakami), 1973; *Echizen Bambo Figure* (Minakami), 1973; *Echigo Tsutsuishi Oya Shirazu* (Minakami), 1974; *Koto of the Lake* (Minakami), 1974; *Gonan-cho Yugiri-roh* (Minakami), 1975; *Nichiren* (Tsugami), 1979; *Yuki-guni* (Miyamoto, after Kawabata), 1980; *Shaka-nai Hitsugi-Uta* (Minakami), 1980; *Hanare-goze Orin* (Minakami), 1980; *Women Who Are Taking Blue Stockings* (Miyamoto), 1983; *Phaedra* (Racine), 1983; *The School for Wives* (Molière), 1983; *Once More, a Shambles* (Miyamoto, after Ozaki), 1985; *The Crucible* (Miller), 1987; *Golden Pond* (Tompson), 1988; *Othello* (Shakespeare), 1988.

Film scores: *Unflyable Silence*, 1966; *A Flame and a Woman*, 1967; *Lover in Cuba*, 1969; *Chi No Mure*, 1970; *Shinobu Gawa*, 1972; *Poem of the Morning Glow*, 1973; *Assassination of Ryoma*, 1974; *Preparation for the Festival*, 1975; *Dojo-ji*, 1976; *Gassan*, 1978; *Darkroom*, 1983; *Yumechiyo's Diary*, 1985; *Sea and Poison*, 1986; *Tomorrow*, 1987; *Downtown Heroes*, 1988; *Senno Rikyu—Honkakubo Ibun/The Death of a Tea Master*, 1989; *Ronin Gai*, 1990.

PUBLICATIONS

By Matsumura: *Matsumura Teizo Ku-shu*, [haiku poems], Tokyo, 1977.

On Matsumura: Kuniharu Akiyama, "TM—Incantation of Multiplying Sounds", in *Ongaku No tomasha* [Japanese Composers Today], 1978; Yoshio Hachimura, "Spirit Incarnated by Sounds—TM", in *Soshia*, 1986; Kazuyuki Toyama, "TM—Mysterious Cosmos", included in anthology of Toyama's musicological works, 1986; Mariko Okayama, "Torrent of the One—TM", in *A Conflict and a Transcendence*, 1990.

* * *

Teizo Matsumura, a student of Tomojiro Ikenouchi and Akira Ifukube, was influenced especially by the latter, whose works accentuate Japanese national elements. From the West Debussy, Ravel and Stravinsky were central in Matsumura's interest. Stravinsky's influence is apparent in Matsumura's preference for ostinato (a perpetually repeated set of notes or chords) structures in his own works, such as the intense *Introduction et Allegro concertante* for orchestra and the even more vigorous *Achime* for soprano solo and chamber orchestra. *Achime* also reflects Matsumura's deep interest in the old Japanese culture by using a text from the ancient "Kagura", a form of sacred Shinto music and dance.

In several works dating from the late 1950s and early 1960s Matsumura put to the test techniques such as dodecaphony and serialism. *Cryptogame* for 13 players—among them a musical saw, a typewriter and a clavioline (an electronic instrument which was widely used later by the early Pink Floyd)—involves dodecaphony and thus provides a strongly atonal image. Except for its central part, the second movement of *Musique pour quatuor à cordes et piano* uses serial techniques. But using current procedures of composition in these works was only an interlude in Matsumura's career; in general he strongly rejected dodecaphony and serialism.

In 1965, after long preparation, he completed one of his major works, the *Symphony* for orchestra, which confirms Matsumura's preference for ostinatos. The ambivalence of beauty and the large masses of sound in this composition are other indicators of his withdrawal from fashionable tendencies of the time.

He began to appreciate Japan's own traditional music by using old Japanese instruments and, in *Prélude* for orchestra by using as a formal model the Netori of Gagaku, the ancient imperial court music of Japan. Matsumura's sense of the beauty of music developed further through his travels to India and Indochina, where he studied native types of music. The influence of Indian music promoted a shift towards tonality in his music, for instance in the beginning of *Piano Concerto No 1*. Over a drone bass representing the central note the piano ornaments the harmonic series of this drone. In Matsumura's music tonality must not be misunderstood as a restoration of Western functional harmony, but rather as the general reference of the sounds to a tonal center, as is the case in nearly all musical cultures of the earth.

From his studies in the histories of many different cultures Matsumura has come to the conclusion that the creative development of music as it appears in its Western form has come to a standstill. In his works and in his practice as a teacher at the Tokyo Academy of Music, Matsumura has worked toward restoring the richness of music. He hopes that new energies might emerge from the encounter of Japanese traditional music with Western music.

—Rolf Klein

MATTHEWS, Colin. British/English; brother of David Matthews, *q. v.* Born in London, 13 February 1946. Educated at University of Nottingham, 1964–67, B.A., M.Phil., 1971; University of Sussex, Brighton, 1975–76, D.Phil., 1977. Married Belinda Lloyd 1977; 3 children. Freelance music editor, from 1970; lecturer, University of Sussex, 1972–3, 1976–7; director, Holst Estate, from 1974; council member, Society for the Promotion of New Music, from 1981; council member, Aldeburgh Foundation, from 1984; trustee, Britten-Pears Foundation, from 1984; collaborated with Benjamin Britten on vocal score of *Death in Venice*, with Deryck Cooke on realisation of Mahler's Tenth Symphony, and with Imogen Holst on edition of Gustav Holst's music. Recipient: Ian Whyte Award, Scottish Orchestra Society (for *Sonata No 4*), 1975; Park Lane Group Composer Award, 1982. Mailing address: Faber Music Ltd., 3 Queen Square, London WC1N 3AU, England.

Publishers: Faber; Novello.

Symphonies/orchestral:

Sonata No 4 "Green and Gold and Blue and White" Op 6 1975; first performed Edinburgh, 2 April 1976.
Night Music Op 10 (small orchestra) 1976–7; first performed London, 22 May 1977.
Sonata No 5: "Landscape" Op 17 1977–81; first performed London, 17 November 1983. Recorded Unicorn-Kanchana DKP 9053.
Little Suite Op 18a (small orchestra) 1979.
Little Suite Op 18b (small orchestra) 1979.
Divertimento Op 21b (double string orchestra) 1982; first performed Aldeburgh, Suffolk, 23 June 1982. Recorded Auracle AUC 1007.
Canonic Overture Op 24a 1983.
Cello Concerto Op 27 1983–4; first performed London, 10 September 1984. Recorded Unicorn Kanchana DKP 9053.
Toccata meccanica Op 24b 1984; first performed Northampton, 30 March 1985.
Monody 1987; first performed Newcastle-upon-Tyne, 25 July 1987.
Two-Part Invention (chamber orchestra) 1987–8; first performed London, 1988.
Cortege 1989; first performed London, 1989.
Quatrain 1989; first performed London, 1989.
Hidden Variables 1989; first performed Birmingham, 1989.

Chamber/instrumental:

Ceres Op 4 (3 flutes, guitar, 2 percussion, 2 cellos, double bass) 1972; first performed Brighton, Sussex, 15 December 1972.
Five Studies Op 5 (piano) 1974–6; first performed London, 14 May 1976.
Partita Op 7 (violin) 1975.
Specula Op 9 (flute, percussion, harp, viola) 1976; first performed Edinburgh, 15 December 1976.
Suite Op 11 1977–9; first performed Hong Kong, 15 December 1983.
Rainbow Studies Op 12 (flute/piccolo, oboe/cor anglais, clarinet/bass clarinet, bassoon, piano) 1977–8; first performed London, 5 July 1978.
String Quartet No 1 Op 16 1979; first performed Aldeburgh, Suffolk, 7 June 1980.
Little Suite Op 18c (harp) 1979; first performed London, 27 December 1980.

Oboe Quartet No 1 Op 19 (oboe, string trio) 1981; first performed Nottingham, 29 November 1981. Recorded Auracle AUC 1007.

Divertimento Op 21a (string octet) 1982; first performed Blythburgh, Suffolk, 23 June 1982.

Triptych Op 25a (piano quintet) 1984; first performed London, 30 May 1984. Recorded Auracle AUC 1007.

Suns Dance (piccolo, oboe, horn, 2 violins, viola, double bass) 1984–5; first performed London, 30 October 1985.

Three Enigmas Op 30 (cello, piano) 1985; first performed Stamford, Connecticut, 10 December 1985.

String Quartet No 2 1985; first performed Stratford-upon-Avon, 16 February 1986; withdrawn for revision.

Four Out of Five Untitled Pieces (flute, piccolo) 1986; first performed London, 8 October 1987.

Five Duos (cello, piano) 1987; first performed London, 29 September 1987.

Eleven Studies in Velocity (piano) 1987; first performed London, 2 October 1987.

Chaconne with Chorale (violin, piano) 1988; first performed London, 23 March 1988.

Moto perpetuo (violin, piano) 1988; first performed London, 10 June 1988.

Fuga (alto flute/piccolo, clarinet/bass clarinet, horn, percussion, piano, viola, cello, double bass) 1988; first performed Huddersfield, Yorkshire, 23 November 1988.

Oboe Quartet No 2 1989; first performed London, 1990.

Three-Part Chaconne (piano quartet) 1990; first performed London, 1990.

Vocal/choral:

Un Colloque sentimental Op 14 (cycle for medium voice, piano; Verlaine, Baudelaire, Nerval) 1971–8; first performed Sydney, 7 September 1978.

Five Sonnets: To Orpheus Op 8 (tenor, harp; Rilke) 1975–6; first performed London, 1 June 1977.

Shadows in the Water Op 15 (high voice, piano; Traherne) 1978–9; first performed Aldeburgh, Suffolk, 11 June 1980.

The Great Journey Op 22 (baritone, flute/alto flute/piccolo, clarinet/bass clarinet, horn, percussion, piano, viola, cello, double bass; Alvar Nuñez Cabeza de Vaca) 1981–8; first performed London, 12 June 1988.

Secondhand Flames Op 20 (unaccompanied SSATB chorus) 1982; first performed Bath, 31 May 1982.

Night's Mask Op 26 (soprano, alto flute/piccolo, bass clarinet/clarinet, horn, harp, piano, viola, cello; Pessoa) 1984; first performed Aldeburgh, Suffolk, 11 June 1984.

Cantata on the Death of Antony (voice and ensemble) 1989; first performed Brighton, Sussex, 1989.

Prometheus-Fragment (unaccompanied SSAATTBB chorus) 1989; first performed London, 1989.

Other:

Five Operetta Excerpts (from J. Strauss, Lehar, Kalman, Wolf, Ferrari; arranged for 2 voices, chamber ensemble) 1985.

Pursuit (ballet for 16 players, extended version of *Suns Dance*) 1987; first performed London, 1987.

Gustav Mahler: *Seven Songs from "Lieder und Gesange"* (orchestrated by Colin and David Matthews) 1964; first performed Cardiff, 12 June 1981.

Hector Berlioz: *Serenade, Hymn and Toccata* (arranged for small orchestra) 1978; first performed London, 28 May 1978.

Puccini: *Tosca—Act I Synthesis* (arranged for chamber orchestra) 1978; first performed 28 May 1978.

Modest Mussorgsky: *Marriage* (1-act opera in 4 scenes arranged for chamber orchestra) 1981; first performed London, 12 December 1981.

Gustav Holst: *The Dream City* (arranged for soprano, orchestra) 1983; first performed London, 1985. Recorded Hyperion CDA 66099.

Franz Schubert: *Ellens Drei Gesange* (arranged for voice, chamber ensemble) 1984; first performed London, 26 July 1984.

PUBLICATIONS

On Matthews: Paul Griffiths, (interview) in *New Sounds, New Personalities: British Composers of the 1980s*, London, 1985.

Colin Matthews comments:

My music is, I think, mainstream, without being conservative, European influenced rather than insular, but openminded about the primacy of colour, shape, harmony and line: every work demands a different approach.

* * *

Colin Matthews's intensely practical training—with Arnold Whittall and Nicholas Maw, and with Deryck Cooke, Benjamin Britten and Imogen Holst—has proved invaluable to his music. The professionalism he experienced while working with Britten has become a hallmark of his own work. As his output would suggest, he is equally fluent in all genres while preserving his compositional personality. His style is made up of very diverse components: the economy and ease of his scoring are perhaps reminiscent of Britten, but his first major orchestral work, the prize-winning *Sonata No 4*, employs shifting repetitive patterns and consonant harmony in a manner clearly influenced by the music of minimalist composers such as Steve Reich, although these patterns are deployed in a richer and more varied context than in Reich's work.

In Matthews's next orchestral work *Night Music* (written in memory of Deryck Cooke), the influence of Mahler begins to be felt, both in the slowness of the pacing and the lugubrious character of the music; but it is in this work that Matthews's personal harmonic idiom emerges. The music is elaborated from two alternating chords and their inversions, both having a strong dominant-with-added-note flavour which pervades the work and gives it its sombre character. This type of rich post-tonal harmony has remained typical of Matthews's music, although he has since developed in several unexpected directions. *Sonata No 5: Landscape* "is a vast, single-movement symphonic poem evolving in three long paragraphs, each more developed than the last; it is more densely contrapuntal than any music Matthews had hitherto composed, with an almost expressionistic intensity and violence of gesture. The harmony is more opaque than before, the orchestration rich and fantastically elaborate, with a complete mastery of form and pacing. It remains one of the most extreme and impressive works of his output.

The *Cello Concerto* is different again. Cast in two movements, it opens with a swift, dream-like scherzo, harmonically simpler than *Landscape* but more volatile in rhythm and texture, with the faintest suggestion of sonata form hovering behind the movement. The second movement is in total contrast, an ominous lament centred on C#, the fleeting melodic scurryings of the first movement slowed down to become a dark, sustained threnody. At the last minute the piece opens out into a fast coda recalling the first movement and ending the work, like *Landscape*, on an unexpected upbeat.

Alongside such ambitious orchestral works, Matthews has composed a large number of works for smaller combinations, including two string quartets, an oboe quartet and a double string quartet, *Divertimento*, all of which demonstrate great expertise in string writing and in creating harmonically articulate, lucid contrapuntal lines. His most substantial chamber work is *The Great Journey*, scored for baritone and eight instruments. It tells of the disastrous abortive expedition of the Spanish explorer Alvar Nuñez Cabeza de Vaca to America, in music of great immediacy and atmosphere, not merely illustrating the text but suggesting the psychological state of the narrator and his ambiguous feelings about the undertaking. The vivid scoring is skillfully handled so as never to drown the voice; indeed one of Matthews's most impressive achievements is to have ensured that every word is clearly audible, whatever the style of vocal delivery.

Matthews has also composed two important works for chamber groups which are more akin in style and form to his orchestral music: *Suns Dance* is a wildly exuberant single movement of brilliantly sustained fast music, contrapuntally and rhythmically almost as complex as *Landscape*, with an immense variety of incident and texture packed into its 17 minutes. Like *Landscape*, it eludes traditional formal classification, evolving as a perpetually developing, self-renewing polyphony propelled by frequent metrical modulation (*Suns Dance* has since been used for a ballet under the title *Pursuit*). The punning *Two-Part Invention* is a continuous running diptych, the music hanging upon a single evolving melodic line for its progress (in the second of the work's two parts, this line is articulated in a cello solo somewhat reminiscent of Matthews's earlier concerto).

The process of elaborating an entire musical texture from a single line also lies behind the orchestral work *Monody*; the work's three sections achieve their contrast through varying the tesitura and articulation of this line, as well as the extent to which it generates the surrounding harmony heterophonically or is contrasted with it. *Monody* is a rare example of a work written for youth orchestra making no concessions to the players, stretching them to the limit without ever becoming impractical.

Matthews's most recent substantial work *Cortege* follows on from *Monody* in a number of respects: it is again highly practically written, playable by a "non-specialist" orchestra without excessive rehearsal, yet not stylistically simplified. Like *Monody*, it includes in its scoring a bass drum for each of the three percussionists—much of the work unfolds against a distant tread of drum-beats. Indeed the scoring, harmony and time-scale all suggest a neo-Mahlerian funeral march, not least at the thunderingly climactic succession of minor triads which close the work.

Despite his versatility, Matthews is clearly most at home in his biggest canvases, in large forms with bold dramatic outlines. His ability to flesh these out with memorable music teaming with substance and invention, together with his flair for vocal writing lead one to wonder whether Matthews may not yet make a fine composer of operas.

—Julian Anderson

MATTHEWS, David (John). British/English; brother of Colin Matthews, *q.v.* Born in London, 5 March 1943. Educated at Bancroft's School, 1954–62; University of Nottingham, 1962–5, B.A. (classics); studied privately under Anthony Milner. Freelance music editor, with Benjamin Britten, 1966–9; musical director, Deal Festival, Kent, since 1988; music adviser, English Chamber Orchestra, since 1988; also freelance book editor (with Faber and Faber); writer; orchestrator of film music. Mailing address: 12 Woodlands, Clapham Common North Side, London SW4 ORJ, England.

Publisher: Faber.

Symphonies/orchestral:

Little Concerto Op 6 (chamber orchestra) 1970–1.
Symphony No 1 Op 9 1975; first performed Stroud, Gloucestershire, 1975.
Symphony No 2 Op 17 1976–9; first performed London, 13 May 1982.
Sonata canonica Op 19 1977; first performed Glasgow, 1982.
September Music Op 24 (small orchestra) 1979; first performed Glasgow, 1980.
White Nights Op 26 (violin, small orchestra) 1980.
Introit Op 28 (2 trumpets, strings) 1981; first performed Windsor, Berkshire, 13 November 1981.
Serenade Op 29 (small orchestra) 1982; first performed Jerusalem, 1982.
Violin Concerto Op 31 1982; first performed Manchester, 1983.
Symphony No 3 Op 37 1983–5; first performed Sheffield, 27 September 1985.
In the Dark Time Op 38 1985; first performed London, 11 December 1985.
Variations for Strings Op 40 1986; first performed Uppingham, Leicestershire, 23 March 1987.
Chaconne Op 43 1986–7; first performed Manchester, 7 October 1988.
Romanza Op 49 1989; first performed London, 1990.
The Music of Dawn Op 50 1990; first performed London, 1990.
Symphony No 4 Op 52 1990; first performed London, 1991.

Chamber/instrumental:

String Quartet No 1 Op 4 1969–70, revised 1980; first performed Dartington, Devon, 31 October 1973.
Fantasia Op 5 (viola) 1970; first performed London, 1970.
Fantasia Op 8 (cello) 1971; first performed Winchester, 1975.
String Quartet No 2 Op 16 1974–6; first performed London, 22 February 1982.
Music of Evening Op 11 (quintet) 1976.
Songs and Dances of Mourning Op 12 (cello) 1976; first performed Nottingham, 1977.
Toccatas and Pastorals Op 13 (2 oboes, bassoon, harpsichord) 1976; first performed Oxford, 1976.
Three Preludes Op 15 (piano) 1976–9; first performed Bristol, 1987.
String Quartet No 3 Op 18 1977–8; first performed York, 7 May 1980.
Etude Op 21 (piano) 1978; first performed Bristol, 1987.
String Quartet No 4 Op 27 1981; first performed Portsmouth, 11 June 1981.
Duet Variations Op 30 (flute, piano) 1982; first performed London, 1982.
Winter Journey Op 32 (violin) 1982–3; first performed London, 3 July 1983.

Piano Trio Op 34 1983–4; first performed London, 11 June 1984.
Clarinet Quartet Op 35 1984; first performed London, 4 July 1984.
String Quartet No 5 Op 36 1984; first performed Sheffield, 23 October 1984.
Three Studies Op 39 (violin) 1985; first performed London, 10 July 1986.
Aria Op 41 (violin, piano) 1985; first performed London, 27 October 1986.
Concertino Op 42 (oboe, string quartet) 1986–7; first performed London, 6 May 1987.
Piano Sonata Op 47 1988; first performed Deal, Kent, 1989.
String Trio Op 48 1989; first performed London, 1989.

Vocal/choral:

Three Orchestral Songs Op 1 (soprano, orchestra; Hugo, Eluard, Baudelaire) 1968–70; first performed London, 1970.
Three Songs Op 2 (baritone, piano; Alun Lewis) 1969–70; first performed London, 1971.
Stars Op 3 (SATB chorus, small orchestra; Holman) 1970; first performed London, 24 October 1970.
Upon Time Op 7 (medium voice, piano) 1970–1; first performed London, 1976.
Ehmals und Jetzt Op 22 (soprano, piano) 1972–9; first performed Cheltenham, Gloucestershire, 1981.
The Book of Hours Op 10 (high voice, piano) 1975–8.
Eclogue Op 14 (soprano, septet) 1975–9.
Four Yeats Songs Op 23 (tenor, piano) 1976–9.
The Golden Kingdom Op 33 (high voice, piano; Raine, Shelley, Blake) 1978–83; first performed Bristol, 1988.
Four Hymns Op 20 (unaccompanied chorus) 1980; first performed London, 1983.
The Company of Lovers Op 25 (unaccompanied SATB chorus) 1980; first performed Australia, 3 August 1981. Recorded Arika AR 002.
Cantiga Op 45 (soprano, chamber orchestra; Maggie Hemingway) 1987–8; first performed London, 27 July 1988.
Marina Op 44 (baritone, basset horn, viola, piano; T.S. Eliot) 1988; first performed Bath, 9 June 1988.

Other:

Emmanuel Chabrier: *Souvenirs de Munich* (arranged for chamber orchestra) first performed Scandinavia, 1978.
Gustav Mahler: *Seven Songs* from *Lieder und Gesange* (with Colin Matthews; arranged for high voice, orchestra) first performed Cardiff, 1981.
Frederick Delius: *Suite* from *A Village Romeo and Juliet* (arranged for orchestra) first performed Watford, Hertfordshire, 1987. Recorded Virgin Classics VC7 90716.
Johannes Brahms: *String Sextet in B♭ Op 18* (arranged for string orchestra) first performed Watford, Hertfordshire, 1987. Recorded (andante only) Virgin Classic VC7 90716.
Francis Poulenc: *Babar the Elephant* (arranged for chamber ensemble) first performed Canterbury, Kent, 1988.
Claudio Monteverdi: *Laudate pueri* (arranged for orchestra) first performed London, 1989.

Film scores (with Peter Sculthorpe): *Manganinnie*, 1980; *Burke and Wills*, 1985.

PUBLICATIONS

By Matthews: *Michael Tippett: An Introduction*, London, 1980; "Act II, Scene I: An examination of the Music", in Cambridge Opera Handbook to Britten's *Peter Grimes*, Cambridge, 1983; "The String Quartets and Some Other Chamber Works", in *The Britten Companion*, London, 1984; "*Death in Venice* and the Third String Quartet", in the Cambridge Opera Handbook to *Death in Venice*, Cambridge, 1987; "Reorientation", in *Salisbury Review*, 5 (3), April 1987; "The Rehabilitation of the Vernacular", in *Music and the Politics of Culture*, edited by Norris, London, 1989; "Peter Sculthorpe at 60", in *Tempo*, 170, September 1989.

On Matthews: Christopher Rowland, "Matthews Brothers, Composers", in *Musical Times*, June 1980; Calum MacDonald, "Symphonic Invention", in *Listener*, 5 December 1985; Paul Griffiths, (interview) in *New Sounds, New Personalities: British Composers of the 1980s*, London, 1985.

David Matthews comments:

My music is closely related to my own life, and to my feelings and emotions. This is romantic, but I am much concerned to try to objectify my feelings by pouring them into classical forms.

My first concern has always been with the symphony (my very first piece was a symphony). I don't just mean the orchestral work with the title "symphony"; rather, the comprehensive, large-scale instrumental piece which has a relation to classical symphonic form, and to classical tonality. I find it natural and right to use such traditions, and I think it important to try to uphold them. Of course, I can't do this unselfconsciously, without being aware of the course of musical history this century. But we are emerging out of a period when the ideas of modernism were dominant, and are rediscovering links with the past, among which the symphonic tradition seems to me one of the most important.

In this connection, I am concerned to use a musical language which is related to the musical vernacular. This was always so in the past, when folksong provided a vernacular basis for the melodies of European classical music. Schoenberg's invention of a non-vernacular language, which has had an enormous influence on subsequent generations of composers, I believe to have been essentially a side-track in musical history. Since we in England no longer have a direct relation with a living folk tradition, we must find its contemporary equivalents. I agree with Tippett that our living vernacular is jazz, blues and especially rock, and that somehow (though with necessary caution) we must find a way to relate ourselves to this contemporary vernacular.

I am wary of minimalism; though it has cheered up post-Darmstadt gloom, it is too simplistic for European composers, with their greater sense of history, to adopt wholesale.

I am happy to think of myself as an English composer, because I believe that all good music will have local roots. The idea of some anonymous Eurostyle appals me. But English composers have always been eclectics, taking from the continent what interested them most. My strongest affinities are still probably with central European composers, who were my first heroes—Mahler above all—and with Sibelius, whose transformation of his symphonic inheritance, and whose personal development from romanticism to classicism, has always seemed to me a paradigm of what a post-romantic composer can achieve.

* * *

"Tonality", David Matthews observed recently, "has survived the death sentence pronounced on it by the modernists, but it must somehow be freed from its current association with nostalgia." For Matthews, communication is essential. Like many of his generation, he found himself increasingly disturbed, upon reaching maturity during the 1960s, by the post-Webernian avant-garde's near stranglehold on contemporary classical music. Matthews identified more closely with composers whose language had vividly impressed itself upon him during the years when he and his younger brother, Colin, used to rifle through hoards of scantily used scores, including Debussy, Ravel (*Daphnis* in particular), Alexander Skriabin's two *Poèmes*, the scintillating First Violin Concerto of Karol Szymanowski and countless others, in an East London public library. Mahler, enjoying his overdue early 1960s revival, was to prove even more important: following his student years studying Classics at Nottingham, Matthews worked with Deryck Cooke on the performing version of Mahler's Tenth Symphony, and this, plus the overwhelming influence of Beethoven, filtered through the string quartets of Britten and Tippett in particular, together with helping prepare vocal and rehearsal scores of Britten's music for the fledgling Faber Music during the later 1960s, was to have a significant bearing on his formal approach and output later on.

But while ruling out of court the more austere dicta of Boulez and Darmstadt, like his elders Matthews has been shrewd enough to learn from rival schools, rendering him not so much *ec*lectic as *syl*lectic. Parts of his intense, extended tone poem *In the Dark Time*, which evidences his skill at handling larger-scale structures, echo the Expressionist melody and timbres that were a feature of his earlier work. Berg is not just a vital influence upon the Dostoevsky-based *Violin Concerto* for the Austrian-born Ernst Kovacic, but infiltrates the Renaissance Spanish, almost Lorca-like drama of the song cycle *Cantiga*, composed for Jill Gomez, which perhaps gives some indication of what could be expected from a Matthews opera. The Raine-Blake-Shelley cycle *The Golden Kingdom*—an alluring lament for past innocence and experience alike, with its studied symmetricality and evocative central passacaglia, has as much a Webernian as an Impressionist delicacy, while parts of the vocal writing echo more elegiac Maxwell Davies. Matthews's fondness for such forms, drawing on not just Britten but Busoni, is reflected in the atmospheric, inexorable unfolding of the double *Chaconne*. Perhaps most important in this context is Schoenberg—not merely by injunction (his treatises on form and counterpoint) but by example: the large-scope, Beethoven-imbued, single-movement *Quartet in D minor* of 1905 has provided a sturdy catalyst for Matthews's own important series of string quartets, to which a sixth, written for the Brindisi Quartet, was recently added.

The confirmation of a British string quartet tradition by Britten and Tippett in the late 1930s, plus the formal explorations (including the piano sonatas) of (in particular) the latter, on whom Matthews has written a detailed monograph, provided further encouragement. Three of the quartets (nos 1, 3 and 5) are penned in a single-movement form: the idea of taking elements from the various classical movements and integrating them almost seamlessly stems also from Sibelius's Seventh Symphony. The remaining three, by way of a reaction, attempt a more traditional pattern.

Matthews's quartets exemplify an unusually diverse talent, whether in their variety and emotional range, or the motoric rhythms of his scherzos, whose bass lines sometimes hint unexpectedly at contemporary non-classical idioms (he carefully differentiates music that is genuinely fast-moving from superficially rapid, static "fast" music). The intricate, often polytonal Third Quartet's simple opening theme in displaced octaves recalls Britten, as do the fanfare-like viola calls of the fourth. Some higher tessitura writing for violin hints at the mysticism of Szymanowski, while more jabbing fragments echo Janáček. (Czechoslovakia, and Brno in particular, has furnished an important "second home" for Matthews, who has acquired a native familiarity with its idioms and found there fecund sources of inspiration.) Particularly striking, and evidence of his command of larger forms, are his finales—the long, eloquent Mahlerian adagio that forms a threnodic close to the Second Quartet, or the repeatedly postponed resolution of the Fourth. His wide-ranging treatment of material and the rich variety of bowing or pizzicato he calls for help maintain unfailing interest for both listener and performer. Recently he added a *String Trio*, alternately energetic, thrusting and reflective, while amid hints of Messiaen's *Quatuor* the *Clarinet Quartet*, like *Quartet No 3*, offers further examples of the strange, tonally uncertain, Maeterlinck-like *Waldmusik* at which he excels.

Matthews has written four symphonies—the most recent, like Maxwell Davies's fourth, for chamber orchestra. His links with the English Chamber Orchestra also occasioned the wide-ranging *Variations for Strings*—again, some Loussier-like jazz rhythms and an effective use of passacaglia—and the *Romanza*, a proxi-symphonic poem for cello and orchestra, written for Mstislav Rostropovich. The latest symphony is in five movements; others, while making use of the single-movement form, opt for an essentially bipartite pattern, interspersed with shorter episodes which often colour his larger-scale structures. As with *In the Dark Time*, material in the symphonies is extensively explored and frequently intense, reflective introductions contrasted with an increasing dynamism, even savagery, while in *September Music* (virtually a reincarnation of *L'Après-midi d'un faune*), the *Serenade* or his *Duet Variations* for flute and piano, despite cascading roulades later on, a more gossamer-like Impressionism predominates. Other works for solo instrument include a *Concertino* for oboe and string quartet, the early *Fantasias* for cello and viola, and the powerful *Three Studies* for solo violin, owing an obvious and welcome debt to both Britten and the Baroque.

Matthews feels no urge to shun the label "romantic": his instrumental palette (including more recent symphonic poems like *The Music of Dawn*) is one of the most fascinating and inventive among contemporary composers, its unashamed neo-*Im*pressionism as bold, in its way, as the *Ex*pressionist shocks of the 1960s. The early-century crisis of tonality and (long pre-Wagner) emotional distensions of chromaticism continue to exercise their fascination upon him, and their re-interpretation poses a continuing challenge. The peroration of his essay "Reorientation" (a reply to Boulez's influential collection entitled *Orientations*) perhaps holds the key to his own attempt at a synthesis: "romanticism is at its most potent when content and form are perfectly balanced, so that, at the highest level, romanticism and classicism become virtually identical." In time, this accolade may come to epitomise Matthews's own achievement.

—Roderic Dunnett

MATUSZCZAK, Bernadetta. Polish. Born in Torun, 10 March 1933. Educated at State Music College, Poznan (piano under Irena Kurpisz-Stefanowa, theory of music under Z. Sitowski), graduated 1958; State Music College, Warsaw (composition under T. Szeligowski and T. Sikorski), graduated 1964; further composition study under Nadia Boulanger, Paris, 1968. Composer. Recipient: Fitelberg Prize (for *Septem tubae*), 1966; Jeunesses Musicales award (for *Musica da camera*), 1967; Young Composers award (for *Canto solenne*), 1967. Mailing address: c/o Union of Polish Composers, Rynek Starego Miasta 27, 00-272 Warsaw, Poland.

Publishers: Polskie Wydawnictwo Muzycne; Moeck.

Symphonies/orchestral:

Per strumenti (bass clarinet, trumpet, percussion, string orchestra) 1969.
Contrasts 1970.

Chamber/instrumental:

Quasi sonata (piano) 1963.
Canto solenne (ensemble) 1965.
Musica da camera (piccolo, 3 flutes, 4 trumpets, 5 tom-toms) 1967.
Aphorisms (flute) 1975.
Pantomime (ensemble) 1976.
Songs Without Words (ensemble) 1978.
Partita (violin, piano) 1979.

Vocal/choral:

Gitanjali (male speaker, soprano, flute, bells; Tagore) 1963.
Dramat kameralny (baritone, taped baritone voice, speaker, bass clarinet, double bass, percussion; Eliot) 1965. Recorded Muza M 3 XW 890.
Septem tubae (chorus, organ, orchestra; Revelation) 1966.
Invocazione (10 solo voices, flute, double bass, theorbo, gong) 1968.
Poésie de chambre (speaker, bass clarinet, vibraphone, 2 harpsichords, tam-tam) 1968.
Canzone (soprano, taped soprano voice, cor anglais, bongos) 1970.
Liebestotenlieder (bass, orchestra; Rilke) 1971.
Salmi (baritone, speaker, percussion, harp, double bass; Psalms) 1971. Recorded Muza S 3 XW 1883.
Elegy for a Polish Boy (soprano, reciter/alto, 2 female choruses, orchestra) 1974.
Apocalypsis (mezzo-soprano, baritone, reciting voices, 2 choruses, orchestra) 1977.
Canticum canticorum (soprano, alto, baritone, bass, orchestra) 1978–9.
Feuer auf der Wladwiese (soprano, alto, instrumental ensemble) 1979.
Epigrams (unaccompanied mixed chorus; Kochanowski) 1980.

Opera/dramatic:

Julia i Romeo (chamber opera; after Shakespeare) 1967; first performed Wiesbaden, 1972.
Humanae voces (operatic oratorio) 1971.
The Mystery of Heloise 1973–4.
The Diary of a Fool (monodrama for actor, baritone, orchestra; after Gogol) 1975.
Prometheus (after Aeschylus) 1981.

* * *

Bernadetta Matuszczak belongs to a particularly gifted group of Polish composers some of whom (like Krzysztof Penderecki) are now well-known internationally. As a group they benefited equally from the rich legacy of Chopin and Karol Szymanowski and from study abroad. Matuszczak studied first in Poznan and Warsaw and then, like so many of her fellow Poles, with the formidable Nadia Boulanger in Paris. Her generation grew up with the horrors of Nazi occupation and the subsequent Stalinist oppression. As with Penderecki, this has given her work a sense of the cataclysmic as well as a certain *gravitas*. Many commentators have found it strange that such a quiet, essentially introverted personality could compose music of such angular aggression.

Matuszczak came to artistic maturity after the cultural "thaw" in Poland which followed the death of Stalin in 1953. During the 1960s, she consolidated her home reputation with a series of works which display her assimilation of numerous sonoristic techniques widely associated with the Polish school. In her best work a fruitful dichotomy exists between "straight" instrumental works and other compositions which reflect an ever-developing literary inspiration. In the last respect, she has not confined herself to Polish writing. Her *Dramat kameralny* is based on T.S. Eliot's "The Hollow Men" and is scored for the unusual combination of baritone soloist, taped narrator, clarinet, double bass, and a wide array of percussion. *Septem tubae* is scored for chorus, organ and orchestra and was the work which brought her to international prominence when it won the Fitelberg Prize. Several more of her works have been taken up abroad, notably the chamber opera *Julia i Romeo* which, following its premiere in Wiesbaden, was produced throughout Germany.

Matuszczak has often returned to the written word after a period of composing strictly instrumental music. *Contrasts* for orchestra was followed by Rilke settings for baritone and orchestra and the striking *The Diary of a Fool*, a monodrama after Gogol for actor, baritone, and orchestra. Her operatic scenes *The Mystery of Heloise* was initially well-received, as was the more haunting *Elegy for a Polish Boy* for the interesting combination of soprano, taped reciter, two women's choruses and orchestra. The text is recited while the orchestra and chorus outline often grim and uncompromising chorales. This is arguably her finest work. The text alone is a memorial to the post-1945 Polish psyche: "My little son, they deprived you of fluttering butterfly dreams/they embroidered your sad eyes with russet blood/they painted landscapes in yellow stitches of war ravages/they seared with hanged men the flowing sea of trees." It is with such a powerful work that Matuszczak will be best remembered, for here is music which unquestionably deserves wider recognition.

—Lyn Davies

MAW, (John) Nicholas. British/English. Born in Grantham, Lincolnshire, 5 November 1935. Educated at Wennington School, Yorkshire, 1945–54; Royal Academy of Music, London (under Lennox Berkeley, for composition, and Paul Steinitz, for theory), 1955–8; studied with Nadia Boulanger and Max Deutsch in Paris on French Government scholarship, 1958–9. Married Karen Graham in 1960; 1 son and 1 daughter. Teacher, Royal Academy of Music, London, 1964–6; Fellow Commoner (composer in residence), Trinity

College, Cambridge, 1966–70; lecturer in music, University of Exeter, Devon, 1972–4; composer in residence, South Bank Summer Music, London, 1973; visiting professor of composition, Yale School of Music, New Haven, Connecticut, 1984, 1985, 1989; visiting professor of music, Boston University, 1986; professor of music, Milton Avery Graduate School of the Arts, Bard College, New York, since 1989; founder member, first chair, Association of Professional Composers. Recipient: Lili Boulanger Prize (for *Nocturne*), 1959; Corporation of London Midsummer Prize, 1980. Mailing address: c/o Faber Music, 3 Queen Square, London WC1N 3AU, England.

Publishers: Boosey & Hawkes; Chester; Faber.

Symphonies/orchestral:

Sinfonia (small orchestra) 1966; first performed Newcastle-upon-Tyne, 30 May 1966. Recorded Argo ZRG676.
Severn Bridge Variations (collaboration with Malcolm Arnold, Michael Tippett, Alun Hoddinott, Grace Williams and Daniel Jones) 1967.
Sonata (2 horns, strings) 1967; first performed Bath, 7 June 1967. Recorded Argo ZRG676.
Concert Music (derived from *The Rising of the Moon*) 1972; first performed London, 19 October 1972.
Odyssey 1972–87; first performed (incomplete) London, 10 August 1987; complete performance Birmingham, October 1990. Recorded EMI CDS7 54277-2.
Life Studies (15 solo strings, 2 groups consisting of 5 violins, viola, cello, double bass; nos II, III, VI VII/VIII may be played by string orchestra) 1973, 1976; original version first performed Cheltenham, Gloucestershire, 9 July 1973; complete version first performed Cheltenham, 7 July 1978. Recorded Argo ZRG899.
Serenade 1973, revised 1977; first performed Singapore, 31 March 1973.
Summer Dances (youth orchestra) 1980; first performed Snape, Suffolk, 27 July 1981.
Spring Music 1982–3; first performed Norwich, Norfolk, 15 October 1982.
Sonata notturna (cello, string orchestra) 1985; first performed King's Lynn, Norfolk, 30 May 1986.
Little Concert (oboe, 2 horns, string orchestra) 1988; first performed Wymondham, Norfolk, 28 May 1988.
The World in the Evening 1988; first performed London, 21 October 1988.
Little Concert (oboe, 2 horns, strings) 1990.
American Games (symphonic wind band) 1990–1; first performed London, 23 July 1991.

Chamber/instrumental:

Sonatina (flute, piano) 1957.
Essay (organ) 1961, revised 1963; first performed Salisbury, Wiltshire, 1961.
String Quartet 1965; first performed Harlow, Essex, 12 July 1965. Recorded Argo ZRG565.
Double Canon for Igor Stravinsky 1967.
Epitaph-Canon in Memory of Igor Stravinsky (flute, clarinet, harp) 1971.
Chamber Music (wind quartet, piano) 1972.
Life Studies (see orchestral) 1973, 1976; II first performed London, 8 March 1976.
Personae (piano) 1973; movements 1 and 2 first performed London, 2 August 1973.
Flute Quartet (flute, string trio) 1981; first performed London, 7 May 1981.
Night Thoughts (flute) 1982; first performed London, 10 June 1982.
String Quartet No 2 1982; first performed London, 13 January 1983.
Personae IV, V, VI (piano) 1985–6; first performed Bath, 7 June 1986.
Ghost Dances (flute/alto flute/piccolo, clarinet/E♭ clarinet/bass clarinet/kazoo, violin/strum stick, cello, piano/kalimba; manjeera for all five players) 1988; first performed New York, 16 May 1988.
Music of Memory (guitar) 1989.

Vocal/choral:

Eight Chinese Lyrics 1956; first performed London, 1958.
Requiem 1957; first performed London, 1957; withdrawn.
Nocturne (mezzo-soprano, chamber orchestra) 1957–8.
Six Chinese Songs 1960; first performed Cheltenham, Gloucestershire, 1960.
Five Epigrams (chorus) 1960.
Our Lady's Song (chorus) 1961. Recorded Argo ZRG5446.
Scenes and Arias (soprano, mezzo-soprano, alto, orchestra; anon., 14th century) 1962, revised 1966; first performed London, 31 August 1962. Recorded Argo ZRG622.
The Angel Gabriel (unaccompanied SATB chorus) 1963.
Round (children's unison chorus, SATB chorus, piano; anon., 15th century) 1963.
Balulalow (chorus) 1964. Recorded Argo ZRG5499.
Six Interiors (high voice, guitar; Hardy) 1966; first performed London, 5 May 1970.
The Voice of Love (mezzo-soprano, piano; Porter) 1966; first performed London, 6 October 1966. Recorded Chandos, 1990.
Five Irish Songs (mixed chorus) 1972; first performed Cork, 4 May 1973.
Te Deum (treble/soprano, tenor, SATB chorus, congregation, organ) 1975; first performed Bruton, Norfolk, 29 May 1975.
Reverdie (unaccompanied TTBarBB chorus; anon., 14th/15th century) 1975; first performed Glasgow, 29 October 1975.
Annes! (chorus) 1976.
Twenty Nonsense Rhymes (children's voices, piano) 1976; first performed Darsham, Suffolk, 4 September 1976.
La vita nuova (soprano, chamber ensemble; Cavalcanti, Boiardo, Tasso, Michelangelo, Stampa) 1979; first performed London, 2 September 1979. Recorded Chandos ABR 1037.
The Ruin (double SSAATTBB chorus, solo horn; Anglo Saxon, translated Alexander) 1980; first performed Edinburgh, 27 August 1980.
Five American Folksongs (high voice, piano) 1988.
Three Hymns (SATB chorus, organ; Beaumont, Hall, Browne) 1989.
Roman Canticle: Two in the Campagna (mezzo-soprano, flute, viola, harp; Browning) 1989.
Motet: One Foot in Eden Still, I Stand (soprano, alto, tenor, bass, 8-part chorus; Muir) 1990.

Opera:

One-Man Show 1964; first performed London, November 1964.
The Rising of the Moon 1967–70; first performed Glyndebourne, Sussex, 19 July 1970.

Other:

The Frontiers of Friction (music for Shell Film Unit) 1962.
Difficulties of a Bridegroom (incidental music to a radio play by Ted Hughes) broadcast BBC Radio, January 1963.
Goldsmiths No 2 (music for Union of Goldsmiths film) 1963.
Les Voyageurs (music for British Petroleum Film Unit) 1965.
Turkey—the Bridge (music for Shell Film Unit) 1966.
The Fate of the Forests (music for Shell Film Unit) April 1982.

PUBLICATIONS

On Maw: articles in *Tempo*, 68, 1964, 71, 1964–5, 92, 1970, 106, 1973, and 125, 1978; Arnold Whittall, "NM", in *British Music Now*, edited by Lewis Foreman, London, 1975; interview with Paul Griffiths, in *New Sounds, New Personalities: British Composers of the 1980s*, London, 1985.

* * *

For a composer who regards himself, and is generally regarded as, an orchestral composer first and foremost, it is curious that Nicholas Maw only turned to producing purely orchestral works over two decades after first appearing on the scene. The orchestra does feature as accompanist in several of his early vocal works, such as the *Nocturne*, *Scenes and Arias* and the operas *One-Man Show* and *The Rising of the Moon*, but in the 1960s and 1970s Maw concentrated on small- or string-orchestral works and chamber music. The excellent piano and wind quintet entitled *Chamber Music* and First String Quartet showed his exceptional instrumental resource early on, but only with the concert overture *Spring Music* did he finally complete a work for a standard late 19th- or 20th-century orchestra.

Starting with *Life Studies* (1972–4), Maw's music began to take on a more expansive, lyrical tone, moving away from his very personal mix of late romanticism and neo-classicism that had characterised the *Sinfonia* for small orchestra and the *Sonata* for strings and two horns of the mid-1960s. The large-boned setting of the ancient Anglo-Saxon poem *The Ruin* exploited this new, more opulent style to the full with the restricted resources of mixed chorus and solo horn, and along with the orchestral song cycle, *La vita nuova*, is fully worthy of comparison with the best word settings of Britten. *Spring Music*, in retrospect something of an off-cut from the then still incomplete *Odyssey*, displayed this new manner in a still trenchant form, but the Second String Quartet and *Sonata notturna* for cello and strings are on an altogether bigger scale. Their mellifluous, long-breathed melodic writing and more passionate style derive ultimately from *Life Studies* and point the way to *Odyssey*. The difference between his earlier and later manners can be heard in conjunction in the two sets of piano pieces which form a kind of ongoing diary, *Personae*. The first of three pieces dates from 1973 and is typical of his style at that time, reflecting certain attributes of more avant-garde piano sound expressed within a modern tonal framework. A second set of three followed in 1986, on a noticeably larger scale and with an expanded emotional range; undoubtedly his most accomplished work for the keyboard the second set shows an enhanced sense of fantasy and generates considerable power.

His magnum opus, though, is still the vast apotheosis of the symphonic poem, *Odyssey*. It towers over his output in both size (it is quite probably the longest continuous piece of orchestral music ever written) and quality. Like *Personae*, its five sections cover a decade and a half of Maw's development, on an even fuller scale. The delay in completion was partly due to problems with the original commission, the work finally appearing in truncated form at the 1987 Proms. The fourth and fifth sections are the longest and account in the main for the great size: the fourth is the crucial experience of the whole, and is framed by two enormous orchestral outbursts, the one catastrophic and the other climactic. In-between comes a long, slow-paced gathering of strength for the confrontation at its close, which evaporates via a magical tintinnabulation into a music of extraordinary, Sibelian generative power moving in paragraphs of Brucknerian length. It is a work, like Havergal Brian's *Gothic Symphony* or Kaikhosru Sorabji's *Opus Clavicembalisticum*, that is not just without parallel, it is beside parallel.

Odyssey not unnaturally has formed a watershed in Maw's compositional career. The expansion of his musical language and its magnificent sustainment on the grandest scale has freed his music to exploit whole new ranges of possibilities. If *The World in the Evening*, written for the orchestra of the Royal Opera House, Covent Garden, was perhaps too close in proximity to its huge precursor and failed to provide the drama necessary to justify its near 40-minute span, his smaller works have continued to break new ground, as can be heard in *Roman Canticle* for voice and ensemble and the *Little Concert* for oboe, two horns and strings which revisits the impressionistic, pastoral music of the early English 20th century in 1990 terms. There can be little doubt that Maw, along with Robert Simpson, is the leading British orchestral composer of his day.

—Guy Rickards

MAYUZUMI, Toshiro. Japanese. Born in Yokohama, 20 February 1929. Educated at Geijutsu Daigaku [National Music Academy], Tokyo (under Kunihiko Hashimoto, Ikenouchi and Ifukube), 1945–51; Conservatoire National Supérieur de Musique, Paris (under Tony Aubin), 1952; study visit to U.S.A., 1960. Organizer, Ars Nova Japonica, Sannin no Kai [Group of Three], with Akutagawa and Dan; composer and broadcaster; presenter of *Untitled Concert*, Ashai Network Television series, since late 1960s. Recipient: Otaka Prize (for *Nehan kokyokyoku* and *Bugaku*), 1959, 1962; Mainichi Music Prize (for *Tokyo Olympics*), 1964. Mailing address: c/o Peters Edition, 10 Baches Street, London N1 6DN, England.

Publishers: Ongaku-no-Tomo Sha, Tokyo; Peters.

Symphonies/orchestral:

Serenade Fantastic 1946.
Rumba Rhapsody 1948.
Symphonic Mood 1950.
Bacchanale 1953.
Ektoplasm 1954; first performed Stockholm, 5 June 1956.
Phonologie symphonique 1957; first performed Tokyo, 28 May 1957.
Nehan kokyokyoku/Nirvana Symphony (with chorus) 1958; first performed Tokyo, 2 April 1958.
Mandala Symphony 1960; first performed Tokyo, 27 March 1960.
Chokoku no ongaku/Music with Sculpture 1961; first performed Pittsburgh, 29 June 1961.

Bugaku (ballet suite) 1962; first performed New York City, 20 March 1963.
Samsara (symphonic poem) 1962; first performed Tokyo, 12 June 1962.
Textures (band) 1962; first performed Pittsburgh, 10 June 1962.
Essay in Sonorities: Mozartiana 1963; first performed Osaka, 21 January 1963.
Essay for Strings 1963.
Hanabi / Fireworks (band) 1963; first performed Pittsburgh, 13 June 1963.
Raihai jokyoku / Ritual Overture (band) 1964; first performed Pittsburgh, 2 July 1964.
Ongaku no tanjo / The Birth of Music 1964; first performed Tokyo, 10 October 1964.
Xylophone Concertino 1965.
Concerto for Percussion and Winds 1966.
Shu / Incantation 1967.
Showa Tempyo Raku / Ancient and Modern Music 1969–70; first performed Tokyo, 31 October 1970.
Tateyama (symphonic poem) 1974.
Aria on G String (violin, orchestra) 1978.

Chamber/instrumental:

Sonata (violin, piano) 1946.
Twelve Preludes (piano) 1946.
Poésie (piano) 1946.
Hors d'oeuvre (piano) 1947.
Divertimento (10 instruments) 1948.
Poem (violin, piano) 1950.
String Quartet 1952.
Sextet (flute, clarinet, bass clarinet, horn, trumpet, piano) 1955.
Tone Pleromas 55 (5 saxophones, musical saw, pianos) 1955.
Mikrokosmos (claviolin, guitar, vibraphone, xylophone, piano, percussion, musical saw) 1957; first performed Karuizawa, 12 August 1957.
Pieces (prepared piano, string quartet) 1957.
A hun (Japanese flute, kotsuzumi, otsuzumi) 1958.
Bunraku (cello) 1960.
Metamusic (violin, saxophone, piano; with conductor) 1961.
Prelude (string quartet) 1961.
Showa Tenpyo-raku (gagaku ensemble) 1970.

Vocal/choral:

Elegy (soprano, piano) 1948.
Sphenogramme (voice, flute, saxophone, marimba, piano—4 hands, violin, cello) 1950; first performed Frankfurt, 25 June 1951.
Shukukon-ka / Wedding Song (chorus, orchestra) 1959.
U so ri (oratorio for soloists, chorus, instruments) 1959; first performed Tokyo, 12 June 1959.
Sange (unaccompanied male voices) 1959.
Geka (Pratidesana) (Buddhist cantata for mixed voices) 1963; first performed Kyoto, 5 September 1963.
Mori (cantata for mixed voices) 1963.
Mandala (voice, tape) 1969.
Nihon sanka / Hymn to Japan (narrator, chorus, orchestra) 1972.

Opera/dramatic:

Omoide o uru otoko / The Souvenir Seller (dance drama) 1953; first performed Tokyo, 1953.
Aoi no ue / Princess Hollyhock (music for *noh*) 1957.
Kawaii onna / A Pretty Woman (musical) 1959; first performed Osaka, 1959.
Bugaku (dance drama) 1962.
Kimi nimo kanemoke ga dekiru / You Can Earn Too (musical) 1962.
Olympics (dance drama) 1966.
Tokaido Yotsuya kaidan / The Yotsuya Ghost Story (music for *kabuki*) 1967.
Kinkakuji / The Golden Pavilion (Mishima) 1976; first performed Berlin, 23 June 1976.

Other:

Boxing (tape) 1954.
X, Y, Z. (tape) 1955.
Mirai no Eve / Eve in the Future (tape) 1955.
Shusaku I / Study I (tape) 1955.
Variations sur 7 (tape; collaboration with Morai) 1957.
Yure wa koko ni iru / The Ghost Is Here (incidental music to Abe) 1958.
Bara to kaizoku / Roses and Pirates (incidental music to Mishima) 1958.
Campanology (tape) 1959.
Campanology Olympica (tape) 1964.
The Bible (film music) 1965.

* * *

In attempting to understand contemporary Japanese music, it is important to recognise the rather special cultural conditions that prevailed in the years immediately preceding World War II. Composers of the generation of Toshiro Mayuzumi and Toru Takemitsu came of age at a time when all Western music (with the sole exception of some German martial music) was officially proscribed by a militaristic establishment which was determined to impose a highly insular and nationalistic cultural orthodoxy. (Takemitsu has said that when he began his collaboration with the movie director Akira Kurosawa on *Ran*, Kurosawa's suggestion of a suitable "modern" score to be used as a model was Mahler's *"Titan" Symphony No 1*!) At the end of the war, the sudden relaxation of this stricture, and the sudden accessibility of large amounts of Western music on record and on the radio stations of the occupation forces made an enormous impact.

Inevitably, initial reactions ranged from a very backward enthusiasm for music that was already considered passé in the West right through to an (over)enthusiastic embrace of the most advanced avant-garde techniques. Though it was in Frankfurt with the performance of his *Sphenogramme* for voice and instrumental group in 1951 that he first came to public notice in the West, unusually for a Japanese Mayuzumi elected to continue his composition studies in France rather than Germany; this may have helped temper his avant-gardist enthusiasms later; he was attracted by Boulez's radicalism, but was perhaps even more profoundly affected by Messiaen's magnificent orchestral language which is the clearest occidental model for his most characteristic work. Mayuzumi's first compositions veered between a lush romanticism, as in the student sonata for violin, and a more adventurous rhythmic language with hints of jazz and an almost obsessive concern for sonority as a spiritual/structural element in its own right.

Less tempted by orthodox serialism than by contemporary developments in electronic music, Mayuzumi created the first documented Japanese *musique concrète* in 1955 with *X, Y, Z.* Later he was to introduce to Japan John Cage's "prepared piano" and philosophy of chance composition, together with elements of Indian and South Asian music, thus extending the Pacific dialectic that is such a vital component of innovative music in the last 40 years. Cage's altered piano stimulated Mayuzumi's interest in unusual sound-colours; in the same period, he experimented with amplified instruments, saxophones, claviolins and the theremin-like effects of musical saw in pieces such as *Ektoplasm* and *Tone Pleromas 55*. In the late 1950s, in *A hun*, he turned back to traditional *noh* instruments, a move which underlines his increasing reliance on native models.

The most significant result of the new change of emphasis was the majestic *Nirvana Symphony*, a work as radical in its development of symphonic structure as Messiaen's *Turangalila-Symphonie*, with *its* Eastward looking rhythms and unusual harmonic patterns. Dominated by the "mixed tones" sonorities of Buddhist templebells, *Nirvana Symphony* marks the clearest move away from heterodox serialism and syncretistic language and towards a style which may be called "personal" in the narrower sense, for it is music of great philosophical and aesthetic abstraction, a curious mixture of Enlightenment logic and reason, and the highly expressionistic qualities of Japanese art. Mayuzumi designates each of its three movements as "campanologies"—a term also used for roughly contemporary tape pieces—which analyse and reconstitute bell-tones in ever more complex ways. A similar combination of resources and philosophies lie behind the slightly later *Mandala Symphony* and *Samsara*, his most significant orchestral works, and also behind the rather misleadingly entitled *Essay in Sonorities: Mozartiana*.

Mayuzumi's compositional career has been very sporadic in more recent years. His success as a composer for the movies (*The Bible* is perhaps the best-known example) deflected some of his energies, but it also channelled his instinct for music and other means of expression which are both highly dramatic and very formalised: *noh* and *kabuki* are obvious examples, but Mayuzumi was also drawn by Yukio Mishima's deliberate mixture of pragmatic logic and ritual excess; *The Golden Pavilion*, the opera Mayuzumi wrote after a break of some years, transforms Mishima's rather unformed and discursive tale into a work of genuinely disturbing power and beauty.

Along with Takemitsu, he is perhaps the most significant Japanese composer of the post-war period, and along with Mishima and Kurosawa, one of the most important artists in any medium. Janus-faced, he looks not just East and West simultaneously, but right across the historical spectrum of modern music.

—Karl Neumann

McCABE, John. British. Born in Huyton, Lancashire, 21 April 1939. Educated at Liverpool Institute High School for Boys; University of Manchester, 1960, B.Mus; Royal Manchester College of Music, 1961–2, A.R.M.C.M.; Hochschule für Musik, Munich, 1964. Married Monica Christine Smith, 31 July 1974. Pianist in residence, University College, Cardiff, 1965–68; director, London College of Music, from 1983. Pianist: has made many recordings. Music Representative on council, Manchester Institute of Contemporary Arts (now defunct), 1958–64; warden, solo performers section, 1978, and president, 1982–3, Incorporated Society of Musicians; member of honorary council of management, from c. 1983, and of programme and executive committee, from c. 1983, Royal Philharmonic Society; chair, Association of Professional Composers, 1985–6; member of general council, and of donations committee, Performing Rights Society, 1985–8; member, from 1987, Wigmore Hall Board; Portsmouth (now London) member of advisory board, from 1988, International String Quartet Competition; vice-president, Luton Music Club, Malvern Music Club, and Ruislip Gramophone Society. Recipient: prizewinner (for piano), Gaudeamus Competition, Holland for interpreters of Contemporary Music, 1969; special award, Composers Guild of Great Britain, for services to British Music, 1975; Ivor Novello Award (for television theme tune *Sam*), 1977; C.B.E. (Commander, Order of the British Empire), 1985. Mailing address: 49 Burns Avenue, Southall, Middlesex UB1 2LR.

Publisher: Novello.

Symphonies/orchestral:

Violin Concerto No 1: "Sinfonia concertante" 1959; first performed Manchester, March 1963.
Concerto funèbre (viola, chamber orchestra) 1962; first performed September 1971.
Concerto for Chamber Orchestra 1962, revised 1968; first performed Manchester, 1962; revised version first performed London, 1968.
Variations on a Theme of Karl Amadeus Hartmann 1964; first performed Manchester, 24 November 1965. Recorded EMI ED 29 12191.
Chamber Concerto (viola, cello, chamber orchestra) 1965.
Concertante (harpsichord, chamber orchestra) 1965; first performed Liverpool, 18 December 1965.
Symphony No 1: "Elegy" 1965; first performed Cheltenham, Gloucestershire, 1966. Recorded Pye TPLS 13005.
Piano Concerto No 1 1966; first performed Southport, Lancashire, May 1967.
Concertino for Piano Duet and Orchestra 1968; first performed Frensham, Surrey, 11 May 1976.
Concertante Music 1968; first performed Bath, 1968.
Metamorphosen (harpsichord, orchestra) 1968; first performed Liverpool, 19 February 1972.
Notturni ed Alba 1970; first performed Hereford, 1970. Recorded EMI ED 29 12191.
Piano Concerto No 2: "Sinfonia concertante" 1970; first performed Middlesbrough, Cleveland, 23 November 1971.
Concertante Variations on a Theme of Nicholas Maw (also version for 11 solo strings) 1970; first performed Bristol, 3 March 1971.
Basse Danse 1970, revised 1973; first performed Guildford, Surrey, 5 May 1975.
Symphony No 2 1971; first performed Birmingham, 26 September 1971. Recorded EMI ASD 2904.
The Lion, The Witch and the Wardrobe: Suite 1971; first performed Stonyhurst, 1971.
Oboe d'Amore Concerto 1972; first performed Portsmouth, 26 April 1972.
Sam 1973, arranged for theme music 1975; first performed London, October 1975.
The Chagall Windows 1974; first performed Manchester, 9 January 1975. Recorded EMI ASD 3096.
Mary Queen of Scots: Ballet Suite No 1 1976; first performed London, 16 March 1987.
Mary Queen of Scots: Ballet Suite No 2 1976; first performed Harlow, Essex, 23 October 1988.
Piano Concerto No 3: "Dialogues" 1976, revised 1977; first performed Liverpool, 5 August 1977.

Sonata on a Motet 1976; first performed Manchester, 20 March 1976.
Clarinet Concerto 1977; first performed Glasgow, 26 June 1978.
Jubilee Suite 1977; first performed (Prelude) London, 17 April 1977; first complete performance London, 14 June 1986.
Mary Queen of Scots: Two Dances (harp, strings) 1977.
Symphony No 3: "Hommages" 1978; first performed London, 11 July 1978.
Images (wind band) 1978; first performed Redlands, California, 14 May 1978.
Nocturne: The Shadow of Light 1979; first performed London, 6 December 1979.
Violin Concerto No 2 1980; first performed Birmingham, 20 March 1980.
Concerto for Orchestra 1982; first performed London, 10 February 1983.
Tuning 1985; first performed s'Hertogenbosch, The Netherlands, 27 July 1985. Recorded Alpha CAPS 367.
Cloudcatcher Fells (brass band) 1985; first performed London, 6 October 1985. Recorded Chandos BBRD 1032/CHAN 8483/BBTD 1032.
Double Concerto (oboe, clarinet, orchestra) 1987–8; first performed London, 25 June 1988.
Fire at Durilgai 1988; first performed Manchester, 13 January 1989.

Chamber/instrumental:

Partita (string quartet) 1960; first performed Manchester, 1960.
Sinfonia (organ) 1961; first performed Leeds, 1961.
Dies Resurrectionis (organ) 1963; first performed Manchester, 1 March 1963. Recorded RCA LVL1 5019; Abbey LPB 665.
Variations (piano) 1963; first performed Newcastle-upon-Tyne, 1983. Recorded RCA RL 25076.
Five Bagatelles (piano) 1964; first performed London, 1966. Recorded PRT GSGC 2069.
Prelude (organ) 1964.
Johannis-Partita (organ) 1964; first performed Pershore, 1965.
Musica notturna (violin, viola, piano) 1964; first performed Manchester, 1964. Recorded Pagecoll S-1.
Symphony (10 winds) 1964; first performed London, December 1964.
Movements (clarinet, violin, cello) 1964, revised 1966; first performed London, 1964.
Three Pieces (clarinet, piano) 1964; first performed Cheltenham, Gloucestershire, 1964. Recorded Coronet 3116.
String Trio 1965; first performed Mannheim, 1966. Recorded Argo ZRG 761.
Bagatelles (2 clarinets) 1965.
Elegy (organ) 1965. Recorded Decca 626.
Miniconcerto (organ, percussion, audience with 485 penny whistles) 1966; first performed London, 1966. Recorded Abbey APR 606.
Partita (cello) 1966; first performed London, 1966. Recorded L'Oiseau Lyre DSLO 18; Pagecoll S-1.
Nocturnal (piano quintet) 1966; first performed Lancaster, 1970.
Fantasy (2 trumpets, horn, trombone) 1967; first performed Salford, Cheshire, 1966.
Dance-Movements (horn, violin, piano) 1967; first performed London, 1967.
Fantasy on a Theme of Liszt (piano) 1967; first performed Cheltenham, Gloucestershire, 1967. Recorded RCA RL 25076.
Intermezzi (piano) 1968; first performed Shrewsbury, Shropshire, 1968.
Oboe Quartet 1968; first performed Cardiff, 11 February 1969.
Rounds (2 trumpets, horn, trombone, tuba) 1968; first performed Salford, Cheshire, 26 February 1968. Recorded Pye GSGC 14114.
Canto (guitar) 1968; first performed Cardiff, 1968. Recorded Deutsche Grammophon DGG 2530 079.
Sonata (clarinet, cello, piano) 1969; first performed Macclesfield, Cheshire, 22 May 1969.
The Greensleeves Ground (harpsichord) 1969.
Capriccio (Study No 1) (piano) 1969; first performed Dublin, 6 June 1969. Recorded RCA RL 25076.
Sostenuto (Study No 2) (piano) 1969; first performed Bath, 19 February 1969. Recorded RCA RL 25076.
Concerto for Piano and Wind Quintet 1969; first performed Birmingham, February 1970.
Gaudi (Study No 3) (piano) 1970; first performed Cardiff, 1970. Recorded RCA RL 25076.
Aubade (Study No 4) (piano) 1970; first performed Harrogate, Yorkshire, 1970. Recorded RCA RL 25076.
Basse Danse (two pianos) 1970; first performed Cardiff, January 1971.
Canzona (wind, percussion) 1970; first performed Frensham, Surrey, May 1971.
Dance-Prelude (oboe d'amore or clarinet, piano) 1971; first performed London, 17 April 1971.
String Quartet No 2 1972; first performed Macclesfield, Cheshire, 17 July 1972.
Maze Dances (violin) 1973; first performed London, 15 May 1974.
Sam: Theme Music 1973, arranged for orchestra 1975.
The Goddess Trilogy (horn, piano) 1973–5.
  The Castle of Arianrhod 1973; first performed Pennsylvania, 1973.
  Floraison 1975; first performed Worcester, 25 August 1975.
  Shape-Shifter 1975; first performed Worcester, 25 August 1975.
Images (version for wind ensemble) 1978; first performed London, 30 March 1978.
Star-Preludes (violin, piano) 1978; first performed Los Angeles, 28 April 1978.
String Quartet No 3 1979; first performed Goodwick, Pembrokeshire, 23 July 1979.
Mary Queen of Scots (Study No 5) (paraphrase for piano) 1979; first performed Kelso, Roxburgh, 11 January 1980.
Mosaic (Study No 6) (piano) 1980; first performed Wales, 25 September 1980.
Portraits (flute, piano) 1980.
Dances (trumpet, piano) 1980.
Desert I: Lizard (flute, oboe, clarinet, bassoon, percussion) 1981; first performed London, 14 March 1983.
Desert II: Horizon (10 brass instruments: piccolo, trumpet, 2 trumpets in C, flugelhorn, horn, 4 trombones, tuba; also version for brass band) 1981; first performed Ripon, Yorkshire, 4 August 1981; London, 12 October 1981; brass band version first performed London, 8 October 1988. Recorded Polyphonic QPRL 039D.
Afternoons and Afterwards (piano) 1981.
Lamentation Rag (piano) 1982; broadcast BBC, 3 March 1982.
Desert III: Landscape (violin, cello, piano) 1982; first performed Armidale, New South Wales, 17 June 1982. Recorded Pagecoll S-1.

String Quartet No 4 1982; first performed London, 20 October 1982.
Desert IV: Vista (solo recorder) 1983; first performed Altrincham, Cheshire, 6 May 1983.
Haydn Variations (piano) 1983; first performed London, 25 October 1983.
Rainforest I (10 players: flute, clarinet, glockenspiel, string quartet, piano trio) 1984; first performed New York, 30 November 1984.
Rainforest II (trumpet and 11 strings) 1987; first performed Ripon, Yorkshire, 3 August 1987.
Concertante Variations on a Theme of Nicholas Maw (11 solo strings, arranged from original version for string orchestra) 1987; first performed Southampton, Hampshire, 7 February 1989.
Caravan (string quartet) 1988; first performed Colchester, Essex, 23 February 1988.

Vocal/choral:

Three Folk Songs (high voice, optional clarinet, piano) 1963; first performed Scotland, 1963. Recorded Cameo Classics GOCLD 9020; Whitetower ENS 153.
Mary Laid Her Child (carol for SATB choir) 1964.
A Hymne to God the Father (anthem for SATB choir) 1966; first performed Northampton, 1967.
Rain Songs (soprano, counter-tenor or alto, cello, harpsichord; Mo-ch'i Yung, Lu Yu, translated Kotewall, Smith) 1966.
Canticles for Salisbury (Magnificat and Nunc Dimittis) (SATB choir, organ) 1966.
Great Lord of Lords (anthem for SATB choir and organ; or SATB choir with brass) 1966; first performed Southport, Cheshire, 1967.
Aspects of Whiteness (SATB choir, piano; Melville) 1967, revised 1969; first performed London, 21 June 1967.
The Morning Watch (SATB choir, organ; Vaughan) 1968.
To Us in Bethlem City (carol for SATB choir) 1969.
Norwich Canticles (Magnificat and Nunc Dimittis) (SATB choir unaccompanied) 1970.
Requiem Sequence (soprano, piano) 1971; first performed London, 7 February 1979.
Voyage (cantata for soprano, mezzo-soprano, counter-tenor, baritone and brass solo, boys' choir, mixed chorus, orchestra; Monica Smith) 1972; first performed Worcester, 30 August 1972.
Das Letzte Gerichte (voice, guitar, percussion; Gryphius) 1973; first performed Nuremberg, 1978.
Times Remembered (soprano, instrumental ensemble; Raleigh, Lionel Johnson, Venantius Fortunatus, Herbert of Cherbury, More) 1973; first performed Malvern, Worcestershire, 4 October 1973.
Upon the High Midnight (3 nativity carols for SATB solo) 1973.
Behold a Silly Tender Babe (SATB choir, organ; Southwell) 1975; first performed Southport, Connecticut, 1975.
Five Folk Songs (high voice, horn, piano) 1976; first performed Derby, 7 July 1979.
Stabat Mater (soprano solo, mixed chorus, orchestra) 1976; first performed Northampton, 28 October 1976.
A Lute-Book Lullaby (carol for SSA choir and flute; Ballett) 1977; first performed Worcester, December 1977.
Reflections of a Summer Night (cantata for mixed chorus and orchestra; Tennyson, HD, Longfellow, de la Mare, Keats) 1977; first performed Fishguard, Dyfed, 26 July 1978.
Motet (SSAATTBB choir) 1979; first performed Chichester, Sussex, 11 July 1979.
Les Soirs Bleus (soprano, recorders—1 player, cello, harpsichord; Rimbaud) 1979; first performed Petworth, Sussex, 15 September 1980.
Mangan Triptych (comprising *Motet*, *Siberia*, *Visions*) (SSAATTBB choir) 1979–83; first performed Harrogate, Yorkshire, 10 August 1984.
Siberia (SATB choir) 1980; first performed Cork, 10 May 1980.
Music's Empire (16 solo voices or SATB solo and chorus, or chorus only, with orchestra; Marvell) 1981; first performed London, 6 October 1982.
Visions (SSAATTBB choir) 1983; first performed Harrogate, Yorkshire, 10 August 1984.
Weaving Song (high voice, piano duet) 1986.
Scenes in America Deserta (6 voices: 2 counter-tenors, tenor, 2 baritones, bass; Rayner Banham) 1986; first performed Houston, Texas, 8 March 1987.

Opera/dramatic:

The Lion, the Witch and the Wardrobe (children's opera in four acts, soprano, baritone, minimum of 9 children, orchestra; Larner, after Lewis) 1968; first performed Manchester, 29 April 1969.
This Town's a Corporation Full of Crooked Streets (entertainment for speaker, tenor, children's choir, mixed choir, instrumental ensemble; Henri, McGough, Patten) 1969; first performed Liverpool, 1970.
Notturni ed Alba (ballet) 1970; first performed Munster, April 1976.
The Teachings of Don Juan (ballet with baritone, chamber ensemble; Smith) 1973; first performed Manchester, 30 May 1973.
The Play of Mother Courage (chamber opera in 5 scenes, mezzo-soprano, 39 other parts, orchestra; Smith, after Brecht) 1974; first performed Middlesbrough, Yorkshire, 3 October 1974.
Die Fenster (ballet to music from *The Chagall Windows*), 1974; first performed Stuttgart, 16 February 1980.
Mary Queen of Scots (ballet in 2 acts with orchestra) 1975; first performed Glasgow, 3 March 1976.
Shadow-Reach (ballet to music from *Symphony No 2*, 1971, with small additions from Hartmann Variations, 1964); first performed Dublin, 19 June 1978.

Other:

Madrigal (instrumental ensemble) 1973.
Arabesque (instrumental ensemble) 1973.
Sam (instrumental ensemble) 1973; for Granada TV drama series, 12 June 1973.
Couples (theme music; piano) 1973; broadcast Thames Television, 14 October 1975.
The Good Soldier (incidental music; instrumental ensemble) 1981; broadcast Granada Television, 15 April 1981.

PUBLICATIONS

By McCabe: *Rachmaninov*, London, 1974; *Bartók's Orchestral Music*, London, 1974; many articles and reviews for *Records & Recordings* and *The Guardian*.

On McCabe: Nick Brenton, "Living British Composers", in *Set to Music*, September/October 1982; Caroline Heslop, "Contemporary Composers", in *Music Teacher*, October 1987; Robert Maycock, "John McCabe's String Quartets", in

Musical Times, July 1989; Stewart R. Craggs, *JM: A Bio-Bibliography*, New York and London, 1991.

* * *

John McCabe's formidable gifts as a pianist, and the international reputation he has acquired as a performer, have tended to overshadow his work as one of Britain's most prolific and consistently fine composers. Although his first big breakthrough came with the richly-scored orchestral song-cycle *Notturni ed Alba*, McCabe's best work is instrumental, particularly that for orchestra. His early works, such as the *Variations on a Theme of Karl Amadeus Hartmann* and the enormously impressive First Piano Concerto and *Concerto for Piano and Wind Quintet*, show how his distinctive language derived first from Bartók and Stravinsky. McCabe has remained largely free of the influence of either Britten or Tippett, learning more from such independent-minded, even alternative, figures such as Alan Rawsthorne and Carl Nielsen. Many of his works up to thc mid-1970s show in varying degrees his individual response to serialism, but since 1976 (during the composition of the *Stabat Mater*) he has eschewed such systematics and trusted more in his inner ear. Unlike a composer such as Robert Simpson who has tended to cultivate the symphony and string quartet in particular, McCabe has diversified, covering most fields including ballet and opera. Although his three orchestral symphonies are unusual and very successful designs, it is the concerto, with its dramatic and dynamic juxtapositions of solo and tutti, which seems to bring out the best in his music, as evidenced by all four piano concertos and the Second Violin Concerto. Even *Notturni ed Alba* positively combines elements of a concerto for mezzo-soprano and orchestra with symphonic song.

As a rare modern example of the composer-pianist (Richard Rodney Bennett and Michael Finnissy are two others), his career compares well with that of the late John Ogdon. If McCabe could not quite match Ogdon's mercurial and stupendous command of the keyboard, as a composer McCabe both set his sights much higher and has achieved far more. Undeniably fine though his own neglected compositions are, no work of Ogdon's can match McCabe's magnificent Third Concerto, *Dialogues*, which is on a truly Beethovenian scale, with form and content in perfect proportion. McCabe has inevitably written much for the piano, including the series of six Alkan-sized Studies and culminating in the formidable *Haydn Variations* of 1983. It is a salutary tribute to his skilful and idiomatic writing for the instrument that several other pianists have taken up both his concertos and solo pieces, whereas Ogdon's lie unplayed. Yet it is odd that being almost a household name for his own recordings of piano music comparatively little of McCabe's own music has found its way into the catalogue.

McCabe's liking for cyclic forms can be heard in several of his scores, not least the Second and Third Symphonies, *The Chagall Windows* (which the composer has described as a single-movement symphony), Violin Concerto No 2 and the highly-praised Concerto for Orchestra. This last score, written for Sir Georg Solti, provided a substantial boost to public awareness of McCabe's music and its subsequent neglect is inexplicable. Since then, however, McCabe has scored two further "hits" at home with his second brass band work, *Cloudcatcher Fells*, and the BBC-commissioned tone poem *Fire at Durilgai*, which has been toured through Europe. In the *Nocturne: The Shadow of Light*, musics of widely divergent character are exuberantly combined, much as in the work of Charles Ives. McCabe's skill is also heard to masterful but deceptively simple effect in *Tuning*, written in 1985 for the National Youth Orchestra of Scotland. With a catalogue of over 130 works constantly being added to, McCabe must be one of the busiest of living composers; his achievement also ranks him as one of the very best.

—Guy Rickards

McGUIRE, Edward. British/Scottish. Born in Glasgow, 15 February, 1948. Educated at Royal Scottish Academy of Music and Drama, Glasgow (flute with David Nicholson), 1964–5; Royal Academy of Music, London (under James Iliff), 1966–70; Royal Academy of Music, Stockholm (under Ingvar Lidholm), 1971. Freelance composer; flautist and arranger with Scottish traditional music group Whistlebinkies, since 1973. Recipient: Hecht Prize, 1968; winner (with *Chamber Music*), National Young Composers Competition, 1969; British Council scholarship, 1971; winner (with *Rant*), in competition to find test piece for Carl Flesch International Violin Competition, 1978; winner (with String Quartet), in competition to find piece for performance at 40th anniversary concert of Society for the Promotion of New Music, 1983. Mailing address: c/o Scottish Music Information Centre, 1 Bowmont Gardens, Glasgow G12, Scotland.

Publisher: self.

Symphonies/orchestral:

Calgacus 1976; first performed Glasgow, October 1976. Recorded BBC Radio 3.
Symphony 1977.
Source (Reflections on Neil Gunn's Novel Highland River) 1979; first performed Kirkwall, Orkney, 15 June 1979.
Flute Concerto 1986.
Guitar Concerto 1988; first performed Glasgow, 1988.
A Glasgow Symphony 1990; first performed Glasgow, 1990. Recorded BBC Radio 3.

Chamber/instrumental:

Three Dialogues (flute, oboe) 1966, revised 1978; revised version first performed Glasgow, 7 June 1981.
Seven Modal Duets (viola, cello) 1966, revised 1975; first performed Glasgow, 22 May 1980.
Three Dialogues (cello, piano) 1966, revised 1982; first performed Toward, Argyll, 1966.
Rebirth (Trilogy Part 1) (flute/alto flute, clarinet/bass clarinet, violin, cello, piano/celeste, percussion) 1967–74; first performed Edinburgh, 1974. Recorded BBC Radio 3.
Trio (flute, oboe, bassoon) 1967–71, revised 1977–81; first performed Glasgow, August 1981.
Chamber Music (3 clarinets, harp, piano) 1968; first performed Liverpool, 1969.
Music for Saxophones (soprano, alto, tenor, baritone saxophones) 1971, revised 1977.
Six Small Pieces in C major (piano) 1971; broadcast Radio Scotland, 14 January 1980.
Twelve Very Small Pieces (piano) 1971; broadcast Radio Scotland, 14 January 1980.

Twelve Studies in C major (piano) 1971; first performed Bracknell, Berkshire 22 July 1979.
Twelve White-Note Pieces for Piano(s) (3 or more pianos, or solo piano with prerecorded tape) 1971; solo version first performed Newcastle-upon-Tyne, December 1980.
Martyr (viola) 1972; first performed Glasgow, 23 April 1974.
Solo for Clarinet(s) (3 or more clarinets, or solo clarinet with tape delay or prerecorded tape) 1972, revised 1982, trio version, 1983; solo version broadcast 9 September 1976, retitled *Prelude 9*, 1982.
Music for Guitar(s) (solo guitar, plus 2 or more others or tape delay) 1973; tape version first performed Cambridge, 23 October 1980.
Music for Low Flutes (3 or more flutes, or solo version with tape delay) 1973; trio version first performed, Glasgow, 8 May 1981.
Interregnum (Trilogy Part 2) (2 flutes/alto flute, clarinet/bass clarinet, viola, cello, percussion, harp) 1974; first performed Edinburgh, 1974. Recorded BBC 3.
Liberation (Trilogy Part 3) (flute/piccolo, clarinet/bass clarinet, viola, harp/clarsach) 1975; first performed Glasgow, 1975. Recorded BBC Radio 3.
Prelude 1 (cello) 1975.
Prelude 2 (bass clarinet) 1975; first performed Jersey, 28 July 1979.
Sounds Around . . . (viola, 2 percussionists) 1976; first performed Glasgow, 13 October 1976. Recorded BBC Radio 3.
Prelude 3 (flute) 1976, revised 1982.
Rant (violin) 1977; test piece for 1978 Carl Flesch Violin Competition. Recorded BBC Radio 3.
Legend (viola, tape) 1978; first performed Glasgow, 1978.
Springsound (clarinet, tape) 1979; first performed Glasgow, 29 March 1979.
Reflections for Two Pianos 1979; first performed Liverpool, 3 May 1979. Recorded Scottish Society of Composers SSC 2.
Movement (flute, viola, harp) 1979; first performed Edinburgh, 2 September 1979.
Divertimento (20 solo violas) 1979; first performed Glasgow, 21 August 1979.
Fast Peace I (piano) 1980.
Wind Octet (2 oboes, 2 clarinets, 2 bassoons, 2 horns) 1980; first performed Glasgow, 23 April 1980. Recorded BBC Radio 3.
Euphoria (flute/piccolo/alto flute, clarinet/bass clarinet, violin, cello, piano, marimba) 1980; first performed Edinburgh, 5 September 1980.
Prelude 4 (organ) 1980; first performed Edinburgh, 17 September 1981.
Quintet (clarinet, violin, viola, cello, piano) 1981; first performed Glasgow, 23 June 1981.
Prelude 5 (guitar) 1981; first performed Edinburgh, 4 September 1981.
Prelude 6 (viola) 1981; broadcast BBC Radio, 15 September 1981.
Improvisations on Calderon (flute, guitar) 1981; first performed London, 11 October 1982. Recorded BBC Radio 3.
Prelude 7 (piano) 1981–2; first performed London, 18 February 1983.
String Quartet 1982; first performed Edinburgh, 20 February 1983. Recorded BBC Radio 3.
Fast Peace II (cello, organ) 1982.
Fast Peace III (viola, guitar) 1982; first performed Glasgow, 15 May 1982.
Fantasy Quartet (violin, viola, cello, piano) 1984; first performed Glasgow, 1984. Recorded Radio Scotland.
Cauldron of Improvisations (flute, viola, guitar) 1986; first performed Glasgow, 1986. Recorded BBC Radio Scotland.
String Trio (violin, viola, cello) 1986; first performed Bracknell, Berkshire, 1986.
Wild Woods (viola, trombone, percussion, tape) 1986; first performed Glasgow, 1987.

Vocal/choral:

Quest (soprano, flute/alto flute, clarinet/bass clarinet, cor anglais/oboe, violin, viola, cello, harp, marimba/percussion; Burns, Trakl, Sassoon, Carey, ancient Chinese, Brecht, Dickinson, Mao) 1978; first performed Edinburgh, 18 October 1978. Recorded BBC Radio Scotland.
Moonsongs (soprano, double bass; Weores, Neruda, Lu Hsun, Holub, García Lorca) 1979; first performed Budapest, 6 January 1980.
Prelude 8 (tenor, with tape delay) 1981; first performed Glasgow, 13 November 1981.
Nameplates I–V (various vocal groupings; settings of names) 1981–2.
Five Songs (female voice, viola, piano; Humberger) 1982; first performed Carnoustie, Fife, 21 March 1982.
Citysongs (baritone, piano) 1982; first performed London, 1983.
Lifesongs (chorus, strings) 1983; first performed Glasgow, 1983.
Pipes of Peace (chorus, bagpipes) 1985; first performed Jerusalem, 1986.
Rhymes (soprano, viola, harp, double bass) 1986; first performed Edinburgh, 1987.
The Web (soprano, flute, viola, guitar, percussion) 1989; first performed Glasgow, 1990.

Opera:

Etain (Carey) 1990; first performed Glasgow, 1990.

Other:

Two Views of Burns (music for television: soprano, tenor, flute, recorder, oboe, violin, cello, harpsichord) 1978; broadcast BBC Television, January 1978.
Let's See Orkney (music for television: flute, clarsach) 1978; broadcast BBC Television, November 1978.
The Annals of the Parish (music for television adaptation of Galt novel; solo flute) 1980; broadcast BBC Television, October/November 1980.
The House with Two Doors (incidental music to play by Calderón de la Barca; 2 flutes, guitar) 1980; first performed Edinburgh, September 1980.
Macbeth (incidental music to Shakespeare; Whistlebinkies group, with viola, percussion) 1981; broadcast BBC Radio Scotland, 25 January 1981.
Beatrice—Inshore Oilfield (audio-visual study: Whistlebinkies group, with electronically treated sounds) 1982.
Peter Pan (ballet music) 1989; first performed Glasgow, 1989. Recorded Scottish Ballet Cassette 1.

Composition/arrangement/recording with Whistlebinkies folk group, 1973–90, Claddagh Records, Dublin, CC 22, 31, 34, 43, 50; also with Ted McKenna, Amiga 8 45 127 VEB Deutsche Schallplatten, Berlin GDR; *Freedom Come All Ye—Songs and Poems of Hamish Henderson*, Claddagh CCA7; David Essex, *Imperial Wizard*, Mercury 9109 616; *Confluence*, 1980; *Glasgow Festival*, Oran Recordings.

PUBLICATIONS

By McGuire: "Aleatoric Methods in Music", BBC Scotland, 4 September 1972; "Composers Workshops", Radio Clyde, 1974; "Composers Portrait", Radio 3, 24 May 1979; interview, "Music in Our Time", Radio 3, 6 April 1982; "John Cage", (interview) in *Cencrastus*, 21, Summer 1985.

On McGuire: Calum MacDonald, "Signals in a Mist", *Listener*, 31 May 1979; Richard McGregor, "EMc", *Musical Times*, June 1979; Paul Hindmarsh, "EMc", in *A Companion to Scottish Culture*, edited by David Daiches, 1980; Kenneth Chalmers, in *The Ethnicity of Scottish Music*, Edinburgh, 1982; Raymond Ross, (interview with EMc) in *Cencrastus*, 14, Autumn 1983; Ailie Munro, in *The Folk Music Revival in Scotland*; Phillip Thorne, (interview with EMc) in *Guitar International*, February 1990.

Edward McGuire comments:

My work had a rebirth in the early 1970s—returning to the freshness of tonality under the influence of practical involvement with Scottish folk music. Since then, influences have included both the minimalism of Steve Reich and the richness of recent complex music. As well as private emotions and relationships, inspirations have sprung from the revolutionary movement ever since my involvement with the anti-Vietnam War campaign of the late 1960s. My *Glasgow Symphony*, for example, is a tribute to the growth and struggle of a great industrial city.

* * *

The influence of Scottish traditional music, itself a widely varied field, has been felt in the work of many contemporary Scottish composers, but none have embraced it quite as ardently, or attempted to reconstruct it quite as vigorously, as Edward McGuire.

McGuire emerged from an early immersion in extremely avant-garde music with a broad understanding of abstract and unconventional idioms, and a growing desire to work in more direct and more communicative modes. That process has been a lengthy one, spanning two decades of patient accretion, all aimed at a gradually forming integration of a range of musical styles.

In the 1970s, McGuire went back to the basics of composition, and worked on a large number of short pieces for soloists or small ensembles, exhaustively investigating the particular qualities of the instruments involved, or working out a particular musical idea, as in the modal miniatures of *Twelve White-Note Pieces for Pianos*. At the same time, he helped form the folk group The Whistlebinkies, dedicated to preserving and extending Scottish traditional music, in which he plays flute.

The folk music McGuire drew on in his early experiments with the form came directly out of that tradition, albeit a tradition he saw as very much a living one. As his work developed into the 1980s, and his use of these idioms alongside a basically atonal musical register (sometimes with a mildly Cage-like provision for instrumentalists to determine what they play within strict bounds) grew more sophisticated, McGuire was able not only to compose new music which reflected the spirit if not the letter of the traditional, but even to imbue music with no immediate folk content, like the *String Quartet*, with the feel of Scottish music.

Two large-scale works from the end of the 1980s would seem to represent some culmination of that process of integration. His music for Scottish Ballet's production of *Peter Pan* works in precisely that synthetic way, combining diverse idiomatic strands into a developed whole. It is indicative of how far down the road into conventional, almost Romantic tonality McGuire is prepared to go in search of direct communication, and how far he has moved from the avant-garde in the process, although without ever quite abandoning it.

The shifting surface and exotic instrumental colouration is beguiling, and much the same might be said of *A Glasgow Symphony*, a work which utilises the full colour and textural palette of a large orchestra (it is scored for 110 players) to trace the historical development of his native city. The opening two movements deploy a wide range of effects in a pictorially suggestive but musically abstract fashion, while the third incorporates a vigorous mêlée of popular tunes intended to capture the spirit of the modern, cosmopolitan city.

It is possible to argue that McGuire's music occasionally suffers in structural terms from this passion for integration, when that integration is not quite achieved. Against that, it consistently exhibits an equally passionate conviction (intimately bound up with his leftwing political beliefs), and a clear determination not only to be widely heard, but widely enjoyed. McGuire is not afraid to be both populist and popular when the work demands it, a trait balanced by an acute awareness of more recondite developments in modern music which still filter through into his composition.

—Kenny Mathieson

MELLERS, Wilfrid (Howard). British/English. Born in Leamington Spa, Warwickshire, 26 April 1914. Educated at Leamington College, 1925–33; Downing College, University of Cambridge (composition under Egon Wellesz and Edmund Rubbra), 1933–8, B.A., 1938, M.A., 1939. Married (1) Vera Muriel Hobbs in 1939 (ended 1947); (2) Peggy Pauline Lewis in 1950 (ended 1976); (3) Robin Stephanie Hildyard in 1985; 3 daughters. College superviser and university lecturer, Downing College, Cambridge, 1945–48; staff tutor in music, extra-mural department, University of Birmingham, 1948–60; Distinguished Andrew Mellon Visiting Professor of Music, University of Pittsburgh, 1960–3; professor of music and founding head of department, University of York, 1964–81, now emeritus; visiting professor of music, City University, London, Keele University, Staffordshire, and the Guildhall School of Music, London, various times since 1980; visiting professor, Tulane University, New Orleans, 1989–90, and others; music editor of periodical *Scrutiny*, 1930s–40s; regular contributor to dictionaries and encyclopaedias, *Times Literary Supplement*, *Music and Musicians*, *Opera Notes*, and *The Independent* and *Guardian* newspapers. Recipient: Mendelssohn Scholarship; grants by Leverhulme Trust and Gulbenkian Trust; honorary D.Mus., University of Birmingham, 1980; honorary D.Phil., City University, London, 1981; Fellow, Guildhall School of Music; O.B.E. (Officer, Order of the British Empire), 1982. Mailing address: 17 Aldwark, York Y01 2BX, England.

Publishers: Novello; Faber; Mills Music, U.S.A.

Symphonies/orchestral:

Sinfonia ricercata 1947.
Alba, in Nine Metamorphoses (solo flute, large orchestra) 1959; first performed Pittsburgh, 1960.
Noctambule and Sun Dance (woodwind, brass and percussion) 1967; first performed Pittsburgh, 1967.
Threnody in Memoriam E.W. (string orchestra) 1976; first performed Edinburgh, 1976.
The Wellspring of Loves (violin and string orchestra) 1981. Recorded UEA 84119.
The Spring of the Year (double string orchestra); first performed Keele, Staffordshire, 1984.
Hortus rosarium (suite for strings); first performed Dartington, Devon, 1985.

Chamber/instrumental:

String Trio (violin, viola, cello); first performed London, 1946.
Sonata (viola, piano) 1947; first performed London, 1947.
Natalis invicti solis (piano) 1969; first performed London, 1969.
De vegetabilibus et animalibus (soprano, clarinet, violin, cello, harp) 1971; first performed York, 1971.
A Blue Epiphany for J.B. (solo guitar) 1972; first performed London, 1973.
Opus alchymicum (organ) 1974; first performed Cheltenham, Gloucestershire, 1975.
Shaman Songs (jazz quartet) 1979; first performed York, 1980.

Vocal/choral:

Canticum felium (soprano, violin, cello, clarinet, bassoon) 1952; first performed London, 1952.
Ygdrasil (cantata for soprano, alto, tenor, bass chamber orchestra) 1954; first performed Bryanston, Dorset, 1954.
Voices and Creatures (declamation for voice, flute, percussion) 1962; first performed Pittsburgh, 1962. Recorded Philips 6589 001.
Rose of May (speaker, soprano, flute, clarinet, string quartet); first performed Cheltenham, Gloucestershire, 1964.
Missa brevis (mixed chorus and organ) 1964; first performed Birmingham, 1964.
May magnificat (mezzo soprano, small orchestra) 1965; first performed York, 1966.
Early Light (2 part songs for SATB chorus, piano) 1966; first performed Cambridge, 1966.
Te Deum (chorus, organ) 1966; first performed Keele, Staffordshire, 1966.
Canticum resurrectionis (16 voices) 1968; first performed Harrogate, Yorkshire, 1969.
Chants and Litanies of Carl Sandburg (male voices, piano, percussion) 1969.
Cloud Canticle (chorus) 1969; first performed Pittsburgh, 1969.
The Word Unborn (double chorus, flute, clarinet, cello, trombone) 1970; first performed Harrogate, Yorkshire, 1970.
The Key of the Kingdom (high soprano, clarinet, piano) 1972; first performed Maine, 1976.
The Gates of the Dream (instrumental and vocal ensemble) 1973; first performed York, 8 May 1974.
Rosae hermeticae (2 sopranos, 2 violins, tenor viola, 2 bass violas, lute) 1977; first performed York, 1977.
The Echoing Green (cantata for female voices, keyboards, viola, cello, percussion) 1989; first performed York, 1989.

Opera/dramatic:

The Tragical History of Christopher Marlowe 1952.
The Shepherd's Daughter (chamber opera with small orchestra) 1954.
The Ancient Wound (one-act monodrama for television) 1970; first performed Vancouver, 1970.
Venery for Six Plus (theatre piece for singing actress, clarinet, violin) 1972; first performed York, 1972.
Life Cycle (ritual theatre for soloists, 3 choirs, two orchestras) 1969; first performed York, 1969. Recorded Philips 6589 001.

PUBLICATIONS

By Mellers: *Music and Society: England and the European Tradition*, London, 1946; *François Couperin and the French Classical Tradition*, London, 1950, revised 1987; *Music in the Making*, London, 1952; *Romanticism in the Twentieth Century*, London, 1957; *The Sonata Principle*, London, 1957; *Man and His Music*, 1957, revised 1987; *Music in a New Found Land*, 1964, revised 1987; *Caliban Reborn: Renewal in Twentieth-Century Music*, New York, 1967; *Twilight of the Gods: The Beatles in Retrospect*, New York, 1973; *Bach and the Dance of God*, New York, 1980; *A Darker Shade of Pale: A Backdrop for Bob Dylan*, New York, 1984; *Beethoven and the Voice of God*, 1984; *Angels of the Night: Popular Female Singers of Our Time*, 1986; *The Masks of Orpheus: 7 Stages in the Story of European Music*, London, 1987; *Vaughan Williams and The Vision of Albion*, London, 1989; *Le Jardin Retrouvé: Homage to Frédéric Mompou*, New York, 1989.

On Meller: Robert Henderson, "The Music of WM: Tradition and Necessity", *Musical Times*, March 1963; Peter Aston, "WM at 70", *Musical Times*, July 1984.

Wilfrid Mellers comments:

Perhaps because I had a literary training at Cambridge before I became a professional musician, I've always been a composer who has been triggered by words and theatre, rather than by "abstract" musical concerns: even my purely instrumental pieces tend to have ritualistic associations. For this reason my later works tend also to embrace "ethnic" material; and for 20-odd years I've been interested in interrelationships between "art" and music and blues, jazz and other folk and pop stylizations. This mishmash seldom worked in the distant days of my youth, but tends to do so nowadays, when barriers between the genre, and the generations, are being broken down. Any future music may have depends, in my view, on precisely this interfusion. I hope my music modestly affirms life, however desperate the odds.

* * *

Wilfrid Mellers is still far better known as a critic and educator than as a composer in his own right. Understandably so, given his enormous contribution to the understanding of music in the United Kingdom. He was founding professor of the highly innovative music department at the University of York, and has been closely associated with other such adventurous departments as those of the University of Keele and the City University, London. His published output is prodigious, combining occasional writing for the British press, and a substantial shelf of important books on subjects as wide-ranging as Couperin, Bach, American music, the contemporary avant-garde, Bob Dylan and the Beatles.

Somewhere across that spectrum, Mellers's own musical enthusiasms and philosophy can perhaps be detected. He has renounced a considerable proportion of his own compositions; what remains is still powerfully achieved and highly individual, combining early polyphony, intriguing elements of 20th-century modernism, and, always, a strong awareness of the dramatic immediacy of popular music.

Taught composition by the remarkable Egon Wellesz, Mellers's *Threnody* for strings in memory of his old teacher is a strikingly beautiful work, expertly orchestrated but without Wellesz's Byzantine complexity and deformation of melodic line. Perhaps Mellers's finest orchestral compositions, though, are the haunting *The Wellspring of Loves*, for solo violin and strings, and *The Spring of the Year* for augmented string orchestra. He has written surprisingly little instrumental chamber music and by far the bulk of his output is for voices in a variety of settings. Perhaps his most important single work is *Life Cycle*, a generously proportioned piece for soloists, three choirs and orchestra, first heard in York in the late 1960s and subsequently recorded. The piece testifies to a new freedom in Mellers's style, or perhaps more accurately a recognition that his earlier, ill-fated attempt to synthesise "high" and popular styles within a single piece had at last met their moment. The 1960s were characterised by a breaking down of the barriers between so-called "serious" and popular musics. Mellers's interest in jazz and in the phenomenon of rock music is well-represented in his writing, but is also evident in his composition as well. A particular facility in vocal setting, a steady pulse and energy levels untypical of most formal concert music are all evident in his work from around 1967 onwards. The slightly stilted formal quality of his earlier work disappears, to be replaced with a freer and—perhaps paradoxically—ritualistic approach very evident in the fine declamatory *Voices and Creatures* and the *Canticum resurrectionis*.

Mellers's music is as distinctively unEnglish and catholic in its resources and priorities as that of the late Sir Lennox Berkeley. It is to be hoped that in future he will receive the same recognition as a composer as he has for his writings. Mellers is an original and his music is an untapped well.

—Richard Stein

MELLNÄS, Arne. Swedish. Born in Stockholm, 30 August 1933. Educated at State College of Music, Stockholm (musical theory, piano, violin, conducting), 1953–9, 1962–3, composition under Lars-Erik Larsson, Karl-Birger Blomdahl, Bo Wallner, 1959–60; Hochschule für Musik, Berlin (composition under Boris Blacher), 1961; private composition studies under György Ligeti (Vienna), Max Deutsch (Paris), 1961–2; also studied electronic music under Gottfried Michael Koenig, Bilthoven, The Netherlands, 1962–3; further study at Tape Music Center, San Francisco, 1964. Military service in signals and radio regiment, 1954–5. Married Marianne Mellnäs, 16 August 1958 (dissolved 1976); 1 son. Teacher of music theory, Stockholm Citizens School, 1961–3; teacher of musical theory, 1963–72, teacher of composition and orchestration, 1972–85, State College of Music, Stockholm; visiting professor of composition, Rice University, Houston, Texas, 1985; freelance composer, since 1985. Member of board, Swedish Composers' Society, 1979–89. Recipient: 1st prize, Gaudeamus composition competition, The Netherlands, 1963; elected member, Royal Academy of Music, 1984; lifetime State Artist's Grant, since 1985. Mailing address: Folkungagatan 142, S-11630 Stockholm, Sweden.

Publishers: Nordiska Musikförlaget/Fazer, Nybrogatan 3, S-11434 Stockholm, Sweden; Edition Reimers, Box 15030, S-16115 Bromma/Stockholm, Sweden.

Symphonies/orchestral:

Concerto for Clarinet and String Orchestra 1956.
Music for Orchestra 1959.
Chiasmos 1961.
Collage 1962; first performed Hilversum, The Netherlands, 1963.
Aura 1964; first performed Malmö, 1964.
Interludier 1970.
Transparence 1972; first performed Malmö, 1972. Recorded Phono Suecia CD 22.
Blow (symphonic wind orchestra) 1974; first performed Karlskrona, 1975. Recorded Caprice, 1991.
Moments musicaux 1977; first performed Lillehammer, Norway, 1978.
Capriccio 1978; first performed Stockholm, 1978.
Incantations (symphonic wind orchestra) 1978; first performed Boras, 1978.
Symphony No 1: Icarus 1986; first performed Stockholm, 1987.
Passages 1989.

Chamber/instrumental:

Sonatina (violin, piano) 1955.
Sonatina (piano) 1955.
Divertimento (flute, clarinet, bassoon) 1955.
Trio (2 violins, viola) 1956.
Sonata (oboe, piano) 1956.
Sonata a tre (homage to Purcell; flute, violin, viola) 1961.
Växlingar (flute/piccolo, clarinet/bass clarinet) 1961.
Per caso (alto saxophone, trombone, 2 percussion, violin, double bass) 1963.
Tombola (horn, trombone, electric guitar, piano—4 hands) 1963.
Tre miniatyrer (piano) 1964.
Gestes sonores (chamber ensemble ad lib) 1964; first performed Oslo, 1965.
Siamfoni (2 trumpets, 2 horns, 2 trombones) 1964.
Drones (alto saxophone/tenor saxophone, alto saxophone/baritone saxophone/clarinet, trumpet/zinka/flute, trombone, percussion, cello, double bass) 1967.
Fixations (organ) 1967; first performed Stockholm, 1967.
Quasi niente (1–4 string trios) 1968; first performed Gothenburg, 1969.
For You and Me (piano) 1969.
Cabrillo (clarinet, trombone, cello, percussion) 1970; first performed Malmö, 1970. Recorded Caprice LP 1070.
Capricorn Flakes (piano, harpsichord, vibraphone/glockenspiel) 1970; first performed Uppsala, 1971.
Agréments (harpsichord) 1970; first performed Stockholm, 1971. Recorded BIS LP 68.
Schizofoni (piano) 1971; first performed Paris, 1971. Recorded Swedish Society SLT 33240.
Disparitions (organ) 1971; first performed Zagreb, 1971. Recorded Phono Suecia CD 31.

Ceremus (flute, clarinet, trumpet, trombone, percussion, double bass) 1973.
Fragments for Flute Family (1–4 flutes) 1973; first performed Stockholm, 1973. Recorded BIS LP 1/50.
Fragile (unspecified instruments) 1973; first performed Graz, Austria, 1973.
The Mummy and the Humming Bird (recorder, harpsichord) 1974; first performed Stockholm, 1975. Recorded BIS LP 78.
Soliloquium IV (bassoon, live electronics) 1976; first performed Stockholm, 1976. Recorded Fylkingen Records LP 1011.
Es laval / Vals (piano) 1977.
Rendez-vous I (clarinet, bass clarinet) 1979; first performed Stockholm, 1980. Recorded Phono Suecia CD 22.
Canzona svedese (harpsichord) 1979.
Riflessioni (clarinet or bass clarinet, tape) 1981; first performed Stockholm, 1981.
Pièces fugitives (flute, violin, bassoon, guitar, harpsichord) 1981; first performed Budapest, 1981.
Apertura (4 trumpets, 4 horns, 4 trombones, 2 tubas) 1982.
31 Variations on CAGE (2 pianos, percussion) 1982. Recorded FYLP 1029.
Rendez-vous 2 (flute, percussion) 1983; first performed Stockholm, 1984. Recorded MAP R-8502.
Expansion & Echoes (piano) 1984; first performed Stockholm, 1984. Recorded Caprice CAP 2021.
Is Not a Bed of Roses (piano) 1984.
Stampede (saxophone quartet) 1985; first performed Basle, 1985. Recorded Caprice, 1991.
Gardens (flute, clarinet, violin, cello, percussion, piano) 1986; first performed New York City, 1988. Recorded Acoustica CD 1010.

Vocal / choral:

Tva sanger (voice, piano; Hinders, Berg) 1956.
Tre sanger (voice, piano; Almgren) 1956.
Vem spelar . . . (unaccompanied male choir; Setterlind) 1958.
Fastepsalm (voice, organ; Forstenson) 1958.
Dagsford och nattharbarge (3 songs for soprano, flute, viola, harp; Hillbäck) 1959.
Missa brevis (unaccompanied mixed chorus) 1959.
Fargernas hjarta (4 soloists, flute, clarinet, violin, cello, percussion, celeste; Key-Åberg) 1961.
Momenti (2-part school choir, violin, piano, percussion) 1962.
Sick transit (2 singers, flute, banjo, guitar, percussion, harmonium, double bass, tape) 1964.
Mumrick for Full hals (canon; Crona) 1964,
Succsim (unaccompanied mixed chorus) 1965; first performed Stockholm, 1965. Recorded Phono Suecia CD 38.
Potpuri: Hommage à Beatles (school choir, instruments, pop group) 1965.
Visa i pojkton (unaccompanied male chorus) 1967.
Spots and Spaces (male chorus, orchestra) 1968.
Tva sanger ur Galgenlieder (voice, piano; Morgenstern) 1968.
Aglaria (unaccompanied 3-part children's chorus; Gabrielsson) 1969.
Aglepta (unaccompanied 3-part children's chorus) 1969; first performed Stockholm, 1970. Recorded Finlandia CD 921; Columbia 5 E 062/34670; Deutsche Grammophon 2530 812.
Pang (Music of Scotland) (sound composition for voices and instruments) 1969.
Ode i skogen (male chorus, tape) 1969.
Inte alltid (voice, piano; Danielsson) 1969.
Dream (unaccompanied mixed chorus) 1970; first performed Stockholm, 1971. Recorded Phono Suecia CD 38.
Der Seufzer (unaccompanied SSA chorus; Morgenstern) 1971.
Noël (2 sopranos, children's chorus, flute, horn, trumpet, trombone, 3 percussion, harp, celeste, piano, strings; cummings) 1971–2.
Omnia tempus habent (soprano) 1972; first performed Visby, 1972. Recorded Ariel LP 4; Phono Suecia CD 37.
Vae . . . (SATB chorus, organ) 1972–3.
Mara mara minne (unaccompanied mixed chorus; Swedish spell) 1973.
Seeker of Truth (unaccompanied mixed chorus; cummings) 1973.
Tre korsatser (choral; Danielsson) 1973.
Sub luna (soprano, flute/oboe, violin, harp) 1973; first performed Stockholm, 1973. Recorded Philips 6519 005.
Bossa buffa (unaccompanied mixed chorus) 1973; first performed Stockholm, 1973. Recorded Caprice LP 3024.
A Wind Has Blown (unaccompanied mixed chorus) 1973; first performed Stockholm, 1975. Recorded SKF 6001.
Forsan (unaccompanied mixed chorus; Vergil) 1973.
Host (unaccompanied mixed chorus; Aspenström) 1973.
Ede, bibe, lude (unaccompanied male chorus) 1976; first performed Uppsala, 1976. Recorded OD 8004.
Merry Go Round (soloists, chorus, instruments ad lib) 1977.
Meditation pa tag (voice, piano; Danielsson) 1978.
Provokationer (2 choruses) 1979.
A Child's Garden of Verses (soprano, flute; R.L. Stevenson) 1979.
Nocturnes (mezzo-soprano, flute, clarinet, viola, cello, piano; Baudelaire, Swedenborg, Blake, Shelley) 1980; first performed Budapest, 1980. Recorded Phono Suecia CD 22.
Japansk danslek (soprano, percussion ensemble) 1980.
Ten Proverbs (unaccompanied mixed chorus; trad.) 1981; first performed Stockholm, 1982.
L'infinito (unaccompanied mixed chorus) 1982; first performed Stockholm, 1983. Recorded Phono Suecia CD 22.
Dementerande (baritone; Hagliden) 1983.
Rostens ansikte (mezzo-soprano, piano; Sonnevi) 1985.
Omnia mutantur (unaccompanied mixed chorus; Ovid) 1987.

Opera:

Minibuff ("A Night in the Department Store"; 2 singers, tape; Kunder) 1967.
Erik den helige (church opera for actors, soloists, 3 choirs, orchestra; Wall) 1975.
The Canterville Ghost (Wilde) 1980; first performed Umea, 1981;
Bed of Roses (Bjornsson) 1984; first performed Copenhagen, 1989.
Doktor Glas / Dr Glass (Söderberg) 1990.

Other:

Intensity 6.5: Edgar Varèse in memoriam (tape) 1966. Recorded HMV CSDS 1088–3.
Pausmusik for TV (tape) 1967.
Conglomerat (tape) 1968. Recorded SR Records LPD 3.
Eufoni (electronic) 1969. Recorded Caprice CAP 35.
Kaleidovision (television ballet; electronic) 1969; broadcast Swedish Television, 1969.
Monotrem (tape) 1969.
Far Out (Portrait of Laura Nyro) (text-sound composition) 1970. Recorded SR Records RELP 1103.
Den bla knappen (theatre music) 1970.
Appassionato (tape) 1970.

OM-Musik (tape) 1970.
Landskapsmusik (tape) 1972.
Measure for Measure (incidental music to Shakespeare) 1979; first performed Stockholm, 1979.

PUBLICATIONS

On Mellnäs: Goran Bergendahl, *Thirty-Three Swedish Composers*, Stockholm, 1972; Rolf Haglund, "AM Shows the Way into the 80s", in *Musikrevy*, 5, 1983; Lennart Reiners, "AM and His Music", in *Musxikrevy*, 6, 1988.

Arne Mellnäs comments:

My place of work during the summer is a cottage on Gotland, an island in the Baltic Sea. Junipers, some windblown and stunted pines. Redshanks, Oystercatchers and curlews. The sea. "I guess you get lots of inspiration there", my friends say. And I start to think: how is the creative artist influenced by nature—or by the outside world in general? What about myself? My experience is unlike Mahler's—"wie ein Naturlaut", " . . . ich habe die Berge wegkomponiert"—even if my experience of nature is surely as intense as his was. When walking on meandering sheep paths, I bring Borges's "Garden of Forking Paths" to mind. Other literary mulch includes: Swedenborg, Blake, Baudelaire, Balzac, Poe. Yes, I think I know what nature does for me. It gives me a push towards the *misterioso*. Towards incantation and magic.

* * *

Arne Mellnäs's *Symphony No 1*, subtitled *Icarus*, represents an obstinate reinterpretation of the classical myth. Following the Swedish poet Erik Lindegren's poem, Mellnäs has Icarus flying alone, apart from his father. His fall into the sea is thereby symbolically transformed into the bursting of the amniotic sac. Mellnäs's music transforms the story further: it begins, with a section called "Since", in the ambivalent "niente" of the labyrinth, with melodic figures built on small intervals; from there it expands, in timbre and dynamics, in the movement "Away" and in the incongruous yearning of "And"; it flies in "Later on", into the "labyrinth of the winds" (with thematic references to the terrestrial labyrinth of the first section), where the gravitation of the earth is overcome; finally, in the fifth movement, "Now", he is reborn through ascent "Allegro e crescendo al ff possibile".

Icarus represents many of the dominant traits of Mellnäs's personality. His music contains elements from many of the stylistic developments of recent decades; however, these were soon integrated into a very personal approach, where a free tonality is combined with very profiled and fresh melodic and timbral ideas. Mellnäs began his composition career with a full hand of cards. He began with a long and taxing period at the College/Conservatory of the State College of Music, studying music education as well as composition. His teachers were the relatively conservative Erland von Koch and Lars-Erik Larsson, as well as the more modernistic Karl-Birger Blomdahl. He then continued with Boris Blacher, Max Deutsch and György Ligeti, in Berlin, Paris and Vienna, and an adventurous course of study in electronic music at Bilthoven.

Before he was 30, then, he had a flavour of the "strict" avant-garde of the 1950s as well as the freedom of the improvising 1960s. He felt no solidarity with any particular trend and communicated in a very fruitful way with such different personalities as Edison Denisov, Alfred Schnittke, Toru Takemitsu and Toshiro Mayuzumi, as well as with the "Darmstadt gang" and the West Coast avant-garde in San Francisco. His compositions from the 1950s and 1960s mirror the breadth of his interests. The chamber pieces *Gestes sonores* and *Aura*, which was performed at the ISCM Festival in Prague in 1967, marked his breakthrough to international recognition in the mid-1960s, while *Succsim* and *Aglepta* from roughly the same period soon became popular fixtures in the choral repertoire.

Mellnäs's eclectic approach means that he is often thinking of a specific performer while he is a working out a musical idea. The solo piece *Soliloquium IV* is closely associated with the bassoon player Kunt Sonsteviold, and the *Rendez-vous* pieces for clarinet and bass clarinet with Harry Sparnaay and Kjell Inge Stevenson. Mellnäs's creativity has focussed on chamber configurations of all sorts. Among his most important works of the 1980s are *Nocturnes* for mezzo-soprano and five players, based on poems by Baudelaire, Swedenborg, Blake and Shelley, *Ten Proverbs*, based on folklore and magical texts, the choral piece *L'infinito*, dedicated to Eric Ericson and the Swedish Radio Choir, and *Stampede* for saxophone quartet. Mellnäs is currently completing the opera *Dr Glass*, commissioned by the Swedish Royal Opera and based on a thrilling story by the Swedish author Hjalmar Söderberg. It is a useful chapter end for a period in Mellnäs's career; as with Söderberg's story, it is impossible to know for sure how Mellnäs's works will end.

—Lennart Reimers

MENOTTI, Gian Carlo. Italian; resident in United States and Scotland. Born in Cadegliano, 7 July 1911. Educated at Milan Conservatory, 1923–7; Curtis Institute of Music, Philadelphia (composition under Rosario Scalero), 1927–33. Has one adopted son. Teacher of music, Curtis Institute of Music, Philadelphia, 1941–5; organizer, Festivals of Two Worlds, Spoleto, Italy, 1958, Charleston, South Carolina, 1977; resident at Yester House, Scotland, from 1974; opera director. Recipient: Guggenheim Fellowship, 1946, 1947; Pulitzer Prize, 1950, 1955 (for *The Medium* and *The Saint of Bleecker Street*); honorary associate, National Institute for Arts and Letters, 1953; Drama Critics' Circle Award, and New York Music Critics' Circle Award (for *The Saint of Bleecker Street*), 1955; Kennedy Center Award for lifetime achievement, 1984; New York City Mayor's Liberty Award, 1986; honorary B.M., Curtis Institute of Music, Philadelphia. Mailing address: c/o Thea Dispeker, 59 East 54th Street, New York, New York 10022, U.S.A.

Publisher: Ricordi.

Symphonies/orchestral:

Pastorale and Dance (piano, string orchestra) 1934.
Prelude (from *Amelia al ballo*) 1937.
Prelude (from *The Old Maid and the Thief*) 1939.
Two Interludes (from *The Island God*) 1942; first performed New York City, February 1942.
Piano Concerto in F 1945; first performed Boston, November 1945.
Sebastian (ballet suite) 1945; first performed New York City, August 1945.

Apocalypse 1951; movements 1 and 2 first performed Pittsburgh, 9 October 1951; first complete performance Philadelphia, 18 January 1952.
Introduction, March and Shepherds' Dance (from *Amahl and the Night Visitors*) 1951.
Violin Concerto 1952; first performed Philadelphia, 5 December 1952.
Triple Concerto a tre (3 trios: piano, harp, percussion; oboe, clarinet, bassoon; violin, viola, cello; orchestra) 1970; first performed New York City, 6 October 1970.
Fantasia (cello, orchestra) 1975; broadcast RAI, Turin, 16 January 1976.
Symphony No 1: The Halcyon 1976; first performed Saratoga, New York, 4 August 1976.
Double Bass Concerto 1983; first performed New York City, 20 October 1983.

Chamber/instrumental:

Variations on a Theme of Schumann (piano) 1931.
Six Compositions (carillon) 1934.
Four Pieces (string quartet) 1936.
Trio for a House-Warming Party (flute, piano, cello) 1936.
Poemetti per Maria Rosa (piano pieces for children) 1937.
Ricercare e toccata (on a theme from *The Old Maid and the Thief*; piano) 1949.
Suite (2 cellos, piano) 1973; first performed New York City, 20 May 1973.
Cantilena scherzo (harp, string quartet) 1977; first performed New York City, 15 March 1977.

Vocal/choral:

Baba's Aria (from *The Medium*; contralto) 1946.
The Black Swan (from *The Medium*; voices) 1946.
Monica's Waltz (from *The Medium*; soprano, orchestra) 1946.
Lucy's Aria (from *The Telephone*; soprano, orchestra) 1947.
Magda's Aria; (from *The Consul*; soprano, orchestra) 1950.
Shepherd's Chorus (from *Amahl and the Night Visitors*; chorus, orchestra) 1951.
The Hero (voice, piano; Horan) 1952.
The Death of the Bishop of Brindisi (cantata for soprano, baritone, children's chorus, mixed chorus, orchestra) 1963; first performed Cincinnati, Ohio, 18 May 1963.
Canti della lontananza (soprano, piano) 1967; first performed New York City, 18 March 1967.
Landscapes and Remembrances (cantata) 1976; first performed Milwaukee, Wisconsin, 14 May 1976.
Missa, o pulchritudo (soprano, alto, tenor, bass, chorus, orchestra) 1979; first performed Spoleto, Italy, Summer 1979.
Four Songs (tenor, piano) 1981; first performed New York City, 21 October 1981.
Notturno (voice, harp, string quintet) 1982.
Muero porque no muero (cantata for soprano, chorus, orchestra; Teresa of Avila) 1982; first performed Washington, D.C., 15 October 1982.

Opera:

Amelia al ballo (opera buffa in 1 act) 1936; first performed Philadelphia, 1 April 1937.
The Old Maid and the Thief (radio opera in 1 act) 1939; broadcast NBC, 22 April 1939; first staged Philadelphia, 11 February 1941.
The Island God (1 act) 1942; first performed New York City, 20 February 1942.
The Medium (tragic opera in 2 acts) 1945; first performed New York City, 8 May 1946.
The Telephone, or L'Amour à trois (opera buffa in 1 act) 1946; first performed New York City, 18 February 1947.
The Consul (musical drama in 3 acts) 1949; first performed Philadelphia, 1 March 1950.
Amahl and the Night Visitors (television opera in 1 act) 1951; broadcast NBC, 24 December 1951; staged Bloomington, Indiana, 21 February 1952. Recorded CDTER/ZCTER 1124.
The Saint of Bleecker Street (opera in 3 acts) 1954; first performed New York, 27 December 1954.
Maria Golovin (music drama in 3 acts) 1958; first performed Brussels, 20 August 1958.
Labyrinth (television opera in 1 act) 1963; broadcast NBC, 3 March 1963.
Le Dernier Sauvage (opera buffa in 3 acts) 1963; first performed Paris, 21 October 1963.
Martin's Lie (children's church opera in 1 act) 1964; first performed Bristol, 3 June 1964.
Help, Help, the Globolinks! (1 act) 1968; first performed Hamburg, 21 December 1968.
The Most Important Man 1971; first performed New York City, 12 March 1971.
Tamu-Tamu (opera in 2 acts) 1973; first performed Chicago, 5 September 1973.
The Egg (church opera for children) 1976; first performed Washington, D.C., 17 June 1976.
The Hero (comic opera) 1976; first performed Philadelphia, 1 June 1976.
The Trial of the Gypsy (children's opera for treble voices, piano) 1978; first performed New York City, 24 May 1978.
Chip and his Dog (children's opera for treble voices, piano, drum) 1979; first performed Guelph, Ontario, 5 May 1979.
La loca (opera in 3 acts) 1979; first performed San Diego, California, 3 June 1979.
A Bride from Pluto (children's opera) 1982; first performed New York City, 14 April 1982.
The Boy Who Grew too Fast (children's opera) 1982; first performed Wilmington, Delaware, 24 September 1982.

Other:

Sebastian (ballet) 1944; first performed New York City, 31 October 1944.
Errand into the Maze (ballet) 1947; first performed New York City, 2 February 1947.
The Unicorn, the Gorgon and the Manticore or The Three Sundays of a Poet (madrigal ballet; 10 dancers, 9 instruments, chorus) 1956; first performed Washington, D.C., 21 October 1956.

PUBLICATIONS

By Menotti: *A Hand of Bridge*, libretto for opera by Samuel Barber, New York, 1960; *Introductions and Goodbyes*, libretto for opera by Lukas Foss, New York, 1961; *Vanessa*, libretto for opera by Samuel Barber, New York, 1964; *The Leper*, stage play, first performed Tallahassee, Florida, 22 April 1970.

On Menotti: Joseph Kerman, *Opera as Drama*, New York, 1956; R. Tricoire, *GCN, l'homme et son oeuvre*, Paris, 1966; D. Ewen, "GCM", in *The World of Twentieth-Century Music*, Englewood Cliffs, New Jersey, 1968; L. Grieb, *The Operas of GCM, 1937–72: A Selective Bibliography*, Metuchen, New

Jersey, 1974; J. Gruen, *M: A Biography*, New York, 1978; George Martin, analyses of *Amelia al ballo, The Consul, The Telephone, The Medium* and *Amahl and the Night Visitors*, in *The Companion to Twentieth-Century Opera*, London, 1979, 1984; J. Ardoin, *The Stages of Menotti*, Garden City, New York, 1985.

* * *

No composer of the post-World War II era has found a broader or more enthusiastic public than Gian Carlo Menotti. Born in Italy, he has resided principally in America for over 50 years. His music is in the Italian operatic tradition, although overlaid with some of the intense expressionism of Richard Strauss. His melodic gift is prodigious, resulting in a wide popular appeal. His one-act *opera buffa*, *Amelia al ballo*, was a great success at the Metropolitan Opera House in New York in 1936, and it was followed by a string of successes over the next decade (*The Old Maid and the Thief*, *The Medium*, *The Telephone*, *The Consul*, *Amahl and the Night Visitors* and *The Saint of Bleecker Street*).

All of those works found an audience, and all found some critical acclaim, even though many berated Menotti for his conservative approach and what they saw as his refusal to develop his own style beyond repeating past successes. It is curious that since *The Saint of Bleecker Street* in 1954, Menotti has not been able to repeat his earlier popular triumphs. His later operas have invariably had fewer productions than his earlier ones, and although he has remained active, when most people think of Menotti they think of his works before 1955.

In his best music, Menotti shows a remarkable grasp of writing for the voice, and a strong sense of musical theatre. His colorful sense of orchestration adds to the overall dramatic impact of his music. One example is the end of Annina's aria in *The Saint of Bleecker Street*, wherein she relives the Crucifixion and experiences the stigmata. At its climactic point, Menotti calls for the striking of an anvil, replicating the sound of the nail being driven in. In describing it here, it sounds melodramatic and somewhat cheap. In performance, however, because of the skill of the orchestral writing and the highly expressive melodic curve of the aria, it is stunningly effective.

Menotti seemed, in the 1940s and 1950s, a logical heir to Puccini, and no other composer from recent generations has reached an operatic public as broad as his. While he has used modern techniques (tape in *Help, Help, the Globolinks!*, for instance), the foundation of his music is its eloquent melodic writing. Menotti has been critical of many composers' tendency "to treat the voice instrumentally, as if composers feared that its texture is too expressive, too human."

Because of his operatic success, Menotti's orchestral music has been undeservedly neglected. His ballet *Sebastian*, his angular *Piano Concerto* and more broadly lyrical *Violin Concerto*, and some of his chamber works reflect the same melodic gift and colorful orchestral style as his operas, and they should be heard more frequently than they are.

In 1958, Menotti started the Spoleto Festival of Two Worlds, which in 1977 he expanded to include Charleston, South Carolina as well. Much of his creative energy has gone into these festivals, administratively and in his directing of plays and operas. He also wrote the librettos of two works by his lifelong friend Samuel Barber, the chamber opera *A Hand of Bridge*, and the grand opera *Vanessa*. He also revised Zeffirelli's libretto for Barber's *Antony and Cleopatra*, making it more compact and effective. One wonders if some of this other activity has distracted him from composing, but it is clear that Menotti is a multi-faceted, multi-talented figure not content to simply sit in a studio and write operas.

In the end, one feels that Menotti will be remembered and performed more frequently in future generations than many of the composers who found a broader critical acceptance during their lives, but one also is left wondering why he has had difficulty repeating his earlier operatic successes. Given the remarkable string of works from 1940 to 1954, one hopes that history will give his later operas the opportunity to be performed and judged.

—Henry Fogel

MESSIAEN, Olivier (Eugène Prosper Charles). French. Born in Avignon, 10 December 1908; family moved to Grenoble, 1914, Nantes, 1918, and subsequently to Paris. Educated: piano lessons, from 1917; Conservatoire National Supérieur de Musique, Paris (harmony under Jewan Gallon, counterpoint and fugue under Georges Caussade, piano accompaniment under C.A. Estyle, organ under Marcel Dupré, composition under Paul Dukas, Greek metrics under Maurice Emmanuel), 1919–30. Married (1) Claire Delbos, 1932 (died 1959), 1 son; (2) the pianist Yvonne Loriod in 1962. Organist, Eglise de la Trinité, Paris, since 1931, public debut 19 February 1931; co-founder (with André Jolivet, Daniel-Lesur and Yves Baudrier), La Jeune France, 1936; teacher of music, Schola Cantorum, from 1936; teacher of music, Ecole Normale de Musique, Paris, 1936–40; military service, medical auxiliary, 1939; captured and imprisoned at Stalag VIIIA, Görlitz, Silesia, May 1940–2; professor of harmony, 1941–7, professor of analysis, aesthetics and rhythm, 1947–1966, and professor of composition, 1966–1978, Paris Conservatoire; first visit to United States, 1947; teacher, Ferienkurse für Neue Musik, Darmstadt, 1949, 1950, 1951; teacher, Berkshire Music Centre, Tanglewood, Massachusetts, 1949; visit to Japan, 1962. Recipient: 2nd prize in harmony, 1924; 1st prize in counterpoint and fugue, 1926, 1st prize in piano accompaniment, 1927, 1st prize in organ, 1929, and 1st prize in composition, 1930, all Paris Conservatoire; elected to Institut de France, 1967; Calouste Gulbenkian Prize, 1969; Erasmus Prize, 1971; Sibelius Prize, 1971; Von Siemens Prize, 1975; associate member, Royal Academy of Science, Literature and Art, Belgium, 1975; Grand Prix National de la Musique, 1977; Leonie Sonning Prize, 1977; Bach Prize, Hamburg, 1979; share of Wolf Foundation Prize, Jerusalem, 1982; Liebermann Priz d'Honneur, 1983; Inamori Prize, Kyoto, 1985; Grand Croix, Légion d'Honneur, 1986; Grand Croix de l'Ordre Nationale du Mérite, 1987. Mailing address: Eglise de la Trinité, 3 rue de la Trinité, 75009 Paris, France.

Publishers: Durand; Leduc; Universal Edition; Lemoine; Broude, New York.

Symphonies / orchestral:

Fugue in D minor 1928.
Le Banquet eucharistique 1928; first performed (by student orchestra), Paris, 1928.
Simple Chant d'un âme 1930.

Les Offrandes oubliées (symphonic meditation) 1930; first performed Paris, 19 February 1931. Recorded Erato STU 70673.

Le Tombeau resplendissant 1931; first performed Paris, 1932.

Hymne au saint sacrament 1932; first performed Paris, 13 March 1933. Recorded Erato STU 70673.

L'Ascension (symphonic meditation; also arranged for organ) 1932–3; first performed Paris, February 1935. Recorded Columbia ML 4214; Erato STU 70673.

Turangalîla-symphonie (piano solo, ondes martenot solo, orchestra) 1946–8; first performed Boston, 2 December 1949. Recorded RCA SB 6761–2; HMV SLS 5117; CBS M2K 42271; EMI CDS7 47463–8.

Réveil des oiseaux (piano solo, orchestra) 1953; first performed Donaueschingen, 11 October 1953. Recorded Supraphon SUA ST 50749.

Oiseaux exotiques (piano solo, orchestra) 1955–6; first performed Paris, 10 March 1956. Recorded Vega C30 A65; Supraphon SUA ST 50749; CBS MK 44762.

Chronochromie 1959–60; first performed Donaueschingen, 16 October 1960. Recorded HMV ALP 2092; ASD 639; ZRG 756.

Sept haikai (Japanese sketches for piano solo, orchestra) 1962; first performed Paris, 30 October 1963. Recorded Ades 16001; Everest SDBR 3192.

Couleurs de la cité céleste (piano solo, orchestra) 1963; first performed Donaueschingen, 17 October 1964. Recorded Erato STU 70302; CBS 72471/MK 44762.

Et exspecto resurrectionem mortuorum 1964; first performed Paris, 7 May 1965. Recorded Erato STU 70302; CBS 72471.

Des Canyons aux étoiles . . . (piano solo, orchestra) 1971–4; first performed New York City, 20 November 1974. Recorded Erato STU 70974/5.

Chamber/instrumental:

La Dame de Shalott (piano) 1917.

La Tristesse d'un grand ciel blanc (piano) 1925.

Esquisée modal (organ) 1927.

Le Banquet céleste (organ; related to *Le Banquet eucharistique* for orchestra) 1928. Recorded EMI 2C I53 16291/6.

L'Hôte aimable des âmes (organ) 1928.

Variations écossaises 1928.

Préludes (piano) 1928–9; first performed Paris, 1931. Recorded Unicorn DKPC 9037.

Diptyque: Essai sur la vie terrestre et l'éternité bienheureux (organ) 1930. Recorded EMI 2C I53 16291/6.

Thème et variations (violin, piano) 1932; first performed Paris, 1932.

Fantaisie burlesque (piano) 1932; first performed Paris, 1932.

Apparition de l'église éternelle (organ) 1932. Recorded EMI 2C I53 16291/6.

Fantaisie (violin, piano) 1933.

L'Ascension (organ) 1933–4. Recorded EMI 2C I53 16291/6.

La Nativité du Seigneur (9 meditations for organ) 1935; first performed Paris, 1935. Recorded EMI 2C I53 16291/6.

Pièce pour le tombeau de Paul Dukas (piano) 1935. Recorded Unicorn DKPC 9037.

Fête des belles eaux (6 ondes martenot) 1937; first performed Paris, 1937.

Deux Monodies en quarts de ton (ondes martenot) 1938.

Les Corps glorieux: Septs Visions brèves de la vie des réssucités (organ) 1939; first performed Chaillot, 15 April 1945. Recorded EMI 2C I53 16291/6.

Quatuor pour la fin du temps/Quartet for the End of Time (violin, clarinet, cello, piano) 1940–1; first performed on damaged instruments, Stalag VIIIa, Görlitz, Silesia, 15 January 1941. Recorded Deutsche Grammophon 2531 093; CBS M2K 42271; Delos D/CD 3043; Philips 422–834 2; RCA GD 87835; HMV CDS7 47463–8.

Musique de scène pour un Oedipe (ondes martenot) 1942.

Rondeau (piano) 1943.

Visions de l'amen (2 pianos) 1943; first performed Paris, 10 May 1943. Recorded Contrepoint CO I-6; Vega C30 A368.

Vingt Regards sur l'Enfant-Jésus (piano) 1944; first performed Paris, 26 March 1945.

Canteyodjaya (piano) 1949; first performed Paris, 23 February 1954. Recorded Vega C30 AI 39; Unicorn DKPCD 9051.

Messe de la Pentecôte (organ) 1949–50; first performed Paris, Pentecost 1951. Recorded EMI 2C I53 16291/6.

Quatre Etudes de rythme (piano) 1949–50; first performed Tunis, 1950. Recorded Columbia LFX 998–9; Erato STU 70433; Denon 33CO-1052.

Ile de feu I/II (piano) 1950.

Le Merle noir (flute, piano) 1951.

Livre d'orgue (organ) 1951; first performed Stuttgart, 23 April 1953. Recorded EMI 2C I53 16291/6.

Catalogue d'oiseaux (piano) 1956–8; first performed Paris, 15 April 1959. Recorded Vega VAL 121; Erato STU 70595–8; Unicorn Kanchana DKPCD 9062.

Verset pour la fête de la Dédicace (organ) 1960.

Méditations sur le mystère de la Sainte Trinité 1969; first performed Washington, D.C., 20 March 1972. Recorded Erato STU 70750–1.

La Fauvette des jardins 1970; first performed Paris, 7 November 1972.

Livre du Saint-Sacrament (organ) 1984; first performed Detroit, Michigan, 1 July 1986.

Petites Esquisses d'oiseaux (piano) 1985; first performed Paris, 26 January 1987.

Un Vitrail et des oiseaux (piano, woodwind, trumpet, percussion) 1986; first performed Paris, 28 November 1988.

La Ville d'en-haut (piano, woodwinds, trumpet, percussion) 1987; first performed Paris, November 1989.

Vocal/choral:

Deux Ballades de Villon (voice, piano) 1921.

Trois Mélodies (voice, piano) 1930; first performed Paris, 1930.

La Mort du nombre (soprano, tenor, violin, piano) 1930; first performed Paris, 1931.

Mass (8 sopranos, 4 violins) 1933.

Vocalise (soprano, piano) 1935.

Poèmes pour Mi (soprano, piano or orchestra) 1936, orchestrated 1937; first performed Paris, 28 April 1937; orchestral version first performed Brussels, 1946. Recorded Everest 3269; (orchestral) Argo ZRG 703.

O sacrum convivium (SATB chorus; or soprano, organ) 1937.

Chants de terre et de ciel (soprano, piano) 1938; first performed Paris, 6 March 1939.

Choeurs pour une Jeanne d'Arc (large and small choruses) 1941.

Trois Petites Liturgies de la Présence Divine (36 women's voices, piano, ondes martenot, celeste, vibraphone, 3 percussion, strings) 1943–4; first performed Paris, 21 April 1945. Recorded Pathe PDT 190–4S.

Harawi (song of love and death for dramatic soprano, piano) 1945; first performed Mâcon, 24 June 1946. Recorded Argo ZRG 606.

Cinq Rechants (3 sopranos, 3 altos, 3 tenors, 3 basses) 1948; first performed Paris, 1949. Recorded Erato STU 70457.

La Transfiguration de Notre-Seigneur Jésus-Christ (SSMsAA-TTBarBB chorus, piano, cello, flute, clarinet, xylorimba, vibraphone, marimba, orchestra) 1965–9; first performed Lisbon, 7 June 1969. Recorded Decca HEAD 1–2.

Opera:

Saint François d'Assise 1975–83; first performed Paris, 28 November 1983.

Other:

Timbres-durées (electronic tape realised by Pierre Henry) 1952; withdrawn.

PUBLICATIONS

By Messiaen: (collaboration with others) *Vingt Leçons de Solfège Moderne*, Paris, 1933; "Ariane et Barbe-Bleue de Paul Dukas", in *Revue Musicale*, 166, 1936; "Le rythme chez Igor Stravinsky", in *Revue Musicale*, 191, 1939; *Vingt Leçons d'Harmonie*, Paris, 1939; *Technique de Mon Langage Musical*, Paris, 1944, (English version) Paris, 1957; "Maurice Emmanuel: Ses 'trente chansons bourguignonnes'", in *Revue musicale*, 206, 1947; *Conférence de Bruxelles*, Paris, 1958; *Conférence de Notre-Dame*, Paris, 1978; *Traité de Rythme*, in progress.

On Messiaen: Claude Rostand, *OM*, Paris, 1957; Antoine Golea, *Rencontres avec M*, Paris, 1960; Pierrette Mari, *OM*, Paris, 1965; Claude Samuel, *Entretiens avec OM*, Paris, 1967, English version London, 1976; Stuart Waumisley, *The Organ Music of OM*, Paris, 1968; Robert Sherlaw Johnson, *OM*, London, 1975, revised 1989; Roger Nichols, *M*, London, 1975; Siegline Ahrens, Hans-Dieter Moller and Almut Rossler, *Das Orgelwerk Ms*, Duisburg, 1976; Paul Borum and Erik Christensen, *M: en handbog*, Copenhagen, 1977; Michèle Reverdy, *L'Oeuvre pour Piano d'OM*, Paris, 1978; Alain Perier, *M*, Paris, 1979; Harry Halbreich, *OM*, Paris, 1980; Paul Griffiths, *OM and the Music of Time*, London, 1985; also many musicological articles and analyses.

* * *

Without ever belonging unequivocally to a perceived mainstream of musical thought, Olivier Messiaen became the outstanding figure in French music between Debussy and Boulez. This commanding position resulted both from his rigorous development of a rich personal style and from his extraordinary influence as a teacher after World War II.

Messiaen's gifts flowered early, in the Paris of the 1920s, where his deeply religious sensibility was far removed from the prevailing aesthetic of Les Six and other prominent composers of the day. Although this difference of approach was to be signalled during the following decade by his brief association with André Jolivet and two lesser-known composers under the banner of "La Jeune France", there was no lasting sense of group identity: Messiaen's commitment to the universal was indeed highly personal, as was his musical language. Deriving in part from Debussy and Skriabin, in part from the French organ tradition of Marcel Dupré and Charles Tournemire, his technique was nevertheless so individual as to give his very earliest works a striking impression of maturity. This was confirmed by the young composer's poetic response to extra-musical ideas, which is intensely mystical even in the secular context of the *Préludes* for piano. Here, in works which otherwise recall Debussy's essays in the same genre, Messiaen replaces the older composer's semblance of detachment with an explicit revelation of the divine majesty which for him underlies the very sights and sounds of man's existence. If the deathly pace of *Le Banquet céleste* is to some extent prefigured in the timelessness of Debussy's *La Cathédrale engloutie*, the ecclesiastical vision is in Messiaen's music no longer picturesquely submerged but fully focused and in command.

Messiaen's religious faith was matched by the single-minded development of his musical style through the synthesis of elements gradually but liberally acquired from elsewhere. His interest in additive rhythms was expanded through a study of mediaeval Indian writings and Greek theories, giving his melodic writing an exotic freedom from the phrase patterns of Western Romantic music. He developed a theory of "modes of limited transpositions" by following through the technical consequences of the whole-tone and octatonic writing found in some works by earlier French and Russian composers, generating a wide-ranging harmonic language encompassing sonorities one might otherwise associate with Berg, Stravinsky or Gershwin. All this was done with a penetrating technical insight which allowed him to codify his procedures in print (*Technique de Mon Langage Musical*) and was to pay dividends in his analysis classes for young composers, which began in 1947.

In no respect was Messiaen's urge towards synthesis more apparent, however, than in his attitude to musical "colour". For him, this was never a metaphor but always a truly synaesthetic phenomenon: he literally sees colours in musical harmonies and timbres. The balancing of dynamics within complex chords allowed him great subtlety in this respect, whether through the stratified textures which come naturally to his own instrument, the organ, or through piano writing often similarly conceived. Writing for the orchestra gave him still greater opportunities for creating effects of this kind.

Both in this context and on account of its huge dimensions, one may reasonably regard the *Turangalîla Symphony* as the culmination of Messiaen's early career. Its orchestra includes not only the conventional instruments but also a solo piano part written for his second wife, Yvonne Loriod, and a prominent part for the ondes martenot—an early electro-acoustic instrument whose exoticism presses home the work's celebration of the transcendent power of human love. The quality of secularisation evident in this and a number of other works of the late 1940s may have resulted from the sublimation of feelings which could not yet be expressed through the productive working relationship he had established with Loriod. Be that as it may, the expansion of his sensibility from a mystical Catholicism towards the Tristan legend and magical beliefs from other cultures allowed Messiaen to bring extra-musical meanings into creative association with the obscure, quasi-serial procedures which entered his music with the *Quatre Etudes de rythme*.

One of these studies, entitled "Mode de valeurs et d'intensités", was to be a catalyst for the "total serialism" of Boulez and the other composers of the Darmstadt circle, many of whom were Messiaen's pupils. But Messiaen himself did not follow this path, nor did he attempt to use serial technique in a post-Schoenbergian manner, as Stravinsky would later do: on the contrary, his own major technical development of the 1950s was an obsessive use of birdsong as a compositional resource. Transcribed within the parameters of his established musical language, birdsong had already played a minor role in *Turangalîla*, and indeed in some earlier works such as the *Quartet for the End of Time*, but this explicit celebration of nature now provided Messiaen with a means to resolve, in renewed accordance with his faith, the gap between technique and expression that had been opened up by the new constructive methods of the *Quatre Etudes* and the *Livre d'orgue*. The vast *Catalogue d'oiseaux* places stylised birdsong in the context of other musical evocations of the divine in nature: night and day, water, mountains and vegetation. By the early 1970s, this varied and striking material—which is sometimes difficult for the listener to treat as entirely musical rather than merely descriptive—had been firmly integrated into the language of works such as *La Fauvette des jardins* and *Des Canyons aux étoiles*.

Messiaen's relentless exploration of new devices continued into old age with the use of ciphers to encode religious texts directly into music—an approach which cannot be said to have been wholly successful. Similarly, the opera *Saint François d'Assise* seemed at first, on account of its lack of overt drama and its resemblance to his earlier music, to be a disappointing summation of a life's work. Subsequent compositions suggested it was by no means the final chapter, but a sense of critical disappointment remained. The composer's musical vigour has remained with him into his eighties, however, and while he has never appeared to be solving anyone's musical problems but his own, time has often before shown the value of his solutions.

—Anthony Pople

MEYER, Krzysztof. Polish. Born in Cracow, 11 August 1943. Educated: piano from age 5; theory and composition with Stanisław Wiechowicz, from 1954; Fryderyk Chopin State Secondary School of Music, Cracow; College of Music, Cracow (composition under Krzysztof Penderecki, theory under Alexander Fraczkiewicz), diploma in composition, 1965, diploma in theory, 1966; study with Nadia Boulanger, Paris, 1964, 1966, 1968. Married Zofia Golab, 25 December 1967. Pianist with contemporary music group, MW2 ensemble, 1965–7; professor of theoretical subjects, 1966–87, and head of department of music theory, 1972–5, State College of Music (now Academy of Music), Cracow; professor of composition, Hochschule für Musik, Cologne, since 1987; guest lecturer in Soviet Union, East and West Germany, Austria, Brazil; president, Union of Polish Composers, 1985–9. Recipient: 1st prize, competition for young composers, France, 1966; 2nd prize (for *Symphony No 1*), 1966, and 1st prize (for *Symphony No 3*), 1968, Young Polish Composers' Competition; Aaron Copland Scholarship, 1966; Grand Prix (for opera *Cyberiada*), Prince Pierre de Monaco International Composers' Competition, 1970; 2 Special Mentions (for *String Quartet No 2* and *String Quartet No 3*), Tribune Internationale des Compositeurs UNESCO, Paris, 1970, 1976; 2nd prize (for *Concerto da camera per oboe, percussione ed archi*), Artur Malawski Composers' Competition, Cracow, 1972; Award of the Minister of Culture and Art, 1973, 1975; 1st prize (for *Symphony No 4*), Karol Szymanowski Competition, Warsaw, 1974; twice, Government of Brazil medal (for *String Quartet No 4* and *Concerto retro*), 1975, 1977; Gottfried von Herder Preis, 1984. Mailing address: Kurt Schumacher Strasse 10/51, 5060 Bergisch Gladbach 1, Germany.

Publishers: PWM Edition, Cracow; Edition Moeck, Celle, Germany; Edition Peters, Frankfurt; Edition Hans Sikorski, Hamburg; Edition Sonoton, Munich.

Symphonies/orchestral:

Concerto da camera Op 6 (flute, percussion, strings) 1964; first performed Cracow, 25 June 1965.
Symphony No 1 Op 10 1964; first performed Cracow, 12 June 1964.
Concerto for Violin and Orchestra Op 12 1965; first performed Poznan, 22 March 1969. Recorded MUZA SXL 1054; MUZA SX 2680; Olympia OCD 323.
Symphony No 2 "Epitaphium Stanisław Wiechowicz in memoriam" Op 14 (mixed choir, orchestra) 1967; first performed Wrocklaw, 15 February 1969.
Symphony No 3 "Symphonie d'Orphée" Op 20 (mixed choir, orchestra) 1968; first performed Warsaw, 16 September 1972.
Concerto for Cello and Orchestra Op 28 1971–2; first performed Poznan, 3 April 1975.
Concerto da camera Op 29 (oboe, percussion, strings) 1972; first performed Zielona Gora, 24 May 1984.
Symphony No 4 Op 31 1973; first performed Zagreb, 14 May 1975. Recorded MUZA SX 1313.
Concerto for Trumpet and Orchestra Op 35 (also piano arrangement) 1973; first performed Poznan, 1976.
Fireballs Op 37 1976; first performed Warsaw, 20 April 1978. Recorded MUZA SX 2077/CK 337/SX 2318.
Symphony in D major in Mozartean Style Op 41 1976; first performed Poznan, 1 April 1977.
Symphony No 5 Op 44 (chamber string orchestra) 1978–9; first performed Bialystok, 17 September 1979. Recorded MUZA SX 1848.
Piano Concerto Op 46 1979, revised 1989; first performed Wroclaw, 21 February 1984.
March (military band) 1979.
Symphony No 6: "Polish" Op 57 1982; first performed Hamburg, 25 November 1982. Recorded (2nd movement) MUZA SX 2418; ISPV 127.
Hommagè a Johannes Brahms Op 59 1982; first performed Hamburg, 15 May 1983.
Concerto for Flute and Orchestra Op 61 1983; first performed Berlin, 1 December 1984.
"Canti Amadei" Op 63 (concerto da camera for cello and orchestra) 1984; first performed Cracow, 19 December 1984.
Concerto da camera Op 64 (harp, cello, string orchestra) 1984; first performed Cologne, 7 October 1987.
Concerto retro Op 39a (flute, violin, harpsichord, string orchestra) 1986; first performed Cracow, 10 April 1988.
Musica incrostata Op 70 1988; first performed Cologne, 6 June 1988.
Caro Luigi Op 73 (4 cellos, double string orchestra) 1989; first performed Stuttgart, 29 September 1989.

Chamber/instrumental:

Sonata Op 1 (cello) 1959–61; first performed Kamien Pomorski, 15 August 1969.
Introspection Op 2 (5 cellos) 1960; first performed Cracow, 28 May 1961.
Aphorisms Op 3 (piano) 1961; first performed Cracow, 20 June 1962.
Music Op 4 (3 cellos, kettledrums, piano) 1962; first performed Cracow, 9 May 1963.
Sonata No 1 Op 5 (piano) 1962; first performed Katowice, 26 April 1962.
Sonata No 2 Op 7 (piano) 1963; first performed Cracow, 3 June 1963. Recorded RBM 3022.
String Quartet No 1 Op 8 1963; first performed Warsaw,

26 September 1963. Recorded MUZA XW 571; ISPV 151.
Interludio statico Op 11 (clarinet, 4 cellos) 1964; first performed Poznan, Poland, 19 April 1967.
Sonata No 3 Op 13 (piano) 1966; first performed Cracow, 18 May 1966.
Hommage à Nadia Boulanger Op 17 (flute, viola, harp) 1967–71; first performed Zagreb, 14 May 1971. Recorded MUZA SX 1654.
Sonata No 4 Op 22 (piano) 1968; first performed Cracow, 5 June 1969. Recorded MUZA SXL 0613.
String Quartet No 2 Op 23 1969; first performed Warsaw, 28 September 1969. Recorded MUZA XW 1188.
Quattro colori Op 24 (clarinet, trombone, cello, piano) 1970.
String Quartet No 3 Op 27 1971; first performed Warsaw, 28 September 1973. Recorded MUZA XW 1886; Veriton SXV 812.
Sonata per clavicembalo Op 30 (harpsichord) 1972–3; first performed Paris, 28 October 1974. Recorded Erato STU 71010.
String Quartet No 4 Op 33 1974; first performed Curitiba, 29 January 1975. Recorded SEEC 004; MUZA SX 1442; ISPV 101.
Sonata No 5 (piano) 1975; first performed Katowice, 19 January 1977.
Sonata per violino solo Op 36 1975; first performed Poznan, 22 April 1977. Recorded ISPV 109.
Concerto retro Op 39 (flute, violin, cello, harpsichord) 1976; first performed Curitiba, 4 February 1977. Recorded SEEC 010.
Moment musical (cello) 1976; first performed Katowice, 1984.
Three Pieces Op 40 (percussion) 1977; first performed Copenhagen, 8 June 1977.
String Quartet No 5 Op 42 1977; first performed Bialystok, 10 March 1978. Recorded SX 1683; ISPV 101.
Twenty-Four Preludes Op 43 (piano) 1978; first performed Stalowa, Wola, 17 May 1979. Recorded ISPV 109.
Interludio drammatico Op 48 (oboe, chamber ensemble) 1980; first performed Leipzig, 19 January, 1981.
Piano Trio Op 50 1980; first performed Wroclaw, 16 April 1985. Recorded Arston ALP 003; ISPV 135.
Sonata Op 52 (flute) 1980; first performed Darmstadt, 30 March 1985. Recorded ISPV 109.
String Quartet No 6 Op 51 1981; first performed Plock, 11 June 1982. Recorded ISPV 114.
Canzona Op 56 (cello, piano) 1981; first performed Cologne, 1 November 1982.
Six Preludes (violin) 1981.
Pezzo capriccioso Op 60 (oboe, piano) 1982; first performed Princeton, New Jersey, 18 April 1983.
Sonata Op 62 (cello, piano) 1983; first performed Klagenfurt, Austria, 22 November 1984. Recorded MUZA SX 2579.
String Quartet No 7 Op 65 1985; first performed Wroclaw, 16 April 1985. Recorded MUZA SX 2427; ISPV 151.
String Quartet No 8 Op 67 1985; first performed Munich, 16 March 1986. Recorded MUZA SX 2460; ISPV 151.
Quartet Op 65a (4 saxophones; arrangement of *String Quartet No 7 Op 65*) 1986; first performed Santa Cruz, California, 24 July 1988.
Clarinet Quintet Op 66 1986; first performed Ulm, Germany, 2 November 1986. Recorded ISPV CD 147.
Capriccio per sei instrumenti Op 69 1987–8; first performed Lanaudière, Canada, 10 July 1989.
Wittener Kammermusik (flute, oboe, clarinet) 1988; first performed Witten, Germany, 22 April 1989.
Monologue (cello) 1990.
Fantazja na organy Op 75 (organ) 1990.

Vocal/choral:

Songs of Resignation and Denial Op 9 (soprano, violin, piano; Szczeblowska) 1963; first performed Prague, 28 April 1966.
Quartettino Op 16 (soprano, flute, cello; Tuwim) 1966; first performed Szczecin, 11 September 1966.
Five Chamber Pieces Op 18 (soprano, clarinet, viola) 1967; first performed Cracow, 17 April 1969.
Polish Chants Op 34 (soprano, orchestra) 1974; first performed Bydgoszcz, 9 September 1977. Recorded MUZA SX 1521.
Lyric Triptych Op 38 (tenor, chamber orchestra) 1976; first performed Aldeburgh, Suffolk, 22 June 1978.
Nine Limericks of Stanisław Jerzy Lec Op 45 (soprano, piano) 1979; first performed Baranow Sandomierski, 7 September 1979.
Sunday Colloquy in the Street Op 54 (baritone, piano; Tuwim) 1981; first performed Cracow, 26 March 1987.
Mass Op 68 (mixed choir, organ) 1987.
Wjelitchalnaja Op 71 (mixed choir) 1988; first performed L'Hermitage, France, 15 May 1989.

Opera:

Cyberiada Op 15 (comic opera; based on novel by Stanisław Lem) 1967–70; first performed Wuppertal, 11 May 1986.
Klonowi bracia / The Maple Brothers Op 73 (children's opera; based on Evgeni Szwarc) 1988–9; first performed Poznan, 3 March 1990.

Other:

Magic Pictures Op 21a (piano music for children) 1975.
Children's Suite Op 25a (piano) 1978.
Hrabina / The Countess Op 49 (ballet based on motifs in Stansław Moniuszko's opera) 1980; first performed Poznan, 14 November 1981.
Igroki / The Gamblers Op 53 (completion of opera by Shostakovitch, after Gogol) 1980–1; first performed Wuppertal, 9 September 1984.
Geigen Kramchen Op 55 (violin, piano; for children) 1981.
Sonatina for the Young Op 55a (violin, piano; for children) 1983.

PUBLICATIONS

By Meyer: "Igor Strawinski", in *Ruch Muzyczny*, 9, 1972; "Paul Hindemith", in *Ruch Muzyczny*, 23, 1973; "D. Shostakovitch in memoriam", in *Ruch Muzyczny*, 19, 1975; "Requiem Canticles of I. Strawinski", in *Ruch Muzyczny*, 20, 1975; "Comments on My *Fourth Symphony*", in *Polish Music*, 1, 1976; "My *24 Piano Preludes*", in *Polish Music*, 1, 1979; *Dmitri Schostakowitsch*, Leipzig, 1979.

On Meyer: Grzegorz Michalski, "Symfonie KM", in *Ruch Muzyczny*, 18, 1971, and "Nadchodzi stabilizacja?", in *Ruch Muzyczny*, 19, 1975; Lidia Rappoport, "Suymfonie KM", in *Muzyka*, 1, 1975; T.A. Zielinski, "Kwartety KM", in *Ruch Muzyczny*, 15, 1976, and "*String Quartet No 4*", in *Polish Music*, 4, 1976; Nigel Osborne, "*Second String Quartet*", in *Music and Letters*, 1, 1979; Lutz Lesle, "KM", in *Neue Zeitschrift für Musik*, 6, 1981, and "*Konzert für Trompette*", in *Das Orchester*, 1, 1985; Walter Labhart, "Polnische Gegenwartsmusik", in *Neue Zurcher Zeitung*, 10 August 1982; Tadeusz Zielinski, "*V Symfonia*", in *Ruch Muzyczny*, 18, 1983.

Krzysztof Meyer comments:

. . . One should do everything to enable art to keep its humanitarian character in our complex and nervous times; one should also do everything to decrease the chasm between contemporary music and its audience . . .

* * *

Krzysztof Meyer soon outgrew the early influences of Krzysztof Penderecki and Nadia Boulanger. Two series of works dominate his compositional output: six symphonies and five piano sonatas. Other sets of works include eight string quartets, of which the most recent is the most important. Played muted throughout, its 12 segments are arranged in a single movement held together by just one motif; only in the ninth segment do all four performers play together. Meyer is also known for numerous articles on contemporary music and a book about Shostakovich (for whose opera *The Gamblers* Meyer produced a full version).

Meyer's piano sonatas typify his non-orchestral works. *Sonata No 1* opens in octaves, and exploits overlapping and extensive polyphony (reminiscent of Tippett's First Sonata). Pedal-points which resolve a perfect fifth downwards precede clusters at the close of the first movement. The score of *Sonata No 2* includes a few "modern" signs. The opening movement's motivic trills lead to non-aggressive clusters in the second movement. When Meyer introduces arrow-notation in the third movement the audience may become aware of some degree of novelty. By *Sonata No 3* earlier techniques are consolidated. Repeated notes are treated as motivic pedal-points, while the right hand is usually given intervals of seconds, thirds or ninths. A set of varying episodes (reminiscent of *Sonata No 1*) ends the work.

Meyer's emphasis on the newest features of a work suggests that he expects his audience to know his earlier keyboard pieces. This emphasis can be felt in *Sonata No 3*, and by *Sonata No 4* is openly evident. *Sonata No 4* also exploits trills, oscillations and the independence of each hand (producing two-part rhythmic counterpoint). Octave writing moves from Tippett-like to quasi-Chopin or Messiaen (whose bird references he includes).

Knowledge of the composer's previous orchestral works is similarly expected in Meyer's symphonies. The slow first movement (played on strings) of *Symphony No 1* exploits one note and its octave transpositions; a faster second movement (played on wind instruments) is orchestrated in long unaltering blocks while copying Bartók in contrapuntal techniques. Melodic ideas centre around a repeated note plus ornaments within a semitone's distance. By the finale, another single pitch predominates. At the mid-point of the next two symphonies, a chorus enters in octaves. The opening low clusters of *Symphony No 2* are eventually overlaid by another single-pitch idea on strings plus brass. Later, xylophone and trumpet playing a minor ninth apart are given fast oscillations while the interval is expanded by strings. The singers make various hissing sounds, and frequently sing descending glissandos at the end of phrases. At two points, "mobiles" are presented: first by a pair of flutes, later by four violins, who perform in any order while the remainder of the orchestra continue playing; otherwise novelty-notation rests with wavy-lines for strings and vibraphone. New effects for Meyer in *Symphony No 3* are again highlighted as the most important elements: he sets the vibraphone gradually vibrating throughout its range by repeating trills and using glissandos; heavy bell chords are followed by multi-canonic quasi-Henze writing countered by slow chorale-like augmented triad arpeggios. *Symphony No 4* is without chorus. Homophonic multi-layered writing contrasts with brief cadenza-like snatches of thin, slow lines plus accompaniment. Eventually the multi-layered side gains some rhythmic counterpoint. By the time he wrote the Fourth Symphony in the mid-1970s, Meyer had become more conservative in method although less self-retrospective; even the notation is predominantly traditional.

—Malcolm J. Hill

MIEREANU, Costin. Romanian; naturalised French. Born in Bucharest, 27 February 1943. Educated at School of Music, Bucharest (piano), B.M., 1960; National Academy of Music, Bucharest, M.F.A., 1966; Ferienkurse für Neue Musik, Darmstadt (under Karlheinz Stockhausen, György Ligeti and E. Karkoschka), 1967–9; further study in musical semiotics, Ecole des Hautes Etudes en Sciences Sociales, Paris, D.M.A., 1978; further research in liberal arts, University of Paris VIII, Ph.D., 1979. Settled in France, 1968; French citizenship, 1977. Visiting professor, Ecole Nationale Supérieure des Arts Décoratifs, Paris, 1977–8; assistant professor, University of Paris VIII, from 1978; co-founder (with Francis Schwartz), Polysensor Group Systems, 1980; visiting professor, University of Puerto Rico, 1981; artistic director, Editions Salabert, since 1981; titular professor in philosophy, aesthetics and art science, Sorbonne, Paris, from 1982; teacher, Ferienkurse für Neue Musik, Darmstadt, from 1982. Recipient: Prix de la Fondation Européene de la Culture, and 1st prize of the Gaudeamus Foundation International Concourse (for *Finis Coronat Opus*), The Netherlands, 1967; Enesco Award, SACEM, France, 1974. Mailing address: c/o Editions Salabert, 22 rue Chauchat, 75009 Paris, France.

Publisher: Salabert.

Symphonies/orchestral:

Monostructures I 1966; first performed Bucharest, 1966.
Finis coronat opus (piano, 6 instrumental groups, from: 3 flutes/piccolo/alto flute, 2 oboes/cors anglais, clarinet, 2 bassoons, 4 trumpets, 4 trombones, tenor saxophone, 4 percussion, 2 electric guitars, strings) 1966; first performed Utrecht, 1967.
Couleur du temps (string orchestra) 1966–8; first performed Paris, 1969.
Espace dernier (version without chorus) 1966–9.
Monostructures II 1967; first performed Lille, 1969.
Rosario (large orchestra, 2 conductors) 1973–6.
Rosenzeit 1980; first performed Metz, Austria, 1982. Recorded Adda.
Miroirs célestes 1981–3. Recorded Adda.
Voyage d'hiver II 1982–5; broadcast Radio France, 1985. Recorded Adda.
Doppel(kammer)konzert (sopranino/soprano/alto/tenor/baritone saxophones—1 player, percussion solo, chamber orchestra) 1985; first performed Metz, 1985.

Chamber/instrumental:

Variantes (clarinet) 1966; first performed Bucharest, 1966. Recorded Electrocord Bucarest ECE 0389.
Cadenza (open form music for piano, or piano—4 hands, or 2 pianos) 1966; first performed Cologne, 1967.

Couleurs du temps (versions for string quartet; or double string quartet, double bass) 1966–8; quartet version first performed Bucharest, 1968.
Sursum corda I (piano, clarinet, violin, viola, cello) 1967–8; first performed Bucharest, 1968.
Sursum corda triplum (flute/piccolo/alto flute/bass flute, percussion, harp, piano/harpsichord, violin, viola, cello) 1967–82; first performed Paris, 1982. Recorded Salabert/Actuel SCD 8803.
Espace au delà du dernier (open-form music for flute/piccolo/alto flute/bass flute, clarinet/bass clarinet, 2 horns, 2 trumpets, 2 trombones, percussion, piano, violin, viola, cello, double bass) 1968; first performed Paris, 1969.
Dans La Nuit des temps (aleatory score for variable ensemble, tape) 1968–9; first performed Madrid, 1969.
Polymorphies 5 × 7 (A) (variable ensemble/minimum 5, tape) 1968–9; first performed Zagreb, 1969.
Polymorphies 5 × 7 (B) (flute/piccolo/alto flute/recorder/bass flute, clarinet/bass clarinet/tenor saxophone, piano, violin, viola, cello, double bass) 1969–70; first performed Paris, 1970. Recorded Erato STU 70630.
Source de juin (flute, clarinet, trumpet, trombone, percussion, electric guitar) 1972; first performed Paris, 1972.
Altar (6 players or singers, tape, visuals ad lib) 1973; first performed Royan, 1973.
Silence tissé (variable ensemble/3–12 instruments and/or voices, tape) 1973–4; first performed Orléans, 1974.
Segundafeira (quartet or orchestra of flutes/piccolos/alto flutes/bass flutes, tape, visuals, ad lib) 1974; first performed Paris, 1974.
Quintafeira (brass quintet, tape, visuals ad lib) 1974; first performed Royan, 1974.
Aquarius (2 pianos/electric organs, 2 percussion/celestes) 1974–80; first performed Paris, 1981. Recorded Salabert/Actuel SCD 8803.
Planetarium (piano, 2 flutes, trombone, 2 percussion/vibraphone) 1975; first performed Gentilly, 1975.
Musiques élémentaires pour la Messe (brass quintet, organ ad lib) 1976; first performed Armagnac, 1976.
Musique élémentaire de concert (flute/piccolo/alto flute/bass flute, oboe/cor anglais/heckelphone ad lib, clarinet/basset horn, percussion, piano, harpsichord/celeste, cello) 1977; first performed Frankfurt, 1977. Recorded Salabert/Actuel SCD 8803.
Attention! Chute de pierres (keyboards) 1977.
Piano-Miroir (piano, polyphonic synthesizer or electric organ, tape, visuals ad lib) 1978; first performed Brussels, 1979. Recorded Poly-Art PAR 4301.
Cuivres do-re (brass quintet, 2 percussion, 3 guitars, piano, strings) 1979; first performed Juvisy, 1979.
Nouvelle Musique élémentaire de concert (flute/piccolo/alto flute/bass flute, bass clarinet, bassoon, trumpet, trombone, 2 percussion, glockenspiel, piano, harpsichord/celeste, string quintet; 2 conductors) 1979; first performed Paris, 1979.
Musique climatique No 2 (variable piano ensemble, percussion, tape ad lib) 1980; first performed San Juan, Puerto Rico, 1981.
Do-Mi-Si-La-Do-Re (soprano/alto/tenor/baritone/bass saxophones/1 player, tape) 1980–1; first performed Paris, 1982. Recorded Salabert SC 003; Poly-Art PAR 5302.
Cuivres célestes (brass quintet, 2 percussion, strings) 1981; first performed Juvisy, 1981.
Sept Minutes autour de moi (2 flutes/piccolo/bass flute, bass clarinet, percussion, ondes martenot, polyphonic synthesizer, cello) 1981; first performed Montpellier, 1982.
Jardins éxotiques (2 electric guitars, 2 polyphonic synthesizers) 1981–3; first performed Paris, 1983.
Aksakor (percussion) 1982; first performed Paris, 1984.
Voyage d'hiver III (3 percussion, tape) 1982; first performed Orléans, 1982.
Variants-invariants (alto or soprano saxophone or bass clarinet/Korg SE 500 echo chamber) 1982; first performed Nice, 1982. Recorded Salabert SC 004; Poly-Art PAR 5302.
Jardins retrouvés (variable ensemble, tape ad lib) 1983; first performed Turin, 1985.
Bucarest-Grenade (guitar) 1983; first performed Massy, 1983. Recorded Poly-Art/Salabert PAR 5307.
Aksax (bass saxophone) 1983; first performed Darmstadt, 1984. Recorded Poly-Art PAR 5302.
Stratus (flute/piccolo/soprano flute/alto flute/bass flute/contrabass flute) 1983–4; first performed Paris, 1984.
Bolero des Balkans (A) (flute(s), saxophone(s), percussion, tape) 1984; first performed Erlangen, 1985.
Bolero des Balkans (C) (saxophone(s), percussion) 1984. Recorded Poly-Art PAR 5302.
La Colline bleue (cor anglais, horn, 2 percussion, piano, viola, tape; also for 1 or more saxophones) 1984; first performed Lugano, 1984; saxophone version first performed Nice, 1985.
Gyrasol I (recorder quartet ATTB/percussion, tape) 1984; first performed Paris, 1984. Recorded Polyart PAR 5305.
Tercafeira (sopranino/soprano/alto saxophones, soprano/alto/tenor/baritone saxophones, soprano/alto/tenor/baritone saxophones, tape) 1984–5.
Kammerkonzert (sopranino/soprano/alto/tenor/bass saxophones—1 player, flute/piccolo, clarinets/bass clarinet, 2 percussion, mandolin, guitar, harp, violin, double bass) 1985; first performed Amsterdam, 1985.
Quatrième Voyage d'hiver (electric guitar, tape) 1985–6.
Ombres lumineuses (clarinet/bass clarinet, horn, 1 or 2 percussion, 2DX7 synthesizers, violin, cello) 1986; first performed Paris, 1986. Recorded Icons Antidogma Records AM I 861–862.
Haute Tension rigoreuse (6 percussion) 1986; first performed Bremen, 1986.
Rumore (clarinet) 1986.
Ondes (alto saxophone) 1986.
Extremis (flute) 1986; first performed Buenos Aires, 1987.
Miroir liquide (sopranino/soprano/alto/tenor saxophones/1 player, bassoon, percussion, harp, piano, double bass) 1986; first performed Erlangen, 1986.
Come nebia al vento (flute/piccolo/bass flute, guitar, piano, DX7 synthesizer; percussion played by all 4) 1986; first performed Rome, 1986.
Tension X (10 percussion) 1986; first performed Paris, 1986.
Clair de biche (flute/piccolo, clarinet, sopranino saxophone/soprano saxophone/tenor saxophone, brass quintet, 5 percussion) 1986.
Tension en cycle (6 percussion, tape) 1986–7; first performed Stockholm, 1987.
Le Mur d'Airain (6 percussion, harp, 2 pianos/celeste) 1987.
Distance zéro (clarinets/alto saxophone/1 player, percussion) 1987; first performed Macerata, 1988.
Trilogie trajectoire (amplified harpsichord) 1987–8.
Bris de sons (bassoon, tape) 1987–8.
Limping Rock (amplified harpsichord) 1988.

Vocal/choral:

Donum sacrum Brancusi (soprano, orchestra) 1963–5; first performed Darmstadt, 1968.
Nacht (mezzo-soprano, mixed chorus) 1965.

Espace dernier (SMsATBarB chorus ad lib, 6 instrumental groups, tape) 1966–9; first performed Royan, 1973.
Alba nuova (SATB chorus/12 voices, 4 percussion) 1970–88.
Alba (12 soloists 3S/3A/3T/3B with percussion, lighting ad lib) 1972; first performed Bordeaux, 1973.
Anfang (variable ensemble: voice, melody instrument(s), piano(s), percussion, tape, slides ad lib) 1972.
Altar (12 or 18 voices SATB/short wave radios, percussion/Thai gongs/bells, tape, visuals ad lib) 1973.
Amurg (soprano, alto, baritone, flute/Melanesian flute, clarinet/Melanesian flute, trombone/Melanesian flute, 3 percussion/kazoos, variable ensemble) 1973.
Domingo (soprano, mezzo-soprano, alto, tenor, bass, tape, visuals ad lib) 1974; first performed Paris, 1974.
Zbor (soprano, alto, baritone, flute/Melanesian flute, clarinet/Melanesian flute, trombone/Melanesian flute, 3 percussion/kazoos, tape, visuals ad lib) 1974; first performed Paris, 1974.
Quartafeira (soprano, flute/piccolo/bass flute, clarinet, trumpet, horn, percussion, piano, cello, tape) 1974, revised 1982; first performed Ferrara, 1982.
Le Jardin des secrets (soprano, alto flute or viola, bass clarinet, trombone, piano, accordion or electric organ) 1980.
Labyrinthes d'Adrien (soprano, flute/piccolo/alto flute/bass flute, bass clarinet, horn, 2 percussion, piano, 2 electric organs/2 ondes martenot/3 synthesizers, 2 electric guitars, cello) 1981; first performed Paris, 1981.
Voyage d'hiver I (soprano, flute, clarinet, horn, percussion, piano, violin, cello, AKS synthesizer, tape) 1982.
Désordre dérisoire (soprano, flute/piccolo/bass flute, clarinet/bass clarinet, horn, 2 percussion, piano, cello; Eluard) 1982–3; first performed Paris, 1983.
Sur la Terre bariolée (5 choruses of equal voices, orchestra) 1984–5; first performed Creteil, 1985.
Enlacements infinis (soprano/crotales/triangles, flute/piccolo/bass flute, 2 clarinets/bass clarinet, horn, trumpet, trombone, 2 percussion, piano/celeste, violin, cello; Blake, Lefebvre) 1985; first performed Rome, 1985.
Le Temps hasardeux (unaccompanied mixed chorus or 4 soloists with sound dispersal system; Emily Brontë) 1986; version with soloists first performed Rome, 1986.

Opera:

L'Avenir est dans les oeufs (after Ionesco) 1980, in progress.

Other:

Night Music (1 or more stereo tapes) 1968; first performed Darmstadt, 1968.
Source de silences (graphic text for musical or conceptual realisation) 1973.
Rainbow-Chess (players, chessboard, slides, fluorescent lighting) 1973.
Amnar (1st "*réécriture spatio-temporelle*" for 9 players or voices, instrumental ensemble, visuals ad lib) 1973.
Rod (2nd "*réécriture spatio-temporelle*" for 9 players and/or voices, tape, 16 mm film, slides, etc) 1973.
Amurg (3rd "*réécriture spatio-temporelle*" for flute, clarinet, trombone, 2 female voices, male voice, 3 percussion, large instrumental ensemble, 16 mm film, slides and "*mise en espace*" ad lib) 1973.
Segundafeira (quartet or orchestra of flutes, tape, film) 1974.
Sempre asuro (strings, 16 mm film) 1975.
Luna cinèse (1 or more tapes) 1975; first performed Paris, 1976. Recorded Cramps CRSLP 6107/CPF Barclay 950514.
Le Temps des cadences (educational music for 2 pianos, variable ensemble) 1976; first performed Champigny, 1976.
Terre de feu (stereo tape of concrete and electronic sounds) 1976; first performed Paris, 1977. Recorded Poly-Art PAR 4303.
Jacques, ou La Soumission (incidental music to Ionesco) 1977; first performed Paris, 1977.
Mini-Sons, grands espaces (musical itinerary for public and Walkmans) 1977.
Musique aquatique élémentaire (tape) 1977.
La Valse des dames (incidental music to Popescu) 1977; first performed Paris, 1977.
Glockenzeit (educational music for variable ensemble) 1977.
Le Royaume de la Reine Pellapouf (stereo tape/synthesizers) 1977–8; first performed Paris, 1978. Recorded Poly-Art International PAI 2701.
Première Coincidence (stereo tape) 1977–8; first performed Paris, 1978. Recorded Poly-Art International PAI 2701.
Pseudo-Final pour Tchekov (scenography, fluorescent lighting, tape) 1977–8.
Douze Musiques transitives élémentaires (environment) 1977–9; installed Paris, 1978.
Finis-Terre (stereo tape) 1978; first performed Paris, 1978. Recorded Poly-Art PAR 5302.
Les Derniers (incidental music to Gorki) 1978; first performed Paris, 1978.
La Maison des coeurs brisés/Heartbreak House (incidental music to Shaw) 1978; first performed Paris, 1978.
Les Trois Soeurs/Three Sisters (incidental music to Chekhov) 1979; first performed Paris, 1979.
Non Stop! 6–24h (large scale audio-visual and socio-musical event) 1979; first performed Juvisy, 17 May 1979.
Le Canard sauvage/The Wild Duck (incidental music to Ibsen) 1979; first performed Paris, 1979.
Musique climatique (stereo tape of reciter, piano, electric organ, percussion) 1979; first performed Paris, 1979. Recorded Poly-Art PAR 4301.
Polyélémentaire (2 tapes, 3 16mm films, 5 video projections) 1979–80; first shown Paris, 1980.
Son Regard l'entend (black and white video) 1980; first shown Paris, 1980.
Quyo qu'on fasse on casse (incidental music to Frayn) 1980; first performed Paris, 1980.
Fata morgana (stereo tape) 1981. Recorded Poly-Art International PAI 2702.
Jardins désertés (stereo tape) 1981. Recorded Poly-Art PAR 4303.
Jardins oubliés (stereo tape) 1981. Recorded Poly-Art PAR 4303.
Miroitements (stereo tape) 1981. Recorded Poly-Art International PAI 2702.
Carrousel (polyphonic synthesizer/stereo tape) 1982. Recorded Poly-Art PAR 4302.
Silence glisse (educational music for flutes and cellos) 1982; first performed Juvisy, 1982.
Nugaes-nuages (stereo tape) 1982. Recorded Poly-Art PAR 4302.
Sur la Terre bariolée (educational music for chorus, orchestra) 1984–5.

Erik Satie: *Sports et divertissements* (arranged for chamber orchestra) 1980; first performed Champigny, 1980.
Claude Debussy: *Chansons* (arrangements of "Coquetterie posthume" after Gauthier and "Musique" after Bourget for soprano, flute, 2 clarinets/bass clarinet, horn, percussion, piano/celeste, violin, cello) 1983; first performed Marseille, 1983.

Film scores: *Aventurile unui punct / Adventures of a Point* (animated film), 1966; *Picatura / The Drop* (animated film), 1966; *Proveste pe geamul inghetat* (animated film), 1967; *Orasul / The Town* (animated film), 1968; *Le Mont Saint-Michel*, 1979; *L'Araignée*, 1980; *Paradis pour tous*, 1982.

PUBLICATIONS

By Miereanu: "Wozzeck—sinteza a muzicli in secolui XX", in *Secolui 20*, 3, 1965; "Webern et G. Trakl", in *Secolui 20*, 2, 1967; *Les Commencements de la Musique Savante en Roumanie*, Bucharest, 1967; "Stil si personalitate in muzica romaneasca", in *Sonda*, 1969; "Dans la Nuit des temps", in *Sonda*, 1970; "Textkomposition—voie zéro de l'écriture musicale", in *Musique en jeu*, 13, 1973; "Une Musique électronique et sa partition: *Artikulation* de György Ligeti", in *Musique en jeu*, 15, 1974; "Décomposons Wagner", in *Musique en jeu*, 2, 1976; "Poly-Art miroirs Fausse fenêtres", in *l'Indicidence*, 2, 1980.

* * *

The overthrow of the repressive Ceausescu regime has led to a curious foreshortening in the world's view of Romania. To read much of the editorial copy dedicated to the democratic revolution [of 1989?], one might gain the impression that Romanian society and culture had lain in an uneasy slumber since the days of Vlad the Impaler, allowing the modern world to pass it by. It should always be remembered that Count Dracula was the invention of an Anglo-Irishman, drawing on rather distant folklore and superstition.

In point of fact, Romania has contributed very materially to modernist culture. Constantin Brancusi is one of the finest sculptors of the century; Mircea Eliade one of the most significant anthropological philosophers; the composers György Ligeti, György Kurtag and Iannis Xenakis were of Romanian background or birth; and Eugene Ionesco is one of the very great dramatists of the modern age. There is, thus, a significant recent tradition of advanced philosophical and aesthetic thought attached to Romania.

Like a great many of the younger generation of Romanian artists, Costin Miereanu escaped the repressions of his native country; like Ionesco, he settled in France, where he has become a highly significant figure on the French music scene. He found in structuralism a fertile soil for his ideas and for his conception of creative activity as an indivisible whole, in which various synaesthetic elements play an active part. Miereanu has been deeply involved in the semiotics of music, the relation of visual notations to audible sounds, the interplay of texts, images and music. Underlying this is a re-evaluation of the spatio-temporal dimensions of music, something like Xenakis's conception of music as a kind of solid architecture, not just linear duration.

Miereanu's musical apprenticeship was served writing scores for animated films, often quite abstract in nature; this was not mimetic, "programme" music, but an attempt at equivalence between aural and visual components of a single piece. His first mature pieces are highly sensuous and chromatic, reminiscent of some strange rapprochement between Satie and Debussy. A fine orchestrator with a gift for text-setting, his earliest important work was the *Donum sacrum Brancusi* which mimics the very tactile but almost mathematically exact dimensions of the Romanian sculptor's work. (To confirm an interest in his native tradition, Miereanu has also written scores for Ionesco plays and has experimented with a ballet based on Eliade.) The 1973 piece *Altar* was presented as "visible music", abetted like many of Miereanu's later works, by film and slides. In recent years, this has led him to experiment with "Poly-Art", an all-inclusive aesthetic principle in which that earlier "musique visible" is much more coherently and organically conceived and by which every piece becomes a single dramatic action with its own "scenography".

Predictably, given his obsession with performance, Miereanu works closely with performers and conductors (notably Paul Mefano and the 2E2M ensemble) and has composed a range of highly virtuosic instrumental works for solo and multiple performance. He has created a very significant body of saxophone music, mostly for the highly gifted Daniel Kientzy, who plays all the saxophones from sopranino to contrabass, and who has developed a range of multiphonic effects and advanced articulations unique in contemporary music.

The distinctive components of his musical imagination are a progressive self-referentiality and a fondness for mirroring (the word appears in a number of titles), "*fausse fenêtres*" and *mise en abîme* effects, which are largely drawn from the visual arts, but translate with remarkable consistency into a music which has steadily gained in complexity and inclusiveness. Works are generated from relatively simple materials so interwoven as to create musical "flying carpets" that defy normal analytical conventions and move with a strange and compelling beauty.

—Tico Bann

MILLS, Richard (John). Australian. Born in Toowoomba, Queensland, 14 November 1949. Educated at Queensland Conservatorium of Music, North Quay, 1964–9; University of Queensland, St. Lucia, 1966–9, B.A.; Guildhall School of Music, London (composition under Edmund Rubbra, percussion under Gilbert Webster), 1969–71. Principal percussionist, Tasmanian Symphony, 1976–9, and Queensland Symphony, 1980–1; lecturer in composition, University of Northern Rivers, Lismore, New South Wales, 1982–4; lecturer in composition and conducting, Queensland Conservatorium, 1985–6; artist in residence, Australian Ballet, 1984, and Australian Broadcasting Corporation, 1989–90; artistic director, Adelaide Chamber Orchestra, 1991–2; artistic consultant, Queensland Symphony, 1991–2. Recipient: Saltzmann Prize, Guildhall School of Music, 1970; Maggs Award, University of Melbourne, 1982; Australian Performing Rights Association Award, most performed serious work (for *Overture with Fanfares*), 1988; National Critics Award, 1989. Mailing address: 22 Gray Road, Hill End, Queensland 4101, Australia.

Publisher: Boosey & Hawkes (Australia).

Symphonies / orchestral:

Toccata 1976.
Music for Strings (soloists, string orchestra) 1977. Recorded EMI ASD 430003.
Fantasia on a Rondel 1981.
Overture with Fanfares 1981. Recorded Festival Australian Orchestras Series 4 238547.

Trumpet Concerto 1982.
Soundscapes (percussion, orchestra) 1983.
Castlemaine Antiphons (brass band, orchestra) 1984.
Bamaga Dipytch 1986. Recorded AMC CD OZM 1002.
Sequenzas / Concertante 1986.
Suite from Snugglepot and Cuddlepie 1987.
Three Dances from Snugglepot and Cuddlepie 1987.
Fantastic Pantomimes (flute, oboe, clarinet, horn, trumpet, orchestra) 1987–8.
Aeolian Caprices 1988.
Seaside Dances (after e.e. cummings; 18 solo strings) 1989.
Concerto for Flute and Orchestra 1990.
Concerto for Cello and Orchestra 1990.

Chamber / instrumental:

Brass Quintet 1986. Recorded Larrikin Records ABWMC 4001.
Sonatina (string quartet; educational) 1986.
Miniatures and Refrains (string quartet; educational) 1986.
String Quartet No 1 1989.

Vocal / choral:

Festival Folksongs (tenor, mezzo-soprano, SATB chorus, children's chorus, 2 optional brass choirs, orchestra) 1985.
Voyages and Visions (soprano, mezzo-soprano, tenor, bass, large SATB chorus, 3 brass bands, 4 percussion, tape, orchestra; McAuley) 1987.
Visionary Fanfare (large SATB chorus, 2 brass bands, 6 trumpets, 6 trombones, orchestra; McAuley) 1988.
Five Mediations on the Poetry of David Campbell (soprano, baritone, SATB chorus, orchestra) 1988.

Other:

Snugglepot and Cuddlepie (ballet, after May Gibbs) 1988. Recorded ANC 422 933 2.

* * *

Two distinct musical styles can be identified in the compositions of Richard Mills, with the division occurring around the seminal work *Bamaga Diptych* (1986) for orchestra; significantly this work was not a commission, but was written solely at the composer's own instigation. One of his first accepted pieces, *Music for Strings* (1977)—he has rejected most of his previous compositions—can be considered typical of his earlier style: the music is clearly diatonic, with an emphasis on colour, melody and rhythm. Its roots can be identified in the music of Barber, Copland, Britten, Holst—with whose pupil, Edmund Rubbra, Mills himself studied composition—and Janáček. While his writing was a valid expression of his musical aesthetic at the time, Mills eventually felt the need to expand his musical idiom, particularly in the areas of harmonic language and counterpoint. Some glimpses of a change in direction can be discerned in *Soundscapes* for percussion and orchestra (1983) and the *Brass Quintet* (1986), but it was *Bamaga Diptych* that most clearly expressed his new concepts of organising pitch and harmony. These were more complex, a move away from triadic harmony partially inspired by Schoenberg's use of hexachords to manipulate harmony: initial chords generate a harmonic or melodic matrix, which determines organisation of pitch. Counterpoint is used as a coloristic device, often with an interplay between free sections and fixed sections, thus developing a more lively surface texture.

Mills has since worked in this stylistic framework, which can perhaps be seen at its most developed in the *Concerto for Cello and Orchestra* (1990), but has not hesitated to divert from it when expressive considerations prompt him to do so. Other stylistic diversions can be seen in his occasional pieces, such as *Festival Folksongs* for the opening of the Performing Arts Complex of the Queensland Cultural Centre and *Voyages and Visions* for the Australian Bicentenary celebrations; these works can be viewed more as social than musical statements. In a similar category is his music for film and dance—the ballet score *Snugglepot and Cuddlepie*, for example—where the nature of the commission largely determined the nature of the music. His belief that a primary purpose of music is to communicate with an audience has also discouraged any venture into stylistic trends such as serialism and minimalism.

Nature is a constant source of musical imagery for Mills; he believes that music can be heard everywhere in the environment. His earlier works expressed this perception, sometimes literally: *Soundscapes* for percussion and orchestra includes a nocturne inspired by sounds heard in a garden at night. Natural images are also found in later works, however; *Bamaga Diptych* provides an almost programmatic impression of the onset of the wet season at that isolated settlement.

His initial experience as a percussion player, both as soloist and orchestral performer, has given Mills a specialist's knowledge of this group of instruments, and his scoring for percussion is both ample and imaginative, not only in virtuoso pieces such as *Soundscapes* but in general orchestral works as well. Conducting, too, has given him firsthand exposure to the characteristics of each instrument, and he credits his orchestral experience with teaching him how to orchestrate effectively. A negative aspect of his dual role is the necessity that he abandon all compositional work while preparing a score to conduct, being unable successfully to divide his concentration between the two activities; nevertheless, his principal allegiance is to his composition, which he has always seen as his prime means of expression.

—Jenny Dawson

MILNER, Anthony. British/English. Born in Bristol, 13 May 1925. Educated at Douai School, Woolhampton, Berkshire; Royal College of Music, London (piano under Herbert Fryer, theory under R.O. Morris); private composition study under Matyas Seiber. Lecturer in music theory and history, Morley College, London, 1947–62; extension lecturer in music, University of London, 1954–65; director and harpsichordist, London Cantata Ensemble, 1954–65; lecturer in music, Royal College of Music, London, 1962–5 (full-time), and until 1980 (part-time); lecturer in music, King's College, University of London, 1965–71; senior lecturer 1971–4, and principal lecturer 1974–80, Goldsmiths' College, University of London; principal lecturer, Royal College of Music, London, from 1980. Lecture tours in United States, 1964, 1966, 1969, 1973–80, 1982–5; composer in residence, Summer School of Liturgical Music, Loyola University, New Orleans, 1965–6, and Liturgical Music Workshop, Boystown, Omaha, 1967; seminars on 20th-century music, and on Purcell and Britten, University of Western Ontario, London, 1976, 1981; lecturer, Summer School, Western Ontario Conservatory of

Music, London, 1980, 1981, 1984. Recipient: Knight of St Gregory, Holy See, Rome (for contributions to Catholic liturgical music), 1985; hon. D.Mus., University of London; Fellow of the Royal College of Music. Mailing address: 147 Heythorp Street, Southfields, London SW18 5BT, England.

Publishers: Universal Edition; Novello; Mayhew-McGrimmon Ltd, 10–12 High Street, Great Wakering, Essex, England; Basil Ramsey, 604 Rayleigh Road, Eastwood, Leigh-on-Sea, Essex, England.

Symphonies/orchestral:

Variations Op 14 1958; first performed Cheltenham, Gloucestershire, 1959.
Overture: April Prologue Op 17 1961; first performed London, 1961.
Divertimento Op 18 (string orchestra) 1961; first performed London, 1961.
Sinfonia Pasquale Op 21 (string orchestra, optional wind and brass) 1963; first performed Dorset, May 1964.
Chamber Symphony Op 25 1968; first performed London, 1968.
Symphony No 1 Op 28 1972; first performed London, 17 January 1973. Recorded Hyperion A 66158.
Symphony No 2 Op 35 (with chorus; texts from Hopkins, St Francis, Bible) 1978; first performed Liverpool, July 1978.
Concerto for Symphonic Wind Band Op 36 1979; first performed Ithaca, New York, 12 October 1979.
Concerto for String Orchestra Op 40 1982; first performed Wells, Somerset, 29 June 1984.
Symphony No 3 Op 45 1986; first performed London, 26 November 1987.

Chamber/instrumental:

Quartet Op 4 (oboe, strings) 1953; first performed Dartington, Devon, Summer 1953.
Rondo saltato Op 6 No 1 (organ) 1955.
Corfu (children's suite for recorders) 1957.
Fugue for Advent (organ) 1958.
Wind Quintet Op 22 1964; first performed Norwich, Norfolk, 4 June 1964.
String Quartet No 1 Op 33 1975; first performed London, 20 June 1975.
Canticle of Joy Op 38 (symphony for organ) 1981; first performed St Albans, Hertfordshire, 1981.

Vocal/choral:

Salutatio angelica Op 1 (cantata for contralto, small chorus, flute, oboe, bassoon, strings) 1948; first performed 1950.
Improperia Op 2 (double chorus, organ, string orchestra) 1949; broadcast BBC Radio, 1952.
Mass Op 3 (unaccompanied mixed chorus) 1951; first performed London, 1952.
The Song of Akhenaten Op 5 (soprano, chamber orchestra; ancient Egyptian) 1954; first performed London, October 1954.
Benedic anima me dominum Op 10 No 1 (motet for unaccompanied mixed chorus) 1954; first performed 1955.
The City of Desolation Op 7 (cantata for soprano, chorus, orchestra) 1955; first performed 1965.
St Francis Op 8 (tenor, SATB chorus, orchestra; Cuddon) 1956; broadcast BBC, December 1957.
The Harrowing of Hell Op 9 (cantata for tenor, baritone, unaccompanied double SATB chorus; Cuddon) 1956; first performed London, 14 May 1964.
Our Lady's Hours Op 11 (song cycle for soprano, piano; 15th century, Hopkins, Belloc) 1957; first performed Attingham Park, Shropshire, Summer 1957.
When All the Angels (unison voices, piano; Bullough) 1957.
Cast Wide the Folding Doorways of the East Op 12 (partsong for Ralph Vaughan Williams's 85th birthday; unaccompanied mixed chorus) 1957.
I Have Surely Built Thee Op 13 No 1 (anthem for chorus, organ) 1958; first performed London, June 1958.
Before Time Beyond Op 13 No 2 (anthem for St Cecilia's Day; chorus, organ; Cuddon) 1958; first performed London, November 1958.
Turbae for the Passion According to St John 1958.
Christus factus est Op 10 No 2 (motet for unaccompanied mixed chorus) 1959.
Praise the Lord of Heaven Op 13 No 3 (anthem for chorus, organ) 1959; first performed Ashwell, Berkshire, August 1959.
Peacock Pie Op 15 (voice, piano; unaccompanied 3-part choruses; de la Mare) 1959.
Out of Your Sleep Arise and Wake (carol for massed 2-part children's chorus, piano; also arranged for 4-part chorus, organ) 1959; first performed London, Christmas 1959.
The Water and the Fire Op 16 (soprano, tenor, baritone, boys' chorus, mixed chorus, orchestra) 1960–1; first performed Hereford, 1964.
Ceremonial Ode: Break to Be Built, O Stone Op 20 (chorus, audience/congregation, orchestra; Ursula Vaughan Williams) 1962; first performed Bristol, November 1962.
Turbae for the Passion According to St Matthew 1962.
Ashmansworth (round for Finzi family; 4 equal voices; *Macbeth*) 1963.
Festival Te Deum (chorus, orchestra) 1967; first performed Leicester, 1967.
I Looked and Behold! Op 26 No 1 (Introit for All Saints' Day; chorus, organ) 1968.
Most Glorious Lord Op 26 No 2 (anthem for chorus, organ) 1968.
Roman Spring Op 27 (cantata for soprano, tenor, chorus, orchestra) 1969.
Blessed Art Thou, O God of Our Fathers Op 23 (anthem for chorus, organ) 1971.
Motet for Peace Op 29 (TTBB chorus, brass ensemble; biblical, St Francis) 1973.
The Leaden Echo and the Golden Echo Op 30 (partsong for unaccompanied mixed chorus; Hopkins) 1974; first performed London, 10 April 1974.
Midway Op 31 (mezzo-soprano, chamber orchestra; Sappho, de la Mare, others) 1974; first performed London, 10 July 1974.
Emmanuel Op 32 (cantata for Christmas; counter-tenor solo, chorus with small parts for soprano/contralto/tenor/bass, congregation/audience, organ, orchestra) 1974; first performed Kingston-on-Thames, Middlesex, 13 December 1975.
O Give Thanks to the Lord Op 34 (festival anthem for chorus, organ) 1976; first performed Leeds, 1976.
Hearken My Son Op 37 (professional for the sesquimillenary of St Benedict's birth; chorus, organ, trumpets, congregational refrains) 1980; first performed London, 11 July 1980.
Send Forth Thy Spirit, O Lord Op 39 (chorus, organ, brass, congregational refrain) 1982; first performed London, 29 May 1982.

O Lord, Our God How Great Is Your Name Op 43 (SATB chorus, organ) 1985; first performed Egham, Surrey, 22 June 1986.
Ode: Gates of Summer Op 47 (soprano, tenor, chorus, strings) 1988.

Other:

Vespers for Sunday Op 20 No 1 1955.
Compline for Congregational Use Op 20 No 2 1956; first performed Hawkesyard, 1956.
Bells, Books and Croziers (music to television film) 1958; broadcast BBC, 1958.
The Book of Philip Sparrow (music for BBC adaptation of Skelton) 1958.
The Egyptian Book of the Dead (music for radio drama) 1960; broadcast BBC, 1960.
Psalm 136 (for congregational use) 1963.
Chants for the Ordinary of the Mass (for congregational use) 1966.
Mary of Nimmegen (incidental music) 1966; broadcast BBC, 1966.
Communion Service (for congregational use) 1969.
Chants for the Ordinary of the Mass Op 41 (for congregational use) 1976.
Congregational Hymns Op 42 1978–82.

PUBLICATIONS

By Milner: *Harmony for Class Teaching*, 2 volumes, Borough Green, 1950; "English Music", in *European Music in the Twentieth Century*, edited by Hartog, 1957; "Music in a Vernacular Liturgy", in *English in the Liturgy*, edited by C.R. Cunliffe, 1960; "Radio and Gramophone", in *Twentieth-Century Music*, edited by Rollo Myers, London, 1961; "Baroque Music", in *Man and His Music*, edited by A. Harmon and W. Mellers, London, 1962; "The Musical Aesthetic of the Baroque", Ferens Memorial Lecture, University of Hull, 1962; "The Water and the Fire", in *The Composer's Point of View: Twentieth-century Composers' Essays on Choral Music*, edited by Robert S. Hines, Oklahoma, 1963; "Sixteenth-Century Music", in *The Pelican History of Music*, edited by Stevens and Robertson, London, 1963; "The Music of Michael Tippett", in *Musical Quarterly*, October 1964; "Music in a Vernacular Catholic Liturgy", in *Proceedings of the Royal Musical Association*, 91, 1964–5; "Liturgy, Church Music and Politics in the Carolingian Empire", in *Studies in Music* 5, 1980; "Britten's Choral Music", in *The Britten Companion*, London, 1983.

On Milner: Arthur Jacobs, "The Music of AM", in *Musical Times*, September 1958; Ernest Bradbury, "The Progress of AM", in *Musical Times*, June 1963; Francis Routh, "AM", in *Contemporary British Music*, London, 1972; James Siddons, *AM: a Bio-Bibliography*, Westport, Connecticut, 1989.

* * *

Composers suffer the cavalier attitude of the public no less than other artistic creators, and frequently the disdain of professional colleagues. Milner's opus 1, the cantata *Salutatio angelica*, was an auspicious debut in 1950. The composer won respect immediately, and curiosity grew about how his music would develop. *Salutatio angelica* was not actually innovative: it was of English stock; it admitted the unshackling of tonality; and its rhythms were no more—or less—sprung than Purcell's. Significantly, the overall impression of a sharply creative talent was not diminished by the absence of startling innovatory features. What became increasingly clear in the light of Milner's subsequent music were the convictions that had been shaped and tried before opus 1 was written. Milner knew at the outset of his journey what he wished to achieve—an entirely personal music entrenched in great traditions, and therefore drawing together unrelated elements by the fusion of his creative drive and mastery of the requisite techniques.

Two other early works for voices and instruments—*Improperia* and *The City of Desolation*—also share with *Salutatio angelica* a sense of drama. Not only is the composer's literary and liturgical understanding extraordinary, but his personal faith is rock-like. Words and music, therefore, are one, and penitence or joyful affirmation are powerfully characterized. While purely instrumental sections are sometimes used to change a mood, the grip of Milner's feeling through music is never in doubt.

And yet early maturity is risky for a composer. Milner's subsequent output has tackled larger forms—three symphonies up to 1986—and extended his use of pantonality (Milner's word for "enlarged tonality") without departing from the fundamentals upon which he launched his opus 1. That one fact provided some critics the word that can kill reputations—"conservative". It is rarely applied correctly, least of all in Milner's case. Always meticulous about the construction of basic material, Milner is then just as resourceful in development. Little can do much in a creative sense. Undeterred, then, Milner continued along the path he chose. His predilection for sets of variations provides some clue to his style. The first purely orchestral work, a set of variations on "Es ist ein Ros", has been the subject of several articles in the musical press. Both *Symphonies Nos 2* and *3* contain sets of variations.

The Second Symphony is for soloists, choir and orchestra. Milner's middle movement is cast as a passacaglia, or a set of variations on a ground bass, and—perhaps uniquely—introduces a tenor solo towards the end. The mood, set by a quotation from Virgil—"There are the tears of things"—is evident by the almost painful tread of the piece as a ground bass slowly unwinds to become the progenitor of melodic and rhythmic embellishment. The vocal line is independent, adding a further thread to the chromatic texture.

Milner wrote his Third Symphony to mark the centenary of the Royal College of Music. It is an abstract work concerned with music and structure, and without extra-musical programmes. The slow movement has six variations on a theme stretching over a two-octave compass, all to a slow crotchet beat. Derived patterns build excitement progressively and then relax into final repose. Milner is more a contrapuntist than a colourist, but in this movement gives much work to a full woodwind chorus, including cor anglais and bass clarinet.

A composer's technical facility is not the only issue at hand, however. No technical device can induce the quintessential emotion that transmutes organised sound into music. Some composers appear lax in technical disciplines and yet convey warmth through their music. A composer such as Milner cannot compose music that stems from his deepest feelings without a precise plan of action in which his humanly acquired skills are tested to the utmost. Milner's music is invariably intense, emotive, and sometimes supremely beautiful.

—Basil Ramsey

MIRZOYAN, Edvard (Mikhail). Armenian. Born in Gori, Georgian S.S.R., 12 May 1921. Educated at Komitas Conservatory, Yerevan (composition), 1935–41; Moscow Conservatory. Military service as infantryman, 1942. Married Elena M. Stepanian, 1 July 1951; 1 daughter and 1 son. Music teacher 1948–65, and professor of composition from 1965; Komitas Conservatory, Yerevan; Member, Communist Party, Soviet Union, since 1952; president, Union of Composers, Armenian S.S.R., from 1957; deputy, Supreme Soviet, Armenian S.S.R., 1959–90; secretary, Union of Soviet Composers, from 1962; member, central committee, Armenian Communist Party, 1964–90; people's deputy, Soviet Union, since 1989; deputy, Supreme Soviet, since 1990; president, Armenian Peace Fund. Recipient: Merited Artist, Armenian S.S.R., 1958; People's Artist, Armenian S.S.R., 1963; People's Artist, U.S.S.R., 1981. Mailing address: ul. Demirchyan 25, dom 9, Yerevan 375002, Armenia, U.S.S.R.

Publisher: none.

Symphonies/orchestral:

Symphonic Poem 1941; first performed Yerevan, 1942.
To the Heroes of War 1944; first performed Tiblisi, 1944.
Symphonic Dance 1945; first performed Yerevan, 1946.
Overture for Symphony Orchestra 1947; first performed Moscow, 1947.
Symphonic Poem 1956; first performed Yerevan, 1957.
Introduction and Perpetual Motion (violin, orchestra) 1957; first performed Yerevan, 1957.
Symphony (strings, timpani) 1962; first performed Yerevan, 1962.
Poem Epitaph for Aram Khatchaturian 1979; first performed Boston, 1988.

Chamber/instrumental:

Themes and Variations (string quartet) 1947; first performed Moscow, 1947.
Sonata (viola, fortepiano) 1967; first performed Moscow, 1967.
Poem (piano) 1970; first performed Yerevan, 1970.
Album for My Granddaughter (piano) 1983; first performed Moscow, 1984.

Vocal/choral:

Soviet Armenia (cantata) 1948; first performed Yerevan, 1948.
Holiday Cantata 1949; first performed Moscow, 1950.
Armenia (cantata) 1950; first performed Yerevan, 1950.
Cantata (collaboration with A. Haratunian; chorus, orchestra) 1950.
Lenin Cantata (collaboration with A. Haratunian; voices, orchestra) 1950.

Other:

Film scores (for Armenfilm): *When Friends Are Next to You*, 1956; *Missak Manouchian*, 1956; *Abval*, 1958; *Pink City*, 1960; *Twelve Satellites*, 1961; *Exile No 11*, 1961; *Difficult Passage*, 1963.

PUBLICATIONS

On Mirzoyan: Teresa Arazian, "EM", in *Heibedhrad*, 1963; Martarit Ter-Simonian, "EM", in *Sovetskaya kompozitor*, 1969.

* * *

Edvard Mirzoyan has combined artistic success with a life in public service to a degree rarely seen in the Western democracies. A member of the Communist Party since just after World War II, and a central committee member of the Party in Armenia, he has been successively a deputy in Armenia, a Soviet people's deputy, and, since 1990, a deputy in the Supreme Soviet of the U.S.S.R. He has in addition taught composition since 1948 at the Sogomon Komitas Conservatory in Yerevan, where he has helped to foster an increasingly influential generation of young Armenian composers.

Mirzoyan's own compositional career has inevitably been complicated by his pedagogical and administrative commitments, but he has nonetheless produced a significant body of work in a clean-limbed neo-classical style which is very much more compelling than the average Soviet standard of the period. Perhaps his finest work, the 1962 *Symphony* for string orchestra and timpani, is a beautifully constructed piece with the same major-minor modulations which Mirzoyan uses to such effect in his cantatas. By no means a programmatic work, it nonetheless breathes with the aspirations of the Armenian people and shows the marked independence of style that characterises the far from mechanical *moto perpetuo* of his exciting violin concerto, *Introduction and Perpetual Motion*.

Mirzoyan's fine *Lenin Cantata* was co-written with his colleague A. Haratunian. Far from being a hagiographical work, it restores the humanity to Vladimir Ilyich Ulyanov and gives a clearer sense than most Soviet works even of the post-XX Congress period of the reality behind the icons; it is clear from Mirzoyan's account that the reality remains impressive even without the careful stage-lighting and air-brushing. His two cantatas about Armenia are rather more personal in inspiration, and have some of the powerful nativist immediacy which was the heritage of Sogomon Komitas, the founding father of modern Armenian music.

Mirzoyan has also written a fine string quartet, some beautiful piano pieces, a fine threnody for Aram Khachaturian, and some highly effective film scores. Though now perhaps a little eclipsed by some of his younger successors, Mirzoyan remains a highly significant figure in post-war Armenian music.

—Oleg Karp

MIYOSHI, Akira. Japanese. Born in Tokyo, 10 January 1933. Educated: piano lessons at Jiyu-Gakuen children's piano group, age 3 to 6; private composition lessons under Tomojiro Ikenouchi, Kozaburo Hirai and Raymond Gallois-Montbrun, 1951–5; further study at Conservatoire National Supérieur de Musique, Paris (composition under Henri Challan, Raymond Gallois-Montbrun and Henri Dutilleux), 1955–7; Tokyo University (French literature), 1957–60.

Independent composer; instructor, Toho Gakuen School of Music, Tokyo, since 1965. Recipient: 1st prize (for *Sonata* for clarinet, bassoon, piano), Japan Music Competition, 1953; Odaka Prize (for *Sinfonia concertante*), 1954; Italia Prize (for *Ondine*) 1950. Mailing address: c/o ISCM, 31–9, 3 chome, Kasu-gacho, Nerima-ku, Tokyo 176, Japan.

Publishers: Kawai Gakufu; Ongaku-no-Tomo-Sha.

Symphonies/orchestral:

Sinfonia concertante (piano, orchestra) 1954.
Symphonic Mutations 1958.
Torse I (chamber orchestra) 1960.
Trois Mouvements symphoniques 1960.
Piano Concerto 1962.
Concerto for Orchestra 1964.
Violin Concerto 1965.
Odes métamorphosées (marimba, vibraphone, celeste, piano, harp, orchestra) 1968.
Concerto for Marimba and Strings 1969.
Ouverture de fête 1969.
Symphony 1971; unfinished.
Leos 1976.
Noesis 1978.

Chamber/instrumental:

Sonata (clarinet, bassoon, piano) 1953.
Sonata (violin, piano) 1955.
Sonata (piano) 1958.
String Quartet No 1 1962.
Conversation (marimba) 1962.
Torse III (marimba) 1964.
Etudes en forme sonate (piano) 1967.
String Quartet No 2 1967.
Huit Poèmes (flute ensemble) 1969.
Transit (percussion, keyboards, tape) 1970.
Hommage à "Musique de chambre '70" I (flute, violin, piano) 1970.
Hommage à "Musique de chambre '70" II (flute, violin, piano) 1971.
Torse IV (quartet of Japanese instruments, string quartet) 1972.
Hommage à "Musique de chambre '70" III (flute, violin, cello) 1972.
Prélude chaîne (piano) 1973.
Nocturne (flute, clarinet, double bass, marimba, percussion) 1973.
Torse V (3 marimbas) 1973.
Hommage à "Musique de chambre '70" IV (flute, violin, piano) 1974.
Litania (double bass, percussion) 1975.
Epitase (guitar) 1975.
Un Deuil (flute, violin, piano) 1976.
Concert étude (2 marimbas) 1977.

Vocal/choral:

Ondine (radiophonic music for voices) 1959.
Torse II (chorus, piano, tape) 1961.
En Blanc (soprano, piano) 1962.
Verre (soprano, piano) 1963.
Trois Occasions (male chorus, piano) 1963.
Duel (soprano, orchestra) 1964.
Saison d'enfants (unaccompanied chorus) 1965.
A Quatre Saisons (unaccompanied chorus) 1966.
Cinq Images enfantines (chorus, piano) 1968.
Requiem (chorus, large orchestra) 1972.
Mittsu no umi no uta / Three Songs of the Sea (unaccompanied chorus) 1974.
Kitsune no uta / The Fox's Song (unaccompanied chorus) 1975.
Henkakan'ei (6 choral groups) 1975.
Kyomon (children's chorus, orchestra) 1984.

* * *

Akira Miyoshi went to the Paris Conservatoire in 1955 to study with Gallois-Montbrun and Dutilleux. Although he received important impulses from Dutilleux Miyoshi later criticized his teacher for his formalism. Back in Japan in 1957 he composed a piano sonata and, in 1958, *Symphonic Mutations* for orchestra. A neo-classicist piece at the surface, its central note E—"mi" (like the composer's signature)—serves as the mirror axis of the gamut of sounds from which the thematic development is derived. The title of the piece already announces the main element of his personal style, which, as Miyoshi states himself, he formulated as his definitive musical grammar by 1960. Until then he had been searching for his own stand within the contemporary musical scene, which, as he believes, is true for most composers at the present time. He did not want to join with the avant-garde movements then popular, but he did not reject the use of some of their common techniques of composition. Processes of mutation, variation and development contribute to Miyoshi's composition style, which does not follow strict principles but might rather be compared to growth and proliferation in nature. *Three Symphonic Movements* for orchestra is a good example for Miyoshi's method of composition, evolving from seven basic cells. Presented by the low strings the first cell is complemented by nos. 2 and 3 in order to develop a slow three-part form in the first movement. The fast second movement uses no. 4 as its main idea. It is counterpointed by nos. 5 and 6, where nos. 4 and 6 are actually derived from 1, and 5 from a combination of 1 and 2. The third movement consists of variations on 7 (derived from 3) and the subsequent superimposition of 1 to 6. This mutational procedure is embedded in a refined, aesthetic musical language with roots in French music.

Miyoshi's First String Quartet came with a formalistic comment by its composer. The harmonic language resembles the consonant atonality of early Schoenberg. His Second String Quartet displayed a more modern language by accentuating the expressive moments with the extended use of dissonant intervals like sevenths and ninths.

After several concertante works (a piano concerto, a concerto for orchestra and a violin concerto) Miyoshi began composing around 1970 several choral works on socialist and pacifist texts. A symphonic project from that time remains unfinished.

His *Requiem* for chorus and large orchestra marked a change in his musical language which until then had been restricted to impressions of order and beauty. Miyoshi's music became more aggressive, and used unusual vocal techniques like *sprechgesang* and a massive apparatus of percussion instruments. In the same year he also introduced the use of traditional Japanese instruments. His preference for writing choral works continued with *Henkakan'ei* for six choral groups and *The Fox's Song* for children's choir, speaker and piano. The latter work continues the radical approach of *Requiem* by the use of clusters in the choir's part.

Miyoshi explicitly states that his style basically has not

changed since 1960; his more recent *Kyomon* for children's choir and orchestra uses the mutational technique as well.

—Rolf Klein

MONK, Meredith (Jane). American. Born in Lima, Peru, 20 November 1942. Piano lessons from age 3 under Gershon Konikow and Marcia Polis Kosinsky. Educated at Sarah Lawrence College, Bronxville, New York (under Meyer Kupferman, Pal Ukena and Bessie Schoenberg), B.A., 1964; studied voice under Vicki Starr, William Horn, John Devers, Jeanette Lovetri, Roland Wyatt, Ethel Raim and Gerald Siena; composition under Ruth Lloyd, Richard Averre and Glenn Mack; piano under Gershon Konikow. Composer, dancer, singer, performer, film-maker, stage director, performing debut New York City, 1964; formed interdisciplinary performance group The House, 1968; teacher Goddard College, Plainfield, Vermont, and New York University, 1970–2; formed Meredith Monk Vocal Ensemble, 1978. Recipient: Obie Awards, 1972 (for *Vessel*), 1976 (for *Quarry*), 1985 (for "sustained achievement"); Guggenheim Fellowships, 1972, 1982; Brandeis University Creative Award in dance, 1974; 1st prize (for *Education of the Girlchild*), Venice Biennale, 1975; Creative Artist Program Service Awards, 1977, 1982; Villager Award for Outstanding Production of the Year (for *Recent Ruins*), 1979; New York Dance Film Festival Merit Award (for *Sixteen Millimetre Earrings*), 1980; Best Recordings of the Year, German record critics, 1981 (for *Dolmen Music*), 1986 (for *Our Lady of Late: Vanguard Tapes*; Atlanta Film Festival Special Jury Prize (for *Ellis Island*), 1981; CINE Golden Eagle Award (for *Ellis Island*, 1981; Grand prize (for *Turtle Dreams [Waltz]*), Video Culture/ Canada Festival, Toronto, 1983; Bessie Award, 1985; New York Foundation for the Arts Fellowship Award in Music composition, 1985; National Music Theater Award, 1986; Sigma Iota Fellowship, MacDowell Colony, 1987; Rockefeller Foundation Distinguished Choreographer Award, 1987; MacDowell Colony Fellow, 1988; Doctor of Arts, Bard College, 1988; Doctor of Fine Arts, University of the Arts, Philadelphia, 1989. Mailing address: 228 West Broadway, New York, New York 10013; or (management) House Foundation for the Arts Inc., 131 Varick Street, Room 901, New York, New York 10013, U.S.A.

Publisher: self.

Works:

Break (theatre piece) 1964.
The Beach (theatre piece) 1965.
Sixteen Millimetre Earrings (voice, guitar) 1966.
Candy Bullets and Moon (collaboration with Don Preston; voice, electric organ, electric double bass, percussion) 1967.
Blueprint: Overload/Blueprint 2 (voice, Echoplex, tape) 1967.
Juice (cantata for 85 solo voices/85 Jew's harps, 2 violins) 1969; first performed New York City, 1979.
Drone for Chorus (60 voices) 1969.
Tour Dedicated to Dinosaurs (theatre piece) 1969.
Porch, Horizon (voice) 1969.
A Raw Recital (voice, electric organ) 1970.
Key: An Album of Invisible Theatre (voice, organ) 1970.
Needle-Brain Lloyd and the Systems Kid (150 solo voices, electric organ, flute, guitar) 1970.
Plainsong for Bill's Bojo (incidental music; electric organ) 1971.
Key (voice, vocal quartet, electric organ, Jew's harp, percussion) 1971.
Vessel (opera epic for 75 solo voices, electric organ, accordion, 2 dulcimers) 1971; first performed New York City, 1972.
Paris (from *Travelogue* trilogy: 2 solo voices, piano) 1972.
Our Lady of Late (voice, wine glass, optional percussion) 1972–3, percussion version arranged 1974. Recorded Wergo SM 1058 50; Minon 1001.
Education of the Girlchild (opera for 6 solo voices, electric organ, piano) 1972–3; first performed New York City, 1973. Recorded ("Biography", "Travelling", "The Tale") ECM 1197.
Chacon (from *Travelogue* trilogy: 25 voices, piano, percussion) 1974.
Anthology and Small Scroll (9 performers) 1974; first performed Amsterdam, 1974.
Fear and Loathing in Gotham (voice, piano) 1975.
Quarry (opera for 38 solo voices, 2 harmoniums, 2 soprano recorders, tape) 1976; first performed New York City, 1976.
Venice/Milan (from *Travelogue* trilogy: 15 solo voices, piano—4 hands) 1976.
Songs from the Hill (voices, pianos, recorder) 1976–7. Recorded Wergo SM 1022.
Tablet (4 solo voices, 2 soprano recorders, piano—4 hands) 1977. Recorded Wergo SM 1022.
The Plateau Series (5 solo voices, tape) 1978; first performed New York City, 1978.
Dolmen Music (6 solo voices, cello, percussion) 1979. Recorded ECM 1197.
Recent Ruins (12 voices, cello) 1979; first performed New York City, 1979.
Specimen Days (Civil War opera for 14 solo voices, 2 pianos, 2 electric organs) 1981; first performed New York City, 1981.
View No 1 (collaboration with Ping Chong; video score for voice, piano, synthesizer) 1981. Recorded ECM 23792.
Ellis Island (2 pianos; film score) 1981–2.
View No 2 (voice, synthesizer) 1982. Recorded ECM 23792
Tokyo Cha-Cha (6 solo voices, 2 electric organs) 1983.
Turtle Dreams (Waltz) (carabet for 4 solo voices, 2 electric organs) 1983. Recorded ECM 23792/1240.
The Games (collaboration with Ping Chong; 16 solo voices, synthesizers, electric keyboards, bagpipes, Flemish bagpipes, Chinese horn, Rauschpfeife) 1983.
Engine Steps (tape collage) 1983. Recorded ECM 23792.
Ester's Song (voice, ensemble) 1983. Recorded ECM 23792.
Two Men Walking (3 solo voices, electric organs) 1983.
Graduation Song (16 voices) 1984.
Panda Chant I (4 voices) 1984.
Panda Chant II (8 voices) 1984.
Book of Days (25 voices, synthesizer; also chamber version) 1985.
Window in 7's (For Nurit) (piano) 1986.
String (unaccompanied solo voice) 1986.
Double Fiesta (solo voice, 2 pianos) 1986.
I Don't Know (voice, piano) 1986.
Scared Song (solo voice, sysnthesizer, piano) 1986.
Do You Be (10 voices, 2 pianos, synthesizer, violin, bagpipes) 1987.

The Ringing Place (12 performers/9 voices) 1987; first performed as work-in-progress, New York City, 1987.
Duet Behaviour (2 voices) 1987.
Processional (piano, voice) 1988.
Parlour Games (2 pianos) 1988.
Cat Song (solo voice) 1988.
Raven (piano) 1988.
Light Wings (solo voice) 1988.
Fayum Music (voice, hammered dulcimer, double ocarina) 1988.
Book of Days (film score; 10 voices, cello, shawm, synthesizer, hammered dulcimer, bagpipe, hurdy-gurdy) 1988.
Facing North (devised with Robert Een; 2 performers) 1990.
Phantom Waltz (2 pianos) 1990.
Book of Days (recorded version: 12 voices, synthesizer, cello, bagpipe, hurdy-gurdy, piano, hammer dulcimer) 1990. Recorded ECM 1399.
Atlas (opera in 3 parts for 18 voices, 2 keyboards, clarinet, bass clarinet, sheng, bamboo sax, 2 violins, viola, 2 cellos, horn, percussion) 1991; first performed 22 February 1991.

PUBLICATIONS

By Monk: "Notes on the Voice", in Banes, *Terpsichore in Sneakers*, Boston, 1980.

On Monk: L. K. Telberg, "MM—Renaissance Woman", in *Musical Journal*, 37 (6), 1979; G. Sandow, "Invisible Theater: The Music of MM", in *The Musical Woman: An International Perspective, 1983*, edited by Zaimont, Westport, Connecticut, 1984.

* * *

At the heart of Meredith Monk's music is what she once described (apropos of *Book of Days*) as a "sense of displacement". Hers is an aesthetic reminiscent of Robert Ashley's but with a deeper focus. It is compounded (sometimes awkwardly) of American comics and fast-zapping multi-channelled television on the one hand and a deep interest in ancient cultures on the other. It is, outwardly at least, an improbable synthesis, but Monk has combined considerable popular success as a recording and concert artist with a reputation as one of the most rigorous and cerebral of the "downtown" avant-garde of late 1960s and 1970s New York.

That reputation is only partly justified. Rigorous she undoubtedly is. Perhaps only the late Cathy Berberian and Joan La Barbara among modern singers have been so wholeheartedly committed to the extension of vocal techniques and to creating a body of music which actualises them. Remarkably, she has achieved popular success without compromise; one might make a comparison with the equally talented Laurie Anderson, surprised into the commercial mainstream by the success of a 1982 single "O Superman". Thanks to a sympathetic contract with the German record label ECM, Monk has not been subjected to the same commercial pressures. It is quite wrong, though, to describe her work as "cerebral". Though early in her career she made a number of self-consciously avant-garde gestures, these were usually also ironic. At the heart of Monk's work is a deep concern with physicality, holistic cultural gestures, and, once again and centrally, movement.

She was born "on the road", while her mother, the popular singer Audrey Marsh, was touring Latin America. Monk has explored some of that background with typical obliqueness, and a characteristic absence of direct autobiographical reference, in the opera *Education of the Girlchild*, while works like the *Travelogue* series develop her interest in geographical as well as physical movement. Her educational background was in performing arts and Monk has sustained an interest in composition (though she is by no means a "pure" composer), radical choreography, theatre and film. Gesture and "body language" are extremely important to her music, which is harmonically minimal, usually dependent on very simple modal melodies or repetitive cells.

Its central thematic concern is a sense of history interpreted as the archaeology of sounds and gestures. An early film, *Ellis Island*, opens with a time-lapse sequence of sunrise-to-dusk on the Hudson River, and juxtaposes tourist commentary on the deserted island where European refugees were "processed" by American immigration officials with "silent" (but soundtracked) black and white dance sequences of the costumed immigrants' arrival in the present-day empty sheds. Objects—inanimate and human—are placed alongside rulers and calibrated surveying rods; static poses are juxtaposed with rapturous dances that combine flight with joy and release. The camera moves in a flat, uninflected security camera pan—left-pause-right-pause-left—which sometimes fails to catch a movement except fleetingly.

The calibration of human to non-human is one of the underlying themes of *Dolmen Music*, a work which has attracted mixed critical response. *Dolmen Music* attempts to reconstruct in sound the socialization of an ancient people. Over minimal cello tones and percussion, the voices explore the primitive definition of harmony (*harmos*) as a coming together. However slight its materials, it is a deeply moving work. At the opposite historical extreme, *The Games* has a more developed and self-consciously modernistic score. It is very much a parallel work, dramatising a people's attempt at reconstitution after a nuclear war; the very density of its musical material, and its dissonance, are an ironic index of how far human society has "progressed".

The later *Book of Days* begins with a similarly apocalyptic moment. The piece has been made as a film, and also recorded as a "vocal concerto" for the Meredith Monk Vocal Ensemble. The film version begins with the blasting of a modern wall and the discovery of a relatively intact medieval village. It then sequences back, using techniques reminiscent of *Ellis Island*, to the story of a young girl, Eva, who undergoes visionary trances in which she sees the products of 20th-century technology, a story-line reminiscent of Alan Garner's *Red Shift*. The instrumentation is a mixture of ancient hurdy-gurdies, dulcimers, pipes and modern synthesizers, and is usually dynamic and motoric for Monk.

In this it recalls some of the more direct passages in *Education of the Girlchild*, notably "Travelling" and "Biography". Monk's interplay of physical and musical movement invites comparison with modern innovations such as Laban-notation (in dance) and Zoltan Kodaly's gestural code for communicating music to deaf children. It is difficult—and undesirable—to discuss her music outside the context of her wider ambitions. These continue to develop into the later 1980s, confirming her status as one of the most important innovative artists in America.

—Brian Morton

MONTAGUE, Stephen (Rowley). American. Born in Syracuse, New York, 10 March 1943; resident in United Kingdom since 1974. Educated at St Petersburg Junior

College, Florida (piano, conducting and composition), A.A., 1963; Florida State University, Tallahassee (theory and composition under Richard Montague, John Boda and Carlisle Floyd), B.M., 1965, M.M., 1967; further study in conducting, Mozarteum, Salzburg, 1966; Ohio State University, Columbus (composition under Marshall Barnes, David Behrman, Herbert Brun and Wolf Rosenberg), D.M.A., 1972; further study in electronic music (Fulbright Fellow), Polish Radio electronic studio, 1972. Married Patricia Mattin, 10 May 1986. Teacher of music, Butler University, Indianapolis, 1967–9; moved to England, 1974; composer in residence, Strider Dance Company, 1974–5; freelance composer, from 1975; founding member, 1980, executive committee 1982–7, and concert director 1983–7, Electro-Acoustic Music Association of Great Britain. Recipient: Gulbenkian Award, 1979; Composers Bursary Award, 1980; Electro-Acoustic Music Award, 1986. Mailing address: 2 Ryland Road, London NW5 3EA; or (management) Magenta Music, 64 Highgate High Street, London N6 5HX, England.

Publishers: Edition Modern, Munich; Theodore Presser, New York; United Music Publishers, New York.

Symphonies/orchestral:

Argalus (youth orchestra) 1968; first performed Columbus, Ohio, 22 November 1971.
Voussoirs (large orchestra, antiphonal tapes) 1970–2; orchestral readings Columbus, Ohio, 1972.
Sound Round (orchestra, electronics) 1973.
At the White Edge of Phrygia (chamber orchestra) 1983; first performed London, 20 June 1983.
From the White Edge of Phrygia 1984; first performed Trossingen, Germany, 26 January 1989.
Prologue 1984; first performed London, 3 January 1985.
Piano Concerto (piano, chamber orchestra) 1988–91; first performed London, 11 June 1988.

Chamber/instrumental:

Christ lag in Todes banden (chamber ensemble) 1970; first performed Columbus, Ohio, 8 December 1970.
Eyes of Ambush (1–5 instruments or voices, digital delay) 1973; first performed Berlin, 18 May 1974.
Caccia (trombone, piano, pre-recorded tape, amplification) 1974; first performed Dartington, Devon, 7 July 1974.
Quiet Washes (3 trombones, 3 pianos or harps or prerecorded tapes) 1974; first performed Dartington, Devon, 7 July 1974.
Strummin' (piano strings, lighting, electronic tape) 1974, revised 1981; first performed Vienna, 2 November 1974.
Inundations I: Trio (3 amplified pianos, 12 pianists, electronics, tape) 1975; first performed Tampa, Florida, 11 January 1976.
Frozen Mirrors (piano, viola, percussion, electronics, tape) 1976; first performed Metz, Austria, 20 November 1976.
E pluribus unum (graphic score for any chamber group) 1976; first performed Holbaek, Denmark, 28 May 1978.
Paramell I (muted trombone, muted piano) 1977; first performed Basle, 7 February 1977. Recorded Lovely Music VR 2041.
Passim (piano, percussion, electronic tape) 1977; first performed London, 30 June 1977.
An "Old Man River" Rendition (trombone, piano, percussion) 1977; first performed Paris, 14 November 1977.
Paramell II: Entity (5 percussion, prepared piano) 1977; first performed Royan, 27 May 1977.
Quintet (graphic score for any instrument, 4-channel prerecorded tape) 1978; first performed London, 8 November 1982.
Trio (graphic score for any instrument, prerecorded stereo tape) 1978; first performed St Petersburg, Florida, 25 May 1978.
Paramell IV/a (tuba or bass trombone, tape) 1979; tuba version first performed Maine, 16 November 1979; bass trombone version first performed London, 5 December 1980.
Gravity's Rainbow (flute, live electronics, tape) 1980; first performed London, 20 June 1980.
Paramell III (piano, prerecorded cassette inside piano, audience hums a drone) 1981; first performed Cambridge, 8 December 1981.
Paramell V (2 pianos, arranged as *Va* for solo piano) 1981; first performed Buffalo, New York, 7 April 1984; solo version first performed Cambridge, 8 December 1981. Recorded (solo version) Lovely Music VR 2041.
Paramell VI (solo piano, flute, clarinet, cello or percussion) 1981; first performed Ohio, 5 April 1984.
Mouth of Anger (bass clarinet, piano, percussion, live electronics, electronic tape) 1981–3; first performed London, 7 December 1983.
Duo (graphic score for any instrument, tape) 1982; first performed Minneapolis, Minnesota, 18 January 1986.
Tongues of Fire (piano, live electronics, tape) 1983–90; first performed Cambridge, 28 October 1983.
Haiku (piano, digital delay, tape) 1987; first performed Cambridge, 26 February 1987.
C Etc. (cello) 1989; first performed Trossingen, Germany, 26 January 1990.
String Quartet: In Memoriam Barry Anderson and Tomasz Sikorski (with live electronics, tape) 1989–91; first performed London, 2 June 1989.
Behold a Pale Horse (organ) 1990–1; first performed Southampton, Hampshire, 20 October 1990.

Vocal/choral:

Three Iberian Sketches (soprano, piano; García Lorca) 1970; first performed Columbus, Ohio, 15 May 1973.
Varshavian Spring (SATB chorus, chamber orchestra) 1973, extended 1980; first performed Hilversum, 10 September 1977; extended version first performed Warsaw, 23 September 1980.
Introduction (vocal feedback, film, tape) 1976; first performed London, 12 December 1976.
Inundations II: Willow (soprano, piano, electronic tape) 1976; first performed Como, Italy, 28 August 1976.
Sotto voce (graphic score for multiphonic chorus, tape recorder, feedback system) 1976; first performed London, 23 April 1979.
Tigida pipa (4, 8, 12 or 16 amplified voices SATB playing woodblocks and claves, tape) 1983, revised 1989; first performed London, 19 February 1983.
Three Temperance Songs (female voice, flute, clarinet, alto saxophone, bassoon, percussion) 1988; first performed Miami, Florida, 8 December 1988.

Other:

A Presto Patch (electronic tape) 1973; first performed Warsaw, 10 January 1974.
Largo con moto (graphic score for dancer, tape; choreography by E. Karczag) 1975.

Criseyde (theatre piece for soprano playing ocarina, slide, tape; text by Chaucer) 1976; first performed Mexico City, 19 October 1976.
Into the Sun (dance by T. Gilbert; 4-channel tape, percussion, prepared piano) 1977; first performed Manchester, 31 October 1977.
Footfalls (dance by Maedee Dupres; tape) 1979; first performed London, 12 October 1979.
I, Giselle (dance by Fergus Early and Jacky Lansley; instruments, tape) 1980; first performed London, 15 March 1980.
Scythia (2-channel electronic tape) 1981; first performed California, 11 November 1984.
Splitter (dance by Maedee Dupres; tape) 1981; first performed Edinburgh, 21 August 1981.
Quartet (graphic score for 4-channel pre-recorded tape) 1982; first performed New York City, 19 April 1982.
Slow Dance on a Burial Ground (*musique concrète* for 2-channel tape) 1982–4; broadcast Belgian Radio, 6 November 1984. Recorded Lovely Music VR 2041.
Median (dance by Jennifer Jackson; consists of *Prologue* and *From the White Edge of Phrygia*) 1984; first performed London, 3 January 1985.
Gravity Is Proving Most Difficult (dance by Sue MacLennan; clarinet/bass clarinet, electronics, tape) 1984; first performed London, 8 August 1984.
The Montague Stomp (dance by Jennifer Jackson) 1984; first performed East Grinstead, Sussex, 10 September 1984.
The West of the Imagination (music for 6-part television series, PBS KERA-TV, Dallas, Texas) 1986.
The Tourist Guide (incidental music) 1986; first performed London, 17 April 1986.
Ceremony (18 dancers, tape) 1986; first performed Eastbourne, Sussex, 26 February 1986.
Bright Interiors (electronic music for Maurice Agis's inflatable sculpture *Colourspace*) 1989; first performed Linz, Austria, 13 September 1989.

PUBLICATIONS

By Montague: articles in *Classical Music*, *Contact* and other magazines and journals.

On Montague: Keith Potter, "A romantic minimalist", in *Classical Music*, London, 6 November 1982; O. Maxwell, "Rhythm Crazy", in *Time Out*, London, 18 February 1983.

* * *

It has been perceptively suggested that the work of Stephen Montague combines the repetitiousness of minimalism with the drama of Romantic music. On his own account, Montague had a more sheltered musical upbringing than most composers of his generation. His first teacher, Carlisle Floyd, wrote opera in the style of Puccini, quite uncynically and with some success; his next teacher was John Boda, a former pupil of Paul Hindemith. Yet around the beginning of the 1970s, as he prepared his doctorate at Ohio State University, Montague began experimenting with serial writing in pieces such as *Christ lag in Todes banden*. He then gravitated towards the dramatic, cluster-based idiom of which Krzysztof Penderecki is the best-known exponent. During a Fulbright Fellowship to Warsaw he composed the uncompromisingly over-scored *Voussoirs*.

This was already the apogee of his atonal work. In his time at Ohio State, Montague was introduced by David Behrman to minimalist music. It made no great impression, but in a festival in Warsaw, Montague heard *Dorian Winds* by Terry Riley, and, set alongside the prevalent heavy cluster compositions, its delicacy and immediacy was refreshing, and intoxicating.

The minimalist influence grew gradually in three successive pieces from 1973, *Varshavian Spring* (for chamber orchestra and chorus, revised 1980), *Sound Round* (orchestra and digital delay) and *Eyes of Ambush* (up to five voices). By *Paramell I* for muted trombone and muted piano (1977) the influence is both important and assimilated.

Montague began to take certain characteristics of minimalism, notably the repetition of motifs derived from scales, and give them shape and structure, and development and climax, the strengths of the 19th-century music he knew from his youth.

Alongside driving rhythms rest gentle colouristic effects, such as the stone shimmering on the piano strings in *Tongues of Fire*, and striking theatrical gestures. In the same piece, the player enters dressed in black, his rosined fingers exciting a length of fish-wire connected to a string in the piano, which thereby seems to ring of its own accord as a pale hand appears from nowhere. *Haiku* should be performed in low light, perhaps with soft blue illumination inside the piano, with "a feeling of ritual".

Montague frequently seeks the blending of timbres. For *Paramell VI* "the flute and cello should be 'inside' the piano sound to colour it", while *Tigida pipa* seeks a "subtle blend and ambiguity of what is live percussion and what is tape". Timbral blending, he insists, is no contradiction of another recurrent concern, for the spatial separation of sound sources (most obviously in *Sound Round*); only a dualism to be broken down.

Since the end of the 1980s, Montague has increasingly deployed clusters in a colouristic dialectic with modal, tonal and scalar materials, to especial effect in *Behold a Pale Horse* for organ solo and the string quartet of 1991.

Montague's music is energetic and direct, with a drive scarce in all musical epochs. Its strength partly resides on his insistence on writing music he would like to hear: music that tells a story. Were it not for the fact that he always wanted to compose, Montague once suggested, he would like to have been a novelist.

—David Revill

MONTSALVATGE (Bassols), Xavier. Spanish. Born in Gerona, 11 March 1912. Educated at Conservatorio Superior Municipal, Barcelona. Married Elena Pérez Fernández, 3 June 1947; 1 son and 1 daughter. Music critic, *La Vanguardia* newspaper, Barcelona, 1960–72; editor, *Destino* weekly newspaper, Barcelona, 1962–70. Recipient: corresponding member, Hispanic Society of America, 1985; Chevalier de l'Ordre des Arts et des Lettres, France, 1957; doctor honoris causa, Free University of Barcelona. Mailing address: c/o Peer Southern, 810 Seventh Avenue, New York, New York 10019, U.S.A.

Publishers: Peer Southern, New York; Union Musical Española, Carrera San Jerónimo 26, Madrid 28014, Spain; Real Musical, Carlos III no 1, Madrid 28013, Spain; Editions Salabert, Paris; Novello.

Symphonies/orchestral:

Concierto breve (piano, orchestra) 1952; first performed Barcelona, 1953. Recorded London FFRR CS 6990.
Partita 1958 1958; first performed Alicante, 1958.
Desintegración morfología de la chacona de Bach 1962; first performed Barcelona, 1962.
Laberinto 1970; first performed Granada, 1971.
Cinco invocaciones al Crucificado 1970.
Reflexus obertura 1974.
Serenade a Lydia de Cadaques (flute, orchestra; also earlier version for flute, piano) 1974.
Concerto capriccio (harp, orchestra) 1975; first performed Madrid, 1975.
Concertino 1 + 13 (violin, chamber string orchestra) 1975; first performed Barcelona, 1975.
Concerto del Albayzin (harpsichord, orchestra) 1977; first performed Granada, 1978.
Metamorfosis de concierto (guitar, orchestra) 1982; first performed Madrid, 1985.
Música per a un diumenge (band) 1984.
Fanfarría para la Alegría de la Paz 1985.
Sinfonía de requiem 1986; first performed Alicante, 1986. Recorded Discobi D 2006.

Chamber/instrumental:

Tres Divertimentos (piano) 1941; first performed Barcelona, 1941.
Cuarteto Indiano (string quartet) 1952; first performed Madrid, 1952.
Sonatine pour Yvette (piano) 1959; first performed Barcelona, 1960. Recorded London FFRR CS 6677.
Sef-parafrasis (clarinet, piano) 1968; first performed Madrid, 1969.
Serenata a Lydia de Cadaques (flute, piano; also version for flute, orchestra) 1969; first performed Cadaques, 1970.
Sonata concertante (cello, piano) 1972; first performed Toledo, 1972.
Aureola (organ) 1973.
Parafrasis concertante (violin, piano) 1975; first performed Barcelona, 1975.
Questions and Answers (brass quintet) 1979; first performed Barcelona, 1980.
Cuadrivio para tres Stradivarius (string trio) 1984; first performed Madrid, 1984.
Si, a Mompou (piano) 1984.
Fantasis para guitarra y arpa (guitar, harp) 1984; first performed New York City, 1984.
Trío (violin, cello, piano) 1987; first performed Madrid, 1988.
Alegoría a la memoria de Joaquín Turina (piano) 1988.
Tres obras para la mana izquierda (piano; "Si, a Mompou", "Berceause a la memoria de Oscar Espla", "Una pagina para Rubinstein") 1988; first performed Barcelona, 1989.

Vocal/choral:

Cinco canciones negras (soprano, piano or orchestra) 1945; first performed Barcelona, 1946.
Canciones para niños (soprano, piano) 1948; first performed Madrid, 1948.
Cant espiritual (mixed chorus, orchestra) 1959; first performed Barcelona, 1960.
Canco amorosa (voice, piano) 1964.
Deshecha de romance que cantaban los seraphines (voice, piano) 1964.
Habaneras de la Costa Brava (melodies with lyrics) 1964.
Cinco invocaciones al Crucifaldo (voice, piano) 1969; first performed Cuenca, 1969.
Homenaje a Manolo Hugue (soprano, orchestra) 1973; first performed Madrid, 1973.
Sum vermis (voice, 2 pianos, 2 percussion) 1974.
Soneto a Manuel de Falla (voice, piano) 1974.
Vocaliso (flute, piano) 1975.
Paisatge del Montseny (voice, piano) 1988.

Opera:

El gato con botas/Puss in Boots (magic opera) 1948; first performed Barcelona, 1948.
Una voce in off 1961; first performed Barcelona, 1962.

Other:

Film scores: *It Is Never Too Late*; *The Glass Prison*; *Rhapsody of Blood*; *Fifth District*; *A Glass of Whiskey*; *Diego Corrientes*; *The Suite of Gold*; *Cristina*; *Velazquez*; *Gaudi*; *The Love of Pleasures*; *Two Years of Vacation*; *Family Story*; *Spain Again*; *La vieja memoria*; *Luces y Somoras*.

PUBLICATIONS

By Montsalvatge: *Papeles Autobiográficos*, Barcelona, 1987.

On Montsalvatge: Enrique Franco, *XM*, Madrid, 1976.

* * *

Xavier Montsalvatge received his musical education at the Barcelona Conservatory, and he has spent much of his career in the Catalán capital, as a music critic and, later, as a teacher. His compositions in many respects typify the theatrical nationalistic tendencies prominent in the work of many 20th-century Spanish musicians. However, his style is deft and witty, exquisitely polished and usually of good taste, so that he rarely descends to the coarser approach of certain "international Spanish" musicians.

Catalonian composers of Montsalvatge's generation tended to receive an education in which the more solid values of late 19th-century Germany were given considerable emphasis. Another, slightly younger composer who built upon the solid technical grounding typical of this tradition to achieve a considerable international career is Carlos Surinach. Certainly, few Spanish musicians of this era were schooled in the radical *fin-de-siècle* ideals of Schoenberg and his followers which, before the rise of European Fascism in the late 1920s and 1930s, had produced potential serialist innovators from Spain, among whom Roberto Gerhard was outstanding. Montsalvatge has remained a tonal composer, though one who sometimes uses astringent dissonance after the manner of neo-classical Stravinsky or Les Six.

During the 1940s and 1950s, Montsalvatge attempted to break away from stereotyped Catalonian music by using an idiom which had been refined (one might more accurately say "refracted") through being exported from Spain to evolve into "West Indian" music. *Cinco canciones negras* comprise his outstanding work in this style. Subsequently, he was to extend his West Indian approach to a number of compositions which seek to view the world through the eyes of children. In the best of them, such as the magical opera, *El gato con botas*, Montsalvatge writes with an immediacy and lack of affectation which at times almost rivals the sublime artlessness with which Schumann and Mussorgsky have evoked childhood.

Montsalvatge's later music has moved away somewhat from this delicate, occasionally unworldly approach. Without abandoning his fundamentally tonal, though sometimes folk-inflected style, he has produced a selection of increasingly extrovert pieces. Sometimes, as in the opera *Una voce in off*, which has been compared with the work of Gian Carlo Menotti, he writes with characteristic Italian *brio*. In common with numerous other prominent modern Spanish musicians, he feels especially comfortable when writing for the piano: the redoubtable Alicia de Larrocha has consistently performed the *Concierto breve* (though it is neither particularly brief nor one of his more characterful works), but Montsalvatge's most successful keyboard work is *Sonatine pour Yvette*, written for his daughter in 1962. The *Sonatine* is no piece of Schumannesque whimsy, despite its subject matter: the character of a young girl is not very successfully portrayed on the whole, but the three movements are a memorable and extremely taxing essay in virtuoso pianism. In places, this music recalls Heitor Villa-Lobos, though its ultimate progenitor (peeping through unmistakably, for example, in the passages of sonorous "blind octaves") is Liszt.

—Paul Horner

MULDOWNEY, Dominic (John). British/English. Born in Southampton, Hampshire, 19 July 1952. Educated at Taunton's Grammar School, Southampton; University of Southampton (composition under Jonathan Harvey); private composition study under Harrison Birtwistle; University of York (composition under Bernard Rands and David Blake), 1971–4. Composer in residence, Southern Arts Association, 1974–6; music director, National Theatre, London, since 1976. Mailing address: c/o Faber Music, 3 Queen Square, London WCIN 3AU, England.

Publishers: Universal Edition; Faber.

Symphonies/orchestral:

Driftwood to the Flow (strings) 1972.
Three-Part Motet 1976.
Piano Concerto 1983; first performed London, 1983. Recorded EMI.
Saxophone Concerto 1984. Recorded EMI.
Sinfonietta (small orchestra) 1986.
Violin Concerto 1989–90.

Chamber/instrumental:

String Quartet No 1 1973.
Klavier-Hammer (1 or more pianos) 1973.
Music at Chartres (ensemble) 1974.
Lovemusic for Bathsheba Everdene and Gabriel Oak 1974.
Solo / Ensemble (sextet) 1974.
Perspectives 1975.
From Arcady I (violin) 1976.
From Arcady III (cor anglais, viola, cello) 1976.
From Arcady IV (4 oboes) 1977.
Double Helix (octet) 1977.
Five Melodies (saxophone quartet) 1978.
Garland of Chansons (6 oboes, 3 bassoons) 1978.
Three Hymns to Agape (3 oboes) 1978.
A First Show (percussion, tape) 1978.
From Arcady II (basset horn, tuba) 1978.
. . . In a Hall of Mirrors . . . (saxophone, piano) 1979.
A Little Piano Book 1979.
Piano Trio 1980.
String Quartet No 2 1980.
Six Chorale Preludes (flute/piccolo, oboe/cor anglais, clarinet, alto saxophone, trombone, harp, violin, viola, cello, tape) 1986.
Ars Subtillor (2 ensembles: alto/soprano saxophones, trumpet, horn, trombone, harp, percussion/2 conductors, 4-track tape) 1987; first performed London, 1987.
Paraphrase on Machaut's Hoquetus David (piano) 1987; first performed London, 1987.
Un Carnaval cubiste (4 trumpets/1 bass trumpet, horn, tuba, 4 trombones) 1989; first performed London, 11 September 1990.

Vocal/choral:

Bitter Lemons (unaccompanied chorus) 1970.
Cantata (voices, instruments) 1975.
Six Psalms (voices, instruments) 1979.
From "Little Gidding" (baritone, treble, piano; Eliot) 1980.
Five Theatre Poems (voice, piano or sextet; Brecht) 1980–1. Recorded (2 poems only) EMI EL 27 0049 1.
In Dark Times (4 voices, quintet; Brecht) 1981.
The Duration of Exile (voice, septet; Brecht) 1983.
A Second Show (voice, trio, tape) 1983.
The Duration of Exile (mezzo-soprano, flute, oboe, clarinet/alto saxophone, trombone, harp, violin, viola; Brecht) 1983.
A Second Show (contralto, harp, violin, alto saxophone, tape) 1983.
Maxims (baritone, treble, 2 flutes, 2 oboes, 2 clarinets, 2 bassoons, 2 horns, 2 trumpets, 2 trombones, harp, vibraphone, 2 violins, viola, cello, double bass; La Rochefoucauld) 1986.
Lonely Hearts (soprano, flute/piccolo, clarinet, alto saxophone, trumpet, trombone, 2 percussion, guitar/banjo, piano, harp, 2 violins, viola, double bass, with 2 conductors; newspaper personal columns) 1988; first performed London, 9 March 1989.
On Suicide (voice, ensemble) 1989; first performed London, 19 November 1989.
Songs from The Good Woman of Szechuan (voice, alto saxophone, piano; Brecht) 1990.
Songs from Out of the East (voices, piano; Fenton) 1990.

Other:

An Heavyweight Dirge (music theatre) 1971.
Da capo al fine (ballet; tape) 1975.
The Earl of Essex's Galliard (music theatre) 1975–6.
Macbeth (ballet; orchestra) 1979.
Baal Songs (after Brecht) 1981.
Carmen (ballet) 1984–5; first performed Edinburgh, 1985.
The Ginger Tree (music for BBC television series) 1989.

Erik Satie: *Sports et divertissements* (arranged for reciter, flute/piccolo, oboe, clarinet, horn, bassoon, violin, viola, double bass, piano) 1981.
Erik Satie: *Geneviève de Brabant* (arrangement of vocal score for voices, ensemble) 1989.

Film scores: *The Ploughman's Lunch*, 1983; *Betrayal*, 1984; *Nineteen Eighty-Four*, 1984.

PUBLICATIONS

On Muldowney: Paul Griffiths, (interview) in *New Sounds, New Personalities: British Composers of the 1980s*, London, 1985.

* * *

Before 1985 and the success of his *Piano Concerto* at the London Proms, Dominic Muldowney was best-known to a wider public for two very different scores: a set of *Baal* songs after Brecht for the rock singer David Bowie; and his moody score to the Ian McEwan film *The Ploughman's Lunch*. Writing incidental music for film, television and theatre (he has been musical director of the National Theatre, London since the mid 1970s) steered Muldowney toward a very direct, uncluttered musical language. His instrumental lines are very distinct and his song settings, mainly of Brecht, but also of La Rochefoucauld and the left-wing British poet James Fenton, have an axiomatic quality. This may have as much to do with his family's socialist background (and a presumable suspicion of avant-garde gestures) as with a general "return to tonality".

The question of Muldowney's tonal language is a key one. Though *The Ploughman's Lunch* is by no means his most important score, it is in many respects his most telling. As with the song-setting, it is unobtrusive, occasionally almost subliminal, but it is also deeply interwoven with the "text" of the film. Its apparent simplicities, and those of Muldowney's large-scale works, are constantly ironised by a harmonic idiom which seems to be continually self-estranging, and is in effect as disturbing as the most extreme atonal music, though far more subtly. The first movement of the *Saxophone Concerto*, which draws too on the populist associations of the solo instrument, depends very largely on deceptively simple modulations around C and on whole-tone progressions which have a outwardly crude abecedarian logic yet lead the listener into remarkable harmonic mazes.

The theme of *The Ploughman's Lunch* is the creation of an ersatz past (the title refers to a packaged bread-and-cheese lunch sold in British bars). Like Harrison Birtwistle and the poet Tony Harrison, who has also been associated with the National Theatre, Muldowney is concerned with the deconstruction and rehabilitation of a pastoral mode. This is evident in the early Hardy-inspired *Lovemusic* and in a number of later pieces. Muldowney's interest in melody—detectable in the number of pieces for wind instruments—is balanced by his remarkably complex juxtaposition of melodic lines and subtle placement of harmonic cruces. The *Arcady* sequence is the best example of his technique boiled down to essentials, romantically individual songs lent a highly ambiguous flavour. It is not emotionless music (the McEwan film was accused of moral anaesthesia) but nor is it expressionistic in the way Birtwistle's savagely inverted pastorals can seem to be.

What Muldowney and his former teacher share is a suspicion of *faux-naïf* simplicities. These are embodied not by Satie (whom both men have arranged very effectively) but of Satie's epigones. Muldowney's scores reveal very little of their own precompositional logic; they are to that extent quite enigmatic, somewhat like some of Ravel's more ambiguous pieces. The architecture of the three important concertos is purely a matter of perspective, shifting with the listeners' point of view. They are ultimately self-supporting pieces, in which the solo instruments play a deceiver's role suggesting ways out of an apparently navigable maze that seems to turn ever inwards upon itself.

Muldowney has not yet written an opera but has expressed an interest in a piece that would pose the question: why sing? His work always begins from a point of initial scepticism; it develops not towards a bland resolution but towards a more coherent contextualisation of that scepticism. Why do we hear certain intervals as right? Why do we hear certain "right" intervals as wrong in certain contexts? What do the gestures of the composer mean? Though not overtly a political composer (he has so far, intriguingly, avoided Brecht's overtly political verse) Muldowney's work and attitudes reflect a profound interest in the politics of new music.

—Brian Morton

MUMMA, Gordon. American. Born in Framingham, Massachusetts, 30 March 1935. Educated at University of Michigan, Ann Arbor, 1952–3; private study of composition, piano and horn. Co-founder, Co-operative Studio for Electronic Music, Ann Arbor, 1958–66; co-director, ONCE Festival/ONCE Group, Ann Arbor, 1960–6; research associate in acoustics and seismics, University of Michigan Institute of Science and Technology, Ann Arbor, 1962–3; composer and performing musician, Merce Cunningham Dance Company, New York City, 1966–74; composer and performing musician, Sonic Arts Union, New York City, since 1966; visiting lecturer in music, Brandeis University, Waltham, Massachusetts, 1966–7; visiting lecturer in music, State University of New York, Buffalo, Winter 1968; lecturer in music, University of Illinois, Urbana, 1969–70; consulting artist and engineer, Experiments in Art and Technology Inc, New York City, 1969–70; technical director, Intermedia Institute, American Foundation on Automation, New York, 1970; visiting lecturer in theatre arts, University of California, Berkeley, Summer 1971; composer-lecturer, New Music in New Hampshire, Chocorua, Summer 1973; lecturer in music, 1973–5, and professor of music, since 1975, University of California, Santa Cruz; visiting lecturer in theatre arts, Wesleyan University, Middletown, Connecticut, Summer 1974; visiting lecturer, Ferienkurse für Neue Musik, Darmstadt, Summer 1974; faculty member, Curso Latinoamericano de Musica Contemporanea, Buenos Aires, January 1975, January 1977, January 1981; Darius Milhaud Professorship, Mills College, Oakland, California, Autumn 1981; visiting professor of music, University of California, San Diego, Autumn 1985, and Winter and Spring 1987; distinguished visiting composer, Mills College, Oakland, Autumn 1989. Mailing address: Porter College, University of California, Santa Cruz, California 95064; or Artservices, 325 Spring Street, New York, New York 10013, U.S.A.

Publisher: Berandol.

Symphonies/orchestral:

Sinfonia (chamber orchestra, magnetic tape) 1958–60; first performed Ann Arbor, Michigan, 4 March 1961.

Le Corbusier (orchestra, organ, magnetic tape, cybersonic concertante) 1965; first performed Dallas, Texas, 13 February 1965.
Aleutian Displacement (chamber orchestra) 1987.

Chamber/instrumental:

Suite (piano) 1959.
Meanwhile, a Twopiece (percussion, tape) 1961.
A Quartet of Four Piece (4 instruments) 1962.
Gestures II (2 pianos) 1962.
Mographs (6 compositions for various combinations of pianos and pianists; consisting of *Large Size Mograph*, *Medium Size Mograph*, *Very Small Size Mograph*, *Small Size Mograph*, *Very Small Size Mograph*, *Medium Mograph* for tape) 1962–4; first performed Ann Arbor, Michigan, 16 February 1963.
Peasant Boy (piano trio) 1964. Recorded ESP 1009.
Horn (horn, cybersonic console) 1965. Recorded Aspen-4; Slowscan Editions 9.
Hornpipe (cybersonic horn, waldhorn) 1967; first performed Davis, California, December 1967. Recorded Mainstream MS 5010.
Beam (violin, viola, cybersonic modification, digital control) 1969; first performed Tokyo, 5 February 1969.
Schoolwork (cross-cut saw, psaltery, piano-melodica) 1970. Recorded Slowscan Editions 9.
Equale—Internal Tempi (3 double horns, 3 snare drums) 1975; first performed Oberlin, Ohio, 1975.
Equale: Zero Crossing (violin, flute, clarinet, saxophone, bassoon, cello, bandoneon) 1976; first performed San Francisco, 20 April 1976.
Eleven-Note Pieces and Decimal Passacaglia (harpsichord) 1978. Recorded Slowscan Editions 9.
Fwyn (bandoneon duo; collaboration with Pauline Oliveros) 1979. Recorded Lovely Communications VR-1092.
Octal Waltz (harpsichord retuned to 8-note equal temperament) 1980.
Los desaparacidos (electric clavichord) 1980.
Faisandange et Galimafree (multi-movement divertimento for trios of diverse instruments) 1984; first performed Santa Cruz, California, 10 June 1984. Recorded Opus One 129.
From the Sixpak Sonatas 1984.
Than Particle (percussion, digital computer) 1985; first performed Los Angeles, 7 November 1985.
Ménages à deux (violin, piano, vibraphone, marimba) 1989.

Electronic/other:

Retrospect (stereophonic electro-acoustical music on magnetic tape) 1962–82; first performed Santa Cruz, California, 6 October 1982. Recorded Slowscan Editions 9.
Five Short Films (soundtrack; collaboration with Robert Ashley, G. Manupelli) 1963.
Greys (film score; collaboration with D. Scaverda) 1963.
Megaton for Wm. Burroughs (performed electronic music for 10 electronic, acoustic and communication channels) 1963; first performed Ann Arbor, Michigan, 28 February 1964. Recorded Vital Records VR-1091.
Music for the Venezia Space Theatre (live-electronic) 1964; first performed Venice, 1 September 1964. Recorded Advance FGR-5; Lovely Music VR-1091.
The Dresden Interleaf: 13 February 1945 (quadrophonic electronic music on magnetic tape) 1965; first performed Ann Arbor, Michigan, 13 February 1965. Recorded JME-1; Vital Records VR-1091.
Mesa (live-electronic music for cybersonic bandoneon) 1966; first performed St Paul de Vence, France, 6 August 1966. Recorded CBS Odyssey 2316 10158; Lovely Communications VR 1092.
Diastasis, as in Beer (2 cybersonic guitars) 1967.
Conspiracy 8 (digital computer and performing musicians) 1970; first performed Massachusetts, 20 February 1970.
Communication in a Noisy Environment (cars, machines, instruments) 1970.
Ambivex (phantom myoelectrical telemetring system with pairs of performing appendages) 1971; broadcast Radio Bremen, 6 May 1972.
Telepos (dancers with telemetry belts and accelerometers) 1971; first performed New York City, 2 February 1972.
Cybersonic Cantilevers (cybersonic electronic system with public participation) 1973; first performed Syracuse, New York, 19 May 1973. Recorded (abridged) Folkways FTS-33904.
Some Voltage Drop (variable-duration theatre with electro-acoustical implementation) 1974; first performed Paris, 13 October 1974.
Passenger Pigeon 116–1976 (live performance cybersonic analog electronic music synthesizer) 1976; first performed Albany, New York, 3 February 1977.
Stressed Space Palindromes (quadrophonic electro-acoustical music on magnetic tape) 1976–82; first performed Santa Cruz, California, 24 April 1982.
Earheart (dancers, electronics; collaboration with Tom Robbins, J. McAuley, D. Cotter) 1977; first performed Portland, Oregon, 9 September 1977.
Echo-BCD (dancers, electronics; collaboration with J. McAuley) 1978; first performed Portland, Oregon, 15 October 1978. Recorded Slowscan Editions 9.
Pontpoint (tape) 1980; first performed Portland, Oregon, 14 March 1980. Recorded Lovely Communications VR 1092.
Epifont (spectral portrait in memoriam George Cacioppo; stereophonic electro-acoustical music on magnetic tape) 1984; first performed Ann Arbor, Michigan, 14 April 1985. Recorded Slowscan Editions 9.
Begault Meandown Sketches (electronic) 1987.
Obit (mouth percussion, Melanesian pidgin text) 1988; first performed Santa Cruz, California, June 1988.

Performer: Mauricio Kagel: *Improvisation ajoutée*, 1958, recorded CBS Odyssey 3216 0158; John Cage: *Solo for Voice*, 1960, recorded CBS Odyssey 3216 0156; David Behrman: *Wavetrain*, 1962, recorded Source 5; George Cacioppo: *Cassiopeia*, 1963, recorded Advance FGR-5; Robert Ashley: *The Wolfman*, 1964, recorded Source 5; Christian Wolff: *Burdocks*, 1970, recorded Wergo WER 60063.

Films/videotape/television: *Twenty Minutes from Now* (television), Michigan, 1963; *John Cage: Variations V*, broadcast Hamburg, 1966; *John Cage* (documentary film), Hamburg, 1966; *498 Third Avenue* (documentary film), broadcast Hamburg, 1967; *Place* (Merce Cunningham dance with Mumma's *Mesa*), broadcast Buffalo, New York, 8 March 1968; *Rainforest* (Merce Cunningham dance), broadcast New York, 21 April 1968; *Assemblage* (colour film of Merce Cunningham dance), broadcast San Francisco, 1968; *Wasserpfeifen in New York; Musikalische Avantgarde zwischen Ideologie und Elektronik* (colour film documentary), broadcast Cologne, 1971; *TV Rerun* (Merce Cunningham dance with Mumma's *Telepos*), broadcast Belgrade, 1972; *Sonic Arts Union* (colour film documentary, includes Mumma's *Some Voltage Drop*), broadcast France, October 1974; *Some Voltage Drop* (2-hour colour videotape), 1976.

Collaborations:

Talk 1 (with Robert Ashley, John Cage, Robert Rauschenberg and David Tudor); performed Ann Arbor, Michigan, 19 September 1965.
Reunion (with David Behrman, John Cage, Lowell Cross, Alexina Duchamp, Marcel Duchamp and David Tudor); performed Toronto, 5 March 1968.
Music of Conlon Nancarrow (with John Cage, Viola Farber, Peter Saul and David Tudor); performed New York City, 18 January 1969.
Conspiracy 8 (with Steven Smoliar); performed Cambridge, Massachusetts, 20 February 1970.
Communication in a Noisy Environment (with David Behrman, Anthony Braxton, Leroy Jenkins and Robert Watts); performed New York City, 20 November 1970.
Loops (with Charles Atlas, Merce Cunningham and Richard Nelson); performed New York City, 3 December 1971.
Real Electric Symphony (with Howard Moscwitz, Ronald Pellegrino and Olly Wilson); performed San Francisco, 12 December 1975.
Fwyynghn (with Beatrice Manley, Pauline Oliveros, Linda Montana, Louise Frazer, Bernard Bachelet and David Robertson); performed Valencia, California, 4 March 1980.
Red Transport (with Robert Ellis Dunn, Norvid Roos and dancers); performed Santa Cruz, 4–8 March 1983.
KhOROS (with Tandy Beal, Lou Harrison, Joanna Lande, Bobby McFerrin, Jon Scoville and John Beal); performed Santa Cruz, California, 17–19 June 1988.

PUBLICATIONS

By Mumma: "An Electronic Music Studio for the Independent Composer", in *Journal of the Audio Engineering Society*, July 1964; "How the Idea of Performance Is Changing", in *Selmer Bandwagon*, November 1965; "Technology in the Modern Arts: Music and Theatre", in *Chelsea*, May 1967; "Alvin Lucier's Music for a Solo Performer", in *Source 2*, 1967; "The ONCE Festival and How It Happened", in *Arts in Society*, 4(2), Summer 1967; "Four Sound Environments for Modern Dance", in *Impulse*, 1967; "The Magnetic Stencils of A.H. Frisch", in *Electronic Music Review*, 1968; "The *Studies for Player Piano* of Conlon Nancarrow", covernotes for Columbia recording CBS MS 7222, reprinted in *Desert Plants*, 1976; "Notes on Cybersonics: Artificial Intelligence in Live Musical Performance", originally published in Polish, 1970, republished in *Guildhall Music and Drama Annual*, 1974; "From Decade 6, Tour Process, Years 6–9", in *John Cage*, edited by Jacques Bekaert, Brussels, 1970; Sun(flower)burst" and "Sound Modifier Console", in *Pavilion*, 1973; "Home Canning—Responsibilities in an Electronic Age", in *Electronic Music: A Listener's Guide*, edited by Elliott Schwartz, New York, 1973; "Witchcraft, Cybersonics and Folkloric Virtuosity", in *Darmstadter Beitrage für Neue Musik*, 1974; "Live Electronic Music", in *The Development and Practice of Electronic Music*, edited by Appleton and Perera, New Jersey, 1974; " . . . from where the circus went . . . ", in *Merce Cunningham*, edited by James Klosty, New York, 1975; "Briefly About Nancarrow", in *Conlon Nancarrow: Studies for Player Piano*, edited by Peter Garland, Berkeley, California, 1977; "Creative Aspects of Live Electronic Music Technology", in *Papers of 33rd National Convention Audio Engineering Society*, October 1977; "Five Composers' Views" (co-author), in *An Ives Celebration: Papers of the Charles Ives Centennial*, edited by H.W. Hitchcock and V. Perlis, Urbana, Illinois, 1977; "Electronic Resources in the Music of Roger Reynolds" (co-authored with Gilbert Chase, Andrew Porter, Ben Johnston and Harvey Sollberger), in *Roger Reynolds: Profile of a Composer*, San Diego, California, 1986; "Sound Recording in the United States", in *The New Grove Dictionary of American Music*, London and New York, 1986; "Recording" (co-author with Barney Kernfeld and Chris Sheridan), in *The New Grove Dictionary of Jazz*, London, 1989.

On Mumma: Michael Nyman, in *Experimental Music*, London, 1974; Joseph Mazo, in *Prime Movers: The Makers of Modern Dance in America*, New York, 1977; B. Schrader, in *Introduction to Electro-Acoustic Music*, Englewood Cliffs, New Jersey, 1981.

* * *

The special talent of Gordon Mumma is his ability to rethink. This can be seen in the electronic works which constitute a good part of his output. He has composed not only for tape, but also by creating circuits for sound creation and manipulation; and in doing so he has explored areas of electronic music which lie outside the usual concern with control, predictability and precision.

Mumma is interested, too, in the creative possibilities of the performance aspect of music. Much of his music can be seen as an exploration of different balances which can be struck between the tendency of electronic music towards fixity, and an emphasis on the variability of live performance.

Several works attempt to combine tape with live performers. *Peasant Boy* matches tape with a jazz band—originally a trio led by pianist-composer Bob James—who imitate the tape sounds. However, interaction of tape and band is one-way, resulting in rather stilted integration.

Mumma's innovative solution was to eliminate prerecorded tape, creating pieces with various live electronic elements. Important here is what he calls cybersonic equipment, which he first developed with William Ribbens. The word derives from the Greek *kybernan* (to steer or guide), the same root as for "cybernetics", thereby implying the interaction of automatic and volitional action. Mumma's equipment features flexible electronic circuitry which responds to, modifies and interrelates a variety of sound sources—live instrumental, ambient and electronically-produced sound and their various transformations.

Diastasis, as in Beer is scored for two cybersonic guitars. *Mesa* employs a cybersonic bandoneon (an accordion-like instrument). Ring modulation produces chordal formations, and the resulting non-harmonic partials yield complex harmonic spectra. The circuitry is controlled from a box slung around the player's neck, so he or she can change settings while playing.

Mumma also attempted to highlight the performance situation by arranging performance movements almost choreographically. In *Gestures II* for two pianos, or *Meanwhile, a Twopiece*, performance indications concern only the movements to be made by the players, and cues to move between instruments at certain points. Mumma explained that the theatrical and improvisatory character of *Meanwhile* . . . was a response to the loss of these elements in "canned" music.

The performer's movement could also be used to link directly live and electronic elements. *Beam*, first performed in Tokyo in February 1969, equips a violin and a viola player with electronic sensors on their bow-arm sleeves. Each movement is translated into pulses of different rates which determine the electronic modification of the instrumental sound and digitalised display of the score.

Another performance variable which Mumma exploited is the acoustics of the performance space. *Hornpipe* marries cybersonic equipment with a French horn equipped with a double reed mouthpiece. The horn slides are also rearranged so the sound will be heared from different parts of the instrument. The settings adjust according to the interplay between the resonances of the performance space and the horn sounds setting them off. An integral part of the music is thus the unique character of the place where it is played. In turn, the player learns which sounds will unbalance and which will rebalance the cybersonics.

In more recent work, Mumma has reproduced this function synthetically. The *Stressed Space Palindromes* use custom-built doppler-shift circuitry to simulate a room whose resonant characteristics rapidly change size and shape.

One further performance resource is the audience. In *Cybersonic Cantilevers*, it becomes the source of control information. Members are invited to bring their own sound, live or recorded, to a control station. Each is equipped with a microphone, an oscilloscope and headphones, and is connected to a central processing system which transforms the input. This is simultaneously recorded, monitored over headphones and broadcast over speakers. Recorded transformations can be recycled later as source material. *Cybersonic Cantilevers* is not a performance by performers, but rather a process by participants. Mumma maximises the ability to influence, but minimises the chance to control.

Designing circuits is the way to discovery for himself and for listeners, a precarious balance between what is known and unknown, with unpredictable results and unexpected hints for future work.

With *Conspiracy 8*, Mumma began to explore the possibilities of the computer as a performance instrument, leading most recently to *Than Particle* for percussion linked with a commercially available computer synthesis system.

Sometimes Mumma's exploration is on an epic scale—as in *Communication in a Noisy Environment*, his 1970 concert for cars, machines and instruments; sometimes it is macrocosmic, such as the 1987 *Begault Meandown Sketches*, derived entirely from one short sound.

His more recent instrumental pieces have cited classical form—*From the Sixpak Sonatas*, the divertimento *Faisandange et Galimafree*, and the *Octal Waltz*, in which the harpsichord is retuned to eight-note equal temperament. *Eleven-Note Pieces and Decimal Passacaglia* was written for Baroque keyboard (ideally harpsichord). Its musical procedures relate to those of the Baroque, but with a 20th-century statistical approach to pitch distribution.

Mumma is that most American character, a workshop composer, an artisan who sets up a situation in order to explore what will happen; an especially clear instance, since composing for Mumma is often the invention of circuits, and the score, as Michael Nyman has suggested, may be nothing more nor less than a circuit diagram.

—David Revill

MURAIL, Tristan. French. Born in Le Havre, 11 March 1947. Educated at Conservatoire Normale Supérieur de Musique, Paris (composition under Olivier Messiaen) 1969–72; further study, Villa Medicis, Rome, 1971–3; further study in computer, IRCAM, Paris, 1981–2. Ondes martenot performing and recording soloist; co-founder (with Gérard Grisey and Michael Levinas), Groupe de l'Intinéraire, 1973; composition courses, Ferienkurse für Neue Musik, Darmstadt, 1980–2, Avignon, 1988, Fontainebleau, 1989, and Royaumont, 1991; teacher of computer-aided composition, Conservatoire de Paris, and at IRCAM, 1990. Recipient: 1st prize for composition, Conservatoire de Paris, 1970; Prix de Rome, 1970. Mailing address: 37 passage le Breton, 93170 Bagnolet, France.

Publisher: Salabert.

Symphonies/orchestral:

Couleur de mer (chamber orchestra) 1969; first performed Le Havre, 13 May 1969.
Altitude 8000 1970; first performed Paris, 18 January 1971.
Au delà du mur du son 1972; first performed Rome, 10 June 1972.
Cosmos privé 1973; first performed Rome, 30 June 1973.
La Dérive des continents (viola, string orchestra) 1973; first performed Royan, 23 March 1974.
Sables 1974; first performed Royan, 22 March 1975.
Les Courants de l'espace (ondes martenot, small orchestra) 1979; first performed Paris, 20 December 1980.
Gondwana 1980; first performed Darmstadt, 21 July 1980. Recorded Salabert Trajectoires SCD 8902.
Sillages 1985, revised for small orchestra 1990; first performed Kyoto, 9 September 1985.
Time and Again 1985; first performed Birmingham, 21 January 1986. Recorded Salabert Trajectoires SCD 8902.
De Terre et de ciel (from *Les Sept Paroles du Christ en croix*) 1986.

Chamber/instrumental:

Où tremblent les contours (2 violas) 1970.
Estuaire (piano) 1971.
Ligne de non-retour (flute/piccolo, clarinet, harp, electric guitar, percussion, viola, double bass) 1971; first performed Paris, 30 September 1971.
Les Miroirs étendus (ondes martenot, piano) 1971.
Mach 2.5 (2 ondes martenot) 1971.
L'Attente (flute, clarinet, harp, 2 violins, viola, cello) 1972; first performed Paris, 1972.
Les Nuages à Magellan (2 ondes martenot, electric guitar, percussion) 1973; first performed Orléans, 23 March 1973.
Tigres de verre (ondes martenot, piano) 1974.
Transahara Express (bassoon, piano) 1974.
C'est un jardin secret, ma soeur, ma fiancée, une fontaine close, une source scellée (viola) 1976; first performed Lisbon, 1978. Recorded Sappho 33T/002.
Mémoire-érosion (solo horn, flute/alto flute, oboe/cor anglais, clarinet/bass clarinet, bassoon, 2 violins, viola, cello, double bass) 1976; first performed Orléans, 5 March 1976. Recorded Sappho 33T/002.
Territoires de l'oubli (piano) 1977; first performed Rome, 22 May 1978.
Tellur (guitar) 1977; first performed Paris, 26 April 1977.
Treize Couleurs du soleil couchant (flute, clarinet, violin, cello, piano, sound projection) 1978; first performed Madrid, 4 December 1979. Recorded Salabert Actuels SCD 8801.
Ethers (flute/piccolo/alto flute/bass flute, with trombone, violin, viola, cello, double bass, maracas) 1978; first

performed Lisbon, 1978. Recorded Sappho 33T/002.
La Conquête de l'Antarctique (ondes martenot) 1982; first performed Paris, 2 March 1984.
Désintégrations (2 flutes/piccolo/alto flute, oboe/cor anglais, 2 clarinets/bass clarinet, bassoon/contrabassoon, horn, trumpet, trombone, 2 percussion, piano, 2 violins, viola, cello, double bass, tape) 1983; first performed Paris, 15 February 1983. Recorded Salabert Trajectoires SCD 8902.
Atlantys (from *Random Access Memory*; version for 2 DX7 synthesizers) 1984.
Vampyr! (from *Random Access Memory*; electric guitar) 1984.
Vision de la cité interdite (from *Random Access Memory*; version for 2 DX7 synthesizers) 1984.
Random Access Memory (electric guitars, percussion, synthesizers, computers; consists of *Le Réveil des machines*, *Sept Degrés du sommeil*, *Atlantys*, *Malédiction*, *Orchestres imaginaires*, *Vampyr!*, *Souffles des éléments*, *Vision de la cité interdite*, *Une Depression dans le continuum*) 1984–7; parts 2, 3, 6, 8 and 9 first performed Metz, 4 October 1984; parts 1, 4, 5 and 7 first performed Helsinki, 8 July 1987.
Vues aeriennes (piano quartet) 1988.
Allégories (flute/piccolo, clarinet, horn, percussion, violin, cello, computers/sound projection) 1989; first performed Brussels, 26 March 1990.
Le Fou à pattes bleues (flutes, piano) 1990.

Vocal/choral:

Les Sept Paroles du Christ en croix (chorus, orchestra; parts may be performed separately) 1986–9; first performed London, 28 October 1989.
Les Sept Paroles (from *Les Sept Paroles du Christ en croix*; chorus, orchestra) 1988–9.

PUBLICATIONS

By Murail: "La Révolution des sons complexes", in *Darmstadter Beitrage*, 80, 1984; "Spectres et lutins", in *Darmstadter Beitrage*, 82, 1984, as "Spectra and Pixies", in *Contemporary Music Review*, 1(1), 1984.

On Murail: Eric Humbertclaude, "Les Modèles perceptuels par simulations instrumentales dans les oeuvres de TM", in *Dissonanz: La Nouvelle Revue Musicale Suisse*, 13, August 1987; various, "Dossier Grisey-Murail", *Revue Entretemps*, 8, 1989.

* * *

Le Groupe de l'Itinéraire, and Tristan Murail in particular, have been credited with the invention and propogation of a new tendency in European music, known as "Spectral music". Crudely speaking, this type of composing takes as its base material the acoustical properties of sounds (or sound "spectra"). These are used as models for large- and small-scale forms, and provide all the harmonic material. As the forms arise directly out of the evolution of the sounds, the distinction between materials and form, between substance and structure, is annulled—they are aspects of the same phenomenon.

This thinking became predominant in Murail's music from 1977 onwards; his earlier works did not display such characteristics, but they do differ markedly from most other French music of the period in their preference for continuously evolving textures, a rich harmonic and instrumental structure, and a persistent use of consonant intervals such as octaves (as in *Altitude 8000* and *Au delà du mur du son*, both for orchestra).

An encounter with the music of the elderly Italian composer Giacinto Scelsi proved a decisive influence on Murail's work; Scelsi's radically static music, focussing upon narrow pitch-bands (often single notes or octaves), its emphasis upon timbre for its own sake, its frequent use of microtones, confirmed Murail's nascent compositional inclinations and led him to question the bases of his art. In the music and theories of his contemporary Gérard Grisey, Murail found a more systematic exploration of similar ideas; Grisey's theories on musical time and psycho-acoustics had a profound effect on Murail, and for a period he and Grisey enjoyed a close exchange of compositional thought which led to a certain degree of stylistic kinship, while the personality of each remained intact.

In his orchestral piece *Sables*, the structure is articulated by recurring harmonic spectra, somewhat as in Grisey's *Périodes* from the same year, but the extreme smoothness of the music and its richly varied harmony are wholly Murail's own. In *Mémoire-érosion* for horn and nine instruments, the structure and details derive from an instrumental simulation of the studio "reinjection loop" technique, in which a live sound is recorded and replayed by being fed through successive tape recorders. In Murail's piece, every note played by the horn is echoed by the ensemble after constantly varying time-delays, which gives the music a constantly fluctuating regularity. Murail also simulates the distortion a repeatedly copied sound undergoes in the "reinjection loop", and the accumulating tape hiss; thus the instrumental material constantly deforms the horn's music, pushing it towards noise and eventually destroying it.

Similar processes of imitation and distortion are found in *Ethers* and *Les Courants de l'espace* but in these works the processes are more complex. In *Ethers*, the flautist sings one note into the instrument while playing another, producing a chord built from the sums and differences of the two notes. In *Les Courants*, the ondes martenot is ring-modulated, which results in a similar complex of sum and difference frequencies. In both cases, the sounds are somewhere between harmony and timbre, an area of ambiguity which especially fascinates Murail and is a feature in much of his music. In order to render such phenomena effectively on acoustical instruments, Murail has abandoned equal temperament in favour of a variety of more exact microtonal approximations of the frequencies (in many of his more recent orchestral works, some of the wind instruments are tuned down a quarter-tone).

Toward the end of the 1970s, Murail composed a sequence of radical works, including those mentioned above, concentrating exclusively upon continuously evolving processes—every element in the music is unstable and constantly mutating. The temporal structure of these works is built upon sliding patterns of perpetual acceleration and deceleration; this in turn is bound up with the evolution of the material—an acceleration may pulverise a slow pulsation into a dense, grainy continuum of sound, while a deceleration may enlarge a single sound into an entire paragraph of music (as at the end of *Les Courants de l'espace*). This sequence of pieces, which includes the piano work *Territoires de l'oubli*, the guitar piece *Tellur*, and the piano quintet *Treize Couleurs du soleil couchant*, culminated in the large orchestral work *Gondwana*, composed for the Darmstadt Summer Courses where Murail was teaching that year. In this piece the harmony is derived from frequency modulation, a technique more commonly associated with computer music, resulting in rich, untempered harmony with a bell-like quality (the technique is often used in digital studios to simulate bell sounds) deployed in a complex structure of greater subtlety and breadth of invention than any Murail had previously composed.

When his next work *Désintégrations*, an IRCAM commission, emerged, a change of direction became apparent. The processes are still present, as are the sliding tempos, but they are placed in a more unpredictable, volatile environment. The piece is scored for ensemble and computer-generated tape; the raw material of each of the work's 11 sections is a different instrumental spectrum. Many spectra were analysed by the computer; the resultant information was treated as the source of the sounds on tape and the instrumental harmony—thus, although the computer does not "imitate" instrumental sounds, an organic link between tape and ensemble is established such that the two fuse and mingle imperceptibly. Each section proceeds to or from a given spectrum, moving between harmonic and inharmonic timbres, but in a more compressed manner than in the earlier music, and silence begins to play a role in the discourse (there is no silence in any Murail work from 1983 to 1991). These new tendencies are confirmed in two subsequent orchestral pieces, *Sillages* and *Time and Again*. Speaking of the latter, Murail says he sought "a more ambiguous architecture of time than in previous works . . . a time rich in flashbacks, premonitions, loops." Elements from past sections return to interrupt the flow of later music, long transformations are abbreviated or distorted, predictable patterns are set up merely to be destroyed. The harmony is still derived from frequency modulation, to which is added a variety of other procedures, including spectral distortion, by which a spectrum can be stretched or distorted in many ways. The notion of stretching and distortion is central to *Vues aeriennes*, written in 1988 for the Nash Ensemble; scored for piano quartet, this consists of the same process heard four times in succession—each version of the process subjects the rhythms and frequencies of the music to a different degree of distortion, with the "original", undistorted process being heard only three-quarters of the way through. A similar process of distortion, of a single harmonic spectrum, is involved in another recent chamber piece *Allégories*, while all of these procedures are applied on the largest scale in the oratorio *Les Sept Paroles du Christ en croix*. The interest of this work, aside from the forceful, almost expressionistic character of some passages, lies in the word-setting and the extra-musical considerations it entails. Processes hitherto of a purely abstract nature, such as spectral distortion, acceleration or deceleration and patterns of accumulation or dispersal, acquire an added dimension through being associated with specific images in the text. The success of this first venture into operatic writing may prove significant for the stage work Murail, by now one of the most influential composers of his generation, is currently contemplating.

—Julian Anderson

MUSGRAVE, Thea. British/Scottish. Born in Barnton, Edinburgh, 27 May 1928. Educated at Moreton Hall, Shropshire; University of Edinburgh (initially in medical faculty), 1947; B.Mus., 1950; private lessons in harmony, counterpoint, music history, composition with Hans Gal, Mary Grierson and Sidney Newman; Boucher Scholar, 1950; Conservatoire National Supérieur de Musique, Paris (with Nadia Boulanger and Aaron Copland), 1950–4. Married violist Peter Mark in 1971. Teacher, Dartington Summer School, Devon, from 1954; coach/pianist, Saltire Singers, from 1954; lecturer, extra-mural department, University of London, 1958–65; scholarship, Tanglewood Summer School, Massachusetts, 1959; visited U.S.S.R. as delegate of Composers' Guild of Great Britain, 1961; visiting professor, University of California, Santa Barbara, 1970; emigrated to the United States, 1973; distinguished professor, Queen's College, City University, New York, 1987. Member, BBC Central Music Advisory Panel, Music Panel for Arts Council of Great Britain, Committee of Awards, Commonwealth Fund of New York, Opera-Music Theatre Panel, and National Endowment for the Arts. Recipient: Boucher Scholarship, 1950; Donald Francis Tovey Prize, 1950; Lili Boulanger Memorial Prize, 1952; Koussevitzky Award, 1972; Guggenheim Fellowship, 1974–5, 1982–3; Hon D.Mus., Council for National Academic Awards, 1976; D.Mus., Smith College, 1979; D.Mus., Old Dominion University, 1980. Mailing address: c/o Virginia Opera Association, P.O. Box 625, Norfolk, Virginia 23501, U.S.A.

Publisher: Novello.

Symphonies/orchestral:

Divertimento (strings) 1957; first performed Edinburgh, 1 September 1957; withdrawn.
Obliques 1958; first broadcast BBC, 8 January 1959.
Perspectives 1961; first performed Stirling, 21 May 1961.
Sinfonia 1963; first performed Cheltenham, Gloucestershire, 3 July 1963.
Festival Overture 1965; first performed Glasgow, 18 September 1965.
Nocturnes and Arias 1966; first performed Zurich, 3 November 1968.
Concerto for Orchestra 1967; first performed London, 8 March 1968. Recorded Decca HEAD 8.
Clarinet Concerto 1968; first performed London, 5 February 1969. Recorded Argo ZRG 726.
Night Music 1969; first performed Cardiff, 24–26 October 1969. Recorded Argo ZRG 702.
Scottish Dance Suite (concert band) 1969; first performed Glasgow, 17 August 1961. Recorded Schirmer cassette 1–7/8.
Memento vitae (homage to Beethoven) 1969–70; first performed Glasgow, 22 March 1970.
Horn Concerto 1971; first performed Glasgow, 1 May 1971. Recorded Decca HEAD 8.
Viola Concerto 1973; first performed London, 13 August 1973.
Orfeo II (flute, 15 strings; based on version for flute and tape) 1975; first performed Pasadena, California, 28 March 1976.
Soliloquy II & III (guitar and strings) 1980.
From One to Another (viola, 15 strings; based on version for viola and tape) 1980; first performed Minneapolis, Minnesota, 17 March 1982.
Peripeteia 1981; first performed London, 2 November 1981.
The Seasons 1988; first performed London, 1988.

Chamber/instrumental:

Piano Sonata in E (No 1) 1951, 1954; first performed London, 4 July 1976.
Piano Sonata No 2 1956; first performed Cheltenham, Gloucestershire, 15 July 1956.
Prelude (organ) 1956; first performed London, 24 March 1956.
String Quintet 1958; first performed Glasgow, 23 April 1958.

Colloquy (violin, piano) 1960; first performed Cheltenham, Gloucestershire, 12 July 1960. Recorded Argo ZRG 5328.
Trio for Flute, Oboe and Piano 1960; first performed London, 8 January 1961. Recorded Delta SDED 18005.
Monologue (piano) 1960; first performed London, 12 December 1960. Recorded Argo ZRG 704.
Serenade (flute, clarinet, harp, viola, cello) 1961; first performed London, 14 March 1962.
Chamber Concerto No 1 (9 instruments) 1962; first performed Glasgow, 26 April 1962.
Chamber Concerto No 2 (flute/piccolo/alto flute, clarinet/bass clarinet, violin/viola, cello, piano) 1966; first performed Dartington, Devon, 5 August 1966. Recorded Delos DEL-25405.
Chamber Concerto No 3 (clarinet, bassoon, string quintet) 1966; first performed London, 16 October 1967.
Music for Horn and Piano 1967; first performed Zagreb, 13 May 1967. Recorded Music Heritage Society MHS 3547.
Impromptu No 1 (flute, oboe) 1967; first performed London, 10 April 1967. Recorded Douglas Whittaker Memorial Record DW1.
Soliloquy I (guitar, tape) 1969; first performed London, 15 March 1972. Recorded Deutsche Grammophon DGG 2530 079.
Elegy (viola, cello) 1970; first performed Goleta, California, 19 May 1970.
From One to Another (viola, tape) 1970; first performed Los Angeles, 30 November 1970.
Impromptu No 2 (flute, oboe, clarinet) 1970; first performed Cardiff, 16 November 1971.
Space Play (flute, oboe, clarinet, horn, bassoon, violin, viola, cello, bass) 1974; first performed London, 11 October 1974.
Orfeo I (flute, tape) 1975; first performed Chichester, Sussex, 4 July 1976.
Fanfare (brass quintet) 1982; first performed Norfolk, Virginia, 3 December 1982.
Pierrot 1985.
The Golden Echo I (horn, tape) 1986.
The Golden Echo II (solo horn, 16 horns) 1986.
Narcissus (solo flute, digital delay system) 1987.
Niobe (oboe, tape) 1987.

Vocal/choral:

Two Songs (baritone, piano; Pound) 1951; first performed Paris, 16 May 1951.
Four Madrigals (unaccompanied SATB chorus; Wyatt) 1953; first performed St Andrews, Fife, 20 March 1953.
Six Songs; Two Early English Poems 1953; first performed Glasgow, 23 April 1953.
A Suite o' Bairnsangs (voice, piano; Lindsay) 1953; first performed Braemar, Aberdeenshire, 21 August 1953.
Cantata for a Summer's Day (solo vocal quartet or small chorus, speaker, flute, clarinet, string quintet; or flute, clarinet, small orchestra; Hume, Lindsay) 1954; first performed Edinburgh, 23 February 1954.
Song of the Burn (from *Cantata for a Summer's Day*) 1954; first performed London, 10 May 1967.
Five Love Songs (soprano, guitar; Parry) 1955; first performed Utrecht, 4 October 1955.
Four Portraits (baritone, clarinet, piano) 1956; first performed London, 10 December 1962.
A Song for Christmas (high voice, piano) 1958; first broadcast BBC Scotland, 16 December 1958.
Triptych (tenor, orchestra) 1959; first performed London, 14 September 1960. Recorded HMV ALP 2279.
Sir Patrick Spens (tenor, guitar) 1961; first performed Aldeburgh, Suffolk, 7 July 1961.
Make Ye Merry for Him That Is to Come (sopranos, altos, children's chorus, optional organ) 1961; first performed London, 8 December 1962.
The Phoenix and the Turtle (small chorus, orchestra) 1962; first performed London, 20 August 1962.
Two Christmas Carols in Traditional Style (soprano, chorus, small orchestra; Nicholson) 1963; first performed Border Television, 29 December 1963.
John Cooke/John Cooke's Grey Mare (unaccompanied SATB chorus) 1963; first performed London, 17 December 1963.
The Five Ages of Man (chorus, orchestra; Hesiod) 1963–4; first performed Norwich, Norfolk, 6 June 1964.
Memento creatoris (unaccompanied SATB chrous; Donne) 1967; first performed Aldeburgh, Suffolk, 6 June 1967.
Primavera (soprano, flute; Alguera) 1971; first performed Zagreb, 19 May 1971. Recorded Caprice RIKS LP 59.
Rorate coeli (unaccompanied chorus; Dunbar) 1973; first performed London, 26 September 1976. Recorded Abbey LPB 798.
Monologues of Mary, Queen of Scots (soprano, orchestra; arranged from the opera) 1977–86; first performed Stirling, 1987.
O caro m'e il sonno (SATB chorus; Michelangelo) 1978; first performed Memphis, Tennessee, 4 December 1982.
The Last Twilight (chorus, 3 horns, 4 trumpets, 4 trombones, percussion; Lawrence) 1980; first performed Santa Fe, New Mexico, 20 July 1980.
Black Tambourine 1985.
For the Time Being (advent for SATB chorus, speaker) 1986.
Echoes Through Time (dramatic work for chorus) 1988.

Opera:

The Abbot of Drimock (chamber; Lindsay) 1955; first performed London, 22 June 1958.
The Decision (Lindsay) 1964–5; first performed London, 30 November 1967.
The Voice of Ariadne (chamber; Alguera, James) 1972–3; first performed Aldeburgh, Suffolk, 11 June 1974.
Mary, Queen Of Scots (Alguera) 1975–7; first performed Edinburgh, 6 September 1977.
A Christmas Carol (after Dickens) 1978–9; first performed Norfolk, Virginia, 7 December 1979. Recorded Moss Music Group MMG 302.
An Occurrence at Owl Creek Bridge (radio opera; Bierce) 1981; first performed BBC, 14 September 1982.
Harriet, The Woman Called Moses 1981–4.

Other:

A Tale of Thieves (ballet) 1953; first performed Oswestry, 15 December 1954.
[Various Scots Songs] (arrangements) 1956; first performed Scotland, 1958.
Suite from A Tale for Thieves (orchestra) 1957; first performed London, 16 May 1957.
Theme and Interludes (youth orchestra) 1962; first performed BBC, 8 January 1962.
Marko the Miser (children's mime; recorders, violin/clarinet, guitar, piano, percussion) 1962; first performed Farnham, Surrey, 16 May 1963.
Suite for Orchestra: Air (collaboration) 1963; first performed London, 23 November 1963.
Excursions (duets for young pianists) 1965; first performed London, 19 April 1967.

Sonata for Three (flute, violin, guitar; for young players) 1966; first performed Winchester, Hampshire, 27 May 1966.
Variations for Brass Band (young players) 1966; first performed St Andrews, Fife, 15 July 1966.
Beauty and the Beast (ballet) 1968–9; first performed London, 19 November 1969.
Variations on "A Happy Birthday" (collaboration; to Sir William Walton on his 70th birthday) 1972.
Scorpius (ballet: arrangement of *Chamber Concerto No 1*) 1972; first performed 19 January 1973.
Scottish Dance Suite (concert band) 1974; first performed Albuquerque, New Mexico, 31 March 1982.

Incidental music: *A Midsummer Night's Dream*, London, 20 December 1960; *A Mummer's Tale*, (Border Television), 16 December 1962; *The Devil and John Brown* (Associated Television), 1963; *Framework for a Nation* (film), 1963; *No Star on the Way Back* (Border Television), 29 December 1963; *Christmas Has Come* (Border Television), 1965; *The Castles of Scotland* (television), 1967; *Golf: Scotland's Royal and Ancient Game* (film), 1967; *The Single Passion* (BBC), 1967.

PUBLICATIONS

By Musgrave: articles in *Musical Times*, *Musical Events* and *The Listener*.

On Musgrave: Jane Weiner LePage, *Women Composers, Conductors and Musicians of the Twentieth Century*, Metuchen, New Jersey, 1980; Donald L. Hixon, *TM: A Bio-Bibliography*, London, 1984; Aaron I. Cohen, *International Encyclopaedia of Women Composers*, 2nd edition, New York and London, 1987.

* * *

40 years' worth of published work reveals Thea Musgrave to be one of the most industriously inventive of post-World War II composers. A capacity for constant self-renewal combined with a shrewd awareness of what is currently happening in musical style have produced an unusually varied and ever-developing series of works.

Musgrave's earliest published work, from the years she spent in Paris studying with Nadia Boulanger, is elegantly lyrical, tonal with an acerbic edge, managing to avoid the territory so comprehensively covered by Britten, thanks, perhaps to a very individual choice of texts (much of the early work is vocal). *A Suite o' Bairnsangs*, for instance, sets deceptively simple Scottish pseudo-folksongs by Maurice Lindsay with a straightforwardness which is both sincere and circumspect; this amalgam of earthiness and elegance is rather rare in Scottish art, and not very common elsewhere.

Bairnsangs is backed up by a sure command of off-tonal harmony; by the time of *Sir Patrick Spens*, which sets another Scottish folksong text (a real one this time), the music has become chromatic, fraught and closer to the continental lingua franca of that period. Such a development might (and for other composers, did) incur the loss of personality, but in the midst of a phase of serial composition in the early 1960s, Musgrave discovered a dynamic which has informed her music ever since: the idea of "dramatic-abstract" music (her term) in which dramatic processes are discovered and enacted in abstract (i.e., non-programmatic) musical settings.

One might mark the beginning of this process in *Colloquy* for violin and piano—whose title explains what goes on. But this idea came to fuller fruition in a fascinating series of concertos which perhaps constitute the most original part of Musgrave's output.

The concertos, including a *Concerto for Orchestra* and concertos for clarinet, horn and viola show the accompanying orchestra as a collection of individuals and smaller groups, as capable of subversion and inner division as of perfectly unanimous tuttis—at times, the comparison with Fellini's film *Prova di orchestra* (which portrays a symphony orchestra as a hotbed of anarchy) is irresistible. In these pieces, soloists lead instrumental sections away from the main tempo and musical direction of the rest of the orchestra; there is a sense of "interference" from the soloist and the "allies" he finds within the orchestral ranks. The drama of the situation is expressed visually: in the *Clarinet Concerto*, the soloist is seen perambulating the orchestral area, stalking orchestral players and even playing music out of their copies. The soloist in the *Horn Concerto* activates and directs an ensemble of the orchestra's horns, who have moved into position around the auditorium.

The idea of spatial deployment of musical forces and of wandering musicians was quite widely current at the time (for instance, Harrison Birtwistle's *Verses for Ensembles*), but Musgrave uses the device with a variety and gusto which sets her "space music" apart from mere vogue.

Musgrave's work since this group of works has centred on a series of operas, which seems an appropriate aftermath to a theatrical inquisition about the orchestra. The first of the operas to gain worldwide attention, *The Voice of Ariadne*, based on Henry James's "The Last of the Valerii" is a deftly lyrical piece whose arias and songlines are a welcome contrast to the ubiquitous wordy arioso of much contemporary opera. The piece is notable for its expert and dramatically justified use of a tape part; like its Jamesian antecedent *The Turn of the Screw* this is a subtle piece about being haunted.

From the 1977 *Mary, Queen of Scots* on, Musgrave has written her own libretti, with workmanlike expertise. *Mary, Queen of Scots* for instance, focuses on a relatively short period in Mary's mature life, thus avoiding the dangers of historical pageant and post-beheading bathos. In *A Christmas Carol* the problem is to concentrate the immense amount of information and incident from the work of a particularly detailed author. Like its successor, *Harriet, The Woman Called Moses*, the opera gains from the inclusion and fluent manipulation (rather than mere quotation) of familiar material—for instance, carols in *A Christmas Carol*, and spirituals in *Harriet*.

Musgrave's career has been characterised by great productive energy, a virtuosic command of a very wide range of techniques, and a fluent musical language which has been activated by an unusual awareness of musical drama.

—Judith Weir

N

NANCARROW, Conlon. American; Mexican citizen. Born in Texarkana, Arkansas, 27 October 1912. Educated at Cincinnati College Conservatory of Music, Ohio, 1929–32; further studies in composition, Boston (under Nicolas Slonimsky, Walter Piston and Roger Sessions), 1933–6. Served with Abraham Lincoln Brigade, Spanish Civil War, 1937–9, passport subsequently confiscated by U.S. authorities. Married (1) Suzanne Stephens; (2) Yoko Nancarrow, 1 son. Jazz and classical trumpeter; occasional reviewer, *Modern Music*, 1939–40; political exile in Mexico since 1940, Mexican citizenship 1956. Recipient: Letter of Distinction, American Music Center, 1982; MacArthur Foundation Fellowship, 1982. Mailing address: Apartado 20-550, Codigo 0100, Mexico.

Publishers: Soundings Press, Washington; Schott; Sylvia Smith.

Works:

Serenade and Scherzo (oboe, bassoon, piano) 1930.
Blues (piano) 1935.
Prelude (piano) 1935.
Toccata (violin, piano) 1935.
Septet 1940.
Sonatina (piano) 1941.
Trio (clarinet, bassoon, piano) 1942.
String Quartet 1942. Recorded Nonesuch 9 79111 1 F.
Suite (orchestra) 1943.
String Quartet 1945.
String Quartet No 3: Canon 3-4-5-6 n.d.

Nancarrow's subsequent output is for player piano. Scores are punched on paper rolls fed through an Ampico reproducing system:

Studies 1–29 (no 21 subtitled *Canon—X*, no 27 subtitled *Canon—5%/6%/8%/11%*) n.d. Recorded (nos 1, 2, 2a, 2b, 7, 10, 15, 23–25) Wergo WER 60166-50; (nos 9, 11–13, 16–19, 27–29) Wergo 60167-50.
Study 30 (prepared player piano) n.d.
Studies 31–38 (no 37 subtitled *Canon—150/160 5/7/168 3/4/180/187 1/2/200/210/225/240/250/262 1/2/281 1/4*) n.d. Recorded (nos 33, 34, 36) Wergo 60166/67-50.
Studies 39–41 (2 player pianos; no 40a subtitled *Canon e/pi*) n.d.
Study 42 n.d. Recorded Wergo 60165-50.
Studies 43 & 44 (2 player pianos) n.d. Recorded (no 43) Wergo WER 60166/67-50.
Studies 45–50 n.d. Recorded (nos 45a/b/c, 46, 47, 48a/b/c, 49a/b/c, 50) Wergo WER 60165-50.
Studies 50–60 n.d.

PUBLICATIONS

By Nancarrow: three works published in *New Music Quarterly*, 1938; *Selected Studies for Player Piano*, edited by Peter Garland, with critical material by Gordon Mumma, Charles Amirkhanian, John Cage, Roger Reynolds and James Tenney, Soundings Book 4, Washington, D.C., 1977.

On Nancarrow: C. Gagne and T. Caras, (interview) in *Soundpieces: Interviews with American Composers*, Metuchen, New Jersey, 1982; Peter Garland, "CN: Chronicle of a Friendship", in *Americas: Essays in American Music and Culture, 1973–80*, Santa Fe, New Mexico, 1982; Roger Reynolds, "CM: Interviews in Mexico City and San Francisco", in *American Music*, 2(2), 1984; P. Carlsen, "The Player Piano Music of CN", dissertation, City University of New York, 1985.

* * *

Conlon Nancarrow is undoubtedly one of the most mysterious and eccentric figures in modern music, devoting his life to composing almost exclusively for the player piano. Only in the last decade has his genius been acknowledged with festivals and concerts—he was recipient of the prestigious McArthur Foundation Fellowship in 1982.

He studied music in Cincinnati and later in Boston with Nicolas Slonimsky, Walter Piston and Roger Sessions. He played trumpet in the school orchestra and later jazz trumpet with a band on board an ocean liner to France.

In 1937 Nancarrow volunteered to join the Abraham Lincoln Brigade against Fascist Spain and for two years he fought in appalling conditions and nearly lost his life. On his return to the United States he refused to recant his politics and chose to live in Mexico instead. In the 1940s he married the artist Suzanne Stephens, friend of Diego Rivera, Frida Kahlo and Anaïs Nin. He now lives on the outskirts of Mexico City in a house designed and decorated by the great muralist, Juan O'Gorman. His present wife, Yoko, is an archaeologist and they have one son.

Nancarrow's consuming musical interest is in rhythm and all its ramifications including counterpoint. He said, "My interest has always been in tempo." His early pieces, *Toccata* for violin and piano and *Sonatina*, were too difficult for players at the time and he searched for an instrument which would not narrow his experiments. Since it was too early to envisage the use of the synthesizer, in the early 1940s Nancarrow picked the player piano and experimented to change the hammers and attacks. He began on a series of *Studies* for player piano and has completed 60 at the time of writing. However, he refuses to date individual works and they are grouped by him according to preference.

Studies 1–12 are based on blues, ragtime, boogie-woogie and betray his training as a jazz trumpeter. Others have a strong Spanish character, for he admits to liking flamenco music and the work of Mexican composer, Carlos Revueltas. The greatest influences are jazz and Bach.

After this early series the works become increasingly more systematic in approach and more streamlined. A significant tool is the canon and its transformations. He also developed metrical and rhythmic scales which he elaborates both horizontally—in duration and speed—and superimposes vertically, sometimes going from one voice to 10 voices in a single work. Each layer may itself be inverted, or gradually slowed down or speeded up at varying rates which he calculates by hand. This gives rise to mirages of texture and colour—epiphenomena of durations, speeds and rhythms, which are very appealing in the warm sonority of the player piano. The instrument allows Nancarrow to realize speeds and densities beyond the physical abilities of a human player. A solitary man with a vast library of books and records, and a large workshop, he labours physically to devise ways of punching rolls: he has spent as long one year composing five minutes of music.

Nancarrow's interest in building structures mathematically and with great precision is enlivened by the fairground charm and resonance of the sound of the player piano. He exploits the vocabulary of ornamentation, very fast glissandos, arpeggios, repeated notes and appogiaturas with grace notes, trills and other figures, stripping them of their historical context to use them as cornerstones of his edifices. In this and in his attitude to constructing a complex structure out of aggregates he shares a similarity with Iannis Xenakis. However, any interest in texture and colour results from the rhythmic elaborations themselves and not from desire to explore other instruments: "I believe that clashes of tempo carry my music."

Nancarrow lives and breathes popular music and culture: the sound world of his pianolas echoes the harp and brass music of the local mariachi players strolling around the Plaza Garibaldi creating simultaneous rhythmic layers and time slices so characteristic of his work. The repetitive momentum of the music generates energy as if to keep the earth spinning and his compositions are among the most accessible and joyful in the 20th century.

—Nouritza Matossian

NEIKRUG, Marc (Edward). American. Born in New York City, 24 September 1946. Educated at Nordwestliche Musikakademie, Detmold, Germany (under Giselher Klebe), 1964–8; State University of New York, Stony Brook, 1969–77, M.M. in composition. Freelance composer; performing pianist; composer in residence, Marlboro Festival, 1972; special consultant, contemporary music, St Paul Chamber Orchestra, Minnesota, 1978–86; director, Melbourne Summer Music, 1986, 1991. Recipient: prizes for best film music (for film version of *Through Roses*), Besançon Film Festival, 1981, and International Film and Television Festival, New York City, 1982. Mailing address: c/o Shirley Kirshbaum Associates, 711 West End Avenue, Suite 5LN, New York, New York 10025, U.S.A.

Publishers: Barenreiter; Salabert; Hansen/Chester.

Symphonies/orchestral:

Piano Concerto 1966.
Clarinet Concerto 1967.
Viola Concerto 1974.
Eternity's Sunrise 1979–80.
Mobile 1981.
Violin Concerto 1982.
Chetro Ketl 1985–6.
Concerto for Two Violins, Viola and Cello 1987.
Flute Concerto 1989; first performed Pittsburgh, 1989.
Symphony No 1 1991.

Chamber/instrumental:

Sonata (cello) 1967.
String Quartet No 1 1969.
String Quartet No 2 1972. Recorded Music Heritage Society MHS 3804.
Suite (cello, piano) 1974.
Rituals (flute, harp) 1976.
Concertino (flute, oboe, clarinet, violin, viola, cello, piano) 1977.
Three Fantasies (violin, piano) 1977.
Continuum (cello, piano) 1978.
Cycle of Seven (piano) 1978.
Kaleidoscope (flute, piano) 1979.
Duo (violin, piano) 1983.
Rosaceae (3 oboes, 3 clarinets, 2 bassoons/1 contrabassoon, 4 horns, 3 trumpets, 3 trombones, 2 percussion) 1986.
Voci (piano, clarinet, violin, cello) 1988.
Stars the Mirror (string quartet) 1989.
Take Me t'Susan's Gift (percussion) 1989.

Vocal/choral:

Nachtlieder (soprano, orchestra) 1988.

Opera/dramatic:

Through Roses (actor, 8 instruments) 1979–80; first performed London, 1980. Recorded Deutsche Grammophon.
Los Alamos 1988; first performed Berlin, 1 October 1988.

* * *

Marc Neikrug grew up in a thoroughly artistic environment. He is the son of the painter and composer Olga Zundel and the eminent cellist George Neikrug, for whom he wrote the intense solo *Sonata*; he has also acted as his father's accompanist. The *Sonata* has all the dense harmonic logic and vigorous rhythmic underpinning of Central European modernism, and particularly Bartók. However, his attraction to large chord clusters and blocks of pure sound ally him to a line that runs between Edgar Varèse and the Danish composer Per Nørgård, who is perhaps Neikrug's most obvious contemporary influence.

He received his education at the music academy in Detmold where he studied composition under Giselher Klebe, author of half a dozen fine operas after Schiller, Kleist, Shakespeare and Balzac, and from whom Neikrug may well have taken his consuming interest in sonorism and large-scale colour effects.

Neikrug's concertante writing is particularly confident. He approaches the awesome technical problems of the *Concerto for Two Violins, Viola and Cello* with great certainty, echoing some of the non-canonical strategies of Klebe's 1954 *Double Concerto*. Neikrug is a fine pianist and premiered his own *Piano Concerto*, his first major work (though a back catalogue of earlier pieces has been withdrawn), with the freedom of articulation that he demands of his soloists and ensemble players. His scores are notoriously uninflected, demanding considerable interpretative intervention by the musicians. On the other hand, they bear no obvious truck with improvisatory or aleatoric conventions; Neikrug maintains a taut control over the harmonic information and the expressive freedom of his superb *Flute Concerto*—written for James Galway—which masks an almost relentless structural logic.

Neikrug's first fully symphonic work has not yet been heard, but promises to combine the same effortless synthesis of apparent contraries. His most significant work in this regard, and in a programmatic sense, is the orchestral *Eternity's Sunrise*, inspired by Blake's intense revelatory simplicities and occasional errors of philosophical tone. The tighter logic of the duo pieces, notably the *Suite* and *Continuum*, both for the very personal medium of cello and piano, avoids any such problems and Neikrug's judgement of tone is perfectly on key in his quite extraordinary theatre piece *Through Roses*. The subject matter, a Jewish violinist's nightmarish recollection of being forced to perform for his Nazi captors, runs a palpable risk of either sentimentality or uncontained expressionist outbursts; in the event, Neikrug achieves something genuinely touching. It seems plausible that, at some pre-compositional point rather than as a direct source, he was thinking about Messiaen, whose *Quatuor pour le fin du temps* was first performed in a German stalag (though for fellow-prisoners, not as a command performance for his guards); *Voci* is for the same forces as the Messiaen piece.

Among his other distinctive chamber pieces, there is *Rosaceae* for winds and percussion, a revelation from a composer who has generally been thought of as a strings specialist, and the punning *Take Me t'Susan's Gift*, a birthday tribute to the Japanese composer Toru Takemitsu, written in a variation of Takemitsu's characteristic percussion idiom so challenging as to raise it above the status of "occasional" writing.

Since *Through Roses*, Neikrug has added a second opera, the large-scale *Los Alamos*, an anti-nuclear work which draws on some of the same ideas and juxtapositions as Godfrey Reggio's and Philip Glass's polemical fantasy about the Hopi, *Koyaanisqatsi*. Combining elements of indigenous music and ritual in the shape of Pueblan drumming, *Los Alamos* is Neikrug's most "American" work to date, almost self-consciously so, and marks a decisive step in the same direction as Varèse's late Americanism. Whether his First Symphony and its successors will continue to pursue that direction remains to be seen.

—Brian Morton

NICULESCU, Stefan. Romanian. Born in Moreni, 21 July 1927. Educated at Academy of Music, Bucharest, 1941–6; Polytechnic Institute, Bucharest, 1946–50; Conservatoire National Supérieur de Musique, Bucharest (harmony and counterpoint under Mihail Jora, composition under Mihail Andricu, orchestration with Rogalski, piano under Muza Germani-Ciomac), 1951–9; further study, Studio Siemens, Munich (electro-acoustic music under Mauricio Kagel), 1966; Ferienkurse für Neue Musik, Darmstadt (under György Ligeti, Karlheinz Stockhausen and Erhard Karkoschka), 1966–8. Married Colette Demetrescu, 22 June 1952. Teacher of piano, Bucharest, 1958–60; head of research, Bucharest Institute of the Arts, 1960–3; lecturer in composition, and subsequently professor of analysis, Bucharest Conservatoire, 1963–87; director, International Festival of New Music, Bucharest, since 1990. Recipient: Enesco Composition Prize, Romanian Academy, 1962; prize (for the book *George Enescu*), French Academy, 1972; prize of the Union of Romanian Composers, 1975, 1977, 1981, 1983, 1985–6, 1988; special prize, Montreux Festival, 1985. Mailing address: Intrarea Sublocotenent Staniloiu 4, 73228 Bucharest 39, Romania.

Publishers: Editura muzicala, Bucharest; Gerig; Salabert; Schott.

Symphonies/orchestral:

Symphony No 1 1956.
Scenes (chamber orchestra) 1962–5; first performed Cluj Napoca, 15 February 1964.
Simfonii (small orchestra/15 soloists) 1963.
Eteromorfie 1967.
Formantji (flexible score for 17 strings or 17 solo strings) 1968; first performed Bayreuth, 15 August 1968.
Unisonos (large orchestra) 1970, revised 1971.
Ison I (large orchestra; also chamber version) 1971–3; first performed La Rochelle, 15 April 1973.
Unisonos II 1972.
Ison II: Concert (winds, percussion) 1975–6; first performed Bucharest, 27 January 1977.
Symphony No 2: Opus Dacicum 1978–80; first performed Timisoara, 29 November 1980.
Snodronniga—La Fée des neiges (small orchestra) 1980.
Synchronie II: Omaggio a Enescu e Bartók (chamber orchestra) 1981.
Cantos (saxophone, orchestra) 1984; first performed Timisoara, 29 November 1984.

Chamber/instrumental:

Sonata (clarinet, piano) 1955.
String Trio 1957; first performed Bucharest, 18 February 1976.
Inventions (clarinet, piano) 1963–5; first performed Bucharest, 29 January 1965.
Inventiuni I (clarinet, piano) 1964.
Sextet (winds; based on *Cantata III*) 1964.
Inventiuni II (viola, piano) 1965.
Tastenspiel (piano) 1968.
Triplum I (flute, cello, piano) 1971; first performed Royan, 8 April 1971.
Ison I (flute, oboe, 3 clarinets, bassoon/contrabassoon, horn, trumpet, trombone, 2 violins, viola, cello, double bass; also version for orchestra) 1971.
Triplum II (clarinet, cello, piano) 1972; first performed Bucharest, 18 April 1973.
Echos (violin) 1977; first performed Bucharest, 21 February 1978.
Syncronie I (2 to 12 instruments ad lib) 1979; first performed Bucharest, 5 November 1979.
Solo (vibraphone, marimba; material from *Syncronie I*) 1979; first performed Bucharest, 14 July 1986.
Sincronie V (wind quintet) 1982.
Duplum (cello, piano or synthesizer) 1984; first performed Bucharest, 7 November 1984.
Ricercare in Uno (clarinet, violin, synthesizer) 1984; first performed Bucharest, 27 March 1984.

Echos II (violin, synthesizer) 1984; first performed Turin, 1 October 1985.
Sincronie III (flute, oboe, bassoon) 1985; first performed Lugar, Spain, 22 February 1986.
Sincronie per quattro (flute, oboe, violin, cello) 1985.
Octoplum (flute, clarinet, soprano saxophone/alto saxophone, percussion, mandolin, guitar, viola, cello) 1985; first performed Den Bosch, The Netherlands, 31 March 1985.
Duplum III (clarinet, piano) 1986; first performed Italy, 1986.
Hétérofonies pour Montreux (flute, cor anglais, clarinet, bassoon, horn) 1986; first performed Vevey, Switzerland, 29 August 1986.
A Due (clarinet, bassoon) 1986.
Sincronie IV (clarinet, piano, percussion) 1987; first performed Bucharest, 21 March 1989.
Monophonie (bassoon) 1988; first performed Bucharest, 4 February 1989.
Chant-son (soprano saxophone/alto saxophone) 1989; first performed Mexico, 24 May 1989.

Vocal/choral:

Cantata I (female and/or children's chorus, orchestra) 1959–74.
Cantata II (tenor, mixed chorus, orchestra) 1960.
Cantata III: Crossing (mezzo-soprano, wind quintet) 1960.
Aphorismes d'Heraclite (unaccompanied mixed chorus/20 voices) 1969; first performed Zagreb, May 1969.
Fragments I (12 voices, flute(s), 5 percussion) 1976; first performed Sarajevo, Yugoslavia, 10 October 1978.
Fragment II (voice, instrumentalists and/or percussion, 12 instruments) 1977.
Fragment III (voice, instrumentalists and/or percussion, 12 instruments) 1977.
Invocatio (12 mixed voices) 1989; first performed Paris, 18 April 1989.

Opera/dramatic:

Le Livre avec Apolodore (children's opera) 1975.

Other:

Fat-Frumos din lacrimae (puppet ballet; 11 instruments) 1982.

PUBLICATIONS

By Niculescu: contributor to *George Enescu*, Bucharest, 1971; *Reflections About Music*, Bucharest, 1980; articles in *Muzica*, *Revue Romaine d'histoire de l'art*, *Arta*, *Studi de Muzicologie*, and other magazines and journals.

On Niculescu: R. Stan, "Cu SN: control si indeterminism in muzica", in *Romania literara*, 2, 1969; V. Cosma, in *Muzicieni romani*, Bucharest, 1970.

* * *

Through his teacher Mihail Jora, Stefan Niculescu imbibed the influence of the Romanian nationalist school, and of George Enesco in particular. In the early 1960s, stimulated by the recent music of Messiaen, Boulez and Stockhausen, Niculescu experimented with the most rigorous forms of total serialisation, resulting in such taut, spare works as the *Inventions* for clarinet and piano, the *Simfonii* for 15 soloists, and the series of three Cantatas for a variety of choral and instrumental formations. He gradually shed the most extreme elements of this style as the decade progressed, and by the time of the orchestral *Eteromorfie* and *Formantji* for strings he had become preoccupied with smoothly transforming textures of greater continuity. He undertook a close study of ethnic music, notably that of his native country, as well as of mathematical logic, which led him to explore a certain degree of aleatory freedom in his music, especially in rhythm. Like many Romanian composers in the 1970s, Niculescu investigated the possibilities of heterophonic writing, as well as attempting to revitalise diatonic harmony in a nontonal context. The result was a striking sequence of works in which the harmonic and melodic material is wholly diatonic, often without any modal changes through a piece: *Ison II: Concert* for winds and percussion, *Fragments I–III* for ensemble, and *Echos* for solo violin. In these works, the rhythm is a free mixture of conducted and aleatoric, while the forms are usually successions of static panels of sound, each with its characteristic instrumentation and tessitura. In *Ison II: Concert*, each section is provided with a pedal tone or group of pedal tones (the *ison* is the drone acompanying the chants in Greek orthodox music) which focus the harmony and assure harmonic contrast between sections, even where there is no change of mode.

In recent years, Niculescu has tried to reintroduce a pronounced melodic element in his music; in a sequence of works entitled *Syncronie* written since 1979, he has devised a formal principle based on "different or identical melodic elements which synchronise or de-synchronise progressively." His harmonic vocabulary has also noticeably expanded, to include elements of sharper contrast and greater dissonance. Investigations into acoustics have led Niculescu to enrich his music with microtonal harmony derived from just intonation and resonance spectra. The Second Symphony combines all the aforementioned techniques and is a summary of Niculescu's styles as it had evolved up to then. The first of the two large sections of the work is predominantly homophonic and harmonic, presenting and varying a small quantity of resonance-type chords in shifting textures; the second section is the most complicated example of the "synchrony" technique in Niculescu's work to date, an elaborate superimposition of melodic strands converging towards the climactic coda, which unites the modal and harmonic threads of the work.

Niculescu's Third Symphony is actually the saxophone concerto *Cantos*, which continues his exploration of modality, resonance chords and microtones (the latter play a melodic as well as a harmonic role) within a typically static succession of sound panels. As in all Niculescu's mature works, the combination of clarity in form, melody and harmony with spontaneity of invention results in music of exceptional freshness.

—Julian Anderson

NIELSEN, Tage. Danish. Born in Frederiksberg, 16 January 1929. Educated at Ribe High School, graduated 1947; University of Copenhagen (musicology and French), 1947–55, M.A.; additional study in France, 1954, Israel, 1972, the United States, 1974, and Italy, 1975. Military service in Danish Army Medical Corps, 1955–6. Married Aase Grue-Sorensen, 14 October 1950; 2 daughters and 1 son. Deputy head of music department, Radio Denmark, Copenhagen, 1957–63; director/professor, Royal Academy of Music, Aarhus, 1963–83; musical adviser, programme committee, Radio Denmark, 1967–71; chair of board, Danish State Art Foundation, 1971–4; member of board, Aarhus Symphony Orchestra, 1974–83; director, Accademica di Danimarca, Rome, 1983–9; chair of board, Society for Publication of Danish Music, since 1989. Recipient: Anker Prize, 1975. Mailing address: Peter Bangs Vej 153, 1.tv., DK-2000 Frederiksberg, Denmark.

Publisher: Samfundet til Udgivelse af Dansk Musik, Valkendorfsgade 3, DK-1151, Copenhagen K, Denmark.

Symphonies/orchestral:

Intermezzo gaio 1952, revised 1963; first performed Copenhagen, 1962.
Four Miniatures (string orchestra) 1963; first performed Aalborg, 1967.
Bariolage 1965; first performed Aalborg, 1967.
Il giardino magico 1967–8; first performed Aarhus, 1969. Recorded point PCD 5083.
Passacaglia 1981; first performed Copenhagen, 1983. Recorded point PCD 5089.

Chamber/instrumental:

String Quartet 1947; first performed Copenhagen, 1949.
Sonata (2 bassoons) 1948.
Sonate (piano) 1949–50.
Toccata (organ) 1951.
Two Nocturnes (piano) 1960–1; first performed Copenhagen, 1962. Recorded SUDM 003.
Variants (alto flute) 1963; first performed Copenhagen, 1964.
Three Small Piano Pieces (for educational use) 1963.
Theme with Variations (for educational use; 3 recorders) 1966.
Two Impromptus (viola, organ) 1967.
Sun, Moon and Stars (for educational use; piano) 1969.
Divertimento: Marker og enge / Fields and Meadows (organ) 1971; first performed Copenhagen, 1972.
Three Character Pieces and an Epilogue (piano) 1972–4; first performed Aarhus, 1977. Recorded Paula 13; point PCD 5089; SUDM 011.
Recitative and Elegy (guitar) 1975; first performed Humlebaek, 1981. Recorded EMI MOAK 30017.
Arrangement and Landscape (flute) 1981. Recorded SUDM 011.
Improvisation and Fugue (clarinet, cello, piano) 1983.
Ballade (glockenspiel, vibraphone, marimba) 1984; first performed Copenhagen, 1985.
Salon Trio (flute, viola, harp) 1984; first performed Copenhagen, 1985.
Paesaggi (2 pianos) 1985; first performed Rome, 1985. Recorded point PCD 5089.
Three Opera Fragments (13 instruments) 1986; first performed Humlebaek, 28 May 1989. Recorded point PCD 5089.
The Frosty Silence in the Gardens (guitar) 1990; first performed Ebertoft, 1990.

Vocal/choral:

Five Songs (mezzo-soprano, piano; Petersen, Hesse, Johannsen, Chenier, anon.) 1946–70; first performed Copenhagen, 1979. Recorded Danica DLP 8056.
Attic Summer (soprano, guitar, percussion; Johannsen) 1974; first performed Copenhagen, 1975. Recorded EMI DOAK 30013.
Eight Choral Songs (1, 2, 3 and 4 voices; Danish poets) 1974.
Three Shakespeare Fragments (soprano, oboe, cello, piano) 1977–8; first performed Egeskov, 1978.
Three Black Madrigals (mixed choir; Plath) 1978; first performed Aarhus, 1978. Recorded point PCD 5089.
Five Poems by William Blake (soprano, vibraphone) 1979; first performed Aarhus, 1980.
Three Mexican Poems (soprano, alto, tenor, bass, piano; Jaime Shelley, Sabines, Zaid) 1982; first performed Aarhus, 1982.
Two Choral Songs (mixed choir; Norbrandt) 1984; first performed Aarhus, 1985.
In tribulatione mea (motet for mixed chorus) 1985.
Ritual (mezzo-soprano, flute, piano, percussion) 1989; first performed Aarhus, 1990.

PUBLICATIONS

By Nielsen: "Musiktheorie als Unterrichtsfach heute", in *Kongressbericht Stuttgart*, 1971; "Rued Langgaard", in *Dansk Musik Tidsskrift*, 43(7/8); "Alban Bergs *Lulu*" in *Dansk Musik Tidsskrift*, 55(1); "Lutosławski i London, Aarhus, og Warszawa", in *Dansk Musik Tidsskrift*, 64(6); "*Wozzeck* i Rom 1942", in *Piranesi*, 4, 1987; "Fra Palestrino til Berio", in *Danmark og Italien*, Copenhagen, 1989.

On Nielsen: Bengt Johnson, "TN", in *Dansk Musik Tidsskrift*, 53(5/6); Erling Kullberg, "En staerk profil—om TN som komponist", in *Dansk Musik Tidsskrift*, 63(5).

Tage Nielsen comments:

After having written a handful of neo-classical works in the late 1940s and early 1950s, I was very much impressed by the "Darmstadt Revolution". The new possibilities of sound, expression and musical structure developed by composers like Boulez, Nono and Berio have left a profound trace on my works from the 1960s onwards.

Even so, I have never believed in serialism. To me, attempts to create musical order and cohesion through predetermination and serial manipulation are a denial of the complex, yet always highly organized way in which human mental processes manifest themselves in works of art. I would define the stylistic orientation which characterizes many of my works from the 1970s and 1980s as something between expressionism and neo-romanticism.

* * *

Tage Nielsen presents an unassuming yet sturdy profile in Danish music. A diversity of cultural activities combined with uncompromising self-criticism have left Nielsen room for no more than a sparse production. In addition, he has always regarded himself as a leisure time composer—although an amateur is the last thing in the world he might be called. Few composers have created such exquisitely refined works—each with its own unique profile, yet all of them with the same fine balance between form and content, the same finely polished detail and natural respiratory movement.

From a stylistic point of view, Nielsen is difficult to categorize. Ever alert to new developments (it was not for nothing that the Jutland Academy of Music flourished as a centre for contemporary music during his tenure as principal there) he has, to a remarkable degree, evinced an ability to assimilate new trends into an integrated personal idiom. The common denominator in his music is a fully exploited precision in the formulation of a concentrated lyrical expression. Not a single note seems superfluous or hesitantly placed in his frequently short works, which seem to have come into being through sheer artistic necessity.

Nielsen first found his footing in neo-classicism, but after a handful of youthful works, he remained silent for most of the 1950s. And when, in 1961, he returned with *Two Nocturnes* for piano, he had become a modernist. The classical Darmstadt idiom, as coined by Boulez in particular, had revealed new possibilities for expression of sound which, for Nielsen, became the essential substance in a sensitive lyrical expressionism. Behind the pianistically refined sound technique we can, however, sense the will to think longitudinally in terms of more or less dynamic types of sequences, a classical reminiscence which was to achieve lasting importance.

Nielsen's principal work of the 1960s is *Il giardino magico* for orchestra in which luminous, atmospherical instrumentation combines with elements of aleatory technique. Quotes from the prelude to Wagner's *Tristan und Isolde* leave no doubt as to which magic garden the composer has in mind. This work of the year of flower power (1967–8) marks the culmination of the seductively colourist in Nielsen—who shortly after came under the influence of the emergent new simplicity in Danish music. In *Attic Summer* crisp, metallic timbres thus provide the framework for almost provocatively simple vocal melodics with few notes and numerous repetitions in a varied strophic form—while *Three Character Pieces and an Epilogue* for piano completed in the same year confront short, static tone pictures with a development form where freer rein is given to the imagination. Alongside a predilection for the character piece in its widest sense—reflected in titles such as "*Intermezzo*", "*Nocturne*", "*Impromptu*", "*Ballade*", etc.—we also meet here a characteristic tendency towards contrasting characters, textures or styles in antithetical forms: *Three Character Pieces and an Epilogue*, *Divertimento: Marker og enge/Fields and Meadows*, *Recitative and Elegy*, *Arrangement and Landscape*, *Improvisation and Fugue*—all works for solo instruments or (in the case of the last mentioned) for a small chamber ensemble.

The 1980s have added neo-romantic trends to Nielsen's increasingly flexible stylistic palette. The orchestral *Passacaglia*, Nielsen's hitherto largest work, and one of the most important, is a sublime fantasy on a variation of the classical "lamento tetrachord" dominated by an almost tragic yet, at the same time, serene gravity. The *Salon Trio* for harps, on the other hand, is an elegant, mildly ironic play on shadows of various traditional forms of expression, while *Paesaggi* for two pianos renounces any thematic substance as such in favour of a sensually luxuriant development of sound. Here we can trace the influence of Nielsen's sojourn in Italy. Finally, *Three Opera Fragments* show a wealth of drastic gesture, vivid imagery and humour suggestive of the stage.

—Jan Jacoby

NIGG, Serge. French. Born in Paris, 6 June 1924. Educated: early musical training with Ginette Martenot, from 1934; Conservatoire National Supérieur de Musique, Paris (fugue and counterpoint under Simone Plé-Caussade, harmony and composition under Olivier Messiaen), 1941–7; further study in twelve-tone technique under René Leibowitz, 1946–8. Married Micheline Nourrit in 1950; 1 daughter. Member, music committee, Radio Française, 1956; founder (with Durey, Roger Desormière and others), Association of Progressive Musicians, 1959; inspector of music (*art lyrique*), Ministry of Culture, 1967–82; professor of composition, 1978–82, and professor of instrumentation and orchestration, 1982–9, Conservatoire National Supérieur de Musique, Paris; president, Société National de Musique, Paris, 1982–9; member, Académie des Beaux Arts, from 1989. Recipient: Prix Blumenthal; Prix Chabrier; Prix Italia (for *L'Etrange Aventures de Gulliver à Lilliput*), 1958; Grand Prix de la Communauté Radiophonique des programmes de langue française, Montreal (for *Histoire d'oeuf*), 1963; Grand Prix Musical de la Ville de Paris, 1974; Grand Prix, SACEM, 1978; Prix Florence Gould, 1976, 1983; Prix René Dumesnil, Académie des Beaux Arts, 1987; 6 Grands Prix du Disque; Chevalier, Légion d'Honneur; Chevalier, l'Ordre National du Mérite; Officier de l'Ordre des Arts et des Lettres; elected to Institut de France, Académie des Beaux Arts, 1989. Mailing address: 15 bis rue Darcel, 92100 Boulogne-sur-Seine, France.

Publishers: Jobert, Paris; Billaudot, Paris.

Symphonies/orchestral:

Timour (symphonic poem) 1944; first performed Paris, 1944.
Concerto for Piano, Strings and Percussion 1947; first performed Brussels, 1947.
Concerto for Piano, Woodwinds, Percussion 1948; first performed Paris, 1948.
Trois Mouvements symphoniques 1948; first performed Paris, 1948.
Pour un Poète captif (symphonic poem) 1950; first performed Prague, 1951.
Piano Concerto No 1 1954; first performed Paris, 10 January 1955.
Violin Concerto 1957; first performed Paris, 27 May 1960.
Musique Funèbre (strings) 1958; first performed Strasbourg, 1959.
Jerôme-Bosch Symphonie 1960; first performed Strasbourg, 21 June 1960. Recorded Chant du Monde 78690.
Concerto for Flute and Strings 1961; first performed Vichy, 1961.
Prémices pour les "Mondes d'Axel" 1966.
Visions d'Axel ("Le Monde visionnaire", "Le Monde passionnel") 1967; first performed Besançon, 4 September 1967. Recorded Inédits ORTF n Barclay 995030.
Fulgur (after Artaud; band, percussion, 2 harps, piano, celeste, chimes) 1968–9; first performed Paris, 9 October 1969.
Piano Concerto No 2 1970–1; first performed Paris, 12 December 1973.
Fastes de l'imaginaire 1974; first performed Paris, October 1974.
Scènes concertantes (piano, strings) 1975; broadcast Radio Française, 26 March 1976.
Mirrors for William Blake (piano, orchestra) 1977; broadcast Radio France, 25 October 1979.
Millions d'oiseaux d'or 1980–1; first performed Boston, 20 March 1981.
Concerto for Viola and Orchestra 1988.
Poème 1989; first performed Quebec, 12 February 1990.

Chamber/instrumental:

Fantaisie (piano) 1942.
Sonata No 1 (piano) 1943; first performed Paris, 1943.
Deux Pièces (piano) 1947; first performed Paris, 1948.
Variations (piano, 10 instruments) 1947; first performed Paris, January 1947.
Quintet (flute, violin, viola, cello, harp) 1953.
L'Etrange Aventure de Gulliver à Lilliput (12 instruments; after Soupault) 1958; first performed Paris, 1960.
Le Tombeau de Jerôme Bosch (piano) 1958.
Sonata No 2 (piano) 1964; first performed Paris, 1964.
Sonata (violin) 1965; first performed New York City, 10 November 1965.
Piece (trumpet, piano) 1972.
String Quartet 1983; first performed Paris, 1983. Recorded REM 311060.
Sonata No 3 (piano) 1984; first performed Paris, 1984.
Arioso (violin, piano) 1987; first performed Paris, 1987. Recorded REM 11055.

Vocal/choral:

Persephone (melodrama) 1942.
Quatre Mélodies (soprano, piano; Eluard) 1948; first performed Abbaye de Royaumont, 1948.
Le Fusille inconnu (voice, speaker, orchestra; Monod) 1949.
Petite Cantate des couleurs (unaccompanied chorus) 1952.
Les Vendeurs d'indulgences (voice, chorus, orchestra; Eluard) 1953.
Prière pour le premier jour de l'été (speaker, chorus, orchestra; Masson) 1956.
La Croisade des enfants (oratorio for radio; children's chorus, mixed chorus, flute, oboe, clarinet, bassoon, horn, trumpet, trombone, violin, cello, piano, celeste, harp, 3 percussion) 1959; first performed Paris, 1959.
Histoire d'oeuf (reciters, 6 percussion, piano) 1961; first performed Strasbourg, January 1962.
Le Chant du dépossédé (baritone, speaker, orchestra; Mallarmé) 1964; first performed Strasbourg, 1964. Recorded Chant du Monde 78690.
Du Clair au sombre (soprano, piano or orchestra; Eluard) 1985–6; first performed Paris, March 1987.

Other:

Billard (ballet for orchestra) 1951; first performed Amsterdam, 1951.

PUBLICATIONS

By Nigg: "Réponse à une enquête", in *Contrepoints* 3, 1946; "Réponse à une enquête: Les Jeunes Musiciens devant le dodécaphonisme", in *Journal musical français* 31, 1954; "La Musique française de Berlioz à nos jours", in *Konzertbuch*, 2, 1960; "Quelques Feuillets de journal", in *Vingtième Siècle: Images de la musique française*, Paris, 1986; "Discours à reception à l'Académie des Beaux Arts", Institut de France, Paris, 1990.

On Nigg: René Leibowitz, in *L'Artiste et sa conscience*, Paris, 1950; Claude Rostand, *La Musique française contemporaine*, Paris, 1952; Bernard Gavoty and Daniel-Lesur, *Pour ou contre la musique moderne*, Paris, 1957; André Golea, "Panorama de la musique française moderne", in *Tendances*, 6, 1960; J. Roy, in *Musique française*, Paris, 1962; G. Brelet, "La Musique contemporaine en France", in *Histoire de la Musique*, edited by Roland-Manuel Paris, 1963.

Serge Nigg comments:

Around 1946, I became one of the very first composers in France to take part in the great adventure of dodecaphony which was to play such a part in music after the war. Later, I changed direction somewhat to attempt a synthesis between that technique and the sensuousness of a native French tradition that is concerned with poetic refinement, lyricism and harmonic beauty.

* * *

Though he has owed a great deal to Maurice Ravel, the first clearly discernible contemporary influence on Serge Nigg's music was that of his teacher Olivier Messiaen (Nigg was later to follow him as professor of composition at the Paris Conservatoire). This is most clearly evident in the richly coloured textures of the early symphonic poem *Timour*. After graduating, though, Nigg went to study with René Leibowitz and, in one of the dramatically sudden conversions that was to mark his career, became a whole-hearted enthusiast for twelve-tone technique. His *Variations* for piano and 10 instruments is often credited as the first French composition in the Schoenbergian style; it is very much a convert's work, rather dryly doctrinaire, slightly mechanical, and very quickly Nigg recognized the limitations of orthodox serial technique.

There was an ideological, not just aesthetic, aspect to his growing scepticism. The hermetic and rather elitist character of serialism ran counter to the populist sympathies already evident in *Le Fusille inconnu*. In the 1950s, in a manner reminiscent of the rather older English composer Alan Bush, Nigg attempted to simplify his music considerably, drawing on folk and popular traditions, and exploring the potential of choral singing and the "affirmative" harmonic language that prevailed in the Soviet bloc. In 1951 another symphonic poem *Pour un Poète captif*, dedicated to the gaoled Turkish writer Nazim Hikmet, was premiered in Prague; there could be no sharper contrast with the lushness of *Timour*. At the end of the decade, Nigg formed a populist-radical Association of Progressive Musicians with the aim of forging a music no longer fettered by the "symbols of the past," but responsive to the imperatives of the present.

Too open-minded and *sympathique* to let himself be fettered by the purely mathematical permutations of serialism, Nigg was also too fine and subtle a craftsman to abandon some of its structural potential and intellectual rigour. Perhaps inevitably, his very finest work represents a synthesis of the two extremes. The compositions of his middle years—the First Piano Concerto and the beautifully articulated *Violin Concerto*—combine a variety of methodological elements lent coherence by Nigg's adamantine structural logic. In the two concertos he gives serial elements a virtually harmonic function in a way which hovers between polytonality and a free, atonal harmony. There are similar elements in the lyrical *Visions d'Axel* and the very remarkable Symphony inspired by Hieronymus Bosch (more by his delicate balance of folk superstition and intellectual faith than by his overvalued exoticism). This has persisted through his work of the 1960s, 1970s and 1980s, though there are suggestions in such "late" pieces as *Millions d'oiseaux d'or*, the Viola Concerto and the *Poème* for orchestra that he is increasingly interested in sound and sound colour as independent compositional elements; if so, this is in keeping with both Messiaen and with a much younger generation of French composers.

Nigg served many years as inspector of music for the

Ministry of Culture, with a special responsibility for vocal music. His own compositions for voice have a very particular power and resonance. Perhaps the clearest spectrum of his career as a whole is the contrast—not as great as one might expect—between the lyrical estrangements of the 1948 Eluard settings and the more rigorously illogical patterns of the recent *Du Clair au sombre*. As with his Bosch Symphony, it is clear that Nigg is not interested in surrealism for its own sake, or merely as a repository of unconventional imagery. Alongside Eluard and the elegant Mallarmé interpretations of *Le Chant d'un dépossédé*, there are settings of the English writers William Blake and Jonathan Swift; reading back from their harshly satirical visions, it becomes clear that Nigg regards surrealism not as a nihilistic and destructive cognition but as a means to the exposure of human frailties, fears and vices, and as a route to human betterment.

—Paul Norman

NOBRE, Marlos. Brazilian. Born in Recife, Pernambuco, 18 February 1939. Educated at Conservatório Pernambuco de Música (piano, musicianship, harmony and counterpoint), graduated 1955; Ernani Braga Institute, University of Recife, graduated 1959; further study under Hans Joachim Koellreutter, Terezópolis, Rio de Janeiro, 1960; also studied anthropology and sociology, University of Brazil, Rio de Janeiro, from 1960; further study under Camargo Guarnieri, São Paulo, 1961–2; further study, Torcuato di Tella Institute, Buenos Aires, (under Alberto Ginastera, Olivier Messiaen, Luigi Dallapiccola, Bruno Maderna, Aaron Copland and Gian Francesco Malipiero, and electronic music under José Vicente Asuar), 1963–4; further study in electronic music, Columbia University, New York City (under Vladimir Ussachevsky), 1969; studied under Alexander Goehr and Gunther Schuller, Berkshire Music Center, Tanglewood, Massachusetts, 1969. Artistic supervisor, Radio Ministerio da Educacao e Cultura, Rio de Janeiro, 1962; music coordinator, Guanabara Tourism Secretariat, from 1965; general coordinator, UNESCO Brazilian Music Council, from 1970; music director, Radio MEC, from 1971; general secretary, Brazilian Musicians' Union, from 1972. Recipient: 1st prize, Music and Musicians of Brazil, 1960; award (for *Nazarethiana*), German American Cultural Society, 1960; Student Composers' Award (for *Tema e variações*), Broadcasting Music Inc., 1961; 1st prize, Jeunesses Musicales International Competition, Rio de Janeiro, 1962; 1st prize, Ernesto Nazareth Competition, Rio de Janeiro, 1963; 1st prize, National Composers' Contest, University of Brazil, Rio de Janeiro, 1963; Torcuato di Tella Award, Buenos Aires, 1963; 1st prize, City of Santos Contest, São Paulo, 1966; UNESCO Prize, Paris, 1974; Gold Medal Pernambuco, 1978; TRIMALCA/UNESCO Prize, Colombia, 1979; Officer of the Order of Merit of Brasilia, 1988; Officer of the Rio Branco Order of the Ministry of Foreign Affairs of Brazil, 1989. Mailing address: Rua Pres. Carlos de Campos 115, BI 2/902, 22231 Rio de Janeiro, Brazil.

Publishers: Tonos, Darmstadt; Vitale, Rua Almte Barrozo 2, 5'andar, 22221 Rio de Janeiro, Brazil; Editions Max Eschig, 48 rue de Rome, 75008 Paris, France; Musica Nova, Caixa Posta 162626, 22257 Rio de Janeiro, Brazil; Ricordi Brasiera SAEC, Rua Conselheiro Nebias 1136, 01203 São Paulo, Brazil.

Symphonies/orchestral:

Concertino Op 1 (piano, string orchestra) 1959.
Divertimento (piano, orchestra) 1963.
Convergências Op 28 1968.
Desafio (viola, string orchestra) 1968.
Desafio VII Op 31 (piano, string orchestra) 1968; first performed Fribourg, Switzerland, 26 May 1980.
Concerto breve Op 33 (piano, orchestra) 1969. Recorded Philips 6598 307.
Ludus instrumentalis Op 34 (chamber orchestra) 1969. Recorded EMI Angel 063 42297.
Biosfera Op 35 (string orchestra) 1970. Recorded Philips 6833 177/8.
Mosaico Op 36 (string orchestra) 1970. Recorded Philips 6833 177/8; 9500 120.
In memoriam Op 39 1973. Recorded EIM/OEA 002.
Concerto for Strings No 1 Op 42 1976.
Concerto for Strings No 2 Op 53 1981.
Concerto for Piano and Strings Orchestra Op 64 1984.
Four Latin American Dances Op 72 (chamber orchestra) 1989.
Concerto for Trumpet and String Orchestra Op 74 1989.
Concertantes do imaginario Op 74 (piano, orchestra) 1989.
Xingu Op 75 1989.

Chamber/instrumental:

Nazarethiana Op 2 (piano) 1960.
Piano Trio Op 4 1960. Recorded Philips 6598 310.
Sixteen Variations Op 8 1962. Recorded Deutsche Grammophon 2584 016.
Variações ritmicas Op 16 (piano, 6 percussion) 1963. Recorded EMI Pathe Marconi 76292791.
Canticum instrumentale Op 25 (flute, harp, piano, timpani) 1967. Recorded EMI Angel 063 270107.
String Quartet No 1 Op 26 1967. Recorded Philips 6598 310.
Rhymetron Op 27 (percussion) 1968. Recorded Philips 6833 177/8; EMI Pathe Marconi 7692791.
Wind Quintet Op 29 1968. Recorded EMI Angel 063 422907.
Tropicale Op 30 (piccolo, E♭ clarinet, piano, percussion) 1968. Recorded EMI Angel 063 422907.
Sonancias Op 37 (piano, percussion) 1972; first performed Munich, 1972. Recorded EMI Pathe Marconi 769 2791.
Homenagem a Arthur Rubinstein Op 40 (piano) 1973. Recorded Deutsche Grammophon 2584 016.
Momentos I Op 41/1 (guitar) 1974. Recorded EMI Angel 063 422921.
Momentos II Op 41/2 (guitar) 1975. Recorded EMI Angel 063 422921.
Momentos III Op 41/3 (guitar) 1976. Recorded EMI Angel 063 422921.
Sonata on a Theme by Béla Bartók Op 45 (piano) 1977.
Homenagem a Villa-Lobos Op 46 (guitar) 1977.
Sonancias II Op 48 (flute, guitar, piano, percussion) 1980.
Sonancias III Op 49 (2 pianos, 2 percussion) 1980. Recorded EMI Pathe Marconi 769 2791.
Momentos IV Op 54 (guitar) 1982. Recorded EMI Angel 063 422921.
Solo I Op 60 (flute) 1984. Recorded EMI Angel 063 270107.
Tango Op 61 (piano) 1984.
Prologo e toccata Op 65 (guitar) 1984. Recorded Hyperion 66203.

Fandango Op 69 (guitar quartet or guitar ensemble) 1985.
Círculos mágicos Op 70 (bass clarinet, percussion) 1989.
Duo Op 71 (guitar, percussion) 1989.
Sonatina Op 76 (2 guitars) 1989.

Vocal/choral:

Três canções Op 9 (high voice, piano) 1962.
Ukrinmakrinkrin Op 17 (soprano, piccolo, oboe, horn, piano; Xucuru) 1964. Recorded EMI Angel 063 422907.
Beiramar / By the Sea Op 21 (voice, instruments) 1967–80.
O canto multiplicado Op 38 (medium voice, string orchestra) 1972. Recorded Philips 6833 177/8.
Yanomani Op 47 (tenor, SATB chorus, guitar) 1980. Recorded EMI Angel 063 422921.
Cantata do chimborazo Op 56 (tenor, baritone, SATB chorus, orchestra) 1982.
Descobrimento da América Op 77 (tenor, baritone, bass, SATB chorus, orchestra) 1990.

PUBLICATIONS

By Nobre: "Notação musical", in *Music in the Americas*, edited by List and Orrego-Salas, Bloomington, Indiana, 1967; "Música brasileina contemporânea", in *Revista de Cultura Brasileina*, 32, 1971.

On Nobre: P. Earls, review article in *Mosaico: Yearbook for InterAmerican Musical Research*, 8, 1973; David P. Appleby, "After *Modernismo*", in *The Music of Brazil*, Austin, Texas, 1983, 1989.

* * *

There is still a tendency in some quarters to see the death of Heitor Villa-Lobos in 1959 as marking the end of the great period in Brazilian music and signalling the arrival of a kind of epigonism, full of diffuse, Europeanised gestures and fundamentally out of touch with native traditions and resources. This is, of course, a misconception. Brazilian musicians had always gone to Europe to complete their training. What was new was a recognition that nationalism was, if not a dead end, then no longer an aesthetic of sufficiency. It remains, however, a constant benchmark in modern Brazilian music, a nourishing dialectical opposite to the internationalist language of serialism, chance, and to the freemasonry of electro-acoustic composition.

By the time of Marlos Nobre's birth, at the beginning of another world war that was to touch Brazil culturally and economically, controversy had been lowered to a gentle simmer (though there was a further outbreak in 1950 when the exiled H.J. Koellreutter and Camargo (or "Mozart") Guarnieri debated the validity of twelve-tone writing in the Brazilian music press). It is significant—or perhaps just tidy—that Nobre's first numbered composition should date from the year of Villa-Lobos's death. The *Concertino* for strings is less overtly nativist than the slightly plodding *Nazarethiana Op 2*. This is a brief piano piece dedicated to the great Brazilian composer Ernesto Nazareth, who died in 1934, leaving behind an influence on his compatriots only a little less dominant than that of Villa-Lobos. *Nazarethiana* is elegantly chromatic and full of folkish elements from Nobre's native North East.

The great virtue of *Nazarethiana* was that it won Nobre a bursary from the German American Cultural Society which enabled him to travel to Terezopolis to study with the influential German–American exile Koellreutter. The defender of Schoenbergian music was by no means blind to the attraction of folk and native elements and was attempting to synthesise them in his own work. It is Koellreutter's influence, rather than that of Guarnieri or Ginastera later that set Nobre on the road towards a highly individualised modernist synthesis which drew on the widest freedoms of an international idiom but preserved the emotional coherence of the native tradition.

Certainly, Nobre's music matured rapidly and gained in depth after 1963. The vital work of this period, up to the hiatus in his compositional output around 1967–8, was the tongue-twisting *Ukrinmakrinkrin*. The piece was scored for soprano with accompaniment of piccolo, oboe, horn and piano, a timbral range increasingly typical of Nobre's work. Its text came from the impenetrable Xucuru Indian tongue. Nobre uses its phonemes in tandem with a modified row and introduces chance and distinctive rhythmic elements in the bass clef which set it apart as one of the most remarkable modern vocal compositions. Nobre's use of ostinato figures gained in confidence over the years. *Beiramar* (the title means "By the Sea") combines a dramatic intensity with a strong hint even in its conservatism of the stylistic restlessness expressed in his more experimental works of the time.

For many of the succeeding years, Nobre was, figuratively, by the sea. There had been a certain apocalyptic exhaustion of his modified serialism, and he was looking out again to the work of the younger European and Asian composers (as well as to figures like Messiaen, who had been a distinguished visitor to Buenos Aires). The work of the 1970s, beginning with the extraordinary *Mosáico* for string orchestra, marks a recombination of the polytonal and free rhythmic qualities that had been drifting apart in his previous works. Nobre was able to give distinctive Brazilian rhythmic patterns an intrinsic, not just decorative, role within an advanced tonal language. *Sonancias* for piano and percussionists is among the most important Latin American works since the end of the war. As a telling instance of the new respect and enthusiasm being shown to South American musicians, it was actually commissioned and premiered in Munich. Nobre's theoretical and polemical underpinning can be found in his influential essay "Música brasileina contemporânea," published in 1971.

Perhaps because his timbral and rhythmic possibilities were still somewhat broader and fresher than those available to most Europeans of his generation, Nobre showed surprisingly little interest in electronic music, a vein that might well have furthered his interest in clusters and extended tonal range. With the 1980s there comes a new neo-classicism and a freedom of conception that comes in part from Ginastera's injunction to write music in the head, not on the keyboard; Nobre's later scores give every impression of being tailored to a specific conception, not constrained to a given range of possibilities. As from the beginning of his career, he is still haunted by the sounds of *frevo* and *maracatu* from his native Pernambuco. His current enthusiasms are recorded as being Mozart, Bartók and Lutosławski, three composers who made a triumphant synthesis of apparently irreconcilable idioms.

Nobre is certainly the most important composer currently working in Latin America. As the continent's colonial and post-colonial past is re-examined, and the quincentenary of Columbus's voyage celebrated, his powerful *Descobrimento da América* is a further reminder that the "discovery" of America was largely a matter of point of view. Equally, the "discoveries" of the European avant-garde were sometimes already enshrined in long-standing nativist traditions where only a species of cultural inferiorism kept them from assuming their true international significance. That is now, thankfully, happening.

—Brian Morton

NONO, Luigi. Italian. Born in Venice, 29 January 1924. Educated at Benedetto Marcello Conservatory, Venice (composition under Gian Francesco Malipiero), 1941–5; concurrently at Padua University, graduated in law, 1946; further study in advanced harmony and counterpoint under Bruno Maderna and Hermann Scherchen, from 1946; Ferienkurse für Neue Musik, Darmstadt, from 1950; further research into electronics, Studio di Fonologia Musicale, 1954–60. Served in Italian Resistance, 1943–5. Married Nuria Schoenberg in 1955; 2 daughters. Member, Italian Communist Party, Central Committee, from 1975. Teacher, Ferienkurse für Neue Musik, Darmstadt, from 1957; composer in residence, Dartington Hall Music Summer School, Devon, 1959, 1960; visits to Soviet Union, 1963, 1973, 1976; organizer, factory and trade union debates, from 1964; visit to Cuba, 1967; visiting lecturer, United States, Soviet Union, Poland, Czechoslovakia, German Democratic Republic, Argentina, Paraguay, Chile, Venezuela, Peru; participant, "*musica-realta*", Federazione Italiana Operai Metalmeccanici, from 1973. **Died March 1991.**

Publisher: Ricordi.

Symphonies/orchestral:

Variazioni canoniche sulla serie dell'op. 41 di A. Schoenberg (chamber orchestra) 1950; first recorded Darmstadt, 27 August 1950.
Composizione No 1 1951.
Y su sangre ya viene cantando (part 2 of *Epitaffio per Federico García Lorca*; flute, chamber orchestra) 1952. Recorded RCA VICS 1313.
Il mantello rosso: Suite No 2 (after the ballet) 1953.
Due expressioni 1953.
Incontri (small orchestra) 1955. Recorded Vega C30 A66.
Varianti (violin, woodwinds, strings) 1957. Recorded Deutsche Grammophon DGG 062030.
Composizione No 2: Diario polacco '58 1958–9.
Per Bastiana Tai-Yang Cheng (L'oriente e rosso) (3 instrumental groups, tape) 1967; first performed Toronto, 31 October 1968. Recorded Wergo 60067.
A Carlo Scarpa architetto, ai suoi infiniti possibili (orchestra with microtones) 1984; first performed Hamburg, 10 March 1985.

Chamber/instrumental:

Polifonica—monodia—ritmica (flute, clarinet, bass clarinet, saxophone, horn, piano, percussion) 1951. Recorded Time Records S/8002.
Canti per tredici (13 instruments) 1954–5.
Notturni-albe (piano, tape) 1974.
. . . sofferte onde serene . . . (piano, tape) 1976; first performed Milan, 17 April 1977. Recorded Deutsche Grammophon DGG 423 248 2.
Con Luigi Dallapiccola (6 percussion, 4 pick-ups, 3 ring modulators, loudspeakers) 1979; first performed Milan, 4 November 1979.
Fragmente-Stille, an Diotima (string quartet) 1980; first performed Bonn, 2 June 1980. Recorded Deutsche Grammophon DG 415 513–2.
A Pierre. Dell'azzurro silenzio, inquietum (contrabass flute, contrabass clarinet, live electronics) 1985; first performed Baden-Baden, 31 March 1985.
Post-Prae-Ludium No 1: Donau (tuba, live electronics) 1987; first performed Donaueschingen, 17 October 1987.
La Lontananza Nostalgica—Futura (violin, 8 tapes) 1988; first performed Berlin, 3 September 1988.
Post-Prae-Ludium No 2: Baab-arr (piccolo) 1988; first performed Berlin, 4 September 1988.

Vocal/choral:

España en el corazon (part 1 of *Epitaffio per Federico García Lorca*; soprano, baritone, small chorus, instruments; Lorca, Neruda) 1952.
Memento: Romance de la guardia civil (part 3 of *Epitaffio per Federico García Lorca*; speaker, speaking chorus, chorus, orchestra; Lorca) 1953.
Il mantello rosso: Suite No 1 (after the ballet; soprano, baritone, chorus, orchestra; Lorca) 1954.
Liebeslied (chorus, ensemble) 1954. Recorded Deutsche Grammophon 429 260 2.
La victoire de Guernica (chorus, orchestra; Eluard) 1954.
Il canto sospeso (soprano, mezzo-soprano, tenor, chorus, orchestra; letters by Italian Resistance partisans) 1955–6.
La terra e la compagna (soprano, tenor, chorus, instruments, Pavese) 1957–8.
Coro di Didone (chorus, percussion; Ungaretti) 1958.
Ha venido: Canciones para Silvia (soprano, 6 unaccompanied female voices; Machado) 1960. Recorded Wergo WER 60038.
Sara dolce tacere (8 unaccompanied solo voices; Pavese) 1960. Recorded Wergo WER 60026.
Canti di vita e d'amore (consists of "Sul ponte di Hiroshima" (Anders), "Djamila Boupacha" (Pacheco), "Tu" (Pavese); soprano, tenor, orchestra) 1962. Recorded Wergo WER 60067; part 2 Wergo WER 60051.
Canciones a Guiomar (soprano, 6 female voices, instruments; Machado) 1962–3. Recorded CBS S 34 61226.
La fabbrica illuminata (voice, tape; Scabia, Pavese) 1964; first performed Venice, 15 September 1964. Recorded Wergo 60038.
A floresta e jovem e cheja de vida (soprano, 3 speakers, clarinet, bronze sheets, tape; Pirelli and others) 1966; first performed Venice, 7 September 1966.
Suite: Intolleranza 1960 (soprano, chorus, live or recorded orchestra) 1969.
Musica-manifesto No 1 ("Un volto e del mare"; voice, tape; Pavese) 1969; first performed Chatillon-sous-Bagneux, 19 May 1969. Recorded Philips 6521027.
Y estonces comprendio (6 female voices, chorus, tape, electronics; Falqui) 1969–70; broadcast RAI, Rome, 21 March 1970. Recorded Deutsche Grammophon DGG 2530436.
Voci destroying muros (4 female voices, speaking voices, chorus, orchestra) 1970, later reworked as part of *Ein Gespenst geht um in der Welt*.
Ein Gespenst geht um in der Welt (soprano, chorus, orchestra; *The Communist Manifesto*, Sanchez, Santamaria) 1970–1; first performed Cologne, 11 February 1971.
Como una ola de fuerza y luz (soprano, piano, orchestra, tape; Huasi) 1971–2; first performed Milan, 28 June 1972.

Recorded Deutsche Grammophon DGG 423 248 2.

Simao la gioventu del Vietnam (unaccompanied unison voices; Federici) 1973.

Io, frammento dal Prometeo (3 sopranos, small chorus, bass flute, contrabass clarinet, live electronics; Cacciari) 1981; first performed Venice, 24 September 1981.

Das atmende Klarsein (small chorus, bass flute, live electronics; Cacciari) 1981; first performed Florence, 30 May 1981. Recorded Finit Cetra Italia 70100.

¿Donde estas hermano? (2 sopranos, mezzo-soprano, contralto; for the "disappeared" of Argentina) 1982; first performed Cologne, 24 November 1982.

Quando stanno morendo: Diario polacco No 2 (4 female voices, flute, cello, live electronics; Milosz, Pasternak, Khlebnikov, Ady, Blok, Cacciari) 1982; first performed Venice, 3 October 1982. Recorded Ricordi CRM 1003.

Guai ai gelidi mostri (2 contraltos, flute/piccolo/bass flute, clarinet/E♭ clarinet/bass clarinet, tuba/piccolo trumpet, viola, cello, double bass, live electronics; Cacciari) 1983; first performed Cologne, 23 October 1983. Recorded Ricordi CRM 1003.

Omaggio a György Kurtag (contralto, flute, clarinet, bass tuba, live electronics) 1983–6; original version first performed Florence, 10 June 1983; revised version first performed Turin, 6 June 1986.

Risonanze errante a Massimo Cacciari (mezzo-soprano, flute, tuba, versions for 4, 5 and 6 percussion, live electronics; Melville, Bachmann) 1986; original version first performed Cologne, 15 March 1986; 2nd version first performed Turin, 6 June 1986; final version first performed Paris, 8 October 1987.

Caminantes . . . Ayacucho (contralto, bass flute, organ, 2 choruses, orchestra with 3 choruses, live electronics; Bruno) 1987; first performed Monaco, 25 April 1987.

Decouvrir la subversion: Hommage à Edmond Jabes (contralto, bass, reciter, bass tuba, horn, flute, live electronics) 1987; first performed Paris, 5 October 1987.

No hay caminos, hay que caminar . . . Andrej Tarkovskij (7 choruses, orchestra) 1987; first performed Tokyo, 28 November 1987.

Opera:

Intolleranza 1960 (Brecht, Eluard, Mayakovsky) 1960; first performed Venice, 1961; revised as *Intolleranza 1970*, Florence, 1974.

Al gran sole carico d'amore / Au Grand Soleil d'amour chargé (Rimbaud, Brecht, Bunke, Castro, Guevara, Dimitrov, Gorky, Gramsci, Lenin, Marx, Michel, Pavese, Sanchez, Santamaria) 1972–4, revised 1977; first performed Milan, 4 April 1975; revised version first performed Milan, 11 February 1978.

Prometeo: Tragedia dell'ascolto (Cacciari) 1981–5; first performed Venice, 25 September 1984.

Other:

Il mantello rosso (ballet; after Lorca) 1953–4; first performed Berlin, 1954.

Omaggio a Emilio Vedova (tape) 1960; broadcast RAI, Rome, 1961. Recorded Wergo WER 60067.

Die Ermittlung (incidental music to play by Weiss; tape) 1965; first performed Berlin, 19 October 1965; new version as *Ricorda coas ti hanno fatto in Auschwitz*, 1966.

Ricorda cosa ti hanno fatto in Auschwitz (tape) 1966; first performed Milan, 17 March 1967. Recorded Wergo WER 60038.

Contrappunto dialettico alla mente (2-track tape; texts by Sanchez, Balestrini, manifesto of the Enraged Women of the Progressive Labour Party, Harlem) 1967–8; first performed Palermo, 27 December 1968. Recorded Deutsche Grammophon DGG 423 248 2.

Musica-manifesto No 1 (part 2: "Non consumiamo Marx"; tape) 1969; first performed Chatillon-sous-Bagneux, 19 May 1969.

Musica per Manzu (tape score to film *Pace e guerra*) 1969.

Für Paul Dessau (tape) 1974; first performed Pisa, 6 May

PUBLICATIONS

By Nono: "Zur Entwicklung der Serientechnik" [also in English], in *Gravesaner Blatter*, 4, 1956; "Die neue Kompositionstechnik", in *Gravesaner Blatter*, 6, 1956; "Der Entwicklung der Reihentechnik", in *Darmstadter Beitrage zur neuen Musik*, 1, 1958; "Diario polacco '58: Bemerkungen eines Komponisten", in *Blatter und Bildung*, Wurzburg, 1960; "Presenza storica nella musica d'oggi", reprinted in *Al gran sole carico d'amore*, edited by Degrada, Milan, 1975, reprinted in German in *Melos*, 27, 1960 and *Darmstadter Beitrage zur neuen Musik*, 3, 1960, in English in *Score*, 27, 1960; "Vorwort zum Kranichsteiner Kompositions-Studio", in *Darmstadter Beitrage zur neuen Musik*, 2, 1960; "Possibilito e necesita di un nuovo teatromusicale", in *Il verri*, Milan, 1963, reprinted in *Al gran sole carico d'amore*, edited by Degrada, Milan, 1975; "Ricordo di due musicisti" [Malipiero and Maderna], in *Cronache musicali Ricordi*, Milan, 1973.

On Nono: Karlheinz Stockhausen, "Sprache und Musik", in *Darmstadter Beitrage zur neuen Musik*, 1, 1958, in English in *Die Reihe*, 4, 1958; U. Unger, "LN", in *Die Reihe*, 4, 1958, in English, in *Die Reihe*, 4, 1960; Roman Vlad, in *Storia della dodecafonico*, Milan, 1958; R. Smith Brindle, "Current Chronicle: Italy", in *Musical Quarterly*, 47, 1961; J.S. Weissmann, "LN und sein Werk", in *Paragone*, 13, 1962; F. D'Amico, "La polemica su LN", in *Paragone*, 13, 1962; Mario Bortolotto, "La missione teatrale di LN", in *Paragone*, 13, 1962; Mario Bortolotto, "New Music in Italy", in *Contemporary Music in Europe*, edited by Lang and Broder, New York, 1965; G.W. Hopkins, "LN", in *Music and Musicians*, 14(8), 1965–6; *LN: Werkverzeichnis*, Schott, Mainz, 1966; M. Barzetti, "A Meeting with LN", in *Recorded Sound*, 24, 1966; R. Smith Brindle, "Current Chronicle: Italy", in *Musical Quarterly*, 53, 1967; Mario Bortolotto, "Le missioni di Nono", in *Fase seconda*, Turin, 1969; G. Pone, "Webern and LN: The Genesis of a New Compositional Morphology and Syntax", in *Perspectives of New Music*, 10(2), 1972; Luigi Pestalozza, "LN—Musik, Text, Bedeutung", in *Melos*, 41, 1974; Jurg Stenzl, "LN and Cesare Pavese", in *Veroffentlichtungen des Institut für neue Musik und Musikerziehung Darmstadt*, 14, 1974; F. Degrada, (interview) in *A gran sole carico d'amore*, Milan, 1975; Jurg Stenzl, *LN—Texte: Studien zur seiner Musik*, Zurich, 1975; Hubert Stuppner, "LN: oder die Manifestation des Absoluten als Reaktion eines gesellschatlich betroffene Ichs", in *Musik-Konzepte*, 20, 1981; Friedrich Spangemacher, "Die elektronische Musik LNs", dissertation, University of Berlin, from 1987.

* * *

A salient feature of Luigi Nono's art is the equilibrium it achieves between abstract constructivism and human values. Furthermore, it is ironic that he should have succeeded in bringing avant-gardism into the orbit of that movement, revolutionary communism, which had studiously ignored and even condemned modernism. Nono's espousal of communism was certainly compatible with a good Italian tendency towards politicizing art and this, combined with his highly developed social commitment, gave to his potentially intractable post-Webern style a dramatically unorthodox quality.

His early studies at the Venice Conservatory profited from the broad interests of his composition teacher Gian Francesco Malipiero, who was an expert on Renaissance music, and it was from such a broad base that Nono became conversant with the techniques of the Second Viennese School, which he learned from Bruno Maderna (who was to be a staunch champion of his work) and Hermann Scherchen. His initial success was with a performance of *Variazioni canoniche sulla serie dell'op. 41 di A. Schoenberg* at Darmstadt in 1950, which established him in Germany long before he was recognized in his native Italy (during much of the 1950s his works were virtually ignored there). The *Variations* employ a strict twelve-tone technique and have characteristically a political undertone which owes much to Schoenberg's obliquely political *Ode to Napoleon* upon which they are modelled. A similar stance is noticeable in a number of succeeding works where one senses an uneasy combination of very strict musical techniques with an impassioned musical testimony, for music that is clearly meant to connect with real life the style for the most part is severe. Other early works, such as the *Polifonica–monodia–ritmica* show how thoroughly he has assimilated many of Webern's techniques and characteristics, yet without adopting the Viennese master's introspection and intimacy. However, his choral piece *Epitaffio per Federico García Lorca* is not at all abstract and fuses elements derived from folksong, liturgical music and the sound of castanets in a manner which convincingly brings together an impassioned emotional expression and dodecaphonic constructivism.

But the most notable synthesis of rational organisation with emotional expression is found in the cantata *Il canto sospeso*, a deeply felt, humanistic work redolent of compassion and tragic eloquence which brought Nono a wider recognition. Scored for soprano, alto and tenor soloists, mixed chorus and orchestra, it is a setting of excerpts from the last letters of members of the European Resistance condemned to death. Although pointillistic in style the unified colour of the chorus gives an aural coherence while the solo parts are powerfully melodic and reflect the inherent lyricism which is often found in Italian avant-garde music. The serial aspect of the work is relatively simple, for the tone row is neither transposed nor used in inversion or retrograde. However, it is not used horizontally in any single vocal or instrumental part but applied to each note as it occurs and in whatever voice. A striking feature is the dispersal of syllables among different voices; some voices sing only vowel sounds and thus focus on the phonetic basis in exploring new areas of expression. But there are also sustained lines, and a historical link is apparent in the curiously insistent repeated notes which identify Nono's vocal writing with that of earlier Venetian masters (in particular the Monteverdian *concitato* style).

The years 1958 to 1960 were transitional ones for Nono and included his first electronic composition, the *Omaggio a Emilio Vedova*. This inaugurated a period of intense devotion to electronic and tape music. Thus his *Suite: Intolleranza 1960* not only shows a new approach to music theatre but makes use of electronic elements (in the form of recorded material). This work, which caused a riot at its premiere in Venice, is a tirade against fascism, the atom bomb, and above all segregation and intolerance in general. Unlike most of his avant-garde contemporaries, who shunned opera as a medium, Nono felt himself drawn inexorably towards it, albeit in a highly unorthodox manner. This became apparent during the 1960s when he rebelled against the middle-class values of the concert hall and produced a number of "portable" tape-based works suitable for performance in informal venues such as factories and small halls. *Al gran sole carico d'amore / Au Grand Soleil d'amour chargé*, however, is an elaborate theatre work, although without a plot, and described by the composer as a "mural" depicting the class struggle in various parts of the world. As it moves from one revolutionary situation to another in compelling fashion, it constantly engages the listener.

A period of reflection after 1974 prompted a change of mood, as is evident in the quiet introspection of *Con Luigi Dallapiccola* and the string quartet *Fragmente-Stille, an Diotima*. In 1980, Nono began working on his monumental "aural drama" *Prometeo: Tragedia dell'ascolto*, the result of a renewed activity with electronics at the Experimentalstudio in Freiburg. This work explores new "aural vistas", making it necessary, in Nono's words, "to listen differently". The work comprises a slow unfolding of literary fragments ranging from Aeschylus to Rilke. Micro-intervals are explored in a soundscape distributed antiphonally on several levels and the whole effect is altered and modulated by live electronics. A concept of sound and space that had always been present in Nono's works is here refined and presented in typically provocative fashion with a new breadth and maturity reflecting the composer's continuing exploration along new paths.

—Richard Elfyn Jones

NORDGREN, Pehr Henrik. Finnish. Born 1944. Educated at Helsinki University, graduated in musicology, 1967; private composition study under Joonas Kokkonen; Tokyo University of Arts and Music (composition and traditional Japanese music), 1970–3. Settled in Kaustinen; independent composer. Recipient: 1st prize (for *Nelja kuolemankuvaa*), 1969. Mailing address: Visatie 16, SF-69600 Kaustinen, Finland.

Publisher: Fazer.

Symphonies / orchestral:

Euphonie I Op 1 1966; first performed Helsinki, 25 February 1967.

Epiphrase Op 4 1966; first performed Aarhus, 1967.

Koko maailma valittanee / The Whole World Will Lament Op 40 1966–74. Recorded Tactus TA 8110.

Euphonie II Op 5 1967; first performed Helsinki, 30 January 1969.

Minore Op 6 1968; first performed Trondheim, February 1969.

Concerto for Violin and Orchestra No 1 Op 10 1969; first performed Helsinki, 12 February 1970.

Concerto for Viola and Orchestra No 1 Op 12 1970; first performed Tampere, 1971.

Concerto for Clarinet, Folk Instruments and Small Orchestra Op 14 1970; first performed Helsinki, 22 April 1971.

The Turning Point Op 16 1972; first performed Helsinki, 12 March 1974.

Autumnal Concerto Op 18 (traditional Japanese instruments,

strings) 1974; first performed Helsinki, 28 August 1974.
Symphony Op 20 1974; first performed Turku, 10 October 1974.
Concerto for Piano and Orchestra Op 23 1975; first performed Helsinki, 22 April 1975.
Euphonie III Op 24 1975; first performed Lahti, 12 April 1975.
Pelimannimuotokuvia / Portraits of Country Fiddlers Op 26 (strings) 1976; first performed Seinajoki, 5 April 1976. Recorded Fuga 3036; Tactus TA 7910.
Concerto for Violin and (String) Orchestra No 2 Op 33 1977; first performed Helsinki, 15 November 1977. Recorded BIS CD 326.
Summer Music Op 34 1977; first performed Kaustinen, 18 July 1977.
Symphony for Strings Op 43 1978; "Adagio" first performed Kalvia, 14 June 1978; first complete performance Kokkola, 14 January 1979. Recorded Tactus TA 8111.
Concerto for Viola and Orchestra No 2 Op 48 1979; first performed Helsinki, 7 December 1979.
Concerto for Cello and (String) Orchestra No 1 Op 50 1980; first performed Kuhmo, 28 July 1980. Recorded FACD 350.
Concerto for Violin and (String) Orchestra No 3 Op 53 1981; first performed Kaustinen, 31 January 1982. Recorded Finlandia FACD 343.
Concerto for Strings Op 54 1982; first performed Kokkola, 27 November 1983.
Concerto for Cello and Orchestra No 2 Op 62 1984; first performed Helsinki, 21 March 1984.
Elegy to Vilho Lampi Op 65 1984; first performed Oulu, 21 February 1985.
Concerto for Kantele and Small Orchestra Op 66 1985; first performed Joensuu, 19 June 1986.
Transe-Choral Op 67 (chamber string orchestra) 1985–6; first performed Kokkola, 6 January 1986.
Concerto for Viola and (Chamber) Orchestra No 3 Op 68 1986; first performed Vaasa, 2 July 1986.
Hate-Love Op 71 (cello, strings) 1987.

Chamber / instrumental:

String Quartet No 1 Op 2 1967; first performed Helsinki, 28 January 1968.
Nachtwache Op 3 (suite from music to radio play by Nelly Sachs; 3 clarinets, horn, 5 percussion, piano, harp, violin, viola, cello) 1967.
String Quartet No 2 Op 7 1968; first performed Trondheim, 1969; subsequently lost.
Nelja kuolemankuvaa / Four Pictures of Death Op 8 (chamber ensemble) 1968; first performed Helsinki, 11 May 1969.
Sonatina per sestetto Op 9 (flute, clarinet, violin, cello, piano, percussion) 1969; first performed Helsinki, 12 March 1969.
Kolme maanitusta / Three Enticements (Wind Quintet No 1) Op 11 (flute, oboe, clarinet, bassoon, horn) 1970; lost.
Ritornello Op 13 (violin, piano) 1970; first performed Helsinki, 18 October 1970.
Ten Piano Ballades to Japanese Ghost Stories by Lafcadio Hearn (piano) 1972–7. Recorded Toshiba LF-91027/91037.
Miminaski-Hoichi Op 17 (piano) 1972; first performed Sendai, Japan, 19 June 1972.
Oshidori Op 25 (piano) 1976; first performed Helsinki, 18 January 1976.
Mugen-Kane Op 28 (piano) 1976; first performed 28 November 1976.
O-tei Op 29 (piano) 1976; first performed Tokyo, 18 January 1977.
Mujina Op 30 (piano) 1976; first performed Helsinki, 13 March 1977.
Yuki-onna Op 31 (piano) 1976; first performed Tokyo, 12 January 1977.
Rokuro-kubi Op 32 (piano) 1976; first performed Tokyo, 12 January 1977.
Akinosuke-no-yume Op 35 (piano) 1977; first performed Helsinki, 29 March 1978.
Jikininki Op 36 (piano) 1977; first performed Jyvaskyla, 6 October 1977.
Jiu-roku-zakura Op 37 (piano) 1977; first performed 18 July 1977.
Quartet No 1 for Traditional Japanese Instruments Op 19 (shakuhachi, shamisen, koto, juschichigen) 1974; first performed Helsinki, 26 August 1974.
As in a Dream Op 21 (cello, piano) 1974.
Wind Quintet No 2 Op 22 (flute, oboe, clarinet, bassoon, horn) 1975; first performed Hasselby, 23 September 1975.
String Quartet No 3 Op 27 1976; first performed Helsinki, 1 September 1976.
Butterflies Op 39 (guitar) 1977; first performed Sydney, 23 October 1977. Recorded BIS LP 207.
In Patches Op 41 (accordion) 1978; first performed Helsinki, 25 October 1978.
Seita (Quartet No 2 for Traditional Japanese Instruments) Op 42 (shakuhachi, 2 kotos, jushichigen) 1978; first performed Helsinki, 1 August 1978.
Piano Quintet Op 44 1978; first performed Edinburgh, 17 October 1978.
A Late Pastorale Op 47 (horn, string quintet) 1979; first performed Jyvaskyla, 27 June 1979.
Piano Trio Op 49 1980; first performed Helsinki, 28 August 1980.
Euphonie IV Op 51 (4 saxophones, 4 trumpets, 3 trombones, piano, drums, double bass) 1980–1; broadcast February 1981.
Equivocations Op 55 (kantele, violin, viola, cello) 1981; first performed Helsinki, 6 April 1981.
String Quartet No 4 Op 60 1983; first performed Joensuu, 20 February 1984.
Epilogue Op 61 (cello, piano) 1983; first performed Espoo, 1984.
String Quartet No 5 Op 69 1986; first performed Kuhmo, 16 July 1986.

Vocal / choral:

Agnus Dei Op 15 (soprano, baritone, mixed chorus, orchestra) 1970; first performed Helsinki, 11 May 1971.
Maan alistaminen / The Subjection of Earth (no opus number; unaccompanied mixed chorus; Kalevala) 1974.
Kuninkaan kammenella / In the Palm of the King's Hand Op 46 (soprano, baritone, mixed chorus, orchestra; Haavikko) 1979; first performed Kokkola, 24 February 1980.
Taivaanvalot / The Lights of Heaven Op 63 (soprano, tenor, mixed chorus, children's chorus, orchestra with folk instruments; Kalevala) 1985; first performed Kaustinen, 3 February 1985.

Opera / dramatic:

Den svarte munken / The Black Monk Op 52 (chamber opera; Saaritsa) 1981; first performed Stockholm, 20 March 1984.
Alex Op 56 (television opera; Saaritsa) 1983; broadcast Finnish Broadcasting Company, 6 September 1986.

* * *

A problem which all Scandinavian composers of our generation must face and solve, either consciously or unconsciously, is that in each of their countries there is one towering figure in the historical background, a single musical personality whose shadow dominates the minds and attitudes of anyone who wishes to compose, and usually a succeeding generation which has split into those that carry on the tradition of "the master" and those who overtly reject it, thus tacitly paying it homage. Nor is it anything so simple as merely a question of musical language or attitudes to national identity, though this would be problem enough (the sound, after all, is the first thing you hear). In the case of Nielsen and Sibelius, both employed systems of rigorous thematic and motivic working, tightly structured harmonic patterns and a highly developed intellectual content that established a definite habit of thought as well as expression. In Finland the problem is compounded by the fact that the dominant tradition is not musical but literary, and that the musical and literary impulses have an uneasy symbiosis so that the spirit of epic is received twice—directly, in its raw state, and processed, via Sibelius and Uuno Klami. The country itself, moreover, was (and to some extent still is) divided—culturally and politically—into Swedish-speakers and "ethnic" Finns, with the Russian bear prowling its borders and gobbling bits up from time to time.

While it contains sharply antagonistic factions, Finland today has two broad schools: the old symphonic tradition is alive and well in the hands of such composers as Joonas Kokkonen, Einojuhani Rautavaara, Aulis Sallinen and Eero Hämeenniemi, while a balancing group of "de-structuralists" and colourists is fast developing behind the banner of Erik Bergman—Kaija Saariaho, Jouni Kaipainen, Magnus Lindberg; bridging the two is the giant figure of Paavo Heininen with his implicitly intellectual statements humanised by his ravishing sound world.

Pehr Henrik Nordgren is a maverick: not because there is anything intrinsically bizarre about his style or subversive in his activities—just the opposite—but because he is a "one-off". He owes allegiance to neither camp, though he did take some lessons privately with Kokkonen, and his music has nothing to do with any larger European movement or the cosmopolitan avant-garde. This is not to suggest that he is uninfluenced: like any creative artist his work is an interaction of his personality with his experience and training, its individuality derived from the degree to which the influences are absorbed and the levels at which they operate. It is possible to be both considerably influenced and totally original: Arvo Pärt is such a composer, Nordgren another, with rather different effect. In Nordgren's case the levels are the most superficial and the most profound. For instance, the outcome of his studies at Tokyo University can be seen in the *Autumnal Concerto* for traditional Japanese instruments and orchestra. Apart from the fact of the instruments and a certain feeling of symbolism and melancholy which might—fancifully—be described as in accordance with the Japanese view of life, the casual listener would be forgiven for failing to see any other overt Japanese musical influence, though the composer has frequently cited his time in Japan as having a more far-reaching influence on his outlook, and thus on his output. With his Finnish consciousness the response is more complex.

Since his return from the Far East, Nordgren has lived in the village of Kaustinen—a sort of Finnish Llangollen—famous for its folk festival and a particular tradition of fiddle-playing. Daily exposure to what one might patronisingly call "ethnic folk-culture" struck a deep chord in his undogmatic mind. Heininen once said that a culture without memory is a culture at risk. Nordgren's standpoint is that tradition is a living thing, looking forward as well as back: you draw from it but you also put back. Nordgren's response to his national roots is twofold. Initially it resulted in an explicit folk influence, in such works as the *Pelimannimuotokuvia / Portraits of Country Fiddlers* and the *Concerto for Kantele and Small Orchestra* (a traditional Finnish instrument). At a deeper level it has provided the basis of much of his recent compositional technique, a sort of freely unfolding, controlled, lyric/epic form with direct parallels in the literary saga tradition.

A significant factor in the composer's work was the series of collaborations with the orchestra of the Ostrobothnian College of Music, later Ostrobothnian Chamber Orchestra, and its director Juha Kangas, resulting in a number of major pieces from the late 1970s onwards. In earlier scores Nordgren's music had shown a fondness for large forces, and a tendency to Shostakovich-derived heroics. From about 1980 onwards we see a process of continuous refinement of expression and growing subtlety of form, a greater integration of style and content, not entirely forced upon him by the (string) orchestra's limited size. His language remains tonal—better, polytonal—in feel, but because forms are built up from within, the triads which pepper the scores serve no diatonic structural purpose. Successive pieces display a growing mood of introspection and restrained scoring, a paring away of anything resembling a gesture, leaving a sort of melancholic nostalgia. Forms are dictated by material and often present a first impression of disjointedness, like a chapter divided into paragraphs but unified by the underlying argument. His group of concertos, for cello, for violin and for strings are particularly characteristic of the trend of his thought at the time, with the solo (which is as likely to be an idea as a particular player) displaying an obstinate individuality rather than a virtuoso display: a figure in a landscape, where the landscape is as important as the figure. As with virtousity for its own sake (though technical difficulties are not lacking) Nordgren rejects what he would regard as spurious academic treatments such as serialism. It does not stop him employing, say, a tone-row, or clusters, to serve his own agenda, to integrate them for their expressive dimensions into his palette or structural needs.

Mood is important to Nordgren, and a sense of place: he is anxious to establish communication through music, that it should be accessible. Movements frequently have emotive subtitles, or are prefaced by quotations, not for programmatic reasons, but to create atmosphere and stimulate the imaginations of (possibly unsophisticated) audiences. Listening to these works, it is not hard to imagine the Ostrobothnian landscape, flat, raw and austere, or its people under the vast sky, their seriousness and obstinate defiance not quite subduing the innate poetry. Nordgren's poetry and humanity are likewise of an oblique kind; it is vernacular music, of the people, but avoiding both the salon and "back woods" romantic nationalism.

—Giles Easterbrook

NORDHEIM, Arne. Norwegian. Born in Larvik, 20 June 1931. Educated at Musikkonservatoriet, Oslo, 1948–52; further composition study under Karl Andersen, Bjarne

Brustad, Conrad Baden and, in Copenhagen, Vagn Holmboe, 1952–5. Music critic, *Dagbladet*, Oslo; visiting lecturer, United States, 1968; worked in electronic Studio Eksperymentalne, Warsaw, 1968; independent composer. Recipient: Bergen International Festival prize, 1960; Nordic Council Music Prize (for *Eco*), 1972. Mailing address: c/o Norwegian Music Information Centre, Toftesgate 69, N-0552 Oslo 5, Norway.

Publishers: Norsk Musikforlag, Oslo; Wilhelm Hansen, Copenhagen; Chester Music, London.

Symphonies/orchestral:

Canzona 1961. Recorded Philips 839 250 AY.
Epitaffio (orchestra, tape) 1963, 1977. Recorded Philips 839 250 AY.
Floating 1970; first performed Graz, Austria, 1970. Recorded Philips 6507 040.
Greening 1973; first performed Los Angeles, 1973. Recorded Decca HEAD 23.
Nachruf (string orchestra) 1975.
Spur (accordion, orchestra) 1975. Recorded Unicorn RHS 357/8.
Polygon 1976.
Tenebrae (cello, orchestra) 1982.
Utposter (24 trumpets, brass, chimes) 1984.
Boomerang (oboe, chamber orchestra) 1984.
Recall and Signals (symphonic band) 1986.
Varder (trumpets, orchestra) 1986.
Rendez-vous (string orchestra) 1987.
Monolith 1990.

Chamber/instrumental:

Essay (string quartet) 1954.
Epigram (string quartet) 1955.
String Quartet 1956.
Partita I (viola, harpsichord, percussion) 1963.
Response I (2 percussionists, tape) 1965. Recorded Philips 839 250 AY.
Colorazione (Hammond X-66 organ, percussion, ring modulators, filter) 1968, 1982. Recorded Philips 854 005 AY.
Partita II (electric guitar) 1969.
Dinosaurus (accordion, tape) 1971. Recorded Philips 6578 016.
Listen (piano) 1971. Recorded NC 3822/4470.
Strender (2 percussionists, tape) 1974.
The Hunting of the Snark (trombone) 1975. Recorded NC 4470.
Response IV (4 percussionists, tape) 1977. Recorded Philips 6514 103.
Clamavi (cello) 1980. Recorded NC 4470.
Partita (6 double basses) 1982.
Response III (organ, 4 percussionists, tape) 1983.
Partita für Paul (violin) 1984.
Flashing (accordion) 1986.

Vocal/choral:

Aftonland/Evening Land (soprano, string quintet, harp, celeste, percussion; version for soprano, chamber orchestra; Lagerkvist) 1957. Recorded Philips 6507 040.
Eco (soprano, SATB chorus, children's chorus, orchestra; Quasimodo) 1968. Recorded HMV CSDS 1087.
Tilitspolka (voice, jazz quartet) 1970.
Solar Plexus (2 voices, jazz group) 1972. Recorded Sonet SLP 1421/22.
Doria (tenor, orchestra) 1975. Recorded Decca HEAD 23.
To One Singing (tenor, harp) 1976.
Ariadne (2 sopranos, orchestra, tape) 1977.
Be Not Afeared (soprano, baritone, harp, piano, 2 percussionists, celeste, tape; Shakespeare) 1977.
Tempora noctis (soprano, mezzo-soprano, orchestra, tape; Ovid) 1979.
Wirklicher Wald (soprano, SATB chorus, cello, orchestra; Rilke, Bible) 1983. Recorded NC 4910.
Venit Rex (SATB chorus, fanfare, organ, orchestra) 1983. Recorded Philips 411 315-1.
Klokkesong (counter-tenor, Renaissance instruments, chorus, chimes) 1984. Recorded Aurora AR 1902.
Aurora (soprano, alto, tenor, bass, crotales, tape; version for soloists, SATB chorus, 2 percussionists, tape) 1984. Recorded Aurora AR 1902; NC 4910.
Tres Lamentationes: Saecundum Hieremias Propheta (unaccompanied SATB chorus) 1984. Aurora AR 1902.
Music to Two Fragments to Music by Shelley (unaccompanied SATB chorus) 1986.
La mia canzone (soprano, piano, percussion; Petrarch) 1987.
Tre voci (soprano, chamber ensemble; Petrarch, Bruno, Ungaretti) 1988.
Johannesgangaren (SSAA chorus, Hardanger fiddle, percussion, emulatorm, 3 trumpets, glockenspiel; Steensen) 1989.

Other:

Katharsis (ballet) 1962.
Favolas (10 dancers, 2 singers, orchestra, tape) 1965.
Evolution (electronic) 1965.
Warzawa (electronic) 1968. Recorded Philips 6507 042.
Solitaire (electronic) 1968. Recorded Philips 854 005 AY.
Pace (electronic) 1970. Recorded Philips 6507 042.
Poly-Poly: Music for Osaka 1970 (electronic music) 1970. Recorded (as *Five Osaka Fragments*) Philips 6507 042.
Ohm (electronic, tape) 1971. Recorded Philips 6529 109.
Lux et tenebrae (electronic) 1971. Recorded Philips 6507 042.
Stages (ballet) 1971.
Minebobler, en Orgelreparators Erindringer 1972.
Morgenraga (electronic) 1972. Recorded Sonet SLP 1421/22.
For Karin Boye (electronic) 1975.
Forbindelser/Connections (5 cities, radio, television) 1975; broadcast 14 December 1975.
Stormen/The Tempest (ballet) 1979. Recorded Philips 9598 043.
Nedstigningen (radiophonic) 1980.

Film and theatre music: *Det Hemmelige Regnskap*, 1957; *Damasktrommen*, 1960; *Sigurd Slembe*, 1960; *Don Juan*, 1960; *Vildanden*, 1960; *Den Lille Prinsen*, 1961; *Isoya Radio Kaller*, 1962; *Krangel ved Bymuren*, 1962; *Kimaere*, 1962; *Hjemkomsten*, 1963; *Her Bor vi sa Gjerne*, 1963; *Laeraren*, 1963; *Fangen i det Bla Tarn*, 1964; *Stoppested*, 1965; *Katteslotte*, 1965; *Nar vi Doge Vagner*, 1965; *Othello*, 1965; *En Gal Manns Dagbok*, 1967; *Don Carlos*, 1967; *Papirfugeln*, 1967; *De Blanke Kanpperne*, 1967; *Hamlet*, 1967; *Faust*, 1967; *Fruen fra Havet*, 1968; *Lille Eyolf*, 1968; *Lillebror-Lillesoster*, 1968; *Mot Bristepunktet*, 1968; *Brand*, 1968; *Hvisomatte*, 1969; *Dagen Vender*, 1969; *Ansiktene*, 1969; *Mandagsbilen*, 1969; *Ingen Himmel for Gunga Din*, 1969; *Myrfolket*, 1969; *Peer Gynt*, 1969; *John Gabriel Borkman*, 1969; *Gjengangere*, 1970; *En Benk i Parken*, 1970; *Vitnene*, 1970; *Vi Pa Alfabulator*, 1970; *En Dag i Ivan Denisovitsjs Liv*, 1970; *Dodsdansen*, 1971; *Kodemus*, 1971; *Macbeth*,

1972; *Dei Kjenslelause*, 1972; *Milkwood*, 1972; *En Havefest*, 1973; *Amaryllis*, 1973; *Aftenen er Stille*, 1973; *Dagny*, 1974; *Forfolgelsen*, 1981; *King Lear*, 1986.

PUBLICATIONS

On Nordheim: Nils Grinde, *Contemporary Norwegian Music, 1920–1980*, Oslo, 1981; Lorentz Reitan, "AN", Chester Music, London, 1985.

* * *

Arne Nordheim effected a quiet revolution in Norwegian music without setting foot in either Nadia Boulanger's classroom or in the sober teaching rooms at Darmstadt. He has never, even in the most radical of his experiments, turned his back on the great well-springs of European music and, indeed, his first significant orchestral work, the *Canzona* for orchestra of 1961, is inspired by Giovanni Gabrielli and the Venetian's almost pointillistic juxtaposition of colour values. This has become an essential component of Nordheim's mature work which distributes melorhythms without any obvious developmental impulse.

Nordheim's first modern influence was certainly Bartók, a presence that can be detected in the early works for string quartet. Already the tonality is quite free and in the vocal work *Aftonland / Evening Land*, based on a Lagerkvist text, it strives to leave harmonic restrictions behind in an altogether more expressionistic manner which begins to lead him away from a fixed pulse and linear melody. Nordheim had incorporated electronic elements into a radiophonic score for Antoine de Saint-Exupéry's fairytale *The Little Prince* as early as 1961; he was to make much more extensive use of such effects in the next two years, notably in the powerful ballet *Katharsis* and in *Epitaffio* for orchestra, a threnody to a flautist friend.

Nordheim's interest in sound developed with the 1960s, and he continued to experiment assiduously with pre-recorded material. Nevertheless, his most significant piece of the decade is without electrophonic material. The prize-winning *Eco* is based on two mordant texts by the great Italian modernist Salvatore Quasimodo and is dedicated to the memory of another musician friend, the Swedish composer Karl-Birger Blomdahl. It evokes an atmosphere of pain and loss, but one curiously dissociated from any single event or occasion, a quality that lends the work its wonderfully floating (Nordheim was to use the word later for an orchestral piece) quality. The much later *Tempora noctis* for two sopranos, orchestra and tape is very similar in treatment and underlines his obsession with death and the metaphysical transitions associated with it.

Nordheim developed his interest in electronics on a study visit to Warsaw in 1968, a trip that yielded an effective electrophonic portrait of the city and helped consolidate his conception of three related pieces called *Response* in which taped sounds derived from keyboards and percussion act as a kind of cantus firmus with which the acoustic instruments call and respond (jazz is another influence on Nordheim's conception). The process is carried a stage further in *Colorazione*. Here, organ and percussion sounds are taped and delayed, interweaving in a complex and non-repetitive way; the same principle lay behind the extraordinary "sound sculpture" designed with Arnold Haukeland for the Blind Centre at Skjeberg. Here the taped materials are programmed with photo-electric switches that respond to Norway's striking extremes of light and dark, producing virtually infinite combinations of sound. A similar principle lay behind Nordheim's music for the World's Fair at Osaka: *Poly-Poly: Music for Osaka 1970* is so devised as only to repeat its pattern exactly every century.

Nordheim drew a concert piece, *Lux et tenebrae*, from the Osaka score which heralded a number of significant orchestral pieces written in the 1970s, a decade when he was much involved with vocal and dance music. These depend on very much the same gentle alternation of musical durations and result in a much more flowing kind of music, which recalls Nordheim's essentially Romantic sensibility. On that score, it is easy to overemphasise Nordheim's experimentalism and commitment to technological solutions to musical questions. The remarkable *Fobindelser / Connections*, by which he attempted to link five cities and over 300 performers by means of radio and television link-ups may seem like hard-boiled experimentalism, but the work is also a celebration of human freedom, drawing its text from the U.N. Declaration on Human Rights. Experiment for its own sake has never appealed to Nordheim. Basically, all of his music, and increasingly as the 1970s gave way to the 1980s, is expressive, highly charged emotionally and passionately humane. *To One Singing*, written for tenor Peter Pears, with harp accompaniment, has an almost unearthly Orphean beauty that surfaces again in the choral Shelley settings and the more complex *Johannesgangaren* of the late 1980s. Words have always been very important to Nordheim, as witness his sensitive handling of Lagerkvist in *Aftonland / Evening Land*, the use of three key words from Quasimodo in the tape part on *Epitaffio* and in the ballet *Stormen / The Tempest*, based on Shakespeare.

He has written surprisingly little instrumental music of real power and most of the solo and small ensemble works sound very much like exercises in instrumental possibility; nonetheless, these can be highly effective, as in *Flashing* for accordion, moving, as in *Clamavi* for cello, and even amusing, as in *The Hunting of the Snark* for solo trombone. The concertante works for solo instrument and orchestra, such as *Spur* (accordion) and *Boomerang* (oboe) develop large areas of sound in a way that is not possible with solo instrumentation (or with tape) and Nordheim has shown little interest in developing a single line of musical argument, as is inevitable on a melody instrument.

This is not to suggest that his work is one-sided or partial. There is a marked bias in the Scandinavian countries towards larger-scale orchestral structures, and Nordheim is a Norwegian through and through, drawing only very implicitly and abstractly on his country's native traditions, but nonetheless conveying a deep understanding of her cultural imperatives, not least in his wonderful theatre scores for Ibsen in the late 1960s. He is the first Norwegian modernist, and, still only in his sixties, may yet become its most important composer of the century. There are those who would accord him that position already.

—Signe Maarten

NØRGÅRD, Per. Danish. Born in Gentofte, near Copenhagen, 13 July 1932. Educated at Royal Danish Conservatory of Music (theory, history of music, and composition under Vagn Holmboe, Finn Høffding and Hjelmborg), 1952–5; further study under Nadia Boulanger, Paris, 1956–7. Music critic, 1958–62; teacher of music, Odense Conservatoire, 1958–61; teacher of music, Royal Danish Academy of Music, 1960–5; professor of music, Royal Academy of Music, Aarhus, since 1965. Recipient: Nordic Council Prize for Music (for *Gilgamesh*), 1974. Mailing address: c/o Danish Music Information Centre, Vimmelskaftet 48, DK-1161 Copenhagen K, Denmark.

Publisher: Wilhelm Hansen, Copenhagen.

Symphonies/orchestral:

Metamorphosis Op 4 (string orchestra) 1952.
Symphony No 1: Sinfonia austera Op 13 1953–5; broadcast Danish Radio, 19 August 1958.
Konstellationer Op 22 (12 string groups, or 12 solo strings) 1958; first performed Copenhagen, 3 November 1958.
Lyse Danse / Bright Dances (divertimento for small orchestra) 1959.
Fragment VI (6 orchestral groups, winds, brass, percussion, harp, pianos, timpani) 1959–61; first performed Aarhus, 12 February 1962.
Det skete i de dage 1960.
Komposition 1966.
Ceremonial Music (wind orchestra) 1967.
Iris 1967; first performed Copenhagen, 19 May 1967. Recorded Caprice RIKS LP 54.
Luna: Four Phases for Orchestra 1967. Recorded Deutsche Grammophon DMA 018.
Recall (accordion, orchestra) 1968.
Doing (variations on a Beatles tune for brass band) 1968. Recorded Danica 8003.
Voyage into the Golden Screen (chamber orchestra) 1968–9. Recorded Caprice RIKS LP 54.
Symphony No 2 in One Movement 1970; first performed Aarhus, 13 April 1970.
Modlys / Backlight 1970.
Symphony No 3 in Two Movements (with double chorus, mezzo-soprano or alto; Latin hymns, Rilke, Ruckert, Scott) 1972–5; first performed Copenhagen, 2 September 1976.
Drømmespil / Dream Play (chamber orchestra) 1975.
Twilight (orchestra, obbligato conga player, dancer ad lib) 1976–7.
Towards Freedom? 1977.
Symphony No 4: Indischer Roosengaarten und Chineesischer Hexensee / Indian Rose Garden and Chinese Witch Lake 1981; first performed Hamburg, 30 October 1981.
For a Change (percussion concerto based on *I Ching*) 1982; first performed January 1983.
Braending (small orchestra) 1983; first performed Copenhagen, August 1983.
Burn (also known as *Illumination*) 1984; first performed Glasgow, 17 September 1984.
Between (3 movements for cello, orchestra) 1985; first performed Copenhagen, 30 August 1985.
Prelude to Breaking (piano, strings) 1986; first performed Gothenburg, 26 September 1986.
Remembering Child (2 movements for viola, chamber orchestra) 1986; first performed St Paul, Minnesota, 12 September 1986.
En lys time 1986.
Helle Nacht (violin concerto) 1986–7; first performed 22 March 1988.
Symphony No 5 1986–90; first performed 1991.
Pastorale (version for string orchestra; from *Babettes Gaestebud*) 1987.

Chamber/instrumental:

Suite (flute, piano) 1952.
Introduction og Toccata (accordion) 1952.
Quartetto breve (string quartet) 1952.
Quintet: Hommage à Marc Chagall Op 1 (flute, violin, viola, cello, piano) 1952–3.
Trio Op 15 (clarinet, cello, piano) 1952–5. Recorded Paula 11.
Sonata in One Movement Op 6 (piano) 1953. Recorded LPWH 3013.
Trifoglio (piano) 1953.
Preludio espansivo e rondo (piano) 1953.
Diptychon (violin, piano) 1953.
Solo intimo Op 8 (cello) 1953–4. Recorded Paula 11.
Quartetto brioso (String Quartet No 1) Op 21 1953–8. Recorded LPWH 3011.
Five Chorales (organ) 1954.
Sonata No 2 (piano) 1957.
Partita concertante (piano) 1958.
Sketches Op 25a (piano) 1959. Recorded LPWH 3013.
Nine Studies Op 25b (piano) 1959. Recorded LPWH 3013.
Three Miniatures (string quartet) 1959.
Four Fragments (piano) 1959–60. Recorded LPWH 3013.
Trompetmusik I and II (2 trumpets) 1960.
Fragment V (violin, piano ad lib) 1961.
Det er ikke til at baere (flute, trumpet, guitar, violin, double bass) 1963.
Rondo (6 percussion) 1964.
Stumspil (flute, trumpet, piano, violin) 1965.
Suite for Martin (3 accordions) 1967.
Anatomic Safari (accordion) 1967. Recorded Philips 6578 106.
Grooving (piano) 1967–8. Recorded LPWH 3013.
Tune In (oboe, electric organ, electric guitar) 1968.
Waves (percussion) 1969. Recorded Cambridge CC 2824.
Dreamscape (string quartet, tape) 1969.
Rejser (piano) 1969.
Musaik (3 trombones, 5 cornets, tape) 1969.
Inscape (string quartet) 1969.
Wawes (percussion) 1969.
Whirls' World (woodwind quintet) 1970. Recorded Philips 6578 007.
Snedronningen (piano) 1970.
Time Is a River Without Banks (chamber duo) 1970.
Arcana (electric guitar, percussion, accordion) 1970.
Canon (organ) 1971.
Lila (flute, 2 clarinets, celeste, 2 harps, piano, xylophone, vibraphone, 3 violins, viola, cello) 1972.
Spell (clarinet, cello, piano) 1973. Recorded Paula 11; EMI MOAK 30012.
Libra (version for recorder) 1973.
Turn (harpsichord or piano) 1973. Recorded BIS LP 68 (harpsichord); EMI CONS 50 (piano).
Returns (guitar) 1976.
Nu daekker sne den hele jord (6 tubas) 1976.
Cantica (piano) 1977.
Mating Dance (flute, guitar) 1977.
In Memory of. . . (guitar) 1978.
Isternia (cimbalom) 1979.
Luftkasteller (flute) 1980.
Frostsalmemusik (organ) 1980.
Vintersalme (organ) 1980.
Marchenfarben (accordion ad lib, percussion ad lib) 1980.
To Mediterrane Meditationer (piano) 1980.

Proteus, Stier og dalestiger og daler (flute, marimba) 1980.
Ghending (chamber ensemble) 1980.
Solo "in Scena" (cello) 1980.
Heyday's Night (alto recorder, cello, harpsichord) 1980–1.
Sonora (flute, harp) 1981.
Sextet (6 percussion) 1981.
Medstrøms og modstrøms (4 percussion; version for piano, percussion) 1981; original version first performed 20 March 1988.
Papalagi (guitar) 1981.
I Ching (percussion) 1982; first performed Denmark, 31 October 1982. Recorded BIS LP 256.
Prelude and Ant Fugue (with a Crab Canon) (violin, double bass, flute, clarinet, percussion, guitar, mandolin) 1982.
Skala Fanfare Variation (trumpet) 1982.
Lille Dans (harp) 1982.
Achilles and the Tortoise (piano) 1983. Recorded Paula 28.
Black and White & In Colours (percussion ensemble) 1983, revised as *Square & Round* for percussion sextet, 1985–6; first performed Copenhagen, 3 March 1986.
Praeludium og Myrefuga (flute, clarinet, mandolin, guitar, piano, violin, double bass) 1982; first performed The Netherlands, December 1982.
Maya (piano; version for percussion, tape) 1983.
Achilles og Skildpadden (piano) 1983.
Forspil ved havet (variable ensemble; strings, piano) 1983–4.
Without Jealousy: Tortoise's Tango (piano) 1984.
The Chase / Jagten (mandolin) 1985.
Nine Friends (accordion) 1985; first performed Humlebaek, 25 October 1985.
Clima 200—Energy Free (percussion) 1985.
In the Mood of Spades (guitar) 1985.
Picture Cards (guitar) 1985.
En lys time (version for percussion ensemble) 1986.
Prelude to Breaking (versions for variable ensemble; and for flute, clarinet, percussion, piano, string quartet) 1986; first performed Brighton, Sussex, 5 April 1986.
Tintinnabulary (string quartet) 1986; first performed Brighton, Sussex, 1987.
Playtime: Hommage à Jacques Tati (3 guitars) 1986.
Energy Fields Forever (percussion) 1986.
String Quartet No 6 1986.
Lin (clarinet, cello, piano) 1986.
Poeme (marimba or other percussion) 1987.
Pastorale (from score to *Babettes Gaestebud*; trio) 1987.
Hut Ab (2 clarinets) 1988.
Og livets sommer sover dybt (8 cellos) 1988.
Lerchesang (flute, cello, piano) 1988.
Trepartita (organ) 1988; broadcast Danish Radio, 17 November 1988.
Syn (2 trumpets, horn, 2 trombones) 1988, revised for 3 trumpets, horn, 2 trombones/euphoniums, 1989.
Majmaneskygger (violin, optional piano, optional cello) 1989.
King, Queen and Ace (harp, wind quintet, trumpet, trombone, percussion, string quartet, double bass) 1989; first performed Humleback, 28 May 1989.
The Colour Is Dark (harp) 1989.
Nemo-dynamo (percussion, computer) 1989; first performed Aarhus, 31 August 1989.
Swan Descending (harp) 1989.
Clubs Among Jokers (guitar) 1989.
Maneskygger (violin, piano) 1989; first performed Rome, October 1989.
Light of a Night (after The Beatles' "Blackbird"; piano) 1989.
Gemini Rising (harpsichord) 1990.
Variationer Soger et Tema (cello, guitar) 1991.
Re-Percussion / Tilbasgeslag (percussion duo) 1991.

Vocal / choral:

Det abne (bass, piano) 1952–5; first performed 27 April 1988.
Aftonland Op 10 (unaccompanied SATB chorus; Lagerkvist) 1954. Recorded Paula 17.
Six Songs Op 14 (voice, piano; Danish and English texts) 1955.
Two Recitatives (voice, cello) 1955.
Nine Danish Songs (voice, piano) 1955–8.
Songs from "Aftonland" Op 17 (alto, flute, violin, cello, harp; Lagerkvist) 1956.
Vintergravejr og ung var (tenor, male chorus) 1957.
Triptychon Op 18 (SATB chorus, organ or orchestra; Psalms, Requiem Mass) 1957–60.
Tivoli (children's chorus, instruments ad lib) 1959.
En Ammehistorie (children's chorus, instruments ad lib) 1959.
Lykkestrejf (unaccompanied male chorus) 1960.
Gron sang (unaccompanied male chorus) 1960.
Strandvalmue (unaccompanied male chorus) 1960.
Af Tue Bentsons sange (baritone, piano) 1960.
Landskabsbillede (mixed chorus, instruments) 1961.
Fuglen hr. Jon (unaccompanied mixed chorus) 1961.
Nocturnes (soprano, piano or small orchestra; Chinese texts/German and Danish translations) 1961–2.
Dommen (mixed chorus, female chorus, children's chorus, 3 flutes, clarinets, 4 trumpets, percussion, tape) 1962.
Tre kaerlighedssange (alto, orchestra) 1963.
Babel (oratorio for soloists, chorus, instruments) 1964; first performed Stockholm, 15 September 1966.
Prisme (song cycle for soprano, tenor, bass, flute, trombone, percussion, violin, double bass) 1964.
L'Amour, La poésie (alto, bass, piano) 1968.
Trois Chansons (alto, flute) 1968.
Sub Rosa (mezzo-soprano, alto, electric guitar) 1971.
Wenn die Rose sich Selbst schuckt . . . (soprano, flute in G, double bass, percussion; Ruckert) 1971. Recorded Caprice RIKS LP 59.
Libra (tenor solo or with 2 SATB choruses, 2 vibraphones or pianos or harps, woodwinds ad lib; Steiner, Psalms) 1973. Recorded EMI PROP 7740.
Singe die Garten, Mein Herz (SSAATTBB chorus, piano; or flute, clarinet, horn, harp, piano, cello, percussion; Rilke) 1974. Recorded EMI MOAK 30013; LPWH 3019.
Nova genitura (soprano, recorder, lute, harpsichord, percussion, violin, viola, double bass) 1975.
Fons laetitiae (soprano or tenor, harp or lute) 1975.
Frostpsalme (16-part unaccompanied mixed chorus; Sarvig) 1975–6.
Vinterkantate (soprano, organ) 1976.
Kredslob (1-, 2-, 4-, 8- and 12-part unaccompanied mixed chorus with percussion; Sarvig) 1977.
Freedom (tenor, guitar) 1977.
Seadrift (soprano, violin, flute/krumhorn, gamba/cello, harpsichord/piano, guitar, percussion; Whitman) 1978. Recorded Sub Rosa 001.
Den afbrudte san Orfeus og Euridike (chorus, percussion, harp, instruments ad lib) 1977.
Mystery (soprano, flute) 1978.
Krystalspejlinger (chorus, instruments ad lib) 1978–9.
Wie ein Kind (unaccompanied SATB chorus; Wolfli, Rilke) 1980.
Drommesange (mixed chorus, percussion ad lib) 1980.
Foraressang (mixed chorus, percussion ad lib) 1980.
Abendlied (unaccompanied mixed chorus) 1980.
Solen er hvid (chorus, gamelan, orchestra) 1980–90; first performed 23 April 1990.

Sla doren op (mixed chorus, children's chorus, instruments ad lib) 1981.
Daggry (soprano, flute in G, guitar) 1981.
Noget andet (SATB chorus, soprano saxophone, tenor saxophone, baritone saxophone, trumpet, trombone, guitar, harp, synthesizer, 4 gamelans, percussion) 1982.
Ordet (4-part unaccompanied mixed chorus; Grundtvig) 1982.
Day and Night (low voice, cello ad lib, piano) 1982.
HIL DI(n)G ROSENBERG (chorus, recitation ad lib) 1982.
Korsalme (SATB chorus, instruments ad lib) 1982.
Plutonian Ode (soprano or baritone, cello; Ginsberg) 1982–4.
Tre Motetter efter Agnus Dei (4-part unaccompanied SATB chorus) 1983; first performed Copenhagen, 18 March 1983.
Afbrudt Hojsang, Skrig- og Drikkevise / Interrupted Hymn, Scream and Drinking Song (unaccompanied SATB chorus; Antz) 1983; first performed 7 November 1983.
Tusind Takker til Tage (dedicated to Tage Nielsen; unaccompanied mixed chorus) 1983.
Floden og dans to store bredder (chorus, synthesizer, percussion; Christensen) 1983; first performed 17 June 1983.
March Macabre (unaccompanied mixed chorus) 1984.
Stov (canon) 1984.
Eclipse (from *Siddhartha*; tenor, chorus, orchestra) 1984.
Den Fjerde Dag: In memoriam Thomas Ring (mixed chorus, chamber orchestra; Sunesson) 1984.
Gondellied (baritone, cello; Nietzsche) 1985; first performed Jyske, 4 September 1986.
Den Foruroligende Aelling ("Kongen af Morket", "Dromhamtare", "D'Monstrantzvögeli"; 12 voices, tape on no 3) 1985; first performed Humlebaek, 31 August 1985.
Entwicklungen (alto, flute, guitar, percussion, cello; Rilke) 1986.
L'Enfant et l'aube (soprano, tenor, chamber ensemble; Rimbaud) 1988; broadcast Radio France, 7 June 1988.
Indvielsessang (soprano, organ; Lundbye) 1988; first performed Copenhagen, 22 February 1989.
Regnnat (mixed chorus; Strunge) 1989.
La Peur As It Were (double chorus; Eluard, Cage) 1989.

Opera:

Labyrinten 1963; first performed Copenhagen, 2 September 1967.
Gilgamesh (opera "in 6 days and 7 nights"; 6 instrumental and vocal groups and tape) 1971–2; first performed Aarhus, 4 May 1973. Recorded EMI DMA 025–026.
Siddhartha: Play for the Expected One (opera-ballet in collaboration with Ole Sarvig; soloists, mixed chorus, children's chorus, dancers, symphony orchestra) 1974–9; first performed Stockholm, 18 March 1983.
Spil for den ventede 1979.
Det Guddommelige Tivoli / Divine Tivoli (after Wolfli, also texts by Hughes, Shakespeare, Nietzsche; 6 soloists, 6 dancers, 6 percussion, amplified cello, synthesizer) 1982.
Den Uendlinge Sange (chamber opera) 1987–8.

Other:

Titanic (tape) 1962.
Pastorale (incidental music for radio; tape) 1963.
Den unge mand skal giftes (ballet; 3 flutes, 3 clarinets, 2 bassoons, 2 horns, 4 trumpets, 3 trombones, percussion, organ, accordion, celeste, guitar) 1964; broadcast 2 April 1965.
Saret (incidental music for radio; organ, accordion, guitar) 1966.
Den rode kappe (film score; chorus, orchestra) 1967.
Tango Chikane (ballet; orchestra) 1967; first performed Copenhagen, 15 October 1967.
Kgs, Enghave (film score for flute, piano, accordion) 1967.
The Enchanted Wood (tape) 1968.
Manden der taenkte ting (film music; tape) 1969.
Nattergalen (tape) 1969.
Ildnatten (tape) 1983.
Kropsdrom (ballet; soprano, flute, percussion/synthesizer, tape) 1984.
Fra de evigt fjernere stjernen / Expanding Space (tape) 1985.
Twitter Machine (tape) 1985.
Ildnatten (ballet; soprano, baritone, percussion, tape) 1986.
Najader (tape) 1986.
Min Babette (score to film *Babettes Gaestebud / Babette's Feast*) 1987.

PUBLICATIONS

On Nørgård: Birgit Bjornum, *PN's Kompositioner: en kronologisk-tematism fortegneise over vaerkerne, 1949–82*, Copenhagen, 1983; Erling Kullberg, "PN", Copenhagen and London, 1983.

* * *

One of the most striking single features of Per Nørgård's work as a whole, perhaps the only feature universally applicable to his large and bewilderingly varied output, is its gradual tendency towards all-inclusiveness. His personal development has thus been only tangentially related to the post-1945 "mainstream" of his generation—by now, virtually any combination of the vast range of stylistic elements available in the late 20th century may be called upon to make a contribution to his own evolving musical character, regardless of their time and place of origin.

What distinguishes this approach from the "post-modern" style-as-quotation attitude is the extent to which the "foreign" elements are integrated into Nørgård's own idiosyncratic systems of thought and composition, which are able to engulf seemingly anything that comes their way. The results thus remain consistent at the most profound level, informed by several unique technical devices, including, most importantly, pitch structures based on Nørgård's "infinity series". This is not so much a type of material as a type of movement, a method whereby chains of pitches extend perpetually while "automatically" generating reflexive features within itself, such as transpositions, inversions and augmentations. Nørgård's Second Symphony (like all except his First, a symphony in name and scale only) is merely an orchestration of the first 4096 notes of such a series, although its use in other works is more subtle and also made to encompass a wide range of harmonic connotations, opening the way for further diversification of his stylistic vocabulary.

The constant state of metamorphosis within an overall sense of balance and consistency engendered by such systems in Nørgård's music can be seen as a radical extrapolation of the motivic transformations found in late Sibelius (an early influence on Nørgård). Comparison with Sibelius also lends a clue to the expressive world to which Nørgård's technical apparatus is harnessed, although the romantically tinged sense of order and poise exemplified, for example, by his Third Symphony has been almost shattered since about 1980 by an alternately latent or explicit tendency towards more "irrational" formal layouts and juxtapositions of irreconcilable materials.

Nørgård has always been receptive to influences from outside music, especially from non-Western philosophies and from scientific concepts: the change from flux to abruptness which characterises his works from the Fourth Symphony onwards is a direct result of his encountering the works of Adolf Wölfli (1864–1930), who, confined to a mental institution for the last 35 years of his life, produced a vast oeuvre of writings, paintings and music (using his own system of notation) showing a constant shifting, in Nørgård's words, "between idyll and catastrophe". This latest stylistic expansion seems to bring Nørgård's music to the brink of surrealism, both his own "hierarchical music" and assortments of often wildly distorted *objets trouvés* acquiring new and disturbing suggestivity through being placed in mutual contact. The visions of a scintillating musical utopia begin to admit chaos and breakdown as if discovering the grim truth of mortality: the graceful equanimity of the earlier works gives way to garish grotesque with perhaps a distant echo of the central movements of Mahler's Ninth Symphony. Introducing his own Fourth, Nørgård cites the Norwegian author Knut Hamsun with words which could equally apply to most of his recent work: "A prisoner on his tumbrel is wheeled to the scaffold. A nail chafes at his behind, he turns over and feels more comfortable."

—Richard Barrett

NØRHOLM, Ib. Danish. Born in Copenhagen, 24 January 1931. Educated at Royal Danish Academy of Music, Copenhagen (composition under Vagn Holmboe, music history under Hjelmborg, form and analysis under Niels Viggo Bentzon and Finn Hoffding), 1950–6, graduated in theory, history, organ, teaching, church music. Music critic, *Information*, Copenhagen, 1957–64; assistant organist, Elsinore Cathedral, 1957; organist, Bethelhemskirke, Copenhagen, from 1964; teacher of theory and history, Odense Conservatory, 1965–73; head of Danish section, ISCM, from 1973; member, Dansk KunstFondet, 1971–4; part-time teacher, from 1961, 1973, now professor, Royal Danish Academy of Music, Copenhagen. Recipient: Carl Nielsen Prize, 1971. Mailing address: c/o Danish Music Information Centre, Vimmelskaftet 48, DK 1161 Copenhagen K, Denmark.

Publishers: Wilhelm Hansen; Samfundet; Engstrøm & Sødring.

Symphonies/orchestral:

Theme and Variations Op 1 1955.
Symphony Op 10 1956–8.
Violin Concerto 1959.
Fluctuations Op 25 (34 solo strings, 2 harps, harpsichord, mandolin, guitar) 1962. Recorded Paula 16.
Relief I and II Op 27 (chamber orchestra) 1963.
Serenade to Cincinnatus Op 28 1964.
Relief III 1964.
Exile Op 29a 1964.
After Icarus Op 39 (orchestral suite) 1967.
Symphony No 2: Isola Bella Op 50 1968–71.
Symphony No 3: Day's Nightmare Op 57 1973.
Skyggen 1974.
Violin Concerto Op 60 1974. Recorded BIS LP 80.
Heretic Hymn Op 62 (fresco for orchestra) 1975.
Symphony No 4: Modskabelse/Decreation Op 76 (with soprano, tenor, bass, 2 SATB choruses, speaker) 1979.
Symphony No 5: Elementerne/The Elements Op 80 1980.
Symphony No 6: Moraliteter—eller maske en der mange kilometer til den naemeste edderkop/Moralities, or There May Be Several Miles to the Nearest Spider Op 85 (with mezzo-soprano, baritone, male and female actors) 1981.
Symphony No 7: Ekliptiske Instinkter/Ecliptic Instincts Op 88 1982. Recorded Polygram EBTL 83.
Spirales (accordion, orchestra) 1986.
At hore Andersen 1987.
Aspects of Sand and Simplicity (string orchestra) 1987.
Cello Concerto 1988–9.
Symphony No 8 (with baritone) 1989–90.

Chamber/instrumental:

Rhapsody (viola, piano) 1955.
String Quartet No 1: In Vere Op 4 1955.
Tombeau Op 7 (cello, piano) 1956.
Sonata Op 9 (organ) 1956.
Sonata Op 12 (violin, piano) 1956–7.
Trio (clarinet, cello, piano) 1957.
Mosaic Fragments in Recitativo Op 15 (flute, string trio) 1958.
Music for Recorder Op 16 (trios, quartet) 1958.
Concertino Op 17 (organ) 1958.
Trio Op 22 (piano, violin, cello) 1959.
Variations (violin, piano) 1959.
Direction inconnue (violin) 1962–4.
String Quartet No 2: Five Impromptus 1965.
Stanzas and Fields/Strofer og Marker Op 33 (piano) 1966.
String Quartet No 3: From My Green Herbarium Op 35 1966.
Three Pieces Op 37a (flute, organ) 1966. Recorded Conservatorium 8.
Three Pieces Op 37b (violin, organ) 1966.
String Quartet No 4: September-October-November Op 38 1966. Recorded EMI Odeon PASK 2006.
Sonata Op 41 (accordion) 1967. Recorded Pyramid TPLP-51.
Two Impressions (accordion) 1967.
Orfeusforvandlinger (6 guitars, 8 strings; variable ensemble) 1967.
Vignettes for the Little Prince (flute) 1968.
Suite (flute) 1968.
In Spring When Snow Is Falling Op 45 (cello, percussion) 1969.
Foresporgsler—overtalelser/Inquiries—Persuasions Op 49 (organ) 1970. Recorded Conservatorium 8.
Signatures from a Province Op 51 (piano) 1970.
Prelude to My Wintry Morning Op 52 (flute, piano, string trio) 1971.
Three Preludes Op 53 (wind quintet) 1971. Recorded Philips 6578007.
Sonata quasi variazioni Op 61 (violin) 1974.
Controversies in Three Courses Op 63 (between guitar and organ) 1975.
Dialogue in Three Courses Op 63b (guitar, accordion, percussion) 1975. Recorded Point PLP 5061.
Quartet for Strings in One Movement (String Quartet No 5) Op 65 1976.
The Funen Cataracts Op 66 (oboe, clarinet, bassoon, piano, violin, viola, cello, double bass) 1976. Recorded Point PLP 5061; Caprice CAP 3013.
Sonata Op 69 (guitar) 1976.
Contrast-Continuum Op 70 (4 flutes) 1977.
Primus inter pares I Op 72 (viola d'amore solo, 2 flutes, horn, trumpet, harpsichord, percussion, 2 violins, cello) 1977.

Skygerne frosner (String Quartet No 6) Op 73 1978.
So to Say Op 74 (flute, percussion) 1978.
Essai prismatique Op 77 (violin, cello, piano) 1979. Recorded SUDM 001.
Idylles d'Apocalypse Op 79 (organ, chamber ensemble) 1980. Recorded Erato STU 71509.
Modlyd / Countersound Op 82 (flute, viola, harp) 1980. Recorded SUDM 020.
Before Silence Op 83 (3 flutes) 1980. Recorded SUDM 001.
A Discourse on Time Op 84 (piano) 1981. Recorded Paula 28.
Haven med stier der deler sig / The Garden of Forking Paths Op 86 (flute, clarinet, piano, guitar, percussion, violin, cello) 1982. Recorded Point PLP 5061.
Immanence Op 87 (flute) 1983.
The Orthodox Dream Op 92 (flute, cello, harpsichord) 1984.
Purple to the People (oboe, cor anglais, trombone, piano, percussion, viola, cello, double bass) 1984.
Turbulence-Laminar Op 93 (piano) 1985.
String Quartet No 7: En passant Op 94 1985.
A Touch of—(Mortality) (oboe, cello, 4 violins, 2 violas, cello, double bass) 1986.
Tea for Tuba 1986.
Essai reflechi (clarinet, cello, piano) 1986–7.
Medusas Skygge (flute, viola, cello, guitar) 1987.
String Quartet No 8: Memories Op 107 1988; first performed London, 13 March 1989.
A Patchwork in Pink Op 109 (oboe, clarinet, horn, bassoon, piano; or 4 saxophones, piano) 1989; first performed Egeskov, 27 August 1989.
Sonata No 2; Summer Op 110 (guitar) 1989; first performed Copenhagen, 12 October 1989.

Vocal / choral:

Four Songs Op 3a (unaccompanied mixed chorus; Rasmussen) 1955.
Three Songs Op 3b (soprano, piano) 1955.
Frels mig Gud / Save Me God Op 5 (motet for soprano, organ) 1955.
Three Songs Op 8a (soprano, piano; *Op 8b* soprano, orchestra; Lagerkvist, Ekelund, Leino) 1956.
Three Madrigals Op 11 (unaccompanied mixed chorus; Rasmussen) 1957.
Three Songs (baritone, piano) 1957.
Sct. Olai Festverspikler (mixed chorus, organ, wind ensemble) 1959.
Three Songs Op 21 (unaccompanied male chorus) 1960–1.
Kenotafium Op 23 (solo voice, chorus, orchestra) 1961.
Three Songs Op 30 (contralto or mezzo-soprano, flute, guitar, percussion, violin, viola, cello; Pedersen) 1965.
Offer / Sacrifice Op 34 (6 songs for unaccompanied mixed chorus; Borum) 1966.
Flowers from the Flora of Danish Poetry Op 36 (8 songs with piano) 1966. Recorded Paula 8.
Summer Sceneries Op 40 (soprano, tenor, female chorus, orchestra) 1967.
Tavole per Orfeo Op 42 (6 songs for mezzo-soprano, guitar) 1967–9. Recorded DMA 036.
Three Songs Op 46 (unaccompanied male chorus; J. Kierkegaard) 1969.
Jongleurs 69 (narrator, voices, mixed chorus; with ensemble or piano or orchestra) 1969.
Still Life Op 44 (5 songs for soprano, guitar, percussion; Borum) 1971. Recorded SUDM 001.
Three Songs Op 54 (contralto, piano; Borum, Ditlevsen, Sarvig) 1971. Recorded Danica DLP 8056.
Lys og Lovsang / Light and Song of Praise Op 55 (mezzo-soprano, 3 basses, 2 mixed chorus, orchestra) 1972.
Day's Nightmare II Op 58 (soprano, tenor, bass, mixed chorus, orchestra) 1973.
Six Songs Op 64 (voice; Borum) 1975.
Proprium Missae Dominicae Pentecostis Op 71 (2 choruses, winds, organ) 1977.
Three Winter Impressions Op 75 (voice; Pedersen) 1979.
Light Op 78 (soprano, flute, cello, harp, percussion; Christensen) 1979.
Phrase-Paraphrase Op 81 (6 duets for soprano, tenor, piano; Borum, Masters) 1980. Recorded SUDM 001.
Americana Op 89 (unaccompanied SATB chorus) 1984.
Lux secunda Op 91 soprano, baritone, mixed chorus, orchestra; Suneson, Christensen) 1984.
Six Folk Songs (soprano, piano) 1985.
Eight Short Motets Op 96 (unaccompanied mixed chorus) 1986.
Lerchenborg Akrostikon (soprano, string quartet) 1986.
Ojet (unaccompanied SATB chorus) 1987.

Opera:

Invitation to a Beheading Op 32 (television opera; Borum, after Nabokov) 1965.
The Young Park Op 48 (Christensen) 1969–70.
The Garden Wall Op 68 (chorus opera for 20 singers, chamber ensemble; Borum) 1976.
Sandhedens Haevn / The Revenge of the Truth Op 95 (2 female singers, 4 male singers, orchestra; Heiner, after Blixen) 1985.

Other:

Rejsekammeraten (film score; orchestra) 1972.
Sange (film score; equal voices, baritone, piano) 1973.
Verandaen (ballet) 1981.

PUBLICATIONS

By Norholm: "Vocale aspekter", in *Dansk musiktidsskrift*, 6 (5), 1962–3.

On Norholm: P. Neilsen, "Der star en hjort ven en skovse—om INs musik", in *Tá*, 1(1), 1967; Svend Aaquist Johansen, "IN", Wilhelm Hansen, Copenhagen, 1985.

* * *

To survey Ib Nørholm's career from a long distance one might be tempted to consider him a pillar of the conventional compositional establishment: he is a composer of a large body of music which has at its core four operas, eight string quartets and eight symphonies, and he is an influential teacher who has returned to the institution where he trained, the Royal Danish Academy of Music in Copenhagen, as senior lecturer in composition. Alter the focus to close-up and one sees that things are not so clear-cut: as Karl Aage Rasmussen has so graphically put it: "you can put as many labels on Nørholm as on a globetrotter's suitcase, they will all bear witness to places he has visited, but they can never tell where he is going." Here then is the key to understanding the bewildering array of styles that make up Nørholm's compositional output.

Nørholm's earliest works, an opera written while at school and the *Symphony Op 10* clearly show the tonal, lyrical legacy left by Nielsen and the influence of his teacher, Vagn

Holmboe. It was not long, however, before he began to be swept up by the radical changes in music outside Denmark and he became involved, along with his contemporary Per Nørgård and other young Danish composers, in a fierce debate on European modernism as it appeared in the music of Schoenberg, Webern, Boulez and others. The work that marks his first turning away from the Danish tradition is the piano *Trio Op 22*—a serial first for both Nørholm and Denmark. In 1960 he attended the ISCM Festival in Cologne (an experience he found both fascinating and alarming) and in subsequent works such as the *Fluctuations Op 25* for thirty-nine string instruments, he shows a technique that is related to Stockhausen, yet in its un-Darmstadtian subtitle, ("The Unseen Pan") perhaps he has not completely relinquished the influence of Carl Nielsen.

The volatile Nørholm did not stay with unadulterated modernism for long. Radical upheavals in New York in the early 1960s, concepts such as "happenings" and the anti-establishment movement, "fluxus", began to make waves in Denmark and brought a cheerful confusion to Nørholm's style in, for example, the theatrical (and appropriately named) *Direction inconnue* for solo violinist and the tongue-in-cheek orchestral happening *Exile Op 29a*. Both Nørholm and Nørgård rediscovered the use of collage techniques and this led to a fusion of styles in such works as *Stanzas and Fields / Strofer og marker Op 33* which marked a new pluralistic stage in his development, and, for a while at least, his music embraced the general spirit of the "new simplicity" movement in Danish Music.

Nørholm likes to describe his nature as dialectical: one takes things apart to analyse and to discover hidden connections and then reassembles them in the hope of discovering new combinations. His growing interest in Ives, the rediscovery of Mahler and music of youth culture, was equally fascinating to him, and it is this open mind and generosity towards other people's music that has made him an inspirational figure to many younger composers, not least Poul Ruders and Rasmussen.

If the 1960s were a period of turmoil stylistically, there was still room for considerable diversion in the 1970s and early 1980s as Nørholm continued to explore and experiment on his way towards a genuinely pluralistic idiom. Six of his eight symphonies were written between 1968 and 1982 and they can be seen as the most variegated in the history of Danish music, both stylistically and technically. *Symphony No 2: Isola Bella Op 50* ranges from pure naivety to avant-garde complexity, while the trilogy of numbers 5, 6 and 7: *Elementerne* (The Elements) *Op 80*, *Moraliteter—eller maske en der mange kilometer til den naemeste edderkop* (Moralities—or There May Be Several Miles to the Nearest Spider) *Op 85*, and *Ekliptiske Instinkter* (Ecliptic Instincts) *Op 88* are three independent and diverse works linked by material based on the musical "alchemy" of playing with the four elements in mixed and transformed states.

So many stylistic *volte faces* might well be indicative of a chameleon or suceptible temperament. Nørholm, however, is fierce in his argument that every choice he has made has been the only possible one in that particular situation. Consequently, as he would wish, his music defies being pigeon-holed: piece follows piece, like a richly coloured kaleidoscope, but whether the music is simple, complicated, tonal or atonal it simply reflects only another facet of Nørholm's imagination.

—Rosemary Johnson

NUNES, Emmanuel. Portuguese. Born in Lisbon, 31 August 1941. Educated at Lisbon Academy of Music (under Fernando Lopes Graça and Benoit); Ferienkurse für Neue Musik, Darmstadt, 1963–5; moved to Paris, 1964; Conservatoire National Supérieur de Musique, Paris (musical aesthetics under Marcel Beaufils), 1964–5; Rheinische Musikhochschule, Cologne (composition under Henri Pousseur and Karlheinz Stockhausen, electronic music under Jaap Spek, phonetics under Georg Heike), 1965–7. Independent composer; composition seminars, University of Pau, 1975–6; DAAD composer in residence, Berlin, 1978–9; composition seminars, Musikhochschule, Freiburg, 1978–9; director, composition seminars, Gulbenkian Foundation, Lisbon, from 1980; teacher, Ferienkurse für Neue Musik, Darmstadt, 1986; visiting professor of composition, Musikhochscule, Freiburg, and Conservatoire National Supérieur de Musique, Paris, since 1986. Recipient: 1st prize, musical aesthetics, Conservatoire National Supérieur de Musique, Paris, 1965. Mailing address: c/o Editions Jobert, 76 rue Quincampoix, 75003 Paris, France.

Publishers: Salabert; Jobert.

[Nunes has organized some of his works into cycles. The first, which is untitled, is indicated by I; the second, known as "The Creation", by II. Works without an appended number belong to neither cycle.]

Symphonies / orchestral:

Seuils I & II (large orchestra) 1966–7; unperformed, subsequently reworked.
Purlieu (21 strings) 1970; first performed Lisbon, 1971.
Fermata [I] (orchestra, stereo tape) 1973; first performed Lisbon, 1974.
Es webt (21 strings, 13 winds, 2 conductors) 1973–5, revised 1977; first performed Paris, 1980.
Ruf [I] (orchestra, tape) 1974–5; first performed Royan and Donaeschingen, 1975.
Seuils (large orchestra) 1977–8.
Tif'ereth [II] (6 orchestral groups, 6 soloists) 1978–85; first performed Paris, 1985.
Chessed II [II] (4 violins, 4 double basses, 4 flutes, 4 clarinets, orchestra) 1979; first performed Munich, 1980.
Nachtmusik II [II] 1981; first performed Donaueschingen, 1981.
Stretti [I] (2 orchestras) 1982–3; first performed Lisbon, 1984.
(38) Sequencias (violin, clarinet, 2 vibraphones, strings, brass) 1986.
Quodlibet (28 instruments, 6 percussion, orchestra, 2 conductors) 1990–1.

Chamber / instrumental:

Degrés (string trio) 1965; first performed Paris, 1970.
Le Voile tangéant (string quartet) 1967; unperformed, subsequently reworked.
Un Calendrier révolu (chamber ensemble) 1968; unperformed, subsequently reworked, 1979.
Litanies du feu et de la mer 1 (piano) 1969; first performed Paris, 1976.
Litanies du feu et de la mer 2 (piano) 1971; first performed Paris, 1976.
Dawn Wo (2 flutes, 2 oboes, 3 clarinets, 2 bassoons, 2 horns, trumpet, trombone) 1971; first performed Lisbon, 1973.
Omens (flute, viola, trumpet, clarinet, violin, trombone,

harp, vibraphone, celeste) 1972, revised 1975; revised version first performed Lisbon, 1981.
Impromptu pour un voyage (trumpet, flute, viola, harp) 1973; first performed Geneva, 1983.
The Blending Season [I] (flute, viola, clarinet, electronic organ, ring modulators) 1973; first performed Paris, 1978.
Impromptu pour un voyage II [I] (alto flute, viola, harp) 1974; first performed Paris, 1976.
73 Oeldorf 75 I [I] (2 electric organs, 3 tapes) 1975; first performed Oeldorf, 1975.
Nachtmusik I [II] (viola, cello, bass clarinet, cor anglais, trombone, 3 synthesizers, tape) 1977–8; first performed Bonn, 1978.
String Quartet 1978.
Chessed I [II] (4 violins, 4 double basses, 4 flutes, 4 clarinets) 1979; first performed Jerusalem, 1979.
Einspielung I [II] (violin) 1979; first performed Berlin, 1979.
Einspielung II [II] (cello) 1980; first performed Lisbon, 1980.
Esquisses (string quartet) 1980, based on 1967 piece; first performed Lisbon, 1983.
Musik der Fruhe [II] (flute/piccolo, oboe, clarinet, 4 trombones, bass clarinet, contrabass clarinet, horn, trumpet, 2 violins, 2 violas, 2 cellos, double bass) 1980–4; 1st version first performed Lisbon, 1980.
Einspielung III [II] (viola) 1981; first performed Lisbon, 1981.
Grund [II] (flute, 8-track tape of flutes) 1982–3; first performed Paris, 1983.
Versus I [II] (violin, clarinet) 1982–4; first performed Lisbon, 1985.
Aura [II] (flute) 1983–6; first performed London, 1986.
Ludi concertati No 1 (bass flute) 1985; first performed Paris, 1985.
Wandlungen [II] (5 passacaglias for 25 instruments, live electronics ad lib) 1986; first performed Donaueschingen, 1986.
Sonata a tre [II] (from *Wandlungen*; violin, voila, cello) 1986.
Versus II (horn, cello) 1987–9.
Versus III (flute, viola) 1987–9.

Vocal/choral:

Voyage du corps [I] (28 mixed voices, ring modulation, tape) 1973–4; first performed Royan, 1975.
Minnesang [I] (12 unaccompanied voices; Boehme) 1975; first performed Paris, 1981.
73 Oeldorf 75 II [I] (6 choruses, 3 tapes) 1976; first performed Pau, France, 1976.
Vislumbre (mixed voices; Carneiro) 1986.

Other:

Nachtmusik III (tape) 1987–8.

* * *

Those who attended the first performance of Emmanuel Nunes's *Conjuntos I*, a work, since withdrawn, which delves into "group theory" and its implications for serial method, could already sense Nunes's striving for precision, strictness and self-control. That first performance, conducted by Jorge Peixinho in Lisbon in 1964, adumbrated the musical profile which gained a harder outline seven years later with the première of Nunes's *Purlieu*.

Nunes explains what happened in between as a "way of initiation," a process by no means incidentally connected to the title and substance of what was to be his Opus 1, the string trio *Degrés*. Between the first and the tenth "degree," order emerges from chaos and musical organization develops step by step from an amorphous mass of undifferentiated sound. Nunes explores and determines the parameters of dynamics, time, speed, metrics, duration, register, pitch, sound colour, texture and the relations of silence and sound, continuity and discontinuity, and relates them in turn to the psychological dimensions of performance technique and the interaction of the interpreting players. The structure of the piece symbolizes staging posts on the "way of initiation."

The process thus corresponds to the mastery of an ever-increasing and extending level of complexity in sound organization. It introduces new sound sources, new organizational parameters and new kinds of interaction between parameters. It develops within each individual work, between one work and the next, in the cycles to which most of the single works belong, and in the "life work" which subsumes all of them. But mastery of complexity does not mean an *a priori* search for complexity; in contrast to a methodological simplification, it allows him to explore fundamentals, to approach sound not just as a compositional element but as something with an "autonomous life", which needs to be "given time" (this may explain the relatively long durations of his works).

In his approximately 40 finished pieces to date, Nunes has written for the most varied instrumental and vocal groupings, often combined with stereo tapes or live electronics. He first employed electro-acoustic transformations in *The Blending Season*, introducing a new cycle of works, but also using materials from previous works. In *Nachtmusik I*, its effect is even more penetrating, the whole structure being based on a reflection upon the phenomenon of "ring modulation", while its exploration of the intersections of rhythm and melody contains basic material for another cycle of works, which Nunes has called "The Creation."

In *Nachtmusik I* Nunes creates tension by eliminating four notes from the scale, restricting the material to C C# D D# F F# B♭ B. The tension is derived from the palpable sense of striving for a chromatic whole, for a balance which can only be achieved within the given sound material as a closed system (comparable to the proposition of entropy in physics). The melodic source for this second cycle of works is to be found in *Einspielung I* (for violin), *Einspielung II* (for cello), and *Einspielung III* (for viola), three pieces which can be played together.

Whereas the first cycle mainly owes its coherence to pitch structure, and to occasional and carefully integrated reminiscences of Schubert and Mahler, the second draws more on a rhythmic matrix. *Impromptu pour un voyage* claims a strictly determined level of freedom for the performers, alternating autonomy and synchronization in a complex multiple process. *Es webt* and *Tif'ereth* were created by combining *Purlieu* and the wind piece *Dawn Wo* to make significant structural use of space. This is also important in *Grund* for solo flute and a prerecorded tape of eight flutes, but is even more intrinsic to the recent *Quodlibet* whose conception and form is based on Lisbon's great 1890 concert hall. Vocal works such as *Minnesang* and *Vislumbre* are partly structured by different textual properties (semantic and morphologic) distributed around the several voices. As different as all these parameters may be, they are relevant only as sound properties; their visual or theatrical dimensions do not affect Nunes's structure.

He has said that he composes for himself as a listener and thereby for anyone else who listens to music. In listening and composing he strives to extinguish his own personality. "Revelation" is the key word to his fundamental orientation, from which it follows that musical creation gives birth to sonorous entities with their own inner life. The musical work is not a vehicle for the composer's expression; the composer is not supposed to use the work according to whim, but should instinctively "serve" the "origin of sound" by selection and restriction.

Nunes belongs to the old tradition of *musicus speculativus*, in which physics, metaphysics, world order and transcendence, cosmos and human consciousness belong on a single plane. Music is not language but order and architecture. Its aesthetic has a living countenance.

—Mário Vieira de Carvalho

NYSTEDT, Knut. Norwegian. Born in Oslo, 3 September 1915. Educated at Oslo Conservatory of Music (organ under Arild Sandvold, composition under Bjarne Brustad), *examen artium*, 1935; further study, organ under Ernest White, composition under Aaron Copland. New York City, 1947. Married Birgit Nystedt, 20 June 1942; 3 children. Organist, debut 1938; conductor, debut with Oslo Philharmonic Orchestra, 1945; organist, Torshov Church, Oslo, 1946–82; conductor, Det Norsk Solistkor/Norwegian Soloists Choir, 1950–90; professor of choral conducting, Oslo University, 1964–85; composer. Recipient: 1st prize (for *Solsong*), Norges Sangerlag, 1953; Knight of the Order of St Olav, 1966; Distinguished Service Citation, Augsburg College, Minneapolis, Minnesota, 1975; Norwegian Council for Cultural Affairs Music Prize, 1980; Norwegian Composers Association "Best Work of the Year" (for *De profundis*), 1984. Mailing address: Vestbrynet 25B, 1160-Oslo 11, Norway.

Publishers: Norsk Musikforlag, Oslo; Edition Lyche, Drammen; Associated, New York; Augsburg, Minneapolis; Hinshaw Music, North Carolina; Roberton Publications, London.

Symphonies/orchestral:

Concerto grosso Op 17 (3 trumpets, strings) 1946; first performed Boston, 1947.
Spenningens Land/The Land of Suspense Op 19 (symphonic fantasy) 1947; first performed Oslo, 1948. Recorded Philips 6507044; RSST-7641A.
Symphony for Strings Op 26 1950; first performed Oslo, 1951.
Concerto for Cor Anglais, Clarinet and Strings Op 29 1952; first performed Oslo, 1954.
The Seven Seals Op 46 1958–60; first performed Hartford, Connecticut, 1960. Recorded Phonogram 839254.
Collocations Op 53 1963; first performed Oslo, 1964.
Entrata festivo Op 60 (symphonic band) 1969; first performed Augsburg, 1969.
Mirage Op 71 1974; first performed Boston, 1975.
Ichthys Op 76 1976; first performed Bergen, 1980. Recorded Norwegian Composers NC 4901.
Exsultate Op 74b 1980; first performed Oslo, 1985.
Mountain Scenes Op 90 (band) 1981; first performed Oslo, 1981.
Masquerade Op 91 (brass band) 1982.
Celebration Op 94 (band) 1982.
Sinfonia del mare Op 97 1983. Recorded NC 4911; Aurora CD 4950.
The Greater Glory Op 105 (band) 1985.
Concerto for Horn and Orchestra Op 114 1986–7.

Chamber/instrumental:

String Quartet No 1 Op 1 1939; broadcast 1939.
Med Jesus Vil Eg Fara Op 4 (organ; variations on a Norwegian folktune) 1940; first performed Oslo, 1941.
Toccata Op 9 (organ) 1941; first performed Notodden, 1941.
Sonata Op 10 (violin, piano) 1941; first performed Oslo, 1942.
Introduzione e passacaglia Op 7 (organ) 1943; first performed Lillestrom, 1944. Recorded Philips 6507056.
Pastorale og Toccata Op 20 (organ) 1947.
Variations Op 21 (piano) 1948.
String Quartet No 2 Op 23 1948; first performed Copenhagen, 1951.
Deus sancta trinitas Op 28 (organ) 1951; first performed Stavanger, 1951.
Barnebilder (piano pieces for children) 1952.
Sonatina Op 35 (piano) 1953.
Fantasia trionfale Op 37 (organ) 1955. Recorded Ark 1094-S; EMI 06137323.
String Quartet No 3 Op 40 1956; first performed Oslo, 1958. Recorded Triola TNLP 4.
Hos Gud er Idel Glede/In Heaven Is Joy Op 44 (partita for organ) 1958. Recorded Kirkelig Kulturverksted JLP 1; Aurora 1912.
Pieta Op 50 (organ) 1961; first performed Vadstena, Sweden, 1961. Recorded Simax PN 2013.
Wedding March (organ) 1964.
String Quartet No 4 Op 56 1966; first performed Oslo, 1967. Recorded Philips 839253 AY.
Pia memoria Op 65 (9 brass) 1971; first performed Oslo, 1971. Recorded NC 3861.
Resurrexit Op 68 (organ) 1973; first performed Tromso, 1973. Recorded Philips 6507061; NC 4911/3861.
Tu es petrus Op 69 (organ) 1973; first performed Bergen, 1974.
Exsultate Op 74 (organ) 1975; first performed Bergen, 1977. Recorded Aurora 1912.
Veni creator spiritus Op 75 (partita for organ) 1976, begun 1957; first performed Oslo, 1976.
Rhapsody in Green Op 82 (brass quintet) 1978; first performed Stockholm, 1978. Recorded NC 4901.
Suite d'orgue Op 84 (organ) 1978; first performed Bergen, 1979. Recorded Simax PN 2013.
Music for Six Trombones Op 87 1980; first performed New York City, 1982.
Crux fidelis Op 96 (organ, with recitation) 1982. Recorded Aurora 1912.
Laudamus Op 105 (hand bells) 1985; first performed Bergen, 1986. Recorded Aurora AR 1912.
String Quartet No 5 Op 115 1988; broadcast 1989.

Vocal/choral:

Four Orheim Songs Op 11 (mezzo-soprano, organ) 1942.
Five Setrom Songs Op 12 (soprano/mezzo-soprano, organ) 1942; first performed Oslo, 1944.
Nadevengen/The Path of Mercy Op 14 (soloists, chorus, orchestra; 13th-century text) 1943–6; first performed Oslo, 1949.
Norge Mitt Land Op 15 (baritone, chorus, piano or orchestra) 1944.
Tru og Saeledrust Op 22 (high voice, organ or piano) 1948.
Solsong/Awakening of Spring Op 33 (chorus, orchestra; Hovden) 1953.

Three Religious Folktunes Op 34 (voice, organ) 1953.
Brennofferet / Burnt Offering Op 36 (recitation, chorus, orchestra; biblical) 1954; first performed Oslo, 1956. Recorded NC 3807/4911; Aurora CD 4950.
Du ska itte tro i graset (mezzo-soprano, organ; Skjaeraasen) 1955.
Six Sonnets Op 38 (high voice, organ; Bjerke) 1955.
Lord God of Israel (chorus) 1957.
Thus Saith the Lord (chorus) 1958.
I Will be as the Dew (chorus) 1958.
Yet a Little While (chorus) 1959. Recorded NC 4911.
Jesu Syv Ord / Seven Words from the Cross Op 47 (chorus) 1960.
Sta Opp Bli Lys Op 51 (cantata for soprano, chorus, organ, congregation) 1962.
The Moment Op 52 (soprano, celeste, percussion; Raine) 1962; first performed Stockholm, 1963. Recorded Philips 839248 AY.
I Stenbrottet (chorus; Bolander) 1962.
Psalm 138 (2 choirs) 1963.
De profundis Op 54 (chorus) 1964; first performed Oslo, 1965. Recorded NC 4911; Sonet SLP 1423.
Peace Be unto You (chorus) 1964.
Six Hymn Tunes (voice, organ) 1965–8.
Praise to God Op 55 1966; broadcast Swedish Radio, 1967. Recorded Augsburg Choir AC 68C.
To Motetter Op 57a (soprano, organ) 1966. Recorded Aurora 1912.
Audi (8 voices) 1968.
Til Deg, Herre (mezzo-soprano, organ; biblical) 1968. Recorded Kirkelig Kulturverksted NKLP 8.
Lucis creator optime Op 58 (soloists, chorus, orchestra; 6th-century, Gregor I) 1968; first performed Minneapolis, Minnesota, 1969. Recorded NC 3861; Philips 6507061.
Sok Herren / Seek Ye the Lord (women's voices) 1969. Recorded Kirkelig Kulturverksted FXLPL 10.
Four Proverbs ("The Path of the Just", "Trust in the Lord", "All the Ways of a Man", "If You Receive My Works"; chorus) 1969–71.
Suoni Op 62 (women's voices, flute, marimba) 1970. Recorded Delta Records DRS 73-330; NC 4901; Aurora CD 4950.
Eight Hymn Tunes (voice, organ) 1971.
Hosttakkefest Op 67 (mass for children's chorus, mixed chorus, recitation, organ, instruments; Ellingsen) 1972.
If You Receive My Words (chorus) 1972.
Shells Op 70a (women's voices) 1973. Recorded NC 4911.
Psalm 77 Op 70b (mixed voices) 1973. Recorded Sonet SLP 1444.
Karlekens Lov Op 72 (women's voices) 1975. Recorded Kirkelig Kulturverksted NKLP 8.
Seven Introits for Eastertide Op 73 (chorus) 1975.
Dies Irae Op 77 (4 choruses, wind, percussion; Sami/Lappish) 1976; first performed Hamar, 1977.
Eg Sokjer deg Tidleg (mezzo-soprano, organ; biblical) 1976. Recorded Aurora 1912.
Sannhetens And (mixed voices, organ) 1976.
I Will Greatly Rejoice (chorus) 1976.
Et Norsk Te Deum Op 78 (chorus, orchestra) 1977; first performed Oslo, 1978.
Tenebrae Op 80a (bass voice, organ; Latin) 1977. Recorded Kirkelig Kulturverksted NKLP 8.
Brodunderet Op 80b (baritone, organ) 1977.
Salme 100 (mixed voices, organ) 1977.
To Orientalske Folkesangen (chorus; Korean and Japanese texts) 1977.
Christmas Carols (chorus, bells) 1977.
O Crux Op 79 (8 voices) 1977. Recorded NC 4911/6008; St Olav Choir E-646.
Listen to Me (chorus) 1977.
Hosanna (women's voices) 1977.
Veni Op 81a (8 voices) 1978.
Gammelvegen Op 81b (8 voices) 1978.
Das Alte Lied Op 83 (chorus, piano) 1978. Recorded NC 4901.
Get You Up (mixed voices) 1978.
Six Songs for Children Op 86 (voice, organ; Saue) 1979.
Beata Nobis Op 88 (male voices) 1979.
Three Songs to Texts by Andre Bjerke Op 85 (voice, organ) 1979–80; first performed Oslo, 1979.
Sing and Rejoice (chorus) 1982. Recorded NC 4911.
A Hymn of Human Rights Op 95 (chorus, organ, percussion; Kaan) 1982. Recorded Aurora 1912.
In Principio (chorus) 1983.
For a Small Planet Op 100 (chorus, string quartet, harp, recitation; Kaan) 1983. Recorded Aurora 1914.
Jag er a Och O (chorus) 1983.
I Will Sing You a New Song (chorus) 1983.
Morro-Vers Op 99 (children's chorus, baritone, flute, piano; Bjerke) 1984.
Hvor er Gud? Op 101 (2-part youth chorus, baritone, flute, piano) 1984.
Missa brevis Op 102 (chorus) 1984.
The Wall Is Down Op 104 (chorus) 1985.
What Does the Lord Require of You? Op 106a (chorus) 1985.
The Lamentations of Jeremiah (chorus) 1985.
Adora te Op 107 (full chorus of mixed voices) 1985.
A Saeleste Stund (chorus) 1985.
Hvilken Venn Vi Har I Jesus (chorus) 1985. Recorded Kirkelig Kulturverksted.
Som en Ceder pa Libanon (3 equal voices) 1986.
Tritten Troll-Trillinger (3 equal voices) 1986.
Brenn Sol! (3 equal voices) 1986.
Ave Maria Op 110 (chorus, violin) 1986.
Teach Me, O Lord (children's chorus, piano, percussion ad lib; Psalm 119) 1986.
Stabat Mater Op 111 (chorus, cello) 1986.
Four Introits for Advent Op 113 (chorus) 1987.

Opera / dramatic:

Spes Mundi / The Hope of the World Op 63 (dramatic mass for chorus, drama group, trumpet, organ, percussion, narrator, congregation; Hillestad) 1970.
Med krone og stjerne / With Crown and Star Op 66 (Christmas opera for television; Johannessen, English version by Ann Saethre, German version by Timmermans) 1972.
Song of Songs Op 116 (church opera; Solomon) 1990; first performed Oslo, January 1991.

Other:

Eyvind Alanes: *Julemotett / Christmas Motet* (arranged for 2 voices, SATB chorus, orchestra) 1940.
J.S. Bach: *Organ Prelude in E♭* (orchestrated) 1943.
J.S. Bach: *Air* (arranged for chamber orchestra) 1943.

PUBLICATIONS

On Nystedt: Bjarne Kortsen, *Contemporary Norwegian Orchestral Music*, Oslo, 1969; Finn Benestad, "KN og hans storverk *Lucis*", in *Norsk Musiktidsskrift*, 1, 1970; Frank Hogberg, "KN's strykekvartetter", Institutt for Musikvitenskap, Oslo, 1970; Anna Alnaes, "Daring Avant-Garde

Composer", in *The Northman*, 2, 1971; Linda Krakowski Spicher, "An Analysis of Selected Choral Works by KN", dissertation, University of Iowa, Iowa City, 1974; Marvin E. Stallcop, "The A Capella Choral Music of KN", dissertation, Arizona State University, Tempe, August 1976; Harald Herresthal, *Festskrift til KN*, Oslo, 1985.

* * *

Knut Nystedt grew up in a highly musical and religious family environment, in which Christian songs and the classical string quartet were a natural part of the daily milieu. At the age of 12, Nystedt became a member of the St Olav Boys' Choir, where he appeared as a successful soprano soloist. He received his advanced musical training at the music conservatory in Oslo.

During World War II, Nystedt made a living as an organist and as a director of several amateur choirs and orchestras. During these years, he had his first compositions published and in 1943 his *Introduzione e passacaglia* for organ received an award. A string quartet, a violin sonata and a number of songs and piano pieces duly attracted attention as well. From a stylistic point of view, Nystedt's compositions were rooted in the prolonged tradition of 1930s nationalist romanticism, characteristic of which is the deliberate use of folkloristic elements and modal harmonies; the oratorio *Nadevengen/The Path of Mercy* is a major work from this modal period.

Shortly after the war, Nystedt gravitated rapidly in the direction of neo-classicism, as expressed in his 1946 *Concerto grosso* for strings and three trumpets. In 1947, after a successful début conducting the Philharmonic Symphony Orchestra in Oslo, he studied with Ernest White and Aaron Copland in the United States. In the years that followed, Nystedt was active in a number of areas. As an organist, he showed great virtuosity, introducing the organ music of Messiaen, Hindemith and Jehan Alain. As a composer, he enjoyed success with his prize-winning orchestral work *Spennigens land/The Land of Suspense*. Nystedt's brilliance as a choirmaster made him the obvious candidate when the Norwegian Soloists' Choir was founded in 1950. In a short time the semi-professional choir developed into a completely indispensable component in Norwegian musical life and became a main inspiration for many of Nystedt's own choral compositions.

In the second half of the 1950s church music was ripe for revival. Nystedt composed his famous collection of evangelical motets and created the first significant American motets. His *Symphony for Strings* and *Concerto for Cor Anglais, Clarinet and Strings* were well-received but one of the highlights of this period was *Brennofferet/Burnt Offering*, in which the description of the Prophet Elijah, in his struggle with the 400 prophets of Baal, ignited Nystedt's colourful orchestral imagination as an emphasis to the dramatic action. The Third String Quartet was considered by many to be his most significant composition of this same period.

The 1960s were exciting years of unrest and upheaval. In the orchestral visions *The Seven Seals*, it was already apparent that Nystedt was in the process of abandoning his neo-classicism. Many of his colleagues adopted the twelve-tone technique, while Nystedt, with his feeling for orchestral colour, was more fascinated by the new sound world that had been developed by György Ligeti and Krzysztof Penderecki. This is reflected in the chamber work *The Moment*, the orchestral work *Collocations*, the *Pia memoria* for brass, and even in such choral compositions as *De profundis* and *Suoni*. After all his experiments in sound and colour, Nystedt created the cantata *Lucis creator optime*, a composition which must be regarded as one of his major productions of the decade. Characteristic of his style was the integration of modern clusters in a tonal framework, with clear ties to the tradition.

In the 1970s, neo-romanticism and pluralism became significant factors in Norwegian music, a development which can in part be traced back to Nystedt's own influence. The years that followed, up to his 70th birthday, are marked by considerable compositional activity in a wide variety of styles. In choral works like *Shells*, *The Law of Love* and the cycle of motets, *Four Proverbs*, his new choral technique is elaborated with some astonishing sound effects.

The orchestral *Mirage*, *Ichthys* and *Sinfonia del mare* all have a more or less pronounced programmatic character. The experimentation of earlier years has receded somewhat into the background, while greater attention is paid to clarity of form and a rich and warm sound. The 1990 church opera *Song of Songs* shows that Nystedt's musical heart is still beating and that he continues to create important music that goes directly to the heart of his listeners.

—Harald Herresthal

O

OHANA, Maurice. French; naturalised, of Spanish descent; dual British-French nationality. Born in Casablanca, Morocco, 12 June 1914. Educated at Bayonne Conservatoire, (piano lessons under Frank Marshall and Lazare-Levy), Barcelona and Paris, early 1930s; Baccalaureat in philosophy; architectural training, Ecole National Supérieur des Arts Déecoratifs, Ecole des Beaux Arts and Ecole National Superiéur, 1932–4; Schola Cantorum, Paris (under Daniel-Lesur), 1937–9; Accademia Santa Cecilia, Rome (under Alfredo Casella), 1944–5. Served in British Army, 1940–46. Married Odile Marcel, 5 May 1976. Co-founder, Groupe Zodiaque, 1947; teacher of music, Schola Cantorum, Paris; founder, Pool de Percussion with Radio France, 1961; chair, Académie M. Ravel, St Jean de Luz, since 1989. Recipient: Prix de la RAI (for *Histoire véridique de Jacotin*), 1961; Grand Prix de L'Académie Charles-Cros (for *Syllabaire / Signes*), 1968; Prix Italia, 1969; Prix du Président de la République (for recording of *Cantigas / Cris*), 1969; Grand Prix du Disque (for recording of *Improvisations pour flûte / Silenciaire / Sibylle*), 1971; Prix du Président de la République (for recording of *24 Préludes pour Piano*), 1974; Prix National Français, 1975; Grand Prix de la Musique Symphonique de la SACEM, 1975; Prix Arthur Honegger, 1982; Commandeur de l'Ordre des Arts et des Lettres, 1984; Prix de l'Académie Charles Cros (for recording of *Lys de Madrigaux / Messe*), 1982; Grand Prix du Disque Contemporain Ritmo, Madrid, 1982; Prix du Disque Lyrique, 1982; Grand Prix de la Ville de Paris, 1983; Prix Maurice Ravel, 1985; Premio Lorenzo il Magnifico, Florence, 1986. Mailing address: 31, rue du Général Delestraint, 75016 Paris, France.

Publishers: Jobert; Billaudot; Amphion/Durand; Schott; Salabert; Editeurs France Musique.

Symphonies / orchestral:

Sarabande (harpsichord, orchestra) 1950. Recorded Club Français du Disque 23; Record Society RS 22; Musidisc RC 697.
Trois Graphiques (guitar, orchestra; occasionally and erroneously also cited separately as "Guitar Concerto") 1950–7; first performed BBC, 1961. Recorded Deutsche Grammophon DG 2530585; Decca SLX 20515; Arion ARN 38240.
La Soirée des proverbes (chamber orchestra) 1953–4; first performed Paris, 30 January 1954.
Synaxix (2 pianos, 4 percussionists, orchestra) 1965–6; first performed Valdagno, Italy, 1966. Recorded Erato 70431.
Chiffres de clavecin (harpsichord, chamber orchestra) 1967–8; first performed La Chaux-de-Fonds, 8 June 1969. Recorded Club Français du Disque 23; Musidisc 697; Erato STU 761548.
Silenciaire (6 percussionists, string orchestra) 1969; first performed Lucerne, 6 September 1969. Recorded ORTF-Barclay 995018.
T'haran-Ngo 1973–4; broadcast Radio France, Paris, 8 October 1975.
Anneau du Tamarit (cello, orchestra) 1976; first performed Orléans, 10 December 1977. Recorded Orchestre National de France.
Livre des prodiges 1978–9; first performed Lyon, 4 October 1979. Recorded Erato STU 71548; Musicfrance.
Crypt (string orchestra) 1980; first performed Chambery, 24 October 1980.
Piano Concerto 1980–1; first performed Nantes, 26 June 1981. Recorded Orchestre National de France.
Cello Concerto 1990; first performed Evian, 1991.

Chamber / instrumental:

Trois Caprices (piano) 1944–54; first performed Paris, 12 June 1948. Recorded BAM 5020/5.863.
Sonatine monodique (piano) 1945; first performed Paris, October 1947. Recorded BAM 5020/5.863.
Tiento (guitar) 1955–7; first performed Paris, 1961. Recorded VSM 2178; Deutsche Grammophon DG 1139 366; CBS 30 A 064; Barclay 991 031; PR 157 128; RS 9014–5.
Quatre Etudes choréographiques (4 or 6 percussionists) 1955; first performed Strasbourg, 8 June 1963. Recorded Philips 834.990.
Carillons (harpsichord) 1960; broadcast 1961. Recorded Erato 70513.
Quatre Improvisations (flute) 1960; broadcast 1962. Recorded ORTF-Barclay 995018.
Cinq Séquences (string quartet) 1963; first performed Mexico, 1964.
Si le Jour paraît . . . (7 pieces for 10-string guitar) 1963–4; first performed La Rochelle, 28 June 1974. Recorded Arion ARN 38261; Deutsche Grammophon DG 2530 307.
Neumes (oboe, piano) 1965; first performed Paris, 1965. Recorded Calliope 1186.
Signes (flute, 2 zithers—1 in ⅓ tones, 1 chromatic/1 player, piano, 4 percussion) 1965; first performed Bordeaux, 23 May 1965. Recorded Erato 70443.
Soron-Ngo (2 pianos) 1969–70; first performed Aix-en-Provence, 22 June 1971. Recorded (1st part) Erato 70810.
Syrtes (cello, piano) 1970; first performed Paris, 15 March 1972.
Sarc (oboe) 1972; first performed Paris, 1 January 1973.
Vingt-quatre Préludes (piano) 1972–3; first performed Paris, 20 November 1973. Recorded Arion 38261.
Planh (guitar) 1974. Recorded Deutsche Grammophon DG 2530 307.
Noctuaire (cello, piano) 1975; first performed Boulogne, 1975.
Sacral d'Ilx (harpsichord, oboe, horn) 1975–6; first performed Royan, 23 March 1976.
Satyres (2 flutes) 1976; broadcast Paris, 15 March 1977.
String Quartet No 2 1980; broadcast Paris, 27 February 1982.
Wamba (carillon or harpsichord) 1980; first performed Paris, 7 December 1980; harpsichord version broadcast Paris, 1 March 1982.
Cadran lunaire (4 pieces for 10-string guitar) 1982; first performed Rome, 9 December 1982.
Etudes d'interprétation (Book I) (piano) 1982; first performed London, 8 April 1983.

Deux Pièces pour clavecin (harpichord) 1980–3; broadcast Paris, 4 January 1984.
Etudes d'interprétation Nos XI & XII (Book II) (piano, percussion) 1984–5; broadcast Radio France, 4 January 1984. Recorded Audivis AV 4831.
Etudes d'interprétation Nos VII–X (Book II) 1984–5; first performed Paris, 29 April 1986.
Kypris (oboe, viola, double bass, piano) 1985; first performed Paris, 5 May 1985.
Anonyme XXème Siècle (2 guitars) 1988; broadcast Radio France, June 1989.
String Quartet No 3 1989; first performed Prague, 13 February 1990.
Miroir de Célestine (harpsichord, percussion) 1990; first performed Munich, October 1990.

Vocal/choral:

Llanto por Ignacio Sanchez Mejias (baritone, reciter, 8–12 female voices, instrumental ensemble; Lorca) 1950; first performed Paris, 22 May 1950. Recorded Club Français du Disque 23; Musidisc 697; Distex L P4; Erato 71136.
Cantigas (soprano/child's voice, mezzo-soprano, 26-voice mixed choir, instrumental ensemble) 1953; first performed Hamburg, 6 February 1957. Recorded Erato 70544.
Récit de l'an zéro (bass, tenor, child's voice, reciter, 12-voice mixed choir; Schehade) 1958–9; first performed Paris, 11 April 1959.
Tombeau de Claude Debussy (soprano, zither tuned in ⅓ tones, piano, chamber orchestra) 1962; first performed Paris, 27 December 1962.
Syllabaire pour Phèdre (coloratura soprano, mezzo-soprano, 3 reciters, mixed choir, piano, harpsichord, harp, 2 zithers—1 in ⅓ tones, 1 chromatic/1 player, 4 percussionists, tape) 1967; first performed Paris, 5 February 1968. Recorded Erato 70443.
Sibylle (soprano, percussion, tape) 1968. Recorded ORTF-Barclay 995018.
Cris (12 mixed voices, SATB) 1968; first performed Berlin, 1 February 1969. Recorded Erato 70544.
Stream (bass, string trio) 1970; first performed Angers, 21 January 1971.
Autodafé (2 sopranos, alto, bass-baritone, 2 reciters, 1 child's voice; 12 choral soloists, 32-voice chorus, 60–80 voice "crowd", jesters, marionettes) 1971–2; first performed Lyon, 23 May 1973.
Office des oracles (3 vocal groups, instrumental ensemble) 1974; first performed La Sainte-Baume, 9 August 1974.
Lys de madrigaux (female choir, piano, organ, 2 zithers—1 in ⅓ tones, 1 chromatic/1 player, percussion) 1975–6; first performed Paris, 1 June 1976. Recorded Erato.
Messe (soprano, mezzo-soprano, choir, instrumental ensemble; liturgical and concert versions) 1977; first performed Avignon, 31 July 1977. Recorded Erato.
Trois Contes de l'honorable fleur (soprano—singing and speaking, instrumental nonet; Marcel) 1977–8; first performed Avignon, 15 July 1978. Recorded Philips 6504 157.
Dies solis (4 choral groups, 2 organs; part of *Lux noctis*) 1981; first performed Lyon, 11 June 1983.
Quatre Choeurs (children's voices) 1987.
Swan Song (12 mixed voices, SATB) 1988; first performed Esch-sur-Alzette, Luxembourg, 7 March 1989.
Lux noctis (4 choirs, including 1 of children's voices) 1988; first performed St Louis-en-l'Ile, 8 December 1988.
Trois Prophéties de la Sibylle (soprano, coloratura soprano, mezzo-soprano, piano, percussion; from the opera *La Célestine*) 1989; first performed London, January 1990.

Opera:

La Célestine (3 sopranos, coloratura soprano, dramatic soprano, alto, 2 baritones, tenor, counter-tenor, bass) 1982–6; first performed Paris, 13 June 1988.
Histoire véridique de Jacotin (opera for children; revision of earlier work as full-scale opera) 1990–1; first performed Paris, April 1991.

Other:

Suite pour un mimodrame (music to *Monsieur Bob'le* by Schehade; chamber orchestra) 1951; first performed Paris, 29 May 1951.
Les Hommes et les autres (music to radio play by Vittorini) 1955.
Images de Don Quichotte (inspired by Cervantes; chamber orchestra) 1956; broadcast BBC, 1960. Recorded Philips 0030.
Le Guignol au gourdin (music to Lorca; chamber orchestra) 1956; first performed Paris, 1956.
Prométhée (ballet; orchestra) 1956; first performed Lyon, July 1956.
Goha (music to film by Schehade and Baratier) 1956.
Fuenteovejuna (music to Lope de Vega; mixed choir, harmony, percussion) 1957; first performed Montaubon, 1957.
Les Dents du singe (music to animated film by Lalou) 1960.
Histoire véridique de Jacotin (radio play with a text by Céla) 1961; broadcast Paris, 1961.
Hélène (music to Euripides; female choir, ensemble) 1963.
Les Héraclides (music to Euripides; mixed choir, harmony, piano, zither, percussion) 1964.
Iphigénie en Tauride (music to Euripides; baritone, bass, vocal ensemble, 4 percussionists, zither, piano) 1965.
Hippolyte (music to Euripides; mixed choir, 4 percussionists, piano, harpsichord, 2 zithers—1 chromatic, 1 in ⅓ tones) 1966.
Suite de ballet 1990; first performed Washington, D.C., 1991.

PUBLICATIONS

By Ohana: "Alfredo Casella", in *Music Review*, 8, 1947; "Deux Oeuvres de Manuel de Falla", in *Journal Musical Français*, 22 October 1953; "Géographie musicale de l'Espagne", in *Journal Musical Français*, March/April 1956; "Erik Satie", in *Présences Contemporaines, Musique Française*, Paris, 1962; "Béla Bartók", in *Ujiras*, July 1965, and *Le Nouvel Observateur*, August 1965; "Micro-Intervals", in *Twentieth-Century Music*: "Experimental Media II", edited by R. Myers, London, 1968; "En el centenario de Manuel de Falla: un revolucionario inconsciente", in *Triunio*, 63, November 1976; "Les Paradoxes de la musique contemporaine", in *Musique en questions*, 1, February 1980; "Ecrire aujourd-hui pour le piano", in *Panorama de la Musique*, March/April 1980; "Sud-Nord", in *20ème Siècle: Images de la Musique Française*, edited by J. P. Derrien, Paris, 1986.

On Ohana: André Gide, in *Journal: 1939–49*, Paris, 1954; C. Rostand, in *La Musique Française Contemporaine*, Paris, 1957; B. Gavoty and D. Lesur, (interview) in *Pour ou Contre la Musique Moderne*, Paris, 1957; J. Roy, in *Présences Contemporaines, Musique Française*, Paris, 1962; R. Myers, in *Modern French Music*, Oxford and New York, 1971; A. Grunenwald, "Conversation avec MO: *T'Haran-Ngo*", in

Arfuyen II, Paris, 1975; F.B. Mache, "Les mal entendus: compositeurs des anneés 1970: MO", in *La Revue Musicale* 314–5, 1976; R. Lyon, "Entretien avec MO", in *Courrier Musical de France*, 62, April 1978; "MO: Essais, études et documentes", *La Revue Musicale*, 351–2, 1982; P. Bolbach, "MO et la guitare", in *La Guitare*, 1982; F. Bayer, "Sous le signe de l'imaginaire: MO", in *L'Esprit*, March 1985; "MO: Miroirs de l'oeuvre", in *La Revue Musicale*, 391–3, 1986; F. Bayer, "Correspondance d'André Gide et MO", in *Bulletin des Amis d'André Gide*, 71, July 1986; C. Paquelet, "La Percussion dans la musique d'O", in *Analyse Musicale*, 8, June 1987; C.A. Rae, "*La Célestine*: MO's Opera in Paris", in *Neue Zeitschrift für Musik*, October 1988, and "The Music of MO", dissertation, University of Oxford, 1989.

Maurice Ohana comments:

My music belongs to no school quotable in current terms. I believe Debussy, de Falla, Ravel and the pre-classical composers have been my constant sources.

I am a complete and perfect stranger to all trends and aesthetic rules originating from Germany and the Vienna School.

* * *

Maurice Ohana was described by André Gide in 1949 as a French Joseph Conrad. Like the Ukrainian-born Pole whose cultural roots were different from his bureaucratic, national identity, Ohana's background is complex and highly cosmopolitan. Born in French Morocco into a family of Spanish origin, he inherited British citizenship from his Gibraltarin father and spent his youth in Morocco, Spain and the Basque country. The southern culture from which he stems reaches beyond the political boundaries of any one country: Ohana often prefers to borrow geographical descriptions from the ancient rather than modern world, and claims as his country of origin the mythical Garden of the Hesperides which embraces both Spain and North Africa. Resident in Paris since 1932, Ohana describes himself as Spanish by birth and upbringing but French by training and adoption, and he can be seen as belonging to the long-established tradition of Spanish musicians, artists and writers who have chosen to travel northwards to exploit their natural heritage.

Ohana's cosmopolitan upbringing has exerted a significant influence on his compositional development. Nurtured into the traditions of Spanish folk music and particularly the Andalusian *cante jondo* from his earliest youth, Ohana looked towards his cultural origins in the development of his musical language and style. Many of his early works choose Spanish subjects and texts, or allude to particular rhythmic and melodic characteristics of Spanish folk music: *Llanto por Ignacio Sanchez Mejias* is a setting of Lorca's poem; *Cantigas* is based on the monodies of King Alphonso "the Wise"; *Tiento* alludes to the traditional form associated with the guitar; and both *Trois Caprices* and *Trois Graphiques* are based on engravings by Goya. While traces of Spanish influence remain in the mature works, including most notably the cello concerto *Anneau du Tamarit* and the opera *La Célestine*, these stylistic elements have been absorbed into the more homogenous musical language of Ohana's mature years. This stems from a variety of eclectic influences including jazz, Afro-Cuban music, Chinese and Japanese theatre music, and much of the Berber and black African tribal music Ohana experienced in his youth. While each of these traditions exerts its influence on melodic as well as harmonic processes, and on much of Ohana's approach to instrumental timbre, African and Afro-Cuban rhythmic features are evident within his technique of superimposing independent layers of ostinatos in sections of aleatory counterpoint. African rhythms and drumming techniques appear in the *Quatre Etudes choréographiques* for solo percussion, as well as the concertos *Synaxis* and *Silenciaire*.

Ohana has contributed to the repertoire of almost every vocal and instrumental genre and has been conspicuous in the revival of interest in the harpsichord. He has been responsible for the invention of two new instruments; the 10-string guitar and the third-tone, micro-interval concert zither. Of particular significance for Ohana's approach to vocal writing was his study of plainsong and much of the Medieval and Renaissance vocal repertoire at the Schola Cantorum with Daniel-Lesur. Ohana has written a large number of vocal works. In addition to *La Célestine* and an opera for children, *Histoire véridique de Jacotin*, Ohana has written two chamber operas: *Syllabaire pour Phèdre* and *Autodafé*. Other dramatic works intended for music theatre setting include *Trois Contes de l'honorable fleur* and *Office des oracles*. There are also two oratorios, a mass and a number of non-dramatic choral works of which *Tombeau de Claude Debussy*, *Cris*, *Sibylle* and *Lys de madrigaux* are particularly important. A feature of his mature vocal works is his disintegration of text into onomatopoeic phonemes. This is often combined with the use of third-tone micro-intervals which are either melodic ornaments or which function as a parallel harmonic system juxtaposed against conventional semitone tuning.

Ohana's fierce independence from Austro-German musical traditions was first established with his founding of the Groupe Zodiaque in 1947. Their aim was to promote folk music and plainsong as the basis for creating a musical language which rejected all pre-compositional systems, but particularly the "new serialism" of their contemporaries. Ohana is a composer for whom Austro-German traditions are irrelevant; his colouristic approach to harmony as timbre and processes of melodic parallelism owe much to Debussy, while the brittle, orchestral acidity of his early works owe much to Manuel de Falla. Commencing with the chamber work *Signes* in 1965, Ohana gave a series of 11 works during the 1960s and 1970s esoteric titles beginning with the letter "S". For Ohana, this was intended to celebrate the proliferation of his mature style into his second 50 years and, with a hidden reference to the reversed Greek sigma, symbolizing "evolution."

—Caroline A. Rae

OLIVER, Stephen. British/English. Born in Liverpool, 10 March 1950. Educated at University of Oxford (composition under Kenneth Leighton), 1968–72. Full-time composer. Recipient: prize (for *Cadenus Observ'd*), GLAA Young Musicians Scheme, 1974. Mailing address: c/o Novello, 8 Lower James Street, London W1R 4DN, England.

Publisher: Novello.

Symphonies/orchestral:

Luv 1975.
Symphony (small orchestra) 1976, revised 1983; first performed Liverpool, 23 May 1976; revised version first performed Finland, 13 October 1983.
O No (brass band) 1976, revised 1985; first performed

London, 10 October 1976.
Concerto for Recorder and Strings (treble recorder) 1988; first performed Aldeburgh, Suffolk, 19 June 1988.

Chamber/instrumental:

Ricercare No 1 (clarinet, violin, cello, piano) 1974; first performed London, 11 January 1974.
Kyoto (organ duet) 1977; first performed London, 22 June 1977.
Sonata (guitar) 1979; first performed Ludwigsburg, Germany, 16 May 1981.
Study (piano) 1979; first performed London, 26 June 1979.
Suite: Nicholas Nickelby (brass quintet) 1980; first performed London, 18 January 1981. Recorded That's Entertainment TER 1029.
Ricercare No 2 (2 oboes, 2 clarinets, 3 bassoons, 2 horns) 1981; first performed Canterbury, Kent, 7 June 1981.
The Lord of the Rings (piano arrangement of incidental music) 1981.
Peter Pan: Three Souvenir Pieces (piano arrangement—with voice in part 3—of incidental music) 1982.
Ricercare No 3 (guitar, viola, cello) 1983; first performed London, 7 January 1984.
Ricercare No 5 (2 trumpets, horn, trombone, tuba) 1986; first performed Sevenoaks, Kent, 15 June 1986.
Character Pieces (after Mozart's *La Clemenza di Tito*; 2 oboes, 2 clarinets, 2 horns, 2 bassoons) 1991; first performed Glyndebourne, Sussex, 12 July 1991.

Vocal/choral:

Overheard on a Saltmarsh (6 male voices; Munro) 1972; first performed Oxford, November 1972.
The Elixir (4 soloists, SATB chorus, melody instrument; Psalm 51, Skelton, Herbert) 1976.
Magnificat and Nunc Dimittis (chorus) 1976.
The Dong with a Luminous Nose (narrator, 5 string quartets; Lear) 1976, revised 1989; first performed Woodfords, 31 July 1976; revised version first performed London, 17 October 1989.
A Dialogue Between Mary and Her Child (soprano, baritone, SATB chorus, unaccompanied; anon. 15th century) 1979.
Ballad of the Breadman (unison voices, piano or guitar; after Causley) 1979.
The Child from the Sea (cantata for treble, SATB chorus, orchestra) 1980; first performed Newcastle-upon-Tyne, 30 October 1980.
From Nicholas Nickelby (overture and vocal music; voices, piano) 1980, revised 1983; first performed London, June 1980. Recorded That's Entertainment TER 1029.
Wedding Anthem: How Blest Are They (arranged from *Nicholas Nickelby*; treble voices, organ; Psalm 128) 1980. Recorded That's Entertainment TER 003.
God Rest You Merry, Gentlemen (SATB chorus, piano; traditional) 1980. Recorded That's Entertainment TER 003.
The Key to the Zoo (narrator, 2 oboes, bassoon, harpsichord; Kington) 1980; broadcast Anglia Television, 5 February 1980; first concert performance Milton Keynes, Hertfordshire, 15 February 1980.
A String of Beads (cantata for SATB chorus, 2 oboes, bassoon, strings) 1980; first performed Milton Keynes, Hertfordshire, 15 February 1981.
Namings (cantata for SATB chorus, brass quintet, timpani; old Scottish riddles) 1981; first performed Edinburgh, 3 September 1981.
Trinity Mass (unaccompanied SSAATTBB chorus) 1981; first performed Norwich, Norfolk, 5 July 1981.
O fons amoris (unaccompanied SSAATTBB chorus; a Kempis) 1981; first performed Norwich, Norfolk, 5 July 1981.
From Blondel (arranged from the musical; voices, piano or guitar; Rice) 1983; first performed Bath, 5 September 1983. Recorded MCA DBL 1.
Running Back for More (arranged from *Blondel*; voice, piano or guitar) 1983. Recorded MCA 845.
This Is the Voice (3-part chorus, organ; Hilton) 1984; first performed Nottingham, 4 July 1984.
Seven Words (cantata for SATB chorus, string orchestra; Bible, How) 1985; first performed Norwich, Norfolk, 15 October 1985.
Forth in Thy Name (soprano, bass, unaccompanied 8-part chorus; Wesley, Psalm 90) 1985; first performed St Albans, Hertfordshire, 5 October 1985.
Festal Magnificat and Nunc Dimittis (SSAATTBB chorus, organ; Evening Canticles, ASB 1980) 1985; first performed Norwich, Norfolk, 6 July 1986.
Two Songs and a Scene from Cymbeline (baritone, piano) 1986; first performed Bromsgrove, Worcestershire, 26 September 1986.
Ricercare No 4 (counter-tenor, 2 tenors, baritone, unaccompanied; Hadrian) 1986.
Prometheus (cantata for chorus, orchestra; after Aeschylus) 1988; first performed Guildford, Surrey, 26 November 1988.
The Vessel (cantata for soprano, tenor, bass, chorus, orchestra) 1990; first performed Nottingham, 19 October 1990.

Opera/dramatic:

Slippery Soules (Christmas drama for treble voices or SATB chorus, violin, percussion, organ, piano) 1969, revised 1976, orchestrated 1988; first performed Oxford, December 1969; orchestrated version first performed London, 12 December 1988.
The Duchess of Malfi (after Webster; 5 principals, 8 supporting roles, chorus, orchestra) 1971, revised 1978; first performed Oxford, 1971; revised version first performed Santa Fe, New Mexico, 5 August 1978.
The Dissolute Punished 1972.
The Three Wise Monkeys 1972.
A Furcoat for Summer 1973.
Three Instant Operas ("Paid Off", "Time Flies", "Old Haunts"; unison voices, optional melody instrument, optional percussion, piano) 1973.
The Donkey 1973.
Sufficient Beauty (short) 1973.
Past Tense (short) 1973.
Cadenus Observ'd (dramatic sketch for solo baritone; after Swift) 1974; first performed London, 26 January 1975.
Perseverance 1974.
Tom Jones (after Fielding; 14 principals, chorus, orchestra) 1974–5; first performed Snape, Suffolk, 6 April 1976.
Bad Times (dramatic sketch for baritone, string quartet) 1975; first performed London, 24 June 1975.
The Waiter's Revenge (short opera for 2 sopranos, counter-tenor, tenor, baritone, bass, male mime) 1976; first performed Nottingham, 15 June 1976.
Il Giardino/The Garden (short opera for soprano, tenor, lute, viola da gamba; or string quartet, harpsichord) 1977; first performed Batignano, Italy, 27 July 1977; English version first performed London, 17 April 1980.

A Stable Home (short opera for 2 soloists, chorus, piano, optional guitar, tuned percussion) 1977; first performed Canada, Winter 1977.
The Girl and the Unicorn (5 soloists, chorus, orchestra or piano, optional guitar and drums) 1978; first performed London, 9 December 1978.
The Dreaming of the Bones 1979.
Jacko's Play (short opera for 3 characters, piano) 1979. Recorded Delyse 7DS 1.
A Man of Feeling (short opera for soprano, baritone, piano; after Schnitzler) 1980; first performed London, 17 November 1980.
Nicholas Nickelby (incidental music to adaptation of Dickens in 2 parts; flute/piccolo, clarinet/bass clarinet, bassoon, horn, 2 trumpets, trombone/tuba, percussion, 2 violins/1 viola, cello, conductor/piano, recorded organ) 1980; first performed London, June 1980. Recorded That's Entertainment TER 1029.
The Lord of the Rings (incidental music for radio; chorus, strings, percussion; Tolkien) 1981. Recorded BBC REH 415.
Euridice (13 soloists, chorus, clarinet/bass clarinet, trumpet, trombone, percussion, piano, banjo/guitar, violin, double bass; after Peri, 1600) 1981; first performed London, 4 March 1981.
Sasha (18 singers, flute, oboe, clarinet, bassoon, horn, trumpet, 2 percussion, piano, 2 violins, viola, cello, double bass; after Ostrovsky) 1982; first performed Banff, Alberta, 7 April 1983.
Peter Pan (incidental music to Barrie play; flexible instrumentation for young and amateur players, plus 2 percussion, piano/synthesizer) 1982; first performed London, 16 December 1982. Recorded Dakota RSP 1.
Blondel (musical for 6 soloists, male quartet, female trio, chorus, violin/viola, clarinet/alto saxophone/baritone saxophone, trumpet, guitar, electric bass guitar, drums, percussion, 2 keyboards/synthesizer; Rice) 1983; first performed Bath, 5 September 1983. Recorded MCA PBL 1.
Britannia Preserv'd (masque for 4 principals, mixed chorus, dancers, flute, oboe, 2 clarinets, bassoon, 2 trumpets, 2 trombones, 2 percussion, guitar/banjo, harp, viola, cello, double bass) 1984; first performed Hampton Court, Middlesex, 30 May 1984.
The Ring (short for 4 singers, orchestra; after *Coronation Street*) 1984; first performed Manchester, 31 May 1984.
La Bella e la bestia / Beauty and the Beast (after de Beaumont; 6 soloists, flute/piccolo, trumpet, B♭ clarinet/E♭ clarinet/bass clarinet, baritone saxophone, cello, guitar/banjo/electric bass guitar, piano/bowed psaltery/Nordic lyre/plucked zither/hurdy-gurdy, 2 percussion, optional synthesizer) 1984; Italiân version first performed Batignano, Italy, 26 July 1984; English version first performed London, 21 June 1985.
Waiting 1985.
Exposition of a Picture (conversation for tenor, baritone, string quartet) 1986; first performed London, 24 June 1986.
Commuting (wordless sketch for counter-tenor, 2 tenors, baritone, 1 other voice, unaccompanied) 1986.
Mario ed il mago / Mario and the Magician (7 principals, 7 supporting roles, flute/piccolo, clarinet, cornet, tuba, 2 percussion, piano/harmonium, viola, 2 cellos; after Mann) 1988; first performed Batignano, Italy, 5 August 1988.
Tables Meet (dramatic sketch for 18 characters) 1990; first performed London, May 1990.
Timon of Athens (9 principals, 2 boys, orchestra; after Shakespeare) 1991; first performed London, 17 May 1991.
L'Oca del Cairo (6 principals, orchestra) 1991; first performed Batignano, Italy, 30 July 1991.

W.A. Mozart: recitatives for *La Clemenza di Tito* 1991; first performed Glyndebourne, Sussex, 28 June 1991.
Aulis Sallinen: translations of: *The Red Line*, 1980, and *The King Goes Forth to France*, 1985.

* * *

There is one hang-over from the romantic period of the arts that has somehow escaped the the general purge—that the "soul of the artist" is sacrosanct and, that music exists for the benefit of composers and performers to express themselves in. Stephen Oliver takes exactly the opposite view: composers exist to write music, and the purpose of such music will vary from one situation to another. We must keep this idea firmly in our minds if we cherish any hope of finding a unity in Oliver's disconcertingly wide range and disparate output. When Stravinsky was taxed with the apparent discontinuity of his own work, he retorted "at one meal I eat fruit, at the next a beefsteak, at the next cream cakes—nobody sees anything wrong with that." It is not that one is better than another, it is a question of appropriateness. Oliver's catalogue bears witness to his lifelong and successful search for and development of a technique that will allow him to deploy a musical idea in the way most appropriate to it rather than to him. It is an unselfish, almost self-effacing attitude which some might find at variance with how they perceive his personality.

Oliver's music reflects the personality of the man in a very real way. His underlying nature is shy, reserved, even diffident, and this is demonstrated by his recurring tendency to supress his own musical ego if it would get in the way of the musical or dramatic idea that is paramount. His manner, however, is forceful, even caustic, as can be seen in the emphatic way he will sometimes express that idea, and his serious music is frequently a blend of the delicate and the forceful. He is a genuine intellectual, and while he may display this with a flourish, the intellect informs his subject at every level. He does not make the music or the story (which may not be theatre, but purely musical) obscure. He tells his story in a straightforward, left-to-right way and in a musical language that places no deliberate obstacles in the path of the listener. The intellectuality shows itself in the way he sees so many implications at so many levels of his material, and seeks to give each a suitable prominence. It is the appropriateness of treatment to idea, and the suitability of the handling to the situation that provides the illusion of diffusion but the fact of continuity.

The other overriding feature of Oliver's music is its utter professionalism and the accuracy of his judgement. He hits the bullseye again and again. He is practical, but it is not always the practicality you expect. When writing for amateurs and young people he never patronises them, but provides something that engages the enthusiasm as well as extends the technique in a purely positive way. People see why they should be developing their techniques, make real efforts to do so, and by so doing move forward. With professionals he expects a professionalism in their field that matches the one he shows in his own, which is only fair, but can be extremely demanding.

To comment on the Oliver "style" is not just impossible, it is not relevant at all. At one level there are influences on the musical style—Britten, Stravinsky and a raft of others—but they get no further than the very surface, and it is not the surface that matters with Oliver outside the area of simple aptness and excellence. His output can be broadly divided into two categories—pastiche and non-pastiche—and thereafter into as many subsections as there are works. He has no "no-go" areas: the idea that something was "beneath him" would strike Oliver as myopic insecurity. Pastiche also has the benefit to composers that jogging has for athletes, and adds an additional element of spontaneity to his work—a characteristic you cannot synthesise by thought—which spills over into his concert scores, to their benefit.

The style of the pastiche is the right one for the situation—epic modality in *The Lord of the Rings* music, Mozartian charm and lightness in *Love's Labours Lost*, cosy Edwardiana for *Peter Pan* and Victoriana for *Nicholas Nickleby*, renaissance dances for period dramas, outright rock for *Blondel*—but always fresh and inventive.

There seems to be a sort of confidence that transfers to the other side of his work. The bravura fioritura and roulades of *Tom Jones* for example, and the claustrophobic prodigality of *The Duchess of Malfi*. The stage is Oliver's natural habitat. His operatic work is distinguished by its sureness of touch, its natural sense of pacing and dramatic structure, its wealth of characterisation and the sense of what works on the stage rather than just on the page. Again and again we find that when it is a choice between the drama and the composer's (supposed) own personality, he will always sacrifice his ego to the needs of the moment. He is constantly redefining integrity, and remaining true to it: it is not a want of individuality, but an expression of strength. Oliver simply has rather unconventional views on the nature of individuality. There seems to be no discrepancy between the wholehearted theatricality of scores like *La bella e la bestia / Beauty and the Beast*, or *Mario ed il mago / Mario and the Magician*, and the effectiveness of the church music. With a composer such as Herbert Howells, the agnosticism permitted him to stand back and permit the poetry of the settings to speak for itself; with Jonathan Harvey, the sheer sincerity of his faith transcends any difficulty of language. With Oliver it is an awareness that what people are doing musically in a religious setting is infinitely more important to them than putting on a concert. They are intended for liturgical use, and as such are perfectly judged. The same considerations also resulted in one of his most beautiful scores, *Seven Words*, so they cannot be lightly dismissed as peripheral.

Nor can the purely concert works. Significantly many carry the title "Ricercare", which the composer is at pains to point out is intended in its purely literal sense, to seek out. Another example of his belief that the composer serves music, not the other way round: he does not explore forms with music, but investigates and expresses ideas and music with forms. This is the common thread running throughout his enormous output, from the briefest score for children to the most ambitious full-evening opera. What separates him from his contemporaries is not a matter of degree (though his fecundity is almost unique), nor of type (though his unique contribution to the theatre is likewise unmatched in 20th-century Britain), but of principle—his basic attitude to why one composes at all. Everything flows from this—the joy of putting notes on the page, the flawless technique, the vibrant orchestration and responsive word setting, the language—depending on tonal centres while avoiding the tyranny of direct tonal implications but with a genuine (if subtle) individuality and flavour derived from the fact that it has established itself from pragmatic concerns; it must work, and it must not confuse, deflect or bore. Humour, tragedy or pathos are a matter of conceptual impulse not rhetorical gesture. His works stand by their substance, not their surface effect.

—Giles Easterbrook

OLIVEROS, Pauline. American. Born in Houston, Texas, 30 May 1932. Educated at University of Houston (composition under Paul Koepke, accordion under William Palmer), 1949–52; San Francisco State College, B.A., 1957; private composition study under Robert Erickson, 1954–60; post-graduate study, University of Toronto (under Hugh Le Caine), 1966. Member, improvising group Sonics, from 1961; co-director (with Ramon Sender and Morton Subotnick), San Francisco Tape Music Center, 1961–5; director, Mills Tape Center, Oakland, California, 1966–7; teacher of music, 1967–79, and professor of music, 1979–81, University of California, San Diego; composer in residence, North Carolina School of the Arts, Walker Art Center, Minneapolis, Cornish School, Seattle, Washington, all 1980, Yellow Springs Institute, Chester Springs, Pennsylvania, 1983, University of Idaho, Moscow, 1985, San Francisco Art Institute Humanities Department, 1986, New School for Dance Development, Amsterdam, 1986–8, The Exploratorium, San Francisco, Bowdoin College, Brunswick, Maine, California College of Arts and Crafts, Oakland, all 1988, and Simon Fraser University, Burnaby, British Columbia, Oberlin Conservatory of Music, Ohio, both 1989; also at Wesleyan University, Middletown, Connecticut, Stanford University, California, Cleveland Museum of Art, Ohio, and Cabrillo Festival; artistic advisor, New Music America Festival, Houston, 1985–6; senior researcher, Institute for Studies in American Music, Brooklyn, New York, 1987; artistic director, "Deep Listening", The Oliveros Foundation, 1988; independent composer and accordionist; karate expert. Recipient: Pacifica Foundation Prize (for *Variations for Sextet*), 1961; Gaudeamus Foundation Award (for *Sound Patterns*), 1962; Beethoven Prize, City of Bonn (for *Bonn Feier*), 1977; black belt, Shotokan karate, 1980; Pauline Oliveros Day and retrospective, Houston, Texas, 1983; National Endowment for the Arts Composer's Fellowship, 1983; honorary doctorate, University of Maryland, 1986; citation, City of Philadelphia Women's History Week, 1987; Artist's Fellowship Award in Music, New York Foundation for the Arts, 1989. Mailing address: 156 Hunter Street, Kingston, New York 12401, U.S.A.

Publisher: Smith.

Symphonies / orchestral:

To Valerie Solanas and Marilyn Monroe in Recognition of their Desperation (orchestra; also version for chamber ensemble) 1970.
Tashi gomang 1981.

Chamber / instrumental:

Trio (clarinet, horn, bassoon) 1955.
Variations for Sextet (flute, clarinet, trumpet, horn, cello, piano) 1960.
Trio (flute, piano, page turner) 1961.
Trio (trumpet, accordion, double bass) 1961.
Outline (flute, percussion, double bass) 1963. Recorded Nonesuch H 71237.
Duo (accordion, bandoneon, optional mynah bird) 1964.
Engineer's Delight (piccolo, 7 conductors) 1967.
Night Jar (viola d'amore) 1968.
Circuitry (5 percussion, lights) 1968.
Wheel of Fortune (clarinet) 1969.
Aeolian Partitions (flute, clarinet, violin, cello, piano) 1969.
1000 Acres (string quartet) 1972.

Sonic Meditations I XXV (optional instruments) 1974.
Horse Sings from Cloud (harmonium, accordion, bandoneon, concertina) 1975. Recorded Love VR 1902.
To Those in Gray Northwestern Rainforests (unspecified ensemble) 1976.
Double X (instrumental duos/similar instruments/overlapping ranges) 1979.
Fwyn (bandoneon duo; collaboration with Gordon Mumma) 1979. Recorded Lovely Communications VR-1092.
The Witness (virtuoso instrumentalists) 1979.
Gone with the Wind 1980 (assorted ensembles) 1980.
Travelling Companions (percussion ensemble) 1980.
Monkey (chamber ensemble) 1981.
Mother's Day (2 concertinos) 1981.
. . . *Jam* (accordion, ensemble) 1982.
Three Meditations (accordion) 1982.
Rattlesnake Mountain (accordion) 1982. Recorded Love VR 1901.
Wind Whirl (accordion) 1982.
Songs and Dance (accordions) 1982.
The Wanderer (accordions) 1982. Recorded Love VR 1902.
The Wheel of Time (string quartet, electronics) 1983.
Gathering Together (piano—8 hands) 1983.
The Seventh Mansion: From The Interior Castle (amplified accordion, effects) 1983.
The Receptive (accordion) 1983. Recorded hat Art 2020; ZOAR SCS 8.
A Secret Relationship (accordion) 1983.
Go (accordion, violin) 1983.
Spiral Mandala (4 clarinets, 8 wine glasses, bass drum, finger cymbals) 1984.
Letting Go (accordion ensemble or solo) 1984.
Tree / Peace (violin, cello, piano) 1984.
Syracuse Meditations (accordion) 1984.
Waking the Heart (accordion or accordion ensemble, with digital delay) 1984.
Wings of a Dove (2 pianos, double wind quintet) 1984.
Earth Ears (accordion, vibraphone, violin) 1984.
Lion's Eye (gamelan or synthesizer) 1985.
Tasting the Blaze (percussion, electronics, trombone, cello, clarinet, 4 accordions, gagaku orchestra) 1985.
The Roots of the Moment (accordion in just intonation, interactive electronic environment) 1987–8. Recorded hat Art CD 6009.

Vocal/choral:

Three Songs (soprano, piano) 1957.
Sound Patterns (chorus) 1961. Recorded Odyssey 32 16 0156; Ars Nova AN 1005.
The C(s) for Once (voices, flutes, trumpets, tape delay system) 1966.
O HA AH (chorus, conductor, 2 percussion) 1968.
*SY*YdY = 1 / The Indefinite Integral of Psi Star Psi d Tau = 1* (4 singers/readers, 4 cellos, 4 bassoons, amplification, heartbeat, shakuhachi) 1969.
AOK (chorus, accordion, violins, conductors, 8 country fiddlers, tape) 1969.
Music for Expo 70 (3 voices, accordion, 2 cellos) 1970.
Music for Tai Chi (voices, accordion, strings, winds, percussion, improvisation) 1970.
Meditations on the Points of a Compass (12 solo voices, chorus, percussion) 1970.
Willow Brook Generations and Reflections (voices, winds, brass) 1976.
Horse Sings from a Cloud (Rose Mountain Slow Runner) (voice, accordion) 1977. Recorded Love VR 1901.
King Kong Sings Along (unaccompanied chorus) 1977.
Rose Moon (chorus, percussion) 1977.
The Wheel of Life (unaccompanied voices) 1978.
El relicario de los animales (soprano, 20 instruments) 1979.
Carol Plantamura (voice, 20 instruments) 1979.
Angels and Demons (chorus, ensemble) 1980.
The Wandering: A Love Song (voice, digital delay) 1983.
The Well: Preponderance of the Great and Gentle Race (voice, flute, alto clarinet, clarinet, accordion, saxophone, violin, percussion; or accordion) 1983. Recorded hat Art 2020.
Drama of the Five Families (narrator, soloist, chorus) 1984.
Song for the Ancestors (voice, shell trumpet, didjeridu) 1984.
Aga (voice, concertina, whistle conch, trumpet, electronics, digital delay) 1984.
A Love Song (voice, accordion) 1984. Recorded Eigelstein ES 2025/6.
Oh Sister Whose Name Is Goddess (voice, digital delay) 1984.
Talking Bottles and Bones (voice, effects, digital delay) 1984.
Open Circuits om mani padme hum for 1984 Summer Olympics 1984.
Rain Music (voice, accordion) 1985.
The Gentle (voice, ensemble) 1985. Recorded hat Art 2020.
Legend (chorus, amplified accordion, percussion, effects) 1985.
The Chicken Who Learned How to Fly (voices, narrator, Fairlight synthesizer) 1985–6.

Opera/dramatic:

Seven Passages (dancer, mobile, 2-channel tape) 1963.
Five (trumpet, dancer) 1964.
Apple Box Concerto (performers, amplified apple boxes) 1964.
George Washington Slept Here Too (theatre piece for amplified violin, film, tape) 1965.
Cat O'Nine Tails (mimes, tape) 1965.
Pieces of Eight (theatre piece for wind octet, tape, props/cash register) 1965.
Seven Sets of Mnemonics (multimedia piece) 1965.
Theater Piece for Trombone Player (garden hoses, tape) 1966.
Hallo Piece for Halloween (mimes, instruments, tapes, lights) 1966.
Aeolian Partitions (theatre piece for flute, clarinet, violin, cello, piano) 1968.
Festival House (mimes, light, film projections, orchestra) 1968.
Evidence for Competing Bimolecular and Thermonuclear Mechanisms in the Hydrochlorination of Cyclohexene (performers, sonic events, audience) 1968.
Double Basses at Twenty Paces (2 double basses, slides, conductor/referee, 2 performers) 1968.
Valentine for SAG (4 card players, amplified sound) 1968.
The Dying Alchemist Preview (narrator, violin, trumpet, piccolo, percussion, slides) 1969.
Please Don't Shoot the Piano Player, He's Doing the Best He Can (theatre piece for ensemble of soloists) 1969.
Why Don't You Write a Short Piece? (theatre piece for 1 performer) 1970.
Link (theatre piece) 1971.
Sonic Meditations (theatre piece for voices, performers, instruments) 1971–2.
Postcard Theater (multimedia event) 1972.
Phantom Fathom (multimedia event, exotic potluck dinner) 1972.
What to Do (performers, sonic and mixed media) 1972.
Phantom Fathom II: From the Theatre of the Ancient Trumpeter (audience participation) 1973.

Crow Two (ceremonial opera) 1974.
Theater of Substitutions 1975.
Theater of Substitutions: Blind / Dumb / Director 1977.
Bonn Feier (theatre piece for actors, dancers, performers) 1977.
The Yellow River Map (theatre piece for 50 or more performers) 1977.
Traveling Companions (theatre piece for dancers and percussion ensemble) 1980.

Other:

Time Perspectives (tape) 1961.
Applebox (sic) 1964.
Bye Bye Butterfly (oscillators, amplifiers, tape) 1965. Recorded Arch S 1765.
Events (film music; tape) 1965.
Winter Light (tape, mobile, figure) 1965.
Light Piece for David Tudor 1965.
Applebox Double 1965.
The Chronicles of Hell (tape) 1965.
Five Thousand Miles (tape, electronics) 1965.
Mnemonics III (tape, electronics) 1965.
Mnemonics IV (tape, electronics) 1965.
Mnemonics V (tape, electronics) 1965.
Before the Music Ends (tape, dancer) 1965.
Rock Symphony (tape) 1965.
Big Mother Is Watching You (tape) 1966.
Applebox Orchestra 1966.
I of IV (tape) 1966.
II of IV (tape) 1966.
III of IV (tape) 1966.
IV of IV (tape) 1966.
V of IV (tape) 1966.
The day I Disconnected the Erase Head and Forgot to Reconnect It (tape, electronics) 1966.
I of IV (2-track tape) 1966. Recorded Odyssey 32 16 0160.
The Bath (soloist, 4 tapes) 1966.
Participle Dangling in Honor of Gertrude Stein (tape, mobile, work crew) 1966.
Beautiful Soop (tape) 1967.
Mills Bog (2-channel tape, electronics) 1968.
Music for Lysistrata (2-channel tape, electronics) 1968.
Live Electronic Piece for Merce Cunningham's Dance 1969.
Events (film music; voices, accordion, cello, instruments) 1969.
Bog Road with Bird Call patch (tape) 1970.
Applebox Orchestra with Bottle Chorus 1970.
Breathe In / Breathe Out (sonic meditations) 1983.

PUBLICATIONS

By Oliveros: *Pauline's Proverbs*, New York, 1976; *Software for People: Collected Writings 1963–80*, New York, 1981; "Karl Kohn: Concerto mutabile", in *Perspectives*, 22; "Tape Delay Techniques for Electronic Music", in *Composer*, 2.

On Oliveros: Morton Subotnick, "PO: *Trio*", in *Perspectives of New Music*, 2(1), 1963; Elinor Kefaias, "PO", in *High Fidelity / Musical America*, 25(6), 1975; W. Zimmermann, (interview) in *Desert Plants: Conversations with 23 American Musicians*, Vancouver, 1976; M. Roth, (interview) in *New Performance*, 1(2), 1977; Z. Cleigh, "All Sounds Are Music", in *San Diego Magazine* 31(9), 1980; Heidi Von Gunden, *The Music of PO*, Metuchen, New Jersey, 1983.

* * *

Pauline Oliveros is an acoustic and electronic composer who has been especially innovative in linking her music with the theatrical, collaborative and socially oriented performing arts.

Her music prior to the mid-1960s was for conventional instruments, neither serial nor indeterminate but based instead on improvisation: "I simply listened until I heard the next sound to write down." This reflected the freedom she had experienced in work with live extemporary groups.

Oliveros collaborated with Buchla in the development of early synthesizer equipment. Her electronic work is characterised by lengthy drones and static sounds. Some have been composed directly on to tape in real time. *I of IV* controls timbre by regulating the density of an initial sound through differently routed feedback loops and delays. Amplified and reverberated signal from a 12-oscillator keyboard passes to one of two tape recorders. It enters input one of the first recorder, is fed into input two, which returns to the first in a double feedback loop. The tape is also fed through to a second machine in playback mode, at such a distance as to create approximately an eight-second delay. The outputs of the second machine are connected to the corresponding inputs of the first, thus giving eight-second delay on the double feedback loop.

Oliveros was one of the originators of what has been dubbed bio-music. Her accompaniment to the Merce Cunningham dance *Loops* was founded on amplification of the heart and respiratory sounds of the solo dancer, transferred by radio to minimise interference with movement.

Many works feature a theatrical dimension. Her second *Trio* is not scored for three instruments, but for flute, piano and page turner. Her work frequently involves mixed-media in the strict sense, often in collaboration. In the 1960s she worked with David Tudor and with dancer-choreographer Elizabeth Harris, and later helped found a women's group for the performance of mixed-media pieces. In 1979 she collaborated with Gordon Mumma on *Fwyyn* for two untreated bandoneons, a five-minute lament for a "dancing princess who has been enchanted unto death" which resuscitates her; it was written for an hour-long theatrical fantasy.

These mixed-media pieces have a conceptual art flavour. Her *Valentine for SAG*, written in 1968 for the Sonic Arts Group, makes playing cards a unifying theme. Its bio-musical core is a game of hearts played onstage; the four players' heartbeats are amplified. A narrator discusses the history of card games while two carpenters build a fence, a croquet player hits a few balls, and giant playing cards are projected.

—David Revill

ORBÓN (de Soto), Julián. Cuban. Born in Aviles, Spain, 7 August 1925; family emigrated to Cuba, 1937. Educated at Conservatory of Oviedo, Spain, from 1935; studied piano under Benjamín Orbón, composition under Jose Ardevol, Havana, 1938–45; Berkshire Music Center, Tanglewood, Massachusetts (composition under Aaron Copland), 1945. Married Mercedes Vicini in 1948; 2 children. Director, Orbon Conservatory, Havana, 1946–60; exiled from Cuba, 1960; work with Carlos Chávez, composition workshop, National Conservatory of Music, Mexico, 1960–3;

settled in New York City, 1964; teacher of music, State University of New York, Purchase, and Washington University, St. Louis, Missouri, 1964–5. Recipient: Juan Landaeta Prize, Latin-American Music Festival, Caracas, 1954; Guggenheim Fellowships, 1958, 1969; Award, American Academy of Arts and Letters, 1967. Mailing address: c/o 6361 SW 16th Terrace, Miami, Florida 33155, U.S.A.

Publishers: Peer Southern; Boosey & Hawkes.

Symphonies/orchestral:

Sinfonía en do / Symphony in C 1945; first performed Havana, 1946.
Homenaje a la tonadilla 1947; first performed Havana, 1950.
Tres versiones sinfónicas 1953; first performed Caracas, 11 December 1954.
Danzas sinfónicas 1955; first performed Miami, 17 November 1957.
Concerto grosso 1958; first performed New York City, 8 November 1961.
Partita No 3 1965; first performed Caracas, 1965.
Partita No 4 (piano, orchestra) 1982–5; first performed Dallas, Texas, 1985. Recorded Olympia Cardinal Classics OCD 351.

Chamber/instrumental:

Tocata (piano) 1943; first performed Havana, 1943.
Concerto da camara (horn, cor anglais, trumpet, cello, piano) 1944; first performed Havana, 1944.
String Quartet 1951; first performed Chicago, 1951. Recorded Elan.
Preludio y danza (guitar) 1951; first performed New York City, 1953. Recorded EMI CDC 749710-2.
Partitas No 1 (harpsichord) 1963; first performed New York City, 1964. Recorded Philips SAL 6505001.
Partita No 2 (harpsichord, vibraphone, celeste, harmonium, string quartet) 1964; first performed Washington, D.C., 1965.
Preludio y fantasia tiento (organ) 1974.

Vocal/choral:

Crucifixus (motet for unaccompanied SATB chorus) 1953.
Hymnus ad galli cantum (soprano, flute, oboe, clarinet, harp, string quartet) 1956; first performed Tanglewood, Massachusetts, 1956. Recorded Heliodor H/HS 25037.
Tres cantigas del rey (soprano, string quartet, harpsichord, percussion) 1960; first performed Santiago de Compostela, Spain, 1961. Recorded Philips SAL 650501.
Monte Gelboe (tenor, orchestra) 1962; first performed Madrid, 1967.
Introito (scared choral) 1967–8.
Oficios / Liturgia de tres dias (chorus, orchestra) 1970–5.
Don canciones folklóricas ("La Llorona" and "The Ballad of Jesse James"; unaccompanied mixed chorus) 1972; first performed New York City, 1972.
Libro de cantares (mezzo-soprano, piano; Asturian texts) 1987; first performed Oviedo, Asturias, Spain, 1988.

PUBLICATIONS

By Orbón: "En la esencia de los estilos", in *Origenes*, 7(25), 1944; "Richard Strauss", in *Origenes*, 6(22), 1949; "Tradición y originalidad en la música hispanoamericana", in *Inter-american Music Bulletin*, 34, March 1963.

On Orbón: R. Parmenter, "Find from Cuba: JO Scores at Composer Forum", in *New York Times*, 7 March 1955; H.C. Schonberg, "Latin Composer", in *New York Times*, 9 November 1961; Alejo Carpentier, *La Música en Cuba*, Mexico City, 1979; Velia Yedra, "JO: An Analytical Study of *Tocata* for Piano and *Partitas* for Harpsichord", dissertation, University of Miami, 1986; Eduardo Mata, "Tres conferencias sobre la música de JO", in *Pauta*, 21, January 1987; Velia Yedra, *JO: A Biographical and Critical Essay*, Miami, 1990.

Julián Orbón comments:

A composer's style is always dictated by the conditions around him. And a true composer remains faithful to those sounds for better or for worse. In my case, these sounds are not limited just to a single type of music or period. For example, I love Latin American popular music, especially that of Cuba, and you'll find that in my writing as well.

* * *

Julián Orbón, who is now in the prime of his artistic productivity, is one of the greatest figures in 20th-century Cuban art music and possibly the most renowned Cuban composer living abroad.

Three major influences are apparent in his music: Spanish popular songs, the music of the "vihuelistas" and the works of Antonio de Cabezón and Tomás Luís de Victoria; African and Spanish-American, mainly Cuban popular music; the Middle Ages, chiefly Gregorian chant.

Regardless of their prevailing influence, all of Orbón's compositions reveal a careful attention to form and rigorous structural design, as well as the use of modes. His works have gradually evolved toward a very personal idiom, the result of the constant streamlining and fusion of elements.

Orbón's best-known work, *Tres versiones sinfónicas*, captures the full gamut of elements that characterize his creation. It is a free interpretation of three musical quotations. The first movement opens with a diatonic theme by Luis de Milán (a Spanish lutenist of the 16th century). Two measures later, a rhythmic pattern, essentially borrowed from the bass line of the *son* (an old Cuban dance), is introduced. A fusion of these two elements prevails in this movement. The musical quotation of the second movement is taken from a conductus of Perotinus (12th century). This movement contains many melismatic passages of Gregorian nature, alternating with fuller modal harmonies. The third movement, "Xilófono", consists of a gradual accumulation of rhythms and orchestral textures based on an original Congolese rhythmic pattern.

Chronologically, four periods are clearly identifiable in Orbón's musical output. The first encompasses his formative years, and bears the strong imprint of Manuel de Falla's and José Ardévol's influence. The second period, commencing after *Sinfonía en do / Symphony in C*, comprises works where Cuban influence is paramount. A third period, more Spanish-American in nature, began in 1955. *Partitas No 1* marks the beginning of the composer's fourth period. The works of this period, such as the *Partita No 4*, feature a more romantic, expansive language.

Orbón has been defined as the most genuine Spanish-American composer, a critical perception based perhaps on the unique way in which the elements from these two cultures are syncretized in his work. Departing from the common tradition of Spanish America, his style of composition has achieved unity, cohesion and individuality; transcending primary nationalistic concepts, his musical output is universal in scope.

—Velia Yedra

ORE, Cecilie. Norwegian. Born in Oslo, 19 July 1954. Educated at Norges Musikhochschule, Oslo (composition and sonology under Lasse Thoresen and Olav Anton Thommessen, postgraduate piano diploma under Liv Glaser, Jens Harald Bratlie and Elisabeth Klein); Institute of Sonology, Utrecht (electro-acoustic composition); Sweelinck Conservatorium, Amsterdam (composition under Ton de Leeuw). Composer, writer and broadcaster. Recipient: mention (for *Im-Mobile*), Concours International de Musique Electro-acoustique, Bourges, 1985; Composition of the Year (*Porphyre*), 1988; prize (for *Etapper*), International Rostrum for Electro-acoustic Music, Stockholm, 1988. Mailing address: Zetlitzgt. 3, 0165 Oslo 1, Norway.

Publishers: Norsk Musikforlag, Oslo; Norwegian Music Information Centre, Oslo.

Symphonies/orchestral:

Strata (string orchestra) 1982.
Porphyre 1986.

Chamber/instrumental:

Camera Lucida (harpsichord, 11 strings) 1983.
Helices (wind quintet) 1984; first performed Bergen, 1985.
Janus (cello) 1985.
Contracanthus (double bass) 1987; first performed Oslo, 1987. Recorded Simax PSC 1039.
Praesens subitus (string quartet) 1989; first performed Oslo, 1989.

Vocal/choral:

Le Tombeau des naïades (soprano, chamber ensemble; Louys) 1981.
Carnatus (soprano, unaccompanied mixed chorus) 1982; first performed Toronto, 1984.
Dream Diary (2 voices, 2 percussion, saxophone; Arasanayagam) 1983.
Ex oculis (2 tenors, baritone, bass) 1985; first performed Bergen, 1986.
Cantus aquatoris (soprano, alto, tenor, bass) 1987; first performed Sima Hydroelectric Plant, Norway, 1987.

Other:

Circe (computer) 1982.
Im-Mobile I/II/III (video; music for sculpture exhibition; electro-acoustic) 1984.
Vacuus (electro-acoustic) 1986.
Kald Verden (electro-acoustic score to film by Jensen and Amundsen) 1986.
Etapper (electro-acoustic) 1988.
Prologos (theatre music) 1990.

PUBLICATIONS

By Ore: *Norwegian Music Institutions and Music Life*, Norwegian Music Information Centre, Oslo, 1981; *Norwegian Pianorama: Piano Music by 25 Norwegian Composers*, Oslo, 1982; "Tid. Teknologi. Tanke.", in *Ballade/Ny Musik*, 2/3, 1988; "Sine qua non", in *Ossia*, 1990; articles in music periodical *Ballade* and literary periodical *Vinduet*.

Cecilie Ore comments:

The concept of time has lost its former coherence. As a consequence, avant-garde music is not based on the idea of linear succession but on the idea of non-linear combinations: different times and different spaces that are combined in a holistic everywhere at every time, an extended present reflecting the past projecting the future.

In my own work I am preoccupied with music as a tissue of temporal relationships, relations giving birth to both colour and form. Through this research I wish to develop further a musical consciousness of a more polycentric nature, a consciousness where a manifold of realities can exist simultaneously.

* * *

The concept of time is a focal point of Cecilie Ore's aesthetics and technical proceedings—different perceptions of time, linearity contra non-linearity, projections of space in relation to time, and simultaneous processes on different levels. She tries to capture the expanded moment and, as a consequence, the dialectic between the static (the being) and the processes (the becoming) stands out as a central field of tension. Her striving to achieve total congruence between the micro- and macro-levels in the works is equally important. The characteristics of the details determine their place and function in the entirety. Ore does not compose her works "from beginning to end", but rather erects them as if they were architecture. Ore's music contains a deliberate paradox in the form of a complementarity, or polycentricity, where courses of events, different by nature, exist simultaneously. The dynamic forces collaborate and counteract one another at the same time.

To capture briefly the compositional thinking of Ore, one could use the words "consistency" and "logic". The strict structure of her works permits no compromises or subjective excesses. No matter which work one chooses as one's point of departure, her entire production reflects the same kinds of problems, exposed in different images.

Aspects of time are already apparent in the title of the string quartet *Praesens subitus*; against a fabric of vibrating sounds, static and yet in constant change, there is the contrast of outbursts of the abrupt present, and in spite of the structural transformations the impression left behind is of something frozen and fixed.

Ore tries to escape from traditional linear melodic development and its resulting causal effects. She replaces it with sonorous/rhythmical structures, evident in works like *Praesens subitus*, the wind quintet *Helices* and the orchestral work *Porphyre*. This work, like most of her compositions, is carved in one piece without clearly defined sections. Here she creates a form that is defined and yet open to different interpretations. The details are ambiguous and polyfunctional, and the foreground–background relations change constantly. Thinnings and thickenings of texture generate the energy of the music.

Electro-acoustic music is an important part of Ore's work. The computer enabled her emancipation from conventional ways of thinking, and has become her main working tool. However, she marks no partition between acoustically and electronically conceived music. Her treatment of the voice, both in *Etapper*, an electro-acoustic work where Ore uses the human voice as sound material, and in her vocal works, has several points in common with the way she works with instruments; the nuances of timbre constitute the fundamental features.

Ore is also preoccupied with science and other arts, which are equally important as a source of inspiration as is the music of other composers. She takes an interest in history and in *Ex oculis*, for four male voices, one finds modern technology combined with the mystics of an ancient ritual.

The style of Ore's music is clearly "international", and her list of works is very homogeneous. Her compositions display apparent similarities in thought, form and expression. However, that is not a result of a planned development, even though the output as a whole is not unimportant for Ore, since it is the individual work that matters most for her.

—Björn Billing

ORR, Robin. British/Scottish. Born in Brechin, Angus, 2 June 1909. Educated at Loretto School, Edinburgh, 1923–4; Royal College of Music London, 1926–9; Pembroke College, University of Cambridge (as organ scholar), 1929–32, Mus.B., M.A. 1938, Mus.D., 1950; Accademia Musicale Chigiana, Siena (under Alfredo Casella), 1934; further composition study under Nadia Boulanger, Paris, 1938. Served as Flight Lieutenant (photographic intelligence), Royal Air Force Volunteer Reserve, 1941–5. Married (1) Margaret Mace in 1937 (dissolved 1979), 2 daughters and 1 son; (2) Doris Winny Meyer in 1979. Director of music, Sidcot School, Somerset, 1933–6; assistant lecturer, University of Leeds, 1936–8; organist and director of music, 1938–51, and Fellow, 1948–56, 1965–76, St John's College, Cambridge; university lecturer, 1947–56, and professor of music 1965–76, University of Cambridge; professor, Royal College of Music, London, 1950–6; Gardiner Professor of music, University of Glasgow, 1956–65; inaugural chair, Scottish Opera, 1962–76; director, Arts Theatre, Cambridge, 1966–76; director, Welsh National Opera, 1977–83. Recipient: Fellow, Royal College of Music, 1965; and Royal Academy of Music, 1966; honorary D.Mus., University of Glasgow, 1972; C.B.E. (Commander, Order of the British Empire), 1972; honorary LL.D., University of Dundee, 1976; Fellow, Royal Scottish Academy of Music and Drama, 1983; honorary fellow, St John's College, Cambridge, 1988; honorary fellow, Pembroke College, Cambridge, 1989; Mailing address: 16 Cranmer Road, Cambridge CB3 9BL, England.

Publishers: Novello; Hinrichsen; Peters; Chappell Music; Anglo-American, 4 Kendall Avenue, Sanderstead CR2 ONH, Surrey, England, Paraclete Press, P.O. Box 1568, Orleans, Massachusetts, MA 02653, U.S.A.; Scottish Music Information Centre.

Symphonies/orchestral:

Overture: The Prospect of Whitby 1948; first performed Glasgow, 1951.
Italian Overture 1952; first performed Birmingham, 1952.
Rhapsody (strings) 1956; first performed Cambridge, 1956.
Symphony in One Movement (Symphony No 1) (full orchestra, piano) 1963; broadcast BBC Scotland, 1963; first concert performance London, 12 December 1963. Recorded HMV ALP 2279.
Symphony No 2 1970–1; first performed Glasgow, 1971.
Symphony No 3 1977–8; first performed Llandaff, Glamorgan, 1978.
Sinfonietta Helvetica 1990–1; first performed Glasgow, 1991.

Chamber/instrumental:

Sonatina (cello, piano) 1938; first performed Edinburgh, 1948.
Two Pieces (piano) 1940.
Sonatina (violin, piano) 1941.
Sonata (viola, piano) 1947; first performed Cambridge, 1947.
Serenade (string trio) 1948; first performed Cambridge, 1948.
Sicilienne and Chaconne (viola, piano) 1949.
Serenade (horn, piano) 1951; first performed 1960.
Duo (violin, cello) 1953, revised 1965.
Toccata alla marcia (organ) 1956; first performed Cambridge, 1956.
Sonata (violin, harpsichord or piano) 1956; first performed Glasgow, 1959.
Three Preludes on Scottish Psalm Tunes (organ) 1958; first performed Glasgow, 1959. Recorded Priory Records 1987.
Sonatina (violin, piano) 1960.
Serenade (horn, piano) 1960; broadcast BBC, 1960.
Elegy (organ) 1968.

Vocal/choral:

Three Songs of Innocence (voice, string quartet) 1932; first performed Halifax, Yorkshire, 1932.
Three Chinese Songs (voice, piano) 1943; first performed London, 1944.
They That Put Their Trust in the Lord 1946; first performed Cambridge, 1946. Recorded Argo RG 340.
Four Romantic Songs (tenor, oboe, string quartet) 1950; first performed London, 1950.
Festival Te Deum (chorus, organ or orchestra) 1950–1; first performed Cambridge, 1951.
Bessie Bell and Mary Gray (unaccompanied SATB chorus) 1951; first performed 1952.
Three Pastorals (soprano, flute, viola, piano) 1951; first performed 1954.
Te Deum and Jubilate in C (chorus, organ) 1952; first performed King's Lynn, 1953.
Seven Scots Songs (voice, piano) 1954.
I Was Glad (unaccompanied chorus) 1955; first performed Norwich, Norfolk, 1955.
Spring Cantata (mezzo-soprano, mixed chorus, piano, timpani, percussion, strings) 1955; first performed Cambridge, 1957.
Colin's Castle (arrangement for unaccompanied SATB chorus) 1956.
Come and Let Yourselves Be Built (SATB chorus, organ) 1961; first performed Cambridge, 1961.
Seven Traditional Scots Airs (voice, piano) 1964.
Magnificat and Nunc Dimittis (Short Service) 1967; first performed Cambridge, 1967.
Sing Aloud (unaccompanied chorus) 1967–8; first performed London, 1968.
From the Book of Philip Sparrow (mezzo-soprano, strings; Skelton) 1969; first performed Glasgow, 1969.

Make a Joyful Noise (treble voices, organ) 1969.
Journeys and Places (mezzo-soprano, string quintet or string orchestra) 1970; first performed Glasgow, 1971.
Liebeslied (after R. Strauss, mezzo-soprano, piano or organ; Rilke) 1972.
Songs of Zion (4 Psalms for unaccompanied SATB chorus) 1978; first performed Wales, 1978.
Versus from Ogden Nash (3 songs for medium voice, strings; 2 arranged for voice, piano) 1978.
O God, Ruler of the World (anthem for SATB chorus, organ) 1982.
Trinity Blessed (unaccompanied SATB chorus) 1987.
Laudate dominum (unaccompanied SATB chorus) 1987.
Jesu, Sweet Son Dear (unaccompanied SATB chorus) 1989.

Opera:

Full Circle (chamber opera; 3 principals, chamber ensemble; Sidney Goodsir Smith) 1968; first performed Perth, Scotland, 10 April 1968.
Hermiston (Bryden, after R.L. Stevenson) 1975; first performed Edinburgh, 1975.
On the Razzle (after Tom Stoppard) 1988; first performed Glasgow, 1988.

Other:

A Winter's Tale (incidental music to Shakespeare; small orchestra) 1947; broadcast BBC, November 1947.
Oedipus at Colonus (incidental music to Sophocles; male chorus, orchestra) 1950; first performed Cambridge, 1950.
Deirdre of the Sorrows (incidental music; full orchestra) 1951; broadcast BBC, 1951.

Fanfares for installation of Chancellor, University of Cambridge, 1968, opening of Theatre Royal, Glasgow, 1975, opening of Corn Exchange concert hall, Cambridge, 1986.

PUBLICATIONS

By Orr: articles on music, literature, food and drink, *Glasgow Herald*, 1958–65.

On Orr: Christopher Grier, "No Mean In-Between", in *The Scotsman*, 11 September 1989.

Robin Orr comments:

As a young student around 1930 I had to make a positive effort to escape the influence of folk song and of Vaughan Williams (whom I nonetheless much admired) because I felt many a young composer has already been caught in what was likely to become a cul-de-sac. So, with the helpful advice of Edward Dent at Cambridge, I went to Alfredo Casella and to Nadia Boulanger, incidentally strengthening my affection for Italian and French music. I had had a thorough grounding in 16th-century polyphony and J. S. Bach. Influences from these rather than the Viennese have remained; but they were followed by Sibelius, Fauré, Stravinsky and Bartók. Powerful stimulus has come from lyric poetry and from drama, hence my three operas, the songs and church music. I am convinced a young musician should be completely familiar with established tradition: take what you care from it, then let development in new directions follow. Live in the present but never ignore the past. There is always rhythm, line and structure.

I am a devoted and loyal Scot, but do not much care to be labelled a "Scottish" composer (nor an "English" one) because the implications of nationalism in music belongs to an earlier age. I find the BBC in London now appears to classify me as a Scottish composer and assumes I am well cared for in Scotland. But the BBC in Glasgow notes that I live in England and evidently believes I am looked after there. Nothing could be further from the truth! This may well be a case of passing the buck; but certainly one falls between two stools, except when it comes to subscriptions to composers' societies, charities, etc., when demands for money descend upon me from all sides. Fortunately, through happy marriage, I now have a foothold in Switzerland (where they know the British are so poor they can't afford anything); but Scotland remains home. Some qualities in my music may be traced to this but it is personality rather than musical style.

Now into my 82nd year, I can look back on many changes: some for the better, but the judgement of some music critics still leaves much to be desired. Until more of them attain to an advanced standard of performance on an instrument, or singing, or attempt to write substantial pieces of music, one can expect little change; but they are adept at the slick phrase and "clever" paragraph. Music publishers, alas, are now so harassed by accountants, take-overs and lack of conviction, that promotion is much reduced—except, it seems, of works that scarcely need it. Hype rules.

* * *

Whatever qualities define a Scot, Robin Orr would seem to have them in full measure: an ability to move without strain between the everyday and the spiritual; a strenuously dialectical mind; a tragic sense balanced by pawky humour; above all, a thoroughgoing pragmatism. Though less well-known in either his native or his first adoptive home, England (he is, in contrast, a considerable presence in his second, Switzerland, where he spends part of each year with his wife), Orr has made a very considerable impact on the music scene north and south of Hadrian's Wall.

In Cambridge, where he returned as professor in 1965, he helped restructure and relocate a music faculty that was conspicuously failing to respond to new educational needs and to the challenge of the continental European schools; Cambridge has returned the compliment with two honorary fellowships and with the establishment of annual lectures in his name and honour. Earlier, while at the University of Glasgow, Orr served as inaugural chair of Scottish Opera, a company that defied Glasgow's residual (and unjustified) reputation as a dourly industrial city grossly unsympathetic to the arts; Orr's own opera *Full Circle*, an outwardly bleak social-realist account of the legendary Clydeside years, is a clever opposition of subject and musical language, transforming a dismal world into something of heroic scale, if not heroic conclusions. *Hermiston*, based on Robert Louis Stevenson's last and unfinished novel, was a Scottish Opera commission for the 1975 Edinburgh Festival. It is a powerful piece, which underlines the distinctive way in which Orr has assimilated and turned to his own highly individual uses native Scottish themes and materials.

Neither a nationalist nor a self-consciously international modernist, Orr has retained a remarkably consistent idiom throughout his long and distinguished career as a composer. His periods of study with Alfredo Casella and Nadia Boulanger failed, as might be expected, to turn him into an avant-gardist, but they did prevent him from retreating into some regressive English pastoral or cultivating a self-consciously Scottish quaintness. Little interested in twelve-tone or serial procedures—though he has used what look suspiciously like rows when these seem appropriate—he combines elements of Monteverdi's vigorous interplay of lines with Fauré's structural magnificence (as in the *Symphony in One Movement (Symphony No 1)*, his best known large-scale non-vocal work), and Bartók's radical transformations of traditional materials. Stravinsky, too, was an influence, as equally might be expected of a Boulanger pupil, but Orr has too direct and personal a voice to be drawn by neo-classicism of any but the most ironic sort.

He has written very little pedestrian journey-work. Even the nominally routine chamber sonatas of the 1940s have an intriguing rhythmic asymmetry and harmonic subtlety that sets them apart from most generic work of the period. The big-boned and jovial *Overture: The Prospect of Whitby* is generously proportioned and expertly orchestrated, its outward "Englishness" conditioned once again by an awareness of continental developments in the harmonic vernacular, its resolutions slightly ambiguous. By contrast, the First Symphony is a darker, almost tragic, piece owing something in its brass voicings and modulation of atmospheres to Sibelius; in a single movement, it has a convincing poetic coherence, and a darkly Nordic vision that is lightened by flashes of irony. The fine Third Symphony, also in a single movement, has a gentler, Mediterranean quality, but the same sinewy strength. Though in recent years Orr has tended to concentrate on vocal and sacred music, much of it of very high standard, he has returned to orchestral writing with the *Sinfonietta Helvetica*, a piece inspired by his new association with Switzerland.

Of his non-operatic vocal work, the finest is *Liebeslied*, settings of Rilke dedicated to his Swiss wife, and the beautiful sequence of *Four Romantic Songs* commissioned in 1950 by the late Peter Pears. The punning *Versus from Ogden Nash* show a lighter side, but like Nash's verses the ease with which ideas are thrown off hides considerable artistry. Orr has never enjoyed or cultivated the patronage of the critical establishment, even when he was himself a leading establishment. "Retirement" has brought a new vigour to his work and has restored some of its youthful edge. He may yet be acknowledged widely as one of the half-dozen truly distinctive British voices of the post-war years.

—Ian Weir

OSBORNE, Nigel. British/English. Born in Manchester, 23 June 1948. Educated at University of Oxford (composition under Kenneth Leighton, serial techniques under Egon Wellesz), 1966–70; Warsaw Academy (under Witold Rudzinski), and Polish Radio Experimental Studio, 1970–1. Lecturer in music, University of Nottingham, 1978–86; editor in chief, *Contemporary Music Review*, since 1984; professor of music, University of Edinburgh, since 1990. Recipient: Osgood Memorial Prize for composition, Oxford, 1970; International Opera Prize, Radio Suisse Normande (for *Seven Words*), 1971; Gaudeamus Prize (for *Heaventree*), 1973; Radcliffe Award (for *I Am Goya*), 1977. Mailing address: Garden Flat, 123 Fordwych Road, London NW2, England.

Publisher: Universal Edition.

Symphonies/orchestral:

Cello Concerto 1977.
Concerto for Flute and Chamber Orchestra 1980. Recorded Unicorn DKP 9031.
Sinfonia 1982.
Sinfonia II 1983.
Esquisse (small string orchestra) 1987; first performed Bath, 5 June 1987.
Stone Garden 1988; first performed London, 18 February 1988.
Esquisse II (small string orchestra) 1988; first performed Frankfurt, 17 April 1988.
Eulogy (for Michael Vyner) (small orchestra) 1990; first performed London, 6 May 1990.
Violin Concerto 1990; first performed London, 21 September 1990.

Chamber/instrumental:

Kinderkreuzzug (flute/alto flute/piccolo, clarinet/bass clarinet, bassoon, trumpet, trombone, piano, 3 percussion, violin, viola, cello, double bass, tape) 1974.
Remembering Esenin (cello, piano) 1974. Recorded Unicorn Kanchana DKP 9031.
Musica da camera (violin, tape, delay, audience) 1975.
Prelude and Fugue (alto flute/flute, clarinet, trumpet, trombone, percussion, piano, violin, viola, cello, double bass) 1975.
Passers By (bass recorder, cello, 3 voices, slides) 1976.
After Night (guitar) 1977. Recorded Bedivere BVR 316.
Kerenza at the Zawn (oboe, 4-channel tape) 1978.
Figure//Ground (piano) 1978, revised 1979.
Quasi una fantasia (cello) 1979.
In Camera (flute, oboe, clarinet, bassoon, horn, trumpet, trombone, 2 violins, viola, cello, double bass, guitar) 1979.
Mythologies (flute, clarinet, trumpet, harp, violin, cello) 1980.
Sonata (piano) 1981.
Fantasia (flute/alto flute, oboe/cor anglais, clarinet in A, bassoon, horn in F, piano, violin, viola, cello, double bass) 1983.
Wildlife (flute/alto flute, clarinet/bass clarinet, horn, trumpet, harp, percussion, violin, viola, cello, double bass, electric bass guitar, optional live electronics) 1984.
Zansa (flute, oboe/cor anglais, clarinet, bassoon, horn in F, trumpet, trombone, percussion, piano, Zansa, 2 violins, viola, cello, double bass) 1985.
Mbira (violin, piano) 1985.
Lumière (string quartet, 4 groups of children) 1986; first performed Devon, 24 September 1986.
The Black Leg Miner (oboe, cor anglais, bassoon, harpsichord) 1987; first performed Southfields, 6 March 1987.
Zone (oboe, clarinet, string trio) 1989.
Canzona (4 trumpets, horn, 4 trombones, tuba) 1990; first performed London, 13 July 1990.

Vocal/choral:

Seven Words (2 tenors, bass, SATB chorus, orchestra with optional ondes martenot; Schutz) 1971.
Heaventree (unaccompanied SATB chorus; texts in 8 languages) 1973.
The Sickle (soprano, orchestra; Esenin, Mayakovsky) 1975. Recorded Unicorn DKP 9031.
Chansonnier ("La Bonne Vie", "Le Bon Vin", "Aube", "La Nonnette", "La Bonne Chanson"; soprano, alto, tenor,

bass, SATB chorus, flute/piccolo, bass clarinet/clarinet, bassoon, trumpet, trombone, piano, percussion, violin, viola, cello, double bass; medieval French ballads) 1975.
Two Spanish Songs (soprano; traditional) 1977.
Vienna. Zurich. Constance. (soprano, violin, cello, 2 clarinets, percussion; Thomas) 1977.
I Am Goya (bass-baritone, flute, oboe, violin, cello; Voznesensky) 1977. Recorded Unicorn DKP 9031.
Orlando furioso (SATB chorus, horn, trumpet, trombone, flute, clarinet, oboe, bassoon, tuba, tenor saxophone, alto saxophone, 2 percussion; after Ariosto) 1978.
Madeleine de la Ste-Baume (soprano, double bass) 1979.
Under the Eyes (voice, percussion, piano, oboe/cor anglais, flute/alto flute; Paulin) 1979.
Songs from a Bare Mountain (unaccompanied SSAA chorus; medieval Polish and Latin) 1979.
Poem Without a Hero (soprano, mezzo-soprano, tenor, bass, live electronics; Akhmatova, translated D.M. Thomas) 1980.
Gnostic Passion (unaccompanied SATB chorus; Nag Hammadi, other Gnostic sources) 1980.
The Cage (tenor, alto flute/piccolo, oboe/oboe d'amore/cor anglais, clarinet/bass clarinet, bassoon, horn, trumpet, violin, viola, cello, optional live electronics; Whiting) 1981.
For a Moment ("The Dawn Verse", "For a Moment", "Tarantella", "What Is a Man Without an Income?", "The Drained Cup"; SSAA chorus, cello, optional Kandyan drum; Lawrence) 1981.
Choralis I (soprano, 2 mezzo-sopranos, tenor, baritone, bass, unaccompanied) 1981.
Choralis II (soprano, 2 mezzo-sopranos, tenor, baritone, bass, unaccompanied) 1981, revised 1982.
Choralis III (soprano, 2 mezzo-sopranos, tenor, baritone, bass, unaccompanied) 1982.
Cantata Piccola ("Professor Klaeber's Nastydream", "The Fair at St Giles's"; soprano, string quartet; Raine) 1982.
Alba ("St-Lo", "Alba", "Musique de l'indifférence", "Roundelay"; mezzo-soprano, flute/alto flute, oboe, clarinet/bass clarinet, horn, trumpet, trombone, percussion, harp, 2 violins, viola, cello, double bass, 3-channel tape; Beckett) 1984.
The Four-Loom Weaver (mezzo-soprano, tape) 1985.
Pornography ("Code Napoleon", "Words on the Page", "City Gent", "Gauguin"; mezzo-soprano, flute, clarinet, horn, percussion, guitar, violin, viola, cello; Raine) 1985.
Tracks (2 SATB choruses, orchestra, wind band) 1990; first performed Rochester, Kent, 21 April 1990.

Opera:

Hell's Angels (chamber opera) 1985; first performed London, 4, 6 January 1986.
The Electrification of the Soviet Union (Raine) 1987; first performed Glyndebourne, Sussex, 5 October 1987.

Other:

Incidental music: Goethe's *Faust*; Malory's *Morte d'Arthur*.

PUBLICATIONS

On Osborne: Niall O'Loughlin, "NO", in *Musical Times*, 121, 1980; Paul Griffiths, (interview) in *New Sounds, New Personalities*, London, 1985.

* * *

The compositional itinerary of Nigel Osborne represents a working-through of the modernism which was his artistic inheritance. He has guided himself by the attempt to forge an equivalence between intellect and emotion, and between theory and practice. "I'm a child of modernism", he once observed, concerned "to crack open the egg of modernism that one was born in." At Oxford he studied serial techniques with Egon Wellesz.

Early music such as *Heaventree* catalogues an experimentation with formal processes in a manner in keeping with the analytical ethos of post-Webernian orthodoxy. The work consists of four movements, divided according to phonetic criteria (frictive, vowel, plosive and nasal sounds), derived from literary fragments in a variety of languages grouped associatively.

Influential from Osborne's early work onwards was his engagement with structuralism, the cultural and linguistic theory emphasising transpersonal, non-historical, isolable regularities of form. One of the earliest examples is the *Prelude and Fugue*, "a transposition into musical terms of a pattern of tensions in the structure" of a South American myth. *Mythologies* uses a Pacific coast Indian myth to explore non-sequential attitudes to narrative. At one level it is a homage to the doyen of French semiology, Roland Barthes.

With *I Am Goya* for baritone and small ensemble, Osborne evinced great strides in the tension and precision of his writing, with enough durability and depth for performances over the years to change character but retain a deeper continuity. His control of musical resources came to express his own temperament rather than doctrinal allegiance. *Alba*, for mezzo-soprano, ensemble and three-channel tape, employs a triangular relation of vocal, instrumental and concrete sound. The tape compounds this; vowels decompose to form pitches and to shape the instrumental harmony, while the consonants break down into sea sounds. The *Concerto for Flute and Chamber Orchestra* derives its inner tension from the conflict of seven metres, superimposed in various combinations, matched by seven sets of pitch relations of varying ambitus.

Osborne independently developed a chord-building technique based on manipulating the overtones of the harmonic series of acoustic sounds. For example, *Zansa* uses harmonies derived from both harmonic and inharmonic spectra, playing off the two in what might be called a tonal dialectic.

His scoring is robust, and well-matched to the instruments, reflecting his hands-on approach as a multi-instrumentalist. The solo flute part of the Flute Concerto or the violin writing of *I Am Goya* are especially good examples.

"It seems", opined Osborne, "that a cycle in the life of modernism is now almost complete." This does not mean it is possible to return to earlier stages of musical development, but it does make more compositional resources available than ever before. This happy post-modernism is most evident in Osborne's opera *The Electrification of the Soviet Union*. "Craig [Raine, librettist] and I felt we had a date to make with lyricism," he recorded, and so wrote "love songs and revolutionary songs frankly and directly, without recourse to irony or pastiche".

Osborne approaches these plural options with an uncommon essentialism, a belief in musical universals. Explaining the numerous models of vocal music deployed in the *Choralis* works, he posited that "there is a 'musicality' common to all human beings, that however different musical cultures may appear to be on the surface, there are certain elements at root which are common". Osborne does not explain this in terms of morphic resonance or archetypes, but the tenet of early structuralism of innate, perhaps physiologically grounded, capacities for certain modes of organisation. He seeks to plumb "musical deep structures and universals . . . deduced from a wide range of ethnic musics". "I'm ultimately seeking a *musica humana*", Osborne has declared, "a comprehensive, physically and mentally liberating music-making, optimistic in spirit and even capable . . . of giving its strength to a weakened society".

Many commentators disqualify Osborne's work as over-intellectual. One could typify his approach, and its musical correlative, as rationalist, in that it possesses a linear clarity. However, what tends to be overlooked is Osborne's fastidious direction of his intellect to the interface with its complement. In other words, he aims to show how in intellect and emotion, or in theory and practice, the highest development of each is indistinguishable from that of its counterpart.

—David Revill

P

PAIK Byung-dong [Paek Pyŏngdong]. Korean. Born in Manchuria, 26 January 1936. Educated at College of Music, Seoul National University, 1955–9, B.A.; Staatliche Hochschule für Musik, Hannover, 1969–71. Married U Hwaja [Woo Hwa-ja], 4 October 1968. Professor, since 1976, and chair of department of composition, 1981–7, College of Music, Seoul National University; chair, Prospective Music Society of Korea, Seoul, since 1989. Recipient: annual New Composers Prize, *Han'guk ilbo/Korean Daily News*, 1962; prize for musical achievement, 5th *Wŏlgan ŭmak/ Monthly Music Journal* awards, 1975; 1st Korean Composers' Prize, Ministry of Information, Seoul, 1977; Seoul Culture Award, Seoul Metropolitan Council, 1983. Mailing address: A-202 Sangdo Villa, Sangdo l-dong, Tongjak-ku, Seoul; or College of Music, Seoul National University, Shilim-dong, Kwanak-ku, Seoul, Korea.

Publishers: Edition Sumun, 349-1, Ulziro 3ga, Joong-ku, Seoul; Christian Music Edition, 39 Chongno 2-ga, Chongno-ku, Seoul, Korea.

Symphonies/orchestral:

Subdued tone 1962; first performed Seoul, 1962.
Three Symphonic Chapters 1963; first performed Seoul, 9 July 1963.
Cello Concerto 1969; first performed Seoul, 30 October 1969.
Viola Concerto 1971; first performed Seoul, 11 October 1971.
Piano Concerto 1974; first performed Seoul, 26 March 1974.
Stimmung 1974; first performed Seoul, 28 March 1974.
Metamorphosen (83 players) 1974; first performed Seoul, 23 October 1974.
Requiescat (3 oboes, orchestra) 1976; first performed Seoul, 11 February 1976.
Intercounter (traditional Korean orchestra) 1977.
Abyss 1978; first performed Seoul, 17 February 1978.
Tchuhung-sa/Ch'uhŭngsa (2 horns, orchestra) 1981; first performed Seoul, 30 May 1981.
Sansudo 1983; first performed Seoul, 22 September 1983.
Pogu 1986; first performed Pusan, 2 May 1986.
In September 1987; first performed Seoul, 1987.
Zweite Kammerkonzert 1987.

Chamber/instrumental:

Seven Variations on a Theme by Hae-Sub Song (piano) 1959; first performed Seoul, 17 June 1966.
Sonata in A, F, C# (violin) 1960; first performed Seoul, 24 October 1960.
Piano Trio in F major 1960; first performed Seoul, 24 October 1960.
Sonata in D major (piano) 1960; first performed Seoul, 24 October 1960.
Sonata No 1 in A major (cello, piano) 1963; first performed Seoul, 15 October 1963.
String Quartet 1963; first performed Seoul, 15 October 1963.
Three Essays (piano) 1963; first performed Seoul, 15 October 1963.
Paraphrase on a Lyrical Theme (cello, piano) 1963; first performed Seoul, 15 October 1963.
Contrast (piano) 1966; first performed Seoul, 17 June 1966.
Sonata No 2 (cello, piano) 1966; first performed Seoul, 17 June 1966.
Chamber Music (kayagum/12-string Korean zither) 1966.
Un-I (oboe, piano) 1970; first performed Seoul, 1971.
Seyub/Seyop (2 voices) 1971; first performed Seoul, 19 November 1971.
Un II (piano) 1972; first performed Seoul, 3 August 1972. Recorded Seongeum Sel-100048.
Chamber Music (kayakum/12-string Korean zither, 6 instruments) 1972; first performed Seoul, 22 June 1972.
Shin Byul-gok (kayakum/12-string Korean zither) 1972; first performed Seoul, 18 April 1972. Recorded SKCD-K-0010.
Eshabe (7 players) 1973; first performed Seoul, 25 May 1973.
Un-III (harp) 1973; first performed Seoul, 25 May 1973.
Irrfahrt (2 harps) 1973; first performed Seoul, 25 May 1973.
Three Bagatelles (piano) 1973; first performed Seoul, 12 November 1974.
Myŏng/Inscription (kayagum/12-string Korean zither) 1975; first performed Seoul, 1975.
Four Pieces (cello) 1976; first performed Seoul, 10 May 1976.
Un-rack/Ollak (traditional Korean ensemble) 1976; first performed Seoul, 1976.
Wind Quintet 1976; first performed Seoul, 12 November 1976.
String Quartet No 2 1977; first performed Seoul, 29 November 1977. Recorded Seongeum Sel-100071.
Classical Suite (7 instruments) 1977; first performed Seoul, 21 November 1977.
Un-IV (violin) 1978; first performed Seoul, 16 May 1978.
Memorandum auf eine Linie (piano) 1978; first performed Seoul, 30 June 1978. Recorded Seongeum Sel-RO 197.
Verknupfung (piano) 1978; first performed Seoul, 30 June 1978.
Epigram (violin, cello, piano) 1978; first performed Seoul, 15 August 1978.
Suite for Children (piano) 1978; first performed Seoul, 30 June 1978.
Intercounter II (taegum/Korean horizontal flute, yanggum/ Korean dulcimer) 1978.
Classical Suite (piano) 1978; first performed Seoul, 30 June 1978.
Ein kleines Nachtlied (violin, piano) 1979; first performed Seoul, 15 March 1979. Recorded Seongeum Sel-100135.
Un-V (horns, strings) 1979; first performed Seoul, 17 May 1979.
Sinaui/Shinawi (shaman improvisation for 5 instruments) 1979; first performed Seoul, 1979.
Passacaglia 1979.
Sori (flute, guitar, cello) 1981; first performed Tokyo, 1981. Recorded Seongeum Sel RO-191.
Memorandum auf eine Linie (piano, 4 hands) 1981; first performed United States, 1981.

Un-VI (flute, piano) 1981; first performed Seoul, 5 October 1981.
Youlmok / Voice of Shadows (strings) 1982; first performed Seoul, 23 June 1982.
Trilogie (flute) 1982; first performed Seoul, 18 November 1982.
For the Soul Disappeared (traditional Korean instruments) 1983; first performed Seoul, 1983.
Passacaglia (viola, chamber ensemble) 1983; first performed Seoul, 26 October 1983.
Guitariana (2 guitars) 1984; first performed Seoul, 23 October 1984. Recorded Seongeum Sel 189.
Piano Trio 1985; first performed Seoul, 30 June 1985.
Sonata-Sonore (piano) 1985; first performed Seoul, 28 November 1985. Recorded Seongeum Sel-RO 197.
Myung / Inscription (flute, clarinet, guitar, viola, double bass) 1987; first performed United States, 11 January 1987.
Byul-gok '87 / Pyolgok '87 / Star Piece '87 (violin, piano) 1987; first performed United States, 1987.
Zweite Kammerkonzert 1988; first performed Seoul, 11 March 1988.
Contra (marimba, 2 percussion) 1988; first performed Tokyo, 1988.
Three Bagatelles (harpsichord) 1988; first performed Seoul, 17 December 1988. Recorded SKCD 0383.
Five Pieces (cello, double bass) 1989; first performed Seoul, 9 March 1989.

Vocal/choral:

Death of a Girl in Budapest (soprano, instruments) 1960.
Jin-Yuh (soprano, orchestra) 1969; first performed Seoul, 7 September 1969.
Drinnen (3 sopranos, 3 instruments, 3 dancers) 1973; first performed Seoul, 26 September 1973.
Morning (soprano, flute) 1975; first performed Seoul, 12 March 1975.
Daesa Deodeum-ki / Taesa todumgi / The Stammering Saint (unaccompanied mixed chorus) 1975; first performed 11 October 1975.
Prologue and Epilogue (female voice, double bass) 1978; first performed Seoul, 20 November 1978.
Cantata: Mountains and Rivers! Morning! (soloists, mixed chorus, orchestra) 1984; first performed Seoul, 3 October 1984.
Three Essays of Gayo (chorus, traditional Korean orchestra) 1986.

Opera:

Sokka tap / Suk-ga tap (operetta) 1968; first performed Seoul, 10 May 1968.
Veranderte Ehepaar 1986; first performed Seoul, 8 October 1986.

Other:

Chun-hyang Jeun (dance music) 1972; first performed Seoul, 1972.
Servants' Documents (theatre music) 1973; first performed Seoul, 19 April 1973.
Veranderte Ehepaar / Ihwa pubu (theatre music) 1977; first performed Seoul, 22 April 1977.
Blue Balloon (music drama for children) 1977; first performed Seoul, 27 November 1977.
Trap (dance music) 1978; first performed Seoul, 2 December 1978.
Ch'angsare pich'in segye ui kurim / Three Pictures Reflected Through a Lattice Window (theatre music) 1980.
The Gong Maker's Letter (dance music) 1981; first performed Seoul, 6 November 1981.
Myth 1900 (theatre music) 1982; first performed Seoul, 19 August 1982.

PUBLICATIONS

By Paik: *Seven Fermatas*, Seoul, 1979; *Sound or Whisper*, Seoul, 1981; *Music for Intelligence*, Seoul, 1985; *Harmony*, Seoul, 1989; *Music Theory*, Seoul, 1989; *Trends in Contemporary Music*, Seoul, 1990.

On Paik: Park Yonggu, "Composer BDP", in *Konggan*; Aekyung Park [Pak Aegyong], "An Analysis of Selected Works by BDP", dissertation, Georgia State University, Atlanta, 1989.

Paik Byung-dong comments:
I am alone. I alone compose music in the style which is my own. I believe that my compositional style comes from Western music; developing tight musical structures is important to me. My personal signature is then imposed on these structures through my use of melody, rhythm and other musical parameters. In Korea, vocal lines are very concentrated: they have much musical meaning enshrined in them. Although I may start with Western structures, my upbringing and consciousness is Korean. Thus, this national identity is stamped on my music primarily through the use of melody. In my music the piano sings, violins, clarinets, sing, all instruments sing with melodies that approach the patriotic. My main personal contribution, then, is to compose music which in terms of vocal melody comes from Korea, but which employs structures derived from the West.

* * *

Paik Byung-dong was born to Korean parents in Manchuria but educated in Korea. Opposition from his parents notwithstanding, Paik entered university to study composition. His early compositions (including four orchestral works, four piano pieces and 19 songs by 1969) show a composer searching for a style. Thus the piano piece, *Seven Variations on a Theme of Hae-Sub Song* is impressionistic, while the *Three Essays* for piano are serial. Nonetheless, two trademarks appear: sectional through-composed structures and melodies which span wide ranges. These are clear in the dramatic song, *Death of a Girl in Budapest*, where the soprano sings across more than two octaves and the structure falls into three contrasted sections (bars 1–16, 17–39, 43–57) plus transition and cadence (bars 40–42 and 58–61). Also in these early pieces a preference for non-functional chromatic harmony is evident.

After the forced imprisonment of Isang Yun in Korea, Paik studied for two years in Germany. Knowledge of Western techniques allowed Paik's mature style to evolve, but also reinforced his academic approach to composition. The results were first demonstrated in the *Un* series. *Un-I* for oboe and piano is again through-composed and utilizes serial techniques (but not strictly). The texture subsumes any notion of functional harmony beneath contrasting contrapuntal, chordal, and solo passages. The work also introduces flexible rhythm, with complex groupings of melodic flurries and ever-changing meters. *Un-II* for piano continues in the same vein, commencing with a fugal passage that leads to a contrapuntal second movement. The *Three Bagatelles* extend the style to virtual pointillism: harmony, melody and rhythm are all non-progressive. Yet Paik is never particularly strict, as is witnessed by the free use of, for example, octaves and tone clusters in his *Sonata-Sonore*.

Paik has written a number of works for Korean instruments. *Shin Byul-gok* for solo zither echoes Yi Sŏngch'ŏn's *Norit'ŏ* and Hwang Pyŏnggi's *Sup*, yet gets caught by awkward fingerwork in semiquaver passages. *Myŏng/Inscription* is much more secure, while later pieces such as *Un-rack Ollak*, have tended to transpose his favoured melodic and rhythmic indeterminancy to a traditional sound world.

In the 1980s, Paik consolidated his musical idiom by both increasing the technical demands made on performers and decreasing the alignment of horizontal and vertical elements. In his concern for the latter, Paik effectively explores the interplay between *yin* and *yang*, the two opposing yet contrasting universal forces. *Sori* for flute, guitar and cello is representative. Metre is replaced with barlines that mark divisions into seconds. Vertical alignment is secondary where musical events are prescribed only approximately (e.g., the use of cells that repeat fast but flexibly (bars 7–9), tones where the length is not determined (bar 5), and beamed accellerando and ritardando (bar 19)). Horizontal alignment between the instruments becomes integral with a crescendo matched to chordal intensification (bar 24), and where cello chords alternate with flute melismas (bar 27). *Byul-gok '87/ Pyolgok '87/Star Piece '87* continues to develop the idiom, initially alternating and opposing vertical piano structures with horizontal violin melismas. Snatches of melody are gradually consolidated as, by the mid-point, the piano imitates the violin's horizontal textures. Finally, the two instruments support each other (from page 9 in the score). The most extreme horizontal/vertical piece to date is *Guitariana*. In this, two guitars have totally separate scores that comprise cells in indeterminate rhythm to be played in any order. The first guitar is *yin*, with horizontal cells; the second is *yang*, with vertical cells. The composer asks for bonding, dispersion and harmonization—that is, carefully managed interplay—leading to a prescribed coda.

—Keith Howard

PAINTAL, Priti. Indian. Born in New Delhi, 2 February 1960. Educated at convent of Jesus and Mary; Delhi University, 1977–82, B.Sc., 1982–5, M.Sc. (anthropology); Royal Northern College of Music, Manchester (composition under Anthony Gilbert), M.Mus., 1987. Married Adrian J. West, 1 February 1985. Director/conductor, Shiva Nova, U.K., since 1988. Recipient: British Council Scholarships for Composition, 1982–4; postgraduate scholarship in composition, Royal Northern College of Music, 1983; nomination, Olivier Award (for opera *Survival Song*), 1990. Mailing address: 84 Dannett Street, Leicester LE3 5RJ, England.

Publisher: none.

Symphonies/orchestral:

Scarlet Mountain Dances: Music for Guilty Lovers 1990; first performed Nottingham, 1990.

Chamber/instrumental:

My Beautiful Valley (flute or cor anglais with echo) 1985; first performed Geneva, 1985.
Ayodhya (flute, clarinet, cello, 2 percussion) 1986; first performed Huddersfield, Yorkshire, November 1986.
Silk Rhythms (string sextet) 1988; first performed London, 21 February 1988.
For Us (flute, cello, sitar, tabla, keyboards, tape) 1988; first performed Huddersfield, Yorkshire, November 1988.
Eurasian Quintet (flute, cello, sitar, tabla, keyboards) 1989; first performed London, 1989.
Bound by Strings of Rhythm (string quartet) 1990; first performed London, 9 December 1990.

Vocal/choral:

A Sanskrit Love Poem (mezzo-soprano, clarinet) 1986; first performed Darmstadt, 1986.
Gondharva Music (mezzo-soprano, piano, 2 percussion) 1987; first performed London, 1987.
Song of Hope (SATB choir) 1987; first performed London, 1987.
Evening Rhythms (mezzo-soprano, flute, cello, sitar, tabla, keyboards) 1988; first performed London, 1988.
Devi (mezzo-soprano, cello) 1989; first performed Heidelberg, 1989.
Was It All Worthwhile? (baritone, piano) 1989; first performed London, 1989.

Opera:

Survival Song 1989; first performed London, 1989.

Priti Paintal comments:

Besides an interest in world music, my special interests lie in the field of Asian music and working with both Asian and Western instruments. I also have a deep interest in music-theatre, hence my work on an opera on the life of Stephen Biko, commissioned by the Royal Opera House, London, "Garden Venture", to be premiered in 1992. I enjoy working in interesting and unique situations and combining untrained voices with trained voices.

* * *

The music by which Priti Paintal has come to be recognised as a distinctive voice on the British, and more recently European, scene includes her 1989 commission for the Royal Opera's Garden Venture Project, *Survival Song*, and pieces for the Eurasian ensemble Shiva Nova, which she founded in 1988. These works are characterised by their direct, open manner, their intense rhythmic vigour, and a melodic eloquence which is especially apparent when she is writing for solo voices. While showing the impact of South Asian and African traditions, and often allowing scope for improvisation, they all exist within basically Western musical and theatrical forms.

Paintal was born in New Delhi, into a family which counted both Indian and Western-trained musicians among its members. Her own music, including an early orchestral piece, had already been played in public there by the time she came to Europe to study composition first at York University and then, with Anthony Gilbert, at the Royal Northern College of Music. In the mid-1980s she began to receive performances and commissions through which the characteristic elements of her style developed: *Ayodhya*, for Lontano, was played at the

1986 Huddersfield Festival, and a string sextet, *Silk Rhythms*, had two South Bank performances by the Park Lane Sextet.

The purpose in setting up Shiva Nova—which consists of flute, cello, keyboards, sitar and tabla—was the opposite of earlier groups' efforts at fusing elements of European and Asian music. It aimed to unite sound worlds, not cultures, and it has worked with composers whose imagination would respond to the purely musical challenge of different tunings, instrumental colours, and performance practices. Paintal's music for the group has developed from the more exploratory world of *Evening Rhythms* (with solo mezzo) and *For Us* (with pre-recorded tape) to the taut and confident forms of the most recent pieces. The *Eurasian Quintet*, like other pieces written around 1989, begins and ends with a catchy theme and exuberant bouts of additive rhythms for the full ensemble (Stravinsky and Africa both in the background), which enclose a series of developments and interpolations, partly improvised: the Asian ambience comes not only from the Indian instruments but from the modal basis of its harmony (slow-changing, in spite of the piece's overall pace), its melodic shapes, and the cross-rhythms of its repeated concluding chords—another typical gesture.

While the ryhthmic insistence has led some listeners to make comparisons with repetitive music, Paintal's practice is much freer: the apparent rondo-like returns in the last of the *Black and White Songs* (for Shiva Nova plus male and female soloists) are always varied, reflecting the kinship with improvisation. This song, for all its popular flavour and clear-cut shape, is one of her most sophisticated pieces, making ingenious use of the same material simultaneously at different speeds. One singer raps the words while the other floats longer lines, and the combination of melodic expansiveness and driving energy recalls parts of *Survival Song*, a short opera widely praised for its dramatic flair and emotional power—the Garden Venture immediately followed its success by commissioning a full-length work from Paintal and librettist Richard Fawkes for 1992, on the life and death of the black African leader Steve Biko.

In the five movements of *Scarlet Mountain Dances: Music for Guilty Lovers* (a commission for the East of England Orchestra), the slow music with its spacious textures, brooding atmosphere and intensely wrought climaxes makes the dominant impact. A string quartet written in 1990, *Bound by Strings of Rhythm*, offers alternative ways of combining quick and slow: sections alternate with manic-depressive effect and culminate in a long fast build-up, heightened by contrapuntal imitation which is all the more effective for its sudden appearance in music of great spontaneous vitality.

—Robert Maycock

PANUFNIK, Andrzej. Polish; naturalized British, 1961. Born in Warsaw, 24 September 1914. Educated at Warsaw State Conservatory, 1932–36; State Academy of Music, Vienna (under Felix Weingartner), 1936–37. Married (1) Scarlett O'Mahoney in 1951, (dissolved), 1 daughter; (2) Camilla Jessel in 1963, 1 son and 1 daughter. Conductor of Cracow Philharmonic Orchestra, 1945–6, and Warsaw Philharmonic Orchestra, 1946–7; vice-president, Polish Composers' Union, 1948–54; vice-chair, International Music Council of UNESCO, 1950–53; settled in England, 1954; musical director, City of Birmingham Symphony Orchestra, 1957–9. Visiting conductor with European and South American orchestras, since 1947. Recipient: 1st prize, Chopin Competition, 1949; Standard of Labour (first class), 1949; State Laureate, 1951, 1952; first prize, Pre-Olympic Competition, 1952; first prize for musical composition Prince Rainier III of Monaco, 1963; Sibelius Centenary Medal, 1965; Knight of Mark Twain, United States, 1966; Prix de Prince Pierre de Monaco, 1984; honorary Fellow of the Royal Academy of Music, 1984; honorary D.Phil., 1985; knighted, 1991. **Died 27 October 1991.**

Publisher: Boosey & Hawkes.

[Works prior to 1944 destroyed, some reconstructed as indicated]

Symphonies/orchestral:

Tragic Overture (orchestra) 1942; first performed Warsaw, 1943; destroyed 1944, reconstructed 1945. Recorded Unicorn RHS 306/UKCD 2016.
Nocturne 1947; first performed Paris, 1948. Recorded Columbia LOU 654, Unicorn RHS 306/UKCD 2016.
Lullaby (29 strings, 2 harps) 1947; first performed Cracow, 1948.
Divertimento (strings, based on trios by Janiewicz) 1947; first performed Cracow, 1948.
Sinfonia Rustica (Symphony No 1) 1948; first performed Cracow, 1949. Recorded Unicorn UNS 257.
Old Polish Suite (strings) 1950; first performed Warsaw, 1951.
Concerto in Modo Antico (trumpet, orchestra) 1951; first performed Cracow, 1951.
Heroic Overture 1952; first performed Helsinki, 1952. Recorded Unicorn RHS 306/UKCD 2060.
Rhapsody 1956; first performed London, 1957.
Sinfonia elegiaca (Symphony No 2) 1957; first performed Houston, Texas, 1957. Recorded Columbia LOU 624.
Polonia 1959; first performed London, 1959.
Piano Concerto 1962; first performed Birmingham, 1962.
Landscape (strings) 1962; first performed Twickenham, Middlesex, 1965. Recorded Unicorn-Kanchana DKP 9016/UKCD 2020.
Autumn Music 1962; first performed Paris, 1968. Recorded Unicorn RHS 306/UKCD 2016.
Two Lyric Pieces 1963; first performed Farnham, Surrey, 1963.
Sinfonia sacra (Symphony No 3) 1963; first performed Monaco, 1964. Recorded Unicorn UNS 257; Nonesuch 79228.
Hommage à Chopin (flute, strings; arranged from vocal piece of 1949) 1966; first performed London, 1966. Recorded HMV ASD 3633; Conifer 182 CD.
Jagiellonian Triptych (strings) 1966; first performed London, 1966.
Katyn Epitaph 1967; first performed New York, 1968. Recorded Unicorn Kanchana DKP 9016/UKCD 2020.
Violin Concerto (violin, string orchestra) 1971; first performed London, 18 July 1972. Recorded EMI EMD 5525; Conifer 182 CD.
Invocation for Peace (orchestra and choir) 1972; first performed Southampton, Hampshire, 1972. Recorded Unicorn UNS 264.
Sinfonia concertante (Symphony No 4) 1973; first performed London, 1974. Recorded EMI EMD 5525.
Sinfonia di Sfere (Symphony No 5) 1975; first performed London, 1976. Recorded Decca HEAD 22.

Sinfonia Mistica (Symphony No 6) 1977; first performed Middlesbrough, Yorkshire, 1978. Recorded Decca HEAD 22.
Metasinfonia 1978; first performed Manchester, 1978. Recorded Unicorn Kanchana DKP 9049.
Concerto festivo 1979; first performed London, 1979. Recorded Unicorn Kanchana DKP 9016/UKCD 2020.
Concertino (timpani, percussion, strings) 1980; first performed London, 1981. Recorded Unicorn Kanchana DKP 9016/UKCD 2020.
Paean for the Eightieth Birthday of Queen Elizabeth, the Queen Mother (brass) 1980; first performed London, 1980.
Sinfonia votiva (Symphony No 8) 1981; first performed Boston, 1982. Recorded Hyperion A 66050/CDA 66050.
A Procession for Peace 1983; first performed London, 1983.
Arbor cosmica (strings) 1983; first performed New York, 1984. Recorded Nonesuch 79228.
Bassoon Concerto: In memoriam Father Jerzy Popieluszko 1985; first performed Milwaukee, Wisconsin, 1986. Recorded Conifer CDCF 182.
Symphony No 9 1986; first performed London, 1987.
Symphony No 10 1988; first performed Chicago, 1990.
Harmony (chamber orchestra) 1989; first performed New York, 1989.

Chamber/instrumental:

Piano Trio 1934; first performed Warsaw, 1935; destroyed 1944; reconstructed 1945.
Twelve Miniature Studies (piano) 1947; first performed Cracow, 1948.
Reflections (piano) 1968; first performed London, 1972.
Three Triangles (3 flutes, 3 cellos) 1972; broadcast BBC, 1972.
String Quartet No 1 1976; first performed London, 1977.
String Quartet No 2: "Messages" 1980; first performed St Asaph, Wales, 1980.
Pentasonata 1984; first performed Aldeburgh, Suffolk, 1989.
String Sextet 1987; first performed London, 1988.

Vocal/choral:

Five Polish Peasant Songs 1940, destroyed 1944, reconstructed 1945; first performed Cracow, 1945.
Hommage à Chopin (original version for soprano, piano) 1949; first performed Paris, 1949.
Song to the Virgin Mary 1964; first performed London, 1964.
Universal Prayer (cantata) 1969; first performed London, 1970. Recorded Unicorn Kanchana DKP 9049.
Thames Pageant (cantata) 1969; first performed Twickenham, Middlesex, 1970. Recorded Unicorn UNS 264.
Winter Solstice (cantata) 1972; first performed Kingston-upon-Thames, Middlesex, 1972.
Dreamscape (mezzo-soprano and piano) 1977; first performed London, 1977. Recorded Unicorn UNS 268.

Other:

Film music for Polish Army Film Unit, including *The Tell-Tale Heart* (after Poe), *The Electrification of the Villages*, 1945–6.

PUBLICATIONS

By Panufnik: *Composing Myself* (autobiography), London, 1987.

* * *

The first impression Andrzej Panufnik makes on the listener may well be of a sheen, a gleam, a tonal lustre—characteristics rare in the official "modern music" of the mid-20th century, though they are surfacing again in the more permissive creative atmosphere of the century's closing years. However, putting it that way suggests a sort of soft-edged neo-romanticism, whereas the outlines in a Panufnik piece are always uncompromisingly crisp and clear, and there is no shirking harsher issues in the interest of a bland Panglossian lyricism.

Panufnik's ability to delineate emotional nuances with an appropriately comprehensive range of sound structures is illustrated even within the relatively modest dimensions of the chamber-orchestral *Autumn Music*. Only 17 minutes in duration, the work paints a loving portrait of a dying friend. The sensuous chains of third-dominated woodwind chords may prompt astonishment that anything so disarmingly euphonious should have been attempted, let alone successfully carried through, in our century. Yet, obviously, the passage could not have been written at any other time; and in between these consolatory paragraphs, and another pair of sections expressive of mankind's panic in the face of death, *Autumn Music* confronts time's inexorable reaping with lucid dignity, in an awesome central section that moves gradually from molto adagio to allegro and back while a single regularly iterated note in the piano's lowest register evokes the unvarying beat of a clock.

Such a technique already hints at what constitutes the radical individuality of Panufnik's language. It is his fresh and absorbing treatment of the relation between sound and time—a relation that is, after all, what distinguishes music at root from the other arts. 20 years before *Autumn Music*, the *Tragic Overture* (Panufnik's first surviving orchestral work) had already begun to envisage a new approach to musical time, one that might replace the frequently changing pulse patterns of earlier styles with a more uniform structure of rhythmic and harmonic progression. For nearly half a century now, by way of works like *Autumn Music* and the 1978 *Metasinfonia* (seventh of the 10 symphonies that constitute the backbone of his oeuvre), right down to the 1989 chamber-orchestral *Harmony*, Panufnik has continued to devise new expressions for this sound/time interplay that remains his fundamental formal interest.

Usually there is something hieratic in the result, a sense of inner order that makes the swirling periodic patterns in *Metasinfonia* or the rare bursts of intensified harmonic change in *Harmony* all the more effective by contrast. In all of this there is a powerful suggestion of mystery, of a numinous other world beneath and behind the world of the senses. That was clearly what the French critic Bernard Gavoty had in mind when, writing about the *Sinfonia Sacra* of 1963, he ascribed to Panufnik "the gift of incantation, of sorcery, without which music is only artifice."

Slowly and painstakingly, with inflexible singleness of purpose and imagination, Panufnik has amassed a body of some 50 works since the whole of his early output was destroyed by fire in the 1944 Warsaw Uprising and he had to begin again (reconstructing the *Tragic Overture* from memory as a first step). There is no lack of variety in what might be called the poetic surface of these works, which range from orchestral and chamber music to an arrestingly granitic setting of Pope's *Universal Prayer* for vocal quartet, chorus, three harps and organ. Panufnik runs the expressive gamut from cosmic grandeur in the esoteric geometric patterns of *Sinfoniá di Sfere* and the nature metaphors of *Arbor cosmica*, through a proud and impassioned patriotic fervor in works like the 1985 *Bassoon Concerto: In memoriam Father Jerzy*

Popieluszko that address the travails of his native Poland, to a beguiling personal tenderness in *Harmony*, a 25th-anniversary present to his wife, Camilla.

However, the unity of his artistic vision is in the end more striking and characteristic than the diversity of its expression. A proverb propagated by Isaiah Berlin after Tolstoy—and the Russians in their turn took it from the Greek fabulist Archilochus—has it that the fox knows many small things, but the hedgehog knows one big thing. Composers come in both shapes: Stravinsky, for instance, was probably a fox; and Panufnik must be counted a hedgehog. His penchant for ambitious formal constructions is in part the product of a continental and Catholic intellectual tradition. That his work has never degenerated into mere system may be due in some degree to the influence the very different empirical tradition of his adopted country, England, has exerted through nearly four decades of his composing life. The quintessential Panufnikian blend of ritual with lyricism, of profound conceptual laws with charming and unexpected turns of expression, is a blend that could perhaps have come only from such a double patrimony. It is a Polish–English confluence that makes his elevation to a knighthood, in the 1991 New Year Honours, an especially apt salute to a life that has harmonised the best of two disparate national and artistic inheritances.

—Bernard Jacobson

PARASKEVAÍDIS, Graciela. Argentinian/Uruguayan. Born in Buenos Aires, 1 April 1940. Educated at Conservatorio Nacional de Música, Buenos Aires (composition), 1958–63; Centro Latinomericano de Altos Estudios Musicales, Instituto Torcuato Di Tella, Buenos Aires, 1965–6; Institut für Neue Musik, Freiburg, 1968–71. Married Coriun Aharonian, 17 December 1975; 1 daughter. Private teacher of music, Buenos Aires, 1958–67, 1975, and Montevideo, Uruguay, 1976–83, 1985–7; member of organizing collective, Cursos Latinomericanos de Música Contemporanea, since 1975; co-founder and member, Nuclea Música Nueva de Buenos Aires, and Montevideo, since 1975; composer in residence, DAAD Kunstlerprogramm, Berlin, 1984–5; professor since 1985, and researcher, since 1988, School of Music, National University, Montevideo; secretary, Sociedad Uruguaya de Música Contemporanea (ISCM), since 1988. Recipient: prize, Asociación Argentina de Compositores, 1961; prize (for *Magma I*), Akademie der Kunste, Berlin, 1970; prize, Municipalidad de la Ciudad de Buenos Aires, 1971. Mailing address: Casilla de correo 1328, U-11.000 Montevideo, Uruguay.

Publishers: Breitkopf & Hartel, Wiesbaden (1 piece); performing rights represented by AGADU, Uruguay.

Symphonies/orchestral:

Música para orquesta 1962; first performed Athens, 2 May 1966.

Chamber/instrumental:

Sonata (piano) 1960; first performed Buenos Aires, 1960.
Cuarteto de cuerdas (string quartet) 1961; first performed Buenos Aires, 1961.
Cinco piezas (piano) 1964; first performed Buenos Aires, 1965.
Parametros (piano, alto saxophone, percussion) 1965; first performed Buenos Aires, 1965.
Combinatoria II (piano, trombone, percussion, tape) 1966, revised 1968; first performed Buenos Aires, 1966; revised version first performed Freiburg, 1968.
Magma I (2 trumpets, 4 horns, 2 trombones, tuba) 1967; first performed Berlin, 1970.
Subliminal I (piano) 1967; first performed San Juan de Puerto Rico, 1968.
Trio (flute, clarinet, bassoon) 1969; first performed Montevideo, 1971.
Magma II (4 trombones) 1969; first performed Santo Domingo, 1969.
Mellonta tauta (accordion) 1970; first performed Freiburg, 1970.
Magma III (flute, trombone, cello, piano) 1974; first performed Freiburg, 1979.
Magma IV (string quartet) 1974; first performed Montevideo, 1981.
Magma V (4 quenas) 1977; first performed Montevideo, 1979.
Magma VI (2 trumpets, 2 trombones) 1979; first performed Bonn, 1979.
Todavía no/Not Yet (3 flutes, 3 clarinets) 1979; first performed Freiburg, 1979.
Y . . . as como todo (2 flutes, 2 clarinets, trumpet, horn) 1981; first performed Montevideo, 1983.
Un lado, otro lado/On the One Hand, On the Other Hand (piano) 1984; first performed Buenos Aires, 1984.
Magma VII (14 wind instruments) 1984; first performed Berlin, 1984. Recorded Tacuabe T/E 17K.
Mas fuerzas tiene/More Strength It Has (clarinet) 1984; first performed La Paz, 1986.
Tres piezas infantiles (piano) 1986; first performed Montevideo, 1987.
Dos piezas para pequeño conjunto (oboe, clarinet, trumpet, claves, piano) 1989; first performed Montevideo, 1990.

Vocal/choral:

Seís canciones (soprano, piano) 1968; first performed Freiburg, 1969.
Liberto va cercando . . . (unaccompanied mixed chorus) 1969; first performed Buenos Aires, 1971.
E desidero solo colori (6 sopranos, 6 altos, unaccompanied; Pavese) 1969; first performed Freiburg, 1970. Recorded Tacuabe T/E 11.
Die Hand voller Stunden (9 solo voices) 1970; first performed Berlin, 1984.
Schatten (soprano, baritone; Kraus) 1971; first performed Freiburg, 1971.
Schattenreich (unaccompanied vocal quartet) 1972; first performed Freiburg, 1973.
Tres poemas de Juan Gelman (voice, piano) 1983; first performed Montevideo, 1983.
El grito en el cielo/The Cry to Heaven (unaccompanied mixed chorus) 1989.

Dramatic:

Aphorismen (music-theatre) 1969; first performed Freiburg, 1970.
Mozart (music-theatre) 1970–2, revised 1974; first performed Freiburg, 1973; revised version first performed Buenos Aires, 1976.

Other:

Huauqui (tape) 1975; first performed Buenos Aires, 1975.
A entera revisacion del publico en general (tape) 1978–81; first performed Montevideo, 1981.

PUBLICATIONS

By Paraskevaídis: "Lulu", in *Tribuna Musical*, 7, November–December 1965; "Entrevista con Iannis Xenakis", in *Tribuna Musical*, 9, August–November 1968; "György Ligeti habla sobre Mahler", in *Tribuna Musical*, 18, 1969; "Pro Musica Nova", in *Tribuna Musical*, 22, June–August 1970; "Die komponierende Frau in Lateinamerika", in *Neue Musik aus Lateinamerika*, Berlin, 1984; "componer es poner en practica la libertad", in *Brecha*, Montevideo, 21 March 1986; "Krzysztof Penderecki", in *Brecha*, 23 October 1987; "La creacion musical femenina, en el centenario de Carmen Barradas", in *Brecha*, 4 November 1988; "La corchea antidilettante, a 70 anos de la muerte de Debussy", in *Brecha*, 4 January 1989; "La función del artista en el Tervcer Mundo, entrevista con Koellreutter", in *Brecha*, 3 February 1989; "Modest Musorgski, a 150 años de su nacimiento", in *La Hora Popular*, 12 August 1989; "Amadeo Roldán, compositór cubano", in *Brecha*, 26 January 1990; "Eduardo Febini y el mensaje sonoro de la tierra, a cuarenta años de su muerte", in *Brecha*, 22 June 1990.

Graciela Paraskevaídis comments:

Composing is an act both of will and consciousness, involving historical, social and personal processes and situations, and determined by philosophical and aesthetic thinking, technical skills, as well as—in the broadest and deepest sense—ideological frontiers and options.

To be a composer (male or female) born under the imposed strong influence and inheritance of western european, white, christian and bourgeois culture, and willingly living in a third world country, implies the assumption of the dangers and challenges of such a choice, a choice defiantly facing culture and music models established by the dominating—first eurocentric and then also north american—imperialistic first world.

Gone should be the days of naive imitation and multiplication of the supposedly only and perfect models from the north. Dependence has always been carefully nourished and supported by the powers imposing these models, from the inside and the outside. There are two kinds of answers to them: comfortable continuation of epigonalism on one hand, confrontation through self-taught awareness on the other. These answers may take different shapes, but the search of possible paths leading to expression and communication through music, here and now, means accepting the challenge and recognizing these most difficult options.

Technique, material, structure, content, have to do with ideology. They always had. Also in music. And this ideological reading—for the past and for today—is defining and meaningful: not of pamphletary actions or fashionable gestures, but of the role culture (and therefore music) played before and should play now.

Music has never been a universal language. It has often and repeatedly been (mis)used as a cultural weapon for dominating purposes, for substitution of one expression for a "better" and "higher" one, for ideological penetration. A struggle going on for centuries in Latin America, now kindly redefined as the "encounter" of two cultures to celebrate 500 years of a continent's "discovery". The dark, cruel, shameless history of physical extermination and spiritual and cultural annihilation of millions of people through humiliation, slavery, greed, deceit, robbery and force should stand as one of the most painful and sorrowful events in the whole history of mankind in general, and of european "civilisation" in particular.

Being aware of this history—not at an end 500 years later—can help to understand the meaning of the absurd option of composing (art) music in Uruguay today. It can become a way of defending and rescuing drowned, forgotten and despised symbols and their right to exist and be listened to, a way of assuming the necessity of a spiritual collective existence through the challenge and risk of music creation.

* * *

The composer, musicologist and teacher Graciela Paraskevaídis belongs to a generation that to constant technical and technological evolution "adds a powerful questioning of the creator's self-existence, the creator's Latin American here-and-now, wonderfully convulsed by the concept of 'new man'".

Her compositional output represents a radical aesthetic, where sound is elaborated as texture in a space–time concept opposed to discursiveness. Her radicalism is expressed first in her use of highly austere material. Pieces germinate and develop in very concrete ideas. They can be intervallic (chords, clusters, melodies) or timbral (instrumentation, treatment of register, amalgams by affinity or opposition), but they all depend on restriction in the organ sound material that provokes the maximum expressive potential in the material itself. *Todavio no / Not Yet* for three flutes and three clarinets is built on an E (unison and octaves), a fourth-cluster, and dense silent blocks; *Un lado, otro latro / On the One Hand, On the Other Hand* for solo piano explores timbral and intervallic perceptions at low and high registers by means of accumulation and resonance-accumulation.

In the structure of Paraskevaídis's music, ideas do not flow or repeat themselves; they rather remain and interpose, creating an abstraction of chronological duration. Each piece of material is allowed to develop organically. If it returns, it does so only as a brief recollection, on which the angle of perception, rather than the motif itself, has changed. Each piece takes place within strict dynamic limits or moves between them abruptly, almost without transition. That is the case in *El grito en el cielo* written for *a capella* mixed chorus with a *pppp* that lasts five minutes. In *Mas fuerza tiene / More Strength It Has* the clarinettist creates a kind of three-handed dialogue among sound characters by means of dynamic indications: *fff*, *mf*, and *ppp*. The second of the *Dos piezas para conjunto* sustains a powerful *ffff* in all participating instruments—piano, trumpet, clarinet, oboe, claves—from beginning to end. Intensity is the basis of Paraskevaídis's appeal to the audience's sensibility: she suffers, she denounces, she claims, she resists.

Since 1960 she has premiered over 30 pieces, mainly chamber music for various, mostly non-conventional, instrumental ensembles, music for solo instruments, for voice, and electro-acoustic music.

Outstanding is the *Magma* series (a seven-piece cycle up to the present), and particularly *Magma I* for brass nonet, and *Magma V* for four quenas, one of the first pieces to accept without qualification the role of the Andean instrument in art music. The *Magma* have, according to the composer, "similar treatment, organized around timbral block-textures", and are inspired by the meaning of the word itself: magma is the hot, permanently moving substance beneath the earth's crust.

The vocal pieces make very particular proposals. *E desidero solo colori*, to a text by Pavese, is an original statement of unisons, intertwinings and mixtures. *Schatten* was composed to be performed in St Albert's Church in Freiburg, Germany, whose strongly resonant acoustics were incorporated into the conception of the piece.

In the electro-acoustic music field, *A entera revisicion del publico en general* is a sound documentary built up with recorded material recorded from the daily environment, revealing, among other things, the world of the merchants' cries in the urban transportation system in Montevideo. The surrounding atmosphere of a city assumes in this music a protagonistic role, not only because of the words' meaning, but also because of their phonetics, rhythm, etc.

The already mentioned *Un lado, otro lado / On the One Hand, On the Other Hand* is perhaps the most representative solo piece to date. The growing and encompassing sound masses are extremely impressive, like few other pieces in the contemporary repertoire, and the work demands unusual performing stamina.

All of Paraskevaídis's works are autonomous in their musical language and support themselves without literary programmes of references. Nevertheless, there is in all of them an intrinsic representation of deep human contents and experience. Without ever becoming programmatic, her work is mostly stimulated by her perception of the surrounding social, political and historical reality. It is music born out of her sensitivity to fact, human experience and circumstances, to life itself. And if the collective memory of this time of horror should ever be lost—as seems to be happening at present—then her music would be an everlasting testimony to what her contemporaries felt about injustice and barbarity. "Anger is the best emotional state to blow this 'magma'. Gather it previously and expel it without fear during the course of the piece . . . " is her instruction to the musicians.

Paraskevaídis is also a significant researcher and musicologist. As in her music, she trespasses over convention and directs her attention to specific Latin American needs. However, she ranges widely, touching on Beethoven, the symphonic work of the important Uruguayan composer Eduardo Fabini, Mozart and Berg, women in music, a large-scale effort dedicated to a "necessity to document and study the musical facts with which our continent tenaciously opens—piece by piece—the way to its own musical identity." Because she is aware of how much Latin America needs its creators and how much creators need their Latin America, freeing themselves from hegemonic processes, Paraskevaídis represents a new spirit among musicians on the continent.

—Cergio Prudencio

PARROTT, Ian. British/English. Born in London, 5 March 1916. Educated: studied harmony under Benjamin Dale, from 1928; Harrow School, Middlesex, 1929–31; Royal College of Music, London, 1932–4, A.R.C.O., 1936; New College, Oxford, 1934–7, D.Mus., 1940, M.A., 1941; associate, Royal College of Organists, 1936. Military service in Royal Signals, 1940–5. Married Elizabeth Olga Cox, 1 June 1940; 2 sons. Lecturer, University of Birmingham, 1946–50; Gregynog Professor of Music, University College of Wales, Aberystwyth, 1950–83. Examiner, Trinity College of Music, London, since 1949. Recipient: 1st prize (for *Luxor*), Royal Philharmonic Society, 1949; fellowship, Trinity College of Music, London, 1953; Bournemouth Orchestra prize (for *Solemn Overture: Romeo and Juliet*), 1957; Harriet Cohen Musicology Award, 1966; fellowship, London College of Music, 1983; J. Rooper Prize (for *String Quartet No 2*), 1983. Mailing address: Henblas Abermad, Aberystwyth, Dyfed SY23 4ES, Wales.

Publishers: Thames Publishing, 14 Barlby Road, London W10 6AR; Oecumuse/Barry Brunton, 51 Eleanor Road, Bounds Green, London N11 2QS, England.

Symphonies / orchestral:

Malvern Music 1937.
Malvern March 1938.
De l'Estuaire à la source 1939.
Russian Dance (small orchestra) 1941; first performed Farnborough, July 1941.
A Dream (small orchestra) 1941.
Scherzo No 2 1941–3; first performed 1949.
Symphony No 1 1943–6.
El Alamein (symphonic prelude) 1944; first performed Guildford, Surrey, October 1945.
Miniature Concerto (violin, small orchestra) 1945.
Luxor 1947; first performed London, 17 October 1950.
Piano Concerto 1948–9.
Maid in Birmingham (ballet suite) 1949; first performed 23 January 1951.
Pensieri (concerto grosso for strings) 1950; first performed Wolverhampton, Staffordshire, 1952.
Solemn Overture: Romeo and Juliet 1951–3; first performed Bournemouth, Hampshire, 24 October 1957.
Overture and Prologue: The Black Ram 1951–2; first performed Aberystwyth, 30 November–1 December 1952.
Two Welsh Tunes (from *The Black Ram*) 1952; first performed Birmingham, 13 March 1953.
Flourish for a Royal Visit (small orchestra) 1955; first performed Cardiff, 8 August 1955.
Orchestral Variations on Dufay's "Se la face ay pale" 1955.
Four Shakespeare Dances 1956; first performed 1962.
Concerto for Cor Anglais and Orchestra 1956; first performed Cheltenham, Gloucestershire, 18 July 1958.
Cwyn Mam Y'mghyfraith (scherzo for orchestra) 1958; first performed 5 June 1958.
Hen Ferchetan / Little Old Maid (gavotte for orchestra) 1958.
Mae Nghariad i'n Fenws / My Love Is Like Venus (sarabande for strings) 1958; broadcast 10 April 1959.
Seithenin (concert overture) 1959.
Symphony No 2: Round the World 1960–1; first performed Glen Ridge, New Jersey, 2 May 1961.
Concerto for Cello and Orchestra 1961; first performed Newtown, 2 May 1963.
Ian Parrot's Attempt (music for string orchestra in the manner of Philidor, Monsigny and Gretry to accompany *The Music of an Adventure*) 1962.
Broncastell (rescored for band) 1964.
Suite (violin, orchestra) 1965; broadcast 25 January 1968.
Symphony No 3 (with obbligato string quartet) 1966; first performed 1972.
Concerto for Trombone and Wind Band (adapted from 1958 *Sonatina*) 1967.
Fantasia on Welsh Tunes (brass band) 1968.
Homage to Two Masters (after Bach and Elgar; also arranged for organ) 1970.

Harrow March (brass) 1970.
Reaching for the Light (harpsichord, piano, 2 oboes, bassoon, 2 horns, glockenspiel, strings) 1971; first performed Attingham Park, 21 August 1971.
Concertino (2 guitars, small orchestra) 1973.
Rumbustuoso VERNONcello Am GRIFFbrett (variations for string orchestra on a theme by Vernon Griffiths) 1974; first performed Christchurch, New Zealand, 1 February 1974.
Sinfonietta (Symphony No 4) 1978.
Symphony No 5 1979; first performed Coventry, Warwickshire, 23 May 1981.

Chamber/instrumental:

Siberian March (piano) 1928.
Sonata (organ) 1933.
Scherzo No 1 in C (piano) 1933; first performed Oxford, June 1936.
Sonatina (flute) 1935.
Sonata (oboe) 1935.
Foursome (piano—4 hands) 1935–9.
Caprice (piano) 1937.
Trio (flute, violin, piano) 1937.
Nocturne (piano) 1937.
Malvern Hills (piano) 1938.
Betinka (piano) 1939.
Westerham (piano) 1940.
Fuga giocosa (piano) 1942.
Berceuse (string quartet) 1942; incorporated into *Three Pieces for String Quartet*, 1946.
Impromptu (piano) 1942.
Theme and Six Variants (piano) 1946; first performed London, 17 October 1946.
Three Pieces (string quartet) 1946; first performed London, 2 May 1950.
Duet (2 flutes) 1946; first performed London, 18 August 1946.
Fantasy and Allegro (2 pianos) 1946; first performed London, 1 May 1947.
Oboe Quartet 1946; first performed Oxford, 19 October 1947.
Wind Quintet 1947–8; first performed Birmingham, 6 May 1949.
Agincourt (organ) 1948.
Fantasy (cello, piano) 1948; first performed Birmingham, 8 October 1948.
Aquarelle (clarinet, piano) 1948.
Fantasy Trio (violin, cello, piano) 1950; first performed Birmingham, 24 May 1951.
Hobos Riding (oboe, oboe d'amore, cor anglais, heckelphone) 1951.
Dafydd y Garreg Wen (viola, piano) 1951; first performed Aberystwyth, October 1951.
The Birds of Glanyrafon (piano) 1953.
Broncastell (piano) 1953; later arranged for band.
By the Ystwyth (piano) 1954.
Little Fugato (piano) 1954.
Three Welsh Airs (2 recorders, piano or harp) 1954.
String Quartet No 2 in G# 1954–5; first performed Swansea, 1956.
Capriccio (trumpet, piano) 1956.
Ceredigion (harp solos and interludes) 1957; first performed Israel, September 1959.
String Quartet No 3 1957; first performed Bangor, May 1961.
Elegy (organ) 1957.
Rhapsody (violin, piano) 1957.
Sonatina (trombone, piano) 1958; first performed Barry, Glamorgan, 20 January 1959.
Fantasy for James Blades (percussion) 1959.
Blackbird Piece (flute/piccolo, oboe, clarinet, horn, bassoon, piano) 1960; first performed Bournemouth, Hampshire, 22 February 1960.
Septet 1962 1961–2; first performed Cheltenham, Gloucestershire, 10 July 1962.
Toccata (organ) 1962; first performed Cambridge, 13 May 1962.
String Quartet No 4 1963; first performed Aberystwyth, September 1964. Recorded Lyrita SRCS 52.
Fantasy (piano) 1964; first performed Bangor, 8 March 1965.
Abergenny (crwth, optional clarinet) 1965.
Big Hat Guy (violin, piano) 1965.
Partita on Two Welsh Tunes (harp) 1967.
Pant Glas (violin, glockenspiel, piano) 1967.
Mosaics (organ) 1968.
Four Silhouettes (flute) 1969; first performed Aberystwyth, 21 May 1969.
Two Dances (flute, harp) 1969.
Wind Quintet No 2: Fresh About Cook Strait 1970; first performed Cardiff, 14 May 1971.
Homage to Two Masters (after Bach and Elgar; arranged for organ) 1971.
Arabesque and Dance (treble recorder, harpsichord or piano) 1972.
Fanfare and March (2 trumpets, trombone, bass tuba) 1973.
Devil's Bridge Jaunt (cello, piano) 1974.
Fantasia (organ) 1974.
Aspects (piano) 1975; first performed Copenhagen, 12 March 1976.
Polished Brass (published as *Gleaming Brass*; brass quintet) 1976.
Duo fantastico (violin, piano) 1976; first performed 1981.
Suite (organ) 1977; first performed London, 1 June 1978.
Rhapsody (trumpet, organ) 1977; first performed Haverfordwest, 11 November 1978.
Arfon (harp) 1978.
Fantasy Sonata (clarinet, piano) 1979; first performed New Haven, Connecticut, October 1986.
Hands Across the Years: In Memoriam Gerald Finzi (organ) 1980; first performed Harrogate, Yorkshire, 8 August 1983.
Reflections (violin, piano) 1982.
Suite for Stefan Popov (cello, piano; "Stefanergico", "Lolargo", "Niccolo", "Diminuendo", "Accalexanderando") 1982; first performed London, 5 February 1985.
Duo (clarinet, trumpet) 1983; first performed London, 17 May 1984.
Autumn Landscape (oboe, piano) 1983; broadcast BBC Radio, 6 March 1986.
Suite No 2 (organ) 1986.
Duo (2 guitars) 1988; first performed Birmingham, 6 November 1988.
Duo fantastico No 2 (violin, piano) 1990.

Vocal/choral:

Two Nature Pieces (chorus, orchestra) 1936–7.
Jolly Good Ale & Old (part song for basses) 1939.
Earth Rejoices (unaccompanied SATB chorus) 1939.
I Heard a Linnet Courting (voice, piano; Bridges) 1940.
O Mieli Moy (Four Songs of Absence) (voice, piano; Lermontov) 1942.
Wie dir, so mir (Four Songs of Absence) (voice, piano; Kerner) 1942.
Absence (Four Songs of Absence) (voice, piano; Donne) 1943; first performed 1991.

How Many Times Do I Love Thee? (Four Songs of Absence) (voice, piano; Beddoes) 1944; first performed London, London, 1 December 1948.
Two Flecker Settings: In Phaecia, & A Ship, an Isle, a Sickle Moon (voice, piano; Flecker) 1945–6; first performed Aberystwyth, November 1954.
Psalm 91 (bass, chorus, orchestra) 1946–7; first performed Belfast, 16 March 1951.
All the Woods Answer (unaccompanied voices; Spenser) 1949.
Voices in a Giant City (male voices, piano; Tesimond—"Money Talks", "Song in a Saloon Bar") 1949; broadcast 27 January 1956.
Three Kings Have Come (female voices or soprano/baritone/SATB chorus, piano, strings; Flecker) 1951; first performed Cambridge, 22 November 1952.
A Child's Hunting Song (soprano, flute, piano; Gododdin/Idris Bell) 1954.
Magnificat and Nunc Dimittis (voices, organ; in Welsh) 1961.
Cantata jubilate Deo (soloists, chorus, orchestra; Psalms, Thomas, Tessimond, Webster, Luther, others) 1963; first performed London, 20 October 1967.
The Three Moorish Princesses (narrator, orchestra; Howard) 1963–4.
The Song of the Stones of St David's (SATB chorus, organ) 1968.
Offertory Motet: Diffusa est gratia in labiis tuis (unaccompanied ATBB chorus) 1968; first performed London, 20 March 1969.
Cymun bendigain (voice(s), organ or piano; guitar and percussion band) 1972; first performed (organ) Bangor, 12 December 1973.
Flamingoes (voice, piano; Wilson) 1972.
Folksong Mass 1972.
Song for Dyfed (2 narrators, chorus, piano) 1973–4.
Surely the Lord Is in this Place (introit) 1974; first performed Llanelli, 22 September 1974.
Master Hugues of Saxe-Gotha (male voices, piano; Browning) 1975.
Three Thoughtful Songs (high voice, piano; Blake, Hopkins, Wilson) 1977; first performed Cardiff, 16 May 1983.
My Cousin Alice (mezzo-soprano, tenor, chorus, piano, tape of birds) 1982; first performed Cardiff, 16 May 1983.
No Complaints (cycle for voice, piano) 1984; first performed Machynlleth, 6 May 1990.
Eastern Wisdom (cycle for voice, chamber orchestra) 1987; first performed Machynlleth, 6 May 1990.
Song of Joy (voice, piano) 1988.
Arglwydd ein lor ni (unaccompanied voices) 1991.

Opera:

The Sergeant-Major's Daughter (burlesque opera) 1942–3.
The Black Ram (Idris Bell) 1951–3; first performed Aberystwyth, 9–11 March 1966.
Once upon a Time (one-act comic opera; Price) 1959; first performed Christchurch, New Zealand, 3 December 1960.
The Lady of Flowers (chamber opera; Cooper, after *Mabinogion*) 1981; first performed Colchester, Essex, 17 September 1982.

Other:

Rosemary Brown: Symphony in F minor (as "inspired" by Beethoven, orchestrated by IP and Alan Hovhaness) 1976.

PUBLICATIONS

By Parrott: "An Aspect of Bach", in *Musical Times*, December 1939; "Musician in the Army", *OCTU Magazine*, May 1941; "Arthur Sullivan, 1842–1900", in *Music & Letters*, July 1942; "Metamorphosis", in *Musical Times*, June 1943; "Encouragement for New Composers" in *Musical Times*, February 1946; "This Schoenbergery", in *Keynote*, August 1947; *Pathways to Modern Music*, London, 1947; "Psychical Research: Experiences of a Composer", in *Birmingham Post*, 31 August 1951; *A Guide to Musical Thought*, London, 1955; "The Group Mind" in *Light*, 79, April 1960; "The Music of William Mathias", in *The Anglo-Welsh Review*, 14(34), Winter 1964–5; *The Music of "An Adventure"*, London, 1966; *The Spiritual Pilgrims*, Narberth, 1969; *Elgar*, London, 1971; "Another Personal Credo", in *Musical Opinion*, October 1975; *Rosemary Brown: Music from Beyond*, 1977; "Grove and the Long-Suffering Celtic Composers", in *Musical Opinion*, April 1983; "The Enigma V [Elgar's Enigma Solved]", in *The Elgar Companion*, edited by Redwood, London, 1983; "Influences on My Music", in *Musical Opinion*, April 1983; "Thirty-Three Years in Welsh Music", in *Welsh Music*, 7(3), 1983; *Cyril Scott and His Piano Music*, London, 1991.

On Parrott: A. Fleighton Thomas, "A Many Sided Composer", in *Western Mail*, 18 November 1961, and "IP at 50", in *Musical Times*, March 1966; Lyn Davies, "IP, 1916– ", in *Y Faner*, Autumn 1977; Kevin Adams, "Welsh Orchestral Music", dissertation, University of Wales, 1980.

Ian Parrott comments:

Being approximately 30% spiritualist, 30% Fundamentalist and 40% independent at the moment, I am inclined to vote Liberal in politics. I believe firmly in inspiration for a creative artist.

Just as a hundred years ago composers may have been inhibited by too many Victorian "rules" of composition, today they live in a permissive world with no limits and therefore insufficient discipline. A composer using electronic "white sound", aleatory methods and minimalism is no better than, say, J.S. Bach, who avoided consecutive fifths. Travel by jet plane and photocopying are no improvement on the stage coach and quill pen when it comes to creativity. We may even be worse off, producing inferior music.

* * *

Ian Parrott's music reflects both his personality and his wide-ranging and diverse interests as a writer on music (particularly 20th-century British composers) as well as psychic research. His musical voice is traditional and virtually the whole of his output is based on the tensions generated between juxtaposed key centres. His musical language eschews the twelve-tone or more freely chromatic idioms of (say) Schoenberg in favour of a freely flowing idiom which often surprises with its sudden harmonic colourations derived from Skriabin and Messiaen, but also from the world of "trad" jazz (as in *Rhapsody and Boogie*). Such elements add spice to a clear-cut neo-classical language which displays some rhythmic affinities with Copland. He has shown little sympathy with the English pastoral school, but his music does embrace elements of Holst (rather than Vaughan Williams), Peter Warlock, Gerald Finzi, Ivor Gurney, Cyril Scott and Elgar. Parrott's generation of English composers was as much moved by the modernism of Warlock's *Curlew* as by the gradual emergence of Bartók (or Webern in the case of Humphrey Searle).

Parrott's quintessentially English background (Harrow, Royal College of Music and Oxford) paradoxically found creative stimulus in Wales. When he became Gregynog Professor of Music at the University College of Wales in 1950, Wales was experiencing great changes in its musical life, not only in the field of instrumental music but also in music education. As a founding member of the Guild for the Promotion of Welsh Music, Parrott played an important role in bringing new music to the fore. He identified himself with Wales to the extent of gaining a proficiency in the language and many of his works since 1950 have reflected his interest in Welsh culture. Parrott's opera, *The Black Ram*, did much to enrich the field of Welsh opera and his fine orchestral overture *Seithenin* was taken up by many of the large professional orchestras, notably the London Philharmonic under Sir Adrian Boult. *Seithenin* is a colourful and often haunting evocation of the night a drunken Cardiganshire nightwatchman failed to lock the floodgates of a town now said to lie underneath the Irish Sea. This vivid music often outlines the tritone in taut melodic curves. Equally colourful is his Welsh *Folksong Mass* and the *Mabinogion* inspired chamber opera *The Lady of Flowers*.

Parrott's choral music communicates directly and much of it has been commissioned for church use. He will probably be remembered best for some striking instrumental works from the powerfully evocative symphonic study *Luxor*, which in many ways sums up the composer's war-time experiences in Egypt, to the fine and cogently argued Cello Concerto, which was first performed by William Pleeth with the Halle Orchestra under Sir John Barbirolli. Similarly many of Parrott's other instrumental works reflect colourful concerns: notably the Cor Anglais Concerto, *Pensieri* for strings, the Second Wind Quintet with its colourful New Zealand bird calls, and *Duo fantastico*, which was performed by Erich Gruenberg and John McCabe. Some impressive organ works (the *Toccata* and the *Fantasia* are fine examples) reflect Parrott's early training as an organist. His *String Quartet No 4* is one of his finest compositions. Here one finds idiomatic string writing coupled with thematic working-out of material in a gripping work which deserves to be more widely known. His five symphonies are worthy of performance (the third is scored for the unusual combination of sting quartet and orchestra while the fifth has some effective jazz-like clarinet material) and many of his smaller-scale instrumental works have a somewhat jaunty sense of humour.

Many of Parrott's songs display a finely tuned sense of poetic rhythm as in the impressionistic *Flamingoes* and the more expansive *Two Flecker Settings: In Phaecia, & A Ship, an Isle, a Sickle Moon* which set the text with sonorous but carefully graded melodic lines.

Parrott's role as a teacher and musical catalyst in Welsh musical life should not be underestimated (one of his earliest pupils was William Mathias) but may have led to the composer falling between several stools. In spite of the commendable way in which Parrott has identified with Wales and things Welsh, to many people he remains a cultured Englishman abroad. He may also have been penalised for removing himself from major centres of music-making in England at such an early age (Parrott was one of the youngest heads of department ever appointed within the University of Wales). The more recent resurgance in tonality may yet show that composers like Parrott will receive the greater recognition that their quietly distinctive musical voices deserve.

—Lyn Davies

PÄRT, Arvo. Estonian; Austrian citizen. Born in Paide, Estonia, 11 September 1935. Educated at Tallinn Conservatory (composition under Heino Eller), graduated 1963. Married in 1972; 2 children. Staff member, Estonian Radio, 1958–67; emigrated to the West, 1980; settled in Berlin, 1980. Recipient: prizes (for *Meie Aed* and *Maailma Samm*), Competition for Young Composers, Moscow, 1962; Estonian Music Prize (for *Tabula rasa*), 1978; Edison Award, The Netherlands, and award of Record Prize Academy, Tokyo (for *Passio* recording). Mailing address: c/o ECM Records, Gleichmannstrasse 10, D-8000 Munich 60, Germany.

Publisher: Universal Edition.

Symphonies / orchestral:

Nekrolog / Obituary 1959.
Perpetuum mobile Op 10 1963. Recorded BIS CD 434.
Symphony No 1: Polyphonic 1963. Recorded BIS CD 434.
Collage von B.A.C.H. 1964.
Pro et contra (cello, orchestra) 1966. Recorded BIS CD 434.
Symphony No 2 1966. Recorded BIS CD 434.
Symphony No 3 1971. Recorded BIS CD 434.
Kui Bach oleks mesilasi pidanud / If Bach Had Been a Beekeeper (harpsichord, electric bass guitar, chamber orchestra, tape; or harpsichord, strings) 1976; 2nd section also arranged by G. Rozhdestvensky as *Silencer*, and included in collaborative work by Rozhdestvensky, Edison Denisov and Alfred Schnittke, entitled *Pas de quatre*.
Cantus in memoriam Benjamin Britten (string orchestra, bell) 1977. Recorded ECM 1275; Chandos 8656.
Tabula rasa (2 violins, prepared piano, string orchestra) 1977. Recorded ECM 1275.
Spiegel im Spiegel (violin, piano, string orchestra) 1980.
Dreiklang Concerto (violin, cello, chamber orchestra) 1981.
Fratres (strings, percussion) 1983.

Chamber / instrumental:

Sonatina No 1 (piano) 1958.
Partita (piano) 1958.
Sonatina No 2 (piano) 1958.
Wind Quintet 1964.
Diagrammid / Diagrams (piano) 1964.
Musica sillabica (12 instruments) 1964.
For Alina (piano) 1976.
Pari intervallo (organ) 1976.
Trivium (organ) 1976.
Fratres (ensemble of early instruments) 1977.
Arbos (7 wind instruments, percussion) 1977. Recorded ECM 1325.
Variations on Arinuschka's Recovery (piano) 1977.
Spiegel im Spiegel / Mirror Within a Mirror (violin, piano) 1978.
Fratres (violin, early instruments) 1980.
Fratres (violin, piano) 1980.
Annum per Annum (organ) 1980.
Pan Intervallo (string quartet or organ) 1980.
Arbos (7 or 8 recorders, 3 triangles) 1980.
Pan Intervallo (4 recorders) 1981.
Fratres (12 cellos) 1982. Recorded ECM 1275.
Sarah Was 91 Years Old (2 pianos, trumpet or soprano) 1984.
Hymn to a Great City (2 pianos) 1984.
Du-o-Du (violin, viola) 1989.
Mein Weg hat Giupfel und Wellentaler / I Walk on the Mountains and in the Valleys (organ) 1989.

Vocal/choral:

Meie Aed / Our Garden (children's chorus, orchestra) 1958.
Maailma Samm / The Stride of the World (oratorio for chorus, orchestra) 1961.
Solfeggio (chorus) 1964.
Credo (mixed chorus, piano, orchestra) 1968.
Laul Armastatule / Song for the Beloved (2 solo voices, chorus, orchestra; Rustaveli) 1973.
Modus (soprano, ensemble) 1976.
In spe (4 voices, 10 instruments) 1976.
Missa sillabica (4 voices or chamber choir, 6 ancient or modern instruments) 1977.
Cantate domino canticum novum (4 voices, 4 ancient or modern instruments) 1977.
Summa (tenor, baritone, 6 instruments; or SATB chorus, 6 instruments) 1980.
De profundis (men's voices, organ, percussion) 1981; first performed Kassel, 1981. Recorded ECM 1325.
Passio domini nostri Jesu Christi secundum Joannem / St John Passion (4 male voices, SATB chorus, organ, instruments) 1981–2. Recorded ECM 1370.
By the Rivers of Babylon (vocal quartet, instruments; arranged from *In spe*) 1984; first performed Witten, 1984. Recorded ECM 1325.
Ein Wallfahrtslied (tenor or baritone, string quartet; Psalm 121) 1984.
Two Slavic Psalms: Lobet den Herrn (Psalm 117), Kindliche Ergebung (Psalm 131) (vocal quintet) 1984; first performed Witten, 1984.
Es Sang für Langen Jahren (alto, violin, viola) 1985.
Stabat mater (vocal and string trios) 1985.
Te Deum (3 choruses, string orchestra, prepared piano, tape/wind-harp) 1985.
Dies irae (chorus, organ, instruments) 1986.
Miserere (vocal quintet, mixed chorus, organ, instruments) 1989.
Magnificat (unaccompanied chorus) 1989.
Nun eile ich zu euch (unaccompanied chorus) 1989.
Berliner Messe (soprano, alto, tenor, bass, organ; or SATB chorus, organ) 1990.
The Beatitudes (soprano, alto, tenor, bass, organ; or SATB chorus, organ) 1990.
Two Antiphons (double chorus) 1990–1.
Carol (chorus) 1990–1.

* * *

A listener hearing the music of the Estonian composer Arvo Pärt for the first time might be forgiven for thinking that he had inadvertently strayed into another century, or had at least been transported to a parallel universe in another galaxy. It has a beauty at once austere and sensuous that seems to be hardly of our time. Yet there can be little doubt that the revelation of his music has been one of the most important factors in the development of a new sensibility in recent music. The early work that he wrote in his native country would hardly prepare us for such an assertion. It was occasionally startling within the confines of Soviet music of the period—the use of serial and aleatoric techniques did cause some difficulty with the authorities from time to time. Even within his atonal music, however, he felt the pull of tonality. The *Symphony No 2*, for example, while being serial has sudden bursts of tonal material (periodic major chords, a melody and accompaniment in A minor) which are not justified by the tone row. He had difficulties of another kind ensuing from his inclusion of overtly religious references, especially in works such as *Credo*, with its words "I believe in Jesus Christ". In this piece he incorporated, too, direct quotation from Bach—the first Prelude (in C major) from the *Well-Tempered Klavier*, associated with Gounod's *Ave Maria*. On other occasions, however, his inclusion of quotation in a piece such as *Kui Bach oleks mesilasi pidanud / If Bach Had Been a Beekeeper* reveals a sense of humour surprising only for those who have not encountered Pärt personally.

Most of the music we now hear from Pärt comes from after he ended a lengthy period of compositional silence in 1976 with a tiny piano piece *For Alina*. In this piece he seems to have discovered a triadic principle that was to guide his future work. This technique he refers to as "tintinnabuli," a word which evokes the pealing of bells, the bells' complex but rich sonorous mass of overtones, the gradual unfolding of patterns implicit in the sound itself, and the idea of a sound that is simultaneously static and in flux. He had studied in depth medieval and Renaissance music, especially Gregorian chant, the School of Notre Dame, Machaut, Ockeghem and Josquin, and he drew on his deep religious feeling and on his roots in the Eastern Orthodox Church. One of the earliest and most famous of his works in the new style, *Fratres*, was first performed by the Estonian ensemble of early music Hortus Musicus. A number of versions of this piece exist (some not authorised by Pärt) and it was the recording of two versions on ECM Records after his move to the West, along with *Cantus in memoriam Benjamin Britten* and the astonishingly subtle *Tabula rasa*, that brought his work quite dramatically to the attention of a worldwide audience. Thereafter his cause has been furthered by subsequent recordings on ECM and above all by his close working relationship with the Hilliard Ensemble, an ensemble with the perfect aesthetic outlook for Pärt's work combining, as they do, remarkable virtuosity in early music with a commitment to contemporary works. Much of his recent work has been vocal, setting religious texts, either unaccompanied or with a sparse but precisely calculated instrumentation. In Estonia he had worked as a composer of music for film and television as well as being recording director for Estonian Radio. This has given him a clear sense of practicality allied to a rare aural sensitivity. His awareness of the most appropriate instrumental nuance can be heard in the perfect blending of vocal trio (soprano, male alto, tenor) and string trio in his exquisite *Stabat mater*, in the use of prepared piano in the double violin concerto *Tabula rasa*, and in the unobtrusive use of electric guitars in *Miserere*. In a way the very term "*Tabula rasa*," with its connotations of the medieval philosophical technique of "wiping the slate clean" and building knowledge from nothing, is very apt when applied to Pärt's musical thought. It can be a metaphor for the way in which his music emerges from silence, quite literally in several pieces, and for the way in which he returns to silence, step by step. Witness the slow stepwise descents at the end of *Tabula rasa*; witness the agonisingly slow falling phrases passed from voice to voice, and instrument to instrument, at the end of *Stabat mater*; and witness the dramatic ending of *Cantus in memoriam Benjamin Britten* where the final *fortissimo* string chord stops to reveal the dying resonance of a solitary bell, struck but not noticed during the climax.

Moments like these, that in any other composer would only be moments, are essentially present throughout Pärt's music, a music of haunting power and beauty that remains with the listener long after the last sound has died away.

—Gavin Bryars

PATTERSON, Paul (Leslie). British/English. Born in Chesterfield, Derbyshire, 15 June 1947. Educated at Royal Academy of Music, London (trombone, and composition under Richard Stoker), 1964–8; further composition study under Richard Rodney Bennett. Married Hazel Wilson in 1981; 1 daughter and 1 son. Freelance composer, from 1968; Manson Fellow in composition, from 1971, Royal Academy of Music, London; head of composition and 20th-century music, since 1985, Arts Council composer-in-association, English Sinfonia, 1969–70; head of electronics, London Sinfonietta, 1970s; director, contemporary music, University of Warwick, 1974–80; composer in residence, South Eastern Arts, 1980–2; composer in residence, Bedford School, 1984–5; composer in residence, Southwark, Exeter (also artistic director) and Bournemouth Festivals, 1991. Recipient: Theodore Holland Scholarship, 1968–9; Royal Philharmonic prize, South West Arts Young Composers Competition; Medal of Honour, Polish Ministry of Culture, 1986. Mailing address: 31 Cromwell Avenue, Highgate, London N6 5HN, England.

Publishers: Josef Weinberger, London; Universal Edition.

Symphonies/orchestral:

Trumpet Concerto Op 3 (trumpet, timpani, string orchestra) 1968; first performed Bristol, 19 November 1969.
Symphonic Study II 1968.
Chamber Concerto 1969.
Partita Op 8 (chamber orchestra: 2 oboes, 2 horns, strings) 1970; first performed Nottingham, 5 March 1970.
Piccola sinfonia Op 10 (string orchestra) 1970; first performed Oakham, 11 March 1971.
Horn Concerto Op 11 (horn, strings) 1971; first performed Nottingham, 21 July 1971.
Fiesta sinfonica Op 12 1971; first performed Nottingham, 22 July 1972.
Sonors Op 17 1972; first performed Southend, 10 January 1973.
Fusions Op 23 (orchestra, tape) 1974; first performed Croydon, Surrey, 9 March 1974.
Chromascope Op 24 (brass band) 1974; first performed Harrogate, Yorkshire, 9 August 1974. Recorded Pye TB 3016.
Count Down Op 28 (brass band) 1974; first performed London, 11 October 1975.
Strange Meeting Op 29 (orchestra, tape) 1975; first performed Croydon, Surrey, 5 May 1975.
Cataclysm Op 30 (brass band) 1975; first performed Hull, Yorkshire, 9 August 1975. Recorded Bedivere BVU K001.
The Circular Ruins Op 31 1975; first performed Exeter, Devon, 10 December 1975.
Wildfire Op 33 (orchestra, tape) 1976; first performed London, 27 March 1976.
Clarinet Concerto Op 34 (clarinet, strings) 1976; first performed London, 19 May 1976.
Concerto for Orchestra Op 45 1981; first performed Birmingham, 13 November 1981. Recorded EMI EL 2706061.
Sinfonia Op 46 (string orchestra) 1982; first performed Warsaw, 22 September 1983. Recorded RPO 8006.
Europhony Op 55 (chamber orchestra) 1985; first performed Cardiff, 11 June 1985. Recorded EMI EL 2706061.
Upside-Down-Under-Variations Op 56 1985; first performed London, 3 March 1985.
Propositions Op 61 (harmonica, strings) 1987; first performed London, 25 April 1987.
White Shadows on the Dark Horizon Op 67 1988; first performed 4 January 1989.
Fanfare for the Future (brass, percussion) 1989; first performed London, 29 October 1989.
Symphony Op 69 1989–90; first performed Cheltenham, Gloucestershire, 1990.

Chamber/instrumental:

Wind Quintet Op 2 1967; first performed San Remo, Italy, 4 August 1967.
Wind Trio Op 4 (flute, oboe, clarinet) 1968; first performed London, 16 October 1968.
Jubilate Op 5 (organ) 1969; first performed Exeter, Devon, 15 July 1969. Recorded HMV CSD 3780.
Monologue Op 6 (oboe) 1969; first performed London, 5 May 1970.
Intrada Op 7 (organ) 1969; first performed London, 18 November 1969. Recorded HMV CSD 3780.
Fanfares for Great Occasions Op 35 (I "Chicester Fanfare", II "Warwick Fanfare", III "St Bartholomew's Fanfare", IV "Exeter Fanfare", 3 trumpets, 2 trombones, bass trombone, tuba) 1969–75; first performed—I Chichester, Sussex, 6 June 1975, II Warwick, 11 September 1974, III London, 21 June 1973, IV Exeter, Devon 15 July 1969.
Visions Op 9 (organ) 1972; first performed London, 6 June 1973. Recorded HMV CSD 3780.
Comedy for Five Winds Op 14 (flute, oboe, clarinet, bassoon, horn) 1972; first performed Mayfield, Sussex, 15 May 1972.
Interludium Op 15 1972; first performed London, 29 September 1972. Recorded HMV CSD 3780.
Intersections Op 20 (instrumental ensemble) 1973; first performed New York City, 8 July 1973.
Fluorescences Op 22 (organ) 1973; first performed Exeter, Devon, 30 July 1973. Recorded HMV CSD 3780; Priory PR 159.
Conversations Op 25 (clarinet, piano) 1974; first performed London, 18 November 1974.
Floating Music Op 26 (flute, clarinet, violin, cello, piano/celeste, percussion) 1974; first performed London, 21 October 1974.
Shadows Op 27 (clarinet, tape) 1975; first performed Cincinnati, Ohio, 6 April 1975.
Diversions Op 32 (saxophone quartet) 1975; first performed 31 July 1976. Recorded SAY DISC SDL 365.
Games Op 37 (organ) 1977; first performed St Albans, Hertfordshire, 6 July 1977.
Cracowian Counterpoints Op 38 (flute/piccolo, oboe, clarinet, bassoon, horn, trumpet, trombone, piano/celeste, percussion, 2 violins, viola, cello, double bass) 1977; first performed London, 3 June 1977.
At the Still Point of the Turning World Op 41 (flute, oboe, clarinet, horn, violin, viola, cello, bass) 1980; first performed Stockholm, 5 January 1980.
Deception Pass Op 43 (horn, 4 trumpets, 3 trombones, bass trombones, tuba) 1980; first performed Cheltenham, Gloucestershire, 5 July 1980.
Spiders Op 48 (harp) 1983; first performed Saint Asaph, Wales, 27 September 1983.
Duologue Op 49 (oboe, piano) 1984; first performed Christchurch, 20 July 1984. Recorded Pearl SHE 591.
Luslawice Variations Op 50 (violin) 1984; first performed Luslawice, Poland, 10 September 1984.
Mean Time Op 53 (brass quintet) 1985; first performed London, 16 June 1985.
String Quartet Op 58 1986; first performed Chester, 24 July 1986.

Memories of Quiberville Op 60 (trombone quartet) 1986; first performed Manchester, 7 February 1987.
Suite Op 62 (cello) 1987; first performed Bristol, 19 November 1987.
Tides of Mananan Op 64 (viola) 1987; first performed Isle of Man, July 1988.
A Tunnel of Time Op 66 1988; first performed London, 17 May 1988.

Vocal/choral:

Rebecca Op 1 (speaker, woodwind, trombone, violin(s), cello, piano, percussion; Belloc) 1965; first performed Dartington, Devon, 21 August 1966.
Kyrie Op 13 (SATB chorus, piano—4 hands) 1971; first performed New York City, 21 March 1972. Recorded HMV CSD 3780.
Time Piece Op 16 (6 unaccompanied male voices; Rose-Price) 1972; first performed London, 10 March 1973. Recorded EMI EMD 5521/ESD 7103.
Gloria Op 21 (SATB chorus, piano—4 hands) 1972. Recorded HMV CSD 3780.
What Shall We Do with the Drunken Sailor? (6 male voices) 1973.
The Abode of the Dead / You'll Never Be Alone Op 18 (voices, woodwind, recorders, brass, percussion, piano, strings) 1973; broadcast BBC, 10 October 1973.
Requiem Op 19 (chorus, boys' chorus, orchestra; liturgical, Ecclesiastes) 1974; first performed Coventry, Warwickshire, 21 June 1975.
Ecclesiastes Op 19a (unaccompanied SATB chorus; drawn from *Requiem Op 19*) 1974.
Spare Parts Op 36 (unaccompanied SATB chorus) 1976; first performed London, 18 January 1978.
Brain Storm Op 39 (soprano, alto, tenor, bass, live electronics; Rose-Price) 1978; first performed London, 9 February 1978.
Voices of Sleep Op 40 (soprano, SATB chorus, orchestra; Rose-Price) 1979; first performed Washington, 19 April 1979.
The Canterbury Psalms Op 44 (SATB chorus, orchestra or organ; Psalms 97, 121, 148) 1981; first performed Canterbury, Kent, 15 April 1981. Recorded Foldback FBR 2852.
Vampireen Op 36a (6 unaccompanied male voices) 1983; first performed St Albans, Hertfordshire, 5 June 1983.
Mass of the Sea Op 47 (soprano, bass, SATB chorus, orchestra; liturgical, Rose-Price) 1983; first performed Gloucester, 22 August 1983. Recorded RPO 8006.
Christ Is the King Op 51 (unaccompanied SATB chorus; Bishop Bell) 1984; first performed Chichester, Sussex, 19 July 1984.
Missa brevis Op 54 (unaccompanied SATB chorus; liturgical) 1985; first performed London, 1985. Recorded EMI EL 2706061.
Stabat mater Op 57 (mezzo-soprano, chorus, orchestra) 1985–6; first performed Huddersfield, Yorkshire, 27 March 1986.
Magnificat and Nunc Dimittis Op 59 (SATB chorus, chorus, organ) 1986; first performed Norwich, Norfolk, 4 July 1986.
The Sorriest Cow of Capricorn Op 63 (soprano, piano; Peake) 1987; first performed Guernsey, 7 September 1987.
Te Deum Op 65 (soprano, SATB chorus, boys' chorus, orchestra) 1988; first performed Hereford, 25 August 1988.
The End (unaccompanied ATB chorus) 1989.

Other:

Film scores: *Mask of Satan*; *Two Faces of Evil*; *Children of the Full Moon*; *Rude Awakening*; *Distant Scream*; *In Possession*; *Black Clarion*; *The Exercise*; *Darwin's Dream*:

Television music: *Country Search*; *Omnibus*; *Dancing Princesses*.

PUBLICATIONS

On Patterson: Andrew Burn, "PP", in *Composer*, Winter 1987, reprinted as introduction to "PP: A Catalogue to Celebrate the Composer's 40th Birthday", London, 1988.

* * *

Paul Patterson spent his formative years in Exeter where his interest in music began to blossom in his early teens. In 1964 he enrolled at the Royal Academy of Music where he studied trombone and composition with Richard Stoker, supplementing the latter's guidance at summer courses with Elizabeth Lutyens, Hans Keller and Harrison Birtwistle. After graduating from the RAM in 1968 Patterson received public recognition for his *Trumpet Concerto*, first performed the following year by John Wilbraham and the Bristol Sinfonia, a rhythmically vital work which bears the influence of Stravinsky and Hindemith. Patterson initially pursued a career as a trombonist, balancing engagements with work on new compositions.

A number of competition prizes and awards, including the Royal Philharmonic Prize and the South West Arts Young Composers Competition, provided added incentive to concentrate on composition, and winning the Theodore Holland Scholarship enabled Patterson to begin private study with Richard Rodney Bennett. In 1971 Patterson was appointed Manson Fellow at the RAM, a post which required him to build the Academy's library of contemporary scores and which allowed him the opportunity to study works by Witold Lutosławski, György Ligeti, Krzysztof Penderecki and Kazimierz Serocki, composers with whom he was shortly after to establish personal contact.

Patterson's acquaintance with the avant-garde was immediately reflected in practical terms in *Kyrie*, in which he adopted the distinct notational and textural procedures of the Polish school. *Kyrie* was followed by a number of other short choral works in similar style including the *Gloria* and *Requiem*, where improvised elements, speech and clapping effects, and tone clusters lie at the heart of the musical language. Other works composed during the 1970s, such as *Chromascope* and *Cataclysm*, both for brass band, *Cracowian Counterpoints* and the *Clarinet Concerto* represent the same complex style extended to instruments. Patterson's characteristic sense of humour can be found in two works commissioned by the King's Singers: *Time Piece* and *Spare Parts* in which the excesses of modernism are gently mocked. As Patterson points out, "having worked for a decade in the area [of the avant-garde], culminating with *Voices of Sleep* in 1979, I eventually felt that it would be nice to write a piece where I didn't have to explain every quarter inch of the score to the performers."

A key element in Patterson's development as composer has been his involvement in education both at the RAM, where he is now head of the strong Composition and 20th-Century Music Department, and in his work as composer in residence at such institutions as King's School, Canterbury and Bedford

School. As a tireless self-publicist and excellent communicator, Patterson has attracted the interest of many festival promoters, being featured composer at the 1985 Llandaff and Greenwich Festivals and composer in residence at the Southwark Festival from 1989. In May 1991 Patterson was appointed Artistic Director of the Exeter Festival, a post which should draw on his experiences as programme director of the RAM's Composer Festivals.

The practical consideration of repeat performances partly influenced Patterson's move to a more "accessible" style of writing; since *Voices of Sleep* he has returned to the use of conventional notation and has written to the strengths of his likely performers. For example, a commission for a new choral work from the traditionally conservative Three Choirs Festival imposed certain conditions, primarily those of lack of rehearsal time, on Patterson's approach and the resulting *Mass of the Sea* scored a popular success with both audience and concert promoters alike. In the Mass and the preceding *Concerto for Orchestra* Patterson exploits the use of small, repeated motivic units to unify individual movements, a technique held over from his earlier works but here allied to a more tonal harmonic and melodic structure. Two other large-scale choral works, the *Stabat mater* and *Te Deum* form with the Mass what Patterson regards as his liturgical trilogy. Echoes of plainsong appear in the *Stabat mater*, although these turn out to be by Patterson himself, whereas the Gregorian *Te Deum* chant appears as a structural device in the eponymous choral work. Elswhere, jazz harmonies, energetic rhythms and vivid orchestration (including off-stage brass bands in the *Te Deum*) add to the appeal of these works.

Since the early 1980s Patterson has composed in what might be fairly termed as a neo-classical style, with obvious influences including Stravinsky, Bartók and Poulenc. However, the striking choral and instrumental textures of the Polish-influenced works is frequently present, as in the "Quando corpus morietur" section of the *Stabat mater* or in the slow movement of the First Symphony. The synthesis of a recondite, uncompromising style with a more traditional musical language has occupied Patterson over the past decade, a process which has earned him a strong public reputation and an impressive list of commissions.

—Andrew Stewart

PAULUS, Stephen (Harrison). American. Born in Summit, New Jersey, 24 August 1949. Educated at Alexander Ramsey High School, Summit, graduated 1967; University of Minnesota, Minneapolis (composition under Paul Fetler and Dominick Argento), B.M., 1971, M.M., 1974, Ph.D. in theory and composition, 1978. Married Patricia Ann Stutzmann, 18 July 1975. Co-founder (with Libby Larsen), 1973–85, and vice-president, from 1983, Minnesota Composer's Forum; composer in residence, Minnesota Orchestra, 1983–7, and Santa Fe Music Festival, 1986. Recipient: Guggenheim Fellowship, 1982. Mailing address: 1710 Jefferson Avenue, St Paul, Minnesota 55105, U.S.A.

Publishers: C. Fischer; European American; Jenson; Shawnee.

Symphonies/orchestral:

Spectra (small orchestra) 1980; first performed Houston, Texas, 12 April 1980.
Translucent Landscapes 1982; first performed August 1982.
Divertimento (youth orchestra) 1982–3.
Concerto for Orchestra 1983.
Seven Short Pieces 1983; first performed Minneapolis, Minnesota, February 1984.
Ordway Overture 1984; first performed St Paul, Minnesota, January 1985.
Reflections: Four Movements on a Theme of Wallace Stevens 1984–5; first performed St Paul, Minnesota, March 1985.
Symphony in Three Movements: Soliloquy 1985–6; first performed Minnesota, January 1986. Recorded Nonesuch 79147 1.
Suite: The Postman Always Rings Twice (from the opera) 1986; first performed Minnesota, July 1986.
Ground Breaker (overture for orchestra and "construction instruments") 1987.
Violin Concerto 1987.

Chamber/instrumental:

Duo (clarinet, piano) 1974.
Exploration (chamber ensemble) 1974.
Colors (brass quintet) 1974.
Village Tales: A Tree of Life (chamber ensemble) 1975.
Wind Suite (flute, oboe, clarinet, bassoon) 1975.
Indefinite Images (clarinet, bassoon) 1976.
Graphics (chamber ensemble) 1977.
Lunar Maria (chamber ensemble) 1977.
Five Translucent Landscapes (piano) 1978.
Music for Contrasts (string quartet) 1980.
Banchetto musicale (cello, piano) 1981.
Courtship Songs for a Summer's Eve (flute, oboe, cello, piano) 1981.
Dance (piano) 1986.
String Quartet No 2 1987.

Vocal/choral:

Three Elizabethan Songs (soprano, piano) 1973.
Three Chinese Poems (unaccompanied SATB chorus) 1973.
Mad Book, Shadow Book: Michael Morley's Songs (tenor, piano; Browne) 1976, arranged for tenor, chamber ensemble, 1978.
Canticles: Songs and Rituals for Easter and the May (soprano, mezzo-soprano, SATB chorus, organ, chamber orchestra; Browne) 1977.
North Shore (mezzo-soprano, baritone, SATB chorus, chamber orchestra; Browne) 1977.
Letters for the Times (soprano, tenor, baritone, SATB chorus, chamber ensemble; 17th-century broadsheets and diaries) 1980.
Lately Arrived from London (arranged from *Letters for the Times* for SATB chorus) 1980.
So Hallow'd Is the Time (treble, soprano, tenor, baritone, SATB chorus, organ, chamber orchestra; Shakespeare) 1980, also arrangements of "This Is the Month and This the Happy Morn", "Run, Shepherds, Run", "A Child My Choice", "Sing Hevin Imperial" for mixed chorus. Recorded Pro Arte PCD 257.
Artsongs (tenor, piano; Rilke, Wilbur, Dasoff, Williams, O'Hara) 1983.
All My Pretty Ones (voice, piano; Browne) 1984; first performed St Paul, Minnesota, 1984.

Bachatelle (homage to J.S. Bach for unaccompanied SATB chorus) 1985.
Madrigali di Michelangelo (unaccompanied SATB chorus) 1987.
Bittersuite (baritone, piano; Nash) 1987; first performed Stockholm, 1987.

Opera:

The Village Singer (Browne, after Freeman) 1979.
The Postman Always Rings Twice (Graham, after Cain) 1982.
The Woodlanders (Graham, after Hardy) 1985.

Other:

Dance a Line (tape) 1976.
Prison Songs (tape) 1976.

PUBLICATIONS

On Paulus: M.A. Feldman, "Triple Header", in *Opera Now*, 49(17), 1985.

* * *

If there is an heir apparent to the user-friendly operatic idiom "pioneered" (if the word can be used of a musical language so thoroughly conventional) by Gian Carlo Menotti in such works as *Amahl and the Night Visitors* and *The Telephone*, it is the young, New Jersey-born Stephen Paulus. Educated at the University of Minnesota, where he was a pupil of the fine dramatic composer Dominick Argento, Paulus achieved a reputation for well-crafted ensemble writing with a body of chamber and vocal pieces in the mid to late 1970s, mostly written before his 30th birthday.

That reputation took a substantial step forward and sideways with the premiere of his first opera *The Village Singer* in 1979, a commission from the Opera Theatre of St Louis with a libretto by Paulus's now longstanding collaborator Michael Dennis Browne and based on a story by Mary Wilkins Freeman. The qualification in his growing recognition as an original voice stems from the selfsame criticism levelled at Menotti: that his operatic writing is conservative to the point of regression, locked into a long outmoded manner which depends heavily on repeated themes and leitmotifs, popular pastiche and dramatic contrivance. Stripped of their negative connotations, these are descriptions rather than criticisms. Paulus indentifies his characters very "literally" and treats his score in an unabashedly illustrative way.

This is particularly noticeable in the second opera, based on James M. Cain's *The Postman Always Rings Twice*. Not immediately promising material for operatic treatment, Cain's hard-boiled *roman noir* comes across in Paulus's version with considerably more menace than in either of its screen adaptations, and in its handling of raw passion bears some comparison with Shostakovich's *Lady Macbeth of Mtsensk District*. Where it palpably differs is that where the Russian composer uses the orchestral score to estrange and ironise the action, Paulus's settings are intended to be relatively neutral contexts for dramatic singing; once again, he uses leitmotifs as a way of identifying characters and situations but manipulates them with considerable subtlety and variation.

His ability as a composer for voice was still evident in the third opera, *The Woodlanders*, based on a Hardy novel. Like *The Village Singer* it has a gentler theme and some melodic and harmonic passages reminiscent of Delius's incorporation of non-canonical materials into his operatic and choral works. Perhaps Paulus's most popular work to date has been the remarkable sequence of Christmas carols from English and Scottish sources *So Hallow'd Is the Time*, which has already gained wide popularity and has been successfully recorded. But Paulus is also a considerable orchestral composer. The *Symphony in Three Movements: Soliloquy* and the *Violin Concerto* are by no means blandly generic, and contain intriguing structural and colouristic elements that lift them beyond the ordinary. The brief 1987 *Ground Breaker* features an ensemble of "construction instruments" and has been a favourite "pops" item since its premiere by the Minneapolis Orchestra, where Paulus and his longstanding Minnesota Composers Forum associate Libby Larsen have both served as composers in residence.

Paulus's virtues are those of his operas: solid construction, an impressively differentiated dramatic spectrum, fine lyrical passages and occasionally startling flourishes. He has not yet written anything with the enduring appeal of Menotti's *Amahl and the Night Visitors* but he is also a more demanding and self-critical craftsman with the benefit of a further two generations of contemporary musical technique at his disposal. Already, he shows no willingness to accept easy answers or ready-made solutions.

—Brian Morton

PAYNE, Anthony (Edward). British/English. Born in London, 2 August 1936. Educated at Dulwich College, London; University of Durham, 1958–61. Married soprano Jane Manning, 24 September 1966. Freelance writer, musicologist, teacher, 1962–73; full-time composer, since 1973. Recipient: Radcliffe Prize, 1975; ISCM nomination (for *Concerto for Orchestra*), Boston, 1976. Mailing address: 2 Wilton Square, London N.1, England.

Publisher: Chester Music.

Symphonies/orchestral:

Suite from a Forgotten Ballet 1955, revised 1986; recorded for broadcast on BBC Radio, 1 February 1989.
Contrapuncti (string quartet, string orchestra) 1958, revised 1979.
Concerto for Orchestra 1974; first performed London, 8 January 1975.
Fire on Whaleness (brass band, percussion) 1976; first performed York, 25 June 1976.
Song of the Clouds (oboe solo, 2 horns, percussion, strings) 1979–80; first performed Cheltenham, Gloucestershire, 29 June 1980.
Spring's Shining Wake 1980–1; broadcast BBC Radio, 21 December 1983.
Songs and Seascapes (string orchestra) 1984; first performed London, 6 June 1984.

The Spirit's Harvest 1985; first performed London, 31 July 1985.
Fanfares and Processional (horn, 4 trumpets, 4 trombones, tuba) 1986; first performed London, 19 September 1986.
Half-Heard in the Stillness 1987; first performed Derby, 17 September 1987.
Echoes of Courtly Love (horn, trumpet, flugelhorn, trombone, tuba) 1987; first performed London, 13 May 1988.
Time's Arrow 1990; first performed London, 24 July 1990.

Chamber/instrumental:

Paraphrases and Cadenzas (clarinet, viola, piano) 1969, revised 1979; first performed London, 20 November 1969.
Sonatas and Ricercars (flute, oboe, clarinet, bassoon, horn) 1970.
Paean (piano) 1971; first performed London, 9 December 1971.
String Quartet 1978; first performed London, 4 December 1978.
Footfalls Echo in the Memory (violin, piano) 1978; first performed 22 August 1980.
The Stones and Lonely Places Sing (flute/piccolo, clarinet/bass clarinet, horn, piano, string trio) 1979; first performed London, 2 September 1979.
Miniature Variations on a Theme of E. L. (piano) 1980; first performed London, 6 March 1981.
A Day in the Life of a Mayfly (flute/piccolo, clarinet, percussion, piano, violin, cello) 1981; first performed London, 25 September 1981.
Relections in the Sea of Glass (organ) 1983.
The Song Streams in the Firmament (clarinet, string quartet, double bass) 1986; first performed New York City, 19 April 1986.
A 1940s Childhood (flute, guitar) 1987; first performed London, 10 April 1987.
Consort Music (2 violins, 2 violas, cello) 1987; first performed Cambridge, 27 July 1987.
Sea-Change (flute, clarinet, harp, string quartet) 1988; first performed London, 12 June 1988.
Amid the Winds of Evening (viola) 1988; first performed London, 26 April 1989.

Vocal/choral:

Phoenix Mass (SATB chorus, 3 trumpets, 3 trombones) 1965, 1972; broadcast BBC Radio, 2 October 1973.
Two Songs Without Words (male voice quintet) 1970; first performed London, 4 February 1971.
A Little Passiontide Cantata (unaccompanied SATB chorus) 1974, revised 1984; first performed London, 22 March 1976.
First Sight of Her and After (16 unaccompanied solo voices SATB; Hardy) 1975; first performed London, 11 December 1975.
The World's Winter (soprano, flute/piccolo, oboe, clarinet/E♭ clarinet/bass clarinet, horn, harp, violin, viola, cello) 1976; first performed Cheltenham, Gloucestershire, 4 July 1976.
The Sea of Glass (SATB chorus, organ) 1977; first performed St Albans, Hertfordshire, 2 July 1977.
A Little Ascensiontide Cantata (unaccompanied SATB chorus) 1977, revised 1984; first performed 29 August 1978.
A Little Whitsuntide Cantata (unaccompanied SATB chorus) 1977, revised 1984.
A Little Christmastide Cantata (unaccompanied SATB chorus) 1983; broadcast BBC Radio, 2 March 1985.
Aleluias and Hockets (based on Machaut's *Hoquetus David*; SATB chorus, 2 oboes, cor anglais, 2 bassoons, 2 trumpets, 3 trombones) 1987.
Adlestrop (soprano, piano; Edward Thomas) 1989; first performed Aldeburgh, Suffolk, 10 June 1984.

PUBLICATIONS

By Payne: *Schoenberg*, London, 1968; *The Music of Frank Bridge*, London, 1984; also contributor to *Tempo*, *Musical Times*, *Music and Musicians*, *The Listener* and other magazines and journals.

* * *

Anthony Payne began his boyhood attempts at composition as a typical, if slightly out-of-date English Romantic. Today, he is once again writing music that fits well within the English Romantic tradition, while also being rich with resonances of the very different experiences that he has taken in his stride in the intervening years. As a whole his works describe a fascinating trajectory away from his roots and then back again, integrating the English tradition to make it understandable within the wider context of European music.

Payne began composing in the late 1950s, but then spent a period simply making the acquintance of music of English composers that at first seemed alien and off-putting. His period of silence was not unfruitful. He made a name for himself as a civilised, educated critic and began work that would lead to books on Schoenberg and Frank Bridge.

Only when Payne married the soprano Jane Manning in 1966 did he feel confident enough to compose again. The result was the touchingly named *Phoenix Mass*, a splendid, earthy fusion of abrasively modern harmony and the ancient rhetoric of the Venetians. With works immediately following the Mass, Payne, showed his interest in rough-hewn block of sound, awkward, sinewy melodic lines and a jerky asymetrical feeling for rhythm that verges, in the slow summation of this period, in an impressive composition, stern in scale and sweep and resolutely untempted by the seductive possibilities of orchestral colour.

After completing this particular score Payne may have felt the need to allow his language to yield, to breath and indulge from time to time. His *String Quartet*, composed to a fascinating collage-like plan in which three movements flow into one another, contains moments of pleasure and a feeling for the medium as a sensual experience. This feeling is more marked in the oboe concerto *Song of the Clouds*, where prowling effects of atmosphere in the lower strings, modal writing for the two horns and a pastoral approach to the solo oboe, all bring Payne's conscious and unconscious ties to an English past to the fore.

But the key work in which Payne really came to grips with his original English Romantic heritage and tried seriously to integrate it with his newer modernist language, was *Spring's Shining Wake*, a piece composed bar by bar on the model of a famous work by Delius. From this point on Payne's course was clear. He has now established himself as one of the few composers who has successfully returned to a more romantic past, while also refusing to give up the benefits of a hard-won present. This achievement is most impressive in his two major orchestral works. *A Spirit's Harvest* is a kind of English symphony, its roots well within the world of Vaughan-Williams or even Elgar. The more recent *Time's Arrow* is inspired originally by the theory of the Big Bang. It traces a powerful formal arch from the greatest speed to absolute stillness and then back again to speed.

Payne's smaller-scale chamber music has also given us ample evidence in recent years of the richness of the particular English soil that he has chosen to plough. Every piece, whether for the largest or the smallest forces, is held together and motivated by Payne's personal and musical qualities of simplicity, honesty and directness.

—Gerard McBurney

PEIXINHO, Jorge (Manuel Rosado Marques). Portuguese. Born in Montijo, 20 January 1940. Educated at Lisbon Conservatoire (piano and composition under Santos and Croner de Vasconcelos), 1951–8; University of Lisbon, 1959; further composition study under Luigi Nono, Venice, 1960; Accademia di S. Cecilia, Rome (under Goffredo Petrassi and Boris Porena), 1960–1; Ferienkurse für Neue Musik, Darmstadt, between 1960 and 1970; further composition study, Basle Academy of Music, (under Pierre Boulez, Karlheinz Stockhausen and Gottfried Michael Koenig), 1962–3. Professor, Conservatoire of Music, Oporto, Portugal, 1965–6; professor of composition, National Conservatoire of Music, Lisbon, since 1985; visiting professor at various times, Viana do Castelo, Vila do Conde (Portugal), Vigo (Spain), Cassine (Italy), Curitiba, São João del Rei and Santos (Brazil); director, Grupo de Música Contemporãnea de Lisboa, since 1970; member, presidential council, ISCM, 1977–81. Recipient: Gulbenkian Prize, 1974; Portuguese Authors' Society, 1975; Portuguese Music Council, 1988; Medal of Cultural Merit, 1988; Portuguese Radio Prize, 1990. Mailing address: rua de S. Bento, 17-1 D, 1200 Lisbon, Portugal.

Publisher: none.

Symphonies/orchestral:

Políptico (chamber orchestra) 1960; first performed Naples, 1961.
Sobreposições 1960; first performed Sintra, 1962.
Concerto for Saxophone and Orchestra 1961; first performed Lisbon, 1973.
Diafonia (harp, harpsichord, piano, celeste, percussion, strings) 1962–5; original version first performed Lisbon, 1962.
Kinetofonias (25 strings, 3 tape recorders) 1965–9; original version first performed Lisbon, 1967.
Nomos 1967; first performed Lisbon, 1972.
Sucessões simétricas II 1971; first performed Lisbon, 1974.
Voix-en-jeux 1972–6; first performed Lisbon, 1976.
Sucessões simétricas III (chamber orchestra) 1974; first performed Lisbon, 1975.
Retrato de Helena 1982; first performed Buenos Aires, 1982.
Concerto de outono (oboe, orchestra) 1983; first performed Lisbon, 1983.
Viagem da natural invenção 1991; first performed Ghent, 1991.

Chamber/instrumental:

Cinco pequeñas peças (piano) 1959; first performed Lisbon, 1959.
Do espressioni (trumpet, harpsichord) 1959; first performed Lisbon, 1959.
Evocação (flute, oboe, clarinet, harp, vibraphone, xylophone) 1960; first performed Lisbon, 1970s.
Episódios (string quartet) 1960; first performed Lisbon, 1970s.
Sucessões simétricas I (piano) 1961; first performed Bayreuth, 1961.
Imagens sonoras (2 harps) 1961; first performed Lisbon, 1962.
Collage (2 pianos) 1962.
Domíno (G flute, percussion) 1963–4; first performed Darmstadt, 1964.
Sequência (G flute, celeste, percussion) 1963–4.
Morfocromia (12 instruments/3 groups) 1963–8; first performed Lisbon, 1978.
Sequência (alto flute, celeste, percussion) 1964.
Situações 66 (flute, clarinet, trumpet, harp, viola) 1966; first performed Sintra, 1970.
Recitativo III (flute, harp, percussion) 1966–9; first performed Lisbon, 1969.
Recitativo V (octet) 1966–74.
Harmõnicos (1 or more pianos, tape recorders) 1967; first performed Funchal, 1967.
As quatro estações (trumpet, harp, piano, cello) 1968–72; first performed Lisbon, 1972.
Estúdio I: Mémoire d'une présence absente (piano) 1969; first performed Madrid, 1969.
C D E (clarinet, violin, cello, piano) 1970.
Estúdio II (piano) 1970–2.
A idade do ouro (2 clarinets, 2 violins, organ, piano, harp, harpsichord) 1970–3.
Recitativo I (harp) 1971; first performed Isle of Man, 1971.
Recit (cello) 1971.
Quatro pecas para setembro vermelho (ensemble) 1972.
Ma Fin est mon commencement: Homage to Machaut (trombone, viol, viola, harp, recorders, piano, celeste) 1972; first performed Royan, 1972.
Welkom (violin, viola) 1972; first performed Funchal, 1972.
Morrer em Santiago (6 percussion) 1973; first performed Lisbon, 1973.
Recitativo IV (8 instruments) 1974; first performed Badasoz, 1974.
". . . e isto é só o início, hein?" (ensemble) 1975.
A aurora do socialismo: madrigale capriccioso (flute, horn, violin, piano, percussion, short wave receiver) 1975; first performed Lisbon, 1975.
Study III in B♭ major (piano) 1976; first performed Montiso, 1976.
Canto da sibila (clarinet, piano, percussion, lights, smells) 1976; first performed Madrid, 1976.
Solo (double bass) 1976; first performed London, 1976.
Elegia (trombone, viola, piano, percussion) 1976; first performed Lisbon, 1976.
Madrigal II (clarinet quintet) 1977; first performed Madrid, 1977.
Música en água e mármore (7 instruments) 1977; first performed Lisbon, 1977.
Lov II (cello, flute, piano, percussion) 1978; first performed Lisbon, 1978.
Faites vos jeux (flute, cello, harp, piano) 1979–81; original version first performed Amsterdam, 1979.
Mémoires . . . miroirs . . . (amplified clavichord, 12 strings) 1980; first performed Lisbon, 1980.

instrumentally partitioned in a similar manner to the prime form. The four forms of the prime row, P-I-PR-IR, form the first large phrase unit. The pattern is repeated six times

Warsaw Workshop Waltz (clarinet, trombone, cello, piano) 1980; first performed Warsaw, 1980.
Ciclo-Valsa (variable instrumental ensemble, percussion, velophonem, music boxes, voices ad lib) 1980–5; original version first performed Lisbon, 1980.
Novo canto da sibila (clarinet, piano, percussion) 1981.
L'oiseau-lyre (guitar) 1982; first performed Lisbon, 1982.
Sax-Blue (alto saxophone/sopranino saxophone, electro-acoustics) 1982–5; original version first performed Lisbon, 1982.
Serenata per A (flutes, guitar, piano, percussion) 1983; first performed Acqui Terme, Italy, 1983.
O jardim de Belisa (7 instruments) 1984; first performed Nice, 1984.
Red Sweet Tango (piano) 1984.
Metaformoses (bass clarinet, 7 instruments) 1984; first performed Amsterdam, 1985.
The Missing Miss (violin) 1985; first performed Lisbon, 1988.
Remake (flute, cello, harp, piano) 1985; first performed Torres Vedras, 1985.
Ougam a soma dos sons que soam (9 instruments) 1986; first performed Milan, 1986.
Villalbarosa (piano) 1987; first performed São Paulo, 1987.
O quadrado azul (oboe, viola, double bass, piano) 1987; first performed Cascals, 1983.
Aquela tarde (piano) 1988; first performed Almada, 1988.
Passage intérieur (saxophone, electric instruments) 1989; first performed Paris, 1989.
Alis (15 instruments) 1990; first performed Toronto, 1990.
Glosa I (piano) 1990; first performed Oporto, 1990.
Glosa II (flute) 1990.
Glosa III (violin) 1990.
Glosa IV (cello) 1990.
Fantasia-impromptu (alto saxophone, piano) 1990; first performed Marseilles, 1990.
Mediterrãnea (7 or 8 instruments) 1991; first performed Alicante, 1991.

Vocal/choral:

Fascinação (soprano, flute, clarinet) 1959; first performed Sintra, 1970.
Alba (soprano, mezzo-soprano, female chorus, 11 instruments) 1959.
Triptico (solo voices, instrumental ensembles) 1959–60; first performed Lisbon, 1977.
A cabeça do grifo (soprano, mandolin, piano) 1960; first performed Lisbon, 1987.
Estrela (soprano or baritone, piano) 1962.
Coração habitado (mezzo-soprano, flute, cello, piano) 1965.
Euridice reamada (solo voices, chorus, orchestra) 1968.
Voix (mezzo-soprano, chamber orchestra) 1972; first performed Lisbon, 1973.
A lira destemperada (soprano, trombone, percussion) 1973.
Madrigal (unaccompanied chorus) 1975; first performed Lisbon, 1979.
A cabeça do grifo (version for soprano, viola, harp, piano) 1980; first performed Madrid, 1980.
Leves veus celam (soprano, flute, viola, harp, marimba) 1980; first performed Madrid, 1980.
Canto para Anna Lívia (3 female voices, 11 instruments) 1981; first performed Estoril, 1981.
A flor das águas verdes (15 voices) 1982; first performed Matosinhos, 1988.
Ulivi aspri e forti (mezzo-soprano, piano; also version for mezzo-soprano, flute, clarinet, trumpet, harp, guitar, viola, cello) 1982, 1984; first performed Lisbon, 1987; ensemble version first performed Sao Paulo, 1984.
Greetings (mezzo-soprano, flute, bassoon, cello, percussion) 1985; first performed Rio de Janeiro, 1985.
Llanto por Mariana (soprano, flute, clarinet, piano, string quartet) 1986; first performed Cagliari, Sardinia, 1986.
Credo (tenor, alto saxophone, piano, double bass, percussion) 1988; first performed Lisbon, 1988.
A capela de Janas (soprano, instrumental ensemble) 1989; first performed Lisbon, 1989.
Memoria de Marília (soprano, baritone, oboe, clarinet, 2 guitars, violin, cello) 1990; first performed Belo Horizonte, 1991.
Cantos de Sophia (unaccompanied mixed chorus) 1990.

Other:

O gebo a sombra (theatre music) 1966.
Recitativo II (music theatre for soprano, mezzo-soprano, harp, percussion) 1966–70.
As quatro estações (theatre music) 1968.
A pousada das chagas (film music) 1970.
Shakespeare's Sonnets (ballet) 1970.
Elegia a Amílcar Cabral (electronic) 1973.
Luis Vaz 73 (electronic) 1973–4.
Con-sequencia (collaboration with Grupo de Música Contemporanea) 1974.
Mariana Pineda (theatre music) 1975.
O Prisoneiro (film music) 1978.
Elecronicolirica (electronic) 1979.
Canto germinal (electronic) 1989.

Publications

By Peixinho: "Memorie e reversibilita", in *La musica, le idee, le cose*, Centro Musicale, Florence, 1981; articles in *Arte Musical*, *Gazeta Musical*, *Jornal de Letras e Artes*, *Diario de Lisboa*, *Seara Nova*.

On Peixinho: Mario Vieira de Carvalho, "JP e o pioneirismo da nova musica", in *Estes Sons, Estes Linguagem*, Estampa, 1978; Paulo Cameiro, "*Memoires . . . Miroirs* . . . de JP", Universidade Nova de Lisboa, 1991.

Jorge Peixinho comments:

The aim of my music is the construction and organisation of a new and personal sound world. I have sought to explore deeply and intensively all the relationships between harmony and timbre in order to build a kind of very dense network of fine sound transformations. The main characteric of my music is a kind of "oneiric sound atmosphere" in which small transformations are made via counterpuntal devices, harmonic and timbral filtering, etc. I also give great importance to the ambiguity between continuity and discontinuity.

* * *

Though one cannot discuss Jorge Peixinho's sound-world without some reference to serialism, except for *Imagense sonoras*, *Collage* and *Kinetofonias*, three strictly serial works from the 1960s, he does not base his compositional method on actual series. Around 1960 his musical language corresponded to a development from "integral" to "virtual" serialism (that is, serial composition without strict series). In the 1960s and 1970s Peixinho combined this comprehensive technical attitude with experimentation in a number of directions: improvisation, aleatoric and open forms, use of prerecorded tape, instrumental theatre, influence of extra-musical or "natural" effects on the shaping of sound, combinations of modern and period instruments, quotation as a structural principle, electro-acoustic music, mixed media, theatre and film music.

Since the late 1970s and during the 1980s Peixinho's musical language has shown a greater concern for harmonic relations in the sense of amalgamations of horizontal and vertical dimensions. There is a transition from undifferentiated intervallic patterns to pure harmony. Descending chromatic passages create planes which become functional elements. At the same time sound colour gains in structural relevance. *Mémoires . . . miroirs . . .* and *Retrato de Helena* are the turning points in this development, representing an accumulation and consolidation of previous innovations.

This process of looking back introspectively is behind *Sine nomine*, a huge work in progress on which Peixinho has been engaged without a break since 1987. The piece is based on vocal or instrumental fragments from previous works, placed in chronological order and transformed according to a logic of mediation. Stylistic changes within the course of his career are isolated, developed and connected up, thereby gradually creating works for independent solo instruments or solo voices. At the same time, he allows each instrument to gloss the material played by others, to read it in a different context. Thus a network of varied relations is developed; when the piano is involved as in Part I then, needless to say, several areas can be glossed at once, including the original material. Dynamics acquire a structural function as never before. Work for solo instruments becomes part of a more extensive work of highly versatile formation by including new instruments or voices which react to the original materials. The intention is to extend the project to all orchestral instruments, including larger formations of similar instruments; electro-acoustic transmission will extend the possible combinations and versions enormously. Between 1987 and the present time, four glosses have been completed, for piano, flute, violin and cello.

Fernando Lopes-Graça suggested in 1961 that Peixinho's expectation of a development and strengthening of Portuguese music as "ethnic cultural reality" was not fulfilled and insisted that "actuality" be applied to the "historical discontinuity" of Portuguese music. Peixinho acknowledged Lopes-Graça as a polemicist and thinker and came to see that the change of style in Lopes-Graça's musical language, especially since 1961, afforded both men an *a posteriori* respect of a certain cultural continuity; this was evident in a mutual respect for the *musicus poeticus*, the professionally and intellectually competent composer with a far-sighted and not estranged conception of cultural creation expressed in political engagement. This is reflected in some of Peixinho's titles as well as in his collaborations with members of the Portuguese avant-garde in the realms of art, poetry, theatre and film. Since the foundation of the Grupo de Musica Contemporanea de Lisboa in 1970, he has increasingly concentrated on chamber music, as both composer and interpreter and has managed to stand apart from and opposed to the conservatism of the musical establishment.

Nearly all of Peixinho's works up to the present time have remained unpublished; some of his most important pieces have still not received premieres and some of his demanding orchestral scores have only been performed without thorough and sympathetic rehearsal. Even after the April Revolution of 1974, he has been denied the sponsorship and critical support his international standing clearly demands. For his 50th birthday, in 1990, though, musicology students at the Universidade Nova de Lisboa organised an exhibition and concert series in his honour.

—Mário Vieira de Carvalho

PELETSIS, Georgy. Latvian. Born in Rīga, 18 June 1947. Educated at Emīls Dārziņš Special Music School, Rīga, graduated 1965; P. Tchaikovsky Conservatoire, Moscow, graduated 1970, post graduate research studentship, until 1977, candidate in history of art, 1981, doctorate in history of art, 1990. Married Marina Pudovska Peletsis in 1967; 2 children. Instructor, 1970–80, reader, 1980–90, and professor since 1990, Jāzeps Vītols Latvian Academy of Music, Rīga; member, Composers' Union of the U.S.S.R., since 1981. Mailing address: 226002 10–2 Templa iela, Riga 2, Latvia.

Publisher: none.

Symphonies/orchestral:

Concerto for Balalaika, Saxophone and Symphony Orchestra 1970.
Concerto for Wind Orchestra 1971.
Grotesque March 1972; first performed Riga, 1972.
New Year Music 1979; first performed Riga, 1979.
Overture: Ave Sol 1983; first performed Riga, 1983.
Festive Overture 1983; first performed Riga, 1983.
Overture: Meeting the Holiday 1987.
Concertino bianco in C (piano, chamber orchestra) 1990.

Chamber/instrumental:

Scherzo-toccata (piano) 1964; first performed Riga, 1970.
Theme and Variations (piano) 1965.
New Year Music (piano) 1977; first performed Riga, 1978.
Suite No 1 (piano) 1980; first performed Riga, 1980.
Quartet: Music from Behind the Wall (violin, viola, cello, bassoon) 1984; first performed Riga, 1984.
Suite No 2 (piano) 1984; first performed Riga, 1984.
Suite No 3 (piano) 1985; first performed Riga, 1985.
Suite No 4 (piano) 1986; first performed Riga, 1986.
String Quartet (Lamento) 1986; first performed Riga, 1986.
Quintet (flute, violin, viola, cello, bassoon) 1987; first performed Riga, 1990.
Sonata (piano) 1988; first performed Riga, 1990.

Vocal/choral:

All the Family Is Singing (25 songs or choruses; various poets) 1963–86.
Squeak of my Cradle (7 poems for unaccompanied mixed chorus; Trjapkin) 1967.
Footprints (oratorio for tenor, mezzo-soprano, mixed chorus, orchestra; Aristov) 1969.
Two Songs (unaccompanied mixed chorus; Smagars) 1983.
On the Boat of Memories (vocal cycle for tenor, piano; Smagars) 1983.
The Poet's Spring Strings (vocal cycle for baritone, piano; Mirsky) 1986.

The Wit Is Longing for Simplicity (cycle for unaccompanied mixed chorus; Sirmbārdis) 1987.
Two Songs (unaccompanied mixed chorus; Saulietis) 1988.
Impressions of Summer (cantata for mixed chorus, orchestra; Austrins) 1988.

Georgy Peletsis comments:

Music is written for one of two main reasons: either to make some intellectual address to the listener, or for the sake of music itself. I feel closer to the second. All my creative inspiration comes from music, the notion of euphony as an embodiment or reflection of the ideal. Aspiration to that ideal is the most important theme of my work.

My musical language is undoubtedly influenced by what I have learned and enjoyed of past musical culture, those expressions of melody, rhythm, harmony which follow a line from the *ars nova* of the 14th century, through the music of 17th-century Italy, Germany, England and France, up to the music of our own time. Folklore also contributes to that fund of understanding.

There is nothing stylized—or even polystylistic—about my music. I have no clear sense of "old" or "contemporary". For me, all great and irresistible music is simply the gleam of the ideal and represents the psychological drama of a mind confronting the unattainability of that ideal. To that extent, and though the inner circumstances are very different, I feel common cause with the Beethoven of the last sonatas.

The word "ideal" may even be too high-flown. It might be simpler to speak of the feelings of joy and delight which can be given by music. I gave the title *All the Family Is Singing* to my collection of songs, in order to give a sense of the joy of shared music-making.

I have no desire to stylize older musics, but simply to give life to music as a principle of euphony and to maintain it as long as possible. In that, I am "contemporary". In any case, the most attractive aspects of older music are usually the most transient, and the best themes in classical music are exhibited only briefly.

My favourite contemporary composer is Arvo Pärt. I also feel a kinship with minimalism and the repetitive style, particularly in the music of Steve Reich. However, such a superficial conception of musical beauty confuses me, and I'm disturbed by the pagan spell-weaving, and narcotic–schizophrenic persistence of musical material which are characteristic of minimalist works.

But I value the extension of musical time and beauty and would love to offer whole concert programmes of works. This is not jealousy or fear of competition. It is simply important to recognize that at a concert, a listener's feelings, far from being confronted by an indivisible aesthetics or united intention, are conditioned from moment to moment by a different creator's point of view. During the concert, the voices of different works and thus different composers mustn't be allowed to crowd out or smother one another.

I hope one day to extend the number of my piano suites to six and to perform them all at one concert. There is also a project for six wind concertos. But revealing long-term plans is a risky (for me) and uninteresting (for you) business. Finished works are quite a different matter . . .

* * *

It is slightly ironic that while composers from the Baltic Republics lag a little way behind those from Armenia and Georgia in terms of international recognition, one of their number, the Estonian Arvo Pärt, should have attained greater fame in the West than almost any other composer from the Soviet Union, except perhaps Alfred Schnittke.

Set Pärt and Schnittke at some distance from one another, and the ground between becomes Georgy Peletsis's identifiable field of operation. Resistant to Schnittke's "polystylistics", Peletsis is nonetheless extremely conscious of the huge available vocabulary of modern and past musics. Unlike Pärt, he appears to regard music-making not as a means to transcendence, but as an act of transcendence in itself, that never loses contact with everyday realities and solidarities. There is a clearly discernible folkloric element in his melodic thinking, and a constant reference back to older, more organic contexts of music making. Peletsis named his album of songs and choruses *All the Family Is Singing* and has expressed an interest in whole-evening programmes of music that will run counter to the fragmentary eclecticism of modern and contemporary concert-programming.

In this regard and in some others, he draws part of his inspiration from the minimalist—or "repetitive" or "process" or "trance"—composers who emerged in the United States in the 1960s and 1970s. As the competing labels suggest, Steve Reich, Philip Glass, Terry Riley and LaMonte Young by no means represented a single, self-consistent musical aesthetic. While their music shares attributes, its emphases are quite different. Peletsis is clearly drawn to the idea of Riley's whole-evening multi-media events without in any way sharing their underlying rationale. He is clearly repelled by the occasional crudities of minimalist music, and its potentially totalitarian implications. He is perhaps closest to the deceptively simple modulations and soaring drama of Steve Reich.

His own music, heard out of context, is remarkably difficult to locate or categorise. Its diatonic folkloristic components are lent considerable tension by ever-wider and more complex harmonic contexts. Though Peletsis is not an adventurous scorer (the Concerto for saxophone and balalaika is far his most *outré* instrumentation), he has a superb grasp of instrumental colour and of dynamics. The cycle of piano suites, which are perhaps his most important single work, have an internal consistency that is reminiscent of some minimalist writing (and even of such younger contemporaries within the Soviet Union as Aleksandr Gugel), but a sweep and dramatic inclusiveness that is redolent of Haydn or even Beethoven. The 1986 *String Quartet* (*Lamento*) certainly recalls Haydn's *Seven Last Words* and has the same balance of unmodulated simplicity and tremendous emotional depth.

Peletsis's orchestral writing is still unfortunately too little known outside his native Latvia, but the *Overture: Ave Sol* and the equally affirmative *New Year Music* deserve wider dissemination. There are, as yet, no symphonies, but Peletsis's handling of the very largest orchestras has a sureness that may yet compensate for his apparent reticence in the field of large-scale symphonic argument. It may be that the continuing struggle for freedom in the Baltic Republics will provide a subject matter commensurate with his technical skill. For the present, Peletsis continues to write music of considerable beauty and some emotional urgency. However, even pieces like *Quartet: Music from Behind the Wall* refuse to yield up any simple one-to-one programmatic purpose; nor do they blandly universalise. It is his rootedness that is most impressive. Peletsis writes in a highly personal idiom that is nonetheless not expressionist or merely idiosyncratic. Its personality comes from his recognition that he stands at a particular intersection in musical and cultural history. Without being conventionally representational, it is iconic, replete with irreducible significations.

—Ivan Karp

PENDERECKI, Krzysztof. Polish. Born in Debica, Cracow district, 23 November 1933. Educated: studied composition privately under F. Skołyszewski; Jagellonian University, Cracow (humanities), 1950; State Higher Music School, Cracow (composition under Artur Malawski and Stanisław Wiechowicz), 1955–8. Married Elzbieta Solecka in 1965; 1 son and 1 daughter. Teacher of music, State Higher Music School, Cracow, 1958–66; professor of composition, Folkwang Hochschule für Musik, Essen, 1966–8; music adviser, Vienna Radio, 1970–1; rector, professor docent, State Higher Music School, Crakow, from 1972; visiting teacher, Yale University, New Haven, Connecticut, 1973–8. Honorary member, Royal Academy of Music, London, 1974; corresponding member, Arts Academy of German Democratic Republic, Berlin, 1975; extraordinary member, Arts Academy of West Berlin, 1975; member, Royal Academy of Music, Stockholm, 1975; honorary member, Accademia di Santa Cecilia, Italy, 1976; corresponding member, Academia Nacional de Bellas Artes, Buenos Aires, 1982. Recipient: 1st, 2nd and 3rd prizes (for *Strophes*, *Emanations* and *From the Psalms of David*), 2nd Competition of Young Polish Composers, Polish Composers' Association, 1959; Fitelberg Prize (for *Threnos*), 1960; UNESCO Award (for *Threnos*), 1961; 1st prize (for *Canon*), Cracow Composition Competition, 1962; Grosser Kunstpreis von Nordrhein-Westphalen (for *St Luke Passion*), 1966; Pax Prize, Poland, 1966; Alfred Jurzykowski Foundation Award, Polish Institute of Arts and Sciences, 1966; Prix Italia, and Sibelius Gold Medal (for *St Luke Passion*), 1967; award of Polish Composers' Association, 1970; Gustav Charpentier Prize, 1971; Gottfried von Herder Preis, and Prix Arthur Honegger (for *Magnificat*), 1977; Grand Medal of Paris, 1982; Sibelius Prize, Wihouri Foundation, Finland, 1983; Order of Banner of Labour (1st Class), 1983; Premio Lorenzo Magnifico, Italy, 1985. Honorary doctorates: University of Rochester, New York, 1972; St Olaf College, Northfield, Minnesota, 1977; Katholieke University, Leuven, 1977; University of Bordeaux, 1979; Georgetown University, Washington, D.C., 1984; University of Belgrade, 1985; University of Madrid, 1986. Mailing addresses: Panstwowa Wyzsza Szkola Muzyczna, ul. Bohaterow Stalingradu 3, 31–038 Cracow; ul. Cisowa 22, 30229 Cracow, Poland; 324 Livingston Street, New Haven, Connecticut 06511, U.S.A.

Publishers: Moeck; Polskie Wydawnictwo Muzyczne; Schott.

Symphonies/orchestral:

Epitafium Artur Malawski (strings, timpani) 1958.
Emanacje/Emanations (2 string orchestras) 1958; first performed Cracow, 1961.
Anaklasis (strings, percussion) 1959–60; first performed Baden-Baden, 16 October 1960.
Tren ofiarom Hirosizmy/Threnody for the Victims of Hiroshima (52 strings) 1960; broadcast Warsaw Radio, 31 May 1961. Recorded HMV CDC7 493162.
Fluorescenje/Flourescence 1961; first performed Baden-Baden, 21 October 1962.
Fonogrammes (flute, chamber orchestra) 1961; first performed Cracow, 1961.
Polymorphia (48 strings) 1961; first performed Hamburg, 16 April 1962.
Kanon (52 strings, 2 tapes) 1962; first performed Warsaw, 20 September 1962.
Sonata (cello, orchestra) 1964; first performed Donaueschingen, 15 October 1964.
De natura sonoris I 1966; first performed Royan, 7 April 1966. Recorded HMV CDC 7 49316 2.
Capriccio No 2 (violin, orchestra) 1967; first performed Donaueschingen, 22 October 1967.
Concerto for Violino Grande and Orchestra (5-stringed instrument) 1967, revised 1968; first performed Ostersund, Sweden, 1 July 1967; revised version first performed Hanover, New Hampshire, 4 August 1968.
Uwertura pittsburska/Pittsburgh Overture (woodwinds, timpani) 1967.
De natura sonoris II 1971; first performed New York City, 3 December 1971.
Partita (harpsichord, electric guitar, bass guitar, harp, double bass, chamber orchestra) 1971; first performed Rochester, New York, 11 February 1972.
Praeludium (woodwinds, double basses, percussion) 1971; first performed Amsterdam, 4 July 1971.
Cello Concerto 1972; first performed Baltimore, Maryland, 8 March 1972.
Symphony No 1 1973; first performed Peterborough, Northamptonshire, 19 July 1973.
Intermezzo (24 strings) 1973; first performed Zurich, 30 November 1973.
Als Jacob erwachte/The Dream of Jacob 1974; first performed Monte Carlo, 14 August 1974. Recorded HMV CDC7 49316 2.
Violin Concerto 1976–7; first performed Basle, 27 April 1977. Recorded Polski Nagrania PNCD 019.
Adagietto (from *Paradise Lost*) 1979; first performed Osaka, 8 April 1979. Recorded Polski Nagrania PNCD 020.
Symphony No 2: Christmas Symphony 1980; first performed New York City, 1 May 1980. Recorded Polski Nagrania PNCD 019.
Cello Concerto No 2 1981–2; first performed Berlin, 11 January 1983. Recorded Polski Nagrania PNCD 020.
Viola Concerto 1982–3; first performed Caracas, 24 July 1983. Recorded Polski Nagrania PNCD 020.
Passacaglia 1988.

Chamber/instrumental:

Three Miniatures (violin, piano) 1959.
String Quartet No 1 1960; first performed Cincinnati, Ohio, 11 May 1962.
Mensura sortis (2 pianos) 1963.
Capriccio No 1 (oboe, 11 strings) 1964; first performed Lucerne, 1965.
String Quartet No 2 1968; first performed Berlin, 30 September 1970. Recorded Olympia OCD 328.
Capriccio per Siegfried Palm (cello) 1968; first performed Bremen, 4 May 1968.
Actions (14 jazz instruments) 1971; first performed Donaueschingen, 17 October 1971.
Capriccio (tuba) 1980; first performed Cracow, June 1980.
Cadenza (viola) 1984; first performed Cracow, 9 September 1984.
Per Slava (cello) 1985–6.

Vocal/choral:

Psalmy Dawida (chorus, percussion; Kochanowski) 1958; first performed Cracow, 26 June 1962.
Strofy/Strophes (soprano, reciter, 10 instruments) 1959; first performed Warsaw, 17 September 1959.
Wymiary czasu i ciszy/Dimensions of Time and Silence (40 voices, instruments) 1960; first performed Warsaw, 18 September 1960.

Stabat mater (3 choruses) 1962.

Passio et mors domini nostri Jesu Christi secundum Lucam / St Luke Passion (soloists, narrator, boys' chorus, mixed chorus, orchestra) 1963–5; first performed Munster, 30 March 1966. Recorded HMV CDC7 49313-2.

Kantata na 600-lecie Uniwersytetu Jagiellonskiego / Cantata in honorem almae matris Universitatis Jagellonicae (chorus, orchestra) 1964.

Piesn zalobna ku czci B. Rutkowskiego / Funeral Song for . . . (unaccompanied chorus) 1964.

Dies irae (soloists, chorus, orchestra) 1967; first performed Cracow, 14 April 1967, and at site of concentration camp Oswiecim-Brzezinka, 16 April 1967.

Utrenia: I—Zlozcnie do grobu / The Laying in the Tomb, II—Zmartwychwstanie / The Resurrection (soloists, chorus, orchestra) 1970; I first performed Altenberg, 8 April 1970; II first performed Munster, 28 May 1971.

Kosmogonia (soprano, tenor, bass, chorus, orchestra) 1970, revised 1971; first performed New York City, 24 October 1970; new version first performed Nuremberg, 22 October 1971.

Canticum Canticorum Salamonis quod hebraice dicitur "Sir hasirim" (chorus, chamber orchestra) 1972; first performed Lisbon, 5 June 1973. Recorded HMV CDC7 49316-2.

Ecloga VIII (6 male voices; Vergil) 1972; first performed Edinburgh, 21 August 1972.

Magnificat (bass, boys' chorus, orchestra) 1974; first performed Salzburg, 17 August 1974. Recorded HMV CDC7 49313-2.

Als Jakob erwachte (voices, orchestra, 12 ocarinas) 1974; first performed Monte Carlo, 14 August 1974.

De profundis (chorus, orchestra) 1977; first performed Graz, 16 October 1977.

Prologue, Visions and Finale (from the opera *Paradise Lost*; 6 soloists, large mixed chorus, orchestra) 1979; first performed Salzburg, 10 August 1979.

Te Deum (solo voices, chorus, orchestra) 1979; first performed Assisi, 27 September 1980.

Lacrimosa (soprano, mixed chorus, orchestra) 1980; first performed Gdansk, 16 December 1980.

Polnisches Requiem (4 soloists, mixed chorus, orchestra) 1980–4; first performed Stuttgart, 28 September 1984.

Agnus Dei (unaccompanied SSAATTBB chorus) 1981.

Opera:

Diably z Loudon / The Devils of Loudun (after Huxley/ Whiting) 1969; first performed Hamburg, 20 June 1969.

Raj utracony / Paradise Lost (C. Fry, after Milton) 1975–8; first performed Chicago, 29 November 1978. "Adagietto" recorded Polski Nagrania PNCD 020.

Die schwarze Maske / The Black Mask (after Hauptmann) 1984–6; first performed Salzburg, 15 August 1986.

Other:

Psalmus (tape) 1961.

Brygada smierci / Brigade of Death (tape) 1963.

Noctiphobie (ballet; based on *Polymorphie*) 1970; first performed Amsterdam, 1970.

PUBLICATIONS

On Penderecki: T. Zielinski, "Technika operowania instrumentami smyczkowymi w utworach KP" [String Techniques in KP's Works], in *Muzyka*, 13(1), 1968; K. Lisicki, *Szkice a KP*, Warsaw, 1973; L. Erhardt, *Spotkania z KP* [Meeting KP], Krakow, 1975; W. Schwinger, *KP: Begegnungen, Lebensdaten, Werkkommentaire*, Stuttgart, 1979.

* * *

Krzysztof Penderecki is the best-known of the modern generation of Polish composers, and arguably, along with Witold Lutosławski, 20 years his senior, the most widely heard outside of his native country. Penderecki's career as a composer blossomed just at the point where the politically imposed retreat from Western ideas and the crime of "formalism" had given way to a new, more liberal artistic climate following the October Revolt of 1956.

The subsequent encouragement of progressive trends fostered a hitherto repressed outbreak of avant-garde composition in Poland, and Penderecki quickly became a leading figure in the new movement, which included elder statesmen like Lutosławski and Grazyna Bacewicz, as well as the younger lions (besides Penderecki, Henryk Gorecki and Wojciech Kilar established international reputations).

Penderecki's entry onto the international stage was most spectacularly heralded by the success of his brittle, emotionally powerful *Tren ofiarom Hirosizmy / Threnody for the Victims of Hiroshima*, a deeply felt work for string orchestra which employed many of the new sonorities then emerging in the work of Stockhausen and Iannis Xenakis, but recast them both in terms of their formal musical application and the ferocity of their expression.

His characteristic use of clusters, massive glissandos, and new string and percussive effects, including non-instrumental devices like typewriters and pieces of wood, iron, glass, or paper, can be heard in other works of the period. *Polymorphia*, which refined the string vocabulary of the Threnody but lacked its raw passion, is a particularly noteworthy example.

As the decade developed, Penderecki grew increasingly interested in vocal music, often with a distinctly theatrical feel, like his celebrated *Passio et mors domini nostri Jesu Christi secundum Lucam / St Luke Passion*, with its distant echoes of Bach, or its sequel Utrenia, a more sombre, less pyrotechnic work. Large-scale choral writing on religious themes has remained a consistent part of his output, including the *Magnificat* and the *Te Deum*.

Those same preoccupations—the voice, theatre, religion—are equally clearly reflected in his operatic works, beginning with *Diably z Loudun / The Devils of Loudun* and *Raj utraconyi / Paradise Lost*, or the more recent *Die Schwarze Maske / The Black Mask*. His orchestral writing, in the meantime, has retreated from his uncompromising early 1960s manner into a more straightforward chromatic idiom, a shift which is well illustrated by his first two symphonies.

While the First Symphony looks back to the powerful expressionism of his 1960s writing, the Second Symphony reflects a more considered, and considerably more conventional, approach to the form. It is widely regarded as almost Brucknerian in both its scope and its relatively simple construction and musical language, at least in relation to 20th-century musical registers and Penderecki's own earlier work. It is a dark, brooding, taut, emotionally intense and rather inward-looking composition, but a distinctly late-Romantic one, and with no hint of parody or pastiche.

Orchestral works from the 1980s, like the *Viola Concerto* and the *Passacaglia* have characteristically drawn on elements from the full range of these styles. The *Passacaglia* is a tense, finely structured piece, building from a persistent ostinato figure in the strings through a series of interlinked, counterpointed variations (a regular feature of his work) for both soloists and ensemble. The piercing tonalities and searing tutti outbursts recall the early, more incisively avant-garde style of the 1960s, but there are also indications of the rather conventional tonalities and orchestration which have increasingly found their place in his work.

The *Viola Concerto* shares these features, together with a pointed use of irregular rhythms. It is not a concerto in the elaborate 19th-century sense, but a spare, carefully contrived one-movement work which takes its unity from a recurring lento tempo and a tonal centre based on D, with the dominant role in opening out the piece falling to the soloist rather than ensemble.

—Kenny Mathieson

PETRASSI, Goffredo. Italian. Born in Zagarolo, near Palestrina, 16 July 1904. Educated at Schola Contorum di S. Salvatore, Lauro, 1913–19; studied piano privately under Alessandro Bustini, from 1920; studied harmony privately under Vincenzo di Donato, from 1925; Conservatorio di S. Cecilia, Rome (composition under Alessandro Bustini, from 1928, diploma, 1932, (organ under Fernando Germani) diploma, 1933, further study in conducting under Bernardino Molinari, 1934–6. Married Rosetta Acerbi in 1961; 1 daughter. Teacher of harmony, counterpoint and choral composition, Accademia di S. Cecilia, Rome, 1934–6; adviser, music section, Ispettorato del Teatro [later Direzione Generale del Teatro], from 1935; secretary, union of music societies, Centro Lirico Italiano, from 1936; general director, La Fenice, Venice, 1937–40; professor of composition, Conservatorio di S. Cecilia, 1939–59; co-founder (with Guido Turchi and others), Musica Viva, 1944; visiting professor, Salzburg Mozarteum, 1951; composer in residence, Berkshire Music Centre, Tanglewood, Massachusetts, 1956; director, advanced composition course, Accademia di S. Cecilia, 1959–74; teacher of composition, Accademia Chigiana, Siena, 1966–7. Recipient: prizewinner (with *Partita*), competition of Sindacali Nazionale dei Musicisti, 1932; 1st prize (for *Partita*), Federation Internationale des Concerts competition, France, 1933. Mailing address: via Fernando di Savoia 3, 00196 Rome, Italy.

Publishers: Ricordi; Suvini Zerboni; Universal.

Symphonies/orchestral:

Preludio e fuga (string orchestra) 1929.
Divertimento 1930.
Concerto for Orchestra 1931.
Ouverture da concerto 1932, revised 1933; first performed Rome, June 1931.
Passacaglia 1932.
Partita 1932; first performed Rome, 2 April 1933.
Concerto for Orchestra No 1 1933–4; first performed Rome, 31 March 1935.
Piano Concerto 1936–9; first performed Rome, 10 December 1939.
Preludio, aria e finale (version for cello, chamber orchestra) 1939; subsequently destroyed.
La follia di Orlando (orchestral suite after the ballet) 1943.
Ritratto di Don Chisciotte (orchestral suite after the ballet) 1945.
Concerto for Orchestra No 2 1951; first performed Basle, 24 January 1952.
Concerto for Orchestra No 3: Recreation concertante 1952–3; first performed Aix-en-Provence, 23 July 1953.
Concerto for Orchestra No 4 (string orchestra) 1954; first performed Rome, 28 April 1956.
Concerto for Orchestra No 5 1955; first performed Boston, 2 December 1955.
Concerto for Orchestra No 6: Invenzione concertata (brass, strings, percussion) 1956–7; first performed London, 9 September 1957.
Saluto augurale 1958.
Flute Concerto 1960; first performed Hamburg, 7 March 1961.
Concerto for Orchestra No 7: Prologo e cinque invenzioni 1961–2, revised 1964; first performed Bologna, 16 March 1965.
Estri (chamber symphony for 15 players) 1966–7; first performed Hanover, New Hampshire, 2 August 1967.
Concerto for Orchestra No 8 1970–2; first performed Chicago, 28 September 1972.

Chamber/instrumental:

Partita (piano) 1926.
Sinfonia, siciliana e fuga (string quartet) 1929.
Siciliana e marcetta (piano—4 hands) 1930.
Sarabanda (flute, piano) 1930.
Introduzione e allegro (violin, piano or 11 instruments) 1933; first performed Rome, 24 February 1934.
Toccata (piano) 1933.
Preludio, aria e finale (cello, piano) 1933; first performed Rome, 20 February 1934.
Piccola invenzione (piano) 1941.
Divertimento scarlattiano (piano) 1942.
Fanfare (3 trumpets) 1944, revised 1976.
Invenzione (piano) 1944.
Invenzione (2 flutes) 1944.
Sonata da camera (harpsichord, 10 instruments) 1948.
Dialogo angelico (based on *Invenzione*; 2 flutes) 1948.
Petite Pièce (piano) 1950, revised 1976.
Cinque duetti (2 cellos) 1952.
Serenata (flute, harpsichord, percussion, viola, double bass) 1958.
String Quartet 1958.
String Trio 1959.
Suoni notturni (guitar) 1959; broadcast RAI, December 1960.
Seconda-serenata trio (harp, guitar, mandolin) 1962.
Musica di ottoni (4 horns, 4 trumpets, 3 trombones, tuba, timpani; material adapted as *Concerto for Orchestra No 7*) 1963.
Tre per sete (piccolo/flute/alto flute, oboe/cor anglais, clarinet/E♭ clarinet) 1964.
Brass Octet (4 trumpets, 4 trombones) 1968.
Souffle (piccolo/flute/alto flute) 1969.
Elogio per un'ombra (violin) 1971.
Nunc (guitar) 1971.
Ala (piccolo/flute, harpsichord) 1972; first performed Siena, 1 September 1973.
Quattro odi (string quartet) 1973–5.
Oh, les beaux jours! (piano; incorporates material from *Piccola invenzione* and *Divertimento scarlattiano*) 1976.
Alias (guitar, harpsichord) 1977.

Grand septuor (clarinet, trumpet, violin, cello, guitar, percussion) 1977–8.
Poems 1977–80.
Violasola 1978.
Romanezetta 1980.
Flou (ensemble) 1980.
Sestina d'autumno 1981–2.

Vocal / choral:

Salvezza (voice, piano) 1926.
Tre liriche antiche italiane (voice, piano) 1929.
Colori del tempo (voice, piano; Cardarelli) 1931; first performed Rome, 5 March 1933.
Tre cori (chorus, orchestra) 1932.
Vocalizzo per addormentare una bambina (voice, piano) 1934.
Benedizione (voice, piano; Genesis) 1934.
Psalm 9 (chorus, brass, percussion, 2 pianos, strings) 1934–6; first performed Turin, 18 December 1936.
Lamento d'Arianna (voice, piano; also version for voice, 11 instruments; Libero) 1936, 1938; first performed Venice, 8 September 1936.
Vocalizzo per addormentare una bambina (arranged for voice, 11 instruments) 1938.
Magnificat (soprano, chorus, orchestra) 1939–40; first performed Rome, 4 May 1941.
Coro di morti (male chorus, brass, 3 pianos, percussion, double basses; Leopardi) 1940–1; first performed Venice, 28 September 1941.
Due liriche di Saffo (voice, piano or 11 instruments; translated Quasimodo) 1941.
Tre liriche (voice, piano) 1944.
Miracolo (baritone, piano) 1944.
Quattro inni sacri (tenor, baritone, organ or orchestra) 1942, orchestrated 1950; orchestral version first performed Rome, 22 February 1950.
Noche oscura (chorus, orchestra; San Juan de la Cruz) 1950–1.
Nonsense (unaccompanied chorus; Lear, translated Izzo) 1952.
Gloria in excelsis Deo (soprano, flute, organ) 1952.
Propos d'Alain (baritone, 12 instruments; Chartrier) 1960.
Sesto non-senso (unaccompanied chorus; Lear, translated Izzo) 1964.
Motetti per la Passione (unaccompanied chorus) 1965.
Beatitudines: in memoriam Martin Luther King (bass-baritone, E♭ clarinet, trumpet, timpani, viola, double bass) 1969; first performed Fiuggi, 17 July 1969.
Orationes Christi (chorus, brass, violas, cellos) 1974–5.
Laudes creaturarum 1982.

Opera / dramatic:

Il cordovano (after Cervantes, translated Montale) 1944–8, revised 1958; first performed Milan, 12 May 1949; revised version first performed Milan, 15 May 1959.
Morte dell'aria (Scialoja) 1949–50; first performed Rome, 24 October 1950.

Other:

Canti della campagna romana (arranged, with Guido Nataletti, for voice and piano) 1927.
O sonni, sonni (arranged for voice, piano) 1934.
La follia di Orlando (ballet, with recitative; Ariosto) 1942–3; first performed Milan, 12 April 1947.
Ritratto di Don Chisciotte (ballet; Milloss) 1945; first performed Paris, 21 November 1947.

PUBLICATIONS

By Petrassi: "Perche i giovani musicisti non scrivono per il teatro", in *Scenario*, 4, 1935; "Il festival internazionale di musica", in *Scenario*, 5, 1936; *Taccuino di musica*, Rome, 1944; "Scuola di composizione", in *Il mondo*, 6, 1945; "Sulla musica religiosa", in *Il campo*, 1, 1946; "La mie avventure con la danza", in *Musica*, 1, 1946.

On Petrassi: G. M. Gatti, "Modern Italian Composers—1: GP", in *Monthly Musical Record*, 67, 1937; L. D'Amico, *GF*, Rome, 1942; Kenneth Gaburo, "GF: The Man and His Music", in *Musical Courier*, 76, 1956; J.S. Weissmann, *GF*, Milan, 1957; Roman Vlad, "La dodecafonia in Italia", in *Storia della dodecafonia*, Milan, 1958, "GFs Orchesterkonzerte", in *Melos*, 26, 1959; J.S. Weissmann, "P's Early Choral Music", in *Ricoriana*, 4(2), 1959, and "GF and His Music", in *Musical Review*, 22, 1961; G.M. Gatti, *L'opera di GF*, Turin, 1964; M. Bortolotto, "Intervista con GF", in *Spettatore musicale*, 1(2), 1966, and "Ps Stil 1960", in *Melos*, 33, 1966; J.C.G. Waterhouse, "The Emergence of Italian Music up to 1940", dissertation, University of Oxford, 1968; special GP issue, *Musica Moderna*, 5, 1969; C. Annibaldi, *GP: catologo delle opere e bibliografia*, Milan, 1971; A.E. Bonelli, "Serial Techniques in the Music of GP", dissertation, University of Rochester, New York, 1971; L. Magini, "L'opera di GP", dissertation, University of Florence, 1973; G. Zosi, *Ricerca e sintesi nell'opera di GP*, Rome, 1978.

* * *

Goffredo Petrassi was one of a generation of Italian composers who rejected such well-established and popular tendencies as the picturesque romanticism of Respighi. Indeed, his music touched on a considerable diversity of styles, sometimes fusing quite different idioms and compositional methods in unexpected ways, though with his own strong artistic personality always in control. His achievement is as great as that of Dallapiccola, his exact contemporary, yet despite his teaching (e.g., in the United States and Austria) and his wide travels as a conductor (e.g., Japan, Argentina) Petrassi's music has been little appreciated outside Italy.

He first made an impression with the orchestral *Partita*, which, though influenced by early Hindemith, late Alfredo Casella and, in the opening *gagliarda*, by jazz, still has a flinty incisiveness of its own, being severly diatonic yet also energetically dissonant, with vigorous contrapuntal lines and urgent rhythms. This manner also shapes works like the *Introduzione e allegro* for violin and 11 instruments but such direct extroversion was not true to Petrassi's real musical character, as his later work showed.

In fact, not all his immediately succeeding compositions made so positive an impression, but outstanding was the first of a series of concertos for orchestra, a form to which he returned later, and *Psalm 9*, his first major choral piece. These naturally had links with the *Partita* yet are less assertive. Any suggestion of jazz disappears, Hindemith's influence diminishes, while the effect of Stravinsky's example, particularly *Les Noces* and the *Symphony of Psalms*, is evident in *Psalm 9*. Here Petrassi also is affected by plainchant and Italian composers from Palestrina onwards. This choral polyphony is married to stringent tonal and rhythmic conflict in the orchestra in a way that is striking and very unusual. Hindemith's influence reasserted itself in the well-made *Piano Concerto*, but a less well-focussed score is the *Magnificat*. While parts of this are straightforwardly diatonic, others are nearly atonal and hint at considerably later developments in Petrassi's music.

Much better integrated is the *Coro di morti*, a setting of Leopardi and a sombre response to Italy's entry into World War II. It also marks a large advance on anything the composer had achieved previously, synthesising an exceptionally wide range of sources, from Renaissance polyphony to the most astringent Stravinskian neo-classicism, into something almost disconcertingly personal. The combination of grimly modal choral writing and highly chromatic, sometimes polytonal, sometimes freely atonal, instrumental parts may seem unlikely, but it parallels the fusing of ancient and modern compositional approaches in Dallapiccola, especially the *Canti di prigionia*, and certain earlier works by Gian Francesco Malipiero. Petrassi's rigorous formal control is the secret, yet *Coro di morti* is often hallucinatory in effect, and decades after its appearance it still seems the expression of an entirely modern sensibility.

It was some years, though, before the advances made here were consolidated, and the composer's wartime stage works to some degree compromised with his earlier achievements. The ballets *La follia di Orlando* and *Ritratto di Don Chisciotte* do not have the emotional power of *Coro di morti* and are again rather noticeably indebted to neo-classicism. Petrassi always rejected that label, however, and both these scores are sufficiently chromatic to subvert the "distancing" effect of neo-classical stylisation and even the security of tonal feeling itself. At the same time instrumental colour becomes more important, hinting at the structural role it will assume later. Similar comments apply to *Il cordovano*, an opera based on Cervantes, and to another opera, *Morte dell'aria*, although these look more positively towards *Noche oscura*.

This deeply moving cantata, a setting of St John of the Cross, marks the real break with Petrassi's early music. It is very chromatic, with only brief tonal references, the supple, oscillating lines and textures being the antithesis of hard-edged and diatonic neo-classical tendencies. Here is one style or idiom rather than a fusion of several, and the atmosphere of *Noche oscura* is truly remarkable, at times almost otherworldly, and the whole piece is most beautifully shaped. After this Petrassi returned to the concerto for orchestra, writing five during 1951–7, each with a distinct character of its own and following-up on *Noche oscura* by going far beyond tonality. Indeed, Concerto No 3 uses a motive from the cantata, as No 5 refers to *Coro di morti*. These works are by no means backward-looking, and though Concerto No 6 quotes from both *Coro di morti* and *Psalm 9* it also has very original orchestral writing and makes extensive use of serial technique. So, less intensively, does No 3, but this was never done with absolute strictness, and Petrassi's involvement with dodecaphony did not lead to his embracing the aesthetics of expressionism.

There were further advances to be made, however, and major scores of the 1960s showed that his music was becoming athematic. There were hints of this in the single-movement *String Quartet*, the form of which is elusive, the opening phrase being the origin, via inversions, retrogrades etc., of most of the piece. There was no more serialism, but instead a free atonality which made great demands on the composer's imagination. These were fully met in works like the *Serenata*, where the use of instrumental colour to articulate the form became central, a point underlined here by *col legno*, flutter-tonguing and an *outré* instrumentation of flute, double bass, percussion, viola and harpsichord. With such pieces as the *Flute Concerto*, whose orchestration advances on that of Concerto No 6, Petrassi began to link up with the post-Webern avant-garde. Certainly in works like *Propos d'Alain* a prominent feature is a drastic, sometimes violent, fragmentation of texture, outward continuity being provided by the vocal line.

The same kind of sombre feeling informs the highly concentrated Concerto No 7, another virtually avant-garde score. It is again completely athematic and has extremely original, often aggressive, orchestral writing, again with instrumental colour having a structural role. *Estri* marked another advance in this last respect, its five groups of three players each having their own particular set of tone colours. The *Brass Octet* likewise explores some of the instruments' fiercest, and most recondite, sounds, and such pieces are true aural kaleidoscopes. So in a different way is *Orationes Christi* for chorus, brass and lower strings, this taking further certain aspects of Concerto No 6, *Coro di morti* and even *Psalm 9*. Though he perhaps never surpassed *Noche oscura*, Petrassi provides the encouraging spectacle of a major artist whose later compositions are among his most creative.

—Max Harrison

PETRIĆ, Ivo. Slovene. Born in Ljubljana, 16 June 1931. Educated at Ljubljana Academy of Music (composition under Lucjan Skerjanc, conducting under Danilo Svara), 1950–8. Has two daughters. Founder and artistic director, Slavko Osterc Ensemble, 1962–82; editor in chief, Edicije Drustva Slovenskih Skladateljev, Association of Slovene Composers, since 1972; artistic director, Slovene Philharmonic, since 1979. Recipient: Preseren Foundation Prize, 1971; 1st prize (for *Sonata* for solo violin), Wieniawski International Competition, Poznan, Poland, 1976; 1st prize (for *Contacts*), Uwharie Contest, U.S.A., 1979; 1st prize (for *The Picture of Dorian Gray*), Oscar Espla International Composition Contest, Spain, 1984. Mailing address: Bilecanska 4, 61000 Ljubljana, Slovenia [Yugoslavia].

Publishers: Edicije DSS, Ljubljana; Peters, Leipzig; Breitkopf & Härtel, Wiesbaden.

Symphonies/orchestral:

Simfonija Goga 1954; first performed Ljubljana, 19 March 1956.
Concerto grosso (string orchestra) 1956; first performed Ljubljana, 27 June 1957.
Divertimento (winds, percussion) 1956.
Symphony No 2 1957; first performed Ljubljana, 20 April 1958.
Flute Concerto 1957; first performed Ljubljana, 4 January 1958.
Clarinet Concerto 1958; first performed Ljubljana, 15 May 1959.
Concerto for Harp and Strings 1959.
Koncertantna suita (bassoon, strings) 1959.
Symphony No 3 1960; first performed Ljubljana, 30 November 1961.
Koncertna uvertura / Concert Overture 1960.

Tre skladba / Three Compositions (horn, orchestra) 1960.
Koncertantna glasba / Musique concertante (woodwind quintet, kettledrums, strings) 1962; first performed Ljubljana, 1 March 1963.
Simfonicne mutacije / Symphonic Mutations 1964; first performed Osaka, 1 October 1964.
Epitaph (clarinet, horn, violin, cello, percussion, strings) 1966; first performed Ljubljana, 7 March 1966.
Integrali v barvi / Integrals in Colour (reflections on verse by Kosovel) 1968; first performed Ljubljana, 9 April 1969.
Intarsia (flute, clarinet, bassoon, chamber orchestra) 1968.
Burlesque pour les temps passés (trumpet, chamber orchestra) 1969; first performed Opatija, November 1970.
Musique concertante (piano, orchestra) 1971.
Dialogues concertantes (cello, orchestra) 1972.
Trois Images (violin, orchestra) 1973; first performed Ljubljana, 26 October 1973.
Nocturnes et jeux 1973; first performed Ljubljana, 20 May 1974.
Fresque symphonique 1973; first performed Ljubljana, 23 November 1973.
Episodes lyriques (oboe, chamber orchestra) 1974; first performed Ljubljana, 6 November 1975.
Gemini Concerto (violin, cello, orchestra) 1975.
Tako je godel Kurent / This Is the Way to Do the Kurent (viola, orchestra) 1976.
Toccata concertante (4 percussion, orchestra) 1978–9; first performed Ljubljana, 28 May 1980.
Groharjeve impresije / Grohar's Impressions 1981; first performed Opatija, 5 November 1982.
Picture of Dorian Gray 1983–4; first performed Alicante, 14 September 1986.
Hommage à Johannes 1984–5.
Concerto for Trumpet and Orchestra 1985–6; first performed Cottbus, East Germany, 12 October 1987.
Adagio 1986; first performed Berlin, February 1990.
Moods and Temperaments (sketches for orchestra) 1987.
After So Many Years 1987.
Dresdener Konzert 1988; first performed Dresden, 21 May 1988.

Chamber / instrumental:

Woodwind Quintet No 1 1953; first performed Ljubljana, 22 June 1954.
Sonata (bassoon, piano) 1954; first performed Ljubljana, 20 May 1954.
Prelude and Scherzino (harp) 1955.
Sonata (oboe, piano) 1955; first performed Ljubljana, 12 December 1956.
Sonata (flute, piano) 1955; first performed Ljubljana, 16 January 1956.
Variations on a Theme of Bartók (violin, piano) 1955.
String Quartet 1956.
Four Pieces (piano) 1956.
Little Suite (winds) 1956.
Sonata (clarinet, piano) 1957; first performed Ljubljana, 24 October 1957.
Woodwind Quintet No 2 1959; first performed Ljubljana, 24 February 1961.
Sonata (horn, piano) 1960; first performed Ljubljana, 25 January 1961.
Sonatina (trumpet, piano) 1961; first performed Ljubljana, 2 May 1962.
Trois Esquisses (flute, string quartet) 1961.
Six Pieces (flute, piano) 1961.
Three Contrasts (violin, piano) 1961; first performed Ljubljana, 1964.
Elégie sur le nom de Carlos Salzedo (harp) 1962; first performed Opatija, 20 October 1962.
Croquis sonores (harp, oboe, bass clarinet, piano, double bass, percussion) 1963; first performed Warsaw, 27 September 1963.
Sept Mouvements (oboe, clarinet, horn, trumpet, harp, violin, cello) 1963.
De profundis (tuba, tam-tam, bass drum) 1963.
Mozaiki (clarinet, trombone, harp, cello, 2 percussion) 1964; first performed Ljubljana, 20 November 1964.
Jeux à trois—jeux à quatre (flute, clarinet, cello, harp, percussion) 1965.
Nuances en couleurs (flute, bassoon, piano, harp, cello) 1966.
Petit concerto de chambre (oboe, cor anglais, bass clarinet, horn, harp, violin, viola, cello, double bass) 1966; first performed Ljubljana, 30 March 1973.
Lirismi (horn, piano) 1969.
Inlaid-Work (flute, clarinet, bassoon, chamber ensemble) 1969; first performed Opatija, 16 November 1969.
Quatuor 1969 (string quartet) 1969; first performed Zagreb, 15 January 1970.
Divertimento for Slavko Osterc (ensemble) 1970; first performed Opatija, 8 November 1970.
Gravures (woodwind trio) 1971.
Meditations (piano trio) 1971; first performed Ljubljana, 20 October 1971.
Gemini Music (cello, piano) 1971; first performed Ljubljana, 14 December 1971.
Les Paysages (piano) 1972; first performed Ljubljana, 20 February 1973.
Capriccio (cello, octet) 1973.
Summer Music (flute, piano) 1973; first performed Ljubljana, 11 December 1973.
Autumn Music (violin, piano) 1974; first performed Ljubljana, 29 October 1974.
Concert Improvisations (oboe, violin, viola, cello) 1974; first performed Deerfield Beach, Florida, 22 January 1975.
Woodwind Quintet No 3 1974; first performed Ljubljana, 4 March 1975.
Dialogi (2 violins) 1975; first performed Radenci, 3 October 1976.
Gemini Concertino (violin, horn, ensemble) 1975.
Cadenza (trombone) 1976; first performed Ljubljana, 26 October 1976.
Capriccio Wannenhorn (flute) 1976; first performed Ljubljana, 1976.
Sonata (violin) 1976; first performed Poznan, Poland, 20 November 1976.
Winter Music (clarinet, piano) 1977; first performed Ljubljana, 5 April 1977.
Trio Labacensis (string trio) 1977; first performed Zitomir, U.S.S.R., 17 November 1977.
Fanfares and Nocturnes (brass quintet) 1978; first performed Ljubljana, 29 May 1978.
Concert for percussion (5 players) 1978; first performed Radenci, 30 September 1978.
Nocturne d'été (violin, guitar) 1978; first performed Ljubljana, 24 April 1979.
Quatuor 1979 (string quartet) 1979; first performed Radenci, 3 October 1982.
Marcimfabialom (cimbalom) 1980; first performed Ljubljana, 22 July 1980.
Contacts Between Clarinet and Percussion 1980; first performed U.S.A., 27 July 1980.
Gemini Cimbalom (2 cimbaloms) 1980; first performed Budapest, 27 February 1981.

Winter Elegy (oboe, piano) 1984; first performed Ljubljana, 6 June 1984.
Leipziger Kammermusik (oboe/cor anglais, trombone, viola, piano, percussion) 1984; first performed 5 February 1985.
Quatuor 1985 (string quartet) 1985; first performed Ljubljana, 14 January 1986.
Rondeau (piano quartet) 1987; first performed Ljubljana, 16 December 1987.

Vocal/choral:

Histoire de Ferdinand (narrator, orchestra) 1959.
Je sais pour le printemps (cantata) 1961.
Pierrot de la mort (chamber cantata) 1962.
Aus den Sonetten an Orpheus (tenor, chamber orchestra; Rilke) 1965.
Games (voice, harp) 1966; first performed Opatija, 14 October 1966.
Tre satiru po Krilovu (chorus, horn, trumpet, trombone, piano, percussion) 1968.

Other:

Jeux II (tape) 1966.
Odisej 67 (dance) 1967.

PUBLICATIONS

On Petrić: A. Rijavec, "Problem forme v delih IP" [Problems of Form in IP's works], in *MZ*, 11, 1975.

Ivo Petrić comments:

Making music is deeply rooted in my way of life. I cannot imagine life without composing or without some other connection to the world of music. Pleasure begins with the first few notes of a new piece and ends with its final bar. That gives way to an unpleasant wait for the first performance, a sense of discomfort that increases during rehearsals and on the day of the premiere itself. Pleasure is restored if the performers play with understanding and with a touch of individuality. Such performances are very rare, and sometimes take many years to achieve.

Apart from orchestral works, which normally begin with some deep inner imperative from my intellectual and emotional nature, the best inspiration is always a commission from a soloist or a conductor.

* * *

Ivo Petrić is the leading Slovenian composer of his generation and, alongside the Croatian Milko Kelemen, the most important important composer in Yugoslavia's short history. His composition training at the Ljubljana Academy under Lucjan Skerjanc was basically conservative and constrained by the prevailing folkloristic style. However, Petrić also studied conducting and acquired a deep understanding of orchestration and instrumental values, which was to pay extraordinary dividends in the years ahead and help him resist the centripetal pull of the Yugoslavian music scene. Unlike Kelemen, though, who quickly became a devotee of the international avant-garde, Petrić has preferred to work with local materials, and has relied very greatly on a close association with the Slavko Osterc Ensemble, an imaginative and adventurous grouping with which he introduced a highly significant repertoire of modern pieces (and premiered new work of his own). Osterc is also the dedicatee of a fine 1970 Divertimento.

This piece represents the first point of rest in the most important single development of Petrić's style. Early pieces had been broadly neo-classical, marked by clean structural values and a superb melodic sense. Perhaps the strongest influence on works like the *Flute Concerto* and *Clarinet Concerto* of the late 1950s was Paul Hindemith, then in the last few years of his life, and a still living exemplar of the principle that work may be in any style, however unfashionable, so long as it is profoundly felt and technically well-executed.

With his association with the Slavko Osterc Ensemble, Petrić acquired a new understanding and outlet for more advanced performance techniques, and though his work remained broadly conservative, poised between its original neo-classicism and a new, freshly Romantic strain, it was increasingly marked by modernist inflections. These were in no way intended as ideological flourishes and were carefully integrated into compositions of remarkable textural consistency and smoothness. In the early 1960s Petrić became somewhat less of an orchestral composer, though his work in that direction continued and resulted in the superb *Simfonicne mutacije/Symphonic Mutatious* concentrating on work for chamber forces and solo instruments. The dearth of piano music would be surprising were it not for the success of his emphasis on melody instruments, notably horn and flute, though Petrić has also written some remarkable scores for harp, notably the Elegy to Carlos Salzedo, the great harpist who died in 1961. Perhaps his finest single piece of this period was *Croquis sonores*, a prize-winning sextet led by harp and built up on the contrasting tonalities of bass clarinet, horn and double bass. The diffidence of the title, "Sketches in Sound," belies the subtlety and imaginative integration of the piece, an observation that applies equally to the slightly later *Sept Mouvements*.

The early *Simfonija Goga* and its successors of the 1950s did not spark off a lasting interest in symphonic language. Petrić's later orchestral pieces, certainly until the work of the 1980s, gave every indication of being no more than amplified chamber works, with an intimacy and freshness of detail that sets them apart from the catch-all symphonic style that swept through the People's Republics. The relation between scale and conception is readily seen in the rather minimal structural contrast between the 1966 chamber piece *Nuances en couleurs* and the larger *Integrali v barvi/Integrals in Colour* written two years later. They share a very natural melodic urge, without contrivance or visible scaffolding, and both are beautifully and unpretentiously argued.

In more recent years, Petrić has shown some signs of returning to an interest in folkloric elements, though these are so carefully blended into the fabric of works like *Marcimfabialom* (one of a couple of works for cimbalom) or *Rondeau* as to be no more than subliminal. The major development since the early to mid-1970s has been a growing interest in conventional and atonal harmony.

Petrić's work as a whole reveals a finely balanced tension between widely divergent influences. Like Hindemith, he is almost impossible to categorise or to locate accurately in the geography of 20th-century music. An undoubted original, he has a convincingly personal voice and a preference for rhythm and melody that communicates well to audiences.

—Curd Frosak

PINKHAM, Daniel (Rogers) Jr. American. Born in Lynn, Massachusetts, 5 June 1923. Educated at Phillips Academy, Andover, Massachusetts (organ and theory under Karl Pfatteicher), 1937–40; Harvard University, Cambridge, Massachusetts (under Walter Piston, Archibald Davison, Aaron Copland and Tillmann Merritt), A.B., 1943, M.A., 1944; studied harpsichord under Putnam Aldrich, Claude-Jean Chiasson and Wanda Landowska; studied organ under E. Power Biggs; further composition study under Arthur Honegger and Samuel Barber, Berkshire Music Center, Tanglewood, Massachusetts; and Nadia Boulanger, Paris. Teacher of music, Boston Conservatory, from 1946; subsequently at Simmons College, Boston, and Harvard University; lecturer in composition, head of department of performance of early music, New England Conservatory of Music, Boston, from 1959; music director, King's Chapel, Boston. Recipient: Fulbright Fellowship, 1950; Ford Foundation Fellowship, 1962; past dean, Boston chapter, American Guild of Organists; member, American Academy of Arts and Sciences; honorary member, Phi Mu Alpha. Honorary degrees: Nebraska Wesleyan University, Litt.D., 1976; Adrian College, Mus.D., 1977; Westminster Choir College, Mus.D., 1979. Mailing address: 150 Chilton Street, Cambridge, Massachusetts 02138, U.S.A.

Publishers: Peters; Schirmer.

Symphonies/orchestral:

Violin Concerto 1956; first performed Falmouth, Massachusetts, 8 September 1956.
Symphony No 1 1961.
Catacoustical Measures 1962.
Symphony No 2 1963; first performed Lansing, Michigan, 23 November 1963.
Signs of the Zodiac (orchestra, optional narrator) 1965.
Violin Concerto No 2 1968.
Organ Concerto 1970.
Serenades (trumpet, winds) 1979.
Symphony No 3 1985.
Symphony No 4 1989.

Chamber/instrumental:

Piano Concertino 1950; first performed Cambridge, Massachusetts, 3 May 1950.
Cantilena and Capriccio (violin, harpsichord) 1956–7.
Partita (harpsichord) 1962.
Concertante No 1 (organ, celeste, 2 percussion) 1963.
Lessons (harpsichord) 1971.
Toccatas for the Vault of Heaven (organ, tape) 1972.
Proverbs (organ) 1974–5.
Blessings (organ) 1977.
Concertante No 2 (2 trumpets, 2 trombones, 2 percussion, organ) 1977–8.
Epiphanies (organ) 1978.
Masks (harpsichord, chamber ensemble) 1978.
Miracles (flute, organ) 1978.
Diversions (organ, harp) 1980.
Concertante No 3 (guitar, harpsichord, percussion, organ or strings) 1980.
Proverbs (organ) 1980.
Holland Waltzes (2 pianos) 1982.
Vigils (harp) 1982.
Brass Quintet 1983.
Psalms (organ, trumpet) 1983.
A Proclamation (organ) 1984.
Reeds (oboe) 1987.

Vocal/choral:

Wedding Cantata (mixed chorus, orchestra) 1956.
Easter Cantata (mixed chorus, orchestra) 1957.
Christmas Cantata (mixed chorus, orchestra) 1957; first performed Boston, 10 December 1957.
Requiem (mixed chorus, orchestra) 1963.
The Song of Jephtha's Daughter (soprano, piano) 1963.
Stabat mater (mixed chorus, orchestra) 1964.
Eight Poems of Gerard Manley Hopkins (baritone, viola) 1964.
St Mark Passion (soloists, chorus, orchestra) 1965.
Letters from St Paul (soprano or tenor, organ) 1965.
Jonah (mezzo-soprano, tenor, bass-baritone, chorus, orchestra) 1966.
Ascension Cantata (mixed chorus, wind, percussion) 1970.
To Troubled Friends (mixed chorus, orchestra; Wright) 1972.
Safe in Their Alabaster Chambers (mezzo-soprano, tape; Dickinson) 1972.
Daniel in the Lions' Den (mixed chorus, orchestra) 1973.
Fanfares (mixed chorus, orchestra) 1975.
Four Elegies (soloists, mixed chorus, orchestra; Herrick, Crashaw, Vaughan, Donne) 1975.
The Passion of Judas (mixed chorus, orchestra) 1976.
Charm Me Asleep (baritone or mezzo-soprano, guitar) 1977.
The Descent into Hell (mixed chorus, orchestra) 1979.
Hezekiah (mixed chorus, orchestra) 1979.
Transitions (mezzo-soprano, bassoon/piano) 1979.
When God Arose (mixed chorus, orchestra) 1979.
Manger Scenes (soprano, piano; Farber) 1980.
Before the Dust Returns (mixed chorus, orchestra) 1981.
The Death of the Witch of Endor (alto, harpsichord, percussion) 1981.
Music in the Manger (soprano, harpsichord or piano; Farber) 1981.
The Conversion of Saul (mixed chorus, orchestra) 1981.
The Wellesley Hills Psalm Book (medium voice, organ) 1983.
Lauds (2 voices, 2 horns, double bass, organ, percussion) 1984.
In Heaven Soaring Up (alto, tenor, mixed chorus, oboe, harp) 1985.
Create a Pure Heart in Me (SATB chorus, organ and piano) 1988.

Opera:

The Dreadful Dining Car (after Twain; mezzo-soprano, actors, soloists, chorus, small ensemble) 1982.

Other:

Arrangements of work by G.F. Handel, Henry Purcell, Franz Schubert, William Selby.

PUBLICATIONS

On Pinkham: M. Johnson, "The Choral Works of DP", dissertation, University of Iowa, Iowa City, 1966; M. L. Crozine, "The Organ Works of DP", dissertation, University of Rochester Eastman School, New York, 1979; L. Raver, "The Solo Organ Music of DP", in *American Organist*, 17(6), 1983; M.E. Stallings, "Representative Works for Mixed Chorus by DP, 1968–83", dissertation, University of Miami, Florida, 1984.

For all his remarkable promise, Daniel Pinkham matured relatively slowly as a composer. His juvenalia give little indication of the remarkable work that was to follow. Having undertaken the *de rigueur* course of study with Nadia Boulanger in Paris, he began to develop in the 1950s a style that easily balances contemporary techniques with earlier musics. He has been a considerable presence as a concert harpsichordist on the early music scene in the United States, and in partnership with the violinist Robert Brink gave several influential performance series of what was then little-known or undervalued repertoire. His interest in Handel and Purcell is evident in his concertante works; as an expert on the performance of early music Pinkham pays considerable attention to the *articulation*, not just structure, of his pieces. They are demanding, but not in the slackly uninflected way which Boulanger disliked so much and which is a mark of much contemporary music. The composer's requirements are always specified and always logically coherent.

He began in an uninventive neo-classical idiom dependent on Boulanger's Stravinskian benchmark, but gradually came to appreciate the potentialities of dodecaphony, constructing melodies which are increasingly chromatic as time passes, but which never entirely leave the bounds of legitimate harmony. The first two symphonies are unquestionably his most conservative works, but they benefit from Pinkham's vigorous polyphonic developments and clearly stated arguments. Nowhere is this seen in sharper relief than in *Catacoustical Measures*, a set of chords commissioned to assess the acoustics in the new Philharmonic Hall at Lincoln Center in 1962.

The same qualities are evident in the capacious *Organ Concerto*, a genre in which it is notoriously difficult to balance solo and orchestral scoring. Pinkham's ability to write very fine, clearly etched organ lines at relatively modest volumes and with a carefully judged use of the more extravagant stops is one of his great stock-in-trade. It is a style which draws on the widest possible range of organ music, from Buxtehude to Vierne and Widor, and with hints of Messiaen's coloristic progressions. Around 1970, Pinkham began to study the uses of combinations of instrumental and vocal music with electronics, which he was studying with his New England Conservatory colleague Robert Ceely. Though little interested in electronic music as such, Pinkham has made imaginative use of an expanded palette of sound colour, notably in such pieces as *Toccatas for the Vault of Heaven*, his most Messiaen-sounding composition.

His choral and vocal music exhibits broadly the same range. The settings of Gerard Manley Hopkins are daring in their unusual viola accompaniment and the *Four Elegies* to English 17th-century poets is a superb example of Pinkham's flexible but disciplined scoring. In *Safe in Their Alabaster Chambers*, the mezzo-soprano's calm enunciation of Emily Dickinson's tranced text is backed by an eerily effective tape. Pinkham's set of cantatas for the sacraments and high days are very individual, but also remarkably impersonal, focussed always on their liturgical significance. Pinkham has returned on a number of occasions to biblical material of a highly dramatic nature, producing scores of considerable economy which allow the original narrative—whether it be Saul's conversation or the Witch of Endor—to occupy the foreground.

Belonging to no school or tendency, Pinkham is remarkably difficult to categorise. He draws on modernist techniques as the need dictates, paying due respect to their underlying philosophies, but never submitting to their more extreme implications.

—Richard Stein

PLESSIS, Hubert (Lawrence) du. South African. Born in Malmesbury District, 7 June 1922. Educated at Porterville High School, 1936–9; University of Stellenbosch (piano under Maria Fismer and Alan Graham), 1940–3, B.A.; Rhodes University College, Grahamstown (under Friedrich Hartmann), 1944–5, B.Mus.; Royal Academy of Music, London (as Performing Rights Society Scholar; composition and orchestration under Alan Bush and Howard Ferguson), 1951–4. Senior demonstrator, Rhodes University College, Grahamstown, 1944–51; lecturer, University of Cape Town, 1955–7; lecturer, University of Stellenbosch, 1956–82; board member, South African Music Rights Organization, since 1962. Recipient: Performing Rights Society Scholarship, 1951; Patron's Fund Award for best composition student of year, Royal College and Royal Academy of Music, London, 1954; Erepenning vir Musiek/Gold Medal, South African Academy for Arts and Sciences, 1963; honorary D.Mus., University of Stellenbosch, 1989. Mailing address: 14 Tinkietinkie Avenue, Stellenbosch 7600, Republic of South Africa.

Publishers: Novello, London; Studio Holland; Gallo; others.

Symphonies/orchestral:

Symphony Op 14 1953–4; first performed Cape Town, 1957.
Musiek by Drie Skilderye van Henri Rousseau/Music After Three Paintings by Henri Rousseau Op 24 (large chamber orchestra) 1962; first performed Johannesburg, 1962.
Feestelike Suite Op 44 (chamber orchestra) 1977–8; first performed Stellenbosch, 1978.

Chamber/instrumental:

Vier Klavierstukke Op 1 (piano) 1943–5, revised 1962.
Ses Miniature Op 3 (piano) 1945–9.
Sonata No 1 Op 8 (piano) 1952. Recorded Gallo VK 1.
Sonata Op 10 (piano duet) 1953.
String Quartet Op 13 1953; first performed London, 1953.
Prelude, Fugue and Postlude Op 17 (piano duet) 1954–5.
Sewe Preludes Op 18 (piano) 1955–6.
Fantasia on an 11th-Century Organum Op 19 1956.
Trio Op 20 (piano, violin, cello) 1957–60; first performed Cape Town, 1960. Recorded HAUM 10961.
Drie stukke Op 25 (flute, piano) 1962–3; first performed Johannesburg, 1963.
Inspiré par mes chats Op 27 (piano) 1963–4.
Vier Klavierstukke Op 28 (piano) 1964–5.
Variasies Op 'n volkswysie Op 31 (harp) 1968; first performed Johannesburg, 1968.
Toe ek 'n kind was Op 33 (piano) 1970–1.
Vier antieke danse Op 35 (flute, harpsichord or piano) 1972, 1974; first performed Stellenbosch, 1981.
Sonata No 2 Op 40 (piano) 1974–5.
Tien klavierstukke vir kinders en jongmense Op 41 1975.
Sonata Op 43 (viola) 1977; first performed Stellenbosch, 1980.
Suite Op 47 (2 clarinets) 1982; first performed Stellenbosch, 1982.
'n Kleine hulde aan Bach Op 50 (2 oboes, bassoon) 1984.

Vocal/choral:

Vier Herfsliedere (no opus number; voice, piano) 1943–4, revised 1978.
Vijf Liedekens Op 2 (voice, piano; Ostaijen) 1946. Recorded Gallo VK 1.

Herbst Op 4 (voice, piano; Rilke) 1946. Recorded Gallo VK 1.
In den Ronde Op 5 (voice, piano; Marsman) 1946–8.
Two Elizabeth Lyrics (no opus number; voice, piano) 1948.
Twee Middelnederlandse Liedere Op 6 (voice, piano 1949–52.
Vreemde Liefde Op 7 (voice, piano; I.D. du Plessis) 1951.
Sechs Galgenlieder Op 9 (voice, piano; Morgenstern) 1952.
Two Christmas Carols Op 11 (unaccompanied SATB chorus) 1953.
Five Invocations Op 12 (voice, piano; Webster, Fletcher) 1953.
Three Sonnets from the Portuguese Op 15 (voice, piano; Browning) 1954, revised 1973.
Two Madrigals Op 16 (voice, piano; Howard, Beddoes) 1954, 1959.
Slamse Beelde / Malay Scenes Op 21 (chorus, clarinet, harp, string orchestra; I.D. du Plessis) 1959; first performed Johannesburg, 1959.
Die Dans van die Reën / The Dance of the Rain Op 22 (chorus, large orchestra; Marais) 1959–60; first performed Bloemfontein, 1960.
Kersliedjie (no opus number; soprano, mezzo-soprano, alto, piano; Opperman) 1960.
Vier Slampamperliedjies Op 23 (voice, piano; Leipoldt) 1961.
Three Diatonic Settings for Twelfth Night Op 26 (voice, piano) 1964.
Suid-Afrika—Nag en Daeraad / Night and Dawn Op 29 (soprano, chorus, orchestra) 1965–6; first performed Pretoria, 1966.
Die Vrou Op 30 (voice, piano; Eybers, Salomo, Marsman, Morgenstern) 1966.
En Boplaas sing Koortaal Op 32 (unacompanied SATB solo; Boerneef) 1970.
Ag wat dis maar 'n hond! Op 34 (SATB chorus, piano; Langenhoven) 1972.
Drie Nokturnes Op 36 (voice, piano; Totius, van Heerden, Marais) 1974.
Drie Liefdesliedere (voice, piano; Bredero, Ostaijen, Samuel) 1974.
Tien Boerneef Toonsettings Op 38 (voice, piano) 1974–5.
Requiem aeternam Op 39 (unaccompanied SATB chorus) 1974–5.
Twee Totius-toonsettings Op 42 (unaccompanied SATB chorus) 1976.
Land van ons vadere Op 46 (unaccompanied SATB chorus; I.D. du Plessis) 1980.
Krokos Op 48 (unaccompanied SATB chorus; Boerneef) 1983.
Drei komische Lieder Op 49 (voice, piano; Morgenstern) 1983.
Hugenote-Kantata Op 51 (soloists, chorus, orchestra) 1986–7; first performed Pretoria, 1988.

Other:

Huberta, the Hippo (music for radio play by Cecil Jubber) 1960.
Die Stem van Suid-Afrika (official orchestrated version of South African national anthem) 1960. Recorded SAUK LP 1735.
Periandros van Korinthe (incidental music to Opperman) 1972.
Die Huis van Bernarda Alba (incidental music to Lorca) 1973.
Die Wintersprokie (incidental music to Shakespeare) 1974.
Ses Afrikaanse volksliedjies (arrangements) 1975. Recorded Brigadiers BCP 1396.
Die Goue Kring (incidental music to Krige) 1976.
Die mal vrou van Chaillot (incidental music to Giraudoux) 1977.
Huit Chansons françaises (arrangements) 1978.

Franz Liszt: *Vallée d'Obermann* (orchestration) 1961.

PUBLICATIONS

By du Plessis: *Johann Sebastian Bach*, 1960; *Dagboek van "Die Dans van die Reën"*, 1970; *Letters from William Bell*, 1973.

On du Plessis: P.J. Krige, "Die Kamermusiek van Hdp", dissertation, 1983; H.H. van der Mescht, "Die Liedere van HdP", dissertation, 1987; Edward Aitchiso, "HdP", in *Composers in South Africa Today*, edited by Peter Klatzow Cape Town, 1987.

Hubert du Plessis comments:

My musical instructional has been traditional, and I have never felt the urge to depart drastically from the traditional concepts of melody, harmony, counterpoint, form, etc. I have been blessed with a natural melodic gift and melody is consequently of prime importance in my compositions. Furthermore, my melodic lines are basically *vocal* in conception—consequently very large leads occur very seldom. I find no reason to abandon *tonality* . . . even in my serial works (such as the *Piano Trio*, the *Rousseau Paintings*, and *Inspiré par mes chats*) a dominating tonal centre prevails; thus my serial works (predominantly derived from series of less than 12 notes—a technique I derived from Stravinsky's *In memoriam Dylan Thomas*) can hardly be distinguished from my "free" compositions. I am allergic to electronic, aleatoric music, and despise all gimmicks of the like. My best compositions are decidedly 20th-century products, but in them my aim has been to achieve the quality of *timelessness*. If an epithet has to be attached, Neo-Romantic suits me perfectly.

* * *

The composer Hubert du Plessis has left an indelible imprint on the musical life of South Africa over a period of more than 40 years. Also as performing artist, lecturer and writer his significance can hardly be overestimated. Together with his contemporaries such as Stefans Grové and the late Arnold van Wyk, he has made a distinguished contribution towards a genuine South African art.

With the exception of opera, oratories and works for organ, du Plessis has ventured into all major and smaller genres of which almost 80 songs for voice and piano, and 50 individual piano works, for example, are the most representative.

Of his song cycles, the following deserve mention: *Vier Slampamperliedjies*, *Die Vrou*, the *Tien Boerneef Toonsettings*, *Drie Kabaretliedere*, and *Drei komische Lieder*. The *Sewe Preludes*, the suite and the *Sonata No 2* are considered the most important of his piano compositions.

Du Plessis's craftmanship and his understanding of the art of musical creation is illustrated further by his large-scale works such as his *Symphony Op 14*, and the patriotic trilogy for soloists, choir and orchestra: *Slamse Beelde / Malay Scenes*, *Die Dans van die Reën / The Dance of the Rain* and *Suid-Afrika—Nag en Daeraad / Night and Dawn*, the latter composed for the Republic Festival of 1966. Another work which belongs to this category is the recent *Hugenote-Kantata* of 1988, a major work in his oeuvre. Apart from the *String Quartet*, the *Trio* for piano, violin and cello features prominently as far as his chamber music works are concerned. For choir *a cappella*, Du Plessis composed a number of important works among others *En Boplaas sing Koortaal*.

In addition to being a very successful lecturer on subjects such as the history of music, harmony and counterpoint, and composition and orchestration, his literary bent has found expression in several publications. In 1960 his book (the first in Afrikaans) on J.S. Bach appeared, while his *Dageboek van "Die Dans van die Reën"* published in 1970, is an autobiographical account of the compositional process involved setting this poem to music. The composer's admiration for his former mentor is documented in *Letters from William Henry Bell*. Furthermore, a treatise in four parts, *The Maintenance of Keyboard Technique*, incorporating finger exercises developed over a period of 30 years, has also been published.

Through concert appearances and broadcasts, and through lecture recitals and radio talks, Du Plessis has actively promoted an appreciation of serious music among his fellow citizens.

—Hans Roosenschoon

POPPY, Andrew. British/English. Born in Chatham, Kent, 29 May 1954. Educated at University of London, B.Mus., 1979; further study under John Cage. Accompanist, Laban Centre of Dance and Movement, London, 1980–2; keyboard player, The Lost Jockey, 1981–3; teacher, Medway College of Design, 1982–3; freelance composer; arranger for various rock/pop artists; pianist—solo and as leader of Andrew Poppy Band. Mailing address: 22c Breakspears Road, Brockley, London SE4 1UW, England.

Publisher: none.

Symphonies/orchestral:

Thirty-Two Frames for Orchestra 1981. Recorded ZTT Records LP/CD *The Beating of Wings*; also remixed 12-inch single.
Matters of Theory (chamber orchestra; electric keyboards and voices/The Lost Jockey) 1981.
The Object Is a Hungry Wolf (chamber orchestra, electric keyboards and voices/The Lost Jockey) 1982. Recorded ZTT Records LP/CD *The Beating of Wings*.

Chamber/instrumental:

Two Chords for Eight Instruments (2 flutes, clarinet, cor anglais, alto saxophone, violin, 2 cellos) 1978.
Music for Chairs to Sit On (flute, clarinet, bass clarinet, soprano saxophone, 2 pianos, bass guitar, guitar, violin, viola, cello) 1980.
Cadenza (piano, electric piano) 1980. Recorded ZTT Records LP/CD *The Beating of Wings*.
Animal Behaviour and Crude Din (keyboards/The Lost Jockey) 1981.
Ribbon (piano) 1982.
45 Is (4 electric keyboards, piano, trombone, soprano saxophone, drum kit, 2 voices) 1985. Recorded ZTT Records LP/CD *Alphabed*.
Elvis Revenged (marimba, vibraphone, 12 tuned roto-toms) 1985.
Charcoal as Fuel (2 violins) 1985.
45 Is (piano) 1987.

Opera:

The Uranium Miners Radio Orchestra Play Scenes from Salome's Revenge (chamber opera) 1989; first performed London, 1989.

Dramatic/dance:

Secret Gardens (incidental music for piano, tape) 1982.
Ribbon (choreographed by Ian Spink) 1982.
On the Beaches (dance piece for piano, vibraphone, xylophone, timpani, electronic percussion, electronic keyboards; choreographed by Sally Owen) 1983.
Objects of Affection (instrumental interludes for cello and bass clarinet) 1983.
The Dead Moon (dance piece for piano, soprano saxophone, bass clarinet/E♭ clarinet, tuba, counter tenor; choreographed by Sally Owen) 1984.
Midday Sun (incidental music for electric keyboards) 1984.
The Songs of the Claypeople (collaborative music theatre project with Impact Theatre; solo piano, high voice, tape, electronic keyboards) 1984.
At the End of the Mechanical Age (collaborative music theatre project with Impact Theatre; studio-processed percussion, brass) 1985.
Candenza (dance piece for piano, electric piano; choreographed by Gaby Agis) 1988.
Forth Fiesta (electric guitar, electronic percussion, keyboards; choreographed by Michael Clark) 1988.
Listening In (choreographed by David Massingham) 1989.
Melody Versus the Brittle Funk (piano, trumpet, tenor saxophone, vibraphone/marimba; choreographed by Siobhan Davies) 1989.

Other:

A Girl in Summer (film score arranged from *Thirty-Two Frames for Orchestra*) 1986.
Mid-Night (arrangements from 7 titles for orchestra) 1988.

Studio compositions: *45 Is*; *Goodbye Mr G*; *The Impossible Net* (released 1986); *The Amusement* (ZTT; released 1987); *The Amusement* remix; *Kink Konk Presto*; *Kink Konk Adagio* (released 1987); *The Passage*; *The Sequence of Violent Actions*; *The Outrage of the Fisherman Is Widely Shared* (recorded 1989).

* * *

Andrew Poppy belongs firmly to a younger generation of classically trained composers who have achieved an unembarrassed rapprochement with rock and pop and the rhythmic intensity of electro-dance music. Central to Poppy's still-developing style are three interrelated considerations. In the first place, he regards pulse and a particular attention to rhythmic articulation as the most obvious way of mitigating the alienating impact of the modern avant-garde and making "serious" music accessible once more. He looks to the example not just of the American Minimalists (to whom he owes his most obvious debt), but also to the senior British composer Harrison Birtwistle, for whom pulse is a central consideration.

Related to this is the conviction Poppy shares with a number of composers who can with some justness and exactitude be called "post-modern" (in the sense that their work represents a conscious and deliberate extension of and distancing from the structural innovations of the serialists) that the majority of untrained listeners hear music imagistically and "nostalgically", as something made up of textures and discontinuous aural scenes, rather than as the product of an identifiable structural logic. The American Minimalists responded to the same recognition by turning away from the complexities of the modern school and restoring a certain *ab ovo* simplicity to harmonic development (or non-development) and virtually all other parameters of music. A typical minimalist piece has an immediately visible exoskeleton (and, some might say, a soft centre) made up of materials which are, ideally, reference-free and make little or no appeal to any but the most fundamental creative associations, purged of the discomforts of "nostalgia".

A final and related element of his compositional approach is a concern for language and text, conceived in the broadest and most continuous sense as a system of gestures, images, spatial relationships. This concern, largely derived from his apparently fruitful apprenticeship with John Cage, has led Poppy into ambitious work in theatre, dance and audio-visual experiments as well as to a generically more conventional approach to musical narrative in his remarkable chamber opera *The Uranium Miners Radio Orchestra Play Scenes from Salome's Revenge*.

The explicit "intertextuality" of this piece and of such instrumental works as the *Thirty-Two Frames for Orchestra* suggest a number of possible influences, from Alfred Schnittke's "inclusive memory" (Poppy traces the Russian composer's "polystylistic" approach back to Charles Ives) and even from Michael Nyman, an English composer whose enormous musicological purview allows him to de-and re-construct musical materials from Purcell, Mozart, Schumann, popular and liturgical resources in a quite radical way.

Like Nyman (and in his categorical way, Philip Glass), Poppy has geared much of his output for the resources of his own performing band. Far from restricting his imagination, this has given it considerable discipline and scope. Between 1981 and 1983 he performed with The Lost Jockey, a now-legendary band on the London avant-rock scene which combined an improvisational approach with formal scores from the likes of Steve Reich, Terry Riley and Philip Glass; they also performed arrangements of Perotin. Like recent British bands such as Man Jumping, The Lost Jockey represented an attempt to create large-scale structures with a modified (i.e., keyboard-dominated) rock instrumentation but which avoided the self-indulgence and whimsicality of keyboard player-composers like Keith Emerson and Rick Wakeman, rock icons of Poppy's student years.

Poppy's most remarkable work to date has been *The Songs of the Claypeople*, a collaborative music theatre project conceived in collaboration with Impact Theatre. With elements suggesting Meredith Monk, video opera composer Robert Ashley and even James Ivory's movie *Savages*, it is nonetheless a stunning work, with a powerful score and staging. The succeeding *At the End of the Mechanical Age* is more discursive, but still effective. A number of Poppy's works have been written or adapted for dance performance, a reviving area of concern among contemporary composers; these are strongly rhythmic and unhackneyed, perfectly responsive to the requirements of the new choreography.

The instrumental performers in *Claypeople* are isolated in plastic booths. This one of several references in Poppy's output to the alienating/liberating implications of the recording studio. He is convinced that contemporary music will not step beyond the not-quite-exhausted resources of modernism until it embraces all the technological and distributional resources associated with rock music; many of Poppy's works have been released in "single" format, and he has written theme music for an influential British television rock programme.

Nonetheless, his work remains equally rooted in the concert format, and he has instinctive skills as an instrumentator. *The Object Is a Hungry Wolf* is a finely judged score and the duo *Charcoal as Fuel*, a "process"-based piece for two violins, makes a significant step beyond its American models. Poppy has suffered a certain amount of critical disparagement for "selling out" to the lucrative blandishments of rock—he signed a contract with ZTT Records, the label responsible for the highly contrived success of the controversial Frankie Goes to Hollywood, and earns an occasional living writing arrangements for the more adventurous British bands—but has clearly survived the supposed transition with his faculties and intelligence quite intact. He is certain to be one of the most exciting British composers of the 1990s.

—Brian Morton

POUSSEUR, Henri (Léon Marie Thérèse). Belgian. Born in Malmedy, 23 June 1929. Educated at Conservatoire de Musique, Liège, 1947–52; Brussels Conservatory, 1952–3; private lessons with Andre Souris and Pierre Boulez. Military service, 1952–3. Married Theresia Schoonbrond, July 1954; 3 daughters and 1 son. Music teacher, Athenée Royal, Eupen, 1951–9; research work in electronic music studios at Cologne, 1954, and Milan, 1957; teacher, Ferienkurse für Neue Musik, Darmstadt, since 1957; professor, INSAS, Brussels, 1962–3, Musikakademie, Basle, 1963–4, and State University of New York, Buffalo, 1966–8; founder, Centre de Recherches Musicales de Wallonie, 1970; professor, 1970–5, and director, since 1975, Conservatoire Royal, Liège; course director, University of Liège, since 1970; director, Institut de Pedagogie Musicale, Paris, 1983–7. Recipient: Prix de la RAI, 1960; doctor honoris causa, University of Metz. Mailing address: 14 Boulevard Frere-Orban, B-4000 Liège, Belgium.

Publishers: Universal Edition, Vienna/London; Suvini Zerboni, Milan.

Symphonies/orchestral:

Rimes pour différentes sources sonores (orchestra, tape) 1959; first performed Donaueschingen, 17 October 1959. Recorded Victrola VIC5-1239.

Couleurs croisées 1967; first performed Brussels, 20 December 1968. Recorded Ricercar RIC 036015.

Les Ephémérides d'Icare 2 (piano, small orchestra) 1970. Recorded harmonia mundi 2021229–7.

L'Effacement du Prince Igor 1971; first performed Brussels, January 1971.

Parade de votre Faust (from the opera) 1974.

Petite Chronique illustrée 1976; first performed Brussels, 12 February 1977.

La Seconde Apothéose de Rameau (chamber orchestra) 1981;

first performed Paris, 9 November, 1981.
Nacht der Nachte (orchestra) 1985; first performed Hamburg, 20 October 1985.

Chamber/instrumental:

Quintette à la mémoire d'Anton Webern (violin, cello, clarinet, bass clarinet, piano) 1955; first performed Donaueschingen, 1955.
Exercices pour piano, variations I (piano) 1956; first performed Cologne, 1957.
Exercices pour Piano, impromptu et variations II (piano) 1956; first performed New York City, 1957.
Symphonies for Fifteen Soloists 1958.
Madrigal I (clarinet) 1958. Recorded Musique Nouvelle MN004.
Mobile (2 pianos) 1958. Recorded Vega C 30 A 278.
Caractères (piano) 1960.
Répons avec son paysage (flute, violin, cello, harp, keyboards, percussion) 1960–5.
Ode (string quartet) 1961.
Madrigal II (antique instruments: flute or violin, violin, viola da gamba or cello, harpsichord) 1961.
Trait (15 strings) 1962.
Madrigal III (clarinet, violin, cello, piano, 2 percussion) 1962. Recorded Everest 3170.
Echo I (from *Votre Faust*; cello) 1965.
Apostrophes et six reflexions (piano) 1966. Recorded Musique Nouvelle MN004.
Mnemosyne I (solo instrument or voice or unison choir) 1968.
Mnemosyne II (improvisation for 1 or more players; later version for piano) 1969, 1973; first performed Bonn, 1970.
Icare apprenti (improvisation for indeterminate number of musicians) 1970; first performed Paris, October 1971.
Icare obstiné (piano) 1972.
Vue sur les jardins interdits (4 saxophones) 1973; first performed Bordeaux, 1974.
Deuxième Vue sur les jardins interdits (organ) 1973–4.
Ballade Berlinoise (piano) 1974–7.
Modèle réduit (bass clarinet or any other melodic instrument of considerable range, piano or other harmonic instrument) 1975. Recorded Musique Nouvelle MN004.
L'Ibéricare (guitar) 1975; first performed Venice, 29 August 1976.
Racine 19 (cello) 1976.
Petite Chronique Berlinoise (string quartet, piano) 1976; first performed London, 9 March 1977.
Flexions I (flute) 1979.
Flexions II (trumpet) 1979.
Flexions III (violin) 1979.
Le Bal de Cendrillon (after Tchaikovsky; piano) 1979.
Flexions IV (viola) 1980.
Flexions V (cello) 1980.
La Patience d'Icarene (harp) 1980.
Fantaisie et fugue (after Schoenberg; cello or bassoon, piano; also version for string quartet) 1980, 1981.
Naturel (horn) 1981.
Variations (after Webern; clarinet, piano) 1981.
La Seconde Apothéose de Rameau (9 woodwinds, 7 brass, 5 muted instruments) 1981.
Hermes I (after Bartók; clarinet) 1982.
Hermes II (after Bartók; violin) 1982.
La paganiana (violin) 1982.
La paganiana secondo (cello) 1982.
Litanie du miel matinal (melody instrument—high) 1983.
Litanie du miel vesperal (melody instrument—low) 1983.
Variations-Caprice (flute or clarinet or violin, harpsichord or piano) 1983.
Cortège des belles ténébreuses au jardin boréal (6 players) 1984; first performed Brussels, 2 November 1984.
Vers l'Ile du Mont Pourpre (flute) 1984.
Un Jardin de passacailles (flute, oboe, clarinet, horn, trombone, bassoon, keyboards, percussion, violin, viola, cello, double bass) 1987.
Figure et ombres (any instrument) 1988.
Mnemosyne obstinée (string quartet) 1988.
At Moonlight, Dowland's Shadow Passes Along Ginkaku-Ji (koto, shamisen, shakuhachi) 1989.
La Lune et les flots (passacaglia for string trio) 1989.

Vocal/choral:

Sept Versets des psaumes de la pénitence (4 mixed voices) 1950. Recorded Wergo 60.026.
Trois Chants sacrés (soprano, violin, viola, cello; Latin text) 1951; first performed Salzburg, 1952. Recorded Candide Vox CE 31.021.
Missa brevis (mixed choir) 1951.
Miroir (from *Votre Faust*; piano, voice ad lib; Butor) 1965.
Portail (from *Votre Faust*; vocal quartet, 12 instruments, tape) 1966.
Phonèmes pour Cathy (voice; Claudel) 1966. Recorded Virgin Classics VC 7 90704-2.
Mnemosyne I (voice or unison choir or solo instrument; Hölderlin) 1968.
Echos de Votre Faust (mezzo-soprano, flute, cello, piano; Goethe, Marlowe, Nerval, Gongora, Petrarch) 1969.
Crosses of Crossed Colours (amplified female voice, 2–5 pianos, electronics; Afro-American/Red Indian texts) 1970; first performed New York City, 19 November 1970.
Invitation à l'utopie (reciter, 2 female voices, 4-voice choir, soloist, orchestra) 1971; first performed Brussels, 25 January 1971.
Pedigree (woman's voice, violin/viola, cello, clarinet/bass clarinet, horn, harp, piano, percussion) 1974–80.
Grande Chronique Berlinoise (string quartet, piano, baritone) 1976; first performed London, 9 March 1977.
Grande Chronique illustrée (baritone, orchestra) 1976.
Humeurs du futur quotidien (2 reciters, orchestra; Butor) 1978; first performed Paris, 12 March 1978.
Vocalise (1–6 mixed voices, piano) 1978.
Les Ruines de Jeruzona (mixed choir, piano/organ, double bass, percussion; Goethe, Nerval, Marlowe, Gongora, Petrarch, Bible, Liturgy) 1978; first performed Brussels, 23 March 1979.
Pour Baudelaire (voice) 1979.
Chevelures du temps (popular oratorio for soloists, vocal ensembles, instruments, noise, amateurs and professionals; Butor) 1979.
Tales and Songs from the Bible of Hell (4 mixed voices, tape, electronics; Dowland, Blake, Poe) 1979; first performed The Hague, June 1979. Recorded Wergo WER 60094.
Canines (female voice, piano; Butor, Hölderlin) 1980.
Cinquième Vue sur les jardins interdits (vocal quartet) 1982; first performed London, June 1982.
La Rose de voix (voices, choir, ensemble) 1982; first performed Naumur, 6 August 1982. Recorded Igloo IGL 028.
Trajets dans les arpents du ciel (soloist, orchestra) 1983; first performed Metz, 18 November 1983.
L'Etoile des langues (mixed choir, reciter; Butor) 1984.
Grande Chronique canine (female voice, 2 pianos) 1984.
Sur le qui-vive (female voice, clarinet, cello, tuba, keyboards) 1985.

Arc-en-ciel de remparts (student orchestra, unison choir; Butor) 1986.
Traverser la forêt (reciter, soprano, baritone, mixed choir, 12 instruments) 1987.
Cinq Soupirs pour un clairière (female voice; Butor, Lorca) 1987–9.
Mnemosyne doublement obstinée (string quartet, female voice; Hölderlin) 1988.
Déclarations d'orages (reciter, soprano, baritone, 3 improvising soloists, orchestra, tape; Butor, Blake, Neruda, Schiller, Mayakovsky) 1988–9.
L'Ecole d'Orphée (speaker, organ, electronics or tape; Butor) 1989.

Opera:

Votre Faust (5 actors, vocal quartet, flute, clarinet, bassoon, tenor saxophone, horn, trumpet, violin, cello, double bass, harp, piano, percussion, tapes; Butor) 1960–8.
Die Erprobung des Petrus Hebraicus (2 reciters, soprano, tenor, counter-tenor, baritone) 1974, adapted into French as *Le Procès du jeune chien*; first performed Berlin, 12 September 1974.

Other:

Scambi (electronic) 1957; first performed Milan, 1957.
Electre (tape; also ballet) 1960.
Trois Visages de Liège (tape; text by Jean Seaux) 1961. Recorded Alpha NR 5.066-5e; CBS S34-61064.
Etudes paraboliques (tape; consisting of *Les Ailes d'Icare*, *Liebesduett*, *Viva Cuba*, *Voyage aux éléments*, *Hymne à Zeus ornithologue*, *Aerial View of Haiphong*, *Massachusetts*, *Mnemosyne disparue*, *An Heinreich*, *Ping-Pong*) 1972.
Quatrième Vue sur les jardins interdits (collaboration with Jean Louis Robert; orchestra) 1974.
Troisième Vue sur les jardins interdits (collaboration with Peter Antony Monk for wind quintet) 1976.
Liège à Paris (tape; text by Butor, Breton) 1977.
Les Iles déchaînées (collaboration with Denis for jazz band, electro-acoustic ensemble, symphony orchestra) 1980; first performed Brussels, 27 November 1980.
Fantaisie et fugue (collaboration with Claude Ledoux after Schoenberg; orchestra) 1981.
Patchwork des tribus americaines (tape) 1984.
Méthodicare (contemporary studies in musical creation, interpretation and understanding: volume 3 *Vingt-quatre petits miroirs à douze faces* 1988; volume 2 *Vingt-six ombres d'une même figure*) 1989; volumes 1 and 4, in preparation.
Methodicare (volume II—*Vingt-huit Etudes assez faciles et un petit labyrinthe* for string ensembles: duos, trios, quartets, indeterminate ensembles) 1989.

PUBLICATIONS

By Pousseur: *Ecrits d'Alban Berg*, selected and translated with a commentary by HP, Monaco, 1956; *Musique sérielle, musique actuelle (fragments théoriques II)*, 1954–78, unpublished; *Quel Enseignement musical pour demain? I: Approches fundamentales*, Paris, 1957; *Fragments théoriques I sur la musique expérimentale*, Brussels, 1970; "A l'Ecoute d'un dialogue", in *Musique en jeu*, Paris, 1971; *Musique sémantique société*, Paris/Tournai, 1972; *La musica elettronica*, Milan, 1976; une esthetique ou un ethique?", "Perspectives d'avenir", Ministry of Culture brochure, Brussels, 1976; "La musique aujourd'hui", in *Socialisme*, 139, 140, 142, 1977; "Webern, de la lettre à l'esprit, une autre mutation", in *Musica/Realta*, 1, 1980; "Le Sacré et la musique aujourd'hui", in *Les Sacré et les formes*, Paris, 1982; "L'héritage dans la musique actuelle", in *Traces et Dires*, 1983; "La Vision de la Rose fait éclore les Voix de Namur", in *La Vision de Namur à l'intention de la Rose des voix*, edited by Michel Butor and HP, Yverdon les Bains, 1983; "Une Expérience de musique microtonale", in *Interface*, 14 (1–2), 1985; "Musique et identité culturelle", in *InHarmonique*, 2, 1987.

On Pousseur: special issue of *Revue Belge de musicologie*, Brussels, 1990; special issue of *Musikkonzepte*, Munich, 1990.

Henri Pousseur comments:

I have been fascinated since the beginning of my professional studies by the work and example of Anton Webern, but also nourished by a multitude of favourite musics, old and recent, "serious" and "popular", Western and exterior to our culture. I am also influenced by the products of other artistic fields (I've been collaborating since 1960 with the French novelist Michel Butor) as well as by (what I can understand of) science and philosophy. And then there are personal preoccupations and pleasures—nature, love, family, friendship.

I am trying to produce a music that is theoretically and practically rooted, that contributes to the emergence of a new form of civilisation, one that is adequate to our contemporary conditions of collective existence. I think that Webern provided the essential key to understanding the most specific 20th-century musical purpose: "multipolarity", an equality of importance of all points, of all associated beings, based on *an unresolved maintenance of tensions*. Through his work we better understand Schoenberg, Debussy, Stravinsky, Varèse and others, but I am also convinced that it would be (or that it was and is) a mistake just to reproduce its literal features, be that in a material multiplication, densification and prolongation of its exterior texture, which he of necessity realised on an extremely narrow, miniaturistic and ascetic level, based on severe, momentaneously indispensible exclusions and negations.

His lesson now understood and fortified, and the environmental conditions considerably changed, we can and must open again our eyes and ears to all sounds of history, geography, nature and urban reality, which to me seems the only way to enlarge and apply this lesson on a broader scale. Only in this way can we effectively explore all the known and unknown regions of our hearable world, from Mozart to the noise of automated industry, from samba to the amplified vibrations of cells and molecules, and communicate its elaborate, joyful comprehension to actual and future people who can learn from its models something about being together in living, vital peace.

* * *

In the golden days of the Darmstadt summer school (the late 1950s and early 1960s) the names of six composers were automatically bracketed together as representative of all that was best and most exciting in avant-garde music. Together with Boulez, Stockhausen, Berio, Nono and Maderna, Henri Pousseur was then at the forefront of post-war musical development—heading the search for new forms of notation as well as expression, doing important work in the early development of electronic music, and contributing widely and extremely articulately to the linguistic theories of the avant-garde as published in *Die Reihe* and other magazines of the period.

His music pursued an equally radical course. Following a complex study of total serialisation in *Symphonies for Fifteen Soloists*, he proceeded to explore less restrictive ways of expressing the same principles. His 1961 *Ode* for string quartet develops a rhythm which is freely notated and variable in performance, while pitch is almost always relative and moving; here, the musical material stems solely from four types of string articulation stated at the outset (tremolo, pizzicato, glissando and arpeggiated chords), features which gradually acquire a quasi-thematic identity of their own, developing a strange and wholly original kind of polyphony built entirely from texture. The even more experimental *Caractères* for piano makes use of various formal options—not only as to the ordering of sections but also as to the appearance or non-appearance of events: "windows" cut in certain pages of the score reveal only parts of other pages placed behind them, and since white and black notes are now used to denote flats and naturals, the rhythmic element is indicated only as relatively faster or slower, rather than in terms of precise durations.

Meanwhile, Pousseur had embarked on his mobile, open-ended opera, *Votre Faust*—which he began in 1960 (long before Berio's influential *Sinfonia*) and completed eight years later. Much influenced by the concept of literary quotation proposed by his collaborator, the French novelist Michel Butor, work on the opera was to have a lasting effect on Pousseur's musical outlook—leaving him free to re-adopt stylistic devices once regarded as anathema by dedicated serialists, himself included. This in turn enabled him to develop the richer and much more relaxed harmonic style characteristic of his present-day music. Always a composer with a highly developed sense of social responsibility, he was even then becoming increasingly aware of the need to cross rather than to erect barriers—between amateur and professional, composer and performer, players and audience, as well as between the various apparently compartmentalised musical styles and genres, both old and new—so that Butor's radical ideas were to prove remarkably in accord with his own.

It was perhaps not entirely coincidental that it was then, during his work on *Votre Faust*, that Pousseur took the decision to retreat from the more competitive aspects of international contemporary music in favour of making a positive social contribution to life in a provincial city: both as Director of the Liège Conservatoire for the past quarter of a century, and as a composer working within and for the community, Pousseur's role and sphere of influence may in this respect be likened to that of Bach in 18th-century Leipzig.

Despite a dearth of international performances over the past decade or so, it would be quite wrong to assume any lack of compositional activity on Pousseur's part: his creativity continues unabated, and although, like others of his generation, he frequently presents alternative versions of existing pieces, their often elaborate reworking evidently relates to the concept of options proposed earlier (most notably in *Votre Faust*, where even the audience is invited to participate in the game of chance). While such works occasionally give evidence of an over-fertile imagination, tantalizingly unable or unwilling to reject the unessential or to pin down particular characters once and for all, the best of his music inhabits sound worlds that explore unusual combinations of timbre in a manner that is both aurally seductive and characteristically exploratory—particularly, now, in its focus on an evolutionary harmony.

—Susan Bradshaw

POWELL, Mel. American. Born in New York City, 12 February 1923. Studied piano under Nadia Reisenberg; jazz pianist, composer and arranger, Glenn Miller Army Air Force Band and with Benny Goodman Orchestra; (concurrently) studied composition under Bernard Wagenaar and Joseph Schillinger, New York, 1937–9; and under Ernst Toch, Los Angeles, 1946–8; Yale University, New Haven, Connecticut, (composition under Paul Hindemith), 1948–52, B.M. Served in United States Army Air Force. Married Martha Scott, 23 July 1946; 2 daughters and 1 son. Teacher of music, Mannes College, New York, and Queens College, City University of New York, 1952–7; president, American Music Center, 1957–60; music faculty, Yale University, 1957–69; founding dean of music 1969–72, provost 1972–6, and Institute Fellow and Roy E. Disney Professor of Musical Composition, since 1978; California Institute of the Arts, Valencia; consultant, National Endowment for the Arts, 1970–3; guest composer, University of Wisconsin, River Falls, 1972; guest composer, Holland Festival, Amsterdam, 1972. Recipient: Guggenheim Fellowship, 1960; Pulitzer Prize (for *Duplicates*), 1990. Mailing address: 14054 Chandler Boulevard, Van Nuys, California 91401, U.S.A.

Publisher: G. Schirmer.

Symphonies/orchestral:

Symphonic Suite 1949.
Cantilena concertante (cor anglais, orchestra) 1949.
Capriccio (symphonic band) 1950.
Stanzas Op 9 1957.
Setting (cello, orchestra) 1961.
Immobiles 1–4 (orchestra and/or tape) 1967.
Modules (intermezzo for chamber orchestra) 1985.
Duplicates: A Concerto for Two Pianos and Orchestra 1987–90.

Chamber/instrumental:

Beethoven Analogs (string quartet) 1948.
Sonatina (piano) 1953.
Recitative and Toccata Percossa (harpsichord) 1953.
Piano Trio 1954. Recorded CRI 121.
Divertimento (violin, harp) 1954. Recorded CRI 121.
Divertimento (wind quintet) 1957.
Miniatures for Baroque Ensemble Op 8 (flute, oboe, violin, viola, cello, harpsichord) 1957.
Piano Quintet 1957.
Etude (piano) 1957.
Filigree Setting (string quartet) 1959. Recorded Son-Nova 1/S-1.
Improvisation (clarinet, viola, piano) 1962. Recorded CRI USD 227.
String Quartet 1982. Recorded Musicmasters MMD 60179Y.
Cantilena (trombone, tape) 1982.
Intermezzo (piano) 1984.
Madrigal (2 pianos) 1985.
Nocturne (violin; new version of *Cantilena*) 1985. Recorded Musicmasters MMD 60179Y.
Woodwind Quintet 1985. Recorded Cambria CD 1044.
Setting (guitar) 1986.
Settings (2 pianos) 1988.
Amy-Abilities (percussion) 1988.
Prelude (piano) 1988.
Three Madrigals (flute; original version *Madrigal for Flute Alone*) 1988. Recorded Musicmasters MMD 60179Y.
Invocation (cello) 1988.

Vocal/choral:

Six Love songs (unaccompanied chorus; anon. 17th century) 1950.
Sweet Lovers Love the Spring (female chorus, piano; Shakespeare) 1953.
Haiku Settings Op 12 (soprano, piano) 1960. Recorded Son-Nova 1/S-1; Nonesuch N78006.
Two Prayer Settings (tenor, oboe, violin, cello; Goodman, Gregory) 1962. Recorded DRI USD 227.
Cantilena (soprano, violin, tape; Hebrew, Chinese, Sanskrit) 1970.
Settings (soprano, chamber ensemble; Joyce, Milton, Euripides, traditional) 1979.
Little Companion Pieces (soprano, string quartet; Baudelaire, William Carlos Williams, Joyce, African and Asian songs) 1980. Recorded Nonesuch N79005.
Strand Settings: Darker (song cycle for mezzo-soprano, electronics) 1983. Recorded Musicmasters MMD 60179Y.
Die Violine (soprano, violin, piano) 1987. Recorded Musicmasters MMD 60179Y.
Letter to a Young Composer (soprano) 1988.

Other:

Electronic Setting (tape) 1961.
Electronic Setting No 2 (tape) 1962.
Events (tape; Hart Crane) 1963. Recorded CRI 227.
Analogs 1–4 (tape) 1966.
Immobiles 1–4 (tape version) 1967.
Immobile 5 (tape, diverse instruments) 1967.
Three Synthesizer Settings 1981.
Computer Prelude (software) 1988. Recorded Musicmasters MMD 60179Y.

Jazz recordings: *The Benny Goodman Band* (Capitol 409); *Clarinade* (Classic Editions CJ8); *Mel Powell and His Orchestra* (Commodore 544); *Mel Powell Bandstand* (Vanguard 8015); *The Return of Mel Powell* (Chiaruscuro 301); *The Unavailable Mel Powell* (Pausa 9023).

PUBLICATIONS

On Powell: Harvey Sollberger, "MP's *Haiku Setting*", in *Perspectives of New Mujsic*, 3, 1964; Les Thimmig, "The Music of MP", in *Musical Quarterly*, 55, 1969; Whitney Balliett, "Whatever Happened to MP?", in *The New Yorker*, 63, 25 May 1987; A. Brandt, "The Absence of Nouns", in *Aperiodical*, 2(1), 1988; D. Perlmutter, "The Private Art of Thoroughly Modern Mel", in *Los Angeles Times*, 29 October 1989; A. Kozinn, "MP's Journey to a Pulitzer Prize", in *The New York Times*, 24 April 1990.

* * *

Mel Powell's route to the composition of complex post-Schoenberg serialism has not been the most direct. Conventionally enough, he started to study music theory and piano at the age of six, but was very soon diverted from the standard classics by the popular big bands of the day. He quickly taught himself to improvise with such virtuosity that, by the age of 16, Benny Goodman had engaged him as a pianist and arranger for his orchestra. During time with the Glen Miller Army Air Force Band he began to compose chamber music and this growing enthusiasm led him to abandon jazz for serious compositional study with Paul Hindemith at Yale University. His early works, for example the *Symphonic Suite*, *Six Love Songs*, the two Divertmentos and the *Piano Trio*, follow the neo-classical style of his teacher, but already these are more than student works, written with a sensitivity, economy and elegance which demonstrate considerable assurance.

Towards the end of the 1950s Powell made a move away from neo-classicism. His first published string quartet, *Filigree Setting*, allows the performers some choice of pitch succession or contour within an otherwise tightly controlled structure. It is a six-minute work in a single movement and owes something in its compression and transparent textures, if not in its language, to the influence of Webern which was beginning to be felt in the United States. By 1961 works such as *Setting* for cello and orchestra and the *Haiku Settings* show that Powell had now firmly abandoned tonality and was moving into an increasingly complex sound world. In *Two Prayer Settings* he goes on to explore the intricacies of counterpoint, while *Stanzas* for orchestra juxtaposes hybrid tonal and atonal structures. During this time Powell pursued similar compositional ideas in the medium of electronic music. In 1961 he had founded an electronic studio at Yale and his first work from this studio, *Events* for tape, is, like the *Two Prayer Settings*, concerned with contrapuntal complexity, and culminates in a 48-part vocal canon. *Immobile 5* for tape and a flexible instrumental combination, and its companion *Immobiles 1–4* for tape and/or orchestra of the same year both strive towards the creation of musical stasis through a variety of methods: uniformity of dynamics and timbre, and harmonic and rhythmic invariance. Intriguingly these new paths were followed by over 10 years of almost complete silence from Powell as a composer. During this time he founded and administered a music school at the California Institute of the Arts, and it was not until 1978, when he left the administration in favour of a chair in composition at the Institute, that he again had the freedom to compose.

The late 1970s and early 1980s were a particularly productive period and show Powell pressing onward with the compositional preoccupations that he had abandoned 10 years previously. The first of the *Little Companion Pieces* for soprano and string quartet explores even further the musical possibilities of stasis, while the richly expressive *String Quartet* is a kaleidoscope of gradually changing, disparate musical events in a single movement work of meticulous craftsmanship. This idea of perpetual change became increasingly important to Powell. In *Modules* and the *Woodwind Quintet* he replaces the single note as a compositional unit with composite modules of chords, pitch sequences and rhythms, which are constantly transformed into a succession of elaborate mazes with resulting expressivity and great dramatic range.

Duplicates: A Concerto for Two Pianos and Orchestra, Powell's first full orchestral work for over 20 years is a consummate work, and satisfyingly, the one which, by winning the 1990 Pulitzer Prize, has brought him most recognition. Like *Modules*, the key to the piece lies in the title. Each of the two solo piano parts can be seen to duplicate the other, while the orchestra also duplicates material given to the pianists. Moreover, throughout the piece, contrasting duos spring up, to imitate by turns the timbre, rhythm and counterpoint of the piano soloists. The whole is an intricate and absorbing musical mosaic, demonstrating why Elliott Carter finds Powell's music "ceaselessly interesting . . . each work is like a travel in a new, fascinating territory full of fresh, often unexpected perspectives."

—Rosemary Johnson

R

RABE, Folke (Alvar Harald Reinhold). Swedish. Born in Stockholm, 28 October 1935. Educated at Royal College of Music, Stockholm (music education, trombone, composition under Valdemar Soderholm, Karl-Birger Blomdahl, Ingvar Lidholm, György Ligeti and Witold Lutosławski), 1957–64; Tape Music Center, San Francisco, 1965. Military service in Swedish Air Force. Married (1) Ursula Hardelin in 1962; (2) Eva Rehnstrom in 1977; 3 children. Jazz musician, from 1950; composer, from 1957; founder (with Jan Bark and others), The Culture Quartet (4 trombones), 1963–73, and New Culture Quartet, from 1983; assistant, Royal College of Music, Stockholm, 1964–8; producer, artist manager, programme director, Rikskonserter/Institute for National Concerts, Stockholm, 1968–80; producer, Swedish National Radio, Stockholm, since 1980; associate/collaborator, Bel-Canto-koren. Mailing address: Birkagatan 1, S-113 36 Stockholm Sweden.

Publishers: Wilhelm Hansen, Copenhagen; Nordiska Musikforlaget, Stockholm; Edition Reimers, Bromma.

Symphonies/orchestral:

Hep-Hep 1966; first performed Gaule, 1967.
Altiplano (wind orchestra; based on Indian tunes) 1982; first performed Murzzuschlag, Austria, 1982.
All the Lonely People . . . (trombone, orchestra) 1990; first performed Vasteras, Sweden, 1990.
Horn Concerto 1991.

Chamber/instrumental:

Seven Variations 1960; first performed Stockholm, 1961.
Bolos (collaboration with Jan Bark; 4 trombones) 1962; first performed Stockholm, 1962. Recorded Artist ALP 102.
Impromptu (clarinet, trombone, cello, piano, percussion) 1962; first performed Stockholm, 1963.
Polonaise (collaboration with Jan Bark; 4 trombones) 1965; first performed Warsaw, 1966.
Basta (trombone) 1981; first performed Stockholm, 1982. Recorded BIS.
Shazam (trumpet) 1984; first performed London, 1985. Recorded BIS.
With Love (piano) 1986; first performed Stockholm, 1986.
Escalations (brass quintet) 1986; first performed Helsinki, 1986.

Vocal/choral:

Notturno (mezzo-soprano, woodwinds) 1959; first performed Copenhagen, 1960.
Piece (collaboration with Lasse O'Mansson; speaking chorus) 1961; first performed Stockholm, 1962. Recorded Artist ALP 102.
Rondes (mixed or male chorus) 1964. Recorded HMV SCLP 1043; RCA VICS 1602.
Joe's Harp (unaccompanied mixed chorus) 1970; first performed Warsaw, 1970. Recorded Philips 6519 001; Proprius Prop 7802.
Two Stanzas (unaccompanied mixed chorus; Sonnevi) 1980; first performed Bergen, Norway, 1981.
To Love (unaccompanied mixed chorus) 1984; first performed Stockholm, 1984.

Other:

Wahrheit/Truth (whole-evening performance) 1966.
Atmospharische Storungen/Atmospheric Disturbances (whole-evening performance) 1966.
Eh?? (electro-acoustic) 1967; first performed Stockholm, 1967. Recorded Wergo WER 60047.
No Hambones on the Moon (film with Culture Quartet) 1971.
Electricity and Trombones (whole evening performance) 1972.
To the Bar Bender (electro-acoustic) 1982; first performed Stockholm, 1982. Recorded Fylkingen FYLP 1029.
Narrskeppet/The Ship of Fools (intermedia show with New Culture Quartet) 1983; first performed Innsbruck, 1983.
Cyclone (electro-acoustic) 1985; first performed Stockholm, 1985.
The World Museum (intermedia show with New Culture Quartet) 1987; first performed Oslo, 1987.
Narragonia (intermedia show with New Culture Quartet) 1989–90; first performed Skinnskatteberg, 1990.

PUBLICATIONS

By Rabe: (with Jan Bark) *Sound Workshop*, Stockholm, 1975.

On Rabe: Lennart Reimers, "FR", in *Musikrevy*, 1, 1989.

* * *

Folke Rabe became known as a composer in the early 1960s, when he emerged with a remarkably broad musical training—in composition, trombone and music education—and with a professional passion for jazz. His studies with Karl-Birger Blomdahl, Ingvar Lidholm, György Ligeti and Witold Lutosławski had made him familiar with the turbulent happenings stirring post-serial music. The same experiences made him aware of the fruitful creative potential of interaction between individual and collective enterprise. He developed a pedagogical "world view" in which music had expanded into a wide concept of "sounds".

Together with Jan Bark and two other trombone players, he founded Kulturkvartetten (The Culture Quartet) and started a close collaboration with Bel Canto-koren and its conductor Karl-Eric Andersson. From the mid 1960s, these two ensembles enjoyed considerable success at many of the major European festivals—ISCM, Donaueschingen, Wiener Festwochen, Warsaw Autumn, Zagreb Biennale, Cheltenham—with *Bolos* and *Polonaise* composed jointly by Rabe and Bark for trombone quartet, and *Piece* with Lasse O'Mansson for speech choir, *Rondes* and *Joe's Harp* for chorus, and a series of powerfully integrated whole-evening performances involving a considerable measure of improvisation, gesture, movement, light and unconventional sound production, in addition to trombones and voices.

From the end of the 1970s Rabe continued to develop highly original expressive combinations: free-tonal music was integrated with light projection, kinetic elements, and references to the "happenings" of the time, as in *Two Stanzas* to a text by Sonnevi, with its memories of 1968; or explorations of the idea of the "show" – *Basta* for trombone begins with the advice "Alert entrance", *Shazam* for trumpet starts with "Check position and foot hold" and ends with a "grand gesture . . . as if throwing a kiss to the audience".

Humoristic elements of this kind must not be misunderstood. The "show" ingredients of Rabe's works are deeply integrated in the artistic totality. The underlying inspiration of the multi-media work *Narrskeppet / The Ship of Fools*, a process-based work begun in 1983, goes back to the medieval tale of those *narren* who try to establish a "normal" human life isolated on the ocean. Their actions are, in Rabe's view, not so irrational, if you see them in relation to the short and passive perspectives of the "solutions" of our time.

Rabe's creative world is above all connected to problems of the *Zeitgeist*, literally what is "in the air", in wind instrument sounds and vocal utterances. Some of his most important works of the last decade contain music that "breathes": *Altiplano* for wind orchestra, *Escalations* for brass quintet, the trombone concerto *All the Lonely People . . .*, the new *Horn Concerto*. One might say that Folke Rabe is searching for an audible blueprint to a silent world.

—Lennart Reimers

RAMEY, Phillip. American. Born in Chicago, Illinois, 12 September 1939. Educated: early piano training; International Academy of Music, Nice (composition under Alexander Tcherepnin), 1959; DePaul University, Chicago (composition under Tcherepnin), 1959–62, B.A.; Columbia University, New York City (composition under Jack Beeson), 1963–5, M.A. Programme annotator, New York Philharmonic Orchestra, since 1977; writer of liner notes, CBS classical Masterworks. Mailing address: 825 West End Avenue, Penthouse F, New York, New York 10025, U.S.A.

Publishers: Boosey & Hawkes; Schirmer; Peters; Marks.

Symphonies / orchestral:

Concert Suite (piano, orchestra) 1962, revised 1983–4.
Piano Concerto No 1 1969–71.
Concerto for Chamber Orchestra 1974.
Piano Concerto No 2 1976.
Concerto for Horn and String Orchestra 1987–9.

Chamber / instrumental:

Incantations (piano) 1960, revised 1982.
Suite (piano) 1960–3.
Sonata (3 timpani) 1961.
Sonata No 1 (piano) 1961.
Capriccio (percussion) 1966.
Toccata breve (percussion) 1966.
Diversions (piano) 1966.
Sonata No 2 (piano) 1966.
Night Music (percussion) 1967.
Epigrams (piano) 1967.
Commentaries (flute, piano) 1968.
Sonata No 3 (piano) 1968.
Sonata No 4 (piano) 1968.
Fantasy (piano) 1969–72.
Suite (violin, piano) 1971.
Leningrad Rag (Mutations on Scott Joplin) (piano) 1972.
Night Songs (piano) 1973.
Sonata No 5 (piano) 1974.
La Citadelle (rhapsody for oboe, piano) 1975.
Arabesque (flute) 1977.
Memorial (piano) 1977.
Fanfare-Sonata (trumpet) 1981.
Echoes (piano) 1981–2.
Cossack Variations (piano) 1981–5.
Canzona (piano) 1982.
Phantasm (flute, violin; or 2 violins) 1984.
Sonata No 6 (piano) 1988.
Canticle (piano, left hand) 1989.
Cantus Arcanus (piano) 1990.
Burlesque-Paraphrase on a Theme of Stephen Foster (piano) 1990.

Vocal / choral:

Cat Songs (soprano, flute, piano; Eliot) 1962, revised 1965–7.
Seven, They Are Seven (incantations for bass baritone, orchestra; Balmont) 1965.
Merlin's Prophecy (high voice, piano; Blake) 1966.
A William Blake Trilogy (soprano, piano) 1980.
Two Moroccan Songs to Poems of Paul Bowles (soprano, piano) 1980–5.

* * *

Phillip Ramey began studying composition with the important Russian composer Alexander Tcherepnin at DePaul University in Chicago in 1959. Tcherepnin once noted, "Phillip Ramey is certainly one of the most gifted composers I've had the pleasure of teaching. His music is not only well-made but it has a great deal of personality. Especially impressive to me is his sure sense of dynamics—not everyone has this to the degree he does." During his early years as a composer, Ramey's major influences were Tcherepnin, Bartók, and Prokofiev, resulting in compositions that emphasize motoristic rhythms, bitonality and percussive piano writing. Works that illustrate these features are: *Sonata* for three unaccompanied timpani, the piano *Sonata No 1*, and the *Concert Suite* for piano and orchestra.

Beginning with the *Incantations* for piano, one starts to find traits that are featured in the works of the 1960s and 1970s. These comprise extremely disjunct textures and lines, complex chord structures, pungent cluster dissonances, and atonality without any consistent serialism. Many works of this time are uncompromising in their harshness and difficulty of execution and require intense concentration from both performers and audiences. These features culminate in the highly discordant *Piano Concerto No 1* and the virtuosic piano *Fantasy*—the latter being one of Ramey's most demanding works.

Many compositions of the 1970s begin manifesting a modified tonality and greater lyricism. Such works as the

Suite for violin and piano, *Piano Concerto No 2*, *Phantasm* for flute and violin, and the recent *Piano Sonata No 6*, *Canticle* for piano, left hand and the piano piece *Cantus Arcanus* are more overtly expressive than those of the previous period. Long arched lines and spacious textures prevail in certain works that grew out of personal experiences—for instance, a trip to Haiti—*La Citadelle*, a rhapsody for oboe and piano, and the death of Tcherepnin—*Memorial* for piano. Ramey's own comments in the scores about the backgrounds of these pieces are important to insure their intelligent performance.

Also characteristic of some works since the early 1970s is a sardonic humor in which popular styles of the past are parodied. Charming instances are the idiosyncratic *Leningrad Rag (Mutations on Scott Joplin)* for piano, written for Vladimir Horowitz, and the witty *Burlesque-Paraphrase on a Theme of Stephen Foster* for piano. In these works quintessentially American models are chosen for musical spoofs within a context of distorting harmonies, textures and rhythms. Interestingly, it is only in these parodies that Ramey shows any easily identifiable "American" influence.

Many of the works mentioned thus far involve the piano, not surprising in a composer who himself is an effective pianist and therefore knows how to test the limits of the instrument. However, in another medium, there is the recent *Concerto for Horn and String Orchestra*, commissioned by the New York Philharmonic to celebrate its 150th anniversary in 1992. This piece requires the utmost virtuosity of the soloist and explores a wide range of color possibilities between the horn and strings.

Ramey is well-known for his work as annotator for the New York Philharmonic and as author of many articles on contemporary music. These activities have put him in close contact with such major figures as Aaron Copland, Samuel Barber, William Schuman, Virgil Thomson and David Diamond. Ramey consequently has a rare perspective on the development of American music and a special knowledge of the complex musical relationships among these composers.

Ramey's own musical roots are clearly, as he puts it, "on the Franco-Russian side." He feels little connection with the Americana style, terming it "a wonderful and probably necessary gimmick from the 1930s and 1940s." However, Ramey does acknowledge Copland's influence on the clear textures, lyric writing and chordal spaciousness of some of his works, and it is germane that Copland once wrote of him as "a composer of real individuality with a flair for dramatic gesture".

In summary, Ramey's music is indeed strikingly individualistic. He has chosen to avoid the clichés of serialism and the changing fashions of aleatory music and minimalism. Instead, he writes music that often challenges the listener because of its complexity and uncompromising rhetoric.

—Enrique Alberto Arias

RANDS, Bernard. British/English; resident in United States since 1975; American citizen since 1983. Born in Sheffield, 2 March 1934. Educated at University College of Wales, Bangor (music and English literature), B.Mus., 1956, M.Mus., 1958; further study under Roman Vlad, Rome, and Luigi Dallapiccola, Florence, 1958–60; further study under Bruno Maderna, Darmstadt, and Luciano Berio, Milan, early 1960s. Composer in residence, Princeton University, New Jersey, from 1966; lecturer in music, University of York, 1970–5; concurrently fellow in creative arts, Brasenose College, Oxford; professor of music, University of California, San Diego, from 1975; professor of composition, Boston University, and simultaneously faculty member, Juilliard School of Music, New York City; composer in residence, Aspen, Colorado, Tanglewood, Massachusetts, and Dartington, Devon; composer in residence, Philadelphia Orchestra, from 1989. Recipient: Harkness Fellowship, 1966; Guggenheim Fellowship, 1982–3; Pulitzer Prize (for *Canti del sole*), 1984. Mailing address: c/o European-American Music Corporation, P.O. Box 850, Valley Forge, Pennsylvania 19482, U.S.A.

Publisher: Universal Edition.

Symphonies/orchestral:

Refractions 1961.
Per esempio (youth orchestra) 1968.
Wildtrack 1 1969.
Agenda (youth orchestra) 1969–70.
Mesalliance (piano, small orchestra/no violins or violas) 1972.
Wildtrack 2 1973.
Ology (jazz orchestra) 1973.
Aum (harp, small orchestra/no violins) 1974; first performed London, 17 April 1974.
Serenata 75B (solo flute, clarinet, celeste, piano, electric piano, electric organ, strings) 1976.
Madrigali (after Monteverdi/Berio) 1977.
Le Tambourin: Suite No 1 (large orchestra) 1984.
Le Tambourin: Suite No 2 (large orchestra) 1984.
Ceremonial 1 1985.
Hiraeth (cello, orchestra) 1987; first performed San Diego, California, 19 February 1987.
. . . Body and Shadow . . . 1988; first performed Boston, 22 February 1989.

Chamber/instrumental:

Tre espressioni (piano) 1960.
Actions for Six (flute, harp, 2 percussion, viola, cello) 1962–3.
Espressione IV (2 pianos) 1964.
Formants 1—Les Gestes (harp) 1965.
Sound Patterns 4 (graphic score for miscellaneous instrumental groups) 1969.
Formants 2: Labyrinth (clarinet, trombone, piano, celeste, 2 percussion, viola, cello) 1969–70.
Tableau ("Monotone", "Epiphanies", "Labyrinthe", "Tutto e sciolto", "Monologue", "Intérieur"; flute/alto flute, clarinet/bass clarinet, piano/celeste, violin, viola, cello) 1970.
Espressioni V-A / V-B (2 pianos) 1970.
Memo 1 (double bass) 1971.
Déjà (flute/alto flute, clarinet/bass clarinet, piano/harp, percussion, viola, cello) 1972.
As All Get Out (indeterminate instrumentation) 1972.
Memo 2 (trombone) 1973.
Response—Memo 1b (2 double basses or double bass, tape) 1973.
Memo 3 (cello) 1974.
Cuaderno (string quartet) 1974.
Etendre—Memo 1c (double bass solo, flute/alto flute, clarinet/bass clarinet, horn, trumpet, trombone, piano/

celeste, electric organ, percussion, violin, viola, cello) 1974.
Scherzi (clarinet, piano, violin, cello) 1974.
Memo 4 (tuba) 1975.
Memo 5 (piano) 1975.
Serenata 75 (flute, clarinet, celeste, piano, electric piano, electric organ, violin, cello) 1976.
Obbligato—Memo 2c (trombone, string quartet) 1980.
Serenata 85 (flute, harp, violin, viola, cello) 1986.
. . . In the Receding Mist . . . (flute, harp, violin, viola, cello) 1988; first performed November 1988.

Vocal/choral:

Sound Patterns 1 (voice, hands) 1967.
Sound Patterns 2 (voices, percussion, miscellaneous instruments) 1967.
Sound Patterns 3 (project for voices) 1969.
Ballad 1 (mezzo-soprano, flute/alto flute, trombone, piano, percussion; Sorrentino) 1970.
Ballad 2 (voice, piano; Sorrentino) 1970.
Metalepsis II (mezzo-soprano, SSAATB chorus, chamber ensemble; Wain, Mao, Requiem Mass) 1971.
Serena (soprano, mime, tape) 1972.
Wildtrack 2 (soprano, narrator, orchestra; Ungaretti) 1973.
Ballad 3 (soprano, tape/bell; Sorrentino) 1973.
Wildtrack 3 (soprano, mezzo-soprano, SATB chorus, narrator, orchestra; 20th-century texts) 1975.
Ballad 4 (2 SATB choruses, 3 clarinets/E♭ clarinet/bass clarinet, 3 trumpets, 2 trombones, bass trombone, electric organ, 2 percussion, harp, 3 violas, 2 cellos, double bass; Sorrentino) 1978.
Déjà (instrumental piece arranged for soprano, flute/alto flute, clarinet/bass clarinet, trumpet, piano/harp, percussion, marimba, viola, cello) 1979.
Canti lunatici (soprano, orchestra or chamber ensemble; 15 poems about the moon) 1980.
Flickering Shadows (2 sopranos, mezzo-soprano, tenor, bass; traditional) 1983–4.
Canti del sole (tenor, orchestra or chamber ensemble; 14 poems about the sun) 1984.
Der Nachsommer (soprano, trumpet, viola) 1985.
Requiescant (soprano, SATB chorus, orchestra) 1985–6.
. . . Among the Voices . . . (SATB chorus, harp) 1988.

Other:

Memo 2b (trombone, female dancer) 1980.
Memo 2d (trombone, string quartet, female dancer) 1980.

PUBLICATIONS

On Rands: C. Small, "BR", in *Musical Times*, October 1967.

* * *

"My main motive in writing music is to put myself in touch with areas of myself that I might not otherwise discover, and to offer audiences a similar experience." Bernard Rands offered that statement of artistic purpose in 1986 at a post-concert "Composer Encounter" for the Philadelphia Orchestra, whose composer in residence he became three years later. It provides a telling insight into the humanity, and the humanism, of this remarkable musician.

There was a time when expressive cordiality was not what came first to mind on encountering a Rands piece. But that was back in the 1960s, when Western music was still largely in thrall to stylistic preconceptions emphasizing intellectual control rather than emotion, when "beauty" was seen by many in the profession as an inadmissible if not a dirty word. Since as far back as *Madrigali*, a tribute to Monteverdi that he composed in 1977, Rands has effected a notable escape from the endemic aridity that dominated other composers in those days and to some degree cramped even his generous communicative urge. The potential for a richer expressive palette was always present in his work, for it was less to the expressionist histrionics of the Second Viennese School than to the more lyrical and vocal serialism of his Italian teacher Dallapiccola that Rands was drawn from the start. His more recent music, from the *Canti lunatici* of 1980 by way of the 1984 *Le Tambourin* suites that will form part of his Van Gogh opera to the 1988 Boston Symphony commission *. . . Body and Shadow . . .* , profits richly from the new stylistic pluralism of our time, besides revealing in ways both musical and more broadly intellectual his "lifelong interest in the writings of Samuel Beckett, and in folksong."

The widespread reaction against mid-century adherence to serial and other doctrinaire systems has been variously dubbed "post-modernism," "neo-romanticism," and "the New Simplicity." The last would be a misleading term for Rands's complex and subtle synthesis. The reconciling of tonal elements with mainstream modernist ones is very far from being a simple musical task. (As the Czech composer Ladislav Kupkovic pointed out a few years ago, moreover, "atonal does not mean complicated, and tonal does not mean simple.") But whatever we call it, there can be little questioning the gain for both composers and listeners from the late-20th-century liberalization of the creative approach, and from the newer music's increasing unwillingness to accept sheer unpleasantness as a necessary corollary of originality and aesthetic value.

Rands does not evade the tough issues in his music. Yet he manages to integrate them into a world view that stresses what makes us all human: a range of qualities that combines strength with tenderness, integrity with humor, and an intense vein of mystery with a respectful attention to the lessons of history. Unlike some of his colleagues, he generally prefers not to indulge in patchworks or potpourris of quasi-historical material; he does not need to. As he said in discussing his approach to a 1991 commission to mark the centenary of Carnegie Hall, when he briefly entertained the notion of incorporating musical ideas from the many works that have been premiered there: "I decided not to do that, because there are lots of problems involved with it. But I think that's in my music anyway, because I relate very much to the music of the past."

More spontaneously and openly than many of his contemporaries, Rands acknowledges classical masters like Mozart, Beethoven, and Brahms, and 20th-century composers like Bartók, as his indispensable meat and drink. Maybe it is to this acknowledgement and the security that goes with it that his own music, not really paradoxically, owes some of its unmistakable originality and sense of identity. But for the real reason we must probably go back to that ultimate ground of humanness, of self, of communication, which as with any creative artist of the highest stature unites Rands the man and Rands the musician.

—Bernard Jacobson

RÁNKI, György. Hungarian. Born in Budapest, 30 October 1907, Educated at Budapest Academy of Music (composition and conducting under Zoltán Kodály, Leó Weiner and Ferencsik), 1926–30; further study in ethnomusicology under Andre Schaeffner, Paris, 1938–9. Married Anna Dekany, 13 November 1940; 1 son and 1 daughter. Musical director, Hungarian Theatre, from 1945; director, music section, Hungarian Radio, 1947–8; worked in Belgium and Italy, 1949; director (UNESCO appointment), National Conservatory of Music, leader of Symphony Orchestra, Guyaquil, Ecuador, 1950–8,; full-time independent composer, resident in Tessin, Switzerland, Vienna and Budapest, since 1958. Recipient: Erkel Prize, 1952, 1957; Kossuth Prize, 1954; Pro Arte Prize, 1970; Merited Artist, Hungary, 1963; Bartók-Pasztory Award, 1987; Outstanding Artist, Hungary, 1988. Mailing address: 36 Gulbaba-Utca, 1023 Budapest; or (management) Artisjus, Vorosmarty-Ter 1, Budapest 1051, Hungary.

Publishers: Edition Musica, Budapest; Universal.

Symphonies/orchestral:

Aristophanes Suite (version for violin, string orchestra) 1947–85.
Kardtanc/Sword Dance 1949.
Magyar tancok a 15. szazadbol/Hungarian Dances from the 15th Century 1950.
Elegiac Variations 1953.
Pomádé kiraly uj ruhaja/King Pomádé's New Clothes: Suites I and II (orchestral suites from the opera) 1954. Recorded LS 759 (I); LP 133 (II); SLPX 12947 (I & II).
Don Quijote y Dulcinea (2 miniatures for oboe, chamber orchestra or harpsichord or piano) 1961. Recorded LPX 11534; Melodiya C10 17655 6.
1514 (fantasy for piano, orchestra; after woodcuts by Derkovits) 1962. Recorded LPX 11481.
Cirkusz/Circus (orchestral suite from dance drama) 1965.
Aurora tempestuosa (prelude for orchestra) 1967. Recorded LPX 11481.
Raga di notte (violin, orchestra) 1974.
A varazsital/The Magic Drink: Suites I and II (orchestral suites from opera) 1975.
Symphony No 1 1977. Recorded SLPX 12434.
Viola Concerto (double string orchestra, percussion, piano) 1979. Recorded SLPX 14234.
Symphony No 2: In memoriam Zoltan Kodaly 1981.
Divertimento (clarinet, strings) 1986.

Chamber/instrumental:

Sonata No 1 (piano) 1931.
Aristophanes Suite (violin, piano) 1947.
Sonata No 2 (piano) 1947.
Easy Variations on a Hungarian Folksong (piano) 1955.
Serenata all 'antiqua (violin, piano) 1956.
Two Hungarian Folksongs (piano duet) 1957.
Pentaerophonia (3 pieces for wind quintet) 1958. Recorded SLPX 31084.
Burlesque (flute/piccolo, oboe, 2 clarinets, 2 bassoons, 3 horns, trumpet, trombone) 1958.
Scherzo Zongorara (piano) 1961.
Pomádé kiraly uj ruhaja/King Pomádé's New Clothes (piano) 1962.
Pas de deux et Galop (piano; from *Circus*) 1966.
Ket bors okrocske/Two Wonder Oxen (arranged for piano duet) 1969.
Two Easy Pieces in Vietnamese Style (violin, piano) 1973.
Seven Easy Pieces on Vietnamese Melodies (piano) 1973.
Concertino (cimbalom, xylophone, timpani, percussion, string quintet) 1978.
A hetfeju sarkany szerenadja/Serenade of the Seven-headed Dragon (brass septet) 1980. Recorded SLPX 31003.
Sonata No 3 (piano) 1980.
String Quartet: in memoriam Béla Bartók 1985.
Ludapo mesei/The Tales of Father Goose (brass septet) 1987.

Vocal/choral:

Emberiseg/Mankind (voice, piano; Jozsef) 1942.
Ket karodban/In Your Arms (voice, piano; Radnoti) 1945.
A varos peremen/At the Outskirts of the City (cantata) 1947.
Medvetanc (voice, piano) 1948.
Magyarorszag az en hazam/Hungary Is My Country (voice, piano; folksongs from 1848) 1948–50.
A szabadsag eneke/Freedom Song (cantata) 1950.
Utkozet bekeben/Battle in Peace (cantata) 1951.
Dal a nepek egyeterteserol/Song on the Concord of Peoples (equal voices, piano; Weöres) 1952.
From *King Pomádé's New Clothes* (2 bass arias; Karolyi) 1953.
A walesi bardok/The Bards of Wales (cantata) 1957.
Sohajtas bekesseg utan/Yearning for Peace (baritone, mixed chorus, piano; Takacs) 1959.
Three Children's Choruses (original and folk texts) 1960.
Bekedal/Peace Song (cantata) 1960.
Six Songs (from *Three Nights*; voice, piano; Hubay, Vas) 1961.
Fekete szolo/Black Grapes (voice, piano; 21 Hungarian folksongs) 1964.
1944 (oratorio for baritone, mixed chorus, chamber orchestra; Radnoti) 1967. Recorded LPX 11481.
Ket bors okrocske/Two Wonder Oxen (tale with music for narrator, 13 instruments) 1969. Recorded LP 1596.
Kodaly emlekezete/Lament in memoriam Zoltan Kodaly (female voice, mixed chorus, cimbalom, harpsichord or organ) 1971.
Fenyben furdik a fold/Earth in Full Light (unaccompanied mixed chorus; Raics) 1971.
A fonix madar/The Phoenix (unaccompanied mixed chorus) 1971.
Cantus urbis (4 soloists, mixed chorus, instrumental ensemble; Déry) 1972.
Ars poetica (unaccompanied mixed chorus) 1972.
Dozsa lelke/Spirit of Dozsa (unaccompanied mixed chorus) 1972.
Csori csuka (3 songs for children's chorus, violin or xylophone; Ivanyi) 1973.
Leverkuhn's Abschied (monodrama for tenor, 10 instruments; after Mann, *Doktor Faustus*) 1979. Recorded SLPX 12455.
Káin es Ábel (soprano, alto, tenor, bass, mixed chorus, orchestra) 1981–9.
Zsoltar gyermekhangra/Psalm for Children's Voices (children's chorus, 3 trumpets; Babits) 1984.
Ket spirituale/Two Spirituals ("The Fifth Commandment", "Canaan"; children's or mixed chorus, 3 trumpets) 1987.
Nyitany a 21. szazadhoz/Overture to the 21st century (chorus, orchestra) 1987.

Opera:

A csendhaborito/The Rioter (musical comedy) 1950, revised 1959; broadcast Budapest Radio, 1950; staged version Budapest, 1959.

Pomádé kiraly uj ruhaja / King Pomádé's New Clothes (Karolyi, after Andersen) 1953, revised 1967; first performed Budapest, 6 June 1953.
A gyoztes ismeretlen / The Winner Is Unknown (operetta) 1961.
Holgyvalasz / Spoon Dance (operetta) 1961.
Egy szerelem harom ejszakája / Three Nights of Love (Hubay, Vas) 1961.
Muzsikus Péter / New Adventures of Peter the Musician or, Peter in Musicland (children's opera; Romhanyi, after Chitz) 1962.
Az ember tragediaja / The Tragedy of Man (mystery opera; after Madách) 1970; first performed Budapest, 4 December 1970. Recorded SLPX 11714.
A holdbeli csonakos / The Boatman of the Moon (opera fantasy; Weöres) 1979.
Vegelszamolas / Terminal (music drama; Karinthy) 1988.

Other:

Hoemberek / Snowmen 1939; first performed London, 1939.
Cirkusz / Circus (symphonic dance drama; after Karinthy) 1965.
A varazsital / The Magic Drink (ballet; after Zola, Keres) 1975.

* * *

György Ránki studied composition with Zoltán Kodály and later became deeply involved with folk music. Much of his creative work has been for the theatre and the cinema. His compositions have always been full of irony and wry humour, but more recently have included a sense of drama.

The song *Medvetanc* starts humorously with bugle references in a quasi-lydian mode. Its verses accumulate extra pitches, resulting in an octatonic fun-song. The pianist's left hand maintains a drone throughout, a feature repeated in Second Piano Sonata. This bustling work is full of multiple-third arpeggios. Frequently, the quick accented notes of the right-hand melody move a semitone while the left hand provides middle C quaver drone repetition. Textural variety is achieved with lively two-part counterpoint and mild syncopations. In the second movement, multiple thirds are used as a delicate waft of sound introducing writing based upon the simultaneous playing of two different triads. The work ends with an exuberant *bulgarese sempre stringendo* movement, built on an inflected bass ostinato.

Many later works exploit the pastiche of national idioms. In *Pentaerophonia* (three pseudo-gamelan pieces for wind quintet) the fastest lines of the Prelude recall Poulenc's cadence rhythms while other voices continue in their own key. Expressive lines of the Fantasia move in the Chabrier mould—a pleasant movement with chromatic inflections. The busy opening of the Rondo is soon thinned in texture for ease of listening, the Fantasia's main melodic compass of a fifth becomes compressed in the Rondo (often into a minor third). Ránki's piano *Scherzo Zongorara* demonstrates typical "Hungarian rhapsodic mood-changes": spiky accompaniment to sprightly tunes when fast; sonoristically rubato when slow, with added-note harmony and well-crafted tension building throughout. This is a totally pianistic encore work, not exploiting figurative runs or arpeggios so much as touch-changes and speed.

Ránki's opera, *Pomádé kiraly uj ruhaja / King Pomádé's New Clothes* was the first important Hungarian opera of the 1950s, and won official esteem and public appreciation. The opera and its associated orchestral suite demonstrates his excellent at pastiche. The introduction, with trumpets and piccolo both playing repeated-note motives in seconds, is answered by a *pesante* tuba, presenting the jovial feeling of this pseudo-Petrushka work: a bombastic movement, full of energy and wit. "Patrol" continues the wit, this time with side drum and third trumpet—similar to Lord Berners's *Neptune*. "Patrol" is followed by "Scottish Dance", "Arabic Dance" and "Chinese Dance", all gloriously skilful pastiches of pre-war burlesque.

Text is treated as all-important in a serious later opera, *Az ember tragediaja / The Tragedy of Man*. Madách's poetic mystery play, from Creation to Destruction in great historical tableaux, suggested that, according to Ránki "the musical reformulation of the play should be approached from the viewpoint of contemporary man, in the tradition of Liszt, Bartók and Kodály". All of the 15 tableaux are retained. Choral interludes are inserted between the individual tableaux to provide a contrasting spectacle to the oratorio character of the drama.

Melodies play an important role in Ránki's more serious works. He illustrates character by using historical styles—sometimes by referential musical quotation. His music is most alive when it describes a historical event, but loses strength at moments of philosophic contemplation. Perhaps for this reason, Ránki claims that his aspiration regarding his music "is to vanish, to merge into the combined effect".

—Malcolm J. Hill

RASKATOV, Alexander. Russian. Born in Moscow, 9 March 1953. Educated at Moscow Conservatoire (composition under Albert Leman), 1972–82. Married Olga Magidenko, October 1978; 2 sons. Freelance composer, member of Union of Soviet Composers, since 1979; and Association for Contemporary Music, from 1990; composer in residence, Stetson University, DeLand, Florida, 1990. Recipient: honorary membership, Pi Kappa Lambda Beta Gamma chapter, Stetson University. Mailing address: ul. Ogareva dom 13, kv. 82, Moscow 103009, U.S.S.R.

Publisher: Sovetskii kompozitor, Moscow.

Symphonies / orchestral:

Concerto for Oboe and Strings 1987; first performed Moscow, 1989.
Six Psalmodies (viola, harp, strings) 1990.

Chamber / instrumental:

Small Triptych (oboe) 1975.
Birinium (7 duets for 2 horns) 1977.
Dramatic Games (cello) 1979; first performed Moscow, 1980.
Sonata (piano) 1980–1; first performed Moscow, 1981.
Invitation to a Concert (percussion) 1981; first performed Moscow, 1982.

Reminiscence of the Alpine Rose (percussion ensemble, music box, tape) 1982; first performed Moscow, 1982.
Night Hymns (piano, 11 instruments) 1984; first performed Leningrad, 1984.
Muta in . . . (3 flutes) 1986; first performed Moscow, 1987.
Sentimental Sequences (13 performers) 1986.
The Road (2 cellos, harpsichord) 1987; first performed Moscow, 1987.
Sonata (viola, piano) 1988; first performed Amsterdam, 1989.
Consolation (piano) 1989; first performed Buffalo, New York, 1989.
Punctuation Marks (harpsichord) 1989.
Glasses (bassoon) 1989.
Illusion (6 percussion) 1990.

Vocal/choral:

Court Songs (cantata for soprano, instrumental ensemble; Japanese verse) 1976. Recorded Melodiya C10 13247 8.
To Those Cured . . . (soprano, piano; Baratynsky) 1980.
Circle of Singing (mezzo-soprano, piano, cello, harpsichord; Zhukovsky, Baratynsky) 1984; first performed Moscow, 1985.
A Book of Spring (tenor, chamber orchestra; Zhukovsky) 1985.
From Spring, from the Grass, from the Heavens (lyrical oratorio for mezzo-soprano, boys' choir, orchestra; Nekrasova) 1987.
Gra-ka-kha-ta (tenor, violin, percussion ensemble; Khlebnikov) 1988; first performed Moscow, 1988.
Stabat mater (high voice, organ) 1988.
Let There Be Light (counter-tenor, string trio; Coleridge) 1989; first performed London, 1989.
Sonnet 66 (soprano, chamber ensemble) 1990; first performed Berlin, 1990.

Opera:

The Pit and the Pendulum (after Poe) 1990.

Other:

Crime and Punishment (theatre music) 1983.
Don Kikhot (theatre music) 1987.
F.I.P. (film score) 1989.
MU-MU (film music) 1989.
N. Roslavetz: *Stuchit* (voice, 6 percussion; arranged and orchestrated). N. Roslavetz: *Chamber Symphony* (arranged and orchestrated).

PUBLICATIONS

On Raskatov: Viktor Ekimovsky, "New Names", in *Music in* the U.S.S.R., October–December 1984; Marina Lobanova, "Poiski sebja", in *Sovetskaya musika*, 11, 1985; Gerard McBurney, "Soviet Discoveries" in *Quarter Notes*, June 1989.

* * *

Alexander Raskatov's music attractively and memorably evades falling into the stylistic orbit of his more famous elders such as Schnittke, Gubaidulina or Denisov. Instead, he has found a language of his own, marked by intense humility and exquisite civilisation. One of his earliest successful compositions is the cycle for voice and instruments, *Court Songs*, based on medieval Japanese poems. Each song is marked by the most refined attention to detail balanced by an attractive emotional openness. It also clearly reflects two technical features that have become almost obsessive concerns of Raskatov's musical imagination.

One of these is a loyalty to modal thinking of a kind that goes straight back in the Russian tradition to figures like Stravinsky and Sriabin and perhaps their predecessors. While modal thinking is hardly an exotic matter these days, Raskatov's approach clearly and subtly establishes and then exploits the particular scalic structures that appeal to him. Modes for him have intrinsic musical lives; they are simply channels to be easily exploited for the way they narrow the field of choice. Raskatov's balletic sense of melodic line is rooted in his awareness of how that line unfolds and breathes life into a particular mode. This is particularly clear in his vocal works such as his *Circle of Singing* and his Coleridge cycle *Let There Be Light.*

The second important element of Raskatov's musical language is his fondness for repetitive patterns, arpeggio accompaniments and various phrases. This might suggest either a neo-romantic or a minimalist temperament label, but neither is accurate. Instead it is a manner of construction, a positive understanding of the decorative as a legitimate approach to form. The care of detail on what seems to be the accompaniment is the sensibility of an applied artist, and indeed Raskatov's work at its most picturesque often suggests the pleasure in ornament, colour and proportion of a jeweller or embroiderer rather than a composer.

But the results of both the modal thinking and the repetition need not be merely charming and beguiling. There is an undercurrent of threat and darkness in Raskatov's music which comes out most forcefully in his chamber concerto for piano and instruments *Night Hymns*, one of his most powerful and successful works to date. Here the sweetness of modality and the charm of making patterns are heard as qualities of life under attack from exterior forces characterised by aggression and brutality.

Another, quite different side to Raskatov's nature delights in boyish high spirits. He shares this quality with the famous Moscow percussionist Mark Perkasky, for whom Raskatov has written several theatrical works designed for fun and games.

Something of both sides of Raskatov's work come together in *Gra-ka-kha-ta*, a setting of texts by the Futurist visionary Velimir Khlebnikov, for Alexei Martynov, a leading Soviet tenor who is also a talented violinist. In Raskatov's piece Martynov is required to play and sing, accompanied by the music of Pekarsky's percussion ensemble. This important work neatly combines a sense of delight in play with the opposed sense of the threat that must always lie behind the play.

—Gerard McBurney

RASMUSSEN, Karl Aage. Danish. Born in Kolding, 13 December 1947. Educated at Royal Academy of Music, Aarhus (composition under Per Nørgård and Pelle Gudmundsen-Holmgreen), diploma in composition and history of music,

1969. Married Charlotte Schioetz, May 1975. Lecturer, Funen Conservatory, 1969–71; lecturer, 1970–9, docent, 1979–88, and full professor, since 1988, Royal Academy of Music, Aarhus; freelance commentator/consultant, Danish Radio, since 1973; co-editor, *Dansk Musiktidsskrift*, 1974–8, and since 1988; artistic director and conductor, The Elsinore Players, since 1975; member, Danish Music Council, 1976–9; artistic director, Numus Festival, 1978–85, and since 1988; artistic director, ISCM Festival, Aarhus, 1983; director, Danish Piano Theatre, 1985–8; chair, Danish Art Foundation, 1987–90. Mailing address: Brokbjerggard, 8752 Oestbirk, Denmark; or via dei Panieri 18, Rome, Italy.

Publisher: Wilhelm Hansen, Copenhagen.

Symphonies/orchestral:

Coralis constantinus 1967.
Symphony for Young Lovers 1967.
Recapitulations 1968.
Symphonie classique 1969.
Symphony: Anfang und Ende 1973; first performed Aarhus, 11 February 1976.
Contrafactum (concerto for cello, orchestra) 1980.
A Symphony in Time 1982.
Movements on a Moving Line (version for small orchestra) 1988.
Doubles 1989; first performed 8 June 1990.

Chamber/instrumental:

Canto serioso (string quartet) 1965.
Aria Grigia (piano—2 and 4 hands) 1966. Recorded (part 1 only) Odeon MOAK 30010.
My Spring Diary I & II (piano—2 and 4 hands) 1967–8.
Afskrift (flute, piano, violin, viola, cello) 1971.
Protocol and Myth (accordion, electric guitar, percussion) 1971.
Genklang/Echo (3 pianos/1 prepared/1 mistuned/4 players, celeste) 1972. Recorded Odeon MOAK 30009.
Als Kind (string quartet) 1972.
Invention (accordion) 1972. Recorded Pyramide TPLP 51.
Antifoni (organ) 1973.
A Ballad of Game and Dream (flute/alto flute/piccolo, clarinet/bass clarinet, electric guitar, percussion, violin, cello) 1974. Recorded DMA 38.
Lullaby (flute, piano) 1976.
Paganini Variations (piano) 1976. Recorded Paula 13.
Lullaby (flute, guitar) 1976–87.
Berio Mask (flute, clarinet, electric guitar, percussion, violin, cello) 1977.
Encore I: Lonesome (guitar) 1977.
Le Tombeau de Père Igor (clarinet, cello, piano) 1977. Recorded DFM 20101.
Parts Apart (flute/piccolo, oboe, string quartet) 1978. Recorded Paula 27.
Capricci e danze (violin, piano) 1979.
Italian Concerto (flute, clarinet, guitar, piano, percussion, violin, cello) 1981.
Ballo in Maschera (wind quintet) 1981.
Pianissimo furioso (flute, clarinet, guitar, piano, percussion, violin, cello) 1982.
A Quartet of Five (2 trumpets, horn, 2 trombones) 1982.
Encore III: Encore for Frances (cello) 1982.
Solos and Shadows (string quartet) 1983.
Encore IV: Match (cello, piano) 1983.
Encore VIIIb (Fuga/Fugue) (piano) 1983–4.
Encore VI: Chains (clarinet) 1983–5.
Encore VII: Strain (piano) 1984.
Toccata (organ) 1984.
Fugue/Fuga (Encore VIII) (clarinet, vibraphone, piano) 1984.
Triple Tango (piano) 1984.
Surrounded by Scales (string quartet) 1985.
Encore II: Join (guitar) 1985.
Encore IX (muted percussion) 1985.
Movements on a Moving Line (version for flute, clarinet, guitar, percussion, piano, violin, cello) 1988.
Still (string quartet) 1989.

Vocal/choral:

Vinter (children's chorus) 1965.
Stilhedens sang (soprano, flute, viola, cello) 1965.
Dette ojeblik/This Moment (haiku for 3 sopranos, flute, percussion) 1966.
Messe (mixed chorus, horn, percussion) 1966.
Nar jeg var lykkelig skrev jeg ingen sange (tenor or baritone, guitar) 1967.
When I Was Happy I Wrote No Songs (6 gipsy lyrics for voice, guitar) 1967. Recorded DMA 36.
Parade (male chorus, electric organ) 1968.
Kaerligheden er i verden/Love Is in the World (male or female singer, guitar, percussion; Aarestrup) 1974–5. Recorded Odeon MOAK 30012.
One and All (voice, piano; Borum) 1976.
Encore V: Ich, nur . . . (voice) 1983.
Liederkreis (soprano, baritone, flute, clarinet, vibraphone, violin, piano) 1985–6.

Opera/dramatic:

Krapp's Last Tape (chamber opera; after Beckett) 1966.
Jephta (3 "playgirls", 3 "playboys", orchestra; Borum) 1976–7.
Majakovskij (scenic concert piece; 2 baritones, flute, clarinet, percussion, piano, violin, cello) 1977–8.
Historien om Jonas (musical play for radio; baritone, mixed chorus, 4 trombones, tuba, 2 percussion, piano, harp, harpsichord/harmonium, guitar/mandolin, cello; Borum) 1978–80.
Vores Hoffmann/Our Hoffmann (2 voices, mime, piano—4 hands, percussion, tape) 1986.
Hvorfor bli'r det nat, mor/Why Will It Be Night, Mother? (music theatre for soprano, electronics) 1988–9.

Other:

Sport og tidsfordriv (ballet; clarinet, bassoon, cornet, trombone, percussion, violin, double bass) 1984.

PUBLICATIONS

By Rasmussen: "Music in the 20th Century", in *The History of Music* [various hands], Copenhagen, 1990; numerous essays in Scandinavian and European journals.

On Rasmussen: Poul Ruders, "KAR", Wilhelm Hansen, Copenhagen, 1985; Margit Nonbo, *The Music of KAR*, Aalborg, 1989.

* * *

Karl Aage Rasmussen made his début as a composer in the mid-1960s, a decade of extensive radical experiments in Danish music. From the very beginning Rasmussen was at the front line of an increasing opposition of the invariable modernistic demands for "new sounds," and a great part of his comprehensive output reflects a most conscious dealing with and thorough exploration of previously existing musical materials.

In his earliest works Rasmussen searched for new means of expression in traditional materials by organizing it in "not-previously-heard-contexts." The building components comprise a wealth of micro-quotations and idioms from different musics intuitively combined in a closely woven montage. This curious merge of micro-elements from a vast diversity of musical expressions imparts to the listener a dualistic experience of seemingly well-known details, but yet a blurred and strange entirety.

The essence of this procedure is shown in *Genklang/Echo* from 1972, a multi-piano work for a mistuned, a prepared, a four-hand piano and a celeste. The mistuned "honky-tonk" piano (with a theme based on the Adagietto from Mahler's Fifth Symphony) actually spells out the dream of Yesterday's World, constantly moulded in the patchy musics of the remaining instruments.

Later on in the 1970s Rasmussen left the completely heterogeneous juxtaposition of material for more connected —often non-musical—sources. In this period a large number of plays, poems, myths and even entire works by other composers were the objects of Rasmussen's unorthodox adaptations and "de-compositions". Through his radical interventions he incessantly asks questions to the music itself and sets forth critical comments on different stylistic, ideological or cultural situations.

Kaerligheden er i verden/Love Is in the World (based on 19th-century poems) is composed of romantic *lied* idioms and literal Schumann quotations coupled with other musics in an abrupt discontinuous course. With an ironic, humorous distance the composer comments on the possible/impossible act of creating a love song on today's terms.

In the radio opera *Historien om Jonas* the dramatic idea is based on a contrast between an ancient Jonas-figure (a "de-composition" from Carissimi's *Oratorio*) and a freely composed modern Jonas; but at the same time this two-fold exposition is a game about the musical expression of its own. The displacements and collisions of different historical layers represent in the work as a whole an ambiguity, which opposes the traditional understanding of coherence in musical material and musical style.

During the 1980s Rasmussen's paramount interest focused on another aspect of the problem about "past" and "present". The paradoxes are transferred to our very experience and perception of time. The concept of time considered as a straight line constantly moving forward is not in accordance with our perception of time, which is often multi-layered. Rasmussen actually composes the complementarity of time and space into his works as part of the very progression of the music.

The outer frames of *A Symphony in Time* are the conventional four movements, each exceeding limits of its own. Intertwining like flash-backs and -forwards in a movie, the movements displace the levels of time, marked by unruly changes of character and of directional energy into enlarged stagnant moments.

In the chamber work *Fugue/Fuga (Encore VIII)* each note is derived from the fugue of Beethoven's "Hammerklavier" Sonata and reorganized for three instruments of related timbre—piano, vibraphone and clarinet. But the music staggers between four different tempos, creating an elastic sensation of strained and squeezed time.

The chamber symphony *Movements on a Moving Line* is partly a fusion of the ideas mentioned above, but with an important addition of the conception of time as a globe. One single "moving line" makes circles within circles throughout the entire work, and the movements run forwards and backwards in a complex "mobile" of different speeds, different times, different spaces.

The development in Rasmussen's music from unhomogeneous towards organic materials, from intuitive composition towards construction has in recent years focused his interest on musical tempo and led him into the self-referential worlds proposed by the theory of chaos and so-called "fractals", which might be his final parting from the previous remains of tradition.

Rasmussen's versatile production displays a leitmotif of always investigating the hows and the whys of contemporary music. Rasmussen never pretends to advance one-sided solutions to musical problems: on the contrary the ambiguity and the paradoxes seem to make us wonder rather than "understand". His music invokes awareness and participation rather than complying with wishes for engaging pleasure.

—Margit Nonbo

RAUTAVAARA, Einojuhani. Finnish. Born in Helsinki, 9 October 1928. Educated at University of Helsinki, 1950–7, M.A.; Sibelius-Academy, Helsinki (under Aare Merikanto), 1950–7, composition diploma; Juilliard School of Music, New York City, and Tanglewood, Massachusetts (under Aaron Copland, Vincent Persichetti and Roger Sessions) 1955–6; study in Switzerland (under Wladimir Vogel), 1957; Kolner Musikhochsschule (under Rudolf Petzold), 1958. Second lieutenant of artillery, Finnish Army, 1953–4. Married Sini Koivisto, 18 August 1984. Lecturer in music theory, 1966–76, artist professor of state, 1971–6, and professor of composition, Sibelius-Academy, 1976–90. Recipient: Arnold Bax Society Medal, 1961; Sibelius Prize, 1965; first prize (for Third String Quartet), Camden Festival Contest, 1965; first prize (for *Ta Tou Theou*), Helsinki Cathedral organ competition, 1967; first prize (for *Itsenaisyyskantaatti*), composition contest in honour of 50th anniversary of Finland's independence, 1966–7; Pro Finlandia Medal, 1968; 1st prize (for *Dithyrambos*), Jean Sibelius Violin Competition, 1970; 1st prize (for *Apollo contra Marsyas*), composition contest, Finnish National Opera, 1970; 1st prize (for *Lapsimessu*), composition contest, city of Espoo, 1973; 1st prize (for *Lorulei*), KUS composition contest, 1973; member, Royal Swedish Academy, 1975; 1st prize (for *Varietude*), Jean Sibelius Violin Competition, 1975; 1st prize (for *Hammarskjold Fragment*), Muntra Musikanterna composition contest, 1975; D.Phhc., 1983; Commander, Order of the Finnish Lion, 1985. Mailing address: Bertil Jungin tie 3, Helsinki 57, Finland.

Publishers: Edition Pan, Vihertie 56C SF-01620 Vantaa, Finland; Edition Fazer; Edition YL; Sulasool; Edition Eres; Breitkopf & Hartel; G. Schirmer.

Symphonies/orchestral:

Pelimannit/The Fiddlers (suite for strings) 1952–72; first performed Helsinki, 11 November 1973. Recorded BIS LP 19; FUGA 3036.
Divertimento (string orchestra) 1953; first performed Helsinki, 1953. Recorded Finnlevy SFX 52.
A Requiem in Our Time (brass orchestra) 1953; first performed Cincinnati, Ohio, 10 May 1954. Recorded Finlandia FA 313; Bluebell BELL 123; JASELP 0008; FACD 009.
Epitaph for Béla Bartók (string orchestra) 1955–86; first performed Helsinki, 27 July 1987.
Symphony No 1 1956, revised 1988; first performed Helsinki, 22 January 1957. Recorded Ondine 740-2.
Symphony No 2 1957, revised 1984; first performed Helsinki, 11 October 1957. Recorded Ondine 740-2.
Praevariata 1957; first performed Strasbourg, 1958.
Modificata 1958, under revision; first performed Helsinki, 25 April 1958.
Canto I (string orchestra) 1960; first performed Helsinki, 7 March 1967.
Canto II (string orchestra) 1960; first performed Helsinki, 7 March 1967.
Symphony No 3 1961; first performed Helsinki, 10 April 1962. Recorded Ondine 740-2.
Symphony No 4 "Arabescata" 1963; first performed Helsinki, 26 February 1963.
Helsinki Fanfare (wind orchestra) 1967, revised 1987; first performed Helsinki, 12 June 1967.
Anadyomene 1968; first performed Helsinki, 30 May 1968.
A Soldier's Mass (wind orchestra) 1968; first performed Finland, 20 November 1968. Recorded Finlandia NEA LP 5.
Concerto for Cello and Orchestra 1968; first performed Helsinki, 26 February 1969.
Concerto for Piano and Orchestra 1969; broadcast 29 May 1970.
Saannollisia Yksikkojaksoja Puolisaannollisessa Tilanteessa/Regular Sets of Elements in Semiregular Situation 1971; first performed Helsinki, 19 April 1972.
Canto III "A Portrait of the Artist at a Certain Moment" (string orchestra) 1972; first performed Jyvaskyla, 27 June 1972.
Cantus arcticus (concerto for birds (tape) and orchestra) 1972; first performed Oulu, 18, October 1972. Recorded Finlandia FA 328; FACD 009.
Concerto for Flute and Orchestra 1973; broadcast 4 May 1974.
Ballad for Harp and Strings (string orchestra or string quintet) 1973, 1980; broadcast 19 October 1976.
Concerto for Violin and Orchestra 1977; broadcast 23 August 1977.
"Annunciations" (organ, symphonic wind orchestra) 1977; first performed Stockholm, 13 September 1977.
Suomalainen myytti (A Finnish Myth) (string orchestra) 1977; first performed Jyvaskyla, 29 April 1978.
Angels and Visitations 1978; first performed Helsinki, 22 January 1978.
Pohjalainen Polska 1980; first performed Vaasa, 11 April 1980.
"Angel of Dusk" (double bass, orchestra) 1980; broadcast 6 May 1981. Recorded FUGA 3035; Finlandia FACD 009.
Hommage à Zoltán Kodály (string orchestra or chamber orchestra) 1982; first performed Helsinki, 16 December 1982. Recorded Finlandia FA 339.
Serenade in Brass (brass orchestra) 1982; first performed Stockholm, 13 March 1983.
Symphony No 5 1985–6; first performed Helsinki, 14 May 1986.
Concerto No 2 for Piano and Orchestra 1989; first performed Munich, 19 October 1989.

Chamber/instrumental:

Three Symmetric Preludes (piano) 1949.
Ikonit (Icons) (piano) 1950. Recorded ODE 710-2; Toshiba TA 60001-4; Finnlevy SFX 45; Musical Heritage 3401.
Pelimannit (The Fiddlers) (piano) 1952. Recorded ODE 710-2.
String Quartet No 1 1952. Recorded EMI HMV 5E063 34444; SJK LP1.
Poytamusiikki Herttua Juhanalle (4 recorders) 1954.
Two Preludes and Fugues (cello, piano) 1955. Recorded EMI HMV 5E061 34017; Da Camera SM 93710.
Partita (piano) 1956–8.
Seven Preludes for Piano 1957.
Quartet for Oboe and String Trio 1957, revised 1965.
String Quartet No 2 1958; first performed Helsinki, 2 April 1959. Recorded Finlandia FACD 355.
Octet for Winds (flute, oboe, clarinet, bassoon, 2 horns, trumpet, trombone) 1962.
String Quartet No 3 1965; first performed London, 1967. Recorded Philips LY 802 855.
Ta Tou Theou (organ) 1967.
Sonata for Bassoon and Piano 1968.
Etudes (piano) 1969. Recorded ODE 710-2; EMI HMV 5E063 34283.
Sonata for Solo Cello 1969.
Piano Sonata No 1: "Christus und die Fischer" 1969. Recorded ODE 710-2; Toshiba 60001-4.
Sonetto/Sonnet (clarinet, piano) 1969. Recorded BIS LP 62.
Piano Sonata No 2: "The Fire Sermon" 1970. Recorded ODE 710-2; Musical Heritage 3401; Finnlevy SFLP 8569.
Dithyrambos (violin, piano) 1970. Recorded RCA-LP 40058; SALP 1.
Toccata per Organo (organ) 1971.
Ugriliainen Dialogi/An Ugrian Dialogue (violin, cello) 1973.
Varietude (violin) 1974. Recorded Finnlevy SFLP 8569; SALP 1.
String Quartet No 4 1975; first performed Espoo, 1975. Recorded BIS LP 66.
Sonata for Flutes and Guitar 1975. Recorded BIS LP 30.
Tarantara (trumpet) 1976. Recorded SOMA 781.
Music for Upright Piano 1976.
Second Music for Upright Piano 1976.
Music for Upright Piano and Amplified Cello 1976.
Polska: Muunelmia Rantasalmelaisesta kansansavelmasta/Variations on a Folk Tune from Rantasalmi (2 cellos, piano) 1977.
Serenades of the Unicorn (guitar) 1977. Recorded BIS LP 207.
Monologues of the Unicorn (guitar) 1980. Recorded BIS LP 207.
Playgrounds for Angels (4 trumpets, 4 trombones, horn, tuba) 1981; first performed Helsinki, 12 September 1981. Recorded Chandos ABTD 1190; JASELP 0008.

Vocal/choral:

Three Sonnets of Shakespeare (voice, piano) 1952. Recorded BIS LP 83.
Pyhia paivia/Sacred Feasts (voice, piano) 1953.
Fünf Sonette an Orpheus (voice, piano or orchestra; Rilke) 1956.

Two Preludes (male chorus; Eliot) 1956–67. Recorded PK LP 10.
Laulaja / The Singer (male chorus) 1956.
Ave Maria (male chorus) 1957. Recorded ACLP 87.
Ludus verbalis (declamatory chorus) 1957. Recorded BIS LP 4; Finnlevy SFLP 8509.
Die Lebenden (voice, piano or orchestra; Rilke) 1958–9.
Missa duodecaphonica (chorus in 3 voices) 1963.
Nattvarden (mixed chorus; Setterlind) 1963. Recorded Philips LY 839 705.
Guds vag / God's Way (voice, piano; Setterlind) 1964.
Itsenaisyyskantaatti / Independence Cantata (soloist, reciter, chorus, orchestra) 1967; first performed Tampere, 10 June 1967.
Praktisch Deutsch (declamatory chorus) 1969. Recorded (in part) SAA CA 8210-1.
Two Psalms (mixed chorus or male chorus) 1970.
True and False Unicorn (reciters, chorus, tape, piano, orchestra; Broughton) 1971; first performed Gothenburg, 1972.
Vigilia (Vigil Commemorating St John the Baptist) (soloists, mixed chorus) 1971–2; first performed Helsinki, 28 August 1971. Recorded EMI HMV 5E063 34516/35016.
The Virgin's Lullasy (SSAA chorus; Broughton—from *True and False Unicorn*) 1971–86.
October (voice, piano; Hellaakoski) 1972.
Elaman Kirja / A Book of Life (soloists, male chorus) 1972. Recorded Finnlevy SFX 327; parts on Finlandia FA 321, EMPS 1019.
Credo (mixed chorus) 1972.
Lorca Suite (mixed chorus or children's chorus; Lorca) 1973. Recorded FUGA 3046; Finnlevy SFX 52; Finlandia FA 327; Ton Art 18.
Lorulei (SSA chorus) 1973.
Viatonten valssi / Waltz of the Innocents (SSA chorus, violin; Hellaakoski) 1973.
Isoo Antti ja Rannanjarvi / Andy from the Big House (male chorus) 1973. Recorded Toshiba TA 60052.
Hallin Janne (male chorus) 1973.
Herran rukous / The Lord's Prayer (mixed chorus) 1973. Recorded Proprius 7803; FGLP 1008.
Lapsimessu / Children's Mass (children's chorus, strings; Latin Mass) 1973; first performed Espoo, 20 December 1973. Recorded BIS LP 94; FUGA 3046.
Hammarskjold Fragment (male chorus; Hammarskjold) 1975.
Lahto / The Departure (mixed chorus; Pekkanen) 1975.
Morsian / The Bride (mixed chorus) 1975.
Puusepan poika / The Carpenter's Son (SSA chorus; Kuusisto) 1975.
Kettu ja sairas kukko / The Fox and the Sick Cock (male chorus; Ganander) 1975.
Sommarnatten / Summer Night (mixed chorus) 1975.
Kainuu (mixed chorus, reciter, percussion) 1975.
Matka / The Journey (voice, piano) 1977.
Serenadi oluelle / Serenade to Beer (male chorus) 1978.
Serenadi kuolemalle / Serenade to Death (male chorus; Baudelaire) 1978.
Joulun virsi—elaman virsi (Christmas Carol) (male chorus or children's chorus; Lounasheimo) 1978.
Serenadi vaimolleni / Serenade to My Wife (male chorus; George) 1978.
Canticum Mariae virginis (mixed chorus) 1978. Recorded SL-1.
Lehdet lehtia / Leaves Are Leaves (male chorus; Haavikko) 1979.
Nirvana Dharma (mixed chorus, soprano, flute; Laing) 1979.
Magnificat (soloists, mixed chorus) 1979. Recorded Finlandia FA 342.
Parantaja / The Healer (reciter, chorus, orchestra) 1981; first performed Helsinki, 29 May 1981.
Rakkaus ei koskaan havia (SSA chorus; Bible) 1983.
Katedralen / The Cathedral (soloists, mixed chorus; Sodergran) 1983.
The First Runo (children's chorus) 1984.
Legenda / A Legend (male chorus; Leino) 1985.
Lyckokatt (voice, piano; Sodergran) 1985.
Mina en puhu mina laulan / I Never Speak But Sing (voice, piano) 1986.

Opera:

Kaivos / The Mine 1957–63; broadcast Finnish television, 10 April 1963.
Apollo contra Marsyas (Wall) 1970; first performed Helsinki, 30 August 1973.
Runo 42 "Sammon ryosto" / The Abduction of the Sampo 1974–81; first performed Helsinki, 8 April 1983.
Marjatta matala neiti / Marjatta, the Lowly Maiden 1975; first performed Espoo, 3 September 1977. Recorded BIS LP 132; Finlandia FACD 921.
Thomas 1985; first performed Joensuu, 21 June 1985. Recorded Ode 704.
Vincent 1987; first performed Helsinki, 17 May 1990.

Other:

Kiusaukset / The Temptations (ballet) 1969; first performed Helsinki, 8 February 1973.
Number 1 (tape music) 1980.
Number 2 (tape music) 1980.
Heureka Musik 1–2 (tape music) 1989.

PUBLICATIONS

By Rautavaara: "Kuorolle Saveltamisesta Tanaan" ("About Choral Writing Today"), Klemetti-Opiston Kamarikuoro, 1984; "Thomas: Analysis of the Tone Material—An Experiment in Synthesis", in *Finnnish Music Quarterly*, 1–2, 1985; "Tyopaivakirja" ("The Birth of Vincent") in *Synteesi*, 3, 1987; "Suomalaisuudesta" ("About Finnishness") in *Synteesi*, 1–2, 1988; "Omakuva" ("Self Portrait"), WSOY Helsinki, 1989.

On Rautavaara: Mikko Heinio, "ER, Aulis Sallinen och ny finsk musik", in *Nutida Musik*, 1, 1986–7, and "A Portrait of the Artist at a Certain Moment", in *Finnish Music Quarterly*, 2, 1988; Juhani Lagerspetz, "The Fire Sermon", in *Finnish Music Quarterly*, 2, 1988; Kalevi Aho, *ER as Symphonist* (also in Finnish and German), Edition Pan 131, 1988.

Einojuhani Rautavaara comments:

There is in my later works a clear interest in the possible interrelated networking of tonal systems and their genealogical hierarchies. Above all, a sympathy for the possibility of synthesis—the need for it and belief in it—has developed gradually through the very varied phases of my composing career. Naturally, the linking together of various (and to some people contradictory) systems must of necessity come to break the taboos of each system. But then I also believe that all artistic taboos are evidence of shortsightedness (in time and space) and often of racism.

* * *

In Einojuhani Rautaraara's music the mixture of traditional and various "modern" attributes for each composition results not from eclecticism but from his wish to keep abreast of current ideas. Up to 1953 he composed in neo-18th-century styles, employing symmetrical writing, complex rhythms, quartal harmonies which often produce free tonality, and chords of extended thirds. His first important work, the cell-organised *A Requiem of Our Time*, copies the primitivism of *Les Noces*. The First Symphony includes techniques from Stravinsky, Shostakovich and Ives. Immediately after this work, Rautavaara turned to serialism.

Rautavaara uses free twelve-tone ideas in the Second Symphony, but although he contrived to be anti-tonal and ultra-modern, Russian influences are still evident. In *Praevariata* the row generates rhythms and form. The composer describes his later serial works as "non-atonal" (Second Quartet, Third Symphony), his most serially organised work being *Symphony No 4 "Arabescata"*. *Ludus verbalis* comprises four short antiphonal movements for speaking choir, with each part written on one of three lines. The Third Symphony is of Brucknerian proportions, based on a "sea" motive. The twelve-tone first subject is given D-minor tonality, transformations following Schoenberg while instrumental doublings resemble earlier models.

The Second String Quartet centres around wide-intervalled lyrical counterpoint, where rhythm creates smooth-flowing lines even when forceful. After a slow quasi-Renaissance fantasia, built around semitone movement and descending perfect intervals, the most idiomatic movement exploits sudden dynamic changes and soaring first violin lines. Variety of texture and tessitura continues in Third String Quartet which is more tonally organised when slow/*espressivo*. Unlike many of his contemporaries, Rautavaara does not start all ideas on the first beat of even changing-time-signature bars.

The Cello Concerto opens with an unaccompanied outburst of double stops, exploiting false relations reminiscent of Walton's Viola Concerto. With the orchestral entry comes the other main motif: a reiterated fifth leading to movement a minor third above and below. While the orchestration is often reminiscent of Joonas Kokkonen, the soloist's second subject has 66 identical rhythms, recalling Elgar's Cello Concerto. The bass ostinato finale recalls the violin concertos of Prokofiev and Walton, before octatonic scales lead to the cadenza.

The early 1970s saw both the Orthodox plainchant-inspired *Vigilia (Vigil Commemorating St John the Baptist)* and the modal *Cantus arcticus* (a concerto for taped birdsong and orchestra, which includes aleatoric polyphony). The first movement of Rautavaara's *Piano Sonata No 1: "Christus und die Fischer"* like that by Barraqué, oscillates between two tempos (one associated with fifths, the other with seconds and thirds). A faster tempo ends the movement, as in the Piano Concerto the right hand plays in fifths while the left arpeggiates. A fast, complex pattern of 3 + 2 + 3 + + 2 + 3 leads into one of Rautavaara's newly acquired clichés: a quickly moving subdivision of 8/8 into 3 + 2 + 3. The Piano Concerto starts, like the Cello Concerto, with the soloist exploiting tonic major/minor, ending with nine loud high non-chromatic 12 voiced chords to bring in the orchestra (the texture then becomes Rachmaninov-like). *Piano Sonata No 2: "The Fire Sermon"* starts and finishes with fast 3 + 2 + 3 grouping, one hand exploiting naturals, the other sharps.

Rautavaara's multi-faceted technique continues with the lighthearted *True and False Unicorn*. After a pseudo-serious opening, the accompaniment gives point and atmosphere, individual vocal lines are well-contrived if not simple. 3 + 2 + 3 is still used at times, and various spirituals and national anthems are humorously parodied.

Rautavaara's later orchestral works, from *Angels and Visitations* to the Fifth Symphony feature numerous strands of *divisi* instrumental motives which repeat rapidly and gradually coalesce into an impressionistic mesh of sound colour, before the texture decreases into triadic writing. The texts of his recent operas, *Thomas* and *Vincent*, create continually differing compositional techniques, each based solely upon characterisation.

—Malcolm J. Hill

REICH, Steve [Stephen] (Michael). American. Born in New York City, 3 October 1936. Educated: piano lessons from age 9; studied percussion under Roland Kohloff, from 1950; Cornell University, Ithaca, New York (philosophy; and music under William Austin), 1953–7; private composition study under Hall Overton, New York City, 1957–8; Juilliard School of Music, New York City (composition under William Bergsma and Vincent Persichetti), 1958–61; Mills College, Oakland, California (composition under Darius Milhaud and Luciano Berio), 1961–3; studied African drumming, University of Accra, Ghana, 1970; studied Balinese music, American Society for Eastern Arts, Seattle, Washington, and Berkeley, California, 1973; studied Hebrew, Torah, cantorial tradition, New York and Jerusalem, 1976–7. Married Beryl Korot, 30 May 1976; 1 son. Composer of music for film and theatre, 1963–5; founder/performer, Steve Reich and Musicians, since 1966; faculty member, New School for Social Research, New York City, 1969–71. Recipient: Grammy (for *Different Trains*), best new composition, 1989. Mailing address: Lynn Garon Management, 1199 Park Avenue, New York, New York 10028, U.S.A.

Publishers: Universal Edition; Boosey & Hawkes.

Symphonies/orchestral:

Music for a Large Ensemble 1979; first performed Amsterdam, June 1979.
Variations for Winds, String and Keyboards (orchestrated from chamber piece) 1980; first performed San Francisco, 14 May 1980. Recorded Philips 412 214.
Eight Lines (orchestral revision of *Octet*) 1983; first performed New York City, 10 December 1983. Recorded Angel DS 37345; EMI EL 27 0291.
Three Movements 1985–6; first performed St Louis, Missouri, 3 April 1986.
Salute 1986; withdrawn.
The Four Sections 1987, version for chamber orchestra in progress; first performed San Francisco, 7 October 1987.

Chamber/instrumental:

Pitch Charts (any instrumentation) 1963.
Music for Three or More Pianos (or piano, tape) 1964; first performed San Francisco, January 1965.

Reed Phase (soprano saxophone, tape) 1966; first performed New York City, 17 March 1967.
Piano Phase (2 pianos or marimbas) 1967; first performed Rutherford, New Jersey, January 1967. Recorded Nonesuch 79169; Hungaroton SLPX 12799.
Violin Phase (violin, tape; or 4 violins) 1967; first performed New York City, April 1969. Recorded Columbia MS 7625; ECM 1168.
Pendulum Music (3 or more microphones, amplifiers, loudspeakers) 1968.
Four Log Drums 1969; first performed New York City, 27 May 1969.
Four Organs (4 electric organs/maracas) 1970; first performed New York City, May 1970. Recorded Disques Shandar 83.511; Angel Records S-36059.
Phase Patterns (4 electric organs) 1970; first performed New York City, May 1970. Recorded Angel Records S-36059.
Drumming (4 pairs of tuned bongos, 3 marimbas, 3 glockenspiels, 2 wordless female voices, whistling, piccolo; 4 parts, each of which may be performed separately) 1971; first performed New York City, 3 December 1971.
Clapping Music (4 hands, no piano) 1972; first performed New York City, April 1973. Recorded Nonesuch 79169.
Music for Pieces of Wood (5 pairs of tuned claves) 1973; first performed New York City, 7 December 1973. Recorded Hungaroton SLPX 12545.
Music for Mallet Instruments, Voices and Organ (4 marimbas, 2 glockenspiels/vibraphone, 3 wordless female voices/2 singing long tones with organ/1 singing melodic patterms with marimbas, electric organ) 1973; first performed New York City, 16 May 1973. Recorded Deutsche Grammophon 2535 463.
Six Pianos (sic) 1973; first performed New York City, 16 May 1973. Recorded Deutsche Grammophon DG 2535 463.
Music for Eighteen Musicians (2 clarinets/bass clarinet, 4 pianos, 3 marimbas/2 xylophones/vibraphone, 4 wordless female voices, violin, cello) 1974–6; first performed New York City, 24 April 1976. Recorded ECM 1129.
Octet (2 flutes/piccolo, 2 clarinets/bass clarinet, 2 pianos, 2 violins, viola, cello) 1979; broadcast Radio Frankfurt, 21 June 1979. Recorded ECM 1168; Hungaroton SLPX 12799.
Variations for Winds, Strings, and Keyboards (3 flutes, 3 oboes, 3 trumpets, 3 trombones, tuba, 2 pianos, 3 electric organs, solo strings—woodwinds and strings amplified) 1979; first performed New York City, 19 February 1980.
Vermont Counterpoint (flute/piccolo/alto flute, tape; ensemble version for 8 flutes/5 piccolos/1 alto, 3 alto flutes) 1982; first performed New York City, 1 October 1982; ensemble version first performed New York City, 10 December 1983. Recorded Agnel DS 37340; EMI EL 27 0291.
Sextet (2 amplified pianos/synthesizers, 2 amplified vibraphones/3 amplified marimbas/tam-tam/click sticks/2 bass drums/crotales) 1984, revised 1985; first performed Paris, 19 December 1984. Recorded Nonesuch 79138.
New York Counterpoint (clarinet, tape; version for 9 clarinets/1 bass clarinet, 2 bass clarinets) 1985; first performed New York City, 20 January 1986; ensemble version first performed Tallahassee, Florida, 21 June 1987. Recorded RCA 5944.
Six Marimbas (version of *Six Pianos*) 1986; first performed New York City, 20 April 1987. Recorded Nonesuch 79138.
Electric Counterpoint (electric guitar, tape; or 11 electric guitars, 2 electric bass guitars) 1987; first performed New York City, 5 November 1987. Recorded Nonesuch Digital 79176.
Different Trains (string quartet or string ensemble, tape) 1988. Recorded Nonesuch Digital 79176.

Vocal/choral:

Tehillim (high soprano, 2 lyric sopranos, alto, flute, piccolo, oboe, cor anglais, 2 clarinets, bassoon, 6 percussion, string quintet—all amplified; Psalms 19, 34, 18, 150, in Hebrew) 1981; movements 1 and 2 first performed Stuttgart, June 1981; first complete performance, New York City, 16 September 1982. Recorded ECM 1215.
The Desert Music (27 amplified voices, orchestra; chamber version for 10 amplified voices, 4 flutes/piccolo, timpani/rototoms, 7 percussion, 2 pianos/4 players/synthesizer, 13 solo strings; William Carlos Williams) 1982–4; broadcast West German Radio, Cologne, 17 March 1984; chamber version first performed Richmond, Virginia, 10 January 1986. Recorded Nonesuch 79101.

Other:

Plastic Haircut (film score; tape) 1963.
Oh Dem Watermelons (film score for 5 voices, piano) 1965; first performed San Francisco, May 1965.
It's Gonna Rain (tape; voice of Brother Walter preaching about the Flood) 1965; first performed January 1965. Recorded Nonesuch 79169.
Come Out (tape; voice of Harlem Six member Daniel Hamm) 1966; first performed New York City, April 1966. Recorded Nonesuch 79169.
Melodica (tape) 1966. Recorded Music from Mills 001.
My Name Is (3 or more tape recorders, performers, audience) 1967; first performed New York, November 1967.
Slow Motion Sound (tape) 1967.

PUBLICATIONS

By Reich: *Writings About Music*, New York, 1974, French translation, 1981.

On Reich: Michael Nyman, (interview) in *Musical Times*, 112, 1971, and "SR: Mysteries of the Phase", in *Music and Musicians*, 20(6), 1972; E. Wasserman, (interview) in *Art Forum*, 10(9), 1972; C. Gottwald, "Signale zwischen Exotik und Industrie: SR auf der Such nach einer neuen Identitat von Kland und Struktur", in *Melos*, 1, 1975; Michael Nyman, (interview) in *Studio International*, 192, 1976, and "SR", in *Music and Musicians* 25(5), 1977; R. Schwarz, "SR: Music as a Gradual Process", in *Perspectives of New Music*, 19, 1980–1; Tim Page, "Framing the River; A Minimalist Primer", in *High Fidelity/Musical America*, 31(11), 1981; C. Gagne and T. Caras, (interview) in *Soundpieces: Interviews with American Composers*, Metuchen, New Jersey, 1982; Wim Mertens, [chapter on SR] in *American Minimal Music*, London, 1983; Keith Potter, "The Recent Phases of SR", in *Contact*, 29, Spring 1985; Ian Macdonald, "What Is the Use of Minimalism?", in *The Face*, 38, March 1987; Ronald Woodley, "Moving Chords: Function and Allusion in SR's *New York Counterpoint*", forthcoming 1991.

* * *

The perpetuation of the commonplace association of Steve Reich with the notion of "minimalism" has by now become all but threadbare. A change of paradigm in discussing his music is imperative in order both to circumvent the dangers of the logocentrist trap, and also to demonstrate some awareness that an important trajectory of Reich's work through the 1970s and 1980s has been its gradual realignment with certain branches of "mainstream" European music, a realignment achieved, however, through radicalisation rather than compliant re-absorption. Viewed from this perspective, the carpet has been slowly but inexorably pulled from under the feet of those critics for whom "from Hippie to Yuppie, Minimalism is a drip-feed pseudo-art for cultural bottle babies" (Ian Macdonald).

Reich can be seen as interrogating tradition in a number of ways. Through his ostensible harmonic conservatism ("Major, minor, Dorian: these are my big three"), his music confronts the post-Renaissance inheritance of harmony as one of the principal means by which "progress" and "originality" have been constructed in Western music, and through which dissonance and chromaticism, in particular, have functioned as an important index to historical placement. A corollary of this confrontation (also evident, *mutatis mutandis*, in other strands of 20th-century music, and partly related to Reich's debt to ethnic and jazz sources) is a rediscovery of the power of the dissonance, particularly in the composer's more recent music, though often as a ludic or structuring element rather than as a vehicle for pathos or resolvable tension. The deliberate use of an apparently conventional harmonic language can also be read as an interrogation through sound of the traditional critical stance of "convention" as a negative attribute in "high art." Related to this is the often criticised re-use of materials (melodic and rhythmic patterns, timbral effects, structural techniques etc.) from one piece to the next. On the one hand this can be viewed as an extension of the notion of "process" from the individual work into the continuum of compositional activity; but it also represents a "de-fetishisation" of the unique, Romantic art-object, and a problematisation of "closure," which relate Reich's music back, through a complex seam of influences, to earlier movements such as Dadaism. A recent, particularly notable instance of comprehensive recomposition is *Electric Counterpoint*, which is, from a structural and textural vantage point, virtually the same piece as *New York Counterpoint*, but refracted through new harmonic and melodic prisms. Furthermore, Reich's characteristic expanding, cellular construction of his melodic materials, and his complex, multi-layered canonic textures, not only challenge traditional notions of the "lyrical," but also act as a *reductio ad absurdum* of organicist theory and motivic analysis. By such means the music invites interpretation (to which Reich's own philosophy training at Cornell may not be unrelated) as covert metacriticism.

Reich's simultaneous critique and repossession of his European musical past—the figures of Bartók and Debussy, perhaps also Janáček and Sibelius, have recently become evident—further invite speculation as to his location within the aesthetics of post-modernism. In so far as assessment is currently possible, it seems that any relationship is at most tangential: while to some extent concerned with reclaiming history, and re-evaluating the relationship between tradition and the present, he seems overtly to eschew that facet of post-modernism which celebrates fragmentation and what Lyotard has described as "incredulity toward meta-narratives." While the dynamics of much of Reich's music relate in a fascinating way to the dynamics of entropy and cybernetics, there seems ultimately—and the composer's increasing exploitation of his Jewish roots are probably deeply significant here—to be no loss of faith in the possibility of progress.

—Ronald Woodley

REIMANN, Aribert. German. Born in Berlin, 4 March 1936. Educated at Hochschule für Musik, Berlin (composition under Boris Blacher, counterpoint under Ernst Pepping, piano under Otto Rausch), 1955–60; further studies in musicology, Vienna, 1958; further study, Italy, 1963. Assistant repetiteur, Studio of Stadtische Oper, Berlin, 1955; freelance composer and accompanist, debut 1957; professor of contemporary song, Akademie der Kunste, Berlin, 1971–83. Recipient: Berlin Arts Award in music, 1962; Prix de Rome, 1963; Schumann Prize, Dusseldorf, 1964; City of Stuttgart Award for young composers, 1966; Critics Award in Music (for total output to date), 1970; elected member, Bayerische Akademie der Schönen Kunste, 1976; elected member, Freie Akademie der Kunste, Hamburg, 1985; Grosses Verdienstkreuz, Verdienstorden, German Federal Republic, 1985; Ludwig Spohr Prize, City of Brunswick, 1985; Prix de la composition musicale de la Fondation Prince Pierre de Monaco, 1986; elected corresponding member, Akademie der Kunste, Berlin, German Democratic Republic, 1986; Bacj Prize, Freie und Hansestadt, Hamburg, 1987; Verdienstorden of the Land Berlin, 1988; Frankfurt Music Award, 1988. Mailing address: c/o B. Schott's Sohne, Weihergarten, Postfach 36 40, D-6500 Mainz 1, Germany.

Publisher: Schott.

Symphonies/orchestral:

Violin Concerto 1959.
Piano Concerto 1961; first performed Berlin, 26 October 1962.
Symphony (from *Ein Traumspiel*) 1964; first performed Darmstadt, 12 December 1976.
Rondes (strings) 1967; first performed Cologne, 25 January 1969.
Loqui 1969; first performed Saarbrücken, 5 December 1969.
Die Vogelscheuchen (orchestral suite from the ballet) 1970; broadcast Bayerisches Rundfunk, 17 November 1972.
Concerto (piano, 19 instruments) 1972; first performed Nuremberg, 12 January 1973. Recorded Wergo WER 60072.
Variations 1975; first performed Zurich, 13 January 1976.
Sieben Fragmente: In memoriam Robert Schumann 1988; first performed Hamburg, 25 September 1988.
Double Concerto (violin, cello, orchestra) 1988–9; first performed Hannover, 13–4 November 1989.

Chamber/instrumental:

Sonata (piano) 1958.
Canzoni e ricercari (flute, viola, cello) 1961; first performed Berlin, 30 September 1961.
Sonata (cello, piano) 1963; first performed Berlin, 11 January 1965.
Dialog I (organ) 1963; first performed Berlin, July 1963.
Nocturnos (cello, harp) 1965; first performed Madrid, April 1966.
Reflexionen (flute, oboe, bassoon, harpsichord, violin, viola, cello) 1966; first performed Berlin, 15 May 1966.
Spektren (piano) 1967; first performed Zagreb, 20 May 1967.
Invenzioni (flute/alto flute/piccolo, oboe/cor anglais, clarinet/bass clarinet, bassoon, horn, trumpet, trombone, 2 violins, viola, cello, double bass) 1979; first performed London, 16 June 1979.
Variationen (piano) 1979; first performed Berlin, 29 November 1982. Recorded Classic Production Osnabruck cpo 999 031-2.

Solo (cello) 1981; first performed Stuttgart, 19 April 1982.
Trio (violin, viola, cello) 1987; first performed Berlin, 11 September 1988.

Vocal/choral:

Auf verschleierten Schaukeln (unaccompanied mixed chorus; Arp) 1957; first performed Berlin, 8 June 1984.
Ein Totenstanz (baritone, chamber orchestra) 1960; first performed Berlin, 29 September 1961.
Fünf Gedichte von Paul Celan (baritone, piano) 1960; first performed Berlin, 4 October 1962.
Kinderlieder (soprano, piano; Reinert—"Wo ist der Vater" "Der Sommer ist fortgeflogen", "Willst du reiten?", "Die Schlange ist gestroben", "Halte den Stein an das Ohr", "Gib mir den Apfel", "Mit meinem Zeigfinger zahle ich die Nacht", "Schlaf' Kind") 1961; I–III, VI–VIII first performed New York City, January 1962; complete cycle first performed Hannover, 2 March 1985. Recorded Wergo WER 60183-50.
Impression IV (soprano, piano; cummings) 1961; first performed Hamburg, 1 February 1985.
Hölderlin-Fragmente (soprano, orchestra) 1963; first performed Berlin, 8 January 1969.
Drei Sonette von William Shakespeare (baritone, piano; "Since Brass, Nor Stone", "When Most Eye Wink", "Thou Blind Fool") 1964; first performed Berlin, 6 December 1964.
Epitaph (tenor, flute, cor anglais, harp, celeste, viola, cello, double bass; Shelley) 1965; first performed Heidelberg, 2 June 1967.
Nachtstück (baritone, piano; Eichendorff—"Wir ziehen treulich auf die Wacht", "Die Voglein, die so frohlich sangen", "Vor dem Schloss in den Baumen es rauschend weht", "Horst du die Grunde rufen", "Hier steh ich wie auf treuer Wacht") 1966; first performed Nurtingen, 27 October 1967. Recorded Wergo WER 60097.
Verra la morte (cantata for soloists, 2 choruses, orchestra; Pavese) 1966; first performed Berlin, 28 February 1967.
Trovers (*Sprechstimme*, clarinet, bassoon, trumpet, trombone, violin, double bass, cimbalom; Troubadour lyrics) 1967; first performed Buenos Aires, 30 July 1967.
Engfuhrung (tenor, piano; Celan) 1967; first performed Berlin, 23 January 1968. Recorded Wergo WER 60072.
Denn Bleiben ist nirgends (*Sprechstimme*, orchestra; Rilke) 1968; first performed Darmstadt, 13 April 1986.
Nenia (after *Denn Bleiben ist nirgends*; *Sprechstimme*, orchestra; anon.16th century) 1968; first performed Kassel, 26 June 1968.
Inane (monologue for soprano, orchestra) 1968; first performed Berlin, 8 January 1969. Recorded Wergo WER 60056.
Lines (soprano, strings; Shelley) 1973; first performed Schwetzinger, 14 May 1973.
Zyklus (baritone, orchestra; Celan) 1974; first performed Nuremberg, 15 April 1971.
Wolkenloses Christfest (requiem for baritone, cello, orchestra; Buthe) 1974; first performed Landau, 2 June 1974.
John 3:16 (unaccompanied 8-part chorus) 1975; first performed York, 12 June 1976. Recorded WER 60056.
Six Poems by Sylvia Plath (soprano, piano; "Words", "Edge", "The Couriers", "Sheep in Fog", "The Night Dances", "Confusion") 1975; first performed Edinburgh, 1 September 1975. Recorded Wergo WER 60097.
Nachtstück 2 (baritone, piano; Eichendorff—"Nachts", "Der Umkehrende", "Wetterleuchten", "Trost", "Auf meaines Kindes Tod") 1978; first performed Berlin, 21 September 1978. Recorded Wergo WER 60097.
Fragment aus Lear (baritone, orchestra) 1979; first performed Zurich, 29 April 1980.
Unrevealed (baritone, string quartet; Byron) 1980; first performed Berlin, 3 September 1981. Recorded Classic Produktion Osnabruck cpo 999 031-2.
Drei Lieder (soprano, orchestra; Poe) 1980–2; first performed Berlin, 5 September 1982.
Requiem (soprano, mezzo-soprano, baritone, mixed chorus, orchestra) 1980–2; first performed Kiel, 26 June 1982.
Nunc dimittis (Canticum Simeonis) (mixed chorus, baritone, bass flute) 1984; first performed Berlin, 30 September 1984.
Tre poemi di Michelangelo (baritone, piano; "Sol io ardendo", "Che fie di me?", "L'alma inquieta e confusa") 1985; II first performed Berlin, 3 February 1985; complete sequence first performed Berlin, 21 September 1986.
Neun Sonette der Louise Labé (mezzo-soprano, piano; "O beaus yeus bruns, o regars destournez", "O long desirs, o esperances vaines", "On voit mourir toute chose animee", "Ie vis, ie meurs, ie me brûle et me noye", "Lut, compagnon de ma calamité", "Oh si i'estois en ce beau sein rauie", "Tant que mes yeux pourront larmes espandre", "Ie fuis la vile, et temples, et tous lieus", "Baise m'encor, rebaise moy et baise") 1986; I–IV first performed Hamburg, 15 June 1987; complete cycle first performed Neuminster, 9 July 1987. Recorded Wergo WER 60183-50.
Ein apokalyptisches Fragment (mezzo-soprano, piano, orchestra; Gunderrode) 1987; first performed Berlin, 27 September 1987.
Nacht-Räume (soprano, piano, 4 hands; Rilke) 1988; first performed Berlin, 11 September 1988. Recorded Wergo WER 60183-50.
Shine and Dark (baritone, piano—left hand; Joyce) 1989; first performed Zurich, 31 May 1991.
Entsorgt (baritone; Born) 1989; first performed Frankfurt, 8 September 1989.

Opera:

Ein Traumspiel (Henius, after Strindberg) 1965; first performed Kiel, 20 June 1965.
Melusine (Henneberg, after Goll) 1970; first performed Schwetzingen, 29 April 1971.
Lear (Henneberg, after Shakespeare) 1978; first performed Munich, 9 July 1978.
Chacun sa chimère ("*poème visuel*" by Baudelaire; tenor, orchestra) 1981; first performed Dusseldorf, 17 April 1982.
Die Gespenstersonate (AR, Schwendel, after Strindberg) 1983; first performed Berlin, 25 September 1984.
Troades (AR, Albrecht, after Euripides/Werfel) 1985; first performed 7 July 1986.

Other:

Stoffreste (ballet) 1957, revised as *Die Vogelscheuchen* (Grass) 1970; first performed Berlin, 7 October 1970.

Robert Schumann: *Gedichte der Maria Stuart Op 135* (arranged for mezzo-soprano, chamber orchestra) 1988; first performed Dusseldorf, 9 September 1988.

PUBLICATIONS

On Reimann: W.-E. von Lewinski, "AR: 'ein Weg in die Freiheit'", in *Melos*, 38, 1971.

* * *

Aribert Reimann has justifiably been called "the singer's composer": he has written many vocal works, often for named performers. For many years his classes in the interpretation of modern vocal music at the State Music High School in Hamburg, and his role as piano accompanist to Dietrich Fischer-Dieskau have contributed to Reimann's fundamental interest in the vocal medium, stimulated by his choir-training father. Reimann's piano accompaniments, especially in *Nachtstück* and *Nacht-Räume* provide a wealth of textural variety.

Reimann's early pointillist style changed from post-Webern to non-strict serial during the mid-1960s. He frequently uses immediate repetition to create emphasis and to increase tension. Sound in one pitch area, consisting of either clusters or figuration, is used to bind lengthy passages together while simultaneously accompanying several other strands of never-crossing texture. These traits are all present in *Rondes* for string orchestra, where numerous brief subsections are contrasted by pitch area and texture; notated rhythmic complexity is normally of the single bar seven-in-the-time-of-six variety; free rhythm notation is placed against held clusters. Another important instrumental work is the single-movement *Solo* for unaccompanied cello, where the composer's natural lyrical style (set in the upper compass of the instrument) is dramatically contrasted with a lower register. This essentially polyphonic work notates rhythm graphically.

Reimann's first opera, *Ein Traumspiel*, incorporates most of his theatrical procedures. Whatever size is used for the orchestra, a string quartet is employed for Shostakovich-like bleakness while more foreground gestures come from the other instruments. In this opera there are only eight other players, who provide many of the ostinatos and text-related tremelandos. In his third opera, *Lear*, an enormous orchestra with additional brass and percussion act similarly, although sometimes their gestures relate to more distant text. The climactic storm interlude in *Lear* demonstrates Reimann's abilities to handle large forces effectively. *Lear* presents formidable orchestration volume problems for the singers. It is only the composer's consummate skill, drawn from a wealth of experience with singers, that permits their histrionic singing techniques to become audible. These two operas are similar in their use of a tenor who has to change during the work into a falsetto alto (the student in *Ein Traumspiel*, Edgar into Mad Tom in *Lear*). In both operas, over 80 minutes of non-stop music consists of a few scenes linked by instrumental interludes.

Three years before *Lear*, Reimann produced the *Variations* for orchestra in which he used graphic notation to differentiate between what he calls the "direct" sounds of normal pitches and the "indirect" sounds caused by quartertone transposition. The latter are applied to the lowest sound-block or held after the direct sounds have vanished in order to produce "shadow sounds". "Mixed sounds" are also employed, where direct and indirect sounds are combined to form a cluster. Reimann does not write linear entities which rely upon quartertone intervals, but merely uses quartertones for effect. All these types were to be incorporated into *Lear* at strategic points. The opera uses two hexachords, often related to character. Later, in *Neun Sonette der Louise Labé*, he takes a cell from the secondmost effective section of *Lear* (bass flute—later plus alto flute—at Tom's entry) to generate a set of variations. This cell of tones and semitones, formed from two ascending intervals and one descending interval which ends on a new pitch, links not only the Sonnets and *Lear*, but also pervades much of Reimann's linear composition.

—Malcolm J. Hill

REVERDY, Michèle. French. Born in Alexandria, Egypt, 12 December 1943. Educated at Conservatoire National Supérieur de Musique, Paris (composition under Olivier Messiaen, analysis under Claude Ballif, counterpoint under Alain Weber); University of Paris, *licence-des-lettres*; further period of study as bursar, Case de Velázquez, Madrid, 1979–81. Divorced; 1 daughter. Professor of analysis, Conservatoire National Supérieur de Musique, Paris, since 1983; producer, Radio France. Recipient: 1st prizes in counterpoint and analysis, prize and special jury mention in composition, Paris Conservatoire; Prix Lili Boulanger, 1979; Prix Philipp Morris, 1982; Prix Salabert, 1982; Prix Jacques Durand, Académie des Beaux-Arts, 1982. Mailing address: 75 rue des Gravilliers, 75003 Paris, France.

Publisher: Salabert.

Symphonies/orchestral:

Espaces (symphony orchestra) 1975; first performed Paris, 4 February 1976.
L'Ile aux lumières (violin, string orchestra) 1983; first performed Juvisy, 23 October 1983.
Le Cercle du vent 1988; first performed Lisbon, 11 May 1989.

Chamber/instrumental:

Kaleidoscope (harpsichord, flute) 1975; first performed Paris, 18 June 1976.
Tetramorphie (viola, percussion) 1976; first performed Paris, 18 November 1976.
Figure (piano) 1976; first performed Paris, 27 April 1977.
Regions (flute/piccolo, clarinet/bass clarinet, bassoon, horn, trumpet, trombone, tuba, harp, harpsichord) 1977; first performed Paris, 27 April 1977; withdrawn.
Number One (guitar; also version for 10-stringed guitar) 1977; first performed Paris, 17 February 1978.
Le Rideau bleu (flute/piccolo/alto flute/bass flute, clarinet/bass clarinet, violin, cello, piano) 1978; first performed Paris, 9 February 1981.
Météores (17 instruments) 1978; first performed Besançon, 11 September 1978. Recorded Salabert Actuels SCD 9001.
Arcane (clarinet, violin, cello, piano, percussion) 1979; first performed Madrid, 20 March 1980.
Wind Quintet 1980; first performed Paris, 2 February 1983.
El corro infrangibile (5 miniatures for flute, oboe, clarinet, bass clarinet, bassoon, horn, trumpet, trombone, violin, viola, cello, double bass) 1982; first performed Madrid, 22 May 1985.
Scenic Railway (16 instruments) 1983; first performed Paris, 30 January 1984. Recorded Salabert Actuels SCD 9001.
Fantasia (alto flute/bass flute/contrabass flute) 1985; first performed Barcelona, 9 January 1986.
Triade (guitar) 1986; first performed Brême, 24 October 1986.
Le Scherzo des petits plats (for a *Souper à la Française*; flute, oboe, bassoon, harpsichord, violin) 1986.
Pas de panique! (piano) 1987.
Cyclades (harpsichord) 1988; first performed Limoges, 16 March 1989.
Messe pour les Blanc-Manteaux (organ) 1990.

Vocal/choral:

Cante Jondo (3 songs for soprano, flute, cor anglais, bass clarinet, 3 percussion; Lorca) 1974, revised 1980; first performed Madrid, 25 May 1981.

Trois Pièces (soprano, bass clarinet, percussion) 1975; first performed Paris, 18 December 1975.
Souci sans soucis (children's chorus, flutes, percussion; Prevel) 1977; first performed Paris, 16 January 1979.
Through the Looking Glass (female voice, clarinet, viola, 2 trombones, piano; Lewis Carroll) 1979; first performed Paris, 20 May 1980.
Trois Fantaisies de Gaspard de la Nuit (mixed chorus or 12 unaccompanied voices; Bertrand) 1987; first performed Paris, 27 October 1987.
Sept Luminaires (soprano, clarinet/bass clarinet, piano, percussion; Poliakoff) 1987; first performed Madrid, 6 December 1988. Recorded Salabert Actuels SCD 9001.
Propos félins (children's chorus, orchestra; Anne Reverdy) 1988; first performed Paris, 17 October 1989.

Opera:

Le Château (9 soloists, men's chorus, children's chorus, orchestra; Kafka) 1980–6.
La Nuit qui suivit notre dernier diner . . . (pocket opera for alto, flute/alto flute/bass flute, cello, piano; Buchard) 1984; first performed Saint-Brieuc, 30 May 1985.
Champs de blé avec corbeaux (soprano, tenor, baritone, children's chorus, mixed chorus, flute, oboe, saxophone, harp, 2 percussion; Siret) 1984; first performed Avignon, 10 April 1986; withdrawn.
Vincent: Sept Paroles de la vie et de la mort to Vincent Van Gogh (soprano, tenor, baritone, children's chorus with treble soloist, mixed chorus, flute, oboe, clarinet, horn, bassoon, harp, 2 percussion, double bass; Gille) 1984–9.
Le Précepteur (coloratura soprano, soprano, mezzo-soprano, alto, 3 tenors, 2 baritones, 3 basses, 20 instruments; Treichel, after Lenz) 1989; first performed Munich, 14 May 1990.

Other:

Mimodrame (3 dancers, 8 percussion, 2 trombones) 1981.
Un Rêve à peain commence . . . (score to film short by Jean-Marc Deschamp; cello, spinet) 1985.

PUBLICATONS

By Reverdy: *L'Oeuvre pour piano d'Olivier Messiaen*, Paris, 1978; *Histoire de la musique occidentale*, Paris, 1985; *L'Oeuvre pour orchestre d'Olivier Messiaen*, Paris, 1990.

On Reverdy: in *20ème Siècle: Images de la musique française*, Paris, 1986.

Michèle Reverdy comments:

The process of creation begins with the choice of a single, deliberately limited piece of material. From there, the work unfolds in several directions simultaneously. On the one hand, I try to work such continuous transformations on the original material and all its components as to give birth to aural images which are apparently entirely new, but which bear signs of common origin. In organizing and controlling the periodicity of this phenomenon, an opportunity presents itself to act on the listener's psyche, exciting in her a buried memory, playing with the accretion of sound-memories in her subconscious. The echos and reprises of the same basic material will provoke a sense of "*déjà entendu*" which will plunge her into a recognizable and accommodating universe, and stir up a desire to become part of the work—such returns are neither blandly familiar nor redundant, and leave intact the excitement of discovery, which maintains the listener's "creative" role: for in order to travel through new music, one must be powerfully possessed of a desire to explore still-virgin territory.

On another side, I try to take account of the world in which we are living: different time scales collapse into one another; space recedes at such velocity that ultimately everything happens simultaneously; every viewpoint is unique. Because it inhabits its own unique frame and axes, music has the ability to give substance to the chimerical notion of absolute ubiquity in time and space. And so the fascination lies in the search for an absolute integration and unfolding of all these universes in a single, coherent process.

Let the many inhabit the one, and track down madly what can only be an expression of the Divine.

* * *

Michèle Reverdy studied under Olivier Messiaen at the Paris Conservatoire. An active educator—notably as professor of analysis at the Conservatoire—she is also a writer and musicologist, with two important books to her credit on Messiaen's piano and orchestral music. Her own music music is a personal synthesis of elements from Messiaen (whose rhythmic freedom and sense of colour she has inherited) with the serialism of Boulez, Betsy Jolas and Gilbert Amy. Her music often alludes to visual phenomena; she conceives of pieces as continually transforming images and landscapes. She has commented that the unity in her music results from "the choice of a single, deliberately limited piece of material" from which the work "unfolds in several directions at once."

Her ensemble work *Scenic Railway* is a case in point; textures of varying stasis and activity for an ensemble rich in high and low instruments (piccolo, E♭ clarinet, contrabass clarinet, contrabassoon) are interspersed with cadenzas for various members of the ensemble. In the earlier piece *Météores*, dedicated to Messiaen on his 80th birthday, the initial material is a six-note chord which is subjected very gradually to permutation and rotation through the ensemble, a process which is constantly disrupted by conflicting elements of a more dramatic nature.

The strong visual and dramatic impulses behind Reverdy's music are exploited fully in her operas *Le Château*, based on Kafka, and *Le Précepteur*, commissioned for the Munich Biennale. She has also composed a large number of smaller chamber and solo pieces, whose construction and imagery are similarly dramatic; one of her best-known and most successful works, *Sept Luminaires*, for soprano, clarinet, piano and percussion, is a lyrical setting of words by the artist Serge Poliakoff, a meditation on time, creativity and the role of the artist in society. Whatever the medium, Reverdy has remained faithful to her wish "to take account of the world we live in" and, by coming to terms with that, to "track down what can only be an expression of the Divine."

—Julian Anderson

REYNOLDS, Roger (Lee). American. Born in Detroit, Michigan, 18 July 1934. Educated at University of Michigan, Ann Arbor, 1952–7, B.S.E. engineering physics; School of

Music, University of Michigan, Ann Arbor (under Ross Lee Finney and Roberto Gerhard), 1957–61, B.M. literature, M.M. composition; further study under Roberto Gerhard, Tanglewood, Massachusetts, 1961; further study in electronic music, West German Radio Electronic Music Studio, Cologne, 1962. Married (1) Sandra Byers in 1957 (ended 1963); (2) Karen Jeanne Hill in 1964; 2 daughters. Co-founder (with Robert Ashley and Gordon Mumma), ONCE group/festival, Ann Arbor, Michigan, 1961; resident in Europe, 1962–6; resident in Japan, 1967–70; Miller Professor, University of Illinois, Urbana, 1971; Regent's Lecturer, 1968, associate professor, 1969–75, director, Center for Music Experiment and Related Research, 1972–7, and professor since 1975, University of California at San Diego, La Jolla, visiting composer, IRCAM, Paris, 1981–3; visiting professor, Yale University, New Haven, Connecticut, 1983; senior fellow, Institute for Studies in American Music, Brooklyn College, New York, 1985; Valentine Professor, Amherst College, Massachusetts, 1988. Recipient: Pulitzer Prize (for *Whispers Out of Time*), 1989. Mailing address: Department of Music, B026, University of California at San Diego, La Jolla, California 92093, U.S.A.

Publisher: Peters, New York.

Symphonies/orchestral:

Graffiti 1964; first performed Seattle, Washington, 2 February 1965.
Threshold 1967; first performed Tokyo, 7 June 1968.
. . . Between . . . (chamber orchestra, ring modulator, sound distribution, function generator) 1968; first performed Chicago, 10 March 1970.
Fiery Wind 1977; first performed New York City, 13 February 1968.
Only Now, and Again (20 winds, piano, 3 percussion) 1977.
Archipelago (chamber orchestra, 4-or 8-channel tape) 1981–2; first performed Paris, 15 February 1983.
Transfigured Wind II 1984; first performed New York City, 4 June 1984.
The Dream of the Infinite Rooms (cello, orchestra, 4-channel tape) 1986.
Symphony: Vertigo (orchestra, computer-generated 4-channel tape) 1987.
Whispers Out of Time (string orchestra) 1988.
Symphony: Myths 1990.

Chamber/instrumental:

Epigram and Evolution (piano) 1959; withdrawn.
Acquaintances (flute, piano, double bass) 1960.
Continuum (viola, cello) 1960.
Situations (cello, piano) 1960.
Mosaic (flute, piano) 1960.
Four Etudes (flute quartet) 1961.
Wedge (2 flutes/piccolo, 2 trumpets, 2 trombones, percussion, piuano, double bass) 1961.
Consequent (alto flute, bassoon, violin, piano) 1961.
String Quartet 1961.
Traces (piano, flute, cello, electronics, 4-or 6-channel tape) 1963.
Fantasy for Pianist 1964.
Quick Are the Mouths of Earth (3 flutes/piccolos, oboe, trumpet, trombone, bass trombone, 2 percussion, piano, 3 cellos) 1964–5.
Gathering (woodwind quintet) 1965.
Ping (flute, piano, percussion, electronics, 4-channel tape after Beckett, projections, film) 1968.
" . . . The Serpent-Snapping Eye" (trumpet, percussion, piano, 4-channel computer-synthesized tape) 1970.
" . . . From Behind the Unreasoning Mask" (trombone, percussion/assistant, 4-channel tape) 1975.
The Promise of Darkness (flute, clarinet, bassoon, trumpet, horn, trombone, piano, percussion, violin, cello, double bass) 1976.
Less than Two (2 pianos, 2 percussion, 4-channel tape) 1976–9.
Shadowed Narrative (clarinet, piano, violin, cello) 1976–9.
Aether (violin, piano) 1983.
Transfigured Wind I 1983.
Summer Island (oboe, 4-channel tape) 1984.
The Behaviour of Mirrors (guitar) 1985.
Transfigured Wind IV (flute, 4-channel tape) 1985.
COCONINO . . . A Shattered Landscape (string quartet) 1985.
Mistral (2 horns, 2 trumpets, 2 trombones, amplified harpsichord, 2 violins, 2 cellos, 2 double basses) 1985.
Autumn Island (marimba) 1986.
Variation (piano) 1988.
Focus a Beam, Emptied of Thinking, Outwards . . . (cello) 1989.
Personae (violin solo, flute/piccolo, clarinet/bass clarinet, horn, bass trombone, percussion, piano, viola, cello, double bass, 2-or 4-channel tape) 1990.

Vocal/choral:

Sky (soprano, alto flute, bassoon, harp) 1961.
A Portrait of Vanzetti (speaker, instruments, tape) 1962–3.
Masks (8-part mixed chorus, orchestra; Melville) 1964.
Ambages (flute) 1966.
Blind Men (24-voice mixed chorus, brass, percussion, piano, projections; Melville) 1966.
Again (2 wordless sopranos, 2 flutes, 2 trombones, 2 percussion, 2 double basses, 4-channel tape, amplification system, lights) 1971–4.
Compass (tenor, bass, cello, double bass, amplification system, 4-channel tape, projections; Borges) 1972–4.
The Palace: Voicespace IV (bass-baritone, 4-channel tape, lights; Borges) 1980.
Sketchbook for "The Unbearable Lightness of Being" (low female voice/piano/electronics; Kundera) 1985.
Not Only Night (soprano, flute/piccolo, E♭ clarinet/bass clarinet, piano, violin, cello, 2-channel tape; Giraud/Hartleben) 1988.

Theatre/dramatic:

The Emperor of Ice Cream (music-theatre for 8 solo voices, percussion, piano, double bass; Stevens) 1961, revised 1974; first performed New York City, 19 March 1975.
I/O: A Ritual (9 female vocalists, 9 male mimes, 2 flutes, clarinet, 2 technician/performers, electronics, projections) 1970; first performed Pasadena, California, 24 January 1971.

Other:

Still: Voicespace I (4-channel tape; Coleridge) 1975.
A Merciful Coincidence: Voicespace II (4-channel tape; Beckett) 1976.
Eclipse: Voicespace III (4-channel tape; texts by Issa, Melville, Stevens, Joyce, Borges, García, Márquez) 1979.

The Tempest (incidental music to Shakespeare; instruments, computer synthesizer, 4-track tape) 1980; first performed Tanglewood, Massachusetts, 30 July 1980.
The Vanity of Words: Voicespace V (2-channel tape; Kundera) 1986.
Vertigo (4-channel tape) 1986.
Versions / Stages I–IV (4-channel tape) 1988.

PUBLICATIONS

By Reynolds: John Cage, "An Interview with RR" [actually *vice versa*], in *John Cage: A Document*, New York City, 1962, and in Childs and Schwartz, *Contemporary Composers on Contemporary Music*, New York City, 1967; *Mind Models: New Forms of Musical Experience*, New York City, 1975; *A Searcher's Path: A Composer's Ways*, New York City, 1987.

On Reynolds: C. Gagne and T. Caras, (interview) in *Soundpieces: Interviews with American Composers*, Metuchen, New Jersey, 1981; Robert Ashley, (interview) in *Music with Roots in the Aether*, New York City, 1982; Don Gillespie, *RR: Portrait of a Composer*, New York City, 1982.

* * *

The diversity of 20th-century music is due in part to the variety of compositional techniques composers have introduced into the language of music. The syntax of Western music has expanded beyond triadic harmonies and diatonic scales to include techniques such as micro-tones, twelve-tone and serial procedures, electronic manipulation of sound, and computer-generated procedures and sounds. While the works of many composers have focused on and explored the potential of a single technique, Roger Reynolds has created a body of work that encompasses nearly every major musical development in the 20th century.

As well as incorporating new techniques into his music, Reynolds is responsible for initiating many of the new developments. The theater piece *The Emperor of Ice Cream*, for instance, became the model for a new genre, and its influence is evident in the numerous imitations it spawned. He was also one of the pioneering composers to use language as the basis of a musical composition; texts are used for their sonic qualities as well as their semantic content. In *Still: Voicespace*, the only materials serving as the basis for musical development are a portion of text taken from Coleridge's "The Wanderings of Cain" and aspirated clicks produced by a vocal ensemble. The text is not sung or recited in any traditional sense, but unfolds in a temporally elongated manner that develops the relationship between the text's sonic quality and its semantic content.

Reynolds's text-based music often contains beautiful and subtle examples of tone painting. In *Whispers Out of Time*, the first section of the first movement is based on the line "a recurring wave of arrival . . ." from a John Ashbery poem. It is divided into three three-measure phrases and one four-measure phrase. Each phrase is articulated by a *luftpause*, has a contacting and expanding dynamic shape, and slightly varies the same pitch material and rhythmic shape, and the first three phrases end with a *rallentando*; as a result the entire passage seems to suggest a "recurring wave" at the moment it reaches its break point.

While programmatic elements are an important feature of Reynolds's expressive style, his goal is not to create a literal illustration of a poem or text, but, in the case of *Whispers*, to evoke (in his words) A "provocative and often disturbing effect."

Besides literature, another major force in Reynolds's music in his use of electronics and computers. These resources add a new dimension to his music, and have also influenced his use of traditional instruments. Of *From Behind the Unreasoning Mask*, Reynolds says "the four-channel tape is the metaphoric 'Mask' of the title behind which the performers act." If one thinks of a mask as a type of filter, then the 4-channel tape should, in some way, alter or influence the instrumental sounds. This appears to be the relationship Reynolds sets up, because the music of the percussion and trombone is virtually a catalogue of special effects that reflect and develop the electronic sounds. This work is also a brilliant example of Reynolds's use of texture as a compositional resource. The ever-evoking textural landscape takes on a motivic as well as structural function.

Reynolds is one of the pioneering composers of his generation, with provocative, expressive work. One can be sure that he will continue to produce interesting works, explore the bounds of human perception, and inspire younger generations of composers.

—Ciro G. Scotto

RIETI, Vittorio. American citizen; Italian parentage. Born in Alexandria, Egypt, 28 January 1898. Educated: studied music under Frugatta, Milan, 1912–17; University of Milan, economics, doctorate 1917; further composition study under Ottorino Respighi and Alfredo Casella, Rome, 1918–20. Military service, Italian Army field artillery, 1917–8. Married Elsie Rappaport, 25 June 1924. Resident in Rome and Paris, 1918–40; co-founder (with Mario Labroca and Massarani), I Tre, 1922–3; founder and co-director, La Serenade ensemble, Paris, 1931–40; emigrated to United States, 1940, citizenship 1944. Visiting professor, Peabody School of Music, Baltimore, Maryland, 1948–50, Chicago Musical College, 1950–3, Queens College, City University of New York, 1956–60, and New York College of Music, New York, 1960–4. Recipient: honorary membership, Accademia di Santa Cecilia, Rome. Mailing address: 1391 Madison Avenue, New York, New York, 10029, U.S.A.

Publishers: Bangiovanni, Bologna; Universal Edition, Vienna; Salabert, Paris; Eschig, Paris; Broude Brothers, New York; Associated Music Publishers, New York; EMI Music Inc, Hollywood; Galaxy Music Corporation, Boston.

Symphonies / orchestral:

Concerto for Winds and Orchestra (5 winds) 1923; first performed Vienna, 1924.
L'arca di Noe (orchestral suite from the ballet) 1923; first performed Vienna, 1925.

Robinson et Vendredi (orchestral suite from the ballet) 1924.
Due pastorali (chamber orchestra) 1925.
Barabau (orchestral suite from the ballet) 1925.
Piano Concerto No 1 1926; first performed Turin, 1927.
Violin Concerto No 1 (Concerto napoletano) 1928; destroyed.
Symphony No 1 1929; first performed Paris, 1930.
Symphony No 2 1930; first performed Brussels, 1931.
Piano Concerto No 2 1930–7; first performed Venice, 1937.
Serenata (violin, chamber orchestra) 1931.
Symphony No 3: Sinfonietta 1932; first performed Paris, 1932.
Cello Concerto No 1 (cello, chamber orchestra) 1934.
Hippolyte (orchestral suite from the ballet) 1937.
Concerto du loup 1938.
Symphony No 4: Sinfonia tripartita 1942; first performed St Louis, Missouri, 1944.
Symphony No 5 1945; first performed Venice, 1947.
Concerto for Two Pianos and Orchestra 1951; first performed Cincinnati, Ohio, 1952.
Harpsichord Concerto (originally for harp) 1952–5, revised 1972; first performed Paris, 1956.
Introduzione e gioco delle ore 1953.
Cello Concerto No 2 1953; first performed New York City, 1954.
Piano Concerto No 3 1955; first performed Brussels, 1955.
Dance Variations (strings) 1956.
La Fontaine 1968.
Violin Concerto No 2 1969.
Triple Concerto (violin, viola, piano, orchestra) 1971.
Symphony No 6 1973; first performed New York City, 1974.
Concerto for String Quartet and Orchestra 1976; first performed New York City, 1976.
Symphony No 7 1977; first performed New Paltz, New York, 1987.
Symphony No 8 1980–1; first performed Lafayette, Indiana, 1988.
Symphony No 9 1983–4; first performed New York City, 1989.

Chamber/instrumental:

Sonatina (flute, piano) 1920.
Poema fiesolana (piano) 1921.
Variations on a Chinese Theme (violin, piano) 1922.
Due studi (piano) 1923.
Sonata (flute, oboe, bassoon, piano) 1924.
Sonatina (piano) 1925.
String Quartet No 1 1926; first performed Paris, 1926.
Suite (piano) 1926.
Madrigale (6 winds, piano, strings) 1927; first performed Brussels, 1927.
Serenata (version for violin, 11 instruments) 1931; first performed Brussels, 1931.
Tre preludi (piano) 1931.
Sei pezzi brevi (piano) 1932.
Sonata in A♭ (piano) 1938.
String Quartet No 2 1941; first performed Chicago, 1943.
Capriccio (violin, piano) 1941.
Second Avenue Waltzes (2 pianos) 1942; first performed New York City, 1943.
Five Little Recital Pieces (for young pianists) 1942.
Partita (harpsichord, flute, oboe, string quartet) 1945; first performed New York City, 1946.
Chess Serenade (2 pianos) 1945.
Rondo variato (violin, piano) 1945.
Sonata all'antica (piano or harpsichord) 1946.
Suite champêtre (2 pianos) 1948.
Academic Variations (piano) 1950.
String Quartet No 3 1951.
New Waltzes (2 pianos) 1956–7.
Quintet (woodwinds) 1957.
String Quartet No 4 1960; first performed New York City, 1961.
Medieval Variations (piano) 1962.
Concertino (flute, viola, cello, harp, harpsichord) 1963.
Variations on When from My Love (flute, clarinet, viola, cello; John Bartlett) 1964.
Pastorale and Fughetta (flute, viola, piano) 1966.
Sonata à cinque (flute, oboe, clarinet, bassoon, piano) 1966; first performed New York City, 1966.
Incisioni (brass quintet) 1967.
Contrasti (piano) 1967.
Siciliana e tarantella (cello, piano) 1967.
Sonata breve (violin, piano) 1967; first performed New York City, 1968.
Silografie (wind quintet) 1967.
Corale, variazioni e finale (2 pianos) 1969.
Three Vaudeville Marches (2 pianos) 1969.
Sonata concertante (violin, piano) 1970.
Valse fugitive (2 pianos) 1970.
String Quartet No 5 1970; first performed New York City, 1990.
Octet (piano, 7 instruments) 1971.
Piano Trio 1972; first performed New York City, 1973.
Chironomes (suite for piano) 1972.
Piano Quartet 1973.
Sestetto pro Gemini (flute, oboe, piano quartet) 1975; first performed Amsterdam, 1976.
Scherzo-March (2 pianos) 1976.
Spiccata 1977–8; first performed New York City, 1982.
Nonetto (woodwinds, strings, piano) 1980; first performed New York City, 1990.
Piano Quintet 1981; first performed New York City, 1990.
Sonata a dieci (woodwinds, trumpet, strings, piano) 1983; first performed New York City, 1984.
Cinquina da camera (woodwinds, strings, piano) 1985; first performed New York City, 1990.

Vocal/choral:

Ulysses Wandering (cantata for chorus) 1939.
Two Songs Between Two Waltzes (voice, piano; Yeats) 1957.
Four Songs (voice, piano; Lawrence) 1960.
Three Choral Songs (unaccompanied mixed chorus) 1963.
Five Elizabethan Songs (voice, piano) 1967.
Missa brevis (voices, organ) 1973.
Sete liriche saffiche (voice, piano) 1974.

Opera/dramatic:

L'arca di Noe (dramatic ballet) 1923.
Robinson et Vendredi (dramatic ballet) 1924.
Barabau (dramatic ballet) 1925; first performed London, 1925.
Orfeo tragedia (Poliziano) 1928; withdrawn.
Le Bal (dramatic ballet) 1929; first performed Monte Carlo, 1929.
Teresa nel bosco (chamber opera) 1933; first performed Venice, 1934.
David triomphant (dramatic ballet) 1937.
Hippolyte (dramatic ballet) 1937.
The Night Shadow (dramatic ballet after Bellini) 1941; first performed New York City, 1946.
Waltz Academy (dramatic ballet based on *Second Avenue Waltzes*) 1944.

The Mute Wife (dramatic ballet on theme by Paganini) 1944.
Trionfo di Bacco e Arianna (dramatic ballet-cantata incorporating material from *Orfeo tragedia*) 1946–7; first performed New York City, 1948.
Don Perimplin (one act) 1949; first performed Paris, 1952.
Viaggio d'Europa (dramatic oratorio for soloists, chorus, orchestra) 1954; first performed Rome, 1955.
The Pet Shop (one act) 1956; first performed New York City, 1956.
Native Dancer (dramatic ballet using material from *Symphony No 5*) 1959.
The Clock 1959–60.
Conundrum (dramatic ballet) 1961.
A Sylvan Dream (dramatic ballet) 1965; first performed Indianapolis, 1984.
Maryam the Harlot (one act) 1966.
Scenes Seen (dramatic ballet) 1975.

PUBLICATIONS

On Rieti: G.Rossi-Doria, "Giovani compositori italiani: Labroca, Massarani, R", in *Il pianoforte*, 5, 1924; Alfredo Casella, "Neue Komponisten in Italien", in *Musikblatter des Anbruch*, 7, 1925, and "VR", in *Cobbett's Cyclopedic Survey of Chamber Music*, London, 1929; D. de'Paoli, *La crisi musicale italiana*, Milan, 1939; J.C.G. Waterhouse, "The Emergence of Modern Italian Music to 1940", dissertation, University of Oxford, 1968; Franco Carlo Ricci, *VR: A Biography*, Naples, 1987.

Vittorio Rieti comments:
Mine's not to reason why; mine's but to do and die (sometime or other).

* * *

It is a well-attested scientific fact that while pure mathematicians rarely achieve any major conceptual breakthroughs after the age of 30, the synapses and conceptual apparatus that go to make up the musical imagination continue to develop right through life. Composers like Alan Bush, the late Jean Langlais, and Vittorio Rieti have continued to produce significant work long past the grand climacteric.

Rieti's biography is a little out of the ordinary. The son of Italian parents, he was born in Egypt, where they were temporarily based. Though essentially self-taught, he studied music with Frugatta while reading for an economics degree in Milan. Subsequently, he was a pupil of Respighi and Alfredo Casella in Rome; it is Respighi, rather than the more orotund Riccardo Malipiero, the other leading Italian composer of the period, who had the greatest impact on his style, which is elegantly melodic, uncomplicatedly expressive, formally controlled and which changed very little in essence for the next 70 years.

Like all young composers, Rieti was initially drawn to the most fashionably revolutionary developments of his time; his early atonal experiments were quickly destroyed and there is no sign that he desired to follow the same individual course through the melodic application of atonality as his slightly younger contemporary Luigi Dallapiccola. Shortly after World War I, Rieti and two like-minded friends—Massarani and Mario Labroca (who had been a pupil of Malipiero) formed a group known as I Tre. The reference to Les Six—a grouping which was just beginning to lose its cohesion at that time—is fairly obvious, though the relative musical achievement may be thought to be rather bathetic. What it did achieve was to align Rieti quite closely with what was going on in France, and he spent much of the next decade, up to his emigration to the United States, moving between Rome and Paris, where he wrote some very significant scores for Sergei Diaghilev's Ballets Russes and for Jouvet's theatre. *Barabou* was premiered in London to considerable applause, and Rieti went on to write some strikingly effective short operas which have much of the unity of theme and mood as the choreographic idiom and scenic design favoured by Balanchine, with whom Rieti worked when he emigrated to the U.S.A. in 1940.

The U.S.A. made no greater impact on his music than an opening up of his already confident structural sense. Like other exiles, such as Ernst Krenek, he remains a European in essentials, and "American" pieces, such as the two-piano *Second Avenue Waltzes* are an outsider's gesture of homage in his own, rather than a borrowed, tongue. Nevertheless, North America welcomed Rieti's compositional talents. He was a respected guest teacher in Baltimore and New York, and has enjoyed considerable success with his own compositions.

His work is fluent, perfectly streamlined, entirely free of unmusical tensions, but full of a strange sense of loss, as if in mourning for an absent tradition. It is hard to conceive of Rieti writing an awkward bar or phrase, but it is equally difficult to hear any of his later works without detecting a calmly accepting nostalgia for the cultural coherence that his own life story seems to belie and for which all of his compositions seem to yearn. He is not a nationalist, but a grandly cosmopolitan figure of the sort that populates Henry James's novels, and there is something of James in his steady diction and quietly ironic humour. There is also an echo of the persistent misprision that has afflicted James in the rather diffident critical response to Rieti's later work, a response not in any way matched by his audiences. In 1990, his Ninth Symphony was premiered in New York City, always a highly significant and symbolic moment in the life of a composer. Rieti seems to have regarded the occasion with typical equanimity, confident that there is still music to be written, but untroubled by any thoughts of fashionable eternity.

—Brian Morton

RIHM, Wolfgang. German. Born in Karlsruhe, 13 March 1952. Educated at Hochschule für Musik, Karlsruhe (theory and composition under Eugen Werner Velte), 1968–72; Ferienkurse für Neue Musik, Darmstadt, from 1970; further study under Karlheinz Stockhausen, Cologne, 1972–3; further composition study under Klaus Huber, musicology under Han Heinrich Eggebrecht, Freiburg, also under Wolfgang Fortner and Humphrey Searle, 1973–6. Teacher, Ferienkurse für Neue Musik, Darmstadt, from 1978; teacher of music 1973–8, and professor since 1985, Musikhochschule, Karlsruhe. Mailing address: c/o Universal Edition, Bosendorferstrasse 12, Postfach 33, A-1015 Vienna, Austria.

Publisher: Universal Edition.

Symphonies/orchestral:

Adagio (strings) 1969.
Symphony No 1 Op 3 1969.
Trakt 1971.
Morphonie, Sektor IV (string quartet, orchestra) 1972.
Magma (large orchestra) 1973.
Dis-Kontur (large orchestra) 1974.
Sub-Kontur 1974–5; first performed Donaueschingen, 26 October 1976.
Symphony No 2 (large orchestra) 1975.
Lichtzwang: In memoriam Paul Celan (violin, orchestra) 1975–6.
Cuts and Dissolves (orchestral sketches) 1976.
Nachtordnung (after Bruch; 15 strings) 1976.
Symphony No 3 (soprano, baritone, mixed chorus, large orchestra; Nietzsche, Rimbaud) 1976–7.
La Musique creuse le ciel (2 pianos, large orchestra) 1977–9; first performed Cologne, 14 November 1980.
Erst Abgesangsszene 1979; first performed Kassel, 8 November 1979.
Fünfte Abgesangsszene 1979; first performed Kiel, 12 January 1981.
Landler (chamber string orchestra) 1979.
Nature Morte—Still Alive (chamber string orchestra) 1979–80.
Walzer I: Sehnsuchtswalzer (part of *Three Waltzes*) 1979–81.
Bratschenkonzert (viola, orchestra) 1979–83; first performed Berlin, 13 November 1983.
Brahmsliebewalzer 1979–88.
Erster Doppelgesang (viola, cello, orchestra) 1980.
Tutuguri I ("*poème danse*" after Artaud) 1981.
Tutuguri III (6 percussion, orchestra) 1981; first performed Karlsruhe, 5 December 1981.
Tutuguri II (large orchestra) 1981–2; first performed Chicago, 3 March 1982.
Zweiter Doppelgesang (clarinet, cello, orchestra) 1981–3; first performed Hitzacker, 7 August 1983.
Zeichen I: Doubles (bass flute/piccolo, contrabass clarinet/clarinet, 2 orchestral groups) 1981, in progress.
Gebild (piccolo trumpet, 2 percussion, 20 strings) 1982–3; first performed Zurich, 15 May 1983.
Monodram (cello, orchestra) 1982–3; first performed Graz, 9 October 1983.
Schwarzer und Roter Tanz (fragment from *Tutuguri*; large orchestra) 1982–3.
Schattenstück (tone poem for orchestra) 1982–4.
Klangbeschreibung I (3 orchestral groups) 1982–7.
Chiffre II: Silence to Be Beaten (percussion, orchestra) 1983.
Vorgefuhle 1984.
Fusées 1984.
Chiffre V 1984.
Spur (orchestral sketch) 1984–5.
Klangbeschreibung III (large orchestra) 1984–7.
Chiffre VII 1985.
Abkehr (notes for large orchestra) 1985.
Dammerung (notes for large orchestra) 1985.
Umriss (notes for large orchestra) 1985–6.
Aufzeichung: Dammerung und Umriss (large orchestra) 1985–6.
Compresenze (draft outlines and processes for large orchestra) 1985–7.
Unbenannt I 1986.
Walzer 2: Drangender Walzer (part of *Three Waltzes*) 1986–7.
Danse 1987.
Splitter (orchestral sketch from *Oedipus*) 1987.
Unbenannt II 1987.
Tutuguri V 1987–8.
Tutuguri VII 1987–8.
Blick 1987–8.
Bruchstück "Die Vorzeichen" (orchestral fragment from *Die Eroberung von Mexico*) 1988–9.
Passim 1989.
Schwebende Begegnung 1989.
Abgewandt (chamber orchestra) 1989.
Ungemaltes Bild 1989–90.
Unbenannt III 1989–90.

Chamber/instrumental:

Contemplatio per organo (organ) 1967.
Drei Fantasien (organ) 1967.
Fantasie (organ) 1968.
Concerto for Piano and Eight Instruments (piano, flute, oboe, bassoon, trumpet, trombone, violin, viola, cello) 1969.
String Quartet No 1 Op 2 1970.
Paraphrase (cello, percussion, piano) 1972.
Deploration (flute, cello, percussion) 1973.
Klavierstück No 4 (piano) 1974.
Siebengestalt (organ, tom-tom) 1974.
Tombeau: Klavierstück No 5 (piano) 1975.
Im Innersten: String Quartet No 3 1976.
Bagatellen: Klavierstück No 6 (piano) 1977–8.
Erscheinung (sketch after Schubert; 9 strings, piano ad lib) 1978.
Music-Hall Suite (clarinet, 2 alto saxophones/tenor saxophones, trumpet, percussion, piano, violin, double bass) 1979.
Mehrere Kurze Walzer (piano—4 hands) 1979, in progress.
Landler (piano) 1979.
String Quartet No 4 1979–81.
Bann, Nachtschwarmerei (organ) 1980.
Klavierstück No 7 (piano) 1980.
Tutuguri VI: Kreuze (6 percussion) 1981.
Musik für Drei Streicher (violin, viola, cello) 1981.
Ohne Titel: String Quartet No 5 1981–3.
Canzona (4 violas) 1982.
Fremde Szene I (violin, cello, piano) 1982.
Chiffre I (piano, clarinet, bassoon, trumpet, trombone, 2 cellos, double bass) 1982; first performed Saarbrücken, 22 April 1983.
Chiffre III (cor anglais, bass clarinet, bassoon/contrabassoon, horn, bass trumpet, trombone, 2 percussion, piano, 2 cellos, double bass) 1983.
Fremde Szene II: Charakterstück (violin, cello, piano) 1983.
Fremde Szene III (violin, cello, piano) 1983.
Chiffre IV (bass clarinet, cello, piano) 1983–4.
Bild (trumpet, horn, trombone, 2 percussion, piano, viola, cello, double bass) 1984.
Blaubuch: String Quartet No 6 1984.
Chiffre VI (bass clarinet/clarinet, contrabassoon, horn, 2 violins, viola, cello, double bass) 1985.
Klavierstück No 8 (piano) 1985, in progress.
Veranderungen: String Quartet No 7 1985.
Maske (2 pianos) 1985.
Sine nomine (brass quintet) 1985.
Chiffre VIII (bass clarinet, contrabassoon, horn, trumpet, piano, 2 cellos, double bass) 1985–8.
Verzeichung—Studie (viola, cello, double bass) 1986.
Brahmsliebewalzer (piano) 1986.
Protokoll, Ein Traum (6 cellos) 1987.
Kein Firmament (bass clarinet, contrabassoon, horn, trumpet, trombone, 2 percussion, piano, 2 violins, viola, 2 cellos, double bass) 1988.
Quintet (clarinet, string quartet) 1988.

String Quartet No 8 1988.
Medea-Spiel (dance theatre for cor anglais, tenor saxophone, bass clarinet, contrabassoon, 2 trumpets, 2 trombones, 2 percussion, harp, piano, 6 violins, 4 cellos, 2 double basses) 1988–9.
Sine nomine II (4 tubas) 1989, in progress.
Stück (bongo, suspended cymbal, wood block) 1989.
Duomonolog (violin, cello) 1989.
Dunkles Spiel (bass clarinet, contrabassoon, 2 horns, 2 trombones, 4 percussion, harp, piano, 2 violas, 4 cellos, 2 double basses) 1990.

Vocal/choral:

Gesange Op 1 (voice, piano; Trakl, George, Heym, Bucheler, Stramm, Loerke, Hölderlin, Rilke) 1968–70.
Sicut cedrvus desiderat ad fontes aquarum Op 7 (soprano, bass clarinet, bassoon, trombone, percussion, piano, organ, cello, double bass) 1970.
Vier Gedichte aus Atemwende (voice, piano; Celan) 1973.
Hervorgedunkelt (mezzo-soprano, flute, harp, vibraphone, cello, organ, 2 percussion) 1974.
O Notte (baritone, small orchestra; Michelangelo) 1975.
Konzertarie ("telepsychogram" for mezzo-soprano, large orchestra; telegram from Ludwig II to Wagner) 1975.
Alexanderlieder (mezzo-soprano/baritone, piano; Herbeck) 1977.
Hölderlin-Fragmente (singer, piano or orchestra) 1977.
Zweite Abgesangsszene (medium voice, orchestra; Nietzsche, Novalis) 1979; first performed Karlsruhe, 5 October 1980.
Neue Alexanderlieder (baritone, piano; Herbeck) 1979.
Dritte Abgesangsszene (baritone, orchestra; Huchel) 1979–80.
Vierte Abgesangsszene (medium voice, orchestra; Nietzsche fragments) 1979.
Fünfte Abgesangsszene (version for mezzo-soprano, baritone, orchestra; Nietzsche) 1979–81.
Lenz-Fragmente (singer, piano or orchestra) 1980.
Wolfli-Liederbuch (bass-baritone, piano, 2 bass drums ad lib) 1980–1.
Umhergetrieben, Aufgewirbelt (mezzo-soprano, baritone, mixed chorus, flutes/1 player; Nietzsche) 1981.
Tutuguri IV (speaker ad lib, large orchestra) 1981–2.
Wolfli-Lieder (baritone, piano or orchestra) 1981–2.
Mit Geschlossenem Mund (2 sopranos, 2 altos, 2 tenors, 2 basses; wordless) 1982.
Lowry-Lieder (singer, orchestra; Wondraschek) 1982–7.
Dies (soprano, alto, tenor, baritone, 2 speakers, children's chorus, speaking chorus, mixed chorus, grand organ, orchestra; da Vinci, Vulgate) 1984.
Umsungen (baritone, A clarinet, bassoon, horn, string quintet; Nietzsche) 1984.
Andere Schatten (high soprano, mezzo-soprano, baritone, speaker, mixed chorus, orchestra; Jean Paul) 1985.
Was Aber . . . (2 female voices, orchestra; Pindar/Hölderlin) 1986.
Raumage (mixed chorus, 8 percussion; Handke) 1986.
Klangbeschreibung II—innere Grenze (4 singers, 5 brass, 6 percussion; Nietzsche) 1986–7.
Nachtwatch (2 sopranos, 2 altos, 2 tenors, 2 basses, SATB chorus, 4 trombones, woodblock played by conductor; biblical) 1987–8.
Départ (mixed chorus, speaking chorus, 22 instruments; Rimbaud) 1988.
Mein Tod. Requiem in memoriam Jane S. (soprano, large orchestra; Wondratschek) 1988–9.
Frau/Stimme (soprano, orchestra; Müller) 1989.
Geheimer Block (soprano, alto, tenor, bass, SATB chorus, orchestra; wordless) 1989.
Engel (2 male voices, cor anglais, tenor saxophone, bass clarinet, contrabassoon, 2 trumpets, 2 trombones, 2 percussion, harp, piano, 2 violins, 2 violas, 2 cellos, 2 double basses; Müller) 1989.
Quo me rapis (2 choruses or 8 solo voices) 1990.

Opera/dramatic:

Faust und Yorick (chamber opera; Tardieu) 1976.
Jakob Lenz (chamber opera; Fröhling, after Büchner) 1977–8; first performed Hamburg, 8 March 1979.
Harlekin 1977, in progress.
Die Hamletmaschine (music theatre; Müller) 1983–6.
Oedipus (music theatre; after Hölderlin, Sophocles, Nietzsche, Müller) 1986–7.
Die Eroberung von Mexico (music theatre) 1987–9.

Other:

Johann Strauss: *Unter Donner und Blitz—Polka Op 324* (arranged for flute, oboe, clarinet, bassoon, 2 violins, viola, cello, piano) 1982.

* * *

From his teacher, Stockhausen, Wolfgang Rihm developed both a technique for manipulating enormous forces and the formation of a *Klavierstück* series of works. From his later teacher, Klaus Huber, he acquired a means of incorporating silence and less-than-extreme contrast into his compositions. Rihm's most successful works precede his chamber operas (*Faust und Yorick* and *Jacob Lenz*); he is best when writing for players whom he knows or when composing Mahler-inspired works for large forces. Most of his music is very loud, with occasional brief quiet backgrounds.

Dis-Kontur is for a large orchestra (including pairs of saxophones, contrabassoons, harps and pianos). A long, loud opening on unpitched percussion is gradually overtaken by rhythmic strings and lower winds. Forcefully disjointed one-bar fragments on standard orchestral groups are pitted against each other throughout. A gruesome march towards the end makes the non-Mahler and non-Weill passages stand out. *Sub-Kontur,* for large orchestra (whose only woodwinds are three contrabassoons) also starts very loudly, with percussion trilling before each rest (rather than *Dis-Kontur*'s single strike plus long rest). Ideas are "melodically conceived," often lasting five or six bars, written in a late-Mahler style, with string glissandos marked at the largest interval. *Sub-Kontur* and the Second Symphony both include marches and transformations from Mahler near their close. The Second Symphony uses a standard large orchestra with organ. There are very brief full-orchestral passages employing either a homophonic colour chord or six or seven simultaneous strands of (often four voiced) polyphony. These surround extended Andante passages of one to four-voiced part-writing. The symphony is seldom more rhythmically complex than five against three; interest comes from long-scale crescendos rather than quick alternations of dynamics.

Rihm's Third Symphony is for an enormous orchestra, chorus and mandolin ad lib. Three Adagios and an Agitato constitute the first of four movements. The symphony starts with tentative violas presenting a neo-romantic view of fugal writing which soon deteriorates into holding notes destined to be a feature of the composition. Held pitches are transformed into single-pitch repetition, where many instruments perform differing rhythms. Varied interjections, often on mallet percussion, are exploited in the second and third Adagios. The music subsides into the brief second movement, where two solo singers are given fragments from Nietzsche to sing homophonically. Taking their ideas from a semitone motif near the work's opening, they are gradually reinforced by the chorus and orchestra. The third movement juxtaposes very loud, complex but normally open-voiced sounds with very soft, held clusters. An even larger ensemble is demanded for *Dies* (including double pairs of percussion units, choruses and soloists), all deployed to display an apocalyptic but godless vision. However, brief references to many historical styles are insufficient to cohese the work or to justify the resources.

Tombeau: Klavierstück No 5, written for Herbert Henck, opens very loudly with a rhythmic set of differing harmonisations below middle C. This pitch becomes central to the work: a texture is built solely below it, against which either faster, higher elements or the whole keyboard can be contrasted. The untitled Fifth String Quartet opens with a single held note, soon answered by a brief rhythmic figure before the first of many outbursts. The piece written for the Arditti Quartet, is essentially a complex tension-arch interspersed with areas of stasis. The similarly opening *Départ* is for two choruses and another typically unusual alignment of 22 players (organ, piccolo, pairs of clarinets, trumpets, trombones, harps, pianos, cellos, contrabasses and six percussionists). One chorus declaims Rimbaud's poetry, the other sings selected vowels. Gestures (which often extend for longer than the norm) create a phrase-structured work in many ways respectably neo-romantic in idiom.

—Malcolm J. Hill

ROCHBERG, George. American. Born in Paterson, New Jersey, 5 July 1918. Educated at Passaic High School; Montclair State Teachers College, New Jersey, 1935–9, B.A.; Mannes School, New York City (under Hans Weisse, George Szell and Leopold Mannes), 1939–42; Curtis Institute of Music, Philadelphia, (studied with Rosario Scaleo and Menotti), 1945–8, B.M.; University of Pennsylvania, Philadelphia, M.A. 1948. Married Gene Rosenfeld, 18 August 1941; 1 son (deceased) and 1 daughter. Faculty Member, Curtis Institute of Music, 1948–54; director of publications, Theodore Presser, 1951–60; chair, music department, 1960–8, professor of composition, 1968–79, and Annenberg Professor of Humanities, University of Pennsylvania, since 1979. Guest composer, State University of New York, Buffalo, 1964, Temple University Institute of Music, Ambler, Pennsylvania, 1969; Festival of Contemporary Music, Oberlin, Ohio, 1970, concert series Testimonium, Jerusalem, Israel, 1970–1, and Conference on Contemporary Music, Aspen, Colorado, 1972. Recipient: American Academy in Rome Fellowship, 1950–1; Fulbright Fellowship, 1950–1; George Gershwin Memorial Award (for *Night Music*), 1952; Society for the Publication of American Music Award (for *String Quartet No 1*), 1956; First Prize, Italian ISCM International Music Competition (for the *Cheltenham Concerto*), 1959; Naumburg Recording Award (for *Symphony No 2*), 1961; National Institute of Arts and Letters Grant, 1962; Honorary Doctor of Music, Montclair State University, New Jersey, 1962, and Musical Academy (now the College for Performing Arts), Philadelphia, 1964; Guggenheim Fellowships, 1956–7, 1966–7; Naumburg Chamber Composition Award (for *String Quartet No 3*), 1972; National Endowment for the Arts Grants, 1972, 1973–4; First Prize, Kennedy Center Friedheim Awards (for *String Quartet No 4*), 1979; Honorary Doctor of Music, University of Michigan, 1980; Distinguished Pennsylvanian, 1981; Honorary Doctorate in Music, University of Pennsylvania, 1985; Member, American Academy and Institute of Arts and Letters, 1985; Gold Medal, Brandeis Creative Arts Award, 1985; elected Fellow of American Academy Arts and Sciences, 1986; Lancaster Symphony Composers Award, 1986; André and Clara Mertens Contemporary Composer Award, University of Bridgeport, Connecticut, 1987; Alfred I du Pont Award for Outstanding Conductors and Composers, Delaware Symphony, Wilmington, Delaware, 1987; Honorary Doctorate, Curtis Institute of Music, 1988. Mailing address: 285 Aronimink Drive, Newtown Square, Pennsylvania 19073, U.S.A.

Publisher: Theodore Presser Co., Presser Place, Bryn Mawr, Pennsylvania 19010, U.S.A.

Symphonies/orchestral:

Night Music (2nd movement of *Symphony No 1*) 1948; first performed 23 April 1953. Recorded Louisville S-634.
Symphony No 1 (3 movements) 1948–57; first performed Philadelphia, 28 March 1958; withdrawn 1977 on revision for 5 movements. Recorded Louisville S-623.
Cantio sacra (small orchestra) 1954; first performed Philadelphia, 1956.
Symphony No 2 1955–56; first performed Cleveland, Ohio, 26 March 1959. Recorded CSP AMS-6379; CRI 492.
Time Span I 1960; first performed St Louis, Missouri, 22 October 1960; withdrawn and revised as *Time Span II*, 1962; revised version first performed Buffalo, New York, 19 January 1964.
Apocalyptica (wind band) 1964; first performed May 1965.
Zodiac (orchestral version of *Twelve Bagatelles* for piano) 1964–5; first performed Cincinnati, Ohio, 8 May 1965.
Music for the Magic Theatre (small orchestra) 1965–9.
Symphony No 3 (double chorus, chamber chorus, soloists and large orchestra) 1966–9; first performed New York City, 24 November 1970.
Fanfares (massed trumpets, horns, trombones) 1968; first performed Philadelphia, 17 March 1968.
Symphony No 1 (revised in 5 movements) 1971–7.
Imago mundi 1973; first performed Baltimore, Maryland, 8 May 1974.
Violin Concerto 1974; first performed Pittsburgh, Pennsylvania, 4 April 1975. Recorded Columbia M-35149.
Transcendental Variations (string orchestra; based on 3rd movement of *String Quartet No 3*) 1975.
Symphony No 4 1976; first performed Seattle, Washington, 15 November 1976.
Oboe Concerto 1983; first performed New York City, 13 December 1984. Recorded New World Records 335.
Symphony No 5 1984; first performed Chicago, 13 March 1986.
Symphony No 6 (large orchestra) 1986–7; first performed Pittsburgh, Pennsylvania, 16 October 1987.
Suite No 1 from "The Confidence Man" 1987–8.

Chamber/instrumental:

Variations on an Original Theme (piano) 1941; first performed New York City, 1942.
Two Preludes and Fughettas (piano) 1946.
Twelve Bagatelles 1952; first performed New York. Recorded Advance 3.
String Quartet No 1 1952; first performed New York City, 10 January 1953. Recorded CRI SD-337.
Chamber Symphony (oboe, clarinet, bassoon, horn, trumpet, trombone, violin, viola, cello) 1953; first performed Baltimore, Maryland, 1955. Recorded Desto 6444.
Duo concertante (violin, cello; also version for violin, piano) 1953; first performed Philadelphia, 1956. Recorded CRI SD-337/ACS 6013; Advance S-6.
Serenata d'estate (flute, harp, guitar, violin, viola, guitar) 1955. Recorded Nonesuch H-71220.
Dialogues (clarinet, piano) 1956; first performed New York, 1956. Recorded Capra 1204; MBS5.
Sonata-Fantasia (piano) 1956; first performed New York, 1958.
Cheltenham Concerto (flute, oboe, clarinet, basson, horn, trumpet, trombone, string quartet) 1958; first performed Philadelphia, 1958.
La bocca della verita (oboe, piano; also version for violin, piano) 1958–9, 1962; first performed Philadelphia, 1960. Recorded CRI SD-423/ACS 6013; Ars Nova/Ars Antigua AN 1008.
Arioso (piano) 1959.
Bartokiana (piano) 1959.
String Quartet No 2 1959–61; first performed Philadelphia, 30 April 1962. Recorded CRI SD-164; Turnabout 34529.
Blake Songs (soprano, chamber ensemble—flute, clarinet, bass clarinet, celeste, harp, violin, viola, cello) 1961; first performed New York City, 1961. Recorded Nonesuch II-71302.
Trio (violin, cello, piano) 1963; first performed Buffalo, New York, 1968. Recorded Turnabout 34520.
Music for the Magic Theatre 1965; first performed Chicago, 1967. Recorded Desto 6444)
Contra mortem et tempus (violin, flute, clarinet, piano) 1965; first performed Maine, 18 August 1965. Recorded CRI SD-231/ACS 6013; MBS5.
Nach Bach (fantasia for harpsichord/piano) 1966; first performed Philadelphia, January 1967. Recorded Grenadilla 1019.
Carnival Music 1969; first performed Philadelphia, 4 May 1972. Recorded Grenadilla 1019.
Fifty Caprice Variations (violin) 1970; first performed New York, 2 April 1970. Recorded Musical Heritage 3719; Deutsche Grammophon 415–484.
String Quartet No 3 1972; first performed New York City, 15 May 1972. Recorded Nonesuch H-71283.
Electrikaleleidoscope (amplified ensemble of flute, clarinet, cello, piano, electric piano) 1972; first performed New York, 19 December 1972. Recorded Smithsonian Collectionin of Recordings No 22.
Ricordanza (cello, piano) 1972; first performed Boston, 1973. Recorded CRI SD-337/ACS 6013.
Ukiyo-E: Pictures of the Floating World (harp) 1973; first performed San Francisco, 1973.
Quintet (piano, string quartet) 1975; first performed New York, 15 March 1976. Recorded Nonesuch H-71396/N1-78011)
Partita-Variations (piano) 1976; first performed Washington, 4 December 1976.
String Quartet No 4 1977; first performed Philadelphia, 20 January 1979. Recorded 2-RCA ARL2-4198.
String Quartet No 5 1978; first performed Philadelphia, 20 January 1979. Recorded 2-RCA ARL2-4198.
String Quartet No 6 1978; first performed Philadelphia, 20 January 1979. Recorded 2-RCA ARL2-4198.
Slow Fires of Autumn: Ukiyo-E II (flute, harp) 1978; first performed New York City, 23 April 1979. Recorded CRI SD-436.
Sonata (viola, piano) 1979; first performed Provo, Utah, 14 July 1979.
Duo (oboe, bassoon) 1979; original version, 1946.
Book of Contrapuntal Pieces (keyboard instuments) 1979.
Octet, A Grand Fantasia (flute, clarinet, horn, piano, violin, viola, cello, bass) 1980; first performed New York City, 25 April 1980.
Trio (clarinet, horn, piano) 1980, revision of 1947 work. Recorded Crystal 731.
String Quintet (with double cello) 1982; first performed Philadelphia, 6 January 1982.
Between Two Worlds: Ukiyo-E III (flute, piano) 1982; first performed Philadelphia, 19 August 1983. Recorded CRI SD-531.
Quartet (piano, violin, viola, cello) 1983; first performed Washington, D.C., 18 June 1985.
Four Short Sonatas (piano) 1984; first performed Rome, 6 June 1984.
To the Dark Wood (woodwind quintet) 1985; first performed Armidale, New South Wales, 3 October 1986.
Trio (piano, violin, cello) 1985; first performed February 1986.
Sonata (violin, piano) 1988; first performed Pasadena, California, 10 April 1989.
Rhapsody and Prayer (violin, piano) 1989; first performed (in competition) Indianapolis, 15–20 September 1990.
Nach Bach II (flute, guitar) 1989.
Muse of Fire (flute, guitar) 1990; first performed 1 February 1991.

Vocal/choral:

Book of Songs (voice, piano) 1937–69.
Four Songs of Solomon (voice, piano) 1946; first performed Philadelphia, 1947.
Three Psalms (unaccompanied mixed chorus; Psalms 23, 43, 150) 1954.
David, The Psalmist (tenor, orchestra) 1954; first performed Pennsylvania, 1965.
Passions According to the 20th Century (singers, jazz quintet, brass ensemble, percussion, piano, tape) 1967.
Tableaux (soprano, 2 actors' voices, small men's chorus, 12 players: alto flute/piccolo, clarinet in A & E♭, trumpet, horn, trombone, percussion, piano, harpsichord, violin, viola, cello, double bass) 1968. Recorded Turnabout 34492.
Tres cantes flamencos (high baritone) 1969.
Eleven Songs (voice, piano; Paul Rochberg) 1969; first performed Oberlin, Ohio, 20 March 1970. Recorded Owl 28.
Two Songs 1969.
Songs in Praise of Krishna 1970; first performed Evanston, Illinois, 16 March 1971. Recorded CRI SD-360.
Sacred Song of Reconciliation (bass-baritone, chamber orchestra) 1970; first performed Jerusalem, 5 January 1971.
Fantasies (voice, piano; Paul Rochberg) 1971; first performed Vancouver, Canada, 1973.
Behold, My Servant (unaccompanied mixed chorus) 1973; first performed 23 October 1973.

Phaedra (monodrama for mezzo-soprano, orchestra; Gene Rochberg, after Robert Lowell) 1973–4; first performed Syracuse, New York, 9 January 1976.
Songs of Inanna and Dumuzi (alto, piano) 1977.
String Quartet No 7 (with baritone voice) 1979; first performed Ann Arbor, Michigan, 27 January 1980. Recorded Nonesuch 78017.
Suite No 2 from "The Confidence Man" (voices, chorus, orchestra) 1987, in progress.

Opera:

The Confidence Man (opera in two parts; after Melville) 1982; first performed Sante Fe, New Mexico, Summer 1982.

Other:

The Alchemist (incidental music to Ben Johnson; 2 flutes, 2 clarinets, 2 trumpets, violin, bass keyboard, 2 percussion, incidental soprano) 1965; first performed New York City, 13 October 1968; concert version first performed Washington, 31 October 1969.
Black Sounds (music for *The Act*; choreography by Anna Sokolow; wind, percussion) 1965; broadcast 24 September 1965; staged Tanglewood, Massachusetts, 1965. Recorded Grenadilla 1019.

W.A. Mozart: *Oboe Concerto in C major K.314* (cadenzas) 1987.

PUBLICATIONS

By Rochberg: *The Hexachord and Its Relation to the Twelve-Tone Row*, 1955; articles in *Journal of Music Theory*, *Perspectives of New Music*, and *The Aesthetics of Survival: A Composer's View of Twentieth-Century Music*, edited by William Bolcom, 1984.

On Rochberg: A. Ringer: "The Music of GR", in *Musical Quarterly*, 52, 1966; J.S. Buccheri, "An Approach to Twelve-Tone Music: Articulation of Serial Pitch Units in Piano Works of Schoenberg, Webern, Krenek, Dallapiccola and GR", dissertation, University of Rochester, New York, 1975; C.L. Sams, "Solo Vocal Writing in Selected Works of Berio, Crumb and GR", dissertation, University of Washington, Seattle, 1975; J.T. Smith, "The String Quartets of GR", dissertation, Eastman School of Music, Rochester, New York, 1976; J. Reise, "R the Progressive", in *Perspectives of New Music*, 19, 1980–1; M. Sokol: "Quartets Nos 4, 5, 6", liner notes, RCA ARL2-4198; C. Gagne and T. Caras, in *Soundpieces: Interviews with American Composers*, Metuchen, New Jersey, 1982; Joan De Vee Dixon, *GR: A Bio-Bibliographic Guide to His Life and Works*, Boston, 1990.

George Rochberg comments:

For many years now I have written works across the spectrum from the tonal to the non-tonal out of the conviction that the language of music itself has been stretched in our time to embrace all possible states of mind, all possible levels of emotional feeling and projections. Given this view of musical speech and its potentially all-embracing range of what a composer can say in and through music, the first thing I have to wrestle with when I face the prospect of a new work is to decide what kind of music I want to compose, whether it will be purely tonal or non-tonal or a mixture of both. This decision—sometimes reasonably conscious, sometimes accompanied by a still-vague, hard-to-define, feeling state—once made will determine the particular range and emotional life of the work, therefore, the kinds of gestures and characters I need to create its tone and atmosphere, its world. For me decisions of this nature are absolutely crucial, especially for large extended works, but they come into play just as much for compositions of a more limited nature.

Once I have made this decision and it feels "right", I begin the search for ideas. It has sometimes happened that an idea itself, already circulating in my head and somehow irrepressible, has had a marked effect on the direction a work took. I have found that ideas seem to have a life of their own and have learned to pay very close attention to what they are telling me. The process of this search is impossible to describe in any clear way. Ideas tend to call up other ideas; and when that begins to happen, I know I've caught something "live". However it works, I need to continue this gathering process until I have in my ear and on paper everything I think I will need to work with, however unconnected the sketches themselves may appear to anyone but myself. As the collection of ideas grows, the shape of the work begins to grow too, so that by the time the gathering process is completed I know pretty much where things will go, what role they will play in the totality, what the overall structure of the work will be.

All of this is done more by "feel" than by logical thought—although I have to add quickly that if the structure begins to feel right to me, I do some hard, cold thinking to make sure that there will be relation, coherence, growth, direction in how the ideas, gestures, and characters unfold in time to make a satisfying whole. I need to feel out the duration as well as carry a sense of the complete work in my mind so that I can "see" all parts of it simultaneously, as though the work were a spatial rather than a purely durational image. Details of execution I leave to the final writing stage where I "fix" everything so that ideas and functions lock into each other firmly and structural coherence becomes the outer skin of the inner emotional scenario I imagine to begin with. When these match in my ear and mind the work is finished and only then will I let it out to lead its own existence in an uncertain world.

* * *

George Rochberg's early works were dominated by tonal models. Several pieces display a tough, sinewy style, sometimes abrasive in harmonic approach and with a strong rhythmic impetus; these qualities have frequently been ascribed to the influence of Hindemith and Stravinsky. However, perhaps Rochberg's most powerful formative influence was Bartók: a fine—and revealingly titled—score from 1948, *Night Music* for orchestra, illustrates a thorough absorption of classic Bartók models from the 1930s and 1940s.

Exposure to the influence of Dallapiccola at the start of the 1950s led to an important self-examination and, eventually, to a wholehearted adoption of serial technique. This change of direction was neither immediate nor effortless: it was achieved after a transitional period involving an intensive study of the works of the Second Viennese School. During the early phase of these studies, Rochberg's most discernible role model continued to be Bartók, as is demonstrated in the self-assured First String Quartet.

As his idiom became permeated with serial procedures, Rochberg adopted compositional titles redolent of the Second Viennese School (*Twelve Bagatelles*, *Chamber Symphony* for nine instruments). Gradually, he felt (as had Boulez when extending the principle to its logical extreme a few years earlier—integral serialism—so that the concept of an imposed mathemetical order is extended from merely pitch classifications to encompass all other facets of the composition, rhythmic groupings, dynamics and even larger-scale form) strongly attracted to Webern's method of condensing the musical argument to an unprecedented extent; thus, all aspects of the composition are governed by the structure of a basic note row or rows. This phase culminated in two of Rochberg's most terse offerings, the Second Symphony and *Cheltenham Concerto*. In the Symphony, Rochberg skilfully adopted a symmetrical tone row, *à la* Webern, to create structural unity. After these pieces, like several other prominent young musicians in the later 1950s, Rochberg appears to have become disillusioned, or perhaps even overawed by the almost monolithic implications of this approach. He attempted to make his work more accessible, first by adopting less rhythmically stringent patterns (as in the Second Quartet), then through a gradually retreat from the entire serial concept during the early 1960s.

Following the piano *Trio*, tonal harmonies begin to reappear in his music and Rochberg embarked upon a much more cosmopolitan phase, attempting to assimiliate elements from a bewildering range of epochs. This approach has rightly been termed "assemblage" rather than "pastiche", because in many cases recognisable styles are presented through a juxtaposition of identifiable quotations from assorted composers. The process is less immediately striking in *Contra mortem et tempus*, where the quotations come from Boulez, Varèse, Ives and Berio (the last three were also not averse to "assemblage", incidentally) than in the *Fifty Caprice Variations* for solo violin, in which some of the models are extremely familiar.

The 50 variations are subtitled "After Paganini" and initially there would appear to be little more to say in reworkings of Paganini's famous A minor caprice; so it transpires, but the charm of this work rests with Rochberg's audacious translation of weightier quotations into Paganini's devillishly virtuosic, occasionally flippant idiom. Of especial note is a breathtaking left-hand pizzicato translation of material from the development section of the first movement of Brahms's Violin Concerto.

Subsequently Rochberg showed a more integrated approch to tonal composition in the Third Quartet, which manages to function less as a collage than as a well-argued return to chromatically inflected tonality. Its cogency recalls Beethoven and the harmonic style has been likened to Mahler's—comparisons which resurface periodically in assessments of Rochberg's subsequent output. The neo-romantic approach of this quartet was followed up in the "Concord Quartets" (numbers 4–6) and in the *Violin Concerto*, though the latter piece, a gentle, elegiac memorial for Rochberg's son, utilises an unusual five-movement form and is notably free of the heroic gestures and conflicts of many 19th-century concertos.

Rochberg's writings on music, though by no means voluminous, are an interesting complement to his lifelong exploration of musical styles. The dilemmas presented in his music are best summed up in his first book, *The Hexachord and Its Relation to the Twelve-Tone Row*, a collection of essays published in 1955. In his more recent compositions, overt quotation tends to be replaced by numerous "reminiscences" of familiar styles. In the *Oboe Concerto*, these range from Tristanesque fragments for cor anglais (in the first section) to emotionally charged outbursts which recall early Berg.

—Paul Horner

ROOSENSCHOON, Hans. South African/Dutch. Born in The Hague, The Netherlands, 17 December 1952; family settled in Pretoria, South Africa, 1953. Educated at Conservatoire of Music, Pretoria, 1969–71, 1974–5; Royal Academy of Music, London (under Paul Patterson), 1977–8; University of Stellenbosch, 1987–9, M.Mus. In composition. Married Linda-Louise Badenhorst, 16 July 1977; 2 sons. Manager, Reel Duplitique, Pretoria, 1971–4; music assistant, 1976–7, producer, 1979–80, and music manager since 1980, South African Broadcasting Corporation, Johannesburg. Recipient: UNISA Composition Prize, 1975; Department of National Education composition prizes, 1975, 1989; Arthur Hinton Prize, 1978; Standard Bank Young Artist Award, 1987. Mailing address: 8 Katzenellenbogen Crescent, Stellenberg 7550, South Africa.

Publishers: Musications, P.O. Box 475, Claremont 7735; Amanuensis Quality Editions, 16 Heseldon Road, Rondebosch, 7700, South Africa.

Symphonies/orchestral:

Katutura 1977.
Palette 1977; first performed Johannesburg, 24 April 1978. Recorded Claremont GSE 604.
" 'n Saaier het uitgegaan om te saai. . . . " 1978.
Mosaiek 1979.
Ghomma 1980; first performed Johannesburg, 2 July 1983.
Ikonografie 1983; first performed Cape Town, 2 November 1989.
Anagram 1983; first performed Cape Town, 29 May 1984. Recorded Claremont GSE 604.
Timbila 1985; first performed Grahamstown, 12 July 1985. Recorded Claremont GSE 1510.
Architectura I 1986; first performed Johannesburg, 8 October 1986.
Chronicles 1987; first performed Grahamstown, 10 July 1987.
Mantis (ballet suite) 1988; first performed Johannesburg, 28 October 1988. Recorded Claremont CDGSE 1510.
Circle of Light 1989; first performed Cape Town, 9 March 1989. Recorded Claremont CDGSE 1510.
Die Sonnevanger 1990.

Chamber/instrumental:

Sonatine (piano) 1974; first performed Johannesburg, 13 May 1977.
Credo (piano) 1975; first performed Johannesburg, 13 May 1977.
Makiette (brass quintet) 1978; first performed London, 1 December 1978. Recorded CDGSE 1510.
Horizon, Night-Sky and Landscape (string ensemble) 1987; first performed Bloemfontein, 18 June 1987.

Fingerprints (piano) 1989; first performed Johannesburg, 1 November 1989. Recorded Teal Trutone Music 200 005-2.

Vocal/choral:

Cantata on Psalm 8 (choir, orchestra) 1976; first performed Johannesburg, 7 July 1977.
Ars poetica (baritone, double chorus, orchestra) 1979; first performed Johannesburg, 9 October 1979. Recorded Claremont GSE 604.
Psalm 23 (unacompanied SATB chorus) 1979.
Firebowl (unaccompanied SATB chorus) 1980; first performed Windhoek, 21 May 1986. Recorded Claremont CDGSE 1510.
Does the Noise in My Head Bother You? (children's choruses, pop group, orchestra) 1988; first performed Cape Town, 29 July 1988.
Tanks Be to Thee (unaccompanied SATB chorus) 1990; first performed Johannesburg, 18 November 1990.

Other:

Kataklisme (electronic) 1980; first performed Johannesburg, 4 July 1983.
Helios (electronic) 1984; first performed Grahamstown, 6 July 1985.
If Music Be (electronic) 1984; first performed Cape Town, 21 November 1984. Recorded Claremont GSE 604.

PUBLICATIONS

On Roosenschoon: A.W. Wegelin, "Music Chronicle", in *Magazine for Human Sciences*, 22(1), 1982; Christopher James, "HR: *If Music Be*", in *South African Journal of Musicology*, 6(1–2), 1986; S.J. Jacobs, "The Compositions of HR", dissertation, University of South Africa, Pretoria, 1987; Peter Klatzow, in *Composers in South Africa Today*, Cape Town, 1987; E. Gerber, "African Influences on Two Works by HR", dissertation, University of South Africa, Pretoria, 1989; Paul Boekkooi, "'Afrikanisme' agtervolg vir HR", in *Insig*, December 1989; Nancy Hofmeyr, "Die Menswees van HR se Musiek", in *Musicus*, 17(1), 1989.

Hans Roosenschoon comments:

Composing is a way of expressing oneself, a way of interacting with the world that one lives in. Through musical creation one expands one's imagination—to create musical events with originality and freshness. Through musical creation one develops an inner sensitivity to the expressiveness of sounds. One's imagination and sensitivity poses challenges which also develop craftsmanship, opening up new ways of expression.

* * *

According to Hans Roosenschoon his style is characterized by three important elements: sound painting, an eclectic approach which creates collages of diverse material, and the presence of African music. His stylistic eclecticism is limited to the use of certain avant-garde techniques and textures; the primary influences come from composers such as Krzysztof Penderecki, Witold Lutosławski and György Ligeti. However, these influences are merely superficial: Roosenschoon's music achieves a remarkable synthesis which in effect is quite individual. While certain parameters of the music apply avant-garde techniques, others are often treated in a more conventional way. For instance, within a highly dissonant texture the composer might use a conventional melodic element. This juxtaposition of new and traditional elements helps to make Roosenschoon's music accessible to the average listener, an accessibility often further enhanced through the quotation of familiar melodic material such as his use of "Frère Jacques" in *Timbila*.

The majority of Roosenschoon's compositions are for orchestra, which is not surprising in view of the composer's preoccupation with tone colour. Since 1977 he has completed 12 orchestral works of which 10 have been commissioned. In addition, there are a number of compositions for choir and orchestra.

Sound painting is already evident in *Palette* for string orchestra, as is the composer's predilection for quoting familiar melodic material. Here he quotes the hymn tune "Melita." In a late orchestral work, *Architectura I*, Roosenschoon uses the folksong "Daar kom die Alibama" as his principal reference. The work is subtitled "A soundscape of Cape Town." Its tripartite structure—probably the composer's favourite formal arrangement—treats the first lines of the song in a fugal, canonic manner in its opening and closing sections. In the opening the imitation is diatonic at the upper fourth. After a lengthy exposition the imitation starts at half-bar intervals, resulting in a masterly passage of contrapuntal complexity. This process is reversed in the final section; a complex texture is gradually reduced to a single statement of the opening lines in the double basses.

Anagram is a short orchestral work commissioned by the SABC. For this Roosenschoon had been asked to produce a work which encapsulated his principal stylistic traits. The work is based on a 14-note set derived from the composer's name; this was achieved by not doubling the Os of his surname. Most of the letters of his name can be spelt in German note names; only N, R and O had to be derived through other means. Although the work is not strictly serial, the set determines the harmonic and melodic material of the piece. The signature unfolds gradually at the opening of the work (B–A–F–E♭ for Hans), until it is fully stated by the first entry of the first flute. In the third final section of the work a transposed version of the signature acts as an ostinato; the signature at actual pitch is used as a counterpoint at the very end.

In two works Roosenschoon set a text in a pop music style. This is done very effectively in *Does the Noise in My Head Bother You?* The work was commissioned by the Cape Performing Arts Board for its Youth Music Festival of 1988. The second composition is *If Music Be* for tape collage. Roosenschoon's interest in electronic music was stimulated by his work as music producer for the SABC. An electronic work like *Kataklisme* has as its referential material the opening four bars of Beethoven's Fifth Symphony and sounds produced in the inside of the piano. *If Music Be* is a collage of speech and electronic and acoustic sounds. The main references are the quote from Shakespeare's *Twelfth Night* and the Crucifixus from Bach's Mass in B minor. The work, which can be seen as a tribute to Bach, also includes the Bach motive as well as quotes from Mozart and Dvořák. The song, which is set in a pop music style, uses the harmony of the Crucifixus opening as its basis.

Roosenschoon's incorporation of African elements in his music has provoked some controversy. It is debatable whether an objective listener will perceive an African flavour in these works; a number of superficial traits of Roosenschoon's music, such as repetitive melodic figurations and rhythms, are found not only in African music but also in many avant-garde works. Of the African-inspired works, *Timbila* is probably Roosenschoon's masterpiece. The composer sees the work as a fusion of traditional African music played on original instruments and the timbre-texture writing of his earlier orchestral pieces. The Chopi, from Southern Mozambique, are well-known for their xylophones (*timbila*), which they combine into large orchestras. A rising tonic-mediant motive is used as a unifying element throughout the work. At the climax of the piece this is expanded into the quotation of "Frère Jacques". However the listener might perceive these African works, they incorporate all of Roosenschoon's best qualities: an innate sense of structure, rhythmic interest, sensitivity to colouristic effect and a strong lyric tendency.

—James W. May

ROREM, Ned. American. Born in Richmond, Indiana, 23 October 1923. Educated at American Conservatory, Chicago (piano and theory under Leo Sowerby), 1938–9; Northwestern University, Evanston, Illinois, 1940–1; Curtis Institute, Philadelphia, 1942–3; Juilliard School of Music, New York City (under Bernard Wagenaar), B.A., 1946, M.A., 1948; privately with Virgil Thomson, 1944; Berkshire Music Centre, Tanglewood, Massachusetts, 1946–7; period in Morocco and France, 1949–58. Composer in residence, University of Buffalo, New York, 1959–60; teacher, University of Utah, Provo, 1966–7; and Curtis Institute, 1980–6. Recipient: George Gershwin Memorial Prize (for *Overture in C*), 1948; Lili Boulanger Award, 1950; Prix de Biarritz, 1951; Eurydice Choral Award, 1954; award of National Institute of Arts and Letters, 1968; ASCAP-Deems Taylor Awards (for *Critical Affairs: A Composer's Journal* and *The Final Diary*), 1971, 1975; Pulitzer Prize (for *Air Music*), 1976; honorary Doctorate of Fine Arts, Northwestern University, 1977; Grammy Award (for recording of *String Symphony*, etc.), 1989; American Guild of Organists Composer of the Year, 1989. Mailing address: Box 764, Nantucket, Massachusetts 02554, U.S.A.

Publishers: Boosey & Hawkes; Southern; Peters; Prosser; Schirmer.

Symphonies/orchestral:

Overture in C 1948.
Piano Concerto No 1 1948; withdrawn.
Piano Concerto No 2 1950; first performed Paris, 1954.
Symphony No 1 1950; first performed Vienna, 1951.
Design 1953; first performed Louisville, Kentucky, 29 May 1953. Recorded Louisville L-57-5.
Symphony No 2 1956; first performed La Jolla, California, 5 August 1956.
Sinfonia (symphonic wind orchestra) 1957; first performed Pittsburgh, Pennsylvania, 1957.
Symphony No 3 1957–8; first performed New York City, 16 April 1959. Recorded Turnabout TV S-34447.
Eagles 1958; first performed Philadelphia, 23 October 1959. Recorded Louisville LS-787; New World NW-353.
Pilgrims (strings) 1958; first performed New York City, 30 January 1959.
Ideas for Easy Orchestra 1961. Recorded Desto DC-6462.
Lions: A Dream 1963; first performed New York City, 28 October 1965. Recorded Orlon ORS-7268.
Water Music (clarinet, violin, orchestra) 1966; first performed Oakland, California, 9 April 1967. Recorded Desto DC-6462.
Concerto in Six Movements (piano, orchestra) 1969; first performed Pittsburgh, Pennsylvania, 3 December 1970. Recorded Louisville LS-73-2.
Solemn Prelude 1973.
Air Music 1974; first performed Cincinnati, Ohio, 5 December 1975. Recorded Louisville LS 787.
Assembly and Fall 1975; first performed Raleigh, North Carolina, 11 October 1975.
Sunday Morning 1977; first performed Philadelphia, 25 August 1978. Recorded New World NW-353.
Remembering Tommy (piano, cello, orchestra) 1979; first performed Cincinnati, Ohio, 1982.
Organ Concerto 1984; first performed Portland, Maine, 19 March 1985.
Violin Concerto 1984; first performed Springfield, Minnesota, 30 March 1985. Recorded Deutsche Grammophon.
String Symphony 1985; first performed Atlanta, Georgia, 31 October 1985. Recorded New World NW-353.
Frolic (fanfare for orchestra) 1986; first performed Houston, Texas, 12 April 1986.
Fantasy and Polka 1988; first performed Evian, France, 4 May 1989.
A Quaker Reader (eight movements for orchestra) 1988; first performed New York City, 8 October 1988.

Chamber/instrumental:

Fantasy and Toccata (organ) 1946.
Concertino da camera (harpsichord, 7 instruments) 1946.
String Quartet No 1 1947; withdrawn.
Sonata (piano) 1948.
Toccata (piano; 4th movement of *Piano Sonata*) 1948.
A Quiet Afternoon (piano) 1948.
Mountain Song (flute/oboe/violin/cello, piano) 1949.
Barcarolles (piano) 1949.
Pastorale (organ; transcription of 2nd movement, *Symphony No 1*) 1949.
Sonata (violin) 1949.
Sonata (piano) 1949.
String Quartet No 2 1950.
Sicilienne (2 pianos) 1950.
Sonata (piano) 1954.
Slow Waltz (piano) 1956.
Eleven Studies for Eleven Players (flute, oboe, clarinet, trumpet, percussion, harp, piano, violin, viola, cello) 1959–60; first performed Buffalo, New York, 17 May 1960.
Trio (flute, cello, piano) 1960.
Lovers (harpsichord, oboe, cello, percussion) 1964; first performed New York City, 15 December 1964. Recorded Desto DL-101108; Serenus 12056.
Spiders (harpsichord) 1968; first performed Waterloo, Ontario, 23 July 1969.
Day Music (8 pieces for violin, piano) 1971; first performed Ames, Iowa, 15 October 1972. Recorded Desto DC-7151.
Night Music (8 pieces for violin, piano) 1972; first performed Washington, D.C., 12 January 1973. Recorded Desto DC-7174.
Book of Hours (flute, harp) 1975; first performed New York City, 29 February 1976. Recorded CRI 362 SD.
Eight Etudes (piano) 1975; first performed Washington, D.C., 13 March 1976.
Sky Music (harp) 1976; first performed Albuquerque, New

Mexico, June 1976.

A Quaker Reader (organ) 1976; first performed New York City, 2 February 1977. Recorded CRI 396; Delos D/CD 3076.

Romeo and Juliet (flute, guitar) 1977; first performed New York City, 1 March 1978. Recorded CRI 394 SD/6007 ACS.

Three Slow Pieces (cello, piano) 1978; first performed New York City, 8 October 1977.

Suite (guitar) 1980; first performed Cuyahoga Falls, Ohio, 25 July 1980. Recorded LPS 3115.

After Reading Shakespeare (9 movements for cello) 1980; first performed New York City, 15 March 1981. Recorded Grenadilla 1065.

Winter Pages (13 movements for clarinet, bassoon, piano, violin, cello) 1981; first performed New York City, 14 February 1982. Recorded Gothic/Delos.

Views from the Oldest House (organ) 1981; first performed Washington, D.C., 29 June 1982. Recorded Delos D/CD 3076.

Dances (cello, piano) 1983; first performed Detroit, Michigan, 5 May 1984.

Picnic on the Marne (7 waltzes for saxophone, piano) 1983; first performed New York City, 14 February 1984.

Septet: Scenes from Childhood (11 movements for string quartet, oboe, horn, piano) 1985; first performed Santa Fe, New Mexico, 11 August 1985.

The End of Summer (clarinet, violin piano) 1985; first performed Bombay, 26 March 1986.

Trio (clarinet, violin, piano) 1985.

Song and Dance (piano) 1986; first performed Maryland, 12–5 July, 1987.

Bright Music (flute, 2 violins, cello, piano) 1987; first performed Bridgehampton, New York, 6 August 1988.

Fanfare and Flourish (2 trumpets, 2 trombones, organ) 1988; first performed New York City, 16 October 1988.

Diversions (brass quintet) 1989; first performed Nantucket, Massachusetts, 11 July 1990.

For Shirley (piano—4 hands) 1989; first performed New York City, April 1989.

Organbook I 1989; first performed New York City, 30 October 1989.

Organbook II 1989; first performed Nantucket, Massachusetts, 7 July 1990.

Organbook III 1989; first performed Nantucket, Massachusetts, 7 July 1990.

Spring Music (violin, cello, piano) 1990; first performed New York City, 8 February 1990.

Vocal/choral:

The 70th Psalm (SATB chorus, orchestra) 1943; first performed Washington, D.C., August 1943.

A Song of David (voice, piano; Psalm 120) 1945.

A Psalm of Praise (voice, piano; Psalm 100) 1945.

Alleluia (voice, piano) 1946. Recorded GSS 104.

On a Singing Girl (voice, piano; Wylie) 1946.

Spring and Fall (voice, piano; Hopkins) 1946. Recorded New World NW 229.

Reconciliation (voice, piano; Whitman) 1946.

Absalom (voice, piano; Goodman) 1946(?), arranged for voice, orchestra, 1947.

A Sermon on Miracles (solo voice, unison voices, strings; Goodman) 1947; first performed Boston, 30 November 1947.

Spring (voice, piano; Hopkins) 1947. Recorded New World NW 229.

Catullus: On the Burial of His Brother (voice, piano; translated Beardsley) 1947.

Mourning Scene from Samuel (medium voice, string quartet; 2 Samuel 1) 1947.

Four Madrigals (unaccompanied SATB choir; Sappho) 1947.

The Lordly Hudson (voice, piano; Goodman) 1947. Recorded GSS 104.

Three Incantations from a Marionette Tale (song cycle for voice and piano; Boultenhouse) 1948.

Echo's Song (voice, piano; Jonson) 1948.

Requiem (voice, piano; Stevenson) 1948.

Rain in Spring (voice, piano; Goodman) 1949. Recorded GSS 104.

The Sleeping Palace (voice, piano; Tennyson) 1949.

Little Elegy (voice, piano; Wylie) 1949. Recorded CRI 238 USD.

What If Some Little Pain (voice, piano; Spenser) 1949.

Fight for Heaven (song cycle for voice and piano; Herrick) 1950; first performed New York City, 19 November 1950.

Lullaby of the Woman of the Mountains (voice, piano; Pearse) 1950. Recorded New World NW 229.

Six Irish Poems (song cycle for voice and orchestra; Darley) 1950; first performed Paris, 1 July 1950.

Philomel (voice, piano; Barnefield) 1950.

Cycle of Holy Songs (voice, piano; Psalms) 1951; first performed Washington, D.C., 24 February 1952.

From an Unknown Past (unaccompanied SATB choir, also arranged for voice, piano; anon. 15th and 16th century) 1951.

From an Unknown Past (song cycle for voice and piano; anon. 15th and 16th century) 1951.

Love in a Life (voice, piano; Browning) 1951.

To a Young Girl (voice, piano; Yeats) 1951.

The Nightingale (voice, piano; anon. 16th century) 1951. Recorded GSS 104.

An Angel Speaks to the Shepherds (voice, piano; Luke 2) 1952.

The Resurrection (voice, piano; Matthew 27) 1952.

The Mild Mother (voice, piano; anon. 15th century) 1952.

Christmas Carol (voice, piano; anon. 16th century) 1952.

Clouds (voice, piano; Goodman) 1953. Recorded GSS 104.

A Far Island (unaccompanied SSA choir; Emslie) 1953.

I Feel Death (unaccompanied TTB choir; Dryden) 1953.

Gentle Visitations (unaccompanied SSA choir; Shelley) 1953.

Five Prayers for the Young (unaccompanied SSA choir; Carroll) 1953.

Epitaph on Eleanor Freeman (voice, piano; anon. 1650) 1953.

Love (voice, piano; Lodge) 1953.

Poèmes pour la paix (voice, piano; Regnier, Ronsard, Magny, Daurat, Baif) 1953, arranged for medium voice and orchestra, 1956; first performed Paris, 23 October 1954.

Six Songs (high voice, orchestra; Browning, Dryden, anon. 16th century) 1953; first performed Paris, November 1954.

Jack l'éventreur (voice, piano; Lauré) 1953.

Sally's Smile (voice, piano; Goodman) 1953. Recorded GSS 104.

The Midnight Sun (voice, piano; Goodman) 1953.

The Tulip Tree (voice, piano; Goodman) 1953. Recorded CRI 238 USD.

The Corinthians (SATB choir, organ) 1953.

For Susan (voice, piano; Goodman) 1953. Recorded GSS 104.

Four Dialogues (soprano, tenor, 2 pianos; O'Hara) 1953–4; first performed Rome, 23 March 1955. Recorded Desto DC-7101.

Abel (voice, piano; Capetanakis) 1954.

Guilt (voice, piano; Capetanakis) 1954.
Youth, Day, Old Age, and Night (voice, piano; Whitman) 1954.
The Land of Fear (voice, piano; Capetanakis) 1954.
The Poet's Requiem (soprano, SATB choir, orchestra; Kafka, Rilke, Cocteau, Mallarmé, Freud, Goodman, Gide) 1954–5; first performed New York City, 15 February 1957.
I Am Rose (voice, piano; Stein) 1955. Recorded GSS 104; New World NW 229.
All Glorious God (unaccompanied SATB choir; anon.) 1955.
Christ the Lord Is Ris'n Today (unaccompanied SATB choir; Wesley) 1955.
Sing My Soul His Wondrous Love (unaccompanied SATB choir; anon. 19th century) 1955.
Early in the Morning (voice, piano; Hillyer) 1955. Recorded GSS 104.
See How They Love Me (voice, piano; Moss) 1956. Recorded GSS 104.
What Sparks and Wiry Cries (voice, piano; Goodman) 1956. Recorded CRI 238 USD; GSS 104.
As Adam Early in the Morning (voice, piano; Whitman) 1957. Recorded Desto DC 7101.
Visits to St Elizabeths (voice, piano; Bishop) 1957. Recorded GSS 104.
The Lord's Prayer (voice, piano) 1957.
Look Down, Fair Moon (voice, piano; Whitman) 1957. Recorded CRI 238 USD; Desto DC 7010.
Conversation (voice, piano; Bishop) 1957. Recorded GSS 104.
Gliding O'er All (voice, piano; Whitman) 1957. Recorded Desto DC 7010.
Gods (voice, piano; Whitman) 1957.
To You (voice, piano; Whitman) 1957. Recorded New World NW-229.
O You Whom I Often and Silently Come (voice, piano; Whitman) 1957. Recorded GSS 104: Desto DC 7010.
Last Day (monodrama for voice, string quartet, wind quartet, piano; Harrison) 1958.
I Strolled Across an Empty Field (voice, piano; Roethke) 1959.
The Waking (voice, piano; Roethke) 1959.
Memory (voice, piano; Roethke) 1959.
Snake (voice, piano; Roethke) 1959. Recorded GSS 104; New World NW 229.
Orchids (voice, piano; Roethke) 1959.
Root Cellar (voice, piano; Roethke) 1959. Recorded New World NW 229; GSS 104.
My Papa's Waltz (voice, piano; Roethke) 1959. Recorded New World NW 229.
Night Crow (voice, piano; Roethke) 1959. Recorded CRI 238 USD.
Miracles of Christmas (SATB choir, organ; Jacob) 1959.
Prayers and Responses (unaccompanied SATB choir) 1960.
King Midas (song cycle for voice, piano; Moss) 1960–1; first performed New York City, 11 March 1962. Recorded Desto DC-6443.
Virelai (unaccompanied SATB choir; Chaucer) 1961. Recorded Boosey & Hawkes SNBH-5001.
Poems of Love and the Rain (voice, piano; Windham, Auden, Moss, Dickinson, Roethke, Larson, cummings, Pitchford) 1962–3; first performed Madison, Wisconsin, 12 April 1964.
Two Psalms and a Proverb (SATB choir, string quintet) 1962.
Ask Me No More (voice, piano; Tennyson) 1963. Recorded GSS 104.
Far-Far-Away (voice, piano; Tennyson) 1963. Recorded GSS 104.
Lift Up Your Heads (The Ascension) (SATB choir, woodwind/brass quinet, organ) 1963; first performed Washington, D.C., 7 May 1964.
Now Sleeps the Crimson Petal (voice, piano; Tennyson) 1963. Recorded GSS 104.
For Poulenc (voice, piano; O'Hara) 1963. Recorded CRI 238.
Laudemus tempus actum SATB choir) 1964; first performed Sioux City, Iowa, 20 April 1974.
Hearing (song cycle for voice, piano; Koch) 1965–6, arranged as stage work, 1976; first performed New York City, 9 May 1967.
Sun (song cycle for voice, orchestra; Ikhnaton, Byron, Goodman, Blake, Morgan, Shakespeare, Whitman, Roethke) 1966; first performed New York City, 1 July 1967.
Love Divine, All Loves Excelling (unaccompanied SATB choir; Wesley) 1966. Recorded Boosey & Hawkes SNBH 5001.
Proper for the Votive Mass of the Holy Spirit (unison voices, organ) 1966.
Truth in the Night Season (SATB choir, organ; Psalm 92) 1966.
Letters from Paris (9 choruses for SATB choir; Flanner) 1966; first performed Ann Arbor, Michigan, 25 April 1969. Recorded Choral Masters GSS106.
He Shall Rule from Sea to Sea (SATB choir, organ; Psalm 71) 1967. Recorded Boosey & Hawkes SNBH 5001.
War Scenes (song cycle for voice, piano; Whitman) 1969; first performed Washington, D.C., 19 October 1969. Recorded Desto DC-7101.
Gloria (soprano, mezzo-soprano, piano) 1970; first performed New York City, 26 November 1972.
Praises for the Nativity (soprano, alto, tenor, bass, SATB choir, organ; Book of Common Prayer) 1970.
Ariel (song cycle for soprano, clarinet, piano; Plath) 1971; first performed Washington, D.C., 26 November 1971.
Canticle of the Lamb (unaccompanied SATB choir) 1971. Recorded Boosey & Hawkes SNBH-5001.
Canticles–Sets 1 & 2 (liturgy; unaccompanied mixed choirs) 1971–2.
Last Poems of Wallace Stevens (soprano, cello, piano) 1971–2; first performed New York, 13 November 1972. Recorded Leonarada LPI-116.
The Serpent (voice, piano; Roethke) 1972. Recorded GSS 104.
Come Pure Hearts (unison chorus, keyboard; traditional) 1973.
Little Prayers (soprano, baritone, SATB choir, orchestra; Goodman) 1973; first performed Sioux City, Iowa, 20 April 1974.
Three Motets (SATB choir, organ; Hopkins) 1973. Recorded Gothic G 78932.
Four Hymn Tunes (2 for mixed chorus, 2 for voice, piano) 1973.
Three Prayers (unaccompanied SATB choir; Goodman) 1973.
In Time of Pestilence (unaccompanied SATB choir; Nashe) 1973.
Missa brevis (soprano, alto, tenor, bass, unaccompanied SATB choir) 1973; first performed Cleveland, Ohio, 17 June 1974. Recorded Vox SVBX 5354.
Prayer to Jesus (unaccompanied SATB choir; Hopkins) 1974.
A Journey (voice, piano; Glaze) 1974.
Where We Came (voice, piano; Garrigue) 1974.
To Jane (voice, piano; Shelley) 1974.
Serenade on Five English Poems (voice, violin, viola, piano; Fletcher, Shakespeare, Tennyson, Hopkins, Campion)

1975; first performed Akron, Ohio, 23 May 1976.
Women's Voices (song cycle for voice, piano; Wylie, Rossetti, Bradstreet, Chudleigh, Pembroke, Coleridge, Rich, Dickinson, Boleyn, Ridge, Mew) 1975–6; first performed New York City, 4 November 1976. Recorded CRI 485 SD.
Surge, illuminare (SATB choir, organ; Isaiah/Draft Proposed Book of Common Prayer) 1977.
O magnum mysterium (unacompanied SATB choir) 1978.
Two Poems of Edith Sitwell (medium-high voice, piano) 1978. Recorded GSS 104.
The Oxen (unaccompanied SATB choir; Hardy) 1978.
Shout the Glad Tidings (unaccompanied SATB choir; Muhlenberg) 1978.
Three Choruses for Christmas (unacompanied SATB choir) 1978.
The Nantucket Songs (voice, piano; Roethke, Williams, Waller, Rossetti, Landor, Ashbery) 1979; first performed Washington, D.C., 30 October 1979. Recorded CRI 6007/485 SD.
The Santa Fe Songs (baritone, piano quartet; Bynner) 1980; first performed Santa Fe, New Mexico, 27 July 1980.
Back to Life (counter-tenor, double bass; Gunn) 1980; first performed Hartford, Connecticut, 28 March 1981.
Give All to Love (2 voices, piano; Emerson) 1981.
Song Album Volumes 1 & 2 (voice, piano; various) 1981.
After Long Silence (song cycle for soprano, oboe, string orchestra; Herbert, Caarew, Burns, Elizabeth I, Hardy, Blake, Dowson, Dickinson) 1981–2; first performed Miami, Florida, 11 June 1982. Recorded Spacio 2079.
Little Lamb, Who Made Thee? (SATB choir, organ; Blake) 1982.
Praise the Lord O My Soul (SATB choir, organ; Psalm 146) 1982.
Three Calamus Poems (voice, piano; Whitman) 1982; first performed New York City, 27 April 1983.
Mercy and Truth Are Met (SATB choir, organ; Psalm 85) 1983.
A Whitman Cantata (male voices, brass) 1983; first performed New York City, 11 September 1983.
An American Oratorio (tenor, SATB choir, orchestra; Lazarus, Poe, Longfellow, Twain, Lanier, Melville, Crane, Whitman) 1983–4; first performed Pittsburgh, Pennsylvania, 4 January 1985.
Pilgrim Strangers (6 male voices; Whitman) 1984; first performed New York City, 16 November 1984.
Seven Motets for the Church Year (unaccompanied mixed chorus; Liber Usualis) 1986.
Three Scenes from the Iliad (4-part mixed chorus, 8 instruments; Homer) 1986.
Five Armenian Love Songs (unaccompanied mixed chorus; Kuckak) 1987; first performed Los Angeles, 17 September 1987.
Three Poems of Baudelaire (unaccompanied mixed chorus) 1987.
Te Deum (mixed chorus, 2 trumpets, 2 trombones, organ; Book of Common Prayer) 1987; first performed Indianapolis, 19 July 1987.
What Is Pink? (treble chorus, piano; Rossetti, Lindsay, Smith, Millay, Robinson) 1987.
The Death of Moses (mixed chorus, organ; Deuteronomy) 1987; first performed New York City, 29 January 1988.
The Schuyler Songs (voice, orchestra) 1987; first performed Fargo, North Dakota, 23 April 1988.
Lead Kindly Light (unaccompanied mixed chorus; traditional) 1988.
Goodbye My Fancy (alto, baritone, mixed chorus, orchestra; Whitman) 1988; first performed Chicago, 8 November 1990.
Love Alone (men's chorus, piano—4 hands; Monette) 1989.
Breathe on Me (unaccompanied mixed choir; Hatch) 1989.
Anna la bonne (voice, piano; Cocteau) 1989.
Are You the New Person? (voice, piano; Whitman) 1989.
The Auden Poems (voice, violin, cello, piano) 1989; first performed Santa Fe, New Mexico, 29 July 1990.
Full of Life Now (voice, piano; Whitman) 1989.
Song Album Volume 3 (voice, piano; various) 1990.
Swords into Plowshares (4 voices, orchestra) 1990; first performed Boston, 12 December 1991.

Opera:

A Childhood Miracle (Stein) 1952.
The Robbers (after Chaucer) 1956; first performed New York, 14 April 1958.
Miss Julie (Elmslie, after Strindberg) 1964–5, revised 1978; first performed New York City, 4 November 1965; New York City, 5 April 1979. Recorded (excerpts) Painted Smiles PS 1338.
Three Sisters Who Are Not Sisters (Stein) 1968; first performed Philadelphia, 24 July 1971.
Bertha (Koch) 1968; first performed New York City, 26 November 1973.
Fables (5 short operas; La Fontaine) 1970; first performed Martin, Tennessee, 21 May 1971.
Hearing (Holmes/Koch) arranged 1976; first performed New York City, 15 March 1977.

PUBLICATIONS

By Rorem: *The Paris Dairy of NR*, New York City, 1966, reprinted 1983; *Music from the Inside Out*, New York City, 1967; *The New York Diary*, New York City, 1967, reprinted 1983; *Music and People*, New York City, 1968; *Critical Affairs: A Composer's Journal*, New York City, 1970; *Pure Contraption: A Composer's Essays*, New York City, 1973; *The Final Dairy: 1961–72*, New York City, 1974, reprinted 1983; *An Absolute Gift: A New Diary*, New York City, 1977; *Setting the Tone: Essays and a Diary*, New York City, 1983; *Paul's Plumes*, New York City, 1984; *The Nantucket Diary of NR, 1973–85*, New York City, 1987; *Settling the Score*, New York City, 1988; autobiography in preparation, 1991.

On Rorem: G. Anderson, "The Music of NR", in *Music Journal*, 21(4), 1963; W.S.W. North, "NR as 20th-Century Song composer", dissertation, University of Illinois, Urbana, 1965; R. Middaugh, "The Songs of NR: Aspects of Musical Style", in *NATS Bulletin*, 24(4), 1968; S.A. Atack, "NR and His Songs", dissertation, University of Nebraska, Lincoln, 1969; M.R. Bloomquist, "Songs of NR: Aspects of the Musical Setting of Songs in English for Solo Voice and Piano", dissertation, University of Missouri, Columbia, 1970; M. Hinson, "The Piano Music of NR", in *the Piano Quarterly*, 110, 1980; P. Ramey, "Not Just a Song Composer", in *Keynote*, 4(3), 1980; R. Miller, "The *NATS Bulletin* Interviews with NR", volume 29(2), 1982; L. Raver, "The Solo Organ Music of NR", in *American Organist* 17(10), 1983; B. Johnson, "Still Sings the Voice: A Portrait of NR", in *Tempo*, 153, 1985.

* * *

It must be ironic for Ned Rorem that his kind of music is today "fashionable", after so many years of being on the outside because of his refusal to follow the latest trends. From his earliest works of the 1940s, Rorem has written lean, elegant and very conservative music. Criticized by many in academic and avant-garde circles through the 1950s and 1960s, Rorem never veered from his course. When, in the 1980s, it became more "acceptable" to write music that spoke directly to audiences, and music with identifiable roots in earlier generations, Rorem found a more hospitable environment for that which he had always been composing.

Because he is also a prolific writer (known in European circles more for his literature than his music), we know a good deal about Rorem and his musical thinking. He speaks of music as being basically divisible into two categories, French and German, and he places himself firmly in the French camp. Transparency of texture, clarity of vision, simplicity of structure and elegance of thought are the hallmarks of Rorem's work. Even his symphonic works are marked by concise themes developed briefly; extensive, complex developmental writing is not in his arsenal.

Rorem himself has noted the influence of Ravel, Debussy, Fauré and Poulenc on his music, and he lived in France for many years. He also observes the role of American jazz in shaping his work. Indeed he is quite open about the importance of the past to his music, claiming that all composers are influenced ("we all grow by taking from our predecessors. To refuse to take from them is itself a taking—an affirmation"). Rorem also says, in "Why I Write as I Do", first delivered as a talk in 1974 and most recently reprinted in his collection of essays *Settling the Score*, " . . . I make no claims to novelty. My sole originality is that I've never sought originality. Though in the end that claim cannot apply to my music, only to a point of view about my music."

The truth, though, is that Rorem's music is more individual and recognizable than those words might imply. Its combination of textural clarity and melodic profile could be no one else. When it comes to setting words, Rorem is virtually without equal among today's composers. His ear is sensitive to both the meaning and the sound of the words in his texts, and he marries those words to music that feels uncannily right to the listener.

Although Rorem's reputation is particularly high as a song composer, he should not be thought of as a miniaturist or a composer limited to the song form. His refined, delicate sense of orchestral color, while not commented on as frequently as is his vocal writing, is another important quality, particularly evident in works like the Third Symphony, *Eagles* and *Goodbye My Fancy*. For over almost half a century he has written successfully in virtually every musical idiom possible, and he is one of the most prolific and consistent composers of the post-World War II era.

—Henry Fogel

ROSING-SCHOW, Niels. Danish. Born in Copenhagen, 14 April 1954. Educated at University of Copenhagen, 1972–9; Royal Danish Academy of Music, diploma in music theory and history, 1984; further composition study under Ib Nørholm, 1984–7. Married to Christine Canals-Frau. Music critic, *Jyllands-Posten*, 1980–2, *Berlingske Tidende*, 1983–6, and *Politiken*, since 1986; chair, Society for Young Music Workers, since 1984; teacher of theory, Royal Danish Academy of Music, since 1984. Recipient: Music Prize, Noilly Prat, 1986. Mailing address: c/o Wilhelm Hansen, Bornholmsgade 1, DK-1266 Copenhagen K, Denmark.

Publisher: Wilhelm Hansen.

Symphonies/orchestral:

Five Preludes (small string orchestra) 1975.
Twofold 1981–2. Recorded SUDM 016.
Chamber Concerto (alto flute, viola, orchestra) 1986–7.

Chamber/instrumental:

Wind Quintet 1973.
String Quartet 1973.
Four Studies (woodwind quintet) 1974, 1985.
Canzona (organ) 1978; first performed 24 March 1985.
Glorie (cello, synthesizer) 1979.
Five Studies (wind quintet) 1979.
E rigidis (violin, piano) 1981.
Trio (flute, viola, harp) 1983. Recorded SUDM 016.
Canon and Chorale (2 flutes, 2 clarinets, horn, 2 trumpets, trombone, accordion, piano, percussion, 2 violins, 2 cellos) 1984.
Metope entre deux (organ) 1984. Recorded SUDM 022.
Turning Points (clarinet, cello, harp, percussion, piano) 1985.
Extraction (oboe, horn, violin, percussion, piano) 1985.
Figura (viola, piano) 1985.
Meeting (oboe, clarinet, bassoon, horn, viola, cello, double bass) 1985.
Sonata a due: Ommagio a Domenico Scarlatti (prepared piano, harpsichord) 1985.
Epiages (flute) 1987.
Double (flute, clarinet, harp, percussion, piano) 1987.
Ritus I (flute, percussion) 1990.
Ritus II (3 percussion) 1990.
Voix intérieures (violin, clarinet, cello, piano) 1990–1; first performed Belfast, 1991.

Vocal/choral:

Three Songs of the Flower Fairies (soprano, flute, cello, piano; Barker) 1974.
Nu (baritone, flute, cello, piano) 1976.
Kinderlieder (women's chorus, flute, clarinet, cornet, harpsichord, percussion, violin, cello; Brecht) 1977.
Three Songs (unaccompanied mixed chorus) 1980.
Three Songs (soprano, flute, viola, piano; Thomsen) 1980. Recorded SUDM 006.
Aria (soprano, flute, oboe d'amore, clarinet, bass clarinet, horn, 2 violins, viola, cello, double bass; Tasso) 1980.
Three Chorus Songs (unaccompanied SSAATTBB chorus; Ecevit) 1980–7.
Reflections (soprano, alto flute, violin, cello, piano) 1981. Recorded SUDM 004.
Sange om traeet/Songs About the Tree (soprano, flute, viola, guitar, piano; Nielsen) 1981. Recorded SUDM 009.
Llanto (soprano, baritone, clarinet, cello, piano, percussion) 1982.
Med sin alabasterkrukke/With Her Alabaster Pot (1 or more voices, piano or organ; Grundtvig) 1983.
Vocabulary (soprano with amplification and digital delay) 1986.
Chants de l'ombre (unaccompanied SATB chorus; Desnos) 1987.

Vintersuite (soprano, alto, tenor, baritone, percussion; Harder) 1988.
Epoke (bass, male chorus, symphony orchestra; Tafdrup) 1988–9.
Combat d'aurore (unaccompanied SATB chorus; Canals-Frau) 1990.

Opera:

Brand (after Ibsen) 1989.

* * *

Like many of his Danish contemporaries, while a student in Copenhagen in the 1970s, Niels Rosing-Schow reacted against the new music establishment of European Modernism and sought to find a language of simplicity and communication. Two unpublished works from this time, the *Three Songs of the Flower Fairies* for soprano and three instruments and the *Kinderlieder* for women's chorus and ensemble with words by Bertolt Brecht, demonstrate this with their simple articulation and tonality and endearing, though perhaps studied, naivity. His works from the early 1980s share the concern of his teacher Ib Nørholm for lyricism, often in vocal works such as *Aria*, a setting of Tasso in the original Italian for mezzo and ensemble and *Reflections* for soprano and four instruments in which the voice sings only phonetic sounds. Both works demonstrate the composer's use of supple melodic lines and impressionistic harmonies.

In 1981–2 he wrote his first orchestral work, *Twofold*, a piece conceived for amateurs and actually playable by them, but without any artistic condescension. This work explores two extremes of the same music—the gestures of extrovert and introvert music—a hallmark which has continued to run through Rosing-Schow's musical language.

Towards the mid-1980s Rosing-Schow appears to have moved away from the his experiments to find a "new simplicity" and supplanted this with a preoccupation with the problems of musical modernism. The first works which demonstrate this are two small ensemble pieces from 1985, *Turning Points* and *Extraction*. Despite the almost fierce modernist gestures of these pieces, he chooses not to abandon totally lyricism and the final bars of the latter piece are a delicate, impressionistic statement of melancholia. It was, perhaps, this leaning towards modernism that encouraged Rosing-Schow to look outside Denmark and in 1987 the Noilly Prat Music Prize enabled him to undertake a period of study in France, a country with which he still has affinities and ties. From this year date two settings of Robert Desnos, *Chants de l'ombre*, for 12 voices written for the Groupe Vocale de France—a piece of sparse textures and harmonies—which led to a second work for mixed chorus in 1990, *Combat d'aurore* this time commissioned by the choir of the Danish Radio and to a text by the composer's wife, Christine Canals-Frau. His time in Paris also gave him the opportunity to explore new areas in electro-acoustic music and at time of writing he is planning a project using the UPIC computer, a system devised by Iannis Xenakis which enables the composer to transform graphic representations into sound.

Returning to Denmark with a more international reputation, Rosing-Schow received a succession of prestigious commissions. His most substantial work to date, *Epoke* for bass solo, male chorus and orchestra, was completed in 1989 and in 1990 his first British commission from the chamber ensemble Capricorn resulted in *Voix intérieures*, which was premiered by them at the 1991 Belfast Sonorities Festival. This work, for the *Quartet for the End of Time* combination, parallels the inner impulses of the mind with the internal parts and relations of the music using a system of gradual transformation of interval patterns, sonorities and dynamics. It may well prove a significant piece for Rosing-Schow and, despite the contrast of his musical voice, win him a place alongside his already frequently performed compatriots, Per Nørgård, Poul Ruders, Hans Abrahamsen and Bent Sørensen in British musical life.

—Rosemary Johnson

ROSTOMIAN, Stepan. Armenian. Born in Kirovakan, April 4 1956. Educated at State Conservatoire, Erevan, 1976–81, graduated in composition and theoretical subjects. Married Svetlana Boyajian, 13 October 1979; 1 daughter and 1 son. Arranger, Armenian State Academic Choir, Erevan, 1981–4; teacher of composition, Music School "Armen Tigranian", Erevan, 1984–9; chief musical instructor, Armenian State Academic Theatre "G. Soundukian", since 1989; lecturer in composition, computer and electronic systems, State Conservatoire, Erevan, since 1990. Member, Composers Union of U.S.S.R., 1984. Recipient: special prize for symphonic music, Armenian Ministry of Culture, 1985–6. Mailing address: st. Israelian 37, apart. 34, Erevan 375015, Armenia.

Symphonies/orchestral:

Symphony No 1 1983; first performed Erevan, 1984.
Symphony No 2 1988; first performed Erevan, 1988.
Symphony No 3 1989; first performed Glasgow, 26 November 1989.

Chamber/instrumental:

String Quartet 1979; first performed Erevan, 1979.
Wind Quintet No 1 1983; first performed Erevan, 1984.
Wind Quintet No 2 1989; first performed Glasgow, 1989.

Vocal/choral:

Tanka (song cycle for voice, piano; Armenian translation of medieval Japanese) 1983; first performed Erevan, 1984.

Other:

Bridge (computer music for film) 1990; first performed Erevan, 1990.
Martiros' Pilgrimage (film music for computer system, with different chamber instrumental and vocal groups) 1990; first performed Erevan, 1990.
Sacrifice (computer music for film) 1990; first performed Erevan, 1990.

PUBLICATIONS

On Rostomian: R. Terterian, "*Tanka*", in *Luis*, 1985; S. Sarkisian, "Young Armenian Composers", in *Rukh Musichui*, 8, 1987; Kenneth Walton, "Republican Overtures", in

Observer (Scotland), 1989; Michael Tumelty, "Paragon", in *Glasgow Herald*, 1989, and "New Beginnings: Music Ends on a Positive Note", in *Glasgow Herald*, 1989; Janet Beat, "Earthquake Eco Proves Festival's Musical Climax", in *Glasgow Herald*, 1989.

* * *

The music of Stepan Rostomian represents a decisive step away from the neo-classicism which has been such a pervasive feature of the response, by composers from the periphery of the European continent, to the central European art music tradition. Instead of the adoption of already existing formal models, whether of the sonata type or the various practices of serialism, Rostomian builds large-scale structures from the methods of melodic line extension and metrical development characteristic of Armenian traditional music. While rooted in an intense national feeling fused with a deep religious faith, he is nevertheless open to the influence of other cultures: in *Tanka*, a song cycle for voice and piano, he manages to convey the peculiar concentration of Japanese poetry (in Armenian translation) without resort either to exoticism or to the employment of formal constraints alien to his own musical language.

The Soviet music education system stresses technical competence and this accent on mastery of the methods of the European classical tradition is one of the sources of latter-day Soviet neo-classicism, where folk-influenced material is often emptied, as it were, into sonata-type receptacles. Even in a work as late as Rostomian's *Wind Quintet No 2* of 1989, it is still possible to hear the tension between formal structures and musical content, as the writing strives to present a more natural and immediate form of instrumental expression than is customary in the wind quintet repertoire. This urge to express the innate voice of each instrument is one of the most important elements of Rostomian's music and can be seen as a development from his experience as a professional violinist and pianist—in this latter role his repertoire includes popular and jazz styles.

This influence was obvious in the composition of his *Symphony No 3*. The work opens with a long double bass solo and, characteristically, Rostomian borrowed an instrument and set to work practising the opening gestures, repeatedly playing the same cells. On the one hand he seemed to be willing the material to open up, to reveal its potential to him, while on the other, he was experiencing the raw physical impact of the instrumental timbre. This extraordinary work, Rostomian's first completed composition after the earthquake which devastated Armenia, is dedicated to its victims, but its elemental power, which created a sensation at the premiere, surely derives from the compositional method of concentration on the initial materials—"cooking" them until the bulk of the composition could be written at intense speed in a final outburst of creative energy. The textures used in the work are built from a small instrumental ensemble and an electronic tape containing "sampled" string and vocal sounds, pre-recorded instrumental sounds which were then electronically treated, and recordings of Armenian church chants and bell sounds. The very diversity of these components embodies Rostomian's rejection of compositional systems as an end in themselves.

—William Sweeney

RUDERS, Poul. Danish. Born in Ringsted, 27 March 1949. Educated at St Annae High School, diploma, 1968; Royal Danish Academy of Music, Copenhagen (organ scholar), graduated 1975; self-taught composer. Married Helene Wanscher, 19 August 1984. Former member, Copenhagen Boys' Choir; organist/choirmaster, Danish Lutheran Church, since 1975; freelance composer; visiting lecturer at Yale University, New Haven, Connecticut, University of Hartford, Connecticut, University of Southern California, Los Angeles, University of California, Santa Cruz, Cornell University, Ithaca, New York, and Berkshire Music Center, Tanglewood, Massachusetts; guest lecturer, Yale University, 1991. Mailing address: 45 Engelstedsgade, DK-2100 Copenhagen O, Denmark.

Publisher: Wilhelm Hansen, Copenhagen.

Symphonies/orchestral:

Pavane 1971.
Capriccio pian'e forte 1978; first performed Odense, 1978.
Recitatives and Arias (piano, orchestra, offstage alto trombone, viola, metal wind chimes) 1978.
Violin Concerto 1981; first performed Copenhagen, 1982.
Manhattan Abstraction 1982; first performed Copenhagen, 1985. Recorded Point CD 5084.
Thus Saw Saint John (Saaledes saae Johannes) 1984; first performed Copenhagen, 1984. Recorded Point CD 5084.
Concerto for Clarinet and Twin-Orchestra 1985; first performed Copenhagen, 1985.
Jubileephony 1986; first performed Houston, Texas, 1986.
Piano Concerto: "Dramaphonia" 1987.
Percussion Concerto: "Monodrama" 1988; first performed Copenhagen, 1988.
Symphony No 1: "Himmelhoch Jauchzen-zum Tode betrubt" 1989; first performed London, 1990.
TUNDRA 1990; first performed Helsinki, 1990.
Cello Concerto: "Polydrama" 1990; first performed Stockholm, 1990.
Psalmodies (guitar, orchestra) 1990.

Chamber/instrumental:

Three Letters from the Unknown Soldier (piano) 1967. Recorded Odeon MOAK 30010.
Requiem (organ) 1970.
Dante Sonata (Piano Sonata No 1) 1970. Recorded Odeon MOAK 30010.
String Quartet No 1: "Der Rastlose Mensch" 1971.
Jargon (guitar) 1973. Recorded EMI MOAK 30017.
Medieval Variations (flute, saxophone, trombone, piano, harpsichord, viola/banjo, cello) 1974.
Rondeau (flute, clarinet, percussion, electric guitar, piano, violin, cello) 1976. Recorded Caprice CAP 1152.
Bravour-Studien (cello) 1976.
Seven Recitatives (piano) 1977. Recorded Danica DLP 8087.
Wind-Drumming (wind quintet, 4 percussionists) 1979.
String Quartet No 2 1979. Recorded RCA RL 70464.
String Quartet No 3: "Motet" 1979. Recorded RCA RL 70464.
Four Compositions (flute, clarinet, horn, piano, 2 violins, viola, cello, double bass) 1980; first performed Copenhagen, 1980. Recorded Paula CD 37.
Carnival (electric alto flute/foot bongos) 1980.
Diferencias (flute, clarinet, vibraphone, guitar, harp, piano, violin, cello) 1980.

Cha Cha Cha (percussion) 1981.

Greeting Concertino (horn, cornet, trombone, percussion, piano, violin, cello, double bass) 1982.

Piano Sonata No 2 1982; first performed Aarhus, 1984. Recorded Paula 28.

Vox in Rama (clarinet, electric violin, piano) 1983; first performed Copenhagen, 1983.

Alarm (percussion) 1983.

Four Dances in One Movement (flute, oboe, clarinet, bassoon, horn, trumpet, trombone, percussion, piano, 2 violins, viola, cello, double bass) 1983; first performed London, 1985.

Break-Dance (piano, 2 trumpets, 3 trombones) 1984; first performed London, 1986. Recorded Teldec.

Regime (3 percussion) 1984.

Tattoo for One (clarinet) 1984.

Tattoo for Three (clarinet, piano, cello) 1984; first performed Buffalo, New York, 1985. Recorded Paula CD 57.

Corpus cum figuris (flute/piccolo, oboe/cor anglais, 2 clarinets/bass clarinets, 2 bassoon/1 contrabassoon, horn, trumpet, trombone, 2 percussion, piano, 2 violins, 2 violas, 2 cellos, double bass) 1985; first performed Copenhagen, 1985. Recorded Point PCD 5084.

Cembal d'Amore (harpsichord, piano) 1986; first performed Copenhagen, 1987.

Nightshade (flute, oboe, contrabass clarinet, contrabassoon, horn, trombone, percussion, piano, violin, double bass) 1987; first performed London, 1987.

Variations (violin) 1989; first performed London, 1989.

Throne (clarinet, piano) 1989; first performed Copenhagen, 1989.

Thirteen Postludes (piano) 1989; first performed Aakirkeby, 3 August 1989.

Vocal/choral:

Stabat mater (SSAATTBBBB choir, "rock" singer, boy soprano, portable organ, tubular bells, tam-tam, saloon piano) 1974.

Pestilence Songs (soprano, guitar, saloon piano; Nashe) 1975.

glOriA (SSAATTBB choir, 4 horns, 4 trumpets, 4 trombones) 1981; first performed Copenhagen, 1983.

Three Motets (SATB, SATTB, SSATBB choirs) 1981–8; first performed Copenhagen, 1982, 1985, 1989. Recorded Kontrapunkt 32016.

Opera:

Tycho (soprano, mezzo-soprano, tenor, 2 basses; clarinet/alto clarinet/bass clarinet, horn, percussion, piano/harpsichord/celeste/synthesizer, harp, amplified acoustic guitar, violin, double bass) 1986; first performed Aarhus, 1987.

PUBLICATIONS

On Ruders: Karl Aage Rasmussen, in *Ten Danish Composers*, Copenhagen, 1990.

Poul Ruders comments:

I employ no specific techniques; what's important to me is the natural balance between emotion and structure—the right and left side of the brain. My only artistic credo is to make a strong emotional impact with the audience and to give my listeners a rich variety of associations.

* * *

Unlike the majority of composers Poul Ruders's biography lacks the conventional study of composition in any formal capacity. His earliest musical experiences were as a chorister in the Copenhagen Boys Choir, followed by conservatory training as an organist. The constant presence of sacred music in his life has undoubted resonances throughout his output, from the Gabrieli-inspired *Capriccio pian'e forte* ("there are not any quotations at all; merely a kind of genre association ping pong") to the unashamed borrowings from Bach's *Christmas Oratorio* in his First Symphony. While lacking any central compositional mentor, Ruders acknowledges inspiration from the Polish avant-garde in his earliest pieces (dating from the late 1960s) and, in the middle of the next decade, to the music theatre works of Peter Maxwell Davies. These influences apart, his self-taught style, combined with his natural eclecticism and magpie habits, has evolved as a ferociously independent and powerful voice.

First acquaintance with Ruders's music can be both exhilarating and disorientating. The ear is assaulted by virtuosity of technique, by musical grotesqueries, by enormous, resonant blocks of sound and by an extraordinary rhythmic propulsion which can be brutally abhorted at the moment one least expects. Taste is not an issue, but elegance is never out of the question.

As well as musical borrowings or starting points, much of Ruders's music contains visual imagery. Indeed, Ruders talks of his role as a film-composer without a film, and sees his music as "acoustic canvases". *Manhattan Abstraction* for large orchestra arose from Ruders's fascination with New York—a city which he regularly visits. He subtitles the piece "a symphonic skyline for large orchestra" and says that it was inspired by "the New York profile seen from Liberty Island, one icy cold, January day with its open, clear sky and dazzling sunlight". The beautiful/ugly metropolis is the perfect metaphor for his music, contrasting as it does the cold, spikily, rhythmic sections (impersonal, monolithic tower blocks) with the fragile "human" voice of the solo violin. Compositionally it is an amalgam of techniques and melodic borrowings from his previous pieces: *Capriccio pian'e forte, String Quartet No 2, Four Compositions* and *Piano Sonata No 2* all make an appearance.

Corpus cum figuris for 20 players, takes its visual inspiration from quite a different world. Aural-visual images (a funeral march, distant Viennese waltzes, glimpses of the Middle Ages, pounding ostinato drums) are juxtaposed and superimposed in ways reminiscent of film and video editing. Each scenario is quite distinct from the one that preceeds it, but all, nonetheless are integrated into a single, powerful 20-minute movement.

Since 1987 the concerto has been the dominant form in Ruders's compositional output. Three linked pieces *Dramaphonia*, *Monodrama* and *Polydrama* feature respectively solo piano, percussion and cello, while most recently a guitar concerto (in reality a suite of short movements) *Psalmodies* has been commissioned by Speculum Musicae for the American guitarist David Starobin. In the "Drama Trilogy" the dialectic of tension is not, as one might expect, created by the solo protagonist in conflict with the instrumental ensemble (indeed in *Monodrama* the instrumental ensemble is texturally and rhythmically wrapped around the solo percussionist so that the whole group emerges as one giant percussion instrument) but each piece is concerned with the drama of an abstract "event" or "events". Ruders invites the listener to make his/her own associations with the music in order to create a personal, private internal theatre.

When offered a major Proms commission by the BBC, the

composer professed himself glad to return to the purely orchestral palette and seized the opportunity of writing a large-scale, four-movement symphony. He also moved away from the abstraction of the "Drama Trilogy" into a very personal expression which mirrors the conflicting tendencies of his own personality. The subtitle, Goethe's *Himmelhoch jauchzend—zum Tode betrubt* encapsulates the zenith of jubilation (represented in the first movement by wholesale borrowings from and imitations of Bach's *Christmas Oratorio*) and the trough of despair (which Ruders deems the "symphonic tundra" of the finale). In between, a static second movement based entirely on two chords and a breathless Scherzo go to their own extremes: a dramatic culmination of 20 years compositional development.

—Rosemary Johnson

RUDZINSKI, Zbigniew. Polish. Born in Czechowice, 23 October 1935. Educated at Warsaw Conservatory (composition under Piotr Perkowski), 1956–62; further composition study, Paris, 1965–6, and in The Netherlands, 1971. Married Ewa Debska, 13 July 1965; 1 daughter. Instructor, 1973–6, assistant professor of composition, theory and conducting, since 1976, head, composition department 1980–1, and rector 1981–4, Frederick Chopin School of Music, Warsaw; president, Warsaw district, 1983–5, and subsequently secretary general, Polish Composers' Union. Recipient: 1st prize (for *Sonata* for string quartets, piano, timpani), Warsaw Conservatory 150th anniversary competition, 1960; 2nd prize (for *Epigramy*), Young Composers' Competition, Warsaw, 1962; Silver Cross of Merit, 1975; Award of the Minister of Culture and Art, 1979, 1985; Award of the Prime Minister of Poland, 1986. Mailing address: ul. Poznanska 23 ul 26, 00-685 Warsaw, Poland.

Publishers: Polskie Wydawnictwo Muzyczne; Schott.

Symphonies/orchestral:

Contra fidem 1964; first performed Warsaw, Autumn 1964. Recorded Polskie Nagrania W-965.
Moments musicaux I 1965. Recorded Polskie Nagrania XL 0336/XW-576.
Moments musicaux II 1967. Recorded Polskie Nagrania XW 889.
Moments musicaux III 1968.
Allegro giocoso 1969.
Symphony (with wordless male chorus) 1969. Recorded Polskie Nagrania XW 1181.
Muzyka noca/Night Music 1970. Recorded Polskie Nagrania XW 1379.

Chamber/instrumental:

Trio (2 clarinets, bassoon) 1958.
Sonata (2 string quartets, piano, timpani) 1960.
String Trio 1964.
Study in C (variable instrumentation) 1964.
Impromptu (3 cellos, 2 pianos, 3 percussion) 1966. Recorded Polskie Nagrania XW 712.
Quartet (2 pianos, 2 percussion) 1969. Recorded Polskie Nagrania XW 1659.
Sonata (piano) 1975. Recorded Polskie Nagrania SX 1253.
Sonata: Pastoral (violin, piano) 1976–8.
Campanella (percussion) 1977. Recorded Polski Nagrania SX 1595/SX 1685.
Tritones (6 percussion) 1979.

Vocal/choral:

Four Songs (baritone, ensemble; Tuwim) 1961.
Epigramy (2 women's choruses, flute, piano, 6 percussion) 1962.
Three Songs (tenor, 2 pianos; Pound, Joyce, Benet) 1969. Recorded Polskie Nagrania SX 1595.
Requiem ofiarom wojen/For the Victims of War (chorus, orchestra, optional speaker) 1971, revised 1974. Recorded Polskie Nagrania SX 1595.
Tutti e solo (soprano, flute, horn, piano) 1973.
Five Romantic Songs (mezzo-soprano, piano trio; Rilke) 1983.
Six Songs (soprano, piano; Bearth) 1986.

Opera:

Antigone (chamber opera after Sophocles; baritone, mime, women's chorus) 1980.
Manekiny/The Mannequins (chamber opera after Bruno Schulz) 1980–1.

PUBLICATIONS

On Rudzinski: T. Kaczynski, "RZ's *Moments musicaux*", in *Ruch muzyczny*, 12, 1966.

* * *

Zbigniew Rudzinski was a prize-winner in the fifth Young Composers' Competition in Warsaw in 1962, and early international success followed with his *Contra fidem* for orchestra. Closed forms and economic use of material give to his music a great coherence. This was apparent as early as the Bartókian *Sonata* for two string quartets, piano and timpani of 1960, and in a rather more expansive way in the choral *Symphony* of 1969, a work which has been widely played in Eastern Europe.

One of Rudzinski's most ingenious pieces is the *String Trio* of 1964, whose formal novelty belies his usual tendency to exert complete structural control. Before performing the piece, the players must decide how the parts are to be distributed; they then read their respective lines in the clef normal to their respective instruments.

One of his most impressive works is the Requiem "for the victims of war", written in 1971 and subsequently revised. The freely arranged text, starting with an uncompromisingly dramatic and disturbing *"in pacem terris"*, gives a highly personal quality to a volatile work. Complex ostinatos are used to evoke anguish and despair. At one point, the notation of the strings represents a crucifix on the page, and towards the close, as the narrator catalogues harrowing events, there are poignant outbursts from various sections of the orchestra and a sorrowful wailing from the chorus. Many of the textures are characteristic of the controlled aleatorism which is common in much contemporary Polish music, and the work as a whole makes a direct and forceful impact.

Uppermost in Rudzinski's mind during the 1970s was the

idea of writing a symbolic music drama—one with a universal dimension, but firmly rooted in the Polish experience. The result was his one-act chamber opera *Manekiny / The Mannequins* based on a number of bizarre short stories by Bruno Schulz (a writer who was shot by the Gestapo in a pogrom in 1942). Schulz's writings are archetypically Polish, and with their sombre and disturbing undertones also evoke characteristic qualities of Jewish life. The opera is the story of a Jewish tailor, Jacob, a man of ideas, who is the creator of a world inhabited by tailors' dummies. His two stupid seamstresses find his philosophical statements incomprehensible. Alongside these living dummies are the failed creations—the handsome Eddie whose legs do not work, Magda the masochistic vamp, Queen Draga and the anarchist Lucheni. The interaction between them and Jacob provides a variety of ironic situations ranging from the bizarre to the whimsical. The opera plays continuously but is structured in three scenes. In the first, Jacob makes pronouncements which no one understands. In the second, his statements are about art, but again they have little effect and are rejected. In the third scene, he makes a last attempt to communicate with his creatures, but to no avail. Here Rudzinski goes beyond the open end of Schulz's original story and provides a dénouement. Just after Jacob's last defeat, when he is abandoned by everybody, he suddenly appears in a dazzling light (representing the grace of God, his inspiration, and in a deep sense his comprehension of the mystery of creation). Jacob's final words "Mystery . . . mystery . . . mystery . . ." provide a Wagnerian apotheosis and a wider dimension that is absent from the original story. Yet the work as a whole remains close to its folk roots, for behind its symbolism and allegory lie deep resonances of Poland's history and economic struggles.

Rudzinski has suggested that composing *Manekiny* was a particularly fulfilling experience because he had previously restricted himself to writing rather abstract instrumental music. He had written for voice before, but on his own admission the texts were rarely a dominating factor; he once said "I used the voice just as an *instrument* with unique colour." The opera is enriched by a great variety of musical devices borrowed from the past and infused with irony. *Sprechstimme*, for instance, is used in a cynical manner to suggest a low level of appreciation, and is associated with the two simple and uncomprehending girls. Musical jokes such as this occur periodically with arresting effect and can be both subtle and elusive (as when accompanying Jacob's private thoughts) or more overtly allusive as in the can-can or in the send-up of operetta.

—Richard Elfyn Jones

RUNSWICK, Daryl (Bernard). British/English. Born in Leicester, 12 October 1946. Educated at Wyggeston Boys' School, Leicester, 1957–63; Corpus Christi College, Cambridge (choral exhibitioner), 1964–7, M.A. Married Elaine Slater in 1969 (dissolved 1990); 1 son and 1 daughter. Double bass player with, *inter alia*, Cleo Laine/John Dankworth, London Sinfonietta, own groups, recorded with Ornette Coleman, Phil Woods, Al Haig, Dizzy Gillespie, Jon Hendricks, others, 1968–84; composer, arranger, record producer with the King's Singers, since 1970; joined Electric Phoenix vocal group as tenor singer, 1983; founder/musical director, Green Light Music Theatre Co, 1990. Recipient: Arts Council of Great Britain bursary, 1982. Mailing address: 34a Garthorne Road, London SE23 1EW, England.

Publisher: Faber.

Symphonies/orchestral:

Fantasy III (trumpet, orchestra) 1980; first performed London, 1981.
World upon World 1984; first performed Bracknell, Hertfordshire, 1985.
Songs of Love and Farewell 1987; first performed London, 1987.

Chamber/instrumental:

Zany (clarinet, trumpet, horn, cor anglais, cello) 1975; first performed London, 1976.
Suite and Low (4 double basses) 1977; first performed London, 1977.
Cool-Warm-Hot (clarinet) 1987; first performed London, 1987.
Dialectic I (flute, cello, sitar, tabla, keyboard) 1990; first performed London, 1990.

Vocal/choral:

One More Day (12 songs for jazz singer) 1979. Recorded DRG Records CDSL 5188.
I Sing the Body Electric (SATB vocal ensemble, tape delay systems; Lawrence, Basho, Pacey, Whitman) 1984; first performed Saintes, France, 12 July 1984.
Lady Lazarus (amplified female voice; Plath) 1985; first performed Reykjavik, 28 September 1986.
Looney Tunes (soprano, alto, tenor, bass, string quartet; President Ronald Reagan) 1986; first performed Darmstadt, 1986.
Patents Pending (6 voices) 1988; first performed London, 1988.

Other:

Gullsandur (film score) 1984.
She Moved Through the Fair (6 voices, SATBarBB; traditional) 1985.
No Surrender (film score) 1986.
By George! (and Ira . . .) (voice, piano; Gershwin arrangements) 1988; first performed Limoges, 1988.
Happy Birthday (soloists, orchestra; arrangement) 1989; first performed London, 1989.
Cabaret Songs (voice, sextet; Britten arrangements) 1989; first performed Aldeburgh, Suffolk, 1990.
Britten's Blues (sextet; Britten arrangements) 1990; first performed Aldeburgh, Suffolk, 1990.

Many television scores, including *Brond* (Recorded Cocteau COQ CD 21), *My Family and Other Animals* (Recorded BBC 12 RSL 220), *We the Accused* (Recorded BBC RESL 83).

PUBLICATIONS

By Runswick: *Boogie for Beginners* (keyboard teaching book), London, 1989; *Play Boogie* (keyboard teaching book), London, 1989.

Daryl Runswick comments:

I grew up at a time when it was almost *de rigueur* to be an integral serialist; that made it hard for me, because integral serialism went against everything I wanted to do musically.

At that time I considered music to be in crisis—"straight" music, that is; the jazz and rock at which I made my living were in a very healthy state! The crisis I could define: it was that the chain between composer, executant and audience had been broken. I saw my task (somewhat grandiosely) as that of reforging the broken links of the chain.

By dictating every last nuance of the music the integral serialist composer is attempting total control. This is not only impossible, it is deeply undesirable. In the attempt the composer usurps the performer's interpretative function, reducing him/her to a cypher intent only on getting the music as accurate as possible. More important, the audience is denied a most important role, that of evaluating the interpretation. They become passive recipients of an *ex cathedra* statement.

That is all old history now, and things have moved on, mostly for the better (even in those days, had I known where to look—to America—I would have seen one way forward). However there is a discipline, improvisation, which finds many performers unprepared and in need of a theoretical basis. My pieces attempt to establish such a basis.

Current tools of my trade are: electronics (especially sampling); microtones; improvisation, text (I am a "words" man); theatre; an eclectic style; and most important, consultation with performers. I attach importance to being a performer myself. I reject harmonic and rhythmic extremism; this is not self-denial, but a challenge to find an expressive language without their use.

Aleatoric techniques got a bad name in the 1960s but, as with improvisation, it was the total absence of controls that made it seem stupid. *Semi*-random elements can challenge the performer to fresh responses. With the advent of microcomputers semi-randomness becomes more creatively manipulable.

I also like to use games which pit my performers against fixed or semi-random accompaniments. I don't want "winners" or "losers" but the dynamics of dialogue and argument. *It is crucial for me that the audience understands this process*, so that (as with, say, baroque ornamentation) they can exercise their critical faculty and join in the dialectic.

"Main line" is a technique where a principal strand (often melodic) runs through the music, the rest of the texture depending from it, a very old idea indeed!

Lastly, "ScaFra" is a process-based idea (I am not a minimalist) where the music repeats-but-moves-on. ScaFra is short for scan/frame advance. A simple, almost simplistic idea, it can be developed to yield complex results. (I'm sure I'm not the originator of this technique, though I did invent my own name for it!)

* * *

The thought of Daryl Runswick's *Looney Tunes* echoing down the still rather chilly and sombre corridors at Darmstadt is an appealing one. Runswick has long set his face against the lockstep of doctrinaire serialism and, more generally, against the idea that to be any good music must hurt a little. A highly entertaining composer, he is also a very able and subtle one. His vocal fantasy on the "wit and wisdom" of Ronald Reagan, a piece looped around the former president's on-mike aside about bombing the U.S.S.R. in five minutes is so beguilingly attractive as to draw attention away from its considerable subtlety.

Runswick has adapted a number of contemporary and older techniques in his music. Underlying many of his most complex scores is a single melodic line, somewhat like the "firm chant" of medieval music. Elsewhere, he manipulates repetitive structures, but less in the carefully "phased" minimalist manner of a Steve Reich, or with the abrupt key and tempo changes of a Philip Glass, than with a constant alteration of melodic content and pace that increases the rate of change quite considerably and produces a musical surface that is both complex and immediately accessible. Runswick's music is melodically and harmonically coherent without ever being conventionally resolved; in more recent years, he has used electronics to increase his timbral resources and to help generate structures which balance freedom and control.

Runswick's entire output is premised on the belief that music is to be enjoyed and digested, not analysed. On the other hand, he believes very strongly that the audience's understanding of the music is an integral component of the performance; his music is never intended to be mystificatory. His enthusiasm for chance procedures (albeit tempered by a insistence on control; he prefers to talk of "semi-random" events) comes from his close involvement with jazz. A bass player and tenor voice of considerable facility, Runswick has written and arranged jazz scores for the British couple John Dankworth and Cleo Laine, performed in improvisational contexts along with such underrated talents as guitarist/composer Ray Russell (who has since made his own transition to the mainstream of popular music), and sings with the innovative vocal group Electric Phoenix.

His attraction to popular forms is less stylistic than sociological, even epistemological. He has long been convinced that the compositional and performance ethos of so-called "legitimate" music establishes a series of necessary conceptual divides between composers, performers and audiences. These are by no means as acute in popular and improvised music and jazz, where the performer (literally) interprets the music and the audience provides an actual (not just passive) ambience for the performance.

He is particularly attracted to texts and has memorably set Sylvia Plath, Walt Whitman and others (in *I Sing the Body Electric*) and has arranged Gershwin and Gershwin in a manner reminiscent of his compatriot Peter Dickinson; recent projects such as his "cabaret" interpretations of Britten songs (bravely undertaken for the summer festivals at Aldeburgh, the Britten heartland) are similarly inspired and similarly successful.

Runswick has brought together a highly personal selection of modern and preclassical idioms to forge a personal style that is both intellectually satisfying and aesthetically palatable. His hostility to much of the output of late modernism has not turned him into a know-nothing populist, but has allowed him to draw on some of the more original phases of contemporary American music as a means of revivifying the rather somnolent English vocal tradition. Runswick's instrumental and orchestral music is less successful, but is nonetheless freshly and imaginatively conceived, and should be better known than it is.

—Ian Weir

RYPDAL, Terje. Norwegian. Born in Oslo, 23 August 1947. Educated: piano from age 5; self-taught guitar player; University of Oslo (musicology); Music Conservatory [now

State Academy of Music], Oslo (composition under Finn Mortensen), 1970–2; further composition study under George Russell. Married to Inger Lise Rypdal. Professional guitarist in rock and jazz ensembles: The Vanguards, 1960s, Dreams, Jan Garbarek Quartet, from 1969, George Russell Sextet/orchestra, late 1960s, and The Chasers; composer. Recipient: Work of the Year (*Undisonus*), 1984. Mailing address: N-6380 Tresfjord, Norway.

Publisher: none.

Symphonies/orchestral:

Capriccio Op 3 (string orchestra) 1970.
Concerto for Double Bass and Orchestra Op 4b 1973.
Symphony No 1 Op 6 1973.
Tumulter Op 7 (percussion, orchestra) 1973.
Krystaller Op 9 (alto flute, orchestra) 1973.
Symphony No 2 Op 11 1977.
Horn Concerto Op 12 1977.
Julemusikk / Christmas Music Op 13 (string orchestra) 1978.
Piano Concerto Op 14 1979.
In Autumn Op 15 (electric guitar, trumpet, orchestra) 1979.
Undisonus Op 23 (violin, orchestra) 1979–81. Recorded ECM 1389.
Shadows Op 16 (image for oboe, 4 trombones, percussion, strings) 1980.
Hulter til Bulter Op 18 1980.
Modulation Op 19 (harmonica, orchestra) 1980.
Symphony No 3 Op 21 1981.
A.B.C. or Adventure–Bedtime Story–Celebration Op 22 (accordion, orchestra) 1981.
Labyrint Op 25 1982.
Vildanden Op 26 (symphonic poem after Ibsen) 1982.
Telegram Op 27 (chamber orchestra) 1982.
Imagi Op 30 (cello, big band) 1983–4.
Patina Op 34 (cello, orchestra) 1984.
Symphony No 4 Op 35 1986.
Bulder og Brak Op 36 (symphonic band) 1986.
Lirumlarum Op 39 (2 rock bands, symphonic band, orchestra) 1987.
Det Bla Folket Op 40 1987.
Gilde (basset horn, small orchestra) 1988.
Over Fjorden Op 45 (symphonic band) 1989.
The Vanguardian Op 46 (jazz guitar, orchestra) 1989.
Soleis Op 49 (pan flute, orchestra) 1990.
Hip som harp (piano, jazz orchestra) 1991.
Adagio von Mozart 1991.
Q.E.D. (jazz orchestra) 1991.

Chamber/instrumental:

String Quartet Op 2 1970.
Woodwind Quintet Op 5 1973.
Whenever I Seem to Be Far Away Op 8 (image for electric guitar, strings, oboe, clarinet) 1974.
Unfinished Highballs (jazz quartet) 1976.
Keyboard Music Op 17 1980.
Concerto ECM (electric guitar, 8 cellos, keyboards, percussion) 1982.
Enigma (2 trumpets, horn, trombone, tuba) 1982.
10 x 10 Op 28 (improvisation ensemble) 1983.
Vidare Op 33 (acoustic/electric violin) 1984.
Crooner Songs Op 37 (clarinet, trumpet, violin, keyboards, percussion) 1986.
Troll Op 38 (electric guitar, flute, clarinet, violin, cello, keyboards) 1986.
Passion Op 41 (harpsichord/synthesizer, vibraphone, fretless electric bass guitar) 1987.
The Illuminator Op 42 (electric guitar, percussion, woodwinds, brass, double bass, keyboards) 1987.
Drommespinn Op 43 (oboe, 2 violins, viola, cello, double bass) 1988.
Arktik (electric guitar/alto flute, trumpet, synthesizer, double bass, percussion) 1988.
Sesam Op 47 (clarinet, trombone, grand piano/synthesizer) 1989.
Inntil Vidare Op 51 (violin, trumpet, electric guitar, bass guitar, percussion) 1990.

Vocal/choral:

Eternal Circulation Op 1 (soprano, chorus, orchestra) 1970.
Spegling Op 20 (mezzo-soprano, orchestra) 1981.
Ineo Op 29 (SATB chorus, electric guitar, orchestra) 1983. Recorded ECM 1389.
Vardoger Op 31 (unaccompanied male chorus) 1984.
Metamorphosis Op 32 (unaccompanied female chorus) 1984.
The Big Bang Op 48 (SA chorus, oboe, clarinet, piccolo trumpet, trumpet, 4 cellos, percussion, 2 electric guitars, synthesizer, electric bass guitar) 1990.

Opera:

Orfeus Op 4 1971.
Freden Op 10 1976.

Other:

Kjaere Maren (film score) 1975.
Undervannsfilm (music for television) 1978.
The Curse (incidental music for television) 1978.
Gruvestreiken (incidental music for television) 1981.
Slaget pa Stiklestad Op 24 (incidental music to Bjornson) 1982.
Syngspillet om Svartedauen (incidental music) 1984.

Large body of recorded jazz, rock and improvisation, mainly on ECM label.

PUBLICATIONS

On Rypdal: Nils Grinde, references in *Contemporary Norwegian Music, 1920–80*, Oslo, 1981.

* * *

Terje Rypdal is well-known as an adventurous electric guitarist whose playing career has run a course from early, Beatles-influenced bands, the pit band in an Oslo production of *Hair!*, accompaniment to the soft rock stylings of his wife Inger Lise Rypdal, to elaborately conceived jazz and improvisational settings. As a member of the quartet led by the very significant Norwegian saxophonist Jan Garbarek, Rypdal has been an important figure in the development of a distinctively "European" idiom in modern jazz; the same thing could also be said of Manfred Eicher's Munich-based recording label ECM, which mainly uses a studio in Oslo, and with whom Rypdal has recorded since the 1970s; his 1982 Concerto for electric guitar, cellos and keyboards, is dedicated to the label.

A growing interest in music deflected Rypdal from a career

in engineering. He studied at the Oslo Conservatory with the veteran modernist Finn Mortensen, but perhaps gained more from his association with the temporarily exiled American composer George Russell, whose *The Lydian Concept of Tonal Organization* is one of the greatest, yet least assimilated, of modern theoretical treatises with a greater impact on jazz players (of whom Russell is also one) than on "legitimate" composers.

Working with Russell undoubtedly gave Rypdal the confidence to ignore such invidious distinctions. Much of his output as serious composer has employed non-canonical ensembles, with a particular emphasis on his own instrument, which he plays with great fleetness and also with a virtuoso control of such devices as sustain, feedback and pedal treatments. His first numbered composition bore the marks of a deep interest in the profound sonorities of Mahler and Krzysztof Penderecki. Using tone-rows in the same heterodox manner as Mortensen, Rypdal has been able to invest music music of basically serial origin a much wider range of associations. He has frequently expressed amused dismay at some of the more banal associations inferred by the critics: "Nordic", "dark", "brooding", redolent of glaciers, midnight sun and the northern *morketid*. The truth is that he is deeply steeped in his country's culture—and now lives in his ancestral district, to the far west of Norway—but as a continuous and active tradition rather than as a set of iconic fixities. The improvisational element in his work, and a marked preference for contexts which place a soloist against a highly textured ensemble or in a *concertante* role with orchestra, suggest his jazz origins, but there is a deeper, technical concern which belies the work's occasionally programmatic and illustrative feel (as in those pieces he calls "images").

"Whenever I Seem to be Far Away," the most striking of these, has a deeply yearning quality, but it is also a powerfully effective exercise in melorhythms and countervailing harmonies, reminiscent like much of Rypdal's output of the Estonian Arvo Pärt, another Baltic composer who has thrown in his lot with the record company ECM and made a highly effective "cross-over" to a younger, more pop-biased audience. The later *Ineo*, where the guitar trails a beautifully arranged choral part, has much of the same impact.

Recent pieces, like the choral *The Big Bang* show an increasing interest in melody and in more strictly tonal methods. It does, though, still derive from very simple materials, as compressed as the title suggests, and is perhaps Rypdal's most ambitious score to date. Of the concertos, special mention must be made of *Undisonus*, a work which cost him considerable effort and which is now increasingly recognised as one of the most significant Norwegian compositions of the last two decades, and also of the earlier *Concerto for Double Bass and Orchestra*, written for Barre Phillips, another player whose roots are in improvisation. The piece may have influenced the British composer Gavin Bryars in his composition *By the Vaar*, a concerto for the jazz bassist Charlie Haden; certainly, Rypdal is accorded considerable respect by his fellow composers.

Rypdal has made it clear that composition is the main focus of his career. It is certainly arguable that being a performer on a modern, electric instrument of considerable timbral range has had an impact on his compositional style. Aside from that, though, Rypdal is deeply and intuitively conscious of the progressions of modern music: from medieval polyphony, through classical harmony, to serialism, to chance operations and pure sound, to the "new tonality." His music is neither reactionary nor self-consciously experimental, but is highly individual and seems certain to grow in significance as the "other" aspect of this very popular musician becomes more widely appreciated.

—Brian Morton

RZEWSKI, Frederic (Anthony). American. Born in Westfield, Massachusetts, 13 April 1938. Educated at Harvard University, Cambridge, Massachusetts (counterpoint under Randall Thompson, orchestration under Walter Piston), B.A., 1958; Princeton University, New Jersey (composition under Roger Sessions and Milton Babbitt), M.F.A., 1960; further composition under Luigi Dallapiccola, Florence, 1960–1; further study under Elliott Carter, 1963–5. Pianist; teacher, Cologne Courses for New Music, 1963–4, 1970; co-founder (with Richard Teitelbaum and Alvin Currar), Musica Elettronica Viva, Rome, 1966; resident in United States, 1971–6; professor of composition, Royal Conservatory of Music, Liège, from 1977; visiting professor of composition, Yale University, New Haven, Connecticut, 1984–5. Recipient: Fulbright Fellowship, 1960. Mailing address: 119 Via Marmorata, 00153 Rome, Italy.

Publishers: Zen-On, Tokyo; others.

Symphonies/orchestral:

Nature morte (small orchestra/25 instruments) 1965.
A Long Time Man (piano, orchestra) 1979.
Satyrica (jazz orchestra) 1983.
Una breve storia d'estate (3 flutes, small orchestra) 1983.

Chamber/instrumental:

Preludes (piano) 1957.
Poem (piano) 1959.
Sonata (2 pianos) 1960.
Study I (piano) 1960.
Study II: Dreams 1961.
Octet (flute, clarinet, trumpet, trombone, piano, harp, violin, double bass) 1961–2.
For Violin 1962.
Self-Portrait (solo performer/unspecified instrumentation) 1964.
Speculum Dianae (any 8 instruments) 1964.
Les Moutons de Panurge (unspecified instrumentation) 1969. Recorded Opus One 20.
Last Judgement (trombone or trombone choir) 1969.
Falling Music (amplified piano, tape) 1971.
What Is Freedom? (any 6 instruments) 1974.
Variations on No Place to Go But Around (piano) 1974.
The People United Will Never Be Defeated! (36 variations on "El pueblo unido jamas sera vencido"; piano) 1975. Recorded Vanguard VSD 71248.
Thirteen Instrumental Studies (unspecified instrumentation) 1977.
Four Pieces (piano) 1977. Recorded Vanguard VA 25001.
Song and Dance (flute, bass clarinet, double bass, vibraphone) 1977. Recorded Nonesuch H-71366.
Four North American Ballads (piano) 1978–9. Recorded (1 only) Vanguard VA 25001; complete on Nonesuch D-79006.

Squares (piano) 1979.
Winnsboro Cotton Mill Blues (2 pianos) 1980.
A Machine (piano) 1984.

Vocal/choral:

Requiem (chorus, ensemble; also arranged for narrator, male chorus, piano, organ, bells, bullroarer, Jew's harp, radio, percussion) 1963–7.
Impersonation (2 voices, 4 track tape, electronics) 1966.
Work Songs (textual compositions) 1967–9.
Jefferson (voice, piano; Declaration of Independence) 1970.
Old Maid (soprano, chorus; Clotiewitz) 1970.
Coming Together (speaker, low instruments, ensemble; letters of Attica prisoner) 1972. Recorded Opus One 20.
Attica (speaker, low instruments, ensemble; letters of Attica prisoner) 1972. Recorded Opus One 20.
Apolitical Intellectuals (voice, piano; Castillo) 1973.
Lullaby: God to a Hungry Child (voice, piano; Hughes) 1974.
No Progress Without Struggle (songs for voice and chamber orchestra; Douglass) 1974.
Nothing Changes (baritone, piano; de Chardin) 1976.
Le Silence des espaces infinis (women's or children's voices, instruments, orchestra, tape) 1980.
The Price of Oil (2 speakers, wind, percussion) 1980.
Antigone-Legend (voice, piano; Brecht) 1982.
Pablo Neruda in Exile (voice, piano) 1983.
The Invincible Persian Army (voice, prepared piano) 1984.

Other:

Composition for Two Players (tapes, 2 amplified glass panes) 1964.
Zoologischer Garten (electronics, tape) 1965.
Projector Piece (electronics, 2 groups, dancers, slides) 1966.
Portrait (dancer-singer, lighting, slides, film, tape, photoresistors) 1967.

Improvisational pieces with Musica Elettronica Viva, recorded on Mainstream MS-5002 and BYG Actuel 529326.

PUBLICATIONS

On Rzewski: W. Zimmermann, (interview) in *Desert Plants: Conversations with 23 American Musicians*, Vancouver, 1976; K. Terry, "FR and the Improvising Avant-Garde", in *Down Beat*, 46(1), 1978; J. Goldberg, "The Art of Political Process", in *Wax Paper*, 4(7), 1979; John Rockwell, "The Romantic Revival and the Dilemma of the Political Composer", in *All American Music: Composition in the Late Twentieth Century*, New York City, 1983.

* * *

Frederic Rzewski has made intermittently fascinating use of material from outside the normal boundaries of composed music, particularly when writing for the instrument on which he himself is a virtuoso performer, the piano. The best-known of these works is the remarkable series of 36 piano variations on the Chilean revolutionary song *The People United Will Never Be Defeated!*, a mammoth work which tests the capabilities of both performer and instrument to the utmost. The theme of that work is characteristic of the increasing degree of political committment evident in his work, as well as the increasingly romantic musical register in which it is framed. His early works tended to concentrate on studies for piano, drawing on extreme tonal and harmonic ideas, as in the *Sonata* for two pianos or *Study I*.

During the 1960s Rzewski was an overtly avant-garde experimentalist, an avenue he was able to explore in some depth in Europe. His work in those years expanded in all directions, taking in composition for larger forces and a wider spread of instruments, electronic music, including co-founding the Musica Electtronica Viva group, improvisation, multimedia projects, and compositions involving the use of spoken texts.

The best-known of these latter works is *Coming Together* for speaker and instrumental octet, written to commemorate the uprising at Attica prison in New York State the previous year. The composer used a text written by a prisoner subsequently killed by the authorities to great emotive effect, while the music set up a contradictory tension through utilising repetitive techniques and skillful but insistently avant-garde textural effects.

The pianist Ursula Oppens commissioned two major piano works which advanced the composer's growing sense of political commitment, *The People United Will Never Be Defeated!* and its sequel, *Four Pieces*, which did not draw upon any popular or folk melodies, but contained echoes of the Spanish flavour which had permeated its predecessor. By this stage, Rzewski seemed committed to a register which, while still highly complex, communicated on a more direct, visceral level than his previous work.

He expanded the idea of using a popular song as the basis for variation form into an orchestral work in *A Long Time Man* for piano and orchestra, based around the prison song "It Makes a Long Time Man Feel Bad." As with *The People United Will Never Be Defeated!*, Rzewski succeeds in maintaining the feel and ethos of the song even through the most far-reaching deviations from it, while still maintaining an acceptable level of internal structural consistency. The *Four North American Ballads* for piano, however, may be the most satisfyingly realised of his works in this vein.

A prolific but highly uneven composer whose work is characterised by great verve and intensity, his willingness to experiment with forms ranging from popular songs to avant-garde jazz often ended in blind alleys. Rzewski will not be seen as a major figure of his generation, but the best of his works deserve a continuing place in the repertoire.

—Kenny Mathieson

S

SAARIAHO, Kaija (Anneli). Finnish. Born in Helsinki, 14 October 1952. Educated at Steiner School; Helsinki University; Sibelius Academy (under Paavo Heininen), graduated 1981; Hochschule für Musik, Freiburg (under Brian Ferneyhough and Klaus Huber), 1981–2; courses in computer music, IRCAM, Paris, 1982. Married to Jean-Baptiste Barrière; 1 son. Freelance composer. Recipient: Finnish Government artist salary, 1984–6, 1988–92; Kranichsteiner Prize, Darmstadt, 1986; Prix Italia, 1988; Prix Ars Electronica, Austria, 1989. Mailing address: 8 rue Bernard de Clairvaux, 75003 Paris, France.

Publisher: Edition Wilhelm Hansen.

Symphonies/orchestral:

Verblendungen 1982–4; first performed Helsinki, 10 April 1984. Recorded BIS LP 307; Finlandia FACD 374.
Du Cristal 1990; first performed Helsinki, 5 September 1990.

Chamber/instrumental:

Canvas (flute) 1978; first performed Helsinki, 1982.
Yellows (horn, percussion) 1980; first performed Copenhagen, 1981.
Im Traume (cello, piano) 1980; first performed Reykjavik, 1982. Recorded JASELP 0010.
Laconisme de l'aile (flute) 1982; first performed Freiburg, 1 March 1983. Recorded BIS LP 307.
Jardin secret II (harpsichord, tape) 1984–6; first performed Helsinki, 12 July 1986; Paris, 21 January 1987. Recorded Finlandia FACD 357.
Lichtbogen (flute, percussion, piano, harp, 2 violins, viola, cello, double bass, live electronics) 1985–6; first performed Paris, 13 May 1986. Recorded Finlandia FACD 361; FACD 374.
Io (2 flutes, bass flute, 2 horns, trombone, tuba, 2 percussion, harp, piano/celeste, 2 violins, viola, cello, double bass, tape, live electronics) 1986–7; first performed Paris, 27 April 1987. Recorded Finlandia FACD 374.
Nymphea (Jardin secret III) (string quartet, live electronics) 1987; first performed New York, 20 May 1987.
Petals (cello, optional electronics) 1988; first performed Bremen, 18 May 1988.

Vocal/choral:

Bruden / The Bride (soprano, 2 flutes, percussion; Södergran) 1977; first performed Helsinki, 1977.
Jing (soprano, cello; Li Ch-ing Chao) 1979; first performed Helsinki, 1979.
Nej och Inte (No and Not) (women's quartet or choir; Bjorling) 1979.
Suomenkielinen sekakuorokappale (mixed choir) 1979; first performed Tampere, 1983.
Preludi-Tunnustus-Postludi (Prelude-Confession-Postlude) (soprano, prepared grand piano; Waltari) 1980; first performed Helsinki, 1980.
Study for Life (female voice, dancer, tape, light) 1980.
Kolme Preludia (Three Preludes) (soprano, organ; Finnish Bible) 1980; first performed Helsinki, 1980.
. . . sah den Vogeln (soprano, flute, oboe, cello, prepared piano) 1981; first performed Helsinki, 1982. Recorded BIS LP 307.
Ju lagre solen (soprano, flute, guitar; Schoultz) 1982, revised 1985 as *Adjo*; first performed Freiburg, 1 March 1983.
Du gick, flog (soprano, piano; Bjorling) 1982; first performed Lappeenranta, 1983.
Grammaire des rêves (soprano, alto, chamber ensemble) 1989; first performed Paris, 23 March 1989.

Other:

Study II for Life (tape) 1981; first performed Helsinki, 1981.
Vers le blanc (tape) 1982; first performed Darmstadt, 1982.
Three Interludes and Other Music for "Skotten in Helsingfors" (tape music for theatre) 1983; first performed Helsinki, 1983.
Kollisionen (tape for theatre) 1984; first performed Linz, 1984.
Jardin secret I (tape) 1984–5; first performed Helsinki, 1985.
Csokolom 1985; first performed Paris, 1985.
Suuri Illusioni (film music) 1985.
Collisions (tape for theatre) 1986; first performed Paris, 1986.
Piipaa (2 singers, tape, live electronics) 1987; first performed Helsinki, 1987.
Stilleben (radiophonic work for tape) 1987–8; first performed Helsinki, 5 July 1988. Recorded Finlandia FACD 374.

PUBLICATIONS

By Saariaho: "Shaping a Compositional Network with Computers", in *Proceedings of the 1984 International Computer Music Conference, Paris*, Berkeley, Computer Music Association, 1985; "Qualities and Functions of Musical Timbre" (with Stephen McAdams), in *Proceedings of the 1985 International Computer Music Conference, Vancouver*, Berkeley, Computer Music Association, 1985; "Timbre and Harmony: Interpolations of Timbral Structures", in *Contemporary Music Review*, 1987; "Timbre et harmonie" in *Le Timbre: Métaphores pour la composition*, edited by J. B. Barrière, Paris, 1988.

On Saariaho: Risto Neiminen, "Kaija Saariahos Besuche im Wunderland", in *Neuland*, 4, 1983–4, "At the Moment Computer and I Belong Together", in *Finnish Music Quarterly*, 3/4, 1985, and "A Portrait of KS", in *Nordic Sounds*, 1986; Jasper Beckman, "De storste begraensinger ligger i fantasien", in *Danske Musik Tidsskrift*, 4, 1984–5; TV1 Finland, "KS, savaltaja Pariisista", (film) 1986; Marc-Andre Dalbavie, "Pour sortir de l'avant-garde", in *Le Timbre: Métaphores pour la composition*, Paris, 1988; Lauri Otonski, "The Grammar of Dreams", in *Finnish Music Quarterly*, 3, 1989.

* * *

Kaija Saariaho's music may occasionally resemble an upper atmospheric phenomenon of late modernism, but it is a music that communicates very powerfully and, for all its adventurous use of computer technology and live electronics, does so with great humanity.

In *Lichtbogen*, a work inspired by the Aurora Borealis and Saariaho's first foray into computer-assisted composition, she underlines that characteristic synaesthesia by calling on the flautist (whose tones are progressively distorted and estranged) to recite single syllables from the English Metaphysical poet Henry Vaughan's "I saw Eternity the Other Night". Saariaho may be considered a metaphysical composer. Her ability to link quite heterogeneous ideas without violence and her unfailing ability to develop very elaborate scores by bringing specific technical decisions and strategies to bear on very simple materials. Most of *Lichtbogen* derives from a computer analysis of a long cello tone of increasing strength. This was then put into a computer-generated grid which affords her a whole range of harmonic and rhythmic refractions.

Writing about Saariaho's exquisite *Jardin secret I*, a computer generated work for tape, her compatriot Risto Nieminen characterised its essential quality as "orchestration in miniature". In places it recalls the extreme refinement of Webern's serialist technique where the tone-row is already giving place to individually articulated sounds of widely differing timbre. In *Verblendungen*, acknowledged as her first genuinely major work, she herself introduces the metaphor of refraction and develops a range of references to light a dark in a way which is not just metaphoric (joy, birth dazzlement, death, shadow, blindness) but also functional. Remarkably, *Jardin secret I* has virtually all the richness of the earlier orchestral piece; the distribution of speakers and musical events places the listener in the midst of a mysterious but somehow never entirely anomalous space, an experience broadly similar to recent experiments with "virtual reality". Saariaho has written two further works with the same title or subtitle, both of them involving instrumental performance, and it is in this direction that her work seems to be developing, extending the tonality and performative resources of existing instruments, rather than leaving them entirely behind.

This is evident in the recent *Petals*, in which the cello may be played untreated or with electronic interventions, but it stretches back as far as the very beautiful *Laconisme de l'aile* in which the solo flute is softly ring-modulated. Saariaho's very earliest work *Bruden / The Bride* and succeeding pieces like . . . *sah den Vogeln* and *Im Traume* are already concerned with the plasticity of sound, the desire to make it move with the almost instantaneous transitions and transformations of light. *Io* is built on the sonorities of bass and bass flute that are transformed in an altogether more forceful way; the title's associations of divine rape and of a distant astronomical mass orbiting round an even more massive, but gaseous and nebulous centre are never allowed to become programmatic, but they do give some sense of the power of the piece.

It is always virtually impossible to characterise any Finnish composer without some reference to Sibelius. In the early *Verblendungen*, Saariaho seemed to echo the great Finn's slow transformations of tempo and very distinctive use of repetition and scalar themes (which were in turn remarkably close to serialist conceptions). Saariaho is an heir in the sense that she has taken that conception one stage further; her sound palette is much purer, her orchestration increasingly miniaturised to the point where it enters the inner space of sub-harmonic and micro-tonal information. In overall impact, she is closer to Henri Dutilleux, whose exact balance of rapture and rigour she seems to share. If her work has a dreamlike quality, then, to use another critic's image, the "grammar" of those dreams has been very exactly worked. Saariaho is unquestionably one of the most significant European composers to emerge in the 1980s.

—Brian Morton

SAEVERUD, Harald (Sigurd Johan). Norwegian. Born in Bergen, 17 April 1897. Educated at Bergen Conservatory (under B. Holmsen), 1915–20; Musikhochschule, Berlin (under F.E. Koch), 1920–1; studied conducting under Clemens Krauss, Berlin, 1935. Member, executive committee, 1946–8, and member, council of experts, 1946–54, 1961–2, Norwegian Composer's Association. Recipient: Norwegian State Artist's Stipend, from 1953. Mailing address: N-5046 Radal, Norway.

Publisher: Norsk Musikforlag.

Symphonies / orchestral:

Early orchestral pieces performed, with Saeverud as conductor, Bergen 12 December 1912.

Symphony No 1 Op 2 1916–9; first performed Bergen, 1923.
Overtura appassionata Op 2b 1920.
Symphony No 2 in C Op 4 1922, revised 1934; first performed Bergen, 22 November 1923; revised version first performed Oslo, 1 April 1935.
Symphony No 3 in B♭ Op 5 1925–6; first performed Bergen, 25 February 1932.
Cello Concerto Op 7 1931.
Cinquante variazioni piccolo Op 8 1931.
Canto ostinato Op 9 1934, revised 1961.
Suite: Lucretia Op 10 (from incidental music to *The Rape of Lucretia*) 1936.
Symphony No 4 Op 11 1937; first performed Oslo, 9 December 1937.
Oboe Concerto Op 12 1938. Recorded Philips 411 081 1; NC 4481.
Divertimento No 1 Op 13 (flute, strings) 1939.
Syljetone [Peasant Heirloom Brooch] Op 14a / 2 (orchestration of piano piece) 1939.
Rondo amoroso Op 14a / 7 (orchestration of piano piece; oboe, bassoon, strings) 1941. Recorded NC 4913.
Bukken og gjetene Op 14a 1941.
Gjaetlevise-variasjoner / Variations on a Shepherd Song Op 15 1941.
Symphony No 5: Quasi una fantasia Op 16 1941; first performed Bergen, 6 March 1941.
Smaafuglvals / The Little Bird's Waltz Op 18a / 2 (orchestration of piano piece) 1941.
Siljuslaatten Op 17a (orchestration of piano piece) 1942.
Sinfonia dolorosa Op 19 1942.
Galdreslaatten Op 20 1942, revised 1955. Recorded NC 4913.
Romanza Op 23 (violin, orchestra) 1942.

Siljustolmarsj Op 22a/2 (orchestration of piano piece) 1943.
Kvernslaatt/Song of the Mill Wheel Op 21a/5 (orchestration of piano piece) 1943.
Den siste baa'nlat/Her Last Lullaby Op 22a/3 (orchestration of piano piece) 1943.
Kjempeviseslaatten/The Song of Struggle Op 22a/5 (orchestration of piano piece) 1943. Recorded Philips A631096 L; NC 4913.
Salme symfoni (Symphony No 7) Op 27 1944–5; first performed Bergen, 1 September 1945. Recorded Triola TNLP 2; Philips 6507 063; NC 3807.
Peer Gynt Op 28 1/2 (2 orchestral suites) 1947. Recorded Philips 6507 006; NC 3806; no 2 also on Philips 6578 101.
Twelve Orchestral Pieces from Peer Gynt Op 28 1947.
Piano Concerto Op 31 1948–50. Recorded Philips 6570 828; NC 4128.
Vade mors Op 38 1955, revised 1956.
Violin Concerto Op 37 1956.
Allegria (Sinfonia concertante) Op 39 1957.
Minnesota Symphony Op 40 1958; first performed Minneapolis, Minnesota, 18 October 1958.
Entrata regale Op 41 1960.
Ridder Blaaskjeggs mareritt/Sir Bluebeard's Nightmare Op 42 (suite, after ballet) 1960.
Haakonshallen Op 43 1961.
Bassoon Concerto Op 44 1963.
Symphony No 9 Op 45 1966. Recorded NC 4913.
Marcia solenne Op 46 1967–8.
Sonata jubilata Op 47 1969.
Fanfare and Hymn Op 48 1970.
Mozart-Motto-Sinfonietta Op 50 1972.

Chamber/instrumental:

Huldredans Jonsonknatt (piano) 1915.
Cinque capricci Op 1 1918–9.
Sonata in G Op 3 (piano) 1921.
Suite Op 6 (piano) 1931.
Lette stykker Op 14 (piano; includes *Siljetone*, *Gjaetle-vise*, *Rondo amoroso*) 1939. Recorded Triola TNLP 3; BIS LP 73; *Rondo amoroso* on HMV 7 PN 7.
Rondo amoroso Op 14/7 (wind quintet; arranged by A. Oscar Haugland) 1939.
Smaafuglvals Op 18 (piano) 1940.
Siljuslaatten Op 17 (piano) 1942. Recorded BIS LP 73.
Slaatter og stev fra Siljustol Opp 21, 22, 24, 25, 26 (5 piano suites) 1942–5. Recorded (Opp 22, 24) Triola TNLP 3; Opp 21, 22 on BIS LP 73; Opp 22/5 on HMV 7 PN 7.
Woodwind Quintet No 1 Op 21a 1943.
Romanza Op 23a (arrangement for violin, piano) 1946.
Peer Gynt Op 28 (piano transcriptions from incidental music) 1947.
Seks sonatiner Op 30 (piano) 1948–50. Recorded Philips 6507 004.
Twenty Little Duets Op 32 (2 violins; also arranged for winds) 1951.
Fuglefloyt-variasjoner/Bird Call Variations Op 36 (piano) 1968.
Grazietta Op 42 (piano; from *Ridder Blaaskjegg's mareritt*) 1970.
String Quartet No 1: Serenade of the Two Rivals Op 49 1970.
String Quartet No 2 1975.
Pastorale: Indian Summer Op 54 1978. Recorded Philips 6579 105; NC 6005.
String Quartet No 3 1978. Recorded VNP 0086 09.
Woodwind Quintet No 2 Op 56 1980.
Andante funebre Op 44/2 (cello, piano) 1981.

Vocal/choral:

Sjaa soli paa Anaripigg Op 35 (chorus) 1952. Recorded Philips 854 001 AY.
Three Peer Gynt Hymns Op 28/4 (voice, piano or organ) 1963.

Other:

Peer Gynt Op 28 (incidental music to Ibsen) 1947; first performed Oslo, 2 March 1948.
Olav og Kari Op 29 (incidental music to Bugge) 1948.
Kejser og Galilaeer Op 34 (incidental music to Ibsen) 1951.
Havratunet Op 33 (film music) 1954.
Ridder Blaskjeggs mareritt/Sir Bluebeard's Nightmare Op 42 (ballet) 1960; first performed Oslo, 4 October 1960.

PUBLICATIONS

On Saeverud: S. Lind, "HS", in *Nordisk musikkultur*, 4, 1952; M. Pergament, "HS", in *Nordens tidning*, 1, 1957; various, *HS [Festschrift]*, Oslo, 1967; Nils Grinde, in *Norsk musikhistorie*, Oslo, 1971; C. Baden, *HS 80 ar*, Oslo, 1977; Nils Grinde, in *Contemporary Norwegian Music, 1920–80*, Oslo, 1981.

* * *

Harald Saeverud has been the doyen of Norwegian musical life for so long now, and his works possessed of such a perennially youthful character, that it is easy to forget that his career stretches back to before World War I. His first three symphonies are as late Romantic as is to be expected from a young composer in Norway at the time, but his later, more mature works show a questing intellect ready to experiment. If he never progressed as far or as persistently into the avant-garde as Fartein Valen was to do (being subsequently overtaken easily by post-War developments), Saeverud nonetheless was quick to see possibilities in atonality, as in works such as the piano *Suite* or the *Cello Concerto*. By the mid-1930s however, in a work such as the *Oboe Concerto*, Saeverud had moved away from expressionism to adopt a more mainstream though still highly personal neo-classicism.

Saeverud's music acquired a deeper, more purposeful mission with the German occupation in 1940. A nationalistic, epic quality emerged reliant on increased polyphony decked out in more sombre hues, most obviously in the principal orchestral works of this period for which he is, perhaps, still best known: the Fifth, Sixth and Seventh symphonies (*Sinfonia quasi una fantasia*, *Sinfonia dolorosa*, *Salme symfoni*) and *Kjempeviseslaatten/The Song of Struggle*. This last was an arrangement of one of the pieces from his four suites of piano pieces, *Siljuslaatten* (named from the composer's country house), various numbers of which have reappeared in assorted arrangements by their composer from wind quintet to full orchestra. For the stage Saeverud composed the ballet *Ridder Blaskjeggs mareritt/Sir Bluebeard's Nightmare* in 1960, premiered in Oslo that same year. In 1935 he produced highly effective incidental music for a production of Shakespeare's *The Rape of Lucretia* which was well-received; the following year he culled from it a "Lucretia Suite" which has been hailed as one of his finest works. His incidental music to Ibsen's *Peer Gynt* caused still more of a stir given its graphic character, much more in keeping with the original play than either Grieg's chocolate-box fancies or Werner Egk's opera.

Basically a miniaturist, Saeverud, unlike Grieg, has been generally successful in larger forms, as in his nine symphonies, the *Allegria (Sinfonia concertante)* and his five concertos, of which that for piano has at times had considerable currency. Of the symphonies, the nationalistic Sixth and Seventh with their wartime associations and modern recordings have become widely known outside Norway; both are very effective single-movement designs and highly emotionally charged. The four-movement Ninth Symphony does not possess the same extra-musical inspiration and is more relaxed, standing in relation to its creator's output much as Prokofiev's Seventh does to his. Since 1970, Saeverud has restricted himself almost exclusively to chamber music, producing various solo works as well as two for wind quintet and three string quartets. One larger-scale work is his *Mozart-Motto-Sinfonietta*.

Saeverud's smaller pieces, though, perhaps best illustrate his essence. The charming "Siljustøl" pieces have deservedly travelled the world, but they are not isolated in his output: if his *Seks sonatiner* do not attempt to scale the heights of either Busoni's or even those of Sibelius, they are nonetheless a most original and important addition to the repertoire for the amateur. In them Saeverud composed short, charming, utterly modern music that does not alienate either by being written-down or possessed of undue technical demands: they are simple, not simplistic, minor gems.

Saeverud's stature as a composer is less easy to define than his music is to appreciate. He is of seminal importance to Norway, of course, as the link between Grieg and the 19th century on the one hand and the systematic atonality of Valen or the dodecaphony of composers such as Finn Mortensen and Klaus Egge on the other. In falling between these two stools his music has tended to be overlooked or dismissed as outmoded, but there can be no denying Saeverud's consummate craftsmanship, nor his prime importance to Norwegian musical life.

—Guy Rickards

SALLINEN, Aulis. Finnish. Born in Salmi, Lake Ladoga [now part of Soviet Russia], 9 April 1935. Educated at Sibelius Academy, Helsinki (composition under Aare Merikanto and Joonas Kokkonen), 1955–60. Teacher of composition, Sibelius Academy, Helsinki, from 1960; administrator, Finnish Radio Symphony Orchestra, 1960–70; secretary, later chair, Finnish Composers Association; board member, Finnish National Opera; Professor of Arts, life appointment by Finnish government, from 1981. Recipient: 1st prize (for *Symphony No 1*), City of Helsinki competition to mark opening of Finlandia House, 1971; Wihuri International Sibelius Prize (jointly with Krzysztof Penderecki), 1983. Mailing address: Ruueberginkatu 37 A 28, SF-00100 Helsinki, Finland.

Publishers: Fazer; Novello.

Symphonies/orchestral:

Two Mythical Scenes 1956.
Concerto for Chamber Orchestra Op 3 1960; first performed Helsinki, November 1960.
Variations (cello, orchestra) 1960–1.
Mauermusik Op 7 1962. Recorded Decca SXL 6431; Finlandia FA 312.
Variations Op 8 1963; first performed as *(Fourteen) Juventas Variaatiota*, June 1963.
Metamorphoses (piano, chamber orchestra) 1964.
Violin Concerto Op 18 1968.
Some Aspects of Peltoniemi Hintrik's Funeral March Op 19 (string orchestra; based on *String Quartet No 3*) 1969.
Chorali Op 22 (wind band) 1970. Recorded BIS LP 41.
Symphony No 1 Op 24 1971; first performed Helsinki, December 1971. Recorded BIS LP 41.
Symphony No 2: Symphonic Dialogue Op 29 (solo percussion, orchestra) 1972; first performed Norrkoping, Sweden, February 1973. Recorded Caprice CAP 1073.
Symphony No 3 Op 35 1975; first performed Helsinki, April 1975.
Chamber Music I Op 38 (string orchestra) 1975; first performed Helsinki, August 1975. Recorded BIS LP 46.
Chamber Music II Op 41 (alto flute, string orchestra) 1976; first performed Helsinki, October 1976. Recorded BIS LP 64.
Cello Concerto Op 44 1976; first performed Lucerne, August 1977.
Symphony No 4 Op 49 1979; first performed Turku, 9 August 1979.
Prelude: Shadows Op 52 (incorporates material from the opera *The King Goes Forth to France*) 1982; first performed Washington, D.C., 30 November 1982.
Symphony No 5: Washington Mosaics Op 57 1985; first performed Washington, D.C., 10 October 1985.
Chamber Music III: The Nocturnal Dances of Don Juanquixote Op 58 1986; first performed Naantali, 15 June 1986.
From a Schoolchild's Diary Op 62 (suite for double children's orchestra/violins, cellos) 1989; first performed Helsinki, August 1990.
Sunrise Serenade Op 63 (2 trumpets in B, piano, string orchestra) 1989; first performed Naantali, 13 June 1990.
Symphony No 6: From a New Zealand Diary 1990; first performed Napier, New Zealand, 6 September 1990.

Chamber/instrumental:

String Quartet No 1 1958.
String Quartet No 2: Canzona 1960.
Serenade (2 wind quartets) 1963.
Elegy for Sebastian Knight Op 10 (cello) 1964. Recorded Scandia SLP 575; BIS LP 64; Da Camera Magna SM 93710.
Quattro per quattro Op 12 (oboe or flute or clarinet, violin, cello, harpsichord) 1965. Recorded BIS LP 64.
Cadenze Op 13 (violin) 1965. Recorded Scandia SLP 575; BIS LP 18.
Notturno Op 14 (piano) 1966. Recorded EMI 5E063 34283.
String Quartet No 3 Op 19 1966. Recorded EMI 5E063 34330; BIS LP 64; Nonesuch K9791111.
Quatre Etudes Op 21 (violin, piano) 1970. Recorded RCA PL 40058.
Chaconne Op 23 (organ) 1970. Recorded BIS LP 12.
String Quartet No 4: Quiet Songs Op 25 1971. Recorded Scandia SLP 575.
Sonata Op 26 (cello) 1971. Recorded Scandia SLP 575.
Metamorfora Op 34 (cello, piano) 1974.
Canto Op 36 (violin) 1975.
Ritornello Op 37 (violin) 1975.
String Quartet No 5: Pieces of Mosaic Op 54 1983; first performed Helsinki, 18 July 1984.
Fanfare Op 59 (brass, percussion) 1986; first performed Houston, Texas, 17 May 1986.

Echoes from a Play Op 66 (oboe, string quartet) 1990; first performed Ravinia, South Dakota, 30 July 1991.
From a Swan Song (cello, piano) 1991; first performed Helsinki, November 1991.

Vocal/choral:

Three Lyrical Songs About Death (baritone, male chorus, orchestra) 1962.
Suita Grammaticale Op 28 (children's chorus, chamber orchestra) 1971.
Four Dreams Songs Op 30 (soprano, orchestra; Haavikko, Binham) 1972.
Songs from the Sea Op 33 (unaccompanied children's choir; folk songs, composer's sons) 1974. Recorded Deutsche Grammophon DGG 2538 812; Finlandia FA 327.
Simppeli Simme ja Hamppari Hamme / Simple Simon and his Dog Op 40 (baritone, piano) 1978. Recorded BIS LP 88.
Die Irae Op 47 (soprano, bass, male chorus, orchestra; Turtiainen) 1978; first performed Budapest, 15 October 1979.
Man, Is-Nothing, Is-No-One Op 48 (baritone, piano; Haavikko, Binham) 1978.
Song Around a Song Op 50 (unaccompanied children's chorus; 4 folk songs in Italian, Japanese, Finnish, English) 1980; first performed Wiesbaden, 16 May 1981.
Suite: Rauta-Aika / The Iron Age Op 55 (soprano, children's chorus, mixed chorus, orchestra; *Kalevala* / television series *The Iron Age*) 1983; first performed Helsinki, 20 March 1985.
The Beaufort Scale Op 56 (humoresque for unaccompanied SATB chorus; wind velocity scale) 1984; first performed Helsinki, June 1984.
Anthem for Ants (unaccompanied SSA chorus) 1988; first performed Tapiola, 16 April 1988.

Opera:

Ratsumies / The Horseman 1973–4; first performed Savonlinna, 17 July 1975. Recorded Finlandia FA 101 LP3.
Punainen Viiva / The Red Line Op 46 (Kianto) 1978; first performed Helsinki, 30 November 1978; English version (translated Stephen Oliver) first performed London, 14 June 1979. Recorded Finlandia FA 102.
Kuningas Lahtee Ranskaan / The King Goes Forth to France Op 53 (Haavikko) 1983; first performed Savonlinna, 7 July 1984; English version (translated Stephen Oliver and Erkki Arni) first performed Santa Fe, New Mexico, 26 July 1986; German version first performed Kiel, 6 April 1986.
Kullervo Op 61 (*Kalevala*) 1988; first performed Los Angeles, February 1992.

Other:

Variations sur Mallarmé (ballet) 1967; first performed Helsinki, 1968.
Midsommernatten (ballet to music from *Symphony No 3*) 1984; first performed Atlanta, Georgia, 29 March 1984.
Himlens hemlighet / Secret of the Heavens (ballet to music from *Symphonies 1, 3, 4*) 1986; broadcast Swedish Television, 20 October 1986.

PUBLICATIONS

On Sallinen: Antony Hodgson, *Scandinavian Music: Finland and Sweden*, Cranbury, New Jersey and London, 1984.

* * *

Aulis Sallinen is one of the foremost post-World War II Finnish composers, and he typifies his generation's struggle to move away from the potent influence of Sibelius, which had tended to stunt the development of a number of the most talented Scandinavian musicians who reached maturity during the inter-war years. In some of his works, even fairly mature pieces like *Chorali*, the influence of Sibelius is very clear, but Sallinen has been able to avoid becoming overwhelmed by this tradition; although he is by no means a trailblazer, he has kept abreast of the latest trends, and his writing is, in consequence, enriched by serial and atonal harmonic procedures, as well as by an advanced and sophisticated style of instrumentation and a marked flair for musico-dramaticism.

The earliest surviving works, dating from the late 1950s and early 1960s are basically serial compositions, though they certainly do not subscribe to the prevailing influences of that time: there is none of the obsessively ordered "integral serialism" of Boulez and other high-profile musicians who had taken their cue from Webern. Neither does Sallinen infuse his serial writing with the hothouse emotionalism of Alban Berg. His pieces are, in the main, relaxed and discursive, even introspective.

During the later 1960s, Sallinen joined the (mostly unconnected) international band of composers who had become dissatisfied with the prognosis for serial music and were seeking ways to renew tonality. Sallinen's conversion was not as dramatic as some and does not appear to have been directly stimulated by external events (as it had been, for example, in the case of George Rochberg). One of the best instances of Sallinen's changing approach at this time is the Third Quartet. This piece was part of the composer's response to an invitation to present his work in Swedish schools, so, naturally, accessibility was an important consideration. He chose to write the Quartet in continuous variation form, based upon a popular Finnish folk violin melody. This theme is never submerged during the variation processes and Sallinen ensures that it is immediately imprinted upon the listener's consciousness: the opening statement is given to first violin and cello, spaced two octaves apart. This unusual sonority was adopted at times by Bartók (not just in orchestral or string quartet contexts—consider the opening solo of his Third Piano Concerto) and the relationship is strengthened because Sallinen reuses other most Bartókian devices for distinguishing his theme, directing that it should be played without vibrato and with slightly different bowings in the two instruments.

Sallinen's music has focused strongly upon traditional genres—opera, string quartet, concerto and symphony. His status has been established, in substantial measure, by the operas and symphonies, which followed the transitional works of the 1960s, in which his style was honed largely through the writing of chamber music. The First Symphony is written in a rather loose harmonic idiom which, despite its emphatically tonal opening and conclusion (and some subject material which has decidedly tonal implications), tends to make its points through isolated effects; in harmonic terms, these include synthetic chords and tone clusters and passages of atonality; a homogeneous approach is not apparent. The Second Symphony, which Sallinen also called "Symphonic Dialogue", is a discourse between solo percussion and the main orchestra and belongs more to the confrontational concerto tradition than to the symphonic mainstream. It is interesting to compare the concept of this piece with the finale of Shostakovich's Second Violin Concerto.

In view of his instinctively theatrical response to the abstract dramatic possibilities of the "symphonic dialogue" format, the success of Sallinen's first opera, *Ratsumies / The Horseman*, should not, perhaps, have occasioned great surprise. The subject was a Symbolist drama, charged with many layers of concealed meaning, which afforded him an excellent chance to create and manipulate an evocative tapestry of motifs. These gifts are seen to no less effect in the more realistic context of the next opera, *Punainen Viiva / The Red Line*.

The international recognition which came to Sallinen in the mid-1970s produced an upsurge in requests for high-profile commissions, but these have not perceptibly altered the composer's approach. The Fourth Symphony, emotionally one of the best-realised and potent works he has completed to date, is entirely consistent with the dark instrumentation and quirky harmonic language of its predecessors; the symphony is punctuated with violent rhythmical interludes and these can even convey a kind of savage humour. The link with the Second Symphony is clear and, again, parallels are also possible with Shostakovitch (not least his Fourth Symphony). Sallinen's third opera, *Kuningas Lahtee Ranskaan / The King Goes Forth to France* and the independent orchestral piece, *Prelude: Shadows*, which has obvious thematic links with the opening of Act III, are further evidence of his motivic control and mastery of sombre tonal palettes.

—Paul Horner

SALMENHAARA, Erkki. Finnish. Born in Helsinki, 12 March 1941. Educated at Sibelius Academy, Helsinki (composition under Joonas Kokkonen), graduated 1963; University of Helsinki (musicology, aesthetics, and theoretical philosophy), Ph.D., 1970. Associate professor of musicology, University of Helsinki, since 1975; chair, Society of Finnish Composers, 1974–6. Mailing address: Telakkakatu 1 C, SF-00150 Helsinki, Finland.

Publishers: Fazer; Jasemusikkii; Ylioppilaskunnan Laulajat; Brahe Djakanar; Sulasol.

Symphonies / orchestral:

Symphony No 1: Crescendi 1962, revised 1963; first performed 11 January 1963.
Symphony No 2 1963, revised 1966; first performed Helsinki, 17 January 1964.
Symphony No 3 1963, revised 1966; first performed Turku, 5 December 1963.
Le Bateau ivre 1965, revised 1966; first performed Helsinki, 1 June 1966.
Suomi—Finland 1966; first performed Helsinki, 31 October 1967.
BFK-83 1967.
Suomi-Finland ("unsymphonic poem") 1967.
La Fille en mini-jupe 1967; first performed Helsinki, 13 February 1968.
Canzonetta per archi (string orchestra) 1971; first performed Savonlinna, 10 July 1972. Recorded Ta 7712; UDCM 93.
Illuminations (after Rimbaud) 1971.
Symphony No 4: Nel mezzo del cammin di nostra vita (after Dante) 1971–2; first performed Helsinki, 13 October 1972.
Concerto for Horn and Orchestra 1973; first performed Oslo, 3 October 1974.
Canzona per piccola orchestra 1974; first performed Kuopio, 26 July 1974.
Poema (violin or viola or cello, string orchestra) 1975; first performed Graz, Austria, 28 May 1976. Recorded Fuga 3054.
Intrada 1975.
Introduction and Chorale (Organ Concerto) 1978; first performed Helsinki, 1 December 1978,
Lamento (string orchestra) 1979; first performed Kokkola, 26 August 1979. Recorded TA 8111.
Concerto for Two Violins and Orchestra 1980; first performed Helsinki, 21 September 1982.
Adagietto 1981; broadcast Finnish Radio, 23 December 1982.
Adagio (oboe, string orchestra) 1981; first performed Porvoo, 13 June 1982.
Concerto for Cello and Orchestra 1983–7; first performed Lahti, 25 March 1988.
Sinfonietta (string orchestra) 1985; first performed Kokkola, 16 February 1986.

Chamber / instrumental:

Seventeen Small Pieces (piano) 1957–60.
Sonata No 1 (cello, piano) 1960, revised 1969; first performed Helsinki, 1960.
Adagio (violin or cello, piano, based on *Sonata*) 1961.
String Trio 1961.
Elegy I (3 flutes, 2 trumpets, double bass) 1963; broadcast Finnish Television, 23 May 1964.
Pan and Echo (4 suspended cymbals, tam-tam; amplified) 1963.
Composition (string quartet) 1963.
Composition (violin, clarinet, guitar, percussion) 1963.
Elegy II (2 string quartets) 1963; first performed Helsinki, 8 June 1964.
Wind Quintet 1964; first performed Hasselby, Sweden, 28 August 1964. Recorded BIS LP 24.
Toccata (organ) 1965; first performed Weimar, 21 October 1965.
Elegy III (cello) 1965; first performed Helsinki, 20 February 1966.
Sonata No 1 (piano) 1965–6; broadcast Finnish Radio, 1966. Recorded EMI SE 063 35065.
Elegy IV (viola) 1967; first performed Helsinki, 1 November 1967.
Prelude, Pop Tune and Fugue (flute) 1967; first performed Stockholm, 31 March 1968. Recorded LRLP 4; BIS LP 88.
Prelude—Interlude—Postlude (organ) 1969; broadcast Finnish Radio 1970. Recorded FA 325.
Etude (harpsichord) 1969.
Trois Scènes de nuit (violin, piano) 1970; first performed Stockholm, 11 April 1970.
Quartet (flute, violin, viola, cello) 1971; first performed Copenhagen, 1972.
Ricercata (organ) 1971; first performed Lahti, 9 August 1977. Recorded LOF V 77/1–2.
Leggenda (harp) 1971; first performed Helsinki, 5 March 1972.
Sonatine: And the Fire and the Rose Are One (2 violins; after Eliot) 1972; first performed Amsterdam, 31 March 1973.
Kocab (piano) 1972; first performed Helsinki, 5 November 1972.
Sonata No 2 (piano) 1973; first performed Hasselby, Sweden, 30 September 1973. Recorded EMI SE 063 35065.
Sonata No 3 (piano) 1975; first performed Helsinki, 13 October 1976.
Thème et variations sur le nom Erik Tawaststjerna (piano)

1976; first performed Kuopio, 11 February 1977.
String Quartet No 1 1977; first performed Jyvaskyla, 29 June 1978.
Oiseaux de nuit (violin, piano) 1977. Recorded RCA PL 40058.
Sonatine (piano) 1979; first performed Helsinki, 22 October 1979.
Sonata No 4 (piano) 1980; broadcast Finnish Radio, 13 July 1982.
Little Suite (piano) 1980.
Adagio (reduction for oboe, piano or organ) 1981. Recorded ML 10.06.
Ballade and Inventio (kantele or harp) 1981.
Sonatina (flute, guitar) 1981.
Sonata (violin, piano) 1982; broadcast Finnish Radio, 11 September 1983.
Sonata No 2 (cello, piano) 1982; first performed Helsinki, 26 June 1986.
Suite (accordion) 1983; first performed Ikaalinen, 12 June 1983.
Sonatella (piano—4 hands) 1983. Recorded FACD 363.
Introduction and Allegro (clarinet or viola, cello, piano) 1985.
Introduction and Toccata (organ) 1985; first performed Helsinki, 9 April 1986.

Vocal/choral:

Joulun kellot (voice, piano; Haahti) 1954, revised 1981; broadcast Finnish Radio, 4 January 1981.
Three Japanese Songs (voice, piano; Takahashi, Miki, Yamamura) 1960, revised 1964. Recorded BIS LP 88.
Lenore (voice, piano; Kosonen) 1962–4; first performed Helsinki, 21 March 1965.
Kuun kasvot/The Face of the Moon (unaccompanied mixed chorus; Saarikoski) 1964. Recorded Philips 839 705 Y; BIS LP 4.
Catullus amans (unaccompanied male voice chorus; Catullus) 1964; first performed Helsinki, 24 May 1965.
Requiem profanum (soprano, alto, baritone, organ or piano or string orchestra; Baudelaire, Espriu, Bible) 1968–9; first performed Helsinki, 24 May 1969.
Syyskuu Romaniassa (voice, piano; Saarikoski) 1970; first performed Helsinki, 21 September 1970.
Da leidet der Hase im Walde not (unaccompanied male voice chorus; Nystrom) 1971; first performed Turku, 18 February 1972.
Satumaisessa metsassa (voice, piano; Juhola) 1974; first performed Helsinki, 27 October 1974.
Missa profana (unaccompanied mixed chorus; Oksala) 1977; first performed Tampere, 3 June 1977.
Selene (voice, piano; Saarikoski) 1977; broadcast Finnish Radio, 25 October 1978.
Kaksi Kiven runoa (unaccompanied mixed chorus; Kivi) 1984; first performed Helsinki, 10 October 1984. Recorded KPLP 114.
Kolme Kantelettaren runoa (unaccompanied male voice chorus; Kanteletar) 1984; first performed Helsinki, 27 October 1985.
Kaukametsa (children's or female chorus, string orchestra; Kivi) 1984; first performed Helsinki, 26 October 1984. Recorded FGLP 1038.
Tva dikter av J.L. Runeberg (unaccompanied mixed chorus) 1985; first performed Helsinki, 23 April 1986.
Tre dikter av J.L. Runeberg (unaccompanied male voice chorus) 1985.
Kakso laulua Aleksis Kiven runoihin (unaccompanied female or children's chorus; Kivi) 1985.

Opera:

Portugalin nainen/The Portuguese Woman (after Musil) 1970–2; first performed Helsinki, 4 February 1976.

Other:

Information Explosion (tape) 1967. Recorded LREP 103.

PUBLICATIONS

By Salmenhaara: "Musikalisk avantgardism", in *Hufvudstadsbladet*, 31 August 1961; "Konstnarligt sokande kannetecknar modern tonkunst", in *Hufvudstadsbladet*, 6 December 1963; "Erik Bergman, Joonas Kokkonen, Tauno Marttinen, Erkki Kurenniemi och hans studio", in *Nutida Musik*, 5, 1963–4; "Sibelius and More Recent Finnish Music", in *Look at Finland*, Spring 1965; "Nagra elegiska anmarkningar", in *Nutida Musik*, 1–2, 1965–6; "Joonas Kokkonen, romantisoituva klassiko", in *Sumomen musiikin vuosikirja*, 1967–8, reprinted in Swedish in *Bilaga till Nomus Nytt*, 5, 1969; *Vuosisatamme musiiki*, Helsinki, 1968; *Sointuanalyysi*, Helsinki, 1968; *Das musikalische Material und seine Behandlung bei Ligeti*, Helsinki and Regensburg, 1969; *Soinnutus*, Helsinki, 1970; *Tapiola* [commentary on Sibelius], Helsinki, 1971; (editor) *Miten savellyskseni ovat syntyneet*, Keuruu, 1976; (editor) *Juhlakirja Erik Tawaststjernalie 10.X.1976*, Keuruu, 1976; "Uber die Anwendung der Volksmusik in der neueren finnischen Kunstmusik", in *Hamburger Jahrbuch der Musikwissenschaft*, 4, 1980; *Tutkielmia Brahmsin sinfonioista*, Hamburg, 1981; *Erik Tawaststjerna als Sibelius-Forscher*, Hamburg, 1981; "The Ostrobothnians—An Opera About Freedom", in *Finnish Music Quarterly*, 2, 1982; *Jean Sibelius: Elamakerta*, Helinski, 1984; "Uuno Klami ja Kaleval", in *Synkooppi*, 20, 1985, in English in *Finnish Music Quarterly*, 1–2, 1985; *Leevi Madetoja: Elamakerta*, Helsinki, 1987; (with Seija Lappalainen) *Leevi Madetojan teokset—The Works of Leevi Madetoja*, Jyvaskyla, 1987; "Toivo Kuula vokaalisaveltajana", in *Synkooppi*, 27, 1987, in English as "Toivo Kuula–Finland's Tragic Romantic", in *Finnish Music Quarterly*, 2, 1987; "Jean Sibelius—Symphonist", in *Finnish Music Quarterly* (Japanese version), 1987.

On Salmenhaara: Kaj Chydenius, "ES", in *Nutida Musik*, 5, 1963–4; Ramin-Jack Dorsch, "Eine neue finnische Oper", in *Neue Zurcher Zeitung*, 17 March 1976; Henri-Claude Fantapie, "Quelques Réflexions pour servir à une interprétation de l'oeuvre d'ES", in *Boréales*, 9–10, 1978; likka Oramo, "ES", in *Musik in Geschichte und Gegenwart*, 16, 1979; Mikki Heinio, "Aikamme suomalaiset saveltajat ja heidan taustansa", in *Musiiki*, 1, 1981, in Swedish as "Var tids finlandska tonsattare och deras bakgrun", in *Hameenlinna*, 1986; Outi Jyrhama, "Behandlingen av tonala element i pianosonat nr 2 H-dur av ES", in *Nordiska musikforskarkongressen*, 8, 1978, and "Nakokulma tyylilliseen synteesiin—ES neljannen pianosonaatin rakenneperiaatteista", in *Musiikki*, 1–2, 1985; Timo Makinen and Seppo Nummi, *Musica fennica*, Helsinki, 1985; Jack Briece, "Today's Finnish Composers", in *Musical America*, May 1986; Juhani Nuorvala, "Minimalism in Finland", in *Finnish Music Quarterly*, 3–4, 1987; Gunnar Sjoqvist, "Mote med finlandsk tonsattare—ES", in *Musikrevy*, 2, 1987.

* * *

Erkii Salmenhaara is internationally recognized both as a lucid musicologist who has specialized in the work of his two teachers, Joonas Kokkonen and György Ligeti, and as a symphonic composer. In his native Finland he is also regarded as a music critic and composer of chamber works titled "Elegy". In the early 1960s, Salmenhaara became one of the Finnish avant-garde. While his early works incorporate polytonality, his symphonies are more akin to the post-Webern school, with the obvious influences of his teachers and the contemporary Polish school seen in the use of parallel triads, long static elements and pedal points.

Salmenhaara's first three symphonies demonstrate an evolution of the composer's style, although the version of the Second Symphony normally heard dates from that of the Third. Salmenhaara shows a progressive interest in linear polyphony while increasingly applying the techniques of Ligeti as well as his particular answer to the legacy of Edgar Varèse and the Polish school. Salmenhaara's individualistic use of free dodecaphonic lines is heard most clearly in the fugue which opens the Second Symphony. The three long movements which constitute the Third Symphony consist of long, complex, overlapping melodic lines contrapuntally set against each other. Salmenhaara's Second and Third symphonies both have main motives which, being essentially based on Sibelius's wailing-songs, frequently centre around the slow, descending figures which permeate much of the works. With little active argument, Salmenhaara's compositions of the mid-1960s tend to rely upon colouristic interest while the slow-moving pieces progress rather than evolve.

Triadic blocks are used with great structural importance in the orchestral work *Le Bateau ivre*. This leads to Salmenhaara's first work where the inevitable tonal implications that result from triadic use force him to use his earlier techniques upon more tonal areas. The underpinning of Salmenhaara's atonal thinking had begun. Meanwhile, the employment of a pseudo-Ligeti style in so many works eventually led to a stylistic crisis. In the 1970s Salmenhaara made an about-face by turning against complexity and incorporating simplistic and even tonal ideas. While being obsessed with sound itself and with the inherent quality of intervals and individual timbres, and wishing to rid his style of all unnecessary elements, Salmenhaara strove to include many different styles and historical idioms. The resulting, more tonal, system is based upon an idiosyncratic use of diatonic triads while exploiting the composer's lyrical and somewhat romantic viewpoint rather than continuing in the avant-garde. Salmenhaara's themes were soon to be divided into motives and small rhythmic cells which are repeated frequently, reminiscent of, if not entirely following, the Minimalist school. Although the first three symphonies were composed according to Ligeti's compositional principles, Fourth Symphony and Fourth Piano Sonata were written in his new tonally based style which acquired the criticism "neo-simplistic". Thematic and motivic material in the Fourth Symphony again suggests the influence of Sibelius.

Just as Salmenhaara's opera, *Portugalin nainen / The Portuguese Woman*, has historical associations, so his works of the early 1970s frequently contain musical quotations from pre-romantic eras. The expansive *Requiem profanum* and the opera are often simple to appreciate because of their long-term melodic structure, where easily recognised themes almost disintegrate into their equally melodic successors. Eventually, Salmenhaara turned slightly from this over-simplification. His more recent works involve far more complicated motives which often produce ideas in a work which are not developed or even recapitulated. His treatment of tonality, however, has become much more traditional.

—Malcolm J. Hill

SANDSTRÖM, Jan. Swedish. Born in Lycksele, Vasterbotten, 25 January 1954. Early interest in rock music; educated at State University of Music, Piteå, 1976–8; Royal Academy of Music, Stockholm (composition and theory under Gunnar Bucht and Brian Ferneyhough), 1978–84. Married Mona Oström, 3 August 1989. Lector of Music, 1982–9, and professor of music, since 1989, State University of Music, Piteå. Recipient: Ernst Johnsson grant, 1984; Tage Book grant, 1984; Sten Broman grant, 1986; Christ Johnson prize, 1989. Mailing address: Vastra Pilgatan 18, S95136 Lulea; or State University of Music, Box 210, S94125 Piteå, Sweden.

Publishers: Nodriska Musikforlaget/Chester Music, Nybrog. 3, S11434 Stockholm; Editions Reimers, Box 150 30, S16115 Bromma; Sveriges Korforbund, Box 140 52, S10440 Stockholm, Sweden.

Symphonies/orchestral:

Era 1982; first performed Reykjavik, 1982.
Formant Mirrors 1983; first performed Oslo, 1983.
Acintyas 1986; first performed Stockholm, 1987.
Trumpet Concerto 1987, substantially revised 1990–1; first performed Gavle, 1987; revised version first performed Belfast, 1991.
Trombone Concerto 1988; first performed Stockholm, 1989. Recorded BIS.
Indri / Cave Canem 1988; first performed Stockholm, 1989.

Chamber/instrumental:

Campane in campi aperti (piano) 1984; first performed Italy, 1985. Recorded Caprice CAP 2021.
Strange Matter (accordion, string quartet) 1985; first performed Germany, 1986.
Short Ride on a Motorbike (trombone, tape) 1989; first performed Umea, 1990.

Vocal/choral:

Tva Korpoem (mixed choir) 1982; first performed Piteå, 1982.
Tva Sonnevisonetter (soprano, flute) 1987; first performed Helsinki, 1988.
Smaa Klanger: en rost (after Goran Sonnevi) 1990; broadcast Swedish television, 1991.

Other:

En Herrgardssagen (ballet; orchestra) 1989; broadcast Swedish television, 1989.

PUBLICATIONS

On Sandström: I. Karkoff, "En upptacksresa", in *Nutida Musik*, 1, 1985–6; J. Jeverud, "JS", in *Nutida Musik* 1, 1988–9.

* * *

Jan Sandström grew up close to Stockholm were he met and played guitar in the same rock band as Anders Hillborg. It was hearing the work of Ingvar Lidholm which awoke in him the desire to develop his own compositions and, at the age of 22, he embarked upon his first serious music studies at the State University of Music at Piteå in northern Sweden. This was followed by six years of compositional and theoretical studies at the Royal Academy of Music in Stockholm where his teachers included Gunnar Bucht (a pupil of Karl-Birger Blomdahl and Max Deutsch) a stylistic traditionalist, and Brian Ferneyhough, a radical complexicist. This was a period of great upheaval in contemporary music and between the two poles represented by his teachers Sandström was allowed considerable latitude: indeed his earlier works with their gradual shifts of detailed rhythmic and tonal patterns show more discernible influence from the American minimalists than from either Bucht or Ferneyhough.

Era for orchestra was the first work to bring him recognition and this and his next large work *Formant Mirrors* for solo septet and string orchestra are examples of what the composer terms "slow-motion music"—shimmering studies in harmonies and transparent textures. Since *Era* Sandström has completed nine further orchestral scores (only seven of these works are still acknowledged) and these form the very heart of his catalogue. It must be unimaginable to British composers of the same generation that economic circumstances can allow a young composer to develop orchestral writing skills so thoroughly, but Sandström obviously recognises the orchestra as his milieu and has revelled in the process of exploiting its potential.

In the late 1980s Sandström was fortunate enough to write concertos for the two most outstanding brass players (arguably in the world, not just in Sweden) of his generation: Håkan Hardenberger and Christian Lindberg. The *Trumpet Concerto* was written in 1987 for the Gävleborg Symphony Orchestra but heavily revised in 1990–1 when the premiere of the new version was given by Hardenberger with the Ulster Orchestra at the Belfast Sonorities Festival. This is far from "slow-motion music". Sudden dynamic changes and pulsating rhythms bring a new sense of drama to his style which is heightened by the use of the orchestra as an extension of the trumpet's resonance and the active and interactive roles played by the solo and orchestral trumpets. In the *Trombone Concerto* theatre is still the key, but this time in the form of unashamed entertainment with the trombone playing a roguishly extrovert role.

Works such as the *Trombone Concerto*, *Indri / Cave Canem* (a frothy orchestral piece from the same year), and *Short Ride on a Motorbike* for trombone and tape demonstrate Sandström's eclecticism and ability to win over audiences to contemporary music, but without ever losing sight of his acute ear or fine compositional mind. In a more serious vein the exquisite sonorities set up in the piano piece *Campane in campi aperti* or the dark orchestral sounds of the massive *Smaa Klanger: en rost*, which sets poems by the Swedish poet Göran Sonnevi, show the breadth of his musical personality as he moves towards compositional maturity. Many would regard him as the great white hope of Swedish new music and with the wealth of performing talent coming out of Sweden the time is ripe for his music to travel. Given how far he has progressed in the first 10 years of his professional career, the next 10 years may well show him firmly established in the international arena.

—Rosemary Johnson

SANTORSOLA (di Bari Bruno), Guido (Antonio). Italian; resident in Uruguay. Born in Canosa di Puglia, 18 November 1904. Educated: early theory lessons with father; Conservatorio Dramatico y Musical, São Paulo (violin under Autuori, harmony and counterpoint under Baldi); further composition study under Baldi; further study under G. Fusella, Naples, and Alfred Mitowsky, Trinity College of Music, London. Married (1) Elisia Sarraf, 20 November 1926; (2) Sarah Bourdillon, 29 March 1941; (3) Carmen Varela Anon, 22 January 1990. Violist, Paulista Quartet, 1925–31; founder, Brazilian Musical Institute; 1st viola, Orchestra of the Teatro Muncipial, Rio de Janeiro; professor of violin, viola and harmony, São Paulo Conservatory; settled in Montevideo, Uruguay; violist, Orquesta Sinfonica del Servicio Oficial de Difusion Radio Electrica (OSSODRE) and SODRE Quartet, from 1931; head of Brazilian musicological survey, 1943; guest conductor, Belo Horizonte Orchestra, 1948; founder, Orchestra of the Uruguayan Cultural Association; founder, Kleiber Quartet, Montevideo; professor of harmony, aesthetics and composition, Montevideo Conservatory. Recipient: 1st prize (for *Improvisso burlesco*), Concursa Ariel, São Paulo, 1929; 1st prize (for *Choro No 1*), Concurso del Ateneo, Montevideo, 1944. Mailing address: Apartado P-41.897, Obligado 1369, Montevideo, Urguay CP 11300.

Publishers: Berben, Ancona, Italy; Compass Communications 48 Tompkins Circle, Staten Island, New York 10301, U.S.A.; Ediciones Musicales, Mexico; Peer Southern, New York.

Symphonies / orchestral:

Canção 1932.
Saudade 1932; first performed Montevideo, June 1936.
Concerto for Viola and Orchestra (viola d'amore, orchestra, chorus) 1933; first performed Montevideo, September 1944.
Preludio y fuga (2 string orchestras) 1937.
Piano concierto 1938–9; first performed Montevideo, October 1946.
Preludio No 1 (string orchestra) 1939.
Adagio y allegro (2 symphonic movements) 1941; first performed Montevideo, November 1947.
Guitar Concertino 1942; first performed Montevideo, 1943.
Sonata de ariosti (viola, chamber orchestra) 1945.
Preludio y fuga (after Bach; string orchestra) 1948.
Cuatro preludios de Bach-Santorsola 1950; first performed Belo Horizonte, 1950.
Triste No 2 1950.
Vida de artigas 1951; first performed Montevideo, November 1955.
Choro No 2 (version for violin or viola, orchestra) 1952; first performed Washington, 1977.
Dos estudios sinfonicos 1953.
Bassoon Concerto 1959.
Carnavál de Venecia (arranged for violin, orchestra) 1959; first performed United States, 1960.
Rapsodia criolla (after Giampietro) 1960; first performed Montevideo, November 1963.
Violin Concerto 1962.
Concierto para orquesta No 1 1964; first performed Montevideo, May 1967.
Concerto for Two Guitars and Orchestra 1966; first performed London, October 1969.
Concerto for Trumpets and Orchestra (or horns) 1967.
Concerto for Four Violins and Strings 1969.
Concerto for Four Guitars and Orchestra 1972; first performed La Plata, Argentina, 1976.

Double Concerto (guitar, harpsichord, chamber orchestra) 1973; first performed Karlsruhe, Germany, January 1975.
Concerto for Two Bandoneons 1976; first performed Montevideo, July 1983.
Concerto No 2 for Guitar and Orchestra 1977.
Concierto para orquesta No 2 1981–2.
Concerto No 3 for Guitar and Chamber Orchestra 1983.

Chamber/instrumental:

Sonata (violin, piano) 1928.
Improvisso burlesco (piano) 1929.
Canción triste y danze brasileña (piano) 1934; first performed Montevideo, 1938.
Cinco poemas siquicos (piano) 1936; first performed Montevideo, 1939.
Preludio y fuga (2 violas, double bass) 1937.
Dos invenciones (piano) 1938; first performed Montevideo, 1939.
Suite infantil (piano) 1942; broadcast SODRE, Montevideo, 1942.
Concertino No 2 (3 guitars, harpsichord or piano) 1943.
Choro No 1 (piano) 1944; first performed Montevideo, 1946.
Preludio (guitar) 1944; broadcast SODRE, Montevideo, 1944.
Sonata de dos movimientos (guitar) 1944; first performed Vienna, 1950.
Quinteto (4 flutes or string quartet, piano) 1945; first performed Montevideo, 1946.
Choro No 1 (violin with or without piano) 1945; first performed Montevideo, 1945.
Suite all'antica (guitar) 1945.
Choro No 2 (violin or viola, piano) 1952; first performed Montevideo, 1970.
Introduccion, tema y variaciones (piano) 1956; broadcast SODRE, Montevideo, 1946.
String Quartet No 1 1957; first performed Montevideo, 1958.
Sonatina (piano) 1958; first performed Montevideo, 1962.
Canción de cuna (piano) 1958; first performed Montevideo, 1958.
Preludio No 2 (guitar) 1959.
Cinco preludio (guitar) 1959.
Tema y variaciones (after *Arroro mi niño*; piano) 1960.
Valsa choro (guitar) 1960; first performed São Paulo, 1962.
Quartet (flute, viola, cello, piano) 1961; first performed Montevideo, 1966.
Sonata a duo No 1 (2 guitars) 1962.
Trio (flute or violin, clarinet, guitar) 1964; first performed Montevideo, July 1973.
Triptico / Tres invenciones (guitar) 1965; first performed Rio de Janeiro, 1972.
Quintet (flute, oboe, clarinet, horn, bassoon) 1966; first performed Montevideo, 9 August 1966.
Concierto a diez (flute, oboe, clarinet, bass clarinet, bassoon, horn, guitar, violin, viola, cello) 1966.
Tres aires de corte (guitar) 1968.
Sonata No 1 (guitar) 1969; first performed Buenos Aires, June 1974.
Trio (flute, viola, piano) 1969; first performed Montevideo, 1970.
Sonata a duo No 2 (2 guitars) 1969.
Cuatro tientos (guitar) 1970; first performed Italy, 1976.
Sugerencias sonoras (3 woodwinds, 3 brasses, string trio) 1970.
Diptico (viola or violin, guitar) 1970.
Sonata No 2: Hispanica (guitar) 1971; first performed New York City, October 1977.
Sonata No 3 (guitar, piano) 1971.
Cuatro piezas latinamericanos (1 or 4 guitars) 1971.
Tre cuadros sinfonicos (choreographic poem) 1972.
Siete estudios preparatorios para la ambientacion armonica de los acordes alterados (guitar) 1973.
Ocho pequeños estudios (guitar) 1973.
Estrellas en Lejania (piano) 1974; first performed Montevideo, 1977.
Sonata No 3 (guitar) 1975.
Sonata a duo No 4 (flute, guitar) 1975; first performed Fairfax, Washington, May 1981.
Seis bagatelas (guitar) 1975.
Sonata a duo No 5 (3 flutes, guitar) 1976.
Sonata No 4: Italiana (guitar) 1977; first performed Montevideo, 6 October 1979.
Concerto a cinque (guitar, string quartet) 1978; first performed Akron, Ohio, April 1979.
Dos momento anímicos (guitar) 1979; first performed Washington, 11 October 1979.
Dos fisonomias sonoras (guitar) 1979.
Espejismo (guitar) 1980.
Diptico (guitar) 1980.
Concertino a la mañera clasica (3 guitars) 1980.
Sonata No 2 (piano) 1980.
Dos momentos musicales (guitar) 1981.
Sonata No 5: Brasileira (guitar) 1981.
Sonata a duo No 6 (mandolin, guitar) 1981.
Cuatro pequeñas piezas (guitar) 1981.

Vocal/choral:

Dos madrigales (unaccompanied mixed chorus) 1928; first performed Montevideo, 1939.
Ocho canciones (voice, piano or orchestra) 1930–5; first performed Montevideo, 1967.
Agonia (contralto, orchestra) 1938–9.
Vida de artigas (unaccompanied mixed chorus) 1951; first performed Montevideo, 1952.
Canto del departamento de artigas (unacompanied mixed chorus) 1953.
Canto del departamento de lavalleja (unaccompanied mixed chorus) 1953.
Canto a Canelones (unaccompanied mixed chorus) 1953.
Canto a treinta y tres (unaccompanied mixed chorus) 1953.
Cantata a artigas (reciter, female chorus, orchestra) 1965.
Os três misterios da noite (voice, reciter, orchestra) 1966; first performed Montevideo, June 1970.
Cinco canciones (voice, guitar; Silva) 1981.

Opera/dramatic:

El juicio final (Edgardo Ubaldo Genta) 1960–1.

Other:

Autuori: *Gavotta all'antica* (arranged for viola d'amore, piano) 1925.
Marais: *Romance* (arranged for viola d'amore, harp) 1942.
Rameau: *Minuet* and *Musette en rondeau* (arranged for viola d'amore, harp) 1942.
Couperin: *Le bavolet flottant* (arranged for viola d'amore, piano) 1942.
Purcell: *Suite Inglesa* (arranged for viola d'amore, piano) 1943.
Vivaldi: *Concierto en re mayor* (arranged for viola d'amore, piano) 1944.
Handel: *Sonata* (arranged for viola d'amore, piano) 1948.

Albinoni: *Concerto en re mayor* (arranged for viola d'amore, piano) 1948.
Beethoven: *Rondino* (arranged for viola d'amore, piano) 1948.

PUBLICATIONS

On Santorsola: references in *Composers of the Americas*, Washington, D.C., 1962.

* * *

After master classes with G. Fusella in Naples and Alfred Mitowsky in London, Guido Santorsola could lay claim to a remarkably broad and catholic musical education. This is evident again and again throughout his long career. Though much of his working life has been spent as an orchestral and solo violist (with a particular interest in the still under-exploited viola d'amore), Santorsola has created an impressive body of composition in a distinctively personal vein that reflects his diverse interests in Baroque counterpoint, Brazilian and Uruguayan folk themes, and the stringencies of the Second Viennese School.

Brought up in São Paulo, Santorsola was exposed early in life to the rhythmic richness of Latin American music and deploys adventurous metrical patterns throughout his mature works, most notably in the concertante pieces of the 1960s. After completing his formal education in Europe, he became violist with the impressively credited Paulista Quartet. While a member of that group, he founded the Brazilian Musical Institute, which afforded him a more formal perspective on the country's immensely complex generic and performing traditions. Having continued his performing career with the Teatro Muncipal Orchestra in Rio, he returned to São Paulo to teach his instrument at the conservatory there, before emigrating to Uruguay as soloist with the influential radio orchestra.

His early works are written in an appealing folk-influenced mode with considerable melodic and rhythmic energy. Pieces like the 1934 *Canción triste y danze brasileña* are evidence of his desire to work within a tradition without resort to pastiche; Santorsola's ability to invest even minor forms with intelligence is very remarkable. He has a considerable body of work for guitar. It is rhythmically very dense, and ranges from sharply percussive passages to episodes of considerable lyrical beauty. The series of guitar sonatas gives a clear impression of the trajectory of his musical interests. The fifth, subtitled *Brasileira*, takes him back to his musical roots. He has experimented with altered chords and with demanding articulations.

Perhaps the finest of his orchestral works are the concertos for one or more guitars and orchestra. The earliest, written in 1942, has the most conventional structure, but is characterised by a clear harmonic argument. The 1966 concerto for two guitars, premiered in the United Kingdom by the London Bach Orchestra, has a restless surface and considerable internal discontinuity that lends it its strongly dramatic impact. The later concerto for four guitars is rather more diffuse and the solo instruments tend to clog the argument slightly, however the subsequent *Double Concerto* for guitar and harpsichord is among Santorsola's finest works and he continued to write for guitar and orchestra into the 1980s.

It may be surprising given his background as a performer that he has not written more for string quartet; the 1978 *Concerto a cinque* adds guitar to great effect. Generally speaking, though, his talents are for solo instruments and for orchestral writing. His use of twelve-tone techniques in larger structures is always individual and almost always has a firm tonal underpinning that seems unaccountably less certain in the scores for small groups. He has written relatively little vocal music, though *Os tres misterios da noite* from the mid-1960s is deeply impressive. His "epic" *El juicio final* summarises most of his compositional interests up to 1960, but has failed to find a place in the operatic repertoire.

Santorsola is now unfortunately little known in his native Europe, but he has many admirers in the United States and his style can increasingly be characterised as "pan-American", drawing as it does on the eclectic (in the non-pejorative sense) approach of modern American composers to the whole spectrum of musical languages and dialects.

—Gena Renk

SANTOS, Ramon (Pagayon). Filipino. Born in Pasig, Manila, 25 February 1941. Educated at Pasig Elementary and Catholic Schools; San Jose Seminary; University of the Philippines, Quezon City (Kalinga music under Benjamin Pangosban, p'ipa under Lao Hong Kio, Javanese music and dance under Sunardi Wisnusubroto), B.Mus. composition and conducting, 1965; Indiana University, Bloomington, M.Mus., 1969; State University of New York, Buffalo, Ph.D., 1972; composition studies under Roque Cordero, Hilarion Rubio, Lucio San Pedro, Thomas Beversdorf, Ramon Fuller and William Kothe; studies in contemporary music under Istvan Anhalt and George Perle; Ferienkurse für Neue Musik, Darmstadt (under Iannis Xenakis, Karlheinz Stockhausen, Christian Wolff and Rolf Gehlhaar). Married Lourdes Yee Wong, 25 October 1969 (deceased 1983); 2 daughters. Horn player, Quezon City Philharmonic Orchestra, 1964–7; instructor in theory and composition, University of the Philippines, Quezon City, 1965–7; assistant secretary, College of Music, University of the Philippines, 1965–7; teaching assistant, Indiana University, Bloomington, 1967–9; teaching assistant and assistant conductor, State University of New York, Buffalo, 1969–72; chair, graduate programme and composition and theory department, 1973–8, chair of artist in residence committee, 1978–84, dean, 1978–84, dean, 1978–88, and professor of composition and theory, since 1987, College of Music, University of the Philippines; professorial lecturer, Philippine Women's University, Manila, 1974–7; acting director, Philippine Music Documentation Center, 1975–8; vice-chair for research, National Music Council of the Philippines, 1978–84; visiting scholar in ethnomusicology, University of Illinois, Urbana, 1988–9. Recipient: Gold Medal, Spanish declamation contest, 1959; 2nd prize (for *Sa Kapurihan at Kapalaran*), Bonfiacio Centennial Composition Contest, 1963; award in recognition of outstanding achievement in music, Minerva Association, 1963; outstanding member award in music, Minerva Association, 1976; Chevalier de l'Ordre des Arts et des Lettres, France, 1987. Mailing address: 16 Juan Lunar Area 2, University of the Philippines, Dimiman, Quezon City, Philippines.

Publishers: NAMCYA Publications, Folk Arts Theater, CCP Complex, Roxas Boulevard, Manila, Philippines; New Day Publications, Quezon City.

Symphonies/orchestral:

The Chant (symphonic poem) 1963.
Four Movements (chamber orchestra) 1968.
Divertimento (chamber orchestra) 1968; first performed Taipei, 1 May 1979.
Concertino Variations 1969.
Parangal Kay S.W. (symphony orchestra, Javanese gamelan) 1971; first performed Philippines, 15 August 1977.
Phenomenon 1980; first performed Philippines, 10 October 1980.
Tin-ig 1982; first performed Philippines, 25 November 1982.
Du-a (large orchestra) 1986; first performed Philippines, 25 November 1986.
Time-Space (2 orchestral groups) 1990.

Chamber/instrumental:

Suite (flute, clarinet, viola, cello, piano) 1968; first performed Bloomington, Indiana, 12 March 1968.
Pied Beauty (tone poem after Hopkins for piccolo, cor anglais, clarinet, bass clarinet, horns, violin, cello) 1968; first performed Philippines, 17 September 1975.
Three Miniatures (oboe, clarinet, bassoon) 1968.
Variations on a Theme by Webern (piano) 1969.
Sequence (violin, cello) 1969.
Music for Nine Instruments 1969; first performed Bloomington, Indiana, 1969.
Time Improvisations (percussion) 1970.
Five Pieces (2 pianos) 1970.
Toccata (piano—4 hands) 1970; first performed Buffalo, New York, 5 December 1971.
Quartet 1971 (string quartet with tape) 1970–1.
Quartet 1974 (string quartet) 1974; first performed Philippines, 4 December 1975.
Para sa intermisyon (percussion ensemble) 1976; first performed Philippines, 18 October 1976.
Singaw (Jew's harp, bamboo flute, takumbo, gongs, violins) 1977; first performed Philippines, 3 September 1977.
Panawagan (3 trumpets, harp, guitar, percussion) 1981; first performed Philippines, 22 December 1981.
Abot-Tanaw I (guitar) 1981; first performed Philippines, 17 October 1983.
Abot-Tanaw II (violin) 1982; first performed Reutlingen, Germany, 25 January 1984.
Klntang (piano) 1982; first performed Brazil, 3 October 1986.
Abot-Tanaw III (piano) 1984.
S'geypo (16 flutes, drums) 1989.

Vocal/choral:

Sa Kapurihan at Kapalaran (symphonic ode for alto, mixed chorus, orchestra) 1963.
Missa brevis (mixed chorus, chamber orchestra) 1964.
Three Songs of Faith (baritone, piano; Hopkins) 1965.
Maikling Misa (unaccompanied chorus) 1965.
Exultatio (unaccompanied chorus) 1968.
Improperia (Good Friday reproaches for soloists, chorus, *Kulintang*, orchestra) 1968.
Canon on a Folk Tune (unaccompanied chorus) 1968.
Two Songs (baritone, alto, flute, double bass, percussion; Housman) 1969.
Magnificat (chorus, woodwinds, strings) 1969.
Five Mountain Songs (unaccompanied chorus; Li Po) 1970.
Mass of the Resurrection (unacompanied chorus) 1970.
Ding Ding Nga Diyawa (unaccompanied chorus) 1970; first performed Philippines, 30 September 1971.
Cuatro Cantos (soprano) 1972.
Dal'wang Sawikaing Pilipino (chorus) 1973; first performed Philippines, 1973.
Tatlong Salmong Pagsamo (chorus) 1973; first performed Philippines, 25 November 1973.
Tagulaylay (baritone, prepared piano) 1973.
Tinig (20 voices, Western and Asian instruments) 1974; first performed Philippines, 17 October 1975.
Kantata: Maliit Na Supling (youth chorus) 1974; first performed Philippines, 1974.
Batang Magalang (chorus) 1974.
Handog Sa Ina (youth chorus) 1974; first performed Philippines, 1974.
Agnus Dei Antifon (unaccompanied mixed chorus) 1976.
Abakada Pahpahla (children's chorus) 1976; first performed Philippines, 1976.
Tong Togodong (children's chorus) 1977; first performed Philippines, 1977.
Maalindog Na Kaliksan (youth chorus) 1977.
Tulog Na (youth chorus) 1978.
Tula-Tula (youth chorus) 1978.
Tatlong Maiikling Awit Pamasko (youth chorus) 1978.
Fyug (youth chorus) 1978.
Dal-Lit (chorus) 1979; first performed Seoul, 13 October 1979.
Balatkayo (voice, 3 clarinets, oboe, trumpet, horn) 1980; first performed Philippines, 8 November 1980.
Awit Ng Ulan (chorus) 1981.
Halina't Umawit (unaccompanied mixed chorus) 1983.
Awit Ng Papuri (unaccompanied chorus) 1983; first performed Philippines, 23 October 1983.
Awit Ng Pagdiriwang (voices, orchestra) 1983; first performed Philippines, 18 June 1983.
He Le (unaccompanied mixed chorus) 1984; first performed Philippines, 22 March 1984.
Panaghoy (voices, gongs, bass drum, guitar; Benigno Aquino Jr) 1985.
Up Law (alumni hymn) 1985.
Ba-dw sa Kapoon-an (3 groups of singers, stones, wood, bamboo percussion, ching) 1987; first performed Philippines, 17 December 1987.

Opera/dramatic:

Ang hardin in Ligaya (opera-tableau) 1965.
Ang Puting Waling-Waling (musico-drama) 1972.
Images (dramatic dance) 1975; first performed Philippines, 3–5 October 1975.
Alamat Ng Araw At Buwan (dance drama; Pagsanjan) 1976; first performed Philippines, 12–14 November 1976.
Siklo (dance theatre for symphony orchestra, singers, tape) 1977; first performed Philippines, 14–16 October 1977.
Yugto-Yugtong Tagpo Na Hinango Sa Makasaysayang Panaginip Ni Antonio Manggagawa 1977; first performed Philippines, 4 March 1977.
Ang Anino ni Saumay (music theatre) 1982.
Awit (drama for dancers, lights, guitars, vocalists, pecussion) 1983; first performed Philippines, 2–3 December 1982.
Anino Ni Saumay (chamber opera) 1983.
Ta-O (multi-media theatre piece) 1985; first performed Philippines, 17–18 October 1985.
Aninag (dancers, orchestra) 1985; first performed Philippines, 1985.
Awit ni Pulau (musical dance drama narrative for children; Maranan) 1990.

Other:

Flight of the Sparrow (film music) 1965.
Nabasag ang banga at iba't-iba pang pinagugpong-ugpong na pananalita sa wikang Philipino para sa labing-anim na tinig (environmental music) 1972.
Radyasyon (improvisational/environmental, with slides) 1974.
Quadrasyon (improvisational/environmental) 1974.
Ritwal ng Pasasalamat (environmental music for bamboo instruments, gamelan, kulintangan, pianos, string quartets, drums, voices, religious ministers) 1976.
Sugapa (film music) 1976.
Likas An (environmental music for bamboo instruments, rotor, plastic tube, hammers, electronics) 1978.

PUBLICATIONS

By Santos: "The Ritual Music of the Iglesia del Ciudad Mistica de Dios: A Preliminary Report", in *Asian Studies*, 1975; "Bagong Kamalayan sa Kontemporaryong Musika sa Pilipinas", in *Musika Jornal*, 1975–6; "Preservation and Enhancement of Traditional Music in Education", in *Proceedings of the Third Asian Pacific Conference on the Preservation of Cultural Properties and Traditions*, Taipei, 1980; "Auswirkungen Kultureller Fremdeinfluesse auf der Musik des Ostens", in *Oesterreichisches Musik Zeitschrift*, February 1982; "Teknolohiya at Musika", in *Agham*, 1984.

On Santos: Helen Samson, "RS", in *Contemporary Filipino Composers*, Quezon City, 1974; Vila S. Felipe, "Kompositor na Pilipino: Konsiyensiya ng Bayan", in *Musika Bulletin*, 3, 1976; Raissa Espinosa, "Understanding the Alien Sound of New Music", in *The Review*, Manila, 3(3), 1980; Ada Dacanay de Leon, "RS: In Search of Truly Filipino Music", in *Celebrity*, November–December 1982; press articles and reviews.

Ramon Santos comments:

My works reflect a continuous search for new directions in contemporary musical expression, wherein the music cultures of South East Asia, their social and aesthetic contexts, serve as the main sources of musical ideologies. These are based on a musical logic and musical organizations that project ambiguities, oppositions and various concepts of mode and musical time. My works have been strongly influenced by Asian performance techniques, the functionality of Asian music and the artistic holismof rituals and other traditional practices.

* * *

As a student, Ramon Santos was fascinated by the music of Mahler and Debussy, and especially intrigued by the avant-gardism and Asian music he heard in concerts arranged by composer-ethnomusicologist Jose Maceda. While at Indiana University, his first works written under the tutelage of Thomas Beversdorf had a neo-classic strain (*Concertino Variations* for orchestra; *Pied Beauty*, a tone poem based on a text by Gerard Manley Hopkins). Studies under Roque Cordero and George Perle heightened his interest in the serial techniques and atonality (*Music for Nine Instruments*; *Variations on a Theme by Webern*; *Canon on a Folk Tune*). Subsequent workshop sessions under Iannis Xenakis introduced him to avant-garde techniques. Using a free medium, he wrote a cantata based on the Lamentations entitled *Improperia* for soloists, chorus, orchestra and *kulintang* (a Philippine indigenous instrument made up of eight graduated bossed gongs laid in a row). While studying with Ramon Fuller and William Kothe he became acquainted with new vocal techniques and electronic and computer music procedures, under the influence of Istwan Anhalt and Lejeran Hiller. Several years later, in 1974, he was further exposed to the various directions of new music in Darmstadt and at the Institute of Sonology in Utrecht.

Upon his return to the Philippines, Santos experienced a deep sense of alienation and conflict between his newly acquired compositional discipline and the reality of life in an Asian society. He took lessons in Chinese Nan Kuan music, Javanese music and dance, and read on the music of Filipino cultural minorities. While his earlier works (*Five Pieces* for two pianos; *Toccata* for one piano (four hands); *Time Improvisations* for percussion) were products of his orientation with Western avant-garde idioms acquired in the United States and Europe, his immersion in indigenous Philippine and Asian musics influenced succeeding works, exhibiting a new phase in his creative output. From a formalistic style of writing, Santos became more interested in open-ended structures of time and space while also exploring the colors provided by local sound sources. *Nabasag ang banga at iba't iba pang pinagugpong-ugpong na pananalita sa wikang Philipino para sa labing-anim na tinig* is a 16-voice choral work consisting of unordered musical events of verses articulated according to tonally exaggerated Filipino accents. *Tinig* is scored for 10 female and 10 male vocalists who move around the stage and play supporting instruments such as whistle flutes, buzzers, sticks, mouth harps, mouth organs, *kulintang*, marimba and piano. *Para sa intermisyon* and *Ritwal ng pasasalamat* show Santos's espousal of the idea of functionality of music. Nature and the various processes of life-forms have also provided conceptual bases for other works such as *Quartet 1974, Siklol* and *Likas An.* In the early 1980s Santos's works still focused on elements in Philippine culture while utilizing Western sound media: *Phenomenon*, *Tin-ig*, and *Du-a* for orchestra, and a series of pieces for solo instruments entitled *Abot-Tanaw I* and *Abot-Tanaw II.* Santos has also shown great partiality towards stage/multimedia works: *Awit, Anino Ni Saumay, Ta-O, Aninag* and *Awit ni Pulau*. In addition to their Asiatic character, they epitomize the Asian concept of an art form, that integrates music, dance, drama and poetry. *Ba-dw sa Kapoon-an* for three groups of singers, stones, wood and bamboo percussion and *ching* was inspired by the poetico-musical expression of the *Ibaloi*, a mountain people from the northern Philippines. It represents the acme of Santos's immersion in old Philippine art forms, capturing as it does the infinite variety of individual and improvisatory nuances within simple melodic formulae. One of his latest works, *Time-Space* is a departure from previous works and may well mark the start of a new creative phase. Scored for two orchestral groups, it portrays a philosophical-psychological interpretation of time perception.

Santos has exerted a strong influence on a group of young composers who took his composition classes at the University of the Philippines. He has ably represented his country in the various composition festivals held over Southeast Asia, Korea and Japan under the Asian Composers' League where he has held important elective posts. Most importantly he has been strongly instrumental in espousing a modern Philippine music rooted in ancient practices and concepts of life in an Asian environment, thus offering an alternative perspective in Philippine culture that has long been smothered by colonial and western influences.

—Corazon C. Dioquino

SATOH, Somei. Japanese. Born in Sendai, 19 January 1947. Educated: self-taught; Nihon University of Art, 1967–9. Married Keiko Satoh, 9 December 1973. Member of "Tone-field" performance group, 1970s. Recipient: Japan Art Festival Prize, 1980; visiting artist's grant from Asian Cultural Council for study in United States, 1983. Mailing address: Minami-Aoyoma 7-5-14-502 Minato-ku, Tokyo, Japan.

Publishers: Ongaku No Tomo Sha Corporation, Kagurazaka 6–30 Shinjuku-ku, Tokyo; Schott Japan, Iidabashi 3-4-3-301 Chiyoda-ku, Tokyo, Japan.

Symphonies/orchestral:

Lyra 1980; first performed Tokyo, 1980.
Sumeru 1981; first performed Tokyo, 1982. Recorded ALM AL-26.
Journey Through Sacred Time 1982; first performed Tokyo, 1983.
Miserere 1989; first performed New York City, 1990.

Chamber/instrumental:

Litania (piano, tape, electronics) 1972; first performed Tokyo, 1973. Recorded ALM AL-11; New Albion NA 008.
Hymn for the Sun (piano) 1973.
Cosmic Womb (piano, tape) 1975; first performed Tokyo, 1975. Recorded ALM AL-23; Denon 6270; Mode 15.
Incarnation II (piano, electronics) 1977; first performed Tokyo, 1978. Recorded ALM AL-23, New Albion NA 008.
Birds in Warped Time (violin, piano) 1980; first performed Tokyo, 1980. Recorded New Albion NA 008.
Shirasagi (string quartet) 1986; first performed San Francisco, 1987.
Uzu (flute, clarinet, harp, percussion, piano) 1988; first performed Tokyo, 1988.
Toki no Mon (violin, percussion, piano) 1988; first performed New York, 1989.
Homa (string quartet) 1988; first performed Tokyo, 1988.
Shunshuka (harp) 1989; first performed Tokyo, 1989. Recorded Fontec FOCD 3253.
A Gate into Infinity (violin, piano, percussion) 1989.

Vocal/choral:

The Heavenly Spheres Are Illuminated by Lights (soprano, percussion, piano; Buddhist chant) 1979; first performed Tokyo, 1979. Recorded New Albion NA 008.
Stabat mater (soprano, chorus) 1987; first performed New York, 1987. Recorded New Albion NA 016.

Other:

Emerald Tablet (tape) 1978; first performed Tokyo, 1978. Recorded ALM AL-23.
Mandala (tape) 1982; first performed Tokyo, 1982. Recorded ALM AL-26.
Mantra (tape) 1987; first performed New York City, 1987. Recorded New Albion NA 016.
Tantra (tape) 1990; first performed Wellington, New Zealand, 1990.

PUBLICATIONS

By Satoh: *Toki O Toku*, Japan, 1987.

* * *

Spiritual clarity peculiarly combined with romantic sensuousness is reflected in Somei Satoh's music from the beginning. Almost totally self-taught as a composer, his great esteem for the Shintoism and Zen Buddhism of Japan has been growing in his spirit since his youth and lies deep in his music concept to this day.

The ideals of Shintoism, such as excessive purity and cleanliness, have been adopted in Japanese arts such as traditional architecture and brush-painting which eliminate ornamentation to the utmost, to present the essence of the subject in genuine beauty of simplicity and clarity. In Satoh's compositions, this Shinto quality can be observed in the simplicity of his minimalistic style with repetitions. Furthermore, the Buddhist element appears in continuous, static sound formation, symbolizing the realization of the infinite, timeless, macrocosmic universe of enlightenment through music.

In the early 1970s, when he was still very much involved in the mixed-media and musical events as a member of "Tone-field", he started to write the first group of compositions for piano that established his name as a composer. *Litania*, *Hymn for the Sun* and others up to *Incarnation II*, written for piano and electronics, are characterized by tremolos of single tone, chords and tone clusters, each of which is repeated by alternating the left and right hand or arm rapidly, emphasizing on different registers, dynamics and colour of sound. The playback of this continuation of sound formation is immediately amplified and slightly delayed by electronic devices and creates sometimes quiet and at other times overwhelming drones without losing static and curiously romantic colouring. The static impression seems to derive from Satoh's deep feeling for religion as well as from the Japanese musical time concept which, unlike Western music, can be continuous and "beatless". His romanticism seems to be related to his longing as a human being to be unified with Shinto gods incarnated in Mother Nature.

His début as a composer coincided with the popularity of minimal music in the early 1970s. Because of his adoption of typical minimalistic techniques, he was very often categorized as simply a minimalist without consideration for his uniquely Japanese musical belief. On the other hand, it was this minimalistic style with Japanese flavour that was recognized and brought him popularity in the United States, where he stayed for one year (1983–4). Yet, before he became known outside of Japan, at the end of the 1970s his music style showed another development, as he introduced modal melody to his composition which was usually supported by harmonic formation by other instruments, first in *The Heavenly Spheres Are Illuminated by Lights* for soprano (text taken from Buddhist chant), piano, percussion and then in *Birds in Warped Time* for violin and piano. The tendency continued with gradually increasing romantic flair and more refined sensuality, especially in his instrumental compositions. One recent example of this development is *A Gate into Infinity* for violin, piano and percussion which shows a desperately romantic side of his music.

Parallel to this series of works that shows his unique characteristics as a Japanese composer, Satoh maintained his strong interest in events and his creation of religiously engraved massive music sound often using electronic means. In 1981, he realized an outdoor music project that involved also a visual effect, locating eight speakers on mountaintops as much as one kilometre apart which transmitted amplified music, together with artificial fog rising from the valley and laser beams running through clouds and fog to create an unforgettable impression. The emphasis on usage of electronic means as well as his religious concern has been proved in such representative work as *Mandala*. The sound material of the piece is the composer's own voice reciting two tone pitches in the traditional Japanese manner of vocalization, filtered, amplified and multiplied from 60 to over 100 times.

—Yukiko Sawabe

SAWER, David (Peter). British/English. Born in Stockport, Lancashire, 14 September 1961. Educated at University of York (composition under Richard Orton), 1979–82, 1985–6, B.A. (hons), M.Phil. (composition), 1984, D.Phil.; Staatliche Hochsschule für Musik Rheinland, Cologne (DAAD scholarship, music theatre under Mauricio Kagel), 1984–5. Performer in music theatre. Recipient: Sony Radio Award (for *Swansong*), 1990. Mailing address: 96 Bermondsey Street, London SE1 3UB, England.

Publisher: Universal Edition.

Chamber/instrumental:

The Force That Through the Green Fuse 1982; withdrawn.
Trompe l'Oeil 1982; withdrawn.
Solo Piano 1983; first performed York, 1983.
Cat's-Eye (2 clarinets/bass clarinets, trumpet, trombone, harp, piano, viola, cello) 1986; first performed London, 1986.
Take Off (flute, 2 clarinets, piano, violin, viola, cello) 1987; first performed Huddersfield, Yorkshire, 1988.
Good Night (flute, harp, violin, viola, cello) 1989; first performed London, 1989.
The Melancholy of Departure (piano) 1989; first performed King's Lynn, Norfolk, 1990.

Other:

Etudes (2–6 actor/musicians, tenor saxophone, 2 trumpets, percussion) 1984; first performed Cologne, May 1985.
Food of Love (actress, piano; Dear) 1988; first performed London, June 1988.
Swansong (radio fantasy; speaker, guitar/harp/accordion/percussion, electric organ/double bass) 1989.
Songs of Love and War (voices) 1990; first performed Cologne, 1990.

* * *

David Sawer is both by nature and by training a theatrical musician. A composer and performer with an innate sense of dramatic values, he greatly benefited from the enlightened music degree course which he undertook at the University of York. There he blossomed both in the writing of music and in the realisation of music-theatre works (e.g., he was soloist in Vic Hoyland's *Michelagniolo* and directed stage performances of Mauricio Kagel's *Pas de cinq*). His fascination with Kagel led him to direct the U.K. première of *Kantrimusik* in 1983, which was repeated at the ICA in London in 1984; he also starred in his own, quite stunning, production of Kagel's monodrama *Phonophonie*. Subsequently, in 1984, he studied with Kagel in Cologne, but this primarily enabled Sawer to burgeon in his own independent way.

In the background to virtually all Sawer's works are visual images, sometimes specific 20th-century art works, together with an implicit dramatic content. This is as much true of the early mixed ensemble work *Trompe l'Oeil* (1982), as it is of a recent piano piece, *The Melancholy of Departure*. In the former we encounter a central shifting image that can never quite be defined or pinned down within the layered textures for the different instrumental groups; while the latter takes its starting-point from a picture by De Chirico. The dramatic basis of another early instrumental piece, *The Force That Through the Green Fuse* was the succession of rituals connected with the sacrifice of a young boy in ancient Crete. This work and *Trompe l'Oeil* do not show quite the formal precision of Sawer's later music and he has withdrawn them.

Two of Sawer's most successful instrumental pieces are *Cat's-Eye* and *Take Off*, both of them essays in surrealist humour. The rhythmic hiccups and hiatuses of *Cat's-Eye* were suggested by the operational quirks of the 18th-century fantascope, a magic-lantern device which conjured fantastic images of spirits and demons, but sometimes broke down. The inspiration for *Take Off* came from photographs of the Wright brothers who made countless attempts at getting airborne before finally succeeding in 1903. Sawer's piece has more of the narrative flow of a mechanical ballet, such as might have been devised in the Bauhaus by Oskar Schlemmer.

So far in his career, Sawer has excelled in small-scale works such as these, and, in purely musical terms, he has developed over a decade or so a more acute sense of structural priorities. His own "voice" has become apparent, too, as he has whittled away the influences from early Stravinsky, Kagel and György Ligeti to reveal his own predilections for bright-hued colours, jaunty rhythms, pointed juxtapositions of material; and his control over larger musical paragraphs is now more assured.

Apart from *Etudes* for six actors/musicians and a quartet of tenor saxophones, two trumpets and percussion—written and performed during his period with Kagel in Cologne—and *Food of Love*, composed for a concert specially devoted his work at the Almeida Festival, Sawer has had relatively few opportunities to show his flair as a theatrical composer. But of all the younger figures selected to write new operatic or music-theatre pieces within schemes such as Covent Garden's The Garden Venture, Sawer would seem an automatic choice. Meanwhile, in *Songs of Love and War*, written for the BBC Singers, Sawer offered a telling reversal of the idea underlying Monteverdi's *Madrigali guerrieri ed amorosi*: instead of depicting love through the imagery of war, the work seeks to express the changing emotional conditions of war (loneliness, uncertainty, anxiety) through the terminology of love; and for this purpose, Sawer's text draws upon 12 World War II songs.

Sawer's biggest enterprise to date, *Swansong*, has been conceived for radio. Lasting about 45 minutes, this is a late 20th-century metamorphosis of the story *Euphonia, or The Musical Town*—an account of a possible musical utopia of the future, as told by one of the players in the operatic orchestra pit during the final evening of Berlioz's *Evenings in the Orchestra*. *Swansong* exhibits a virtuoso handling of its huge musical forces from the intimacy of the guitar music accompanying Berlioz's narrative, to the interpolations by other soloists, children's choir, chorus and orchestra; it communicates on many levels—from the most intimate to the most grandiose, from documentary to fantasy: altogether manifesting a multi-facetedness that portends a composer of some significance.

—Meirion Bowen

SAXTON, Robert (Louis Alfred). British/English. Born in London, 8 October 1953. Educated at Bryanston School, 1967–71; St Catharine's College (under Robin Holloway), Cambridge, 1972–5, B.A. (M.A.); Worcester College, Oxford, 1975–6, B.Mus.; studied privately with Elisabeth Lutyens, 1970–4, and Luciano Berio, 1976–7. Visiting tutor, University of Sussex, Brighton, 1979, and Oxford University, 1980–2; composition tutor, 1979–84, and head of composition department since 1986, Guildhall School of Music, London; assistant to Peter Maxwell Davies, Dartington Summer School, Devon 1983 and 1984; lecturer, University of Bristol, 1984–5; Fulbright visiting fellow, Princeton University, New Jersey, 1986; teacher of composition (with Oliver Knussen), Tanglewood, Massachusetts, 1986. Recipient: 1st prize, Gaudeamus International Music Week, The Netherlands, 1975; Fulbright Arts Award, 1985–6; honorary fellow, Guildhall School of Music and Drama, 1987. Mailing address: c/o Chester Music, 8–9 Frith Street, London WI, England.

Publisher: Chester Music.

Symphonies/orchestral:

Reflections of Narziss and Goldmund 1975; first performed Royan, 1977.
Choruses to Apollo 1980; first performed London, 1980.
Traumstadt 1980; first performed Harrogate, Yorkshire, 1980.
The Ring of Eternity 1982; first performed London, 1983. Recorded EMI CDC7499152.
Concerto for Orchestra 1984; first performed London, 13 August 1984. Recorded EMI CDC7499152.
The Circles of Light 1985; first performed London, 1986. Recorded EMI CDC7499152.
Viola Concerto 1986; first performed Cheltenham, Gloucestershire, 9 July 1986.
Birthday Piece for RRB (small string orchestra) 1986; first performed London, 1986.
In the Beginning 1987; first performed London, 31 January 1988.
Birthday Music for Sir William Glock (small orchestra) 1988; first performed London, 13 February 1989.
Elijah's Violin 1988; first performed London, 13 February 1989.
Music to Celebrate the Resurrection of Christ 1988; broadcast BBC television, 26 March 1989. Recorded Collins Classics.
Violin Concerto 1989; first performed Leeds, 1990.
Trumpet Concerto 1990–1.
Cello Concerto 1991–2.

Chamber/instrumental:

Ritornelli and Intermezzi (piano) 1972; first performed London, 1972.
Krystallen (flute, piano) 1973; broadcast BBC Radio, 1975.
Echoes of the Glass Bead Game (wind quintet) 1975; first performed London, 1977.
Two Pieces for Piano 1976; first performed London, 1977.
Sonatas for Two Pianos 1977; first performed London, 1977.
Arias (oboe, piano) 1977; first performed London, 1978.
Toccata (cello) 1978; first performed Burnham Market, Norfolk, 1979.
Canzona in memoriam Igor Stravinsky (flute, oboe, clarinet, horn, harp, string trio) 1978; first performed Newcastle-upon-Tyne, 1979.
Sonata: In Memory of Béla Bartók (piano) 1981; first performed Cambridge, 1981.
Processions and Dances (flute/piccolo/alto flute, oboe/cor anglais, piano, harp, string trio) 1981; first performed London, 1981.
Piccola musica per Luigi Dallapiccola (flute, oboe, viola, cello, piano/celeste) 1981; first performed Montepulciano, 1981.
Chiaroscuro (percussion solo) 1981; first performed Keele, Staffordshire, 1981.
Fantasiestück (accordion) 1982; first performed Nottingham, 1982.
The Sentinel of the Rainbow (flute, clarinet, piano, violin, cello) 1984; first performed London, 24 October 1984. Recorded EMI-CDC7499.
Night Dance (guitar) 1986; first performed London, 1987. Recorded Bridge Records, New Music with Guitar, volume 4.
Fanfare (brass, percussion) 1987; first performed Porvoo, Finland, 18 June 1987.
Chacony (piano, left hand) 1987; first performed Aldeburgh, Suffolk, 20 June 1988.
Paraphrase on Mozart's Idomeneo (wind octet) 1990–1; first performed Glyndebourne, Sussex, 15 June 1991.
Invocation, Dance and Meditation (viola, piano) 1991; first performed Litchfield, Hampshire, 5 July 1991.

Vocal/choral:

La Promenade d'automne (soprano, flute, clarinet, percussion, piano, string trio) 1972; first performed Lancaster, 1972.
Where Are You Going To, My Pretty Maid? (arranged for soprano, flute, clarinet, harp, guitar, violin, cello) 1973; first performed Cambridge, 1974.
What Does the Song Hope For? (soprano, flute, oboe, piano, string trio, tape) 1974; first performed Hilversum, 1975.
Brise marine (soprano, piano, tape) 1976; first performed Sweden, 1976.
Cantata on Poems by Hölderlin (tenor, counter-tenor, piano) 1979; first performed London, 1979.
Cantata No 2 (tenor, oboe, piano) 1980; first performed London, 1980.
Eloge (soprano, flute, oboe, clarinet, horn, piano, string quartet) 1980; first performed London, 1980.
Cantata No 3 (2 sopranos, tape delay) 1981; first performed London, 1981.
Chaconne (double SATB choir) 1981; first performed London, 1981.
Child of Light (carol; sopranos, organ) 1984; first performed Westonbirt, Gloucestershire, 1987.
I Will Awake the Dawn (double SATB choir) 1987; first performed London, 1987.
Rex gloriae (anthem; female voices, organ) 1988; first performed Westonbirt, Gloucestershire, 1988.

Opera:

Caritas (Wesker) 1990; first performed Huddersfield, Yorkshire, November 1991.

PUBLICATIONS

By Saxton: "Elisabeth Lutyens", in *New Music*, Oxford, 1988; "Lend Me Your Ears", in *The Independent*, September 1989.

On Saxton: Paul Griffiths, "RS", in *Musical Times*, 1985; Paul Griffiths, (interview) in *New Sounds, New Personalities*, London, 1985; David Wright, "RS", in *The Listener*, 1989.

Robert Saxton comments:

My music, especially since about 1979, has aimed at creating large structures, achieved by controlling long-range background harmonic areas. Many of my pieces, as can be seen from their titles, are concerned with religious/philosophical concepts, especially the idea of progressing from darkness to light. These ideas are inseparable in my mind from the harmonic workings of the music and the pieces' overall movement. Many of my works contrast dance, as celebration, with sustained, slower music. Perhaps my most prominent ambition has been, and is, to create a flexible and varied sense of pacing by means of rates of harmonic change, making clear to the listener marked differences between music of different speeds but unified harmonic direction.

* * *

Viewed from abroad, composers like John Casken, Oliver Knussen, Nigel Osborne and Robert Saxton, with the slightly younger George Benjamin, Simon Holt and Mark-Anthony Turnage consitiute an identifiable English School, cultivated partly by the commissioning policy and performing style of expert new music ensembles like the London Sinfonietta. In reality, these composers have distinct voices but similar roots, put down in gentler soil it seems than the acidic medium of Edgar Varèse, Schoenberg, Stravinsky, post-war serialism and rediscovered medieval music which earlier nurtured the young Harrison Birtwistle and Peter Maxwell Davies. Components of Saxton's style are the linear and lyrical qualities of Britten and Tippett combined with the decorative exuberance and iridescent textures of Berio, Boulez and Witold Lutosławski. For Saxton, as for many younger British composers, it would seem that Debussy has replaced Schoenberg or Stravinsky as the seminal 20th-century figure. But if the initial influences upon his music were predominantly French, they have been assimilated into a style which is confidently and clearly his own.

The exceptional technical and expressive assurance of his earliest music won him a first prize at the International Gaudeamus Music Week for *What Does the Song Hope For?* composed in 1974 when he was still an undergraduate at Cambridge. Through a series of accomplished ensemble and then orchestral works Saxton's subsequent development has been meteoric. Their most striking aspect is the skillful manipulation of a highly-charged texture, like a constantly shifting musical landscape through which more defined thematic shapes move forward slowly and remorselessly. The music proceeds in successive surges of energy generated by whirling, volatile patterns undergoing ceaseless transformation. Layers of perspective arise from the animated velocity of the foreground set against a more sustained polyphonic background. And in the larger mature scores, like *The Ring of Eternity*, the inherent drama is intensified by contrasting instrumental forces, opposing densities and different types of linear movement vying with each other for dominance.

Rhythmically assymetric and chromatically inflected, Saxton's restless textures never fall into the repetitive cycles of minimalism. Where they solidify into overt rhythmic or melodic statements, the effect is powerful. Essentially, however, his structures are articulated through harmony, characteristic interval groups, pedals and chordal progressions generating immense dynamic tension. All his music is powerfully directional.

His ensemble works range from the eight instruments of the *Canzona in memoriam Igor Stravinsky*, via the widely acclaimed chamber symphony *The Circles of Light*, to the sophisticated symphonic arch of the *Concerto for Orchestra*. Even in the *Toccata* for solo cello, Saxton achieves an impression of textural interplay, and a convincing synthesis of idiomatic, intuitive and logical processes, resulting in a composition as virtuoso to perform as it is a dazzling example of integrated musical craftsmanship. An outcome of this emphasis upon instrumental music is the trilogy of concertos for string soloist and orchestra, for viola in 1986, for violin in 1989 with a future cello concerto newly commissioned by Mstislav Rostropovitch and the London Symphony Orchestra.

From around 1980 are several pieces for solo voices with piano, tape or small ensemble which, with their elegance of line and astringent, tremulous atmosphere, provide pointers to his opera, jointly commissioned by Huddersfield Contemporary Music Festival and Opera North and premiered in November 1991. *Caritas*, which sets a libretto adapted from an existing play by Arnold Wesker, tells the story of a young girl who becomes an anchoress against the turbulent background of the Peasants' Revolt of 1381. In this impressive first stage work Saxton has found an intensity of musical resonance and a depth of subject matter appropriate to his considerable dramatic gifts. It is the summation of all he has achieved in two decades.

—Richard Steinitz

SCHAFER, R(aymond) Murray. Canadian. Born in Sarnia, Ontario, 18 July 1933. Educated at Royal Conservatory of Music, Toronto, 1951–3, L.R.S.M. in piano, 1952; University of Toronto Faculty of Music (composition under John Weinzweig, piano under Alberto Guerrero, harpsichord under Getra Kraus), 1953, expelled for insubordination; moved to Europe to pursue private study in music, literature, languages and philosophy, 1955–61. Married (1) mezzo-soprano Phyllis Mailing, 1 July 1960 (dissolved); (2) Jean Elliott, September 1975. Cataloguer, Canadian Music Center, Toronto, 1961–3; founder, Ten Centuries Concerts, Toronto, 1961; teacher of music and artist in residence, Memorial University, St John's Newfoundland, 1963–5; founding faculty, Simon Fraser University, Vancouver, British Columbia, 1965–75; founder, World Soundscape Project, 1969–75; resident as freelance composer, lecturer, writer, Monteagle Valley, Maynooth, Bancroft, Ontario, 1975–84; lived briefly in St Gall, Switzerland, 1984; resident, Indian River, Peterborough, Ontario, from 1987. Recipient: Fromm Foundation Award (for *Gita*), 1972; William Harold Moon Award, 1974; Guggenheim Fellowship, 1974; Canadian Music Council, first Composer of the Year Award, 1977; first Jules Leger Prize for New Chamber Music (for *String Quartet No 2*), 1978; Prix International Arthur Honegger (for *String Quartet No 1*), 1980; Donald Cameron Medal, Banff School of Fine Arts, 1985; Glenn Gould Award, 1987. Honorary doctorates: Carleton University, Ottawa, and Trent University, Peterborough, Ontario. Mailing address: c/o Arcana Editions, P.O. Box 425, Station K, Toronto, Ontario M4P 2G9, Canada.

Publishers: Berandol; Arcana Editions (self).

Symphonies/orchestral:

In memoriam: Alberto Guerrero (string orchestra) 1959; first performed Vancouver, 1962.
Partita (string orchestra) 1961.

Dithyramb (string orchestra) 1961; withdrawn.
Canzoni for Prisoners 1962; first performed Montreal, 1963.
Invertible Material (youth orchestra) 1963; withdrawn.
Untitled Composition No 1 1963; first performed Toronto, 3 November 1966.
Untitled Composition No 2 1963.
Statement in Blue (youth orchestra) 1964; first performed Toronto, 1965. Recorded Melbourne SMLP 4017.
Festival Music (small orchestra) 1966; first performed Charlottetown, Prince Edward Island, 1966.
Son of Heldenleben (orchestra, tape) 1968; first performed Montreal, 13 November 1968. Recorded Select CC 15–101; RCI 387; ACM 3.
No Longer than Ten Minutes 1970; first performed Toronto, 16 November 1971.
East 1973; first performed Bath, May 1973. Recorded RCI 434; ACM 3.
North / White (orchestra, snowmobile) 1973; first performed Vancouver, 17 August 1973.
Train (youth orchestra) 1976; first performed Toronto, 1979.
Cortège 1977; first performed Ottawa, 6 December 1977.
Flute Concerto 1984; first performed Montreal, 1984. Recorded CBC SM 5000 series.
Ko wo kiku / Listen to the Incense 1985; first performed Kyoto, 1985.
Dream Rainbow Dream Thunder 1986; first performed Kingston, Ontario, 1986. Recorded CBC SM 5000.
Harp Concerto 1987; first performed Toronto, 1988.
Guitar Concerto 1989; first performed Toronto, 1990.
Scorpius 1991; first performed Toronto, March 1991.

Chamber / instrumental:

Polytonality (piano) 1952.
Trio (clarinet, cello, piano) 1953; first performed Toronto, 1958; withdrawn.
Concerto for Harpsichord and Eight Winds (2 flutes, oboe, clarinet, bass clarinet, 2 bassoons, horn) 1954; first performed Montreal, 1958. Recorded CMC C3488.
Sonatina (flute, harpsichord or piano) 1958; first performed London, 1959.
Sonorities (brass sextet, tape) 1966; first performed St John's, Newfoundland, 1967.
Minimusic (any combination of performers) 1969; first performed Maryland, Summer 1970.
String Quartet No 1 1970; first performed Vancouver, 16 July 1970. Recorded Guilde internationale du disque SMS 2902; Melbourne SMLP 4026; ACM 3; CMC CD 39/4090.
String Quartet No 2: Waves 1976; first performed Vancouver, 24 November 1976. Recorded Melbourne WRC 1–1120; ACM 3; CMC CD 39 4090.
The Crown of Ariadne (harp, percussion) 1979; first performed Toronto, 11 May 1979. Recorded Aquitaine MS 90570; Marc MC 20485.
Music for Wilderness Lake (12 trombones, small lake) 1979; first performed O'Grady Lake, Ontario, 26 September 1979.
Situational Music (brass quintet) 1981; first performed Stratford, Ontario, July 1981.
String Quartet No 3 1981; first performed Boston, 26 September 1981. Recorded CMC CD 39 4090.
Theseus (harp, string quartet) 1983; first performed Toronto, 28 January 1986.
Buskers (formerly *Rounds* from *Patria III*; flute, violin, viola) 1985; first performed Toronto, 26 January 1986.
Le Cri de Merlin (guitar, tape) 1987; first performed Toronto, 23 June 1987.
String Quartet No 4 1989; first performed Vancouver, 18 April 1989. Recorded CMC CD 39 4090.
String Quartet No 5: Rosalind 1989; first performed (privately) Toronto, 17 December 1989; first public performance Toronto, 9 January 1990. Recorded CMC CD 39 4090.

Vocal / choral:

Three Contemporaries (3 songs for medium voice, piano) 1956; first performed Toronto, 1958.
A Music Lesson (voice, piano) 1958; first performed Toronto, 1958.
Kinderlieder (9 songs for soprano, piano) 1958; first performed Toronto, January 1959.
Protest and Incarceration (mezzo-soprano, orchestra) 1960; first performed Toronto, 10 March 1968.
Brebeuf (cantata for baritone and orchestra) 1961; first performed Toronto, 17 November 1966.
The Judgement of Jael (cantata for soprano, mezzo-soprano, orchestra) 1961; withdrawn.
Five Studies on Texts by Prudentius (soprano, 4 flutes) 1962; first performed Toronto, 1963.
Four Songs on Texts of Tagore (SA chorus) 1962.
Opus One (SATB chorus, tape) 1962; withdrawn.
The Geography of Eros (soprano, chamber orchestra) 1963; first performed Toronto, 5 April 1964.
Modesty (from *Loving*; soprano, chamber orchestra) 1965.
Air Ishtar (from *Loving*; soprano, chamber orchestra) 1965.
Vanity (from *Loving*; soprano, chamber orchestra) 1965.
Requiems for the Party Girl (arias from *Patria II*; mezzo-soprano, chamber orchestra) 1966; first performed Vancouver, 21 November 1968. Recorded Melbourne SNLP 4026; Musique d'aujourd'hui RCI 298 301; CRI SD 245.
Threnody (speakers, chorus, youth orchestra, tape) 1967; first performed Vancouver, 11 June 1967. Recorded Melbourne SMLP 4017.
Gita (SATB chorus, 3 trumpets, 3 horns, 3 trombones, tuba, tape) 1967; first performed Tanglewood, Massachusetts, 10 August 1967.
Epitaph for Moonlight (SATB chorus, bells) 1968; first performed Vancouver, 1968. Recorded SM 274; ACM 3; Melbourne SMLP 4017.
From the Tibetan Book of the Dead (soprano, SATB chorus, flute, clarinet, tape) 1968; first performed Vancouver, 1968.
Two Anthems (formerly *Yeowe and Pax*) (SATB chorus, organ, tape) 1969.
Sappho (mezzo-soprano, harp, piano, guitar, percussion) 1970; first performed Washington, 31 October 1970; subsequently withdrawn.
Divan i Shams i Tabriz (part 1 of *Lustro*; 7 voices, orchestra, tape) 1970; first performed Toronto, 12 April 1972.
Music for the Morning of the World (part 2 of *Lustro*; soprano, tape) 1970; first performed Montreal, 25 February 1971. Recorded Melbourne SMLP 4035/6.
In Search of Zoroaster (150 voice SATB chorus, percussion) 1971; first performed Hanover, New Hampshire, May 1973.
Enchantress (soprano, exotic flute, 8 cellos) 1971; first performed Vancouver, 21 September 1972.
Miniwanka, or The Moments of Water (unaccompanied SA or SATB chorus) 1971; first performed Toronto, 1973. Recorded RCI 434; ACM 3.
Beyond the Great Gate of Light (part 3 of *Lustro*; 8 voices, orchestra, tape) 1972.
Lustro (8 voices, orchestra, tape) 1972; first performed Toronto, 31 May 1973.

Arcana (14 songs for soprano, chamber or full orchestra) 1972; first performed Montreal, 1973. Recorded RCI 434; ACM 3.

Psalm (formerly *Tehillah*; SATB chorus, percussion) 1972; first performed Vancouver, 1975. Recorded RCI 434; ACM3.

Adieu, Robert Schumann (contralto, piano, orchestra, tape) 1976; first performed Ottawa, 14 March 1978. Recorded CBC BR SM 364.

Hymn to Night (portion of *Patria V*; soprano, full orchestra, tape) 1976; first performed Toronto, 8 January 1978. Recorded CBC BR SM 364.

La Testa d'Adriane (soprano, free-bass accordion) 1977; first performed Toronto, 11 March 1978. Recorded Melbourne SMLP 4017.

Hear Me Out (portion of *Patria III*; 4 voices) 1979; first performed Maynooth, Ontario, July 1979.

Felix's Girls (9 songs, vocal quartet or SATB chorus) 1979; first performed Toronto, 26 April 1980. Recorded Grouse 101.

Gamelan (4 voices) 1979. Recorded Grouse 100/101.

Hear Me Out (from *Patria III*; 4 speaking voices) 1979; first performed Maynooth, Ontario, July 1979.

Beauty and the Beast (portion of *Patria III*; contralto, string quartet) 1980; first performed Montreal, 1 April 1981.

Wizard Oil and Indian Sagwa (portion of *Patria III*; speaker, clarinet) 1981.

The Garden of the Heart (contralto, full orchestra) 1981; first performed Ottawa, May 1981.

Snowforms (unaccompanied SA chorus; Eskimo words for snow) 1981, revised 1983; first performed Vancouver, 18 January 1981.

Sun (from *The Princess of the Stars*; unaccompanied SATB chorus; word for sun in 36 languages) 1982; first performed Toronto, 13 September 1982. Recorded CMC 14/1584; Grouse 101.

A Garden of Bells (unaccompanied SATB chorus) 1983. Recorded Grouse 101.

The Star Princess and the Waterlilies (narrator, children's chorus, light percussion) 1984; first performed Toronto, 23 December 1984.

Sun-Father Sky-Mother (from *And Wolf Shall Inherit the Moon*; solo voice in mountain setting, nearwater and forest) 1986; first performed Spray Lake, near Canmore, Alberta.

Fire (from *Patria V*; SATB chorus, light percussion) 1986; first performed Vancouver, 1986.

Tantrika (from *Patria III*) 1986; first performed St John's, Newfoundland, 11 July 1986.

Letters from Mignon (mezzo-soprano, orchestra) 1987; first performed Calgary, Alberta, 1987.

Magic Songs (unaccompanied SATB or TTBB chorus) 1988; first performed Sweden, 1990.

The Death of Buddha (mixed chorus, gongs, bell tree) 1988; first performed Toronto, 6 June 1989.

Opera/dramatic:

Loving (4 voices, 2 actors, dancers, orchestra, tape) 1965; first performed Montreal, 24 May 1966. Recorded Melbourne SMLP 4035/6.

Patria (12-part cycle) 1966, in progress.

Dream Passage (mezzo-soprano, chorus, actors, dancers, chamber orchestra, tape; revised as *Patria II*) 1969; first performed Vancouver, 27 May 1969.

Patria II: Requiems for the Party-Girl (mezzo-soprano, SATB chorus, actors, dancers, chamber orchestra, tape) 1972; first performed Stratford, Ontario, 23 August 1972.

Patria I: The Characteristics Man (later renamed *The Wolfman*; mezzo-soprano, SATB chorus, actors, chamber orchestra, tape) 1974.

Apocalypsis (consisting of *John's Vision*—3 sound poets, 5 singers, dancers, mime artists, men's chorus, women's chorus, children's chorus, 2 mixed choruses, speech chorus, 4 instrumental groups, organ, tape, 7 conductors, text from *Revelation*; *Credo*—12 choruses, tape or synthesizer, optional string and/or synthesizer, text from Bruno) 1977–8; first performed London, Ontario, 28 November 1980.

Jonah (SATB chorus, actors, children, flute, clarinet, organ, percussion) 1979; first performed Maynooth, Ontario, 29 August 1979.

The Princess of the Stars (prologue to *Patria*; 4 sound poets or actors, soprano, 6 dancers, flute, clarinet, brass quartet, 4 percussion, canoeists, small lake) 1981; first performed Heart Lake, Ontario, 1981.

Patria VI: Ra (7 singers, 9 actors, 9 dancers, belly dancers, extras, 8 voice male chorus, violin, harp, percussion, ud, qanum, darabukkah, Middle Eastern percussion, tape by Bentley Jarvis, electronic sounds, participatory audience of 75; *Litany of Re*, *Egyptian Book of the Dead*) 1983; first performed Toronto, 1983.

Patria III: The Greatest Show (120 actors and singers, chamber orchestra) 1987; first performed Peterborough, Ontario, 1988.

Patria IV: The Black Theatre of Hedrmes Trismegistos (11 actors, 7 singers, 2 optional dancers, 8–16 voice chorus, chamber ensemble; alchemical and gnostic texts) 1988; first performed Liège, Belgium, 1989.

Patria V: The Crown of Ariadne in progress.

Patria VII: Asterion in progress.

Patria VIII: The Enchanted Forest in progress.

Patria IX: The Spirit Garden in progress.

Patria X: The Kingdom of the Cinnabar Phoenix in progress.

Patria: Conclusion—And the Wolf Shall Inherit the Moon in progress.

Other:

Kaleidoscope (multi-track tape) 1967.

Dream Passage (radio version of *Patria II: Requiems for the Party Girl*; mezzo-soprano, chamber ensemble, tape) 1969; broadcast CBC Radio, 27 May 1969.

Okeanos (quadrophonic tape; collaboration with Bruce Davis and Brian Fawcett) 1971; first performed Vancouver, March 1972.

Bing, Bang, Boom (film music) 1975.

Ontario Variations (1 movement for set of piano variations by several hands on a theme of Jack Behrens) 1979.

Music for Wilderness Lake (film music) 1980.

Harbour Symphony (fog horns) 1983; first performed St John's Newfoundland, Canada, July 1983.

A Carnival of Shadows (film adaptation of *Patria III: The Greatest Show*) 1989.

PUBLICATIONS

By Schafer: "The Limits of Nationalism in Canada", in *Tamarack Review*, 18, Winter 1961; "Ezra Pound and Music", in *Canadian Music Journal*, 5, Summer 1961, reprinted in *Ezra Pound: A Collection of Critical Essays*, Englewood Cliffs, New Jersey, 1963; "The Canadian String Quartet", in *Canadian Music Journal*, 6, Spring 1962; *British Composers in Interview*, London, 1963; "Short History of

Music in Canada", in *Catalogue of Orchestral Music at the Canadian Music Centre*, Toronto, 1963; "What Is This Article About?", in *Canadian Forum*, 44, December 1964; *The Composer in the Classroom*, Scarborough, Ontario, 1965; *Ear Cleaning*, Scarborough, Ontario, 1967; "The Future of Music in Canada", in *Proceedings and Transactions of the Royal Society of Canada*, 5 June 1967; "Cleaning the Lenses of Perception", in *Arts Canada*, 25, October–November 1968; *The New Soundscape*, Scarborough, Ontario, 1969; "A Basic Course", in *Source: Music of the Avant-Garde*, 3, January 1969; "The City as a Sonic Sewer", in *Vancouver Sun*, 11 March 1969; *The Book of Noise*, Wellington, New Zealand, 1970; *When Words Sing*, Scarborough, Ontario, 1970; "A Middle East Sound Diary", in *Focus on Musicology*, 1, 1970; *A Survey of Community Noise By-Laws in Canada*, Soundscape Document 4, Vancouver, 1972; *The Public of the Music Theatre: Louis Riel—A Case Study*, Vienna, 1972; *The Music of the Environment*, Vienna, 1973, reprinted in *Cultures*, 1, 1973; *The Vancouver Soundscape*, Document No 5, Vancouver, 1974; *Rhinoceros in the Classroom*, London, 1975; *E.T.A. Hoffmann and Music*, Toronto, 1975; *Creative Music Education*, New York, 1976; *Smoke* [novel], Vancouver, 1976; *The Tuning of the World*, Toronto, 1977; *Music in the Cold*, Toronto, 1977; *A Chaldean Inscription*, Toronto, 1978; *R. Murray Schafer: A Collection*, Bancroft, Ontario, 1979; *The Sixteen Scribes*, Bancroft, Ontario, 1981; "For Composers to Become Acoustic Designers", in *Musicworks*, 25, Winter 1984; *On Canadian Music*, Bancroft, Ontario, 1984; *Diacamus and Labyrinthos: A Philologist's Notebook*, Bancroft, Ontario, 1984; "McLuhan and Acoustic Space", in *Antigonish Review*, 62, Summer/Fall 1985; *The Thinking Ear: Complete Writings on Music Education*, Toronto, 1986; *Patria and the Theatre of Confluence*, Indian River, Ontario, 1991, also available as special issue of *Descant*, 22(2), Spring 1991; many more.

On Schafer: Dulan Barber, (interview) in *Times Educational Supplement*, London, 18 June 1971; in *Contemporary Canadian Composers/Compositeurs canadiens contemporains*, edited by Keith MacMillan and John Beckwith, Toronto; Keith Potter and John Shepherd, (interview) in *Contact*, 13, Spring 1976; Ulla Colgrass, "MS" in *Music Magazine*, 3, January 1980; Keiko Torigoe, "A Study of the World Soundscape Project", dissertation, York University, Toronto, 1982; Stephen J. Adams, *RMS*, Canadian Composer Series 4, Toronto, 1983; Tina Pearson, "Beyond *RA*: RMS in person", (interview) in *Musicworks*, 25, Autumn 1983; Susan Bradley, "Extra-Musical References in the Works of RMS", dissertation, University of Alberta, Edmonton, 1983; Stephen J. Adams, "MS's *Patria*: The Greatest Show on Earth?" in *Journal of Canadian Studies*, 23, Spring/Summer 1988; Kirk MacKenzie, "Influences of Soundscape Theory on the Compositions of RMS", dissertation, University of Cincinnati, Ohio, 1988, and "A Twentieth-Century Musical/Theatrical Cycle: RMS's *Patria*", doctoral dissertation, University of Cincinnati, 1991.

* * *

Even in this age of specialisation, there are composers who have made significant contributions also to architecture, engineering, mathematics and to the visual arts. Yet generally we have had to accept that the Renaissance ideal of the Universal Man, epitomised by Leonardo da Vinci, is no longer achievable. Nevertheless, there is something Leonardo-like about R. Murray Schafer who, in a many-faceted career, has demonstrated an impressive integration of artistic, scientific, metaphysical and intellectual activity. Composer, pedagogue, philosopher, writer, literary and linguistic scholar, graphic artist, acoustician, theatrical creator and impresario—Schafer is all of these yet, paradoxically, by inclination a recluse. Gentle and retiring, it is more through the vision of an extraordinary imagination that he has moved mountains and inspired others than by any authoritarian personality. He is Canada's most original and internationally distinguished composer and yet also peculiarly Canadian. From the conflicting creeds of the 1950s and early 1960s he made his own synthesis, forging a unique and individual course increasingly removed from that of Europe and similarly distinct from new trends in the United States. He is respected worldwide as a stimulating educator, for his pioneering research into the sounds of the environment, and as the creator of a new genre of epic, multi-dimensional music-theatre. But sadly, because of the exceptional demands of these major multi-media works, performances, particularly outside Canada, are less frequent than Schafer deserves.

Even in his purely instrumental works, Schafer has overturned convention. *Son of Heldenleben* parodies orchestral repertoire, *North/White* introduces a snowmobile on stage, *Cortège* requires the orchestra to process through the auditorium while *Lustro* scatters instrumentalists and singers around the audience. Schafer has written normal concert music like his early *Concerto for Harpsichord and Eight Winds* and the recent *Flute Concerto*, wherein a dazzling contemporary instrumental technique is combined with a Romantic aesthetic. But the theatrical is seldom far absent. It can be most affecting when most discreet, unfolding purely through musical means as in *Threnody*, a stark and disturbing memorial to the victims of Nagasaki, and *Adieu, Robert Schumann*, which draws on the diary kept by Clara Schumann during her husband's last years in an asylum, and which floats stylistically between snatches of Schumann's own music and the language of 20th-century Expressionism.

In the huge diversity of Schafer's work, it can be the smaller pieces whose simple poetry seems to touch the infinite. *Snowforms* for unaccompanied chorus is such a piece. Indeed, Schafer's short choral compositions are among his finest and deserve to be in every good amateur choral repertory. Graphic notation, clusters, sonorous effects and other contemporary vocal techniques are used alongside simple melodies and harmonies. The results are original and practical, challenging maybe, but enormously rewarding. Indeed, Schafer has provided generously for amateurs and young musicians ever since his important contribution to the new creative music educational movement of the 1960s, which influenced classroom attitudes throughout the world.

The core of his professional instrumental works are his five magnificent string quartets which chart his thoughts since 1970, over the same period as his massive *Patria* cycle. Without satirising the conventions of the medium, Schafer characteristically develops both its technical and expressive possibilities. The beautiful Second Quartet, *Waves*, is based on the fluctuating frequency patterns of ocean waves and derives from a serious scientific study, part of the World Soundscape Project, which he founded to study the sonic environment and which resulted in his most important book, *The Tuning of the World*.

It is the multi-dimensional works created for specific environments that are Schafer's most individual and controversial achievement. It was his first audio-visual work, *Loving*, commissioned by CBC television in 1966, that brought him to prominence in Canada. Since then he has been engaged in an ongoing series of dramatic spectacles involving music, acting, dance, myth, ritual and allegory, unconventional performance conditions and spectacular outdoor environments. In these ambitious, labyrinthian creations Schafer seeks to open wide the shutters of our imagination and to overcome the numbing anesthesia of materialism. Via more-or-less elaborate metaphors and symbols, he argues for the reinstatement of human and spiritual values and a unification of Man's fragmented spirit with "natural" rhythms and timeless archetypes.

A remarkable example of this unique vision is *The Princess of the Stars*, originally performed in 1981 on a wilderness lake in the Rocky Mountains to a total audience of around 5000. Part Indian pageant, part creation-legend, *The Princess of the Stars* commences in the dark one hour before sunrise, utilising the natural acoustic amplification of water and mountains and, as dawn breaks, reveals canoes of masked singers and dancers whose accompanying musicians are concealed around the shore. *Apocalypsis*, on the other hand, based on the Book of Revelation, is a monumental music-drama for indoors involving several choirs, soloists, sound poets, dancers, speech chorus, orchestra and tape. *The Characteristics Man* and *Requiems for a Party Girl* are the first two in the *Patria* series on which Schafer has been working for many years. Its third part, *Patria* series on which Schafer has been working for many years. Its third part, *The Greatest Show*, is another outside extravaganza in which assorted musical "side-shows" are mysteriously integrated in the context of a huge fairground.

Ra is the most outlandish of these epic works. Here an audience of exactly 75 people is invited to participate in an all-night sequence of tasks and ordeals, initiation rites, artistic and quasi-religious experiences. The ancient Egyptian myth of the sun god's passage through the netherworld is used to symbolise a spiritual journey from death to rebirth and into the centre of life and self. Musically, *Ra* uses coptic chants, incantation and authentic middle-Eastern instruments. But the attempt to recreate ancient purification rituals for contemporary society demands, perhaps, too great a suspension of disbelief. It is vulnerable to the intrusions of modern culture and to accusations of incongruity, even gimmickry. If *Ra* cannot entirely succeed, its failure is attendant upon an exceptional idealism. Schafer, indeed, is one of those brave adventures, kindred spirit to those who first crossed continents and circumnavigated the globe, a doer of deeds, to borrow the words of Roosevelt, "whose face is marred by dust and sweat and blood; who strives valiantly, who errs and comes short again and again; who knows the great enthusiasms; who at best knows the triumph of high achievement; and who, at the worst, if he fails, at least fails while daring greatly, so that his place shall never be with those cold and timid souls, who know neither victory nor defeat."

—Richard Steinitz

SCHAT, Peter. Dutch. Born in Utrecht, 5 June 1935. Educated at Utrecht Conservatory (composition under Kees van Baaren), 1952–8; further study under Van Baaren and piano under Jaap Callenbach, Royal Conservatory, The Hague; further composition study under Matyas Seiber, London, 1959, and Pierre Boulez, Basle, 1960–2. Participant, Studio for Electro-Instrumental Music, Amsterdam, from 1967, and Nutcracker movement, 1969; founder, Amsterdam Electrisch Circus, 1973; teacher of composition, Royal Conservatory, The Hague, 1974–83; subsequently full-time composer. Recipient: AVRO Award (for *Septet*), 1957; Matthijs Vermeulen Prize (for *To You*), 1972; Joost van den Vondel Prize, Westfalische Wilhelmsuniversitatat, Munster (for exemplary achievement in the Dutch and Low German cultural area), 1990. Mailing address: c/o Donemus, Paulus Potterstraat 14, 1071 CZ Amsterdam, The Netherlands.

Publisher: Donemus.

Symphonies/orchestral:

Mozaiken 1959.
Concerto da camera (2 clarinets, percussion, piano, strings) 1960.
Entelechie I (5 instrumental groups) 1961.
Dansen uit het Labyrinth (orchestral suite; from the opera) 1962.
On Escalation (6 percussion, orchestra) 1968.
Symphony No 1 1978. Recorded Composers Voice CV 7901.
Symphony No 2 1983, revised 1984. Recorded Composers Voice CVS 1986/1.
Serenade (strings) 1984.
De Hemel/Heaven 1989–90; first performed Amsterdam, June 1991.
Opening Op 38 1991.

Chamber/instrumental:

Passacaglia and Fugue (organ) 1954.
Introductie en adagio in oude stijl (string quartet) 1954.
Septet (flute, oboe, bass clarinet, horn, piano, percussion, cello) 1956. Recorded Composers Voice CV 7901.
Octet (wind quintet, 2 trumpets, trombone) 1958.
Inscripties (piano) 1959.
Due pezzi (flute, trumpet, percussion, violin) 1959.
Improvisations and Symphonies (flute, bassoon, horn) 1960.
Sextet (3 record players, 3 musicians) 1961.
Signalement (6 percussion, 3 double basses) 1961.
Collages (organ) 1962.
First Essay on Electrocution (violin, guitar, percussion) 1966.
Clockwise and Anticlockwise (16 winds) 1967.
Anathema (piano) 1968.
Hypothema (recorder; recorder, tape) 1969.
Thema (oboe, 18 winds, 4 electric guitars, electric organ) 1970.
Polonaise (piano) 1981.

Vocal/choral:

Cryptogamen (baritone, orchestra; Achterberg) 1959.
The Fall (16 voices) 1960. Recorded Composers Volice CV 7902.
Entelechie II (soprano, flute, clarinet, trumpet, harp, piano, percussion, vibraphone, violin, viola, cello) 1961.
Choirs from Labyrinth (chorus; from the opera) 1962.
Stemmen uit het Labyrinth (3 voices, orchestra) 1963.
Improvisations from the Labyrinth (3 voices, bass clarinet, piano, percussion, double bass) 1964.
Scenes uit het Labyrinth (narrator, 3 voices, chorus, orchestra) 1964.
To You (mezzo-soprano, 6 electric guitars, 3 bass guitars, 4 electric pianos, 2 electric organs, 6 electric humming tops; Mitchell) 1972. Recorded Composers Voice 7475/1.
Canto general (mezzo-soprano, violin, piano) 1974. Recorded Composers Voice CV 7475/1.
Mei '75: eenlied van bevrijding (mezzo-soprano, baritone, orchestra) 1975.
Houdini symfonie (soprano, mezzo-soprano, tenor, baritone, chorus, orchestra) 1976.

De briefscene (mezzo-soprano, tenor, piano) 1976.
Kind en kraai (soprano, piano; Mulsich) 1977.
De Trein/The Train (from the opera *Symposion*; 5 male voices, orchestra) 1985.

Opera/dramatic:

Labyrinth (de Boer, after Boon) 1961–2.
Reconstructie (collaboration with Louis Andriessen, Reinbert de Leeuw, Misha Mengelberg and J. van Vlijmen; text by Mulisch and Claus) 1969.
Het vijde seizoen/The Fifth Season (music theatre) 1973.
Houdini (circus opera; Mitchell) 1974–6; first performed Amsterdam, 29 September 1977. Recorded Composers Voice CVS 1977.
Aap verslaat de knekelgeest/Monkey Subdues the White-Bone Demon (strip opera) 1980; first performed Amsterdam, 1980.
Symposion (Komrij) 1990–1; first performed Brussels, 1992.

Other:

I Am Houdini (ballet; tenor, chorus, 2 pianos) 1976.

PUBLICATIONS

By Schat: "*Labyrinth*: A Kind of Opera", in *Opera 66*, London, 1966; *De Toonklok* (essays and interviews), Amsterdam, 1984.

On Schat: Reinbert de Leeuw, "S's *Labyrinth*: An Opera of Sorts", in *Sonorum speculum*, 27, 1966; E. Vermeulen, "Compositions by LA and PS Incorporating Quotations", in *Sonorum speculum*, 35, 1969.

* * *

Along with Louis Andriessen, with whom he and others collaborated on the "morality" opera *Reconstructie*, Peter Schat is probably the most significant Dutch composer since the death of Willem Pijper. In the same year as *Reconstructie* was finished and staged, Schat joined the so-called "Nutcracker" movement aimed at injecting life into the moribund post-war Dutch music scene. By that time, aged only 34, he was already an established composer, having won international recognition a decade before at the 1958 ISCM Festival with the superb *Septet*.

A one-time pupil of Boulez, Schat was initially drawn to a rather heterodox brand of serialism. The tone-row in his first orchestral essay *Mozaiken* is subjected to a shifting grid which frees it from any rigidity or constraint on choice; the effect is remarkably similar to some of the earlier experiments of American minimalism. In the conservative-sounding *Concerto da camera* he breaks the row into smaller units, but subjects all other parameters of the piece—rhythm, durations etc—to serial procedures; the results are unsettling, but unquestionably powerful.

At the same time as this deceptively rigid system, Schat was experimenting with improvisational techniques, notably in the ambitious *Improvisations and Symphonies* for winds, in which the composer's control over the music shifted from the notes played to the physical disposition of the performers. Something of the same concern for the spatial distribution of sound was evident in the Stockhausen-influenced *Entelechie I* for five instrumental groups. This interest in the "conquest of space" became one of the essential components of the multi-media operatic *Labyrinth*, a highly complex work which has not yet been fully assimilated, and which is best known by virtue of several abstracted concert pieces which adumbrate its main elements and concerns.

One of the main motifs of this period is Schat's growing interest in what he calls "shadow-objects", a device which links the more dogmatic procedures of dogmatic serialism with Schat's highly politicised desire for an aesthetic of very exact mediations and material juxtapositions. There are elements of it already in the *Concerto da camera*, but it reaches maturity in *Entelechie I* and in the curious *Clockwise and Anticlockwise*, which is Schat's first experiment with a "tone clock" which will transcend the chromatic scale and open up new but controllable areas of harmonic and post-harmonic language. In *Clockwise and Anticlockwise*, the players are again distributed spatially, this time in the shape of a clock-face. The references range from Renaissance ratios, to the advent of chromaticism, to twelve-tone composition, to Stockhausen's zodiacal concerns.

Though he had helped establish the Amsterdam Studio for Electro-Instrumental Music in 1967, Schat showed surprisingly little interest in electronics as a direct alternative to conventional instrumentation. There is no sign of a development towards something like the American Morton Subotnick's notion of "shadow" scoring. On the other hand, Schat's populist radicalism helped draw him toward a rapprochement with rock music and some of his best scores of the 1970s, beginning with *Thema*, made extensive use of electric guitars and bass guitars. This is most effective in *To You*, a setting of texts by the British poet Adrian Mitchell which uses no less than nine electric guitars, a pair of electronic keyboards, and a row of electric spinning tops (a Kagelish *coup de théâtre* which suits Mitchell's intentions perfectly).

To You is, perhaps, Schat's best work; it is certainly one of the most frequently revived. Its legacy is evident in the remarkable First and Second Symphonies and in the related group of works on the subject of the escapologist Houdini, who becomes a kind of iconic representation of the modern composer handcuffed and chained by one or another of the modern dogmatisms, and whose "entertainment value" is largely in his evasion of those constraints.

Schat has perhaps not yet entirely fulfilled the extraordinary promise of his early work and of the new direction suggested by *Thema* and *To You*, but it is clear that his conception of a new tonal system is not yet fully articulated. As he moves into a fourth decade as a vanguard composer, it is clear that there are major discoveries still to be made.

—Henk Maarten

SCHERCHEN, Tona (Tona Scherchen-Hsiao). French. Born in Neuchâtel, Switzerland, 12 March 1938; resident in China, 1950–60. Educated: *Baccalaureat* in arts and letters, Peking, 1957; Peking Conservatory (traditional Chinese music and pipa), 1958–60; also studied at Shanghai Music Academy; Gravesano Studio Switzerland (under Hermann Scherchen), 1960–1; Mozarteum, Salzburg (under Hans Werner Henze), 1961–3; Conservatoire National Supérieur de Musique, Paris (composition under Olivier Messiaen), 1963–6; private composition study under György Ligeti, Vienna, 1966–7; also studied ethnology, ethnomusicology, psychology, INALCO, Paris, mid-1970s; self-taught in electronic music and computers, United States, 1980s. Independent composer, since 1968; guest professor of ethnomusicology, universities of Basle and Zurich, 1969–71; visiting lecturer, Denmark, 1972; DAAD artist in residence, Berlin, 1977; resident in United States, 1979–84; visiting research associate, Yale University, New Haven, Connecticut, 1979–81; freelance radio producer, Paris, since late 1970s. Recipient: 1st prize, Paris Conservatoire, 1964; 1st prize (for *Tzang*), Gaudeamus Foundation Composers' Competition, 1967; Prix Stéphane-Chapelle-Clergue-Gabriel-Marie, SACEM, 1972; Koussevitzky Award, "in recognition of her valuable contribution to the music of our time", 1979; Grand Priz Hervé Dugardin, 1973; laureate, Foundation de France, 1983. Mailing address: 33 rue de Nevers, 75006 Paris, France.

Publishers: Universal Edition; Boosey & Hawkes; Amphion.

Symphonies/orchestral:

Tzang (chamber orchestra) 1966; first performed The Netherlands, 1967.
Khouang 1966–8; first performed Strasbourg, 1972.
Tao (viola, orchestra) 1971; first performed Graz, Austria, 1976.
Vague-Tao 1974–5; first performed Paris, 1976.
"*S . . .* " 1975; first performed St Paul, Minnesota, 1976.
Oeil de chat 1976–7; first performed Paris, 1976.
L'Invitation au voyage (chamber orchestra) 1977; first performed Paris, 1978.
L'illégitime (orchestra, tape) 1985–6; first performed Saarbrücken, 1986.

Chamber/instrumental:

In/Sin (2 pieces for flute) 1965; first performed Darmstadt, 1966.
Hsun (oboe, trumpet, trombone, percussion, 2 cellos) 1968; first performed Copenhagen, 1971.
Shen (6 percussion) 1968; first performed Amsterdam, 1969. Recorded Philips 6521 030 ST.
Tzoue (clarinet, cello, harpsichord; version for flute, double bass, harpsichord) 1970; first performed Copenhagen, 1971.
Yun-Yu (violin or viola, vibraphone) 1972; first performed Strasbourg, 1972.
Bien (clarinet/bass clarinet, horn, trumpet, trombone, 2 percussion, piano, 2 violins, viola, cello, double bass) 1972–3; first performed New York City, 1973.
Lien (viola) 1973; first performed Paris, 1973. Recorded Finnadar.
Tjao-Hjouen (flute, oboe, piano, viola, cello, 3 percussion) 1973; first performed Lucerne, 1973.
Yi (large marimba/2 players) 1973; first performed Strasbourg, 1973. Recorded Prodisc Apostrophe AS 37334.
Ziguidor (wind quintet) 1977; first performed Baden-Baden, 1978.
Lo (trombone, 12 strings) 1978–9; first performed Tanglewood, Massachusetts, 1980.
Tzing (brass quintet) 1979; first performed Paris, 1980.
Once upon a Time (harp) 1979; first performed Paris, 1979.
Escargots volants (clarinet) 1979; first performed Orléans, 1979.
Radar (piano) 1980; first performed New York City, 1983.
Tarots (harpsichord, 3 clarinets, trumpet, trombone, violin, double bass) 1981–2.
Lustucru (6 short pieces for variable instrumentations) 1983.

Vocal/choral:

Wai (mezzo-soprano, string quartet) 1966–7; first performed Donaueschingen, 1968.
Tzi (16 unaccompanied voices tuning fork, gong) 1969–70; first performed Baden-Baden, 1971.
La Larme de crocodile (solo voice) 1977; first performed Strasbourg, 1978.
Fuite? (voice, clarinet/bass clarinet, double bass, percussion, tape) 1987.

Other:

Tzan-Shen (ballet version of *Shen*) 1970–1; first performed Strasbourg, 1972.
Between (*son et lumière*/architectural spectacle) 1978–86; music realised in New York City and Geneva; first presented Lille, 1986.
Eclats obscurs (electro-acoustic music for cello, piano, percussion, tape and speaker with a poem by St-John Perse for radiophonic presentation) 1982; first presented Paris, 1983.
Portières castor (tape music for film) 1982.
Man Ray (tape music for film) 1983.
Cancer, Solstice '83 (music for Space Installation) 1983–7; music for main area realised New York City, 1983; music for access tunnel realised Geneva and presented New York City, 1986; audio-visual version of main area music realised Paris, 1987; first presented Witten, 1987.
Spaceflight/Fou-Fou (electronic) 1987; first performed Lyon, 1987.
Lude pour Alice!!V (fantasy film, with music for mezzo-soprano, tuba, SYTER computer, tape) 1988–9.
Le Jeu de pogo (radiophonic work) 1990; in progress.

PUBLICATIONS

By Scherchen: articles in *Ear Magazine*, 1984, DAAD catalogue *French Artists in Berlin*, 1984, and *L'alfabeto urbano*, 1987.

On Scherchen: Brigitte Shiffer, "TS", in *Tempo*, 117, 1976.

Tona Scherchen comments:

According to the ancient Greeks music is ordered time. The axiom holds good down to our times.

In itself, sound is energy, movement, part of the cosmic order; in physics, the sound wave is the phenomenon of particles moving through space in vibrating cycles at a speed of 340 kilometres per second.

While our auditory perceptions are limited to a small band of frequencies and sounds detectable to the human ear, our nervous system does react to much larger areas of the sonic spectrum.

Mankind is therefore only conscious of a minute part of the formidable cosmic energy of sound, a part which it manipulates according to cultural and aesthetic needs and aspirations.

As a composer, it is that cosmic energy which is vital to me and central to my work. I am fascinated by the relationships and correspondences between sound and light, and this is why, during the 1980s, I've dedicated myself to research in this field.

* * *

The richness of Tona Scherchen's style owes much to her unshakable commitment to a remarkably single-minded and unitary musical exploration. If one can unpack her oriental background—her composer mother Hsiao She-sien married the Swiss conductor Hermann Scherchen—through such characteristics as the use of silence, asymmetrical phrasing and cellular development, it emerges most clearly in her work in a universalised conception of music in which the primary intention is to deploy micro and macro dimensions in specific temporal proportions that retain the music's beauty and lyrical sonority.

Scherchen's music is largely grounded in the law of proportions, in which area of inquiry, coming from science and the plastic arts, she has concentrated most of her theoretical explorations, but also her awareness of how musical work is perceived. The results are for the most part quite audibly located in the vanguard of new musical thought.

She works with essentially simple materials, turning instinctively in the direction of minimalism, but traversing the extremes of sonority. Her basic materials may be as divergent as a simple tempered note or the most recherché acoustic effects. Whatever their nature, though, such materials are always directed toward an essentially dramatic conception of music, underlined by her exploitation of very different realms of musical discourse.

Scherchen, indeed, likes to work at and with limits: the limits of possible performance (as witness the problematic vocal parts in *Wai* or of *Lien*, which demands four simultaneous melodic lines of the violist), the limits of the specific sonority she has chosen (as in *Tzi*, for 16 unaccompanied voices, tuning fork and gong), and also those which she constantly extends: the limits of temporal organization.

It is possible to distinguish two distinct periods in her career. Up to 1979, Scherchen attempted to develop a primarily instrumental language (in *Wai*, *Tzi*, *Yun-Yu*, *Lien* and also in *Bien*, a piece for 12 performers that imposes considerable difficulty of realisation). She organised her essentially dramatic progress by means of cellular development, a process which favours the linking of quite diverse musical realms. She deployed techniques such as chance, minimalism and spectral modulation quite instinctively and undogmatically.

Her subsequent progress is most particularly evident in *Radar*, her only piece for piano to date, in which she moves toward an altogether more unified conception. Pieces such as *Ziguidor, Lo, Oeil de chat*, and *L'Invitation au voyage* mark a transitional phase, stripped of the earlier concern with sonority, in which she develops a counterpoint that alternates binary and ternary rhythms. With *Radar* she attempts to perfect her articulation of sonorities. In the first movement particularly, the attack is organized round a high chord marked *sffz*, and recombinant sequences of two, three or four sound events. The majority of these groups are followed by one or more others, as a kind of resonance. Attacks, dynamics and pedal marks play an important part in the contours of the piece. Such abstraction is even more evident, following Scherchen's five-year sojourn in the United States, during which she devoted herself to multidisciplinary research, in a piece like *Le Jeu de pogo (Pogo Interstellaire)*, which is based on polyrhythms and a greatly expanded conception of musical time.

Parallel with her formally scored concert music, Scherchen has also undertaken various audio-visual works (sonic sculpture, *son et lumière*, performance pieces and film) in which she invests electro-acoustic resources with considerable poetry. One might have cited *Between* as a concert piece, exploiting the sonorities of flux and reflux and combining them with those of solo trombone. The piece is perfectly balanced between a conception based on temporal concerns and one based on sonorities, and it is on this middle ground that Scherchen places such emphasis, balancing purely compositional innovations with an awareness of the intrinsic potentialities of pure sound.

This in turn relates back to Scherchen's inheritance of a double culture which has opened up for her a musical field both virtually unlimited and profoundly original in its disposition of resources. One should add that her preference for the number five and even more for the number seven renders the co-existence in the natural order of the unitary, the binary and the ternary, an aspect which lends Scherchen's music its characteristic complexity and equilibrium.

—Christine Paquelet

SCHNEBEL, Dieter. German. Born in Lahr, Baden, 14 March 1930. Educated: studied music privately under Wilhelm Sibler, 1942–5; studied piano privately under Wilhelm Resch, 1945–9; Musikhochschule, Freiburg (music history under Eric Doflein) 1949–52; Ferienkurse für Neue Musik, Darmstadt (composition under Ernst Krenek, Hermann Scherchen, Edgar Varèse, Theodor Adorno, Hans Werner Henze, Luigi Nono and Pierre Boulez), from 1950; University of Tübingen (theology, philosophy and musicology under Walter Gerstenberg), 1952–6; further piano study under Hans von Besele, Stuttgart, 1953–5; passed theological examinations, 1955; entered ministry, 1956. Married (1) Camilla Riegger in 1956, 1 son and 1 daughter; (2) Iris von Kaschnitz in 1970. Minister, teacher of theology and religious studies, Kaiserlautern, 1957–63; teacher of philosophy, psychology and religious studies, Theological Seminary, Frankfurt, 1963–70; teacher, Oscar von Miller Gymnasium, Munich, from 1970; professor of experimental music and musical research, Hochschule der Kunste, Berlin, from 1976; visits to United States, Brazil, Israel and East Asia, 1979–81. Mailing address: c/o B. Schott's Sohne, Weihergarten Postfach 36 40, D-6500 Mainz 1, Germany.

Publisher: Schott.

[Schnebel's work-list is divided into cycles of broadly similar works, which can be performed individually or alone.]

Works:

Versuche 1953–6, 1964.
- I *Analysis* (string instruments, percussion) 1953; first performed Brussels, 12 December 1964.
- II *Stücke* (string quartet or string instruments) 1954–5; first performed Rome, June 1968.
- III *Fragment* (chamber ensemble, voices) 1955; first performed Witten, 22 April 1972.
- IV *Compositio* (orchestra) 1955–6, revised 1964; first performed Venice, 13 September 1971.

Für Stimmen (. . . missa est) 1956–69.
- I *Dt 31* (12 vocal groups) 1956–8; first performed Stuttgart, 5 November 1965.
- II *Amn* (7 vocal groups/speaking) 1958, 1966–7; first performed Kassel, 31 March 1967.
- III *:! (madrasha 2)* (3 choral groups) 1958, 1967–8; first performed Bremen, 5 May 1968.
- IV *Choralvorspiele I/II* (organ, supporting instruments, tape) 1966, 1968–9; first performed Bremen, 29 May 1970. Recorded Wergo WER 60075.

Projekte 1958–61.
I *Raum—zeit y* (variable instrumentation) 1958, in progress; first performed Palermo, 6 October 1963.
II *Das Urteil (after Franz Kafka)* (voices, instruments, sound-sources, audience) 1959; first performed Paris, 21 October 1966.
III *Glossolalie* (speaker, instruments) 1959–60; first performed Paris, 21 October 1966.
IV *Glossolalie 61* (3–4 speakers, 3–4 instrumentalists) 1960–1; first performed Palermo, 6 October 1963.
Abfälle I 1960–2.
I *reactions* (instrumentalist, audience) 1960–1; first performed Padua, 29 April 1961.
II *visible music I* (conductor, instrumentalist) 1960–2; first performed Palermo, 7 October 1962.
Modelle (Ausarbeitungen) 1961–6.
I *Nostalgie* (conductor) 1962; first performed Wiesbaden, 1962.
II *Espressivo* (musical drama for pianist/any harmony instruments) 1961–3.
III *Concert sans orchestre* (pianist, audience) 1964; first performed Zurich, 13 June 1970.
IV *Fall <-> out* (vocalist, audience) 1965, in progress.
V *Anschlage—ausschlage* (flute, cello, harpsichord) 1965–6; first performed Zurich, 5 January 1970.
Räume 1963–77.
I *Ki-no* (projectors, listeners) 1963–7. First performed Munich, 10 July 1967.
II *Mo-no* ("music to read") 1969; realised Cologne, 1969.
III *Gehörgänge* (environmental) 1972.
IV *Drei-Klang* (3 different spatially disposed ensembles) 1976–7.
Abfälle II 1964, in progress.
I *Stoj* (3 instrumentalists) 1964, in progress.
II *Lections* (4 speakers, listener) 1964–74.
Produktionsprozesse 1968, in progress.
Maulwerke (mouths, electronics) 1968–74; first performed Donaueschingen, 20 October 1974.
Atemzuge (breath) 1970–1; first performed Rome, 3 November 1971. Recorded Wergo WER 60075.
Mundstücke (mouth) 1972; first performed Munich, 29 August 1972.
Kehlkopfspannungen & Gurgelrollen (throat, larynx) 1974; first performed Munich, 23 June 1975.
Zungenschlage & Lippenspiel (tongue, lips) 1974; first performed Munich, 23 June 1975.
Radiophonien 1969, in progress.
Horfunk (5 parts) 1969–70.
No (*hörspiel*) 1979–80.
Bearbeitungen 1972–80.
I *Bach-Contrapuncti* (voices) 1972–6; *Contrapunctus I* first performed Frankfurt, 19 May 1973; *Contrapunctus XI* first performed Zurich, 10 July 1976.
II *Beethoven-Sonate* (percussion) n.d.
III *Webern Variationen* (variable instrumentation) 1972; first performed Paris, 20 October 1973.
IV *Wagner-Idyll* (chamber ensemble, voice) 1980; first performed Berlin, 9 September 1980.
V *Schubert-Fantasie* (large orchestra) 1977–8; first performed Frankfurt, 16 March 1979.
Schulmusik 1973, in progress.
Blasmusik 1973; first performed Grunstadt, 23 November 1973.
Gesums 1974; first performed Munich, 22 March 1974.
Klange 1975; first performed Munich, 20 June 1978.
Kontrapunkt 1975; first performed Paris, 25 October 1975.
Rhythmen 1977; first performed Munich, 20 June 1978.
Harmonik 1979; first performed Metz, 16 November 1979.
Orchestra (OPXH TPA) (mobile music) 1974, in progress.
Tradition 1975, in progress.
I *In motu proprio* (7 equal instruments) 1975; first performed Paris, 24 October 1975.
II *Diapason* (13 unequal instrumental groups) 1977; first performed Tübingen, 7 October 1977.
III *B-Dur Quintett* (2 pieces for string quartet and piano; or other groupings) 1976–7; first performed Darmstadt, 17 April 1978.
IV *Thanatos-Eros* (large orchestra, voices) 1979–82; first performed Graz, 5 November 1982.
V *Jowaegerli* (vocal and instrumental sounds, percussion; Hebel) 1983.
VI *Toccata und Fuge* (organ) 1980–2.
VII *Missa* 1983–7.
Handwerke-Blaswerke (speech organs) 1977, in progress; first performed Frankfurt, 16 April 1978.
Soli.
Pan (flue, accompaniment) 1978; first performed Zurich, 25 January 1980.
Lieder ohne Worte (voice, accompaniment) 1980–2.
Korper-Sprache (3–9 participants) 1979–80; first performed Metz, 20 November 1980.
Laut—Gesten—Laute I-II (language/body compositions) 1981–5, 1988.

PUBLICATIONS

By Schnebel: "Studien zur Dynamik Arnold Schönbergs", dissertation, University of Freiburg, 1955; *Karlheinz Stockhausen: Texte*, Cologne, 1963–71; *Mauricio Kagel—Musik, Theater, Film,* Munich, 1970; *Denkbare Schriften, Schriften 1952–72*, edited by Zeller, Cologne, 1972.

On Schnebel: F.C. Reininghaus, *Zwolf Thesen zu DSs "mono"*, Stuttgart, 1970; U. Sturzbecher, "Das grosse Fragezeichen hinter einer gesellschaftspolitischen Funktionder Musik", in *Melos*, 39, 1972; D. Erler, "Textgestalterische Grundzuge in einem chorwerk Ss und dessen Verwendbarkeit zur Werkbetrachtung", dissertation, Hanover Musikhochschule, 1973; special DS issue of *Melos*, 16, 1974; Erhard Karkoschka, "Ss Musik zum Lesen", in *Melos*, 41, 1974.

* * *

Dieter Schnebel had divided his list of works into several cycles, each with certain common aspects. The works of one cycle can be performed together or alone. In most cases the composition of the cycles was extended over a decade or longer, since the composer always worked on several cycles at a time.

Versuche were composed from 1953–6 and in 1964. These works are generally characterized by serial technique of composition, very complicated temporal structures, and the introduction of space with large distances between the performers. No II, the *Stücke* for string quartet, consists of five movements, each with only 12 notes. Here, Webern's tendency of extreme concentration is applied to the twelve-tone technique with only one complete presentation of a row. (In 1952 Schnebel wrote the first extensive study on one of Webern's works [*Variations for Piano Op 27*], which had considerable impact on international serialism.)

Being also a protestant theologian, Schnebel has made important contributions to contemporary religious music, part of which is collected under the title *Für Stimmenl*

(. . .*Missa est*). The three vocal works on prayers and verses for the Bible focus on the liberation of voices expanding the realm of vocal techniques, while *Choralvorspiele I/II* experiment with new techniques on the organ.

As early as 1958–61 Schnebel explored Cage's indeterminacy concepts in the cycle *Projekte*. Musical processes are not explicitly composed but only verbally defined. Another group of cycles *Abfälle I* and *Abfälle II* and *Modelle (Ausarbeitungen)* concentrated on the theatrical aspects of music. Historical models of musical performance are investigated with respect to their dramatic, visual elements such as the behavior of a conductor (*Nostalgie* for a solo conductor) or of a concert pianist and his audience (*Concert sans orchestre* for a pianist and audience).

Schnebel's tape music primarily refers to the way of listening to radio broadcasts (*Radiophonien*) in two *Hörspiele* using environmental and typical radio sounds and processes.

Compositions dealing with spatial moments of music are collected under the title *Räume*. *Ki-no*, night music for projectors and listeners, is mainly optical music. Silent motion pictures and slides are projected onto several screens. Verbal descriptions of sound and notes produce imaginative music within the consciousness of the listeners. *Mo-no* is a version of *Ki-no* for readers and is published in the form of a book. *Gehörgänge* is a concept for the musical and acoustical exploration of a specially prepared building. The listeners are invited to follow their own "paths of listening".

Produktionsprozesse is a series which concentrates on the various ways of producing sounds. Thus, it is not the result of a sound producing action that is notated but rather the physical action itself. *Maulwerke* is the major work of this series. The performers exercise different actions with their speech organs, movements of the breathing organs, throat, tongue, etc. In later stages the actions are elaborated into musical developments and communicative cooperation between the performers. Schnebel continued these experimental "language and body" compositions with *Laut–Gesten–Laute I-II*.

Schnebel also has made a number of arrangements of traditional works (*Bearbeitungen*) in order to transform the conventional way of listening to them. *Tradition* applies a similar concept to traditional musical forms with works like *Diapason* which presents a canon of 13 voices, and *Missa* including a number of historical techniques in a "non-postmodern" environment. Currently a great symphonic project is in progress.

—Rolf Klein

SCHNITTKE, Alfred. Russian; German descent. Born in Engels, near Saratov, German Volga Republic, 24 November 1934. Family moved to Vienna; early musical study there, including piano under Charlotte Ruber, 1946–8; moved to Moscow, choirmaster's diploma, 1948–53; Moscow Conservatoire (counterpoint and composition under Yevgeny Golubev, instrumentation under Nikolai Rakov), 1953–8; additional study under Philipp Herschkowitz. Married (1) Galina Koltsina in 1956 (dissolved 1958); (2) Irina Katayeva in 1961, 1 son. Teacher of instrumentation, Moscow Conservatoire, 1962–72; member, Federation of Composers, since 1961; member, Federation of Cinematographers, since 1970; guest teacher, Hochschule für Musik und Darstellende Kunst, Vienna, 1980; serious illness impeded work, 1985. Recipient: elected member, Akademie der Kunste, German Democratic Republic; elected member, Bayerische Akademie der Schonen Kunste, 1981; State Prize, R.S.F.S.R., 1986. Mailing address: ulitsa Vavilova 48, dom 419, 117333 Moscow, U.S.S.R.

Publishers: Sovetskii kompozitor, Moscow; Hans Sikorski, Hamburg; Ricordi, Milan.

Symphonies/orchestral:

Concerto No 1 for Violin and Orchestra (2nd movement, "Presto", may be omitted) 1957, revised 1962; first performed Moscow, 29 November 1963.
Concerto for Piano and Orchestra 1960; first performed Moscow, 1960.
Suite for Children (small orchestra) 1962; first performed Moscow, 1962.
Music for Piano and Orchestra 1964; first performed Warsaw, September 1965.
Concerto No 2 for Violin and Chamber Orchestra 1966; first performed Leningrad, 20 February 1968. Recorded Melodiya Eurodisc 27 393 XGK; Philips 411 107 1.
Pianissimo 1968; first performed Donaueschingen, 19 October 1969.
Sonata (violin, chamber orchestra) 1968; first performed Moscow, 5 February 1986.
Symphony No 1 1969–72; first performed Gorky, 9 February 1974. Recorded Melodiya.
Double Concerto (oboe, harp, strings) 1971; first performed Zagreb, May 1972. Recorded BIS CD 377.
In memoriam (orchestral version of *Piano Quintet*) 1972–8; first performed Moscow, 20 December 1979.
Concerto grosso No 1 (2 violins, harpsichord, prepared piano, strings) 1977; first performed Leningrad, 21 March 1977. Recorded Melodiya C 10 21225 004; Melodiya Eurodisc S 10 13135 6; BIS CD 377.
Concerto No 3 for Violin and Chamber Orchestra 1978; first performed Moscow, 27 January 1979. Recorded Eurodisc 201234 405; Melodia C 10 15681 000.
Symphony No 2: St Florian (with chamber chorus; Latin text) 1979; first performed London, 23 April 1980. Recorded Melodiya C 10 23085 00.
Concerto for Piano and Strings 1979; first performed Leningrad, 10 December 1979. Recorded Panton 8 111 0496 ZA; Melodia C 10 228 45 004; BIS CD 377.
Passacaglia 1979–80; first performed Baden-Baden, 8 November 1981.
Gogol Suite (from incidental music to production of *The Dead Souls Register*; orchestrated by Rozhdestvensky) 1980; first performed London, 5 December 1980. Recorded Melodiya C 10 15262 2.
Symphony No 3 1981; first performed Leipzig, 5 November 1981. Recorded Melodiya.
Concerto grosso No 2 (violin, cello, orchestra) 1981–2; first performed Berlin, 11 September 1982. Recorded Melodiya.
Concerto No 4 for Violin and Orchestra 1984; first performed Berlin, September 1984.
Symphony No 4 (soprano, alto or counter-tenor, tenor, bass, chamber or full orchestra; also version with alto or counter-tenor, tenor, SATB chorus) 1984; chamber version first performed Moscow, 16 March 1986; 2nd version first performed Moscow, 12 April 1984. Recorded Melodiya.
Ritual: In Memory of the Victims of the Second World War 1984–5; first performed Novosibirsk, 15 March 1985.

Concerto grosso No 3 (2 violins, chamber orchestra) 1985; first performed Moscow, 20 April 1985.
(K)Ein Sommernachtstraum (not after Shakespeare) 1985; first performed Salzburg, August 1985.
Concerto for Viola and Orchestra 1985; first performed Amsterdam, 9 January 1986.
Concerto for Cello and Orchestra 1985–6; first performed Munich, 7 May 1986. Recorded Melodiya.
Epilogue from "Peer Gynt" (orchestra, tape of mixed chorus) 1987; first performed Hamburg, 27 April 1987.
Quasi una sonata (violin, chamber orchestra; orchestral version of *Sonata No 2* for violin, piano) 1987; first performed Milan, 10 June 1987.
Trio-sonata (chamber orchestra; version of *String Trio*) 1987; first performed Moscow, 13 May 1987.
Four Aphorisms 1988; first performed Berlin, 18 September 1988.
Concerto grosso No 4—Symphony No 5 1988; first performed Amsterdam, 10 November 1988.
Concerto for Piano (Four Hands) and Orchestra 1988; first performed Moscow, 18 April 1990.
Monologue (viola, string orchestra) 1989; first performed Bonn, 4 June 1989.
Concerto No 2 for Cello and Orchestra 1990; first performed Evian, France, 27 May 1990.

Chamber/instrumental:

Prelude and Fugue (piano) 1963; first performed Moscow, 1965.
Sonata No 1 (violin, piano) 1963; first performed Spring 1964. Recorded Melodiya C 10 15537 8; Chandos ABRD 1089; GOST K 28961 33 D 020372; BIS CD 364.
Dialogue (cello, flute, oboe, clarinet, cor anglais, trumpet, piano, percussion) 1965; first performed Warsaw, September 1967.
Improvisation and Fugue (piano) 1965; first performed Moscow, April 1973. Recorded Panton 77 07 30.
Variations of One Chord (piano) 1965; first performed Moscow, 1966.
String Quartet No 1 1966; first performed Moscow, 1967. Recorded Melodiya Eurodisc 27 393XGX.
Sonata No 2: Quasi una sonata (violin, piano) 1968; first performed Kazan, February 1969. Recorded Philips 6514 102.
Serenade (violin, clarinet, double bass, piano, percussion) 1968; first performed Moscow, Spring 1969.
Canon in memoriam Igor Stravinsky 1971; first performed London, 1971. Recorded Orfeo S 009 844.
Four Pieces ("Folk Tune", "In the Mountains", "Cuckoo and Woodpecker", "Tune"; piano) 1971; first performed Moscow, December 1971.
Suite in Old Style (violin, piano or harpsichord) 1972; first performed Moscow, 1973. Recorded Melodiya 33 C 10 09937 8; Melodiya 33 C 10 08673 4; Melodiya C 10 202 23 005; Chandos ABRD 1089.
Piano Quintet 1972–6; first performed September 1976. Recorded Melodiya Eurodisc 28384 KK; Philips 411 107 1; Le Chant du Monde LDX 78675.
Hymns (I—cello, harp, timpani; II—cello, double bass; III—cello, bassoon, harpsichord, bells or timpani; IV—cello, double bass, bassoon, harpsichord, harp, timpani, bells/2 performers) 1974–9; first performed Moscow, 26 May 1979. Recorded (III, IV) Opus 9111 1277.
Cantus perpetuus (keyboard instrument, 1–4 percussionists ad lib) 1975; first performed Moscow, 14 December 1975.
Prelude in memoriam Dmitri Shostakovich (2 violins; or violin, tape) 1975; first performed December 1975. Recorded Victor 2064; Philips 6504 102; Melodiya/Le Chant du Monde LDX 78675; Melodiya Eurodisc 28 752 KK.
Moz-Art (2 violins; after sketches by Mozart, K.416d) 1976; first performed Vienna, February 1976. Recorded Melodiya Eurodisc 200 083 405; Melodiya/Le Chant du Monde LDX 786 75; Melodiya C 10 18173 74.
Moz-Art à la Haydn (2 violins, 2 string quintets, double bass, conductor) 1977; first performed Tbilisi, 30 December 1983.
Sonata (cello, piano) 1978; first performed Moscow, January 1979. Recorded Melodiya C 10 18359 60; Melodiya C 10 19237 38; BIS CD 336.
Stille Nacht (German carol arranged for violin, piano) 1978; first performed Leningrad, January 1978. Recorded Eurodisc 201264 366.
Stille Musik (violin, cello) 1979; first performed Paris, 1979.
Polyphonic Tango (flute, oboe, clarinet, bassoon, horn, trumpet, trombone, piano, percussion, strings) 1979; first performed Moscow, 15 September 1979.
Dedication to Igor Stravinsky, Sergey Prokofiev and Dmitry Shostakovich (piano—6 hands) 1979; first performed Moscow, 28 December 1979. Recorded Melodiya C 10 15262 2.
Two Short Pieces (organ) 1980; first performed Vienna, 1980.
String Quartet No 2 1980; first performed Evian, France, May 1980. Recorded Preciosa Aulos 68 508.
Moz-Art (oboe, harpsichord, harp, violin, cello, double bass) 1980; first performed Lockenhaus, July 1981.
Septet (flute, 2 clarinets, violin, viola, cello, harpsichord or organ) 1981–2; first performed Moscow, 14 November 1982.
Lebenslauf (4 metronomes, 3 percussion, piano) 1982; first performed Witten, 25 April 1982.
A Paganini (violin) 1982; first performed Leningrad, 29 September 1982. Recorded Melodiya C 10 21869 001; Deutsche Grammophon 415 484 1.
Schall und Hall (trombone, organ) 1983; first performed Moscow, 22 May 1983.
String Quartet No 3 1983; first performed Moscow, 8 January 1984.
String Trio 1985; first performed Moscow, 2 June 1985.
Music to an Imaginary Play (4 flutes/piccolo, trumpet, trombone, percussion/vibraphone, piano—2 or 4 hands, violin, double bass) 1985; first performed Moscow, 7 November 1985.
Sonata (piano) 1988; first performed New York City, 22 May 1988.
Piano Quartet 1988; first performed Kuhmo, 29 July 1988.
Klingende Buchstaben (cello) 1988; first performed Moscow, 28 December 1988.
3 × 7 (clarinet, horn, trombone, harpsichord, violin, cello, double bass) 1989; first performed Witten, 22 April 1989.
String Quartet No 4 1989; first performed Vienna, 21 October 1989.
Drei Fragmente (harpsichord) 1990; first performed Hamburg, 14 June 1990.
Moz-Art (8 flutes, harp) 1990; first performed Salzburg, 2 August 1990.

Vocal/choral:

Nagasaki (oratorio for mezzo-soprano, SATB chorus, orchestra; Sofronov, Fere, Eisaku, Toson) 1958; first performed Moscow, 1959.
Songs of War and Peace (cantata for soprano, SATB chorus, orchestra; Leontiev, Pokrovsky, modern Russian folk songs) 1959; first performed Moscow, 1960.

Three Poems by Marina Tsvetayeva (mezzo-soprano, piano) 1965; first performed Moscow, 1966.
Voices of Nature (10 female voices, vibraphone; wordless) 1972; first performed Moscow, Spring 1975.
Requiem (from the stage music to Schiller's *Don Carlos*; 3 sopranos, alto, tenor, SATB chorus; trumpet, trombone, organ, piano, celeste, electric guitar, bass guitar, percussion) 1975; first performed Budapest, Autumn 1977.
Der Sonnengesang des Franz von Assisi (2 mixed choruses, organ, celeste, timpani, tam-tam, vibraphone, bells) 1976.
Three Madrigals (soprano, violin, viola, double bass, vibraphone, harpsichord; Tanzer) 1980; first performed Moscow, 10 November 1980. Recorded Melodiya C 10 18403 4; ORF 0120 618.
Three Scenes (soprano, vibraphone/6 performers, bass drum, cymbal/1 or 2 performers, glockenspiel or violin and double bass behind scenery) 1980; first performed Moscow, 1981.
Minnesang (52 voices; 12th-, 13th-century *Minnesingers*) 1980–1; first performed Graz, Austria, 21 October 1981. Recorded ORF 0120 618.
Seid nuchten und wachet (contralto, counter-tenor, tenor, bass, SATB chorus, orchestra; *Historia von D. Johannen Fausten*) 1983; first performed Vienna, 19 June 1983.
Concerto (unaccompanied mixed chorus; narekatsi) 1984–5; 3rd movement only performed Istanbul, 14 July 1984; first complete performance, Moscow, 1986.
Busslieder (4-part unaccompanied mixed chorus) 1988; first performed Moscow, 26 December 1988.
Eroffnungsvers zum ersten Festspielsonntag (4-part mixed chorus, organ) 1989; first performed Lockenhaus, 2 July 1989.

Opera/dramatic:

The Eleventh Commandment (Churova, Ansimov, AS) 1962.
Der gelbe Klang ("scenic composition" for pantomime, mixed chorus on tape, clarinet, trumpet, trombone, violin, double bass, 3 percussion, harpsichord, celeste, 2 pianos, ionika, electric guitar; Kandinsky) 1973–4; first performed Saint Bomme, France, 1974.
The Life of an Idiot 1990–1.

Other:

Charleston (score to film *Adventures of a Dentist*; light music ensemble) 1965.
Stream (electronic) 1969.
Labyrinths (ballet by Vasilyev in 5 episodes; 3 percussion, harpsichord, celeste, strings) 1971; 1st episode only performed Moscow, 1972; first complete performance, Leningrad, 7 June 1978.
Two Fragments (from score to film *How Tsar Peter Got the Black Man Married*; small orchestra) 1976.
Endstation Sehnstucht (ballet by Neumeier after Williams *A Streetcar Named Desire*; music by Prokofiev and Schnittke: from *Symphony No 1*) 1983; first performed Stuttgart, 3 December 1983.
Sketches (choreographic fantasia by Petrov, after Gogol; episodes 2–10 by Gennadi Rozhdestvensky; episodes 1 and 11, "Nevsky Prospekt" and "Long Live Gogol!" by Schnittke, Rozhdestvensky, Sofia Gubaidulina and Edison Denisov) 1985; first performed Moscow, 16 January 1985.
Peer Gynt (ballet by Neumeier, after Ibsen; orchestra, SATB chorus on tape) 1986; first performed Hamburg, January 1989.
W. A. Mozart: cadenzas to *Piano Concerto in C minor K.491* (1975; recorded Melodiya C 10 14751), *Piano Concerto in C major K.467* (1980), *Piano Concerto in C major K.503* (1983), *Concerto for Bassoon and Orchestra* (1983).
Ludwig van Beethoven: cadenza to *Violin Concerto* 1975–7. Recorded Philips 65 14 075.
Dmitri Shostakovich: *Five Preludes for Piano* (1 and 2 transcribed for small orchestra) 1976.
Scott Joplin: *Ragtime* (orchestrated) 1984; first performed Moscow, 1 December 1984.
Adolf Jensen: *Serenade* (orchestrated) 1984; first performed Moscow, 17 February 1984.
Friedrich Nietzsche: *Beschworung* (orchestrated) 1984; first performed Moscow, 17 February 1984.
Alban Berg: *Canon: an das Frankfurter Opernhaus* (arranged for 9 strings) 1985; first performed Moscow, 2 April 1985.

Film music: *Introduction*, 1962; *Aim the Barrage at Us*, 1963–4; *Adventures of a Dentist*, 1965; *Just a Little Joke*, 1966; *Day Stars*, 1966; *The Commissar/In the Town of Berdichev*, 1967, 1986; *House and Owner*, 1967; *The Angel/The Commissar*, 1968; *The Sixth of July*, 1968; *The Glass Accordion*, 1968; *Used Cartridge Cases*, 1968; *The Night Call*, 1968; *The Waltz*, 1969; *Sick at Heart*, 1969; *A Ballerina Aboard*, 1969; *Uncle Vanya*, 1970; *Sport, Sport, Sport*, 1970; *The Seagull*, 1970; *Our Gagarin*, 1971; *The Last Run of the Albatross*, 1971; *You and Me*, 1971; *A Cottage in Kolomna*, 1971; *The Wardrobe*, 1971; *Where the Arbat Crosses Bubulinas Street*, 1972; *Chile Fights and Hopes*, 1972; *Cheer Up, the Worst Is Yet to Come*, 1972; *The Butterfly*, 1972; *Hot Snow*, 1972; *The Right to Jump*, 1972; *The World Today/And Yet I Believe*, 1972–4; *In Fableworld*, 1973; *Cities and Years*, 1973; *The Arduous Roads of Peace/The Balance of Terror*, 1973; *The Agony*, 1974; *Selecting a Target*, 1974; *Autumn*, 1974; *Ricky-Ticky-Tavi*, 1975; *Travka's Adventures*, 1975; *The White Steamer*, 1975; *How Tsar Peter Got the Black Man Married*, 1976; *The Life Story of an Unknown Actor*, 1976; *Trainers*, 1976; *Clowns and Kids*, 1976; *The Ascent*, 1976; *Father Serghy*, 1978; *My Memories Take Me to You*, 1978; *Paradoxes of Evolution*, 1979; *Little Tragedies*, 1979; *The Plane Crew*, 1980; *I Am with You Again*, 1980; *The Leave-Taking* (co-written with Artyomov), 1980; *Larisa*, 1980; *The Fancies of Faryatev*, 1981; *Eugene Onegin*, 1981; *Sturdy Boy*, 1981; *Autumn*, 1981; *A Tale of Travels*, 1982; *Star Fall*, 1983; *Dead Souls*, 1983; *The White Poodle*, 1984.

Theatre music: G.B. Shaw: *Caesar and Cleopatra*; Schiller: *Don Carlos*; Pushkin: *Boris Godunov*; Brecht: *Turandot*; Vampilov: *A Duck Shooting Party*; Gogol: *The Dead Souls Register*; Blok: *The Rose and the Cross*; *Mayakovsky's Debut*.

PUBLICATIONS

By Schnittke: "Notes on the Orchestral Polyphony in Dmitri Shostakovich's Fourth Symphony", in *Muzyka i sovremennost* [Music and the Present Age], 4, 1966; "Some Features of the Orchestral Harmonisation of Themes in Dmitri Shostakovich's Symphonic Works", in *Dmitri Shostakovich*, Moscow, 1967; "The Orchestral Harmonisation of Themes in the Early Works of Stravinsky", in *Muzyka i sovremennost*, 5, 1967; "Edison Denisov", in *Res facta*, 6, 1972; "Paradoxicality as a Feature of Stravinsky's Musicallogic", in *I.F. Stravinsky*, Moscow, 1973; "Collage and polystylistics", in *Muzykalniye kultury narodov. Traditsii i sovremennost* [Musical Culture of Different Peoples. Tradition and the Present Age], 1973; "Special Features of Sergey Prokofiev's Orchestral Harmonisation of Themes", in *Muzyka i sovremennost*, 8, 1974; "Circles of Influence", in *Dmitry Shostakovich*, Moscow, 1976; "Embodying a New Idea", in *Problemy traditsii i novatoorstva v sovremennooi muzyke* [Problems of Tradition and Innovation in Modern Music], 1982; also in manuscript—"Overcoming Metre by Rhythm", "Ligeti's Orchestral Micropolyphony", "Stereophonic Tendencies in Modern Orchestral Thinking", "Static Form: A New Conception of Time", "The Third Movement of Luciano Berio's Sinfonia: Stylistic Counterpoint, Thematic and Formal Unity in the Context of Polystylistics—Expansion of the Concept of Theme", "Klangfarbenmelodie", "Infinitely Interlocking Timbre Ties in a Fugue (Ricercata) by Bach-Webern", "Timbre Modulations in Bartók's *Music for Strings, Percussion and Celeste*", and "Timbre Affinity and Its Functional Utilisation; Timbre Scale".

* * *

Dramatic to the point of theatricality, Alfred Schnittke's music has wit, exuberance, enormous energy, and also a darker side of affecting beauty, sorrow and catastrophe. It flows from a deep vein of humanity marked by intense anguish born of very real suffering. And in the 1990s, it strikes us as uncannily representative of the times, particularly, of course, of the political turbulence, contradictions and crisis of identity in Eastern Europe ushered in by *glasnost*. Its host of stylistic references is positively schizophrenic. Through the multiplicity of experience these evoke, the return to a human (rather than an abstract) expression (whether of extrovert extravagance or intimate reflection); through an attempt to integrate acute cultural and stylistic differences in a music which is both very unified and very Russian, yet also strangely ambivalent and homeless—Schnittke has given artistic and spiritual expression to the perplexing confusion of modern life. He has spoken of the Ivesian kaleidoscope of different musical cultures which constantly envelops us. The polystylistic nature of his own music, both disturbing and stimulating, is a reflection of our divided musical consciousness, with deeper implications.

For many years Schnittke's music has embodied the disintegrative qualities of a creative personality who grew up in Vienna, was drawn to the Western avant-garde, yet has had to compose for most of his life under the restrictive political pressures of Soviet Russia. The variety of style is an acknowledgement of these diverse roots and, to some extent, an allegory of conflicting human forces and political creeds. This is made clear by his music for the animation film *The Glass Accordion* in which the style of 18th-century music and art symbolises humanity, freedom and *joie de vivre*, while a dissonant surreal music conveys faceless repression. Repeatedly in his concert music, Schnittke starts with an imitation of Classical or Baroque music whose innocence is gradually overwhelmed by multiple distorting mirrors (superimposed canons, perhaps) and by adverse forces. Works like the first Concerto Grosso and *(K)Ein Sommernachstraum* maintain an enigmatic balance between sardonic humour and music that is decidedly threatening. Schnittke shares with Peter Maxwell Davies and György Ligeti an interest in showing that things are not what they may at first seem.

After graduating from the Moscow Conservatory and inspired by the visit to Russia of Luigi Nono in 1962, Schnittke became actively interested in the European avant-garde and for some five years utilised serial techniques, a stance which surrounded him in controversy. Denied concert performances of his work, he turned to film music as a matter of economic necessity; but it offered also a stimulating and congenial forum for experiment. Through some 60 film scores he developed the polyglot characteristics of his style as well as its enormous iconographic power, and learned also to apply cinematic cross-cutting techniques to concert music. Gradually Schnittke's innovatory daring came to be admired by younger Russian composers. His music was played more widely, but for many years life was not easy.

It is in the last 15 years, since the death of the composer's mother, that the emotional intensity that strikes one so forcibly in Schnittke's personality has deepened and filled. The earlier works, although expressively motivated, are more inclined to be abstract, technically adroit or, as in the case of the First Symphony, daringly experimental—a condition inevitably frowned on by the authorities. The premiere of the First Symphony in 1974 was banished (like Andrei Sakharov) to Gorky; not until 1985 was this crucial work performed in Moscow. For years, it seems, Schnittke was something of an outcast and it was through the courageous championship of such outstanding artists as Gidon Kremer, Yuri Bashmet and Gennadi Rozhsdestvensky that his music became known in Russia and the West. Indeed, his close musical relationship with so many great solo performers is almost without precedent; for them he has written a remarkable series of concertos and other solo works. There are now also five symphonies, several concertos for chamber orchestra, a full-length ballet *Peer Gynt*, whose recent premiere in Hamburg was a sensational success, an opera called *The Life of an Idiot* for The Netherlands Opera and another projected on Faust. The Swedish BIS are recording his entire production. Since the mid-1980s the official attitude to Schnittke's music in Russia has changed for the better too.

In the First Symphony, Schnittke dramatises the opposite poles of the serious and the absurd, of vulgar hotchpotch and the spiritually sublime. His music has become increasingly programmatic and symbolic, for he is a skillful delineator of character, whether mephistophelean or angelic, and a composer who enjoys and can write genuine musical humour. But since the severe, near fatal illness which afflicted him a few years ago, his overriding urge has been to say strongly and clearly things which are deeply felt. With its fortitude and sense of conveying momentous events, his music conveys also an awareness of mortality and a prevailing introspection. In this it comes close to Shostakovich; indeed the breadth, honesty and very nobility of Schnittke's art ally it to a great Russian tradition.

—Richard Steinitz

SCHULLER, Gunther (Alexander). American. Born in New York City, 22 November 1925. Educated: private flute study, from 1937; St Thomas Choir School, 1938–44; Manhattan School of Music, New York City (horn under Robert Schulze, theory and counterpoint), 1939–41. Married Marjorie Black, 8 June 1948; 2 sons. Horn player, New York City Ballet Theater Orchestra, 1943; principal horn, Cincinnati Symphony Orchestra, Ohio, 1943–5, and Metropolitan Opera Orchestra, 1945–59; teacher, Manhattan School of Music, 1950–63; ceased performing professionally, 1962; conductor and organizer, Twentieth-Century Innovations concert series, New York City, 1962–5; teacher of composition, Yale School of Music, New Haven, Connecticut, 1964–7; teacher of composition, 1963–84, head of contemporary music activities,

1965–84, artistic co-director, 1969–74, and director 1974–84, Berkshire Music Center, Tanglewood, Massachusetts; president, New England Conservatory, Boston, 1967–77; broadcaster on modern music, WBAI radio, New York City; special adviser, composer-in-residence programme, Lyric Opera of Chicago, from 1984; artistic adviser and principal conductor, Spokane Symphony Orchestra, from 1984; artistic director, Sandpoint Festival, Idaho, since 1984. Recipient: Creative Arts Award, Brandeis University, 1960; Darius Milhaud Award (for best film score in 1964, *Yesterday in Fact*), 1964; Mark Horblitt Award, Boston Symphony Orchestra, 1966; elected member, National Institute of Arts and Letters, 1967; Ditson Conducting Award for contributions to contemporary music, 1970; Rodgers and Hammerstein Award (for contributions to theatre in Boston), 1971; 3 Grammy Awards, 1973, 1976, 1985; elected member, American Academy and Institute of Arts and Letters, 1980; Gustavus Adolphus College Fine Arts Award, 1980; American Music Center Letter of Distinction, 1980; George Peabody Medal (for services to music in America), 1982; William Schuman Award for lifetime achievement, 1989; Boston Music Award (for best jazz album, *Jumpin' in the Future*), 1990. Honorary degrees: Northeastern University, 1967; University of Illinois, 1968; Colby College, 1969; Williams College, 1975; Cleveland Institute of Music, 1977; New England Conservatory of Music, 1978; Rutgers University, 1980; Oberlin College, 1989. Mailing address: Margun Music, 167 Dudley Road, Newton Centre, Massachusetts 02159, U.S.A.

Publishers: Margun; Associated; Belwin-Mills; Big Three; Dramatic: E.B. Marks; Malcolm; MCA; McGinnis & Marx; Merion; MJQ; Oxford University Press; Presser; Rongwen; Schott, Shawnee; Universal.

Symphonies/orchestral:

Horn Concerto No 1 1944; first performed Cincinnati, Ohio, 6 April 1945.
Cello Concerto 1945, revised 1985.
Suite (chamber orchestra) 1945; first performed New York City, 1959.
Vertige d'Eros 1945; first performed Madison, Wisconsin, 14 October 1967.
Symphonic Study 1947–8; first performed Cincinnati, Ohio, May 1949.
Symphony for Brass and Percussion 1950; first performed Cincinnati, Ohio, 2 February 1950. Recorded Argo ZRG 731; Golden Crest CRS 4214; Columbia CL 941.
Dramatic Overture 1951; first performed Darmstadt, August 1954. Recorded Louisville LOU 666.
Recitative and Rondo (Op 21) (violin, orchestra) 1953; first performed Chicago, 16 July 1967.
Symphonic Tribute to Duke Ellington 1955; first performed Tanglewood, Massachusetts, 19 August 1976.
Little Fantasy 1957; first performed Englewood, New Jersey, 7 April 1957.
Contours (chamber orchestra) 1958; first performed Cincinnati, Ohio, 31 December 1959. Recorded Odyssey Y 34141.
Spectra 1958; first performed New York City, January 14 1960.
Concertino (jazz quartet, orchestra) 1959; first performed Baltimore, Maryland, 2 January 1960. Recorded Atlantic 1359.
Seven Studies on Themes of Paul Klee 1959; first performed Minneapolis, Minnesota, 27 November 1959. Recorded Mercury SRI 75116; RCA Victor LSC 2879; Mercury SR 90282.
Capriccio (tuba, orchestra) 1960; first performed New York, 17 January 1963. Recorded CM 2004 C.
Contrasts (wind quintet, orchestra) 1960; first performed Donaueschingen, October 1961.
Journey to the Stars 1962; first performed Toledo, Ohio, 1 December 1962.
Movements (flute, strings) 1962; first performed Dortmund, 29 May 1962.
Piano Concerto No 1 1962; first performed Cincinnati, Ohio, 26 October 1962.
Composition in Three Parts 1963; first performed Minneapolis, Minnesota, 29 March 1963.
Diptych (brass quintet, band or orchestra) 1963; first performed Ithaca, New York, 22 March 1964; orchestral version first performed Boston, 31 March 1967.
Meditation (band) 1963; first performed Greensboro, North Carolina, 7 March 1963.
Threnos (oboe, orchestra) 1963; first performed Cologne, 29 November 1963.
Five Bagatelles 1964; first performed Fargo, North Dakota, 22 March 1964. Recorded Louisville LS 686.
American Triptych: A Study in Textures 1965; first performed New Orleans, 9 March 1965.
Symphony 1965; first performed Dallas, 8 February 1965. Recorded Turnabout TV 34412S.
Concerto No 1: Gala Music 1965–6; first performed Chicago, 20 January 1966.
Five Etudes 1966; first performed New Haven, Connecticut, 19 March 1967.
Study in Textures (band) 1966; first performed Fort Worth, Texas, August 1967. Recorded Century Records 28297.
Triplum I 1967; first performed New York City, 28 June 1967. Recorded Columbia MS 7052.
Colloquy (2 pianos, orchestra) 1968; first performed Berlin, 6 June 1968.
Concerto for Double Bass and Chamber Orchestra 1968; first performed New York City, 27 January 1968.
Fanfare for St Louis 1968; first performed St Louis, Missouri, 26 January 1968.
Shapes and Designs 1969; first performed Hartford, Connecticut, 26 April 1969.
Consequents 1969; first performed New Haven, Connecticut, 16 December 1969.
Museum Piece (Renaissance instruments, orchestra) 1970; first performed Boston, 11 December 1970.
The Visitation (orchestral suite from the opera) 1970; first performed Chicago, 26 July 1970.
Concerto da camera (chamber orchestra) 1971; first performed Rochester, New York, 24 April 1971.
Capriccio stravagante 1972; first performed San Francisco, 6 December 1972.
Three Nocturnes 1973; first performed Interlochen, Michigan, 15 July 1973.
Four Soundscapes: Hudson Valley Reminiscences 1974; first performed Poughkeepsie, New York, 2 March 1975.
Triplum II 1975; first performed Baltimore, Maryland, 26 February 1978.
Violin Concerto (orchestra of instrumental trios) 1975–6; first performed Lucerne, Switzerland, 25 August 1976.
Concerto No 2 1976; first performed Washington, D.C., 12 October 1976.
Horn Concerto No 2 1976; first performed Budapest, 12 February 1977.
Contrabassoon Concerto 1978; first performed Washington, D.C., 16 January 1979.
Trumpet Concerto (trumpet, chamber orchestra) 1979; first performed Jefferson, New Hampshire, 25 August 1979.
Eine kleine Posaunemusik (trombone, orchestra) 1980; first

performed Norfolk, Connecticut, 18 July 1980. Recorded GM 2009.

In Praise of Winds (symphony for large wind orchestra) 1981; first performed Ann Arbor, Michigan, 13 February 1981. Recorded Silver Crest D-81-CBDNA 7.

Piano Concerto No 2 1981; first performed Mainz, Germany, 24 November 1982.

Alto Saxophone Concerto 1983; first performed Pittsburgh, 19 February 1984.

Concerto quaternio (violin, flute, oboe, trumpet, orchestra) 1984; first performed New York City, 21 November 1984.

Concerto festivo (brass quintet, orchestra) 1984; first performed Trier, Germany, 29 November 1984.

Jubilee Music 1984; first performed Dayton, Ohio, 7 March 1984.

Viola Concerto 1984; first performed New Orleans, 17 December 1984.

Bassoon Concerto: Eine kleine Fagottmusik 1985; first performed Washington, D.C., 16 May 1985.

Farbenspiel (Concerto for Orchestra No 3) 1985; first performed Berlin, 8 May 1985.

Concerto for String Quartet and Orchestra 1988; first performed Madison, Wisconsin, 20 February 1988.

Concerto for Flute and Orchestra 1988; first performed Chicago, 13 October 1988.

On Winged Flight (divertimento for symphonic band) 1989; first performed Tallahassee, Florida, 4 March 1989.

Fanfare pour Wolf Trap (16 brass, percussion, timpani) 1989; first performed Vienna, Virginia, 14 July 1989.

Concerto for Piano Three Hands (2 pianos—3 hands, chamber orchestra) 1989; first performed Springfield, Illinois, 20 January 1990.

Song and Dance (violin, band) 1990; first performed Minnesota, 23 February 1990.

Chamber/instrumental:

Romantic Sonata (clarinet, horn, piano) 1941, revised 1983. Recorded Crystal S 731.

Trois Hommages ("Intermezzo" for Delius, "Pavanne" for Ravel, "Chanson" for Milhaud; 1 or 2 horns, piano) 1942–6. Recorded GM 2010.

Blues (brass quartet, double bass, drums) 1945.

Suite (woodwind quintet) 1945. Recorded Orion ORS 79345.

Fantasia concertante No 1 (3 oboes, piano) 1947.

Fantasia concertante No 2 (3 trombones, piano) 1947; first performed Nashville, Tennessee, 31 May 1983.

Quartet (4 double basses) 1947; first performed New York City, 8 April 1960. Recorded GM 2004; Turnabout TV 34412 S.

Trio (oboe, horn, viola) 1948; first performed New York City, 1948. Recorded CRI 423.

Perpetuum mobile (4 muted horns, bassoon/tuba) 1948.

Jumpin' in the Future (Atonal Jazz Study) (12 instruments) 1948.

Duo Sonata (clarinet, bass clarinet) 1948–9; first performed New York City, 23 October 1953. Recorded Crystal S 355.

Sonata (Op 17) (oboe, piano) 1948–51; first performed New York City, February 1952. Recorded Desto DC 7116.

Fantasy (Op 19) (cello) 1951; first performed New York City, 1952.

Five Pieces (5 horns) 1952; first performed New York City, 1953.

Adagio (flute, violin, viola, cello) 1953; first performed New York City, 30 November 1958.

Recitative and Rondo (Op 21) (arranged for violin, piano) 1953; first performed New York City, 23 October 1953.

Twelve by Eleven (flute, clarinet/tenor saxophone, bassoon, horn, trombone, harp, vibraphone, piano, bass, drums) 1955; first performed New York City, 19 November 1955.

Abstraction (alto saxophone, string quartet, 2 double basses, guitar, percussion) 1955; first performed New York City, 16 May 1960. Recorded Atlantic SD 1365; GM 3005.

Transformation (flute, clarinet/tenor saxophone, bassoon, horn trombone, harp, vibes, piano, bass, drums) 1957; first performed Waltham, Massachusetts, 7 June 1957. Recorded New World NW 216; Columbia C2S CS 8909–8910; Columbia WL 127.

Symbiosis (violin, piano, percussion, optional dancer) 1957; first performed New York City, 6 October 1957. Recorded GM 2007.

String Quartet No 1 1957; first performed Urbana-Champaign, Illinois, 29 March 1957. Recorded Golden Crest NEC 115; University of Illinois CR 5.

Woodwind Quintet 1958; first performed Cologne, Autumn 1962. Recorded Vox Box SVBX 5307; Concert Disc CM 1229.

Fantasy Quartet (4 cellos) 1958; first performed New York City, 26 December 1959. Recorded CRI 144.

Fantasy (harp) 1959; first performed Israel, 1959.

Conversations (jazz quartet, string quartet) 1959; first performed New York City, 25 September 1959. Recorded Atlantic 1345.

Lines and Constants (16 horns) 1960; first performed Los Angeles, 23 October 1960. Recorded Angel S 36036.

Curtain Raiser (flute, clarinet, horn, piano) 1960; first performed New York City, 8 April 1960.

Lifelines (flute, guitar, percussion) 1960.

Variants on a Theme of John Lewis ("Django"; flute, alto saxophone/flute, vibraphone, guitar, string quartet, 2 double basses, drums) 1960; first performed New York City, 16 May 1960.

Variants on a Theme of Thelonious Monk ("Criss-Cross"; flute, alto saxophone/flute/bass clarinet, vibes, guitar, piano, 2 double basses, drums, string quartet) 1960; first performed New York City, 16 May 1960.

Double Quintet (brass quintet, wind quintet) 1961.

Music for Brass Quintet 1961; first performed Washington, D.C., 13 January 1961. Recorded McGill University Records 80012; Keyboard Jr Recordings KPL 57; CRI 144.

Fanfare (4 trumpets, 4 trombones) 1962; first performed Madison, Wisconsin, 20 November 1963.

Duets (2 horns) 1962. Recorded Crystal S 371.

Music for Carillon 1962; arranged for harpsichord or organ; and for organ, glockenspiel, vibraphone/marimba, chimes; first performed Chicago, 27 June 1962.

Densities No 1 (clarinet, harp, vibraphone, double bass) 1962; first performed New York City, 13 March 1963. Recorded DM 3005; Cambridge CRS 1820.

Studies (horn) 1962.

Night Music (bass clarinet, guitar, 2 double basses, drums) 1962; first performed New York City, 29 April 1978. Recorded Cambridge CRS 1820; GM Recordings GM 3005.

Music from Yesterday in Fact (flute, horn, trumpet, alto saxophone, bass clarinet, violin, cello, double bass, piano, drums) 1963.

Little Brass Music (trumpet, horn, trombone, tuba) 1963; first performed New York City, January 1963.

Episodes (clarinet) 1964; first performed Venice, September 1964. Recorded Mark MRS 32645.

String Quartet No 2 1965; first performed Iowa City, 4 March 1966.

Teardrop (flute, clarinet/alto saxophone, baritone saxophone, horn, trumpet, trombone, tuba, guitar, double bass,

drums) 1966; first performed Boston, 10 October 1983.
Aphorisms (flute, string trio) 1967; first performed New York City, May 1971.
Tre invenzioni (5 instrumental groups: piccolo, flute, oboe, alto clarinet, bass clarinet; cor anglais, alto saxophone, bass clarinet, bassoon, contrabassoon; trumpet in D, trumpet in C, trumpet in B♭, trombone, bass trombone; flugelhorn, 2 horns, baritone horn, tuba) 1972; first performed Tanglewood, Massachusetts, 8 August 1972. Recorded Odyssey Y34141.
Five Moods (4 tubas) 1973; first performed Bloomington, Indiana, 25 May 1973. Recorded Crystal S 221.
Triptych (organ) 1976; first performed Boston, June 1976.
Sonata serenata (clarinet, violin, cello, piano) 1978; first performed New York City, 28 September 1979.
Octet (clarinet, horn, bassoon, 2 violins, viola, cello, double bass) 1979; first performed New York City, 2 November 1979.
Symphony (organ) 1981; first performed St Paul, Minnesota, 8 November 1981.
Duologue (violin, piano) 1983; first performed Washington, D.C., 31 July 1984.
On Light Wings (piano quartet) 1984; first performed Atlanta, Georgia, 20 May 1984.
Piano Trio 1984; first performed St Paul, Minnesota, May 1984.
String Quartet No 3 1985–6; first performed New York City, 3 May 1987.
Orglewalzer (organ) 1986; first performed New York City, 10 March 1986.
The Sandpoint Rag (brass sextet or ragtime ensemble) 1986; first performed Pasadena, California, 15 November 1986.
String Quartet No 3 1986; first performed Syracuse, New York, 15 November 1986.
Sextet (bassoon, piano, string quartet) 1986; first performed Sandpoint, Idaho, 2 August 1987.
Franfare (6 trumpets) 1986; first performed Boston, 1986.
Chimeric Images (chamber ensemble) 1988; first performed New York City, 21 June 1988.
A Bouquet for Collage (clarinet, flute, violin, cello, piano, percussion) 1988; first performed Cambridge, Massachusetts, 21 March 1988.
Sonata (horn, piano) 1988.
The Trial (Third Stream chamber ensemble) 1989; first performed Amherst, Massachusetts, 30 April 1989.
Five Impromptus (cor anglais, string quartet) 1989; first performed Baltimore, Maryland, 9 December 1990.
Phantasmata (violin, marimba) 1989; first performed Boston, 21 April 1990.
Impromptus and Cadenzas (oboe, clarinet, bassoon, horn, violin, cello) 1990; first performed Tarrytown, New York, 24 March 1990.
Hommage à Rayechka (8 cellos) 1990; first performed Tempe, Arizona, 15 June 1990.
A Trio Setting (piano, violin, clarinet) 1990; first performed Michigan, 11 July 1990.

Vocal/choral:

O Lamb of God (SATB chorus, optional organ) 1941.
O Spirit of the Living God (SATB chorus, optional organ) 1942.
Six Early Songs (lyric soprano, piano; Li-Po) 1943–4; orchestrated 1973; first performed Boston, 4 May 1973.
Blumenstrauss (soprano, piano) 1944.
Schreie der Raben (soprano, piano) 1946.
Meditations (soprano, piano; Gertrude Stein) 1960; first performed New York City, 19 December 1963.
Journey into Jazz (narrator, jazz quintet, orchestra; collaboration with Nat Hentoff) 1961; first performed Washington, D.C., 2 June 1961.
Six Renaissance Lyrics (tenor, septet: Shakespeare, De la Cruz, Vogelweide, Petrarch, Ronsard, Michelangelo) 1962.
Five Shakespearean Songs (baritone, orchestra) 1964; first performed Poughkeepsie, New York, 2 March 1975.
Sacred Cantata (SATB chorus, chamber orchestra: Psalm 98) 1966; first performed Atlanta, Georgia, June 1966.
The Power Within Us (oratorio for baritone, narrator, chorus, orchestra; Long) 1971; first performed Atlanta, Georgia, March 1972.
Poems of Time and Eternity (chorus, 9 instruments; Dickinson) 1972; first performed Boston, 24 June 1976.
Deai (Encounters) (7 voices, 3 orchestras) 1978; first performed Tokyo, 17 January 1978.
Music for a Celebration (chorus, audience, orchestra) 1980; first performed Springfield, Massachusetts, 26 September 1980.

Opera/dramatic:

The Visitation (after Kafka) 1966; first performed Hamburg, 12 October 1966.
The Fisherman and his Wife (children's opera in 13 scenes by Updike, after Grimm; chamber orchestra) 1970; first performed 7 May 1970.
Treemonisha (orchestration of 1911 opera by Scott Joplin) 1975; first performed Houston, Texas, 23 May 1975. Recorded Deutsche Grammophon 2707083.

Other:

The Traitor (dance piece based on *Symphony for Brass and Percussion*) 1954; first performed New London, Connecticut, 19 August 1954.
Variants (ballet by Balanchine; jazz quartet, orchestra) 1960; first performed New York City, 4 January 1961.
Automation (film score) 1962.
Journey to the Stars (film score) 1962.
Yesterday in Fact (film score) 1963.

Charles Ives: *Ann Street* (arranged for flute, trumpet in C, trombone, glockenspiel, piano), *At Sea* (arranged for cor anglais, optional horn celeste, piano or glockenspiel, 3 violins), *Chromamelodtune* (arranged for oboe, clarinet, bassoon, horn, trumpet, trombone, tuba, piano, 3 violins, viola, cello, double bass), *Gen'l Slocum* (arranged and orchestrated), *The Indians* (arranged for trumpet in C, Indian drum, string quartet, double bass, piano), *The Last Reader*, *A Lecture*, *Luck and Work* (arranged for flute, cor anglais, percussion, piano, 3 violins, viola, cello, double bass), *The New River*, *Premonitions*, *Set No 1*, *Set No 2*, *Set No 3*, *Yale-Princeton Football Game* (all arranged).

Scott Joplin: *Chrysanthemum: An Afro-American Intermezzo*, *Combination March* (arranged for band; orchestrated), *The Easy Winners: A Ragtime Two-Step* (arranged for piccolo, clarinet, cornet, trombone, tuba, optional string quartet), *The Entertainer: A Ragtime Two-Step* (arranged), *Euphonic Sounds: A Syncopated Novelty* (arranged), *Maple Leaf Rag*, *Solace: A Mexican Serenade, Wall Street Rag* (arranged).

Ornette Coleman: transcriptions of "Forerunner", "Congeniality", "Peace", "Free", "Lonely Woman", "Face of the

Bas", "Chronology", "Bird Food", "Focus on Sanity", "Una Muy Bonita", 1961.

Franz Josef Haydn: horn passages in the symphonies, compiled by Thomas Haunton, edited by GS, 1980.

Domenico Dragonetti: *Concerto in A major for Double Bass* (arranged and orchestrated).

Arrangements of works by Arban, J.S. Bach, Eubie Blake, Carriker, Converse, Dede, Dvořak, Europe, Farina, Fauré, Fischer, Giovanni Gabrieli, Gesualdo, Gottschalk, Grapelli, Hartmann, J.P. Johnson, Key, Lamb, Laufer, Matthews, Mendelssohn, Monteverdi, Mozart, Ockeghem, Cole Porter, Rosas, Tallis, Weill, Wiedoeft, and others.

As conductor: recordings of work by Bazelon, Berlioz, Harbison, Helps, Ives, McKinley, Paine, Schaffer, Schoenberg, Sessions, Sollberger, Richard Strauss, Stravinsky, Whiteman.

As horn player: various recordings with Miles Davis, Gil Evans, John Lewis, Metropolitan Wind Quintet.

Publications

By Schuller: *Horn Technique*, New York, 1962; *Early Jazz: Its Roots and Musical Development*, New York, 1968; *Musings*, New York, 1986; many contributions to journals.

On Schuller: R.L. Larson, "A Study and Comparison of Samuel Barber's *Vanessa*, Robert Ward's *The Crucible*, and GS's *The Visitation*", dissertation, University of Indiana, Bloomington, 1971; B. Persia, "Two Works [*Conversations* and *Concertino*] for Jazz Quartet and Ensemble by GS", dissertation, Eastman School of Music, Rochester, New York, 1973; F. Batisti, "GS and His Many Worlds of Music", (interview) in *The Instrumentalist*, 32(11), 1978; P. Spurling, "A Conducting Analysis of *Symphony for Brass and Percussion* by GS", dissertation, Stanford University, California, 1979; J. Hasse, "An Interview with GS", in *Jazz Studies*, 1, 1982; J. Tassel, "GS: Composer, Conductor and Musical Conscience", in *Ovation*, 6(10), 1985; *GS: A Bio-Bibliography*, Westport, Connecticut, 1988.

* * *

As well as being an accomplished and prodigious composer, Gunther Schuller is a renowned conductor who has worked with major orchestras in Europe and the United States. Besides conducting the standard repertoire, his unselfish promotion of the music of other composers, such as Milton Babbitt, have made him a champion of contemporary music. Schuller's deep understanding of 20th-century compositional techniques and his expertise as a conductor have produced some of the best performances and recordings of this repertoire in the world. Although he is a champion of works by other composers, there are also many fine recordings of Schuller conducting his own compositions.

In addition to his work as a composer and performer, Schuller has written many articles on music (*Musings* is a collection of his articles published in book form), edited editions of works by Ives and other composers, and taught at several institutions. He also had a long association with the Berkshire Music Center as composition teacher and artistic director. Since 1984 he has been artistic director of The Festival at Sandpoint in Idaho.

Although he has accomplished much in the world of "classical" music, Schuller's achievements in the world of jazz are no less significant. He has published important works on the subject, such as *Early Jazz: Its Roots and Musical Development*, and he has worked with many ensembles, such as the Modern Jazz Quartet. Schuller's compositions have been influenced by his interest in both types of music; he often integrates "classical" compositional techniques with the rhythmic vigor and improvisational techniques of jazz. He coined the term "third stream" to represent a separate music that draws on both traditions, while allowing the first and second streams to "go their own way unaffected by attempts at fusion." For Schuller, third stream is "a way of composing, improvising, and performing that brings musics together rather than segregating them." Since his initial conception of a third stream music, Schuller has expanded the idea to include non-Western music as well.

Schuller's compositions have benefited from his vast musical experience. His output is diverse, and each composition explores new techniques that have entered his musical world. He has written symphonies, operas, concertos for many instruments, overtures, compositions for solo instruments and many chamber works. Besides jazz, the works of Schoenberg, Ives, Webern, Berg, Stravinsky and Babbitt have influenced Schuller's compositional techniques. Although he is primarally a pitch-oriented composer, his music exhibits a keen awareness of the timbral potentialities in orchestras and ensembles of every imaginable combination, such as the unusual ensemble of four double basses in *Quartet*. *Episodes* for solo clarinet explores the timbral resources of this instrument by means of registeral extremes, dynamic contrast, and the use of multiphonics.

Episodes is also a beautifully expressive work featuring many of the compositional issues important to Schuller. It has a strong melodic direction as well as being rich thematically. While not in the 19th-century tradition, the melodies and themes have a communicative power and developmental potential. The listening experience created by this type of melodic drive is analogous to traveling on a road where the scenery constantly changes, and the present view is a subtle permutation of what came before. The melodic content of the work, however, is not merely an interesting succesion of notes; the linear motion is firmly grounded in, and is an expression of, its harmonic content. Melodies project chordal areas. The same type of writing can be heard in the violin part from the *Recitative and Rondo* for violin and piano.

Although Schuller is primarily a twelve-tone composer, he has also written works that are more traditionally tonal, such as *Six Early Songs*. His twelve-tone works often exhibit a unique application of this technique to composition, especially when he uses the principles of twelve-tone composition in his third stream works. While his earlier works often use successions of single-row forms, from which a variety of harmonic and melodic structures are extracted, his later compositions use combinatorial set relations, such as the pairing of inversionally related row forms to create secondary sets from the first hexachords of each row. Furthermore, a row often influences the form of a work.

The symmetrical ABA form of *Abstraction*, for strings, alto saxophone, guitar and percussion, is directly related to a row and its transformations. The prime form (P) of the row is D, F#, D#, G, B, F, E, C#, C, A#, A and G#. The work begins with violas playing the first four notes of the row, followed by the next six in the first violins, and the A and G# then follow in the second violins. The row is followed by its inversion (I), the retrograde of the prime (PR), and then the retrograde of the inversion (IR). Each transformation is beginning on a different transposition of the prime form. Each large phrase is articulated by a timbral change. For instance, the guitar is heard for the first time at the beginning of second group of rows, while the alto saxophone is not heard until the fifth group. The first note of the prime form from each group of rows taken in the order of their entrance form a hexachord (D, A#, C#, A, F, and B) that is inversionally related to the first hexachord of (P). Since the transposition level of each group of rows is determined by the intervallic structure of the inversion, the order of entrances follows a plan that is analogous in function to fugal entrances in tonal counterpoint. The six groups of rows form the A section of the work.

The B section begins with a seventh group of P-I-PR-IR rows starting on the note C (the first note from the second hexachord of the inversion). Rather than entering in succession, the row entrances form a stretto played by the violins, violas and cellos. The saxophone and basses improvise over the string stretto. The strettos and improvisations continue throughout the B section. When the A section returns, it is a retrograde version of the opening A section.

Abstraction makes a beautiful progression from its sparse opening textures in the A section to the dense and dramatic textures, punctuated by a saxophone cadenza, in the B section that gradually returns to the sparse textures that began the work. The types of instrumental sounds and pitch strategies used in *Abstraction* exemplify much of Schuller's music.

Schuller's contribution to contemporary music has been enormous. His compositions reflect a keen musical mind that continues to be excited by the possibilities of musical expression. The enthusiasm and demand for his compositions can be measured by the number of commissions and performances he receives. Many of Schuller's works, such as *Seven Studies on Themes of Paul Klee*, are already part of the standard repertoire. His compositions will continue to generate interest among musicians and audiences of today and of the future.

—Ciro G. Scotto

SCHULTZ, Andrew (Noel). Australian. Born in Adelaide, 18 August 1960. Educated at University of Queensland, St Lucia (composition under Colin Brumby), 1978–81, 1982–6, B.Mus., PhD., 1987; University of Pennyslvania, Philadelphia (composition under George Crumb), 1983; King's College, University of London (composition under David Lumsdaine), 1985–6, M.Mus. Composer fellowship, Australia Council, Brisbane, 1982; tutor/lecturer, University of Queensland, St Lucia, 1982–5; Fulbright Fellow, AAEF, Philadelphia, 1983; senior lecturer, University of Wollongong, since 1986; composer fellowship, Australia Council, since 1991. Recipient: University of Queensland Medal, 1981; Dalley Scarlett Award, Queensland, 1984; Albert H. Maggs Composition Award, Melbourne, 1985; Hilda Margaret Watts Prize, King's College, University of London, 1986; Australia National Composers Opera Award, 1988. Mailing address: School of Creative Arts, University of Wollongong, P.O. Box 1144, Wollongong, New South Wales 2500, Australia.

Publisher: Sounds Australian, P.O. Box 49, Broadway, New South Wales 2007, Australia.

Symphonies/orchestral:

Garotte 1981; first performed Sydney, 1982. Recorded OZM 1002.
Solace 1981; first performed Sydney, 1981.
Summer Pieces (string orchestra) 1982.
Cloud Burning 1986; first performed Brisbane, 1986.
Concerto for Orchestra 1986.

Chamber/instrumental:

Three Pieces (2 pianos) 1979.
With a View to Infinity . . . (flute, percussion, piano) 1982.
Sonata (piano) 1982; first performed Brisbane, 1990.
Septet (flute, clarinet, trombone, percussion, piano, violin, cello) 1983.
L'Oiseau fantastique (clarinet, violin, cello, piano) 1983; first performed Brisbane, 1984.
B-Bouncing (3 clarinets) 1984; first performed London, 1986.
L'Oiseau fantastique II (string quartet, piano) 1984; first performed Brisbane, 1984.
Shadow's Dance (clarinet, violin, piano) 1985.
Study after Figaro (E♭ clarinet) 1985.
Study After Septet (bass clarinet) 1985.
Spherics (flute, trombone or bass clarinet, percussion, synthesizer, piano, cello) 1985; first performed Sydney, 1985.
String Quartet (string quartet) 1986; first performed Hobart, Tasmania, 1991.
Etudes espace (3 inventions for organ) 1986.
Babel Canons (flexible scoring/4 or more players) 1987.
Sea-Change (piano) 1987; first performed London, 1987.
Stick Dance (clarinet, marimba, piano) 1987; first performed Brisbane, 1987.
Barren Grounds (clarinet, viola, cello, piano) 1988; first performed Brisbane, 1988.
Sea Call (2 trumpets, trombone) 1988.
Machine (4 percussion) 1989; first performed Sydney, 1989.
Stick Dance II (clarinet, viola, piano; arranged by N. Saintilan) 1989.
Mephisto (flute, clarinet, violin, viola, double bass, guitar) 1990; first performed Melbourne, 1991.
Attack (viola) 1990.
Collide (bass clarinet, marimba) 1990.
Duo Variations (viola, piano) 1990.

Vocal/choral:

Elegy (tenor, 2 violins, viola, double bass) 1978.
Mulga Bill's Bicycle (SABar chorus, flute, clarinet, trumpet, 2 percussion, piano—4 hands, violin, cello; Banjo Patterson) 1979; first performed Brisbane, 1980.
How Twinkle Police Jelly Fish, Miss? (soprano, piano) 1980.
All Flesh Is Grass (SATB chorus, brass quartet, organ; sacred) 1981; first performed Brisbane, 1981.
Ode on a Grecian Urn Summarized (female voices, Skirow) 1982.
Ditties (baritone, guitar) 1983.
Reading a View (2 sopranos, SATB chorus, orchestra; Malouf) 1985.
O Oriensis (SATB chorus, marimba, piano, organ) 1986; first performed Sydney, 1987.
Seafarer (baritone, bass clarinet, horn, trumpet, marimba, harp; MacLeish) 1986.

Where the Dead Men Lie (SATB chorus, orchestra) 1987.
Ekstasis (2 sopranos, alto, tenor, baritone, bass; sacred) 1990; first performed Sydney, 1990.

Opera/dramatic:

Black River (one-act opera) 1988; first performed Sydney, 1989.
Fast Talking: The Last Words of Dutch Schultz (solo male voice) 1988; first performed Perth, 1989.
A Distant Shore (song cycle or staged version; baritone, horn, trumpet, trombone, percussion, piano, harp, string quintet; Nowra) 1989; first performed Newcastle, 1991.
Going into Shadows (Julianne Schultz) 1990–1.

PUBLICATIONS

By Schultz: "*Sequenze I–VII* by Luciano Berio: Compositional Idea and Musical Action", dissertation, University of Queensland, St Lucia, 1987; "Forget the Philistines—What About the Critics?", in *Sounds Australian*, 20, Summer 1988; analytical essays in *Anthology of Australian Music on Disc*, Canberra, 1989; "The Specialization Dilemma", in *Sounds Australian*, 21, Summer 1989; "Identity and Memory: Temporality and the Music of David Lumsdaine", in *Studies in Music*, 14, 1991; "Other Places, Whose Music?", in *Sounds Australian*, 27, Winter 1991; "Writing for Performance by Children", in *Proceedings of the 1988 Australian National Composers Conference*, 1991.

On Schultz: James Murdoch, in *Australian Musicians*, Sydney, 1983; *AS: Australian Composers Series 20*, Sydney, 1989, 1991; Nicole Saintilan, "AS: A Musical and Biographical Sketch", in *Fifty Australian Composers*, edited by Broadstock.

Andrew Schultz comments:

We live in an age in which music has become a commodity, a thing to be manufactured and sold like mouthwash and aftershave. Music is used to appease and placate us in supermarkets, in restaurants and while on the telephone. Yet, as a composer I cling to the knowledge that music has the power to strike the listener dumb with terror or grief and open inner worlds of astonishing beauty and exhilaration. My work is concerned with finding a means of expression that is at once direct and subtle; that is, balancing communicative and technical features to achieve the creation of involving and satisfying works for myself, the listener and the performer.

* * *

The music of Andrew Schultz propounds a widespread eclecticism, in which ideas can be borrowed from the entire musical field; his strong rhythmic sense derives from flamenco, Asian and even pop (rap) music. The natural environment, too, provides a source of ideas in the songs of birds and environmental sounds. There is some influence of Stravinsky evident in the earlier works; later pieces reveal elements traceable to Messiaen—*Spherics* for instrumental ensemble—and Berio—*Ekstasis* for an ensemble of six solo voices.

Schultz has resisted adopting specific musical styles, but is alert to the concepts behind various trends. The two versions of *L'Oiseau fantastique* for instrumental ensemble provide an exposition of the minimalistic concept that an idea may be worked out by constant repetition, with variations gradually occurring in an almost organic manner. This can also be discerned in *Sonata* and *Sea-Change* for piano, in *Barren Grounds* for instrumental ensemble, and to a lesser extent in *Spherics*. Repetition is less a feature of Schultz's later works, in which there is a stronger use of structural form to achieve a similar purpose.

Post-serial techniques and ideas have had a noticeable influence upon his compositional development. Earlier pieces tended to incur a great deal of complex pre-compositional work on sketches, notes and jottings, but his more recent tendency has been towards a gradual simplification and clarification of ideas and methods. Works such as *Ekstasis*, a setting of erotic love poetry from the biblical *Song of Songs*, are much more intuitive in their conception and exposition. The finished product is still complex, but its compositional process has been less so.

A somewhat offbeat sense of humour is a recurring feature of Schultz's output. Sometimes this is expressed verbally: either being a characteristic of the chosen text, as in *Mulga Bill's Bicycle*—a choral setting of A.B. ("Banjo") Patterson's wry bush ballad—and the setting of Desmond Skirrow's succinct *Ode on a Grecian Urn Summarized* for female voices, or being a felicitous title, such as *How Twinkle Police Jelly Fish, Miss?*, comprising key or title words from each song in the cycle. Other humour is strictly and rather esoterically musical, as in the orchestral *Garotte*, where an inoffensive Baroque gavotte is warped and fragmented during the course of the piece. The borrowing of this device from Berlioz is duly acknowledged by musical reference to that composer's *Symphonie fantastique*.

The one-hour opera *Black River* is a highly significant work for several reasons. Schultz's first attempt in this genre, it was promptly given seasons by two different opera companies, and plans made for a film version. Dealing with the controversial issue of Australian Aboriginal deaths in police custody, it posed a specific musical puzzle: how to integrate the central character, an Aboriginal woman, successfully into the peculiarly European standard operatic framework. The composer, himself keenly interested in the politics of race relations, approached the problem with a blend of sung and spoken lines, preserving a natural speech pattern and accent and also incorporating traditional elements of wailing and lamenting. The overall dramatic success of the work can be gauged by its receiving the Australian National Composers Opera Award for 1988, and the 1989 Sounds Australian National Music Critics' Award for best performance in Australian music theatre.

Despite his strongly cerebral approach to the technique of composition, Schultz believes that it is a function of music to communicate with the soul of both the performer and the listener: while the creative process may be largely intellectual, its reception should be emotional.

—Jenny Dawson

SCHUMAN, William (Howard). American. Born in New York City, 4 August 1910. Popular composition and jazz performance, c.1926–34. Educated at School of Commerce, New York University, 1928–30; studied harmony privately under Max Persin, from 1930; studied counterpoint privately under Charles Haubiel; summer courses, Juilliard School of Music, New York City (under Bernard Wagenaar and Adolf Schmid), 1932, 1933; Columbia University Teachers College,

New York City, 1933–7, B.S., M.A; studied conducting, Salzburg Mozarteum, 1935; summer course, Juilliard School (under Roy Harris), 1936; further private composition study under Harris, 1936–8. Married Frances [Frankie] Prince, 27 March 1936. Teacher of music and chorus conductor, Sarah Lawrence College, Bronxville, New York, 1935–45; director of publications, 1945–8 and special consultant, until 1952, G. Schirmer, New York City; president, Juilliard School, 1952–62; president, 1962–9, thereafter President Emeritus, Lincoln Center for the Performing Arts, New York City; full-time composer and honorary administrator, since 1969. Recipient: 1st Town Hall League of Composers Award (for *String Quartet No 3*) 1940; 1st New York Music Critics' Circle Award (for *Symphony No 3*) 1941; 1st Pulitzer Prize in music (for *A Free Song*), 1943; New York Music Critics Circle Award (for *Judith*), 1951; 1st Brandeis University Creative Arts Award in music, 1957; citation of merit, State University of New York, Buffalo, 1963; Gold Medal of Honor, National Arts Club, New York City, 1964; Brandeis Medal for Distinguished Service to Higher Education, 1965; Composer's Award, Lancaster [Pennsylvania] Symphony Orchestra, 1965; Handel Medallion, City of New York, 1967; Certificate of Merit, Sigma Alpha Iota, 1967; Concert Artist Guild Award, 1967; American Music Center Letter of Distinction, 1967; Findley Award, City University of New York, 1968; MacDowell Colony Medal, 1971; Horblit Award, Boston Symphony Orchestra and Harvard University, 1980; 1st William Schuman Award, Columbia University, 1981, subsequently given annually to a composer; Gold Medal, American Academy of Arts and Letters, 1982; Pulitzer Prize special citation for career achievement, 1985; George Peabody Medal for outstanding contributions to American music, Peabody Conservatory, 1985; Gold Baton, American Symphony Orchestra League, 1985; Chamber Music America Award, 1986; 1st Alfred I. DuPont Award, 1986; American Eagle Award, National Musical Council, 1989; Kennedy Center Honor (for lifetime contribution to American culture), 1989. Honorary degrees: Chicago Musical College, 1946, University of Wisconsin, 1949, Philadelphia Conservatory of Music, 1952, Cincinnati College of Music, 1953, Columbia University, 1954, Hartt College of Music, 1956, Colgate University, 1960, Allegheny College, 1961, Dartmouth College, 1962, New York University, 1963, Adelphi College, 1963, Northwestern University, 1963, University of New Mexico, 1964, University of Rhode Island, 1965, Bates College, 1966, Fordham University, 1970, Ashland College, 1970, Peabody Conservatory, 1971, University of Rochester Eastman School of Music, 1972, State University of New York, 1974, University of North Carolina, 1980, New England Conservatory of Music, 1981, Johns Hopkins University, 1985, State University of New York at Potsdam, 1986, Juilliard School of Music, 1987, Yale University, 1988, Manhattanville College, 1990. Mailing address: 888 Park Avenue, New York, New York 10021, U.S.A.

Publishers: Associated; Schirmer; Boosey & Hawkes; Presser; Merion; Hendon; Carl Fischer; Peer International.

Symphonies/orchestral:

Potpourri 1932; withdrawn.

Symphony No 1 (small orchestra) 1935; first performed New York City, 21 October 1936; withdrawn.

Prelude and Fugue 1937; withdrawn.

Symphony No 2 1937; first performed New York City, 25 May 1938; withdrawn.

Piano Concerto 1938; revised 1942; first performed New York City, 13 January 1943. Recorded Turnabout TVS 34733.

American Festival Overture 1939; first performed Boston, 6 October 1939. Recorded RCA Victor 18511; American Recording Society ARS 28/ARS 115/Desto 6404E; Deutsche Grammophon DG 253 2085.

Symphony No 3 1941; first performed Boston, 17 October 1941. Recorded Columbia MS 7442/CMS 6245/M1 4413.

Newsreel, in Five Shots (concert band) 1941; first performed University Park, Pennsylvania, 1942; version for orchestra first performed New York City, 15 July 1942. Recorded (orchestral version) Pro Arte PAD 102.

Symphony No 4 1941; first performed Cleveland, Ohio, 22 January 1942. Recorded Louisville S 692.

Prayer in Time of War 1943; first performed Pittsburgh, Pennsylvania, 26 February 1943. Recorded Louisville S 721.

Symphony No 5: Symphony for Strings 1943; first performed Boston, 12 November 1943. Recorded Columbia MS 7442; Concert Hall CHS 1078; Capitol P 8212.

Overture: William Billings 1943; first performed New York City, 17 February 1944; withdrawn.

Variations on a Theme by Eugene Goossens (5th of a set by different composers) 1944; first performed Cincinnati, Ohio, 23 March 1945.

Circus Overture (Side Show) (full or small orchestra) 1944; first performed with small orchestra Philadelphia, 17 December 1944; first performed with full orchestra, Pittsburgh, 7 January 1945.

Undertow (choreographic episodes for orchestra) 1945; first performed Los Angeles, 29 November 1945. Recorded New World 253; Mercury MG 10088.

Violin Concerto 1947, revised 1954, 1958–9; first performed Boston, 10 February 1950; 1st revised version first performed New York City, 26 February 1956; 2nd revised version first performed Aspen, Colorado, 9 August 1959. Recorded Deutsche Grammophon DGG 253 0103; Angel CDC 49464.

Symphony No 6 1948; first performed Dallas, 27 February 1949. Recorded Columbia CML 4922; CRI SD 477.

George Washington Bridge (concert band) 1950; first performed Interlochen, Michigan, 30 July 1980. Recorded Mercury MG 40006; KOCD 3562.

Credendum, Article of Faith 1955; first performed Cincinnati, Ohio, 4 November 1955. Recorded Columbia ML 5185; CRI S-308.

New England Triptych 1956; first performed Miami, Florida, 26 October 1956.

Chester Overture (from *New England Triptych*; concert band) 1956; first performed Louisville, Kentucky, January 1957. Recorded RCA IM 2677; Vogt CSR V 2503; Cornell CUWE 10; Decca DL 8633; Vanguard VRS 9119/VSD 2124.

When Jesus Wept (from *New England Triptych*; concert band) 1958. Recorded Cornell CUWE 9.

Symphony No 7 1960; first performed Boston, 21 October 1960. Recorded Turnabout TVS 34447.

A Song of Orpheus (based on *Orpheus and His Lute*; cello, orchestra) 1961, arranged for chamber orchestra 1978; original version first performed Indianapolis, 17 February 1962; revised version first performed 8 November 1978. Recorded Columbia MS 6338.

Symphony No 8 1962; first performed New York City, 4 October 1962. Recorded Odyssey Y 34140.

Variations on "America" (after Ives; also arranged for band) 1963; first performed New York City, 20 May 1964. Recorded RCA Victor LSV 2893; Columbia MS 7289; Louisville 651; London SPC 21178.

The Orchestra Song 1963; first performed New York City, 11 April 1964.
Symphony No 9: Le Fosse ardéatine 1968; first performed Philadelphia, 10 January 1969. Recorded CRI SD 477.
Dedication Fanfare (concert band) 1968; first performed St Louis, Missouri, 4 July 1968.
To Thee Old Cause (evocation for oboe, brass, timpani, piano, strings) 1968; first performed New York City, 3 October 1968. Recorded Columbia MS 7392.
In Praise of Shahn (canticle for orchestra) 1969; first performed New York City, 29 January 1970. Recorded Columbia M 30112; New World NW 368.
Anniversary Fanfare (brass band, percussion) 1969; first performed New York City, 13 April 1970.
Voyage 1972; first performed Rochester, New York, 27 October 1972. Recorded Columbia CML 4987; Etcetera ETC 1036.
Concerto on Old English Rounds (viola, orchestra, female chorus) 1974; first performed Boston, 29 November 1974. Recorded Columbia M 35101.
Prelude for a Great Occasion (brass band, percussion) 1974; first performed Washington, D.C., 1 October 1974.
Symphony No 10: American Muse 1975; first performed Washington, D.C., 6 April 1976.
Be Glad, Then (from *New England Triptych*; concert band) 1975. Recorded Cornell CUWE 19.
Amaryllis (strings) 1976; first performed Philadelphia, 27 July 1976.
Three Colloquies ("Rumination", "Renewal", "Remembrance"; horn, orchestra) 1979; first performed New York City, 24 January 1980. Recorded New World NW 326.
American Hymn (orchestral variations; also arranged for band) 1980; first performed St Louis, Missouri, 24 December 1982. Recorded Elektra/Nonesuch 1-79072.
Showcase (short display for orchestra) 1986; first performed Houston, Texas, 26 September 1986.
Let's Hear It for Lenny! (variations on "New York, New York" for Leonard Bernstein's 70th birthday) 1988; first performed Boston, 28 August 1988.

Chamber/instrumental:

Canon and Fugue (piano trio) 1934; withdrawn.
Two Pastorales (I—2 violas or violin and cello or alto and clarinet; II—flute, oboe or violin, clarinet) 1934; I broadcast 1942; withdrawn.
String Quartet No 1 1936; first performed New York City, 21 October 1936; withdrawn.
String Quartet No 2 1937; first performed New York City, Spring 1938.
Quartettino (4 bassoons) 1939. Recorded New Music Quarterly 1415.
String Quartet No 3 1939; first performed New York City, 27 February 1940. Recorded RCA Victor LSC 2481; Vox SVBX 5305.
Three-Score Set (piano) 1943; first performed New York City, 29 August 1943. Recorded Educo 3105.
String Quartet No 4 1950; first performed Washington, D.C., 28 October 1950. Recorded Columbia ML 4993.
Voyage (piano) 1953; first performed Chicago, 18 August 1953.
Three Moods (piano) 1958; first performed Athens, Greece, 2 December 1958.
Amaryllis (variations for string trio) 1964; first performed Washington, D.C., 21 October 1964.
XXV Opera Snatches (trumpet) 1978; first performed New York City, 10 January 1979.
Night Journey (variable ensembles; from the ballet) 1980; first performed New York City, 30 March 1981. Recorded CRI SD 500.
American Hymn (brass quintet) 1980; first performed New York City, 30 March 1981.
Dances (wind quintet, percussion) 1984; first performed New York City, 1 October 1985.
Awake, Thou Wintry Earth (clarinet, violin, arranged for flute, bassoon) 1986.
Cooperstown Fanfare (2 trumpets, 2 trombones) 1987; first performed Cooperstown, New York, 28 June 1987.
String Quartet No 5 1987; first performed New York City, 21 June 1988.
Chester: Variations (piano) 1988; first performed Fort Worth, Texas, 2 June 1989.

Vocal/choral:

God's World (voice, piano; Millay) 1932.
Four Canonic Choruses ("Epitaph" (Millay), "Epitaph for Conrad" (Cullen), "Night Stuff" (Sandburg), "Come Not" (Tennyson)); unaccompanied SATB chorus. 1932–3; first performed New York City, 3 May 1935.
Pioneers! (unaccompanied SSAATTBB chorus; Whitman) 1937; first performed Princeton, New Jersey, 23 May 1938; withdrawn.
Choral Etude (unaccompanied SATB vocalise) 1937; first performed New York City, 16 March 1938. Recorded Columbia C 17139D.
Prologue (SATB chorus, orchestra; Taggard) 1939; first performed New York City, 7 May 1939.
The Orchestra Song (any voices; Farquhar, traditional) 1939.
Prelude (soprano, unaccompanied female or SATB chorus; Wolfe) 1939; first performed New York, 24 April 1940. Recorded Concordia S-6; GSS 110.
This Is Our Time: Secular Cantata No 1 (SATB chorus, orchestra; Taggard) 1940; first performed New York City, 4 July 1940.
Requiescat (female or SATB chorus, piano) 1942; first performed New York City, 4 April 1942.
Holiday Song (female voices or SATB chorus or solo voice, piano) 1942; first performed New York City, 13 January 1943.
A Free Song: Secular Cantata No 2 (SATB chorus, orchestra; Whitman) 1942; first performed Boston, 26 March 1943.
Orpheus with His Lute (voice, piano; Shakespeare) 1944. Recorded Turnabout TBS 34727; GSS 110.
Te Deum (unaccompanied SATB chorus) 1944; first performed Cambridge, Massachusetts, April 1945. Recorded Aspen 1511.
Truth Shall Deliver (unaccompanied male chorus; Farquhar, after Chaucer) 1946; first performed New Haven, Connecticut, 7 December 1946.
Choruses from The Mighty Casey (SATB chorus, piano—4 hands; from the opera) 1953.
The Lord Has a Child (unaccompanied SATB or female chorus; or voice, piano; Hughes) 1956, revised 1990; first performed New York City 16 June 1990.
Five Rounds on Famous Words ("Health", "Thrift", "Caution", "Beauty", "Haste"; unaccompanied treble voices or SATB chorus) 1956–69. Recorded GSS 110.
Carols of Death ("The Last Invocation", "The Unknown Region", "To All, to Each"; unaccompanied SATB chorus; Whitman) 1958; first performed Canton, New York, 20 March 1959. Recorded GSS 110; Everest 3129.
Deo ac veritati (unaccompanied male chorus) 1963; first performed Hamilton, New York, 19 April 1963.

Declaration Chorale (unaccompanied SATB chorus; Whitman) 1971; first performed New York, 30 April 1972.
Mail Order Madrigals (unaccompanied SATB chorus; Sears Roebuck catalogue of 1897) 1971; first performed Ames, Iowa, 12 March 1972. Recorded GSS 110.
To Thy Love (choral fantasy for unaccompanied SSA chorus; old English rounds) 1973.
The Young Dead Soldiers (soprano, horn, woodwinds, strings; MacLeish) 1975; first performed Washington, D.C., 6 April 1976. Recorded CRI SD 439.
Casey at the Bat (cantata for soprano, baritone, chorus, orchestra; based on the opera) 1976; first performed Washington, D.C., 6 April 1976.
In Sweet Music (based on *Orpheus and His Lute*; mezzo-soprano, flute, viola, harp) 1978; first performed New York City, 29 October 1978. Recorded CRI SD 439.
Time to the Old (voice, piano; MacLeish) 1979.
Esses (short suite for unaccompanied SATB chorus; words beginning with S) 1982; first performed Ithaca, New York, 13 November 1982. Recorded GSS 110.
Perceptions (cycle for unaccompanied SATB chorus; Whitman) 1982; first performed Greenwich, Connecticut, 9 January 1983. Recorded GSS 110.
On Freedom's Ground (cantata for baritone, chorus, orchestra; Wilbur) 1985.

Opera/dramatic:

The Mighty Casey (Gury, after Thayer) 1951–3; first performed Hartford, Connecticut, 4 May 1953. Recorded (excerpts) Premiere PRCD 1009.
A Question of Taste (after Roald Dahl) 1988; first performed Cooperstown, New York, 24 June 1989.

Other:

Steeltown (film score).
Undertow (ballet by Tudor) 1945; first performed New York City, 10 April 1945. Recorded Mercury MG 10088; New World 253.
Night Journey (ballet by Graham) 1947; first performed Cambridge, Massachusetts, 3 May 1947.
Judith (ballet by Graham) 1949; first performed Louisville, Kentucky, 4 January 1950. Recorded Mercury MG 10008; CRI SD 500.
Voyage for a Theater (ballet by Graham) 1953; first performed New York City, 17 May 1953.
The Earth Is Born (film score) 1959.
The Witch of Endor (ballet by Graham) 1965; first performed New York City, 2 November 1965; withdrawn.

PUBLICATIONS

On Schuman: Paul Rosenfeld, "Copland, Harris, S", in *Musical Quarterly*, 25, 1939; Leonard Bernstein, "WS", in *Musical Monthly*, 19, 1942; N. Broder, "The Music of WS", in *Musical Quarterly*, 31, 1945; F.R. Schreiber and V. Persichetti, *WS*, New York City, 1954; J.F. Weber, *Carter and S*, Discography series 19, Utica, New York, 1978; H. Wiley Hitchcock, "WS: Musical All-American", in *Keynote*, 4(6), August 1980; C. Rose, *A WS Documentary*, New York, 1980; H. Gleason and W. Becker, "WS", in *Twentieth-Century American Composers*, Bloomington, Indiana, 2nd edition 1981; D. Hall, " A Bio-Discography of WS", in *Ovation*, 6, 1985.

* * *

William Schuman's symphonies are the backbone of his output and they neither echo 19th-century Romanticism like those of Samuel Barber or Howard Hanson nor are they overtly American like Roy Harris's or Aaron Copland's works in this genre. He did tackle American subjects, as in *The Mighty Casey*, a baseball opera (revised as a cantata, *Casey at the Bat*, in 1976), the *Circus Overture* (*Side Show*) and *Newsreel, in Five Shots*, this last for band; and there are occasional oblique echoes of jazz, as in the *Vigoroso* of *Symphony No 7.* Yet despite his early involvements in the world of popular entertainment Schuman, perhaps rather disappointingly, never attempted a synthesis of America's numerous musical idioms.

Harris was his most significant teacher, however, and the long, freely ranging lines of pieces such as the older man's *Symphony No 3* were continued, if to rather different ends, by Schuman. In fact he had greater sophistication than Harris, technical and otherwise, though he always said that melody was the chief element in his music. Certainly his large orchestral scores are built not from symphonically aphoristic themes but with sustained, quasi-vocal melodic paragraphs, often modal in contour, plastic in rhythm, with further growth arising from motives recurring in new shapes. Rather than deriving from the concept of sonata form, Schuman's tendencies are polyphonic, hence the monistic structures of *Symphony No 3*, whose two large sections are titled *Passacaglia and Fugue*, *Chorale and Toccata*. Fugal subjects often undergo much change during the course of development, and melodic and particularly harmonic repetitions are rhythmically displaced to renew their impact.

Much stamina is needed to compose works that grow with seeming inevitability from sustained melody, and at his best Schuman has this. At such times it is with exhilarating skill that he pursues his arguments, for example in handling the shifting stresses between the modal configurations of his melodies and resonant triadic harmony, which usually contains many false relations. The melodies are often supported by rhythmically irregular chords and the vocabulary of these ranges from non-functional triadic harmony to polytonal combinations; there is plentiful dissonance but also a strong sense of underlying tonality.

The development of this buoyant and large-boned style is best followed in the symphonies, though not all of them can be mentioned here. The opening *Passacaglia* of *Symphony No 3* gives rise to all the work's themes, and the strong-sinewed lyricism of the *Chorale* should be contrasted with the acutely expressive tenderness of the *Cantabile intensamente* of *Symphony No 7.* In the Fifth Symphony, for strings only, Schuman makes a more frequent use of polytonal chords than hitherto, but the full, very active textures are relieved with unison passages. For instance the opening theme of the initial *Molto agitato* is first heard as a powerful unison on the G strings of the first and second violins, unaccompanied. All subsequent themes, again, derive from this, and there are other linking relationships, for example between the polytonal chords that open the central *Larghissimo* and the climax of the previous movement.

As it happens, the outer movements of the Fifth Symphony do have respectively sonata and rondo forms in their backgrounds, but *Symphony No 6*, one of Schuman's finest works, is altogether different, being a single movement, as polyphonic as ever and full of major–minor chords, in six sections. After this came such pieces as the ballet *Judith*, *String Quartet No 4* and the choral *Carols of Death*, which are among the most remarkable of all Whitman settings. *Symphony No 7*, *Symphony No 8* and *Symphony No 9* were linked in the composer's mind, perhaps because they were written in the same decade, in 1960, 1962 and 1968 respectively. They yield nothing in orchestral verve or developmental energy to Schuman's earlier music yet they represent full maturity. The Seventh Symphony, in four movements played without a break, picks up some of the initiatives uncovered by the *Carols of Death*, with slow and sad thoughts predominating, especially among the dark colours of the opening *Largo assai*. This mood recurs in *Symphony No 9*.

Schuman's orchestral writing is often demanding—the trumpet parts in the *Fugue* of *Symphony No 3*, for example, or the percussion in the finale of *Symphony No 7*—and although the textures remain clear, his more declamatory passages, as in *Credendum, Article of Faith*, can be rather overwhelming with their huge sonorities. There is greater restraint in the orchestration of his ballets, for instance *Undertow*, despite the grimness of the story in this particular case. Another striking work is the *New England Triptych*, an orchestral setting of three vocal pieces by William Billings, the inspired 18th-century American primitive composer. If Schuman can here fuse contemporary techniques with this old music it is partly because Billings bypassed so much of traditional procedure.

While the symphonies embody the main line of his development, other scores such as the moving *Three Colloquies* for horn and orchestra should not be neglected. There were a considerable number of vocal works in the 1970s, some of them quite unusual, like the *Mail Order Madrigals*—1972 settings from the 1897 Sears Roebuck catalogue—and the *Concerto on Old English Rounds* for viola and women's voices.

Naturally the polyphonic aspects of Schuman's thinking are prominent in his chamber music. The first movement, titled *Sinfonia*, of *String Quartet No 2* is an early instance of his successfully basing an entire piece on the steady expansion of a single melodic idea. The following movement, a passacaglia, has a quasi-serial structure yet retains tonal feeling, while the concluding fugue has a characteristic theme built on fourths. There is much quiet dissonance in the opening *Adagio* of *String Quartet No 4*, as in the later *Andante*. And again there are hints of serial technique in the intervening *Allegro con fuoco*, much rhythmic interest in the development section of the finale *Presto*.

Schuman's later music should be seen not so much as backward-looking as an act of unification, a return to forms, styles and even materials that had occupied him in earlier years. It is fairly typical, for instance, that the serenade *In Sweet Music* is a recomposition and extension of the 1944 song *Orpheus and His Lute*. He returned to Whitman also, for the *Declaration Chorale* and in particular for the 1982 *Perceptions*.

—Max Harrison

SCHURMANN, (Edward) Gerard. Dutch and British. Born in Kertosono, Java, 19 January 1924 [several sources cite 1928; *Baker's* cites 23 January]; emigrated to England. Educated: studied composition with Alan Rawsthorne, piano with Kathleen Long, conducting with Franco Ferrara. Aircrew, 320 Squadron, Royal Air Force, 1941–6. Married (1) Vivien Hind in 1948; (2) Carolyn Nott, 26 May 1973; 1 daughter. The Netherlands Cultural Attaché, London, 1945–7; resident orchestral conductor, The Netherlands Radio, Hilversum, 1947–9; freelance pianist/composer/conductor, since 1949; emigrated to the United States, 1981. Mailing address: 3700 Multiview Drive, Los Angeles, California 90068, U.S.A.

Publisher: Novello.

Symphonies/orchestral:

Six Studies of Francis Bacon 1968; first performed Dublin, January 1969. Recorded Chandos ABR 1011.
Variants 1970; first performed Guildford, Surrey, March 1971. Recorded Chandos ABR 1011.
Attack and Celebration 1971; first performed London, 1971. Recorded Silva Screen/Cloud Nine.
Piano Concerto 1972–3; first movement first performed Dublin, 14 January 1973; first complete performance Portsmouth, 21 November 1973.
Violin Concerto 1975–8; first performed Liverpool, 26 September 1978.
The Gardens of Exile (cello, orchestra) 1989–90; first performed Poole, Dorset, 20 March 1991.

Chamber/instrumental:

Bagatelles (piano) 1945; first performed Amsterdam, November 1945. Recorded HMV ESD 7144.
Fantasia (cello, piano) 1963, revised 1965.
Wind Quintet 1964, revised 1976.
Fantasia (formerly *Dialogue*; cello, piano) 1967; first performed Paris, March 1968.
Sonatina (flute, piano) 1968; first performed Rome, 1968.
Serenade (violin) 1969; first performed Dublin, 7 January 1970.
Contrasts (piano) 1973; first performed London, 21 May 1973.
Leotaurus (piano) 1975; first performed Canberra, Australia, September 1975.
Two Ballades (in Homage to Janáček): Hukvaldy / Brno (piano) 1981–3; first performed Los Angeles, 19 September 1983.
Duo (violin, piano) 1983–4; first performed Washington, D.C., 23 March 1984.
Quartet for Piano and Strings 1986; first performed Cheltenham, Gloucestershire, 20 July 1986.
Ariel (oboe) 1987; first performed Valencia, California, 30 November 1988.

Vocal/choral:

Nine Songs of William Blake (tenor, piano) 1950s; unreleased.
Carceri (baritone, orchestra; 15th-century Italian) begun 1958.
Chuench'i (high voice, piano; also high voice, orchestra; Waley) 1966, 1967; first performed London, May 1966. Recorded (piano version) Pye GSGC 14105; Nonesuch H-71209.
Summer Is Coming (unaccompanied SATB chorus; Guinness) 1970; first performed Cork, May 1970.
The Double Heart (unaccompanied SATB chorus; Marvell) 1976; first performed London, 28 March 1977. Recorded BBC TS 554.
Piers Plowman (cantata for soprano, alto, tenor, bass, chorus, orchestra; Langland) 1979–80; first performed Gloucester, 22 August 1980.
Slovak Folk Songs (high voice, piano/orchestra) 1987, orchestrated 1988.

Other:

Film scores: *The Long Arm*; *Man in the Sky*; *Lease of Life*; *Camp on Blood Island*; *The Two-Headed Spy*; *The Ruthless One*; *Horrors of the Black Museum*; *Konga*; *The Headless Ghost*; *Cone of Silence*; *The Living Earth*; *Dr Syn*; *The Ceremony*; *The Bedford Incident*; *Attack on the Iron Coast*; *The Lost Continent*; also orchestrations for *Lawrence of Arabia*, *Exodus*, *The Vikings*.

PUBLICATIONS

By Schurmann: "GS Writes About His Work 'Variants'", in *The Listener*, April 1971; introduction to 3 volumes on *Alan Rawsthorne*, London, 1984; "GS in Conversation with Francis Routh", in *The Composer*, January 1989; "A Reply to Maurice Jarre About *Lawrence of Arabia*", in *The Cue Sheet*, July 1990.

On Schurmann: Kenneth Loveland, "The Music of GS", in *The Musical Times*, May 1970; Richard Cooke, "An Unfashionable Form?" (piano concerto), in *Music and Musicians*, November 1973; Margaret Campbell, "New Violin Concerto for a Veteran Virtuoso", in *The Strad*, September 1978; Michael Oliver, "S's Violin Concerto", in *Music and Musicians*, September 1978; Robert Matthew-Walker, "GS and Piers Plowman", in *The Musical Times*, August 1980; "The Music of GS", in *Halle*, Autumn 1980, and "A Note of GS's New Piano Quartet", in *Music and Musicians*, July 1986; Gerard Victory, "*Chuench'i*: An Analysis of GS's Song-Cycle", in *The Music Review*, 3, 33.

Gerard Schurmann comments:

I feel that as a composer I matured late in life. Earlier on, after the first flush of unselfconscious writing had subsided, my main preoccupation seems to have been with the manipulation of technique. A basic lack of confidence in trusting one's own instinct had to be overcome very gradually, until almost exactly the opposite is now true.

When I write I listen very intensely, and try to respond emotionally in the most direct way possible.

* * *

Gerard Schurmann was born within a year or so of both Pierre Boulez and Hans Werner Henze: the latter, though more prolific, offers the better parallel. Eschewing the more puritan rigours of strict dodecaphonic writing, Schurmann has nonetheless applied related techniques and used a similar structurally self-critical approach to serve his own expressive ends, marrying rare inventiveness and technical skill with remarkable powers as an orchestrator to create a highly individual voice.

Schurmann's work is approachable through two main avenues: the few brilliant, highly coloured orchestral canvases, whose expressionism touches both extremes—in *Six Studies of Francis Bacon* unbridled violence (such as by 1968 among English musicians only Birtwhistle (*Punch and Judy*) and Davies (*Revelation and Fall*) had unleashed, and a balancing calm and serenity, most obvious in the accompanied vocal works; or the concise chamber miniatures, hailing especially from the 1970s.

A thirst for technical assurance drove the young Schurmann to early lessons with Alan Rawsthorne and helped him emerge as perhaps one of the finest technicians of all. An occasional terseness may offset the expressiveness; more usually, this control of his material enables the music to flower. Hans Keller's claim to have been able to analyse *Variants*, an 18-minute piece for Schubert-sized orchestra and one of his most obviously attractive achievements, back to its single, ambivalent opening hexachord—Stravinskian in gesture—makes ample sense: it reflects the way the composer spins all his works, be they a concerto with the prescribed sheen (two, for piano and violin, spring from the 1970s); his expressive new cello work, *The Gardens of Exile*, was premièred in spring 1991), or the range of meticulously wrought chamber items—the flute *Sonatina* or solo violin *Serenade*, piano pieces like *Leotaurus* and above all, the longer three-movement Piano Quartet of 1986, with its canonic opening *Ricercar* and thrusting central *Capriccio*, dedicated appropriately to Keller's memory.

In the *Six Studies of Francis Bacon*, material is cleverly filtered through delicate (and here even highly *in*delicate), minute transformations, just as in the close-worked soprano song cycle *Chuench'i*: short poems taken (in translation) from the Chinese, whose expressionist, tritonic intensity and shifting tonalities most obviously suggest Berg's *Lulu* or the moonstruck texts of *Pierrot Lunaire*, chart a young girl's transition through youthful spring towards philosophic acceptance of decline and dissolution. Schurmann achieves balance between the movements and textures especially light scherzando for "Plucking the Rushes"; a somnolent, fragrant Ophelia-like quality in "Flowers and Moonlight" or "Self-Abandonment"; and in the final poem, visionary acceptance and embracement, akin to Peter Maxwell Davies's subsequent *Into the Labyrinth*. With its shimmering piano part, *Chuench'i* remains one of the most powerful products of the 1960s neo-Expressionist surge.

Oriental flavouring—including occasional hints of Javanese music, which had a wider impact (after Debussy) on Messiaen's succeeding generation—recalls Schurmann's Dutch East Indies origin, but reflects rather the impact, especially on the chamber pieces, of Bartók, with whom his mother, born of Hungarian parents, studied piano in Budapest. Russian and Magyar influences surface in his use of the pentatonic or related scales and dervish-like rhythmic patterns, as also in the brilliant vocal challenge of *The Double Heart*, his densely scored *a capella* cantata for double chorus (a kind of *tour de force* of canonic counterpoint) with text from Andrew Marvell. East Europe resurfaces in the Concerto for piano, German Romanticism in that for violin—both of which, in two movements, match exterior display with that gradually unveiling dynamic intensity found throughout Schurmann's work; while the Stravinskian input—plus Prokofiev, notably in the Piano Quartet and Flute Sonatina—extends well beyond the explicit neo-classicism of *Variants* (whose seminal chord also features elsewhere).

The equality of roles Schurmann allots to his chamber music performers consistently sharpens the dialogue: this is particularly true of the *Duo* for violin and piano of 1984—a work that reveals some of the most personal characteristics of his individual style; whereas in the recent arrangements of nine *Slovak Folk Songs*, finely judged orchestral accompaniments serve to colour in the warmth of the original vocal lines—wit for "Ja Parobok z Kapušan", Neapolitan rapture in "Trebišov", an unutterably lovely, sensual Szymanowskian opening to "Hej, pofukuj". All Schurmann's best qualities seem to fuse in his 1980 "opera-cantata" *Piers Plowman:* immense spareness and concision (the entire 55-minute work derives from a five-note opening motif), dramatic power, deft orchestral colourings and weaving of solo vocal lines of a rare beauty. Its neat, pared-down text, extracted by the composer from Langland's acerbic view of 14th-century English bourgeois morality, offers, like the later Piano Quartet, a splendid route into Schurmann's carefully controlled, richly varied output.

—Roderic Dunnett

SCHWARTZ, Elliott (Shelling). American. Born in Brooklyn, New York, 19 January 1936. Educated at Columbia University, New York City (composition under Otto Luening and Jack Beeson), B.A., 1957, M.A., 1958, Ed.D., 1962; private composition study under Paul Creston; private piano study under Alton Jones; Bennington Composers (further study under Chou Wen-chung, Stefan Wolpe, Edgar Varèse and Henry Brant), summers 1961–9. Married Dorothy Feldman, 26 June 1960; 1 son. Lecturer in music, University of Massachusetts, Amherst, 1960–4; visiting lecturer, Trinity College of Music, London, 1967; visiting lecturer in music, University College of California, Santa Barbara, 1970; lecturer in music, 1975–8, and since 1981, now chair of music department, Bowdoin College, Brunswick, Maine; founder, Bowdoin College Music, and Bowdoin Music Festival; vice-president, American Music Center, 1983; national chair, American Society of University Composers, 1984–6; distinguished visiting professor, Ohio State University, Columbus, 1985–6. Recipient: Gaudeamus Prize, The Netherlands, 1970. Mailing address: Music Department, Bowdoin College, Brunswick, Maine 04011, U.S.A.

Publishers: ACA; Bowdoin College Music Press; Fischer; Margun; Media.

Symphonies/orchestral:

Works include *Islands*, *The Harmony of Maine*, *Four Ohio Portraits*, *K Janus*, *Celebrations/Reflections*.

Chamber/instrumental:

Oboe Quartet 1963.
Suite (viola, piano) 1963.
Trio (flute, cello, piano) 1964.
Four Studies (2 clarinets) 1964.
Concert Piece for Ten Players (wind quintet, string trio, double bass, percussion) 1965.
Interruptions (wind quintet, tape) 1965.
Soliloquies (flute, clarinet, violin, piano) 1965.
Dialogue No 1 (double bass) 1966.
Essays (trumpet, trombone) 1966.
Mini Concerto (flute, oboe, string trio) 1969.
Music for Napoleon and Beethoven (trumpet, piano, 2 tapes) 1969.
Music for Prince Albert (piano, 2 tapes) 1969.
Divertimento No 2 (2 horns, 2 keyboards) 1970.
Options 1 (trombone, percussion, optional tape) 1970.
Options 2 (clarinet, percussion, tape) 1970.
Eclipse I (2 clarinets, 2 bassoons, trumpet, trombone, violin, cello, percussion, keyboard) 1971.
Memorabilia (cello, tape) 1971.
Octet (flute, oboe, clarinet, violin, cello, 2 keyboards) 1972.
The Decline and Fall of the Sonata (violin, piano) 1972.
Echo Music I (clarinet, viola, tape) 1973.
Grand Concerto (piano, tape) 1973.
Mirrors (piano, tape) 1973.
Echo Music II (wind quintet, tape) 1974.
Prisms (organ, tape) 1974.
Cycles and Gongs (trumpet, organ, tape) 1975.
Extended Clarinet (clarinet, tape) 1975.
Extended Oboe (oboe, tape) 1975.
Five Mobiles (flute, harpsichord, organ, tape) 1975.
Archaeopteryx (trombone, piano) 1976.
Ziggurat (flute, tape) 1976.
Chamber Concerto II (clarinet, 9 instruments) 1977.
Divertimento No 3 (organ, percussion) 1977.
Extended Piano (piano, tape) 1977.
Pentagonal Mobile (piano, tape/5 pianos, audience) 1978.
Souvenir (clarinet, piano) 1978.
Bellagio Variations (string quartet) 1980.
Divertimento No 4 ((flute, double bass, piano) 1980.
Dream Piece (violin, piano) 1980.
Jet Piece (keyboards, 3 instruments) 1980.
Chamber Concerto IV (saxophone, 10 instruments) 1981.
Dream Music with Variations (piano quartet) 1983.
Octagon (8 percussion) 1984.

Vocal/choral:

Septet (voice, piano, 5 instruments) 1969.
A Bowdoin Anthology (narrator, instruments, tape) 1976.

Mixed media/dramatic:

Elevator Music (unspecified instrumentation) 1967.
Areas (flute, clarinet, violin, cello, trombone, piano, 2–4 dancers) 1968.
Gibson Hall (keyboards, synthesizers) 1969.
Music for Soloist and Audience 1970.
Telly (5 woodwinds/brass, 4 percussion, 3 television sets, tape) 1972.
Scales and Arpeggios (tape) 1973.
Spaces (tape) 1974.
A Dream of Beats and Bells (piano, audience) 1977.
California Games (4–6 players, tapes, audience) 1978.
Radio Games (duet for performers in radio studio, listeners) 1980.

PUBLICATIONS

By Schwartz: *The Symphonies of Ralph Vaughan Williams*, Amherst, Massachusetts, 1964; *Contemporary Composers on Contemporary Music* (with Barney Childs), New York City, 1967; *Electronic Music: A Listener's Guide*, New York City, 1973, 2nd edition, 1976; *Music: Ways of Listening*, New York City, 1982.

* * *

The idea of a "university composer" is one which does not pertain in Britain or Europe to anything like the extent it does in the United States, where a campus position is one of the few ways that a relatively independent and integral composing career can be sustained outside Tin Pan Alley or Hollywood. However, few composers more fully embody the role than Elliott Schwartz. His music is only academic in the sense that it is deeply cogitated and researched, analysed and re-explored constantly. It is not academic in the sense of being hermetic or hidebound, or excessively cerebral. Above all, Schwartz is a communicator. A fine writer on music, he also transformed the music department at Bowdoin College in Maine, founding an influential music press there and launching a contemporary music festival which has had a significant impact on new music performance in northern New England.

After studying under Otto Luening and Jack Beeson in New York City (and taking private composition lessons under the maverick Paul Creston, the adopted name of Giuseppe Guttoveggio), Schwartz launched himself on a career of quite remarkable individuality. Though his work draws quite freely from all branches of the modern tradition, it is virtually impossible to quantify his influences in a straightforward way. It might be said that his greatest single influence, on the *spirit* of his music, rather than its content, was Erik Satie, whose sonority and offbeat classicism have made a profound impact on Schwartz.

His music is basically instrumental, with a few works in other genres, but he has developed a particular interest in interactive and mixed media works, often with ludic elements like audience participation. This is very much in keeping with his spirit as a demystifier of music—his textbooks *Music: Ways of Listening* and *Electronic Music: A Listener's Guide* are models of their kind—who wishes to break down some of the more oppressive hierarchies in an effort to open music out to an audience which may not ordinarily consider itself musically literate.

His greatest contribution as an instrumental composer is his exploration of instrumental sound. His series of "extensions" on conventional instrumental ranges by means of tape are impressive not least in that they do precisely what their titles suggest. Schwartz makes a new range of sonority available to the instrument; he does not wrap the instrument in alien sounds. He draws on a wide range of contemporary techniques, using openly conceived serial structures, hints of jazz tonality, popular and folk forms greatly transformed. Works like *Archaeopteryx* use taped backings as a context for highly original instrumental argument while *The Decline and Fall of the Sonata* manages to prove the opposite! (or at least that the conventional sonata has to accommodate itself to a more open-ended conception).

A distinguished educationist, Schwartz has served as chair of the American Society of University Composers, during which time he was highly effective as a spokesman for creative musical artists within the academic environment. In his own career, he has proven that such a position is by no means an ivory tower, but a constant challenge.

—Russell Kane

SCHWEINITZ, Wolfgang von. German. Born in Hamburg, 7 February 1953. Educated at American University, Washington, D.C. (composition and music theory under Esther Ballou), 1968–9; Staatlichen Hochschule für Musik, Hamburg (composition under Ernst Gernot Klussmann), 1970–3; further composition study under György Ligeti, Hamburg, 1973–5, diploma; research fellow, Centre for Computer Research in Music and Acoustics, Stanford University, California, 1975–6; further study, Studienstiftung des Deutschen Volkes scholarship, German Academy, Villa Massimo, Rome, 1978–9. Independent composer, since 1976. Recipient: Bach Prize, Hamburg, 1975; Forderungspreis (for *Variationen uber ein Thema von Mozart Op 12*), Stuttgart, 1976; Rotary Scholarship, Hamburg, 1979–80; Forderungspreis Musik, Academy of Fine Arts, Berlin, 1981; Schneider-Schott Music Prize, Mainz, 1986. Mailing address: D-2241 Tielenhemme, Germany.

Publishers: Boosey & Hawkes, London; Hans Sikorski, Hamburg.

Symphonies/orchestral:

Cosmic Harmony Op 1 (large orchestra) 1970–2.
Symphony No 1 Op 2 1972–3.
Opus 6 (flute, alto flute, strings) 1973; first performed Hilversum, 28 October 1974.
Symphony No 2 Op 8 1974.
Variation über ein Thema von Mozart Op 12 (large orchestra) 1976; first performed Saarbrücken, 20 May 1977.
Piano Concerto Op 18 1978–9; first performed Saarbrücken, 1979.
Konzertouverture Op 19 (large orchestra) 1979–80; first performed Darmstadt, 5 July 1980.

Chamber/instrumental:

Vier Variationen (2 flutes, 2 clarinets, cello) 1972; first performed Hamburg, 18 February 1973.
Bagatelle Op 3 (flute, alto flute, clarinet, basset horn, cello) 1973; first performed Braunschweig, 7 November 1973.
Canon perpetuus I Op 4 (string sextet) 1973.
Canon perpetuus II Op 5 (flute, alto flute, 2 clarinets, harp, guitar, piano, violin or viola, cello) 1973; first performed Darmstadt, 5 April 1974.
Motetus Op 7 (alto flute, basset horn, alto trombone, violin, cello) 1974; first performed Sindelfingen, 20 June 1974.
Wind Quintet Op 9 1975; first performed Hamburg, 18 November 1976.
Septett Op 11 (viola solo, piccolo, oboe, bass clarinet, bassoon, trumpet, trombone) 1976; first performed Bremen, May 1978.
String Quartet Op 13 1976–7.
Sonata Op 14 (violin) 1977–8; first performed Darmstadt, 1978.
String Sextet: Hommage à Franz Schubert Op 16 1978; first performed Baden-Baden, 1978.
String Trio Op 17 1978; first performed Darmstadt, 1978.
Adagio Op 22 (cor anglais, basset horn, horn, bassoon) 1981; first performed Berlin, 11 February 1981.
Drei Etuden Op 23 (piano) 1983–4; first performed Hamburg, 24 February 1984.
Englische Serenade Op 24 (2 clarinets, 2 bassoons, 2 horns) 1984; first performed Hamburg, 27 March 1985.
Musik für vier Saxophon Op 25 (saxophone quartet) 1985; first performed Witten, 27 April 1986.

Vocal/choral:

Die Brücke Op 14 (bass-baritone, orchestral; Kafka) 1977.
Papiersterne/Paper Stars Op 20 (15 songs for mezzo-soprano, piano; Kirsch) 1980–1; first performed Berlin, 22 September 1981.
Mass Op 21 (soloists, chorus, orchestra) 1981–3; first performed Berlin, 8 July 1984. Recorded Wergo 60504 50.
Sechs Alte Lieder (6 arrangements of German folksongs for children's chorus SA, 2 soprano recorders, 2 alto recorders,

2 trumpets, 3–4 percussion) 1984; first performed Krieglach, 18 October 1985.

Opera:

Patmos ("*azione musicale*" in 7 acts; Sattler, after Book of Revelation) 1989; first performed Munich, 28 April 1990.

PUBLICATIONS

By von Schweinitz: "Standort", in *Neue Zeitschrift für Musik*, January-February 1979; "Von Komponieren", in *Darmstadter Beitrage zur Neuen Musik*, 18, 1980.

* * *

When sufficient time has passed for assessments of music since 1950 to be independent of the personalities, the cultural politics and the media publicity peculiar to our own day, the world premiere of Wolfgang von Schweinitz's "Azione musicale" *Patmos* at the Munich Biennale on 28 April 1990 may or may not be seen as an important and even historic event. If it is not so seen, it will be a reflection on the state of music at that future date; if on the other hand the event is at least recognized for what it was, there can only be astonishment at the original reception in the German press.

In review after review—with only a handful of exceptions—Schweinitz's two outstanding achievements were reduced to their lowest common denominators: instead of appreciation of the structural strength and genuine complexity of a large-scale form in which every detail is functional, there were glib and often exaggerated references to duration (about 140 minutes); and instead of tributes to the assurance and consistency of a musical language whose originality derives from a highly personal synthesis of post-Boulez modernism with a "North German" tradition that stretches back through Brahms to Bach and, in a sense fundamentally, to Schütz, there were reach-me-down references to "influences".

The text of *Patmos* is the entire *Revelation of St John the Divine*, set in Luther's German (with the King James version as an English alternative), and arranged for the stage by the Hölderlin pioneer D.E. Sattler, who has taken more than the title from Hölderlin's poem "Patmos". The figure of John is divided into two distinct roles, while the communities he is addressing, together with his spiritual and symbolic adversaries on the one hand and the heavenly host on the other, are sung, acted, danced and mimed.

As for the music, the composer himself maintained, with characteristic modesty, that it is from first to last subservient to "the word". But that is true only in the sense that it is composed as a "reading" of the text, almost in the natural speech tempo. It therefore denies itself the luxury of (post-) Romantic expression: never is there any lingering for conventionally contemplative effect, and hardly ever does the orchestra offer a commentary of its own. Yet the massive interlocking of many-faceted tonal, modal and non-tonal forms is compellingly dramatic in its progress towards the seventh and last of the "Acts", a Utopian vision achieved in the teeth of the work's profound disquiet about the world we live in, and the future of mankind.

Patmos is the culmination of Schweinitz's slow and painstaking progress since he emerged as one of the key figures in the generation of composers that first attracted attention in West Germany during the latter half of the 1970s. Together with Wolfgang Rihm, Detlef Müller-Siemens, and Hans Jürgen von Bose, he was misleadingly identified in the musical press with Neo-Romanticism, and either praised or blamed for rejecting the so-called avant-garde. In truth there has been no such rejection, either on his part or on that of his colleagues, although his continuing debt to modernism is as different from theirs (in kind and in musical effect) as is his relation to tradition.

How close Schweinitz remains to his teacher György Ligeti and yet how firmly he occupies his own ground, is perhaps most apparent in those recent works where there are generic similarities—notably the *Mass*, which post-dates Ligeti's *Requiem*, and the *Drei Etuden* for piano, which pre-date Ligeti's piano studies. But the orchestral Mozart Variations, which made his name in 1977, already inhibit a highly personal sound-world, where post-Ligetian microtonal and clustered harmony, together with related rhythmic and melodic structures, act upon and react to the Mozart of the *Masonic Festival Music* K.477 in such a way as to suggest (in the composer's own words) that "if new expressive possibilities are to be derived from our experience of Classical tonality, it could only be on the understanding that any return to the tonal paradise itself is illusory".

That such a work has found a place in the non-specialist repertory of his native Germany testifies to the ideals of communication which Schweinitz has always cherished, and which are no less influential in the more obviously modernist Kafka setting, *Die Brücke*, which followed soon after the Mozart Variations. The manner in which it too seeks to "bridge" our schizoid culture without response to Expressionist cliché is already so distinctive that it might well be regarded as *the* quintessential Schweinitz composition. With its doubled protagonist it is clearly a forebear of *Patmos*, and hence a milestone in the development of one of Germany's most important yet least celebrated living composers.

—David Drew

SCHWERTSIK, Kurt. Austrian. Born in Vienna, 25 June 1935. Educated at Academy of Music, Vienna (composition under Joseph Marx and Karl Schiske, also horn), 1949–57; composition studies under Karlheinz Stockhausen, Darmstadt and Cologne, 1955–9; research bursary, Austrian Cultural Institute, Rome, 1960–1; private analysis studies under Josef Polnauer, 1964–5, and Oswald Jonas, 1966. Married to mezzo-soprano Christa Schwertsik; 2 children. Horn player, Nieder Osterreichisches Tonkunstler Orchester, 1955–9, 1962–8; co-founder, with Friedrich Cerha, *die reihe* new music ensemble, 1958; co-founder (with Otto M. Zykan), Salonkonzerte and MOB art & tone ART ensemble, 1965; teacher of composition, University of California, 1966; appointed 2nd horn, Vienna Symphony Orchestra, 1968; teacher of composition, City of Vienna Conservatory, 1979. Mailing address: Hockegasse O, A-1180 Vienna, Austria.

Publishers: Ariadne; Doblinger; Edition Modern; Universal Edition; Boosey & Hawkes.

Symphonies/orchestral:

. . . *für Audifax & Avachum Op 8* (symphony for large orchestra) 1963–70.

Dracula Haus–& Hofmusik Op 18 (Transylvanian symphony for strings) 1968.
Symphonie im MOB-Stil Op 19 1971.
Alphorn Concerto: In the Celtic Manner Op 27 1975; first performed Vienna, 15 May 1977. Recorded Amadeo/ Polygram 419 556 1.
Wiener Chronik Op 28 (3 suites for orchestra; may be performed separately) 1976–7.
Violin Concerto Op 31 1977; first performed Graz, 9 October 1977. Recorded ORF 0120 239.
Epilog zur Rosamunde Op 33 1978; first performed (privately) Vienna, 31 May 1978; first public performance, Detroit, Michigan, 7 November 1978.
Tag-und Nachtweisen Op 34 1978; first performed Salzburg, 25 August 1978.
Guitar Concerto Op 35 1979.
Irdische Klange Op 37 (symphony for large orchestra) 1980; first performed Vienna, 16 April 1980.
Instant Music Op 40 (flute, wind orchestra) 1981, revised 1983; first performed Vienna, 28 November 1982.
Verwandlungsmusik (Transformation-Scenes) (from the opera *Das Marchen von Fanferlieschen Schönefüsschen*) 1982–3; first performed Vienna, 6 December 1985.
Der Irdische Klange 2: teil, nämlich Fünf Naturstücke / Five Nature Pieces Op 45 1984; first performed Vienna, 4–5 December 1985. Recorded Amadeo/Polygram 419 556 1.
Concerto for Tom-Tom and Orchestra Op 51 1987–8; first performed Vienna, 5 July 1988.
Ein emfindsames Konzert Op 56 (double bass, orchestra) 1989; first performed Heidelberg, 29 April 1989.

Chamber/instrumental:

Sonata Op 1 (horn, piano) 1952.
Duo and Double Op 2 1957.
Trio Op 3 (violin, horn, piano) 1960.
String Quartet Op 4 1961.
Salotto romano Op 5 (12 bass instruments) 1961.
Eden-Bar-Seefeld Op 6 (piano) 1961.
Liebesträume Op 7 (7 instruments) 1963.
Eichendorff Quintet Op 9 (winds) 1964.
Five Nocturnes Op 10b (piano) 1964; first performed Paris, Autumn 1965.
Proviant Op 11 (wind sextet) 1965.
Five Nocturnes Op 10c (cello, piano) 1966; first performed Tokyo, 1966.
Quershnitt durch eine Operette Op 13 (wind quintet) 1966.
Austrian Quodlibet Op 14 (flute/piccolo, bassoon, trumpet, tuba, percussion, harp, guitar, harmonium, violin, double bass) 1967; first performed Montreal, 28 April 1967.
Musik vom Mutterland Mu Op 22 ("reconstruction" for 11 instruments) 1974.
Skizzen und Entwurfe Op 25 (string quartet) 1974; first performed Hamburg, 13 September 1974. Recorded Amadeo/Polygram 419 556 1.
Twilight Music Op 30 ("Celtic serenade" for clarinet, bassoon, horn, 2 violins, viola, cello, double bass) 1976; first performed Hall, Tyrol, 25 August 1977.
Kleine Blasmusik Op 32 (5 short movements for 2 trumpets, 2 trombones) 1977; first performed Graz, 16 October 1977.
Moment Musical (clarinet, piano) 1978.
Bagatellen: in stark wechseinder Laune / In Abruptly Changing Moods Op 36 (piano trio) 1979; first performed Vienna, 12 December 1979.
Sotto voce (Gedampte Unterhaltung) Op 39 (flute, violin, cello, guitar) 1980; first performed Stuttgart, 3 October 1980.
Blechpartie im neuesten Geschmack Op 43 (brass quintet) 1982, revised 1986; first performed Innsbruck, 8 November 1982.
Fantasy Piece (trumpet, piano) 1982.
Hornpostille Op 46 (4 pieces for 4 horns) 1983; first performed Vienna, September 1983.
Strecken & gahnen (trumpet) 1985.

Vocal/choral:

Shal-i-mar Op 17 (7 songs for baritone, orchestra; Artmann) 1962–72.
Stuckwerk Op 12 (soprano, cor anglais, bass clarinet, contrabassoon, trombone, piano, double bass; Zettl) 1966; first performed Vienna, 30 January 1967.
Blattlause, Schnecken, Ohrenkreiser Op 16 (songs after Bletschacher, Fried, Hardekopf) 1967.
da uhu schaud me so draurech au . . . Op 20 (5 Viennese songs; Artmann) 1969.
Kurt Schwertsiks lichte momente Op 21 (album of unpublished songs) 1971. Recorded BASF 20 21605 5.
Brautigan Songbook Op 23 (voice, piano) 1971; first performed Vienna, June 1985.
Manchmal vertrodelt Christa S. den Tag Op 26 (album of unpublished songs) 1975. Recorded Jeunesses Musicales 1012.
Ich sein Blumenbein Op 38 (11 songs for voice, piano; or voice, guitar, keyboards; Jandl) 1980; first performed Vienna, June 1980.
Starckdeutsche Lieder und Tanze Op 44 (baritone, orchestra; Koeppel) 1980-2; first performed Vienna, 13 February 1986.
Kurze Geschichte der Bourgeoisie Op 41 (3 choruses for mixed choir; Enzensberger) 1981.
. . . & was ist dann Friede? Op 47 (6 songs for voice, guitar; Friede) 1983; first performed Vienna, June 1983.
Starker Tobak Op 48 (humorous cantata for soprano, 7 instruments) 1983.
Iba di gaunz oaman Fraun Op 49 (8 songs for soprano, piano, double bass, drums; Nostlinger) 1983; first performed Vienna, January 1984.
Cinq Chansons cryptiques Op 50 (voice, piano; texts after Satie) 1985; first performed Vienna, June 1986. Recorded Amadeo/Polygram 419 556 1.
Güte nacht, Güten Morgen Op 51 (8 songs for voice, piano; Mayrocker) 1985; first performed Vienna, 26 October 1986.
Das Leben Op 52 (8 songs for mezzo-soprano, Celtic natural horn; Walser) 1986; first performed Bregenz, 21 August 1986.
Gedichte an Ljuba Op 53 (5 songs by KS, 1 by Hanns Wisler; voice, piano; Altenberg) 1986; first performed Vienna, 5 February 1987.

Opera/dramatic:

Der lange Weg zur Grossen Mauer Op 24 (after Bletschacher) 1974; first performed Ulm, 13 May 1975.
Das Märchen von Fanferlieschen Schoenefusschen / The Wonderful Tale of Fanferlizzy Sunnyfeet Op 42 (Karin and Thomas Korner, after Brentano) 1982; first performed Stuttgart, 24 November 1983.

Other:

Veranderungen Op 10a (montage by F. Achleitner for speaker, piano, projector) 1964.

Ur-Faust (music for the play by Goethe) 1976.
Wiener Chronik 1848 Op 28 (ballet after *Walzerträume*; orchestra) 1976–7; first performed (as *Walzerträume*) Cologne, 16 February 1977.
Kaiser Joseph und die Bahnwarterstochter Op 29 (incidental music for play by Herzmanovsky-Orlando) 1977.
Macbeth (dance theatre; piano, percussion/natural sound effects) 1988; first performed Hiedelberg, 10 February 1988.

Hervé: *Der Bekloppte Komponist* (orchestration of musical entertainment) 1984.

* * *

A salient feature of Kurt Schwertsik's reticent and sensitive music is its way of presenting conventional tonal means in new guises, reformed according to Schwertsik's own views, so that a balance is struck between imitated and discovered expression. Its character was well-described by the composer himself when he once referred to its "pleasing superficies", a term which in its German original has a double resonance which encapsulates on the one hand, the aesthetic criteria of surfaces and depths, and on the other hand the pejorative implications of superficiality.

During the early 1960s, some years after he and Cerha founded the *die reihe* ensemble, he became disaffected with the Darmstadt avant-garde, a break which was marked by *Liebesträume* for seven instruments, in which Schwertsik attempted to write non-tonal music with triads. In this work, he cut up a simplified version of Liszt's *Liebesträume No 3* and re-assembled it so that familiar sounds underwent unfamiliar developments. Soon afterwards he co-founded with Otto Zykan the Vienna Salon Concerts and the MOB art & tone ART ensemble with the aim of bringing back entertainment from its discredited position. This reaction against what he believed to be "haphazard" and "uncouth" elements emanating from the avant-garde is well-represented by the *Eichendorff Quintet* for winds, a work which he maintains was the first in which he "really wrote tonally from the heart". Also, since 1965 he has been collecting and listening to pop music and frequenting pop concerts, experiences which have clearly reinforced his pluralistic stance and which have self-evidently nourished his very simple aim, which is just to "sing a song".

Like his mentor Satie he has remained true to his inner voice and, as a result, he has often been accused of crankiness. Yet if his path of self-discovery seems a well-trodden one his gently ironic pastiche of (mainly) Viennese models has a very fresh (if recherché) quality.

Extended movements often turn out to be a succession of self-contained vignettes, a series of miniature songs, sometimes disarmingly naive but never boring. The *Skizzen und Entwurfe* for string quartet, for instance, brings together within its seven movements a range of contradictory elements, including a cryptic waltz, a severe and questioning *Lied*, Mahlerian inflections, surprise interruptions and mock-contrapuntal references to Beethoven—all done with affection and good humour. Aiming for simplicity sometimes descends into a rather contrived naiveté, as in the *Alphorn Concerto* of 1975, a work "in the Celtic manner". In the first movement, the stringing together of miniatures is very apparent. Elsewhere, replication of different styles and a certain formal disorder make this one of his more strikingly tongue-in-cheek pieces. Not surprisingly, when the avant-garde Tanz Forum in Cologne presented Schwertsik's ballet *Walzerträume* in 1977 the work occasioned a scandal because of its 19th-century lyricism and wistful blandness. Perhaps those who know his opera *Der lange Weg zur Grossen Mauer* expected more dissonance, for that work certainly has a harmonic grittiness and parts of it are highly chromatic.

The first piece of *Der Irdische Klange 2: Teil, nämlich Fünf Naturstücke / Five Nature Pieces* for orchestra shows how beautiful Schwertsik's music can be in its Mahler-without-the-angst sumptuousness. This five-movement piece provides a compendium of his harmonic and textural procedures. Repetition is important and so is quasi-minimal ostinato. The impressionists opening of "Wasser" is particularly eccentric in employing real water sounds, which Schwertsik justified as follows: "Before the music of human beings, there were sounds of water, of stones, of the earth, of conflagrations, of volcanos, and so forth. Marinetti and the Futurists created an aesthetic of wars as the symphony of our century. Cage an individual aesthetic out of everyday noises; now, after the Futurists and after Cage, the sounds of nature can perhaps by deprives of some of their romantic overtones (which are certainly still present in this account!), and may be regarded more as material."

Schwertsik's attitude sometimes is not far removed from the minimalists, and some of his music, notably the fourth movement of the *Violin Concerto*, the first movement of *Twilight Music*, and the second movement of the slightly later *Irdische Klange* show influences from minimal music. In general, though, the minimalists' attitude to tonality is too primitive for Schwertsik, while minimalism's other-worldly formalization tends, in his view, to "turn creative craftsmanship into carpet-making."

One of Schwertskik's great achievements is the second opera *Das Märchen von Fanferlieschen Schoenefusschen / The Wonderful Tale of Fanferlizzy Sunnyfeet*. It is based on one of Clemens Brentano's Italian fairytales, a parable of imagination and piety against enlightenment and revolution which the librettists Karin and Thomas Korner tightened and modernized. This Christian tale was turned into a political parable which, in its 10 short scenes, has a sweeping vitality and rare accessibility. The music is simple and often has a brooding quality, but with a clear C major at the opening and at the close. Echoes of other composers abound, from Satie, the Orff of *Die Klüge*, the Prokofiev of *Peter and the Wolf*, to Hindemith, Copland and, above all, Stravinsky. But Schwertsik's synthesis has originality both dramatically in the characterization and musical in the novel sonorities. It is a confirmation of the composer's serenely good-natured pluralism and of his role as a so-called serious composer who sees his colleagues rather "like giant saurians who have not noticed that their species has died out". It may be an oversimplification to take Schwertsik's avowed aim ("to move people") at face value, for in one place in his writings he asserts that "it is not sufficient to say 'Look, that is what the world is like!' Our music is only the mirror we hold in front of human beings. Art must show that it is possible to raise oneself, to take decisive steps, perhaps even to float."

—Richard Elfyn Jones

SCIARRINO, Salvatore. Italian. Born in Palermo, Sicily, 4 April 1947. Began composing at age 12; general classical education; composition and theory lessons from Antonino Titone, Franco Evangelisti and Turi Belfiore; Accademia di

Santa Cecilia, Rome (electronic music under Franco Evangelisti), 1969. Formerly artistic director, Teatro Communale, Bologna; has taught at Milan, Florence and Perugia Conservatoires. Recipient: ISCM Award, 1971; Taormina Prize, 1971; Guido Monaco Prize, 1972; Cassado Prize, 1974; Dallapiccola Prize, 1974; Annod Discografico award, 1979; Psacaropoulos Prize, 1983; Abbiati Prize 1983; Premio Italia, 1984. Mailing address: c/o Ricordi, via Berchet 2, Milan, Italy.

Publisher: Ricordi.

Symphonies/orchestral:

Berceuse 1967–8; first performed (as *Ancora*) Venice, 13 September 1969.
Berceuse variata (revised and expanded version) 1967–8, 1977; first performed Milan, 2 November 1977.
Concerto for Double Bass and Orchestra (includes *Scherzo sinfonico*) 1968.
L'eco (strings) 1969.
Due romanze 1969.
Da a da da (fragment for orchestra) 1970; first performed Venice, 12 September 1970.
Grande sonata de camera 1971; first performed Paris, 21 February 1972.
Sonata da camera (small orchestra) 1971; first performed Rome, 31 October 1971.
Rondo (flute concertante, 2 oboes, 2 horns, strings) 1972; first performed Naples, 6 April 1973.
Romanza (viola d'amore, orchestra) 1973; first performed Florence, 20 October 1973.
Variazioni (cello, orchestra) 1974; first performed Saarbrücken, 23 May 1974.
Clair de lune Op 25 (piano, orchestra) 1976; first performed Milan, 12 February 1976.
Il paese senz'alba 1977; first performed Naples, 18 June 1977.
Che sai guardiano, della notte? (clarinet, small orchestra) 1979; first performed Paris, 19 June 1979. Recorded Fonit Cetra Italia LMA 3002.
Autoritratto nella notte 1982; first performed Lugano, 17 March 1983.
Allegoria della notte (violin, orchestra) 1985; first performed Venice, 1 October 1985.
Sui poemi concentrici I (cello, orchestra) 1987; first performed Turin, 8 April 1988.
Sui poemi concentrici II (flute, clarinet, cello, orchestra) 1987; first performed Turin, 8 April 1988.
Sui poemi concentrici III (flute, violin, viola d'amore, orchestra) 1987; first performed Turin, 8 April 1988.
Lettura da lontana (fragment for double bass, orchestra) 1989; first performed Milan, 21 October 1989.

Chamber/instrumental:

Sonata (2 pianos) 1966; first performed Brescia, June 1969.
Quartetto II (string quartet; from *Sei quartetti brevi*) 1967; first performed Rome, 17 June 1968.
Prelude (piano) 1969; first performed Trieste, 19 February 1970.
. . . da un Divertimento (III—"Romanza", IV—"Scherzo"; flute, oboe, clarinet, bassoon, horn, string quintet) 1969–70; III first performed Como, 5 October 1969; IV first performed Zurich, June 1970.
De o de do (harpsichord) 1970; first performed Brescia, June 1970. Recorded Finlandia FACD 357.
Arabesque (2 church organs—4 players) 1971; first performed Venice, 10 August 1971.
De la Nuit (piano) 1971; first performed Como, 23 September 1971.
Esercizio (piano) 1971; first performed Rovereto, September 1971.
In memoriam (2 harpsichords) 1971.
Sonatina (violin, piano) 1974; first performed Milan, 19 January 1975.
Due studi (cello) 1974; first performed Florence, December 1974.
Danse (2 violins, viola) 1975; first performed Monaco, 14 May 1976.
Per Mattia (violin) 1975; first performed Florence, 21 November 1980.
Siciliano (flute, harpsichord) 1975; first performed Brescia, 5 June 1975.
Toccata (harpsichord) 1975; first performed Brescia, 19 May 1976.
Trio (violin, cello, harpsichord) 1975; first performed Rome, 19 December 1975.
Esercizio (piano) 1975.
Tre notturni brillanti (viola) 1975; first performed Florence, March 1975. Recorded Fonit Cetra Italia ITL 70038.
String Quartet No 2 1975.
Sei Capricci (violin) 1976; first performed Siena, 27 August 1976. Recorded Fonit Cetra Italia ITL 70061.
Prima sonata (piano) 1976; first performed Brescia, 19 May 1976.
Quintettino No 1 (clarinet, string quartet) 1976; first performed Venice, 19 September 1976.
Di Zefiro e Pan ("poemetta" for 2 flutes, 2 oboes, 2 clarinets, 2 bassoons, 2 horns) 1976; first performed Utrecht, 3 September 1976. Recorded Rusty Records RRCL 606619.
Etude de concert (piano) 1976; first performed Brescia, 19 May 1976.
All'aure in una lontananza (flute or alto flute or bass flute) 1977; first performed Naples, 19 July 1977. Recorded Philips LP 411 066 1.
Quintettino No 2 (flute, oboe, clarinet, bassoon, horn) 1977; first performed Perugia, 29 May 1977. Ricordi CRMCD 1010.
Attraverso i cancelli (flute, oboe, 2 clarinets, bassoon, horn, trombone, celeste, wind quintet) 1977.
Ai limiti della notte (viola; version for cello) 1979; first performed Spoleto, 8 July 1979; cello version first performed Milan, December 1980.
L'addio a Trachis (harp) 1980; first performed Lanciano, 23 August 1980. Recorded Fonit Centra Italia CTL 70072.
D'un Faune (flute, piano) 1980; first performed Citta di Castello, 1 September 1980.
L'addio a Trachis II (transcribed for guitar) 1980, 1989; first performed Macerata, 19 June 1989.
Fauno che fischia a un merlo (flute, harp) 1980; first performed Florence, 14 September 1980.
Anamorfosi (piano) 1980; first performed Alessandria, 19 December 1981.
La Malinconia (violin, viola) 1981; first performed Siena, 19 August 1983.
Melancolia I (cello, piano) 1981; first performed Rome, 7 May 1985.
Introduzione all'oscuro (flute, oboe, clarinet, bassoon, horn, trumpet, trombone, wind quintet) 1981; first performed London, 29 June 1981.
Let Me Die Before I Wake (clarinet) 1982; first performed Venice, 30 September 1982.
Nox apud Orpheum (2 organs, 3 flutes, 3 horns, 3 trumpets, 3 trombones, percussion) 1982; first performed Bologna, 24

September 1982.

Codex purpureus (string trio) 1983; first performed Cologne, 22 October 1983.

Sonata II (piano) 1983; first performed Florence, 9 June 1983. Recorded Frequenz LP 011.012.

Centauro marino (clarinet, violin, viola, cello, piano) 1984; first performed Foggia, 18 November 1984.

Rafigurar narciso al fonte (2 flutes, 2 clarinets, piano) 1984; first performed Citta di Castello, 27 August 1984.

Codex purpureus II (2 violins, viola, cello, piano) 1984; first performed Cremona, 12 September 1984.

Hermes (flute) 1984; first performed Chiusi, 22 July 1984.

Canzona di ringrazamiento (flute) 1985; first performed Latina, 13 June 1985. Recorded Europa Musica 350.229.

Il tempo con l'obelisco (flute, clarinet, bassoon, violin, viola, cello) 1985; first performed Milan, 20 April 1985.

Lo spazio inverso (flute, clarinet, celeste, violin, cello) 1985; first performed Venice, 23 September 1985.

Come vengono prodotti gli incantesimi? (flute) 1985; first performed Milan, 21 April 1985. Recorded Europa Musica 350.229.

Appendice all perfezione (14 bells) 1986; broadcast RAI television, 3 July 1986.

La ragione delle conchiglie (2 violins, viola, cello, piano) 1986; first performed Naples, 19 December 1986.

Esplorazione del bianco I (double bass) 1986; first performed Macerata, 2 July 1986.

Esplorazione del bianco II (flute, bass clarinet, guitar, violin) 1986; first performed Amsterdam, 20 June 1986.

Esplorazione del bianco III (jazz percussion) 1986; first performed Milan, 30 September 1986.

Il motivo degli oggetti di vetro (2 flutes, piano) 1986–7; first performed (incomplete, as *Frammento*) Erice, 23 August 1986; first complete performance Fermo, 24 July 1989.

III Sonata (piano) 1987; first performed Citta di Castello, 26 August 1990.

Trio No 2 (violin, cello, piano) 1987; first performed Amsterdam, 3 December 1988.

Fra i testi dedicati alle nubi (flute) 1989; first performed Rome, 12 November 1990.

Il silenzio degli oracoli (wind quintet) 1989; first performed New York City, 30 May 1989.

L'orizzonte luminoso di Aton (flute) 1989; first performed Siena, 22 August 1989.

Venere che le Grazie la fioriscino (flute) 1989; first performed Macerata, 17 June 1989.

Variazione su uno spazio ricurvo (piano) 1990; first performed Genoa, 26 February 1990.

Vocal/choral:

Aka Aka to I, II, III (soprano, flute, horn, trombone, chamber organ, 4 percussion, 2 violins, 2 cellos; Basho) 1967–8; first performed Palermo, 28 December 1968.

Musiche per "I bei colloqui" di Aurelio Pes (unaccompanied mixed chorus) 1970.

Introduzione e Aria "Ancora il duplice" (from *Amore e Psiche*; mezzo-soprano, orchestra) 1973–6; first performed Venice, 9 September 1976.

Un'immagine di Arpocrate (chorus, piano, orchestra; Goethe, Wittgenstein) 1974–9; first performed Donaueschingen, 19 October 1979. Recorded Fonit Cetra Italia ITL 70088.

Il paese senza tramonto (soprano, orchestra; Marino) 1977.

Due melodie (soprano, piano; "Occhi stillanti" and "Occhi stellanti" by Mariano) 1978; first performed ("Occhi stillanti") Naples, 17 June 1978; first complete performance Turin, 11 February 1980.

Kindertotenlied (soprano, tenor as echo, small orchestra; Ruckert) 1978; first performed Venice, 7 October 1979.

Aspern Suite (soprano, 2 flutes/piccolo/alto flute/bass flute, percussion, harpsichord, viola, cello; Da Ponte) 1979; first performed Citta di Castello, 6 September 1979.

Due nuove melodie (baritone, piano; on fragments by Bob Dylan, Pier Paolo Pasolini) 1979–82; first performed Siena, 5 August 1987.

Le donne di Trachis (6 pieces for soprano, mezzo-soprano, alto soloists, female chorus; Sophocles) 1980; first performed Florence, 1 October 1988.

Efebo con radio (voice, orchestra) 1981; first performed Florence, 28 May 1981.

Canti degli specchi (voice, piano; Aragon) 1981; first performed Perugia, 31 May 1981.

Flos florum, ovvero Le trasformazioni della materia sonora (chorus, orchestra; various sources) 1981; first performed Turin, 30 April 1981.

La perfezione di uno spirito sottile (voice, flute, percussion) 1985; first performed Pantelleria, 12 August 1985.

Tutti i miraggi delle acque (unaccompanied mixed chorus) 1987; first performed Rome, 1 April 1988.

Morte di Borromini (reader, orchestra) 1988; first performed Milan, 18 October 1988.

Due arie marine (mezzo-soprano, real-time electronics; Laforgue) 1990; first performed Turin, 27 October 1990.

Opera/dramatic:

Amore e Psiche (Pes) 1973; first performed Milan, 2 March 1973.

Aspern (after Henry James) 1978; first performed Florence, 1978.

Cailles en Sarcophage: atti per un museo delle ossesioni (Marini) 1979; first performed 26 September 1979.

Vanitas ("still life" in 1 act for mezzo-soprano, cello, piano; various sources) 1981; first performed Milan, 11 December 1981. Recorded Ricordi CRMCD 017.

Lohengrin (after Laforgue) 1982–4; first performed (as *Melodramma*) Milan, 15 January 1984; definitive version first performed Catanzaro, 9 September 1984. Recorded Ricordi CRM 1001.

Macbeth 1983.

Perseo e Andromeda ("invisible drama" for soloist, instruments and voices) 1990; first performed Stoccarda, 27 January 1991.

Other:

I bei colloqui (incidental music to Pes; chorus, electronics) 1970; broadcast RAI, 1971.

Anonymous: *Dodici canzoni da battello* (completed and arranged for soprano, Venetian melody instruments) 1977; first performed Rovereto, 7 September 1978. Recorded Fonit Centra Italia ITL 70030.

All'uscita (incidental music to Pirandello; radiophonic and film versions for voices, orchestra) 1978, 1985; broadcast RAI 26 November 1979; broadcast RAI television, 13 December 1985.

Blue Dream (selection and arrangement of material by Mercer, De Rose, Porter, Sciarrino, Gray, Brown, Ellington, Perkins, Gershwin, Carmichael, Hanley, Dameron) 1980; first performed Alessandria, 19 December 1981.

Trachinie (incidental music to Sophocles; female chorus, tape) 1980; first performed Syracuse, May 1980.

La voce dell'inferno (incidental music to Dante; tape) 1981; broadcast RAI, 2 September 1981.

Lectura Dantis (incidental music to Carmelo Bene; ancient instruments, tape) 1981; first performed Bologna, 2 August 1981.

La Divina Commedia (incidental music to Dante) 1987; broadcast RAI television, 11 April 1988.

Guillaume de Machaut: *Rose Liz* (voices, flute, clarinet, bassoon, viola, cello) 1984; first performed, 19 December 1984.

Various: *Conque canzoni del XX secolo* (arranged for orchestra) 1985–7; first performed Trento, 25 November 1988.

Ary Barroso: *Epigraphe fenicienne du Brazil* (arranged for piccolo, clarinet, bassoon, horn, harp, violin, viola, cello, double bass) 1988; first performed Trento, 14 November 1988. Recorded Ricordi CRM 1009.

Gioachino Rossini: *Giovanni d'Arco* (orchestrated from piano original) 1989; first performed Pesaro, 31 August 1989. Recorded Claves 50/9016.

W.A. Mozart: cadenzas to *Piano Concerti* K.467, K.482, K.491, K.503, K.537, cadenzas to *Flute Concerti* K.313–315; cadenza to *Oboe Concerto* K.314 (289d). Recorded CD Nuovo Era 6902/6926/6938.

PUBLICATIONS

By Sciarrino: "Ancora il duplice", Venice Biennale, 1976; "Di una musica d'oggi", Florence, 1979; "Le cosmesi di Glauco", in *Stravinsky oggi*, 1982; "Annali del mio tavolo", manuscript, 1985; "Appunti di viaggio", in *Quartetto della maledizione*, 1985; "Como vengono prodotti gli incantesimi?", in *Intorno al flauto Magico*, 1985; "L'immagine del suono grafici", Latina, 1985; "La fabrica degli incantesimi", in *Settimana Musicale Senese*, 1989; "Mozart svelato", in *Do maggiore*, 1990; other writings and analytical notes.

On Sciarrino: Mario Bortolotto, (interview) in *Lo Spettatore Musicale*, November–December 1972; Mya Tannenbaum, "S crede ancoranei chiari di luna", (interview) in *Il Mondo*, 19 February 1976; Claudio Tempo, "Utopia di un uomo in ascolto", (interview) in *Il Secolo XIX*, 23 September 1983; Antonio Poce, "Il processo compositivo di SS e la musica per strumento solo", dissertation, Universita La Sapienza, Rome, 1988; Renato Rivolta, (interview) in *Syrinx*, 1(3), September–October 1989; Marco Mazolini, (interview) in *Sonus*, 3, 1990; various, *SS* [includes interview], special issue of *Entretemps*, 9, 1991; Renato Chiesa, *SS*, Milan, 1991; other interviews, reviews and press articles.

* * *

The most strikingly constant features of Salvatore Sciarrino's music are its unprecedented timbral characteristics. Often only the most rarefied of sounds occur, often at the limits of audibility: breath sounds, harmonics and fluttering of keys on wind instruments, delicate scrapings and harmonic glissandos on strings, veiled, resonant traceries on piano and so on, blended into textures or spinning out spiderweb-like solo lines.

The possession of an immediately recognisable sound world, and a seeming obsession with charting its landscapes as thoroughly as possible, lays a composer open to, on the one hand, endless unthinking imitation by less single-minded musical personalities, and, on the other hand, marginalisation or pigeon-holing as a "specialist" with a restricted musical range. Sciarrino is a good example of both of these unfortunate tendencies. First, he is, along with Donatoni, among the most influential composers in Italy: the "Sciarrino sound" is probably now heard more often in second-hand form, lacking the sense of *necessity* without which its originator's work would be almost as impoverished. Second, it is all-important when encountering Sciarrino's music to appreciate that an enormous range of allusion and expressivity is to be found within its diaphanous and indistinct sounds.

Many of the titles of his compositions (*Clair de lune*, *Kindertotenlied*, *D'un Faune*, as well as the numerous sonatas notturnes and so on) relate to the musical past and specifically the Romantic past. In the *Sei capricci* for solo violin, for example, the ghostly presence of Paganini is constantly evoked, in a reckless virtuosity made all the more narcissistic by its *pianissimo* reticence and inwardness. Sciarrino's relationship with 19th-century music is not the rationalised, critical and engaged attitude of, say, Lachenmann (who, although using many of the same sound elements, creates with them an almost diametrically opposed effect), but rather a hopeless (and hopelessly "romantic") nostalgia for lost means of expression. Sounds and gestures from the past appear like sepia photographs bleached out by the passage of time or by some more cataclysmic event. Their flickering presence carries a memory of their original emotional weight, as well as reminding of the skull placed in "Vanitas" still lives as a *memento mori* (made explicit in Sciarrino's own *Vanitas*).

The results are beautiful rather than ghoulish (unlike George Crumb's meditations on mortality, seemingly inspired by cheap horror movies), creative rather than parasitic. This is the result of Sciarrino's subtle and sophisticated handling of his materials, never allowing a descent into mere "anecdotal" treatment but more often hovering on the *brink* of quotation, the music invariably leaving an impression of rigorous consistency. The stratospheric filigrees of Sciarrino's work are a perfect delineation of one of the few genuinely romantic musical personalities in the late 20th century (although one not untouched by irony). In developing an authentic stylistic framework for his almost decadent recreations (in both senses), he has also created a whole repertoire of sounds and forms whose capacity to fascinate and move the listener is matched by their icy delicacy.

—Richard Barrett

SCULTHORPE, Peter (Joshua). Australian. Born in Launceston, Tasmania, 29 April 1929. Educated at University of Melbourne, B.Mus., 1950; Wadham College, Oxford (composition under Egon Wellesz and Edmund Rubbra), 1958–60. Lecturer in music, 1963–9, and reader, from 1970, University of Sydney; composer in residence and Harkness Fellow, Yale University, New Haven, Connecticut, 1965–7; visiting professor of music, University of Sussex, Brighton, 1971–2. Recipient: M.B.E. (Member, Order of the British Empire), 1970; Australia Council Composers Award, 1975–8; O.B.E. Officer, Order of the British Empire), 1977; Australian Film Award, 1980; hon. D.Litt., University of Tasmania, 1982; APRA Award for most performed Australasian serious work, 1985. Mailing address: 91 Holdsworth Street, Woollahra, New South Wales 2025, Australia.

Publisher: Faber.

Symphonies/orchestral:

To Meadows (string orchestra) 1949.
Overture (theatre orchestra) 1949.
Irkanda IV (violin, percussion, strings) 1961. Recorded WRC R00028; SCCD 1016; ABC 426481 2.
King's Cross Overture 1963; withdrawn.
Small Town (from *The Fifth Continent*; chamber orchestra) 1963, revised 1976. Recorded EMI OASD 7604; ABC 426481 2.
Sun Music I 1965. Recorded WRC R00028; Odyssey 32 16 0150; EMI OASD 7604.
Sun Music II 1966, revised 1969. Recorded ABC RRCS 134; ABC 760023–4; EMI OASD 7604.
Sun Music III: Anniversary Music 1967. Recorded HMV OASD 7547; Louisville First Editions LS 735; EMI OASD 7604.
Sun Music IV 1967. Recorded ABC RRC 401; EMI OASD 7604.
From Tabuh Tabuhan (strings, 2 percussion) 1968. Recorded ABC RRC 72.
Autumn Song (arranged for string orchestra) 1968, arranged 1986.
The Stars Turn (from *Love 200*; arranged for string orchestra) 1970–6.
Music for Japan 1970. Recorded HMV SOELP 9721.
Rain 1970; withdrawn.
Overture for a Happy Occasion 1970.
Lament (string orchestra) 1976. Recorded MBS2; SCCD 1016.
Port Essington (string trio, string orchestra) 1977. Recorded SCCD 1016.
Mangrove 1979. Recorded ABC TS AC 1053.
Guitar Concerto 1980; withdrawn.
Little Suite (string orchestra) 1983.
Piano Concerto 1983. Recorded ABC TS AC 1074.
Sonata (string orchestra) 1983. Recorded SCCD 1016.
Sun Song 1984.
Earth Cry 1986. Recorded ABC 426481.
Sonata No 2 (string orchestra) 1988.
At the Grave of Isaac Nathan 1988; withdrawn.
Two Grainger Arrangements ("Beautiful Fresh Flower", "Faroe Island Song"; percussion, strings) 1989. Recorded ABC 426989 2.
Nourlangie (guitar, percussion, strings) 1989.
Nourlangie Dreaming 1990.
Little Nourlangie (organ, orchestra) 1990.

Chamber/instrumental:

Nocturne (piano) 1945.
Puppet Show (piano) 1945.
Suite (2 violins, cello) 1946.
Five Scherzos (piano) 1946.
Siesta (piano) 1946.
Sonatina (bassoon, piano) 1946.
Siesta (piano) 1946.
Two Evocations (piano) 1946.
Two Short Pieces (piano) 1946.
String Quartet No 1 1947.
Reverie (piano) 1948.
String Quartet No 2 1948.
String Quartet No 3 1949.
Two Nocturnes (piano) 1949.
String Quartet No 4 1950.
Seascapes (2 preludes for piano) 1950.
Sonata (violin) 1954.
The Loneliness of Bunjil (string trio) 1954.
Sonatina (piano) 1954. Recorded HMV OASD 7567; Electric ELEC 4334; Move MS 3031; Discourses ABM 30.
Irkanda I (violin) 1955. Recorded MBS 10.
Irkanda II (String Quartet No 5) 1955; withdrawn.
Three Movements (jazz band) 1957; withdrawn.
Left Bank Waltz (piano) 1958. Recorded W & G SB 5589; Move MS 3031.
Sonata (cello) 1959; withdrawn, incorporated into *Sonata* for viola, percussion.
Sonata (viola, percussion) 1960. Recorded ABC PRX 5599; Halcyon PM 102.
Irkanda II (piano trio) 1961; withdrawn, incorporated into *String Quartet No 6*.
Small Town (from *The Fifth Continent*; arranged for string quartet by David Matthews) 1963, arranged 1980.
Sonata (piano) 1963; withdrawn, incorporated into *String Quartet No 6*.
Callabonna (piano) 1963, revised 1989.
String Quartet No 6 1964–5. Recorded WRC A601; RCA Victor VX79.
Five Night Pieces (piano) 1965–71. Recorded Move MS 3031; HMV OASD 7567.
String Quartet No 7: Red Landscape 1966. Recorded HMV OASD 7563.
Tabuh Tabuhan (wind quintet, 2 percussion) 1968. Recorded ABC RRCS 378; Philips 6508001.
Sea Chant (arranged for piano) 1968. Recorded Move MS 3031.
String Quartet No 8: String Quartet Music 1969. Recorded Argo ZRG 672; ABC RRCS 1468; HMV OASD 7563; Nonesuch 79111; SWC 8201.
Dream (variable instrumentation) 1970.
Overture for a Happy Occasion (arranged for organ) 1970, arranged 1980.
Landscape I (amplified piano, prerecorded tape loop) 1971. Recorded HMV OASD 7567; Festival L 42015; Move MS 3031.
How the Stars Were Made (6 percussion) 1971. Recorded Great Island Records LP 003.
Koto Music I and II (amplified piano, prerecorded tape loop) 1973, 1976. Recorded Move MS 3031; RCA VRL 10083.
String Quartet No 9 1975. Recorded Cherry Pie CPF 1030.
Alone (violin) 1976.
Sun Song (recorded quartet SATB) 1976.
Little Serenade (string quartet) 1977. Recorded Cherry Pie CPF 1034.
Colonial Dances (arranged for 2 pianos) 1977.
Dua Chant (3 recorders/SAB) 1978.
Landscape II (piano quartet) 1979. Recorded MBS 16.
Four Pieces (piano duet) 1979. Recorded MBS 16.
Requiem (cello) 1979. Recorded MBS 16.
Cantares (flamenco guitar, classical guitars, jazz guitars, string quartet) 1980.
Nocturne (from *Guitar Concerto*; solo guitar) 1980.
Tailitnama Song (flute, percussion, violin, cello) 1981. Recorded MBS 16.
Nocturnal (piano) 1981.
Mountains (piano) 1981. Recorded MBS 16.
String Quartet No 10 1983.
Djilile (arranged for piano; cello, piano) 1986. Recorded MBS 16.
Songs of Sea and Sky (clarinet, piano; flute, piano) 1987. Recorded MBS 13.
Sun Songs (percussion) 1989.
The Rose Bay Quadrilles (piano) 1989.
Irkanda IV (string quartet arranged for flute, string trio) 1990.

String Quartet No 11 1990–1.
String Quartet No 12 1990–2.

Vocal/choral:

Winter Landscape (speaker, piano) 1945.
Chamber Suite (high voice, bassoon) 1946.
Elegy for a Clown (high voice, piano) 1946.
Three Shakespeare Songs (medium voice, piano) 1946.
Trio (3 voices) 1948.
Reverie (high voice, piano) 1948.
Three Songs (medium voice, piano) 1948.
The White Bird (high voice, piano) 1952.
Prophecy (medium voice, piano) 1958; withdrawn.
Sun (cycle for high voice, piano) 1958; withdrawn.
South by Five (girls' voices, instruments; Covell) 1965; withdrawn.
Night Piece (SATB chorus, piano—1 or 2 players; Wallace-Crabbe) 1966.
Sun Music (SATB chorus, 3 percussion) 1966. Recorded ABC RRCS 134.
Morning Song for the Christ Child (unaccompanied SATB chorus; Covell) 1966. Recorded ABC RRC 65; SAR 1; HMV HQS 1308; HMV OASD 7563.
Sea Chant (unison voices, piano, optional high instruments, optional percussion; also arranged for orchestra; Covell) 1968, orchestrated 1975.
Autumn Song (unaccompanied SATBarB chorus; Covell) 1968.
Love 200 (2 singers, rock band: winds, keyboard, bass guitar, drums; or orchestra; Morphetti) 1970. Recorded ABC RRCS 1466.
The Stars Turn (from *Love 200*; arranged for AATBarBarB chorus by David Matthews; also arranged for high voice, piano or string orchestra) 1970, arranged 1972.
Boat Rise (from *Love 200*; arranged for high voice and piano by Michael Hannan) 1970, arranged 1980. Recorded Larikan TC LRF 153.
Ketjak (6 male voices, tape echo) 1972.
The Song of Tailitnama (high voice, 6 cellos, 2 percussion; also arranged for medium voice, piano) 1974. Recorded ABC TS AC 1062.
Eliza Frazer Sings (soprano, flute, piano; Blackman) 1978.
East of India (from *Quiros*; high voice, piano; Bell) 1982.
Saibai (unison voices, organ; Milgate) 1986.
Child of Australia (soprano, chorus, narrator, orchestra; Kenneally) 1987.
The Birthday of Thy King (unaccompanied SATB chorus) 1988.
It's You (arrangements after Gershwin for unaccompanied SATB chorus) 1989.

Opera/dramatic:

Rites of Passage ("Rites", Chorales, "Rebirth"; theatre work for soloists, chorus, orchestra, dancers; Aboriginal, Boethius) 1972–3. Recorded (Chorales and "Rebirth" only) WRC R 03074.
Quiros (soloists, chorus, orchestra; Bell) 1982.
Tatea (music theatre piece for soloists, chamber ensemble; after Berlioz) 1990–1.

Other:

Sun Music (ballet, based on the series) 1968. Recorded EMI OASD 7604.
Burke and Wills (film score; brass or symphonic band) 1985. Recorded AGCD 900.

Film music: *They Found a Cave*, 1962; *The Splendour and the Peaks*, 1963; *The Troubled Mind*, 1964; *Age of Consent*, 1968; *Essington*, 1974; *Exploration North*, 1978; *Manganinnie*, 1980.

Theatre music: *Much Ado About Nothing*, 1951; *The Miser*, 1952; *The Girl Who Couldn't Quite*, 1953; *Life With Father*, 1954; *Junius on Horseback*, 1956; *Twelfth Night*, 1956; *Ulterior Motifs*, 1956; *Cross Section*, 1957; *King Lear*, 1959.

Radio music: *Song of the Morning,* 1957; *Don't Listen, Ladies,* 1957; *Some New Moon,* 1958; *The Fifth Continent,* 1963; *The Body Is a Concert of Sensation,* 1976; *Love Thoughts of a Lady,* 1977.

PUBLICATIONS

By Sculthorpe: in *The Composers and Their Works*, Canberra, 1969; "S on S" [autobiographical], in *Music Now,* 1(1), February 1969; "Some Thoughts upon the Idea of a Pacific Culture", in *Canzona*, 6(18), December 1984; "From Corroboree to 'Corroboree'", lecture broadcast on 2MBS-FM, 1985 or 1986; "The Asian Influence upon Australian Music", in *The Asian Composers Conference Australia*, 1985; "Peggy Glanville-Hicks", (orationb) in *University of Sydney News*, 2 May 1987; *Sun Mist* [autobiography], in progress.

On Sculthorpe: Max Oldaker, "Two Australian Composers" [PS, Margaret Sutherland], in *The London Magazine*, 2(6), 1962; Kenneth Hince, "Composer's Search for an Australian Music", in *The Australian*, 22 August 1964; Robert Henderson, "PS", in *The Musical Times*, 1481, July 1966; Donald Peart, "Some Recent Developments in Australian Composition", in *Composer*, Spring 1966; Roger Covell, *Australia's Music*, Melbourne, 1967; Malcolm Williamson, "How Australian Can Australian Music Become?", in *Music Now*, 1(4), 1971; David Hush, (interview) in *Quadrant*, December 1979; Michael Hannan, *PS: His Music and Ideas, 1929–79*, Queensland, 1982.

* * *

An early interest in literature may largely be credited with shaping Peter Sculthorpe's attitude to music composition. The philosophical contemplation of what his musical style should be, rather than a purely emotional response to the sounds of music, resulted in a deliberate rejection of some forms and methods and the seeking out of others. To this end, after some experimentation with idioms which he came to believe were alien to him, he determined to make a conscious attempt to write "Australian" music, developing his own theories about the nature of such music. He attempted to eliminate from his writing qualities that he perceived as "European"—a tonal approach to harmony, and the complex development usually associated with large-scale musical structures—and to use Asian influences to replace these characteristics: repetitive rhythmic patterns, melodies (often pentatonic) of limited range, considerable use of percussion instruments, and variation in tone colour rather than the use of polyphony and extended melodic invention. He determined to work with limited musical material, restricting the dramatic growth of a piece and concentrating upon timbre and sonority. As a consequence, his works were mainly of relatively short duration, relying upon repetition and variation rather than harmonic and melodic development. This could be considered as an aural interpretation of a common visual perception of the Australian landscape: a vast, extensive sameness.

Sculthorpe's work includes a number of sets or series of pieces, the names of which reflect this attitude: the *Sun Music* series—the sun being harsh and relentless rather than friendly and life-giving—and the *Irkanda* series, named after an Aboriginal word for "a remote and lonely place." *Irkanda IV*, for example, is a lament expressing the composer's feelings upon the death of his father, depicting in musical terms the loneliness of grief. On the other hand, the work for voice, six cellos and percussion *The Song of Tailitnama* is almost programmatic in its portrayal of the Central Australian scene described by its Aranda (an Aboriginal language) text. A similar atmosphere pervades *Child of Australia*, a setting for large forces of a text by Thomas Keneally, written for Australia's Bicentennial celebrations.

The opera *Rites of Passage* was commissioned for the opening of the Sydney Opera House, but in the event was not performed until later. It was not only Sculthorpe's first opera, and—with a few minor exceptions—his first vocal work, but it was also the largest work upon which he had embarked. It was designed to be presented upon two planes or levels: chorales, by one group of performers, and rites, by another, which could be split from each other and performed as separate entities.

Much of Sculthorpe's music is for stringed instruments, and he has constantly sought new techniques and effects from string players. Some, such as layers of string glissandos, have become identifiably characteristic of his work: the String Quartets and *Mangrove*. His musical development can perhaps be seen most easily in his works for strings. The *String Quartet No 6* used minimal motivic material, expanded simply and directly in a mood of sustained mournfulness. By the *String Quartet No 8* his style clearly displayed a strong Asian influence, while the *String Quartet No 9* used some techniques which the composer had found in Australian Aboriginal music; there was also more energy and rhythmic vitality to be found in the music. This can be heard even more clearly in *Port Essington* for strings, drawn from music for the feature film *Essington*. Despite Sculthorpe's rejection of European methods and styles as inappropriate and irrelevant, some influences remain and recur: some elements of Mahler, the emotional response of Ernest Bloch, and a persistent Bartókian approach to rhythm.

In a number of cases Sculthorpe has withdrawn, re-used, or renamed his compositions, leading to some confusion in identifying the works. The original *Sun Music II* for voices and percussion was renamed, and its title given to an orchestral work previously known as *Ketjak*; there is also a vocal work *Ketjak*. The orchestral composition *Anniversary Music* was retitled *Sun Music III* after the piece which originally carried this name was withdrawn and incorporated into *Sun Music IV*. The *String Quartet No 6* included portions of the earlier works *Irkanda II*, *Irkanda III*, and *Sun*; while many compositions, for example *Irkanda IV* and *The Song of Tailitnama*, have been rescored for different instrumental forces.

—Jenny Dawson

SEGERSTAM, Leif (Selim). Finnish. Born in Vaasa, 2 March 1944. Educated at Sibelius Academy, Helsinki (violin, conducting), 1952–63; Juilliard School of Music, New York City (conducting under Jean Morel, violin under Louis Persinger), 1963–5, diploma and postgraduate diploma in conducting. Military service, 1967–8. Married Hannele Angervo, 13 September 1964; 2 children. Violinist, debut 1962; conductor, Finnish National Opera, Helsinki, and concurrently director of orchestral courses, Klemetti Institute of Music, 1965–8; conductor, later first conductor and *chef de musique*, Swedish Royal Opera, Stockholm, 1968–72; chief conductor, Deutsche Oper, Berlin, 1972–3; and Austrian Radio Symphony Orchestra (ORF), Vienna, 1975–82, chief conductor, 1977–87, and subsequently principal guest conductor, Finnish Radio Symphony Orchestra; general musical director, Staatsphilharmonie Rheinland-Pfalz, Germany, 1983–9; chief conductor, Danish Radio Symphony Orchestra, since 1988; musical adviser, Tampere Symphony Orchestra, since 1989. Recipient: 1st prize, Maj Lind piano competition, 1962. Mailing address: Takojantie 1K, SF-02130 Espoo, Finland; or Danish Broadcasting Corporation, Danish Radio Symphony Orchestra, Channel 2, 22 Rosenoerns Alle, DK-1999 Frederiksberg C, Denmark.

Publishers: Finnish Music Information Centre; Schirmer; Universal Edition, Vienna; Fazer, Helsinki; Jasemusiikki, Hameenlinna; Doblinger, Vienna; Hans Busch, Sweden.

Symphonies/orchestral:

A Legend: Nils-Eric Fougstedt in memoriam (string orchestra) 1960; first performed Helsinki, 1961.
Divertimento (string orchestra; based on *String Quartet No 2*) 1963; first performed Helsinki, 1964. Recorded BIS LP 19.
Pandora (essay for orchestra; also ballet score) 1967; first performed Helsinki, 1967.
Concerto serioso (violin, orchestra) 1967; first performed Helsinki, 1968. Recorded BIS LP 84.
Skizzen aus Pandora 1967, 1971; first performed Berlin, 1971. Recorded BIS LP 84.
Cappriccio (sopranino, small orchestra: flute, cor anglais, clarinet, trumpet, strings) 1967; first performed Helsinki, 1968.
Seven Red Moments (trumpet, orchestra) 1967; first performed Helsinki, 1968. Recorded Austro Mechanica 120 589.
Nocturne (from *Seven Red Moments*) 1967; first performed Helsinki, 1968. Recorded Austro Mechanica 0120279.
Patria 1973; first performed Stockholm, 1974. Recorded BIS LP 84.
. . . Aroundwards . . . Towards . . . (2 pianos, large orchestra with 2 string sections) 1974; first performed Helsinki, 1974.
Helsinki, 1974.
Screams and Visions 1975.
Visions of Inner Time (piano, string orchestra) 1976.
Concerto No 1 for Piano and Orchestra (Thoughts 1978) 1977; first performed Helsinki, 1977. Recorded Austro Mechanica 120 539.
Concertino-Fantasia (violin, piano, small orchestra) 1977; first performed Vienna, 1979. Recorded Austro Mechanica 0120279.
Orchestral Diary Sheets Nos 33, 34, 36 (Symphony of Slow Movements) 1977–8; first performed Stockholm, 1979. Recorded Austro Mechanica 120 359.
Plays for Two Cellos, Amplified if Possible and Necessary, Percussion and Small Orchestra (also for 2 violas) 1978; first performed Vienna, 1978. Recorded Austro Mechanica 0120279.
Plays for Percussion and String Orchestra 1978; first performed Helsinki, 1979.
Orchestral Diary Sheet No 22 (Symphony No 2) 1980; first

performed Helsinki, 1981.

Orchestral Diary Sheet No 23 (Symphony No 3) 1981; first performed Helsinki, 1981.

Orchestral Diary Sheets Nos 24, 25, 26 (Symphony No 4) (in 3 movements which may be played separately) 1981; first performed Turku, 1981; Vienna, 1982; Vienna, 1982. Recorded (No 25) Austro Mechanica 120 589.

Orchestral Diary Sheet No 11a (Cello Concerto No 1) 1981; first performed Stockholm, 1982.

Orchestral Diary Sheet No 11b (Violin Concerto No 2) 1981; first performed Lahti, 1982.

Orchestral Diary Sheet No 11c (violin, cello, orchestra) 1981; first performed Helsinki, 1982.

Orchestral Diary Sheet No 11d (Piano Concerto No 2) 1981; first performed Frankfurt, 1984.

Orchestral Diary Sheet No 11e (organ, orchestra) 1981; first performed Vienna, 1982. Recorded Austro Mechanica 120 589.

Orchestral Diary Sheet No 11f (trombone, orchestra) 1981; first performed Helsinki, 1982.

Orchestral Diary Sheet No 11g (clarinet in D, orchestra) 1981; first performed Helsinki, 1982.

Orchestral Diary Sheet No 11h (alto saxophone, orchestra) 1981; first performed Helsinki, 1982.

Orchestral Diary Sheet No 11i (tuba, orchestra) 1981; first performed Helsinki, 1982.

Orchestral Diary Sheet No 11j (flute/piccolo, double bass, orchestra) 1981; first performed Helsinki, 1982.

Orchestral Diary Sheet No 12 (Symphony No 5) 1982; first performed Helsinki, 1983.

Orchestral Diary Sheet No 7 (Sinfonia piccola No 6) 1982; first performed Lahti, 1982.

Orchestral Diary Sheet No 15 (Symphony No 7) 1982; first performed Helsinki, 1983.

Orchestral Diary Sheet No 14a (Cello Concerto No 2) 1983; first performed Helsinki, 1985.

Orchestral Diary Sheet No 14b (Violin Concerto No 3) 1983; first performed Oulu, 1985.

Orchestral Diary Sheet No 14c (Trumpet Concerto) 1983; first performed Tampere, 1985.

Orchestral Diary Sheet No 14d (Concerto No 2 for Two Pianos and Orchestra) 1983; first performed Mainz, 1984.

Orchestral Diary Sheet No 14e (Clarinet Concerto No 2) 1983; first performed Lahti, 1984.

Violin Concerto No 4 1983, later versions for flute or viola, 1985; first performed Hagen, 1986; flute version first performed Ludwigshafen, 1985.

Orchestral Diary Sheet Nos 1, 2 (Symphony No 8) (may be played separately) 1984.

Orchestral Diary Sheet No 3 (Sinfonia piccolo No 9) 1985; first performed Joensuu, 1986. Recorded FACD 403.

Orchestral G-A-L-A Music (with B-A-S-F) 1985; first performed Mannheim, 1985.

So It Feels . . . 1985; may be realised as *Violin Concerto No 5* (Kuopro, 1986), or *Oboe Concerto* (Zweibruchen, 1986), or *Cello Concerto No 3*, or *Viola Concerto*, or *Piano Concerto No 3* (Mannheim, 1989), or *Concerto No 3 for Two Pianos and Orchestra* (2nd piano *tacet*), or *Trumpet Concerto No 2* (Helsinki, 1990). Recorded (*Piano Concerto No 3*) BIS CD 484.

A Last Melodioso (violin, orchestra) 1985; first performed Helsinki, 1986. Recorded BIS CD 326.

Orchestral Diary Sheet No 5 (Small Symphony No 11) 1986; first performed Verlzen, 1986. Recorded BIS CD 483.

Symphony No 10: Three Times . . . (horn, orchestra) 1986; first performed Helsinki, 1987.

Violin Concerto No 6: Feelings and Visions 1986; first performed Copenhagen, 1988.

Symphony No 12: Nach der Sindflut (Orchestral Diary Sheet No 9) (also shorter version: *Orchestral Diary Sheets Nos 9a, 9b, 9c 9d*) 1986; first performed Nuremberg, 1989. Recorded FACD 403.

Symphony No 13 (Orchestral Diary Sheet No 13) (percussion, piano, strings) 1987; first performed Ludwigshafen, 1988. Recorded BIS CD 484.

Thoughts 1987 (Orchestral Diary Sheet No 49) 1987; first performed Ludwigshafen, 1987.

Symphony No 14: Moments of Peace III (Orchestral Diary Sheet No 44) (high baritone or ondes martenot or C trumpet or trombone or synthesizer, orchestra; John Gracen Brown) 1987; first performed Stockholm, 1989. Recorded BIS CD 484.

Thoughts 1988 (Orchestral Diary Sheet No 19) 1988; first performed Wellington, New Zealand, April 1989.

Thoughts 1989 (Orchestral Diary Sheet No 18) 1989; first performed Helsinki, 1989.

Monumental Thoughts: Martti Talvela in memoriam 1989; first performed Copenhagen, 1989. Recorded FACD 403.

Symphony No 15: Ecliptic Thoughts 1990.

Symphony No 16: Thoughts at the Border 1990.

Thoughts 1990 (string quartet, orchestra) 1990.

Murmurs and Screams from Soulful Old Stones (Mostly of Granite) (symphonic wind orchestra) 1990; first performed Copenhagen, 1990.

Chamber/instrumental:

String Quartet No 1 1962.

Five Pedagogical Duets (2 violins) 1963.

Three Sketches (piano) 1964; first performed Helsinki, 1966.

String Quartet No 2 1964; first performed New York City, 1964. Recorded EMI HMV 5E063 35038.

Three Sketches (2 violins) 1965.

Three Meditations (piano) 1965; first performed Helsinki, 1966.

Improvisandum (violin) 1965.

Myriasm (2 violins) 1965; first performed Helsinki, 1965.

String Quartet No 3 1965–6.

Poem (violin or cello, piano) 1966; first performed Helsinki, 1967. Recorded BIS LP 18.

Nocturne (piano) 1966.

String Quartet No 4 1966; first performed Stockholm, 1969. Recorded SLT Electra 33222.

String Quartet No 5: Three Hundred Sixty Degrees/The "Lemming" Quartet 1970; first performed Stockholm, 1970. Recorded SLT Electra 33222.

Seven Questions to Infinity (piano) 1970; first performed Helsinki, 1970. Recorded EMI 5E063 34283.

Three Moments of Parting (violin, piano; or violin, cello, piano; or flute, clarinet, bassoon, violin, viola, cello, piano) 1973; first performed Helsinki, 1973. Recorded BIS LP 39.

A NNNNOOOOOWWW (wind quintet) 1973; first performed Helsinki, 1975. Recorded BIS LP 11.

String Quartet No 6 1974; first performed Helsinki, 1974. Recorded BIS LP 20.

At the Border (violin or viola or cello or double bass, piano) 1974; first performed Helsinki, 1975.

String Quartet No 7 1974–5; first performed Helsinki, 1976. Recorded BIS LP 39.

Moments Kept Remaining (flute, cello or clarinet, piano) 1975; first performed Berlin, 1975.

ANOTHER OF MANY NNNNOOOOOWWWS (wind quintet) 1975; first performed Helsinki, 1976.

Why Yes or No (violin) 1975; first performed Helsinki, 1977.
String Quartet No 8 1975–6; first performed Helsinki, 1978. Recorded Finnlevy SFX 54.
String Quartet No 9 1976; first performed Espoo, 1979.
String Quartet No 10: Homage to Charles Ives's Title "A Contemplation of a Serious Matter" 1976; first performed Helsinki, 1979. Recorded Austro Mechanica 0 120 219.
Thoughts 1977 (piano) 1976; first performed Helsinki, 1977.
Thoughts (piano) 1976; first performed Helsinki, 1977.
Tensions (piano) 1976; first performed Helsinki, 1977.
Tranquil Traumas Nos 1, 4, 5 (2 violins) 1976–7; first performed Espoo, 1978.
Tranquil Traumas Nos 2, 3 (2 double basses) 1976; first performed Lund, 1978.
Music for Four Friends (violin, trumpet, horn, percussion) 1976; first performed Helsinki, 1977.
Adagio–Tensions (violin, piano) 1976; first performed Helsinki, 1976.
A Last Melodioso (violin, piano) 1976; first performed Helsinki, 1976.
Trio (violin, cello, piano) 1976; first performed Vienna, 1977.
Visions of Inner Time (violin, viola, cello, piano) 1976; first performed Stockholm, 1977.
Trio No 2 (violin, cello, piano) 1977; first performed Helsinki, 1979.
String Quartet No 11: Voces con visiones 1977.
Epitaph (cello) 1977; first performed Espoo, 1978.
String Quartet No 12 1977. Recorded Austro Mechanica 0 120 219.
String Trio No 1 1977.
Epitaph No 2a (violin, piano) 1977; first performed Lemi, 1989.
Epitaph No 2b (cello, piano) 1977.
Epitaph No 2c (alto saxophone, piano) 1977; first performed Helsinki, 1978.
Epitaph No 2d (bass clarinet, piano) 1977.
Noem (violin or cello, piano) 1977.
Another Melodioso (violin, piano) 1978.
String Trio No 2 1978.
Episode Nos 8, 11 (guitar) 1978.
String Trio No 3 1978.
String Quartet No 13 1978.
String Quartet No 14 1978.
String Quartet No 15 1978.
Noem No 2 (violin, piano) 1978.
Signature (3 trumpets/1 assistant to relieve players as necessary) 1978.
Episode No 1 (2 violins) 1978.
Episode No 2 (recorder, flute, guitar) 1978.
A Moment of Brasstime (2 trumpets, 2 trombones) 1978; first performed Helsinki, 1979.
Noem No 3 (violin or cello, piano) 1979.
Noem No 4 (violin or cello, piano) 1979; first performed Helsinki, 1979.
Noem No 5 (violin, piano) 1979.
String Quartet No 16: A Moment of String Time 1979.
String Quartet No 17 1979.
Episode No 4 (percussion, 8 horns) 1979; first performed Helsinki, 1979.
Episode No 5 (flute, piano) 1979; first performed Turku, 1980.
Episode No 6 (flute, piano) 1979.
Episode No 7 (percussion, alto saxophone) 1979; first performed Helsinki, 1981.
Episode No 9 (6 trumpets, 3 horns, 2 baritone horns, 3 trombones, 2 tubas, percussion) 1979; first performed Stockholm, 1979.
String Quartet No 18 1979; first performed Joroinen, 1984.
String Quartet No 19 1979.
Noem No 6 (violin or cello, piano) 1980; first performed Helsinki, 1983.
Episode No 10 (oboe, bassoon, violin, viola, cello) 1980.
String Quartet No 20 1980.
String Quartet No 21 1980.
String Quartet No 22 1980.
String Quartet No 23 1980.
Noem No 7 (violin, piano) 1980; first performed Mannheim, 1987.
Episode No 12 (12 violins) 1980.
Episode No 13 (trombone, piano) 1980; first performed Vienna, 1980.
Episode No 22 (cello or viola, harp) 1980.
Epitaph No 3 (violin, piano) 1981.
Episode No 14 (2 trumpets, horn, trombone, tuba) 1981; first performed Stockholm, 1987.
Episode No 15 (woodwind quintet, trombone) 1981; first performed Ludwigshafen, 1985.
Episode No 16 (trumpet in C, 4 percussion) 1981; first performed Helsinki, 1983.
Two Movements (each movement may be played separately; clarinet, violin, cello, piano) 1982.
String Quartet No 24 1982.
Episode No 17 (flute or violin, guitar) 1982; first performed Helsinki, 1983.
Episode No 18 (clarinet, cello) 1982.
Episode No 23 (percussion, harp) 1982.
String Quartet No 25: (Another) Mad Song (with mezzo-soprano; text by Blake) 1982; first performed Helsinki, 1985.
Episode No 24 (bassoon, harpsichord or piano) 1982; first performed Helsinki, 1990.
Episode No 5a (flute, oboe, piano) 1983.
Episode No 5b (flute, trombone, piano) 1983.
Episode No 6a (flute, oboe, piano) 1983.
Episode No 6b (flute, trombone, piano) 1983.
Episode No 20 (violin, horn in F, piano) 1983; first performed Ludwigshafen, 1985.
Episode No 21 (violin, horn in F, piano) 1983.
The Bells Are Ringing / For a Certain Time (piano) 1983; first performed Helsinki, 1983.
Sounds and Visions (from *Symphony No 7*; organ, piano, 5 percussion) 1983; first performed Helsinki, 1985.
Episode No 19 (oboe) 1985.
Noem No 8 (cello, piano) 1986.
String Quartet No 26 (I–"For Four . . . or One & Three", II–"For Two & Two Mostly . . . ") 1986; I first performed Zagreb, 1989.
Mininoem (violin, piano) 1986.
String Quartet No 27 1990.
Double Thoughts at the Border (Trio No 3) (violin, cello, piano) 1990.
At Another Border (violin or cello, piano) 1990.
Noem No 11 (cello) 1990.

Vocal/choral:

Three Songs (soprano, piano; Sandelin) 1960–1; first performed Stockholm, 1961.
Morgonen / The Morning (unaccompanied chorus; Kihlman) 1963; first performed Vaasa, 1975. Recorded Finnlevu SFLP 8454.
Missa piccola (3-part unaccompanied mixed chorus) 1964.
Three American Songs (voice, piano, Frost, Pound) 1964–5; first performed Helsinki, 1966.

Reincarnation (unaccompanied female chorus; Josefsson) 1965.
Three Leaves of Grass (voice, piano; Whitman) 1966; first performed London, 1967. Recorded Philips 802855LY.
Youth Cantata (unison chorus of 100–200 singers, orchestra) 1967; first performed Tampere, 1967.
Seven Red Moments (soprano, orchestra; Renwall, Bjorling) 1967; first performed Helsinki, 1968.
3+/or 4 NNNNOOOOOWWWS (voice, small orchestra; Bjorling) 1968–72; first performed Copenhagen, 1972.
Tre bilder/Three Pictures (chamber chorus, flute, bass clarinet, viola, vibraphone, glockenspiel) 1970; first performed Stockholm 1971.
Six Songs of Experience (soprano, large orchestra; Blake, Auden) 1970–1; first performed Stockholm, 1974. Recorded BIS LP 83.
Three Songs of Parting (bass voice with extreme range, piano; Whitman) 1971–2; first performed Helsinki, 1973.
Kvarhallna ogonblick/Gehaltene Augenblicke (mezzo-soprano, piano; Bjorling) 1973.
Nagra nur i allts/Some Nows in All's (high baritone, piano; Bjorling) 1974.
Visions of Inner Time (high or medium voice, piano; Bjorling) 1975; first performed Helsinki, 1977.
Jalkeen pain, Tulitikkulaatikot, Asema II/Afterwards, Matchboxes, Station II (voice, piano; Saarikoski) 1976; first performed Helsinki, 1977.
Host, Alla hus med graa ogon, Manes gront/Autumn, Grey the Eyes, Moon's Green (mezzo-soprano, piano) 1976.
Grona kronors, Nar det vaxer nypon, Hjartatsgata/Green Crowns, When Rosebuds Are Growing, Heart's Road (high voice or mezzo-soprano, piano; Bjorling) 1976.
Chinese Diary (mezzo-soprano, flute, violin, piano; Po Chi-Cu, Nieminen) 1977; first performed Helsinki, 1977.
Tre ganger/Three Times (mezzo-soprano, piano; Bjorling) 1978.
Med sommar/With Summer (soprano or mezzo-soprano, piano; Bjorling) 1978.
Two Korean Birds (mezzo-soprano, piano; "The Lark", "The Kite"; Cho Byung-hwa, O'Bourke) 1979.
Three Last Songs ("Stroke of Midnight", "Credo", "Before Rebirth"; voice, piano; Martin) 1979.
Mad Song (soprano or mezzo-soprano, piano; Blake) 1981.
Three Times or Two Times (versions for medium, high or low voices, orchestra; Bjorling) 1982.
Two Songs (voice, piano; Bjorling) 1983.
Moments of Peace IV (voice, piano) 1987.

Leif Segerstam comments:

As a "summer composer" like Gustav Mahler, I have been writing in a so-called "free pulsative" style since about 1970 . . . Inspirative expressive music of complex tonality, a touch of Nordic post-expressionism . . . Nature's closeness providing most of the stimulus for music caught in a notation flexible enough for the next generation's instinct for a rich immediacy . . .

* * *

Like that of his younger compatriot Esa-Pekka Salonen, Leif Segerstam's prodigious compositional output has been been somewhat eclipsed by his genius with the conductor's baton. Since joining the Finnish National Opera as associate conductor in 1965, Segerstam has been one of the most significant interpreters of modern and contemporary music in Northern Europe, a figure to set alongside such other composer-conductors as Gilbert Amy, Pierre Boulez, Giuseppe Sinopoli and Oliver Knussen.

Like Knussen, Segerstam has a feel for orchestral language that is pure and instinctive. Unlike Knussen's, it has been put to the very fullest use. At first glance, Segerstam's oeuvre gives an impression of rather fissiparous insubstantiality. A great many of his works are free variants of other works, and he prefers to write in long, rather discontinuous series, which appear to work discursively rather than organically. There are the chamber *Noems, Episodes, Epitaphs*, 27 string quartets to date, and the often confusing symphonic note-books, the *orchestral Diary Sheets*, from which he has drawn all of his symphonies to date.

Since 1970, most of Segerstam's compositions have been conceived in what he himself has called a "free pulsative style", which restores to individual performers a considerable responsibility for determining the exact rhythm. This is adopted in a very different manner from the semi-aleatory idiom of Segerstam's Danish colleague, the fantastically productive Nils Viggo Bentzon. Where Bentzon's use of freedom and chance is largely based on jazz and improvisation, Segerstam's is closer to a recognition of the mediating contingencies of the natural world.

Segerstam has called himself a "summer composer", likening himself in the process to Gustav Mahler. While he shares Mahler's profound expressionism, it is of an altogether tougher sort. Stripped of much of its attendant emotionalism, it is a nature mysticism that suggests Darwin or Hobbes, nature as a *bellum omnium contra omnia*, the chaos of *Revelation* rather than the edenic peace of *Genesis*. In fact, this is a conception of nature which is part and parcel of the Scandinavian cultures, detectable in Ibsen, Strindberg, Munch, the Finnish *Kalevala*, the writings of Tarjei Vesaas. In the recent *Symphony No 15: Ecliptic Thoughts*, Segerstam, who has always attempted to explain his works either at concerts or on record, suggests an inspiration that takes place at the zenith of the northern summer, an oneiric-analytical exploration of the birth of harmony in the primitive clash of great blocks of orchestral sound (like much of his work, the Fifteenth Symphony balances great violence and great calm).

The landscape he suggests is chaotic, but constantly declares its own history, just as most of his works constantly declare their own motives and origins. He describes a forest apocalyptically shorn, but thus showing the sensitive, vibratory growth-rings on their suddenly naked trunks, and their echo of the solar and lunar discs above. As always, growth and destruction move side by side in his work. In *Symphony No 16: Thoughts at the Border*, the matrix has been extended even further. The musical material is sent "out" at a fantastic rate, inducing a type of Doppler or recessional effect, but then bringing back "messages" from the "borders" of tonality and audibility. A number of analogies suggest themselves, not in the circumstances too far-fetched: there is a suggestion of astronomical exploration by means of radio-electronic pulses, either bouncing back or receiving "answers" from unknowable sources; and there is a culturally older reference to the sending out from the Ark of a raven and a dove, and the return of a message of hope and renewed growth from across the devastated landscape. Segerstam has described the sensibility required to experience such effects as "hysterically super-sensitive" and indeed as the potentialities exposed by Segerstam's proliferating method appear to approach infinity, there is a suspicion that only the most highly strung of natures will resonate in tune with his remarkable imagination. However, individual works are considerably more accessible than seems possible when the work-list is viewed *in toto*. The chamber music is less compelling, partly because, though an accomplished violinist, Segerstam's true instrument is the orchestra. He has, however, written superbly for voices, from the early—and typically grandiose—*Youth Cantata* for up to 200 voices and full orchestra, to the sublimely beautiful bass settings of Whitman's *Three Songs of Parting*, a part for the remarkable Finnish bassist Martti Talvela whose untimely death inspired one of Segerstam's most direct orchestral works. *Monumental Thoughts: Martti Talvela in memoriam*, the stately First Symphony and the single-movement second, third and fifth are among the finest orchestral works since the death (or silence) of Sibelius and seem to contain within them something like that delicate balance of utterance and withdrawal which was Sibelius's profoundest legacy to his compatriots.

—Henk Maarten

SHAPERO, Harold. American. Born in Lynn, Massachusetts, 29 April 1920. Educated at Malkin Conservatory, Boston (composition under Nicolas Slonimsky), 1936–7; composition study under Ernst Krenek, 1937; piano study under Eleanor Kerr; Harvard University, Cambridge, Massachusetts (composition under Walter Piston), 1938–41; Berkshire Music Center, Tanglewood, Massachusetts (composition under Paul Hindemith), 1940; Longy School (composition under Nadia Boulanger), 1942–3; further study in Rome, 1949–50. Married Esther Geller in 1945. Founding professor (with Arthur Berger, Irving Fine and Leonard Bernstein), music department, Brandeis University, Waltham, Massachusetts, 1952–85. Recipient: George Arthur Knight Prizes, 1938, 1940; Prix de Rome, 1941; Naumburg Fellowship, 1942; Gershwin Prize, 1946; Bearns Prize, 1946; Guggenheim Fellowships, 1947, 1948. Mailing address: c/o Department of Music, Brandeis University, 415 South Street, Waltham, Massachusetts 02254, U.S.A.

Publisher: Southern.

Symphonies/orchestral:

Nine-Minute Overture 1940; first performed New York City, 8 June 1941.
Serenade in D (string orchestra) 1945; 1st movement performed New York City, 1946.
Symphony for Classical Orchestra 1947; first performed Boston, 30 January 1948.
The Travellers Overture (Sinfonia in C) 1948; first performed Houston, Texas, 1948.
Concerto for Orchestra 1950.
Credo 1955; first performed Louisville, Kentucky, 19 October 1955.
Lyric Dances 1955.
Partita in C (piano, small orchestra) 1960; first performed Detroit, Michigan, 1961.
On Green Mountain (orchestrated from ensemble piece) 1981.

Chamber/instrumental:

String Trio 1938.
Three Pieces for Three Pieces (flute, clarinet, bassoon) 1939.
Sonata (trumpet, piano) 1940.
Sonata (piano—4 hands) 1941.
String Quartet 1941.
Sonata (violin, piano) 1942.
Three Amateur Sonatas (piano) 1944.
Variations in C (piano) 1947.
Sonata in F (piano) 1948.
American Variations (piano) 1950.
On Green Mountain (jazz group) 1957.
Three Improvisations in B (piano, synthesizer) 1968.
Three Studies in C# (piano, synthesizer) 1969.
Four Pieces in B♭ (piano, synthesizer) 1970.

Vocal/choral:

Four Baritone Songs (voice, piano; cummings) 1942.
Two Psalms (unaccompanied SATB chorus; adapted from Psalms 100, 117, 146) 1952.
Hebrew Cantata (soprano, alto, tenor, baritone, mixed chorus, flute, trumpet, violin, harp, organ) 1954.
Two Hebrew Songs ("They Who Sow at Night"—Shalom, "Will There Yet Come Days of Forgiveness"—Goldberg; tenor, piano) 1973, orchestrated 1973.

PUBLICATIONS

By Shapero: "The Musical Mind", in *Modern Music*, 23, 1946.

On Shapero: Elliott Carter, "The Changing Scene", in *Modern Music*, 17, 1939–40; Irving Fine, "S Symphony Given Premiere", in *Musical America,* 68(4), 1948; Aaron Copland. "1949: The New 'School' of American Composers", in *New York Times Magazine*, 14 March 1948, reprinted in *Copland on Music*, New York, 1963; Arthur Berger, "Stravinsky and the Younger American Composers", in *The Score*, 12, 1955; A. Cohn, "HS", in *The Collector's Twentieth-Century Music in the Western Hemisphere*, New York, 1961; Wilfrid Mellers, in *Music in a New Found Land*, London, 1964.

* * *

Harold Shapero had the advantage of much excellent teaching, from Ernst Krenek, Walter Piston, Paul Hindemith and Nadia Boulanger. He also won a number of prizes, especially during the 1940s, and received several commissions, for instance from the Koussevitsky Foundation. Among the prizes was the American Prix de Rome, for his *Nine-Minute Overture*, a typical example of one kind of piece, usually lasting about 10 minutes, that American composers were then producing. Other cases were Robert Palmer's *Poem*, David Diamond's *Pslam* (both 1938) and William Schuman's *American Festival Overture* (1939), and they often served as steps towards writing the Great American Symphony. There were other American composers like this, usually well trained conservatives, and several of them, such as Peter Mennin, Vincent Persichetti and again Diamond, were indeed persistent symphonists. Shapero's closer associates, however, were Arthur Berger, Leonard Bernstein and Irving Fine, all fellow pupils of Piston, and they followed a rather different path—in Shapero's case leading in strongly neo-classical directions.

Good instances are the *Three Amateur Sonatas* for piano of 1944, in a sort of modernisation of rococo, the chief model being Haydn via Stravinsky, perhaps with something also from Scarlatti and C.P.E. Bach. Shapero is an excellent pianist, the music he writes for the instrument is unfailingly effective, a pleasure to play, and in this case surprisingly appealing, even memorable. Its precise, elegant lyrical freshness is reminiscent of Prokofiev—of, for example, the Gavotte and Rigaudon from the Russian composer's *Episodes* Op 12. With his *Symphony for Classical Orchestra* and *Variations in C* for piano Shapero went further in the same direction, but more questionably using Beethoven as a model, or mask, as Stravinsky used several composers. But he stays closer to his models than Stravinsky (or Piston) ever did, and the "distancing" effect of neo-classical stylisation is sometimes unduly evident. Piston's influence is clear in the *String Quartet*, with its fourth-founded harmony and dissonant counterpoint, and an earlier *String Trio* reflects Krenek's applications of serial technique. Another model is Schubert, in the separate F minor Piano Sonata of 1948.

A fluent improviser at the piano, Shapero was interested both in jazz and pre-rock popular music, and wrote dance band arrangements. This finds an occasional echo in his orchestration, but a weightier result is *On Green Mountain*, a "third stream" piece for jazz group. Again he turned to the past, and this is an imaginative recomposition of Monteverdi's *Zefiro torna* with striking ensemble textures and plenty of room for improvisation. Comparable to this exploration of jazz techniques is Shapero's adaptation of Renaissance procedures in *Two Psalms*, of serialism in the *Partita in C* for piano and small orchestra and even the use of electronic media in *Three Studies in C#* a rather simple work for synthesizer and piano. But, as his list of compositions proves, Shapero has written less and less as the decades have passed, and most of the pieces which made any considerable impression date from the 1940s. It has to be acknowledged that expectations raised by the commendations of Stravinsky and Copland were not fulfilled.

—Max Harrison

SHAPEY, Ralph. American. Born in Philadelphia, 12 March 1921. Educated: studied violin under Emmanuel Zeitlin, composition under Stepan Wolpe. Assistant conductor, National Youth Symphony Orchestra, 1938–47; founder and director, Contemporary Chamber Players, University of Chicago, 1954; teacher of music, University of Pennsylvania, Philadelphia, 1963–4; teacher of composition and conducting, University of Chicago, 1964–85; withdrew all works from performance, 1969–76; distinguished professor of music, Queens College, New York City, 1985. Recipient: MacArthur Prize, 1982; 1st prize, Kennedy Center Friedheim Competition, 1990. Mailing address: 5532 South Shore Drive, 18D Chicago, Illinois 60637, U.S.A.

Publisher: Presser.

Symphonies/orchestral:

Fantasy 1951; withdrawn.
Challenge: The Family of Man 1955.
Ontogeny 1958.
Invocation (concerto for violin and orchestra) 1959.
Rituals 1959. Recorded CRI 275.
Double Concerto (violin, cello, orchestra) 1983.
Grotou (3 movements for youth orchestra) 1984.
Symphonie concertante 1985; first performed Philadelphia, 1987.
Concerto for Cello, Piano and String Orchestra 1986.

Chamber/instrumental:

String Quartet No 1 1946.
Quintet (2 violins, viola, cello, piano) 1946–7.
Three Essays on Thomas Wolfe (piano) 1948–9.
String Quartet No 2 1949.
Sonata (violin, piano) 1949–50.
String Quartet No 3 1950–1.
Seven Little Pieces (piano) 1951.
Sonata (oboe, piano) 1951–2. Recorded CRI SD 501.
Suite (4 pieces for piano) 1952.
Quartet (oboe, violin, viola, cello) 1952.
Sonata (cello, piano) 1953.
String Quartet No 4 1953.
Piano Trio 1953–5.
Sonata Variations (piano) 1954.
Concerto (clarinet solo, horn, percussion, piano, violin, cello) 1954.
Mutations I (piano) 1956.
Duo (viola, piano) 1957.
Rhapsodie (oboe, piano) 1957. Recorded CRI 423.
String Quartet No 5 (with female voice) 1957–8.
Form (piano) 1959.
Evocation No 1 (violin, piano, percussion) 1959. Recorded CRI 141.
De profundis (double bass solo, violin, piccolo/flute, oboe/cor anglais, clarinet/bass clarinet/alto saxophone, horn) 1960.
Movements (flute, oboe, clarinet, bassoon, horn) 1960.
Five (violin, piano) 1960.
Discourse (flute, clarinet, piano, violin) 1961.
Birthday Piece (piano) 1962.
Piece (violin, oboe, clarinet, bassoon, horn, trumpet, trombone, percussion, cello) 1962.
Chamber Symphony (flute, oboe, cor anglais, horn, trumpet, percussion, piano, violin, cello, double bass) 1962.
Convocation (2 oboes, 2 trumpets, 2 trombones, bass trombone, 2 violins, double bass) 1962.
Seven (piano—4 hands) 1963. Recorded Friends of Four Hand Music.
String Quartet No 6 1963. Recorded CRI 275.
Brass Quintet 1963. Recorded New World Records NW 377 2.
Sonance (carillon) 1964.
Configurations (flute, piano) 1965. Recorded New World Records NW 254.
String Trio 1965.
Mutations II (piano) 1966.
Poeme (viola, percussion) 1966.
Partita (violin) 1966.
Partita (violin, flute, oboe, clarinet, bassoon, horn, trumpet, trombone, 2 percussion, violin, viola, cello, double bass) 1966.
Partita-Fantasia (cello, 2 flutes, 2 oboes, 2 clarinets, 2 bassoons, horn, trumpet, trombone, 2 percussion, violin, viola, double bass) 1966.
Fromm Variations (piano) 1966, 1972–3. Recorded CRI 428.
Deux (piano—4 hands) 1967.
Reyem (Musical Offering) (flute, violin, piano) 1967.
For Solo Trumpet 1967.
String Quartet No 7 1972. Recorded CRI 391.
Three Concert Pieces (young string players; violin, viola, cello, percussion) 1972.

Sonata No 1 (violin; based on *String Trio*) 1977.
Twenty One Variations (piano) 1978. Recorded CRI SD 496.
Evocation No 2 (cello, percussion, piano) 1979.
Three for Six (violin/viola, cello, flute/piccolo, clarinet/bass clarinet, percussion, piano) 1979. Recorded CRI SD 509.
Four Etudes (violin) 1980.
Concerto grosso (woodwind quintet) 1981.
Evocation No 3 (viola, piano) 1981.
Fanfares (brass quintet) 1981.
Passacaglia (piano) 1982.
Fantasy (violin, piano) 1983. Recorded New World NW 333.
Krosnick soli (cello) 1983.
Discourse No 2 (violin, piano, clarinet, cello) 1983.
Mann Duo (violin, viola) 1983.
Harmaxiemanda (piano) 1984.
Gottlieb Duo (percussion, piano) 1984.
Concertante No 1 (trumpet solo, flute, oboe, clarinet, bassoon, horn, percussion, strings) 1984. Recorded New World Records NW 355-2.
Variations (organ) 1985.
Korshlish Sonate (cello, piano) 1985.
Variations on a Cantus (piano) 1987.
Theme + 10 (harpsichord) 1987.
Variations (viola solo, flute/piccolo/bass flute, E♭ clarinet, clarinet/alto clarinet, bass clarinet, piano, violin, viola, cello, percussion) 1987.
Concertante No 2 (alto saxophone solo, flute/piccolo/bass flute, oboe/cor anglais, clarinet/E♭ clarinet/bass clarinet, bassoon/contrabassoon, horn, trumpet/piccolo trumpet, trombone/bass trombone, 3 percussion, solo strings) 1987.
Soli (percussion duo) 1989.

Vocal/choral:

Cantata (soprano, tenor, bass, narrator, orchestra) 1951; revised as *String Quartet No 5*, 1957–8.
Walking Upright (8 songs for female voice, violin; Klement) 1958.
Soliloquy (narrator, string quartet, percussion) 1959.
This Day (female voice, piano; Klement) 1960.
Dimensions (wordless soprano, flute, oboe, tenor saxophone, horn, trumpet, piano, 7 percussion, timpani, double bass) 1960.
Incantations (wordless soprano, alto saxophone, horn, trumpet, 2 percussion, piano, cello) 1961. Recorded CRI 232.
Praise (bass-baritone, double chorus, 2 oboes, 2 trumpets, 3 trombones, 4 percussion, 2 violins, viola, cello, double bass) 1962–71. Recorded CRI 355/SD 275.
Songs of Ecstasy (soprano, percussion, tape; Bible, Joyce, Shakespeare, Benton) 1967. Recorded Desto Records DC 7124.
Songs of Eros (soprano, orchestra, tape; Whitman, Joyce, Louys, Bible) 1973–5.
O Jerusalem (soprano, flute) 1974–5. Recorded Opus One 121.
The Covenant (soprano, flute, oboe, clarinet, bassoon, horn, trumpet, trombone, tuba, 2 percussion, piano, 2 2-track tapes, 2 violins, viola, cello, double bass; Whitman, Bible, others) 1977. Recorded CRI 435.
Trilogy: Song of Songs I–III (soprano, baritone, orchestra) 1979–80.
Songs (soprano, piano; 25 poets) 1982. Recorded Opus One 106.
Psalm No 1 (soprano, oboe, piano) 1984.
Psalm No 2 (soprano, chorus, oboe, viola, cello, double bass, piano) 1984.
Songs No 2 (soprano, violin, clarinet, cello, piano) 1984.
Songs of Joy (soprano, piano) 1987.
In memoriam (soprano, baritone, 9 players) 1987.
Songs of Life (soprano, cello, piano) 1988.
Songs of Love (soprano, piano) 1989.

PUBLICATIONS

By Shapey: liner notes to *Praise*, recorded CRI 355/SD 275.

On Shapey: Shulamit Ran, "An Angry Composer Forbids His Music to Be Performed", in *New York Times*, 8 May 1977; C. Gagne and T. Caras, in *Soundpieces: Interviews with American Composers*, Metuchen, New Jersey, 1982; John Rockwell, "Romantic Defiance: Enlightened Patronage and Misanthropy in the Midwest", in *All-American Music: Composition in the late 20th century*, New York City, 1983.

* * *

Ralph Shapey has always been a controversial figure. This is partly because of his temperament—to describe it as "stormy" would be like calling a cobalt bomb in your backyard "disquieting"—and partly because his music offers no easy options to the listener or the performer unwilling to sweat for his satisfactions.

Yet, through all the controversy and the occasional maverick bouts of polemic, it is hard not to perceive the sheer granitic honesty that lies beneath, or to admire and love the man's warmth and positively quixotic generosity. It is impressive for example to see how, over the years, he has programmed the most comprehensive range of new works with his University of Chicago Contemporary Chamber Players, explaining (when asked whether he really liked one piece he had been rehearsing) that it was his responsibility as director of such an ensemble to afford a hearing to the full spectrum of current styles whether he happened to like them or not.

Then there is the music itself. I described it once, when I was the critic of the *Chicago Daily News,* as "the finest and most substantial body of music by any American composer of our time", a judgment that in the intervening years has been quoted assentingly at least twice in the *New York Times,* and that now, three decades later, I find no reason to disown.

There was a period of several years, beginning in 1969, when Shapey's bitterness at what he saw as the corruption of the world in general and the musical world in particular reached such a pitch that he declared a moratorium on performances of his work. "I seriously considered burning it all", he told his younger colleague and friend, the Israeli-born composer Shulamit Ran, "but my compositions are my children, and I love my children. How can I destroy that which I love?" Fortunately for the rest of us, that time came to an end. It would be perilous, to speak of Shapey mellowing. But certainly his music, now numbering more than 100 works, has blossomed again since then. Shapey himself seems to have attained at least a modicum of personal tranquillity, and recognition of his stature too has grown.

What, then, is this music like? A National Institute of Arts and Letters citation honored Shapey for "his exciting and dynamic music, full of rugged power and high originality, developed over a number of years in response to an intensely personal vision, uninfluenced by changing fashion." Those words do suggest something of the music's character. The word "granitic" too, used above in connection with his personal qualities, is a clue to his music also. Shapey himself has spoken of music as "an object in time and space . . .

aggregate sounds sculpted into concrete sculptured forms". He once observed:

> There was a point in my life, in the 1950s, when I got fed up—really fed up—with so-called modern music. I quit composing for a whole year; I went back and studied the old mastery, trying to discover what their secrets were. What were their secrets? The music is graven in rock. In stone. It cannot be destroyed. I said to myself, "thou shalt not make graven images." I'LL MAKE GRAVEN IMAGES!

That statement offers a hint of the almost tangible physical reality of Shapey's music, and it also reveals the respect for the past that animates this dazzlingly original creator. What is likely to make his work difficult for an unaccustomed listener is its fearless use of dissonance and, even more, its often unrelenting intensity of expression. The texture and structure are complex, but not, be it noted, needlessly complicated. The complexity is the product of relatively simple elements assembled in kaleidoscopically shifting combinations and recombinations—almost a kind of minimalism raised to the maximal point of ingenuity and intellectual integrity. Tiny thematic motifs, often no more than three or four notes in length, are the core of the music, and they are developed with a consuming single-mindedness that leaves no room for merely decorative elements.

The parallel with Brahms's uncompromisingly organic structures may not be apparent to the ear at first encounter, but it imposes itself as one gets to know Shapey's music better. And the rewards of taking the trouble to do that are enormous, for the values he celebrates are deeply and universally human. They are the ageless values of beauty and truth, of love and tolerance and awe before the infinite. They are as evident in an "abstract" piece like the 1987 *Symphonie concertante* as they are in Shapey's explicitly religious works, such as *The Covenant* for soprano and 16 players and the large-scale oratorio *Praise*. "Pure music", Shapey says, "cannot be philosophical. But the philosophical ideas are part of my inspiration, if I may call it that. Part of myself, as a human being."

—Bernard Jacobson

SHCHEDRIN, Rodion (Konstantinovich). Russian. Born in Moscow, 16 December 1932. Educated at Moscow Choral College, 1945–50; Moscow State Conservatory (piano under Y. Flier; composition under Yuri Shaporin), 1950–5, post-graduate studies 1955–9. Married Maya Plisetskaya, 2 October 1958. Professor of composition, Moscow State Conservatory, 1965–9; president, Union of Composers, Russian Federation, Moscow (in succession to Dmitri Shostakovitch), 1973–90. Recipient: State Prize of the U.S.S.R., 1972; associate member, Bayerische Akademie der Schonen Kunste, 1976; honorary member, Liszt Society, 1978; People's Artist, 1981; member, Deutsche Akademie der Kunste, 1983; Lenin Prize, 1984; honorary member, International Music Council, 1985; Berliner Akademie der Kunste, 1989. Mailing address: ul. Tverskaya Gorky 25, dom 31, 103050 Moscow, U.S.S.R.

Publishers: Sovetskii kompozitor, Moscow; Ricordi, Milan.

Symphonies/orchestral:

Piano Concerto No 1 1954, re-orchestrated in 1974; first performed Moscow, 7 November 1954; revised version first performed Moscow, 5 May 1974. Recorded Melodiya C10 05135006.
The Little Humpback Horse (orchestral suite from the ballet) 1955; first performed Moscow, 1956.
Symphony No 1 1958; first performed Moscow, 6 December 1958. Recorded Melodiya C10 05135006; SUK 7786.
Concerto No 1 for Orchestra: Naughty Limericks 1963; first performed Moscow, 17 November 1963. Recorded Melodiya CM 02917–8; Capitol R SR40011.
Not for Love Alone (symphonic suite from the opera) 1964.
Symphony No 2 (Twenty-Five Preludes) 1965; first performed Moscow, 11 April 1963. Recorded Melodiya C10 01099-006.
The Little Humpback Horse (second orchestral suite from the ballet) 1965.
Piano Concerto No 2 1966; first performed Moscow, 5 January 1967. Recorded Melodiya C10 09417000; EMI C065 94464; Ariola S87468 XG.
Symphonic Fanfares (festive overture for orchestra) 1967; first performed Moscow, 6 November 1967.
Concerto No 2 for Orchestra: Chimes 1968; first performed New York City, 11 January 1968. Recorded Melodiya C10 10941008.
Anna Karenina (romantic music from the opera) 1972; first performed Moscow, 24 October 1972. Recorded CBS XUS 478 MK; Melodiya C10 12657000.
Piano Concerto No 3 1973; first performed Moscow, 5 May 1974. Recorded Melodiya C10 05135006; Victor 2149.
Solemn Overture (symphonic salute for the 60th anniversary of the U.S.S.R.) 1982; first performed Moscow, December 1982.
Self-Portrait 1984; first performed Moscow, 1984. Recorded Melodiya A10 00207004.
Music for Strings, Oboes, Horns and Celeste 1985; first performed Leningrad, 1986.
Music for the City of Kothen (chamber orchestra) 1985; first performed Berlin, 1985. Recorded Melodiya A10 00207004; Melodiya SUCD 10 00133.
Stykhiza 1986–7; first performed Washington, D.C., 1988. Recorded Erato 2292 45343 2.
Old Russian Circus Music: Concerto for Orchestra No 3 1988; first performed Chicago, 1990.
Khorovody / Round Dances: Concerto for Orchestra No 4 1988; first performed Tokyo, 1989.
Flagollets for Toru Takemitsu 1990.

Chamber/instrumental:

Two Etudes (piano) 1949.
Festivity on a Collective Farm (piano) 1951; first performed Moscow, 1951.
Suite (clarinet, piano) 1951; first performed Moscow, 1952.
Piano Pieces 1952–61.
Poem (piano) 1954.
Four Pieces from The Little Humpback Horse (piano) 1955.
Variations on a Theme of Glinka (piano) 1957.
Toccatina (piano) 1958.
Humoresque (piano) 1959.
Troika (piano) 1959.
Chamber Suite (20 violins, harp, accordion, 2 double basses) 1961; first performed Moscow, 1962. Recorded Melodiya C10 02723 004.

Sonata (piano) 1962; first performed Moscow, 24 April 1968. Recorded Melodiya C10 18131 004.
Two Polyphonic Pieces (piano) 1962.
Ala Albeniz (piano) 1963.
Twenty-Four Preludes and Fugues: Volumes I and II (piano) 1964–70; I first performed Moscow, 20 April 1965; II first performed Moscow, 27 January 1971. Recorded Melodiya C10 0277500.
Polyphonic Notebook (25 pieces for piano) 1972; first performed Moscow, 31 March 1973. Recorded Melodiya C10 04685000.
The Frescoes of Dionysus (flute, cor anglais, horn, clarinet, percussion, cello, viola, cello) 1981; first performed Moscow, October 1981. Recorded Melodiya A10 007100 Y.
Notebook for Youth (15 piano pieces) 1981; first performed Moscow, March 1982. Recorded Melodiya A10 000712004.
Musical Offering (organ, 3 flutes, 3 horns, 3 trombones) 1983; first performed Moscow, 1983.
Hommage à Chopin (4 pianos) 1983; first performed Munich, 1983.
Echo-Sonata (violin) 1984; first performed Cologne, 1985. Recorded Olympia OCD 140; col legno 5507.
The Geometry of Sound (chamber ensemble) 1986; first performed Moscow, 1987.
Three Shepherds (flute, oboe, clarinet) 1987; first performed Kuhmo, Finland, 1987.
Russkie Naigzishy (cello) 1989; first performed Paris, 1990.

Vocal/choral:

The Ukrainian Night Is Quiet (unaccompanied children's chorus; Pushkin) 1950.
Collection of Russian Folk Songs (arranged for piano duet with A. Flyarovsky) 1950.
Choruses Written over a Number of Years (unaccompanied mixed chorus; Pushkin, Tvardovsky, Voznesensky, Kharabarov) 1950–70. Recorded CO 4585 6; C10 16759 009.
Songs and Ditties of Varvara (arranged from *Not for Love Alone* for mezzo-soprano, piano) 1961.
Bureaucratiade (satirical cantata for soprano, mezzo-soprano, tenor, bass, chorus, small symphony orchestra; Rules for those staying at the Kurpaty Boarding House) 1963; first performed Moscow, 24 February 1965.
Three Solfege Exercises (high voice, piano) 1965; first performed Moscow, 13 October 1967. Recorded Melodiya DO 21821 2.
Laments (voice, piano; traditional) 1965; first performed Moscow, 31 January 1966.
Poetoria (concerto for narrator, soprano, mixed chorus, symphony orchestra; Voznesensky) 1968; first performed Moscow, 24 February 1968. Recorded Melodiya C10 07943 007.
Lenin Lives in the People's Heart (oratorio for 3 soloists, mixed chorus, symphony orchestra; traditional) 1969; first performed Moscow, 6 February 1970. Recorded Eurodisc 89045 KK.
Supplice de Pougatchev (unaccompanied mixed chorus; Pushkin) 1981; first performed Talin, March 1983.
Stanzas from Eugene Onegin (unaccompanied mixed chorus; Pushkin) 1981; first performed Moscow, May 1982.
Concertino (unaccompanied chorus) 1982; first performed Moscow, 1983.
The Sealed Angel (mixed chorus, reed pipe) 1987; first performed Moscow, 1988. Recorded Melodiya SU 10 000004.

Opera:

Not for Love Alone (Katanyan, after Antonov) 1961, revised version for chamber orchestra, 1971; first performed Moscow, 25 December 1961; revised version first performed Moscow, 20 January, 1972. Recorded Melodiya C10 06847007.
Dead Souls (after Gogol) 1976; first performed Moscow, 7 June 1977. Recorded Melodiya C10 17683003.

Other:

The Little Humpback Horse (ballet by V. Vainonen and P. Malyarevsky, after Yershov) 1955; first performed Moscow, 4 March 1960. Recorded (parts only) MCD 219A; video Corinth 1988 1204; Pony Video VAC 1039.
Carmen Suite (ballet after Bizet by Alicia Alonso) 1967; first performed Moscow, 20 April 1967. Recorded EMI ASD 2448; Angel SR 40067/CDC 7 47198 2; video Video Arts International VAI RB 7.
Anna Karenina (ballet by B. Lvov-Anokhin, after Tolstoy) 1971; first performed Moscow, 10 June 1972. Recorded Ariola Eurodisc LPS 869967 XK; video Pony Video V 98F 1421; Corinth 1988 1203.
The Seagull (ballet by RS and V. Levental, after Chekhov) 1979; first performed Moscow, 1980. Recorded Melodiya C10 17683003.
The Lady with a Lapdog (ballet after Chekhov) 1985; first performed Moscow, 1985. Recorded Melodiya SUCD 10 00133.
Nina and the Twelve Months (musical) 1988; first performed Tokyo, 1988.

Film scores: *The Height*, 1957; *The Communist*, 1957; *People on the Bridge*, 1959; *Normandie-Neman*, 1960; *What if It Is Love?*, 1961; *The Bath-House*, 1961; *Anna Karenina*, 1968; *The Subject for a Short Story*, 1969.

PUBLICATIONS

By Shchedrin: "Folk Songs in Life and at the Conservatory", in *Sovetskaya muzyka*, 2, 1954; "For Creative Daring", in *Sovetskaya muzyka* 7, 1955; "At a Concert of the Academic Russian Chorus", in *Sovetskaya muzyka* 7, 1956; "Hungarian Music" in *Sovetskaya muzyka* 5, 1957; "A Feast of Music" [on Aram Khatchaturian, in *Sovetskaya Kuttura*, 23 April 1959; "A Teacher and a Friend" [Yuri Shaporin], in *Sovetskaya muzyka*, 11, 1962; "Contemporary Opera: What Should It Be?", in *Moskovskaya pravda*, 21 July 1964; "Prokofiev's Music Is with Us", in *Literaturnaya Rossia*, 23 April 1971; "Variations on Contemporary Themes" [dialogue with Gennady Rozhdestvensky], in *Literaturnaya gazeta*, 7, 1973; *D. D. Shostakovich* [collection of articles]. Moscow, 1976; "Recollections of Nikolai Anosov", in *N. P. Anosov*, Moscow, 1978; many other articles and essays.

On Shchedrin: J. Lichatcheva, *Musikalni Teatr RS*, Moscow, 1977; W. Komissinsky, *O dramaturgicheskich principach tvorchestra RS*, Moscow, 1978; M. Tarakanov, *Tvorchestro RS*, Moscow, 1980; Hannelore Gerlach, *Zum Schaffen von RS*, Berlin, 1982; Istvan Balazs, "RS. Die Toten Seelen. Aspekte zum Problem der Operadramaturgie", in *Melos*, 1, 1988.

Rodion Shchedrin comments:
I would define my position in contemporary music as "post-

avant-garde". What does this mean? All avant-garde codes, with their ascetic constraints on the intonational, rhythmic and substantive content of the music, have exhausted their hold on both listeners and musicians; they have alienated potential enthusiasts for contemporary music and limited the range available to those who remain.

This is very annoying, expecially if we compare the interest of the public at large in contemporary literature, theatre, painting, cinema and architecture. For me, the post-avant-garde means that all constraints and restrictions are lifted. The birds are let out of the cage. It is essential to write as one feels . . . and yet, the resources of modern composition are enriched and multiplied by the great discoveries of the avant-garde, discoveries we have lived through, painfully experienced and stored away.

* * *

Rodion Shchedrin, whose wife is the celebrated ballerina Maya Plesetskaya, is himself a political ballet-dancer of no mean talent. His extraordinary career has seen him leaping from position to position as he has successfully attempted to reconcile a career as an official senior figure in the Union of Soviet Composers with that of an avant-garde composer with plenty of concerts in foreign lands. As a result his name has become a by-word for extra-musical manoeuvre. But an unsavoury reputation should not allow one to dismiss this man's music out-of-hand. He is a talented composer with a fluent and often theatrical streak, and if his music is not remarkable for depth and sincerity of feeling, it has the nonetheless commendable qualities of panache and colour.

Shchedrin has written prolifically and competently for the ballet and many of his collaborations with his wife have remained prize shows of the Bolshoi Theatre, such as the officially popular and accessible dance versions of the classics *Anna Karenina* and *The Seagull*. (However, when more closely examined, much of the music for the more recent of these ballets is in a clearly modernist idiom. Shchedrin has also written several operas including the widely performed *Dead Souls*, as well as a more recent quasi-Broadway musical for a Japanese department store. These, like the ballets, reveal a knack for dramatic effect and the setting of a scene or a mood.)

Although Shchedrin is probably first and foremost a theatrical composer, he has written a great deal for the concert hall, including three piano concertos which effectively reflect his own no-nonsense piano-playing, and a number of orchestral works. His early works, like those indeed of his more persecuted contemporaries, are written in a thoroughly orthodox Soviet idiom. But there is a certain secondhand tunefulness about pieces like *The Little Humpback Horse* which seems well-aimed towards the official concept of the popular. It is perhaps the first indication of Shchedrin's chameleon-like capacity to anticipate his audience's expectations, whether of Soviet officials or Western festival goers.

In the 1960s Shchedrin, like many of his contemporaries, began incorporating different styles of music, such as Neo-classicism and pop music, or, as in his Second Piano Concerto, jazz. But it was in the 1970s that Shchedrin found his personal synthesis. He owes much to Lutosławski and the other Polish composers, frequently employing the same sorts of heterophonic devices and having the same fondness for a single line. One of the best works in this idiom is the Third Piano Concerto, marked by a clear, witty and uncluttered sense of form and direction.

In more recent years Shchedrin has sometimes sacrificed clarity to a greater urge to experiment. If the results are unpredictable, Shchedrin's desire not repeat himself is impressive. *Self-Portrait*, for example, is a somewhat cloudy exercise in cinematic expressionism, while *The Geometry of Sound* is a piece of euphonious minimalism. In honour of Bach's Tricentenary Shchedrin wrote his *Musical Offering*, a vast and sprawling meditation for organ and instruments in a harmonic style approaching Schnittke at his most opaque. In all these recent pieces Shchedrin has still stuck to his underlying techniques. At the very least he is a composer with a remarkable sense of the boundaries of his ability. In that he is remarkably different from the other, far less talented official composers with whom his name has so often been linked.

—Gerard McBurney

SHCHETINSKY, Alexander. Ukrainian. Born in Kharkov, 22 June 1960. Educated at Kharkov Art Institute (composition under V. Borisov), 1978–83. Teacher of composition, children's Music School, Kharkov, 1982–90; member of Union of Composers, Soviet Union, since 1986; participant, Summer Courses for Young Composers, Kazimierz Dolny, Poland, 1990; participant, computer Music Course, Cracow, Poland, 1991; contributor to television and radio as music journalist. Recipient: main prize and special prize (for *Glossolalie*), Kazimierz Serocki, Composers' Competition, Poland, 1990. Mailing address: ul. Uborevicha 24–103, Kharlkov 310144, U.S.S.R.

Publisher: none.

Symphonies/orchestral:

Pro memoria (chamber orchestra) 1980.
Concerto for Cello and Orchestra 1982; first performed Kharkov, 1983.
Intersections (oboe, orchestra) 1988; first performed Kharkov, 1989.
Glossolalie (chamber orchestra) 1989; first performed Warsaw, 1990.

Chamber/instrumental:

Music (piano or organ or accordion or synthesizer) 1981, 1989.
Sonata (clarinet, piano) 1982.
Intermezzo (flute, piano) 1983.
Sonata (bayan/key button accordion) 1983; first performed Moscow, 1984.
Antiphons (cello, piano) 1983; first performed Kharkov, 1984.
Sumna pisnya/Sad Song (bayan) 1984; first performed Moscow, 1985.
Four Inventions (bayan/key button accordion) 1985; first performed Moscow, 1986.
Quintet (flute, oboe, clarinet, bassoon, horn) 1985–7.
Sonata (viola) 1985–7; first performed Minsk, 1988.
Suite (clarinet, piano) 1987–90.
Praise Ye the Name of the Lord (piano) 1988; first performed

London, 1989.
Cryptogram (vibraphone) 1989; first performed London, 1989.
Sonata (violin, piano) 1990.
Prayer for the Cup (piano) 1990.
Lamento (flute, oboe, clarinet, bassoon, horn, vibraphone, piano, violin, viola, cello) 1990.
On the Eve (brass quintet) 1990.
Way to Meditation (flute, clarinet, violin, cello, piano) 1990; first performed Amsterdam, 1991.
Romantic Music (flute, oboe, clarinet, bassoon, horn, trumpet, trombone, 2 percussion, harp, piano, violin, viola, cello, double bass) 1991.
String Quartet 1991.
Poco misterioso (bayan) 1991.

Vocal/choral:

From Pavlo Movchan's Poetry (cycle for baritone, piano) 1984.
Svet vo otcroveniye/Light to Lighten (sacred cantata for unaccompanied mixed chorus, 2 bells) 1989.
The Preacher's Word (soprano, string quartet; Ecclesiastes, Psalms 85, 86) 1991.

Other:

Near the Entrance (electronic) 1991.

PUBLICATIONS

By Shchetinksy: "Valentin Bibik's music", in *Composers of the Union Republics*, 7, 1991.

Alexander Shchetinsky comments:

I do not know why I write music. Perhaps what I am doing is trying to adhere to that which I find most precious in art. In concrete terms, that amounts to the careful and accurate handling of sound, as such. I like listening to sound, listening attentively to its inner life (its pitch, its rhythm, its timbre, etc); I like discovering its possibilities, its aspirations, what it is drawn to and what it repels. I do not like sound to be treated violently. I prefer it when an artist sets up a democratic regime in his work, rather than an authoritarian one. It seems to me that creativity, as a part of the Creation, and refracted through the prism of the composer's mind, should by no means be an excuse for the artist to demonstrate his technical or other skills. A higher goal exists and that is the unity of the artist with his Creator. For me, every good composition is a universe in miniature, or rather a fragment of the Universe, and has to submit to certain common laws. When I write music therefore, I try not to think about myself, but about God.

One cannot get away from European individualism, however. Having been brought up in the European tradition, we are doomed to swing like a pendulum between art as religious service, and art as self-expression. This oscillation gives our culture its particular intensity.

I am trying at the moment to understand the essence of Oriental culture. Its metaphysical and meditative qualities could breathe new life into us. But it is unlikely that we would be able to interpret and experience Oriental culture without fundamentally distorting it. That is something too difficult for someone from the West, because we would have to give up too much. The most important part of past cultures for me, therefore, is always going to be Western civilization with all its pluses and minuses.

I believe that European modernism and the avant-garde have not yet exhausted all their possibilities. I foresee some highly interesting results from their merging with the Slavic mentality. I hope that the new Ukrainian music will be able to integrate with Western achievements and become interesting to other nations.

* * *

Alexander Shchetinsky's formation as a composer occurred under the influence of the ideas of European musical universalism. He was never inspired by stylistic seclusion and national introversion, despite the fact that this ran exactly counter to what the cultural situation in the Soviet Union was fostering in musical composition, with conservatism and simplified folklore being encouraged, and American and European music of the second half of the 20th century remaining only poorly known. More accessible proved to be the Soviet avant-garde of the 1960s and 1970s, as well, to some degree, as the music of the Polish school. It was through these influences that the composer came to know many of the contemporary stylistic ideas.

Among the composers whom Shchetinsky has named as having influenced him are Shostakovich, Webern, Morton Feldman, and Aarvo Pärt. Treating music as a spiritual message rather than as a pure structure is one of Shostakovich's aspirations which Shchetinsky values highly. From Webern he has studied how to intensify intonation and give each sound full meaning. His interest in Feldman is for his meditativeness and beauty of phonation, while Pärt has attracted him with his unconventional attitude towards dominant aesthetic tendencies. Also close to Shchetinsky are the plasticity of Edison Denisov's form, Alfred Shnittke's gravitation towards spiritually meaningful themes, the paradoxicality of Sofia Gubaidulina's thinking, and the refined contemplativeness and aestheticism of the music of Valentin Silvestrov. Shchetinsky has acquired many principles from the compositions of the Kharkov composer Valentin Bibik, who has also exerted a major personal influence on him.

Nevertheless, in Shchetinsky's scores we rarely find any concrete influence in a pure form. He attempts to construct a language of his own, gravitating towards monostyle without, generally, accepting eclecticism as a concept, although he does occasionally use a stylistic mixture.

One of the composer's leading aesthetic ideas is that of a new spiritual music, arising at the intersection between various cult and genre traditions of Christianity. In his spiritual compositions we come across elements of stylization of cult melodies and their interpretation through the adoption of contemporary language. These works are unhurried in their development and distinguished by their prayerful absorption. In "Antyphons" and "Intersections" we sense a comparison of religious and secular cultures expressed in the dialogue of the linguistic systems—by the diatonic modality and the free atonality. Stylistically more even are *Praise Ye the Name of the Lord*, *Prayer for the Cup* for piano, and the vocal opuses *Light to Lighten* and *The Preacher's Word*. While the spiritual theme is dominant in these works, they are meant exclusively for concert performance and are not linked to divine service.

Another of Shchetinsky's important ideas, especially from the beginning of 1989, is the contemplation of musical sound, a meditative admiration for the material which actually produces sound. The form becomes finer and the musical thought comes across forcefully and laconically. We sense a tension of intonation that is romantic in the character of its expression.

Without adopting stylistic variegation the composer does, nevertheless, use a mixed technique. For example, the high-pitched arrangement in the Violin Sonata, *Glossolalie* and *Way to Meditation* blend both the overtone relationship of sounds and the dodecaphonic scale and the operation with the melodic structures. In *Praise Ye the Name of the Lord* there is a balancing between tonality, modality and atonality.

Rhythm in Shchetinsky's works is most often suggested by overcoming accentuation with the help of polyrhythm and the irrational division of musical units. The fragments where regular accentuation is preserved serve as a means of dramaturgical contrast in *Praise Ye the Name of the Lord*, *Lamento* and *Romantic Music*. The texture in certain of the works has been assiduously detailed to alternate with the aleatoric episodes. Such alternation in *Glossolalie* is an important dramaturgical instrument. The composer has assimilated the genre's diversity of meanings for himself. The specific genre definitions (for example, the Violin Sonata) seem openended enough, but as a rule they are most commonly replaced by the programme titles.

Shchetinsky's music is distinguished by its refined intellectualism, its contemplativeness and lyrical expressiveness, and its balance of concentration and latent energy.

—Aleksandr Grinberg

SHEFF, Robert (Nathan). Stage name "Blue" Gene Tyranny. American. Born in San Antonio, Texas, 1 January 1945. Educated: studied composition under Otto Wick and Frank Hughes; studied piano under Meta Hertwig and Rodney Hoare. Member, ONCE Festival Group, Ann Arbor, Michigan, 1962–70; technician and lecturer in keyboard and jazz improvisation, Mills College, Oakland, California, 1970–81; subsequently independent composer and performer. Recipient: BMI Student Composers Award, 1962. Mailing address: c/o Performing Artservices Inc, 325 Spring Street, New York, New York 10013, U.S.A.

Publisher: none.

Works:

How Things That Can't Exist May Exist (theatre music) 1958.
Ballad: A Method for Making Pathways (graphic score for 1–40 sound sources) 1960.
Sonata (piano) 1962.
Just Walk on In (performance piece) 1965.
A Method for Discovering (and Inventing) Music in Your Daily Life (improvisational score) 1967.
Now That I Am 66 Years Old, A Retired Railroad Engineer and at the End of My Rope (film and score) 1968.
Portraits (score to film by G. Manuypelli) 1968.
Live and Let Live (video, live electronics, improvisation) 1972.
Remembering (voice, electronics) 1974.
My Song (score to film by Mary Ashley) 1974.
33 Yoyo Tricks (score to film by D. White) 1976.
David Kopay: Portrait (unspecified instrumentation) 1976.
Perfect Lives (Private Parts) (incidental music to video opera by Robert Ashley) 1977.
Harvey Milk: Portrait (tape) 1978.
The White Night Riot (tape, dancers ad lib) 1979.
The Country Boy Dog Concert for Improvisors and Electronics (unspecified instrumentation; also arranged as *Variations* for soloists and chamber orchestra) 1980.
The Intermediary (improvisation; also arranged for electronics, computer, piano ad lib) 1981.
Le Chant de la rue du poulet qui chante (electric keyboard) 1981.
The World's Greatest Piano Player (electric keyboard) 1981.
Music for Dance 1983–6.
Letter from Home (cantata) 1986.

* * *

The retiring composer Robert Sheff meets his public in the extravagant persona of "Blue" Gene Tyranny. Together, they represent a significant presence on the contemporary new music/performance scene. Born symbolically on the first day of the first year of what was to become (as the result of experiments being finalised not so far from San Antonio) the "post-war age", Sheff concentrates many of the central questions and issues of contemporary composition and performance. Though he spent a fruitful decade at the innovative Mills College in Oakland, Sheff has largely avoided academic entanglements and his professional resumé more closely resembles a rock musician's than a "serious" composer. However, the existence of "Blue" Gene adds a Mr Hyde dimension to Sheff's patiently thoughtful exploration of natural and physical phenomena, language, performance gestures and multi-media creativity.

Privately trained in piano and composition, Sheff won a BMI student composers award with an essentially academic sonata for piano. He was, though, already involved in theatrical and improvisational activity, and has only rarely written for conventional forces since, preferring to devise ephemeral and largely improvisatory scores for mixed-media settings. Powerfully interested by the nascent revolution in popular music, Sheff incorporated elements of rock and southern country styles into his work, notably *The Country Boy Dog Concert / Variations*. This approach is also evident in his later solo pieces for electric keyboards, like *The World's Greatest Piano Player*.

Much concerned with the processes of time, Sheff wrote what he describes as a "time travel piece" *Remembering*, which explores the "internal language" of cognition and memory, with all its shifts and sudden gaps and absences. *Remembering*, subsequently incorporated into a video sequence by the performance artist and singer Mary Ashley, is the clearest objectification of Sheff's understanding of language as the highest and most refined constituent of musical composition. In this regard, he considerably influenced Ashley's composer husband Robert Ashley, who had been a fellow member of the influential ONCE Group in Michigan. It was Sheff, in the Liberace-meets-Elvis-in-Hades persona of "Blue" Gene who provided the incidental music to Ashley's ambitious video opera for television *Perfect Lives (Private*

Parts). His rambling bar-room score, largely improvised, is a perfect correlative to the fractured imagery of Ashley's "libretto".

Active in the gay community, and a member of the Society for Gay and Lesbian Composers, Sheff has developed interesting insights into the relationships between homosexuality and creativity, and this is a current that runs through his compositional work. His "portraits"—*à la* Virgil Thomson—of friends and acquaintances are both moving and acute, most particularly that of the murdered Californian public official Harvey Milk, whom Sheff memorialised in a remarkable tape piece.

There are few figures who more ambitiously straddle the ever-widening gap between popular and "serious" composition and performance. Sheff's contribution is remarkably difficult to pin down, because it is not limited to an orderly sequence of opus numbers, but it is unquestionably considerable.

—Russell Kane

SHERLAW JOHNSON, Robert. British/English. Born in Sunderland, County Durham, 21 May 1932. Educated at Gosforth Grammar School, Newcastle-upon-Tyne; King's College, University of Durham, 1950–3, B.A, B.Mus., 1959; Royal Academy of Music, London, 1953–7, licentiate in piano, associate; further composition study under Nadia Boulanger and Jacques Fevrier, and some classes under Olivier Messiaen, Paris, 1957–8; University of Leeds, M.A., 1970; University of Oxford, M.A., 1970. Married Rachel Maria Clarke, 28 July 1959; 2 daughters and 3 sons. Concert and recording pianist (mainly 20th-century repertoire, but also Liszt); assistant lecturer in music, University of Leeds, 1961–3; director of music, Bradford Girls' Grammar School, Yorkshire, 1963–5; lecturer in music, University of York, 1965–70; university lecturer in music, University of Oxford, and tutorial fellow, Worcester College, Oxford, from 1970; vice-chair, Composers' Guild of Great Britain, 1979–81; visiting professor of composition, Eastman School of Music, Rochester, New York, 1985. Recipient: Charles W. Black Award for composition, 1957, 1959; Radcliffe Award for composition, 1969. Mailing address: Malton Croft, Woodlands Rise, Stonesfield, Oxford OX7 2PL, England.

Publisher: Oxford University Press.

Symphonies/orchestral:

Piano Concerto 1983.
Clarinet Concerto 1986; first performed Oxford, 1986.
Sinfonietta concertante 1989; first performed Birmingham, 19 January 1990.

Chamber/instrumental:

Sonata No 1 (piano) 1963; first performed Attingham Park, Shropshire, 1963. Recorded Argo ZRG 694.
String Quartet No 1 1966; first performed Stour Valley, Kent, 1966.
Sonata No 2 (piano) 1967; first performed Harrogate, Yorkshire, 1967. Recorded EMI ASC 2551.
Seven Short Pieces (piano) 1968; first performed Liverpool, 1969. Recorded ARG ZRG 694.
String Quartet No 2 1969; first performed Brighton, Sussex, 1969. Recorded Argo ZRG 622.
Astereogenesis (piano) 1973; first performed Oxford, 1973..
Quintet (clarinet, violin, viola, cello, piano) 1974; first performed Lancaster, 1975.
Sonata (alto flute, cello) 1975; first performed London, 1975.
Sonata No 3 (piano) 1976; first performed Norwich, Norfolk, 1976. Recorded ECR 001.
Homage to Haydn (piano) 1982.
Projections (flute, viola, guitar, piano) 1985; first performed Oxford, 1985.
Cantilena (clarinet) 1987; first performed London, January 1988.
Encounters (clarinet, string quartet, piano) 1988; first performed London, 28 October 1988.
Intersections (viola, piano) 1988–9; first performed London, 13 January 1989.

Vocal/choral:

Amores (soprano, clarinet, piano) 1965; first performed London, 1965.
The Resurrection of Feng-Huang (soprano, unaccompanied mixed voices) 1968; first performed London, 1969.
The Praises of Heaven and Earth (soprano, electronic tape, piano) 1969; first performed London, 1969.
Incarnatio (unaccompanied SSA and TB choruses) 1970.
Green Whispers of Gold (voice, electronic tape) 1971; first performed Oxford, 1971.
Christus Resurgens (unaccompanied SATB chorus) 1972; first performed London, 1972.
Anthem for the Trinity (SSA chorus, organ) 1971.
Carmina vernalia (soprano, flute, oboe, clarinet, horn, trumpet, trombone, piano, violin, viola, cello) 1972, revised 1980; first performed London, 1972.
Festival Mass of the Resurrection (SATB chorus, small orchestra or organ) 1974, revised 1986.
Anglorum feriae (soprano, tenor, chorus, 2 oboes, 2 trumpets, timpani, strings; Peele) 1977; first performed London, 1977.
The Manger (SATB chorus, organ; Southwell) 1981.
Veritas veritatem (vocal sexet) 1981; first performed Spode, Staffordshire 1981.
Muniments (baritone, piano) 1984; first performed Wales, 1984.
Hymn to the Seasons (soprano, clarinet, piano) 1990; first performed Oxford, 30 November 1990.

Opera:

The Lambton Worm (11 solo roles, chorus, orchestra; Ridler) 1978; first performed Oxford, 1978.

Other:

Kyisi (Fairlight CMI/electronic) 1982.
Fractal in Ab (Atari computer, Yamaha TX812) 1990.
Other liturgical music.

PUBLICATIONS

By Sherlaw Johnson: *Messiaen*, 1975, 1989; "The European Tradition", in *How Music Works*, London, 1981; "Olivier Messiaen and Pierre Boulez", in *Heritage of Music: Music in the Twentieth Century IV*, Oxford, 1989; "Analysis and the Composer", in *A Compendium of Contemporary Musical Thought*, London, 1991.

On Sherlaw Johnson: Peter Aston, "RSJ", in *Musical Times*, March 1968.

Robert Sherlaw Johnson comments:

My early work was to some extent technically influenced by Messiaen, Boulez, Stockhausen and Varèse. I used serial methods to some extent in the mid-1960s but had abandoned these by the early 1970s. This did not entail a return to tonality in any traditional sense, although my work tends to be structured around certain "key" notes, which are often defined at specific registers. To give a somewhat oversimplified example: a movement, or part of a movement, may have middle C as a central note, for instance, other Cs being excluded from an equal role.

Although part of my work as a musician has been given to piano recitals, only a small proportion of my total output is for piano solo. In addition to my mainstream composition, I have composed functional pieces for use in the new Roman liuturgy (in English) and have been influenced to some extent, in these and other religious works, by both Western and Eastern chant.

* * *

Robert Sherlaw Johnson has travelled over a wide musical orbit, initially studying the piano and composition. In Paris he attended some of Messiaen's classes and like Messiaen, Sherlaw Johnson's music is profoundly radical, serious in intent, and often has a deeply religious feeling.

He has written several works for the Music Week of Spode House, a Roman Catholic conference centre in Staffordshire. Some of these are specifically liturgical such as his *Festival Mass of the Resurrection*. Having been appointed to a music fellowship at Worcester College, Oxford (two previous fellows were also composers—Edmund Rubbra and Kenneth Leighton) Sherlaw Johnson composed an *In nomine* for piano for Rubbra. By coincidence, Sherlaw Johnson has something in common with Rubbra in choice of religious and mystical subjects (though not in musical style). Sherlaw Johnson has often been the piano exponent in first performances of his own compositions.

Sherlaw Johnson is a composer who has specialised in works for small groups of performers. He has not succumbed to the temptation to be too prolific but has produced only 59 opus numbers over 20 years—an average of about three works a year. Much of his music comprises settings of words, many religious, for solo voice or chamber choir.

Among his works is his joyful *The Resurrection of Feng-Huang* for unaccompanied voices, including spoken, chant-like sections, whose oriental subject and asceticism suggests the influence of Messiaen.

In the mystical, rapturous *The Praises of Heaven and Earth*, a setting of a psalm for soprano and piano, the addition of a tape to the performers gives a wider range of possibilities. This work was written for Noelle Barker who has frequently been the soloist in the first performances of his compositions.

Noelle Barker again features as the soloist in *Carmina vernalia* for soprano and chamber orchestra 1972, revised in 1980. Latin titles often give contemporary music a strikingly detached and often hieratic quality. Early on in his career Sherlaw Johnson incorporated Latin titles or texts in several works associated with the Roman Catholic liturgy such as "Liturgiae redemptionis nostrae", "Veni sancte spiritus", "Sedit angelus", "Christus resurgens", Anglorum feriae and Veritas veritatem.

The opera *The Lambton Worm*, based on a famous folk legend, reflects Sherlaw Johnson's personal links with North-eastern England. (Lambton is the family name of the earldom of Durham.) The opera was produced at Oxford University Opera Club in 1978 and represents a new departure into theatre music. This was perhaps a natural progression since Sherlaw Johnson's music has a vividly imaginative quality. The OUOC has a tradition of performing new or unfamiliar operas.

He has made a welcome addition to the relatively sparse repertory of English piano concertos. His *Sinfonietta concertante* suggests a reversion to the early classical form for chamber orchestra. He is a profoundly thoughtful and serious-minded composer.

—Michael Dawney

SHINOHARA, Makoto. Japanese. Born in Osaka, 10 December 1931. Educated at Tokyo Geijitsu Daigaku [Tokyo National University of Fine Arts and Music] (piano under Kazuko Yasukawa, conducting under Akeo Watanabe, composition under Tomojiro Ikenouchi), 1952; Ecole National Supérieur de Musique, Paris (composition under Tony Aubin, musical aesthetics under Olivier Messiaen, counterpoint and fugue under Simone Plé-Caussade, harmony under Pierre Revel, conducting under Louis Fourrestier), 1954–9; studied concrete music, Groupe de Recherches Musicale, French Radio, 1959–60; Hochschule für Musik, Munich, and researcher, Siemens electronic studio, Munich, 1960–2; Hochschule für Musik, Cologne (further composition study under Bernd Alois Zimmermann, electronic music under Gottfried Michael Koenig), 1962–5; further composition study under Karlheinz Stockhausen, Cologne, 1963–5; further research in electronic music, Columbia-Princeton Electronic Music Center, New York City, 1971–2; further research in electronic music, electronic music studio, Japan National Radio (NHK), 1974. Assistant to Karlheinz Stockhausen, 1965; technical researcher, Institute of Sonology, Utrecht, 1965–6, 1973, 1975–6, 1978–80; DAAD artist in residence, Berlin, 1966; visiting professor in Japanese Music and electronic music, Faculty of Music, McGill University, Montreal, 1978. Recipient: composition prize (for *Sonata* for violin and piano), Paris Conservatoire, 1958; also prizes for aesthetics, fugue, counterpoint and harmony; prize (for *Consonancew*), International Composition Competition, Rome, 1968. Mailing address: c/o Yukogakuen, Mukaaigahara

17, Fukakusa, Kyoto, Japan 612; or c/o Osada, Yarai-cho 1, Shinjuku-ku, Tokyo, Japan 162; or Gildstraat 149, NL-3572 EM Utrecht, The Netherlands.

Publishers: Leduc, Paris; Moeck, Germany; Gerig/Breitkopf, Germany; Schott, London; Zen-on, Tokyo; Ongaku-no-tomo-sha, Tokyo; The Japan Federation of Composers.

Symphonies/orchestral:

Rondo 1953.
Solitude 1961; first performed Utrecht, 1964.
Vision II 1970; first performed Tokyo, 1970.

Chamber/instrumental:

Trio d'anches (oboe, clarinet, bassoon) 1956; first performed Berlin, 1974.
Sonata (violin, piano) 1958; first performed Paris, 1958. Recorded Victor (Japan) VX 105.
Kassouga (flute, piano) 1959; first performed Paris, 1960. Recorded Golden Crest RE 7048; Sheridan Music Press SMP 209.
Trois Pièces concertantes (flute, piano) 1959.
Obsession (oboe, piano) 1960. Recorded CBS S 34 61142; EMI 5 c 053 24 585.
Alternance (percussion ensemble) 1962; first performed (incomplete) Darmstadt, 17 July 1962; first complete performance New York City, 5 March 1963. Recorded Philips 836.991 DSY; Philips SFI 8538.
Tendance (piano) 1963, revised 1969. Recorded Crown SWS 1–2; RCA SRA 2941.
Consonance (flute, horn, vibraphone, marimba, harp, cello) 1967; first performed Berlin, 1968.
Fragmente (tenor recorder) 1968; first performed Tokyo, 1970. Recorded Principal PLP 1029; BIS LP 48; CBS 71102.
Reflexion (oboe) 1970.
Relations (flute, piano) 1970; first performed New York City, 1971.
Rencontre (percussion, tape) 1972.
Kyudo/In Quest of Enlightenment (shakuhachi) 1973; first performed Shiraz/Persepolis, Iran, 1973.
Egalisation (piccolo, flute, alto flute, oboe, cor anglais, clarinet, bass clarinet, bassoon, contrabassoon, horn, trumpet, trombone, tuba, piano, celeste, harpsichord, harp, guitar, vibraphone, marimba, percussion, violin, viola, cello, double bass) 1975; first performed Paris, 1976.
Relation (flute, piano) 1976.
Elevation (organ) 1976; first performed Zurich, 1976.
Liberation (20 strings) 1977; first performed Shiraz/Persepolis, Iran, 1977.
Nagre/Flow (shamisen) 1981; first performed Haarlem, 1982. Recorded Victor SJL 2401 A.
Jushichigen-no-umare/Birth of the Bass Koto (jushichigen) 1981; first performed Tokyo, 1981. Recorded Camerata CMT 1101.
Play (flute, alto flute, oboe, clarinet, bass clarinet, bassoon, horn, trumpet, trombone) 1982; first performed Kusatsu, 1982.
Turns (violin, koto; or violin solo) 1983; first performed Amsterdam, 1983.
Passage (stereo amplified bass flute; or flute or alto flute) 1986; first performed London, 1986.
Evolution (cello) 1986; first performed Tokyo, 1987.
Cooperation (nokan, shakuhachi, hichikiri, shō, kito, shamisen, biwa, kokyu, cor anglais, clarinet, trumpet, trombone, percussion, piano, violin, cello) 1990.

Vocal/choral:

Tayutai/Fluctuation (1 or 2 voice(s), koto, percussion) 1972; first performed Berlin, 1973. Recorded Victor KVX 1102.
Tabiyuki/On Travel (mezzo-soprano, flute, oboe, clarinet, bassoon, horn, trumpet, trombone, percussion, violin, viola, cello, double bass; Basho) 1984; first performed Montreal, 1984.

Other:

Visions I (4-channel tape) 1964; first performed Utrecht, 1966.
Memoires (4-channel tape) 1966; first performed Hilversum, 1966. Recorded Philips 836.993 DSY.
Personnage (mime, lights, tape; or tape alone) 1973; first performed Utrecht, 1973.
Broadcasting (stereo electronic music tape) 1974; first performed Bourges, 1974.
City Visit (slides, tape; or tape alone) 1979; first performed Utrecht, 1980.

PUBLICATIONS

By Shinohara: articles in *Ongaku-geijutsu*, *Asahi-shinbun*, *TranSonic*, *Interface*, *Neue Zeitung für Musik*.

On Shinohara: Kuniharu Akiyama, in *Nihon-no-sakkyokuka-tachi* [Japanese Composers], Tokyo, 1979; Leigh Landy, "An Analysis of *Tayutai*", in *Interface*, 16, 1987; Satoru Takaku, "List of S's Works, Their Recordings and Performances in Japan", in *Volksrant and Trouw*, The Netherlands, 1989.

* * *

One of Makoto Shinohara's first compositions, the *Rondo* for orchestra, was composed during his studies at the Tokyo Arts University. Though it was written in the key of F major, tonality was veiled by a complicated harmonic and melodic structure. Until 1958 he did not proceed much beyond the academic style he was taught in Tokyo and, from 1954 on, at the Paris Conservatoire. His *Sonata* for violin and piano showed him under influence of Stravinsky, Bartók, and his teacher Messiaen. At that time he came to realize that he had not known anything about avant-garde music, which then reached its climax with Boulez's Third Piano Sonata, Cage's *Concert for Piano and Orchestra*, and Stockhausen's *Gruppen* for three orchestras.

By frequently visiting Darmstadt, the West German center of serial and aleatory music, Shinohara updated his musical consciousness and turned his compositional work into a new direction. A first result of these efforts was *Solitude* for orchestra in which he used charts and lists for a serially determined organization of the music. *Alternance* for six percussion players established Shinohara's aleatory style, which did not loosen the composer's control like Cage's indeterminacy, but rather followed Boulez's example. The players could select the order of structural parts within restrictions given by the composer. This composition was characterized by a great richness of timbres, strong dynamic contrasts, and gave the impression of a sensitive listening to the instrumental possibilities.

The piano composition *Tendance* consisted of 21 parts

divided into six parts and applies rules of macro-aleatory (the arbitrary order of formal sections rather than single notes) to the procedures of performance. The title alluded to the tendency of composition, which was then clearly defined by Shinohara after several years of search. *Consonance* for flute, horn, vibraphone, marimba, harp and cello refined the aleatory concept by combining determined and indeterminate movements of sounds within a dedicated set of "if . . . then . . . "–directions to the performers. Ten structural sequences can be brought into any order with the exception of the beginning and the end parts. The simplicity and delicate shortness of this work, which reminded Western listeners of Japanese haiku poems, can also be recognized in *Fragmente* for tenor recorder. Its 14 particles provide insights into the different sound possibilities of the instrument which sometimes sounds like electronic music or like a *shakuhachi* (Japanese bamboo flute).

Vision II for orchestra gave up aleatory in favour of a freely composed alternation of different techniques of composition. Glissandos of the strings, chromatic lines in the wind instruments, chaotic punctual structures or chordal accents are clearly organized, first successively, then simultaneously (post-serialism is the appropriate name for this style). *Rencontre* for percussionist and tape music contrasted Shinohara's controlled way of composing by a verbal notation for the percussionist. The performer uses hundreds of different instruments, mainly folk instruments, and interacts with the sounds from the tape which include percussion sounds themselves. The electronic compositions by Shinohara like *Memoires* and *City Visit* did not restrict themselves to the asceticism of the other compositions but the composer clearly sees their background in the elegance of Japanese Noh theatre.

Japanese critics see Shinohara's compositions for Japanese instruments as his main strength. In *Tayutai / Fluctuation* for *koto* (long zither) the instrument is played with unconventional techniques like using stones as plectrum or the player's responding to the instrument with interjections of normal speech. This preference for unconventional playing techniques is also eminent in more recent works like *Passage* for stereo amplified bass flute and *Evolution* for cello.

—Rolf Klein

SHOOT, Vladislav. Russian. Born in the Soviet Union, 1941. Educated at Gnesin Musical-Pedagogic Institute (composition under N. Peiko). Editor, Sovetskii kompozitor, 1967–82; freelance composer, since 1982. Mailing address: ulitsa Generala Ermolova, dom 2, kv.214, 121293 Moscow, U.S.S.R.

Publisher: VAAP, Moscow.

Symphonies / orchestral:

Sinfonia da camera No 3 (flute, oboe, 2 string groups, percussion) 1978.
Romantic Messages (bassoon, strings, flute, prepared piano) 1979. Recorded Melodiya S 10 15747 8.
Largo-Sinfonia (chamber orchestra, organ) 1981.
Warum? 1986.
Ex animo 1988.

Chamber / instrumental:

Cuckoo Ditties (children's album of violin and piano pieces) 1969.
Youth Album (violin, piano) 1971.
Sinfonia da camera No 1 (4 cellos, double bass, timpani) 1973.
Silhouettes (11 piano miniatures) 1973.
Talyanochka (piano piece for children) 1974.
Sinfonia da camera No 2 (flute, oboe, clarinet, saxophone, bassoon, viola, cello, double bass) 1975.
Ten Children's Pieces (horn, piano) 1976.
Sonata breve (flute) 1977.
Trio (bassoon, cello, percussion) 1978.
Solo per fagotto (bassoon) 1978.
Metamorphoses (alto saxophone, harp, double bass, percussion) 1979.
Two Lyrical Miniatures (flute, piano) 1980.
Trio (2 clarinets, bass clarinet) 1982.
Parable (percussion ensemble) 1983.
Espressivo (flute, oboe, violin, cello, piano) 1984.
A Little Suite (children's pieces for alto saxophone(s)) 1987.
A Little Partita (alto saxophone piece for children) 1987.
Scherzo (alto saxophone piece for children) 1987.
Four Versions (bassoon, string quartet) 1990.

Vocal / choral:

Six Poems (tenor, piano; Gorodetsky) 1967.
Four Poems (high voice, piano; Gorodetsky) 1970.
Gleam of the Light (medium voice, piano; Pasternak) 1988.

Vladislav Shoot comments:

The combination and interplay of something new and of something easily recognizable, of unreal and real, imaginary and practical have always appealed to me. Learning to master new means and systems led as if dialectically to a nostalgia for tonal expressiveness. The two strands come together in different proportions in my works. Sometimes, especially in the pieces marked by neo-romantic tendencies, the pseudo-tonal systems that emerge are actually based on a foundation of polyserial clusters.

* * *

Vladislav Shoot is on the surface the great eccentric among the middle generation of Soviet composers. His works are startling for their wilful oddness, their apparently misshapen and sometimes even ugly forms, their absurd contradictions of style and syntax. Yet behind the surface of Shoot's music is a highly personal and unified vision, as joltingly unexpected in the Russian world to which he belongs as it would be in the West, where, as yet, his music is hardly known. Shoot's distinctiveness may be best observed in the cycle of orchestral works which leads from his *Sinfonia da camera No 1* of 1973 through to his symphony *Ex animo*.

The former is scored for the peculiar combination of four cellos, double bass and timpani. The atmosphere is by turns mournful and ludicrous, the images veering wildly between obvious evocations and religious chant and fragments that sound like the purest doodling. This feeling of uncertainty and the accidental was evidently very important to Shoot at this period. However, when examined closely the apparently uncertain turns out often to be quite deliberate. A closely-wrought handling of connections of motive, voice and proportion all the time hold the piece together.

The same atmosphere pervades *Sinfonia da camera No 2*,

scored for five woodwinds, viola, cello and double bass. Here a first movement suggestive of Schoenberg at his most awkward is suddenly cut off by a scherzo of quite a different sort, in a sort of Stravinskian manner but severely hobbled to avoid momentum. There then follow two long movements, both heterophonic in character and vague in their absence of harmonic or rhythmic definition. A fifth movement is a microscopic interlude for string trio alone (marked lagrimose), while the sixth takes the heterophonic discoveries of the third and fourth and builds them into a dreamlike processional that seems to go on for the rest of the piece.

Sinfonia da camera No 3 brings these ideas into much sharper focus. It is scored for two antiphonal groups of strings, a single flute and oboe and percussion. After a Prologue dramatising the spacial lay-out of these instruments, the first movement is a lengthy adagio, in which typical passages of heterophonic vagueness are interrupted and pinned down by choric writing for the strings of considerable beauty. A second movement must be one of Shoot's most active and fluent pieces of composition up to this point in his career. But here too the fast music is gradually interrupted and brought to a halt by the chorus of strings. An epilogo returns us to the opening.

Largo-Sinfonia, scored for a large ensemble, is a further advance in Shoot's range and articulacy. This work is particularly impressive for its considerable mastery of unusual colour, especially in its mixtures of instruments and extraordinary combinations of different chord structures, and for its ability to galvanise such heterogeneous ideas and materials into a real feeling of an organically unfolding structure.

But Shoot's most impressive work, and the turning point in his development, is the Symphony for large orchestra, *Ex animo*. In *Ex animo* the oddities of Shoot's harmonic language, the wrinkles in his melodies and unexpected leaps and turns of texture take their place within a wider scheme, a passionately felt and almost extrovertly driven symphonic utterance. *Ex animo* makes a deep impression in the concert hall and deserves wide performance.

A number of other smaller-scale works in Shoot's output also deserve attention. In particular the solo pieces for bassoon and flute are attractive, as well as the trio for clarinets, demonstrating Shoot's imaginative grasp of how to write for woodwinds. The chamber orchestral *Romantic Messages*, with its witty and affectionate handling of a very famous moment from Mozart's music, is testimony too to the warmth and humanity that lie under the apparent surface whimsy of Shoot's music.

—Gerard McBurney

SIMPSON, Robert (Wilfred Levick). British/English. Born in Leamington Spa, Warwickshire, 2 March 1921. Educated at Westminster City School, London; began and subsequently abandoned medical training; studied harmony and counterpoint under Herbert Howells, London, 1941–4; University of Durham, D.Mus., 1951. Married to Angela Musgrave. Music producer, BBC, 1951–80. Recipient: Carl Nielsen Gold Medal, Denmark, 1956; Kilenyi Medal of Honour, Bruckner Society of America, 1962; *Gramophone* award (for *Symphony No 9*). Fellow, Royal Astronomical Society. Mailing address: Stochain, Killeton, near Camp, Tralee, County Kerry, Ireland.

Publishers: Lengnick; Faber; Boosey & Hawkes; Rosehill, Beaconsfield, Buckinghamshire.

Symphonies/orchestral:

Symphony No 1 1951; first performed Copenhagen, 11 June 1953. Recorded HMV HQM 1010.
Allegro deciso (string) 1954.
Symphony No 2 1956; first performed Cheltenham, Gloucestershire, 16 July 1957.
Canzona (brass) 1958.
Symphony No 3 1962; first performed Birmingham, 14 March 1963. Recorded Unicorn Kanchana UNS 225.
Piano Concerto 1967; first performed Cheltenham, Gloucestershire, 14 July 1967.
Energy (brass band) 1971.
Symphony No 4 1972; first performed Manchester, 26 April 1973.
Symphony No 5 1972; first performed London, 3 May 1973.
Symphony No 6 1977; first performed London, 8 April 1979. Recorded Hyperion KA 66280.
Symphony No 7 1977; first performed Liverpool, 20 October 1984. Recorded Hyperion KA 66280; CDA 66280.
Volcano (brass band) 1979.
Symphony No 8 1981; first performed London, 10 November 1982.
Suite: The Four Temperaments (brass band) 1982.
Variations on a theme of Carl Nielsen 1983.
Introduction and Allegro on a Bass by Max Reger (brass band) 1986.
Symphony No 9 1986; first performed Poole, Dorset, 8 April 1987. Recorded Hyperion KA 66299.
Symphony No 10 1988.
Vortex (brass band) 1989.
Flute Concerto 1989.
Bach Variations (strings) 1991.
Symphony No 11 1991.

Chamber/instrumental:

Sonata (piano) 1946.
Variations and Finale on a Theme of Haydn (piano) 1948.
String Quartet No 1 1952. Recorded Hyperion CDA 66419.
String Quartet No 2 1953. Recorded Hyperion CDA 66386.
String Quartet No 3 1954. Recorded Hyperion CDA 66376.
Variations and Fugue (recorder, string, quartet) 1959; unpublished.
Trio (clarinet, cello, piano) 1967.
Quintet (clarinet, string quartet) 1968. Recorded Unicorn Kanchana UKCD 2028.
String Quartet No 4 1973. Recorded Hyperion CDA 66419.
String Quartet No 5 1974. Recorded Hyperion CDA 66386.
String Quartet No 6 1975. Recorded Hyperion CDA 66376.
Quartet (horn, violin, cello, piano) 1975.
String Quartet No 7 1977. Recorded Hyperion CDA 66117.
String Quartet No 8 1979; first performed Uxbridge, Middlesex, 21 June 1980. Recorded Hyperion CDA 66117.
Sonata (2 pianos) 1979.
Quintet (clarinet, bass clarinet, string trio) 1981.
String Quartet No 9 (variations and fugue on a theme by Haydn) 1982; first performed London, 6 October 1982. Recorded Hyperion A 66127.
String Quartet No 10 (For Peace) 1983. Recorded Hyperion CDA 66225.
String Quartet No 11 1984. Recorded Hyperion CDA 66225.
Sonata (violin, piano) 1984.

Trio (horn, violin, piano) 1984.
Eppur si muove (ricercar and passacaglia for organ) 1985.
String Quartet No 12 1987. Recorded Hyperion.
String Quintet 1987.
String Trio: Prelude, Adagio and Fugue 1987.
Trio (violin, cello, piano) 1988–9.
String Quartet No 13 1989.
String Quartet No 14 1990.
Variations on a Theme by Beethoven (piano) 1990.
String Quartet No 15 1991.

Vocal/choral:

Meddia morte in vita sumus (unaccompanied SATB chorus) 1975.
Tempi (unaccompanied SATB chorus) 1987.

Other:

The Pretenders (incidental music to Ibsen) 1965.
Samson Agonistes (incidental music to Milton) 1975.

PUBLICATIONS

By Simpson: *Carl Nielson, Symphonist,* London, 1952, revised 1979; *Bruckner and the Symphony*, London, 1960; *Sibelius and Nielsen*, London, 1965; *The Essence of Bruckner*, London 1966, 1978; (editor) *The Symphony*, Harmondsworth, Essex, 1966, 1967, 1969, 1972; *The Beethoven Symphonies*, London, 1970; "Symphonies", in *The Listener*, 89, 1973; *The Proms and Natural Justice: A Plan for Renewal*, London, 1981; numerous articles in musical journals.

On Simpson: H. Ottaway, "RS's First Symphony", in *Musical Times*, 97, 1956; *RS: Essays*, edited by E. Johnson, London, 1971.

Robert Simpson comments:

My work aims at recapturing the momentum to be found in classical music and at direct human communication. It is not "atonal" and most of it is not (in the classical sense) "tonal", but seeks to release the energy locked in the basic intervals and resonances. This, too, is an essentially human rather than academic aim. I have been described as "an avant-garde radical" and I suppose that hits the nail on the head. I have no interest in trends or fashions.

* * *

Although a composer from the outset, Robert Simpson first came to public notice as a scholar; his special interest in Bach, the Viennese classics, Bruckner, Nielsen and Sibelius gave him considerable knowledge of composition which has deeply affected his whole outlook. But he is essentially an artist first and a theorist second, with much greater insights into music than are vouchsafed to most people. Many of these insights are enshrined in his books and articles. In addition, Simpson has spent much of his working life promoting neglected masterpieces and unjustly underrated composers: it is owing to his efforts that the works of, for example, Bruckner and Nielsen are now in the standard repertoire. A watershed in Simpson's life came when he resigned his post at the BBC following dissatisfaction with its cultural policies: since then he has dedicated most of his time to composition, an activity he now feels more valuable than analytical essay-writing. It is not surprising that the public began almost immediately to be acutely aware of him as a composer: the distinctive characteristic of his writing and broadcasting—to communicate complex musical processes so that the lay-person might understand them—was apparent in his own music. Recordings and performances of Simpson's music began to multiply, culminating in a prestigious *Gramophone* award for the recording of his *Symphony No 9*.

Though one can find traces of the influence of—and, indeed, sometimes deliberate, if brief quotations from—Haydn, Bruckner and Neilsen in Simpson's music, one cannot maintain that he imitates any of these composers, yet the influences have affected him profoundly. "Energy" is a word that constantly crops up in his discussion of music: he much admires the muscular rhythmic control of the Viennese classics, pointing out that most contemporary composers have lost the ability to handle the groundswell of rhythm in this way. In a similar fashion he finds himself in sympathy with Nielsen's remark that music is nothing unless it has a "current": Simpson is a pacifist humanitarian and while this makes him pessimistic about the future of the human race, it nevertheless results in life-affirming music. He believes passionately that even if the future seems hopeless, the artist must behave positively. This causes him to pursue the idea of growth in his music—the same kind of growth found in the symphonic processes of Beethoven and Sibelius, expressed in his own individual language. He has been consistently absorbed by the possibilities of large-scale tonality, and believes it to be a fundamental resource that is far from exhausted. In the 1980s he began to concentrate on the interacting resonances of intervals for the generation of structural tensions.

Most of Simpson's output is instrumental (he has not so far produced much vocal music): the backbone is found in string quartets (15 to date) and symphonies (11 to date), in which fields he is one of the leading composers of the 20th century. There is great variety of form and character in these works—no two are structurally alike, or even similar in feeling. In contrast to the relatively short and somewhat classical Second Symphony is the massive Ninth Symphony—the longest Western work ever written over a single basic pulse. Contrasting with the single-movement Seventh Quartet is the almost hour-long Ninth; since this latter, subtitled "*Variations and Fugue on a Theme by Haydn*", is based on a theme whose second-half is a mirror version of the first, each variation is also *al rovescio*.

Simpson's early experiences as a brass player have led him to write expertly for brass bands, and each of his handful of works for this medium has enjoyed considerable acclaim in the brass band world from its very first appearance.

—Lionel Pike

SIMS, Ezra. American. Born in Birmingham, Alabama, 16 January 1928. Educated at Birmingham Conservatory of Music, 1945–8; Birmingham Southern College, B.A., 1947; Yale University School of Music, New Haven, Connecticut (under Quincy Porter), B. Mus., 1952; U.S. Army Language School (Chinese), 1953; Mills College, Oakland, California (under Leon Kirchner and Darius Milhaud), M.A., 1956; Berkshire Music Center, Tanglewood, Massachusetts, 1960. "General dogsbody", programmer and music cataloguer,

Loeb Music Library, Harvard University, Cambridge, Massachusetts, 1958–62, 1965–74; music director, New England Dinosaur Dance Theatre, 1968–78; member, theory faculty, New England Conservatory of Music, Boston, 1976–8; guest composer, 23rd annual Contemporary Music Festival, Illinois Wesleyan University, Bloomington, 1977; president ("i.e., figurehead"), Dinosaur Annex Music Ensemble, 1977–81. Recipient: Sagalyn Prize, Tanglewood, 1960; Guggenheim Fellowship, Japan, 1962–3; National Endowment for Arts fellowships, 1976, 1978. Mailing address: 1168 Massachusetts Avenue, Cambridge, Massachusetts 02138; or (management) Rosalie Calabrese, 170 West 74th Street, New York, New York 10023, U.S.A.

Publishers: Composers Facsimile Edition; Merion; American Composers Alliance; Broadcast Music, Inc; Diapason Press.

[Most of Sims's non-electronic works after 1971 employ a microtonal 18–24-note scale in a 72-note division of the octave—exceptions using conventional 12-note equal division of scale are indicated.]

Symphonies/orchestral:

Le Tombeau d'Albers (conventional notation) 1959.
Longfellow Sparrow (5 flutes, 5 clarinets, 3 trumpets, 5 trombones) 1976.
Yr Obedt Servt (2 clarinets, violin, cello, with 2 clarinets, horn, trombone, violin, viola, double bass, 2 marimbas) 1977; first performed Boston, January 1978.
Yr Obedt Servt II (enlarged version; 2 clarinets, violin, cello, with flute, alto flute, 2 bassoons, 2 horns, 2 trombones, 2 marimbas, 4 or 5 violins, 2 violas, cello, double bass) 1981.
Pictures for an Institution (chamber orchestra) 1983; first performed Massachusetts, June 1983.
Night unto Night (3 flutes, 2 oboes, 2 clarinets, 2 bassoons, 3 horns, 2 trombones) 1984.

Chamber/instrumental:

Sonatine (piano; conventional notation) 1957.
Sonata (cello, piano; conventional notation) 1957; first performed New York City, 1959.
Twelve Arabesques (cello, piano; conventional notation) 1957.
Grave Dance (piano; conventional notation) 1958, see also version 1975.
String Quartet (conventional notation) 1959; first performed New York City, 1960.
Buchlein for Lyon (piano; conventional notation) 1962; first performed New York City, 1962.
Grave Dance (version of 1958 piece; 2 violins, viola/violin, cello, piano; conventional notation) 1975; first performed Boston, January 1978.
Slow Hiccups [sic] (2 equal melody instruments; conventional notation) 1975; first performed Cambridge, Massachusetts, November 1976.
Sonate concertante (quarter-tone music; consisting of *Five Sonate* for string quartet; *Five Sonatine* for oboe, viola, cello, double bass; octet version or may be played separately) 1961.
Third Quartet (quarter-tone music; string quartet) 1962; first performed New York City, 1965. Recorded CRI 223.
"String Quartet No 2" (flute [sic], clarinet [sic], violin, viola, cello) 1962; first performed February 1976. Recorded CRI 377.
Octet for Strings (double string quartet) 1964.
From an Oboe Quartet (oboe, violin, viola, cello) 1971.
Oboe Quartet 1971–5.
II—Variations (oboe, violin, viola, cello) 1973; first performed Boston, May 1974.
Second Thoughts (1, 2 or many double basses, with or without magnetic tape) 1974; first performed Massachusetts, February 1974.
Flourish (oboe, violin, viola, cello) 1975; first performed Boston, March 1976.
Twenty Years After (violin, clarinet) 1978; first performed Boston, October 1978.
Midorigaoka (2 violins, 2 violas, cello) 1978; first performed Tokyo, February 1979.
—And, As I Was Saying . . . (viola) 1979; first performed Boston, June 1979. Recorded Northeastern NR 224.
All Done from Memory (violin) 1980; first performed Ernen, July 1980. Recorded Northeastern NR 224.
Ruminations (clarinet) 1980; first performed Brunswick, Maine, February 1988.
Two for One (violin, viola) 1980; first performed Somerville, Massachusetts, March 1981. Recorded NR 224.
Sextet (clarinet, alto saxophone, horn, violin, viola, cello) 1981; first performed Boston, March 1982. Recorded Northeastern NR 224.
Phenomena (flute, clarinet, violin, viola, cello) 1981; first performed Cambridge, Massachusetts, January 1982.
Solo after Sextet (saxophone) 1981.
Quartet (flute, violin, viola, cello) 1982; first performed Boston, January 1983.
Tune & Variations (1 or 2 horns) 1983.
Sextet@ (version of *Sextet* for 3 clarinets, violin, viola, cello) 1983; first performed Boston, 14 October 1984.
Brief Elegies (flute, zoomoozophone, clarinet, bassoon, trombone, double bass) 1983; first performed New York City, April 1985.
This Way to the Egress, or: Manners Makyth Man (violin, viola, cello) 1983; first performed Boston, February 1984.
String Quartet No 4 1984.
Wedding Winds (3 clarinets) 1986.
Quintet (clarinet, 2 violins, viola, cello) 1987; first performed Boston, March 1988.
Chase (clarinet) 1987.
Solo in Four Movements (cello) 1987; first performed New York City, May 1988.
AEDM in memoriam (cello) 1988; first performed Providence, Rhode Island, August 1989.
Flight (flute, electronics) 1989; first performed Haarlem, The Netherlands, May 1989.
Night Piece: In girum inus nocte et consumimur igni (flute, clarinet, viola, cello, electronics) 1989; first performed Boston, October 1989.

Vocal/choral:

Chanson d'aventure; Nou sprinkes the sprai (tenor, harpsichord or piano; conventional notation) 1951, revised 1975; first performed New Haven, Connecticut, 1951.
Chamber Cantata on Chinese Poems (tenor, flute, clarinet/bass clarinet, viola, cello, harpsichord; conventional notation) 1954; first performed New York City, 1959. Recorded CRI 186.
Mass (unaccompanied SSAATB choir; conventional notation) 1955.
Two Folk Songs (baritone, piano; conventional notation) 1958; first performed New York City, 1972.
Three Cradle Songs (mezzo-soprano, guitar, 2 clarinets;

conventional notation) 1958, revised 1977; first performed Boston, January 1978.
Music for the "Kubla Khan" of Coleridge (reciter, gamelan, chamber ensemble; also tape) 1959.
Brief Glances into Contemporary French Literature (4 countertenors, piano; Stacton; conventional notation) 1959; first performed 1975.
What God Is Like to Him I Serve? (unaccompanied SATB choir; Bradstreet; conventional notation) 1959; first performed Birmingham, Alabama, 1976.
Sieben Spencer-Lieder (soprano, keyboard; conventional notation) 1960; first performed New York City, 1960.
Three Songs (tenor, orchestra; Marvell, Herrick, Jonson; conventional notation) 1960.
Cantata III (quarter-tone music; mezzo-soprano, percussion) 1963.
In memoriam Alice Hawthorne (tenor, baritone, narrator, 4 clarinets, horn, marimba—4 hands or 2 marimbas; Gorey) 1967; first performed Massachusetts, January 1977.
The Bewties of the Futeball (5-part children's chorus, optional recorders, piano, metal idiophones; or SSATB choir, optional flute, horn, trombone, 2 pianos, metal idiophones; anon., Scottish 15th-century; conventional notation) 1974; first performed Boston, May 1977.
Madame Mim's Work Song (soprano, piano; White; conventional notation) 1975; first performed London, 1975.
The Temptations at the Siege of Air and Darkness (voices, piano, optional instruments; White; conventional notation) 1975; "Fourth Temptation" first performed London, May 1975.
Celebration of Dead Ladies (voice, alto flute, basset horn, clarinet in A, viola, cello, percussion; Higgins) 1976; first performed Boston November 1989.
Elegie—nach Rilke (soprano, flute, clarinet, violin, viola, cello; Rilke) 1976; first performed Boston, November 1976. Recorded CRI 377.
Aeneas on the Saxophone (soprano, alto, tenor, bass, 2 clarinets, horn, trombone, viola, double bass; Lancaster) 1977; first performed Boston, January 1978.
Come Away (mezzo-soprano, viola, clarinet, alto flute, horn, trombone, double bass; Campion, Fletcher, Hardy, Whitman; "Lullaby" rewritten for soprano, 2 alternative viola accompaniments) 1978; first performed Boston, March 1979. Recorded CRI CD 577.
Five Songs (alto, viola; Nashe, Herrick, Fletcher, Ford, Donne) 1979.
Song (mezzo-soprano, clarinet, viola; Auden) 1980.
The Conversions (SSAATTBB soli; Mathews) 1985; first performed Berkeley, California, June 1986.

Other:

The Trojan Women (theatre music; chamber orchestra; conventional notation) 1955; first performed Oakland, California, 1955.
Masque (dance music; chamber orchestra or 2 pianos; conventional notation) 1955; first performed San Francisco, 1957.
The Ticklish Acrobat (theatre music; oboe, celeste, xylophone; conventional notation) 1957; first performed San Francisco, 1957.
Music for the "Kubla Khan" of Coleridge II (reciter, tape collage) 1959.
Sakoku (music to television drama by Oda Makoto; electronic/*musique concrète*) 1963; broadcast April 1963.
Antimatter: Three Dances for Today (dance music; tape collage) 1968; first performed Boston, June 1968.
McDowell's Fault, or The Tenth Sunday After Trinity (dance music; tape collage) 1968; first performed Boston, August 1968.
Alec (dance music; collage/*musique concrète*) 1968; first performed Boston, November 1968.
A Frank Overture. Four Dented Interludes. And Coda (dance music; tape collage) 1969; first performed Massachusetts, 1969.
Cat's Cradle (theatre music to text by Vonnegut; chorus, 2 flutes, 2 clarinets, trumpet, trombone, percussion; conventional notation) 1969; first performed Cambridge, Massachusetts, March 1969.
The Duchess of Malfi; Toby Armour Her Toy (dance music; *musique concrète*) 1969; first performed Boston, August 1969.
Warts & All (dance music; tape collage) 1969.
Commonplace Book or A Salute to Our American Container Corp (*musique concrète*) 1969; first performed Boston, 1973.
Lion at the Door (dance/theatre music to text by Nemchinova; unaccompanied voice(s); conventional notation) 1969; first performed Cambridge, Massachusetts, March 1969.
Real Toads (dance music; *musique concrète*) 1970; first performed New York City, 1970.
Mugs McGhee's Last Song (theatre music to text by Williams; mezzo-soprano, piano, page-turner; conventional notation) 1970; first performed New York City, April 1970.
Pastorale (dance music; "combine tape") 1970; first performed Boston, June 1970.
Summer Piece: Homage to Gene Krupa (dance music; *musique concrète*) 1970.
Clement Wenceslaus Lothaire Nepomucene, Prince Metternich (1773–1859) IN MEMORIAM (dance music; "combine tape") 1970; first performed Boston, July 1970.
Landscape II: 7 July 70 (Parker 470) (*musique concrète*) 1970.
More Overture and Another Interlude (dance music; collage/*musique concrète*) 1970; first performed Pennsylvania, October 1970.
Elina's Piece (dance music; computer, *musique concrète*) 1970; first performed Boston, November 1970.
. . . Including the . . . (dance music; *musique concrète*) 1970; first performed Massachusetts, November 1970.
Interlope (dance music; collage/*musique concrète*) 1970; first performed Boston, December 1970.
Dreams for Sale (theatre music to text by Williams; mezzo-soprano, baritone, piano; conventional notation) 1970; first performed Boston, September 1979.
Temptation (introduction to and interludes between 4 recorded tangos; "combine tape") 1971; first performed New England, 1972.
Tango Variations ("combine tape") 1971; first performed Boston, January 1973.
Two Toby Minutes I, II and III ("combine tape") 1971.
Five Toby Minutes plus 49.5" (dance music which includes *Two Toby Minutes I*; "combine tape") 1971; first performed New England, December 1971.
Ground Cover (dance music; "combine tape") 1972; first performed New York City, 1972.
Museum Piece (ambient music for exhibit of New Guinea artifacts; tape collage) 1972; first performed Boston, June 1972.
Wall to Wall (collage/musique concrète) 1972; first performed Boston, 1972.
Where the Wild Things Are (choreography to story/drawings by Sendak; narrator, "combine tape") 1973; first performed New England, October 1973.
After Lyle or Untitled (dance music; *musique concrète*) 1975;

first performed New England, April 1975.

Behold Icarus (dance music; "combine tape") 1975; first performed Cambridge, Massachusetts, May 1975.

The Owl and the Pussycat (theatre/dance music to text by Lear; bass, chromatic harmonica, electric guitar; conventional notation) 1975; first performed Massachusetts, December 1975.

The Walrus and the Carpenter (theatre/dance music to text by Carroll; speaker, 6 woodblocks; conventional notation) 1975; first performed Massachusetts, December 1975.

When the Angels Blow Their Trumpets (theatre music to text by Williams; 2 mezzo-sopranos, baritone; conventional notation) 1976; first performed New York City, November 1976.

Collage XIII (The Inexcusable) (dance music; tape collage) 1977; first performed Illinois, March 1977.

PUBLICATIONS

By Sims: "Microtones" and related entries, in *Harvard Dictionary of Music* 1964, 1969; "A 72-Note Just Computer Music System", in *1/1*, 5(1); "Yet Another 72-Noter . . . ", in *Computer Music Journal*, 12(4); "A Question of Microtonal Notation", in *Xenharmonikon*, 11, Autumn 1987; "Harmonic Ordering in *Quintet 1987*", in Hesse (ed), *Mikrotone III: Bericht über das 3. Internatationale Symposium in Salzburg 1989*, edited by Hesse, Innsbruck, 1990; analytic liner notes to recordings of *Cahmber Cantata on Chinese Poems*, *Third Quartet*, *String Quartet No 2/Elegie—nach Rilke*.

Ezra Sims comments:

For 30 of the 36 years I've been letting the music I write go out and cross the street by itself, I've been writing microtonal music. I'm surprised to realise this—I had been used to thinking it this new thing that I had finally given up and started to do.

And "given up" is the proper phrase; at the time I did so, it seemed the most quixotic and lunatic fringe of enterprises, but it had also become apparent that either I would write microtonal music or nothing—my ear would provide me with nothing else. And I wasn't about to stop composing, unless absolutely forced to by powers outside my control.

I have been very lucky to have been associated, through much of that time, with two new music groups in Boston: Dinosaur Annex, which I helped found, and Boston Musica Viva. The most of my music has been written for, and admirably performed by, them.

The most is strongly tonal and firmly constrained by the relations of the harmonic series. After a period of uncertain fumbling, it has come to use an 18-or 24-note (per octave) scale in a matrix of atotal chromatic of 72 notes (per octave) as tonal music used the diatonic scale in a matrix of the 12-note chromatic. It generally eschews the triad, building its consonances out of the adjacent pitches of the 6th to the 12th harmonics—but (as my Flute Quartet and string trio *This Way to The Egress* make obvious) it can accommodate itself to and appropriate to itself the materials and usages of traditional tonal practice, just as tonal music could make use of the materials and ways of modal counterpoint.

* * *

"Yet another 72-noter . . .": Ezra Sims remains engagingly diffident and ironic about his most significant musical innovation. For 20 years, he has concentrated almost exclusively on microtonal composition and on a highly personal synthesis of *musique concrète* materials and collage methods which he calls "combine tape". He belongs squarely to a well-attested American tradition of aesthetic self-sufficiency, inventing or synthesising where mechanisms appropriate to his needs are not to hand, following the logic of his own procedures without a glance at fashion or tradition.

It may be that fashion has caught up a little with Sims. Microtonal writing is now, largely via electronic techniques, firmly established as part of the composer's available resources. It certainly did not begin with Sims. Another great original, Charles Ives, and the latterly Americanized Bartók experimented with microtones, and the possibilities of extended microtonal writing (as opposed to occasional, incidental effects) were explored by the Mexican Julian Carrillo, who died in relative obscurity in 1965. What is distinctive about Sims is the thoroughgoing nature of his interest in the method.

Since 1971 most of his non-electronic work has utilised an equal-tempered scale of 18 or 24 notes within a 72-note division of the octave. Though computer technology has allowed him to use these scales with absolute (sometimes deadeningly absolute) strictness, Sims frequently makes further microtonal modifications that allow him to compose in an approximation to conventional just intonation with its unequal spacings. Though his basic compositional instincts are friendly, and often humorous, it is the tonal adaptability of his scale which allows so much of his music to remain accessibly "familiar" even without triads, with no disturbing excess of chromaticism.

Clearly, music of this type requires a certain flexibility from its performers and most of Sims's microtonal pieces have been written for and premiered by the innovative Boston Musica Viva and by his own ensemble Dinosaur Annex. A pupil of Quincy Porter (who may have stimulated an underlying interest in polytonality) and of Darius Milhaud, Sims's earliest scores show very little of the "uncertain fumbling" he has spoken of. The First String Quartet is neat and energetic with some signs of dissatisfaction at its own limited vocabulary. The second and third are clearly "transitional"; the former carries its own self-protective quote marks for it is probably the only extant string quartet in which the first violin part is scored for flute and clarinet. The third is written in quarter-tones, and already marks a significant step toward the microtonal epiphanies that came with the decade's end. It was another dozen years before Sims turned to those forces again. Sims's work contemporary with the Fourth String Quartet has a remarkable certainty and consistency, giving off something of the impression one receives from John Cage's first venture in the medium, that of hearing early but quite conventional music being played by alien performers, or of English spoken by someone with absolutely no knowledge of English phonetics or stress patterns. Sims himself singles out his 1982 *Quartet* for flute and strings as the best example of a work in which the microtonal scale is put to (relatively) conventional tonal use; it is a very beautiful and affecting work, more restrained in formal conception than near-contemporary pieces like the *Sextet* or *Brief Elegies*.

Sims studied Chinese at a U.S. Army language school and fostered a close interest in Chinese literature. The early, conventionally notated *Chamber Cantata on Chinese Poems* is an excellent example of his musical base-point: implicitly contrapuntal, fighting against tonal restrictions, vigorously voiced. This is even more evident in the daring "Kubla Khan" music, and in the absolutely astonishing *Brief Glances into Contemporary French Literature*, written in 1959 but only performed in 1975. The high point of Sims's vocal writing, though, is the 1976 *Elegie—nach Rilke*, a deeply moving piece for soprano and "string quartet" which exactly captures the poet's alternation of lyrical immediacy and profound alienation, qualities also found in the novelist Harry Mathews, whose *The Conversions* Sims has recently set.

This is perhaps the key to his aesthetic. He can be playful, as in *Slow Hiccups* (words printed upside down), poignantly beautiful, as in his setting of Anne Bradstreet (*What God is Like to Him I Serve?*) and in *In memoriam Alice Hawthorne*, and often quite capricious. His music is inherently dramatic, because it enacts its processes in a remarkably open and unselfconscious way, but also because Sims has felt a great affinity for theatre and dance. Like Ives and Harry Partch and Lou Harrison, he is a great individual, a term often and quite wrongly used as a euphemism for marginality. Sims is by no means an eccentric or crank. What he has done is fundamentally in and of the American experimental tradition; or to put it more precisely, if "the American tradition" is an essentially experimental one, in the sense of constantly rewriting its own language and values, then Sims is central to it.

—Brian Morton

SINGLETON, Alvin (Elliott). American. Born in Brooklyn, New York, 28 December 1940. Educated at New York University (composition and music education), B.M., 1967; Yale University, New Haven Connecticut, (composition under Mel Powell and Yehudi Wyner), M.M.A., 1971; Accademia di Santa Cecilia, Rome (composition under Goffredo Petrassi), 1971–2. Independent composer; resident in Graz, Austria, 1973–5; composer in residence, Atlanta Symphony Orchestra, Georgia, 1985–8, and Spelman College, Atlanta, Georgia, from 1988. Recipient: Darmstadt Kranichsteiner Musikpreis (for *Be Natural*), 1974. Mailing address: c/o European American Music, P.O. Box 850, Valley Forge, Pennsylvania 19482-0850, U.S.A.

Publisher: European American.

Symphonies/orchestral:

Kwitana (piano, double bass, percussion, chamber orchestra) 1974.
Again (chamber orchestra) 1979; first performed London, October 1979.
A Yellow Rose Petal 1982; first performed Houston, Texas, 1982. Recorded Nonesuch 9 79231 2.
Shadows 1987; first performed Atlanta, Georgia, May 1987. Recorded Nonesuch 9 79231 2.
Eine Idfee is ein Stueck Stoff (string orchestra) 1988.
After Fallen Crumbs 1988. Recorded Nonesuch Elektra 9 79231 2.
Sinfonia Diaspora 1991; first performed 5 May 1991.
Even Tomorrow 1991; first performed October 1991.

Chamber/instrumental:

Mutations (piano) 1966.
Woodwind Quintet 1968–9.
Clinque (piano) 1969.
Argoru I (piano) 1970.
Argoru II (cello) 1970.
Argoru III (flute) 1971.
Be Natural (3 strings) 1974.
Extension of a Dream, in Memory of Steve Biko (2 percussion) 1977.
Argoru IV (viola) 1978.
Le Tombeau du Petit Prince (harpsichord) 1978.
Such a Nice Lady (clarinet, violin, viola, cello, piano) 1979.
Et nunc (alto flute, bass clarinet, double bass) 1980.
La Flora (flute/alto flute, clarinet, 2 percussion, violin, cello) 1983.
Inside-Out (piano—4 hands) 1984.
Apple (clarinet quintet) 1984.
Argoru Va (bass clarinet) 1984.
Argoru Vb (alto flute) 1984.
Out of Necessity (double bass) 1984.
Akwaaba (flute, clarinet, bassoon, piano, percussion, violin, cello) 1985.
Agoru VI (marimba) 1987–8.
Quartet Isabella (string quartet) 1988.

Vocal/choral:

Epitaph (unaccompanied double chorus; Raleigh) 1966; first performed Vienna, January 1987.
A Seasoning (female or male voice/percussion, alto saxophone/percussion, trombone/percussion, double bass/percussion, 1 percussionist) 1971.
Messa (soprano, chorus, flute, 2 guitars, electric organ, cello, double bass) 1975; first performed Vatican, May 1985.
Alleluia (unaccompanied female chorus) 1987; first performed Atlanta, Georgia, October 1987.
Fallen Crumbs (unaccompanied male chorus) 1987; first performed Atlanta, Georgia, October 1987.
Between Sisters (soprano, piano, alto flute, vibraphone; Dove) 1990.

Opera/dramatic:

Dream Sequence '76 1976.
Necessity Is a Mother (drama without words for 3 actresses/singers, amplified double bass) 1981; first performed Tanglewood, Massachusetts, August 1981.

* * *

Sharing as he does the surname of one of the greatest drummers in jazz, Zutty Singleton, it is no surprise to find a concern with rhythm at the heart of Alvin Singleton's music. His work places a heavy reliance on loosely metrical harmonic passages, largely constructed out of triads, interspersed with more freely-pulsed episodes of considerable dissonance. It is clear that modern jazz has played a considerable role in the development of his style; he has dedicated a solo work, *Out of Necessity*, to the great jazz double bassist, composer and bandleader Charles Mingus, who memorably defined jazz as the classical music of Black Americans.

Encouraged by Mel Powell, Singleton has preserved the dynamics of jazz performance in his large- and small-scale compositions, even when his structural concerns have moved in the direction of an essentially European, post-serial idiom. In the 1970s, like so many Afro-Americans, though for perhaps rather different motives and reasons, Singleton settled in Europe, where he worked as a freelance composer. His reputation was perhaps first established in Europe where performances at Darmstadt, and the ISCM Festivals in Graz and Brussels, and a fine piece for the innovative London Sinfonietta attracted considerable critical attention.

In 1985, he was appointed composer in residence at the Atlanta Symphony Orchestra, a position that gave him access to full-scale orchestral forces for the first time. The resultant *A Yellow Rose Petal* and *Shadows* are masterful contemporary scores. *Shadows* in particular is marked by great blocks of sound, often quite dark in timbre as befits the title, but with considerable freedom of articulation left to the conductor and individual players, which gives the work its dramatic impact. *Such a Nice Lady* for quintet is a fiercer score, with less immediate appeal, but it is instantly recognizable as by the same hand.

Singleton has written one opera *Dream Sequence '76*, offering an unorthodox perspective on the American Bicentennial and one "wordless drama", punningly entitled *Necessity Is a Mother*. In a sense, though, all his works are inherently dramatic. His *Mass*, commissioned for a Vatican ordination, restores much of the sense of ritual that has leached out of contemporary liturgical writing. *Alleluia* is deceptively simple, but subtly scored, and for all its acclamatory verve, rather sombre in effect. The early setting of Raleigh, apparently written while Singleton was still a student in New York, is full of the unexpected harmonic and rhythmic shifts which he disposes to greater effect later in his career.

Among his instrumental pieces, the most important are the prize-winning (and also punning) *Be Natural* for three bowed instruments, and the sequence of solo pieces known as *Argoru*, which represent his most sustained examination of instrumental values. *Be Natural* constantly evades the tug of one construction of its title, the centripetal B natural, in order to fulfil another. That concern of freedom, and specifically freedom *in time*, is the essence of Singleton's quest. It emerges thematically in the recent *Sinfonia Diaspora*, and in the moving tribute to the murdered South African activist Steve Biko where Singleton again returns to percussion.

Singleton is, along with the slightly older Olly Wilson, perhaps the most significant Black American composer of formal music. That is not to separate either man from the tradition of extended composition begun by Duke Ellington and extended, almost to the point of entropy in Mingus's chaotic *Epitaph*. Singleton is always conscious of that continuum, works proudly within it but also against its self-imposed limitations and obsessions. Independent of spirit, eclectic, adventurous, anti-elitist, improvisational, he is an American composer *par excellence*.

—Richard Washington

SKEMPTON, Howard. British/English. Born in Chester, 31 October 1947. Educated at Birkenhead School, Cheshire, 1959–66; Ealing Technical College, London, 1967–70; studied composition privately under Cornelius Cardew, 1967–8; Morley College, London (composition under Cornelius Cardew), 1968–71. Married in 1984; 1 son. Co-founder (with Cornelius Cardew and Michael Parsons), Scratch Orchestra, 1969; music editor, Faber Music, 1971–6; performing duo with Michael Parsons, from 1974; music editor, Boosey & Hawkes, 1977–9; freelance music editor, from 1979; editor, G.I. Holst, Ltd, 1982–5; visiting lecturer in composition, department of music studies, University of Adelaide, 1991.

Mailing address: Flat 11, 11 Warwick Place, Leamington Spa, Warwickshire CV32 5BS, England.

Publishers: self; Oxford University Press.

[Many pieces originally performed privately; details of first performances not available]

Symphonies/orchestral:

May Pole (open score) 1971.
Chorales 1980.
Two Preludes (string orchestra) 1986.
Little Suite for Strings (string orchestra) 1986.
Chorales 2 1987.
Lento 1990.

Chamber/instrumental:

A Humming Song (piano) 1967.
Snowpiece (piano) 1968.
September Song (piano) 1968.
Piano Piece 1969 1969.
African Melody (cello) 1969.
Two Highland Dances (piano) 1970.
North Wind (soprano saxophone) 1970.
Waltz (piano) 1970.
First Prelude (piano) 1971.
Prelude (horn) 1971.
One for Molly (piano) 1972.
Quavers (piano) 1972.
Simple Piano Piece 1972.
Lament (open score) 1972.
Intermezzo (piano) 1973.
Sweet Chariot (piano) 1973.
Riding the Thermals (piano) 1973.
Eirenicon (piano) 1973.
Rumba (piano) 1973.
Slow Waltz (piano—3 hands) 1973.
Bends (cello) 1973.
One for Martha (piano) 1974.
Quavers 2 (piano) 1974.
Senza licenza (piano) 1974.
Invention (piano) 1974.
Tender Melody (piano) 1974.
Gentle Melody (accordion) 1974.
Equal Measures (2 drums) 1974.
Drum Canon (2 drums) 1974.
Second Gentle Melody (piano) 1975.
Colonnade (piano) 1975.
Quavers 3 (piano) 1975.
Passing Fancy (piano) 1975.
Deeply Shaded (accordion) 1975.
Summer Waltz (accordion) 1975.
Ada's Dance (accordion) 1975.
Surface Tension (flute, cello, piano) 1975.
Surface Tension 2 (flute, cello, piano) 1975.
Two Drum Trios 1975.
Prelude (flute, string trio) 1975.
Chorale (piano) 1976.
Surface Tension 3 (piano) 1976.
One for the Road (accordion) 1976.
Duet (piano, woodblocks) 1976.
Drum Canon 2 (2 drums) 1976.
Acacia (2 drums) 1976.
Impromptu (2 baritone horns) 1976.

Autumn Waltz (2 baritone horns) 1976.
Hornplay (2 baritone horns) 1976.
June '77 (piano) 1977.
Eirenicon 2 (piano) 1977.
Saltaire Melody (piano) 1977.
Children's Dance (accordion, piano) 1977.
Eirenicon 3 (piano) 1978.
Postlude (piano) 1978.
Memento (piano) 1978.
Merry-Go-Round (accordion) 1978.
Pendulum (accordion) 1978.
Summer Sketches (accordion) 1978.
Tuba da caccia (tuba) 1978.
Intermezzo (viola, horn) 1978.
Air Melody (open score) 1978.
Friday's Child (piano) 1979.
Air (piano) 1979.
Melody for a First Christmas (flute) 1979.
Melody (horn) 1979.
Scherzo (2 horns) 1979.
Trio (3 horns) 1979.
Trace (piano) 1980.
Break (2 drums) 1980.
Fabric (2 sdrums) 1980.
Preamble (2 drums) 1980.
Campanella (piano) 1981.
Outline (piano—3 hands) 1981.
Breather (cello) 1981.
Campanella (piano) 1982.
Well, Well, Cornelius 1982.
Seascape (piano) 1982.
Campanella 3 (piano) 1982.
Suite (accordion) 1982.
Prelude (violin) 1982.
Highland Melody (open score) 1982.
Beginner (piano) 1983.
Breathing Space (accordion) 1983.
Call (clarinet) 1983.
Wedding Tune (violin, autoharp) 1983.
Lullaby (clarinet, cello) 1983.
Recessional (open score) 1983.
Christmas Melody (open score) 1983.
Quavers 5 (piano) 1984.
Twin Set and Pearls (accordion) 1984.
Cakes and Ale (accordion) 1984.
A Card for Lucy (clarinet) 1984.
May Fair (bassoon) 1984.
Fanfare and Caprice (guitar) 1984.
Lyric (cello, piano) 1984.
The Durham Strike (piano) 1985.
Piano Piece for Trevor Clarke 1985.
Campanella 4 (piano) 1985.
Eirenicon 4 (piano) 1985.
Second Suite (accordion) 1985.
Third Suite (accordion) 1985.
Small Change (accordion) 1985.
Home and Abroad (accordion) 1985.
Bagatelle (flute) 1985.
Song Without Words (horn, accordion) 1985.
Agreement (2 drums) 1985.
Pineapple Melody (horn, accordion, double bass) 1985.
Alone and Together (clarinet, bassoon, piano) 1985.
The Mold Riots (piano) 1986.
Resolution (piano) 1986.
Something of an Occasion (accordion) 1986.
Axis (accordion) 1986.
Axis 2 (accordion) 1986.
Two Interludes (accordion, vibraphone) 1986.
Finding Home (clarinet, cello, glockenspiel, piano) 1986.
Toccata (piano) 1987.
Solo and Duet (violin, piano) 1987.
Aria (string quartet) 1987.
Pendulum 2 (piano) 1988.
Study (piano) 1988.
Even Tenor (piano) 1988.
Lament and Farewell (oboe, cello, piano) 1988.
Images (piano) 1989.
No Great Shakes (piano duet) 1989.
Prelude 2 (violin) 1989.
After-Image (piano) 1990.
After-Image 2 (piano) 1990.
After-Image 3 (piano) 1990.
Maestoso (piano) 1990.
Axis 90 (piano) 1990.
Half Moon (flute, piano) 1990.
The Beauty of the Morning (peking, aaron and gender—gamelan) 1990.
A Perugia (piano) 1991.
Low (tuba, piano) 1991.

Vocal/choral:

Not-Very-Long Song (voice, accordion) 1972.
Gentle Melody (2 voices) 1974.
Embers 2 (2 voices) 1974.
Song at the Year's Turning (4-part mixed chorus; R.S. Thomas) 1980.
Alice Is One (voice, piano) 1982.
Tree Sequence ("From the Palm Trees", "Willow", "Laburnum", "Mountain Ash", Duet; voice, piano, woodblocks) 1982. Recorded Practical 3.
Second Tree Sequence ("Tree, Leafless", "Under the Elder", "Aspen Trees"; voice, piano) 1983. Recorded Practical 3.
Pigs Could Fly (voice, piano) 1983.
The Gipsy Wife's Song (mezzo-soprano, flute, oboe, vibraphone, piano; Bevan Jones, after Lawrence) 1983.
Two Voices (male voices) 1986.
From Waterloo Bridge (mixed chorus, 2 pianos; Mackie) 1986.
Three Poems of D.H. Lawrence (soprano, clarinet) 1989.
How Slow the Wind (soprano, 2 clarinet, viola, cello, double bass; Dickinson) 1989.
Five Poems of Mary Webb (3-part female chorus) 1989.
The Maldive Shark (baritone, piano; Melville) 1990.
Colomen (soprano, clarinet, piano; Webb) 1990.
The Witches' Wood (soprano, flute, clarinet, violin, cello, piano; Coleridge) 1990.
Rose-Berries (3-part female chorus; Webb) 1990.

PUBLICATIONS

By Skempton: *Piano Music* [album], Faber Music, London, 1974; *Lament*, *Eirenicon*, *Prelude* for horn, *Gentle Melody* for accordion, published in *Soundings*, 10, 1976.

On Skempton: Michael Nyman, *Experimental Music: Cage and Beyond*, London, 1974 [includes *Snowpiece*]; Parsons, article on HS, *Contact*, 21, Autumn 1980 [includes *One for Martha*, *Quavers 2*, *Autumn Waltz* for 2 baritone horns, *One for the Road*, *Air*]; Walter Zimmermann, article on HS, *MusikTexte*, 3, February 1984 [includes *Waltz* for piano, *Pendulum* for accordion, *Beginner* for piano]; Kevin Volans, (interview) in *Summer Gardeners: Conversations with Com-*

posers, Durban, 1985 [includes *Well, Well, Cornelius*, *Cakes and Ale*]; Keith Potter, article on HS, *Musical Times*, March 1991.

Howard Skempton comments:

Most of my pieces, certainly my most characteristic, are short. Many are occasional. It is in the company of such music that I feel most at home.

* * *

The music of Howard Skempton has always been touched by a cleanliness of line and proportion. His early influences were primarily Morton Feldman and Anton Webern. Most of Skempton's music from 1967 to 1983 has the sparseness of much of Feldman's work, with the focus on individual notes and simple combinations of notes, while relying on structure more architecturally pure than Webern's. Skempton's interest in clarity of line and sonority extends even to the cleanliness of manuscript and notation. In this strict style, Skempton uses mostly barred and unbarred semi-breves to emphasize the superiority of the sonorities, to make clear the classic proportions inherent in his work.

In *A Humming Song*, black notes do not indicate shorter durations; rather they indicate that the player hum the pitches to help sustain the sonority. The piece is built out of several combinations of single notes and two, three or four note simultaneities, which Skempton arranged by chance procedures, a method of organization he used regularly through the mid-1970s. Skempton then places this progression of notes in a framework which emulates the proportion of Greek architecture—a system of division of events which are mathematically symmetrical. In early works such as *A Humming Song* and *September Song*, this framework is made apparent through Skempton's use of barlines.

Proportion exists in later unbarred pieces. *Campanella* consists of 32 chords separated into four sections of eight. Each section begins with the same pitches in the right hand. *Beginner* consists only of 16 pitches grouped as four sets of four pitches each. Like Feldman, Skempton abandoned random procedures for pitch determination, and now uses the kind of sonorities engendered by the earlier technique in an empirical way.

From 1970, Skempton's musical ouput follows two methods: the sonorous, classically proportioned pieces as those mentioned above, and what Skempton has referred to as "occasional pieces". These works are miniatures, usually tonally based or at least having more of an emphasis on melody. In Skempton's much-anthologized *Waltz*, which Michael Nyman claims is "the first experimental tonal piece to be conceived in terms of a connected melodic and harmonic sequence . . . ", the 32-bar melody is broken into sections of eight bars. *One for Molly* has a *Gymnopédies*-like tune. His voice piece "Mountain Ash" has an almost Asian simplicity, but because of the melodic movement it exists as one of the second type of pieces. Skempton has also written extensively for the accordion, which he plays, and pieces can be classic, or tuneful (as his *Cakes and Ale*).

There is a danger in performing Skempton's work of being misled by the simplicity of its notation. Technically the piano pieces could be played by a child, but this sonic world is so fragile that much specialised training and innate musicianship is required to perform the works properly. Michael Finnessy and John Tilbury are two of the pianists who have been able to approach these pieces; Janet Sherbourne, with her straight, almost folk-like tone, is the dedicates for most of the vocal works. Michael Parsons has collaborated with Skempton in performance of percussion works, and as both a performer and writer has an intimate knowledge of Skempton's style.

In the last decade Skempton has brought a fusion of architectonic and occasional styles to larger works, such as his orchestral music and large ensembles. One such piece is *The Gipsy Wife's Song*, in which Skempton sets words by Bevan Jones (based on the D.H. Lawrence story "The Virgin and the Gipsy") to a gentle polymetric melody, which is then echoed at the end by wind instruments. The prelude recalls his more architectonic work in a kind of *klangfarbenmelodie* of some mystery.

—Virginia Anderson

SKOUEN, Synne. Norwegian. Born in Oslo, 1950. Educated at Hochschule für Musik und darstellende Kunst, Vienna (theory of composition under Alfred Uhl and Erwin Ratz, experimental composition in electronic music studio under Dieter Kaufmann and Friedrich Cerha), 1969–73; Norwegian State Academy of Music, Oslo (composition under Finn Mortensen), 1973–6, diploma in composition. Member of experimental music theatre group, *Die Fremden*, from 1970; editor, *Ballade*, 1977–86; music critic, *Arbeiderbladet*, Oslo; full-time composer, since 1986. Recipient: Prix Italia (for *Gull Eaters*), 1983. Mailing address: c/o Norwegian Music Information Centre, Toftesgate 69, N-0552 Oslo 5, Norway.

Publisher: Norsk Musikforlag.

Symphonies/orchestral:

Tombeau to Minnona (large orchestra) 1976.
Nattstykke / Nightpiece 1987.
Intonazione—Quasi una fantasia (orchestra, tape) 1987.
Canto delle Balene (orchestra, tape) 1988.
Kjaere Mozart! 1991.

Chamber/instrumental:

Et Sviskekomplott / The Evergreen Conspiracy (from the score to *Formynderne*; flute, clarinet, violin, cello, piano, percussion, tape) 1978.
Hils Domitila! (piano) 1980. Recorded Danica DLP 8017.
P.s.: pianissimo (piano) 1980. Recorded Norwegian Composers NC 4903.
Uten tittel (viola) 1985.
Angrboda's Datter (flute/piccolo, violin, viola, cello, harp) 1986.

Vocal/choral:

Hva sa Schöpenhauer . . . ? Et partiturinlegg / What Did Schöpenhauer Say . . . ? An Argument (actor/actress, flute, clarinet/bass clarinet/tenor saxophone, percussion, violin, cello, tape) 1977.
Rug / Rye (female voice, cello, grand piano; Obstfelder, Loveid) 1982–4.
Rosa (soprano, grand piano, tape) 1984.
Two Children's Songs from "Peter Pan" (Barrie, Vagsas) 1984.

Oatas Eimi (female chorus, melodica, tablas, large pebbles, Tibetan finger cymbals) 1985.
Tre haner galer (2 sopranos, 2 altos, orchestra) 1985.
Balladen om Anna Roggloy (melodrama for tenor, bass, actress, orchestra) 1990.

Opera/dramatic:

Dusj/Shower (video opera for 2; soprano, tenor/oboe, flute, cello, percussion, tape; Loveid, Heske) 1984.
Froskeprinsen/The Frog Prince (television fable for tenor, soprano, electronics) 1988–9.

Other:

Formynderne/The Guardians (film score; Nicole Mace, after Amalie Skram) 1978.
Evergreen (ballet by Kari Blakstad for television; flute, oboe, clarinet, bassoon, trumpet, percussion, violin, viola, cello, double bass, tape) 1979.
Reise Gjennom Ukjent Land—Gravid (score to audio-visual work on 16-mm film) 1979–81.
Makespisere/Gull Eaters (incidental music to play by Cecile Loveid) 1981.
Love Letters on Blue Paper (incidental music to play by Wesker) 1982.
Vinteren Rivnar (incidental music to play by Loveid) 1983.
My Life, Your Life (incidental music to play by Andersen) 1984.
Reiser til Begjaer/Journeys to Desire (collaborative work with poet Inger Elisabeth Hansen and painter Inger Sitter; incorporates *uten tittel*, with portable radio) 1985.
Minotauros Is Dead (incidental music to play by Nicole Mace) 1986.
Balansedame (incidental music to play by Loveid) 1986.
Bluey (incidental music to play by Wesker) 1987.
Volven (ballet by Kjersti Alveberg) 1987–8.
Fodsel er Musikk/Birth Is Music (incidental music to play by Loveid) 1988.

* * *

Synne Skouen occupies a highly significant place in Norwegian contemporary life. Under her editorship, the adventurous new music journal *Ballade* became an indispensable guide to the newest developments in composition. It may even be that her skills as an editor have tended to eclipse her reputation as one of the finest young composers in Norway. However, since the mid-1980s, Skouen has been writing music full-time, and has created a substantial body of highly individual and impressive music.

She opted initially to study abroad, a not infrequent recourse for Norwegian composers, and a sharp contrast to their colleagues in Finland, Sweden and Denmark, who appear, initially at least, to find sufficient support and inspiration closer to home. However, one of the things that is most striking about young Norwegian musicians is the degree to which they seem to return to native resources. Like Terje Rypdal and Ase Hedstrøm, Skouen is unmistakably Norwegian, but is so without any overt use of folkloric elements or explicit allusions to earlier musics.

Like Rypdal again, she benefited considerably from a period of study with Finn Mortensen, the most significant and daring of the Norwegian modernists. Mortensen favoured an open-ended construction of serial technique, an absence of dogmatism that is clearly reflected in Skouen's free atonal approach and unembarrassed recourse to melodic or harmonic passages when these are required. There are echoes of Bartók in some of her pieces, notably the orchestral *Nattstykke/Nightpiece* and the remarkable *Uten tittel* for solo viola, but the essential logic of her most recent composition seems to be entirely self-generated and directed towards an expressive and inherently dramatic compositional aesthetic.

Skouen has long been interested in and involved with fringe drama experiments. While studying in Vienna, where she was a pupil of Dieter Kaufmann and Friedrich Cerha, she joined an ambitious performance group known as *Die Fremden*; the reference to foreignness or strangeness in the title underlines a constant characteristic of her stage works, a powerful sense of alienation and separation which nonetheless does not render her work uncommunicative or inaccessible. In *Makespisere/Gull Eaters* and in the remarkable orchestral *Canto delle Balene*, she has shown how to reconcile a thoroughgoing strangeness with a coherent and perfectly realised musical language. Her very recent bicentennial tribute to Mozart suggests that her stylistic perspective is not limited to the 20th century, and indeed there is a hint of the "long 18th century" in the formal precision and carefully modulated instrumental groupings or her larger scale works.

Skouen has enjoyed collaboration with choreographers such as Kjersti Alveberg, writers such as Cecilie Loveid, theatre directors and painters. Outwardly at least, hers is not "pure" or "absolute" music, even in those pieces for solo performance. It is most certainly not closet music. Association with particular performers or soloists—most notably perhaps the soprano Anna Mahler-Werfel, whose name suggests another possible parameter of influence—is of great significance for her. Lacking all methodological dogmatism, her works express the unities of time, space and mood that are defining characteristics of great drama. They are not simply scores, blandly encoded ideas or matrices; they are scripts, written in order to be enacted.

—Signe Maarten

SLAVICKÝ, Klement. Czechoslovak. Born in Tovačov, Moravia, 22 September 1910. Educated at Prague Conservatoire (composition under K.B. Jirák, conducting under P. Dědeček and V. Talich, piano under R. Kuržova, viola under F. Stupka), 1927–33; further composition study under Josef Suk and V. Talich, 1934–5. Administrator, Umělecká Beseda, 1939–72; producer, dramaturge, Czech Radio, until 1951; administrator, Union of Czechoslovak Composers, 1949–69; otherwise full-time composer. Recipient: Artist of Merit, Czechoslovak People's Republic, 1967; United Nations Gold Medal (for *Sinfonietta No 4 (Pax hominibus in universo orbi)*, 1985. Mailing address: c/o Czech Music Fund, Music Information Centre, Besedni 3, 118 00 Prague 1, Czechoslovakia.

Publishers: Panton; Supraphon.

Symphonies/orchestral:

Fantasia (piano, orchestra) 1931.
Sinfonietta No 1 (large orchestra) 1940.
Moravian Dance Fantasy 1951. Recorded Supraphon.

Rhapsodic Variations 1953. Recorded Supraphon.
Sinfonietta No 2 (large orchestra) 1962.
Sinfonietta No 3 (Concerto for Orchestra) (large orchestra) 1980. Recorded Supraphon.
Sinfonietta No 4 (Pax hominibus in universo orbi) (strings, keyboard, percussion, solo voice, reciter, organ) 1982.

Chamber/instrumental:

String Quartet No 1 1932.
Two Compositions (cello, piano) 1936.
Wind Trio (oboe, clarinet, bassoon) 1937.
Three Compositions (piano) 1947.
Frescoes (organ) 1957. Recorded Supraphon.
Sonata: Reflection upon Life (piano) 1958. Recorded Supraphon.
On the Black. On the White (piano) 1958.
Piano and Youth (piano) 1958.
Suite (oboe, piano) 1959.
Invocation (organ) 1963. Recorded Panton.
Partita (violin) 1963. Recorded Panton.
Twelve Small Etudes (piano) 1964.
Etudes and Essays (piano) 1965.
Intermezzi mattutini (flute, harp) 1965.
Trialogue (violin, clarinet, piano) 1966.
Capricci (horn, piano) 1967.
Musica monologica (harp) 1973.
Suite (piano—4 hands) 1969.
The Song, the Home and Furiant (piano—4 hands) 1971.
String Quartet No 2 1972.
Poema a rondo (cello, piano) 1973.
Sonata: Friendship (violin, piano) 1974.
Senteze (trumpet, piano) 1976.
Intermezzo lyrico (piano) 1987.
Rapsodia (viola) 1987.

Vocal/choral:

Spiritual Songs (voice, piano; Latin texts) 1942.
To Nature (2 symphonic songs for high voice, orchestra) 1942.
To My Mother (unaccompanied male chorus; Sladek) 1942.
Song of My Native Country (Moravian songs for tenor, piano) 1942.
Lidice (double chorus of male voices; Halas) 1945.
Vonicka (12 songs; Urbankova) 1948.
Sohaje (cycle of love poetry for soloists, female chorus; Moravian folk poetry) 1948.
Oh My Heart (high voice, piano; Moravian folk poetry) 1954. Recorded Supraphon.
Madrigals (unaccompanied mixed chorus; Czech, Moravian and Slovak love poetry) 1959. Recorded Supraphon.
The Spring Merry Go Round (children's chorus for voice, flute, piano; Vaclav Fischer) 1969.
Psalmi (soloists, mixed chorus, organ; Old Testament Latin) 1970.
Calling You, Sun (songs about children and for children; Vaclav Fischer) 1974.
Road to Light (dramatic fresco for reciter, male chorus, solo voice; Mahen) 1980.
Summer Day (cycle of children's choruses with piano acompaniment; Vaclav Fischer) 1983.
Bird Year (cycle of children's choruses with piano acompaniment; Ivo Fischer).

Other:

Some film music, folk song arrangements.

PUBLICATIONS

On Slavický: J. Berkovec, "Nova komorni hudba", in *H Ro*, 7, 1954; J. Seda, "Nad dilem KS", in *H Ro*, 14, 1961.

* * *

Klement Slavický has a special place among contemporary Czech composers because he unifies two apparently antagonistic tendencies that determined the course of Czech music between the wars: the Moravian tendency founded and represented by the dominant figure of Leoš Janáček, and the Czech one represented by V. Novák and Josef Suk. It was in fact Suk and Novák who dominated contemporary music; far more pupils passed through their hands at the Prague Conservatoire than were handled by Janáček's rather more isolated master class at Brno.

Slavický was a student at the Prague Conservatoire (where his composition teachers were Suk and K.B. Jirák), but he was born in Moravia, deeply influenced by Janáček, and brought with him a longstanding family interest in and love of folklore. He combines in his compositional style a powerfully expressive side with a deep and concentrated interest in musical structure that starts in local detail and develops into consistent form. The virtuosity evident in the majority of his works is a direct result of those characteristics of his basic musical language.

During the 1930s his music was in contemporary, even modernistic idioms, often articulated as toccata-like instrumental stylizations. The events of the World War II suggested a turn to partriotic themes as well as to a simpler compositional idiom, an orientation most clearly seen in the vocal works written around that time, the symphonic songs *To Nature*, *Song of My Native Country* and *Lidice*. This development led perfectly logically to the folklorism of the 1950s, but in addition to satisfying the prevailing ideals of the period, Slavický continued to develop some of his youthful dispositions in the area of melodic colour and rhythm. The pieces from this period are among his most frequently performed works

Towards the latter half of the 1950s, a new creative period began; Slavický abandoned folklore and turned back as if to his artistic starting point. This is evident in such compositions as the organ *Frescoes* and the piano *Sonata: Reflection upon Life* which was written two years before his 50th birthday. Slavický's chamber compositions from the 1960s place a high demand on the performer's technical sophistication and ability to convey a serious message by means of absolute musical values. This is equally true of his large orchestral pieces, which he has always preferred to label *Sinfoniettas.* The third of these, subtitled *Concerto for Orchestra* captivates by virtue of its unprecedented concision; the single movement is divided into introduction, main part, slow part, finale and coda, and makes remarkable use of contract between timbrally transparent areas and orchestrally dense blocks of sound. The fourth, with the theme *Pax hominibus in universo orbi*, was dedicated to the 40th anniversary of the United Nations, and won Slavický a UN Gold Medal.

Slavický is not a composer whose work can be easily overviewed and theorised; on the contrary, he draws in listener and performer alike; for all the technical demands of his work it has an impact which is as immediate as it is profound.

—Jan Dehner

SMALLEY, Denis (Arthur). New Zealander. Born in Nelson, 16 May 1946. Educated at Nelson College, 1957–63; University of Canterbury, Christchurch, 1957–63, B.Mus., Dip.Mus.; Victoria University of Wellington, 1968–9, B.Mus.; Conservatoire National Supérieur de Musique, Paris, 1971–2, diplome de musique electro-acoustique et de recherche musicale; "Stage", Groupe de Recherches Musicales, Radio-diffusion Television Française, Paris, 1971–2; University of York, 1972–5; Licentiate, Royal Schools of Music; Licentiate, Trinity College, London. Divorced; 1 son. Head of music, Wellington College 1969–71; northern music critic, *The Guardian*, 1972–5; composition fellow, 1975–6, lecturer in music and director of the recording and electro-acoustic music studio 1976–88, and senior lecturer, since 1988, University of East Anglia, Norwich, Norfolk. Recipient: Fylkingen Prize for Electronic Composition, Sweden, 1975; 2nd prize, Bourges Electro-Acoustic Awards, France, 1977; 1st prize, Bourges Electro-Acoustic Awards, France, 1983; special prize, International Confederation for Electro-Acoustic Music, 1983; 2nd prize, Newcomp Award for Computer Music Composition, United States, 1984; Prix Ars Electronica, 1988. Mailing address: Music Centre, University of East Anglia, University Plain, Norwich NR4 7TJ, Norfolk, England.

Publisher: none.

Works:

Gradual (tape, amplified clarinet) 1974. Recorded Fylkingen FYLP 1012.
Pentes (tape) 1974; first performed France, 1975. Recorded UEA 81063.
Ouroboros (tape) 1975.
Pneuma (amplified voices, percussion) 1976, revised 1981; first performed York, 1976. Recorded Hyperion A 66060.
Darkness After Time's Colours (tape) 1976.
Chanson de geste (amplified voice, amplified clavichord) 1978. Recorded UEA 81063.
The Pulses of Time (tape) 1979; first performed London, 1979. Recorded UEA 81063.
Berne Mobiles (tape) 1980.
Word Within (2 amplified voices) 1981; first performed Bath, 1981.
Vortex (tape) 1982; first performed London, 1982.
Tides (tape) 1984; first performed France, 1984.
Clarinet Threads (amplified clarinet, tape) 1985; first performed Norwich, Norfolk, 1985. Recorded Wergo, 1990.
O Vos Omnes (8-part chorus, treble, alto, tenor, tape) 1986; first performed Norwich, Norfolk, 1986.
Wind Chimes (tape) 1987; first performed London, 1987. Recorded Wergo, 1990.
New Work (piano, tapes) 1990; first performed Norwich, Norfolk, 1990.

PUBLICATIONS

By Smalley: "Spectromorphology and Structuring Processes", in *The Language of Electro-Acoustic Music*, edited by Simon Emmerson, London, 1986; "The Listening Imagination: Listening in the Electro-Acoustic Era", in *The Compendium of Musical Thought*, London, 1991.

* * *

The work of Denis Smalley is primarily electronic and electro-acoustic. His few pieces for other media manifest the same concentrated attitude in evidence there. After leaving his native New Zealand in 1971, he studied with the Groupe de Recherches Musicales in Paris, which initiated an interest in the use of concrete sounds in electronic music. In 1974 he produced *Pentes* using transformed instrumental sounds; the only instrument which becomes recognisable is the Northumbrian small-pipes. The focus of the piece is the tiny pulsed shifts of the harmonic spectrum. A progression slowly evolves which resolves on to the drone of the pipes, and from that a traditional piper's melody emerges.

Smalley moved to England, having decided to concentrate on electro-acoustic composition. Having been scathingly partisan in his advocacy of concrete composition, he made a truce with analogue synthesis in *Darkness After Time's Colours*.

Vortex is concerned with movement, with types of motion suggested by the title—not literal spatial movement, but elements of sound with analogous effects, an "invisible kinetic sculpture". Graphics-based computer programmes were employed to specify sound objects and sequences which were modified and developed using a versatile editing programme. Final changes, some made live, were added during recording, and natural sounds developed for inclusion.

Concrete sounds remain prominent in Smalley's tape pieces. *Tides*, a large-scale work, employs digital transformation of water and sea sounds. *Wind Chimes* transforms the sound of ceramic aeolian chimes from New Zealand. With both of these pieces, as with *Pentes*, he discovered the sound-source by accident.

A small cache of Smalley's work pairs tape with live performance: *Gradual* for amplified clarinets and tape, and *Clarinet Threads*, "a series of interlocked electro-acoustic environments in which the clarinet's sound repertory could be integrated". *Word Within*, for two amplified voices and tape, deploys extended vocal techniques on a word clipped from a Petrarchan sonnet, "sospirando" ("sighing"), heard in over a hundred ways which investigate the interior of the word. Other pieces involve performers with live electronics, such as *Pneuma* for amplified voices and tape.

Chanson de geste combines extended vocal techniques for female voice and a subsidiary voice with clavichord sounds, and a tuning fork, wooden ruler and a pair of stones. Amplification is used to magnify sounds which would otherwise be inaudible, and to hone the sound-balance. Much more spacious than Smalley's other work, the piece explores the voice as a collection of sound-sources based on various means of producing consonants and vowels, and the clavichord, which "ideally matches the voice", chosen for the subtle profusion of its sounds.

Smalley's work with live performance feeds back into tape work. *The Pulses of Time*, for instance, uses the clavichord vocabulary developed in *Chanson de geste* in an exploration of periodicity ("pulses", as Smalley puts it) in sound, from form to metre to the mathematical acceleration of pulses in the sound of bouncing objects, and their internal behaviour.

"The medium of electro-acoustic music on tape allows me to explore and use sounds in ways otherwise impossible," writes Smalley. The complexity of the sounds of bouncing in *The Pulses of Time*, for example, could only be explored in the way Smalley wished by the use of electronics. He also characterises his approach by stating, "traditional pitch and rythmic values are not to be discarded but incorporated in an expanding sound medium where a more comprehensive approach to the audio-spectrum and its temporal behaviour has changed and is changing human perception of the nature of sound and music".

Smalley's rigorous technical standards make his tape work

very clean, and there could be said to be a somewhat cold precision to his music. However, he intends it to be "dramatically expressive": *Wind Chimes* is a "narrative", the voice in *Chanson de geste* "traverses a variety of emotional qualities" to furnish a sensitive shape for the music's "expressive interior".

—David Revill

SMIRNOV, Dmitri (Nikolayevich). Russian. Born in Minsk, 2 November 1948. Educated in Frunze, 1956–65; Music Technicum, Frunze, 1964–7; Moscow Conservatory (composition under Nikolai Sidelnikov, orchestration under Edison Denisov, analysis under Yuri Kholopov), 1967–72; further study under Philip Gershkovich, 1970, 1980–9. Married Elena Firsova, *q.v.*, 19 August 1972; 1 son and 1 daughter. Editor, Sovetskii kompozitor publishers, Moscow, 1973–80; member, Union of Soviet Composers, since 1974, and Association for Contemporary Music, Moscow, from 1990. Recipient: 1st prize (for *Solo*), International Week of the Harp, The Netherlands, 1976; 2nd prize (for *Serenade*), 5th International Marcel Josse Composers Competition, France, 1981. Mailing address: c/o Dartington College of Arts, Totnes, Devon TQ9 6JE, England.

Publishers: Boosey & Hawkes; Hans Sikorski, Hamburg; Schirmer; VAAP, Moscow.

Symphonies/orchestral:

Two Ricercares Op 40 (string orchestra) 1969–83; first performed Moscow, 11 April 1983.
Piano Concerto No 1 Op 8 1971; first performed Moscow, 21 June 1972.
Clarinet Concerto Op 14 1974, revised 1977.
Pastorale Op 15 1975; first performed Leningrad, 14 February 1977. Recorded Opus Stereo 9110 1448.
Triple Concerto Op 21 (alto saxophone, double bass, piano, orchestra) 1977; first performed Moscow, 26 December 1977.
Fanfares (symphonic poem) 1978.
Piano Concerto No 2 Op 24 1978; first performed Moscow, 25 December 1978.
Symphony No 1: The Seasons (in Memory of William Blake) Op 30 1980; first performed Riga, 8 October 1981.
Symphony No 2 Op 36 (soloists, mixed chorus, orchestra; Hölderlin) 1982; first performed Moscow, 1990.
Tiriel-Prologue Op 41a (from the opera) 1983; first performed Moscow, 30 October 1984.
Mozart-Variations Op 47 1987; first performed Moscow, 2 February 1988.
Concerto for Violin and Chamber Strings Op 54 (13 strings) 1990.

Chamber/instrumental:

Twelve Melancholic Waltzes (piano) 1965–85.
Two Pieces (piano) 1966.
Sonata No 1 Op 1 1967, revised 1977; first performed Frunze, 5 June 1967.
Nine Pieces (piano) 1967–79.
Monologue Op 3 (clarinet) 1968.
Five Little Pieces Op 4 1968; first performed Moscow, 13 March 1971.
Sonata No 1 Op 5 (violin, piano) 1969, revised 1971; first performed Moscow, 20 April 1970.
Suite in Baroque Style (piano or harpsichord) 1969–80.
Magic Casket (album of piano pieces for children) 1969–85.
Two Fugues Op 6 (violin) 1970; first performed Moscow, 1970.
String Trio Op 7 1970; first performed Moscow, 28 February 1971.
Two Magic Quadrates ("Magic", "The Bells"; piano) 1971.
Toccata (Kirgiz) (piano) 1972; first performed Moscow, 21 June 1972.
Cradle Song (oboe, piano) 1972.
String Quartet No 1 Op 11 1973.
Sonata Op 16 (flute, harp) 1975; first performed Moscow, 6 October 1975.
Mirages Op 17 (saxophone quartet) 1975; first performed Moscow, 6 May 1976. Recorded Melodiya C10 15159–60.
Lyrical Composition Op 18 (flute, oboe, violin, cello, harpsichord) 1975; first performed Moscow, 11 May 1977.
Canon-Humoresque (3 saxophones) 1975, revised 1985.
The Melancholic Minute (clarinet, piano) 1975.
Solo for Harp Op 19 1976; first performed Limburg, The Netherlands, August 1976. Recorded Mobile Fidelity 906.
Nine Children's Pieces (horn, piano) 1976–9.
Sonata Op 22 (bassoon, piano) 1977; first performed Moscow, 30 January 1978.
Three Dances (xylophone) 1977.
Piano Trio Op 23 1977; first performed Moscow, 11 October 1980.
Sonata Op 25 (cello, piano) 1978; first performed Moscow, 24 February 1979.
Two Pieces (harp) 1978.
Two Pieces ("Alarming News", "Song without Words"; cello, piano) 1978–9.
Sonata No 2 Op 26 (violin, piano) 1979; first performed Moscow, 26 December 1979.
Children's Concerto (cello, piano) 1980.
Sonata No 2 Op 29 (piano) 1980; first performed Moscow, 8 December 1980.
Dirge Canons in memoriam Igor Stravinsky Op 33 (flute, oboe, clarinet, bassoon, horn, trumpet, trombone, tuba, percussion, string quartet) 1981; first performed Moscow, 14 December 1981.
Serenade Op 34 (oboe, alto saxophone, cello) 1981; first performed Moscow, 25 May 1981.
Three Equale (trumpet, horn, trombone, piano) 1981.
Ballade Op 35 (alto saxophone, piano) 1982; first performed Moscow, 14 April 1982. Recorded Melodiya C10 20849 004.
Forest Pictures (harp) 1982.
The Farewell Song Op 37 (viola, harp) 1982; first performed Moscow, 4 October 1982.
Fantasia Op 38 (saxophone quartet) 1982; first performed Moscow, 12 December 1983.
Titriel Op 41b (from the opera; baritone saxophone, piano) 1983; first performed Moscow, 25 April 1984.
Titriel Op 41c (cello, piano; after Blake) 1984; first performed Kishinev, 5 March 1987.
String Quartet No 2 Op 42 (2nd movement is a meditation on Blake's "Cradle Song") 1985; first performed Moscow, 22 October 1985.

Music Greeting to H.S. (trumpet) 1985; first performed Hamburg, 16 October 1985.
Partita Op 43 (violin) 1985; first performed New York City, 7 December 1987.
Epitaph to Emil Gilels Op 44 (piano, organ) 1985.
Seven Melancholic Waltzes (alto saxophone, piano) 1985; first performed Kiev, 22 February 1986.
Thel-Prologue Op 45a (after the opera; flute, oboe, clarinet, bassoon, horn, trumpet, trombone, 2 percussion, harp, celeste, string quartet) 1985.
Two Moods (guitar) 1987.
Two Intermezzi (piano) 1987.
The Seven Angels of William Blake Op 50 (piano) 1988; first performed Glasgow, 23 November 1989.
The Moonlight Story Op 51 (after a Blake engraving; piccolo, bass clarinet, violin, viola, cello, double bass) 1988; first performed London, 8 June 1989.
Evening Song Op 56 (alto or tenor saxophone, piano) 1990.
Trinity Music Op 57 (clarinet, violin, piano) 1990.
Jacob's Ladder (large ensemble) 1990–1; first performed London, 17 April 1991.

Vocal/choral:

The Handful of Sand Op 2 (voice, 12 players; Op 2a for voice, piano; Takuboku) 1967, revised 1983; piano version first performed Moscow, 6 January 1971.
Twelve Chorales (unaccompanied mixed chorus; biblical) 1968–72.
Two Choruses (unaccompanied mixed chorus; Blok) 1968.
About Mr Trullalinski (children's song for voice, piano; Tuvim) 1969; first performed Frunze, January 1969.
The Ominous Stink (cantata for bass, mixed chorus, orchestra; Yesenin) 1969–70.
Six Poems by Alexander Blok Op 9 (voice, orchestra or piano) 1972.
Eternal Refuge Op 10 (voice, organ, strings, percussion; Bulgakov) 1972, revised 1981; first performed Tula, 31 January 1982.
Six Haiku of Kabajasi Issa Op 12 (voice, flute, piano) 1973.
Cantata in memoriam Pablo Neruda Op 13 (soprano, tenor, mixed chorus, strings, percussion) 1974.
The Sorrow of Past Days Op 20 (voice, flute, violin, cello, percussion; Pushkin) 1976; first performed Moscow, 30 November 1977.
Two Poems by Alexander Pushkin (voice, piano) 1976.
Four Poems by Arseni Tarkovski Op 27 (voice, piano) 1979.
The Seasons Op 28 (voice, flute, viola, harp; Blake) 1979; first performed Moscow, 10 March 1980.
Lyrical Epigrams (unaccompanied children's chorus; Marshak) 1979.
Songs of Fate Op 31 (voice, organ; Hölderlin) 1980; first performed Moscow, 21 November 1981.
Wonderful Stories (children's songs for voice, piano; English nursery rhymes, translated Marshak) 1980–6.
Six Poems by William Blake Op 32 (voice, organ) 1981; first performed Moscow, 10 March 1986.
The Night Rhymes Op 39 (voice, orchestra or piano; Pushkin) 1982; first performed Moscow, 24 November 1986.
Cock and Bull Stories (children's song for voice, piano; Kruzhkov) 1983.
The Horse (unaccompanied mixed chorus; Pushkin) 1984.
Song of the Learned Cat (children's song for voice, piano; Pushkin) 1984–8.
Magic Boat Op 46 (voice, piano; Tjutchev) 1986; first performed Moscow, 6 June 1988.
The Visions of Coleridge Op 48 (voice, flute, clarinet, horn, percussion, string quintet) 1987; first performed London, 14 February 1988.
Songs of Love and Madness Op 49 (voice, clarinet, celeste, harp, string trio; Blake) 1988.
The Initial Time Op 52 (voice, piano; Pasternak) 1988.
Eight-Line Poems Op 53 (voice, flute, horn, harp, string trio; Mandelstam) 1989.
From Evening to Morning Op 55 (unaccompanied mixed chorus; Blake) 1990.

Opera:

Tiriel Op 41 (after Blake) 1983; first performed Freiburg, 28 January 1989.
The Lamentations of Thel Op 45 (chamber opera after Blake) 1985–6; first performed London, 9 June 1989.

Other:

Adagiosissimo (transcribed from J.S. Bach: *Capricio sopra la lontananza . . . BWB 992* for piano) 1982.
Capriccio on Departure . . . (transcribed and arranged from J.S. Bach's BWV 992: flute, oboe, clarinet, bassoon, horn, trumpet, trombone, percussion, celeste, harp, string quartet) 1982; first performed Moscow, 6 November 1982.

Arrangements/transcriptions of: Dmitri Shostakovitch: *Preparations (Pantomime)* (from *Hamlet*; clarinet, piano) 1975; *Football* (from *The Age of Gold*; piano) 1980; Modest Mussorgsky: *Khovanschina* (final scene; after Stravinsky) 1983; Alexander Skriabin: *Op 57* (15 players) 1990.

Film music: *Heritage: The Art of Ancient Greece / The Art of Ancient Rome / The Art of the Middle Ages* [collaboration with Elena Firsova], 1979; *He*, 1980; *Chronicle of Moon Nights*, 1983; *Mystery of Atmospheric Whirlwinds*, 1984; *Atlas of Micro-World*, 1984; *Atomic Scientists*, 1986; *Nickolaj Bukharin*, 1989.

PUBLICATIONS

By Smirnov: "*Tiriel* von William Blake und meine Oper", and "Mein musikalischer Weg", Freiburg Theatre programme notes, 1989; "Philip Gershkovich", in *Tempo*, 1990.

On Smirnov: Robert Henderson, "New Voices from Russia", in *The Daily Telegraph*, 16 February 1988; Gerard McBurney, "Smirnov's *Tiriel*", Tempo, 1969, June 1989; Robert Maycock, "Blake Experienced", *The Independent*, 12 June 1989.

Dmitri Smirnov comments:

I do not find it a problem to choose which technique to use, which instruments to limit myself to, or which style to follow. It could be any technique, or maybe several all at once: a hybrid or fusion of techniques. And the musical and expressive means I draw from can also be incredibly varied—the widest possible range. The style need not be sterile, but can absorb into itself elements of various styles from very different epochs. None of this should be all that important nor should it be an end in itself, as it is all only an *instrument* helping one to achieve the main aim, which is the clearest possible expression of the musical idea.

It is not easy to say where my musical ideas come from. The discussions Socrates held with his Genius gave birth to philosophy. Blake "copied down" his spiritual visions and what resulted was either poetry or painting. I am convinced that music also has its source in that same mysterious world, which I see as a world of infinite beauty, harmony and perfection. To be able to hear this world spiritually is a great joy, and an even greater joy if we are able even partially to convey what we hear in our music.

* * *

Together with his wife, Elena Firsova, Dmitri Smirnov is among the first of the middle generation of composers from the Soviet Union to find wide recognition and appreciation in the West. Smirnov's music is open, direct and unafraid of nostalgia and excitement. His idiom, founded originally on the lyrical and heterophonic modernism of his teacher and mentor Edison Denisov, has since taken on board Smirnov's own private rediscovery of the great late Romantic composers, especially Mahler and Ricard Strauss. From them Smirnov has garnered an appealing strain of yearning (and strongly tonal) melody, a fondness for the delayed resolution of old-fashioned passing-notes and a sometimes wickedly rich orchestral palette.

The dominating impulse behind Smirnov's work for the last decade and a half has been his love for the life and work of William Blake. Smirnov first encountered Blake's poetry, in Russian translation, in the late 1970s. Since then he has composed more than 20 works, operatic and orchestral, vocal and instrumental, inspired either by Blake's poetry or by his paintings and drawings. He has also published his own translations of Blake into Russian verse.

The first piece to be inspired by the English poet was *The Seasons*, a song cycle on Blake's four early lyrics. It was specifically in this piece that Smirnov first allowed the inflections of late 19th-century music to creep back into his own language. On all levels the composition of this charming work represented for Smirnov the opening of an important door into the less-than-conscious. A year later Smirnov confirmed this new direction by orchestrating *The Seasons* and calling it *Symphony No 1*. What was once the vocal line is now the orchestral *haupstimme* and in a form expanded and coloured beyond the original intentions.

The chief products of Smirnov's exploration of Blake are probably his two operas *Tiriel* and *The Lamentations of Thel. Tiriel* is a substantial work, a realisation of the poet's early prophetic vision as an apocalyptic symbolic drama in the Wagnerian mould. The action is slow and grand as the King Lear-like eponymous hero wanders across a blasted and friendless landscape vividly evoked by the long elegiac orchestral accompaniment. Although using some of the same ideas and much the same language, the chamber opera *The Lamentations of Thel* is cast in a much smaller and more intimate form. The chamber orchestral writing is sweet and filled with the ringing of bells, and the vocal parts include a child treble and a counter-tenor. *Thel* is written not as continuous melo-declamation but as a series of clearly defined numbers, each with its own form and character.

Smirnov's father was an opera singer and the composer was brought up in the atmosphere of the typical repertoire of the provincial Soviet opera house. Perhaps that is why he has so strongly turned away from that kind of theatre-music towards the Wagnerian–Straussian tradition that is almost completely unfamiliar to most Russian audiences. It may be that Smirnov was so appalled by the spiritual and artistic devastation brought about by the Soviet system that he felt the need to draw his strength from as far away as possible in order adequately to express his feelings. That he has managed such a feat is a tribute both to his serious artistry and to the resilient, upright character so apparent in his music.

—Gerard McBurney

SOHAL, Naresh. Indian. Born in Harsipind, Punjab, 18 September 1939. Educated at University of Punjab (mathematics and physics); emigrated to United Kingdom, 1962; further study, City Literary Institute, London, and London College of Music; private music study under Jeremy Dale Roberts; further study, Leeds University (under Alexander Goehr), 1972–4. Music copyist, Boosey & Hawkes, London; independent composer, resident in Edinburgh since 1983; member, BBC Central Music Advisory Committees, London and Scotland. Recipient: Padma Shri (Order of the Lotus), President of India, 1987. Mailing address: 50 Spottiswoode Street, Edinburgh EH9 1DG, Scotland.

Publishers: Novello; Music Production Company, 28 Harcourt Street, London WI, England.

Symphonies/orchestral:

Concerto for Harmonica, Percussion and Strings 1966.
Aalaykhyam I 1970; first performed London, 27 November 1971.
Aalaykhyam II 1972; first performed London, 5 February 1973.
Indra-Dhanush 1973.
Dhyan I (cello, small orchestra) 1974; first performed London, 27 January 1975.
Tandava Nritya/Dance of Destruction and Recreation 1984.
Concerto for Violin and Orchestra 1986.

Chamber/instrumental:

Hexad (flute/piccolo, horn/cymbal, percussion, violin, cello, double bass) 1971; first performed London, 13 July 1971.
Chiaruscuro I (2 trumpets, horn, trombone, tuba) 1971; broadcast BBC 1975–6.
Oblation (violin, piano) 1971; first performed London, 10 December 1971.
Octal (flute/piccolo, oboe, clarinet/bass clarinet, trumpet, horn, electric guitar/cymbal, electric double bass/tam-tam, electronics) 1972; first performed Durham, 23 July 1972.
A Mirage (piano) 1974; first performed Birmingham, 23 October 1974.
Shades (soprano saxophone) 1974; broadcast BBC 28 May 1974.
Shades II (flute) 1975; first performed London, 4 June 1978.
Hexahedron (flute, oboe, clarinet/bass clarinet, bassoon, horn, piano) 1975; first performed Portsmouth, Hampshire, 4 June 1975.
Chiaruscuro II (string quartet) 1976; first performed Middleburg, The Netherlands, 8 July 1978.
Monody (cello) 1976; first performed Leicester, 18 September 1976.
Undulation (cello, piano) 1976; first performed London, 17 May 1983.
Shades III (cello) 1978; first performed Calcutta, 7 January 1979.

Chakra (piano) 1979; first performed Croydon, Surrey, 13 November 1979.
Shades IV (viola) 1983; first performed Toronto, December 1983.
Brass Quintet No 2 1983; first performed London, 26 March 1984.
Shades V (guitar) 1988.
Trio (violin, cello, piano) 1988.

Vocal/choral:

Ashit Prahar (soprano, orchestra) 1965; first performed London, 17 January 1970.
Kavita I (soprano, flute, oboe, clarinet, bassoon, trombone, piano, violin/percussion, cello/percussion; Tagore) 1970; first performed Birmingham, 13 July 1970.
Poems of Tagore I (soprano, piano; Tagore) 1970; first performed London, 15 October 1970.
Surya (soprano, alto, tenor, baritone, bass, 24 voices, flute, 3 percussion; Kalida, Rig Veda) 1970; first performed London, 16 February 1971.
Night's Poet (2 clarinets/bass clarinet, percussion, piano/celeste; Tagore) 1971; first performed Bradford, Yorkshire, 5 November 1974.
Kavita II (soprano/cymbal, flute, piano; Donne) 1972; first performed London, 28 January 1972.
Kavita III (soprano/cymbal, electric double bass; Marvell) 1972; first performed Bristol, 7 December 1972.
Poets to Come (baritone, unaccompanied SATB chorus; Whitman) 1975; first performed London, 20 February 1976.
Poems of Tagore II (1 or 2 mezzo-sopranos, cello) 1977; first performed London, 1 May 1977.
Inscape (soprano, mezzo-soprano, alto, tenor, baritone, bass, flute, percussion, electronics; Tagore) 1979; first performed London, 18 November 1979.
The Wanderer (baritone, SATB chorus, orchestra; Anglo Saxon) 1981; first performed London, 23 August 1982.
From Gitanjali (bass-baritone, orchestra; Tagore) 1985; first performed New York City, 12 September 1985.
Madness Lit by Lightning (soprano, mezzo-soprano, tenor, baritone, bass, flute/piccolo, clarinet/bass clarinet, bassoon/contrabassoon, horn, trumpet, piano, percussion, violin, cello, double bass; Preston) 1989.

Other:

Sir William in Search of Xanadu (music for television) 1983.
End of Empire (music for television) 1985; broadcast Granada TV, 25 April 1985.
Apartheid (music for television) 1986.
Gautama Buddha (ballet) 1987; first performed Edinburgh, 1989.
The World at Your Feet—Zanskar (music for television) 1988.
Monarchy—The Enchanted Glass (music for television) 1988.

PUBLICATIONS

On Sohal: "S at 50", in *Music Current*, 11, September 1989.

* * *

Remarkably, Naresh Sohal is the first composer from the Indian subcontinent to establish an international reputation for composition in a Western idiom; only the film composer Vanraj Bhatia had preceded him on the journey West. There is, though, nothing about his work of that bland "East-West" synthesis which is the almost routine response of composers of Asian origins who have settled in the West. If its philosophical underpinnings and subject matter are identifiably Asian (he has, for instance, a strong interest in the poetry of Rabindranath Tagore, whom he has set in *From Gitanjali* and other pieces), its basic compositional strategies represent a highly personal and expressive engagement with the modernist tradition in Western music. Indeed, almost ironically, Sohal was selected to represent the West at Musicultura, an East/West music conference convened in Queekhoven in The Netherlands.

Sohal set out studying science and mathematics at the University of Punjab, destined, it was thought, for a career in electronic engineering. His interests, though, lay in the direction of music, and Western music. His father, a well-known Urdu poet, opposed the move (not altogether strenuously), but Sohal emigrated to London in 1962. He made a modest living as a music copyist and furthered his studies at the City Literary Institute, a justly renowned adult education centre specially devoted to the arts, and under Jeremy Dale Roberts. In 1972, with a grant from the Arts Council of Great Britain, he moved to Leeds to research micro-tonal composition under Alexander Goehr.

Sohal's first completed score was the orchestral tone poem *Ashit Prahar*, in which an evocation of the passage of a day and a night is subjected to the darkly evocative and highly textural approach which is typical of his ensemble writing. Sohal does not write melodically as such, but his scoring creates harmonic patterns which fulfil very much the same role as conventional melody. He writes very dramatically, with sudden alterations of tone and instrumental sequence, as in the ballet *Gautama Buddha* and his remarkable setting of the Anglo-Saxon poem, *The Wanderer*, the work which established his reputation. His dramatic piece *Madness Lit by Lightning* incorporates elements as far afield as *Don Giovanni* and the Theatre of Cruelty. Written for essentially the same forces as Stravinsky's *The Soldier's Tale*, it is a furiously concentrated piece which may sit rather uncomfortably alongside its intended concert partner.

Sohal's chamber and instrumental writing has a fluidity of line which recalls the extended improvisations of Indian Music, but it is here, ironically, that he is most completely "Western", concerning himself very directly with linear development (albeit idiosyncratically), and an ambitious post-serial approach to tonal development. The early *Concerto for Harmonica* (the first Western instrument he encountered) is a perfect example of his ability to look at a familiar, not to say hackneyed, idiom from a startlingly fresh point of view, and the same is true of his instrumental sequence *Shades* in which familiar instruments speak with the voices of their shadow sides. *Shades* is one of the most adventurous and convincing instrumental sequences of recent years. Micro-intervals are given a structural, not just cosmetic, function in his best scores.

Essentially self-taught, Sohal seems to be working towards ever-larger principles of organisation. His debut score was a remarkable act of confident self-expression and though Sohal has written nothing quite as startlingly impressive since, there are clear signs that he is entering the most productive phase of his career to date, writing in a fully developed and mature style.

—Sukphal Mody

SONDHEIM, Stephen (Joshua). American. Born in New York City, 22 March 1930. Educated at Williams College, Williamstown, Massachusetts, 1946–50, B.A.; further composition study under Milton Babbitt. Independent composer; president, Dramatists Guild, 1973–81, and subsequently council member; visiting professor of drama, and fellow of St Catherine's College, Oxford, 1990. Recipient: New York Drama Critics Circle Awards (for *Company*, *Follies*, *A Little Night Music*, *Sweeney Todd*, *Into the Woods*, *Pacific Overtures*, *Sunday in the Park with George*); Tony Awards for best score to a musical (for *Company, Follies, A Little Night Music, Sweeney Todd, Into the Woods*); honorary doctorate, Williams College, 1971; elected to American Academy and Institute of Arts and Letters, 1983; Pulitzer Prize for drama (for *Sunday in the Park with George*), 1985; London *Evening Standard* Best Musical Award (for *Follies*), 1987; SWET Laurence Olivier Award (for *Follies*), 1988. Mailing address: c/o Flora Roberts Inc., 157 West 57th Street, New York, New York 10019, U.S.A.

Publishers: Chappell; Hansen; Revelation; Valando.

Musical plays (score and lyrics by Sondheim):

A Funny Thing Happened on the Way to the Forum (libretto by Shevelove and Gelbart, after Plautus, orchestrated by Kostal and Ramin, directed by Abbott) 1961–2; first performed New York, 8 May 1962; filmed 1966. Recorded Capitol SW 1717.
Anyone Can Whistle (libretto and direction by Laurents, orchestrated by Walker) 1963; first performed New York City, 4 April 1964.
Evening Primrose (television musical; libretto by Goldman, orchestrated by Paris, directed by Bogart) 1966; first shown New York, 16 November 1966.
Company (libretto by Furth, orchestrated by Tunick, directed by Prince) 1969–70; first performed New York City, 26 April 1970. Recorded Columbia OS 3550.
Follies (libretto by Goldman, orchestrated by Tunick, directed by Prince) 1969–70; first performed New York, 4 April 1971, revived in London, 1987. Recorded Capitol SO 761.
A Little Night Music (libretto by Wheeler, orchestrated by Tunick, directed by Prince) 1972; first performed New York City, 23 February 1973. Recorded Columbia JS 32265.
The Frogs (libretto and directed by Shevelove, after Aristophanes, orchestrated by Tunick) 1973–4; first performed New Haven, Connecticut, 20 May 1974.
Pacific Overtures (libretto by Weidman and Wheeler, orchestrated by Tunick, directed by Prince) 1975; first performed New York, 11 January 1976. Recorded RCA ARL1 1367.
Sweeney Todd, the Demon Barber of Fleet Street (libretto by Wheeler, orchestrated by Tunick, directed by Prince) 1978; first performed New York City, 1 March 1979; produced for television, 1982. Recorded RCA CBL2 3379.
Merrily We Roll Along (libretto by Furth, orchestrated by Tunick, directed by Prince) 1981; first performed New York, 16 November 1981. Recorded RCA CBL1 4197.
Sunday in the Park with George (libretto and direction by Lapine, orchestrated by Starobin) 1983; first performed New York City, 2 May 1984.
Into the Woods (libretto by Lapine) 1986; first performed New York City, 5 November 1987. Recorded RCA RD 86796; RD 60752.
Assassins (libretto by Goldman) 1990; first performed New York City, January 1991.

As lyricist:

West Side Story (music by Leonard Bernstein) 1957; first performed New York City, 26 September 1957; filmed 1961.
Gypsy (music by Jules Styne) 1958–9; first performed New York, 8 May 1959; filmed 1963.
Do I Hear a Waltz? (music by Richard Rodgers) 1964; first performed New York City, 18 March 1965.
Candide (music by Bernstein, additional lyrics by SS) revised 1973; first performed New York City, 20 December 1973.

Other:

Rag Me That Mendelssohn March (song in Kober and Oppenheimer, *A Mighty Man Is He*) 1955.
The Girls of Summer (incidental music to N.R. Nash) 1956.
Invitation to a March (incidental music to Laurents) 1961.
Twigs (incidental music) 1971.
The Enclave (incidental music to Laurents) 1973.
The Last of Sheila (collaboration on film script) 1973.
Stavisky (film score) 1974.
Side by Side by Sondheim (compilation of songs) 1976, revised 1983; revised version first performed (as *A Stephen Sondheim Evening*) New York City, 3 March 1983. Recorded (revised version) RCA CBL2 1851.
I Never Do Anything Twice (song in film *The Seven Per Cent Solution*) 1977.
Reds (film score) 1981.
Marry Me a Little (compilation of songs) 1981. Recorded RCA ABL-4159.

PUBLICATIONS

By Sondheim: *The Hansen Treasury of Stephen Sondheim Songs*, New York City, 1977; *The Stephen Sondheim Songbook*, London, 1979; *All Sondheim*, New York City, 1980.

On Sondheim: Charles Michener, "Broadway's Music Man", in *Newsweek*, 23 April 1973; Gerard Bordman, *American Musical Theatre: A Chronicle*, Oxford, 1978, and *American Operetta from HMS Pinafore to Sweeney Todd*, Oxford, 1981; S.B. Wilson, "Motivic, Rhythmic and Harmonic Procedure of Unification in SS's *Company* and *A Little Night Music*", dissertation, Ball State University, Muncie, Indiana, 1983; D.J. Cartmell, "SS and the Concept Musical", dissertation, University of California, Santa Barbara, 1983; Craig Zadan, *Sondheim & Co*, New York, 2nd edition, 1984; John Rockwell, "Urban Popular Song, the Broadway Musical, the Cabaret Revival and the Birth Pangs of American Opera: SS", in *All-American Music: Composition in the Late 20th Century*, New York City, 1985.

* * *

The musical comedy has arguably been North America's most significant contribution to the development of the theatre in the 20th century, and has fostered a long line of important song and lyric writers, from Cole Porter through George and Ira Gershwin to Rodgers and Hammerstein. Stephen Sondheim is widely held to be the most significant heir to that tradition in current musical comedy, although his work has often attracted hostile attention precisely for breaking with those traditions.

Sondheim was a protégé of Oscar Hammerstein, and he has gone on record as saying that Hammerstein, a family friend, was almost a second father to him as a teenager ("if he had been a geologist rather than a lyricist, I would have become a geologist too"). Hammerstein was among the first to break with the old idea of songs as simple colourful interjections in the musical, and Sondheim's subsequent development of them as an integral part of the action had its roots in Hammerstein's teaching.

More significantly, he learned how to structure each song "in the manner of a one-act play", a lesson which Sondheim was able to combine with a musical language derived from his studies under Milton Babbitt in New York. His first significant theatrical contribution came when he was invited to write lyrics for Leonard Bernstein's epic *West Side Story*, including the celebrated "Maria" and "Tonight".

He also contributed memorable songs to Jules Styne's *Gypsy*, and later Richard Rodgers's *Do I Hear a Waltz?*. His first show in which he composed both music and lyrics was *A Funny Thing Happened on the Way to the Forum*. This adaptation of Plautus is the most conventional of his shows, but its success established him as a major name, and it proved to be the springboard for more radical developments to come.

His subsequent works increasingly deviated from the well-established show-business norms of musical comedy, and many of them contained an implicit—and even an explicit—critique of those norms, often in the form of highly expert pastiche, as in *Follies*, which, like *Company*, tends to develop themes rather than a plot.

Sondheim's major development of the form has lain in his overwhelming interest in character, and his insistence that the placement, structure and nature of the song should be devoted to bringing out or revealing elements of character or character relationships, while at the same time being fully integrated into the sometimes complex, and even rather abstract, thematic and plot developments.

Partly as a consequence of this approach, and partly because of the idiosyncratic and highly complex nature of the songs, Sondheim's work has not been widely absorbed into the popular or jazz repertoire, as was common with his predecessors. The only real exception is "Send in the Clowns", a haunting but very simple melody specifically composed for a non-singing actress in the ambitious *A Little Night Music* adapted from Ingmar Bergman's *Smiles of a Summer Night*).

Sondheim's songs are generally through-composed, and draw on a wide range of musical styles and forms, often distinguished by a degree of tonal ambiguity and an insistent rhythmic structure. He is a master of pastiche, and an intricate lyricist of great wit and sometimes dazzling wordplay, often laced with an astringent cynicism which is not common in the genre.

His later works include *Sweeney Todd, the Demon Barber of Fleet Street* and *Sunday in the Park with George*, based on the work of artist George Seurat, and particularly his famous pointillist painting "A Sunday Afternoon on the Island of La Grande Jatte", indicative of Sondheim's penchant for untypical subjects. He has also written for television and film, but his reputation as an innovator will rest on his work for the theatre.

—Kenny Mathieson

SØRENSEN, Bent. Danish. Born in Borup, Denmark, 18 July 1958. Educated at Royal Academy of Music, Copenhagen (composition under Ib Norholm, 1983–7. Freelance composer. Mailing address: 48 Gevinge, 4000 Roskilde, Denmark.

Publisher: Wilhelm Hansen.

Symphonies/orchestral:

Lachrimae 1984, revised 1986; first performed 26 April 1985.

Chamber/instrumental:

Three Pieces (piano) 1976.
String Quartet 1978.
Three Escapades (violin) 1981.
Troldspil (clarinet) 1982.
Ulvetime (flute, clarinet, violin, viola, double bass) 1982.
Sirernes Sange og Nokkens Spil (wind quintet, string quartet, double bass) 1982.
Angelus (piano) 1982, revised 1985.
Klamulan (violin) 1983.
Trotto (oboe, bassoon, horn, violin, cello) 1983.
Alman (String Quartet No 1) 1983–4.
Madelein (flute, oboe, clarinet, bassoon, horn) 1985.
Lais (organ) 1985.
Les Tuchins (2 trombones, 2 electric guitars, 2 cellos) 1986.
Impromptu (clarinet) 1986.
Adieu (String Quartet No 2) 1986.
Clairobscur (flute, oboe, clarinet, bassoon, horn, 2 violins, viola, cello, double bass) 1987.
The Lady of Shalott (viola) 1987.
Camelot by Night (bass flute, guitar) 1988.
Angels' Music (String Quartet No 3) 1988.
Minnewater (2 flutes, oboe, clarinet, 2 horns, trumpet, trombone, 2 percussion, string quartet, double bass) 1988.
Shadowland (flute, oboe, clarinet, bassoon, horn, 2 violins, viola, cello, double bass) 1988–9.
Funeral Procession (chamber ensemble) 1989.
The Shadows of the Shepherds (oboe) 1990.
The Masque of the Red Death (piano) 1990.
The Deserted Churchyards (flute, clarinet, percussion, piano, violin, cello) 1990.
The Bells of Vineta (trombone) 1990.

Vocal/choral:

Diapsalmata (unaccompanied mixed chorus) 1982.
Cyprianus (3 female singers, 2 clarinets, 2 percussion; old Danish spells) 1982.
Donne (voice, violin, guitar; John Donne) 1983.
Garnet to Garnet (voice, guitar, percussion; Shakespeare, Dickinson) 1985.
Lacrimosa (unaccompanied mixed chorus) 1985.
Three Motets (unaccompanied mixed chorus; Psalms) 1985.
Pop sange (tenor, piano; Strunge) 1990.

* * *

Unlike that of most of his compatriots, Bent Sørensen's work is often multi-layered with a wealth of implications which show him embracing elements of "mainstream" modernism. Combined with his delicacy of touch and nuance this gives him a highly distinctive voice which, nonetheless, the outside ear recognises as Danish, not least through his preoccupation with other musics. In Sørensen's case this preoccupation has centred largely on medieval and Renaissance music and often provides a starting point for the beautiful, evocative titles which he gives his compositions.

These titles often prove tantalisingly difficult for a listener to relate to the content of each specific piece—the composer says that they occur to him usually quite early in the compositional process and refer generally not to the content or programme of each work, but more to an image or tangential idea that he had at the time of composition. Nonetheless, they are not merely decorative, but taken together can provide some insight into the mind of this private and most talented young composer.

The three string quartets written between 1983 and 1988 are at the heart of his output to date, with the homogeneous, instrumental colour providing an ideal canvas for the intricate subtleties of his compositional palette. The first, *Alman*, was given its title because Sørensen had a copy of the *Fitzwilliam Virginal Book* by the side of his desk while working on the piece. An alman is a dance, an old form of allemande, but the influence of the original in this work only appears momentarily, as if in a dream. In actuality the dramatic form of this three-movement piece is characterised by the composer as "curve", "mosaic" and "climax" and the three movements together form one long, integrated, harmonic progression.

Adieu is a shorter, one-movement work and shows more preoccupation with melody: heightening and simultaneously blurring melodic possibilities with the fine nuances of quartertones, glissandos and polyrhythms. The title "Adieu" has no reference to Beethoven, but rather to the composer's private image of medieval monks in grey habits and white cowels in a funeral procession—the opening is a solemn, chorale-like music and the pervasive mood is dark and expressionistic. This image and sonority has, from time to time, surfaced in successive works of the composer, most recently and overtly in his ensemble piece *Funeral Procession* of 1989 in which reminiscences of the funeral chorales permeate in all directions.

His third and most recent quartet, *Angels' Music*, was begun during a period of time in Rome and tiny Italian references find their way into the music in an almost pointillistic way: reminiscences of the mediaeval trotto dance, rich Pucciniesque harmony in the most expressive part, and the little songs (angel songs) of the countless golden angels that he saw adorning frescoes and altars. The idea of these songs being created, played and dying out became the overall pattern of the whole work and Sørensen translates this into three corresponding sections: pre-echo, culmination and echo. The whole is a constantly shimmering, shifting piece with harmonies, which although largely rooted in diatonicism, are constantly altered with microtones.

Moving away from the string quartet, Sørensen's recent time has been devoted to works for large ensemble and he has been commissioned by ensembles from four different European countries, the resulting works being *Minnewater* for the Ensemble Modern (Germany), *Funeral Procession* for the Sonanza Ensemble (Sweden), *Clairobscur* for the Esbjerg Ensemble (Denmark) and most recently *Shadowland* for the London Sinfonietta. Progressing from the ideas he explored in the string quartets the four connected movements of *Shadowland* again show glimpses and flashes of ideas shyly emerging from behind the melodies and trills of the foreground. However, the remarkable control Sørensen exercises over the numerous climaxes and the original way in which the material is focused and interlocked makes this a most vivid and compelling piece and marks a new stage in his compositional maturity.

—Rosemary Johnson

STEINBERG, Carolyn. American. Born in San Antonio, Texas, 17 May 1956. Educated at North Texas State University, Denton, B.M. (theory), 1978; Manhattan School of Music, New York City, M.M. (composition), 1980; private study with Cathy Berberian, 1980–1; Accademia Chigiana, Siena, 1981–2; Staatliche Hochsschule für Musik, Freiburg, 1983; private studies (conducting) with Francis Travis, 1985–6; Juilliard School of Music, New York City, 1987–9, D.M.A.; studies with Ludmila Ulehla, Franco Donatoni, Brian Ferneyhough and Bernard Rands. Married Brian Ferneyhough, *q.v.*, in 1984 (dissolved 1989). Teacher of sight-reading, ear-training, rhythmic skills, Freiburg Hochsschule, 1984–6; private tutor in music theory, since 1987; teaching artist, Lincoln Centre Institute, New York City, since 1988; Tanglewood Music Center composition fellow, Massachusetts, 1989; lecturer, New York Philharmonic Education Department, 1990. Recipient: Stipendium Prize, Darmstadt, 1986; Arthur Ross Foundation Scholarship, Juilliard, 1987; Irving Ruckens Composition Scholarship, Juilliard, 1988; Goddard Lieberson, American Academy and Institute of Arts and Letters, 1990. Mailing address: 405 East 12th Street, No 7, New York, New York 10009, U.S.A.

Publisher: none.

Symphonies/orchestral:

Fluchtpunkte/Vanishing Points (chamber orchestra) 1987; first performed Donaueschingen, 1988.
Flute Concerto (large orchestra) 1988–9.
Chamber Symphony 1990.

Chamber/instrumental:

Smara (piano quartet) 1979.
Shaku (flute) 1981.
Panegyric (cello) 1982; first performed Milan, 1982.
14 + K (2 trumpets, 2 trombones, tuba) 1982.
Variations (violin) 1982; first performed Milan, 1983.
2.1.3-5 Alice (clarinet, alto saxophone, cor anglais, trumpet, violin) 1983.
Ventaglio (cor anglais) 1984.
String Quartet No 1 1985; first performed Darmstadt, 1986.
Nature Studies (piano) 1986.
Rauhreif/Frost (flute, oboe, clarinet; violin, viola, cello; piano) 1987; first performed Darmstadt, 1988.
Brass Quintet No 2 (2 trumpets, horn, trombone, tuba) 1989.

Vocal/choral:

Fiesta (soprano, clarinet, bass clarinet; violin, cello, marimba) 1981, 1984.
Four Love Madrigals (soprano, alto, tenor, bass solo; or small unaccompanied chorus) 1988.
Three Songs (soprano, piano) 1990.

Opera:

Cors de chasse 1990; first performed New York City, 8 June 1990.

Carolyn Steinberg comments:

Through the various stages of initial efforts to the beginning stages of mature work (which is the point I consider myself to have attained now) there are several characteristics of my compositions which continue to emerge in my work naturally, and which I have cultivated. These characteristics will probably remain true of my work throughout my life.

Early works (1977–80, pre-Europe) account for some 20 compositions of chamber, vocal and orchestral music. Most of these pieces made an effort to be "about" something, often relying on timbral colour for local interest, or upon a harmony/melody disposition of lines. In 1980, at the age of 24, I went to Europe, a move which was to have profound effects upon my life and work. Beginning with the cello solo of 1982 and reaching an extreme in *Fluchtpunkte* and *Rauhreif*, I came to control an ever-increasing number of parameters with micro-and macro-structural devices which originated with a germ idea (*Einfall*) for the piece and which permeated the work. Numbers were especially useful in measuring constituent elements and reapplying those quantitites and propositions in a variety of ways. The results of these techniques can vary greatly: *Rauhreif* sounds very different from *Fluchtpunkte*. Such diversity of mood and character will be an asset in writing operas, where rigour and relaxation may all find roles to play.

Another quality which has endured is a striving towards beauty of sound. Timbre and unusual timbral combinations are often used to create a heightened sensitivity to the phenomena of sound. In *Fluchtpunkte*, the number of instruments playing, both being rotated and pivoted in crystalline ways, in keeping with the original image for the piece (*Rauhreif* = frost). In addition, the pitches are organized in modes, themselves crystalline, which are fractured, pivoted and attached to each other, thus furthering the imagery frost. In the *Flute Concerto*, however, instrumentation as the definer of forms finds more sectional and less global application. In this work, the flute provides the core line which is then danced around, covered, exposed or decorated.

Along with what might be called the emancipation of the consonance, my music for the theatre allows melody, which I consider essential when writing for operatically-trained voices. Lyricism has always been a part of my music, and since I am discovering a talent for writing extended melodies, I will not eliminate these powerful musical entities from my vocabulary; I have no party line to support. The melodies of my chamber opera *Cors de chasse* make passing use of tonality (employing open fifths, and major and minor thirds), diversionary tactics from tonality via deceptive leading tones (an expected half-step might become a major second), freely interpolated whole-tone segments which destroy the tonality, and clusters. Tonal references are short-lived: all of the above devices are called into play in rapid succession. The effect is not one of free atonality because the vocabulary of diversionary tactics is larger. The purpose of using these elements is to allow a linear order of pitches to be related to one another in a perceptible though enigmatic way. The line of pitches should breathe. Historically, this grouped length has been called a phrase, the necessity of which originally was not to fill a certain number of bars but rather to create a perceptible unit of information, and to breath, both literally and metaphorically.

Writing music is a personal, spiritual process of growth in which I continuously recombine experiences, skill, sensation, thought and emotion with the creative organization of sound.

* * *

Carolyn Steinberg has continued to clarify for herself, through her compositions, her creative integration of earlier influences. She neither eschews her pedagogical heritage nor restates others' aesthetics. Rather, she is consciously and meticulously building a well-informed foundation in order to construct a vital, spiritual language.

At first listening, most of Steinberg's seminal works seem very diverse in character, and, to some ears, in style. *String Quartet No I* has a twittering, tense surface through which glimpses of lyricism tentatively seek presence, finally emerging more predominantly and, indeed, cathartically, at the end. *Rauhreif*, on the other hand, is built upon five wholesome-sounding, invented modes which, when coupled with constant eight-note repetitions, result in a cheerful, clean declamation of straightforward intent. In *Fluchtpunkte / Vanishing Points* one is struck by the complexity of interlocking timbral, rhythmic and textural designs; lyricism does not play a major role in the piece. In contrast, the chamber opera *Cors de chasse*, which is basically a numbers opera with improvised sections, contains several songs that are deeply lyrical. These songs are characterized by beautiful melodies notated in uncomplicated ways (bars of 2/4 and 3/4, with few irrational subdivisions) and supported by transparent chords of few pitches. Tonality is not absent in *Cors de chasse*, and this fact makes the work sound radically different from the above-mentioned compositions.

Cors de chasse is not so much different from the other pieces as it is a heightened manifestation of a lyricism that is covertly present in all her works. *Rauhreif* contains interesting examples of the distinction between melody with and without lyricism, questioning the point at which one perceives lyricism emerging from melody. The oboe line (bars 25–30, 99–120, 223–32) provides exceptionally good examples here, emerging as melodic foreground despite the rather mechanical generation of its pitches. The Second Brass Quintet also discusses this question. An extended, lyrical melody in the first trumpet was broken into its constituent parts and randomly reordered via computer. This generated material provided a continuation of the original, freely composed melody. Though this process could be construed as a motivic one, its main function was to call to question the nature of lyricism. The generated material did not sound radically different from the intuitive melody and provided an excellent bridge from the melody-accompaniment disposition to the chorale-like harmonies which close the movement. The difference, however, between the free melody and the generated material lies within a certain immediacy. Steinberg's confrontation with the problem of putting a more sensual, human or emotional element into the modernist vocabulary offers some interesting alternatives to the more radical division into camps such as are evident today.

In virtually all of Steinberg's works, there are elaborate designs for the formal disposition of instruments. The most rigorous application of the link between form and instrumentation might be in *Rauhreif*, in which groups of instruments rotate according to an autonomous design. In other works such systematic patterning does not define the limits of the piece but rather is employed within a larger framework. The approach is unique, however, in *Fluchtpunkte / Vanishing Points*, which "makes more striking timbral 'objects', and the total instrumentation of the piece is the sum of instruments necessary to make these 'objects'" (Steinberg). Such organizational strategies do not detract from Steinberg's innate ability to hear subtle timbral combinations, this being a striking feature of her music. Some of the more arresting moments in this regard are to be found in the *Flute Concerto*, especially its accompanied cadenza and coda section; the clarinet–violin–viola trio in *Rauhreif*; the opening of the second section of *Fluchtpunkte / Vanishing Points*, and the oboe d'amore/alto flute duet in the third section of that work; and in numerous portions of the recent *Chamber Symphony*.

In several recent works (since 1988) it seems that Steinberg is allowing acoustic phenomena to achieve a complexity previously sought by invention. The *Chamber Symphony* is full of examples, of which one is the woodwind writing in bars 29–33. Here, an almost minimalist patterning creates, due to register and dynamics, a blasting sound, whereas in *Rauhreif* (bars 11–14) a similar effect is created using far greater rhythmic complexity. The song "Mansion", of *Cors de chasse*, written for mezzo-soprano, Oberheim four-voice synthesizer and contrabass, arrives at some very rich, complex sounds which would not have been noticed or appreciated had there been greater rhythmic complexity. It is as if the composer herself has gained a greater appreciation for an intuitive understanding of individual sonorities. It remains to be seen how this composer will integrate these Dyonisian tendencies with those more Apollian practices which have informed so many of her works.

The *Chamber Symphony* may well prove to be a seminal work in Steinberg's integration of the two opposing tendencies. The pervasive use of simple meters and regular pulses result nevertheless in surprisingly complex sonic events. Gestures are still treated as objects but are not obliged to be part of a larger system; their weight is balanced intuitively in the flow of the music. The third movement reflexively reorganizes material of the first in an elaborate rereading game, and citations of lyricism in the form of gestural units are placed strategically along the pathway of the measures. A rondo of instrumentations emerges (from bar 89), and nervous string textures are followed by long, forceful notes as accompaniment to kaleidoscopic instrumentations. A vocabulary from previous works is drawn to the service of a spontaneous urgency that moves this composition.

—C. Bryan Rulon

STEPTOE, Roger. British/English. Born in Winchester, Hampshire, 25 January 1953. Educated at University of Reading, Berkshire, 1971–74, B.A.; Royal Academy of Music, London, 1974–77. Composer in residence, Charterhouse, Surrey, 1976–79; professor of composition, since 1980, and administrator (also International Composer Festivals) since 1986, Royal Academy of Music London; pianist, accompanist and lecturer internationally. Recipient: all major composition prizes, Royal Academy of Music. Mailing address: 7 Jeffrey's Street, London NW1 9PS, England.

Publisher: Stainer and Bell, London.

Symphonies/orchestral:

Two Miniatures (string orchestra) 1977; first performed Oxford, 29 May 1982.
Sinfonia concertante (violin, viola, cello, strings) 1981; first performed London, 26 June 1982.
Concerto for Oboe and Strings (also arranged for oboe, piano) 1982; first performed London, 3 May 1984.
Concerto for Tuba and Strings (also arranged for tuba, piano) 1983; first performed London, 27 October 1986.
Rapsodia sinfonica (violin, orchestra) 1987.
Symphony 1988.
Clarinet Concerto 1989; first performed Ripon, Yorkshire, 2 August 1989.
Organ Concerto (organ, brass, percussion) 1990; first performed Gloucester, 13 July 1990.

Chamber/instrumental:

String Quartet No 1 1976; first performed London, 5 January 1977. Recorded Phoenix DGS 1001.
Three Preludes (piano) 1976; first performed London, 7 June 1984.
Suite (cello) 1977; first performed London, 6 October 1977.
Study (violin) 1978; first performed Charterhouse, Surrey, 12 February 1979.
Two Impromptus (clarinet) 1978; first performed Cambridge, 21 November 1978. Recorded Phoenix DGS 1017.
Sonata No 1 (piano) 1979; first performed London, 8 May 1980.
Quintet (clarinet, string quartet) 1980; first performed Birmingham, 9 February 1981. Recorded Phoenix DGS 1017.
Study (guitar) 1981.
Equinox (piano) 1981; first performed London, 28 April 1981.
The Knight of the Sun (brass quintet) 1982; first performed London, 17 December 1982.
Three Pieces (viola, piano) 1982; first performed Rugby, Warwickshire, 9 October 1983.
Sonata No 1 (violin, piano) 1983; first performed London, 25 October 1985.
Two Studies (bassoon, piano) 1983; first performed Huddersfield, Yorkshire, 7 November 1983.
Four Sonnets (brass quintet) 1984; first performed London, 7 June 1984.
String Quartet No 2 1985; first performed Aberystwyth, Powys, 5 May 1986.
Sonata No 2 (violin, piano) 1986; first performed London, 7 May 1986.
Sonata No 2 (piano) 1988; first performed Lisbon, 7 December 1988.
Quartet (oboe, strings) 1988; first performed Berlin, 18 April 1989.
Five Poems: In the White and the Walk of the Morning (4 guitars) 1989; first performed Pulborough, Sussex, August 1989.

Vocal/choral:

Two Madrigals (unaccompanied SATB chorus; Jonson, Shakespeare) 1976; first performed Spain, 1981.
Two Introits (SATB chorus, organ) 1977–85; first performed Bristol, 1988.
Aspects (high voice, piano; Ursula Vaughan Williams) 1978; first performed London, 17 May 1978.
The Looking Glass (soprano, oboe, piano) 1980. Recorded Phoenix DGS 1001.
A Little Music (baritone, piano; Wolfe) 1981; first performed London, 24 January 1983.
Chinese Lyrics, Set One (soprano, piano; Tang, translated Helen Waddell) 1982; first performed Oxshott and Cobham, Surrey, 21 October 1982.
Chinese Lyrics, Set Two (mezzo-soprano or counter-tenor, piano; Chinese verse, translated Kotewall and Smith) 1983; first performed Croydon, Surrey, 31 January 1984.
Another Part of the Forest (baritone, violin, 4 voices, piano; Shakespeare) 1983; first performed London, 22 February 1983.
The Bond of the Sea (baritone, piano; Conrad) 1983; first performed London, 22 April 1983.
In Winter's Cold Embraces Dye (mezzo-soprano, tenor, mixed chorus, orchestra; Congreve) 1985; first performed Harrow, Middlesex, 7 March 1987.
Two Folk Songs (bass, baritone, piano) 1986.

An Elegy on the Death and Burial of Cock Robin (counter-tenor, 11 solo strings; traditional) 1988. Recorded Meridien CDE 84158.

Five Rondos (soprano, baritone, piano; Ursula Vaughan Williams) 1989; first performed London, 16 June 1989.

Opera:

King of Macedon (libretto by Ursula Vaughan Williams) 1979; first performed Charterhouse, Surrey, 1979.

Other:

As pianist: *Two Shelley Songs* (with David Wilson), Phoenix DGS 1001; *Songs of Vaughan Williams* (included *Four Last Songs*; with Peter Savidge), Trax Classique TRXC 116; Walton: *Piano Quartet*, and Bridge: *Phantasy Piano Quartet*, Phoenix DGS 1047; Bach: *Ave Maria*, *Anna Magdalena Suite*, Trax Classique TRX LP119.

Roger Steptoe comments:

I write slowly, with ideas forming themselves over a long period of time. I generally start at the beginning of a piece and work through to the end, in sequence. My music has always been lyrical, hence a number of vocal pieces and the demand and interest of chamber music. Stylistically, it is seen as English, without the pastoral romanticism yet being entirely contemporary. Works tend to go in groups, with each work of a particular group using and developing certain melodic or harmonic ideas or procedures. This does not mean that each work sounds identical, but each piece being part of a larger pattern but also being self contained.

* * *

Although Roger Steptoe is best known for a sequence of concertos that includes works for oboe, tuba, clarinet and cello, he has also composed an extensive list of chamber music and of song. In addition to a pair of string quartets, there is a Clarinet Quintet, an Oboe Quartet, and two brass quintets, *The Knight of the Sun* and *Four Sonnets*. Vocal works include *Aspects*, a song-cycle for high voice and piano on texts by Ursula Vaughan Williams, two sets of *Chinese Lyrics*, and the unusual *Elegy on the Death and Burial of Cock Robin* for counter-tenor and 11 solo strings.

The spread of genres is significant. For above all Steptoe is a composer who continues to stand by the traditional forms, and is prepared to renew his artistic personality by submitting to the challenge of their archetypal vitality and discipline. Inseparable from this position is his wholehearted acceptance of established notions of musicianship, whether as a composer or as a senstitive and gifted pianist. The superficially modern has no place in his music; but neither do elements of the archaic, or pedantic, that might impede the essential integrity of utterance. Such an attitude places him in an oblique relationship to current notions of the avant-garde. Yet it insures that when a genuine breakthrough is achieved, it is one of substance rather than gesture.

Central to Steptoe's thinking is the role of melody and cadence, and therefore the function of harmonic colour, weight and tension as a means of creating structure. In themselves his chords, though often subtly altered in quality by presence of added notes, can generally be categorized as familiar structures of thirds, with clear origins in the music not only of British but also of French 20th-century masters. Instinctively, however, he tends to dissolve line in harmony, and vice versa, so that the resulting tonality is powerfully idiosyncratic, skilfully exploiting the potential for tonal ambiguity to achieve its strength and character.

In the Clarinet Concerto (perhaps Steptoe's most intimate and personal work to date), this mutual generation of melody and harmony is witnessed in the organic growth of the first movement—apparently seamless, yet unfolding from the relaxed counterpoint of the opening to a fierce climax which is also the point of greatest harmonic concentration and focus. The Concerto's germinal intervals, thirds and sevenths, find a different context in the finale, where a central cadenza presents in linear form the same harmonic patterns heard in the rapt chord of the surrounding meditations for strings. A similar principle applies in the grandly rhetorical Cello Concerto: in the third movement, which offers increasingly rich harmonisations of a quiet, modal melody initially heard unaccompanied; and in the larger relationship between motive and structure that binds the first movement, scherzo and fourth-movement finale into a unified design through the all-pervading presence of intense thematic variation and development.

Steptoe's undoubted mastery of means and ends in these mature instrumental works can be traced back not only to the nocturnal Oboe Concerto, but also to the two violin sonatas and the *Three Pieces* for viola and piano. Theme and harmony in all four works can be attributed to a simple form of serial working—inspired, no doubt, by the composer's instinctive need to coordinate horizontal and vertical aspects of his music. But their most impressive feature is simply the eloquent communication of intense emotional states in a way which is inseparable from the technical means involved. This, in effect, is the true strength of Steptoe's work: a shared identity of form and content, whether on the level of the phrase or entire movement, that displays itself in the form of a controlled and highly personal lyricism.

It places him firmly in the category of the operatic composer. And it is no coincidence that his first major score was also full-length opera: *King of Macedon*, composed to a libretto by Ursula Vaughan Williams, and produced at Charterhouse School in 1979, during the composer's time there as first composer in residence. Its sweep and urgency marked a turning point in his development, and the lessons of its choral writing were subsequently put to good account in the cantata on texts by William Congreve, *In Winter's Cold Embraces Dye*, and a large work written in 1992 to commemorate the bicentenary of the birth of Shelley.

When it comes, Steptoe's next opera is likely to mark another important stage in his compositional development. Meanwhile, each new work continues to reveal new facets of his artistic personality, while confirming the position he has come to occupy through his work as pianist, lecturer and administrator at the Royal Academy of Music, as a highly respected figure in British musical life today.

—Nicholas Williams

STOCKHAUSEN, Karlheinz. German. Born in Modrath, Cologne, 22 August 1928. Educated at secondary school in Burschied; boarder, teacher training college, Xanten, Lower Rhine, 1942–4 [other sources cite 1941]; classical academy, Bergisch Gladbach, February 1946–March 1947; Staatliche Hochschule für Musik, Cologne (piano under Hans Otto Schmidt-Neuhaus, composition lessons after 1950 under Frank Martin), 1947–51; University of Cologne (musicology, philosophy and philology, educational music, and music theory under Hermann Schroeder), 1947; passed with distinction civil service examination (piano teaching in high schools), October 1951; International Summer School, Darmstadt-Kranichstein, 1951; Conservatoire National Supérieur de Musique, Paris (under Olivier Messiaen), 1952–3; also research in studio for *musique concrète*, French Radio; Bonn University (phonetics and communication under Werner Meyer-Eppler), 1954–6. Army stretcher-bearer, Bedbrug, Erft, October 1944–March 1945. Married (1) Doris Andrae, 29 December 1951, 1 son and 3 daughters; (2) Mary Bauermeister, 3 April 1967, 1 son and 1 daughter. Permanent collaborator, from 1953, artistic director, 1963–73, Westdeutsche Rundfunk electronic music studio; lecturer, Darmstadt International Summer School, 1953–74; co-editor, "Die Reihe", Universal Edition series on serial music, 1954–9; professor of composition, University of Basle, 1962–3; founder/artistic director, Cologne Courses for New Music, 1963–8; founded ensemble for live electronic music, 1964; guest professor of composition, University of Pennsylvania, Philadelphia, 1965; guest professor, University of California, Davis, 1966–8; professor of composition, College of Music, Cologne, 1971–7. Recipient: Nordrhein-Westfalen Prize for Music, 1968; member, Akademie der Künste, Hamburg, 1968, Kungl. Musikaliska Akademie, Sweden, 1970, and Akademie der Künste, Berlin, 1973; Bundesverdienstkreuz 1st class, 1974; member, American Academy and Institute of Arts and Letters, 1977, Accademia Filarmonica Romana, 1979, and Académie Européenne des Sciences, des Arts et des Lettres, 1980; honorary member, Royal Academy of Music, London, 1987; many other prizes and awards. Mailing address: Stockhausen Verlag, 5067 Kürten, Germany.

Publishers: Stockhausen Verlag; Universal Edition.

[Numbering is Stockhausen's own; certain pieces are in multiple form, as indicated.]

Symphonies/orchestral:

Formel [No 1/6] 1951. Recorded Deutsche Grammophon 2707111.
Spiel [No 1/4] 1952.
Punkte [No 1/2] 1952, revised 1962; first performed Donaueschingen, 20 October 1963.
Gruppen [No 6] (3 orchestras) 1955–7; first performed Cologne, 24 March 1958. Recorded Deutsche Grammophon DGG 137002.
Carré [No 10] (4 orchestras and choruses) 1959–60; first performed Hamburg, 28 October 1960. Recorded Deutsche Grammophon 137002.
Mixtur [Nos 16/16½] (orchestra, sine-wave generators, ring modulators, loudspeakers; also chamber ensemble version) 1964, revised 1967; first performed Hamburg, 9 November 1965; revised version first performed Frankfurt, 23 August 1967. Recorded Deutsche Grammophon 137012.
Stop [Nos 18/18½ "Paris Version"] 1965, 1969. Recorded Deutsche Grammophon 2530442.
Hymnen [no 22⅔] (orchestral version) 1969. Recorded Deutsche Grammophon 2707039.
Fresco [No 29] (wall sounds for meditation for 4 orchestral groups) 1969.
Sternklang [No 34] ("park music" for 5 groups) 1971. Recorded Polydor 2612031.
Trans [No 35] 1971. Recorded Deutsche Grammophon 2530276.
Inori [No 38] (1 or 2 soloists, orchestra) 1973–4. Recorded Deutsche Grammophon 2707111.
Tierkreis [No 41⅞] (version for chamber orchestra; clarinet, horn, bassoon, strings) 1977.
Jubiläum [No 45] 1977.
Der Jahreslauf [No 47] (scene from opera *Dienstag aus LICHT*; originally for dancers, orchestra and tape; or for orchestra and tape) 1977.
Michaels Reise um die Erde (from second act of *Donnerstag aus LICHT* [No 48]; trumpet, orchestra) 1978.
Luzifers Tanz [No 53] (from *Samstag aus LICHT*; bass/trumpet/euphonium, piccolo trumpet, wind orchestra/symphony orchestra; with stilt dancer, dancer, ballet/mimes) 1983.
Botschaft [No 58½] (from *Evas Zauber* from *Montag aus LICHT*; version for basset horn, alto flute, modern orchestra) 1984–5.
Der Kinderfänger [No 58⅔ and ¾] (from *Evas Zauber* from *Montag aus LICHT*; alto flute/piccolo, modern orchestra) 1986.

Chamber/instrumental:

Sonatine [No 1/8] (violin, piano) 1951. Recorded Deutsche Grammophon 2530827.
Kreuzspiel [No 1/7] (oboe, bass clarinet, piano, 3 percussionists) 1951; broadcast Cologne December 1951; first performed Darmstadt, 21 July 1952; Recorded Deutsche Grammophon 2530443.
Schlagtrio/quartett [No ⅓] (piano, 2 x 3 timpani) 1952; first performed Munich, 23, 24 March 1953; broadcast Hamburg, 12 March 1953. Recorded Deutsche Grammophon 2530827.
Kontra-Punkte [No 1] (10 instruments) 1952–3; first performed Cologne, 26 May 1953. Recorded RCA Victrola VICS 1239; Vega C 30 A 66.
Klavierstücke I–IV [No 2] (piano) 1952–3; first performed Darmstadt, 21 August 1954. Recorded CBS 72591-2; Wergo 60136.
Klavierstücke V–X [No 4] (piano) 1954–5, IX and X revised 1961; (V–VIII first performed Darmstadt, 1 June 1955. Recorded CBS 72591-2; VI—Vega C 30 A278; VIII—Vox STGBY 637; Wergo 60136.
Zeitmasse [No 5] (woodwind quintet) 1955–6; first performed Paris, 15 December 1956. Recorded Odyssey 321 60154; Vega C 30 A 139.
Klavierstück XI [No 7] (piano) 1956; first performed Darmstadt, 28 July 1957. Recorded CBS 72591-2; Philips 6500 101; Wergo 60136.
Zyklus [No 8] (1 percussionist) 1959; first performed Darmstadt, 25 August 1959. Recorded Heliodor Wergo 2549016; Mainstream 5003; Columbia MS 7139; Erato STU 70603; Sonc 16 012.
Refrain [No 11] (3 players; originally piano/woodblocks, celeste/antique cymbals, vibraphone/cowbells/glockenspiel) 1959; first performed Berlin, 2 October 1959. Recorded Vox STGBY 638; Mainstream 5003.
Kontakte [No 12½] (electronic sounds, piano, percussion) 1959–60; first performed Cologne, 11 June 1960. Recorded Vox STGBY 638; Wergo 60009.
Mikrophonie I [No 15] (tam-tam, 2 microphones, 2 filters, 2 potentiometers; 6 players) 1964; first performed Brussels, 9 February 1964. Recorded CBS 72647.
Solo [No 19] (melody instrument, tape recorder feedback) 1965–6; flute, trombone versions first performed Japan, 1966; oboe version first performed Basle, 2 May, 1967. Recorded Deutsche Grammophon DGG 104992.
Adieu für Wolfgang Sebastian Mayer [No 21] (wind quintet) 1966; first performed Calcutta, 30 January 1967.
Prozession [No 23] (tam-tam, viola, electronium, piano, microphones, filters, potentiometers) 1967; broadcast Radio

Helsinki, 21 May 1967. Recorded Vox STGBY 615; Fratelli Fabri mm-1098.

Kurzwellen [No 25] (4–5 instrumentalists with short wave receivers, sound projectionist) 1968; first performed Bremen, 5 May 1968. Recorded Deutsche Grammophon 139461.

Aus den sieben Tagen [No 26] (15 compositions of textual/ intuitive music for ensemble, or with voices as indicated; performable separately; "Richtige Dauern" for 4 speakers; "Unbegrenzt"; "Verbindung"; "Treffpunkt"; "Nachtmusik"; "Abwärts"; "Aufwärts"; "Oben und Unten", theatre piece for man, woman, child, 4 instrumentalists; "Intensität"; "Setz die Segel zur Sonne"; "Kommunion", "Litanei", for speaker or choir; "Es"; "Goldstaub"; "Ankunft", for speaker or speaking choir) 1968. Recorded (parts) Harmonia Mundi MV 30795; Nuits de la Fondation Maeght; others.

Spiral [No 27] (soloist, with short-wave receiver) 1968. Recorded (oboe version) Deutsche Grammophon 2561109; electric recorder version—Wergo 325; electronium version—Nuits de la Fondation Maeght.

Für kommende Zeiten [No 33] (17 compositions of textual/ intuitive music for large or small ensemble, or as indicated; "Übereinstimmung"; "Verlängerung"; "Verkürzung"; "Über die Grenze", for small ensemble; "Kommunikation", for small ensemble; "Intervall", piano duo—4 hands; "Ausserhalb", for small ensemble; "Innerhalb", for small ensemble; "Anhalt", for small ensemble; "Schwingung"; "Spektren", for small ensemble; "Wellen"; "Zugvogel"; "Vorahnung", for 4–7 interpreters; "Japan"; "Wach", "Ceylon", for small ensemble) 1968–70.

Dr K-Sextett [No 28] (flute, cello, tubular bells, vibraphone, bass clarinet, viola, piano) 1969.

Pole [No 30] (2 players/singers with short wave receivers) 1969–70.

Expo [No 31] (3 players/singers with short wave receivers) 1969–70.

Mantra [No 32] (2 pianists, also with wood blocks, antique cymbals, ring modulators) 1970. Recorded Deutsche Grammophon DGG 2530208.

Alphabet für Liege [No 36] (13 scenes of visible music for soloists and duos) 1972.

Ylem [No 37] (19 players/singers) 1972. Recorded Deutsche Grammophon 2530422.

Herbstmusik [No 40] (4 players) 1974.

Laub und Regen [No 40½] (clarinet, viola) 1974.

Musik im Bauch [No 41] (6 percussionists, with musical boxes) 1975. Recorded Deutsche Grammophon 2530913.

Tierkreis [No 41½] (12 melodies on the Zodiac, for one melody and one harmony instrument) 1975–6. Recorded Deutsche Grammophon 2530913.

Tierkreis [No 41 ⁸⁄₉] (clarinet, piano) 1975, 1981.

Tierkreis [No 41 ⁹⁄₁₀] (clarinet, flute/piccolo, trumpet, piano) 1975, 1983.

Harlekin [No 42] (clarinet) 1975. Recorded Deutsche Grammophon 2531006.

Der kleine Harlekin [No 42½] (clarinet) 1975. Recorded Deutsche Grammophone 2531006.

Amour [No 44] (5 pieces for clarinet) 1976. Recorded Deutsche Grammophon 423378 2.

Aries [No 43½] (trumpet, electronics) 1977, 1980.

Libra [No 43⅔] (bass clarinet, electronics) 1977.

In Freundschaft [No 46] (individual versions for clarinet, flute, recorder, oboe, bassoon, basset horn or bass clarinet, violin, cello, saxophone, horn, trombone) 1977. Recorded Deutsche Grammophon 423378 2.

Piccolo [ex. No 47] (from *Der Jahreslauf*) (piccolo) 1977.

Eingang und Formel [ex. No 48] (from *Michaels Reise* from *Donnerstag aus LICHT*; trumpet) 1978.

Halt [ex. No 48] (from *Michaels Reise* from *Donnerstag aus LICHT*; trumpet, double bass) 1978.

Kreuzigung [ex. No 48] (from *Michaels Reise* from *Donnerstag aus LICHT*; trumpet, with basset horn/clarinet; also with basset horn, 2 horns, 2 trombones, tuba, electric organ) 1978.

Mission und Himmelfahrt [ex. No 48] (from *Michaels Reise* from *Donnerstag aus LICHT*; trumpet, basset horn) 1978.

Donnerstags-Gruss [No 48½] (from *Donnerstag aus LICHT*; 8 brass, 3 piano, 3 percussionists) 1978.

Michaels Ruf [ex. No 48½] (from *Donnerstag aus LICHT*; variable ensemble/8 orchestral players) 1978.

Michaels Reise [No 48⅔] (from *Donnerstag aus LICHT*; trumpet, 9 co-players, sound projectionist) 1978, 1984; first performed Bremen, 8 May 1986.

Tanze Luceva! [1 ex. No 49½] (from *Michaels Jugend* from *Donnerstag aus* LICHT; basset horn or bass clarinet) 1978–9.

Bijou [2 ex. No 49½] (from *Michaels Jugend* from *Donnerstag aus LICHT*; alto flute, bass clarinet) 1978–9.

Klavierstück XII [ex. No 49¾] (from *Donnerstag aus LICHT*; piano) 1978–9.

Drachenkampf [1 ex. No 50½] (from *Michaels Heimkehr* from *Donnerstag aus LICHT*; trumpet, trombone, electric organ/synthesizer; 2 dancers ad lib, 1 percussionist ad lib) 1980.

Knabenduett [2 ex. No 50½] (from *Michaels Heimkehr* from *Donnerstag aus LICHT*; 2 soprano saxophones or other instruments) 1980.

Donnerstag-Abschied [No 50¾] (from *Michaels Abschied* from *Donnerstag aus LICHT*; 5 trumpets, or trumpet with 5-track playback recording) 1980.

Klavierstück XIII [No 51½] (from *Luzifers Traum* from *Samstag aus LICHT*; piano) 1981.

Traum-Formel [No 51⅔] (from *Luzifers Traum* from *Samstag aus LICHT*; basset horn) 1981. Recorded Deutsche Grammophon 423378 2.

Kathinkas Gesang als Luzifers Requiem [Nos 52, 52½, 52⅔] (from *Samstag aus LICHT*; flute, 6 percussionists; also for solo flute; versions for flute, electronics, flute, piano) 1982–3.

Linker Augenbrauentanz [1 ex. No 53] (from *Luzifers Tanz* from *Samstag aus LICHT*; flutes, basset horn(s), percussion, synthesizer) 1983.

Rechter Augenbrauentanz [2 ex. No 53] (from *Luzifers Tanz* from *Samstag aus LICHT*; clarinets, bass clarinet(s), percussion, synthesizer) 1983.

Linker Augentanz [3 ex. No 53] (from *Luzifers Tanz* from *Samstag aus LICHT*; saxophone, percussion, synthesizer) 1983.

Rechter Augentanz [4 ex. No 53] (from *Luzifers Tanz* from *Samstag aus LICHT*; oboes, cors anglais, bassoons, percussion, synthesizer) 1983.

Linker Backentanz [5 ex. No 53] (from *Luzifers Tanz* from *Samstag aus LICHT*; trumpets, trombones, percussion, synthesizer) 1983.

Rechter Backentanz [6 ex. No 53] (from *Luzifers Tanz* from *Samstag aus LICHT*; trumpets, trombones, percussion, synthesizer) 1983.

Nasenflügeltanz [7 ex. No 53] (from *Luzifers Tanz* from *Samstag aus LICHT*; percussion, synthesizer; or percussion solo) 1983.

Oberlippentanz ("Protest") [8 ex. No 53] (from *Luzifers Tanz* from *Samstag aus LICHT*; piccolo trumpet; or piccolo trumpet, trombone/euphonium, 2 percussion, 4 or 8 horns) 1983.

Zungenspitzentanz [9 ex. No 53] (from *Luzifers Tanz* from *Samstag aus LICHT*; piccolo; or piccolo, 2 euphoniums, percussion, ad lib percussion, ad lib dancer) 1983.
Kinntanz [10 ex. No 53] (from *Luzifers Tanz* from *Samstag aus LICHT*; euphonium, percussion, synthesizer; or euphonium, percussion, alto trombone(s), baritone/tenor saxhorn(s), tuba(s)) 1983.
Samstags-Gruss [No 53½] (from *Luzifers Tanz* from *Samstag aus LICHT*; 26 wind instruments, 2 percussion) 1983.
Montags-Gruss [No 55] (from *Montag aus LICHT*; multiple basset horns, electric keyboard instruments) 1984, 1988.
Klavierstück XIV [ex. No 57⅔] (from *Geburtstag-Formel* from *Montag aus LICHT*; piano) 1984.
Botschaft [No 58½] (from *Evas Zauber* from *Montag aus LICHT*; basset horn, alto flute; other versions) 1984.
Evas Spiegel [1 ex. No 58½] (from *Evas Zauber* from *Montag aus LICHT*; basset horn) 1984.
Susani [2 ex. No 58½] (from *Evas Zauber* from *Montag aus LICHT*; basset horn) 1984.
Susanis Echo [3 ex. No 58½] (from *Evas Zauber* from *Montag aus LICHT*; alto flute) 1985.
Xi [1 and 2 ex. No 55] (from *Montags-Gruss* from *Montag aus LICHT*; versions for basset horn and alto flute/flute; with microtones) 1986.
Wochenkreis [ex. No 57¾] (from *Evas Zweitgeburt* from *Montag aus LICHT*; basset horn, electric keyboards) 1986.
Entführung [ex. 58¾] (from *Evas Zauber* from *Montag aus LICHT*; piccolo) 1986.
Willkommen [1 ex. No 60] (from *Dienstags-Gruss* from *Dienstag aus LICHT*; 9 trumpets, 9 trombones, 2 synthesizers) 1988.
Quitt [1 ex. No 59] (from *Evas-Abschied* from *Montag aus LICHT*; 3 instrumentalists, with microtones) 1989.
Ypsilon [2 ex. No 59] (from *Evas-Abschied* from *Montag aus LICHT*; melody instrument, with microtones) 1989.
Su-Kat [2 ex. No 60] (from *Dienstags-Gruss* from *Dienstag aus LICHT*; basset horn, alto flute) 1989.
Flautina [ex. No 56½] (from *Montag aus LICHT*; flute, piccolo, alto flute) 1989.

Vocal/choral:

Chore für Doris [No 1/11] (unaccompanied chorus) 1950. Recorded Deutsche Grammophon 2530461.
Drei Lieder [No 1/10] (alto, chamber orchestra) 1950. Recorded Deutsche Grammophon 2530827.
Choral [No 1/9] (4-part unaccompanied chorus) 1950. Recorded Deutsche Grammophon 2530827.
Momente [No 13] (soprano, 4 choral groups, 13 instruments) 1962–4. Recorded Wergo 60024; Deutsche Grammophon 2709055.
Mikrophonie II [No 17] (12 voices, Hammond organ, 4 ring modulators, tape) 1965. Recorded Deutsche Grammophon 2530583.
Stimmung [No 24] (6 singers) 1968. Recorded Harmonia Mundi DMR 1019 21; Hyperion A 66115.
Am Himmel Wandre Ich . . . [No 36½] (Indian songs for 2 voices) 1972. Recorded Deutsche Grammophon 2530876.
Vortrag über HU [No 38½] (1 voice) 1974.
Atmen gibt das Leben [No 39] (choral opera; with orchestra or tape) 1974–7. Recorded Deutsche Grammophon 410857 1/2530641.
Tierkreis [No 41⅔–6/7] (voice/soprano/high soprano/tenor/high tenor/mezzo-soprano/alto/low tenor/baritone/bass, harmony instrument) 1975–6. Recorded Deutsche Grammophon 2530913; Music Boxes ACANTA 23531.
Michael Jugend [No 49] (from *Donnerstag aus LICHT*; tenor, soprano, bass, trumpet, basset horn, trombone, piano, electric organ, 3 dance-mimes, taped chorus and instruments) 1978–9.
Kindheit [No 49½] (from *Donnerstag aus LICHT*: tenor, soprano, bass, trumpet, basset horn, trombone, dancers, tapes) 1978–9.
Mondeva [No 49⅔] (from *Donnerstag aus LICHT*; tenor, basset horn, with soprano, bass, trombone, mime, electric organ, tapes ad lib) 1978–9.
Examen [No 49¾] (from *Donnerstag aus LICHT*; tenor, trumpet, dancers, basset horn, piano, with "jury" of soprano, bass, 2 dance-mimes, 2 tapes) 1978–9.
Michaels Heimkehr [No 50] (from *Donnerstag aus LICHT*; tenor, soprano, bass, trumpet, trombone, 2 soprano saxophones, electric organ or synthesizer, 3 dance mimes, alto, chorus, orchestra, tapes) 1980.
Argument [3 ex. No 50½] (from *Donnerstag aus LICHT*; tenor, bass, electric organ or synthesizer) 1980.
Vision [No 50⅔] (from *Donnerstag aus LICHT*; tenor, trumpet, dancers, Hammond organ or synthesizer, tape) 1980.
Luzifers Traum [No 51] (from *Samstag aus LICHT*; bass, piano) 1981.
Luzifers Abschied [No 54] (from *Samstag aus LICHT*; male chorus, organ, 7 trombones/live or on tape) 1982.
Luzifers Tanz [No 53] (from *Samstag aus LICHT*; bass, piccolo trumpet, piccolo, harmony orchestra or symphony orchestra, dancers/mimes) 1983.
Evas Zauber [No 58] (from *Montag aus LICHT*; chorus, children's chorus, modern orchestra) 1984–6; first performed Metz, 20 November 1986.
Evas Zweitgeburt [No 57] (from *Montag aus LICHT*; 7 solo singers, basset horn, 3 bass clarinets, piano, chorus/live or on tape, girls' chorus, modern orchestra) 1984–7.
Evas Lied [No 57¾] (from *Montag aus LICHT*; 7 voices or female chorus, basset horns, 3 bass clarinets, modern orchestra) 1986; first performed Berlin, 3 September 1986.
Evas Erstgeburt [No 56] (from *Montag aus LICHT*; 3 sopranos, 3 tenors, bass, actor, chorus/live or on tape, children's chorus, modern orchestra) 1987.
Geburtsfest, Quelle des Lebens, Kinderspiel, Trauer mit Humor [ex No 56] (from *Montag aus LICHT*; chorus, tape) 1987.
In Hoffnung [No 56½ and ⅔] (from *Montag aus LICHT*; 3 sopranos, chorus/live or on tape, modern orchestra) 1987.
Geburts Arien I, II [No 56¾] (from *Montag aus LICHT*; 3 sopranos, 3 tenors, chorus/live or on tape, children's voices ad lib, modern orchestra) 1978.
Knabengeschrei [No 56⅘] and [⅚] (from *Montag aus LICHT*; (3 sopranos, bass, actor, chorus/live or on tape, children's chorus, modern orchestra) 1987.
Luzifers Zorn [ex No 56⅚] (from *Montag aus LICHT*; bass, actor, synthesizer, tape) 1987.
Das grosse Geweine [No 56 6/7] (from *Montag aus LICHT*; 3 sopranos, bass, chorus/live or on tape, modern orchestra) 1987.
Mädchenprozession [No 57½] (from *Montag aus LICHT*; girls' chorus, piano, chorus/live or on tape, modern orchestra) 1987.
Friedens Gruss [No 60] (from *Dienstag aus LICHT*; soprano, chorus, 9 trumpets, 9 trombones, 2 synthesizers) 1988.

Opera:

LICHT: Die sieben Tage der Woche (operatic cycle in 7 parts) begun 1977, in progress.
Donnerstag aus LICHT [Nos 48–50] (3 soloists, 8 instru-

mentalists, 3 dancers, chorus, orchestra, tape) 1978–80; first performed Milan, 1981. Recorded Deutsche Grammophon 2740272/423379–2.
Samstag aus LICHT [Nos 51–54] (solo voice, 10 instrumentalists, 2 dancers, harmony orchestra, ballet or mime, men's chorus, organ) 1981–3; first performed Milan, 1984. Recorded Deutsche Grammophon 4235956.
Montag aus LICHT [Nos 55–59] (14 voices, 5 instrumentalists, actor, chorus, children's chorus, modern orchestra) 1984–8; first performed Milan, 1988.
Dienstag aus LICHT [Nos 60–] in progress.

Other:

Etude [No ⅕] (concrete music) 1952.
Studie I [No 3/I] (electronic music) 1953.
Studie II [No 3/II] (electronic music) 1954.
Gesang der Jünglinge [No 8] (electronic music; with boy soprano) 1955–6.
Kontakte [No 12] (electronic sounds) 1959–60. Recorded Schwann 310 020.
Originale [No 12⅔] (music theatre with *Kontakte*) 1961.
Telemusik [No 20] (electronic music) 1966. Recorded Deutsche Grammophon 137012.
Hymnen [No 22] (electronic and concrete music; version [No 22½] for electronics, soloist) 1966–7.
Unsichtbare Chore [ex. No 49] (from *Donnerstag aus LICHT*; electronic processed voices) 1978–9. Recorded Deutsche Grammophon 419432 1/419432 2.

PUBLICATIONS

By Stockhausen: *Texte zur Musik*, 6 volumes, DuMont Buchverlag, Cologne, 1963–89.

On Stockhausen: Karl H. Worner, *S: Life and Work*, London, 1973; Jonathan Cott, *S: Conversations with the Composer*, New York, 1973, London, 1974; Jonathan Harvey, *The Music of S*, London, 1975; Mya Tannenbaum, *Conversations with S*, Oxford, 1987; *S on Music: Lectures and Interviews*, edited by Robin Maconie, London, 1988, 2nd edition London, 1989; Michael Kurtz, *S: eine Biographie*, Kassel and Basle, 1988.

* * *

Karlheinz Stockhausen must be accounted among the most important of the European avant-garde composers whose innovations made a vital contribution to composition after World War II. He is also one of the few musical figures of the period of modernism that thrived in the 1950s and 1960s to have found, at least until recently, a wider reputation beyond a small circle of enthusiasts.

Stockhausen's output of the 1950s and 1960s and the theoretical speculation that accompanied it have much higher claims both to innovative influence and to lasting significance in their own right than his work of the last 20 years. Nevertheless, many would still assert Stockhausen as the *most* important of that group of avant-gardists—Pierre Boulez and Luciano Berio arguably also pre-eminent within it—who were among both the first and the best composers to exploit the significance of total serialism and electronics for musical composition. He was also important, sometimes pre-eminent, among those who later made contributions to the development of indeterminacy and musical notation as a compositional resource, of new fusions of music and language, of post-serial techniques and the reincorporation of melody into radical composition, and of several other areas.

It is in works dating from 1951 onwards that we find the beginnings of Stockhausen's radicalism, founded on a totally fresh exploration of the potential of the twelve-note method and inspired in particular by the music of Anton Webern. *Kreuzspiel* for oboe, bass clarinet, piano (and woodblock) and three percussionists (1951) is Stockhausen's first work to attempt the serialisation of parameters other than pitch; it does this in part by means of an ingenious "crossplay" (the work's title) involving several parameters: instrumentation, pitch register, speed and dynamics being the most important. *Kreuzspiel*'s radical, "post-Webern" stance—in which, for once, at least the essentials of the elaborate structural schemes employed stand some chance of being perceived by the attentive listener—puts the work squarely in the radical context of current work being done not only by Europeans such as Messiaen, Boulez and the Belgian Karel Goeyvaerts, but by Milton Babbitt, John Cage, Morton Feldman and others in the United States.

At first, Stockhausen was interested in inventing an entirely new compositional universe by constructing what he once called a "fantastic music of the stars" out of "points" of sound, essentially single notes; for him, at this time a Catholic, even serialism itself had religious aspirations, which makes the choice of the "Benedicite" as the text the boy soprano sings in *Gesang der Jünglinge* ("Song of the Youths"), one of the classics of tape composition, less surprising. *Gesang* is already a mature demonstration of Stockhausen's conviction that the extreme "pointillism" of works such as *Punkte* ("Points") was of limited value; 10 years later Stockhausen drastically revised this orchestral composition, filling out many of the "gaps" between the "points" by building constellations, or "groups", of notes around them.

More immediately, works such as *Kontra-Punkte* for 10 instruments marked the point of departure, as it were, from "points" to "groups" by placing more emphasis on its overall shape: a gradual reduction from the opening full ensemble to a final piano solo, in which continuity is more important than any note-by-note "sound for sound's sake". Perhaps surprisingly, however, *Kontra-Punkte* also achieved the kind of total serialisation at which Stockhausen had been aiming. The techniques he had now discovered for himself became the basis of his instrumental music for almost the next 10 years, culminating in important works such as *Gruppen* ("Groups", perhaps the finest composition using this formal approach) for three orchestras, *Carré* ("Square") for four choirs and four orchestras, and several of the early piano pieces.

During this same decade, however, two further examples of Stockhausen's modernist concern insistently to renew the ideas, materials and forms of music first informed and then crucially began to transform his musical methods and general approach. The first of these is the already alluded to use of electronics. His contributions to both the theory and practice of sound synthesis with electronically-generated materials soon made so-called *elektronische Musik* a rival to the already-established *musique concrète* methods of those such as Boguslaw Schaeffer. This is not to say that Stockhausen became a dogmatic proponent of *elektronische Musik*: the already-mentioned boy's voice in *Gesang* was combined with electronically synthesized material to create the first undisputed masterpiece of electronic music. In bringing the two previously opposed types of electronic music together, Stockhausen was, as so often, ahead of most of his colleagues.

He was also among the first to put the fruits of such research at the service of both wider theoretical speculation and practical experimentation, notably in considering the correspondence between duration and pitch, and in allowing all these new discoveries to influence his approach to purely instrumental composition. This was evident at least as early as *Gruppen*, but is particularly crucial in both the conception and realisation of *Kontakte* ("Contacts") for piano, percussion and tape.

By this time, Stockhausen had moved so far away from post-Webernian serialism that experimentation with the techniques, if not the original aesthetic intentions, of what had previously been considered its own opposite—indeterminacy as developed from the beginning of the 1950s by Cage—seemed only natural. This second example of fresh developments in Stockhausen's music during the 1950s saw its beginnings as early as 1955–6, with the notational freedoms of *Zeitmasse* (sometimes translated as "Tempi") for woodwind quintet and the 19 freely-ordered fragments of *Klavierstück XI*; these ideas were continued in the more notationally experimental *Zyklus* ("Cycle") for solo percussionist and *Refrain* for three players.

The possibilities of reapportioning the responsibilities of composer and performer that indeterminacy offers only became of central and more permanent importance to Stockhausen's music, however, with the clear move from "groups" to "moments" in the 1960s and the greater freedoms this inspired. A "moment" is, essentially, a section of music which—however rigorously determined and notated in itself—has no fixed place in the sequence of "moments" that now makes up a composition but must, with all the others, be ordered differently from performance to performance. For Stockhausen, the importance of this approach lay in its encouragement of a new way of listening: "Unity and continuity", he wrote, "are less the outcome of obvious similarities than of an immanent concentration on the present, as uninterrupted as possible." *Momente* ("Moments" for soprano, four choral groups and 13 instrumentalists—which its composer offers in several different forms fixed by himself, owing to the work's complexity—is at once the chief begetter and best example of this widely imitated "moment form".

Any remnants of the conventional bonds between technique and expression now having been rendered irrelevant, the way was open for Stockhausen to explore a wide variety of approaches: "plus/minus" notation (in which signs such as "+" and "−" provide the basic notation for "form schemes" which may be applied to many different kinds of musical "contents") and "intuitive music" (in which all conventional notation is finally abandoned in favour of various kinds of text, usually of a somewhat mystic nature, as the basis for performance) are just two which he explored during the following decade. Such radical re-evaluations of notation were often accomplished with the aid of electronic resources: now not often resulting in pieces for tape alone, but rather in the increasingly sophisticated use of live electronics, in which sound production and transformation both occur at the moment of performance.

By this time, Stockhausen no longer considered himself a composer in the conventional sense; indeed, he now insisted that he never had been. Inspired by a range of Oriental philosophy in general and the writings of Sri Aurobindo in particular, he asserted, in one of the text compositions of *Aus den sieben Tagen*, "that/I do not make MY music, but/only relay the vibrations I receive". Compositions of, especially, the late 1960s as well as his extensive work with his own performing group (now internationally famous) demonstrated Stockhausen's concern to write "not 'my' music, but music of the whole world". Now deeply immersed in his new-found religious preoccupations, he became, at a time peculiarly susceptible to such influences, a guru not only for many other composers but for at least some among a young generation earnestly seeking enlightenment through contact with Eastern mysticism. Perhaps the best instance of these concerns in practice is *Stimmung* ("Tuning") for six vocalists, which draws on a variety of Oriental sources both textual and musical.

In terms of musical techniques, this period arguably came to a fairly abrupt end in 1970 with the composition of *Mantra* for two pianists. This marks not only a return to essentially conventional notation, but the use of a single melodic statement divided into clearly separate phrases as the basis of an entire composition. Stockhausen had always been capable not only of a wide technical range but of employing apparently divergent methods during the same period and even within the same work, often to uncannily fresh effect: *Stimmung*, for instance—for all its mystic aspect and indeed its fundamental departure from the European avant-garde's norm of dissonance at the time of its composition—is said to be as rigorously serial as any work of the 1950s.

Yet the compositional method of *Mantra*, based on what the composer himself calls a melodic "formula", which he had used as far back as the orchestral *Formel* ("Formula"), now became not only the prime element in Stockhausen's music of the 1970s and 1980s, but the point of entry for its more wide-ranging re-engagement with the expressive as well as technical means of the past. Works to pursue this trend include *Am Himmel Wandre Ich* ("In the Sky I Am Wandering", otherwise known as "Indianerlieder"), 12 songs based on American Indian poems for two voices, and the several works for unaccompanied clarinet composed in the mid-1970s and later. The inspirational starting points as well as techniques employed remain typically diverse during these years, however, as demonstrated by *Trans* for orchestra—based on a dream and inventively exploring its symbology—and *Inori* ("Adorations") for soloists and orchestra—with its ingenious transmutation of prayer into movement and its elaborately analytical timbral construction. All four of these works have an important theatrical aspect.

But as even the titles of these works show, Stockhausen's aesthetic aims continued to have an important mystic dimension. The significance of this for his output right up to the time of writing can best be illustrated by reference to *LICHT* ("Light"), the major operatic project on which he has been engaged since 1977 and of which all his compositions from that time, no matter for what vocal and instrumental forces, are destined to form part. When complete (its composer estimates that it will take well into the 1990s), this operatic cycle will consist of seven complete evenings of highly varied music-theatre, each evening's performance given the name of the appropriate day of the week. Drawing extensively on a wide variety of sources—including Jewish and Christian hagiography as well as an important autobiographical element—*LICHT* is, amidst much else, about the journey of a creative soul through the cosmos. It provides an appropriately grand summation of Stockhausen's life, thought and work even if, as many consider, his most significant contributions to composition in the 20th century were made during his first two creative decades.

—Keith Potter

STOKER, Richard. British/English. Born in Castleford, Yorkshire, 8 November 1938. Educated at Breadalbane House School, 1943–52; Huddersfield School of Music and School of Art, Yorkshire, 1953–8; studied composition under Eric Fenby; Royal Academy of Music, London (composition under Lennox Berkeley), 1958–62; further composition study under Nadia Boulanger, Paris, 1962–3. Married Gillian Patricia Watson, 10 July 1986. Professor 1963–85, and tutor 1970–81, Royal Academy of Music, London; editor, *Composer* magazine, 1969–80; member, executive committee, Composers' Guild, 1969–80; member, steering group, and treasurer, Lewisham Arts Festival, London, 1990. Recipient: associate of the Royal College of Music, 1961; Dove Prize, Royal Academy of Music, 1962; Mendelssohn Scholarship, 1962–3; associate, 1969, Fellow 1979, Royal Academy of Music. Mailing address: 38 Lee Road, London SE3 9RU; or c/o Ricordi & Co, The Bury, Church Street, Chesham, Buckinghamshire, England.

Publishers: Ricordi, Chesham; Boosey & Hawkes; Brietkopf, Fentone, Berben, Corby, Northamptonshire; Associated Board Edition, 14 Bedford Square, London WC1 3JG; Leeds Music, 144 Piccadilly, London W1; Oecumuse, 51 Eleanor Road, London N11 2QS, England.

Symphonies/orchestral:

Suite: After Purcell 1959; first performed London, 1961.
Overture: Antic Hay Op 2 1960; first performed London, 1962.
Petite Suite Op 1 1961.
Suite: Four Countries Op 11c 1964.
French Suite Op 11d 1964.
Chorale for Strings Op 18b 1966; first performed 1970.
Permutations Op 19 1967.
Passacaglia Op 17 1967.
Interludes and Arias from "Johnson Preserv'd" Op 30b 1967; first performed London, 1967.
Overture: Feast of Fools Op 34 1968; first performed London, 1969.
Little Symphony Op 23 1969; first performed London, 1970.
Suite: Four Countries Op 11c 1970.
Serenade Op 33 1971; first performed London, 1971.
Suite from "The Garden Party" Op 33c 1971; first performed London, 1971.
Suite: French Suite Op 11d 1971.
Antiphons and Responses Op 23b (recorder quartet, orchestra) 1974.
Variations, Passacaglia and Fugue Op 10 1974; first performed 1981.
Piano Concerto Op 54 1978.
Movement from "Bouquet for Lennox" 1983; first performed Cheltenham, Gloucestershire, 1983.
Locations Op 62 1986.

Chamber/instrumental:

Five Nocturnes Op 9 (piano) 1959; first performed London, 1961.
Trio Op 3 (flute, oboe, clarinet) 1960; first performed London, 1962.
String Quartet No 1 Op 11 1961; first performed Buxton, Yorkshire, 1962. Recorded Gaudeamus GRS 8.
Festival Suite (trumpet, piano) 1961.
Wind Quintet Op 6 1962; first performed London, 1963.
String Quartet No 2 Op 18 1962; first performed Harlow, Essex, 1965. Recorded Gaudeamus GRS 8.
Sonata No 1 Op 15 (violin, piano) 1963; first performed London, 1966.
Sextet Op 16 (clarinet, horn, bassoon, string trio) 1963; first performed Cheltenham, Gloucestershire, 1966.
Piano Trio No 1 Op 24 1963; first performed London, 1964.
Little Suite Op 36 (2 treble instruments) 1963.
Sonatina Op 5 (clarinet, piano) 1964; broadcast BBC Radio, 1980.
Four Miniatures Op 8 (flute, clarinet, piano) 1964.
Triptych Op 13 (clarinet or bass clarinet) 1964; first performed Chichester, Sussex, 1967.
Soliloquy Op 13b (flute) 1964; first performed London, 1966.
Sonatina Op 21b (violin, viola) 1964; first performed Canada, 1965.
Three Inventions Op 12b (2 bass instruments) 1965.
Conversations Op 12c (2 bass instruments) 1965.
Concertino No 1 Op 49 (flute, violin) 1965; first performed Cheltenham, Gloucestershire, 1966.
Miniature String Trio Op 80 1965. Recorded Gaudeamus GRS 8.
Zodiac Variations Op 7 (guitar) 1966.
Terzetto Op 32 (clarinet, viola, piano) 1966; first performed Harlow, Essex, 1968.
Rounds and Canons Op 3b (3 treble instruments) 1967.
Prelude and Toccata Op 22 (violin, piano) 1967; first performed London, 1974.
Sonata Op 26 (piano) 1967; broadcast Radio Dublin, 1970.
Three Epigrams Op 29b (cor anglais, piano) 1967; first performed London, 1968.
Improvisation Op 42b (guitar) 1967. Recorded Fonal MMS 56.
Pastoral Op 42c (guitar) 1967.
Nocturnal Op 37 (horn, violin, piano) 1967; first performed Cheltenham, Gloucestershire, 1970.
An Oboe Method 1967.
Music for Three Op 5b (3 oboes) 1968.
Music for Two and Little Dance Suite Op 13 (recorders) 1968–9.
Sonatina Op 21 (flute, piano) 1968; broadcast BBC Radio, 1984.
String Quartet No 3 Op 36 1968; first performed London, 1969.
Piano Trio No 2 Op 35 1968; first performed London, 1969.
Diversions on a Theme of Mikis Theodorakis Op 46 (guitar) 1968.
A Little Organ Book Op 27 1968; first performed London, 1969.
A Poet's Notebook Op 7 1968; first performed London, 1972.
Sonatina Op 42 (guitar) 1969.
Partita Op 28 (organ) 1969; first performed Wolverhampton, Staffordshire, 1970.
Three Pieces Op 29 (oboe) 1969; first performed London, 1970.
Three Improvisations Op 31 (organ) 1970; first performed London, 1973.
Contemporary Organ Technique Op 31c 1970; first performed Oxford, 1979.
Polemics Op 40 (oboe, string trio) 1970; first performed London, 1971.
Sonata No 2 Op 43 (violin, piano) 1971; first performed London, 1972.
Variations Op 45 (piano) 1971; first performed London, 1973.
Monologue Op 13c (violin) 1972.
Sinfonia for Sax Op 38b (saxophone quartet) 1972; first performed London, 1973.
Litany, Sequence and Hymn Op 12 (brass quartet) 1974; first performed Peterborough, Cambridgeshire, 1976.

Facets Op 38 (flute, violin, cello, harpsichord) 1974; first performed London, 1975.
Diversions on a Theme of Berkeley Op 46 (2 pianos) 1974; first performed London, 1975.
Duologue Op 47 (2 pianos) 1974; first performed London, 1975.
Concertino No 2 Op 49b (violin, cello) 1974; first performed London, 1975.
Two Jazz Preludes Op 63 (piano) 1976; first performed London, 1982.
Prelude and Scherzando (flute) 1976.
Variants Op 31b (organ) 1976; first performed Leeds, Yorkshire, 1978.
Chant and Danse (oboe, piano) 1976.
Air and Danse (bassoon, piano) 1976.
Chaconne and Rondo (horn, piano) 1976.
Melody and Concert Piece (trombone, piano) 1976.
Sonata Op 55 (2 guitars) 1977; first performed London, 1977. Recorded KRS 33.
Concerto Op 56 (2 guitars, tape) 1978; first performed London, 1978. Recorded KRS 33.
Pieces for Polita Op 57 (guitar) 1979.
Organ Symphony Op 58 1979; first performed Wimborne, Dorset, 1980.
Trio Sonata Op 60 (flute, violin, organ) 1979; first performed London, 1980.
Piano Trio No 3 Op 59 1980; first performed London, 1980.
Three Pieces Op 31d (organ) 1980; first performed London, 1982.
Air and Dance (cello, piano) 1980.
Sonata Op 61 (violin) 1982; first performed London, 1982.
Dance Movements Op 66 (guitar or lute) 1983; first performed London, 1984.
Partita Op 65 (clarinet, piano) 1984; first performed London, 1985.

Vocal/choral:

Ecce Homo Op 14 (speaker, tenor, baritone, chorus, orchestra) 1962; first performed London, 1966.
The Canticle of the Rose Op 4 (high voice, clarinet, cello, piano) 1963.
Magnificat and Nunc Dimittis Op 20b (unaccompanied SATB chorus) 1963.
Requiescat and Songs of Spring Op 20d/e (unaccompanied SATB chorus) 1965; first performed Lothbury, 1988.
Proverbs Op 20 (SATB chorus, organ or ensemble) 1966.
Visits of Truth (unaccompanied SATB chorus) 1966.
O Be Joyful Op 20c (unaccompanied SATB chorus) 1967; first performed London 1979.
Glora in Excelsis Deo Op 20b (unaccompanied SATB chorus) 1967; first performed Fairfax, Virginia, 1970.
Jubilate deo Op 20c (unaccompanied SATB chorus) 1967; first performed Fairfax, Virginia, 1970.
Music That Brings Sweet Sleep Op 25 (voice, piano) 1967; first performed Maidstone, Kent, 1968.
Aspects I in III Op 39 (voice, piano) 1968; first performed London, 1970.
Six Folk Song Arrangements (voice, piano) 1968.
The World's Way (unison voices, piano or ensemble) 1968.
Sailaway (unison voices, piano or instruments) 1968.
The Glory of the Dove Op 41a (unaccompanied SATB chorus) 1970.
Noble Nature and Truth Op 41c (unaccompanied SATB chorus) 1970; broadcast BBC Radio, 1974.
A Supplication (unaccompanied SAB chorus) 1970.
Missa brevis (unaccompanied SAB chorus) 1970.
Make Me a Willow Cabin Op 44 (soprano, mezzo-soprano, piano; Shakespeare) 1972; first performed London, 1973.
Aspects of Flight Op 48 (voice, piano) 1973; first performed London, 1974. Recorded KRS 33.
Benedictus Op 51 (SATB chorus, organ or orchestra) 1974; first performed London, 1975.
Portrait of a Town Op 52 (speaker, 2 pianos) 1975; first performed Huddersfield, Yorkshire, 1976.
A Landscape of Truth Op 41b (unaccompanied SATB chorus) 1978; broadcast BBC Radio, 1982.
Four Yeats Songs Op 64 (voice, piano) 1980; first performed 1988.
Four Shakespeare Songs Op 57 (voice, piano) 1988; first performed Oxford, 1989.

Songs: *Can You Feel Love*, 1980, recorded Royal JB 306, Royal MS 100, JJ EP 117; *Waiting for You*, 1980, recorded Royal JB 306, Royal MS 100, JJ EP 117; *No Longer Cry, No Longer Sing*, 1980, recorded Royal JB 306; *Fine and Mellow*, 1980, recorded JSO 181.

Opera:

Johnson Preserv'd Op 30 1966–7; first performed London, 1967.
Therese Raquin Op 50 1978; in preparation.

Other:

The End of the Line (film score) 1959.
Lysistrata (incidental music to Aristophanes) 1963.
Troilus and Cressida (incidental music to Shakespeare) 1964.
Macbeth (incidental music to Shakespeare) 1965.
Garden Party Op 33b (ballet by Ashton) 1971; first performed London, 1971.
My Friend, My Enemy (ballet) 1971; first performed London, 1971.
Portrait of a Town (film score) 1982.

PUBLICATIONS

By Stoker: "Bennett in Baltimore", in *Composer*, 1971; *Portrait of a Town* [poetry], 1977; "Recollections of Genius" [on Nadia Boulanger], in *Books and Bookmen*, January 1977; "Dedicated Artist", in *Records and Recording*, October 1978; "Nature, Purpose and Destiny", in *Records and Recording*, January 1979; "Player's Viewpoint", in *Records and Recording*, July 1979; "The First Six Years", in *Records and Recording*, August 1979; *Words Without Music* [poetry], 1980; *Screened: Take Five* [play], 1981; "One Man and Many", in *Composer*, Winter 1984; *Open Window, Open Door* [autobiography], London and New York, 1985; "Compositions of a Marathon Man", in *The Guardian*, 29 November 1989.

On Stoker: Elizabeth Brophy, "RS's "Dr Johnson" Opera", in *Opera*, July 1967; Richard Townend, "The Music of RS", in *Musical Times*, May 1968; Judyth Knight, "RS's Modern Music for Dance", in *Dancing Times*, May 1970; Brian Schlotel, "RS's Music for Young People", in *Music Teacher*, January 1975; Michael Dawney, "RS's Easy Music", in *Making Music*, 1975; Christopher Norris, "RS", in *Music and Musicians*, February 1975; Hilary Thomson, "RS's Music", in *Guitar*, September 1982; Malcolm Stewart, "Composer's Portrait", in *Composer*, Spring 1984; John Gardner, "RS's Autobiography", in *Composer*, Summer 1986; Michael Dawney, "RS at 50", in *Musical Opinion*, February 1989; Ruth Franks, "Contemporary Composer RS", in *Coda*, April 1989.

Richard Stoker comments:

Communication is vital in the arts generally, and in music in particular. Without communication, there is no point in composing. I approach writing (in words), painting and composing in just the same way, hoping my inspiration is strong enough to write or paint something moving and memorable whatever the medium. There is an overlap from "serious" music to popular music and I think this is a very good thing. Most talented composers work in the commercial field as well as the so-called "serious" fields. Anything political in composition is not possible without words. I believe that the "dedicated professionals", together with the "elderly senior members" suffer most in our society today. Commercialism is killing originality in art. The spiritual qualities are receding from all our lives. Popular music, however, the best and not the most commercial, has made rapid strides forward, due mainly to television, radio and electronic technology, together with a few extremely gifted composers and arrangers. We live in a purely materialistic nation, that has little time for the arts. There is no indication that this will change, either. Nothing is lost for the artist, however; to quote Muriel Spark, "Time is always redeemed, nothing is lost for him and wonders never cease."

As far as so-called serious music is concerned, I try to compose "absolute" music, whether there is a descriptive title to the work or not. Form is all-important for me and this helps to make the movements cohesive. The movement can often find its own form and when this happens it is a good thing. When I have used serial techniques in my music, they have always been my own version of this technique and the works have always had tonal elements. I have always liked exploring the "circle of fifths" for the tonal sections of my movements. I prefer to use the same material throughout a longer work as I attempt to "unify" my music at all times. A short work for solo instruments can be just as important to me as a full-size orchestral work.

I owe a great deal to my lessons with Eric Fenby as far as my orchestration is concerned. I never met anyone who understood the orchestra better. The string quartet is my favourite medium, with the piano trio a very close second. My favourite instrument is the guitar and I feel some of my best pieces are written for this, the noblest of instruments.

My love of and interest in music began early. In the war, at the age of four, my father took me to Italian prisoner-of-war camps situated throughout Yorkshire, where I would stay with the Italian men all day. My father took me in by hiding me under the dashboard of the car when he showed his pass at the various barriers. The Italians love children, so they fussed over me, playing games with me and singing extracts from Verdi, Puccini and Italian folk music, accompanying each other on the harmonica and the accordion. They were happy to be out of the war and I remember them continually singing. I think it was also at these camps that my love of the tenor voice—perhaps the most beautiful sound in the world—was nourished. To compose a fine violin concerto is a dream of mine, but it would have to stand with the Elgar, the Mendelssohn, the Tchaikovsky, and the Sibelius, not to mention Bartók, Stravinsky and Prokofiev—a daunting thought. You can see I am firmly rooted in tradition.

* * *

In his autobiography *Open Window, Open Door*, published in 1985, Richard Stoker writes, "A performer's love of his own instrument is catching and this enthusiasm—which has to be genuine—can pass to a willing composer and stay with him for a very long time." This statement of musical faith is very much the key to Stoker's compositional output, for over the years the majority of his pieces have either been conceived for or commissioned by particular performers known to him and his response has always been to write music carefully and sympathetically crafted to match their particular instrumental abilities. Works that particularly come to mind include the Second String Quartet composed in 1962 for the Alberni Quartet (a work which also displays his cunning way with fugue and canon, for each movement is a study in these forms which are so well-suited to the string quartet), and of the series of pieces for guitarists like Hector Quine (*Pastoral Op 42c*), Angelo Gilardino (*Improvisation Op 42b*), and Gabriel Estarellas (*Sonatina Op 42*), and of the series of organ pieces (*A Little Organ Book Op 27* and *Three Pieces Op 31d*) written for Richard Townend. In these, as in so many other instances, he has understood the medium completely and exploited the sonorities of the instruments in a new and totally convincing fashion without recourse to extravagant technical demands on the performers. Perhaps the success of his chamber music (intimate music for a smaller number of people both performers and listeners than large orchestral canvasses) is bound up with his great love of people and his philosophy that "Art is only a complement to life's imperfections and it's my belief that these very imperfections could be put right by more social interaction, awareness and interest."

Another of the clear influences in Stoker's music is his wide breadth of interest in painting and sculpture: it was the line drawings and circus paintings of Picasso which inspired the *Wind Quintet Op 6*, and the painting of Christ wearing the Crown of Thorns by Guido Reni which led to the composition of the cantata *Ecce Homo Op 14*.

Stylistically Stoker's music though it often has serial leanings is more freely organised and, without overt dissonance, is quite easily accessible to the ordinary listener. Though his technical grasp of all classical forms is always evident in the careful plans of his works it is never used to force a compositional point, but rather to give structure to the musings of a free mind which enjoys exploring the possibilities of "new" musical forms and sound patterns without confusing the average listener or pandering to a modernist pastiche.

Stoker's three-act chamber opera *Johnson Preserv'd*, first performed in 1967, is deftly scored for small chamber orchestra with well-drawn characterisations in the five vocal parts. It makes one wish not only that this work might be revived, but also that he might receive a commission to write a large-scale opera which would draw out his talent for setting 20th-century writers like Emerson and Whitman, to whom he has already responded so warmly in his choral work *Visits of Truth* and the three songs *Aspects I in III Op 39*.

Stoker has established himself as a composer whose originality has endeared him to performers and listeners alike because he has used his creative imagination to produce works that are both stimulating and challenging without overwhelming with transient modernism. As he himself has said, "Artists do have an influence on life. Music clears people's minds."

—Richard Townend

SUBOTNICK, Morton (Leon). American. Born in Los Angeles, California, 14 April 1933. Educated at the University of Denver, Colorado, B.A., 1958; Mills College, Oakland, California (composition under Darius Milhaud and Leon

Kirchner), M.A., 1960. Military service, 1955–7. Married (1) Linn Pottle in 1953 (dissolved 1971), 1 son and 1 daughter; (2) Doreen Nelson in 1976 (dissolved 1977); (3) Joan La Barbara, *q.v.*, in 1979, 1 son. Fellow, Institute for Advanced Musical Studies, Princeton University, New Jersey, 1959–60; teacher of composition, Mills College, Oakland, California, 1959–66; co-founder (with Ramon Sender) and co-director, San Francisco Tape Center, 1961–5; music director, Anne Halprin Dance Company, 1961–7; teacher of composition and artist in residence, New York University School of the Arts, 1966–9; music director, Lincoln Center Repertory Theater, New York City, 1967–8; director of electronic music, Electric Circus, St Mark's Place, New York City, 1967–8; visiting professor of composition, University of Maryland, College Park, 1968; visiting professor of composition, University of Pittsburgh, 1969; teacher of composition, and subsequently head of composition department, California Institute of the Arts, Valencia, since 1969; vice-president, American Music Center, 1979–82; visiting professor, Yale University, New Haven, Connecticut, 1980, 1982; visiting professor, Brooklyn College, New York, 1983–4; DAAD composer in residence, Berlin, 1979–80, and Massachusetts Institute of Technology, Cambridge, 1986. Recipient: Brandeis University Creative Arts Award, 1983. Mailing address: 121 Coronado Lane, Santa Fe, New Mexico 87501, U.S.A.

Publishers: Theodore Presser, New York; European/American.

Symphonies/orchestral:

Play! No 2 (orchestra, conductor, tape) 1964; first performed St Louis, Missouri, March 1964.
Laminations (orchestra, electronic sounds) 1967; first performed Buffalo, New York, February 1968. Recorded Turnabout TBS 34428.
Two Butterflies (amplified orchestra) 1974; first performed Los Angeles, 17 April 1975.
Before the Butterfly (amplified trumpet, amplified trombone, amplified percussion, amplified harp, amplified violin, amplified viola, amplified cello, orchestra) 1975; first performed Los Angeles, April 1976.
Place 1979; first performed Portland, Oregon, March 1979.
Axolotl (cello, chamber orchestra, electronic ghost score) 1982; first performed Los Angeles, 15 February 1982.
Liquid Strata (piano, orchestra, electronic ghost score) 1982.
The Key to Songs (chamber orchestra, synthesizer; 1985, also version for orchestra, 2 MIDI grand pianos) 1990–2; first performed Aspen, Colorado, 1985.
In Two Worlds (concerto for saxophone, electronic wind controller, orchestra) 1988; first performed New Mexico, 1988.
A Desert Flowers (orchestra, computer, MIDI baton) 1988; first performed Cleveland, Ohio, 1988.

Chamber/instrumental:

Prelude No 1: The Blind Owl (piano) 1956.
Prelude No 2: The Feast (piano) 1956.
Serenade No 1 (clarinet, flute, vibraphone, cello, piano, mandolin) 1959.
Serenade No 2 (clarinet, horn, piano, percussion) 1961.
Prelude No 3 (piano, tape) 1962.
Ten (flute, oboe, trumpet, trombone, 3 percussion, piano, viola, double bass) 1963, revised 1976; first performed San Francisco, November 1963.
Prelude No 4 (piano, tape) 1966. Recorded Fiction FC 001.
Serenade No 3 (flute, clarinet, violin, piano, tape) 1968.
Liquid Strata (version for piano, electronic ghost score) 1977; first performed Ojai, California, May 1977. Recorded Town Hall S-24.
Parallel Lines (piccolo, electronic ghost score, oboe/cor anglais, clarinet/bass clarinet, trumpet, trombone, horn, 2 percussion, viola, cello) 1978; first performed Valencia, California, March 1979. Recorded CRI SD 458.
The Wild Beasts (trombone, piano, electronic ghost score) 1978; first performed Valencia, California, March 1978. Recorded Nonesuch 78012.
Passages of the Beast (clarinet, electronic ghost score) 1978; first performed Toronto, June 1978.
After the Butterfly (trumpet, 2 clarinets, 2 trombones, 2 cellos, percussion, electronic ghost score) 1979; first performed Los Angeles, October 1979. Recorded Nonesuch N-78001.
The First Dream of Light (tuba, electronic ghost score) 1980; first performed Los Angeles, February 1980. Recorded Crystal S-398.
Ascent into Air (from *The Double Life of Amphibians Part I*; 2 cellos, clarinet, bass clarinet, trombone, bass trombone, 4 percussion, 2 pianos, computer) 1981; first performed Paris, 18 January 1982. Recorded Nonesuch.
The Fluttering of Wings (from *The Double Life of Amphibians Part III*; string quartet with or without electronic ghost score) 1981; first performed Washington, D.C., 14 October 1982. Recorded Nonesuch.
Axolotl (cello, electronic ghost score; also version with chamber ensemble—flute, clarinet, bass clarinet, trumpet, percussion, piano, 6 further cellos) 1981, 1982; solo version first performed Washington, D.C., 13 February 1981. Recorded (solo version) Nonesuch N-78012.
An Arsenal of Defence (viola, electronic ghost score) 1982; first performed San Francisco, 7 November 1982.
And the Butterflies Begin to Sing (chamber ensemble, computer) 1988; first performed Santa Fe, New Mexico, 1988.

Vocal/choral:

Two Life Histories (male voice, clarinet, electronic ghost score) 1977; first performed Los Angeles, April 1977. Recorded Wizard Records.
The Last Dream of the Beast (soprano, electronic ghost score; also versions with 6 cellos and with chamber orchestra score) 1979, 1982, 1982; original version first performed Washington, D.C., February 1979; orchestral version first performed Los Angeles, 6 December 1982. Recorded Nonesuch.
Jacob's Room (monodrama for soprano, string quartet) 1984; first performed San Francisco, January 1985.

Opera:

Hungers (electronic media opera in collaboration with Ed Emshwiller) 1986–7; first performed Los Angeles, 1987.
Jacob's Room (opera version) 1987, in progress.

Other:

Mr & Mrs Discobolos (clarinet, violin, cello, narrator, mime, tape) 1958.
The Balcony (incidental music on tape) 1960.
King Lear (incidental music on tape) 1960.
Sound Blocks (heroic vision for violin, cello, xylophone, marimba, tape, lights, narrator) 1961.

Mandolin (mixed media work for viola, tape, film) 1961–3; first performed San Francisco, October 1963.
Play! No 1 (mixed media work for woodwind quintet, piano, tape, film) 1963; first performed San Francisco, November 1963.
The Five Legged Stool (dance score on tape) 1963.
Galileo (incidental music on tape) 1964.
Play! No 3 (mixed media work for pianist/mime, tape and 16mm film by Tony Martin) 1965; first performed Pasadena, California, March 1965.
Play! No 4 (mixed media work for soprano, vibraphone, cello, 4 game players, 2 game conductors, two 16mm films by Tony Martin) 1965; first performed Seattle, Washington, Spring 1965.
The Caucasian Chalk Circle (music to Brecht; male narrator-singer, 3 female singers, percussion, mandolin, accordion) 1965.
Danton's Death (incidental music on tape) 1965–6.
Silver Apples of the Moon (electronic) 1967. Recorded Nonesuch 71174.
Parades and Changes (dance score on tape) 1967.
Reality I/II (electronic) 1968.
The Wild Bull (electronic) 1968. Recorded Nonesuch 71208.
Touch (electronic) 1969. Recorded Columbia Records.
Sidewinder (electronic) 1971. Recorded Columbia M 30683.
Four Butterflies (electronic sounds, 3 16mm films) 1973. Recorded Columbia M 32741.
Until Spring (electronic) 1975. Recorded Odyssey Y 34158.
Ice Floe (electronic) 1978.
A Sky of Cloudless Sulphur (electronic) 1978.
Return: The Triumph of Reason (computer) 1985–6; first performed (in celebration of Halley's Comet, with planetarium show) Los Angeles, 17 March 1986. Recorded New Albion NA 010.

PUBLICATIONS

On Subotnick: R. Norton, "The Vision of MS", in *Musical Journal*, 28(1), 1970; H.W. Whipple, "Beasts and Butterflies: MS's Ghost Scores", in *Musical Quarterly*, 69, 1983.

* * *

Morton Subotnick is one of the United States' premier composers of electronic music. Most of his music calls for a tape part, or live electronic processing; his oeuvre utilizes many of the important technological breakthroughs in the history of the genre.

The work which brought Subotnick celebrity was *Silver Apples of the Moon*. Written in 1967 using the Buchla modular synthesizer (an instrument Donald Buchla built utilizing suggestions from Subotnick and Ramon Sender), this work contains synthesized tone colours striking for its day, and a control over pitch that many other contemporary electronic composers had relinquished. There is a rich counterpoint of gestures, in marked contrast to the simple surfaces of much contemporary electronic music. There are sections marked by very clear pulses, another unusual trait for its time; *Silver Apples of the Moon* was used as dance music by several companies. It was commissioned by Nonesuch Records, marking the first time an original large-scale composition had been created specifically for the disc medium—a conscious acknowledgment that the home stereo system constituted a present-day form of chamber music. Subotnick wrote this piece (and subsequent record company commissions) in two parts to correspond to the two sides of an LP. The exciting, exotic timbres and the dance-inspiring rhythms caught the ear of the public—the record was an American bestseller in the classical music category, an extremely unusual occurrence for any contemporary concert music at the time.

The next eight years saw the production of several more important compositions for LP, realized on the Buchla synthesizer: *The Wild Bull*, *Touch*, *Sidewinder* and *Four Butterflies*. All of these pieces are marked by sophisticated timbres (for their time), contrapuntally rich textures, and sections of continuous pulse suggesting dance.

In 1975, fulfilling another record company commission, Subotnick composed *Until Spring*, a work for solo synthesizer. In this work, changes in settings which Subotnick made in real time on the synthesizer were stored as control voltages on a separate tape, enabling him to duplicate any of his performance controls, and to subsequently modify them if he felt the desire to do so. While the use of control voltages was nothing new, it suggested to Subotnick a means to gain exact control over real-time electronic processing equipment.

The next step in Subotnick's use of control voltages was the development of the "ghost" box. This is a fairly simple electronic device, consisting of a pitch and envelope follower for a live signal, and the following voltage-controlled units: an amplifier, a frequency shifter, a ring modulator, and a frequency shifter. The control voltages for the ghost box are stored on a tape. A performer, whose miked signal is sent into the ghost box, can then be processed by playing back the pre-recorded tape containing the control voltages. As the tape produces no sound, Subotnick refers to it as a "ghost score". By providing the performer with exact timings, co-ordination between performer and the ghost score is possible.

Two Life Histories was the first piece involving an electronic ghost score; the bulk of Subotnick's output for the next six years was devoted to compositions involving performers and ghost scores. Some of the more notable works in this series include *Liquid Strata* (piano), *Parallel Lines* (piccolo accompanied by nine players), *The Wild Beasts* (trombone and piano), *Axolotl* (for cello), and *The Fluttering of Wings* (for string quartet). The subtlety, sophistication and control over real time electronic processing that Subotnick demonstrated in these innovative works secured his reputation as one of the world's most important electronic music composers.

Subotnick reached the apex of live electronic processing in his work *Ascent into Air*. Written for the powerful 4C computer at IRCAM, this piece involved many of the techniques which Subotnick had developed in his ghost scores. In addition to the processing normally available to him with his ghost boxes, Subotnick was able to spatially locate sounds in a quadraphonic field and to modulate the timbres of the instruments. But perhaps the most significant aspect of this work is its use of live performers to control the computer music; the live performers, in effect, serve as "voltage controls" to influence where a sound is placed, how it is modulated and by how much, etc.—the reverse situation of the ghost score compositions. Even more remarkable is the ability of traditional musical instruments to control computer-generated sounds. The sophistication of this control is currently unavailable using the commercial MIDI devices which many electronic musicians, including Subotnick, favor today.

Since 1985, Subotnick has been using commercially available MIDI gear in works such as *The Key to Songs* and *Return*. His more recent pieces are also marked not only by pulse-driven rhythms, but also by clear diatonic melodies and harmonies.

—Christian Hertzog

SURINACH, Carlos. Spanish; American citizen. Born in Barcelona, 4 March 1915. Educated at Barcelona Conservatoire (piano under José Camirals); studied composition privately (while in uniform) under Enrique Morera, Barcelona, 1936–9; further composition study, Musikhochschule Robert Schumann, Dusseldorf (under Hugo Balzer), from 1940; studied conducting under Pabst, Kölnische Musikhochscule, 1941; further composition study under Max Trapp, seminars under Richard Strauss, Prussian Academy, Berlin, 1941–2; returned to Spain, 1942. Conductor, Orquesta Filarmónica de Barcelona and Gran Teatro del Liceo, Barcelona, 1942–7; resident in France, 1947–51; emigrated to United States, 1951, American citizenship, 1959; visiting professor of composition, Carnegie-Mellon University, Pittsburgh, Pennsylvania, 1966–7, and Queens College, City University of New York, 1974–6. Recipient: Bax Society Medal for Non-Commonwealth Composers, 1966; Knight Commander, Order of Isabella I of Castile, 1972. Mailing address: 111 Park Street, No 9D, New Haven, Connecticut 06511, U.S.A.

Publishers: Associated; Peer; Peters; Ricordi.

Symphonies/orchestral:

Passacaglia-Symphony 1945.
Danza andaluza (chamber orchestra) 1946.
Symphony No 2 1949–50; first performed Paris, 29 January 1950.
Sinfonietta flamenca 1953–4; first performed Louisville, Kentucky, 9 January 1954.
Doppio concertino (violin, piano, small chamber orchestra) 1954.
Fandango 1954; first performed Utica, New York, 4 April 1961.
Hollywood Carnival (chamber orchestra) 1954.
Concertino (piano, strings, cymbals) 1956; first performed New York City, 9 February 1957.
Feria mágica (overture) 1956; first performed Louisville, Kentucky, 14 March 1956.
Madrid 1890 (chamber orchestra) 1956.
Sinfonía chica 1957; first performed La Jolla, California, 6 August 1957.
Concerto for Orchestra 1959.
Paeans and Dances of Heathen Iberia 1959.
Symphonic Variations 1962.
Drama jondo (overture) 1965; first performed Milwaukee, Wisconsin, 4 October 1965.
Melorhythmic Dramas 1966; first performed Rochester, Michigan, 16 August 1966.
Jota (concert band; from *Suite espagnole*) 1970.
Sinfonietta flamenca (transcribed for concert band) 1971.
Soleriana (concert band; after *Fandango* by Soler) 1972.
Piano Concerto 1973; first performed Minneapolis, Minnesota, 13 November 1974.
The Trumpets of the Seraphim (overture) 1973; first performed Muncie, Indiana, 5 December 1973.
Harp Concerto 1978; first performed Grand Rapids, Michigan, 15 February 1979.
Concerto for String Orchestra 1978.
Violin Concerto 1980.

Chamber/instrumental:

Piano Quartet 1944.
Flamenquerias (2 pianos) 1951.
Trois Chansons et danses espagnoles (piano) 1951.
Tres cantos berberes (flute, oboe, clarinet, viola, cello, harp) 1952.
Ritmo jondo (original version for clarinet, trumpet, tamburo, xylophone, timpani, hand claps) 1952; first performed New York City, 5 May 1952.
Tientos (harp or harpsichord or piano, cor anglais, timpani) 1953; first performed New York City, 11 November 1953.
Tales from the Flamenco Kingdom (piano for children) 1955.
Sonatina (guitar) 1960.
Flamenco cyclorhythmia (violin, piano) 1967.
Bolero (guitar; from *Suite espagnole*) 1970.
Una rosa en cada galta / Red Cheeks (2 guitars) 1973.
String Quartet 1974; first performed Las Palmas, Canary Islands, 21 May 1975.

Vocal/choral:

Tres canciones / Three Songs of Spain (soprano, piano or chamber orchestra) 1945.
Romance, oración y saeta (soprano, piano or orchestra) 1958.
Tres cantares (soprano, piano or orchestra) 1958.
Cantata de San Juan (SATB chorus, percussion) 1963; first performed New York City, 23 June 1963.
Songs of the Soul (unaccompanied SATB chorus) 1964; broadcast CBS Television, 15 November 1964.
Flamenco Meditations (voice, piano; E.B. Browning) 1965.
The Missions of San Antonio (male voices, orchestra) 1969; first performed San Antonio, Texas, 25 January 1969.
Via Crucis (voices, guitar) 1972; broadcast CBS Television, 2 April 1972.
Prayers (voice, guitar; Quoist) 1972–3.
Celebraciones medievales (SATB chorus, concert band) 1977.

Dance:

Monte Carlo (choreographed by Goube) 1945; first performed Barcelona, 1945.
Ritmo jondo / Deep Rhythm (Humphrey; orchestra or chamber orchestra or concert band) 1953; first performed New York City, 15 April 1953.
Embattled Garden (Graham; orchestra) 1958; first performed New York City, 3 April 1958.
Hazana (based on *tientos*) 1959; first performed London, 25 May 1959.
La sibila (music from *Concertino* for piano, strings, cymbals) 1959; first performed Spoleto, Italy, 13 July 1959.
Acrobats of God (Graham; orchestra) 1960; first performed New York City, 27 April 1960.
Córdoba (music from *Iberia Suite* after Albeniz) 1960; first performed Barcelona, 1 May 1960.
David and Bath-Sheba (Butler; orchestra) 1960; broadcast CBS Television, 15 May 1960.
A Place in the Desert (music as for *David and Bath-Sheba*) 1961; first performed London, 25 July 1961.
Apasionada (Lang; small orchestra) 1961–2; first performed New York City, 5 January 1962.
Feast of Ashes (choreographed to *Doppio concertino* and *Ritmo jondo*) 1963; first performed Lisbon, 30 November 1962.
Celebrants (music from *Concertino* for piano, strings, cymbals) 1963; first performed Tel Aviv, 25 November 1963.
Los renegados (Anduze; orchestra) 1964–5; first performed San Juan, Puerto Rico, 27 May 1965.
Venta quemada (Skibine) 1966; first performed Cannes, 12 March 1966.
Agathe's Tale (Taylor; orchestra) 1967; first performed New London, Connecticut, 12 August 1967.

Suite española (Udaeta) 1969–70; first performed Barcelona, 6 October 1970.
Chronique (Graham; guitar, timpani) 1974; first performed New York City, 1974.
The Owl and the Pussycat (Graham; orchestra or reduced orchestra) 1977; first performed New York City, 26 June 1978.
Blood Wedding (Terekhov) 1979; first performed Oklahoma, 1979.

Opera:

El mozo que caso con mujer brava 1947; first performed Barcelona, 10 January 1948.

Other:

Albeniz: *Iberia Suite* (orchestrated; parts called "Almeria", "Eritana", "Jerez", "Lavapies", "Malaga", "El Polo", "Rondena") 1955; first performed Philadelphia, 16 February 1956.

* * *

Although Carlos Surinach spent an 18-month period of post-graduate study in war-time Germany, the Spanish influences upon his style were already indelible. Evidence of this background is apparent in *Tres canciones / Three Songs of Spain*, his first published work, which was written in the year before his German visiting scholarship and is based upon texts by Lorca and Mached. However, his time in Germany undoubtedly helped to polish Surinach's technical ability, which has always been most apparent in his exuberant and assured orchestration—Richard Strauss and Carl Orff were prominent among those composers whose work he heard in Germany and he also attended some of Strauss's lecture-seminars.

The apprentice pieces which Surinach composed at about this time, including the *Piano Quartet* and *Passacaglia-Symphony*, conform in many respects to the structural tendencies of Germanic late Romanticism best exemplified by Brahms and his followers; but the harmonic language sets Surinach's efforts apart. Tentative use of the eighth-note "flamenco" scale is already evident (flamenco music, indigenous to the Andalusia region of Southern Spain, is strongly associated with the Phrygian mode, from which the distinctive descending pattern A–G–F–E—or its transposed equivalents—has been extracted for use with "flamenco" scale patterns) and this device was to assume greater importance in some later works.

After the war, when Surinach returned to Barcelona and began to develop a European career as a conductor, he continued to compose, albeit on a reduced scale. Two works from these years, the ballet, *Monte Carlo* and *Symphony No 2*, give a strong hint of the colourful theatricality which characterises much of his subsequent career. The Symphony was well received in the United States, which has proved to be a highly congenial setting for Surinach's talents: after settling there in 1951, his ability to turn a striking phrase was initially used for the production of television advertising jingles, but his assured, strongly flavoured Spanish idiom was soon much in demand and he prospered as a composer of ballet scores.

Surinach's ballet scores were enthusiastically taken up by some prominent performers, such as Martha Graham and the Robert Joffrey Ballet Company and he has continued to write for this medium, often to fulfill prestigious international commissions, throughout his subsequent career. From the early 1950s onwards, his instrumental music (such as the *Ritmo jondo* for clarinet, trumpet and percussion, which was expanded for balletic use in *Ritmo jondo / Deep Rhythm* and presented by the José Limon Company) was also frequently choreographed. His reputation as a symphonic composer was thereby enhanced and he was a natural choice of Albeniz's heirs as the orchestrator of the *Iberia Suite*, an arrangement which has been widely performed and has to some extent superceded the instrumentation of five of the movements by Fernandez Arbos.

The vivid, distinctly cinematic Spanish nationalism which characterises much of Surinach's output is well-illustrated by his piano music. A number of his keyboard works have been championed by Alicia de Larrocha, who commissioned and recorded the *Piano Concerto*, an effective, though somewhat meandering essay. De Larrocha has also recorded some of Surinach's solo pieces, including the *Trois Chansons et danses espagnoles* which were written in New York during the composer's earliest months in the U.S. At their best, these pieces follow the traditions of Isaac Albéniz and Enrique Granados—seldom strikingly original in language or material, but well-fashioned and piquant. Unfortunately, elsewhere in this collection, Surinach's main failings as a composer are illustrated too. In particular, the basic structures are quite stereotypical, and this predictability seems to augment the impression of anonymity which is an all-too-frequent by-product of his language of conventional exoticism.

Surinach has produced several quite impressive concert works, among which the *Symphonic Variations* are outstanding, but he is definitely at his best when writing for the stage or screen. A theatrical challenge seems to stimulate his technically dazzling and attractively exotic talent to the full.

—Paul Horner

SUSLIN, Viktor. Russian. Born in Miass, Ural region, 1942. Educated: piano study from age 4; Music School, Kharkov (composition, music; piano under W. Topilin), 1950–61; Gnessin Institute, Moscow (composition under N. Pejko, piano under A. Wedernikov), 1962–6. Music editor, Muzyka publishing house, Moscow, from 1966; docent in instrumentation and orchestration, Moscow Conservatory, 1972–4; co-founder (with Sofia Gubaidulina, *q.v.* and V. Artyomov, *q.v.*), improvisation ensemble Astraea, 1975–81; emigrated to Germany, 1981; music editor, Internationale Musikverlage Hans Sikorski, Hamburg, since 1981; docent in instrumentation, Musikhochschule, Lubeck, since 1981. Mailing address: c/o Internationale Musikverlage Hans Sikorski, Postfach 132001, 2000 Hamburg 13, Germany.

Publisher: Hans Sikorski.

Symphonies: / orchestral:

Piano Concerto 1966.
Concerto for Violin and Chamber Orchestra 1969.

Sinfonia piccola 1970.
Etuden (24 strings) 1972.
Lebwohl 1982.

Chamber/instrumental:

String Quartet No 1 1963.
Five Pieces (piano) 1965.
Sonata (piano) 1968.
Trio Sonata (flute, guitar, cello) 1971.
[24] Triaden (harpsichord) 1973.
Patience (2 pianos) 1974.
Gioco appassionato (card game for 4 string instruments) 1974.
Mitternachtmusik (violin, harpsichord/live electronics, double bass) 1977.
Ave Marcus (percussion; 2 versions) 1977.
Poco a poco (Sonata No 1) (organ) 1978. Recorded Aulos 66022 AUL.
Terrarium (6 percussion) 1978.
Capriccio uber die Abreise (2 violins) 1979.
Sonata (cello, percussion) 1983. Recorded Schwann VMS 1064.
In My End Is My Beginning (Sonata No 2) (organ) 1983. Recorded Aulos PRE 66022 AUL.
Chanson contre raison (sonata for cello solo) 1984.
Sonata capricciosa (viola, harpsichord) 1986.
Lamento (organ) 1989.
Grenzubertritt (viola, cello, double bass) 1990.

Vocal/choral:

Japanese Songs (baritone, piano) 1965.
Cycle of Songs after Daniil Charms (unaccompanied mixed chorus) 1972.

PUBLICATIONS

By Suslin: essays on Sofia Gubaidulina and Galina Ustvolskaya, Internationale Musikverlage Hans Sikorski, Hamburg, 1988, 1990.

On Suslin: Detlev, Gohowy, "Wenn einer in Moskau Schakopf spielt. Der russische Komponist in Westen", in *Die Welt*, 15 May 1982; Michael Kurtz, (interview) in *Zeitung für Musik*, 1, 1989.

* * *

Viktor Suslin was once one of the more interesting of the younger generation of post-war Soviet composers. Since his emigration to Germany more than a decade ago, he has become one of the most serious and individual composers working in Germany today.

Suslin's early compositions reflected his keen interest in the German and Austrian modernists of earlier this century. Unlike most of his contemporaries Suslin was lucky enough to study privately with Philip Herschkovich, the Romanian musician and pupil of Webern, who by tragic mischance found himself in 1940 stuck inside the Soviet Union and unable to find a way out until 1988, right at the end of his life. Herschkovich's concentration on the structural thinking of Beethoven was liberating for young Soviet musicians. Herschkovich refused to teach the 12-tone method, declaring it to be a natural consequence of a full knowledge of the classics.

The second great influence on Suslin was, and still is, his friendship with Sofia Gubaidulina. Together with Viacheslav Artyomov they founded the improvisation group Astreia to explore the kinds of musical and acoustic freedoms that seemed so refreshingly new in Moscow at that time.

From his German influences Suslin took an intense respect for organic integration and coherence. From the shared experience of improvisation he gained a refined awareness of the minutiae of sound and silence, of the slightest change of instrumental colour. As a result he has developed a musical tongue combining extreme refinement with a powerful original sense of form and development.

Suslin's personal voice can first be heard in the works immediately preceding his emigration, such as the impressive and menacing *Mitternachtmusik* for harpsichord, violin and double-bass, or the First Organ Sonata, *Poco a Poco 11*. In these and other pieces of the time the fundamental technical premises of Suslin's later work are clearly heard. These premises depend in particular on a serial organisation not of pitches alone but of the 24 keys around the circle of fifths. The music is not tonal, but the raw materials of tonality, usually in the shape of the fundamental triads, are picked up and handled as whole elements of several different but related series. The results are very impressive. One might characterise the music as the narration of an almost endless variety of adventures within a bizarre imaginary world. The dislocation implied by such a world in which the surface preoccupation with triads and the like takes place within a quite un-tonal framework obeying often arcane structural principles, lends to this music something of the dream-like quality of Lewis Carroll or even the nightmare feeling of a Russian absurdist like Daniel Kharms.

Since his emigration Suslin has written a great deal of chamber music, including a powerful Sonata for cello and two percussionists and a second sonata for the organ. Chamber music suits the essentially private nature of Suslin's communication. But he has also written on a larger scale, most notably in the deeply impressive symphonic epigraph *Lebwohl*, a work in which the composer proves by a mastery of the larger dramatic effect and a richly wrought tapestry of orchestral invention, that he is capable of speaking to the wider public without diminishing the subtlety and precision of what he wishes to say. One may hope that he ventures again into the orchestral domain as *Lebwohl* gives promise of much to be achieved in this field.

—Gerard McBurney

SVIRIDOV, Georgy (Yuriy Vasilyevich). Russian. Born in Fatezh, Kursk, 15 December 1915. Educated at Children's Music School, Kursk (piano), 1929–32; Central Music College, Leningrad, 1932–6; Leningrad Conservatory (composition under Dmitri Shostakovitch), 1936–41. Military service, 1936–41. Married Elza Gustavovna Klazer, 28 November 1953; 1 son. Composer; pianist; member, since 1936, and secretary, since 1962, Union of Composers, Soviet Union; 1st secretary, Russian Federation Union of Composers, 1968–73. Recipient: State Prizes, 1946, 1968, 1980; Lenin Prize, 1960;

Order of Lenin, 1965, 1971, 1975, 1985; People's Artist of the Soviet Union, 1970; Hero of Socialist Labour, 1975. Mailing address: ultisa Bolshaya Gruzinskaya dom 36, kv. 62, 123056 Moscow, U.S.S.R.

Publishers: Sovetskii kompozitor, Moscow; Muzyka, Moscow.

Symphonies/orchestral:

Symphony (string orchestra) 1940; first performed Leningrad, 1940.
Music (chamber orchestra) 1964; first performed Moscow, 12 September 1964. Recorded Melodiya SR 04224.
Suite: Time, Forward! 1965; first performed Moscow, 1965. Recorded Melodiya S10 06383 009.
Little Triptych 1965; first performed Moscow, 5 February 1966. Recorded Melodiya SM 01943 03542; Le Chant du Monde LDX 78481.
Music Illustrations (to Pushkin's *Snow Storm*) 1975; first performed Moscow, 1975. Recorded S10 06383 009.

Chamber/instrumental:

Sonata (piano) 1944; first performed Leningrad, 1944. Recorded Melodiya S10 03141 004.
Trio (piano, violin, cello) 1945; first performed Leningrad, 1945. Recorded Melodiya S10 03141 004/16871 009.
Two Partitas (in E minor and F minor; piano) 1947; first performed Leningrad, 1947. Recorded Melodiya S10 02511 002; E minor only, S10 17129 001; F minor only, S10 19487 006.
Album of Pieces for Children (piano) 1948; first performed Leningrad, 1948. Recorded S50 15909 000.

Vocal/choral:

Six Romances (high, voice, piano; Pushkin) 1936; first performed Leningrad, 1936. Recorded Melodiya S10 21191 004/11981 008/11345 009/13539 008; etc.
Eight Romances (voice, piano; Lermontov) 1937; first performed Leningrad, 1937. Recorded Melodiya S10 11981 008.
Peasant Lyrics (alternating tenor and baritone, piano; Prokofiev) 1938; first performed Leningrad, 1938. Recorded Melodiya S10 16587 002.
From Shakespeare (bass/1 song for mezzo-soprano, piano) 1942. Recorded Melodiya S10 11981 008; S10 06689 009; parts only.
The Land of My Fathers (tenor and/or bass, piano; Isaakyan) 1953; first performed Leningrad, 25 November 1953. Recorded S10 11981 008/11345 009.
Burns Songs (bass, piano) 1955; first performed Leningrad, 28 November 1955. Recorded Melodiya S10 06689 009.
Poem to the Memory of Sergei Yesenin (tenor, mixed chorus, orchestra) 1956; first performed 31 May 1956. Recorded Melodiya S10 05799 006; Le Chant du Monde LDX 78563.
Five Choruses (unaccompanied mixed chorus; Russian poets) 1958; first performed Moscow, October 1958. Recorded Melodiya SM 01021 01944.
Pathetic Oratorio (bass, mezzo-soprano, mixed chorus, orchestra; Mayakovsky) 1959; first performed Moscow, 15 October 1959. Recorded Melodiya S10 05861 004; Le Chant du Monde LDXA 78464.
My Father Is a Peasant (tenor, baritone, piano; Yesenin) 1960. Recorded Melodiya S10 21191 004.
Kursk Songs (mixed chorus, orchestra; folk lyrics) 1964; first performed 13 June 1964. Recorded Melodiya SM 01021 01944; Angel SR 40224; Marconi S063 90280.
Wooden Russia (tenor, male chorus, symphony orchestra; Yesenin) 1965; first performed 5 February 1966. Recorded Melodiya SM 01943 03542; Le Chant du Monde LDX 78481.
The Snow Is Falling (female chorus, boys' chorus, symphony orchestra; Pasternak) 1966; first performed 21 December 1966. Recorded Melodiya S10 11533 009; Le Chant du Monde LDXA 78481.
Two Choruses (baritone, 4-and 12-part unaccompanied male chorus; Yesenin) 1967; first performed Moscow, 17 November 1967. Recorded Melodiya SM 01943 03542; Le Chant du Monde LDX 78481.
Petersburg Songs (soprano, mezzo-soprano, baritone, bass, piano, violin, cello; Blok) 1969; first performed Moscow, December 1969.
Spring Cantata (mixed chorus, orchestra; Yesenin) 1972; first performed 7 July 1972. Recorded Melodiya S10 06461 007.
Three Choruses (unaccompanied mixed chorus; Tolstoy) 1973; first performed Moscow, 23 October 1973. Recorded Melodiya S10 06461 007.
Concerto in Memory of A.A. Yurlov (unaccompanied mixed chorus) 1973; first performed Moscow, 1973. Recorded Melodiya S10 07119 001; Le Chant du Monde LDX 78656.
Three Miniatures (unaccompanied mixed chorus; Blok) 1975; first performed Moscow, 1975. Recorded Melodiya S10 06461 007; Columbia M 34525.
The Pushkin Wreath (large mixed chorus, celeste, harp, piano, clog-box, cymbals, bass drum, vibraphone) 1978; first performed Moscow, 5 April 1979. Recorded Melodiya S10 15903 004.
Three Poems (unaccompanied mixed chorus; Pushkin) 1979. Recorded Melodiya S10 18857 009.
Night Clouds (mixed chorus, celeste, piano, percussion; Blok) 1979; first performed Melodiya S10 15907 009.
Hymns to the Motherland (unaccompanied mixed chorus; Sologub) 1979. Recorded Melodiya S10 18857 009.
Ladoga (bass, mixed chorus, 2 bayans, piano, cymbals, clog box, tambourine, side drum; Prokofiev) 1979; first performed 31 January 1980.
Songs of Hard Times (mezzo-soprano, mixed chorus, electric organ or harmonium; Blok) 1980; first performed Moscow, 23 December 1980.
Romances and Songs (mezzo-soprano, soprano, piano; Blok) 1980; first performed Moscow, 23 December 1980. Recorded Melodiya S10 20793 007.
Russia Launched (voice, piano) 1982; first performed Moscow, 1982. Recorded Melodiya S10 20695 006.
Three Old Russian Songs of the Kursk Region (2 mezzo-sopranos, mixed chorus, 2 pianos, ocarina, percussion) 1983; first performed Moscow, 1983.

Other romances and songs to lyrics by Pushkin, Blok Lermontov, Yesenin, Kornilov, Isaakyan Mayakovsky, Khlebnikov, Prokofiev. Recorded Melodiya S10 11981 008/ 11345 009/13539 008/ 14047 003.

PUBLICATIONS

On Sviridov: M.-R. Hofmann, *La Musique russe des origines à nos jours*, Paris, 1968; A. Sokhor, *GS*, Moscow, 2nd edition, 1972; *GS*, edited by D. Frishman, [collection of articles], Moscow 1971; *GS*, edited by R. Ledenev, Moscow, 1979; A.A. Zolotov, *A Book About S: Reflections, Opinions, Articles*, Moscow, 1983; *GS's Musical World*, edited by A. Belonenko, [collection of articles], Moscow, 1990.

Georgy Sviridov comments:

Russian music, indeed all Russian art, has for most of its history been closely bound up with the Orthodox outlook and philosophy. This is the tap-root of our culture, its originality and individuality. During the last century, that connection was severed. Will it be possible to restore it? Not only the destiny of our culture depends on it, but the very existence of Russians as a nation, with a place and a voice in world history. The restoration of this spiritual connection is the most difficult task facing our society. Only by taking this path do I see any future for Russian art.

* * *

In his youth Georgy Sviridov was a pupil of Shostakovich and held a place in the affections of the older composer. But as his career progressed, and especially after the appearance of the *Pathetic Oratorio* in 1959, he increasingly provoked his former teacher's disapproval and even wrath. Shostakovich has not been the only person to take offence; for many of the younger generation Sviridov has long represented a retrospective pernicious side of Soviet music. The official awards and honours that he has received, as well as his many compositions in honour of Lenin, would seem to confirm their worst fears.

However, Sviridov also has his staunch supporters and defenders. For example, the former experimental composer Roman Ledenyov has written that he considers Sviridov to be, in essence, the most important composer in Russia today. And there is certainly a specific audience for concerts of Sviridov's works in his native land.

To understand Sviridov and his appeal one must have some idea of the history of Slavophilia in our century. It was always characteristic of the Slavophiles to wish to see a Russia free from dependence—whether political, intellectual, religious, economic or artistic—on the outside world. And since Russia has notably failed to produce a continuous form of development (in almost any sphere) of the kind highly regarded in the West, so Slavophilia, wishing to restore true Russianness in all domains of life, is a most extreme form of idealistic conservatism.

Ironically, given its revolutionary premise, the Soviet regime has consistently attempted to court and incorporate the Slavophile tradition. Stalinism desperately needed emotional sanction as the new true path of the Russian peoples, isolated, purified and quick to crush the enemy. But Slavophilia was never entirely won over by the state organs. As cracks have appeared in the edifice of Soviet power, so Slavophilia has quickly gathered new strength, feeding on the longing to return to a nostalgic (and imaginary) past before the Communist curse.

Sviridov is the composer laureate of the Slavophiles of our time. His music is not just written in an olden style as a matter of taste. It is in fact the deliberate recreation of an imagined univeral idiom of 100 hundred years ago or more, a synthetic generalisation drawn from a mixture of characteristic manners and procedures common to Glinka, Dargomyshzky, the Mighty Handful, Tchaikovsky and Rachmaninov. It also takes in Orthodox liturgical music and Russian folk music. Not surprisingly, most of Sviridov's music is vocal or choral. His careful use of great Russian poetry, his reliance on the characteristic sound and intonation of the Russian voice, and his word-setting, with its stress on the acoustic texture of the individual phonemes (a nostalgic matter for a Russian speaker and a matter of exclusive indifference to anyone else), all contribute to the desired effect.

There are many reasons to dislike what Sviridov does. One might object to his point of view, either for its political implications or for its grotesque naivety. One might find the music an appalling example of generalised kitsch. One might, like Shostakovich, hear the music as a moral failure, the work of a man who does not wish to think anymore. But to those who love Sviridov's music, all such criticisms are merely sanctimonious resistance to its obvious truths and beauties. And certainly, even to an outsider, there is something curiously skilful in the intensity of Sviridov's identification with his chosen models. To listen to, say, *The Pushkin Wreath*, can be, almost against one's will, to be caught up in a mysterious kind of time-travel, where historical continuity is dissolved into a selective equality of past and present.

—Gerard McBurney

SWAYNE, Giles. British/English. Born 30 June 1946. Educated: early piano lessons under Gordon Green; University of Cambridge (under Raymond Leppard and Nicholas Maw), 1963–8; Accademia Chigiana, Siena, Summer 1968; Royal Academy of Music, London (piano under Gordon Green, composition under Harrison Birtwistle, Alan Bush and Nicholas Maw), 1968–71; Conservatoire National Superiéur de Musique, Paris (some composition classes under Olivier Messiaen), 1976–7; study visit to The Gambia and southern Senegal, 1981–2. Repetiteur, Wexford Festival, and Glyndebourne, Sussex, 1972–4; temporary director of music, St Paul's Girls' School, London, 1976–7; composer in residence, London Borough of Hounslow, 1980–3. Recipient: Greater London Arts Young Composers' Prize (for *String Quartet No 1*), 1972; 1st prize (for *Canto*), Lancaster University competition for new violin work, 1974. Mailing address: 43 Victor Road, London NW10 5XB, England.

Publisher: Novello.

Symphonies/orchestral:

Orlando's Music 1974; first performed Liverpool, 3 February 1976.
Charades (school orchestra) 1975; first performed (as *Charade*) London, 1976–7.
Pentecost Music 1977; first performed Manchester, 8 April 1981.
Symphony (small orchestra) 1984; first performed London, 1 June 1984.
Naotwa Lala 1984; first performed Manchester, 4 December 1984.
The Song of Leviathan 1988; first performed London, 10 October 1988.

Chamber/instrumental:

Sonata (string quartet) 1968.
Phoenix Variations (piano) 1968–1979; broadcast BBC, 23 July 1980.
Chamber Music for Strings (2 violins, 2 violas, 2 cellos, harp) 1970; first performed London, 1971.

Four Lyrical Pieces (cello, piano) 1970; first performed Aldeburgh, Suffolk, 16 June 1971.
String Quartet No 1 1971; first performed Bromsgrove, Worcestershire, 18 April 1972.
Paraphrase (organ; after a theme of Thomas Tallis) 1971.
Trio (flute, oboe, piano) 1972.
Canto (guitar) 1972; first performed London, 26 October 1972. Recorded L'Oiseau Lyre DSL03.
Canto (piano) 1973; broadcast 1974; first concert performance, 23 November 1976.
Canto (violin) 1973; first performed Lancaster, 7 February 1974.
Synthesis (2 pianos) 1974; first performed York, 27 October 1976.
Scrapbook (12 short piano pieces for children) 1974.
Canto (clarinet) 1975; first performed London, 4 January 1982.
Three Pieces (string quartet) 1975.
Duo (violin, piano) 1975; first performed Birmingham, 7 January 1976.
Suite (guitar) 1976.
String Quartet No 2 1977; first performed Manchester, 30 October 1978.
The Three Rs (recorders, tuned and untuned percussion, 3 violin parts, cello; for schoolchildren) 1980.
Freewheeling (viola, baryton, cello) 1980; first performed Kuhmo, Finland, 25 July 1980.
Canto (cello) 1981; first performed London, 6 January 1982.
Rhythm Study I (2 xylophone players, 2 marimba players; for children) 1982.
Rhythm Study II (6 child percussionists) 1982.
Riff-Raff (organ) 1983; first performed St Albans, Hertfordshire, 9 July 1983. Recorded Priory PR 188.
A Song for Haddi (flute, clarinet, viola, cello, double bass, percussion) 1983; first performed 4 June 1983.
Small Song for Miss Brown (clarinet, optional drum) 1983.
Solo (guitar) 1986.
Into the Light (clarinet/E♭ clarinet/bass clarinet, bassoon, trumpet, trombone, violin, double bass, percussion) 1986; first performed near Canterbury, Kent, 28 June 1986.
Time Passes (piano; from *God-Song*) 1986.
PP (flute, oboe, clarinet, bassoon, horn, trumpet, trombone, percussion, celeste, 2 violins, viola, cello, double bass) 1987; first performed London, 10 February 1987.
Tonos (flute, harp, violin, viola, cello) 1987; first performed London, 20 February 1987.
Songlines (flute, guitar; after Bruce Chatwin) 1987; first performed Turkey and Greece, January 1988.
The Coming of Saskia Hawkins (organ) 1987; first performed Norwich, Norfolk, 20 June 1989.
Harmonies of Hell (flute/2 piccolos, oboe, clarinet/2 bass clarinets, bassoon, horn, 2 percussion, strings) 1988; first performed Harrogate, Yorkshire, 7 August 1988.
A Memory of Sky (brass quintet) 1989; first performed Hungerford, Berkshire, 16 May 1989.

Vocal/choral:

Three Shakespeare Songs (soloists, unaccompanied SATB chorus) 1969; first performed London, 16 February 1971.
The Good Morrow (mezzo-soprano, piano; Donne) 1971; first performed London, 11 January 1979.
Alleluia! (narrator, SSA chorus, harp, piano, 3 percussion; Jerusalem Bible, medieval drama) 1976; first performed London, 14 December 1976.
Cry (28 amplified solo voices; consists of 7 movements which may be performed separately—"Void—Light—Darkness", "Sky", "Sea—Dry Land—Vegetation", "Sun—Moon—Stars", "Creatures of the Air and Water", "Creatures of the Dry Land", "Rest") 1979; first performed (unamplified) London, 23 July 1980; first public performance (amplified but without electronic treatments) London, 9 October 1980; first definitive performance The Hague, 22 October 1982. Recorded BBC Enterprises RF 550.
Count-Down (16-part chorus, 2 percussion) 1981; first performed Merton, Devon, 23 May 1982.
Magnificat (unaccompanied SSAATTBB chorus) 1982; first performed Oxford, 4 July 1982.
Missa tiburtina (unaccompanied SATB chorus) 1985, enlarged 1986; first performed London, 21 July 1985; first complete performance (with "Gloria") Norwich, Norfolk, 5 July 1986.
God-Song (mezzo-soprano, flute, trombone, cello, piano; York Mysteries) 1985, enlarged 1986; first performed London, 7 December 1985; first complete performance London, 4 December 1986.
Nunc dimittis (SATB chorus, organ) 1986; first performed Norwich, Norfolk, 3 July 1986.
O magnum mysterium (3-part boys' chorus, organ) 1986; first performed London, 10 December 1986.
Veni Creator I (SATB chorus, organ; 9th century) 1987.
Veni Creator II (SATB chorus, organ; 9th century) 1987; first performed Windsor, Berkshire, August 1987.
No Quiet Place (60–70 children's or women's voices, 2 soloists, 6–12 xylophones, violin, viola, cello) 1989; first performed Milgavie, Strathclyde, 17 June 1990.
No Man's Land (bass, SATB chorus, bass clarinet, percussion, violin, cello, double bass, harpsichord; *Jabberwocky*, Breytenbach) 1990; first performed Manchester, 14 October 1990.

Opera:

Le nozze di cherubino (12 singers and continuo: 2 harpsichords, cello, double bass) 1984; 1st act first performed Birmingham, 11 July 1984; first complete performance London, 22 January 1985.

Other:

A World Within (ballet on life of Brontës; multi-tracked tape of horn) 1978; first performed Stoke-on-Trent, 2 June 1978.
Floating Off (incidental music for Stephen Davis play) 1983; broadcast BBC, 24 August 1983.
Crime Inc (incidental music for television documentary series) 1984; broadcast ITV, from 18 July 1984.

* * *

Acutely aware of the contemporary composer's uneasy position on the fringes of society, Giles Swayne has increasingly sought for ways to communicate sophisticated musical thought in terms which would neither exclude nor deter the vast majority of mankind—whether they be children, or amateurs, or simply the huge, untapped audience which listens avidly to pop music but never sets foot in a concert hall.

Swayne has certainly come close to achieving his impossible dream, particularly with *Cry*, his stupendous tone-poem for 28 solo voices. An hour-long song without words, depicting the seven days of Creation, *Cry* communicates on as many levels as there are ears to hear—not only as a wonderfully colourful and profoundly moving evocation of the birth of the world, but as a musical structure of the most intellectually absorbing kind. Right from the outset, Swayne's work has revealed a fascination with structure as a basis for, rather than as the outcome of, his musical ideas. No matter what "style" he chooses to adopt for a particular piece, or how apparently free-flowing its inspiration, the amount of detailed pre-compositional planning from which it springs varies only in kind.

Despite his refusal to be stylistically pigeon-holed, a retrospective survey of his output reveals a striking consistency, particularly with regard to gesture. His early *String Quartet No 1* already shows a typically energetic handling of ostinato refrains interspersed with the cadenza-like figurations that have since become a notable feature of his style. More significantly, a childlike dance motif (first heard in the *Trio* for flute, oboe and piano) was to recur in various guises in several works of the period, culminating in *Orlando's Music*, while the five *Cantos* for solo instruments introduced the equally characteristic song element—eventually to blossom into the extended orchestral aria of *Naotwa Lala*.

Swayne seems instinctively to have rejected the classical Austro-German concepts of counterpoint and harmonic voice-leading, so that the more toughly abstract works of the mid-1970s (such as *Synthesis* for two pianos) represent an important stage in the formation of a clearly founded alternative—with areas of tension or relaxation no longer necessarily related to an ongoing harmonic development. Thus they already hint at the harmonic simplification first used to large-scale effect in *Pentecost Music*.

Scored for huge orchestra, the single-movement *Pentecost Music* is based on a series of modal cells centred around and intermittently returning to the note D, so giving the music a harmonic focus that was to be developed on a still more extended time scale in *Cry* and in his most recent orchestral work, *The Song of Leviathan*—as too were the numerically-based proportions linking its vividly characterised internal divisions.

Then, following the overwhelming success of *Cry*, Swayne felt himself at a turning point. He had already paid the first of several visits to Africa, and this experience, together with that of working with the untrained talents of London schoolchildren, forced him to submit to a radical self-questioning vis-à-vis his wider musical purpose. Focusing on melody and on a feelable, danceable rhythm, he wrote a succession of immediately attractive, relatively small-scale pieces, mostly intended for children or amateurs, but including the virtuoso *Canto* for cello and the chamber orchestral *Symphony*. Yet Swayne's stylistic restlessness is in no sense negative: both the chamber music *God-Song* and the huge orchestral piece, *The Song of Leviathan* (written for amateurs, but without pulling any musical punches), show him at full stretch—again pushing himself to the limits of his commanding musical intellect.

—Susan Bradshaw

SWEENEY, William (John). British/Scottish. Born in Glasgow, 5 January 1950. Educated at Knightswood Secondary School, 1961–7; Royal Scottish Academy of Music, 1967–70, diploma, 1970; Royal Academy of Music, London, 1970–3. Married Susannah Margaret Conway, 6 July 1977; 1 son and 1 daughter. Woodwind tutor, Central Regional Council, Scotland, 1975–85; composition teacher, University of Glasgow, since 1988, and Douglas Academy, Strathclyde, since 1989. Member, executive committee, Musicians' Union of Great Britain, 1989. Recipient: Aeleph Prize, 1981; McEwen Memorial Commission, University of Glasgow, 1981, 1989. Mailing address: 37 Lawrence Street, Glasgow G11 5HD, Scotland.

Publisher: none.

Symphonies/orchestral:

Maqam 1984; first performed Glasgow, 1984.
Glasgow 1985; first performed Glasgow, 1985.
Sunset Song 1986; first performed Glasgow, 1986.
Cumha (Elegy) 1987; first performed Orkney, 1987.
An Rathad Ur (The New Road) 1989; broadcast BBC, 1989.
Seann Orain (Old Songs) 1989; first performed Ullapool, Northwestern Scotland, 1989.
Air, Strathspey and Reel 1990; first performed Glasgow, 1990.

Chamber/instrumental:

Nine Days (clarinet) 1977; first performed Aberdeen, 1977.
Paraphrases on Poems by Rilke (piano) 1978; first performed Edinburgh, 1978.
An-og Mhadainn (basset horn, piano) 1979; first performed Yorkshire, 1979. Recorded Nato 257.
String Quartet 1981; first performed Glasgow, 1981.
Landscape (guitar(s)) 1982; first performed Glasgow, 1982.
Trio (clarinet, viola, piano) 1982; first performed Wentworth Woodhouse, Yorkshire, 1982.
Sextet (clarinet, string quartet, piano) 1982; first performed Londonderry, 1982.
Fantasias (2 flutes, 2 oboes, 2 clarinets, 2 bassoons, contrabassoon, 4 horns) 1986; first performed Edinburgh, 1986.
Life Studies (clarinet, piano) 1987. Recorded nato 1180.
Sweeney Astray (2 clarinets) 1987; first performed Glasgow, 1987.
Springburn (clarinet, electronics) 1987; first performed Glasgow, 1987.
Sonata for Viola, Marimba and Claves 1988; first performed Edinburgh, 1988.
Glean Fadamach (2 clarinets, piano, percussion) 1988. Recorded Watercourse 001.
Sharakan (flute, clarinet, viola, cello, double bass, electronics) 1989; first performed Glasgow, 1989.
Hallaig (organ) 1990; first performed Dunblane, 1990.

Vocal/choral:

Three Poems from Sangschaw (soprano, 3 clarinets, piano; MacDiarmid) 1977; first performed Aberdeen, 1977.
Two Concert Arias (soprano, orchestra) 1978; broadcast BBC, 1978.
A Vision of Scotland (soprano, orchestra) 1979; first performed Hidden Valley, California, 1979.
The Heights of Maccu Piccu (soprano, flute, viola, harp, percussion) 1980; first performed Glasgow, 1980.
Sonata with Some Pine Trees (2 sopranos, ensemble) 1981; first performed Edinburgh, 1981.
Salm an Fhearainn (18 voices) 1987; first performed Glasgow, 1987.
Scenes from Old Stirling (soprano, orchestra) 1987; first performed West Germany, 1987.
An Seachnadh (16 voices) 1988; first performed Glasgow, 1988.

Three Poems of William Soutar (chorus, orchestra) 1989; first performed Kirkcaldy, 1989.
El pueblo (baritone, ensemble) 1989; first performed Glasgow, 1989.

Other:

Voyage of Discovery (opera for primary schools) 1980; first performed Glasgow, 1980.
Bagpipe Music (educational; chamber orchestra and children's ensemble(s)) 1986; first performed Edinburgh, 1986.
The Elements Danced . . . (educational; multiple string and wind ensemble) 1988; first performed Glasgow, 1988.
All Change (television music; flute, clarinet, trumpet, cello, double bass, percussion) 1989; broadcast ITV, 1989.
Uncle Fishknife Song (television music; flute, clarinet, harp, cello, double bass) 1989; broadcast ITV, 1989.

PUBLICATIONS

By Sweeney: "The Heights of Maccu Piccu", in *Stretto*, Autumn 1985; "Prague Diary", in *Stretto*, Autumn 1986.

William Sweeney comments:

I try to write the kind of music I have always liked—well-defined gestures, non-traditional tonality, metrical organization as a base for rhythmic freedom and primary tone-colours.

As well as Scottish traditional music, I listen to a wide range of ethnic music—I like its directness, earthy colours and rhythmic élan. Also important is jazz—not only for the element of improvisation, but for the brooding lyricism of, for example, Gil Evans, or the intellectual fervour of John Coltrane.

I am not interested in private, coded messages nor in obvious propaganda, but I do hope that my music can play some part on the side of common humanity against the cynics, sell-outs, exploiters, racists and other enemies of culture.

* * *

Like that of his fellow Glaswegian composer Edward McGuire, the work of William Sweeney has drawn extensively on Scottish traditional music, both for specific musical registers, as in the *Air, Strathspey and Reel* for orchestra, and as a more generalised influence, often giving shape and flow to a piece without recourse to direct quotation or writing drawn from a particular style.

Sweeney points out the range of his musical interests in his statement, and those shadings are all evident in his composition. The bold sweep of a composition like *An Rathad Ur (The New Road)*, one of the most successful of all his works, owes much to a skilful integration of the jazz based saxophonist Tommy Smith within a work which utilises the orchestral palette in a vibrant synthesis.

The echo of bagpipe music can be detected in many of Sweeney's compositions, almost irrespective of instruments. The keening wail of his clarinet (Sweeney is a highly accomplished performer on the instrument) in *Springburn*, a work for clarinet and computer-generated tape, reveals that influence as surely as those works which draw more overtly on the musical traditions of the instrument, such as the pibroch *Nine Days*, also for clarinet.

Sweeney's work for voice is in many respects an extension of that interest in traditional musical forms, beginning with the *Three Poems from Sangschaw* by the poet Hugh MacDiarmid, through to *Three Poems of William Soutar*, although it may be most evident in the large *a cappella* works *Salm an Fhearainn* and *An Seachnadh*, with their echoes of the ancient Gaelic tradition of unaccompanied singing.

The former is a splendid example of Sweeney's ability to bring together two very distinct musical strands, allowing a register derived from the cacophonous, asynchronous congregational singing of the Free Kirk (using a text composed by poet Aonghas MacNeacail, also a collaborator in *Glean Fadamach* for two clarinets, piano, percussion and voice) to clash headlong with contemporary choral music exhibiting a high degree of melodic and harmonic sophistication. The resulting mix avoids any sense of parody or pastiche in reconciling these poles.

While steeped in both the music and culture of his native Scotland, however, Sweeney is in no sense a parochial composer. His musical registers reveal a familiarity with the ebbs and flows of contemporary musical thought, and where he does draw on traditional material, it is subsumed within a distinctly non-traditional tonal and rhythmic language.

His fascination with the music, history, art and culture of South America and Africa have found vivid expression in works like *The Heights of Maccu Piccu*, *El pueblo* and *I Will Wait*, a composition inspired by South African poet Mongane Wally Serote, which fuses orchestra, jazz quartet and choir, although not as seamlessly as in the earlier *An Rathad Ur (The New Road)*.

As in much of his adaptation of Scottish modes, Sweeney attempts to capture the traditional parallel harmonies of African choirs, but without recourse to directly borrowing any African material. Ethnic music has provided a rich vein of tonal colour and unorthodox sonorities in his work, and one which he has mined with great skill and sensitivity.

—Kenny Mathieson

SWIFT, Richard (G.). American. Born in Middlepoint, Ohio, 24 September 1927. Educated at University of Chicago (under Leland Smith, Grosvenor Cooper and Leonard Meyer), 1953–6, M.A. (music); Princeton University Institute for Advanced Musical Studies, New Jersey, 1959–60. Served in United States Army, 1950–2. Married Dorothy Zackrisson, 10 February 1951; 3 sons. Teaching assistant, University of Chicago, 1954–6; professor of music since 1956, and chair department of music, 1963–71, University of California, Davis; visiting professor of music, Princeton University, 1977; University of California Faculty Research lecturer, 1982–3. Recipient: Rockefeller Foundation/Louisville Orchestra Young Composers Award, 1955; Composers' Forum Concert Award, 1961; Rockefeller Foundation Performance Award, 1968; Macdowell Foundation fellowship, 1971; Composers String Quartet Award, 1973; National Endowment for the Arts Award, 1976–7; American Institute-Academy of Arts and Letters Award, 1978. Mailing address: Department of Music, University of California, Davis, California 95616, U.S.A.

Publisher: Presser.

Symphonies/orchestral:

A Coronal 1954; first performed Louisville, Kentucky, 1956.
The Pleasures of Merely Circulating (band) 1959.
Concerto No 1 (piano, chamber orchestra) 1961; first

performed Davis, California, 1961.
Extravaganza 1962; first performed Mexico City, 1966.
Violin Concerto 1965.
Tristia 1967; first performed Oakland, California, 1968.
Symphony 1970; first performed Davis, California, 1971.
Concerto No 2 (piano, chamber orchestra) 1980.
Some Trees 1982; first performed Williamsburg, Virginia, 1983.

Chamber / instrumental:

Sonata (flute) 1951.
String Quartet No 1 1955; first performed San Francisco, 1957.
Serenade concertante (piano, wind quintet) 1956.
Nine Stravaganzas (various) 1956–78.
Sonata (clarinet) 1957; first performed Chicago, 1958.
Sonata (violin) 1957; first performed San Francisco, 1960. Recorded Orion ORS 74147.
Trio (violin, cello, piano) 1957.
String Quartet No 2 1958.
Domains II (percussion) 1963.
Domains III (ensemble) 1963.
String Quartet No 3 1964; first performed Iowa, 1964.
Summer Notes (piano) 1965; first performed Iowa, 1965. Recorded CRI 412.
Music for a While I (3 instruments) 1965.
Thrones (alto flute, double bass) 1966.
Music for a While II (3 instruments) 1969.
String Quartet No 4 1973; first performed Boston, 1974. Recorded Golden Crest NEC-115.
Music for a While III 1975.
Prime (saxophone, chamber ensemble) 1975; first performed Davis, California, 1975. Recorded Perspectives of New Music CD PNM 26.
Mein blaues Klavier (piano) 1978.
String Trio 1979–80.
String Quartet No 5 1982; first performed Berkeley, California, 1983.
Elective Affinities (cello, piano) 1983.
Domains IV (piano) 1986.
Things of August (piano) 1986; first performed Davis, California, 1987.
A Stitch in Time (guitar) 1988; first performed Tucson, Arizona, 1989.

Vocal / choral:

Eve (soprano, chamber orchestra) 1959.
Domains I (baritone, ensemble; Lowell) 1963; first performed Davis, California, 1963.
Carmina archilochi (soprano, ensemble) 1965.
Thanatopsis (mezzo-soprano, chorus, ensemble; Lucretius) 1971.
Specimen Days (soprano, orchestra; Whitman) 1976–7.
Great Praises (soprano, piano; Eberhart) 1977; first performed Davis, California, 1978. Recorded CRI 412.
The Garden (mezzo-soprano, flute, clarinet, viola; Marvell) 1984; first performed Davis, California, 1985.

Opera:

The Trial of Tender O'Shea (D. Swift) 1964; first performed San Francisco, 1964.

Other:

Large body of theatre / incidental music.

PUBLICATIONS

By Swift: "Demonstrations of J.K. Randall", in *Perspectives of New Music* 2(2), 1964; "Some Aspects of Aggregate Composition", in *Perspectives of New Music*, 1976; "1/XII/99: Tonal Relations in Schoenberg's *Verklaerte Nacht*", in *19th-Century Music*, 1977, reprinted in Garland Library of the History of Music, 1985, also in anthology of articles from *19th-Century Music*, 1990; "A Tonal Analog", in *Perspectives of New Music*, 1980–1.

On Swift: Karl Kohn, "RS: Concerto", in *Perspectives of New Music*, 1964; John Graziano, "RS: *Stravaganza VII*", in *Contemporary Music Newsletter*, 1971; John Peck, "Alkman's Guest", in *Margins*, 1975; Robert Bloch, "RS's *String Quartet IV*", in *Contemporary Music Newsletter*, 1975; Thomas Stauffer, "RS's *Summer Notes*", in *Perspectives of New Music*, 1977.

Richard Swift comments:

It is my hope that I make music that attempts to be, as Milton Babbitt has said, as much as music can be. Pitch and interval complexes are projected in the musical space by temporal, timbral and registral delineation to form clusters of memorable associations. Such contextual "tropes" and their various transformations are most easily recognized at the surface of the music, but at a deeper level they generate the global shape of each composition.

* * *

Richard Swift is an active and influential music theorist and critic as well as an accomplished composer. The insights offered by Swift about the music of other composers demonstrate his deep understanding of the compositional process. Consequently, his theoretical writings indirectly reveal aspects of his own compositional style. Swift's compositions run the gamut of genres; his compositional interests range from the operatic to the instrumental solo and everything in between. The majority of his work, however, has been written for chamber ensembles (including voice) and instrumental solos.

A continuous thread running through Swift's music is his use of twelve-tone and serial techniques. His compositional output can be characterized as an exploration into the vast resources of the twelve-tone system. He communicates his sense of adventure to the listener and performer through the many innovative aspects of his compositions, and uses serial techniques in other domains besides pitch. For this reason his serial compositions can be considered his most influential.

General aspects of Swift's compositional style include formal cohesiveness, exploration of timbre, extended harmonic content, lyrical lines and a powerful rhythmic character. Swift's earlier works, from the 1960s, contain elements of improvisation that are perhaps influenced by his association with the New Music Ensemble and by his work as a bass player in a jazz ensemble. Even in later music, where aspects of form are much more rigorous, the music maintains an air of spontaneity.

Specifically, his compositions are rigorous in form without being formulaic; form is always a consequence of the underlying pitch structures. The relationships that group pitches also form the basis of how groups of pitches form sections. Each section of a work naturally evolves from that work's unique compositional premise. For instance, two works from the 1960s, which received much attention, *Concerto* for piano and chamber orchestra and *Summer Notes* for piano, share many formal characteristics with two later works, *Prime* for saxophone and chamber ensemble and *Domains IV* for piano. Phrases, sections and movements in each of these works are clearly differentiated by means of texture, tempo, motivic and rhythmic character, figuration and intervallic content. However, the form of each work is uniquely determined not only by the articulatory devices themselves, but by the pitch structures associated with those devices. The articulatory devices thus underscore the twelve-tone and serial pitch relationships.

In the *Concerto*, the pitch material is generated by a "source set" consisting of two complementary hexachords. From the source set Swift extracts subsets that have a particular intervallic make-up. The movement from one collection of intervals to another becomes a form defining feature. The pitch material of *Summer Notes* is generated by six trichords that each contain a different pairing of intervals. The entire trichord collection contains 11 of the 12 possible intervals (the octave is the excluded interval). Sectional divisions are differentiated by the trichord that forms a section's harmonic basis. Movements are similarly differentiated, although they are dominated by pairs of trichords.

Following the lead of Milton Babbitt, Swift's later compositions use pitch arrays, matrices of rows and columns in which the rows are twelve-tone rows and the columns form aggregates (the total chromatic). *Prime*, for instance, is a one-movement work consisting of 12 sections, and each section is a pitch array. Articulatory devices emphasize the movement from one array to the next and thus underscore each array's unique harmonic configuration.

Extended timbral resources and techniques, such as the addition of bongos and maracas to a traditional orchestra in the composition *Some Trees*, and the bowings behind the bridge in the composition *Prime*, are never merely foreground sound effects, but function as integral parts of the structural whole, drawing attention to shifts in harmonic structure and sectional divisions.

Swift's music is impressive because of his attention to detail, his provocative sonic landscapes, his inventiveness, and because of his rethinking of what creates form in music. His music has and will continue to generate interest among performers, theorists and audiences.

—Ciro G. Scotto

SZOKOLAY, Sándor. Hungarian. Born in Kunágota, 30 March 1931. Educated: early musical training at Bekestarhos Music College; Budapest Academy of Music (composition under Ferenc Szabo and Ferenc Farkas), 1950–7. Teacher, Municipal Music School, 1952–5; music reader and producer, Hungarian Radio, 1955–9; teacher of composition, 1959–66, and professor of composition, since 1966, Budapest Academy of Music; musical adviser, Hungarian Television; president, Hungarian Kodály Society. Recipient: World Youth Festival prize in composition (for *Sonatina* for piano), 1955; distinction (for *Allegro de concert*), Wieniawski International Competition, Warsaw, 1956; 1st prize (for *Sonata* for solo violin), World Youth Festival, Moscow, 1057; 1st prize (for *Two Ballads*), World Youth Festival, Vienna, 1959; Erkel Prize, 1960, 1965; Kossuth Prize, 1966; Golden Star of the Best Score (for *Ballad of Horror*), 5th International Dance Festival, 1967; Merited Artist, Hungarian People's Republic, 1976; Hungarian Radio Prize for New Hungarian Music (for *Tabernakulum*), 1985; Outstanding Artist, Hungarian People's Republic, 1986; Bartók-Pásztory Award, 1987; 5 Grand Prix du Disque (for *Blood Wedding* and *Samson*). Mailing address: c/o Budapest Academy of Music, Liszt Ferenc ter 8, 1061 Budapest, Hungary.

Publishers: Editio Musica; Universal Edition.

Symphonies/orchestral:

Violin Concerto Op 13 1956–7.
Piano Concerto Op 17 1958.
Ballata sinfonica Op 29 1967–8.
Trumpet Concerto Op 32 1968.
Archaikus nyitany / Archaic Overture Op 62 1977.
Rapszodia Op 68 (chamber orchestra) 1978.
Concerto for Orchestra Op 84 1982.

Chamber/instrumental:

Gyermek-kvartett / Quartet for Children Op 5 (2 violins, cello, piano) 1954.
Sonata Op 11 (violin) 1956.
String Quartet No 1: In Memory of Zoltán Kodály Op 40 1972. Recorded SLPX 11754.
Sirato es kultikus tanc / Lament and Ritual Dance Op 42 (cimbalom, celeste, piano, percussion, harp) 1974. Recorded SLPX 11686.
Sestetto d'ottoni Op 47 (3 trumpets, 2 trombones, tuba) 1975.
Ket portre / Two Portraits Op 49 (piano) 1975.
Sonata Op 51 (flute) 1975.
Quattro lamenti Op 52 (cimbalom) 1976. Recorded SLPX 1189.
Miniature per ottoni Op 56 (brass sextet) 1976.
Improvvisazione Op 57a (harp) 1977.
Alliteraciok / Alliterations Op 61 (brass quintet) 1977.
Jatek a hangkozokkel / Playing with Intervals Op 64 (5 cimbalom duos; or piano) 1978. Recorded SLPX 12064.
Bagatellen Op 67 (harpsichord, harp; or 2 pianos) 1978.
Al fresco Op 70 (organ) 1978.
Sonata Op 66 (cello) 1979. Recorded SLPX 12139.
Archaikus szvit Op 72 (brass sextet) 1979.
Polimorfia Op 76 (violin, cello, harpsichord or piano) 1980.
Hommage à Bartók Op 81 (divertimento for brass quintet) 1981. Recorded Panton M 8011 0271.
String Quartet No 2: In Memory of Béla Bartók Op 82 1982. Recorded SLPX 12139.
Gregorian valtozatok / Gregorian Variations Op 86 (5 miniatures for brass quintet) 1983.
Harom trefas miniatur / Three Funny Miniatures Op 90 (brass quintet) 1983.
Variacio egy sirato-dallamra / Variation on a Lament Melody Op 94 (6 percussion) 1986.
Musica Transylvanica Op 104 (13 variations for organ) 1988.

Vocal/choral:

Vizimesek Op 14 (cantata for children; soprano, children's chorus, chamber orchestra; Weöres) 1957.

Ket ballada / Two Ballads Op 16 (mixed chorus, 2 pianos, percussion; Bulgarian and Bantu folk texts) 1957. Recorded LPX 1166.
Mesteremberek / Artisans (cantata for voices, orchestra) 1958.
A tuz marciusa / Fiery March Op 18 (oratorio for mixed chorus, children's chorus, soprano, alto, tenor, baritone, bass, narrator, organ, 2 pianos, orchestra; Ady) 1958–9.
Vilagok vetelkedese / Rivalry of Worlds Op 19 (cantata for soprano, alto, baritone, mixed chorus; Bartók) 1959.
Istár pokoljarasa / Isthar's Descent into Hades Op 21 (oratorio for soprano, alto, baritone, bass, mixed chorus, orchestra; Weöres) 1960–1.
Magikus dalok / Magic Songs (oratorio for soprano, chamber orchestra; Weöres) 1960.
Due motetti Op 22 (unaccompanied mixed chorus) 1962. Recorded SLPX 12113.
Neger kantata / Negro Cantata Op 24 (cantata for alto, mixed chorus, orchestra; Guillen) 1962.
Miniatur kantata, madrigal stilusban / Miniature Cantata in Madrigal Style Op 24a (mixed chorus, piano or strings) 1963.
Deploration: Concerto da requiem in memory of Francis Poulenc (mixed chorus, piano, chamber ensemble) 1964. Recorded SLPX 12442.
Revelation Op 27 (voices, organ or 6 winds; Musset) 1966. Recorded SLPX 12388.
Vitezi enek / Song of Heroes Op 33 (cantata for alto, bass, male chorus, orchestra; Balasi) 1970.
Magyar korus-szimfonia Op 34 (mixed chorus, orchestra; Ady) 1970.
Karácsonyi pasztoral / Christmas Pastoral Op 35 (cantata for mixed chorus, organ, orchestra; Bible, folk liturgy) 1970.
Apokalipsziss Op 36 (cantata after Dürer for mixed chorus, orchestra) 1971.
Pünkösdi enek / Pentecostal Song Op 38 (cantata for soprano, baritone, organ, orchestra) 1972.
Odon enek / Ancient Song Op 39 (cantata for mixed chorus, woodwind, horns, kettle-drum, harp, string orchestra; Csanadi) 1972.
Dalok imadsag helyett / Songs for Prayers Op 44 (soprano, piano; Nagy) 1974.
Hodolat Kodálynak / Homage to Kodály Op 45 (cantata for voices, orchestra; Illyes) 1975.
Ady kantata Op 46 (mixed chorus, orchestra) 1975.
Kantata a galyarabok emlekere / In Memory of the Galley Slaves Op 48 (narrator, baritone, mixed chorus, organ, orchestra; 17th-century texts) 1975.
Musica notturna Op 50 (female chorus; Babits) 1975.
Three Epigrams Op 54 (3-part male chorus or children's chorus; Pannonius) 1976.
Anakreóni dalok / Anacreontic Songs Op 55 (soprano, piano) 1976.
A minden titkok titka / The Secret of All Secrets Op 57 (soprano, flute, clarinet, harp, piano, cimbalom, violin; Ady) 1977.
A zengo csuda-erdo balladaja / The Ballad of the Miraculous Echoing Forest Op 59 (unaccompanied mixed chorus; folk texts) 1977.
Aforizmak / Aphorisms Op 60 (unaccompanied mixed chorus; Weöres) 1977.
Himnusz-toredek / Hymn Fragment Op 63 (versions for mixed chorus and for women's or children's chorus; Juhasz) 1978.
Tiz Jószef toredek / Ten Attila Joszef Fragments Op 69 (mixed chorus) 1978–9. Recorded SLPX 12388.
Joslat / Prophecy Op 70 (unaccompanied mixed chorus; Vorosmarty) 1979.
Libellus Ungaricus Op 71 (archaic cantata for soprano, alto, tenor, baritone, bass, mixed chorus, organ, orchestra; Bornemisza) 1979.
Orbis Pictus Op 73 (cantata for soprano, flute, string quartet; Weöres) 1979.
Jeremiada Op 74 (cantata for soprano, flute, harpsichord, cello; biblical 1979. Recorded SLPX 12139.
Tabernakulum Op 75 (unaccompanied mixed chorus; Pilinszky) 1980.
Confessio augustana Op 77 (cantata in 10 movements for baritone, mixed chorus, organ, orchestra; Latin texts) 1980. Recoded SLPX 12644.
Nevcsufolo-abece / Mocking Alphabet Op 78 (children's or female chorus; folk texts) 1980.
Negy archaikus enek / Four Archaic Songs Op 83 (soprano, piano; Latin texts) 1982.
Luther-Kantate Op 85 (baritone, mixed chorus, chamber orchestra, organ) 1983. Recorded SLPX 12644.
Nursery Rhymes Op 88 (unaccompanied children's or female chorus) 1983. Recorded JAMAC R 870004.
Quattro madrigali Op 89 (unaccompanied female chorus; Petrarch, Michelangelo, Leopardi, Carducci) 1983.
Missa pannonica Op 96 (6-part mass for mixed chorus) 1987. Recorded POKER K. SZ.
Jelesnapi kantalok / Holiday Chants Op 99 (unaccompanied mixed chorus; liturgical and folk texts) 1987. Recorded POKER K. SZ.
Aeternitas temporis Op 100 (cantata for soprano, string quartet; Pandula) 1988.
Ima rontas ellen / Prayer Against Evil Op 102 (versions for mixed chorus and for equal voices) 1988.
Archaikus himnusz Op 102a (unaccompanied mixed chorus; Szechenyi) 1988.
Leben—Natur—Liebe Op 103 (cantata for soprano, string orchestra; Frick) 1988.
Szabo Istvan Te Deuma Op 105 (unaccompanied mixed chorus; biblical) 1988.
Ave Maria Op 105a (3-part female chorus) 1988.

Opera:

Vernasz / Blood Wedding Op 26 (after Lorca) 1962–4. Recorded LPX 1262/3.
Hamlet Op 31 (Arany, after Shakespeare) 1965–8.
A tavaszhozo kisleany / The Spring Bearing Maiden Op 30 (fairytale opera; Balassy, after Mora) 1967.
Sámson Op 41 (Nemeth) 1971–3. Recorded SLPX 11738/9.
Csaloka Peter / Sly Peter Op 58 (radio opera; Weöres) 1978.
Ecce homo Op 92 (passion-opera after Kazantzakis) 1984. Recorded SLPX 12967/8/9.
Szavitri Op 101 (after Illes) 1987–8.

Other:

Orban es az ordog / Urban and the Devil Op 8 (ballet; Arnany) 1958.
Az iszonyat balladaja / The Ballad of Horror Op 20 (ballet) 1960.
Extazis Op 27a (ballet) 1970.
Az aldozat / The Sacrifice Op 31 (dance oratorio) 1970–1.

PUBLICATIONS

On Szokolay: I. Foldes, (interview) in *Harmincasok*, Budapest, 1969; György Kroo, *A magyar zeneszerzes harminc eve* [Thirty Years of Hungarian Music], Budapest, 1975.

* * *

Since the premiere of his sombre setting of Lorca's *Vernasz / Blood Wedding* in 1964 Sándor Szokolay has become the international representative of Hungarian opera. *Vernasz / Blood Wedding*, Szokolay's first opera, followed several large-scale oratorio-type works which formulated his dramatic outlook. He uses melismata of confined compass, straight from Hungarian speech and the embellishments of Hungarian folk music. He has always stressed the primary role of singable melody in opera, and uses only easily recognizable variants when creating larger formal units such as rondo, sonata and passacaglia. Szokolay does not work with definite leitmotifs as such, but the same themes or motifs link various characters in similar emotional states. Rather, as in his later opera *Hamlet*, he uses thematic recurrence to underline the connections between dramatic and psychological situations rather than to identify characters or to mark their entry.

Hamlet, with the unwieldy cast of 16 male and only two female soloists, signals a significant stylistic change. Serial technique is incorporated, mostly in a leitmotif sense, harmony being determined more by the intervallic content of the melody. There is less sustained melody, but leaps are wide. Szokolay uses primary triads at the outset of a new mood, then adds an accompanimental figure that eventually destroys the nature of the harmony. *Hamlet* is unified by a simple motif (a descending minor third followed by a held ascending major seventh), long pedal points (often of low clusters), accompaniment reminiscent of *Bluebeard's Castle* and lengthy orchestral interludes. The interlude leading to Hamlet's death is reminiscent of Debussy's Cello Sonata; other interludes are based on ostinatos (resulting in a Frank Martin-like style).

In the neo-Romantic *Violin Concerto*, Szokolay employs a lydian second subject which is treated to flattening the seventh and transposing whole bars a perfect fourth in order to perform unexpected cadences. After this tonally inflected virtuosic opening, and an octatonic Adagio (a rolling 6/8 with a raucous central outburst), the third movement is generated from one-bar ideas, with rhythms changing at the bar-line. The one-movement *String Quartet No 1: In Memory of Zoltán Kodály* is a set of textural variants which frequently suggests a single line with sets of canons in varying numbers of voices and dynamics, countered by some less polyphonic passages which act as coalescing agents (at the opening, at cadences etc.).

Szokolay had already used Bantu poems and pseudo-African drumming, before composing *Neger kantata / Negro Cantata*, which sets a ballad-form translation full of popular symbolism and rhythmic tension. While "African" ideas come from the poly-ostinatos of the percussion parts, much stylized Hungarian choral writing typical of Bartók's *Cantata profana* is also present. Effects such as vocal acciaccaturas taken over by the accompaniment, unison chorus, and accompanying rhythmic ostinatos built from a single bar are featured. Frequently a melodramatic syncopation of repeated descending semitones depicting moaning is predominant. In the slow third movement, an alto solo is given neo-baroque ornamentation against a naive vibraphone tune and a simplistic piano part. Lengthy vocalizations of anguish are all taken by the chorus in octaves during a lengthy build-up crescendo.

The opera *Sámson* is more concerned with the rebirth from defeat, and the significance of Samson's revenge, than with the loss of his strength. Musically, Szokolay does not exploit the dramatic situation; apart from the choral tableaux, he builds the dramatic and musical material upon dialogue. Both the central characters and specific situations are indicated by what he calls "visiting card themes", used in the opposite manner from the recurrence technique of his earlier operas. The whole dramatic course of the opera is built on these short normally sung themes while the dominant feature of the opera is the use of fragments of dodecaphonic music.

—Malcolm J. Hill

SZYMANSKI, Pawel. Polish. Born in Warsaw, 28 March, 1954. Educated at F. Chopin Academy of Music, Warsaw (composition under Wlodimierz Kotonski), M.A., 1978; Ferienkurse für Neue Musik, Darmstadt, 1978, 1980, 1982; further study under Tadeusz Baird, Warsaw; further composition study under Roman Haubenstock-Ramati, Vienna, 1984–5. Married Anna Jordan in 1975. Freelance composer; DAAD artist in residence, Berlin, 1987–8. Recipient: 1st prize (for *Gloria*), Young Polish Composers Competition, 1979; prize (for *Lux Aeterna*) in composers' competition for sacred music, Stuttgart Internationale Bachakademie, 1985; award from Deutscher Akademischer Austauschdienst, Berliner Kunstlerprogramm, 1987–8; prize, Benjamin Britten Composers' Competition, Aldeburgh, Suffolk, 1988. Mailing address: Sluzby Polsce 3 m57, 02 784 Warsaw, Poland.

Publishers: Chester Music, London; PWM, Cracow; Authors Agency, Warsaw; Moeck, Celle.

Symphonies / orchestral:

K. 1972; first performed Warsaw, 1973.
Partita I 1976.
Partita II 1977–8; first performed Opole, 1978.
Partita III (harpsichord, orchestra) 1985–6; first performed Warsaw, 1986. Recorded Polskie Nagrania SX 2466.
Partita IV 1986; first performed Belfast, 1987.
Through the Looking Glass I (chamber orchestra) 1987.
A Study of Shade 1989; first performed Aldeburgh, Suffolk, 1989.
Quasi una sinfonietta (chamber orchestra) 1990; first performed London, 1990.
Sixty Odd Pages (chamber orchestra) 1991; first performed Warsaw, September 1991.

Chamber / instrumental:

Suite (flute, piano, 2 violins, viola, cello) 1969; first performed Warsaw, 1970.
Epitaph (2 pianos) 1974; first performed Warsaw, 1974.
Limericks (violin, harpsichord) 1975; first performed Warsaw, 1976.
String Quartet 1975; first performed Warsaw, 1975.
Intermezzo (chamber ensemble) 1977; first performed Warsaw, 1977.
Ten Pieces (string trio) 1979; first performed Baranow, 1980.
Limericks (flute, violin, cello) 1979; first performed Darmstadt, 1980.
Sonata (9/27 violins, 1/3 double basses, 2 percussionists) 1982; first performed Warsaw, 1982. Recorded Polskie Nagrania SX 2176.
Two Pieces (string quartet) 1982; first performed Zakopane, 1989.
Appendix (small flute, instruments) 1983; first performed Warsaw, 1984. Recorded Polskie Nagrania SX 2409.

Two Illusory Constructions (clarinet, cello, piano) 1984; first performed Lerchenberg, Denmark, 1984.
Trope (piano) 1986; first performed Lerchenberg, Denmark, 1990.
Two Studies (piano) 1986; first performed Warsaw, 1990.
A Kaleidoscope for MCE (cello) 1989; first performed Wroclaw, 1989.

Vocal/choral:

Kyrie (boys' choir, orchestra) 1977; first performed Warsaw, 1978.
Gloria (women's choir, instrumental ensemble) 1979; first performed Warsaw, 1979. Recorded Polskie Nagrania SX 1845.
Four Liturgical Pieces (soprano, instrumental ensemble) 1980–1; first performed Poznan, 1986.
Villanelle (alto, tenor, 2 violas, harpsichord) 1981; first performed Luslawice, 1983.
Lux aeterna (voices, instruments) 1984; first performed Warsaw, 1985. Recorded Polskie Nagrania SX 2430.

Other:

La Folia (tape) 1979.
. . . *Under the Plane Tree* (tape) 1979.
Crux fidelis (sound background for "The Sign of the Cross in Art", Church of Divine Mercy, Warsaw) 1983.
Through the Looking Glass II (tape) 1988.

PUBLICATIONS

On Szymanski: Andrzej Chlopecki, "In Search of Lost Order", in *Polish Music*, 3–4, 1984; "Unravelling a Puzzle", (interview) in *Polish Music*, 1–2, 1987.

* * *

If there is no generally accepted definition of the phenomenon—or group of phenomena—known as "post-modernism", it is clear that Pawel Szymanski shares at least some of its informing characteristics: a rejection of historicism, a concern with process, an almost ideological suspicion of ideology, fragmentation, a deceptive use of polystylistic quotation, and an enormous variation in tone. His music is in a very particular sense "through the looking glass" (a title he has used for two pieces), deeply concerned with dualities.

Partita II for orchestra marks his full maturity as a composer. Like many of his pieces, it deploys devices from Baroque music such as canon and contrapuntal variation, but in such a way as to suggest that musical history and tradition are not a continuous flow, but an interference pattern. Szymanski omits notes, shifts chords laterally, breaks up rhythmic patterns without apparent rationale, but retains a clear sense of logic and structure, almost like a dim memory of some prior audition of the piece. The violence that is one of the less understood aspects of the Baroque (but brilliantly theorised by no less than André Malraux) is evident too in *Partita III* which features a prominent solo part for amplified harpsichord. Again, the piece creates very specific disjunctions and alienations, constantly referring back to a "shadow score" or to implicit pre-compositional perceptions and assumptions.

Through the looking glass, reality acquires a dream-like specificity. Most of Szymanski's scores are, on the surface, remarkably "simple". The 1982 pieces for string quartet rather resemble Cage's first experiments in the medium, and the sense they give of a very ancient music played (somewhat imperfectly) from memory, with the transitions improvised in a makeshift contemporary idiom. Szymanski's logic, though, is watertight, and irruptions of older styles are absorbed into his structures without irony (such as we might find in Alfred Schnittke's magpie pieces) and without strain. The later chamber piece *Appendix* develops the collage method almost as far as Szymanski has so far been able to take it. The solo piccolo moves in a landscape from which all pastoral associations have been stripped; it is a mechanized world, constantly receiving signals from the past and from outlying areas of its own idiom; as such, it represents an appendix or footnote to a whole tradition, deconstructing it mercilessly.

Szymanski's use of texts is similarly dissective. Liturgical texts are broken down into "meaningless" phonemes and eidetic fragments which nevertheless retain, as in the *Kyrie* and the magnificent *Lux aeterna* (by no means the only echo of György Ligeti in his output), some memory of their original sense and context. Since these associations are even stronger than more purely musical ones, Szymanski's freedom of movement is greatly enhanced, not always to complete advantage. *Lux aeterna* is a triumph of exact control over the violently centripetal and even fissile material, which is broken down into the smallest quantifiable constituents. In a non-vocal work like *Partita IV* the performance is required to be more explicit and locates a fully formed—and very beautiful—canonic theme in the midst of a harsh, brass-laden score that is much more obviously self-referential than the vocal piece.

Still under 40, Szymanski is one of the most significant younger composers working in Europe. His music is both demanding and disturbingly beautiful. Unlike the "paper music" of the Darmstadt School, on whom he firmly but respectfully turned his back in the early 1980s, it never fails to register awareness of the listeners' presence. It may be a clinching proof of a post-modernist sensibility that it insists on the listener's presence, not just in the concert hall, but in the processes and interstices of the piece itself.

—Gena Renk

T

TAKEMITSU, Toru. Japanese. Born in Tokyo, 8 October 1930. Educated at Keika High School, graduated 1948; studied composition (under Yasuji Kiyose); self-taught. Organised Jitsuken Kohbo (Experimental Workshop), 1951; composer in residence, Canberra Festival, 1968; designer of "Space Theatre", musical director, Expo '70, 1970; main composer (with Stravinsky, Stockhausen and Jean-Claude Eloy) at SMIP (International Contemporary Music Week), Paris, 1971; organizer and artistic director, annual "Music Today" festival, Tokyo, since 1973; visiting professor, Yale University, New Haven, Connecticut, 1975; guest composer, "Meet the Modern" series, Brooklyn Philharmonic Orchestra, New York, 1975; Japanese delegate, International Friendship of the People's Republic of China, 1976; jury member, Concours de Flûte, 6th Rencontres Internationales d'Art Contemporain, La Rochelle, and of International Competition for Excellence in the Performance of American Music, Washington, D.C., 1978; aristic director, Festival d'Automne, Paris, 1978; jury member, Canadian Broadcasting Commission National Competition for Young Composers, Vancouver Music Festival, 1980; regent lecturer, University of California, San Diego, 1981; composer in residence, California Art Festival, 1981; guest lecturer, Yale University, Harvard University, Cambridge, Massachusetts, and Boston University, 1983; composer in residence, Colorado Music Festival, 1983; and Aldeburgh Festival, Suffolk, 1984; featured composer, Tanglewood Festival of Contemporary Music, Massachusetts, 1986; supervisor, annual Suntory International Program for Music Composition, Tokyo, 1986; jury member, International Society of Contemporary Music, Hong Kong, 1987. "Takemitsu Festival", Tokyo, 1974; "The Music of Toru Takemitsu", Buffalo, New York, 1977. Recipient: first prize (for *Le Son calligraphie I*), Competition for Contemporary Music Composition, 1958; Prix Italia (for *Kuroi kaiga / Tableau noir*), 1958; Incentive Prize, Japan (for *Solitude sonore*), 1958; German Ambassador's Prize, Tokyo (for *Requiem for Strings*), 1960, (for *Ring*) 1961; 5th prize, International Rostrum of Composers, UNESCO (for *Coral Island*), 1963; Prize for Top Excellence, International Rostrum of Composers (for "Textures", *Arc-Part II*), 1965; Prize of the Music Critics in the West Coast, San Francisco (for *Dorian Horizon*), 1967; Otaka Prize, Japan (for *Quatrain*), 1976; prize of the Japan Art Academy, 1980; Otaka Prize (for *Far Calls, Coming, Far!*), 1981; 11th Mobil Music Prize, 1981; honorary member, American Academy and Institute of Arts and Letters, 1984; Asahi Prize, 1985; membre de l'Ordre des Arts et des Lettres, France, 1985; honorary member, Académie des Beaux Arts, France, 1986; Los Angeles Film Critics Award (for *Ran*), 1987. Mailing address: c/o Schott Japan Co Ltd, no 301, 3-4-3 Iibidashi, Chiyoda-ku, Tokyo 102, Japan.

Publishers: Schott; Editions Salabert; Universal Edition; Zen-On, Japan.

Symphonies / orchestral:

Requiem for Strings 1957; first performed Tokyo, June 1957. Recorded Victor KVX 5513; Philips 6527002; RCA SB6814; King SKF 3004.

Solitude sonore 1958.

Scene (cello, string orchestra) 1959; first performed Tokyo, December 1959.

Music of Trees 1961. Recorded Columbia OW7837; Victor JVCD 1009.

Arc—Part I (piano, orchestra) 1963–6, revised 1976; first performed Tokyo, May 1966; revised version first performed New York City, January 1977. Recorded Victor VX69; Victor VDC 5507; Philips 6527002; Varese 81060.

Arc—Part II (piano, orchestra) 1964–6, revised 1976; first performed Tokyo, July 1966; revised version first performed New York City, January 1977. Recorded Victor VDC 5507; Philips 6527002; Varese 81060.

Dorian Horizon (17 strings) 1966; first performed San Francisco, February 1967. Recorded CBS 58DC282-3; Columbia MS7281; Victor KVX 5513.

Green 1967; first performed Tokyo, 3 November 1967. Recorded RVC RX2355; RCA SB6814.

Asterism (piano, orchestra) 1967. Recorded RVC RX2355.

November Steps (biwa, shakuhachi, orchestra) 1967; first performed New York City, 9 November 1967. Recorded RVC SX2015; King GT9330; Philips 32CD3109; CBS 50AC1994.

Eucalypts (flute, oboe, harp, string orchestra) 1970; first performed Tokyo, November 1970. Recorded Polydor MG2411; Deutsche Grammophon 2530407.

Gemeaux (oboe, trombone, 2 orchestras) 1971–86; first performed Tokyo, October 1986.

Winter 1971; first performed Paris, October 1971. Recorded Victor SJX 9567; Victor VDC 1071.

Cassiopeia (percussion solo, orchestra) 1971; first performed Chicago, July 1971. Recorded Toshiba EAC 70205; EMI AA8872.

Autumn (biwa, shakuhachi, orchestra) 1973; first performed Tokyo, September 1973. Recorded (excerpt only) Polydor MG 1056.

Gitimalya (marimba, orchestra) 1974; first performed Rotterdam, November 1975. Recorded Victor VDC 1071.

Quatrain (clarinet, violin, cello, piano, orchestra) 1975; first performed Tokyo, September 1975. Recorded Polydor MG1272; Deutsche Grammophon 2531210.

Marginalia 1976; first performed Tokyo, October 1976. Recorded Victor VDC 1071.

A Flock Descends into the Pentagonal Garden 1977; first performed San Francisco, November 1977. Recorded Polydor MG1272; Deutsche Grammophon 2531210; CBS 58DC282-3.

Far Calls, Coming, Far! (violin, orchestra) 1980; first performed Tokyo, May 1980.

Dreamtime 1981; first performed Sapporo, June 1982. Recorded CBS 58DC282-3.

A Way a Lone II (string orchestra) 1981; first performed Sapporo, June 1982. Recorded RVC RCL 8342.

Toward the Sea II (alto flute, harp, string orchestra) 1981; first performed Sapporo, June 1982. Recorded RVC RCL 8342; Bridge BDG 2004.

Star-Isle 1982; first performed Tokyo, October 1982. Recorded Deutsche Grammophon F33G20015.

Rain Coming (chamber orchestra) 1982; first performed

London, October 1982.

To the Edge of Dream (guitar, orchestra) 1983; first performed Liège, March 1983.

Orion and Pleiades (cello, orchestra) 1984; first performed Paris, May 1984. Recorded CBS 58DC282-3.

Vers, l'arc en ciel, Palma (guitar, oboe d'amore, orchestra) 1984; first performed Birmingham, October 1984.

Riverrun (piano, orchestra) 1984; first performed Los Angeles, January 1985.

Dream/Window 1985; first performed Kyoto, September 1985.

I Hear the Water Dreaming (flute, orchestra) 1987; first performed Indianapolis, April 1987.

Nostalgia: In Memory of Andrei Tarkovskij (violin, string orchestra) 1987; first performed Edinburgh, August 1987.

Twill by Twilight; In Memory of Morton Feldman 1988; first performed Tokyo, March 1988.

Tree Line (chamber orchestra) 1988; first performed London, May 1988.

A String Around Autumn (viola, orchestra) 1989; first performed Paris, 29 and 30 November 1989.

Visions 1990; first performed Chicago, 8, 9, 10 and 13 March, 1990.

Chamber/instrumental:

Lento in due movementi (piano) 1950; first performed Tokyo, December 1950. Recorded Fontec FOCD 3202.

Distance de fée (violin, piano) 1951; first performed Tokyo, November 1951.

Uninterruped Rest (Pause interrompue) (piano) 1952–9; 1st movement first performed Tokyo, August 1952; first complete performance Tokyo, December 1959. Recorded Toshiba EAC 60153; Decca Head 4; Polydor MG2408.

Le Son calligraphie I and III (4 violins, 2 violas, 2 cellos) 1958–60; I first performed Karuisawa, August 1958; III first performed Tokyo, April 1960. Recorded Victor JVCD 1008; Philips 6527003; complete version I, II, III, Polydor MG1047.

Mask (2 flutes) 1959–60; 1st and 3rd movements first performed Karuisawa, August 1959; first complete performance Tokyo, April 1960. Recorded Trio RSA 1011; Victor JVCD 1008; CBS SONC 16019.

Landscape (string quartet) 1960; first performed Tokyo, April 1960.

Ring (flute, terz guitar, lute) 1961; first performed Osaka, August 1961. Recorded MG2139.

Piano Distance (piano) 1961; first performed Tokyo, October 1961. Recorded Toshiba EAC 60153; Victor JVCD 1008; Decca Head 4; Fontec FONC 5043.

Corona for Pianist(s) (graphic work) 1962; first performed Tokyo, February 1962. Recorded MG2408; Decca Head 4; Victor JVCD 1008.

Sacrifice (alto flute, lute, vibraphone) 1962. Recorded Polydor MG2139.

Crossing (graphic work for piano(s)) 1962; first performed Tokyo, March 1962. Recorded RVC 2325.

Corona II (graphic work for string(s)) 1962; first performed Honolulu, Hawaii, April 1964.

Arc for Strings (graphic work; flexible instrumentation) 1963; first performed Honolulu, Hawaii, 1964.

Valeria (violin, cello, guitar, electric organ, 2 piccolos obligato) 1965; first performed Tokyo, November 1965. Recorded Polydor MG2139.

Eclipse (biwa, shakuhachi) 1966; first performed Tokyo, May 1966. Recorded Polydor MG1056; Victor JVCD 1008; Philips 6527003.

Hika (violin, piano) 1966; first performed Osaka, November 1966. Recorded Polydor MG1047; Victor JVCD 1008; Trio PA1156–7.

Munari by Munari (percussion solo) 1967; first performed Paris, October 1971. Recorded Polydor MG2476; RVC RDC9; Victor JVCD 1008.

Cross Talk (2 bandoneons, tape) 1968; first performed Tokyo, June 1968. Recorded Philips 6527003.

Seasons (graphic work for 4 percussionists or percussionist and tape) 1968; first performed Osaka, August 1970. Recorded Polydor MG2476; L'Oiseau-Lyre DSL01; King SLA 1032.

Stanza I (guitar, piano/celeste, harp, vibraphone, female voice) 1969; first performed Tokyo, February 1969. Recorded Polydor MG2139.

Voice (flute) 1971; first performed Tokyo, June 1971. Recorded Polydor MG2411; Fontec FONC 5042.

Stanza II (harp, tape) 1971; first performed Paris, October 1971. Recorded Polydor MG2411; Deutsche Grammophon 2530407; Columbia OW7845.

Eucalypts II (flute, oboe, harp) 1971; first performed Paris, October 1971. Recorded Polydor MG2411; Deutsche Grammophon 2530407.

Distance (oboe with/without shō) 1972; first performed London, May 1973. Recorded Polydor MG2411.

For Away (piano) 1973; first performed London, May 1973. Recorded Toshiba EW-CC33-332; Decca Head 4; Fontec FOCD 3202.

Voyage (3 biwas) 1973; first performed Tokyo, September 1973. Recorded Polydor MG2457.

In an Autumn Garden (gagaku ensemble) 1973; first performed Tokyo, October 1973. Recorded MG2457.

Folios (guitar) 1974; first performed Tokyo, July 1974. Recorded Polydor MG1047; Alfa ALR 28038.

Garden Rain (divided brass ensemble: I—horn, 2 trumpets, trombone, tuba; II—2 trumpets, 2 trombones, bass trombone) 1974; first performed Tokyo, November 1974. Recorded Polydor MG1047; Decca Head 14.

Bryce (flute, 2 harps, 2 percussion) 1976; first performed Toronto, March 1976. Recorded RVC RCL 8342.

Waves (clarinet solo, with horn, 2 trombones, bass drum) 1976; first performed Tokyo, June 1976. Recorded RVC 2290.

Quatrain II (clarinet, violin, cello, piano) 1977; first performed Boston, March 1977. Recorded RVC 2290.

Twelve Songs for Guitar (transcriptions of Irish traditional, Arlen, Gershwin, Nakada, Cosma, Converse, Fain, Lennon/McCartney, Degeyter) 1977. Recorded Toshiba TA72039; Pavane ADW 7037.

Waterways (clarinet, violin, cello, piano, 2 harps, 2 vibraphones) 1978; first performed Tokyo, June 1978. Recorded RVC 2290.

In an Autumn Garden (complete version) (gagaku orchestra) 1979; first performed Tokyo, September 1979. Recorded Victor VDC 506.

Les Yeux clos (piano) 1979; first performed Tokyo, September 1979. Recorded Fontec FOCD 3202; RVC RCL 8377.

A Way a Lone (string quartet) 1981; first performed New York, February 1981. Recorded RVC RCL 8342.

Toward the Sea (alto flute, guitar) 1981; 1st part first performed Toronto, February 1981; first complete performance Tokyo, May 1981. Recorded RVC RCL 8342; Bridge BDG 2004.

Rain Tree (2 marimbas, vibraphone, or 3 keyboard players) 1981; first performed Tokyo, May 1981. Recorded RVC RCL 8342; CBS 32DC673.

Rain Tree Sketch (piano) 1982; first performed Tokyo, January 1983. Recorded Fontec FOCD 3202.

Rain Spell (flute, clarinet, harp, piano, vibraphone) 1982; first performed Yokohama, January 1983.
Rocking Mirror Daybreak (2 violins) 1983; first performed New York, November 1983.
From Far Beyond Chrysanthemums and November Fog (violin, piano) 1983; first performed Tokyo, December 1983. Recorded Fontec FONC 5070.
Orion (cello, piano) 1984; first performed Vienna, March 1984. Recorded CBS 32DC570.
Entre-temps (oboe, string quartet) 1986; first performed Tokyo, May 1986.
Rain Dreaming (harpsichord) 1986; first performed Washington, D.C., June 1986.
Day Signal; Signals from Heaven I (2 brass groups: I—3 trumpets in C, 3 trombones; II—piccolo trumpet, trumpet, 2 horns in F, trombone, tuba) 1987; first performed Tokyo, July 1987.
All in Twilight (guitar) 1987.
Night Signal: Signals from Heaven II (2 brass groups: I—B♭ cornet, trumpet in C, 2 horns in F, trombone, tuba; II—trumpet in C, 2 horns in F, 2 trombones) 1987; first performed Glasgow, September 1987.
Itinerant: In Memory of Isamu Noguchi (flute) 1989; first performed New York, 7 February 1989.
Les Yeux clos II (piano) 1989; first performed New York, 11 November 1989.
Litany: In Memory of Michael Vyner (piano) 1990; first performed London, 6 May 1990.

Vocal/choral:

Kuroi kaiga/Tableau noir (narrator, orchestra) 1958.
Kaze no Uma (Wind Horse) (SATB chorus; Akiyama) 1961–6; 1st 2 pieces first performed Tokyo, November 1962; first complete performance Tokyo, October 1966. Recorded Victor SJX 1069.
Coral Island (soprano, orchestra) 1962. Recorded Victor JVCD 1009; RCA VCCS 1334.
Grass (male chorus; Tanikawa/Merwin) 1982; first performed Tokyo, December 1982.
Uta (mixed chorus: traditional, Tanikawa, Takemitsu, Kawaji, Izawa, Akiyama) 1983; first performed Tokyo, October 1983. Recorded Victor VDC 1074.
Handmade Proverbs—Four Pop Songs (6 male voices: Takiguchi/Kennith Lyons) 1987; first performed Tokyo, January 1987.
My Way of Life: in memory of Michael Vyner (baritone, mixed chorus, orchestra) 1990; first performed Leeds, Yorkshire, 30 June 1990.

Other:

Static Relief (magnetic tape) 1955; first performed Tokyo, February 1956. Recorded Universal PBU1.
Vocalism AI (magnetic tape) 1956; broadcast Shin-Nippon Hoso, May 1956. Recorded Universal PBU1; Victor JVCD 1009; RCA VCCS 1334.
Sky, Horse and Death (magnetic tape) 1958; first performed San Francisco, January 1960. Recorded Victor SJV 1515; Philips 6527003.
Water Music (magnetic tape) 1960; first performed Tokyo, April 1960. Recorded Victor JVCD 1009; RCA VCCS 1334.
Blue Aurora for Toshi Ichiyanagi (musical event) 1964; first performed Tokyo, April 1964.
Kwaidan (magnetic tape, from the sountrack) 1964; first performed Tokyo, 1964. Recorded Victor JVCD 1009.
Toward (magnetic tape) 1970; first performed Paris, October 1971. Recorded Polydor MG2331.
Wavelength (2 percussion, 2 dancers, installation) 1984, in progress; first performed Tokyo, June 1984.
A Minneapolis Garden (environmental music for tape) 1986; first performed Minneapolis, Minnesota, March 1986.
The Sea Is Still (environmental music for tape) 1986; first performed San Diego, California, April 1986.

Film scores: *Kurutta Kajitsu/Crazed Fruit*, 1956; *Shu to Midori/Red and Green*, 1956; *Tsuyu no Atosaki/The Rainy Season*, 1956; *Doshaburi/Cloudburst*, 1957; *Kaoyaku/The Country Boss*, 1958; *Haru o Matsu Hitobito/Waiting for Spring*, 1959; *Kiken Ryoko/Dangerous Trips*, 1959; *Itazura/Joking*, 1959; *Jose Torres*, 1959; *Kawaita Mizuumi/Dry Lake*, 1960; *Mozu/The Shikes*, 1961; *Furyo Shonen/Bad Boys*, 1961; *Hannyo/Woman of Tokyo*, 1961; *Ningen Dobutsuen*, 1961; *Mitsareta Seikatsu/A Full Life*, 1962; *Karami-Ai/The Inheritance*, 1962; *Otoshiana/The Pitfall*, 1962; *Namida o Shishi no Tategami ni/Tears in the Lion's Mane*, 1962; *Seppuku/Harakiri*, 1962; *Koto/Two Sisters of Kyoto*, 1963; *Kanojo to Kare/She and He*, 1963; *Taiheiyo Hitoribocchi/Alone on the Pacific*, 1963; *Subarashii Akujo/A Marvellous Kid*, 1963; *Shiro to Kuro/White and Black*, 1963; *Love*, 1963; *Kawaita Hana/Pale Flower*, 1964; *Suna no Onna/Woman of the Dunes*, 1964; *Ni ju-issai no Chichi/Our Happiness Alone*, 1964; *Shiro Asa/The White Dawn*, 1964; *Ansatsu/The Assassin*, 1964; *Nihon Dasshutsu/Nippon Escape*, 1964; *Kwaidan*, 1964; *Te o Tsunagu Kora/Children Hand in Hand*, 1964; *Nyotai/The Female Body*, 1964; *Jidosha Dorobo/The Car Thief*, 1964; *Utsukushisa to Kanamishimi to/With Beauty and Sorrow*, 1965; *Bwana Toshi no Uta*, 1965; *Saigo no Shinpan/Last Judgement*, 1965; *Ibun Sarutobi Sasuke/Samurai Spy*, 1965; *Kemono Michi/Beast Alley*, 1965; *Yotsuya Kaidan/Illusion Island*, 1965; *Sahjokei no Shima/Punishment Island*, 1966; *Ki no Kawa/The Kii River*, 1966; *Tanin no Kao/The Face of Another*, 1966; *Akogare/Once a Rainy Day*, 1966; *Akanegumo/Clouds at Sunset*, 1967; *Joi-uchi/Rebellion*, 1967; *Izu no Odoriko/Izu Dancer*, 1967; *Midaregumo/Bellowing Clouds*, 1967; *Meguriai/The Encounter*, 1968; *Moetsukita Chizu/The Ruined Map*, 1968; *Nihori no Seishun/Hymn to a Tired Man*, 1968; *Kyo*, 1968; *Shinju Ten no Amishima/Double Suicide*, 1969; *Dankon/The Bullet Wounded*, 1969; *Taiyo no Karyudo/The Sun's Hunter*, 1970; *Tokyo Sesnso Sengo Hiwa/The Man Who Left His Will on Film*, 1970; *Dodes'ka-Den*, 1970; *Yomigaeru Daichi/The Earth Is Born Again*, 1971; *Gishiki/The Ceremony*, 1971; *Inochi Bo ni Furo/Inn of Evil*, 1971; *Chinmoku/Silence*, 1971; *Summer Soldiers*, 1972; *Natsu no Mori/Dear Summer Sister*, 1972; *Kaseki no Mori/The Forest of Fossils*, 1973; *Seigen-ki/Time Within Memory*, 1973; *Himiko*, 1974; *Shiawase/Happiness*, 1974; *Sakura no Mori no Mankai no Shita/Under the Blossoming Cherry Tree*, 1975; *Kaseki/The Fossil*, 1975; *Sabita Honoo/Incandescent Flame*, 1977; *Hanare Goze Orin/Banished*, 1977; *Ai no Borei/Empire of Passion*, 1978; *Moeru Aki/Burning Autumn*, 1978; *Kataku/House of Blaze*, 1979; *Tenpyo no Iraka*, 1979; *Minimata no Zu*, 1981; *Renyo to sono Haha/Renyo the Priest and His Mother*, 1981; *Tokyo Saiban/Tokyo Trial*, 1982; *Yogen/Prophecy*, 1982; *Antonio Gaudi*, 1984; *Hi-Matsuri/Fire Festival*, 1984; *Ran*, 1985; *Shokutaku no Nai le/The Empty House*, 1985; *Yari no Gonza/Gonza, a Spear Man*, 1985; *Hiroshima to iu Na no Shonen*, 1987; *Arashi-ga-Oka/Onimaru*, 1988; *Kuroi Ame*, 1989; *Rikyu*, 1989.

* * *

Largely self-taught, Toru Takemitsu absorbed numerous influences from contemporary Western music during his formative years. His lack of formal training, together with an enthusiasm for traditional Japanese and other Asian musics, have contributed significantly to the development of one of the most unusual voices in contemporary music.

Takemitsu has observed that he came to recognise his own Japanese cultural inheritance first through his study of modern Western music. Having recognised his indigenous tradition, Takemitsu's attention was drawn to other Far Eastern musical cultures—Chinese, Korean, Indian and Indonesian—which have their own individualities, despite having undergone various cross-fertilisations.

During his association with the Shin Sakkyokuha Kyōkai Group in the early 1950s, Takemitsu's first compositions were premiered; they display an already sophisticated approach to rhythm (especially in the highly irregular *Uninterrupted Rest* which dispenses with bar-lines) and some extremely dissonant, yet sensitively calculated, harmony. Whereas the first generation of Japanese composers to espouse Western idioms (a group which attained prominence in the post-World War I period and whose prime representative was Kôsçak Yamada) had been most influenced by German late Romanticism, Takemitsu and his contemporaries were more directly affected by an intermediary group—of whom Michio Miyagi was typical—which had been inspired by the French Impressionists. Among Takemitsu's more contemporary influences during this phase, Webern and Stravinsky are perhaps most significant; the period culminated in a Chamber Concerto for 13 instruments (*Shitsunai kyōsō-kyoku*), after which Takemitsu turned briefly to electronic music.

His most accomplished and interesting electronic piece is *Vocalism A–I* (the letters make up the word "Ai", or "love" in Japanese), in which the two speech-sounds of the title are pronounced in various ways by two actors as part of the structural process. The result, in parts, resembles certain effects from Stockhausen's *Stimmung*, a considerably later piece but one in which a mystical evocation of the Far East is attempted with the aid of an almost equally restricted range of pitches.

International recognition came swiftly for Takemitsu in the late 1950s, first with Stravinsky's fulsome praise for his first extended composition, the *Requiem for Strings*, and then with the prizes awarded to three works: the miniscule *Le Son calligraphie I*, *Kuroi kaiga / Tableau noir* and *Solitude sonore*. At about this time, the Eastern influences which had long been apparent in Messiaen's work, and especially in the music and philosophies of John Cage, began to be widely appreciated and adopted by the Western avant-garde and Takemitsu found himself increasingly regarded as a seminal figure; his compositions were lauded and his lecture series with Cage in 1964 assisted in the creation of a popular perception of Takemitsu as an ambassador between musical cultures.

At about the same time, Takemitsu developed an interest in traditional Japanese instruments (he had used them first in 1962, for the film score *Seppuku*) which was to prove invaluable for his nascent career as a composer of film and incidental music. Two of his most accomplished and successful concert works, *Eclipse* and *November Steps*, feature traditional Japanese instruments, the biwa (a kind of lute) and shakuhachi (a form of bamboo flute, developed in the 17th century). Despite the sometimes apparently unstructured nature of its harmonies and instrumentation, the orchestral writing of *November Steps* (which is now one of Takemitsu's best-known works) owes as much to Western models like Debussy and Boulez—albeit that they fed to some extent upon Oriental sources—as to any Japanese forebear. In this, Takemitsu resembles some other Far Eastern musicians who have found favour in the West, notably the Korean, Isang Yun. Indeed, Takemitsu has deliberately set out to write European-style music for Japanese instruments, despite the clear links between some of his formal and rhythmic practices and the Japanese musical tradition, which have helped him to fuse elements from both cultures into an individual approach. However, the non-diatonic effects typical of shakuhachi repertoire from the Edo period (i.e., of works written before about 1850) and achieved through assorted half-holing techniques and variations of embouchure, are used to great effect by Takemitsu in *November Steps* and are partly responsible for the work's exotic façade and enduring popularity.

Takemitsu has become one of the most popular of contemporary composers with international commissioning bodies; they are unable to resist his appeal as a figure able to transcend disparate cultures. The composer himself is intensely aware of the dramatic effect which the sudden infusion of Western culture had upon Japanese art about a century ago, but confesses to personal doubts as to how to interpret this collision through music. In 1984, he said that he was interested neither in adopting traditional Japanese music into the Western art, nor in a blending of the two forms, but would prefer to concentrate upon creating an individualist art capable of illuminating the human condition. Takemitsu feels both excited and disorientated by the shattering of the pre-eminence of the European musical tradition: excited because it is now possible to treat this tradition as part of a number of sources capable of partaking in the continuous renewal necessary for artistic progress, but disorientated by his belief that if the old mainstream cannot participate as well in this renewal, it will stagnate and, ultimately, ossify.

—Paul Horner

TANAKA, Karen. Japanese. Born in Tokyo, 7 April, 1961. Educated: music lessons from age 4; composition lessons from age 10; Toho Gakuen School of Music (under Akira Miyoshi) 1982–6, B.A.; further study (under Tristan Murail), IRCAM, Paris, since 1986; Advanced Music Studies, Banff Centre, Alberta, Canada, 1989. *Stagiaire*, IRCAM, Paris, since 1986; freelance composer. Recipient: prizes at Viotti and Trieste competitions; Japan Symphony Foundation Award, 1986; International Gaudeamus Prize, Amsterdam (for *Anamorphose*), 1987; Nadia and Lili Boulanger Foundation scholarship, 1990–1. Mailing address: 7 Cité du Cardinal Lemoine, 75005 Paris, France.

Publisher: Chester.

Symphonies/orchestral:

Prismes 1984; first performed Tokyo, 1984. Recorded BIS CD, June 1990.

Anamorphose (piano, orchestra) 1987; first performed Amsterdam, 1987.

Chamber/instrumental:

Tristesse (flute, violin, piano) 1982; first performed Tokyo, 1983.
Monodrama (flute) 1984; first performed Tokyo, 1985.
Crystalline (piano) 1988; first performed Tokyo, 1988.
Lilas (cello) 1988; first performed Amsterdam, 1988.
Jardin des herbes (harpsichord) 1989; first performed Tokyo, 1989.

Vocal/choral:

Quatuor (soprano, violin, viola, cello) 1984; first performed Tokyo, 1985.

* * *

Karen Tanaka's as yet small opus shows a delicacy and quest for perfection which even at this early stage of her career has served to win her some considerable standing in the contemporary music world, both across Europe and in her native Japan. Following her studies at the Toho Gakuen School of Music, her first international success came with the performance of her orchestral work *Prismes* which was premiered by the Tokyo Philharmonic in Tokyo in 1984 and then two years later played at the ISCM World Music Days in Budapest. This work has subsequently been performed widely in Europe and recorded by the Swedish record label BIS. Fascinated by the effects of light through a prism, Tanaka says that she set out to demonstrate these various phenomena in sound using the different instrumental colours of the orchestra. Central to the whole piece are the two notes B♭ and E and the overall structure is that of a spiral, obtained by subjecting the original motif to numerous transfigurations, so that it circulates and rises to a peak.

Tanaka claims to have been inspired to use this process of gradual transfiguration through circular transformation by Edgar Allen Poe's "The Raven", and she employs a similar technique in the construction of her other work from this period, the trio *Tristesse*. The tristesse of the title, however, is a much more fragile entity than Poe's black undercurrents, more a poignant sadness for the inevitability of death. The language of these two early works clearly owes much to Toru Takemitsu, undoubtedly the dominant influence in Japan, and perhaps also to the instrumental colours of Olivier Messiaen. While the simplicity and delicacy of language have stayed with Tanaka in more recent compositions, one can not help but feel that her move to Paris in 1986 was partly, at any rate, motivated by the necessity of finding her own voice. Her initial studies in Paris with Tristan Murail were funded by a French Government Scholarship and she also worked as a *stagiaire* at IRCAM. Her experience at IRCAM does not seem to have overtly affected her musical language, and to date all her pieces have been for conventional acoustic instruments without any kind of electronic enhancement; nor does she anticipate deviating from this in projected works.

Tanaka's residency in Europe rapidly opened up access to new audiences for her music which over the next four years was performed in the Netherlands, Spain, the U.K., France, Italy, Poland (where she was featured in an ISCM/Polish Television film on international composers), Germany, Norway and Sweden. Indeed her first work composed in Paris, *Anamorphose*, a piano concerto, won the Gaudeamus Prize at the International Music Week in Amsterdam in 1987. "Anamorphose" is a word taken from the technology of optics meaning a distorted figuration, and Tanaka has attempted to transpose this distortion into musical terms, by distorting both timbres and structure. The 15-minute piece is in three sections, and again she uses a two-note motif which is constantly transfigured. The glassy hard sounds demanded of the pianist obviously held a particular fascination for her and she went onto explore these possibilities further in the solo piano piece *Crystalline*.

Still in search of her own voice, Tanaka has continued to study. In 1988 she went to the Banff Centre in Canada to take part in the Advanced Musical Studies Course, and more recently she has had rewarding lessons with Luciano Berio. The consolidation of these experiences has yet to reveal itself in her work. Since 1987 she has only acknowledged three short solo pieces, one for cello, *Lilas*, composed for Frances-Marie Uitti, *Crystalline* for piano, and a little suite, largely tonal, for harpsichord, *Jardin des herbes*. Each is admirably concise, exquisitely crafted and richly expressive. They are a tantalising foretaste of a more mature voice and one looks forward with increasing anticipation to the newly commissioned orchestral piece from the Tokyo Philharmonic, promised in 1993.

—Rosemary Johnson

TARNOPOLSKY, Vladimir. Russian. Born in Dneproetrovsk, Ukraine, 30 April 1955. Educated at Moscow Conservatoire, 1973–8, postgraduate study, 1978–80. Married musicologist Irene Snetkova in 1975; 1 son. Assistant, department of composition, Moscow Conservatoire, 1979–80; teacher of composition, Higher Musical College "Ippolitov Ivanov", Moscow, 1980–5; member, Union of Composers, since 1981; independent composer, since 1985; organizer, Society for Contemporary Music, from 1990. Recipient: prizes, All Union Young Composer Competition, 1978, 1980. Mailing address: ulitsa Vorontovskie Prudi, dom 9, kv 16, Moscow 117630, U.S.S.R.

Publisher: Sovetskii kompozitor, Moscow.

Symphonies/orchestral:

Symphonic Prologue 1978.
Concerto for Cello and Orchestra 1980; first performed 1982.
Symphony 1982.
Double Portrait Against a Landscape (concerto for 2 violins, orchestra) 1990.

Chamber/instrumental:

Scoring (piano) 1972.
Variations in the Style of Bartók (piano) 1973.
Moments (piano) 1974.
Sonata (piano) 1975.
Woodwind Quintet 1975.
Chamber Harmony (harp, celeste, double bass) 1976; first performed Prague, 1979.
String Trio 1977; first performed Moscow, 1978.
Three Pictures by Joan Miró (piano) 1979.
Echoes of the Passing Day (piano) 1990; first performed Huddersfield, Yorkshire, 1990.

La crimoso (in memoriam Luigi Nono) (percussion ensemble) 1990.

Vocal/choral:

Maiden Songs (female chorus; folk songs) 1973; first performed 1975.
The Pipe Plays (soprano, flute, violin; Blok) 1973; first performed Dnepropetrovsk, 1973.
Italian Cycle (soprano, piano; Blok) 1977; first performed 1978.
In memoriam Dmitri Shostakovich (musical collage for reciter, chamber orchestra) 1983.
Jesus Deune Teufen Wunden (choral prelude for 17 performers) 1987; first performed Cologne, 1987.
Brooklinskii Bridge (soprano, tenor, orchestra or ensemble; Mayakovsky) 1988; first performed San Diego, California, 1989.
On Reading Musical Outlines by Mussorgsky (chorus, soloist, chamber orchestra, reciter) 1989.
Impression-Expression 1989; first performed Dortmund, 1989.
Troisti musika (voice, piano trio; Skorovoda) 1989; first performed Dortmund, 1989.
Psalmus poenitentialis (concerto for chorus, violin, reciter, orchestra) 1990; first performed Oxford, 1990.

Opera:

The Three Graces (opera-parody; Beber) 1987.

Other:

Transcriptions/arrangements of Arnold Schoenberg *Opus 19* (piano); Claude Debussy: *Prelude* (piano); Sergei Prokofiev: *Navozdeni* (piano); Dmitri Shostakovich: preludes.

PUBLICATIONS

By Tarnopolsky: articles and reviews in *MusikTexte*, and other magazines and journals.

On Tarnopolsky: "Portrait", BBC Russian Service, 1989; T. Parval, "Die Alternative Komponisten Generation in Moskau", in *Sovietische Musk im Licht der Perestroika*, 1990; S. Savenko, an introduction to VT's recordings, 1991.

Vladimir Tarnopolsky comments:

My aim is to search not just for new means of expression, but for an individualistic conception that will allow every new work to be conceived afresh, on its own terms. In contrast to a purely technical approach, mine is cultural and conceptual; I make use of symbols and semiotic systems—often medieval in origin but deployed in a new context.

Schoenberg says "not style but idea". I'd like to change that to read "style *and* idea".

* * *

Vladimir Tarnopolsky is one of the youngest of that generation of Moscow composers that includes such figures as Elena Firsova, Dmitri Smirnov, Alexander Raskatov and others. Although he was born in the Western Ukraine, he found his way to Moscow through the help and encouragement of Edison Denisov. Through the older composer too Tarnopolsky has come to take a prominent position as one of the most active and energetic young figures working in Moscow today.

Tarnopolsky's earliest works are on the larger scale and tend to expressionism. Although the results, especially in the Cello Concerto, are powerful and show a considerable mastery of orchestral colour, they failed to find favour with their own creator, who in more recent years has distanced himself from what he feels to be these works' rather naive emotionalism.

Tarnopolsky is by nature an experimentalist who tends to treat every new piece as an individual proposition to be approached on its own terms. In this way he may be the nearest to a Post-Modernist the younger Russians have yet produced, although he himself prefers the equally hideous description "culturological", a word he uses with a wry smile. Tarnopolsky regards the act of composition not as a matter of expression, but of engagement with many different sources, mostly from the past, but also from alien cultures. He clearly reflects the intellectual confusion and hunger so characteristic of Russia and Russians in the wake of the collapse of Communism. But he is not merely reflecting it; he is also trying to take advantage of the latent energy and excitement generated by the peculiar situation in which the people of his country find themselves.

A strong vein of humour in Tarnopolsky's work has so far brought a great deal of attention. Among the most successful of the comic pieces are a fantasy reconstruction of a (practically) non-existent opera by Weber and a very jolly setting of some of Mayakovsky's picture-postcard impressions of America as a kind of hooligan's cantata, *Brooklinsky Bridge*.

But, like most young people in his country, Tarnopolsky has a great interest in religion. One of the best of his pieces with a strong religious bent is his *Psalmus poenitentialis*, a magnificently dark-hued setting of Psalm 31 for chorus, solo violin, organ and tam-tam. Other religious pieces are not direct settings of sacred texts but rather symbolic or instrumental dramas analogous to particular religious experiences or rituals—for instance the "choral prelude" *Jesus Deune Teufen Wunden*, in which two percussionists advance like penitents down a long line of instruments by the playing of which they are scourged and purified.

Other more recent works explore quite different areas of experience. For example, his Trio for clarinet, violin and piano, *Echoes of the Passing Day* is an affectionate tribute to such emblematic masters of early Modernism as Proust and Joyce, as well as to the sort of "Modern Music" that flourished at festivals like those of Darmstadt and Warsaw in the early 1960s.

—Gerard McBurney

TAVENER, John (Kenneth). British/English. Born in London, 28 January 1944. Educated at Highgate School London; Royal Academy of Music, London (composition under Lennox Berkeley and David Lumsdaine), 1961–5. Married Victoria Marangopoulou in 1974. Independent composer; professor of music, Trinity College of Music, London, from 1969. Received into Greek Orthodox Church, 1976. Mailing address: c/o Chester Music, 8–9 Frith Street, London W1V 5TZ, England.

Publisher: Chester.

Symphonies/orchestral:

Piano Concerto 1962–3; first performed London, 6 December 1963.
Chamber Concerto (chamber orchestra) 1965, revised 1968; first performed London, 12 June 1968.
Variations on Three Blind Mice 1972; broadcast BBC Television, 1 February 1973.
Palintropos (piano, orchestra) 1978; first performed Birmingham, 1 March 1979.
Towards the Son: Ritual Procession (orchestra, includes 33 tenor bowed psalteries, 3 offstage trebles, handbells) 1982; first performed Cheltenham, Gloucestershire, 12 July 1982.
The Protecting Veil (cello, strings) 1987; first performed 1989.
The Repentant Thief (dance lament for clarinet, percussion, timpani, strings) 1990; first performed London, 19 September 1991.

Chamber/instrumental:

Grandma's Footsteps (oboe, bassoon, horn, 5 music boxes, double string quartet) 1967–8; first performed London, 1968.
In memoriam Igor Stravinsky (2 alto flutes, organ, hand bells) 1971; first performed Little Missenden, Buckinghamshire, 1971.
Palin (piano) 1977; first performed London, 24 November 1980.
Greek Interlude (flute, piano) 1979; first performed Little Missenden, Buckinghamshire, 10 October 1979.
My Grandfather's Waltz (piano duet) 1980; first performed Little Missenden, Buckinghamshire, 1980.
Mandelion (organ) 1981; first performed Dublin, 27 June 1982.
Trisagion (brass quintet) 1981; first performed Huddersfield, Yorkshire, 25 November 1985.
Mandoodles (pieces for young pianist) 1982.
Little Missenden Calm (oboe, clarinet, bassoon, horn) 1984; first performed Little Missenden, Buckinghamshire, 13 October 1984.
Chant (guitar) 1984; first performed London, 17 May 1984.
In Memory of Cats (piano) 1986; first performed London, 31 January 1988.
The Hidden Treasure (string quartet) 1989; first performed Keele, February 1991.
Threnos (cello) 1990.

Vocal/choral:

Three Holy Sonnets (baritone, 2 horns, 2 trombones, strings; Donne) 1962; first performed London, 1962.
Three Sections from T.S. Eliot's The Four Quartets (high voice, piano) 1963–4; first performed London, 11 November 1965.
The Whale (mezzo-soprano, baritone, children's chorus, SATB chorus, speakers, 6 male actors, orchestra/no violins, Hammond organ, 8 percussion, amplified piano, grand organ, celeste, tape) 1965–6; first performed London, 24 January 1968. Recorded Sapcor 15/Ring o' Records 2320 104.
Three Surrealist Songs (mezzo-soprano, tape, piano/bongos) 1967–8; broadcast BBC, Autumn 1968. Recorded Caprice CAP 1112.
In alium (high soprano, Hammond organ/2 players, optional grand organ) 1968; first performed London, 12 August 1968.
Introit for March 27th, the Feast of St John Damascene (soprano, alto, SATB chorus, orchestra) 1968; first performed London, 27 March 1968.
Celtic Requiem (soprano, children's chorus, SATB chorus, 3 orchestral groups) 1969; first performed London, 16 July 1969.
Coplas (soprano, alto, tenor, bass, SATB chorus/16 voices, tape) 1970; first performed Cheltenham, Gloucestershire, 9 July 1970.
Nomine Jesu (mezzo-soprano, double SSAATTBB chorus, 2 alto flutes, organ/2 players, 5 male speaking voices) 1970; first performed Dartington, Devon, August 1970.
Responsorium in Memory of Annon Lee Silver (2 mezzo-sopranos, SATB chorus, 2 flutes ad lib) 1971; first performed Birmingham, 20 September 1971.
Ma Fin est mon commencement (4-part tenor chorus, 4 trombones, percussion, 4 cellos) 1972; first performed London, 1972.
Canciones españoles (2 counter-tenors or sopranos, 2 flutes, organ, harpsichord, percussion) 1972; first performed London, 8 June 1972. Recorded RCA LRL1 5104.
Little Requiem for Father Malachy Lynch (SATB chorus, 2 flutes, trumpet, organ, strings) 1972; first performed Winchester, Hampshire, 29 July 1972.
Ultimos ritos (soprano, alto, tenor, bass, 5 SATB choruses, orchestra) 1972; first performed Haarlem, 22 June 1974.
Requiem for Father Malachy (2 counter-tenors, tenor, 2 baritones, bass, large ensemble) 1973; first performed London, 10 June 1973. Recorded RCA LRL1 5104.
Canticle of the Mother of God (soprano, SATB chorus) 1976; first performed Rye, Sussex, 22 April 1977.
Lamentation, Last Prayer and Exaltation (soprano, handbells or piano) 1977; first performed Rye, Sussex, 28 April 1978.
Kyklike Kinesis (soprano, cello solo, SATB chorus, large ensemble) 1977; first performed London, 8 March 1978.
Six Russian Folksongs (soprano, flute/piccolo, bassoon, trumpet, piano, domra, 2 violins, cello) 1978; first performed London, 15 January 1978.
The Liturgy of St John Chrysostom (unaccompanied SATB chorus) 1978; first performed London, 1978. Recorded IKOS 8E.
The Immurement of Antigone (dramatic mezzo-soprano, orchestra; Gerard McLarnon) 1978; first performed London, 30 March 1979.
Akhmatova: Requiem (soprano, baritone, orchestra) 1979–80; first performed Edinburgh, 20 August 1981.
Six Abbasid Songs (tenor, 3 flutes/alto flutes, percussion) 1979–80; first performed Snape, Suffolk, 18 June 1980.
Sappho: Lyrical Fragments (2 sopranos, strings) 1980; first performed London, 25 April 1981.
Risen! (SATB chorus, orchestra) 1981; first performed Bedford, 19 October 1981.
The Great Canon of St Andrew of Crete (unaccompanied SATB chorus) 1981; first performed Winchester, Hampshire, 1981. Recorded Gimell 1585 02.
Prayer for the World (16 unaccompanied solo voices, SATB) 1981; first performed London, 11 October 1981.
Funeral Ikos (unaccompanied SATB chorus) 1981; first performed Winchester, Hampshire, 1981. Recorded Ikon C IKO 21; Gimell 1585–05.
Doxa (unaccompanied SATB chorus) 1982; first performed London, 12 September 1982.
Lord's Prayer (unaccompanied SATB chorus; English and Russian) 1982; first performed London, 12 September 1982.
The Lamb (unaccompanied SATB chorus; Blake) 1982; first performed Winchester, Hampshire, 22 December 1982. Recorded Gimell 1585–05.

He Hath Entered the Heaven (trebles, optional handbells) 1982; first performed Oxford, 16 January 1983.
To a Child Dancing in the Wind (soprano, flute, harp, viola; Yeats) 1983; first performed Little Missenden, Buckinghamshire, 16 October 1983.
Mini Song Cycle for Gina (soprano, piano; Yeats) 1984; first performed London, 3 April 1986.
Ikon of Light (SATB chorus, string trio; St Symeon) 1984; first performed Cheltenham, Gloucestershire, 8 July 1984. Recorded Gimell 1585–05.
Orthodox Vigil Service (SATB chorus, handbells) 1984; first performed Oxford, 17 May 1985. Recorded Ikon Records IKO 16/17.
A Nativity (unaccompanied SSSAA chorus; Yeats) 1984; first performed London, December 1987.
Sixteen Haiku of Seferis (soprano, tenor, percussion, bells, strings) 1984; first performed St David's, Wales, 16 May 1984.
Angels (SATB chorus, organ) 1985; first performed Basingstoke, Hampshire, 3 November 1985.
Love Bade Me Welcome (unaccompanied SATB chorus; Herbert) 1985; first performed Winchester, Hampshire, 28 June 1985.
Two Hymns to the Mother of God (unaccompanied SATB chorus; liturgy of St Basil) 1985; first performed Winchester, Hampshire, 14 December 1985.
Ikon of St Cuthbert of Lindisfarne (unaccompanied SATB chorus; Mother Thekla) 1986; first performed Durham, 20 March 1987. Recorded Ikon C IKO 21.
Magnificat and Nunc Dimittis (Collegium Regale) (unaccompanied SATB chorus) 1986; first performed Cambridge, 24 April 1987.
Meditation on the Light (counter-tenor, guitar, handbells) 1986.
Panikhida (unaccompanied SATB chorus) 1986; first performed London, 21 June 1986. Recorded Ikon C IKO 21.
Akathist of Thanksgiving (soloists, SATB chorus, bells, percussion, massed strings; Petrov, translated Mother Thekla) 1986–7; first performed London, 21 November 1988.
Prayer (for Szymanowski) (bass, piano; *Hamlet*) 1987; first performed Warsaw, Autumn 1987.
Wedding Prayer (unaccompanied SATB chorus; Orthodox Holy Rite of Matrimony) 1987; first performed London, April 1987.
Many Years (unaccompanied SATB chorus) 1987; first performed Frinton-on-Sea, Essex, 22 August 1987.
Acclamation (unaccompanied SATB chorus) 1987; first performed Canterbury, Kent, 8 December 1987.
God Is with Us (unaccompanied SATB chorus, organ) 1987; first performed Winchester, Hampshire, 22 December 1987.
Hymn to the Holy Spirit (unaccompanied SATB chorus) 1987; first performed London, 30 June 1988.
The Tyger (unaccompanied SATB chorus; Blake) 1987.
Apolytikion for St Nicholas (unaccompanied SATB chorus) 1988. Recorded IKON C IKO 21.
The Call (unaccompanied SATB chorus) 1988; first performed Northampton, 23 September 1988.
Ikon of St Seraphim (baritone solo, 4 bases, SATB chorus, solo violin, orchestra; Mother Thekla) 1988; first performed St Endellion, Cornwall, 7 August 1988.
Let Not the Prince Be Silent (2 antiphonal choruses; St Clement of Alexandria) 1988; first performed Sherborne, Dorset, May 1989.
The Uncreated Eros (treble, unaccompanied SATB chorus) 1988.
Lament of the Mother of God (soprano, unaccompanied SATB chorus) 1988; first performed Norwich, Norfolk, 28 June 1989.
Today the Virgin (unaccompanied SATB chorus; Mother Thekla) 1989; first performed London, 27 December 1989.
Eonia (unaccompanied SATB chorus) 1989; first performed Cork, 6 May 1990.
Psalm 121 (unaccompanied SATB chorus) 1989; first performed London, 8 July 1990.
Resurrection (soloists, actors, SATB and male choruses, recorders, 3 trumpets, 5 trombones, timpani, percussion, tam-tam, organ, string quartet; Mother Thekla) 1989; first performed Glasgow, 17 April 1990.
Thunder Entered Her: A Divine Allegory (SATB chorus, organ, male chorus, handbells in distance) 1990; first performed St Albans, Hertfordshire, 15 June 1991.
Ikon the Trinity (unaccompanied SATB chorus) 1990.
Do Not Move (unaccompanied SATB chorus; Seferis) 1990.
A Christmas Round (unaccompanied SATB chorus; Greek text) 1990.

Opera/dramatic:

The Cappemakers (music drama; after the York Mysteries) 1964, revised 1965; first performed Alfriston, Sussex, 14 June 1964.
Cain and Abel (music drama; Vulgate, York Mysteries) 1965; first performed London, 21 November 1966.
Therèse (Gerard McLarnon) 1973–6; first performed London, 1 October 1979.
A Gentle Spirit (chamber opera; McLarnon, after Dostoevsky) 1977; first performed Bath, 6 June 1977.
Eis Thanaton (ritual by Andreas Kalvos) 1986; first performed Cheltenham, Gloucestershire, 5 July 1987.
Mary of Egypt (chamber opera) 1990–1; first performed Aldeburgh, Suffolk, 1992.

PUBLICATIONS

On Tavener: Paul Griffiths, articles on JT, in *Musical Times*, 115, 1974, and 120, 1979; P. Phillips, "JT", in *Contact*, 26, 1983; (interview) in *New Sounds, New Personalities: British Composers of the 1980s*, London, 1985.

* * *

The essence of John Tavener's music is what he calls the "uncreated light", a non-numinous essence that exists prior to and throughout creation. This conviction is in keeping with Tavener's remarkably Orthodox views—he was received into Greek Orthodox worship in 1976—and his work reflects that essentially mystical philosophy very thoroughly, rejecting polyphonic development, making extensive use of common chords, incorporating silence, and constantly suggesting a hermetic, ritual quality which, because of its constant urge to transcendence, is as far beyond introspection as it is beyond conventionally concert-oriented composition. One senses that the dividing lines in Tavener's mind are the Renaissance and the northern shore of the Mediterranean, but he has also shown an interest in the traditions of the Celtic church, as in his magnificent *Celtic Requiem*. Perhaps the only modern composer he closely resembles is the Estonian Arvo Pärt; *Akhmatova: Requiem* is the closest thing to Pärt yet written by an Englishman.

For all his pre-Renaissance and Byzantine leanings, Tavener is an Englishman, with a deceptively pragmatic and robust approach to composition; he may even claim distant kinship with his 17th-century near-namesake, the composer John Taverner. His pieces are constructed, sometimes over long periods, in an essentially empirical way; when the need arises he has used modern techniques like his personalised version of total serialism, and electronics. Tavener studied with Lennox Berkeley at the Royal Academy of Music, and allowed the experience to crystallise his developing interest in Catholic liturgy (surprisingly, Messiaen has been much less of an influence) and mystical expression. His classes with the Australian composer David Lumsdaine were, if anything, even more significant. Lumsdaine's interest in natural and ambient sound contributed very significantly to Tavener's thinking, and also opened up for him a way through the modern avant-garde.

Unlike Pärt, who traced a path through orthodox modernism before arriving at his present pre-modern style, Tavener tended to draw his inspiration directly from the music of the distant past. Probably the only modern genius to influence him was Stravinsky, in whose *Canticum sacrum* Tavener claims to hear distinctively Byzantine elements. There are clear Stravinskyan elements in the early dramatic piece *The Cappemakers*, based on the York Mystery Plays. However, the work that really brought him to the attention of critics and public was his dramatic cantata *The Whale*, a remarkable reworking of the Jonah story for voices, chorus and an orchestra that incorporates electric keyboards and tape and alternates huge blocks of sound with startling silence.

To a large extent, all of Tavener's work is dramatic, most of it in the sense that all liturgical music is essentially dramatic. He has written liturgies specifically for the Orthodox Church, notably *The Liturgy of St John Chrysostom*, the *Funeral Ikos* for the burial of priests, and also a long ecumenical Vigil Service for a combined Anglican/Orthodox congregation. His ritualised opera *Therèse* dramatises the dying agonies (spiritual, rather than physical) of St Theresa of Lisieux. In the massive *Ultimos ritos*, based on the Crucifixion meditations of San Juan de la Cruz, he deploys the musicians in the shape of the Cross, a rather more obvious reification of his musical intent.

He works equally well on a much smaller scale. The *Ikon of Light* for chorus and string trio is perhaps his finest and most approachable single work. It has all the profound, mystical resonance of the larger works, but in a simpler and less forbidding vein. Its yearning quality makes it instantly appealing, and it has been effectively recorded.

He has written within a more secular tradition as well. *Grandma's Footsteps* is an early reminder of his background and there are a number of non-religious Greek-inspired pieces, notably *The Immurement of Antigone* and the Sapphic fragments, which make for an interesting comparison with Harrison Birtwistle's mysterious . . . *agm* . . . The setting of William Blake's *The Lamb*, though patently religious in association, is direct, simple and communicative.

Critically, Tavener suffers from the same unsubstantiated presuppositions that are routinely directed against Messiaen. Neither man is a "difficult", withdrawn mystic. Both have their fleshly side; both are master technicians; and Tavener, 30 years younger, may yet approach the Frenchman's altitude.

—Brian Morton

TCHAIKOVSKY, Boris (Alexandrovich). Russian. Born in Moscow, 10 September 1925. Educated at Gnessin Music Institute, Moscow (composition, piano), 1935–41; Moscow Conservatoire (composition under Dmitri Shostakovich, Vladimir Shebalin and Nikolai Miaskovsky), 1942–9. Married Janina Moshinskaya in 1953. Composer; member, Moscow Union of Composers, since 1950. Recipient: State Prize of the Soviet Union, 1959; People's Artist, 1985. Mailing address: ultisa Studencheskaya 44/28, kv. 125, 121165 Moscow, U.S.S.R.

Publisher: Sovetskii kompozitor, Moscow.

Symphonies/orchestral:

Symphony No 1 1947; first performed Moscow, 1962.
Fantasia on Russian Folk Themes 1950; first performed Moscow, 1951.
Sinfonietta (string orchestra) 1953; first performed Moscow, 1954.
Capriccio on English Themes 1954; first performed Moscow, 1954.
Concerto for Clarinet and Chamber Orchestra 1964. Recorded Melodiya C 10 24171 007.
Cello Concerto 1964; first performed Moscow, 1964.
Symphony No 2 1967; first performed Moscow, 1967. Recorded Melodiya CM 02281-82.
Chamber Symphony 1967; first performed Moscow, 1967. Recorded Melodiya C 10 01899 002/ C 10 24141 006.
Violin Concerto 1968; first performed Moscow, 1970. Recorded Melodiya CM 04175 6.
Theme and Eight Variations 1969; first performed Dresden, 1974. Recorded Melodiya M 10 42733 005.
Piano Concerto 1969; first performed Moscow, 1971. Recorded Melodiya C 10 06427 28.
Six Studies (organ, strings) 1974; first performed Leningrad, 1979.
Sebastopol Symphony 1980; first performed Moscow, 1981. Recorded Melodiya C 10 20245 002.
Siberian Wind 1982; first performed Moscow, 1984.
Raw Youth (poem for orchestra after Dostoevsky) 1984; first performed Moscow, 1985.
Four Preludes (chamber orchestra) 1985; first performed Moscow, 1985.
Music for Orchestra 1986; first performed Moscow, 1987.

Chamber/instrumental:

Early piano pieces, 1937–46.
Sonata (piano) 1942; first performed Moscow, 1944.
Sonatina (piano) 1942; first performed Moscow, 1946.
Suite (cello) 1955; first performed Moscow, 1961. Recorded Melodiya C 10 07669 000.
Piano Trio 1956; first performed Moscow, 1956. Recorded Melodiya C 10 0697 001.
String Quartet No 1 1956; first performed Moscow, 1958.
Sonata (cello, piano) 1957; first performed Moscow, 1958. Recorded Melodiya C 10 0697 001.
Sonata (violin, piano) 1958; first performed Moscow, 1958.
Piano Quintet 1960; first performed Leningrad, 1962. Recorded Melodiya C 10 07567.
String Quartet No 2 1961; first performed Moscow, 1962.
Partita (cello colo, chimes, xylophone, vibraphone, timpani, cymbals, electric guitar, harpsichord, piano, percussion) 1966; first performed Moscow, 1967. Recorded Panton 11 0420G.

String Quartet No 3 1967; first performed Moscow, 1968. Recorded Melodiya C 10 11141 009.
Sonata (2 pianos) 1967; first performed Moscow, 1967.
String Quartet No 4 1972; first performed Moscow, 1973. Recorded Melodiya C 10 06087 001.
String Quartet No 5 1974; first performed Moscow, 1975. Recorded Melodiya C 10 10919 003.
String Quartet No 6 1975; first performed Moscow, 1976.

Vocal/choral:

Two Poems (soprano, piano) 1940; first performed Moscow, 1940.
Pushkin's Lyrical Poems (soprano, piano) 1969; first performed Moscow, 1972. Recorded Melodiya C 10 1129 005.
Signs of the Zodiac (soprano, harpsichord, strings) 1974; first performed Leningrad, 1976. Recorded Melodiya C 10 11141 009.
The Last Spring (mezzo-soprano, flute, clarinet, piano; Zabolotsky) 1982; first performed 1983.
Four Poems (soprano, piano; Brodsky) 1987; first performed Boston, 1988.

Other:

19 film scores for Mosfilm, 1956–77.
3 film scores for Lenfilm, 1958–64.
7 television scores, 1961–84.
9 radio dramas, 1951–6.
13 radio scores for children, 1957–79.
5 theatre scores, 1954–86.

PUBLICATIONS

On Tchaikovsky; M. Yakubov, "BT" in *Musical Life*, 24, 1974; V. Kelle, "BT", in *Music in the U.S.S.R., 10–12, 1985.*

* * *

Boris Tchaikovsky is an impressive exponent of modern tonality, writing large and expansive scores which constantly flirt with the boundaries of orthodox harmony without ever stepping fully outside them. His most characteristic pieces are characterised by strong motivic development, with a robust rhythmic structure, and carefully managed climaxes.

His symphonic writing is among the most impressive to have emerged in the post-World War II Soviet Union, matching that of Boris Tischenko and occasionally even, as in the case of the magnificent *Sebastopol Symphony*, Dmitri Shostakovich. The *Sebastopol Symphony* is essentially affirmative, but with strong elements of tragedy and thus powerfully recalls Shostakovich's darker scores. Tchaikovsky's orchestration is as always absolutely watertight and perfectly balanced. As in his chamber and instrumental writing, he continues to make use of folk and traditional themes, though these are more deeply etched into the fabric of his own musical discourse than when he was a younger composer. In a work like the chamber *Partita* he uses a vivid and very modern instrumentation to great effect.

Fantastically talented, Tchaikovsky wrote his first piano pieces when he was only 13 or 14. Perhaps spurred by his famous surname (though he is not a descendant of Peter Ilyich Tchaikovsky), he has dedicated himself to composition from the outset. Study under Shostakovich and Nikolai Miaskovsky, the latter particularly, taught him how far the harmonic system could be stretched in the direction of a open-ended polytonality without losing its anchoring. The piano pieces are highly inventive, rhythmically more subtle than at first appears, marked by alternations of triple and double time and large-scale chord progressions which are reminiscent of Janáček, and, less often, Bartók.

Tchaikovsky's vocal music occupies a rather less prominent position in his output but is nonetheless significant. His settings of Joseph Brodsky and Lermontov are of particular interest, and there is the fascinating *Signs of the Zodiac* for soprano, harpsichord and strings. Tchaikovsky has also written extensively for film and theatre, and is one of the most highly respected senior composers in the Soviet Union.

—Kyril Maslin

THOMSON, Virgil (Garnett). American. Born in Kansas City, Missouri, 25 November 1896. Educated: piano from age 5 (later under Heinrich Gebhard), organ from age 13 (under Wallace Goodman); Central High School, Kansas City, 1908–13; Junior College, Kansas City, 1915–7, completed 1919; Harvard University, Cambridge, Massachusetts (orchestration and modern music history under Edward Burlingame Hill, choral conducting under Archibald Davison, composition under S. Foster Damon), 1919–23; further study in organ and counterpoint under Nadia Boulanger, Paris, 1921–2; further study in counterpoint and composition under Rosario Scalero, conducting under Chalmers Clifton, New York City, 1923–5. Military service, Field Artillery, United States Army, 1917–18, commissioned Fort Sill, Oklahoma; further training as radio operator, Columbia University, New York City. Church organist, Calvary Baptist Church, Kansas City, before World War I, and in Northhampton, Massachusetts, from 1919; early critical pieces published in *Boston Evening Transcript*, 1921; assistant conductor and accompanist, Harvard Glee Club, 1920–3; resident in Paris, 1925–40; music critic, *New York Herald Tribune*, 1940–54; visiting lecturer, distinguished professor and artist in residence, many institutions, 1950s–1970s; member, ASCAP board of review, 1960–8, board of directors 1975–83. Recipient: Chevalier 1947, Officer 1951, Légion d'Honneur; Pullitzer Prize (for score to film *Louisiana Story*), 1948; elected to National Institute of Arts and Letters, 1948; elected to American Academy of Arts and Letters, 1959; Guggenheim Fellowship, 1960; Gold Medal for Music, American Academy and Institute of Arts and Letters, 1966; Creative Arts Award, Brandeis University, 1968; Handel Medallion, City of New York, 1971; Edward MacDowell Award, 1977; Carnegie Hall 90th anniverary award, 1981; Deems Taylor Award, 1982; National Book Critics Circle Award (for *A Virgil Thomson Reader*), 1983; Kennedy Center Honor, 1983; National Music Council Award, 1984; foreign corresponding member, Académie des Beaux Arts, France. Honorary degrees: Syracuse University, 1949; Rutgers University, 1956; Park College, 1966; Roosevelt University, 1971; University of Missouri, 1971, 1980; Columbia University, 1978; Johns Hopkins University, 1978; Fairfield University, 1978; Emerson College, 1981; University of Windsor, 1981; Brooklyn College, 1981; Bard College, 1982; Harvard University, 1982; Manhattanville College, 1983; University of Connecticut at Storrs, 1985; New England Conservatory of Music, 1986; New School for Social Research, 1986; William Jewell College, 1986. **Died 30 September 1989.**

Publishers: Boosey & Hawkes; Belwin-Mills; C. Fisher; Peters; Presser; Schirmer; Southern.

Symphonies/orchestral:

Two Sentimental Tangos (arranged from piano piece) 1923.
Symphony on a Hymn Tune 1928; first performed New York City, 22 February 1945.
Symphony No 2 (arranged from *Sonata No 1* for piano) 1931, revised 1941; first performed Seattle, Washington, 17 November 1941.
The John Moser Waltzes (used in ballet *Filling Station*) 1935, orchestrated 1937.
Meditation . . . Jere Abbott 1935, orchestrated 1944; first performed Vancouver, 21 November 1948.
The Plow That Broke the Plains (orchestral suite from film score) 1936; first performed Philadelphia, 2 January 1943.
Filling Station (orchestral suite from the ballet) 1937; broadcast WNYC, 2 February 1941; first concert performance New York City, 14 December 1941.
The River (orchestral suite from film score) 1937; first performed Brooklyn, New York, 12 January 1943.
Bugles and Birds . . . Pablo Picasso 1940, orchestrated 1944; first performed Philadelphia, 17 November 1944.
Cantabile for Strings . . . Nicholas de Chatelain 1940, orchestrated 1944; first performed Philadelphia, 17 November 1944.
Fanfare for France . . . Max Kahn 1940, arranged for woodwinds 1944; first performed Cincinnati, Ohio, 15 January 1943.
Fugue . . . Alexander Smallens 1940, orchestrated 1944; first performed Philadelphia, 17 November 1944.
Tango Lullaby . . . Mlle Alvarez de Toledo 1940, orchestrated 1944; first performed Philadelphia, 17 November 1944.
Percussion Piece . . . Jessie K. Lasell 1941, orchestrated 1944; first performed Philadelphia, 17 November 1944.
Insistences . . . Louise Crane 1941, arranged for band as *Study Piece: Portrait of a Lady*, 1969; first performed Cambridge, Massachusetts, Spring 1973.
Parades . . . Florine Stettheimer 1941, arranged for band as *Metropolitan Museum Fanfare: Portrait of an American Artist* 1969; first performed New York City, 16 October 1969.
Canons for Dorothy Thompson 1942; first performed New York City, 23 July 1942.
The Mayor La Guardia Waltzes 1942; first performed Cincinnati, Ohio, 14 May 1942.
Aaron Copland, Persistently Pastoral 1942, orchestrated as *Pastorale* 1944; first performed New York City, 15 March 1945.
Fugue and Chorale on Yankee Doodle (from the film score *Tuesday in November*) 1945; first performed Atlanta, Georgia, 16 April 1969.
The Seine at Night 1947; first performed Kansas City, Missouri, 24 February 1948.
Acadian Songs (from the film score *Louisiana Story*) 1948; first performed Philadelphia, 11 January 1951.
Louisiana Story (orchestral suite from film score) 1948; first performed Philadelphia, 26 November 1948.
Wheat Field at Noon 1948; first performed Louisville, Kentucky, 7 December 1948.
At the Beach (concert waltz arranged for trumpet, band from *Le Bains-var*) 1949; first performed New York City, 21 July 1950.
The Mother of Us All (orchestral suite from the opera) 1949; first performed Knoxville, Tennessee, 17 January 1950.
A Solemn Music (band) 1949, orchestrated 1961; first performed New York City, 17 June 1949; first performance of orchestral version, New York City, 15 February 1962.
Cello Concerto (also arranged for cello, piano) 1950; first performed Philadelphia, 24 March 1950.
Sea Piece with Birds 1952; first performed Dallas, 10 December 1952.
Concerto . . . Roger Baker (flute, harp, string, percussion; version for flute, piano) 1954; first performed Venice, 14 September 1954.
Eleven Chorale Preludes (after Brahms Op 122) 1956; first performed New Orleans, 25 March 1957.
The Lively Arts Fugue 1957.
Fugues and Cantilenas (from the film score *Power Among Men*) 1959; first performed Ann Arbor, Michigan, 2 May 1959.
A Joyful Fugue (also arranged for band) 1962; first performed New York City, 1 February 1963.
Autumn (concertino for harp, strings, percussion; arranged from *Homage to Marya Freund and to the Harp* and from *Sonata No 2* for piano) 1964; first performed Madrid, 19 October 1964.
Pilgrims and Pioneers (from the film score *Journey to America*; also arranged for band) 1964; first performed New York City, 27 February 1961.
Ode to the Wonders of Nature (brass, percussion) 1965; first performed Washington, D.C., 16 September 1965.
Fantasy in Homage to an Earlier England 1966; first performed Kansas City, Missouri, 27 May 1966.
Edges . . . Robert Indiana 1966, arranged for band 1969; first performed Cambridge, Massachusetts, Spring 1973.
Symphony No 3 1972; first performed New York City, 26 December 1976.
Thoughts for Strings 1981.
Dead Pan: Mrs Betty Freeman 1981, orchestrated as *A Love Scene* 1982.
Intensely Two: Karen Brown Waltuck 1981, orchestrated 1982.
Loyal, Steady and Persistent: Noah Creshevsky 1981, orchestrated 1982.
Something of a Beauty: Anne-Marie Soullière 1981, orchestrated 1982.
David Dubal in Flight 1982.
A Double Take (orchestrated from *John Houseman: No Changes*) 1984.
Major Chords (orchestrated from *Tony Tommasini: A Study in Chords*) 1985.

Chamber/instrumental (excluding keyboard):

Sonata da chiesa (clarinet, trumpet, horn, trombone, viola) 1926, revised 1973; first performed Paris, 5 May 1926.
Portraits for Violin Alone ("Senorita Juanita de Medina Accompanied by her Mother", "Madame Martine", "Georges Hugnet, Poet and Man of Letters", "Miss Gertrude Stein as a Young Girl", "Clicquet-Pleyel in F", "Mrs C[hester] W[hitlin] L[asell]", "Sauguet, from Life", "Ruth Smallens") 1928–40; first performed (in part) Paris, 14 November 1928.
Five Portraits (4 clarinets; "Portrait of Ladies: A Conversation", "Portrait of a Young Man in Good Health: Maurice Grosser with a Cold", "Christian Berard as a Soldier", "Christian Berard in Person") 1929; first performed Boston, 1929.
Le Bains-var (violin, piano; also arranged for 2 violins, cello, double bass, piano) 1929, arranged for trumpet, piano or band as *At the Beach*, 1940.
Sonata (violin) 1930; first performed Paris, 24 January 1931.

Portraits (violin, piano; "Alice Toklas", "Mary Reynolds", "Anne Miracle", "Yvonne de Casa Fuerte") 1930–40; published, with the addition of *Cynthia Kemper, a Fanfare*, as *Five Ladies*.
Serenade (flute, violin) 1931; first performed New York City, 13 November 1935.
String Quartet No 1 1931, revised 1957; first performed Paris, 15 June 1931.
String Quartet No 2 1932, revised 1957; first performed Hartford, Connecticut, 14 April 1933.
Sonata (flute) 1943.
Barcarolle for Woodwinds: A Portrait of Georges Hugnet (arranged from piano piece for flute, oboe, cor anglais, clarinet, bass clarinet, bassoon) 1944; first performed Pittsburgh, Pennsylvania, 29 November 1946.
Party Pieces (Sonorous and Exquisite Corpses) (20 pieces, collaboratively written as a game of "Consequences" by VT, John Cage, Henry Cowell and Lou Harrison) 1945; arranged for flute, clarinet, bassoon, horn, piano by Hughes.
At the Beach (version for trumpet, piano) 1949; first performed New York City, 19 February 1949.
Etude: Lamentations (accordion) 1959.
Variations (koto) 1961.
Etude . . . Frederic James (cello, piano) 1966.
Family Portrait ("A Fanfare: Robin Smith", "At 14: Annie Barnard", "A Portrait of Howard Rea", "Scherzo: Priscilla Rea", "Man of Iron, Willy Eisenhart"; 2 trumpets, horn, 2 trombones) 1974; first performed New York City, 24 March 1975.
For Lou Harrison and His Jolly Games Sixteen Measures (Count 'Em) (unspecified instrumentation) 1981.
A Short Fanfare (2 or 3 trumpets, optional drums) 1981.
Bell Piece (2–4 players) 1983.
Cynthia Kemper: A Fanfare 1983.
Lili Hastings (violin, piano) 1983.
A Portrait of Two [Benjamin Zifkin and Joelle Armar] 1984.
Jay Rosen: Portrait and Fugue (bass tuba, piano) 1984–5.
Stockton Fanfare (3 trumpets, 2 drums) 1985.

Keyboard (piano, except where otherwise stated; VT's piano "Portraits" were published in 7 albums; for key to appended numbers, see PUBLICATIONS):

Prelude 1921.
Fanfare (organ) 1922.
Passacaglia (organ) 1922, revised 1974.
Pastorale on a Christmas Plainsong 1922.
Prelude (organ) 1922.
Two Sentimental Tangos 1923.
Five Chorale-Preludes ("O Sacred Head, Now Wounded", "The New-Born Babe" in 3 variations, "Praise God, Ye Christians Everywhere"; organ) 1924.
Synthetic Waltzes (2 pianos or piano—4 hands) 1925.
Five Two-Part Inventions 1926.
Ten Easy Pieces and a Coda 1926.
Variations on Sunday School Tunes ("Come, Ye Disconsolate", "There's Not a Friend Like the Lowly Jesus", "Will There Be Any Stars in My Crown?", "Shall We Gather at the River?"; organ) 1926–7.
Sonata No 1 1929.
Sonata No 2 1929.
Travelling in Spain . . . Alice Woodfin Branliere [6] 1929.
Alternations . . . Maurice Grosser [1] 1929.
Catalan Waltz . . . Ramon Senabre [2] 1929.
Madame Dubost chez elle [5] 1930.
Sonata No 3 1930.
Pastoral . . . Jean Ozenne [3] 1930.
Russell Hitchcock Reading [5] 1930.
Clair Leonard's Profile [6] 1930.
Meditation . . . Jere Abott [2] 1935.
Sea Coast . . . Constance Askew [2] 1935.
A Portrait of R. Kirk Askew [2] 1935.
The Hunt . . . A. Everett Austin Jr [4] 1935.
Helen Austin at Home and Abroad [5] 1935.
Souvenir . . . Paul Bowles [3] 1935.
Connecticut Waltzes . . . Harold Lewis Cook [6] 1935.
Hymn . . . Josiah Marvel [4] 1935.
Tennis . . . Henry McBride [4] 1935.
The John Moser Waltzes (used in ballet *Filling Station*) 1935.
Prelude and Fugue . . . Miss Agnes Rindge [3] 1935.
An Old Song . . . Carrie Stettheimer [1] 1935.
Ettie Stettheimer [5] 1935.
A Day Dream . . . Herbert Whiting 1935.
Maurice Bavoux; Young and Alone [6] 1938.
Portrait of Claude Biais 1938.
A French Boy of Ten: Louis Lange [5] 1938.
Tango Lullaby . . . Mlle Flavie Alvarez de Toledo [1] 1940.
Wedding Music (organ) 1940, revised 1978.
With Trumpet and Horn. . . . Louise Ardant 1940.
Poltergeist . . . Hans Arp [4] 1940.
Stretching . . . Jamie Campbell [6] 1940.
Cantabile . . . Nicolas de Chatelain [3] 1940.
Duet . . . Clarita, Comtesse de Forceville [6] 1940.
In a Bird Cage . . . Lise Deharme [2] 1940.
Sonata No 4: Guggenheim jeune 1940.
Barcarolle . . . Georges Hugnet [1] 1940.
Aria . . . Germaine Hugnet [2] 1940.
Invention: Theodore Johnson Busy and Resting [6] 1940.
Fanfare for France . . . Max Kahn [2] 1940.
Five Finger Exercise . . . Leon Kochnitzky [2] 1940.
Awake or Asleep . . . Pierre Mabille [5] 1940.
The Bard . . . Sherry Mangan [3] 1940.
Canons with Cadenza . . . Andre Ostier [3] 1940.
Bugles and Birds . . . Pablo Picasso [1] 1940.
Dora Maar, or the Presence of Pablo Picasso [1] 1940.
Lullaby Which Is Also a Spinning Song . . . Howard Putzel [4] 1940.
The Dream World of Peter Rose-Pulham [3] 1940.
Fugue . . . Alexander Smallens [1] 1940.
Swiss Waltz . . . Sophie Tauber-Arp [4] 1940.
Eccentric Dance . . . Madame Kristians Tonny 1940.
Pastoral . . . Tristan Tzara [5] 1940.
Toccata . . . Mary Widney [3] 1940.
Insistences . . . Louise Crane [4] 1941.
With Fife and Drums . . . Mina Curtiss [1] 1941.
Percussion Piece . . . Jessie K. Lasell 1941.
Parades . . . Florine Stettheimer [6] 1941.
James Patrick Cannon, Professional Revolutionary [6] 1942.
Aaron Copland, Persistently Pastoral [6] 1942.
Scottish Memories: Peter Monro Jack [6] 1942.
Prisoner of the Mind: Schuyler Watts [5] 1942.
Wedding Music . . . Jean Watts Schuyler [4] 1942.
Five Finger Exercise . . . Briggs Buchanan 1943.
Ten Etudes ("Repeating Tremolo/Fanfare", "Tenor Lead/Madrigal", "Three Fingered Fifths/Canon", "Fingered Glissando/Aeolian Harp", "Double Glissando/Waltz", "For the Weaker Fingers/Music Box Lullaby", "Oscillating Arm/Spinning Song", "Five Finger Exercise . . . Briggs Buchanan", "Nine Parallel Chords/Tango", "Ragtime Bass") 1943–4.
Solitude . . . Lou Harrison [1] 1945.
Chromatic Double Harmonies . . . Sylvia Marlowe 1951.
Nine Etudes ("With Trumpet and Horn . . . Louise Ardant",

"Pivoting on the Thumb", "Alternating Octaves", "Double Sevenths", "The Harp", "Chromatic Major Seconds/The Wind", "Chromatic Double Harmonies . . . Sylvia Marlowe", "Broken Arpeggios/The Waltzing Waters", "Guitar and Mandolin") 1951.
For a Happy Occasion / Happy Birthday Mrs Zimbalist 1951.
Homage to Marya Freund and to the Harp [6] 1956.
A Study in Stacked-up Thirds [5] 1958; revised as *For Eugene Ormandy's Birthday*, 1969.
Pange lingua (organ) 1962.
Edges . . . Robert Indiana 1966.
Man of Iron . . . Willy Eisenhart 1972.
Franco Assetto: Drawing VT [7] 1981.
Gerald Busby: Giving Full Attention [7] 1981.
Sam Byers: With Joy [7] 1981.
Christopher Cox: Singing a Song [7] 1981.
Noah Creshevsky: Loyal, Steady and Persistent [7] 1981.
Barbara Epstein: Untiring [7] 1981.
Norma Flender: Waltzing [7] 1981.
Richard Flender: Solid Not Stolid [7] 1981.
Dead Pan: Mrs Betty Freeman [7] 1981.
Morris Golde: Showing Delight [7] 1981.
Buffie Johnson: Drawing VT in Charcoal [7] 1981.
Bill Katz: Wide Awake [7] 1981.
Round and Round: Dominique Nabokov [7] 1981.
Craig Rutenberg: Swinging [7] 1981.
Anne-Marie Soullière: Something of a Beauty [7] 1981.
Karen Brown Waltuck: Intensely Two [7] 1981.
Scott Wheeler: Free-Wheeling [7] 1981.
John Wright: Drawing [7] 1981.
Theme for an Improvisation by McNeil Robinson (organ) 1981.
Dennis Russell Davies: In a Hammock 1982.
Molly Davies: Terminations 1982.
David Dubal: In Flight 1982.
Dona Flor: Receiving 1982.
Rodney Lister: Music for a Merry-Go-Round 1982.
Dr Marcel Roche: Making a Decision 1982.
Paul Sanfacon: On the Ice [7] 1982.
Mark Beard: Never Alone 1983.
Power Boothe: With Pencil 1983.
Charles Fussell: In Meditation 1983.
Glynn Boothe Harte: Reaching 1983.
Bennett Lerner: Senza espressione 1983.
Peter McWilliams: Firmly Spontaneous 1983.
Malitte Matta: In the Executive Style 1983.
Phillip Ramey: Thinking Hard 1983.
Louis Rispoli: In a Boat 1983.
Vasilis Voglin: On the March 1983.
Brendan Lemon 1984.
John Houseman: No Changes 1984, revised 1985.
Lines: For and About Ron Henggeler 1984.
Boris Baranovic: Whirling 1984.
Tony Tommasini: A Study in Chords 1984.
Christopher Beach Alone 1985.
Danyal Lawson: Playing 1985.
Jane Bowles Early and as Remembered 1985.
Philip Claflin: Dans le Temps très noceur 1985.
Robin Holloway 1985.
A Suite of Voluntaries (organ) 1985.

Vocal / choral:

The Sunflower (voice, piano; Blake) 1920.
De profundis (unaccompanied SATB chorus; Psalm 30) 1920, revised 1951.
Vernal Equinox (voice, piano; Lowell) 1920.
O My Deir Hart (unaccompanied SATB chorus) 1921, revised 1978.
Sanctus (unaccompanied TTBB chorus) 1921.
Tribulationes civitatum (unaccompanied SATB chorus) 1922; first performed Boston, 1922.
Three Antiphonal Psalms (unaccompanied SA or TB chorus; Psalms 123, 133 and 136) 1922–4; first performed New York City, 1923.
Agnus Dei (3 equal voices) 1924.
Three Sentences from The Song of Solomon (voice, piano) 1924.
Missa brevis (unaccompanied TTBB chorus) 1924.
Fete polonais (TTBB chorus, piano; after Chabrier, *Le Roi malgré lui*) 1924; first performed Boston, 1925.
Agnus dei (unaccompanied TTBB chorus) 1925.
Benedictus (unaccompanied TTBB chorus) 1926.
Susie Asado (voice, piano; Stein) 1926.
The Tiger (voice, piano; Blake) 1926.
Sanctus (unaccompanied TTBB and children's choruses) 1926.
Five Phrases from The Song of Solomon (soprano, percussion) 1926; first performed Paris, 30 May 1928.
Capital, Capitals (4 male voices, piano; Stein) 1927, revised 1968; first performed France, 30 May 1928.
Preciosilla (voice, piano; Stein) 1927.
La Valse grégorienne (voice, piano; Hugnet) 1927, revised 1971.
Le Berceau de Gertrude Stein, ou Le Mystère de la rue de Fleurus (voice, piano; Hugnet) 1928.
Commentaire sur St Jerome (voice, piano; de Sade) 1928.
Les Soirées bagnolaises (voice, piano; Hugnet) 1928.
Trois Poèmes de la Duchesse de Rohan (voice, piano) 1928.
Portrait of F.B. [Frances Blood] (voice, piano; Stein) 1929.
Air de Phèdre (voice, piano; Racine) 1930.
Deux Soeurs qui ne sont pas soeurs (voice, piano; Stein) 1930.
Oraison funèbre de Henriette-Marie de France, reine de Grande Bretagne (voice, piano; Bossuet) 1930, revised 1934.
Le Singe et le léopard (voice, piano; La Fontaine) 1930.
Stabat mater (soprano, string quartet or string orchestra; Jacob) 1931, arranged for voice, piano, 1960; revised 1981; first performed Paris, 15 June 1931.
La Belle en dormant (voice, piano; Hugnet) 1931.
Chamber Music (voice, piano; Kreymbourg) 1931.
Mass (2 solo voices, chorus) 1934; first performed New York City, 10 April 1935.
Seven Chorus from the Medea of Euripides (SSAA chorus, percussion) 1934; first performed New York City, 16 December 1942.
Pigeons on the Grass Alas (from *Four Saints in Three Acts*; arranged for baritone, piano or orchestra) 1934.
Go to Sleep, Alexander Smallens (unaccompanied voice) 1935.
My Shepherd Will Supply My Need (unaccompanied SATB chorus; Watts, Psalm 23) 1937, arranged for voice, piano, 1959.
Go to Sleep, Pare MacTaggett Lorentz (unaccompanied voice) 1937.
Scenes from the Holy Infancy According to St Matthew ("Joseph and the Angel", "The Wise Men", "The Flight into Egypt"; tenor, baritone, bass, SATB chorus) 1937; first performed New York City, 12 December 1937.
Dirge (voice, piano, Webster) 1939.
The Bugle Song (unison children's voices, piano; Tennyson) 1941.
Surrey Apple-Howler's Song (round for children's chorus) 1941.

Welcome to the New Year (2-part children's chorus or SATB chorus, piano; Farjeon) 1941.
Hymns from the Old south ("Morning Star", "Green Fields", "Death, 'Tis a Melancholyday"; unaccompanied SATB or SSA chorus) 1949.
Four Songs to Poems of Thomas Campion ("Follow Your Saint", "There Is a Garden in Her Face", "Rose Cheek'd Laura, Come", "Follow Thy Fair Sun"; mezzo-soprano, clarinet, viola, harp) 1951, arranged for mezzo-soprano and piano, and for SATB chorus and piano, 1955, first performed New York City, 11 February 1952.
Five Songs from William Blake ("The Divine Image", "Tyger Tyger!", "The Land of Dreams", "The Little Black Boy", "And Did Those Feet"; baritone, orchestra or piano) 1951, arranged for TTBB chorus, piano, 1955; first performed Louisville, Kentucky, 6 February 1952.
Kyrie Eleison (unaccompanied SATB chorus; later included in *Missa pro defunctis*) 1953.
Never Another / Praise Him That Makes Us Happy (unaccompanied SATB chorus; Van Doren) 1955.
At the Spring (voice, piano; Fisher) 1955.
The Bell Doth Toll (voice, piano; Heywood) 1955.
Consider, Lord (voice, piano; Donne) 1955.
The Holly and the Ivy (voice, piano) 1955; arranged for SATB chorus, piano, 1963.
If Thou a Reason Dost Desire to Know (voice, piano) 1955, 1958.
John Peel (voice, piano; Graves) 1955.
Look, How the Floor of Heav'n (voice, piano; Shakespeare) 1955.
Remember Adam's Fall (voice, piano) 1955.
Song for the Stable / It Seems That God Bestowed Somehow (unaccompanied SATB chorus; Hall) 1955.
Shakespeare Songs (voice, piano) 1956–7.
Tres estampas de Niñez (voice, piano; Rivas) 1957.
Crossing Brooklyn Ferry (SSATB chorus, piano or orchestra; Whitman) 1958, orchestrated 1961.
Collected Poems of Kenneth Koch (soprano, baritone, orchestra or piano) 1959.
Mostly About Love (Songs for Alice Estey) (voice, piano; Koch) 1959.
Missa pro defunctis (double chorus, orchestra; Requiem Mass) 1960.
Mass (voice or unison voices, piano) 1962, orchestrated 1969.
Dance in Praise (unaccompanied SATB chorus; *Gaudeamus igitur*, translated Symonds) 1962.
Five Auvergnat Folk Songs (SATB chorus, piano or orchestra; after Canteloube) 1962, 1964.
Praises and Prayers (voice, piano; St Francis, Crashaw, anon.) 1963; arranged SATB or SSA chorus, piano, 1963.
Two by Marianne Moore (voice, piano) 1963.
When I Survey the Bright Celestial Sphere (unison voices, organ or piano; Habbingdon) 1964.
The Feast of Love (baritone, orchestra; *Pervigilium veneris*) 1964; first performed Washington, D.C., 1 November 1964.
The Nativity as Sung by the Shepherds (alto, tenor, bass, SATB chorus, orchestra; Crashaw) 1966–7; first performed Chicago, 7 May 1967.
How Will Ye Have Your Partridge Today (round for 4 unaccompanied voices; Brown) 1967.
From Byron's Don Juan (tenor, orchestra) 1967; first performed New York City, 11 April 1968.
Hymn for Pratt Institute (unaccompanied SATB chorus; Fjelde) 1968.
Landing Variations (voice, piano; O'Hara) 1972.
Cantata on Poems of Edward Lear (soprano, 2 baritones, SATB chorus, piano; "The Owl and the Pussycat", "The Jumblies", "The Pelican Chorus", "Half an Alphabet", "The Akond of Swat") 1973, revised 1974; first performed Baltimore, Maryland, 18 November 1973.
The Courtship of the Yongly Bongly Bo (from *Cantata*; voice, piano; Lear) 1973–4.
The Peace Place (SATB chorus, piano; Larson) 1979, revised as *Fanfare for Peace* with brass 1983.
What Is It? (voice, piano or guitar; Campion) 1979.
Go to Sleep, Gabriel Liebowitz (unaccompanied voice) 1979.
The Cat (voice, piano; Larson) 1980.
A Prayer to Venus (SATB chorus, piano; Fletcher) 1981.
Cantantes eamus (TTBB chorus, piano, optional brass; Maro) 1982.
Southern Hymns ("How Bright Is the Day!", "Mississippi", "Death of General Washington", "Convention"; SATB chorus, piano) 1984.

Opera:

Four Saints in Three Acts (Gertrude Stein) 1927–8, orchestrated 1933; first performed Hartford, Connecticut, 8 February 1934. Recorded Nonesuch 5 79035 1.
The Mother of Us All (Stein) 1947; first performed New York City, 7 May 1947.
Lord Byron (Larson) 1961–8; first performed New York City, 20 April 1972.

Other:

Le Droit de Varech (incidental music to Hugnet) 1930.
A Bride for the Unicorn (incidental music to Johnston) 1934.
The Plow That Broke the Plains (film score; Lorentz) 1936; first performed New York City, 25 May 1936.
Hamlet (incidental music to Shakespeare) 1936.
Horse Eats Hat (orchestration of Paul Bowles's incidental music to Labiche) 1936.
Injunction Granted: A Living Newspaper (incidental music) 1936.
Macbeth (incidental music) 1936.
Filling Station (ballet by Christensen) 1937; first performed New York City, 18 February 1938; version with piano accompaniment first performed Hartford, Connecticut, 6 January 1938.
The River (film score; Lorentz) 1937; first performed New Orleans, 29 October 1937.
Antony and Cleopatra (incidental music to Shakespeare) 1937.
The Spanish Earth (film score collaboration with Marc Blitzstein using collage of Spanish folk melodies; Ivens) 1937.
Androcles and the Lion (incidental music to Shaw; piano score only) 1938.
The Trojan Women (incidental music to Euripides) 1940.
The Life of a Careful Man (incidental music) 1941.
Oedipus Tyrannos (incidental music to Sophocles) 1941.
Tuesday in November (film score incorporating *Fugue and Chorale on Yankee Doodle, Pastorale* and *Walking Song*; Houseman) 1945.
Louisiana Story (film score; Flaherty) 1948; first performed Edinburgh, Scotland, 22 August 1948.
The Harvest According (ballet by De Mille; arranged from *Symphony on a Hymn Tune, Cello Concerto* and *Suite: Mother of Us All*) 1952; first performed New York City, 1 October 1952.
The Grass Harp (incidental music to Capote) 1952.
King Lear (incidental music to Shakespeare) 1952.

Bayou (choreographed from *Acadian Songs and Dances*) 1952.
Measure for Measure (incidental music to Shakespeare) 1956.
King John (incidental music to Shakespeare) 1956.
The Goddess (film score; Chayevsky) 1957; first performed Brussels, June 1958.
The Merchant of Venice (incidental music to Shakespeare) 1957.
Much Ado About Nothing (incidental music to Shakespeare) 1957.
Othello (incidental music to Shakespeare) 1957.
Power Among Men (film score; Dickinson and Sheers) 1958; first performed New York City, 5 March 1959.
Bertha (incidental music to Koch) 1959.
Journey to America (film score; Houseman) 1964; first performed New York City, July 1964.
Parson Weems and the Cherry Tree (ballet) 1975; first performed Amherst, Massachusetts, 1 November 1975.
Hurrah! (choreographed from *Symphony No 2* by Hawkins) 1975.

PUBLICATIONS

By Thomson: *The State of Music*, New York, 1939, revised 1961; *the Musical Scene* [writings from *New York Herald Tribune*], 1945; *The Art of Judging* [writings from *New York Herald Tribune*], 1948; *Portraits for Piano Solo: Album 1*, New York City, 1948 [1]; *Portraits for Piano Solo: Album 2*, New York City, 1949 [2]; *Portraits for Piano Solo: Album 3*, New York City, 1950 [3]; *Music Right and Left* [writings from *New York Herald Tribune*], 1951; *Portraits for Piano Solo: Album 4*, New York City, 1953 [4]; *Virgil Thomson*, New York, 1966; *Music Reviewed, 1940–54* [reviews and articles from *New York Herald Tribune*], New York City, 1967; *American Music Since 1910*, New York, 1971; *Nine Portraits for piano Solo,* New York City, 1974; *A Virgil Thomson Reader*, New York, 1981; *Thirteen Portraits for Piano Solo*, New York City, 1981; *Nineteen Portraits for Piano Solo,* New York City, 1983 .

On Thomson: Aaron Copland, "Our Younger Generation: Ten Years Later", in *Modern Music*, 13(4), 1936; S. Barlow, "American Composers XVII: VT", in *Modern Music*, 18, 1940–1; C. Smith, "Gertrude S., Virgil T., and Susan B." in *Theatre Arts*, 31(7), 1947; Peggy Glanville-Hicks, "VT", in *Musical Quarterly*, 35, 1949; B.H. Hagin, "VT as Critic", in *The Nation*, 173, 22 September 1951; M.G. Field, "VT and the Maturity of American Music", in *The Chesterian*, 28, 1953–4; K. Hoover and John Cage, *VT: His Life and Music*, New York City, 1959; R. Jackson, "The Operas of Gertrude Stein and VT", dissertation, Tulane University, New Orleans, 1962; M. Steinberg, "Musician as Writer", in *Commentary*, 43(5), 1967; "A Tribute to VT on His 81st Birthday", in *Parnassus: Poetry in Review*, 5(2), 1977; K.M. Ward, "An Analysis of the Relationship Between Text and Musical Shape and an Investigation of the Relationship Between Text and Surface Rhythmic Detail in *Four Saints in Three Acts* by VT", dissertation, University of Texas, Austin, 1978; H. Gleason and W. Becker, "VT", in *Twentieth-Century American Composers*, Bloomington, Indiana, 2nd edition, 1981; M. Meckna, "The Rise of the American Composer-Critic: Aaron Copland, Roger Sessions, VT, and Elliot Carter in the Periodical *Modern Music*, 1924–46", dissertation, University of California, Santa Barbara, 1984; A.C. Tommasini, *The Musical Portraits of VT*, New York City, 1985.

* * *

Though normally of marked simplicity, Virgil Thomson's music is always recognisable as his, and this is because of the specific nature of that simplicity and the ways in which it is arrived at. Thomson's harmony in particular sounds as if it is straight out of hymn books and popular songs, often amounting to a roving non-functional diatonicism. As such it seems distinctly odd in relation to what was going on elsewhere in music during the composer's lifetime.

Thomson received an elaborate education, first at Harvard and then as one of Nadia Boulanger's earliest American pupils. In Paris he met Cocteau, Les Six and most importantly Satie, to some of whose work—and some of Gertrude Stein's—Thomson had been introduced by one of his Harvard teachers. The survival of a childlike state of consciousness is suggested by dislocations of grammar and musical logic, and these work in part, as with Satie, by juxtaposing highly disparate elements such as academic counterpoint and café music, plainsong and parlour ballads. Indeed Thomson, notwithstanding his long residence in Paris, remained fully in touch with the American musical past—on its vernacular rather than its cultivated side—and he appeared often to aim at folklike directness rather than at art. Hence his quotations are always more literal than those found in, for example, Ives: for the older man the familiar religious and secular melodies of Americana are symbolic and undergo much distortion, whereas for Thomson they are part of the trivia of everyday life.

His *Stabat mater* for soprano and string quartet has quasi-archaic counterpoint reminiscent of Satie, and the early unaccompanied choral pieces relate to the music of that composer's Rosicrucian period. Also strongly suggestive of Satie's influence are the sentimental tangos and synthetic waltzes. The waltz genre recurs frequently in Thomson's music, perhaps most surprisingly in the double glissando piece of his *Ten Etudes* for piano, and tangos are another favourite. There is even a waltz in *String Quartet No 2*, which otherwise, like *String Quartet No 1*, could in manner almost be the work of a minor 18th-century composer. Far less innocent is *Sonata da chiesa*, where, although he described it as a graduation piece to mark the conclusion of his studies with Boulanger, the desire to defy convention is just a little too evident. This is for trumpet, trombone, clarinet, french horn and viola, and again there is a sort of archaicism in the opening chorale's organum-like consecutive fifths and ninths. The following tango is both nostalgic and modern with its alternation between 4/4 and 5/4, and the finale is a fugue worked with ironically academic strictness. Often the instruments are written for in exaggerated and deliberately unsuitable ways, and the piece demonstrates Thomson's willingness to use almost any kind of musical material. It is also very American.

So too are his amusing *Variations on Sunday School Tunes* for organ and other such pieces, but perhaps the main point of this casual, improvisatory, artless music is that it is so well-adapted to the setting of specifically American speech. Thomson's first Gertrude Stein setting was of *Susie Asado*, followed by *Capital, Capitals*, which might be called a dialogue between four cities except that the text contains no questions, no answers. With its incessant C major clichés—process without progress—the music is simplified almost to the point of self-effacement yet embodies a strikingly close equivalent to Stein's literary techniques with their repetition and irrationality.

The first of two major collaborations, *Four Saints in Three Acts* is both an opera and a choreographic spectacle, and has more than three acts, many more than four saints, although the chief ones are St Teresa of Avila and St Ignatius Loyola.

Rooted in American vernacular music, the work completely bypasses all concepts of 19th-century dramaturgy and grandiose symphonic gestures that had hitherto afflicted the operatic essays of American composers. At the same time it is unique and unrepeatable, elusive yet of great charm. It is impossible to interpret but cannot be dismissed as meaningless: here the irrational and matter-of-fact are one. The initial 19-piece orchestration is dominated by an accordion and this gives reedy emphasis to the simplicity of music which, for all its Parisian chic, is, again, quintessentially American. In fact it pointed to the "new simplicity" of American serious music in the 1930s as typified by Copland's ballets and other works.

Palpably the work of the same composer and librettist, *The Mother of Us All*, Stein's last completed text, is only in relatively superficial ways different from *Four Saints in Three Acts*, yet it never produces the same almost magical effect. Again there is no real sequence of events on stage and no long-term continuity to music which sounds extremely familiar even though it includes only one quotation ("London Bridge Is Falling Down") as against the earlier work's numerous quotations. The opera centres on Susan B. Anthony, a pioneer feminist, and other historical American personages are brought in too, sometimes anachronistically. In the background is 19th-century Americana, its banalities accepted, once more, for their own sake. A different expression of innocence, without a hint of parody, is found in Thomson's remarkable William Blake settings, but his final opera, *Lord Byron*, takes quite another line. This is his most ambitious piece and among his least-known, the result of seven years work with his librettist Jack Larson. It has lyrical richness, emotional depth and seriousness which separate it from the rest of his vast output and as such is hard to account for.

Thomson's Requiem Mass for double chorus and orchestra, designed for liturgical use, might seem to be of a similar order but in the event has a curiously ambiguous impact. This is because it is dominated by the very stable major third employed without any evident feeling of tonal stability or direction, the interval's constant presence resulting in whole-tone harmonies and frequent modulations. The composer said that this arose from his "wish to express the idea, constantly present in the text of, 'eternal light'".

There is something disconcerting again in a work like the homespun *Cello Concerto*, whose finale, titled "Children's Games", quotes both a Sunday school hymn and Beethoven's *Piano Sonata Op 10 No 2*. Thomson's willingness to adopt any style comes into play in his more than 100 "portraits" of individuals, which take on a great diversity of manners and presumably were prompted by Stein's exploitation of the same idea in literature. He also composed what remains some of the finest of all film music, avoiding the Hollywood dream factory and writing scores for documentaries such as Pare Lorentz's *The Plow That Broke the Plains* and *The River* and Robert Flaharty's *Louisiana Story*. These make a telling use of traditional melodies of several kinds, underlining and interpreting the stories with rare sensitivity. Thomson's longstanding affinity with the folksy atmosphere of such films is indicated by the score for *The River* including much of his earlier *Symphony on a Hymn Tune*, not greatly altered.

Besides a huge quantity of music in virtually all genres, Thomson wrote a great deal of compulsively readable criticism, was a fair pianist, a good conductor and an entertaining lecturer.

—Max Harrison

TIPPETT, (Sir) Michael (Kemp). British. Born in London, 2 January 1905. Educated at Brookfield Preparatory School, Dorset; Fettes College, Edinburgh; Stamford Grammar School, Lincolnshire; Royal College of Music, London (under R.O. Morris, 1930), 1923–8, 1930, B.Mus.; studied under Charles Wood, C.H. Kitson, Malcolm Sargent and Adrian Boult; director of madrigal choir, later Oxted and Limpsfield Players, Oxted, Surrey, from 1924; French teacher, Hazelwood School, Limpsfield, Surrey, 1929–32; member of various workers' music groups, from 1932; organizer/director, South London Orchestra, Morley College, from 1933; joined Communist Party, 1935; adult education work for London County Council; director, choirs of Royal Arsenal Co-Operative Society education departments, 1937; director, Morley College, 1940–51; joined Peace Pledge Union, 1940; imprisoned for two months from 21 June, 1943 for refusing non-combatant military service; moved to Tidebrook Manor, Sussex, 1951; composer in residence, Aspen Festival, Colorado, 1965; further visits to United States, 1968, 1969, 1974; artistic director, Bath Festival, 1969–74; president, Kent Opera, since 1979. Recipient: Cobbett Medal, 1948; Honorary Member, Royal Academy of Music, 1959; C.B.E., (Commander, Order of the British Empire), 1959; Fellow, Royal College of Music, 1961; Knight of the British Empire, 1966; honorary member, American Academy of Arts and Letters, 1973; extraordinary member, Akademie der Kunste, Berlin, 1976; gold medal, Royal Philharmonic Society, 1976; foreign honorary member, American Academy of Arts and Sciences, 1978; Companion of Honour, 1979; honorary liveryman, Worshipful Company of Musicians, 1982; Incorporated Society of Musicians Distinguished Musician Award, 1982; honorary member, Guildhall School of Music and Drama, 1982; Order of Merit, 1983; president, London College of Music, 1983; honorary fellow, Royal Northern College of Music, 1984; Prix de Composition, Fondation Prince Pierre de Monaco, 1984; Commandeur de l'Ordre des Arts et des Lettres, France, 1988. Honorary degrees: Cambridge, Mus.D., 1964; Trinity College, Dublin, Mus.D., 1964; University of Leeds, D.Mus., 1965; University of York, D.Univ., 1966; University of Oxford, D.Mus., 1967; University of Leicester, D.Mus., 1968; University of Wales, D.Mus., 1968; University of Bristol, D.Mus., 1970; University of Bath, D.Litt., 1972; University of Warwick, D.Litt., 1974; University of London, D.Mus., 1975; University of Sheffield, D.Mus., 1976; University of Birmingham, D.Mus., 1976; University of Lancaster, D.Mus., 1977; University of Liverpool, D.Mus., 1981; Royal College of Music, D.Mus., 1982; University of Melbourne, D.Mus., 1984; University of Keele, D.Mus., 1986; University of Aberdeen, D.Mus., 1987; University of Hartford, D.Mus., 1989; University of Western Australia, D.Mus., 1990. Mailing address: c/o Schott & Co, 48 Great Marlborough Street, London W1V 2BN, England.

Publisher: Schott & Co.

Symphonies/orchestral:

Symphony in B♭ 1933, revised 1934; first performed London, 1933.

Concerto for Double String Orchestra 1938–9; first performed London, 21 April 1940. Recorded Virgin VC 7 90701 2; HMV C7926/8; CFP 414489-1; Argo ZRG 680; HMV ALP 1961.

Fantasia on a Theme by Handel 1939–41; first performed London, 7 March 1942.

Symphony No 1 1944–5; first performed Liverpool, 10

November 1945. Recorded Philips 9500 107; Philips 414 091-1.

Little Music (string orchestra) 1946; first performed London, 9 November 1946. Recorded CBC SM 124; Argo ZRG 680; Decca D26D4; Chandos ABRD 1208.

Suite for the Birthday of Prince Charles 1948; broadcast London, 15 November 1948. Recorded Philips 9500 107; Decca SXDL 7546.

Fantasia Concertante on a Theme of Corelli 1953; first performed Edinburgh, 29 August 1953. Recorded HMV ASD 637; Argo ZRG 680; ASV CD DCA518.

Ritual Dances from "The Midsummer Marriage" 1953; first performed Basle, February 1953. Recorded Nimbus Ni 5217; Pye CCL 30114/5; Philips 6580 093; EMI EL 27 0273-1.

Divertimento on "Sellinger's Round" 1953–4; first performed Zurich, 5 November 1954. Recorded Decca LXT 2798.

Concerto for Piano and Orchestra 1953–5; first performed Birmingham, 30 October 1956. Recorded HMV ASD 621; EMI EX 29 0228-3.

Symphony No 2 1956–7; first performed London, 5 February 1958. Recorded Argo RG 535; Philips 414 091-1.

Concerto for Orchestra 1962–3; first performed Edinburgh, 28 August 1963. Recorded Philips SAL 3947; Philips 420 781-2.

Braint 1966; first performed Swansea, 11 January 1967.

Symphony No 3 1970–2; first performed London, 22 June 1972. Recorded Philips 6500 662; Philips 414 091-1.

Symphony No 4 1976–7; first performed Chicago, 6 October 1977. Recorded Decca 425 646 2; Philips 414 091 1.

Triple Concerto (violin, viola, cello, orchestra) 1978–9; first performed London, 22 August 1980. Recorded Philips 6514 209.

Water Out of Sunlight (string orchestra arrangement by Meirion Bowen of *String Quartet No 4*) 1988; first performed London, 15 June 1988.

Chamber/instrumental:

Jockey to the Fair (piano solo) 1929–30; first performed Oxted, Surrey, 5 April 1930.

String Trio in B♭ 1932; first performed London, 13 January 1965.

String Quartet No 1 1934–5; first performed London, 9 December 1935. Recorded Decca 425 645 2; Waverley LLP 1027; EMI EX 29 0228-3; Pye GSGC 14079; L'Oiseau Lyre DSLO 10.

Sonata for Piano No 1 1936–8, revised 1942, 1954; first performed London, 11 November 1938. Recorded Lyrita RCS 5; Musical Heritage Society 7022; HMV ASD 2322; EMI EX 0228-3; CRD1130/1; Philips 6500 534.

String Quartet No 2 1941–2; first performed London, 27 March 1943. Recorded Decca 425 645 2; HMV ALP 1302; Pye GSGC 14130; L'Oiseau Lyre DSLO 10.

Fanfare No 1 (4 horns, 3 trumpets, 3 trombones) 1943; first performed Northampton, 21 September 1943. Recorded Argo ZRG 870; RCA RL 25081.

String Quartet No 3 1945–6; first performed London, 27 March 1946. Recorded Pye GSGC 14079; Factory FACD 246; Decca 425 645 2; L'Oiseau Lyre DSLO 10.

Preludio al Vespro di Monteverdi (organ) 1946; first performed London, 5 July 1946. Recorded Argo RG 528; Argo 414 647-1; Exon EAS 18.

Fanfare No 2 (4 trumpets) 1953; first performed St Ives, Cornwall, 6 June 1953.

Fanfare No 3 (3 trumpets) 1953; first performed St Ives, Cornwall, 6 June 1953.

Four Inventions (descant and treble recorders) 1954; first performed London, 1 August 1954.

Sonata (4 horns) 1955; first performed London, 20 December 1955. Recorded Argo RG 535.

Praeludium (brass, bells, percussion) 1962; first performed London, 14 November 1962.

Sonata for Piano No 2 1962; first performed Edinburgh, 3 September 1962. Recorded HMV ALP 2073; Pye GSGC 14085; Philips 6500 534; CRD 1130/1.

In memoriam magistri (flute, clarinet, string quartet) 1971; first performed London, 17 June 1972.

Sonata for Piano No 3 1972–3; first performed Bath, 26 May 1973. Recorded Philips 6500 534; Musicon TAM 0639; CRD 1130/1.

String Quartet No 4 1977–8; first performed Bath, 20 May 1979. Recorded ASV CD DCA 608.

Wolf Trap Fanfare (3 trumpets, 2 trombones, tuba) 1980; first performed Vienna, Virginia, 29 June 1980.

The Blue Guitar (solo guitar) 1982–3; first performed Pasadena, California, 9 November 1983. Recorded Pearl SHE CD 9609; Chandos CHAN 8784.

Festal Brass with Blues (brass band) 1983; first performed Hong Kong, 6 February 1984. Recorded CRDC 4144; CRD 3444.

Sonata for Piano No 4 1984; first performed Los Angeles, 14 January 1985. Recorded CRD 1130/1.

Vocal/choral:

A Child of Our Time (soprano, alto, tenor, bass, SATB chorus, orchestra) 1939–41; first performed London, 19 March 1944. Recorded Pye CCL 30114/5; Philips 6500 985; RPO/ASV 8005; Decca 425 158 2; RPO CDRPO 8005; excerpts on L'Oiseau Lyre DSLO 25, etc.

The Source (SATB chorus) 1942; first performed London, 17 July 1943. Recorded L'Oiseau Lyre DSLO 25.

The Windhover (SATB chorus; Hopkins) 1942; first performed London, 17 July 1943. Recorded DSLO 25.

Boyhood's End (tenor, piano; Hudson) 1943; first performed London, 5 June 1943. Recorded Argo RG 15; L'Oiseau Lyre DSLO 14.

Plebs angelica (double chorus) 1943–4; first performed Canterbury, Kent, 16 September 1944. Recorded Grosvenor GRS 1030; HMV ESD 7172; L'Oiseau Lyre DSLO 25.

The Weeping Babe (soprano, SATB chorus; Sitwell) 1944; first performed London, 24 December 1944. Recorded L'Oiseau Lyre DSLO 25.

The Heart's Assurance (song cycle for high voice, piano; Keyes, Lewis) 1950; first performed London, 7 May 1951. Recorded Argo DA 34; L'Oiseau Lyre DSLO 14.

Dance, Clarion Air (unaccompanied SSATB chorus) 1952; first performed London, 1 June 1953. Recorded Columbia 33CX 1063; RCA GL 25062; L'Oiseau Lyre DSLO 25.

Bonny at Morn (unison voices, 3 recorders) 1956; first performed Trogen, Switzerland, April 1956. Recorded L'Oiseau Lyre DSLO 25.

Four Songs from the British Isles (SATB chorus) 1956; first performed Royaumont, Seine-et-Oise, France, 6 July 1958. Recorded Argo ZRG 5496.

Crown of the Year (SSA chorus, recorders, oboe, clarinet, trumpet, percussion, piano, string quartet; Fry) 1958; first performed Bristol, 25 July, 1958.

Lullaby (alto solo, SSTTB chorus; Yeats) 1959; first performed London, 31 January 1960. Recorded L'Oiseau Lyre DSLO 25.

Music (voices, strings, piano) 1960; first performed Tunbridge Wells, Kent, 26 April 1960. Recorded L'Oiseau Lyre DSLO 25.

Words for Music Perhaps (speaker(s), bass clarinet, trumpet, gong, xylophone, violin, cello, piano) 1960; first performed London, 8 June 1960.
Magnificat and Nunc Dimittis (SATB chorus, organ) 1961; first performed Cambridge, 13 March 1962. Recorded Argo ZRG 5340; L'Oiseau Lyre DSLO 25.
Songs for Achilles (tenor, guitar) 1961; first performed Aldeburgh, Suffolk, 7 July 1961. Recorded DSLO 14.
Songs for Ariel (medium voice and piano or harpsichord; also ensemble arrangement; Shakespeare) 1962, 1964; first performed London, 21 September 1963. Recorded Argo ZRG 5349; L'Oiseau Lyre DSLO 14; Unicorn RHS 316.
The Vision of St Augustine (baritone, SATB chorus, orchestra) 1963–5; first performed London, 19 January 1966. Recorded RCA SER 5620; RL 89498.
The Shires Suite (SATB chorus, orchestra) 1965–70; first performed Cheltenham, Gloucestershire, 8 July 1970. Recorded Argo ZRG 685.
Songs for Dov (tenor, orchestra) 1969–70; first performed Cardiff, 12 October 1970. Recorded Argo ZRG 703.
The Mask of Time (soprano, mezzo-soprano, tenor, bass/baritone, chorus, orchestra) 1980–2; first performed Boston, 5 April 1984. Recorded EMI EX 27 0567-3; EMI CDS 7 47705 8.

Opera:

The Midsummer Marriage 1946–52; first performed London, 27 January 1955. Recorded Philips 6500 125/127.
King Priam 1958–61; first performed Coventry, Warwickshire, 29 May 1962. Recorded Decca D246D3; excerpts Decca SET 392–3; London OSA 1276.
The Knot Garden 1966–9; first performed London, 2 December 1970. Recorded Philips 6500 552/553.
The Ice Break 1973–6; first performed London, 7 July 1977.
New Year 1988; first performed Houston, Texas, October 1989.

Other:

The Village Opera (realisation of 1729 work by Charles Johnson) 1927–8; first performed Oxted, Surrey, 19 April 1928.
Don Juan (incidental music to play by Flecker) 1930; first performed Oxted, Surrey, February 1930.
Robin Hood (folk song opera) 1934.
Robert of Sicily (children's opera) 1938.
Voice and Keyboard: Original Compositions for Voice and Figured Bass (various composers, mainly Purcell) 1947–66.
Incidental Music for Shakespeare's The Tempest (flute/piccolo, clarinet, bass clarinet, horn, trumpet, trombone, 2 percussionists, harp, harpsichord, 4 singers) 1962; first performed London, 29 May 1962.

Henry Purcell: *Come Ye Sons of Art* (SAAB, SATB chorus, orchestra; edition) 1951.
Henry Purcell: *The Golden Sonata* (2 violins, basso continuo; edition) 1953.
Henry Purcell: *Ode for St Cecilia's Day (1692)* (SAATBB, SATB chorus, orchestra; edition) 1955.

PUBLICATIONS

By Tippett: "*A Child of Our Time*", in *The Listener*, 33, 18 January 1945; *Moving into Aquarius* (broadcasts and essays), London, 1959, expanded edition, St Albans, Hertfordshire, 1974; "The Gulf in Our Music", in *Observer*, 14 May 1961, translated as "Die Spaltung unserer Musik", in *Neue Zeitschrift für Musik*, 123, February 1962; "*King Priam*: Some Questions Answered", in *Opera*, 13, May 1962; "An Englishman Looks at Opera", in *Opera News*, 29, 2 January 1965; "*The Knot Garden*", in *About the House*, 3(7), 1970; *Music of the Angels: Essays and Sketchbooks of Michael Tippett*, selected and edited by Meirion Bowen, London, 1980; "*The Mask of Time*", *Music and Musicians*, 35, June 1987.

On Tippett: Murray Schafer, "MT", in *British Composers in Interview*, London, 1963; *MT: A Symposium on His 60th Birthday*, edited by Ian Kemp, London, 1965; Richard Elfyn Jones, "The Operas of MT", dissertation, University of Wales, Cardiff, 1976; Richard Earl Rodda, "The Symphonies of MT", dissertation, Case Western Reserve University, Cleveland, Ohio, 1979; Eric Walter White, *T and His Operas*, London, 1979; David Matthews, *MT: An Introductory Study*, London, 1980; Meirion Bowen, *MT*, London, 1982; Ian Kemp, *T: The Composer and His Music*, London, 1984; *MT: A Celebration*, edited by Geraint Lewis, Tunbridge Wells, Kent, 1985.

Michael Tippett comments:

I have been writing music for 60 years. During those years there have been huge and world-shattering events in which I have been inevitably caught up. Whether society has felt musical valuable or needful I have gone on writing because I must. And I know that my true function within a society which embraces all of us is to continue an age-old tradition, fundamental to our civilization, which goes back into prehistory and will go forward into the unknown future. This tradition is to create images from the depths of the imagination and to give them form whether visual, intellectual or musical. For it is only through images that the inner world communicates at all. Images of the past, shapes of the future. Images of vigour for a decadent period, images of calm for one too violent. Images of reconciliation for worlds torn by division. And in an age of mediocrity and shattered dreams, images of abounding, generous, exuberant beauty.

* * *

Michael Tippett belongs to a generation of British composers who reached maturity in the 1930s. Like others whose sensibilities were at least as strongly social as musical—Alan Bush and Imogen Holst, to name but two—he felt a supreme necessity, in that politically momentous decade, to define his creativity in terms of its social and moral functions. Matters of style and technique were subordinate, in contrast to the work of his precocious junior contemporary, Benjamin Britten.

At the same time, Tippett's career as a composer suffered a false start that was only rectified through a seminal period of study with the theorist R.O. Morris. Under Morris, Tippett developed a way of working that was founded on a close technical study of English 16th-century music, Bach and Beethoven. His characteristic ability to manipulate elements of these and other styles for expressive purposes comes from this training. But in keeping with his humanist convictions, Tippett's expression is one of ideas and purposes rather than Romantic emotions, even if the sheer power of those visions he has sought to encompass in music has frequently led to a ruggedness that provokes an emotional response in the listener.

Tippett's earliest well-known work, the *Concerto for Double String Orchestra*, gives evidence of his willingness to stretch technical ingenuity and stylistic allusion beyond conventional notions of discipline. The obsessive counterpoint of the outer movements has a transcendental vigorous quality that one associates with the very act of liberation, in keeping with his teacher's credo that the composer should first learn rules in order to break them. While the style of this work is reminiscent of the English pastoralism of other Morris pupils such as Gerald Finzi, Tippett's individuality was securely and immediately won with the oratorio *A Child of Our Time*, in which black American music was added to his range of stylistic resources. The result was a work in which integration was shunned: its power comes from a jarring conjunction of ideas which demand the listener's active participation if they are to be resolved. The pieces which followed in the 1940s suggested that, for the present, Tippett needed the stimulus of a humanitarian drama to sustain this approach, which was only later to find its place in his instrumental compositions.

During his middle years, while British critics debated the comparative merits of Vaughan Williams and Britten, Tippett was not a prominent figure. Those who saw Britten's technical fluency as evidence of a mundane professionalism in the age of the gentleman amateur were set against those who found Vaughan William's sensibilities parochial and his technique slipshod. When, during the 1960s, Tippett began to be bracketed with Britten as a great figure, the lack of integration in his technique allowed this old debate to run again. But within a few years it was accepted that Tippett's willingness to place striking images in conflict, and to write torrents of notes which jostled against each other in apparent violation of technical propriety, came not from an inability to smooth the rough edges of his compositions but from a desire to identify his music with ideas which could not be sanitised without losing their urgent meaning.

Tippett's new reputation was founded on his opera *The Midsummer Marriage*, which Norman Del Mar revived for the BBC in 1963. This was the culminating work of the composer's early career; its liberating quality is firmly rooted in the pastoralism that attracted its audience. But the music transcends this, in keeping with the self-knowledge attained by the stage protagonists, Jenifer and Mark, so that the "marriage" of drama and music is exquisitely achieved. By the time the opera returned triumphantly to Covent Garden in 1968 under Colin Davis—a conductor who did much to habilitate Tippett's music in Britain and the United States—the composer's more recent music was also reaching a wide audience which has remained with him to the present day.

In all his philosophical and dramatic works, from *A Child of Our Time* through *The Vision of St Augustine* to *New Year*, Tippett has pursued his arguments through the interactions of archetypal characters and ideas, in line with his Jungian belief in the power of such images to tap the depths of the collective unconscious. If this, and his willingness to evoke the musical vernacular of jazz and blues, have sometimes led him near to cliché, these pillars of familiarity have also served to support his listeners in their discovery of music in which the bonds of harmony and tonality have been continually loosened. Close study reveals nevertheless that in works such as the Third Symphony and the Fourth Piano Sonata there is a fine technical control behind the sustained equivocation which simultaneously projects and undermines the musical bedrock of familiar forms, styles and textures. The vigour which Tippett has retained in old age despite failing eyesight suggests that he has more to give; one hopes the message of his idealism will not be lost amidst the pluralistic indifference that today threatens his professed reasons for composing.

—Anthony Pople

TISHCHENKO, Boris (Ivanovich). Russian. Born in Leningrad, 23 March 1939. Educated at Musical College, Leningrad, 1954–7; Leningrad Conservatoire (composition and piano under Salmanov, Voloshinov and Evlakhov), 1957–63, postgraduate study (under Dmitri Shostakovich), 1962–5. Married Irina Donskaya, 26 February 1977; 3 sons. Member of Composers Union, Leningrad, since 1962; teacher of music, 1965–72, lecturer, 1972–84, and professor, since 1984, Leningrad Conservatoire; performing pianist. Recipient: 1st prize, International Competition for Young Composers, Prague, 1966; Glinka State Award, Russian Republic, 1978; People's Artist, 1987. Mailing address: Rimsky Korsakoff Avenue dom 10, kv. 79, St Petersburg, U.S.S.R.

Publisher: Sovetskii kompozitor, Moscow.

Symphonies/orchestral:

Concerto for Violin and Orchestra No 1 Op 9/29 1958. Recorded Melodiya C 10 08788.
Symphony No 1 Op 20 1961.
Concerto for Piano and Orchestra Op 21 1962. Recorded Melodiya CM 02069.
Concerto for Cello No 1 Op 23 (solo cello, 17 winds, percussion, harmonium) 1963; orchestrated by Shostakovich, 1969. Recorded Melodiya C 10 22267 009.
Octaves 1963.
Symphony No 2 Op 28 (with chorus, Tsvetayeva) 1964.
Palekh Op 28 1965.
Symphony No 3 Op 36 (chamber orchestra) 1966. Recorded Melodiya CM 01973 4.
The Death of Pushkin Op 38 1967.
Concerto No 2 for Cello Op 44/1 (solo cello, 48 cellos, 12 double basses, percussion) 1969, version Op 44/2 for string orchestra, percussion, 1979.
Simfonia robusta Op 46 1970.
Concerto for Flute, Piano, and String Orchestra Op 54 1972. Recorded Melodiya C 10 08193 4.
Symphony No 4 Op 61 (with narrator; Turgenev) 1974.
Suite: A Lark Op 62 (suite after incidental music to Anouilh) 1974.
Symphony No 5 Op 67 1976. Recorded Melodiya C 10 25287 005.
Concerto for Harp and Orchestra Op 69 1977.
Concerto No 2 for Violin and Orchestra Op 84 1981.
Symphony: The Siege Chronicles Op 92 1984.
Symphony No. 6 Op 105 (with soprano, contralto, large orchestra; Naiman, Akhmatova, Tsvetaeva) 1988.

Chamber/instrumental:

Variation Op 1 (piano) 1956.
Rondo Op 2 (violin, piano) 1956.
Sonata No 1 Op 3 (piano) 1957.
Sonata No 1 Op 4 (piano; in 6 parts) 1957.
Sonata No 1 Op 5 (violin) 1957.
Suite No 2 Op 6 (piano) 1957.
String Quartet No 1 Op 8 1957. Recorded Melodiya C 10 07200.
A Muleteer Op 11 (piano) 1957.
String Quartet No 2 Op 13 1959.
Sonata No 2 Op 17 (piano) 1960. Recorded Melodiya CM 02070.
Sonata No 1 Op 18 (cello) 1960. Recorded Melodiya C 10 08194.
Three Riddles Op 19/1 (piano) 1960.

Twelve Inventions Op 27 (organ) 1964. Recorded Melodiya C 10 16844.
Capriccio Op 31 (violin, piano) 1965.
Sonata No 3 Op 32 (piano) 1965.
Northern Exercises Op 42 (ensemble) 1968.
Two Pieces (percussion) 1970.
String Quartet No 3 Op 47 1970. Recorded Melodiya C 10 07199.
Sonata No 4 Op 53 (piano) 1972.
Sonata No 5 Op 56 (piano) 1973.
Sonata No 2 Op 63 (violin) 1975.
Sonata No 6 Op 64 (piano) 1976.
Sonata No 2 Op 76 (cello) 1979. Recorded Melodiya C 10 23279.
String Quartet No 4 Op 77 1980. Recorded Melodiya C 10 19639.
Sonata No 7 Op 85 (piano, with bells) 1982. Recorded Melodiya C 10 20091 004.
String Quartet No 5 Op 90 1984.
Quintet Op 93 (2 violins, viola, cello, piano) 1985.
Sonata No 8 Op 99 (piano) 1986.
The Dog's Heart Op 104 (chamber ensemble) 1988.
Concerto alla marcia Op 106 (16 soloists) 1989.
Concerto for Clarinet and Piano Trio Op 109 1990.

Vocal/choral:

A White Stork Op 10 (medium voice, piano; Shestinsky) 1958.
Yuaffu Op 14/1 (unaccompanied chorus; ancient Chinese texts) 1959. Recorded Melodiya C 10 07808.
Energy Op 14/2 (fugue for unaccompanied mixed chorus; Law of the Conservation of Energy) 1959.
The Wedding Song Op 16 (unaccompanied female chorus) 1959.
Lenin Is Alive Op 15 (cantata for mixed chorus; after Mayakovsky) 1959.
Sad Songs Op 22 (soprano, piano) 1962.
Suzdal (suite for soprano, tenor, chamber orchestra) 1964. Recorded Melodiya CM 01974.
Requiem Op 35 (soprano, tenor, symphony orchestra; Akhmatova) 1966.
Three Songs Op 48 (voice, piano or guitar; Tsetayeva) 1970. Recorded Melodiya C 10 07801.
Five Songs Op 57 (medium voice, piano; Driz) 1974.
Hard Frost Op 60 (mezzo-soprano, orchestra; Tendriakov) 1974.
The Will Op 96 (soprano, harp, organ; Zabolocky) 1986.
To My Brother Op 98 (soprano, flute, harp; Lermontov) 1986.
The Garden of Music Op 101 (cantata for soprano, contralto, baritone, violin, cello, piano; Koushner) 1987.

Opera/dramatic:

The Stolen Sun Op 40 (after Chukhovsky) 1968.
A Cockroach Op 41 (musical comedy) 1968.

Other:

Newly Ploughed Virgin Soil Op 16 (incidental music to Sholokhov) 1959.
The Twelve Op 25 (Jacobson, after Blok) 1963.
On One Planet Op 33 (film score) 1965.
Fly-Bee Op 39 (ballet, after Chukhovsky) 1968.
The Birth of a Ship Op 43 (film score) 1969.
The Pier of That Shore Op 49 (film score) 1971.
The Choices Op 51 (incidental music to Arbuzov) 1972.
Etenraku, Rasori (transcription of Japanese *gagaku*) 1972.
The One Who Gets a Slap Op 56 (incidental music to Andreev) 1973.
Jaroslavna Op 58 (ballet) 1974. Recorded Melodiya C10 07823 6.
The Day of Reception on Personal Issues Op 59 (film score) 1974.
Advice and Love Op 60 (incidental music to Tendriakov) 1974.
The Lark Op 62 (incidental music to Anouilh) 1974.
Rosa Bernd Op 65 (incidental music to Gauptman) 1976.
The Children of the Sun Op 66 (incidental music to Gorky) 1976.
An Ignoramus Op 68 (incidental music to Fonvizin) 1976.
The Children as Children Op 71 (film score) 1978.
Ivanov Op 72 (incidental music to Chekhov) 1978.
Am Emigrant from Brisbane Op 73 (incidental music to Shekhade) 1978.
Richard III Op 74 (incidental music to Shakespeare) 1978.
A Shore Op 75 (incidental music to Bondarev) 1979.
Excuse Me Op 78 (incidental music to Astafiev) 1980.
Light in a Window Op 79 (film score) 1980.
Sergei Ivanovich Is Retiring Op 80 (film score) 1980.
Continuation of Don Juan Op 82 (incidental music to Radzinsky) 1980.
Fans and Talents Op 83 (incidental music to Ostrovsky) 1980.
Rumours Op 88 (incidental music to Salinsky) 1983.
Such a Long Winter Op 89 (incidental music to Voronov) 1984.
Fires Op 91 (film score) 1984.
Light but not Heat Op 95 (incidental music to Ostrovsky) 1986.
Igor Savvovich Op 100 (film score) 1986.
Three Sisters Op 102 (incidental music to Chekhov) 1987.
The Dog's Heart Op 103 (incidental music to Bulgakov) 1988.
The Time Which Has Passed Out of Mind Op 107 (film score) 1989.

Claudio Monteverdi: *L'Incoronazione di Poppea* (orchestrated and adapted) 1967.
Sergei Prokofiev: *Boris Godunov* (orchestration and choruses for the music after Pushkin) 1972.
Dmitri Shostakovich: *Satires* (orchestration of vocal cycle) 1980. Recorded Melodiya C10 22267 009.
Dmitri Shostakovich: *Trio No 1* (completed) 1980.
Dmitri Shostakovich: *Four Poems by Captain Lebjadkin* (orchestrated) 1986.
Dmitri Shostakovich: *Antiformalistic Paradise* (orchestrated) 1989.

PUBLICATIONS

By Tishchenko: "Reflections on Opp 142 and 143 by D. Shostakovich", in *Soviet Music*, 9, 1974; "D. Shostakovich"s *Viola Sonata*", in *Soviet Music*, 11, 1975; "Study for a Portrait", in *D. Shostakovich, Articles and Materials*, Moscow, 1976; "Her Own Words in Music" [liner notes on Galina Ustvolskaya], Leningrad, 27 December 1976; "Orest Evlakhov", in *Orest Evlakhov: Composer and Teacher*, Moscow 1981; "*Madonna and Soldier* by M. Vainberg", in *Muzizin*, 16, 1986; "My Conservatoire", in *Memories of Leningrad Conservatoire*, Leningrad, 1987.

On Tishchenko: Vaclav Kucera, in *New Trends in Soviet Music*, Prague, 1967; Marina Nestjeva, "BT's First Cello Concerto", in *Problems of Musicology*, Moscow, 1975;

Valery Syrov, "BT and His Symphonies", in *Composers of the USSR*, Moscow, 1976; Mark Aranovsky, in *Symphonic Searchings*, Leningrad, 1979; Gennady Belov, "The Symphonies by Calling", in *Neva*, 6, 1979; Michael Byalik, "BT", in *Music of Russia*, Moscow, 1982; Boris Katz, *On BT's Music*, Moscow, 1986.

* * *

Boris Tishchenko was Shostakovich's favourite pupil and an intimate confidant. Perhaps not surprisingly his recent music has come to sound disturbingly like his master's voice. But in earlier years at least and, interestingly, while Shostakovich was still alive, Tishchenko's music sometimes showed a distinctly more individual streak.

Tishchenko's earlier reputation as something of a daring modernist had much to do with his large-scale setting of Anna Akhmatova's *Requiem*, a poem of political and artistic importance equal (in the field of verse) to the works of Solzhenitsyn (in prose). It was, when Tishchenko set it, a banned and dangerous text, and his decision to put it to music must have taken considerable courage. The resulting composition is, not surprisingly, intensely tragic, and often violent and dramatic. But, notably towards the end, a few beautiful rays of light brighten the gloom. Tishchenko said that when he wrote the work he never actually expected to hear it performed; but under the new political dispensation, *Requiem* has recently been performed several times in the composer's native city.

Another example of Tishchenko's more experimental frame of mind at this early period is the Third Symphony. This ungainly but striking work is scored for a large mixed chamber ensemble and consists of two extremely and oddly contrasted movements. The first one—*Meditation*—is concerned with the attempted integration of highly contrasted images and even to some extent with their development. However, between the more dynamic episodes there are also several recitative-like passages for one or more instruments. These recitatives, breaking up the music's flow and destroying almost any sense of long-term rhythm, were to become an important feature of Tishchenko's music for a number of years. The second movement is even odder. Disarmingly named *Postludium*, it is in fact far longer than the first movement and also much more of a single idea. Plaintive and almost entirely unadorned melodic lines, often suggestive of primitive liturgical music with an element of folk-song, wend their way on and on, passing from one instrument to the next without significant change or development. It can be difficult to listen to, but if played with the correct degree of intensity, it can evoke a primeval, meditational stillness.

While he never abandoned the fundamental aesthetic position inherited from Shostakovich, Tishchenko did for a time in the 1960s turn his experimental instinct towards some of the new modernist ideas and techniques coming from the West such as dodecaphony. He also claimed to have been touched by Iannis Xenakis's music, perhaps by the viscerally expressive power of Xenakis's superficially random-sounding and highly dissonant textures, clusters, glissandos and the like.

However, the native tradition, in particular the strong Russian belief in intrinsic emotional truth poured out in spontaneous invention, does not allow much room for the rigours of systematic organicism of the kind that most Western modernism has deemed essential. This contradiction may explain why, towards the end of Shostakovich's life, Tishchenko was already retreating to more familiar ground. The odd and genuinely surprising qualities in his music became fewer. Within the last few years Tishchenko's symphonies, concertos and piano sonatas have not added a great deal to his individual reputation and have too frequently irritated many by their embarrassing closeness to the Shostakovichian models that are so clearly the lodestone of Tishchenko's personal world. Yet to dismiss them altogether would be to miss the fact that Tishchenko's talent and natural musicianship are indeed very great, and that his own personal characteristics—his genuine naivety and innocent prolixity as well as his fondness for a virtuosic style of piano writing—all mean that his music has an energy and a sense of space that are well worth the attention of a sympathetic ear.

—Gerard McBurney

TON-THAT Tiet. Vietnamese/French. Born in Hue, Vietnam, 18 October 1933. Educated at Ecole Normale de Musique, Paris (harmony and counterpoint), 1958–60; Conservatoire National Supérieur de Musique, Paris (counterpoint, fugue and composition), 1960–6; composition pupil of Jean Rivier and André Jolivet. Military service, Vietnamese Army, 1954–6. Married Tam-Quy, 25 July 1969; 2 children. High school professor of music, Hue, 1950s; conservatory lecturer in music, University of Paris. Recipient: Viotti Prize; Lili Boulanger Prize; SACEM Prize, 1972; Ministry of Culture bursary, 1981. Mailing address: 16 rue du Dauphine, 94100 Saint Maur, France.

Publishers: Jobert, Paris; Transatlantiques, Paris; Salabert, Paris; Billaudot, Paris.

Symphonies/orchestral:

Concerto for violin and orchestra 1964–5.
Multi cordi (string orchestra) 1966; broadcast Radio France, 1969.
Ngu Hanh II 1973; broadcast Radio France, 1974.
Vo Vi (string orchestra; or 12 strings) 1974; broadcast Radio France, 1974.
An Tuong 1974–5; broadcast Radio France, 1975.
Cello Concerto 1985; first performed Nice, 1986.
Chu Ky VII (harp, chamber orchestra) 1986; first performed Paris, 1987.

Chamber/instrumental:

Five Pieces for Oboe and Piano 1965; first performed Paris, 1966.
Sonata for Solo Violin 1965; first performed Paris, 1966.
String Quartet No 2 1966; first performed Paris, 1967.
Incarnations structurales (flute, viola/cello, harp) 1967; first performed Paris, 1970. Recorded Erato STU 70706.
Ba Doan Khuc (piano) 1967; first performed Paris, 1970. Recorded Calumet Fr Cal 3732.
Tu Dai Canh (flute, oboe, clarinet, bassoon, piano) 1968; broadcast Radio France, 1969.
Hy Vong 267 (cor anglais, harpsichord) 1970; broadcast Radio France, 1971. Recorded CBS Moot S 3461142.
Hy Vong 14 (cor anglais, horn, harpsichord, 12 strings) 1971; first performed Paris, 1973.
Ai Van I (harpsichord) 1972; broadcast Radio France, 1973.
Ai Van II (bass recorder, harpsichord) 1972; first performed Paris, 1973.

Tuong Niem (flute, viola, 2 harps) 1973; first performed Paris, 1974. Recorded GL.B GLB010.
Niem (flute in G, harp) 1974; first performed Gargilesse, 1975.
Chu Ky I (string trio) 1976; first performed Paris, 1978. Recorded Erato CD 2292 45019 2.
Chu Ky II (brass quintet) 1976; first performed Armagnac, 1976.
Chu Ky III (harp) 1977; first performed Paris, 1977. Recorded Erato STU 71160.
Bao La (clarinet) 1977; first performed Paris, 1978.
Chu Ky IV (4 percussionists) 1977; first performed Paris, 1979.
Tranh (Celtic harp, tape) 1980.
Trung Dzuong (piano) 1980; first performed Paris, 1980. Recorded REM 11009.
Terre-feu (viola) 1981; first performed Saint Gervais, 1981. Recorded CRI-ACS 6017.
VO (flute, harp) 1981; broadcast Radio France, 1984.
Metal-terre-eau (violin) 1982; first performed Nice, 1983.
Bois-terre (cello) 1982; first performed Nice, 1983.
Jeu des cinq éléments I (violin, cello) 1982; first performed Nice, 1983.
Jeu des cinq éléments II (bassoon) 1982; first performed Paris, 1982.
Chu Ky V (flute, electronic tape) 1983; first performed Paris, 1983.
Jeu des cinq éléments III (harp, string trio) 1984; first performed Paris, 1985.
Strasbourg 85 (organ) 1986; first performed Paris, 1988.
DZAO (9 preludes for harpsichord) 1987; first performed Tokyo 1988.
Les Jardins d'autre-monde (flute, oboe, clarinet, bassoon, harp, percussion, string trio) 1987; first performed Paris, 1988.
Trois Intermezzi (bassoon, percussion, harp) 1987.
Kim Co (alto recorder) 1988; first performed Paris, 1988.
Doi Dzien (tenor recorder, electronic tape) 1988.
Préludes à un dialogue (2 guitars) 1989; first performed Paris, 1989.
Dang Phung Vu (flute, bass clarinet, piano/synthesizer, percussion, viola, cello) 1989.
Moments rituels (tenor saxophone, percussion, synthesizer) 1989.

Vocal/choral:

Vang Bong Thoi Xua (soprano, with flute, oboe, clarinet, bassoon, horn, trumpet, trombone, 4 percussion, piano, celeste, 2 violins, viola, 2 cellos) 1969; first performed Paris, 1971.
Bodhi (1 male, 1 female voice, electric guitar) 1974.
Kiem Ai (mixed choir, children's choir, orchestra) 1978; broadcast Radio France, 1982.
Image lointaine II (soprano, orchestra) 1979–80; first performed Lille, 1981.
Prajna Paramita (2 high tenor/altos, tenor, baritone, 2 basses, flute, oboe, clarinet, horn, trombone/percussion/violin/cello) 1988; first performed Paris, 1988.
Le Chant de l'espérance (children's choir) 1989.

Other:

Ngu Hanh I (ensemble of ancient instruments) 1971; first performed Paris, 1973.
Le Chemin du Bouddha (ballet for bass, chorus, orchestra) 1990.

Ton-That Tiet comments:

I received a traditional upbringing, highly influenced by the teachings of Confucianism, Taoism and Buddhism. At first I was attracted by European culture, but in the end came back to oriental ways of thinking. In fact, most of my works are inspired by oriental philosophy, in particular Hinduism and the Yi King. In some of my works, however, I want to revive the spirit of the traditional sacred and court music of Vietnam.

The two major ideas on which most of my works are based are "Man and the Universe"—as in the seven-part *Chu Ky* cycle—and "Man and Mankind", of which *Kiem Ai* is the main expression.

* * *

The trajectory of Ton-That Tiet's career is typical of a generation of Asian musicians who were raised in a relatively traditional way but who then were intensively exposed to Western culture. His earliest works, notably the Violin Concerto and the very fine *Multi cordi* for string orchestra are written in a highly adaptive modern romantic idiom reminiscent of Henri Dutilleux, though on a generally smaller scale. Harmonies are lush, but also slightly acidulous, and there is a tension in the rhythmic structure which suggests a non-Western provenance.

Studies under Jean Rivier and André Jolivet, whose broadly based nationalism went hand in hand with a concentrated attention to musical texture, widened Ton-That's horizons very considerably and even some of his most recent chamber pieces bear strong marks of Jolivet's influence. With an irony that neatly summarises the whole "post-colonial" predicament, Ton-That became even more of a "Vietnamese" composer once he had removed to France, where the musics of former colonies were being absorbed into a complex new tradition.

Ton-That brings with him a whole range of acoustic effects and structural devices which render shifts from polyphony to diatony to full-blown chromaticism largely irrelevant. Ton-That draws heavily on the old Viet court music tradition, which was centred on his birthplace Hue, the ancient capital. Though he has written for traditional instrumentations, as in *Ngu Hanh I*, premiered in Paris in 1973, the greater bulk of his work is for Western forces lent a profoundly alienating cadence by their unusual distribution. The early *Incarnations structurales* is typical of his use of instrumental sound; elsewhere, he makes extensive use of harpsichord, Celtic harp, recorders and the cor anglais, only relatively recently beginning to experiment with electronic means. In the later 1980s he has used keyboard synthesizers, much as Jolivet used the ondes martenot to such effect. The extreme chromaticism towards which the court tradition appears to lead is constantly mitigated by a more sparsely logical progress, sometimes of whole tones, sometimes of triads, though in the ambitious and almost Messiaen-like *Les Jardins d'autre-monde* the compositional logic is so highly specific as to seem almost autotelic.

The most important chamber pieces are in the sequence *Chu Ky*, dedicated, as are so many of Ton-That's remarkably eclectic scores, to an examination of the broadest ontological and epistemological questions. In this he follows the Buddhist identification of music and philosophy, or rather the belief that music-making is a form of philosophising. The wider ramifications of the short sequence of pieces dedicated to the elements are made quite explicit, while the choral piece *Kiem Ai* is a significant expression of Ton-That's objectification of the relationship between man and his environment, which in the East Asian tradition always includes music as a kind of "fifth element".

Now very much established in the contemporary French music scene, Ton-That brings with him a whole range of cultural references that express an eclectic blend of philosophies. He draws on orthodox Hinduism and also the I Ching (from which he takes his conception of controlled chance), on Taoism and Zen. Pieces like *Terre-feu* and *Boisterre* are beautifully articulated and thoroughly grounded in both Eastern and Western form. With the apparent culmination of the *Chu Ky* sequence in a major work for harp and chamber orchestra, Ton-That has emerged as a highly significant modern voice who has contributed substantially to a phenomenon that receives considerably more lip service than actual attention: the rapprochement of Eastern and Western culture, as expressed in music.

—Charles Lao

TOWER, Joan. American. Born in La Rochelle, New York, 6 September 1938; childhood to 1955 spent in South America. Educated at Bennington College, Vermont, 1958–61; Columbia University, New York City (composition under Jack Beeson, Ben Boretz, Chou Wen-chung, Oto Luening, Alan Sapp, Ralph Shapey, Vladimir Ussachevsky and Charles Wuorinen), M.A. in theory and history of music, 1967, D.M.A. in composition, 1978; further composition study under Henry Brant, Louis Calabro, Darius Milhaud, and Wallingford Riegger, 1968–71. Founder and pianist, Da Capo Chamber Players, 1969–84; assistant professor, Bard College, Annandale-on-Hudson, New York, from 1972; composer in residence, St Louis Symphony Orchestra, Missouri, from 1985. Recipient: Naumburg Award (with Da Capo Chamber Players), 1973; MacDowell Colony Fellowship, 1974; Grawemeyer Award (for *Silver Ladders*), 1990. Mailing address: c/o G. Schirmer Inc./Associated Music Publishers Inc., 24 East 22nd Street, New York, New York 10010, U.S.A.

Publishers: G. Schirmer/Associated Music Publishers.

Symphonies/orchestral:

Amazon II 1979; first performed New York, 10 November 1979.
Sequoia 1981; first performed New York City, 18 May 1981. Recorded Nonesuch Digital 9 79118-1F.
Music for Cello and Orchestra 1984; first performed New York City, 29 September 1984. Recorded Nonesuch.
Island Rhythms 1985; first performed Florida, 29 June 1985.
Piano Concerto: Homage to Beethoven 1985; first performed New York, 31 January 1986.
Silver Ladders 1986; first performed St Louis, Missouri, 9 January 1987. Recorded Nonesuch.
Concerto for Clarinet and Orchestra 1988; first performed New York City, 10 April 1989.
Island Prelude 1989; first performed St Louis, Missouri, 1989.
Concerto for Flute and Orchestra 1989; first performed New York City, 28 January 1990.
Concerto for Orchestra 1991; first performed St Louis, Missouri, 16 May 1991.

Chamber/instrumental:

Pillars (2 pianos, percussion) 1961.
Percussion Quartet 1963, revised 1969; first performed Chicago, 17 August 1963.
Circles (piano) 1964.
Brimset (flute, percussion) 1965.
Fantasia (piano) 1966.
Opa Eboni (oboe, flute) 1967.
Movements (flute, piano) 1968; first performed 9 May 1968. Recorded Advance Recording FGR 24S.
Prelude for Five Players (flute, oboe or violin, clarinet, bassoon or cello, piano) 1970; first performed 22 October 1971. Recorded CRI 302.
Six Variations (cello) 1971.
Hexachords (flute) 1972; first performed 26 February 1972. Recorded CRI S-354.
Breakfast Rhythms I and II (solo clarinet, flute/piccolo, violin, cello, piano, percussion) 1974–5; first performed 30 April 1975. Recorded CRI S-354.
Black Topaz (solo piano, flute, clarinet/bass clarinet, trumpet, trombone, 2 percussion) 1976; first performed 15 November 1976.
Platinum Spirals (violin) 1976; first performed 21 April 1976. Recorded CRI SD 517.
Red Garnet Waltz (piano) 1977. Recorded Nonesuch D-79011.
Amazon I (flute, clarinet, violin, cello, piano) 1977; first performed 11 January 1977. Recorded CRI SD 517.
Petrouschkates (flute, clarinet, violin, cello, piano) 1980. Recorded CRI SD 411.
Wings (clarinet) 1981; first performed 14 December 1981. Recorded CRI SD 517.
Noon Dance (flute, clarinet, violin, cello, piano, percussion) 1982; first performed 28 February 1983. Recorded CRI SD 517.
Snow Dreams (flute, guitar) 1983; first performed 18 April 1983.
Fantasy . . . Harbor Lights (clarinet, piano) 1983; first performed 4 November 1983.
Clocks (guitar) 1985; first performed 3 August 1985.
Fanfare for the Uncommon Woman (4 horns, 3 trumpets, 3 trombones, tuba, 4 timpani, 2 percussion) 1986; first performed Houston, Texas, 10 January 1987. Recorded Nonesuch.
Island Prelude (chamber versions for oboe and string or wind quintet) 1989.
Second Fanfare for the Uncommon Woman (brass, timpani) 1989; first performed New York City, 28 January 1990.
Third Fanfare for the Uncommon Woman (2 brass quintets) 1990; first performed New York City, 5 May 1991.

PUBLICATIONS

On Tower: C. Ammer, in *Unsung: A History of Women in American Music*, Westport, Connecticut, 1980; V. O'Brien, "JT: Musician of the Month", in *High Fidelity/Musical America*, 31(9), 1982; L. Koplewitz, "JT: Building Bridges for New Music", in *Symphony Magazine*, 34(3), 1983.

* * *

Although born in New York, Joan Tower grew up in South America and steeped herself in the rhythms and colours of the native music there. It is perhaps this influence, above all, which has led her to the energy and dynamism of her own music. She is, also, an eminently practical musician and her career as a pianist has not only influenced the course she pursued as a composer but also provided her with a special understanding of performers' problems.

In 1969, after receiving a doctorate in composition from Columbia University, Tower formed the Da Capo Chamber Players with whom she continued to play for 15 years before leaving to devote more time to composition and teaching. Symptomatically, her works from this period are nearly exclusively for chamber forces and those from the late 1960s and early 1970s such as *Movements* for flute and piano and *Prelude for Five Players* are clearly influenced by the rhythmically complex serial music which formed much of Da Capo's repertoire at this time. Nonetheless, one can perceive almost tantalising glimpses of the compositional preoccupations that were to emerge in Tower's later music: energy, colour and the balancing of compositional gestures. *Breakfast Rhythms I and II* for clarinet and five instruments is a significant landmark: after writing the work's loosely serial first movement, Tower stopped composing for a year. Obviously a considerable compositional re-think took place and the second movement, *Breakfast Rhythms II*, is far less dissonant, more colourful and more impressionistic, yet Tower is able to retain a stylistic unity of the whole through the strong directional motion of each movement.

Amazon I for five instruments is Tower's first attempt at creating a seamless whole; its sections are linked without strong demarcations and the evocation of the Amazon River, a tribute to her South American childhood, underscores the fluidity of the whole. In 1979 Tower rescored the work for chamber orchestra as *Amazon II*, but it was not until *Sequoia* that she was to undertake the composition of work specifically conceived for orchestra. The abstract programme behind this much-performed piece is the striking contrast between the majestic height of the giant redwood tree, the sequoia, and its tiny needles. Rather than creating a seamless structure the composer has concentrated on the complex layering and balancing of compositional elements (line, rhythms, pedal points, dynamics).

Since leaving the Da Capo Chamber Players Tower has been able to concentrate more exclusively on large-scale works, writing concertos for piano and cello in 1984 and 1985 respectively and *Island Rhythms* for the Florida Orchestra. In 1985 she was pursued this experience further when she was appointed to a three-year term as composer in residence for the St Louis Symphony. The first fruits of this residency was *Silver Ladders*, her first work for large orchestra and her longest to date. The piece's varying textures depict alternately the heavy properties of solid silver and the lightness of molten silver, juxtaposed against a panorama of huge rising symmetrical scales or "ladders". It is a piece of tremendous physical momentum which has great impact in performance—so much so that it attracted the attention of the jury of the 1990 Grawemeyer Award, who gave Tower this most prestigious of compositional prizes.

This success looks set to keep Tower writing for orchestra, at least in the forseeable future: a further work for the St Louis Symphony, a violin concerto and a piece for the centenary of Carnegie Hall are all promised. It will be interesting to see whether the prestige of the award will bring her music wider currency in Europe, where, at the time of writing, her works have been performed very little.

—Rosemary Johnson

TRUSCOTT, Harold. British/English. Born in Ilford, Essex, 23 August 1914. Educated at Ilford County High School, 1925–30; Bretton Hall Teacher Training College, Yorkshire, 1935–7. Married Eleanor Margaret Madge, 9 August 1948; 3 children. Teacher, Blackheath Conservatry, London, 1948–54; music teacher, Sandwich Secondary Modern, Kent, 1954–6; assistant, later principal and lecturer, Huddersfield Polytechnic, Yorkshire, 1957–79. Mailing address: 16 Claremont Road, Deal, Kent, England.

Publishers: Lynwood Music; Bardic Edition.

Symphonies / orchestral:

Symphony in E major 1948–9.
Piano Concerto 1950; incomplete.
Fantasy (string orchestra; originally entitled *A Window on Infinity*) 1960; first performed Huddersfield, Yorkshire, 1961.
Suite in E minor (string orchestra) 1961; unfinished.
Symphony in A minor 1962–8; unfinished.
Suite in G major 1966.
Symphony in A minor 1967–72; unfinished.
Oboe Concerto 1968; unfinished.

Chamber / instrumental:

Sonata No 1 in D♭ major (piano) 1945; first performed London, 1947.
Sonata No 2 in C major 1945–7; first performed London, March 1948.
Sonata No in F# minor (violin, piano) 1946.
Sonata in One Movement (violin) 1946; first performed (privately) 22 January 1951; first public performance London, 9 October 1989.
Sonata No 3 in G# minor (piano) 1947–8; first performed London, September 1981. Recorded Altarus AIR 2 900 8.
Sonata No 4 in E♭ major (piano) 1948–9; first performed London, 24 October 1989.
Sonata No 2 in G# minor (violin, piano) 1948–9; broadcast BBC, 1954.
Suite No 1 (piano) 1949.
Trio in A major (flute, violin, viola) 1950; broadcast BBC, 25 April 1955; first public performance, London, 9 October 1989.
Sonata No 5 in B minor: In Memory of Nicolas Medtner (piano) 1951–5; first performed London, September 1982. Recorded Altarus AIR 2 900 2.
Sonata No 6 in E major (piano) 1955–6; first performed London, September 1984.
Sonata No 7 in C (piano) 1956; broadcast BBC, 30 August 1969; first public performance London, 1983. Recorded Altarus AIR 2 900 8.
Toccata in A minor (organ) 1956; first performed Huddersfield, Yorkshire, June 1965.
Two Preludes and Fugues (piano) 1957; first performed London, September 1982. Recorded Altarus AIR 2 900 2.
Sonata No 8 in E minor 1958–60; first performed London, 24 October 1989.
Sonata No 3 in C major (violin, piano) 1959; first performed Huddersfield, Yorkshire, 1959.
Sonata No 1 in C major (clarinet, piano) 1959; first performed Huddersfield, Yorkshire, 1960.
Sonata No 4 in A major (violin, piano) 1959; unfinished.
Sonata No 5 in E major (violin, piano) 1960; unfinished and withdrawn.

Sonata No 9 in E minor (piano) 1960; first performed London, September, 1983. Recorded Altarus AIR 2 900 3.
Sonata No 10 in E minor 1962; broadcast BBC, 30 August 1969.
Suite No 2 (piano) 1962.
Sonata No 11 in A minor (piano) 1964; first performed London, September 1981. Recorded Altarus AIR 2 900 8.
Sonata No 2 in D major (clarinet, piano) 1965.
Sonata (oboe, piano) 1965; first performed Huddersfield, Yorkshire, 1971 or 1972.
Sonata No 3 in F# minor (clarinet, piano) 1966.
Variations and Fugue on an Original Theme in B minor (piano) 1967.
Sonata No 12 in C major (piano) 1967; first performed London, September 1982. Recorded Altarus AIR 2 900 2.
Sonata No 13 (piano) 1967; first performed London, September 1983. Recorded Altarus AIR 2 900 3.
Sonata No 14 in G major (piano) 1967.
Trio Sonata in E♭ major (organ) 1972.
Variations on a Minuet of Schubert (4 clarinets, 2 bass clarinets) 1974.
Sonata in E♭ major (horn, piano) 1975–81.
Sonata No 15 in B minor (piano) 1981; first performed London, September 1983. Recorded Altarus AIR 2 900 3.
Sonata No 16 in E♭ major (piano) 1981; revision in progress.
Sonata No 17 in G minor (piano) 1982; first performed (privately) London, September 1984; first public performance London, 9 October 1989.
Sonata (cello, piano) 1982–7.
Sonata No 18 in A♭ major (piano) 1982; in progress.
Meditations on Themes from Emmanuel Moor's Suite for Four Cellos (cello solo) 1985.

Vocal/choral:

Two Songs (voice, piano; "The Vision"—Mary Webb, "I Love all Beauteous Things"—Bridges) 1946.
Five Songs (voice, piano; Hood, Emily Brontë, Belloc, Tennyson, Francis Thompson) 1956.
Two Songs (voice, piano; "An Epitaph upon a Virgin"—Herrick, "Praise of Good Women"—Mannyng) 1971.

PUBLICATIONS

By Truscott: articles in *Music Survey*, 1949–52, *The Listener*, *The Chesterian*, *Music Review*, 1950–78, *Tempo*, 1960–87; *Beethoven's Late String Quartets*, London, 1968; *The Music of Franz Schmidt: The Orchestral Music*, London, 1984; "Panufnik's Symphonies", in *Musical Times*, 1988; *The Music of Felix Mendelssohn*, in preparation.

On Truscott: David J. Brown, "Altarus First Releases", in *Tempo*, 153, 1985, and "New Altarus Releases", in *Tempo*, 158, 1986; Jack Greenhalgh, "T Piano Sonatas", in *Classical Music*, 1986; *HT: 75th Birthday Celebration*, edited by G.S. Rickards, Havergal Brian Society, London, 1989; G.S. Rickards, (review article) in *Tempo*, 171, 1989; Calum Macdonald, (review article) in *Havergal Brian Society Newsletter*, 87, 1990.

Harold Truscott comments:

The sonata always has been and still is for me the most fruitful vehicle of musical thought. This is not today a fashionable attitude, but that is unimportant. I compose as I must. Not all my music is sonata-based, but the bulk is. Nor is there much vocal music: a total of about nine songs. Beethoven once said that when he thought of a theme, he always heard it on an instrument, never a voice. The same applies to me.

* * *

Harold Truscott has a deserved reputation as one of the clearest, most open-minded and knowledgeable writers on music since World War II. His renown as a musical polymath is widespread: his reputation of apparently knowing all classical music is matched by an ability to reproduce at the piano almost any music that is placed before him. What few have realised is that he has been writing music of great integrity himself which has been utterly neglected: several works have never been completed due to the absence of any performances, most of the rest either never being performed at all or just once.

Truscott's music is vigorously contrapuntal, unashamedly (though not unadventurously) tonal and possesses a calm integrity and Bachian timelessness that make it quite unique. After conquering an initial desire to compose in a Beethovenian style, he has completed about 50 works, including an orchestral *Suite in G major*, a *Fantasy* for strings and a *Symphony in E major* (only the final movement has ever been performed—once, in 1961), though at least two others have remained unfinished. The voice is always distinctively his own, and if occasionally reminiscent of the music of Havergal Brian (with whom he was well-acquainted, Truscott dedicating the short bravura Seventh Piano Sonata of 1956 to him), is quite dissimilar in its internal processes and artistic aims; other influences do appear, but betray only the vast range of his sympathies (e.g., Bach, Jan Ladislav Dussek, Beethoven, Schubert, Nikolay Karlovich Medtner). One feature of his style that has been present throughout his career is the seemingly casual nature of the material that he uses to build his complex movements; the almost burlesque or pop-ish character of the openings of the Fourth, Sixth, Seventh and Seventeenth Sonatas, for example, tease one's expectations and the ordeal-by-counterpoint that they endure belies their apparent innocence. As with the work of both Brian and Elizabeth Maconchy, Truscott's later music has assumed a more compressed, highly individual mode of thought, moving away from its earlier, expansive style. The works say what they need to without padding of any kind, yet often give the impression of far greater length (some barely last into the teens of minutes) and scale than is actually the case.

The majority of his compositional effort has been for the piano, with 17 completed sonatas (an eighteenth has not been completed)—surely, the finest set ever written by an Englishman—plus two preludes and fugues, a set of variations and fugue on an original theme, as well as two suites of miniatures. The Sixth Sonata in E major is large (over 40 minutes), and is partly a recomposition of movements from a Suite written (and withdrawn) in 1949. Despite a calm and quiet opening, it generates tremendous power during its four movements. All of Truscott's consummate craftsmanship is exhibited in a work that is not a note too long. The deeper and more elusive Eighth Sonata is a marvellous work in three movements betraying his deep love and understanding of Russian music and constitutes one of his finest creations. The tiny Seventeenth Sonata in G minor is the shortest: just five minutes in length. The composer Robert Simpson described it as a "black dwarf", and there is a sense of a large work compressed overwhelmingly into a short span about it.

The only substantial piece of chamber music is the divertimento-like *Trio in A major*, which shows Truscott's disarming sense of humour to full effect, as does the deadpan

Fourth Piano Sonata, which plays blind-man's-bluff with the Classical tradition and has a splendidly drunken minuet constantly trying to be dignified only to giggle at the wrong moment. The first of Truscott's three sonatas for clarinet and piano is an eloquent and superbly poised work, most idiomatically written for the instrument, and builds from a serene opening through moments of great drama and tension to an impassioned and brilliant conclusion. Like much of his music, the cello *Sonata* in A minor is ferociously difficult: concise yet lyrical, contrapuntally exacting while never dry or academic. There are few enough top rank British cello sonatas, but this is definitely one of them.

The appearance in the 1980s of three Altarus records by Peter Jacobs of eight piano sonatas began to put an end to decades of shameful neglect. The first retrospective of his music in live performance was mounted by the Havergal Brian Society at the British Music Information Centre in October 1989, two months after the composer's 75th birthday. This, and the recordings eventually emanating from it, has served at long last to do a little more justice to this fine composer.

—Guy Rickards

TURNAGE, Mark-Anthony. British/English. Born in Essex in 1960. Educated at the Royal College of Music, London (composition under Oliver Knussen and John Lambert); further study under Gunther Schuller and Hans Werner Henze, Tanglewood, Masachussetts, 1983. Freelance composer; composer in residence, National Centre for Orchestral Studies, 1985–6; composer in association, City of Birmingham Symphony Orchestra, 1989–92. Recipient: composition prizes, Royal College of Music; Guinness Prize (for *Night Dances*) 1981; Mendelssohn Scholarship, 1983; Benjamin Britten Composition Prize (for *Let Us Sleep Now*), 1983; BMW prizes for best opera and best libretto, Munich Biennale, 1988. Mailing address: c/o Schott & Co, 48 Great Marlborough Street, London W1V 2BN, England.

Publisher: Schott.

Symphonies/orchestral:

Let Us Sleep Now (chamber orchestra) 1979, revised 1982; first performed Snape, Suffolk, 14 June 1983.
Night Dances 1981–2; first performed London, 1 February 1982.
Kind of Blue 1981–2; first performed London, 21 March 1982.
Ekaya 1984; first performed London, 29 March 1985.
Gross Intrusion (amplified string quartet, string orchestra, 14 players) 1987; first performed Glasgow, 19 September 1987; subsequently withdrawn for revision.
Three Screaming Popes 1989; first performed Birmingham, 5 October 1989.
Momentum 1990–1; first performed Birmingham, 12 June 1991.

Chamber/instrumental:

And Still a Softer Morning (flute, vibraphone, harp, cello) 1978, revised 1983; revised version first performed Montepulciano, 31 July 1984.
Entranced (piano) 1982; first performed Huddersfield, Yorkshire, 25 November 1982.
After Dark (wind quintet, string quintet) 1982–3; first performed London, 13 April 1983.
On All Fours (flute/bass flute, oboe/cor anglais/optional bass oboe, clarinet/bass clarinet, bassoon, trumpet in C/ flugelhorn/percussion/desk bell, alto saxophone/soprano saxophone/percussion, trombone/percussion, percussion, piano/optional electric piano, violin/woodblock, viola, cello, double bass; or with string section) 1985; first performed London, 4 February 1986.
Sarabande (soprano saxophone, piano) 1985; first performed London, 10 January 1986.
Release (soprano/large and nasty-sounding ratchet, alto saxophone/soprano saxophone/bass clarinet, bass clarinet, trumpet in C/percussion, tenor trombone, percussion, piano, amplified double bass) 1987; broadcast BBC Radio 4 December 1988.
Kai (cello solo, flute, soprano saxophone/alto saxophone, alto saxophone/soprano saxophone, bass clarinet/clarinet, bassoon/contrabassoon, 2 trumpets, trombone, piano, harp, bass guitar, 2 violins, viola, cello, double bass) 1989–90; first performed Birmingham, 18 December 1990.
Three Farewells (flute, clarinet, string quartet) 1990; first performed London, 8 July 1990.

Vocal/choral:

Lament for a Hanging Man (soprano/percussion, soprano saxophone/lead pipe, bass clarinet/soprano saxophone/ tom toms, bass clarinet/tom toms, percussion, harp/syn drum; Jeremiah, Plath) 1983; first performed Durham, 4 February 1984.
One Hand in Brooklyn Heights (16 mixed voices, 2 large triangles, 2 hyoshigis; Berkoff) 1986; first performed Bath, 3 June 1986.
Beating About the Bush (mezzo-soprano, flute, cor anglais, horn, harp, viola, cello) 1987; first performed 14 June 1987.
Greek Suite (mezzo-soprano, tenor, flute/piccolo/alto flute/ bodhran, 2 oboes/cors anglais/percussion, 2 clarinets/2 bass clarinets/E♭ clarinet, soprano, saxophone/alto saxophone/baritone saxophone/ratchet, trumpet in C/percussion, 2 horns, trombone, percussion, viola, 2 cellos, double bass) 1989; first performed Frankfurt, 20 March 1989.
Some Days (mezzo-soprano, orchestra) 1989; first performed London, 21 July 1991.
Greek Songs (mezzo-soprano, viola, ensemble) 1990; first performed Aldeburgh, Suffolk, 22 June 1990.

Opera:

Greek (after Steven Berkoff) 1986–8; first performed Munich, 17 June 1988.

PUBLICATIONS

On Turnage: *Release*, film on MAT, directed by Philip Bonham-Carter, broadcast BBC Radio "Sound on Film" series, November 1988.

* * *

Mark-Anthony Turnage believes that music must be accessible to a wide public, rather than the limited audience often reached by new contemporary works. Like his contemporaries Steve Martland and James MacMillan, he has drawn on the direct rhythmic and emotional appeal of popular music as a constituent in that process, although his own introduction to non-classical music did not arrive until his late teens.

This pattern is evident in one of the earliest compositions to gain him wide attention, and one of the earliest he still includes in his list of published works. *Night Dances* was intended to evoke what the composer describes as "the feelings and emotions aroused by my first encounter with Black music", and is built around a constantly manipulated four note cell and samba-like rhythmic pattern, while the central section of the work is based on the Miles Davis ballad "Blue in Green". A later piece is named for the record on which it appears, *Kind of Blue*.

There is a slightly undigested feeling to this borrowing which is less evident in his more recent work, perhaps because the influences have become less directly stated, and more fully incorporated into the composer's developing voice. That more personal, less diffuse voice arguably begins to emerge around the period of *Lament for a Hanging Man*, his setting of the lamentations of Jeremiah and poems by Sylvia Plath.

Turnage confesses he is attracted to dark themes rather than bright ones, although the colourful percussion assembled for *Ekaya* may be an early exception. The harder, more austere edge which his music was developing continued in the chamber piece *On All Fours* and *One Hand in Brooklyn Heights* for 16 mixed voices.

His liking for contrasting motifs and violent juxtapositions, however, was crystallised in his music for Steven Berkoff's controversial opera *Greek*, initially in *Beating About the Bush*, for mezzo-soprano and chamber ensemble, and *Gross Intrusion*, both of which set some of his sketches for the opera, then in *Greek* itself, and subsequently in *Greek Suite* and *Greek Songs*. The two-act opera translated the Oepidus story to a modern telling in the East End of London, and its controversial treatment of sexual and violent themes called for a stark, strident score which set up wrenching contrasts between the outbrusts of violence and the calmer, more lyrical interludes.

Rhythmic directness and an almost lush orchestration are utilised in a somewhat similar fashion in his orchestral composition *Three Screaming Popes*, which is inspired by Francis Bacon's famous series of portraits. Some commentators have found a distinct edge of menace and even outrage in this work, but it can be considered to be a perfectly uncontroversial welding together of the composer's major preoccupations. It has a strong but somewhat complex rhythmic directness which alludes to rock and soul's regular pulse without overtly employing it, allied to an orchestral scoring which is strong on colouration and instrumental textures, but far from radical or threatening in its use of dissonances. It is an ideal example of Turnage's determination to write music which will break down audience as much as musical barriers, while avoiding the banality or simple compromise which constantly attends such ambitions.

—Kenny Mathieson

U

UNG, Chinary. American. Born in Cambodia, 24 November 1942. Educated at University of Fine Arts, Pnomh Penh, diploma, 1964; Manhattan School of Music, New York City, B.M., 1967, M.M., 1968; Columbia University, New York City, D.M.A. (with distinction), 1974. Married Susan Lee Pounders, 4 August 1984; 2 daughters. Performer on *roneat-ek* [Cambodian xylophone]; assistant professor of music, Northern Illinois University, DeKalb, 1977–9; assistant professor, Connecticut College, New London, 1979–84; assistant professor, University of Pennsylvania, Philadelphia, 1984–7; associate professor, 1987, and full professor, since 1990, Arizona State University, Tempe; chair of the board, since 1983, and president, since 1986, Khmer Studies Institute. Recipient: Margaret Grant Memorial Composition Prize, Tanglewood (for *Anicca*), 1970; Boris and Ida Rapaport Prize, Columbia University (for *Tall Wind*), 1971; finalist (with *Khse Buon*) Politis International Music Composition Competition, 1980; American Academy and Institute of Arts and Letters (Goddard Lieberson Fellowship), 40th annual award, 1981; Honored Citizens' Committee for Immigration Reform, 1982; Chicago Society of Composers' Cello Competition (for *Khse Buon*), 1982; elected, American Academy and Institute of Arts and Letters, 1988; first prize, Kennedy Center Friedheim Award (for *Spiral I*), 1989; University of Louisville Grawemeyer Award for Music (for *Inner Voices*), 1989. Mailing address: 1833 East La Donna Lane, Tempe, Arizona 85283, U.S.A.

Publisher: Peters.

Symphonies/orchestral:

Anicca 1970; first performed DeKalb, Illinois, 1979.
Inner Voices 1986; first performed Philadelphia, 1986.

Chamber/instrumental:

Por (5 percussionists) 1967; first performed New York City, 1968.
Khse Buon (cello or viola) 1980.
Child Song (flute, violin, cello, piano) 1984; first performed Chicago, 1984.
Spiral I (cello, piano, percussion) 1987; first performed Boston, 1987.
String Quartet No 1 1990; first performed Chicago, 1990.

Vocal/choral:

Tall Wind (soprano, flute, oboe, cello, guitar) 1970; first performed Tanglewood, Massachusetts, 1970.
Mohori (mezzo-soprano, flute, oboe, cello, guitar, harp, 2 percussion) 1973; first performed New York City, 1975.
Spiral (mezzo-soprano, piano, tuba) 1989; first performed Tempe, Arizona, 1989.

Other:

Three recordings of *Cambodia: Traditional Music*: I & II compiled and annotated by CU, Folkways Records Inc, III performed and annotated by CU, Khmer Studies Institute.

PUBLICATIONS

By Ung: "More Than Pitch and Rhythm: Approaches to the Understanding of Contemporary Music", in *International Musicological Society Report of the Twelfth Congress*, Berkeley, California, 1981; "The Regeneration of Khmer Music and the Performing Arts in the US", State University of New York/ Genesco Foundation, 1989.

Chinary Ung comments:

Rather than succumbing to descriptions of my music as "East-West", I prefer to say the following: if the East can be characterized as the color blue and the West as the color yellow, then perhaps my music is green. Although I spent the first 21 years of my life in Cambodia, I had all my formal training in the United States, and did not become intimate with the traditional music of Cambodia until about 1980. It was then that I taught myself the *roneat-ek*, or high xylophone, used for the court dance of Cambodia, and became familiar with the techniques and structure of various musics of Southeast Asia and elsewhere. Certainly, my music grew out of formal Western training, yet it evokes an Asian ambiance and color.

* * *

The trend of cross-fertilization of Eastern and Western music has continued unabated since the successful absorption of Eastern musical elements into Debussy's work. This cultural middle ground also has proven fertile for Chinary Ung, an Indo-Chinese American who lived his first 21 years in Cambodia. His years spent among its native music, his experience of the long brutal war, his eventual exposure to Western music (at age 16 when he first heard French band music) and the subsequent tutelage under Chou Wen-chung were pivotal to the formation of a unique musical personality and idiosyncratic approach to composition.

To the Western ear, Ung's music projects a tinge of exoticism that results from a sensitive deployment of harmony and instrumental coloring. Although the music sounds vaguely tonal in the Western sense, its inspiration appears to have come from Cambodian sources rather than from the West. This is revealed particularly by a penchant for prominent modality, which often involves an interplay of the major and minor third intervals that is generated by an ascending major third followed by a descending minor second. There is also a feeling of tonal centricity that comes from the use of the minor seventh chord, which is derived at least in part from the harmonic series. In addition, the strong linear tendency of the melodies is a manifestation of an inherent lyricism that owes much to Cambodian music. This indebtedness is evidenced by a consistent reinforcement of melodies at the octave or by unison doublings. In his mature works, Ung pays regular homage to Cambodian music by evoking its ambience without resorting to quotation of specific Cambodian melodies.

An undercurrent of dramatic tension exists on different levels in his music and comes from a direct confrontation of opposing impulses. On one level, tension is achieved through a juxtaposition of disparate Eastern and Western elements, including such tangibles as melody and scale, and also such intangibles as cultural sensibility. On another level, this subtle yet palpable conflict manifests itself in the changeable tendency toward both dispersion and coalescence of the various melodic lines within the total texture.

A characteristic texture of the music resembles an intricate tapestry of prismatic colors. His orchestral work *Inner Voices*, which has a genuine symphonic dimension, contains such representative texture. A predilection for intricacy of this kind is seen in his chamber works as well. Even his solo cello work *Khse Buon* conjures up the image of a complex weave. In addition, the sliding portamento, a feature prominent in Asian music, has become integral to his style since the composition of *Khse Buon*.

This richly textured music favors bright timbres and reveals the composer's unabashed delight in attractive sonorities. The use of percussion is thus aimed at creating a kaleidoscope of colors, and less at generating climaxes. In his scores, one finds bells of all kinds, and also the metallic timbre of the gong, suspended cymbal etc. Along with these bright instruments he employs the mellower marimba, a Western substitute of sort for the Cambodian xylophone *roneat-ek*. A skillful practitioner on the *roneat-ek*, Ung seeks to reinterpret the sound of this instrument and the melodic and harmonic peculiarities of the music of his native land in his own work through the use of Western instruments—an approach to evocation emblematic of his music.

—David Tsang

USTVOLSKAYA, Galina. Russian. Born in Petrograd, 17 June 1919. Educated at Leningrad Arts School, 1937–9; Leningrad Conservatoire (composition under Dmitri Shostakovich and Maximilian Steinberg), 1940–1, 1945–7, post-graduate study (including composition study under Georgy Rimsky-Korsakov), 1947–50. Married Konstantin Makukhin, 23 December 1966. Teacher of composition, Music College of Leningrad Conservatoire, 1948–77; composer. Mailing address: prospekt Gagarina 27-2, St Petersburg 196135, U.S.S.R.

Publishers: Muzyka, Moscow; Sovetskii kompozitor, St Petersburg; Hans Sikorski, Hamburg.

Symphonies/orchestral:

Concerto for Piano, Timpani and String Orchestra 1946; first performed 1968 or 1969.
Suite No 1 1948.
Suite No 2 1950.
Pioneer Suite 1951.
Symfonietta 1951.
Suite No 3 1952.
Symphony No 1 (with 2 boys' voices) 1955; first performed Spring 1966.
Children's Suite 1955. Recorded Melodiya 04430/31.
Podvig geroya (symphonic poem) 1957.
Ogni v stepi 1958.
Sportivnaya Suite 1958.
Symphony No 2: True and Eternal Bliss (orchestra, solo voice; Hermannus Contractus) 1979; first performed Leningrad, 8 October 1980.
Symphony No 3: Jesus Messiah, Save Us! (orchestra, solo voice; Hermannus Contractus) 1983; first performed Leningrad, 1 October 1987.
Symphony No 4: Prayer (trumpet, tam-tam, piano, contralto; Hermannus Contractus) 1985–7; first performed Heidelberg, 24 June 1988.
Symphony No 5: Amen (oboe, trumpet, tuba, violin, percussion /thick plywood cube with wooden hammers, voice) 1989–90.

Instrumental:

String Quartet 1945.
Sonata No 1 (piano) 1947; first performed Leningrad, 20 February 1974. Recorded Melodiya C 10 23 283 007.
Sonata (violin, piano) 1947.
Sonatina (violin, piano) 1947.
Trio (clarinet, violin, piano) 1949; first performed Leningrad, 11 January 1968.
Sonata No 2 (piano) 1949; first performed Leningrad, 14 December 1977.
Octet (2 oboes, 4 violins, timpani, piano) 1949–50; first performed Leningrad, 17 November 1970. Recorded Melodiya C 10 0 715 152.
Sonata No 3 (piano) 1952; first performed Leningrad, 16 February 1972. Recorded Melodiya C 10 0 715 152.
Sonata (violin, piano) 1952; first performed Leningrad, 5 March 1961.
Twelve Preludes (piano) 1953; first performed Leningrad, 20 March 1968.
Sonata No 4 (piano) 1957; first performed Leningrad, 4 April 1973. Recorded Melodiya C 10 23 282 007.
Grand Duet (cello, piano) 1959; first performed Leningrad, 14 December 1977. Recorded Melodiya C 10 23 283 077.
Duet (violin, piano) 1964; first performed Leningrad, 23 May 1968.
Composition No 1: Dona nobis pacem (piccolo, tuba, piano) 1970–1; first performed Leningrad, 19 February 1975.
Composition No 2: Dies irae (8 double basses, percussion/ thick plywood cube with wooden hammers, piano) 1972–3; first performed Leningrad, 14 December 1977.
Composition No 3: Benedictus, qui venit (4 flutes, 4 bassoons, piano) 1974–5; first performed Leningrad, 14 December 1977.
Sonata No 5 (piano) 1986.
Sonata No 6 (piano) 1988.

Vocal/choral:

The Dream of Stenka Razin (bass, orchestra) 1948.
Hail, Youth (chorus, orchestra; Lebedev-Kumach) 1950.
Dawn over the Fatherland (children's chorus, orchestra; Gleisarov) 1952.
The Man from the High Mountain (soloist, chorus, orchestra; Gleisarov) 1952.

Other:

Boldinsky Autumn (film score; orchestra) 1951.
Mordvin Autonomous Soviet Socialist Republic (film score) 1952.
Russian Museums (film score) 1954.
Gogol (film score) 1954.

PUBLICATIONS

On Ustvolskaya: A. Sanin, "GU", in *Soviet Music*, 10, 1990.

Galina Ustvolskaya comments:

My works are not religious in a liturgical sense, but they are infused with a religious spirit, and to my mind they are best suited to performance in a church, without scholarly introductions and analyses. In the concert hall, that is, in "secular" suroundings, the music sounds different . . .

* * *

The external facts of Galina Ustvolskaya's biography can convey only little of her work. Ustvolskaya is a recluse, in whose life it is fruitless to seek dramatic incidents. Her biography seems as restrained, as laconic and as difficult as her art. Her lack of compromise either in her work or in her life is the lack of compromise of a person totally absorbed in her work.

Though her relationship with Dmitri Shostakovich, her teacher, seems at first glance quite straightforward—a great master with an exceptional pupil—it is in fact rather more complicated. Shostakovich did indeed send Ustvolskaya his manuscripts for her inspection (according to her, it was "really very difficult to pronounce one's opinion on his pieces"), but even beyond that quoted from her works, notably in the ninth part of his suite *The Sonnets of Michelangelo Buonarotti*. His words, "I believe that Ustvolskaya's music will acquire world recognition by all those who value genuine musical creativity", speak for themselves. But perhaps another statement he made is deserving of particular attention: "It's not you who is under my influence, it's me who is under your influence."

One of the most distinguishing characteristics of Ustvolskaya is her absolute independence. In all things, she draws from inner resources, without ever leaning on any other authority. She has therefore not had to overcome the influence of Shostakovich or any other composer.

One can call her art neither traditional nor avant-garde. It lies outside stylistic trends and in comparing her work with someone else's, points of contact (however inevitable these might be in view of the limited means of her music) are of far less significance than the differences. There are no bar-lines in her manuscripts, and this method of notation seems the only one possible for the simultaneous expression of both the clarity and multiplicity of her structures.

In each of her works a special world is created anew that is always filled with great strength, giving the composer the right to maintain that, "no composition, even a solo sonata, can be a chamber work". The very concept of "chamber music" presupposes a hermetic, motionless piece of space, while the tectonics of Ustvolsakya's music are a moving and indivisible unity, a cosmic religious rite, or as the composer Viktor Suslin has defined it, "the colossal victory for the spirit over matter".

Ustvolskaya unquestionably occupies a unique position in 20th-century art. Her pieces of the 1940s and 1950s, first published and performed in the 1970s, still manage to sound as if they were freshly written then. World criticism, for whom, Ustvolskaya's name was almost unknown until recently, has called the performance of her works "sensational". In Russia, the words of one critic, writing in 1988, continue to hold true: "Her life is led in obscurity, her name is not known to a wide public."

—A. Sanin

UZOIGWE, Joshua. Nigerian. Born in Nigeria, 1 July 1946. Educated at University of Nigeria, Nsukka, 1970–3, diploma in music; Guildhall School of Music and Drama, London, 1973–7, licentiate in piano, 1974, graduate in piano and composition, 1977; Queen's University of Belfast (ethnomusicology under John Blacking), 1977–81, M.A., 1978, Ph.D., 1981. Military service with Biafran Army during Nigerian civil war, 1967–9. Married Joanne McGuckin in 1982 (deceased 1990); 3 children. Lecturer, department of music, Alvan Ikoku College of Education, Owerri, 1979–81; senior lecturer, department of music, Obafemi Awolowo University, Ile-Ife, Oyo State, since 1981. Recipient: composition prize, African Studies Center, University of California, Los Angeles, 1973; composition prize, Guildhall School of Music and Drama, London, 1974. Mailing address: Department of Music, Obafemi Awolowo University, Ile-Ife, Oyo State, Nigeria.

Publisher: none.

Symphonies/orchestral:

Lustra Variations Op 4 1977; first performed London, 1977.
Royal Procession Op 7 (European and African instruments) 1980; first performed Belfast, 1980.

Chamber/instrumental:

Four Nigerian Dances Op 2 (flute, clarinet, violin, viola, cello) 1976; first performed London, 1976.
A Collection of Works for Piano Solo Op 5 1977; first performed London, 1977.
Masquerade Op 6 (African tension drum, piano) 1979; first performed Aba, 1979.
Fanfare (brass ensemble) 1981.
Sketch Op 8 (trombone, piano) 1986; first performed Ife, 1986.
Five Sketches Op 10 (piano) 1990; first performed Ife, 1990.
Talking Drums (piano) 1990.

Vocal/choral:

Four Igbo Songs Op 1 (voice, piano) 1973; first performed Nsukka, 1973.
Two Songs Op 3 (unaccompanied mixed chorus) 1976; first performed London, 1976.
Watermaid Op 9 (bass, orchestra) 1989.

Other:

Nigerian Art: Kindred Spirits (music for documentary film) 1990.

PUBLICATIONS

By Uzoigwe: "Akin Euba: The Life and Work of a Nigerian Composer", dissertation, Queen's University, Belfast, 1978; "The Compositional Techniques of Ukom Music in South-eastern Nigeria", dissertation, Queen's University, Belfast, 1981; "The Problems of Analysing Traditional Music", *Studies in Traditional Music and Dance*, edited by Cooke, Edinburgh, 1981; "A Cultural Analysis of Akin Euba's Musical Works", in *Odu: Journal of West African Studies*, 1983; "The Creative Experience of an Igbo Master Musician", in *The Black Perspective in Music*, 14(2), 1986; "Tonal Organisation in Ukom Drum Performance", in *Nigerian Magazine*, 54(3), 1986; "Operational and Hierarchical Forms of Creativity in Igbo Music", in *Ife: Annals of the Institute of Cultural Studies*, 2, 1988; "Nigerian Composers and Their Works", in *Daily Times* (Lagos), 25 August, 1 September 1990.

On Uzoigwe: Gary Weltz, "Three Songs", in *African Arts*, 7(3), Spring 1974; Olabode Omojola, "Compositional Style and African Identity: A Study of Modern Art Music", dissertation, University of Leicester, 1987.

Joshua Uzoigwe comments:

Most of my works have been influenced by my analytical studies of the ethnography of musical performance in African societies. They therefore involve the utilization of traditional African elements and techniques, as well as a positive assimilation of qualitative and useful foreign musical ideas and creative methodologies.

* * *

Joshua Uzoigwe's works, like those of most of his contemporaries, are very much influenced in varied degrees by three main musical cultures: European, African and ethnic or tribal. Thus, most of his works could be considered as being a synthesis of these cultures. However, observation shows that while at the conceptual level his compositions have their strongest roots in his Igbo/African cultural background his mode of realizing them, in terms of tonal organisation and instrumentation, suggests a European musical influence.

Invariably, his works derive their themes from cultural and traditional musical elements that one associates mainly with the Igbos of Nigeria, his ethnic group, as well as other neighbouring groups. Titles such as "royal procession", "Nigerian dances" and "talking drums", serve as a pointer to his source of creative inspiration.

The style of his earlier works, such as *Four Igbo Songs* and *Four Nigerian Dances*, for chamber orchestra, have strong African traditional musical influence. The use of modal harmony, rich percussive sounds and complex rhythms associated with African music are manifested vividly in these and other works of his early period.

Recently Uzoigwe has developed his style through Schoenbergian techniques; he uses twelve-tone language in a personal way, combining it freely with melodic-rhythmic elements drawn from African musical traditions. Heralding this new style are *Royal Procession* and *Masquerade*, for African tension drum and piano. *Talking Drums*, for piano, is based on a row of 10 tones which in Igbo tradition is associated with the *ukom aria nkwa*, a set of 10 membrane drums, with each drum having only one pitch sound. This work is one of the best representatives of Uzoigwe's compositional approach.

Royal Procession, for an orchestra consisting of a combined African and European instruments, exemplifies Uzoigwe's attempt to evoke the presence of "total art", the latter being reminiscent of scenes in an African festival. This work highlights Uzoigwe's approach to the problems of rhythm, harmony, texture and form. The piece consists of 52 melodic-rhythmic patterns of different phrase lengths; each pattern is derived from a well-known time-line pattern which, in its complete form, is assigned to a twin metal gong with two pitches and which repeats the pattern constantly throughout the entire duration of the performance of the piece. Each player dwells on each pattern as long as he choses, moving progressively from one pattern to another in the order presented in the score and taking his bearing from the main pulse established by the gong. The result of all these activities is an interplay of rhythmic patterns, textures and waves of dissonant harmonies, giving one the aural impression of a fusion of sounds from different ensembles in a festive musical procession—hence the title. The free form in which this piece is cast suggests Uzoigwe's leaning towards the use of a type of perpetual variation technique called *ilulu nkwa* (musical proverb) in Igbo musical practice. The dynamic contrasts between instruments result mainly from the pitching of the tonal strength of one instrument against the other. This music reveals the workings of a fertile mind and places Uzoigwe among the leading composers from Africa.

—P.A.F. Dixon

V

VAN de VATE, Nancy (professional name of Nancy Jean Hayes Van de Vate Smith; has used pseudonyms Helen Huntley and William Huntley). American; resident in Austria. Born in Plainfield, New Jersey, 30 December 1930. Piano study under Anton Rovinsky, New York City, 1947–8; Eastman School of Music, Rochester, New York (piano under Cecile Genhart), 1948–9, Summer 1950; Wellesley College, Massachusetts (music theory; piano under David Barnett), 1949–51, A.B., 1952; further piano study under Albion Metcalf, Boston, 1951–2; Yale School of Music, New Haven, Connecticut (piano study under Bruce Simonds), 1954; studied composition under Arthur Kreutz, 1956–8; University of Mississippi, University (composition), M.M., 1958; further composition study under John Boda, 1963–4, 1967–8; Florida State University, Tallahassee (composition), D.Mus., 1968; further study in electronic music, Dartmouth College, Hanover, New Hampshire, and University of New Hampshire, Durham, Summer 1972. Married (1) Dwight Van de Vate Jr, 9 June 1952 (dissolved 1976), 3 children; (2) Clyde Arnold Smith, 23 June 1979. Performing pianist, debut 1946; private piano teacher, Oxford, Mississippi, 1957–63, and Tallahassee, Florida, 1963–4; instructor in music, University of Mississippi, University, 1960; assistant professor of music, Memphis State University, Tennessee, 1964–6; secretary and newsletter editor, 1965–8, 1970–3, and president 1973–5, Southeastern Composers League; instructor in music, University of Tennessee, 1967; associate professor of music, 1968–9, and lecturer in music, 1971–2, Knoxville College, Tennessee; lecturer in music, Maryville College, Tennessee, 1973–4; visiting associate professor of music, University of Hawaii, Manoa, 1975–6; founder, chair and newsletter editor, International League of Women Composers, 1975–82; music critic, *Hawaii Observer*, 1976–7; lecturer in Music, University of Hawaii, Honolulu Community College, 1976–9; lecturer in music, 1977–8, associate professor in music, 1978–80, and dean of academic affairs, 1979, Hawaii Loa College; resident in Indonesia, 1982–5; resident in Vienna, since 1985; composer in residence, Pittsburg State University, Kansas, 1987. Recipient: First Place Award (for *Quintet for Brass*), Delius Composition Contest, 1975; 1st prize (for *Quintet*), Los Alamos Chamber Music Competition, 1979; Maryland State Arts Council Composers Fellowship and work-in-progress award, 1988–9; Koussevitzky International Recording Award (for *Chernobyl*), 1989. Mailing address: c/o Vienna Associates, Margaretenstrasse 125/15, A-1050 Vienna, Austria.

Publishers: Vienna Masterworks (self); North/South Editions, P.O. Box 5081, Albany, New York 12205-0081; Arsis Press, 170 N.E. 33rd Street, Fort Lauderdale, Florida 33334; Montgomery Music Inc., Box 157, Niagara Square Station, Buffalo, New York 14202; Southern Music Company, P.O. Box 329, San Antonio, Texas, 78292, U.S.A.; Waterloo Music Company Ltd, 3 Regina Street North, Waterloo, Ontario, Canada.

Symphonies/orchestral:

Adagio 1957; first performed Tuscaloosa, Alabama, 18 April 1958.

Variations (chamber orchestra) 1958; first performed Hattiesburg, Mississippi, 13 March 1960.

Concerto for Piano and Orchestra 1968; first performed Tuscaloosa, Alabama, 26 April 1969.

Concertpiece (cello, small orchestra) 1978; first performed Boston, 29 April 1979. Recorded Conifer CDCF 147.

Dark Nebulae 1981; first performed Columbus, Ohio, 29 June 1983. Recorded Conifer CDCF 147.

Gema Jawa (string orchestra) 1984; first performed Washington, D.C., 20 November 1984.

Journeys 1984; first performed Eugene, Oregon, February 1985. Recorded Conifer CDCF 147.

Distant Worlds (violin, orchestra) 1985; first performed Cracow, Poland, 20 June 1987. Recorded Conifer CDCF 147.

Concerto for Violin and Orchestra 1986; first performed Pittsburg, Kansas, 15 November 1987. Recorded Conifer CDCF 168.

Pura Besakih 1987; first performed San Francisco, 6 February 1988.

Chernobyl 1987. Recorded Conifer CDCF 168.

Krakow Concerto (percussion, orchestra) 1988; first performed Cracow, 28 November 1989. Recorded Conifer CDCF 185.

Concerto for Viola and Orchestra 1990.

Chamber/instrumental:

Short Suite (brass quartet) 1960; first performed Atlanta, Georgia, 9 November 1963.

Diversion (brass) 1964; first performed Atlanta, Georgia, 14 November 1964.

Sonata (viola, piano) 1964; first performed Memphis, Tennessee, 16 February 1966. Recorded Vienna Modern Masters CD 2001.

Woodwind Quartet 1964; first performed Interlochen, Michigan, Autumn 1964.

String Quartet No 1 1969; first performed Lancing, Tennessee, July 1971. Recorded VMM CD 2001.

Six Etudes (violin) 1969; first performed Pittsburg, Kansas, 12 November 1987.

Sonata (oboe, piano) 1969; first performed Knoxville, Tennessee, January 1970.

Six Etudes (viola) 1969; first performed New York City, 24 December 1974.

Sonata (clarinet, piano) 1970.

Three Sound Pieces (brass, percussion) 1973; first performed Atlanta, Georgia, 23 February 1974.

String Trio 1974; first performed Stowe, Vermont, August 1975.

Brass Quintet 1974, revised 1979; first performed Jacksonville, Florida, 25 February 1975.

Suite (viola) 1975.

Suite (violin) 1975; first performed New York City, 3 December 1976.

Quintet (flute, violin, double bass, clarinet, cello or piano) 1975; first performed Honolulu, Hawaii, 12 January 1976.

Music for Viola, Percussion and Piano 1976; first performed

Honolulu, Hawaii, 27 February 1977. Recorded VMM 2001.

Nine Preludes (piano) 1978; first performed Los Angeles, 2 April 1982. Recorded Opus One SN 118; VMM 2001.

Sonata No 1 (piano) 1978; first performed Columbus, Ohio, Autumn 1981. Recorded Coronet LPS 3105.

Trio (bassoon, percussion, piano) 1980; first performed Honolulu, Hawaii, 7 December 1980.

Sonata (harpsichord) 1982; first performed Davis, California, 12 November 1983.

Fantasy (harpsichord) 1982; first performed Ann Arbor, Michigan, 6 May 1983.

Trio (violin, cello, piano) 1983; first performed Mexico City, 24 March 1984.

Sonata No 2 (piano) 1983; first performed Mexico City, 23 March 1984. Recorded Coronet LPS 3206.

Contrasts (2 pianos—6 hands) 1984; first performed Djakarta, Indonesia, 23 May 1984.

Music for Max (mixed ensemble) 1985; first performed New York City, 10 February 1989.

Teufelstanz (percussion) 1988; first performed Munich, 24 February 1989.

Seven Fantasy Pieces 1989; first performed Vienna, 19 July 1991.

Twelve Pieces on One to Twelve Notes (piano) 1989; first performed Vienna, 19 July 1990.

Vocal/choral:

Psalm 121 (chorus) 1958; first performed Knoxville, Tennessee, 30 June 1974.

How Fares the Night? (chorus; anon. Chinese 5th century) 1959; first performed Honolulu, Hawaii, 29 May 1977.

Youthful Age (high voice; Greek 6th century B.C.) 1960.

Death Is the Chilly Night (voice, piano; Heine) 1960; first performed Oxford, Mississippi, Autumn 1960.

Loneliness (voice, piano; Rilke) 1960; first performed Oxford, Mississippi, Autumn 1960.

Cradlesong (voice, piano; Brentano) 1962; first performed Hattiesburg, Mississippi, 2 February 1963.

The Earth Is So Lovely (voice, piano; Heine) 1962; first performed Oxford, Mississippi, Autumn 1962.

Make a Joyful Noise to the Lord (written under pseudonym William Huntley; chorus) 1963.

Four Somber Songs (voice, piano; Trakl, Poe, Blake, Verlaine) 1970; first performed Oak Ridge, Tennessee, 21 October 1973.

The Pond (chorus; Annette von Droste-Hulsoff) 1970; first performed Tampa, Florida, 30 January 1971.

An American Essay (chorus; Whitman) 1972; first performed Knoxville, Tennessee, 16 May 1972.

To the East and to the West (voice, piano; Whitman) 1972; first performed Knoxville, Tennessee, 16 May 1972.

Letters to a Friend's Loneliness (voice, string quartet; Unterecker) 1976; first performed Johnson City, Tennessee, 8 November 1976.

Cantata for Women's Voices (chorus) 1979; first performed Los Angeles, 1 April 1982.

A Night in the Royal Ontario Museum (voice, tape; Atwood) 1983; first performed College Park, Maryland, 13 April 1984.

Songs for the Four Parts of the Night (voice, piano; Owl Woman) 1983; first performed Paris, 25 October 1984. Recorded Cambria CD 1037.

The Saga of Cocaine Lil (vocal ensemble) 1986; first performed Frankfurt, 22 April 1988.

Katyn (chorus, large orchestra) 1989; first performed Cracow, Poland, 28 November 1989. Recorded Conifer CDCF 185.

Opera:

Death of the Hired Man (chamber opera) 1960; first performed Tupelo, Mississippi, 8 February 1960.

In the Shadow of the Glen (chamber opera) 1961.

Nemo: Jenseits von Vulkania in progress.

All Quiet on the Western Front in progress.

Other:

Invention No 1 (tape) 1972; first performed Knoxville, Tennessee, 20 May 1973.

Wind Chimes (electronic) 1972; first performed Knoxville, Tennessee, 20 May 1973.

Satellite Music (electronic) 1973; first performed Knoxville, Tennessee, 20 May 1973.

Educational piano pieces published under pseudonym Helen Huntley (except first and last four): *Twilight*, *Hoe-Down*, *Topsy Turvy*, *Syncopated Solidier*, *Mississippi Twilight*, *Bicycle Ride*, *A Quiet Exchange*, *Up or Out*, *Shifting Shadows*, *Clusterphobia*.

PUBLICATIONS

By Van de Vate: "Every Good Boy (Composer) Does Fine", in *Symphony News*, 24(6), December 1973–January 1974; "The American Woman Composer: Some Sour Notes", in *High Fidelity/Musical American*, June 1975; "Women in Music: The Second Stage", keynote address to Second International Congress on Women in Music, Los Angeles, 2 April 1982, published in *International Congress on Women in Music Newsletter*, 1(1), January 1983; "Is There Life After Fifteen? Some observations on the League", in *International League of Women Composers Journal*, Autumn 1989.

On Van de Vate: Ev Grimes, (interview) in *Music Educators Journal*, October 1986; Jane Weiner LePage and Clyde Smith, *The Life and Music of NVdV*, Metuchen, New Jersey and London, 1991; Ev Grimes (producer), "The Music of NVdV", 1-hour radio programme, American Public Radio stations, 1990–1.

Nancy Van de Vate comments:

Although my music is not stylistically conservative, I do regard it as growing out of and continuing the mainstream tradition of Western music which has been with us for more than a thousand years. I make no effort to eliminate those elements which have marked Western music during most of its history—melody, coherent rhythm, structure, vertical sonority, tension—resolution relationships, idiomatic use of instruments and voices, and the intention of being expressive.

I do not regard myself primarily as an innovator or an inventor looking for altogether new ways to express my ideas. At the same time, I have never wanted to compose totally serialized music, although I do occasionally write twelve-tone pieces. I have made use of virtually every contemporary compositional technique, always with the aim of writing dramatic, understandable and expressive music.

Foreign elements have influenced my music since 1975 when I moved to Hawaii and first had substantial exposure to

Asian music. My six years there were followed in 1982 by nearly four years in Indonesia, where gamelan and other vivid tone colours pervade one's daily existence. In Indonesia I travelled widely, often to distant areas to observe practices remote from Western musical traditions. In 1983, I began travelling from Jakarta to Polish and Czechoslovakian music festivals, broadening my exposure to the music of East European composers in particular. In December 1985 I moved permanently to Vienna.

Composers whose music has especially influenced my own work are Bartók, Stravinsky, Varèse and Penderecki. In recent years I have also been interested in the music of other contemporary Polish composers as well as that of Giya Kancheli and Sofia Gubaidulina of the Soviet Union. I am particularly drawn to music of great emotional intensity and value that quality in my own works.

Certain of my pieces are politically inflected. *An American Essay, Katyn, Krakow Concerto* and my opera-in-progress, *All Quiet on the Western Front*, have anti-war themes. These works reflect events or concerns which moved me but they are not primarily didactic or programmatic in nature. The largest part of my output up until 1990 is absolute music.

Since my study of electronic music in 1972 and my introduction to Asian and exotic music in 1975, I have become increasingly interested in timbre. My mature works are also characterized by a concern with dramatic contrast (dynamic, textural, rhythmic, etc) interest in the large forms—in particular, extended one-movement forms—and movement among varying levels of dissonance. For example, large extremely dissonant clusters often alternate with lyric melodies which may contain archaic elements such as modality or movement in parallel fifths. Since the late 1970s I have composed primarily for large ensemble.

* * *

Nancy Van de Vate has fashioned diverse, eclectic modes into an individual, strong musical voice and has emerged as one of the most internationally active and prolifically recorded American composers. She turned fulltime to composition rather late in her music career, but since 1981, with the appearance of her orchestral piece *Dark Nebulae*—the first work to embody most of the identifiable characteristics of her mature style—she has created an impressive catalogue of virtuosic, colorfully dissonant scores that often display an intense concern for the human condition.

Van de Vate's early music gives few clues to what her style would become. Her music of the 1960s incorporates some expressionistic features—nonserial twelve-tone themes, dissonant counterpoint—and shows a fondness for arch forms. However, by the mid-to late-1970s, her compositions had become more extroverted, and new traits are discernible in three major works from that period.

In *Music for Viola, Percussion and Piano* the prominence given to percussion became more than a one-time novelty; this often dancelike and jazzy score, with its playfully imitative counterpoint and hypnotic "night music" middle movement, seemed to awaken in Van de Vate an interest in instrumental color. Since then percussion instruments became an important component in her music, especially in her programmatic orchestral compositions of the 1980s, where the percussion section serves as both a forceful exclamation point for her observations and a melodic complement—whether it is used as a solo unit in itself or as a timbral counterpoint behind frequent ruminative solo instrumental lines. Her *Nine Preludes* for piano are notable for a dramatic application of clustered sound and extremes in dynamics; delicately shaded preludes are alternated with hammered-out, perpetuum-mobile ones, and such sharply contrasted sound has been an organizational feature in her compositions ever since. Finally, her *Sonata No 1* for piano exhibits the sweeps, swells, emotionalism and harmonic language associated with late Romanticism and with the bravura of Prokofiev and Shostakovich.

Yet it is with orchestral works that Van de Vate has made her greatest impact. Her 1957 *Adagio* and 1968 Piano Concerto were her only pre-1980 large-scale works, and then *Dark Nebulae* appeared, breaking that nearly 12-year silence and inaugurating a series of quite remarkable full orchestral scores of a uniquely personal nature. *Dark Nebulae* confirms immediately the composer's transformation to sonorism, wherein staggered blocks of sound supplant customary thematic development—a change hinted at by her chamber pieces of the 1970s; it marks Van de Vate's first use of the extremely dense clustering typical of Penderecki and the modern Polish School of composition. Dissonant behemoths rise seemingly from nowhere and form chilling, almost tactile pillars of sound and then cease, only to form again a few moments later while trumpets sound desperate warnings of unspecified calamity.

Journeys is another important marker in Van de Vate's output. Begun in Bali in 1981 and completed in Jakarta nearly four years later—after intermediate stops in Washington, Poland and Czechoslovakia—the work's title reflects both external and internal movement: her "wanderings" around the globe and her absorption of various cultures, and the music's traversal through several contrasting episodes, with a colossal, percussion-laden aleatory outburst forming the work's climax. There is a Southeast Asian "sound" to much of the score; some stretches of the music have an unhurried timbral suspension, permitting the listener's ears to savor the emotional aspects of her autobiographical showcase. *Distant Worlds*, with its solo violin protagonist, continues the composer's self-professed "great love of travel to obscure places" by presenting an almost surreal space and time travelogue.

Since 1985 there has been a tendency for Van de Vate's music to sound alarms—alerting listeners to be watchful and concerned citizens of the world. Sometimes the alarm is programmatically direct, as in the symphonic "tragic landscapes" of *Chernobyl, Katyn,* and the *Krakow Concerto* for percussion and orchestra; in other works such as *Dark Nebulae*, *Distant Worlds*, and the First Violin Concerto, the call to attention is more abstract but no less visceral, as solemnly hopeful solo lines are seemingly caught off guard and buffeted by sudden, crushingly dissonant episodes.

In all, Van de Vate's music has become the embodiment of fearful times—a music of dauntless immediacy that does not sacrifice satisfying compositional precepts.

—Stephen W. Ellis

VEGA, Aurelio de la. Cuban; American citizen. Born in La Habana, 28 November 1925. Educated at De La Salle College, Havana, 1940–4, B.A. in humanities; University of Havana, 1944–6, M.A. in diplomacy; private music study under Ernst Toch, Los Angeles, 1947–8; Ada Iglesias Music Institute, Havana, 1951–8, M.A. in musicology, 1956, Ph.D. in composition, 1958. Married Sara Lequerica, 26 January

1947. Music critic, *Alerta*, Havana, 1952–7; president, Cuban Council of Music, 1952–5; professor of music and chair of music department, University of Oriente, Santiago de Cuba, 1953–9; advisor, National Institute of Culture, Havana, 1955–9; guest professor of music, University of Southern California, Los Angeles, Summer 1959; distinguished professor of music and director, Electronic Music Studio, California State University, Northridge, since 1959; Andrew Mellon Fellow, University of Pittsburgh, Pennsylvania, 1963; president, Los Angeles Chapter, National Association of Composers, 1964–7. Recipient: Virginia Colliers Chamber Music Award, Washington, D.C., 1955; Medal of the Order of the Sociedad Económica de Amigos del Pais, Havana, 1955; Havana Lyceum Award, 1957; Medal of the Order Eloy Alfaro, Bogota, 1961; Outstanding Professor Award, California State University and Colleges, 1971; Distinguished Professor Award, California State University, 1974; National Federation of Music Clubs Award, Washington, D.C., 1975; Juan J. Remos Award, Miami, 1978; City of Los Angeles Commendation, Office of the Mayor, 1978; Kennedy Center Friedheim Award, Washington, D.C., 1978, 1984; California State Senate Commendation, Sacramento, 1979; Honor Distinction for Creativity, Patronata Jose Marti, Los Angeles, 1979; Creativity Award, California State University, Northridge, 1984; Fulbright Research Award, Washington, D.C., and Rio de Janeiro, 1985; Jose de la Luz y Caballero Award, Miami, 1986. Mailing address: 18800 Stare Street, Northridge, California 91324, U.S.A.

Publishers: Southern; Belwin Mills-Columbia Pictures Publications, Miami; Facsimile Editions, Northridge, California.

Symphonies/orchestral:

Overture to a Serious Farce 1950; first performed Havana, 1951.
Introduction and Episode 1952; first performed Havana, 1953.
Elegy (string orchestra) 1954; first performed London, 1954.
Divertimento (violin, piano, cello, string orchestra) 1956; first performed Redlands, California, 1958.
Symphony in Four Parts 1960; first performed Washington, D.C., 1961.
Intrata 1972; first performed Los Angeles, 1972.
Adiós 1977; first performed Los Angeles, 1978.

Chamber/instrumental:

Rondo (piano) 1948; first performed Havana, 1948.
The Death of Pan (violin, piano) 1948.
Trio (violin, cello, piano) 1949; first performed Havana, 1952.
Soliloquy (viola, piano) 1950; first performed Havana, 1951.
Leyenda del Ariel Criollo (cello, piano) 1953; first performed Havana, 1954. Recorded Panart 4001.
Epigram (piano) 1953; first performed Washington, D.C., 1955.
String Quartet in Five Movements: In memoriam Alban Berg 1957; first performed Washington, D.C., 1958.
Toccata (piano) 1957; first performed Northridge, California, 1960.
Wind Quintet 1959; first performed Los Angeles, 1961.
Trio (flute, oboe, clarinet) 1960; first performed Northridge, California 1961.
Structures (piano, string quartet) 1962; first performed Washington, D.C., 1964.
Segments (violin, piano) 1964; first performed Berkeley, California, 1964.
Exametron (flute, cello, 4 percussion) 1965; first performed Los Angeles, 1965.
Interpolation (clarinet, tape) 1965; first performed Los Angeles, 1966. Recorded Orion 76239.
Exospheres (oboe, piano) 1966; first performed Los Angeles, 1968. Recorded Orion 76239.
Antinomies (piano) 1967; first performed Los Angeles, 1969. Recorded Orion 80397.
Labdanum (flute, vibraphone, viola) 1970; first performed Los Angeles, 1970.
Tangents (violin, tape) 1973; first performed Los Angeles, 1974. Recorded Orion 73128.
Para-Tangents (trumpet, tape) 1973; first performed Los Angeles, 1974. Recorded Crystal S-366.
Septicilium (solo clarinet, flute, harp, piano/celeste, percussion, violin, cello) 1974.
Olep ed Arudamot (variable instrumentation) 1974; first performed Tujunga, 1974.
Andamar-Ramadna (variable instrumentation) 1975; first performed Mexico City, 1977.
The Magic Labyrinth (variable instrumentation) 1975.
Sound Clouds (guitar) 1975; first performed Los Angeles, 1978. Recorded Klavier 565.
The Infinite Square (variable instrumentation) 1975; first performed Northridge, California, 1976.
Astralis (variable instrumentation) 1977; first performed Buenos Aires, 1979.
Nones (variable instrumentation) 1977; first performed San Francisco, 1979.
Corde (variable instrumentation) 1977.
Undici colori (bassoon, colour slides) 1981; first performed Los Angeles, 1982.
Galandiacoa (clarinet, guitar) 1982; first performed Los Angeles, 1983.
Tropimapal (flute, clarinet, bassoon, trombone, percussion, violin, viola, cello, double bass) 1983; first performed Los Angeles, 1983. Recorded Opus One S 134.
Homenagem: In memoriam Heitor Villa Lobos (piano) 1987; first performed São Paulo, 1987.

Vocal/choral:

La fuente infinita (song cycle for soprano, piano) 1944; first performed Havana, 1945.
Cantata (2 sopranos, contralto, 21 instruments) 1958; first performed Washington, D.C., 1964.
Inflorescencia (soprano, bass clarinet, tape) 1976; first performed Los Angeles, 1976. Recorded Orion 78302.
Asonante (soprano, flute, trumpet, trombone, piano, violin, cello, double bass) 1985; first performed Los Angeles, 1987.

Other:

Vectors (1-track tape) 1963.
The Magic Labyrinth (graphic score) 1975.
Extrapolation (tape) 1981; first performed Los Angeles, 1981.

PUBLICATIONS

By de la Vega: *Arnold Schoenberg and the Atonalists*, 1947; *The Negative Emotion*, 1950; *The New Romanticism*. 1951; "Por que Mozart?" [Why Mozart?] in *Revista del Instituto National de Cultura*, 1(2), Havana, March 1956; "La musica de Norteamerica hoy" [U.S. Music Today], in *Buenos Aires Musical* (special issue), December 1959; "Mozart ahora" [Mozart Now], in *Revista Musical Chilena,* 16(80), April–June 1962; "Music as a Reflection of Latin America", in *Musical Journal Annual Anthology*, New York, 1963; "En torno a la musica electronica" [Regarding Electronic Music], in *Revista Musical Chilena*, 19(94), October–December 1965; "The Artist in Latin America", in *Journal of the Canadian Association of University Schools of Music*, 8(2), Autumn 1978; "Latin American Composers in the U.S.A", in *Latin American Music Review*, 5(2), Spring-Summer 1983; "Alejo Carpentier's Musical Phases", in *Inter American Club Magazine*, 1984; "Unas musicas extranas" [Some Strange Musics], in *Linden Lane Magazine*, 4(2), April-June 1985; "La necesaria transformación del crítico músical" [The Needed Transformation of the Music Critic], in *Heterfonia* 18(3), July-September 1985; "El arista en latinoamerica" [The Artist in Latin America], in *Arte Plural*, 4(9), 1985; "A Quick Encounter with Brazil's Art Music", in *latin American Music Review*, 8(1), 1987; "Os musicológicos tem tido pouca visão", in *Encontros sob Música*, edited by José E. Martins, São Paulo, 1990; "Anotaciones para la historia músical de más tarde" [Annotations for Tomorrow's Music History], in *Linden Land Magazine* (special issue), 9(4), October-December 1990.

On de la Vega: James Ramsen Schortt, "AV, un compositor de las Americas", in *Revista Musical Chilena*, 17(84), April–June 1963; Alice Ramsay, "AV: His Life and Works", dissertation, California State University, Northridge, 1963; Andres Pardo-Tovar, "AV, Músico de las Américas", in *Boletín de la Radio-TV National de Colombia,* July 1964; Lester Trimble, "Critical Comments on *Structures*", in *Musical Quarterly*, 50(4), October 1964; Gilbert Chase, "A Cuban in California", in *America's Music*, 2nd edition, New York City, 1966; Gerard Béhague, comments on various works, in *Music of Latin America*, New York City, 1979; Ronald Erin, "Cuban Elements in the Music of AV", in *Latin American Music Review*, 5(1), 1984; Mercedes Otero, (interviews) in *La Autocrítica Insaciable*, Mexico City, 1985.

Aurelio de la Vega comments:

The 20th century, with all its fascinating and multi-faceted explorations of new parameters of artistic creativity, novel discoveries in science, untrodden and varied expansions of philosophical and political propositions, and the reordering of myriads of structural and ethical parameters applied to all levels of human thought, remains a paradoxically often troubled and confused period of humanity. Powerful expansive forces created far-reaching revolutions in the arts, and acted as a revamping of postures and concepts which, at least theoretically, would parallel the deep changes, expansions and transformations projected by science. Yet, these upheavals were somehow unable to create a new methodology which could harness coherently the unleashed energy, Imagination ran wild—often movingly, valiantly, fearlessly—destroying in its process of expansion so many viable languages and structural blueprints that incoherence replaced communication. Particularly in music (already an art so abstract in itself that it required more than others reiteration, summarization and recapitulation of sound patterns) a deep and evergrowing abyss soon separated the composer from his audience. The end of our century has proposed various solutions to re-establish a healthy dialogue between the music creator and the public for whom he writes, no matter how idealistically or theoretically expressed the composer's message would be. From minimalism to neo-tonality, from incorporation of pop elements to constant proselytizing through carefully orchestrated explanatory verbalization, the aim was to change for the better the negative prevailing climate which had turned the composer of "art" music into a social and cultural pariah. However, several of the proposed solutions to the crisis may prove in the long run to be, however welcome, merely transitory mirages.

Personally, I feel a need to reinstate a workable musical language which would permit, without a loss of individuality and without an easy return to a secure past, a renewed possibility of intelligibility. Again for me, said language is to be based on elements which have evolved from those that formed and underlined my own cultural origin, transformed into an aesthetical experience which, without renouncing the positive technical advances that have shaped the structural and conceptual forms of 20th-century music, is once more capable of establishing a colloquy between composer and hearer. Then, the effort of creativity will become again a happy artistic event, removed from perpetual "angst", faceless internationalism, mere scientific explanations and occasional political crutches. This way, somehow, the audience will listen again.

* * *

From his earliest works, Aurelio de la Vega exhibited certain concerns and characteristics that shaped and defined his musical vocabulary. Stylistically, some of his early works such as the song cycle *La fuente infinita* display a chromatic, post-impressionist harmonic language while simultaneously utilizing Afro-Cuban rhythmic devices. However, it is important to note that even from the beginning de la Vega rejected overt nationalist colloquialisms in his style and publicly denounced such compositional practices, against the prevailing folk-based neo-romanticism of Cuban music at the time. Internationalist in harmonic language and structure, Afro-Cuban in rhythmic awareness, the early pieces of the late 1940s and early 1950s also display his predilection for virtuosic statement, vigorous rhythmic drive, dramatic contrapuntal line and highlighted instrumental color—elements which continue to be important throughout his stylistic evolution.

The mid-1950s displayed a new stylistic direction for de la Vega, exemplified in his *String Quartet in Five Movements: In memoriam Alban Berg*. Given the highly chromatic vocabulary and European influences of his earlier work, the progression to serialism was inevitable considering his previous direction. At the same time de la Vega was developing a more personal free atonal language that is still apparent in his more recent works. His last work constructed on serial procedures was *Exametron* scored for flute, cello and four percussionists.

By the mid-1960s, de la Vega's stylistic concerns had changed to include chance procedures, open forms, graphic notation, more fluid melodic emphasis, electronics and abandonment of serialism. Whereas during the 1950s, the Cuban elements in his style had been kept to an absolute minimum, his music during the late 1960s began to display more of the synthesis between national and international vocabularies. The works began to exhibit four facets of Cuban music: Afro-Cuban rhythmic patterns, call and answer construction (antecedent-consequent), rhythmic counterpoint and an emphasis on percussive instrumental color. Just as serialism and its abandonment was for him a natural progression of his harmonic and organizational principles, the use of national elements became more evident and increasingly more important in his music at this point. Examples of this early synthesis include *Antinomies* for solo piano and the two chamber works *Exospheres* and *Labdanum*.

During the 1970s the national gestures reached an apogee in de la Vega's compositional concerns. Folk themes are quoted directly as in the chamber work *Septicilium* and Afro-Cuban rhythms take on programmatic functions in *Inflorescencia* written for soprano, bass clarinet and tape. It is from this period that two of his most well-known works were written, both for orchestra: *Intrata* and *Adiós*. At the same time, de la Vega continued to develop his interest in electronic music, aleatoric procedures, and the combination of visual and sound elements through graphic scores, as in *The Magic Labyrinth*.

However, since the early 1980s, de la Vega has de-emphasized some of the stylistic elements of the 1970s. In general, his music has become less experimental, less aggressive, more lyrical and personal, with a predilection for vocal chamber music. Although Cuban elements continue to be included in his compositional process, their importance and frequency has decreased form his works of the 1970s. From national and modernist elements, he has developed a unique personal style—a highly dramatic pantonality with an elemental rhythmic drive.

—Ronald F. Erin

VICTORY, Gerard. Irish. Born in Dublin, 24 December 1921. Educated at Belvedere College, Dublin; National University of Ireland. B.A.; Trinity College, University of Dublin, B.Mus. Married Geraldine Herity, 14 April 1948; 5 children. Administrative officer, Irish Civil Service, Dublin, 1943–8; actor, radio repertory, Irish Radio Service, 1948–53; radio producer, 1953–61, television producer, 1961–2, deputy director of music, 1962–7, and director of music, 1967–82, Radio Telefis Eireann; President, UNESCO Rostrum of Composers, 1981–4; freelance composer and conductor, since 1944. Recipient: Oirgachtas Composition Prize, 1961; honorary Mus.D., University of Dublin, 1972; Chevalier de l'Ordre des Arts et des Lettres, France, 1975; Verdienstkreuz (Order of Merit), Germany, 1975; Hamilton Harty Bursary, Irish Arts Council, 1981. Mailing address: 29 Lawnswood Park, Stillorgan, County Dublin, Ireland.

Publishers: Vanderbeek and Imrie, 15 Marvig, Lochs, Isle of Lewis PA86 9QP, Scotland; Cranz; Basil Ramsey; Fairfield-Novello; Cary; Curwen; Walton; Barenreiter; Bosworth, Leduc; McCullough-Pigott; Mozart Edition.

Symphonies/orchestral:

Piano Concerto No 1 1955; first performed Dublin, 1955.
Symphony No 1: Short Symphony 1960; first performed Dublin, 1961.
Five Mantras (string orchestra) 1963.
Ballade 1964; first performed Dublin, 1964.
Overture: Treasure Island 1966; first performed Dublin, 1966.
Overture: Rapparee 1967.
Homage to Petrarch (string orchestra) 1969.
Four Tableaux 1969; first performed Dublin, 1969.
Accordion Concerto 1969; first performed Dublin, 1970.
Overture: Cyrano de Bergerac 1970; first performed Dublin, 1971.
Miroirs (chamber orchestra) 1970; first performed Dublin, 1970. Recorded Nwe Irish Recording Company NIR 004.
Concerto for Harp and Chamber Orchestra 1971.
Piano Concerto No 2 1971; first performed Dublin, 1973.
Jonathan Swift (symphonic portrait) 1971; first performed Dublin, 1972. Recorded New Irish Recording Company NIR 011.
Suite: Spirit of Molière 1972.
Capriccio (violin, orchestra) 1975.
Symphony No 2: Il ricorso 1977; first performed Dublin, 1978.
Concerto for Accordion and Orchestra 1978.
Nine Variations on "An Carabhat" 1979.
Overture: Olympic Festival 1980.
Six Epiphanies of the Author: A Symphonic Study in Memory of James Joyce 1981; first performed Dublin, 1984.
Symphony No 3: Refrains 1982; first performed Dublin, 1982.
Tableaux sportifs (Overture; "Le Patinage", "Karate", "Le Croquet", "La Corrida", "A la voile", "Les Courses", Finale: March; orchestra or wind band) 1985.
Marche bizarre (wind band or brass band) 1985.
Tightrope (circus fantasy for wind band or brass band) 1985.
Fantasy Overture: Monte Cristo 1985–6.
Symphony No 4 1985–7.
Concertino à la grecque ("Triton", "Leander", "Proteus", "Centaur"; 4 evocations for trombone, orchestra; also version for trombone, piano) 1987.

Chamber/instrumental:

Wind Quintet 1957.
String Quartet 1963; first performed Dublin, 1984.
Compensations (cor anglais, tape) 1963; first performed Dublin, 1970. Recorded New Irish Recording Company NIR 002.
Prelude and Toccata (piano) 1963; first performed Dublin, 1963. Recorded New Irish Recording Company NIR 001.
Rodomontade (woodwind quintet) 1964.
Sémantiques (flute, piano) 1967.
Five Correlations (piano) 1969; first performed Dublin, 1971.
Three Legends (clarinet, piano, violin, cello) 1969; first performed Dublin, 1969.
Trio (accordion, guitar, percussion) 1970; first performed Dublin, 1971.
Piano Quintet 1971; first performed Dublin, 1974.
Sonatina (alto saxophone, piano) 1973; first performed Bordeaux, 1974.
Capriccio (version for violin, piano) 1975.
Adest hora (violin, cello, clarinet, percussion, piano) 1976; first performed Dublin, 1978.
Verona Preludes (piano) 1979; first performed Dublin, 1980.
String Trio 1981; first performed Dublin, 1982.
Five Exotic Dances (brass sextet) 1981; first performed Dublin, 1981.
Tableaux sportifs (chamber version for 2 flutes/piccolo, oboe, 2 clarinets, bassoon, 2 horns, 2 trumpets, 2 trombones, timpani, 2 percussion, harp, 2 pianos, double bass) 1985.
Runic Variations (flute, clarinet) 1987; first performed Dublin, 1988.
Moresca (violin, cello, harp) 1989; first performed Dublin, 1990.

Vocal/choral:

The River of Heaven (cantata for soprano, tenor, SATB chorus, orchestra; Lafcadio Hearn, after the Japanese) 1964; first performed Dublin, 1965.

Hymnus Vespertinus (unaccompanied SATB chorus) 1965; first performed Berlin, 1965.
Quartetto (narrator, SATB chorus) 1966; first performed Cork, 1966.
Kriegslieder (tenor, chorus, trumpet, percussion) 1966.
Voyelles (soprano, flute, percussion, string orchestra) 1966.
Five Ember Songs (mezzo-soprano, orchestra; Ibsen) 1967; first performed Dublin, 1968.
Civitas nova (SATB chorus, organ; Apocalypse, in Latin) 1968; first performed Dublin, 1970.
The Passionate Pilgrim (song cycle after Shakespeare) 1969.
Four Idylls from Theocritus (alto solo, unaccompanied SATB chorus) 1971.
Processus (SATB chorus, flute, oboe, clarinet, bassoon, 4 horns, 3 trumpets, 3 trombones, bassoon, 4 percussion, 2 pianos, string; medieval alchemists) 1972; first performed Dublin, 1976.
Seven Songs of Experience (unaccompanied SATB chorus; Blake) 1978.
Five Songs by James Joyce (soprano, tenor, SATB chorus, orchestra) 1978; first performed Dublin, 1982.
Ultima rerum (symphonic requiem for soprano, alto, tenor, bass, small and large chorus, orchestra, optional organ) 1982; first performed Dublin, 1984.
In paradisum (drawn from *Ultima rerum*; unaccompanied SATB chorus) 1982.
King Sweeney (tenor, SATB chorus, small instrumental ensemble; Irish folk tale) 1984.
Songs from Lyonnesse (chorus) 1985.
The Land of Lilliput (SSA chorus, piano, 2 percussion; Swift) 1987.

Opera:

An fear a phos balbhan / The Silent Wife 1953; first performed Dublin, 1953.
Iomrall Aithne 1956.
The Music Hath Mischief 1964.
Chatterton (after de Vigny) 1968–70; first performed Paris, 1971.
Eloise and Abelard 1972.
An Evening for Three 1976; first performed Dublin, 1976.
The Rendezvous 1988–9; first performed Dublin, 1989.

Other:

Four Plays for Dancers (incidental music to Yeats; chamber ensemble, voices) 1963; first performed Dublin, 1963. Recorded Argo PLP 1091.
Victor Frankenstein (film score for full orchestra) 1978; first shown Stockholm, 1978.

Film scores: *Oliver Twist*, *Ghost Stories*, *From the Pickwick Papers*, *Les Miserables*, *The Phantom of the Opera*, *A Tale of Two Cities*, 1987–9; first broadcast on American television.

PUBLICATIONS

By Victory: *Ri-cheol agus Romansaiocht* [Study of Romantic Composers; in Irish], Dublin, 1963; "Folklore vor dem Mikrophon", in *50 Jahre Rundfunk*, Vienna, 1973; "Sean O'Riada", in *Written on the Wind*, Dublin, 1976.

On Victory: Anne Murphy, *The Requiem in the Twentieth Century* [contains detailed analysis of *Ultima rerum*], Maynooth, 1989; David Wright, *GV*, forthcoming, 1991.

Gerard Victory comments:

My work has covered a wide variety of genres over the years from light concert to "intellectual" and experimental works. The degree of searching and questing implied in this is linked to a strong desire to communicate to as wide an audience as possible in a way that would combine diversion and stimulation of the ear with as much underlying sincerity of purpose as I could summon up. I think in my works since 1980, especially the symphonies, I have achieved a better synthesis of these objectives.

* * *

Gerard Victory is an eclectic composer. While he was director of music for Radio Telefis Eireann (RTE), the enterprising broadcasting station of the Republic of Irleand, he encouraged the performance of new music by contemporary composers, both Irish and from abroad. He is a prolific composer and has written works in a wide range of styles for almost every conceivable medium, including, naturally, incidental music for radio and TV programmes.

At RTE, Victory was fortunate to have a group of musicians at hand who were able to perform his works. His compositions of the last 20 years have not featured the traditional training ground of Irish composers (i.e., arrangements or Irish folk dance and folk song, though one Irish tune appears in his *Six Epiphanies of the Author*) but ventured further afield.

The works of the last 20 years display a very wide variety and include several for orchestra and/or choir. His *Processus* is a short cantata with a text based on alchemical writings of the Middle Ages. It suggests the influence of Stravinksy via Orff, recalling the atavistic, exuberant spirit of Orff, something in the spirit of Orff's vivid *Carmina Burana*.

Victory's extrovert and ceremonial *Overture: Olympic Festival*, written for the Olympic games in Montreal in 1975, is in the zestful spirit of athleticism and a more popular style. Accordion concertos are very unusual in the orchestral field. Victory's concerto of 1978 successfully solves the problems of balance between the soloist and the orchestra and is dynamic.

The curiously titled *Six Epiphanies of the Author* is explained by the subtitle "A Symphonic Study in Memory of James Joyce". The orchestral work was composed in 1981 for Joyce's centenary year in 1982. The work is extremely vivid. "Epiphany" (usually associated with Christ) may be translated as the manifestation of a human being. Victory has successfully attempted to depict different side of Joyce's life and work which he clearly finds fascinating. This composition is in six sections with a prologue and epilogue. It is based upon a twelve-note row, which is not stated explicitly in its entirety until the end of the piece. Here Victory's music, like Joyce's literary style, often consists of an all-embracing collage of different elements (e.g., a Habanera, a medieval chorale, a music hall song "The Yorkshire Girl", an Irish melody "The Shores of Amerikay", a marche macabre etc.). This is one of the most interesting and approachable of Victory's works.

Victory's *Symphony No 3: Refrains* is a vivid, trenchant and powerful work. The thematic material of the opening section has something in common with Shostakovich.

By contrast, Victory's *Tableaux sportifs* is a frothy piece in the joyful spirit of Chabrier, and an example of the best kind of entertaining light music.

In Victory's short one-act opera, *The Rendezvous*, based on a short story by Maurice Renard, Victory managed to capture the fantastic, passionate and Francophile aura of this story. The opera reaches a great climax. This very effective opera perhaps suggests that the composer should work in the direction of theatre music.

Victory's music is marked by vivid and effective orchestration and often a francophile elegance. He is a versatile Irish composer with essentially European perspectives.

—Michael Dawney

VIERU, Anatol. Romanian. Born in Iasi (Jassy), 8 June 1926. Educated at Bucharest Conservatory (harmony under Paul Constantinescu, orchestration under Theodor Rogalski, composition under Leon Klepper, conducting under Constantin Silvestri), 1946–51, P.I. Tchaikovsky Conservatory, Moscow (composition under Aram Khachaturian), 1951–4, postgraduate course, 1958; G. Dima Conservatory, Cluj-Napoca (Koloszvar), doctorate in musicology, 1978. Married Nina Shutikova in 1954; 1 daughter and 1 son. Conductor, National Theatre, Bucharest, 1947–50; editor, *Muzica* magazine, 1950–1; teacher of orchestration, later composition, Ciprian Porumbescu Conservatory, Bucharest, since 1953; founder/conductor, "Muzici paralele" concert series, George Enescu Philharmonic, Bucharest, from 1970; composer in residence, Deutscher Akademischer Austauschdienst, Berlin, 1973; guest lecturer, Juilliard School, New York City, Sarah Lawrence College, Bronxville, New York, P.I. Tchaikovsky Conservatory, Moscow, and Rubin Academy of Music, Jerusalem. Recipient: 2nd place, George Enescu Composition Prize, 1946; State Prize, Romania, 1949; Order of Work, Romania, 1959; Reine Marie José Composition Prize, Geneva, 1962; Koussevitzky Composition Prize, Washington, D.C., 1966; George Enescu Prize, Romanian Academy, 1967; Order of Cultural Merit, 1969; prizes of Union of Composers and Musicologists, Romania, 1973, 1977, 1979; Herder Prize, Vienna, 1986. Mailing address: Str Stirbei-Voda 68 ap 3, Bucharest 70734, Romania.

Publishers: Editura Muzicala, Bucharest; Editions Salabert, Paris.

Symphonies/orchestral:

Suite in Ancient Style (string orchestra) 1945.
Concerto for Orchestra 1955; first performed Bucharest, April 1966.
Concerto for Flute and Orchestra 1958; first performed Bucharest, December 1961.
Concerto for Cello and Orchestra 1962; first performed Geneva, March 1963.
Symphony (15 instrumentalists, mezzo-soprano) 1962; first performed Cluj-Napoca, December 1965.
Jocuri/Jeux (piano, orchestra) 1963; first performed Iasi, March 1966.
Concerto for Violin and Orchestra 1964; first performed Cluj-Napoca, April 1967.
Oda tacerii/Ode to Silence (Symphony No 1) 1967; first performed Bucharest, 26 March 1968.
Museum Music (harpsichord, 12 strings) 1968; first performed Paris, July 1970.
Clepsydra I (Sonnenuhr) (trumpet, orchestra) 1968; first performed Donaueschingen, October 1969.
Ecran/Screen 1970; first performed Royan, April 1970.
Symphony No 2 1973; first performed Berlin, 1978.
Sinfonietta 1975; first performed Prague, May 1977.
Concerto for Clarinet and Orchestra 1975; first performed Iasi, January 1978.
Symphony No 3 1976–8; first performed Bucharest, March 1978.
Iosif Si Fratii Sai/Joseph and His Brothers (11 instrumentalists, tape) 1979; first performed Metz, November 1979.
Concerto for Violin, Cello, Orchestra 1979; first performed Bucharest, June 1980.
Scoica/Shell (15 strings) 1981; first performed Timisoara, 5 November 1982.
Symphony No 4 1982; first performed Cluj-Napoca, 15 May 1983.
Symphony No 5 (orchestra, choir) 1984–5; first performed Bucharest, 30 January 1986.
Narration II (saxophone, orchestra) 1985; first performed Nice, 9 February 1986.
Sinfonia Concertante (cello, orchestra) 1987; first performed Bucharest, 1988.
Symphony No 6 1989.

Chamber/instrumental:

String Quartet No 1 1955.
String Quartet No 2 1956.
Quintet (clarinet, string quartet) 1957.
Din Lumea Copiilor/From the Children's World (piano) 1958.
Sonata (cello) 1963, version *Clockworks* for cello, percussion ad lib 1977.
Trepte ale Tacerii/Steps of Silence (string quartet, percussionist) 1966.
Nautilos (piano, tape) 1968.
Sita lui Eratostene/Erastothene's Sieve (clarinet, violin, viola, cello, piano) 1969.
Nasterea Unui Limbaj/The Birth of a Language (piano—4 hands) 1971.
Mozaicuri (3 percussion) 1972.
String Quartet No 3 (with soprano, second movement) 1973.
Narration (organ) 1975.
Sonata (piano) 1976.
String Quartet No 4 1980.
String Quartet No 5 1982.
Double Duos (alto saxophone/bass clarinet, vibraphone/marimba) 1983.
Ma-Jo-R Music (harp obbligato, flute, clarinet, string quartet) 1984; first performed Geneva, 30 April 1985.
Soroc I (six etudes for solo percussion and winds) 1984; first performed Bucharest, 16 June 1984.
Duo (violin, cello) 1984–5; first performed Bucharest, 7 April 1987.
Metaksax (alto saxophone, "envelope follower") 1984; first performed Nice, February 1985.
Doux Polysson (alto saxophone) 1984; first performed Timisoara, May 1985.
Pelinarium (Korg DW-8000 synthesizer) 1986.
String Quartet No 6 1986; first performed Bucharest, 7 April 1987.
String Quartet No 7 1987; first performed Turin, 29 September 1988.
Trinta (saxophone(s), percussion) 1987; first performed Bucharest, 25 September 1989.
Diaphonie (cello, double bass) 1988; first performed Cologne, 28 June 1988.
Dar I (flute) 1988.
Dar II (cello) 1989.
Giusto (saxophone, synthesizer, percussion, electric guitar, bass guitar) 1989; first performed Berlin, February 1990.

Vocal/choral:

Cinci Coruri/Five Choirs (folk verse) 1954.
Miorita/The Ewe (soloists, choir, orchestra; folk verse) 1957;

first performed Bucharest, April 1958.

Muzica Pentru Bacovia Si Labis / Music for Bacovia and Labis (3 cycles for voice, piano, instrumental interludes; *Luptu cu Inertia / Struggles Against Inertia*—violin, clarinet, piano; *Noptile lui Bacovia / Bacovia's Nights*—mezzo-soprano, piano; Trio II; *Ode*—tenor, piano; Trio III; *Nocturnes*—soprano or tenor, piano; *Rezonante Bacovia*—flute, tape ad lib; *Destinderi / Relaxations*—mezzo-soprano, piano) 1959–63.

Cantata Anilor Lumina / Cantata of the Light Years (choir, orchestra; Cassian) 1960; first performed Bucharest, May 1986.

Scène nocturne / Nocturnal Scenes (2 unaccompanied choirs; Lorca) 1964.

Vocale / Vowels (female choir; Ungaretti) 1965.

Clepsydra II (choir, orchestra, panpipe, cimbalom; folk verse) 1971; first performed Bucharest, October 1972.

Discul Lui Newton / Newton's Disc (12 solo voices) 1972.

Patru Unghiuri din Care am Bazut Florenta / Four Angles to See Florence (soprano, piano/harpsichord, 1–2 percussion) 1973.

Comorile din Stafida / The Treasures from the Raisin (children's choir, orchestra; Vlad Vieru) 1982; first performed Brasov, 2 July 1982.

Psalm 91 (baritone, organ, cello, double bass) 1983; first performed Berlin, 15 November 1984.

Waage (recitation, instruments; Heidegger, Urmuz, Bacovia) 1986; first performed Bucharest, 23 November 1986.

Hohelied I: Sage Mir An (mezzo-soprano, wind quintet) 1986. Recorded Electrocord ST-CS0218.

Hohelied II: O If You Were Like a Brother (vocal octet) 1986.

Hohelied III: Siehe, du bist schon (mezzo-soprano, alto saxophone) 1987. Recorded Electrocord ST-CS0218.

Hohelied IV: Ja, nartsis jaronskij (unaccompanied choir) 1987.

Opera:

Iona / Jonah (Sorescu) 1972–6; first performed Bucharest, 31 October 1976.

Praznicul calicilor / The Feast of the Cadgers (Sorbul) 1978–81.

Telegrame, Tema, si Variazioni / Telegrams, Themes and Variations (micro-operas; Caragiale) 1982–3; first performed Bucharest, 8 November 1983.

Other:

Tara de Piatra / Stone Country (electronic) 1972.

Orlandus Lassus: *Cantiones sine textu* (arranged for flute, clarinet, bassoon, viola, double bass, vibraphone) 1970; first performed Bucharest, April 1970.

Film scores: *Cind Primavara e Fierbinte / When Spring Is Hot*, 1960; *Ciucurencu*, 1964; *Procesul Alb / The White Trial*, 1965; *Brancusi at Tirgu-Jui*, 1966; *Soarele Negru / Black Sun*, 1968; *Romanta Aspra / Harsh Romance*, 1969; *O Suta de Lei / One Hundred Lei*, 1972; *Felix and Otilia*, 1974; *Marele Singuratic / The Great Lonesome*, 1976; *Intoarcerea lui voda Lapusneanu / Lapusneanu's Return*, 1979; *Surorile / The Sisters*, 1984; *Anotimpul Iubirii*, 1985; *Iacob*, 1988.

PUBLICATIONS

By Vieru: "Prezentarea Lucarii Elemente ale Unei Teorii Generale a Modurilor/Elements of a General Theory of Modes", in *Cercetari de Muzicologie*, 2, 1968; "Silence and the Sculpture of Sound", in *Muzica*, 3, 1970; "Beethoven Azi/Today", in *Muzica*, 12, 1970; "Insemnari Muzicale/ Musical Items" in *Romania literara*, 4, 1970; "Muzeu Muzical, Viziune Asupra Istoriei Orchestrei Simfonice/Musical Museum, A Vision of the History of the Symphony Orchestra", in *Romania literara*, 12 August 1971; "In Domeniul formei Muzicale/In the Field of Musical Form", in *Studiki de Muzicologie*, 8, 1972; "Des Modes, vers un modèle de la pensée musicale intervallique", in *Muzica*, 9, 1975; "Marii Isolati/The Great Isolated Ones", in *Béla Bartók si Muzica Romaneasca*, 1976; "Les Nouvelles Tendances musicales: vers la simplicité", in *Cadmos*, 2(6), 1979; *Cartea modurilor / The Book of Modes*, Bucharest, 1980; "Insemnari Muzicale/ Musical Items", in *Ramuri*, Craiova, 1980; "Modalism—'Third World'", in *Perspectives of New Music*, Spring–Summer 1985; "En forant le domaine" (with Dan Vuza), in *Muzica*, 1985; "Palindromes musicaux", in *Muzica*, 3, 1989; *Cuvinte Despre Sunete / Words About Sounds*, Bucharest, 1990; *Dela moduri la timpul muzical / From Modes Towards Musical Time*, Bucharest, 1990.

On Vieru: Mila Contini, "Il primo premio e stato viato dal compositore Romeno AV", in *Domenica del Corriere*, 14 April 1963; Irving Lowens, "Romania", in *The Musical Quarterly*, April 1965; Peter Pirie, "Broadcasting", in *The Musical Times*, 2, 1965; Nicholas Slonimsky, "Modern Composition in Romania", in *The Musical Quarterly*, 51(1), 1965; Alan Kriegsmann, "Steps Born of Romanian Composer's Own Kind of Silence", in *Washington Post*, 10 March 1968; Octav Nemescu, "Vonvorbire cu AV", (interview) in *Romania literara*, 3 April 1969; Edgar Elian, "Concerte de Bach cu clavire convorbire cu AV", (interview) in *Muzica*, 5, 1977; Fred Popovici, "AV", in *Muzica*, 4, 1981; Dan Vuza, "Aspects mathématiques dans la théorie modale d'AV", in *Revue Roumaine de Mathématiques Pure et Appliquées*, 1982–3; Solomon Marcus, "Gindirea Modala: Dialogul Vieru-Vuza", in *Arta si Stiinta*, 1986; Zoe Dumitrescu-Busulenga, "Timpul—Destin Intr-o Grava Meditatie Muzicala", in *Secolul XX*, 1987.

Anatol Vieru comments:

I refuse to be called a "vanguard composer" (sometimes I am ahead of the vanguard and sometimes behind it). My musical life and evolution have been full of adventures, suprising at first sight but somehow always validated by the work that results. I am open-hearted, and have received suggestions from art, nature, science, blending them into music with a personal grammar and structures.

Starting from the neo-modal example of the new generation of Romanian composers, I have developed it and built out of it the microstructures of my own music. *The Book of Modes* gives coherence of system to my findings and offers new suggestions for the future. In *Eratosthene's Sieve* I blended periodicities, and in *Clepsydra* superposed "ephemerides" on a "perpetuum" that was subtly elaborated.

My ambition in my mature work is to generate complex musics with an ever restricted vocabulary. I organize musical events by regulating their *conspicuousness* in the light of their frequency of occurrence; this is especially noticeable in the "sieves" (*Cribles*) and in my concertante work, in the relation between the solos and the tutti.

To be properly understood, any composer's music must be known whole.

* * *

Anatol Vieru is a maverick. In his language and form, there is a defining refusal to submit to fixed categories, but rather a pursuit of individual truth in the body of the music itself. This is not to suggest that he considers his art *sub specie* abstraction or that he ruthlessly excludes all external significations. Such conscientious objection to doctrinaire recruitment makes Vieru difficult to locate; if one insists on a formula, then one might say that he is a post-modernist before the fact of post-modernism, or even of modernism. This has never prevented him engaging with the problems of modernity, or posing, work by work, new questions of articulation and language (chance in *Jocuri / Jeux*, collage in *Sita lui Eratostene / Erastothene's Sieve*, the "perforated" language of *Museum Music*) but to which the conclusion is nevertheless not contained in the premises. In fact, for all its apparent stylistic breaks, Vieru's output is stable, faithful to itself.

Since the Fifth Symphony his music has had an almost archaic element, but its logic makes no explicit reference to the past and there is nothing nostalgic in its expression. Vieru alternates rapidly between inductive and deductive reasoning and the change of focal length makes his surface effects extremely deceptive. In this way he rationalises the strangest of associations (as in the third movement of the same symphony). The ambiguity of his language has its origin in the diversity of his articulation. If the mechanisms are often simple in detail or when reduced to a deep structure, the grammar which generates its functional rules are, by contrast, complex. So if the music is transparent, it is nonetheless unpredictable (see, for example, the transformation of scattered harmonic and then melodic cells in the Second Symphony).

Vieru frequently invents forms particular to a composition. Some of these he has called "sieves" (as in *Eratosthene's Sieve*, some symphonic movements, and *Oda tacerii / Ode to Silence*, a significant work for the manner in which a technical procedure generates a narrative argument). The formal characteristic of a "sieve" is the co-existence of different elements in which each has its own periodicity (often in inverse ratio to its impact). Other forms he calls "clepsydres"; their essence lies in the unfolding of a long-wave structure, on top of which the composer sets brief flashes ("ephemerides") which, by the suddenness and unpredictability, but also by their intense self-identification, exclude themselves from the basic pulse and from the logic of the basic form.

A music as strongly individual as this must almost of necessity steer its maker towards theatre. The theatrical component can be identified in Vieru's music even before the two operas proper, *Iona / Jonah* and *Praznicul calicilor / The Feast of the Cadgers*. One thinks of *Scène nocturne / Nocturnal Scenes*, of *Eratosthene's Sieve*, and of *Waage*, a piece based on texts by Heidegger and the Romanian writers Urmuz and Bacovia. If one looks for a common thematic thread running through all his work it maybe found in that recognition of the absurd which is particular to artists living under authoritarian regimes.

Though he refuses to be pigeon-holed as a theoretician, Vieru is nevertheless also the author of two important theoretical works, *Cartea modurilor / The Book of Modes*, and *Dela moduri la timpul muzical / From Modes Towards Musical Time*. Closely bound up with his musical work and constantly feeding back into it, Vieru's theoretical output constitutes an important summation of contemporary thinking on modes, confirming an "ensemblist" logic of musical perception, in which the operation of hitherto separate realms—the modal, the tonal and the serial—is unified on a yet higher plane.

—Costin Cazaban

VIÑAO, (Raul) Alejandro. Argentinian. Born in Buenos Aires, 4 September 1951. Educated: initially studied composition under Jacobo Fischer, guitar and conducting, Buenos Aires; studied architecture, University of Buenos Aires; Royal College of Music, London; City University, London, B.Sc., 1979, Ph.D. in computer and electronic music, 1988. Teacher of electronic music composition, City University, London, from 1979; composer in residence, Massachusetts Institute of Technology, Cambridge, Massachusetts, Spring 1987; independent composer. Recipient: Cobbett Prize, 1978; 2nd prize (for *Una orquesta imaginaria*), International Competition for Electro-Acoustic Music, Bourges, 1979; 1st prize (for *Go*), International Competition for Electro-Acoustic Music Unesco World Music Council, 1984; honorary tant work of the year, International Rostrum of Electro-acoustic Music Unesco World Music Council, 1984; honorary mention for *Triple Concerto*, Prix Ars Electronica, 1987; 2nd prize (for *Son entero*), Priz Ars Electronica, 1989. Mailing address: 24 Coolhurst Road, London N8 8EL, England.

Publisher: Crew Studios (self).

Works:

Una orquesta imaginaria (tape) 1979; first performed London, 1979.
Go (tape) 1981; first performed London, 1981. Recorded Fylkingen FYLP 1026.
Hendrix Haze (computer) 1983; first performed London, 1983. Recorded Crew Studios Cassette.
Triple Concerto (flute, cello, piano, computer) 1984; first performed Paris, 1984. Recorded Wergo WER 2019-50.
Son entero (soprano, alto, tenor, bass, computer-controlled synthesizers) 1985–8; first performed London, 27 May 1988. Recorded Wergo WER 2019–50.
Toccata del mago (4 violins, 2 violas, cello, double bass, computer-controlled synthesizers) 1986–7; first performed Boston, 1987. Recorded Wergo WER 2031-50.
Algebra on Fire (orchestra, computer; chamber and symphony versions) 1988–90.
Tumblers (violin, marimba, computer-controlled synthesizers) 1989; first performed Boston, 21 April 1990.
Chant d'ailleurs (soprano, tape) 1991.

PUBLICATIONS

By Viñao: "An Old Tradition We Have Just Invented", in *EMAS Journal*, 4(1–2), 1989; "Shaken, Not Stirred", in *Radio* (Radio Academy quarterly), 2, February 1990.

Alejandro Viñao comments:

European serious music is highly developed in all areas except rhythm. From the rhythmic point of view it lags behind other musical traditions. In my music I seek to create large-scale form by developing new rhythmic processes. I learn from the great rhythmic traditions of the Middle and Far East, Africa, Latin America and from the computer, which has no tradition and knows nothing about rhythm but allows the mind to explore the unimaginable.

* * *

As an ambassador for electronic and computer music there are few who have equalled Alejandro Viñao's success in promoting its message to wider contemporary audiences. Despite relatively few compositions in his portfolio, Viñao's music is regularly performed in the Americas, Scandinavia, the U.K. and continental Europe, receiving many important electro-acoustic composition prizes and commissions. *Go* was voted the most important work of 1984 by the Unesco World Music Council and since the early 1980s his music has been featured at many international festivals, including Bergen, Tanglewood, Warsaw Autumn, BBC Proms and Ultima (Oslo). Viñao has worked extensively in many countries, particularly France, where he is frequently invited to use the studio facilities of IRCAM.

Viñao has pioneered new computer composition techniques, synthesizing acoustic and synthetic sound properties in a wholly original way, and in a "live" concert environment. *Triple Concerto* (for flute, cello, piano and computer) was completed in 1984 and explores the relationship between phrasing and timbre in contrasting instrumental resources, and the transformation of metre, from the mechanical to more flexible patterns. The computer part extends the instrumental sound possibilities of harmonics and "scraped" sounds, for example, and allows the instruments to articulate their strongest natural sounds.

Viñao's concern for precise synchronicity and practical computer applications in live performance (the temporal rigidity of tape compositions when incorporating instruments can be very restrictive) reaches a high degree of sophistication in *Algebra on Fire*, for orchestra and computer-controlled synthesizers, his first mature orchestral composition. He overcomes the problem of rhythmic synchronicity with pre-recorded tape material by introducing a MIDI keyboard player who controls the tempo of the computer-originated material. It is the first work to permit a computer facility to "perform" alongside instrumentalists and follow a conductor's beat—a technique that is sure to become widely known in future.

There is a strong Latin American influence in several of his works. Viñao utilises both the language and inherent rhythms to great effect in *Son entero*. Inspired by the poems of Cuban writer Nicolas Guillen the composer's text is a collation of words and phrases taken from the collection of poems entitled "El son entero". The music develops the dramatic possibilities of the text and is scored for four unaccompanied voices and computer.

In addition to his instrumental and electro-acoustic music compositions Viñao has been involved with writing and playing rock music, the creation of multi-media works, and has composed music for over 20 films. He has also broadcast several programmes for the BBC, presenting his own music and that of other composers who share similar aesthetic and technological interests.

Viñao has already made a significant contribution to electroacoustic music, both in the innovative way he has overcome the limitations of "live" electronics and in developing a highly distinctive compositional voice.

—Sean Rourke

VINE, Carl (Edward). Australian. Born in Perth, Western Australia, 8 October 1954. Educated at Hale and Guildford schools, Perth, 1963–71; University of Western Australia, Nedlands (piano under Stephen Dornan, composition under John Exton), 1972–5. Trainee sound recording engineer, BBC tape transcription unit, 1972; pianist, West Australian Symphony Orchestra, 1973–5; sponsored participant, Australia Council "Young Composers' Training Scheme", 1975; free-lance performer with Australia Ensemble, AZ Music, Seymour Group, Mused Performance Ensemble, The Ashes of Sydney, etc., 1975–80; accompanist, Sydney Dance Company, 1975–8; resident composer, SDC, 1978; guest performer, "Music Rostrum '78", 1978; guest conductor, Seymour Group, 1978; guest resident composer, conductor and pianist, London Contemporary Dance Theatre, 1979; co-director, pianist and conductor with Flederman contemporary music ensemble, 1979–88; lecturer in electronic music composition, Queensland Conservatorium of Music, North Quay, 1980–2; participant, Australian "Composers' Summer School", ABC Sinfonietta, 1980; musical director, Australia/New Zealand Choreographic School, 1984; resident composer, New South Wales State Conservatorium, 1985; guest conductor, Australian Chamber Orchestra, 1985–7; resident composer, ACO, 1987; guest conductor, Sydney Philharmonia Society, 1987; resident composer, EVOS Pty Ltd (Perth), Western Australian University, Western Australian Academy for the Performing Arts, 1989. Recipient: first prize (under-18), Australian Society for Music Education Composers' Competition, 1970; A.Mus.A. (with distinction), Australian Music Examinations Board, 1972; winner, open instrumental solo division, Perth Music Festival, 1972; winner, Australian Broadcasting Commission instrumental and vocal competition, 1974; Adams Award for outstanding contribution to music for dance in Australia, 1983. Mailing address: 39 Evans Street, Balmain, New South Wales 2041, Australia.

Publisher: Chester.

Symphonies/orchestral:

Curios 1980; first performed Sydney, 5 February 1980.
Canzona (string orchestra) 1985; first performed Sydney, 1985.
Micro Symphony 1986; first performed Sydney, 17 August 1986.
Percussion Concerto (with orchestra or tape) 1987; first performed Perth, 1987.
Legend 1988; first performed Perth, 8 July 1988.
Symphony No 2 1988; first performed Melbourne, 23 April 1988.
Concerto grosso (violin, flute, oboe, horn, strings) 1989.
Symphony No 3 1990; first performed Adelaide, 5 March 1990.

Chamber/instrumental:

Miniature I (viola) 1973; first performed Perth, 1974.
Miniature II (2 violas) 1974.
Tergiversative Blues (lute) 1977.
Free Game (tuba, electronics) 1979.
Occasional Poetry (tuba, piano) 1979.
Images (flute, trombone, cello, piano, harpsichord, percussion) 1981; first performed Melbourne, 1981.
Sinfonia (flute, clarinet, violin, cello, piano, percussion) 1982; first performed Sydney, 1982.
Miniature III (flute, tuba, piano, percussion) 1982; first performed Las Vegas, Nevada, 1983. Recorded MBS 14 CD.
String Quartet No 2 1984; first performed Sydney, 1985.
Occasional Poetry (piano) 1984.
Café Concertino (flute, clarinet, violin, viola, cello, piano) 1984; first performed Sydney, 1984.

Elegy (flute, cello, trombone, piano—4 hands, percussion) 1985; first performed Melbourne, 1985. Recorded MBS 14 CD.
Love Song (trombone, tape) 1986; first performed Melbourne, 1986.
Defying Gravity (percussion quartet) 1987; first performed Sydney, 1987.
Miniature IV (flute, clarinet, violin, viola, cello, piano) 1988; first performed Perth, 1988.
Sonata (piano) 1991.

Vocal/choral:

Aria (soprano, flute, cello, piano, celeste, percussion; White) 1984; first performed Sydney, 1984.
After Campion (SSAATTBB, 2 pianos) 1989; first performed Sydney, 1989.

Other:

BBC Exercises (tape) 1974.
Tape Piano Piece (tape) 1976.
Poppy (dance; flute, clarinet, bassoon, horn, trumpet, trombone, piano, percussion, tape) 1978; first performed Sydney, 1978.
Knips Suite (dance; string quartet) 1979; first performed London, 1979.
Scene Shift (dance; trombone, double bass, 2 pianos) 1979; first performed London, 1979.
Heavy Metal (tape and improvisation) 1980.
Kondallila Mix (tape and improvisation) 1980.
Donna Maria Blues (dance; electronic tape) 1981; first performed London, 1981.
Hate (dance; horn, trombone, 2 pianos, percussion) 1982; first performed Sydney, 1982.
Intimations of Immortality (computer tape) 1985.
A Christmas Carol (dance; orchestra) 1988; first performed Brisbane, 1983.
Legend (dance; orchestra) 1988; first performed Perth, 1988.
On the Edge (dance; tape) 1989; first performed Adelaide, 1989.

Carl Vine comments:

My music seems to be growing more and more accessible. An earlier preoccupation with overlayered rhythms and developing "metric modulation" are now being tempered by a fascination with tonality; how keenly tonal centres can be perceived and what, exactly, constitutes a shift in tonal centre. My style remains, however, rather volatile, as I like to view every project as a move into unknown territory.

* * *

Carl Vine is arguably one of Australia's most versatile musicians. He has worked as a pianist and conductor, was co-founder and a member of Australia's leading contemporary music group, Flederman, between 1979–89 and has a compositional output that embraces many different genres including music for the concert hall, theatre, cinema, television, electronics and, particularly because of its rhythmic vibrancy and energy, for dance.

While Vine himself cites the exotic influence of the musics of Sri Lanka, Africa and South America on specific pieces, the most pervasive influence on his work is undoubtedly that of North America. Since the early 1970s he has moved from pieces which briefly reflected a kind of Cageian experimental aesthetic, through a New York "up-town" complexity more akin to Carter and Wuorinen, from the mid-1980s onward, to a style which, without losing anything of its rhythmic dynamism, is increasingly tonal and more approachable and perhaps, to continue the North American analogy, closer to John Adams.

Vine's experimental works date from the early 1970s and were written for a number of alternative dance and performance companies while he was employed as a pianist for the Sydney Dance Company. By 1976 he had moved away from experimentalism, but dance was becoming more the focus of his compositional output. A grant from Australia Council enabled him to attend the Gulbenkian Choreographic Summer School in England in 1976 and these intensive two weeks proved to be a deciding point in his career. Certainly a BBC Documentary made about the course had far-reaching consequences as it brought his work to the attention of several British choreographers and led to collaborations with Mischa Bergese, Kathy Lewis and the London Contemporary Dance Company, and with Ian Spink for Basic Dance Space in Edinburgh. In tandem with his success in the U.K. his reputation also increased in Australia. When he returned there he was commissioned to write a number of works for the Australian Dance Theatre and took up a residency with the Sydney Dance Company; the most notable product of this time was the highly acclaimed instrumental score *Poppy*, which, with choreography by Graeme Murphy, subsequently toured world-wide.

While Vine has continued to write dance scores, the early 1980s saw him concentrating more on music for the concert hall as the ensemble Flederman began to grow in size and importance. The idiosyncratic line-up (flute, cello, trombone, keyboards, percussion) is often discernible among the works of this decade. One such work, *Miniature II*, composed for the 1983 American tour of the group, is a work in three sections each of which explores respectively the expansion, contraction and interruption of a constantly varying rhythmic pulse: in the first, continuous semiquavers are grouped in a variety of ways to create a constantly changing pulse; the second section is based on a fragment of Sri Lankan dance music and maintains a constant 2/4 metre over which finger cymbals accentuate complex subdivisions of the beat; while the third and most simple is based on a 3/4 and 3/16 rhythmic ostinato in conjunction with metric modulation to give an effect of dazzling rhythmic intricacy.

This work marks the height of Vine's flirtation with complexity but already by such works as *Café Concertino* and *Aria* and *Elegy* he had found a simpler and more direct voice. *Café Concertino* revolves around the treatment of a simple cycle of fifths and while the overall structure may be academic, many of the gestures of the piece are gleaned, not always reverently, from 19th-century chamber music. *Aria*, Flederman commission, this time with the addition of a soprano, shows Vine's talent for the theatrical: the text, by Patrick White follows the wandering mind of a "woman of fashion and distinction" as she sits at her hairdressers and it is beautifully heightened by the dry and never overstated wit of Vine's music, while *Elegy*, by complete contrast is a very personal statement which chronicles the composer's reaction to the unexpected death of a friend. It is a single-movement work in four sections, and, particularly in the solo cello passages, exemplifies Vine's increased concern with lyricism.

In recent years, as Vine has continued to refine his harmonic language, he has had the opportunity to work more and more with the full orchestra. By the end of the decade works such as the *Percussion Concerto*, *Legend*, a substantial orchestral score for the West Australian Ballet, and his two most recent symphonies, *No 2* and *No 3* show a bold new simplicity. Whether or not this is a permanent state of affair remains to be seen. Given Vine's openness to new sounds and ideas it seems likely that the 1990s will reveal yet another facet of the composer's personality.

—Rosemary Johnson

VOLANS, Kevin. South African. Born in Pietermaritzburg, 26 July 1949. Educated at University of the Witwatersrand, Johannesburg, 1972; University of Aberdeen, 1972–3; Musikhochschule, Cologne (further composition study under Karlheinz Stockhausen, music-theatre under Mauricio Kagel, piano under Aloys Kontarsky), 1973–81. Freelance composer, 1973–81; teaching assistant to Karlheinz Stockhausen, Musikhochschule, Cologne, 1973–5; field trips recording African music, WDR, Cologne; radio programmes for WDR, Belgian Radio and Deutsche Welle; co-editor (with Johannes Fritsch), Feedback Papers; teacher of music, University of Natal, Durban, 1982–4; resident in Paris, 1984–5; board of professors, Ferienkurse für Neue Musik, Darmstadt, 1984–6; resident in Ireland, from 1986; composer in residence, Queen's University, Belfast, 1986–9; composer in residence, Princeton University, New Jersey, from 1992. Mailing address: Greenfoet, Kerry Keel, Letter Kenny, County Donegal, Ireland.

Publisher: Chester.

Symphonies/orchestral:

One Hundred Frames 1991; first performed Ulster, 6 December 1991.

Chamber/instrumental:

Monkey Solo (piano) 1977.
Nine Beginnings (2 pianos) 1979, revised 1981.
Matepe (2 harpsichords, rattles) 1980.
Mbira (harpsichord, rattles) 1980.
Renewed Music / Reviewed Music (8 percussion) 1981.
Newer Music (piano) 1981.
White Man Sleeps (2 harpsichords, viola da gamba, percussion) 1982.
Journal (Walking Song) (2 pianos, 2 flutes, clarinet, bassoon, trumpet, violin, double bass; version for flute, fiedel, plucked fiedel, vibraphone, marimba) 1983, 1984; both withdrawn.
Leaping Dance (fiedel, marimba, harpsichord) 1984.
Leaping Dance (2 pianos) 1984.
Walking Song (flute, harpsichord, 2 handclappers) 1984.
Ways of History (Part One) (piano, violin, cello) 1984; withdrawn.
Kneeling Dance (2 pianos) 1985.
She Who Sleeps With a Small Blanket (percussion solo) 1985–6.
White Man Sleeps: String Quartet No 1 1986. Recorded Nonesuch 79163.
Into Darkness (piano, clarinet, trumpet, violin, cello, marimba, vibes) 1987.
Hunting: Gathering: String Quartet No 2 1987. Recorded Nonesuch 79253.
Notes d'un peintre (movement for string quartet) 1987.
The Songlines: String Quartet No 3 1988.
The Ramanujan Notebooks: String Quartet No 4 1990.

Vocal/choral:

Delay in Glass (2 singers, 2 pianos, Irish harp, tape) 1979.
Monkey Music (speaker, piano) 1981.

Opera:

L'Homme aux semelles de vent (chamber opera for 4 voices, 16 instruments) 1988–90; provisional title.
Correspondences (dance opera for baritone, string quartet) 1990.

Other:

Graphik (graphic score) 1969.
Die Reisen vom Berge (incidental music to Pirandello; solo, instrumental, orchestral) 1980.
Kwazulu Summer Landscape (tape) 1980.
Studies in Zulu History (electronic) 1980.
Cover Him with Grass (tape) 1982.
Chevron (ballet; small orchestra) 1989, revised 1990.

PUBLICATIONS

By Volans: *Summer Gardeners: Conversations with Composers*, Durban, 1984.

* * *

As a student in South Africa between 1968–71, Kevin Volans, though relatively isolated from mainstream contemporary events in Europe and the U.S.A., discovered the work of the post-war avant-garde through records and scores, and subsequently decided to go to Cologne to study with Stockhausen. His earliest acknowledged piece, and the only one remaining from this period, is a graphic score. The first important work in his output is *Nine Beginnings* which dates from his association with the "New Simplicity" movement, a term coined by the German composer Walter Zimmermann who along with Michael von Biel were the other composers in this group. Their intention was to return to the "vigour and rigour", as Volans calls it, of the 1950s and 1960s, and to get away from the pseudo-intellectualism of the early 1970s. But they also wanted to re-establish rhythmic symmetry, combined with a renewed interest in tonality and harmony. *Nine Beginnings* demonstrates this new approach to functional harmony in its use of interlocking whole-tone scales.

His association with Zimmermann also led to the most significant turning point in Volans's career. While the German composer returned to his native Bavaria to study the traditional music there, Volans returned to his native Natal in South Africa to do likewise, and prepared programmes for German radio. Among the first fruits of his research were two tape pieces, *Studies in Zulu History* in which the electronic sounds deliberately imitate or paraphrase the natural sounds, and *Kwazulu Summer Landscape* consisting exclusively of natural outdoor sounds recorded in Zululand.

Wishing to take African music into the realm of Western chamber music, Volans chose Shona *mbira* music which had been transcribed by Andrew Tracey. In the first two of his "African Paraphrases", as he chose to call this initial group of 13 works, the *mbira* tunes provided the basis for his own variations, in which the chord pattern and cycle of chords remains unchanged, while both the configuration of notes and rhythm undergo variations. While a Shona-based tuning (roughly seven equal steps to the octave) is employed for the harpsichords he acknowledges that in transcribing the music for different instruments the result is already "non-folk" or "art music". This became particularly apparent when he started writing for string quartet and for two pianos, where not only equal temperament prevailed, but the musical tradition of the new medium too. Some passages in the quartets sound very much like parts of the classical quartet repertoire.

In his First String Quartet, a transcription for the Kronos Quartet of *White Man Sleeps*, the five movements are drawn from a range of South African musical sources, including Tswana and Nyanga panpipe music, San bow music and Basotho lesiba music. However, the importance of baroque music, particularly French—for Volans' musical taste has always leaned towards the French, right through to Debussy, Stravinsky and Morton Feldman—should not be overlooked, illustrated by Volans's choice of harpsichords and viola da gamba together with their attendant period performers, and use of transparent textures.

The Second String Quartet, *Hunting: Gathering*, is a kind of autobiographical work of sorts, incorporating at least 15 different pieces of music into its three movements or "Expeditions". The string quartet writing reaches a new level of sophistication here—inhabiting the quartet worlds of Bartók and Terry Riley—and the treatment of the African sources is also approached with a greater originality. For here he is already at work on the second series of African pieces—"Translations from the European", in which he wanted to approach European music through the eyes of an African. This had already begun with the mixed ensemble piece *Into Darkness*, in which, at the outset, he wanted to move away from the paraphrase technique, and particularly to use all 12 notes of the chromatic scale once again. The first movement of *Into Darkness*, described as a kind of *Totentanz*, is effectively a piano piece with textural elaboration by the other five instruments and harmonic pointing by the vibraphone. Continuing the textural preoccupations of the "paraphrases" in which instruments play a note or combination of notes alternately, he creates an elaborate gamelan-like interlocking of all the instruments. The second movement is, by contrast, a sparse, pointillistic piece in which instrumental colour plays an important role: the chords are differently orchestrated each time they appear, and even the colour on each pitch changes.

Volans's recent involvement with choreographers led to the commissioning of *Chevron* which, however, did not have a brief. With no idea of what form the piece would take, he started writing at bar one, and literally waited to see what would happen next. The zig-zagging, which is a feature of the music, gave the piece its title. Harmonically, the piece derives from his interest in the years 1912–3, and the music of Skriabin, early Schoenberg and late Mahler, as well as Debussy's *Jeux* and Stravinsky's *Rite of Spring*. The scoring and lay-out of the chords is reminiscent of Stravinsky's *Symphonies for Wind Instruments,* and the relentless unvaried repetition of chords or whole bars recalls the late pieces of Morton Feldman.

Volans spoke of a third series of pieces to be called "Slow Homecoming", in which he intended to return to Africa musically, at least. But until the premiere of his opera, which is still in progress, one will not really be able to tell if the second series has been concluded yet. Volans has emerged as the one of the major South African composers of his generation, and certainly the most performed. Probably no other composer has created such a bold confrontation between Europe and Africa in music and ideas.

—Michael Blake

VRIES, Klaas de. Dutch. Born in Terneuzen, 14 July 1944. Educated at Rotterdam Conservatory (piano and composition); Royal Conservatory, The Hague (composition under Otto Ketting); further study under Milko Kelemen, Germany. Teacher of analysis and instrumentation, Rotterdam Conservatory. Recipient: Matthijs Vermeulen Prize (for *Discantus*), 1984. Mailing address: c/o Donemus, Paulus Potterstraat 14, 1071 CZ Amsterdam, The Netherlands.

Publisher: Donemus.

Symphonies/orchestral:

Refrains (2 pianos, orchestra) 1968.
Follia (brass, percussion, electronic instruments, 5 solo strings) 1973.
Moeilijkheden/Difficulties (winds, piano; for orchestra De Volharding) 1977.
Tombeau (string orchestra) 1980.
Discantus 1982.

Chamber/instrumental:

Three Pieces (wind quintet) 1968.
Chain of Changes (piano) 1969.
Organum (3 amplified pianos, 4 trombones) 1971.
Five-Part Fantasy (flute ensemble) 1971.
Mars (tenor saxophone, piano) 1972.
Kwartet (strings, electronics) 1973.
Twee Koralen (saxophone quartet) 1974.
Echo (piano) 1974.
Bewegingen (15 instruments) 1979.
Drei Harpisten (3 pieces for 3 small harps) 1979.
Kotz (11 instruments) 1979.
Das Lebewohl? Oder . . . das Wiedersehen (2 violins, viola, cello) 1979.
Rondo (horn, piano) 1980.
Murder in the Dark (harpsichord) 1985.
Sonata No 1: Melancholie (piano) 1986.
Diafonia, la creación (ensemble) 1988.
. . . sub nocte per umbras . . . (large ensemble) 1989.

Vocal/choral:

Tegenzangen (4-part mixed chorus, orchestra, speaking chorus, percussion ensemble) 1973.
Areas (soloists, chorus, orchestra) 1980.
Phrases (soprano, 4-part chorus, ensemble, orchestra) 1986.

Opera:

Erendira 1984.

* * *

An embittered Dutch musician once described Klaas de Vries grudgingly as "almost a *very* good composer". The list of names already dismissed by him rendered this statement praise indeed. What the critic missed in the music (without realising it) was the element of ideology; what he fails to realise is that it is this very absence of ideology that gives the music its unique qualities and its special strengths.

De Vries has always been unswerving in his commitment to the practice of composition. He gets real pleasure and satisfaction from the very act of composing, rather than the fact of having composed (as do many of his contemporaries). It is not an accident, but a manifesto: scores appear because he writes them by arguing through an idea or set of ideas in an organic way where the idea prescribes the material and the material determines the process, or form. He does not explore forms with music; he expresses music with forms.

The idea for a de Vries work may be a musical one, or something quite different, say literary, which suggests to him the glimmerings of an entire piece, which dim outline in turn gives birth to appropriate material. Only after long consideration do they reach the sketch paper. "It is then", says the composer "that I discover what the piece is really about." The growth of the work is then on purely musical lines. The constituent parts are worked simultaneously and feed off each other—colour, thematic identity and its expansion, harmonic voicing and instrumental deployment, all completely complementary and integrated; the work, in a sense, discovers itself, and the role of the composer is almost that of arranger. De Vries is very open about this third stage of the writing process. Sections which seem too simplistic or bare are telescoped with others, often layered and superimposed to give his characteristic richness and massive effects. At this stage he impresses his personality on ideas that are almost self-generating (by selection, discipline and organisation) to make the piece speak as he would wish.

Such a method of working contains both risks and compensating virtues. If you are always on the inside of a piece and looking out, you deny yourself certain options. You will find very little whimsy or caprice in his work—nothing irresponsible or just fun. What you will find is a tremendous sense of growth and cohesion, of consistency and integration. De Vries tends to overestimate the complexity of some of his work and wonders if certain sections are too involved, where they are strong, fresh and individual. The enormous richness retains its vibrancy because it is a result of the coinciding of a number of events, not a colouristic device or gesture. Rhythm, as distinct from pitch, still remains an intuitive area for de Vries, and this provides an almost alien element of sponteneity. Of course he is also an extremely distinguished performer, a pianist of great insight, and this has itself affected his creative side by restoring a few drops of humanity that might have gone with the rigour of his working practice. At a more immediate level it has given him an insight into the importance of using instruments most effectively in the hall rather than on the page. It has also given him a very fine ear for sound and pitch relationships as well as an ingrained sense of pacing and timing. Even the most rigorous working is subconsciously adjusted. However massive the sound becomes, it is never inpenetrable: complexities exist in the head, never in the ear.

De Vries's stylistic development has been steady and continuous. His basic sound world has not changed so very much since his earliest acknowledged works (unlike his harmonic base) and can be traced to Stravinsky, particularly *Agon* (note particularly the use of wind and the voicing of certain chords). Stravinsky's attitude of "daring to be simple" is also seen in de Vries's basic conceptual approach, and it is the clarity of the Russian's approach to serialism, rather than the afflatus of Schoenberg's romantic expressionism that dignifies such early scores as *Refrains* and *Organum*. It also found him ensnared by the "tyranny of sevenths and ninths" which besets many with a terror of tonal associations. The works immediately following find him overcoming his intervallic concerns and loosening up his approach to tonality. They also show, in for example a piece like *Follia*, a personal use of the juxtaposition of blocks and lines, or sustained and ornamented material layered to present a feel of rich, resonating stasis. His rhythmic development achieves its most extreme point in *Moeilijkheden / Difficulties* written for De Volharding. Catering for this group's style of naked aggression and dynamic forthrightness also taught him to identify and emphasise what was crucial to the individual piece, even to the extent of sacrificing nuances. Thereafter de Vries concerned himself again with refinement, narrowing the gap between aggression and lyricism either by transition or contrast without disturbing the flow of the music. This sense of oscillation producing variety within continuity occurs very plainly in *Bewegingen*, his best work of the period. Another idea which exercised his mind from about the late 1970s was the concept of breaking the forces down into separate parts, maybe individual lines, and distributing them throughout the available space, including the audience who would thus enter into the creative process by identifying with their chosen aspect and following it. In practice it was possible only in a modified form, but the results of the thought can be seen in *Areas*, *Phrases* and *Discantus* particularly, with the extreme degree of separation and (complementary) independence of lines and sharply differentiated types of material, layering compression with expansion.

The extraordinary, vast Piano Sonata marks a much more fundamental breakthrough. His earlier block and layer construction did not permit the sustaining of a work over extended time scales appropriate to the implied weight of the intrinsic material. The solution he discovered to this problem was almost an employment of classical forms; to analogise, he changed his angle of view from looking through a work in sections, to looking along it in elevation. Material is no longer grouped in respect of time, but in respect of its nature to leave it generically unpolluted in self-contained packets. These packets are then organised into an organic cohesive shape—say sonata form—to impart not only greater freedom of layout but developmental strength and thrust. In a sense, each block in the piece is a microcosm of what would previously have been an entirely separate work. As well as providing the wherewithal for much more substantial pieces, the effect has been to make his language more relaxed—it breathes more—though with no reduction in invention.

Subconsciously de Vries has also perceived that classical forms deny him the use of colour as a specific ingredient, which dimension he is seeking to restore by turning to works for the stage and to electronic originated pieces. He is not, and never has been, concerned with breaking down orthodoxy or doing bizarre things with instruments, but has been compelled to the realisation that the precise achieving of his aims sometimes necessitates unconventional, though never impractical, handling. That it is possible to combine classical austerity with inventive richness in a contemporary language without loss of freedom or colour is graphically illustrated by *. . . sub nocte per umbras . . .*, a most beautiful sounding and scrupulously organised piece.

—Giles Easterbrook

WEIR, Judith. British. Born in Cambridge, 11 May 1954. Educated at Wembley Grammar School, London, 1966–72; composition lessons under John Tavener; King's College, Cambridge (composition under Robin Holloway), 1973–6. Composer in residence, Southern Arts Association, 1976–9; Cramb Fellow, University of Glasgow, 1979–82; Fellow Commoner, Trinity College, Cambridge, 1983–5; composer in residence, Royal School of Art, Music and Drama, Glasgow, 1988–91. Mailing address: c/o Chester Music, 8–9 Frith Street, London, WIV 5TZ, England.

Publisher: Chester.

Symphonies/orchestral:

Isti mirant stella 1981; first performed Orkney, 23 June 1981.
The Ride over Lake Constance 1984.
Variation on "Summer Is Icumen In" (contribution to collaborative work) 1987; first performed Aldeburgh, Suffolk, 13 June 1987.
Music Untangled 1991.

Chamber/instrumental:

Out of the Air (flute, oboe, clarinet, horn, bassoon) 1975; first performed London, 8 February 1975.
King Harald Sails to Byzantium (flute/piccolo, clarinet/bass clarinet, violin, cello, piano, marimba/glockenspiel) 1979; first performed Orkney, 18 June 1979.
Several Concertos (flute/alto flute/piccolo, cello, piano) 1980; first performed Dundee, 21 January 1981.
An Mein Klavier (piano) 1980; first performed Bracknell, Berkshire, 20 July 1980. Recorded NMCD 002.
Music for 247 Strings (violin, piano) 1981; first performed London, 5 October 1981.
Wild Mossy Mountains (organ) 1982; first performed Edinburgh, 10 September 1982.
Spij Dobrze (Pleasant Dreams) (double bass, tape) 1983; first performed Kazimierz Dolny, Poland, 8 September 1983.
The Art of Touching the Keyboard (piano) 1983; first performed London, 31 May 1983. Recorded Merlin MRFD 891706.
Sketches from a Bagpiper's Album (clarinet, piano) 1984; first performed Huddersfield, Yorkshire, 8 June 1984. Recorded Nato CD1180.
Ettrick Banks (organ) 1985; first performed Edinburgh, 28 August 1985.
Michael's Strathspey (piano or organ) 1985; first performed London, 17 December 1985. Recorded NMCD 002.
The Bagpiper's String Trio (violin, viola, cello; arranged from the above) 1985; first performed Cambridge, 19 May 1985.
Airs from Another Planet (flute/piccolo, oboe, clarinet, bassoon, horn, piano) 1986; first performed St Andrews, Fife, 14 October 1986.
Gentle Violence (piccolo, guitar; based on postures of Ta Chi Chuan martial art) 1987; first performed London, 10 April 1987.
Sederunt Principles (flute, oboe, 2 clarinets, bassoon, horn, trombone, xylophone, harp, piano, 3 violins, 2 violas, cello, double bass) 1987; first performed London, 1 September 1987.
Mountain Airs (flute, oboe, clarinet) 1988; first performed Tunbridge Wells, Kent, 25 February 1988.
Distance and Enchantment (piano, violin, viola, cello) 1989; first performed London, 26 September 1989.
String Quartet 1990; first performed Liverpool, 2 October 1990.
Ardnamurchan Point (2 pianos) 1990; first performed London, 18 October 1990.

Vocal/choral:

Black Birdsong (baritone, flute, oboe, violin, cello; traditional) 1977; first performed Oxford, 5 November 1977.
Ballad (baritone, orchestra) 1981; first performed Glasgow, 17 September 1981.
Thread! (narrator, flute/alto flute/piccolo, clarinet/bass clarinet, 2 violins, viola, cello, piano, percussion; text from Bayeux Tapestry) 1981; first performed Stirling, 2 March 1981.
Scotch Minstrelsy (tenor or soprano, piano; traditional) 1982; first performed Glasgow, 14 May 1982. Recorded Abacus ABA 109 2.
Ascending into Heaven (SATB chorus, organ; Hildebert de Lavardin) 1983; first performed St Albans, Hertfordshire, 5 July 1983.
A Serbian Cabaret (narration by quartet: violin, viola, cello, piano) 1984; first performed Bath, 8 June 1984.
Illuminare, Jerusalem (SATB chorus, organ; 15th-century Scottish) 1985; first performed Cambridge, 24 December 1985. Recorded Hyperion CDH 88031; AFKA SK516.
Songs from the Exotic (low voice, piano) 1987; first performed Cambridge, 7 October 1987.
Lovers, Learners and Libations (scenes from 13th-century Parisian life; early music consort) 1987; first performed Glasgow, 12 February 1988.
A Spanish Liederbooklet (soprano, piano) 1988; first performed Cheltenham, Gloucestershire, 6 July 1988.
Missa del Cid (SAAATTTBBB, speaker) 1988; broadcast BBC 1988.
HEAVEN ABLAZE in His Breast (SSATBB, 2 pianos, 8 dancers) 1989; first performed Basildon, Essex, 5 October 1989.
The Romance of Count Arnaldos (soprano, 2 clarinets, viola, cello, double bass) 1989; first performed Brighton, Sussex, 13 May 1989.
Don't Let That Horse (soprano, horn; Ferlinghetti) 1990; first performed Glasgow, 16 September 1990.
Ox Mountain was Covered by Trees (soprano, counter-tenor, baritone, orchestra) 1990; first performed Canterbury, Kent, 30 September 1990.

Opera/dramatic:

King Harald's Saga (soprano, 8 singing parts; after *Heimskringla* saga) 1979; first performed Dumfries, Scotland,

17 May 1979. Recorded Novello NVLCD 1909.

The Black Spider (2 soloists, chorus; optionally 3 clarinets 2 trumpets or wind/string alternatives, acoustic guitar, piano/optional organ; Gotthelf, *Times* news report from Poland) 1984; first performed Canterbury, Kent, 6 March 1985.

The Consolations of Scholarship (soprano, flute/alto flute/piccolo, oboe, clarinet, bassoon, horn, violin, cello, piano, percussion; Chinese Yuan drama, 13th/14th century) 1985; first performed Durham, 5 May 1985. Recorded Novello NVLCD 109.

A Night at the Chinese Opera (10 singers, orchestra; JW, after 13th-century *The Chao Family Orphan*) 1987; first performed Cheltenham, Gloucestershire, 8 July 1987.

The Vanishing Bridegroom (5 principals, SSAATTBB chorus, orchestra; J.F. Campbell of Islay, *Popular Tales of the West Highlands*) 1990; first performed Glasgow, 17 October 1990.

PUBLICATIONS

By Weir: article on contemporary music, *Times Higher Education Supplement*, March 1982; "A Note on a Chinese Opera", in *Musical Times*, July 1987.

On Weir: Tom Morgan, "JW", in *New Music 88*, Oxford, 1988.

* * *

Judith Weir has withdrawn most of her earliest pieces, clearly dissatisfied with their attempted complexities and no longer tolerant of her own solutions. Since 1975, when her catalogue now effectively begins, she has produced a substantial body of work in all genres (except, so far, the large-scale orchestral) and with a particular emphasis on deceptively simple but frequently virtuosic instrumental pieces and vocal/dramatic works.

Though born in England, Weir's family roots are in Scotland, and she draws on that both for her themes and subject matter (though she has an equal interest in medieval and Chinese subjects) and for her general orientation to music, which is opposed to the giantism of contemporary concert performance and promotion and much closer to a folkish approach to music-making. Much of her work is thus chamber music in the strictest sense, usually written with specific performers (often close friends) centrally in mind.

The Scottish element is evident in some of the technical aspects of her work, in some of the rhythmic structures she adopts, in a leaning to plainly diatonic harmonies, even in the use of "Scotch snaps" at moments of transition, but it would be mistaken to gather from this that her music is naive or regressive. The Scottish tradition also offers a "great music" replete with microtonal complexities and highly chromatic harmonies, and in a piece like *Scotch Minstrelsy* Weir juxtaposes a straightforwardly lyrical vocal line with a complex scoring that continually deconstructs the listener's expectations.

Some of these devices appear to considerable effect in the *Sketches from a Bagpiper's Album*. They are also transposed to an even more elevated context in *Airs from Another Planet*, an echo of Stefan George (and, by extension, of Schoenberg), where the complex surface of Highland "*ceol mhor*" is transferred to music which descends in all other particulars from the Second Viennese School.

Weir's compositional approach is inherently dramatic; even a piece like the orchestral *The Ride over Lake Constance* has a charged narrative pre-text, which is an important, but not programmatic component of the music. She wrote three short operas, and uncategorisable entertainments like *A Serbian Cabaret* before embarking on *A Night at the Chinese Opera*. The faint echo of the Marx Brothers is undoubtedly deliberate, but what Weir has done in this extraordinary piece, the work that established her reputation firmly as one of the most significant of the younger generation in Britain, is to take the declamatory recitative style of Chinese opera and turn it into an extended exploration of what it means to convey words by music. She had already explored similar ground in *The Consolations of Scholarship*, a work based on Yuan opera rather than on Boethius and she has extended the technique in *The Vanishing Bridegroom*.

In the operas, she is able to substitute a kind of literalism for the normal motivic development which she seems to have abandoned in her instrumental pieces as well. There are elements of minimalist practice in her use of ostinato (as in the marvellous *Music for 247 Strings*) but these also recall the late 19th-century nationalists, and influences as distinct as Sibelius and Peter Maxwell Davies (to whom *Isti mirant stella*, with its evocation of the 11th-century return of Halley's Comet, is dedicated).

Weir's sensitivity to the "long 19th century" of basically harmonic music does not camouflage a timidity in the face of newer procedures and practices. Like Maxwell Davies, she has combined old and new techniques and philosophies, and done so seamlessly, in a voice entirely her own. In terms of public and critical response, she is one of the most successful young composers to have emerged in Britain since World War II.

—Brian Morton

WELIN, Karl-Erik. Swedish. Born in Genarp, Lund, 31 May 1934. Educated at Musikhochschule, Berlin, 1955; State Academy of Music, Stockholm, 1956–60; studied organ under Alf Linder, composition under Gunnar Bucht and Ingvar Lidholm, piano under Sven Brandel and David Tudor. Military service, sergeant, Signal Corps. Has one son. Concert and recording pianist, modern and contemporary repertoire; producer, Swedish Broadcasting Corporation, 1960–8; visiting professor in the United States, Germany, The Netherlands and Sweden, 1966–71; board member, Society of Swedish Composers, 1969–75; teacher of music, State College of Music, Stockholm, mid-1970s. Mailing address: E-07110 Bunyola, Mallorca, Spain.

Publisher: Wilhelm Hansen, Copenhagen.

Symphonies/orchestral:

Pereo (35 strings) 1964; first performed Stockholm, 11 September 1965.

Ben fatto (version for small orchestra) 1968; first performed Stockholm, 27 August 1968.

Jeux à l'occasion d'une fête (chamber orchestra) 1976; first performed Trelleborg, 17 October 1976.

Min femte (*String Quartet No 5*; string quartet, orchestra) 1977; first performed Norrkoping, 18 March 1980.

Symphony No 1 1985–6; first performed Malmo, 22 October 1987.
Concertino No 1 (clarinet, violin, piano, orchestra) 1987.

Chamber/instrumental:

Three Miniatures (piano) 1956.
Introduction och fuga (organ) 1956.
Fyra bagateller (viola, cello) 1957.
Sermo modulatus (flute, clarinet) 1960; first performed Oslo, February 1961.
Nummer 3 (flute, oboe, 2 clarinets/bass clarinet, horn, trumpet, trombone, violin, double bass) 1961.
Manzit (clarinet, trombone, piano, percussion, cello) 1962; broadcast Swedish Radio, 11 February 1963.
Esservecchia (horn, trombone, electric guitar, piano) 1963; first performed Malmo, 30 November 1963.
Warum Nicht? (flute, vibraphone, xylophone, tam-tam, violin, cello) 1964; first performed Stockholm, 22 April 1965.
Kazimir (4 flutes) 1965.
L'Essai du pianiste (pianist) 1965.
Visoka 12 (2 horns, 2 violins, 2 cellos) 1965; first performed Malmo, 2 February 1966.
Etwas für . . . (wind quintet) 1966; first performed Stockholm, 12 November 1966.
Eigentlich nicht: String Quartet No 1 1967; first performed Stockholm, 28 January 1868.
Ben fatto (1 or more instruments) 1968.
Ancora (4 flutes) 1969.
Hommage à . . . (organ) 1969.
Improvisations (organ) 1969.
PC-132: String Quartet No 2 1970; first performed Stockholm, 18 April 1971. Recorded Caprice CAP 1024.
Frammenti (cello) 1972. Recorded Caprice CAP 1190.
Harmonies (clarinet, trombone, piano, cello) 1972; first performed Warsaw, September 1972.
Pagabile (ensemble) 1972.
Recidivans: String Quartet No 3 1972; first performed Norrkoping, 17 March 1972.
Residuo: String Quartet No 4 1974; first performed Stockholm, 24 April 1976.
Eurytmi (string quartet, piano) 1979; first performed Stockholm, 29 August 1979.
Denby–Richard (flute, cello) 1981.
String Quartet No 6 1982; first performed Munich, 19 October 1982.
Variazioni sopra Laudi (after Ingvar Lidholm; organ) 1982; first performed Stockholm, 27 October 1982. Recorded PROP 9914.
Solo (oboe) 1983; first performed Rotterdam, 15 April 1984.
Solo (flute) 1983; first performed Rotterdam, 15 April 1984.
Solo (bassoon) 1983; first performed Rotterdam, 15 April 1984.
Poème (horn in F, piano) 1983; first performed Rotterdam, 15 April 1984.
String Quartet No 7 1984; first performed Stockholm, 22 January 1985.
Tema con 36 variazioni (piano) 1984; first performed Stockholm, 2 December 1985. Recorded Caprice CAP 2021.
String Quartet No 8 1986–7; first performed Lund, 6 September 1988.
EssAEG (2 pianos, electronics) 1988; first performed Jonkoping, 21 October 1988.
Suite (piano) 1988; first performed Vikingsberg, 5 February 1989.
Viriditas per Omnibus (2 flutes, 2 oboes, 3 clarinets, 2 bassoons, 2 horns, double bass) 1988; first performed Uppsala, 18 June 1989.

Vocal/choral:

Fyra kinesiska dikter (unaccompanied chorus; Wang Wei, translated Luboff) 1956.
Dikter (unaccompanied mixed chorus; Grave) 1957; broadcast Swedish Radio, 8 March 1968.
Van, i forodelsens stund/Friend in the Hour of Devastation (unaccompanied chorus; Stagnelius) 1958; broadcast Swedish Radio, 4 May 1959.
Fem dikter (unaccompanied mixed chorus; Setterlind) 1958. Recorded BIS LP 4.
Cantata (children's voices, 3 instruments; Diktonius) 1960.
Renovationes (soprano, flute, violin, mandolin, celeste, percussion; biblical) 1960; first performed Stockholm, 4 December 1961.
Glazba/Music (soprano, 3 flutes, bassoon) 1967–8.
Another Piece (4-part children's chorus, Orff instruments; Noren) 1969–76.
Helg/Festival (unaccompanied chorus) 1970; first performed Gothenburg, 11 August 1971.
Sex kompositioner (unaccompanied mixed chorus) 1970–5.
A New Map of Hell (unaccompanied chorus) 1971; first performed Stockholm, 21 November 1971.
Natalino/Christmas (unaccompanied chorus) 1971.
Ayer la forza di . . . (mixed chorus, string orchestra) 1972; first performed Vasteras, 6 May 1972.
Pagabile (mixed chorus, orchestra) 1972.
Joergen (unaccompanied chorus; Wiborg) 1973; first performed Stockholm, 25 November 1973.
Fyra japanska dikter (unaccompanied chorus; translated Wahlund) 1974. Recorded PROP 9926.
Viso (unaccompanied chorus) 1975; first performed Bergen, 1 June 1976.
En bukett japanska sanger om att aldras i skonhet (soprano, 3 recorders) 1975; first performed Stockholm, 18 March 1976.
I vanten pag (radiophonic composition for tenor, bass, flute, double bass, harp, organ) 1976; broadcast Swedish Radio, 18 October 1976.
Ett svensk rekviem/A Swedish Requiem (tenor, baritone, chorus, orchestra; Linne) 1976; first performed Stockholm, 14 December 1977.
Sonett (soprano, flute, cello, piano; Shakespeare) 1979; first performed Stockholm, 22 July 1980.
Flying Safe (soprano, flute, mixed chorus; von Heidenstam) 1980; first performed Graz, Austria, 12 October 1982.
Sorgesang (voice, organ; Setterlind) 1980; first performed Stockholm, 10 April 1980.
In silvis cum libro (unaccompanied male chorus; Ekelund) 1980; first performed Lund, 4 May 1980.
L'aveu (soloists, chorus, orchestra; Gellerfelt) 1982–3; broadcast Swedish Radio, 15 December 1984.
Lamento Op 41 (unaccompanied mixed chorus; Shakespeare) 1986.
Avsked (unaccompanied male chorus) 1987.
Maxi–Mini (unaccompanied mixed chorus; George, Persson) 1987; first performed Copenhagen, 26 November 1988.
I Am Nobody Op 51 (male chorus, flute, 3 percussion; Dickinson) 1989.
Luna llena, violeta Op 60 (tenor, flute, mixed chorus; Verdera) 1989; first performed Bunyola, Mallorca, 22 September 1990.
Tre kinesiska dikter Op 61 (unaccompanied mixed chorus; Hwang Tsu-Yu, translated Henrikson) 1990.

Opera:

Dummerjöns / Silly Jöns (children's television opera; Hellberg) 1966–7; broadcast 10 May 1967.
Drottning Jag / I, the Queen (soloists, mixed chorus, orchestra; Claesson) 1972; first performed Stockholm, 17 February 1973.

Other:

Coppelius (ballet; orchestra) 1968.
Ondine (incidental music to Giraudoux) 1968.
Danton's Tod (incidental music to Buchner; soprano, flute, vibraphone, tam-tam, drums, percussion) 1971.
Britannicus (incidental music to Racine; electronic) 1974.
Luddkolts aventyr (music for children's theatre) 1977; first performed Stockholm, 11 February 1963.
John Bauer (incidental music to marionettes) 1979; first performed Stockholm, 3 November 1979.

PUBLICATIONS

By Welin: "Arbetsbok" [Workbook], in *Nutida musik*, 6(8), 1963; "Fore konserten upplever jag mig sjalv som en kinesisk ask" [Before a Concert I Imagine I Have Become a Chinese Box], in *Konsertnytt*, 5, 1965–6; "Den svenske tonsattarens situation", in *Nutida musik*, 14(2), 1970; "Tonsattarna ska anvandas" [Composers Must Be Used], in *Tonfallet*, 8, 1973.

On Welin: J. Cederholm, "Aleatorik med lyckliga forveck-lingar" [Aleatory and Fortuitous Complications], in *Nutida musik*, 11(1–2), 1967; H. Connor, (interview) in *Samtal med tonsattare*, Stockholm, 1968.

* * *

The man, rather than the artifacts, constitutes the work of art: so Karl-Epik Welin postulates. In consequence, virtually all his activites and statements have become inherently introspective—an exhibitionism almost amounting to eccentric narcissism. He regards his own compositions almost as by-products of his inner striving. His works are personal confessions—"All my compositions, from opus 1 onwards, are about myself". He composes according to traditional concepts of beauty, seeking the poetical and aiming at the utmost expressivity. The dreamlike fragile art of his compositions is contrary to the fierce extravaganza of his performances.

In Welin's artistry we encounter striking antitheses; as a composer he is the unobtrusive, sensitive romantic, and as a musician/actor (i.e., when facing the audience) he is the frenzied member of avant-garde, whose name has been closely connected with "happening" and "instrumental theater". The determining impulse for exploring these fields was the contact he made with David Tudor at the Darmstadt festivals in the early 1960s.

During that decade Welin's performances were calculated to provoke the Swedish concert establishment—he sawed up a piano (injuring himself in the process), beat up eggs, combed a teddy bear, crawled into a grand piano. The visual element was important, even dominant at these concerts, in which Welin moved from exaltation to tranquillity and from absurdity to profundity. The use of symbolism was intended to polemicize against cliché in the music culture of the West. Welin's dramatic abilities made him world renowned as an interpreter, resulting in a number of works dedicated to him by György Ligeti, Mauricio Kagel, Sylvano Bussotti, Ingvar Lidholm and others. When performing the music of others, Welin tries to visualize the personality of the composer, the image of whom becomes "the final inspiration for expressing that individual".

Welin's first opus, *Fyra kinesiska dikter*, is still his most frequently performed work. Tonally based, these choral pieces are uncomplicated and tenderly lyrical. With the chamber works *Manzit* and *Warum Nicht?* Welin demonstrated his reaction against the complexity of the deterministic music of the time. With the intention of sharpening the listeners' attention Welin avoided great dynamic contrasts and gave the pauses an intrinsic value. In these works the basic material and expensive means are the sound qualities of each instrument respectively, realized in a sparing transparent texture.

Pereo for string orchestra differs from the earlier works, revealing new stylistic traits. The alternation between the minor and major triad forms the foundation for this work, into which a quotation of Monteverdi is inserted towards the end. Quotations, preferably of Romanticists like Beethoven and Reger, have become a recurring feature of Welin's music, as in the Brahusian *Ett svensk rekviem / A Swedish Requiem*.

During the 1960s Welin worked with complementary forms juxtaposing fragmentary sections. In his recent compositions, such as *Maxi–Mini* for choir, he works with traditionally conveyed linear forms, and uses a tonal language reminiscent of Wagner.

The ethical aspects of art has long been of major concern to Welin, who believes that art should always be constructive and positive in its attitude to life. He considers a conservative academical approach "anti-musical". However, this posture does not prevent Welin from emphasizing that in order to avoid dillettantism, a thorough craftsmanship together with stylistic historical awareness is a necessity.

—Björn Billing

WERNICK, Richard (Frank). American. Born in Boston, Massachusetts, 19 January 1934. Educated at Brandeis University, Waltham, Massachusetts (composition under Irving Fine, Harold Shapero and Arthur Berger), 1952–5, B.A.; Berkshire Music Centre, Tanglewood, Massachusetts (composition under Boris Blacher, Aaron Copland and Ernst Toch, conducting under Leonard Bernstein and Seymour Lipkin), 1954–5; Mills College, Oakland, California (under Leon Kirchner), 1956–7, M.A. Married Beatrice Messina, 15 July 1956; 2 sons. Music director and composer in residence, Royal Winnipeg Ballet, Manitoba, 1957–8; freelance composer and arranger, theatre, television and film, 1959–64; part-time instructor, Metropolitan Music School, New York, 1959–62; assistant professor and music coordinator, Centre for the Creative and Performing Arts, State University of New York, Buffalo, 1964–5; assistant professor of music, University of Chicago, 1965–8; assistant professor, from 1968, professor of music, from 1977, and Irving Fine Professor of Music, from 1986, University of Pennsylvania, Philadelphia; conductor Penn Contemporary Players; consultant on contemporary music, Philadelphia Orchestra, from 1983. Recipient: 1st prize (for *Four from Tulips and Chimneys*), Brookline Music Library Association, 1963; Naumburg Recording Award (for *Cadenzas and Variations III*), 1976; Guggenheim Fellowship,

1976; Pulitzer Prize (for *Visions of Wonder and Terror*), 1977; Kennedy Center Friedheim Award (for *Violin Concerto*), 1986. Mailing address: Music Department, University of Pennsylvania, 201 South 34th Street, Philadelphia, Pennsylvania 19104, U.S.A.

Publishers: Mills Music; Presser.

Symphonies/orchestral:

Concert Overture (band) 1962.
Hexagrams (chamber orchestra) 1962.
Snapshots (band) 1963.
Aevia (large orchestra) 1964; first performed Chicago, December 1966; broadcast WYYW TV, Chicago, February 1967.
Introits and Canons (chamber orchestra) 1978.
Cello Concerto 1980.
Fanfare for a Festive Occasion (antiphonal brass choirs) 1981; first performed Philadelphia, 23 October 1981.
Violin Concerto 1984; first performed Philadelphia, 17 January 1986.
Viola Concerto: Do Not Go Gentle . . . 1986; first performed 8 May 1987.
Symphony No 1 1988–9.

Chamber/instrumental:

String Quartet 1953; withdrawn.
Four Pieces (string quartet) 1955.
Divertimento (clarinet, bassoon, viola, cello) 1956.
Duo concertante (cello, piano) 1960.
Trio (clarinet, violin, piano) 1961–2; first performed Waltham, Massachusetts, 7 December 1962.
String Quartet No 2 1963; first performed Philadelphia, 8 February 1974.
Music (viola d'amore) 1964.
Stretti (clarinet, violin, viola, guitar) 1965; first performed Buffalo, New York, 25 April 1965.
Cadenzas and Variations I (viola, piano) 1967.
Three Pieces (string trio) 1967.
Cadenzas and Variations II (violin) 1970; first performed Philadelphia, Autumn 1970. Recorded New World Records 313.
Cadenzas and Variations III (cello) 1972; first performed Philadelphia, Spring 1973.
String Quartet No 3 1973.
Introits and Canons (flute, clarinet, bassoon, horn, percussion, violin, viola, cello, double bass) 1977, revised 1981; first performed New York City, January 1978.
Partita (violin) 1978; first performed New York City, September 1978.
In Praise of Zephyrus (oboe, string trio) 1980.
Concerto for Cello and Ten Players (cello solo, oboe, bass clarinet, contrabassoon/bassoon, horn, trumpet, trombone, violin, double bass, harp, percussion) 1980.
Formula: P— —m (violin, cello) 1981; first performed Chicago, 22 January 1982.
Fanfare for a Festive Occasion (brass, 8 timpani) 1981.
Sonata: Reflections of a Dark Light (piano) 1982; first performed Washington, D.C., 15 January 1983. Recorded Bridge Records BC5 7003.
Sonata: Portraits of Antiquity (cello) 1982; first performed New York City, 5 December 1983.
Musica Ptolemaica (brass quintet) 1987; first performed Philadelphia, 13 October 1987.
String Quartet No 3 1988.

Vocal/choral:

Four from Tulips and Chimneys (baritone, orchestra; cummings) 1956, arranged for baritone, piano 1957; first performed Brookline, Massachusetts, April 1963.
Full Fadom Five (SATB chorus, chamber ensemble; Shakespeare) 1964.
what if a much of a which of a wind (SATB chorus, prepared piano—4 hands; cummings) 1964.
Lyrics from I × I (soprano, double bass, percussion; cummings) 1966; first performed Chicago, December 1966.
Haiku of Basho (soprano, flute, clarinet, violin, double bass, 2 percussion, piano, tape) 1968; first performed Chicago, 1 March 1968. Recorded CRI S-379.
Moonsongs from the Japanese (soprano, tape) 1968; first performed Philadelphia, Spring 1969. Recorded CRI S-379.
Kaddish-Requiem (cantor, mezzo-soprano, flute/piccolo, clarinet/bass clarinet, violin, cello/sitar, 2 percussion, piano, tape) 1971; first performed Philadelphia, Autumn 1971. Recorded Nonesuch 71303.
A Prayer of Jerusalem (mezzo-soprano, percussion) 1971; first performed Philadelphia, Spring 1972. Recorded CRI S-344.
Kee el Asher (unaccompanied SATB chorus; biblical) 1972.
Songs of Remembrance (4 songs for mezzo-soprano, shawm/cor anglias/oboe) 1973; first performed Philadelphia, 1974. Recorded Nonesuch 71342.
Visions of Wonder and Terror (mezzo-soprano, orchestra; Bible, Koran) 1976; first performed Aspen, Colorado, July 1976.
Contemplations of the Tenth Muse: Books I–II (soprano, piano; Bradstreet) 1977–9; first performed New York City, 1977.
And on the Seventh Day . . . (sacred service for cantor, 4 percussion) 1979, revised 1985; first performed Bridgeport, Connecticut, April 1979.
A Poison Tree (soprano, flute, clarinet, violin, cello, piano; Blake) 1980; first performed Syracuse, New York, January 1980. Recorded Spectrum SR 183.
Oracle of Shimon Bar Yochai (soprano, cello, piano) 1983; first performed New York City, 8 December 1983.
Oracle II (soprano, oboe, piano) 1985; first performed Baltimore, Maryland, 18 January 1987.
The Eleventh Commandment: A Silly Piece with a Serious Message (SATB chorus, piano, organ) 1987; first performed Ithaca, New York, 14 November 1987.

Opera:

Maggie (Stephen Crane) 1959.

Other:

The Trojan Women (incidental music) 1953.
Thieves Carnival (incidental music to Anouilh; clarinet) 1955; first performed Waltham, Massachusetts, April 1955.
Oedipus Rex (incidental music) 1956.
The Twisted Heart 1957.
Le Bourgeois Gentilhomme (incidental music) 1957.
The Emperor's Nightingale 1958.
The Geranium Hat 1959.
The Nativity 1961.

* * *

Richard Wernick's music is immediately reminiscent of his favourite literary source, the poet e.e. cummings. There are the same alternations of complexity and almost naive simplicity, dissonant intervals and fractured syntax, a vocabulary of sounds and instrumental gestures suddenly pulled loose from their familiar associations. Wernick's prize-winning setting of verse from *Tulips and Chimneys* is an excellent example of his early style, still somewhat constrained by teachers such as Aaron Copland and Leonard Bernstein (who was Wernick's conducting tutor at the Berkshire Music Center, but made a clearly audible impact on his compositional style as well). That is still evident in the two Japanese settings of 1967 and 1968. Wernick approaches Basho much as he approaches cummings, relishing the semantic space and strightforward ostensive approach, comfortable with a text that imposes no strict metrical constraints.

Like Bernstein, Wernick manages to convey profound and often quite disturbing visions in remarkably palatable forms. Where he differs fundamentally from cummings is that his musical texts—and texts are very important to Wernick—are always striving for some sort of transcendence, usually a spiritual or religious one. An early experiment with opera (not so far repeated, surprisingly) used the short and much-bowdlerised novel *Maggie: A Child of the Streets* by the novelist Stephen Crane (and not the poet Hart Crane, as American *Grove* suggests) to create a touching parable of suffering and secular redemption. Wernick has continued to write within that broadly secular tradition, producing a non-sectarian *Kaddish-Requiem* for the victims of the Vietnam War, while his finest work to date is the Pulitzer Prize-winning *Visions of Wonder and Terror*, which draws on both the Judaeo-Christian and Islamic traditions in a work of considerable ecumenical significance.

The bell-tones that introduce "The Vision from Judah", the first part of the *Visions*, are typical of Wernick's heightened sensitivity to instrumental colour. Though the *haiku* are for relatively conventional forces disposed somewhat unconventionally, Wernick increasingly made use of unconventional instrumentations, and sometimes electronics; the following year, he added a multi-tracked tape of a soprano voice to *Moonsongs from the Japanese*. Typical gestures are the inclusion of a shawm, doubling with English horn and oboe, in *Songs of Remembrance*, a work written for the great mezzo-soprano Jan DeGaetani, and the addition of a (not quite authentic) sitar, doubling with cello, in the *Kaddish-Requiem*. He has also used a version of Cage's prepared piano in a further cummings setting, and has an early piece for the under-exploited viola d'amore.

Wernick's vocal and instrumental music is highly textured, full of surprising shifts and alternations, highly wrought. By contrast, his orchestral music is less compelling. The key to his larger-scale approach may be found in miniature in the concerto for cello and 10 players, a piece that gives free rein to his dramatic alternations of consonance and dissonance. The *Violin Concerto* is a powerful, free-ranging work, with a highly dramatic and evocative disposition of orchestral forces, daring chordal progressions, and intermittent glimpses of the whole history of the form.

Wernick is a warmly humane teacher, and his work is not without humour. In 1987, he joined those daring enough to write an Eleventh Commandment. Wernick's was set to the text "No, though shalt not Xerox music".

—Ian Grey

WHITE, (Edward) John. British. Born in Berlin, 5 April 1936. Educated: private piano study under Helene Gipps, from 1943; St Paul's School, London, 1949–51; private composition study under Elisabeth Lutyens, 1954; Royal College of Music, London (composition under Bernard Stevens and Humphrey Searle), 1955–8. Married choreographer Pat Garrett in 1980. Professor of composition, Royal College of Music, London, 1961–6; performer, Promenade Theatre Orchestra, 1970–2, Hobbs-White Duo, 1972–6, Garden Furniture Music Ensemble, 1977–9, Farewell Symphony Orchestra, 1979–80, Nordic Reverie Trio, 1980, Instant Dismissal Symphony Orchestra, 1983–4, Lower Edmonton Latin Lovers Choral Society, 1988, and Edouard Ratt and Live Batts!, 1988; teacher of composition and improvisation, Menuhin School, Cobham, 1974–8; head of piano studies, Leicester Polytechnic, 1980–6. Mailing address: 16 Queens Road, Edmonton, London, N9 ORB, England.

Publishers: Leduc, Paris; Forward, London.

Orchestral:

Overture (2 orchestras/2nd orchestra entirely percussion) 1958.
Concerto for Piano and Strings 1960–1.
Piano Concerto 1963; first performed London, 18 October 1963.
Concerto for Harpsichord and Brass 1964.
Concerto for Eleven Brass 1964.
37 Orchestra Snapshots (based on piano sonatas 53–69) 1973; first performed Richmond, Surrey, July 1973.

Symphonies [all for small ensembles or for solo performance with "user-friendly" live electronics]:

Symphony for Solo Piano 1961.
Symphony for Organ and Six Tubas 1965; first performed London, 6 October 1965.
Symphony No 3 (2 clarinets/saxophones, cello, double bass, tuned and untuned percussion) 1981; first performed Birmingham, 5 November 1981.
Symphony No 4 (2 clarinets/saxophones, cello, double bass, tuned and untuned percussion) 1981; first performed Birmingham, 5 November 1981.
Symphony No 5 (2 clarinets/saxophones, cello, double bass, tuned and untuned percussion) 1981; first performed Birmingham, 5 November 1981.
Symphony No 6 (2 clarinets/saxophones, cello, double bass, tuned and untuned percussion) 1981; first performed Birmingham, 5 November 1981.
Symphony No 7: Pandora's Box (electric keyboards, sequencers) 1982; first performed Paris, 26 October 1982.
Symphony of a Thousand: Symphony No 8 (Casio Veltones, pre-recorded tape backing track) 1983; first performed Milan, 24 March 1983.
Symphony No 9: Topless Wolf Whistle (2 Roland micro-composers, 2 toy electric keyboards, voice) 1983; first performed Amsterdam, 29 September 1983.
Symphony No 10 (voices, tuned and untuned percussion, keyboards) 1984, revised version for synthesizers 1986; original version first performed Northampton, 11 May 1984; revised version first performed The Hague, 29 May 1986. Recorded Musica Nova 3.
Symphony No 11 (sequenced material, live electronics) 1984; first performed Cologne, 29 September 1984.

Symphony No 12 ("Plainsong", "Bells"; Yamaha CX5/1 synthesizer) 1985; first performed London, October 1985.
Symphony No 13: Toccata, Adagio and Idleburger Salsa (CX5/1) 1986. Recorded Musica Nova 3.
Symphony No 14 (2 violins, clarinet, alto saxophone, trumpet, tubular bells, piano duet) 1986; first performed Leicester, 6 May 1986.
Symphony No 15 ("A Survivor from Vienna" and "The Crematorium Organist's Favourite Chords"; CX5/1) 1986; first performed The Hague, 30 May 1986.
Symphony No 16 ("The Jake's Ladder", "Veltone Ripple", "Codetta Improvisation"; CX5/1, sampler) 1986; first performed London, 7 November 1987.
Symphony No 17 ("Cosmic Banjo I–II", "Aeolian Boogie"; CX5/2) 1986; first performed The Hague, 25 May 1987.
Symphony No 18: The Alpine (CX5/2, live electronics) 1987; first performed The Hague, 25 May 1987.
Symphony No 19: The Whistlers and Their Mothers (CX5/2, live electronics) 1987; first performed London, 7 November 1987. Recorded Musica Nova 3.
Symphony No 20 (CX5/2, Yamaha TX81Z sound module) 1988.
Symphony No 21: The Sea (electric keyboard, Vocoder, optional soprano trombone, speaker) 1989; first performed London, 15 June 1989.

Chamber/instrumental (excluding piano):

Divertimentissimo (bassoon, horn, piano) 1956; first performed London, 1957.
Chorale Dirge on the Agincourt Song (string quartet, harp, xylophone) 1957; first performed London, 1957.
Trio (flute, oboe, piano) 1958; first performed London, 11 November 1961.
Quintet No 1 (flute, oboe, bassoon, double bass, piano) 1958; first performed London, 1958; used in ballet *Disenchantment*.
Sonata (violin) 1958; first performed London, 10 November 1960.
Four Pastorales ("héroïque", "cosmique", "sportif", "pastorale", violin, piano) 1958; first performed 4 October 1962.
Diversions on Lilliburlero (violin, piano) 1958.
Septet (flute, oboe, violin, horn, 3 trombones) 1959; first performed London, 1959.
Quintet No 2 (flute, oboe, violin, cello, piano) 1959; used for ballet *Pelleas and Melisande*.
Duettino (flute, piano) 1960.
Two Pieces (oboe, piano) 1960.
Toccata (organ) 1961; first performed Guildford, Surrey, 16 May 1961.
Conte (clarinet, piano) 1961.
Sonatina No 1 (2 tubas) 1964; first performed London, 1964.
Carillons (bass trombone, piano) 1964; first performed London, 6 December 1964.
Combine Piece (tuba, piano strings) 1964; first performed London, 18 June 1964.
Sonata No 1 (tuba, piano) 1964; first performed London, 1964.
Sonatina No 2 (2 tubas) 1965; first performed London, 1 February 1965.
Sonata No 2 (tuba, piano) 1965; first performed London, 1965.
Sonatina (bass trombone, piano) 1965; first performed London, 12 July 1965.
Untitled (flugelhorn, horn, tuba) 1965; first performed London, 16 May 1991.
Souvenir of Lake Constance (alto melodica, tuba, piano) 1965; first performed London, 1965.
Scene (Snaefell) (trombone, piano) 1965; first performed 10 May 1965.
Trombone Quartet 1966; first performed London, 1966.
Five Chimes (2 trumpets, 2 trombones, bass trombone/tuba) 1966; first performed New York City, 2 April 1969.
Bell Machine (trombone, tuba, piano) 1968; first performed London, 17 October 1968.
Machine (cello, tuba) 1968; first performed London, April 1968.
Air (2 trumpets, horn, trombone, tuba; from "The Four Elements", other movements written by Richard V. Hill, Gordon Rose, Ian Lake) 1969. Recorded Deutsche Grammophon DGG 2530032.
P.T. Machine (contrabassoon, swanee whistle, gongs, goat bells) 1969; first performed London, 18 October 1970.
Autumn Countdown Machine (any number of groups containing 2 similarly low-pitched wind or string instruments, percussion, bell-metronomes) 1971; first performed Liverpool, 15 October 1971. Recorded Obscure OBS 8.
Concert Duos (7 pieces for tuba, piano; 1 "Dance of Changing Metres", 5 "Interrupted Romance", 6 "Christmas Carol", 7 "Dreaming Spires"; others untitled) 1975; first performed Egham, Surrey, 8 February 1976.
Three Pieces (bassoon, piano) 1976.
Sonata No 3: Basingstoke (tuba, piano) 1976; first performed London, 4 February 1979.
Menuhin School Machines (string sextet or 12 strings, 2 pianos—8 hands) 1976–7; first performed 16 May 1991.
WUT (violin, 2 violas, cello, clarinet, tuba vibraphone, marimba, piano duet, percussion) 1987; first performed London, 5 March 1987.
Not WUT (violin, soprano saxophone, bass clarinet, cornet) 1987; first performed London, 17 May 1987.
Incantation (viola or massed violas) 1987; broadcast BBC Radio, 25 September 1990.
Not WUT Again (No Way, Shitface!) (2 violas, 2 E♭ clarinets, piano) 1988; first performed London, 4 July 1988.
Two Nocturnes (violin, piano) 1988.
True Romance (4 clarinets, bass clarinets) 1988; first performed Redlands, California, 1988.
A Little Souvenir from Costa Mijas (bass clarinet, piano) 1989; first performed London, 27 April 1989.
100 Snapshots (bass trombone, electric keyboard, drum machine) 1989; first performed Schwaz, Austria, 11 April 1990.
Holiday Snapshots (version of *100 Snapshots*; trombone, piano) 1989; first performed Redlands, California, 1989.
Les Enfants de Salieri (2 trumpets, horn, trombone, tuba) 1990; first performed Hali-in-Tirol, Austria, 8 January 1991.
Aerobic Chant (organ) 1990; first performed London, 16 December 1990.
Conversation Piece (clarinet) 1990; first performed Redlands, California, 13 February 1991.
SUN Reader (violin, viola, cello, bass clarinet, tuba, vibraphone, marimba, piano, percussion) 1991; first performed London, 18 March 1991.
Three Voluntaries (single manual organ or harmonium) 1991; first performed Austria, 10 January 1991.

Piano:

Five Preludes 1956; first performed London, 29 May 1957.
Variations 1958; first performed London, 11 November 1960.
Sonatina No 1 1959.
Sonatina No 2 1959.

Sonatina No 3 1960.
Eight Etudes 1960; first performed Paris, 9 December 1960.
Sonatina No 4 1960.
Sonatina No 5 1960; first performed Richmond, Surrey, 6 June 1962.
Sonatina No 6 1960; first performed London, early 1960s.
Sonatina No 7 1961; first performed London, 10 November 1961.
Sonatina No 8 (includes *Symphony to the Memory of Charles-Valentin Morhange [Alkan]*) 1961; first performed (in part) London, 1964.
Machine (harpsichord, piano) 1970.
Four Mantras (toy piano) 1970; first performed Gillingham, 1970.
Piano Duets: First Set 1974–5; first performed London, 24 March 1975.
Piano Duets: Second Set 1975; first performed London, 24 October 1976 and 4 February 1979.
Edwardian Snapshots (2 pianos) 1979; first performed Amsterdam, 26 January 1980.
Machine (4 pianos) 1979; first performed Milan, 23 June 1979.
A Serene Greeting to the People of York (piano—6 hands) 1988; first performed York, 1988.
Robust Melody (2 pianos) 1988; first performed Leicester, 24 November 1988.
Grand Hotel Suite (with tape) 1989; first performed London, 18 January 1989.

The Sonatas:
1—1956; broadcast BBC Radio, 21 January 1959. Recorded Lyrita RCS 18.
2—1957; first performed London, 18 March 1960.
3—1958; first performed Australia, 1959.
4—1959; first performed London, 26 November 1959. Recorded Lyrita RCS 18.
5—1959; first performed Bristol, 27 April 1960.
6—1959; first performed London, 11 June 1961.
7—1960.
8—1960; first performed London, January 1962.
9—1960; first performed Leicester, February 1961. Recorded Lyrita RCS 18.
10—1960; first performed Cheltenham, Gloucestershire, 7 July 1962.
11—1960.
12—1960; to be played together with No 13.
13—1960; to be played together with No 12.
14—1960.
15—1962; subtitled "Traumatic Rural Rape"; first performed London, 17 October 1963. Recorded MIOT/LP1.
16—1962.
17—1962; first performed Richmond, Surrey, 6 June 1962.
18—1963.
19—1963.
20—1963; first performed London, 6 December 1964.
21—1964; first performed London, 15 May 1964.
22—1965; first performed London, 18 October 1967.
23—1965; first performed London, 16 May 1991.
24—1965.
25—1965.
26—with optional part for alto trombone, 1965; first performed London, 5 October 1966.
27—1966.
28—1966.
29—1966; first performed London, 16 May 1991.
30—1966.
31—1967; broadcast BBC Radio, 13 September 1967.
32—1967.
33—1967.
34—1967; first performed London, 21 September 1967.
35—1968; first performed London, 16 October 1968.
36—1968.
37–49—all 1969.
50—1969; first performed London, 16 May 1991.
51—1970; broadcast BBC Radio, 8 December 1970.
52—1970; first performed London, 14 April 1986.
53—1972; first performed London, 24 January 1973.
54—1972; first performed London, 24 January 1973.
55—1972; first performed London, 24 January 1973.
56—1972; first performed London, 7 August 1983.
57—1973; first performed Hall-in-Tirol, 13 March 1989.
58—1973.
59—1973; first performed London, 7 August 1983.
60—1973.
61—1973.
62—1973; first performed London, 7 August 1983.
63—1973.
64—1973; first performed London, 24 October 1976.
65—1973; first performed London, 12 May 1987.
66—1973.
67—1973.
68—1973; first performed London, 12 May 1987.
69—1973; first performed London, 7 August 1983.
70—1973.
71—1973; first performed Egham, Surrey, 8 March 1973.
72—1973.
73—1973.
74—1973.
75—1973; first performed London, 11 January 1977.
76—subtitled "The Rustic", 1973; first performed London, 5 January 1974.
77—1973.
78—1973; first performed London, 24 October 1976.
79—1973.
80—1973.
81—1973; first performed London, 5 January 1974.
82—1973; first performed London, 1 July 1986.
83—1973; first performed London, 30 September 1987.
84—1973; first performed London, 7 August 1983.
85—1973; first performed London, 1 July 1986.
86—1973; first performed London, December 1973.
87—1973; first performed London, December 1973.
88—1973.
89—1973; first performed London, 7 August 1983.
90—1973; first performed London, 5 January 1974.
91—1975–6; first performed Egham, Surrey, 8 March 1978.
92—1976.
93—1976; first performed London, 24 October 1976.
94—1976; first performed Redlands, California, 9 September 1982.
95—1977; first performed Valetta, Malta, 20 April 1977.
96—1977; subtitled "The Caledonian"; first performed Egham, Surrey, 8 March 1978.
97—1978; first performed Egham, Surrey, 8 March 1978.
98—1978; first performed Egham, Surrey, 8 March 1978.
99—1978.
100—1980; first performed London, 27 June 1986.
101—1980; first performed London, 7 August 1983.
102—1980; first performed London, January 1981.
103—1980; first performed London, 7 March 1986.
104—1980; first performed London, 7 August 1983.
105—1980; first performed London, January 1981.
106—1980; first performed London, January 1981.
107—1981; first performed London, 30 September 1987.

108—1983; first performed London, 7 August 1983.
109—1984; first performed Ipoh, Malaysia, 24 June 1984.
110—1986; first performed London, 27 June 1986.
111—1987; first performed London, 30 September 1987.
112—1987; first performed London, 30 September 1987.
113—1987; first performed London, 30 September 1987.
114—1987; first performed London, 30 September 1987.
115—1987; first performed London, 30 September 1987.
116—1987; first performed Hall-in-Tirol, Austria, 13 March 1989.
117—1988; first performed London, 29 September 1989.
118—1989; first performed London, 29 September 1989.
119—1990; first performed Chicago, 22 April 1990.
120—1991; first performed London, 24 January 1991.
121—1991; first performed London, 16 May 1991.
122—1991; first performed London, 16 May 1991.

Vocal/choral:

Praeludium (contralto, piano; Morgenstern) 1957; first performed London, 16 May 1991.
Verses from the Revelation of St John (high voice, flute, oboe, harp, trombone or double bass, piano) 1958; first performed London, 1958.
Introit, Hymn and finale (SATB chorus, 2 oboes, cor anglais) 1958; first performed London, 1958.
Fantasia on Easter Hymn from Goethe's Faust (voice, string quartet, piano) 1963; first performed London, 24 March 1963.
Nightpiece (baritone, bass trombone; Joyce) 1964; first performed London, June 1964.
Three Morgenstern Songs (baritone, 2 tubas) 1967; broadcast BBC Radio, 18 October 1967.
Humming and Ahing Machine (unaccompanied SATB chorus) 1971; first performed London, 20 February 1976.
The Chairman's Enemies' Favourite Things (4 vocal groups/each with 1 percussion) 1971; first performed 1 July 1986.
Nine Morgenstern Songs (voice, tuba) 1975; first performed Egham, Surrey, 8 February 1976.
Stella Avis (voice, CX5/1, drum machine) 1985; first performed London, 5 February 1985.
Pagina tres puella (male voices, violin, piano, pre-recorded tape backing track) 1985; first performed Zurich, 28 April 1985.
La Mentation (SSAATTBB chorus, organ, electric keyboard, drum machine, rock drummer) 1989–90.

Opera:

Stanley and the Monkey-King (Barson) 1975; first performed London, 24 March 1975.
Orpheus-Euridice (Barson) 1976; first performed London, 6 April 1976.
Alfred (Carter) 1981; first performed London, June 1981.
Gartenzwergdiebe/Gnomesnatchers 1991, in progress.

Dance:

Disenchantment (3 versions: piano; piano duet; *Quintet No 1*; Roope) 1958; first performed London, 1958.
Disenchantment 2 (piano or piano duet; Roope) 1959; first performed London, 1959.
Pelleas and Melisande (to *Quintet No 2*; Roope) 1959.
St George en Provence (piano) 1960.
Glove (percussion; Thatcher) 1980; first performed London, 1980.
A Day in the Life of a Romantic Novelist (voices; Thatcher) 1980; first performed London, 1980.
Classical Snapshots (piano duets; Garrett) 1980; first performed Edinburgh, 17 August 1980.
From a Celestial Clock Factory (percussion; Garrett) 1980; first performed Edinburgh, 17 August 1980.
They Are Not Like Us (piano/*Sonata 107*; Taylor) 1980; first performed Edinburgh, 16 August 1981.
Pythagoras's Trousers (Casio 202; Thatcher) 1981; first performed London, 1981.
Earthbound/Airbound (*Air*; Garrett) 1981; first performed Bishop's Stortford, Hertfordshire, 1981.
Postchoch (Casio Keyboard; Garrett) 1981; first performed Hemel Hempstead, Hertfordshire, 29 September 1981.
Gothick Satires (Casio 202; Garrett) 1982; first performed London, 23 February 1982.
Festival Solo (piano; Garrett) 1982; first performed East Grinstead, Sussex, 15 May 1982.
Tens into Five in Black (Casio 202; Garrett) 1982; first performed London, 26 June 1982.
Underworld (2 synthesizers; Garrett) 1983.
Mambos to Murder By (drum machine, synthesizer, flanger; Garrett) 1983; first performed London, 5 October 1983.
Tellab (2 synthesizers; Garrett) 1984; first performed London, 20 March 1984.
Chrome baroque (synthesizer; Garrett) 1984; first performed London, 5 June 1984.
Mouth of the Night (CX5/1, synthesizer; Micha Bergese) 1985.
Witness to the Unpresentable (synthesizer; various) 1986.
Man-Machine Interface (clarinet, 2 synthesizers, 2 drum machines, sequencer; Garrett) 1990.

Other:

Promenade Theatre Orchestra (works for read organs, toy pianos, winds, percussion, psalteries, Jew's harps, etc) 1970–2.
Hobbs-White Duo (works for percussion and other instruments) 1972–6.
Garden Furniture Music Ensemble (works for viola, baritone horn, tuba, piano, percussion) 1977–9.
Farewell Symphony Orchestra (works for trumpets, clarinets, flutes, saxophones, double bass, percussion, piano) 1979–80.
Nordic Reverie Trio (piano, glockenspiel, double bass) 1980.
Instant Dismissal Symphony Orchestra (electronic; including *Faberge Curate's Egg, The Merry Samurai's Return from Work, Breakfast Time at the Academy of Martial Arts, Calligraphic Trip, Ricercare*) 1984–5.
Lower Edmonton Latin Lovers Choral Society (electronic works; including *Nil carborundum*) 1988.
Edouard Ratt (electronic works; including *ER's Farting Tape, ER Goes Latin!, Now Play Some of Your Own Music, ER*) 1988–90.
Other *Machines*, process-based pieces for improvisatinal performance (e.g., *Cello and Tuba Machine*, *Drinking and Hooting Machine*, etc.).
Other electronic works and music for film and theatre (including *Calderon, Mayor of Salomea*).

PUBLICATIONS

On White: Brian Dennis, "The Music of JW", in *Musical Times* 1959, May 1971; Dave Smith, "JW and His Piano Sonatas", in *Contact*, 21, Autumn 1980, and "JW: A Catalogue of His Works", unpublished, 1991 [the editors would like to thank Dave Smith for his help in preparing this entry].

John White comments:
I just work here.

* * *

The flux of John White's musical thinking throughout his life is reflected in his piano sonatas. White says these works are "like entries in a diary [which] reflect the sort of musical interests of the moment. They're nearly all about music almost more than about me." Musical interests that pop up from time to time include a lifetime obsession with composers of the late 19th century, including Alkan, Nikolay Karlovich Medtner, Ferruccio Busoni, Satie and Bruckner. Musical problems and questions occur to White in the study of the works of these composers and others; musical directions in his other works and concerns from his theatre music; suggestions, passing comments, or works by friends; and White makes note of and comments upon these problems most closely in the sonatas, in the same way a diarist might work through philosophical concerns in a journal. Dave Smith says White's sonatas "conjure up an imaginary musical seance at which 'friends' of the composer make brief appearances."

This practice of composition as a form of argument, of language, occurs in White's other music. White is the inventor of *Machines*, an early systemic procedure in which he used random processes such as dart boards and chess moves to determine the note-to-note procedure of repetition or occurrence of events. His cello and tuba *Machine*, written for himself and Cornelius Cardew, could take up to five hours to perform. Random procedures indicate in *Drinking and Hooting Machine* the number and order of swigs, gulps, sips and hoots on bottles of "a favoured drink".

White's concerns with musical problems are directly affected by his work with colleagues. He was the first to perform "perverse" or opposite readings in early performances of Cardew's *Treatise*. His collaboration with Christopher Hobbs (in the Promenade Theatre Orchestra, the Hobbs-White Duo, and Live Batts!), Gavin Bryars and Benedict Mason (in Garden Furniture Music) and Jamie Crofts (in more recent collaborations) have added to his use of technique to reflect his musical concerns. White influenced the jokey tenor of the Promenade Theatre Orchestra, his concern with strict systemic processes stems from his percussion music for the Hobbs-White Duo, and his use of toy sheep calls and whistles in Garden Furniture Music recall Spike Jones's nuttier hits. The rock elements in many of White's newer electric music arise from White's brother-in-law's interest in European techno-pop.

One example of White's mode of working can be found in his Third, Fourth, Fifth and Sixth Symphonies. All four symphonies are meant to be played contiguously; their total performance time is only a little over 20 minutes. The Third Symphony has a rather traditional order of introductory movement, scherzo, song form and rousing finale. White then created the next symphonies in the way that he perceived his work with the director Michael Bogdanov for *Calderon, Mayor of Salomea*. White found, when writing music for this director and many others, that it was a process of writing a theme to a verbal description, and then almost blindly altering to more vague descriptions, such as "too Spanish . . . more medieval . . . too metrical . . . more Celtic." Rather than a simple variation of each movement of the Third Symphony in each movement of succeeding symphonies, White directed himself to make alterations, some every minute, such as adding another stroke of a sheep call at the end of the scherzo of the Fourth Symphony instead of one, to very large alterations, such as scrapping the entire scherzo in the Fifth Symphony for another, slower one. The finale of the Fourth Symphony was directed to be "more popular", so White wrote a theme with the feel of that of *Dick Barton: Special Agent*.

Directions apply to many of White's electric music, from his *Spanish Sketchbook*, a set of daily recordings White made while on holiday in Spain on a set of small cheap Casios, a flanger pedal, a mixer and a portable tape recorder, to his Alpine Symphony, the second movement of which evokes a pair of rock guitarists playing to each other from neighbouring peaks, in the manner of the shepherds in the third movement of *Symphonie fantastique*.

White's work with music as a form of communication pervades all of his output, from his theatre work, to his ballets (many with his wife, the choreographer Pat Garrett) to the massive dance multimedia evening *Man-Machine Interface*, as well as his symphonies, electric works, sonatas and chamber works. This communication takes the form of conversation, direction, psychic revelation, and gestures, both sacred and profane.

—Virginia Anderson

WHITEHEAD, Gillian. New Zealander. Born in Hamilton, 23 April 1941. Eucated at University of Auckland, 1959–62; University of Wellington, 1963, B.Mus., 1964; University of Sydney (composition under Peter Sculthorpe), 1964–5, M.Mus., 1966; University of Adelaide, (composition under Peter Maxwell Davies), 1966; subsequent private composition study under Maxwell Davies, London, 1967. Freelance composer, 1967–78; composer in residence, Northern Arts, Newcastle-upon-Tyne, 1978–80; visiting lecturer, 1981, lecturer, 1982–90, and head, department of composition, since 1990, Sydney Conservatorium of Music [alternate years to be spent as full-time composer]. Recipient: New Zealand Broadcasting Corporation String Quartet Prize, 1971. Mailing address: 7 Neale Street, Katoomba, New South Wales 2780, Australia.

Publishers: Price Milburn, New Zealand; Musica Dei Gloria; Wai-te-ata Press; LaTrobe University Press.

Symphonies/orchestral:

Punctua solis 1971.
Te Tangi a Apakura (string orchestra) 1975; first performed London, 1976.
Tirea (oboe, violin, cello, harpsichord, strings) 1978; first performed London, 1978.
Hoata (chamber orchestra) 1979; first performed Newcastle-upon-Tyne, 1979.
Resurgences 1988; first performed Wellington, 1989.

Chamber/instrumental:

Fantasia on Three Notes (piano) 1966.
Okuru (violin, piano) 1968; first performed Auckland, 1981.
Aria (cello) 1969.

Te-akua-te-atarangi (string quartet) 1970.
Piano Trio 1972.
Trio (harpsichord, violin, cello) 1974.
La cadenza sia corta (piano) 1974; first performed London, 1974.
Voices of Tane (piano) 1975; first performed Auckland, 1976.
Ricercare (viola) 1976.
Antiphons (3 trumpets, 2 horns, 3 trombones, tuba) 1979; first performed Newcastle-upon-Tyne, 1980.
Tamatea Tutahi (piano) 1980; first performed Auckland, 1980.
Ahotu (flute, trombone, cello, 2 keyboards, percussion) 1984; first performed Adelaide, 1984.
Windstreams (solo percussion) 1985; first performed Sydney, 1986.
Manutaki (flute, clarinet, violin, viola, cello, piano) 1985–6; first performed Wellington, 1986. Recorded 2MBS FM.
Napier's Bones (improvising piano, 24 percussion) 1989; first performed Sydney, 1990.
String Quartet No 3 1991.
Angels Born at the Speed of Light (string quartet) 1991.

Vocal/choral:

Missa brevis (unaccompanied SSAATTB chorus) 1963; first performed Sydney, 1965. Recorded Kiwi SLD 56.
Qui natus est (unaccompanied SATB chorus) 1966; first performed Auckland, 1967. Recorded Kiwi SLD 31.
Pakuru (soprano, flute, clarinet, viola, cello, harpsichord, percussion) 1967; first performed Berlin, 1968.
Six Songs of Umberto Saba (soprano, clarinet) 1968.
Whaka-tau-ki (medium voice, flute, oboe, clarinet, horn, trumpet, trombone, violin or viola, cello, double bass, percussion) 1970.
Three Songs of Janet Frame (soprano, oboe, clarinet/bass clarinet, horn, trumpet, trombone, guitar, double bass, piano) 1972; first performed London, 1972.
Christmas Music (mixed chorus) 1972.
Riddles (soprano, piano; Manhire) 1973, revised version for mezzo-soprano, marimba, guitar, harpsichord; first performed Wellington, 1978.
Laudate spirituale: Five Songs of Hildegard von Bingen (unaccompanied SATB chorus) 1976; first performed Sydney, 1984.
The Inner Harbour (Adcock) 1979.
Bright Forms Return (mezzo-soprano, string quartet; Raine) 1980; first performed Lake District, 1980.
Hotspur (soprano, mezzo-soprano, 2 clarinets, violin, cello, percussion; Adcock) 1980; first performed Durham, 1981.
Low Tide, Aramoana (large SATB chorus, 3 trumpets, 2 trombones, timpani; McQueen) 1981; first performed Auckland, 1982.
Pao (soprano, piano, clarinet) 1981; first performed Newcastle-upon-Tyne, 1982.
Requiem (mezzo-soprano, organ) 1981; first performed Wellington, 1987.
These Isles Your Dream (mezzo-soprano, viola, piano) 1983; first performed Carlisle, England, 1983.
Out of This Nettle, Danger (mezzo-soprano, flute, clarinet, trumpet, cello, piano, percussion; Mansfield/Adcock) 1984; first performed Sydney, 1984.
Tongues, Swords, Keys (SSAATTBB chorus, 4 percussion; Stow) 1985; first performed Sydney, 1985.
Eleanor of Aquitaine (mezzo-soprano, chamber orchestra; Adcock) 1987; first performed Sydney, 1988.
The Virgin and the Nightingale (unaccompanied SATB chorus) 1988; first performed Auckland, 1989.

Opera:

Tristan and Iseult (chamber opera; Hill, Crowthers) 1975; first performed Auckland, 1978.
The King of the Other Country (chamber opera; Adcock) 1983; first performed Sydney, 1984.
The Pirate Moon (chamber opera; dell'Oso) 1985; first performed Auckland, 1986.
Bride of Fortune (chamber opera; dell'Oso) 1990; first performed Perth, 1991.

Other:

Marduk (mezzo-soprano, mime dancers, instruments) 1973.

PUBLICATIONS

On Whitehead: Noel Sanders, "GW in Discussion", in *NMA Magazine*, 1986; Jane Weiner LePage, "GW", in *Women Composers, Conductors and Musicians of the Twentieth Century*, Metuchen, New Jersey, 1988; Elizabeth Kerr, interview in *Music in New Zealand*, 6, Spring 1989.

Gillian Whitehead comments:

Composition has seemed to me different things at different times—an expression of philosophy, meditation, a form of sculpture, the realisation of a natural soundscape, a woven pattern, an outlet for drama, humour or anger, or just play. Sometimes it flows easily, sometimes not, but whatever else, it is life-giving and a total commitment.

* * *

Gillian Whitehead is a strong composer—she seems to have sprung ready-made into the profession, with her own unmistakable voice. From her very earliest works, like the *Fantasia on Three Notes*, for solo piano in 1966, to the monodrama *Out of This Nettle, Danger* for chamber ensemble and voice in 1984, she has shown a firm structure, a clear texture built on extremely economic means, and a breadth of expression that is deep and fulfilling. Her quiet personality and slight frame belie the force of her music. She can weave compelling and mystic phrases with creative power and intensity.

Her life has been cosmopolitan with many sojourns of residence and work in England and Europe, and later in Australia in various posts. All these events have influenced her work. But her roots are in her much-loved homeland of New Zealand, where, at the age of 17, as a first-year student of music at the University of Auckland, she wrote home with a much-quoted description of the music she wanted to write: Debussy-like harmony, Webernian orchestration and a Dufay-like structure. 15 years later, this adequately described her music and has remained the lynchpin of further development.

The two teachers who particularly inspired her were Ron Tremain at Auckland University, and Peter Maxwell Davies in Adelaide and England. They helped her to acquire a strong technique based on medieval and serial-related practices, yet flexible enough to absorb and reflect future experiences.

An important award for Whitehead was as Northern Arts inaugural composer-in-residence in England, between 1978 and 1980. Here she wrote nine works ranging through chamber pieces of various forces to solo pieces, including *Bright Forms Return* for string quartet and mezzo-soprano in 1980, *Hoata* for chamber orchestra in 1979, *Hotspur* for chamber orchestra and soprano in 1980 and *Tamatea Tutahi* for piano in 1980. These works invoked the spirit of the place as she often used local folktunes as threads in the tapestry of her music.

The range of her works is impressive as her natural and assured technique can tackle all idioms. *Tristan and Iseult* is a puppet opera, written for instrumental ensemble, four singers mimes and puppets; *Windstreams* is for solo percussion, *Antiphons* is for brass ensemble; there are many other chamber or orchestral pieces for strings, wind, chorus, voice and combinations of all.

Whitehead particularly enjoys setting words, and has had a fruitful collaboration over many years with the writer. Fleur Adcock, with she has produced *The Inner Harbour*, *Hotspur*, *Eleanor of Aquitaine*, *Out of This Nettle, Danger* and *The King of the Other Country*. She has recently finished the opera *Bride of Fortune*, which is about Italian arranged marriages in Melbourne in the 1950s. The excitement of adapting the abstract language of music to the dramatic goals of the stage inspires her with the true vision of the operatic composer; a fusion of text, drama and music, hopefully adding up to more than the sum of its parts.

—Sally Mays

WILLIAMSON, Malcolm (Benjamin Graham Christopher). Australian. Born in Sydney, 21 November 1931. Educated at Sydney Conservatorium (horn, violin; composition under Eugene Goossens, piano under Sverjensky), 1943–50; studied composition privately under Elisabeth Lutyens, London, 1950; settled in London, 1953; further composition study under Lutyens and Erwin Stein, 1953–7. Organist, 1955–60; full-time composer, from 1960; composer in residence, Westminster Choir College, Princeton, New Jersey, 1970–1; 19th Master of the Queen's Musick, from 1975; president, Royal Philharmonic Orchestra, from 1977. Recipient: C.B.E. (Commander, Order of the British Empire), 1976. Mailing address: c/o Simon Campion, Rooks Nest House, Weston Road, Old Stevenage, Hertfordshire SG1 4DE, England.

Publishers: Weinberger; Campion; Agape, Illinois; Almqvist & Wiksell Forlag AB, Stockholm; Editions Mario Bois, Paris; Boosey & Hawkes, London and New York; Chappell Music, London; Edward B. Marks/Belwin-Mills, New York and Croydon, Surrey; Novello, London; Oxford University Press.

Symphonies/orchestral:

Theme and Variations, Lento, Scherzo 1947–9; unpublished.
Symphony No 1: Elevamini 1956–7; first performed (privately) London, June 1957; first public performance Melbourne, 13 November 1963. Recorded EMI SLS 5085.
Overture: Santiago de Espada 1957; first private performance London, June 1957; broadcast BBC, 8 February 1958. Recorded EMI SLS 5085; ABC RRCS 384.
Piano Concerto No 1 1957–8; first performed Cheltenham, Gloucestershire, 15 July 1958. Recorded ABC PRX 4716.
Sinfonia concertante (formerly *Symphony No 2: Laudes*; 3 trumpets, piano, strings) 1958–62; first performed Glasgow, 21 May 1964. Recorded EMI SLS 5085; ABC RRCS 127.
Piano Concerto No 2 (string orchestra) 1960; first performed Perth, 1962. Recorded EMI SLS 5080; ABC RRCS 127.
Organ Concerto 1961; first performed London, 8 September 1961.
Piano Concerto No 3 1962; first performed Sydney, June 1964. Recorded MHS 3586; Lyrita SRCS 79; ABC PRX 5584.
Our Man in Havana (orchestral suite) 1963; first performed Glasgow, 6 January 1966.
The Display (concert suite from the dance symphony) 1963–4; first performed Adelaide, 14 March 1964. Recorded WRC S 5264; EMI SLS 5085.
Sinfonietta (Prelude, Toccata, Elegy, and Tarantella) 1965–7; broadcast BBC, 21 March 1965; Prelude first performed Stratford-upon-Avon, 10 February 1967. Recorded VRL 1-0192; RCA GL 40542.
Concerto grosso 1965; first performed London, 28 August 1965.
Symphonic Variations 1965; first performed Edinburgh, 9 September 1965.
Serenade and Aubade (movements II and III of *Symphonic Variations*) 1965.
Violin Concerto (in memory of Dame Edith Sitwell) 1965; first performed Bath, 15 June 1965. Recorded EMI SLS 5085; WRC S 4930.
Two Epitaphs for Edith Sitwell (arranged for string orchestra from organ work) 1966; first performed London, April 1972. Recorded EMI EMD 5520.
Symphony No 2: Pilgrim pa havet 1968–9; first performed Bristol, 29 October 1969.
A Word from Our Founder (for the Hoffnung Festival) 1969.
Concerto for Two Pianos and Strings 1973; first performed Melbourne, 1972. Recorded EMI EMD 5520.
Music for a Quiet Day (movement IV of *Mass of a Medieval Saint*; concert band) 1973.
Untitled Orchestral Work 1973–4.
Concerto for Harp and Orchestra: Au Tombeau du martyr juif inconnu 1973–6; first performed London, 17 November 1976.
Two Pieces (nos 3 and 7 from *The Bridge That Van Gogh Painted*; string orchestra) 1975.
Symphony No 4 1977; unfinished.
Fiesta 1978; first performed Geneva, 14 March 1978.
Ochre (orchestra; or organ, strings) 1978; first performed London, 2 September 1978. Recorded RCA PL 25123.
Azure (movement IV of *Mass of a Medieval Saint*; arranged for string orchestra by Brown) 1978. Recorded RCA PL 25123.
Fanfarade 1979; first performed London, 10 May 1979.
Symphony No 5: Aquero 1979–80; first performed London, 23 April 1980.
Lament in Memory of Lord Mountbatten of Burma (violin, string orchestra) 1980; first performed Edinburgh, 5 May 1980.
Ode for Queen Elizabeth (string orchestra) 1980; first performed (privately), Edinburgh, 3 July 1980; first public performance Edinburgh, 25 August 1980.
Symphony No 6 1982; broadcast ABC FM radio, Australia, 29 September 1986.
In Thanksgiving—Sir Bernard Heinze 1982; first performed Sydney, 1 July 1982.
Himna Titu 1984.
Lento (strings) 1985.
Symphony No 7 1986.

Chamber/instrumental:

Minuet (violin, piano) 1947; unpublished.
Two-Part Invention (piano) 1947; unpublished.

Study (horn) 1947; unpublished.
String Quartet No 1: Winterset 1947–8; unpublished.
Nonet (strings, wind, harp) 1949; unpublished.
Variations (piano) 1953; unpublished.
Piece (7 wind instruments, piano) 1953; unpublished.
String Quartet No 2 1954; unpublished.
Sonata No 1 (piano) 1955–6; first performed Aldeburgh, Suffolk, 1956. Recorded Pye GSGC 1.
Fons amoris (organ) 1955–6; first performed London, 21 April 1956. Recorded Mirosonic DRE 1008.
Epithalamium (organ) 1957; unpublished.
Sonata No 2 (piano; formerly *Janua coeli*) 1957, revised 1970–1; first performed Cheltenham, Gloucestershire, 1957. Recorded Argo ZRG 704.
Sonata No 3 (piano) 1958; unpublished.
Variations on Veni Creator (organ) 1959; unpublished.
Resurgence du feu (organ) 1959.
Symphony (organ) 1960; first performed Canterbury, Kent 1961. Recorded Chalfont C77 015; AUR 5033.
Travel Diaries (impressions of famous cities for piano) 1960–1. Recorded ABC 2XS 2935.
Vision of Christ-Phoenix (organ) 1961; first performed Coventry, Warwickshire, 27 May 1962. Recorded Chalfont C77-015; AUR 5033.
Sonata No 4 (piano) 1963.
Variations (cello, piano) 1964; first performed London, 21 November 1964. Recorded Tower BLM 1002; MIOTLP 2.
Elegy—J.F.K. (organ) 1964; first performed Wyton, 1964. Recorded EMI SLS 3001; Weldon WS 165.
Concerto (for Alan Rawsthorne's 60th birthday concert; wind quintet, 2 pianos—8 hands) 1965; first performed London, 9 April 1965.
Five Preludes (piano) 1966; first performed Cheltenham, Gloucestershire, 11 July 1966. Recorded Argo ZRG 682; Discourses ABM 30.
Two Epitaphs for Edith Sitwell (organ) 1966; first performed Aldeburgh, Suffolk, 17 June 1966. Recorded EMI CSD 3657; EMI HQS 1376; EMI SLS 3001.
Serenade (flute, piano quartet) 1967; first performed London, 8 March 1967.
Sonata (2 pianos) 1967; first performed Cheltenham, Gloucestershire, 16 July 1967. Recorded Argo ZRG 704; HMV SLS 868.
Pas de quatre (flute, oboe, clarinet, bassoon, piano) 1967; first performed Newport, Rhode Island, 21 August 1967. Recorded Argo ZRG 682.
Piano Quintet 1967–8; first performed Birmingham, 23 March 1968.
Peace Pieces (organ) 1971; first performed Washington, D.C., 22 October 1971. Recorded EMI SLS 3001.
Partita on Themes of Walton (viola) 1972; broadcast BBC television, 29 March 1972.
Little Carols of the Saints (5 pieces for organ) 1972; first performed London, 10 January 1973. Recorded EMI SLS 3001.
Mass of a Medieval Saint (organ) 1973; first performed New York City, 23 September 1973. Recorded EMI SLS 3001.
Adelaide Fanfare (2 trumpets, 2 horns, 2 trombones, tuba, organ) 1973.
Haifa Watercolours (piano) 1974.
Untitled Wedding Piece (organ) 1975.
Fantasy on This Is My Father's World (organ) 1975.
Fantasy on O Paradise (organ) 1975; first performed Santillana del Mar, 13 March 1976.
The Bridge That Van Gogh Painted and the French Camargue (album for the young pianist) 1975.
Ritual of Admiration (piano) 1976.
Piano Trio 1976; first performed Wyoming, 22 June 1976.
The Lion of Suffolk (organ) 1977; first performed London, 10 March 1977.
Konstanz Fanfare (brass, percussion, organ) 1980; first performed Konstanz, Germany, 26 October 1980.
Richmond Fanfare (brass, percussion, organ) 1980; first performed Konstanz, Germany, 29 March 1981.
Fontainebleau Fanfare (brass, percussion, organ) 1981; first performed Konstanz, Germany, 29 March 1981.

Vocal/choral:

Two Songs (middle voice, piano) 1947; unpublished.
A Cycle of Love Songs (mezzo-soprano, piano) 1947; unpublished.
Two Motets ("Tantum ergo", "Pange Lingua"; unaccompanied 3- and 4-part chorus; St Thomas Aquinas) 1954.
Aye, Flattering Fortune (unaccompanied tenor) 1956; unpublished.
Meditations (unaccompanied SATB chorus) 1957; unpublished.
Mass (unaccompanied SATB chorus) 1957; unpublished.
Concerto (soprano, oboe, cor anglais, cello, organ) 1957; unpublished.
A Vision of Beasts and Gods (song cycle for soprano or tenor, piano; Barker) 1958; broadcast BBC Radio, October 1968.
Adoremus (Christmas cantata for alto, tenor, chorus, organ; Latin, Old English) 1959. Recorded ABC AC 1019.
Dawn Carol (unaccompanied SATB chorus or unison voices, organ or piano; Gradual and Alleluia in the Second Mass of Christmas, the Mass of Dawn) 1960.
Ode in Solitude (baritone, piano) 1960; unpublished.
Tu es Petrus (cantata for speaker, SATB chorus, organ; Vulgate, ordinary of Mass, Toplady) 1961.
Agnus Dei (soprano, SATB chorus, organ) 1961. Recorded Abbey LPB 796/805.
Dignus est Agnus (motet for soprano, SATB chorus, organ) 1961. Recorded Abbey LPB 796/734; ABC RRCS 1470.
Ascendit Deus (SATB chorus, organ) 1961.
Procession of Palms (SATB chorus, organ or piano; SSA chorus, organ or piano) 1961. Recorded Abbey LPB 805.
Ye Choirs of New Jerusalem (Easter carol for SATB chorus, organ; St Fulbert of Chartres, translated Neale) 1962.
Symphony for Voices ("Invocation", "Terra Australis", "Jesus", "Envoi", "New Guinea"; contralto, unaccompanied SATB chorus; McAuley) 1962; first performed London, 2 May 1962. Recorded HMV WRC S 690; Argo ZRG 758; ABC RRCS 384.
Planctus (monody for men's voices: Abelard) 1962.
Twelve New Hymn Tunes (unison voices, piano or organ) 1962.
Harvest Thanksgiving (SATB chorus, organ) 1962. Recorded ABC RRCS 400.
Let Them Give Thanks (SATB chorus, massed unison voices, organ) 1962. Recorded Abbey LPB 796.
Wrestling Jacob (soprano, SATB chorus, organ; Wesley) 1962. Recorded Abbey ABY 817.
The Morning of the Day of Days (Easter cantata for soprano, tenor, SATB chorus, organ) 1962. Recorded Abbey LPB 805.
Te Deum (unison voices, piano or organ) 1963.
An Australian Carol (Nativity) (SATB chorus, organ; McAuley) 1963.
Celebration of Divine Love (cantata for soprano or tenor, piano; McAuley) 1963; first performed London, 8 April 1963.
Our Man in Havana (concert suite for soprano, tenor, bass, SATB chorus, orchestra) 1963; first performed Munich,

October 1963.

Hasselbacher's Scena (from *Our Man in Havana*; bass, piano or orchestra) 1963.

Epiphany Carol (unison voices, piano or organ; soprano or treble voices, SATB chorus, organ; Bishop Heber) 1963. Recorded Gothic 57979803.

Six Christmas Songs for the Young (unison voices, piano, optional percussion) 1963.

Mass of Saint Andrew (unison voices, piano or organ) 1964.

English Eccentrics (after the chamber opera; choral suite for unaccompanied double chorus) 1964.

Three Shakespeare Songs ("Come Away, Death", "Full Fathom Five", "Fear No More the Heat of the Sun"; soprano or tenor, guitar or piano) 1964; first performed Edinburgh, 1964.

Six Evening Hymns (unison voices, piano or organ) 1964.

A Christmas Carol (low voice, piano; Chesterton) 1964.

The Boar's Head (unaccompanied SATB chorus; traditional) 1964. Recorded Argo ZRG 5446.

A Young Girl (unaccompanied SATB chorus; E. Sitwell) 1964. Recorded ABC AC1019.

Four North Country Songs (voice, chorus ad lib, piano or orchestra) 1965; first performed London, 19 May 1966. Recorded Argo ZRG 5496; Decca SPA 321.

A Psalm of Praise (unison voices, organ; Psalm 148) 1965.

The Brilliant and the Dark (choral-operatic sequence for female voices, orchestra; Ursula Vaughan Williams) 1966; first performed London, 3 June 1969. Recorded RDS 9351 2.

Six English Lyrics (alto or baritone, piano or string orchestra; SATB chorus, piano; Waller—"Go Lovely Rose", Tennyson—"Crossing the Bar", "Sweet and Low", Christina Rosetti—"A Birthday", "When I Am Dead", Leigh Hunt—"Jenny Kiss'd Me") 1966; piano version first performed London, 19 May 1966; orchestral version first performed Liverpool, 17 February 1969. Recorded Abbey ABY 810.

Each Afternoon (Berthe's aria from Act I of *The Violins of Saint-Jacques*; soprano, orchestra) 1966.

A Canon for Stravinsky (unaccompanied SATB chorus) 1967; published in *Tempo*, Summer 1967, as part of "Homage to Stravinsky". Recorded ABC RRC 68.

Mowing the Barley (SATB chorus, orchestra) 1967; first performed London, 1 March 1967.

From a Child's Garden (song cycle for soprano or tenor, piano; Stevenson) 1968; first performed Cardiff, 24 April 1968. Recorded Argo ZRG 682; Unicorn RHS 316.

Angels Made a Little Crown (carol) 1968; unpublished.

Schluss-Szene (final scene from *The Growing Castle*; soprano, orchestra) 1968.

Sonnet: On Hearing the Dies Irae Sung in the Sistine Chapel (unaccompanied SATB chorus; Wilde) 1969; first performed Cork, 3 May 1969.

Hallo Everybody (24 songs for students beginning English; Carl-Axel Axelsson, Michael Knight, Kerstin Sundin) 1969. Recorded (in part) A & W 7109–10.

Dear Ocean Hail (aria from Act III of *Lucky Peter's Journey*; baritone, orchestra) 1969.

I Will Lift up Mine Eyes (anthem for chorus, echo chorus, organ; Psalm 121) 1970; first performed Sydney, 3 May 1970. Recorded HMV OXLP 7526.

Cantate domino (SATB chorus, organ; Psalm 98) 1970; first performed Princeton, New Jersey, 21 October 1970.

In Place of Belief (I Stallet for Tro) (6-part chorus, piano—4 hands; Lagerkvist) 1970; first performed Washington, D.C., 15 January 1971.

Te Deum (SATB chorus, organ, optional brass) 1971.

Six Wesley Songs for the Young (unison voices, piano) 1971.

The Death of Cuchulain (5 male voices/percussion; Yeats) 1971; first performed London, 6 November 1971.

The Icy Mirror (Symphony No 3) (cantata for soprano, mezzo-soprano, 2 baritones, chorus, orchestra; Ursula Vaughan Williams) 1972.

O Jerusalem (unison chorus, congregation, organ; Psalm 122) 1972.

The King of Love (unison chorus, congregation, organ; Psalm 23) 1972.

Who Is the King of Glory (unison chorus, congregation, organ) 1972.

Together in Unity (unison chorus, congregation, organ: Psalm 133) 1972.

The Musicians of Bremen (6 male voices; after Grimm and Grimm) 1972; first performed Sydney. Recorded EMI EMD 5521.

Love, the Sentinel (unaccompanied SATB chorus; Tennyson) 1972; first performed Scunthorpe, Lincolnshire, 19 February 1972.

Ode to Music (chorus, echo chorus, orchestra; Ursula Vaughan Williams) 1972–3; first performed London, 3 February 1973.

Pietà (soprano, oboe, bassoon, piano; Lagerqvist) 1973; first performed London, 31 October 1973.

Canticle of Fire (SATB chorus, chorus, organ; 13th-century hymn, Bible) 1973; first performed New York City, 20 May 1973.

The World at the Manger (Christmas cantata for soprano, baritone, SATB chorus, organ or piano duet) 1973; first performed Leicester, 6 December 1973. Recorded Abbey ABY 805.

Hammarskjold Portrait (song cycle for soprano, string orchestra) 1974; first performed London, 30 July 1974.

Vocalise (mezzo-soprano, piano) 1974; unpublished.

Communion Hallelujahs (unison children's chorus, unison male chorus, organ) 1974–5.

Sixteen Hymns and Pastorals (unison voices, piano or organ) 1975.

Love Chorales (voices, piano or organ or guitar) 1975.

Dove Chorales (voices, piano or organ) 1975.

Above Chorales (voices, piano or organ) 1975.

Psalms of the Elements ("Air Psalms", "Water Psalms", "Earth Psalms", "Fire Psalms"; 20 responsorial psalms for unison chorus, congregation, organ) 1975.

Mass of St James (unison voices, piano or organ) 1975.

Les Olympiques (mezzo-soprano, string orchestra; Montherlant) 1976; first performed Meyer, Germany, 19 June 1977.

Jubilee Hymn (unison chorus, SATB chorus, orchestra or piano; Betjeman) 1977; first performed London, 6 February 1977.

Setting of Poems by Mary Wilson (SATB chorus, strings; unison voices, piano) 1977–8; unpublished.

Mass of Christ the King (lyric soprano, dramatic soptrno, tenor, baritone, echo chorus, mixed chorus, orchestra) 1977, orchestrated 1978; first performed Gloucester, 25 August 1977; first complete performance London, 3 November 1978.

This Christmas Night (SATB chorus, piano; Wilson) 1977.

Kerygma (anthem for SATB chorus, organ; Philippians) 1979; first performed London, 11 March 1979. Recorded Abbey HMP 2280.

Little Mass of St Bernadette (unbroken voices, organ or instruments) 1980; first performed London, 26 November 1980.

Mass of St Margaret of Scotland (congregation, optional SATB chorus, organ) 1980.

Three Choric Hymns (unaccompanied SATB chorus; Sarum Primer 1558, Whitman, Hilton Young) 1980, 1 and 3 begun 1947; first performed Konstanz, Germany, 26 October 1980.
Josip Broz Tito (a tribute in music for baritone, orchestra or piano; Whitman) 1980–1; first performed Skopje, Yugoslavia, 9 March 1981; first performance with piano, Tunbridge Wells, Kent, 22 March 1981.
Mass of the People of God (voices, organ) 1980–1; first performed Bromsgrove, Worcestershire, 29 April 1981.
Now Is the singing Day (chorus, strings; voice, piano trio) 1981; unpublished.
Songs for a Royal Baby (soprano, alto, tenor, bass or chorus, piano or string orchestra; Wilson) 1983.
The Feast of Eurydice (mezzo-soprano, piano, flute, percussion) 1983.
White Dawns (medium voice, piano; Ratsoin) 1984.
Vocalise (medium voice, piano) 1984.
The Fly (high voice, piano) 1984.
A Pilgrim Liturgy (cantata for mezzo-soprano, baritone, chorus, orchestra) 1984–5.
The Mower to the Glowworms (low voice, piano; Marvell) 1985.
The White Island or Place of the Blessed (low voice, piano; Herrick) 1986.
Day That I Have Loved (low voice, piano) 1986.
The True Endeavour (speaker, SATB chorus, orchestra) 1988.
The Dawn Is at Hand (choral symphony) 1989.
Mass of St Ethelreda (missa brevis on themes by Lennox Berkeley; SATB chorus, organ) 1990.

Opera/dramatic:

Our Man in Havana (Gilliat, after Graham Greene) 1963; first performed London, 2 July 1963.
English Eccentrics (chamber opera; Dunn, after E. Sitwell) 1964; first performed Aldeburgh, Suffolk, 11 June 1964.
The Happy Prince (children's opera; after Wilde) 1965; first performed Farnham, Surrey, 22 May 1965. Recorded Argo ZNF 5.
Julius Caesar Jones (children's opera; Dunn) 1965–6; first performed London, 4 January 1966. Recorded Argo ZRG 529.
The Violins of St Jacques (Chappell, after P. Leigh) 1966; first performed London, 29 November 1966.
The Moonrakers (cassation for audience and orchestra) 1967; first performed Brighton, Sussex, 22 April 1967.
Dunstan and the Devil (Dunn) 1967; first performed Cookham, Berkshire, 19 May 1967.
Knights in Shining Armour (cassation for audience, piano) 1968; first performed Brighton, Sussex, 29 April 1968.
The Snow Wolf (cassation for audience, piano) 1968; first performed Brighton, Sussex, 29 April 1968.
The Growing Castle (chamber opera; after Strindberg) 1968; first performed Dynevor Castle, 13 August 1968.
Lucky Peter's Journey (Tracey, after Strindberg) 1969; first performed London, 18 December 1969.
Genesis (cassation for audience and instruments) 1971; first performed Black Montain, North Carolina, June 1971.
The Stone Wall (cassation for audience, orchestra or piano) 1971; first performed London, 18 September 1971.
The Red Sea 1972; first performed Dartington, Devon, 14 April 1972.
The Winter Star (cassation for audience, instruments or orchestra) 1973; first performed Holm Cutram, 19 June 1973.
The Glitter Gang (cassation for audience, orchestra or piano) 1973–4; first performed Sydney, 23 February 1974.
La Terre des rois (cassation for audience, orchestra or piano) 1974.
The Valley and the Hill (cassation in 8 scenes for audience, orchestra or piano) 1977; first performed Liverpool, 21 June 1977.
Le Pont du diable (cassation for SSA voices, piano) 1982; first performed Angoulême, March 1982.

Other:

No Bed for Bacon (musical) 1958–9.
The Display (ballet by Helpmann) 1964; first performed Adelaide, 14 March 1964.
The Merry Wives of Windsor (incidental music to Shakespeare; flute/piccolo, clarinet/tenor saxophone, trumpet, percussion, double bass, piano) 1964; first performed Stratford-upon-Avon, 17 December 1964.
Spectrum (ballet to variations for cello, piano) 1964; first performed Bury St Edmunds, Suffolk, 21 September 1967.
Sun into Darkness (ballet by Rudkin) 1966; first performed London, 13 April 1966.
BigfellaTootsSquoodgeandNora (ballet to *Pas de quatre*) 1967; first performed Manchester, 25 September 1976.
Persynthyon (ballet) 1974; first performed Adelaide, 1974.
Churchill's People (music to BBC television series) 1974–5.
The House of Windsor (music to BBC television series) 1977.
Watership Down (title music and prologue to film) 1978. Recorded CBS 70161.
National Anthem: God Save the Queen (arranged for SATB chorus, full or string orchestra; and for full orchestra) 1979–80.

Film scores: *The Brides of Dracula*, 1960; *Crescendo*, 1969; *The Horror of Frankenstein*, 1969; *Nothing But the Night*, 1970; *Thunder in Heaven*; *North Sea Strike*; *September Spring*; *Inland with Stuart*; *The Timber Getters*; *Rio Tinto Zinc*.

Radio and television music: includes *Bald Twit Lion*; *Choice*; *Strange Excellency*; *Gallery*; *Chi Ming/Jackanory*; *The Golden Salamander*.

PUBLICATIONS

On Williamson: C. Mason, "The Music of MW", in *Musical Times*, 103, 1962; S. Walsh, "MW the Many-Sided", in *Music and Musicians*, 13(11), 1965, and "A Memory of Violins", in *Opera*, 17, 1966; A. McCredie, in *Musical Composition in Australia*, Canberra, 1969; Anthony Payne, "MW's Second Symphony", in *Tempo*, 91, 1969–70; S. Walsh, "MW's Organ Symphony", in *Musical Times*, 112, 1971; C. Raney, "MW", in *Music Magazine*, 7(2), 1973.

* * *

Technically Malcolm Williamson's affinities lie with Europe, for which he left Australia early in the 1950s. But he is happy to admit his "essentially Australian identity"—of which a directness, freshness and unstuffiness perhaps form a part. More than 30 years separate Williamson's first essays in those fundamentally European forms, the piano concerto and the symphony, from the striking Sixth Symphony and two large-scale works written for the Australian Bicentenary in 1988, *The True Endeavour* and *The Dawn Is at Hand*. The last amounts to a hymn of hope and freedom, in part a requiem.

Its Aboriginal-inspired settings (including a stunning "Curlew" movement) underline his own deeper yearnings and aspirations for the homeland from which he ventured forth, exchanging it for the more advanced artistic establishments of France and England.

Despite championing by Benjamin Britten, Williamson was, prior to his operatic successes, sometimes censured for bestriding several styles while attaching himself to none. Trained under Erwin Stein and Elizabeth Lutyens, he soon assimilated the essentials of serialism, taking as his model late Stravinsky and the French as much as Vienna, and simultaneously drawing other strands into his vocabulary: in particular, Stravinsky and Messiaen—influences he has never lost. The almost demonic thrust ("Toccata" or "Tarantella" are favourite headings) of the early piano concertos—something one associates with the present younger generation like Steve Martland or James MacMillan—acquires in each slow movement a warm, more traditional ring: Ravel (No 1), the French Organ School (the plainsong-like No 2) or Romanticism (No 3, later made into a North American ballet). By contrast, his *Symphony No 1: Elevamini*, premiered in 1956 by Sir Adrian Boult, with its vast, slow-unfolding, sometimes almost static first movement (the Symphony includes two Lentos) showed not just an early grasp of Sibelius but a deeper response to the larger symphonic canvases of Shostakovich and the then still unfashionable Mahler.

Since 1970, large-scale vocal and choral pieces have been central to his output. *The Icy Mirror (Symphony No 3)*, for four soloists and orchestra to a text by Ursula Vaughan Williams, is a case in point; the *Hammarskjold Portrait*, settings for soprano and strings of contemplative poetry by the Swedish statesman, was stunningly premiered by Soderström at the Proms in 1974. The dazzling Borges symphonic song cycle, *Next Year in Jerusalem*, a recent Proms commission for soprano and larger orchestra, honouring the Argentinian poet's tenet that we are all "Jews of the Spirit", merges in one that sense of ghetto desolation, scapegoatism and an almost Blakean vision of temporal and spiritual resurrection which infuses power into much of Williamson's writing for voice or organ. This includes larger-scale works like the extended *Mass of Christ the King*, a piece of almost Verdian dimensions, for which responsory psalms and hymns are all set by the composer.

Williamson has written extensively for the organ. *The Vision of Christ Phoenix*, written for the opening of Coventry Cathedral, offers a similar message of reconciliation and hope; a weighty early *Organ Concerto* employs as its thematic launch-pad the "ACB" initials of Boult, one of his unfailing champions. Other works, like the solo *Organ Symphony*, liturgically reflective *Mass of a Mediaeval Saint* or 1971 *Peace Pieces* for Washington, turn Williamson's debt to Messiaen (no less acknowledged in the *Sinfonietta* or his powerful dance symphony, *Perisynthion*) to good effect.

The *Two Epitaphs for Edith Sitwell* were later adapted for strings, for which forces Williamson has produced some of his best efforts: the recent *Symphony No 7*; the *Hammarskjold Portrait* and his Montherlant soprano cycle *Les Olympiques*; the *Ode for Queen Elizabeth*; plus several concertos, including the *Concerto for Harp and Orchestra: Au Tombeau du martyr juif inconnu*—one of three works forming a decisive point for Williamson in the mid-1970s, which, like the earlier, strikingly Stravinskian *Sinfonia concertante*, or the *Concerto for Two Pianos and Strings*, with its intricate serialised double name-motif, sets in relief his personal modifications of serial technique.

Chamber works include the challenging, highly effective and inventive *Piano Quintet*, with extended central quasi-scherzo, the *Piano Trio*, two sonatas and and several inventive miniatures for piano. The *Violin Concerto* for Yehudi Menuhin, dedicated to the memory of Edith Sitwell and infused with a delicacy and poignancy akin to the concerto of Alban Berg, is one of his happiest creations.

Most stage works enjoyed significant early success: *Our Man in Havana* offered a life-enhancing, "Caribbean" outlet to his place-in-the-sun yearnings (a recurrent theme), Graham Greene's skilled juxtaposition of sacred and profane, portentous and absurd, meshing remarkably with his own outlook. The pastiche chamber opera *English Eccentrics*, based on Sitwell, was well-received a year later. The catastrophe-climaxed *The Violins of Saint-Jacques* clearly invites revival, while *The Growing Castle* and *Lucky Peter's Journey*, both after Strindberg, recall an important, lasting affinity with Scandinavia. The ballets include not just Ashton's characterful adaptation of the *Sinfonietta*, but a colourful *cause célèbre*, *The Display*, first boldly choreographed by Helpmann for the Australian Ballet, and the more perturbing *Sun into Darkness*.

In *The Display* Williamson suggests a continuum between civilisation and the wild, man, beast and immortal, a preoccupation that recurs in several of his 10 (mainly shorter) works for children and small forces (or piano) known as "cassations", notably *The Snow Wolf*, *La Terre des rois*, *The Devil's Bridge* and a longer biblical sequence based on Psalm 23, *The Valley and the Hill*. The notion of the scapegoat, powerfully encountered in *Sun into Darkness*, is brilliantly echoed in his second children's opera, *Julius Caesar Jones*, which, with its companion piece, *The Happy Prince*, must rank among the most inspired compositions of that period for young performers.

—Roderic Dunnett

WILSON, Olly (Woodrow). American. Born in St Louis, Missouri, 7 September 1937. Educated: self-taught in piano and double bass; Washington University, St Louis, Missouri, B.Mus., 1959; University of Illinois, Urbana, M.Mus., 1960; University of Iowa, Iowa City (composition under Robert Sykes, Robert Kelley and Phillip Bezanson), Ph.D., 1964; further study in electronic music, Illinois Studio for Experimental Music, 1967; field study of African music, Nigeria and Ghana, 1971–2. Jazz double bassist; double bass player, St Louis Philharmonic Orchestra and Cedar Rapids Symphony Orchestra; teacher of music, Florida Agricultural and Mechanical University, 1960–2; teacher of music, Oberlin College, Ohio, 1965–70; professor of music, University of California, Berkeley, since 1970; visiting artist, American Academy, Rome, 1977–8. Recipient: prize (for *Cetus*), International Electronic Music Competition, 1967; Guggenheim Fellowships, 1971, 1977. Mailing address: c/o GunMar Music Inc., 167 Dudley Road, Newton Centre, Massachusetts 02159, U.S.A.

Publisher: GunMar.

Symphonies/orchestral:

Structure 1960.
Three Movements 1964.

Akwan (piano, electric piano, orchestra) 1972. Recorded Columbia M-33434.
Reflections 1978.
Trilogy 1979–80.
Lumina 1981.
Sinfonia 1983–4. Recorded New World NW 331.
Houston Fanfare 1986.

Chamber/instrumental:

Prelude and Line Study (flute, clarinet, bassoon, bass clarinet) 1959.
Trio (flute, cello, piano) 1959.
String Quartet 1960.
Sonata (violin, piano) 1961.
Dance Suite (woodwind ensemble) 1962.
Soliloquy (double bass) 1962.
Dance Music I (wind ensemble) 1963.
Sextet (flute, clarinet, basson, horn, trumpet, trombone) 1963.
Dance Music II (wind ensemble) 1965.
Piece for Four (flute, trumpet, double bass, piano) 1966.
Piano Piece 1969.
Echoes (clarinet, tape) 1974–5. Recorded CRI S-367.
Trio (violin, cello, piano) 1977.
Expansions (organ) 1979.

Vocal/choral:

Two Dutch Poems (alto, piano; Holst, Ostaijen) 1960.
Gloria (unaccompanied chorus) 1961.
Wry Fragments (tenor, percussion; Cunningham) 1961.
And Death Shall Have No Dominion (tenor, percussion; Thomas) 1963.
Chanson innocente (alto, 2 bassoons; cummings) 1965.
Biography (soprano, chorus; Jones) 1966.
In memoriam Martin Luther King Jr (chorus, electronics) 1968.
Spirit Song (soprano, double chorus; spirituals) 1973.
Sometimes (tenor, electronics; spiritual) 1974–5. Recorded CRI S-370.
No More (tenor, flute, clarinet/bass clarinet, violin, cello, harp, piano, percussion; Brutus, Mackay) 1985.

Other:

Cetus (electronic) 1967.
The Eighteen Hands of Jerome Harris (ballet; electronic score) 1969–70.
Black Mass (incidental music to Jones; electronic score) 1971.
Black Martyrs (electronic) 1972.

PUBLICATIONS

On Wilson: W. Logan, "OW: Piece for Four", in *Perspectives of New Music*, 9(1), 1970; E. Southern, in *The Music of Black Americans: A History*, New York City, 1971, 2nd edition, 1983, and (interview) in *The Black Perspective in Music*, 5, 1977; in *The Black Composer Speaks*, edited by S.N. Baker, L.M. Belt and H.C. Hudson, Metuchen, New Jersey, 1978; C. Oliver, "Selected Orchestral Works of Thomas J. Anderson, Arthur Cunningham, Talib Rasul Hakim and OW", dissertation, Florida State University, Tallahassee, 1978.

* * *

Given that all such distinctions are invidious and that there are so many very significant contenders on the "popular" side of the imaginary divide, it is difficult to claim that Olly Wilson is the single most significant black American composer of his generation. In terms of formal concert music, he undoubtedly is, the only serious rival being the slightly younger Alvin Singleton. Sadly, the death of Duke Ellington has once again sundered black music. However significant the contribution of figures like George Russell and Anthony Braxton to advanced music, and however respected by fellow musicians, they have once more fallen foul of the essentially racialist recording industry and been consigned to the still under-valued "jazz" category.

Wilson was brought up at the very epicentre of modern jazz, in St Louis, and it is clear that the cadences of jazz play a central role in his work, not just in the matter of a few blues-based tonalities, but as an informing spirit that sustains his concern with rhythm, with music as a vehicle for particular kind of emotion, with (literally) ec-centric resolutions. He received his musical training in the Midwest, where it has traditionally been easier to forge an idiosyncratically personal style without falling foul of restrictively received stylistic dogma. In due course, Wilson was to become a music teacher and professor at Florida A and M University, and at the famously free-thinking Oberlin College in Ohio, before finding his niche at Berkeley, where he remains. But his finishing school was undoubtedly the research trip he made to West Africa at the onset of the 1970s, an experience that finds its most direct reflection in the magnificent *Akwan*.

Akwan was written in the same year as the pinnacle of trumpeter Miles Davis's jazz-rock experiment *Live-Evil*, and has much of Davis's deceptive stealth. Its pairing of acoustic and amplified piano over a strongly pulsed orchestral backing is very contemporary, and though Wilson tended to revert to rather more conventional structures in the later 1970s and beyond, his understanding of musical texture was profoundly altered.

Wilson's understanding of texture, however, is not restricted to the superficial metrical count of a passage, but to a more deeply engrained pattern which is instinctive with his often complex but always solidly effective compositional means. Wilson began his musical career as a double bass player, moving between jazz ensembles and symphony orchestras. In his compositions, from the fine *Sinfonia* down to chamber scores like the classic jazz-influenced *Piece for Four*, and to solo works like *Soliloquy*, he builds his musical argument around premises solidly grounded in the bass clef and proceeding in progressions that may be straightforwardly intervallic or more subtly chromatic. Whatever their origins and development, Wilson's always emerge with a hint of drama and declamation.

In 1967, he studied electronic music at the Illinois Studio for Experimental Music, an experience that immediately inspired the prize-winning *Cetus*, one of the finest electronic works of the decade and a significant turning point in American work in the medium. Electronics opened a new range of musical resources to Wilson. Perhaps most striking were his threnody to the assassinated Martin Luther King Jr, and the spiritual *Sometimes*. The latter is a good example of Wilson's ability to transform and personalise traditional materials and forms without in any way distorting the spirit of the original. This is a version of the distinctive black aesthetic of imitation, transformation and destruction articulated by Imamu Amiri Baraka. Wilson set some of Baraka's earlier work—as LeRoi Jones—to powerful effect. The contained ferocity of *No More*, based on a Dennis Brutus poem, depends on a more conventional instrumentation, but is nonetheless disturbing in its power. If the cultural legacy of black people in the U.S.A. is to be fairly assessed, it has to be seen to include not just those who fall within the comfortably marketable categories of popular music, but also those like Wilson who have made their way within and against not one but two sometimes antagonistic.

—Richard Washington

WILSON, Thomas (Brendan). British. Born in Colorado, 10 October 1927. Educated at Blairs College, 1940–5; University of Glasgow, 1948–54, M.A., B.Mus. (Hons); Royal College of Music, London, 1955, A.R.C.M. (composition). Royal Air Force, 1945–8. Married Margaret Rayner, 20 September 1952; 3 sons. Lecturer, 1957–71, reader, 1971–7, professor, 1977–84, now professor emeritus, University of Glasgow. Executive and advisory positions in The Arts Council, the New Music Group of Scotland, Society for the Promotion of New Music, Composers Guild of Great Britain (former chair), Scottish Society of Composers (president). Recipient: Goudie Prize, 1946; McEwen Composition Prize (for *String Quartet No 3*), 1958; C.B.E. (Commander, Order of the British Empire), 1990. Mailing address: 120 Dowanhill Street, Glasgow G12 9DN, Scotland.

Publishers: Queensgate Music, Glasgow; Boosey & Hawkes; Berben; Schott; Chappell Music.

Symphonies/orchestral:

Early works withdrawn.
Toccata 1959.
Variations for Orchestra 1960; first performed Glasgow, 1960.
Pas de quoi (strings) 1964; first performed Edinburgh, 1964.
Symphony No 2 1965.
Concerto for Orchestra 1967; first performed Edinburgh, 1967.
Touchstone 1967; first performed London, 1967.
Sinfonietta (brass band) 1967; first performed St Andrews, Fife, 1967.
Cartoon (cornet, band) 1969.
Threnody 1970; first performed Glasgow, 1970.
Ritornelli per archi (string orchestra, or 11 solo strings) 1972; first performed Edinburgh, 1972.
Refrains and Cadenzas 1973; first performed Cheltenham, Gloucestershire, 1973.
Symphony No 3 1979; first performed Glasgow, 1979.
Mosaics (flute/alto flute, harpsichord, polyphonic synthesizer, strings) 1981.
Introit (Towards the Light . . .) 1982; first performed Stirling, 1982.
Concerto for Piano and Orchestra 1984; first performed Manchester, 1985.
St Kentigern Suite 1986.
Viola Concerto 1987.
Passeleth Tapestry 1988.
Chamber Symphony 1990.
Toccata Festevole 1990.

Chamber/instrumental:

Early works withdrawn.
Sonatina (piano) 1956.
String Quartet No 3 1958; first performed Glasgow, 1958.
Sonata (piano) 1959–64; first performed Edinburgh, 1964.
Violin Sonata 1961.
Sonatina (clarinet, piano) 1962.
Three Pieces (piano) 1964.
Fantasia (cello) 1964; first performed Glasgow, 1964.
Concerto da Camera (flute, oboe, violin, cello, piano) 1965.
Piano Trio 1966; first performed Montrose, 1966.
Sinfonia (clarinet, bassoon, horn, string quartet) 1968; first performed Glasgow, 1968.
Soliloquy (guitar) 1969; first performed Glasgow, 1969.
Sonata (cello, piano) 1971; first performed Glasgow, 1971.
Three Pieces (guitar) 1971; first performed Glasgow, 1971.
Ritornelli per Archi (11 solo strings) 1972; first performed Edinburgh, 1972.
Canti Notturni (flute/alto flute, clarinet/bass clarinet, violin, viola, cello, piano) 1972; first performed Glasgow, 1972.
Coplas del Ruisenor (guitar) 1972; first performed Italy, 1972.
Complementi (clarinet/bass clarinet, violin, cello, piano) 1973; first performed Glasgow, 1973.
String Quartet No 4 1978; first performed Glasgow, 1978.
Canción (guitar) 1982; first performed Glasgow, 1982.
Incunabula (piano) 1983; first performed London, 1983.
Dream Music (guitar) 1983; first performed Glasgow, 1983.
Chamber Concerto (flute, clarinet, horn, trumpet, trombone, 2 percussion, piano, violin, cello) 1986.

Vocal/choral:

Carmina sacra (high voice, harp, strings) 1964; first performed Glasgow, 1964.
Night Songs (unaccompanied SATB choir) 1967; first performed Glasgow, 1967.
Ave Maria / Pater Noster (unaccompanied SATB choir) 1967; first performed Glasgow, 1967.
A Babe Is Born (unaccompanied SATB choir) 1967; first performed Glasgow, 1967.
My Soul Longs for Thee (unaccompanied SSA choir) 1967.
Missa pro nobi conturbato (chamber choir, percussion, harp, strings) 1970.
Te Deum (large chorus, orchestra) 1971.
Sequentiae passionis (large chamber choir, orchestra) 1971.
There Is No Rose (unaccompanied SATB choir) 1974; first performed Cambridge, 1974.
Ubi caritas et amor (2 tenor, 2 baritone, 2 bass) 1976; first performed London, 1976.
Songs of Hope and Expectation (chamber choir, electric piano, harpsichord, strings) 1977.
One Foot in Eden (mezzo-soprano, flute, clarinet, harp, electric piano, percussion, violin, viola, cello; also for voice, piano) 1977, 1980; version with piano acompaniment first performed Birmingham, 1980.
Three Orkney Songs (soprano, baritone, flute, oboe, violin, cello, piano) 1980; first performed Edinburgh, 1980.
The Willow Branches (mezzo-soprano, small orchestra) 1983; first performed London, 1983.

Opera:

The Charcoal Burner (Morgan) 1968; broadcast BBC Radio, 1968.
The Confessions of a Justified Sinner (Currie/Hogg) 1974; first performed York, 1974.

Other:

Embers of Glencoe (ballet; percussion) 1973; first performed Nottingham, 1973.

Television/film/radio scores: including *The Splendid Silent Sun*; *The Voyage of St Brandon*; *Sunset Song*; *Cloud Howe*; *Grey Granite*.

PUBLICATIONS

On Wilson: John Maxwell Gaddes, "TW", in *Composer*, Winter 1983; Ian Robertson, "TW", in *Stretto*, Autumn 1987; Kenneth Walton, "TW", in *Classical Music*, 24 October 1987.

Thomas Wilson comments:

My works have been heard in most countries of the world, and cover most forms (symphonies, concertos, chamber works of all kinds, vocal and choral works, pieces for string orchestra, brass band, and many works for different solo instruments, some involving various electronic aspects). Though there is no doubt a Scottish dimension to my music (I have lived most of my life in Glasgow), it is not of an obvious or ethnic kind. Early influences such as Bartók and Berg have led through serialism, aleatorism, and various other expressionist and mystical aspects to a mature style which is almost "classical" in its lucidity.

* * *

Thomas Wilson is widely regarded as Scotland's most distinguished senior composer, a reputation grounded in a large and satisfyingly consistent body of work which betrays a serious and single-minded determination not to be swayed by musical fashion or the ebb and flow of institutional favour.

He withdrew many early works from performance, but his mature canon dates at least from the Third String Quartet, one of the earliest allowed to stand. The music of those years is generally more expressionistic, and often more experimental (including his only sustained exploration of serialism, the *Violin Sonata*) than in his subsequent development.

Wilson has acknowledged his admiration for the verve and rhythmic drive of Bartók, Stravinsky and Berg, and that strongly etched sense of purpose is continually evident in his work. He is not a composer to play with effects simply for the sake of it, or to clutter up a score with superfluous technical complexities, but aims always at clarity of both intention and expression.

At the same time, he has remained alive to developments in the wider musical sphere, including, for example, occasional use of aleatoric methods and even electronics, prompted by the explorations of Boulez and Stockhausen. These have been restricted, however, to minor colourings in an already vivid palette.

His best work has always been revealed by its lucidity of structure, argument and purpose, by his sharp ear for telling use of colouration, whether for orchestral or chamber forces, and his ability to write expressive and communicative music in all of the many forms he has attempted, including song cycles, sacred choral works and opera.

Religious subjects have prompted some of his most impressive writing, among which the eloquent and beautiful *Sequentiae passionis* stands out, although the very different *Te Deum*, with its considerably darker vision of the Deity, is no less impressive.

Wilson's two essays into opera have both tilted around the battle between light and dark, good and evil. *The Charcoal Burner*, with a libretto by poet Edwin Morgan, was written for radio, but can be staged. His major venture into the field to date, however, is a mature and finely realised version of James Hogg's classic novel, *The Confessions of a Justified Sinner*, in which that theme is writ large.

Wilson's overt use of contrapuntal forms has lessened, but his musical register has moved increasingly toward a greater lyrical warmth, as in the *Introit (Towards The Light . . .)*, the *St Kentigern Suite*, one of his most widely performed scores, or the *Viola Concerto*.

With that warmth has come a shift in the nature of the abstract musical strategies of his work, resulting in a more dramatic unravelling of the thematic material of the composition. Examples of this shift could be found through a stylistic comparison of the Third String Quartet with the Fourth, or the Second Symphony with the Third.

Like many composers, Wilson often uses one piece of music as a springboard to a subsequent work, as in one of his most admired later compositions, the *Piano Concerto* of 1984. It had its genesis in the song cycle *The Willow Branches*, by way of a solo piano piece entitled *Incunabula*. The rhythmic élan and sophisticated colouristic effects of the Concerto are developed in the context of a dialectical discussion between piano and orchestra, which eventually finds a harmonious conclusion.

—Kenny Mathieson

WISHART, Trevor. British/English. Born in Leeds, 11 October 1946. Educated at University of Oxford, 1965–8, B.A.; University of Nottingham, 1968–9, M.A.; University of York, 1969–73, D.Phil.; further study in computer music, IRCAM, Paris, 1981. Married Jacqueline Joan Everett in 1971; 2 daughters. Independent composer, since 1973; composer in residence, New South Wales Conservatorium, Sydney, 1976; composer in the community, Manchester, 1979; Hinrichsen composer in residence, York, 1980; part-time lecturer in music and sound, Sheffield Polytechnic, 1981–6; composer in residence, University of Texas, Austin, 1982; Queens guest visiting scholar, Queens University, Kingston, Ontario, 1983; Amelia Cummins Nancy visiting scholar, Girton College, Cambridge, 1985; special professor of music, University of Nottingham, 1989–90; sound designer, Jorvik Viking Centre multimedia museum, York; founder, Composers Desktop Project. Recipient: prize for (*Red Bird*), Bourges International Electro-acoustic Music Festival, 1978; prize, Gaudeamus International Composers Competition, 1979; honourable mention, New England Computer Music Competition, 1983; prize, Ars Electronica, Linz, Austria, 1989. Mailing address: 83 Heslington Road, York Y01 5AX, England.

Publisher: self; distributed through Universal Edition, London.

Symphonies/orchestral:

Kaleidoscope 1969; first performed Nottingham, 1969.
Dance-Music 1990.

Chamber/instrumental:

Polysaccharides (8 clarinets) 1969; first performed London, 1970.

Vocal/choral (with or without electronics):

Machine 2 (small chorus, taped machine sounds) 1970.
Passion (SSAATTBB chorus, 4 percussion, 3 trumpets, tape, 150 children) 1978.
Anticredos (6 amplified voices—2 female and 4 male, percussion) 1980. Recorded Hyperion.
Vox I (4 amplified voices—SATB, 4-channel tape) 1982; first performed Paris, 1985. Recorded Virgin Classics VC7 91108 2.
Vox II (4 amplified voices—SATB, live electronics, stereo tape) 1984; first performed Paris, 1985. Recorded Virgin Classics VC7 91108 2.
Vox III (4 amplified voices/SATB polyrhythmic click-track tape) 1985; first performed Boston, 1986. Recorded Virgin Classics VC7 91108 2.
Vox IV (4 amplified voices—SATB, 4-channel and click tape) 1987; first performed Huddersfield, Yorkshire, 1987. Recorded Virgin Classics VC7 91108 2.
Vox VI (4 amplified voices—SATB, stereo tape with or without backing voices) 1988; first performed London, 1988. Recorded Virgin Classics VC7 91108 2.

Dramatic/environmental:

Bicycle Music (bicycles) 1970; first presented York, 1970.
Carnival (community arts carnival) 1970; first performed York, 1970.
Landscape (environmental event) 1970; first performed Hebden Bridge, Yorkshire, 1970.
Seaside (environmental event) 1971; first performed Filey, Yorkshire, 1971.
Official Gazetteer (multimedia project) 1974; first performed York, 1974.
Ecological Enterprises (performance art) 1974; first performed Scunthorpe, Lincolnshire, 1974.
Fidelio (flute or clarinet, mime, 6 suitcases, 6 cassette players, 6 prerecorded cassettes) 1976; first performed York, 1976.
Son et lumière domestic (performance art) 1976; first performed London, 1976.
Beach Singularity (sound/visualevent devised for English holiday beach; brass, percussion, pre-recorded tape collage based on seaside and circus music) 1977; first presented Lancashire beaches, 1977.
Forest Singularity (sound/visual event for woodland at dusk; illuminated and visually transformed tree) 1977; first presented Sussex woods, 1977.
Tuba mirum (tuba, tape, props, 3 mimes) 1979; first performed The Netherlands, 1979.
Pastorale (flute, tuba, tape, slides, set with stuffed animals, magician's vanishing cabinet) 1980; first performed London, 1980.

Electronic:

Machine (tape) 1970; first performed London 1970.
Journey into Space (tape) 1972; first performed York, 1973.
Menagerie (tape assemblages) 1975; first performed Birmingham, 1975.
Fanfare and Contrapunctus 1976; first performed Sydney, 1976.
Red Bird (tape) 1977; first performed Ghent, Belgium, 1977. Recorded Recommended Records.
Anna's Magic Garden (tape) 1982; first performed Huddersfield, Yorkshire, 1982.
Vox V (4-channel tape of computer-transformed vocal and environmental sounds) 1986; first performed France, 1987. Recorded Virgin Classics VC7 91108 2.

PUBLICATIONS

By Wishart: *Sun I—Creativity and Environment*, 1974; *Sun II—A Creative Philosophy*, 1977; *Sounds Fun 1 & 2* (educational music programmes) 1974, 1975; *Whose Music?*, London, 1976, U.S.A., 1978; *On Sonic Art*, York, 1985.

Trevor Wishart comments:

My attitude to the arts is strongly influenced by my origins in an ordinary working class home in Yorkshire. Although my work has now achieved international recognition, I continue to hold the view that serious art has to relate to the wider context of human life and meaning, and not merely to the concerns of its professional practitioners.

As a composer, I enjoy both the research and discovery involved in exploring new approaches to music making, and the challenge of relating these to this wider context. My work usually explores new areas of musical discourse (environmental and performance art projects in the 1970s, music theatre pieces like *Tuba mirum* where the soloist is an imprisoned psychiatric patient and his tuba magically transformed by props and electronics; the *Vox* cycle, exploring the human voice from experimental multiphonics and polyrhythm, through imaginary theatre, to popular disco idioms), and is often challenging for the performers. However, I have no interest in either boring or outsmarting my audience, as music is, in the end, what other people make of it.

I have also been involved in music education, community-oriented workshops and accessible technology (the Composers Desktop Project) as I believe that creative activity is a valuable human activity per se and should be accessible to anyone.

* * *

Of all the titles Trevor Wishart has borne in a strikingly independent career, "artist in the community" is the one that sits best on him. He has shown a remarkable interest thorughout his nearly 20 years as a full-time composer in the community implications of art. The opposite of a "pure" or "absolute" composer, he devises works which are specifically and powerfully interactive; his consultancy at the Jorvik Viking Museum in York may be one of the most prominent achievements of any contemporary British artist. Earlier in his career, he drew on much the same performance-art tradition as Gavin Bryars to create a series of very individual environmental and dramatic pieces which conspicuously lacked the avant-gardist self-consciousness of much performance art of the period. Where Bryars's early pieces were mannered to the point of preciosity, Wishart's performance pieces, and notably the haunting *Forest Singularity*, were marked by the unpretentious directness of statement and lack of irony that persists in his mature compositions.

Rather than turning away from these roots, Wishart has built on his performance background. Virtually all his music is in some sense dramatic. In the 1980s he wrote a series of sometimes astringent, sometimes consciously sentimental music-theatre works, which combine the collage effects of *Menagerie* and a growing interest in advanced instrumental and vocal techniques. The extraordinary *Tuba mirum*, commissioned by the virtuosic brass player Melvyn Poore, presents a patient in some psychiatric way-station to hell, exploring the bounds of normalcy and redemption. *Pastorale* from 1980 follows *Menagerie* in transforming the "native wood notes wild" of English Romanticism into something altogether more modern and troubled, but which preserves something of its longer tradition.

The high point of Wishart's output to date—and along with Giles Swayne's *Cry*, the most distinctive British vocal work of the past 25 years—is the *Vox* cycle, six pieces for voice and electronics initially commissioned by the innovative vocal quartet Electric Phoenix. The individual pieces explore the outer reaches of vocal technique. *Vox III* explores, by means of a pre-recorded click track, the problems and potentialities of singing polyrhythmically. Elements of the same concern are visible in Wishart's remarkable cantata for the schoolchildren of Soweto township in South Africa, *Passion*, a work of barely disguised sorrow and anger that utilises the exuberant cross-rhythm of voices as a point of escape from violence and oppression.

Wishart's orientation is non-elitist and non-academic. He is dedicated to the propagation of music as an activity rather than as a consumer item. In recent years, he has been involved in "desktop" music publishing, opening the means of musical production to the widest possible constituency. His work in the community and his educational projects receive the same attention as works for IRCAM. There is nothing deflationary about his approach. It is grounded in a formidable musical grasp, but one which remains unimpressed by musical fashions. Wishart regards low-level technology—and notably microcomputers—as a substantial step forward in the liberation of music from the publishing and critical establishment. He is, in the words of his own work in progress, a pantomime Orpheus.

—Ian Grey

WOLFF, Christian. American. Born in Nice, France, 8 March 1934; emigrated to U.S.A., 1941. Self-taught as composer. Educated at Harvard University, Cambridge, Massachusetts (classics), B.A., Ph.D. Lecturer in Greek and Latin, Harvard University, 1962–76; professor of classics and music, and subsequently Strauss Professor of Music, 1976–9, Dartmouth College, Hanover, New Hampshire. Recipient: American Academy and Institute of Arts and Letters award. Mailing address: c/o C.F. Peters, 373 Park Avenue South, New York, New York 10016, U.S.A.

Publisher: Peters.

Symphonies/orchestral:

Burdocks (1 or more orchestral groups or variable size) 1970–1.
Exercise 23/24 (J.C.'s Bread and Roses) (chamber orchestra) 1983–6.
Exercise 25 (Liyashizwa) 1986.

Chamber/instrumental:

Duo (2 violins) 1950.
For Prepared Piano 1951.
Nine (flute, clarinet, horn, trumpet, trombone, celeste, piano, 2 cellos) 1951.
Trio I (flute, trumpet, cello) 1951.
For Piano I 1952.
For Piano II 1952.
Suite I (prepared piano) 1954.
For Piano with Preparations 1955.
Duo for Pianists I 1957.
Sonata (3 pianos) 1957.
Duo for Pianists II 1958.
For Pianist 1959.
Music for Merce Cunningham (violin, viola, trumpet, trombone, piano, double bass) 1959.
Duet I (piano duet) 1960.
Suite II (horn, piano) 1960.
Duet II (horn, piano) 1961.
Duo for Violinist and Pianist 1961.
Summer (string quartet) 1961.
Trio II (piano duet, percussion) 1961.
For Five or Ten People (unspecified instrumentation) 1962.
In Between Pieces 1963.
For One, Two or Three Players (unspecified instrumentation) 1963.
Septet (7 players, conductor) 1964.
Electric Spring I (horn, contrabassoon, electric guitar, electric double bas) 1966.
Quartet (4 horns) 1966.
Electric Spring II (tenor recorder/alto recorder, trombone, guitar, electric guitar, electric double bass) 1966–70.
Electric Spring III (violin, horn, electric guitar, electric double bass) 1967.
Edges (unspecified instrumentation) 1968.
Pairs (duos; unspecified instrumentation) 1968.
Toss (8 or more players) 1968.
Prose Collection (unspecified instrumentation) 1968–9.
Tilbury (unspecified instrumentation) 1969.
Tilbury 2 and 3 (unspecified number of amplified instruments) 1969.
Snowdrop (harpsichord and/or other instruments) 1970.
Burdocks (1 or more ensembles/5 players in each) 1970–1.
Accompaniments (unspecified instrumentation) 1972.
Lines (string quartet or other string groups) 1972.
Variations (Extracts) on the Carman's Whistle Variations of Byrd (keyboard or other instruments) 1972.
Changing the System (unspecified instrumentation) 1972–3.
Exercises 1–14 (any 3 or more instruments) 1973–4.
Studies (piano) 1974–6.
String Quartet Exercises Out of Songs 1974–6.
String Bass Exercise Out of "Bandiera rosa" (double bass) 1975.
Exercises 15–18 (keyboard, trombone, any instruments) 1975.
Bread and Roses (piano) 1976.
Dark as a Dungeon (clarinet; also for trombone, double bass) 1977.
The Death of Mother Jones (violin) 1977.
Braverman Music (instrumental ensemble) 1978.
Cello Song Variations 1978.
Hay una mujer desaporscida (piano; after Near) 1979.
Stardust Pieces (cello, piano) 1979.
Three Pieces: Rock About, Instrumental, Starving to Death on a Government Claim (violin, viola) 1979–80.
Exercises 19 (Harmonic Tremors) and 20 (Acres of Clams) (2 pianos) 1980.
Preludes 1–11 (piano) 1980–1.
Exercise 21 (piano—4 hands) 1981.
Isn't This a Time (saxophone) 1981.
Exercise 22 (Bread and Roses, for John, 1982) (piano—4

hands) 1982; orchestrated as *Exercise 24* 1983.
Eisler Pieces: I (For Cornelius), II (Dig a Hole in the Meadow) (clarinet/bass clarinet, violin, cello, piano) 1983.
Piano Song (I Am a Dangerous Woman) 1983.
Peace March I (Stop Using Uranium) (flute) 1983–4.
Peace March 2 (flute, clarinet, cello, percussion, piano) 1984.
Peace March 3 (The Sun Is Burning) (flute, cello, percussion) 1984.
Piano Trio 1985.
Bowery Preludes (flute/alto flute/piccolo, trombone, percussion, piano) 1986.
Black Song Organ Preludes 1987.
Long Peace March (flute/piccolo, oboe, clarinet/bass clarinet, bassoon/contrabassoon, alto saxophone, horn, trombone, percussion, viola) 1987.
For Morty (2 percussion, piano) 1987.
Digger Song (for John Cage's 76th Birthday) (violin, cello, piano) 1988.
27/28 (percussion) 1988.
Emma (viola, cello, piano) 1989.
Rosas (piano, percussion) 1990.

Vocal/choral:

Songs (unison voices) 1973–4.
Wobbly Music (mixed chorus, instruments: World War I texts) 1975–6.
I Like to Think of Harriet Tubman (female voice, any treble instrument, any alto instrument, any bass instrument) 1984.
Leaning Forward (soprano, baritone, clarinet/bass clarinet, cello; Paley) 1988.

Other/electronic:

For Magnetic Tape 1952.

PUBLICATIONS

By Wolff: "Uber Form", in *Die Reihe*, 7, 1960; "Questions", in *Collage*, 1964; "Electricity and Music", in *Collage* 8, 1968; "Edges", in *Source*, 3(1), 1969.

On Wolff: J. Birke, *CWs Metaphysik und die zeitgenossische Literatur und Musiktheorie*, Berlin, 1966; Michael Nyman, "CW" in *Music and Musicians*, 20(8), 1972, and in *Experimental Music*, London, 1974; Walter Zimmermann, (interview) in *Desert Plants: Conversations with 23 American Musicians*, Vancouver, 1976; M. Barry, "CW", in *Music and Musicians*, 26(7), 1978; T. DeLio, *Circumscribing the Open Universe: Essays on Cage, Feldman, CW, Ashley and Alvin Lucier*, Washington, D.C., 1984.

* * *

The early pieces of Christian Wolff are musically laconic. Pitch material is contained within a tiny range; the *Duo* for violins uses only three notes (D, E♭ and E natural). This narrowness tends to encourage concentration on individual sounds and their combinations rather than on progressions. Indeed, attention often moves from pitch to timbre, and from rhythm to time perceived non-metrically.

Later in the 1950s, Wolff began writing pieces which incorporated variable elements. The *Duo for Pianists II* has no score, only various parts, and the clef assignations for *Tilbury 2 and 3* are not fixed. His timbral resources were frequently adventurous; the *Duo* employs pizzicato and other effects inside a piano, and his later *Electric Spring* series makes use of electric guitar and bass.

Wolff was an early experimenter with text scores, where performance instructions are given in words. His *Prose Collection* is a precursor of similar works by, for example, Stockhausen and Cardew, but is more prosaic than many of its descendants: "allow various spaces between playing (2, 5 seconds, indefinite) . . . At some point or throughout use electricity".

From the late 1950s, Wolff began preparing scores which involve the players in game activity. Often they involve a kind of puzzle: reference letters for transforming material (in *For Pianist* for example) which have an algebraic appearance ("4 ½:lb"), or links between notes, as in the *Duet II* for horn and piano which is reminiscent of a molecular diagram. Sometimes the game is akin to sport, passing notes from one player to another as if playing basketball. Wolff also employs "cueing" technique, where one performer's decisions are influenced by what another has played. The ensuing chains of action and reaction give the music an improvisatory quality.

At the turn of the 1970s, Wolff began to move away from the objectivist abstraction of this early music, writing instead music with a more or less direct political message. The pieces often derive from folk material. The *String Bass Exercise Out of "Bandiera rosa"* employs an Italian revolutionary song, which serves as point of reference for the nature and spirit of performance. *The Death of Mother Jones* for violin is based on a West Virginian song from the early 1930s; *Three Pieces* for violin and viola utilise two Civil War songs. Some works are derived from the work of specific songwriters: *Hay una mujer desaporcida*, for piano, from a Holly Near song, *Dark as a Dungeon*, for clarinet from a Merle Travis number about Kentucky miners.

Other pieces set political texts: either proletarian poetry ("When all the workers stand with hand in hand/The world with all its wealth will be at their command"—*Wobbly Music*) or political writing. *Changing the System* uses Tom Hayden's reflections on the failures of the counterculture; *Accompaniments* draws on Myrdal and Kessler's *China: The Revolution Continued* ("many people have come to realize that latrines, too, are a political question").

Like much contemporary music, the Wolff's work is innovative in notation and aural result, and it has an educative side—whether in the discipline, disinterest and focus of the earlier pieces or the revolutionary commitment which follows. It also evidences rare modesty, whether in the simplicity of the sounds, or the unpretentious character of his simply typed or handwritten titles and directions.

—David Revill

WOOLRICH, John. British. Born in Cirencester, Gloucestershire, 3 January 1954. Educated at University of Manchester, 1972–5, B.A.; University of Lancaster (composition under Edward Cowie), 1975–7, M.Litt. Northern Arts Fellow in Composition, University of Durham, 1982–5; composer in residence, National Centre for Orchestral Studies, London, 1985–6; visiting lecturer, Goldsmith's College, University of London, 1986–7; tutor in performance and communication skills, Guildhall School of Music, London, since 1990. Mailing address: 80 Highworth Road, London N11 2SH, England.

Publisher: Faber.

Symphonies/orchestral:

Songbook II 1984; first performed Stockton, Lancashire, 1985.
The Barber's Timepiece (large orchestra) 1986; first performed London, 13 June 1986.
The Ghost in the Machine 1989; first performed Tokyo, 1990.

Chamber/instrumental:

La Bonne Vaux (string sextet) 1980; first performed London, 1981.
Stone Dances (octet) 1980; first performed York, 1980.
The Dark Spring (sextet) 1981; first performed London, 1981.
Spalanzani's Daughter (octet) 1982; first performed London, 1983.
Night Machines (sextet) 1986; first performed London, 1987.
Vaucanson's Machine (woodwinds, horns) 1987.
Dartington Doubles (alto flute, soprano saxophone, horn, trumpet, piano, boo bams, bass drum, violin, viola, cello) 1988; first performed London, 10 April, 1988.
The Kingdom of Dreams (oboe, piano) 1989; first performed Cheltenham, Gloucestershire, 7 July, 1989.
Barcarolle (alto flute/flute/piccolo, oboe, harp, violin, cello, percussion) 1989; first performed London, 20 April 1989.
Lending Wings (16 players) 1989; first performed Birmingham, 1989.
Ulysses Awakes (after Monteverdi; for viola, with 6 violins, viola, 2 cellos, double bass) 1989; first performed Dartington, Devon, 11 August, 1989.

Vocal/choral:

Four Songs After Hoffman (soprano, clarinet in E♭ and C/bass clarinet; soprano also plays assorted percussion) 1981; first performed Feltham, Surrey, 16 April 1982.
Cascades (soprano, clarinet, percussion, piano, viola, cello and assorted additional percussion; Italian folk sources) 1983; first performed Newcastle-upon-Tyne, 26 January 1984.
Harlequinade (soprano, clarinet/bass clarinet, piano, violin, cello and assorted percussion; anon.) 1983; first performed Washington, Tyne and Wear, 10 May, 1984.
Black Riddle (soprano, large chamber ensemble; anon.) 1984; first performed London, 8 September 1984.
Three Macedonian Songs (soprano, clarinet, piano, tam-tam, violin, viola, cello, double bass; translated Harvey) 1984; first performed Durham, 30 November 1984.
Figures in a Landscape (chorus, large orchestra) 1986; first performed Brighton, Sussex, 1987.
Light and Rock (soprano, bassett horn, piano; Serbian, translated Harvey) 1988; first performed in Ilkley, Yorkshire, 7 September, 1988.
The Turkish Mouse (soprano, soprano saxophone, bass clarinet, viola, cello, double bass) 1988; first performed Brighton, Sussex, 13 May 1989.
Berceuse (soprano, 5 instruments) 1990; first performed Nether Alderley, 1990.
Favola in Musica (concert aria after Monteverdi) 1990.

Other:

Machaut: *Hoquetus David* (arrangement) 1987.

PUBLICATIONS

On Woolrich: David Wright, "Compact Risks", in *The Listener*, 18 May 1989.

* * *

The very individual music that John Woolrich writes shuns heroic or portentous gestures, avoids inflated textures and has no complicated "systems". Yet neither is it *faux naïf*, for one source of the music's strength is its unselfconscious manner. In general terms the pieces are straightforward, the ear readily drawn to a point of musical focus which provides the perspective for the varied gestures which surround it. But these events, whose effect is sometimes local rather than long-range, frequently intrigue, as—wheezing and ticking—they entice the listener into Woolrich's often gothic world. Some tease by their very understatement—perhaps a laconic aside, whose meaning strikes later—and some just because they sound fascinating, but which vanish before their patterns can be satisfactorily deduced. Much of the impact comes from their placement within the work as a whole, and Woolrich has a striking ability to pace events.

Woolrich's output is concentrated in three areas. First are the sets of pieces for voice and instrumental ensemble, second are the compositions for chamber ensemble alone, while third are the works involving orchestra. The titles of his pieces reveal some consistent preoccupations, in particular, a delight in the fantasy tales of E.T.A. Hoffmann and a fondness for the plangent qualities of folk poetry. Some recent works have shown an interest in the possibilities of compositions coming out of other music, and the arrangement of Machaut's *Hoquetus David* has been the starting point for newer ventures such as *Ulysses Awakes* (after Monteverdi) and *Favola in Musica* which takes the literary themes of loss and waiting in Monteverdi's madrigal *O sia tranquillo il mare* and through them goes on to make musical contact with Mozart and Wagner.

Woolrich's enthusiasm for Hoffmann opens a way into his musical world. Hoffmann's automata represent the opposition between controlled precision (or mechanised restriction) and spontaneous freedom, effectively a metaphor for the compositional process itself and so a basis for Woolrich's fascination. Tip the balance too far, and the search for musical order becomes the obsession with system that produces something grotesque in the Hoffmann sense.

The treatment of texts drawn from folk sources reflects the influence of Berio and Stravinsky rather than of Vaughan Williams. Their timeless validity apart, the potency of these texts rests in expression which is often direct rather than just simple. Woolrich builds on this feature in settings such as *Harlequinade*, *Cascades* and *Three Macedonian Songs*, whose pithy compactness point their qualities of delicacy and wit.

In *The Barber's Timepiece*, the eponymous *meccanico* percussion gestures also provide the caesuras to separate the three prolonged melodic arches that constitute the work's second basic element. These melodies in their turn generate the surrounding heterophonic textures. Although melody has always featured in his music, the construction of such expanded arcs reflects Woolrich's belief in their potential to bear the structural weight of a composition.

The Ghost in the Machine makes conscious use of the medieval technique of isorhythm, based on the repetition of a central melodic core. The structure of the piece becomes clear as the transposed melodic line is passed, like a baton, across the orchestra. Behind this is a steady process of diminution, with the progressive reduction of section lengths which effectively speeds up the piece. However the regularity of the scheme, with its seemingly inevitable, and mechanical, drive to the conclusion is thrown off course by the slower tempo of the coda, and its presentation of fragmented snatches of preceding material. In fact, the suppleness of the work's total effect makes any rigidity of the structural scaffold more apparent than real.

—David Wright

WU Zuqiang. Chinese. Born in Beijing, 24 July 1927. Educated at Central Conservatory of Music, Beijing (compos ition), graduated 1952; Tchaikovsky Conservatory of Music, Moscow, graduated 1958. Married Zheng Liqin, 29 January 1953; 1 son and 1 daughter. Teacher, 1952–62, senior lecturer, 1962–78, deputy president, 1978–82, president, 1982–8, professor, since 1983, and supervisor of doctoral work, since 1988, Central Conservatory of Music, Beijing; head of composition section, Central Philharmonic Orchestra, Beijing, 1972–5; vice-chair and director of composition committee, Chinese Musicians Association, since 1985; council member, Chinese People's Association for Friendship with Foreign Countries, since 1985; council member, Soong Ching Ling Foundation, 1986; co-executive chair, China Federation of Literary and Art Circles, since 1988; member, Art and Education Committee, under State Education Commission, from 1987; member, board of directors, Copyright Agency Corporation, China, since 1988; member, Standing Committee of Chinese Peoples Political Consulatative Conference, since 1988. Recipient: National Outstanding Textbook Prize (for *Analysis of Musical Forms and Works*), 1987. Mailing address: Central Conservatory of Music, 43 Baojia Street, Beijing 100031, China.

Publisher: China Record Company, The People's Music Press, Beijing.

Works for Western or mixed forces:

String Quartet 1957.
The Mermaid (dance drama) 1958.
Red Women's Detachment (ballet) 1964.
Young Sisters of the Grassland (pipa concerto) 1973–6.
Moon Reflected in the Erquan Pool (string orchestra) 1976.

PUBLICATIONS

By Wu: *Analysis of Musical Forms and Works*, Beijing, 1987.

* * *

Wu Zuqiang is a well-known Chinese composer, theorist and educator. He is now a professor of composition and was formerly president of the Central Conservatory of Music in Beijing. During his tenure at the conservatory, Wu has brought up many outstanding young musicians in China.

Wu is from an intellectual family. He was interested in music, literature and fine arts when he was young and received his degrees in composition from the Central Conservatory of Music, Beijing and Tchaikovsky Conservatory of Music, Moscow. During his study, he published his *String Quartet* which combined his well-trained traditional Western music technique with Chinese folk melodies.

After Wu returned to China from Moscow, he cooperatively composed *The Mermaid* (music for dance drama) and *Red Women's Detachment* (music for ballet). Both orchestral works are performed and well-received at home and abroad, and have had a significant influence on the younger generation in China, in the way of using diatonicism in developing melodies in the style of Chinese folk music. Wu was the first composer to employ Chinese traditional instrumental melodies in new music composition. In the 1970s he arranged some instrumental pieces of Chinese traditional classical music for Western orchestra, and composed music for Chinese traditional instruments with Western orchestra. *Moon Reflected in the Erquan Pool* for string orchestra, arranged from a solo piece of erhu, a Chinese string instrument, and *Young Sisters of the Grassland*, a concerto for pipa, a Chinese plucked instrument and Western orchestra, have been performed by major orchestras throughout the world.

Wu is a music critic for several newspapers and has written extensively for journals and magazines. His book *Analysis of Musical Forms and Works* is an important textbook for composition students in China.

—Chen Yi

WUORINEN, Charles. American. Born in New York City, 9 June 1938. Educated at Columbia University, New York City (composition under Otto Luening, Vladimir Ussachevsky and Jack Beeson), 1956–63, B.A., 1961, M.A., 1963. Conductor and pianist; co-founder and co-artistic director (with Harvey Sollberger), since 1962, and president, since 1984; Group for Contemporary Music; instructor, 1964–9, and assistant professor, 1969–71, Columbia University; consultant, Manhattanville Music Curriculum Project, 1967; visiting lecturer, New England Conservatory, Boston, 1968–71; member, editorial board, *Perspectives of New Music*, 1968–72; visiting lecturer, Princeton University, New Jersey, 1969–71; visiting lecturer, University of Iowa, Iowa City, 1970; visiting composer in residence, University of South Florida, Tampa, 1971; director, American Music Center, 1971; visiting lecturer, Manhattan School of Music, New York City, 1971–9; composer in residence, Chamber Music Northwest Festival, 1978, and Grand Teton Music Festival, 1979; visiting professor, Yale University, New Haven, Connecticut, 1983; professor, Rutgers University, New Brunswick, New Jersey, since 1984; visiting professor, State University of New York, Buffalo, since 1989, New York University, Spring 1990. Recipient: New York Philharmonic Young Composers Award, 1954; Bearns Prize, 1958, 1959, 1961; Alice M. Ditson Fellowship, 1959; Phi Beta Kappa, 1960; Lili Boulanger Memorial Award, 1961, 1962; elected to American Academy of Arts and Letters, 1967; Guggenheim Fellowships, 1968, 1972; Pulitzer Prize (for *Time's Enconium*), 1970; Brandeis University Creative Arts Citation in Music, 1970; special citation, Koussevitzky International Recording Award, 1970; Phoebe Kethum Thorn Honorary Award, 1973; Creative Artists Public Service Award, 1976; Arts and Letters Award, Finlandia Foundation, 1976; Rockefeller Foundation Fellowships, 1979, 1981, 1982; MacArthur

Foundation Fellowship, 1986–91. Mailing address: c/o Howard Stokar Management, 870 West End Avenue, New York, New York 10025, U.S.A.

Publishers: Peters, New York; McGinnis and Marx; Schirmer; Presser; Music for Percussion; New Music Edition; Composers Facsimile Editions.

Symphonies/orchestral:

Concertpiece (piano, strings) 1956; first performed Bennington, Vermont, 18 August 1956.
Music for Orchestra 1956; first performed New York City, 1 December 1956.
Alternating Currents (chamber orchestra) 1957; first performed Bennington, Vermont, August 1957.
Concertante I (violin, strings) 1957; first performed Middlebury, Vermont, 7 July 1957.
Symphony No 1 1958; first performed New York City, 7 May 1958.
Summer Music (violin, chamber orchestra) 1958; withdrawn.
Violin Concerto No 1 1958; withdrawn.
Concertante IV (violin, piano, chamber orchestra) 1959; first performed Bennington, Vermont, 29 August 1959.
Symphony No 2 1959; first performed New York, 27 February 1959.
Symphony No 3 1959; first performed New York City, 11 November 1959.
Concertone (brass quintet, orchestra) 1960; first performed Iowa City, 19 February 1964.
An Educator's "Wachet Auf" (chamber orchestra) 1961.
Evolution transcripta (chamber orchestra) 1961; first performed Bennington, Vermont, 19 August 1961.
Orchestral and Electronic Exchanges (orchestra and synthesized sound) 1965; first performed New York City, 30 July 1965.
Piano Concerto 1966; first performed Iowa City, 4 May 1966. Recorded CRI 239.
Contrafactum 1969; first performed Iowa City, 19 November 1969.
Grand Bamboula (string orchestra) 1971; first performed Iowa City, 30 September 1972. Recorded Nonesuch H 71319.
Concerto for Amplified Violin 1972; first performed Tanglewood, Massachusetts, 5 August 1972. Recorded University of Iowa Press 8319.
Piano Concerto No 2 (amplified piano, orchestra) 1974; first performed New York City, 6 December 1975.
A Reliquary for Igor Stravinsky (based on Stravinsky's last sketches and drafts) 1975; first performed Ojai, California, 13 June 1975.
Percussion Symphony (24 percussion players) 1976. Recorded Nonesuch 9 79150 2/H 71353.
Two-Part Symphony 1978; first performed New York, 11 December 1978. Recorded CRI 410.
Ancestors (chamber orchestra) 1978; first performed Portland, Oregon, 17 August 1978.
Tashi (clarinet, violin, cello, piano, orchestra) 1979.
The Magic Art (orchestral suite) 1979.
Ecclesiastical Symphonies (orchestral movements from *The Celestial Sphere*) 1981.
Short Suite 1981; first performed Purchase, New York, 13 February 1983.
Piano Concerto No 3 1983; first performed Albany, New York, 4 May 1984. Recorded Nonesuch 9 79185 2.
Rhapsody (violin, orchestra) 1983; first performed San Francisco, 16 January 1985.
Bamboula Squared (orchestra, electronic sound) 1984; first performed New York City, 4 June 1984.
Movers and Shakers 1984; first performed Cleveland, Ohio, 13 December 1984.
Overture 1984.
Crossfire 1984; first performed Baltimore, Maryland, 9 May 1985.
Prelude to Kullervo (tuba, orchestra) 1985; first performed New York City, 21 November 1985.
Fanfare for the Houston Symphony 1986.
The Golden Dance 1986; first performed San Francisco, 10 September 1986. Recorded Nonesuch 9 79185 2.
Galliard (chamber orchestra) 1987; first performed Cleveland, Ohio, 27 September 1987.
Five (concerto for amplified cello, orchestra) 1987.
Overture: Bamboula Beach 1987.
Another Happy Birthday 1988; first performed 4 February 1988.
Machault Mon Chou (after the *Messe de Notre Dame*) 1988; first performed San Francisco, 24 May 1989.
Astra 1990.

Chamber/instrumental:

Scherzo (piano) 1953.
Hommage à Bach (organ) 1955.
Prelude and Fugue (4 percussion) 1955.
Into the Organ Pipes and Steeples (piccolo, clarinet, saxophone, timpani, 2 pianos, 2 violas, 2 cellos, double bass) 1956.
Song and Dance (piano) 1956.
Two Tranquil Pieces (piano) 1956.
Sonatina (flute, oboe, clarinet, bassoon) 1956.
Subversion (string septet) 1956.
Woodwind Quintet 1956.
Three Mass Movements (violin) 1957.
String Quartet 1957.
Triptych (violin, viola, percussion) 1957.
Concertante II (violin, chamber ensemble) 1958.
Sonata (piano) 1958.
Three Prepositions (piano) 1958.
Movement (wind quintet) 1958.
Spectrum (violin, brass quintet, piano) 1958.
Three Pieces (string quartet) 1958.
Concertante II (oboe, harpsichord, violin, viola, cello) 1959.
Musica duarum partium ecclesiastica (brass quintet, timpani, piano, organ) 1959.
Trio concertante (oboe, violin, piano) 1959.
Consort (4 trombones) 1960.
Eight Variations (violin, harpsichord) 1960.
Sonata (flute, piano) 1960.
Turetzky Pieces (flute, clarinet, double bass) 1960.
Concert (double bass) 1961.
Evolutio (organ) 1961.
Tiento sobre Cabezon (transcription of Antonio de Cabezon's *Tiento del primer tono*; flute, oboe, harpsichord, piano, violin, viola, cello) 1961.
Trio No 1 (flute, cello, piano) 1961.
Bearbeitungen über das Glogauer Liederbuch (flute/piccolo, clarinet/bass clarinet, violin, double bass) 1962.
Duuiensela (cello, piano) 1962.
Invention (5 percussion, piano) 1962.
Liederbuch (flute, clarinet, violin, double bass) 1962.
Octet (oboe, clarinet, horn, trombone, piano, violin, cello, double bass) 1962.
Trio No 2 (flute, cello, piano) 1962.
Chamber Concerto (cello solo, flute, oboe, clarinet, bassoon, 2 percussion, piano, violin, viola, double bass) 1963.

Recorded Nonesuch H 71263.
Variations (piano) 1963.
Variations I (flute) 1963. Recorded Nonesuch HB 73028.
Chamber Concerto (flute solo, 4 percussion, harp, guitar, piano, harpsichord, celeste, double bass) 1964. Recorded CRI 230.
Composition (violin solo, 2 oboes, 2 bass clarinet, 2 horns, 2 trombones, percussion, piano, double bass) 1964.
Variations à deux (flute, piano) 1964.
Chamber Concerto (oboe solo, tuba, 5 percussion, timpani, harp, piano, double bass) 1965.
Composition (oboe, piano) 1965.
Bicinium (2 oboes) 1966.
The Bells (carillon) 1966.
Harpsichord Division 1966.
Duo (violin, piano) 1966.
Janissary Music (percussion) 1966. Recorded CRI 231.
Making Ends Meet (piano—4 hands) 1966.
Salve Regina: John Bull (chamber ensemble) 1966.
Variations II (flute) 1968. Recorded Nonesuch HB 73028.
String Trio 1968.
Adapting to the Times (cello, piano) 1969.
Sonata No 1 (piano) 1969. Recorded CRI SD 306.
The Long and the Short (violin) 1969. Recorded Bridge BCD 9008.
Nature's Concord (trumpet, piano) 1969.
Chamber Concerto (tuba solo, 12 winds, 12 drums) 1970. Recorded CRI SD 491.
Ringing Changes (12 percussion) 1970. Recorded Nonesuch H 71263.
Variations I (cello) 1970.
Canzona (*to the Memory of Igor Stravinsky*) (12 instruments) 1971; first performed 31 January 1972.
Variations (harp, violin, viola, cello) 1971; first performed 17 April 1971.
String Quartet No 1 1971; first performed 11 October 1971.
Variations (bassoon, harp, timpani) 1972. Recorded New World NW 209.
On Alligators (flute, oboe, clarinet, bassoon, string quartet) 1972; first performed Florida, 22 April 1973.
Speculum speculi (flute, oboe, bass clarinet, percussion, piano, double bas) 1972; first performed 14 January 1973. Recorded Nonesuch H 71300.
Trio No 3 (flute, cello, piano) 1972; first performed 28 March 1973.
Variations (violin) 1972.
Arabia felix (flute, bassoon, piano, electric guitar, vibraphone, violin) 1973; first performed 23 February 1974. Recorded CRI SD 463.
Grand Union (cello, drums) 1973; first performed Tanglewood, Massachusetts, 5 January 1974.
Twelve Short Pieces (piano) 1973.
Fantasia (violin, piano) 1974. Recorded Bridge BCD 9008.
Hyperion (12 instruments) 1975; first performed 21 March 1976.
Tashi (clarinet, violin, cello, piano, orchestra ad lib) 1975; first performed 15 January 1976.
Variations II (cello) 1975.
Sonata No 2 (piano) 1976.
Fast Fantasy (cello, piano) 1977; first performed 13 February 1979. Recorded New World NW 385.
Six Pieces (violin, piano) 1977; first performed 18 April 1978. Recorded Bridge BCD 9008.
Self-Similar Waltz (piano) 1977.
Wind Quintet No 1 1977; first performed 24 February 1978.
The Winds (8 winds, piano) 1977; first performed 19 May 1977. Recorded New World NW 306.
Archaeopteryx (bass trombone, 10 performers) 1978; first performed 1 July 1982.
Archangel (bass trombone, string quartet) 1978; first performed 18 December 1978.
Fortune (clarinet, violin, cello, piano) 1979; first performed Bonn, 1980.
Joan's (flute, clarinet, violin, cello, piano) 1979. Recorded CRI SD 441.
Duo (mallet instruments, piano) 1979; first performed 20 October 1979. Recorded CRI SD 459.
String Quartet No 2 1979; first performed 1 August 1979.
Beast 708 for Humans (chamber ensemble) 1980.
The Blue Bamboula (piano) 1980; first performed 29 May 1981. Recorded Bridge BCD 9008.
Horn Trio 1981.
Trio for Bass Instruments (double bass, bass trombone, tuba) 1981.
Capriccio (piano) 1981.
New York Notes (flute, clarinet, violin, cello, percussion, piano) 1982. Recorded GM 2028.
Divertimento (alto saxophone, piano) 1982; first performed New York City, 6 March 1983.
Divertimento (string quartet) 1983.
Piano Trio 1983; first performed 1 October 1983.
Concertino (2 flutes/piccolo, 2 oboes, 4 clarinets/E♭ clarinet/bass clarinet/contrabass clarinet, 2 bassoons/contrabassoon, 4 horns, solo double bass, optional strings) 1984; first performed New York City, 5 February 1985.
Spinoff (violin, double bass, 4 congas) 1984. Recorded Bridge BCD 9008.
Horn Trio Continued 1985.
Natural Fantasy (organ) 1985.
Trombone Trio 1985; first performed New York City, 6 November 1986.
Double Solo (horn trio) 1985; first performed New York City, 16 May 1986.
Fanfare for Rutgers University (2 trumpets, 2 horns, 2 trombones) 1986.
A Doleful Dompe on Deborah's Departure as Well as Borda's Bawdy Badinage (cor anglais, violin, cello) 1986.
Sonata No 3 (piano) 1986.
String Quartet No 3 1987. Recorded New World NW 385.
Bagatelle (piano) 1988.
Ave Christe (Josquin motet remade for piano) 1988.
Sonata (violin, piano) 1988; first performed Washington, D.C., 25 November 1988.
String Sextet 1989; first performed New York City, 4 November 1989.

Vocal/choral:

Te decet hymnuys (mezzo-soprano, bass, piano, organ, timpani) 1954.
Be Merry All That Be Present (mixed voices, organ or 4 instruments; medieval carol) 1957.
Dr Faustus Lights the Lights (narrator, clarinet, saxophone, bassoon, piano, percussion, cello; Stein) 1957.
Wandering in This Place (unaccompanied mezzo-soprano; anon.) 1957.
Madrigale spirituale sopra Salmo Secundo (tenor, baritone, 2 oboes, double bass ad lib, 2 violins, cello, double bass) 1960.
Two Songs ("The Door in the Wall", "On the Raft"—2 mezzo-sopranos, piano) 1960.
Symphonia sacra (tenor, baritone, bass, 2 oboes, 2 violins, double bass, organ) 1961.
The Prayer of Jonah (chorus, string quintet) 1962.

Super salutem (men's voices, 9 brass, percussion, piano) 1964.
A Message to Denmark Hill (baritone, flute, cello, piano; Howard) 1970.
A Song to the Lute in Musicke (soprano, piano; Edwards) 1970.
Mannheim 87. 87. 87 (chorus, organ) 1973.
An Anthem for Epiphany (chorus, organ, trumpet) 1974.
Six Songs (counter-tenor or alto, tenor, chamber ensemble; Britten) 1977.
Psalm 39 (baritone, guitar) 1979.
Three Songs ("Morning", "Noon", "Night"; tenor, piano) 1979.
The Celestial Sphere (oratorio for mixed chorus, orchestra; Fuller) 1980.
Mass (soprano, chorus, violin, organ) 1982.
Genesis (oratorio for chorus, orchestra) 1989.
A solis ortu (unaccompanied SATB chorus) 1989.
Twang (mezzo-soprano, piano; Stevens) 1989.

Opera/dramatic:

The Politics of Harmony (masque for alto, tenor, bass, 2 flutes, tuba, 3 percussion, piano, 2 harps, 2 violins, 2 double basses; Monaco) 1967; first performed New York, 28 October 1968.
The W. of Babylon (baroque burlesque for 8 singers, 1 speaker, 44–48 players) 1975.
The Magic Art (instrumental masque after Purcell) 1979.

Other:

Consort from Instruments and Voices (electronic) 1961.
Times Enconium (electronic) 1969. Recorded Nonesuch H 71225.

PUBLICATIONS

On Wuorinen: W. Hibberd, "The Politics of Harmony", in *Perspectives of New Music*, 7(2), 1969; B. Boretz, (interview) in *Contemporary Music Newsletter* 3(7–8), 1969; T. Caras and C. Gagne, (interview) in *Soundpieces: Interviews with American Composers*, Metuchen, New Jersey, 1982.

* * *

Charles Wuorinen is one of the most significant American composers of his generation. Widely performed, extremely prolific and highly articulate. Wuorinen has done more than any other composer since Aaron Copland to advocate the idea of concert music composition as an earnest profession in the United States.

His music can be viewed as the logical continuation of early 20th-century European musical ideals, transplanted to the U.S.A. during the wave of immigrant European composers during the 1930s and 1940s: this sets him apart from many of his contemporaries, who have been influenced by the American experimentalist tradition of Ives, Cowell, and Cage, or by non-European music. His spiritual grandfathers can be seen to be Schoenberg and Stravinsky (especially late Stravinsky); unlike many American composers who have gravitated towards one of the other. Wuorinen has managed to synthesize both influences into a powerful, highly personal musical language.

Although Wuorinen has composed several important vocal and choral works, including an undeservedly neglected opera *The W. of Babylon*, the bulk of his output consists of abstract instrumental music. His writing celebrates virtuosity, and he has created works to showcase nearly every instrument.

Wuorinen was for many years pigeonholed as a "twelve-tone" composer, but his catalogue reveals a variety of compositional techniques. He has used fractals in composing *Bamboula Squared* and *New York Notes*; *Beast 708 for Humans* is a "transcription of computer output". Many of his recent works were composed using more intuitive means. Additionally, Wuorinen has written a number of arrangement or recompositions of earlier composers' music whom he admires, including the *Bearbeitungen über das Glogauer Liederbuch; The Magic Art*, an evening-long orchestral piece drawn from Purcell's music; and *Machaut Mon Chou* for orchestra. *A Reliquary for Igor Stravinsky* incorporates Stravinsky's last sketches for an orchestral piece.

There is some justification for Wuorinen's "twelve-tone" reputation. Many of his works from the 1960s and 1970s were written in an idiom he developed which had its roots in Milton Babbitt's pioneering work in twelve-tone composition. Babbitt found a rhythmic analogue to the twelve-tone row by equating a rhythmic value with the size of each adjacent interval in the row. Wuorinen extended Babbitt's "time point" system by applying these values to sections and subsections of a composition, so that the rhythmic proportions of a given row are reflected in the larger formal structures as well. Wuorinen has lucidly documented these techniques in *Simple Composition*, a book which, for better or worse, has helped contribute to the uninformed general perception of him as being exclusively a "twelve-tone" composer.

In early pieces such as the *Chamber Concerto for Cello* or the *Chamber Concerto for Flute*, the disjunct, angular melodies, the extreme contrasts of dynamics within a single melodic line, the kaleidoscopic use of instruments, and a rapid circulation of all 12 pitches characterized Wuorinen's idiom.

Several years later, Wuorinen refined this vocabulary through the use of strong pitch centers, typically at the beginnings and ends of pieces, as can be seen by the repeated Gs in the *String Trio*. Wuorinen also began to display a predilection for octave reinforcements of pitches for reasons of both formal articulation and personal orchestrational preference; this can be seen in works such as the First String Quartet and *Speculum speculi*.

Many critics have noted the emergence of a new style for Wuorinen over roughly the last decade. Its features include a marked clarification of rhythm (there is usually a readily perceptible underlying pulse to his recent works) and orchestration, and the use of broader, less disjunct melodic gestures. However, many of these elements can be seen in works two decades old such as the *Grand Bamboula* for strings.

Pieces typically cited as displaying Wuorinen's newer style are usually drawn from the impressive list of substantial orchestral works he has composed in the last ten years: the Third Piano Concerto; the *Rhapsody for Violin and Orchestra*; *Bamboula Squared* for orchestra and computer-generated tape; *Movers and Shakers*; *The Golden Dance*; and *Five* for amplified cello and orchestra. A partial list of the more notable chamber works from this period includes the *Horn Trio* and its sequel, *Horn Trio Continued*; *New York Notes* for six players; *Spinoff*, for violin, contrabass, and conga drums; the *Sonata for Violin and Piano*; and the *String Sextet*. All of these works display the ebullient, propulsive rhythms, the sharp, unclouded textures, and the long, clearly-directed melodic lines which have become associated with his more recent music.

—Christian Hertzog

XENAKIS, Iannis. Greek; French citizen. Born Braila, Romania, 29 May 1922. Educated at Anargyrios and Koryalenios School, Spetzai, from 1932; music study under Aristotle Koundourov, from 1934; Athens Polytechnic (preparatory course, engineering), 1938; active in Greek Resistance, severely wounded, December 1945, subsequently condemned to death; emigrated to France, 1947; Ecole Normale de Musique, Paris (composition under Darius Milhaud and Arthur Honegger); Conservatoire National Supérieur de Musique, Paris (composition under Oliver Messiaen), 1950–2; further composition study under Hermann Scherchen, Gravesano, Switzerland. Married Francoise Gargouil, 3 December 1953; 1 daughter. Architect, collaborator with Le Corbusier, 1947–60: designed L'Unité d'habitation de Nantes-Reze, 1949, urbanization plan, Chandigarth, Punjab, 1951, Couvent Sainte Marie de La Tourette, Eveux sur l'Arbresle, 1953, l'Unité d'habitation de Briey en Forêt and l'Unite d'Habitation de Berlin-Charlottenburg, 1954, Philips Pavilion, Brussels World Fair, 1956, Sports and Cultural Centre, Baghdad, 1957, competition for urbanization of Berlin and of Meaux region, 1958; subsequently designed Polytope French pavilion, Montreal Expo, 1967, music and light spectacle, Persepolis, 1971, and Polytope de Cluny, Paris, 1972–4; founder and director, Centre d'Etudes de Mathématique et Automatique Musicales, Paris, since 1966; associate professor and director, Centre for Mathematics and Automated Music, Indiana University, Bloomington, 1967–72; membre, Centre National de Recherche Scientifique, 1970–2; professor, University of Paris I; Gresham Professor, City University, London. Recipient: Diploma of Merit, World Festival of Youth and Students for Peace and Friendship, Bucharest, 1953; Prize of the European Foundation for Culture, Geneva, 1957; Manos Hadjidakis Prize, Athens, 1963; Grand Prix du Disque, Paris, 1965, 1968, 1970, 1977; 1st prize, Computer Composed Music Competition, International Federation for Informatic Processing, Edinburgh, 1968; Bax Society Prize (Harriet Cohen International Awards), London, 1968; Modern Music Prize, Japanese Recording Academy, Nippon Academy Award, Tokyo, 1971; honorary member, British Computer Arts Society, London, 1972; Maurice Ravel Gold Medal, 1974; honorary member, American Academy of Arts and Letters, 1975; D.Litt.Hum., University of Paris I, Sorbonne, 1976; Grand Prix National de la Musique, Paris, 1976; Beethoven Prize, 1977; Edison Prize for best record of contemporary music, Amsterdam, 1977; elected member, European Academy of sciences and of arts and letters; elected member, National Council of Hellenic Resistance, Greece, 1980; elected member, French Institute, 1983, elected member, Acadéemie des Beaux Arts, 1984; Officer de l'Ordre des Arts et des Lettres; Officier, l'Ordre National du Merite; Chevalier, Légion d'Honneur. Mailing address: 9 rue Chaptal, 75009 Paris, France.

Publishers: Salabert; Boosey & Hawkes.

Symphonies/orchestral:

Metastaseis (61 instruments) 1953–4; first performed Donaueschingen, 15 October 1955. Recorded Le Chant du Monde LDX A 8368; Vanguard Cardinal 10030.

Pithoprakta (50 instruments) 1955–6; first performed Munich, 8 March 1957. Recorded Le Chant du Monde LDX A 8368; Vanguard Cardinal 10030; Nonesuch 7120; Lyra 251; Neuauflage 32.818.

ST/48 1,240162 (48 musicians; numbers relate to stochastic composition [ST], number of players [48], number of work for these forces [1], date of realisation [24 January 1962]; also applies to chamber works below) 1956–62.

Duel (game for 2 orchestras) 1959; broadcast Radio Hilversum, October 1971.

Syrmos (18 or 36 strings) 1959. Recorded Erato STU 70526; Candide 31049; Neuauflage 9088.

Hiketides (from the stage work; concert suite for 2 trumpets, 2 trombones, strings) 1962.

Terretektorh (88 instruments dispersed through audience) 1965–6; first performed Royan, 3 April 1966. Recorded Erato STU 70529; Neuauflage 9119.

Nomos Gamma (98 instruments dispersed through audience) 1967–8. Recorded EratoSTU 70529; Neuauflage 9119.

Synaphai (piano, orchestra) 1969. Recorded Decca HEAD 13.

Eridanos (2 horns, 2 trumpets, 2 tubas, strings) 1973; first performed La Rochelle, 1973.

Erikthon (piano, orchestra) 1974; first performed Paris, May 1974.

Noomena (large orchestra) 1974; first performed Paris, 16 October 1964.

Empreintes 1975; first performed La Rochelle, 29 June 1975.

Jonchaies (108 instruments) 1977. Recorded Performance PER 84061; Decca 411610 1.

Pour les Baleines (large string orchestra) 1982.

Shar (large string orchestra) 1983.

Lichens (orchestra) 1984.

Thallein 1985.

Alax (3 orchestral groups) 1985.

Keqrops (piano, 92 instruments) 1986; first performed New York City, 13 November 1986.

Horos (89 instruments) 1986; first performed Tokyo, 24 October 1986.

Tracées (large orchestra) 1987; first performed Paris, 17 September 1987.

Ata (large orchestra) 1987; first performed Lisbon, 3 May 1988.

Chamber/instrumental:

Achorripsis (large ensemble/21 instruments) 1956–7; first performed Brussels, 20 July 1958. Recorded EMI CO63 10011; Angel S 36656; Mainstream MS 5008.

ST/4 (string quartet) 1956–62. Recorded EMI CVC 2086; HMV S-ASD 2441; RCA RS 9009/RL 25444.

ST/10 1,080262 (10 instruments) 1956–62. Recorded EMI CO63 1001; Angel S-36656; EMI Columbia SCXG 55.

Morsima-Amorsima (piano, violin, cello, double bass) 1956–62. Recorded EMI CVC 2086; HMV S-ASD 2441; Barclay 920217; Musicdisc RC 16.013.

Analogiques (9 string instruments, 4-channel electronic tape)

1959. Recorded Philips 835487.
Herma (piano) 1960–1. Recorded Mainstream 50001 Jeugden Muziek BVHAAST 007; EMI CVB 2190; EMI Angel EAA 85013 5.
Eonta (piano, 5 brass) 1963–4. Recorded Le Chant du Monde LDX A 8368; Lyra 251; Jeugden Muziek BVHAAST 007.
Akrata (16 winds) 1964–5; first performed Oxford, 28 June 1966. Recorded EMI CO63 1001; Angel S-36656; CBS 34 61226; Nonesuch H-71201.
Nomos Alpha (cello) 1966. Recorded EMI CVC 2086; Deutsche Grammophon 2530562.
Anaktoria (octet) 1969. Recorded Barclay 920217; Musicdisc RC 16-013; EMI HMB CSDG 63.
Persephassa (6 percussionists dispersed around perimeter of audience) 1969. Recorded Philips 652 1020.
Charisma (clarinet, cello) 1971.
Aroura (12 string instruments or other multiples) 1971. Recorded Decca HEAD 13.
Mikka (violin) 1971. Recorded RCA RS 9009; ADDA 81042.
Linaia-Agon (horn, tenor trombone, tuba) 1972.
Evryali (piano) 1973. Recorded Heugden Muziek BVHAAST 007; Denon OX 7063; Toshiba TA 72034.
Gmeeorh (organ) 1974.
Phlegra (11 instruments) 1975; first performed London, 28 January 1976. Recorded Nieuwe Muziek 004.
Psappha (percussion) 1975. Recorded Erato STU 71.106; CBS Sony 32DC673.
Theraps (double bass) 1975–6.
Khoai (harpsichord) 1976. Recorded Erato STU 71.266.
Retours-Windungen (12 cellos) 1976.
Epei (6 wind and brass) 1976. Recorded Nieuwe Muziek 004.
Mikka "S" (violin) 1976. Recorded RCA RS 9009; ADDA 81042.
Dmaathen (oboe, percussion) 1976. Recorded Eterna 827906.
Kottos (cello) 1977. Recorded RCA RS 9009/RL 25444..
Ikhoor (string trio) 1978. Recorded RCA RS 9009/RL 25444.
Pleiades (6 percussion) 1978. Recorded CBS Sony 32 DC 691.
Palimpsest (quintet) 1979. Recorded Nieuwe Muziek 004.
Dikthas (violin, piano) 1979. Recorded RCA RS 9009/RL 25444.
Mists (piano) 1980. Recorded Hungaroton SLPX 12569; Harmonia Mundi HMC 6172.
Embellie (viola) 1980. Recorded RCA RS 9009/RL 25444.
Khall Perr (brass quintet, percussion) 1983.
Tetras (string quartet) 1983.
Naama (harpsichord) 1984.
A l'Ile de Gorée (amplified harpsichord, flute/piccolo, oboe, clarinet, bassoon, horn, trumpet, trombone, 2 violins, viola, cello, double bass) 1986; first performed Amsterdam, 4 July 1986.
Akea (piano, string quartet) 1986; first performed Paris, 15 December 1986.
Keren (trombone) 1986; first performed Strasbourg, 19 September 1986.
Jalons (flute/piccolo, oboe, clarinet/bass clarinet/contrabass clarinet, bassoon/contrabassoon, horn, trumpet, trombone, tuba, 2 violins, viola, cello, double bass) 1986; first performed Paris, 26 January 1987.
Xas (saxophone quartet) 1987; first performed Lille, 17 November 1987.
Air (hommage à Ravel) (piano) 1987; first performed Montpellier, 2 August 1987.
Rebonds A (percussion) 1987–9; first performed Rome, 1 July, 1988.
Waarg (flute/piccolo, oboe, clarinet, bassoon, horn, trumpet, trombone, tuba, 2 violins, viola, cello, double bass) 1988; first performed London, 6 May 1988.
Oophaa (amplified harpsichord, percussion) 1989; first performed Warsaw, 17 September 1989.
Okho (3 djembes, large African drum) 1989; first performed Paris, 20 October 1989.
Rebonds B (percussion) 1989; first performed Avignon, 24 July 1989.
Echange (bass clarinet, flute, oboe, clarinet, bassoon, horn, trumpet, trombone, 2 violins, viola, cello, double bass) 1989; first performed Amsterdam, 26 April 1989.
Epicycles (cello solo, flute, oboe, clarinet, bassoon, horn, trumpet, trombone, tuba, 2 violins, viola, double bass) 1989; first performed London, 18 May 1989.

Vocal/choral:

Polla ta Dhina (children's chorus, orchestra) 1962. Recorded EMI C063 1001.
Oresteia (from the stage work; concert suite for mixed chorus, chamber orchestra) 1965–6. Recorded Erato STU 70656.
Nuits (12 unaccompanied mixed voices) 1967. Recorded Erato STU 70457. MHS 1187.
Cendrées (mixed chorus/72 voices, orchestra) 1973.
N'Shima (2 mezzo-sopranos, horns, 2 trombones, cello) 1975.
Akanthos (2 sopranos, flute, clarinet, 2 violins, viola, cello, double bass, piano) 1977.
A Colonne (men's chorus, horn, trombone, double bass; version for male or female chorus, 3 horns, 3 trombones, 3 cellos, 3 double basses) 1977.
Anemoessa (chorus/80 voices, orchestra) 1979.
Ais (baritone, percussion, orchestra) 1980.
Nekuia (chorus, large orchestra) 1981.
Serment-Orkos (mixed chorus; Hippocrates) 1981.
Pour la Paix (mixed chorus, electronic tape, narrators; also version for unaccompanied mixed chorus) 1982.
Pour Maurice (baritone, piano) 1982.
Chant des Soleils (mixed chorus, children's chorus, brass, percussion) 1983.
Idmen A (mixed chorus, 4 percussion) 1985.
Idmen B (chorus ad lib, 6 percussion) 1985.
Nyuyo (Sunset) (voice, shakuhachi, 2 kotos) 1985.
Kassandra: Oresteia II (amplified baritone/20 string psaltery, percussion) 1987; first performed Gibellina, Italy, 21 August 1987.
Knephas (unaccompanied mixed chorus/32 voices or multiples) 1990; first performed London, 24 June 1990.

Dramatic:

Hiketides (women's chorus, instrumental ensemble) 1964.
Oresteia (mixed chorus, chamber orchestra) 1965–6.
Medea (men's chorus, instrumental ensemble) 1967. Recorded Erato STU 70526; Candide 31049; Erato DLEV 523; MHS 1187.

Other:

Diamorphoses (4-channel electronic tape) 1957.
Concret PH (4-channel electronic tape) 1958. Recorded Philips 835487.
Orient-Occident (4-channel electronic tape) 1960. Recorded Philips 836897.
Bohor (8-channel electronic tape) 1962. Recorded Erato STU 70530; Nonesuch H 71245.
Polytope of Montreal (light and sound show for 4 orchestras) 1967. Recorded Erato STU 70526.

Kraanerg (ballet music for 4-channel tape, orchestra) 1968–9; first performed Ottawa, 2 June 1969. Recorded Erato STU 70527/28.
Hibiki-Hana-Ma (12-channel electronic tape for light and sound show; also 4-channel version) 1969–70. Recorded RCA Victor Japan JRZ 2501.
Persepolis (light and sound show with 8-channel electronic tape; also 4-channel version) 1971. Recorded Philips T 652 1045; NipponPhonogram SFX 8683.
Antikthon (ballet; orchestra) 1971; first performed Bonn, 21 September 1974. Recorded Decca HEAD 13.
Polytope of Cluny (sound and light space with 7-channel electronic tape; also 4-channel version) 1972.
The Legend of Er (7-channel electronic tape for the Diatope sound and light environment) 1977.
Mycenae A (computer-generated stereo tape) 1978.
Taurhiphanie (computer-generated stereo tape) 1987; first performed Arles, 13 July 1988.
Voyage absolu des Unari vers Andromede (computer-generated stereo tape) 1989; first performed Osaki, 1 April 1989.

PUBLICATIONS

By Xenakis: "La Couvent de La Tourette", in Le Corbusier, *Modulor 2*, Paris, 1955; *Gravesaner Blatter* (includes "The Crisis of Serial Music", 1955, "Letter to Hermann Scherchen", 1956, "Probability Theory and Music", 1956, "Le Corbusier's Electronic Poem—The Philips Pavilion", 1957, "In Search of a Stochastic Music", 1958, "Elements of Stochastic Music I-IV", 1960–1, "Stochastic Music", 1962, "Who Is IX", 1962, "Free Stochastic Music", 1965, "Towards a Philosophy of Music", 1966), Gravesano, Ticino, Switzerland, 1955–66; "Genèse de l'architecture du pavillon: Le Pavillon Philips à l'Exposition universelle de Bruxelles", in *Revue technique Philips* (special issue), 1958; "La Musique stochastique: Eléments sur les procèdes probabilistes de composition musicale", in *Revue d'esthétique*, 14(3–4), 1961; *Musique formelle*, Paris, 1963; "Towards a Metamusic", in *Tempo*, 93, 1970; *Musique architecture*, Tournai, 1971, Tokyo, 1976; *Formalized Music*, Bloomington, Indiana, 1971; *Arts/Sciences: Alliages*, Paris, 1979, New York City, 1981.

On Xenakis: Daniel Charles, *La Pensée de X*, Boosey & Hawkes, Paris, 1968; Tim Souster, "X's *Nuits*", in *Tempo*, 85, 1968; Michel Perrot, (interview) in *La Revue musicale*, 1969; [various] *IX*, Paris, 1972; David Halperin, "The Musical Oeuvre of IX", dissertation, University of Jerusalem, 1975; Nouritza Matossian, *X*, Paris, 1981, London, 1986, 2nd edition, 1990; various, *Regards sur IX*, Paris, 1981; Balint Andras Varga, *IX* [interviews], Budapest, 1982.

* * *

The composition of Iannis Xenakis has been a singular force in shaping the landscape of post-World War II music. Free-standing and independent, it has created a new prototype against which other works must be measured. He is the only living composer with a background in the sciences and a distinguished career in a completely different discipline: engineering and architecture. Indeed his musical career began at a tangent to this main occupation.

Xenakis was educated in boarding-school in Spetsai, then went on to Athens to study engineering during World War II. He was a leader in the resistance movement, was severely wounded and lost an eye; he was subsequently sentenced to death. This background gave him a combative and uncompromising attitude to composition only relaxed in certain choral works.

After escaping to Paris with a false passport, Xenakis worked with Le Corbusier on Les Habitations de Marseilles, Le Couvent Sainte Marie de la Tourette and the Philips Pavilion. He welded expertise in mathematics and a raw musical talent to his grasp of philosophy. He viewed the world of music as a neutral space and began to redesign it. Not influenced by styles, he took up cudgels against serialism and argued as early as 1954 that serialism led to an impasse and he wished to open the horizons of composition to larger mass events and new techniques of combining the different characteristics of sound, pitch, rhythm, timbre, duration. This fierce acultural perspective brought him into conflict with the composers of his time. Fortunately he came into contact with Olivier Messiaen, Hermann Scherchen and Edgar Varèse, gaining vital artistic support for his own ideas.

He continued to explore and introduce new theoretical structures simultaneously in architecture and composition. Inspired by the music of nature—thunder, rainstorms, lightning—he regarded music as an extension of the cosmos. He embraced the rough and primitive qualities of textures to dramatize movement and conflicts in the compositional space. He coined the term "stochastic" music for the probabilistic methods using random theory to plot the path of each instrument of the orchestra within a vast configuration in which it would play a part like a gigantic moving tapestry of sound. *Metastaseis*, *Pithoprakta* and *Terretektorh* have become modern classics.

Xenakis was accurate in predicting the application of computers in music and in 1957 based a whole series of compositions on one programme.

He adapted mathematical concepts and functions to pitch, duration, timbre, to create new musical entities using logic; *Herma*, *Eonta* for piano and brass, *Nomos Alpha*, *Nomos Gamma* for orchestra, whose pitches were ordered by set theory and presented a new aesthetic.

At the same time Xenakis devised multi-media shows, called "Polytopes", using light and sound in an architectural space and in the open air: the *Polytope of Montreal*, *Persepolis*, *Polytope of Cluny* and *Mycenae A*.

His Greek roots became manifest with his interest in Byzantine music; he set up a series of classical Greek tragedies to music for stage performance: *Oresteia*, *Medea*, *Kassandra: Oresteia II*, as well as using Greek texts for vocal works such as *Polla to Dhina*, *Serment-Orkos*. Xenakis has also orchestrated the voice creating his own proto-language in major choral works, *Nuits*, *Cendrées*, *Anemoessa*, *Ais* and *Nekuia*.

The 1970s found him integrating mathematical functions such as Poisson's Law, Brownian walk, fractals (*Mikka*, *Noomena, Erikthon*), in a more organic way. He developed a computer drawing-board, the UPIC, as a tool, both for composing and education, and went on to invent a new approach for synthesising sound.

In the last decade he has been reluctant to talk about his systems and methods, yet his music has gained from a more integrated approach, *Horos*, *Keqrops*, *Ata* and *Knephas*. "I look at the empty page and I try to move from what I don't already know. It is the problem of originality in art and behind that is always the quest for freedom."

—Nouritza Matossian

Y

YI Sanggyu. Korean. Born in Kyonggi province, 6 October 1944. Educated at Korean Traditional Music High School, Seoul, 1961–4; College of Music, Hanyang University, Seoul, 1973–7, B.A., thereafter in graduate school, 1979–81, M.A. Married. *Taegŭm* (horizontal flute) player, Seoul Municipal Traditional Music Orchestra, 1965–6; *taegŭm* player, Korean Traditional Performing Arts Centre, Seoul, 1969–81; instructor, Ch'ugye Arts University, Seoul, 1977–85; instructor, Seoul Arts University, 1981–2; assistant professor, Hanyang University, Seoul, since 1982; music director and conductor, Korean Broadcasting System Traditional Orchestra, since 1985; editor, Bulletin of the College of Music, Hanyang University; director, Han'guk chŏngagwŏn/Korean Court Music Institute; Master for Intangible Cultural Asset 1, the Rite of Royal Ancestors. Recipient: new composers award, *Chosŏn ilbo* [Korean Daily News], 1962; new composition award, Korean Traditional Performing Arts Centre, 1963, 1964, 1965; Seoul Culture Prize, 1970; prizes for work on Rite of Royal Ancestors, 1972, 1973, 1975; first Korean Composer's Prize, 1977; Film Music Prize, Korean Ministry of Information, 1978; President's Prize for Composition, 1978. Mailing address: College of Music, Hanyang University, 17 Haengdong, Sŏngdong-ku, Seoul, Korea.

Publisher: none.

[All works are scored for Korean instruments and were first performed in Seoul in the year shown.]

Orchestral:

Ch'unaengjŏn / The Story of Ch'unaeng 1965.
Shinawi / Shaman Improvisation 1967.
Yŏmyŏng / Dawn 1967.
Hapchugok 7 / Ensemble Piece 7 1969.
Chŏng / Justice 1970.
Kojŏn / Tradition 1971.
Chajin hanip (oboe, orchestra) 1972.
Pyŏk / Rock 1972.
Kiak 1974.
Insŏng / Humanity 1974.
Taebaram sori / The Sound of the Big Wind (horizontal flute, orchestra) 1978.
Sunabwi / Waterfly (2-string fiddle, orchestra) 1982.
Hasŏngjo / Hasong Mode 1981.
San / Mountain 1982.
Pada sori / Sound of the Sea 1985.

Chamber/instrumental:

Shillaeak 6-chungju (piece for 6 instruments) 1966.
Kwanak 5-chungju (piece for 4 instruments) 1966.
Chul karak (melodies for strings) 1967.
Tanso-e ŭihan seak 1-chang / Invitation (flute) 1969.
Piece for Kayagŭm (12-string long zither) 1971.
(16-)kye t'aakirŭl wihan shinawi / Shaman Improvisation (16 percussion) 1971.
Sŏgin / Stone Statue (horizontal flute) 1972.
Seak (piece for 3 instruments) 1972.
Yŏm / Rocky Island (horizontal flute) 1972.
Shillaeak 4 chungju (music for 4 instruments) 1974.
Sohoe / Cherished Thoughts 1975.
Haegŭm tokchugok (piece for 2-string fiddle) 1975.
San / Mountain (percussion ensemble) 1976.
Taegŭmŭl wihan 3-chungju (piece for 3 horizontal flutes) 1976.
Piece in Three Movements (horizontal flute, zither) 1977.
Taebi / Comparisons 1980.
T'obun (piece for horizontal flute) 1980.
Piece for T'aep'yŏngso [shawm] and Ensemble 1982.
Piece for Flute and Zither 1983.
Piece for Flute and Oboe 1983.
Piece for Kayagŭm and Kŏmun'go (12-and 6-string zithers) 1983.
First Piece for Kŏmun'go Solo (6-string zither) 1983.

Vocal/choral:

Sanbangilgi / Freedom on the Mountain 1969.
Sandohwa / Mountain Flower 1969.
Yŏrishi oshin tangshin / You Who Are Coming 1980.
Ŭm / Folk Song (chorus) 1980.
Somogok / Yearning Piece 1981.

Opera:

Hŭngboga / The Story of the Two Brothers (arrangement for Korean opera of solo sung story) 1977.
Kwangdaega / Entertainers in Old Korea 1979.

Other:

Sarang ŭi chŏnsŏl / Love's Legend (dance) 1975.
Macbeth (incidental music) 1976.
Emille Chŏng / The Emille Bell (incidental music) 1978.
Pukpŏl / Expedition to Conquer the North (incidental music) 1978.
Sagye / The Four Seasons (dance) 1979.
Kaeksa / Dying in a Strange Land (incidental music) 1979.
Munyŏdo / The Shaman (incidental music) 1979.
Tara, tara, palgŭn tara / Moon, Moon, Bright Moon (incidental music) 1979.
Piece for Kim Maeja (dance) 1979.
P'urhun huk ui yon'ga / Love Song of the Blue Earth (dance) 1979.
Muŏn'ga / Silent Tale (incidental music) 1980.
Nangnangdong / The Place Nangnang (incidental music) 1980.
Aeoraji / Somewhat (incidental music) 1980.
Maŭi t'aeja / The Crown Prince's Demon (dance) 1981.
Pomi omyŏn . . . / When Spring Comes . . . (incidental music) 1981.
Pul pora / Looking at Fire (incidental music) 1981.
Koryŏjang / The Koryo Dynasty (dance) 1984.
Yennal yech'ŏge . . . / Times Gone, Like Then . . . (incidental music) 1985.

PUBLICATIONS

By Yi: dissertation on folk music in Kangwŏn province, Hanyang University, Seoul, 1981.

Yi Sanggyu comments:

From the very first day I composed I have had the same, very simple thoughts about my music. First, I am a Korean. My music should always reflect this: it should always be nationalistic. At the same time, I live in the present. My music should always be contemporary. It should reflect the culture, society and politics of today. These two things give identity to my music. Nonetheless, I do not want to compose music which is merely commonplace or ephemerally popular. I want to create musical structures which will last, which will endure. This is my philosophy.

* * *

Yi Sanggyu is probably the most prolific of living Korean composers. In high school he learned much—though composition was not part of the curriculum—from Kim Kisu (1916–86), the first modern composer of music for traditional Korean instruments. In 1962 he entered a composition concours and carried off first prize. He then spent 15 years combining paid work as a performer of the horizontal flute (*taegŭm*) with the hard work of composition, before entering university. Not surprisingly, his expertise and energy have been directed solely towards the world of Korean music, performing the traditional canon and attempting to create a new legacy. Yi claims not to have been influenced by Western composers, though he admits the value of studying their music for formal and structural procedures. And he claims only indirect influence from Korean composers. Recently, his prodigious output has been stemmed somewhat, but this reflects less a lack of ideas than the demands of his two current occupations, as a professor at Hanyang University and as orchestral director at the state broadcasting network.

Yi spends much time waiting for inspiration: when he starts to write a piece he claims to have the whole musical structure in his head. Critical thought thus precedes writing, and Yi rarely changes a page after the initial transcription. Further, while this gives some clue to his reluctance to admit influences, Yi respects the musical traditions of both court and folk. He sees himself very much as a continuation, thus melodies are sometimes taken from old pieces. *Chajin hanip* for oboe and orchestra is a good example, taking a movement from the court chamber piece *Yŏngsan hoesang* as its basis. It opens with a typical slow introduction which, from bar 15 onwards plays with snippets of the original melody. Similarly, his two operas, *Hŭngboga / The Story of the Two Brothers* and *Kwandaega / Entertainers in Old Korea*, continue with the style of *ch'anggŭk*, a native operatic tradition which emerged in the early 20th century, and *Ŭm / Folk Song*—the title takes the Chinese character for music—transcribes a folksong for chorus. Typically, in solo and small ensemble pieces, Yi never offers a completely new style. Here, the influence of Kim Kisu, as a steadying hand arguing that tradition must be respected, is most apparent.

Yi sees the Korean orchestra as contrasting its Western counterpart. Winds, with the bamboo oboe (*p'iri*) as leader, provide basic melodies; strings, notably the *kayagŭm* and *kŏmun'go* (plucked long zithers) and the *ajaeng* (bowed long zither), offer harmonic depth. The fiddle (*haegŭm*), most surely a counterpart of violins, retains something of its traditional role of go-between: it has strings yet produces long, nasal sounds close to the winds. Interestingly, harmony is seen to evolve from melodic ornamentation, hence in *Chajin hanip* octaves and fourths feature more than Western tritonic chords. Yi's style is summed up by *Sunabwi / Waterfly*: a slow introduction in octaves builds to snippets of melody—neither entirely Korean nor Western. A solo fiddle moves through a central movement marked by a light but cliché-ridden 6/8 to a long cadenza. The cadenza starts by gradually opening up ascending pitch registers, breaks into a tune, then closes with a perfect cadence. *Taebaram sori / The Sound of the Big Wind* is structurally identical, except that the fiddle is replaced by the *taegŭm* (horizontal flute) and the underlying melody comes from a court solo, *Ch'ŏngsŏnggok*.

Melodically, Yi provides a mix of East and West. Nowhere is this more true than in his piece for 3 flutes, *Taegŭmŭl wihan 3-chungju,* one of his most adventurous pieces to date. But it is in terms of rhythm that he is considered unique. The traditional concept of rhythmic cycles (*changdan*), used as a constantly repeating metric frame, to Yi should be considered as a set of sounds with contrasting intensity and timbre. The idea of percussion colour thus replaces any notion of support. *(16-)kye t'aakirŭl wihan shinawi / Shaman Improvisation* for 16 percussion instruments is representative, exploring percussive sounds in a manner that reflects the instruments' supposed order of invention—earth, wood, skin and iron.

—Keith Howard

YI Sŏngch'ŏn. Korean. Born in North Hamgyŏng province, 28 May 1936. Educated at Catholic Medical College, Seoul, 1955–9; College of Music, Seoul National University, 1961–5, B.A.; graduate school, Seoul National University, 1965–7, M.A. Married Ch'oe Yŏngsuk, 12 February 1980; 1 son and 3 daughters. Assistant, 1967–9, instructor, 1969–79, assistant professor, 1982–6, and associate professor, since 1986, College of Music, Seoul National University; assistant professor, 1979–81, and associate professor, 1981–2, Sungshin Women's University, Seoul; chair, Han'guk kugak Kyoyuk Hakhoe / Korean Traditional Music Education Society, since 1984, and Tongyang ŭmak yŏn'guhoe / Asian Music Research Institute, 1988–90. Recipient: New Musician Prize (for *Norit'ŏ*), Ministry of Culture and Information, Seoul, 1965; Korean Academic Prizes, *Sŏul shinmun / Seoul Daily News*, 1969, 1971; Korean Music Prize, Korean Broadcasting System, 1985. Mailing address: Apt. 801-1004, Purim-dong, Kwach'on-si, Kyŏnggi-do, Seoul, Korea.

Publisher: Sumumdang, 349-1 Ŭlchiro 3-ga, Chung-ku, Seoul, Korea.

[All pieces first performed in Seoul]

Orchestral:

P'iri / Oboe (orchestral ensemble) 1968.
Ch'ŏngsonyŏnŭl wihan kugak kwanhyŏnak immun / Young Person's Guide to the Korean Traditional Orchestra 1974.
Kwanhyŏn shigok: Naŭi noguk / Poem: My Fatherland:
  Part I—*Koyohan ach'im ŭi nara / Land of Morning Calm* 1981.
  Part II—*Sanhwa / Mountains and Rivers* 1983.
  Part III—*Minjok ŭi songga / Ode of the People* 1985.

Prelude (*kayagŭm*/zither, orchestra) 1987.
Sasŏng chiak / *Music of the Four Saints* 1988.
Orchestral Ensemble No 6 1989.

Chamber/instrumental:

Mixed Quintet (Western instruments) 1964.
Norit o / *The Playground* (piano, revised for *kayagŭm*) 1965.
Piece for Korean Strings 1969.
Chamber Piece for Korean Winds 1969.
Chamber Variations (winds) 1970.
Shinawi (fantastic dance suite for clarinet, piano) 1971.
Two Studies (piano) 1975.
Fantasy (Korean instruments) 1975.
Supsok ŭi iyagi / *Talking of the Forest* (*kayagŭm*) 1977.
Shigol p'unggyŏng / *Village Landscapes* (percussion) 1981.
Pada / *Sea* (21-string *kayagŭm*) 1986.
Owŏl ŭi norae / May Song (*kayagŭm*) 1989.
Hahyŏn ŭi pyŏnyŏng / *Variations of Hahyon* (ensemble) 1989.

Vocal/choral:

Iyagi / *Talking* (voice, Korean instruments) 1975.
Samogok (voice, Korean instruments) 1976.
Elli, Elli / *Eli, Eli* (mixed chorus, ensemble) 1980.
Kyrie (female chorus, ensemble) 1981.
Sasŭm / *The Deer* (baritone, piano or instrumental ensemble) 1986.
Sagye / *Four Seasons* (vocal duet, instruments) 1988.
Kugak tongyo (songs for children) 1989.

Other:

Hodong wangja / *Prince Hodong* (dance) 1973.
P'ansori inhyŏnggŭk Hŏsaengjŏn / *Husaeng's Story* (puppet show) 1975.
Pyŏllak (lyric song; arranged for ensemble) 1987.
P'yŏnsudaeyŏp (lyric song; arranged for lute) 1989.

Three collections of compositions and arrangements: *Norit'o* (Seoul, 1977), *Supsok ui iyagi* (Seoul, 1977), *Pada* (Seoul, 1987).

Arrangements for kayagŭm of pieces by Mills, Daquin, Shop, Beethoven and Korean composers, 1987.

PUBLICATIONS

By Yi: *Theory of Music, with Exercises*, Seoul, 1971; *Ear Training and Sight Singing I, II*, Seoul, 1972, 1973; *The Aesthetics of Music*, Seoul, 1974; *Young Person's Guide to the Korean Traditional Orchestra*, Seoul, 1974; *History of Korean Music*, Seoul, 1976; *The Analysis of Musical Form*, Seoul, 1976; *Fundamental Musical Exercises*, Seoul, 1979; "Meaning of Disuniformity in Korean Traditional Music", in *Minjok ŭmakhak* / *Journal of the Asian Music Research Institute*, 9, 1987; "Hyang pip'a, tang pip'a, wŏlgŭm ŭi pogwŏn'ga kaeryange" [On the Restoration of the Three Korean Lutes], in *Kugakki kaeryang chonghap pogosŏ*, 1989.

On Yi: Alan Hovhaness, "Variations by Theme of Chongsunggok", in *University News*, 1963; Yi Sangman, "Ensemble for P'iri and Percussion", in *Chosŏn ilbo*, 26 September 1967; Hwang Pyonggi, "Second Composition Recital", in *Umak segye* / *World Music*, 1977; Ko Chingman, "Modification of Kayagŭm Important to Preserve Original Sound", in *Korea Times*, 1986; Sŏn Kwangju, "The 21-String Zither", in *Umak tonga*, 33, 1986; Pak Yongsu, "The Improvement and Restoration of Korean Lutes", in *Sports Seoul*, 1384, 1989.

Yi Sŏngch'ŏn comments:

I am a Korean composer, and I think that it is important for me to remain faithful to Korean idioms in my compositions. I tend to employ traditional instruments—or in the cases of kayagŭm (12-string long zither), komun'go (6-string fretted long zither) and pip'a (lute), developments of them which I have designed myself—taking as my starting point the pitch, rhythm and melodies of traditional music.

Initially I studied Western art music, but my home is in Korea. So, first I must be faithful to the sound worlds of Korea. Since Koreans today are often unaware of their own heritage, I have considered it my duty to make traditional music more accessible to all through my more than 150 compositions. In addition to reworking instruments, I have become involved in writing children's songs and arranging old music in contemporary idioms. But I live in a contemporary world. Thus, in the future I hope to create a new sound world which is neither East Asian nor Western—yet which is also both.

* * *

Yi Sŏngch'ŏn studied under Chŏng Hoegap and Kim Talsŏng at Seoul National University. There was no course in Korean music composition so, despite Yi's strong nationalistic outlook, he was only able to study Western music. His first piece to achieve success, *Norit'ŏ* / *The Playground*, was thus initially written as a piano suite. It was awarded a national prize, for promise among new musicians, in 1965.

Norit'ŏ also brought notoriety when in 1966, responding to the dearth of new music for the Korean 12-string zither (*kayagŭm*), Yi rearranged it. Much criticism followed Yi Chaesuk's first performance of the new suite. The problems concerned musical grammar. Many—the scholar-composers Hwang Pyŏnggi and Kim Kisu among them—considered that new music for Korean instruments should reflect a tradition dating back many centuries. Others, including several performers, argued that a new grammar was needed if Korean music was to be contemporary. *Norit'ŏ* hardly fitted under fingers trained for old court and folk music, thus Yi's new grammar involved learning techniques. These, although alien to Korea, were essentially common in Japanese *koto* music—glissandos and arpeggios, chords, and ostinato passages. The composer was not trying to imitate; he simply wanted the zither to produce his imagined music. Nonetheless, Hwang Pyŏnggi's *Sup* / *The Forest* is directly quoted in the suite's fourth movement (bar 30 onwards) and one can hear echoes of the old folk genre, *sanjo* (e.g., second movement, bars 19–20). Since much of the criticism came from senior figures, Yi's radical approach to Korean music was dampened.

There followed 15 relatively fallow composition years. Yi published many academic and educational handbooks, but allowed his compositions to stay within a derivative mould. Only gently did he push at the boundaries of "tradition". This can be seen in songs inspired by the age-old lyric song repertory (e.g., *Iyagi* / *Talking*, *Samogok*, and the suite for zither, *Supsok ŭi iyagi* / *Talking of the Forest*). The 1980s saw much greater creativity. Arguably, as a senior figure, Yi no longer needs to heed advice concerning respect for the "tradition". Yet maturity has arrived not so much in compositions which were entirely new in outlook, but in pieces where Yi balances the new with a mastery of traditional language. The three parts of the orchestral poem *Kwanhyŏn shigok: Naŭi nogok* / *Poem: My Fatherland, Sasŏng chiak / Music of Four Saints* and *Sasŭm / The Deer* are representative examples.

The relative lack of creativity in Yi's output during the 1970s was counterbalanced by the development of other concerns. On one hand, education came to the fore. Yi saw the need to introduce students brought up with Western music to their own traditions. Hence, the successful attempt to imitate Britten in the *Young Person's Guide to the Korean Traditional Orchestra*. More recently, Yi has contributed children's songs written with Korean melodic contours and accompanied by Korean instruments to volumes published and recorded by the Korean Traditional Performing Arts Centre. At the same time, and perhaps initiated by the depression caused by the criticism of *Norit'ŏ / The Playground*, Yi has worked to restore lutes—absent for several centuries from Korean court ensembles—and develop new forms of zithers. He has reworked the 12-string *kayagŭm*, for instance, to create both a larger instrument with 21 strings more suitable for theatre and solo work, and a smaller instrument more practical for children's limited hand spans.

With *Pada / Sea*, Yi's large-scale piece for solo 21-string *kayagŭm*, the composer has come full circle. Simple melodies spanning a wide range (four octaves) in the first three movements are balanced with writing in the latter three movements where the zither favours almost orchestral textures, offering a melody supported by solid triadic harmony. The techniques which were new in *Norit'ŏ / The Playground* have all returned, but now they are played on an instrument for which Yi—as inventor—defines the tradition.

—Keith Howard

YU, Julian Jing-Jun. Chinese; Australian citizen. Born in Beijing, 2 September 1957; emigrated to Australia, 1985. Educated at Central Conservatory of Music, Beijing, 1973–7, diploma, 1977; Tokyo College of Music (under Joji Yuasa and Schin-ichiro Ikebe), 1980–2, postgraduate studies certificate, 1982; Queensland Conservatorium of Music, graduate diploma in music, 1987; La Trobe University, Melbourne, 1988–91, M.A., 1991; Melbourne Summer Music School for Advanced Musical Studies, 1988; (Australian) Composers' National Orchestral School, 1988. Married Marion Hazel Gray, 9 November 1984. Conductor, amateur Chinese music ensemble, Beijing, 1974–80, 1982–5; assistant lecturer, composition department, Central Conservatory of Music, Beijing, 1977–80, 1982–5; part-time teacher of composition, Balaklava High School, Melbourne, 1986; conductor, Adelaide Chinese Music Ensemble, 1986; piano teacher/accompanist, "Die Musiker Studio" music school, Adelaide, 1986; part-time teacher, Queensland Conservatorium of Music, 1987; fellow in composition, Tanglewood, Massachusetts, 1988; conductor, Chao Feng Chinese Orchestra, Melbourne, 1988–9; guest lecturer, La Trobe University, Melbourne, 1990. Recipient: 2nd prize, 56th Japan Music Concours (for *Scintillation II*), 1987; Prix d'Encouragement Voya Toncitch, Paris, 1987; 1st prize, Northern Rivers CAE Young Composers' Competition (for *Scintillation I*), 1987; Award of Merit, International New Music Composers' Competition (for *Scintillation I*), 1987; 3rd prize, 35th Premio Musicale, Citta di Trieste, Italy, 1988; Albert H. Maggs Award for Composition, Australia, 1988; Koussevitzky composition prize, 1988; 2nd prize, International New Music composers' Competition, U.S.A. (for *Wu-Yu*), 1988; Jacobena Angliss Music Award, Astra Chamber Music Society, Melbourne, 1989; 2nd prize, 10th Irino Prize Foundation International Composers' Competition, Japan (for *Great Ornamented Fuga Canonica*), 1989; Musical Excellence Award, International New Music Composers' Competition, 1989–90. Mailing address: 4/53 Kellett Street, Northcote, Victoria 3070, Australia.

Publisher: Universal Edition.

Symphonies / orchestral:

Wu-Yu 1987; first performed Melbourne, 2 February 1989.
Great Ornamented Fuga Canonica 1988; first performed Melbourne, 30 January 1988.
Hsiang-Chi 1990.
First Australian Suite (chamber orchestra) 1990; first performed Melbourne, 1990.

Chamber / instrumental:

Quintet (flute, clarinet, harp, violin, cello) 1981; first performed Tokyo, 29 March 1982.
Sol la do re (string trio) 1982; first performed Tokyo, 1982.
Four Pieces (wind quintet) 1982; first performed Tokyo, 1982.
Impromptu (piano) 1982; first performed Melbourne, 14 August 1987.
Crossing (flute) 1986; first performed Adelaide, 1 August 1986.
Scintillation I (piano) 1987; first performed Lismore, New South Wales, 1988.
Scintillation II (piano, 2 vibraphones, glockenspiel) 1987; first performed Tokyo, 12 October 1987.
Scintillation III (flute, piano) 1987.
Medium Ornamented Fuga Canonica (wind quintet) 1988; first performed Melbourne, 30 January 1988.
Mini Symphony (flute, clarinet, piano, viola, double bass) 1988; first performed Tanglewood, Massachusetts, July 1988.
Reclaimed Prefu (2 pianos) 1989; first performed Melbourne, 5 September 1989.

Vocal / choral:

Three Haiku (mezzo-soprano, piano) 1987.
Haiku (soprano, piano) 1988; first performed Tanglewood, Massachusetts, 18 August 1988.
In the Sunshine of Bach (unaccompanied mixed choir) 1990; first performed Melbourne, 24 August 1990.
Reclaimed Prefu II (SATB choir, 2 pianos) 1990; first performed Melbourne, 25 May 1990.

Opera:

The White Serpent (puppet opera; instrumentation—clarinet/bass clarinet, trumpet, trombone, percussion, piano/celeste, violin/viola, double bass) 1989; first performed Munich, May 1990.

Other:

A Changing Picture (music for cartoon, China Central Television: flute, clarinet, 3 trombones, harp, strings) 1985.

Alban Berg: *Sonate* (arranged for orchestra) 1981, revised 1989.

PUBLICATIONS

By Yu: "A Brief Introduction to the Symbols Used in the Notation of Contemporary Music", in *Journal of the Central Conservatory of Music*, 12(3), 1983.

Julian Jing-Jun Yu comments:

I believe that quality and beauty in music come from something much deeper than the sound effect produced; they lie in the pattern of thought, the inner laws or structure, and it is this inner pattern that gives to music integrity and individual character. The sound is only a result, a physical phenomenon, and the inner pattern is not always readily discernible at first hearing.

Notation is another physical form reflecting the musical idea. The written form is a surer guide to the quality of a piece of music than its sound, as the ear always lags behind the eye and needs to be guided by intellect and/or intuition.

I see value in writing music that I cannot "hear", in order gradually to broaden my limits of aural comprehension—provided that what I am writing "makes sense" on some inner plane.

* * *

Julian Jing-Jun Yu's approach to composition has undergone a radical change over the past few years, a change exceeding that of the normal evolution expected of a student aspiring to mature composer status. In the 1970s China was still isolated from the most important musical developments in 20th-century Europe; for example, theoretical studies of Western music were concerned exclusively with tonality and the only work of Arnold Schoenberg to be found in the Beijing Conservatory music library at the time was *Verklärte Nacht/Transfigured Night*. In 1979 Alexander Goehr was invited to give a series of lectures at the Beijing Conservatory where he introduced works of latter-day European composers to the music students. Yu was overwhelmed and seized the opportunity to acquaint himself further with the new music by winning a scholarship to undertake postgraduate work at the Tokyo College of Music where, from 1980 to 1982, he studied with Joji Yuasa. He thus became familiar with serial and other techniques as well as the compositional methods of his Japanese mentors. Three works represent this period in Yu's development: *Quintet* for two woodwinds, two strings and harp; *Sol la do re* for string trio, and *Four Pieces* for wind quintet, all premiered at the Tokyo College of Music in 1982. On his return to Beijing, Yu was besieged by commissions to write music for various television, radio and live theatre plays and ballets. During this time Yu began to make his name on the international scene by distinguishing himself in various competitions. Performances during this period included *Scintillation II* by members of the NHK (Japan Broadcasting Corporation) Symphony Orchestra, Tokyo, and two versions of *Ornamented Fuga Canonica*: the *Medium Ornamented Fuga Canonica* for wind quintet performed in Melbourne and Tanglewood, and the *Great Ornamented Fuga Canonica* performed in Hobart and London by the Tasmanian and BBC symphony orchestras. Yu's growing reputation won him a three-year publishing contract with Universal Edition and several commissions, the most important of which was a 40-minute puppet opera, *The White Serpent*, with libretto by the composer, commissioned by Hans Werner Henze and the City of Munich and performed at the second Munich Biennale International New Music Theatre Festival, May 1990. In the *Ornamented Fuga Canonica,* Yu adopted an approach to composition based on traditional teaching practices in his own country combined with western techniques. In the teaching of folk music in China a beginner learns a simple piece which is practised until the learner is capable, through improvisation, of embellishing the piece in an individual way. The embellished version then serves as the basis for further improvisation and the process continues until the piece, now unrecognisable in comparison with the original, becomes the learner's own composition—thus the beginnings of a personal style are forged. In *Reclaimed Prefu* Yu has applied this "additive" technique to Bach's *Prelude and Fugue No 1*. The first version for two pianos was performed in 1989 at La Trobe University by Kim Bastin and Lawrence Whiffin, and the second version for two pianos and choir was performed in 1990 in Melbourne by the legendary Astra Chamber Music Society under John McCaughey. The embellishments in the two-piano version of *Reclaimed Prefu* consist of systematically adding tones foreign to the original harmonies and sounded together with them, the result serving as the basis for the second version with choir tracing the work's implied melodic outlines. Yu also uses Chinese scales in his additive technique and it is this curious but effective way of blending characteristic Chinese idioms with European atonality wedded to a fine sense of instrumental colour, that has brought him to the fore among today's composers.

—Laurence Whiffin

YUN Isang. Korean; German citizen. Born in Tongyong, 17 September 1917. Early training in cello and Western-style composition, Korea, 1935–7, later in Japan, 1941–3; imprisoned due to opposition to Japanese occupation of Korea, released 1945; teacher of music, Korea, 1945–56; emigrated to Europe, 1956; further composition study in Paris and under Boris Blacher and Joseph Rufer, Berlin, 1956–9; settled in Berlin, 1964; abducted with his wife by South Korean secret police, 17 June 1967; arraigned on charges of sedition and treason, Seoul, and sentenced to life imprisonment [3 years imprisonment for his wife]; freed after campaign led by prominant musicians; teacher of music, Hannover State College of Music, 1969–70; professor of composition, Hochschule für Musik, Berlin, since 1970; German citizenship, 1971. Recipient: honorary member, Akademie der Kunste, Hamburg and Berlin; honorary doctorate, Tübingen University. Mailing address: c/o Bote & Bock GmbH, Hardenbergstrasse 9a, D-1000 Berlin 12, Germany.

Publisher: Bote & Bock.

Symphonies/orchestral:

Bara 1960; first performed Berlin, 19 January 1962.

Symphonische Szenen 1960; first performed Darmstadt, 7 September 1961.

Colloides sonores (string orchestra) 1961; first performed Hamburg, 12 December 1961.

Fluktuationen 1964; first performed Berlin, 10 February 1965. Recorded Harmonia Mundi DMR 1019 1021.

Reak 1966; first performed Donaueschingen, 23 October 1966. Recorded Wergo 60034.

Dimensionen 1971; first performed Nuremberg, 22 October 1971.

Konzertante Figuren 1972; first performed Hamburg, 30 November 1973.
Ouverture 1973, revised 1974; first performed Berlin, 4 October 1973.
Harmonia (winds, harp, percussion) 1974; first performed Herford, 22 January 1975.
Concerto for Cello and Orchestra 1976; first performed Royan, France, 25 March 1976.
Concerto for Flute and Small Orchestra 1977; first performed Hitzacker, 30 July 1977.
Double Concerto (oboe, harp, small orchestra) 1977; first performed Berlin, 26 September 1977. Recorded Camerata CMT 4024.
Muak (dance fantasy for large orchestra) 1978; first performed Monchengladbach, 9 November 1978. Recorded Camerata CMT 4014.
Fanfare and Memorial 1979; first performed Munster, 18 September 1979.
Exemplum in memoriam Kwangju 1981; first performed Cologne, 8 May 1981.
Concerto for Clarinet and Orchestra 1981; first performed Munich, 29 January 1982. Recorded Camerata CMT 1084.
Concerto for Violin and Orchestra No 1 1981; 1st and 2nd movements first performed Frankfurt, 29 April 1982; first complete performance, 25 November 1982. Recorded Camerata CMT 4004.
Symphony No 1 1983; first performed Berlin, 15 May 1984. Recorded Camerata 32 CM 26.
Concerto for Violin and Orchestra No 2 (in three parts) 1983–6; "Festliches Praludium" (1984) first performed Siegen, 30 March 1984; "Dialog Schmetterling und Atombombe" (1983) first performed Tokyo, 8 July 1983; "Adagio und Finale" (1986); first performance of complete work, Stuttgart, 20 January 1987.
Symphony No 2 1984; first performed Berlin, 9 December 1984.
Gong-Hu (harp, strings) 1984; first performed Lucerne, 22 August 1985.
Symphony No 3 in One Movement 1985; first performed Berlin, 26 September 1985.
Mugung-Dong (invocation for winds, percussion, double bass) 1986; first performed Hamburg, 22 June 1986. Recorded Harmonia Mundi HM 855 D.
Symphony No 4: Im Dunkeln singen 1986; first performed Tokyo, 13 November 1986.
Impression (small orchestra) 1986; first performed Frankfurt, 9 February 1987. Recorded Harmonia Mundi HM 855-2.
Symphony No 5 (baritone, orchestra; Sachs) 1987; first performed Berlin, 17 September 1987.
Duetto concertante (oboe/cor anglais, cello, strings) 1987; first performed Rottweil, 8 November 1987.
Chamber Symphony No 1 1987; first performed Gutersloh, 18 February 1988.
Konturen 1989; first performed Braunschweig, 18 March 1990.

Chamber/instrumental:

Fünf Klavierstücke (piano) 1958; first performed Bilthoven, 6 September 1959.
String Quartet No 3 [nos 1 and 2 withdrawn] 1959; first performed Cologne, 15 June 1960. Recorded cpo 999 075-2.
Musik für sieben Instrumente (flute, oboe, clarinet, bassoon, horn, violin, cello) 1959; first performed Darmstadt, 4 September 1959. Recorded Time 8006.
Loyang (flute, oboe, clarinet, bassoon, harp, 4 percussion, violin, cello) 1962; first performed Hannover, 23 January 1964.
Gasa (violin, piano) 1963; first performed Prague, 2 October 1963. Recorded Wergo 60034; Mainstream MS 5016.
Garak (flute, piano) 1963; first performed Berlin, 11 September 1964. Recorded Gaudeamus 73002; Da Camera Magna; EMI 1 C 065 30834.
Nore (cello, piano) 1964; first performed Bremen, 3 May 1968.
Shao Yang Yin (harpsichord) 1966; first performed Freiburg, 12 January 1968.
Tuyaux sonores (organ) 1967; first performed Hamburg, 11 March 1967. Recorded Wergo 60034; Cantate 658229.
Riul (clarinet, piano) 1968; first performed Erlangen, 26 July 1968. Recorded Camerata CMT 1084.
Images (flute, oboe, piano, cello) 1968; first performed Oakland, California, 24 March 1969. Recorded Camerata CMT 4024.
Glissees (cello) 1970; first performed Zagreb, 8 May 1971. Recorded Deutsche Grammophon DGG 2530562.
Piri (oboe or clarinet) 1971; first performed Bamberg, 25 October 1971. Recorded Denon OX 7031 ND; Camerata CMT 1084; col legno 5515/429 354 2.
Trio (flute/alto flute, oboe, violin) 1972–3; first performed Mannheim, 18 October 1973.
Trio (violin or viola, cello, piano) 1972–5; first performed Berlin, 23 February 1973.
Etuden (1 or more flutes) 1974; first performed Kyoto, 16 July 1974.
Rondell (oboe, clarinet, bassoon) 1975; first performed Bayreuth, 30 September 1975.
Fragment (organ) 1975; first performed Hamburg, 17 May 1975.
Pièce concertante (flute/alto flute, clarinet/bass clarinet, piano, percussion, violin, viola, cello, double bass) 1976; first performed Hamburg, 15 June 1976. Recorded Camerata CMT 4014.
Duo (viola, piano) 1976; first performed Rome, 3 May 1977.
Konigliches Thema (after J.S. Bach; violin) 1976; first performed Dusseldorf, 1 April 1977. Recorded Toshiba TL 1006; Thorofon MTH 180; col legno 5515.
Salomo (from *Der weisse Mann*; alto flute or flute) 1977–8; first performed Kiel, 30 April 1979. Recorded Attacca Babel 9056 3.
Octet (clarinet/bass clarinet ad lib, bassoon, horn, string quintet) 1978; first performed Paris, 10 April 1978. Recorded Harmonia Mundi HM 855–2.
Sonata (oboe/oboe d'amore ad lib, harp, viola or cello) 1979; first performed Saarbrücken, 6 July 1979. Recorded Camerata 32 CM 22.
Novellette (flute/alto flute, harp ad lib, violin, cello or viola) 1980; first performed Bremen, 5 February 1981. Recorded attacca babel 9056–3.
Interludium A (piano) 1982; first performed Tokyo, 6 May 1982.
Concertino (accordion, string quartet) 1983; first performed Trossingen, 6 November 1983. Recorded cpo 999 075-2.
Sonatina (2 violins) 1983; first performed Tokyo, 15 December 1983. Recorded Camerata CMT 4014.
Monolog (bass clarinet) 1983; first performed Melbourne, 9 April 1983. Recorded Attacca Babel 8635–4.
Inventionen (2 oboes or flutes) 1983; first performed Witten, 29 April 1984. Recorded (flute version) Attacca Babel 9056–3.
Monolog (bassoon) 1983–4; first performed Nice, 2 February 1985.
Duo (cello, harp or piano) 1984; first performed Ingelheim,

27 May 1984. Recorded col legno 5515/429 354-2.
Quintett (clarinet, string quartet) 1984, version for clarinet 1986; first performed Kusatsu, Japan, 24 August 1984. Recorded col legno 5515/429 354 2; Camerata 32 CM 70.
Li-Na im Garten (5 pieces for violin) 1984–5; first performed Berlin, 28 November 1985.
Rencontre (clarinet, harp or piano, cello) 1986; first performed Hitzacker, 2 August 1986. Recorded col legno 5515/429 354-2.
Quartet (2 piccolos, 4 flutes, 2 alto flutes, 2 bass flutes) 1986; first performed Berlin, 27 August 1986. Recorded Attacca Babel 9056–3; DIV 31007.
Quintet (flute, string quartet) 1986; first performed Paris, 17 January 1987.
Tapis (string quintet) 1987; first performed Mannheim, 20 November 1987. Recorded cpo 999 075-2.
In Balance (harp) 1987; first performed Hamburg, 8 April 1987.
Kontraste (2 pieces for violin) 1987; first performed Hamburg, 10 April 1987. Recorded Camerata 32 CM 70.
Pezzo fantasioso (2 flutes or oboes or clarinets or violins, with bass instrument—bass flute, bassoon, double bass, etc) 1988; first performed Chiusi, 10 July 1988. Recorded Attacca Babel 9056–3.
Quartet (flute, violin, cello, piano) 1988; first performed Erlangen, 1989.
Distanzen (flute, oboe, clarinet, bassoon, horn, string quintet) 1988; first performed Berlin, 9 October 1988.
Intermezzo (cello, accordion) 1988; first performed Erlangen, 1989.
String Quartet No 4 1988; first performed Wurzburg, 28 November 1988. Recorded cpo 999 075-2.
Contemplation (2 violas) 1988; first performed Berlin, 9 October 1988.
Sori (flute) 1988; first performed New York City, 7 November 1988.
Together (violin, double bass) 1989; first performed Aarhus, 28 April 1990.
Rufe (oboe, harp) 1989; first performed Ravensburg, 10 November 1989.
Kammerkonzert I 1990; first performed Amsterdam, 16 June 1990.
Kammerkonzert II 1990; first performed Berlin, 21 October 1990.
String Quartet No 5 1990.

Vocal/choral:

Om mani padme hum (cycle for soprano, baritone, chorus, orchedstra; Buddhist, translated Neumann and Rogosky) 1964; first performed Hannover, 30 January 1965.
Ein Schmetterlingstraum (mixed chorus, percussion ad lib; Ma Chi-Yuan) 1968; first performed Hamburg, 8 May 1969.
Namo (3 sopranos, orchestra; Buddhist texts) 1971, version for solo soprano, orchestra, 1975; first performed Berlin, 4 May 1971; solo version first performed Munster, 10 May 1976.
Gagok (voice, guitar, percussion) 1972, version for voice, harp, 1985; first performed Barcelona, 25 October 1972.
Memory (3 voices, percussion) 1974; first performed Rome, 3 May 1974.
Schamanengesange aus Geisterliebe (alto, chamber orchestraa; Kunz) 1969–70, orchestrated by Erwin Koch-Raphael 1977; first performed Berlin, 16 December, 1977.
Vom Tao (chorus from *Sim Tjong*; mixed chorus, organ, percussion) 1972, revised and expanded 1982; first performed Hamburg, 21 May 1976; revised version first performed Vienna, 6 November 1986.
An der Schwelle (baritone, female chorus, organ, flute, oboe, trumpet, trombone, 2 percussion; Haushofer) 1975; first performed Kassel, 5 April 1975.
Der weisse Mann (cantata for baritone, mixed chorus, orchestra; Salomo, Lao Tse) 1977; first performed Berlin, 9 June 1977.
Teile dich Nacht (soprano, flute, oboe, clarinet, bassoon, horn, percussion, harp or piano, strings; Sachs) 1980; first performed Witten, 26 April 1981. Recorded Kojima CLM 2002; Harmonia Mundi HM 855-2.
O Licht . . . (chorus, violin, percussion; Sachs, Buddhist texts) 1981; first performed Nuremberg, 21 June 1981.
Der Herr ist mein Hirte (chorus, trombone; Psalm 23, Sachs) 1981; first performed Stuttgart, 14 November 1982.

Opera:

Der Traum des Liu-Tung (Hans Rudelsberger and Winfried Fauernfeind, after Ma Chi-Yuan) 1965; first performed Berlin, 25 September 1965.
Traume (consists of *Der Traum des Liu-Tung* and *Die Witwe des Schmetterlings*) 1965–8; first performed Nuremberg, 23 February 1969.
Die Witwe des Schmetterlings / Butterfly Widow (Harald Kunz, after 16th-century Chinese tale) 1968; first performed Nuremberg, 23 February 1969; English version first performed Evanston, Illinois, 27 February 1970.
Geisterliebe (Kunz) 1969–70; first performed Kiel, 20 June 1971.
Sim Tjong (Kunz) 1971–2; first performed Munich, 1 August 1972.

PUBLICATIONS

On Yun: Luise Rinser, IY: *der verwundte Drache,* Frankfurt, 1977; Hans Werner Heister, Walter-Wolfgang Sparrer, *Der Komponist IY*, Munich, 1987.

* * *

Isang Yun's position in contemporary music is often attributed partly to his arrest, abduction and imprisonment by the south Korean regime in 1967. His sentence—for supposed spying—was reduced from life to 10 years and, after a petition signed by Stravinsky, Stockhausen, Boulez, Otto Klemperer and others, he was released in poor health after just two. Expressions of his suffering later featured in his works. In *Piri* for solo oboe or clarinet represents the voice of the prisoner (the Korean oboe referred to in the title has traditionally been considered an instrument of the soul). The extraordinary *Concerto for Cello and Orchestra* was inspired in jail when Yun heard a monk's wooden gong intoning to announce the death of a fellow prisoner. The choral piece *An der Schwelle* adds biblical verses—"Fear not for I am with you"—to a sonnet by Albrecht Haushofer in which the author considers suicide. Memories turn to politics in *Exemplum in memoriam Kwangju*, where Yun offers a large-scale orchestral piece that portrays a 1980 populist uprising, and its barbaric repression, in the south Korean city of Kwangju: "In *Exemplum*, I am a humble servent of the people who suffered. I take on their feelings and enable them to be expressed before the whole world."

The politics of Japanese colonialisation and its aftermath meant Yun became a successful composer only in middle age.

From 1956–9 he studied in Paris and Berlin—in the latter place with Josef Rufer and Boris Blacher. His *Musik für sieben Instrumente* was accepted for Darmstadt and his *Fünf Klavierstücke* was performed at Gaudeamus. While his third acknowledged piece, *String Quartet No 3*, demonstrates a mastery of European techniques, it is cast in the ascendent serial mould of its time, a mould which Yun then questioned. He doubted that the experiments of John Cage were worthwhile and suggested that strict dodecophony might also stifle creativity. The chamber piece *Loyang* and the pieces leading to *Reak* fleshed out a stylistic solution: Yun sought to create music which was neither Korean nor Western and yet which was both. *Loyang*, while adhering to serial techniques, in its contrasts suggests allegiance to what later becomes Yun's "central tone" practice: in East Asia tones have identity independent of melodic context, identity enhanced by ornamentation and dynamic changes. *Gasa* for violin and piano and *Garak* for flute and piano take titles from a Korean lyric song repertory and a term for "fingers of melody". Again, although serialism is retained, Yun begins to offer long and elastic melodies.

Both individual tones and elastic melodies were absorbed from Korean court music, and this is demonstrated best by *Reak*, a piece whose title refers to the Sino-Korean characters for such music (*Aak*). Premiered at Donaueschingen, *Reak* opens with a percussive clap, the director's *pak* (clappers) from Korean court ensembles. The large orchestra is divided into three blocks—strings (soft, steady), brass (brash, thrusting) and woodwind (flickering, uneasy)—a characteristic of Yun's music to this day (*Kammerkonzert I* recently provided confirmation). From the opening, each block builds a chord, each instrument either keeping one pitch or adding something reminiscent of court ornamentation (rising and falling tones, acciaccaturas, brief trills, and so on). The end is the climax. Strings, then winds, conclude *fortissimo*, the strings rising in pitch, and the percussion echoes the rattled ending of Korea's court ritual pieces. The blend of East and West is most apparent in *Muak*—the title means "dance music"—yet we would do well to remember that Yun's music is never overtly Korean in its orientation.

The opposition of blocks represents Yun's conception of *yin* (strings) and *yang* (brass), positive and negative, opposing yet complementary. *Piri* demonstrates, suggesting that the oboe goes between the two, representing—continuing with Chinese philosophy—the colour black, wind, and breathing. At the beginning, long, held pitches are introduced with a melismatic flurry and conclude with a gently rising portamento: again, tone identity from Korea. The streams of melodies which eventually build seem to come from the cosmos. Indeed, Yun has described music as an endless flow, a flow he taps into as he writes, then interrupts as he concludes.

During the 1970s, Yun continued to develop his style, moving away from serialism towards his "central tone" concept. Each central tone has its own character and is used to underpin a melisma or solo melody, or to strengthen or pivot orchestral movement. Juxtaposed, central tones offer contrasts or oppositions along the philosophical lines of *yin* and *yang*. And in the same vein, they create much of the energy (in Korean, *chi*) invested in the music. The 1980s saw more stylistic consolidation. The cosmic nature of music—that endless flow—gave ceaseless material, while Yun's poor health spurred him to prolific writing. Five Symphonies appeared annually from 1983 in a design which, if played in sequence, would create a single piece. *Symphony No 2* explores the world of timbre, taking individual tones and adding *yang* ornamentation, and creating central tones. In contrast *Symphony No 3* is more concerned with melody, exploring the opposing *yin* and *yang* nature of conflict in the three orchestral blocks. Taken together, these works demonstrate well how Yun continues to refine his own unique musical style.

—Keith Howard

Z

ZAIDEL-RUDOLPH, Jeanne. South African. Born in Pretoria, 9 July 1948. Educated at Pretoria High School for Girls, 1961–5; University of Pretoria, Brooklyn (under Johann Potgieter, Arthur Wegelen and Stefans Grove), 1966–79, B.Mus (*cum laude*), 1969; M.Mus. (*cum laude*), 1972; D.Mus., 1979; Royal College of Music, London, (piano under John Lill, composition under John Lambert, electronic music under Tristram Carey), advanced postgraduate diploma, 1973; studied (under Sir Peter Maxwell Davies), Dartington Summer Course, Devon, 1973; Hochsschule for Musik Hamburg (advanced composition under György Ligeti), 1974; Darmstadt Summer Course, 1974, 1976; also research in Boston, Massachusetts, 1977. Married Michael Rudolph, 14 September 1976; 4 daughters. Lecturer in harmony, counterpoint, composition, 1975–82, and senior lecturer in composition techniques and form, since 1985, University of the Witwatersrand, Johannesburg, temporary/part-time lecturer, University of Pretoria, 1980; head of music, Performing Arts Workshop, Johannesburg, 1983, 1984; piano recitalist, solist; permanent organist, Sydenham/Highlands North Synagogue. Recipient: piano Licentiate of Royal Schools of Music, London, 1969; piano Licentiate of the Trinity College, London, 1969; Fellowship of the Trinity College, London, 1979; Ernest Oppenheimer Memorial Trust Scholarships, 1979, 1973; University of South Africa Performers Licentiate, 1971; R.O. Morris and Cobbett Prize for composition, Royal College of Music, 1973; 1st prize (for *Tempus fugit*), Total Oil Music Competition for Original composition, 1986. Mailing address: 17 Thelma Crescent, Bagleyston, 2192 Johannesburg, South Africa.

Publishers: Seesaw Music Publishing, New York; S.A. Broadcasting Corporation, Private Bag XI, Auckland Park; UNISA (University of South Africa), P.O. Box 392, 0001 Pretoria, South Africa; Zaidel-Rudolph Publisher (address as above).

Symphonies/orchestral:

Concert Overture 1979.
Five Chassidic Melodies (small orchestra) 1981.
Construction Symphony (youth orchestra) 1985.
Fanfare Festival Overture 1985; first performed Johannesburg, 1986. Recorded EMCJ 4061831/4061834.
Tempus fugit 1986; first performed Johannesburg, October 1986. Recorded EMCJ 4061831/4061834.
At the End of the Rainbow (symphonic poem) 1988.
Symphony for Wind, Brass, and Strings 1990.

Chamber/instrumental:

Sonata No 1 (piano) 1969; first performed Cape Town, 1976. Recorded EMCJ 4061831/4061834.
Seven Variations on an Original Theme (piano) 1971.
Kaleidoscope (wind instruments, percussion) 1971. Recorded EMCJ 4061831/4061834.
Canonetta for Four (trumpet, bassoon, viola, vibraphone) 1973.
Reaction (piano, cello, percussion) 1973; first performed London, 1973.
Tango for Tim (guitar) 1973.
Three Dimensions (piano) 1974. Recorded EMCJ 4061831/4061834.
Chamber Concertino (11 instruments) 1979.
The Fugue That Flew Away (flute, piano) 1981; first performed Johannesburg, 1981.
Three Chassidic Pieces (flute, violin, cello) 1982.
Four "Minim" (cello, piano) 1982; first performed Johannesburg, 1983.
Brass Quintet—and All That Jazz (2 trumpets, horn, trombone, tuba) 1983.
Margana (flute, violin, cello, 2 percussion) 1985; first performed Pretoria, October 1985.
Mereko (marimba) 1985; incomplete.
Virtuoso I (piano) 1987. Recorded EMCJ 4061831/4061834.
Mixed Feelings: For Sara (piano) 1988.
Mosaic (piano) 1989.
Masada (string quartet, bassoon) 1989; first performed Potchefstroom, 16 May 1989.
Five African Sketches (guitar) 1990.
Sextet 1990–1.

Vocal/choral:

Settings of a Selection of Afrikaans Poems (soprano, piano) 1968.
Dialogue of Self and Soul (speech chorus, 8 soloists) 1971.
Setting of the Swaziland National Anthem (chorus, piano) 1974.
Five Pieces (soprano, woodwind quartet) 1976; first performed Cape Town, 1976.
Boy on a Swing (female choir, piano, percussion) 1983.
Back to Basics (narrator, piano, prepared piano) 1983; first performed Johannesburg, July 1983.
It's a Woman's World (choir, piano) 1985.

Opera:

Animal Farm (overture, prologue, act I) 1978.
A Rage in a Cage (rock opera for soloists, chorus, chamber group) 1983; first performed Johannesburg, 1983.

Other:

The River People—Abantubomlambo (ballet; chamber orchestra, electronic tape, baritone) 1987; first performed Durban, 1987. Recorded L4 BCP 1832.
African Dream (feature film score; electronic tape) 1988; first performed Johannesburg, 1988.
Psalms of David—Hallel 1989.

Arrangements for overseas visiting singers of religious music, Avraham Fried, Mordechai ben David.

PUBLICATIONS

By Zaidel-Rudolph: "First International Congress on Women in Music", in *S.A. Journal of Musicology*, 1, 1981; "Thomas Rajna: Preludes for Piano", in *S.A. Journal of Musicology*, 8–9, 1988–9; "A Tribute to Witold Lutosławski", in *Musicus*, 17(2), 1989.

On Zaidel-Rudolph: Penelope Jane Clough, "JZ—A Contemporary Woman in Music", dissertation, University of the Witwatersrand, Johannesburg, 1981; D. Springer, "Rainier, Gerstman, Z-R—Their Lives, Times and Music", dissertation, University of the Witwatersrand, Johannesburg, 1984; Lea Lesicnik, "An Analytical Study of *Four Minim* for Cello and Piano by JZ-R", dissertation, University of South Africa, Pretoria, 1985; Margaret Nabarro, "JZ-R", in *Scenaria*, November 1985; "*Scenaria* Interviews JZ-R", in *Scenaria*, 89, June 1988.

Jeanne Zaidel-Rudolph comments:

My work so far can be divided into three periods: the early student period from 1965 to 1973, mostly devoted to piano composition; the five years from 1974 to 1979 dominated by György Ligeti, both as a teacher and as an influence; a third period blending Western and African influences in an attempt to integrate ethnic and folk elements found in African music with a mature symphonic style.

Composing in a changing South Africa, at the meeting point of First and Third World cultures, is *very* exciting. Nothing is as it seems: "primitive" is complex; "sophisticated" is simplistic.

The essence of my own music remains the serious search for spiritual integrity.

* * *

Jeanne Zaidel-Rudolph is one of South Africa's foremost composers. Her oeuvre is wide-ranging in its styles and genres; yet it is expressive of a highly individual compositional voice.

Early works reveal her interest in the experiments of the post-World War II avant-garde, particularly those of her teacher, the Hungarian composer György Ligeti. From him she inherited her love for unusual and bold instrumental colourings, as well as a predilection for linear rather than vertical pitch structuring.

Although a student composition, the Piano Sonata of 1969 shows great conceptual clarity in its extrapolation of the essential structural processes of the classical sonata form. *Kaleidoscope*, is strictly serial in construction; but it is its exotic timbral and textural juxtapositions rather than its intellectual rigour that determine its aural surface.

The piano has remained a compositional catalyst for Zaidel-Rudolph. In *Three Dimensions* she uses the instrument both to make a personal statement in relation to the world around her and to explore different indigenous and "environmental" sonic materials.

The Fugue That Flew Away, for flute and piano, is a lighthearted parody of Baroque contrapuntal techniques. The opening fugue subject (a note row) is cast in a wide-ranging pointillistic pitch frame, with Webernesque timbral and dynamic markings. There follows a veritable essay in conventional fugal techniques, until the flute, like a bird released from its cage, flies dizzily out of control, despite the piano's efforts to bring it to fugal order.

However, Zaidel's most important works of the 1980s are characterized by their fusion of indigenous African materials with contemporary Western syntax. *Margana*, scored for flute, violin, cello and percussion, incorporates elements of African responsorial chant. The *Fanfare Festival Overture*, commissioned to celebrate the 1985 Johannesburg centenary, paints a lively sonic picture of a thriving first-world/third-world metropolis, erupting at its apex into a coil-sprung marimba (African xylophone) solo, that is taken up by the whole orchestra in a vibrant celebration of Africa.

Tempus fugit explores images of time in relation to contemporary Southern Africa. These images are given aural expression primarily as a montage of metres, polyrhythms and accentuations; however the work's harmonic, textural and timbral conceptions also reflect the literal and metaphorical layerings of time, linked by the evocative colour and idiom of the marimba.

Zaidel-Rudolph's ballet, *The River People—Abantubomlambo*, premiered in 1987, concerns the mythical long-haired river people who protect the morals of the tribe, the birds who are an ill omen, and the python who represents the supernatural powers of the ancestors. The music of *The River People* pulses with the rhythms of Africa, in complex metrical juxtapositions, additive note values and polyrhythmic layerings. But, as is generally the case in Zaidel-Rudolph's music, it is its colouristic aspect that is most distinctive. An electronic soundscape provides the basis, ranging from the strange insinuating atmospheres of white noise to simulations of a wide range of Western and African instruments. Above it are imposed a choir and solo baritone voice, which both articulate the narrative aspect of the music and emphasize its concern with humanity.

In the late 1980s and early 1990s Zaidel-Rudolph has become increasingly concerned with modern man's connection with a historical and mythical past and his need for spiritual generation. The symphonic poem, *At The End Of The Rainbow* was inspired by the biblical account of The Flood, and is an aural metaphor for the inherent sin in man as well as his search for redemption. A chamber work, *Masada*, for string quartet and bassoon, is a vivid sonic account of the bitter meshing of tragedy and courage of that most painful episode in the history of the Jewish people. And yet while its modal inflections, nasal timbral overlay, and alternations of driving with rhapsodic rhythms have a palpably middle-Eastern flavour, it too is ultimately a contemplation of man's spiritual essence.

Zaidel-Rudolph's conceptual and sonic worlds are thus primarily concerned with the deeper and more universal aspects of human existence, but she also has a sense both for the contemporary and the popular: her rock opera *A Rage in a Cage* drew enthusiastic audiences both in South Africa and Israel.

—Mary Rörich

ZHOU Long. Chinese. Born in Beijing, 8 July 1953. Educated at Central Conservatory of Music, Beijing, 1978–83, B.A.; Columbia University, New York City, since 1985. Married Chen Yi, 20 July 1983. Composer and conductor, ZhangJiaKou Song and Dance Company, Hebei, China, 1973–8; composer, China Broadcasting Symphony Orchestra, Beijing, 1983–5. Recipient: 2nd and 1st prize, 4th Chinese National Composition Competition, 1983, 1985; 1st prize,

International Ensemble Composition Competition, Monchengladbach, 1990. Mailing address: 500 West 122nd Street, Apartment 2G, New York, New York 10027, U.S.A.

Publisher: none.

Symphonies/orchestral:

Fishjerman's Song 1981; first performed Beijing, 1982. Recorded China Record Company AL 52.
Dong Shi (ballet suite) 1983. Recorded China Record Company AL 52.
Guang Ling San Symphony 1983; first performed Beijing, 1983. Recorded China Record Company AL 52.
Chinese Rhapsody 1984; first performed Beijing, 1985.
Da Qu (percussion concerto) 1989; first performed Hong Kong, 1991.
The Defeated King of Chu Taibei (pipa concerto) 1991.
Secluded Orchid (erhu concerto) 1991.

Chamber/instrumental:

Song of the Ch'in (string quartet) 1983; first performed Berkeley, Calfornia, 1985.
Wu Kui (piano) 1983; first performed Berkeley, California, 1985.
Valley Stream (Chinese quartet) 1984; first performed Belo Horizonte, 1985. Recorded CRC RL 29.
Su (flute, ch'in) 1984; first performed Belo Horizonte, 1985. Recorded CRC RL 29.
Green (flute, pipa) 1984; first performed Scotland, 1989. Recorded CRC RL 29.
Triptych of Bell-Drum Music 1984; first performed Beijing, 1984. Recorded CRC RL 29.
Taiping Drum 1985; first performed New York City. 1986.
The Moon Rising High (Chinese ensemble) 1985; first performed New York City, 1986.
Wu Ji (piano, tape) 1986; first performed Illinois, 1988.
Soul (string quartet) 1986; first performed Illinois, 1988.
Heng (Chinese ensemble) 1987; first performed New York City, 1987.
Ding (clarinet, percussion, double bass) 1989; first performed Monchengladbach, Germany, 1991.
Dhyana (flute, clarinet, violin, cello) 1990; first performed Sapporo, Japan, 1991.

Vocal/choral:

Words of the Sun (unaccompanied chorus) 1984; first performed Beijing, 1984.
Shi Jing (cantata for soprano, large ensemble) 1989; first performed Boston, 1990.
Li Sao (cantata for soprano, large ensemble) 1989; first performed Boston, 1990.
Ballad of the Sea (soprano, piano) 1990; first performed Toronto, 1990.

Other:

The Comsic Light (electronic ballet score) 1984; first performed Beijing, 1984.
Dan Huang (electronic dance score) 1986; first performed New York City, 1987.
The Lute Song (theatre music) 1989; first performed Tanglewood, Massachusetts, 1989.
The Bacchae (theatre music) 1989; first performed New York City, 1990.
Sheng Sheng Man (dance music) 1989; first performed New York City, 1989.
The Tablet (dance music) 1989; first performed New York City, 1990.

PUBLICATIONS

By Zhou: [works published and annotated in] *Musical Works* journal—*Valley Stream*, 1(121), 1984; *Wu Kui*, 3(127), 1985; *Song Under the Moon*, 4(132), 1986, and in *Journal of the Central Conservatory of Music—Song of the Ch'in*, 2(15), 1984; *Triptych of Bell-Drum Music*, 1(18), 1985; *Su*, 1(22), 1986; *Ding*, 2(35), 1989.

On Zhou: Fan Zu-yin, "ZL's String Quartet *Song of the Ch'in*", in *Journal of the Central Conservatory of Music*, 4, 1984; Jin Jian-min, "Amazing Taste: An Appreciation of the String Quartet *Song of the Ch'in*", in *People's Music*, 10, 1985; Fan Zu-yin, "Critical study of *Triptych of Bell-Drum Music*", in *Journal of the Central Conservatory of Music*, 4, 1985; Wu Gan-bo, "New Wave Chinese Music: *Valley Stream*", in *Daily News* (Hong Kong), 7 February 1986; Fan Zu-yin, "Rich Traditional Soil Brought up the New Seedling: A Critical Study of ZL's Compositions", in *People's Music*, 1, 1988; Vai Meng Lei, "*Wu Ji* for Piano and Synthesized Sounds", doctoral dissertation, University of Illinois, Urbana, 1990.

Zhou Long comments:

I am very interested in different approaches to creativity. My own preference is to abstract the quintessences of various cultures and then assimilate them into new work rather than to make scissors-and-paste imitations which are supposed to "carry on and develop traditional culture".

* * *

Zhou Long was born into an artistic family. Strongly influenced by his parents, who painted and taught vocal music, he began piano lessons when still very young. Unfortunately, he was unable to escape the fate of most of his generation in China whose education was stopped during the Cultural Revolution. He was sent to a state farm in a remote area where the natural scene—roaring winds and fierce land fires—made a profound impression on him. Though life was very hard, music helped him to survive for nearly four years. When the school system was resumed in 1977, Zhou enrolled in the Beijing Central Conservatory to restart his professional composition training; he also studied musical theory, conducting and choral composition. After graduation, he worked as resident composer with the China Broadcasting Symphony Orchestra for two years.

Zhou's enforced close contact with the Chinese motherland has meant that he is profoundly influenced by Chinese traditional culture; he has studied Chinese music systematically at the Conservatory and in the field and many of his pieces are inspired by traditional sources; his prize-winning string quartet *Song of the Ch'in* is one clear example. In writing Chinese instrumental music Zhou has experimented with different instrumental combinations and has dealt a blow to the established formulas that have prevailed in Chinese music over the last 30 years. The first collection of such pieces employing new ideas and experimental compositional techniques was released by the China Record Company in 1984 and there have been successful recitals on concert stage, radio and television.

Since emigrating to New York in 1985, Zhou has been more directly concerned with the merging of Eastern and Western cultures. Much as Buddhism crept into Chinese culture during the Tang dynasty, Zhou has been incorporating Western compositional values and has been writing music for Western chamber ensembles. The most recent of these—*Wu Ji*, *Heng*, *Ding* and *Dhyana*—are related to Buddhist thought and use a combination of instrumental and electronic resources. The literal meaning of *ding* (or *samadhi* in Sanskrit) is the perfect absorption of thought into the object of meditation and this is the key to Zhou's aesthetic. The quintet *Dhyana* derives its inspiration from the "cultivation of thought" in Buddhism. Zhou bases his compositional approach on the concept of "knowing with a clear mind", a shift from existence into nothingness. There are complex textures in the piece, and the performers are required to combine a high degree of concentration with great spiritual awareness.

In his cantatas *Shi Jing* and *Li Sao*, Zhou experimented in setting Chinese words to a combination of Beijing opera recitative and free atonal writing. In the recent *Da Qu* for percussion and Chinese orchestra, he took an ancient Chinese song and dance form and re-applied the principles of folk percussion ensemble music to his own distinctive ends.

—Chen Yi

ZIMMER, Ján. Slovak. Born in Ružomberk, northern Slovakia, 16 May 1926. Educated at State Conservatory, Bratislava (organ, piano and composition under Suchon), 1941–8; further composition study, High School of Music, Budapest, 1948–9; Salzburg Seminar in American Studies, 1949. Divorced; son Richard is chief conductor, State Philharmonia, Kosice. Music manager, Czech Broadcasting corporation, Bratislava, 1945–8; professor of piano and composition, State Conservatory, Bratislava, 1948–52, subsequently demoted and redeployed to manufacturing industry by Communist authorites; full-time composer, since 1952, but many works not published. Mailing address: Letecka 10, 831 03 Bratislava, Czechoslovakia.

Publisher: Slovenksy hubodny fond [Slovak Music Fund], Fučikova 29, 811 02, Bratislava, Czecholsovakia.

Symphonies/orchestral:

Piano Concerto No 1 Op 5 1949; first performed Bratislava, 1950.
Concerto grosso Op 7 (2 pianos, 2 string orchestras, percussion) 1951; first performed Bratislava, 1952.
Piano Concerto No 2 Op 10 1952; first performed Bratislava, 1953.
Suite: The Tatras I Op 11 1952; first performed Bratislava, 1954.
Violin Concerto Op 15 1953; first performed Bratislava, 1954.
Rhapsody Op 18 (piano, orchestra) 1955; first performed Bratislava, 1955.
Concertino Op 19 (piano, strings) 1955; first performed Bratislava, 1956.
Symphony No 1 Op 21 1955; first performed Bratislava, 1956.
Suite: The Tatras II Op 25 1956; first performed Bratislava, 1957.
Symphony No 2 Op 26 1958; first performed Bratislava, 1959.
Concerto for Organ, Strings and Percussion Op 27 1958; first performed Bratislava, 1958.
Piano Concerto No 3 Op 29 1958; first performed Bratislava, 1959.
Symphony No 3 Op 33 1959; first performed Bratislava, 1960.
Symphony No 4 Op 37 (soprano, tenor, mixed chorus, orchestra) 1959; first performed Prague, 1961.
Strecno (symphonic poem) 1959.
Piano Concerto No 4 Op 36 1960; first performed Bratislava, 1961.
Symphony No 5 Op 44 1961; first performed Bratislava, 1962.
Concerto da camera Op 47 (oboe, strings) 1961; first performed Bratislava, 1961.
Piano Concerto No 5 Op 50 (piano—left hand, orchestra) 1964; first performed Bratislava, 1965.
Symphony No 6: Improvisata Op 51 1965; first performed Bratislava, 1966.
Symphony No 7 Op 54 1966; first performed Prague, 1967.
Concerto for Two Pianos and Orchestra Op 57 1967; first performed Bratislava, 1968.
French Suite Op 62 (chamber orchestra) 1968; first performed Bratislava, 1969.
Songs Without Words Op 67 (string orchestra) 1970; first performed Bratislava, 1971.
Symphony No 8 Op 68 1971; first performed Bratislava, 1971.
Piano Concerto No 6 Op 71 1972; first performed Bratislava, 1973.
Symphony No 9: Dedicated to the 30th Anniversary of the Slovak National Uprising Op 72 1973; first performed Bratislava, 1974.
Music from Old Bratislava Op 80 1975; first performed Bratislava, 1976.
Symphony No 10: Hommage à J. Haydn Op 82 1979; first performed Bratislava, 1977.
Concerto Prelude Op 96 1981; first performed Bratislava, 1981.
Symphony No 11 Op 98 1981; first performed Kosice, 1982.
Chamber Concerto Op 104 (chamber organ, strings) 1984; first performed Bratislava, 1984.
Piano Concerto No 7 Op 106 1986; first performed Bratislava, 1988.
Symphony No 12 Op 107 1986; first performed Kosice, 1987.
Concerto Poliphonico Op 108 1987; first performed Bratislava, 1988.
Three Dancing Pieces Op 112 (piano, orchestra) 1988; first performed Bratislava, 1989.
Concertino for Viola and Chamber Orchestra Op 117 1989.

Chamber/instrumental:

Sonata No 1 Op 4 (piano) 1948; first performed Bratislava, 1948.
Suite: The Tatras I Op 11 (version for piano) 1952. Recorded Opus 9111 0039.
Prelude and Fugue Op 13b (organ) 1952; first performed Bratislava, 1952.
Sonata No 1 Op 16 (2 pianos) 1954; first performed Bratislava, 1955.
Concerto for Piano Without Orchestra Op 23 1956; first performed Bratislava, 1956.
Suite: The Tatras II Op 25 (version for piano) 1956.
Suite Op 30 (violin, piano) 1958; first performed Bratislava, 1958.
Sonata Op 31 (viola, piano) 1958; first performed Bratislava, 1958.
Phantasy and Toccata Op 32 (organ) 1958; first performed Bratislava, 1958.

Sonata No 2 Op 35 (2 pianos) 1958; first performed Bratislava, 1959.
Two Slovak Dances Op 38 (violin, piano) 1959; first performed Bratislava, 1961.
String Quartet 1960.
Concerto in D Op 42 (organ) 1960; first performed Bratislava, 1960.
Sonata No 2 Op 45 (piano) 1961; first performed Bratislava, 1962.
Sonata No 3 Op 53 (2 pianos) 1965; first performed Bratislava, 1965.
Sonata No 3 Op 45 (piano) 1966; first performed Bratislava, 1967.
Wind Quintet Op 61 1968.
Sonata No 1 Op 65 (organ) 1970; first performed Bratislava, 1971.
Sonata No 4 Op 69 (piano) 1971; first performed Bratislava, 1972.
Sonata No 4 Op 73 (2 pianos) 1972; first performed Bratislava, 1973.
Two Romantic Pieces Op 81 (piano) 1975; first performed Bratislava, 1975.
Ballade and Burlesque Op 84 (viola) 1976; first performed Bratislava, 1976.
Poetical Sonata Op 85 (violin, piano) 1976; first performed Bratislava, 1977.
Three Small Preludes Op 86 (organ) 1977; first performed Bratislava, 1978.
Variations Op 87 (2 violins, viola) 1977.
Sonata No 5 Op 90 (piano) 1978; first performed Bratislava, 1979.
Sonata Op 91 (flute) 1978.
Trio Op 93 (flute, violin, piano) 1979.
Sonata No 6 Op 94 (piano) 1979; first performed Bratislava, 1981.
Sonata No 2 Op 97 (organ) 1981; first performed Bratislava, 1982.
String Quartet No 2 Op 100 1982.
Bagatelles Op 103 (piano) 1983; first performed Bratislava, 1985.
Introductions and Toccata Op 109 (piano) 1986; first performed Bratislava, 1989.
Sonata No 7 Op 113 (piano) 1987; first performed Bratislava, 1988.
Four Pieces Op 116 (piano—4 hands) 1988; first performed Bratislava, 1989.

Vocal/choral:

Spring in the Valley Op 3 (cycle of songs for soprano, piano) 1947.
Magnificat Op 9 (cantata for mixed chorus, orchestra) 1952; suppressed by Communist authorities; unperformed.
Peace Op 14 (symphonic poem for mixed chorus, orchestra) 1954.
Holubica pokoja / The Dove of Peace (cantata) 1960.
Three Songs (voice, piano; Wolker) 1961.
Four Motets 1967.
Death Shall Have No Dominion Op 60 (oratorio for soloists, mixed chorus, orchestra) 1968.
Emerald Op 64 (cycle of songs for soprano, piano) 1969.
Songs of Spring Op 67 (tenor, piano) 1970.
Svatoboj Op 75 (Slovak madrigal; after Stur) 1973.
Phantasy Op 83 (male chorus, piano, orchestra) 1975.

Opera/dramatic:

Heracles Op 70 (opera ballet) 1972; broadcast 1982.
Oedipus Rex Op 48 1973; broadcast 1974.
The Broken Line Op 76 1974.

Other:

Film music: *Banska Stiavnica*; *Grafik Hloznik*; *Pionieri*; *Geologicka cinnost ladu*; *Kysucky lekar*; *Na brehoch Dunajca*; *Narodna galeria*; *Ocami kamery*; *Samo Chalupka*; *Sestra*; *Pamatniky slavy*; *Tovaren na Dunaji*; *Trat volna*; *Travetin*; *Vlna je na horach*; *Spisske mesta*; *Kamena kronika Bratislavy*; *V hodine dvanostej*; *Jergus Lapin*; *Bratia*; *Organ*; *Zivy bic*; *Generacia*; *Stopy na Sitne*; *Skryty pramen* (all orchestral).

Ján Zimmer comments:

My musical philosophy is based on a metaphysical and idealistic exploration of our personal lives and of the world in which we live.

* * *

Whatever his emphasis on solid technical construction, Ján Zimmer's music always makes a direct appeal to the listener's emotions. His attention to form is meticulous and thorough and his ideas are always carefully controlled, directed to the main arguments of a piece. He uses melody, harmony and counterpoint in a quite traditional way with a strong influence from all the classic periods of European music, from the Baroque to Romanticism; but Zimmer is also concerned with the individual possibilities and specific properties of instruments, and this concern also plays a prominent role.

In character, Zimmer is impulsive, and this is the quality of much of his music as well. His compositions are full of dramatic tension (even in lyrical passages) but even when he is alternating moods quite freely, he manages to sustain a consistently balanced form. He is not by nature an experimenter; though he has dabbled to some extent with twelve-tone composition and its four basic variations, he does quite freely and undogmatically, preferring on the whole a kind of motivic development in which the formal structure of a piece is made absolutely specific. Though Zimmer's basic orientation is toward "pure" or "absolute" music, he is frequently moved—either directly or indirectly—by extra-musical events and experiences, and, of course, by earlier musics.

His compositional method has remained fairly fixed and consistent from the outset, developing and maturing slowly, rather than undergoing dramatic revelatory shifts. Zimmer's earliest compositions were for piano—on which he is an expert performer—and the instrument has remained central to his interests. There are now seven piano sonatas and seven piano concertos; they share a fresh inventiveness, are often technically demanding and require considerable stamina from the performer.

Zimmer has now also completed 12 symphonies. Solidly constructed and unrelentingly dramatic, with a colourful approach to instrumentation, they are by no means always conventionally resolved, either in the number of movements or their arrangement within the overall architecture, but this is only part of their considerable appeal. Folkloric elements are implicit rather than directly quoted; each of the symphonies—even the choral Fourth—develops its own internal resources with impressive enterprise and cohesion.

In his organ works Zimmer develops the traditions of Baroque and classical composition—voice-leading, counterpoint, sonata form—in a lively and individual way, enriching tradition rather than slavishly following it. The results are highly expressive and unmistakably individual.

Zimmer's vocal compositions combine demanding solo

parts with complex and richly developed piano accompaniments. In the *Four Motets* and elsewhere, he simplifies his musical language as much as possible in order to achieve a tremendous concentration and depth of utterance. He has written extensively for film and played a pioneering role in the development of television opera in Eastern Europe. His work with and for children is appropriately acknowledged even at times when his mainstream composition has been brutally marginalised. Zimmer is a courageous and single-minded composer, a major figure in the Slovak tradition and a model of artistic resolve in deeply troubled times.

—Brian Morton

ZOHRABIAN, Ashot. Armenian. Born in Yerevan, 29 January 1945. Educated at Music School, Yerevan, 1961–5; Sogomon Komitas State Conservatory, Yerevan (composition under Grigory Egiazaryan), 1965–71. Married Panian Larisa in 1971; 2 children. Lecturer in music, State Conservatory, Yerevan, since 1972. Mailing address: Norskii massiv I, 48/49 kv 11, 375056 Yerevan, Armenia.

Publisher: Leduc, Paris.

Symphonies/orchestral:

Variations 1971; first performed Yerevan, 1972.
Symphonic Poem 1975.
Elegy (concerto for strings) 1979.
An Offering to Metsarents (string quartet, chamber orchestra) 1981.
Symphonia Metsaroz (flute, 2 oboes, 2 horns, chamber orchestra) 1985; first performed Yerevan, 1986.
Violin Concerto (chamber orchestra) 1989; first performed Yerevan, 1991.

Chamber/instrumental:

Piano Quintet 1968.
Three Pieces (2 flutes, oboe, 2 clarinets, piano) 1969.
Septet (2 flutes, 2 oboes, 2 clarinets, piano) 1970.
Boomerang Games: Book 1 (flute, oboe, clarinet, string quartet, piano) 1972; first performed Yerevan, 1973.
Boomerang Games: Book 2 (chamber ensemble) 1973; first performed Yerevan, 1973.
Sonata No 1 (cello, piano) 1975; first performed Yerevan, 1975.
Sonata No 2 (cello, piano) 1977; first performed Yerevan, 1977.
Sonata (piano) 1980; first performed Yerevan, 1983.
Elegy (6 violins, 3 violas, 3 cellos) 1982; first performed Yerevan, 1982.
Serenade (flute, oboe, clarinet, bassoon, trumpet, trombone, horn, piano, 2 violins, viola, cello, double bass) 1983; first performed Moscow, 1983.
Chant Matinal (wind quintet) 1984; first performed Prague, 1984.

Vocal/choral:

Circles (cycle for voice, bass flute, oboe, clarinet, piano; Metsarents, Varuzhan) 1972.
Madrigal (voice, chamber ensemble; Metsarents) 1972.
The Red Loaves (song cycle for voice, chamber ensemble; Metsarents) 1973.
Three Poems by Metsarents (mezzo-soprano, 2 violins, cello, piano) 1983.
Night Songs (cycle to words by Varuzhan and Metsarents) 1985.

PUBLICATIONS

On Zohrabian: Svetlana Sarkisyan, "Composer AZ", in *Music in the USSR*, 2, 1984; Tatjana Porwoll, "Schwingungen des Kosmos. Zeitgenossische Musik in Armenien", in *Musik-Texte*, 32, 1989; Svetlana Sarkisyan, "Bekenntnis zur armenischen Tradition bei AZ", in *Sowjetische Musik*, 1990.

* * *

The late 1960s and early 1970s were a period of profound self-examination in Armenian music, a period when new ideas began to be absorbed and fundamentally new directions undertaken. Ashot Zohrabian was at the time one of a group of young composers searching for their own musical language, and for an identifiable place in the continuum of modern music. The questions he was asking were those that occupied his young and not so young colleagues: how should Armenian music develop? What traditions of the past and what trends of the present should it accept or discard?

Zohrabian concentrated on instrumental music from the outset of his career, showing a marked preference for chamber genres. While still a pupil of Professor Grigory Egiazaryan at the Komitas Conservatory in Yerevan, Zohrabian began experimenting with different instrumental combinations, confining hiself to chamber music in order to be able to concentrate on every detail, polish his musical language, and attain the profound inner harmony he values so highly. These qualities are evident in almost all his work since.

Like a researcher in his laboratory, Zohrabian was never satisfied with preliminary results, but repeated his experiments in his desire to grasp the fundamental laws and values of musical process and to devise ways of making outworn techniques breathe again. Quite simply, he was seeking forms adequate to the expression of his ideas, and in some of his student works he achieved some convincing solutions. Particularly successful were the *Septet* for woodwinds and piano, the song cycle *Circles*, the first of several pieces to words by Metsarents and Varuzhan, and its successor *The Red Loaves* (the two pieces can be performed together as a solo cantata).

His ideas found their most graphic realisation in the two sets of *Boomerang Games* for instrumental ensemble, which were written some time after his graduation. Performed in Yerevan and at the Centre Georges Pompidou in Paris, they summed up almost seven years of restless inquiry. Their mosaic texture, elaborate rhythmic patterns and what may be described as a rarefied musical atmosphere was to be characteristic of Zohrabian's later works as well, though these tend to be free of his former harshness and project a greater expressiveness and lyricism. As time goes by, Zohrabian's music acquires a more natonalist coloration.

The lyrical and expressive aspects of his approach are particularly in evidence in his piano and two cello sonatas, and it is noteworthy that he called his 1979 concerto for string orchestra *Elegy*. This has been one of his most successful works; after its Yerevan premiere, it was performed in Byelorussia, Moscow, Tbilisi and the Baltic Republics. Its appeal can be attributed not only to its remarkable stylistic purity and exquisite finish of form, but also to its meditative quality and lyricism.

The imagery of the *Elegy* is also present—albeit treated somewhat differently—in *An Offering to Metsarents* for string quartet and chamber orchestra, a work favourable received at the Plenary Session of the Armenian Union of Composers. In his inspired tribute to an original Armenian poet who lived in the late 19th century, Zohrabian has managed to produce music that virtually sparkles with fascinating instrumental colours.

Zohrabian has reached artistic maturity with a respectable number of published works to his credit. His compositions have been performed by the likes of cellist Medea Abramyan and the Yerevan Chamber Orchestra. He is an original talent, writing accessible and very beautiful music, which is nonetheless demanding on performer and listener alike.

—Svetlana Sarkisyan

ZWILICH, Ellen Taaffe. American. Born in Miami, Florida, 30 April 1939. Educated at Florida State University, Tallahassee (under John Boda and Carlisle Floyd), B.M., 1956, M.M., 1962; Juilliard School of Music, New York City (composition under Elliott Carter and Roger Sessions), D.M.A., 1975; also studied violin under Richard Burgin and Ivan Galamian. Married Joseph Zwilich, 22 June 1969. College teacher; violinist, American Symphony Orchestra (under Leopold Stokowski); independent composer. Recipient: Marion Freschl Prize, 1971, 1972, 1975; Elizabeth Sprague Coolidge Chamber Music Prize, 1974; Gold Medal (for *Sonata in Three Movements*), 26th Annual G.B. Viotti Composition Competition, 1975; Guggenheim Fellowship, 1980–1; Ernst von Dohnanyi Citation, Florida State University, 1981; Pulitzer Prize (for *Symphony No 1: Three Movements for Orchestra*), 1983 [first female winner]; award, American Academy of Arts and Letters, 1984; Arturo Toscanini Music Critics Award (for recording of *Symphony No 1*), 1986; 3 prizes, Florida Composers League. Mailing address: 600 West 246th Street, Riverdale, New York 10471, U.S.A.

Publishers: Margun; Merion/Presser; Music Associates of America.

Symphonies/orchestral:

Symposium 1973.
Symphony No 1: Three Movements for Orchestra 1982.
Prologue and Variations (string orchestra) 1983.
Celebration 1984.
Symphony No 2: Cello Symphony 1985.
Concerto grosso (after Handel, *Sonata in D* for violin and continuo) 1985; first performed Washington, D.C., 1985.
Concerto for Piano and Orchestra 1986.
Images (2 pianos, orchestra) 1986.
Symbolon 1988; first performed Leningrad, 1988.
Concerto for Trombone and Orchestra 1988; first performed Chicago, 1989.
Concerto for Bass Trombone, Strings, Timpani and Cymbals 1989.
Concerto for Flute 1990.
Concerto for Oboe 1990.

Chamber/instrumental:

Sonata in Three Movements (violin, piano) 1973–4.
String Quartet 1974.
Clarino Quartet (4 trumpets) 1977.
Chamber Symphony (flute/piccolo, clarinet/bass clarinet, violin, viola, cello, piano) 1979.
String Trio 1982.
Divertimento (flute, clarinet, violin, cello) 1983.
Fantasy (harpsichord) 1983.
Intrada (flute/piccolo, clarinet, violin, cello, piano) 1983.
Chamber Concerto (trumpet, flute/piccolo, bass clarinet/clarinet, double bass, piano, percussion) 1984.
Double Quartet (strings) 1984.
Trio (piano, violin, cello) 1987.
Praeludium (organ) 1987; first performed Boston, 1988.
Clarinet Quintet 1990.

Vocal/choral:

Einsame Nacht (song cycle for baritone, piano; Hesse) 1971.
Im Nebel (alto, piano; Hesse) 1972.
Trompeten (soprano, piano; Trakl) 1974.
Emlekezet (soprano, piano; Petofi) 1978.
Passages (soprano, flute/alto flute/piccolo, clarinet/bass clarinet, violin, viola, cello, percussion; Ammons) 1981; orchestrated 1982.
Thanksgiving Song (SATB chorus, piano) 1986.

Other:

Tanzspiel (ballet; orchestra) 1987.

PUBLICATIONS

On Zwilich: Tim Page, "The music of ETZ", in *New York Times Magazine*, 14 July 1985.

* * *

Ellen Taaffe Zwilich vaulted into prominence among American composers by winning the Pulitzer Prize for Music in 1983 for her *Symphony No 1*. Since then her career has developed with remarkable speed by way of commissions, recordings, critical commentary, lectures and a steady stream of performances. Her catalogue has grown rapidly, exhibiting a concentration on music for orchestra that reflects the importance of that medium in the work of so many American composers.

Her First Symphony, a terse work lasting a little over 17 minutes, is cast in three movements. Like others of Zwilich's multi-movement works the Symphony shows a predilection for the long lyric line, frequent ostinatos and pedal-points at times suggesting minimalist procedures, clean-limbed and uncomplicated orchestration and an overall tone of seriousness that manages to avoid both pretension and psuedo-profundity.

Her style is direct, tonal yet untraditional, rhythmically inventive and always appealing to the ear and distinctly personal. If it can be connected to American music of the past, perhaps its nearest ancestor might be the robust, forthright music of such American masters as Roy Harris, Walter Piston, the early Roger Sessions, one of Zwilich's mentors, and others who came to prominence in the 1930s. It is an honorable tradition in American music, especially for its address to a wider audience than the university-based clique that so often has seemed the only market for the music of recent decades.

Since her *Symphony No 1* Zwilich has enlarged her catalogue with the *Prologue and Variations* for orchestra, commissioned by the Chattanooga Symphony Orchestra, *Celebration* for orchestra, commissioned by the Indianapolis Symphony, *Symbolon*, commissioned by the New York Philharmonic for its tour of the Soviet Union where the work received its world premiere, *Symphony No 2* concertos for piano and trombone, and the *Trio* for violin, cello and piano. Earlier works still in circulation include the *Clarino Quartet* and *Passages*.

Zwilich began her musical studies as a violinist and for a time was a member of the American Symphony Orchestra under Leopold Stokowski's direction. She is therefore well-acquainted with the performer's side of music, an insight that enhances her writing for instruments, which is invariably idiomatic, its technical demands exhibiting a full understanding of instrumental capacities, and deeply concerned with the sound qualities of instruments and instrumental textures. Her music often relies upon bell sounds or bell-like sonorities, and is unfailingly open, clear and resonant. It is music for the ear, not the eye.

The year 1990 proved especially productive for Zwilich. Among the works either completed or premiered in that year are her Flute Concerto, Bass Trombone Concerto, Concerto for Oboe, and Quintet for clarinet and string quartet. All were commissions from some of the most distinguished musical organizations in the United States. In recent years Zwilich has made it something of a habit to write concertos for principal soloists of major American orchestras, an enterprise serving both artistic and practical ends. Among her projects now underway are a Double Concerto for violin and cello and her Third Symphony, the latter another commission from the New York Philharmonic.

Zwilich in her combination of artistic imagination, professional skill, and business acumen has forged a major career among American composers. Her determination has been crowned with success, proof of her gifts and a sign that musical composition enjoys a condition of good health in the United States.

—Frederic Goossen

APPENDICES

APPENDIX I

Major music publishers — head offices and main subsidiaries only. Small and independent publishers' addresses are given with the relevant composers' entries.
(Telephone and telefax numbers should be prefixed with the relevant national and/or international dialling code.)

Ars Polona
Krakowskie Przedmiescie 7
00068 Warsaw
Poland
Tel: (22) 26 12 01

Bärenreiter Verlag
Heinrich-Schütz Allee 35
Kassel-Wilhelmshöhe
Germany
Tel: (561) 31050

Boosey & Hawkes Music Publishers Ltd
295 Regent Street
London W1R 8JH
England
Tel: (71) 580 2060
Fax: (71) 435 5675
Telex: 89 54 613

Boosey & Hawkes Inc.
24 East 21st Street
New York, NY 10010–7200
U.S.A.
Tel: (212) 228 3300
Fax: (212) 473 5730

Boosey & Hawkes (Australia) Pty Ltd
Unit 12/6 Campbell Street
Artarmon, NSW 2064
Australia
Tel: (2) 439 4144
Fax: (2) 439 2912

Bote & Bock
Hardenbergstrasse 9a
D-1000 Berlin 12
Germany
Tel: (30) 311 0030
Fax: (30) 312 4281
Telex: 1 86 055 bote d

Breitkopf & Härtel
Walkmühlstrasse 52
Postfach 1707
D-6200 Wiesbaden 1
Germany
Tel: (6121) 49030

Cesky Hubedni Fond
Czech Music Foundation
Parizska 13
110 00 Prague 1
Czechoslovakia
Tel: (2) 324060

Chester Music Ltd
8/9 Frith Street
London W1V 5TZ
England
Tel: (71) 434 0066
Fax: (71) 439 2848
Telex: 21892 MSLDNG

Doblinger
Postfach 882
Dorotheergasse 10
A-1011 Vienna
Austria
Tel: (222) 515030

Donemus Amsterdam
Paulus Potterstraat 14
1071 CZ Amsterdam
The Netherlands
Tel: (20) 764 436
Fax: (20) 733 588

Editions Durand
215 rue de Faubourg St Honoré
F-75008 Paris
France
Tel: (1) 42 89 17 13

European American Music
P.O. Box 850
Valley Forge, PA 19482-9985
U.S.A.
Tel: (215) 648 0506
Fax: (215) 889 0242

Faber Music Ltd
3 Queen Square
London WC1N 3AU
England
Tel: (71) 278 7436
Fax: (71) 278 3817
Telex: 299633 FABER G

Fazer Music Inc.
P.O. Box 169
SF-02102 Espoo
Finland
Tel: (0) 435011
Fax: (0) 4552162

Edition Wilhelm Hansen AS
Gothersgade 9–11
DK-1123 Copenhagen K
Denmark
Tel: (1) 11 78 88
Fax: (1) 14 81 78
Telex: 19912 musik dk

Edition Jobert
76 rue Quincampoix
F-75003 Paris
France
Tel: (1) 42 72 83 43
Fax: (1) 42 72 27 67

Alfred A. Kalmus Ltd
Universal Edition (London) Ltd
2/3 Fareham Street
London W1V 4DU
England
Tel: (71) 437 6880

Alphonse Leduc
175 rue Saint-Honoré
F-75001 Paris
France
Tel: (1) 42 96 89 11

Margun/GunMar
167 Dudley Road
Newton Centre, MA 02159
U.S.A.
Tel: (617) 332 6398
Fax: (617) 969 1079

Edition Modern
Elisabethstrasse 38
Munich
Germany
Tel: (89) 271 3781

Edition Moeck
Postfach 143
D-3100 Celle
Germany
Tel: (5141) 88530

Music Sales Corporation
225 Park Avenue South
18th Floor
New York, NY 10003
U.S.A.
Tel: (212) 254 2100
Fax: (212) 254 2013

Editio Musica Budapest
P.O. Box 322
1370 Budapest
Hungary
Tel: (1) 118 4190

Nordiska Musik Forlaget
Nybrogatan 3
S-11434 Stockholm
Sweden
Tel: (8) 679 8240
Fax: (8) 611 2167

Novello & Co. Ltd
8–10 Lower James Street
London W1R 3PL
England
Tel: (71) 287 5060
Fax: (71) 287 0816

Oxford University Press
Ely House
37 Dover Street
London W1XC 4AH
England
Tel: (71) 493 2661
Telex: 262749

Panton
Ricni 12
118 00 Prague 1
Czechoslovakia
Tel: (2) 538151

Peer-Southern Concert Music
810 Seventh Avenue
New York, NY 10019
U.S.A.
Tel: (212) 265 3910
Fax: (212) 489 2465

Edition Peters
(C.F. Peters Corporation)
373 Park Avenue South
New York, NY 10016
U.S.A.
Tel: (212) 686 4147
Fax: (212) 689 9412

Peters Edition Limited
10–12 Baches Street
London N1 6DN
England
Tel: (71) 253 1638
Fax: (71) 490 4921

Theodore Presser Co.
Presser Place
Bryn Mawr, PA 19010
U.S.A.
Tel: (215) 525 3636

G. Ricordi & C.S.p.A.
via Berchet 2
20121 Milan
Italy
Tel: (2) 8881
Fax: (2) 8881 ext. 270

Editions Salabert
22 rue Chauchat
75009 Paris
France
Tel: (1) 48 24 55 60

E.C. Schirmer (Boston)
138 Ipswich Street
Boston, MA 02215
U.S.A.
Tel: (617) 236 1935

G. Schirmer Inc.
225 Park Avenue South
New York, NY 10003
U.S.A.
Tel: (212) 254 2100

Schott & Co. Ltd
48 Great Marlborough Street
London W1V 2BN
England
Tel: (71) 437 1246
Fax: (71) 437 0263

B. Schott's Söhne
Weihergarten 5
6500 Mainz
Germany
Tel: (6131) 2460
Fax: (6131) 246211
Telex: 007414187821

Hans Sikorski
(Internationale Musikverlage Hans Sikorski)
Postfach 132001
Johnsallee 23
2000 Hamburg 13
Germany
Tel: (40) 414 1000

Slovensky Hubodny Fond
Fucikova 29
811 01 Bratislava
Czechoslovakia
Tel: (7) 333 569

Sovetskii kompozitor
ul. Sadovay Triumfalnaya 14–12
Moscow 103006
U.S.S.R.
Tel: (095) 209 2384/4105/1942

Stainer & Bell Ltd
P.O. Box 110
Victoria House
23 Gruneisen Road
London N3 1DZ
England
Tel: (81) 343 3303
Fax: (81) 343 3024

Edition Suecia/Svensk Musik
Box 27327
Sandhamnsg. 79
S-102 54 Stockholm
Sweden
Tel: (8) 783 8800

Supraphon
Palackeho 1
112 99 Prague 1
Czechoslovakia
Tel: (2) 264051

Editioni Suvini Zerboni
via Quintiliano 40
Milan
Italy
Tel: (2) 50841

United Music Publishers Ltd
42 Rivington Street
London EC2A 3BN
England
Tel: (71) 729 4700
Fax: (71) 739 6549

Universal Edition A.G.
Bösendorferstrasse 12
A-1015 Vienna
Austria
Tel: (222) 505 86 95
Fax: (222) 505 27 20
Telex: 111397

VAAP
B. Bronnaia 6A
Moscow 103670 K-104
U.S.S.R.
Tel: (095) 203 4599

Joseph Weinberger Ltd
12–14 Mortimer Street
London W1N 7RD
England
Tel: (71) 580 2827
Fax: (71) 436 9616

Zen-On Music Company Ltd
3–14 Higashi Goken-cho
Shinjuku-ku
Tokyo 162
Japan
Tel: (3) 3269 0121

APPENDIX II

Contemporary music information — useful addresses and telephone numbers.
***ISCM = International Society for Contemporary Music national divisions.**
(Telephone and telefax numbers should be prefixed with the relevant national and/or international dialling code.)

Argentina

*Fundación Encuentros Internacionales de Música Contemporánea/ISCM
CC 1008 Correo Central
1000 Buenos Aires
Argentina
Tel: (1) 831383
Fax: (1) 774 1016
Telex: 18390 UZAL AR

Australia

Australian Music Centre
P.O. Box N690
Grosvenor Place
Sydney, NSW 2000
Australia
Tel: (2) 247 4677
Fax: (2) 241 2873

*ISCM
c/o Department of Music
University of Sydney
Sydney, NSW 2006
Australia
Tel: (2) 692 2923
Telex: UNISYD 26169

Austria

A.K.M. staatl. genehmigte Gesellschaft der Autoren, Komponisten und Musikverleger
(Performing Rights Society)
Baumannstrasse 10
A-1030 Vienna
Austria
Tel: (222) 713 1550

*IGNM/ISCM
Ungargasse 9/3
A-1030 Vienna
Austria
Tel: (222) 713 3040

Österreichische Gesellschaft für Musik
Hanuschgasse 3
A-1010 Vienna
Austria
Tel: (222) 524299

Belgium

*ISCM
c/o André Laporte
22 Langeheide
B-3052 Ottenburg
Belgium
Tel: (2) 649930
Fax: (2) 646 2997

Brazil

*Sociedade Brasileira de Música Contemporânea/ISCM
Super Quadras Sul 105-Bloco B-Apto 506
70344 Brasilia DF
Brazil
Tel: (61) 2429036

Canada

Canadian Music Centre
Chalmers House
20 St Joseph Street
Toronto, Ontario M4Y 1J9
Canada
Tel: (415) 961 6601

*ISCM
c/o Louise Ostiguy
1906 Henri Bourassa Est
Apt 405
Montreal, Quebec H2B 1S1
Canada

Chile

*Asociación Nacional de Compositores de Chile
Pío Nono 140
Santiago de Chile
Chile
Tel: (2) 5516974/371204

Czechoslovakia

*Zvaz Ceskoslovenskych Skladatelov
Skroupovo Nam. 9
130 00 Prague
Czechoslovakia

Denmark

Danish Music Information Centre
Vimmelskaftet 48
DK-1161 Copenhagen K
Denmark
Tel: 33 11 20 66
Fax: 33 32 20 16

*ISCM
c/o DUT
Valkendorfsgade 3
DK-1151 Copenhagen K
Denmark
Tel: 33 91 01 09

Finland

Finnish Music Information Centre
& *ISCM
Runeberginkatu 15 A 6 & 11
00100 Helsinki
Finland
Tel: (0) 409 134/445 589
Fax: (0) 409 634

France

Centre du Documentation de
la Musique Contemporaine/SACEM
225 avenue Charles-de-Gaulle
F-92521 Neuilly-sur-Seine Cedex
France
Tel: 47 47 56 50/47 15 47 15
Telex: Musica 630 312 F

*ISCM
c/o 112 rue Michel Angel
F-75016 Paris
France

Germany

Institut für Neue Musik und Musikerziehung
Grafenstrasse 35
D-6100 Darmstadt
Germany
Tel: (6151) 23062

*Gesellschaft für Neue Musik
Schirn
Bendergasse 3
D-6000 Frankfurt M
Germany
Tel: (69) 20038
Fax: (69) 20081
Telex: 4170016 JDPH D

Greece

*ISCM
c/o KSYME
7 Agamemnos Street
Holargos
GR-155 61 Athens
Greece
Tel: (1) 6525887/6536863

Hungary

*Magyar Zenemuveszek Szovetsege
P.O. Box 47
H-1364 Budapest
Hungary
Tel: (1) 184243/179598

Iceland

Iceland Music Information Centre
Box 978
1 Freyjugotu
IS-121 Reykjavik
Iceland
Tel: (1) 12322

Ireland

*Association of Irish Composers
Room 604 Liberty Hall
Dublin 1
Ireland
Tel: (1) 740070

Music Division
Radio Telefis Eireann
Donnybrook
Dublin 4
Ireland
Tel: (1) 643111

Israel

*Israel Composers League
P.O. Box 45068
Tel Aviv 61450
Israel
Tel: (3) 440395

Italy

*Societa Italiana Musica Contemporanea
via F. Juvara 11
I-20129 Milan
Italy
Tel: (2) 70600837

Japan

*ISCM
31-9, 3 Chome, Kasugacho
Nerima-ku
Tokyo 179
Japan
Tel: (3) 9702895

Republic of Korea

*ISCM
c/o Korean Development Institute
92-06 Umyeon-dong
Seocho-gu
Seoul 137-791
Korea
Tel: (2) 572 5121 ext. 216-8
Fax: (2) 572 7261

Mexico

*Sociedad Mexicana de Música
Nueva S.C.
Apartado Postal 11–626
Mexico D.F.
Mexico
Tel: (5) 584 3204/554 7266
Fax: (5) 548 1507

The Netherlands

Gaudeamus Foundation (*International Foundation for Contemporary Music)
Swammerdamstraat 38
1091 RV Amsterdam
The Netherlands
Tel: (20) 694 7349

Society of Dutch Composers
Professor E.M. Meijerslaan 3
P.O. Box 725
1180 AS Amsterdam
The Netherlands
Tel: (20) 540 7911
Fax: (20) 540 7496

Donemus Foundation
Paulus Potterstraat 14
1071 CZ Amsterdam
The Netherlands
Tel: (20) 764 436
Fax: (20) 733 588

New Zealand

Archive of New Zealand Music
Alexander Turnbull Library
P.O. Box 12–349
Wellington
New Zealand
Tel: (4) 743000

Norway

Norwegian Music Information Centre
Toftesgate 69
0552 Oslo 5
Norway
Tel: (2) 37 09 09
Fax: (2) 35 69 38

Poland

*Polski Towarzystwo Muzyki Wspolczesnej
ul. Mazdwiecka 11
PL-00 052 Warsaw
Poland
Tel: (2) 276981

Portugal

*Sociedade Portuguesa de Música Contemporânea
c/o Escola Superior de Música
Av. dos Caetanos 29
1200 Lisbon
Portugal

Spain

*Sociedad Internacional de Música Contemporánea
Avenida de América 58–5 Dcha
E-28028 Madrid
Spain
Tel: (1) 2463621

Sweden

Swedish Music Information Centre/ *Society of Swedish Composers
Sandhamnsgatan 79
Box 27327
102 54 Stockholm
Sweden
Tel: (8) 783 8800
Fax: (8) 662 6275

Switzerland

*Association des Musiciens Suisses
Case Postale 177
CH-100 Lausanne 13
Switzerland
Tel: (21) 266371

Taiwan

*ISCM
7F, No. 230,
Sec. 1 Da-An Road
10652 Taipei
Taiwan
Tel: (2) 707 4198
Fax: (2) 708 0182

United Kingdom

International Society for Contemporary Music
c/o SPNM
1 West Heath Yard
174 Mill Lane
London NW6 1NT
England
Tel: (71) 431 3752

The Performing Rights Society Ltd
29–33 Berners Street
London W1P 4AA
England
Tel: (71) 580 5544

Welsh Music Information Centre
University College
P.O. Box 78
Cardiff CF1 1XL
Wales
Tel: (222) 874000 ext. 5126

Scottish Music Information Centre
1 Bowmont Gardens
Glasgow G12 9LR
Scotland
Tel: (41) 334 6393

U.S.A.

American Composers Alliance
170 West 74th Street
New York, NY 10023
U.S.A.
Tel: (212) 362 8900

American Music Center Inc./
*League of Composers
30 West 26th Street, Suite 1001
New York, NY 10010–2011
U.S.A.
Tel: (212) 366 5260

Meet the Composer Inc.
212 Broadway, Suite 505
New York, NY 10023
U.S.A.
Tel: (212) 787 3601

International League of Women Composers
P.O. Box 42
Three Mile Bay, NY 13693
U.S.A.

Uruguay

*Sociedad Uruguaya de Música Contemporánea
Casilla de Correo 1328
U-11000 Montevideo
Uruguay

U.S.S.R.

House of Composers
ul. Nezdanova 8–10
Moscow
U.S.S.R.
Tel: (095) 229 1365/8101/4890

Venezuela

*ISCM
c/o El Penon.
Calle Andromeda
Qta. Chepina
Caracas 1080
Venezuela

Yugoslavia

*ISCM
c/o SOKOJ
P.O. Box 213
YU-11000 Belgrade
Yugoslavia
Tel: (11) 3347713

NOTES ON ADVISERS AND CONTRIBUTORS

ADAMS, Byron. Musicologist and freelance writer. **Essay:** Karel Husa.

ANDERSON, Julian. Conductor, musicologist and freelance writer. **Essays:** Alain Bancquart; Claude Ballif; Hugues Dufourt; Pascal Dusapin; Gérard Grisey; Robin Holloway; Michaël Levinas; Jonathan Lloyd; Colin Matthews; Tristan Murail; Stefan Niculescu; Michèle Reverdy.

ANDERSON, Virginia. Writer and educator. Contributor to *Contact, ClariNetwork* and various newspapers. **Essays:** Christopher Hobbs; Howard Skempton; John White.

ARIAS, Enrique Alberto. Chair of Graduate Studies, American Conservatory of Music, Chicago. Author of *Alexander Tcherepnin: A Bio-Bibliography,* and of articles in *Music Review, Latin American Music Review, Clavier, NATS Journal, Anuario Musical* and other journals. **Essays:** Roque Cordero; Phillip Ramey.

ÅSTRAND, Hans. Professor and Perpetual Secretary Emeritus, Royal Swedish Academy of Music, Stockholm. Author of *Bird's Eye Perspectives on North American Music Life,* 1983, *The Principle of Truth and the Principle of Beauty: Towards an Aesthetic of Contemporary Swedish Music* (with Gerd Schönfelder), 1984, and articles in *ARTES, Nutida Musik, Musikrevy, Revista de Occidente* and other journals. **Essay:** Luís de Pablo.

BANN, Tico. Computer and musicologist. **Essay:** Costin Miereanu.

BARRETT, Richard. See his own entry. **Essays:** Aldo Clementi; Brian Ferneyhough; Michael Finnissy; Heinz Holliger; Helmut Lachenmann; Ivo Malec; Per Nøgård; Salvatore Sciarrino.

BENNETT, Richard Rodney. See his own entry. **Essay:** Irwin Bazelon.

BILLING, Björn. Member of the Department of Musicology, University of Gothenburg, Sweden. Contributor to *Nutida Musik.* **Essays:** Egil Hovland; Maurice Karkoff; Cecilie Ore; Karl-Erik Welin.

BIRKIN, Kenneth. Musical scholar, reviewer and librettist. Author of *Richard Strauss's Arabella,* 1989, *Friedenstag & Daphne: An Interpretative Study,* 1989, articles on Strauss, Joseph Gregor, Stefan Zweig, John Joubert and other subjects, record sleeve notes, and reviews of records, books and performances. Editor of *Stefan Zweig/Joseph Gregor: Briefwechsel 1921-1938,* 1991. **Essay:** John Joubert.

BLAKE, Michael. Composer and pianist; artistic director, London New Music. **Essays:** Gerald Barry; Bunita Marcus; Kevin Volans.

BOTHA, Amanda. Journalist. Author of *Phyllis Spira: A Ballerina,* 1988, essays for *World Ballet and Dance* and *Opera Companies of the World,* 1991, and articles in *De Kat, Lantern* and *Leadership.* **Essay:** Johann Cloete.

BOURSIN, Paul. Retired teacher of violin. **Essays:** Alexander Brott; Levon Chaushian.

BOWEN, Meirion. Music critic, *The Guardian,* London; freelance musician. Author of *Michael Tippett,* 1981. Editor of *Michael Tippett: Music of the Angels,* 1980. **Essays:** Martin Butler; David Sawer.

BRADSHAW, Susan. Pianist, writer and broadcaster on music; piano tutor, Goldsmiths' College, University of London. Contributor to *Pierre Boulez: A Symposium,* 1986, and author of articles in *Musical Times, Tempo, Contact* and *Music and Musicians.* Translator of *Boulez on Music Today,* 1971. **Essays:** Richard Rodney Bennett; John Buller; Edison Denisov; Brian Elias; Henri Pousseur; Giles Swayne.

BRAMANI, Lidia. Musicologist and freelance writer. **Essay:** Ivan Fedele.

BRASK, Peter. Composer and Professor of literary analysis and theory, Roskilde University Center, Denmark. Author of *The Basic Structure of Twelve-Tone Music* (in Danish), 1973, *Text and Interpretation* (in Danish), 1974, and articles in *Danish Semiotics* and *The Nordic Mind.* Composer of orchestral and choral works, songs, and chamber music. **Essay:** Jan Maegaard.

BRINDLE, Reginald Smith. See his own entry.

BRINER, Andres. Musicologist; president of the Hindemith Foundation. Author of *Paul Hindemith,* 1971, *Paul Hindemith: Leben und Werk in Bild und Text* (with others), 1988, and articles in *Schweizerische Musikzeitung, Dissonanz, Melos, Neue Zeitschrift für Musik* and other journals. **Essay:** Rudolf Kelterborn.

BROWN, Cynthia Clark. Alma Dark Howard Chair of Church Music, Campbell University, Buies Creek, North Carolina. Contributor to *Southern Baptist Church Music Journal.* **Essay:** Emma Lou Diemer.

BRYARS, Gavin. See his own entry. **Essays:** Harold Budd; Ladislav Kupkovič; Arvo Pärt.

CALDWELL, Eleanor. Teacher and freelance writer. **Essays:** Dominick Argento; Elsa Barraine; David Blake; William Bolcom; Geoffrey Burgon; Joel Chadabe; Charles Chaynes; John Corigliano; Edward Cowie; James Drew.

CAZABAN, Costin. Composer, journalist and teacher at the University of Paris I. Compositions include *Still Life with Instruments and Composers, Naturalia* and *Zig-Zag.* Music critic for *Le Monde de la Musique* and *Le Monde.* **Essay:** Anatol Vieru.

CHEN Yi. See her own entry. **Essays:** He Lu-ting; Wu Zuqiang; Zhou Long.

CHEW Shyh-ji. Musician and musicologist. **Essays:** Hsu Tsang-houei; Ma Shui-long; Jose Maceda.

CHOU Wen-chung. See his own entry.

CLARK, Thomas. Professor of music, University of North Texas, Denton. Author of *Learning to Compose,* 1989, and *Arrays: Musical Patterns for Aural Development,* 1992. Contributor to *Perspectives of New Music, Computer Music Journal* and *In Theory Only.* Compositions published by the American Composers Alliance. **Essays:** Larry Austin; Leslie Bassett; Lukas Foss; Andrew Imbrie.

COLE, Hugo. Composer and critic. Author of *Sounds and Signs,* 1974, *The Changing Face of Music,* 1978, and *Malcolm*

Arnold: An Introduction to His Music, 1989; contributor to *The Musical Companion* and *How Music Works,* and critic for the *Guardian, The Listener* and *Country Life.* **Essay:** Malcolm Arnold.

COLLINS, Pamela. Freelance writer. Co-author of *Women in Music,* 1992. Editor, with Brian Morton, of *Contemporary Composers,* 1991. **Essays:** Simon Bainbridge; Howard Blake; Gordon Crosse; Lucia Dlugoszewski; Libby Larsen.

DAHLSTEDT, Sten. Research fellow, Institute of Musicology, University of Uppsala, Sweden. Contributor to *Sohlman's Dictionary of Music, Nutida Musik, Artes* and *Svensk Tidskrift för Musikforskning.* **Essay:** Mikael Edlund.

DAVIES, Lyn. Lecturer, Department of Extra Mural Studies, University College of Wales, Aberystwyth. Contributor to *Tempo, Musical Times, Welsh Music Journal* and other periodicals. **Essays:** Henryk Górecki; Bernadetta Matuszczak; Ian Parrott.

DAWNEY, Michael. Freelance writer on music; also composer, lecturer and pianist. Editor of three books of folksongs — *Doon the Waggon Way,* 1973, *The Iron Man,* 1974, and *The Ploughboy's Glory,* 1977 — and author of an essay in *Edmund Rubbra: A Symposium* and articles in *Musical Opinion* and other journals. **Essays:** Christopher Brown; Robert Sherlaw Johnson; Gerard Victory.

DAWSON, Jenny. Freelance musician and musicologist. Contributor to *Australian Journal of Music Education, Australia and New Zealand Association of Teachers of Singing Newsletter* and other journals. **Essays:** Alison Bauld; Betty Beath; Colin Brumby; Barry Conyngham; George Dreyfus; Ross Edwards; Jennifer Fowler; Mary Mageau; Richard Mills; Andrew Schultz; Peter Sculthorpe.

DEHNER, Jan. Musicologist; member of the Department for the Research of the Czech Theatre, Czechoslovak Academy of Sciences, Prague. Contributor to *Enzyklopädie des Musiktheaters,* and to the journals *Lidové noviny, Hudební rozhledy, Opus musicum, Scéna, Divadelní revue* and *Hudební věda.* **Essays:** Petr Eben; Viktor Kalabis; Marek Kopelent; Ivana Loudova; Klement Slavický.

DIOQUINO, Corazon C. Member of the music research faculty, University of the Philippines College of Music, Quezon City. **Essay:** Ramon Santos.

DIXON, P.A.F. Professor of pharmacology, Obafemi Awolowo University, Ife, Nigeria. **Essay:** Joshua Uzoigwe.

DREW, David. Music publisher. **Essay:** Wolfgang von Schweinitz.

DUNNETT, Roderic. Freelance writer. Contributor to *The Financial Times, The Strad, Opera Now, Agenda, P.N. Review* and *Musical Times.* **Essays:** Luciano Chailly; Michael Hurd; David Matthews; Gerard Schurmann; Malcolm Williamson.

EASTERBROOK, Giles. Publisher, writer, composer, lecturer, arranger and editor. Director of "Maecenas (Contemporary) Composers". **Essays:** Anders Eliasson; Hans Henkemans; Otto Ketting; Tristan Keuris; Theo Loevendie; Pehr Henrik Nordgren; Stephen Oliver; Klaas de Vries.

ELLIS, Stephen W. Senior textbook editor. Contributor to *The New Grove Dictionary of American Music, Baker's Biographical Dictionary of Musicians* and *Music Since 1900*; record and book reviewer for *Fanfare.* **Essay:** Nancy Van de Vate.

EMMERSON, Simon. See his own entry.

ERIN, Ronald F. Graphic artist and printer. Author of program notes and of articles in *Latin American Music Review.* **Essay:** Aurelio de la Vega.

EUBA, Akin. See his own entry.

FEINBERG, Alan. Performing pianist, with particular interest in the contemporary repertoire. **Essay:** George Edwards.

FELZER, Oleg. Composer and musicologist; choirmaster and organist, St Ignatus Church, New York. Author of articles in *Soviet Music, Farazh Karayev* and other collections and journals. **Essay:** Faraj Karayev.

FERNEYHOUGH, Brian. See his own entry.

FLEISCHMANN, Aloys. Retired teacher. **Essay:** Brian Boydell.

FOGEL, Henry. Executive director, Chicago Symphony Orchestra. Reviewer for *Fanfare*; contributor to *Symphony, High Fidelity, American Record Guide, Keynote* and other magazines. **Essays:** John Harbison; Karel Husa; Gian Carlo Menotti; Ned Rorem.

FROSAK, Curd. Cellist and musicologist. **Essay:** Ivo Petrić.

GILBERT, Anthony. See his own entry. **Essay:** David Lumsdaine.

GILLIS, Patrick. Musicologist, specializing in 19th-century French music. Author of programme notes for the Théâtre du Châtelet and the Paris Opera, and contributor to *Avant-Scène Opéra, Dossiers du Musée d'Orsay* and *La Lettre du Musicien.* **Essay:** Noel Lee.

GLIGO, Nikša. Senior Lecturer, Department of Musicology, University of Zagreb. Author of *Vrijeme Glazbe* (Time of Music), 1977, *Varijacije Razvojnog Kontinuiteta: Skladatelj Natko Devčić* (The Variations of Developmental Continuity: Composer Natko Devčić), 1985, and *Problemi Nove Glazbe 20.Stoljeca* (Problems of the 20th-Century New Music), 1987. **Essay:** Milko Kelemen.

GOLDBERG, Loretta. Musician and writer on music. **Essay:** Sorrel Hays.

GOOSSEN, Frederic. Professor of music and Director of Graduate Studies in Music, University of Alabama, Tuscaloosa. Composer of some 150 works of music in all genres. Editor of *Thinking About Music: The Collected Writings of Ross Lee Finney,* 1991. **Essays:** Ross Lee Finney; Ellen Taaffe Zwilich.

GREY, Ian. Former co-director of the new music ensemble Phlogiston. **Essays:** Richard Wernick; Trevor Wishart.

GRINBERG, Aleksandr. Musicologist. **Essay:** Alexander Shchetinsky.

HARRISON, Max. Musicologist. Author or co-author of *Charlie Parker,* 1960, *Unpleasant for the Peasants,* 1966, *The*

Lieder of Brahms, 1972, *Modern Jazz: The Essential Records 1945–1970,* 1975, *A Jazz Retrospect,* 1976, *The Essential Jazz Records 1–2,* 1984–92, *The New Grove Gospel, Blues, and Jazz,* 1987, and *The Music of Scriabin,* 1992. **Essays:** Milton Babbitt; Arnold Cooke; Norman Dello Joio; David Diamond; Howard Ferguson; Jean Françaix; Peter Racine Fricker; Morton Gould; Iain Hamilton; Donald Martino; Goffredo Petrassi; William Schuman; Harold Shapero; Virgil Thomson.

HERRESTHAL, Harald. Teacher and writer. **Essay:** Knut Nystedt.

HERSH, Howard. Composer, performer and writer. **Essay:** Richard Feliciano.

HERTZOG, Christian. Doctoral candidate in composition, University of California, San Diego. Music critic, La Jolla *Light,* California; contributor to San Diego *Tribune.* **Essays:** Curtis O.B. Curtis-Smith; Donald Erb; Morton Subotnick; Charles Wuorinen.

HEUREUX, Pierre. Musicologist. **Essay:** Essay: Jacqueline Fontyn.

HILL, Malcolm J. Member of the faculty, Royal Academy of Music, London. **Essays:** Kalevi Aho; Sven-Erik Bäck; Sándor Balassa; Erik Bergman; Einar Englund; Joonas Kokkonen; György Kurtág; Ingvar Lidholm; Tauno Marttinen; Krzysztof Meyer; György Ránki; Einojuhani Rautavaara; Aribert Reimann; Wolfgang Rihm; Erkki Salmenhaara; Sándor Szokolay.

HOOPEN, Christiane ten. Musician and musicologist; research assistant, Department of Music, University of Amsterdam. Author of articles in *MusikTexte, Les Cahiers du CREM, Avant Garde* and *Proceedings of the Second European Music Analysis Conference.* **Essays:** Simon Emmerson; Ton de Leeuw.

HORNER, Paul. Advances analyst, Central Advances Department, Barclays Bank. Formerly editor of *Soundings.* **Essays:** Lennox Berkeley; Peter Maxwell Davies; Zsolt Durko; Henri Dutilleux; Alun Hoddinott; Vagn Holmboe; Daniel Jones; György Ligeti; William Mathias; Xavier Montsalvatge; George Rochberg; Aulis Sallinen; Carlos Surinach; Toru Takemitsu.

HOWARD, Keith. Lecturer, School of Oriental and African Studies, University of London. Author of *Korean Musical Instruments: A Practical Guide,* 1988, *Bands, Songs, and Shamanistic Rituals: Folk Music in Korean Society,* 1989, *The Sounds of Korea,* 1990, and articles in *Ethnomusicology, Cahiers de Musique Traditionelles, World of Music, Journal of Ritual Studies* and other journals. **Essays:** Hwang Byung-ki; Kang Sukhi; Kim Young Dong; Paik Byung-dong; Yi Sanggyu; Yi Sŏngch'ŏn; Isang Yun.

HUGILL, Andrew. Composer; Head of Music, Leicester Polytechnic. Compositions include *Simon & Ennoia,* 1983, *Catalogue de Grenouilles,* 1987, *Brisset Rhymes,* 1990, *Bachelor Machine,* 1991, and *One Hundred Thousand Billion Songs.* Contributor to *Musical Times, Contact, Monitores du Cymbalum Pataphysicum* and *Archive de la Fondation Erik Satie.* **Essays:** Gavin Bryars; Roger Marsh.

JACOBSON, Bernard. Artistic leader, The Hague Philharmonic. Author of *The Music of Johannes Brahms,* 1977, *Conductors on Conducting,* 1979, articles in *The New Grove Dictionary of Music and Musicians, Dictionary of 20th-Century Music,* and *The Chopin Companion,* and reviews in *The Times, The Guardian, Musical Times* and other periodicials; also song lyricist and translator of operas by Henze and Mathus. **Essays:** Hans Werner Henze; Wilfred Josephs; Andrzej Panufnik; Bernard Rands; Ralph Shapey.

JACOBY, Jan. Freelance writer. **Essay:** Tage Nielsen.

JOHNS, Lana Kay. Doctoral student, Florida State University School of Music, Tallahassee. **Essay:** Jindřich Feld.

JOHNSON, Rosemary. International Promotion Manager, Chester Music, London. Contributor to *New Music '87* and *'88,* and to *Kaleidoscope* radio programme. **Essays:** Bo Holten; Leon Kirchner; Magnus Lindberg; Ib Nørholm; Mel Powell; Niels Rosing-Schow; Poul Ruders; Jan Sandström; Bent Sørensen; Karen Tanaka; Joan Tower; Carl Vine.

JONES, Richard Elfyn. Composer; Lecturer in music, University of Wales College of Cardiff; musical director, Welsh Chamber Choir. Author of *The Music of David Wynne,* 1978, and articles on Tippett and on the metaphysics of music in *Welsh Music, Efrydiau Athronyddol* and other publications. Composer of numerous choral works. **Essays:** HK Gruber; Jonathan Harvey; Alexander Lasoń; Luigi Nono; Zbigniew Rudzinski; Kurt Schwertsik.

KANE, Russell. Freelance musician and music writer. **Essays:** Vic Hoyland; Kent Kennan; Ezra Laderman; Marcel Landowski; Benjamin Lees; Tod Machover; Elliott Schwartz; Robert Sheff.

KARP, Ivan. Freelance writer. **Essay:** Georgy Peletsis.

KARP, Oleg. Builder of electronic synthesizers. **Essay:** Edvard Mirzoyan.

KLEIN, Rolf. Musicologist; research fellow, Japan Society for the Promotion of Science. Author of *Die Intervallehre in der deutschen Musiktheorie des 16. Jahrhunderts,* 1989, and articles in *Contemporary Music Review.* **Essays:** Komei Abe; Roland Kayn; Gottfried Michael Koenig; Jo Kondo; Yori-Aki Matsudaira; Yoritsune Matsudaira; Teizo Matsumura; Akira Miyoshi; Dieter Schnebel; Makoto Shinohara.

KLÜPPELHOLZ, Werner. Professor of music education, University of Siegen, Germany. Author of *Sprache als Musik,* 1976, *Modelle zue Didaktik der Neuen Musik,* 1981, *Mauricio Kagel 1970–1980,* 1981. Editor of *Kagel,* 1991. **Essays:** Vinko Globokar; Mauricio Kagel.

KRONES, Hartmut. Musicologist. **Essays:** Francis Burt; Friedrich Cerha; Gottfried von Einem; Ivan Eröd.

LAO, Charles. Freelance piano teacher and writer on contemporary music. **Essay:** Ton-That Tiet.

LION, Margaret. Freelance pianist and teacher. Composer of incidental music for plays. **Essays:** David Farquhar; Douglas Lilburn.

LOCK, Graham. Freelance journalist. Author of *Forces in Motion: Anthony Braxton and the Meta-Reality of Creative Music,* 1988. **Essays:** Henry Brant; Anthony Braxton.

LOSSEFF, Nicola. Research student, King's College, London. Contributor to *Contemporary Music Review* and *The Garland Encyclopedia of Medieval England.* **Essay:** Erika Fox.

LOUBET, Emmanuelle. Musicologist, radio producer and writer. Author of the radio work *Tokyo im Rennschritt: Ein Sound-Polaroid,* 1990, and contributor to *Larousse de la Musique,* 1982. **Essay:** Mesias Maiguashca.

MAARTEN, Henk. Ethnomusicologist, specialising in the music of Northern Europe. **Essays:** Hans Abrahamsen; Louis Andriessen; Gunnar Bucht; Violeta Dinescu; Friedhelm Döhl; Ulf Grahn; Åse Hedstrøm; Anders Hillborg; Peter Schat; Leif Segerstam.

MAARTEN, Signe. Pianist and ethnomusicologist. **Essays:** Jouni Kaipainen; Arne Nordheim; Synne Skouen.

MACKAY, Neil. Composer and lecturer; Scottish music correspondent, *The Guardian.* Contributor to *The New Grove's Dictionary of Music and Musicians,* and to *Tempo.* Editor of *Francis George Scott: Centenary Album,* 1980. **Essay:** Haflidi Halgrimsson.

MARTINEZ, Odaline de la. Composer and condutor. Author of two forthcoming books, *Mendelssohn's Sister* and *Latin American Music.*

MASLIN, Kyril. Freelance writer. **Essay:** Boris Tchaikovsky.

MATHIESON, Kenny. Freelance writer. Contributor to *Wire* and *Scotland on Sunday.* **Essays:** John Adams; Janet Beat; Leonard Bernstein; Elliott Carter; Aaron Copland; Lyell Cresswell; George Crumb; James Dillon; John Maxwell Geddes; Philip Glass; Edward Harper; Oliver Knussen; Witold Lutoslawski; James MacMillan; Edward McGuire; Krzysztof Penderecki; Frederic Rzewski; Stephen Sondheim; William Sweeney; Mark-Anthony Turnage; Thomas Wilson.

MATOSSIAN, Nouritza. Writer and film producer. Author of *Iannis Xanakis,* 1981, and *Xenakis,* 1986, and associate producer of a radio documentary on Xenakis, *Something Rich and Strange,* 1991. Contributor to *Tempo, Music and Musicians, The Independent,* and *Harpers and Queen.* **Essays:** Rolf Gehlhaar; Conlon Nancarrow; Iannis Xenakis.

MATTHEW-WALKER, Robert. Author of *Rachmaninoff,* 1976, *Muhammad Ali: His Fights in the Ring,* 1978, *Elvis Presley: A Study in Music,* 1978, *Simon and Garfunkel,* 1984, *David Bowie: Theatre of Music,* 1985, *Madonna,* 1989, *The Authentic Gershwin,* 1989, *Edvard Grieg,* 1990, *Alun Hoddinott on Record,* 1990, *The Keller Column,* 1990, *The Symphonies of Robert Simpson,* 1991, and *Rachmaninoff's Piano Music,* 1991. **Essays:** Nicola LeFanu; Elizabeth Maconchy.

MATTHEWS, Michael. Composer, conductor and teacher. **Essay:** Violet Archer.

MAY, James W. Member of the Faculty of Music, University of Cape Town. **Essays:** Peter Klatzow; Hans Roosenschoon.

MAYCOCK, Robert. Music editor, *The Independent,* London; chair, Society for the Promotion of New Music; artistic adviser to the King's Lynn Festival, Norfolk. Contributor to *Classic CD* and *Classical Music* (editor, 1977 – 86). **Essay:** Priti Paintal.

MAYS, Sally. Concert pianist and chamber player, and teacher. Editor of *Australian Piano Music,* 7 vols., from 1990. **Essays:** Edwin Carr; Gillian Whitehead.

McBURNEY, Gerard. Freelance composer and writer about music. Author of an essay in *The Music of Howard Ferguson,* 1989, and articles in *Tempo, Musical Times, The Listener, The Independent, The Guardian, Sovetskaya Muzyka* and *Moskovskii Komsomoletz.* **Essays:** Franghiz Ali-Zadeh; Vyacheslav Artyomov; Georgy Dmitriev; Elena Firsova; Simon Holt; Leonid Hrabovsky; Giya Kancheli; Nikolai Karetnikov; Yuri Kasparov; Alexander Knaifel; Elena Konshina; Nikolai Korndorf; Roman Ledenyov; Vassily Lobanov; Tigran Mansurian; Anthony Payne; Alexander Raskatov; Rodion Shchedrin; Vladislav Shoot; Dmitri Smirnov; Viktor Suslin; Georgy Sviridov; Vladimir Tarnopolsky; Boris Tishchenko.

MILNE, Hamish. Pianist and Professor, Royal Academy of Music, London. Author of *Bartók,* 1982, and contributor to *Heritage of Music,* 1989. Has made numerous recordings and broadcasts, and given concerts throughout Europe. **Essay:** John Gardner.

MIVAL, William. Composer and Professor of musicianship, Royal College of Music, London. Contributor to *Tempo* and broadcaster on Radio 3. **Essay:** York Höller.

MODY, Sukphal. Freelance guitarist and sitarist. **Essay:** Naresh Sohal.

MORTON, Brian. Full-time writer. Features then literary editor, *Times Higher Education Supplement,* London, 1981-91; has taught at the University of East Anglia, Norwich, and the University of Tromso, Norway. Editor, with Pamela Collins, of *Contemporary Composers,* 1992. **Essays:** Robert Ashley; Antonio Bibalo; Anthony Burgess; Alan Bush; Chou Wen-chung; David Del Tredici; Peter Dickinson; Ketil Hvoslef; Johan Kvandal; Annea Lockwood; Meredith Monk; Dominic Muldowney; Marc Neikrug; Marlos Nobre; Stephen Paulus; Andrew Poppy; Vittorio Rieti; Terje Rypdal; Kaija Saariaho; Ezra Sims, John Tavener; Judith Weir; Ján Zimmer.

MUELLER, R. Peter. Composer and teacher. **Essays:** Martin Bresnick; Jacob Druckman (with Rachel Myers); Alexander Goehr (with Rachel Myers).

MUSA, Isaac. Serving soldier and musician. **Essay:** Akin Euba.

MYERS, Rachel. Freelance editor and writer. **Essays** (with R. Peter Mueller): Jacob Druckman; Alexander Goehr.

NEFF, Severine. Associate Professor of music theory, University of Cincinnati Conservatory of Music, Ohio. Contributor to *New Music, Theory and Practice* and *Current Musicology.* Editor of two forthcoming works by Schoenberg, *Der musikalische Gedanke und die Logik, Technik und Kunst seiner Darstellung* and *Zusammenhang, Kontrapunkt, Instrumentation, Formenlehre.* **Essay:** Otto Luening.

NEUMANN, Karl. Architect and amateur conductor of contemporary music. **Essay:** Toshiro Mayuzumi.

NEWMAN, Michael. Freelance lecturer and violinist; co-director of Forward Music. Reviewer for *The Strad* and *Musical Times.* **Essay:** Barney Childs.

NOLLER, Joachim. Musicologist. Author of *Engagement und Form: Giacomo Manzonis Werk in kulturtheoretischen und musikhistorischen Zusammenhängen,* 1987, and many articles on 20th-century culture and music in German and Italian journals. **Essays:** Cristobal Halffter; Giacomo Manzoni.

NONBO, Margit. Member of the Faculty of Music, Aalborg University Center, Denmark. Author of *Karl Aage Rasmussen: Historie, Aestetik, Analyse,* 1990. **Essay:** Karl Aage Rasmussen.

NORGAARD, Helmer. Musicologist. **Essay:** Bent Lorentzen.

NORMAN, Paul. Retired civil servant. **Essay:** Serge Nigg.

ONDISHKO, Denise. Computer programmer. **Essay:** Paul Lansky.

ORGASS, Stefan. Teacher at the Folkwang-Hochschule, Essen, and at a secondary school in Herne, Germany. Contributor to *Enzyklopädie des Musiktheaters.* **Essay:** Nicolaus A. Huber.

PAQUELET, Christine. Musiologist and writer on music. **Essay:** Tona Scherchen.

PERLIS, Vivian. Director, Oral History, American Music, Yale University School of Music, New Haven, Connecticut. Author of *Charles Ives Remembered: An Oral History,* 1974, *Copland: 1900 Through 1942,* 1984, and *Copland: Since 1943,* 1989; contributor to the New York *Times* and to music journals and newsletters. **Essay:** Betsy Jolas.

PERONE, James E. Adjunct Professor of music, Canisius College, Buffalo, New York. Contributor to *Flutist Quarterly, ClariNetwork, Journal of the Science and Practice of Music* and *Interface.* **Essays:** William Albright; Petr Kotik; Anestis Logothetis.

PIKE, Lionel. Dean, Faculty of Music, University of London; Senior Lecturer in music, Royal Holloway and Bedford New College, Egham, Surrey; also organist. Author of *Beethoven, Sibelius and "the Profound Logic",* 1978, and articles in *Music and Letters, Tempo, Tonic* and *Musical Times.* **Essay:** Robert Simpson.

POPLE, Anthony. Lecturer in music, Lancaster University; editor of the journal *Musicus: Computer Applications in Music Education.* Author of *Skrybian and Stravinsky: Studies in Theory and Analysis,* 1988, *Berg: Violin Concerto,* 1991, and articles in *Music Analysis, Music and Letters, Musical Times* and other journals. Co-editor of *Computer Models and Representations in Music* (forthcoming). **Essays:** Pierre Boulez; Olivier Messiaen; Michael Tippett.

POTTER, Keith. Lecturer in Music, Goldsmiths' College, University of London. **Essay:** Karlheinz Stockhausen.

PRUDENCIO, Cergio. Composer, conductor, musicologist and teacher. Contributor to *Presencia,* La Paz, Bolivia, *La Del Taller,* Montevideo, Uruguay, and *Derives,* Quebec. **Essay:** Graciela Paraskevaídis.

RADIC, Thérèse. Australian Research Council Fellow, Department of Music, Monash University, Melbourne. Author of *G.W.L. Marshall-Hall: Portrait of a Lost Crusader,* 1982, *A Treasury of Favourite Australian Songs,* 1983, *Melba: The Voice of Australia,* 1986, *Bernard Heinze,* 1986, *Songs of Australian Working Life,* 1989, *Whitening the Songlines,* 1991, and many articles in journals and collections; also author of four plays — *Some of My Best Friends Are Women,* 1983, *A Whip Round for Percy Grainger,* 1984, *Madame Mao,* 1986, and *Peach Melba: Melba's Last Farewell,* 1990. **Essay:** Helen Gifford.

RAE, Caroline. Lecturer in music, University of Wales College of Cardiff. Author of *The Music of Maurice Ohana* (forthcoming), and articles in *Musical Times, Die Neue Zeitschrift für Musik, Les Cahiers du Centre Internationale de Recherches en Esthétique Musicale,* and other publications. **Essay:** Maurice Ohana.

RAMSEY, Basil. Editor, *Musical Times,* London. Author of articles in *Organists' Review* and *The Guardian,* and of programme notes. **Essays:** Charles Camilleri; Anthony Milner.

RAVNKILDE, Sven. Librarian. Regular contributor to *Dansk Musik Tidsskrift,* and author of articles on Carl Nielsen. **Essay:** Pelle Gudmundsen-Holmgreen.

REIMERS, Lennart. Professor of music, University of Stockholm; publisher, Edition Reimers, Stockholm. Author of *A Swedish St John's Passion from the 17th Century,* 1962, *Konst och musikhistoria* (with Gerd Reimers), 1967, *10 Musikanalyser,* 1968, *Alice Tegner's barnvisor,* 1983, and articles in *Musik und Bildung, Nutida Musik, Musikrevy* and other journals. **Essays:** Arne Mellnäs; Folke Rabe.

RENK, Gena. Music teacher. **Essays:** Guido Santorsola; Pawel Szymanski.

REVILL, David. Freelance writer and musician. Compositions include *Harihara* (for guitar) and electronic music for a music theatre project, *Les Tentations d'Antoine.* Author of *The Roaring Silence* (forthcoming biography of John Cage) and articles in *Paragraph, The Times, Times Higher Education Supplement, Times Literary Supplement,* and *The Guardian.* **Essays:** Richard Barrett; François Bayle; Pierre Bernard; Earle Brown, Jr; John Cage; John Casken; Luc Ferrari; Lejaren A. Hiller, Jr; Toshio Ichiyanagi; Joan La Barbara; Alvin Lucier; François-Bernard Mâche; Stephen Montague; Gordon Mumma; Pauline Oliveros; Nigel Osborne; Denis Smalley; Christian Wolff.

REZNEK, Renée. Concert pianist and lecturer. Has given many first performances of works written for her by Robert Saxton, George Nicholson and other composers. **Essay:** David Earl.

RICH, Alan. Freelance music critic; member of the music faculty, University of California, Los Angeles, and California Institute of the Arts, Valencia. Author of *Music, Mirror of the Arts,* 1969, *The Simon and Schuster Listener's Guide to Music,* 3 vols., 1980, *The Lincoln Center Story,* 1984, and articles in *Entertainment Weekly, L.A. Style, Opera News* and other journals. **Essay:** Aaron Jay Kernis.

RICKARDS, Guy. Freelance computer consultant; vice-chair, Havergal Brian Society. Contributor to *Tempo,* Havergal Brian Society *Newsletter, Classic CD* and *Journal of the British Music Society.* **Essays:** Bengt Hambraeus; Paavo Heininen; Nicholas Maw; John McCabe; Harald Saeverud; Harold Truscott.

ROOSENSCHOON, Hans. See his own entry. **Essay:** Hubert du Plessis.

RÖRICH, Mary Elizabeth. Senior Lecturer, School of Music, University of the Witwatersrand, Johannesburg. Author of *Composers in South Africa Today,* 1987, *The Women in Richard Strauss's Operas* (forthcoming), and articles in *Ars Nova, South African Journal of Musicology* and *World of Music.* **Essay:** Jeanne Zaidel-Rudolph.

ROURKE, Sean. Managing director, STR Music Marketing and Management; director, Forward Music Ltd. publisher. Compositions include *Waterloo Approach* (piano solo), 1984, *Berberis Darwinii* (horn quartet), 1985, *Nocturne for Organ,* 1985, *Purl One* (ensemble), 1988, and *Bede's Death Song* (choir), 1988. Compiler of *Franz Lehár Thematic Index,* 1985, and contributor to *Music Teacher* and *Musical Times.* **Essay:** Alejandro Viñao.

RULON, C. Bryan. Teacher and writer on music. **Essay:** Carolyn Steinberg.

SAHL, Michael. Musicologist. **Essay:** Beth Anderson.

SANIN, A. Musicologist. **Essay:** Galina Ustvolskaya.

SARKISYAN, Svetlana. Musicologist. **Essays:** Martin Israelyan; Ashot Zohrabian.

SAWABE, Yukiko. Musicologist and freelance writer. **Essay:** Somei Satoh.

SCARPONE, Guido. Retired physician. **Essays:** Sylvano Bussotti; Franco Donatoni; Carlos Jiménez-Mabarak.

SCHOOF, Dieter. Pianist, conductor and writer on Latin American music. **Essay:** Rolf Liebermann.

SCHULMAN, Paul R. Professor of government, Mills College, Oakland, California. Author of *Large-Scale Policy-Making,* 1980, and articles in *American Political Science Review, Journal of Politics, Administration and Society* and *Liberal Education.*

SCOTTO, Ciro G. Lecturer in composition, University of California, Santa Barbara. Contributor to *Perspectives of New Music.* **Essays:** Lou Harrison; Alan Hovhaness; Roger Reynolds; Gunther Schuller; Richard Swift.

SHANAHAN, Ian. Composer and performer; president, Fellowship of Australian Composers. Compositions on CD include *Earth Spirit* and *Times Remembered.* Author of *Recorder Unlimited* (forthcoming), and articles in *Ossia, Sounds Australian* and *The Recorder.* **Essay:** Eric Gross.

SHEARER, Ivan. Freelance writer on music and science. **Essay:** Dmitri Kapyrin.

SHIRAISHI, Miyuki. Freelance writer. **Essay:** Toshio Hosokawa.

SINKER, Mark. Assistant editor, *Wire,* London. Author of *The Electric Storm* (forthcoming), and contributor to *Cultural Icons,* 1990, and *The Village Voice, Marxism Today* and *The Face.* **Essay:** Steve Martland.

SMITH, Geoff. Composer. With Nicola Walker Smith author of *Something About the Music 1: Interviews with Seventeen American Experimental Composers,* 1992, and contributions to *Contemporary Music Review.* **Essay** (with Nicola Walker Smith): James Fulkerson.

SMITH, Nicola Walker. Vocalist, specializing in contemporary repertoire. With Geoff Smith author of *Something About the Music 1: Interviews with Seventeen American Experimental Composers,* 1992, and contributions to *Contemporary Music Review.* **Essay** (with Geoff Smith): James Fulkerson.

STEIN, Richard. Pianist, conductor and freelance writer. **Essays:** Michael Gielen; Alexander Gugel; Ernst Krenek; Otomar Kvěch; George Lloyd; Wilfrid Mellers; Daniel Pinkham.

STEINITZ, Richard. Professor of music, Huddersfield Polytechnic, Yorkshire; director and founder, Huddersfield Contemporary Music Festival; also composer and broadcaster. Contributor to *Towards a Cosmic Music,* 1989, and *The Messiaen Companion* (forthcoming). **Essays:** Luciano Berio; Harrison Birtwistle; Ge Gan-ru; Sofia Gubaidulina; Robert Saxton; R. Murray Schafer; Alfred Schnittke.

STEVENSON, Robert. Professor of musicology, University of California, Los Angeles. Author of more than 25 books, including studies of the music of Mexico, Spain, Peru and the Caribbean, and works on opera. **Essay:** Blas Galindo.

STEWART, Andrew. Retired teacher; now music copyist and accompanist. **Essay:** Paul Patterson.

SWANSTON, Roderick. Principal Lecturer, Royal College of Music, London; academic adviser in music, Birkbeck College, University of London. Frequent broadcaster on Radio 3, and contributor to *Musical Times, Classic CD, Opera Now* and *Classical Music.* **Essay:** Geoffrey Bush.

SWEENEY, William. See his own entry. **Essay:** Stepan Rostomian.

THOMERSON, Kathleen. Lecturer in music, Southern Illinois University, Edwardsville. Author of *Jean Langlais: A Bio-Bibliography,* 1988, and articles in *American Organist, The Diapason* and *Choice.* **Essay:** Jean Langlais.

TOWNEND, Richard. Freelance writer. **Essay:** Richard Stoker.

TSANG, David. Musicologist. **Essays:** Earl Kim; Chinary Ung.

VIEIRA de CARVALHO, Mário. Professor of musicology, New University of Lisbon. Author of *Para um dossier Gulbenkian,* 1974, *A música e a luta ideológica,* 1976, *Estes sons, esta linguagem,* 1978, *O essencial sobre Fernando Lopes-Graça,* 1989, *O Teatro de São Carlos na mudança de sistemas sociocomunicativos,* 1991, and articles in *Beiträge zur Musikwissenschaft, Boletim da A.P.E.M., Colóquio-Letras, Diário de Lisboa, Jornal des Letras, Oper Heute, Revista Portuguesa de Musicologia, Penélope, Seara Nova, Vértice* and other journals. **Essays:** Fernando Lopes-Graça; Emmanuel Nunes; Jorge Peixinho.

WASHINGTON, Richard. Jazz musician and freelance writer. **Essays:** Alvin Singleton; Olly Wilson.

WEIR, Bea. Historian of music, currently writing a critical study of women's music. **Essays:** Vivian Fine; Janice Giteck; Barbara Kolb; Anne LeBaron; Gudrun Lund.

WEIR, Ian. Music editor and freelance writer. **Essays:** Robin Orr; Daryl Runswick.

WEIR, James. Composer and reeds player. **Essays:** Carlos Roqué Alsina; Gilbert Amy; Boris Arapov; David Bedford; George Benjamin; Nils Viggo Bentzon; Michael Berkeley; Glenn Branca; Reginald Smith Brindle.

WEIR, Judith. See her own entry. **Essay:** Thea Musgrave.

WHIFFIN, Lawrence. Senior Lecturer in composition, La Trobe University, Melbourne; pianist: has performed throughout Europe and Australia; composer. Author of *Counterpoint of the Species* (textbook), 1986, a forthcoming 3-volume study of counterpoint and an article in *Musicology Australia.* Editor of *Contemporary Australian Piano,* 1986, and *Contemporary Australian Violin,* 1991. **Essays:** Keith Humble, Julian Jing-Jun Yu.

WILLIAMS, Nicholas. Publisher and writer. Contributor to *The Independent, Classical Music, Musical Times* and the collection *Music and the Politics of Culture.* **Essays:** Anthony Gilbert; Roger Steptoe.

WOLPE, Michael. Musician. **Essay:** Haim Alexander.

WOODLEY, Ronald. Lecturer in music, University of Newcastle-upon-Tyne. Author of *John Tucke: A Case Study in Early Tudor Music,* 1991, *Moving Chords; Function and Allusion in Steve Reich's New York Counterpoint* (forthcoming), and articles in *Journal of the American Musicology Society, Early Music History, Renaissance Studies* and other journals. **Essay:** Steve Reich.

WRIGHT, David. Musicologist and writer; part-time lecturer, Goldsmiths' College, University of London. Author of *Faber Music: The First 25 Years 1965–1990,* 1990, and articles in *Musical Times, Tempo, The Listener* and *The Independent.* **Essay:** John Woolrich.

YEDRA, Velia. Concert pianist, writer and lecturer. Author of *Julián Orbón: A Biographical and Critical Essay,* 1990. **Essay:** Julián Orbón.

ZHOU Long. See his own entry. **Essay:** Chen Yi.

ZURABIAN, Jean. Assistant Professor of music history, Yerevan State Conservatory, Armenia. Author of several articles for republician journals and newspapers on the creative work of modern Armenian composers. **Essay:** Simon Hovanessian.